KW-554-582

6

WHO WAS WHO

VOLUME XIII

2011–2015

WITHDRAWN
FROM STOCK
PARLIAMENTARY
ARCHIVES

WHO'S WHO

An annual biographical dictionary
first published in 1849

WHO WAS WHO

Volume I	1897–1915
Volume II	1916–1928
Volume III	1929–1940
Volume IV	1941–1950
Volume V	1951–1960
Volume VI	1961–1970
Volume VII	1971–1980
Volume VIII	1981–1990
Volume IX	1991–1995
Volume X	1996–2000
A CUMULATED INDEX 1897–2000	
Volume XI	2001–2005
Volume XII	2006–2010
Volume XIII	2011–2015

WHO WAS WHO VOLUME XIII

WHO WAS WHO

2011–2015

A COMPANION TO

WHO'S WHO

CONTAINING THE BIOGRAPHIES
OF THOSE WHO DIED DURING
THE PERIOD 2011–2015

A & C BLACK
AN IMPRINT OF
B L O O M S B U R Y
LONDON • OXFORD • NEW YORK • NEW DELHI • SYDNEY

A&C Black
An Imprint of Bloomsbury Publishing Plc

50 Bedford Square
London
WC1B 3DP
UK

1385 Broadway
New York
NY 10018
USA

www.bloomsbury.com

A&C BLACK and the 'WHO'S WHO PUBLISHED ANNUALLY SINCE 1849' belt logo are trademarks of Bloomsbury Publishing Plc

© Bloomsbury Publishing Plc, 2016

Entries from Who's Who may not be reproduced, in any form whatsoever, without the written permission of the publishers.

All rights reserved. No part of this publication may be reproduced or used in any form or by any means—graphic, electronic or mechanical, including photocopying, recording, taping or information storage and retrieval systems—without the written permission of the publishers.

The publishers make no representation, express or implied, with regard to the accuracy of the information contained in this book and cannot accept any legal responsibility for any errors or omissions that may take place.

British Library Cataloguing-in-Publication Data
A catalogue record for this book is available from the British Library.
ISBN: HB: 978-1-472-92432-2
www.ukwhoswho.com

2 4 6 8 10 9 7 5 3 1

Printed and bound in Great Britain by
Bell and Bain Ltd, Glasgow

To find out more about our authors and books visit www.bloomsbury.com. Here you will find extracts, author interviews, details of forthcoming events and the option to sign up for our newsletters.

PREFACE

This, the thirteenth volume of biographies removed from *Who's Who* on account of death, contains the entries of those who died between 2011 and 2015. Those whose deaths occurred before the end of 2010, but were not reported until after the volume of *Who Was Who* covering the years 2006–2010 had been published, are listed as Addenda at the beginning of the biographical section.

The entries are as they last appeared in *Who's Who*, with the date of death added and in some cases further information, such as posthumous publications. It has not always been possible to ascertain the exact date of death, and the editors will welcome such information for inclusion in the next edition of this volume.

WITHDRAWN FROM STOCK
PARLIAMENTARY ARCHIVES

CONTENTS

ABBREVIATIONS USED IN THIS BOOK

Some of the designatory letters in this list are used merely for economy of space and do not necessarily imply any professional or other qualification.

A

AA Anti-aircraft; Automobile Association; Architectural Association; Augustinians of the Assumption; Associate in Arts
AAAL American Academy of Arts and Letters
AA&QMG Assistant Adjutant and Quartermaster-General
AAAS American Association for the Advancement of Science
AAC Army Air Corps; Amateur Athletic Club
AACE Association for Adult and Continuing Education
AAFCE Allied Air Forces in Central Europe
AAG Assistant Adjutant-General
AAIL American Academy and Institute of Arts and Letters (*now see* AAAL)
AAM Association of Assistant Mistresses in Secondary Schools
A&AEE Aeroplane and Armament Experimental Establishment
AAS American Astronomical Society
AATSE Australian Academy of Technological Sciences and Engineering
AAUQ Associate in Accountancy, University of Queensland
AB Bachelor of Arts (US); able-bodied seaman; airborne; Alberta (postal)
ABA Amateur Boxing Association; Antiquarian Booksellers' Association; American Bar Association
ABC Australian Broadcasting Commission; American Broadcasting Companies; Amateur Boxing Club; Associate, Birmingham Conservatoire; Accredited Business Communicator
ABCC Association of British Chambers of Commerce
ABM Advisory Board of Ministry
ABPsS Associate, British Psychological Society
ABRC Advisory Board for the Research Councils
ABTA Association of British Travel Agents
AC Companion, Order of Australia; *Ante Christum* (before Christ)
ACA Associate, Institute of Chartered Accountants
Acad. Academy
ACARD Advisory Council for Applied Research and Development
ACAS Advisory, Conciliation and Arbitration Service; Assistant Chief of the Air Staff
ACC Association of County Councils; Anglican Consultative Council
ACCM Advisory Council for the Church's Ministry (*now see* ABM)
ACDS Assistant Chief of Defence Staff
ACE Association of Consulting Engineers; Member, Association of Conference Executives; Allied Command Europe
ACertCM Archbishops' Certificate in Church Music
ACF Army Cadet Force
ACFA Army Cadet Force Association
ACI Airports Council International (Europe)
ACIArb Associate, Chartered Institute of Arbitrators
ACIB Associate, Chartered Institute of Bankers
ACII Associate, Chartered Insurance Institute
ACIS Associate, Institute of Chartered Secretaries and Administrators (*formerly* Chartered Institute of Secretaries)
ACM Association of Computing Machinery
ACMA Associate, Chartered Institute of Management Accountants (*formerly* Institute of Cost and Management Accountants)
ACMI Associate, Chartered Management Institute
ACNS Assistant Chief of Naval Staff
ACORD Advisory Committee on Research and Development
ACOS Assistant Chief of Staff
ACOST Advisory Council on Science and Technology
ACPO Association of Chief Police Officers
ACRE Action with Rural Communities in England
ACS American Chemical Society; Additional Curates Society
AcSS Member, Academy of Learned Societies for the Social Sciences
ACT Australian Capital Territory; Australian College of Theology; Associate, College of Technology; Association of Corporate Treasurers
ACU Association of Commonwealth Universities
aD ausser Dienst
AD Dame of the Order of Australia; *Anno Domini* (in the year of the Lord); Air Defence
ADAS Agricultural Development and Advisory Service
ADB Asian Development Bank; Associate of the Drama Board (Education)
ADC Aide-de-camp; Association of District Councils
ADCM Archbishop of Canterbury's Diploma in Church Music
ADGMS Assistant Director-General of Medical Services
Adjt Adjutant
Adm. Admiral
ADMS Assistant Director of Medical Services
ADP Automatic Data Processing
Adv. Advisory; Advocate
AE Air Efficiency Award
AEA Atomic Energy Authority; Air Efficiency Award (*now see* AE); American Economic Association
AEC Agriculture Executive Council; Army Educational Corps (*now see* RAEC); Atomic Energy Commission
AEE Atomic Energy Establishment
AEEU Amalgamated Engineering and Electrical Union
AEI Associated Electrical Industries
AELTC All England Lawn Tennis Club
AER Army Emergency Reserve
AERE Atomic Energy Research Establishment (Harwell)
AEU Amalgamated Engineering Union (later AEEU)
AFAIAA Associate Fellow, American Institute of Aeronautics and Astronautics
AFASIC Association for All Speech Impaired Children
AFC Air Force Cross; Association Football Club
AFCENT Allied Forces in Central Europe
AFOM Associate, Faculty of Occupational Medicine

AFRC Agricultural and Food Research Council (*now see* BBSRC)
AG Attorney-General
AGAC American Guild of Authors and Composers
AGARD Advisory Group for Aerospace Research and Development
AGC Adjutant General's Corps
AGI Alliance Graphique Internationale; Associate, Institute of Certificated Grocers
AHA Area Health Authority; American Hospitals Association; Associate, Institute of Health Service Administrators (later AHSM)
AHA(T) Area Health Authority (Teaching)
AHQ Army Headquarters
AHRB Arts and Humanities Research Board (*now see* AHRC)
AHRC Arts and Humanities Research Council
AHSM Associate, Institute of Health Services Management
AIA Associate, Institute of Actuaries; American Institute of Architects; Association of International Artists
AIAA American Institute of Aeronautics and Astronautics
AIAgrE Associate, Institution of Agricultural Engineers
AIB Associate, Institute of Bankers (*now see* ACIB)
AIDS Acquired Immunity Deficiency Syndrome
AIEE Associate, Institution of Electrical Engineers
AIF Australian Imperial Forces
AIIA Associate, Insurance Institute of America; Associate, Indian Institute of Architects
AIL Associate, Institute of Linguists
AIM Associate, Institution of Metallurgists (later MIM); Australian Institute of Management; Alternative Investment Market; Advanced Institute of Management Research
AInstP Associate, Institute of Physics
AITP Associate, Institute of Town Planners, India
AJAG Assistant Judge Advocate General
AK Knight, Order of Australia; Alaska (postal)
AKC Associate, King's College London
AL Alabama (postal)
Ala Alabama
ALA Associate, Library Association (*now see* MCLIP); Association of London Authorities
ALCD Associate, London College of Divinity
ALCS Authors Lending and Copyright Society
ALI Argyll Light Infantry; Associate, Landscape Institute
ALP Australian Labor Party
ALS Associate, Linnean Society; Amyotrophic Lateral Sclerosis
Alta Alberta
AM Albert Medal; Member, Order of Australia; Master of Arts (US); Alpes Maritimes
AMA Association of Metropolitan Authorities; Assistant Masters Association; Associate, Museums Association; Australian Medical Association
Amb. Ambulance; Ambassador
AMBIM Associate Member, British Institute of Management
AMCT Associate, Manchester College of Technology
AMF Australian Military Forces
AMICE Associate Member, Institution of Civil Engineers (*now see* MICE)
AMIEE Associate Member, Institution of Electrical Engineers (later MIEE)
AMIERE Associate Member, Institution of Electronic and Radio Engineers
AMN Ahli Mangku Negara (Malaysia)
AMP Advanced Management Program; Air Member for Personnel
AMS Assistant Military Secretary; Army Medical Services
AMTRI Advanced Manufacturing Technology Research Institute
Anat. Anatomy; Anatomical
ANC African National Congress
ANU Australian National University
ANZAAS Australian and New Zealand Association for the Advancement of Science
Anzac Australian and New Zealand Army Corps
AO Officer, Order of Australia; Air Officer
AOA Air Officer in charge of Administration
AOC Air Officer Commanding
AOC-in-C Air Officer Commanding-in-Chief
AOE Alberta Order of Excellence
APACS Association of Payment and Clearing Systems
APEX Association of Professional, Executive, Clerical and Computer Staff
APHA American Public Health Association
APMI Associate, Pensions Management Institute
APS Aborigines Protection Society; American Physical Society
AQ Administration and Quartering
AQMG Assistant Quartermaster-General
ARA Associate, Royal Academy; Armada de la República Argentina
ARAD Associate, Royal Academy of Dancing
ARAeS Associate, Royal Aeronautical Society
ARBS Associate, Royal Society of British Sculptors
ARC Architects' Registration Council; Agricultural Research Council (later AFRC); Aeronautical Research Council; Arthritis and Rheumatism Council
ARCA Associate, Royal College of Art; Associate, Royal Canadian Academy
ARCM Associate, Royal College of Music
ARCO Associate, Royal College of Organists
ARCS Associate, Royal College of Science; Accreditation Review and Consulting Service (*now see* ISI)
ARCUK Architects' Registration Council of the United Kingdom (*now see* ARB)
ARCVS Associate, Royal College of Veterinary Surgeons
ARE Associate, Royal Society of Painter-Printmakers (*formerly* of Painter-Etchers and Engravers); Arab Republic of Egypt; Admiralty Research Establishment
ARIAS Associate, Royal Incorporation of Architects in Scotland
ARIBA Associate, Royal Institute of British Architects (*now see* RIBA)
ARIC Associate, Royal Institute of Chemistry (*now see* MRSC)
ARICS Professional Associate, Royal Institution of Chartered Surveyors (*now see* MRICS)
ARPS Associate, Royal Photographic Society
ARSA Associate, Royal Scottish Academy
ARSCM Associate, Royal School of Church Music
ARSM Associate, Royal School of Mines
ARWS Associate, Royal Society of Painters in Water-Colours
AS Anglo-Saxon
ASA Associate Member, Society of Actuaries; Associate of Society of Actuaries (US); Australian Society of Accountants; Army Sailing Association; Advertising Standards Authority; Alment Aksjeselskap
ASBAH Association for Spina Bifida and Hydrocephalus
ASC Administrative Staff College, Henley
ASCAP American Society of Composers, Authors and Publishers
ASCE American Society of Civil Engineers
ASD Armament Supply Department
ASEAN Association of South East Asian Nations

ASH Action on Smoking and Health
ASIAD Associate, Society of Industrial Artists and Designers
ASLEF Associated Society of Locomotive Engineers and Firemen
Aslib Association for Information Management (*formerly* Association of Special Libraries and Information Bureaux)
ASM Association of Senior Members; Australian Service Medal
ASME American Society of Mechanical Engineers; Association for the Study of Medical Education
Asst Assistant
ASTMS Association of Scientific, Technical and Managerial Staffs (subsequently part of MSF)
ASVU Army Security Vetting Unit
ASWE Admiralty Surface Weapons Establishment
ATA Air Transport Auxiliary
ATAF Allied Tactical Air Force
ATD Art Teacher's Diploma
ATI Associate, Textile Institute
ATII Associate Member, Chartered Institute (*formerly* Incorporated Institute, then Institute) of Taxation
ATS Auxiliary Territorial Service (later WRAC)
ATV Associated Television (*formerly* Association TeleVision)
AUA American Urological Association; Association of University Administrators
AUS Army of the United States
AUT Association of University Teachers
AVCM Associate, Victoria College of Music
AVR Army Volunteer Reserve

B

b born; brother
BA Bachelor of Arts
BAA British Airports Authority; British Accounting Association
BAAS British Association for the Advancement of Science
BAC British Aircraft Corporation
BAe British Aerospace
BAFTA British Academy of Film and Television Arts
BAI *Baccalarius in Arte Ingeniaria* (Bachelor of Engineering)
BAO Bachelor of Art of Obstetrics
BAOMS British Association of Oral and Maxillo-Facial Surgeons
BAOR British Army of the Rhine (*formerly* on the Rhine)
BAOS British Association of Oral Surgeons (*now see* BAOMS)
BARC British Automobile Racing Club
BArch Bachelor of Architecture
BASCA British Academy of Songwriters, Composers and Authors
BBA British Bankers' Association; Bachelor of Business Administration
BBC British Broadcasting Corporation
BBFC British Board of Film Classification
BBS Bachelor of Business Studies
BBSRC Biotechnology and Biological Sciences Research Council
BC Before Christ; British Columbia; Borough Council
BCC British Council of Churches (later CCBI)
BCE Bachelor of Civil Engineering; Before the Christian Era
BCh or **BChir** Bachelor of Surgery
BCL Bachelor of Civil Law
BCMF British Ceramic Manufacturers' Federation
BCMS Bible Churchmen's Missionary Society
BCOF British Commonwealth Occupation Force
BCom or **BComm** Bachelor of Commerce
BComSc Bachelor of Commercial Science
BCS Bengal Civil Service; British Computer Society; Bachelor of Combined Studies
BCURA British Coal Utilization Research Association
Bd Board
BD Bachelor of Divinity
BDA British Dental Association; British Deaf Association; British Dyslexia Association
Bde Brigade
BDS Bachelor of Dental Surgery
BE Bachelor of Engineering; British Element
BEA British East Africa; British European Airways; British Epilepsy Association
BEAMA Federation of British Electrotechnical and Allied Manufacturers' Associations (*formerly* British Electrical and Allied Manufacturers' Association)
BE&A Bachelor of Engineering and Architecture (Malta)
BEc Bachelor of Economics
BEd Bachelor of Education
Beds Bedfordshire
BEF British Expeditionary Force; British Equestrian Federation
BEM British Empire Medal
BEMAS British Educational Management and Administration Society
BEng Bachelor of Engineering
Berks Berkshire
BERR Department for Business, Enterprise and Regulatory Reform
BESO British Executive Service Overseas
BFI British Film Institute
BGS Brigadier General Staff
BHF British Heart Foundation
BI British Invisibles
BICC British Insulated Callender's Cables
BICERA British Internal Combustion Engine Research Association (*now see* BICERI)
BIEC British Invisible Exports Council (*now see* BI)
BIM British Institute of Management
BIR British Institute of Radiology
BIS Bank for International Settlements; British Interplanetary Society; Department for Business, Innovation and Skills
BISPA British Independent Steel Producers Association
BISRA British Iron and Steel Research Association
BITC Business in the Community
BJSM British Joint Services Mission
BKSTS British Kinematograph, Sound and Television Society
BL Bachelor of Law; British Library
BLA British Liberation Army
BLESMA British Limbless Ex-Servicemen's Association
BLitt Bachelor of Letters
BM British Museum; Bachelor of Medicine; Brigade Major; British Monomark
BMA British Medical Association
BMet Bachelor of Metallurgy
BMG British Military Government
BMH British Military Hospital
BMJ British Medical Journal
BMRA Brigade Major Royal Artillery
Bn Battalion
BNEC British National Export Council
BNF British National Formulary
BNFL British Nuclear Fuels Ltd

BNOC British National Oil Corporation; British National Opera Company
BNP Banque Nationale de Paris; British National Party
BOAC British Overseas Airways Corporation
BoT Board of Trade
BOTB British Overseas Trade Board
Bp Bishop
BPA British Paediatric Association; Bachelor of Performing Arts
BPharm Bachelor of Pharmacy
BPMF British Postgraduate Medical Federation
BPsS British Psychological Society
BR British Rail
Br. Branch
BRB British Railways Board
BRCS British Red Cross Society
Brig. Brigadier
BRIT British Recording Industry Trust
BRNC Britannia Royal Naval College
BS Bachelor of Surgery; Bachelor of Science; British Standard
BSA Bachelor of Scientific Agriculture; Birmingham Small Arms; Building Societies' Association
BSAS British Society of Animal Science
BSc Bachelor of Science
BSC British Steel Corporation; Bengal Staff Corps
BScEcon Bachelor of Science in Economics
BScEng Bachelor of Science in Engineering
BScSoc Bachelor of Social Sciences
BSE Bachelor of Science in Engineering (US); Bovine Spongiform Encephalopathy
BSES British Schools Exploring Society
BSI British Standards Institution
BSJA British Show Jumping Association
BSME Bachelor of Science in Mechanical Engineering; British Society of Magazine Editors
BSRA British Ship Research Association
BSS Bachelor of Science (Social Science)
Bt Baronet; Brevet
BT Bachelor of Teaching; British Telecommunications
BTA British Tourist Authority (*formerly* British Travel Association)
BTC British Transport Commission
BTech Bachelor of Technology
BTh Bachelor of Theology
Btss Baronetess
Bucks Buckinghamshire
BURA British Urban Regeneration Association
BV Besloten Vennootschap
BVA British Veterinary Association; British Video Association
BVI British Virgin Islands
BVSc Bachelor of Veterinary Science

C

c child; cousin; *circa* (about)
C Conservative; 100
CA Central America; County Alderman; Chartered Accountant (Scotland and Canada); California (postal)
CAA Civil Aviation Authority
CAB Citizens' Advice Bureau; Centre for Agricultural and Biosciences (*formerly* Commonwealth Agricultural Bureau)
CABE Commission for Architecture and the Built Environment
CAF Charities Aid Foundation
CAFCASS Child and Family Court Advisory and Support Service
Calif California
CAM Communications, Advertising and Marketing
Cambs Cambridgeshire
C&G City and Guilds of London Institute
Cantab *Cantabrigiensis* (of Cambridge)
CAP Common Agricultural Policy
Capt. Captain
CARE Cottage and Rural Enterprises
Carms Carmarthenshire
CAS Chief of the Air Staff
CATE Council for the Accreditation of Teacher Education
CB Companion, Order of the Bath; County Borough
CBC County Borough Council
CBE Commander, Order of the British Empire
CBI Confederation of British Industry
CBIM Companion, British Institute of Management (later CIMgt)
CBiol Chartered Biologist
CBNS Commander British Navy Staff
CBS Columbia Broadcasting System
CBSI Chartered Building Societies Institute (*now see* CIB)
CC Companion, Order of Canada; City Council; County Council; Cricket Club; Cycling Club; County Court
CCAB Consultative Committee of Accountancy Bodies
CCBE Commission Consultative des Barreaux de la Communauté Européenne
CCBI Council of Churches for Britain and Ireland (*now see* CTBI)
CCC Corpus Christi College; Central Criminal Court; County Cricket Club
CCF Combined Cadet Force
CChem Chartered Chemist
CCHMS Central Committee for Hospital Medical Services
CCIA Commission of Churches on International Affairs
CCIPD Companion, Chartered Institute of Personnel and Development
CCJ Council of Christians and Jews
CCLRC Council for the Central Laboratory of the Research Councils
CCMI Companion, Chartered Management Institute
CCPR Central Council of Physical Recreation
CCRE Commander Corps of Royal Engineers
CCSU Council of Civil Service Unions
CCTA Commission de Coöpération Technique pour l'Afrique; Central Computer and Telecommunications Authority
CD Canadian Forces Decoration; Commander, Order of Distinction (Jamaica); Civil Defence; Compact Disc
CDC Centers for Disease Control and Prevention
CDipAF Certified Diploma in Accounting and Finance
Cdo Commando
Cdre Commodore
CDS Chief of the Defence Staff
CDU Christlich-Demokratische Union
CE Civil Engineer
CEC Commission of the European Communities
CECD Confédération Européenne du Commerce de Détail
CECG Consumers in European Community Group
CEDR Centre for Effective Dispute Resolution
CEED Centre for Economic and Environmental Development
CEFIC Conseil Européen des Fédérations de l'Industrie Chimique

CEGB Central Electricity Generating Board
CEI Council of Engineering Institutions
CEMR Council of European Municipalities and Regions
CEng Chartered Engineer
Cento Central Treaty Organisation
CEnv Chartered Environmentalist
CEO Chief Executive Officer
CERN Organisation (*formerly* Centre) Européenne pour la Recherche Nucléaire
CET Council for Educational Technology
CF Chaplain to the Forces; Companion, Order of Fiji; Corporate Finance; Corporate Financier
CFE Central Fighter Establishment
CFM Cadet Forces Medal
CFS Central Flying School; Chronic Fatigue Syndrome
CGA Community of the Glorious Ascension; Country Gentlemen's Association
CGeol Chartered Geologist
CGIA Insignia Award of City and Guilds of London Institute (*now see* FCGI)
CGLI City and Guilds of London Institute (*now see* C&G)
CGRM Commandant-General Royal Marines
CGS Chief of the General Staff
CH Companion of Honour
Chap. Chaplain
CHAR Campaign for the Homeless and Rootless
ChB Bachelor of Surgery
CHB Companion of Honour of Barbados
CHC Community Health Council
(CHM) *see under* ARCO(CHM), FRCO(CHM)
ChM Master of Surgery
Chm. Chairman or Chairwoman
ChStJ Chaplain, Most Venerable Order of the Hospital of St John of Jerusalem
CI Imperial Order of the Crown of India; Channel Islands
CIA Chemical Industries Association; Central Intelligence Agency
CIArb Chartered Institute of Arbitrators
CIB Chartered Institute of Bankers
CIBSE Chartered Institution of Building Services Engineers
CIC Chemical Institute of Canada; Community Interest Company
CICAP Criminal Injuries Compensation Appeal Panel
CICB Criminal Injuries Compensation Board
CID Criminal Investigation Department
CIE Companion, Order of the Indian Empire; Confédération Internationale des Etudiants
CIFE Council (*formerly* Conference) for Independent Further Education
CIGRE Conférence Internationale des Grands Réseaux Electriques
CIGS Chief of the Imperial General Staff (*now see* CGS)
CIHR Canadian Institutes of Health Research
CIMgt Companion, Institute of Management (*now see* CCMI)
C-in-C Commander-in-Chief
CIPD Companion, Institute of Personnel and Development (*now see* CCIPD); Chartered Institute of Personnel and Development
CIPFA Chartered Institute of Public Finance and Accountancy
CIPM Companion, Institute of Personnel Management (later CIPD)
CIRP Collège Internationale pour Recherche et Production
CIT Chartered Institute of Transport; California Institute of Technology
CIWEM Chartered Institution of Water and Environmental Management
cl *cum laude*
Cl. Class
CLA Country Land & Business Association (*formerly* Country Landowners' Association)
CLIC Cancer and Leukemia in Childhood
CLit Companion of Literature (Royal Society of Literature Award)
CLJ Commander, Order of St Lazarus of Jerusalem
CLP Constituency Labour Party
CLRAE Congress (*formerly* Conference) of Local and Regional Authorities of Europe
CLY City of London Yeomanry
CM Member, Order of Canada; Congregation of the Mission (Vincentians); Master in Surgery; Certificated Master; Canadian Militia
CMA Canadian Medical Association; Cost and Management Accountant (NZ); Competition and Markets Authority
CMath Chartered Mathematician
CMB Central Midwives' Board
CME Continuing Ministerial Education
CMF Commonwealth Military Forces; Central Mediterranean Force
CMG Companion, Order of St Michael and St George
CMJ Commander, Supreme Military Order of the Temple of Jerusalem
CMO Chief Medical Officer
CMS Church Mission (*formerly* Church Missionary) Society; Certificate in Management Studies
CNAA Council for National Academic Awards
CND Campaign for Nuclear Disarmament
CNOCS Captain Naval Operational Command Systems
CNRS Centre National de la Recherche Scientifique
CNZM Companion, New Zealand Order of Merit
CO Commanding Officer; Commonwealth Office (after Aug. 1966) (*now see* FCO); Colonial Office (before Aug. 1966); Conscientious Objector; Colorado (postal); Congregation of the Oratory
Co. County; Company
COHSE Confederation of Health Service Employees
COI Central Office of Information
CoID Council of Industrial Design (*now* Design Council)
Col Colonel
Coll. College; Collegiate
Colo Colorado
Comd Command
Comdg Commanding
Comdr Commander
Comdt Commandant
Commn Commission
Commnd Commissioned
CompICE Companion, Institution of Civil Engineers
CompIERE Companion, Institution of Electronic and Radio Engineers
Comr Commissioner
CON Commander, Order of the Niger
Conn Connecticut
Const. Constitutional
Co-op. Co-operative
COPA Comité des Organisations Professionels Agricoles de la CEE
COPUS Committee on the Public Understanding of Science
Corp. Corporation; Corporal
COS Chief of Staff; Charity Organization Society
CoSIRA Council for Small Industries in Rural Areas
COSLA Convention of Scottish Local Authorities

COSPAR Committee on Space Research
CP Central Provinces; Cape Province; Congregation of the Passion
CPA Commonwealth Parliamentary Association; Chartered Patent Agent; Certified Public Accountant (USA)
CPAS Church Pastoral Aid Society
CPC Conservative Political Centre
CPEng Chartered Professional Engineer (of Institution of Engineers of Australia)
CPFA Member or Associate, Chartered Institute of Public Finance and Accountancy
CPhys Chartered Physicist
CPL Chief Personnel and Logistics
CPM Colonial Police Medal
CPR Canadian Pacific Railway
CPRE Campaign to Protect Rural England (*formerly* Council for the Protection of Rural England)
CPRW Campaign for the Protection of Rural Wales
CPS Crown Prosecution Service; Certificate in Pastoral Studies
CPSA Civil and Public Services Association; Church of the Province of South Africa
CPSU Communist Party of the Soviet Union
CPsychol Chartered Psychologist
CPU Commonwealth Press Union
CQ Chevalier, National Order of Quebec
cr created or creation
CRA Commander, Royal Artillery
CRAC Careers Research and Advisory Centre
CRAeS Companion, Royal Aeronautical Society
CRC Cancer Research Campaign (*now see* CRUK); Community Relations Council
CRE Commander, Royal Engineers; Commission for Racial Equality; Commercial Relations and Exports; Conference of Rectors of European Universities (*formerly* Association of European Universities)
CRMP Corps of Royal Military Police
CRNCM Companion, Royal Northern College of Music
CRO Commonwealth Relations Office (*now see* FCO)
CRUK Cancer Research United Kingdom
CS Civil Service; Clerk to the Signet; Companion, Order of Samoa
CSA Confederate States of America; Child Support Agency
CSAB Civil Service Appeal Board
CSCE Conference on Security and Co-operation in Europe
CSci Chartered Scientist
CSD Civil Service Department; Co-operative Secretaries Diploma; Chartered Society of Designers
CSEU Confederation of Shipbuilding and Engineering Unions
CSI Companion, Order of the Star of India; Cross, Order of Solomon Islands
CSIR Commonwealth Council for Scientific and Industrial Research (*now see* CSIRO); Council of Scientific and Industrial Research, India
CSIRO Commonwealth Scientific and Industrial Research Organization (Australia)
CSO Chief Scientific Officer; Chief Signal Officer; Chief Staff Officer; Central Statistical Office
CSSB Civil Service Selection Board
CStat Chartered Statistician
CSTI Council of Science and Technology Institutes
CStJ Commander, Most Venerable Order of the Hospital of St John of Jerusalem
CSV Community Service Volunteers
CSW Certificate in Social Work
CT Connecticut (postal)
CTA Chaplain Territorial Army; Chartered Tax Adviser
CTBI Churches Together in Britain and Ireland
CU Cambridge University
CUF Common University Fund
CUP Cambridge University Press
CVCP Committee of Vice-Chancellors and Principals of the Universities of the United Kingdom (*now see* UUK)
CVO Commander, Royal Victorian Order
CVS Council for Voluntary Service
CWA Crime Writers Association
CWGC Commonwealth War Graves Commission
CWS Co-operative Wholesale Society

D

d died; daughter
D Duke
DA Dame of St Andrew, Order of Barbados; Diploma in Anaesthesia; Diploma in Art; Doctor of Arts
DAA&QMG Deputy Assistant Adjutant and Quartermaster-General
DAAD Designers and Art Directors Association
DAAG Deputy Assistant Adjutant-General
DAC Development Assistance Committee; Diocesan Advisory Committee
DACG Deputy Assistant Chaplain-General
DACOS Deputy Assistant Chief of Staff
DADOS Deputy Assistant Director of Ordnance Services
DADST Deputy Assistant Director of Supplies and Transport
DAgr Doctor of Agriculture
D&AD Design and Art Direction (*formerly* Designers and Art Directors Association)
DAQMG Deputy Assistant Quartermaster-General
DArt Doctor of Art
DArts Doctor of Arts
DAvMed Diploma in Aviation Medicine, Royal College of Physicians
DBA Doctor of Business Administration
DBE Dame Commander, Order of the British Empire
DC District Council; District of Columbia
DCAe Diploma of College of Aeronautics
DCH Diploma in Child Health
DCL Doctor of Civil Law; Dr of Canon Law
DCLG Department for Communities and Local Government
DCLI Duke of Cornwall's Light Infantry
DCLJ Dame Commander, Order of St Lazarus of Jerusalem
DCnL Doctor of Canon Law
DCNZM Distinguished Companion, New Zealand Order of Merit
DCom Doctor of Commerce
DCP Diploma in Clinical Pathology; Diploma in Conservation of Paintings
DCS Deputy Chief of Staff; Doctor of Commercial Sciences
DCSG Dame Commander, Order of St Gregory the Great
DCSO Deputy Chief Scientific Officer
DCVO Dame Commander, Royal Victorian Order
DD Doctor of Divinity
DDes Doctor of Design
DDGAMS Deputy Director General, Army Medical Services
DDMS Deputy Director of Medical Services
DDPH Diploma in Dental Public Health
DDR Deutsche Demokratische Republik

DDS Doctor of Dental Surgery; Director of Dental Services
DDSc Doctor of Dental Science
DE Doctor of Engineering; Delaware (postal)
DEA Department of Economic Affairs; Diplôme d'Etudes Approfondies
DEc Doctor of Economics
DECC Department of Energy and Climate Change
decd deceased
DEcon Doctor of Economics
DEconSc Doctor of Economic Science
DEd Doctor of Education
DEFRA Department for Environment, Food and Rural Affairs
Deleg. Delegate
(DemU) Democratic Unionist
DEng Doctor of Engineering
DenM Docteur en Médicine
Dep. Deputy
DERA Defence Evaluation and Research Agency
DES Department of Education and Science (later DFE); Dr in Environmental Studies
DèsL Docteur ès lettres
DesRCA Designer of the Royal College of Art
DETR Department of the Environment, Transport and the Regions
DFA Doctor of Fine Arts
DFAS Decorative and Fine Art Society
DFC Distinguished Flying Cross
DFE Department for Education
DFEE Department for Education and Employment
DfES Department for Education and Skills
DFH Diploma of Faraday House
DFM Distinguished Flying Medal
DfT Department for Transport
DG Director General; Directorate General; Dragoon Guards
DGAA Distressed Gentlefolks Aid Association
DGMS Director-General of Medical Services
DH Doctor of Humanities; Doctor of Health
DHA District Health Authority
DHL Doctor of Humane Letters; Doctor of Hebrew Literature
DHM Dean Hole Medal
DHSS Department of Health and Social Security
DHum Doctor of Humanities
DHumLit Doctor of Humane Letters
DIC Diploma of the Imperial College
DIH Diploma in Industrial Health
Dio. Diocese
DipAD Diploma in Art and Design
DipArch Diploma in Architecture
DipBS Diploma in Fine Art, Byam Shaw School
DipEcon Diploma in Economics
DipEd Diploma in Education
DipHSM Diploma in Health Services Management
DipHum Diploma in Humanities
DipLib Diploma of Librarianship
DipPsych Diploma in Psychology
DipSoc Diploma in Sociology
DipTh Diploma in Theology
DipTP Diploma in Town Planning
Div. Division; Divorced
DJStJ Dame of Justice, Order of St John of Jerusalem (*now see* DStJ)
DK Most Esteemed Family Order (Brunei)
DL Deputy Lieutenant; Democratie Libérale
DLaws Doctor of Laws
DLC Diploma of Loughborough College
DLI Durham Light Infantry
Dlit or **DLitt** Doctor of Literature; Doctor of Letters
DLO Diploma in Laryngology and Otology
DM Doctor of Medicine
DMA Diploma in Municipal Administration
DMed Doctor of Medicine
DMin Doctor of Ministry
DMJ Diploma in Medical Jurisprudence
DMRD Diploma in Medical Radiological Diagnosis
DMS Director of Medical Services; Decoration for Meritorious Service (South Africa); Diploma in Management Studies
DMSc Doctor of Medical Science
DMus Doctor of Music
DNB Dictionary of National Biography
DNH Department of National Heritage
DNZM Dame Companion, New Zealand Order of Merit
DO Diploma in Ophthalmology
DObstRCOG Diploma of Royal College of Obstetricians and Gynaecologists (*now see* DRCOG)
DoE Department of the Environment
DoH Department of Health
DoI Department of Industry
DOMS Diploma in Ophthalmic Medicine and Surgery
DOR Director of Operational Requirements
DPA Diploma in Public Administration; Discharged Prisoners' Aid; Doctor of Public Administration
DPh Doctor of Philosophy
DPH Diploma in Public Health
DPhil Doctor of Philosophy
DPM Diploma in Psychological Medicine; Diploma in Personnel Management
DPP Director of Public Prosecutions
DPS Director of Postal Services; Director of Personal Services; Doctor of Public Service; Diploma in Pastoral Studies
Dr Doctor
DRA Defence Research Agency (later DERA)
DRCOG Diploma of Royal College of Obstetricians and Gynaecologists
DS Directing Staff; Doctor of Science
DSA Diploma in Social Administration
DSAC Defence Scientific Advisory Council
DSAO Diplomatic Service Administration Office
DSc Doctor of Science
DSC Distinguished Service Cross
DSc(Eng) Doctor of Engineering Science
DSIR Department of Scientific and Industrial Research (later SRC; then SERC)
DSM Distinguished Service Medal
DSO Companion of the Distinguished Service Order
DSocSc Doctor of Social Science
DSS Department of Social Security; Doctor of Sacred Scripture
DSSc Doctor of Social Science
DStJ Dame of Grace, Most Venerable Order of the Hospital of St John of Jerusalem; Dame of Justice, Most Venerable Order of the Hospital of St John of Jerusalem
DTA Diploma in Tropical Agriculture
DTech Doctor of Technology
DTh or **DTheol** Doctor of Theology
DThPT Diploma in Theory and Practice of Teaching
DTI Department of Trade and Industry
DTLR Department for Transport, Local Government and the Regions
DTM&H Diploma in Tropical Medicine and Hygiene
DU Honorary Doctor of the University
Dunelm *Dunelmensis* (of Durham)
DUniv Honorary Doctor of the University
DVetMed Doctor of Veterinary Medicine
DVM&S Doctor of Veterinary Medicine and Surgery
DVO Driver, Vehicle and Operator

DVSc Doctor of Veterinary Science
DWP Department for Work and Pensions

E

e eldest
E East; Earl; England; E-mail
EA Environment Agency
EAA Edinburgh Architectural Association
EBC English Benedictine Congregation
EBRD European Bank for Reconstruction and Development
EBU European Broadcasting Union
EC Etoile du Courage (Canada); European Community; European Commission; Emergency Commission
ECAFE Economic Commission for Asia and the Far East
ECCTIS Education Courses and Credit Transfer Information Systems
ECE Economic Commission for Europe
ECGD Export Credits Guarantee Department
ECHR European Court of Human Rights
ECSC European Coal and Steel Community
ed edited
ED Efficiency Decoration; Doctor of Engineering (US); European Democrat
EdB Bachelor of Education
EDC Economic Development Committee
EDG European Democratic Group; Employment Department Group
Edin. Edinburgh
Edn Edition
Educ Educated
Educn Education
EEC European Economic Community (*now see* EC); Commission of the European Communities
EEF Engineering Employers' Federation; Egyptian Expeditionary Force
EETS Early English Text Society
EFTA European Free Trade Association
EIB European Investment Bank
E-in-C Engineer-in-Chief
EIS Educational Institute of Scotland
EIU Economist Intelligence Unit
ELBS English Language Book Society
EMBL European Molecular Biology Laboratory
EMBO European Molecular Biology Organisation
EMI European Monetary Institute
Eng. England
Engr Engineer
ENO English National Opera
ENSA Entertainments National Service Association
ENT Ear Nose and Throat
EO Executive Officer
EP European Parliament
EPP European People's Party
EPSRC Engineering and Physical Sciences Research Council
ER Eastern Region (BR); East Riding
ERA Electrical Research Association
ERD Emergency Reserve Decoration (Army)
ESA European Space Agency
ESART Environmental Services Association Research Trust
ESCP-EAP Ecole Supérieure de Commerce de Paris-Ecole des Affaires de Paris
ESF European Science Foundation
ESL English as a Second Language
ESRC Economic and Social Research Council; Electricity Supply Research Council
ESU English-Speaking Union
ETA Engineering Training Authority
ETH Eidgenössische Technische Hochschule
ETUC European Trade Union Confederation
EU European Union
Euratom European Atomic Energy Community
EurChem European Chemist
EUROM European Federation for Optics and Precision Mechanics
Ext Extinct; external

F

FA Football Association
FAA Fellow, Australian Academy of Science; Fleet Air Arm
FAAAS Fellow, American Association for the Advancement of Science
FABE Fellow, Association of Building Engineers
FACC Fellow, American College of Cardiology
FACD Fellow, American College of Dentistry
FACE Fellow, Australian College of Educators (*formerly* of Education)
FACM Fellow, Associaton of Computing Machinery
FACOG Fellow, American College of Obstetricians and Gynæcologists
FACP Fellow, American College of Physicians
FACR Fellow, American College of Radiology
FACRM Fellow, Australian College of Rehabilitation Medicine
FACS Fellow, American College of Surgeons
FAHA Fellow, Australian Academy of the Humanities; Fellow, American Heart Association
FAI Fellow, Chartered Auctioneers' and Estate Agents' Institute (*now* (after amalgamation) *see* FRICS); Fédération Aéronautique Internationale
FAIA Fellow, American Institute of Architects; Fellow, Association of International Accountants
FAIAA Fellow, American Institute of Aeronautics and Astronautics
FAIB Fellow, Australian Institute of Bankers
FAICD Fellow, Australian Institute of Company Directors
FAIM Fellow, Australian Institute of Management
FAIP Fellow, Australian Institute of Physics
FAMI Fellow, Australian Marketing Institute
FAMINZ(Arb) Fellow, Arbitrators and Mediators Institute of New Zealand
FANY First Aid Nursing Yeomanry
FAO Food and Agriculture Organization of the United Nations
FAOrthA Fellow, Australian Orthopaedic Association
FAPA Fellow, American Psychiatric Association
FAPM Fellow, Association for Project Management (*formerly* of Project Managers)
FARELF Far East Land Forces
FASA Fellow, Australian Society of Accountants (*now see* FCPA)
fasc. fascicule
FASME Fellow, American Society of Mechanical Engineers
FASSA Fellow, Academy of the Social Sciences in Australia
FAusIMM Fellow, Australasian Institute of Mining and Metallurgy
FAWT Farm Animal Welfare Trust
FBA Fellow, British Academy; Federation of British Artists
FBC Fellow, Birmingham Conservatoire
FBCS Fellow, British Computer Society
FBEng Fellow, Association of Building Engineers
FBHA Fellow, British Hospitality Association

FBHI Fellow, British Horological Institute
FBI Federation of British Industries (*now see* CBI); Federal Bureau of Investigation
FBIDST Fellow, British Institute of Dental and Surgical Technologists
FBIM Fellow, British Institute of Management (later FIMgt)
FBIPP Fellow, British Institute of Professional Photography
FBNA Fellow, British Naturalists' Association
FBOA Fellow, British Optical Association
FBPsS Fellow, British Psychological Society
FBS Fellow, Building Societies Institute (later FCBSI; *now see* FCIB)
FBSM Fellow, Birmingham School of Music (*now see* FBC)
FC Football Club
FCA Fellow, Institute of Chartered Accountants; Fellow, Institute of Chartered Accountants in Australia; Fellow, New Zealand Society of Accountants; Federation of Canadian Artists
FCAM Fellow, CAM Foundation
FCBSI Fellow, Chartered Building Societies Institute (merged with Chartered Institute of Bankers; *now see* FCIB)
FCCA Fellow, Chartered Association of Certified Accountants
FCCP Fellow, American College of Chest Physicians
FCGI Fellow, City and Guilds of London Institute
FCIArb Fellow, Chartered Institute of Arbitrators
FCIB Fellow, Corporation of Insurance Brokers; Fellow, Chartered Institute of Bankers
FCIBS Fellow, Chartered Institution of Building Services; Fellow, Chartered Institute of Bankers in Scotland
FCIC Fellow, Chemical Institute of Canada (*formerly* Canadian Institute of Chemistry)
FCIHT Fellow, Chartered Institution of Highways & Transportation
FCIL Fellow, Chartered Institute of Linguists
FCILA Fellow, Chartered Institute of Loss Adjusters
FCILT Chartered Fellow, Chartered Institute of Logistics and Transport
FCIM Fellow, Chartered Institute of Marketing; Fellow, Institute of Corporate Managers (Australia)
FCIOB Fellow, Chartered Institute of Building
FCIPD Fellow, Chartered Institute of Personnel and Development
FCIPR Fellow, Chartered Institute of Public Relations
FCIPS Fellow, Chartered Institute of Purchasing and Supply
FCIS Fellow, Institute of Chartered Secretaries and Administrators (*formerly* Chartered Institute of Secretaries)
FCIT Fellow, Chartered Institute of Transport (*now see* FCILT)
FCIWEM Fellow, Chartered Institution of Water and Environmental Management
FCLIP Fellow, Chartered Institute of Library and Information Professionals
FCMA Fellow, Chartered Institute of Management Accountants (*formerly* Institute of Cost and Management Accountants); Fellow, Communications Management Association
FCMI Fellow, Chartered Management Institute
FCNA Fellow, College of Nursing, Australia
FCO Foreign and Commonwealth Office
FCollP Fellow, College of Preceptors
FCOphth Fellow, College of Ophthalmologists (*now see* FRCOphth)
FCOptom Fellow, College of Optometrists
FCP Fellow, College of Preceptors
FCPA Fellow, Australian Society of Certified Practising Accountants
FCPS Fellow, College of Physicians and Surgeons
FCQI Fellow, Chartered Quality Institute
FCSD Fellow, Chartered Society of Designers
FCSI Fellow, Chartered Institute for Securities & Investment
FCSM Fellow, Cambridge School of Music
FCSSA Fellow, College of Surgeons, South Africa
FCS(SoAf) Fellow, College of Surgeons, South Africa
FD Doctor of Philosophy
FDS Fellow in Dental Surgery
FDSRCS Fellow in Dental Surgery, Royal College of Surgeons of England
FDSRCSE Fellow in Dental Surgery, Royal College of Surgeons of Edinburgh
FE Far East; Further Education
FEA Fellow, English Association
FEAF Far East Air Force
FEANI Fédération Européenne d'Associations Nationales d'Ingénieurs
FEBS Federation of European Biochemical Societies; Fellow, European Board of Surgery
FEFC or **FEFCE** Further Education Funding Council for England
FEI Fédération Equestre Internationale; Fellow, Energy Institute
FEIS Fellow, Educational Institute of Scotland
FEng Fellow, Royal Academy (*formerly* Fellowship) of Engineering (*now see* FREng)
FESC Fellow, European Society of Cardiology
FF Fianna Fáil; Field Force
FFA Fellow, Faculty of Actuaries (in Scotland); Fellow, Institute of Financial Accountants
FFAEM Fellow, Faculty of Accident and Emergency Medicine
FFARCS Fellow, Faculty of Anaesthetists, Royal College of Surgeons of England (*now see* FRCA)
FFARCSI Fellow, Faculty of Anaesthetists, Royal College of Surgeons in Ireland
FFB Fellow, Faculty of Building
FFCM Fellow, Faculty of Community Medicine (*now see* FFPH); Fellow, Faculty of Church Music
FFCS Founding Fellow, Contemporary Scotland
FFFP Fellow, Faculty of Family Planning & Reproductive Health Care of the Royal College of Obstetricians and Gynaecologists (*now see* FFSRH)
FFOM Fellow, Faculty of Occupational Medicine
FFPH Fellow, Faculty of Public Health
FFPHM Fellow, Faculty of Public Health Medicine (*now see* FFPH)
FFPM Fellow, Faculty of Pharmaceutical Medicine
FFSRH Fellow, Faculty of Sexual and Reproductive Healthcare of the Royal College of Obstetricians and Gynaecologists
FFSSoc Fellow, Forensic Science Society
FG Fine Gael
FGA Fellow, Gemmological Association
FGCM Fellow, Guild of Church Musicians
FGS Fellow, Geological Society; Fellow, Guildhall School of Music and Drama
FGSM Fellow, Guildhall School of Music and Drama (*now see* FGS)
FHCIMA Fellow, Hotel Catering and International (formerly Institutional) Management Association (*now see* FIH)
FHEA Fellow, Higher Education Academy
FHKCP Fellow, Hong Kong College of Physicians
FHKIE Fellow, Hong Kong Institution of Engineers
FHSA Family Health Services Authority

FHSM Fellow, Institute of Health Services Management
FIA Fellow, Institute and Faculty of Actuaries (formerly Institute of Actuaries)
FIAAS Fellow, Institute of Australian Agricultural Science
FIAE Fellow, Irish Academy of Engineering
FIAL Fellow, International Institute of Arts and Letters
FIAM Fellow, International Academy of Management
FIAS Fellow, Institute of Aeronautical Sciences (US) (*now see* FAIAA)
FIASc Fellow, Indian Academy of Sciences
FIB Fellow, Institute of Bankers (*now see* FCIB)
FIBiol Fellow, Institute of Biology (later FSB, *now see* FRSB)
FIBMS Fellow, Institute of Biomedical Sciences
FIC Fellow, Institute of Chemistry (then FRIC; *now see* FRSC); Fellow, Imperial College, London; Fellow, Institute of Consulting
FICA Fellow, Commonwealth Institute of Accountants; Fellow, Institute of Chartered Accountants in England and Wales (*now see* FCA)
FICD Fellow, Institute of Civil Defence; Fellow, Indian College of Dentists; Fellow, International College of Dentists
FICE Fellow, Institution of Civil Engineers
FICeram Fellow, Institute of Ceramics (later FIM)
FICFM Fellow, Institute of Charity Fundraising Managers
FICFor Fellow, Institute of Chartered Foresters
FIChemE Fellow, Institution of Chemical Engineers
FICS Fellow, Institute of Chartered Shipbrokers; Fellow, International College of Surgeons
FIEAust Fellow, Institution of Engineers, Australia
FIEE Fellow, Institution of Electrical Engineers (*now see* FIET)
FIEEE Fellow, Institute of Electrical and Electronics Engineers (NY)
FIEI Fellow, Institution of Engineering Inspection (later FIQA); Fellow, Institution of Engineers of Ireland
FIEJ Fédération Internationale des Editeurs de Journaux et Publications
FIEnvSc Fellow, Institution of Environmental Sciences
FIERE Fellow, Institution of Electronic and Radio Engineers (later FIEE)
FIES Fellow, Illuminating Engineering Society; Fellow, Institution of Engineers and Shipbuilders, Scotland
FIET Fédération Internationale des Employés, Techniciens et Cadres; Fellow, Institution of Engineering and Technology
FIFA Fédération Internationale de Football Association
FIFireE Fellow, Institution of Fire Engineers
FIFP Fellow, Institute of Freight Professionals
FIFST Fellow, Institute of Food Science and Technology
FIGasE Fellow, Institution of Gas Engineers (*now see* FIGEM)
FIGD Fellow, Institute of Grocery Distribution
FIGEM Fellow, Institution of Gas Engineers and Managers
FIH Fellow, Institute of Housing; Fellow, Institute of the Horse; Fellow, Institute of Hospitality
FIHE Fellow, Institute of Health Education
FIHort Fellow, Institute of Horticulture
FIHT Fellow, Institution of Highways & Transportation (*now see* FCIHT)
FIIE Fellow, Institution of Incorporated Engineers in Electronic, Electrical and Mechanical Engineering (*now see* FIET)
FIIM Fellow, Institution of Industrial Managers
FIInfSc Fellow, Institute of Information Scientists (*now see* FCLIP)
FIIP Fellow, Institute of Incorporated Photographers (*now see* FBIPP)
FIL Fellow, Institute of Linguists (*now see* FCIL)
FILT Fellow, Institute of Logistics and Transport (*now see* FCILT)
FIM Fellow, Institute of Materials (*formerly* Institution of Metallurgists, then Institute of Metals) (*now see* FIMMM)
FIMA Fellow, Institute of Mathematics and its Applications
FIMarE Fellow, Institute of Marine Engineers (*now see* FIMarEST)
FIMarEST Fellow, Institute of Marine Engineering, Science and Technology
FIMBRA Financial Intermediaries, Managers and Brokers Regulatory Association
FIMC Fellow, Institute of Management Consultants
FIMechE Fellow, Institution of Mechanical Engineers
FIMgt Fellow, Institute of Management (*now see* FCMI)
FIMH Fellow, Institute of Materials Handling; Fellow, Institute of Military History
FIMI Fellow, Institute of the Motor Industry
FIMinE Fellow, Institution of Mining Engineers
FIMLS Fellow, Institute of Medical Laboratory Sciences (*now see* FIBMS)
FIMMM Fellow, Institute of Materials, Minerals and Mining
FIMS Fellow, Institute of Mathematical Statistics
FInstAM Fellow, Institute of Administrative Management
FInstBiol Fellow, Institute of Biology (later FIBiol)
FInstD Fellow, Institute of Directors
FInstE Fellow, Institute of Energy (*now see* FEI)
FInstM Fellow, Institute of Meat; Fellow, Institute of Marketing (*now see* FCIM)
FInstMC Fellow, Institute of Measurement and Control
FInstP Fellow, Institute of Physics
FInstPet Fellow, Institute of Petroleum (*now see* FEI)
FInstPS Fellow, Institute of Purchasing and Supply (*now see* FCIPS)
FInstTT Fellow, Institute of Travel & Tourism
FINucE Fellow, Institution of Nuclear Engineers
FIOB Fellow, Institute of Building (*now see* FCIOB)
FIPA Fellow, Institute of Practitioners in Advertising; Fellow, Insolvency Practitioners Association
FIPD Fellow, Institute of Personnel and Development (*now see* FCIPD)
FIPEM Fellow, Institute of Physics and Engineering in Medicine
FIPENZ Fellow, Institution of Professional Engineers, New Zealand
FIPM Fellow, Institute of Personnel Management (later FIPD)
FIPR Fellow, Institute of Public Relations (*now see* FCIPR)
FIProdE Fellow, Institution of Production Engineers
FIPSM Fellow, Institute of Physical Sciences in Medicine (*now see* FIPEM)
FIQA Fellow, Institute of Quality Assurance (*now see* FCQI)
FIRM Fellow, Institute of Risk Management
FIRSE Fellow, Institute of Railway Signalling Engineers
FISITA Fédération Internationale des Sociétés d'Ingénieurs des Techniques de l'Automobile
FISTC Fellow, Institute of Scientific and Technical Communicators
FIStructE Fellow, Institution of Structural Engineers

FITD Fellow, Institute of Training and Development (later FIPD)
FIWE Fellow, Institution of Water Engineers
FIWEM Fellow, Institution of Water and Environmental Management (*now see* FCIWEM)
FIWM Fellow, Institution of Works Managers (*now see* FIIM); Fellow, Institute of Wastes Management
FIWSc Fellow, Institute of Wood Science
FJI Fellow, Institute of Journalists
FKC Fellow, King's College London
FL Florida (postal)
Fla Florida
FLA Fellow, Library Association (*now see* FCLIP)
FLAS Fellow, Chartered Land Agents' Society (*now* (after amalgamation) *see* FRICS)
FLCM Fellow, London College of Music
FLI Fellow, Landscape Institute
FLS Fellow, Linnean Society
FLSW Fellow, Learned Society of Wales
Flt Flight
FM Field-Marshal
FMA Fellow, Museums Association
FMedSci Fellow, Academy of Medical Sciences
FMI Foundation for Manufacturing and Industry
FNA Fellow, Indian National Science Academy
FNECInst Fellow, North East Coast Institution of Engineers and Shipbuilders
FNI Fellow, Nautical Institute; Fellow, National Institute of Sciences in India (*now see* FNA)
FNZIE Fellow, New Zealand Institution of Engineers (*now see* FIPENZ)
FNZIM Fellow, New Zealand Institute of Management
FO Foreign Office (*now see* FCO); Field Officer; Flag Officer; Flying Officer
FODC Franciscan Order of the Divine Compassion
FONAC Flag Officer, Naval Air Command
FOR Fellowship of Operational Research
For. Foreign
FPA Family Planning Association
FPC Family Practitioner Committee (later FHSA); Financial Planning Certificate
FPS Fellow, Pharmaceutical Society (*now also* FRPharmS); Fauna Preservation Society
FRA Fellow, Royal Academy
FRACGP Fellow, Royal Australian College of General Practitioners
FRACI Fellow, Royal Australian Chemical Institute
FRACMA Fellow, Royal Australian College of Medical Administrators
FRACOG Fellow, Royal Australian College of Obstetricians and Gynaecologists
FRACP Fellow, Royal Australasian College of Physicians
FRACS Fellow, Royal Australasian College of Surgeons
FRAD Fellow, Royal Academy of Dancing
FRAeS Fellow, Royal Aeronautical Society
FRAgS Fellow, Royal Agricultural Societies (*ie* of England, Scotland and Wales)
FRAI Fellow, Royal Anthropological Institute of Great Britain & Ireland
FRAIA Fellow, Royal Australian Institute of Architects
FRAIC Fellow, Royal Architectural Institute of Canada
FRAIPA Fellow, Royal Australian Institute of Public Administration
FRAM Fellow, Royal Academy of Music
FRAPI Fellow, Royal Australian Planning Institute
FRAS Fellow, Royal Astronomical Society; Fellow, Royal Asiatic Society
FRASE Fellow, Royal Agricultural Society of England
FRBS Fellow, Royal Society of British Sculptors; Fellow, Royal Botanic Society
FRCA Fellow, Royal College of Art; Fellow, Royal College of Anaesthetists
FRCCO Fellow, Royal Canadian College of Organists
FRCEM Fellow, Royal College of Emergency Medicine
FRCGP Fellow, Royal College of General Practitioners
FRCM Fellow, Royal College of Music
FRCN Fellow, Royal College of Nursing
FRCO Fellow, Royal College of Organists
FRCO(CHM) Fellow, Royal College of Organists with Diploma in Choir Training
FRCOG Fellow, Royal College of Obstetricians and Gynaecologists
FRCOphth Fellow, Royal College of Ophthalmologists
FRCP Fellow, Royal College of Physicians, London
FRCPA Fellow, Royal College of Pathologists of Australasia
FRCPath Fellow, Royal College of Pathologists
FRCPC Fellow, Royal College of Physicians of Canada
FRCPCH Fellow, Royal College of Paediatrics and Child Health
FRCPE or **FRCPEd** Fellow, Royal College of Physicians Edinburgh
FRCPGlas Fellow, Royal College of Physicians and Surgeons of Glasgow
FRCPI Fellow, Royal College of Physicians of Ireland
FRCPSGlas Hon. Fellow, Royal College of Physicians and Surgeons of Glasgow
FRCPsych Fellow, Royal College of Psychiatrists
FRCR Fellow, Royal College of Radiologists
FRCS Fellow, Royal College of Surgeons of England
FRCSCan Fellow, Royal College of Surgeons of Canada
FRCSE or **FRCSEd** Fellow, Royal College of Surgeons of Edinburgh
FRCSGlas Fellow, Royal College of Physicians and Surgeons of Glasgow
FRCSI Fellow, Royal College of Surgeons in Ireland
FRCVS Fellow, Royal College of Veterinary Surgeons
FREconS Fellow, Royal Economic Society
FREng Fellow, Royal Academy of Engineering
FRES Fellow, Royal Entomological Society of London
FRFPSG Fellow, Royal Faculty of Physicians and Surgeons, Glasgow (*now see* FRCPGlas)
FRG Federal Republic of Germany
FRGS Fellow, Royal Geographical Society
FRHistS Fellow, Royal Historical Society
FRHS Fellow, Royal Horticultural Society
FRIAS Fellow, Royal Incorporation of Architects of Scotland; Royal Institute for the Advancement of Science
FRIBA Fellow, Royal Institute of British Architects (*and see* RIBA)
FRIC Fellow, Royal Institute of Chemistry (*now see* FRSC)
FRICS Fellow, Royal Institution of Chartered Surveyors
FRIN Fellow, Royal Institute of Navigation
FRINA Fellow, Royal Institution of Naval Architects
FRIPA Fellow, Royal Institute of Public Administration (the Institute no longer has Fellows)
FRIPHH Fellow, Royal Institute of Public Health and Hygiene (*now see* FRSPH)
FRMCM Fellow, Royal Manchester College of Music
FRMetS Fellow, Royal Meteorological Society

FRMIA Fellow, Retail Management Institute of Australia
FRNCM Fellow, Royal Northern College of Music
FRNS Fellow, Royal Numismatic Society
FRPharmS Fellow, Royal Pharmaceutical Society
FRPS Fellow, Royal Photographic Society
FRPSL Fellow, Royal Philatelic Society, London
FRS Fellow, Royal Society
FRSA Fellow, Royal Society of Arts
FRSAI Fellow, Royal Society of Antiquaries of Ireland
FRSAMD Fellow, Royal Scottish Academy of Music and Drama
FRSB Fellow, Royal Society of Biology
FRSC Fellow, Royal Society of Canada; Fellow, Royal Society of Chemistry
FRS(Can) Fellow, Royal Society of Canada (used when a person is also a Fellow of the Royal Society of Chemistry)
FRSCM Hon. Fellow, Royal School of Church Music
FRSE Fellow, Royal Society of Edinburgh
FRSGS Fellow, Royal Scottish Geographical Society
FRSH Fellow, Royal Society for the Promotion of Health (*now see* FRSPH)
FRSL Fellow, Royal Society of Literature
FRSN Fellow, Royal Society of New South Wales
FRSNZ Fellow, Royal Society of New Zealand
FRSocMed Fellow, Royal Society of Medicine
FRSPH Fellow, Royal Society for Public Health
FRSSAf Fellow, Royal Society of South Africa
FRSTM&H Fellow, Royal Society of Tropical Medicine and Hygiene
FRTPI Fellow, Royal Town Planning Institute
FRTS Fellow, Royal Television Society
FRWCMD Fellow, Royal Welsh College of Music and Drama
FS Field Security
FSA Fellow, Society of Antiquaries; Financial Services Authority
FSAE Fellow, Society of Automotive Engineers; Fellow, Society of Art Education
FSAScot Fellow, Society of Antiquaries of Scotland
FSASM Fellow, South Australian School of Mines
FSB Fellow, Society of Biology (*now see* FRSB)
FSCA Fellow, Society of Company and Commercial Accountants
FSDC Fellow, Society of Dyers and Colourists
FSE Fellow, Society of Engineers
FSIAD Fellow, Society of Industrial Artists and Designers (*now see* FCSD)
FSLCOG Fellow, Sri Lankan College of Obstetrics and Gynaecology
FSLTC Fellow, Society of Leather Technologists and Chemists
FSNAME Fellow, American Society of Naval Architects and Marine Engineers
FSQA Fellow, Scottish Qualifications Authority
FSRHE Fellow, Society for Research into Higher Education
FSRP Fellow, Society for Radiological Protection
FSS Fellow, Royal Statistical Society
FSTD Fellow, Society of Typographic Designers
FSVA Fellow, Incorporated Society of Valuers and Auctioneers (*now see* RICS)
FTC Flying Training Command; Full Technological Certificate, City and Guilds of London Institute
FTCL Fellow, Trinity College of Music, London
FTI Fellow, Textile Institute
FTII Fellow, Chartered Institute (*formerly* Incorporated Institute, then Institute) of Taxation
FTS Fellow, Australian Academy of Technological Sciences and Engineering (*now see* FTSE); Flying Training School; Fellow, Tourism Society
FTSE Fellow, Australian Academy of Technological Sciences and Engineering
FUCEB Fellow, University of Central England in Birmingham
FUMIST Fellow, University of Manchester Institute of Science and Technology
FVRDE Fighting Vehicles Research and Development Establishment
FWAAS Fellow, World Academy of Arts and Sciences
FWCMD Fellow, Welsh College of Music and Drama (*now see* FRWCMD)
FWeldI Fellow, Welding Institute
FZS Fellow, Zoological Society

G

Ga Georgia
GA Geologists' Association; Gaelic Athletic (Club); Georgia (postal)
GAPAN Guild of Air Pilots and Air Navigators
GATT General Agreement on Tariffs and Trade (*now* World Trade Organisation)
GB Great Britain
GBA Governing Bodies Association
GBE Knight or Dame Grand Cross, Order of the British Empire
GBM Grand Bauhinia Medal (Hong Kong)
GBS Gold Bauhinia Star (Hong Kong)
GC George Cross
GCB Knight or Dame Grand Cross, Order of the Bath
GCBS General Council of British Shipping
GCCF Grand Commander, Companion Order of Freedom (Zambia)
GCHQ Government Communications Headquarters
GCIE Knight Grand Commander, Order of the Indian Empire
GCLJ Grand Cross, Order of St Lazarus of Jerusalem
GCMG Knight or Dame Grand Cross, Order of St Michael and St George
GCSE General Certificate of Secondary Education
GCSG Knight Grand Cross, Order of St Gregory the Great
GCSI Knight Grand Commander, Order of the Star of India
GCSL Grand Cross, Order of St Lucia
GCStJ Bailiff or Dame Grand Cross, Most Venerable Order of the Hospital of St John of Jerusalem
GCVO Knight or Dame Grand Cross, Royal Victorian Order
GDBA Guide Dogs for the Blind Association
GDC General Dental Council
Gdns Gardens
GDR German Democratic Republic
GDST Girls' Day School Trust
Gen. General
Ges. Gesellschaft
GHQ General Headquarters
GLA Greater London Authority
GLC Greater London Council
Glos Gloucestershire
GM George Medal; Grand Medal (Ghana); genetically modified
GMB (Union for) General, Municipal, Boilermakers
GmbH Gesellschaft mit beschränkter Haftung
GMC General Medical Council; Guild of Memorial Craftsmen; General Management Course (Henley)

GNZM Knight or Dame Grand Companion, New Zealand Order of Merit
GOC General Officer Commanding
GOC-in-C General Officer Commanding-in-Chief
GOE General Ordination Examination
GOQ Grand Officer, National Order of Quebec
GOSK Grand Officer, Order of the Star and Key of the Indian Ocean (Mauritius)
Gov. Governor
Govt Government
Gp Group
GP General Practitioner; Grand Prix
GPDST Girls' Public Day School Trust (*now see* GDST)
GPO General Post Office
GR General Reconaissance
GS General Staff; Grammar School
GSM General Service Medal; (Member of) Guildhall School of Music and Drama
GSMD Guildhall School of Music and Drama
GSO General Staff Officer
GTCL Graduate, Trinity College of Music
GTS General Theological Seminary (New York)
GWR Great Western Railway

H

HA Historical Association; Health Authority
HAA Heavy Anti-Aircraft
HAC Honourable Artillery Company
Hants Hampshire
HAT Housing Action Trust
HBM His (or Her) Britannic Majesty (Majesty's); Humming Bird Gold Medal (Trinidad)
HCF Honorary Chaplain to the Forces
HCIMA Hotel, Catering and International (*formerly* Institutional) Management Association
HCSC Higher Command and Staff Course
HE His (or Her) Excellency; His Eminence; Higher Education
HEA Health Education Authority
HEFCE Higher Education Funding Council for England
HEFCW Higher Education Funding Council for Wales
HEQC Higher Education Quality Council
Herts Hertfordshire
HG Home Guard
HH His (or Her) Highness; His Holiness; Member, Hesketh Hubbard Art Society
HHA Historic Houses Association
HHD Doctor of Humanities (US)
HIV Human Immunodeficiency Virus
HKSAR Hong Kong Special Administrative Region
HLD Doctor of Humane Letters
HLI Highland Light Infantry
HM His (or Her) Majesty, or Majesty's
HMC Headmasters' and Headmistresses' (*formerly* Headmasters') Conference; Hospital Management Committee
HMCS His (or Her) Majesty's Canadian Ship
HMI His (or Her) Majesty's Inspector
HMMTB His (or Her) Majesty's Motor Torpedo Boat
HMNZS His (or Her) Majesty's New Zealand Ship
HMOCS His (or Her) Majesty's Overseas Civil Service
HMP His (or Her) Majesty's Prison
HMS His (or Her) Majesty's Ship
HMSO His (or Her) Majesty's Stationery Office
HNC Higher National Certificate
Hon. Honourable; Honorary
HPA Health Protection Agency
HQ Headquarters
HQA Hilali-Quaid-i-Azam (Pakistan)
HR Human Resources
HRA Horseracing Regulatory Authority
HRH His (or Her) Royal Highness
HRHA Honorary Member, Royal Hibernian Academy
HRSA Honorary Member, Royal Scottish Academy
HRSW Honorary Member, Royal Scottish Water Colour Society
HSE Health and Safety Executive
HSH His (or Her) Serene Highness
HSS Health and Social Services
Hum. Humanity; Humanities (Classics)
Hunts Huntingdonshire

I

I Island; Ireland
i/c in charge; in command
IA Indian Army; Iowa (postal)
IAC Indian Armoured Corps; Institute of Amateur Cinematographers
IAEA International Atomic Energy Agency
IAM Institute of Advanced Motorists; Institute of Aviation Medicine
IAML International Association of Music Libraries
IAS Indian Administrative Service; Institute for Advanced Studies; International Academy of Science
IATA International Air Transport Association
IAU International Astronomical Union
IBA Independent Broadcasting Authority; International Bar Association
IBG Institute of British Geographers (now part of RGS)
IBRD International Bank for Reconstruction and Development (World Bank)
IBRO International Bank Research Organisation; International Brain Research Organisation
ICA Institute of Contemporary Arts; Institute of Chartered Accountants in England and Wales (*now see* ICAEW)
ICAEW Institute of Chartered Accountants in England and Wales
ICAI Institute of Chartered Accountants in Ireland
ICAO International Civil Aviation Organization
ICC International Chamber of Commerce; International Cricket Council (*formerly* International Cricket Conference)
ICE Institution of Civil Engineers
ICED International Council for Educational Development
ICFTU International Confederation of Free Trade Unions
IChemE Institution of Chemical Engineers
ICI Imperial Chemical Industries
ICL International Computers Ltd
ICMA Institute of Cost and Management Accountants
ICOM International Council of Museums
ICOMOS International Council on Monuments and Sites
ICRC International Committee of the Red Cross
ICRF Imperial Cancer Research Fund (*now see* CRUK)
ICS Indian Civil Service
ICSID International Council of Societies of Industrial Design; International Centre for Settlement of Investment Disputes
ICSTM Imperial College of Science, Technology and Medicine, London
ICSU International Council for Science (*formerly* International Council of Scientific Unions)
ID Independence Decoration (Rhodesia); Idaho (postal)

idc completed a course at, or served for a year on the Staff of, the Imperial Defence College (*now see* rcds)
IDC Imperial Defence College (*now see* RCDS); Inter-Diocesan Certificate
IDRC International Development Research Centre
IEA Institute of Economic Affairs
IEE Institution of Electrical Engineers (*now see* IET)
IEEE Institute of Electrical and Electronics Engineers (NY)
IEEIE Institution of Electrical and Electronics Incorporated Engineers
IERE Institution of Electronic and Radio Engineers
IES Indian Educational Service; Institution of Engineers and Shipbuilders in Scotland; International Electron Paramagnetic Resonance Societ
IET Institution of Engineering and Technology
IFAD International Fund for Agricultural Development (UNO)
IFC International Finance Corporation
IFPI International Federation of the Phonographic Industry
IGasE Institution of Gas Engineers
IGU International Geographical Union; International Gas Union
IIExE Institution of Incorporated Executive Engineers
IIM Institution of Industrial Managers
IISI International Iron and Steel Institute
IISS International Institute of Strategic Studies
IL Illinois (postal)
ILEA Inner London Education Authority
Ill Illinois
ILO International Labour Office; International Labour Organisation
ILR Independent Local Radio; International Labour Review
ILT Institute for Learning and Teaching in Higher Education
IM Individual Merit
IMA International Music Association; Institute of Mathematics and its Applications
IMCO Inter-Governmental Maritime Consultative Organization (*now see* IMO)
IMechE Institution of Mechanical Engineers
IMEDE Institut pour l'Etude des Méthodes de Direction de l'Entreprise
IMF International Monetary Fund
IMGTechE Institution of Mechanical and General Technician Engineers
IMinE Institution of Mining Engineers
IMO International Maritime Organization
Imp. Imperial
IMRO Investment Management Regulatory Organisation
IMS Indian Medical Service; Institute of Management Services; International Military Staff
IMunE Institution of Municipal Engineers (now amalgamated with Institution of Civil Engineers)
IN Indian Navy; Indiana (postal)
Inc. Incorporated
Ind. Independent
Inf. Infantry
INSA Indian National Science Academy
INSEAD Institut Européen d'Administration des Affaires
Insp. Inspector
Inst. Institute
Instn Institution
InstSMM Institute of Sales and Marketing Management
INTELSAT International Telecommunications Satellite Organisation
IOC International Olympic Committee; Intergovernmental Oceanographic Commission
IOM Isle of Man; Indian Order of Merit
IOP Institute of Painters in Oil Colours
IoW Isle of Wight
IP Intellectual Property
IPC International Property Corporation
IPCS Institution of Professional Civil Servants
IPFA Member or Associate, Chartered Institute of Public Finance and Accountancy (*now see* CPFA)
IPI International Press Institute; Institute of Patentees and Inventors
IPM Institute of Personnel Management (later CIPD)
IPPR Institute for Public Policy Research
IProdE Institution of Production Engineers (later Institution of Manufacturing Engineering)
IPU Inter-Parliamentary Union
IRC Industrial Reorganization Corporation; Interdisciplinary Research Centre
IRRV (Fellow/Member of) Institute of Revenues, Rating and Valuation
Is Island(s)
ISABE International Society for Air Breathing Engines
ISC Imperial Service College, Haileybury; Indian Staff Corps; Independent Schools Council
ISCO Independent Schools Careers Organisation
ISI International Statistical Institute; Independent Schools Inspectorate
ISIS Independent Schools Information Service (*see now* ISCis)
ISM Incorporated Society of Musicians
ISO Imperial Service Order; International Organization for Standardization
IStructE Institution of Structural Engineers
ISVA Incorporated Society of Valuers and Auctioneers
IT Information Technology; Indian Territory (US)
ITA Independent Television Authority (later IBA)
ITB Industry Training Board
ITC International Trade Centre; Independent Television Commission
ITCA Independent Television Association (*formerly* Independent Television Companies Association Ltd)
ITN Independent Television News
ITO International Trade Organization
ITU International Telecommunication Union
ITV Independent Television
IUA International Union of Architects
IUC Inter-University Council for Higher Education Overseas (*now see* IUPC)
IUCN International Union for Conservation of Nature (*formerly* International Union for the Conservation of Nature and Natural Resources, then World Conservation Union)
IUGS International Union of Geological Sciences
IUPAC International Union of Pure and Applied Chemistry
IUPAP International Union of Pure and Applied Physics
IUPS International Union of Physiological Sciences
IVS International Voluntary Service
IWA Inland Waterways Association
IWM Institution of Works Managers (*now see* IIM)

J

JCD *Juris Canonici* (or *Civilis*) *Doctor* (Doctor of Canon (or Civil) Law)
JCI Junior Chamber International
JCO Joint Consultative Organisation (of AFRC, MAFF, and Department of Agriculture and Fisheries for Scotland)
JD Doctor of Jurisprudence
JDipMA Joint Diploma in Management Accounting Services
JISC Joint Information Systems Committee, Higher Education Funding Council
JMN Johan Mangku Negara (Malaysia)
JP Justice of the Peace
Jr Junior
jsdc completed a course at Joint Service Defence College
JSDC Joint Service Defence College
JSM Johan Setia Mahkota (Malaysia); Master of the Science of Jurisprudence
JSPS Japan Society for the Promotion of Science
jssc completed a course at Joint Services Staff College
JSSC Joint Services Staff College
jt or **jtly** joint, jointly
Jun. Junior

K

KAR King's African Rifles
KBE Knight Commander, Order of the British Empire
KC King's Counsel
KCB Knight Commander, Order of the Bath
KCH King's College Hospital; Knight Commander, Hanoverian Order
KCHS Knight Commander, Order of the Holy Sepulchre
KCIE Knight Commander, Order of the Indian Empire
KCL King's College London
KCLJ Knight Commander, Order of St Lazarus of Jerusalem
KCMG Knight Commander, Order of St Michael and St George
KCSG Knight Commander, Order of St Gregory the Great
KCSHS Knight Commander with Star, Order of the Holy Sepulchre
KCSI Knight Commander, Order of the Star of India
KCSJ Knight Commander, Sovereign Order of St John of Jerusalem (Knights Hospitaller)
KCVO Knight Commander, Royal Victorian Order
KG Knight, Order of the Garter
KGB Komitet Gosudarstvennoi Bezopanosti (Committee of State Security, USSR)
KHS Hon. Surgeon to the King; Knight, Order of the Holy Sepulchre
KJSJ Knight of Justice, Sovereign Order of St John of Jerusalem (Knights Hospitaller)
KLJ Knight, Order of St Lazarus of Jerusalem
KM Knight of Malta
KNZM Knight Companion, New Zealand Order of Merit
KOSB King's Own Scottish Borderers
KOYLI King's Own Yorkshire Light Infantry
KRRC King's Royal Rifle Corps
KSC Knight of St Columba
KSG Knight, Order of St Gregory the Great
KSJ Knight, Sovereign Order of St John of Jerusalem (Knights Hospitaller)
KSLI King's Shropshire Light Infantry
KStJ Knight, Most Venerable Order of the Hospital of St John of Jerusalem
Kt Knight
KT Knight, Order of the Thistle
KUOM Companion of Honour, National Order of Merit (Malta)
Ky Kentucky

L

L Liberal
La Louisiana
LA Los Angeles; Library Association; Liverpool Academy; Louisiana (postal)
LAA Light Anti-Aircraft
Lab Labour
LAMDA London Academy of Music and Dramatic Art
LAMSAC Local Authorities' Management Services and Computer Committee
Lance-Corp. Lance-Corporal
Lancs Lancashire
Lautro Life Assurance and Unit Trust Regulatory Organisation
LBC London Broadcasting Company; London Borough Council
LCAD London Certificate in Art and Design (University of London)
LCC London County Council (later GLC)
LCD Lord Chancellor's Department
LCL Licentiate of Canon Law
LDDC London Docklands Development Corporation
Ldr Leader
LDS Licentiate in Dental Surgery
LDV Local Defence Volunteers
LEA Local Education Authority
LG Lady Companion, Order of the Garter
LGA Local Government Association
LHD *Literarum Humaniorum Doctor* (Doctor of Literature)
LHSM Licentiate, Institute of Health Services Management
LI Light Infantry; Long Island
Lieut Lieutenant
LIFFE London International Financial Futures and Options Exchange
Lincs Lincolnshire
Lit. Literature; Literary
Lit.Hum. *Literae Humaniores* (Classics)
LitD or **LittD** Doctor of Literature; Doctor of Letters
LLB Bachelor of Laws
LLC Limited Liability Company
LLD Doctor of Laws
LLM Master of Laws
LLP Limited Liability Partnership
LM Licentiate in Midwifery
LMBC Lady Margaret Boat Club
LMCC Licentiate, Medical Council of Canada
LMR London Midland Region (BR)
LMRTPI Legal Member, Royal Town Planning Institute
LP Limited Partnership
LPh Licentiate in Philosophy
LPO London Philharmonic Orchestra
LPTB London Passenger Transport Board (later LTE)
LRAM Licentiate, Royal Academy of Music
LRCP Licentiate, Royal College of Physicians, London
LRCPE Licentiate, Royal College of Physicians, Edinburgh
LRCPI Licentiate, Royal College of Physicians of Ireland

LRCSE Licentiate, Royal College of Surgeons, Edinburgh
LRPS Licentiate, Royal Photographic Society
LRT London Regional Transport
LSA Licentiate, Society of Apothecaries; Licence in Agricultural Sciences
LSC Learning and Skills Council
LSE London School of Economics and Political Science
LSHTM London School of Hygiene and Tropical Medicine
LSO London Symphony Orchestra
Lt Lieutenant; Light
LTA Lawn Tennis Association
LTB London Transport Board (later LTE)
LTCL Licentiate of Trinity College of Music, London
LTE London Transport Executive (later LRT)
LTh Licentiate in Theology
LVO Lieutenant, Royal Victorian Order (*formerly* MVO (Fourth Class))
LWT London Weekend Television

M

m married
M Marquess; Member; Monsieur
MA Master of Arts; Military Assistant; Massachusetts (postal)
MACM Member, Association of Computing Machines
MAE Member, Academia Europaea
MAFF Ministry of Agriculture, Fisheries and Food
Man Manitoba
MAP Ministry of Aircraft Production
MArch Master of Architecture
MASME Member, American Society of Mechanical Engineers
Mass Massachusetts
Math. Mathematics; Mathematical
MB Medal of Bravery (Canada); Bachelor of Medicine; Manitoba (postal)
MBA Master of Business Administration
MBC Metropolitan/Municipal Borough Council
MBCS Member, British Computer Society
MBE Member, Order of the British Empire
MBIM Member, British Institute of Management (later MIMgt)
MC Military Cross; Missionaries of Charity
MCC Marylebone Cricket Club; Metropolitan County Council
MCD Master of Civic Design
MCh or **MChir** Master in Surgery
MCIArb Member, Chartered Institute of Arbitrators
MCIM Member, Chartered Institute of Marketing
MCIPR Member, Chartered Institute of Public Relations
MCIT Member, Chartered Institute of Transport
MCLIP Member, Chartered Institute of Library and Information Professionals
MCMI Member, Chartered Management Institute
MCom Master of Commerce
MCP Member of Colonial Parliament; Master of City Planning (US)
MCS Malayan Civil Service
MCSD Member, Chartered Society of Designers
MCSI Member, Chartered Institute for Securities & Investment
MCSP Member, Chartered Society of Physiotherapy
MCT Member, Association of Corporate Treasurers
Md Maryland
MD Doctor of Medicine; Military District; Maryland (postal)
MDC Metropolitan District Council
MDiv Master of Divinity
MDS Master of Dental Surgery
ME Mining Engineer; Middle East; Master of Engineering; Maine (postal); Myalgic Encephalomyelitis
MEAF Middle East Air Force
MEc Master of Economics
MEC Member of Executive Council; Middle East Command
MECAS Middle East Centre for Arab Studies
Mech. Mechanics; Mechanical
MEd Master of Education
MED Master of Environmental Design
Med. Medical
MEF Middle East Force
MEIC Member, Engineering Institute of Canada
MELF Middle East Land Forces
Mencap Royal Society for Mentally Handicapped Children and Adults
MEng Master of Engineering
MEP Member of the European Parliament
MFA Master of Fine Arts
MFCM Member, Faculty of Community Medicine (later MFPHM)
MFH Master of Foxhounds
MFOM Member, Faculty of Occupational Medicine
MFPHM Member, Faculty of Public Health Medicine
Mgr Monsignor
MHA Member of House of Assembly; Master of Health Administration
MHCIMA Member, Hotel Catering and International (*formerly* Institutional) Management Association (*now see* MIH)
MHR Member of the House of Representatives
MHSM Member, Institute of Health Services Management
MI Military Intelligence; Michigan (postal)
MIAgrE Member, Institution of Agricultural Engineers
MICE Member, Institution of Civil Engineers
Mich Michigan
MIChemE Member, Institution of Chemical Engineers
MIED Member, Institution of Engineering Designers
MIEE Member, Institution of Electrical Engineers (*now see* MIET)
MIEEE Member, Institute of Electrical and Electronics Engineers (NY)
MIES Member, Institution of Engineers and Shipbuilders, Scotland
MIET Member, Institution of Engineering and Technology (*formerly* Member, Institute of Engineers and Technicians)
MIEx Member, Institute of Export
MIFA Member, Institute of Field Archaeologists
MIFF Member, Institute of Freight Forwarders
MIH Member, Institute of Housing; Member, Institute of Hospitality
MIHT Member, Institution of Highways and Transportation
Mil. Military
MIM Member, Institute of Materials (*formerly* Institution of Metallurgists, then Institute of Metals)
MIMarE Member, Institute of Marine Engineers (*now see* MIMarEST)
MIMarEST Member, Institute of Marine Engineering, Science and Technology
MIMC Member, Institute of Management Consultants
MIMechE Member, Institution of Mechanical Engineers

MIMgt Member, Institute of Management (*see now* MCMI)
MIMinE Member, Institution of Mining Engineers
Min. Ministry
Minn Minnesota
MInstAM Member, Institute of Administrative Management
MInstCE Member, Institution of Civil Engineers (*now see* FICE)
MInstD Member, Institute of Directors
MInstM Member, Institute of Marketing (*now see* MCIM)
MInstP Member, Institute of Physics
MInstPet Member, Institute of Petroleum
MInstRE Member, Institution of Royal Engineers
MInstTA Member, Institute of Transport Administration
MInstW Member, Institute of Welding
MIPD Member, Institute of Personnel and Development
MIPlantE Member, Institution of Plant Engineers
MIPM Member, Institute of Personnel Management (later MIPD)
MIS Member, Institute of Statisticians
MISI Member, Iron and Steel Institute (later part of Metals Society)
Miss Mississippi
MIT Massachusetts Institute of Technology
MITI Member, Institute of Translation & Interpreting
MLA Member of Legislative Assembly; Modern Language Association; Master in Landscape Architecture; Museums, Libraries and Archives Council
MLC Member of Legislative Council; Meat and Livestock Commission
MLitt Master of Letters
Mlle Mademoiselle
MLO Military Liaison Officer
MLR Modern Language Review
MM Military Medal; Merchant Marine
MMA Metropolitan Museum of Art
MMB Milk Marketing Board
MMD Movement for Multi-Party Democracy
Mme Madame
MME Master of Mining Engineering
MMS Member, Institute of Management Services
MMus Master of Music
MN Merchant Navy; Minnesota (postal)
MNAS Member, National Academy of Sciences (US)
MO Medical Officer; Military Operations; Missouri (postal)
MoD Ministry of Defence
Mods Moderations (Oxford)
MOH Medical Officer(s) of Health
MOI Ministry of Information
MOM Member, Order of Merit (Malta)
MOMI Museum of the Moving Image
Mon Monmouthshire
Mont Montgomeryshire
MoT Ministry of Transport
MP Member of Parliament
MPA Master of Public Administration; Member, Parliamentary Assembly, Northern Ireland
MPBW Ministry of Public Building and Works
MPH Master of Public Health
MPhil Master of Philosophy
MPO Management and Personnel Office
MPS Member, Pharmaceutical Society (*now see* MRPharmS)
MRAC Member, Royal Agricultural College
MRAeS Member, Royal Aeronautical Society
MRC Medical Research Council
MRCA Multi-Role Combat Aircraft
MRCGP Member, Royal College of General Practitioners
MRCOG Member, Royal College of Obstetricians and Gynaecologists
MRCP Member, Royal College of Physicians, London; Member, Royal College of Physicians, United Kingdom
MRCPath Member, Royal College of Pathologists
MRCPE Member, Royal College of Physicians, Edinburgh
MRCPGlas Member, Royal College of Physicians and Surgeons of Glasgow
MRCPI Member, Royal College of Physicians of Ireland
MRCPsych Member, Royal College of Psychiatrists
MRCS Member, Royal College of Surgeons of England
MRCVS Member, Royal College of Veterinary Surgeons
MRI Magnetic Resonance Imaging; Member, Royal Institution
MRIA Member, Royal Irish Academy
MRIAI Member, Royal Institute of the Architects of Ireland
MRICS Member, Royal Institution of Chartered Surveyors
MRIN Member, Royal Institute of Navigation
MRSC Member, Royal Society of Chemistry
MRSocMed Member, Royal Society of Medicine
MRTPI Member, Royal Town Planning Institute
MS Master of Surgery; Master of Science (US); Mississippi (postal); Multiple Sclerosis; Motor Ship
MS Manuscript, Manuscripts
MSA Master of Science, Agriculture (US); Mineralogical Society of America; Motor Sports Association
MSc Master of Science
MSC Manpower Services Commission; Missionaries of the Sacred Heart
MSF (Union for) Manufacturing, Science, Finance
MSI Member, Securities Institute (later Securities & Investment Institute, *now see* MCSI)
MSIA Member, Society of Industrial Artists
MSIAD Member, Society of Industrial Artists and Designers (*now see* MCSD)
MSN Master of Science in Nursing
MSS Manuscript, Manuscripts
MSt Master of Studies
MSTD Member, Society of Typographic Designers
MSzP Magyar Szocialista Párt
Mt Mount; Mountain
MT Mechanical Transport; Montana (postal)
MTB Motor Torpedo Boat
MTCA Ministry of Transport and Civil Aviation
MTh Master of Theology
MTS Master of Theological Studies; Ministerial Training Scheme
MUniv Honorary Master of the University
MusB Bachelor of Music
MusD Doctor of Music
MV Merchant Vessel, Motor Vessel (naval)
MVEE Military Vehicles and Engineering Establishment
MVO Member, Royal Victorian Order
MW Master of Wine

N

N Nationalist; Navigating Duties; North
NA National Academician (America)
NAAFI Navy, Army and Air Force Institutes
NAAS National Agricultural Advisory Service

NAB National Advisory Body for Public Sector Higher Education
NABC-CYP National Association of Boys' Clubs - Clubs for Young People
NAC National Agriculture Centre
NACAB National Association of Citizens' Advice Bureaux
NACCB National Accreditation Council for Certification Bodies
NACETT National Advisory Council for Education and Training Targets
NACF National Art-Collections Fund
NACRO National Association for the Care and Resettlement of Offenders
NADFAS National Association of Decorative and Fine Arts Societies
NAE National Academy of Engineering
NAHAT National Association of Health Authorities and Trusts
NAMH MIND (National Association for Mental Health)
NAMMA NATO MRCA Management Agency
NAS National Academy of Sciences
NASA National Aeronautics and Space Administration (US)
NASDIM National Association of Security Dealers and Investment Managers (later FIMBRA)
NATFHE National Association of Teachers in Further and Higher Education (combining ATCDE and ATTI)
NATO North Atlantic Treaty Organisation
NATS National Air Traffic Services
NAYC Youth Clubs UK (*formerly* National Association of Youth Clubs)
NB New Brunswick; Nebraska (postal)
NBC National Book Council (later NBL); National Broadcasting Company (US)
NBL National Book League
NBPI National Board for Prices and Incomes
NC National Certificate; North Carolina
NCB National Coal Board
NCC National Computing Centre; Nature Conservancy Council; National Consumer Council
NCCI National Committee for Commonwealth Immigrants
NCD National Capital District, Papua New Guinea
NCET National Council for Educational Technology
NCH National Children's Homes
NCVCCO National Council of Voluntary Child Care Organisations
NCVO National Council for Voluntary Organisations
NCVQ National Council for Vocational Qualifications
ND North Dakota
NDA National Diploma in Agriculture
NDC National Defence College; NATO Defence College
NDD National Diploma in Dairying; National Diploma in Design
NDP New Democratic Party
NE North-east
NEAC New English Art Club
NEB National Enterprise Board
NEC National Executive Committee
NECInst North East Coast Institution of Engineers and Shipbuilders
NEDC National Economic Development Council; North East Development Council
NEDO National Economic Development Office
NEH National Endowment for the Humanities
NERC Natural Environment Research Council
NESTA National Endowment for Science, Technology and the Arts
NFC National Freight Consortium (*formerly* Corporation, then Company)
NFER National Foundation for Educational Research
NFHA National Federation of Housing Associations
NFS National Fire Service
NFT National Film Theatre
NFU National Farmers' Union
NFWI National Federation of Women's Institutes
NH New Hampshire
NHBC National House-Building Council
NHS National Health Service
NI Northern Ireland; Native Infantry
NICG Nationalised Industries Chairmen's Group
NIESR National Institute of Economic and Social Research
NIH National Institutes of Health (US)
NIHR National Institute of Health Research
NIMR National Institute for Medical Research
NJ New Jersey
NL National Liberal; No Liability; Newfoundland and Labrador
NM New Mexico (postal)
NMC Nursing and Midwifery Council
NNOM Nigerian National Order of Merit
NO Navigating Officer
Northants Northamptonshire
Notts Nottinghamshire
NP Notary Public
NPA Newspaper Publishers' Association
NPG National Portrait Gallery
NPL National Physical Laboratory
NRA National Rifle Association; National Recovery Administration (US); National Rivers Authority
NRDC National Research Development Corporation
NS Nova Scotia; New Style in the Calendar (in Great Britain since 1752); National Society; National Service
NSF National Science Foundation (US)
NSM Non-Stipendiary Minister
NSPCC National Society for Prevention of Cruelty to Children
NSW New South Wales
NT New Testament; Northern Territory (Australia); Northwest Territories (Canada); National Theatre; National Trust
NTO National Training Organisation
NUBE National Union of Bank Employees
NUI National University of Ireland
NUJ National Union of Journalists
NUM National Union of Mineworkers
NUR National Union of Railwaymen (*now see* RMT)
NUS National Union of Students; National University of Singapore
NUT National Union of Teachers
NUU New University of Ulster
NV Nevada (postal)
NW North-west
NWFP North-West Frontier Province
NWT North-Western Territories
NY New York
NYC New York City
NYO National Youth Orchestra
NYT National Youth Theatre
NZ New Zealand
NZTF New Zealand Territorial Force

O

o only
OAM Medal of the Order of Australia
OAS Organisation of American States; On Active Service
OBE Officer, Order of the British Empire
OC Officer, Order of Canada (equivalent to former award SM)
OC Officer Commanding
OCC Order of the Caribbean Community
OCF Officiating Chaplain to the Forces
OCS Officer Candidates School; Officer Cadet School
OCTU Officer Cadet Training Unit
OCU Operational Conversion Unit
ODA Overseas Development Administration
ODI Overseas Development Institute
ODM Ministry of Overseas Development
OECD Organization for Economic Co-operation and Development
OEEC Organization for European Economic Co-operation (*now see* OECD)
OF Order of the Founder, Salvation Army
OFMConv Order of Friars Minor Conventual (Franciscans)
OFR Order of the Federal Republic of Nigeria
OGS Oratory of the Good Shepherd
OH Ohio (postal)
OJ Order of Jamaica
OLM Officer, Legion of Merit (Rhodesia); Ordained Local Minister
OM Order of Merit; Order of Manitoba
ON Order of the Nation (Jamaica); Ontario (postal)
OND Ordinary National Diploma
Ont Ontario
ONZ Order of New Zealand
ONZM Officer, New Zealand Order of Merit
OOnt Order of Ontario
OP *Ordinis Praedicatorum* (of the Order of Preachers (Dominican)); Observation Post
OPS Office of Public Service
OQ Officer, National Order of Quebec
ORGALIME Organisme de Liaison des Industries Métalliques Européennes
OSB Order of St Benedict (Benedictine)
OSCE Organisation for Security and Co-operation in Europe
OSMTH Ordo Supremus Militaris Templi Hierosolymitani (Supreme Military Order of the Temple of Jerusalem)
OSNC Orient Steam Navigation Co.
OST Office of Science and Technology
OStJ Officer, Most Venerable Order of the Hospital of St John of Jerusalem
OT Old Testament
OTC Officers' Training Corps
OU Oxford University; Open University
OUBC Oxford University Boat Club
OUDS Oxford University Dramatic Society
OUP Oxford University Press; Official Unionist Party
Oxon Oxfordshire; *Oxoniensis* (of Oxford)

P

PA Pakistan Army; Personal Assistant; Pennsylvania (postal)
P&O Peninsular and Oriental Steamship Co.
PAO Prince Albert's Own
PC Privy Counsellor; Police Constable; Perpetual Curate; Peace Commissioner (Ireland); Progressive Conservative (Canada)
PCC Parochial Church Council; Protected Cell Company (Guernsey); Private Cell Company
PCEF Polytechnic and Colleges Employers' Forum
PCFC Polytechnics and Colleges Funding Council
PCL Polytechnic of Central London
PCNZM Principal Companion, New Zealand Order of Merit
PCT Primary Care Trust
PDSA People's Dispensary for Sick Animals
PE Procurement Executive; Prince Edward Island (postal)
PEI Prince Edward Island
PEN Poets, Playwrights, Editors, Essayists, Novelists (Club)
Penn Pennsylvania
PEP Political and Economic Planning (*now see* PSI)
PES Party of European Socialists
PF Procurator-Fiscal
pfc Graduate of RAF Flying College
PGA Professional Golfers' Association
PGCA Post Graduate Certificate of Adjudication
PGCE Post Graduate Certificate of Education
PHAB Physically Handicapped & Able-bodied
PhD Doctor of Philosophy
Phil. Philology; Philological; Philosophy; Philosophical
PHLS Public Health Laboratory Service
Phys. Physical
PITCOM Parliamentary Information Technology Committee
PJK Pingkat Jasa Kebaktian (Malaysia)
PLA Port of London Authority
plc or **PLC** public limited company
PLP Parliamentary Labour Party; Progressive Liberal Party (Bahamas)
PMD Program for Management Development
PMN Panglima Mangku Negara (Malaysia)
PMO Principal Medical Officer; Princess Mary's Own
PNG Papua New Guinea
PNP People's National Party
PO Post Office
POB Presidential Order of Botswana
POUNC Post Office Users' National Council
POW Prisoner of War; Prince of Wales's
PPA Periodical Publishers Association
PPARC Particle Physics and Astronomy Research Council
PPCSD Past President, Chartered Society of Designers
PPE Philosophy, Politics and Economics
PPP Private Patients Plan; Psychology, Philosophy and Physiology
PPRA Past President, Royal Academy
PPRIBA Past President, Royal Institute of British Architects
PPRSA Past President, Royal Scottish Academy
PPRSW Past President, Royal Scottish Society of Painters in Water Colours
PPRTPI Past President, Royal Town Planning Institute
PPRWA Past President, Royal Watercolour Association
PPRWS Past President, Royal Society of Painters in Water Colours
PPS Parliamentary Private Secretary
PQ Province of Quebec
PR Public Relations; Parti républicain
PRCA Public Relations Consultants Association
Preb. Prebendary

Prep. Preparatory
Pres. President
Prin. Principal
PRO Public Relations Officer; Public Records Office
Proc. Proctor; Proceedings
Prof. Professor; Professional
PRORM Pay and Records Office, Royal Marines
ProtU Protestant Unionist Party
Prov. Provost; Provincial
PRS President, Royal Society; Performing Right Society Ltd
PRSW President, Royal Scottish Water Colour Society
psa Graduate of RAF Staff College
PSA Property Services Agency; Petty Sessions Area
psc Graduate of Staff College († indicates Graduate of Senior Wing Staff College); Personal Services Company
PSD Petty Sessional Division; Social Democratic Party (Portugal); Panglima Setia Diraja
PSI Policy Studies Institute
PSM Panglima Setia Mahkota (Malaysia)
PSO Principal Scientific Officer; Personal Staff Officer
PTA Passenger Transport Authority; Parent-Teacher Association
PTC Personnel and Training Command
ptsc passed Technical Staff College
Pty Proprietary
PWO Prince of Wales's Own
PYBT Prince's Youth Business Trust

Q

Q Queen
QARNNS Queen Alexandra's Royal Naval Nursing Service
QBD Queen's Bench Division
QC Queen's Counsel; Quebec (postal)
QCA Qualifications and Curriculum Authority
QCB Queen's Commendation for Bravery
QEH Queen Elizabeth Hall
QFSM Queen's Fire Service Medal for Distinguished Service
QHC Honorary Chaplain to the Queen
QHDS Honorary Dental Surgeon to the Queen
QHNS Honorary Nursing Sister to the Queen
QHP Honorary Physician to the Queen
QHS Honorary Surgeon to the Queen
Qld Queensland
Qly Quarterly
QMC Queen Mary College, London
QMG Quartermaster-General
QMUL Queen Mary, University of London
QMW Queen Mary and Westfield College, London (*now see* QMUL)
QO Qualified Officer
QOY Queen's Own Yeomanry
QPM Queen's Police Medal
QS Quarter Sessions; Quantity Surveying
QSO Queen's Service Order (NZ)
QUB Queen's University, Belfast

R

RA Royal Academician; Royal Academy; Royal (Regiment of) Artillery
RAAF Royal Australian Air Force
RAAMC Royal Australian Army Medical Corps
RAC Royal Automobile Club; Royal Agricultural College; Royal Armoured Corps
RACI Royal Australian Chemical Institute
RACP Royal Australasian College of Physicians
RACS Royal Australasian College of Surgeons; Royal Arsenal Co-operative Society
RAD Royal Academy of Dance
RADA Royal Academy of Dramatic Art
RADC Royal Army Dental Corps
RAE Royal Australian Engineers; Royal Aerospace Establishment (*formerly* Royal Aircraft Establishment); Research Assessment Exercise
RAEC Royal Army Educational Corps
RAEng Royal Academy of Engineering
RAeS Royal Aeronautical Society
RAF Royal Air Force
RAFA Royal Air Forces Association
RAFO Reserve of Air Force Officers
RAFVR Royal Air Force Volunteer Reserve
RAI Royal Anthropological Institute of Great Britain & Ireland; Radio Audizioni Italiane
RAM (Member of) Royal Academy of Music
RAMC Royal Army Medical Corps
RAN Royal Australian Navy
R&D Research and Development
RANR Royal Australian Naval Reserve
RANVR Royal Australian Naval Volunteer Reserve
RAOC Royal Army Ordnance Corps
RAPC Royal Army Pay Corps
RARDE Royal Armament Research and Development Establishment
RARO Regular Army Reserve of Officers
RAS Royal Astronomical Society; Royal Asiatic Society; Recruitment and Assessment Services
RASC Royal Army Service Corps (*now see* RCT)
RASE Royal Agricultural Society of England
RAU Royal Agricultural University
RAuxAF Royal Auxiliary Air Force
RBK&C Royal Borough of Kensington and Chelsea
RBL Royal British Legion
RBS Royal Society of British Sculptors
RBY Royal Bucks Yeomanry
RC Roman Catholic
RCA Member, Royal Canadian Academy of Arts; Royal College of Art; (Member of) Royal Cambrian Academy
RCAF Royal Canadian Air Force
rcds completed a course at, or served for a year on the Staff of, the Royal College of Defence Studies
RCDS Royal College of Defence Studies
RCGP Royal College of General Practitioners
RCHME Royal Commission on Historical Monuments of England
RCM (Member of) Royal College of Music
RCNC Royal Corps of Naval Constructors
RCO Royal College of Organists
RCOG Royal College of Obstetricians and Gynaecologists
RCP Royal College of Physicians, London
RCPath Royal College of Pathologists
RCPE or **RCPEd** Royal College of Physicians, Edinburgh
RCPI Royal College of Physicians of Ireland
RCPSG Royal College of Physicians and Surgeons of Glasgow
RCPsych Royal College of Psychiatrists
RCR Royal College of Radiologists
RCS Royal College of Surgeons of England; Royal Corps of Signals; Royal College of Science
RCSE or **RCSEd** Royal College of Surgeons of Edinburgh
RCSI Royal College of Surgeons in Ireland
RCT Royal Corps of Transport

RCVS Royal College of Veterinary Surgeons
Rd Road
RD Rural Dean; Royal Naval and Royal Marine Forces Reserve Decoration
RDC Rural District Council
RDI Royal Designer for Industry (Royal Society of Arts)
RE Royal Engineers; Fellow, Royal Society of Painter-Printmakers (*formerly* of Painter-Etchers and Engravers); Religious Education
REACH Retired Executives Action Clearing House
REconS Royal Economic Society
Regt Regiment
REME Royal Electrical and Mechanical Engineers
REOWS Royal Engineers Officers' Widows' Society
Res. Resigned; Reserve; Resident; Research
Rev. Reverend; Review
RFC Royal Flying Corps (*now* RAF); Rugby Football Club
RFCA Reserve Forces and Cadets Association
RFD Reserve Force Decoration
RFH Royal Festival Hall
RFU Rugby Football Union
RGI Royal Glasgow Institute of the Fine Arts
RGJ Royal Green Jackets
RGN Registered General Nurse
RGS Royal Geographical Society
RHA Royal Hibernian Academy; Royal Horse Artillery; Regional Health Authority
RHASS Royal Highland and Agricultural Society of Scotland
RHB Regional Hospital Board
RHBNC Royal Holloway and Bedford New College, London
RHC Royal Holloway College, London (later RHBNC)
RHG Royal Horse Guards
RHistS Royal Historical Society
RHR Royal Highland Regiment
RHS Royal Horticultural Society; Royal Humane Society
RI (Member of) Royal Institute of Painters in Water Colours; Rhode Island
RIA Royal Irish Academy
RIAS Royal Incorporation of Architects in Scotland
RIASC Royal Indian Army Service Corps
RIBA (Member of) Royal Institute of British Architects
RIBI Rotary International in Great Britain and Ireland
RIC Royal Irish Constabulary; Royal Institute of Chemistry (*now see* RSC)
RICS (Member of) Royal Institution of Chartered Surveyors
RIE Royal Indian Engineering (College)
RIIA Royal Institute of International Affairs
RILEM Réunion internationale des laboratoires d'essais et de recherches sur les matériaux et les constructions
RIM Royal Indian Marines
RIN Royal Indian Navy
RINA Royal Institution of Naval Architects
RIPA Royal Institute of Public Administration
RIPH Royal Institute of Public Health (*now see* RSPH)
RIPH&H Royal Institute of Public Health and Hygiene (later RIPH; *now see* RSPH)
RLSS Royal Life Saving Society
RM Royal Marines; Resident Magistrate; Registered Midwife
RMA Royal Marine Artillery; Royal Military Academy Sandhurst (*now* incorporating Royal Military Academy, Woolwich)
RMB Rural Mail Base
RMC Royal Military College Sandhurst (*now see* RMA)
RMCS Royal Military College of Science
RMetS Royal Meteorological Society
RMFVR Royal Marine Forces Volunteer Reserve
RMIT Royal Melbourne Institute of Technology
RMLI Royal Marine Light Infantry
RMO Resident Medical Officer(s)
RMP Royal Military Police
RMPA Royal Medico-Psychological Association
RMS Royal Microscopical Society; Royal Mail Steamer; Royal Society of Miniature Painters; Royal Mail Ship
RMT National Union of Rail, Maritime and Transport Workers; Registered Massage Therapist
RN Royal Navy; Royal Naval; Registered Nurse
RNAS Royal Naval Air Service
RNC Royal Naval College
RNCM (Member of) Royal Northern College of Music
RNEC Royal Naval Engineering College
RNIB Royal National Institute of Blind People (*formerly* Royal National Institute for the Blind, then Royal National Institute of the Blind)
RNID Royal National Institute for Deaf People (*formerly* Royal National Institute for the Deaf)
RNLI Royal National Life-boat Institution
RNR Royal Naval Reserve
RNSA Royal Naval Sailing Association
RNSC Royal Naval Staff College
RNT Registered Nurse Tutor; Royal National Theatre
RNVR Royal Naval Volunteer Reserve
RNVSR Royal Naval Volunteer Supplementary Reserve
RNZAF Royal New Zealand Air Force
RNZNVR Royal New Zealand Naval Volunteer Reserve
ROF Royal Ordnance Factories
RoSPA Royal Society for the Prevention of Accidents
RP (Member of) Royal Society of Portrait Painters
RPC Royal Pioneer Corps
RPF Rassemblement pour la France
RPMS Royal Postgraduate Medical School
RPO Royal Philharmonic Orchestra
RPR Rassemblement pour la République
RPSGB Royal Pharmaceutical Society of Great Britain
RRC Royal Red Cross; Rapid Reaction Corps
RRE Royal Radar Establishment
RRS Royal Research Ship
RSA Royal Scottish Academician; Royal Society of Arts; Republic of South Africa
RSAA Royal Society for Asian Affairs
RSAMD Royal Scottish Academy of Music and Drama
RSAS Royal Surgical Aid Society
RSC Royal Society of Canada; Royal Society of Chemistry; Royal Shakespeare Company
RSCM (Member of) Royal School of Church Music
RSCN Registered Sick Children's Nurse
RSE Royal Society of Edinburgh
RSGS Royal Scottish Geographical Society
RSH Royal Society for the Promotion of Health (*now see* RSPH)
RSL Royal Society of Literature; Returned Services League of Australia
RSM Royal School of Mines
RSM Royal Society of Medicine
RSO Rural Sub-Office; Railway Sub-Office; Resident Surgical Officer
RSocMed Royal Society of Medicine

RSPB Royal Society for Protection of Birds
RSPCA Royal Society for Prevention of Cruelty to Animals
RSPH Royal Society for Public Health
RSTM&H Royal Society of Tropical Medicine and Hygiene
RSW Member, Royal Scottish Society of Painters in Water Colours
RTE Radio Telefis Eireann
RTPI Royal Town Planning Institute
RTR Royal Tank Regiment
RTS Religious Tract Society; Royal Toxophilite Society; Royal Television Society
RU Rugby Union
RURAL Society for the Responsible Use of Resources in Agriculture & on the Land
RUSI Royal United Services Institute for Defence and Security Studies (*formerly* Royal United Service Institution)
RVC Royal Veterinary College
RWA (Member of) Royal West of England Academy
RWAFF Royal West African Frontier Force
RWF Royal Welch Fusiliers
RWS (Member of) Royal Society of Painters in Water Colours
RYA Royal Yachting Association

S

(S) (in Navy) Paymaster; Scotland
s son
S Succeeded; South; Saint
SA South Australia; South Africa; Société Anonyme; Society of the Atonement
SABC South African Broadcasting Corporation
SACEUR Supreme Allied Commander Europe
SACLANT Supreme Allied Commander Atlantic
SACRO Scottish Association for the Care and Resettlement of Offenders
SAE Society of Automobile Engineers (US)
Sarum Salisbury
SAS Special Air Service
Sask Saskatchewan
SASO Senior Air Staff Officer
SATRO Science and Technology Regional Organisation
SB Bachelor of Science (US)
SBAC Society of British Aerospace Companies (*formerly* Society of British Aircraft Constructors)
SBStJ Serving Brother, Most Venerable Order of the Hospital of St John of Jerusalem
sc student at the Staff College
SC Star of Courage (Canada); Senior Counsel; South Carolina
SCAA School Curriculum and Assessment Authority
ScD Doctor of Science
SCF Senior Chaplain to the Forces; Save the Children Fund
Sch. School
SCI Society of Chemical Industry
SCM State Certified Midwife; Student Christian Movement
SCOB Supreme Counsellor of Baobab (South Africa)
SCONUL Standing Conference of National and University Libraries
Scot. Scotland
SCOTVEC Scottish Vocational Education Council
SDI Strategic Defence Initiative
SDLP Social Democratic and Labour Party
SDP Social Democratic Party
SE South-east
SEAC South-East Asia Command
SEALF South-East Asia Land Forces
SEATO South-East Asia Treaty Organization
Sec. Secretary
SEP Stanford Executive Program
SEPA Scottish Environmental Protection Agency
SERC Science and Engineering Research Council
SESO Senior Equipment Staff Officer
SFA Securities and Futures Authority
SFTA Society of Film and Television Arts (*now see* BAFTA)
SG Solicitor-General
Sgt Sergeant
SHA Secondary Heads Association; Special Health Authority
SHAEF Supreme Headquarters, Allied Expeditionary Force
SHAPE Supreme Headquarters, Allied Powers, Europe
SHEFC Scottish Higher Education Funding Council
SHHD Scottish Home and Health Department
SHO Senior House Officer
SIAD Society of Industrial Artists and Designers (*now see* CSD)
SIAM Society of Industrial and Applied Mathematics (US)
SIB Shipbuilding Industry Board; Securities and Investments Board (*now see* FSA)
SICA-FICA Foundation for International Commercial Arbitration
SIMA Scientific Instrument Manufacturers' Association of Great Britain
SIS Secret Intelligence Service
SITPRO Simpler Trade Procedures Board (*formerly* Simplification of International Trade Procedures)
SJ Society of Jesus (Jesuits)
SJAB St John Ambulance Brigade
SJD Doctor of Juristic Science
SK Saskatchewan (postal)
SLAC Stanford Linear Accelerator Centre
SLC St Lucia Cross
SLS Society of Legal Scholars
SM Medal of Service (Canada) (*now see* OC); Master of Science; Officer qualified for Submarine Duties
SME School of Military Engineering
SMMT Society of Motor Manufacturers and Traders Ltd
SMN Seri Maharaja Mangku Negara (Malaysia)
SMO Senior Medical Officer; Sovereign Military Order
SMP Senior Managers' Program
SMRTB Ship and Marine Requirements Technology Board
SNAME Society of Naval Architects and Marine Engineers (US)
SNP Scottish National Party
SO Staff Officer; Scientific Officer; Symphony Orchestra
SOAS School of Oriental and African Studies
Soc. Society; Socialist (France, Belgium)
SOE Special Operations Executive; Society of Operations Engineers
SOM Society of Occupational Medicine; Saskatchewan Order of Merit (Canada)
SOSc Society of Ordained Scientists
SOTS Society for Old Testament Study
SpA Società per Azioni
SPAB Society for the Protection of Ancient Buildings
SPCA Society for the Prevention of Cruelty to Animals
SPCK Society for Promoting Christian Knowledge

SPCM Darjah Seri Paduka Cura Si Manja Kini (Malaysia)
SPD Salisbury Plain District; Sozialdemokratische Partei Deutschlands
SPMB Seri Paduka Makhota Brunei
SPMO Senior Principal Medical Officer
SPNM Society for the Promotion of New Music
SPSO Senior Principal Scientific Officer
SPTL Society of Public Teachers of Law (*now see* SLS)
sq staff qualified
Sq. Square
SQA Sitara-i-Quaid-i-Azam (Pakistan)
Sqdn or **Sqn** Squadron
SR Special Reserve; Southern Railway; Southern Region (BR)
SRC Science Research Council (later SERC); Students' Representative Council
SRHE Society for Research into Higher Education
SRN State Registered Nurse
SS Saints; Straits Settlements; Steamship
SSAFA Soldiers, Sailors, Airmen and Families Association (*formerly* Soldiers', Sailors', and Airmen's Families Association, then Soldiers, Sailors, Airmen and Families Association Forces Help)
SSC Solicitor before Supreme Court (Scotland); Sculptors Society of Canada; *Societas Sanctae Crucis* (Society of the Holy Cross); Short Service Commission
SSEB South of Scotland Electricity Board
SSEES School of Slavonic and East European Studies
SSF Society of St Francis
SSO Senior Supply Officer; Senior Scientific Officer
SSRC Social Science Research Council (*now see* ESRC)
St Street; Saint
STC Senior Training Corps
STD *Sacrae Theologiae Doctor* (Doctor of Sacred Theology)
STh Scholar in Theology
STL *Sacrae Theologiae Lector* (Reader or a Professor of Sacred Theology)
STM *Sacrae Theologiae Magister* (Master of Sacred Theology)
STSO Senior Technical Staff Officer
SUNY State University of New York
Supt Superintendent
Surg. Surgeon
SW South-west
SWET Society of West End Theatre
SWO Staff Warfare Officer

T

T Telephone; Territorial
TA Telegraphic Address; Territorial Army
TA&VRA Territorial Auxiliary and Volunteer Reserve Association (*now see* RFCA)
TAF Tactical Air Force
T&AFA Territorial and Auxiliary Forces Association
T&AVR Territorial and Army Volunteer Reserve
TARO Territorial Army Reserve of Officers
TAS Torpedo and Anti Submarine Course
TAVRA Territorial Auxiliary and Volunteer Reserve Association (*now see* RFCA)
TCD Trinity College, Dublin (University of Dublin, Trinity College)
TCPA Town and Country Planning Association
TD Territorial Efficiency Decoration; Efficiency Decoration (T&AVR) (since April 1967); Teachta Dala (Member of the Dáil, Eire)
TE Technical Engineer
TEC Technician Education Council; Training and Enterprise Council
TEFL Teaching English as a Foreign Language
TEM Territorial Efficiency Medal
TEMA Telecommunication Engineering and Manufacturing Association
Temp. Temperature; Temporary
Tenn Tennessee
TES Times Educational Supplement
TGO Timber Growers' Organisation (*now see* TGEW)
TGWU Transport and General Workers' Union
ThD Doctor of Theology
THES Times Higher Education Supplement
ThL Theological Licentiate
TLS Times Literary Supplement
TMA Theatrical Management Association
TPI Town Planning Institute (*now see* RTPI)
TQ Teaching Qualification
Trans. Translation; Translated
TRH Their Royal Highnesses
TRIC Television and Radio Industries Club
Trin. Trinity
TRRL Transport and Road Research Laboratory
TS Training Ship
TSB Trustee Savings Bank
TSSA Transport Salaried Staffs' Association
TUC Trades Union Congress
TV Television
TWA Thames Water Authority
TX Texas (postal)

U

u uncle
U Unionist
U3A University of the Third Age
UAE United Arab Emirates
UAR United Arab Republic
UBI Understanding British Industry
UC University College
UCAS Universities and Colleges Admissions Service
UCD University College Dublin
UCE University of Central England
UCET Universities Council for Education of Teachers
UCH University College Hospital (London)
UCL University College London
UCLA University of California at Los Angeles
UCNS Universities' Council for Non-academic Staff
UCNW University College of North Wales
UCRN University College of Rhodesia and Nyasaland
UCS University College School
UCSB University of California at Santa Barbara
UCSD University of California at San Diego
UCSF University of California at San Francisco
UCW University College of Wales; Union of Communication Workers
UDC Urban District Council; Urban Development Corporation
UDF Union Defence Force; Union pour la démocratie française
UDR Ulster Defence Regiment; Union des Démocrates pour la Vème République (later RPR)
UEA University of East Anglia
UFC Universities' Funding Council
UGC University Grants Committee (later UFC)
UHI University of the Highlands and Islands (*formerly* University of the Highlands and Islands Millennium Institute)

UIAA Union Internationale des Associations d'Alpinisme
UK United Kingdom
UKAEA United Kingdom Atomic Energy Authority
UKLF United Kingdom Land Forces
UKMF(L) United Kingdom Military Forces (Land)
UKMIS United Kingdom Mission
UKPIA United Kingdom Petroleum Industry Association Ltd
UMDS United Medical and Dental Schools
UMIST University of Manchester Institute of Science and Technology
UMP Union pour un Mouvement Populaire (*formerly* Union pour la Majorité Présidentielle)
UN United Nations
UNA United Nations Association
UNCAST United Nations Conference on the Applications of Science and Technology
UNCTAD United Nations Commission for Trade and Development
UNDP United Nations Development Programme
UNEP United Nations Environment Programme
Unesco or **UNESCO** United Nations Educational, Scientific and Cultural Organisation
UNHCR United Nations High Commissioner for Refugees
UNICE Union des Industries de la Communauté Européenne
UNICEF United Nations Children's Fund (*formerly* United Nations International Children's Emergency Fund)
UNIDO United Nations Industrial Development Organisation
Univ. University
UNRWA United Nations Relief and Works Agency
URC United Reformed Church; Urban Regeneration Company
URSI Union Radio-Scientifique Internationale
US United States
USA United States of America
USAAF United States Army Air Force
USAF United States Air Force
USAID United States Agency for International Development
USAR United States Army Reserve
USC University of Southern California
USN United States Navy
USNR United States Naval Reserve
USPG United Society for the Propagation of the Gospel
USS United States Ship
USSR Union of Soviet Socialist Republics
UTS University of Technology, Sydney
UU Ulster Unionist
UUK Universities UK
UUUC United Ulster Unionist Coalition
UWCC University of Wales College of Cardiff
UWE University of the West of England
UWIC University of Wales Institute, Cardiff
UWIST University of Wales Institute of Science and Technology

V

v *versus* (against)
v *vide* (see)
V Five (Roman numerals); Version; Vicar; Viscount; Vice
Va Virginia
VA Virginia (postal)
V&A Victoria and Albert
VAT Value Added Tax
VC Victoria Cross; Voluntary Controlled
VCT Venture Capital Trust
VD Royal Naval Volunteer Reserve Officers' Decoration (*now* VRD); Volunteer Officers' Decoration; Victorian Decoration
Ven. Venerable
Vet. Veterinary
VG Vicar-General
Vic Victoria
VMH Victoria Medal of Honour (Royal Horticultural Society)
Vol. Volume; Voluntary; Volunteers
VQMG Vice-Quartermaster-General
VRD Royal Naval Volunteer Reserve Officers' Decoration
VSO Voluntary Service Overseas
Vt Vermont
VT Vermont (postal)

W

W West; Website
WA Western Australia; Washington (postal)
WAAF Women's Auxiliary Air Force (later WRAF)
Wash Washington State
WCC World Council of Churches
WCMD Welsh College of Music and Drama
WDA Welsh Development Agency
WEA Workers' Educational Association; Royal West of England Academy
WEU Western European Union
WHO World Health Organization
WI West Indies; Women's Institute; Wisconsin (postal)
Wilts Wiltshire
WIPO World Intellectual Property Organization
Wis Wisconsin
Wm William
WNO Welsh National Opera
WO War Office; Warrant Officer
Worcs Worcestershire
WR West Riding; Western Region (BR)
WRAC Women's Royal Army Corps
WRAF Women's Royal Air Force
WRNS Women's Royal Naval Service
WRVS Women's Royal Voluntary Service (*now see* RVS)
WS Writer to the Signet
WSAVA World Small Animal Veterinary Association
WSPA World Society for the Protection of Animals
WTO World Trade Organisation
WV West Virginia (postal)
WVS Women's Voluntary Services (later WRVS)
WWF World Wide Fund for Nature (*formerly* World Wildlife Fund)

XY

X Ten (Roman numerals)
XO Executive Officer
y youngest
Yeo. Yeomanry
YMCA Young Men's Christian Association
Yorks Yorkshire
yr younger
yrs years
YWCA Young Women's Christian Association

ADDENDA

The following biographies are of those whose deaths occurred before 31 December 2010, but were not reported until after the volume of *Who Was Who* covering the years 2006–2010 had been published.

ALEXANDER, Rt Rev. Mervyn Alban Newman, DD; Bishop of Clifton, (RC), 1974–2001, then Bishop Emeritus; Parish Priest, St Joseph, Weston-super-Mare, 2001–07; *b* London, 29 June 1925; *s* of William Paul Alexander and Grace Evelyn Alexander (*née* Newman). *Educ:* Bishop Wordsworth School, Salisbury; Prior Park College, Bath; Gregorian University, Rome (DD 1951). Curate at Pro-Cathedral, Clifton, Bristol, 1951–63; RC Chaplain, Bristol University, 1953–67; Parish Priest, Our Lady of Lourdes, Weston-super-Mare, 1967–72; Auxiliary Bishop of Clifton and Titular Bishop of Pinhel, 1972–74; Vicar Capitular of Clifton, 1974. Hon. LLD Bristol, 2001. *Address:* St Angela's Convent, 5 Litfield Place, Bristol BS8 3LU. *T:* (0117) 973 0717. *Died 14 Aug. 2010.*

ALGOSAIBI, Dr Ghazi Abdulrahman; Minister for Labour, Saudi Arabia, since 2004; *b* 2 March 1940; *s* of Abdul Rahman and Fatma; *m* 1968, Sigrid Presser; three *s* one *d*. *Educ:* primary and secondary schs, Bahrain; Cairo Univ. (LLB 1961); Univ. of Southern California (MA Internat Relations 1964); Univ. of London (PhD 1970). King Saud University, Riyadh: Lectr, Faculty of Commerce, 1965–70, Asst Prof., 1970–74; Dean, Faculty of Commerce, and Hd, Pol Sci. Dept, 1971–73; Dir Gen., Saudi Railways, 1974–75; Minister: Industry and Electricity, 1975–82; Health, 1982–84; Ambassador to Bahrain, 1984–92, to UK and Ireland, 1992–2002; Minister for Water, 2002–04. Numerous foreign awards. *Publications:* in Arabic: A Life in Poetry, 1980; From Here and There, 1981; Arabian Essays, 1982 (also in English); In My Humble Opinion, 1983; A Hundred Rose Petals, 1986; Development Face to Face, 1989; To Return to California as a Tourist, 1990; Cultural Invasion and Other Essays, 1991; Poems I Liked, 1992; The Gulf Crisis: an attempt to understand, 1992 (also in English); Poets Followed by Sinners: who are they?, 1994; An Apartment Called Freedom (novel), 1994 (trans. English 1996); The Dilemma of Development, 1995 (also in English); A Very Hot Political Dialogue, 1996; Al Asforiya, 1996; Conciliation, Fallacies and Other Issues, 1997; The Two of Them, 1997; The Myth, 1997; Voice from the Gulf, 1997; With Nagi and With Her, 1998; The Golden Cage (play), 1998; Yes, (Saudi) Minister!: a life in administration (autobiog.), 1999 (also in English); Seven (novel), 1999 (also in English); Thursday Break, 2000; Abu Shalaq, 2000; Dansko, 2000; *poetry:* Drops of Thirst; Battle Without Flag; Love Verses; You are Riyadh; Fever; Return to Old Places; The Complete Works of Poetry, 1960; Inside a Poet's Tent, 1988; Flowers in Sana's Braids, 1989; Necklace of Stones, 1991; Obituary of a Former Knight, 1992; Lyrics from Arabia, 1993 (also in English); From the Orient and the Desert, 1994; A Hundred Jasmine Flowers, 1995; Dusting the Colour from Roses, 1995 (also in English); Souhaim, 1996; Reading London's Face, 1997; Poems from the Pearl Islands; trans. Joseph Frankel, International Relations; anthologies. *Recreations:* swimming, fishing, table tennis. *Address:* Ministry of Labour, Omar bin Al-Khatab Street, Riyadh 11157, Saudi Arabia. *Clubs:* Brooks's, Travellers, Army and Navy (Hon. Mem.). *Died 15 Aug. 2010.*

ARMSTRONG, John Archibald, (Jack), OC 1983; retired; Chief Executive Officer, 1973–82, and Chairman, 1974–82, Imperial Oil Ltd; *b* Dauphin, Manitoba, 24 March 1917; *m* June Keith (*d* 1986); three *s* one *d* (and one *s* one *d* decd). *Educ:* Univ. of Manitoba (BSc Geol.); Queen's Univ. at Kingston (BSc Chem. Engrg). Worked for short time with Geol Survey of Canada and in mining industry; joined Imperial Oil Ltd as geologist, Regina, 1940; appts as: exploration geophysicist, western Canada, and with affiliated cos in USA and S America; Asst Reg. Manager, Producing Dept, 1949; Asst Co-ordinator, Producing Dept of Standard Oil Co. (NJ), New York; Gen. Man., Imperial's Producing Dept, Toronto, 1960; Dir, 1961; Dir resp. for Marketing Ops, 1963–65; Exec. Vice-Pres., 1966, Pres. 1970, Chief Exec. Officer, 1973, Chm., 1974. Chm., Commonwealth Study Conf. Assoc. Life Mem., Fraser Inst. Hon. LLD: Winnipeg, 1978; Calgary, 1980. *Died 26 Dec. 2010.*

ASHFORD, William Stanton, OBE 1971; HM Diplomatic Service, retired; *b* 4 July 1924; *s* of Thomas and May Ashford; *m* 1957, Rosalind Anne Collett; two *s*. Served RAF, 1943–47; Air Ministry, 1948; Commonwealth Relations Office, 1961; Director of British Information Services, Sierra Leone, 1961, Ghana, 1962; Acting Consul-General, Tangier, 1965; Regional Information Officer, Bombay, 1966; Head of Chancery, British Government Office, Montreal, 1967; seconded to Northern Ireland Office, 1972; FCO, 1974; Consul-General, Adelaide, 1977; High Comr, Vanuatu, 1980–82. *Recreations:* 18th Century music, gardening. *Died 3 June 2006.*

AUNG, U Win; Minister for Foreign Affairs, Myanmar, 1998–2005; *b* 28 Feb. 1944; *m* 1972, Daw San Yone; two *s* one *d*. *Educ:* Yangon Univ. (BSc). 2nd Lieut, 1964; Major 1978; joined Foreign Service, 1985; Chargé d'Affaires: Laos, 1986–88; Singapore, 1988–90; Ambassador to Germany, 1990–96; Ambassador to the Court of St James's, 1996–98. Naing Ngan Daw Sit Smu Htan Tazeik; Pyi Thu Wun Htan Gaung Tazeik. *Publications:* Nation of the Gold and Selected Articles, 1996; articles in periodicals in Myanmar. *Recreation:* music. *Address:* c/o Ministry of Foreign Affairs, Pyay Road, Yangon, Union of Myanmar. *Died 4 Nov. 2009.*

AYERST, Rev. Edward Richard; a Chaplain to the Queen, 1987–95; *b* 21 Oct. 1925; *m* 1959, Pauline Clarke; one *s* two *d*. *Educ:* Coopers' Company's School; Leeds Univ. (BA Hons 1951); College of the Resurrection, Mirfield. Vicar of St Mary with St John, Edmonton, N18, 1960–66; Rector of East Cowes with Whippingham, IoW, 1966–77; Vicar of Bridgwater, 1977–90. Mem., Philosophical Soc., 1981. *Recreations:* sailing; helping the Sea Cadet Corps. *Address:* 56 Maple Drive, Burnham-on-Sea, Somerset TA8 1DH. *T:* (01278) 780701. *Died 2 Oct. 2009.*

BAIRD, Charles Fitz; Chairman and Chief Executive Officer, Inco Ltd, 1980–87, retired; *b* 4 Sept. 1922; *s* of George White and Julia (Fitz) Baird; *m* 1947, Norma Adele White; two *s* two *d*. *Educ:* Middlebury Coll. (BA); New York Univ. (Grad. Sch. of Bus. Admin); Harvard Univ. (Advanced Management Program). US Marine Corps, 1943–46, 1951–52 (Capt.). Standard Oil Co. (NJ), now Exxon, 1948–65: Dep. European Financial Rep., London, 1955–58; Asst Treas., 1958–62; Dir, Esso Standard SA Française, 1962–65; Asst Sec., Financial Man., US Navy, 1965–67, Under Secretary, 1967–69; Internat. Nickel Co. of Canada Ltd (Inco Ltd): Vice Pres. Finance, 1969–72, Sen. Vice Pres., 1972–76; Dir, 1974–93; Vice Chm., 1976–77; Pres., 1977–80. Director: Bank of Montreal, 1975–93; Aetna Life and Casualty Co., 1982–93. Nat. Advr, Council on Oceans and Atmosphere, 1972–74; Member: Presidential Commn on Marine Sci. Engrg and Resources, 1967–69; Council on Foreign Relations. Mem., Bd of Trustees, Bucknell Univ., 1969–95 (Chm., 1976–82); Trustee, Center for Naval Analyses, 1990–2002 (Chm.,

1992–97). Hon. LLD Bucknell Univ. 1976. US Navy Distinguished Civilian Service Award, 1969. *Recreations:* tennis, platform tennis, golf. *Clubs:* Chevy Chase (Washington, DC); Maidstone (E Hampton, NY); Bridgehampton (NY). *Died 26 Dec. 2009.*

BALL, Prof. John Geoffrey, CEng; consultant metallurgist; Professor of Physical Metallurgy, Imperial College, University of London, 1956–80, then Emeritus (Head of Metallurgy Department, 1957–79; Senior Research Fellow, 1980–86); *b* 27 Sept. 1916; *s* of late I. H. Ball and Mrs E. M. Ball; *m* 1941, Joan C. M. (*d* 2007), *d* of late Arthur Wiltshire, JP, Bournemouth. *Educ:* Wellington (Salop) High Sch.; Univ. of Birmingham. British Welding Res. Assoc., 1941–49; Sen. Metallurgist, 1945–49; AERE, Harwell, 1949–56; Head of Reactor Metallurgy, 1953–56. Min. of Tech. Visitor to British Non-Ferrous Metals Res. Assoc., 1962–72. Dean, Royal Sch. of Mines, Imperial Coll., 1962–65 and 1971–74; Dean, Faculty of Engineering, Univ. of London, 1970–74. Chairman: Res. Bd, 1964–74, and Mem. of Council Br. Welding Res. Assoc., 1964–81; Engrg Physics Sub-Cttee, Aeronautical Res. Council, 1964–68; Metallurgy Bd, CNAA, 1965–71; Metallurgy and Materials Cttee and Univ. Science and Technology Bd, SRC, 1967–70; Engrg Bd, SRC, 1969–71; Manpower Utilisation Working Party, 1967–69; Mem., Light Water Reactor Pressure Vessel Study Gp, Dept of Energy, 1974–77. Consultant on Materials, SERC, 1983–84. President: Inst. of Welding, 1965–66; Instn of Metallurgists, 1966–67 (Mem. Council 1951–56, 1958–70); Member: Council, Br. Nuclear Forum, 1964–71; Manpower Resources Cttee, 1965–68; Council, Inst. of Metals, 1965; Council, Iron and Steel Inst., 1965; Council, City Univ., 1966–90; Brain Drain Cttee, 1966–67; Public Enquiry into loss of "Sea Gem", 1967; Materials and Structures Cttee, 1967–70; Technology Sub-Cttee of UGC, 1968–73; Chartered Engineer Section Bd, CEI, 1978–83; Mem., Group IV Exec. Cttee, Engineering Council, 1983–94. Governor, Sir John Cass Coll., 1958–67. Hon. ARSM 1961. Brooker Medal, Welding Inst., 1979; Freedom of Inst. and Distinguished Service Award, Indian Inst. of Technology, Delhi, 1985. *Address:* 3 Sylvan Close, Limpsfield, Surrey RH8 0DX. *Died 14 Dec. 2010.*

BARRACK, William Sample, Jr; Senior Vice-President, Texaco Inc., NY, 1983–92; *b* 26 July 1929; *s* of William Sample Barrack and Edna Mae Henderson; *m* 1953, Evelyn Irene Ball; one *s* one *d*. *Educ:* Pittsburgh Univ. BSc (Eng) 1950. Comdr, USN, 1950–53. Joined Texaco Inc., 1953; marketing and management positions in USA, 1953–67; in Europe, 1967–71; Vice-President: in NY, 1971–80; Marketing Dept, Europe, 1971–76; Producing Dept, Eastern Hemisphere, 1976–77; Personnel and Corporate Services Dept, 1977–80; Chm. and Chief Exec., Texaco Ltd, London, 1980–82. Director: Caltex Petroleum Corp.; Texaco Foundn Inc.; Standard Commercial Corp.; Consolidated Natural Gas Corp. Governor, Foreign Policy Assoc.; Member: US Naval War College Foundn; Bd of Visitors, Univ. of Pittsburgh. Trustee, Manhattanville College. *Clubs:* Woodway Country; Ox Ridge Hunt; Ida Lewis Yacht; North Sea Yacht (Belgium); Clambake (Newport, RI); New York Yacht. *Died 17 April 2008.*

BASS, Bryan Geoffrey; Headmaster, City of London School, 1990–95; *b* 23 March 1934; *s* of Leslie Horace Bass and Mary Joyce Light; *m* 1956, Cecilia Manning; one *s* two *d*. *Educ:* Wells Cathedral School; Christ Church, Oxford (BA Hons English 1956; MA 1983). Teacher, Manchester Grammar School; Headmaster, Hymers College, Hull, 1983–90. Mem., NE London Educn Assoc., 1995–96. *Recreations:* making music, cooking with friends. *Address:* Flat 79, Putney Wharf, 25 Brewhouse Lane, Putney, SW15 2JX. *Died 23 Dec. 2010.*

BAYDA, Hon. Edward Dmytro; Chief Justice of Saskatchewan, 1981–2006; *b* 9 Sept. 1931; *s* of Dmytro Andrew Bayda and Mary Bilinski; *m* 1953, Marie-Thérèse Yvonne Gagné (decd); one *s* six *d*; *m* 2002, Lorraine Bethell. *Educ:* Univ. of Saskatchewan (BA 1951, LLB 1953). Called to the Bar, Saskatchewan, 1954; QC (Sask) 1966. Senior Partner, Bayda, Halvorson, Scheibel & Thompson, 1966–72. Judge, Court of Queen's Bench, 1972; Justice, Court of Appeal, 1974. Hon. LLD: Saskatchewan, 1989; Regina, 2006. KM 1975. *Address:* 3000 Albert Street, Regina, SK S4S 3N7, Canada. *T:* (306) 5862126. *Died 2 April 2010.*

BIRCHENOUGH, (John) Michael, BSc, PhD; Visiting Professor, School of Education, Open University, 1986–89; *b* 17 Jan. 1923; *s* of John Buckley Birchenough and Elsie Birchenough; *m* 1945, Enid Humphries; two *s*. *Educ:* Ashford Grammar Sch., Kent; Chiswick County Sch.; London Univ. Chemist, May & Baker Ltd, 1943–45; teaching posts, 1946–60; HM Inspector of Schools, 1960; Staff Inspector, 1966; Chief Inspector, 1968–72; Chief Inspector, ILEA, 1973–83; Res. Fellow, Sch. of Educn, Univ. of Bristol, 1983–86. Pres., Educn Section, BAAS Annual Meeting, Stirling, 1974. *Publications:* contribs to Jl of Chem. Soc. and other scientific jls. *Address:* 46B Sandfield Road, Arnold, Nottingham NG5 6QB. *Died 9 Sept. 2010.*

BLAIR, Prof. Gordon Purves, CBE 1995; PhD, DSc; FREng, FIMechE, FSAE; Professor of Mechanical Engineering, Queen's University of Belfast, 1976–96, then Emeritus; Senior Associate, Professor Blair and Associates, since 2002; *b* 29 April 1937; *s* of Gordon Blair and Mary Helen Jones Blair; *m* 1964, Norma Margaret Millar; two *d*. *Educ:* Queen's Univ. of Belfast (BSc; PhD 1962; DSc 1978). CEng, FIMechE 1977; FSAE 1979; FREng (FEng 1982). Asst Prof., New Mexico State Univ., 1962–64; Queen's University of Belfast: Lectr, 1964–71; Sen. Lectr, 1971–73; Reader, 1973–76; Head of Dept of Mechl and Industrial Engrg, 1982–89, and of Dept of Mechl and Manufacturing, Aeronautical and Chemical Engrg, 1987–89; Dean, Faculty of Engrg, 1985–88; Pro-Vice-Chancellor, 1989–94. Chm., Automobile Div., IMechE, 1991. *Publications:* The Basic Design of Two-Stroke Engines, USA, 1990; Design and Simulation of Two-Stroke Engines, 1996; Design and Simulation of Four-Stroke Engines, 1999; wide pubn in IMechE and SAE Jls on design and develt of internal combustion engines. *Recreations:* golf, fishing, motorcycles. *Address:* 9 Ben Madigan Park South, Newtownabbey, N Ireland BT36 7PX. *T:* (028) 9037 0368. *Clubs:* Cairndhu Golf; Royal Portrush Golf. *Died 21 Oct. 2010.*

BLAYNEY, Elizabeth Carmel, (Eily); Head of Library and Records Department and Departmental Record Officer (Assistant Secretary), Foreign and Commonwealth Office, 1977–85; *b* 19 July 1925; *d* of William Blayney, MRCS, LRCP, Medical Practitioner (previously County Inspector, RIC) of Harrold, Beds, and Mary Henrietta *d* of John Beveridge, sometime Town Clerk of Dublin. *Educ:* St Mary's Convent, Shaftesbury; The Triangle, S Molton Street. Chartered Librarian. Served War, WTS(FANY) in UK, India and Ceylon (Force 136), 1944–46. Library Asst, Hampstead Borough Libraries, 1947–50; Assistant Librarian: RSA, 1950–52; CO/CRO Jt Library, CRO, 1953; Head of Printed Library, FO, 1959–68; Librarian i/c, ODM, 1968–69; Librarian, FCO, 1969–77. *Address:* 6 Bamville Wood, East Common, Harpenden, Herts AL5 1AP. *T:* (01582) 715067. *Died 23 June 2010.*

BODDY, Prof. Keith, CBE 1998 (OBE 1989); PhD, DSc; FRSE; Professor of Medical Physics, University of Newcastle upon Tyne, and Head of Regional Medical Physics Department, Northern Regional Health Authority, 1978–98; *b* 1 Nov. 1937; *s* of late Ernest Boddy and Edith Mary Boddy; *m* 1960, Sylvia Mary (*née* Goodier); two *s*. *Educ:* Liverpool Univ. (BSc 1959); St Bartholomew's Hosp. Med. Coll. (MSc 1961); Glasgow Univ. (PhD 1971); Strathclyde Univ. (DSc 1976). FRSE 1980; FInstP 1969; FIPEM (FIPSM 1988). Head of Health Physics, AEI Res. Lab., Aldermaston Court, 1959–63; Lectr, 1963–67, Sen. Lectr, 1967–78, and Head of Health Physics and Nuclear Medicine Unit, Scottish Univs Res. and Reactor Centre. Numerous eponymous lectures. Member: Radioactive Waste Mgt Adv. Cttee, 1989–2003; Cttee on Med. Aspects of Radiation in the Envmt, 1991–2000; Ionising Radiations Adv. Cttee, 1995–2001; Chm., Dounreay Particles Adv. Gp, 2003–09, Particles Retrieval Adv. Gp (Dounreay), 2009–, SEPA. President: Hosp. Physicists Assoc., 1986–88; Inst. of Physical Scis in Medicine, 1986–88; Internat. Orgn for Med. Physics, 1994–97; Internat. Union for Physical and Engrg Scis in Medicine, 1997–2000; Hon. Member: British Nuclear Medicine Soc., 1980; RCR, 1981; BIR,

1997; European Fedn of Med. Physics, 2002. Hon. FIPEM 1998; Hon. FSRP 1999. Hon. DSc De Montfort, 1997. Glazebrook Medal and Prize, Inst. of Physics, 1991; Hon. Distinction Medal, Univ. of Ioannina, Greece, 1997; Skinner Medal, RCR, 1999; Merit Award, Internat. Union for Phys. and Engrg Scis in Medicine, 2000. *Publications:* numerous papers, lectures, contribs to books; contribs to reports of nat. cttees. *Recreations:* walking, gardening, crosswords, logic puzzles, music, family activities, stray animals. *Address:* 2 Eppleton Hall, Colliery Lane, Hetton-le-Hole, Tyne and Wear DH5 0QZ. *T:* and *Fax:* (0191) 526 4315. *Died 19 Sept. 2010.*

BOYERS, (Raphael) Howard, DFC 1945; Regional Chairman of Industrial Tribunals, Sheffield, 1984–87, retired 1988; *b* 20 Oct. 1915; *yr s* of late Bernard Boyers and Jennie Boyers; *m* 1st, 1949, Anna Moyra Cowan (*d* 1984); three *d*; 2nd, 1985, Estelle Wolman (*née* Davidson), JP; two step *s* one step *d*. *Educ:* King Edward VI Grammar School, Retford. Admitted Solicitor, 1939. Served War, RAF, 1940–45; 130 Sqdn, 10 Gp Fighter Comd, 1941; 51 Sqdn, 4 Gp Bomber Comd, 1944–45. Sen. Partner, Boyers Howson & Co., 1944–72. Clerk of the Peace, City of Sheffield, 1964–71; Chairman: VAT Tribunals, 1972–75; Industrial Tribunals, 1975–80; acting Regional Chm., 1980–84. Pres., Rep. Council of Sheffield and Dist Jews, 1963–67 and 1973–74. *Recreations:* theatre, music, watching football. *Address:* 8 Paragon Court, Holders Hill Road, Hendon, NW4 1LH. *T:* (020) 8343 4651. *Club:* Royal Air Force. *Died 8 April 2010.*

BRIGHTLING, Peter Henry Miller; Assistant Under Secretary of State, Ministry of Defence, 1973–81; *b* 12 Sept. 1921; *o s* of late Henry Miller Brightling and Eva Emily Brightling (*née* Fry); *m* 1951, Pamela Cheeseright; two *s* two *d*. *Educ:* City of London Sch.; BSc(Econ), London. War of 1939–45: Air Ministry, 1939–40; MAP, 1940–41; served in RAF, 1941–46. Ministry of: Supply, 1946–59; Aviation, 1959–67; Technology, 1967–70; Aviation Supply, 1970–71; MoD (Procurement Executive), 1971. *Address:* 39 Thetford Road, New Malden, Surrey KT3 5DP. *Died 8 Oct. 2009.*

BROOKS, Most Rev. Francis Gerard, DD, DCL; Bishop of Dromore, (RC), 1976–99, then Bishop Emeritus; *b* 14 Jan. 1924. Ordained, 1949; priest of Dromore, 1949–75. Formerly President, St Colman's Coll., Violet Hill, Newry. *Address:* Drumiller House, Jerrettspass, Newry, Co. Down BT34 1TF. *T:* (028) 3082 1508, (028) 3082 1367. *Died 4 Sept. 2010.*

BROWNING, (David) Peter (James), CBE 1984; MA; Chief Education Officer: Southampton, 1969–73; Bedfordshire, 1973–89; *b* 29 May 1927; *s* of late Frank Browning and Lucie A. (*née* Hiscock); *m* 1953, Eleanor Berry, *d* of late J. H. Forshaw, CB, FRIBA; three *s*. *Educ:* Christ's Coll., Cambridge (Engl. and Mod. Langs Tripos); Sorbonne; Univs of Strasbourg and Perugia. Personal Asst to Vice-Chancellor, Liverpool Univ., 1952–56; Teacher, Willenhall Comprehensive Sch., 1956–59; Sen. Admin. Asst, Somerset LEA, 1959–62; Asst Dir of Educn, Cumberland LEA, 1962–66; Dep. Chief Educn Officer, Southampton LEA, 1966–69. Member: Schools Council Governing Council and 5–13 Steering Cttee, 1969–75; Council, Univ. of Southampton, 1970–73; C of E Bd of Educn Schools Cttee, 1970–75; Council, Nat. Youth Orch., 1972–77; Merchant Navy Trng Bd, 1973–77; British Educnl Administration Soc. (Chm., 1974–78; Founder Mem., Council of Management); UGC, 1974–79; Taylor Cttee of Enquiry into Management and Govt of Schs, 1975–77; Governing Body, Centre for Inf. on Language Teaching and Research, 1975–80; European Forum for Educational Admin (Founder Chm., 1977–84); Library Adv. Council (England), 1978–81; Bd of Governors, Camb. Inst. of Educn (Vice-Chm., 1980–89); Univ. of Cambridge Faculty Bd of Educn, 1983–92; Council of Management, British Sch. Tech., 1984–87, Trust Dir, 1987–92; Lancaster Univ. Council, 1988–97 (Treas., 1993–97); Dir, Nat. Educnl Resources Inf. Service, 1988–91; Member: Carlisle Diocesan Bd of Educn, 1989–97 (Chm., 1992–97); Council, Open Coll. of NW, 1991–94; Cumbria Arts in Educn Trust, 1992–95 (Chm., 1992–95); Chairman: Carlisle DAC for Care of Churches, 1993–2000; Armitt (Liby and Mus.) Trust, 1994–2000 (Mem., 1992–2002); Armitt Liby and Mus. Centre Co., 1996–2000 (Mem., 1996–2001); Armitt Centre Enterprises Co., 1997–2001. Dir, Wordsworth Meml Lects and Rydal Bach Celebrity Concerts, 1993–95. Governor: Gordonstoun Sch., 1985–92; Lakes Sch., Windermere, 1988–92; Charlotte Mason Coll. of Higher Educn, Ambleside, 1988–92; London Coll. of Dance, 1990–93. Consultant, Ministry of Education: Sudan, 1976; Cyprus, 1977; Italy, 1981. Sir James Matthews Meml Lecture, Univ. of Southampton, 1983. FRSA 1981–93. Cavalier, Order of Merit (Republic of Italy), 1985; Médaille d'honneur de l'Oise, 1988; Commandeur, Ordre des Palmes Académiques (Republic of France), 1989 (Officier, 1985). *Publications:* Editor: Julius Caesar for German Students, 1957; Macbeth for German Students, 1959; contrib. London Educn Rev., Educnl Administration jl, and other educnl jls. *Recreations:* music, theatre, travel, conversation, walking. *Address:* Park Fell, Skelwith Bridge, near Ambleside LA22 9NP. *T:* (015394) 33978. *Died 13 Feb. 2010.*

CALLENDER, Dr Maurice Henry; Ministry of Defence, 1977–80; *b* 18 Dec. 1916; *s* of Harry and Lizbeth Callender; *m* 1941, Anne Kassel; two *s*. *Educ:* Univ. of Durham (MA, PhD). Commissioned: Royal Northumberland Fusiliers, 1939–41; RAF, 1941–45. Lectr, Huddersfield Technical Coll., 1945–47; Research, Univ. of Durham, 1947–49; Lectr, Bristol Univ. Extra-Mural Dept, 1949–53; MoD, 1953–62; Joint Services Staff Coll., 1959–60; Cabinet Office, 1962–64; MoD, 1964–70; Cabinet Office, 1970–73; Counsellor, Canberra, 1973–77. *Publications:* Roman Amphorae, 1965; various articles in archaeological jls. *Recreations:* oil painting, golf, bridge. *Address:* 24 Glanleam Road, Stanmore, Middx HA7 4NW. *T:* (020) 8954 1435. *Club:* Aldenham Golf and Country. *Died 2 Oct. 2010.*

CAMMELL, John Ernest; Head, Manufacturing and Technology (formerly Mechanical Engineering and Manufacturing Technology) Division, Department of Trade and Industry, 1986–92; *b* 14 Nov. 1932; *s* of Ernest Alfred Cammell and Gladys Clara (*née* Burroughes); *m* 1976, Janis Linda Moody. *Educ:* Highfield Coll., Leigh-on-Sea, Essex. Mil. Service, Royal Signals. Joined Victualling Dept, Admiralty, 1952; DSIR, 1963; Min. of Technology, 1964; DTI, 1967; Dept of Industry, 1973; Dir, National Maritime Inst., 1981–84. British Standards Institution: a Dir, 1992–2000; Consultant, 2000–02. Part-time Lectr, Warwick Manufg Gp, Warwick Univ., 1993–2005. FIET (Companion, IProdE, 1988); FRSA. *Recreations:* amateur theatre, golf, cricket, eating. *Address:* 41 Cunnington Street, Chiswick, W4 5ER. *T:* (020) 8995 6937. *Died 5 March 2010.*

CARR, William Compton; *b* 10 July 1918; *m*; two *s* one *d*. *Educ:* The Leys Sch., Cambridge. Admitted Solicitor, 1950; MP (C) Barons Court, 1959–64; PPS to Min. of State, Board of Trade, 1963; PPS to Financial Sec. to the Treasury, 1963–64. *Recreations:* reading, theatre-going, skin diving, eating, dieting. *Died Dec. 2000.*

CARRICK, 10th Earl of, *cr* 1748; **David James Theobald Somerset Butler;** Viscount Ikerrin 1629; Baron Butler (UK) 1912; *b* 9 Jan. 1953; *s* of 9th Earl of Carrick, and his 1st wife, (Mary) Belinda (*d* 1993), *e d* of Major David Constable-Maxwell, TD; *S* father, 1992; *m* 1975, Philippa J. V. (marr. diss. 2002), *yr d* of Wing Commander L. V. Craxton; three *s* (including twin *s*). *Educ:* Downside. *Heir: s* Viscount Ikerrin, *b* 1 Sept. 1975. *Died 8 Jan. 2008.*

CHANTRY, Dr George William, CEng, FIET; CPhys, FInstP; Director, European Operations, 1990–93, Senior Vice-President Europe, 1994–99, Carnahan & Associates; Consultant to Ministry of Defence on Strategic Defence Initiative Technology Transfer, 1990–98; *b* 13 April 1933; *s* of George William Chantry and Sophia Veronica (*née* Johnston); *m* 1956, Diana Margaret Rhodes (*née* Martin); two *s* one *d*. *Educ:* Christ Church, Oxford (DPhil 1959, MA 1960). CEng, FIET (FIEE 1976); FInstP 1974. Res. Associate, Cornell Univ., 1958; National Physical Lab., Dept of Industry: Sen. Res. Fellow, 1960; Sen. Scientific Officer, 1962; Principal Sci. Officer, 1967; Sen. Principal Sci. Officer, 1973; Dep. Chief Sci. Officer, DoI HQ, 1982, seconded to FCO; Counsellor (Sci. and Tech.), Bonn and Berne, 1982; Res. and Technol. Policy Div., DTI, 1985; seconded to MoD as Asst Dir for Industry in SDI Participation Office, 1985. Past Chm., European Molecular Liquids Gp; Mem., Science Educn and Technol. Bd, IEE, 1980–82. Editor, Proc. IEE, Science, Measurement and Technology (formerly Part A), 1981–2001 (Guest Editor, 2001–02). *Publications:* Submillimetre Spectroscopy, 1971; High-Frequency Dielectric Measurement, 1972; Submillimetre Waves and their Applications, 1978; Modern Aspects of Microwave Spectroscopy, 1980; Long-Wave Optics, 1983; papers in learned literature. *Recreations:* philately, bridge, gardening, music. *Died 24 Sept. 2010.*

CHINUBHAI, Sir Udayan, 3rd Bt *cr* 1913, of Shahpur, Ahmedabad, India; *b* 25 July 1929; *s* of 2nd Bt and Tanumati (*d* 1970), *d* of Javerilal Mehta; *S* father, 1990; grandfather, 1st Bt, was only member of Hindu Community to receive a baronetcy; *m* 1953, Muneera Khodad Fozdar; one *s* three *d*. Arjuna Award, 1972. *Heir: s* Prashant Ranchhodlal [*b* 15 Dec. 1955; *m* 1977, Swati Hrishikesh Mehta; three *d*]. *Clubs:* Willingdon, Cricket of India (Bombay). *Died 1 Sept. 2006.*

CLERKE, Sir John Edward Longueville, 12th Bt *cr* 1660; Captain Royal Wilts Yeomanry, RAC, TA; *b* 29 Oct. 1913; *er s* of Francis William Talbot Clerke (killed in action, 1916), *e s* of 11th Bt, and late Albinia Mary, *er d* of Edward Henry Evans-Lombe (who *m* 3rd, 1923, Air Chief Marshal Sir Edgar Rainey Ludlow-Hewitt, GCB, GBE, CMG, DSO, MC); *S* grandfather, 1930; *m* 1948, Mary (marr. diss. 1987; she *d* 1998), *d* of late Lt-Col I. R. Beviss Bond, OBE, MC; one *s* two *d*. *Heir: s* Francis Ludlow Longueville Clerke [*b* 25 Jan. 1953; *m* 1982, Vanessa Anne, *o d* of late Charles Cosman Citron and of Mrs Olga May Citron, Mouille Point, Cape Town; one *s* one *d*]. *Died 1 Oct. 2009.*

CRAGGS, Prof. James Wilkinson, BSc, PhD; Professor of Engineering Mathematics, University of Southampton, 1967–81; *b* 3 Feb. 1920; *s* of Thomas Gibson Craggs and Margaret (*née* Wilkinson); *m* 1946, Mary Baker; two *s* one *d*. *Educ:* Bede Collegiate Sch., Sunderland; University of Manchester (BSc 1941, PhD 1948); PhD Cambridge, 1953. Junior Lectr, Royal Military Coll. of Science, 1941–45; Asst Lectr, University of Manchester, 1947–49; Lecturer, Queen's Coll., Dundee, 1951–52; King's Coll., Newcastle upon Tyne: Lectr, 1952–56; Senior Lecturer, 1956–60; Reader in Mathematics, 1960–61; Prof. of Mathematics, University of Leeds, 1961–63; Prof. of Applied Mathematics, Melbourne Univ., 1963–67. *Publications:* contrib. learned journals regarding the mechanics of solids and fluids. *Recreation:* Methodist lay preacher. *Address:* 23 Redhill, Bassett, Southampton SO16 7BR. *Died 17 Feb. 2008.*

CUNNINGHAM, Alexander Alan; Executive Vice President, General Motors, 1984–86, retired; *b* Bulgaria, 7 Jan. 1926; naturalised citizen, US; *m* 1955, Dorothy Irene; one *s* three *d*; *m* 1976, Mary Helen. *Educ:* General Motors Inst., Michigan. BSc (Industrial Engrg) 1951. Served War of 1939–45, navigation electronics radar specialist, RAF. General Motors: Jun. Process Engr, Frigidaire Div., 1951; Asst to Frigidaire Man., NY, Gen. Motors Overseas Ops, 1952; Prodn Planning Technician for Adam Opel AG, Germany, 1953; Exec. Asst to Man. Dir, GM Ltd, London, 1956; Master Mechanic, Gen. Motors do Brasil, 1957, Works Man., 1958; Works Man., Gen. Motors Argentina SA, 1962; Man. Dir, Gen. Motors do Brasil, 1963; Man., Adam Opel's Bochum plant, 1964; Asst Gen. Manufg Man., Adam Opel AG, 1966, Gen. Manufg Man., 1969; Man. Dir, Adam Opel AG, 1970; Gen. Dir, European Organisations, Gen. Motors Overseas Corp., 1974–76; Vice Pres., Group Exec. Overseas, 1978; Group Exec., Body Assembly, 1980. Exec. Vice-Pres., N American Cars, 1982. Trustee, Detroit SO, 1983. *Address:* 70–671 Oroville Circle, Rancho Mirage, CA 92270–3414, USA. *T:* (760) 3288621. *Clubs:* Thunderbird Country, Mission Hills Country (Rancho Mirage); Center (Orange County). *Died 5 Sept. 1996.*

DAVIES, John Duncan, OBE 1984; DSc, PhD; Director, Polytechnic of Wales, 1978–92, then University of Glamorgan, Jan.–Oct. 1992, now Emeritus Professor; *b* 19 March 1929; *s* of Ioan and Gertrude Davies; *m* 1949, Barbara, *d* of Ivor and Alice Morgan; three *d*. *Educ:* Pontardawe School; Treforest School of Mines. BSc, MSc, PhD, DSc, Univ. of London. Junior Engineer, Consulting Engineers, 1949; Site Engineer, Cleveland Bridge Co., 1950–54; Royal Engineers, 1952–53; Design Engineer, Local Authority, 1955–56; Asst Lectr, Manchester Univ., 1957–58; University College, Swansea: Lecturer, 1959; Senior Lecturer, 1965; Reader, 1968; Professor of Civil Engineering, 1971–76; Dean, 1974–76; Principal, West Glamorgan Inst. of Higher Education, 1976–77. Member: Open University Delegacy, 1978–83; OU Cttee, 1987–90; Manpower Services Cttee (Wales), 1980–83; Wales Adv. Bd for Public Sector Higher Educn, 1982–83, 1986–89; Council, CNAA, 1985–93; Chm., Coleg Powys Corp., 1994–98. Hon. Fellow, Univ. of Wales, 1996. Hon. DTech Glamorgan, 1995. *Publications:* contribs to Structural Mechanics. *Died 22 Nov. 2005.*

DAVIES, Stanley Mason, (Sam), CMG 1971; Director, ACM (formerly Alliance) International Health Care Fund (formerly Trust), 1986–2002 (Consultant, 1984–86); *b* 7 Feb. 1919; *s* of late Charles Davies, MBE and Constance Evelyn Davies; *m* 1943, Diana Joan (*née* Lowe); three *d*. *Educ:* Bootle Grammar School. War Service, UK and W Europe, 1939–46; Royal Army Dental Corps, 1939–41 (Sgt); Corps of Royal Engineers, 1941–46 (Staff Captain). Clerical Officer, Min. of Labour, 1936; Exec. Officer, Inland Revenue, 1938; Higher Exec. Officer, Min. of Pensions, 1946–53; Min. of Health, 1953–68; Asst Sec., DHSS, 1968–75; Under Sec., Industries and Exports Div., DHSS, 1975–76. Consultant: Monsanto Health Care, 1977–85; Sterling Winthrop Drug, 1977–86. FSAScot. Croix de Guerre (France), 1944. *Recreations:* reading, archæology, philately. *Address:* 31 Leverstock Green Road, Hemel Hempstead, Herts HP2 4HH. *T:* (01442) 217142. *Died 24 July 2010.*

de MARCO, Prof. Guido, KUOM 1999; LLD; President of Malta, 1999–2004; Lecturer and Professor of Criminal Law, University of Malta, since 1967; *b* 22 July 1931; *s* of Emanuele de Marco and Giovanna (*née* Raniolo); *m* 1956, Violet Saliba; one *s* two *d*. *Educ:* St Joseph High Sch.; St Aloysius Coll.; Royal Univ. of Malta (BA Philosophy, Econs and Italian 1952; LLD 1955). Warrant of Advocate, Superior Courts of Malta, 1956; Crown Counsel, 1964–66. MP (Nat.) Malta, 1966–99; Dep. Prime Minister and Minister of Interior and Justice, 1987–90; Dep. Prime Minister and Minister of Foreign Affairs, 1990–96; Shadow Minister and Opposition Spokesman on Foreign Affairs, 1996–98; Dep. Prime Minister and Minister of Foreign Affairs, 1998–99. Nationalist Party: Sec. Gen., 1972–77; Dep. Leader, 1977–99. Rep. of Maltese Parlt, Council of Europe, 1967–87 and 1996–98 (Chm., Monitoring Cttee, 1997–98); Pres., UN Gen. Assembly (45th Session), 1990. Hon. LLD Seconda Università degli Studi di Napoli, 1999. *Publications:* A Presidency with a Purpose: United Nations General Assembly 45th Session, 1991; Malta's Foreign Policy in the Nineties: its evolution and progression, 1996; (with M. Bartolo) A Second Generation United Nations: for peace in freedom in the 21st century, 1997; Momentum, 2001; Momentum II, 2004; The Politics of Persuasion, 2008. *Recreations:* reading, travelling. *Address:* L'Orangerie, Mile End Street, Hamrun, Malta. *Died 12 Aug. 2010.*

DOSSER, Prof. Douglas George Maurice; Professor of Economics, University of York, 1965–81; retired, 1981; *b* 3 Oct. 1927; *s* of George William Dosser; *m* 1954, Valerie Alwyne Elizabeth, *d* of Leslie Jack Lindsey; three *d*. *Educ:* Latymer Upper School; London School of Economics. Lecturer in Economics, Univ. of Edinburgh, 1958–62; Vis. Prof. of Economics, Univ. of Washington, Seattle, 1960; Vis. Res. Prof. of Economics, Columbia Univ., NY, 1962; Reader in Economics, Univ. of York, 1963–65. *Publications:* Economic Analysis of Tax Harmonisation, 1967; (with S. Han) Taxes in the EEC and Britain, 1968; (with F. Andic) Theory of Economic Integration for Developing Countries, 1971; European Economic Integration and Monetary Unification, 1973; (with K. Hartley) The Collaboration of Nations, 1981; articles in Economic Jl, Economica, Rev. of Economic Studies. *Recreation:* art and antiques. *Died 9 Feb. 2010.*

FERGUSON, Ernest Alexander; Under-Secretary and Accountant-General, Department of Employment, 1973–77; *b* 26 July 1917; *s* of William Henry and Lilian Ferguson; *m* 1940, Mary Josephine Wadsworth; two *s*. *Educ:* Priory Sch., Shrewsbury; Pembroke Coll., Cambridge (Scholar, 1935–39; MA 1944). Served War, RA (Captain), 1940–45. Entered Ministry of Labour, 1945; Principal, 1948; Asst Sec., 1962. Chm., Central Youth Employment Executive, 1967–69; Sec. to NEDC, 1971–73; Dep. Chm., Central Arbitration Cttee, 1977–87. *Recreations:* sport, hill walking, reading. *Address:* 164 Balcombe Road, Horley, Surrey RH6 9DS. *T:* (01293) 432138. *Club:* Civil Service. *Died 31 July 2010.*

FINLAY, Alexander William; Planning Director, BOAC and British Airways, 1971–78; *b* 28 Nov. 1921; *s* of late Robert Gaskin Finlay and Alice Finlay; *m* 1949, Ona Margaret Lewis; no *c*. *Educ:* Tottenham County School. Flt-Lt RAF, 1941–47; various posts, BOAC and British Airways, 1947–71. Chm., Soc. for Long Range Planning, 1978–79; Mem. Council, Sussex Trust for Nature Conservation, 1982–89; Trustee, Charitable Trust, 1983–2001. Active interest in support for crime victims, 1989–2001. FCILT. *Recreations:* conservation, photography, gardening. *Club:* Royal Air Force. *Died 27 Nov. 2009.*

FITZPATRICK, John Ronald; Solicitor and Parliamentary Officer, Greater London Council, 1977–85, Consultant, 1985–86; *b* 22 Sept. 1923; *s* of Henry Fitzpatrick and Mary Lister; *m* 1952, Beryl Mary Newton; two *s* one *d*. *Educ:* St Bede's Coll., Manchester; Univ. of Manchester (LLB). Served War, RAF, navigator (Flt Lt), 1942–46. Admitted Solicitor, 1947; LMRTPI 1951. Asst Solicitor: Burnley, 1947; Stockport, 1948–51; Asst/Principal Asst Solicitor, Middx CC, 1951–65; Asst Clerk/Asst Dir-Gen., GLC, 1965–69; Asst Dir, 1969–72, Dir, 1972–77, Planning and Transportation, GLC. *Recreations:* golf, bridge. *Address:* Courtlands, 2 Langley Grove, New Malden, Surrey KT3 3AL. *T:* (020) 8942 8652. *Died 1 Oct. 2006.*

FOURNIER, Jean, OC 1987; CD 1972; Agent General for the Province of Quebec in London, 1971–78; *b* Montreal, 18 July 1914; *s* of Arthur Fournier and Emilie Roy; *m* 1942, May Coote (*d* 2008); five *s*. *Educ:* High Sch. of Québec; Laval Univ. (BA 1935, LLB 1938). Admitted to Bar of Province of Quebec, 1939. Royal Canadian Artillery (NPAM) (Lieut), 1935; Canadian Active Service Force Sept. 1939; served in Canada and overseas; discharged 1944, Actg Lt-Col. Joined Canadian Foreign Service, 1944; Third Sec., Canadian Dept of External Affairs, 1944; Second Sec., Canadian Embassy, Buenos Aires, 1945; Nat. Defence Coll., Kingston, 1948 (ndc); Seconded: to Privy Council Office, 1948–50; to Prime Minister's Office, Oct. 1950–Feb. 1951; First Sec., Canadian Embassy, Paris, 1951; Counsellor, 1953; Consul Gen., Boston, 1954; Privy Council Office (Asst Sec. to Cabinet), 1957–61; Head of European Division (Political Affairs), Dept of External Affairs, 1961–64; Chm., Quebec Civil Service Commn, 1964–71. Mem., Canadian Metric Commn, 1981–85. Pres., Inst. of Public Administration of Canada, 1966–67; Pres., Centre Québecois de Relations Internationales; Chm. Bd, Canadian Human Rights Foundn, 1982–90; Member: Canadian Inst. of Strategic Studies; Canadian Inst. of Internat. Affairs. Freedom, City of London, 1976. Pres., Canadian Veterans Assoc. of the UK, 1976–77. *Address:* Apt 206, 4430 Sainte-Catherine Ouest, Westmount, QC H3Z 3E4, Canada. *T:* (514) 9328633. *Died 28 Nov. 2010.*

FRIEDMANN, Jacques-Henri; Grand Officier, Légion d'Honneur, 2006 (Commandeur, 1996); Chevalier, Ordre du Mérite, 1970; Honorary Chairman, Musée du Quai Branly, since 2005 (Chairman, Planning Committee, 1999–2005); *b* Paris, 15 Oct. 1932; *s* of André Friedmann and Marie-Louise Bleiweiss; *m* 1962, Cécile Fleur; two *s* one *d*. *Educ:* Inst. d'Etudes Politiques, Paris (law degree). Student, Ecole Nat. d'Admin, 1957–58; Inspector of Finance, 1959; Lectr, Inst. d'Etudes Politiques, 1964–68; Special Asst 1964, Tech. Advr, 1965–66, Deptl Staff of Valéry Giscard d'Estaing, Minister of Finance; Special Asst, Gen. Directorate of Domestic Trade and Pricing, 1966; Actg Dep. Sec. Gen., Interministerial Cttee on Eur. Econ. Co-op., 1966–67; Hd, Finance Dept, French Planning Org., 1967–68; Chief Executive Secretary: to Jacques Chirac, Sec. of State for Econ. Affairs and Finance, 1969–70, and Minister responsible for liaison with Parlt, 1971; Hd of Dept of Gen. Inspectorate of Finances and of Central Dept of Gen. Inspectorate for the Nat. Economy, 1971–72; Advr on Econ. and Financial Affairs to Pierre Messmer, Prime Minister, then Chief Exec. Sec., 1972–74; Special Asst to Jacques Chirac, Prime Minister, 1974; Chm., Co. Générale Maritime, 1974–82; Inspector Gen. of Finance, 1980; Chm. and Man Dir, Co. Parisienne de Chauffage Urbaine, 1983–87; Special Asst to Edouard Balladur, Minister of Econ. Affairs, Finance and Privatisation, 1986–87; Chairman: Caisse d'Epargne de Paris, 1985–95; Air France, 1987–88; SAGI, 1989–93; UAP, 1993–97; Supervisory Bd, AXA, 1997–2000. *Address:* 80 avenue de Breteuil, 75015 Paris, France. *T:* (1) 47340459; 222 Rue de l'Université, 75343 Paris, Cedex 07, France. *T:* (1) 56617001. *Died 15 Dec. 2009.*

GALVIN, Bernard Vincent Joseph, CB 1991; Secretary to the Treasury, New Zealand, 1980–86; *b* 15 March 1933; *s* of Eustace Bartholemew Galvin and Margaret Jean (*née* Lenihan); *m* 1st, 1960, Beverly Ann Snook (marr. diss. 1977); three *s* one *d*; 2nd, 1980, Margaret Clark. *Educ:* Univ. of NZ (BSc 1954); Victoria Univ. of Wellington (BA Hons 1959); Harvard Univ. (MPA 1961). Joined Treasury, NZ, 1955; Harkness Fellow, USA, 1960–61; Econ. Counsellor, NZ High Commn, London, 1965–68; Treasury Dir, 1969; Asst Sec., 1972; Dep. Sec., 1974; Perm. Head of PM's Dept, 1975–80. Chm., Econ. Develt Commn, 1986–89. Alternate Gov., World Bank, 1976–86. Chm., Ministerial Wkg Pty on Disability and Accident Compensation, 1991. Vis. Fellow, Inst. of Policy Studies, 1989–98. Mem. Council, Victoria Univ. of Wellington, 1989–98 (Treas., 1990–96). *Publications:* Policy Co-ordination, Public Sector and Government, 1991; chapters in books on NZ government; articles in public admin jls. *Recreations:* beach house, gardening, reading, walking. *Address:* 10 Jellicoe Towers, 189 The Terrace, Wellington, New Zealand. *T:* (4) 4728143. *Club:* Wellington (Wellington, NZ). *Died 2 June 2010.*

GARCIA, Arthur, CBE 1989; JP; Judge of the High Court, Hong Kong, 1979–89; Commissioner for Administrative Complaints, Hong Kong, 1989–94; *b* 3 July 1924; *s* of late F. M. Garcia and of Maria Fung; *m* 1948, Hilda May; two *s*. *Educ:* La Salle Coll., Hong Kong; Inns of Court Sch. of Law. Called to the Bar, Middle Temple, 1957. Jun. Clerk, Hong Kong Govt, 1939–41; Staff Mem., British Consulate, Macao, 1942–45; Clerk to Attorney Gen., Hong Kong, 1946–47; Asst Registrar, 1951–54; Colonial Develt and Welfare Scholarship, Inns of Court Sch. of Law, 1954–57; Legal Asst, Hong Kong, 1957–59; Magistrate, 1959; Sen. Magistrate, 1968; Principal Magistrate, 1968; Dist Judge, 1971. Member: Preliminary Working Cttee, HKSAR, 1994–95; Preparatory Cttee, HKSAR, 1996–97. JP Hong Kong, 1991. *Recreations:* photography, swimming. *Address:* 15 Briar Avenue, Hong Kong. *Club:* Hong Kong Jockey (Hong Kong). *Died 16 Dec. 2010.*

GLASSER, Cyril, CMG 1999; Consultant, Sheridans, Solicitors, since 2001; *b* 31 Jan. 1942; *s* of late Phillip and Eva Glasser. *Educ:* Raine's Foundn Grammar Sch., London; London Sch. of Econs (LLB 1963; LLM 1966). Admitted solicitor, 1967; Sheridans, Solicitors: Partner, 1977–2001; Hd, Litigation Dept, 1977–99; Managing Partner, 1989–2001; Sen. Partner, 2001. Consultant on solicitors' costs to NBPI, 1967; Co-founder and Dir, Legal Action Gp, 1972–74; Legal Advr to ANC during Commn on Rhodesian Opinion, 1972; attached to Lord Chancellor's Dept as Special Consultant, Legal Aid Adv. Cttee, 1974–77. Vis. Prof. of Law, UCL, 1987–. Mem., Wkg Party to Review Legal Aid Legislation, 1974–77; Chm., Legal Aid Provisions Wkg Party, 1975–77; Mem., Social Scis and the Law Cttee, SSRC, 1979–83. Mem. Council, Law Soc., 1997–2001; Dir, Law Soc. Trustees Ltd, 1999–2005. Mem., Jt Tribunal on Barristers' Fees, 1998–2001. Advr, Experts' Cttee on Efficiency of Justice, Council of Europe, 1998–2000. Trustee, Legal Assistance Trust, 1985–2004. FRSA 1995; Fellow, Soc. Advanced Legal Studies, 1998. Member: Legal Practice Course Bd, 1999–2005 (Vice-Chm., 2000–01); Bar/Law Soc. Jt Academic Stage Bd, 2004–05; Common Professional Examination Bd, 2003–05

(Chm., 2004–06). Member: Mgt Cttee, Inst. Judicial Admin, Birmingham Univ., 1984–; Adv. Bd, Centre of Advanced Litigation, Nottingham Trent Univ., 1991–2002. London School of Economics: Gov., 1996–2007; Mem. Council, 1999–2005; Emeritus Gov., 2008; Trustee, LSE Legal Activities Trust, 2008–. Member, Editorial Board: Modern Law Rev., 1992–; Internat. Jl Evidence and Proof, 1996–2002; Mem., Editl Adv. Bd, Litigator, 1994–98. Hon. LLD London Guildhall, 2002. *Publications:* contribs to legal jls, books, etc. *Address:* Sheridans, Whittington House, Alfred Place, WC1E 7EA. *T:* (020) 7079 0100. *Died 5 May 2010.*

HARDY, Herbert Charles; Director, Evening Standard, 2001; Deputy Chairman, The Scotsman Publications Ltd, 1995–99; *b* 13 Dec. 1928; *s* of Charles John Hardy and Margaret Elizabeth (*née* Burniston); *m* 1st, 1959, Irene Burrows (marr. diss. 1992); one *d*; 2nd, 1999, Janet Goldsmith. *Educ:* RMA Sandhurst. With Mirror Gp; Chief Exec., News Internat.; Dir, London Weekend Television; Chief Exec., Associated Newspapers Ltd, 1989–94; Chm., Evening Standard Co. Ltd, 1989–94; Chief Exec., The European, 1995–98; Chief Exec. and Dep. Chm., 1995–99, Dir, 1999–2000, Press Hldgs; Director: Channel 4 Television Corp., 1992–98 (Dep. Chm., 1997–98); Channel One TV, 1994–95; Teletext Holdings, 1995–96; Accord Hldgs, 2000–01. *Recreations:* golf, horse racing. *Died 10 March 2009.*

HARRIS, Frank; *see* Harris, W. F.

HARRIS, Maurice Kingston, CB 1976; Secretary, Northern Ireland Ministry of Home Affairs, 1972, seconded to Northern Ireland Office, 1974–76; *b* 5 Oct. 1916; *s* of Albert Kingston Harris and Annie Rebecca Harris (*née* Hakes); *m* 1948, Margaret, *d* of Roderick Fraser and Gertrude McGregor; one *s* three *d*. *Educ:* The Perse Sch.; London Univ. 1st cl. Hons Mod. Langs, 1939. Served in Indian Army, 8th Punjab Regt, 1942–46. Colonial Office, 1946–47. Entered Northern Ireland Civil Service, 1947, and served in various Ministries; retired 1976. *Recreations:* music, walking. *Address:* Apt 1, Marlborough Manor, 48 Marlborough Park South, Belfast BT9 6HS. *T:* (028) 9068 1409. *Died 28 June 2010.*

HARRIS, (Walter) Frank; Business Planning Executive, Dunlop Ltd (UK Tyre Group), 1979–81; *b* 19 May 1920; *m* Esther Blanche Hill; two *s* two *d*. *Educ:* King Edward's Sch., Birmingham; University of Nottingham (BCom (Hons) 1949); BSc (1st cl. Hons) Open Univ., 1994. Served Royal Air Force, 1939–46. University, 1946–49. Ford Motor Company, 1950–65; Principal City Officer and Town Clerk, Newcastle upon Tyne, 1965–69. Comptroller and Dir, Admin, Massey-Ferguson (UK), 1969–71; Finance Dir, Dunlop SA Ltd, 1972–79. *Recreation:* astrophysics. *Address:* Acomb High House, Northumberland NE46 4PH. *T:* (01434) 602844. *Died 13 Dec. 2010.*

HASHMI, Dr Farrukh Siyar, OBE 1974; FRCPsych; Consultant Psychiatrist: All Saints' Hospital, Birmingham, 1969–92; Woodbourne Priory Hospital (formerly Woodbourne Clinic), Edgbaston, 1992–2007; Psychotherapist, HM Prison, Stafford, 1973–92; *b* Gujrat, Pakistan, 12 Sept. 1927; *s* of Dr Ziaullah Qureshi and Majida Qureshi; *m* 1972, Shahnaz; one *s* two *d*. *Educ:* King Edward Med. Coll., Lahore (Punjab Univ.). MB BS; MRCPsych; DPM; FRCPsych 1979. Mayo Hosp. and King Edward Med. Coll., Lahore, March–Sept. 1953; New End Hosp., Hampstead, 1954; Children's Hosp., Birkenhead, 1954–55; Sen. House Officer, Brook Gen. Hosp., Woolwich, 1955–56; Snowdon Road Hosp., Bristol, 1956; Asst MOH, Co. Berwicks, 1957; Scholar, Volkart Foundn, Switzerland, 1958–60; psychiatric medicine: Registrar, Uffculme Clinic and All Saints Hosp., Birmingham, 1960–63, Sen. Registrar, 1966–69; Research Fellow, Dept of Psychiatry, Birmingham Univ., 1963–66. Chairman: Psychiatric Div., West Birmingham Health Dist, 1977–83 and 1988–92; Woodbourne Clinic Hosp. Management Team, 1989–2003; Member: Race Relations Bd, W Midlands Conciliation Cttee, 1968–81; Community Relations Working Party, NAYC, 1968–81; Home Secretary's Adv. Cttee on Race, 1976–81 (formerly Mem., HO Adv. Cttee on Race Relations Research); CRE, 1980–86; Working Party on Community and Race Relations Trng, HO Police Trng Council, 1982–83; Wkg Gp on Ethnic Minorities, W Midlands RHA, 1982–92; Mental Health Services Cttee, RHA, 1976–92; Council, Mind (NAMH), 1976–81; UK Cttee, World Fedn for Mental Health, 1978–81; Health and Welfare Adv. Panel, NCCI, 1966–81; Cttee of Inquiry into Educn of Children from Ethnic Minority Gps (Swann Cttee), 1982–85; Warley Area Social Services Sub-Cttee, 1973–81; Central DHA, Birmingham, 1982–90; BBC Regl Adv. Council, 1970–77; GMC, 1979–84 (GMC Mem., Tribunal on Misuse of Drugs, 1983–84); Parole Board, 1981–85; Alternate Mem., Economic Social Cttee, EEC, 1985; Advisory Consultant, C of E Bd for Social Responsibility, 1984–87; consultant psychiatrist in eating disorders, St Michael's Hosp., Warwick, 1994–98. President: Pakistan Med. Soc., UK, 1974–76; Overseas Doctors Assoc., UK, 1975–79; Founder and Chm, Iqbal Acad., Coventry Cathedral, 1972–86. Member Editorial Board: New Community, 1972–82; Medicos, 1977–81. Involved in clinical trials and psycho-pharmacological studies, e.g. assessing effects of drugs in anxiety states and neurotic illness, incl. antidepressants. *Publications:* Pakistan Family in Britain, 1965; Mores, Migration and Mental Illness, 1966; Psychology of Racial Prejudice, 1966; Community Psychiatric Problems among Birmingham Immigrants, 1968; In a Strange Land, 1970; Measuring Psychological Disturbance in Asian Immigrants to Britain, 1977. *Recreations:* writing, reading, music. *Address:* Shahnaz, 5 Woodbourne Road, Edgbaston, Birmingham B15 3QJ. *Died 25 Dec. 2010.*

HEAD, Audrey May; Member, Monopolies and Mergers Commission, 1986–89; Director, 1973–85, Managing Director, 1976–85, Hill Samuel Unit Trust Managers Ltd; *b* 21 Jan. 1924; *d* of Eric Burton Head and Kathleen Irene Head. *Educ:* St Catherine's Sch., Bramley, Surrey. Chartered Auctioneers' and Estate Agents' Institute, 1949–58; Hill Samuel Group, 1958–85, a Manager, 1968; Director: Hill Samuel Investment Management, 1974–86; Hill Samuel Life Assurance, 1983–86; Trade Union Unit Trust Managers Ltd, 1983–85. Chm., Unit Trust Assoc., 1983–85. Non-exec. Mem., Royal Surrey and St Luke's NHS Trust, 1991–93. Chm. Governing Body, St Catherine's Sch., Bramley, 1988–96. Nominated as Business Woman of the Year, 1976. Silver Jubilee Medal, 1977. *Recreations:* golf, gardening. *Address:* West Chantry, 4 Clifford Manor Road, Guildford, Surrey GU4 8AG. *T:* (01483) 561047. *Died 11 Aug. 2010.*

HEGLAND, David Leroy, DFC 1944; Director: Kemtron Ltd; Galena; Massey-Ferguson Holdings (Australia) Ltd; Carlton and United Breweries Holdings Ltd; Plessey Pacific Pty Ltd; cattle grazier; *b* 12 June 1919; *s* of Lee and Jennie Hegland; *m* 1944, Dagmar Cooke; two *s* one *d*. *Educ:* Whitman Coll., Washington, USA (BA). Served War, 1942–45; USN aircraft pilot in Pacific Ocean areas; Lt Comdr USNR, 1945. Managing Director: GM International, Copenhagen, 1956–58; GM South African, Port Elizabeth, 1958–61; GM Holden's Pty Ltd, Melbourne, 1962–65; Chm. and Man. Dir, Vauxhall Motors Ltd, Luton, 1966–70; Dir, General Motors Ltd, London, 1966–70; Chm., GKN Australia Ltd, and Dir, Ajax GKN Holdings Pty Ltd, and Guest, Keen & Nettlefolds (Overseas) Ltd 1972–80. Member: Albury-Wodonga Develt Corp., 1980–81; Industry Forum, Aust. Acad. of Science, 1972; Aust. Inst. of Dirs; Delta Sigma Rho. FIMI. Richard Kirby medal for production engrg, 1964. *Recreations:* flying, tennis, riding. *Address:* 300 Hot Springs Road #A30, Santa Barbara, CA 93108–2038, USA. *Clubs:* Royal & Ancient Golf (St Andrews); Melbourne, Victoria Racing (Melbourne); Albury (Albury, NSW). *Died 26 Nov. 2005.*

HINCHLIFF, Stephen, CBE 1976; Chairman and Managing Director, Dexion Group, 1976–91; *b* 11 July 1926; *s* of Gordon Henry and Winifred Hinchliff; *m* 1987, Ann Fiona Maudsley; one *d*, and one *s* one *d* from a previous marriage. *Educ:* Almondbury Grammar Sch., Huddersfield; Boulevard Nautical Coll., Hull; Huddersfield Coll. of Technology; Cranfield Inst. of Technology (MSc). FIMechE, FIET. Production Engr, Dowty Auto Units Ltd, 1953–54; Dowty Seals Ltd: Chief Prodn Engr, 1953–54; Works Manager, 1954–56; Dir, 1956–76; Dep. Man. Dir,

1966–67; Man. Dir, 1967–76; Dep. Chm., Dowty Gp Ltd, 1973–76; Man. Dir, Dowty Gp Industrial Div., 1973–76. CCMI; FRSA. *Recreations:* reading, spectator sports, family. *Address:* Cedar House, Little Gaddesden, Berkhamsted, Herts HP4 1PE. *T:* (01442) 843728. *Died 10 April 2010.*

HOARE, John Michael; *b* 23 Oct. 1932; *s* of Leslie Frank Hoare and Gladys Hoare; *m* 1963, Brita Hjalte; one *s* one *d*; *m* 2000, Susan C. D. Faulkner. *Educ:* Raynes Park; Christ's Coll., Cambridge (BA). Asst Sec., United Bristol Hosps, 1961; House Governor, St Stephen's Hosp., 1963; Asst Clerk, St Thomas' Hosp., 1965; Administrator, Northwick Park Hosp., 1967; Wessex Regional Health Authority: Administrator, 1974–84; Gen. Man., 1984–89; Quality Advr, 1989–90. *Died 26 April 2010.*

HOLLAND, Sir Clifton Vaughan, (Sir John), AC 1988; Kt 1973; BCE; CPEng, FTSE, Hon. FIEAust, FAIM, FAIB; Chairman, John Holland Holdings Limited, 1963–86; *b* Melbourne, 21 June 1914; *s* of Thomas and Mabel Ruth Elizabeth Holland; *m* 1st, 1942, Emily Joan Atkinson (*d* 1999); three *s* one *d*; 2nd, 2003, Suzanne Wharton, *d* of Hector Desbrowe-Annear and Gladys Heron. *Educ:* Flinders State Sch.; Frankston High Sch.; Queen's Coll., Univ. of Melbourne (BCE); Monash Univ. (Hon. DEng 1978). Junior Engineer, BP, 1936–39. Served War of 1939–45, RAE and 'Z' Special Force, Middle East, SW Pacific (Lt-Col). Construction Engr, BP Aust. 1946–49; Founder, John Holland (Constructions) Pty Ltd, 1949, Man. Dir 1949–73, Chm., 1949–86; Chm., Process Plant Constructions Pty Ltd, 1949–82; Director: T & G Life Soc., 1972–82; Aust. and NZ Banking Gp, 1976–81. Foundn Pres., Australian Fedn of Civil Contractors (Life Mem., 1971); Chm., Nat. Construction Industry Conf. Organising Cttee, 1982; Mem., Construction Industry Res. Bd, 1982. Chm., Econ. Consultative Adv. Gp to the Treasurer, 1975–81; Mem., Rhodes Scholar Selection Cttee, 1970–73; Mem. Bd, Royal Melbourne Hosp., 1963–79; Nat. Chm., Outward Bound, 1973–74, Chm. Victorian Div., 1964–77; Councillor, Inst. of Public Affairs, 1980; Mem., Churchill Fellowship Selection Cttee, 1968–82; Director: Winston Churchill Meml Trust, 1976–82 (Chm., Vic. Br., 1977–82); Child Accident Prevention Foundn of Australia, 1979–81; Chairman: La Trobe Centenary Commemoration Council, 1975–76; Matthew Flinders Bi-Centenary Council, 1973–75; History Adv. Council of Victoria, 1975–85; Loch Ard Centenary Commemoration Cttee, 1976–78; Citizens' Council, 150th Anniversary Celebrations, Victoria, 1979–82; Victorian Cttee for Anzac Awards, 1982–; Nat. Chm., Queen's Silver Jubilee Trust for Young Australians, 1981–87 (Vic. Chm., 1977–80; Life Mem., 1992); Mem., Centenary Test Co-ordinating Cttee, 1976–77. Dep. Chm., Melbourne Univ. Engineering Sch. Centenary Foundn and Appeal Cttee, 1982–90. Director: Corps of Commissionaires (Victoria) Ltd, 1978–89; Australian Bicentenary Celebrations, 1980–82 (Vic. Chm., 1980–82). Pres., Stroke Res. Foundn, 1983–90; Patron: Bone Marrow Foundn, 1992–; Voluntary Euthanasia Soc. of Victoria, 1996–; Children First Foundn, 2000–. Construction projects include: Jindabyne pumping station; Westgate Bridge; Tasman Bridge restoration, New Parliament House. Foundation Fellow, Australian Acad. of Technological Scis. Hon. Fellow, AATSE, 2004. Hon. DEng Monash, 1976. Peter Nicoll Russell Meml Medal, 1974; Kernot Meml Medal, Univ. of Melbourne, 1976; Consulting Engineers Advancement Soc. Medal, 1983; Dist. Constructor Award, Qld Univ. of Technol., 2000; Australian Constructors' Assoc. Medallion, 2000; Australian Centenary Medal, 2003. *Recreations:* golf, music, gardening, cricket. *Address:* Hurst Lodge II, 33 George Road, Flinders, Vic 3929, Australia. *Clubs:* Australian, Naval and Military (Melbourne); Royal Melbourne Golf, Flinders Golf (Patron). *Died 31 May 2009.*

HOLLIS, Most Rev. Reginald; Rector, St Paul's Church, New Smyrna Beach, Florida, 1994–97; *b* 18 July 1932; *s* of Jesse Farndon Hollis and Edith Ellen Lee; *m* 1957, Marcia Henderson Crombie; two *s* one *d*. *Educ:* Selwyn Coll., Cambridge; McGill Univ., Montreal. Chaplain and Lectr, Montreal Dio. Theol Coll., 1956–60; Chaplain to Anglican Students, McGill Univ.; Asst Rector, St Matthias' Church, Westmount, PQ, 1960–63; Rector, St Barnabas' Church, Pierrefonds, PQ, 1963–70; Rector, Christ Church, Beaconsfield, PQ, 1971–74; Dir of Parish and Dio. Services, Dio. Montreal, 1974–75; Bishop of Montreal, 1975; Metropolitan of the Ecclesiastical Province of Canada and Archbishop of Montreal, 1989–90; Asst Bishop, Dio. of Central Florida and Episcopal Dir, Anglican Fellowship of Prayer, 1990–94. Hon. DD 1975. *Publications:* Abiding in Christ, 1987. *Address:* 303–1175 Newport Avenue, Victoria, BC V8S 5E6, Canada. *Died 8 Nov. 2010.*

JACK, Hon. Sir Alieu (Sulayman), Grand Commander, 1972, and Chancellor, 1972–83, National Order of The Gambia; Kt 1970; Speaker, House of Representatives of the Republic of The Gambia, 1962–72, and 1977–83; *b* 14 July 1922; *m* 1946, Yai Marie Cham; four *s* four *d* (and one *d* decd). *Educ:* St Augustine's School. Entered Gambia Civil Service, 1939; resigned and took up local appt with NAAFI, 1940–44; Civil Service, 1945–48; entered commerce, 1948; Man. Dir, Gambia National Trading Co. Ltd, 1948–72. Mem., Bathurst City Council, 1949–62. Minister for Works and Communications, The Gambia, 1972–77. Represented The Gambia Parlt at various internat. gatherings. Comdr, National Order of Senegal, 1967; Comdr, Order of Merit of Mauritania, 1967; Commander, Order of Fed. Republic of Nigeria, 1970; Kt Grand Band, Liberia, 1977. *Recreation:* golf. *Address:* PO Box 376, Banjul, The Gambia. *T:* (home) 4392204, (office) 4227486. *Club:* Bathurst (Banjul). *Died 27 Dec. 2010.*

JACK, Prof. Robert Barr, CBE 1988; Partner, McGrigor Donald, Solicitors, Glasgow, Edinburgh and London, 1957–93 (Joint Senior Partner, 1986–90; Senior Partner, 1990–93); *b* 18 March 1928; *s* of Robert Hendry Jack and Christina Alexandra Jack; *m* 1958, Anna Thorburn Thomson; two *s*. *Educ:* Kilsyth Acad.; High Sch., Glasgow; Glasgow Univ. MA 1948, LLB 1951. Admitted a solicitor in Scotland, 1951; Prof. of Mercantile Law, Glasgow Univ., 1978–93. Member: Company Law Cttee of Law Society of Scotland, 1971–95 (Convener, 1978–85); Scottish Law Commn, 1974–77. Scottish observer on Dept of Trade's Insolvency Law Review Cttee, 1977–82; Mem., DoT Adv. Panel on Company Law, 1980–83; Chm., Review Cttee on Banking Services Law, 1987–89. Lay Member: Council for the Securities Industry, 1983–85; Stock Exchange Council, 1984–86; Independent Mem. Bd, Securities Assoc., later SFA, 1987–94; Mem. Bd, SIB, 1994–97; UK Mem., Panel of Arbitrators, ICSID, 1989–95; Member: Takeover Panel, 1992–2001; Financial Law Panel, 1993–2001; MCSI (MSI 1993). Chairman: Brownlee plc, Timber Merchants, Glasgow, 1984–86 (Dir, 1974–86); Joseph Dunn (Bottlers) Ltd, Soft Drink Manufacturers, Glasgow, 1983–2003; Scottish Mutual Assce 1992–98 (Dir, 1987–98); Dep. Chm., Scottish Metropolitan Property, 1991–98 (Dir, 1980–98); Director: Clyde Football Club Ltd, 1980–96; Bank of Scotland, 1985–96; Gartmore Scotland Investment Trust, 1991–2001; Glasgow Develt Agency, 1992–97. Pres., Scottish Nat. Council of YMCAs, 1983–98 (Chm., 1966–73). Mem., SHEFC, 1992–96. Chm., The Turnberry Trust, 1983–; Mem., Cttee of Mgt, Malin Housing Assoc., Turnberry, 1971–; Governor, Hutchesons' Educational Trust, Glasgow, 1978–87 (Chm. 1980–87); Mem. Bd of Govs, Beatson Inst. for Cancer Res., Glasgow, 1989–2004; Chm., Audit Cttee, Glasgow Univ., 1996–2003. Mem., W of Scotland Adv. Bd, Salvation Army, 1995–. Trustee, Football Trust, 1998–2000. DUniv Glasgow, 2001. *Publications:* lectures on various aspects of company, insolvency and banking law and financial services regulation law. *Recreations:* golf (latterly unhappily on a non-playing basis), hopeful support of one of Scotland's less fashionable football teams; an erstwhile dedicated lover of Isle of Arran. *Address:* 50 Lanton Road, Newlands, Glasgow G43 2SR. *T:* (0141) 637 7302. *E:* Robertjack75@aol.com. *Clubs:* Caledonian; Western (Glasgow); Pollok Golf; Shiskine Golf and Tennis (Isle of Arran) (Captain 1973–75). *Died 25 Oct. 2010.*

JACKSON, Roy Arthur; Assistant General Secretary, Trades Union Congress, 1984–92; *b* 18 June 1928; *s* of Charles Frederick Jackson and Harriet Betsy (*née* Ridewood); *m* 1956, Lilian May Ley; three *d*. *Educ:* North Paddington Central Sch.; Ruskin Coll., Oxford (DipEcon Pol Sci (Distinction)); Worcester Coll., Oxford (BA Hons, PPE). Post Office Savings Bank, 1942; RN, Ord. Signalman, 1946–48. Trades Union Congress: joined

Educn Dept, 1956; Dir of Studies, 1964; Head of Educn, 1974–84. Member: Albemarle Cttee of Youth Service, 1958–60; Open Univ. Cttee on Continuing Educn, 1975–76; Adv. Cttee for Continuing and Adult Educn, 1977–83; Schools Council Convocation, 1978–82; Further Educn Unit, DES, 1980–; Employment Appeal Tribunal, 1992–99; TUC Comr, MSC, 1987–88. Non-exec. Dir, Remploy Ltd, 1992–99. *Recreations:* walking, reading, gardening. *Address:* 27 The Ryde, Hatfield, Herts AL9 5DQ. *T:* (01707) 890566. *Died 11 Dec. 2010.*

JANSEN, Sir Ross (Malcolm), KBE 1989 (CBE 1986); Chairman, Local Government Commission, New Zealand, 1998–2001; Mayor of Hamilton City, New Zealand, 1977–89; *b* 6 Sept. 1932; *m* 1957, Rhyl Robinson; three *s* three *d. Educ:* Horowhenua Coll., Levin (Dux *proxime accessit* 1950); Victoria Univ., Wellington (LLB 1957); Univ. of Waikato (DPhil 1994). NZ Univ. Law Moot Prize, 1956. Practised law in partnership. Hamilton, 1958–77. Hamilton City Council: Mem., 1965–74, 1977–89; Chairman: Planning Cttee, 1965–68; Works Cttee, 1968–74; Dep. Mayor, 1971–74. Chairman: Waikato United Council, 1986–89; Hamilton Industrial Develt Prog., 1966–68; NZ Bldg Industry Commn, 1986–89; Lottery Community Facilities Cttee, 1989–91; Waikato Regl Council, 1989–91; Midland Regl HA, 1992–98. President: Municipal Assoc. of NZ, 1984–89; NZ Local Govt Assoc., 1988–89. Mem. Council, Univ. of Waikato, 1977–99. Winston Churchill Trust Fellowship in Town Planning, 1968. FRSA; ACIArb. Hon. Dr Waikato Univ., 1984. Hon. Chieftain of Western Samoa (for services to the Samoan Community). Commemoration Medal, NZ, 1990. *Recreations:* reading (poetry and history), tennis, gardening. *Address:* Apartment 12, 232 Hibiscus Coast Highway, Orewa, Rodney, New Zealand. *Died 14 Dec. 2010.*

JEANES, Leslie Edwin Elloway, CBE 1982; Chief of Public Relations, Ministry of Defence, 1978–81; *b* 17 Dec. 1920; *er s* of late Edwin Eli Jubilee Jeanes and of Mary Eunice Jeanes; *m* 1942, Valerie Ruth, *d* of Ernest and Ethel Vidler; one *d. Educ:* Westcliff High Sch. Entered Civil Service, 1939; Inf. Officer, DSIR, 1948–65; Chief Press Officer, Min. of Technol., 1965–68; Dep. Head of Inf., MoT, 1968–70; Head of News, DoE, 1970–73; Chief Inf. Officer, MAFF, 1973–78. *Recreations:* gardening, motoring, DIY. *Address:* 14 Whistley Close, Bracknell, Berks RG12 9LQ. *T:* (01344) 429429. *Died 15 Aug. 2010.*

JONES, Charles Beynon Lloyd, CMG 1978; Chairman of Directors, David Jones Ltd, 1963–80; Consul General of Finland in Sydney, 1971–88; *b* 4 Dec. 1932; *s* of late Sir Charles Lloyd Jones and Lady (Hannah Beynon) Lloyd Jones, OBE. *Educ:* Cranbrook Sch., Sydney; Univ. of Sydney (not completed). Joined David Jones Ltd, 1951; Alternate Director, 1956; Director, 1957; Joint Managing Director, 1961. President: Retail Traders Assoc., NSW, 1976–78; Bd of Trustees, Art Gall. of NSW, 1980–83 (Trustee, 1972; Vice-Pres., 1976–80). Governor, London House for Overseas Graduates, 1983–92. Officer, Order of Merit, Republic of Italy (Cavaliere Ufficiale); Comdr, Order of the Lion, Finland. *Address:* Summerlees Farm, Yarramalong, NSW 2259, Australia. *Died 11 July 2010.*

JONES, Glynn, CBE 1992; Circuit Administrator, Western Circuit, Lord Chancellor's Department, 1987–93; *b* 5 March 1933; *s* of late Bertie Jones and Alice Maud Jones (*née* Griffiths); *m* 1957, Crystal Laura, *d* of late Edward William Kendall and Ivy Irene Kendall; one *s* one *d. Educ:* state schs in Monmouthshire; BA Open. Local Govt service, 1950–71; Lord Chancellor's Department: Crown Court, Newport, 1972, Winchester, 1973; Courts Administrator: Nottingham Group of Courts, 1976; South Wales Group of Courts, 1980. *Recreations:* Rugby Union football, golf. *Address:* 17 Rockfield Glade, Penhow, Newport, S Wales NP26 3JF. *T:* (01633) 400835. *Clubs:* Civil Service; St Pierre Golf and Country, Newport Golf. *Died 6 April 2010.*

JONES, Prof. Kathleen; Professor of Social Policy, University of York, 1981–89 (Professor of Social Administration, 1965–81), then Emeritus Professor; *b* 7 April 1922; *d* of William Robert Savage and Kate Lilian Barnard; *m* 1944, Rev. David Gwyn Jones (*d* 1976); one *s* decd. *Educ:* North London Collegiate Sch.; Westfield Coll., Univ. of London (BA, PhD). Research Asst in Social Administration, Univ. of Manchester, 1951–53, Asst Lectr 1953–55; Sen. History Teacher, Victoria Instn, Kuala Lumpur, 1956–58, also Asst Lectr in History, Univ. of Malaya (part-time); Lectr in Social Administration, Univ. of Manchester, 1958–62, Sen. Lectr 1962–65. Chm., Social Scis Cttee, UK Commn for UNESCO, 1966–69. Mem., Gen. Synod of C of E, 1975–80; Member: Archbishops' Commn on Church and State, 1966–71; Lord Gardiner's Cttee on NI, 1974–75; Archbishops' Commn on Marriage, 1976–78; Mental Health Act Commn, 1983–86 (NE Chm., 1983–85). Chm., Assoc. of Psychiatric Social Workers, 1968–70; Chm., Social Admin Assoc., 1980–83. Hon. FRCPsych, 1976. *Publications:* Lunacy, Law and Conscience, 1955; Mental Health and Social Policy, 1960; Mental Hospitals at Work, 1962; The Compassionate Society, 1965; The Teaching of Social Studies in British Universities, 1965; A History of the Mental Health Services, 1972; Opening the Door: a study of new policies for the mentally handicapped, 1975; Issues in Social Policy, 1978; (ed) Living the Faith: a call to the Church, 1980; Ideas on Institutions, 1984; Eileen Younghusband: a biography, 1985; Experience in Mental Health, 1988; The Making of Social Policy, 1991; Asylums and After, 1993; Poems of St John of the Cross, 1993; (ed) Butler's Lives of the Saints: June, 1997; December, 1999; Women Saints, 1999; Saints of the Anglican Calendar, 2000; A Basic Dictionary of Saints, 2001; Who are the Celtic Saints?, 2002; Songs of the Isles, 2004; Challenging Richard Dawkins, 2007; (series editor) International Library of Social Policy, 1968–85; (ed) Year Book of Social Policy in Britain, 1971–76. *Address:* 44 West Moor Lane, Heslington, York YO10 5ER. *T:* (01904) 411579. *Died 13 Oct. 2010.*

KIRK, Rt Hon. Herbert Victor; PC (N Ireland) 1962; Member (U) for South Belfast, Northern Ireland Assembly, 1973–75; *b* 5 June 1912; *s* of Alexander and Mary A. Kirk; *m* 1944, Gladys A. Dunn; three *s. Educ:* Queen's Univ., Belfast (BComSc). FCA 1940. MP Windsor Div. of Belfast, NI Parlt, 1956–72; Minister of Labour and Nat. Insce, Govt of N Ireland, 1962–64; Minister of Education, 1964–65; Minister of Finance, 1965–72, Jan.–May 1974, resigned. *Recreation:* golf. *Clubs:* Royal Portrush Golf, Belvoir Park Golf. *Died 2006.*

LAWSON, James Robert; Regional Nursing Officer, Mersey, 1985–89; *b* 29 Dec. 1939; *s* of James and Grace Lawson; *m* 1962, Jean; two *d. Educ:* Keswick High School; Royal Albert Hosp. (Registered Nurse of Mentally Handicapped); Cumberland Infirmary (Registered Gen. Nurse). Chief Nurse, 1972; Area Nurse, Personnel, 1974; Divl Nursing Officer, 1976; District Nursing Officer, 1982–85. *Recreations:* fell walking, caravanning, active sports. *Address:* 11 Hazelgarth, Church Road, Allithwaite, Grange-over-Sands, Cumbria LA11 7RS. *Died 12 July 2008.*

LEE, Rt Rev. Paul Chun Hwan, Hon. CBE 1974; Bishop of Seoul, 1965–83; *b* 5 April 1922; unmarried. *Educ:* St Michael's Theological Seminary, Seoul; St Augustine's College, Canterbury. Ordained deacon, 1952 (Pusan Parish), priest, 1953 (Sangju and Choungju Parish). Dir, Yonsei University, Seoul, 1960– (Chm., Bd of Trustees, 1972–; Hon. DD 1971). Chairman: Christian Council of Korea, 1966–67; Christian Literature Soc. of Korea, 1968–83; Korean Bible Soc., 1972–83 (Vice-Pres., 1969–72); Nat. Council of Churches in Korea, 1976–78. Hon. LLD Korea, 1978 *Recreation:* reading. *Address:* 104–401 Dae Woo Apt, Bang Bae 3 Dong, 981, So'cho-Ku, Seoul 137–063, Korea. *Died 26 March 2010.*

LEHMAN, Prof. Meir, (Manny), DSc, PhD; FREng, FBCS, FIET, FIEEE, FACM; Professor, School of Computer Science, and Consultant, Middlesex University, 2002–07, then Professor Emeritus; Professor of Computer Science, Jerusalem College of Technology, 2002 and since 2006; *b* 24 Jan. 1925; *s* of late Benno and Theresa Lehman; *m* 1953, Chava Robinson; three *s* two *d. Educ:* Letchworth Grammar Sch.; Imperial Coll. of Science and Technol. (BSc Hons 1953, PhD 1956, ARCS, DIC); DSc (London) 1987. FIET (FIEE 1972; StuIEE 1947); FIEEE 1985 (MIEEE 1974); FBCS 1986 (MBCS 1956); FREng (FEng 1989);

FACM 1994 (MACM 1953). Murphy Radio, 1941–50; Imperial Coll., 1950–56; London Labs, Ferranti, 1956–57; Scientific Dept, Israeli Defence Min., 1957–64; Res. Div., IBM, 1964–72; Department of Computing, Imperial College: 1972–84 (part-time 1984–87); Prof. of Computing Sci., 1972–84, then Emeritus; Hd of Dept, 1979–84; Sen. Res. Fellow, 1989–2002; Sen. Res. Investigator, 1998–2002; Principal Investigator, Feedback Evolution and Software Technology, EPSRC Project, 1996–98 and 1999–2001; Imperial Software Technology Ltd: Founder, 1982; Chm., 1982–84; Dir, 1984–87; Exec. Dir, 1987–88; Man. and Tech. Dir, Lehman Software Technology Associates Ltd, 1985–2003. Vice-Chm. of Exec., Kisharon Day Sch. for Special Educn and Vice-Chm. of Trustees and Gov., 1976–2000. *Publications:* Software Evolution—Processes of Program Change, 1985; over 250 refereed pubns and 20 book chapters. *Recreations:* family, Talmudic studies, classical orchestral music, DIY. *Address:* 17 Rehov Mitudela, Rechavia, Jerusalem 92305, Israel; Department of Computing, Machon Lev, Jerusalem College of Technology, Jerusalem, Israel. *E:* mml@onetel.com, mannyml@netvision.net.il. *Died 29 Dec. 2010.*

LEITCH, Sir George, KCB 1975 (CB 1963); OBE 1945; Chief Executive (Permanent Secretary), Procurement Executive, Ministry of Defence, 1974–75; *b* 5 June 1915; *er s* of late James Simpson and Margaret Leitch; *m* 1942, Edith Marjorie Maughan (*d* 2003); one *d. Educ:* Wallsend Grammar Sch.; King's Coll., University of Durham. Research and teaching in mathematics, 1937–39. War Service in Army (from TA), 1939–46 (despatches, OBE): Lt-Col in charge of Operational Research in Eastern, then Fourteenth Army, 1943–45; Brigadier (Dep. Scientific Adviser, War Office), 1945–46; entered Civil Service, as Principal, 1947; Ministry of Supply, 1947–59 (Under-Secretary, 1959); War Office, 1959–64; Ministry of Defence: Asst Under-Secretary of State, 1964–65; Dep. Under-Sec. of State, 1965–71; Procurement Executive, MoD: Controller (Policy), 1971–72; 2nd Permanent Sec., 1972–74. Chm., Short Brothers Ltd, 1976–83. Chm., Adv. Cttee on Trunk Rd Assessment, 1977–80. Commonwealth Fund Fellow, 1953–54. Hon. DSc Durham, 1946. *Address:* 5 West Avenue, Gosforth, Newcastle upon Tyne NE3 4ES. *T:* (0191) 285 2619. *Died 16 March 2010.*

LEVENE, Ben, RA 1986 (ARA 1975); painter; *b* 23 Dec. 1938; *s* of late Mark Levene and Charlotte (*née* Leapman); *m* 1st (marr. diss. 1977); two *d*; 2nd, 1978, Susan Margaret Williams; one *s. Educ:* St Clement Danes Grammar Sch.; Slade School of Fine Art (DFA 1960). Boise Scholarship, 1961; lived in Spain, 1961–62; Vis. Lectr, taught painting and drawing, Camberwell Sch. of Art, 1963–89; Visiting Tutor: RA Schs, 1980–95; City & Guilds, 1990–95; Curator, RA Schs, 1995–98. Exhibited at: Thackeray Gall., 1973–81 (one man shows, 1973, 1975, 1978, 1981); Browse & Darby, London, 1986– (one man shows, 1988, 1993, 2001); one man show, Friends Room, RA, 2006; group exhibitions incl.: regular exhibitor, RA Summer Exhibn; Jasper Galls, Houston and NY; works in various private collections in England and America. *Recreation:* gardening under the supervision of my wife. *Address:* c/o Royal Academy of Arts, Piccadilly, W1V 0DS. *T:* (020) 7300 8000. *Died 15 Sept. 2010.*

LEWIS, H(erbert) J(ohn) Whitfield, CB 1968; Chief Architect, Ministry of Housing and Local Government, 1964–71; *b* 9 April 1911; *s* of Herbert and Mary Lewis; *m* 1963, Pamela (*née* Leaford); one *s* three *d. Educ:* Monmouth Sch.; Welsh Sch. of Architecture. Associate with Norman & Dawbarn, Architects and Consulting Engineers; in charge of housing work, 1945–50; Principal Housing Architect, Architects Dept, London County Council, 1950–59; County Architect, Middlesex County Council, 1959–64. FRIBA; DisTP 1957. *Recreations:* music, electronics. *Address:* 8 St John's Wood Road, NW8 8RE. *Died 29 March 2010.*

LLOYD JONES, Charles Beynon; *see* Jones, Charles B. L.

LUCAS, Christopher Charles; Under Secretary, Community and International Policy Division, Department of Energy, 1977–80; *b* 5 June 1920; *s* of Charles Edwin Lucas and Mabel Beatrice Read; *m* 1945, Beryl June Vincent; two *d. Educ:* Devonport High Sch.; Balliol Coll., Oxford (Newman Exhibnr). Min. of Fuel, 1946; Central Econ. Planning Staff, 1948; HM Treasury, 1950–70; Cabinet Office, 1970–72; Sec., NEDC, 1973–76; Under-Sec., Dept of Energy, 1976–80. *Recreation:* riding. *Address:* Orchard Croft, Withycombe, near Minehead, Somerset TA24 6PT. *T:* (01643) 821551. *Died 8 Nov. 2009.*

McDONALD, F(rancis) James; Chairman, Beaumont Hospital Board of Trustees, 1992–96 (Chairman, Beaumont Hospital Foundation, 1987–92); President and Chief Operating Officer, General Motors, 1981–87; *b* Saginaw, Mich, 3 Aug. 1922; *s* of Francis and Mary McDonald; *m* 1944, Betty Ann Dettenthaler; two *s* one *d. Educ:* General Motors Inst.; Yale Univ. Served USN Submarine Service, 1944–46 (Lieut). Joined Saginaw Malleable Iron Plant, 1946; Transmission Div., Detroit, 1956–65; Pontiac Motor Div., 1965–68; Dir, Manufacturing Operations, Chevrolet Motor Div., 1968–69; Vice-Pres., and Mem. Admin Cttee, Gen. Motors, 1969; General Manager: Pontiac Motor Div., 1969–72; Chevrolet Motor Div., 1972–74; Exec. Vice-Pres. and a Dir, 1974; Mem. Finance Cttee, 1979; Chm., Exec. and Admin Cttees, 1981. Holder of hon. degrees from univs and colls in the US, incl. Michigan State Univ. and Notre Dame Univ. *Died 13 June 2010.*

McLOUGHLIN, George Leeke, CB 1988; Deputy Director of Public Prosecutions for Northern Ireland, 1982–87; *b* 2 July 1921; *e s* of Charles M. McLoughlin and Rose W. McLoughlin (*née* Leeke); *m* 1953, Maureen Theresa McKaigney (*d* 1998); two *s* six *d. Educ:* St Columb's College, Londonderry; Queen's Univ. Belfast (BA). Barrister, N Ireland, practised 1945–58; joined HMOCS 1958; Resident Magistrate, 1958, Crown Counsel, 1958–63, Northern Rhodesia; Parly Draftsman, Zambia, 1965; Solicitor General, Zambia, 1968–70, retired; Office of Law Reform, N Ireland, 1971–72; Sen. Asst Dir of Public Prosecutions, NI (Under Secretary, NI Civil Service), 1973–82. *Recreations:* photography, armchair sports following. *Address:* 27 Tullymacnous Road, near Killyleagh, Toye, Downpatrick, Co. Down, Northern Ireland BT30 9PW. *Died 4 Feb. 2005.*

MANZINI, Raimondo, Hon. GCVO 1969; Italian Ambassador to the Court of St James's, 1968–75; *b* Bologna, 25 Nov. 1913. *Educ:* Univ. of California (Berkeley); Clark Univ., Mass. (MA); Dr of Law, Bologna Univ. Entered Diplomatic Service, 1940; served San Francisco, 1940–41; Lisbon, 1941–43; Min. of Foreign Affairs in Brindisi, Salerno, Rome, 1943–44; London, 1944–47; Consul General for Congo, Nigeria and Gold Coast, 1947–50; Consul General, Baden Baden, 1951–52; Head of Information Service, CED, Paris, 1952–53; Ministry of Foreign Affairs, 1953–55; Adviser to the Minister of Foreign Trade, 1955–58; Chef de Cabinet of Minister for Foreign Affairs, 1958; Diplomatic Adviser to the Prime Minister, 1958–59; Advr to Minister of Industry, 1960–64; Perm. Rep. to OECD, Paris, 1965–68; Sec.-Gen., Min. of Foreign Affairs, 1975–78. Gran Croce, Ordine Merito Repubblica, 1968; Commandeur, Légion d'Honneur (France), 1976. *Address:* Villa Bellochio, 83 Boulevard de Garavan, Menton, France. *Died 12 Nov. 2010.*

MASSEVITCH, Prof. Alla Genrikhovna; Chief Scientist of the Astronomical Institute of the Russian Academy of Sciences, since 1988 (Vice-President, 1952–88); Professor of Astrophysics, Moscow University, since 1946; *b* Tbilisi, Georgia, USSR, 9 Oct. 1918; *d* of Genrick Massevitch and Natalie Zhgenti; *m* 1942, Joseph Friedlander; one *d. Educ:* Moscow Univ. Lectured at the Royal Festival Hall, London, and at the Free Trade Hall, Manchester, etc., on The Conquest of Space, 1960; in charge of network of stations for tracking Sputniks, in Russia, 1957–93. Pres. Working Group 1 (Tracking and Telemetring) of COSPAR (Internat. Cttee for Space Research) 1961–66. Pres., Commission 35 (Internal Structure of Stars) of the IAU, 1967–70; Dep. Sec. Gen., UNISPACE 82 (UN Conf. on Exploration and Peaceful Uses of Outer Space), Vienna, 1981–83. Chm., Space Science Studies Cttee, Internat. Acad. of Astronautics, 1983–86; Associate Editor, Astrophysics and Space Science, 1987–94; Mem. Editorial Bd, Astrophysics (Russian), 1985–; Editor of series: Vital Problems of Astrophysics, 1987–99; Vital Problems of Space Research, 1987–99. Foreign Member: Royal

Astronomical Soc., 1963; Indian Nat. Acad. of Sciences, 1979; Austrian Acad. Scis, 1985; Internat. Acad. Astronautics, 1964. Vice-President: Inst. for Russian-American Relations (formerly Soviet-American Relations), 1967–; USSR Peace Cttee, 1977–92 (Mem. Bd, 1965–92); Mem. Bd, Internat. Peace Cttee, 1965–92. Hon. Mem., Russian Acad. of Cosmonautics, 1996. Internat. Award for Astronautics (Prix Galabert), 1963. Medals of 2nd World War; Govtl decorations, USSR, Sign of Honour, 1963, Red Banner, 1975; Govt Order with Star (Poland), 1985; USSR State Prize, 1975. Hon. Scientist Emeritus, 1978. *Publications:* Use of Satellite Tracking Data for Geodesy (monograph), 1980; Physics and Evolution of Stars (monograph), 1988; 159 scientific papers on the internal structure of the stars, stellar evolution, and optical tracking of artificial satellites, in Russian and foreign astronomical and geophysical journals. *Address:* 48 Pyatnitskaya Street, Moscow 119017, Russia. *T:* (095) 2313980, *Fax:* (095) 2302081. *E:* vmyakutin@inasan.rssi.ru. *Club:* Club for Scientists (Moscow). *Died 6 May 2008.*

MENDEL, Paul David, MBE 2000; Director, Council of Christians and Jews, 1992–98; broadcaster and speaker; *b* 14 Oct. 1930; *s* of late Eric Lazarus Mendel and Esther (*née* Graber); *m* 1st, 1952, Marion Leigh (marr. diss. 1967); one *s* one *d*; 2nd, 1967, Ada Marianne Levinson (marr. diss. 1983); 3rd, 1989, Rosalind Alder. *Educ:* St Christopher Sch., Letchworth. Nat. Service, 1949–51, Capt. RMP. Former Member: Middx CC; Barnet BC. Dep. Dir, Defence and Gp Relns, Bd of Deputies of British Jews, 1982–84; Council of Christians and Jews: Asst Dir, 1985–87; Dep. Dir, 1987–92. Mem., Interfaith Network Exec., 1987. JP Juvenile and W Central PSD, 1955–83 (sometime Chm.). *Recreations:* travel, reading, people. *Address:* 100 Lyncroft Mansions, Lyncroft Gardens, NW6 1JY. *T:* (020) 7794 6989. *Died 25 March 2010.*

MITCHELL, Alexander Graham, CBE 1973; DFM 1945; Governor, Turks and Caicos Islands, 1973–75 (Administrator, 1971–73); *b* 2 Nov. 1923; *s* of Alexander Mitchell and Evelyn Mitchell (*née* Green); *m* 1954, Pamela Ann Borman; three *d*. *Educ:* Dulwich College; Downing Coll., Cambridge (BA 1946; MA 1951). Served RAF, 1942–45. Sudan Government Civil Service, 1951–55; HM Overseas Civil Service, 1955; Western Pacific High Commission: various posts in British Solomon Islands Protectorate and British Residency, New Hebrides, 1955–71; Sec., Financial Affairs, British Residency, 1968–71; retired June 1977. Clerk to Governors, Dame Allan's Schools, Newcastle, 1977–88. *Recreation:* ancient and military history. *Address:* 2 Corchester Towers, Corbridge, Northumberland NE45 5NP. *Club:* Royal Over-Seas League. *Died 18 July 2010.*

MONCEL, Lt-Gen. Robert William, OC 1968; DSO 1944; OBE 1944; CD 1944; Vice-Chief of the Defence Staff, Canada, 1965–66; *b* 9 April 1917; *s* of René Moncel and Edith Brady; *m* 1939, Nancy Allison (decd), *d* of Ralph P. Bell; (one *d* decd). *Educ:* Selwyn House Sch.; Bishop's Coll. Sch. Royal Canadian Regt, 1939; Staff Coll., 1940; Bde Major 1st Armd Bde, 1941; comd 18th Manitoba Dragoons, 1942; GSO1, HQ 2 Canadian Corps, 1943; comd 4th Armd Bde, 1944; Dir Canadian Armd Corps, 1946; Nat. War Coll., 1949; Canadian Jt Staff, London, 1949–54; Comdr 3 Inf. Bde, 1957; QMG, 1960; GOC Eastern Comd, 1963; Comptroller Gen., 1964. Col, 8th Canadian Hussars. Chm., Fishermen's Memorial Hosp., 1980–84; Dir, Nova Scotia Rehabilitation Center, 1986. Mem. Bd of Regents, Mount Allison Univ., 1983. Croix de Guerre, France, 1944; Légion d'Honneur, France, 1944. Hon. LLD Mount Allison Univ., 1968. *Recreations:* fishing, sailing, golf. *Club:* Royal Nova Scotia Yacht. *Died 10 Dec. 2007.*

MOORTHY, Arambamoorthy Thedchana; Sri Lanka Foreign Service, retired; private academic research and writing, since 1984; *b* 10 Aug. 1928; *s* of late Mr Arambamoorthy and Mrs Nesamma Arambamoorthy; *m* 1959, Suseela T. Moorthy (*d* 2005), *d* of Justice P. Sri Skanda Rajah; one *s* two *d*. *Educ:* Univ. of Ceylon (BAEcon Hons 1948). Called to Bar, Gray's Inn, 1965. Entered Foreign Service of Ceylon (later Sri Lanka), 1953; Second Secretary: Indonesia, 1955–57; China, 1957–59; First Secretary: London, 1961–63; Federal Republic of Germany, 1964–66; Chargé d'Affaires, *ai*, Thailand, and Permanent Representative of Ceylon to Economic Commn for Asia and Far East, 1969; Chargé d'Affaires, *ai*, Iraq, 1970; Ambassador in Pakistan, 1978–Dec. 1980, and concurrently, Jan.–Dec. 1980, Ambassador to Iran with residence in Islamabad; High Comr in London, 1981–84. *Address:* 39 Gladstone Road, Wimbledon, SW19 1QU. *T:* (020) 8544 9537. *Died 1 April 2008.*

MURPHY, Cornelius McCaffrey, (Neil Murphy), MBE 1982; Chairman, New Life Venues Ltd, 1992–95, retired; *b* 31 May 1936; 2nd *s* of Edward and Annie Murphy, Glasgow; *m* 1st, 1963, Joan Anne, *d* of William Tytler (marr. diss.); two *d*; 2nd, 1992, Carmel Murphy; two *s*, and two step *d*. *Educ:* Holyrood Sch.; Univ. of Glasgow (MA 1958). Joined The Builder Group, 1962, following spells of teaching and management trng: Editor, 1974–83, Editor-in-Chief, 1983–87, Building Magazine; Dir, 1979–92; Man. Dir, Building (Publishers) Ltd, 1981–90, Group Man. Dir, 1990–92. *Recreations:* reading, golf. *Died Nov. 2010.*

NAIRN, Margaret, RGN, SCM; Chief Area Nursing Officer, Greater Glasgow Health Board, 1974–84; *b* 20 July 1924; *d* of James R. Nairn and Anne G. Nairn. *Educ:* Aberdeen Academy. Nurse Training: general: Aberdeen Royal Infirmary, to 1945 (RGN); midwifery: Aberdeen Maternity Hosp., until 1948 (State Certified Midwife); Health Visitors: Aberdeen Coll. for Health Visitors, until 1952 (Health Visitors Cert.); administrative: Royal Coll. of Nursing, London, to 1959 (Nursing Admin Cert.); 6 months study in USA as British Commonwealth and Empire Nurses Scholar, 1956. Ward Sister and Night Supt, Aberdeen Maternity Hosp., 1945–52; Director of Nursing Services in Aberdeen and Glasgow, 1952–74. *Publications:* articles in medical and nursing press: A Study of 283 Families with Rent Arrears; Liaison Services between Hospital and Community Nursing Services; Health Visitors in General Practice. *Recreations:* reading, gardening, swimming, travel. *Address:* 12 Countesswells Terrace, Aberdeen AB1 8LQ. *Died 12 May 2010.*

NEWTON, David Alexander; Chairman, Carr's Milling Industries, 1997–2005 (Director, 1996–2005); *b* 6 Oct. 1942; *s* of Alexander and Hazel Newton; *m* 1965, Kathleen Mary Moore; one *s* one *d*. *Educ:* Morecambe Grammar Sch.; Wyvern Coll. Mgt trainee, J. Bibby & Sons Ltd, UK, 1964–67; Area Manager, Cobb Breeding Co., 1967–69; Gen. Manager and Dir, Anglian Food Gp, 1969–72; Agricl Dir, Sovereign Chicken Ltd, 1972–82; Ops Dir, Ross Poultry Ltd, 1982–84; Chief Exec. Officer and Dir, Buxted Poultry Ltd, 1984–85; Hillsdown Holdings: Dir, 1985–96; Chief Operating Officer, 1992–93; Chief Exec. Officer, 1993–96; Chm., Maple Leaf Mills Ltd, Toronto, 1987–90; Pres. and Chief Exec. Officer, Canada Packers Inc., 1990–92. Director: Bernard Matthews Hldgs Ltd, 1996; Bodfari, 1996–2005; MRCT, 1997–2005; Chm., Firstan Ltd. FCMI (FBIM 1984); FInstD 1984. *Recreations:* golf, music, watching sports. *Club:* Diss Golf (Norfolk). *Died 15 Jan. 2007.*

NGAIZA, Christopher Pastor; Chairman and Managing Director, Kamachumu Inn Ltd, Tanzania, since 2001; *b* 29 March 1930; parents decd; *m* 1952, Thereza; three *s* two *d* (and one *s* decd). *Educ:* Makerere University Coll.; Loughborough Co-operative College. Local Courts Magistrate, 1952–53; Secretary/Manager, Bahaya Co-operative Consumer Stores, 1955–57; Loughborough Co-operative Coll., 1957–59; Auctioneer and Representative of Bukoba Native Co-operative Union, Mombasa, 1959–61; joined Tanzanian Foreign Service, 1961; Counsellor, Mission to UN, 1961–62; Counsellor, Tanganyika High Commn, London, 1962–63; High Commissioner for United Republic of Tanganyika and Zanzibar in London, 1964–65; Tanzanian Ambassador: to Netherlands, 1965–67, to Arab Republic of Egypt, 1972–77; Mem., E African Common Market Tribunal, 1968–69; Tanzania's first High Comr to Zambia, 1969–72; Special Personal Assistant to Pres. of Tanzania, 1977–83; Comr for Kagera River Basin Orgn, 1978–83. Chm. and Man. Dir, PES Consultants Ltd, 1986–2000. *Recreations:* music, tennis. *Address:* Kamachumu Inn Ltd, PO Box 59, Kamachumu, Tanzania. *Died March 2010.*

NIELSEN, Aksel Christopher W.; *see* Wiin-Nielsen.

NORGARD, John Davey, AO 1982; Chairman, Australian Broadcasting Commission, 1976–81; Executive General Manager, Operations, BHP Co. Ltd, and Chairman, Associated Tin Smelters, until 1970; *b* 3 Feb. 1914; *s* of John Henry and Ida Elizabeth Norgard; *m* 1943, Irena Mary Doffkont; one *s* three *d*. *Educ:* Adelaide Univ. (BE); SA Sch. of Mines (FSASM). Part-time Chm., Metric Conversion Bd, Australia, 1970–81; Chairman: Commonwealth Employment Service Review, 1976–77; Pipeline Authority, 1976–81; Mem., Nat. Energy Adv. Cttee, 1977–80. Dep. Chancellor, La Trobe Univ., 1972–75. Chm., Grad. Careers Council of Australia, 1979–86. *Address:* 29 Montalto Avenue, Toorak, Victoria 3142, Australia. *T:* (3) 98274937. *Clubs:* Australian, Royal Melbourne Golf (Melbourne). *Died 4 Oct. 2010.*

OLIVER, Benjamin Rhys; Stipendiary Magistrate for Mid-Glamorgan, 1983–95; a Recorder of the Crown Court, 1972–93; *b* 8 June 1928; *m* 1955, Gwynneth (decd); one *s* one *d*. *Educ:* Llandovery and Aberystwyth. Called to the Bar, Inner Temple, 1954. An Asst Recorder, Swansea, Cardiff and Merthyr Tydfil QS, 1967–71. A Chm., Med. Appeal Tribunals and Vaccine Damage Tribunals, 1981–83. *Recreation:* golf. *Died 31 Oct. 2007.*

O'REILLY, William John, CB 1981; OBE 1971; FCPA; Commissioner of Taxation, Australian Taxation Office, 1976–84; *b* 15 June 1919; *s* of William O'Reilly and Ruby (*née* McCrudden). *Educ:* Nudgee Coll., Brisbane, Qld; Univ. of Queensland (AAUQ 1950). FCPA 1990 (FASA 1983). Served RAAF, 1942–44. Joined Australian Public Service, 1946; Australian Taxation Office: Brisbane, 1946–55; Melbourne, 1955–61; Canberra, 1961–84; Asst Comr of Taxation, 1963; First Asst Comr of Taxation, 1964; Second Comr of Taxation (Statutory Office), 1967. *Recreations:* reading, walking. *Address:* 62/1321 Anzac Avenue, Kallangur, Qld 4503, Australia. *Clubs:* Commonwealth, Canberra (Canberra). *Died 2 Nov. 2010.*

PALMES, Peter Manfred Jerome; Principal Assistant Director, Public Prosecutions Department, 1979–81; *b* 28 Feb. 1920; *s* of late Manfred Palmes and Gwendoline Robb; *m* 1st, 1945, Sylvia Theodor (decd); 2nd, 1969, Brenda Laban; one step *d*. *Educ:* Charterhouse; Worcester Coll., Oxford. Served War of 1939–45: Oxford and Bucks LI and 1/8th Gurkha Rifles, 1940–45. Called to Bar, Inner Temple, 1948. Public Prosecutions Dept: Legal Assistant, 1948; Sen. Legal Asst, 1958; Asst Solicitor, 1969; Asst Director, 1977. Jubilee Medal, 1977. *Address:* Chapel Lodge, Cross Colwood Lane, Bolney, West Sussex RH17 5RY. *Died 11 Jan. 2010.*

PARKER, Keith John, OBE 1993; Director, MNA Broadcasting Ltd, 2005–09; *b* 30 Dec. 1940; *s* of late Sydney John Parker and Phyllis Mary Parker; *m* 1962, Marilyn Ann Edwards; one *s*. Various editorial appointments; Editor, Shropshire Star, 1972–77; Editor, 1977–95, Gen. Manager, 1995, Express & Star, Wolverhampton; Man. Dir, Shropshire Newspapers, 1996–2002; Ed., Shropshire Mag., 1997–2002; Man. Dir, Express & Star Ltd, Wolverhampton, 2002–05. Director: Midland News Assoc. Ltd, 1996–2005; Telford Radio Ltd, 1998–2009; Chairman: Kidderminster Radio Ltd, 2005–09; Shrewsbury and Oswestry FM Ltd, 2005–09. President: Guild of British Newspaper Editors, 1987–88 (Vice-Pres., 1986–87; Chm., Parly and Legal Cttee, 1991–94); Midland Newspaper Soc., 1999–2000; Chm., Newspaper Qualifications Council, 2004–07; Member: Press Complaints Commn, 1992–94; Data Protection Tribunal, 1996–2006; Parly, Editl and Regulatory Cttee (formerly Govt and Legal Affairs Cttee), 1997–2005, Council, 2002–04, Newspaper Soc. Director: Shropshire Chamber of Commerce, Trng and Enterprise, 2000–01; Black Country Consortium, 2004–05. Trustee, Ironbridge Gorge Mus. Develt Trust, 2000–02. *Recreations:* reading, travel. *Address:* 94 Wrottesley Road, Tettenhall, Wolverhampton, West Midlands WV6 8SJ. *T:* (01902) 758595. *Died 31 July 2010.*

PERRY, George Henry; *b* 24 Aug. 1920; *s* of Arthur and Elizabeth Perry; *m* 1944, Ida Garner; two *d*. *Educ:* elementary sch. and technical college. Engineering Apprentice, 1934–41. Naval Artificer, 1941–46 (Atlantic and Italy Stars; 1939–45 Star). Railway Fitter, 1946–66. Derby Town Councillor, 1955–66. Chairman: Derby Water Cttee, 1957–61; S Derbys Water Board, 1961–66; Derby Labour Party, 1961–62; Secretary, Derby Trades Council, 1961–66. Contested (Lab) Harborough, 1964; MP (Lab) Nottingham South, 1966–70. *Recreation:* walking. *Address:* 123 Hawthorn Street, Derby DE2 8BB. *Died 1998.*

PETO, Sir Henry (George Morton), 4th Bt *cr* 1855; *b* 29 April 1920; *s* of Comdr Sir Henry Francis Morton Peto, 3rd Bt, RN, and Edith (*d* 1945), *d* of late George Berners Ruck Keene; *S* father, 1978; *m* 1947, Frances Jacqueline, JP, *d* of late Ralph Haldane Evers; two *s*. *Educ:* Sherborne; Corpus Christi College, Cambridge. Served War with Royal Artillery, 1939–46. Manufacturing industry, 1946–80. *Heir:* *s* Francis Michael Morton Peto [*b* 11 Jan. 1949; *m* 1974, Felicity Margaret, *d* of late Lt-Col John Alan Burns; two *s*]. *Died 17 Dec. 2010.*

PIX WESTON, John; *see* Weston.

PROBINE, Dr Mervyn Charles, CB 1986; FRSNZ; FInstD; FNZIM; company director and consultant, since 1986; *b* 30 April 1924; *s* of Frederick Charles and Ann Kathleen Probine; *m* 1949, Marjorie Walker; one *s* one *d*. *Educ:* Univ. of Auckland (BSc); Victoria Univ. of Wellington (MSc); Univ. of Leeds (PhD). Physicist, DSIR, 1946–67; Dir, Physics and Engineering Lab., 1967–77; Asst Dir-Gen., DSIR, 1977–79; State Services Commission: Comr, 1979–80; Dep. Chm., 1980–81; Chm., 1981–86. Chm., GEC (NZ), 1986–95; Dir, Fujitsu (NZ), 1986–2000. Chairman: Legislation Adv. Cttee, 1991–96; Insurance and Savings Ombudsman Commn, 1994–98. Trustee, Nat. Library of NZ, 1992–98. FRSNZ 1964; FNZIM 1985; FInstD 1993 (Dist. Fellow, 2004). *Publications:* numerous scientific research papers and papers on application of science in industry. *Recreations:* bridge, sailing, angling. *Address:* 10A Rodney Road, Northcote, Auckland, New Zealand. *T:* (9) 4198140. *Club:* Wellington (Wellington, NZ). *Died 17 April 2010.*

PRYCE, Rt Rev. (James) Taylor; a Suffragan Bishop of Toronto (Area Bishop of York-Simcoe), 1985–2000; *b* 3 May 1936; *s* of James Pryce and Florence Jane (*née* Taylor); *m* 1962, Marie Louise Connor; two *s* one *d* (and one *s* decd). *Educ:* Bishop's Univ., Lennoxville, Quebec (BA, LST). Ordained deacon, 1962, priest, 1963; Asst Curate, Church of the Ascension, Don Mills, 1962–65; Incumbent: St Thomas' Church, Brooklin, Ont, 1965–70; St Paul's, Lorne Park, 1970–75; Christ Church, Scarborough, 1975–82; St Leonard's, North Toronto, 1982–85. Hon. DD Wycliffe Coll., 1986. *Address:* 12 Walnut Drive, RR#2, Shanty Bay, ON L0L 2L0, Canada. *Died 1 Aug. 2010.*

RAJ, Prof. Kakkadan Nandanath, Padma Vibhushan 2000; Hon. Emeritus Fellow, Centre for Development Studies, Trivandrum, Kerala State, since 1983 (Fellow, 1973–84); National Professor, since 1992; *b* 13 May 1924; *s* of K. N. Gopalan and Karthiayani Gopalan; *m* 1957, Dr Sarasamma Narayanan; two *s*. *Educ:* Madras Christian Coll., Tambaram (BA (Hons), MA, in Economics); London Sch. of Economics (PhD (Econ); Hon. Fellow, 1982). Asst Editor, Associated Newspapers of Ceylon, Nov. 1947–July 1948; Research Officer, Dept of Research, Reserve Bank of India, Aug. 1948–Feb. 1950; Asst Chief, Economic Div., Planning Commn, Govt of India, 1950–53; University of Delhi: Prof. of Economics, Delhi Sch. of Economics, 1953–73; Vice-Chancellor, 1969–70; Nat. Fellow in Economics, 1971–73; Jawaharlal Nehru Fellow, 1987–88. Mem., Economic Adv. Council to Prime Minister of India, 1983–91. Visiting Prof., Johns Hopkins Univ., Jan.-June, 1958; Vis. Fellow, Nuffield Coll., Oxford, Jan.–June, 1960. Corresp. Fellow, British Academy, 1972. Hon. Fellow, Amer. Economic Assoc. *Publications:* The Monetary Policy of the Reserve Bank of India, 1948; Employment Aspects of Planning in Underdeveloped Economies, 1956; Some Economic Aspects of the Bhakra-Nangal Project, 1960; Indian Economic Growth-Performance and Prospects, 1964; India, Pakistan and China-Economic Growth and Outlook, 1966; Investment in Livestock in Agrarian Economies, 1969; (ed jtly) Essays on the

Commercialization of Indian Agriculture, 1985; Organizational Issues in Indian Agriculture, 1990; also articles in Economic Weekly, Economic and Political Weekly, Indian Economic Review, Oxford Economic Papers. *Address:* Nandavan, Kumarapuram, Trivandrum 695011, Kerala State, India. *T:* (home) (471) 443309, (office) (471) 448881, 448412. *Died 10 Feb. 2010.*

RAMA RAU, Santha; free-lance writer, since 1945; English teacher at Sarah Lawrence College, Bronxville, NY, since 1971; *b* Madras, India, 24 Jan. 1923; *d* of late Sir Benegal Rama Rau, CIE and Lady Dhanvanthi Rama Rau; *m* 1st, 1951, Faubion Bowers (marr. diss. 1966); one *s*; 2nd, 1977, Gurdon W. Wattles (*d* 1995). *Educ:* St Paul's Girls' School, London, England; Wellesley College, Mass, USA. Feature writer for the Office of War Information, New York, USA, during vacations from college, 1942–45. Hon. doctorate: Bates College, USA, 1961; Russell Sage College, 1965; Phi Beta Kappa, Wellesley College, 1960; Roosevelt Coll., 1962; Brandeis Univ., 1963; Bard Coll., NY, 1964. *Publications:* Home to India, 1945; East of Home, 1950; This is India, 1953; Remember the House, 1955; View to the South-East, 1957; My Russian Journey, 1959; A Passage to India (dramatization), 1962; Gifts of Passage, 1962; The Adventuress, 1971; Cooking of India, 1971 (2 vols); A Princess Remembers (with Rajmata Gayatri Devi of Jaipur), 1976; An Inheritance (with Dhanvanthi Rama Rau), 1977; many articles and short stories in New Yorker, Art News, Horizon, Saturday Evening Post, Reader's Digest, National Geographic, etc. *Address:* 508 Leedsville Road, Amenia, NY 12501, USA. *Died 21 April 2009.*

RANCHHODLAL, Sir Chinubhai Madhowlal; *see* Chinubhai, Sir U.

RAU, Santha Rama; *see* Rama Rau, S.

REID, Whitelaw; President, Reid Enterprises; *b* 26 July 1913; *s* of late Ogden M. Reid and Mrs Ogden M. Reid; *m* 1st, 1948, Joan Brandon (marr. diss. 1959); two *s*; 2nd, 1959, Elizabeth Ann Brooks; one *s* one *d*. *Educ:* Lincoln Sch., NYC; St Paul's Sch., Concord, New Hampshire; Yale Univ. (BA). New York Herald Tribune: in various departments, 1938–40; foreign correspondent, England, 1940; Assistant to Editor, 1946; Editor, 1947–55; Pres., 1953–55; Chm. of Bd, 1955–58; Director, 1946–65; Dir, 1946–65, Pres., 1946–62, Herald Tribune Fresh Air Fund. Served War of 1939–45, 1st Lieut naval aviator, USNR. Formerly Director: Farfield Foundn; Freedom House; Golden's Bridge Hounds Inc., 1970–83; Dir, Yale Westchester Alumni Assoc. Chm., NY State Cttee on Public Employee Security Procedures, 1956–57. Ambassador to inauguration of President Ponce, Ecuador, 1956. Member: Nat. Commn for Unesco, 1955–60; President's Citizen Advisers on the Mutual Security Program, 1956–57; Yale Alumni Board (Vice-Chm., 1962–64), Yale Univ. Council (Chm., Publications Cttee, 1965–70; Sec., Class of Yale 1936, 1986–91, 2004–; Co-Chm., Class 65th Reunion); Nat. Inst. of Social Sciences, 1959–95; Mem., Council on Foreign Relations, 1941–94. District Comr, Purchase Pony Club, 1964–70; Pres., New York State Horse Council (formerly Empire State Horsemen's Assoc.), 1975–80. Fellow, Pierson Coll., Yale, 1949–. *Address:* (home and office) Reid Enterprises, Ophir Farm North, 73 West Patent Road, Bedford Hills, NY 10507, USA. *Clubs:* Century, Overseas Press, Silurians, Pilgrims, Yale, Amateur Ski (New York); Metropolitan (Washington); Bedford Golf and Tennis; St Regis Yacht. *Died 18 April 2009.*

RICHARDSON, (Henry) Anthony; a Recorder of the Crown Court, 1978–96; a Deputy Traffic Commissioner and a Deputy Licensing Authority, North Eastern Traffic Area, 1989–93; *b* 28 Dec. 1925; *er s* of late Thomas Ewan Richardson and Jessie (*née* Preston), Batley, W Yorks; *m* 1954, Georgina (*née* Lawford) (*d* 2004), *d* of late Rosamond Bedford and step *d* of late Gp Captain G. R. Bedford, MB, ChB, RAF retd. *Educ:* Giggleswick Sch.; Leeds Univ. (LLB 1950, LLM 1956). Called to the Bar, Lincoln's Inn, 1951; North-Eastern Circuit; Dep. Circuit Judge, 1972–78. Chm., a Police Disciplinary Appeal Tribunal, 1983. *Publications:* articles in legal periodicals. *Recreations:* listening to music, British history. *Died 3 Dec. 2010.*

RUTTER, Prof. Arthur John; Professor of Botany, 1967–79, then Emeritus, and Head of Department of Botany and Plant Technology, 1971–79, Imperial College, University of London; *b* 22 Nov. 1917; *s* of late W. Arthur Rutter, CBE, FRIBA and Amy, *d* of William Dyche, BA, Cardiff; *m* 1944, Betsy Rosier Stone (*d* 1978); two *s* one *d*. *Educ:* Royal Grammar Sch., Guildford; Imperial Coll. of Science and Technology. BSc, PhD. ARCS; FSB. Mem., ARC team for selection of oil-seed crops and develt selective herbicides, 1940–45; Asst Lectr, Imperial Coll., 1945, Lectr 1946; Reader in Ecology, Univ. of London, 1956. Vis. Prof., Univ. of the Panjab, Pakistan, 1960–61. *Publications:* papers, mainly in Annals of Botany, Jl of Ecology, Jl of Applied Ecology on water relations of plants, forest hydrology and effects of atmospheric pollution on trees. *Recreations:* gardening, walking. *Address:* 10 Thursby Road, Woking, Surrey GU21 3NZ. *T:* (01483) 765009. *Died 1 Nov. 2010.*

SABATINI, Lawrence John; Assistant Under Secretary of State, Ministry of Defence, 1972–79; *b* 5 Dec. 1919; *s* of Frederick Laurence Sabatini and Elsie May Sabatini (*née* Friggens); *m* 1947, Patricia Dyson; one *s* one *d*. *Educ:* Watford Grammar School. Joined HM Office of Works, 1938. Army service, 1940–46: commnd in RTR, 1943: service in NW Europe with 5 RTR. Asst Principal, Min. of Works, 1947; Asst Private Sec. to Minister of Works, 1948–49; Principal, 1949; Principal Private Sec. to Ministers of Defence, 1958–60; Asst Sec., MoD, 1960; Defence Counsellor, UK Delegn to NATO, on secondment to Diplomatic Service, 1963–67. *Recreations:* gardening, photography, music. *Address:* 44a Batchworth Lane, Northwood, Middx HA6 3DT. *T:* (01923) 823249. *Club:* MCC. *Died 10 July 2010.*

SALTHOUSE, Leonard; Assistant Under Secretary of State, Ministry of Defence, 1977–87; *b* 15 April 1927; *s* of late Edward Keith Salthouse and Dorothy Annie (*née* Clark); *m* 1950, Kathleen May (*née* Spittle); one *s* one *d*. *Educ:* Queen Elizabeth Grammar Sch., Atherstone, Warwickshire; University Coll. London (BScEcon). Home Civil Service: Asst Principal, Min. of Fuel and Power, 1950–55; Principal, Air Min., then Min. of Defence, 1955–66; Asst Sec., 1966–77. *Recreations:* gardening, music. *Address:* Highfield, 115 Cross Oak Road, Berkhamsted, Herts HP4 3HZ. *T:* (01442) 877809. *Died 28 Dec. 2010.*

SAMUELS, Prof. Michael Louis, FRSE; Professor of English Language, University of Glasgow, 1959–89; *b* 14 Sept. 1920; *s* of late Harry Samuels, OBE, MA, barrister-at-law, and Céline Samuels (*née* Aronowitz), London; *m* 1950, Hilary, *d* of late Julius and Ruth Samuel, Glasgow; one *d*. *Educ:* St Paul's School; Balliol College, Oxford (Domus Exhibnr in Classics, 1938–40 and 1945–47; MA 1947 (1st Cl. Hons English Lang. and Lit.)). Worked for Air Ministry (Maintenance Command), 1940–45. Res. Fellow, Univ. of Birmingham, 1947–48; Asst in English Language, 1948–49, Lectr in English Language, 1949–59, Univ. of Edinburgh. Chm., Scottish Studentships Selection Cttee, 1975–88. FRSE 1989. Hon. DLitt Glasgow, 2006. *Publications:* Linguistic Evolution, 1972; (ed jtly) A Linguistic Atlas of Late Medieval English, 1987; (jtly) Middle English Dialectology, 1989; (with J. J. Smith) The English of Chaucer, 1989; contribs to: Approaches to English Historical Linguistics, 1969; So Meny people Longages and Tonges (presented to A. McIntosh), 1981; Middle English Studies (presented to N. Davis), 1983; Proc. 4th Internat. Conf. on English Historical Linguistics, 1985; Explanation and Linguistic Change, 1987; A Companion to Piers Plowman, 1988; (jtly) The Historical Thesaurus of the Oxford English Dictionary, 2009; articles and reviews in linguistic and literary jls. *Died 24 Nov. 2010.*

SCHOLTENS, Sir James (Henry), KCVO 1977 (CVO 1963); Director, Office of Government Ceremonial and Hospitality, Department of the Prime Minister and Cabinet, Canberra, 1973–80; Extra Gentleman Usher to the Queen, since 1981; *b* 12 June 1920; *s* of late Theo F. J. Scholtens and Grace M. E. (*née* Nolan); *m* 1945, Mary Maguire, Brisbane; one *s* five *d*. *Educ:* St Patrick's Marist Brothers' Coll., Sale, Vic. Served War, RAAF, 1943–45. Joined Aust. Public Service, 1935; PMG's Dept, Melbourne, 1935; Dept of Commerce, Melb., 1938; transf. to Dept of Commerce,

Canberra, 1941; Dept of Prime Minister, Canberra: Accountant, 1949; Ceremonial Officer, 1954; Asst Sec., Ceremonial and Hospitality Br., 1967. Dir of visits to Australia by the Sovereign and Members of the Royal Family, Heads of State, Monarchs and Presidents, and by Heads of Govt and Ministers of State. *Address:* Unit 24, 33 Burkitt Street, Page, Canberra, ACT 2614, Australia. *T:* (2) 62542661. *Clubs:* Canberra, Southern Cross (Canberra). *Died 26 July 2010.*

SHEPHERD, Archie; HM Diplomatic Service, retired; Counsellor and Head of Migration and Visa Department, Foreign and Commonwealth Office, 1977–80; *b* 2 Nov. 1922; *s* of William Shepherd and Edith (*née* Browning); *m* 1959, Dorothy Annette Walker (*d* 2000); one *s*. *Educ:* Torquay Grammar Sch. Prison Commission, 1939; served War, RAF, 1942–46. Foreign Office, 1949; Asst Political Agent and Vice Consul, Muscat, 1951–53; FO, 1954–55; Second Sec., UK Delegn to United Nations, Geneva, 1956–57; HM Consul: Warsaw, 1958–60; Rabat, 1960–62; FO, 1963–67; Consul, Cape Town, 1968–72; First Sec. (Commercial), Beirut, 1973–75. *Recreations:* tennis, gardening. *Address:* 9 Oaks Way, Kenley, Surrey CR8 5DT. *T:* (020) 8660 1299. *Clubs:* Civil Service, Royal Commonwealth Society. *Died 9 Jan. 2010.*

SPEELMAN, Sir Cornelis Jacob, 8th Bt *cr* 1686; BA; *b* 17 March 1917; *s* of Sir Cornelis Jacob Speelman, 7th Bt and Maria Catharina Helena Castendijk; *S* father, 1949; *m* 1972, Julia Mona Le Besque (*d* 1978); *m* 1986, Irene Agnes van Leeuwen; two step *c*. Education Dept, Royal Dutch Army, 1947–49; with The Shell Company (Marketing Service Dept), 1950. Student, Univ. of Western Australia, 1952; formerly Master of Modern Languages at Clifton Coll., Geelong Grammar Sch.; Exeter Tutorial Coll. *Died 23 April 2005 (dormant or ext).*

STEWART, Sir James (Douglas), Kt 1983; agricultural consultant; Principal, Lincoln University College of Agriculture, 1974–84; *b* 11 Aug. 1925; *s* of Charles Edward Stewart and Edith May Stewart (*née* Caldwell); *m* 1953, Nancy Elizabeth Dunbar; one *s* three *d*. *Educ:* Lincoln UC (Dip. Valuation and Farm Management); Canterbury Univ. (MA); Reading Univ. (DPhil). Lectr in Farm Management, Lincoln Coll., NZ, 1951–59; Research Fellow, Reading Univ., 1959–61; Sen. Lectr, Lincoln Coll., 1962–64; Prof. of Farm Management, Lincoln Coll., 1964–74, then Emeritus. Chairman: NZ Vice-Chancellors Cttee, 1981–82; NZ Wheat Bd, 1986–87 (Dep. Chm., 1984–86); NZ Nat. Educn Qualifications Authority, 1989–95. Chm., Pyne Gould Guinness Internat. Ltd, 1987–95; Director: Pyne Gould Corp., 1982–95; Alpine Dairy Products Ltd, 1985–91. Chairman: Canterbury Develt Corp., 1983–89 (Dir, 1983–85); Christchurch Sch. of Medicine, 1987–88; NZ Crown Res. Insts Implementation Cttee, 1991–. Silver Jubilee Medal, 1977. *Publications:* contrib. Jl Agricl Econs, Jl Farm Econs, Econ. Record, etc. *Recreations:* swimming, part-time farming. *Address:* 75/95 Grants Road, Papanui, Christchurch, New Zealand. *Died 19 Feb. 2010.*

STOW, (Julian) Randolph; writer; *b* Geraldton, W Australia, 28 Nov. 1935; *s* of Cedric Ernest Stow, barrister, and Mary Stow (*née* Sewell). *Educ:* Guildford Grammar Sch., W Australia; Univ. of Western Australia. Lecturer in English Literature: Univ. of Leeds, 1962; Univ. of Western Australia, 1963–64; Harkness Fellow, United States, 1964–66; Lectr in English and Commonwealth Lit., Univ. of Leeds, 1968–69. Reviewer, TLS, 1976–2002. Britannica Australia Award, 1966; Patrick White Literary Award, 1979. *Publications: poetry:* Act One, 1957; Outrider, 1962; A Counterfeit Silence, 1969; *novels:* A Haunted Land, 1957; The Bystander, 1957; To The Islands, 1958 (Miles Franklin Award, 1958), rev. edn 1981; Tourmaline, 1963; The Merry-go-round in the Sea, 1965; Visitants, 1979; The Girl Green as Elderflower, 1980; The Suburbs of Hell, 1984; *music theatre* (with Peter Maxwell Davies): Eight Songs for a Mad King, 1969; Miss Donnithorne's Maggot, 1974; *for children:* Midnite, 1967. *Address:* c/o Sheil Land Associates Ltd, 52 Doughty Street, WC1N 2LS. *Died 29 May 2010.*

SUMMERSCALE, Peter Wayne; HM Diplomatic Service, retired; Consultant to Central America Direct (conservation volunteers), since 2005; *b* 22 April 1935; *s* of Sir John Summerscale, KBE; *m* 1st, 1964, Valerie Turner (marr. diss. 1983); one *s* two *d*; 2nd, 1985, Cristina Fournier (marr. diss. 1986); 3rd, 1989, Elizabeth Carro. *Educ:* Rugby Sch.; New Coll., Oxford Univ. (Exhibnr; 1st Cl. Hons Modern History); Russian Res. Centre, Harvard Univ. FO, 1960–62; Pol Residency, Bahrain, 1962–65; 1st Sec., Tokyo, 1965–68; FCO, 1968–69; Cabinet Office, 1969–71; 1st Sec. and Head of Chancery, Santiago, Chile, 1971–75; Head of CSCE Unit, FCO, 1976–77; Dep. Leader, UK Delegn, Belgrade Rev. Conf., 1977–78; Counsellor and Head of Chancery, Brussels, 1978–79; Vis. FCO Res. Fellow, RIIA, Chatham House, 1979–81; Head of Civilian Faculty, Nat. Defence Coll., 1981–82; Ambassador to Costa Rica, 1982–86, and concurrently (non-resident) to Nicaragua; Dep. Leader, UK Delegn to CSCE, 1986–89; Exec. Sec., London Information Forum, 1989. Hd, EU Monitoring Mission, Zagreb, 1992; Belgrade, 1995; UK expert, EU Programme for Human Rights in Central America, 1992–99. *Publications:* (jtly) Soviet—East European Dilemmas, 1981; The East European Predicament, 1982; articles on E Europe and communism. *Recreations:* tennis, ski-ing, walking. *Address:* 25B Lady Somerset Road, NW5 1TX. *Died 9 Dec. 2010.*

SUTHERLAND, John Menzies, Eur Ing, CEng, FICE, FIStructE; Secretary, Joint Board of Moderators, Institution of Civil Engineers, 1985–93; *b* 19 June 1928; *s* of John Menzies and Margaret Rae Sutherland; *m* 1962, Margaret Mary (*née* Collins); one *s* one *d*. *Educ:* Royal Technical Coll., Glasgow. FIStructE 1962; CEng, FICE 1968; Eur Ing 1988. Indentured Civil Engineer, City Engineer, Glasgow, 1945–51; Engineer, Costains Group, 1952–56; Site Agent, Pakistan and Chief Engineer, Middle East, Gammon Group, 1956–61; Engineer Adviser (Colombo Plan), new capital city, Islamabad, Pakistan, 1962–66; Associate Partner, Bullen & Partners, 1966–69; Chief Civil Engineer, overseas plant construction, Union International Co. (Vestey Gp Holding Co.), 1970–74; Board Dir and Dir Engineering Projects, Internat. Military Services Ltd, 1974–83 (2 years Malaysia); Gen. Manager, BTR-Swire Projects, Singapore, 1983–85. *Publications:* Naval Bases and Infrastructure, 1979. *Recreations:* music, collecting Victorian ceramics. *Address:* 6 Fursefield Close, Chislehurst, Kent BR7 5DE. *Clubs:* Royal Over-Seas League; Chislehurst Golf. *Died 2 Jan. 2008.*

THOMAS, Elizabeth Marjorie; Secretary General, 1979–83, Literary Consultant, 1984–85, The Authors' Lending and Copyright Society; *b* 10 Aug. 1919; *d* of Frank Porter and Marjorie Porter (*née* Pascall); *m* 1941, George Thomas; one *s* one *d*. *Educ:* St George's Sch., Harpenden; Girton Coll., Cambridge (BA 1st Cl.; MA 1998). Journalist, 1951–59 and Literary Editor, 1959–71, Tribune; Asst Literary Editor, New Statesman, 1971–76; Political Adviser to Rt Hon. Michael Foot, MP, Lord Pres. of the Council and Leader of the House of Commons, 1976–79. Mem., Arts Council, 1974–77 (Mem., Literature Panel, 1971–77); Chm., Literature Panel, Eastern Arts Assoc., 1978–84; Mem., British Council Bd, 1982–88. *Publications:* (ed) Tribune 21, 1959. *Address:* Oakhaven, 136 Hales Road, Cheltenham, Glos GL52 6TB. *T:* (01242) 250310. *Died 5 April 2010.*

THOMAS, Rt Rev. Maxwell McNee, ThD; Warden of St Paul's College, University of Sydney, 1985–94; Lecturer in History and Thought of Christianity, University of Sydney, 1986–94; *b* 23 Aug. 1926; *s* of Rev. Charles Elliot Thomas, ThL, and Elsie Frances Thomas (*née* McNee); *m* 1952, Elaine Joy Walker; two *s* one *d*. *Educ:* St Paul's Coll., Univ. of Sydney (MA, BD); General Theological Seminary, New York (ThD). Lectr in Theology and Greek, St John's Coll., Morpeth, NSW, 1950; deacon, 1950; priest, 1952; Curate: St Peter's, E. Maitland, 1951–52; St Mary Magdalene, Richmond, Surrey, 1952–54; All Saints', Singleton, NSW, 1955. Priest-in-Charge and Rector, The Entrance, NSW, 1955–59; Fellow and Tutor, General Theol. Seminary, NY, 1959–63; Hon. Chaplain to Bishop of New York, 1959–63, Chaplain, 1963–64; Chaplain, Univ. of Melbourne and of Canterbury Fellowship, 1964–68; Consultant Theologian to Archbishop of Melbourne, Stewart Lectr in Divinity, Trinity Coll. and Chaplain of Canterbury Fellowship, 1968–75; Bishop of Wangaratta, 1975–85. Member: Gen. Synod's Commn on Doctrine, 1970–92 (Chm., 1976–92); Faith and Order Commn,

WCC, 1977–79; Internat. Commn for Anglican-Orthodox Theol Dialogue (formerly Anglican-Orthodox Jt Doctrinal Discussion Gp), 1978–2007. *Address:* Martha's Point, 27/165 Osborne Drive, Mount Martha, Vic 3934, Australia. *Fax:* (3) 59754060. *Died 8 Oct. 2008.*

THOMAS, Sir Michael; *see* Thomas, Sir W. M. M.

THOMAS, Roger Lloyd; Senior Clerk (Acting), Committee Office, House of Commons, 1979–84 and Clerk, Select Committee on Welsh Affairs, 1982–84; *b* 7 Feb. 1919; *er s* of Trevor John Thomas and Eleanor Maud (*née* Jones), Abercarn, Mon; *m* 1945, Stella Mary, *d* of Reginald Ernest Willmett, Newport, Mon; three *s* one *d.* *Educ:* Barry County Sch.; Magdalen Coll., Oxford (Doncaster Schol.; Heath Harrison Trav. Schol.). BA 2nd Mod. Langs, 1939; MA 1946. Pres., OU Italian Soc., 1938–39. Served 1939–46, RA and Gen. Staff (Major GSO2) in India, Middle East, N Africa, Italy and Germany. Civil Servant, 1948–70: Min. of Fuel and Power, Home Office, Treasury, Welsh Office and Min. of Housing and Local Govt; Private Sec. to Perm. Under-Sec. of State, Home Office, 1950 and to successive Parly Under-Secs of State, 1951–53; Sec., Interdeptl Cttee on powers of Subpoena, 1960; Asst Sec., 1963; Sec., Aberfan Inquiry Tribunal, 1966–67; Chm., Working Party on Building by Direct Labour Organisations, 1968–69; Gen. Manager, The Housing Corporation, 1970–73; Asst Sec., DoE, 1974–79. *Publications:* sundry reports. *Recreation:* growing flowers. *Address:* 5 Park Avenue, Caterham, Surrey CR3 6AH. *T:* (01883) 342080. *Club:* Union (Oxford). *Died 12 June 2010.*

THOMAS, Sir (William) Michael (Marsh), 3rd Bt *cr* 1918, of Garreglwyd, Anglesey; *b* 4 Dec. 1930; *s* of Sir William Eustace Rhyddlad Thomas, 2nd Bt, and Enid Helena Marsh; *S* father 1957; *m* 1957, Geraldine Mary (*d* 2002), *d* of Robert Drysdale, Anglesey; three *d.* *Educ:* Oundle School, Northants. Formerly Man. Dir, Gors Nurseries Ltd. *Died 2009 (ext).*

THOMPSON, James Craig; Chairman, MD Presscom Ltd, 1997–2007; *b* 27 Oct. 1933; *s* of Alfred Thompson and Eleanor (*née* Craig); *m* 1957, Catherine (*née* Warburton); one *s* one *d.* *Educ:* Heaton Grammar Sch., Newcastle upon Tyne; Rutherford Coll., Newcastle upon Tyne. Commercial Exec., Belfast Telegraph, Newcastle Chronicle and Journal, Scotsman Publications, Liverpool Post and Echo, 1960–76; Advertising and Marketing Manager, Kent Messenger Gp, 1976–79, Dir, 1972–79; Man. Dir, South Eastern Newspapers, 1975–79; Chm. and Man. Dir, 1973–89, Consultant Dir, 1989–92, Adverkit Internat. Ltd; Chm. and Man. Dir, Harvest Publications Ltd, 1983–95; Director of Policy: Maidstone and Mid Kent Chamber of Commerce and Industry Ltd, 1994–2003; Kent Gateway Chamber of Commerce, 2001–03. Dir, Weekly Newspaper Advtg Bureau, 1977. Director: Ad Builder Ltd, 1971–89; MLO Ltd, 2000–; Business Point Maidstone Ltd, 1996–2002; Maidstone Enterprise Agency Ltd, 1998–2002; Associated Kent Chambers, 2001–03. Chm., Otham Parish Council, Kent, 2005–. Life Governor, Kent County Agricl Soc., 1974. Hon. Life Mem., Kent CCC, 1978; Mem., Catenian Assoc. (Pres., Maidstone Circle, 1974–75). Chm., Maidstone United Football Club, 1970–92; Chm., Southern Football League, 1977–79 (Life Mem., 1985); Pres., The Football Conf. Ltd, 1989–2008; Mem. Council, Football Assoc., 1982–92. FInstD; MInstM; MCMI. Freeman, City of London; Liveryman, Co. of Stationers and Newspaper Makers. Distinguished Service Award, Internat. Classified Advertising Assoc., Baltimore, 1968. *Publications:* numerous articles on commercial aspects of newspaper publishing and Association football. *Recreations:* walking, Northumbrian history. *Address:* Greenlands, Honey Lane, Otham, Maidstone, Kent ME15 8RJ. *T:* (01622) 861606. *Clubs:* MCC; Maidstone (Maidstone) (Life Mem., Pres., 1997). *Died 16 Jan. 2009.*

THOMPSON, William John; former politician, Northern Ireland; *b* 26 Oct. 1939; *s* of William H. Thompson and Catherine Thompson; *m* 1962, Violet Joyce Armstrong; one *s* two *d.* *Educ:* Edenderry Primary Sch.; Deverney Primary Sch.; Omagh Acad. With Tyrone CC, 1957–66; radio and TV retailer, 1966–97. Member: NI Assembly, 1973–74 and 1982–85; NI Convention, 1975–76; Omagh DC, 1981–93. MP (UU) Tyrone West, 1997–2001; contested same seat, 2001. Methodist local preacher, 1962–. *Recreations:* reading, occasional round of golf. *Address:* 129 Donaghanie Road, Beragh, Co. Tyrone, N Ireland BT79 0XE. *Died 12 Dec. 2010.*

TINSTON, Robert Sydney, CBE 2001; Regional Director, NHS Executive North West, 1996–2002; Vice Chair, Western Cheshire Primary Care Trust, since 2009; *b* 29 March 1951; *s* of Sydney Tinston and Rita (*née* Jardine); *m* 1975, Catherine Mary Somers; one *s* one *d.* *Educ:* Stockport Sch.; Edinburgh Univ. (BSc). DipHSM 1979; MHSM 1979. Assistant Sector Administrator: Withington Hosp., Manchester, 1976–78; King's Coll. Hosp., London, 1978–79; Hosp. Sec., Cookridge Hosp., Leeds, 1979–83; Commissioning Officer, Clarendon Wing, Leeds, 1983–86; Gen. Manager, Leeds General Infirmary, 1986–89; Chief Exec., Royal Liverpool Hosp., 1989–91; Dep. Chief Exec., then Chief Exec., Mersey RHA, 1991–94; Chief Exec., NW RHA, 1994–96. Non-exec. Dir, NHS Western Cheshire, 2006–08 and 2009–; Interim Chm., Robert Jones and Agnes Hunt Hosp., 2008–09. FRSA 1994; CCMI (CIMgt 1997). Hon. Vis. Prof., Univ. of Manchester, 1996–. *Recreations:* astronomy, genealogy, Stockport County Football Club. *Address:* The Thatched Cottage, Utkinton, Tarporley, Cheshire CW6 0LL. *Died 7 Feb. 2010.*

TRIPP, (John) Peter, CMG 1971; HM Diplomatic Service, retired; Consultant, Al-Tajir Bank, since 1986; *b* 27 March 1921; *s* of Charles Howard and Constance Tripp; *m* 1948, Rosemary Rees Jones; one *s* one *d.* *Educ:* Bedford Sch.; Sutton Valence Sch.; L'Institut de Touraine. Served War of 1939–45, Royal Marines, 1941–46. Sudan Political Service, 1946–54; Foreign (subsequently Diplomatic) Service, 1954–81; Political Agent, Trucial States, 1955–58; Head of Chancery, Vienna, 1958–61; Economic Secretary, Residency Bahrain, 1961–63; Counsellor 1963; Political Agent, Bahrain, 1963–65; sabbatical year at Durham Univ., 1965; Amman, 1966–68; Head of Near Eastern Dept, FCO, 1969–70; Ambassador to Libya, 1970–74; High Comr in Singapore, 1974–78; Ambassador to Thailand, 1978–81. Political Adviser, Inchcape Gp, 1981–86; Chm., Private Investment Co. for Asia (UK), 1981–84. County Councillor (Ind.), Powys, 1985–87. Chairman: Anglo-Thai Soc., 1983–88; Montgomeryshire Br., CPRW, 1990–94. *Recreations:* theatre, gardening. *Address:* 43 Kempe Road, NW6 6SP. *Died 11 Dec. 2010.*

TUPPER, Sir Charles Hibbert, 5th Bt *cr* 1888, of Armdale, Halifax, Nova Scotia; *b* 4 July 1930; *o s* of Sir James Macdonald Tupper, 4th Bt, formerly Assistant Commissioner, Royal Canadian Mounted Police, and Mary Agnes Jean Collins; *S* father, 1967; *m* 1959, Bernice Yvonne Quinn (marr. diss. 1976); one *s.* *Heir:* *s* Charles Hibbert Tupper [*b* 10 July 1964; *m* 1987, Elizabeth Ann Heaslip; one *d*]. *Address:* 955 Marine Drive, Apt 1101, West Vancouver, BC V7T 1A9, Canada. *Died 25 May 2008.*

WALKER, Prof. Thomas William, ONZM 2000; DSc; ARCS; DIC; Professor of Soil Science, Lincoln College, New Zealand, 1961–79, then Emeritus; *b* 22 July 1916; *m* 1940, Edith Edna Bott; four *d.* *Educ:* Loughborough Grammar School; Royal College of Science. Royal Scholar and Kitchener Scholar, 1935–39; Salter's Fellow, 1939–41; Lecturer and Adviser in Agricultural Chemistry, Univ. of Manchester, 1941–46. Provincial Advisory Soil Chemist, NAAS, 1946–51; Prof. of Soil Science, Canterbury Agric. Coll., New Zealand, 1952–58; Prof. of Agric., King's Coll., Newcastle upon Tyne, 1958–61. Bledisloe Medal, Lincoln Univ., 1997; Gold (later Rutherford) Medal, Royal Soc. of NZ, 1998; Inaugural Jubilee Medal, NZ Inst. Agricl Sci., 2003. *Publications:* Vegetable Growers Handbook for New Zealanders, 1992; numerous research. *Recreations:* fishing, gardening. *Address:* 843 Cashmere Road, Christchurch 3, New Zealand. *Died 8 Nov. 2010.*

WALKINE, Herbert Cleveland, CMG 1990; CVO 1994; OBE 1985; Secretary to the Cabinet, Bahamas, 1987–94; *b* 28 Nov. 1929; *s* of late Herbert Granville Walkine and Rebecca Walkine; *m* 1966, Julliette Pam Maria Sherman; three *d.* *Educ:* Government High Sch., Nassau; Bahamas Teachers' Coll.; Univ. of Manchester. Started career as teacher; served as District Commissioner, 1958–68; Asst

Sec., 1968, First Asst Sec., 1969, Dep. Perm. Sec., 1970, Under Sec., 1972, Perm. Sec., 1974–87, Bahamas. Chm., Public Disclosure Commn. *Recreations:* fishing, reading, watching boxing matches. *Address:* PO Box CB 13333, Nassau, Bahamas. *T:* 3255979. *Died 20 Aug. 2009.*

WATTLES, Santha; *see* Rama Rau, S.

WATTS, William Arthur, ScD; MRIA; Provost, Trinity College, Dublin, 1981–91; *b* 26 May 1930; *s* of William Low Watts and Bessie (*née* Dickinson); *m* 1954, Geraldine Mary Magrath; two *s* one *d*. *Educ:* Trinity Coll., Dublin (MA, ScD). Lecturer in Botany, Univ. of Hull, 1953–55; Trinity College, Dublin: Lectr in Botany, 1955–65; Fellow, 1970; Professor of Botany, 1965–80; Prof. of Quaternary Ecology, 1980–81. Adjunct Prof. of Geology, Univ. of Minnesota, 1975–. Pres., RIA, 1982–85. Governor: National Gallery of Ireland, 1982–85; Marsh's Library, 1981–91; Member: Dublin Inst. for Advanced Studies, 1981–91; Scholarship Exchange Bd, Ireland, 1982–. Chairman: Federated Dublin Voluntary Hosps, 1983–89; Mercer's Hosp., 1975–83; Mercer's Hosp. Foundn, 1983–; Health Res. Bd, Ireland, 1987–89; Fota Trust, Co. Cork, 1992–; Dublin Dental Hosp., 1999–2007. Hon. LLD QUB, 1990; Hon. DSc NUI, 1991. *Publications:* numerous articles on aspects of quaternary ecology. *Recreations:* walking, conservation studies, music. *Address:* Room 24.02, Trinity College, Dublin 2, Ireland. *T:* (home) (1) 2887130. *Died 26 April 2010.*

WESTON, John Pix, BSc(Eng), BSc(Econ); CEng, FIET; investment consultant, since 1984; *b* 3 Jan. 1920; *s* of John Pix Weston and Margaret Elizabeth (*née* Cox); *m* 1948, Ivy (*née* Glover); three *s*. *Educ:* King Edward's Sch., Birmingham, 1931–36; Univ. of Aston, 1946–50 (BScEng, Hons); Univ. of London (LSE), 1954–57 (BScEcon, Hons). CEng 1953, FIET (FIEE 1966); FSS 1958; FREconS 1958. Mil. Service, 1939–46, S Africa and Albania. City of Birmingham: Police Dept, 1936–39; Electricity Supply Dept, 1939–48; Midlands Electricity Bd, 1948–50; English Electricity Co., 1950–51; NW Elec. Bd, 1951–58; Eastern Elec. Bd, 1958–60; Dep. Operating Manager, Jamaica Public Services Co., 1960–61; Principal Asst Engr, Midlands Elec. Bd, 1961–64; Asst Ch. Commercial Officer, S of Scotland Elec. Bd, 1964–66; Sen. Econ. Adviser to Mrs Barbara Castle, MoT, 1966–69; Sen. Econ. and Chartered Engr, IBRD, 1968–70; Michelin Tyre Co., France, 1970–72; Dir of Post Experience Courses, Open Univ., 1972–75; Dir Gen., RoSPA, 1975–77; Gen. Sec., Birmingham Anglers' Assoc., 1977; Industrial Develt Officer, Argyll and Bute, 1977–79; Health, Safety and Welfare Officer, Newcastle Polytechnic, and Central Safety Advr, Northants CC, 1979; Chief Admin. Officer and Clerk to Governors, W Bromwich Coll. of Commerce and Tech., 1979–85. Hon. Sec. and Treasurer, Assoc. of Coll. Registrars and Administrators (W Midlands), 1982–85. Council Mem., Midlands Counties Photographic Fedn, 1984–86; Hon. Prog., Competition and Outings Sec. and Council Mem., Birmingham Photographic Soc., 1981–86; MIES 1963; Mem., Assoc. of Public Lighting Engrs, 1962. FCMI (FBIM 1977). Chm., Upper Marlbrook Residents' Assoc., 1982–87; Treasurer, Laugharne Cons. Assoc., 1991–94 (Asst Treasurer, 1990–91). Member: Narberth and Dist Probus Club, 1988–96; St Clears Probus Club, 1989–96 (Pres., 1990–91); Tenby Probus Club, 1990–96. Page Prize, IEE, 1950; Rosebery Prize, Univ. of London, 1957. SBStJ 1962. *Publications:* papers, reports and other contribs on electricity, highways, educn (espec. function and progress of the Open University), safety, etc, to public bodies, congresses and conferences, UK and abroad. *Recreations:* cine photography, gardening, swimming, fell walking. *Address:* Brook Mill & Woodside, Brook, Pendine, Carmarthenshire SA33 4NX. *T:* (01994) 427477. *Clubs:* Farmers, St John House; Birmingham Press. *Died 26 Aug. 2010.*

WHITFIELD LEWIS, Herbert John; *see* Lewis.

WIIN-NIELSEN, Aksel Christopher, Fil.Dr; Secretary-General, World Meteorological Organization, 1980–83; Professor, Geophysical Institute, University of Copenhagen, 1988–94, then Emeritus; *b* 17 Dec. 1924; *s* of Aage Nielsen and Marie Petre (*née* Kristoffersen); *m* 1953, Bente Havsteen (*née* Zimsen); three *d*. *Educ:* Univ. of Copenhagen (MSc 1950); Univ. of Stockholm (Fil.Lic. 1957; Fil.Dr 1960). Danish Meteorol Inst., 1952–55; Staff Member: Internat. Meteorol Inst., Stockholm, 1955–58; Jt Numerical Weather Prediction Unit, Suitland, Md, USA, 1959–61; Asst Dir, Nat. Center for Atmospherical Research, Boulder, Colorado, 1961–63; Prof., Dept of Atmospheric and Oceanic Sci., Univ. of Michigan, 1963–73; Dir, European Centre for Medium-Range Weather Forecasts, Reading, 1974–79; Dir, Danish Meteorol Office, 1984–87. Pres., European Geophysical Soc., 1988–90; Vice-Pres., Danish Acad. of Technical Scis, 1989–92 (Mem., 1984–); Member: Finnish Acad. of Arts and Scis; Royal Swedish Acad. of Sci.; Danish Royal Soc., 1986–; Hon. Member: RMetS; Amer. Meteorol Soc., 1994; European Geophysical Soc., 1998. Hon. DSc: Reading, 1982; Copenhagen, 1986. Buys Ballot Medal, Royal Netherlands Acad., 1982; Wihuri Internat. Prize, Finland, 1983; Rossby Prize, Sweden, 1987; Friedman Rescue Award, Friedman Foundn, Calif., 1993. *Publications:* Dynamic Meteorology, 1970; Predictability, 1987; Fundamentals of Atmospheric Energetics, 1993; over 100 scientific publications. *Address:* Kirstinedalsvej 11, Room 302, 2000 Frederiksberg, Denmark. *Died 26 April 2010.*

WILLIAMS, David Claverly, CVO 1970; CBE 1977; *b* 31 July 1917; *s* of late Rev. Canon Henry Williams, OBE, and Ethel Florence Williams; *m* 1944, Elizabeth Anne Fraser (*d* 2010); three *d*. *Educ:* Christ's Coll., Christchurch, NZ; Victoria Univ. of Wellington. Professional Exam. in Public Administration. Inland Revenue Dept, 1936–39. Served War, NZTF, 1939–41, 2NZEF, Pacific and Middle East, 1941–46. NZ Forest Service, 1946–60; Official Sec. to the Governor-General of NZ, 1960–77; Sec./Manager, The Wellington Club (Inc.), 1978–82. *Address:* 20 Bellbird Crescent, Woodlands, Waikanae 5036, New Zealand. *Club:* Wellington (Wellington). *Died 7 Aug. 2010.*

WILLIAMS, Geoffrey Guy; Public Works Loan Commissioner, 1990–98; *b* 12 July 1930; *s* of late Captain Guy Williams, OBE, and Mrs Margaret Williams (*née* Thomas). *Educ:* Blundell's Sch.; Christ's Coll., Cambridge (BA 1952; MA 1961; LLB 1953; LLM 1988). Slaughter and May, Solicitors, 1952–66, Partner 1961; Dir, J. Henry Schroder Wagg & Co. Ltd, 1966–90, Vice-Chm. 1974, Dep. Chm., 1977–90. Chm., National Film Finance Corp., 1976–85 (Dir, 1970). Director: Bass plc, 1971–91; Schroders plc, 1976–90; John Brown plc, 1977–85; Standard Chartered plc, 1990–94. Chm., Issuing Houses Assoc., 1979–81. *Recreations:* reading, theatre, cinema. *Address:* 18G Eaton Square, SW1W 9DD. *T:* (020) 7235 5212. *Club:* Brooks's. *Died 7 July 2010.*

WILSON, Geoffrey; Chairman, Wells, O'Brien & Co., 1972–82; *b* 11 July 1929; *m* 1962, Philomena Mary Kavanagh; one *s* one *d*. *Educ:* Bolton County Grammar Sch.; Univ. of Birmingham; Linacre Coll., Oxford. PE Consulting Group, 1958–63; British Railways, 1963–71; Mem., BR Bd, 1968–71, Chief Exec. (Railways), 1971. Member: Council, Royal Inst. of Public Admin, 1970–71; Council, Inst. of Transport, 1970–71. *Recreations:* golf, gardening, painting. *Address:* 10 Montpellier Grove, Cheltenham, Glos GL50 2XB. *Died 26 Jan. 2010.*

WILSON, (Katherine) Muriel (Irwin), OBE 1985; Chairman and Chief Executive, Equal Opportunities Commission for Northern Ireland, 1981–84; *b* 3 Dec. 1920; *d* of Francis Hosford and Martha Evelyn (*née* Irwin); *m* 1949, William George Wilson; one *s*. *Educ:* Methodist Coll., Belfast; The Queen's University of Belfast (DPA). Northern Ireland Civil Service, 1939–49; N Ireland Health Service, 1949–73: Eastern Special Care Management Cttee (Services for the Mentally Handicapped): Asst Sec., 1963–71; Gp Sec. and Chief Admin. Officer, 1971–73; Asst Chief Admin. Officer (Personnel and Management Services), Northern Health and Social Services Board, 1973–81. Chm. NI Div., 1977–79, National Vice-Pres. 1979–81, United Kingdom Fedn of Business and Professional Women; Member: Bd, Labour Relations Agency (NI), 1976–81; Fair Employment Agency for NI, 1981–84; NI Adv. Cttee, IBA, 1978–83; NI Council, RIPA, 1985–88; Women's Forum, NI, 1990–. Dir, Ulster

Telethon Trust, 1989–2000. Chairman, Board of Governors: Glenravel Special Sch., Belfast, 1987–93; Hill Croft Sch., Newtownabbey, 1987–89; Glenveagh Sch., Belfast, 1993–97; Chm., Whiteabbey Hosp. League of Friends, 1989–92. MCMI. *Recreations:* swimming, reading. *Died 26 Feb. 2010.*

WOOD, Leslie Walter; General Secretary, Union of Construction, Allied Trades and Technicians, 1978–85; Member, TUC General Council, 1979–85; *b* 27 Nov. 1920; *s* of Walter William Wood and Alice Bertha Wood (*née* Clark); *m* 1945, Irene Gladys Emery; two *d. Educ:* Birmingham Central Technical Coll.; Ruskin Coll., Oxford. Apprenticed carpenter and joiner, 1935; RAF, 1939–45; Asst Workers' Sec., Cadbury's Works Council, 1948–49; full time employment in Union, 1953–85; Asst Gen. Sec., Amalgamated Soc. of Woodworkers, 1962. Mem. Council, ACAS, 1980–85. *Publications:* A Union to Build (history of Building Trades Unionism), 1979. *Recreations:* golf, swimming, bridge. *Address:* 67 Chestnut Grove, South Croydon, Surrey CR2 7LL. *T:* (020) 8657 7852. *Died 11 Oct. 2010.*

WRIGHT, Rt Rev. Benjamen; Bishop of Bendigo, 1992–93; former Priest in charge, Heathridge, Western Australia; *b* 15 March 1942; *s* of Clarice and Herbert Wright; *m* 1966, Annette Jennifer Dunne; two *s* one *d. Educ:* Slade Sch., Warwick, Qld; Murdoch Univ., Perth (ThL, BA). Ordained deacon, 1964, priest, 1965; Asst Curate, Applecross, 1964–67; Priest-in-charge, 1967–69, Rector, 1969–71, Narembeen; Army Reserve Chaplain, 1971–76; Rector, Alice Springs and Chaplain, St Mary's Child and Welfare Services, dio. of NT, 1976–80; Rector, Scarborough, 1980–88; Archdeacon of Stirling, 1986–88; Rector, Kalgoorlie, Boulder, 1988; Asst Bishop, dio. of Perth (Goldfields Region), 1988–91; Archdeacon of Goldfields, 1988–89; Archdeacon of O'Connor, 1990; Rector of Busselton, WA, 1993. Hon. Canon of Christ Church Cathedral, Darwin, 1979–80. *Recreations:* fishing, gardening. *Address:* PO Box 785, Joondalup, WA 6919, Australia. *Died 22 Jan. 2010.*

YOUNG, John Richard Dendy; Attorney of Supreme Court, South Africa, 1984; *b* 4 Sept. 1907; 5th *s* of James Young and Evelyn Maud Hammond; *m* 1946, Patricia Maureen Mount; four *s* two *d. Educ:* Hankey, Cape Province, SA; Humansdorp, CP, SA; University, South Africa (External). Joined Public Service, S Rhodesia, 1926; resigned to practise at Bar, 1934; joined Military Forces, 1940; active service, North Africa, Sicily and Italy; commissioned in the field; demobilised, 1945. QC 1948; MP Southern Rhodesia, 1948–53; Member Federal Assembly, 1953–56; Judge of the High Court of Rhodesia, 1956–68; Chief Justice, Botswana, 1968–71; Advocate of Supreme Court of SA, 1971–84; Sen. Counsel, 1979–84; Judge of Appeal, Lesotho, Swaziland, Botswana, 1979–84. *Recreations:* swimming, walking. *Address:* 8 Tulani Gardens, Greenfield Road, Kenilworth, Cape, 7700, South Africa. *Died 11 July 1998.*

A

ABBADO, Claudio; Artistic Director, Berlin Philharmonic Orchestra, 1989–2002; Generalmusikdirektor of Vienna, since 1987; *b* Milan, 26 June 1933; *m* 1st, 1956, Giovanna Cavazzoni (marr. diss. 1968); one *s* one *d*; 2nd, Gabriella Cantalupi; one *s*. Music Dir, La Scala, Milan, 1968–86; Principal Conductor, LSO, 1979–88; Music Director, Vienna State Opera, 1986–91. Founder, European Community Youth Orch., 1978; Artistic Advr, Chamber Orchestra of Europe, 1981–; Founder and Artistic Director: Gustav Mahler Jugend Orchester, 1988; Festival, Wien Modern, 1988; Artistic Dir, Salzburg Easter Fest., 1994; Chief Conductor and Music Dir, Lucerne Fest. Orch., 2003. Dr *hc*: Aberdeen, 1986; Ferrara, 1990; Cambridge, 1994. Mozart-Medaille, Mozartgemeinde, Vienna, 1973; Goldmedaille der Internat. Gustav Mahler Gesellschaft, Vienna, 1985; winner of major international prizes for recordings. Ehrenring, City of Vienna, 1994. Gran Croce d'Italia, 1984; Cross, Légion d'Honneur; Bundesverdienstkreuz (Germany), 1992; Praemium Imperiale Award (Japan), 2003. *Address:* c/o Askonas Holt Ltd, Lincoln House, 300 High Holborn, WC1V 7JH. *Died 20 Jan. 2014.*

ABBOTT, Adm. Sir Peter (Charles), GBE 1999; KCB 1994; Vice Chief of the Defence Staff, 1997–2001; Commissioner, Commonwealth War Graves Commission, 2001–06; *b* 12 Feb. 1942; *s* of late Lieut-Col Dennis Abbott, Royal Garwhal Rifles and Delphine McConaghey; *m* 1965, Susan Phillippa Grey; three *d*. *Educ:* St Edward's Sch., Oxford; Queens' College, Cambridge (MA 1966). Articled Clerk, Blackburn, Robson Coates, 1963; 2nd Lieut, RMFVR 1963; Sub Lieut, RN 1964; Commanding Officer, HM Ships Chawton, 1972, Ambuscade, 1976, Ajax, 1983 (and First Frigate Sqdn); RCDS 1985; Flag Officer, Flotilla Two, 1989; ACNS, 1991–93; Dep. SACLANT, 1993–95; C-in-C Fleet, C-in-C Eastern Atlantic Area and Comdr Naval Forces N Western Europe, 1995–97. Chairman: Trustees, 2003–10, Mgt Bd, 2010–, Royal Naval Mus.; Bd of Dirs, Nat. Mus. of Royal Navy, 2008–10. King of Arms, Order of the British Empire, 2010–. Officer, US Legion of Merit, 1995. *Died 28 Sept. 2015.*

ABDY, Sir Valentine (Robert Duff), 6th Bt *cr* 1850; European Representative, Smithsonian Institution, Washington, 1983–95 and 1998 (Member, National Board, 1995–98); *b* 11 Sept. 1937; *s* of Sir Robert Henry Edward Abdy, 5th Bt, and Lady Diana Bridgeman (*d* 1967), *e d* of 5th Earl of Bradford; *S* father, 1976; *m* 1971, Mathilde Coche de la Ferté (marr. diss. 1982); one *s*. *Educ:* Eton. Formerly: Administrator, Musée des Arts Décoratifs, Paris; Dir, Sotheby's (opened Sotheby's Paris, 1967, Sotheby's Munich, 1970). Member: Art Adv. Bd, Artemis, 1973–75; Scientific Committee, Conservatoire Nationale des Arts et Métiers, 1992; Special Advr, Internat. Fund for Promotion of Culture, UNESCO, 1991–97. Mem., Organising Cttee, Cité de l'Espace, Toulouse, 1999. FRSA 1998. Chevalier des Arts et des Lettres (France), 1995. *Heir: s* Robert Etienne Eric Abdy, *b* 22 Feb. 1978. *Address:* 2 New Square, Lincoln's Inn, WC2A 3RZ. *Died 27 June 2012.*

ABER, Prof. Geoffrey Michael, FRCP; Professor of Renal Medicine, University of Keele, 1982–93; *b* 19 Feb. 1928; *s* of David and Hilda Aber; *m* 1964, Eleanor Maureen; one *s* one *d*. *Educ:* Leeds Grammar School; University of Leeds (MB, ChB, MD with distinction); PhD Birmingham. Leeds Gen. Infirmary, 1952–54; RAMC, 1954–56; Queen Elizabeth Hosp., Birmingham (Univ. of Birmingham), 1956–57, 1958–65; Brompton Hosp., London, 1957–58; Research Fellow: Univ. of Birmingham (Depts of Exptl Path. and Medicine), 1958–59 and 1960–64; McGill Univ., 1959–60; Wellcome Sen. Res. Fellow in Clinical Sci., 1964–65; Keele University: Prof. and Adviser in Clinical Res., 1979–82; Head of Dept of Postgrad. Medicine, 1982–89; Dean of Postgrad. Medicine, 1989–91. *Publications:* contribs to: Recent Advances in Renal Medicine, 1983; Postgraduate Nephrology, 1985; Textbook of Genitourinary Surgery, 1985; scientific papers in learned jls. *Recreations:* music, sport, motor cars. *Address:* Mill Green House, Stone Rings Grange, Harrogate HG2 9HU. *T:* (01423) 871737. *E:* g.aber@btopenworld.com. *Died 15 March 2014.*

ABRAHAMS, Anthony Claud Walter; advocate and solicitor, Brunei Darussalam, 1987–2000; *b* 16 June 1923; *s* of late Rt Hon. Sir Sidney Abrahams, QC, and of Ruth Bowman; *m* 1st, 1950, Laila Myking (marr. diss.); two *s* one *d*; 2nd, 1982, Elizabeth, *d* of late Comdr A. E. Bryant, RN. *Educ:* Bedford Sch.; Emmanuel Coll., Cambridge (MA). Barrister-at-law. Served War: Wavell Cadet, Bangalore, 1942–43; commnd 3/12 Royal Bn, Frontier Force Regt, 1943–45; India, N Africa, Italy, Greece (despatches). Called to the Bar, Middle Temple, 1951; practised Midland Circuit, 1951–64. Gov., 1966–88, Chm., 1978–88, Harpur Trust (the Bedford Charity). Centre for British Teachers: Founder, 1964; Dir, 1973–82; Life Pres., 1982. Mem., Educn Cttee, British-Malaysian Soc., 1986–96. Liveryman, Glaziers' Co., 1976. Kt, Order of Uggla (Norway), 1962. *Recreations:* golf, watching cricket and Rugby, wine, travel. *Address:* Berry Cottage, Southey Green, Sible Hedingham, Halstead, Essex CO9 3RN. *Club:* Garrick. *Died 22 April 2011.*

ABRAHAMS, Ivor, RA 1991 (ARA 1989); FRBS 1996; sculptor; Professor of Sculpture, Royal Academy Schools, 2008–11; *b* 10 Jan. 1935; *s* of Harry Abrahams and Rachel Kalisky; *m* 1st, 1965, Victoria Taylor; (one *s* decd); 2nd, 1974, Evelyne Horvais; one *s*. *Educ:* Wigan Grammar Sch.; St Martin's and Camberwell Schools of Art. NDD(ScSp). Visiting Lecturer: Birmingham College of Art, 1960–63; Coventry College of Art, 1963–66; RCA, Slade Sch., 1980–82. *Major Exhibitions:* Kölnischer Kunstverein, Cologne, 1973; Ikon Gall., Birmingham, 1976; Yorkshire Sculpture Park, Wakefield, 1984. *Public Collections:* Arts Council of GB; Bibliothèque Nat., Paris; Brit. Council; Denver Mus., Colorado; Metropolitan Mus., NY; Nat. Gall. of Australia, Canberra; Tate Gall.; Mus. of Modern Art, NY; V&A Mus.; Wilhelm Lembruck Mus., Duisburg, W Germany; Boymans Mus., Rotterdam; Leeds City Art Gall., etc. Winston Churchill Fellow, 1990. *Publications:* E. A. Poe: poems and tales (foreword Norbert Lynton), 1976; Oxford Garden Sketchbook (foreword Robert Melville), 1977; *relevant publication:* The Life and Work of Ivor Abrahams, ed by Andrew Lambirth, 2012. *Recreations:* reading, digital photography. *Address:* c/o Royal Academy, Burlington House, W1J 0BD. *W:* www.ivorabrahams.com. *Clubs:* Chelsea Arts, Arts. *Died 6 Jan. 2015.*

ABSE, Dr Dannie, CBE 2012; FRSL; Specialist in charge of chest clinic, Central Medical Establishment, London, 1954–89; writer; *b* 22 Sept. 1923; *s* of Rudolph Abse and Kate (*née* Shepherd); *m* 1951, Joan Mercer (*d* 2005), art historian; one *s* two *d*. *Educ:* St Illtyd's Coll., Cardiff; University Coll., Cardiff; King's Coll., London (FKC 2009); Westminster Hosp., London. MRCS, LRCP. First book of poems accepted for publication, 1946. Qualified at Westminster Hosp., 1950; RAF, 1951–54, Sqdn Ldr; Sen. Fellow of the Humanities, Princeton Univ., 1973–74. Pres., Poetry Soc., 1978–92. FRSL 1983; Fellow, Welsh Acad. of Letters, 1992 (Pres., 1995). Hon. Fellow, Univ. of Wales Coll. of Med., 1999. Hon. DLitt: Wales, 1989; Glamorgan, 1997. *Publications: poetry:* After Every Green Thing, 1948; Walking Under Water, 1952; Tenants of the House, 1957; Poems, Golders Green, 1962; A Small Desperation, 1968; Funland and other Poems, 1973; Collected Poems, 1977; Way Out in the Centre, 1981; Ask the Bloody Horse, 1986; White Coat, Purple Coat, 1989; Remembrance of Crimes Past, 1990; Selected Poems, 1994; On the Evening Road, 1994; Welsh Retrospective, 1997; Arcadia, One Mile, 1998; New and Collected Poems, 2003; Running Late, 2006; New Selected Poems, 2009; Two for Joy, 2010; Speak, Old Parrot, 2013; *prose:* A Strong Dose of Myself, 1983; Journals from the Ant Heap, 1986; Intermittent Journals, 1994; The Two Roads Taken, 2003; The

Presence, 2007; Dannie Abse: a sourcebook, 2010; *novels:* Ash on a Young Man's Sleeve, 1954; Some Corner of an English Field, 1957; O. Jones, O. Jones, 1970; There Was a Young Man from Cardiff, 1991; The Strange Case of Dr Simmonds and Dr Glas, 2002; *autobiography:* A Poet in the Family, 1974; Goodbye, Twentieth Century, 2001, 2nd edn 2011; *plays:* House of Cowards, (first prod.) Questors Theatre, Ealing, 1960; The Dogs of Pavlov, (first prod.) Questors, 1969; Pythagoras, (first prod.) Birmingham Rep. Th., 1976; Gone in January, (first prod.) Young Vic, 1978; *anthologies edited:* (with Howard Sergeant) Mavericks, 1957; Modern European Verse, 1964; (with Joan Abse) Voices in the Gallery, 1986; (with Joan Abse) The Music Lover's Literary Companion, 1988; The Hutchinson Book of Post-War British Poets, 1989; Twentieth Century Anglo-Welsh Poetry, 1997; Homage to Eros, 2003. *Recreations:* chess, watching Cardiff City FC. *Address:* 85 Hodford Road, NW11 8NH. *Died 28 Sept. 2014.*

ACHEBE, Prof. Chinua, FRSL 1983; author; Professor Emeritus, University of Nigeria, since 1984; Charles P. Stevenson Professor of Languages and Literature, Bard College, Annandale, 1990–2009; David and Marianna Fisher University Professor and Professor of Africana Studies, Brown University, since 2009; *b* 16 Nov. 1930; *s* of Isaiah and Janet Achebe; *m* 1961, Christiana Okoli; two *s* two *d. Educ:* Univ. of Ibadan. Nigerian Broadcasting Corp.: Talks Producer, 1954; Controller, 1959; Dir, 1961–66. Rockefeller Fellowship, 1960; Unesco Fellowship, 1963; Professor of English: Univ. of Massachusetts, 1972–75; Univ. of Connecticut, Storrs, 1975–76; Univ. of Nigeria, Nsukka, 1973–81; Pro-Chancellor and Chm. Council, Anambra State Univ. of Technol., Enugu, 1986–88. Fulbright Prof., Univ. of Massachusetts, 1987–88; Vis. Distinguished Prof. of English, City Coll., City Univ. of NY, 1989; Vis. Fellow and Ashby Lectr, Clare Hall, Cambridge, 1993. Chairman: Soc. of Nigerian Authors, 1966; Assoc. of Nigerian Authors, 1982–86. Hon. Vice-Pres., Royal Africa Soc., 1999. Member: Council, Univ. of Lagos, 1966; Exec. Cttee, Commonwealth Arts Orgn, London, 1981. Neil Gunn Internat. Fellowship, Scottish Arts Council, 1975; Hon. Fellow: Modern Language Assoc. of America, 1975; Amer. Acad. of Arts and Letters, 1982; Amer. Acad. of Arts and Scis, 2002. Editor, Okike, 1971–84. Patron, Writers and Scholars Educnl Trust, London, and Writers and Scholars Internat., 1972–90; Governor, Newsconcern Internat. Foundn, London, 1983–90. Goodwill Ambassador, UN Population Fund, 1999–2006. Hon. DLitt: Dartmouth Coll., 1972; Southampton, 1975; Ife, 1978; Nigeria, 1981; Kent, 1982; Guelph and Mount Allison, 1984; Franklin Pierce Coll., 1985; Ibadan, 1989; Skidmore Coll., 1990; Harvard, 1996; Syracuse, 1998; Brown, 1998; Witwatersrand, Cape Town, 2000; Toronto, 2006; DUniv: Open, 1989; Stirling, 1975; Hon. LLD Prince Edward Island, 1976; Hon. DHL: Massachusetts, 1977; Westfield Coll., 1989; Georgetown Univ., 1990. Jock Campbell New Statesman Award, 1965; Commonwealth Poetry Prize, 1972; Commonwealth Foundn Sen. Vis. Practitioner Award, 1983; Man Booker Internat. Prize, 2007. Nigerian Nat. Order of Merit, 1979; Order of the Fed. Repub. (Nigeria), 1979. *Publications: fiction:* Things Fall Apart, 1958; No Longer at Ease, 1960; Arrow of God, 1964; A Man of the People, 1966; Girls at War (short stories), 1972; Anthills of the Savannah, 1987; *essays:* Morning Yet on Creation Day, 1975; The Trouble with Nigeria, 1983; Hopes and Impediments, 1987; Beware Soul-brother (poems), 1971; (with Robert Lyons) Another Africa (poetry, prose and photographs), 1998; Home and Exile, 2000; Collected Poems, 2004; The Education of a British-Protected Child, 2010; *for children:* Chike and the River, 1966; (jtly) How the Leopard Got its Claws, 1971; The Flute, 1978; The Drum, 1978; *memoir:* There was a Country: a personal history of Biafra, 2012. *Recreation:* music. *Address:* Bard College, PO Box 41, Annandale-on-Hudson, NY 12504, USA. *Died 21 March 2013.*

ADAM, Brian James; Member (SNP) Aberdeen Donside, Scottish Parliament, since 2011 (North East Scotland, 1999–2003, Aberdeen North, 2003–11); *b* 10 June 1948; *s* of James Pirie Adam and Isabel Adam (*née* Geddes); *m* 1975, Dorothy McKillip Mann; four *s* one *d. Educ:* Keith Grammar Sch.; Aberdeen Univ. (BSc, MSc). Principal Biochemist: City Hosp., Aberdeen, 1973–88; Aberdeen Royal Infirmary, 1988–99. Mem. (SNP) Aberdeen CC, 1988–99. Joined SNP, 1974. Contested (SNP): Gordon, 1992; Aberdeen N, 1997. Minister for Parly Business and Chief Whip, Scottish Parlt, 2011–12. *Died 25 April 2013.*

ADAMS, Ernest Victor, CB 1978; Deputy Secretary and Commissioner, Inland Revenue, 1975–81; *b* 17 Jan. 1920; *s* of Ernest and Amelia Adams; *m* 1st, 1943, Joan Bastin, Halesworth, Suffolk (*d* 1985); one *s* one *d*; 2nd, 1987, Mavisse Evelyn Surtees, Henley-on-Thames. *Educ:* Manchester Grammar Sch.; Keble Coll., Oxford (MA). HM Forces, RA, 1940–45. Inland Revenue Dept, 1947; Sen. Inspector of Taxes, 1956; Principal Inspector of Taxes, 1961; Sen. Principal Inspector of Taxes, 1966; Dep. Chief Inspector of Taxes, 1969. *Address:* 5 Northfield Court, Henley-on-Thames RG9 2LH. *T:* (01491) 572586. *Club:* Phyllis Court (Henley). *Died 29 Oct. 2011.*

ADAMS, Prof. John Norman; Professor of Intellectual Property, University of Sheffield, 1994–2005, then Emeritus; Adjunct Professor of Law, University of Notre Dame London Centre, since 2005; *b* 24 Dec. 1939; *s* of Vincent Smith Adams and Elsie Adams (*née* Davison), Gateshead. *Educ:* Newcastle upon Tyne Royal GS; Univ. of Durham. Called to the Bar, Inner Temple, 1984. Solicitor in private practice, 1965–71; Lectr in Law, Univ. of Sheffield, 1971–79; Sen. Lectr, 1979–87, Prof. of Commercial Law, 1987–94, Univ. of Kent. Dir, Intellectual Property Inst., 1991–99. *Publications include:* (with K. V. Prichard-Jones) Franchising, 1981, 5th edn (with K. V. Prichard-Jones and J. Hickey) 2005; (with G. Averley) A Bibliography of Eighteenth Century Legal Literature, 1982; Character Merchandising, 1987, 3rd edn (with J. Hickey and G. Tritton) 2007; (with R. Brownsword) Understanding Contract Law, 1987, 5th edn 2007; Commercial Hiring and Leasing, 1989; (with R. Brownsword) Understanding Law, 1992, 4th edn 2005; (with R. Brownsword) Key Issues in Contract, 1995; (ed) Atiyah's Sale of Goods, 11th edn 2005, 12th edn (ed with H. L. MacQueen), 2010. *Recreations:* music, walking. *Address:* 26 Priory Terrace, NW6 4DM. *T:* (020) 7328 8676; 49 Endcliffe Hall Avenue, Sheffield S10 3EL. *T:* (0114) 268 7311. *Clubs:* Savage, Lansdowne. *Died 14 April 2012.*

ADAMS, Major Kenneth Galt, CVO 1979; CBE 1989; Hon. Industry Fellow, Comino Foundation, since 1997; *b* 6 Jan. 1920; *s* of late William Adams, OBE, and Christina Elisabeth (*née* Hall); *m* 1988, Sally, *d* of late Col John Middleton and *widow* of Douglas Long; one step *s* one step *d. Educ:* Doncaster Grammar Sch.; Staff Coll., Camberley (psc 1953). Served RASC, 1940–59: War Service, ME and N Africa; DADST WO, 1946–48; DAA&QMG, Aldershot, 1952; DAQMG HQ Northern Comd, 1954–56; Sen. Instr, RASC Officers Sch., 1956–59. Sec., S London Indust. Mission, 1959–61; Proprietors of Hay's Wharf Ltd, 1960–70, Exec. Dir, 1966–70; non-exec. dir and consultant, other cos, until 1985. St George's House, Windsor Castle: Dir of Studies, 1969–76; Fellow, 1976–82; Hon. Fellow, 1990–. Comino Fellow, RSA, 1979–89; Industry Fellow, Comino Foundn, 1989–96. Chairman: S London Indust. Mission, 1971–74; Indust. Christian Fellowship, 1977–86; Vice Chairman: Archbishops' Council on Evangelism, 1965–77; Southwark Cathedral Council, 1967–70; Member: Indust. Cttee, Bd for Social Responsibility of C of E, 1973–81; Bldg EDC, NEDC, 1977–81; Prof. Standards Cttee, BIM, 1976–81; Dept of Employment's Services Resettlement Cttee for SE England, 1967–77; Adv. Cttee, Christian Assoc. of Business Execs, 1975–96 (Pres., 2004–); Adv. Cttee, Inst. of Business Ethics, 1986–96; Hon. Mem., Foundn for Manufg and Industry (Chm., 1993); Trustee, Industrial Trng Foundn, 1980–91. Lay Steward, St George's Chapel, Windsor, 1969–. Freeman: City of London, 1967; Cooks' Co., 1967; Liveryman, Pattenmakers' Co., 1976–96. CCMI (CBIM 1972); FRSA 1979. MA Lambeth, 1979; Hon. DPhil Internat. Management Centres, 1991. Templeton Award, 1996. *Publications:* lectures and papers on developing an affirmative cultural attitude to industry in Britain, and on Christianity and wealth creation. *Recreations:* 19th century novels, pilgrimages. *Address:* 8 Datchet Road, Windsor, Berks SL4 1QE. *T:* (01753) 869708. *Died 1 July 2012.*

ADCOCK, Robert Wadsworth, CBE 1992; DL; solicitor; Chief Executive and Clerk, Essex County Council, 1976–95; *b* 29 Dec. 1932; *s* of Sir Robert Adcock, CBE; *m* 1957, Valerie Colston Robins; one *d* (one *s* decd). *Educ:* Rugby Sch. Solicitor. Assistant Solicitor: Lancs CC, 1955–56; Manchester City Council, 1956–59; Sen. Solicitor, Berks CC, 1959–63; Asst Clerk, later Dep. Clerk, Northumberland CC, 1963–70; Dep. Chief Exec., Essex CC, 1970–76. Assoc. of County Councils: Advisor, Police Cttee, 1976–83; Advisor, Policy Cttee, 1983–95; Chm., Officers Adv. Gp, 1987–95. Hon. Sec., Assoc. of County Chief Executives, 1983–90 (Chm., 1991–92); Chm., Officers Adv. Panel, SE Regional Planning Conference, 1984–88. DL Essex, 1978. *Recreations:* gardening, ornithology. *Address:* The Christmas Cottage, Great Sampford, Saffron Walden, Essex CB10 2RQ. *T:* (01799) 586363. *Club:* Royal Over-Seas League. *Died 4 July 2014.*

ADEANE, Hon. (George) Edward, CVO 1985; an Extra Equerry to HRH the Prince of Wales, since 1985; *b* 4 Oct. 1939; *s* of Baron Adeane, GCB, GCVO, PC and Lady Adeane. *Educ:* Eton; Magdalene College, Cambridge (MA). Called to Bar, Middle Temple, July 1962. Page of Honour to HM the Queen, 1954–55; Plebiscite Supervisory officer, Southern Cameroons, 1960–61; Private Sec. and Treas. to HRH the Prince of Wales, 1979–85; Treas. to TRH the Prince and Princess of Wales, 1981–85; Private Sec. to HRH the Princess of Wales, 1984–85. Director: Guardian Royal Exchange plc, 1985–99; Hambros plc, 1992–98; Hambros Bank Ltd, 1986–98 (Exec. Dir, 1991–98); BNP Paribas UK Holdings Ltd, 1998–2005. Mem., British Library Bd, 1993–99. Trustee: Leeds Castle Foundn, 1991–2004; Lambeth Palace Liby, 1991–2002. *Address:* B4 Albany, Piccadilly, W1J 0AN. *T:* (020) 7734 9410. *Died 20 May 2015.*

ADETILOYE, Most Rev. Joseph Abiodun; Metropolitan Archbishop and Primate of Nigeria, 1988–99; Bishop of Lagos, 1985–99; *b* 25 Dec. 1929; *m* 1967 (decd); one *s*. *Educ:* Melville Hall, Ibadan; King's Coll., London (BD); Wycliffe Hall, Oxford. Ordained, dio. of Lagos, 1954; Bossey Ecumenical Inst., 1961–62; Lectr, 1962, Vice Principal, 1963–66, Immanuel Coll., Ibadan; Provost, Ibadan Cathedral, 1966–70; Bishop of Ekiti, 1970–85. Mem., Eames Commn; Chm., Anglican Encounter in the South, 1994–. DD Gen. Theol Seminary, NY, 1993. *Address:* c/o PO Box 13 (Bishopscourt, 29 Marina), Lagos, Nigeria. *Fax:* (1) 2636026, 2635681. *Died 14 Dec. 2012.*

ADRIEN, Hon. Sir Maurice L.; *see* Latour-Adrien.

AGNEW, Sir John (Keith), 6th Bt *cr* 1895, of Great Stanhope Street, London; *b* 19 Dec. 1950; *er s* of Major Sir (George) Keith Agnew, 5th Bt, TD, and Anne Merete Louise, *yr d* of Baron Johann Schaffalitzky de Muckadell, Fyn, Denmark; *S* father, 1994. *Educ:* Gresham's Sch., Holt. *Heir: b* George Anthony Agnew, *b* 18 Aug. 1953. *Address:* Rougham Estate Office, Rougham, Bury St Edmunds, Suffolk IP30 9LZ. *Died 27 June 2011.*

AILSA, 8th Marquess of, *cr* 1831; **Archibald Angus Charles Kennedy;** Baron Kennedy 1452; Earl of Cassillis 1509; Baron Ailsa (UK) 1806; *b* 13 Sept. 1956; *er s* of 7th Marquess of Ailsa, OBE and Mary, 7th *c* of John Burn; *S* father, 1994; *m* 1979, Dawn Leslie Anne Keen (marr. diss. 1989); two *d*. *Recreations:* shooting, ski-ing, cadets and youth-work. *Heir: b* Lord David Thomas Kennedy [*b* 3 July 1958; *m* 1991, Anne Kelly; one *s* one *d*]. *Club:* New (Edinburgh). *Died 15 Jan. 2015.*

AJAYI, Prof. (Jacob Festus) Ade, NNOM 1986; OFR 2000; Professor of History, University of Ibadan, 1963–89, then Emeritus; *b* 26 May 1929; *s* of late Chief Ezekiel Adeniyi Ajayi and Mrs Comfort F. Bolajoko Ajayi; *m* 1956, Christie Aduke Martins; one *s* four *d*. *Educ:* University College, Ibadan; University College, Leicester; Univ. of London; BA 1st Cl. Hons, PhD (London). Research Fellow, Inst. of Historical Research, London, 1957–58; Lectr, Univ. of Ibadan, 1958–62, Sen. Lectr, 1962–63; Dean, Faculty of Arts, 1964–66; Asst to Vice-Chancellor, 1966–68. Fellow, Centre for Advanced Study in the Behavioural Sciences, Stanford, Calif, 1970–71; Vice-Chancellor, Univ. of Lagos, 1972–78; Pro-Chancellor, Ondo State Univ., Ado-Ekiti, 1984–88. Member: UN University Council, 1974–80 (Chm., 1975–77); Nat. Archives Cttee, Nigeria, 1961–72; Nat. Antiquities Commn, Nigeria, 1970–74; Exec. Council, Internat. African Inst. London, 1971– (Chm., 1975–87); Exec. Bd, Assoc. of African Univs, 1974–80; Admin. Bd, Internat. Assoc. of Univs, 1980–90; Pres., Historical Soc. of Nigeria, 1972–81; Pres., Internat. Congress of African Studies, 1978–85. Director: BCN plc, 1988–92; SOWSCO, 1994–. Chm., Jadeas Trust, 1989–. Mem. Governing Bd, Nigerian Nat. Order of Merit, 1996–2000. Hon. LLD Leicester, 1975; Hon. DLitt: Birmingham, 1984; Ondo State Univ., Ado-Ekiti, 1992. Hon. Fellow, SOAS, Univ. of London, 1994. Fellow, Hist. Soc. of Nigeria, 1980; Overseas FRHistS, 1982. Traditional titles, Bobapitan of Ikole-Ekiti and Onikoyi of Ife, 1983. *Publications:* Milestones in Nigerian History, 1962; (ed with Ian Espie) A Thousand Years of West African History, 1964; (with R. S. Smith) Yoruba Warfare in the Nineteenth Century, 1964; Christian Missions in Nigeria: the making of a new elite, 1965; (ed with Michael Crowder) A History of West Africa, vol. I, 1972; vol. II, 1974; (ed with T. N. Tamuno) The University of Ibadan, 1948–73, 1973; (ed with Bashir Ikara) Evolution of Political Culture in Nigeria, 1985; (ed with M. Crowder) A Historical Atlas of Africa, 1985; (ed) Africa in the Nineteenth Century until the 1880s, vol. VI of Unesco General History of Africa, 1989; History and the Nation, and other Addresses, 1990; (with Peter Pugh) Cementing a Partnership: the story of WAPCO 1960–1990, 1990; A Patriot to the Core: Samuel Ajayi Crowther, 1992, 2nd edn, subtitled Bishop Ajayi Crowther, 2001; History of the Nigerian Society of Engineers, 1995; (jtly) The African Experience with Higher Education, 1996; Kayode Eso: the making of a judge, 2002; contribs to Jl Historical Soc. of Nigeria, Jl of African History, etc. *Recreations:* dancing, tennis. *Address:* 1 Ojobadan Avenue, Bodija, Ibadan, Nigeria; PO Box 14617 UI, Ibadan, Nigeria. *Died 9 Aug. 2014.*

AKERS, John Fellows; Chairman, International Business Machines Corp., 1986–93; *b* 28 Dec. 1934; *m* 1960, Susan Davis; one *s* two *d*. *Educ:* Yale Univ. (BS). International Business Machines Corp., 1960–93: Pres., Data Processing Div., 1974–76; Vice Pres., Asst Gp Exec., plans and controls, Data Processing Product Gp, 1976–78; Vice Pres., Gp Exec., Data Processing Marketing Gp, 1978–81, Inf. Systems and Communications Gp, 1981–82, Sen. Vice Pres., 1982–83; Dir, 1983–93; Pres., 1983–89; Chief Exec. Officer, 1985–93. Director: New York Times Co., 1985; PepsiCo. Inc.; W. R. Grace; Lehmann Bros; Hallmark Cards. Formerly Mem., President's Educn Policy Adv. Cttee. Former Trustee, MMA; former Chm. Bd of Governors, United Way of America. *Died 22 Aug. 2014.*

ALAIN, Marie-Claire Geneviève; organist; Lecturer, Conservatoire National de Région Rueil-Malmaison, Paris, 1978–98; *b* 10 Aug. 1926; *d* of Albert Alain and Magdeleine Alain (*née* Alberty); *m* 1950, Jacques Gommier (*d* 1992); one *d* (one *s* decd). *Educ:* Institut Notre Dame, Saint-Germain-en-Laye; Conservatoire Nat. Supérieur de Musique, Paris. Lectr, Summer Acad. for Organists, Haarlem, Netherlands, 1956–72; Dir, Internat. Summer Acad. for Organists, Saint-Donat, 1978–92. Numerous concerts and recitals worldwide, 1955–; more than 250 recordings, incl. works of Jehan Alain, complete organ works of J. S. Bach, César Franck, Handel, Buxtehude and Mendelssohn. Prix Léonie Sonning, Copenhagen; Buxtehude Prize, Lübeck, 1976; Prix Franz Liszt, Budapest, 1987; 15 Grands Prix du Disque. Hon. doctorates: Colorado, 1972; Southern Methodist, Dallas, 1990; Sibelius Acad., 1997; Boston Conservatory, 1999; McGill, 2001; John Hopkins, 2006. Grand Officier, Légion d'honneur (France) (Commandeur, 1997); Commandeur: Ordre Nat. du Mérite (France), 1998; Officier des Arts et des Lettres (France), 1999. *Publications:* Notes critiques sur l'oeuvre d'orgue de Jehan Alain, 2001. *Address:* 4 rue Victor Hugo, 78230 Le Pecq, France. *Died 26 Feb. 2013.*

ALBEMARLE, Diana, Countess of, (Diana Cicely), DBE 1956; Chairman: Development Commission, 1948–74; The Drama Board, 1964–78; *b* 6 Aug. 1909; *oc* of John Archibald Grove; *m* 1931, 9th Earl of Albemarle, MC (*d* 1979); one *d*. *Educ:* Sherborne Sch. for Girls. Norfolk County Organiser, WVS, 1939–44. Chairman: Exec.

Cttee, Nat. Fedn of Women's Institutes, 1946–51; Departmental Cttee on Youth Service, 1958–60; Nat. Youth Employment Council, 1962–68. Vice-Chm., British Council, 1959–74. Member: Arts Council, 1951; Royal Commn on Civil Service, 1954; Harkness Fellowship Cttee of Award, 1963–69; UGC, 1956–70; Standing Commn on Museums and Galleries, 1958–71; English Local Govt Boundary Commn, 1971–77; Youth Develt Council, 1960–68; Council, Univ. of E Anglia, 1964–72. Life Trustee, Carnegie UK Trust (Chm., 1977–82); Trustee of: The Observer, until 1977; Glyndebourne Arts Trust, 1968–80. RD Councillor, Wayland, Norfolk, 1935–46. Hon. DLitt Reading, 1959; Hon. DCL Oxon, 1960; Hon. LLD London, 1960. *Recreations:* gardening, reading. *Address:* c/o Leuchie, North Berwick, East Lothian EH39 5NT. *Died 6 May 2013.*

ALBERY, Prof. (Wyndham) John, FRS 1985; FRSC; Master, University College, Oxford, 1989–97; *b* 5 April 1936; *s* of late Michael James Albery, QC, and Mary Laughton Albery. *Educ:* Winchester Coll.; Balliol Coll., Oxford (MA, DPhil). Weir Jun. Research Fellow, 1962, Fellow, 1963–78, University Coll., Oxford; Lectr, Phys. Chem., Univ. of Oxford, 1964–78; Imperial College, London: Prof., Phys. Chemistry, 1978–89; Staff Orator, 1980–83; Dean, RCS, 1986–89. Vis. Fellow, Univ. of Minnesota, 1965; Vis. Prof., Harvard Univ., 1976. Tilden Lectr, RSC, 1979; Sherman Fairchild Schol., Calif. Inst. of Tech., 1985. Chairman: SERC Chemistry Cttee, 1982–85; Electrochem. Gp, RSC, 1985–89. Mem. Council, Royal Instn, 1985–88; Pres., Chemistry Section, British Assoc., 1992. Writer for television series That Was The Week That Was, 1963–64; also (with John Gould) two musicals, Who Was That Lady?, and On The Boil. Curator, Oxford Playhouse, 1974–78; Gov., Old Vic, 1979–89; Chm., Burton Taylor Theatre Management Cttee, 1990–93. Gov., Rugby Sch., 1987–2000; Fellow, Winchester Coll., 1989–2000. Hon. DSc Kent, 1990. *Publications:* Ring-Disc Electrodes, 1971; Electrode Kinetics, 1975; papers in jls: Faraday I, Nature, and Jls of Electrochemical Soc., Electroanalytical Chemistry, etc. *Recreations:* theatre, cruising. *Address:* 35 Falmouth House, Clarendon Place, Hyde Park Street, W2 2NT. *T:* (020) 7262 3909. *Died 3 Dec. 2013.*

ALDERSON, John Cottingham, CBE 1981; QPM 1974; writer and commentator on police and penal affairs; Chief Constable of Devon and Cornwall, 1973–82; *b* 28 May 1922; *e s* of late Ernest Cottingham Alderson and Elsie Lavinia Rose; *m* 1948, Irené Macmillan Stirling (*d* 2008); one *s*. *Educ:* Barnsley Elem. Schs and Techn. College. Called to Bar, Middle Temple. British Meml Foundn Fellow, Australia, 1956; Extension Certif. in Criminology, Univ. of Leeds. Highland LI, 1938–41 (Corp.); Army Phys. Trng Corps, N Africa and Italy, 1941–46 (Warrant Officer). West Riding Constabulary as Constable, 1946; Police Coll., 1954; Inspector, 1955; Sub-Divisional Comd, 1960; Sen. Comd Course, Police Coll., 1963–64; Dep. Chief Constable, Dorset, 1964–66; Metropolitan Police, Dep. Comdr (Admin and Ops), 1966; 2nd-in-comd No 3 Police District, 1967; Dep. Asst Comr (Trng), 1968; Comdt, Police Coll., 1970; Asst Comr (Personnel and Trng), 1973. Consultant on Human Rights to Council of Europe, 1981–. Member: BBC Gen. Adv. Council, 1971–78; Royal Humane Soc. Cttee, 1973–81; Pres., Royal Life-Saving Soc., 1974–78. Vis. Prof. of Police Studies, Strathclyde Univ., 1983–89; Res. Fellow, Inst. of Police and Criminol Studies, Univ. of Portsmouth, 1994–2000. External Examiner, Leadership Studies, Univ. of Exeter, 1994–. Fellow Commoner, Corpus Christi Coll., Cambridge, 1982; Fellow, Inst. of Criminology, Cambridge, 1982; Gwilym Gibbon Res. Fellow, Nuffield Coll., Oxford, 1982–83; Australian Commonwealth Fellow, Australian Govt, 1987; Hon. Res. Fellow, Centre for Police Studies, Univ. of Exeter, 1987–95. Contested (L) Teignbridge, Devon, 1983. Hon. LLD Exeter, 1979; Hon. DLitt Bradford, 1982. *Publications:* (contrib.) Encyclopedia of Crime and Criminals, 1960; (ed jtly) The Police We Deserve, 1973; Policing Freedom, 1979; Law and Disorder, 1984; Human Rights and the Police, 1984; Principled Policing, 1998; articles in professional jls and newspapers. *Recreations:* reading, writing, keeping fit. *Died 7 Oct. 2011.*

ALEXANDER, Andrew Clive; columnist; City Editor, Daily Mail, 1984–2000; *b* 12 May 1935; *s* of Ronald and Doreen Alexander. *Educ:* Lancing College; Univ. of Life (2.2). Leader Writer, Yorkshire Post, 1960–65; Parly Sketch-Writer, Daily Telegraph, 1966–72; Parly Sketch-Writer and Columnist, Daily Mail, 1972–84. Director: Associated Newspapers plc, 1992–2000; Underoneroof Ltd, 2000–01; OneStopCarShop Ltd, 2000–02. Contested (C) Colne Valley, March 1963, 1964. Specialist Writer of the Year, British Press Awards, 1976, 1977; Political Journalist of the Year, What the Papers Say awards, 1977; Jt Financial Journalist of the Year, Baltic Trent Award, 1986; Sen. Financial Journalist of the Year, Wincott Foundn, 1991. *Publications:* The Making of the Prime Minister (with Alan Watkins), 1970; America and the Imperialism of Ignorance, 2011. *Recreations:* music, gardening, history. *Club:* Reform. *Died 5 July 2015.*

ALEXANDER, Thomas John; Senior Research Fellow, Department of Education (formerly of Educational Studies), University of Oxford, since 2000; Director for Education, Employment, Labour and Social Affairs (formerly Social Affairs, Manpower and Education), OECD, Paris, 1989–2000; *b* 11 March 1940; *s* of late John Alexander and Agnes Douglas Stewart (*née* Creedican); *m* 1961, Pamela Mason; two *s* one *d*. *Educ:* Royal High Sch., Edinburgh. Entered FO, 1958; MECAS, 1961; Third Sec. (Commercial), Kuwait, 1963; Asst Private Sec. to the Minister of State, FO, 1965; Second Sec. (Commercial), Tripoli, 1967; seconded to industry (ICI), 1970; Vice Consul (Commercial), Seattle, 1970; First Sec., FCO, 1974; special unpaid leave to act as Private Sec. to Sec.-Gen. of OECD, Paris, 1977–82; Counsellor and Head of Chancery, Khartoum, 1982–83; Dep. Head of Planning, 1984, Head of Private Office of Sec.-Gen., 1984–89, OECD. Mem., Higher Educn Bd, 1999–2009, Gen. Educn Bd, 2002– (Chm., 2002–03, 2007–), Open Soc. Foundns (formerly Open Soc. Inst.), Budapest. *E:* tomalexander231@btinternet.com. *Clubs:* Oriental; Phyllis Court (Henley-on-Thames). *Died 22 Jan. 2012.*

ALEXANDER, William Gemmell, MBE 1945; Chairman, W. H. Stott & Co. Ltd, 1979–83 (Director, 1968–83); *b* 19 Aug. 1918; *s* of Harold Gemmell Alexander and Winifred Ada Alexander (*née* Stott); *m* 1945, Janet Rona Page Alexander (*née* Elias) (*d* 1992); three *s* one *d* (and one *s* decd). *Educ:* Tre Arddur Bay Sch.; Sedbergh Sch.; Brasenose Coll., Oxford (MA). Served War of 1939–45 (despatches, war stars and clasps): Driver Mechanic, 2nd Lieut, Lieut, Capt., Maj.; served in France, S Africa, Eritrea, Egypt, Middle East, Sicily, Italy, Algeria, NW Europe. HM Overseas Civil Service, 1946–59: Gilbert and Ellice Is, 1946–51; Mauritius, 1951–55; Cyprus, 1955–59; Man., Cooperative Wholesale Soc., Agricultural Dept, 1960–63; Dir, Internat. Cooperative Alliance, 1963–68; Dir-Gen., RoSPA, 1968–74; County Road Safety Officer, W Yorks MCC, 1974–78. Mem., BSI Quality Assurance Council, 1975–83. Member: Bradford Dio. Bd of Finance, 1985–91; Ewecross Deanery Synod, 1985–99; Dent PCC, 1978–2008. Clerk, Dent Parish Council, 1980–86. Chm., Bd of Govs, Dent GS. ACMI (AMBIM 1963). *Recreations:* all sports, long distance walking. *Address:* Pear Tree House, The Green, Cropredy, near Banbury, Oxon OX17 1NH. *Club:* Royal Commonwealth Society. *Died 10 June 2014.*

ALEXANDER-SINCLAIR of Freswick, Maj.-Gen. David Boyd, CB 1981; Commandant, Staff College, 1980–82; *b* 2 May 1927; *s* of late Comdr M. B. Alexander-Sinclair of Freswick, RN and Avril N. Fergusson-Buchanan; *m* 1958, Ann Ruth, *d* of late Lt-Col Graeme Daglish; two *s* one *d*. *Educ:* Eton. Commnd into Rifle Bde, 1946, served in Germany, Kenya, Cyprus; ADC to GOC South Malaya District and Maj.-Gen. Bde of Gurkhas, 1950–51; psc 1958; Bde Major, 6th Inf. Bde Gp, 1959–61; GSO2 (Dirg Staff) Staff Coll., 1963–65; comdg 3rd Bn Royal Green Jackets, 1967–69; MoD, 1965–67 and 1969–71; Comdr, 6th Armd Bde, 1971–73; Student, RCDS, 1974; GOC 1st Division, 1975–77; COS, UKLF, 1978–80. *Died 7 Feb. 2014.*

ALFRED, (Arnold) Montague; Deputy Chairman: Ward Lock Educational Co. Ltd, 1985–88; BLA Publishing Ltd, 1985–88; Ling Kee (UK) Ltd, 1985–88; *b* 21 March 1925; *s* of Reuben Alfred and Bessie Alfred (*née* Arbesfield); *m* 1st, 1947, Sheila Jacqueline Gold (*d* 2009); three *s*; 2nd, 2010, Naureen Nathan. *Educ:* Central Foundation Boys' Sch.; Imperial Coll., London; London Sch. of Economics. Head of Economics Dept, Courtaulds Ltd, 1953–69; Director, Nylon Div., Courtaulds Ltd, 1964–69; Dir, BPC Ltd, 1969–81; Chairman: BPC Publishing Ltd, 1971–81; Caxton Publishing Holdings Ltd, 1971–81; Second Permanent Sec., and Chief Exec., PSA, DoE, 1982–84. *Publications:* Discounted Cash Flow (jointly), 1965; Business Economics (jointly), 1968. Numerous articles in: Accountant, Textile Jl, Investment Analyst, etc. *Recreation:* Jewish community affairs. *Died 26 July 2011.*

ALLAN, Andrew Norman; Chairman, Codeworks, since 2005; *b* 26 Sept. 1943; *s* of Andrew Allan and Elizabeth (*née* Davison); *m* 1st, 1969, Wendy Wilson (marr. diss.); two *d*; 2nd, 1978, Joanna Forrest (marr. diss.); two *s* one *d*; partner, Phoebe Lambert. *Educ:* Birmingham Univ. (BA). Presenter, ABC Television, 1965–67; Producer: ITN, 1968; Thames Television, 1969–77; Head of News, Thames TV, 1977–78; Tyne Tees Television: Dir of Progs, 1978–82; Dep. Man. Dir, 1982–83; Man. Dir, 1983–84; Dir of Progs, Central Ind. TV, 1984–90; Managing Director: Central Broadcasting, 1990–93; Central Ind. TV, 1993–94; Chief Exec., 1994–95, Dir of Progs, 1996–98, Carlton TV. Chairman: Birmingham Rep. Theatre, 2000–05; Route4 plc, 2001–05. *Recreations:* theatre, music, reading, dining. *Address:* Cheviot View, Hedley, Stocksfield, Northumberland NE43 7SW. *Died 28 Nov. 2011.*

ALLAN, Rt Rev. Hugh James Pearson, DD; Assistant Bishop of Nova Scotia, 1991–94; *b* 7 Aug. 1928; *s* of Hugh Blomfield Allan and Agnes Dorothy (*née* Pearson); *m* 1955, Beverley Edith Baker; one *s* three *d*. *Educ:* St John's Coll., Univ. of Manitoba (LTh 1955, BA 1957). Deacon 1954, priest 1955; Assistant: St Aidan's, Winnipeg, 1954; All Saints, Winnipeg, 1955; Missionary, Peguis Indian Reserve, 1956–60; Rector, St Mark's, Winnipeg, 1960–68; Hon. Canon, Diocese of Rupert's Land, 1967; Rector, St Stephen's Swift Current, Sask., 1968–70; Rural Dean of Cypress, 1968–70; Dean of Qu'Appelle and Rector of St Paul's Cathedral, Regina, Sask., 1970–74; Bishop of Keewatin, 1974–91. Hon. DD, St John's Coll., Univ. of Manitoba, 1974. *Recreations:* ornithology, boating, Canada. *Died 26 June 2013.*

ALLAN, Ian, OBE 1995; Chairman, Ian Allan Group Ltd, 1962–2010; *b* Horsham, 29 June 1922; *s* of George A. T. Allan, OBE, and Mary Louise (*née* Barnes); *m* 1947, Mollie Eileen (*née* Franklin); two *s*. *Educ:* St Paul's Sch. Joined Southern Railway Co., 1939. Founded Ian Allan Ltd, Publishers, 1945; other cos co-ordinated into Ian Allan Group Ltd, 1962. Dir, Dart Valley Light Railway PLC, 1968–2004 (Chm., 1976–87). Governor, Christ's Hosp., 1944, Almoner, 1980–89; Chm., King Edward's Sch., Witley, 1983–95 (Governor, 1975–95); Treas., Bridewell Royal Hosp., 1983–95. Vice President: Transport Trust, 1979–; Assoc. of Ind. Rlys, 1997– (Chm., 1987–97); Heritage Rly Assoc., 1996–; Mem., Transport Users Consultative Cttee for London, 1982–84. Pres., Main Line Steam Trust (Great Central Rly), 1995–. Patron, Mid Hants Rly plc, 1994–. Freeman, City of London, 1986. Hon. Freeman, Borough of Spelthorne, 2001. FCIT 1992. *Publications:* compiled and edited many books on railways and transport subjects, 1939–; Driven by Steam (autobiog.), 1992. *Recreations:* swimming, touring, miniature railways, Freemasonry. *Address:* The Jetty, Middleton-on-Sea, Bognor Regis, W Sussex PO22 7TS. *T:* (01243) 593378. *Died 28 June 2015.*

ALLAN, Richard Andrew; Director, Regional Policy and Local Governance, Office of the Deputy Prime Minister (formerly Department for Transport, Local Government and the Regions), 2001–05; *b* 28 Feb. 1948; *s* of late Kenneth and of Mary Allan; *m* 1975, Katharine Mary Tait; one *s* one *d*. *Educ:* Bolton Sch.; Balliol Coll., Oxford (MA Mod. Hist.); York Univ. (MA Railway Studies and Transport Hist. 2011). VSO, Nigeria, 1970. Asst Principal, DTI, 1970; Asst British Trade Comr, Hong Kong, 1973; Department of Industry: Private Sec. to Perm. Sec., 1974–75; Principal, 1975–79; First Sec. (Civil Aviation and Shipping), Washington, 1980–84; Department of Transport: Asst Sec., 1984; Principal Private Sec. to Sec. of State for Transport, 1985–87; Under Sec., 1988; seconded to BRB, 1988–90; Dir of Personnel, 1990–94; Head, Urban and Local Transport Directorate, 1994–97; Dir, London Transport Directorate, DETR, 1997–98; Dir, New London Governance, Govt Office for London, 1998–2000; Dir, Regl Policy and Regeneration, DETR, 2000–01. *Recreations:* choral singing, theatre, walking. *Address:* 1 Ellerton Road, SW18 3NG. *Died 17 July 2011.*

ALLANBRIDGE, Hon. Lord; William Ian Stewart; a Senator of the College of Justice in Scotland, 1977–95; *b* 8 Nov. 1925; *s* of late John Stewart, FRIBA, and Mrs Maysie Shepherd Stewart (*née* Service), Drimfearn, Bridge of Allan; *m* 1955, Naomi Joan Douglas (*d* 2005), *d* of late Sir James Boyd Douglas, CBE, and Lady Douglas, Barstibly, Castle Douglas; one *s* one *d*. *Educ:* Loretto; Glasgow and Edinburgh Univs. Sub-Lt, RNVR, 1944–46. Called to the Bar, 1951; QC (Scot.) 1965; Advocate-Depute, 1959–64; Mem., Criminal Injuries Compensation Bd, 1969–70, 1976–77; Home Advocate-Depute, 1970–72; Solicitor-General for Scotland, 1972–74; Temp. Sheriff-Principal of Dumfries and Galloway, April–Dec. 1974; Justice of Appeal, Republic of Botswana, 1996–99. *Address:* 60 Northumberland Street, Edinburgh EH3 6JE. *T:* (0131) 556 2823. *Club:* New (Edinburgh). *Died 21 June 2012.*

ALLASON, Lt-Col James Harry, OBE 1953; *b* 6 Sept. 1912; *s* of late Brigadier-General Walter Allason, DSO; *m* 1946, Nuala Elveen (marr. diss. 1974; she *d* 2008), *d* of late J. A. McArevey, Foxrock, Co. Dublin; two *s*. *Educ:* Haileybury; RMA, Woolwich. Commissioned RA, 1932; transferred 3rd DG, 1937; War Service India and Burma, 1939–44; retired 1953. Member Kensington Borough Council, 1956–65. Contested (C) Hackney Central, General Election, 1955; MP (C) Hemel Hempstead, 1959–Sept. 1974; PPS to Sec. of State for War, 1960–64. *Publications:* Ringside Seat, 2007. *Address:* 82 Ebury Mews, SW1W 9NX. *T:* (020) 7730 1576. *Clubs:* White's; Royal Yacht Squadron. *Died 16 June 2011.*

ALLDAY, Coningsby, CBE 1971; CEng, FIChemE; BSc (Hons); Chairman and Chief Executive, British Nuclear Fuels plc, 1983–86 (Managing Director, 1971–83); *b* 21 Nov. 1920; *s* of late Esca and Margaret Allday; *m* 1st, 1945, Iris Helena, (Bobbin), Adams (*d* 1990); one *s* one *d*; 2nd, 1993, Rosalind Roberts. *Educ:* Solihull Sch.; BSc (Hons) Chemistry, London. CEng 1979; FIChemE 1979. ICI, 1939–59; UKAEA, 1959–71: Chief Chemist, Technical Dir, Commercial Dir, Dep. Man. Dir; Mem. UKAEA, 1976–86. Chairman, NIMTECH NW, 1986–90; Director: North Region, National Westminster Bank, 1985–92; Sonomatic Ltd, 1988–90. FRSA. Hon. DSc Salford, 1985. Chevalier, Légion d'Honneur, 1983. *Died 30 Nov. 2011.*

ALLDIS, Air Cdre Cecil Anderson, CBE 1962; DFC 1941; AFC 1956; RAF (retd); *b* 28 Sept. 1918; 2nd *s* of John Henry and Margaret Wright Alldis, Birkenhead; *m* 1942, Jeanette Claire Tarrant (*d* 2010), *d* of Albert Edward Collingwood and Aida Mary Tarrant, Johannesburg; no *c*; *m* 2013, Shirley Jean Russell (*née* Hilder); one step *d*. *Educ:* Birkenhead Institute; Emmanuel Coll., Cambridge (MA). Served War, 1939–45 (despatches, DFC): Pilot, Wing Comdr, RAF, Bomber Command. Asst Air Attaché, Moscow, 1947–49; Flying and Staff appts, RAF, 1949–59; Dir of Administrative Plans, Air Ministry, 1959–62; Air Attaché, Bonn, 1963–66. Retd from RAF and entered Home Civil Service, 1966; MoD, 1966–69; seconded to HM Diplomatic Service, 1969; Counsellor (Defence Supply), HM Embassy, Bonn, 1969–80; retired from Home Civil Service, 1980. Sec. Gen., The Air League, 1982–90. *Recreations:* walking, reading. *Address:* Tudor Cottage, Oxshott Way, Cobham, Surrey KT11 2RU. *T:* (01932) 866092. *Died 5 Oct. 2014.*

ALLEN, Gary James, CBE 1991; DL; Chairman, IMI plc, 2001–04 (Chief Executive, 1986–2001); *b* 30 Sept. 1944; *s* of Alfred and Alice Allen; *m* 1966, Judith Anne Nattrass; three *s*. *Educ:* King Edward VI Grammar School, Aston, Birmingham; Liverpool University (BCom). FCMA. Managing Dir, IMI Range, 1973–77; Dir, IMI, 1978–2004; Asst Man. Dir, IMI, 1985–86; Chairman: Optilon, 1979–84; Eley, 1981–85; (non-exec.) Nat.

Exhibition Centre Ltd, 1989–2006; Dep. Chm., Marley, 1993–97 (Dir, 1989–97); non-executive Director: NV Bekaert SA, Belgium, 1987; Birmingham European Airways, 1989–91; London Stock Exchange, 1994–2007; Temple Bar Investment Trust, 2001–07. Mem. Council, CBI, 1986–99 (Mem., W Midlands Regional Council, 1983–89); Mem. Council, Birmingham Chamber of Industry & Commerce, 1983–98 (Pres., 1991–92). Lord's Taverners: Pres., W Midlands Regl Cttee, 1994–2006; Nat. Trustee, 1995–2001; Mem., Nat. Council, 1992–2001. Mem. Council, Univ. of Birmingham, 1985–90 (Hon. Life Mem., Court, 1984–). Mem. Bd, Birmingham Royal Ballet, 1993–2003. Pres., Midlands Club Cricket Conf., 1995–96. Chm., Birmingham Children's Hosp. Appeal, 1995–2000. DL 1993; High Sheriff, 2002–03, West Midlands. CCMI; FRSA. Hon. DSc Birmingham Univ., 2003. Midland Businessman of the Year, 1989. Officer, Order of Leopold II (Belgium), 2002. *Recreations:* sport, reading, gardening. *Clubs:* Royal Automobile, Lord's Taverners. *Died 19 Nov. 2011.*

ALLEN, James Hendricuss; QC 1995; a Recorder, 1995–2011; a Deputy High Court Judge, 2000–11; *b* 19 Sept. 1949; *s* of James Ede Allen and Anna Catarina Allen; *m* 1st, 1974, Heather Boocock (marr. diss. 1994); one *s* two *d*; 2nd, 1996, Melanie Jane Williamson; one *s* one *d*. *Educ:* Morley Grammar Sch.; Newcastle upon Tyne Poly. (BA Hons Law). Called to the Bar, Gray's Inn, 1973. An Asst Comr, Boundary Commn for England, 2000–11; an Acting Deemster, 2008–09, Deemster, 2009–11, High Court of IoM. *Recreations:* theatre, opera, foreign travel, shooting, tennis, bridge. *Died 26 Nov. 2013.*

ALLEN, Sir John (Derek), Kt 1994; CBE 1987; FCIOB; Board Member, since 1998, and Vice Chairman, 1998–2000, Welsh Development Agency; Member, Land Authority for Wales, 1976–98 (Deputy Chairman, 1988–98); *b* 6 Nov. 1928; *s* of late William Henry Allen and Lalla Dorothy Allen (*née* Bowen); *m* 1951, (Thelma) Jean Hooper; one *s*. *Educ:* Cardiff High Sch.; Cardiff Coll. of Technology (BA). FCIOB 1979. Civil Engr, then Chm. and Man. Dir, John Morgan Gp, Cardiff, 1947–79; Mgt Consultancy Practice, 1979–86. Dep. Chm., then Chm., Cwmbran Develt Corp., 1979–88; Chm., Housing for Wales, 1988–96. Pres., Nat. Fedn of Building Trade Employers, 1979 (Treas., 1980–83). FCMI (FIMgt 1980). Hon. Fellow, UWIC, 2000. Freeman, City of London, 1980. *Recreations:* fly-fishing, golf, gardening. *Address:* 5 Cotswold Court, Cyncoed Place, Cardiff CF23 6SL. *T:* (029) 2075 3688. *Club:* Cardiff Golf. *Died 24 Oct. 2014.*

ALLEN, Very Rev. John Edward; Provost of Wakefield, 1982–97, then Emeritus; *b* 9 June 1932; *s* of Rev. Canon Ronald and Mrs Isabel Allen; *m* 1957, Eleanor (*née* Prynne); one *s* three *d*. *Educ:* Rugby; University Coll., Oxford (MA); Fitzwilliam Coll., Cambridge (MA); Westcott House. Colonial Service, Kenya, 1957–63; Sales and Marketing, Kimberly-Clark Ltd, 1963–66; Theological College, 1966–68; Curate, Deal, Kent, 1968–71; Senior Chaplain to Univ. of Bristol and Vicar of St Paul's, Clifton, 1971–78; Vicar of Chippenham, Wilts, 1978–82. Mem., Gen. Synod of C of E, 1985–97. Vice Chm., Partnership for World Mission, 1987–96. Dir, Wakefield HA, 1991–97; Chm., Scarborough and NE Yorks Healthcare NHS Trust, 1997–2001. Chm., Local Research Ethics Cttee, 1992–97; Mem., Northern and Yorks Reg. Multi-Centre Res. Ethics Cttee, 1997–2001 (Vice-Chm., 1997–99). Religious Advr, Yorkshire TV, 1994–96. Gov., Queen Elizabeth GS, Wakefield, 1983–97; Chm. of Govs, Cathedral High Sch., 1993–97. Trustee and Dir, Public Arts, 1997–99. Pres., Scarborough Cavaliers Rotary Club, 2001–02. *Recreations:* travel, people, genealogy, family history. *Address:* The Glebe Barn, Sawdon, near Scarborough, N Yorks YO13 9DY. *T:* (01723) 859854. *E:* jeallen70@btinternet.com. *Died 9 Sept. 2015.*

ALLENBY, 3rd Viscount *cr* 1919, of Megiddo and of Felixstowe; **Michael Jaffray Hynman Allenby;** Lieutenant-Colonel, The Royal Hussars, retired 1986; a Deputy Speaker, House of Lords, since 1993; *b* 20 April 1931; *s* of 2nd Viscount Allenby and of Mary Lethbridge Allenby (*d* 1988), *d* of Edward Champneys; *S* father, 1984; *m* 1965, Sara Margaret, *d* of Lt-Col Peter Milner Wiggin; one *s*. *Educ:* Eton; RMA Sandhurst. Commnd 2/Lieut 11th Hussars (PAO), 1951; served Malaya, 1953–56; ADC to Governor, Cyprus, 1957–58; Bde Major, 51 Brigade, Hong Kong, 1967–70; comd Royal Yeomanry (TA), 1974–77; GSO1 Instructor, Nigerian Staff Coll., Kaduna, 1977–79. Chm., Quickrest Ltd, 1987–90. Elected Mem., H of L, 1999; Mem., Admin and Works Cttee, H of L, 2006–. Vice Pres., Internat. League for Protection of Horses, 1999–2006 (Chm., 1997–99). *Recreations:* horses, sailing. *Heir:* *s* Hon. Henry Jaffray Hynman Allenby [*b* 29 July 1968; *m* 1996, Louise, *yr d* of Michael Green; two *s*]. *Died 3 Oct. 2014.*

ALLISON, John, CBE 1975; company director; *b* 4 Oct. 1919; *m* 1st, 1948, Elvira Gwendoline Lewis (*d* 1992); one *s* two *d*; 2nd, 1997, Barbara Mary Tarrant. *Educ:* Morriston Elementary Sch.; Glanmor Secondary Sch.; Swansea Tech. Coll. In family business of quarrying until 1968, and musical instrument retailing, 1957–89. Mem. (Lab) Swansea City Council, 1957–74, Leader, 1967–74 (Dep. Mayor, 1966–67 and 1972–73); Mem. (Lab) W Glamorgan County Council, 1974–89, Leader, 1977–89 (Chm., 1975–76); Chm., ACC, 1986–88. Contested (Lab) Barry, 1970. Chm., S Wales Police Authority, 1987–89. DL W Glam, subseq. Swansea, 1975; JP Swansea, 1966. *Recreations:* fishing, gardening. *Club:* Morriston Golf. *Died 25 May 2012.*

ALLOTT, Air Cdre Molly Greenwood, CB 1975; *b* 28 Dec. 1918; *d* of late Gerald William Allott. *Educ:* Sheffield High Sch. for Girls. Served War of 1939–45: joined WAAF, 1941; served in: Egypt, Singapore, Germany. Staff of AOC-in-C: RAF Germany, 1960–63; Fighter Command, 1963–66; Training Command, 1971–73; Dir, WRAF, 1973–76; ADC 1973–76. Nat. Chm., Girls' Venture Corps, 1977–82; Member: Council, Union Jack Club, 1977–91; Main Grants Cttee, RAF Benevolent Fund, 1977–82. Raised funds for bldg of Battle of Britain Mus., Hendon, 1977–79. *Recreations:* travel, fine and decorative arts. *Address:* St George's, De La Warr Road, Milford-on-Sea, Lymington, Hants SO41 0NE. *Club:* Royal Air Force. *Died 12 Dec. 2013.*

ALLOTT, Robin Michael; Under-Secretary, Departments of Industry and Trade, 1978–80; *b* 9 May 1926; *s* of late Reginald William Allott and Dorothy (*née* Dobson). *Educ:* The Oratory Sch., Caversham; New Coll., Oxford; Sheffield Univ. Asst Principal, BoT, 1948; UK Delegn to OECD, Paris, 1952; Private Sec. to Sec. for Overseas Trade, 1953; Principal, Office for Scotland, Glasgow, 1954; UK Delegn to UN Conf. on Trade and Develt, Geneva, 1964; Asst Sec., BoT, 1965; Counsellor, UK Delegn to EEC, Brussels, 1971; sabbatical year, New Coll., Oxford, 1974–75; Dept of Industry (motor industry), 1975; Under-Sec., Dept of Trade, 1976. Member: European Sociobiol Soc., 1992; NY Acad. of Scis, 1995; AAAS, 1996. Herder/Jan Wind Prize Essay, 2015. *Publications:* The Physical Foundation of Language, 1973; The Motor Theory of Language Origin, 1989; (ed) Studies in Language Origins 3, 1994; (ed jtly) Dorothy Dobson's Commonplace Book, 2000; The Natural Origin of Language, 2000; The Great Mosaic Eye, 2001, 2nd edn as The Great Mosaic Eye: embodied language, evolution and society, 2012; The Child and the World, 2005; contrib. Jl of Social and Evolutionary Systems; contrib. collections on lang. and origin of semiosis, sound symbolism, syntax, etc. *Recreations:* studying the evolutionary relation of language, perception and action and language acquisition. *Address:* 5 Fitzgerald Park, Seaford, East Sussex BN25 1AX. *T:* (01323) 492300. *Died 22 Oct. 2015.*

ALLPORT, Denis Ivor; Chairman, 1979–85 and Chief Executive, 1977–85, Metal Box Ltd (Director, 1973–85, Managing Director, 1977–79, Deputy Chairman, 1979); *b* 20 Nov. 1922; *s* of late A. R. Allport and E. M. Allport (*née* Mashman); *m* 1949, Diana (*née* Marler); two *s* one *d*. *Educ:* Highgate School. Served War, Indian Army, 1941–46; joined Metal Box Ltd, 1946; various appts in UK, Singapore and Pakistan; Man. Dir, Metal Box Co. of India, 1969–70; Dir, Metal Box Overseas Ltd, 1970–74. Chairman: Castle Underwriting Agents Ltd, 1989–94 (Dir, 1988–94); Devonshire Underwriting Agents Ltd, 1991–93; Director: Beecham Gp plc, 1981–88; Marley plc, 1985–91. Member: Nat. Enterprise Bd, 1980–83; NRDC, 1981–83; Neill Cttee of Enquiry into Regulatory Arrangements at

Lloyd's, 1986. Gov., Highgate Sch., 1981–94. CCMI (FBIM 1977). *Recreation:* golf. *Address:* 26 Great Maytham Hall, Rolvenden, Cranbrook, Kent TN17 4NE. *T:* (01580) 241909. *Clubs:* MCC, Oriental. *Died 30 Dec. 2012.*

ALSTON, John Alistair, CBE 1988; DL; Chairman, Norfolk Health Authority, 1996–2002; *b* 24 May 1937; *s* of late David Alston and Bathia Mary (*née* Davidson). *Educ:* Orwell Park, Sherborne; RAC, Cirencester. Norfolk County Council: Mem., 1973–97; Leader, 1981–87 and 1989–93; Vice-Chm., 1987–88; Chm., 1988–89. Chairman: Norwich, then E Norfolk HA, subseq. Norfolk Health Commn, 1994–96; Chm., Broads Bill Steering Cttee, 1984–87; Member: Broads Authority, 1988–95; Council, Morley Res. Station, 1981–97; Council, UEA, 1986–2002 (Vice Chm., 1997–2002). Chairman: Norfolk Connections, 2000–02; Norfolk County Strategic Partnership, 2002–07; Norfolk Cttee, Queen's Diamond Jubilee, 2010–12. Pres., Norfolk Athletics Assoc., 1997–2007. DL 1991, High Sheriff, 2004–05, Norfolk. Hon. DCL UEA, 2004. *Recreations:* gardening, shooting, fishing. *Address:* Besthorpe Hall, Attleborough, Norfolk NR17 2LJ. *T:* (01953) 450300. *Died 22 Feb. 2015.*

ALSTON, Prof. Robin Carfrae, OBE 1992; FSA; Professor of Library Studies, London University, 1990–98, then Professor Emeritus, University College London; Hon. Senior Research Fellow, English Studies, London University, since 1998; *b* 29 Jan. 1933; *s* of late Wilfred Louis Alston; *m* 1st, 1957, Joanna Ormiston (marr. diss. 1996; she *d* 2009); one *s* one *d* (and one *s* decd); 2nd, 1996, Janet Pedley-King (marr. diss. 1999); 3rd, Conceição Neves da Silva Colella. *Educ:* Rugby Sch.; Univs of British Columbia (BA 1954), Oxford (MA 1956), Toronto (MA 1958) and London (PhD 1964). Teaching Fellow, University Coll., Toronto, 1956–58; Lectr, New Brunswick Univ., 1958–60; Lectr in English Lit., Leeds Univ., 1964–76; Consultant to British Library, 1977–; Editor-in-Chief, 18th Century Short Title Catalogue, 1978–89; Advr to Develt and Systems Office, Humanities and Social Scis (formerly Ref. Div.), British Library, 1984–; Editl Dir, The Nineteenth Century, series of microfiche texts 1801–1900, 1985–. Dir, Sch. of Library, Archive and Information Studies, UCL, 1990–95; Course Dir, History of the Book, Sch. of Advanced Studies, London Univ., 1995–98. Hon. Res. Fellow, UCL, 1987–. Klein Vis. Prof., Univ. of Texas, 1990; Vis. Prof., Univ. of Malta, 1994. David Murray Lectr, Univ. of Glasgow, 1983; Guest Lectr, Univ. of London, 1983, Sorbonne, 1984, Tokyo Symposium on micro-reproduction, 1984; Cecil Oldman Lectr, Leeds Univ., 1988, 1989; Morris Meml Lectr, Royal Instn, 1991. Jt Editor, Leeds Studies in English and Leeds Texts and Monographs, 1965–72; Editor, Studies in Early Modern English, 1965–72; Jt Editor, The Direction Line, 1976–; Editor: Special Pubns, Bibliographical Soc., 1983–; Libraries and Archives (series), 1991–. Founder, Chm. and principal Editor, Scolar Press Ltd, 1966–72, Man. Dir, 1984–; Founder, Janus Press, devoted to original art prints, 1973. Member: Adv. Cttee, British Library, 1975–; Adv. Cttee, MLA of America for the Wing Project, 1980–; Adv. Panel, Aust. Research Grants Cttee, 1983–; Adv. Bd, Cambridge Hist. of the Book in Britain, 1989–. Member: Organising Cttee, 18th Century Short Title Catalogue, 1976–; Cttee, British Book Trade Index, 1984–. Mem. Council, Bibliographical Soc., 1967– (Vice-Pres., 1978–88, Pres., 1988–90); Founding Mem. Council, Ilkley Literature Festival, 1973–; Jt Founder, Frederic Madden Soc., 1989–. Consultant, Consortium of Univ. Research Libraries, 1985–86; Adviser to: Govt of Pakistan on estabt of Nat. Liby of Pakistan, 1988; UC of Barbados, 2005–. FSA 1987; Hon. FLA 1986. Hon. DLitt London, 2005. Samuel Pepys Gold Medal, Ephemera Soc., 1984; Smithsonian Instn award, 1985; Walford Medal, Library Assoc., 1993; Gold Medal, Bibliographical Soc., 1996. *Publications:* An Introduction to Old English, 1961 (rev. edn 1966); A Catalogue of Books relating to the English Language (1500–1800) in Swedish Libraries, 1965; English Language and Medieval English Literature: a Select Reading-List for Students, 1966; A Bibliography of the English Language from the Invention of Printing to the Year 1800: Vol. I, 1965; Vols V and VIII, 1966; Vols VII and IV, 1967; Vol. II, 1968; Vol. VI, 1969; Vol. III, 1970; Vol. IX, 1971; Vol. X, 1972; Vol. XI, 1978; Vol. XII part 1, 1987; Vol. XII part 2, 1988; Vol. XIII, 1999; Vol. XIV, 2000; Vol. XV, 2001; Vol. XVI, 2002; Vol. XVII, 2003; Vol. XVIII, 2004–06; Vol. XIX part 1, 2007; Vol. XXI part 1, 2008; Vol. XX, 2010; Vol. XIX part 2, 2011; Vol. XXI part 2, 2011; Vol. XXII, 2012; Alexander Gil's Logonomia Anglica (1619): a translation into Modern English, 1973; (jtly) The Works of William Bullokar, Vol. I, 1966; English Studies (rev. edn of Vol. III, Cambridge Bibl. Eng. Lit.), 1968; English Linguistics 1500–1800: a Collection of Texts in Facsimile (365 vols), 1967–72; European Linguistics 1500–1700: a Collection of Texts in Facsimile (12 vols), 1968–72; A Checklist of the works of Joseph Addison, 1976; Bibliography MARC and ESTC, 1978; Eighteenth-Century Subscription Lists, 1983; ESTC: the British Library Collections, 1983; The arrangement of books in the British Museum Library 1843–1973, and the British Library 1973–1985, 1987; The Nineteenth Century: subject scope and principles of selection, 1987; Index to Pressmarks in use in the British Museum Library and the British Library, 1987; Index to the Classification Schedules of the Map Collections in the British Library, 1987; Computers and Libraries, 1987; The British Library: past, present, future, 1989; Women Writers of Fiction, Verse and Drama: a checklist of works published between 1801 and 1900 in the collections of the British Library, 1990; Handlist of unpublished finding aids to the London Collections of the British Library, 1991; Handlist of catalogues and book lists in the Department of Manuscripts, British Library, 1991; Books with Manuscript: a catalogue, 1994; Books printed on vellum in The British Library, 1996; A Catalogue of Book Sales, 1676–1800, 2009; numerous articles, printed lectures, reviews, etc. *Recreations:* music, photography. *Address:* 202 Alameda Linhares, Jardim Santa Rosa, Foz do Iguaçu-PR, 85.869–110, Brazil. *E:* robina95@gmail.com. *Died 29 June 2011.*

ALVES, Colin, OBE 1990; General Secretary: General Synod Board of Education, 1984–90; National Society for Promoting Religious Education, 1984–90; *b* 19 April 1930; *s* of Donald Alexander Alves and Marjorie Alice (*née* Marsh); *m* 1953, Peggy (*née* Kember); two *s* one *d*. *Educ:* Christ's Hospital, Horsham; Worcester Coll., Oxford (MA). School teaching, 1952–59; Lectr, King Alfred's Coll., Winchester, 1959–68; Head of Dept, Brighton Coll. of Educn, 1968–74; Dir, RE Centre, St Gabriel's Coll., 1974–77; Colleges Officer, General Synod Bd of Educn, 1977–84. Mem., Durham Commn on RE, 1967–70; Chm., Schs Council RE Cttee, 1971–77; Jt Sec., RE Council of England and Wales, 1974–77; Sec., Assoc. of Voluntary Colls, 1978–84; Member: Adv. Cttee on Supply and Educn of Teachers, 1980–85; Nat. Adv. Body for Public Sector Higher Educn, 1983–88; Voluntary Sector Consultative Council, 1984–88. Pres., Inter-Eur. Commn on Church and Schs, 1977–82; Review Officer, Churches Together in England, 1993–94. Governor: Christ Church Coll., Canterbury, 1981–95; Haywards Heath Coll., 1982–99; Digby Stuart Coll., 1990–96; Trustee: Shoei Coll., Winchester, 1982–94; St Gabriel's Trust, 1984–2009; St Pierre Internat. Youth Trust, 1990–96; St Gregory's Trust, 1991–99. MLitt Lambeth, 1989. *Publications:* Religion and the Secondary School, 1968; The Christian in Education, 1972; The Question of Jesus, 1987; Free to Choose, 1991; contrib. various symposia on RE. *Recreations:* music, walking, gardening. *Address:* 9 Park Road, Haywards Heath, W Sussex RH16 4HY. *T:* (01444) 454496. *Died 2 June 2014.*

AMBRASEYS, Prof. Nicholas, FREng; FICE; Professor of Engineering Seismology, University of London, at Imperial College, 1973–94, then Emeritus; Senior Research Fellow, since 1995, and Senior Research Investigator, since 1996, Imperial College; *b* 19 Jan. 1929; *s* of Neocles Ambraseys, Athens, and Cleopatra Jambany; *m* 1955, Xeni, *d* of A. Stavrou. *Educ:* National Technical Univ. of Athens (DipEng); Univ. of London (DIC; PhD; DSc 1980). Lectr in Civil Engineering, Imperial Coll., 1958–62; Associate Prof. of Civil Engrg, Univ. of Illinois, 1963; Prof. of Hydrodynamics, Nat. Tech. Univ., Athens, 1964; Imperial College: Lectr, 1965–68; Univ. Reader in Engrg Seismology, 1969–72; Hd, Engrg Seismology Sect., 1969–95. Chm., British Nat. Cttee for Earthquake Eng., 1961–71; Dir, Internat. Assoc. for Earthquake Engrg, 1961–77; Vice-Pres., European Assoc. for Earthquake

Engrg, 1964–75; Mem., 1969–78, Vice-Chm., 1979–81, Unesco Internat. Adv. Cttee of Earthquake Risk; leader, UN/Unesco earthquake reconnaissance missions to Pakistan, Iran, Turkey, Romania, Jugoslavia, Italy, Greece, Algeria, Nicaragua, East and Central Africa; Chm., Internat. Commn for earthquake protection of historical monuments, 1977–81; consultant to UN/Unesco. Member: European Acad., 2002; Acad. of Athens, 2003. FREng (FEng 1985); FCGI 2000. Hon. Fellow, Internat. Assoc. for Earthquake Engrg, 1992; Hon. Mem., Earthquake Res. Inst., USA, 2001. Dr Eng *hc* Nat. Tech. Univ. of Athens, 1993. Decennial Award, European Assoc. for Earthquake Engrg, 1975; Busk Medal, RGS, 1975; William Smith Medal, Geological Soc. of London, 2002; Seismological Soc. of America Medal, 2006. Freedom of City of Skopje, 1999. *Publications:* (with C. Melville) A History of Persian Earthquakes, 1982; (with C. Melville) Seismicity of Arabia & Red Sea, 1994; (with C. Finkel) Seismicity of Turkey, 1995; (with R. Sigbjörnsson) Re-appraisal of the Seismicity of Iceland, 2000; (with R. D. Adams) The Seismicity of Central America, 2001; Earthquakes in the Mediterranean and the Middle East: a multidisciplinary study of seismicity up to 1900, 2009; papers on engrg seismology, soil mechanics, tectonics, historical seismicity. *Recreations:* history, philately. *Address:* Imperial College London, SW7 2BU. *T:* (020) 7589 5111; 19 Bede House, Manor Fields, SW15 3LT. *T:* (020) 8788 4219. *Died 28 Dec. 2012.*

AMBROZIC, His Eminence Cardinal Aloysius Matthew; Archbishop of Toronto, (RC), 1990–2006; *b* 27 Jan. 1930; *s* of Aloysius Ambrozic and Helena (*née* Pecar). *Educ:* St Augustine's Seminary, Scarborough, Ont; Angelicum, Rome (STL); Biblicum, Rome, 1957–60 (SSL); Univ. of Würzburg, Germany (ThD). Ordained, 1955; Curate, St Teresa's, Port Colborne, Ont, 1955–57; Professor: St Augustine's Seminary, Scarborough, Ont, 1960–67; Toronto Sch. of Theol., 1970–76; Auxiliary Bishop of Toronto, 1976–86; Coadjutor Archbishop of Toronto, 1986–90. Cardinal, 1998. *Publications:* The Hidden Kingdom, 1972; Remarks on the Canadian Catechism, 1974; Oče, posvečeno bodi tvoje ime, 1980; Oče, zgodi se tvoja volja, 1996; Če hoče kdo hoditi za menoj, 2001. *Recreations:* hiking, swimming. *Died 26 Aug. 2011.*

AMPTHILL, 4th Baron *cr* 1881; **Geoffrey Denis Erskine Russell,** CBE 1986; PC 1995; Deputy Speaker, House of Lords, since 1983; Deputy Chairman: Express Newspapers, 1989–98 (Director, 1985–98); United Newspapers, 1991–96 (Director, 1981–96); *b* 15 Oct. 1921; *s* of 3rd Baron Ampthill, CBE, and Christabel, Lady Ampthill (*d* 1976); *S* father, 1973; *m* 1st, 1946, Susan Mary (marr. diss. 1971; she *d* 2001), *d* of late Hon. Charles John Frederic Winn; two *s* one *d* (and one *s* decd); 2nd, 1972, Elisabeth Anne Marie (marr. diss. 1987), *d* of late Claude Henri Gustave Mallon. *Educ:* Stowe. Irish Guards, 1941–46; 2nd Lt 1941, Captain 1944. Gen. Manager, Fortnum and Mason, 1947–51; Chairman, New Providence Hotel Co. Ltd, 1951–64; Dir, Dualvest plc, 1981–87. Managing Director of theatre owning and producing companies, 1953–81. Dep. Chm., 1980–92, Chm., 1992–94, of Cttees, H of L; Chairman: Select Cttee on Channel Tunnel Bill, 1987; Select Cttee on Channel Tunnel Rail Link Bill, 1996; elected Mem., H of L, 1999. Chm., London Helicopter Emergency Service, 1991–96. Dir, Leeds Castle Foundn, 1980–82. *Heir: s* Hon. David Whitney Erskine Russell [*b* 27 May 1947; *m* 1st, 1980, April McKenzie Arbon (marr. diss. 1998), *y d* of Paul Arbon, New York; two *d*; 2nd, 2002, Christia, *widow* of Prince Rostislav Romanoff and *d* of Harold Noregaard Ipsen]. *Address:* 6 North Court, Great Peter Street, SW1P 3LL. *Died 23 April 2011.*

ANDERSON, Rev. David; Principal Lecturer in Religious Studies, Hertfordshire College of Higher Education (formerly Wall Hall College), Aldenham, Herts, 1974–84 (Senior Lecturer, 1970–74); *b* 30 Oct. 1919; *s* of William and Nancy Anderson, Newcastle upon Tyne; *m* 1953, Helen Finlay Robinson, 3rd *d* of Johnson and Eleanor Robinson, Whitley Bay, Northumberland; one *s* two *d*. *Educ:* Royal Grammar Sch., Newcastle upon Tyne; Selwyn Coll., Cambridge. Served in RA, 1940–42, Intelligence Corps, 1942–46, Lieut. Ordained deacon, 1949, priest, 1950; Curate of parish of St Gabriel, Sunderland, 1949–52; Tutor of St Aidan's Coll., Birkenhead, 1952–56; Warden of Melville Hall, Ibadan, Nigeria, 1956–58; Principal of: Immanuel Coll., Ibadan, Nigeria, 1958–62; Wycliffe Hall, Oxford, 1962–69. Chaplain, Heswall Nautical Trng Coll., 1952–53. Examining Chaplain: to Bishop of Liverpool, 1969–75; to Bishop of St Albans, 1972–80. *Publications:* The Tragic Protest, 1969; Simone Weil, 1971; contributed: Religion and Modern Literature, 1975; William Golding: some critical considerations, 1978; The Passion of Man, 1980. *Recreations:* listening to music, hi-fi gramophones. *Address:* 16 Manor Park, Borrowash, Derby DE72 3LP. *T:* (01332) 664426. *Died 30 Dec. 2014.*

ANDERSON, David; Chairman: Reclaim Fund, 2010–14; Vice Chairman, NFU Mutual Insurance Society, 2012–14 (non-executive Director, 2010–14); *b* 23 Oct. 1955; *s* of Donald and Gweneth Anderson; *m* 1980, Fiona Ellen Hamilton; one *s* one *d*. *Educ:* Cheadle Hulme Sch.; St Edmund Hall, Oxford (MA PPE). Graduate trainee, Aveling Barford Ltd, construction equipment manufr, 1977–80; Dun and Bradstreet, 1980–83; PA Mgt Consultants, 1983–87; Dep. Gen. Manager (Mkting), 1987–90, Dir, 1990–2003, Chief Exec., 1996–2003, Yorkshire Building Soc.; Chief Executive: Jobcentre Plus, DWP, 2003–05; Co-operative Financial Services Ltd, 2005–09. Non-exec. Dir, John Lewis Partnership, 2011–14. *Recreations:* golf, sailing. *Died 24 Sept. 2015.*

ANDERSON, Gerry, MBE 2001; film producer, director, and writer; Managing Director, Anderson Entertainment Ltd, since 2001; *b* 14 April 1929; *s* of Joseph and Deborah Anderson; *m* 1st, 1952, Betty Wrightman; two *d*; 2nd, 1961, Sylvia Thamm; one *s*; 3rd, 1981, Mary Robins; one *s*. *Educ:* Willesden County Secondary Sch. Entered film industry as Colonial Film Unit Trainee, 1943; Asst Editor, Gainsborough Pictures, 1945–47; dubbing editor, various ind. cos, 1949–53; Film Dir, Polytechnic Films, 1954–55; Co-Founder: Pentagon Films, 1955; AP Films, 1956; AP Merchandising, 1961; Chm., Century 21 Orgn, 1966–75; Dir of TV Commercials, 1961, 1988–92; Man. Dir, Inimitable Ltd, 1989–97. *Puppet films/series* include: director: The Adventures of Twizzle, 1956; Torchy the Battery Boy, 1957; producer: Four Feather Falls; Supercar, 1959–60; Fireball XL5, 1962; Stingray, 1963–65; Thunderbirds, 1966–67; Captain Scarlet and the Mysterons, 1967–68, re-make with computer-generated images as New Captain Scarlet, 2003; Joe 90, 1968–69; The Secret Service, 1969; Terrahawks, 1981–85; *live action series* include: UFO, 1969; The Protectors, 1971; Space: 1999, 1973–75, 1977–78; Space Precinct, 1993–95; *stop motion series:* Dick Spanner, 1987; Lavender Castle, 1997; *feature films:* executive producer: Thunderbirds are Go (puppet); Thunderbird 6 (puppet); producer, Journey to the far side of the Sun (live action). Hon. Fellow, BKSTS. *Recreations:* gardening, walking, DIY. *Died 26 Dec. 2012.*

ANDERSON, Gordon Alexander, CBE 2000; CA, FCMA; *b* 9 Aug. 1931; *s* of Cecil Brown Anderson and Janet Davidson Bell; *m* 1958, Eirené Cochrane Howie Douglas; two *s* one *d*. *Educ:* High School of Glasgow. Qualified as Chartered Accountant, 1955; FCMA 1984. National Service, RN, 1955–57. Partner: Moores Carson & Watson, 1958 (subseq. McClelland Moores & Co., Arthur Young McClelland Moores & Co., Arthur Young (Chm., 1987–89), and Ernst & Young (Dep. Sen. Partner, 1989–90)); McLintock Moores & Murray, 1963–69. Chairman: Bitmac Ltd, 1990–96 (Dir, 1984–96); TSB Bank Scotland, 1994–99 (Dir, 1991–99); Director: Douglas Firebrick Co. Ltd, 1961–70; Lloyds TSB Group (formerly TSB Group), 1993–99; Merchants House of Glasgow, 1996–2002. Mem., Scottish Milk Marketing Bd, 1979–85. Mem., Council on Tribunals, 1990–96 (Mem., Scottish Cttee, 1990–96). Institute of Chartered Accountants of Scotland: Mem. Council, 1980–84; Vice-Pres., 1984–86; Pres., 1986–87. Dir, 1975–81 and 1990–92, Chm. of Govs, 1992–2001, High Sch. of Glasgow. *Club:* Glasgow Golf. *Died 31 Jan. 2013.*

ANDERSON, Prof. Joan Mary, (Jan), FRS 1996; FAA; Adjunct Professor, Division of Plant Sciences, Research School of Biology (formerly Photobioenergetics Group, Research School of Biological Sciences), Australian

National University, since 1996; *b* 12 May 1932; *d* of William Arthur Anderson, OBE and Mary Anderson (*née* Lee). *Educ:* Univ. of Otago, NZ (BSc 1954; MSc 1st Cl. Hons 1956); Univ. of California, Berkeley (PhD 1959). Div. of Plant Industry, CSIRO, 1962–, Chief Res. Scientist, 1962–97. Fellowships: King George VI Meml, NZ, 1956; Carnegie Inst., Stanford, 1966; Kettering, Dayton, Ohio, 1967; Harvard, 1973; Newnham Coll., Cambridge, 1973–74; Vis. Spring Prof., Univ. of California, Berkeley, 1982; Vis. Swedish Natural Sci. Res. Council Prof., Lund, 1986. FD *hc* Umeå, Sweden, 1998. Lemberg Medal, Aust. Soc. of Biochem., 1983; Australian Citation Laureate in plant and animal sci., 2004; Lifetime Achievement Award, Internat. Soc. of Photosynthesis Res., 2007. *Publications:* 213 articles on photosynthesis research. *Recreations:* music, art, water colour painting. *Address:* Division of Plant Sciences, Research School of Biology, Australian National University, Canberra, ACT 2601, Australia. *T:* (2) 61255895, *Fax:* (2) 61258056. *E:* jan.anderson@anu.edu.au. *Died 28 Aug. 2015.*

ANDERSON, Prof. John Russell, CBE 1980; Professor of Pathology at the Western Infirmary, Glasgow University, 1967–83; *b* 31 May 1918; *s* of William Gregg Anderson and Mary Gordon Adam; *m* 1956, Audrey Margaret Shaw Wilson; two *s* one *d* (and one *d* decd). *Educ:* Worksop Coll.; St Andrews Univ. (BSc 1939; MB, ChB 1942; MD 1955); MRCP 1961; FRCPGlas 1965; FRCPath 1966; FRSE 1968. RAMC, 1944–47 (Emergency Commn). Lecturer and Senior Lecturer in Pathology, Glasgow Univ., 1947–65; George Holt Prof. of Pathology, Liverpool Univ., 1965–67. Rockefeller travelling fellowship in Medicine, at Rochester, NY, 1953–54. Pres., RCPath, 1978–81 (Vice-Pres., 1975). Hon. FRCPI, 1981. Hon. LLD Dundee, 1981. *Publications:* Autoimmunity, Clinical and Experimental (jtly), 1967; (ed) Muir's Textbook of Pathology, 9th edn 1971 to 12th edn 1985; various papers on immunopathology in scientific jls. *Recreations:* golf, arboriculture, gardening. *Address:* 3 Connell Crescent, Milngavie, Glasgow G62 6AR. *Died 30 Oct. 2011.*

ANDERSON, Reginald, CMG 1974; *b* 3 Nov. 1921; *s* of late Herbert Anderson and Anne Mary (*née* Hicks); *m* 1945, Audrey Gabrielle Williams; two *d. Educ:* Palmers, Grays, Essex. Cabinet Office, 1938–40. Served War, RAF, Flt Lt, 1941–46. Ministry of: Supply, 1947–57; Supply Staff, Australia, 1957–59; Aviation, 1960–67; Counsellor, British Embassy, Washington, 1967–70; Asst Under-Sec. of State, 1970–76, Dep. Under-Sec. of State, 1976–81, MoD. *Club:* Royal Air Force. *Died 2 Jan. 2012.*

ANDREOTTI, Giulio; Life Senator, Chamber of Deputies, since 1992; Prime Minister (President of the Council of Ministers) of Italy, 1972–73, 1976–79 and 1989–92; *b* 14 Jan. 1919; *s* of Filippo and Rosa Andreotti; *m* 1945, Livia Danese; two *s* two *d. Educ:* Univ. of Rome. Mem. for Rome Latina Viterbo Frosinone, Chamber of Deputies, 1946–92. Under Sec. of State, Council of Ministers, 1947–54; Minister of Interior, 1954; Minister of Finance, 1955–58; Minister of the Treasury, 1958–59; Minister of Defence, 1959–65; Minister of Industry and Commerce, 1966–68; Chm., Christian Democrats, 1968–72; Minister of Defence, March–Oct. 1974; Minister for Budget and Economic Planning, 1974–76; Minister of Foreign Affairs, 1983–89. Founder, and Editor, Concretezza (political weekly), 1955–76. Hon. Dr: Sorbonne; Loyola Univ., Chicago; Copernican Univ. of Torun, Poland; La Plata; Salamanca; St John's, NY; Warsaw; Univ. of Sci. and Technol., Beijing; New York; Jewish Theol Seminary, NY. Bancarella Prize, 1985. *Publications* include: Pranzo di magro per il cardinale, 1954; De Gasperi e il suo tempo, 1965; La Sciarada di Papa Mastai, 1967; Ore 13: il Ministro deve morire, 1975; Ad Ogni morte di Papa, 1980; Il diario 1976–79, 1981; De Gasperi visto da vicino, 1986; Visti da vicino (4 vols of profiles): Onorevole, stia zitto, 1987, vol II, 1992; L'URSS vista da vicino, 1988, Gli USA visti da vicino, 1989; Il potere logora … ma è meglio non perderlo, 1990; Governare con la crisi, 1991; The USA Up Close, 1992; Cosa Loro, 1995; De Prima Repubblica, 1996; many articles. *Address:* Senato della Repubblica, Piazza Madama, 00816 Rome, Italy. *Died 6 May 2013.*

ANDREW, His Honour Herbert Henry; QC 1982; a Circuit Judge, 1984–99; *b* 26 July 1928; *s* of Herbert Henry Andrew and Nora Andrew (*née* Gough); *m* 1966, Annette Josephine Colbert; two *s* two *d. Educ:* Preston Grammar Sch.; Queens' Coll., Cambridge (BA). Called to the Bar, Gray's Inn, 1952; practised on Northern Circuit, 1953–84; a Recorder, 1978–84. *Recreation:* fell walking. *Club:* Liverpool Racquet. *Died 25 Dec. 2014.*

ANDREW, Sydney Percy Smith, FRS 1976; FREng, FIChemE, MIMechE; consultant chemical engineer; ICI Senior Research Associate, 1976–88; *b* 16 May 1926; *s* of Harold C. Andrew and Kathleen M. (*née* Smith); *m* 1986, Ruth Harrison Kenyon (*née* Treanor). *Educ:* Barnard Castle Sch.; King's Coll., Durham Univ. (Open Schol.; BSc); Trinity Hall, Cambridge (Schol. and Prizeman; MA). Joined ICI Billingham Div., 1950; Chemical Engrg Res., 1951; Plant Engr, 1953; Section Manager: Reactor Res., 1955; Process Design, 1959; Gp Man., Catalysts and Chemicals Res., 1963–76. Vis. Prof., Univ. of Bath, 1988–. Chm., Res. Cttee, IChemE. FREng (FEng 1976). Hon. DSc Leeds, 1979. Soc. of Chemical Industry Medal, 1989. *Publications:* Catalyst Handbook, 1970; various papers in chemical engrg, applied chemistry and plant physiology. *Recreations:* archaeology, ancient and medieval history. *Address:* 1 The Wynd, Stainton in Cleveland, Middlesbrough TS8 9BP. *T:* (01642) 596348. *Died 2 Nov. 2011.*

ANDREWS, Prof. Kenneth Raymond, FBA 1986; Professor of History, University of Hull, 1979–88 (part-time, 1986–88), then Emeritus; *b* 26 Aug. 1921; *s* of Arthur Walter and Marion Gertrude Andrews; *m* 1969, Ottilie Kalman (*d* 2000), Olomouc, Czechoslovakia; two step *s. Educ:* Henry Thornton Sch., Clapham; King's College London (BA 1948, PhD 1951). Lectr, Univ. of Liverpool, 1963–64; Lectr and Sen. Lectr, Univ. of Hull, 1964–79. *Publications:* English Privateering Voyages to the West Indies, 1959; Elizabethan Privateering, 1964; Drake's Voyages, 1967; The Last Voyage of Drake and Hawkins, 1972; The Spanish Caribbean, 1978; Trade, Plunder and Settlement, 1984; Ships, Money and Politics, 1991; articles in learned jls. *Died 6 Jan. 2012.*

ANGELOU, Marguerite Annie, (Maya); writer, singer and actress; *b* St Louis, 4 April 1928; *d* of Bailey Johnson and Vivian Baxter Johnson; one *s. Educ:* George Washington High Sch., San Francisco; California Labor Sch. Yale Univ. Fellowship, 1970; Rockefeller Foundn Scholar, 1975; Reynolds Prof. of Amer. Studies, Wake Forest Univ., 1981–. Writer, director, or actor: *stage:* Cabaret for Freedom, 1960; Medea, 1966; The Least of These, 1966; Gettin' Up Stayed On My Mind, 1967; Ajax, 1974; And Still I Rise, 1976; Look Away, 1975; Moon and Rainbow Shawl, 1988; *films:* Georgia, Georgia, 1972; All Day Long, 1974; Poetic Justice, 1993; How to Make an American Quilt, 1996; *television:* Black, Blue, Black, 1968; Roots, 1977; Sister, Sister, 1982. Awards include: Amer. Revolution Bicentennial, 1975; Woman of the Year in Communications, 1976; Horatio Alger, 1992. *Publications: autobiography:* I Know Why the Caged Bird Sings, 1970 (televised, 1979); Gather Together in My Name, 1974; Singin' and Swingin' and Gettin' Merry Like Christmas, 1976; The Heart of a Woman, 1981; All God's Children Need Travelling Shoes, 1986; Wouldn't Take Nothing for my Journey Now, 1993; (jtly) My Painted House, My Friendly Chicken and Me, 1994; A Song Flung to Heaven, 2002; Hallelujah! the Welcome Table, 2005; Mom & Me & Mom, 2013; *essays:* Lessons in Life, 1993; Letter to My Daughter, 2009; *poetry:* Just Give Me a Cool Drink of Water 'Fore I Diiie, 1971; Oh Pray My Wings are Gonna Fit Me Well, 1975; Shaker, Why Don't You Sing?, 1983; Now Sheba Sings the Song, 1987; I shall not be Moved, 1990; On the Pulse of Morning, 1993 (delivered personally at Presidential Inauguration); Complete Collected Poems of Maya Angelou, 1995; Amazing Peace, 2005; *fiction:* Even the Stars Look Lonesome, 1998; *short stories:* All Day Long. *Died 28 May 2014.*

ANGLESEY, 7th Marquess of, *cr* 1815; **George Charles Henry Victor Paget;** Baron Paget, of Beau Desert, 1549; Earl of Uxbridge, 1784; Bt 1730; Lord-Lieutenant of Gwynedd, 1983–89; *b* 8 Oct. 1922; *o s* of 6th Marquess of

Anglesey, GCVO, and Lady Victoria Marjorie Harriet Manners (*d* 1946), *d* of 8th Duke of Rutland; *S* father, 1947; *m* 1948, Elizabeth Shirley Vaughan Morgan, DBE, LVO; two *s* three *d*. *Educ:* Wixenford, Wokingham; Eton Coll. Major, RHG, 1946. Div. Dir, Wales, Nationwide Building Soc., 1973–89. President: Anglesey Conservative Assoc., 1948–83; Nat. Museum of Wales, 1962–68; Friends of Friendless Churches, 1966–84; Ancient Monuments Soc., 1979–84. Treasurer, Danilo Dolci Trust (Britain), 1964–86. Vice-Chm., Welsh Cttee, Nat. Trust, 1975–85; Member: Historic Buildings Council for Wales, 1953–92 (Chm., 1977–92); Royal Fine Art Commn, 1965–71; Redundant Churches Fund, 1969–78; Royal Commn on Historical Manuscripts, 1984–92; Council, Soc. of Army Historical Research; Trustee: Nat. Portrait Gall., 1979–91; Nat. Heritage Memorial Fund, 1980–92. Hon. Prof., UCW, 1986. FSA 1952; FRSL 1969; Hon. FRIBA, 1971; FRHistS, 1975. Anglesey: CC, 1951–67; JP, 1959–68, 1983–89; DL, 1960, Vice-Lieut, 1960. Hon. Fellow, Royal Cambrian Acad. Freeman of the City of London. Hon. DLitt Wales, 1984. Octavia Hill Bronze Medal, Nat. Trust, 2002. CStJ 1984. *Publications:* (ed) The Capel Letters, 1814–1817, 1955; One-Leg: the Life and Letters of 1st Marquess of Anglesey, 1961, repr. 1996; (ed) Sergeant Pearman's Memoirs, 1968; (ed) Little Hodge, 1971; A History of the British Cavalry 1816–1919 (Chesney Gold Medal, RUSI, 1997): vol. I, 1816–1850, 1973; vol. II, 1851–1871, 1975; vol. III, 1872–1898, 1982 (Templer Medal, Nat. Army Mus., 1982); vol. IV, 1899–1913, 1986; vol. V, 1914–1919: Egypt, Palestine and Syria, 1995; vol. VI, 1914–1918: Mesopotamia, 1996; vol. VII, 1914: The Curragh Incident and the Western Front, 1996; vol. VIII, The Western Front, 1915–1918, and Epilogue, 1919–1939, 1997. *Recreations:* gardening, music. *Heir:* *s* Earl of Uxbridge, *b* 13 Nov. 1950. *Address:* Plâs-Newydd, Llanfairpwll, Anglesey LL61 6DZ. *T:* (01248) 714330. *Died 13 July 2013.*

ANNESLEY, 11th Earl *cr* 1789, of Castelwellan, co. Down; **Philip Harrison Annesley;** Baron Annesley 1758; Viscount Glerawly 1766; *b* 29 March 1927; 2nd *s* of 9th Earl Annesley and Nora, *y d* of Walter Harrison; *S* brother, 2001; *m* 1951, Florence Eileen (*d* 1995), *o d* of John Arthur Johnston. *Heir:* *b* Hon. Michael Robert Annesley [*b* 4 Dec. 1933; *m* 1956, Audrey Mary Goodwright; two *s* one *d*]. *Died 18 March 2011.*

ANSON, Vice-Adm. Sir Edward (Rosebery), KCB 1984; FRAeS 1982; Senior Naval Adviser, British Aerospace plc, 1989–91; Aerospace Consultant (part-time), I.A.D. Aerospace Ltd, Worthing, 1991–93; *b* 11 May 1929; *s* of Ross Rosebery Anson and Ethel Jane (*née* Green); *m* 1960, Rosemary Anne Radcliffe; one *s* one *d*. *Educ:* Prince of Wales Sch., Nairobi, Kenya; BRNC, Dartmouth; Empire Test Pilots Sch., Farnborough (grad. 1957). Served, 1952–64: Naval Air Sqdns, and 700X and 700Z Flts (Blackburn Aircraft Ltd, 1959–61); comd HMS Eskimo, 1964–66; Commander (Air): RNAS Lossiemouth, 1967–68; HMS Eagle, 1969–70; comd Inter Service Hovercraft Trials Unit, 1971; Naval and Air Attaché, Tokyo and Seoul, 1972–74; comd HMS Juno and Captain F4, 1974–76; comd HMS Ark Royal, 1976–78; Flag Officer, Naval Air Command, 1979–82; C of S to C-in-C Fleet, 1982–84. Exec. Dir, Sales, BAe Bristol Div., 1985–86; Pres. and Chief Exec. Officer, BAe, Washington, 1986–89. *Recreations:* walking, golf, photography. *Address:* c/o Lloyds, 9 High Street, Yeovil, Som BA20 1RN. *Died 22 Sept. 2014.*

ANTALPÉTER, Tibor; Chairman, Supervisory Board, Danubius Hotels Group, since 2002 (Member, 2000–02; Director, 1996–2000); *b* 4 Feb. 1930; *s* of late István Antalpéter and Viktória Dobai; *m* 1956, Adél Máthé; two *d*. *Educ:* Univ. of Economics, Budapest; graduated 1954. Importtex, foreign trade co., 1954; Commercial Sec. in London, 1956–60; Department of International Commercial Relations, Ministry of Foreign Trade: Head of Section, 1960; Dir of Dept, 1964; Dep. Dir-Gen., 1968–73; Dir-Gen. of Dept, 1977–88; Commercial Counsellor, London, 1973–77, 1988–90; Ambassador to UK, 1990–94. Director: Hungarian Investment Co. Ltd, 1995–2001; Linamar Hungary Rt (formerly Mezőgép) Orosháza, 1997–2011; Mem., Supervisory Bd, Weslin, Oroszlány, 2000–03. Vice-Chm., CAB Internat., 1992–94. Internat. volley-ball player, 1947–56; Chm., Hungarian Volley-ball Assoc. and Mem., Hungarian Olympic Cttee, 1980–86. Hon. FRSA 1992. Order of Merit for Labour, Bronze 1966, Gold 1979; Order of Merit of Hungarian Republic, Middle Cross, 1995. Order of the Finnish Lion, 1st Cl., 1969; Comdr, Order of Prince Henry the Navigator (Portugal), 1979; Order of Merit, Grand Silver Grade (Austria), 1983. *Recreations:* sport, music. *Address:* Kavics u. 11, 1025 Budapest, Hungary. *Died 15 Sept. 2012.*

ANTON, Alexander Elder, CBE 1973; FBA 1972; *b* 2 July 1922; *m* 1949, Doris May Lawrence; one *s*. *Educ:* Aberdeen Univ. (MA, LLB with dist.; Hon. LLD 1993). Solicitor, 1949; Lectr, Aberdeen, 1953–59; Prof. of Jurisprudence, Univ. of Glasgow, 1959–73. Hon. Vis. Prof., 1982–84, Hon. Prof., 1984, Aberdeen Univ. Mem., Scottish Law Commission, 1966–82. Literary Dir, Stair Soc., 1960–66; Chm., Scottish Rights of Way Soc., 1988–92. *Publications:* Private International Law, 1967, 2nd edn (with P. R. Beaumont), 1990; Civil Jurisdiction in Scotland, 1984; The Speyside Way, 2002; contribs to legal and historical jls. *Recreation:* hill walking. *Address:* 5 Seafield Drive West, Aberdeen AB15 7XA. *Died 6 June 2011.*

APEL, Dr Hans Eberhard; Member (SPD) of Bundestag, 1965–90; Minister of Defence, Germany, 1978–82; *b* Hamburg, 25 Feb. 1932; *m* 1956, Ingrid Schwingel; two *d*. *Educ:* Hamburg Univ. Diplom-Volkswirt, 1957, Dr rer. pol., 1960. Apprentice in Hamburg export and import business, 1951–54; Sec., Socialist Group in European Parlt, 1958–61; Head of Economics, Finance and Transportation Dept of European Parlt, 1962–65. MEP, 1965–69; Chm., Bundestag Cttee on Transportation, 1969–72; Parly Sec. of State, Min. for Foreign Affairs, Germany, 1972–74; Federal Minister of Finance, 1974–78. Joined Social Democratic Party (SPD), 1955: Dep. Chm., Parly Gp, 1969–72; Mem. Nat. Bd, 1970–88. Hon. Prof. in Econ. Dept, Rostock Univ., 1993. *Publications:* Edwin Cannan und seine Schüler (Doct. Thesis), 1961; Raumordnung der Bundesrepublik, in: Deutschland 1975, 1964; Europas neue Grenzen, 1964; Der deutsche Parlamentarismus, 1968; Bonn, den Tagebuch eines Bundestagsabgeordneten, 1972; Der Abstieg, 1990; Die deformierte Demokratie, 1991; Der kranke Koloss, 1994. *Recreations:* sailing, soccer. *Address:* Rögenfeld 42c, 22359 Hamburg, Germany. *Died 6 Sept. 2011.*

APPLETON, Brig. John Roper, OBE 2000; CEng, FIMechE; Director and Trustee: Smallpeice Trust, since 1998 (Chairman, 2001–07); Arkwright Scholarships Trust, since 2000 (Chairman, 2001–07); *b* 29 April 1938; *s* of late John Jackson Appleton and Ada Mary Appleton (*née* Roper); *m* 1st, 1959, Jenifer Jane Worman; one *s* one *d*; 2nd, 1978, Elizabeth Ann Cullen; two *d*. *Educ:* Liverpool Collegiate Sch.; Alun Grammar Sch., Mold; RMA Sandhurst; RMC Shrivenham. BScEng. Commnd REME, 1958; regtl and staff appts in UK, BAOR, Cyprus, Canada, 1961–78; MoD, 1978–79; Comdr REME, 1st Armd Div., BAOR, 1979–82; British Liaison Officer, HQ US Army, Pentagon, 1982–83; MoD, 1983–84; Asst Dir, Defence Commitments Staff, MoD, 1984–87, retired 1987. Fellowship, subseq. Royal Academy, of Engineering: Head of Engineering Affairs, 1987; Head of Corporate Affairs, 1991; Exec. Sec., 1993–2000; Hon. FREng 2000. Liveryman, Engineers' Co., 1996–. *Recreations:* gardening, garden construction. *Address:* 1 Beeches Drive, Great Bookham, Surrey KT23 4EQ. *Died 18 Feb. 2014.*

ARAUCARIA; *see* Graham, Rev. J. G.

ARBUTHNOTT, 16th Viscount of, *cr* 1641; **John Campbell Arbuthnott,** KT 1996; CBE 1986; DSC 1945; FRSE 1984; Lord-Lieutenant, Grampian Region (Kincardineshire), 1977–99; Her Majesty's Lord High Commissioner to General Assembly, Church of Scotland, 1986, 1987; *b* 26 Oct. 1924; *e s* of 15th Viscount of Arbuthnott, CB, CBE, DSO, MC, and Ursula Collingwood (*d* 1989); *S* father, 1966; *m* 1949, Mary Elizabeth Darley (*née* Oxley) (*d* 2010); one *s* one *d*. *Educ:* Fettes Coll.; Gonville and Caius Coll., Cambridge (BA Estate Mgt 1949; MA 1967). Served RNVR (Fleet Air Arm), 1942–46; Near and Far East, British Pacific Fleet,

1945. Chartered Surveyor and Land Agent; Agricultural Land Service, 1949–55; Land Agent (Scotland), The Nature Conservancy, 1955–67. Chm., Aberdeen and Northern Marts, 1986–91 (Dir, 1973–91); Director: Scottish Widows' Fund and Life Assurance Soc., 1978–94 (Dep. Chm., 1982–84, 1987–88; Chm., 1984–87); Scottish Northern Investment Trust, 1979–85; Clydesdale Bank, 1985–92 (Northern Area, 1975–85); Britoil, 1988–90; Scottish Adv. Bd, BP, 1990–96. Member: Countryside Commn for Scotland, 1967–71; Aberdeen Univ. Court, 1978–84; Royal Commn on Historical MSS, 1987–94; Chm., Red Deer Commn, 1969–75; President: British Assoc. for Shooting and Conservation (formerly Wildfowlers Assoc. of GB and Ireland), 1973–92; The Scottish Landowners' Fedn, 1974–79 (Convener, 1971–74); Royal Zool Soc. of Scotland, 1976–96; Scottish Agricl Orgn Soc., 1980–83; RSGS, 1983–87; Fedn of Agricl Co-operatives (UK) Ltd, 1983–87; Dep. Chm., Nature Conservancy Council, 1980–85, Chm., Adv. Cttee for Scotland, 1980–85. Hon. Air Cdre, 612 Co. of Aberdeen Sqn, RAuxAF, 1998–. FRSA. Hon. LLD Aberdeen, 1995. GCStJ 1994; Prior of Scotland, OStJ, 1983–95. *Recreations:* countryside activities, historical research. *Heir: s* Master of Arbuthnott, *b* 18 July 1950. *Address:* Arbuthnott House, by Laurencekirk, Kincardineshire, Scotland AB30 1PA. *T:* (01561) 361226. *Clubs:* Army and Navy; New (Edinburgh). *Died 14 July 2012.*

ARCHER OF SANDWELL, Baron *cr* 1992 (Life Peer), of Sandwell in the County of West Midlands; **Peter Kingsley Archer;** PC 1977; QC 1971; a Recorder of the Crown Court, 1982–98; *b* 20 Nov. 1926; *s* of Cyril Kingsley Archer and May (*née* Baker); *m* 1954, Margaret Irene (*née* Smith); one *s*. *Educ:* Wednesbury Boys' High Sch.; LSE; University Coll., London (Fellow 1978). Called to Bar, Gray's Inn, 1952; Bencher, 1974; commenced practice, 1953. MP (Lab) Rowley Regis and Tipton, 1966–74, Warley West, 1974–92. PPS to Attorney-Gen., 1967–70; Solicitor General, 1974–79; chief Opposition spokesman on legal affairs, 1979–82, on trade, 1982–83, on N Ireland, 1983–87. UK Deleg. to UN Gen. Assembly (Third Cttee), 1969. Chairman: Council on Tribunals, 1992–99; Enemy Property Claims Assessment Panel, 1999–; Inquiry into Contaminated Blood, 2007–09; Mem., Privy Council Review of Intercept Evidence, 2007–08 (Mem., Adv. Gp, 2008–11). Chairman: Amnesty International (British Section), 1971–74; Parly gp for World Govt, 1970–74; Soc. of Labour Lawyers, 1971–74, 1979–93 (Jt Pres., 1993–); Mem., Exec. Cttee, Fabian Soc., 1974–86 (Chm., 1980–81; Pres., 1993–). Ombudsman for Mirror Group Newspapers, 1989–90. President: Uniting for Peace (formerly World Disarmament Campaign), 1993–; One World Trust, 1993–. Pres., Methodist Homes for the Aged, 1992–. *Publications:* The Queen's Courts, 1956; ed Social Welfare and the Citizen, 1957; Communism and the Law, 1963; (with Lord Reay) Freedom at Stake, 1966; Human Rights, 1969; (jtly) Purpose in Socialism, 1973; The Role of the Law Officers, 1978; contributions to: Trends in Social Welfare, 1965; Atkin's, Court Forms, 1965; The International Protection of Human Rights, 1967; Renewal, 1983; Fabian Centenary Essays, 1984; (ed) More Law Reform Now, 1984. *Recreations:* music, writing, talking. *Address:* House of Lords, SW1A 0PW. *Died 14 June 2012.*

ARCHER, Albert, MBE 1980; Member, Royal Commission on Environmental Pollution, 1981–85; *b* 7 March 1915; *s* of Arthur Archer and Margaret Alice Norris; *m* 1st, 1939; two *s*; 2nd, 1975, Peggy, *widow* of John F. Marsh; two step *s*. *Educ:* Manchester Grammar Sch.; Manchester Coll. of Technology. Fellow, Instn of Environmental Health Officers, 1961. Chief Public Health Inspector, Bor. of Halesowen, 1943–73; City of Birmingham: Envmtl Protection Officer, 1973–75; Dep. City Envmtl Officer, 1975–76; City Envmtl Officer, 1976–80. Mem., govt working parties on air pollution. Pres., Inst. of Environmental Health Officers, 1979–83. *Publications:* articles on air pollution in technical jls. *Recreation:* watching cricket. *Address:* 10 Peppard Road, Maidenbower, Crawley, West Sussex RH10 7QS. *T:* (01293) 884068. *Died 19 Aug. 2011.*

ARCHIBALD, Liliana, OBE 1997; Chairman: Adam Brothers Contingency Ltd, 1991–92 (Director, 1957–73 and 1977–85); Wilton Park Academic Council, 1992–99; *b* 25 May 1928; *d* of late Noah and Sophie Barou; *m* 1951, George Christopher Archibald (marr. diss. 1965). *Educ:* Kingsley Sch.; Geneva University. Univ. Lectr, Otago Univ., 1952–55; Director: Const & Co. Ltd, 1955–73, 1977–83; Credit Consultants Ltd, 1957–73, 1977–85; Fenchurch Gp Internat., 1985–88; Holman Wade, 1989–92; CLM Insurance Fund, 1993–99. Head of Division (Credit Insurance and Export Credit), EEC, 1973–77; EEC Advr to Lloyd's and the British Insurance Brokers Assoc., 1978–85; Internat. Affairs Advr to Lloyd's, 1981–85; Advr to Internat. Gp of Protection & Indemnity Clubs, 1980–85. Frequent lecturer on insurance-related problems. Member: Liberalisation of Trade in Services Cttee, British Invisible Exports Council, 1981–95; British Export Finance Adv. Council, 1982–91; Action Resource Centre, 1986–91; Govt Inquiry into Shops Act - Sunday and Late-Night Trading, 1984–85; Review Cttee, Banking Law Services, 1987–88; Lord Chancellor's Adv. Cttee on Legal Educn and Conduct, 1991–94; Vice-Chm., ICC Insurance Commn, 1982–87; Chm., Insurance Cttee, British Nat. Cttee, ICC, 1983–87. Member of Lloyd's, 1973–94. *Publications:* (trans. and ed) Peter the Great, 1958; (trans. and ed) Rise of the Romanovs, 1970; contrib. Bankers Magazine. *Recreations:* driving fast cars, gardening. *Address:* 21 Langland Gardens, NW3 6QE. *Died 1 June 2014.*

ARDEN, Rt Rev. Donald Seymour, CBE 1981; Assistant Bishop, Willesden Episcopal Area, 1981–93; an Honorary Assistant Bishop, Diocese of London, 1994–2011; Honorary Assistant Priest, St Alban's, North Harrow, 1986–2011; *b* 12 April 1916; *s* of Stanley and Winifred Arden; *m* 1962, Jane Grace Riddle; two *s*. *Educ:* St Peter's Coll., Adelaide; University of Leeds (BA); College of the Resurrection, Mirfield. Deacon, 1939; Priest, 1940. Curate of: St Catherine's, Hatcham, 1939–40; Nettleden with Potten End (and Chaplain, Charing Cross Hosp., Ashridge Park), 1941–43; Asst Priest, Pretoria African Mission, 1944–51; Dir, Usuthu Mission, Swaziland, 1951–61; Canon, St Michael and All Angels Cathedral, Zululand, 1959–61; Bishop of Nyasaland, 1961–64 (name of diocese changed, when Nyasaland was granted independence, July 1964); Bishop of Malaŵi, 1964–71, of Southern Malaŵi, 1971–81; Archbishop of Central Africa, 1971–80; Priest-in-charge, St Margaret's, Uxbridge, 1981–86. *Publications:* (with Richard Herrick) Youth's Job in the Parish, 1939; Out of Africa Something New, 1976. *Address:* 28 Mill Lane, Romsey, Hants SO51 8EU. *T:* (01794) 524171. *E:* ardendj@yahoo.co.uk. *Died 18 July 2014.*

ARDEN, John; novelist and playwright; *b* 26 Oct. 1930; *s* of C. A. Arden and A. E. Layland; *m* 1957, Margaretta Ruth D'Arcy; four *s* (and one *s* decd). *Educ:* Sedbergh Sch.; King's Coll., Cambridge; Edinburgh Coll. of Art. *Plays produced include:* All Fall Down, 1955; The Life of Man, 1956; The Waters of Babylon, 1957; Live Like Pigs, 1958; Serjeant Musgrave's Dance, 1959; Soldier, Soldier, 1960; Wet Fish, 1962; The Workhouse Donkey, 1963; Ironhand, 1963; Armstrong's Last Goodnight, 1964; Left-Handed Liberty, 1965; The True History of Squire Jonathan and his Unfortunate Treasure, 1968; The Bagman, 1970; Pearl, 1978; To Put It Frankly, 1979; Don Quixote, 1980; Garland for a Hoar Head, 1982; The Old Man Sleeps Alone, 1982; Little Novels of Wilkie Collins, 1997; Woe Alas, the Fatal Cashbox, 1999; Wild Ride to Dublin, 2003; Poor Tom, Thy Horn is Dry, 2003; Scam, 2007; *with Margaretta D'Arcy:* The Business of Good Government, 1960; The Happy Haven, 1960; Ars Longa Vita Brevis, 1964; Friday's Hiding, 1966; The Royal Pardon, 1966; The Hero Rises Up, 1968; Island of the Mighty, 1972; The Ballygombeen Bequest, 1972; The Non-Stop Connolly Cycle, 1975; Vandaleur's Folly, 1978; The Little Gray Home in the West, 1978; The Manchester Enthusiasts, 1984; Whose is the Kingdom?, 1988; A Suburban Suicide, 1994. *Publications:* (with Margaretta D'Arcy) To Present the Pretence (essays), 1977; Silence Among the Weapons (novel), 1982; Books of Bale (novel), 1988; (with Margaretta D'Arcy) Awkward Corners (essays, etc.), 1988; Cogs Tyrannic (novellas), 1991; Jack Juggler and the Emperor's Whore (novel), 1995; The Stealing Steps (short stories), 2003; Gallows (short stories), 2009. *Recreations:* antiquarianism, mythology. *Address:* c/o Casarotto Ramsay Ltd, Waverley House, 7–12 Noel Street, W1F 8GQ. *Died 28 March 2012.*

ARMSTRONG, Rear Adm. John Herbert Arthur James, (Louis), CBE 2004; Chief Executive, Royal Institution of Chartered Surveyors, 1998–2010; Chairman, Spada Ltd, since 2011; *b* 4 Sept. 1946; *s* of John William Armstrong and Marie Helen (*née* Clark); *m* 1st, 1973, Marjorie Anne Corbett (marr. diss. 2006); one *s* one *d*; 2nd, 2011, Miriam Meyer Lowe. *Educ:* King's Sch., Canterbury; BRNC Dartmouth; Magdalen Coll., Oxford (MA Law). Served in HM Ships Fife, Intrepid and Zulu, 1970–75; called to the Bar, Middle Temple, 1976; Staff Legal Advr to Flag Officer, Plymouth, 1977–79; HM Yacht Britannia, 1979–81; Comdr 1981; HMS Raleigh, 1981–83; Naval Secretary's Staff, 1983–85; HMS Illustrious, 1985–87; Capt. 1987; seconded to Cabinet Office, 1987–89; Asst Dir, Sea Systems' Operational Requirements, MoD, 1989–91; RCDS 1992; Director: Naval Manpower Planning, 1993; Naval Personnel Plans and Progs, 1994; Cdre, 1994; Comdt, RNSC, Greenwich, 1994–95; Rear Adm., 1996; Sen. Naval Directing Staff, RCDS, 1996–98. Director: SNT Media Networks, 2010–; Hyperoptic Ltd, 2012–. Chm., Professions for Good, 2011–; Dir, Inst. of Leadership and Mgt, 2006–. Mem. Council, C&G, 2005–. Liveryman, Co. of Chartered Surveyors, 2007–. Hon. FCGI 2009; Hon. Mem. RICS 2010. *Recreations:* the arts, ski-ing, tennis, parties. *Address:* c/o Spada Ltd, Lion House, Red Lion Street, WC1R 4NA. *Club:* Reform. *Died 31 Dec. 2014.*

ARMSTRONG, Neil A.; Chairman, EDO Corporation, 2000–02, then Emeritus; formerly NASA Astronaut (Commander, Apollo 11 Rocket Flight to the Moon, 1969; first man to step on to the Moon, 20 July 1969); *b* Wapakoneta, Ohio, USA, 5 Aug. 1930; *s* of Stephen and Viola Armstrong, Wapakoneta; *m* 1st, 1956, Janet Shearon (marr. diss. 1994); two *s* (one *d* decd); 2nd, Carol Knight. *Educ:* High Sch., Wapakoneta, Ohio; Univ. of Southern California (MS); Purdue Univ. (BSc). Served in Korea (78 combat missions) being a naval aviator, 1949–52. He joined NASA's Lewis Research Center, 1955 (then NACA Lewis Flight Propulsion Lab.) and later transf. to NASA High Speed Flight Station at Edwards Air Force Base, Calif, as an aeronautical research pilot for NACA and NASA; in this capacity, he performed as an X-15 project pilot, flying that aircraft to over 200,000 feet and approximately 4,000 miles per hour; other flight test work included piloting the X-1 rocket airplane, the F-100, F-101, F-102, F-104, F5D, B-47, the paraglider, and others; as pilot of the B-29 "drop" aircraft, he participated in the launches of over 100 rocket airplane flights. Selected as an astronaut by NASA, Sept. 1962; served as backup Command Pilot for Gemini 5 flight; as Command Pilot for Gemini 8 mission, launched 16 March 1966; he performed the first successful docking of 2 vehicles in space; served as backup Command Pilot for Gemini 11 mission; assigned as backup Comdr for Apollo VIII Flight, 1969; Dep. Associate Administrator of Aeronautics, NASA HQ, Washington, 1970–71; University Prof. of Aerospace Engrg, Univ. of Cincinnati, 1971–79; Chairman: Cardwell International Ltd, 1980–82; AIL Systems Inc., 1989–2000. Mem., Nat. Acad. of Engrg. Fellow, Soc. of Experimental Test Pilots; FRAeS. Honours include NASA Exceptional Service Medal, and AIAA Astronautics Award for 1966; RGS Gold Medal, 1970. Presidential Medal for Freedom, 1969. *Died 25 Aug. 2012.*

ARMSTRONG, Sir Patrick (John), Kt 2002; CBE 1989; JP; Chairman, Police Authority of Northern Ireland, 1996–2001; *b* 16 Sept. 1927; *s* of Andrew and Hannah Armstrong; *m* 1949, Agnes Carson; two *s* two *d*. *Educ:* Ruskin Coll., Oxford (DipEcon and Pol Sci.); Queen's Univ., Belfast (BA, Dip. Social Studies); Univ. of Newcastle upon Tyne (Dip. Applied Social Studies). Factory worker, 1947–57; Dep. Co. Welfare Officer, 1966–71, Chief Welfare Officer, 1971–73, Co. Antrim; Dep. Chief Inspector of Social Services for NI, 1973–83, Chief Inspector of Social Services, 1983–89. Vice-Chm., Police Authy for NI, 1994–96. JP 1994. *Recreations:* walking, cycling, reading. *Address:* 13 North Parade, Belfast BT7 2GF. *T:* (028) 9064 3616. *Club:* Ulster Reform (Belfast). *Died 30 June 2014.*

ARMYTAGE, Captain David George, CBE 1981; Royal Navy, retired; Secretary General, British Diabetic Association, 1981–91; *b* 4 Sept. 1929; *e s* of late Rear-Adm. Reginald William Armytage, GC, CBE and Sylvia Beatrice Armytage; *heir* to Sir (John) Martin Armytage, 9th Bt; *m* 1954, Countess Cosima Antonia de Bosdari; two *s* one *d*. *Educ:* RNC, Dartmouth. Comd Motor Torpedo Boats, 1952–53; Direction Officer: 809 Sqn, 1956–58; HMS Chichester, 1958–59; Action Data Automation Project Team, 1959–64; Direction Officer, HMS Eagle, 1964–66; Directorate, Navigation and Tactical Control, 1966–68; comd HMS Minerva, 1968–70; Defence Policy Staff, 1970–72; Naval Asst to First Sea Lord, 1972–74; Internat. Mil. Staff, Brussels, 1975–76; comd, HMS Scylla, 1976 and HMS Jupiter, 1977–78; Capt., 7th Frigate Sqn, 1976–78; Dep. Dir, Naval Warfare, 1978–80; comd, NATO Standing Naval Force Atlantic, 1980–81. ADC to the Queen, 1981. Master Mariner, 1967. *Recreations:* sailing, gardening, shooting. *Address:* Sharcott Manor, Pewsey, Wilts SN9 5PA. *T:* (01672) 563485. *Clubs:* Oriental, Royal Naval Sailing Association; Royal Channel Islands Yacht. *Died 8 Feb. 2015.*

ARNOLD, Eve, Hon. OBE 2003; photographer and writer; *b* Philadelphia, 21 April 1912; *m* 1948, Arnold Arnold (marr. diss.); one *s*. Took a 6-week photography class with Alexei Brodovitch, at New Sch. for Social Research, NY, 1948, after receiving a 40 Rolleicord as her first camera; first photographs in Picture Post, followed by Ladies Home Jl, Life, Time, Look, Stern, Paris Match, Harpers, Queen, Sunday Times; joined Magnum Photos agency, 1951; work in USA, UK, Africa, China, Russia, Afghanistan, Arab countries; portrait photographs include Royalty, film stars and politicians. Exhibitions: Brooklyn Mus., NY, 1980; Nat. Portrait Gall., 1991; (retrospective) Barbican, 1996; Marilyn Monroe by Eve Arnold, Halcyon Gall., London, 2005; In China, Asia House, London, 2007. *Films:* Behind the Veil, 1973; special production photographer on 31 films. *Publications:* The Unretouched Woman, 1976; Flashback!: the 50s, 1978; In China, 1980; In America, 1984; Marilyn Monroe: an appreciation, 1987; Private View: inside Baryshnikov's American Ballet Theatre, 1988; All in a Day's Work, 1989; Eve Arnold in Britain, 1991; Eve Arnold: in retrospect, 1996; Eve Arnold: Film Journal, 2002; Handbook (with Footnotes), 2004; Marilyn Monroe, 2005; Eve Arnold's People, 2009. *Address:* Flat 3, 26 Mount Street, W1K 2RS. *Died 4 Jan. 2012.*

ARNOTT, Prof. Struther, CBE 1996; FRS 1985; Principal and Vice-Chancellor, University of St Andrews, 1986–2000, then Emeritus; *b* 25 Sept. 1934; *s* of Charles McCann and Christina Struthers Arnott; *m* 1970, Greta Edwards, BA, DLitt; two *s*. *Educ:* Hamilton Academy, Lanarkshire; Glasgow Univ. (BSc, PhD). FRSC 1970; FRSE 1988. King's College London: scientist, MRC Biophysics Research Unit, 1960–70; demonstrator in Physics. 1960–67; dir of postgraduate studies in Biophysics, 1967–70; FKC 1997; Purdue University: Prof. of Molecular Biology, 1970–; Head, Dept of Biol Scis, 1975–80; Vice-Pres. for Research and Dean, Graduate Sch., 1980–86; Oxford University: Sen. Vis. Fellow, Jesus Coll., 1980–81; Nuffield Res. Fellow, Green Coll., 1985–86. Haddow Prof., Inst. of Cancer Res., 2000–03; Vis. Prof. and Sen. Res. Fellow, Imperial Coll., London, 2002–; Vis. Prof., Sch. of Pharmacy, UCL (formerly Univ. of London), 2003–. Guggenheim Meml Foundn Fellow, 1985. Hon. ScD St Andrews, Laurinburg, USA, 1994; Hon. DSc Purdue, USA, 1998; Hon. LLD St Andrews, 1999. *Publications:* papers in learned jls on structures of fibrous biopolymers, especially nucleic acids and polysaccharides, and techniques for visualizing them. *Recreations:* bird watching, botanizing. *Address:* Number One Yorkshire, South Parade, Bawtry DN10 6JH. *E:* no1yorkshire@btinternet.com. *Clubs:* Athenæum; Royal and Ancient (St Andrews). *Died 20 April 2013.*

ARRINDELL, Sir Clement Athelston, GCMG 1984; GCVO 1985; Kt 1982; QC; Governor-General, St Christopher and Nevis, 1983–95 (Governor, St Kitts-

Nevis, 1981–83); *b* Basseterre, 19 April 1931. *Educ:* private school; Basseterre Boys' Elementary Sch.; St Kitts-Nevis Grammar Sch. (Island Scholar). Called to the Bar, Lincoln's Inn, 1958. Post-grad. studies; in practice as barrister and solicitor, 1959–66; Acting Magistrate, 1964–66; Magistrate, 1966–71; Chief Magistrate, 1972–78; Judge, WI Associated States Supreme Court, 1978–81. *Recreations:* piano-playing, classical music, gardening. *Address:* The Lark, Bird Rock, St Kitts, West Indies. *Died 27 March 2011.*

ARTHUR, His Honour John Rhys, DFC 1944; JP; a Circuit Judge, 1975–93; *b* 29 April 1923; *s* of late John Morgan Arthur and Eleanor Arthur; *m* 1951, Joan Tremearne Pickering (decd); two *s* one *d*. *Educ:* Mill Hill; Christ's Coll., Cambridge (MA). Commnd RAF, Bomber Command, 1943, demobilised 1946. Cambridge, 1946–48; called to Bar, Inner Temple, 1949. Asst Recorder, Blackburn QS, 1970; Dep. Chm., Lancs County QS, 1970–71; a Recorder, 1972–75. JP Lancs, 1970. *Address:* Orovales, 135 Caldy Road, Wirral CH48 1LP. *T:* (0151) 625 8624. *Clubs:* MCC, Old Millhillians; Athenæum (Liverpool); Cardiff Athletic. *Died 17 Jan. 2014.*

ARTRO MORRIS, John Evan; District Judge, Principal Registry of the Family Division (formerly a Registrar of the Supreme Court, Family Division), 1977–95; *b* 17 Feb. 1925; *s* of Tudor and Mabel Artro Morris; *m* 1961, Karin Ilsa Alida Russell (*d* 1999); two *s*. *Educ:* Liverpool Inst.; Liverpool Coll.; The Queen's Coll., Oxford (MA). Served RN, 1943–47; Acting Stores Chief Petty Officer. Called to the Bar, Middle Temple, 1952; practised at the Bar, 1952–77. *Recreations:* television, reading, contemplation. *Address:* 59 Chesnut Avenue, Ewell, Surrey KT19 0SY. *Died 15 April 2014.*

ASH, Raymond; Director, Business and Trade Statistics Ltd, 1986; *b* 2 Jan. 1928; *s* of late Horace Ash and Gladys Ash; *m* 1947, Mavis (*née* Wootton); two *s* one *d*. *Educ:* Wolverhampton Grammar Sch. Civil Service, 1949–86: professional statistician and senior manager working on health, labour, overseas trade, and business statistics. *Publications:* contrib. learned jls. *Recreations:* country walks, tourism, historical studies. *Address:* 20 Taliesin Close, Rogerstone, Newport, Gwent NP10 0DD. *T:* (01633) 663814. *Died 9 Oct. 2012.*

ASHCOMBE, 4th Baron *cr* 1892; **Henry Edward Cubitt;** late RAF; former Chairman, Cubitt Estates Ltd; *b* 31 March 1924; *er s* of 3rd Baron Ashcombe; *S* father, 1962; *m* 1955, Ghislaine (marr. diss. 1968), *o d* of Cornelius Willem Dresselhuys, Long Island, New York; *m* 1973, Hon. Virginia Carington, LVO, *yr d* of Baron Carrington, KG, GCMG, CH, MC, PC; *m* 1979, Mrs Elizabeth Dent-Brocklehurst. *Educ:* Eton. Served War of 1939–45, RAF. Consul-General in London for the Principality of Monaco, 1961–68. *Heir: cousin* Mark Edward Cubitt [*b* 29 Feb. 1964; *m* 1992, Melissa Mary, *o d* of Maj. Charles Hay; two *s*]. *Address:* Sudeley Castle, Winchcombe, Cheltenham, Glos GL54 5JD. *Club:* White's. *Died 4 Dec. 2013.*

ASHCROFT, Philip Giles; Solicitor, British Telecommunications, 1981–87; *b* 15 Nov. 1926; *s* of Edmund Samuel Ashcroft and Constance Ruth Ashcroft (*née* Giles); *m* 1st, 1968, Kathleen Margaret Senior (marr. diss. 1983); one *s*; 2nd, 1985, Valerie May Smith, *d* of late E. T. G. Smith. *Educ:* Royal Grammar Sch., Newcastle upon Tyne; Durham Univ. Admitted solicitor, 1951. Joined Treasury Solicitor's Dept, 1955; Asst Legal Adviser, Land Commn, 1967; Asst Treasury Solicitor, 1971; Under-Sec. (Legal), DTI, 1973; Legal Adviser, Dept of Energy, 1974–80; Dep. Solicitor to the Post Office, 1980–81. Legal Consultant, Registry of Friendly Socs and Building Socs Commn, 1988–96. *Recreations:* reading, listening to music. *Died 1 Nov. 2015.*

ASHLEY OF STOKE, Baron *cr* 1992 (Life Peer), of Widnes in the County of Cheshire; **Jack Ashley,** CH 1975; PC 1979; *b* 6 Dec. 1922; *s* of John Ashley and Isabella Bridge; *m* 1951, Pauline Kay Crispin (*d* 2003); three *d*. *Educ:* St Patrick's Elem. Sch., Widnes, Lancs; Ruskin Coll., Oxford; Gonville and Caius Coll., Cambridge (Hon. Fellow). Labourer and cranedriver, 1936–46; Shop Steward Convenor and Nat. Exec. Mem., Chemical Workers' Union, 1946; Scholarship, Ruskin Coll., 1946–48 and Caius Coll., 1948–51 (Chm. Cambridge Labour Club, 1950; Pres. Cambridge Union, 1951); BBC Radio Producer, 1951–57; Commonwealth Fund Fellow, 1955; BBC Senior Television Producer, 1957–66; Mem., General Advisory Council, BBC, 1967–69, 1970–74. Councillor, Borough of Widnes, 1945. MP (Lab) Stoke-on-Trent, South, 1966–92. Parliamentary Private Secretary: to Sec. of State for Econ. Affairs, 1967–68; to Sec. of State, DHSS, 1974–76. Mem., Lab. Party Nat. Exec. Cttee, 1976–78. Co-Chm., All-Party Disablement Gp. President: Deafness Res. UK (formerly Hearing and Speech, subseq. Defeating Deafness, Trust), 1985–; RNID, 1987–; Royal Coll. of Speech and Language Therapists, 1995–2001. Chancellor, Staffordshire Univ., 1993–2002. Holds 13 hon. degrees. *Publications:* Journey into Silence (autobiog.), 1973; Acts of Defiance (autobiog.), 1992. *Address:* House of Lords, SW1A 0PW. *Died 20 April 2012.*

ASHMORE, Dr Alick, CBE 1979; Director, Daresbury Laboratory, Science Research Council, 1970–81; *b* 7 Nov. 1920; *s* of Frank Owen Ashmore and Beatrice Maud Swindells; *m* 1947, Eileen Elsie Fuller; two *s* three *d*. *Educ:* King Edward VII Sch., Lytham; King's Coll., London. Experimental Officer, RRDE, Malvern, 1941–47; Lecturer in Physics, University of Liverpool, 1947–59; Queen Mary Coll., London: Reader in Experimental Physics, 1960–64; Prof. of Nuclear Physics, 1964–70, also Head of Physics Dept, 1968–70. *Publications:* research publications on nuclear and elementary-particle physics in Proc. Phys. Soc., Nuclear Physics, Physical Review. *Recreations:* walking, travel. *Address:* Farnham House, Hesket Newmarket, Wigton, Cumbria CA7 8JG. *T:* (01697) 478414. *Died 28 Feb. 2014.*

ASHTON, George Arthur, CEng; FIMechE; engineering and management consultant; *b* 27 Nov. 1921; *s* of Lewis and Mary Ashton; *m* 1st, 1948, Joan Rutter (decd); (one *s* decd); 2nd, 1978, Pauline Jennifer Margett. *Educ:* Llanidloes Grammar Sch.; Birmingham Central Tech. Coll. Student Engrg Apprentice, Austin Motor Co., 1939–42. HM Forces, 1943–47 (Major, REME). Works Dir, Tubes Ltd, 1958; Tech. Dir, 1962, Dep. Man. Dir, 1966, TI Steel Tube Div.; Dir, Tube Investments, 1969; Man. Dir, Machine Div., 1974, Technical Dir and Business Area Chm., 1978–84, TI Group plc; Chm., Seamless Tubes Ltd, 1983–86. Dir, A. Lee & Sons plc, 1981–91. Consultant, Welsh Develt Agency, 1984–87. Pres., BISPA, 1974–75; Vice-Pres., AMTRI, 1986– (Chm. Council, 1982–86). CBIM 1981. FRSA 1981. *Recreation:* theatre-going. *Address:* Barn Cottage, Longford, Ashbourne, Derbys DE6 3DT. *T:* (01335) 330561. *Club:* Royal Over-Seas League. *Died 23 Jan. 2013.*

ASHTON, Prof. Robert, PhD; Professor of English History, University of East Anglia, 1963–89, then Emeritus; *b* 21 July 1924; *s* of late Joseph and Edith F. Ashton; *m* 1946, Margaret Alice Sedgwick (*d* 2010); two *d*. *Educ:* Magdalen Coll. Sch., Oxford; University Coll., Southampton (1942–43, 1946–49); London Sch. of Economics (1949–52). BA 1st Cl. hons (London) 1949; PhD (London) 1953. Asst Lectr in Economic History, Univ. of Nottingham, 1952; Lectr, 1954; Senior Lectr, 1961; Vis. Associate Prof. in History, Univ. of California, Berkeley, 1962–63; Prof. of English History, 1963, and Dean of Sch. of English Studies, 1964–67, Univ. of East Anglia. Vis. Fellow, All Souls Coll., Oxford, 1973–74 and 1987; James Ford Special Lectr in History, Oxford, 1982; Leverhulme Emeritus Fellow, 1989–91. FRHistS 1960 (Vice-Pres., 1983–86). *Publications:* The Crown and the Money Market, 1603–1640, 1960; Charles I and the City, in Essays in the Economic and Social History of Tudor and Stuart England in honour of R. H. Tawney (ed F. J. Fisher), 1961; James I by his Contemporaries, 1969; The Civil War and the Class Struggle, in The English Civil War and After 1642–1658 (ed R. H. Parry), 1970; The English Civil War: Conservatism and Revolution 1603–49, 1978, 2nd edn 1989; The City and the Court 1603–1643, 1979; Reformation and Revolution 1558–1660, 1984; Counter-Revolution: the second Civil War and its origins, 1646–8, 1994; articles in learned periodicals. *Recreations:* music, looking at old buildings, exploring Italy and things Italian, wine. *Address:* The Manor House, Brundall, Norwich NR13 5JY. *T:* (01603) 713368. *Died 9 Feb. 2013.*

ASHWORTH, Prof. Graham William, CBE 1980; DL; Visiting Professor: of Environmental Policy, University of Salford, 2004–12; International Baptist Theological Seminary, Prague, 2003–12; *b* 14 July 1935; *s* of Frederick William Ashworth and Ivy Alice Ashworth; *m* 1960, Gwyneth Mai Morgan-Jones; three *d*. *Educ:* Devonport High Sch., Plymouth; Univ. of Liverpool (Master of Civic Design, BArch). RIBA, PPRTPI, FRSA, FIEnvSc, FCMI. LCC (Hook New Town Project), 1959–61; consultancy with Graeme Shankland, 1961–64; architect to Civic Trust, 1964–65; Dir, Civic Trust for North-West, 1965–73 (Chm., Exec. Cttee, 1973–87); Prof. of Urban Envmtl Studies, Univ. of Salford, 1973–87; Director: Univ. of Salford Environmental Inst., 1978–87; CAMPUS (Campaign to Promote Univ. of Salford), 1981–87; Dir Gen., Keep Britain Tidy, then Tidy Britain, Gp, 1987–2000. Chairman: Going for Green, 1994–2000; World of Glass, 2000–09; Envmtl Campaigns, 2000–03. Member: Skeffington Cttee on Public Participation in Planning, 1969; North-West Adv. Council of BBC, 1970–75 (Chm.); NW Economic Planning Council (and Sub-gp Chm.), 1968–79; Countryside Commn, 1974–77; Merseyside Urban Develt Corp., 1981–92; (non-exec.) North Western Electricity Bd, 1985–88; Chairman: Ravenhead Renaissance, 1988–2002; Rural Recovery Trust, 2002–04. Governor, Northern Baptist Coll., 1966–82; President: RTPI, 1973–74; Foundn for Envmtl Educn, 1988–2004 (Pres., 1996–2004); Vice-Pres., Chartered Inst. of Envmtl Health, 2000–. Chm., Instn of Environmental Sciences, 1980–82. Member: Council, St George's House, Windsor, 1982–88; Council, Baptist Union, 1983– (Pres., 2000–01). Trustee: Manchester Mus. of Science and Industry, 1988–90; Tatton Trust, 2002–. Chm., Samlesbury and Cuerdale Parish Council, 2007–. Editor, Internat. Jl of Environmental Educn, 1981–2001. DL Lancs, 1991. *Publications:* An Encyclopædia of Planning, 1973; Britain in Bloom, 1991; The Role of Local Government in Environmental Protection, 1992. *Recreations:* gardening, painting, church and social work. *Address:* Spring House, Preston New Road, Samlesbury, Preston PR5 0UP. *E:* ashworth260@btinternet.com. *Died 18 Sept. 2015.*

ASKEW, Barry Reginald William; journalist, broadcaster and public relations consultant; *b* 13 Dec. 1936; *s* of late Reginald Ewart Askew and Jane Elizabeth Askew; *m* 1st, 1958, June Roberts (marr. diss. 1978), *d* of late Vernon and Betty Roberts; one *s* one *d*; 2nd, 1980, Deborah Parker (marr. diss. 1989), *d* of Harold and Enid Parker. *Educ:* Lady Manners Grammar Sch., Bakewell, Derbys. Trainee reporter upwards, Derbyshire Times, 1952–57; Reporter and sub-ed., Sheffield Telegraph, 1957–59; reporter, feature writer and broadcaster, Raymonds News Agency, Derby, 1959–61; Editor, Matlock Mercury, 1961–63; Industrial Correspondent, Asst Ed., Dep. Ed., Sheffield Telegraph, later Morning Telegraph, Sheffield, 1964–68; Associate Ed., The Star, Sheffield, 1968; Editor, 1968–81, Dir, 1978–81, Lancashire Evening Post; Editor, News of the World, 1981. Presenter and anchor man: ITV, 1970–81; BBC Radio 4, 1971–72; BBC1, 1972; BBC2, 1972–76. Consultant in TV, radio, PR and commerce, 1982–95. Mem., Davies Cttee to reform hosp. complaints procedures in UK, 1971–73. Campaigning Journalist of 1971, IPC Nat. Press Awards; Journalist of 1977, British Press Awards; Crime Reporter of 1977, Witness Box Awards. *Recreations:* Rugby, bridge, reading military history. *Address:* 14 Sunningdale, Woodplumpton Road, Broughton, Preston, Lancs PR4 0AX. *T:* (01772) 863021. *Died 16 April 2012.*

ASKEW, Rev. Canon Reginald James Albert; Dean of King's College, London, 1988–93; Canon Emeritus, Salisbury Cathedral, since 1988; *b* 16 May 1928; *s* of late Paul Askew and Amy Wainwright; *m* 1953, Kate, *yr d* of late Rev. Henry Townsend Wigley; one *s* two *d*. *Educ:* Harrow; Corpus Christi Coll., Cambridge (MA); Lincoln Theological College. Curate of Highgate, 1957–61; Tutor and Chaplain of Wells Theol Coll., 1961–65, Vice-Principal 1966–69; Priest Vicar of Wells Cath., 1961–69; Vicar of Christ Church, Lancaster Gate, London, 1969–73; Principal, Salisbury and Wells Theol Coll., 1973–87; Canon of Salisbury Cathedral and Prebendary of Grantham Borealis, 1975–87. Proctor in Convocation for London Univ., Gen. Synod of C of E, 1990–93. Chaplain, Merchant Taylors' Co., 1996–97. Trustee, Christian Evidence Soc., 1988–2002. Mem., Corrymeela Community, 1990–. Pres., Bath and Wells Clerical Soc., 1998–. *Publications:* The Tree of Noah, 1971; Muskets and Altars: Jeremy Taylor and the last of the Anglicans, 1997. *Recreations:* music, gardening, making wood-cuts and lino-cuts. *Address:* Carters Cottage, North Wootton, Shepton Mallet, Somerset BA4 4AF. *T:* (01749) 890728. *Club:* Athenæum. *Died 9 April 2012.*

ASKONAS, Brigitte Alice, (Ita), PhD; FRS 1973; immunologist, Weatherall Institute of Molecular Medicine (Molecular Immunology), John Radcliffe Hospital, Oxford, since 1989 (part-time); Visiting Professor, Leucocyte Biology, National Heart and Lung Institute (formerly Department of Biology, subseq. of Biological Sciences, later Department of Molecular and Cellular Biology), Imperial College London, since 1995 (part-time); *b* 1 April 1923; *d* of late Charles F. Askonas and Rose Askonas. *Educ:* McGill Univ., Montreal (BSc, MSc); Cambridge Univ. (PhD; Hon. Fellow, New Hall and Girton Coll.). Research student, Sch. of Biochemistry, Univ. of Cambridge, 1949–52; Immunology Div., NIMR, 1953–89 (Head of Div., 1977–88); Dept of Bacteriology and Immunology, Harvard Med. Sch., Boston, 1961–62; Basel Inst. for Immunology, Basel, Switzerland, 1971–72. Vis. Prof., Dept of Medicine, St Mary's Hosp. Med. Sch., London, 1988–94. Mem. Council, Royal Soc., 1988–90 and 2002–03 (Vice Pres., 1989–90). Founder FMedSci 1998; FIC 2000. Hon. Member: Amer. Soc. of Immunology; Soc. française d'Immunologie; German Ges. für Immunologie; Foreign Associate, US NAS, 2007. Hon. DSc: McGill, 1987; Oxford, 2010. Robert Koch Gold Medal, Robert Koch Foundn, 2007. *Publications:* contrib. scientific papers to various biochemical and immunological jls and books. *Recreations:* art, travel. *Address:* Leucocyte Biology, National Heart and Lung Institute, Imperial College London, Sir Alexander Fleming Building, Imperial College Road, SW7 2AZ. *T:* (020) 7594 5405, *Fax:* (020) 7584 2056. *Died 9 Jan. 2013.*

ASPIN, Norman, CMG 1968; HM Diplomatic Service, retired; Adviser and Secretary, East Africa Association, 1981–84; *b* 9 Nov. 1922; *s* of Thomas and Eleanor Aspin; *m* 1948, Elizabeth Irving; three *s*. *Educ:* Darwen Grammar Sch.; Durham Univ. (MA). War Service, 1942–45, Lieut RNVR. Demonstrator in Geography, Durham Univ., 1947–48; Asst Principal, Commonwealth Relations Office, 1948; served in India, 1948–51; Principal, Commonwealth Relations Office, 1952; served in Federation of Rhodesia and Nyasaland, 1954–57; HM Treasury, 1958–60; British Deputy High Commissioner in Sierra Leone, 1961–63; Commonwealth Relations Office, 1963–65; British Embassy, Tel Aviv, 1966–69; IDC 1970; Head of Personnel Policy Dept, FCO, 1971–73; Under-Sec., FCO, 1973–76; Comr, British Indian Ocean Territory, 1976; British High Comr in Malta, 1976–79; Asst Under-Sec. of State, FCO, 1979–80. *Recreations:* sailing, tennis. *Address:* Mounsey Bank, Dacre, Cumbria CA11 0HL. *Died 25 July 2011.*

ASPINWALL, Jack Heywood; author; company director; *b* 5 Feb. 1933; *m* 1954, Brenda Jean Aspinwall; one *s* two *d*. *Educ:* Prescot Grammar School, Lancs; Marconi College, Chelmsford. Served RAF, 1949–56. Director: family retail business, 1956–66; food distribn co., 1966–71; investment co., 1971–96. Mem., Avon CC, 1973–80. Contested (L) Kingswood, Feb. and Oct. 1974; MP (C) Kingswood, 1979–83, Wansdyke, 1983–97. *Publications:* (comp.) Kindly Sit Down!: best after-dinner stories from both Houses of Parliament, 1983; Hit Me Again, 1992; Tell Me Another, 1994. *Died 19 May 2015.*

ASSCHER, Sir (Adolf) William, Kt 1992; MD, FRCP; Principal (formerly Dean) and Professor of Medicine, St George's Hospital Medical School, London University, 1988–96; Consultant Physician, St George's Hospital; *b* 20 March 1931; *s* of William Benjamin Asscher and Roosje van der Molen; *m* 1st, 1959, Corrie van Welt (*d* 1961); 2nd, 1962, Dr Jennifer Lloyd, (*d* 2006), *d* of Wynne Llewelyn Lloyd, CB; two *d*. *Educ:* Maerlant Lyceum, The Hague; London Hosp. Med. Coll. BSc 1954; MB 1957; MD 1963; MRCP 1959, FRCP 1971; FFPM 1992. Nat. service, Lieut RE, 1949–51. Jun. appts, London Hosp., 1957–59; Lectr in

Medicine, London Hosp. Med. Coll., 1959–64; Welsh National School of Medicine, later University of Wales College of Medicine: Sen. Lectr, 1964–70, and Hon. Cons. Physician, Royal Inf., Cardiff; Reader, 1970–76; Prof. of Medicine, 1976–80; Head of Dept of Renal Medicine, 1980–88. Chairman: Cttee on Review of Medicines, DHSS, 1985–87; Cttee on Safety of Medicines, Dept of Health (formerly DHSS), 1987–92 (Mem., 1984–87); Member: Medicines Commn, DHSS, 1981–84; SW Thames RHA, 1987–90; Jt Consultants Cttee, 1992–96; Med. Adv. Cttee, Royal Hosp. for Neuro-Rehabilitation, Putney, 1995–97; Welsh Arts Council, 1985–88. Chm., Morriston Hosp. NHS Trust, Swansea, 1996–99; non-executive Director: Wandsworth DHA, 1991–93; St George's Health Care Trust, 1993–96; Vanguard Media plc, 1996–2002; Cancer Research Ventures, 1999–2001. Chairman: Med. Benefit Risk Foundn UK, 1993–96; Welsh Med. Technology Forum, 1993–; BMA Bd of Sci. and Educn, 1998–2002; UK Co-ordinating Cttee on Cancer Res., 1998–2002; Working Party on Therapeutic Uses of Cannabinoids, RPharmS, 1998–2000. Royal College of Physicians: Regl Advr, 1976–79; Mem. Council, 1977–80; Pres., Faculty of Pharmaceutical Medicine, 1995–97. Examr, Final MB, Wales, London, Bristol and Edinburgh. Pres., Renal Assoc., 1986–89. Hon. Fellow: St George's Hosp. Med. Sch., 1996; QMW, 1998. DUniv Kingston, 1996. Gold Medal, BMA, 2002. *Publications:* (with W. Brumfitt) Urinary Tract Infection, 1973; The Challenge of Urinary Tract Infections, 1980; (with D. B. Moffat and E. Sanders) Nephrology Illustrated, 1982; (with D. B. Moffat) Nephro-Urology, 1983; (with W. Brumfitt) Microbial Diseases in Nephrology, 1986; (with S. R. Walker) Medicines and Risk-Benefit Decisions, 1986; (with J. D. Williams) Clinical Atlas of the Kidney, 1991; papers on nephrology and drug regulation in learned jls. *Recreation:* visual arts. *Address:* 10 The Paddock, Cowbridge, Vale of Glamorgan CF71 7EJ. *Club:* Cardiff and County (Cardiff). *Died 20 July 2014.*

ASSHETON, Hon. Nicholas, CVO 2002; FSA; Treasurer and Extra Equerry to the Queen Mother, 1998–2002; *b* 23 May 1934; *yr s* of 1st Baron Clitheroe, KCVO, PC, FSA and Sylvia Benita Frances, Lady Clitheroe, FRICS (*d* 1991), *d* of 6th Baron Hotham; *m* 1960, Jacqueline Jill, *d* of Marshal of the Royal Air Force Sir Arthur Harris, 1st Bt, GCB, OBE, AFC; one *s* two *d*. *Educ:* Eton; Christ Church, Oxford (MA). FSA 1984. 2nd Lieut, Life Guards, 1954; Lieut, Inns of Court Regt, 1954–57. Joined Montagu, Loebl, Stanley & Co. (Stockbrokers), 1957: Partner, 1960; Sen. Partner, 1978–86; Chm., 1986–87; Coutts & Co.: Dir, 1987–99; Dep. Chm., 1993–99; Chm., SG Hambros Bank & Trust Ltd, 2000–07. Mem., Stock Exchange, 1960–92 (Mem. Council, 1969–87). Dir, United Services Trustee, 1981–2002, Chm., 1997–2002. Treas., Corp. of Church House, 1988–2002. Chm., 2004–07, Vice Pres., 2007–, Heritage of London Trust. Mem. Council, Soc. of Antiquaries, 1998–2001. Chief Hon. Steward, Westminster Abbey, 2002–06. Liveryman, Vintners' Co., 1955. *Address:* 15 Hammersmith Terrace, W6 9TS. *Clubs:* White's, Pratt's, Beefsteak. *Died 27 Nov. 2012.*

ASTON, Dr Margaret Evelyn, (Hon. Mrs Buxton), CBE 2013; FSA, FRHistS; FBA 1994; historian; *b* 9 Oct. 1932; *d* of 1st Baron Bridges, KG, GCB, GCVO, MC, PC, FRS and Katharine Dianthe, *d* of 2nd Baron Farrer; *m* 1st, 1954, Trevor Henry Aston (marr. diss. 1969; he *d* 1985); 2nd, 1971, Paul William Jex Buxton (*d* 2009); one *d* (and one *d* decd). *Educ:* Downe House; Lady Margaret Hall, Oxford (BA, MA; DPhil 1962). FRHistS 1962; FSA 1987. Lectr, St Anne's Coll., Oxford, 1956–59; Theodor Heuss Schol., W Germany, 1960–61; Res. Fellow, Newnham Coll., Cambridge, 1961–66; Res. Fellow, Folger Shakespeare Liby, and teaching post, Catholic Univ. of America, Washington, 1966–69; Hon. Sen. Res. Fellow, QUB, 1984–85. Pres., Ecclesiastical History Soc., 2000–01. DUniv York, 2001. *Publications:* Thomas Arundel: a study of church life in the reign of Richard II, 1967; The Fifteenth Century: the prospect of Europe, 1968, repr. 1994; Lollards and Reformers: images and literacy in late medieval religion, 1984; England's Iconoclasts: laws against images, 1988; Faith and Fire: popular and unpopular religion 1350–1600, 1993; The King's Bedpost: reformation and iconography in a Tudor group portrait, 1994; (ed) The Panorama of the Renaissance, 1996; (ed jtly) Lollardy and Gentry in the Later Middle Ages, 1997; (ed jtly) Much Heaving and Shoving: late-medieval gentry and their concerns, 2005; Broken Idols of the English Reformation, 2014; contrib. learned jls. *Address:* Castle House, Chipping Ongar, Essex CM5 9JT. *T:* (01277) 362642. *Died 22 Nov. 2014.*

ASTON, Prof. Michael Antony, FSA; FRGS; Professor of Landscape Archaeology, University of Bristol, 1996–2004, then Emeritus; *b* 1 July 1946; *s* of Harold and Gladys Aston; one *s* by Carinne Allinson, and one step *d*; partner, Teresa Hall. *Educ:* Univ. of Birmingham (BA 1967). FSA 1976; MiFA (MIFA 1983); FRGS 2010. Field Officer, Oxford City and County Mus., 1970–74; County Archaeologist, Somerset CC, 1974–78; Tutor, Ext. Studies Dept, Univ. of Oxford, 1978–79; University of Bristol: Staff Tutor in Archaeol., 1979–89; Reader in Archaeol., 1989–96. Hon. Prof., Dept of Archaeol., Univ. of Durham, 2004–; Hon. Vis. Prof., Dept of Archaeol., Univ. of Exeter, 2004–. Jt Presenter, Time Team series, TV, 1994–2012. Hon. DLitt: UC Winchester, 2004; Durham, 2010; Hon. MA Worcester, 2007. *Publications:* (with Trevor Rowley) Landscape Archaeology, 1974; (with James Bond) The Landscape of Towns, 1976; Interpreting the Landscape, 1985; Mick's Archaeology, 2000; Monasteries in the Landscape, 2000; (with Victor Ambrus) Recreating the Past, 2001; (with Tony Robinson) Archaeology is Rubbish, 2002; Interpreting the Landscape from the Air, 2002; (with Christopher Gerrard) The Shapwick Project, Somerset: a rural landscape explored, 2007. *Recreations:* walking, camping in my camper van, music (classical concerts), pottery, painting, landscape gardening, visiting archaeological sites, churches, etc. *Address:* Department of Archaeology and Anthropology, University of Bristol, 43 Woodland Road, Bristol BS8 1UU. *Died 24 June 2013.*

ASTON, Prof. Peter George, DPhil; Professor and Head of Music, University of East Anglia, 1974–98, Professor Emeritus, since 2001; *b* 5 Oct. 1938; *s* of late George William Aston and Elizabeth Oliver Aston (*née* Smith); *m* 1960, Elaine Veronica Neale; one *s*. *Educ:* Tettenhall Coll.; Birmingham Sch. of Music (GBSM); Univ. of York (DPhil); FTCL, ARCM. Lectr in Music, 1964–72, Sen. Lectr, 1972–74, Univ. of York; Dean, Sch. of Fine Arts and Music, 1981–84, Professorial Fellow, 1998–2001, UEA. Director: Tudor Consort, 1958–65; Morley Consort of Voices, 2009–; Conductor: English Baroque Ensemble, 1968–70; Aldeburgh Festival Singers, 1975–88; Principal Guest Conductor: Sacramento Bach Fest., USA, 1993–2001; Incontri Corali Internat. Choral Fest., Italy, 1996; Schola Cantorum Gedanensis, Poland, 1999; Jt Artistic Dir, Norwich Fest. of Contemporary Church Music, 1981–; Chorus Master, Norfolk and Norwich Triennial Fest., 1982–88. Composer-in-residence, Combe Bank Sch., Kent, 2006–10. Chairman: Eastern Arts Assoc. Music Panel, 1976–81; Norfolk Assoc. for the Advancement of Music, 1990–93 (Pres., 1993–98); Acad. Bd, Guild of Church Musicians, 1996–2011; President: Trianon Music Gp, 1984–96; Bury St Edmunds Bach Soc., 2005–. Royal School of Church Music: Chm., Norfolk and Norwich Area Cttee, 1998–2006; Mem., Adv. Bd, 2000–, Press Editl Bd, 2003–. Patron, Lowestoft Choral Soc., 1986–. Gen. Editor, UEA Recording Series, 1979–98; Editor, Peter Aston Editl Liby, Pavane Publishing, USA, 2001–. Hon. Lay Canon and Mem. Council, Norwich Cathedral, 2002–. FRSA 1980; FRSCM 1999. Hon. Fellow, Curwen Inst., 1987; Hon. RCM 1991; Hon. FGCM 1995. *Compositions:* song cycles, chamber music, choral and orchestral works, church music, opera. *Publications:* George Jeffreys and the English Baroque, 1970; The Music of York Minster, 1972; Sound and Silence (jtly), 1970, German edn 1972, Italian edn 1979, Japanese edn 1982; (ed) The Collected Works of George Jeffreys, 3 vols, 1977; (jtly) Music Theory in Practice, vol. 1, 1992, vols 2 and 3, 1993; (jtly) Music and Musicians of Norwich Cathedral, 2013; contrib. to internat. music jls. *Recreations:* Association football, cricket, bridge, chess. *Address:* University of East Anglia, Music Centre, School of Music, Norwich NR4 7TJ. *T:* (01603) 592452. *Clubs:* Athenæum; Norfolk (Norwich). *Died 13 Sept. 2013.*

ATHOLL, 11th Duke of, *cr* 1703; **John Murray;** Lord Murray of Tullibardine 1604; Earl of Tullibardine 1606; Earl of Atholl 1629; Marquess of Atholl, Viscount of Balquhidder, Lord Murray, Balvenie and Gask, 1676; Marquess of Tullibardine, Earl of Strathtay and Strathardle, Viscount Glenalmond and Glenlyon, 1703 – all in the peerage of Scotland; professional land surveyor; *b* 19 Jan. 1929; *s* of Maj. George Murray (*d* 1940), and Joan (*d* 2000), *d* of William Eastwood; *S* cousin, 1996; *m* 1956, Margaret Yvonne, *o d* of Ronald Leonard Leach; two *s* one *d*. KStJ 2010. *Heir: s* Marquess of Tullibardine, *b* 6 April 1960. *Died 15 May 2012.*

ATKINSON, Sir Alec; *see* Atkinson, Sir J. A.

ATKINSON, David Anthony; *b* 24 March 1940; *s* of late Arthur Joseph Atkinson and of Joan Margaret Atkinson (*née* Zink); *m* 1968, Susan Nicola Pilsworth (marr. diss.); one *s* one *d*. *Educ:* St George's Coll., Weybridge; Coll. of Automobile and Aeronautical Engrg, Chelsea. Diplomas in Auto. Engrg and Motor Industry Management. Member: Southend County Borough Council, 1969–72; Essex CC, 1973–78. MP (C) Bournemouth East, Nov. 1977–2005. PPS, 1979–87, to Rt Hon. Paul Channon, MP (Minister of State, Civil Service Dept, 1979–81, Minister for the Arts, 1981–83, Minister of State, DTI, 1983–86, Sec. of State for Trade and Industry, 1986–87). Introduced Licensing (Occasional Permissions) Act 1983. Mem., Council of Europe and WEU, 1979–86, 1987–2005 (Special Rapporteur for Soviet Union, then Russian Fedn, 1989–2005; Leader, Conservative delegn, 1997–2005; Chm., EDG, 1998–2005). Nat. Chm., Young Conservative Orgn, 1970–71; Life Vice Pres., Christian Solidarity Internat. (UK), 1996 (Chm., 1979–83; Pres., 1983–96). *Recreations:* mountaineering, art and architecture, travel. *Address:* c/o Bournemouth East Conservative Association, Haviland Road West, Bournemouth BH1 4JW. *Died 22 Jan. 2012.*

ATKINSON, Air Marshal Sir David (William), KBE 1982; FFOM; FRCPE; FFPH; Director-General, Stroke (formerly Chest, Heart and Stroke) Association, 1985–93; Director-General, RAF Medical Services, 1981–84; *b* 29 Sept. 1924; *s* of late David William Atkinson and Margaret Atkinson; *m* 1948, Mary (*née* Sowerby) (separated); one *s*. *Educ:* Edinburgh Univ. (MB, ChB 1948). DPH and DIH, London; FFPH (FFCM 1976); MFOM 1978, FFOM 1983; FRCPE 1983. Joined RAF, 1949; med. officer appts, UK, Jordan and Egypt, 1949–63; Student, RAF Staff Coll., 1963–64; SMO, RAF Brüggen, Germany, 1964–67; Dep. PMO, HQ Air Support Comd, 1967–70; PMO, HQ Brit. Forces Gulf, Bahrain, 1970–71; OC RAF Hosp., Wegberg, Germany, 1971–73; Dir of Health and Research (RAF), 1974–78; QHP 1977–84; PMO, RAF Strike Command, 1978–81. Freeman, City of London, 1984; Liveryman, Soc. of Apothecaries. CStJ 1981. *Publications:* (jtly) Double Crew Continuous Flying Operations: a study of aircrew sleep patterns, 1970. *Recreations:* walking, gardening, reading, looking at pictures. *Address:* Rosedene, Woodside Lane, Lymington, Hants SO41 8FJ. *Club:* Royal Air Force. *Died 28 June 2013.*

ATKINSON, Frank, CBE 1995 (OBE 1980); FSA; FMA; Director, Beamish North of England Open Air Museum, 1970–87; *b* 13 April 1924; *s* of Ernest Atkinson and Elfrida (*née* Bedford); *m* 1953, Joan Peirson; three *s*. *Educ:* Holgate Grammar Sch., Barnsley; Sheffield Univ. (BSc). Director: Wakefield City Art Gall. and Mus., 1949; Halifax Museums, 1951; Bowes Mus. and Durham Co. Mus. Service, 1958. Member: Working Party on Preservation of Technol Material, 1970–71; Wright Cttee on Provincial Museums and Galls, 1971–73; Working Party of Standing Commn on Museums and Galls (Drew Report), 1975–78; Museums and Galleries Commn, 1987–94 (Chm., Registration Cttee, 1988–94). Chairman: Thomas Bewick Birthplace Trust, 1985–91; Northumbrian Tourism Co-ordination Gp, 1989–93; Thomas Bewick (Newcastle) Trust, 1996–2001; Juvenile Autism in the NE Wkg Gp, 1996–99; Friends of Beamish Mus. Ltd, 1996–. Pres., Museums Assoc., 1974–75. Hon. MA Newcastle upon Tyne, 1971; Hon. DCL Durham, 1987. *Publications:* Aspects of the 18th century Woollen and Worsted Trade, 1956; The Great Northern Coalfield, 1966, 3rd edn 1979; Industrial Archaeology of North East England, 1974; Life and Traditions in Northumberland and Durham, 1977, 3rd edn 2001; North East England: people at work 1860–1950, 1980; Victorian Britain: North East England, 1989; Northern Life, 1991; The Man Who Made Beamish: an autobiography, 1999; The Story of Ovingham on Tyne, 2001; contribs to Trans Newcomen Soc., Antiquaries Jl, Museums Jl, etc. *Recreations:* pot-holing (later only in retrospect), computer programming, village history. *Died 30 Dec. 2014.*

ATKINSON, Prof. James; Founder Director, Centre for Reformation Studies, Sheffield, 1983–2006; Professor of Biblical Studies, University of Sheffield, 1967–79, then Emeritus; *b* 27 April 1914; *s* of Nicholas Ridley Atkinson and Margaret (*née* Hindhaugh); *m* 1939, Laura Jean Nutley (*d* 1966); one *s* one *d*. *Educ:* Tynemouth High Sch.; Univ. of Durham. MA 1939, MLitt 1950 Durham; DrTheol, Münster, Germany, 1955. Curate, Newcastle upon Tyne, 1937; Precentor, Sheffield Cath., 1941; Vicar, Sheffield, 1944; Fellow, Univ. of Sheffield, 1951; Canon Theologian: Leicester, 1954–70; Sheffield, 1971–93; Reader in Theology, Univ. of Hull, 1956; Vis. Prof., Chicago, 1966; Public Orator, Univ. of Sheffield, 1972–79; Consultant Prof. with Evangelical Anglican Res. Centre, Latimer House, Oxford, 1981–84; Special Prof. in Reformation Theol., Univ. of Nottingham, 1993–2001. Examining Chaplain to: Bp of Leicester, 1968–79; Bp of Derby, 1978–95. Member: Anglican-Roman Catholic Preparatory Commission, 1967–72; Gen. Synod of Church of England, 1975–80; Marriage Commn, 1976–78. Pres., Soc. for Study of Theology, 1978–80; Mem., Acad. Internat. des Sciences Religieuses, 1980–2006. Hon. DD Hull, 1997. *Publications:* Library of Christian Classics, Vol. XVI, 1962; Rome and Reformation, 1965; Luther's Works, Vol. 44, 1966; Luther and the Birth of Protestantism, 1968; (trans. Spanish 1971, Italian 1983); The Reformation, Paternoster Church History, Vol. 4, 1968; The Trial of Luther, 1971; Martin Luther: Prophet to the Church Catholic, 1983; The Darkness of Faith, 1987; (contrib.) The Bible, the Reformation and the Church, ed W. P. Stephens, 1994; Faith Lost-Faith Regained, 2005; Understanding the Incarnation, 2008; contribs to learned jls, also essays and parts of books. *Recreations:* gardening, music. *Address:* Leach House, Hathersage, Derbyshire S32 1BA. *T:* (01433) 650570. *Died 30 July 2011.*

ATKINSON, Sir John Alexander, (Sir Alec), KCB 1978 (CB 1976); DFC 1943; Second Permanent Secretary, Department of Health and Social Security, 1977–79; *b* 9 June 1919; *yr s* of late Rev. R. F. Atkinson and Harriet Harrold Atkinson, BSc (*née* Lowdon); *m* 1945, Marguerite Louise Pearson, MA (*d* 2004); one *d*. *Educ:* Kingswood Sch.; Queen's Coll., Oxford. Served in RAF, 1939–45. Asst Prin., 1946, Prin., 1949, Min. of Nat. Insce; Cabinet Office, 1950–52; Prin. Private Sec. to Minister of Pensions and Nat. Insce, 1957–58; Asst Sec., 1958; Under-Sec., Min. of Social Security, later DHSS, 1966–73; Dep. Sec., DHSS, 1973–76. Member: Panel of Chairmen, CSSB, 1979–88; Occupational Pensions Bd, 1981–88. Chm., Working Gp on Pensions and Divorce, Pensions Management Inst. with Law Soc., 1992–93. Pres., Kingswood Assoc., 1983. *Address:* Bleak House, The Drive, Belmont, Sutton, Surrey SM2 7DH. *T:* (020) 8642 6479. *Club:* Oxford and Cambridge. *Died 7 Aug. 2015.*

ATKINSON, Norman; *b* 25 March 1923; *s* of George Atkinson, Manchester; *m* 1948, Irene Parry. *Educ:* elementary and technical schs. Served apprenticeship, Metropolitan Vickers Ltd, Trafford Park. Member of Manchester City Council, 1945–49. Chief Design Engineer, Manchester University, 1957–64. Contested (Lab) Wythenshawe, 1955, Altrincham and Sale, 1959. MP (Lab) Tottenham, 1964–87. Treasurer, Labour Party, 1976–81. Mem., Governing Body, Imperial Coll., London, 1975–89. Hon. MA Manchester, 1997. *Publications:* Sir Joseph Whitworth: the world's best mechanician, 1996; Old Merrypebbles (play), 2005; political pamphlets. *Recreations:* walking, cricket, football, oil painting. *Club:* Arts. *Died 8 July 2013.*

ATKINSON, Sir Robert, Kt 1983; DSC 1941; RD 1947; FREng; Chairman, British Shipbuilders, 1980–84; *b* 7 March 1916; *s* of Nicholas and Margaret Atkinson; *m* 1st, 1941, Joyce Forster (*d* 1973); one *d* (one *s* decd); 2nd, 1977, Margaret Hazel Walker. *Educ:* London Univ. (BSc(Eng) Hons). FIMechE, CEng, FREng (FEng 1983). Served War 1939–45 (DSC 1941 and two Bars, 1st, 1943, 2nd, 1944, mentioned in Despatches, 1943). Managing Director: Wm Doxford, 1957–61; Tube Investments (Eng), 1961–67; Unicorn Industries, 1967–72; Chm., Aurora Holdings, Sheffield, 1972–84; Dir, Stag Furniture Hldgs, 1973–92. Chm., Engrg and Shipbuilding Cttee, BSI, 1984–87. James Clayton Medal, NECInst, 1961. *Publications:* The Design and Operating Experience of an Ore Carrier Built Abroad, 1957; The Manufacture of Doxford Crankshafts, 1960; Some Crankshaft Failures: investigations into causes and remedies, 1960; British Shipbuilders Offshore Division, 1982; booklets: The Development and Decline of British Shipbuilding; Some Experiences of an Ancient Mariner; pamphlets and technical papers. *Recreations:* salmon fishing, walking, gardening. *Address:* Southdowns, 1 Little Hayes Lane, Itchen Abbas, Winchester SO21 1XA. *Club:* Royal Thames Yacht. *Died 25 Jan. 2015.*

ATKINSON, Prof. Thomas, PhD, DSc, DEng; FREng; Professor and Head of Department of Mining Engineering, Nottingham University, 1977–88, then Emeritus; Adjunct Professor, University of British Columbia, since 1997; *b* 23 Jan. 1924; *s* of Thomas Bell and Elizabeth Atkinson; *m* 1948, Dorothy; one *d*. *Educ:* Imperial Coll., London. DIC; PhD London, 1973; DSc Nottingham, 1988; DEng Witwatersrand, 1989. FREng (FEng 1987); FIMMM, FIMinE, FIET, FIMechE. Served RN, 1942–46. Charlaw and Sacriston Collieries Ltd, Durham, 1938–42; NCB, 1946–49; Andrew Yule, India, 1949–53; KWPR, Australia, 1953–56; Mining Engr, Powell Duffryn Technical Services Ltd, 1956–68; Sen. Lectr, Imperial Coll., 1968–73; Head of Coal Mining Div., Shell Internat. Petroleum Maatschappij BV, Holland, 1973–77. Dir, British Mining Consultants Ltd, 1969–88; Chm., Consolidated Coalfields Ltd, 1986–91. Chm., Nat. Awards Tribunal, British Coal (formerly NCB), 1984–92. FRSA. *Publications:* contribs to Mining Engrg, Mineral Econs, Mine Electrics, etc. *Recreation:* painting. *Club:* Chaps. *Died 6 Dec. 2014.*

ATTENBOROUGH, Baron *cr* 1993 (Life Peer), of Richmond upon Thames, in the London Borough of Richmond upon Thames; **Richard Samuel Attenborough,** Kt 1976; CBE 1967; actor, producer and director; Goodwill Ambassador for UNICEF, since 1987; Chancellor, University of Sussex, 1998–2009 (Pro-Chancellor, 1970–98); *b* 29 Aug. 1923; *s* of late Frederick Levi Attenborough and Mary Attenborough (*née* Clegg); *m* 1945, Sheila Beryl Grant Sim; one *s* one *d* (and one *d* decd). *Educ:* Wyggeston Grammar Sch., Leicester. Leverhulme Schol. to Royal Acad. of Dramatic Art, 1941 (Bancroft Medal). First stage appearance as Richard Miller in Ah Wilderness, Intimate Theatre, Palmers Green, 1941; Ralph Berger in Awake and Sing, Arts Theatre (West End début), 1942; Sebastian in Twelfth Night, Ba in Holy Isle, Murder in the Red Barn, Arts Theatre; The Little Foxes, Piccadilly Theatre, 1942; Brighton Rock, Garrick, 1943. Joined RAF 1943; seconded to RAF Film Unit for Journey Together, 1944; demobilised, 1946. Returned to stage in The Way Back (Home of the Brave), Westminster, 1949; To Dorothy, a Son, Savoy, 1950, Garrick, 1951; Sweet Madness, Vaudeville, 1952; The Mousetrap, Ambassadors, 1952–54; Double Image, Savoy, 1956–57, St James's, 1957; The Rape of the Belt, Piccadilly, 1957–58. *Film: appearances:* In Which We Serve (screen début), 1942; School for Secrets, The Man Within, Dancing With Crime, Brighton Rock, London Belongs to Me, The Guinea Pig, The Lost People, Boys in Brown, Morning Departure, Hell is Sold Out, The Magic Box, Gift Horse, Father's Doing Fine, Eight O'Clock Walk, The Ship That Died of Shame, Private's Progress, The Baby and the Battleship, Brothers in Law, The Scamp, Dunkirk, The Man Upstairs, Sea of Sand, Danger Within, I'm All Right Jack, Jet Storm, SOS Pacific; The Angry Silence (also co-prod), 1959; The League of Gentlemen, 1960; Only Two Can Play, All Night Long, 1961; The Dock Brief, The Great Escape, 1962; Séance On a Wet Afternoon (also prod; Best actor, San Sebastian Film Fest. and British Film Acad.), The Third Secret, 1963; Guns at Batasi (Best actor, British Film Acad.), 1964; The Flight of the Phœnix, 1965; The Sand Pebbles (Hollywood Golden Globe), 1966; Dr Dolittle (Hollywood Golden Globe), The Bliss of Mrs Blossom, 1967; Only When I Larf, 1968; The Last Grenade, A Severed Head, David Copperfield, Loot, 1969; 10 Rillington Place, 1970; And Then There Were None, Rosebud, Brannigan, Conduct Unbecoming, 1974; The Chess Players, 1977; The Human Factor, 1979; Jurassic Park, 1993; Miracle on 34th Street, 1994; The Lost World: Jurassic Park, 1997; Elizabeth, 1998; Puckoon, 2001; *produced:* Whistle Down the Wind, 1961; The L-Shaped Room, 1962; *directed:* Young Winston (Hollywood Golden Globe), 1972; A Bridge Too Far (Evening News Best Drama Award), 1976; Magic, 1978; A Chorus Line, 1985; In Love and War, 1997; Closing the Ring, 2007; *produced and directed:* Oh! What a Lovely War (16 Internat. Awards incl. Hollywood Golden Globe and SFTA UN Award), 1968; Gandhi (8 Oscars, 5 BAFTA Awards, 5 Hollywood Golden Globes, Dirs' Guild of America Award for Outstanding Directorial Achievement), 1980–81; Cry Freedom (Berlinale Kamera; BFI Award for Technical Achievement), 1987; Chaplin, 1992; Shadowlands, 1993 (Alexander Korda Award for Outstanding British Film of the Year, BAFTA); In Love and War, 1997; Grey Owl, 2000. Formed: Beaver Films with Bryan Forbes, 1959; Allied Film Makers, 1960. Chairman: Goldcrest Films & Television Ltd, 1982–87; Channel Four Television, 1987–92 (Dep. Chm., 1980–86); Capital Radio, 1972–92 (Life Pres., 1992–); Duke of York's Theatre, 1979–92. Dir, Chelsea Football Club, 1969–82 (Life Vice Pres., 1993–). Chairman: Actors' Children's Trust (formerly Actor's Charitable Trust), 1956–88 (Pres., 1988–); Combined Theatrical Charities Appeals Council, 1964–88 (Pres., 1988); BAFTA (formerly SFTA), 1969–70 (Vice-Pres., 1971–94; Chm. Trustees, 1970); RADA, 1972–2002 (Mem. Council, 1963; Pres., 2002–); UK Trustees, Waterford-Kamhlaba Sch., Swaziland, 1976– (Gov., 1987–); BFI, 1981–92; Cttee of Inquiry into the Arts and Disabled People, 1983–85; British Screen Adv. Council, 1987–96 (Hon. Pres., 1996); European Script Fund, 1988–96 (Hon. Pres., 1996); Member: British Actors' Equity Assoc. Council, 1949–73; Cinematograph Films Council, 1967–73; Arts Council of GB, 1970–73. Trustee: Tate Gall., 1976–82 and 1994–96 (Tate Foundn, 1986); Foundn for Sport and the Arts, 1991. Pres., Nat. Film Sch., 1997– (Gov., 1970–81); Dir, Young Vic, 1974–84. Pres., Muscular Dystrophy Gp of GB, 1971, then Hon. Life Pres. (Vice-Pres., 1962–71); Chm., Help a London Child; Gov., Motability, 1977. Patron: Kingsley Hall Community Centre, 1982–; RA Centre for Disability and the Arts, Leicester, 1990–. President: The Gandhi Foundn, 1983–; Brighton Festival, 1984–95; British Film Year, 1984–86; Arts for Health, 1989–; Gardner Centre for the Arts, Sussex Univ., 1990– (Patron, 1969–90). Fleming Meml Lect., RTS, 1989; Cameron Mackintosh Vis. Prof. of Contemporary Theatre, Oxford Univ., 1996. Fellow: BAFTA, 1983; BFI, 1992. Freeman, City of Leicester, 1990. FKC 1993; Hon. Fellow: Univ. of Wales, 1997; Nat. Film and Television Sch., 2001; Univ. of Leicester, 2006. Hon. DLitt: Leicester, 1970; Kent, 1981; Sussex, 1987; Hon. DLit Amer. Internat. Univ., London, 1994; Hon. DCL Newcastle, 1974; Hon. LLD Dickinson, Penn., 1983. Evening Standard Film Award, 40 years service to British Cinema, 1983; Award of Merit for Humanitarianism in Film Making, European Film Awards, 1988; Shakespeare Prize, FVS Foundn, Hamburg, 1992; Praemium Imperiale, Japan Art Assoc., 1998; Outstanding Achievement in the Arts Award, South Bank Awards, 2006. Martin Luther King, Jr Peace Prize, 1983. Padma Bhushan (India), 1983; Commandeur, Ordre des Arts et des Lettres (France), 1985; Chevalier, Légion d'Honneur (France), 1988. *Publications:* In Search of Gandhi, 1982; Richard Attenborough's Chorus Line, 1986; Cry Freedom, A Pictorial Record, 1987. *Recreations:* collecting paintings and sculpture, listening to music, watching football. *Clubs:* Garrick, Beefsteak. *Died 24 Aug. 2014.*

AUDET, Daniel; Senior Vice-President, Conseil du patronat du Québec, since 2007; *b* 6 April 1961; *s* of Marc Audet and Gisèle (*née* Bédard); *m* 1995, Nathalie Chalifour; one *d*. *Educ:* Univ. of Ottawa (philosophy); Univ. of Montreal (law); Montreal Bar school. Freelance journalist,

Montreal, 1986–90; attorney, Lapointe Rosenstein, Montreal, 1990–94; COS for Quebec Dep. Premier and Minister of State for Economy and Finance, Quebec, 1994–97; Vice Pres., Corporate Affairs, Videotron Inc., Montreal, 1997–2000. Columnist, Jl de Montréal, 2008–. Member Board: Canadian Customs and Revenue Agency, 1999–2000; Horizon Scis and Technologies Inc., 1999–2000; Agent Gen. of Quebec in London, 2000–03; Man. Partner, Nat. Public Relations Inc., Montreal, 2003–07. Chm. Bd, Fondation jeunesse du monde, 1998–2000; Mem. Exec., Montreal Internat. Ambassador Club, 1999–2000. *Recreations:* arts in general, economics and the digital revolution. *Address:* Conseil du patronat du Québec, Suite 510, 1010 Sherbrooke Street W, Montreal, QC H3A 2R7, Canada. *Died 18 June 2012.*

AUDUS, Prof. Leslie John, MA, PhD, ScD Cantab; FSB; Hildred Carlile Professor of Botany, Bedford College, University of London, 1948–79; *b* 9 Dec. 1911; *m* 1938, Rowena Mabel Ferguson (*d* 1987); two *d. Educ:* Downing Coll., Cambridge Univ. Downing Coll. Exhibitioner, 1929–31; Frank Smart Research Student (Cambridge Univ.), 1934–35; Lecturer in Botany, University Coll., Cardiff, 1935–40. Served War of 1939–45: RAFVR (Technical, Radar, Officer), 1940–46; PoW South Pacific, 1942–45. Scientific Officer, Agricultural Research Council, Unit of Soil Metabolism, Cardiff, 1946–47; Monsanto Lecturer in Plant Physiology, University Coll., Cardiff, 1948. Recorder, 1961–65, Pres., 1967–68, Section K, British Assoc. for the Advancement of Science. Vis. Prof. of Botany: Univ. of California, Berkeley, 1958; Univ. of Minnesota, Minneapolis, 1965. Vice-Pres. Linnean Soc. of London, 1959–60 (Hon. FLS 1995); Life Mem. New York Academy of Sciences, 1961. Editor, Journal Exp. Botany, 1965–74. *Publications:* Plant Growth Substances, 1953, 3rd edn 1972; (ed) The Physiology and Biochemistry of Herbicides, 1964; (ed) Herbicides: physiology, biochemistry and ecology, 1976; Spice Island Slaves, 1996; original research on plant respiration, hormones, responses to gravity, soil micro-biology in relation to pesticides, etc. in Annals of Botany, New Phytologist, Nature, Journal of Experimental Botany, Weed Research, etc. *Recreations:* furniture construction and restoration, electronics, amateur radio. *Address:* 11 Crossborough Hill, Basingstoke, Hants RG21 4AG. *Died 5 May 2011.*

AVERY, (Francis) John; Chairman, Averys of Bristol, since 2002 (Managing Director, 1975–2002); *b* 27 Dec. 1941; *s* of Ronald Avery and Linda Avery (*née* Jackson); *m* 1967, Sarah Midgley; one *s* three *d. Educ:* Clifton Coll.; Lincoln Coll., Oxford (MA Agricl Sci. 1965). MW 1975. Mem., Wine Selection Cttee for Govt Hospitality, 1997–; Wine Advr to Grocers' Co., 1997–. Pres., Internat. Wine and Food Soc., 2008– (Chm., 1996–2000); Chm., Inst. of Masters of Wine, 2000–01. Liveryman, Vintners' Co. (Master, 2004–05); Master: Soc. of Merchant Venturers, Bristol, 1995–96; Antient Soc. of St Stephen's Ringers, Bristol, 1994–95; President: Anchor Soc. of Bristol, 1990; Colston Soc. of Bristol, 2010; Mem., Cook Soc., 2011–. Judge, Australian and NZ Wine Shows, 1978–; Chief Judge, Winpac Wine Comp., Hong Kong, 1989–2003. Mem., Commanderie de Bordeaux. *Recreations:* ski-ing, cricket, Rugby (watching only!). *Address:* Apartment 10, The Grove, West Hay Road, Wrington, Bristol BS40 5NS. *Clubs:* Garrick, Savile, Saintsbury, MCC; Ski Club of GB; Marden's, Kandahar Ski. *Died 23 March 2012.*

B

BACALL, Betty Joan, (Lauren Bacall); actress; *b* NYC, 16 Sept. 1924; *d* of William Perske and Natalie Perske (*née* Weinstein, later Bacal); adopted stage name, Lauren Bacall; *m* 1st, 1945, Humphrey Bogart (*d* 1957); one *s* one *d*; 2nd, 1961, Jason Robards (marr. diss. 1969; he *d* 2000); one *s*. *Educ:* Julia Richman High Sch., NY; Amer. Acad. of Dramatic Arts, NY. *Plays:* on Broadway: Franklin Street, 1942; Goodbye Charlie, 1959; Cactus Flower, 1965; Applause, 1970 (Tony Award for Best Actress in a Musical, 1970), London, 1972; Wonderful Town, 1977; Woman of the Year, 1981 (Tony Award for Best Actress in a Musical, 1981); Sweet Bird of Youth, 1983, London, 1985; Waiting in the Wings, 1999; Visit, Chichester Fest., 1995; *films* include: To Have and Have Not, 1944; Confidential Agent, 1945; The Big Sleep, 1946; Dark Passage, 1947; Key Largo, 1948; Young Man with a Horn, Bright Leaf, 1950; How to Marry a Millionaire, 1953; Woman's World, 1954; The Cobweb, Blood Alley, 1955; Written on the Wind, 1956; Designing Woman, 1957; The Gift of Love, 1958; North West Frontier, 1959; Shock Treatment, Sex and the Single Girl, 1964; Harper, 1966; Murder on the Orient Express, 1974; The Shootist, 1976; Health, 1980; The Fan, 1981; Appointment with Death, Mr North, 1988; Tree of Hands, 1989; Misery, 1990; A Star for Two, All I Want for Christmas, 1991; A Foreign Field, 1993; Prêt-à-Porter, 1994; The Mirror Has Two Faces (Screen Actors Guild Award, Golden Globe Award, 1997), My Fellow Americans, 1996; Day and Night, 1997; Diamonds, The Venice Project, Presence of Mind, 1999; The Limit, Dogville, 2003; Birth, 2004; Manderlay, 2005; These Foolish Things, 2006; The Walker, 2007; Wide Blue Yonder, 2010; numerous television appearances. Cecil B. DeMille Award, Golden Globe Awards, 1993; Hon. Academy Award, 2009. Comdr, Ordre des Arts et Lettres (France), 1995. *Publications:* Lauren Bacall By Myself, 1978; Lauren Bacall Now, 1994; By Myself and Then Some, 2005. *Address:* c/o HarperCollins Publishers, 10 East 53rd Street, New York, NY 10022, USA. *Died 12 Aug. 2014.*

BACON, Prof. George Edward, MA, ScD Cantab, PhD London; Professor of Physics, University of Sheffield, 1963–81, then Emeritus; *b* 5 Dec. 1917; *s* of late George H. Bacon and Lilian A. Bacon, Derby; *m* 1945, Enid Trigg (*d* 2003); one *s* one *d*. *Educ:* Derby Sch.; Emmanuel Coll., Cambridge (Open and Sen. Schol.). CPhys. Air Ministry, Telecommunications Research Estabt, 1939–46. Dep. Chief Scientific Officer, AERE, Harwell, 1946–63; Dean, Faculty of Pure Science, Sheffield Univ., 1969–71. Leverhulme Emeritus Fellow, 1988. FInstP (Guthrie Medal, 1999). Hon. DSc Sheffield, 1998. *Publications:* Neutron Diffraction, 1955; Applications of Neutron Diffraction in Chemistry, 1963; X-ray and Neutron Diffraction, 1966; Neutron Physics, 1969; Neutron Scattering in Chemistry, 1977; The Architecture of Solids, 1981; Fifty Years of Neutron Diffraction, 1987; many scientific pubns on X-ray and neutron crystallographic studies in Proc. Royal Society, Acta Cryst., etc. *Recreations:* gardening, photography, genealogy. *Address:* Windrush Way, Guiting Power, Cheltenham GL54 5US. *T:* (01451) 850631. *Died 18 March 2011.*

BACON, Sir Sidney (Charles), Kt 1977; CB 1971; BSc(Eng); CEng, FREng, FIMechE, FIET; Managing Director, Royal Ordnance Factories, 1972–79; Deputy Chairman, Royal Ordnance Factories Board, 1972–79; *b* 11 Feb. 1919; *s* of Charles and Alice Bacon. *Educ:* Woolwich Polytechnic; London Univ. Military Service, 1943–48, Capt. REME. Royal Arsenal, Woolwich, 1933–58; Regional Supt of Inspection, N Midland Region, 1958–60; Asst Dir, ROF, Nottingham, 1960–61; Director, ROF: Leeds, 1961–62; Woolwich, 1962–64; Birtley, 1965; idc, 1964; Dir of Ordnance Factories, Weapons and Fighting Vehicles, 1965–66; Dep. Controller, ROFs, 1966–69; Controller, ROFs, 1969–72. Dir, Short Brothers, 1980–89. Pres., IProdE, 1979; Mem. Council, CGLI, 1979–91. Hon. FCGI 1991. *Recreations:* golf, listening to music. *Address:* 228 Erith Road, Bexleyheath, Kent DA7 6HP. *Club:* Shooters Hill Golf. *Died 14 Feb. 2012.*

BADIAN, Ernst, FBA 1965; Professor of History, 1971–82, John Moors Cabot Professor of History, 1982–98, Harvard University, then Emeritus; *b* 8 Aug. 1925; *s* of Joseph and Sally Badian (*née* Horinger); *m* 1950, Nathlie Anne (*née* Wimsett); one *s* one *d*. *Educ:* Christchurch Boys' High Sch.; Canterbury Univ. Coll., Christchurch, NZ; University Coll., Oxford (Hon. Fellow 1987). MA (1st cl. hons), NZ, 1946; LitD, Victoria, NZ, 1962. University of Oxford: Chancellor's Prize for Latin Prose, 1950; Craven Fellow, 1950; Conington Prize, 1959; BA (1st cl. hons Lit. Hum.) 1950; MA 1954; DPhil 1956. Asst Lectr in Classics, Victoria University Coll., Wellington, 1947–48; Rome Scholar in Classics, British Sch. at Rome, 1950–52; Asst Lectr in Classics and Ancient History, Univ. of Sheffield, 1952–54; Lectr in Classics, Univ. of Durham, 1954–65; Prof. of Ancient History, Univ. of Leeds, 1965–69; Prof. of Classics and History, State Univ. of NY at Buffalo, 1969–71. Editor, Amer. Jl of Ancient History, 1976–2001. John Simon Guggenheim Fellow, 1985; Fellow, Nat. Humanities Center, 1988. Visiting Professor: Univs of Oregon, Washington and California (Los Angeles), 1961; Univ. of S Africa, 1965, 1973; Harvard, 1967; State Univ. of NY (Buffalo), 1967–68; Heidelberg, 1973; Univ. of California (Sather Prof.), 1976; Univ. of Colorado, 1978; Univ. of Tel-Aviv, 1981; Martin Classical Lectr, Oberlin Coll., 1978; lecturing visits to Australia, Canada, France, Germany, Holland, Israel, Italy, NZ, Switzerland, and S Africa. Fellow: Amer. Acad. of Arts and Sciences, 1974; Amer. Numismatic Soc., 1987; Corresponding Member: Austrian Acad. of Scis, 1975; German Archaeol Inst., 1981; Foreign Mem., Finnish Acad. of Sci. and Letters, 1985. Hon. Mem., Soc. for Promotion of Roman Studies, 1983. Hon. LitD: Macquarie, 1993; Canterbury, NZ, 1999. Austrian Cross of Honour for Sci. and Art, 1999. *Publications:* Foreign Clientelae (264–70 BC), 1958; Studies in Greek and Roman History, 1964; (ed) Ancient Society and Institutions, 1966; (ed) Polybius (The Great Histories Series), 1966; Roman Imperialism in the Late Republic, 1967, 2nd edn 1968; Publicans and Sinners, 1972 (trans. German (expanded) 1997); (ed) Sir Ronald Syme, Roman Papers, Vols 1–2, 1979; From Plataea to Potidaea, 1993; contribs to collections, dictionaries and encyclopaedias and to classical and historical journals. *Recreation:* parrots. *Address:* Department of History, Harvard University, Cambridge, MA 02138, USA. *Died 1 Feb. 2011.*

BAGIER, Gordon Alexander Thomas; DL; *b* 7 July 1924; *m* 1949, Violet Sinclair; two *s* two *d*. *Educ:* Pendower Secondary Technical Sch., Newcastle upon Tyne. Served RM, 1941–45. Signals Inspector, British Railways; Pres., Yorks District Council, NUR, 1962–64. Mem. of Keighley Borough Council, 1956–60; Mem. of Sowerby Bridge Urban Council, 1962–65. MP (Lab) Sunderland South, 1964–87. PPS to Home Secretary, 1968–69. Chm., Select Cttee on Transport, 1985–87. DL Tyne and Wear, 1988. *Recreation:* golf. *Address:* Nesta, 89 Whaggs Lane, Whickham, Newcastle upon Tyne NE16 4PQ. *Clubs:* Victory Services; Holmeside Hall Working Men's; Westerhope Golf (Newcastle upon Tyne), Dunston and Whickham Glebe Sports. *Died 8 April 2012.*

BAILEY, Sir Richard (John), Kt 1984; CBE 1977; Chairman, British Ceramic Research Limited, 1982–83 and 1987–90; Director, Central Independent Television plc, 1986–94; *b* 8 July 1923; *s* of Philip Bailey and Doris Margaret (*née* Freebody); *m* 1945, Marcia Rachel Cureton Webb; one *s* three *d*. *Educ:* Shrewsbury. FICeram 1955. Served RNVR 1942–46. Doulton Fine China Ltd: Technical Dir, 1955–63; Man. Dir, 1963–72; Dir, Doulton & Co. Ltd, 1967–82; Chairman: Royal Crown Derby Porcelain Co. Ltd, 1983–87; Royal Doulton Ltd, 1983–87. Jt Chm., Ceramics Industry Nat. Jt Council, 1969–84; Mem., Ceramic Industry Training Bd, 1967–70; Dir, W

Midlands Industrial Develt Assoc., 1983–87; President: BCMF, 1973–74; British Ceramic Soc., 1980–81; Chm., North Staffs Business Initiative, 1981–91. Pres., North Staffs Med. Inst., 1987–99. Hon. Freeman, City of Stoke-on-Trent, 1987. FRSA 1977. Hon. Fellow, Staffordshire Univ. (formerly Poly.), 1988. MUniv Keele, 1983. *Recreations:* golf, walking, gardening. *Died 18 Jan. 2011.*

BAILLIE, William James Laidlaw, CBE 1998; PPRSA (RSA 1979; ARSA 1968); PPRSW (PRSW 1974; RSW 1963); painter; President, Royal Scottish Academy, 1990–98 (Treasurer, 1980–90); *b* 19 April 1923; *s* of James and Helen Baillie; *m* 1961, Helen Gillon; one *s* two *d*. *Educ:* Dunfermline High Sch.; Edinburgh College of Art (Andrew Grant Schol., 1941–50; Dip. Drawing and Painting 1950). Studies interrupted by war service with Royal Corps of Signals, mainly in Far East, 1942–47. Taught in Edinburgh schools, 1951–60; Mem., Teaching Staff, Edin. College of Art, 1960–88, Sen. Lectr, 1968–88; Visiting Tutor, National Gallery of Canada Summer Sch., near Ottawa, 1955. Exhibitions at Albemarle Gall., London, but mostly in Scotland, mainly at Scottish Gall., Edinburgh; first retrospective exhibn in Kirkcaldy Art Gallery, 1977; numerous private commns. HRA; RGI. Hon. DLitt Heriot-Watt, 1997. *Recreations:* music, travel. *Address:* 6A Esslemont Road, Edinburgh EH16 5PX. *T:* (0131) 667 1538. *Died 21 May 2011.*

BAIN, Neville Clifford, FCA, FCIS; Chairman: Hogg Robinson plc, 1997–2007; Institute of Directors, 2006–12; *b* 14 July 1940; *s* of Charles Alexander Bain and Gertrude Mae Bain; *m* 1987, Anne Patricia (*née* Kemp); one step *d*, and one *s* one *d* by previous marriage. *Educ:* King's High Sch., Dunedin, NZ; Otago Univ., Dunedin (BCom Acctcy 1964; BCom Econ 1966; MCom Hons 1968). CMA; ACA 1959, FCA 1989; FCIS 1962. Trainee Inspector, Inland Revenue, NZ, 1957–59; Manager, Anderson & Co., Chartered Accountants, NZ, 1960–62; Cadbury Schweppes Hudson: Cost Accountant, subseq. Financial Controller, and Co. Sec., NZ, 1963–68; Finance Dir, NZ, 1968–75; Cadbury Schweppes: Group Chief Exec., S Africa, 1975–80; Group Strategic Planning Dir, 1980–83 (apptd to Main Bd, 1981); Managing Director: Cadbury Ltd, 1983–86; Cadbury World Wide, 1986–89; Dep. Group Chief Exec. and Finance Dir, Cadbury Schweppes Plc, 1989–90; Gp Chief Exec., Coats Viyella PLC, 1990–97; Chm., Post Office, later Consignia, 1997–2001. Chairman: SHL Gp, 1998–2003 (non-exec. Dir, 1997–2003); Gartmore Split Capital Opportunities Trust, 1999–2001; Hogg Robinson Pension Fund, 2000–; Scottish Newcastle Pension Trustees, 2007–; Director: London Internat. Gp, 1988–93; Gartmore Scotland Investment Trust, 1992–2001; Safeway plc (formerly Argyll Group), 1993–2000; Scottish & Newcastle, 1997–; non-executive Director and Chair, Audit Committee: Biocon Ltd (India), 2000–; Provexis Ltd, 2003–. FInstD 1995 (Councillor, 1997–2012; Chm., Audit Cttee, 1999–2012). FRSocMed 1995. Hon. LLD Otago, NZ, 1993. *Publications:* Successful Management, 1995; (with D. Band) Winning Ways through Corporate Governance, 1996; (with Bill Mabey) The People Advantage, 1999; The Effective Director, 2008; (with Roger Barker) The Successful Board, 2010. *Recreations:* sport, walking, music. *Died 22 May 2012.*

BAINS, Lawrence Arthur, CBE 1983; DL; formerly Director: Bains Brothers Ltd; Crowland Leasings Ltd; Bains Finance Management Ltd; *b* 11 May 1920; *s* of late Arthur Bains and Mabel (*née* Payn); *m* 1954, Margaret, *d* of late Sir William and Lady Grimshaw; two *s* one *d*. *Educ:* Stationers' Company's School. Served War, 1939–46: Middlesex Yeomanry, 1939; N Africa, 1940; POW, 1942, escaped Italy, 1943. Hornsey Borough Council: Mem., 1949–65; Dep. Leader, 1958–64; Mayor, 1964–65; Council, London Borough of Haringey: Mem., 1964–74; Finance Chm., 1968–71; Greater London Council: Chm., 1977–78; Mem. for Hornsey/Haringey, 1967–81; Chm., South Area Planning Bd, 1970–73; Dep. Leader, Housing Policy Cttee, 1979–81; Chm., GLC/Tower Hamlets Jt Housing Management Cttee, 1979–81; Mem., Lee Valley Regional Park Authority, 1968–81 (Chm., 1980–81); Chm., Haringey DHA, 1982–93. Chm., N London Coll. of Health Studies, 1991–95. Trustee, Help the Homeless, 1979–2012. Liveryman, Basketmakers' Co., 1978– (Mem., Ct of Assts, 1995–). DL Greater London, 1978 (Rep. DL for Borough of Barnet, 1983–95). *Recreation:* being a grandfather. *Address:* Flat 14, Southgate Beaumont, 15 Cannon Hill, Old Southgate, N14 7DJ. *T:* (020) 8886 4679. *Died 5 Dec. 2015.*

BAIRD, Joyce Elizabeth Leslie, OBE 1991; Joint General Secretary, Assistant Masters and Mistresses Association, 1978–90; *b* 8 Dec. 1929; *d* of Dr J. C. H. Baird and Mrs J. E. Baird. *Educ:* The Abbey School, Reading; Newnham College, Cambridge (MA); secretarial training. FEIS 1987. Sec. to Ernő Goldfinger, architect, 1952; Secretary to Sir Austin Robinson and editorial assistant, Royal Economic Soc., 1952–60; Senior Geography Mistress, Hertfordshire and Essex High School, Bishop's Stortford, 1961–77 (Dep. Head, 1973–75). President: Assoc. of Assistant Mistresses, 1976–77; Internat. Fedn of Secondary Teachers, 1981–85; Vice Pres., NFER, 1991–2010. Mem., Cambridge City Council, 1992–96. Bd Mem., Granta Housing Soc., 1992–2006. Trustee, Cambridge Preservation Soc., 1998–2008. Gov., Alleyn's Sch., Dulwich, 1993–2003. *Recreations:* opera, thinking about gardening, travel. *Address:* 14 Gretton Court, High Street, Girton, Cambridge CB3 0QN. *T:* (01223) 277666. *Died 3 Oct. 2015.*

BAKER, Howard Henry, Jr; Senior Counsel, Baker, Donelson, Bearman, Caldwell & Berkowitz, PC, since 2005; Senior Advisor, Citigroup, since 2005; *b* 15 Nov. 1925; *s* of Howard H. Baker and Dora Ladd; *m* 1st, 1951, Joy Dirksen (*d* 1993); one *s* one *d*; 2nd, 1996, Hon. Nancy Landon Kassebaum. *Educ:* McCallie Sch.; Tulane Univ.; Univ. of Tennessee (LLB 1949). Served USN, 1943–46. Dir, Pennzoil; Chm. of Bd, Newstar Inc. US Senate: Senator from Tennessee 1967–85; Minority Leader, 1977–81; Majority Leader, 1981–85; former Co-Chm., Senate Select Cttee on Presidential Campaign Activities, and mem. other Senate cttees; Chief of Staff, White House, 1987–88. Senior Partner: Baker, Worthington, Crossley, Stansberry & Woolf, Knoxville, Tenn, 1985–87 and 1988–95; Baker, Donelson, Bearman & Caldwell, Washington, 1995–2001; US Ambassador to Japan, 2001–05. Mem., Bd of Regents, Smithsonian Instn. Mem., Amer. Bar Assoc. Presidential Medal of Freedom, 1984. *Publications:* No Margin for Error, 1980; Howard Baker's Washington, 1982; Big South Fork Country, 1993; Scott's Gulf, 2000. *Address:* (office) 920 Massachusetts Avenue, NW, Suite 900, Washington, DC 20001, USA. *Died 26 June 2014.*

BAKER, Rt Rev. John Austin; Bishop of Salisbury, 1982–93; an Hon. Assistant Bishop, Diocese of Winchester, since 1994; *b* 11 Jan. 1928; *s* of George Austin Baker and Grace Edna Baker; *m* 1974, Gillian Mary Leach (MBE 1997). *Educ:* Marlborough; Oriel Coll., Oxford (MA, MLitt). Asst Curate, All Saints', Cuddesdon, and Lectr in Old Testament, Cuddesdon Theol Coll., 1954–57; ordained priest, 1955; Asst Curate, St Anselm's, Hatch End, and Asst Lectr in NT Greek, King's Coll., London, 1957–59; Official Fellow, Chaplain and Lectr in Divinity, Corpus Christi Coll., Oxford, 1959–73, Emeritus Fellow, 1977; Lectr in Theology, Brasenose and Lincoln Colls, Oxford, 1959–73; Hebrew Lectr, Exeter Coll., Oxford, 1969–73; Canon of Westminster, 1973–82; Treas., 1974–78; Sub-Dean and Lector Theologiae, 1978–82; Rector of St Margaret's, Westminster, and Speaker's Chaplain, 1978–82. Governor of Pusey House, Oxford, 1970–78; Exam. Chaplain to Bp of Oxford, 1960–78, to Bp of Southwark, 1973–78. Governor: Westminster Sch., 1974–81; Ripon Coll., Cuddesdon, 1974–80; Westminster City Sch., 1978–82; Dorset Inst. of Higher Educn, 1982–86; Bishop Wordsworth's Sch., 1982–93; Sherborne Sch., 1982–93; Salisbury & Wells Theological Coll., 1982–93; Pres. of Council, Marlborough Coll., 1982–93; Trustee, Harold Buxton Trust, 1973–79. Dorrance Vis. Prof., Trinity Coll., Hartford, Conn, USA, 1967; Vis. Prof., King's Coll., London, 1974–77; Hulsean Preacher, Univ. of Cambridge, 1979; Select Preacher, Univ. of Oxford, 1983; Stephenson Lectr, Univ. of Sheffield, 1994; Warburton Lectr, Inns of Court, 1994. Chairman: Defence Theol Working Party, C of E Bd for Social Responsibility, 1980–82; C of E Doctrine Commn, 1985–87 (Mem., 1967–76, 1977–81, 1984–87); House of Bps Working Party

on Nature of Christian Belief, 1985–86, on Issues in Human Sexuality, 1990–91; Member: Faith and Order Advisory Gp, C of E Bd for Mission and Unity, 1976–81; Cttee for Theological Education, 1982–85; Standing Commn, WCC Faith and Order Commn, 1983–87; Exec. Cttee, CCJ, 1995–97; Vice-President: Nat. Family Mediation, 1993–; Sudan Church Assoc., 1994–. Pres., Anglican Soc. for Welfare of Animals, 1998–2008. Chaplain, Playing Card Makers' Co., 1977. DD Lambeth, 1991. *Publications:* The Foolishness of God, 1970; Travels in Oudamovia, 1976; Prophecy in the Church, 1976; The Living Splendour of Westminster Abbey, 1977; The Whole Family of God, 1981; The Right Time, 1981; Evidence for the Resurrection, 1986; Christian Civilisation and Common Security, 1990; The Faith of a Christian, 1996; contrib. to: Man: Fallen and Free (ed Kemp), 1969; Thinking about the Eucharist (ed Ramsey), 1972; Church Membership and Intercommunion (ed Kent and Murray), 1973; What about the New Testament? (ed Hooker and Hickling), 1975; Man and Nature (ed Montefiore), 1975; Studia Biblica I, 1978; Religious Studies and Public Examinations (ed Hulmes and Watson), 1980; Believing in the Church, 1981; Hospice: the living Idea (ed Saunders, Summers and Teller), 1981; Darwin: a Commemoration (ed R. J. Berry), 1982; Unholy Warfare (ed D. Martin and P. Mullen), 1983; The Challenge of Northern Ireland, 1984; Lessons before Midnight (ed J. White), 1984; Feminine in the Church (ed M. Furlong), 1984; Dropping the Bomb (ed J. Gladwin), 1985; Theology and Racism, I (ed K. Leech), 1985; Peace Together (ed C. Barrett), 1986; Working for the Kingdom (ed J. Fuller), 1986; Faith and Renewal (ed T. F. Best), 1986; Church, Kingdom, World (ed G. Limouris), 1986; Women Priests? (ed A. Peberdy), 1988; For the Love of Animals (ed B. and M. Annett), 1989; Liberating Life (ed S. McFague *et al*), 1990; The Extended Circle (ed J. Wynne Tyson), 1990; Praying for Peace (ed M. Hare Duke), 1991; The Church, Medicine and the New Age (ed J. Watt), 1995; The Warburton Lectures 1985–94, 1995; Community-Unity-Communion: essays in honour of Mary Tanner (ed C. Podmore), 1998; Act of Synod—Act of Folly? (ed M. Furlong), 1998; *translations:* W. Eichrodt, Theology of the Old Testament, vol. 1 1961, vol. 2 1967; T. Bovet, That They May Have Life, 1964; J. Daniélou, Theology of Jewish Christianity, 1964; H. von Campenhausen, Ecclesiastical Authority and Spiritual Power, 1969; H. von Campenhausen, The Formation of the Christian Bible, 1972; J. Daniélou, Gospel Message and Hellenistic Culture, 1973; (with David Smith) J. Daniélou, The Origins of Latin Christianity, 1977. *Recreation:* music. *Address:* 4 Mede Villas, Kingsgate Road, Winchester, Hants SO23 9QQ. *T:* (01962) 861388.
Died 4 June 2014.

BAKER, His Honour Paul Vivian; a Circuit Judge, 1983–96; *b* 27 March 1923; *er s* of Vivian Cyril Baker and Maud Lydia Baker; *m* 1957, Stella Paterson Eadie, *d* of William Eadie, MD; one *s* one *d*. *Educ:* City of London Sch.; University Coll., Oxford (BCL, MA). RAF Wireless Operator and Navigator, 1941–46. Called to Bar, Lincoln's Inn, 1950, Bencher, 1979; QC 1972. Editor, Law Quarterly Review, 1971–87. Chm., Incorporated Council of Law Reporting for England and Wales, 1992–2001. *Publications:* (ed) Records of the Hon. Society of Lincoln's Inn, vol. 6 (1914–1965), 2001. *Recreation:* growing old gracefully. *Address:* 6 Redgrave Court, Patron's Way East, Denham Garden Village, Uxbridge, Middx UB9 5NT. *T:* (01895) 833631. *Clubs:* Athenæum, Authors'. *Died 26 Aug. 2012.*

BAKER, His Honour Peter Maxwell; QC 1974; a Circuit Judge, 1983–2000; *b* 26 March 1930; *s* of late Harold Baker and of Rose Baker; *m* 1st, 1954, Jacqueline Mary Marshall (*d* 1986); three *d*; 2nd, 1988, Sandra Elizabeth Hughes. *Educ:* King Edward VII Sch., Sheffield; Exeter Coll., Oxford (MA). Called to Bar, Gray's Inn, 1956 (Holker Senior Exhibitioner); Junior, NE Circuit, 1960; a Recorder of the Crown Court, 1972–83. *Recreations:* fishing, shooting, yachting, music, watching others garden. *Address:* c/o North-Eastern Regional Director, 18th Floor, West Riding House, Albion Street, Leeds LS1 5AA.
Died 27 Nov. 2015.

BALDERSTONE, Sir James (Schofield), AC 1992; Kt 1983; Chairman: Australian Mutual Provident Society, 1990–93 (Director, 1979–93); Chase AMP Bank, 1990–91 (Director, 1985–91); Broken Hill Proprietary Co. Ltd, 1984–89 (Director, 1971–89); Stanbroke Pastoral Co., 1982–93 (Managing Director, 1964–81); *b* 2 May 1921; *s* of late James Schofield and Mary Essendon Balderstone; *m* 1946, Mary Henrietta Tyree (*d* 2011); two *s* two *d*. *Educ:* Scotch College, Melbourne. Service with RANR, WWII, 1940–45. General Manager for Aust., Thos Borthwick & Sons, 1953–67; Dep. Chm., Westpac Banking Corp., 1992–93 (Dir, 1981–84); Director: NW Shelf Develt Pty, 1976–83; Woodside Petroleum, 1976–83; ICI (Australia), 1981–84. Founding Chm., Australian Meat Exporters' Fed. Council, 1963–64; Mem., Australian Meat Bd, 1964–67. Chairman: Commonwealth Govt Policy Discussion Gp on Agriculture, 1981–82; Scotch Coll. Council, 1991–95. Mem. Council, Aust. War Meml, 1994–99; Dir, Aust. War Meml Foundn, 1996–99. Pres., Inst. of Public Affairs (Vic.), 1981–84. DUniv Newcastle, NSW, 1985. Commander's Cross, Order of Merit (Germany), 1991. *Recreations:* farming, reading, sport. *Address:* 115 Mont Albert Road, Canterbury, Vic 3126, Australia. *T:* (3) 98363137. *Clubs:* Australian, Melbourne (Melbourne); Union (Sydney); Queensland (Brisbane). *Died 15 Oct. 2014.*

BALDWIN, Maj.-Gen. Peter Alan Charles, CBE 1994; Company Secretary, Television Corporation, 1997–2006 (Consultant, 1996); *b* 19 Feb. 1927; *s* of Alec Baldwin and Anne Dance; *m* 1st, 1953, Judith Elizabeth Mace; 2nd, 1982, Gail J. Roberts. *Educ:* King Edward VI Grammar Sch., Chelmsford. Enlisted 1942; commnd R Signals 1947; early service included Berlin, 1948–49 (during airlift), and Korean War, 1950; Staff Coll., 1960; JSSC, 1964; Borneo operations (despatches, 1967); Directing Staff, Staff Coll., 1967–69; Comdr, 13 Signal Regt, BAOR, 1969–71; Sec. for Studies, NATO Defence Coll., 1971–74; Comdr, 2 Signal Group, 1974–76; ACOS Jt Exercises Div., Allied Forces Central Europe, 1976–77; Maj.-Gen. and Chief Signal Officer, BAOR, 1977–79. Dep. Dir of Radio, 1979–87, Dir of Radio, 1987–90, IBA; Chief Exec., Radio Authy, 1991–95. Mem., Bd, Crimestoppers, 2003–06. Trustee: Eyeless Trust, 1996–2007 (Chm., 2002–07); CSV, 1997–2009; D'Oyly Carte Opera Co., 2000–12. Fellow, Radio Acad., 1992; FRSA 1993. *Recreations:* cricket, music, theatre. *Address:* c/o Lloyds Bank, Cox's and King's Branch, 8–10 Waterloo Place, SW1Y 4BE. *Club:* Army and Navy.
Died 15 Sept. 2015.

BALES, Kenneth Frederick, CBE 1990; Regional Managing Director, West Midlands Regional Health Authority, 1984–92; *b* 2 March 1931; *s* of Frederick Charles Bales and Deborah Alice Bales; *m* 1958, Margaret Hazel Austin; two *s* one *d*. *Educ:* Buckhurst Hill Grammar Sch.; LSE; Univ. of Manchester. BScSoc; DipSocAdmin; AHSM. Hosp. Sec., Newhall & Hesketh Park Hosps, 1958–62; Regional Trng Officer, Birmingham Regional Hosp. Bd, 1962–65; Regional Staff Officer, Birmingham Regional Staff Cttee, 1965–68; Group Sec., W Birmingham HMC, 1968–73; Regional Administrator, W Midlands RHA, 1973–84. Vice Pres., Disability W Midlands, 1999–2006 (Chm., 1996–98). *Recreations:* painting, sport, bridge. *Address:* Stronefield, 4 St Catherine's Close, Blackwell, near Bromsgrove, Worcestershire B60 1BG. *T:* (0121) 445 1424. *Died 20 Jan. 2011.*

BALFOUR OF INCHRYE, 2nd Baron *cr* 1945, of Shefford; **Ian Balfour;** *b* 21 Dec. 1924; *s* of 1st Baron Balfour of Inchrye, PC, MC and Diana Blanche (*d* 1982), *d* of Sir Robert Grenville Harvey, 2nd Bt; *S* father, 1988; *m* 1953, Josephine Maria Jane (*d* 2007), *d* of late Morogh Percy Wyndham Bernard and of the Hon. Mrs Bernard; one *d*. *Educ:* Eton, spasmodically, and Magdalen College, Oxford (MA). Business consultant, gemological author and composer of 9 operas, and numerous orchestral and instrumental works. Performances include: In Memoriam II (oboe, harp, percussion and strings), Dublin, 1982; Suite No 1 for 'Cello, Edinburgh, 1984, London, 1986; Oxford Memories (orch.), Oxford, London, 1996; Millennium Surprise (orch.), Esterhazy, Leipzig, Moscow, Prague, Hanover, Bratislava, 2000. *Publications:* Famous Diamonds, 1987, 5th edn 2008. *Recreations:* watching cricket and Association football, walking, writing, thinking, drinking, dreaming. *Address:* 4 Marsh End, Ferry Road, Walberswick, Suffolk IP18 6TH. *Club:* Garrick. *Died 14 April 2013* (ext).

BALFOUR, Peter Edward Gerald, CBE 1984; Chairman, Charterhouse plc, 1985–90; a Vice-Chairman, Royal Bank of Scotland, 1985–90 (Director, 1971–90); Director, 1978–91, Vice-Chairman, 1981–91, Royal Bank of Scotland Group; *b* 9 July 1921; *y s* of late Brig. Edward William Sturgis Balfour, CVO, DSO, OBE, MC and Lady Ruth Balfour, CBE, MB; *m* 1st, 1948, Grizelda Davina Roberta Ogilvy (marr. diss. 1967); two *s* one *d*; 2nd, 1968, Diana Rosemary Wainman; one *s* one *d*. *Educ:* Eton College. Scots Guards, 1940–54. Joined Wm McEwan & Co. Ltd, 1954; Chm. and Chief Exec., Scottish & Newcastle Breweries, 1970–83. Director: British Assets Trust Ltd, 1962–91; Selective Assets Trust (formerly Edinburgh American Assets Trust), 1962–92 (Chm., 1978–92); First Charlotte Assets Trust, 1980–92 (Chm., 1981–92). Chm., Scottish Council for Develt and Industry, 1978–85. Mem., Hansard Soc. Commn on Electoral Reform, 1975–76. *Address:* Scadlaw House, Humbie, East Lothian EH36 5PH. *T:* (01875) 833252. *Club:* Cavalry and Guards. *Died 19 July 2013.*

BALFOUR, Raymond Lewis, LVO 1965; HM Diplomatic Service, retired; Counsellor, Kuwait, 1979–83; *b* 23 April 1923; *s* of Henry James Balfour and Vera Alice (*née* Dunford); *m* 1975, Vanda Gaye Crompton. RMA Sandhurst, 1942; commnd RAC; served with IV Queen's Own Hussars, 1942–47. Diplomatic Service, 1947–87; served at Munich, Beirut, Gdansk (Poland), Baghdad, Khartoum, Geneva, Damascus; Counsellor, Tripoli, 1976–79. Order of the Two Niles, Sudan, 1965. *Recreations:* travel, gardening. *Address:* 4 Foxglove Close, Wyke, Gillingham, Dorset SP8 4TW. *Died 27 Feb. 2013.*

BALL, Air Marshal Sir Alfred (Henry Wynne), KCB 1976 (CB 1967); DSO 1943; DFC 1942; Vice-Chairman (Air), Council of Territorial, Auxiliary and Volunteer Reserve Associations, 1979–84; *b* 18 Jan. 1921; *s* of Captain J. A. E. Ball, MC, BA, BE, Chief Engineer, Bengal Nagpur Railway, 1937; *m* 1942, Nan McDonald (*d* 2006); three *s* one *d*. *Educ:* Campbell Coll., Belfast; RAF Coll., Cranwell; idc, jssc, psc, pfc. Served War of 1939–45 (despatches twice; US Air Medal 1943); Sqdn Ldr 1942; Wing Comdr 1944; air operations, Lysanders, Spitfires, Mosquitoes; commanded: 4 Photo. Reconn. Unit; 682, 542, 540 and 13 Photo. Reconn. Sqdns in N Africa, UK, France and Middle East; E Africa, 1947; RAF Staff Coll., 1952; Canberras, RAF Wyton, 1953; RAF Flying Coll., Bomber Comd, 1956; jssc 1959; BJSM, Washington, 1959; Comdr, Honington V Bomber Base, 1963–64; Air Officer, Administration, Aden, 1965; IDC, 1967; Dir of Operations, (RAF), MoD, 1967–68; Air Vice-Marshal, 1968; ACOS, Automatic Data Processing Div., SHAPE, 1968–71; Dir-Gen. Organisation (RAF), 1971–75; Air Marshal, 1975; UK Rep., Perm. Mil. Deputies Gp, Cento, 1975–77; Dep. C-in-C, RAF Strike Command, 1977–79, retired 1979. Mil. Affairs Advr, Internat. Computers Ltd, 1979–83. Hon. Air Cdre, No 2624 (Co. of Oxford) RAuxAF Regt Sqdn, 1984–90. Hon. FBCS 1984 (Hon. MBCS 1974). *Recreations:* golf, bridge. *Clubs:* Royal Air Force; Phyllis Court (Henley). *Died 25 Jan. 2012.*

BALL, Denis William, MBE 1971; industrial and financial consultant; *b* 20 Oct. 1928; *er s* of late William Charles Thomas and Dora Adelaide Ball, Eastbourne; *m* 1972, Marja Tellervo Lumijärvi (*d* 1987), *er d* of late Osmo Kullervo and Leila Tellervo Lumijärvi, Toijala, Finland; two *s* one *d*. *Educ:* Brunswick Sch.; Tonbridge Sch. (Scholar); Brasenose Coll., Oxford (MA). Sub-Lt, RNR, 1953; Lieut 1954; Lt-Comdr 1958. Asst Master, 1953–72, Housemaster, 1954–72, The King's Sch., Canterbury; Headmaster, Kelly Coll., 1972–85 (Governor, 1997–2004). Director: Perkins Foods, 1987–96 (founder Dir); James Wilkes, 1987–88; Western Bloodstock, 1987–92; Redbridge Properties, 1990–96; Kelly Enterprises, 1997–2002; Bamboo Travel, 2008–; Cons., Throgmorton Investment Management, 1987–88. Trustee, Tavistock Sch., 1972–85; Vice-Chm. of Governors, St Michael's Sch., Tawstock Court, 1974–93 (Hon. Gov., 1993–; Headmaster during interregnum, 1986); Mem., Political and PR Sub-Cttee, HMC, 1979–84. Hon. Treasurer: Ickham PCC, 1990–2010; Ickham-Uganda, 2005–. Mem., Johnson Club, 1987–98. *Recreations:* Elizabethan history, cryptography, literary and mathematical puzzles, cricket, Real tennis (played for MCC and Jesters), squash (played for Oxford Univ. and Kent), golf, ballet, poverty in Uganda. *Address:* Ickham Hall, Ickham, Canterbury, Kent CT3 1QT. *Clubs:* MCC, Jesters. *Died 2 Jan. 2011.*

BALLESTEROS, Severiano; professional golfer, 1974–2007; *b* Santander, Spain, 9 April 1957; *s* of Baldomero Ballesteros; *m* 1988, Carmen Botin (marr. diss. 2004); two *s* one *d*. Won Spanish Young Professional title, 1975, 1978; French Open, 1977, 1982, 1985, 1986; Japan Open, 1977, 1978; Swiss Open, 1977, 1978, 1989; German Open, 1978, 1988; Open Champion, Lytham St Anne's, 1979 and 1988, St Andrews, 1984; won US Masters, 1980, 1983; World Matchplay Champion, Wentworth, 1981, 1982, 1984, 1985; Australian PGA Championship, 1981; Spanish Open, 1985, 1995; Dutch Open, 1986; British Masters, 1991; PGA Championship, 1991; Internat. Open, 1994; numerous other titles in Europe, USA, Australasia; Mem. Ryder Cup team, 1979, 1983, 1985, 1987, 1989, Captain, 1997. Prince of Asturias prize for sport, 1989; Lifetime Achievement Award, BBC Sports Personality of the Year, 2009. *Publications:* (with Robert Green): Trouble-shooting, 1996; Seve: My Life and Golf, 2002. *Address:* c/o Fairway SA, C1 Pasaje de Peña, 2–4ª Planta, 39008 Santander, Spain. *Died 7 May 2011.*

BALLYEDMOND, Baron *cr* 2004 (Life Peer), of Mourne in the County of Down; **Edward Enda Haughey,** OBE 1987; JP; Chairman, Norbrook Laboratories Ltd, Norbrook Holdings BV and 20 subsidiary companies, since 1980; Member, Senate of Ireland, 1994–2002 (Government spokesman for Northern Ireland); *b* 5 Jan. 1944; *s* of Edward Haughey and Rose Haughey (*née* Traynor); *m* 1972, Mary Gordon Young; two *s* one *d*. *Educ:* Christian Brothers Sch., Dundalk, Ireland. Bd Mem., Warrenpoint Harbour Authy, 1986–89; Dir, Adv. Bd, Bank of Ireland, 1987–99; Chairman: Ballyedmond Castle Farms Ltd, 1991–; Haughey Air, 2000–; Cumberland Breweries Ltd, 2009–. Member: Forum for Peace and Reconciliation, 1996–; Oireachtas Cttee for For. Affairs, 1997–; British-Irish Inter-Parly Body, 1997–; Inst. of British/Irish Studies, 2000–. Trustee: Dublin City Univ., 1995–2000; RCVS, 2001– (Perm. Vice-Pres.; Hon. ARCVS). Perm. Vice-Pres., Anglo-Chilean Soc., 1995; Hon. Consul for Chile in NI and N of England, 1997. JP NI 1986. FInstD; FIAM. Dist. Fellow, Griffith Coll., Dublin; Fellow Entrepreneurship, RVC, Univ. of London, 2004. Hon. Associate: BVA, 2004; RCVS, 2005; NI Veterinary Assoc., 2008. Hon. Fellow, Irish Mgt Inst.; Hon. FRCSI 1998; Hon. FRSC 2008; Hon. FRCVS, 2008. Hon. Col, 2nd Bn Royal Irish Regt, 2008–13. Freeman, City of London, 2014. Hon. DBA Internat. Mgt Centres, 1992; Hon. LLD NUI, 1997; Hon. DSc Ulster, 2008. Order of Bernardo O'Higgins (Chile), 1995. *Recreations:* fishing, shooting. *Address:* Ballyedmond Castle, Rostrevor, Co. Down, Northern Ireland BT34 3AG. *T:* (028) 3026 9824; Corby Castle, Great Corby, Cumbria CA4 8LR; 64 Fitzwilliam Square, Dublin 2, Ireland; 9 Belgrave Square, SW1X 8PH; Villa Le Belvoir, Cannes, France. *Clubs:* Carlton, Savage; Reform (Belfast); Kildare Street and University (Dublin). *Died 13 March 2014.*

BALSTON, His Honour Antony Francis; a Circuit Judge, 1985–2005; *b* 18 Jan. 1939; *s* of late Comdr Edward Francis Balston, DSO, RN, and Diana Beatrice Louise Balston (*née* Ferrers); *m* 1966, Anne Marie Judith Ball; two *s* one *d*. *Educ:* Downside; Christ's Coll., Cambridge (MA). Served Royal Navy, 1957–59; Univ. of Cambridge, 1959–62; admitted Solicitor, 1966. Partner, Herington Willings & Penry Davey, Solicitors, Hastings, 1967–85; a Recorder of the Crown Court, 1980–85; Hon. Recorder, Hastings, 1984–2005. *Recreation:* gardening. *Club:* Farmers. *Died 10 Dec. 2014.*

BAMBER, Helen, OBE 1997; Co-Founder and Clinical Director, Helen Bamber Foundation, 2005–14, then Director Emeritus; *b* 1 May 1925; *d* of Louis and Marie Balmuth; *m* 1947, Rudi Bamberger (marr. diss. 1970); two *s*. Mem., Relief and Rehabilitation Assoc., UN, 1945–47; Mem., Cttee for the Care of Children from Concentration

Camps, 1947; health and social work in various hospitals and orgns; joined Amnesty Internat., 1961 (Mem. Exec. Council, and Sec., Med. Gp, 1974, British section); Founder and Dir, Med. Foundn for the Care of Victims of Torture, 1985–2002. Consultant and supervisor, Family Trauma Centre, Belfast. Hon. DCL Oxon, 2000. *Address:* Helen Bamber Foundation, Bruges Place, 15–20 Baynes Street, Camden, NW1 0TF. *Died 21 Aug. 2014.*

BAMFORD, Alan George, CBE 1985; Principal, Homerton College, Cambridge, 1985–91; *b* 12 July 1930; *s* of James Ross and Margaret Emily Bamford; *m* 1954, Joan Margaret, *e d* of Arthur W. Vint; four *s*. *Educ:* Prescot Grammar School; Borough Road College, London; Liverpool University (DipEd, MEd); MA Cantab; Cert. Ed. London. Teacher and Dep. Headmaster, Lancashire primary schs, 1952–62; Lectr in Primary Educn, Liverpool Univ., 1962–63; Sen. Lectr in Educn, Chester Coll., 1963–66; Principal Lectr and Head of Educn Dept, S Katharine's Coll., Liverpool, 1966–71; Principal, Westhill Coll., Birmingham, 1971–85. Pres., Birmingham Council of Christian Educn, 1972–74, Vice-Pres., 1974–91; Vice-Pres., Colls of Educn Christian Union, 1965–86, Pres., 1966–67, 1972–73; Chm., Birmingham Assoc. of Youth Clubs, 1972–85, Vice-Pres., 1985–; Member: Standing Conf. on Studies in Educn, 1974–91 (Exec. Cttee and Editl Bd, 1978–87, Sec., 1982–84); Council of Nat. Youth Bureau, 1974–80 (Exec. Cttee, 1978–80); Adv. Cttee on religious broadcasts, BBC Radio Birmingham, 1972–80; Educn Cttee, Free Church Fed. Council, 1978–89; BCC Standing Cttee on Theol Educn, 1979–82; Council, British and Foreign School Soc., 1979–85; Exec. Cttee, Assoc. of Voluntary Colls, 1979–86; Standing Cttee on Educn and Training of Teachers, 1985–91 (Vice-Chm., 1988; Chm., 1989); Cttee, Standing Conf. of Principals and Dirs of Colls and Insts of Higher Educn, 1986–91; Voluntary Sector Consultative Council, 1987–88; Cambridge HA, 1987–90 (Trustee, 1988–90); Chairman: Colls Cttee, NATFHE, 1981–82; Central Register and Clearing House Cttee, 1981–82 (Mem. Council of Management, 1982–92). Gov., London Bible Coll., 1981–89. JP Birmingham 1977–85. Hon. MA Birmingham, 1981. *Publications:* articles on educn and church-related subjects. *Recreations:* travel, photography. *Died 18 June 2011.*

BAND, His Honour Robert Murray Niven, MC 1944; QC 1974; a Circuit Judge, 1978–91; *b* 23 Nov. 1919; *s* of Robert Niven Band and Agnes Jane Band; *m* 1948, Nancy Margery Redhead; two *d*. *Educ:* Trinity Coll., Glenalmond; Hertford Coll., Oxford (MA). Served in Royal Artillery, 1940–46. Called to the Bar, Inner Temple, 1947; Junior Treasury Counsel in Probate Matters, 1972–74; Chm. Family Law Bar Assoc., 1972–74; a Recorder of the Crown Court, 1977–78. Chm., St Teresa's Hosp., Wimbledon, 1969–83. *Recreations:* the countryside, gardens, old buildings, treen. *Died 20 Dec. 2013.*

BANFIELD, Ven. David John; Archdeacon of Bristol, 1990–98; *b* 25 June 1933; *s* of Norman Charles Banfield and Muriel Gladys Honor Banfield (*née* Pippard); *m* 1967, Rita (*née* Woolhouse); three *d*. *Educ:* Yeovil Sch.; London Coll. of Divinity, London Univ. (ALCD). RAF, 1951–53. Ordained deacon, 1957, priest, 1958; Curate, Middleton, Manchester, 1957–62; Chaplain and Asst Warden, Scargill House, Yorks, 1962–67; Vicar of Addiscombe, Croydon, 1967–80; Vicar of Luton, Beds, 1980–90; RD, Luton, 1989–90; Hon. Canon, St Alban's, 1989–90; Chm., St Alban's Diocesan House of Clergy, 1989–90. *Recreations:* travel, walking, music, gardening. *Address:* 47 Avon Way, Stoke Bishop, Bristol BS9 1SL. *T:* (0117) 968 4227. *Died 2 Oct. 2014.*

BANHAM, Belinda Joan, CBE 1977; JP; Independent Assessor, Office of the Commissioner for Public Appointments, 2000; independent consultant, health care services, since 1996; *b* 1917; *d* of late Col Charles Unwin and Winifred Unwin (*née* Woodman Wilson); *m* 1939, Terence Middlecott Banham (*d* 1995); two *s* two *d*. *Educ:* privately; West Bank Sch.; Brussels; BSc Hons, Dip. Social Studies London; Dip. PhilMed Soc. of Apothecaries. RGN. Work in health services, 1937–; work in theory and practice on aspects of social deviance and deprivation, Cornwall CC, 1954–67; Mem., SW RHB, 1965–74; Chairman: Cornwall and Isles of Scilly HMC, 1967–74 (Mem., 1964–77); Cornwall and Isles of Scilly AHA, 1974–77; Kensington, Chelsea and Westminster FPC, 1979–85 (Mem., 1977–79); Paddington and N Kensington DHA, 1981–86; Mem., Lambeth, Southwark and Lewisham FPC, 1987–90; Chm., Lambeth, Southwark and Lewisham FHSA, 1993–96 (Vice-Chm., 1990–93); Vice-Chm., Lambeth, Southwark and Lewisham Health Commn, 1993–96. Lay Chm., and Convenor, NHS Complaints Procedure, London Reg., 1999–2003; Chm., Prof. Adv. Gp, Enfield, Barking, Haringay and Camden PCTs, 2003–05. Mem., MRC, 1980–87 (Chm., Standing Cttee on Use of Medical Inf. in Research, 1980–87). Mem., Industrial Tribunals, 1974–87. Marriage Guidance Councillor, 1960–72. A Vice-Chm., Disabled Living Foundn, 1984–91 (Dir, then Hon. Dir, 1977–83); Vice President: Friends of St Mary's Hosp., Paddington, 2000– (Pres., 1983–90); KIDS, 1987– (Chm., 1982–87); AFASIC, 1990–. Mem. Delegacy, KCH Med. Sch., 1996–99. Pres., Wytham Hall, 2005– (Trustee, 1985–97; Vice Chm., 1990–99). Mem. Bd of Trustees, Carrick CAB; Member and caseworker: RBL; SSAFA, Cornwall. JP Cornwall, 1972. Special interests: social deprivation and deviance, Health Service management and use of resources. *Publications:* Snapshots in Time: some experiences in health care 1936–1991, 1991; General Practice in the NHS: or, football round the mulberry bush 1918–1995, 1995; (jtly) (paper) Systems Science in Health Care (NATO Conf., Paris, 1977); (jtly) (report) Partnership in Action: a study of healthcare services for elderly and physically handicapped in Newcastle, 1989; (jtly) Care and Understanding of People in a Multi-Cultural Multi-Faith Society: a quick reference guide, 2008. *Recreations:* gardening, plant biology, medical ethics, theatre. *Died 13 Oct. 2014.*

BANKS, Iain; writer; *b* Fife, Scotland, 16 Feb. 1954; *m* 1992, Annie (marr. diss. 2007; she *d* 2009); *m* 2013, Adele Hartley. *Educ:* Stirling Univ. Technician: British Steel, 1976; IBM, Greenock, 1978; Costing Clerk, Denton, Hall & Burgin, London, 1980. *Publications:* The Wasp Factory, 1984; Walking on Glass, 1985; The Bridge, 1986; Espedair Street, 1987; Canal Dreams, 1989; The Crow Road, 1992 (televised, 1996); Complicity, 1993 (filmed, 2000); Whit, 1995; A Song of Stone, 1997; The Business, 1999; Dead Air, 2002; The Steep Approach to Garbadale, 2007; Transition, 2009; Stonemouth, 2012; The Quarry, 2013 (posthumous); *as Iain M. Banks*: Consider Phlebas, 1987; The Player of Games, 1988; Use of Weapons, 1990; The State of the Art, 1991; Against a Dark Background, 1993; Feersum Endjinn, 1994; Excession, 1996; Inversions, 1998; Look to Windward, 2000; The Algebraist, 2004; Matter, 2008; Surface Detail, 2010; *non-fiction:* Raw Spirit, 2003; (with Ken MacLeod) Poems, 2015 (posthumous). *Address:* c/o Little, Brown, 100 Victoria Embankment, EC4Y 0DY. *Died 9 June 2013.*

BANNSIDE, Baron *cr* 2010 (Life Peer), of North Antrim in the County of Antrim; **Rev. Ian Richard Kyle Paisley;** PC 2005; Member (DemU) Antrim North, 1998–2011, and First Minister, 2007–08, Northern Ireland Assembly; Minister, Martyrs Memorial Free Presbyterian Church, Belfast, 1946–2012; *b* 6 April 1926; 2nd *s* of late Rev. J. Kyle Paisley and Mrs Isabella Paisley; *m* 1956, Eileen Emily Cassells, (Baroness Paisley of St George's); two *s* three *d* (incl. twin *s*). *Educ:* Ballymena Model Sch.; Ballymena Techn. High Sch.; S Wales Bible Coll.; Reformed Presbyterian Theol. Coll., Belfast. Ordained, 1946; Moderator, Free Presbyterian Church of Ulster, 1951–2008; Pres., Whitefield Coll. of the Bible, 1979–. Commenced publishing The Protestant Telegraph, 1966. Contested (ProtU) Bannside, NI Parlt, 1969; MP (ProtU), Bannside, Co. Antrim, NI Parlt, 1970–72; Leader of Opposition, 1972; Chm., Public Accounts Cttee, 1972. MP N Antrim 1970–2010 (ProtU 1970–74, DemU 1974–2010; resigned seat Dec. 1985 in protest against Anglo-Irish Agreement; re-elected Jan. 1986). Co-Founder, Democratic Unionist Party, NI, 1972, Leader, 1972–2008. Mem. (Democratic Unionist), N Antrim, NI Assembly, 1973–75; Mem. (UUUC), N Antrim, NI Constitutional Convention, 1975–76; Mem. (DemU) N Antrim, NI Assembly, 1982–86. MEP (DemU) NI, 1979–2004. Hon. DD Bob Jones Univ., SC. FRGS. Mem., Internat. Cultural

Soc., Korea, 1977. *Publications:* History of the 1859 Revival, 1959; Christian Foundations, 1960; Ravenhill Pulpit, Vol. 1, 1966, Vol. 2, 1967; Exposition of the Epistle to the Romans, 1968; Billy Graham and the Church of Rome, 1970; The Massacre of St Bartholomew, 1972; America's Debt to Ulster, 1976; (jtly) Ulster—the facts, 1981; No Pope Here, 1982; Dr Kidd, 1982; Those Flaming Tennents, 1983; Mr Protestant, 1985; Be Sure, 1986; Paisley's Pocket Preacher, 1987, vol. II, 1988, vol. III, 1989, vol. IV, 1990; Jonathan Edwards: the theologian of revival, 1987; Union with Rome, 1989; The Soul of the Question, 1990; The Revised English Bible: an exposure, 1990; What a Friend We Have in Jesus, 1994; Understanding Events in Northern Ireland: an introduction for Americans, 1995; Ian Paisley Library, 10 vols, 1997–99. *Address:* House of Lords, SW1A 0PW; The Parsonage, 17 Cyprus Avenue, Belfast BT5 5NT. *Died 12 Sept. 2014.*

BARBER, Alan Vincent Heys, OBE 2009; freelance consultant in urban greenspace management, since 1992; *b* 11 June 1942; *s* of late Harold Heys Barber and of Mary McLean Barber; *m* 1965, Angela Janice Alton; two *d. Educ:* King George V Grammar Sch., Southport; Royal Botanic Gdns, Kew. Parks Manager, Bristol CC, 1974–92. Member: Govt Urban Green Spaces Taskforce, 2000–02; CABE, 2003–08. Simon Res. Fellow, Univ. of Manchester, 2003–. Pres., Inst. of Leisure and Amenity Mgt, 1997–98 (Hon. Fellow, 2004); Hon. ALI 1995. DUniv Essex, 2005. *Publications:* Green Future: a study of the management of multifunctional urban green spaces in England, 2005. *Recreations:* writing, music, grandchildren. *Address:* 9 Shipham Close, Nailsea, Bristol BS48 4YB. *T:* (01275) 854851. *E:* alan.barber@blueyonder.co.uk. *Died 16 Feb. 2011.*

BARBER, Giles Gaudard; Librarian, Taylor Institution, University of Oxford, 1970–96; Fellow, Linacre College, Oxford, 1963–96, then Emeritus (Vice-Principal, 1988–90); *b* 15 Aug. 1930; *s* of Eric Arthur Barber and Madeleine Barber (*née* Gaudard); *m* 1st, 1958, Monique Fluchère (*d* 1969); one *d*; 2nd, 1970, Gemma Miani (marr. diss. 1997); two *s* one *d*; 3rd, 1997, Lisa Jefferson; one step *d. Educ:* Dragon Sch., Oxford; Leighton Park Sch.; St John's Coll., Oxford (MA, BLitt). Asst, Bodleian Library, 1954–70; Univ. Lectr in Continental Bibliography, Oxford, 1969–96. Pres., Oxford Bibliographical Soc., 1992–96 and 1999–2000; Vice-Pres., Bibliographical Soc., 1983–93; Chm., Voltaire Foundn, 1987–89; Mem. Council, Internat. Soc. for 18th Century Studies, 1979–83. Vis. Lectr, Univ. of Paris IV (Sorbonne), 1980; Lectures: 1st Graham Pollard Meml, 1984; Moses Tyson Meml, Manchester Univ., 1985; Panizzi, British Library, 1988; First Founders' Library Lectr, Univ. of Wales, Lampeter, 1996; Sandars Reader in Bibliography, Cambridge Univ., 1997–98. Corresp. Mem., Soc. Archéologique du Midi de la France, 2004. Gordon Duff Prize in Bibliography, 1962. Commandeur, Ordre des Arts et des Lettres (France), 2002 (Officier, 1992). *Publications:* (ed jtly) Fine Bindings 1500–1700, 1968; A checklist of French printing manuals, 1969; Textile and embroidered bookbindings, 1971; (ed) Book making in Diderot's Encyclopédie, 1973; (ed) Contat, Anecdotes typographiques, 1980; (ed jtly) Buch und Buchhandel in Europa im achtzehnten Jahrhundert, 1981; Daphnis and Chloe, 1989; Studies in the booktrade of the European Enlightenment, 1994; Arks for Learning, 1995; Les Rues de Saint-Girons, 2004; articles in learned jls. *Recreations:* book-collecting, gardening. *Address:* La Mandro, 09420 Lescure, France. *E:* giles.barber@wanadoo.fr. *Died 12 March 2012.*

BARBER, Prof. James Peden, PhD; Master, Hatfield College, Durham, 1980–96; Professor of Politics, Durham University, 1992–96, then Emeritus; *b* 6 Nov. 1931; *s* of John and Carrie Barber; *m* 1955, Margaret June (*née* McCormac); three *s* one *d. Educ:* Liverpool Inst. High Sch.; Pembroke Coll., Cambridge (MA, PhD); The Queen's Coll., Oxford. Served RAF, 1950–52 (Pilot Officer). Colonial Service, Uganda: Dist Officer, subseq. Asst Sec. to Prime Minister and Clerk to the Cabinet, 1956–63; Lectr, Univ. of NSW, Australia, 1963–65; Lectr in Govt, Univ. of Exeter, 1965–69 (seconded to University Coll. of Rhodesia, 1965–67); Prof. of Political Science, 1969–80, Pro-Vice-Chancellor, 1970–73, Open Univ.; Pro-Vice-Chancellor, 1987–92 and Sub-Warden, 1990–92, Durham Univ. Associate Fellow, Centre of Internat. Studies, Cambridge Univ., 1996; Res. Fellow, South African Inst. of Internat. Affairs, 1996. Advr, Commons Select Cttee on Foreign Affairs, 1990–91. Mem. RIIA; Part-time Dir, Chatham House study, Southern Africa in Conflict, 1979–81; Course Tutor, U3A, Cambridge, 1996–. Member: Amnesty International, 1985–; Parkinson's Disease Soc., 1997–. President: Durham Univ. Soc. of Fellows, 1988; Durham Univ. Hockey Club, 1981–96. JP Bedford, 1977–80. *Publications:* Rhodesia: the road to rebellion, 1967; Imperial Frontier, 1968; South Africa's Foreign Policy, 1973; European Community: vision and reality, 1974; The Nature of Foreign Policy, 1975; Who Makes British Foreign Policy?, 1977; The West and South Africa, 1982; The Uneasy Relationship: Britain and South Africa, 1983; South Africa: the search for status and security, 1990; The Prime Minister since 1945, 1991; Forging the New South Africa, 1994; South Africa in the Twentieth Century: a political history, 1999; Mandela's World, 2004. *Recreations:* watching sport, listening to music. *Address:* 14 North Terrace, Midsummer Common, Cambridge CB5 8DJ. *T:* (01223) 313453. *Died 24 July 2015.*

BARBOUR, Very Rev. Prof. Robert Alexander Stewart, KCVO 1991; MC 1945; Professor of New Testament Exegesis, University of Aberdeen, 1971–82; Master of Christ's College, Aberdeen, 1977–82; an Extra Chaplain to the Queen in Scotland, since 1991 (Chaplain-in-Ordinary to the Queen, 1976–91); Dean of the Chapel Royal in Scotland, 1981–91; Prelate of the Priory of Scotland of the Order of St John, 1977–93; *b* 11 May 1921; *s* of George Freeland Barbour and Helen Victoria (*née* Hepburne-Scott); *m* 1950, Margaret Isobel Pigot; three *s* one *d. Educ:* Rugby Sch.; Balliol Coll., Oxford (MA 1946); Univ. of St Andrews (BD 1952); Yale Univ. (STM 1953). Sec., Edinburgh Christian Council for Overseas Students, 1953–55; Lectr and Sen. Lectr in NT Lang., Lit. and Theol., Univ. of Edinburgh, 1955–71. Hensley Henson Lectr, Univ. of Oxford, 1983–84. Moderator, Gen. Assembly of Church of Scotland, 1979–80. Chm., Scottish Churches' Council, 1982–86. Hon. Sec., Studiorum Novi Testamenti Societas, 1970–77. Chm. Governors, Rannoch Sch., 1973–79. Hon. DD St Andrews, 1979. *Publications:* The Scottish Horse 1939–45, 1950; Traditio-Historical Criticism of the Gospels, 1972; What is the Church for?, 1973; articles in various jls. *Recreations:* music, walking, forestry. *Address:* Old Fincastle, Pitlochry, Perthshire PH16 5RJ. *T:* (01796) 473209. *Club:* New (Edinburgh). *Died 18 Oct. 2014.*

BARCLAY, Christopher Francis Robert, CMG 1967; Secretary, Government Hospitality Fund, 1976–80; *b* 8 June 1919; *s* of late Captain Robert Barclay, RA (retired) and Annie Douglas Dowdeswell Barclay (*née* Davidson); *m* 1st, 1950, Clare Justice Troutbeck (marr. diss., 1962); two *s* one *d*; 2nd, 1962, Diana Elizabeth Goodman; one *s* one *d. Educ:* Eton Coll.; Magdalen Coll., Oxford (MA). 2nd Lieut The Rifle Bde, 1940; Capt. 1942; Major 1943; served in Middle East; Political Officer, Northern Iraq, 1945; Brit. Embassy, Baghdad, 1946. Foreign Office, 1946; Second Sec., British Embassy, Cairo, 1947; First Sec., Foreign Office, 1950; Brit. Embassy, Bonn, 1953; FO, 1956; Regional Information Officer, Beirut, 1960; FO, 1961; Counsellor and Head of Information Research Dept, 1962–66; Head of Personnel Dept (Training and General), FCO, 1967–69; Asst Sec., CSD, 1969–73, DoE, 1973–76. Chm., Jt Nat. Horse Educn and Trng Council, 1988–90. Mem. Council, City Univ., 1976–84. Master, Saddlers' Co., 1983–84. FRSA 1984. *Address:* Croft Edge, Painswick, Glos GL6 6XH. *T:* (01452) 812332. *Died 20 March 2015.*

BARCLAY, Hugh Maben, CB 1992; Clerk of Public Bills, House of Commons, 1988–91; *b* 20 Feb. 1927; *s* of late William Barclay, FRCS, and Mary Barclay; *m* 1956, Hilda Johnston; one *s* one *d. Educ:* Fettes Coll., Edinburgh (exhibnr); Gonville and Caius Coll., Cambridge (schol.). Served Royal Artillery, 1948. House of Commons: Asst Clerk, 1950; Sen. Clerk, 1955; Dep. Principal Clerk, 1967; Principal Clerk, 1976; Clerk of Standing Cttees, 1976; Clerk of Private Bills, 1982. *Address:* South Hayes Care Home, 101 London Road, Worcester WR5 2DZ. *Died 22 May 2012.*

BARCLAY, Sir Peter (Maurice), Kt 1992; CBE 1984; Chairman, 1996–2001, Trustee, 1972–2001, Joseph Rowntree Foundation (formerly Joseph Rowntree Memorial Trust); *b* 6 March 1926; *s* of George Ronald Barclay and Josephine (*née* Lambert); *m* 1953, Elizabeth Mary, *d* of late Herbert H. S. Wright; one *s* two *d*. *Educ:* Bryanston Sch.; Magdalene Coll., Cambridge (MA). Served RNVR, 1944–46. Admitted Solicitor, 1952; Senior Partner, 1964–74, Partner, 1974–88, Beachcroft & Co. Chm., The Family Fund Trust, 1973–97. Chairman: Cttee on Roles and Tasks of Social Workers, 1981–82; Social Security Adv. Cttee, 1984–93; Nat. Family Mediation, 1994–96. Non-exec. Mem., DSS Deptl Bd, 1994–97. Pres., National Inst. for Social Work, 1988 (Chm., 1973–85); Chm., Horticultural Therapy, 1989–94; Pres., St Pancras and Humanist Housing Assoc., 2000– (Vice Pres., St Pancras Housing Assoc., 1994–2000; Mem., 1971–93, Chm., 1983–91, Management Cttee). Governor, Bryanston Sch., 1972–88; Council Mem., PSI, 1989–95; Trustee, Nat. Family and Parenting Inst., 1999–2005. DUniv: Stirling, 1994; York, 1996. *Recreations:* gardening, painting. *Address:* Mulberry House, Sion Hill, Bath BA1 2UL. *T:* (01225) 424868. *E:* barclayem@gmail.com. *Died 29 June 2014.*

BARDSLEY, Andrew Tromlow; JP; General Manager and Chief Executive, Harlow Development Corporation, 1973–80; *b* 7 Dec. 1927; *o s* of Andrew and Gladys Ada Bardsley; *m* 1954, June Patricia (*née* Ford) (*d* 2002); one *s* one *d*. *Educ:* Ashton-under-Lyne Grammar Sch.; Manchester Coll. of Art. CEng, FICE. Royal Navy, 1947–49. Entered Local Govt (Municipal Engrg), 1950; various appts leading to Borough Engr and Surveyor, Worksop MB, 1962–69; Director of Technical Services: Corby New Town, 1969–71; Luton CBC, 1971–73; Principal, Westgate Develt Consultancy, 1981–93. Gen. Comr of Taxes in England and Wales, 1987–92. JP Essex, 1975 (Dep. Chm., Harlow Bench, 1987–92). *Recreations:* golf, music, gardening, most spectator sports. *Club:* Bournemouth Bowling (Past Pres.). *Died 12 Aug. 2013.*

BARKER, Anthony; QC 1985; a Recorder, since 1985; *b* 10 Jan. 1944. *Educ:* Newcastle-under-Lyme High Sch.; Clare Coll., Cambridge (BA Hons). Called to the Bar, Middle Temple, 1966, Bencher, 1997. Asst Recorder, 1981. Mem. Faculty, Nat. Inst. for Trial Advocacy, Gainesville, Houston, Berkeley and Colorado, USA, 1985–90. Mem., Internat. Soc. of Barristers, 2000. *Recreations:* gardening, walking, music. *Address:* Ty Fry, Rhoscefnhir, Pentraeth, Gwynedd LL75 8YT. *Died 14 March 2012.*

BARKER, Sir Colin, Kt 1991; Chairman, British Technology Group Ltd, 1983–93 (Chief Executive, 1983–85); *b* 20 Oct. 1926; *m* 1951, Beryl; three *s* one *d*. *Educ:* Hull Grammar Sch.; London Univ.; Edinburgh Univ. Ford UK, 1960–67 (Finance Dir, 1967); Finance Director: Blue Circle, 1968–70; STC, 1970–80; British Steel Corp., 1980–83. Chairman: CIN Management, 1985–93; British Investment Trust, 1985–93; MCD (UK), 1990–95; Anglian Group (formerly Anglian Windows), 1991–95; Director: Reed Internat., 1983–92; British Coal Corp., 1984–91; Edinburgh Fund Managers, 1988–93. *Address:* 12 Clune Court, Hutton Road, Shenfield, Essex CM15 8NQ. *Died 10 June 2015.*

BARKER, David; QC 1976; a Recorder of the Crown Court, 1974–98; *b* 13 April 1932; *s* of late Frederick Barker and of Amy Evelyn Barker; *m* 1957, Diana Mary Vinson Barker (*née* Duckworth); one *s* three *d*. *Educ:* Sir John Deane's Grammar Sch., Northwich; University Coll., London; Univ. of Michigan. 1st cl. hons LLB London; LLM Michigan. RAF, 1956–59. Called to Bar, Inner Temple, 1954, Bencher, 1985; practised Midland and Oxford Circuit; a Dep. High Court Judge, 1993–98. Mem., Senate of Inns of Court and the Bar, 1981–84. Member: Criminal Injuries Compensation Bd, 1990–2000; Criminal Injuries Compensation Appeals Panel, 1997–2007. Mem., Woodhouse Parish Council, 2003–10 (Chm., 2005–10). Contested (Lab) Runcorn, 1955. *Recreations:* gardening, walking, sailing. *Address:* 17 Nanhill Drive, Woodhouse Eaves, Leics LE12 8TL. *T:* (01509) 890224. *Club:* Reform. *Died 9 Nov. 2013.*

BARKER, Prof. David James Purslove, CBE 2006; MD, PhD, DSc; FRCP; FRS 1998; Professor of Clinical Epidemiology, University of Southampton, since 1979 (Director, Medical Research Council Environmental Epidemiology Unit, 1983–2003); *b* 29 June 1938; *s* of Hugh Purslove and Joye Frances Barker; *m* 1st, 1960, Angela Beatrice Coddington (*d* 1980); three *s* two *d*; 2nd, 1983, Janet Elizabeth Franklin; one step *s* two step *d*. *Educ:* Oundle Sch.; Guy's Hosp. Med. Sch., London Univ. (BSc 1st Cl. Hons, 1959; MB BS 1962; PhD 1966; MD 1973). FRCP 1979. University of Birmingham: Research Fellow in Social Medicine, 1963–66; Lectr in Medicine, 1966–69; Lectr in Preventive Medicine, Makerere Univ., Uganda, 1969–72; Sen. Lectr in Clinical Epidemiology and Consultant Physician, Univ. of Southampton, 1972–79. Founder FMedSci 1998. Hon. FRCOG 1993; Hon. FRCPCH 2003. Hon. DSc Birmingham 2003. Royal Soc. Wellcome Gold Medal, 1994; Feldberg Foundn Prize, 1995; Prince Mahidol Award, Prince Mahidol Award Foundn, Thailand, 2001; Danone Internat. Nutrition Award, 2005; Archbp Gandarillas Medal, Chile, 2006; Fondation Ipsen Award, Paris, 2007; Butterfield Award, Nat. Inst. of Child Health and Human Develt, 2007; Agnes Higgins Award, March of Dimes, 2010; Richard Doll Prize, Internat. Epidemiol. Assoc., 2011. *Publications:* Practical Epidemiology, 1973, 4th edn 1992; (with G. Rose) Epidemiology in Medical Practice, 1976, 5th edn (with C. Cooper and G. Rose) 1998; (with G. Rose) Epidemiology for the Uninitiated, 1979, 5th edn 2003; Fetal and Infant Origins of Adult Disease, 1992; Mothers, Babies and Disease in Later Life, 1994, 2nd edn 1998; The Best Start in Life, 2003; Nutrition in the Womb, 2008. *Recreations:* writing, drawing, golf, fishing, craic. *Address:* Manor Farm, East Dean, near Salisbury, Wilts SP5 1HB. *T:* (01794) 340016. *Died 27 Aug. 2013.*

BARKER, John Francis Holroyd, CB 1984; Consultant, Cabinet Office, 1985–93; *b* 3 Feb. 1925; *s* of Rev. C. H. Barker and B. A. Barker (*née* Bullivant); *m* 1954, Felicity Ann (*née* Martindale); three *d*. *Educ:* King Edward's School, Stourbridge; Oriel College, Oxford. RNVR, 1943–46. Director of Music, Abingdon School, 1950–54; War Office/Ministry of Defence, 1954–85. *Recreation:* music. *Address:* c/o Coutts & Co., 440 Strand, WC2R 0QS. *Club:* Athenæum. *Died 27 Dec. 2012.*

BARKER, Ronald Hugh, PhD; BSc; CEng, FIET, FIMechE; Deputy Director, Royal Armament Research and Development Establishment, 1965–75; *b* 28 Oct. 1915; *s* of E. W. Barker and L. A. Taylor; *m* 1943, W. E. Hunt; two *s*. *Educ:* University of Hull. Physicist, Standard Telephones and Cables, 1938–41; Ministry of Supply, 1941–59; Dep. Dir, Central Electricity Research Laboratories, 1959–62; Technical Dir, The Pullin Group Ltd, 1962–65. Inventor of Barker Code to check synchronization and framing of received data. *Publications:* various, on servomechanisms and control systems. *Died 7 Oct. 2015.*

BARKER, Thomas Christopher; HM Diplomatic Service, retired; *b* 28 June 1928; *s* of Rowland Francis Barker and Katheen Maude Barker (*née* Welch); *m* 1960, Griselda Helen Cormack; two *s* one *d*. *Educ:* Uppingham (Schol.); New Coll., Oxford (Schol.; MA Lit. Hum., 1952; Gaisford Prize for Greek Verse). 2nd Lt, 1st Bn, The Worcestershire Regt, 1947–48. HM Foreign Service, 1952; Third Sec., Paris, 1953–55; Second Sec., Baghdad, 1955–58; FO, 1958–62; First Sec., Head of Chancery and Consul, Mexico City, 1962–67; FO, 1967–69; Counsellor and Head of Chancery, Caracas, 1969–71; FCO, 1971–75; seconded as Under Sec., NI Office, Belfast, 1976. Curator, 1978–87, Secretary to Trustees, 1987–93, Scottish Nat. War Meml, Edinburgh. *Died 11 Jan. 2014.*

BARLOW, Sir (George) William, Kt 1977; BSc Tech, FREng, FIMechE, FIET; President, Royal Academy of Engineering (formerly Fellowship of Engineering), 1991–96; *b* 8 June 1924; *s* of Albert Edward and Annice Barlow; *m* 1948, Elaine Mary Atherton (*née* Adamson); one *s* one *d*. *Educ:* Manchester Grammar Sch.; Manchester Univ. (Kitchener Schol., Louis Atkinson Schol.; BSc Tech. 1st cl. Hons Elec. Engrg, 1944). Served as Elec. Lt, RNVR, 1944–47. Various appts, The English Electric Co.

Ltd (in Spain, 1952–55, Canada, 1958–62); Gen. Manager, Liverpool and Netherton, 1964–67; Managing Director: English Electric Domestic Appliance Co. Ltd, 1965–67; English Electric Computers Ltd, 1967–68; Gp Chief Exec., 1969–77, Chm., 1971–77, Ransome Hoffman Pollard Ltd; Chm. and Chief Exec., Post Office, 1977–80, organized separation of Post Office and British Telecom, 1980; Chairman: Thorn EMI Engrg Gp, 1980–84; Ericsson, 1981–94; BICC, 1984–91 (Dir, 1980–91); SKF (UK), 1990–92; Barking Power Ltd, 1992–93; Kennedy and Donkin, later Parsons Brinckerhoff, 1997–2002; Director: Vodafone Group, 1988–98; Chemring Gp, 1994–97. Chm., NICG, 1980. Member: Industrial Develt Adv. Bd, 1972–79; Council, IEE, 1969–72 (Vice-Pres., 1978–80, Dep. Pres., 1983–84; Hon. Fellow, 1990); Council, IMechE, 1971–74; National Electronics Council, 1982–94; President: BEAMA, 1986–87; ORGALIME, 1990–92; Vice Pres., City and Guilds of London Inst., 1982–92. Chairman: Design Council, 1980–86; Engineering Council, 1988–90. Pres., Assoc. of Lancastrians in London, 1981 and 1992. Trustee, Brain Res. Trust, 1987–99. Governor, London Business Sch., 1979–92 (Hon. Fellow, 1991). Master, Worshipful Company of Engineers, 1986–87. FREng (FEng 1979). Hon. FUMIST 1978; Hon. FIET (Hon. FIEE 1990); Hon. FICE 1991; Hon. FIMechE 1993; Hon. FCGI 1996. Hon. DSc: Cranfield, 1979; Bath, 1986; Aston, 1988; City, 1989; Hon. DTech: CNAA, 1988; Loughborough, 1993; Hon DEng UMIST, 1996. *Recreations:* golf, racing. *Address:* 4 Parkside, Henley-on-Thames, Oxon RG9 1TX. *T:* (01491) 410550. *E:* william@barlowpark.co.uk. *Clubs:* Brooks's; Leander (Henley-on-Thames); Huntercombe Golf. *Died 19 May 2012.*

BARNETT, Baron *cr* 1983 (Life Peer), of Heywood and Royton in Greater Manchester; **Joel Barnett;** PC 1975; JP; *b* 14 Oct. 1923; *s* of Louis and Ettie Barnett, both of Manchester; *m* 1949, Lilian Goldstone (*d* 2011); one *d.* *Educ:* Derby Street Jewish Sch.; Manchester Central High Sch. Certified accountant. Served RASC and British Military Govt in Germany. Mem. of Prestwich, Lancs, Borough Council, 1956–59; Hon. Treas. Manchester Fabian Society, 1953–65. Contested (Lab) Runcorn Div. of Cheshire, Oct. 1959; MP (Lab) Heywood and Royton Div., Lancs, 1964–83. Member: Public Accounts Cttee, 1965–71 (Chm., 1979–83); Public Expenditure Cttee, 1971–74; Select Cttee on Tax Credits, 1973–74; Chm. Parly Labour Party Economic and Finance Group, 1967–70 and 1972–74 (Vice-Chm., 1966–67); Opposition Spokesman on Treasury matters, 1970–74; Chief Sec. to the Treasury, 1974–79 (Cabinet Mem., 1977–79); Opposition spokesman on the Treasury in House of Lords, 1983–86. Vice-Chm., Bd of Govs, BBC, 1986–93. Chm., British Screen Finance Ltd (formerly British Screen Finance Consortium), 1985–97. Mem., Internat. Adv. Bd, Unisys, 1989–96. Chm., Building Societies' Ombudsman Council, 1987–96. Trustee, V&A Museum, 1984–97. Mem., Hallé Cttee, 1982–93. Chm., Birkbeck Coll. Appeal Cttee, 1990–96; Trustee, Open Univ. Foundn, 1994–2003. Chm., Hansard Soc. for Parly Govt, 1984–90. Pres., RIPA, 1989–92. Hon. Fellow, Birkbeck Coll., London, 1992. JP Lancs 1960. Hon. LLD Strathclyde, 1983. *Publications:* Inside the Treasury, 1982. *Recreations:* walking, conversation and reading, good food. *Address:* Flat 92, 24 John Islip Street, SW1P 4LG; 7 Hillingdon Road, Whitefield, Manchester M45 7QQ. *Died 1 Nov. 2014.*

BARON, Hon. Dame Florence (Jacqueline), DBE 2004; **Hon. Mrs Justice Baron;** a Judge of the High Court of Justice, Family Division, since 2003; Liaison Judge, South Eastern Circuit, 2008–11; *b* 7 Oct. 1952; *d* of Jose Baron and Ellen Elizabeth Jane Baron (*née* McLennan); partner, 1974, *m* 2013, John Tonna. *Educ:* Jersey Coll. for Girls; St Hugh's Coll., Oxford (BA Juris.; Hon. Fellow 2004). Called to the Bar, Middle Temple, 1976, Bencher, 2002; QC 1995; a Recorder, 1999–2003; a Dep. High Court Judge, 2000–03. *Recreation:* relaxing. *Address:* Royal Courts of Justice, Strand, WC2A 2LL. *Died 9 Dec. 2013.*

BARON, Sir Thomas, Kt 1992; CBE 1983. FRICS 1948. Former Chairman, Stockbridge Village Trust, Merseyside. *Address:* Lightoaks Hall, Glazebury, Warrington WA3 5PX. *Died 22 Dec. 2014.*

BARRATT, Sir Lawrence Arthur, (Sir Lawrie), Kt 1982; FCIS; Life President, Barratt Developments PLC, and subsidiary companies, 1989–91 and since 1997 (Managing Director, 1962–88; Chairman, 1962–88 and 1991–97); *b* Newcastle, 14 Nov. 1927; *m* 1st, 1951 (marr. diss. 1984); two *s*; 2nd, 1984, Mary Sheila (*née* Brierley). Founded Barratt Developments, as a private co., 1958. *Recreations:* golf, shooting, sailing. *Address:* Barratt Developments, Rotterdam House, 116 Quayside, Newcastle upon Tyne NE1 3DA. *Died 18 Dec. 2012.*

BARRATT, Sir Richard (Stanley), Kt 1988; CBE 1981; QPM 1974; HM Chief Inspector of Constabulary, 1987–90; *b* 11 Aug. 1928; *s* of Richard Barratt and Mona Barratt; *m* 1952, Sarah Elizabeth Hale; one *s* two *d.* *Educ:* Saltley Grammar Sch., Birmingham. CCMI. Birmingham City Police (Constable to Chief Inspector), 1949–65; Dir, Home Office Crime Prevention Centre, Stafford, 1963; seconded to Home Office (Res. and Develt), 1964; Sen. Comd Course, Police Coll., 1964; Supt, Cheshire Constab., 1965, Chief Supt, 1966; Asst Chief Constable, Manchester City Police, 1967; Asst Chief Constable, Manchester and Salford Police, 1968, Dep. Chief Constable, 1972; Dep. Chief Constable, Greater Manchester Police, 1974; Chief Constable, S Yorks Police, 1975–78; HM Inspector of Constabulary, 1978–87. Review of the Royal Bahamas Police, 1985. Led Police delegns to China, 1987, Pakistan, 1990. Assessor, Guildford and Woolwich Inquiry, 1990–94. Mem., Gaming Bd for GB, 1991–95. CStJ 1996. *Died 5 May 2013.*

BARRETT, Rev. Prof. Charles Kingsley, DD; FBA 1961; Professor of Divinity, Durham University, 1958–82; *b* 4 May 1917; *s* of Rev. F. Barrett and Clara (*née* Seed); *m* 1944, Margaret E. Heap (decd), Calverley, Yorks; one *s* one *d.* *Educ:* Shebbear Coll.; Pembroke Coll., Cambridge (Hon. Fellow, 1995); Wesley House, Cambridge. DD Cantab, 1956. Asst Tutor, Wesley Coll., Headingley, 1942; Methodist Minister, Darlington, 1943; Lecturer in Theology, Durham Univ., 1945. Lectures: Hewett, USA, 1961; Shaffer, Yale, 1965; Delitzsch, Münster, 1967; Cato, Australia, 1969; Tate-Willson, Dallas, 1975; McMartin, Ottawa, 1976; Sanderson, Melbourne, and West-Watson, Christchurch, NZ, 1983; Alexander Robertson, Univ. of Glasgow, 1984; K. W. Clark, Duke, USA, 1987; Ryan, Asbury Seminary, Kentucky, 1988; Dominion-Chalmers, Ottawa, 1990; Woodruff Vis. Prof., Emory Univ., Atlanta, 1986; Gunning Fellow, Edinburgh Univ., 1994. Vice-Pres., British and Foreign Bible Soc.; Pres., Studiorum Novi Testamenti Societas, 1973; Mem., Royal Norwegian Soc. of Scis and Letters, 1991; Hon. Mem., Soc. of Biblical Literature, USA. Hon. DD: Hull, 1970; Aberdeen, 1972; Hon. DrTheol Hamburg, 1981. Burkitt Medal for Biblical Studies, 1966; von Humboldt Forschungspreis, 1988. *Publications:* The Holy Spirit and the Gospel Tradition, 1947; The Gospel according to St John, 1955, 2nd edn 1978; The New Testament Background: Selected Documents, 1956, 2nd edn 1987; Biblical Preaching and Biblical Scholarship, 1957; The Epistle to the Romans, 1957, 2nd edn 1991; Westcott as Commentator, 1959; Yesterday, Today and Forever: The New Testament Problem, 1959; Luke the Historian in Recent Study, 1961; From First Adam to Last, 1962; The Pastoral Epistles, 1963; Reading Through Romans, 1963; History and Faith: the Story of the Passion, 1967; Jesus and the Gospel Tradition, 1967; The First Epistle to the Corinthians, 1968; The Signs of an Apostle, 1970; Das Johannesevangelium und das Judentum, 1970; The Prologue of St John's Gospel, 1971; New Testament Essays, 1972; The Second Epistle to the Corinthians, 1973; The Fourth Gospel and Judaism, 1975; (ed) Donum Gentilicium, 1978; Essays on Paul, 1982; Essays on John, 1982; Freedom and Obligation, 1985; Church, Ministry and Sacraments in the New Testament, 1985; The Acts of the Apostles, vol. I (Internat. Critical Commentary series), 1994, vol. II, 1998; Paul: an introduction to his thought, 1994; Jesus and The Word, 1995; (jointly) Jesus, Paul and John, 1999; (jtly) Conflicts and Challenges in Early Christianity, 1999; The Acts of the Apostles: a shorter commentary, 2002; On Paul, 2003; contributions to learned journals and symposia in Britain, the Continent, Australia and USA. *Address:* 22 Rosemount, Durham DH1 5GA. *T:* (0191) 386 1340. *Died 26 Aug. 2011.*

BARRETT, Edmond Fox, OBE 1981; HM Diplomatic Service, retired; First Secretary, Foreign and Commonwealth Office, 1986–88; *b* 24 Aug. 1928; *s* of late Edmond Henry Barrett and Ellen Mary Barrett (*née* Fox); *m* 1959, Catherine Wendy Howard (*née* Slater). *Educ:* St Brendan's Coll., Bristol. Dominions Office, 1946; Royal Navy, 1947–49; CRO, 1949–50; Karachi, 1950–52; New Delhi, 1952–54; CRO, 1954–55; Admiralty, 1955–60; Foreign Office, 1960–63; Bucharest, 1963–65; Rio de Janeiro, 1965–68; Boston, 1968–70; Mexico City, 1971–73; FCO, 1973–76; Santo Domingo, 1976–79; Tehran, 1979–81; Consul Gen., Bilbao, 1981–86. *Recreations:* reading, gardening. *Address:* 10 Greenheys Place, Woking, Surrey GU22 7JD. *Died 24 Jan. 2011.*

BARRETT, Rt Rev. Peter Francis; Bishop of Cashel and Ossory, 2003–06; *b* 8 Feb. 1956; *s* of Alexander Barrett and Kathleen (*née* Aldred); *m* 1980, Anne (*née* Davidson) (marr. diss. 2011); two *s* one *d*. *Educ:* Avoca Kingstown Sch.; TCD (BA 1978, MA 1981, DipTh 1981, MPhil 1984). Ordained deacon, 1981, priest, 1982; Curate Assistant: Drumachose, 1981–83; St Ann and St Mark with St Stephen, 1983–85; Rector: Conwal Union with Gartan, 1985–90; St George's, Belfast, 1990–94; Dean of Residence and Chaplain, TCD, 1994–98; Rector, Waterford with Killea, Drumcannon and Dunhill, 1998–2003; Dean of Waterford, 1998–2003. Minor Canon, 1994–96, Succentor, 1996–98, St Patrick's Cathedral, Dublin; Precentor: Lismore Cathedral, 1998–2003; Cashel Cathedral, 1998–2003. Reviews Ed., Search: a C of I Jl, 1994–98. *Publications:* Love's Redeeming Work (Irish Consultant), 2001; The Measure and the Pledge of Love, 2003; Symbols of Service, 2004; contrib. jl Scripture in the Church. *Recreations:* music, ornithology, sport, especially hockey. *Address:* 4 Pembroke Gardens, Ballsbridge, Dublin 4, Ireland. *Club:* Monkstown Hockey. *Died 28 Oct. 2015.*

BARRITT, Rev. Dr Gordon Emerson, OBE 1979; Principal, National Children's Home, 1969–86; President of the Methodist Conference, 1984–85; *b* 30 Sept. 1920; *s* of Norman and Doris Barritt; *m* 1947, Joan Mary Alway (*d* 1984); two *s* one *d*; *m* 1993, Karen Lesley Windle (marr. diss. 1999); *m* 2003, Eileen Marjorie Smith. *Educ:* William Hulme's Grammar Sch., Manchester; Manchester Univ.; Cambridge Univ. (Wesley House and Fitzwilliam Coll.). Served War, RAF, 1942–45 (despatches). Methodist Minister: Kempston Methodist Church, Bedford, 1947–52; Westlands Methodist Church, Newcastle-under-Lyme, 1952–57; Chaplain, Univ. of Keele, 1953–57. Dir, Enfield Counselling Service, 1986–89; Treasurer, 1969–86, Chm., 1970–72, Nat. Council of Voluntary Child Care Organisations; Member: Home Office Adv. Council on Child Care, 1968–71; Brit. Assoc. of Social Workers, 1960–95; Nat. Children's Bureau, 1963–2000 (Treasurer, 1989–95; Vice Pres., 1997–2000); Internat. Union for Child Welfare, 1969–86; Chm., Kids, 1986–93; Gov., CAF, 1996–2000. Vice Chm. of Council, Selly Oak Colls, Birmingham, 1991–2000 (Fellow, 1987); Governor: Farringtons Sch., 1986–94 (Chm. of Govs, 1986–93); Queenswood Sch., 1986–93. DUniv Keele, 1985. *Publications:* The Edgworth Story, 1972; (ed) Many Pieces—One Aim, 1975; (ed) Family Life, 1979; Residential Care, 1979; contrib.: Caring for Children, 1969; Giving Our Best, 1982; Thomas Bowman Stephenson, 1996. *Recreations:* music, walking. *Address:* 1 Pitcairne Court, 5 Donovan Place, N21 1RZ. *T:* (020) 8360 8687, *Fax:* (01582) 792658. *Died 11 Nov. 2015.*

BARRON, Sir Donald (James), Kt 1972; DL; Chairman, Joseph Rowntree Foundation, 1981–96; *b* 17 March 1921; *o s* of Albert Gibson Barron and Elizabeth Macdonald, Edinburgh; *m* 1956, Gillian Mary, *o d* of John Saville, York; three *s* two *d*. *Educ:* George Heriot's Sch., Edinburgh; Edinburgh Univ. (BCom). Member, Inst. Chartered Accountants of Scotland. Joined Rowntree Mackintosh Ltd, 1952; Dir, 1961; Vice-Chm., 1965; Chm., 1966–81. Dir, 1972, Vice-Chm., 1981–82, Chm., 1982–87, Midland Bank plc. Dep. Chm., CLCB, 1983–85; Chm., Cttee of London and Scottish Bankers, 1985–87. Director: Investors in Industry, subseq. 3i, Gp, 1980–91; Canada Life Assurance Co. of GB Ltd, 1980–96 (Chm., 1991–94; Dep. Chm., 1994–96); Canada Life Unit Trust Managers Ltd, 1980–96 (Chm., 1982–96); Canada Life Assurance Co., Toronto, 1980–96; Canada Life Assce (Ireland), 1992–96; Clydesdale Bank, 1986–87. Mem., Bd of Banking Supervision, 1987–89. Dir, BIM Foundn, 1977–80 and Mem. Council, BIM, 1978–80; Trustee, Joseph Rowntree Foundn (formerly Meml Trust), 1966–73, 1975–96 (Chm., 1981–96); Treasurer, 1966–72, a Pro-Chancellor, 1982–95, York Univ.; Member: Council of CBI, 1966–81 (Chm., CBI Educn Foundn, 1981–85); SSRC, 1971–72; UGC, 1972–81; Council, PSI, 1978–85; Council, Inst. of Chartered Accountants of Scotland, 1980–81; NEDC, 1983–85. Governor, London Business Sch., 1982–88. Chm., York Millennium Bridge Trust, 1997–2003. DL N Yorks (formerly WR Yorks and City of York), 1971–96. Hon. doctorates: Loughborough, 1982; Heriot-Watt, 1983; CNAA, 1983; Edinburgh, 1984; Nottingham, 1985; York, 1986. *Recreations:* travelling, golf, tennis, gardening. *Address:* Greenfield, Sim Balk Lane, Bishopthorpe, York YO23 2QH. *T:* (01904) 705675, *Fax:* (01904) 700183. *Club:* Athenæum. *Died 30 Dec. 2015.*

BARROT, Jacques; Member and Vice-President, European Commission, 2004–10; Member, Constitutional Council of the French Republic, since 2010; *b* 3 Feb. 1937; *s* of Noël Barrot and Marthe Barrot (*née* Pivot); *m* 1982, Florence Cattani; one *s* two *d*. *Educ:* Coll. d'Yssingeaux; Faculté de Droit, Paris; Inst. d'Etudes Politiques, Paris. Deputy for Haute-Loire, National Assembly, France: (Union Centriste) 1967–78; (UDF) 1981–2002; (Union pour un mouvement populaire) 2002–04. Sec. of State, Min. of Equipment, 1974–78; Minister: of Commerce and Wkg Classes, 1978–79; of Health and Social Security, 1979–81; of Labour, Social Dialogue and Participation, 1995; of Labour and Social Affairs, 1995–97. Mem., 1974–2004, Pres., 1976–2004, Conseil-Gen., Haute-Loire; Mayor of Yssingeaux, 1989–2001. *Publications:* Les Pierres de l'avenir, 1978; (jtly) Notre contrat pour l'alternance, 2002; L'Europe n'est pas ce que vous croyez, 2007. *Address:* Constitutional Council, 2 rue de Montpensier, 75001 Paris, France. *Died 3 Dec. 2014.*

BARROW, Prof. Geoffrey Wallis Steuart, FBA 1976; Sir William Fraser Professor of Scottish History and Palæography, University of Edinburgh, 1979–92, then Professor Emeritus; *b* Headingley, Leeds, 28 Nov. 1924; *s* of late Charles Embleton Barrow and Marjorie, *d* of Donald Stuart; *m* 1951, Heather Elizabeth, *d* of James McLeish Lownie; one *s* one *d*. *Educ:* St Edward's Sch., Oxford; Inverness Royal Acad.; St Andrews Univ.; Pembroke Coll., Oxford. FRSE 1977. Lecturer in History, University Coll., London, 1950–61; Prof. of Mediaeval Hist., King's Coll., Univ. of Durham, later Univ. of Newcastle upon Tyne, 1961–74; Prof. of Scottish History, Univ. of St Andrews, 1974–79. Mem., Royal Commn on Historical MSS, 1984–90. Ford's Lectr, Univ. of Oxford, 1977; Rhind Lectr, Soc. of Antiquaries of Scotland, 1985. Vice Pres., Commn Internationale de Diplomatique, 1994–2005. Hon. DLitt: Glasgow, 1988; Newcastle, 1994. *Publications:* Feudal Britain, 1956; Acts of Malcolm IV, King of Scots, 1960; Robert Bruce and the Community of the Realm of Scotland, 1965; Acts of William I, King of Scots, 1971; Kingdom of the Scots, 1973; (ed) The Scottish Tradition, 1974; The Anglo-Norman Era in Scottish History, 1980; Kingship and Unity, 1981; Scotland and its Neighbours, 1992; The Charters of David I, 1999; contrib. Scottish Historical Review, etc. *Address:* 12A Lauder Road, Edinburgh EH9 2EL. *Died 14 Dec. 2013.*

BARROW, Captain Michael Ernest, CVO 2002; DSO 1982; RN; Assistant Chief of Staff (Operations) to Commander, Allied Naval Forces Southern Europe, Naples, 1978–80; *b* 21 May 1932; *s* of late Captain Guy Runciman Barrow, OBE, RN and Barbara Barrow (*née* Heinekey); *m* 1962, Judith Ann (*née* Cooper); two *s* one *d*. *Educ:* Wellesley House; RNC, Dartmouth. Served in HM Ships: Devonshire, Liverpool; Agincourt, Euryalus, 1950–54; HM Yacht Britannia, 1954–56; Camperdown, 1958–59; Flag Lt to Cdre Hong Kong, 1956–58; commanded: Caunton, 1960; Laleston, 1961–62; Mohawk, 1963–64; Torquay, 1967–69; Diomede, 1973–75; Glamorgan, 1980–83 (Falkland Is conflict); RN Staff Course, 1966; Staff Flag Officer, Malta, 1970–71; Comdr RNC, Dartmouth, 1971–73; Dep. Dir, Recruiting, 1975–77; ADC to the Queen, 1982–83; retired RN 1983.

Clerk to the Worshipful Co. of Haberdashers, 1983–95, Hon. Assistant, 1995–. Gentleman Usher to Her Majesty, 1984–2002, Extra Gentleman Usher, 2002–. Trustee, Falkland Is Meml Chapel, 1992–2006; Dir, Union Jack Club, 1996–2011. *Recreations:* sailing, gardening. *Address:* 1 Lake House, 27 Heath Road, Petersfield, Hampshire GU31 4EH. *T:* (01730) 264198. *Clubs:* Army and Navy; Royal Naval Sailing. *Died 28 April 2013.*

BARRY, John; *see* Prendergast, J. B.

BARRY, Michael; *see* Bukht, M. M. J.

BARSTOW, Stan, FRSL; writer; *b* 28 June 1928; *s* of Wilfred Barstow and Elsie Gosnay; *m* 1951, Constance Mary Kershaw; one *s* one *d*. *Educ:* Ossett Grammar Sch. Employed in Engineering Industry, 1944–62, mainly as Draughtsman. Best British Dramatisation, Writers' Guild of GB, 1974; Royal TV Soc. Writers' Award, 1975. FRSL 1999; Fellow, Welsh Acad., 2008. Hon. Fellow, Bretton Coll., 1985. Hon. MA Open Univ., 1982. *Radio: dramatisations:* A Kind of Loving, 1964; The Pity of it All, 1967; Bright Day, 1968; The Watchers on the Shore, 1971; We could always fit a sidecar, 1974; The Right True End, 1978; The Apples of Paradise, 1988; Foreign Parts, 1990; My Son, my Son, 1993. *Television: dramatisations:* A Raging Calm, 1974; South Riding, 1974; Joby, 1975; The Cost of Loving, 1977; Travellers, 1978; A Kind of Loving (from A Kind of Loving, The Watchers on the Shore, The Right True End), 1982; A Brother's Tale, 1983; The Man Who Cried, 1993; (with Diana Griffiths) Calon Gaeth (A Small Country), 2007. *Publications:* A Kind of Loving, 1960; The Desperadoes, 1961; Ask Me Tomorrow, 1962; Joby, 1964; The Watchers on the Shore, 1966; A Raging Calm, 1968; A Season with Eros, 1971; The Right True End, 1976; A Brother's Tale, 1980; A Kind of Loving: The Vic Brown Trilogy, 1982; The Glad Eye, 1984; Just You Wait and See, 1986; B-Movie, 1987; Give Us This Day, 1989; Next of Kin, 1991; In My Own Good Time, 2001; *plays*: Listen for the Trains, Love, 1970; Joby (TV script), 1977; An Enemy of the People (ad. Ibsen), 1978; The Human Element, and Albert's Part (TV scripts), 1984; (with Alfred Bradley): Ask Me Tomorrow, 1966; A Kind of Loving, 1970; Stringer's Last Stand, 1972. *Address:* c/o The Agency, 24 Pottery Lane, W11 4LZ. *Died 1 Aug. 2011.*

BARTLES-SMITH, Ven. Douglas Leslie; Archdeacon of Southwark, 1985–2004, then Emeritus; Chaplain to the Queen, 1996–2007; *b* 3 June 1937; *s* of late Leslie Charles and Muriel Rose Bartles-Smith; *m* 1967, Patricia Ann Coburn; two *s* one *d*. *Educ:* Shrewsbury School; St Edmund Hall, Oxford (MA); Wells Theol Coll. Nat. Service (2nd Lieut, RASC), 1956–58. Curate of St Stephen's, Rochester Row, SW1, 1963–68; Curate-in-charge, St Michael and All Angels with Emmanuel and All Souls, Camberwell, 1968–72; Vicar, 1972–75; Vicar of St Luke, Battersea, 1975–85; Rural Dean of Battersea, 1981–85. Hon. Freeman, London Bor. of Southwark, 2004. *Publications:* (co-author) Urban Ghetto, 1976; Opportunities for a Strong Church, 1993; Fighting Fundamentalism, 2007; How the Prime Minister Saved the Church of England, 2013. *Recreations:* Shrewsbury Town Football Club, reading, walking, travel. *Address:* 18 Vane Road, Shrewsbury SY3 7HB. *Died 5 June 2014.*

BARTLETT, (Harold) Charles, RE 1961 (ARE 1950); RWS 1970 (ARWS 1959); painter and printmaker; President, Royal Society of Painters in Water Colours, 1987–92; *b* Grimsby, 23 Sept. 1921; *s* of Charles Henry and Frances Kate Bartlett; *m* 1st, 1947, Elizabeth Robertson (marr. diss.); (one *s* decd); 2nd, 1970, Olwen Jones, RE, RWS. *Educ:* Eastbourne Grammar Sch.; Eastbourne Sch. of Art; Royal College of Art (ARCA 1949). Sen. Lectr in Drawing and Painting, Harrow College of Art, 1960–70. First one man exhibition in London, 1960; major retrospective, Bankside Gall., London, 1997. *Recreations:* music, sailing. *Address:* St Andrews House, Chapel Road, Fingringhoe, near Colchester, Essex CO5 7BG. *T:* (01206) 729406. *Died 19 Dec. 2014.*

BARTLETT, Henry Francis, CMG 1975; OBE 1964; HM Diplomatic Service, retired; *b* 8 March 1916; *s* of F. V. S. and A. G. Bartlett, London; *m* 1940, Amanda D. Roy (*d* 2004). *Educ:* St Paul's Sch.; Queen's Coll., Oxford; Ruskin Sch. of Drawing; Univ. of California (Commonwealth Fellow). Min. of Inf., 1940–45; Paris, 1944–47; Vice-Consul, Lyons, 1948–49; FO, 1949–50; Vice-Consul, Szczecin, 1950; Second, later First, Sec., Warsaw, 1951–53; FO, 1953–55; First Sec. (Commercial), Caracas, 1955–60; First Sec. (Inf.), Mexico City, 1960–63; Consul, Khorramshahr, 1964–67; Dep. High Comr, Brisbane, 1967–69; Counsellor, Manila, 1969–72 (Chargé d'Affaires, 1971); Ambassador to Paraguay, 1972–75. Hon. Prof., Nat. Univ. of Asunción, 1975. Exec. Officer, Utah Foundation, Brisbane, 1976–89. Exhibitions of painting: Paris, 1947; London, 1950; Caracas, 1957, 1959; Mexico City, 1962; Brisbane, 1969, 1978, 1981, 1983, 1985, 1988, 1990, 1992, 1994, 1996. Represented: Commonwealth Art Bank; Queensland and S Aust. State Galleries; Queensland Univ. of Technol.; Brisbane Civic Art Gall.; Bendigo Art Gall. Trustee: Queensland Art Gallery, 1977–87; Qld Cultural Centre Trust, 1980–87. *Recreation:* painting. *Address:* 14 Bowen Place, 341 Bowen Terrace, New Farm, Brisbane, Qld 4005, Australia. *Died 17 Feb. 2014.*

BARTON, Prof. (Barbara) Anne, PhD; FBA 1991; Professor of English, Cambridge University, 1984–2000; Fellow of Trinity College, Cambridge, since 1986; *b* 9 May 1933; *d* of Oscar Charles Roesen and Blanche Godfrey Williams; *m* 1st, 1957, William Harvey Righter (marr. diss.); 2nd, 1969, John Bernard Adie Barton, CBE. *Educ:* Bryn Mawr College, USA. BA 1954 (*summa cum laude*); PhD Cantab 1960. Lectr in History of Art, Ithaca Coll., NY, 1958–59; Girton College, Cambridge: Rosalind Lady Carlisle Research Fellow, 1960–62; Official Fellow in English, 1962–72; Dir of Studies in English, 1963–72; Univ. Asst Lectr, later Univ. Lectr in English, Cambridge, 1962–72; Hildred Carlile Prof. of English and Head of Dept, Bedford Coll., London, 1972–74; Fellow and Tutor in English, New Coll., Oxford and CUF Lectr, 1974–84. Lectures: British Acad. Chatterton, 1967; Alexander Meml, Univ. Coll., Toronto, 1983; British Acad. Shakespeare, 1991; Northcliffe, UCL, 1994; Clark, Cambridge, 2003. MAE 1995. Hon. Fellow: Shakespeare Inst., Univ. of Birmingham, 1982; New Coll., Oxford, 1989. Member Editorial Advisory Boards: Shakespeare Survey, 1972–99; Shakespeare Quarterly, 1981–2004; Studies in English Literature, 1976–; Romanticism, 1995–. *Publications:* Shakespeare and the Idea of the Play, 1962, 4th edn 1977, trans. Japanese 1982; Ben Jonson, Dramatist, 1984; The Names of Comedy, 1990; Byron: Don Juan, 1992; Essays, Mainly Shakespearean, 1994; essays and studies in learned jls. *Recreations:* opera, fine arts. *Address:* Trinity College, Cambridge CB2 1TQ. *T:* (01223) 338466. *Died 11 Nov. 2013.*

BARTRAM, George Christopher, TD 1960; Vice Lord-Lieutenant of Co. Durham, 1997–2002; *b* 23 Aug. 1927; *s* of Robert Appleby Bartram and Winifred Hannah (*née* Murray); *m* 1969, Josephine Anne Ker Staveley; two *s*. *Educ:* Rugby Sch.; St Catharine's Coll., Cambridge (MA). Served DLI, 1945–48; TA service, DLI, 1948–64; Hon. Col, 7th Bn (Durham) LI, 1989–94. Bartram & Sons Ltd, Ship Builders, 1952–63; Colvilles Ltd, Steel Mfrs, 1964–72; trainee, Paddington Churches Housing Assoc., 1974; Chief Exec., Endeavour Housing Assoc., 1975–92. Pres., Co. Durham SSAFA Forces Help, 1987–2002. High Sheriff, 1982, DL 1990, Co. Durham. *Recreations:* swimming, combatting litter, family history research. *Address:* Eldon House, Heighington, Newton Aycliffe, Co. Durham DL5 6PP. *T:* (01325) 312270. *Club:* Victory Services. *Died 18 Oct. 2013.*

BARWELL, David John Frank; international business consultant; *b* 12 Oct. 1938; *s* of James Howard and Helen Mary Barwell; *m* 1968, Christine Sarah Carter; one *s*. *Educ:* Lancing College; Trinity College, Oxford; Institut des Hautes Etudes Internationales, Geneva. FCO, 1965; served: Aden, 1967; Baghdad, 1968; Bahrain, 1971; Cairo, 1973; FCO, 1976; Nicosia, 1982; Paris, 1985; FCO, 1989–93; Consultant, Control Risks Gp, 1994–2002; FCO Regl Advr, Central Africa, 2002–03; Dir, Coalition Provisional Authy, Baghdad, 2003. Mem., Methodology Soc., 2002–. Trustee, Kidnap Victim Support, 2002–07. *Recreations:* gardening, singing. *Club:* Athenæum. *Died 29 Aug. 2011.*

BARZUN, Jacques; University Professor Emeritus, Columbia University; *b* 30 Nov. 1907; *s* of Henri Barzun and Anna-Rose Martin; *m* 1st, 1931, Lucretia Mueller (marr. diss. 1936); 2nd, 1936, Mariana Lowell (*d* 1979); two *s* one *d*; 3rd, 1980, Marguerite Lee Davenport. *Educ:* Lycée Janson de Sailly; Columbia Univ. Instructor in History, Columbia Univ., 1929; Research Fellow, American Council of Learned Socs, 1933–34; Columbia University: Asst Prof., 1938; Associate Prof., 1942; Prof. of History, 1945–75; University Prof., 1967; Dean of Grad. Faculties, 1955–58; Dean of Faculties and Provost, 1958–67. Dir Emeritus, Council for Basic Educn; Dir, NY Soc. Library; Mem. Adv. Council, Univ. Coll. at Buckingham. Membre Associé de l'Académie Delphinale, Grenoble, 1952; Member: Amer. Acad. of Arts and Letters, USA (President, 1972–75, 1977–79); Amer. Acad. of Arts and Sciences; American Historical Assoc.; Amer. Philos. Soc.; FRSA, USA (Benjamin Franklin Fellow); FRSL. Seth Low Prof. of History, Columbia Univ., 1960; Extraordinary Fellow, Churchill Coll., Cambridge, 1961–. Literary Advisor, Charles Scribner's Sons Ltd, 1975–93; Mem. Bd of Editors, Encyclopaedia Britannica, 1962–. Chevalier de la Légion d'Honneur. *Publications:* The French Race: Theories of its Origins, 1932; Race: A Study in Superstition, 1937 (revd, 1965); Of Human Freedom, 1939 (revd, 1964); Darwin, Marx, Wagner, 1941 (revd, 1958); Teacher in America, 1945 (revd, 1981); Berlioz and the Romantic Century, 1950, 4th edn 1982; Pleasures of Music, 1951, rev. edn 1977; Selected Letters of Byron, 1953, 2nd edn 1957; Nouvelles Lettres de Berlioz, 1954, 2nd edn 1974; God's Country and Mine, 1954; Music in American Life, 1956; The Energies of Art, 1956; The Modern Researcher (with Henry F. Graff), 1957, 5th edn 1993; The House of Intellect, 1959, 2nd edn 1961; Classic, Romantic and Modern, 1961; Science: The Glorious Entertainment, 1964; (ed) Follett's Modern American Usage, 1967; The American University, 1968, 3rd edn 1992; (with W. H. Taylor) A Catalogue of Crime, 1971, rev. edn 1989; On Writing, Editing and Publishing, 1971; Berlioz's Evenings with the Orchestra, 1956, 2nd edn 1973; The Use and Abuse of Art, 1974; Clio and the Doctors, 1974; Simple and Direct, 1975; Critical Questions, 1982; A Stroll with William James, 1983; A Word Or Two Before You Go, 1986; The Culture We Deserve, 1989; Begin Here, 1991; An Essay on French Verse for Readers of English Poetry, 1991; From Dawn to Decadence, 2001; What is a School?, 2002; A Jacques Barzun Reader, 2002; contrib. to leading US journals. *Address:* 18 Wolfeton Way, San Antonio, TX 78218–6045, USA. *Club:* Century (New York). *Died 25 Oct. 2012.*

BATCHELOR, Prof. (John) Richard; Professor of Immunology, Royal Postgraduate Medical School, Hammersmith Hospital, 1979–94, then Professor Emeritus; *b* 4 Oct. 1931; *s* of B. W. Batchelor, CBE and Mrs C. E. Batchelor; *m* 1955, Moira Ann (*née* McLellan) (*d* 2015); two *s* two *d*. *Educ:* Marlborough Coll.; Emmanuel Coll., Cambridge; Guy's Hospital, London. MB, BChir Cantab, 1955; MD Cantab 1965. FRCPath 1991; FRCP 1995. Nat. Service, RAMC, 1957–59; Dept of Pathology, Guy's Hospital: Res. Fellow, 1959–61; Lectr and Sen. Lectr, 1961–67; Prof. of Transplantation Research, RCS, 1967; Dir, McIndoe Res. Unit, Queen Victoria Hosp., East Grinstead, 1967–78. European Editor, Transplantation, 1964–97. Pres., Transplantation Soc., 1988–90 (Hon. Sec., then Vice-Pres. (E Hemisphere), 1976–80); Member Council, Nat. Kidney Res. Fund, 1979–86; Chm., Scientific Co-ord. Cttee, Arthritis and Rheumatism Council, 1988–96. Trustee: Kennedy Inst. for Rheumatology Trust, 1997– (Dep. Chm., 1997–2014; Hon. Vice Pres., 2014–); Sir Jules Thorn Charitable Trust, 1999–2004. MRSocMed. Mem. Court, Skinners' Company. Hon. Fellow, Faculty of Medicine, Imperial Coll. London, 2002. *Publications:* scientific articles upon tissue transplantation research in various special jls. *Recreations:* Real tennis and lawn tennis, walking. *Address:* Little Ambrook, Nursery Road, Walton-on-the-Hill, Tadworth, Surrey KT20 7TU. *T:* (01737) 812028. *Club:* Queen's. *Died 21 Dec. 2015.*

BATE, Sir David (Lindsay), KBE 1978 (CBE 1968); Chief Judge, Benue and Plateau States of Nigeria, 1975–77; Senior Puisne Judge, High Court of Justice, Northern States of Nigeria, 1968–75 (Puisne Judge, 1957–68); *b* 3 March 1916; *m* 1948, Thadeen June, *d* of late R. F. O'Donnell Peet; two *s*. *Educ:* Marlborough; Trinity Coll., Cambridge. Called to Bar, Inner Temple, 1938. Commissioned, Royal Artillery, 1939 and served, Royal Artillery, 1939–46. Entered Colonial Legal Service, 1947; Crown Counsel, Nigeria, 1947–52; Senior Crown Counsel, Nigeria, 1952–54; Senior Crown Counsel, Northern Nigeria, 1954–56; Solicitor-Gen., Northern Nigeria, 1956. *Recreations:* shooting, fishing. *Address:* PO Box 1339, Howick 3290, Natal, South Africa. *Died 4 June 2011.*

BATES, Alfred; Research Assistant, Union of Shop, Distributive and Allied Workers, 1991–2000; *b* 8 June 1944; *s* of Norman and Alice Bates; single. *Educ:* Stretford Grammar Sch. for Boys; Manchester Univ. (BSc); Corpus Christi Coll., Cambridge. Lectr in Maths, De La Salle Coll. of Educn, Middleton, 1967–74. MP (Lab) Bebington and Ellesmere Port, Feb. 1974–1979; PPS to Minister of State for Social Security, 1974–76; Asst Govt Whip, 1976–79; a Lord Comr, HM Treasury, 1979. Researcher and presenter, 1980–87, and an assistant producer, 1983–87, BBC TV; freelance media consultant, 1987–91. Mem., Trafford MBC, 1992–2000 (Chm., Licensing Cttee, 1996–97, 1998–2000; Chm., Public Protection Cttee, 1997–98). Mem., Exec. Cttee, Assoc. of Former Members of Parlt, 2007–. Mem. Bd of Dirs, Hallé Concerts Soc., 1996–98. *Recreations:* cricket umpiring, philosophical reading. *Address:* 116 Jackson Street, Stretford, Manchester M32 8BB. *Died 17 Dec. 2013.*

BATEY, Mavis Lilian, MBE 1986; FSA; President, Garden History Society, 1985–2000; *b* 5 May 1921; *d* of Frederick Lever and Lily Lever; *m* 1942, (John) Keith Batey (*d* 2010); one *s* two *d*. *Educ:* Convent of Ladies of Mary, Croydon; University Coll. London. Worked at Bletchley Park, breaking German Enigma codes, 1940–45. Tutor (part time), Oxford Dept of External Studies, 1970–92. Mem., Historic Parks and Gardens Panel, English Heritage, 1984–94. Hon. Sec., Garden History Soc., 1971–85. FSA 2002. Veitch Meml Medal, RHS, 1985. *Publications:* Alice's Adventures in Oxford, 1980; Oxford Gardens, 1982; Historic Gardens of Oxford and Cambridge, 1989; (with D. Lambert) The English Garden Tour, 1990; Arcadian Thames, 1994; Privy Garden at Hampton Court, 1995; Regency Gardens, 1995; Jane Austen and the English Landscape, 1996; Alexander Pope: the poet and the landscape, 1999; (jtly) Indignation!, 2000; (ed) A Celebration of John Evelyn, 2007; Dilly: the man who broke Enigmas, 2009. *Recreations:* walking, bird-watching, reading. *Died 12 Nov. 2013.*

BATHURST, 8th Earl *cr* 1772; **Henry Allen John Bathurst;** DL; Baron Bathurst of Battlesden, Bedfordshire, 1712; Baron Apsley of Apsley, Sussex, 1771; Earl Bathurst of Bathurst, Sussex, 1772; Capt. Royal Gloucestershire Hussars (TA); TARO, 1959; *b* 1 May 1927; *s* of Lord Apsley, DSO, MC, MP (killed on active service, 1942) and Lady Apsley, CBE, MP for Bristol Central 1943–45 (*d* 1966); *g s* of 7th Earl; *S* grandfather, 1943; *m* 1st, 1959, Judith Mary (marr. diss. 1977; she *d* 2001), *d* of Mr and Mrs A. C. Nelson, Springfield House, Foulridge, Lancs; two *s* one *d*; 2nd, 1978, Gloria, *widow* of David Rutherston and *o d* of Harold Edward Clarry, Vancouver, BC. *Educ:* Ridley Coll., Canada; Eton; Christ Church, Oxford, 1948–49. Lieut 10th Royal Hussars (PWO), 1946–48. Capt., Royal Glos Hussars, TA, 1949–57. Hon. Sec. Agricultural Cttee (Conservative), House of Lords, 1957; a Lord-in-Waiting, 1957–61; Joint Parliamentary Under-Sec. of State, Home Office, 1961–July 1962. Governor, Royal Agricultural Coll.; Pres. Glos Branch CPRE. Chancellor, Primrose League, 1959–61. Dir, Forestor Gp, 1986–92. Member: CLA Council, 1965 (Chm., Glos Branch of CLA, 1968–71); Timber Growers' Organisation (TGO) Council, 1966; President: Royal Forestry Soc., 1976–78; InstSMM, 1982–92; Assoc. of Professional Foresters, 1983–87, 1995–98. Master, 1950–64, Jt Master, 1964–66, Vale of White Horse (Earl Bathurst's) Hounds. DL County of Gloucester, 1960. *Heir:* *s* Lord Apsley, *b* 11 March 1961. *Address:* Cirencester Park, Cirencester, Glos GL7 2BT. *Clubs:* White's, Cavalry and Guards. *Died 16 Oct. 2011.*

BATHURST, Sir (Frederick) John (Charles Gordon) Hervey-, 7th Bt *cr* 1818, of Lainston, Hants; *b* 23 April 1934; *o s* of Sir Frederick Peter Methuen Hervey-Bathurst, 6th Bt and of Maureen Eley (*née* Gordon); *S* father, 1995; *m* 1957, Caroline, *d* of Lt-Col Sir William Starkey, 2nd Bt; one *s* two *d*. *Educ:* Eton; Trinity Coll., Cambridge (MA). Grenadier Guards, 1952–54. Lazard Brothers & Co. Ltd, 1957–91. *Heir: s* Frederick William John Hervey-Bathurst [*b* 18 Sept. 1965; *m* 1991, Annabel Warburg; one *s* one *d*]. *Address:* East Wing, Somborne Park, Stockbridge, Hants SO20 6QT. *T:* (01794) 388322. *Died 5 Dec. 2011.*

BATTEN, Sir John (Charles), KCVO 1987; MD, FRCP; Physician to the Queen, 1974–89 (Physician to HM Royal Household, 1970–74), and Head of HM Medical Household, 1982–89; Physician: King Edward VII Hospital for Officers, 1968–89; King Edward VII Hospital, Midhurst, 1969–89; Hon. Physician to: St George's Hospital, since 1980; Royal Brompton Hospital (formerly Brompton Hospital), since 1986; *b* 11 March 1924; *s* of late Raymond Wallis Batten, JP and Gladys (*née* Charles); *m* 1950, Anne Mary Margaret (*d* 2007), *d* of late John Oriel, CBE, MC; one *s* two *d* (and one *d* decd). *Educ:* Mill Hill School; St Bartholomew's Medical School. MB, BS 1946 London Univ.; MRCP 1950; MD London 1951; FRCP 1964. Junior appts, St George's Hosp. and Brompton Hosp., 1946–58. Surgeon Captain, Royal Horse Guards, 1947–49. Physician: St George's Hospital, 1958–79; Brompton Hosp., 1959–86. Dep. Chief Med. Referee, 1958–74, CMO, 1974–95, Confederation Life. Dorothy Temple Cross Research Fellow, Cornell Univ. Medical Coll., New York, 1954–55. Examiner in Medicine, London Univ., 1968; Marc Daniels Lectr, RCP, 1969; Croonian Lectr, RCP, 1983. Member: Board of Governors, Brompton Hosp., 1966–69; St George's Hosp. Medical School Council, 1969; Council, RSocMed, 1970; Royal College of Physicians: Censor, 1977–78; Senior Censor, 1980–81; Vice-Pres., 1980–81. President: Cystic Fibrosis Trust, 1986–2003; British Lung Foundn, 1987–95; Medical Protection Soc., 1988–97. Life Vice-Pres., RNLI, 2000. *Publications:* contributions to medical books and journals. *Recreations:* music, sailing. *Died 7 Oct. 2013.*

BAWDEN, Nina Mary, (Mrs A. S. Kark), CBE 1995; MA; FRSL; JP; novelist; *b* 19 Jan. 1925; *d* of Charles and Ellalaine Ursula May Mabey; *m* 1st, 1946, Henry Walton Bawden; one *s* (and one *s* decd); 2nd, 1954, Austen Steven Kark, CBE (*d* 2002); two step *d* (and one *d* decd). *Educ:* Ilford County High Sch.; Somerville Coll., Oxford (BA; Hon. Fellow, 2001). Asst, Town and Country Planning Assoc., 1946–47. JP Surrey, 1968. Mem., ALCS. Pres., Soc. of Women Writers and Journalists. *Publications: novels:* Who Calls the Tune, 1953; The Odd Flamingo, 1954; Change Here for Babylon, 1955; The Solitary Child, 1956; Devil by the Sea, 1958, 2nd edn 1972 (abridged for children, 1976); Just Like a Lady, 1960; In Honour Bound, 1961; Tortoise by Candlelight, 1963; Under the Skin, 1964; A Little Love, a Little Learning, 1965; A Woman of My Age, 1967; The Grain of Truth, 1969; The Birds on the Trees, 1970; Anna Apparent, 1972; George beneath a Paper Moon, 1974; Afternoon of a Good Woman, 1976 (Yorkshire Post Novel of the Year, 1976); Familiar Passions, 1979; Walking Naked, 1981; The Ice House, 1983; Circles of Deceit, 1987 (televised, 1990); Family Money, 1991 (televised, 1997); A Nice Change, 1997; Ruffian on the Stair, 2001; *for children:* The Secret Passage, 1963; On the Run, 1964; The White Horse Gang, 1966; Squib, 1966; A Handful of Thieves, 1967; The Witch's Daughter, 1968; The Runaway Summer, 1969; Carrie's War, 1975 (Phoenix Award, 1995); The Peppermint Pig, 1975 (Guardian award, 1976); Rebel on a Rock, 1978; The Robbers, 1978; Kept in the Dark, 1982; The Finding, 1985; Princess Alice, 1985; Keeping Henry, 1987; The Outside Child, 1989; Humbug, 1992; The Real Plato Jones, 1993; Granny the Pag, 1995; Off the Road, 1998; *non-fiction:* Dear Austen, 2005; *autobiography:* In My Own Time, 1994. *Recreations:* travelling, reading, politics, friends. *Address:* 22 Noel Road, N1 8HA. *T:* (020) 7226 2839; 19 Kapodistriou, Nauplion 21100, Greece. *Clubs:* Oriental, PEN, Society of Authors. *Died 22 Aug. 2012.*

BAYLEY, Prof. John Oliver, CBE 1999; FBA 1990; Warton Professor of English Literature, and Fellow of St Catherine's College, University of Oxford, 1974–92; *b* Lahore, India, 27 March 1925; *s* of F. J. Bayley; *m* 1st, 1956, Dame Jean Iris Murdoch, DBE, CLit (*d* 1999); 2nd, 2000, Audhild Villers. *Educ:* Eton; New Coll., Oxford. 1st cl. hons English Oxon 1950. Served in Army, 1943–47. Mem., St Antony's and Magdalen Colls, Oxford, 1951–55; Fellow and Tutor in English, New Coll., Oxford, 1955–74. *Publications:* The Romantic Survival: A Study in Poetic Evolution, 1956; The Characters of Love, 1961; Tolstoy and the Novel, 1966; Pushkin: A Comparative Commentary, 1971; The Uses of Division: unity and disharmony in literature, 1976; An Essay on Hardy, 1978; Shakespeare and Tragedy, 1981; The Order of Battle at Trafalgar, 1987; The Short Story: Henry James to Elizabeth Bowen, 1988; Housman's Poems, 1992; Iris: a memoir of Iris Murdoch, 1998; Iris and the Friends: a year of memories, 1999; Widower's House, 2001; Hand Luggage (anthology), 2001; The Power of Delight: a lifetime in literature, 2005; *fiction:* In Another Country, 1954; trilogy: Alice, 1994; The Queer Captain, 1995; George's Lair, 1996; The Red Hat, 1997. *Died 12 Jan. 2015.*

BAYLEY, Peter Charles; Emeritus Professor, University of St Andrews; Emeritus Fellow, University College, Oxford; *b* 25 Jan. 1921; *y s* of late William Charles Abell Bayley and Irene Evelyn Beatrice (*née* Heath); *m* 1951, Patience (marr. diss. 1980), *d* of late Sir George (Norman) Clark and Lady Clark; one *s* two *d*. *Educ:* Crypt Sch., Gloucester; state scholarship, 1939; University Coll., Oxford (Sidgwick Exhibnr; MA 1st Cl. Hons English, 1947). Served RA (anti-tank) and Intell. Corps (India), 1941–46. Jun. Res. Fellow, University Coll., Oxford, 1947; Fellow and Praelector in English, 1949–72 (at various times Keeper of Coll. Buildings, Domestic Bursar, Tutor for Admissions, Librarian; Editor of University Coll. Record, 1949–70); Univ. Lectr in English, 1952–72; Proctor, 1957–58; Founder Master of Collingwood Coll. and Lectr, Dept of English, Univ. of Durham, 1971–78; Berry Prof. and Head of Dept of English, Univ. of St Andrews, 1978–85. Vis. Reader, Birla Inst., Pilani, Rajasthan, India, 1966; Vis. Lectr, Yale Univ., and Robert Bates Vis. Fellow, Jonathan Edwards Coll., 1970; Brown Distinguished Vis. Prof., Univ. of the South, Sewanee, Tenn, 1978; Brown Distinguished Vis. Lectr in British Studies, Vanderbilt Univ., Univ. of the South, Sewanee, etc, 1985. Oxford Univ. Corresp., The Times, 1960–63. Sen. Mem., OUDS, 1958–69; Chairman: Oxford Univ. Theatre Fund, 1959–61; Oxford Playhouse Mgt Cttee, 1961–65; Founder Mem., Cherwell Family Housing Trust, later Cherwell Housing Trust, Oxford, 1967. *Publications:* Edmund Spenser, Prince of Poets, 1971; 'Casebook' on Spenser's The Faerie Queene, 1977; Poems of Milton, 1982; An ABC of Shakespeare, 1985; University College, Oxford: a guide and brief history, 1992; edited: Spenser, The Faerie Queene: Book II, 1965; Book I, 1966; Loves and Deaths: short stories by 19th century novelists, 1972; contributed to: Patterns of Love and Courtesy, 1966; Oxford Bibliographical Guides, 1971; C. S. Lewis at the Breakfast Table, 1979; Encyclopaedia of Oxford, 1988; Literature East and West, 1995; Sir William Jones 1746–94, 1998; Fancy's Images: 'faerie' and romance in Chaucer, Spenser and Shakespeare, in Festschrift for Prof. V. Kostić, Belgrade Univ., 2000; articles in TLS, Rev. of English Studies, Essays in Criticism, Critical Qly. *Recreations:* nature, art. *Died 3 Nov. 2015.*

BAYLY, Sir Christopher (Alan), Kt 2007; LittD; FRHistS; FRSL; FBA 1990; Vere Harmsworth Professor of Imperial and Naval History, 1992–2012, then Emeritus, and Director, Centre of South Asian Studies, 2006–14, Cambridge University; Fellow of St Catharine's College, Cambridge, 1970–2012, then Emeritus (Honorary Fellow, 2014); Professor of History, Queen Mary University of London, since 2014; *b* Tunbridge Wells, 18 May 1945; *s* of Roy Ernest and Elfreda Madeleine Bayly; *m* 1981, Susan Banks Kaufmann. *Educ:* Skinners' School, Tunbridge Wells; Balliol College, Oxford (MA; Hon. Fellow 2014); St Antony's, Oxford (DPhil 1970); LittD Cantab. FRSL 2006. Stanhope Prize, Oxford, 1965. Cambridge University: Dir of Studies in History, St Catharine's Coll., 1970–92 (Tutor, 1977–80); Smuts Reader in Commonwealth Studies, 1981–87; Reader in Modern Indian History, 1988–91; Prof. of Modern Indian Hist., 1991–92. Sen. Scholar, Kluge Center, Library of Congress, Washington, 2006. Directeur d'Etudes associé, CNRS, Ecole des Hautes Etudes, Paris, 1986. Vis. Prof., Univ. of Virginia, Charlottesville, 1975; Humanitas Vis. Prof., Univ. of Oxford, 2013; Vivekananda Vis. Prof., Univ. of Chicago, 2014–15. Trustee, British

Mus., 2008–. MAE. DUniv KCL, 2014. Wolfson Prize for History, Wolfson Foundn, 2005; Royal Asiatic Soc. Medal, 2008. *Publications:* The Local Roots of Indian Politics: Allahabad 1880–1920, 1975; Rulers, Townsmen and Bazaars: North Indian society in the age of British Expansion 1770–1870, 1983, 2nd edn 1988; Indian Society and the Making of the British Empire, 1988; Imperial Meridian: the British Empire and the world 1780–1830, 1989; (ed) The Raj: India and the British 1600–1947, 1990; Empire and Information: intelligence gathering and social communication in India 1780–1870, 1996; Origins of Nationality in South Asia, 1998; The Birth of the Modern World: global connections and comparisons 1780–1914, 2003; (with Tim Harper) Forgotten Armies: the fall of British Asia 1941–1945, 2004; (with Tim Harper) Forgotten Wars: the end of Britain's Asian Empire, 2007; Recovering Liberties: Indian thought in the age of liberalism and empire, 2011; contribs to jls. *Recreation:* travelling. *Club:* Reform. *Died 19 April 2015.*

BEACHAM, Prof. Arthur, OBE 1961; MA, PhD; Deputy Vice-Chancellor, Murdoch University, Western Australia, 1976–79 (Acting Vice-Chancellor, 1977–78); *b* 27 July 1913; *s* of William Walter and Maud Elizabeth Beacham; *m* 1938, Margaret Doreen Moseley (*d* 1979); one *s* one *d*. *Educ:* Pontywaun Grammar Sch.; University Coll. of Wales (BA 1935); Univ. of Liverpool (MA 1937); PhD Belfast 1941. Jevons Res. Student, Univ. of Liverpool, 1935–36; Leon Res. Fellow, Univ. of London, 1942–43; Lectr in Economics, Queen's Univ. of Belfast, 1938–45; Sen. Lectr, University Coll. of Wales, 1945–47; Prof. of Indust. Relations, University Coll., Cardiff, 1947–51; Prof. of Economics, University Coll. of Wales, Aberystwyth, 1951–63; Vice-Chancellor, Univ. of Otago, Dunedin, New Zealand, 1964–66; Gonner Prof. of Applied Econs, Liverpool Univ., 1966–75. Chairman: Mid-Wales Industrial Develt Assoc., 1957–63; Post Office Arbitration Tribunal, 1972–73; Member: Advisory Council for Education (Wales), 1949–52; Transp. Consultative Cttee for Wales, 1948–63 (Chm. 1961–63); Central Transp. Consultative Cttee, 1961–63; Economics Cttee of DSIR, 1961–63; North West Economic Planning Council, 1966–74; Merseyside Passenger Transport Authority, 1969–71; Council, Royal Economic Soc., 1970–74. Chm., Cttees on Care of Intellectually Handicapped, Australia, 1982–85; Dir, Superannuation Scheme for Aust. Univs, 1982–83. Hon. LLD Otago, 1969; Hon. DUniv Murdoch, 1982. *Publications:* Economics of Industrial Organisation, 1948, 5th edn 1970; Industries in Welsh Country Towns, 1950; articles in Econ. Jl, Quarterly Jl of Economics, Oxford Econ. Papers, etc. *Recreations:* golf, gardening. *Address:* 10 Mannersley Street, Carindale, Qld 4152, Australia. *T:* (7) 33986630. *Clubs:* Dunedin (Dunedin, NZ); Cricketers' (Qld). *Died 4 June 2012.*

BEALES, Peter Leslie, MBE 2005; Chairman and Managing Director, Peter Beales Roses, since 1967; *b* 22 July 1936; *s* of E. M. Howes; *m* 1961, Joan Elizabeth Allington (*d* 2012); one *s* one *d*. *Educ:* Aldborough School, Norfolk; Norwich City Tech. Coll. FIHort. Apprenticed E. B. LeGrice Roses (1st apprentice, Horticultural Apprentice Scheme), 1952–57; Nat. Service, RA, 1957–59; Manager, Rose Dept, Hillings Nurseries, Chobham, 1959–66; founded Peter Beales Roses, 1967. Lecturer, UK and overseas, 1985–. Pres., Royal Nat. Rose Soc., 2003–05. Chm., Attleborough Chamber of Commerce, 1988–89. Chm., Norfolk and Norwich Horticultural Soc., 1998–2001 (Pres., 1997–98); President: Norfolk Br., Gardening with Disabilities, 1999–; Attleborough Horticl Soc., 2000–; Patron, E Anglia in Bloom, 2010–. Hon. Life Mem., Bermuda Rose Soc., 1987; Life Mem., N Ireland Rose Soc., 1985. Freeman, City of London; Liveryman, Gardeners' Co. Lester E. Harrell Award for significant contrib. to heritage roses, USA, 1988; DHM, Royal Nat. Rose Soc., 1997; VMH 2003; Queen Mother's Internat. Rose Award, Royal Nat. Rose Soc., 2006; Gold Medal, World Fedn of Rose Societies, 2006; Lifetime Achievement Award, Garden Media Guild, 2009. *Publications:* Georgian and Regency Roses, 1981; Early Victorian Roses, 1981; Late Victorian Roses, 1981; Edwardian Roses, 1981; Classic Roses, 1985; Twentieth-Century Roses, 1988; Roses, 1992; Visions of Roses, 1996; New Classic Roses, 1997; A Passion for Roses, 2004; Rose Petals and Muddy Footprints (autobiog.), 2008. *Recreations:* photography, rose breeding, travelling, sport, book collecting. *Address:* Peter Beales Roses, London Road, Attleborough, Norfolk NR17 1AY. *T:* (01953) 454707. *Died 26 Jan. 2013.*

BEALEY, Prof. Frank William; Professor of Politics, University of Aberdeen, 1964–90, then Emeritus; *b* Bilston, Staffs, 31 Aug. 1922; *er s* of Ernest Bealey and Nora (*née* Hampton), both of Netherton, Dudley; *m* 1960, Sheila Hurst; one *s* two *d*. *Educ:* Hill Street Elem. Sch.; King Edward VI Grammar Sch., Stourbridge; London Sch. of Economics (BSc Econ 1948); DSc Econ London, 1990. Able Seaman in RN, 1941–46. Finnish Govt Scholar, 1948–49; Research Asst for Passfield Trust, 1950–51; Extra-Mural Lectr, University of Manchester (Burnley Area), 1951–52; Lectr, later Sen. Lectr, University of Keele, 1952–64. Vis. Fellow, Yale, 1980. Treas., Soc. for Study of Labour Hist., 1960–63. Organiser, Parly All-Party Gp, Social Sci. and Policy, 1984–89. Trustee, Jan Hus Educnl Foundn, 1981–2003; Co-ordinator of Jt European Project 0276 (Political Sci. in Czechoslovakia), 1991–93. FRHistS 1974. *Publications:* (with Henry Pelling) Labour and Politics, 1958, 2nd edn 1982; (with J. Blondel and W. P. McCann) Constituency Politics, 1965; The Social and Political Thought of the British Labour Party, 1970; The Post Office Engineering Union, 1976; (with John Sewel) The Politics of Independence, 1981; Democracy in the Contemporary State, 1988; (jtly) Elements in Political Science, 1999; The Blackwell Dictionary of Political Science, 1999; Power in Business and the State, 2001; articles in academic jls. *Recreations:* reading poetry, eating and drinking, watching football and cricket. *Address:* 11 Viewforth Terrace, Edinburgh EH10 4LH. *T:* (0131) 229 8313. *Clubs:* Economicals Association Football, Economicals Cricket. *Died 18 Jan. 2013.*

BEARD, Allan Geoffrey, CB 1979; CBE 1994; Under Secretary, Department of Health and Social Security, 1968–79 (Ministry of Social Security 1966–68); *b* 18 Oct. 1919; *s* of late Major Henry Thomas Beard and Florence Mercy Beard; *m* 1945, Helen McDonagh (*d* 2012); one *d*. *Educ:* Ormskirk Grammar Sch. Clerical Officer, Air Min., 1936; Exec. Off., Higher Exec. Off., Asst Principal, Assistance Board, 1938–47; Army Service, 1940–46 (Capt., RE); Principal, Nat. Assistance Board, 1950; Asst Sec., 1962. Life Vice-Pres., Motability, 2000– (Governor, 1981–99, Hon. Treasurer, 1985–98). *Publications:* Motability: the road to freedom, 1998. *Recreation:* reading the classics. *Address:* Collins Farm, Abson, Wick, Bristol BS30 5TT. *T:* (0117) 937 2920. *Died 5 Jan. 2015.*

BEARD, Prof. Richard William, MD 1971; FRCOG 1972; Professor and Head of Department of Obstetrics and Gynaecology, St Mary's Hospital Medical School, 1972–96, then Emeritus Professor of Obstetrics and Gynaecology, Imperial College School of Medicine; *b* 4 May 1931; *s* of late William and Irene Beard; *m* 1st, 1957, Jane; two *s*; 2nd, 1979, Irène Victoire Marie de Marotte de Montigny; one *s*, and one step *d*. *Educ:* Westminster Sch.; Christ's Coll., Cambridge (MA, MB BChir); St Bartholomew's Hosp. Obstetrician and Gynaecologist, RAF Changi, Singapore, 1957–60; Chelsea Hosp. for Women, 1961–62; UCH, 1962–63; Senior Lecturer/Hon. Consultant: Queen Charlotte's and Chelsea Hosps, 1964–68; King's Coll. Hosp., 1968–72. Dir, Pelvic Pain Clinic, Northwick Park Hosp., 1996–2000. Advr to Social Services Select Cttee, H of C (2nd Report on Perinatal and Neonatal Mortality), 1978–80; Civilian Consultant in Obstetrics and Gynaecology to RAF, 1983–2001; Consultant Advr in Obsts and Gynaecol. to DoH (formerly DHSS), 1985–91. Pres., Eur. Bd and Coll. of Obsts and Gynaecol., 1996–99. Trustee, Sheffield Inst. Foundn for Motor Neurone Disease, 2007–. Mem., Acad. Royale de Médecine de Belgique, 1983. Gov., Downe House Sch., Newbury, 1991–96. *Publications:* Fetal Physiology and Medicine, 1976, 2nd edn 1983; contribs to learned jls. *Recreations:* tennis, sailing, perinatal medicine. *Address:* 64 Elgin Crescent, W11 2JJ. *T:* (020) 7727 3129; Lough Ine House, Ballyisland, Skibbereen, Co. Cork, Eire. *T:* (28) 21934. *Club:* Garrick. *Died 13 Jan. 2012.*

BEASLEY, Michael Charles, IPFA, FCA, FCCA; County Treasurer, Royal County of Berkshire, 1970–88; *b* Hereford City, 20 July 1924; *y s* of late William Isaac Beasley and Mary Gladys (*née* Williams), Ipswich, Suffolk; *m* 1955, Jean Anita Mary, *o d* of late Reginald John Shedrick Webber and Margaret Dorothy (*née* Rees), Penarth, S

Glamorgan; one *s.* *Educ:* Northgate Grammar Sch., Ipswich; BScEcon London. Treasurer's Dept, East Suffolk County Council, 1940–48; served Royal Navy, 1943–46; Treasurer's Dept, Staffordshire CC, 1948–51; Educn Accountant, Glamorgan CC, 1951–54; Asst County Treasurer, Nottinghamshire CC, 1954–61; Dep. County Treasurer, Royal County of Berkshire, 1961–70, Acting Chief Exec., 1986. Examiner, CIPFA, 1963–66; Financial Adviser, Assoc. of County Councils and former County Councils Assoc., 1971–87; Hon. Treasurer, Soc. of County Treasurers, 1984–88 (Hon. Sec., 1972–80, Vice-Pres., 1980–81, Pres., 1981–82); member of various central and local govt cttees. Member Council: Local Authorities Mutual Investment Trust, 1974–75; RIPA, 1976–82. *Publications:* (ed) Charging for Local Authority Services, 1984; contribs to jls on local govt finance and computers. *Recreations:* cultivating indolence, pottering and pondering, encouraging anti-theism. *Address:* 39 Imperial Court, Reading Road, Wokingham RG41 1AB. *T:* (0118) 977 5493. *Died 2 Sept. 2012.*

BEATTIE, (George) Anthony; academic, consultant and executive coach; UK Permanent Representative to the UN Food and Agriculture Agencies in Rome, 1997–2004, with personal rank of Ambassador, 2002–04; *b* 17 April 1944; *s* of James Ellison Beattie and Christine Beattie; *m* 1973, Janet Frances Dring; one *s.* *Educ:* Stationers' Company's Sch., London; Trinity Coll., Cambridge (MA). Economic Planning Div., Office of the President, Malawi, 1966–69; Overseas Development Administration: Economic Planning Staff, 1969–78; Admin. Group, 1978; Dir, Tropical Develt and Res. Inst., 1986; Dir, Overseas Develt Natural Resources Inst., 1987–90; Chief Exec., Natural Resources Inst., 1990–96; seconded to Efficiency and Effectiveness Gp, OPS, Cabinet Office, 1996–97; Internat. Div., Dept for Internat. Develt, 1997; Minister (UN Agencies and Aid Affairs), Rome, 1997 (on secondment). Vis. Prof., Univ. of Geneva, 2005–; Visiting Fellow: Henley Business Sch., 2006–; Ashridge Business Sch., 2008–. *Recreations:* music, books (especially history), editing the parish magazine, pottering in the country, dog-walking. *Address:* Middle Standen, Benenden, Cranbrook, Kent TN17 4LA. *Died 31 March 2014.*

BEAUMONT, Capt. Hon. Sir (Edward) Nicholas (Canning), KCVO 1994 (CVO 1986; LVO 1976); DL; Vice Lord-Lieutenant of Berkshire, 1989–94; *b* 14 Dec. 1929; 3rd *s* of 2nd Viscount Allendale, KG, CB, CBE, MC and Violet (*d* 1979), *d* of Sir Charles Seely, 2nd Bt; *m* 1953, Jane Caroline (*d* 2007), *d* of Alexander Lewis Paget Falconer Wallace, of Candacraig, Strathdon, Aberdeenshire; two *s.* *Educ:* Eton. Joined Life Guards, 1948; Captain 1956; retired 1960. Assistant to Clerk of the Course, Ascot, 1964; Clerk of the Course and Sec. to Ascot Authy, 1969–94. Pres., Berks SJAB, 1988–94. DL Berks 1982; DL Northumberland, 1996. KStJ 1994. *Address:* Low Shield House, Sparty Lea, Allendale, Northumberland NE47 9UD. *T:* (01434) 685037. *Died 22 June 2011.*

BEAUMONT, Sir George Howland Francis, 12th Bt *cr* 1661; late Lieutenant 60th Rifles; *b* 24 Sept. 1924; *s* of Sir George Arthur Hamilton Beaumont, 11th Bt and Renée Muriel (*d* 1987), 2nd *d* of late Maj.-Gen. Sir Edward Northey, GCMG, CB; *S* father, 1933; *m* 1949, Barbara Singleton (marr. annulled, 1951); *m* 1963, Henrietta Anne (marr. diss. 1986), *d* of late Dr A. Waymouth and Mrs J. Rodwell, Riverside Cottage, Donnington, Berks; twin *d.* *Educ:* Stowe Sch. *Address:* Stretton House, Stretton-on-Fosse, near Moreton-in-Marsh, Glos GL56 9SB. *T:* (01608) 662845. *Club:* Lansdowne. *Died 23 March 2011 (ext).*

BEAUMONT, Hon. Sir Nicholas; *see* Beaumont, Hon. Sir E. N. C.

BECKE, Mrs Shirley Cameron, OBE 1974; QPM 1972; Vice-Chairman, 1976–83 and Regional Administrator, London Region, 1974–79, Women's Royal Voluntary Service; *b* 29 April 1917; *er d* of late George L. Jennings, AMIGasE and Marion Jennings; *m* 1954, Rev. Justice Becke, MBE, TD, FCA (*d* 1990); no *c.* *Educ:* privately; Ealing Co. GS. Trained in Gas Engineering, 1935–40. Joined Metropolitan Police as Constable, 1941; served in various ranks; Woman Commander, 1969–74. OStJ 1975. *Recreations:* reading, bridge. *Address:* 4 North Close, St Martin's Square, Chichester PO19 1NU. *T:* (01243) 784295. *Died 25 Oct. 2011.*

BECKER, Prof. Gary Stanley, PhD; University Professor, Departments of Economics and Sociology, Chicago Booth School of Business, University of Chicago, since 1983; *b* 2 Dec. 1930; *s* of Louis William Becker and Anna (*née* Siskind); *m* 1st, 1954, Doria Slote (*d* 1969); two *d*; 2nd, 1979, Guity Nashat; two step *s.* *Educ:* Princeton Univ. (AB *summa cum laude* 1951); Univ. of Chicago (AM 1953; PhD 1955). Asst Prof., Univ. of Chicago, 1954–57; Columbia University: Asst and Associate Prof of Econs, 1957–60; Prof. of Econs, 1960–68; Arthur Lehman Prof. of Econs, 1968–69; University of Chicago: Ford Foundn Vis. Prof. of Econs, 1969–70; Prof., 1970–83, Chm., 1984–85, Dept of Econs. Member: Domestic Adv. Bd, Hoover Instn, 1973–91 (Sen. Fellow, 1990–); Acad. Adv. Bd, Amer. Enterprise Inst. for Public Policy Res., 1987–91; Associate Mem., Inst. Fiscal and Monetary Policy, Min. of Finance, Japan, 1988–; Res. Associate, Econs Res. Center, Nat. Opinion Res. Center, 1980–; Affiliate, Lexecon Corp., 1990–2002; Dir, UNext.com, 1999–2003. Columnist, Business Week, 1985–2004. Member: American Economic Association: Vice-Pres., 1974; Pres., 1987; Distinguished Fellow, 1988; Mont Pelerin Society, 1971–: Exec. Bd, 1985–96; Vice-Pres., 1989–90; Pres., 1990–92; Editl Bd, Amer. Econ. Rev., 1968–71; Amer. Statistical Assoc. (Fellow 1965); Econometric Soc. Member: Nat. Acad. Scis, 1975–; Internat. Union for Scientific Study of Population, 1982–; Amer. Philosophical Soc., 1986–; Founding Mem., Nat. Acad. Educn (Vice-Pres., 1965–67). Fellow: Amer. Acad. Arts and Scis, 1972; Nat. Assoc. of Business Economists, 1993; Pontifical Acad. of Sci., 1997. Hon. degrees: PhD: Hebrew Univ., Jerusalem, 1985; Palermo, 1993; LLD: Knox Coll., Ill, 1985; Dr of Arts, Illinois, 1988; DSc: SUNY, 1990; Rochester, 1995; DHL: Princeton, 1991; Columbia, 1993; Hofstra, 1997; DBA: Miami, 1995; Aix-Marseilles, 1999; DEconSc Warsaw Sch. of Econs, 1995; Dr: Prague Univ. of Econs, 1995; Athens, 2002; DLaws Harvard, 2003. John Bates Clark Medal, Amer. Econ. Assoc., 1967; Frank E. Seidman Dist. Award in Pol Econ., 1985; Merit Award, NIH, 1986; John R. Commons Award, Omicron Delta Epsilon, 1987; Nobel Prize for Economics, 1992; US Nat. Medal of Sci., 2000; Phoenix Prize, Univ. of Chicago, 2001; Amer. Acad. of Achievement, 2001; Heartland Prize, Chicago Tribune, 2002; Nat. Inst. of Child Health and Human Develt Hall of Honor, 2003; Hayek Award, Frederic A. von Hayek-Gesellschaft Awards, Germany, 2003; Von Neumann Lecture Award, Rajk Coll., Corvinus Univ., Budapest, 2004; Arrow Award, Internat. Health Econs Assoc., 2005; Provost's Teaching Award, Univ. of Chicago, 2006. Medal of the Italian Presidency, 2004; Presidential Medal of Freedom (USA), 2007; Bradley Prize, Lynde and Harry Bradley Foundn, 2008. *Publications:* The Economics of Discrimination, 1957, 2nd edn 1971; Human Capital, 1964, 3rd edn 1993 (trans. Japanese 1975, Spanish 1984, Chinese 1987, Romanian 1997); Human Capital and the Personal Distribution of Income: an analytical approach, 1967; Economic Theory, 1971 (trans. Japanese 1976); (ed jtly) Essays in the Economics of Crime and Punishment, 1974; (with G. Ghez) The Allocation of Time and Goods Over the Life Cycle, 1975; The Economic Approach to Human Behaviour, 1976 (trans. German 1982, Polish 1990, Chinese 1993, Romanian 1994, Italian 1998); A Treatise on the Family, 1981, expanded edn 1991 (trans. Spanish 1987, Chinese 1988); Accounting for Tastes, 1996; (with Guity Nashat) The Economics of Life, 1996 (trans. Chinese 1997, Czech 1997, German 1998, Japanese 1998, Spanish 2002); (with Kevin M. Murphy) Social Economics, 2000; (with Richard Posner) Uncommon Sense: economic insights from marriage to terrorism, 2009; The Challenge of Immigration, 2011; contrib. chaps in numerous books and articles in jls incl. Jl Pol Econ., Qly Jl Econs, Amer. Econ. Rev., Jl Law and Econs, Jl Labor Econs, Business Econs, etc. *Address:* Department of Economics, University of Chicago, 1126 East 59th Street, Chicago, IL 60637, USA. *T:* (773) 7028168. *Died 3 May 2014.*

BECKETT, Bruce Probart, FRIBA, FRIAS, FRTPI, FCIOB; Chartered Architect, Town and Country Planner and Building Consultant in private practice, 1984–97; *b* 7

June 1924; *s* of J. D. L. Beckett and Florence Theresa (*née* Probart); *m* 1957, Jean McDonald (*d* 2009); two *s* three *d* (incl. twin *s* and *d*). *Educ:* Rondebosch Boys' High Sch., Cape Town; Univ. of Cape Town (BArch with distinction, 1950); University Coll. London (Diploma in Town Planning, 1963). Active Service SA Navy, 1943; Midshipman, 1943; Sub-Lieut, 1944; seconded RN, 1944; Lieut, 1946. ARIBA 1950, FRIBA 1968; FRIAS 1968. Mem. Inst. S African Architects, 1950; FRTPI (AMTPI 1966); FCIOB 1979. Private practice in S Africa, 1952–59, London, 1960. Sen. Architect, War Office, 1961; Superintending Grade Archt, Directorate-Gen. of Res. and Development, 1963–67; Chief Architect, 1967–84 and Dir of Bldg, 1978–84, Scottish Office, retd. Partner, Hutchison Locke & Monk, 1984–87. Dep. Leader, Timber Trade Mission to Canada, 1964. A Vice-Pres., RIBA, 1972–73, 1975–76, 1976–77; Hon. Librarian, 1976–78. Sec. of State for Scotland's nominee on ARCUK, 1970–85, RIBA nominee, 1985–97; Member Council: EAA, 1970–78; RIAS, 1971–78, 1984–87; RIBA, 1972–78; Member: Sec. of State for Environment's Construction and Housing Res. Adv. Council, 1968–79; Building Res. Estabt Adv. Cttees in England and Scotland, 1970–84; York Adv. Cttee for continuing educn for building professions, 1975–80. Assessor, to Scottish Cttee of Design Council, 1974–84; Civic Trust Adjudicator, 1985–87. *Publications:* papers on industrialised building, contract procedure, etc, in various jls; HMSO publications on Scottish housing, educational and health buildings. *Recreations:* sailing, walking. *Address:* 20 Thamespoint, Fairways, Teddington, Middx TW11 9PP. *T:* (020) 8943 8843. *Clubs:* Arts; New (Edinburgh); Kelvin (Kelvin Grove, Cape Town). *Died 8 Feb. 2012.*

BECKETT, Sir Terence (Norman), KBE 1987 (CBE 1974); Kt 1978; DL; Managing Director and Chief Executive, 1974–80 and Chairman, 1976–80, Ford Motor Co. Ltd; Director General, Confederation of British Industry, 1980–87 (Member, Council, 1976–80); *b* 13 Dec. 1923; *s* of late Horace Norman Beckett, MBE and Clarice Lillian (*née* Allsopp); *m* 1950, Sylvia Gladys Asprey (*d* 2012); one *d*. *Educ:* Wolverhampton and S Staffs Tech. Coll. (Engrg Cadetship Diploma); London Sch. of Econs (BScEcon, Hon. Fellow, 1994). FIMechE, CEng, FIMI, FREng. Captain REME, British Army (UK, India, Malaya), 1945–48; RARO, 1949–62. Company Trainee, Ford Motor Co. Ltd, 1950; Asst in office of Dep. Chm. and Man. Dir, 1951; Man., Styling, Briggs Motor Bodies Ltd (Ford subsid.), 1954; Admin Man., Engrg, Briggs, 1955; Manager, Product Staff, 1955; Gen. Man., Product Planning Staff, 1961 (responsible for Cortina, Transit Van, 'D' series truck); Manager, Marketing Staff, 1963; Dir, Car Div., 1964; Exec. Dir, Ford Motor Co. Ltd, 1966 and Dir of Sales, 1968; Vice-Pres., European and Overseas Sales Ops, Ford of Europe Inc., 1969–74; Chm., Ford Motor Credit Co. Ltd, 1976–80; Director: ICI, 1976–80; Automotive Finance Ltd, 1974–77. Dep. Chm., CEGB, 1990 (Dir, 1987–90). Advr to Jt Cttee of MMB and Dairy Trade Fedn, 1987–94. Member: NEDC, 1980–87; Engineering Industries Council, 1975–80; BIM Council, 1976–77; Top Salaries Review Body, 1987–92; Grand Council, Motor and Cycle Trades Benevolent Fund (BEN), 1976–80; SMMT Council and Exec. Cttee, 1974–80; Council, Automobile Div., IMechE, 1979–80; Vice Pres. and Hon. Fellow, Inst. of the Motor Industry, 1974–80; Vice-Pres., Conference on Schs, Sci. and Technol., 1979–80; Chm., Governing Body, London Business Sch., 1979–86; Mem. Court, Cranfield Inst. of Technology, 1977–82; Governor, NIESR, 1978–; Governor and Mem. Court, LSE, 1978–99; Pro-Chancellor, Univ. of Essex, 1989–98 (Mem. Court, 1985–; Chm. Council, 1989–95). Mem. Court of Assts, Worshipful Co. of Engineers, 1983–85. DL Essex, 1991. Pres., IVCA, 1987–91. Patron: MSC Award Scheme for Disabled People, 1979–80; AIESEC, 1985. Lectures: Stamp, London Univ., 1982; Pfizer, Kent at Canterbury Univ., 1983. CCMI; FRSA 1984. Hon. Fellow: Sidney Sussex Coll., Cambridge, 1981; London Business Sch., 1988; Hon. DSc: Cranfield, 1977; Heriot-Watt, 1981; Hon. DSc (Econ.) London, 1982; Hon. DTech: Brunel, 1991; Wolverhampton, 1995; DU Essex, 1995; Hon. DLitt Anglia Poly., 1998. Hambro Businessman of the Year, 1978; BIM Gold Medal, 1980. *Recreations:* travel, music. *Address:* c/o Barclays Bank plc, 74 High Street, Ingatestone, Essex CM4 9BW. *Died 2 May 2013.*

BEDDARD, His Honour Nicholas Elliot; a Circuit Judge, 1986–2003; *b* 26 April 1934; *s* of Terence Elliot Beddard and Ursula Mary Hamilton Howard; *m* 1964, Gillian Elisabeth Vaughan Bevan, 2nd *d* of Llewellyn and Molly Bevan; two *s* one *d*. *Educ:* Eton; Univ. of Essex (BA Eng. Lit. 2008). National Service, 1952–54; commissioned, Royal Sussex Regt, 1953; TA (Royal Sussex Regt), 1955–64. United Africa Co., 1955–58; Asst Public Policy Executive, RAC, 1958–68; called to the Bar, Inner Temple, 1967; a Recorder, 1986. *Recreations:* choral singing, ski-ing, golf. *Address:* The Old School, Sudbourne, Woodbridge, Suffolk IP12 2BE. *T:* (01394) 450468. *Clubs:* Lansdowne; Aldeburgh Golf. *Died 12 Jan. 2011.*

BEDFORD, David, FRAM, FTCL; Composer in Association, English Sinfonia, 1993–2005 (Youth Music Director, 1986–93); *b* 4 Aug. 1937; *s* of late Leslie Herbert Bedford and Lesley Florence Keitley Duff; *m* 1st, 1958, Maureen Parsonage; two *d*; 2nd, 1969, Susan Pilgrim; two *d*; 3rd, 1994, Allison Powell; one *s* two *d*. *Educ:* Lancing College; Royal Acad. of Music (ARAM; FRAM 1997); Trinity Coll. London (LTCL; FTCL 1998). Guy's Hosp. porter, 1956; teacher, Whitefield Sch., Hendon, 1965; teacher, 1968–80, and composer-in-residence, 1969–81, Queen's Coll., London; Assoc. Vis. Composer, Gordonstoun, 1983–88; Imogen Holst Composer in Residence, Dartington Coll. of Arts, 1996–97. Mem. Exec. Cttee, SPNM, 1982–88; Pres., British Music Information Centre, 1988–89; Chm., Assoc. of Professional Composers, 1991–93; Chairman: PRS, 2002–04 (Dep. Chm. (writer), 1999–2001); PRS Foundn, 2000–02. Patron, Barnet Schs Music Assoc., 1987. Numerous compositions, many commissioned by major London orchestras and BBC; numerous recordings. *Recreations:* tennis, table tennis, cricket, astronomy, ancient history, philosophy, horror films. *Address:* 12 Oakwood Road, Bristol BS9 4NR. *T:* (0117) 962 4202. *E:* dvbmus@aol.com. *Died 1 Oct. 2011.*

BEDINGFELD, Sir Edmund George Felix P.; *see* Paston-Bedingfeld.

BEECHAM, Sir John Stratford Roland, 4th Bt *cr* 1914; *S* father, 1982, but his name does not appear on the Official Roll of the Baronetage. *Educ:* Winchester; Queen's Coll., Oxford. *Heir:* *b* Robert Adrian Beecham [*b* 6 Jan. 1942; *m* 1969, Daphne Mattinson; one *s* one *d*]. *Died 5 Jan. 2011.*

BEEDHAM, Brian James, CBE 1989; Associate Editor, The Economist, 1989–2002; *b* 12 Jan. 1928; *s* of James Victor Beedham and Nina Beedham (*née* Zambra); *m* 1960, (Ruth) Barbara Zollikofer. *Educ:* Leeds Grammar Sch.; Queen's Coll., Oxford. RA, 1950–52. Asst Editor, Yorkshire Post, 1952–55; The Economist, 1955–2002: Washington correspondent, 1958–61; Foreign Editor, 1964–89. Commonwealth Fellowship, 1956–57. Fellow, Royal Geographical Society. *Recreations:* music, Kipling, Wodehouse, cats. *Address:* Coombe Hill Manor, Flat 301, 190–196 Coombe Lane West, Kingston-upon-Thames KT2 7EQ. *Club:* Travellers. *Died 11 May 2015.*

BEESTON, Richard Nicholas; Foreign Editor, The Times, since 2008; *b* London, 18 Feb. 1963; *s* of William Richard Charles Beeston and Moyra Alice Beeston (*née* Salmon); *m* 1989, Natasha Fairweather; one *s* one *d*. *Educ:* Westminster Sch.; Nat. Council for Trng of Journalists. Reporter, Financial Mail, Johannesburg, 1983–84; freelance corresp., Beirut, 1984–86; The Times: foreign reporter, 1986–91; Jerusalem corresp., 1991–94; Moscow corresp., 1994–98; Foreign News Ed., 1998–2000; Diplomatic Ed., 2000–07. *Recreations:* fishing, poker. *Address:* c/o The Times, 3 Thomas More Square, E98 1XY. *T:* (020) 7782 5234, *Fax:* (020) 7782 5140. *E:* richard.beeston@thetimes.co.uk. *Club:* Frontline. *Died 19 May 2013.*

BEETHAM, Marshal of the Royal Air Force Sir Michael (James), GCB 1978 (KCB 1976); CBE 1967; DFC 1944; AFC 1960; DL; Chief of the Air Staff, 1977–82; Air ADC to the Queen, 1977–82; *b* 17 May 1923; *s* of Major G. C. Beetham, MC; *m* 1st, 1945, June Anne Southorn (marr. diss. 1956); 2nd, 1956, Patricia Elizabeth Lane; one *s* one *d*. *Educ:* St Marylebone Grammar School. Joined RAF, 1941; pilot trng, 1941–42; commnd 1942; Bomber Comd: 50, 57 and 35 Sqdns, 1943–46; HQ Staff, 1947–49; 82 (Recce) Sqdn, E Africa, 1949–51; psa 1952; Air Min. (Directorate Operational Requirements), 1953–56; CO 214 (Valiant) Sqdn Marham, 1958–60; Gp Captain Ops, HQ Bomber Comd, 1962–64; CO RAF

Khormaksar, Aden, 1964–66; idc 1967; Dir Ops (RAF), MoD, 1968–70; Comdt, RAF Staff Coll., 1970–72; ACOS (Plans and Policy), SHAPE, 1972–75; Dep. C-in-C, Strike Command, 1975–76; C-in-C RAF Germany, and Comdr, 2nd Tactical Allied Air Force, 1976–77. Hon. Air Cdre, 2620 (Co. of Norfolk) Sqdn, RAuxAF Regt, 1983–2001; Pres., Bomber Comd Assoc., 1986–. Chm., GEC Avionics Ltd, 1986–90 (Dir, 1984–91); Dir, Brixton Estate PLC, 1983–93. Chm. Trustees, 1983–99, Pres. Soc. of Friends, 1999–, RAF Museum; Pres., RAF Historical Soc., 1993–. Governor: Cheltenham Coll., 1983–89; Wymondham Coll., 1990–98. FRSA 1979. DL Norfolk, 1989. Hon. Liveryman, Hon. Co. of Air Pilots (formerly GAPAN), 1983. Polish Order of Merit, 1998. *Recreations:* golf, tennis. *Clubs:* Royal Air Force (Pres., 1992–2002, Vice Patron, 2003–); Royal West Norfolk Golf. *Died 24 Oct. 2015.*

BELICH, Sir James, Kt 1990; Mayor of Wellington, New Zealand, 1986–92; *b* 25 July 1927; *s* of Yakov Belich and Maria (*née* Batistich); *m* 1951, Valerie Frances Anzulovich; one *s* two *d*. *Educ:* Otahuhu Coll.; Auckland Univ.; Victoria Univ. of Wellington (BA Hons Econs); IBM Teaching Fellow, Massey Univ. Consular/Internat. Trade, Auckland, Sydney, Wellington, 1948–56; Economist, Market Res. Manager, Dir, Chief Exec. and Chm., Research, Marketing, Public Relns, Advertising, 1956–86. Member: Wellington Harbour Bd; Wellington Regional Council. Director: Air NZ, 1987–89; Lambton Harbour Overview Ltd (Chm.); Wellington Internat. Airport. Pres. and Exec., various orgns incl.: Pres., UNA, Wellington and NZ; Founder Pres., UNICEF, NZ. FInstD; Fellow, Inst. of Advertising. *Recreations:* reading, walking, bowls. *Address:* 4 Indus Street, Khandallah, Wellington 4, New Zealand. *T:* (4) 4793339. *Clubs:* Wellington, Wellington Central Rotary (Wellington). *Died 13 Sept. 2015.*

BELL, His Honour Alistair Watson; a Circuit Judge, 1978–97; *b* Edinburgh, 31 March 1930; *s* of Albert William Bell and Alice Elizabeth Watson; *m* 1957, Patricia Margaret Seed; one *s* two *d*. *Educ:* Lanark Grammar Sch.; George Watson's Coll.; Univs of Edinburgh (MA) and Oxford (MA, BCL). 2nd Lieut RASC, 1955. Called to Bar, Middle Temple, 1955; Harmsworth Scholar, 1956; entered practice, Northern Circuit, 1957; a Recorder of the Crown Court, 1972–78. Hon. Recorder, Carlisle, 1990–98. Contested (L) Chorley, 1964 and Westmorland, 1966. *Recreations:* hill walking, with or without golf clubs, political history and economics. *Address:* c/o Courts of Justice, Carlisle. *Died 2 Aug. 2012.*

BELL, David John, CB 1998; FRICS; Commissioner of Valuation for Northern Ireland, 1988–98; Chief Executive, Valuation and Lands Agency, 1993–98; *b* 17 March 1938; *s* of James Bell and Elizabeth Bell; *m* 1962, Agnes Mona Eileen; two *d*. *Educ:* Regent House GS. FRICS 1981. Sen. Valuation Asst, Valuer I, Valuation Office, 1963–70; Department of the Environment, Northern Ireland: Divl Estates Surveyor (Belfast), 1975–80; Superintending Estates Surveyor, 1980–82; Chief Lands Officer, Lands Service, 1982–84; Asst Comr, 1984–87, Dep. Comr, 1987–88, Valuation and Lands Office, Dept of Finance and Personnel, NI. *Recreations:* reading, gardening, church work, golf. *Address:* 1 Rockmount, Dundonald, Belfast BT16 2BY. *T:* (028) 9048 4241. *Died 22 May 2012.*

BELL, Guy Davies; Director, BAA plc, 1988–89; Managing Director, Gatwick Airport Ltd, 1985–89; *b* 19 May 1933; *s* of Percival and Margaret Bell; *m* 1958, Angela Mary Joan Bickersteth; two *s* one *d* (and one *s* decd). *Educ:* Sedbergh Sch. British Transport Docks Bd, 1963–68; British Airports Authority, 1968–86, Engrg Dir, 1977–85; BAA, 1986–89. *Recreations:* gardening, open air, music. *Club:* Royal Automobile. *Died 10 May 2012.*

BELL, Leslie Gladstone, CEng, FRINA; RCNC; Director of Naval Ship Production, Ministry of Defence, 1977–79; *b* 20 Oct. 1919; *s* of late John Gladstone Bell and Jessie Gray Bell (*née* Quigley); *m* 1963, Adriana Agatha Jacoba van den Berg; one *s* one *d*. *Educ:* Portsmouth Dockyard Tech. Coll.; Royal Naval Engineering Coll., Keyham; Royal Naval Coll., Greenwich. Staff Constructor Comdr, Home Fleet, 1953–56; Aircraft Carrier Design, 1956–59; Chief Constructor, Weapon Development, 1959–67; IDC, 1968; Asst Dir, Submarine Design, 1969–72; Dir, Submarine Project Team, 1972–77. *Recreations:* gardening, golf, music. *Address:* Haytor, Old Midford Road, Bath, Avon BA2 7DH. *T:* (01225) 833357. *Club:* Bath Golf. *Died 4 April 2012.*

BELL, Sir Stuart, Kt 2004; MP (Lab) Middlesbrough, since 1983; Second Church Estates Commissioner, 1997–2010; barrister; *b* High Spen, Co. Durham, 16 May 1938; *s* of Ernest and Margaret Rose Bell; *m* 1st, 1960, Margaret (marr. diss.), *d* of Mary Bruce; one *s* one *d*; 2nd, 1980, Margaret, *d* of Edward and Mary Allan; one *s*. *Educ:* Hookergate Grammar Sch. Formerly colliery clerk, newspaper reporter, typist and novelist. Called to the Bar, Gray's Inn, 1970. Conseil Juridique and Internat. Lawyer, Paris, 1970–77. Member: Newcastle City Council, 1980–83 (Mem., Finance, Health and Environment, Arts and Recreation Cttees; Chm., Youth and Community Cttee; Vice-Chm., Educn Cttee); Educn Cttee, AMA; Council of Local Educn Authorities; Newcastle AHA (T), 1980–83. Contested (Lab) Hexham, 1979. PPS to Dep. Leader of Opposition, Rt Hon. Roy Hattersley, 1983–84; Opposition front bench spokesman: on NI, 1984–87; on trade and industry, 1992–97. Chm., Finance and Services Select Cttee, 2000–10; Mem., H of C Commn, 2000–10; Mem., Speaker's Cttee, Ind. Parly Standards Authy, 2009–10. Founder Mem. and Vice Chm., British-Irish Inter Parly Body, 1990–93; Sec., Franco-British Parly Relns Gp, 2010– (Chm., 2005–08); Chm., Labour First Past the Post Gp, 2010–. Freeman, City of London, 2003. Member: Fabian Soc.; Soc. of Lab. Lawyers; GMB. Chevalier de la Légion d'Honneur (France), 2006. *Publications:* How to Abolish the Lords (Fabian Tract), 1981; Valuation for United States Customs Purposes, 1981; When Salem Came to the Boro: the true story of the Cleveland child abuse crisis, 1989; Annotation of The Children Act, 1989; Raising the Standard: the case for first past the post, 1998; Where Jenkins Went Wrong, 1999; Pathway to the Euro, 2002; An Ever Closer Union—The Forward March, 2007; What Future the European Left?, 2011; Why Labour Must Say NO to AV, 2011; *autobiography:* Tony Really Loves Me, 2000; Lara's Theme, 2004; Softly in the Dusk, 2004; *fiction:* Paris 69, 1973; Days That Used To Be, 1975; Binkie's Revolution, 2002; The Honoured Society, 2002; The Ice Cream Man and Other Stories, 2007; The Ice Cream Man: an afterthought, 2011. *Recreation:* writing. *Address:* House of Commons, SW1A 0AA. *Died 13 Oct. 2012.*

BELL, William Edwin, CBE 1980; Deputy Chairman, Enterprise Oil plc, 1991–97 (Chairman, 1984–91); *b* 4 Aug. 1926; *s* of late Cuthbert Edwin Bell and Winifred Mary Bell (*née* Simpson); *m* 1952, Angela Josephine Vaughan; two *s* two *d*. *Educ:* Birmingham University (BSc Civil Eng.); Royal School of Mines, Imperial College. Joined Royal Dutch Shell Group, 1948; tech. and managerial appts, Venezuela, USA, Kuwait, Indonesia; Shell International Petroleum Co. (Middle East Coordination), 1965–73; Gen. Man., Shell UK Exploration and Production and Dir, Shell UK, 1973; Man. Dir, Shell UK, 1976–79; Middle East Regional Coordinator and Dir, Shell International Petroleum Co., 1980–84, retired; non-exec. Dir, Costain Group, 1982–92. Pres., UK Offshore Operators Assoc., 1975–76. *Publications:* contribs to internat. tech. jls, papers on offshore oil industry develts. *Recreations:* golf, sailing. *Address:* Fordcombe Manor, near Tunbridge Wells, Kent TN3 0SE. *Club:* Nevill Golf. *Died 18 Oct. 2015.*

BELL, William Lewis, CMG 1970; MBE (mil.) 1945; Information Officer, University of Oxford, 1977–84; *b* 31 Dec. 1919; *s* of Frederick Robinson Bell and Kate Harper Bell (*née* Lewis); *m* 1943, Margaret Giles (*d* 2003); one *s* one *d*. *Educ:* Hymers Coll., Hull; Oriel Coll., Oxford. Served The Gloucestershire Regt (Major), 1940–46. Colonial Administrative Service, Uganda, 1946–63: Dep. Sec. to the Treasury, 1956–58; Perm. Sec., Min. of Social Services, 1958–63; Fellow, Economic Develt Inst., World Bank, 1958. Chm., Uganda National Parks, 1962; Pres., Uganda Sports Union, 1961–62. Director, Cox & Danks Ltd (Metal Industries Group), 1963–64. Sec. to the Governors, Westfield Coll., Univ. of London, 1964–65; Founding Head of British Develt Div. in the Caribbean, ODA, 1966–72; UK Dir, Caribbean Develt Bank, 1970–72; Founding Dir-Gen., Technical Educn and

Training Org. for Overseas Countries, 1972–77. *Recreations:* cricket, Caribbeana. *Address:* c/o Owl House, Poundgate, E Sussex TN22 4DE. *Clubs:* MCC; Vincent's (Oxford). *Died 12 Sept. 2013.*

BELLAMY, Rear-Adm. Albert John, CB 1968; OBE 1956; CMath, FIMA; first Deputy Director, Polytechnic of the South Bank, 1970–80; *b* Upton-on-Severn, 26 Feb. 1915; *s* of late A. E. Bellamy and Mrs A. E. Bellamy; *m* 1942, Dorothy Joan Lawson (decd); one *s* one *d*. *Educ:* Hanley Castle Grammar Sch.; Downing Coll., Cambridge (Buchanan Exhibitioner; 1st cl. hons Pts I and II, Math. tripos, MA 1939). FIMA 1960; CMath 1992. Asst master, Berkhamsted Sch., 1936–39. Joined RN, 1939, as Instructor Lieut; Fleet Instr and Meteorological Officer, America and WI, 1948–50 (HMS Glasgow); Instr Comdr, 1950; Headmaster, RN Schs, Malta, 1951–54; HMS Ark Royal, 1955–56; Dean of the College, RN Engineering Coll., Manadon, Plymouth, 1956–60; Instr Capt., 1958; staff of Dir, Naval Educn Service, 1960–63; Dir of Studies, RN Electrical, Weapons and Radio Engineering Sch., HMS Collingwood, 1963–65; Instr Rear-Adm., 1965; Dir, Naval Educn Service and Hd of Instructor Branch, MoD, 1965–70. Mem., Home Office Extended Interview non-Service Mems Panel, 1980–87. *Recreations:* gardening, show jumping, crosswords, parish council work, keeping old age at bay (not very successfully) by being involved. *Address:* The Cottage, Kington Magna, Gillingham, Dorset SP8 5EG. *T:* (01747) 838668. *Died 3 July 2012.*

BELLANY, Prof. Ian; Professor of Politics, University of Lancaster, 1979–2006, then Emeritus; *b* 21 Feb. 1941; *s* of James Bellany and Jemima Bellany (*née* Emlay); *m* 1965, Wendy Ivey, *d* of Glyndwr and Bronwen Thomas; one *s* one *d*. *Educ:* Preston Lodge, Prestonpans; Firth Park Grammar Sch., Sheffield; Balliol Coll., Oxford (State Scholar, MA, DPhil). Foreign and Commonwealth Office, 1965–68; Res. Fellow in Internat. Relations, ANU, 1968–70; University of Lancaster: Lectr, later Sen. Lectr in Politics, 1970–79; Dir, Centre for Study of Arms Control and Internat. Security, 1979–90; Head, Dept of Politics, 1985–86. Leverhulme Res. Fellow, 1982 and 2003; NATO Instnl Fellow, 1989–90. Examr in Internat. Relations, LSE, 1985–88 and 1999–2002, in Internat. Studies, Birmingham Univ., 1990–93, in Internat. Relations, Aberdeen Univ., 1995–99. Founding Editor, Arms Control: Journal of Arms Control and Disarmament, 1980–91. Trench Gascoigne Essay Prize, RUSI, 2002. *Publications:* Australia in the Nuclear Age, 1972; A Basis for Arms Control, 1991; Reviewing Britain's Defence, 1994; The Environment in World Politics, 1997; Curbing the Spread of Nuclear Weapons, 2006; edited jointly: Antiballistic Missile Defences in the 1980s, 1983; The Verification of Arms Control Agreements, 1983; The Nuclear Non-Proliferation Treaty, 1985; New Conventional Weapons and Western Defence, 1987; Terrorism and Weapons of Mass Destruction, 2007; contribs to jls. *Recreations:* broadcasting, coarse carpentry, computing. *Address:* 11 Spruce Avenue, Lancaster LA1 5LB. *T:* (01524) 68157. *Died 17 July 2011.*

BELLANY, John, CBE 1994; RA 1991 (ARA 1986); artist (painter); *b* Scotland, 18 June 1942; *s* of Richard Weatherhead Bellany and Agnes Craig Bellany; *m* 1st, 1964, Helen Margaret Percy (marr. diss. 1974); two *s* one *d*; 2nd, 1980, Juliet Gray (*née* Lister) (*d* 1985); 3rd, 1986 (for 2nd time), Helen Margaret Bellany. *Educ:* Cockenzie Public Sch., Scotland; Preston Lodge Sch., Scotland; Edinburgh Coll. of Art (DA); Royal Coll. of Art (MA Fine Art; ARCA). Lectr in Fine Art in various art colls and univs in Gt Britain, incl. Winchester Coll. of Art, Goldsmiths' Coll., London Univ., RCA; Artist in Residence, Victorian Coll. of the Arts, Melb., 1982. *One man exhibitions:* Nat. Portrait Gall., 1986; Fischer Fine Art, London, 1988–89, 1991; Scottish Nat. Gall. of Modern Art, 1989; Raab Gall., Berlin and Ruth Siegel Gall., NY, 1990; Fitzwilliam Mus., Cambridge, 1991; Kelvingrove Art Gall. and Mus., Glasgow, 1992; Beaux Arts Gall., London, 1997, 1998, 2000, 2001, 2006, 2010; Galeria K, Mexico City, 1997; Elaine Baker Gall., Florida, 1999; Soloman Gall., London, 2000; many others in Britain, USA, Australia, Europe; *retrospective exhibitions:* Scottish Nat. Gall. of Modern Art, Edin., and Serpentine Gall., London, 1986; Kunsthalle, Hamburg, 1988; Scottish Nat. Gall., 2012. Works represented in major museums and private collections throughout the world, incl. Tate Gall., V&A Mus., Mus. of Modern Art, NY, Metropolitan Mus., NY, Nat. Gall. of NSW, Melbourne. Sen. Fellow, RCA, 1999. Hon. Fellow Commoner, Trinity Hall, Cambridge, 1988. Hon. RSA 1987. Dr (*hc*) Edinburgh, 1996; Hon. DLitt Heriot-Watt, 1998. *Relevant publications:* John Bellany, by Victor Musgrave and Philip Rawson, 1982; John Bellany, a Retrospective, by Douglas Hall, 1986; John Bellany (Portraits) (The Maxi Hudson Collection), by Robin Gibson, 1986; John Bellany, by Richard Cork, 1986; John Bellany, Retrospective, by Prof. D. Werner Hofmann and Keith Hartley, 1988; John Bellany, by John McEwen, 1994. *Recreation:* climbing to and fro across Hadrian's Wall. *Address:* 2 Windmill Drive, SW4 9DE. *T:* (020) 8675 7909, *Fax:* (01799) 542062; 19 Great Stuart Street, Edinburgh EH3 7TP. *T:* (0131) 226 5183; Beaux Arts Gallery, 22 Cork Street, W1S 3NA. *T:* (020) 7437 5799; Berkeley Square Gallery, 23A Bruton Street, W1X 7DA. *T:* (020) 7493 7939. *Clubs:* Chelsea Arts; Scottish Arts (Edinburgh). *Died 28 Aug. 2013.*

BELLOTTI, David Frank; Member (Lib Dem), Bath and North East Somerset Council, 2003–15 (Chairman, 2008–09; Cabinet Member for Community Resources, 2011–15); *b* 13 Aug. 1943; *s* of Patrick Frank Bellotti and Elsie (*née* Venner); *m* 1st, 1965, Sheila (*née* Jones) (marr. diss.); one *s* one *d*; 2nd, 1973, Jennifer (*née* Compson) (marr. diss.); one *s*; 3rd, 1996, Josephine (*née* Brown); one *s* one *d*. *Educ:* Exeter Sch.; YMCA National Coll. (Diploma in Youth Service); Brighton Polytechnic (Diploma in Counselling); Univ. of Sussex (MA). Civil Service, 1961–64; Young Men's Christian Association: student, Nat. Coll., 1964–65; Sec., St Helens, Llanelli, Norwich and Lewes, 1965–76; Regional Sec., South-East, 1977–81; Dir, Hove, 1981–90. Dep. Chm. and Chief Exec., Brighton and Hove Albion FC, 1993–97. Mem. (L, then Lib Dem), E Sussex CC, 1981–97 (Chm., 1993–94). Chm., Sussex Police Authy, 1993–95. Mem., Cttee of the Regions, EU, 1994–98. MP (Lib Dem) Eastbourne, Oct. 1990–1992; contested same seat, 1992. Contested (Lib Dem), European Parliamentary elections: E Sussex and Kent S, 1994; SE Reg., 1999. *Recreations:* Association Football, politics. *Address:* 12 Kipling Avenue, Bath BA2 4RB. *Club:* National Liberal. *Died 10 June 2015.*

BELTRAM, Geoffrey; Under-Secretary, Department of Health and Social Security, 1973–81; *b* 7 April 1921; *s* of George and Beatrice Dorothy Beltram; *m* 1945, Audrey Mary (*née* Harkett); one *s* one *d*. *Educ:* Dame Alice Owen's School. Tax Officer, Inland Revenue, 1938; served in RAF, 1941–46; Exec. Officer and Higher Exec. Officer, Min. of Town and Country Planning, 1947–51; Asst Principal, Nat. Assistance Bd, 1951–55; Principal 1955–63; Asst Sec. 1963–73 (NAB 1963–66, Min. of Social Security 1966–68, DHSS 1968–73). Vis. Res. Associate, LSE, 1981–84. Vis. social worker, Ind. Living Fund, 1988–93. *Publications:* Testing the Safety Net: a study of the Supplementary Benefit scheme, 1984. *Recreations:* literature, listening to music, opera, ballet, theatre, walking. *Died 30 Oct. 2011.*

BENACERRAF, Prof. Baruj; Fabyan Professor of Comparative Pathology, Harvard Medical School, 1970–91, Professor Emeritus, since 1991; President: Dana-Farber, Inc., 1991–96; Dana-Farber Cancer Institute, Boston, 1980–91; *b* 29 Oct. 1920; *m* 1943, Annette Dreyfus (*d* 2011); one *d*. *Educ:* Lycée Janson, Paris (BèsL 1940); Columbia Univ. (BS 1942); Medical Coll. of Virginia (MD 1945). Served US Army, 1946–48. Intern, Queens Gen. Hosp., NY, 1945–46; Res. Fellow, Dept of Micro-biol., Coll. of Physicians and Surgeons, Columbia Univ., 1948–49; Chargé de Recherches, CNRS, Hôpital Broussais, Paris, 1950–56; New York University School of Medicine: Asst Prof. of Pathol., 1956–58; Assoc. Prof. of Pathol., 1958–60; Prof. of Pathol., 1960–68; Chief, Lab. of Immunol., Nat. Inst. of Allergy and Infectious Diseases, NIH, Bethesda, 1968–70. Scientific Advr, WHO; Chm., Scientific Adv. Cttee, Centre d'Immunologie de Marseille, CNRS-INSERM; Member: Immunology A Study Sect., NIH, 1965–69; Adv. Council, National Inst. of Allergy and Infectious Disease, 1985–88; Scientific Adv. Cttee, Basel Inst. of Immunology, 1985–89; Member Scientific

Advisory Board: Trudeau Foundn, 1970–76; Mass Gen. Hosp., 1971–74. President: Amer. Assoc. of Immunologists, 1973–74; Fedn of Amer. Socs for Exptl Biol., 1974–75; Internat. Union of Immunol Socs, 1980–83. Fellow, Amer. Acad. of Arts and Scis, 1972. Correspondent Emérite, Institut National de la Santé et de la Recherche Scientifique, 1988. Member: Nat. Acad. of Scis, 1973; Nat. Inst. of Med., 1981; Amer. Assoc. of Pathologists and Bacteriologists; Amer. Soc. for Exptl Pathol.; British Assoc. for Immunol.; French Soc. of Biol Chem.; Harvey Soc. Lectures: R. E. Dyer, NIH, 1969; Harvey, 1971, 1972; J. S. Blumenthal, Univ. of Minnesota, 1980. Hon. MD Geneva, 1980; Hon. DSc: Virginia Commonwealth Univ., 1981; NY Univ., 1981; Yeshiva Univ., 1982; Univ. Aix-Marseille, 1982; Columbia Univ., 1985; Adelphi Univ., 1988; Weizmann Inst., 1989; Harvard Univ., 1992; Univ. Bordeaux, 1993; Univ. Vienna, 1995. Rabbi Shai Shacknai Lectr and Prize, Hebrew Univ. of Jerusalem, 1974; T. Duckett Jones Meml Award, Helen Hay Whitney Foundn, 1976; Waterford Biomedical Science Award, 1980; (jtly) Nobel Prize for Physiology or Medicine, 1980; Rous-Whipple Award, Amer. Assoc. of Pathologists, 1985; Nat. Medal of Science, US, 1990. *Publications:* (with D. Katz) Immunological Tolerance, 1974; Immunogenetics and Immunodeficiency, 1975; (with D. Katz) The Role of Products of the Histocompatibility Gene Complex in Immune Responses, 1976; Textbook of Immunology, 1979; 650 articles in professional journals. *Recreations:* music, art collecting. *Address:* 111 Perkins Street, Boston, MA 02130–4313, USA. *Died 2 Aug. 2011.*

BENAUD, Richard, OBE 1961; international sports consultant, journalist and media representative; television commentator, Nine Network, Australia, since 1977; *b* 6 Oct. 1930; *s* of Louis Richard Benaud and Irene Benaud; *m* 1967, Daphne Elizabeth Surfleet; two *s* by previous marriage. *Educ:* Parramatta High Sch. Captain, Australian Cricket Team, 28 Tests, played for Australia 63 Tests, Tours to England, 1953, 1956, 1961; first cricketer to achieve Test double, 2000 runs, 200 wickets, 1963. TV commentator: BBC, 1960–99; Channel 4, 1999–2005. *Publications:* Way of Cricket, 1960; Tale of Two Tests, 1962; Spin Me a Spinner, 1963; The New Champions, 1965; Willow Patterns, 1972; Benaud on Reflection, 1984; The Appeal of Cricket, 1995; Anything but… An Autobiography, 1998; My Spin on Cricket, 2005; Over but Not Out, 2010. *Recreation:* golf. *Address:* (office) 19/178 Beach Street, Coogee, NSW 2034, Australia. *T:* (2) 96641124. *Died 10 April 2015.*

BENN, Rt Hon. Anthony Neil Wedgwood, (Rt Hon. Tony); PC 1964; *b* 3 April 1925; *er* surv. *s* of 1st Viscount Stansgate, DSO, DFC, PC, former Labour MP and Cabinet Minister (*d* 1960); unsuccessfully attempted to renounce his right of succession, 1955 and 1960, won a bye-election in May 1961 only to be prevented from taking seat; instigated Act to make disclaimer possible, and disclaimed title for life, 1963; *m* 1949, Caroline Middleton De Camp, MA (*d* 2000); three *s* one *d*. *Educ:* New Coll., Oxford (Hon. Fellow, 2005). Served: RAFVR, 1943–45; RNVR, 1945–46. Joined Labour Party, 1943; Mem., NEC, 1959–60, 1962–93 (Chm., 1971–72); candidate for leadership of Labour Party, 1976, 1988, and for dep. leadership, 1971, 1981. MP (Lab): Bristol SE, Nov. 1950–1960 and Aug. 1963–1983; Chesterfield, 1984–2001; Postmaster-Gen., 1964–66; Minister of Technology, 1966–70, assumed responsibility for Min. of Aviation, 1967 and Min. of Power, 1969; opposition spokesman on Trade and Industry, 1970–74; Sec. of State for Industry, 1974–75; Sec. of State for Energy, 1975–79. Pres., EEC Council of Energy Ministers, 1977. Pres., Campaign Gp, subseq. Socialist Campaign Gp of Lab. MPs, 1987–2001. Contested (Lab) Bristol East, 1983. Vis. Prof. of Govt, LSE, 2001–03. Pres., Stop the War Coalition, 2004–. Freedom: of H of C, 2001; of City of Bristol, 2003. Awarded 11 hon. doctorates from univs in UK and USA. *Publications:* The Privy Council as a Second Chamber, 1957; The Regeneration of Britain, 1964; The New Politics, 1970; Speeches, 1974; Arguments for Socialism, 1979; Arguments for Democracy, 1981; (ed) Writings on the Wall: a radical and socialist anthology 1215–1984, 1984; Out of the Wilderness, Diaries 1963–1967, 1987; Fighting Back: speaking out for Socialism in the Eighties, 1988; Office Without Power, Diaries 1968–72, 1988; Against the Tide, Diaries 1973–76, 1989; Conflicts of Interest, Diaries 1977–80, 1990; A Future for Socialism, 1991; The End of an Era, Diaries 1980–1990, 1992; (jtly) Common Sense, 1993; Years of Hope: Diaries, Letters and Papers 1940–1962, 1994; The Benn Diaries 1940–1990, 1995; Free at Last!: Diaries 1990–2001, 2002; Free Radical, 2003; Dare to Be a Daniel, 2004; More Time for Politics: diaries 2001–2007, 2007; Letters to my Grandchildren, 2009; A Blaze of Autumn Sunshine: the last diaries, 2013; numerous pamphlets, videos and audio tapes. *Address:* Flat 11, Chartwell House, 12 Ladbroke Terrace, W11 3PQ. *E:* tony.benn@btinternet.com. *Died 14 March 2014.*

BENN, Edward, CMG 1981; Minister (Defence Research and Development, later Defence Equipment), British Embassy, Washington, 1978–82; *b* 8 May 1922; *s* of John Henry Benn and Alice (*née* Taylor); *m* 1947, Joan Taylor; one *d*. *Educ:* High Storrs Grammar Sch., Sheffield; Sheffield Univ. (BEng; 1st Cl. Hons Civil Engrg; Mappin Medal, 1943). Operational Research with Army, 1943–48; India and Burma, 1944–46 (Major); entered War Office, 1948; tank research and war studies, Army Op. Res. Gp, 1948–52; Consultant, US Ops Res. Office, Washington, DC, 1952–53; Supt Special Studies, and later Dep. Dir, Army Op. Res., 1954–60 (created and directed AORG War Game in which sen. army comdrs were able to study how the develt of tactical nuclear weapons, and their possible future use, might affect ops in the event of a land battle in NW Europe); Advr to Dir of Combat Develt, War Office, 1960–61; Asst Sci. Adviser to SACEUR, Paris, 1962–65; Dep. Chief Sci. Adviser, Home Office, 1966–68; Dir, Defence Policy, MoD, 1968–75; Under Sec. and Dep. Chief Scientist (RAF), MoD, 1975–78. *Recreation:* golf. *Address:* 7 Hiatt Road, Minchinhampton, Glos GL6 9DB. *T:* (01453) 883005. *Club:* Minchinhampton Golf. *Died 7 June 2013.*

BENN, Rt Hon. Tony; *see* Benn, Rt Hon. A. N. W.

BENNETT, Dudley Paul; His Honour Judge Dudley Bennett; a Circuit Judge, since 1993; *b* 4 Aug. 1948; *s* of late Patrick James Bennett and of Mary Bennett (*née* Edmondson); *m* 1986, Patricia Ann Martin; two *d*. *Educ:* Bradfield Coll.; LSE (LLB). Called to the Bar, Inner Temple, 1972; Recorder of the Crown Court, 1988–93. *Recreations:* travel, gardening, Afghan Hounds. *Address:* The Crown Court, Canal Street, Nottingham NG1 7EJ. *Club:* United Services (Nottingham). *Died 25 Dec. 2012.*

BENNETT, His Honour Harry Graham; QC 1968; a Circuit Judge, 1972–91; Designated Circuit Judge, Leeds, 1988–91; *b* 19 Sept. 1921; *s* of Ernest and Alice Mary Bennett, Cleckheaton, Yorks; *m* 1987, Elizabeth, *widow* of Judge Allister Lonsdale. *Educ:* Whitcliffe Mount Grammar Sch., Cleckheaton; King's Coll., London. Royal Artillery, 1943–47. Called to Bar, Gray's Inn, 1948. Recorder: Doncaster, 1966–68; York, 1968–71 (Hon. Recorder, 1972–93); Crown Court, 1972; Dep. Chm., ER of Yorks QS, 1964–71. Chm., Agricl Land Tribunal (N Area), 1967–72; Chm., Cttee of Inquiry into Police Interrogation Procedures in NI, 1978–79. *Died 13 Feb. 2011.*

BENNETT, Ralph Featherstone; Chairman: London Transport International, 1976–80; London Transport Executive, 1978–80; *b* 3 Dec. 1923; *o s* of late Mr and Mrs Ralph J. P. Bennett, Plymouth, Devon; *m* 1948, Delia Marie, *o d* of late Mr and Mrs J. E. Baxter, Franklyns, Plymouth; two *s* two *d*. *Educ:* Plympton Grammar Sch.; Plymouth Technical Coll. Articled pupil to City of Plymouth Transport Manager, 1940–43; Techn. Asst, Plymouth City Transp., 1943–54; Michelin Tyre Co., 1954–55; Dep. Gen. Man., City of Plymouth Transp. Dept, 1955–58; Gen. Manager: Gt Yarmouth Transp. Dept, 1958–60; Bolton Transp. Dept, 1960–65; Manchester City Transp., 1965–68; London Transport Executive (formerly London Transport Board): Mem., 1968–71; Dep. Chm., 1971–78; Chief Exec., 1975–78. Pres., Confedn of Road Passenger Transport, 1977–78; Vice-President: Internat. Union of Public Transport, 1978–81; CIT, 1979–82. CEng; FIMechE; FCILT; FRSA. *Address:* 12 The Beeches, Harrowbeer Lane, Yelverton, Devon PL20 6EF. *T:* (01822) 853269. *Died 10 Nov. 2015.*

BENNETT, Sir Richard Rodney, Kt 1998; CBE 1977; composer; Visiting Professor of Composition, Royal Academy of Music, since 1995; *b* 29 March 1936; *s* of H. Rodney and Joan Esther Bennett. *Educ:* Leighton Park Sch., Reading; Royal Academy of Music. Works performed, 1953–, at many Festivals in Europe, S Africa, USA, Canada, Australia, etc. Writer of music for numerous films including: Indiscreet; The Devil's Disciple; Only Two Can Play; The Wrong Arm of the Law; Heavens Above; Billy Liar; One Way Pendulum; The Nanny; Far from the Madding Crowd; Billion Dollar Brain; Secret Ceremony; The Buttercup Chain; Figures in a Landscape; Nicholas and Alexandra; Lady Caroline Lamb; Voices; Murder on the Orient Express (SFTA award; Academy Award Nomination; Ivor Novello award, PRS); Permission to Kill; Equus (BAFTA Nomination); The Brinks Job; Yanks (BAFTA Nomination); Return of the Soldier; Four Weddings and a Funeral; Swann; also the music for television series: The Christians; L. P. Hartley trilogy; The Ebony Tower; Tender is the Night; The Charmer; Poor Little Rich Girl; The Hiding Place; The Story of Anne Frank; Gormenghast (Ivor Novello award). Commissioned to write 2 full-length operas for Sadler's Wells: The Mines of Sulphur, 1965, A Penny for a Song, 1968; commnd to write opera for Covent Garden: Victory, 1970; other compositions include: Symphony No 1, 1965; Symphony No 2, 1967; (children's opera) All the King's Men, 1969; Guitar Concerto, 1970; Spells (choral work), 1975; Sonnets to Orpheus, 1979; Symphony No 3, 1987; Concerto for Stan Getz, 1990; Concerto for Trumpet, 1993; Partita, 1995; Reflections on a 16th Century Tune, 1999; Rondel (for large jazz ensemble), 1999; On Christmas Day (choral work), 1999; Seven Country Dances (for oboe and strings), 2000; Songs Before Sleep, 2003; Reflections on a Scottish Folk Song, 2004. *Publications include:* chamber music, orchestral music, educational music, song cycles, etc; articles for periodicals, about music. *Recreations:* cinema, modern jazz, painting. *Address:* c/o Novello & Co., 14–15 Berners Street, W1T 3LJ. *Died 24 Dec. 2012.*

BENNETT, Seton John, CBE 2006; PhD; Metrology Adviser, National Physical Laboratory, 2009–12 (Deputy Director, 2002–09); *b* 10 July 1945; *s* of John and Joyce Bennett; *m* 1966, Lesley Downs; two *s*. *Educ:* Norfolk House Primary Sch., Barnet; Queen Elizabeth's Grammar Sch., Barnet; Oriel Coll., Oxford (BA 1967); Imperial Coll., London (PhD 1973). CPhys; FInstP 1982. Res. Scientist, Nat. Physical Lab., 1967–85; Dep. Dir, 1985–90, Chief Exec., 1990–2001, Nat. Weights and Measures Lab. Chairman: WELMEC, 1990–2001; EUROMET, 2004–06; Mem., Internat. Cttee for Weights and Measures, 2002–11. Chm., Keychange Charity, 2008–13. Warden Emeritus, Scientific Instrument Makers' Co., 2013. *Recreation:* reading. *E:* setonb@hotmail.com. *Died 14 Sept. 2015.*

BENNETTS, Rt Rev. Colin James; Bishop of Coventry, 1998–2008; *b* 9 Sept. 1940; *s* of James Thomas Bennetts and Winifred Florence Bennetts (*née* Couldrey); *m* 1965, Veronica Jane Leat; two *s* two *d*. *Educ:* Battersea Grammar Sch.; Jesus Coll., Cambridge (Exhibnr); Ridley Hall, Cambridge. MA (Cantab); MA (Oxon) by incorporation. Assistant Curate: St Stephen, Tonbridge, 1965–69; St Aldates, Oxford, 1969–73; Chaplain to Oxford Pastorate, 1969–73; Chaplain, Jesus Coll., Oxford, 1973–80; Vicar, St Andrew, Oxford, 1980–90; RD of Oxford, 1984–90; Canon Residentiary of Chester Cathedral, 1990–94; Canon Librarian and Diocesan Director of Ordinands, Chester, 1990–94; Area Bishop of Buckingham, 1994–98. Co-Chm., Springboard, 1995–2001; Vice-Chm., Liturgical Commn, 2001–. Chm., Bible Reading Fellowship, 1999–2001 (Vice-Chm., 1994–98). *Recreations:* mediaeval music, woodcutting. *Address:* 23 Brox Road, Ottershaw, Surrey KT16 0HG. *Died 10 July 2013.*

BENNION, Francis Alan Roscoe; barrister and writer; *b* 2 Jan. 1923; *o s* of Thomas Roscoe Bennion, Liverpool; *m* 1st, 1951, Barbara Elisabeth Braendle (separated 1971, marr. diss. 1975); three *d*; 2nd, 1977, Mary Field. *Educ:* John Lyon Sch., Harrow; Balliol Coll., Oxford. Pilot, RAFVR, 1941–46. Gibbs Law Scholar, Oxford Univ., 1948. Called to Bar, Middle Temple, 1951 (Harmsworth Scholar); practised at Bar, 1951–53, 1985–94. Lectr and Tutor in Law, St Edmund Hall, Oxford, 1951–53; Office of Parly Counsel, 1953–65, and 1973–75; Dep. Parly Counsel, 1964; Parly Counsel, 1973–75; seconded to Govt of Pakistan to advise on drafting of new Constitution, 1956; seconded to Govt of Ghana to advise on legislation and drafting Constitution converting the country into a Republic, 1959–61. Sec., RICS, 1965–68; Governor, College of Estate Management, 1965–68. Co-founder and first Chm., Professional Assoc. of Teachers, 1968–72; Founder: Statute Law Soc., 1968 (Chm., 1978–79); Freedom Under Law, 1971; Dicey Trust, 1973; Towards One World, 1979; Statute Law Trust, 1991; founder and first Chm., World of Property Housing Trust (later Sanctuary Housing Assoc.), 1968–72 (Vice-Pres., 1986–); Co-founder, Areopagitica Educnl Trust, 1979. *Publications:* Constitutional Law of Ghana, 1962; Professional Ethics: The Consultant Professions and their Code, 1969; Tangling with the Law, 1970; Consumer Credit Control, 1976–2001; Consumer Credit Act Manual, 1978, 3rd edn 1986; Statute Law, 1980, 3rd edn 1990; Statutory Interpretation, 1984, 5th edn 2008; Victorian Railway Days, 1989; The Sex Code: Morals for Moderns, 1991; Statutes, in Halsbury's Laws of England, 1996; Understanding Common Law Legislation, 2001; The Blight of Blairism, 2002; Poemotions: Bennion undraped (poems), 2002; Sexual Ethics and Criminal Law, 2003; articles and contribs to books on legal and other subjects. *Recreation:* maintaining my website (with webmaster's help). *Address:* 29 Pegasus Road, Oxford OX4 6DS. *T:* (01395) 442265. *E:* fb@fbennion.com. *W:* www.francisbennion.com. *Club:* MCC. *Died 28 Jan. 2015.*

BENSON, Prof. Frank Atkinson, OBE 1988; DL; BEng, MEng (Liverpool); PhD, DEng (Sheffield); FIET, FIEEE; Professor and Head of Department of Electronic and Electrical Engineering, University of Sheffield, 1967–87, then Emeritus; *b* 21 Nov. 1921; *s* of late John and Selina Benson; *m* 1950, Kathleen May Paskell (*d* 2006); two *s*. *Educ:* Ulverston Grammar Sch.; Univ. of Liverpool. Mem. research staff, Admty Signal Estab., Witley, 1943–46; Asst Lectr in Electrical Engrg, University of Liverpool, 1946–49; University of Sheffield: Lectr 1949–59, Sen. Lectr 1959–61, in Electrical Engrg; Reader in Electronics, 1961–67; Pro-Vice Chancellor, 1972–76. DL South Yorks, 1979. *Publications:* Voltage Stabilizers, 1950; Electrical Engineering Problems with Solutions, 1954; Voltage Stabilized Supplies, 1957; Problems in Electronics with Solutions, 1958; Electric Circuit Theory, 1959; Voltage Stabilization, 1965; Electric Circuit Problems with Solutions, 1967; Millimetre and Submillimetre Waves, 1969; Fields, Waves and Transmission Lines, 1991; many papers on microwaves, gas discharges and voltage stabilization in learned jls. *Died 23 Nov. 2014.*

BENTALL, Hugh Henry, MB; FRCS; Professor of Cardiac Surgery, Royal Postgraduate Medical School, University of London, 1965–85, then Professor Emeritus at Imperial College School of Medicine at Hammersmith Hospital; *b* 28 April 1920; *s* of late Henry Bentall and Lilian Alice Greeno; *m* 1944, Jean, *d* of late Hugh Cameron Wilson, MD, FRCS; three *s* one *d*. *Educ:* Seaford Coll., Sussex; Medical Sch. of St Bartholomew's Hospital, London. RNVR, Surg. Lieut, 1945–47. Consultant Thoracic Surgeon, Hammersmith Hosp., 1955–85; Lecturer in Thoracic Surgery, Postgraduate Medical Sch., London, 1959; Reader, 1962–65. Order of Yugoslav Flag with Gold Leaves, 1984. *Publications:* books and papers on surgical subjects. *Recreations:* sailing, antique horology. *Address:* Imperial College School of Medicine at Department of Surgery, Hammersmith Hospital, Ducane Road, W12 0NN. *T:* (020) 8743 2030. *Club:* Royal Naval Sailing Association (Portsmouth). *Died 9 Sept. 2012.*

BENTLEY, His Honour David Ronald; QC 1984; a Circuit Judge, 1988–2005; Designated Civil Judge, South Yorkshire, 1998–2005; *b* 24 Feb. 1942; *s* of Edgar Norman and Hilda Bentley; *m* 1978, Christine Elizabeth Stewart; two *s*. *Educ:* King Edward VII Sch., Sheffield; University Coll. London (LLB (Hons) 1963); LLM and Brigid Cotter Prize, London Univ., 1979; PhD Sheffield, 1994; MA Leeds, 2008. Called to the Bar, Gray's Inn, 1969 (Macaskie Scholar). In practice at the bar, 1969–88; a Recorder,

1985–88. *Publications:* Select Cases from The Twelve Judges' Notebooks, 1997; Criminal Justice in Nineteenth-Century England, 1998; Victorian Men of Law, 2000; The Sheffield Hanged 1750–1864, 2002; Sheffield Murders 1865–1965, 2003; Crimes and Misdemeanours, 2005; Capital Punishment in Northern England 1750–1900, 2008. *Recreations:* legal history, watching Sheffield United.
Died 1 March 2012.

BENTON, Rev. Canon Michael John; Priest-in-charge, Kingsclere, 1996–2003; Chaplain to the Queen, 1998–2008; *b* 3 Nov. 1938; *s* of William James Benton and Violet May Benton (*née* Pearse); *m* 1960, Frances Elizabeth Margaret Joyce Harris; two *s* one *d*. *Educ:* Chichester High Sch. for Boys; University Coll. London (BSc Hons 1960); Fitzwilliam House, Cambridge (CertEd 1961). Asst Biology Master, Alleynes GS, Stevenage, 1961–63; Head of Biology, Perse Sch., Cambridge, 1963–69; Lectr and Sen. Lectr, Biol Scis, King Alfred's Coll., Winchester, 1969–76. Theol study, Salisbury Theol Coll. and St George's Coll., Jerusalem, 1972–74; ordained deacon and priest, 1974; Hon. Curate, Weeke, 1974–76; full time priest in C of E, 1976–2003; Curate, Bursledon, 1976–78; Rector, Over Wallop with Nether Wallop, 1978–83; Rector, St Lawrence and St Maurice with St Swithun, Winchester, 1983–90; Dir of Educn, Dio. of Winchester, 1979–95; Hon. Canon, Winchester Cathedral, 1989–2003, then Canon Emeritus. *Publications:* regular Christian comment column for Hampshire Chronicle, 1988–2002; occasional papers and articles. *Recreations:* reading, science and faith debate (Mem. SOSc), history, bird-watching, growing shrub roses, watching vintage aircraft (Mem. Spitfire Soc.), archaeology. *Address:* South Lodge, Auchterarder, Perthshire PH3 1ER. *Died 15 June 2013.*

BENYON, Sir William (Richard), Kt 1994; DL; landowner, since 1964; Vice Lord-Lieutenant, Berkshire, 1994–2005; *b* 17 Jan. 1930; *e s* of late Vice-Adm. Richard Benyon, CB, CBE (*né* Shelley, name changed to Benyon by deed poll, 1964), and of Mrs Benyon, The Lambdens, Beenham, Berkshire; *m* 1957, Elizabeth Ann Hallifax; two *s* three *d*. *Educ:* Royal Naval Coll., Dartmouth. Royal Navy, 1947–56; Courtaulds Ltd, 1956–64. Mem., Berks CC, 1964–74. MP (C) Buckingham, 1970–83, Milton Keynes, 1983–92. PPS to Minister of Housing and Construction, 1972–74; Conservative Whip, 1974–76. Chairman: Peabody Trust, 1993–98; Ernest Cook Charitable Trust, 1993–2004. JP 1962–78, DL 1970, High Sheriff 1995, Berks. *Address:* Wimbletons Barn, Englefield, Reading, Berkshire RG7 5EH. *T:* (0118) 930 5229. *E:* benyon@englefield.co.uk. *Clubs:* Boodle's, Pratt's, Beefsteak. *Died 2 May 2014.*

BERESFORD-PEIRSE, Sir Henry Grant de la Poer, 6th Bt *cr* 1814; *b* 7 Feb. 1933; *s* of Sir Henry Campbell de la Poer Beresford-Peirse, 5th Bt, CB, and Margaret (*d* 1995), *d* of Frank Morison Seafield Grant, Knockie, Inverness-shire; *S* father, 1972; *m* 1966, Jadranka, *d* of Ivan Njerš, Zagreb, Croatia; two *s*. *Heir:* *s* Henry Njerš de la Poer Beresford-Peirse [*b* 25 March 1969; *m* 2005, Joanna Tamlyn; two *s* one *d*]. *Died 24 Jan. 2013.*

BERG, Adrian, RA 1992; *b* 12 March 1929; *s* of Charles Berg, MD, DPM and Sarah (*née* Sorby). *Educ:* Charterhouse; Gonville and Caius Coll., Cambridge (MA); Trinity Coll., Dublin (HDipEd); St Martin's Sch. of Art (Intermediate Arts & Crafts); Chelsea Sch. of Art (NDD); Royal Coll. of Art (ARCA; Hon. FRCA 1994). Nat. Service, 1947–49. Taught at various art schools, esp. Central Sch. of Art and Design and Camberwell Sch. of Arts and Crafts, 1961–78; Sen. Tutor, RCA, 1987–88. One-man exhibitions include: Arthur Tooth & Sons Ltd, London, 1964, 1967, 1969, 1972 and 1975; Galleria Vaccarino, Florence, 1973; Galerie Burg Diesdonk, Düsseldorf, 1976; Waddington and Tooth Galls, London, 1978; Waddington Galls, Montreal and Toronto and Grace Hokin, Inc., Chicago, 1979; London: Waddington Galls, 1981 and 1983; Serpentine Gall., 1973, 1984 and 1986; Piccadilly Gall., 1985, 1988, 1989, 1991, 1993, 1999 and 2002; Concourse Gall., Barbican Centre, 1993; Friends' Room, RA, 1999, 2009; Walker Art Gall., Liverpool, 1986; Victoria Art Gall., Bath, 1993; Plymouth City Mus. and Art Gall., 1993; Newport Mus. and Art Gall., Gwent, 1993; Mappin Gall., Sheffield, 1993; Hatton Gall., Newcastle, 1994; Royal Botanic Gdn, Edinburgh, 1994; Rye Art Gall., 1994; (contrib.) Art of the Garden, Stourhead, 2004; Richmond Hill Gall., 2008. Lorne Scholarship, 1979–80. Gold Medal, Florence Biennale, 1973; minor and major prizes, John Moores Nat. Exhibns, 1980 and 1982; Major Prize, 3rd Tolly Cobbold, Eastern Arts Nat. Exhibn, 1981; Foundn for Art Award, NT, 1987; First Prize, RWS Open, 2001. *Recreations:* imaginative reading, criticism. *Address:* Royal Academy of Arts, Piccadilly, W1J 0BD. *Died 22 Oct. 2011.*

BERGERSEN, Dr Fraser John, AM 2000; FRS 1981; FAA 1985; Visiting Fellow, Division of Biochemistry and Molecular Biology, School of Life Sciences, 1994–2002, and University Fellow, 1996–98, Australian National University; *b* 26 May 1929; *s* of Victor E. and Arabel H. Bergersen; *m* 1952, Gladys Irene Heather; two *s* one *d*. *Educ:* Univ. of Otago, New Zealand (BSc, MSc (Hons)); Univ. of New Zealand (DSc 1962). Bacteriology Dept, Univ. of Otago, 1952–54; Div. of Plant Industry, CSIRO, Canberra, Aust., 1954–94, Chief Res. Scientist, 1972–94; formerly engaged in scientific research in microbiology, with special reference to symbiotic nitrogen fixation in legume root-nodules. Foreign Sec., Aust. Acad. of Science, 1989–93. David Rivett Medal, CSIRO Officers' Assoc., 1968. *Publications:* Methods for Evaluating Biological Nitrogen Fixation, 1980; Root Nodules of Legumes: structure and functions, 1982; over 160 articles and chapters in scientific journals and books. *Recreations:* music, gardening. *Address:* PO Box 4287, Manuka, ACT 2603, Australia. *Died 3 Oct. 2011.*

BERNARD, Joan Constance, MA, BD; FKC; Principal of Trevelyan College, University of Durham, and Honorary Lecturer in Theology, 1966–79; *b* 6 April 1918; *d* of late Adm. Vivian Henry Gerald Bernard, CB, and Eileen Mary Bernard. *Educ:* Ascham Sch., Sydney, NSW; St Anne's Coll., Oxford Univ. (BA Lit. Hum. 1940, MA 1943); King's Coll., London (BD 1961). War Service, ATS, 1940–46; AA Comd, 1940–44; SO Air Def. Div., SHAEF, 1944–45 (mentioned in despatches 1945); Special Projectile Ops Gp, July–Nov. 1945. Dep. Admin. Officer, NCB, 1946–50; Asst Sec., Educn, Music and Drama, NFWI, 1950–57; full-time student, 1957–61; Warden, Canterbury Hall, Univ. of London, and part-time Lectr, Dept of Theol., KCL, 1962–65; FKC 1976. Mem., Ordination Candidates' Cttee, ACCM, 1972–91; Examining Chaplain to Bishop of Southwark, 1984–94. Mem., Fabric Adv. Cttee, Southwark Cathedral, 1992–97. FRSA 1984. *Recreations:* music (assisted John Tobin in Handel research for many years); mountaineering, photography, travel. *Address:* 89 Rennie Court, Upper Ground, SE1 9NZ.
Died 1 Aug. 2012.

BERRIDGE, (Donald) Roy, CBE 1981; FREng; Chairman, South of Scotland Electricity Board, 1977–82 (Deputy Chairman, 1974–77); *b* 24 March 1922; *s* of Alfred Leonard Berridge and Pattie Annie Elizabeth (*née* Holloway); *m* 1945, Marie (*née* Kinder); one *d*. *Educ:* King's Sch., Peterborough; Leicester Coll. of Art and Technology. FREng (FEng 1979); FIMechE 1962. Taylor, Taylor & Hobson Ltd, Leicester, 1940; James Gordon & Co., 1946; British Electricity Authority, 1948; seconded to AERE, Harwell, 1952; Reactor Design Engr, CEGB, 1962; Chief Generation Design Engr, 1964–70; Dir-Gen., Gen. Develt Constr. Div., CEGB, 1970–72; Dir of Engrg, SSEB, 1972–74. Dir, Howden Gp, 1982–88. Member: N of Scotland Hydro-Electric Bd, 1977–82; Scottish Economic Council, 1977–83; CBI (Scottish Council), 1977–83. *Address:* East Gate, Chapel Square, Deddington, Oxon OX15 0SG. *Died 3 Jan. 2011.*

BERRY, Rt Rev. (Robert Edward) Fraser; Bishop of Kootenay, 1971–89; *b* Ottawa, Ont, 21 Jan. 1926; *s* of Samuel Berry and Claire Hartley; *m* 1951, Margaret Joan Trevorrow Baillie; one *s* one *d*. *Educ:* Sir George Williams Coll., Montreal; McGill Univ., Montreal; Montreal Diocesan Theological Coll. Assistant, Christ Church Cathedral, Victoria, BC, 1953–55; Rector: St Margaret's, Hamilton, Ont, 1955–61; St Mark's, Orangeville, Ont, 1961–63; St Luke's, Winnipeg, Manitoba, 1963–67; St Michael and All Angels, Kelowna, BC, 1967–71. Chaplain:

RCAF Assoc. 883 (Kelowna) Wing, 1988–; Royal Canadian Legion 23 (Kelowna) Br., 1994–; Royal Canadian Mounted Police Okanagan Div., 1995– (Chaplain, Veterans' Assoc., 1989–); (on call), Kelowna Gen. Hosp., 1992–, Asst (on call), St Andrew's, Okanagan Mission, Kelowna, 1992–. Hon. DD Montreal Diocesan Theol Coll., 1973. *Recreations:* reading, boating, angling, swimming, walking, computer communications. *Address:* 13–1101 Cameron Avenue, Kelowna, BC V1Y 8V6, Canada. *T:* (250) 7622923. *Clubs:* Vancouver (Vancouver); Kelowna Yacht. *Died 25 Oct. 2011.*

BERTHOUD, Prof. Jacques Alexandre; Professor of English, Department of English and Related Literature, University of York, 1980–2002, then Emeritus (Head of Department, 1980–97; Deputy Vice-Chancellor, 1987–90); *b* 1 March 1935; *s* of Alexandre L. Berthoud and Madeleine (*née* Bourquin); *m* 1958, Astrid Irene (*née* Titlestad); one *s* two *d*. *Educ:* Univ. of the Witwatersrand, Johannesburg (BA and BA Hons). Lectr, English Dept, Univ. of Natal, Pietermaritzburg, 1960–67; Lectr, subseq. Sen. Lectr, English Dept, Univ. of Southampton, 1967–79. Vis. Fellow Commoner, Trinity College, Cambridge, 1990–91. British Chm., Amnesty Internat., 1978–80. *Publications:* (with Dr C. van Heyningen) Uys Krige, 1966; Joseph Conrad, the Major Phase, 1978; Joseph Conrad: au cœur de l'œuvre, 1992; (ed jtly) 'Twixt Land and Sea, 2007; (ed) books for OUP and Penguin Books; articles in jls. *Recreation:* music. *Address:* 30 New Walk Terrace, Fishergate, York YO10 4BG. *T:* (01904) 629212. *Died 29 Oct. 2011.*

BEST, Sir Richard (Radford), KCVO 1990; CBE 1989 (MBE 1977); HM Diplomatic Service, retired; *b* 28 July 1933; *s* of Charles and Frances Best (*née* Raymond); *m* 1st, 1957, Elizabeth Vera Wait (*d* 1968); two *d*; 2nd, 1969, Mary Hill (*née* Wait); one *s*. *Educ:* Worthing High Sch.; University Coll. London (BA Hons). Home Office, 1957–66; HM Diplomatic Service, 1966–91: CO (formerly CRO), 1966–68; Lusaka, 1969–72; Stockholm, 1972–76; FCO, 1976–79; New Delhi, 1979–83; FCO, 1983–84; Dep. High Comr, Kaduna, 1984–88; Ambassador to Iceland, 1989–91; FCO, 1991. Chm., Friends of Clapham and Patching Churches, 1996–2006. BBC 'Brain of Britain', 1966. Life Mem., Kaduna Br., Nigeria-Britain Assoc. Grand Cross, Order of Icelandic Falcon, 1990. *Recreation:* gardening. *Address:* Holly Howe, The Street, Patching, near Worthing, West Sussex BN13 3XF. *Died 7 March 2014.*

BEST-SHAW, Sir John (Michael Robert), 10th Bt *cr* 1665; *b* 28 Sept. 1924; *s* of Sir John James Kenward Best-Shaw, 9th Bt, Commander RN, and Elizabeth Mary Theodora (*d* 1986), *e d* of Sir Robert Hughes, 12th Bt; *S* father, 1984; *m* 1960, Jane Gordon, *d* of A. G. Guthrie; one *s* one *d* (and two *s* decd). *Educ:* Lancing; Hertford Coll., Oxford (MA); Avery Hill Coll., London (Teachers' Cert.). Captain, Royal West Kent Regt, 1943–47. Royal Fedn of Malaya Police, 1950–58; church work, 1958–71; teaching, 1972–82. *Recreations:* bridge, writing. *Heir: s* Thomas Joshua Best-Shaw [*b* 7 March 1965; *m* 1992, Emily Susan, *d* of Vivian Rubin; two *s*]. *Address:* Belmont, 104 High Street, West Malling, Kent ME19 6NE. *T:* (01732) 843823. *Club:* Commonwealth. *Died 22 April 2014.*

BETHEL, Dr Keva Marie, CMG 1995; Scholar-in-Residence, College of the Bahamas, since 2009 (President, 1995–98, President Emerita, 2005); *b* 18 Aug. 1935; *d* of late Sidney Alexander Eldon and Rowena Beatrice Eldon (*née* Hill); *m* 1962, E. Clement Bethel (*d* 1987); one *s* one *d*. *Educ:* Girton Coll., Cambridge (BA, MA); Univ. of Alberta (PhD 1981). Government High School, Nassau, Bahamas: Asst Mistress, Spanish and French, 1959–66; Head, Mod. Langs Dept, 1966–72; Dep. Headmistress, 1972–75; College of the Bahamas: Chm., Div. of Humanities, 1975–77; Dean, Acad. Affairs, 1977–78; Vice Principal, 1979–81; Actg Principal, Jan.–June 1982; Principal, 1982–95. Hon. LLD Univ. of W Indies, 1998. *Publications:* (contrib.) Handbook of World Education, ed Walter Wickremasinghe, 1991; (contrib.) Educational Reform in the Commonwealth Caribbean, ed Errol Miller, 1999; (contrib.) Bahamas: independence and beyond, ed W K. Jones and D. G. Saunders, 2003. *Recreations:* reading, music. *Address:* PO Box N1232, Nassau, New Providence, Bahamas. *Died 15 Feb. 2011.*

BEVAN, Prof. Peter Gilroy, CBE 1983; MB, ChB; FRCS; Consultant Surgeon, Dudley Road Hospital, Birmingham, 1958–87; Professor of Surgery and Postgraduate Medical Education, University of Birmingham, 1981–87, then Emeritus Professor; *b* 13 Dec. 1922; *s* of Rev. Thomas John Bevan and Norah (*née* Gilroy); *m* 1st, 1949, Patricia Joan (*née* Laurie) (*d* 1985); one *s* one *d*; 2nd, 1990, Beryl Margaret (*née* Perry). *Educ:* King Edward VI High Sch., Birmingham; Univ. of Birmingham Medical Sch. (MB, ChB 1946; ChM 1958). LRCP MRCS 1946, FRCS 1952; Hon. FRCSI 1984; Hon. FBIDST 2002. Served RAMC, BAOR, 1947–49 (Captain). Demonstrator in Anatomy, Univ. of Birmingham, 1949–51; Resident Surgical Officer, Birmingham Children's Hosp., 1954–55; Lectr in Surgery and Sen. Surgical Registrar, Queen Elizabeth Hosp., Birmingham, 1954–58; WHO Vis. Prof. of Surgery to Burma, 1969; Director, Board of Graduate Clinical Studies, Univ. of Birmingham, 1978–87; Birmingham Medical Institute: Postgrad. Tutor, 1987–94; Organiser, GP Surg. Workshops, 1994–2004; Pres., 1994–2003. Royal College of Surgeons: Vice-Pres., 1980–82; Member: Council, 1971–83; Court of Patrons, 1988–; Bd of Hunterian Trustees, 1990–; Dir, Overseas Doctors Training Scheme Cttee, 1986–90. Founder Chm., W Midlands Oncology Assoc., 1974–79; Vice-Pres., Brit. Assoc. of Surgical Oncology, 1975–78; President: Pancreatic Soc. of GB, 1977; British Inst. of Surgical Technologists, 1980–95 (Hon. Fellow, British Inst. of Surgical and Dental Technologists, 1999); Assoc. of Surgeons of GB and Ireland, 1984–85 (Fellow, 1960–; Mem. Council, 1975–85); W Midlands Surgical Soc., 1986; Nat. Assoc. of Theatre Nurses, 1992–94. EEC: UK representative: on Monospecialist Section of Surgery, 1975–84; on Adv. Cttee on Medical Trng, 1980–85. Civil Consultant Advr in Gen. Surgery to RN, 1973–84; Med. Adviser, Midlands Div., Ileostomy Assoc., 1976–87. Chm., Adv. Cttee of Deans, 1986–88. Chairman: Steering Gp on Operating Theatres, Dept of Health, 1988–89; Jt Planning Adv. Cttee, Dept of Health, 1990–95; Medical Mem., Pensions Appeal Tribunals, 1987–89; Mem., Medical Appeals Tribunal, 1989–95. Former Member: Jt Planning Adv. Cttee; Central Manpower Cttee; Jt Consultants Cttee; Council for Postgraduate Med. Educn. Pres., Sands Cox Soc., 2003. Mem. Editl Bd, Health Trends, 1990–97. *Publications:* Reconstructive Procedures in Surgery, 1982; Handbook of General Surgery, 1992; various surgical papers in BMJ, Brit. Jl Surgery, Lancet, Annals of RCS; papers on illnesses of classical composers. *Recreations:* inland waterways, golf, photography, music, gardening. *Address:* 10 Russell Road, Moseley, Birmingham B13 8RD. *T:* (0121) 449 3055. *Clubs:* Royal Navy Medical; Edgbaston Golf (Birmingham). *Died 11 Sept. 2011.*

BEWLEY, Edward de Beauvoir; Judge of the High Court of Hong Kong, 1980–96; Commissioner, Supreme Court of Brunei, since 1996 (with desig. Hon. Mr Justice Bewley); *b* 12 March 1931; *s* of Harold de Beauvoir Bewley and Phyllis Frances Cowdy; *m* 1st, 1956, Sheelagh Alice Brown; one *s*; 2nd, 1968, Mary Gwenefer Jones; three *d*. *Educ:* Shrewsbury School; Trinity College, Dublin (BA, LLB). Called to the Bar, Gray's Inn, 1956. Administrative Officer, Northern Rhodesia, 1956–59; English Bar, 1960–61; Resident Magistrate, Nyasaland, 1961–64; Magistrate, Hong Kong, 1964–76, District Judge, 1976–80. *Recreations:* golf, reading, wine. *Address:* Ysgubor Fawr, Llanfairpwll, Ynys Môn LL61 6PX. *T:* and *Fax:* (01248) 430162. *Clubs:* Hong Kong; Holyhead Golf, Hong Kong Golf. *Died 19 May 2012.*

BEXON, Roger, CBE 1985; Chairman: Laporte plc, 1986–95; Goal Petroleum, 1990–96; Managing Director, British Petroleum Co., 1981–86, and Deputy Chairman, 1983–86; *b* 11 April 1926; *s* of late MacAlister Bexon, CBE, and Nora Hope Bexon (*née* Jenner); *m* 1951, Lois Loughran Walling; one *s* one *d*. *Educ:* Denstone Coll. (schol.); St John's Coll., Oxford (MA); Tulsa Univ. (MS). Geologist and petroleum engineer with Trinidad Petroleum Development Co. Ltd, 1946–57; management positions with British Petroleum Co., E Africa, 1958–59; Libya, 1959–60; Trinidad, 1961–64; London, 1964–66; Manager, North Sea Operations, 1966–68; Gen. Manager, Libya, 1968–70; Regional Coordinator, Middle East, London, 1971–73; Gen. Manager, Exploration and Production, London, 1973–76; Managing Director, BP Exploration Co. Ltd, London, 1976–77; Dir and Sen. Vice Pres., 1977–80, and Dir, 1982–86, Standard Oil Co. of Ohio; Director: BP Canada Inc., 1983–87; BICC, 1985–92; Lazard Bros, 1986–91; Fenner plc, 1986–89; Cameron Iron Works, 1987–89; Astec (BSR) PLC, 1989–95. Mem. Council, British-N American Res. Assoc., 1986–95. *Publications:* general and technical contribs to internat. jls on oil and energy matters. *Recreations:* swimming, reading, crossword puzzles. *Died 4 March 2014.*

BEYNON, Ernest Geoffrey; Joint General Secretary, Assistant Masters and Mistresses Association, 1979–87; *b* 4 Oct. 1926; *s* of late Frank William George and Frances Alice Pretoria Beynon; *m* 1956, Denise Gwendoline Rees; two *s* one *d*. *Educ:* Borden Grammar Sch., Kent; Univ. of Bristol, 1944–47, 1949–50 (BSc (Hons Maths) 1947, CertEd 1950). National Service, Royal Artillery, 1947–49. Mathematics Master, Thornbury Grammar Sch., Glos, 1950–56; Mathematics Master and Sixth Form Master, St George Grammar Sch., Bristol, 1956–64; Asst Sec., Assistant Masters Assoc., 1964–78. Last Chm., Teachers' Panel, Burnham Primary and Secondary Cttee, 1985–87. Mem., Univ. of Bristol Court, 1986–2002; Trustee and Manager, Muntham House Sch., 1979–97. Mem., Exec. Cttee, Welwyn Garden City Soc., 1987–2010 (Treas., 1988–2005); Treas., Welwyn Garden Decorative and Fine Arts Soc., 1992–99; Dir, Digswell Lake Soc., 1987–2010 (Co. Sec., 1992–2008). Tower Captain, St John's, Lemsford, 1982–2001. Hon. FCP, 1985. *Publications:* many reports/pamphlets for AMA, incl. The Middle School System, Mixed Ability Teaching, Selection for Admission to a University. *Recreations:* family, campanology, puzzles, visits to HPB and other sites in UK by car, books. *Address:* 3 Templewood, Welwyn Garden City, Herts AL8 7HT. *T:* (01707) 321380. *Died 21 Oct. 2012.*

BEYNON, Prof. John Herbert, DSc; FRS 1971; Professor Emeritus, University of Wales, since 1991; *b* 29 Dec. 1923; British; *m* 1947, Yvonne Lilian (*née* Fryer) (*d* 2009); no *c*. *Educ:* UC Swansea, Univ. of Wales (BSc (1st cl. hons Physics); DSc 1960). CPhys; FInstP; CChem; FRSC; CSci. Experimental Officer, Min. of Supply, Tank Armament Research, 1943–47; ICI Ltd (Organics Div.), 1947–74: Associate Research Manager i/c Physical Chemistry, 1962–70; Sen. Res. Associate, 1965–74; University College of Swansea, University of Wales, subseq. University of Wales Swansea, then Swansea University: first Hon. Professorial Fellow, and Lectr in Chemistry, 1967–74; Royal Soc. Res. Prof., 1974–86; Res. Prof., Depts of Physics and Chemistry, 1987–. Boomer Meml Fellow, Univ. of Minnesota, 1955; Prof. of Chemistry, Purdue Univ., Indiana, 1969–75; Associate Prof. of Molecular Sciences, Univ. of Warwick, 1972–74; Vis. Prof., Univ. of Essex, 1973–74, 1982–; Hon. Prof., Univ. of Warwick, 1977–; Associate, Institut Jožef Stefan, Ljubljana, 1980–. Chm., Schs Curriculum Develt Cttee, Cttee for Wales, 1983–88; Pres., Assoc. for Sci. Educn, Wales, 1985–86. Founder Chm., British Mass Spectrometry Soc., 1960 (Hon. Mem. 1988); Founder Pres., Eur. Mass Spectrometry Soc., 1993–97. Hon. Member, Mass Spectrometry Societies: Japan, 1967; Yugoslavia, 1977; China, 1986; Italy, 1990. Hon. Life Mem., Swansea Camera Club; Mem., Athenæum, 1972–86. Editor, Internat. Jl of Mass Spectrom. Ion Processes, 1983–85; Founder Editor-in-Chief, Rapid Communications in Mass Spectrom., 1987–97. Hon. DSc: Purdue, USA, 1995; Babeş-Bolyai, Romania, 1997. Sigma-Xi Res. Award, Purdue Univ., USA, 1973; Hasler Award of Applied Spectroscopy, USA, 1979; Medal, Serbian Chemical Soc., 1981; Techmart Trophy, British Technol. Gp, 1984; Jan Marc Marci Medal, Czechoslovak Spectrometry Soc., 1984; Field and Franklin Medal, Amer. Chem. Soc., 1987; Gold Medal: Internat. Mass Spectrometry Soc., 1985; British Mass Spectrometry Soc., 1987; Italian Mass Spectrometry Soc., 1992. *Publications:* Mass Spectrometry and its Applications in Organic Chemistry, 1960; Mass and Abundance Tables for use in Mass Spectrometry, 1963; The Mass Spectra of Organic Molecules, 1968; Table of Ion Energies for Metastable Transitions in Mass Spectrometry, 1970; Metastable Ions, 1973; An Introduction to Mass Spectrometry, 1981; Current Topics in Mass Spectrometry and Chemical Kinetics, 1982; Application of Transition State Theory to Unimolecular Reactions, 1983; papers in Proc. Royal Soc., Nature, Jl Sci. Inst., Jl Applied Physics, Chem. Soc., JACS, Trans Faraday Soc., Int. Jl Mass Spectrom. and Ion Physics, Org. Mass Spectrom., Anal. Chem., etc. *Recreations:* photography, golf. *Address:* Brynfield Manor Nursing Home, 42 Brynfield Road, Langland, Swansea SA3 4SX. *T:* (01792) 363180. *Clubs:* Swansea Cricket and Football (Bd Mem., 1990–92), Swansea Sports (Chm., 1988–93); Glamorgan County Cricket (Life Vice Pres.); Bristol Channel Yacht; Buxton and High Peak Golf (Captain, 1965). *Died 24 Aug. 2015.*

BIANCHERI, Boris, Hon. GCVO 1990; Chairman, Agenzia Nazionale Stampa Associata, since 1997; President, Institute for International Political Studies, Milan, since 1998; *b* 3 Nov. 1930; *s* of Augusto and Olga Wolff von Stomersee; *m* 1979, Flavia Arzeni; one *s* one *d*. *Educ:* Univ. of Rome (Law Degree). Joined Min. of Foreign Affairs, 1956; served Athens, 1959; Economic Dept, Min. of Foreign Affairs, 1964–67; Sec.-Gen., Commn for 1970 Osaka Exhibn, 1968; First Counsellor, Cultural Relations, Min. of Foreign Affairs, 1971; Political Counsellor, London, 1972–75; Chef de Cabinet, Sec. of State for Foreign Affairs, 1978; Minister, 1979; Ambassador, Tokyo, 1980–84; Dir Gen., Political Affairs, Min. of Foreign Affairs, 1985; Ambassador: UK, 1987–91; USA, 1991–95; Sec.-Gen., Min. of Foreign Affairs, 1995–97. Gran Croce, Ordine al Merito della Repubblica Italiana; numerous foreign orders. *Publications:* Accordare il mondo: la diplomazia nell'età globale, 1999. *Recreations:* gardening, boating, swimming. *Address:* Agenzia Nazionale Stampa Associata, Via delle Dataria 94, 00187 Rome, Italy. *Club:* Circolo Della Caccia (Rome). *Died 19 July 2011.*

BICESTER, 3rd Baron *cr* 1938, of Tusmore; **Angus Edward Vivian Smith;** *b* 20 Feb. 1932; *s* of Lt-Col Hon. Stephen Edward Vivian Smith (*d* 1952) (2nd *s* of 1st Baron) and Elenor Anderson, *d* of Edward S. Hewitt, New York City; *S* uncle, 1968. *Educ:* Eton. *Heir: b* Hugh Charles Vivian Smith, *b* 8 Nov. 1934. *Died 11 Dec. 2014.*

BIDWELL, Sir Hugh (Charles Philip), GBE 1989; Deputy Chairman, ITE Group plc (formerly International Trade & Exhibitions J/V Ltd), 1996–2003; Lord Mayor of London, 1989–90; *b* 1 Nov. 1934; *s* of late Edward and Elisabeth Bidwell; *m* 1st, 1962, Jenifer Celia Webb (*d* 2001); two *s* one *d*; 2nd, 2003, Priscilla Pode (*née* Hunter). *Educ:* Stonyhurst College. Nat. Service, 1953–55; commissioned E Surrey Regt, seconded to 1st Bn KAR, based Nyasaland. Viota Foods, 1956–70 (Dir, 1962–70); Dir, Robertson Foods, 1969–70; Chairman: Pearce Duff & Co. Ltd, 1970–84; Gill & Duffus Foods Ltd, 1984–85; British Invisibles, 1991–94; Chief Exec., Allied Lyons Eastern, 1985–91; non-executive Chairman: Riggs AP Bank Ltd, 1989–92; Julius Gp Ltd (formerly Octavian Gp Ltd), 1993–97; non-exec. Dep. Chm., London Forum, 1992–93; non-executive Director: Argyll Group plc, 1990–95; Rothschild Asset Mgt Ltd, 1992–98; Fleming Geared Income and Assets Investment Trust plc, 1993–97; Alpha Airports Gp plc, 1994–2003. Chm., London Tourist Bd, 1992–93; Member: Exec. Cttee, London Chamber of Commerce and Industry, 1976–85; Food from Britain Council, 1983–89 (Chm., Export Bd, 1983–86); European Trade Cttee, 1989–91; British-Soviet Chamber of Commerce, 1989–92; China-Britain (formerly Sino-British) Trade Gp, 1989–94; E European Trade Gp, 1991–92; BOTB, 1992–94. Pres., British Food Export Council, 1980–87; Dep. Pres., Food and Drink Fedn, 1985–86. Gov., Berkhamsted Schs, 1984–91. Trustee, Canterbury Cathedral Trust Fund, 1997–2003. Alderman, Billingsgate Ward, 1979–96; Sheriff of the City of London, 1986–87. Master, Grocers' Co., 1984–85. President: Billingsgate Ward Club; Fishmongers' & Poulterers' Instn, 1980–98. KStJ 1989; KCSG 1991. *Recreations:* golf, fishing, tennis, cricket, shooting. *Address:* Rose Cottage, 38 New Street, Sandwich, Kent CT13 9AB. *Clubs:* White's, City of London, MCC; Royal & Ancient; Denham Golf; Swinley Forest Golf, Royal St George's. *Died 7 Dec. 2013.*

BIGGAR, (Walter) Andrew, CBE 1980 (OBE 1967); MC 1945; TD 1995; FRAgS; farming, since 1956; *b* 6 March 1915; *s* of Walter Biggar and Margaret Sproat; *m* 1945, Patricia Mary Irving Elliot (*d* 2007); one *s* one *d*. *Educ:* Sedbergh Sch., Cumbria; Edinburgh Univ. (BScAgric). FRAgS 1969. Commnd Royal Signals, 1938; War Service, 51st Highland Div., 1939–46; POW, Germany, 1940–45. Rowett Res. Inst., 1935–54. Director and Trustee: Scottish Soc. for Research in Plant Breeding, 1958–88; Animal Diseases Res. Assoc., 1966–96. Member: Farm Animals Welfare Adv. Cttee, 1967–77; ARC, 1969–80; Scottish Agricultural Develt Council, 1971–82; JCO Consultative Bd, 1980–84; Chm., Animals Bd, JCO, 1973–80. Chm., Moredun Animal Health Trust, 1988–94; Dir, Moredun Foundn, 1996–98. Governor: St Margaret's Sch., Edinburgh, 1960–81; Grassland Res. Inst., 1962–81 (Hon. Fellow, 1981); Scottish Crop Res. Inst., 1980–83. *Recreation:* photography. *Address:* Magdalenehall, St Boswells, Roxburghshire TD6 0EB. *T:* (01835) 823741. *Died 16 Nov. 2012.*

BIGGS, Sir Norman (Parris), Kt 1977; Chairman, Esso Petroleum Company Ltd, 1968–72 (Director, 1952–66); *b* 23 Dec. 1907; *s* of John Gordon Biggs and Mary Sharpe Dickson; *m* 1936, Peggy Helena Stammwitz (*d* 1990); two *s* one *d*. *Educ:* John Watson's Sch., Edinburgh. Bank of England, 1927–46; Dir, Kleinwort Sons & Co. Ltd, 1946–52; Chairman: Williams & Glyn's Bank Ltd, 1972–76; United International Bank Ltd, 1970–79; Deputy Chairman: National and Commercial Banking Gp Ltd, 1974–76; Privatbanken Ltd, 1980–83; Director: Royal Bank of Scotland, 1974–76; Gillett Bros Discount Co. Ltd, 1963–77; Banco de Bilbao, 1981–87. Mem., Bullock Cttee on Industrial Democracy, 1976. *Address:* Northbrooks, Danworth Lane, Hurstpierpoint, Sussex BN6 9LW. *T:* (01273) 832022. *Died 25 July 2011.*

BILBY, Prof. Bruce Alexander, BA, PhD; FRS 1977; Professor of the Theory of Materials, University of Sheffield, 1966–84, then Emeritus; *b* 3 Sept. 1922; *e s* of late George Alexander Bilby and Dorothy Jean (*née* Telfer); *m* 1st, 1946, Hazel Joyce (*née* Casken); one *s* (and one *s* one *d* decd); 2nd, 1966, Lorette Wendela (*née* Thomas); two *s*. *Educ:* Dover Grammar Sch.; Peterhouse, Cambridge (BA); Univ. of Birmingham (PhD). Admiralty, 1943–46. Research, Birmingham, 1946–51; Univ. of Sheffield: Royal Soc. Sorby Res. Fellow, 1951–57; J. H. Andrew Res. Fellow, 1957–58; Reader in Theoretical Metallurgy, 1958–62, Prof., 1962–66. Made contributions to theory of dislocations and its application to the deformation, transformation and fracture of metallic crystals. Rosenhain Medal, Inst. of Metals, 1963; Griffith Medal, European Structural Integrity Soc., 1994. *Publications:* contribs to learned jls. *Address:* 32 Devonshire Road, Sheffield S17 3NT. *T:* (0114) 236 1086; Department of Mechanical Engineering, The University, Mappin Street, Sheffield S1 3JD. *T:* (0114) 222 7713. *Died 20 Nov. 2013.*

BILGER, Pierre, Hon. CBE 2002; Chairman and Chief Executive Officer, 1998–2003, Chairman of the Board, 2003, Alstom; *b* Colmar, 27 May 1940; *s* of Joseph Bilger and Suzanne Gillet; *m* 1966, Eliane Oyon; two *s* three *d*. *Educ:* Institut d'Etudes Politiques; Ecole Nationale d'Admin, Paris. Sen. posts at French Min. of Econ. and Finance (Inspection Générale des Finances and Budget Dept), 1967–82; sen. posts with Cie Générale d'Electricité, subseq. Alcatel Alsthom, then Alcatel, 1982–87 (Dep. Man. Dir, 1987); joined Alsthom, 1987; Pres. and CEO, GEC Alsthom, 1991–98. Mem. Bd, Eurotunnel, 2007–. Chm., Stichting Preference Shares Renault-Nissan Foundn, 2002–. Advr, Proudfoot Consulting, 2005–. Officier de la Légion d'Honneur (France), 2002; Commandeur de l'Ordre National du Mérite (France), 1995. *Publications:* Quatre millions d'euros, le prix de ma liberté, 2004; Causeurs à bâtons rompus, 2007. *Address:* 7 rue de l'Assomption, 75016 Paris, France. *Died 4 March 2011.*

BILK, Bernard Stanley, (Acker), MBE 2001; musician (jazz clarinettist) and composer; band leader, since 1951; *b* 28 Jan. 1929; *s* of William and Lillian Bilk; *m* 1954, Jean Hawkins; one *s* one *d*. *Educ:* Pensford Sch., Somerset. Nat. Service, RE, 1948. Founder, Bristol Paramount Jazz Band, 1951; with Ken Colyer's Band, London, as clarinettist, 1952–53; numerous recordings; singles include: Summer Set, 1960; Stranger on the Shore, 1961 (first No 1 simultaneously in UK and USA; BMI award for over 4 million broadcasts, 2004); A Taste of Honey, 1963; Aria, 1976; albums include: Blue Acker, with the Stan Tracey Big Brass, 2005; tours worldwide, incl. Europe, Scandinavia, Australia, NZ, Far East, ME, USA, Canada and Ireland. Hon. MA Bristol, 2005. Silver Medal for Lifetime Achievement, Musicians' Co., 2008. *Recreation:* oil painting. *Address:* c/o Acker's Agency, 53 Cambridge Mansions, Cambridge Road, SW11 4RX. *Died 2 Nov. 2014.*

BILLOT, Barbara Kathleen; Deputy Director (Under-Secretary), Department for National Savings, 1974–80; *b* 26 May 1920; *d* of Alfred Billot and Agnes Billot (*née* Hiner). *Educ:* Petersfield County High Sch. for Girls. Post Office Savings Bank: Clerical Officer 1938; Exec. Off. 1939; Higher Exec. Off. 1946; Sen. Exec. Off. 1953; Chief Exec. Off. 1957; Principal, Post Office Headquarters, 1960; Sen. Chief Exec. Off., PO Savings Dept, 1961; Principal Exec. Off. (Estabt Off.), 1969; Asst Sec., Dept for Nat. Savings, 1971. *Recreations:* reading, theatre-going. *Address:* 6 Springbank, Chichester, W Sussex PO19 6BX. *T:* (01243) 776295. *Died 24 Sept. 2011.*

BILLS, David James, CBE 2001; President, Commonwealth Forestry Association, 2004–10; *b* 9 Feb. 1948; *s* of Nigel Bills and Sue Bills; *m* 1970, Michele Clutha Ellis; one *s* two *d*. *Educ:* Australian Nat. Univ. (BSc Forestry); MIT (SMP 1991). FICFor. Research Scientist, Australian Forest Res. Inst., 1970–74; Officer, Dept of Primary Industry, Australian Govt, 1974–77; various posts with Associated Pulp & Paper Mills and North Broken Hill Ltd, 1977–95 (Gen. Manager, Forest Products and Dir, 1986–95); Dir Gen., Forestry Commn, 1995–2004. Non-exec. Dir, South African Forestry Co., 2006. Vice Pres., Australian Forest Develt Inst., 1982–86; Pres., Nat. Assoc. Forest Industries, 1992–95. Warden, Hobart Marine Bd, 1992–95. *Publications:* contribs to various scientific jls and to Australian Forestry Conf. Proc. *Recreations:* sailing, classic cars, ski-ing. *Died 30 March 2014.*

BILSTON, Baron *cr* 2005 (Life Peer), of Bilston in the county of West Midlands; **Dennis Turner;** *b* 26 Aug. 1942; *s* of Mary Elizabeth Peasley and Thomas Herbert Turner; *m* 1976, Patricia Mary Narroway; one *s* one *d*. *Educ:* Stonefield Secondary Modern School, Bilston; Bilston College of Further Education; Bilston Black Country. Office boy, salesman, market trader, steel worker, partner in worker co-operative. Mem. (Lab), Wolverhampton BC, 1966–86 (Chairman of Committees: Social Services, 1972–79; Educn, 1979–86; Econ. Develt, 1982–85; Housing, 1985–86). MP (Lab and Co-op) Wolverhampton SE, 1987–2005. An Opposition Whip, 1993–97; PPS to Sec. of State for Internat. Develt, 1997–2001. Mem., Educn Select Cttee, 1989–94; Chairman: All Party Gp on Further Educn, 1988–2005; H of C Catering Cttee, 1997–2005; W Midlands Gp Parly Lab MPs, 2001–05. Vice Pres., LGA. Chm., Wolverhampton Fair Trade Partnership. Patron, Wolverhampton Interfaith. Freedom, City of Wolverhampton, 2007. Hon. DLitt Wolverhampton, 2006. *Address:* House of Lords, SW1A 0PW; Aubyn, 16 King Street, Bradley, Bilston, W Midlands WV14 8PQ. *Club:* Springvale Sports and Social (Bilston). *Died 25 Feb. 2014.*

BINCHY, Maeve, (Mrs Gordon Snell); writer; *b* Dublin, 28 May 1940; *d* of William Binchy and Maureen Blackmore; *m* 1977, Gordon Snell, writer and broadcaster. *Educ:* Holy Child Convent, Killiney, Dublin; University College, Dublin. History teacher in girls' schs, 1960–68; columnist, Irish Times, 1968–2000. *Publications: novels:* Light a Penny Candle, 1982; Echoes, 1985; Firefly Summer, 1987; Circle of Friends, 1990 (filmed, 1995); Copper Beech, 1992; The Glass Lake, 1994; Evening Class, 1996; Tara Road, 1998 (filmed 2005); Scarlet Feather, 2000; Quentins, 2002; Nights of Rain and Stars, 2004; Whitethorn Woods, 2006; Heart and Soul, 2008; Minding Frankie, 2010; *novella:* Star Sullivan, 2006; *short stories:* Central Line, 1978; Victoria Line, 1980; Dublin 4, 1982; The Lilac Bus, 1984; Silver Wedding, 1988; This Year It Will Be Different, 2007 (How About You filmed 2007);

The Return Journey, 2010; *non-fiction:* Aches and Pains, 1999; The Maeve Binchy Writers' Club, 2008. *Recreations:* reading, theatre, very bad bridge, gardening. *Address:* Dalkey, Co. Dublin, Ireland. *Died 30 July 2012.*

BINNIE, David Stark, OBE 1979; General Manager, British Rail, London Midland Region, 1977–80; *b* 2 June 1922; *s* of Walter Archibald Binnie and Helen (*née* Baxter), Bonkle, Lanarkshire; *m* 1947, Leslie Archibald; one *s* one *d.* *Educ:* Wishaw High School. British Railways: Gen. and Signalling Asst to Gen. Manager Scottish Region, 1955; Asst District Operating Supt 1961, District Operating Supt 1963, Glasgow North; Divisional Movements Manager, Glasgow Div., 1965; Movements Manager, Scottish Region, 1967; Divisional Manager, SE Div., Southern Region, 1969; Asst Gen. Manager, Southern Region, 1970, Gen. Manager, 1972; Exec. Dir, Freight, BR Board, 1974–76. Lt-Col Engineer and Railway Staff Corps, RE (T&AVR). OStJ. *Recreation:* Dartmoor and Highland life. *Address:* Above Ways, Lower Knowle Road, Lustleigh, Devon TQ13 9TR. *T:* (01647) 277386.

BIRCH, Prof. Anthony Harold, PhD; FRSC 1988; Professor of Political Science, University of Victoria, British Columbia, 1977–89, then Emeritus; *b* 17 Feb. 1924; *o s* of late Frederick Harold Birch and Rosalind Dorothy Birch; *m* 1953, Dorothy Madeleine Overton, Bayport, New York; one *s* one *d.* *Educ:* William Ellis Sch.; University Coll., Nottingham; London Sch. of Economics. BSc (Econ) London, with 1st cl. hons, 1945; PhD London, 1951. Asst Principal, Board of Trade, 1945–47; University of Manchester: Asst Lectr in Govt, 1947–51; Lectr, 1951–58; Senior Lectr in Government, 1958–61; Prof. of Political Studies, Univ. of Hull, 1961–70; Prof. of Political Sci., Exeter Univ., 1970–77. Commonwealth Fund Fellow at Harvard Univ. and University of Chicago, 1951–52. Consultant to Government of Western Region of Nigeria, 1956–58. Vis. Prof. Tufts Univ., 1968; Vis. Fellow, ANU, 1987. Vice-Pres., Internat. Political Sci. Assoc., 1976–79. Sir Isaiah Berlin Prize, Political Studies Assoc., 2002. *Publications:* Federalism, Finance and Social Legislation, 1955; Small-Town Politics, 1959; Representative and Responsible Government, 1964; The British System of Government, 1967, 10th edn 1998; Representation, 1971; Political Integration and Disintegration in the British Isles, 1977; Nationalism and National Integration, 1989; The Concepts and Theories of Modern Democracy, 1993, 3rd edn 2007; articles in various journals. *Recreations:* reading, music, bridge. *Address:* 1901 Fairfield Road, Victoria, BC V8S 1H2, Canada. *Died 13 Dec. 2014.*

BIRCH, Dennis Arthur, CBE 1977; DL; Councillor, West Midlands County Council, 1974–77; *b* 11 Feb. 1925; *s* of George Howard and Leah Birch; *m* 1948, Mary Therese Lyons (*d* 2012); one *d.* *Educ:* Wolverhampton Municipal Grammar Sch. Wolverhampton County Borough Council: elected, 1952; served, 1952–74; Alderman, 1970–73; Mayor, 1973–74; Leader, 1967–73. Elected (following Local Govt reorganisation) Chm. West Midlands CC, 1974–76. DL West Midlands, 1979. *Address:* 3 Tern Close, Wolverhampton Road East, Wolverhampton WV4 6AU. *T:* (01902) 883837. *Died 15 Dec. 2012.*

BIRCH, Frank Stanley Heath; public sector consultant; Commander, London District, St John Ambulance, 1992–2002 (Deputy Commander, 1990–92); *b* 8 Feb. 1939; *s* of late John Stanley Birch, CEng and Phyllis Edna Birch (*née* Heath), BA; *m* 1963, Diana Jacqueline Davies, BA; one *d.* *Educ:* Weston-super-Mare Grammar Sch. for Boys; Univ. of Wales (BA); Univ. of Birmingham (Inst. of Local Govt Studies). IPFA; MBIM. Entered local govt service, 1962; various appts, City Treasurer and Controller's Dept, Cardiff, 1962–69; Chief Internal Auditor, Dudley, 1969–73; Asst County Treasurer, 1973–74, Asst Chief Exec., 1974–76, W Midlands CC; Chief Exec., Lewisham, 1976–82; Town Clerk and Chief Exec., Croydon, 1982–90. Hon. Clerk, Gen. Purposes Cttee, 1982–90, Principal Grants Advr, 1983–86, London Boroughs Assoc.; Sec., London Co-ordinating Cttee, 1985–86. Dir, Croydon Business Venture Ltd, 1983–92. Chm., Lifecare NHS Trust, 1994–98. Freeman, City of London, 1980. FRSA 1980. KStJ 1997 (OStJ 1988; CStJ 1992); Mem. Council, Order of St John, London, 1986–2006; Vice-Pres., London SJAB, 1988–90. *Publications:* various articles on public admin and local govt management. *Recreations:* music, walking, the countryside, France and all things French. *Address:* The Old Liberal Club, 5 Lower Lane, Chinley, Derbys SK23 6BE. *Died 12 March 2013.*

BIRCH, John Anthony, MA, DMus; FRCM, FRCO(CHM), LRAM; Curator-Organist, Royal Albert Hall, since 1984; Professor, Royal College of Music, 1959–97, then Consultant; Organist: to the Royal Choral Society, since 1966; of the Royal Philharmonic Orchestra, since 1983; *b* 9 July 1929; *s* of late Charles Aylmer Birch and Mabel (*née* Greenwood), Leek, Staffs; unmarried. *Educ:* Trent Coll.; Royal Coll. of Music (ARCM; Pitcher Schol. of RCO). Nat. Service, Royal Corps of Signals, 1949–50. Organist and Choirmaster, St Thomas's Church, Regent Street, London, 1950–53; Accompanist to St Michael's Singers, 1952–58; Organist and Choirmaster, All Saints Church, Margaret Street, London, 1953–58; Sub-Organist, HM Chapels Royal, 1957–58; Organist and Master of the Choristers, Chichester Cathedral, 1958–80; Organist and Dir of Choir, Temple Church, 1982–97. With the Cathedral Organists of Salisbury and Winchester re-established the Southern Cathedrals Festival, 1960; Musical Advr, Chichester Festival Theatre, 1962–80; Choirmaster, Bishop Otter Coll., Chichester, 1963–69. Rep., 1950–66, and Man. Dir, 1966–73, C. A. Birch Ltd, Staffs. Accompanist, Royal Choral Soc., 1965–70; Examr to Associated Bd, Royal Schs of Music, 1958–77; a Gen. Ed., Novello & Co., 1967–77. Univ. Organist, 1967–94 and Vis. Lectr in Music, 1971–83, Univ. of Sussex. Special Comr, Royal Sch. of Church Music; Royal College of Organists: Mem. Council, 1964–2003, 2005–09; Pres., 1984–86; Vice-Pres., 1986–; Hon. Treas., 1997–2002. Pres. Emeritus, Burgon Soc. (Hon. Fellow, 2001; Pres., 2001–11). Fellow, Corp. of SS Mary and Nicolas (Woodard Schs), 1973–99; Governor: Hurstpierpoint Coll., 1974–93; St Catherine's, Bramley, 1981–89; Mem. Council, Corp. of Cranleigh and Bramley Schs, 1981–90. Trustee, Ouseley Trust, 1989–. Waywarden, Liberty of the Close, Salisbury Cathedral, 1997–2004. Made concert appearances in France, Belgium, Italy, Austria, Germany, Poland, Romania, Switzerland, Netherlands, Spain, Portugal, Scandinavia, Japan, USA, Mexico and Far East; recital tours: Canada and US, 1966 and 1967, Australia and NZ, 1969, S Africa, 1978. Underwriting Mem., Lloyds, 1976–2002. Hon. Bencher, Middle Temple, 1998. Freeman; City of London, 1991; Liveryman, Co. of Glaziers and Painters of Glass, 2007. DMus Lambeth, 1989; Hon. MA Sussex, 1971. *Address:* 2 The Chantry, Canon Lane, Chichester, W Sussex PO19 1PZ. *T:* (01243) 537333, *Fax:* (01243) 537377. *E:* DrJohnBirch@aol.com. *Clubs:* Garrick; New (Edinburgh). *Died 28 April 2012.*

BIRDWOOD, 3rd Baron *cr* 1938, of Anzac and of Totnes; **Mark William Ogilvie Birdwood;** Bt 1919; Chairman, Martlet Ltd, since 1986; *b* 23 Nov. 1938; *s* of 2nd Baron Birdwood, MVO, and Vere Lady Birdwood, CVO (*d* 1997); *S* father, 1962; *m* 1963, Judith Helen, *e d* of late R. G. Seymour Roberts; one *d.* *Educ:* Radley Coll.; Trinity Coll., Cambridge. Commnd RHG. Director: Wrightson Wood Ltd, 1979–86; Du Pont Pixel Systems (formerly Benchmark Technology); Comac plc, 1988–92; Scientific Generics, 1989–97; Terra Firma, 1990–95; Fiortho plc, 1995–2001 (Chm.); The Character Gp (formerly Toy Options) plc, 1995–; IMS plc, 1997–2000; Steeltower Ltd, 2001–. Mem., Select Cttee on Science and Technol., H of L, 1998–99. Associate, LSE Centre for Philosophy of Nat. and Social Sci., 2001–. Trustee of charities. Liveryman, Glaziers' Co. *Address:* 5 Holbein Mews, SW1W 8NW; Russell House, Broadway, Worcs WR12 7BU. *Clubs:* Brooks's, Pratt's. *Died 11 July 2015 (ext).*

BIRKETT, 2nd Baron *cr* 1958, of Ulverston; **Michael Birkett;** Co-Chairman, Donatella Flick Conducting Competition, since 2008 (Chairman, 1990–2008); *b* 22 Oct. 1929; *s* of 1st Baron Birkett, PC and Ruth Birkett (*née* Nilsson, she *d* 1969); *S* father, 1962; *m* 1st, 1960, Junia Crawford (*d* 1973); 2nd, 1978, Gloria Taylor (*d* 2001); one *s.* *Educ:* Stowe; Trinity Coll., Cambridge. Asst Dir at Ealing Studios and Ealing Films, 1953–59; Asst Dir, 1959–61, on films including: The Mark; The Innocents; Billy Budd; Associate Producer: Some People, 1961–62;

Modesty Blaise, 1965; Producer: The Caretaker, 1962; Marat/Sade, 1966; A Midsummer Night's Dream, 1967; King Lear, 1968–69; Director: The Launching and The Soldier's Tale, 1963; Overture and Beginners, the More Man Understands, 1964; Outward Bound, 1971. Vice Pres., British Bd of Film Classification, 1985–97. Dep. Dir, National Theatre, 1975–77; Consultant to Nat. Theatre on films, TV and sponsorship, 1977–79; Dir for Recreation and Arts, GLC, 1979–86; Adviser to South Bank Bd, 1986–89; Exec. Dir, Royal Philharmonic Soc., 1989–90; Dir, Olympic Festival 1990, Manchester, 1990. Chairman: Children's Film & TV Foundn, 1981–99; Theatres Adv. Council, 1986–2002; Adv. Cttee, Nat. Sound Archive, 1993–2003; Music Adv. Cttee, British Council, 1994–2001. Chm., Management Cttee, Park Lane Gp, 1991–2005. Chm. Governors, BRIT Sch. for Performing Arts and Technology, 1990–2001. Master, Curriers' Co., 1975–76. *Recreations:* music, printing, horticulture. *Heir:* *s* Hon. Thomas Birkett, *b* 25 July 1982. *Address:* Great Allfields, Balls Cross, Petworth GU28 9JU. *Died 3 April 2015.*

BIRLEY, James Leatham Tennant, CBE 1990; FRCP, FRCPsych, DPM; Consultant Psychiatrist, Bethlem Royal and Maudsley Hospitals, 1969–90, Emeritus Psychiatrist, 1990; President, British Medical Association, 1993–94; *b* 31 May 1928; *s* of late Dr James Leatham Birley and Margaret Edith (*née* Tennant); *m* 1954, Julia Davies; one *s* three *d*. *Educ:* Winchester Coll.; University Coll., Oxford; St Thomas' Hosp., London. Maudsley Hospital: Registrar, 1960; Sen. Registrar, 1963; Mem. Scientific Staff, MRC Social Psychiatry Research Unit, 1965; Dean, Inst. of Psychiatry, 1971–82. Dean, 1982–87, Pres., 1987–90, RCPsych. *Publications:* contribs to scientific jls. *Recreations:* music, gardening. *Address:* Upper Bryn, Longtown, Hereford HR2 0NA. *Died 6 Oct. 2013.*

BIRLEY, Michael Pellew, MA (Oxon); Housemaster, 1970–80, Assistant Master, 1980–84, Marlborough College; *b* 7 Nov. 1920; *s* of late Norman Pellew Birley, DSO, MC, and Eileen Alice Morgan; *m* 1949, Ann Grover (*née* Street); two *s* two *d*. *Educ:* Marlborough Coll.; Wadham Coll., Oxford (1st class Classical Honour Moderations, 1940; 1st class *Literae Humaniores*, 1947; MA 1946). Served War of 1939–45 with the Royal Fusiliers; joined up, Sept. 1940; commissioned, April 1941; abroad, 1942–45 (despatches); demobilised, Jan. 1946. Taught Classics: Shrewsbury Sch., 1948–50; Eton Coll., 1950–56; Headmaster, Eastbourne College, 1956–70. Member Council: Ardingly Coll., 1981–90; Marlborough Coll., 1985–90. Fellow, Woodard Corp., 1983–90. *Recreations:* gardening, wine-making. *Address:* Long Summers, Cross Lane, Marlborough, Wilts SN8 1LA. *T:* (01672) 512830. *Died 2 Jan. 2012.*

BIRO, Bálint Stephen, (Val); illustrator, painter, and author of children's books; *b* Budapest, 6 Oct. 1921; *s* of late Dr Bálint Biro and Margaret Biro (*née* Gyulaházi); *m* 1st, 1945, Vivien Woolley (marr. diss. 1970; she *d* 1991); one *d*; 2nd, 1970, Marie-Louise Ellaway; one step *s* one step *d*. *Educ:* Cistercian Sch., Budapest; Central Sch. of Art, London. Nat. Fire Service, London, 1942–45; Studio Manager, Sylvan Press, 1944–46; Production Manager, C. & J. Temple, 1946–48; Art Dir, John Lehmann, 1948–53; weekly illustrations for Radio Times, 1951–72; freelance illustrator and children's author, 1953–. Mem., Chesham UDC, 1966–70. Vice Chm., Bosham Assoc., 1989–91; Member: Soc. of Authors, 1970; Vintage Austin Register, 1961. Chm. of Govs, Amersham Coll. of Art and Design, 1974–84. *Publications:* author and illustrator of over ninety books, including: Bumpy's Holiday, 1943; 36 Gumdrop titles, incl. Gumdrop: the adventures of a vintage car, 1966, Gumdrop's School Adventure, 2001; Hungarian Folk Tales, 1981 (trans. Spanish 1991); The Magic Doctor, 1982; The Hobyahs, 1985; Tobias and the Dragon, 1989; Peter Cheater, 1989; Look and Find ABC, 1990; Miranda's Umbrella, 1990; Rub-a-Dub-Dub Nursery Rhymes, 1991; Three Billy Goats Gruff, 1993; Lazy Jack, 1995; Jasper's Jungle Journey, 1995; Bears Can't Fly, 1996; Hansel and Gretel, 1996; Goldilocks and the Three Bears, 1998; Little Red Riding Hood, 2000; The Joking Wolf, 2001; Aesop's Fables (18 titles), 2002; Hans Christian Andersen Fairy Tales, 2005; Grimm's Fairy Tales, 2008; Charles Perrault's Tales of Mother Goose, 2010; Tales from the Arabian Nights, 2013; illustrator of numerous books, including: Denys Val Baker, Worlds Without End, 1945; H. E. Todd, 15 children's picture books, 1954–88; Jean Plaidy, historical novels, 1960–74; Anthony Hope, The Prisoner of Zenda, 1961; L. Frank Baum, Wizard of Oz books, 1965, 1967; Lord Tweedsmuir, One Man's Happiness, 1968; Eric Shipton, That Untravelled World, 1969; J. H. B. Peel, Country Talk books, 1970–81; The Good Food Guide, 1971; The Robert Carrier Cookery Course, 1974; Kenneth Grahame, Wind in the Willows, 1983; Margaret Mahy, The King's Jokes, 1987; My Oxford Picture Word Book, 1994; Ted Wragg, The Flying Boot reading scheme, 1994–95; Christina Butler, The Dinosaur's Egg, 1994; Anthony Trollope, The Landleaguers, 1995; Golden Lion of Grandpere, 1997; G. K. Chesterton, Father Brown Stories, 1996; Michael Hardcastle, Carole's Camel, 1997; Anthony Buckeridge: Jennings Sounds the Alarm, 1999; Jennings Breaks the Record, 2000; Jennings Joins the Search Party, 2001; Jennings and the Old Rattletrap, 2003; 100 Bible Stories for Children, 2002; 100 New Testament Stories for Children, 2003; Enid Blyton, Secret of the Lost Necklace, 2003; Dot Meharry, The Dinosaur Dance, 2005; Macmillan Primary Integrated Studies (Jamaica), 3 pts, 2005–06; Enid Blyton, The Secret Valley, 2009. *Recreations:* vintage car rallies, painting, photography. *Address:* Bridge Cottage, Brook Avenue, Bosham, West Sussex PO18 8LQ. *T:* (01243) 574195. *E:* v.biro@btinternet.com. *Club:* Vintage Sports-Car (Chipping Norton). *Died 4 July 2014.*

BISHOP, Alan Henry, CB 1989; HM Chief Inspector of Prisons for Scotland, 1989–94; *b* 12 Sept. 1929; *s* of Robert Bishop and May Watson; *m* 1959, Marjorie Anne Conlan; one *s* one *d*. *Educ:* George Heriot's Sch., Edinburgh; Edinburgh Univ. (MA Hons Econ. Sci., 1951, History, 1952). Served RAF Educn Br., 1952–54. Asst Principal, Dept of Agric. for Scotland, 1954; Private Sec. to Parly Under-Secs of State, 1958–59; Principal, 1959; First Sec., Agric. and Food, Copenhagen and The Hague, 1963–66; Asst Sec., Commn on the Constitution, 1969–73; Asst Under-Sec. of State, 1980–84, Principal Establishment Officer, 1984–89, Scottish Office. *Recreations:* contract bridge (Pres., Scottish Bridge Union, 1979–80), theatre. *Address:* Beaumont Court, 19/8 Wester Coates Gardens, Edinburgh EH12 5LT. *T:* (0131) 346 4641. *Clubs:* New (Edinburgh); Melville Bridge. *Died 22 Aug. 2015.*

BISHOP, Anthony; *see* Bishop, K. A.

BISHOP, Dr John Edward Lucas; freelance musician; *b* 23 Feb. 1935; *s* of late Reginald John Bishop and of Eva Bishop (*née* Lucas). *Educ:* Cotham Sch., Bristol; St John's Coll., Cambridge (Exhibnr; MA, MusB); Reading Univ. (DipEd (Dist.)); Edinburgh Univ. (DMus). FRCO (CHM); ADCM; Hon. FBC. John Stewart of Rannoch Schol. (Univ. prize) 1954. Organist and Asst Dir of Music, Worksop Coll., Notts, 1958–69; Dir of Music, Worksop Coll., 1969–73; Birmingham School of Music: Dir of Studies, 1973–74; Sen. Lectr, 1974–79; Principal Lectr, Head of Organ Studies and Head of Admissions, 1979–87. Dir of Music, Cotham Parish Church, Bristol, 1976–90; Hon. Dir of Music, St Paul's Church, Birmingham, 1986; Dir, Bristol Highbury Singers, 1978–90; Consultant, Wells Cathedral Sch., 1986–93; Organist, St Augustine's Chapel, 2004–, and Hon. Dir of Music, 2006–09, St Monica Trust. Organ recitalist (incl. many broadcasts) and choral conductor (Conductor, 1997–2000, Pres., 2000–05, Portishead Choral Soc.), pianist, coach and adjudicator, 1960–. Former Pres., Sheffield, Birmingham and Bristol Organists' Assocs; Member: Council, ISM, 1991–97; Music Adv. Panel, Henleaze Concert Soc., 1995–2002; Bd of Mgt, Emerald Chamber Players, 1997–2002. *Publications:* various articles on history and practice of church music and 19th century organ design. *Recreations:* food and friends, walking, ecclesiology, savouring the countryside, cities and towns, railways, architecture. *Address:* 38 Westfield House, Cote Lane, Westbury-on-Trym, Bristol BS9 3TJ. *T:* (0117) 949 4838. *Died 14 Aug. 2013.*

BISHOP, (Kenneth) Anthony, CMG 1998; OBE 1973; HM Diplomatic Service, retired; *b* 22 Jan. 1938; *s* of Charles William Bishop and Mary Ann Bishop (*née* Bell); *m* 1962, Christine Mary Pennell; one *s* one *d*. *Educ:* Wade Deacon GS, Widnes; Emmanuel Coll., Cambridge (BA

Hons Mod. Langs 1961). Nat. Service, RAF, 1956–58. Joined Foreign Office, 1961; Principal Conf. Interpreter, 1968–98, Res. Counsellor, 1981–98, FCO Research Department: Moscow, 1963–65; Berlin Four-Power Negotiations, 1970–71; Bonn, 1971–72; Geneva Comprehensive Test Ban Talks, 1978–81; Royal Visit to Russia, 1994; Russian State Visit, 2003; Anglo-Soviet/Russian summits, 1961–2004. Medal for Outstanding Contribution to the UK/USA Intelligence Relationship, CIA, 1997. *Recreations:* church-based charity work in Russia, hill walking, choral singing. *Address:* 33 Lansdowne Road, Sevenoaks, Kent TN13 3XU. *T:* (01732) 452718. *Died 3 Aug. 2012.*

BISHOP, Prof. Peter Orlebar, AO 1986; DSc; FRS 1977; FAA; Professor Emeritus, Australian National University, since 1983; Hon. Research Associate, Department of Anatomy and Histology, University of Sydney, since 1987; *b* 14 June 1917; *s* of Ernest John Hunter Bishop and Mildred Alice Havelock Bishop (*née* Vidal); *m* 1942, Hilare Louise Holmes (*d* 2011); one *s* two *d*. *Educ:* Barker Coll., Hornsby; Univ. of Sydney (MB, BS, DSc). Neurol Registrar, Royal Prince Alfred Hosp., Sydney, 1941–42; Surgeon Lieut, RANR, 1942–46; Fellow, Postgrad. Cttee in Medicine (Sydney Univ.) at Nat. Hosp., Queen Square, London, 1946–47 and Dept Anatomy, UCL, 1947–50; Sydney University: Res. Fellow, Dept Surgery, 1950–51; Sen. Lectr, 1951–54, Reader, 1954–55, Prof. and Head, Dept Physiology, 1955–67; Prof. and Head of Dept of Physiology, John Curtin School of Medical Res., ANU, 1967–82; Vis. Fellow, ANU, 1983–87. Visiting Professor: Japan Soc. for Promotion of Science, 1974, 1982; Katholieke Universiteit Leuven, Belgium, 1984–85; Guest Prof., Zürich Univ., 1985; Vis. Fellow, St John's Coll., Cambridge, Jan.–Oct. 1986. FAA 1967; Fellow: Aust. Postgrad. Fedn in Medicine, 1969; Nat. Vision Res. Inst. of Australia, 1983. Hon. Member: Neurosurgical Soc. of Aust., 1970; Ophthalmol Soc. of NZ, 1973; Aust. Assoc. of Neurologists, 1977; Australian Neuroscience Soc., 1986; Aust. Physiol and Pharmacol Soc., 1987. Hon. MD Sydney, 1983. (Jtly) Australia Prize, 1993; Centenary Medal, Australia, 2003. *Publications:* contribs on physiological optics and visual neurophysiology. *Recreation:* bushwalking. *Address:* Department of Anatomy and Histology, University of Sydney, NSW 2006, Australia. *Died 3 June 2012.*

BLACH, Rolf Karl, MD; FRCS, FRCOphth; Ophthalmologist, St Dunstan's, 1967–2004; Consultant Surgeon, Moorfields Eye Hospital, 1970–95; Dean, Institute of Ophthalmology, London University, 1985–91; *b* 21 Jan. 1930; *s* of Paul Samuel Blach and Hedwig Jeanette Blach; *m* 1960, Lynette Cecilia Sceales; two *s* one *d*. *Educ:* Berkhamsted Sch.; Trinity Coll., Cambridge (Sen. Schol.; MA); St Thomas' Hosp. MD 1965; FRCS 1962; FRCOphth (FCOphth 1989). Capt. RAMC, 1957–58. Jun. medical appts, St Thomas' Hosp. and Moorfields Eye Hosp., 1955–62; Sen. Registrar, Middlesex Hosp., 1962–63; Consultant Ophthalmic Surgeon, St Mary's Hosp., 1963–70; Hon. Consultant Ophthalmologist, RPMS, Hammersmith, 1967–70. Dep. Master, Oxford Ophthalmol Congress, 1985. Vice Chm., British Council for Prevention of Blindness, 1996–2004. Vice-Chm., Harpsden Parish Council, 2007–10 (Mem., 2003–10). Liveryman, Soc. of Apothecaries, 1970. *Publications:* articles on ophthalmology, esp. medical and surgical retina. *Recreations:* my family, aspects of history and PPE. *Address:* Summers, Northfield Avenue, Lower Shiplake, Henley-on-Thames, Oxon RG9 3PB. *T:* (0118) 940 4549. *E:* rblach@waitrose.com. *Club:* Phyllis Court (Henley-on-Thames). *Died 1 Nov. 2013.*

BLACK, Alastair Kenneth Lamond, CBE 1989; DL; Under Sheriff of Greater London, 1974–94; Clerk, Bowyers' Company, 1985–94; *b* 14 Dec. 1929; *s* of Kenneth Black and Althea Joan Black; *m* 1st, 1955, Elizabeth Jane (*d* 1995), *d* of Sir Henry Darlington, KCB, CMG, TD; one *s* two *d*; 2nd, 1997, Mrs Susan Mary Miller (*d* 2009); 3rd, 2010, Mrs Jenny Adams. *Educ:* Sherborne Sch.; Law Soc. Coll. of Law. Admitted solicitor, 1953. Nat. Service, Intelligence Corps, 1953–55, Lieut. Partner in Messrs Burchell & Ruston, Solicitors, 1953–94. Dep. Sheriff, Co. of London, then Greater London, 1953–74; DL Greater London, 1978. Mem. Council, Shrievalty Assoc., 1985–91; Vice-Pres., Under Sheriffs Assoc., 1985–87, Pres., 1987–93. Member: House of Laity, Gen. Synod, 1982–97; (a Chm., Gen. Synod, 1991); Dioceses Commn, 1986–91; Ecclesiastical Fees Adv. Commn, 1986–96; Bd of Social Responsibility, 1992–96. Lay Reader, 1983–97. Founder Mem. and Trustee, Ted Russell Charitable Trust, 1987–. Governor, St Matthew's C of E Infant Sch., Cobham, 1995–97. *Publications:* contributions to: Halsbury's Laws of England, 4th edn, vols 25, 1978 (rev. edn 1994), and 42, 1983 (rev. edn 1999); Atkin's Court Forms, 3rd edn, vols 19, 1972 (rev. edn 1985), 22, 1968, and 36, 1977 (rev. edn 1988); Enforcement of a Judgement, 8th edn, 1993. *Recreations:* horseracing, gardening, travel. *Address:* The Bothy, Hawkley Hurst, near Liss, Hants GU33 6NS. *T:* (01420) 538404. *Died 19 Oct. 2013.*

BLACK, Cilla, OBE 1997; entertainer; *b* 27 May 1943; *née* Priscilla Maria Veronica White; *d* of John and Priscilla White; *m* 1969, Bobby Willis (*d* 1999); three *s*. *Television series include:* Cilla (8 series), 1968–76; Cilla's World of Comedy, 1976; Surprise, Surprise, 1984–99; Blind Date, 1985–2003; The Moment of Truth, 1998–2001; Soapstar Superstar, 2005; *films:* Ferry Cross the Mersey, 1964; Work is a Four-Letter Word, 1968; *recordings include:* (singles): Love of the Loved, 1963; Anyone Who Had a Heart, 1964; You're My World, 1964; It's For You, 1964; You've Lost that Lovin' Feeling, 1965; Love's Just a Broken Heart, 1966; Alfie, 1966; Don't Answer Me, 1966; Step Inside Love, 1968; Surround Yourself With Sorrow, 1969; Conversations, 1969; Something Tells Me, 1971; (albums): Cilla, 1965; Cilla Sings a Rainbow, 1966; Sher-oo!, 1968; Beginnings, 2003. Top TV Female Personality, Sun Awards, 1970, 1971, 1972, 1973 and 1974 (including a Gold Award); Favourite Female Personality on TV Awards, TV Times, 1986, 1988, 1989 and 1990; Top Female Comedy Star, Writers' Guild of GB, 1975; Variety Club Showbusiness Personality, 1991; Lew Grade Award, BAFTA, 1995; Special Television Award, BAFTA, 2014. *Publications:* Step Inside, 1985; Through the Years: my Life in Pictures, 1993; What's It All About?, 2003. *Died 2 Aug. 2015.*

BLACK, Adm. Sir (John) Jeremy, GBE 1991 (MBE 1963); KCB 1987; DSO 1982; Stia Negara Brunei 1963; Vice Admiral of the United Kingdom and Lieutenant of the Admiralty, 2001–03 (Rear Admiral of the United Kingdom, 1997–2001); *b* 17 Nov. 1932; *s* of Alan H. Black and Gwendoline Black; *m* 1958, Alison Pamela Barber; two *s* one *d*. *Educ:* Royal Naval College, Dartmouth (entered 1946). Korean War and Malayan Emergency, 1951–52; qualified in gunnery, 1958; commanded HM Ships: Fiskerton, 1960–62 (Brunei Rebellion, 1962); Decoy, 1969 (Comdr 1969, Captain 1974); Fife, 1977; RCDS 1979; Director of Naval Operational Requirements, Naval Staff, 1980–81; commanded HMS Invincible (Falklands), 1982–83; Flag Officer, First Flotilla, 1983–84; ACNS (Policy), Oct.–Dec. 1984; ACNS, 1985–86; Dep. CDS (Systems), 1986–89; C-in-C Naval Home Comd, 1989–91; Flag ADC, 1989–91. Chairman: Remy and Associates (UK) Ltd, 1992–96; Applied Visuals Ltd, 1998–2000; Berry Birch & Noble, 1999–2002; Director: Devonport Management Ltd, 1992–97; Macallan-Glenlivet plc, 1993–96; Global Emerging Markets Europe Ltd, 1993–96; St Davids Investment Trust, 1996–98; Gosport Seaport Ltd, 1993–96; Consultant: Shorts, 1992–98; British Aerospace, 1993–97; Krug Champagne, 1996–99. Trustee, Imperial War Mus., 1991–97; Chm., Britain at War Mus., 1999–2010; Dir, Nat. Army Mus., 2004–10. Mem. Council, RUSI, 1987–89. Gov., Wellington Coll., 1992–2003; Chm. Govs, Eagle House, 1998–2003. Chairman: Whitbread Round the World Race Cttee, 1990–94; Royal Navy Club of 1765 and 1785, 1992–95; Governor, Ocean Youth Club, 1991–95 (Chm., World Voyage, 1994–97). Life Vice Cdre, RNSA, 1991 (Cdre, 1989–91). *Publications:* There and Back (autobiog.), 2005. *Recreations:* sailing, history. *Clubs:* Boodle's; Royal Yacht Squadron. *Died 25 Nov. 2015.*

BLACK, Timothy Reuben Ladbroke, CBE 1994; Founder, 1975, Chief Executive, 1975–2006, and Trustee, since 2007, Marie Stopes International; *b* 7 Jan. 1937; *s* of late Stephen Joscelyn Ladbroke Black and Dorothy Joyce (*née* Bedford, later Fletcher); *m* 1962, Jean Carter; two *d*. *Educ:* Dartington Hall Sch., Devon; Brighton Tech. Coll.;

St George's Hosp., London Univ. (MB BS); Univ. of Northern Carolina (MPH 1970). MRCS 1962; LRCP 1962, MRCP 1966; DTM&H 1968; CDipAF 1989. Jun. House Officer, Harare Hosp., Salisbury, Rhodesia, 1962–63; Sen. House Officer, Croydon General and Mayday Hosps, 1963–64; Medical Registrar, Harefield Hosp., 1964–65; Consultant Physician, Rabaul and E Sepik Reg., New Guinea Med. Service, 1967; GP, NZ, 1968; Population Studies Fellow, Population Council and Ford Foundn, Univ. of N Carolina, 1969–70; Population Services International: Co-founder, 1970; Vice-Pres., 1970–75; Africa Regl Dir, Nairobi, Kenya, 1972–74. Chm., Options Consultancy Services Ltd, 1992–2007 (Dir, 2007–); Vice Pres., DKT Internat., 1985–. FRSTM&H 1970; FCMI (FIMgt 1985); FCIM 1989; FFSRH (FFFP 2006). *Publications:* numerous articles in population/family planning jls covering service delivery, contraceptive social marketing and mgt issues. *Recreations:* gardening, geese, hill-walking, trees, reading. *Address:* Gorsedene, Lower Beeding, Sussex RH13 6PX. *Club:* Royal Society of Medicine. *Died 11 Dec. 2014.*

BLACKBURN, Mark Alistair Sinclair, PhD, LittD; FSA; Keeper of Coins and Medals, Fitzwilliam Museum, since 1991, and Reader in Numismatics and Monetary History, since 2004, University of Cambridge; Fellow, Gonville and Caius College, Cambridge, since 2005; *b* 5 Jan. 1953; *y s* of late Neil Blackburn and Joan Wallace Blackburn; *m* 1980, Fiona Anne Haigh; two *s* one *d.* *Educ:* Skinners' Sch.; St Edmund Hall, Oxford (BA Juris. 1975; MA 1978); Gonville and Caius Coll., Cambridge (PhD 1994; LittD 2011). Called to the Bar, Middle Temple, 1976; in practice, 1976–78; Kleinwort Benson Ltd, 1978–82; Res. Associate, 1982–86, Sen. Res. Associate, 1986–91, Faculty of Hist., Univ. of Cambridge; Bye-Fellow, Gonville and Caius Coll., Cambridge, 1990–91. Mem. British Acad. Cttee, Sylloge of Coins of the British Isles, 1980– (Jt Editor, 1980–87; Gen. Editor, 1987–); Dir, Corpus of Early Medieval Coin Finds from British Isles proj., 1996–. Pres., British Numismatic Soc., 2003–08 (Ed., British Numismatic Jl, 1983–87); FRNS 1976 (Editor, Numismatic Chronicle, 1992–98); FSA 1983; FRHistS 1989. Member Editorial Board: Studies in Anglo-Saxon History, 1985–98; Anglo-Saxon England, 1991–; Revue Belge de Numismatique, 2007–; Gen. Ed., Medieval Eur. Coinage series, 1998–. Gov., Skinners' Sch., 2007–10. Liveryman, Skinners' Co., 2008. Société Française de Numismatique Medal, 1991; Royal Numismatic Soc. Medal, 2008; Sanford Saltus Medal, British Numismatic Soc., 2008; Derek Allen Prize, British Acad., 2011. *Publications:* (ed jtly) Viking-Age Coinage in the Northern Lands, 1981; (jtly) Early Medieval Coins from Lincoln and its Shire c. 770–1100, 1983; (jtly) Medieval European Coinage 1: the Early Middle Ages (5th–10th Century), 1986; (ed) Anglo-Saxon Monetary History, 1986; (ed jtly) Kings, Currency and Alliances, 1996; Viking Coinage and Currency in the British Isles, 2011; contrib. books and learned jls. *Recreation:* travelling off the beaten track. *Address:* Fitzwilliam Museum, Trumpington Street, Cambridge CB2 1RB. *T:* (01223) 332900. *E:* mab1001@cam.ac.uk. *Died 1 Sept. 2011.*

BLACKETT-ORD, His Honour Andrew James, CVO 1988; a Circuit Judge, 1972–87; Vice-Chancellor, County Palatine of Lancaster, 1973–87; *b* 21 Aug. 1921; 2nd *s* of late John Reginald Blackett-Ord, Whitfield, Northumberland; *m* 1945, Rosemary Bovill; three *s* one *d.* *Educ:* Eton; New Coll., Oxford (MA). Scots Guards, 1943–46; called to Bar, 1947, Bencher, Lincoln's Inn, 1985; County Court Judge, 1971. Mem. Council, Duchy of Lancaster, 1973–87. Chancellor, Dio. of Newcastle-upon-Tyne, 1971–98. *Recreations:* reading, art, shooting, country life, travel. *Address:* Helbeck Hall, Brough, Kirkby Stephen, Cumbria CA17 4DD. *T:* (017683) 41323. *Clubs:* Garrick, Lansdowne. *Died 21 Feb. 2012.*

BLACKSHAW, Alan, OBE 1992; VRD 1970; President, Union Internationale des Associations d'Alpinisme, 2005; *b* 7 April 1933; *s* of late Frederick William Blackshaw and Elsie (*née* MacDougall); *m* 1st, 1956, Jane Elizabeth Turner (marr. diss. 1983); one *d*; 2nd, 1984, Dr Elspeth Paterson Martin, *d* of late Rev. Gavin C. Martin and Agnes Martin; one *s* two *d.* *Educ:* Merchant Taylors' Sch., Crosby; Wadham Coll., Oxford (MA). Royal Marines (commnd), 1954–56, and RM Reserve, 1956–76. Entered Home Civil Service, Min. of Power, 1956; 1st Sec., UK Delegn to OECD, Paris, 1965–66; Principal Private Sec. to Minister of Power, 1967–69; with Charterhouse Gp on loan, 1972–73; Dept of Energy: Under Sec., 1974; Offshore Supplies Office, 1974–78 (Dir-Gen., 1977–78); Coal Div., 1978–79; Consultant, NCB, 1979–86. Consultant Dir, Strategy Internat., 1980–91; Director: Paths for All Partnership, 1996–97; Badenoch, Moray and Strathspey Enterprise, 1998–2000. Member: Scottish Council for Develt and Industry, 1974–78; Offshore Energy Technol. Bd, 1977–78; Ship and Marine Technol. Requirements Bd, 1977–78; Scottish Sports Council, 1990–95; Scottish Natural Heritage, 1992–97 (Chairman: Task Force on Access, 1992–94; Audit Cttee, 1994–97); Adventure Activities Licensing Authy, 1996–2005; Bd, Cairngorms Partnership, 1998–2003 (Chm., Recreational Forum, 1998–2003); Rights of Way Survey Steering Gp, Countryside Agency, 2000–02. University of Highlands and Islands Project: Academic Advr, 1997–2001; Chm., Working Gp on Tourism and Leisure, 1998–99; Mem., Scis and Envmt Faculty Bd, 1999–2004. Libel damages against Daily Telegraph (upheld in Ct of Appeal, 1983) and Daily Mail, 1981. Pres., Oxford Univ. Mountaineering Club, 1953–54; Climbers' Club: Sec., 1956–61; Vice-Pres., 1973–75; Hon. Mem., 1998; Alpine Club: Editor, Alpine Jl, 1968–70; Vice-Pres., 1979–81; Trustee, 1980–90; Hon. Mem., 1998; Pres., 2001–04; British Mountaineering Council: Pres., 1973–76; Patron, 1979–; Chairman: Standing Adv. Cttee on Mountain Trng Policy, 1980–86 and 1990–93; Ski Touring and Mountaineering Cttee, 1981–91. Chairman: Sports Council's Nat. Mountain Centre (formerly Nat. Centre for Mountain Activities), Plas y Brenin, 1986–95; Mountaineering Cttee, UIAA, 1990–2000 (Mem., 1985–89; Dep. Chm., 1989–90); UIAA Gp on competitions in mountain areas, 1993–96, on mountain access, 1995–99; UK Mountain Trng Bd, 1991–94; Scottish Adventure Activities Forum, 1999–2007; Interim Wkg Gp on Leadership in Outdoor Activities, Sports Council, 1990–91; Leader, British Alpine Ski Traverse, 1972; UIAA Special Representative: UN Inter-Agency Gp on Mountains, 1996–2005; UN Year of Mountains 2002, 2000–03; Adviser on public access to land: Scottish Envmt Link, 1994–2010; CCPR, 1997–2003; Hon. Advr, Mountaineering Council of Scotland, 1994–. Pres., Snowsport Scotland (formerly Scottish Nat. Ski Council), 1994–2000 (Chm., 1991–94); Ski Club of Great Britain: Vice-Pres., 1977–80, 1983–85; Pres., 1997–2003; Pery Medal, 1977; Hon. Mem., 1992; Pres., Eagle Ski Club, 1979–81 (Hon. Mem., 1982); British Ski Federation: Vice-Pres., 1983–84; Chm., 1984–86. Sec., Edinburgh Br., Oxford Soc., 1989–98. Hon. Advr, Venture Scotland, 1995–2004. Freeman, City of London. Award for voluntary service to sport and Olympism, IOC, 2001. *Publications:* Mountaineering, 1965, 3rd revision 1975. *Recreations:* mountaineering, ski-ing, sailing. *Address:* Rhu Grianach, Kingussie Road, Newtonmore, Inverness-shire PH20 1AY. *T:* (01540) 673239; Les Autannes, Le Tour, Argentière, 74440, France. *T:* 450541220. *Died 4 Aug. 2011.*

BLAIR, Lt-Gen. Sir Chandos, KCVO 1972; OBE 1962; MC 1941 and bar, 1944; GOC Scotland and Governor of Edinburgh Castle, 1972–76; *b* 25 Feb. 1919; *s* of Brig.-Gen. Arthur Blair and Elizabeth Mary (*née* Hoskyns); *m* 1947, Audrey Mary Travers (*d* 1997); one *d* (and one *s* decd). *Educ:* Harrow; Sandhurst. Commnd into Seaforth Highlanders, 1939; comd 4 KAR, Uganda, 1959–61; comd 39 Bde, Radfan and N. Ireland. GOC 2nd Division, BAOR, 1968–70; Defence Services Secretary, MoD, 1970–72. Col Comdt, Scottish Div., 1972–76; Col, Queen's Own Highlanders, 1975–83. *Recreations:* golf, fishing, shooting. *Died 22 Jan. 2011.*

BLAKE, Sir Alfred (Lapthorn), KCVO 1979 (CVO 1975); MC 1945; DL; Director, The Duke of Edinburgh's Award Scheme, 1967–78; Consultant with Blake Lapthorn, Solicitors, Portsmouth and area, 1985–2000 (Partner, 1949–85, Senior Partner, 1983–85); *b* 6 Oct. 1915; *s* of late Leonard Nicholson Blake and Nora Woodfall Blake (*née* Lapthorn); *m* 1st, 1940, Beatrice Grace Nellthorp (*d* 1967); two *s*; 2nd, 1969, Alison Kelsey Dick, Boston, Mass, USA. *Educ:* Dauntsey's Sch. LLB (London), 1938. Qual. Solicitor and Notary Public, 1938. Royal Marines Officer, 1939–45: Bde Major 2 Commando Bde, 1944; Lieut-Col comdg 45 (RM) Commando and Holding Operational Commando, 1945 (despatches). Mem., Portsmouth CC, 1950–67 (Past Chm., Portsmouth Educn Cttee); Lord Mayor of Portsmouth, 1958–59. Mem., Youth Service Development Council, 1960–66; Pres., Portsmouth Youth Activities Cttee, 1976–2007; Patron: Elizabeth Foundn, 1984–; Portsmouth Family Welfare, 1987–. Lay Canon, Portsmouth Cathedral, 1962–72. DL Hants, 1991. Hon. Fellow, Portsmouth Univ. (formerly Poly.), 1981. Hon. Freeman, City of Portsmouth, 2003. *Recreation:* golf. *Address:* 59 Shipwright Circle, Port Royal, SC 29935–1100, USA. *T:* (843) 5251310. *Died 17 Nov. 2013.*

BLAKENEY, Hon. Allan Emrys, OC 1992; SOM 2000; PC (Can.) 1982; QC (Sask) 1961; FRSC; Visiting Scholar, University of Saskatchewan, Saskatoon, since 1992 (Professor of Law, 1990–92); *b* Bridgewater, NS, 7 Sept. 1925; *m* 1st, 1950, Mary Elizabeth (Molly) Schwartz (*d* 1957), Halifax, NS; one *s* one *d*; 2nd, 1959, Anne Gorham, Halifax; one *s* one *d*. *Educ:* Dalhousie Univ. (BA, LLB); Queen's Coll., Oxford (MA). FRSC 2001. Univ. Medal for Achievement in Coll. of Law, Dalhousie; Rhodes Schol. Sec. and Legal Adviser, Saskatchewan Crown Corps, 1950; Chm., Saskatchewan Securities Commn, 1955–58; private law practice, 1958–60 and 1964–70. MLA, Saskatchewan, 1960–88; formerly Minister of Educn, Provincial Treas. and Health Minister; Chm., Wascana Centre Authority, 1962–64; Opposition Financial Critic, 1964–70; Dep. Leader, 1967–70; Federal New Democratic Party President, 1969–71; Saskatchewan NDP Leader and Leader of Opposition, 1970; Premier, 1971–82; Leader of Opposition, Sask, 1982–87. Prof. of Public Law, Osgoode Hall Law Sch., York Univ., Toronto, 1988–90. Hon. DCL Mount Allison; Hon. LLD: Dalhousie; York; Western Ontario; Regina; Saskatchewan. *Publications:* Political Management in Canada (with Sandford Borins), 1992, 2nd edn 1998; An Honourable Calling: political memoirs, 2008. *Recreations:* reading, swimming, formerly ice hockey and badminton. *Address:* 1752 Prince of Wales Avenue, Saskatoon, SK S7K 3E5, Canada; College of Law, 15 Campus Drive, University of Saskatchewan, Saskatoon, SK S7N 5A6, Canada. *Died 16 April 2011.*

BLANDINO, Elizabeth Assunta, (Betty), (Mrs E. A. Jones); studio potter (self employed) and writer, since 1973; *b* 12 Sept. 1927; *d* of Pietro Pierino Blandino and Marie Bradlaugh; *m* 1973, Gwyn Owain Jones, CBE (*d* 2006); two step *d*. *Educ:* St Aloysius Convent Sch., London NW1; Univ. of Reading (Teacher's Cert. 1947); Goldsmiths Coll. of Art, London Univ. (Painting and Ceramics 1958); Postgrad. Dip Art Educn, London Univ., 1973. Teacher, all levels, 1947–58; Asst Dir, 1958–61, Dir, 1961–67, Upper Gall., Whitechapel (ILEA); County Art Advr, E Sussex Educn Authy, 1967–71. Pres., Oxfordshire Craft Guild, 1990–93; Mem., Oxford Art Soc. *Exhibitions include:* solo/sole potter: Commonwealth Inst., London, 1975; Oriel, Welsh Arts Council Gall., Cardiff, 1976; Oxford Gall., 1978; Peter Dingley Gall., Stratford-upon-Avon, 1980; Beaux Arts, Bath, 1982; Prescote Gall., Cropredy, 1983; Primavera, Cambridge, 1986; Galerie L, Hamburg, 1988; Sheila Harrison Fine Art, London, 1991; Blue Gall., London, 1995; Manor House Gall., Chipping Norton, 1999; Abingdon Mus., 2008; group: New Faces, British Crafts Centre, London, 1977; Handbuilt Ceramics, Casson Gall., London, 1981; Keramik aus England, Marianne Heller Galerie, Heidelberg and Galerie Handwerk, Munich, 1989; Gall. North, Kirkby Lonsdale, 1990; Crafts in the City, Bluecoat Display Centre, Liverpool, 1992; South Bank Centre, RFH, London, 1993; Focus, V&A Mus., 1998; Spring Fever, Focus, Contemp. Applied Arts, London, 2000; Internat. Clay Works, Carlin Gall., Paris, 2000; work in public and private collections including: Ashmolean Mus., Oxford; Bristol Mus. and Art Gall.; Buckinghamshire Co. Mus.; Cheltenham Art Gall. and Mus.; Cleveland Crafts Centre, Middlesbrough; Fitzwilliam Mus., Cambridge; Hereford City Mus. and Art Gall.; Merseyside Co. Mus., Liverpool; Nat. Mus. and Art Gall. of Wales, Cardiff; Southampton City Art Gall.; V&A Mus., London; York City Art Gall., Yorkshire Mus., York; Mus. Bellerive, Zurich; Mus. of Applied Arts, Cologne; Mus. für Kunst und Gewerbe, Hamburg. *Publications:* Coiled Pottery, 1984, revd edn 1997, colour edn 2003; The Figure in Fired Clay, 2001. *Recreations:* essentially sober cultural activities, life drawing and painting, gardening, food. *Address:* 12 Squitchey Lane, Oxford OX2 7LB. *T:* (01865) 510363. *E:* Bettyablandino@btinternet.com. *Died 10 Sept. 2011.*

BLANDY, Prof. John Peter, CBE 1995; MA, DM, MCh, FRCS, FACS; Consultant Surgeon: The Royal London (formerly London) Hospital, 1964–92; St Peter's Hospital for the Stone, 1969–92; Professor of Urology, University of London, 1969–92, then Emeritus; *b* 11 Sept. 1927; *s* of late Sir E. Nicolas Blandy, KCIE, CSI, ICS and Dorothy Kathleen (*née* Marshall); *m* 1953, Anne, *d* of Hugh Mathias, FRCS, Tenby; four *d*. *Educ:* Clifton Coll.; Balliol Coll., Oxford (Hon. Fellow, 1992); London Hosp. Med. Coll. BM, BCh 1951; MA 1953; FRCS 1956; DM 1963; MCh 1963; FACS 1980. House Phys. and House Surg., London Hosp., 1952; RAMC, 1953–55; Surgical Registrar and Lectr in Surgery, London Hosp., 1956–60; exchange Fellow, Presbyterian St Luke's Hosp., Chicago, 1960–61; Sen. Lectr, London Hosp., 1961; Resident Surgical Officer, St Paul's Hosp., 1963–64. McLaughlin-Gallie Vis. Prof., Royal Coll. of Physicians and Surgeons of Canada, 1988. Member: BMA; RSM (Hon. FRSocMed 1995); Council, RCS, 1982–94 (Hunterian Prof., 1964; Hunterian Orator, 1991; a Vice-Pres., 1992–94); GMC, 1992–96; Internat. Soc. Pædiatric Urol. Surg.; Internat. Soc. of Urological Surgeons; British Assoc. Urological Surgeons (Pres., 1984); President: European Assoc. of Urology, 1986–88; European Bd of Urology, 1991–92. Chm., Nat. Confidential Enquiry into Perioperative Deaths, 1992–97. Fellow, Assoc. of Surgeons; Hon. FRCSI 1992; Hon. Fellow, Urological Society: of Australasia, 1973; of Canada, 1986; of Denmark, 1986; of Germany, 1987; of The Netherlands, 1990; of Romania, 1991; of Japan, 1991; Hon. Fellow: Mexican Coll. of Urology, 1974; Amer. Urol Assoc., 1989. Maurice Davidson Award, Fellowship of Postgrad. Med., 1980; St Peter's Medal, British Assoc. of Urol Surgs, 1982; Francisco Diaz Medal, Spanish Urol Assoc., 1988; Grégoir Medal, Eur. Assoc. of Urology, 2001. Ed., Lives of the Fellows of the Royal College of Surgeons, 1985–2010. *Publications:* (with A. D. Dayan and H. F. Hope-Stone) Tumours of the Testicle, 1970; Transurethral Resection, 1971, 5th edn (with R. G. Notley and J. M. Reynard) 2004; (ed) Urology, 1976, 2nd edn (with C. G. Fowler) 1995; Lecture Notes on Urology, 1976; Operative Urology, 1978; (ed with B. Lytton) The Prostate, 1986; (with J. Moors) Urology for Nurses, 1989; (ed with R. T. D. Oliver and H. F. Hope-Stone) Urological and Genital Cancer, 1989; (ed with J. S. P. Lumley) History of the Royal College of Surgeons, 2000; papers in surgical and urological jls. *Recreation:* painting. *Address:* 362 Shakespeare Tower, Barbican, EC2Y 8NJ. *T:* (020) 7638 4095. *Died 23 July 2011.*

BLATCHLY, John Marcus, MBE 2007; MA, PhD; FSA 1975; Headmaster, Ipswich School, 1972–93; *b* 7 Oct. 1932; *s* of late Alfred Ernest Blatchly and Edith Selina Blatchly (*née* Giddings); *m* 1955, Pamela Winifred, JP, *d* of late Major and Mrs L. J. Smith; one *s* one *d*. *Educ:* Sutton Grammar Sch., Surrey; Christ's Coll., Cambridge (Natural Scis Triposes; BA, MA, PhD). Instr Lieut RN, 1954–57. Asst Master and Head of Science Dept: King's Sch., Bruton, 1957–62; Eastbourne Coll., 1962–66; Charterhouse, 1966–72 (PhD awarded 1967 publication of work carried out with Royal Society grants at these three schools). Sen. Vis. Fellow in History, 2011–14, Hon. Wolsey Prof. of History, 2014–, Univ. Campus Suffolk. Pres., Suffolk Inst. of Archaeology and History, 1975–2001; Chm., Suffolk Records Soc., 1988–2013. Editor, Conference and Common Room (Journal of HMC Schools), 1987–92; Hon. Treas., 1990–92, Hon. Associate Mem., 1993, HMC; lead inspector to HMC schs, 1994–2000. Co-ed., Bookplate Jl, 1994–98. Hon. Res. Associate, Oxford DNB, 2001. Gov. of several schs, 1993–2005. President: Old Ipswichian Club, 2011; Bookplate Soc., 2012–. Hon. LittD UEA, 1993. *Publications:* Organic Reactions, vol. 19, 1972 (jtly, with J. F. W. McOmie); The Topographers of Suffolk, 1976, 5th edn 1988; (with Peter Eden) Isaac Johnson of Woodbridge, 1979; Eighty Ipswich Portraits, 1980; (ed) Davy's Suffolk Journal, 1983; The Town Library of Ipswich: a history and catalogue, 1989; The Bookplates of Edward Gordon Craig, 1997; Some Suffolk and Norfolk

Ex-Libris, 2000; (jtly) The Journal of William Dowsing, 2001; The Bookplates of George Wolfe Plank, 2002; A Famous Antient Seed-Plot of Learning: a history of Ipswich School, 2003; John Kirby's Suffolk: his maps and roadbooks, 2004; (with Peter Northeast) Decoding Flint Flushwork on Suffolk and Norfolk Churches, 2005; East Anglian Ex-Libris, 2008; (with Martin Sanford) Thomas Fella's Book of Divers Devices, 2012; (with Diarmaid MacCulloch) Miracles in Lady Lane: the Ipswich Shrine at the Westgate, 2013; Isaac Johnson of Woodbridge, Georgian Surveyor and Artist, 2014; many papers in chemical, educnl, archaeological and antiquarian jls. *Recreations:* East Anglian history, music, books. *Address:* 11 Burlington Road, Ipswich, Suffolk IP1 2HS. *Club:* East India. *Died Sept. 2015.*

BLAUG, Prof. Mark, PhD; FBA 1989; Professor of the Economics of Education, University of London Institute of Education, 1967–84, then Professor Emeritus; *b* 3 April 1927; *s* of Bernard Blaug and Sarah (*née* Toeman); *m* 1st, 1946, Rose Lapone (marr. diss.); 2nd, 1954, Brenda Ellis (marr. diss.); one *s*; 3rd, 1969, Ruth M. Towse; one *s*. *Educ:* Queen's Coll., NY (BA); Columbia Univ. (MA, PhD). Asst Prof., Yale Univ., 1954–62; Sen. Lectr, then Reader, Univ. of London Inst. of Educn, 1963–67; Lectr, LSE, 1963–78. Consultant Prof., Univ. of Buckingham, 1984–92, then Prof. Emeritus; Visiting Professor: Exeter Univ., 1989–2001; Univ. of Amsterdam, 1999–2008; Erasmus Univ., Rotterdam, 2000–07. Guggenheim Foundn Fellow, 1958–59. Dist. Fellow, Hist. of Econs Soc., 1988. Editl Consultant, Edward Elgar Publishing, 1986–. Foreign Hon. Mem., Royal Netherlands Acad. of Arts and Scis, 1984. Hon. DSc Buckingham, 1993. *Publications:* Ricardian Economics, 1958; Economic Theory in Retrospect, 1962, 5th edn 1996; (jtly) The Causes of Graduate Unemployment in India, 1969; Introduction to the Economics of Education, 1970; Education and the Employment Problem in Developing Countries, 1973; (jtly) The Practice of Manpower Forecasting, 1973; The Cambridge Revolution?, 1974; The Methodology of Economics, 1980, 2nd edn 1992; Who's Who in Economics, 1983, 4th edn (jtly) 2003; Great Economists Since Keynes, 1984, 2nd edn 1998; Great Economists Before Keynes, 1986; Economic History and the History of Economics, 1986; The Economics of Education and the Education of an Economist, 1987; Economic Theories: True or False?, 1990; Keynes: Life, Ideas and Legacy, 1990; (jtly) Appraising Economic Theories, 1991; (jtly) Quantity Theory of Money, 1995; Not Only an Economist, 1997; (jtly) Great Figures and Diagrams in Economics, 2010. *Recreations:* talking, walking, sailing. *Address:* Langsford Barn, Peter Tavy, Tavistock, Devon PL19 9LY. *T:* (01822) 810562. *Died 18 Nov. 2011.*

BLESSLEY, Kenneth Harry, CBE 1974 (MBE 1945); ED; Valuer and Estates Surveyor, Greater London Council, 1964–77; *b* 28 Feb. 1914; *s* of Victor Henry le Blond Blessley and Ellen Mary Blessley; *m* 1946, Gwendeline MacRae (*d* 2005); two *s*. *Educ:* Haberdashers' Aske's Hampstead Sch.; St Catharine's Coll., Cambridge (MA); Coll. of Estate Management. FRICS. Private practice, West End and London suburbs. Served War of 1939–45, TA Royal Engrs, Persia, Middle East, Sicily, Italy (despatches 1942 and 1944). Sen. Property Adviser, Public Trustee, 1946–50; Dep. County Valuer, Middx CC, 1950–53; County Valuer, Middx CC, 1953–65. Mem. Urban Motorways Cttee, 1970–72; Chm., Covent Garden Officers' Steering Gp, 1970–77; Chm., Thamesmead Officers' Steering Gp, 1971–76; Pres., Assoc. of Local Authority Valuers and Estate Surveyors, 1962 and 1972; Mem. Gen. Council, RICS, 1972–78, Pres., Gen. Practice Div., 1976–77. Pres., Old Haberdashers' Assoc., 1963 (Pres. RFC, 1966–68); Vice-Pres., Cambridge Univ. Land Soc., 1985–86. *Publications:* numerous articles and papers on compensation, property valuation and development. *Recreations:* music, drama, sport, motoring. *Address:* Sun Rise, Christchurch Road, Virginia Water, Surrey GU25 4BE. *Died 10 April 2012.*

BLOWERS, Dr Anthony John, CBE 1985; JP, DL; CBiol; FIBMS; Commissioner, Mental Health Act Commission, 1987–95; Director, Ogilvy Public Relations Worldwide, 1999; *b* 11 Aug. 1926; *e s* of late Geoffrey Hathaway and Louise Blowers; *m* 1948, Yvonne Boiteux-Buchanan; two *s* one *d*. *Educ:* Sloane Sch., Chelsea; Sir John Cass Coll.; Univ. of London; Univ. of Surrey (PhD 1982). FIMLS 1983; CBiol 1984. Served War, RCS, 1944–45; served: RAMC, 1945–46; RWAFF, 1946–48. Min. of Agriculture, 1948–59, Exptl Officer, 1953–59; Sandoz Pharmaceuticals, 1959–91; Sen. Res. Officer, 1973–87; Psychopharmacology Consultant, 1987–91; Consultant in Bacteriology, Mansi Labs, 1973–90. Dir, Corporate Affairs, Magellan Medical Communications, 1990–99. Vis. Res. Fellow, Roehampton Inst., 1998; Vis. Lectr, Dept of Psychiatry of Addictive Behaviour, St George's Hosp. Med. Sch., 1999. Chairman: W Surrey and NE Hants HA, 1981–86; Mental Health and Learning Disabilities Monitoring Gp, SW Surrey HA, 1991–95; Member: Surrey AHA, 1973–80 (Vice Chm., 1976–77); SW Thames RHA, 1980–81; Mental Health Review Tribunal, 1975–99; Nat. Standing Cttees on Consent to Treatment and Community Care, 1992–95. Admin. Sec., All-Party Parly Gp on R & D in Fertility and Contraception, 1994. Member: Chertsey UDC, 1964–74 (Chm., 1969–70, 1973–74); Runnymede BC, 1973–84 (Chm., 1973–74); Surrey CC, 1970–85 (Vice Chm., Social Services Cttee, 1973–77); Surrey Police Authority, 1973–90 (Chm., 1981–85); Chairman: Runnymede and Elmbridge Police Community Liaison Cttee, 1983–94; Surrey Drug Action Team, 1995–2001. Chm. SE Region, and Mem. Nat. Adv. Council, Duke of Edinburgh's Award, 1990–98; Chm., Surrey Magistrates' Soc., 1988–94; Member: Council, Magistrates' Assoc., 1986–91; Bd of Visitors, Coldingley Prison, 1978–93; Court, Surrey Univ., 1986; Surrey Scout Council, 1991; Pres., Runnymede Scout Council, 1970–84. Vice-President: Hosp. Saving Assoc., 1994; Parkinson's Disease Soc., 1995 (Actg Chief Exec., 1995); Mem. Council, 1986, Trustee, 1995, Psychiatry Res. Trust; Chm., Knight Foundn for Cystic Fibrosis Appeal, 1997. Mem., CGA, 2000–09. Governor: Fullbrook Sch., 1967–85 (Chm., 1981–85); Ottershaw Sch., 1975–81 (Chm., 1979–81). Liveryman, Worshipful Soc. of Apothecaries, 1988– (Yeoman, 1983–88); Freeman, City of London, 1983; Hon. Freeman, Bor. of Runnymede, 1985. JP 1970, DL 1986, High Sheriff, 1990–91, Surrey. St John Ambulance: Asst Dir Gen., 1985–91; Dir Gen., 1991–94; Actg Chief Comdr, 1991–92; Comdr, Surrey, 1987–91; Nat. Chm., 1995–2001, Vice-Pres., 2001–05, Life Patron, 2006, St John Fellowship. KStJ 1991 (Mem., Chapter-Gen., 1991–99; Mem. Priory, England and the Islands, 1999–2001). *Publications:* The Isolation of Salmonellae, 1978; Tardive Dyskinesia, 1982; Certificate in Drugs: prevention and education, 2002; contribs to med. and scientific books and jls. *Recreations:* tackling drug misuse; fund-raising, gardening. *Died 30 March 2014.*

BLUCK, Duncan Robert Yorke, CBE 1990 (OBE 1984); Chairman: British Tourist Authority, 1984–90; English Tourist Board, 1984–90; Director, John Swire & Sons, 1984–99; *b* 19 March 1927; *s* of Thomas Edward Bluck and Ida Bluck; *m* 1952, Stella Wardlaw Murdoch; one *s* three *d*. *Educ:* Taunton Sch. RNVR, 1944–47. Joined John Swire & Sons, 1948; Dir, 1964–99, Chief Exec., 1971–84, Chm., 1980–84, Cathay Pacific Airways; Chairman: John Swire & Sons (HK) Ltd, 1980–84; Swire Pacific Ltd, 1980–84; Swire Properties Ltd, 1980–84. Dir, Hongkong and Shanghai Banking Corp., 1981–84. Chairman: English Schools Foundn (Hongkong), 1978–84; Hongkong Tourist Assoc., 1981–84; Kent Economic Develt Bd, 1986–91; Cystic Fibrosis Trust, 1996–2003 (Pres., 2003–11). Governor, Marlborough House Sch., 1986–2007; Mem. Ct, Univ. of Kent, 1991–2001. JP Hong Kong, 1981–84. *Recreation:* sailing. *Address:* 2 West Cross, Tenterden, Kent TN30 6JL. *T:* (01580) 766729. *Clubs:* Hong Kong, Sheko (Hong Kong). *Died 6 Oct. 2015.*

BLUMBERG, Prof. Baruch Samuel, MD, PhD; Distinguished Scientist, and Senior Advisor to the President, Fox Chase Cancer Center, since 1989; Distinguished Scientist, Lunar Institute, NASA, Ames Research Center, California (Director, Astrobiology Institute, 1999–2002); *b* 28 July 1925; *s* of Meyer Blumberg and Ida Blumberg; *m* 1954, Jean Liebesman Blumberg; two *s* two *d*. *Educ:* Union Coll. (BS Physics, 1946); Columbia University Coll. of Physicians and Surgeons (MD 1951); Balliol Coll., Oxford (PhD Biochemistry, 1957; Hon.

Fellow, 1977). FRCP 1984. US Navy, 1943–46 (Lieut JG). US Public Health Service (rank of med. dir, Capt.), and Chief, Geographic Medicine and Genetics Sect., Nat. Insts of Health, Bethesda, Md, 1957–64; Associate Dir for Clinical Res., then Vice-Pres. for Population Oncology, Fox Chase Cancer Center, 1964–89; Univ. Prof. of Medicine and Anthropol., Univ. of Pennsylvania, 1977–; Clin. Prof., Dept of Epidemiology, Univ. of Washington Sch. of Public Health, 1983–89; Master of Balliol Coll., Oxford, 1989–94. Sen. Advr to Adminr, NASA, Washington, 2000–01. George Eastman Vis. Prof., Oxford Univ., 1983–84; Lokey Vis. Prof., Program in Human Biology, Stanford Univ., 1997–98; Fellow, Center for Advanced Study in Behavioural Scis, Stanford Univ. Mem. Nat. Acad. of Sciences, Washington. Pres., Amer. Philosophical Soc., 2005–; Mem., Soc. of Mars Explorers. Hon. DSc: Univ. of Pittsburgh, 1977; Union Coll., Schenectady, NY, 1977; Med. Coll. of Pa, 1977; Dickinson Coll., Carlisle, Pa, 1977; Hahnemann Med. Coll., Philadelphia, Pa, 1977; Indian Acad. of Scis, 1977; Elizabethtown Coll., Pa, 1988; Ball State Univ., Muncie, 1989; Dr *hc* Univ. of Paris VII, 1978. (Jt) Nobel Prize in Physiology or Medicine, 1976. *Publications:* (ed) Genetic Polymorphisms and Geographic Variations in Disease, 1961; (ed jtly) Medical Clinics of North America: new developments in medicine, 1970; (ed jtly) Hepatitis B: the virus, the disease and the vaccine, 1984; Hepatitis B: the hunt for a killer virus, 2002; *chapters in:* McGraw-Hill Encyclopedia of Science and Technology Yearbook, 1962; The Genetics of Migrant and Isolate Populations, ed E. Goldschmidt, 1963; Hemoglobin: its precursors and metabolites, ed F. W. Sunderman and F. W. Sunderman, Jr, 1964; McGraw-Hill Yearbook of Science and Technology, 1970; (also co-author chapter) Viral Hepatitis and Blood Transfusion, ed G. N. Vyas and others, 1972; Hematology, ed W. J. Williams and others, 1972; Progress in Liver Disease, Vol. IV, ed H. Popper and F. Schaffner, 1972; Australia Antigen, ed J. E. Prier and H. Friedman, 1973; Drugs and the Liver, ed. W. Gerok and K. Sickinger, 1975 (Germany); *(jtly) chapters in:* Progress in Medical Genetics, ed A. G. Steinberg and A. G. Bearn, 1965 (also London); Viruses Affecting Man and Animals, ed M. Sanders and M. Schaeffer, 1971; Perspectives in Virology, 1971; Transmissable Disease and Blood Transfusion, ed T. J. Greenwalt and G. A. Jamieson, 1975; Physiological Anthropology, ed A. Damon, 1975; Hepatite a Virus B et Hemodialyse, 1975 (Paris); Onco-Developmental Gene Expression, 1976; contrib. symposia; over 460 articles in scientific jls. *Recreations:* cycling, kayaking, cattle raising. *Club:* Explorers (New York). *Died 5 April 2011.*

BLUMER, Rodney Milnes, (Rodney Milnes), OBE 2002; Chief Opera Critic, The Times, 1992–2002; *b* 26 July 1936; *s* of Charles Eric Milnes Blumer and Kathleen Bertha Croft. *Educ:* Rugby School; Christ Church, Oxford (BA Hons Hist.). Editorial Dir, Rupert Hart-Davis Ltd, 1966–68; Music Critic, Queen magazine, later Harpers and Queen, 1968–87; Opera Critic: The Spectator, 1970–90; Evening Standard, 1990–92; Opera magazine: contribs, 1971–; Editl Bd, 1973; Associate Editor, 1976; Editor, 1986–99. Pres., Critics' Circle, 1988–90. Trustee, British Youth Opera, 2010–12. Hon. RAM 2002. Kt, Order of White Rose (Finland). *Publications:* numerous opera translations. *Recreation:* travel. *Address:* c/o Opera Magazine, 36 Black Lion Lane, W6 9BE. *Died 4 Dec. 2015.*

BLUNDELL, John; Distinguished Senior Fellow, Institute of Economic Affairs, since 2010 (Director General (formerly General Director), 1993–2010, and Ralph Harris Fellow, 2007–10); *b* 9 Oct. 1952; *s* of James Blundell and Alice Margaret Blundell (*née* Taylor); *m* 1977, Christine Violet Lowry; two *s*. *Educ:* King's Sch., Macclesfield; London Sch. of Econs, Univ. of London. Head of Press, Parly Liaison and Res. Office, Fedn of Small Businesses, 1976–82; Councillor (C), Lambeth BC, 1978–82; Institute for Humane Studies, George Mason University: Dir, Public Affairs, 1982–85; Exec. Vice-Pres., 1985–88; Pres., 1988–91; Trustee, 1991–; Atlas Economic Research Foundation, Washington, DC (formerly Fairfax, VA): Pres., 1987–91; Chm., Exec. Cttee, 1991–2005; Chm., Inst. Develt & Rels Bd Cttee, 2005–08; Co-Chm., Finance and HR, 2008–; Director: Inst. for Economic Studies, Europe (formerly Inst. for Humane Studies Europe), Paris, 1988–2002; Fraser Inst., Vancouver, 1987–92; Humane Studies Foundn, 1988–91; Atlas Economic Res. Foundn (UK), 1993–2001; Centre for the New Europe, Brussels, 1998–2003; Internat. Policy Network (UK), 2001–10; Founder Director: Inst. for Justice, Washington, 1991–93; Athens Inst., Alexandria, Va, 1992–2000; Founder Trustee, Buckeye Inst. for Public Policy Solutions, Dayton, Ohio, 1989–; Pres., Charles G. Koch and Claude R. Lambe Charitable Foundns, Washington DC, 1991–93. Co-founder and Chm., Inst. for Children, Cambridge, Mass, 1993–98. Advr, Business Wise, 1993–98; Member: Adv. Bd, Inst. de Libre Empresa, Peru, 2000–; Adv. Council, TaxPayers' Alliance, 2003–; Council of Reference, OPLAN Foundn, 2005–10. Mem. Council, 1998–2006, Mem., Adv. Bd, 2006–10, Fairbridge. Member: Mont Pelerin Soc., 1990– (Mem. Bd, 1998–2004; Vice Pres., 2002–04; Chm., London Host Cttee, 2002); Philadelphia Soc., 1994– (Bd Mem., 2006–10); Scientific Cttee, Adam Smith Soc., Milan, 2003–. Hon. Mem., Hayek Soc., LSE. Pres., Bd of Regents, Congressional Schs of Virginia, 1988–92. Vis. Fellow, Heritage Foundn, Washington, DC, 2010–. Associate Ed. for Internat. Business, Mid-Atlantic Jl of Business, 1996–2006. Member: Bd of Scholars, Centre for Civil Soc., New Delhi, 2001–; Selection Cttee, Milton Friedman Prize for Advancing Liberty, Cato Inst., 2002–08; Bd, Center for Freedom and Prosperity, Washington, 2005–; Bd, F. A. Hayek Inst., Vienna, 2005–10; Founder, and Founder Judge, Sir Antony Fisher Meml Awards, 1990–93. CCMI 2003–10. Nat. Free Enterprise Award, Aims of Industry, 2000. Hon. Mem., Templeton World Charity Foundn (formerly John Templeton Foundn), 2001–09. Hon. DSc Buckingham, 2010; Hon. DSSc Francisco Marroquin, Guatemala City, 2010 (Hon. Prof., 2010–). *Publications:* Fundraising for a Free Society, 1987; (with Brian Gosschalk) Beyond Left and Right, the New Politics of Britain, 1998; (with Colin Robinson) Regulation Without the State, 1999; (with Colin Robinson) Regulation Without the State…The Debate Continues, 2000; Waging the War of Ideas, 2001, 3rd edn 2007; (jtly) A Tribute to Peter Bauer, 2002; (with Gerald Frost) Friend or Foe?: what Americans should know about the European Union, 2004; Margaret Thatcher: a portrait of the Iron Lady, 2008; Ladies for Liberty: women who made a difference in American history, 2011, 2nd expanded edn 2013; (ed and annotated) Remembering Margaret Thatcher: commemorations, tributes and assessments, 2013; Female Force (series of comics): Margaret Thatcher, 2010; Ayn Rand, 2011; papers, contribs to jls, forewords, introductions, newspaper columns and magazine articles. *Recreations:* cricket, golf, genealogy, Morgan sports cars, minimising the role of the state and maximising individual liberty. *Address:* PO Box 3819, Placida, FL 33946, USA. *T:* (941) 916 2991; 171 Greenbrier Lane, Alpine Lake, Terra Alta, WV 26764, USA. *T:* (304) 789 2115. *Died 22 July 2014.*

BLUNDEN, Sir George, Kt 1987; Deputy Governor, Bank of England, 1986–90 (Executive Director, 1976–84, non-executive Director, 1984–85); Joint Deputy Chairman, Leopold Joseph Holdings, 1984–85 and 1990–94; *b* 31 Dec. 1922; *s* of late George Blunden and Florence Holder; *m* 1949, Anne, *d* of late G. J. E. and Phyllis Bulford; two *s* one *d*. *Educ:* City of London Sch.; University Coll., Oxford (MA). Royal Sussex Regt, 1941–45. Bank of England, 1947–55; IMF, 1955–58; Bank of England: rejoined 1958; Dep. Chief Cashier, 1968–73; Chief of Management Services, 1973–74; Head of Banking Supervision, 1974–76. Director: Eagle Star Hldgs, 1984–85; Portals Hldgs, 1984–86; Grindlays Hldgs, 1984–85. Advr, Union Bank of Switzerland in London, 1990–94. Chairman: Group of Ten Cttees, BIS, Basle, on Banking Regulations and Supervisory Practices, 1974–77, on Payments Systems, 1981–83; cttee to oversee estabt and operation of Code of Banking Practice, 1990–94; London Pensions Fund Authy, 1989–92. Chm. Governors, St Peter's Gp of Hosps, 1978–82; Chm., St Peter's Hosps Special Trustees, 1982–96; Chm., Inst. of Urology, 1982–88 (Hon. Treasurer, 1975–78); Mem. Council, Imperial Cancer Res. Fund, 1981–94 (Treas., 1988–91; Chm., 1991–94). Chairman: Samuel Lewis Housing Trust, 1985 (Trustee, 1980–85); Centre for Study of Financial

Innovation, 1995–98. President: Inst. of Business Ethics, 1994–96; British-Malaysia Soc., 1989–94. Member: Court, Mermaid Theatre Trust, 1979–84; Council, RCM, 1983–89 (Dep. Chm., 1990–97; Hon. FRCM 1987). Mem., Livery, Goldsmiths' Co., 1987. Hon. Fellow, UEA, 1997. *Address:* Ashdale, Gunthorpe, Melton Constable, Norfolk NR24 2NS. *T:* (01263) 860359. *Clubs:* Reform; Norfolk (Norwich). *Died 3 March 2012.*

BLYE, Douglas William Alfred, CMG 1979; OBE 1973; Secretary for Monetary Affairs, Hong Kong Government, 1977–85; *b* 15 Dec. 1924; *s* of William Blye and Ethel Attwood; *m* 1955, Juanita, (June), Buckley. *Educ:* King's Road Sch., Herne Bay; Maidstone Polytechnic. ACMA. Served War, RAF, 1941–46. Various commercial and industrial appts in UK, 1947–55; Govt of Fedn of Malaya, 1955–58; Hong Kong Govt, 1958–85; Econ. and Financial Advr, Govt of Dubai, 1986–87. *Recreations:* squash, walking. *Address:* Middlefield, The Street, Goodnestone, Canterbury, Kent CT3 1PG. *T:* (01304) 842196. *Club:* Royal Automobile. *Died 22 July 2011.*

BLYTH, John Douglas Morrison, CMG 1981; HM Diplomatic Service, retired; *b* 23 July 1924; *s* of late William Naismith Blyth and Jean (*née* Morrison); *m* 1st, 1949, Gabrielle Elodie (*née* Belloc) (*d* 1971); three *s* two *d*; 2nd, 1973, Lucy Anne (*née* Alcock), JP; one *s* one *d*. *Educ:* Christ's Coll.; Lincoln Coll., Oxford (MA); Downing Coll., Cambridge (MA). Served War, RNVR, 1942–46. Editor, The Polar Record (publd by Scott Polar Res. Inst., Cambridge), 1949–54; joined FO, 1954; served: Geneva, 1955; Athens, 1959; Leopoldville, 1963; Accra, 1964; FO, 1966; Athens, 1968; FCO, 1972; Vienna, 1974; FCO, 1977. Pres., Hélène Heroys Literary Foundn, 1975–2004. Hon. Sec., Suffolk Preservation Soc., 1985–94. *Publications:* articles in The Polar Record. *Recreations:* gardening, military history, enjoying wine. *Address:* Crownland Hall, Walsham-le-Willows, Suffolk IP31 3BU. *T:* (01359) 259369. *Died 30 July 2011.*

BODDINGTON, Ewart Agnew; JP; DL; Chairman, The Boddington Group PLC (formerly Boddingtons' Breweries), 1970–88 (President, 1989–95); *b* 7 April 1927; *m* 1954, Vine Anne Clayton (*d* 1989); two *s* one *d*. *Educ:* Stowe Sch., Buckingham; Trinity Coll., Cambridge (MA). Jt Man. Dir, Boddingtons', 1957. Dir, Northern Bd, National Westminster Bank, 1977–92. Pres., Inst. of Brewing, 1972–74; Chm., Brewers' Soc., 1984–85; Mem., Brewers' Co., 1980–. JP Macclesfield, 1959; High Sheriff of Cheshire, 1978–79; DL Cheshire 1993. Chetham's School of Music: Feoffee, 1953–2009 (Chm., 1969–92; Hon. Feoffee, 2009); Gov., 1953–99 (Chm., 1969–83). Trustee, NSPCC, 1993–2002. Hon. MA Manchester, 1977. *Recreations:* bridge, fishing, music. *Address:* Fanshawe Brook Barn, Henbury, Macclesfield, Cheshire SK11 9PP. *T:* (01260) 224387. *Died 3 Dec. 2015.*

BOGLE, Dr Ian Gibb, CBE 2003; FRCGP; Chairman of Council, British Medical Association, 1998–2003; general practitioner, Priory Medical Centre, Liverpool, 1962–2000; *b* 11 Dec. 1938; *s* of Dr John G. Bogle and Muriel Bogle (*née* Stoll); *m* 1962, Dorothy Edwards; two *d*; *m* 2001, Julie Coulson. *Educ:* Liverpool Coll.; Liverpool Univ. (MB ChB 1961). FRCGP 1997. Member: Liverpool Exec. Health Council, 1972–74; Liverpool FPC, 1974–90 (Vice Chm., 1987–88); Liverpool AHA, 1978–90; Section 63 Wkg Party, DHSS, 1985; Standing Med. Adv. Cttee, DoH, 1991–2003; NHS Modernisation Bd, 2000–03. Secretary: Liverpool Div., BMA, 1978–82 (Pres., 1977); Jt Cttee on Post Graduate Trng for Gen. Practice, 1985–90; Chairman: Anfield CAB, 1970–74; Gen. Med. Services Cttee, 1990–97. Chm., Anfield Youth Club, 1968–74. Chm. Govs, Pinehurst Jun. Sch., 1968–73. Hon. MD Liverpool, 1999. Gold Medal, BMA, 2004. *Recreations:* football, golf, photography, travel, music. *Address:* Peach Cottage, Burnt Oak Corner, East Bergholt, Suffolk CO7 6TJ. *T:* (01206) 298073. *Died 21 June 2014.*

BOHAN, William Joseph, CB 1988; Assistant Under Secretary of State, Home Office, 1979–89; *b* 10 April 1929; *s* of John and Josephine Bohan; *m* 1955, Brenda Skevington (*d* 1995); one *s* (one *d* decd). *Educ:* Finchley Catholic Grammar Sch.; Cardinal Vaughan Sch., Kensington; King's Coll., Cambridge (Chancellor's Classical Medallist, 1952). Home Office: Asst Principal, 1952; Principal, 1958; Sec., Cttee on Immigration Appeals, 1966–67; Asst Sec., 1967. Chm., European Cttee on Crime Problems, 1987–89. *Recreations:* languages and literature, visiting the opera. *Address:* 16 Mostyn Road, SW19 3LJ. *T:* (020) 8542 1127. *Died 11 Aug. 2013.*

BOILEAU, Sir Guy (Francis), 8th Bt *cr* 1838; antique dealer; *b* 23 Feb. 1935; *s* of Sir Edmond Charles Boileau, 7th Bt, and of Marjorie Lyle, *d* of Claude Monteath D'Arcy; *S* father, 1980; *m* 1962, Judith Frances, *d* of George Conrad Hannan; two *s* three *d*. *Educ:* Xavier College, Melbourne; Royal Military Coll., Duntroon, Australia. Lieut, Aust. Staff Corps, 1956; Platoon Comdr, 3rd Bn, Royal Aust. Regt, Malaysia, 1957–58; Observer, UN Mil. Observer Gp in India and Pakistan, 1959–60; Instructor, Aust. Army Training Team, Vietnam, 1963–64; attached US Dept of Defence, Washington, DC, 1966–68; Security Adviser, Dept of the Administrator, Territory of Papua-New Guinea, 1970–71; CO, Army Intelligence Centre, 1972–74; Directing Staff (Instructor), Aust. Staff Coll., 1975–76; SO1 Personnel, HQ Third Mil. Dist, 1979. *Recreations:* boating, fishing. *Heir:* *s* Nicolas Edmond George Boileau, *b* 17 Nov. 1964. *Club:* The Heroes (Toorak, Victoria). *Died 8 Feb. 2013.*

BOLES, Sir Jeremy John Fortescue, 3rd Bt *cr* 1922; *b* 9 Jan. 1932; *s* of Sir Gerald Fortescue Boles, 2nd Bt, and Violet Blanche (*d* 1974), *er d* of late Major Hall Parlby, Manadon, Crown Hill, S Devon; *S* father, 1945; *m* 1st, 1955, Dorothy Jane (marr. diss. 1970), *yr d* of James Alexander Worswick; two *s* one *d*; 2nd, 1970, Elisabeth Gildroy Willis Fleming (marr. diss. 1981; she *d* 2009), *yr d* of Edward Phillip Shaw; one *d*; 3rd, 1982, Marigold Aspey, *e d* of Donald Frank Seckington. *Heir:* *s* Richard Fortescue Boles [*b* 12 Dec. 1958; *m* 1990, Allison Beverley, *d* of Brian MacDonald; one *s* one *d*]. *Address:* Heriots, Brendon Close, Roadwater, Watchet TA23 0RG. *Died 15 Feb. 2014.*

BOLES, Sir John Dennis, (Sir Jack), Kt 1983; MBE 1960; DL; Director General of the National Trust, 1975–83; *b* 25 June 1925; *s* of late Comdr Geoffrey Coleridge Boles and Hilda Frances (*née* Crofton); *m* 1st, 1953, Benita (*née* Wormald) (*d* 1969); two *s* three *d*; 2nd, 1971, Lady Anne Hermione, DL, *d* of 12th Earl Waldegrave, KG, GCVO. *Educ:* Winchester Coll. Rifle Brigade, 1943–46. Colonial Administrative Service (later Overseas Civil Service), North Borneo (later Sabah), 1948–64; Asst Sec., National Trust, 1965, Sec., 1968; Mem., Devon and Cornwall Regl Cttee, Nat. Trust, 1985–95. Dir, SW Region Bd, Lloyds Bank plc, 1984–91. Devon: DL 1991; High Sheriff 1993–94. *Address:* Rydon House, Talaton, near Exeter, Devon EX5 2RP. *Died 1 July 2013.*

BOLINGBROKE, 8th Viscount *cr* 1712, **AND ST JOHN,** 9th Viscount *cr* 1716; **Henry Fitzroy St John;** Bt 1611; Baron St John of Lydiard Tregoze, 1712; Baron St John of Battersea, 1716; *b* 18 May 1957; *s* of 7th Viscount Bolingbroke and 8th Viscount St John and Patricia Mary McKenna; *S* father, 2010. *Educ:* Rudolf Steiner Sch., Christchurch, NZ. *Heir:* *half b* Hon. Nicholas Alexander Mowbray St John, *b* 1974. *Died 21 May 2011.*

BOLT, Air Marshal Sir Richard (Bruce), KBE 1979 (CBE 1973); CB 1977; DFC 1945; AFC 1959; Chairman, Pacific Aerospace Corporation of New Zealand, 1982–95; *b* 16 July 1923; *s* of George Bruce Bolt and Mary (*née* Best); *m* 1st, 1946, June Catherine South (*d* 1984); one *s* one *d*; 2nd, 1987, Janice Caroline Tucker. *Educ:* Nelson Coll., NZ. Began service with RNZAF in mid 1942; served during 2nd World War in RAF Bomber Command (Pathfinder Force); Chief of Air Staff, NZ, 1974–76; Chief of Defence Staff, NZ, 1976–80. *Recreations:* fly fishing, golf, horse racing. *Club:* Wellington (Wellington, NZ). *Died 27 July 2014.*

BOLTON, Prof. Geoffrey Curgenven, AO 1984; DPhil; Chancellor, Murdoch University, 2002–06 (Pro-Chancellor, 2000–02); Professor of History, Edith Cowan University, 1993–96, then Emeritus; *b* 5 Nov. 1931; *s* of Frank and Winifred Bolton, Perth, W Australia; *m* 1958, (Ann) Carol Grattan; two *s*. *Educ:* North Perth State Sch.; Wesley Coll., Perth; Univ. of Western Australia; Balliol Coll., Oxford, (DPhil). FRHistS 1967; FAHA 1974;

FASSA 1976. Res. Fellow, ANU, 1957–62; Sen. Lectr, Monash Univ., 1962–65; Prof. of Modern Hist., Univ. of Western Australia, 1966–73; Prof. of History, 1973–82 and 1985–89, and Pro-Vice-Chancellor, 1973–76, Murdoch Univ.; Prof. of Australian Studies, Univ. of London, 1982–85; Prof. of Australian Hist., Univ., of Queensland, 1989–93. Vis. Fellow, All Souls Coll., Oxford, 1995; Sen. Scholar in Residence, Murdoch Univ., 1997–. Mem. Council, Australian Nat. Maritime Museum, Sydney, 1985–91; Trustee, Western Australian Mus., 2005–12. Boyer Lectr, Australian Broadcasting Corp., 1992. FRSA. General Editor, Oxford History of Australia, 1987–91. DUniv Murdoch, 1995. Western Australia Citizen of the Year, 2003. *Publications:* Alexander Forrest, 1958; A Thousand Miles Away, 1963; The Passing of the Irish Act of Union, 1966; Dick Boyer, 1967; A Fine Country to Starve In, 1972; Spoils and Spoilers: Australians Make Their Environment, 1981; Oxford History of Australia, vol. 5, 1990; Daphne Street, 1997; Claremont: a history, 1999; Edmund Barton, 2000; May It Please Your Honour, 2005; Land of Vision and Mirage: Western Australia since 1826, 2008; Paul Hasluck: a life, 2014; articles in learned jls. *Recreation:* sleep. *Address:* PO Box 792, Claremont, WA 6910, Australia. *Club:* Athenæum. *Died 4 Sept. 2015.*

BOMPAS, Donald George, CMG 1966; Secretary, United Medical and Dental Schools of Guy's and St Thomas's Hospitals, 1984–86; *b* 20 Nov. 1920; *yr s* of Rev. E. Anstie Bompas; *m* 1946, Freda Vice, *y d* of F. M. Smithyman, Malawi; one *s* one *d.* *Educ:* Merchant Taylors' Sch., Northwood; Oriel Coll., Oxford (MA Oxon 1947). Overseas Audit Service, 1942–66: Nyasaland, 1942–47; Singapore, 1947–48; Malaya, later Malaysia, 1948–66; Deputy Auditor-General, 1957–60; Auditor-General, Malaya, later Malaysia, 1960–66, retired. Dep. Sec., Guy's Hosp. Med. and Dental Schools, 1966–69, Sec., 1969–82; Dep. Sec., UMDS of Guy's and St Thomas's Hosps, 1982–83 (Hon. Fellow, 1996). Chm., Univ. of London Purchasing Gp, 1976–82. Mem. Exec., Federated Pension Schemes, 1979–86. Man. Exec., Philip and Pauline Harris Charitable Trust, 1986–2005. Mem. Council and Exec. Cttee, Technology (formerly City Technology) Colls Trust, 1990–2000; Trustee, Bacon's Coll., 1991–2005; Gov., St Olave's and St Saviour's Grammar Sch. Foundn, 1992–2001. FKC 1998. Liveryman, Merchant Taylors' Co., 1951. JMN (Hon.) Malaya, 1961. *Address:* 3 Chesil House, St Paul's Cray Road, Chislehurst, Kent BR7 6QF. *T:* (020) 8467 3340. *E:* dbompas@btinternet.com. *Club:* Royal Commonwealth Society. *Died 18 Jan. 2013.*

BOND, Alan; Founder: Madagascar Oil, 2002; Global Diamond Resources plc, 2002; World Gold Corporation plc, 2002; *b* 22 April 1938; *s* of Frank and Kathleen Bond; *m* 1st, 1956, Eileen Teresa Hughes (marr. diss. 1992); two *s* one *d* (and one *d* decd); 2nd, 1995, Diana Bliss (*d* 2012). *Educ:* Perivale Sch., Ealing, UK; Fremantle Boys' Sch., W Australia. Chairman, Bond Corporation Holdings Ltd, 1969–90 (interests in property, brewing, electronic media, oil and gas, minerals, airships); Chairman: North Kalgurli Mines Ltd, 1985–89; Gold Mines of Kalgoorlie Ltd, 1987–89; Dallhold Investments Pty, 1987. Director: Strategic Asset Investments, 2012–; Capital Asset Enterprises, 2012–. Founder, Bond Univ., Qld, 1991. Syndicate Head, America's Cup Challenge 1983 Ltd; Australia II Winners of 1983 America's Cup Challenge, following three previous attempts: 1974 Southern Cross, 1977 Australia, 1980 Australia. Australian of the Year, 1977; America's Cup Hall of Fame, 2005. AO 1984. *Publications:* (with Rob Mundle) Bond (autobiog.), 2004. *Recreation:* yachting. *Address:* GPO Box H555, Perth, WA 6001, Australia. *Clubs:* Royal Ocean Racing; Young Presidents Organisation, Royal Perth Yacht, Cruising Yacht, Western Australian Turf (WA). *Died 5 June 2015.*

BONE, Rt Rev. John Frank Ewan; Area Bishop of Reading, 1989–96; an Honorary Assistant Bishop, Diocese of Oxford, since 1996; *b* 28 Aug. 1930; *s* of Jack and Herberta Blanche Bone; *m* 1954, Ruth Margaret Crudgington; two *s* two *d* and one adopted *s.* *Educ:* Monkton Combe School, Bath; St Peter's Coll., Oxford (MA); Ely Theological Coll.; Whitelands Coll. of Education (Grad. Cert. in Education). Ordained, 1956; Assistant Curate: St Gabriel's, Warwick Square, 1956–60; St Mary's, Henley on Thames, 1960–63; Vicar of Datchet, 1963–76; Rector of Slough, 1976–78; Rural Dean of Burnham, 1974–77; Archdeacon of Buckingham, 1978–89. Mem. of General Synod, 1980–85. *Recreations:* collecting maps, topographical books and prints, classical music, walking. *Address:* 4 Grove Road, Henley-on-Thames, Oxon RG9 1DH. *Died 5 July 2014.*

BONSALL, Sir Arthur (Wilfred), KCMG 1977; CBE 1957; *b* Middlesbrough, 25 June 1917; *s* of late Wilfred Bonsall and Sarah Bonsall; *m* 1941, Joan Isabel Wingfield (*d* 1990); four *s* three *d.* *Educ:* Bishop's Stortford Coll.; St Catharine's Coll., Cambridge. 2nd Cl. Hons Mod. Langs. Joined Govt Code and Cypher Sch., 1940; transf. to Govt Communications HQ, 1946; IDC, 1962; Dir, Govt Communications HQ, 1975–78. *Publications:* contrib. to Bletchley Park Reports. *Recreation:* balcony gardening. *Address:* Chapel Cottage, Faithfull House, Suffolk Square, Cheltenham, Glos GL50 2DT. *Died 26 Nov. 2014.*

BONSALL, Prof. Frank Featherstone, FRS 1970; Professor of Mathematics, University of Edinburgh, 1965–84, then Emeritus; *b* 1920; *s* of late Wilfred Bonsall and Sarah Bonsall; *m* 1947, Gillian Patrick. *Educ:* Bishop's Stortford Coll.; Merton Coll., Oxford. *Publications:* (all with J. Duncan): Numerical Ranges of Operators on Normed Spaces and of Elements of Normed Algebras, 1971; Numerical Ranges II, 1973; Complete Normed Algebras, 1973. *Recreation:* walking. *Died 22 Feb. 2011.*

BOOKER-MILBURN, Donald; Sheriff of Grampian, Highland and Islands, 1983–2005; *b* Dornoch, 20 May 1940; *s* of late Captain Booker Milburn, DSO, MC, Coldstream Guards, and Betty Calthrop Calthrop; *m* 1963, Marjorie Lilian Elizabeth Burns; one *s* one *d.* *Educ:* Trinity College, Glenalmond; Grenoble Univ.; Jesus Coll., Cambridge (BA); Edinburgh Univ. (LLB). Admitted to Faculty of Advocates, 1968; Standing Junior Counsel to RAF, 1977–80; Sheriff of Lothian and Borders, 1980–83. *Recreations:* golf, ski-ing. *Clubs:* Royal & Ancient Golf (St Andrews); Royal Dornoch Golf. *Died 29 May 2012.*

BOORMAN, Edwin Roy Pratt, OBE 2002; DL; President, Kent Messenger Group, since 2006 (Managing Director, 1965–86; Chief Executive, 1986–2002; Chairman, 1986–2005); *b* 7 Nov. 1935; *s* of late H. R. P. Boorman, CBE and Enid (*née* Starke); *m* 1st, Merrilyn Ruth Pettit (marr. diss. 1982); four *d*; 2nd, 1983, Janine Craske; one *s.* *Educ:* Rydal; Queens' Coll., Cambridge (MA Econ. History). National Service, 1954–56. Cambridge Univ., 1956–59; Kent Messenger, 1959; Editor: South Eastern Gazette, 1960–62; Kent Messenger, 1962–65. Pres., Newspaper Soc., 2001–02 (Vice-Pres., 2000–01). Chm., Royal British Legion Industries, 2001– (Pres., RBL, Kent, 1998–2003). Chairman: N Kent Success, 1993–96; Kent River Walk, 1998–. Dep. Pres., Kent Youth and Kent Youth Trust, 2001–; Pres., Maidstone Sen. Cadets, 2004–. Trustee: Chatham Historic Dockyard, 1992–97; Kent Air Ambulance, 1993–2005. Chm., Kent Council, Order of St John, 1997–2004. Patron: Kent Child Witness Service, 1999–; Kent County Playing Fields Assoc., 2009–. Governor: Sutton Valence Sch., 1976–2002; Canterbury Christ Church Coll., 1996–2005; Mid Kent Coll., 2005–. Stationers' and Newspapermakers' Co.: Liveryman, 1960–86; Mem., Ct of Assts, 1987–2000 (Ct Emeritus list, 2000–). High Sheriff, Kent, 1997; DL Kent, 2001. Hon. DCL Kent, 2004. *Recreation:* sailing. *Address:* Messenger House, New Hythe Lane, Larkfield, Kent ME20 6SG. *Clubs:* Carlton; Maidstone; Veteran Car (Ashwell, Herts); Royal Yachting Association, Medway Yacht, Ocean Cruising. *Died 14 March 2012.*

BOOTH, Sir Christopher (Charles), Kt 1983; Harveian Librarian, Royal College of Physicians, 1989–97; *b* 22 June 1924; *s* of Lionel Barton Booth and Phyllis Petley Duncan; *m* 1st, 1959, Lavinia Loughridge, Belfast; one *s* one *d*; 2nd, 1970, Soad Tabaqchali; one *d*; 3rd, 2001, Joyce Singleton. *Educ:* Sedbergh Sch., Yorks; University of St Andrews (MB 1951, MD 1958 (Rutherford Gold Medal)). Served War, RNVR, 1942–46. Junior appointments at Dundee Royal Infirmary, Hammersmith Hosp. and Addenbrooke's Hosp., Cambridge; successively Medical Tutor, Lecturer in Medicine and Senior Lecturer, Postgraduate Medical School of London; Prof. and Dir of Dept of Medicine,

RPMS, London Univ., 1966–77; Dir, Clin. Res. Centre, MRC, 1978–88. Member: Adv. Bd to Res. Councils, 1976–78; MRC, 1981–84; Chm., Medical Adv. Cttee, British Council, 1979–85; President: British Soc. of Gastroenterology, 1978–79; BMA, 1986–87; RSocMed, 1988; Johnson Soc., 1987–88; Soc. Social History of Medicine, 1990; Friends Historical Soc., 2005. Hon. Prof., UCL, 2001. Chm., Royal Naval Personnel Cttee, 1985–91. Trustee, Coeliac Soc., 1968–93 (Chm., 1968–83). FRCP 1964; FRCPEd 1967; Hon. FACP 1973; Hon. FRSocMed 1991; Hon. FMedSci 2002. For. Mem., Amer. Philosophical Soc., 1981. Docteur (*hc*): Paris, 1975; Poitiers, 1981; Hon. LLD Dundee, 1982; Laurea (*hc*) Bologna, 1991. Dicke Gold Medal, Dutch Soc. of Gastroenterology, 1973; Ludwig Heilmeyer Gold Medal, German Soc. for Advances in Internal Medicine, 1982; Gold Medal, BMA, 1992; Fothergillian Medal, Med. Soc. of London, 2007. Chevalier de l'Ordre National du Mérite (France), 1977. *Publications:* (with Betsy C. Corner) Chain of Friendship: Letters of Dr John Fothergill of London, 1735–1780, 1971; (with G. Neale) Disorders of the Small Intestine, 1985; Doctors in Science and Society, 1987; A Physician Reflects, 2003; John Haygarth, FRS, 1740–1827, 2005; papers in med. jls on relationship of nutritional disorders to disease of the alimentary tract, and on medical history. *Recreations:* fishing, history. *Address:* Swakeley's Cottage, 2 The Avenue, Ickenham, Middx UB10 8NP. *T:* (01895) 677811. *Died 13 July 2012.*

BOOTH, Sir Gordon, KCMG 1980 (CMG 1969); CVO 1976; HM Diplomatic Service, retired; *b* 22 Nov. 1921; *s* of Walter and Grace Booth, Bolton, Lancs; *m* 1944, Jeanne Mary Kirkham; one *s* one *d*. *Educ:* Canon Slade Sch.; London Univ. (BCom). Served War of 1939–45: Capt. RAC and 13/18th Royal Hussars, 1941–46. Min. of Labour and Bd of Trade, 1946–55; Trade Comr, Canada and West Indies, 1955–65; Mem. HM Diplomatic Service, 1965–80; Counsellor (Commercial), British Embassy in Copenhagen, 1966–69; Dir, Coordination of Export Services, DTI, 1969–71; Consul-General, Sydney, 1971–74; HBM Consul-Gen., NY, and Dir-Gen. of Trade Develt in USA, 1975–80; Chm., SITPRO Bd, 1980–86. Chairman: London Clubs Internat. plc, 1992–95; Ritz Hotel Casino Ltd, 1998–2002. Director: Hanson PLC (formerly Hanson Trust), 1981–89; Bechtel Ltd, 1983–92; Allders Internat. Ltd, 1992–96. *Recreation:* gardening. *Address:* 27 Chartcombe, 162/164 Canford Cliffs Road, Canford Cliffs, Poole, Dorset BH13 7EJ. *T:* (01202) 929761. *Died 13 June 2014.*

BOOTH, Graham Harry; Member (UK Ind) South West Region, England, European Parliament, Dec. 2002–Sept. 2008; *b* 29 March 1940; *s* of Harry Booth and Dinx Booth; *m* 1st, 1961 (marr. diss. 1969); two *s*; 2nd, 1982, Pamela Jones; one step *s* two step *d*. *Educ:* Torquay Boys' Grammar Sch. Lloyds Bank, 1956–60; family holiday business, 1960–. Mem. NEC, UK Independence Party, 1997–2006. *Recreations:* golf, poetry, astronomy, coin collecting. *Address:* 41 Oyster Bend, Paignton, Devon TQ4 6NL. *T:* and *Fax:* (01803) 557433. *E:* mrgrahambooth@aol.com. *Club:* Farmers. *Died 14 Dec. 2011.*

BOOTHMAN, Derek Arnold, CBE 2003; FCA; Deputy Chairman, Central Manchester Development Corporation, 1988–96; non-executive Director, Remploy Ltd, 1987–2004; *b* 5 June 1932; *s* of Eric Randolph Boothman and Doris Mary Boothman; *m* 1958, Brenda Margaret; one *s* one *d*. *Educ:* William Hulme's Grammar Sch., Manchester. Mem., ICA, subseq. ICAEW, 1954. Articled to J. Needham & Co., 1948; National Service, RAF, 1954–56; Partner: J. Needham & Co., and successor cos (later part of Binder Hamlyn), 1957–74; Binder Hamlyn, Chartered Accts, 1974–88. President: Manchester Chartered Accountants Students Soc., 1967–68; Manchester Soc. of Chartered Accountants, 1968–69; Institute of Chartered Accountants in England and Wales: Council Member, 1969–91; Treasurer, 1981–83; Vice-Pres., 1983–85; Dep. Pres., 1985–86; Pres., 1986–87. Member, Accounting Standards Cttee, 1974–82. Gov., William Hulme's Grammar Sch., 1982–2002 (Chm., 1988–99); Mem. Ct, Univ. of Manchester, 1990–99. Chm., Prestbury Probus, 2006–07. Liveryman, Worshipful Company of Chartered Accountants, 1976–. *Publications:* contribs to professional press and lectures on professional topics, internationally. *Recreations:* cricket, gardening, travel. *Address:* Ashworth Dene, Wilmslow Road, Mottram St Andrew, Cheshire SK10 4QH. *T:* (01625) 829101. *Clubs:* St James's (Manchester) (Vice Pres., 2013–); Withington Golf (Manchester) (past Captain). *Died 7 Aug. 2014.*

BORG COSTANZI, Prof. Edwin J., MOM 1999; Rector, University of Malta, 1964–80 and 1988–91; *b* 8 Sept. 1925; 2nd *s* of late Michael Borg Costanzi and M. Stella (*née* Camilleri); *m* 1948, Lucy Valentino; two *s* one *d*. *Educ:* Lyceum, Malta; Royal University of Malta (BSc, BE&A); Balliol College, Oxford (BA 1946, MA 1952); Malta Rhodes Scholar, 1945. Professor of Mathematics, Royal University of Malta, 1950–64; Vis. Fellow, Univ. of Southampton, 1980–82; Professorial Res. Fellow, 1982–85, Hd of Dept of Computer Sci., 1985–87, Brunel Univ. Chm., 1976–77, Mem., 1965–66, 1968–69, 1972–74, 1977–78, Council of ACU. Chairman: Public Service Reform Commn, 1988–89; Public Service Commn, Malta, 1991–95. Hon. DLitt Malta, 1993. *Address:* 35 Don M. Rua Street, Sliema, SLM 1883, Malta. *Club:* Casino Maltese (Valletta, Malta). *Died 14 May 2013.*

BOSCAWEN, Rt Hon. Robert Thomas, MC 1944; PC 1992; *b* 17 March 1923; 4th *s* of 8th Viscount Falmouth and Dowager Viscountess Falmouth, CBE; *m* 1949, Mary Alice (*d* 2013), JP London 1961, *e d* of Col Sir Geoffrey Ronald Codrington, KCVO, CB, CMG, DSO, OBE, TD; one *s* two *d*. *Educ:* Eton; Trinity College, Cambridge. Served Coldstream Guards, 1941–50 (with 1st (armoured) Bn Coldstream Guards, Normandy to N Germany, wounded 1945); NW Europe, 1944–45; attached to British Red Cross Civilian Relief Orgn in occupied Europe, 1946–47. Mem., London Exec. Council, Nat. Health Service, 1954–65; Underwriting Mem. of Lloyd's, 1952–99. Contested Falmouth and Camborne (C), 1964, 1966; MP (C) Wells, 1970–83, Somerton and Frome, 1983–92. An Asst Govt Whip, 1979–81; a Lord Comr of HM Treasury, 1981–83; Vice-Chamberlain of HM Household, 1983–86, Comptroller, 1986–88. Mem., Select Cttee on Expenditure, 1974; Vice-Chm., Conservative Parly Health and Social Security Cttee, 1974–79. Mem. Parly Delegns, USSR 1977, Nepal 1981; led Parly Delegn to UN Assembly, 1987, to Canada, 1991. *Publications:* Armoured Guardsmen: a war diary, 2001. *Recreations:* sailing, shooting. *Address:* Ivythorn Manor, Street, Somerset BA16 0TZ. *Clubs:* Pratt's; Royal Yacht Squadron. *Died 28 Dec. 2013.*

BOSNICH, Prof. Brice, PhD; FRS 2000; Gustavus F. and Ann M. Swift Distinguished Service Professor in Chemistry, University of Chicago, 2004, then Emeritus (Professor of Chemistry, 1987–2004); *b* 3 June 1936; *s* of Frank Bosnich and Zorka (*née* Setimo); *m* 1992, Jayne Seberling. *Educ:* St Gregory's Coll., Australia; Univ. of Sydney (BSc); ANU (PhD 1962). DSIR Fellow, 1962–63, ICI Fellow, 1963–66, Lectr, 1966–69, UCL; University of Toronto: Associate Prof., 1969–75; Prof., 1975–87; Killam Fellow, 1979–81. Noranda Award in Inorganic Chem., CIC, 1978; Organometallic Award, 1994, Nyholm Award Medal, 1995, RSC; Award in Inorganic Chem., ACS, 1998. *Publications:* Asymmetric Catalysis, 1993; contrib. numerous papers to learned scientific jls. *Recreations:* art, Asian collection. *Address:* c/o Department of Chemistry, University of Chicago, 5735 South Ellis Avenue, Chicago, IL 60637, USA. *Died 13 April 2015.*

BOSSY, Prof. John Antony, PhD; FRHistS; FBA 1993; Professor of History, University of York, 1979–2000, then Emeritus; *b* 30 April 1933; *s* of Frederick James Bossy and Kate Louise Fanny Bossy (*née* White). *Educ:* St Ignatius Coll., London; Queens' Coll., Cambridge (BA 1954; PhD 1961). FRHistS 1975. Res. Fellow, Queens' Coll., Cambridge, 1959–62; Lectr in Hist., Goldsmiths' Coll., London, 1962–66; Lectr, then Reader, in Mod. Hist., QUB, 1966–78. Mem., Editl Bd, Past and Present, 1972–2003. *Publications:* The English Catholic Community 1570–1850, 1976; Christianity in the West 1400–1700, 1984; Giordano Bruno and the Embassy Affair, 1991; Peace in the Post-Reformation, 1998; Under the Molehill, 2001. *Recreations:* chess, piano. *Address:* 80 Stockton Lane, York YO31 1BS. *T:* (01904) 424801. *Died 23 Oct. 2015.*

BOSTON OF FAVERSHAM, Baron *cr* 1976 (Life Peer), of Faversham, Kent; **Terence George Boston;** QC 1981; barrister; a Deputy Speaker, House of Lords, 1991–2008; *b* 21 March 1930; *yr* surv. *s* of late George T. Boston and Kate (*née* Bellati); *m* 1962, Margaret Joyce (Member: SE Metropolitan Regional Hospital Board, 1970–74; Mental Health Review Appeals Tribunal (SE Metropolitan area), 1970–74; market research consultant), *er d* of late R. H. J. Head and Mrs E. M. Winters, and step *d* of late H. F. Winters, Melbourne, Australia. *Educ:* Woolwich Polytechnic Sch.; King's Coll., University of London. Dep. President, University of London Union, 1955–56. Commnd in RAF during Nat. Service, 1950–52; later trained as pilot with University of London Air Sqdn. Called to the Bar, Inner Temple, 1960. BBC News Sub-Editor, External Services, 1957–60; Senior BBC Producer (Current Affairs), 1960–64; also Producer of Law in Action series (Third Programme), 1962–64. Chm., TVS Entertainment, 1980–90. Joined Labour Party, 1946; contested (Lab) Wokingham, 1955 and 1959; MP (Lab) Faversham, Kent, June 1964–70; PPS to: Minister of Public Building and Works, 1964–66; Minister of Power, 1966–68; Minister of Transport, 1968–69; Asst Govt Whip, 1969–70; Minister of State, Home Office, 1979; opp. front bench spokesman on home affairs, 1979–84, on defence, 1984–86; Prin. Dep. Chm. of Cttees, 1992–94, Chm. of Cttees, 1994–2000, H of L. UK Deleg. to UN Gen. Assembly, XXXIst, XXXIInd and XXXIIIrd Sessions, 1976–78. Member: Executive Cttee, International Union of Socialist Youth, 1950; Select Cttee on Broadcasting Proceedings of Parliament, 1966; Speaker's Conference on Electoral Law, 1965–68. Trustee, Parly Lab. Party Benevolent Fund, 1967–70. Founder Vice-Chm., Great Britain-East Europe Centre, 1967–69; Chm., The Sheppey Gp, 1967–. Trustee, Leeds Castle Foundn, 1991–2010; Chm., Leeds Castle Enterprises Ltd, 2005–10. *Recreations:* opera (going, not singing), fell-walking. *Address:* House of Lords, SW1A 0PW. *Died 23 July 2011.*

BOSWORTH, Prof. Clifford Edmund, FBA 1992; Professor of Arabic Studies, Manchester University, 1967–90, then Emeritus; *b* 29 Dec. 1928; *s* of Clifford Bosworth and Gladys Constance Gregory; *m* 1957, Annette Ellen Todd; three *d*. *Educ:* St John's College, Oxford (MA Mod. Hist.); Edinburgh Univ. (MA Arabic, Persian, Turkish; PhD). Dept of Agriculture for Scotland, 1952–54; Lectr in Arabic, St Andrews Univ., 1956–67. Vis. Associate Prof., Univ. of Toronto, 1965–66; Vis. Prof., UCLA, 1969; Center for Humanities Fellow, Princeton, 1984; Vis. Prof., Inst. of Arabic and Islamic Studies, Exeter Univ., 2004–13. Pres., British Soc. for Middle Eastern Studies, 1983–85. Hon. Mem., Hungarian Acad. of Scis, 2004. Avicenna Silver Medal, UNESCO, 1998; Dr Mahmud Afshar Foundn Award, Tehran, 2001; Royal Asiatic Soc. Award, 2004; Levi Della Vida Medal, UCLA, 2010. *Publications:* The Ghaznavids, 1963; The Islamic Dynasties, 1967, 2nd edn as The New Islamic Dynasties, 1996; Sistan under the Arabs, 1968; The Book of Curious and Entertaining Information, 1968; The Medieval Islamic Underworld, 1976; The Later Ghaznavids, 1977; Al-Maqrizi's Book of contention and strife, 1981; Medieval Arabic Culture and Administration, 1982; The History of al-Tabari (annotated trans.), vols 5, 30, 32–3, 1987–99; The History of the Saffarids of Sistan and the Maliks of Nimruz, 1994; The Arabs, Byzantium and Iran, 1996; (ed) A Century of British Orientalists 1902–2001, 2001; An Intrepid Scot: the travels of William Lithgow 1609–21, 2006; (ed) The Turks in the Early Islamic World, 2007; (ed) Historic Cities of the Islamic World, 2007; The History of the Seljuq State, 2011; The Ornament of Histories: a history of the Eastern Islamic Lands, 2011; The History of Beyhaqi, 2011; Eastward Ho! Diplomats, travellers and interpreters of the Middle East and beyond 1600–1940, 2012. *Recreations:* walking, listening to music, collecting detective fiction. *Address:* 1 Parsons Gate, Castle Cary, Som BA7 7JS. *T:* (01963) 350621. *Died 28 Feb. 2015.*

BOSWORTH, Sir Neville (Bruce Alfred), Kt 1987; CBE 1982; Consultant, Grove Tompkins Bosworth, Solicitors, Birmingham, since 1989; *b* 18 April 1918; *s* of W. C. N. Bosworth; *m* 1945, Charlotte Marian Davis (*d* 2003); one *s* two *d*. *Educ:* King Edward's Sch., Birmingham; Birmingham Univ. LLB. Admitted Solicitor, 1941; Sen. Partner, Bosworth, Bailey Cox & Co., Birmingham, 1941–89. Birmingham City Council, 1950–96; County Bor. Councillor (Erdington Ward), 1950–61; Alderman, 1961–74; Dist Councillor (Edgbaston Ward), 1973–96; Hon. Alderman, 1996; Lord Mayor of Birmingham, 1969–70; Dep. Mayor, 1970–71; Leader of Birmingham City Council, 1976–80, 1982–84; Leader of Opposition, 1972–76, 1980–82 and 1984–87; Cons. Gp Leader, 1972–87 (Dep. Gp Leader, 1971–72); Chairman: Gen. Purposes Cttee, 1966–69; Finance Cttee, 1976–80, 1982–84; National Exhibn Centre Cttee, 1976–80. Chm., W Midlands Police Bd, 1985–86. County Councillor (Edgbaston Ward), W Midlands CC, 1973–86; Chm., Legal and Property Cttee, 1977–79; Vice-Chm., Finance Cttee, 1980–81. Chm., Sutton Coldfield Cons. Assoc., 1963–66; Vice-Chm., Birmingham Cons. Assoc., 1972–87; Mem., Local Govt Adv. Cttee, National Union of Cons. and Unionist Assocs, 1973–87; Pres., Edgbaston Constituency Cons. Assoc., 1992–. Vice Chm., Assoc. of Metropolitan Authorities, 1978–80, and Mem. Policy Cttee, 1976–80; Vice-Pres., Birmingham and Dist Property Owners Assoc.; Dir, Nat. Exhibn Centre Ltd, 1970–72, 1974–96; Mem., W Midlands Econ. Council, 1978–79. Trustee, several charitable trusts; Mem. Council, Birmingham Univ., 1962–91; Governor, King Edward VI Schs, Birmingham, 1970–87 (Dep. Bailiff, 1979–80). Hon. Freeman, City of Birmingham, 1982. *Recreations:* politics, football, bridge. *T:* (office) (0121) 236 9341. *Died 25 Dec. 2012.*

BOTHWELL, Rt Rev. John Charles, DD; Archbishop of Niagara and Metropolitan of Ontario, 1985–91; *b* 29 June 1926; *s* of William Alexander Bothwell and Anne Bothwell (*née* Campbell); *m* 1951, Joan Cowan; three *s* two *d*. *Educ:* Runnymede Public School; Humberside Coll. Inst., Toronto; Trinity Coll., Univ. of Toronto (BA 1948, LTh 1951, BD 1952; DD 1972). Asst Priest, St James' Cathedral, Toronto, 1951–53; Sen. Assistant at Christ Church Cathedral, Vancouver, 1953–56; Rector: St Aidan's, Oakville, Ont, 1956–60; St James' Church, Dundas, Ont, 1960–65; Canon of Christ Church Cathedral, Hamilton, Ont, 1963; Dir of Programs for Niagara Diocese, 1965–69; Exec. Dir of Program, Nat. HQ of Anglican Church of Canada, Toronto, 1969–71; Bishop Coadjutor of Niagara, 1971–73; Bishop of Niagara, 1973–85. Chancellor, Trinity Coll., Univ. of Toronto, 1991–2003. Hon. Sen. Fellow, Renison Coll., Univ. of Waterloo, 1988. Hon. DD: Huron Coll., Univ. of Western Ont, 1989; Wycliffe Coll., Univ. of Toronto, 1989. *Publications:* Taking Risks and Keeping Faith, 1985; An Open View: keeping faith day by day, 1990; Old Time Religion or Risky Faith: the challenge and the vision, 1993. *Recreations:* golf, cross-country ski-ing, swimming. *Died 28 Jan. 2014.*

BOTTOMLEY, Sir James (Reginald Alfred), KCMG 1973 (CMG 1965); HM Diplomatic Service, retired; *b* 12 Jan. 1920; *s* of Sir (William) Cecil Bottomley, KCMG, and Alice Thistle Bottomley (*née* Robinson), JP; *m* 1941, Barbara Evelyn Vardon (*d* 1994); two *s* two *d* (and one *s* decd). *Educ:* King's College Sch., Wimbledon; Trinity Coll., Cambridge. Served with Inns of Court Regt, RAC, 1940–46. Dominions Office, 1946; Pretoria, 1948–50; Karachi, 1953–55; Washington, 1955–59; UK Mission to United Nations, 1959; Dep. High Commissioner, Kuala Lumpur, 1963–67; Asst Under-Sec. of State, Commonwealth Office (later FCO), 1967–70; Dep. Under-Sec. of State, FCO, 1970–72; Ambassador to South Africa, 1973–76; Perm. UK Rep. to UN and other Internat. Organisations at Geneva, 1976–78; Dir, Johnson Matthey plc, 1979–85. Mem., British Overseas Trade Bd, 1972. *Recreation:* formerly golf. *Address:* 22 Beaufort Place, Thompson's Lane, Cambridge CB5 8AG. *T:* (01223) 328760. *Died 5 June 2013.*

BOULTER, Prof. Donald, CBE 1991; FSB; Head of Department of Biological Sciences, University of Durham, 1988–91 (Professor of Botany and Head of Department of Botany, 1966–88); Director of Durham University Botanic Garden, 1966–91; *b* 25 Aug. 1926; *s* of late George Boulter and Vera Boulter; *m* 1956, Margaret Eileen Kennedy; four *d*. *Educ:* Portsmouth Grammar Sch.; Christ Church, Oxford (BA, MA, DPhil). FSB (FIBiol 1970). Served RAF, 1945–48. Sessel Fellow, Yale Univ., 1953–54; Asst Lectr in Botany, King's Coll., London, 1955–57; Lectr 1957–64,

Sen. Lectr 1964–66, Liverpool Univ. Vis. Prof., Univ. of Texas, Austin, 1967. Chm., Plant Science Res. Ltd, Cambridge Lab., John Innes Centre, 1992–94. Member: AFRC, 1985–89; Biological Scis Sub-Cttee, UFC (formerly UGC), 1988–89; Chm., Plants & Soils Res. Grant Bd, 1986–89; Pres., Sect. K, BAAS, 1981. Dep. Chm. Governing Body, AFRC Inst. of Horticultural Res., 1987–90; Member, Governing Body: Scottish Crop Res. Inst., 1986–92; AFRC Inst. of Plant Sci. Res., 1989–92; Trustee, John Innes Foundn, 1994–97. Mem., Exec. Cttee, Horticultural Res. Internat., 1990–97. FRSA 1972. Tate & Lyle Award for Phytochem., 1975. *Publications:* (ed) Chemotaxonomy of the Leguminosae, 1971; (ed) Encyclopedia of Plant Physiology, vol. 14B: Nucleic Acids and Proteins, 1982; papers in sci. jls on molecular evolution, genetic engrg of crops, biochem. and molecular biol. of seed develt. *Recreation:* travel. *Address:* 5 Crossgate, Durham DH1 4PS. *T:* (0191) 386 1199. *Died 8 June 2012.*

BOULTON, Sir Clifford (John), GCB 1994 (KCB 1990; CB 1985); DL; Clerk of the House of Commons, 1987–94; *b* 25 July 1930; *s* of Stanley Boulton and Evelyn (*née* Hey), Cocknage, Staffs; *m* 1955, Anne, *d* of Rev. E. E. Raven, Cambridge; one adopted *s* one adopted *d. Educ:* Newcastle-under-Lyme High School; St John's Coll., Oxford (exhibnr). MA (Modern History). National Service, RAC, 1949–50; Lt Staffs Yeomanry (TA). A Clerk in the House of Commons, 1953–94: Clerk of Select Cttees on Procedure, 1964–68 and 1976–77; Public Accounts, 1968–70; Parliamentary Questions, 1971–72; Privileges, 1972–77; Clerk of the Overseas Office, 1977–79; Principal Clerk, Table Office, 1979–83; Clerk Asst, 1983–87. A school Governor and subsequently board mem., Church Schools Company, 1965–79; Trustee, Oakham Sch., 1998–2010. Trustee, Industry and Parliament Trust, 1991–95. Mem., Standing Cttee on Standards in Public Life, 1994–2000. Chairman: Standards Cttee, Rutland CC, 2000–05; Rutland Historic Churches Preservation Trust, 2004–12. DL Rutland, 1997. Hon. LLD Keele, 1993. *Publications:* (ed) Erskine May's Parliamentary Practice, 21st edn, 1989; contribs to Halsbury's Laws of England, 4th edn, and Parliamentary journals. *Recreations:* visual arts, the countryside. *Address:* 2 Main Street, Lyddington, Oakham LE15 9LT. *T:* (01572) 823487. *Died 25 Dec. 2015.*

BOULTON, Prof. James Thompson, FBA 1994; FRSL; Director, 1987–99, Deputy Director, 1999–2006, then Director Emeritus, Institute for Advanced Research in Arts and Social Sciences (formerly Institute for Advanced Research in the Humanities), University of Birmingham (Fellow, 1984); *b* 17 Feb. 1924; *e s* of Harry Boulton, MM and Annie M. P. Boulton; *m* 1949, Margaret Helen Leary; one *s* one *d. Educ:* University College, Univ. of Durham; Lincoln Coll., Oxford. BA Dunelm 1948; BLitt Oxon 1952; PhD Nottingham 1960. FRSL 1969. Served as pilot in RAF, 1943–46 (Flt-Lt). Lectr, subseq. Sen. Lectr and Reader in English, Univ. of Nottingham, 1951–64; John Cranford Adams Prof. of English, Hofstra Univ., NY, 1967; Prof. of English Lit., Univ. of Nottingham, 1964–75, Dean, Faculty of Arts, 1970–73; University of Birmingham: Prof. of English Studies and Head of Dept of English Lang. and Lit., 1975–88, Prof. Emeritus, 1989; Dean of Faculty of Arts, 1981–84; Public Orator, 1984–88. Hon. Prof., Sch. of English, Bangor Univ., 2007–. Chm. of Govs, Fircroft Coll., Selly Oak, 1985–92. Editor, Renaissance and Modern Studies, 1969–75, 1985. General Editor: The Letters of D. H. Lawrence, 1973–2001; The Works of D. H. Lawrence, 1975–2013. Hon. DLitt: Dunelm, 1991; Nottingham, 1993. *Publications:* (ed) Edmund Burke: A Philosophical Enquiry into…the Sublime and Beautiful, 1958, rev. edn 1987, repr. 2008; (ed) C. F. G. Masterman: The Condition of England, 1960, repr. 2009; The Language of Politics in the Age of Wilkes and Burke, 1963, 2nd edn 1975, repr. 2010; (ed) Dryden: Of Dramatick Poesy etc., 1964; (ed) Defoe: Prose and Verse, 1965, 2nd edn 1975, repr. 2010; (with James Kinsley) English Satiric Poetry: Dryden to Byron, 1966; (ed) Lawrence in Love: Letters from D. H. Lawrence to Louie Burrows, 1968; (ed) Samuel Johnson: The Critical Heritage, 1971; (with S. T. Bindoff) Research in Progress in English and Historical Studies in the Universities of the British Isles, vol. 1, 1971, vol. 2, 1976; (ed) Defoe: Memoirs of a Cavalier, 1972, rev. edn 1991; (ed) The Letters of D. H. Lawrence, vol. 1, 1979, vol. 2 (jtly), 1982, vol. 3 (jtly), 1984, vol. 4 (jtly), 1987, vol. 5 (jtly), 1989, vol. 6 (jtly), 1991, vol. 7 (jtly), 1993, vol. 8, 2000, Selected Letters, 1997 (trans. Japanese 2011), Further Letters, (annually) 2006–10; (ed jtly) The Writings and Speeches of Edmund Burke, vol. 1, The Early Writings, 1997; D. H. Lawrence: man of learning, 2000; D. H. Lawrence, Philip Heseltine and Three Unpublished Letters, 2001; (ed) D. H. Lawrence: Late Essays and Articles, 2004; (ed jtly) James Boswell: An Account of Corsica, 2006; (ed jtly) News from Abroad: letters written by British Travellers on the Grand Tour 1728–1771, 2012; *contributed to:* The Familiar Letter in the 18th Century, 1966; Renaissance and Modern Essays, 1966; D. H. Lawrence, 1980; Renaissance and Modern Studies, 1985; D. H. Lawrence in Italy and England, 1999; papers in Durham Univ. Jl, Essays in Criticism, Renaissance and Modern Studies, Modern Drama, Jl of D. H. Lawrence Soc., etc. *Recreations:* reading, looking at the garden. *Address:* Tyn y Ffynnon Cottage, Nant Peris, Caernarfon, Gwynedd LL55 4UH. *Club:* Royal Air Force. *Died 18 July 2013.*

BOURKE, Christopher John; Metropolitan Stipendiary Magistrate, 1974–96; *b* 31 March 1926; *e s* of late John Francis Bourke of the Oxford Circuit and Eileen Winifred Bourke (*née* Beddoes); *m* 1956, Maureen (*d* 2000), *y d* of late G. A. Barron-Boshell; two *s* one *d. Educ:* Stonyhurst; Oriel Coll., Oxford. Served Army, 1944–48: commnd Glos Regt; served BAOR and Jamaica (ADC to Governor). Called to Bar, Gray's Inn, 1953; Oxford Circuit, 1954–55; Dir of Public Prosecutions Dept, 1955–74. *Recreations:* landscape painting, ballet. *Died 5 April 2013.*

BOURN, James; HM Diplomatic Service, retired; *b* 30 Aug. 1917; *s* of James and Sarah Gertrude Bourn; *m* 1st, 1944, Isobel Mackenzie (*d* 1977); one *s*; 2nd, 1981, Moya Livesey (*d* 1993). *Educ:* Queen Elizabeth's Grammar Sch., Darlington; Univ. of Edinburgh (MA Hons 1979). Executive Officer, Ministry of Health, 1936. War of 1939–45; served (Royal Signals), in India, North Africa and Italy; POW; Captain. Higher Exec. Officer, Ministry of National Insurance, 1947; Asst Principal, Colonial Office, 1947; Principal, 1949; Secretary to the Salaries Commission, Bahamas, 1948–49; Private Sec. to Perm. Under-Sec., 1949; seconded to Tanganyika, 1953–55; UK Liaison Officer to Commn for Technical Co-operation in Africa (CCTA), 1955–57; Commonwealth Relations Office, 1961; seconded to Central African Office, 1962; Dar es Salaam, 1963; Deputy High Commissioner in Zanzibar, Tanzania, 1964–65; Counsellor and Dep. High Comr, Malawi, 1966–70; Ambassador to Somalia, 1970–73; Consul-General, Istanbul, 1973–75. *Address:* c/o National Westminster Bank, 20 Market Place, Richmond, North Yorks DL10 4QF. *Club:* Royal Commonwealth Society. *Died 2 Jan. 2012.*

BOURNS, Prof. Arthur Newcombe, OC 1982; FRSC 1964; FCIC; President and Vice-Chancellor, 1972–80, Professor of Chemistry 1953–81, then Emeritus, McMaster University; *b* 8 Dec. 1919; *s* of Evans Clement Bourns and Kathleen Jones; *m* 1943, Marion Harriet Blakney; two *s* two *d. Educ:* schs in Petitcodiac, NB; Acadia Univ. (BSc); McGill Univ. (PhD). Research Chemist, Dominion Rubber Co., 1944–45; Lectr, Acadia Univ., 1945–46; Asst Prof. of Chemistry, Saskatchewan Univ., 1946–47; McMaster University: Asst Prof., 1947–49; Associate Prof., 1949–53; Dean, Faculty of Grad. Studies, 1957–61; Chm., Chemistry Dept, 1965–67; Vice-Pres., Science and Engrg Div., 1967–72; Actg Pres., 1970. Nuffield Trav. Fellow in Science, University Coll., London, 1955–56. Chm., Gordon Res. Conf. on Chem. and Physics of Isotopes (Vice-Chm. 1959–60; Chm., 1961–62); Nat. Res. Council of Canada: Mem. Chem. Grant Selection Cttee, 1966–69 (Chm. 1968–69); Mem. Council, 1969–75; Mem. Exec. Cttee, 1969–75; Mem. or Chm. various other cttees; Natural Scis and Engrg Res. Council: Member: Council, 1978–85; Exec. Cttee, 1978–85; Allocations Cttee, 1978–86; Cttee on Strategic Grants, 1978–83; Chm., Grants and Scholarships Cttee, 1978–83; Mem., Adv. Cttee on University/Industry Interface, 1979–83; Vis. Res. Officer, 1983–84. Member: Ancaster Public Sch. Bd, 1963–64; Bd, Royal Botanic Gdns, 1972–80 (Vice-Chm.); Cttee on Univ. Affairs, Prov. Ontario; Canadian Cttee for Financing Univ. Res., 1978–80; Council of Ontario Univs,

1972–80; Bd of Dirs and Exec. Cttee, Assoc. of Univs and Colleges of Canada, 1974–77; Mohawk Coll. Bd of Dirs, 1975–82; Council, Canadian Inst. for Advanced Research, 1983–89; Chm., Internat. Adv. Cttee, Chinese Univ. Develt Project, 1985–92; Pres. and Chm. Exec. Cttee, Canadian Bureau for Internat. Educn, 1973–76. McMaster Univ. Med. Centre: Member: Bd of Trustees, 1972–80; Exec. Cttee, 1972–80. Director: Nuclear Activation Services, 1978–80; Slater Steel Industries Ltd, 1975–79. British Council Lectr, 1963. Assoc. Editor, Canadian Jl Chemistry, 1966–69; Mem. Editorial Bd, Science Forum, 1967–73. FCIC 1954 (Chm. Hamilton Section, 1952–53; Mem. Educn Cttee, 1953–59; Mem. Council, 1966–69; Montreal Medal, 1976). Hon. Prof., Jiangxi Univ., China, 1989. Hon. DSc: Acadia, 1968; McGill, 1977; New Brunswick, McMaster, 1981; Hon. LLD Brock, 1980. *Address:* No 1411, 100 Burloak Drive, Burlington, ON L7L 6P6, Canada. *T:* (905) 6396964. *E:* abourns2@cogeco.ca. *Died 29 May 2015.*

BOWDEN, Logan S.; *see* Scott-Bowden.

BOWEN, Prof. David Aubrey Llewellyn, FRCP, FRCPE, FRCPath; Professor of Forensic Medicine, University of London, 1977–89, then Emeritus; Head of Department of Forensic Medicine and Toxicology, Charing Cross Hospital Medical School, 1973–89 (Charing Cross and Westminster Medical School, 1985–89); Hon. Consultant Pathologist, Charing Cross Hospital, 1973–89; *b* 31 Jan. 1924; *s* of late Dr Thomas Rufus Bowen and Catherine (*née* Llewellyn); *m* 1st, 1950, Joan Rosemary Davis (*d* 1973); two *s* one *d*; 2nd, 1975, Helen Rosamund Landcastle. *Educ:* Caterham Sch.; Garw Secondary Sch., Pontycymmer; University College of Wales, Cardiff; Corpus Christi Coll., Cambridge (MA); Middlesex Hosp. Med. Sch. (MB BChir 1947); DipPath 1955; DMJ Soc. of Apoth. of London 1962. FRCPE 1971; FRCPath 1975; FRCP 1982. Ho. posts at W Middlesex Hosp. and London Chest Hosp., 1947 and 1950; RAMC, 1947–49; Jun. Resident Pathologist, Bristol Royal Inf., 1950–51; Registrar in Path., London Chest Hosp., 1951–52; Registrar and Sen. Registrar in Clin. Path., National Hosp. for Nervous Diseases, 1952–56; Asst Pathologist and Sen. Registrar, Royal Marsden Hosp., 1956–57; Demonstr 1957–63, Lectr 1963–66, in Forensic Medicine, St George's Hosp. Med. Sch.; Sen. Lectr 1966–73, Reader 1973–77, in Forensic Medicine, Vice-Dean 1974–78, Charing Cross Hosp. Med. Sch.; Lectr in Forensic Medicine, Oxford Univ., 1974–89. Chairman: Div. of Pathology, Charing Cross Hosp., 1976–78; Apptd and Recog. Teachers in Path., Charing Cross Hosp. Med. Sch., 1980–82; Examiner: Univ. of Riyadh, Saudi Arabia, 1978–81; on Forensic Med., RCPath, 1976–90; for Diploma of Med. Jurisprudence, Soc. of Apothecaries of London, 1970–93; for MD (Forensic Medicine) and Diploma in Legal Medicine, Univ. of Sri Lanka, 1985. Lectr, Metropolitan Police Trng Coll., Hendon, 1976–84; W. D. L. Fernando Oration to Medical Legal Soc. of Sri Lanka, 1985. Chm., Quality Assce and Scientific Standards Cttee, Adv. Bd for Forensic Pathol., Home Office, 1990–96. Vice-President: Medico-Legal Soc., 1977–90; Medical Defence Union, 1979–91; President: British Assoc. in Forensic Med., 1977–79; W London Medico-Chirurgical Soc., 1987–88; Member: British Academy in Forensic Sci. and Forensic Sci. Soc., 1960–91 (Mem. Council, 1965–67); British Div. of Internat. Acad. of Path., 1974–93; Acad. Internat. de Médecine Légale et de Méd. Sociale, 1976–90; RCPath Adv. Cttee on Forensic Path., 1973–76 and 1980–82. Liveryman, Apothecaries' Soc., 1972–. Vice-Pres., Old Caterhamians Assoc., 1987–88. *Publications:* Body of Evidence (autobiog.), 2003; sci. papers in numerous med., forensic med. and path. jls. *Recreations:* travel, writing. *Address:* 19 Letchmore Road, Radlett, Herts WD7 8HU. *T:* (01923) 856936. *Died 31 March 2011.*

BOWEN, Sir Geoffrey (Fraser), Kt 1977; Managing Director, Commercial Banking Company of Sydney Ltd, Australia, 1973–76 (General Manager, 1970–73); *b* 23 June 1912; *m* 1st, Ruth (decd), *d* of H. E. Horsburgh; two *s* one *d*; 2nd, Isabel, *d* of H. T. Underwood. *Address:* Apt 35/36 The Cotswolds, 28 Curagul Road, North Turramurra, NSW 2074, Australia. *Died 28 Feb. 2012.*

BOWEN, Hon. Lionel Frost, AC 1991; MHR (Lab) Kingsford-Smith, NSW, 1969–90; Attorney-General of Australia, 1984–90; Chairman, National Gallery, Canberra, 1990–95; *b* 28 Dec. 1922; *m* 1953, Claire Clement; five *s* three *d*. *Educ:* Sydney Univ. (LLB). Alderman, 1948, Mayor, 1949–50, Randwick Council; MLA, NSW, 1962–69; Postmaster Gen., 1972–74; Special Minister of State, 1974–75; Minister for Manufacturing Industry, 1975; Dep. Leader, Opposition, 1977–83; Minister for Trade, 1983–84; Dep. Prime Minister, 1983–90. *Recreations:* surfing, reading. *Address:* 24 Mooramie Avenue, Kensington, NSW 2033, Australia. *Died 1 April 2012.*

BOWEN, Sir Mark Edward Mortimer, 5th Bt *cr* 1921, of Colworth, Co. Bedford; *b* 17 Oct. 1958; *s* of Sir Thomas Frederic Charles Bowen, 4th Bt and Jill, *d* of Lloyd Evans; *S* father, 1989; *m* 1983, Kerry Tessa, *d* of Michael Moriarty; one *s* one *d*. *Heir:* *s* George Edward Michael Bowen, *b* 27 Dec. 1987. *Address:* Church House, Cucklington, Somerset BA9 9PT. *Died 27 Feb. 2014.*

BOWERING, Ven. Michael Ernest; Archdeacon of Lindisfarne, 1987–2000; *b* 25 June 1935; *s* of Hubert James and Mary Elizabeth Bowering; *m* 1962, Aileen (*née* Fox); one *s* two *d*. *Educ:* Barnstaple Grammar Sch.; Kelham Theological Coll.; York St John University Coll. (MA 2006 Univ. of Leeds). Curate: St Oswald, Middlesbrough, 1959–62; Huntington with New Earswick, York, 1962–64; Vicar, Brayton with Barlow, 1964–72; RD of Selby, 1971–72; Vicar, Saltburn by the Sea, 1972–81; Canon Residentiary of York Minster and Secretary for Mission and Evangelism, 1981–87. *Recreation:* crosswords. *Address:* Robin's Nest, Crabmill Lane, Easingwold, York YO61 3DD. *T:* (01347) 823682. *Died 25 April 2015.*

BOWES, Richard Noel; Deputy Chairman, Willis Faber plc and Chairman, Willis Faber and Dumas, 1985–88; *b* 17 Dec. 1928; *m* 1961, Elizabeth Lyle; one *s* two *d*. *Educ:* Epsom College; Worcester Coll., Oxford (MA). Called to the Bar, Gray's Inn, 1950. RN, 1950–53. Willis Faber and Dumas, 1953–88. *Died 24 May 2014.*

BOWMAN-SHAW, Sir (George) Neville, Kt 1984; DL; Chairman, Samuk Ltd, since 1995; *b* 4 Oct. 1930; *s* of George Bowman-Shaw and Hazel Bowman-Shaw (*née* Smyth); *m* 1962, Georgina Mary Blundell; two *s* one *d* (and one *s* decd). *Educ:* Caldicott Preparatory Sch.; then private tutor. Farming Trainee, 1947; Management Trainee in Engineering Co., 1948. Commissioned in 5th Royal Inniskilling Dragoon Guards, 1950. Sales Manager: Matling Ltd, Wolverhampton, 1953; Materials Handling Equipment (GB) Ltd, London, and Matbro Ltd, London, 1955; Chairman: Boss Trucks Ltd, 1959–95; Lancer Boss Gp Ltd, 1966–94; FOREXIA (UK) Ltd, 1994–97. Member: Development Commn, 1970–77; Design Council, 1979–84; BOTB, 1982–85. High Sheriff, Bedfordshire, 1987–88; DL Bedfordshire, 2002. *Recreations:* shooting, vintage tractors. *Address:* Goose Farm, North Street, Fritwell, Oxfordshire OX27 7QS. *Clubs:* Cavalry and Guards, MCC. *Died 11 July 2015.*

BOWN, Jane Hope, (Mrs M. G. Moss), CBE 1995 (MBE 1985); Photographer for The Observer, since 1950; *b* 13 March 1925; *d* of Charles Wentworth Bell and Daisy Bown; *m* 1954, Martin Grenville Moss, CBE (*d* 2007); two *s* one *d*. *Educ:* William Gibbs Sch., Faversham. Chart corrector, WRNS, 1944–46; student photographer, Guildford School of Art, 1946–50. Hon. DLitt: Bradford, 1986; Southampton, 2009; DUniv Open, 2009. Barry Award, What the Papers Say, 1995. *Publications:* The Gentle Eye: a book of photographs, 1980; Women of Consequence, 1986; Men of Consequence, 1987; The Singular Cat, 1988; Pillars of the Church, 1991; Jane Bown: Observer, 1996; Faces, 2000; Rock, 2003; Unknown Bown, 2007; Exposures, 2009. *Recreations:* restoring old houses, chickens. *Died 21 Dec. 2014.*

BOWRING, Peter, CBE 1993; Chairman, C. T. Bowring & Co. Ltd, 1978–82; Director, Marsh & McLennan Cos Inc., New York, 1980–85 (Vice-Chairman, 1982–84); *b* 22 April 1923; *e s* of Frederick Clive Bowring and Agnes Walker (*née* Cairns); *m* 1st, 1946, Barbara Ekaterina Brewis (marr. diss.; she *d* 2005); one *s* one *d*; 2nd, 1979, Carol Gillian Hutchings (marr. diss.); 3rd, 1986, Mrs Carole Dear.

Educ: Abberley Hall; Shrewsbury Sch. Served War, 1939–45: commnd Rifle Bde, 1942; served in Egypt, N Africa, Italy, Austria (mentioned in despatches, 1945); demobilised 1946. Joined Bowring Group of Cos, 1947: Dir, C. T. Bowring & Co. Ltd, 1956–84, Dep. Chm. 1973–78; Chairman: C. T. Bowring Trading (Holdings) Ltd, 1967–84; Bowmaker (Plant) Ltd, 1972–83; Bowring Steamship Co. Ltd, 1974–82; Bowmaker Ltd, 1978–82; C. T. Bowring (UK) Ltd, 1980–84. Director: City Arts Trust Ltd, 1984–94 (Chm., 1987–94); Independent Primary and Secondary Educn Trust, 1986–2006. Mem. of Lloyd's, 1968–98. Chm., Help the Aged Ltd, 1977–87, Pres., 1988–2000. Dir, Centre for Policy Studies, 1983–88. Vice Pres., Aldeburgh Foundn, 1989– (Chm., 1982–89). Chairman: Inter-Action Social Enterprise Trust, 1989–91; Bd of Governors, St Dunstan's Educnl Foundn, 1977–91; Dulwich Picture Gall. Consultative Cttee, 1989–96; Mem. Bd of Governors, Shrewsbury Sch., 1969–97. Chm., Transglobe Expedition Trust, 1993–2012; Trustee: Ironbridge Gorge Mus. Develt Trust, 1989–93; Spry Trust (formerly Upper Severn Navigation Trust), 1989–2010; Third Age Challenge (formerly ReAction Trust), 1991–96; Wakefield (Tower Hill, Trinity Square) Trust, 1986–2007 (Chm., 2002–05). Mem., Guild of Freemen of City of London; Liveryman, Co. of World Traders (Master, 1989–90); Freeman, Co. of Watermen and Lightermen. FRSA; FZS; FInstD. *Publications:* The Last Minute, 2000; A Thicket of Business, 2007. *Recreations:* motoring, listening to music, photography, cooking, travel. *Address:* Flat 79, New Concordia Wharf, Mill Street, SE1 2BB. *T:* (020) 7237 0818; Flint Cottage, Walnut Tree Farm, Benhall, Saxmundham, Suffolk IP17 1JB. *T:* (01728) 602707. *Club:* Royal Green Jackets. *Died 1 Dec. 2012.*

BOWRON, John Lewis, CBE 1986; solicitor; Secretary-General, The Law Society, 1974–87; *b* 1 Feb. 1924; *e s* of John Henry and Lavinia Bowron; *m* 1950, Patricia, *d* of Arthur Cobby; two *d*. *Educ:* Grangefield Grammar Sch., Stockton-on-Tees; King's Coll., London (LLB, FKC 1976). Principal in Malcolm Wilson & Cobby, Solicitors, Worthing, 1952–74. Member of the Council of the Law Society, 1969–74. Chm. (part-time), Social Security Appeal Tribunals, 1988–96; Agent (part-time) Crown Prosecution Service, 1988–93. *Address:* Hurworth, Sanctuary Lane, Storrington, Pulborough, West Sussex RH20 3JD. *T:* (01903) 746949. *Died 6 July 2011.*

BOWYER, (Arthur) William, RA 1981 (ARA 1974); NEAC, RWS; landscape and portrait painter; Head of Fine Art, Maidstone College of Art, 1971–82; *b* Leek, Staffs, 25 May 1926; *s* of Arthur and Emma Bowyer; *m* 1951, Vera Mary Small; two *s* one *d*. *Educ:* Burslem School of Art; Royal College of Art (ARCA). Former Hon. Sec., New English Art Club. Retrospective exhibn, Messum's, London, W1, 2003. *Recreations:* cricket (Chiswick and Old Meadonians Cricket Clubs), snooker. *Address:* 12 Cleveland Avenue, Chiswick, W4 1SN. *T:* (020) 8994 0346. *Club:* Arts. *Died 1 March 2015.*

BOX, Prof. George Edward Pelham, BEM 1946; FRS 1985; Emeritus Professor of Statistics and Engineering, since 1992, and Director of Research, Center for Quality and Productivity, since 1990, University of Wisconsin-Madison; *b* 18 Oct. 1919; *s* of Harry and Helen (Martin) Box; *m* 1st, 1945, Jessie Ward; 2nd, 1959, Joan Gunhild Fisher; one *s* one *d*; 3rd, 1985, Claire Louise Quist. *Educ:* London University (BSc Maths and Statistics 1947, PhD 1952, DSc 1961). Served War of 1939–45 in Army; res. at Chemical Defence Exptl Station, Porton. Statistician and Head Statistician, Statistical Res. Section, ICI, Blackley, 1948–56; Dir, Stats Tech. Res. Group, Princeton Univ., 1956–60; Prof. of Stats, 1960–92, and Vilas Res. Prof., Dept of Stats, 1980–92, Univ. of Wisconsin-Madison. Res. Prof., Univ. of N Carolina, 1952–53; Ford Foundn Vis. Prof., Harvard Business Sch., 1965–66; Vis. Prof., Univ. of Essex, 1970–71. President: Amer. Statistical Assoc., 1978; Inst. of Mathematical Statistics, 1979. Fellow, Amer. Acad. of Arts and Scis, 1974. Hon. DSc: Rochester, NY, 1975; Carnegie Mellon, 1989; Don Carlos III, Madrid, 1995; Waterloo, Canada, 1999; Conservatoire nat. des arts et métiers, Paris, 2000. Numerous medals and awards. *Publications:* Statistical Methods in Research and Production, 1957; Design and Analysis of Industrial Experiments, 1959; Evolutionary Operation: a statistical method for process improvement, 1969; Time Series Analysis Forecasting and Control, 1970; Bayesian Inference in Statistical Analysis, 1973; Statistics for Experimenters, 1977; Empirical Model Building and Response Surfaces, 1986; Statistical Control by Monitoring and Feedback Adjustment, 1997; Box on Quality and Discovery, 2000; *posthumous publication*: An Accidental Statistician: the life and memories of George E. P. Box, 2013. *Address:* 911 Western Road, Madison, WI 53705–2128, USA. *T:* (608) 4419905. *Died 28 March 2013.*

BOYCE, Joseph Frederick, JP; FRICS; General Manager, Telford Development Corporation, 1980–86; *b* 10 Aug. 1926; *s* of Frederick Arthur and Rosalie Mary Boyce; *m* 1953, Nina Margaret, *o d* of A. F. Tebb, Leeds; two *s*. *Educ:* Roundhay Sch., Leeds; Leeds Coll. of Technology. Articled Pupil and Sen. Assistant, Rex Procter & Miller, Chartered Quantity Surveyors, 1942–53; Sen. Quantity Surveyor, Bedford Corp., 1953–55; Group Quantity Surveyor, Somerset CC, 1955–60; Principal Quantity Surveyor, Shropshire CC, 1960–64; Telford Development Corporation: Chief Quantity Surveyor, 1964–71; Technical Dir, 1971–76; Dep. Gen. Manager, 1976–80. JP Shrewsbury, 1975. *Publications:* technical articles and publications on new towns, in learned journals. *Recreations:* gardening, hill walking, music, fine wine. *Address:* Grasse, Alpes-Maritimes, France. *Died July 2013.*

BOYCE, Michael David; DL; FRWCMD; Chief Executive, Cardiff Bay Development Corporation, 1992–2000; *b* 27 May 1937; *s* of Clifford and Vera Boyce; *m* 1962, Audrey May Gregory; one *s* one *d*. *Educ:* Queen Elizabeth's Sch., Crediton. DMA 1962; Dip. in French, UC Cardiff, 1984. Admitted Solicitor, 1968. Asst Solicitor, 1968–69, Sen. Asst Solicitor, and Asst Clerk of the Peace, 1969–71, Exeter CC; Dep. Town Clerk, 1971–73, Dep. Chief Exec., 1973–74, Newport, Gwent; County Solicitor, S Glam, 1974–87; Chief Exec., S Glam CC, and Clerk to Lieutenancy, 1987–92. Mem., Home Office Adv. Council on Fire Service Pensions, 1976–87; Sec., Lord Chancellor's Adv. Cttee, 1987–92. Director: Cardiff Marketing Ltd, 1990–94; Cardiff Business Technology Centre Ltd, 1979–87; S Glam Youth Opportunities Ltd, 1979–87; New Openings Ltd, 1979–87; S Glam Investments Ltd, 1979–87. Member: Prince's Trust, 1987–92; Bd, S Glam TEC, 1987–95; Cardiff Chamber of Commerce & Trade, 1987–2000; S and Mid Glam Area Manpower Bd, 1976–79; Council, Cardiff Common Purpose, 1995–2000; Bd, Sgrîn Media Agency for Wales, 2002–04. Dir, Earthfall Dance Co. Ltd, 2003–08. Advr, ACC, 1976–87; Legal Adviser: Assembly of Welsh Counties, 1976–87; Council of Museums in Wales, 1979–85; Hon. Solicitor, S Glam Probation and After-care Cttee, 1974–85. Member: Sports Council for Wales, 1980–82; BBC Wales Ind. Assessment Panel on Sport, 1997; Legal Advr, BBB of C, 2003–12. Trustee: Glam County History Trust Ltd, 1974–85; S Wales Community Foundn, 1996–99; Trustee and Hon. Legal Advisor: STAR Recreation Trust, 1982–2002; Millennium Stadium Charitable Trust, 2002–04; Trustee and Presenter, Hosp. Radio Glamorgan, 2002–12; Chm., Old St Mellons Community Council, 2000–08; Pres., Rotary Club of Cardiff St Davids, 2009–10. Mem. Council, Univ. of Wales Coll. of Cardiff, 1987–93; Governor: Royal Welsh Coll. of Music and Drama, 1992–98; St Mellons Ch in Wales Primary Sch., 2003–12. Chm., Cardiff City AFC, 1993–95. Mem., TAVRA (Wales), 1987–92. FRWCMD (FWCMD 1999). DL S Glam, 1993. *Recreations:* France and French, Association Football, music, railways, travel. *Address:* 1 White Oaks Drive, Old St Mellons, Cardiff CF3 5EX. *T:* (029) 2079 1927. *Died 2 Feb. 2013.*

BOYD, Dame Vivienne (Myra), DBE 1986 (CBE 1983); Vice Chairperson, Hutt Diabetic Foundation, 1992; *b* 11 April 1926; *d* of Hugh France Lowe and Winifred May Lowe (*née* Shearer); *m* 1948, Robert Macdonald Boyd (*d* 2004); three *d* (one *s* decd). *Educ:* Eastern Hutt Sch.; Hutt Valley High Sch.; Victoria Coll., Univ. of New Zealand (MSc (Hons)). President: Dunedin Free Kindergarten Assoc., 1965; NZ Baptist Women's League, 1966; Nat. Council of Women of NZ, 1978–82; NZ Baptist Union of Churches and Missionary Soc., 1984–85; Wellington Br., NZ Epilepsy Assoc., 1994–96; Hutt Valley Br., NZ Fedn of Graduate Women, 2002–04. Member: Royal Commn on Nuclear Power Generation, 1976–78; Equal Opportunities Tribunal, 1979–89; Advertising Standards Council, subseq. Advertising Standards Complaints Bd, 1988–97; Envmtl Choice Mgt Adv. Cttee, 1990–98; chaired: Abortion Supervisory Cttee, 1979–80; Women and Recreation Conf., 1981; Review of Preparation and Initial Employment of Nurses, 1986–92; Consumer Council, NZ, 1983–88 (Mem., 1975–88); Consumers' Inst. of NZ Inc., 1988–89 (Mem. Bd, 1989–90); Convener, Internat. Council of Women Standing Cttee on Social Welfare, 1982–88. Chm., Taita Home and Hosp. for the Elderly, 1989–92. Trustee, Celebrating Women Trust, 1998–2003. Silver Jubilee Medal, 1977. *Recreation:* reading. *Died 13 July 2011.*

BOYES, Kate Emily Tyrrell, (Mrs C. W. Sanders); Chairman, Civil Service Selection Boards, 1978; *b* 22 April 1918; *e d* of S. F. Boyes, Sandiacre, Derbyshire; *m* 1944, Cyril Woods Sanders, CB; one *s* three *d*. *Educ:* Long Eaton Grammar Sch.; (Scholar) Newnham Coll., Cambridge. Economics Tripos, 1939; MA (Cantab). Administrative Class, BoT, Home Civil Service, 1939; Private Sec. to Parly Sec., 1942–45; Principal, 1945; Sec. to Council on Prices, Productivity and Incomes, 1958–60; Asst Sec., 1961; Speechwriter to President of BoT, 1963–64; Under-Sec., Europe, Industry and Technology Div., DTI, later Dept of Trade, 1972–78. Member: Council, National Trust, 1967–79; Exec., Keep Britain Tidy Gp, 1980. *Recreations:* climbing, sailing, ski-ing, archæology. *Address:* 41 Smith Street, SW3 4EP. *T:* (020) 7352 8053; Giles Point, Winchelsea, Sussex TN36 4AA. *T:* (01797) 226431; Canower, Cashel, Connemara, Ireland. *Clubs:* Ski Club of Gt Britain; Island Cruising (Salcombe). *Died 15 Nov. 2012.*

BOYSON, Rt Hon. Sir Rhodes, Kt 1987; PC 1987; *b* 11 May 1925; *s* of Alderman William Boyson, MBE, JP and Mrs Bertha Boyson, Haslingden, Rossendale, Lancs; *m* 1st, 1946, Violet Burletson (marr. diss.); two *d*; 2nd, 1971, Florette MacFarlane. *Educ:* Haslingden Grammar Sch.; UC Cardiff; Manchester Univ. (BA, MA); LSE (PhD); Corpus Christi Coll., Cambridge. Served with Royal Navy. Headmaster: Lea Bank Secondary Modern Sch., Rossendale, 1955–61; Robert Montefiore Secondary Sch., Stepney, 1961–66; Highbury Grammar Sch., 1966–67; Highbury Grove Sch., 1967–74. Chm., Nat. Council for Educnl Standards, 1974–79. Chm., Churchill Press and Constitutional Book Club, 1969–79. Councillor: Haslingden, 1957–61; Waltham Forest, 1968–74 (Chm. Establishment Cttee, 1968–71); Chm., London Boroughs Management Services Unit, 1968–70. Formerly Youth Warden, Lancs Youth Clubs. Contested (C) Eccles, 1970. MP (C) Brent North, Feb. 1974–1997; contested (C) same seat, 1997. Vice-Chm., Cons Parly Educn Cttee, 1975–76; Hon. Sec. Cons. Adv. Cttee on Educn, 1975–78; Opposition spokesman on educn, 1976–79; Parly Under-Sec. of State, DES, 1979–83; Minister of State: for Social Security, DHSS, 1983–84; NI Office, 1984–86; for Local Govt, DoE, 1986–87. Non-executive Dir, Black's Leisure, 1998–2001. *Publications:* The North-East Lancashire Poor Law 1838–1871, 1965; The Ashworth Cotton Enterprise, 1970; (ed) Right Turn, 1970; (ed) Down with the Poor, 1971; (ed) Goodbye to Nationalisation, 1972; (ed) Education: Threatened Standards, 1972; (ed) The Accountability of Schools, 1973; Oversubscribed: the story of Highbury Grove, 1974; Crisis in Education, 1975; (jt ed) Black Papers on Education, 1969–77; (ed) 1985: An Escape from Orwell's 1984, 1975; Centre Forward, 1978; Speaking My Mind (autobiog.), 1995; Boyson on Education, 1996. *Recreations:* reading, writing, talk, hard work, meeting friends, inciting the millennialist Left in education and politics. *Address:* 71 Paines Lane, Pinner, Middx HA5 3BX. *T:* (020) 8866 2071. *Clubs:* Carlton; Churchill (N Wembley), Wembley Conservative. *Died 28 Aug. 2012.*

BRABHAM, Sir John Arthur, (Sir Jack), Kt 1979; AO 2008; OBE 1966; retired, 1970, as professional racing driver; Director, Engine Developments Ltd, 1964–2002; *b* Sydney, Australia, 2 April 1926; *m* 1st, 1951, Betty Evelyn Beresford (marr. diss. 1994); three *s*; 2nd, 1996, Margaret Taylor. *Educ:* Hurstville Technical Coll., Sydney. Served in RAAF, 1944–46. Started own engineering business, 1946; Midget Speedway racing, 1947–54; several championships (Australian, NSW, South Australian); numerous wins driving a Cooper-Bristol, Australia, 1953–54; to Europe, 1955; Australian Grand Prix, 1955, 1963 (debut of Repco Brabham) and 1965; World Champion Formula II, 1958, also many firsts including Casablanca, Goodwood, Brands Hatch, NZ Grand Prix (three times), Belgian Grand Prix; Formula II Champion of France, 1964–66. World Champion Driver: (after first full Formula I Season with 2·5-litre car), 1959–60, 1960–61, 1966. First in Monaco and British Grandes Epreuves, 1959; won Grand Prix of: Holland, Belgium, France, Britain, Portugal, Denmark, 1960; Belgium, 1961. Elected Driver of the Year by Guild of Motoring Writers, 1959, 1966 and 1970, Sportsman of the Year by Australian Broadcasting Co., 1959; left Cooper to take up building own Grand Prix cars, 1961; debut, 1962; first ever constructor/driver to score world championship points, 1963; cars finished first: French GP; Mexican GP, 1964; Formula II and Formula III cars world-wide success, 1963; awarded Ferodo Trophy, 1964 and again, 1966; British Saloon Car Championship, 1965; won French Grand Prix and British Grand Prix, 1966; won French Grand Prix, 1967. Patron, Kidney Health Australia, 2008–. RAC Gold Medal, 1966; BARC Gold Star, 1959, 1960 and 1966; Formula I Manufacturers' Championship, 1966, 1967. *Publications:* Jack Brabham's Book of Motor Racing, 1960; When the Flag Drops, 1971; The Jack Brabham Story, 2004; contribs to British journals. *Recreations:* reading, documentaries, driving trips. *Address:* Suite 404, Bag no 1, Robina Town Centre, Qld 4230, Australia. *Clubs:* Royal Automobile, British Racing and Sports Car, British Racing Drivers'; Australian Racing Drivers'; Royal Automobile, Victorian Historic Racing Register (Vic). *Died 19 May 2014.*

BRACEGIRDLE, Dr Brian, FSA, FRPS, FRSB; Research Consultant in microscopy, and Fellow, Science Museum, 1990–2005; *b* 31 May 1933; *oc* of Alfred Bracegirdle; *m* 1st, 1958, Margaret Lucy Merrett (marr. diss. 1974); one *d*; 2nd, 1975, Patricia Helen Miles; no *c*. *Educ:* King's Sch., Macclesfield; Univ. of London (BSc); PhD 1975 (UCL). DipRMS 1975. FRPS 1969; FBIPP (FIIP 1970); FRSB (FIBiol 1976); FSA 1981. Technician in industry, 1950–57; Biology Master, Erith Grammar Sch., 1958–61; Sen. Lectr in Biol., S Katharine's Coll., London, 1961–64; Head, Depts of Nat. Science and Learning Resources, Coll. of All Saints, London, 1964–77; Science Museum: Keeper, Wellcome Mus. of Hist. of Medicine, 1977; Head of Dept of Med. Scis, and Head of Collections Management Div., 1987–89; Asst Dir, 1987–89. Hon. Lectr in History of Medicine, UCL, 1978–90; Hon. Res. Fellow in Hist. of Sci., Imperial Coll., 1990–93. Hon. Treasurer, ICOM (UK), 1978–89. Chm., Inst. of Medical and Biological Illustration, 1973–74; President: Assoc. Européenne de Musées de l'Histoire des Sciences Médicales, 1983–90; Quekett Microscopical Club, 1985–88; Vice-Pres., Royal Microscopical Soc., 1988–90. Ed., Quekett Jl of Microscopy, 1998–2012. *Publications:* Photography for Books and Reports, 1970; The Archaeology of the Industrial Revolution, 1973; The Evolution of Microtechnique, 1978, 1987; (ed) Beads of Glass: Leeuwenhoek and the early microscope, 1984; Scientific Photomacrography, 1995; Notes on Modern Microscope Manufacturers, 1996; Microscopical Mounts and Mounters, 1998; A Catalogue of the Microscopy Collections at the Science Museum, 2005; A History of Photography with the Light Microscope, 2010; The Quekett Microscopical Club 1865–2015, 2016; (with W. H. Freeman): An Atlas of Embryology, 1963, 1978; An Atlas of Histology, 1966; An Atlas of Invertebrate Structure, 1971; An Advanced Atlas of Histology, 1976; (with P. H. Miles): An Atlas of Plant Structure, vol. I, 1971; An Atlas of Plant Structure, Vol. II, 1973; Thomas Telford, 1973; The Darbys and the Ironbridge Gorge, 1974; An Atlas of Chordate Structure, 1977; (with J. B. McCormick) The Microscopic Photographs of J. B. Dancer, 1993; (with S. Bradbury): Modern Photomicrography, 1995; Introduction to Light Microscopy, 1998; papers on photography for life sciences, on scientific topics, and on history of science/medicine. *Recreations:* walking, music, travel, shouting at the television set. *Address:* 22 Montpellier Spa Road, Cheltenham, Glos GL50 1UL. *T:* (01242) 517478. *Died 16 Dec. 2015.*

BRADBOURN, Philip Charles, OBE 1994; Member (C) West Midlands Region, European Parliament, since 1999; *b* 9 Aug. 1951; *s* of Horace and Elizabeth Bradbourn. *Educ:* Tipton Grammar Sch.; Worcester Coll. of Higher Educn; Wulfrun Coll. of Further Educn, Wolverhampton (DMA 1972). Local govt officer, 1967–87; Advr to Leader of Opposition, Wolverhampton BC, 1987–99. *Recreation:* gardening. *Address:* (office) 285 Kenilworth Road, Balsall Common, Coventry, Warwickshire CV7 7EL. *T:* (01676) 530621. *Died 19 Dec. 2014.*

BRADBURY, Ray Douglas; author; *b* Waukegan, Ill, USA, 22 Aug. 1920; *s* of Leonard S. Bradbury and Esther Moberg; *m* 1947, Marguerite Susan McClure (*d* 2003); four *d. Educ:* Los Angeles High Sch. First Science-Fiction stories, 1941–44; stories sold to Harpers', Mademoiselle, The New Yorker, etc., 1945–56. Stories selected for: Best American Short Stories, 1946, 1948, 1952, 1958; O. Henry Prize Stories, 1947, 1948; and for inclusion in numerous anthologies. *Screenplays:* Moby Dick, 1954; Icarus Montgolfier Wright, 1961; The Martian Chronicles, 1964; The Picasso Summer, 1968; The Halloween Tree, 1968; The Dreamers; And The Rock Cried Out. Benjamin Franklin Award for Best Story Published in an Amer. Magazine of General Circulation, 1954; 1000 dollar Grant from Inst. of Arts and Letters, 1954. *Publications: novels:* Dark Carnival, 1947; Fahrenheit 451, 1953 (filmed); (for children) Switch on the Night, 1955; Dandelion Wine, 1957; Something Wicked This Way Comes, 1962 (filmed 1983; adapted for stage, 1986); The Small Assassin, 1973; Mars and the Minds of Man, 1973; The Mummies of Guanajuato, 1978; The Ghosts of Forever, 1981; Death is a Lonely Business, 1986; The Toynbee Convector, 1989; A Graveyard for Lunatics, 1990; Green Shadows, White Whale, 1992; From the Dust Returned, 2001; Let's All Kill Constance, 2003; Farewell Summer, 2006; Now and Forever: somewhere a band is playing and Leviathan '99, 2007; *short stories:* The Martian Chronicles, 1950 (English edn, The Silver Locusts, 1957); The Illustrated Man, 1951 (filmed with The Day It Rained Forever); The Golden Apples of the Sun, 1953; The October Country, 1955; A Medicine for Melancholy (English edn, The Day It Rained Forever), 1959; (for children) R Is For Rocket, 1962; (for children) S Is For Space, 1962; The Machineries of Joy, 1964, repr. 2010; The Autumn People, 1965; The Vintage Bradbury, 1965; Tomorrow Midnight, 1966; Twice Twenty-Two, 1966; I Sing the Body Electric!, 1969; Long After Midnight, 1976; Quicker than the Eye, 1998; Driving Blind, 1998; One More for the Road, 2001; (for children) The Cat's Pajamas, 2004; A Sound of Thunder and other stories, 2005; The Homecoming, 2006; The Stories of Ray Bradbury, 2010; *general:* Zen and the Art of Writing, 1973; Bradbury Speaks: too soon from the cave, too far from the stars, 2005; *poems:* When Elephants Last in the Dooryard Bloomed, 1973; Where Robot Mice and Robot Men Run Round in Robot Towns, 1977; This Attic where the Meadow Greens, 1980; The Haunted Computer and the Android Pope, 1981; *plays:* The Meadow, 1947; The Anthem Sprinters (one-act), 1963; The World of Ray Bradbury (one-act), 1964; The Wonderful Ice Cream Suit and Other Plays (one-act), 1965; Any Friend of Nicholas Nickleby's is a Friend of Mine, 1968; Pillar of Fire, 1975. *Recreations:* oil painting, ceramics, collecting native masks. *Address:* 10265 Cheviot Drive, Los Angeles, CA 90064, USA. *Died 6 June 2012.*

BRADBY, Prof. David Henry, PhD; Professor of Drama and Theatre Studies, 1988–2007, then Emeritus, and Dean of Arts, 2000–02, University of London, at Royal Holloway (formerly Royal Holloway and Bedford New College); *b* 27 Feb. 1942; *s* of late Edward Lawrence Bradby; *m* 1965, Rachel Anderson, writer; three *s* one *d. Educ:* Rugby Sch.; Trinity College, Oxford (MA); PhD Glasgow; CertEd Bristol. Lectr, Glasgow Univ., 1966–70; University of Kent at Canterbury: Lectr, 1971; Sen. Lectr, 1979–85; Reader in French Theatre Studies, 1985–88; Prof. of Theatre Studies, Univ. of Caen, 1983–84. Dir, Orange Tree Theatre, Richmond, 1990–2002. Ed., Contemporary Theatre Review, 2003–. Chevalier des Arts et des Lettres (France), 1997. *Publications:* People's Theatre (with John McCormick), 1978; The Theatre of Roger Planchon, 1984; Modern French Drama 1940–1980, 1984, 2nd edn, as Modern French Drama 1940–1990, 1991; (with David Williams) Directors' Theatre, 1988; Le Théâtre Français Contemporain, 1990; The Theatre of Michael Vinaver, 1993; (with Annie Sparks) Mise en Scène: French theatre now, 1997; Beckett: Waiting for Godot, 2001; Le Théâtre en France de 1968 à 2000, 2007. *Recreation:* forestry. *Address:* Lower Damsels, Northrepps, Cromer NR27 0LJ. *Died 17 Jan. 2011.*

BRADFIELD, Sir John (Richard Grenfell), Kt 2007; CBE 1986; PhD; Senior Bursar, Trinity College, Cambridge, 1956–92; Founder, and Manager, Cambridge Science Park, 1970–92; *b* 20 May 1925; *s* of Horace and Ada Bradfield; *m* 1951, Jane Wood; one *s. Educ:* Trinity Coll., Cambridge (schol. 1942; MA, PhD). Research Fellow in Cell Biology, Trinity Coll., Cambridge, 1947; Commonwealth (Harkness) Fellow, Chicago, 1948; Jun. Bursar, Trinity Coll., Cambridge, 1951. Director: Cambridge Water Co., 1965–95; Cambridge Building Soc., 1968–95; Biotechnology Investments, 1989–2000; Anglian Water, 1989–93 (Bd Mem., 1975–89); 3i Bioscience Investment Trust, 2000–02 (Consultant, 2002–04); Chm., Abbotstone Agricl Property Unit Trust, 1975–2002. Chairman: Addenbrooke's NHS Trust, 1993–96; Commn for the New Towns, 1995–98. Darwin College, Cambridge: proposed foundn, 1963; Hon. Fellow, 1973. Hon. LLD Cambridge, 1992. FRSA 1990. *Publications:* scientific papers on cell biology. *Recreations:* walking, arboretum-visiting. *Address:* Trinity College, Cambridge CB2 1TQ. *T:* (01223) 338400. *Died 13 Oct. 2014.*

BRADFORD, Prof. Eric Watts, MDS (Sheffield); DDSc (St Andrews); Professor of Dental Surgery, 1959–85, then Emeritus, and Pro-Vice-Chancellor, 1983–85, University of Bristol; *b* 4 Nov. 1919; *e s* of E. J. G. and C. M. Bradford; *m* 1946, Norah Mary Longmuir; two *s* three *d. Educ:* King Edward VII Sch., Sheffield; High Storrs Grammar Sch., Sheffield; Univ. of Sheffield (Robert Styring Scholar). LDS, Sheffield, 1943; BDS, Sheffield, 1944; MDS, Sheffield, 1950; DDSc St Andrews, 1954. Lieut, Army Dental Corps, Nov. 1944; Capt., Nov. 1945. Lectr, Univ. of Sheffield, 1947–52; Senior Lectr, Univ. of St Andrews, 1952–59; Dean, Faculty of Medicine, Bristol University, 1975–79. Mem., Gen. Dental Council, 1979–85. *Publications:* many papers on dental anatomy in British and other journals. *Address:* 9 Cedar Court, Glenavon Park, Sneyd Park, Bristol BS9 1RL. *T:* (0117) 968 1849. *Died 21 March 2013.*

BRADLEY, Prof. Donald Charlton, CChem, FRSC; FRS 1980; Professor of Inorganic Chemistry, 1965–87, and Head of Chemistry Department, 1978–82, Fellow, 1988, Queen Mary College, University of London; Emeritus Professor, University of London, since 1988; *b* 7 Nov. 1924; *m* 1st, 1948, Constance Joy Hazeldean (*d* 1985); one *s*; 2nd, 1990, Ann Levy (*née* MacDonald). *Educ:* Hove County School for Boys; Birkbeck Coll., Univ. of London (BSc 1st Cl. Hons Chemistry, PhD, DSc; Fellow, 2006). Research Asst, British Electrical and Allied Industries Research Assoc., 1941–47; Asst Lectr in Chemistry, 1949–52, Lectr in Chemistry, 1952–59, Birkbeck Coll.; Prof. of Chemistry, Univ. of Western Ontario, Canada, 1959–64. Univ. of London: Chm., Bd of Studies in Chemistry and Chemical Industries, 1977–79; Mem. Senate, 1981–87. MRI 1979 (Mem. Council, 1987–93; Hon. Sec., 1988–93); Royal Society of Chemistry: Pres. Dalton Div., 1983–85; Ludwig Mond Medal and Lectr, 1987. Exec. Editor, Polyhedron, 1982–97. Gov., Haberdashers' Aske's Schs, Elstree, 1973–95. Freeman: Haberdashers' Co., 1995; City of London, 1996. Member: Samuel Pepys Club, 1995–; Aldersgate Ward Club, 1996–. FRSA 1982. Royal Medal, Royal Soc., 1998. *Publications:* (jtly) Metal Alkoxides, 1978; Alkoxo and Aryloxo Derivatives of Metals, 2001; numerous pubns on synthesis and structure of metallo-organic compounds, co-ordination chemistry and inorganic polymers, mainly in Jl of Chemical Soc. *Recreations:* travelling, theatre, listening to music, amateur interest in archaeology. *Address:* 171 Shakespeare Tower, Barbican, EC2Y 8DR. *Died 20 Dec. 2014.*

BRADLEY, Edgar Leonard, OBE 1979; Metropolitan Stipendiary Magistrate, 1967–83; *b* 17 Nov. 1917; 2nd *s* of Ernest Henry and Letitia Bradley, W Felton, Oswestry; *m* 1942, Elsa, *o d* of Colin and Elizabeth Matheson,

Edinburgh; two *s* three *d*. *Educ:* Malvern Coll.; Trinity Hall, Cambridge. BA 1939; MA 1942. Called to Bar, Middle Temple, 1940. Served 1940–46, RA; Capt. and Adjt, 1943–45; Major, GSO2, Mil. Govt of Germany, 1946. Practised at Bar, 1946–51, SE Circuit, Central Criminal Ct, S London and Surrey Sessions. Legal Dept of Home Office, 1951–54. Sec., Departmental Cttee on Magistrates' Courts Bill, 1952; Sec. of Magistrates' Courts Rule Cttee, 1952–54; Clerk to Justices: Wrexham and Bromfield, 1954–57; Poole, 1957–67. Justices' Clerks Society: Mem. Council, 1957–67; Hon. Sec., 1963–67. Mem., Nat. Adv. Council on Trng of Magistrates, 1965–67; Magistrates' Association: Vice Pres., 1984–; Mem. Council, 1968–84; Chm. Legal Cttee, 1973–82. Adv. tour of Magistrates' Courts in Ghana, 1970. *Publications:* (with J. J. Senior) Bail in Magistrates' Courts, 1977; articles in legal jls. *Recreations:* visiting Perthshire, music. *Address:* 55 St Germains, Bearsden, Glasgow G61 2RS. *T:* (0141) 942 5831. *Died 11 Oct. 2015.*

BRADLEY, Richard Alan; Headmaster, Rivers Country Day School, Massachusetts, USA, 1981–91; *b* 6 Oct. 1925; *s* of late Reginald Livingstone Bradley, CBE, MC, and of Phyllis Mary Richardson; *m* 1950, Meryll J. Braddy; one *s* two *d*; *m* 1971, Mary Ann Vicary. *Educ:* Marlborough Coll.; Trinity Coll., Oxford (Scholar). 2nd cl. hons Mod. History. Royal Marines, 1944–46; Oxford, 1946–48; Club Manager, Oxford and Bermondsey Club, 1949. Asst Master: Dulwich Coll., 1949–50; Tonbridge Sch., 1950–66 (Head of History Dept, 1957–66; Housemaster of Ferox Hall, 1961–66); Warden of St Edward's Sch., Oxford, 1966–71; Headmaster, Ridley Coll., Canada, 1971–81. *Recreations:* games, dramatics, mountains. *Address:* 10 Carver Hill Court, South Natick, MA 01760–5531, USA. *Club:* Vincent's (Oxford). *Died 25 March 2015.*

BRAGG, Stephen Lawrence, MA, SM; FREng; FIMechE; Administrator, Cambridge Office, American Friends of Cambridge University, 1988–93; Fellow, Wolfson College, Cambridge, 1982–91, then Emeritus Fellow; *b* 17 Nov. 1923; *e s* of Sir Lawrence Bragg, CH, OBE, MC, FRS and Lady Bragg, CBE; *m* 1951, Maureen Ann (*née* Roberts); three *s*. *Educ:* Rugby Sch.; Cambridge Univ.; Massachusetts Inst. of Technology. BA 1945, MA 1949 (Cambridge); SM 1949 (MIT). FREng (FEng 1981). Rolls-Royce Ltd, 1944–48; Commonwealth Fund Fellow, 1948–49; Wm Jessop Ltd, Steelmakers, 1949–51; Rolls-Royce Ltd, 1951–71: Chief Scientist, 1960–63; Chief Research Engineer, 1964–68; Dir, Aero Div., 1969–71. Vice-Chancellor, Brunel Univ., 1971–81. Eastern Region Broker, SERC, 1981–83. Dir in Industrial Co-operation, Cambridge Univ., 1984–87. Chm., Cambridge DHA, 1982–86. Member: Univ. Grants Cttee, 1966–71; Aeronautical Research Council, 1970–73; Court of ASC, Henley, 1972–81; SRC Engineering Bd, 1976–79; Airworthiness Requirements Bd, 1979–81; Chm., Adv. Cttee on Falsework, 1973–75. Pres., Railway and Canal Histl Soc., 1998–2000. Corresp. Mem., Venezuelan Acad. Sci., 1975. Hon. DEng Sheffield, 1969; Hon. DTech Brunel, 1982. *Publications:* Rocket Engines, 1962; articles on Jet Engines, Research Management, University/Industry Collaboration, etc. *Recreation:* railway history. *Address:* 22 Brookside, Cambridge CB2 1JQ. *T:* (01223) 362208. *Club:* Athenæum. *Died 15 Nov. 2014.*

BRAHAM, Allan John Witney, PhD; Keeper and Deputy Director, National Gallery, 1978–88; *b* 19 Aug. 1937; *s* of Dudley Braham and Florence Mears; *m* 1963, Helen Clare Butterworth (marr. diss. 2004); two *d*. *Educ:* Dulwich Coll.; Courtauld Inst. of Art, Univ. of London (BA 1960, PhD 1967). Asst Keeper, National Gall., 1962, Dep. Keeper, 1973. Arts Council Exhibn (with Peter Smith), François Mansart, 1970–71; National Gall. Exhibitions: (co-ordinator and editor) The Working of the National Gallery, 1974; Velázquez, The Rokeby Venus, 1976; Giovanni Battista Moroni, 1978; Italian Renaissance Portraits, 1979; El Greco to Goya, 1981; Wright of Derby "Mr and Mrs Coltman", 1986. *Publications:* Dürer, 1965; Murillo (The Masters), 1966; The National Gallery in London: Italian Painting of the High Renaissance, 1971; (with Peter Smith) François Mansart, 1973; Funeral Decorations in Early Eighteenth Century Rome, 1975; (with Hellmut Hager) Carlo Fontana: The Drawings at Windsor Castle, 1977; The Architecture of the French Enlightenment, 1980 (Hitchcock Medal, Banister Fletcher Prize; French edn 1982); National Gall. catalogues: The Spanish School (revised edn), 1970, and booklets: Velázquez, 1972; Rubens, 1972; Architecture, 1976; Italian Paintings of the Sixteenth Century, 1985; contrib. prof. jls, etc. *Recreation:* history of architecture. *Address:* 1 Catherine Lodge, 40 Woodside Park Road, N12 8RP. *Died 3 March 2011.*

BRAIN, 2nd Baron *cr* 1962, of Eynsham; **Christopher Langdon Brain;** Bt 1954; *b* 30 Aug. 1926; *s* of 1st Baron Brain, MA, DM, FRS, FRCP and Stella, *er d* of late Reginald L. Langdon-Down; *S* father 1966; *m* 1953, Susan Mary (*d* 2007), *d* of George P. and Ethelbertha Morris; three *d*. *Educ:* Leighton Park Sch., Reading; New College, Oxford. MA 1956. Royal Navy, 1946–48. Liveryman, 1955, Upper Warden, 1974–75, Asst, 1980–2000, Renter Bailiff, 1983–84, Upper Bailiff, 1984–85, Worshipful Co. of Weavers. Chm., Rhone-Alps Regional Council, British Chamber of Commerce, France, 1967. ARPS 1970. *Recreations:* bird watching, fly-fishing. *Heir: b* Hon. Michael Cottrell Brain, MA, DM, FRCP, FRCP Canada, Prof. of Medicine, McMaster Univ. [*b* 6 Aug. 1928; *m* 1960, Dr the Hon. Elizabeth Ann Herbert, *e d* of Baron Tangley, KBE; one *s* two *d*]. *Address:* 4 Penny Long Lane, Leicester LE3 3LE. *Club:* Oxford and Cambridge Sailing Society. *Died 15 Aug. 2014.*

BRANDON, (David) Stephen; QC 1996; *b* 18 Dec. 1950; *s* of late James Osbaldeston Brandon and Dorothy Brandon (*née* Wright); *m* 1982, (Helen) Beatrice Lee; one *d*. *Educ:* Univ. of Nottingham (BA); Univ. of Keele (LLM). Lectr in Law, Univ. of Keele, 1975–85; called to the Bar, Gray's Inn, 1978; in practice at Revenue Bar, 1981–. Mem., Group Bd, United Church Schs Trust/United Learning Trust, 2011–. *Publications:* Taxation of Non-Resident and Migrant Companies, 1989; Foreign Companies and the Problem of UK Residence, 1991; Taxation of Non-UK Resident Companies and Their Shareholders, 2003; various articles. *Recreations:* art (esp. collecting early woodcuts), opera, nurturing woodlands. *Address:* 15 Old Square, Lincoln's Inn, WC2A 3UE; Clopton Manor, Clopton, Northants NN14 3DZ. *Died 15 Feb. 2015.*

BRANDT, His Honour (Paul) Nicholas; a Circuit Judge, 1987–2003; *b* 21 Nov. 1937; *s* of late Paul Francis and Barbara Brandt. *Educ:* St Andrew's Sch., Eastbourne; Marlborough Coll.; New Coll., Oxford (BA 2nd Cl. Hons Sch. of Jurisprudence). Called to the Bar, Gray's Inn, 1963; a Recorder, 1983–87. Chm., Polstead Parish Council, 2007–. *Recreations:* sailing, shooting, Rugby football. *Address:* c/o Colchester County Court, Falkland House, 25 Southway, Colchester, Essex CO3 3EG. *Clubs:* Royal Harwich Yacht (Woolverstone, Suffolk), Bar Yacht. *Died 22 Feb. 2012.*

BRANSON, Rear Adm. (Cecil Robert) Peter (Charles), CBE 1975; Assistant Chief of Naval Staff (Operations), Ministry of Defence, 1975–77; *b* 30 March 1924; *s* of Cecil Branson and Marcelle Branson; *m* 1945, Sonia Moss (*d* 2010); one *d*. *Educ:* RNC, Dartmouth. Served, HMS Dragon, W Africa, S Atlantic, Indian Ocean and Far East (present during time of fall of Singapore and Java), 1941–42; Sub-Lieut's Courses, 1943; qual. as submarine specialist, served in HM S/M Sea Rover, Far East, 1944–45; various appts in S/Ms, 1945–49; First Lieut, HMS Defender, 1953–55; jssc; CO, HMS Roebuck, Dartmouth Trng Sqdn, 1958; Staff, Flag Officer Flotillas Mediterranean, 1959–60; Jt Planning Staff, MoD, 1960–62; Exec. Officer, HMS Victorious, Far East, 1962–64; CO, HMS Rooke, Gibraltar, 1964–65; NATO Def. Coll., 1965; Defence Planning Staff, MoD, 1966–68; CO, HMS Phoebe, and Captain (D) Londonderry Sqdn, 1968–70; Naval Attaché, Paris, 1970–73; CO, HMS Hermes, 1973–74 (Hermes headed RN task force evacuating Brit. and foreign subjects from Cyprus beaches after Turkish invasion, 1973). Man. Dir, UK Trawlers Mutual Insurance Assoc., 1977–85. *Died 1 Jan. 2011.*

BRANSON, Edward James, MA; public relations and publicity services; a Metropolitan Stipendiary Magistrate, 1971–87; barrister-at-law; *b* 10 March 1918; *s* of late Rt

Hon. Sir George Branson, PC, sometime Judge of High Court, and Lady (Mona) Branson; *m* 1949, Evette Huntley, *e d* of late Rupert Huntley Flindt; one *s* two *d*. *Educ:* Bootham Sch., York; Trinity Coll., Cambridge. Served War, 1939–46, Staffordshire Yeomanry: Palestine, Egypt, and Western Desert, 1941–42; GSO3 (Ops) attd 2 NZ Div. for Alamein, 1942; GSO2 (Ops), attd 6 (US) Corps for Salerno and Anzio landings, 1943–44; subseq. GSO2 (Ops) 53 (W) Div. in Germany. Called to the Bar, Inner Temple, 1950; practised London and SE Circuit. *Recreations:* shooting, fishing, archaeology. *Address:* Cakeham Manor, West Wittering, W Sussex PO20 8LG. *Died 19 March 2011.*

BRANSON, Rear Adm. Peter; *see* Branson, Rear Adm. C. R. P. C.

BRANT, Colin Trevor, CMG 1981; CVO 1979; HM Diplomatic Service, retired; *b* 2 June 1929; *m* 1954, Jean Faith Walker; one *s* two *d*. *Educ:* Christ's Hospital, Horsham; Sidney Sussex Coll., Cambridge (MA). Served Army, 4th Queen's Own Hussars, active service, Malaya, 1948–49; Pilot, Cambridge Univ. Air Squadron, 1951–52. Joined Sen. Br., Foreign Office, 1952; MECAS, Lebanon, 1953–54; Bahrain, 1954; Amman, 1954–56; FO, 1956–59; Stockholm, 1959–61; Cairo, 1961–64; Joint Services Staff Coll., Latimer, Bucks, 1964–65 (jssc); FO, 1965–67; Head of Chancery and Consul, Tunis, 1967–68; Asst Head, Oil Dept, FCO, 1969–71; Counsellor (Commercial), Caracas, 1971–73; Counsellor (Energy), Washington, 1973–78; Ambassador to Qatar, 1978–81; FCO Fellow, St Antony's Coll., Oxford, 1981–82; Consul Gen., and Dir Trade Promotion for S Africa, Johannesburg, 1982–87. Internat. business consultant, 1990–96. Donation Governor, Christ's Hosp., 1980–, Almoner, 1989–95; Cttee Mem., Oxfordshire Sect., Christ's Hosp. Club, 1999–2010 (Chm., 2002–04). *Recreations:* music, painting, history. *Address:* Apt 4, 15 Vittoria Walk, Montpellier, Cheltenham, Glos GL50 1TL. *Club:* Royal Over-Seas League. *Died 28 Dec. 2015.*

BRASSEY OF APETHORPE, 3rd Baron *cr* 1938, of Apethorpe; **David Henry Brassey,** OBE 1994; Bt 1922; JP; Vice Lord-Lieutenant of Northamptonshire, 2000–07; *b* 16 Sept. 1932; *er s* of 2nd Baron Brassey of Apethorpe, MC, TD, and Lady Brassey of Apethorpe; *S* father, 1967; *m* 1st, 1958, Myrna Elizabeth (*d* 1974), *o d* of late Lt-Col John Baskervyle-Glegg; one *s*; 2nd, 1978, Caroline, *y d* of late Lt-Col G. A. Evill; two *d*. Commissioned, Grenadier Guards, 1951; Major, 1966, retired, 1967. JP 1970, DL 1972, Northants. *Heir: s* Hon. Edward Brassey [*b* 9 March 1964; *m* 2003, Joanna, *e d* of Julian Pardoe; one *s* one *d*]. *Address:* The Manor House, Apethorpe, Peterborough PE8 5DL. *T:* (01780) 470231. *Club:* White's. *Died 7 May 2015.*

BRAY, Charles; artist, mainly in glass; *b* 26 Feb. 1922; *s* of Charles and Minnie Bray; *m* 1955, Margaret Ingram; four *s*. *Educ:* Goldsmiths' Coll., London. University of Sunderland: Principal Lectr in 3D Design, 1962–81; Hd, Glass and Ceramics, 1981. *Solo exhibitions,* including: Ancrum Gall., Fountain Fine Arts, Llandeilo, Carlisle City Art Gall., 1991; Invetro Galerie, Hanover, 1992; Galerie H. D. Nick, Montpellier, 1993; Pilkington Glass Mus., 1994; Castlegate Gall., Cockermouth, 2001; Sultan Gall., Lancaster, 2002; Red Barn Gall., Melkinthorpe; Garden Sculpture, Quenington, Cirencester; work in *group exhibitions,* including: England Glass, The Hague, Eur. Glass Sculpture, Liege, Sculpteurs de Lumière, Nimes, 1993; Glass Objects, Art Centre Internat., Holland, 1994; British Glass, Nat. Glass Centre, Sunderland, 1998; Thompson Gallery: Aldermaston, 2000, 2001 and 2002; Stow on the Wold, 2000, 2001 and 2002; Marylebone High St, 2000, 2001 and 2002; work in *collections,* including: Turner Collection, Sheffield; Shipley Art Gall., Gateshead; Ulster Mus., Belfast; Kelvingrove Mus., Glasgow; Royal Scottish Mus., Edinburgh; Glass Mus., Ebeltoft, Denmark; Corning Mus. of Glass, NY. Fellow, Univ. of Sunderland, 1990. Fellow, Soc. of Glass Technol., 1970. FRSA 1965. *Publications:* A Dictionary of Glass, 1995, 2nd edn 2001; Ceramics and Glass: a basic technology, 2000; Glass Blowing, 2003, 2nd edn 2006. *Address:* Prospect House, Farlam, Cumbria CA8 1LA. *T:* and *Fax:* (01697) 746203. *E:* charlesbray@btinternet.com. *Died 22 July 2012.*

BRAY, Maj.-Gen. Paul Sheldon, CB 1991; Paymaster-in-Chief and Inspector of Army Pay Services, 1989–92; *b* 31 Jan. 1936; *s* of Gerald Bray and Doris (*née* Holt); *m* 1958, Marion Diana Naden; one *s* two *d*. *Educ:* Purbrook Park County High Sch.; RMA Sandhurst; Southampton Univ. (BA 1995; MA 1998). ndc, psc†, sq, pfc. Commissioned RA 1956; served BAOR, Cyprus, UK; transf. RAPC 1965; served Malaya, N Wales, MoD, HQ UKLF, HQ Scotland, HQ NE District; OC RAPC Training Centre, 1976–77; NDC 1978; DS RMCS Shrivenham, 1979–82; MoD 1982; Chief Paymaster, Army Pay Office (Officers' Accounts), 1982–83; Comdt, Defence ADP Training Centre, 1983–85; Chief Paymaster ADP, RAPC Computer Centre, 1985–89. Governor, King's Sch., Winchester, 1992– (Chm., 1998–). *Recreations:* music, theatre, travel, oenology, digging the allotment. *Address:* c/o Corps HQ, RAPC Worthy Down, Winchester, Hants SO21 2RG. *Died 9 Sept. 2012.*

BRENCHLEY, Dr Thomas Frank, CMG 1964; HM Diplomatic Service, retired; *b* 9 April 1918; *m* 1946, Edith Helen Helfand (*d* 1980); three *d*. *Educ:* privately and at Sir William Turner's Sch., Coatham; Merton Coll., Oxford (Modern History postmastership; Classical Hon. Mods, 1938; MA Philos. and Ancient Hist., 1946; Mem., Sen. Common Room, 1987; Hon. Fellow 1991; DPhil 2001); Open Univ. (BA 1986; BSc 1996). CS quals in Arabic, Norwegian and Polish. Served with Royal Corps of Signals, 1939–46; Major on Staff of Military Attaché, Ankara, 1943–45; Director, Telecommunications Liaison Directorate, Syria and Lebanon, 1945–46. Civil Servant, GCHQ, 1947; transferred to Foreign Office, 1949; First Secretary: Singapore, 1950–53; Cairo, 1953–56; FO, 1956–58; MECAS, 1958–60; Counsellor, Khartoum, 1960–63; Chargé d'Affaires, Jedda, 1963; Head of Arabian Department, Foreign Office, 1963–67; Assistant Under-Secretary of State, Foreign Office, 1967–68; Ambassador to: Norway, 1968–72; Poland, 1972–74; Vis. Fellow, Inst. for Study of Conflict, 1974–75; Dep. Sec., Cabinet Office, 1975–76. Dep. Sec. Gen. and Chief Exec., Arab-British Chamber of Commerce, 1976–83; Chairman: Institute for Study of Conflict, 1983–89; Res. Inst. for Study of Conflict and Terrorism, 1989–94; Pres., Internat. Inst. for Study of Conflict, Geneva, 1989–91. Dir, Center for Security Studies, Washington DC, 1988–90. *Publications:* New Dimensions of European Security (ed), 1975; Norway and her Soviet Neighbour: NATO's Arctic Frontier, 1982; Diplomatic Immunities and State-sponsored Terrorism, 1984; Living With Terrorism: the problem of air piracy, 1986; Britain and the Middle East: an economic history 1945–87, 1989; Aegean Conflict and the Law of the Sea, 1990; Britain, the Six-Day War and its Aftermath, 2005. *Recreation:* collecting (and sometimes reading) books. *Address:* 19 Ennismore Gardens, SW7 1AA. *Club:* Travellers (Chm., 1991–94). *Died 7 July 2011.*

BRENNAN, John James Edward, OBE 1990; Chairman, Associated Textiles Co. Ltd, Bradford, since 1970; Vice Lord-Lieutenant, West Yorkshire, since 2004; *b* 14 Nov. 1941; *s* of Joseph Edward Brennan, KSG and Mary Jane Brennan; *m* 1984, Claire Elizabeth Linnell; two *s* one *d*. *Educ:* Ampleforth; Keble Coll., Oxford; Barcelona Univ. Mem. (C), Bradford CC, 1965–68. Chm., Bradford Conservative Fedn, 1978–98. Yorkshire Agricultural Society: Mem. Council, 1997–; Chairman: Finance Cttee, 2001–06; Audit and Investment Cttee, 2006–; Remuneration Cttee, 2010–; Trustee, 2006–. Chm., British Wool Fedn, 1996–98. Pres., Leeds Business Br., RNLI, 2003–; Vice Pres., Hosp. Heartbeat Appeal, Leeds, 2008–12. DL 1991, High Sheriff, 1998–99, W Yorks. *Recreations:* reading, music, antiques, gardening, golf. *Address:* Lieutenancy Office, Bowcliffe Hall, Bramham, W Yorks LS23 6LP. *Clubs:* White's; Alwoodley Golf (Chm., 2006–12), Swinley Forest Golf. *Died 16 July 2012.*

BRETT, Baron *cr* 1999 (Life Peer), of Lydd in the county of Kent; **William Henry Brett;** *b* 6 March 1942; *s* of William Joseph Brett and Mary Brett (*née* Murphy); *m* 1st, 1961, Jean Valerie (marr. diss. 1986); one *s* one *d*; 2nd, 1994, Janet Winters (marr. diss. 2006); two *d*; 3rd, Amanda Milne. *Educ:* Radcliffe Secondary Technical College, Manchester. British Railways, 1958–64; TSSA, 1964–66; NW

Organiser, NUBE (then AMICUS, previously UNIFI), 1966–68; E Midlands Divl Officer, ASTMS, 1968–74; Institution of Professionals, Managers and Specialists (formerly IPCS): Asst Sec.; Asst Gen. Sec., 1980; elected Gen. Sec., 1988, Gen. Sec., 1989–99. A Lord in Waiting (Govt Whip), 2008–10. Mem., Gen. Council, TUC, 1989–99. Exec. Sec., Internat. Fedn of Air Traffic Electronic Assocs, 1984–92; Mem. Public Services Internat. Exec. Cttee, 1989–99. International Labour Organisation: Mem. Governing Body, Geneva, 1991–2002 (Vice Pres., 1993–2002); Pres., Worker Group, 1993–2002; Chm., Governing Body, 2002–03; Dir, 2004–08. FRSA. Hon. Sen. Fellow, Sullivan Univ., Louisville, Kentucky, 2004– (Hon. DBA, 2004). *Publications:* International Labour in the 21st Century, 1994. *Recreations:* travelling, reading. *Address:* 310 Nelson House, Dolphin Square, SW1V 3NY. *E:* billbrett70@hotmail.com. *Died 29 March 2012.*

BREWIS, Marion Teresa, CVO 2014; JP; Lord-Lieutenant for Wigtown, 2006–14; *b* 5 Sept. 1939; *d* of Robert and Anna Anderson; *m* 1981, Francis Roger Mactaggart Brewis (*d* 2014). *Educ:* Convent of Sacred Heart High Sch., Hammersmith. Civil Servant, resigned 1989 to move to Scotland to assist in running Ardwell Estates; Dir, Ardwell Estates, 1997–. Lay Chm., NHS Appeals Tribunal, 1993. JP Wigtown, 1991. *Recreations:* walking, singing, cooking. *Address:* Ardwell House, Ardwell, by Stranraer, Wigtownshire DG9 9LY. *T:* (01776) 860227, *Fax:* (01776) 860288. *Club:* New (Edinburgh). *Died 31 Dec. 2014.*

BRIDGEMAN, (John) Michael, CB 1988; Chief Registrar of Friendly Societies and Industrial Assurance Commissioner, 1982–91; First Commissioner (Chairman), Building Societies Commission, 1986–91; *b* 26 April 1931; *s* of late John Wilfred Bridgeman, CBE and Mary Bridgeman (*née* Wallace); *m* 1958, June Forbes (CB 1990); one *s* four *d*. *Educ:* Marlborough Coll.; Trinity Coll., Cambridge. Asst Principal, BoT, 1954; HM Treasury, 1956–81, Under Sec., 1975–81. *Address:* Bridge House, Culverden Park Road, Tunbridge Wells, Kent TN4 9QX. *Died 19 April 2013.*

BRIDGES, Rt Rev. Dewi Morris; Bishop of Swansea and Brecon, 1988–98; *b* 18 Nov. 1933; *s* of Harold Davies Bridges and Elsie Margaret Bridges; *m* 1959, Rhiannon Williams; one *s* one *d*. *Educ:* St David's University College, Lampeter (BA 1954, 1st cl. Hons History); Corpus Christi Coll., Cambridge (BA 1956 II 1, Pt 2 Theol Tripos, MA 1960); Westcott House, Cambridge. Assistant Curate: Rhymney, Gwent, 1957–60; Chepstow, 1960–63; Vicar of St James', Tredegar, 1963–65; Lectr and Senior Lectr, Summerfield Coll. of Education, Kidderminster, 1965–69; Vicar of Kempsey, Worcester, 1969–79; RD of Upton-upon-Severn, 1974–79; Rector of Tenby, Pembs, 1979–88; RD of Narberth, 1980–82; Archdeacon of St Davids, 1982–88. Member: Court, 1989–98, and Council, 1989–95, UCW, Swansea; Council, Univ. of Wales, Lampeter (formerly St David's UC, Lampeter), 1992–98. *Recreations:* walking, gardening, photography. *Address:* 11 Wimbledon Court, St Florence Parade, Tenby, Pembrokeshire SA70 7DX. *T:* (01834) 844087. *Died 18 May 2015.*

BRIDGES, Ven. Peter Sydney Godfrey; Archdeacon of Warwick, 1983–90, then Emeritus; Canon-Theologian of Coventry Cathedral, 1977–90, then Emeritus; *b* 30 Jan. 1925; *s* of Sidney Clifford Bridges and Winifred (*née* Livette); *m* 1952, Joan Penlerick (*née* Madge); two *s*. *Educ:* Raynes Park Grammar Sch.; Kingston upon Thames Sch. of Architecture; Lincoln Theol College. ARIBA 1950, Dip. Liturgy and Architecture 1967. Gen. and ecclesiastical practice, 1950–54; Lectr, Nottingham Sch. of Architecture, 1954–56. Deacon, 1958; Priest, 1959. Asst Curate, Hemel Hempstead, 1958–64; Res. Fellow, Inst. for Study of Worship and Religious Architecture, Univ. of Birmingham, 1964–67 (Hon. Fellow, 1967–72 and 1978); Warden, Anglican Chaplaincy and Chaplain to Univ. of Birmingham, 1965–68; Lectr, Birmingham Sch. of Arch., 1967–72; eccles. architect and planning consultant, 1968–75; Chm., New Town Ministers Assoc., 1968–72; Co-Dir, Midlands Socio-Religious Res. Gp, 1968–75; Dir, Chelmsford Diocesan R&D Unit, 1972–77; Archdeacon of Southend, 1972–77; Archdeacon of Coventry, 1977–83. Advr for Christian Spirituality, Dio. of Coventry, 1990–93. Mem., Cathedrals Advisory Commn for England, 1981–86. Chm., Painting and Prayer, 1989–94. *Publications:* Socio-Religious Institutes, Lay Academies, etc, 1967; contrib. Church Building, res. bulletins (Inst. for Study of Worship and Relig. Arch.), Clergy Review, Prism, Christian Ministry in New Towns, Cathedral and Mission, Church Architecture and Social Responsibility. *Recreations:* architecture, singing, painting. *Address:* Saint Clare, 25 Rivermead Close, Romsey, Hants SO51 8HQ. *T:* (01794) 512889. *Died 24 Jan. 2015.*

BRIDLE, Ronald Jarman; private consultant and inventor, Cardiff University Industry Centre, 1989, and Hon. Professor, Cardiff University, 1991; *b* 27 Jan. 1930; *s* of Raymond Bridle and Dorothy (*née* Jarman); *m* Beryl Eunice (*née* Doe); two *d*. *Educ:* West Monmouth Grammar Sch.; Bristol Univ. (BSc). FREng (FEng 1979); FICE, FIHE. Graduate Asst, Monmouthshire CC, 1953–55; Exec. Engr, Gold Coast Govt, 1955–57; Sen. Engr, Cwmbran Develt Corp., 1957–60; Principal Designer, Cardiff City, 1960–62; Project Engr, Sheffield-Leeds Motorway, West Riding CC, 1962–65; Dep. County Surveyor II, Cheshire CC, 1965–67; Dir, Midland RCU, DoE, 1967–71; Dep. Chief Highway Engr, 1971–73, Under-Sec., Highways 1, 1973–75, Chief Highway Engr, 1975–76, DoE; Chief Highway Engr, Dept of Transport, 1976–80; Controller of R&D, Dept of Transport, and Dir, Transport and Road Res. Lab., 1980–84; Dir, Key Resources Internat., 1984–87. Dir (Technology and Develt), Mitchell Cotts PLC, 1984–86; Chm., Permanent Formwork Ltd, 1987–89. FRSA. Former Member: Council, ICE; EDC for Civil Engrg; Past Pres., IHE; Mem. Bd, BSI, 1979–85; Chm., Building and Civil Engineering Council, BSI, 1979–85. *Publications:* papers in jls of ICE, IHE and internat. confs. *Recreations:* golf, painting. *Address:* Parsonage Farm, Kemeys Commander, Usk, Gwent NP15 1JU. *T:* (01873) 880929. *E:* ron@kolvox.net. *Club:* Royal Automobile. *Died 2 Sept. 2015.*

BRIERS, Richard David, CBE 2003 (OBE 1989); actor, since 1955; *b* 14 Jan. 1934; *s* of Joseph Briers and Morna Richardson; *m* 1957, Ann Davies; two *d*. *Educ:* Rokeby Prep. Sch., Wimbledon; Ridgeway Sch., Wimbledon. RADA, 1954–56 (silver medal). First appearance in London in Gilt and Gingerbread, Duke of York's, 1959. *Plays:* (major parts in): Present Laughter, Queen's, 1964; Arsenic and Old Lace, Vaudeville, 1965; Relatively Speaking, Duke of York's, 1966; The Real Inspector Hound, Criterion, 1968; Cat Among the Pigeons, Prince of Wales, 1969; The Two of Us, Garrick, 1970; Butley, Criterion, 1972; Absurd Person Singular, Criterion, 1973; Absent Friends, Garrick, 1975; Middle Age Spread, Lyric, 1979; The Wild Duck, Lyric, Hammersmith, 1980; Arms and the Man, Lyric, 1981; Run for Your Wife, Shaftesbury, 1983; Why Me?, Strand, 1985; The Relapse, Chichester, 1986; Twelfth Night, Riverside Studios, 1987 (televised 1988); Midsummer Night's Dream, and King Lear, Renaissance Theatre world tour, 1990; Wind in the Willows, Nat. Theatre, 1991; Uncle Vanya, Lyric, Hammersmith, 1991; Coriolanus, Chichester, 1992; Home, Wyndham's, 1994; A Christmas Carol, Lyric, Hammersmith, 1996; The Chairs, Duke of York's and NY, 1997; Spike, Southampton, 2001; Bedroom Farce, Aldwych, 2002; The Tempest, nat. tour, 2002; London Assurance, NT, 2010. *Television series:* Brothers-in-Law; Marriage Lines; The Good Life; OneUpManShip; The Other One; Norman Conquests; Ever-Decreasing Circles; All In Good Faith; Monarch of the Glen. *Films:* Henry V, 1989; Much Ado About Nothing, Swan Song, 1993; Mary Shelley's Frankenstein, 1994; In the Bleak Midwinter, 1995; Hamlet, 1997; Love's Labours Lost, 1999; Peter Pan, 2003; As You Like It, 2007. *Publications:* Natter Natter, 1981; Coward and Company, 1987; A Little Light Weeding, 1993; A Taste of the Good Life, 1995. *Recreations:* reading, gardening. *Address:* c/o Hamilton Hodell Ltd, Fifth Floor, 66–68 Margaret Street, W1W 8SR. *Died 17 Feb. 2013.*

BRINK, Prof. André Philippus, DLitt; Professor of English, University of Cape Town, 1991–2005, Professor Emeritus, since 2006; *b* 29 May 1935; *s* of Daniel Brink and Aletta Wilhelmina Wolmarans; *m*; three *s* one *d*. *Educ:*

Potchefstroom Univ. (MA Eng. Lit. 1958, MA Afr. Lit. 1959); Rhodes Univ. (DLitt 1975). Rhodes University: Lectr, 1961; Sen. Lectr, 1975; Associate Prof., 1977; Prof. of Afrikaans and Dutch Literature, 1980–90. Hon. DLitt: Witwatersrand, 1985; Univ. of Free State, 1997; Pretoria, 2003; Paul Valéry Univ. of Montpellier, 1998; Rhodes Univ., 2001. CNA Award, 1964, 1978, 1982; Prix Médicis étranger, 1981; Martin Luther King Meml Prize, 1981; Monismanien Prize for Human Rights, Univ. of Uppsala, 1992; Premio Mondello, Italy, 1997; Hertzog Prize, 2000, 2001; Commonwealth Prize for Literature, Africa Reg., 2003; Jan Rabie/Marjorie Wallace Award for Literature, 2010. Silver, Order of Ikhamanga (SA); Commandeur, l'Ordre des Arts et des Lettres (France), 1992; Officier de la Légion d'honneur (France), 2005. *Publications:* in Afrikaans: Die meul teen die hang, 1958; over 40 titles (novels, plays, travel books, literary criticism, humour); in English: Looking on Darkness, 1974; An Instant in the Wind, 1976; Rumours of Rain, 1978; A Dry White Season, 1979; A Chain of Voices, 1982; Mapmakers (essays), 1983; The Wall of the Plague, 1984; The Ambassador, 1985; (ed with J. M. Coetzee) A Land Apart, 1986; States of Emergency, 1988; An Act of Terror, 1991; The First Life of Adamastor, 1993; On the Contrary, 1993; Imaginings of Sand, 1996; Reinventing a Continent (essays), 1996; Devil's Valley, 1998; The Rights of Desire, 2000; The Other Side of Silence, 2002; Before I Forget, 2004; Praying Mantis, 2005; A Fork in the Road: a memoir, 2009; Other Lives, 2010; Philida, 2012. *Died 6 Feb. 2015.*

BRINTON, Michael Ashley Cecil, CVO 2012; JP; Director, 1970–2011, Chairman, 1991–2008, and Honorary President, 2008–11, Brintons Ltd; Lord-Lieutenant of Worcestershire, since 2001; *b* 6 Oct. 1941; *s* of Maj. Sir (Esme) Tatton (Cecil) Brinton and Mary Elizabeth Brinton (*née* Fahnestock); *m* 1966, Angela Elizabeth Ludlow; two *s* one *d*. *Educ:* Arden House, Henley in Arden; Eton; lang. studies at univs of Vienna, Perugia and Aix-en-Provence. Joined Brintons Ltd, 1962. Chm., Export Council, 1984–95, Vice Pres., 1996–98, Pres., 1998–2000, British Carpet Manufr's Assoc.; President: Confedn Internat. de Tapis et Tissus d'Ameublement, 1987–91; Qualitas Council, 1992–94. Chm., Hereford and Worcester, CBI, 1998–. High Sheriff, 1990–91, DL 1991–2001, Hereford and Worcs; JP Worcs, 2008. KStJ 2002. *Recreations:* shooting, fishing, old cars. *Address:* The Old Rectory, Pudleston, Leominster, Herefordshire HR6 0RA. *E:* macbrinton@hotmail.co.uk. *Died 23 April 2012.*

BRITNELL, Prof. Richard Hugh, PhD; FBA 2005; FRHistS; Professor of History, University of Durham, 1997–2003, then Professor Emeritus; *b* 21 April 1944; *s* of Ronald Frank Britnell and Edith Britnell (*née* Manson); *m* 1973, Jennifer Joan Beard (*d* 2011); two *s*. *Educ:* Sir William Borlase Sch.; Bedford Modern Sch.; Clare Coll., Cambridge (BA 1964; PhD 1970). FRHistS 1988. University of Durham: Lectr in Econ. Hist., 1966–85; Lectr in Hist., 1985–86; Sen. Lectr, 1986–94; Reader in Hist., 1994–97. Jt Ed., Surtees Soc., 1999–. *Publications:* Growth and Decline in Colchester 1300–1525, 1986; The Commercialisation of English Society 1000–1500, 1993, 2nd edn 1996; The Closing of the Middle Ages? England 1471–1529, 1997; Britain and Ireland 1050–1530: economy and society, 2004; (ed) Records of the Borough of Crossgate, Durham, 1312–1531, 2008; Markets, Trade and Economic Development in England and Europe, 1050–1550, 2009; (with J. Mullan) Land and Family: trends and local variations in the peasant land market on the Winchester bishopric estates, 1263–1415, 2010. *Recreations:* acting with Durham Shakespeare Group, keyboard playing (clavichord, piano, organ), cooking, membership of Durham Bede Rotary Club (Pres., 2009–10). *Address:* 25 Orchard House, New Elvet, Durham DH1 3DB. *T:* (0191) 383 0409. *E:* R.H.Britnell@durham.ac.uk. *Died 17 Dec. 2013.*

BRITTAN OF SPENNITHORNE, Baron *cr* 2000 (Life Peer), of Spennithorne in the County of North Yorkshire; **Leon Brittan,** Kt 1989; PC 1981; QC 1978; DL; Vice-Chairman, UBS Investment Bank (formerly UBS Warburg), 2000–14 (on secondment as Trade Adviser to the Prime Minister, 2010–11); Member, 1989–99, a Vice-President, 1989–93 and 1995–99, European Commission (formerly Commission of the European Communities); *b* 25 Sept. 1939; *s* of late Dr Joseph Brittan and Mrs Rebecca Brittan; *m* 1980, Diana Peterson (Lady Brittan of Spennithorne, DBE); two step *d*. *Educ:* Haberdashers' Aske's Sch.; Trinity Coll., Cambridge (MA); Yale Univ. (Henry Fellow). Chm., Cambridge Univ. Conservative Assoc., 1960; Pres., Cambridge Union, 1960; debating tour of USA for Cambridge Union, 1961. Called to Bar, Inner Temple, 1962; Bencher, 1983. Chm., Bow Group, 1964–65; contested (C) North Kensington, 1966 and 1970. MP (C): Cleveland and Whitby, Feb. 1974–1983; Richmond, Yorks, 1983–88. Editor, Crossbow, 1966–68; formerly Mem. Political Cttee, Carlton Club; Vice-Chm. of Governors, Isaac Newton Sch., 1968–71; Mem. European North American Cttee, 1970–78; Vice-Chm., Nat. Assoc. of School Governors and Managers, 1970–78; Vice-Chm., Parly Cons. Party Employment Cttee, 1974–76; opposition front bench spokesman on Devolution, 1976–79, on employment, 1978–79; Minister of State, Home Office, 1979–81; Chief Sec. to the Treasury, 1981–83; Sec. of State for Home Dept, 1983–85; Sec. of State for Trade and Industry, 1985–86. Chm., Cons. Gp for Europe, 2000–03. Consultant, Herbert Smith, 2000–06; non-exec. Dir, Unilever, 2004–10 (Adv. Dir, 2000–04). Distinguished Vis. Scholar, Yale Univ., 2000–02. Chancellor, Univ. of Teesside, 1993–2005. Chm., Soc. of Cons. Lawyers, 1986–88. DL N Yorks, 2001. Hon. DCL: Newcastle, 1990; Durham, 1992; Hon. LLD: Hull, 1990; Bath, 1995; Dr *hc* Edinburgh, 1991; Hon. DLitt Bradford, 1992; Hon. DEc Korea, 1997. *Publications:* Defence and Arms Control in a Changing Era, 1988; Hersch Lauterpacht Memorial Lectures, 1990; European Competition Policy, 1992; The Europe We Need, 1994; Globalisation *vs* Sovereignty (Rede Lect., 1997); A Diet of Brussels, 2000; (contrib.) The Conservative Opportunity; pamphlets: Millstones for the Sixties (jtly), Rough Justice, Infancy and the Law, How to Save Your Schools, To spur, not to mould, A New Deal for Health Care, Discussions on Policy, Monetary Union. *Recreations:* opera, art, cricket, walking. *Address:* c/o House of Lords, SW1A 0PW. *Clubs:* White's, Pratt's, MCC. *Died 21 Jan. 2015.*

BRITTENDEN, (Charles) Arthur; Senior Consultant, Bell Pottinger (formerly Lowe Bell) Communications Ltd, 1988–2003; Director of Corporate Relations, News International, 1981–87; General Manager (Editorial), Times Newspapers, 1982–87; Director, Times Newspapers Ltd, 1982–87; *b* 23 Oct. 1924; *o s* of late Tom Edwin Brittenden and Caroline (*née* Scrivener); *m* 1st, 1953, Sylvia Penelope Cadman (marr. diss. 1960); 2nd, 1966, Ann Patricia Kenny (marr. diss. 1972); 3rd, 1975, Valerie Arnison (*d* 2002). *Educ:* Leeds Grammar School. Served in Reconnaissance Corps, 1943–46. Yorkshire Post, 1940–43, 1946–49; News Chronicle, 1949–55; joined Sunday Express, 1955: Foreign Editor, 1959–62; Northern Editor, Daily Express, 1962–63; Dep. Editor, Sunday Express, 1963–64; Exec. Editor, 1964–66, Editor, 1966–71, Daily Mail; Dep. Editor, The Sun, 1972–81. Dir, Harmsworth Publications Ltd, 1967–71; Man. Dir, Wigmore Cassettes, 1971–72. Dir, Dowson-Shurman Associates Ltd, 1990–. Mem., 1982–86, Jt Vice-Chm., 1983–86, Press Council. *Address:* 22 Park Street, Woodstock, Oxon OX20 1SP. *Died 25 April 2015.*

BRITTLE, (Benjamin) Cliff; Chairman, Management Board, Rugby Football Union, 1996–98; *b* 11 Jan. 1942; *s* of Benjamin James Brittle and Amy Brittle; *m* (marr. diss.). *Educ:* Longton High Sch., Stoke-on-Trent. With NCR, 1960–62; started business, 1962, retd 1987. FCMI. *Recreations:* golf, Rugby. *Address:* The Hollies, Main Road, Baldrine, Isle of Man IM4 6DQ. *T:* (01624) 861011. *Died 11 Sept. 2011.*

BROCK, Michael George, CBE 1981; Warden of St George's House, Windsor Castle, 1988–93; *b* 9 March 1920; *s* of late Sir Laurence George Brock and Ellen Margery Brock (*née* Williams); *m* 1949, Eleanor Hope Morrison; three *s*. *Educ:* Wellington Coll. (Schol.); Corpus Christi Coll., Oxford (Open Schol.; First Cl. Hons Mod. Hist. 1948; MA 1948); DLitt Oxon 2002. FRHistS 1965; FRSL 1983. War service (Middlesex Regt), 1940–45. Corpus Christi Coll., Oxford: Jun. Res. Fellow, 1948–50;

Fellow and Tutor in Modern History and Politics, 1950–66, Fellow Emeritus, 1977; Hon. Fellow, 1982; Oxford University: Jun. Proctor, 1956–57; Univ. Lectr, 1951–70; Mem., Hebdomadal Council, 1965–76, 1978–86; Vice Pres. and Bursar, Wolfson Coll., Oxford, 1967–76; Prof. of Educn and Dir, Sch. of Educn, Exeter Univ., 1977–78; Warden of Nuffield Coll., Oxford, 1978–88; Pro-Vice-Chancellor, Oxford Univ., 1980–88. Church Comr, 1990–93. Hon. Fellow: Wolfson Coll., Oxford, 1977; Nuffield Coll., Oxford, 1988; Hon. FSRHE 1986–2006. Hon. DLitt Exeter, 1982. *Publications:* The Great Reform Act, 1973; (ed with Eleanor Brock) H. H. Asquith: Letters to Venetia Stanley, 1982; (ed with M. Curthoys) The History of the University of Oxford, vols vi and vii: Nineteenth-Century Oxford, Part 1, 1997, Part 2, 2000; (ed with Eleanor Brock) Margot Asquith's Great War Diary 1914–1916: the view from Downing Street, 2014; many articles on historical topics and on higher education. *Address:* Flat 1, Ritchie Court, 380 Banbury Road, Oxford OX2 7PW. *Club:* Oxford Union. *Died 30 April 2014.*

BROCK, Prof. William Ranulf, FBA 1990; Fellow of Selwyn College, Cambridge, since 1947; Professor of Modern History, University of Glasgow, 1967–81, then Emeritus; *b* 16 May 1916; *s* of Stewart Ernst Brock and Katherine Helen (*née* Temple Roberts); *m* 1950, Constance Helen (*née* Brown) (*d* 2000); one *s* one *d*. *Educ:* Christ's Hosp.; Trinity Coll., Cambridge (MA, PhD). Prize Fellow 1940 (in absentia). Military service (Army), 1939–45; Asst Master, Eton Coll., 1946–47. Commonwealth Fund Fellow, Berkeley, Calif, Yale and Johns Hopkins, 1952–53, 1958; Vis. Professor: Michigan Univ., 1968; Washington Univ., 1970; Maryland Univ., 1980; Charles Warren Fellow, Harvard Univ., 1976; Leverhulme Emeritus Fellow, 1981. Hon. LittD Keele, 1978. *Publications:* Lord Liverpool and Liberal Toryism, 1941; The Character of American History, 1960; An American Crisis, 1963; The Evolution of American Democracy, 1970; Conflict and Transformation 1844–1877, 1973; The Sources of History: the United States 1790–1890, 1975; Parties and Political Conscience, 1979; Scotus Americanus, 1982; Investigation and Responsibility, 1985; Welfare, Democracy and the New Deal, 1988; (with P. H. M. Cooper) Selwyn College: a history, 1994; contrib. New Cambridge Mod. History, Vols VII and XI; articles and reviews in Proc. of British Acad., Jl Amer. Studies, Jl Amer. Hist., Amer. Nineteenth Cent. Hist., etc. *Recreation:* antiques. *Address:* 49 Barton Road, Cambridge CB3 9LG. *T:* (01223) 529655. *E:* wrb20@cam.ac.uk. *Died 12 Nov. 2014.*

BROCKLEHURST, Prof. John Charles, CBE 1988; FRCP, FRCPE, FRCPGlas; Professor of Geriatric Medicine, University of Manchester, 1970–89, then Emeritus; Associate Director, Research Unit, Royal College of Physicians, 1989–98; *b* 31 May 1924; *s* of late Harold John Brocklehurst and Dorothy Brocklehurst; *m* 1956, Susan Engle; two *s* one *d*. *Educ:* Glasgow High Sch.; Ayr Academy; Univ. of Glasgow (MB ChB 1947; MD Hons 1950). Christine Hansen Research Scholar, Glasgow Univ., 1948–49; RAMC (to rank of Major), 1949–51; Medical Registrar, Stobhill Hosp., and Asst Lectr, Dept of Materia Medica and Therapeutics, Glasgow Univ., 1952–53 and 1958–59; MO, Grenfell Mission, Northern Newfoundland and Labrador, 1955–57; Cons. Geriatrician, Bromley Hosp. Gp and Cray Valley and Sevenoaks Hosp. Gp, 1960–69; Cons. in Geriatric and Gen. Med., Guy's Hosp., London, 1969–70. Dir, Univ. of Manchester Unit for Biological Aging Research (formerly Geigy Unit for Res. in Aging), 1974–89. Chm., Age Concern England, 1973–77, Hon. Vice-Pres., 1980–; Governor, Research into Ageing (formerly British Foundn for Age Research), 1980–97; President: Soc. of Chiropodists, 1977–83; British Geriatrics Soc., 1984–86; Trustee, Continence Foundn, 1992–97. Vis. Professor of Geriatric Med. and Chm., Div. of Geriatric Med., Univ. of Saskatchewan, Canada, 1978–79. Hon. Fellow, Manchester Med. Soc. Hon. MSc Manchester 1974. Bellahouston Gold Medal, Univ. of Glasgow, 1950; Willard Thomson Gold Medal, Amer. Geriatrics Soc., 1978; Sandoz Prize, Internat. Assoc. of Gerontology, 1989; Founder's Medal, British Geriatrics Soc., 1990. *Publications:* Incontinence in Old People, 1951; The Geriatric Day Hospital, 1971; ed and part author, Textbook of Geriatric Medicine and Gerontology, 1973, 7th edn 2010; Geriatric Care in Advanced Societies, 1975; (jtly) Geriatric Medicine for Students, 1976, 3rd edn, 1986; (jtly) Progress in Geriatric Day Care, 1980; (jtly) Colour Atlas of Geriatric Medicine, 1983, 2nd edn 1991; (ed and part author) Urology: the elderly, 1985; Geriatric Pharmacology and Therapeutics, 1985; (jtly) British Geriatric Medicine in the 1980s, 1987; 125 Years an Art Club: the ups and downs of the Manchester Graphic Club 1876–2001, 2001. *Recreations:* painting, the mandoline. *Address:* Apt 14, Oakmere, Spath Lane, Handforth, Wilmslow, Cheshire SK9 3NS. *Club:* East India and Devonshire. *Died 27 June 2013.*

BRÖDER, Ernst-Günther, DEcon; German economist and financial executive; international consultant; *b* Cologne, 6 Jan. 1927. *Educ:* Univs of Cologne, Mayence, Freiburg and Paris. Corporate staff, Bayer AG Leverkusen, 1956–61; Projects Dept, World Bank, 1961–64; Kreditanstalt für Wiederaufbau, 1964–84: Manager, 1969–75; Mem., Bd of Management, 1975–84; Bd of Management Spokesman, 1980–84; European Investment Bank: a Dir, 1980–84; Pres., and Chm. of Bd of Dirs, 1984–93; Hon. Pres., 1993–; Chm., 1994–96, 1998–99, Mem., 1997–98, 1999, Inspection Panel, World Bank. Member: Special Adv. Gp, Asian Develt Bank, 1981–82; Panel of Conciliators, Internat. Centre for Settlement of Investment Disputes, 1976–. *Address:* Büelstrasse 12, 6052 Hergiswil NW, Switzerland. *Died 13 Dec. 2013.*

BROMLEY, Lance Lee, MA; MChir; FRCS; Director of Medical and Health Services, Gibraltar, 1982–85; Honorary Consultant Cardiothoracic Surgeon, St Mary's Hospital, W2; *b* 16 Feb. 1920; *s* of late Lancelot Bromley, MChir, FRCS, of London and Seaford, Sussex, and Dora Ridgway Bromley, Dewsbury, Yorks; *m* 1952, Rosemary Anne Holbrook; three *d*. *Educ:* St Paul's School; Caius Coll., Cambridge. Late Capt. RAMC. Late Travelling Fell. Amer. Assoc. for Thoracic Surgery. Consultant Thoracic Surgeon, St Mary's Hosp., 1953–80; Consultant Gen. Surgeon, Teddington Hosp., 1953–80. *Publications:* various contributions to medical journals. *Recreations:* sailing, golf. *Address:* 26 Molyneux Street, W1H 5HW. *T:* (020) 7262 7175. *Club:* Royal Ocean Racing. *Died 25 April 2013.*

BROMLEY, Prof. Peter Mann; Professor of English Law, University of Manchester, 1985–86 (Professor of Law, 1965–85), then Professor Emeritus; *b* 20 Nov. 1922; *s* of Frank Bromley and Marion Maud (*née* Moy); *m* 1963, Beatrice Mary, *d* of Eric Charles Cassels Hunter and Amy Madeleine (*née* Renold). *Educ:* Ealing Grammar Sch.; The Queen's College, Oxford (MA 1948). Called to the Bar, Middle Temple, 1951. Served War, Royal Artillery, 1942–45. University of Manchester: Asst Lectr 1947–50, Lectr 1950–61, Sen. Lectr 1961–65; Dean, Faculty of Law, 1966–68, 1972–74 and 1981–83; Pro-Vice-Chancellor, 1977–81; Principal, Dalton Hall, 1958–65. Vis. Prof. of Law, Univ. of Buckingham, 1987–88. Chm., Cttee on Professional Legal Educn in NI, 1983–85; Member: Adv. Cttee on Legal Educn, 1972–75; University Grants Cttee, 1978–85 (Chm., Social Studies Sub-cttee, 1979–85); Commonwealth Scholarship Commn, 1986–92. Editor, Butterworths Family Law Service, 1983–96. *Publications:* Family Law, 1957, 8th edn with N. V. Lowe, 1992; (contrib.) Parental Custody and Matrimonial Maintenance, 1966; (contrib.) Das Erbrecht von Familienangehörigen, 1971; (contrib.) The Child and the Courts, 1978; (contrib.) Adoption, 1984; (contrib.) Children and the Law, 1990; (contrib.) Droit Sans Frontières, 1991; articles in various legal jls. *Recreations:* walking, theatre, listening to music. *Address:* 7A Hawthorn Avenue, Wilmslow, Cheshire SK9 5BR. *T:* (01625) 526516. *Club:* Oxford and Cambridge. *Died 6 March 2013.*

BRONFMAN, Edgar Miles; Chairman, The Seagram Company Ltd, 1975–2000; *b* 20 June 1929; *s* of late Samuel Bronfman and of Saidye Rosner; *m* 1st, 1953, Ann Loeb (marr. diss. 1973); four *s* one *d*; 2nd, 1973, Lady Carolyn Townshend (marr. diss. 1974); 3rd, 1975, Rita, (later Georgiana) Webb (marr. diss., later re-married, then marr. diss.); two *d*; 5th, 1994, Jan Aronson. *Educ:* Trinity College Sch., Port Hope, Ont., Canada; Williams Coll., Williamstown, Mass, US; McGill Univ., Montreal (BA

1951). Chm., Joseph E. Seagram & Sons, Inc. (Pres., 1957); Pres., 1971, CEO, 1975–94, The Seagram Company Ltd; Dir, E. I. duPont de Nemours & Co. Pres., World Jewish Congress, 1980–2007. Hon. LHD Pace Univ., NY, 1982; Hon. Dr Laws Williams Coll., Williamstown, 1986. *Address:* 375 Park Avenue, 17th Floor, New York, NY 10152–0192, USA. *T:* (212) 572719. *Died 21 Dec. 2013.*

BROOKE, Prof. Christopher Nugent Lawrence, CBE 1995; MA; LittD; FSA; FRHistS; FBA 1970; Dixie Professor of Ecclesiastical History, University of Cambridge, 1977–94, then Dixie Professor Emeritus; Fellow, Gonville and Caius College, Cambridge, 1949–56 and since 1977 (Life Fellow, 1994); *b* 23 June 1927; *y s* of late Professor Zachary Nugent Brooke and Rosa Grace Brooke; *m* 1951, Rosalind Beckford (*d* 2014), *d* of Dr and Mrs L. H. S. Clark; two *s* (and one *s* decd). *Educ:* Winchester College (Scholar); Gonville and Caius College, Cambridge (Major Scholar). BA 1948; MA 1952; LittD 1973. Army service in RAEC, Temp. Captain 1949. Cambridge University: College Lecturer in History, 1953–56; Praelector Rhetoricus, 1955–56; Asst Lectr in History, 1953–54; Lectr, 1954–56; Prof. of Mediæval History, University of Liverpool, 1956–67; Prof. of History, Westfield Coll., Univ. of London, 1967–77. Member: Royal Commn on Historical Monuments (England), 1977–83; Reviewing Cttee on Export of Works of Art, 1979–82. Vice-Pres., Soc. of Antiquaries, 1975–79, Pres., 1981–84. Corresp. Fellow, Medieval Acad. of America, 1981; Corresponding Member: Monumenta Germaniae Historica, 1988; Bavarian Acad. of Scis, 1997. DUniv York, 1984. Lord Mayor's Midsummer Prize, City of London, 1981. *Publications:* The Dullness of the Past, 1957; From Alfred to Henry III, 1961; The Saxon and Norman Kings, 1963, 3rd edn 2001; Europe in the Central Middle Ages, 1964, 3rd edn 2000; Time the Archsatirist, 1968; The Twelfth Century Renaissance, 1970; Structure of Medieval Society, 1971; Medieval Church and Society (sel. papers), 1971; (with W. Swaan) The Monastic World, 1974, new edn as The Age of the Cloister, 2004, as The Rise and Fall of the Medieval Monastery, 2006; (with G. Keir) London, 800–1216, 1975; Marriage in Christian History, 1977; (with R. B. Brooke) Popular Religion in the Middle Ages, 1000–1300, 1984; A History of Gonville and Caius College, 1985; The Church and the Welsh Border, 1986; (with J. R. L. Highfield and W. Swaan) Oxford and Cambridge, 1988; The Medieval Idea of Marriage, 1989; (jtly) David Knowles Remembered, 1991; A History of the University of Cambridge, vol. IV, 1870–1990, 1993, (jtly) vol. II, 1546–1750, 2004; Jane Austen: illusion and reality, 1999; (with R. B. Brooke) Churches and Churchmen in Medieval Europe (selected papers), 1999; (jtly) A History of Emmanuel College, Cambridge, 1999; part Editor: The Book of William Morton, 1954; The Letters of John of Salisbury, vol. I, 1955, vol. II, 1979; Carte Nativorum, 1960; (with A. Morey) Gilbert Foliot and his letters, 1965 and (ed jtly) The Letters and Charters of Gilbert Foliot, 1967; (with D. Knowles and V. London) Heads of Religious Houses, England and Wales 940–1216, 1972, 2nd edn 2001; (with D. Whitelock and M. Brett) Councils and Synods, vol. I, 1981; (with Sir Roger Mynors) Walter Map, De Nugis Curialium (revision of M. R. James edn), 1983; (with M. Brett and M. Winterbottom) Hugh the Chanter, History of the Church of York (revision of C. Johnson edn), 1990; (with D. Knowles) The Monastic Constitutions of Lanfranc, 2002; (jtly) English Episcopal Acta, vol. 33, Worcester 1062–1185, 2007, vol. 34, Worcester 1186–1218, 2008; (with D. Greenway and J. Denton) J. Le Neve, Fasti Ecclesiae Anglicanae 1066–1300, vol. 11, Coventry and Lichfield, 2012; contributed to: A History of St Paul's Cathedral, 1957; A History of York Minster, 1977; A Portrait of Gonville and Caius College, 2008; general editor: Oxford (formerly Nelson's) Medieval Texts, 1959–87; A History of the University of Cambridge, 4 vols 1988–2004; Nelson's History of England, etc.; articles and reviews in English Historical Review, Cambridge Historical Journal, Studies in Church History, Bulletin of Inst. of Historical Research, Downside Review, Traditio, Bulletin of John Rylands Library, Jl of Soc. of Archivists, etc. *Address:* Gonville and Caius College, Cambridge CB2 1TA. *Died 27 Dec. 2015.*

BROOKE, (Christopher) Roger (Ettrick), OBE 2005; Chairman, Candover Investments plc, 1991–99 (Chief Executive, 1980–90); *b* 2 Feb. 1931; *s* of late Ralph Brooke and Marjorie (*née* Lee); *m* 1958, Nancy Belle Lowenthal; three *s* one *d*. *Educ:* Tonbridge; Trinity Coll., Oxford (MA). Served HM Diplomatic Service: Bonn, 1955–57; Southern Dept, FO, 1958–60; Washington, 1960–63; Tel Aviv, 1963–66. Dep. Man. Dir, IRC, 1966–69; Man. Dir, Scienta SA, 1969–71; Dir, Pearson Gp, 1971–79; Gp Man. Dir, EMI, 1979–80. Chm., Audit Commn, 1995–98. Director: Slough Estates plc, 1980–2001; Lambert Fenchurch Gp (formerly Lowndes Lambert Gp Holdings) PLC, 1991–99; Tarmac plc, 1994–99; Wembley PLC, 1995–99; Ethos Private Equity (South Africa), 1998–2007; Beeson Gregory Gp, 2000–02; IP Gp (formerly IP2IPO) plc, 2001–; Prolitec Inc. (USA), 2002–; RL Automotive, 2007–, and various other cos; Dep. Chm., Carillion plc, 1999–2001; Chairman: Innisfree Gp Ltd, 1995–2006; Accord plc, 1999–2005; Foresight 4VCT, 2004–. Mem., Southampton Univ. Develt Trust, 2006–; Royal Soc. Enterprise Fund, 2008–. *Publications:* Santa's Christmas Journey, 1985. *Recreations:* theatre, reading, travel. *Address:* Water Meadow, Swarraton, near Alresford, Hants SO24 9TQ. *T:* (01962) 732259. *Died 11 Dec. 2012.*

BROOKE, His Honour Michael Eccles Macklin; QC 1994; a Circuit Judge, 2004–10; *b* 8 May 1942; *s* of late Reginald Eccles Joseph Brooke and Beryl Cicely Brooke (*née* Riggs); *m* 1st, 1972, Annie Sophie (marr. diss. 1985), *d* of André Vautier; three *s*; 2nd, 1996, Mireille, *d* of late Colin Colahan; two step *d*. *Educ:* Froebel Sch., Datchet; Lycée Français de Londres; Edinburgh Univ. (LLB). Called to the Bar, Gray's Inn, 1968 (Bencher, 2002); in practice, 1968–2004; a Recorder, 2000–04; Avocat, Cour d'appel, Paris, 1987–2004. Chevalier, Légion d'Honneur (France), 2011. *Recreations:* boating, travelling, comparing England and France. *Club:* Bar Yacht. *Died 8 June 2014.*

BROOKE, Sir Richard (David Christopher), 11th Bt *cr* 1662, of Norton Priory, Cheshire; *b* 23 Oct. 1938; *s* of Sir Richard (Neville) Brooke, 10th Bt and Lady Mabel Kathleen Brooke (*d* 1985), *d* of 8th Earl of Roden; *S* father, 1997; *m* 1st, 1963, Carola Marion (marr. diss. 1978), *e d* of Sir Robert Erskine-Hill, 2nd Bt; two *s*; 2nd, 1979, Lucinda, *d* of John Frederick Voelcker. *Educ:* Eton College. MCSI. Lt, Scots Guards, 1957–58. Partner, Rowe & Pitman, 1968–86; Dir, S. G. Warburg Gp and Dep. Chm., S. G. Warburg Securities, 1986–90; Pres. and Chm., S. G. Warburg (USA) Inc., 1988–90; Chm., J. O. Hambro & Partners, 1990–97. Director: Potter Partners, 1987–90; Govett Atlantic Investment Trust plc, 1990–92; Contracyclical Investment Trust, 1990–96; J. O. Hambro & Co., 1990–97; Exeter Preferred Capital Investment Trust plc, 1991–2000; Gartmore American Securities plc, 1991–95; Govett American Smaller Companies Investment Trust plc, 1992–98; HCG Lloyd's Investment Trust plc, 1994–96; Templeton Emerging Markets Investment Trust plc, 1994–2003; Templeton Latin America Investment Trust plc, 1994–2001; Templeton Central and Eastern European Investment Trust plc, 1995–98; Avocet Mining plc, 1995–2010; Fidelity Special Values plc, 1995–2009; Exeter Selective Assets Investment Trust, 1996–2001; Chairman: Armstrong International Ltd, 1990–2001; N Atlantic Smaller Cos Investment Trust plc, 1993–98; Govett Global Smaller Cos Investment Trust plc, 1994–97; Tai Chi Fund Ltd, 2006–; Johim IDF LLC, 2006–; Pepin Fund Ltd, 2008–. Member: Internat. Capital Mkts Adv. Bd, NY Stock Exchange, 1987–89; Cttee, Soc. of Merchants Trading into Europe, 1988–2005; National Association of Securities Dealers Inc.: Chm., Internat. Markets Adv. Bd, 1991–95; Vice Chm. Bd of Governors, 1994–95. *Recreations:* travel, antiques and fine art, wines, boating. *Heir: er s* Richard Christopher Brooke [*b* 10 July 1966; *m* 1st, 1995, Sophie Scott (marr. diss. 1997); one *d*; 2nd, 2002, Sarah Montague; three *d*]. *Address:* Château Rouzaud, St Victor-Rouzaud, 09100 Pamiers, France. *Clubs:* Boodle's (Chm., 1998–2001), Pratt's, Pilgrims; Tarporley Hunt (Cheshire); Society of Merchants. *Died 24 Oct. 2012.*

BROOKE, Roger; *see* Brooke, C. R. E.

BROOKE-ROSE, Prof. Christine; novelist and critic; Professor of English Language and Literature, University of Paris, 1975–88 (Lecturer, 1968–75); *b* 16 Jan. 1923; *m* 1st, 1944, Rodney Bax (marr. diss); 2nd, 1953, Jerzy Pietrkiewicz (marr. diss. 1975; he *d* 2007); 3rd, 1981, Claude Brooke (marr. diss. 1982). *Educ:* Somerville Coll., Oxford (MA 1953; Hon. Fellow, 1997); PhD London 1954. WAAF Intelligence Officer, Bletchley Park Decoding Centre, 1942–45. Research and criticism, 1955–. Reviewer for: The Times Literary Supplement, The Times, The Observer, The Sunday Times, The Listener, The Spectator, and The London Magazine, 1956–68; at Univ. of Paris VIII, Vincennes, 1968–88. Broadcasts in book programmes on BBC, and on 'The Critics', and ABC Television. Hon. LittD East Anglia, 1988. Travelling Prize of Society of Authors, 1964; James Tait Black Memorial Prize, 1966; Arts Council Translation Prize, 1969. *Publications: novels:* The Languages of Love, 1957; The Sycamore Tree, 1958; The Dear Deceit, 1960; The Middlemen, 1961; Out, 1964; Such, 1965; Between, 1968; Thru, 1975; Amalgamemnon, 1984; Xorandor, 1986; Verbivore, 1990; Textermination, 1991; Remake, 1996; Next, 1998; Subscript, 1999; Life, End of, 2006; *criticism:* A Grammar of Metaphor, 1958; A ZBC of Ezra Pound, 1971; A Rhetoric of the Unreal, 1981; Stories, Theories and Things, 1991; Invisible Author, last essays, 2002; *short stories:* Go when you see the Green Man Walking, 1969; short stories and essays in various magazines, etc. *Recreations:* people, books. *Address:* c/o Cambridge University Press, PO Box 110, Cambridge CB2 3RL. *Died 21 March 2012.*

BROOKE TURNER, Alan, CMG 1980; HM Diplomatic Service, retired; Director, British Association for Central and Eastern Europe (formerly Great Britain/East Europe Centre), 1987–95; *b* 4 Jan. 1926; *s* of late Arthur Brooke Turner, MC; *m* 1954, Hazel Alexandra Rowan Henderson; two *s* two *d*. *Educ:* Marlborough; Balliol Coll., Oxford (Sen. Schol.). 1st cl Hon. Mods 1949; 1st cl. Lit. Hum. 1951. Served in RAF, 1944–48. Entered HM Foreign (subseq. Diplomatic) Service, 1951; FO, 1951; Warsaw, 1953; 3rd, later 2nd Sec. (Commercial), Jedda, 1954; Lisbon, 1957; 1st Sec., FO, 1959 (UK Delegn to Nuclear Tests Conf., Geneva, 1962); Cultural Attaché, Moscow, 1962; FO, 1965; Fellow, Center for Internat. Affairs, Harvard Univ., 1968; Counsellor, Rio de Janeiro, 1969–71; Head of Southern European Dept, FCO, 1972–73; Counsellor and Head of Chancery, British Embassy, Rome, 1973–76; Civil Dep. Comdt and Dir of Studies, NATO Defense Coll., Rome, 1976–78; Internat. Inst. for Strategic Studies, 1978–79; Minister, Moscow, 1979–82; Ambassador to Finland, 1983–85. Member: Council, Anglican Centre, Rome, 1976–77; Anglican Synod Wkg Gp on Peacemaking, 1986–88; Southwark Diocesan Synod, 2000–06. Mem. Council, SSEES, 1987–95 (Chm., 1989–92). *Recreation:* enjoyment of family and friends. *Address:* Poultons, Moor Lane, Dormansland, Lingfield, Surrey RH7 6NX. *E:* alan.brooketurner@btopenworld.com. *Club:* Travellers. *Died 5 Oct. 2013.*

BROOKES, Beata Ann, CBE 1996; *b* 21 Jan. 1931. *Educ:* Lowther College, Bodelwyddan; Univ. of Wales, Bangor; studied politics in USA (US State Dept Scholarship). Former social worker, Denbighshire CC; company secretary and farmer. Contested (C) Widnes, 1955, Warrington, 1963, Manchester Exchange, 1964. Contested (C) N Wales, European Parly Elecn, 1989. MEP (C) N Wales, 1979–89; Hon. MEP, 1989. Mem., European Econ. and Social Cttee, 1993–98. Chm., Wales Cons. Party Nat. Exec., 1994–97; Vice-Pres., N Wales and NW Fedn of Cons. Clubs, 2008–. Chm., Wales Consumer Council, 1992–94; Mem., Nat. Consumer Council, 1992–98. Formed B. A. Brookes Properties, 1997. *Died 18 Aug. 2015.*

BROOKING, Maj.-Gen. Patrick Guy, CB 1988; CMG 1997; MBE 1975; DL; Director General, Army Manning and Recruiting, 1990; *b* 4 April 1937; *s* of late Captain C. A. H. Brooking, CBE, RN, and G. M. J. White (*née* Coleridge); *m* 1964, Pamela Mary Walford; one *s* one *d*. *Educ:* Charterhouse Sch.; Alliance Française, Paris, 1955. Commnd 5th Royal Inniskilling Dragoon Guards, 1956; early career served in England, W Germany, NI, Cyprus (UN); Staff Coll., Camberley, 1969; Mil. Asst to Comdr 1st British Corps, 1970–71; Bde Major 39 Bde, Belfast, 1974–75; comd his regt, 1975–77; Instr Army Staff Coll., 1978; COS, 4 Armd Div., 1979–80; RCDS 1981; Comdr 33 Armd Bde, Paderborn Garrison, 1982–83; Dep. COS, HQ UKLF, 1984–85; Commandant and GOC Berlin (British Sector), 1985–89. Chief Exec. Officer, Worldwide Subsidiaries, KRONE AG, Berlin, 1991–97. Colonel: 5th Royal Inniskilling Dragoon Guards, 1991–92; Royal Dragoon Guards (on foundn), 1992–94. Chm., British-German Assoc., 2000–04; Life Pres., Internat. Club, Berlin, 2001 (Chm., 1994–2001). Mem., Salisbury Cathedral Chapter, 2001–07. Freeman, City of London, 1964; Liveryman, Broderers' Co., 1964– (Master, 2003–04). DL Wilts, 1997. Verdienstorden des Landes, Berlin, 1996; Bundesverdienstkreuz 1st cl. (Germany), 2004. *Recreations:* golf, choral singing, painting. *Address:* c/o National Westminster Bank, PO Box 411, 34 Henrietta Street, WC2E 8NN. *Club:* Cavalry and Guards. *Died 22 Jan. 2014.*

BROOKS, Douglas; Chairman, Ledbury Poetry Festival Ltd, 2001–08; *b* 3 Sept. 1928; *s* of Oliver Brooks and Olive Brooks; *m* 1952, June Anne (*née* Branch); one *s* one *d*. *Educ:* Newbridge Grammar Sch.; University Coll., Cardiff (Dip. SocSc.). CCIPD. Girling Ltd: factory operative, 1951–53; Employment Officer, 1953–56; Hoover Ltd: Personnel Off., 1956–60; Sen. Personnel Off., 1960–63; Dep. Personnel Man., 1963–66; Indust. Relations Advr, 1966–69; Gp Personnel Man., 1969–73; Personnel Dir, 1973–78; Group Personnel Manager, Tarmac Ltd, 1979–80; Director: Walker Brooks and Partners Ltd, 1980–91; Flexello Castors & Wheels plc, 1987–91; Consultant, Douglas Brooks Associates, 1992–98. Member: Council, SSRC, later ESRC, 1976–82; BBC Consultative Gp on social effects of television, 1978–80; Hon. Soc. Cymmrodorion, 1981– (Mem. Council, 1992–). Vis. Fellow, PSI, 1982–84. Vice-Pres., IPM, 1972–74. Chm., Wooburn Fest. Soc. Ltd, 1978–86. *Publications:* (with M. Fogarty) Trade Unions and British Industrial Development, 1986; various articles in professional jls. *Recreations:* talking, music, reading, cooking, theatre. *Address:* 5 Queensholme, Pittville Circus Road, Cheltenham, Glos GL52 2QE. *Club:* Reform. *Died 6 Sept. 2014.*

BROOKS, Prof. Nicholas Peter, DPhil; FSA, FRHistS; FBA 1989; Professor of Medieval History, University of Birmingham, 1985–2004, then Emeritus; *b* 14 Jan. 1941; *s* of late W. D. W. Brooks, CBE; *m* 1967, Chloë Carolyn Willis; one *s* one *d*. *Educ:* Winchester Coll.; Magdalen Coll., Oxford (Demy; MA DPhil). FRHistS 1970; FSAScot 1970–85; FSA 1974. Lectr in Medieval Hist., 1964–78, Sen. Lectr, 1978–85, St Andrews Univ.; Birmingham University: Chm., Sch. of History, 1987–89; Chm., Jun. Year Abroad prog., 1988–95; Dean, Faculty of Arts, 1992–95; Hd, Dept of Medieval History, 1985–2001. Chm., British Acad./RHistS Anglo-Saxon Charters Project, 1994–2013. General Editor: Studies in the Early Hist. of Britain, 1978–2000; Studies in Early Medieval Britain, 1999–2008. *Publications:* (ed) Latin and the Vernacular Languages in Early Medieval Britain, 1981; The Early History of the Church of Canterbury, 1984; (ed) St Oswald of Worcester, 1996; Anglo-Saxon Myths: State and Church 400–1066, 2000; Communities and Warfare 700–1400, 2000; (ed) St Wulfstan and his World, 2005; (ed) Early Medieval Studies in Memory of Patrick Wormald, 2009; numerous articles in festschriften, Medieval Archaeology, Anglo-Saxon England, Trans of RHistS, etc. *Recreations:* gardening, bridge, walking. *Address:* Department of Medieval History, University of Birmingham, Edgbaston, Birmingham B15 2TT. *T:* (0121) 414 5736. *Died 2 Feb. 2014.*

BROOKS, Sir Timothy (Gerald Martin), KCVO 2003; JP; farmer; Lord-Lieutenant of Leicestershire, 1989–2003; *b* 20 March 1929; *s* of late Hon. Herbert William Brooks, *s* of 2nd Baron Crawshaw, and of Hilda Muriel (*née* Steel); *m* 1951, Hon. Ann Fremantle, *d* of 4th Baron Cottesloe, GBE, TD and late Lady Elizabeth Harris; three *s* two *d*. *Educ:* Eton; RAC, Cirencester (NDA). Set up farm and garden centre, Wistow, 1953; Dir, Thomas Tapling & Co. Ltd, 1963–2007. Mem., Harborough DC, 1975–89 (Chm.,

1983–84). Chm. Governors, Wyggeston's Hosp., Leicester, 1988–96. Churchwarden, St Wistan's, Wistow. JP 1960, High Sheriff, 1979–80, Leics. Hon. DLitt Loughborough, 1997; Hon. LLD: De Montfort, 1997; Leicester, 2002. KStJ 1992. *Recreations:* arts, travel. *Address:* Garden Cottage, Wistow, Leicester LE8 0QF. *Died 2 May 2014.*

BROWN, Rt Rev. Arthur Durrant; a Suffragan Bishop of Toronto, 1981–93 (Bishop of York-Scarborough); *b* 7 March 1926; *s* of Edward S. Brown and Laura A. Durrant; *m* 1949, Norma Inez Rafuse (*d* 2005); three *d.* *Educ:* Univ. of Western Ontario (BA 1949); Huron College (LTh 1949). Ordained deacon, 1949; priest, 1950, Huron. Rector: of Paisley with Cargill and Pinkerton, 1948–50; of Glenworth and St Stephen, London, Ont., 1950–53; of St John, Sandwich, Windsor, Ont., 1953–63; of St Michael and All Angels, Toronto, 1963–80; Canon of Toronto, 1972–74; Archdeacon of York, Toronto, 1974–80. Member: Nat. Exec. Council, Anglican Church of Canada, 1969–81; Judicial Council of Ontario, 1978–85; Multi-Cultural Council of Ontario, 1985–87; Press Council of Ontario, 1986. Hon. Chm. Adv. Bd, Canadian Foundn on Compulsive Gambling (Ontario), 1983–; Chairman: Canadian Friends to West Indian Christians, 1982–; Royal Visit Children's Fund, 1984–. Columnist, Toronto Sunday Sun, 1974–86. Mem., Corp. of Huron Coll., 1961–86; Chancellor, Renison Coll., 1994–2001, Chancellor Emeritus, 2001. City of Toronto Civic Award, 1981. Hon. DD: Huron Coll., 1976; Wycliffe Coll., 1981; Trinity Coll., 1999. Distinguished Service Award, 5th Caribbean Anglican Consultation, 1999. *Died 2 May 2011.*

BROWN, Dr Daniel McGillivray, BSc, PhD, ScD; FRS 1982; FRSC; Emeritus Reader in Organic Chemistry, Cambridge University, since 1983; Fellow of King's College, Cambridge, since 1953; Attached Scientist, MRC Laboratory of Molecular Biology, 1983–2002; *b* 3 Feb. 1923; *s* of David Cunninghame Brown and Catherine Stewart (*née* McGillivray); *m* 1953, Margaret Joyce Herbert; three *d* (one *s* decd). *Educ:* Glasgow Acad.; Glasgow Univ. (BSc); London Univ. (PhD); Cambridge Univ. (PhD, ScD). FRSC 2001. Res. Chemist, Chester Beatty Res. Inst., 1945–53; Asst Dir of Res., 1953–58, Lectr, 1959–67, Reader in Org. Chem., 1967–83, Cambridge Univ.; Vice-Provost, King's Coll., Cambridge, 1974–81. Vis. Professor: Univ. of Calif, LA, 1959–60; Brandeis Univ., 1966–67. *Publications:* scientific papers, mainly in chemical and molecular biology jls. *Recreations:* modern art, gardening. *Address:* 60 Hartington Grove, Cambridge CB1 7UE. *T:* (01223) 245304. *Died 24 April 2012.*

BROWN, Prof. David Clifford; writer on music; Professor of Musicology, Southampton University, 1983–89, then Professor Emeritus; *b* 8 July 1929; *s* of Bertram and Constance Brown; *m* 1953, Elizabeth (*née* Valentine); two *d.* *Educ:* Sheffield Univ. (BA, MA, BMus); PhD Southampton Univ. LTCL. RAF 1952–54. Schoolmaster, 1954–59; Music Librarian, London Univ., 1959–62; Southampton University: Lectr in Music, 1962; Sen. Lectr, 1970; Reader, 1975. Many broadcast talks and scripts incl. series: Tchaikovsky and his World, 1980; Tchaikovsky: a fateful gift, 1984; A Sympathetic Person, 1989–90. Mem. Editl Cttee, Musica Britannica, 1980–2005. City of Southampton Award, 2009. *Publications:* (ed jtly) Thomas Weelkes: collected anthems, 1966; Thomas Weelkes, 1969; Mikhail Glinka, 1974; John Wilbye, 1974; Tchaikovsky, vol. 1, 1978, vol. 2, 1982 (Derek Allen Prize, British Acad.), vol. 3, 1986, vol. 4, 1991 (Yorkshire Post Music Book Award, 1991); Tchaikovsky Remembered, 1993; Musorgsky, 2003; Tchaikovsky: the man and his music, 2006; contribs to jls and periodicals. *Address:* Braishfield Lodge West, Braishfield, Romsey, Hants SO51 0PS. *T:* (01794) 368163. *Died 20 June 2014.*

BROWN, Hon. Sir Douglas (Dunlop), Kt 1989; a Judge of the High Court of Justice, Queen's Bench Division, 1996–2005 (Family Division, 1989–96); Judge of Employment Appeal Tribunal, 2001–05; *b* 22 Dec. 1931; *s* of late Robert Dunlop Brown, MICE, and Anne Cameron Brown; *m* 1960, June Margaret Elizabeth McNamara; one *s.* *Educ:* Ryleys Sch., Alderley Edge; Manchester Grammar Sch.; Manchester Univ. (LLB). Served in RN, 1953–55; Lieut, RNR. Called to Bar, Gray's Inn, 1953; Bencher, 1989; practised Northern Circuit from 1955; Mem. General Council of Bar, 1967–71; Asst Recorder, Salford City QS, 1971; a Recorder of the Crown Court, 1972–80; QC 1976; a Circuit Judge, 1980–88; Family Div. Liaison Judge, Northern Circuit, 1990–95; Presiding Judge, Northern Circuit, 1998–2001. Mem., Parole Bd for England and Wales, 1985–87. *Recreations:* cricket, golf, music. *Address:* c/o Royal Courts of Justice, Strand, WC2A 2LL. *Club:* Wilmslow Golf. *Died 21 Dec. 2015.*

BROWN, Rev. Canon Geoffrey Harold; Vicar of St Martin-in-the-Fields, 1985–95; *b* 1 April 1930; *s* of Harry and Ada Brown; *m* 1963, Elizabeth Jane Williams; two *d.* *Educ:* Monmouth Sch.; Trinity Hall, Cambridge (MA). Asst Curate, St Andrew's, Plaistow, 1954–60; Asst Curate, St Peter's, Birmingham and Sub-Warden of Pre-Ordination Training Scheme, 1960–63; Rector: St George's, Newtown, Birmingham, 1963–73; Grimsby, 1973–85. Hon. Canon, Lincoln Cathedral, 1978; Canon Emeritus, 1985. FRSA 1991. *Recreations:* the countryside, photography, theatre. *Address:* Greenacres, Little Shurdington, Cheltenham, Glos GL51 4TX. *Died 27 May 2015.*

BROWN, Gillian Margaret S.; *see* Stuart-Brown.

BROWN, John, CMG 1989; HM Diplomatic Service, retired; *b* 13 July 1931; *s* of John Coultas Scofield Brown and Sarah Ellen Brown (*née* Brown); *m* 1955, Christine Ann Batchelor; one *d.* Export Credits Guarantee Dept, 1949; Nat. service, Grenadier Guards, 1949–51; Board of Trade, 1967; seconded to HM Diplomatic Service, 1969; Diplomatic Service, 1975; First Secretary and Head of Chancery, Accra, 1977; FCO, 1979, Counsellor, 1981; Counsellor (Commercial) and Dir of Trade Promotion, British Trade Develt Office, NY, 1984; Consul-Gen., Toronto, and Dir, Trade Promotion and Investment, 1989–91. *Recreations:* walking, public speaking. *Club:* Royal Over-Seas League. *Died 24 Sept. 2014.*

BROWN, Rt Rev. John Edward; Bishop in Cyprus and the Gulf, 1987–95; Episcopal Canon, St George's Cathedral, Jerusalem, 1987–95; an Assistant Bishop, Diocese of Lincoln, since 1995; *b* 13 July 1930; *s* of Edward and Muriel Brown; *m* 1956, Rosemary (*née* Wood); one *s.* *Educ:* Wintringham Grammar Sch., Grimsby; Kelham Theological Coll., Notts; BD London. Ordained deacon 1955, priest 1956; Master, St George's School, Jerusalem; Curate, St George's Cathedral, Jerusalem; Chaplain of Amman, Jordan, 1954–57; Curate-in-Charge, All Saints, Reading, 1957–60; Missionary and Chaplain, All Saints Cathedral, Khartoum, Sudan, 1960–64; Vicar: Stewkley, Buckingham, 1964–69; St Luke's, Maidenhead, 1969–73; Bracknell, Berkshire, 1973–77; Rural Dean of Sonning, 1974–77; Archdeacon of Berkshire, 1978–86; Rural Dean, Grimsby and Cleethorpes, 2003–04. *Publications:* A Way in the Wilderness: a bishop's prayer journey through the Arabian Peninsula, 2008. *Recreations:* writing; Middle East and African studies. *Address:* 130 Oxford Street, Cleethorpes DN35 0BP. *T:* (01472) 698840. *E:* bishopjohnsaints@tiscali.co.uk. *Died 23 Oct. 2011.*

BROWN, John Russell; Honorary Visiting Professor, University College London, 2008–13, then Emeritus; *b* 15 Sept. 1923; *yr s* of Russell Alan Brown and Olive Helen Brown (*née* Golding), Coombe Wood, Somerset; *m* 1961, Hilary Sue Baker; one *s* two *d.* *Educ:* Monkton Combe Sch.; Keble Coll., Oxford. Sub-Lieut (AE) RNVR, 1944–46. Fellow, Shakespeare Inst., Stratford-upon-Avon, 1951–55; Lectr and Sen. Lectr, Dept of English, Birmingham Univ., 1955–63; Prof. and Hd of Dept of Drama and Theatre Arts, Univ. of Birmingham, 1964–71; Prof. of English, Sussex Univ., 1971–82; Prof. of Theatre Arts, State Univ. of NY at Stony Brook, 1982–85; Prof. of Theatre, Univ. of Michigan, Ann Arbor, 1985–97, then Emeritus Prof. of English and Theatre; Artistic Dir, Project Theatre, Michigan Univ., 1985–89. Reynolds Lectr, Colorado Univ., 1957; Vis. Prof. Graduate Sch., New York Univ., 1959; Mellon Prof. of Drama, Carnegie Inst., Pittsburgh, 1964; Vis. Prof., Zürich Univ., 1969–70; Univ. Lectr in Drama, Univ. of Toronto, 1970; Vis. Prof., Columbia Univ., NY, 1998 and 2002; Research Consultant, 1994–2000, Vis. Prof. of Theatre, 2000–08,

Middlesex Univ. Robb Lectr, Univ. of Auckland, 1976; Lansdowne Visitor, Univ. of Victoria, BC, 1990. Associate, NT, 1973–88. Member: Adv. Council of Victoria and Albert Museum, 1980–83; Adv. Council of Theatre Museum, 1974–83 (Chm., 1979–83); Arts Council of GB, 1980–83, and Chm. Drama Panel, 1980–83 (formerly Dep. Chm.). Hon. Fellow, British Shakespeare Assoc., 2014. Medal of Honour, Free Univ. of Brussels, 1992. *Theatre productions include:* Twelfth Night, Playhouse, Pittsburgh, 1964; Macbeth, Everyman, Liverpool, 1965; The White Devil, Everyman, 1969; Crossing Niagara, Nat. Theatre at the ICA, 1975; They Are Dying Out, Young Vic, 1976; Old Times, British Council tour of Poland, 1976; Judgement, Nat. Theatre, 1977; Hamlet (tour), 1978; Macbeth, Nat. Theatre (co-director), 1978; The Vienna Notes and The Nest, Crucible, Sheffield, 1979; Company, Nat. Theatre, 1980; Faith Healer, Nat. Theatre and Santa Fe, 1982, and, with Candida, British Council tour of India, 1983; The Double Bass, Nat. Theatre, 1984; The Daughter-in-Law, Antique Pink, Oedipus, Waiting for Godot, Don Juan, Every Good Boy, Project Theater, Ann Arbor, Mich, USA, 1985–89; Richard II, Nat. Theatre, Educn Project Tour, 1987; Much Ado About Nothing, Playhouse, Cincinnati, 1989; Burn This, 1989, On the Verge, 1991, Dunedin, NZ; Arden of Faversham, Empty Space, Seattle, 1991; Life Sentences, Group Theater of Mich, 1994. General Editor: Stratford-upon-Avon Studies, 1960–67; Stratford-upon-Avon Library, 1964–69; Theatre Production Studies, 1981–2002; Theatre Concepts, 1992–95; Shakespeare Handbooks, 2002–12. *Publications:* (ed) The Merchant of Venice, 1955; Shakespeare and his Comedies, 1957; (ed) The White Devil, 1960; Shakespeare: The Tragedy of Macbeth, 1963; (ed) The Duchess of Malfi, 1965, rev. edn 2009; (ed) Henry V, 1965; Shakespeare's Plays in Performance, 1966; Effective Theatre, 1969; Shakespeare's The Tempest, 1969; Shakespeare's Dramatic Style, 1970; Theatre Language, 1972; Free Shakespeare, 1974; Discovering Shakespeare, 1981; Shakespeare and his Theatre, 1982; A Short Guide to Modern British Drama, 1983; Shakescenes, 1993; (ed) Oxford Illustrated History of Theatre, 1995; William Shakespeare: writing for performance, 1996; What is Theatre?, 1997; New Sites for Shakespeare: theatre, the audience and Asia, 1999; Shakespeare: the Tragedies, 2001; Shakespeare and the Theatrical Event, 2002; Shakespeare Dancing: a theatrical study of the plays, 2004; (ed) Directors' Shakespeare, 2008; (ed) Actors' Shakespeare, 2011; On Stage Shakespeare, 2014; articles in Shakespeare Survey, Critical Quarterly, Tulane Drama Review, Studies in Bibliography, New Theatre Qly, Theatre Res. Internat., etc. *Recreations:* gardening, travel. *Died 25 Aug. 2015.*

BROWN, Joseph Lawler, CBE 1978; TD 1953; DL; FCIM; Chairman and Managing Director, The Birmingham Post & Mail Ltd, 1973–77; *b* 22 March 1921; *s* of late Neil Brown; *m* 1950, Mabel Smith, SRN, SCM (*d* 2000); one *s* one *d*. *Educ:* Peebles; Heriot-Watt Coll., Edinburgh. BA Hons Open Univ. FCIM (FInstM 1976); CCMI (FBIM 1978). Served War, The Royal Scots, 1939–47 (Major). The Scotsman Publications Ltd, 1947–60; Coventry Newspapers Ltd: Gen. Man., 1960; Jt Man. Dir, 1961; Man. Dir, 1964–69; The Birmingham Post & Mail Ltd: Dep. Man. Dir, 1970; Man. Dir, 1971. Director: Cambridge Newspapers Ltd, 1965–69; Press Assoc., 1968–75 (Chm. 1972); Reuters Ltd, 1972–75; BPM (Holdings) Ltd, 1973–81. Pres., Birmingham Chamber of Industry and Commerce, 1979–80. Exec. Chm., Birmingham Venture, 1981–85. Mem., Bromsgrove and Redditch DHA, 1982–84; Mem., Hereford and Worcester Family Practitioner Cttee, 1982–83. Mem. Council, Regular Forces Employment Assoc., 1983–87; Warden, Neidpath Castle, Peebles, 1983–84. Mem., Peebles Guildry Corp., 1991–97. Life Mem., Court, Birmingham Univ., 1980–2013; Bailiff, Schs of King Edward the Sixth in Birmingham, 1987–88. Hon. Callant of Peebles, 2007. FRSA 1975. DL County of W Midlands, 1976. Kt, Mark Twain Soc., 1979. Commendatore, Order Al Merito Della Repubblica Italiana, 1973. *Publications:* (with J. C. Lawson) History of Peebles 1850–1990, 1990. *W:* www.lawlerbrown.com. *Died 22 May 2015.*

BROWN, Air Vice-Marshal Michael John Douglas; consulting engineer; *b* 9 May 1936; *s* of late N. H. B. Brown, AMIERE; *m* 1st, 1961, Audrey (*d* 1994); one *s*; 2nd, 1997, Ruth, *d* of late H. G. Willey, Weobley, Herefordshire. *Educ:* Drayton Manor, W7; RAF Technical Coll., Henlow; Trinity Hall, Cambridge (MA). CEng 1968; CMath, FIMA 1991; FRIN 1998; FRAeS 2000; CSci 2005. Commnd RAF Technical Br., 1954; Cambridge Univ. Air Sqdn, 1954–57; RAF pilot trng, 1958–59; served in Bomber Comd, 1959–61; signals duties in Kenya (also assisted with formation of Kenya Air Force), 1961–64; advanced weapons course, 1965–66; Defence Operational Analysis Estabt, 1966–69; RAF Staff Coll., 1970; MoD Operational Requirements Staff, 1971–73; RAF Boulmer, 1973–75; USAF Air War Coll., 1975–76; HQ RAF Strike Comd, 1976–78; Comdr, RAF N Luffenham, 1978–80; rcds 1981; Dir, Air Guided Weapons, MoD (PE), 1983–86; Dir Gen., Strategic Electronic Systems, MoD (PE), 1986–91. Non-exec. Dir, CSE International Ltd, 1993–2002. Mem. Council, Royal Inst. Navigation, 2006–09 (Mem. Finance Cttee, 2008–). Vice-Chm., Herefordshire RBL, 1997–2000; Vice-President: SSAFA, Powys, 1993–2001; RAFA, Hereford, 1997–2001; Regl Rep. for S Wales, SSAFA Nat. Council, 1997–2001; Pres., RAFA, Peterborough, 2002–09. Chairman: Cambridge Soc., Peterborough, 2002–09; Peterborough Astronomical Soc., 2004–09; Peterborough Art Soc., 2006–09; Lichfield Art Soc., 2011–. Freeman, City of London, 2000; Freeman, 2000, Liveryman, 2001, Engineers' Co. *Club:* Royal Air Force. *Died 21 July 2011.*

BROWN, Ralph, RA 1972 (ARA 1968); sculptor; *b* 24 April 1928; *m* 1st, 1952, Margaret E. Taylor (marr. diss. 1963); one *d* (and one *s* decd); 2nd, 1964, Caroline Ann Clifton-Trigg; one *s*. *Educ:* Leeds Grammar School. RAF, 1946–48. Studied Royal College of Art, 1948–56; in Paris with Zadkine, 1954; travel scholarships to Greece 1955, Italy 1957. Tutor, RCA, 1958–64. Sculpture Prof., Salzburg Festival, Summer 1972. Work exhibited: John Moores, Liverpool (prizewinner 1957), Tate Gallery, Religious Theme 1958, Arnhem Internat. Open Air Sculpture, 1958; Middelheim Open Air Sculpture, 1959; Battersea Park Open Air Sculpture, 1960, 1963, 1966, 1977; Tokyo Biennale, 1963; British Sculptors '72, RA, 1972; Holland Park Open Air, 1975; Sculpture of the Century, Salisbury Cathedral and Canary Wharf, London, 1999. One man shows: Leicester Galls, 1961, 1963; Archer Gall., 1972; Salzburg 1972; Munich 1973; Montpellier 1974; Marseilles 1975; Oxford 1975; Taranman Gall., 1979; Browse & Darby Gall., 1979; Beaux Arts, Bath, 1983, 1987; Charles Foley Gall., Columbus, US, 1984; Lloyd Shine Gall., Chicago, 1984; Falle Gall., Jersey, 1995; Bruton Gall., Leeds, 1999; Number 9 the Gall., Birmingham, 2005; Retrospective: Leeds City Art Gall. and Warwick Arts Centre, 1988; Pangolin London, 2009. Work in Collections: Tate Britain, Arts Council, Contemp. Art Society, Kröller-Müller, Gallery of NSW, Stuyvesant Foundation, City of Salzburg, Nat. Gallery of Wales, Allbright-Knox Gall., and at Leeds, Bristol, Norwich, Aberdeen, etc; public sculpture in Harlow New Town Market Square and Jersey Zoo. Hon. RWA 1990. *Relevant publication:* Social, Savage, Sensual: the sculpture of Ralph Brown, ed by Gillian Whiteley, 2009. *Address:* Southanger Farm, Chalford, Glos GL6 8HP. *T:* (01285) 760243. *E:* caroline@ralphbrown.co.uk. *W:* www.ralphbrown.co.uk. *Died 3 April 2013.*

BROWN, Rt Rev. Mgr Ralph, JCD; Vicar General, Archdiocese of Westminster, 1977–99; *b* 30 June 1931; *s* of John William and Elizabeth Josephine Brown. *Educ:* Highgate Sch.; St Edmund's Coll., Old Hall Green, Herts; Pontifical Gregorian Univ., Rome (LCL 1961; JCD 1963). Commnd Middlesex Regt, 1949; Korea, 1950. Ordained priest, Westminster Cathedral, 1959; Vice-Chancellor, Vice Officialis, Dio. of Westminster, 1964–69; Officialis, 1969–76, Officialis, subseq. Judicial Vicar, 1988–2006, Westminster; Judicial Vicar, Oslo, 2006–; Mem., Oslo Coll. of Consultors, 2007–; Canonical Adviser: to British Mil. Ordinariate, 1987–95; to Polish Catholic Mission in England and Wales, 2002–08. Pres., Canon Law Soc. of GB and Ireland, 1980–86, Sec., 1986–89. Apptd Papal Chamberlain, 1972; National Co-ordinator for Papal Visit to England and Wales, 1982; Prelate of Honour to HH the Pope, 1987; Protonotary Apostolic, 1999. Elected to Old Brotherhood of English Secular Clergy, 1987 (Sec., 1989; Pres., 2009). Hon. Member: Canon Law Soc. of Aust. and NZ, 1975; Canadian Canon Law Soc., 1979; Canon Law Soc. of America, 1979; Canon Law Soc. of GB and Ireland, 2006. KHS 1985; KCHS 1991 (Prior, Westminster sect., 1996–2008). Silver Palm of Jerusalem, 1999; Cross, Pro Piis Meritis, Order of Malta, 2000; Comdr, Order of the Republic of Poland, 2004. *Publications:* Marriage Annulment, 1969, rev. edn 1990; (ed) Matrimonial Decisions of Great Britain and Ireland, 1969–; co-translator, The Code of Canon Law in English Translation, 1983; (ed jtly) The Canon Law: Letter and Spirit: a practical guide to the Code of Canon Law, 1995; articles in Heythrop Jl, Studia Canonica, Theological Digest, The Jurist. *Address:* St Wilfrid's Convent, 29 Tite Street, Chelsea, SW3 4JX. *T:* (020) 7565 5838. *Club:* Sloane. *Died 6 Jan. 2014.*

BROWN, Sir Robert C.; *see* Crichton-Brown.

BROWN, Russell; *see* Brown, J. R.

BROWNE, Sir Anthony Arthur Duncan M.; *see* Montague Browne.

BROWNE, Bernard Peter Francis K.; *see* Kenworthy-Browne.

BROWNE, Sir Nicholas (Walker), KBE 2002; CMG 1999; HM Diplomatic Service, retired; Ambassador to Denmark, 2003–06; *b* 17 Dec. 1947; *s* of Gordon Browne and late Molly (*née* Gray); *m* 1969, Diana Aldwinckle; two *s* two *d*. *Educ:* Cheltenham Coll.; University Coll., Oxford (Open Scholar) (BA). Third Sec., FCO, 1969–71; Tehran, 1971–74; Second, later First Sec., FCO, 1974–76; on loan to Cabinet Office, 1976–80; First Sec. and Head of Chancery, Salisbury, 1980–81; First Sec., FCO, 1981–84; First Sec. (Envmt), Office of UK Rep., Brussels, 1984–89; Chargé d'Affaires, Tehran, 1989; Counsellor, FCO, 1989–90; Counsellor (Press and Public Affairs), Washington, and Hd of British Information Services, NY, 1990–94; Hd of Middle East Dept, FCO, 1994–97; Chargé d'Affaires, Tehran, 1997–99; Ambassador to Iran, 1999–2002; Sen. Dir (Civil), RCDS, 2002–03. *Recreations:* travel, theatre, log fires. *Died 13 Jan. 2014.*

BROWNE, Peter K.; *see* Kenworthy-Browne.

BROWNE, Sheila Jeanne, CB 1977; Principal, Newnham College, Cambridge, 1983–92; *b* 25 Dec. 1924; *d* of Edward Elliott Browne. *Educ:* Lady Margaret Hall, Oxford (MA; Hon. Fellow 1978); Ecole des Chartes, Paris. Asst Lectr, Royal Holloway Coll., Univ. of London, 1947–51; Tutor and Fellow of St Hilda's Coll., Oxford and Univ. Lectr in French, Oxford, 1951–61, Hon. Fellow, St Hilda's Coll., 1978; HM Inspector of Schools, 1961–70; Staff Inspector, Secondary Educn, 1970–72; Chief Inspector, Secondary Educn, 1972; Dep. Sen. Chief Inspector, DES, 1972–74, Senior Chief Inspector, 1974–83. Member: CNAA, 1985–93; Franco-British Council, 1987–95; Marshall Aid Commemoration Comr, 1987–92. Trustee, Gladstone Meml Trust, 1991–2010. Chairman: Council, Selly Oak Colls, 1992–93; Govs, Morley Coll., 2000–04. Hon. Fellow: Thames Valley Univ. (formerly Ealing Tech. Coll., later Poly. of W London), 1984; RHBNC, 1987; Lancashire Polytechnic, 1989; Univ. (formerly Poly.) of N London, 1989. Hon. DLitt Warwick, 1981; Hon. LLD: Exeter, 1984; Birmingham, 1987. *Recreations:* medieval France, enjoying Oxford. *Address:* 23 Ritchie Court, 380 Banbury Road, Oxford OX2 7PW. *T:* (01865) 557063. *Died 27 Aug. 2015.*

BROWNE-CAVE, Sir Robert C.; *see* Cave-Browne-Cave.

BROWNLOW, James Hilton, CBE 1984; QPM 1978; Adviser on Ground Control, Football Association, 1990–94; HM Inspector of Constabulary for North Eastern England, 1983–89; *b* 19 Oct. 1925; *s* of late Ernest Cuthbert Brownlow and Beatrice Annie Elizabeth Brownlow; *m* 1947, Joyce Key; two *d*. *Educ:* Worksop Central School. Solicitor's Clerk, 1941–43; served war, RAF, Flt/Sgt (Air Gunner), 1943–47. Police Constable, Leicester City Police, 1947; Police Constable to Det. Chief Supt, Kent County Constabulary, 1947–69; Asst Chief Constable, Hertfordshire Constabulary, 1969–75; Asst to HM Chief Inspector of Constabulary, Home Office, 1975–76; Dep. Chief Constable, Greater Manchester Police, 1976–79; Chief Constable, S Yorks Police, 1979–82. Mem., Parole Bd, 1991–94. Queen's Commendation for Brave Conduct, 1972. Officer Brother OStJ 1981. *Recreations:* golf, gardening. *Died 25 Oct. 2012.*

BROWNLOW, Peter; Managing Director and Financial Director, Border Television plc, 1996–2000; *b* 4 June 1945; *s* of Frederick and Margaret Brownlow; *m* 1971, Judith Margaret Alton; two *s*. *Educ:* Rothwell Grammar Sch.; Leeds Poly. ACMA 1970. Company Accountant: John Menzies plc, 1967–70; United Newspapers, 1970–82; Co. Sec., Border Television plc, 1982–84; Financial Dir, 1984–96, non-exec. Dep. Chm., 1995–2006, Cumberland Building Soc. Director: Century Radio Ltd, 1993–2000; Century Radio 106 Ltd, 1996–2000; Century Radio 105 Ltd, 1997–2000; Sun FM Ltd, 1997–2000; Border Radio Hldgs, 1997–2000. *Recreations:* sailing, fell walking, gardening. *Address:* Quarry Bank, Capon Hill, Brampton, Cumbria CA8 1QN. *Died 16 April 2014.*

BRUBECK, David Warren; jazz musician, composer; Chairman, Brubeck Institute, University of the Pacific, since 2000; *b* Concord, Calif, 6 Dec. 1920; *s* of Howard Brubeck and Elizabeth Ivey; *m* 1942, Iola Whitlock; four *s* one *d* (and one *s* decd). *Educ:* Univ. of the Pacific (BA); graduate study with Darius Milhaud, Mills Coll. Leader, Dave Brubeck Octet, and Trio, 1946–; formed Dave Brubeck Quartet, 1951; played colls, fests, clubs and symphony orchs; 3 month tour of Europe and Middle East (for US State Dept) and tours in Aust., Japan, USSR and S America. Numerous recordings. Composed: *ballet:* Points on Jazz, 1962; Glances, 1976; *orchestral:* Elementals, 1963; They All Sang Yankee Doodle, 1976; *flute and guitar:* Tritonis, 1979; *piano:* Reminiscences of the Cattle Country, 1946; Four by Four, 1946; *oratorios:* The Light in the Wilderness, 1968; Beloved Son, 1978; The Voice of the Holy Spirit, 1985; *cantatas:* Gates of Justice, 1969; Truth is Fallen, 1971; La Fiesta de la Posada, 1975; In Praise of Mary, 1989; *chorus and orchestra:* Pange Lingua Variations, 1983; Upon This Rock Chorale and Fugue, 1987; Lenten Triptych, 1988; Joy in the Morning, 1991; *mass:* To Hope!, a celebration, 1980; *SATB Chorus:* I See Satie, 1987; Four New England Pieces, 1988; Earth is our mother (with chamber orch.), 1992; *jazz opera*: Cannery Row Suite, 2006; over 250 *jazz* compositions incl. Blue Rondo à la Turk; In Your Own Sweet Way; The Duke. Duke Ellington Fellow, Yale Univ., 1973. Hon. PhD: Univ. of Pacific; Fairfield Univ.; Bridgeport Univ., 1982; Mills Coll., 1982; Niagara Univ., 1989; Kalamazoo Coll., 1991. Hollywood Walk of Fame. Winner, jazz polls conducted by Downbeat, Melody Maker, Cashbox, Billboard and Playboy magazines, 1952–55; Broadcast Music Inc. Jazz Pioneer Award, 1985; Compostela Humanitarian award, 1986; Connecticut Arts award, 1987; American Eagle award, Nat. Music Council, 1988; Pantheon of the Arts, Univ. of the Pacific, 1989; Gerard Manley Hopkins Award, Fairfield Univ., 1990; Distinguished Achievement Award, Simon's Rock Coll., 1991; Connecticut Bar Assoc. Award, 1992; Nat. Medal of the Arts, USA, 1994; Lifetime Achievement Award, Nat. Acad. of Recording Arts and Scis, 1996; Kennedy Center Honor, 2009. Officier de l'Ordre des Arts et des Lettres (France), 1990. *Address:* Derry Music Co., PO Box 150270, San Rafael, CA 94915, USA. *Died 5 Dec. 2012.*

BRUCE, Hon. James Michael Edward, CBE 1992; Founder and Chairman, Scottish Woodlands Ltd, 1967–93; *b* 26 Aug. 1927; *s* of 10th Earl of Elgin, KT, CMG, TD and Hon. Katherine Elizabeth Cochrane, Countess of Elgin, DBE (*d* 1989); *m* 1st, 1950, Hon. (Margaret) Jean Dagbjørt Coats (marr. diss. 1974), *d* of 2nd Baron Glentanar; two *s* one *d* (and one *s* decd); 2nd, 1975, Morven-Anne Macdonald (*d* 1994); two *s* two *d*; 3rd, 2000, Mrs Mary Elizabeth Hamilton. *Educ:* Eton; RAC, Cirencester (Goldstand Medal). Served Scots Guards, 2nd Lieut. Mem., Home Grown Timber Adv. Cttee, 1969–93; Dir, Forest Industry Cttee, 1989–93. Vice-Pres., Scottish Opera,

1985–94. Trustee, Scottish Opera Endowment Trust, 1979–2009. FRSA (Council Mem., 1988–95); Hon. Fellow: Game Conservancy, 1993; Scottish Council for Development and Industry, 1993. JP Perth, 1962–2002. *Recreations:* gardens, boats. *Address:* Dron House, Balmanno, Perth PH2 9HG. *T:* (01738) 812786. *Died 22 April 2013.*

BRÜGGEN, Frans; conductor; formerly recorder player; Founder and conductor, Orchestra of the Eighteenth Century, since 1981; *b* Amsterdam, 30 Oct. 1934; *m* Machtelt Israëls; two *d. Educ:* Conservatory and Univ. of Amsterdam. Prof., Royal Hague Conservatoire, 1955; formerly: Erasmus Prof., Harvard Univ.; Regents Prof., Univ. of Calif, Berkeley. Artistic Dir, Stavanger Symphony Orch., 1990–94; Principal Guest Conductor, Orchestre de Paris, 1998–2000; former Chief Conductor, Radio Kamer Filharmonie, later Conductor Emeritus; guest conductor: Concertgebouw Orch., Amsterdam; Vienna Philharmonic Orch.; Rotterdam Philharmonic Orch.; Orch. of the Age of Enlightenment; City of Birmingham Symphony Orch.; Royal Stockholm Philharmonic Orch. Hon. RCM. UNESCO Music Prize, 1997; Gold Medal for Arts and Scis, Order of House of Orange (Netherlands), 2010. *Address:* c/o Askonas Holt Ltd, Lincoln House, 300 High Holborn, WC1V 7JH. *Died 13 Aug. 2014.*

BRUNNER, Sir John Henry Kilian, 4th Bt *cr* 1895; *b* 1 June 1927; *s* of Sir Felix John Morgan Brunner, 3rd Bt, and Dorothea Elizabeth, OBE, *d* of Henry Brodribb Irving; *S* father, 1982, but his name does not appear on the Official Roll of the Baronetage; *m* 1955, Jasmine Cecily, *d* of late John Wardrop Moore; two *s* (one *d* decd). *Educ:* Eton; Trinity Coll., Oxford (BA 1950). Served as Lieut RA. On staff, PEP, 1950–53; Talks producer, 1953; Economic Adviser, Treasury, 1958–61; Asst Manager, Observer, 1961. *Heir: s* Nicholas Felix Minturn Brunner, *b* 16 Jan. 1960. *Died 18 Nov. 2015.*

BRUNSKILL, Ronald William, OBE 1990; MA, PhD; FSA; lecturer and author; Professor, Centre for Conservation Studies, School of Architecture (formerly School of the Built Environment), De Montfort University, 1995–2001; *b* 3 Jan. 1929; *s* of William Brunskill and Elizabeth Hannah Brunskill; *m* 1960, Miriam Allsopp; two *d. Educ:* Bury High Sch.; Univ. of Manchester (BA Hons Arch. 1951, MA 1952, PhD 1963). Registered Architect and ARIBA, 1951; FSA 1975. National Service, 2nd Lieut RE, 1953–55. Studio Asst in Arch., Univ. of Manchester, 1951–53; Architectural Asst, LCC, 1955; Asst in Arch., Univ. of Manchester, 1955–56; Commonwealth Fund Fellow (arch. and town planning), MIT, 1956–57; Architect to Williams Deacon's Bank, 1957–60; Manchester University: Lectr, 1960–73; Sen. Lectr, 1973–84; Reader in Architecture, 1984–89; Hon. Fellow, Sch. of Architecture, 1989–95; Architect in private practice, 1960–66; Partner, Carter, Brunskill & Associates, chartered architects, 1966–69, Consultant, 1969–73. Vis. Prof., Univ. of Florida, Gainesville, 1969–70; Hon. Vis. Prof., De Montfort Univ., 1994–95. President: Vernacular Arch. Gp, 1974–77; Cumberland and Westmorland Antiquarian and Archaeol Soc., 1990–93 (Vice-Pres., 1975–90); Friends of Friendless Churches, 1999–2009 (Chm., 1990–98); Ancient Monuments Soc., 2004–09 (Hon. Architect, 1983–88; Vice-Chm., 1988–90; Chm., 1990–2000; Vice-Pres., 2000–04); Vice-Pres., Weald and Downland Museum Trust, 1980–; Chm., Urban Parks Adv. Panel, Heritage Lottery Fund, 1995–99; Member: Historic Bldgs Council for England, 1978–84; Royal Commn on Ancient and Historical Monuments of Wales, 1983–97 (Vice Chm., 1993–97); Historic Buildings and Monuments Commn (English Heritage), 1989–95 (Member: Historic Buildings Adv. Cttee, 1984–95 (Chm., 1989–95); Ancient Monuments Adv. Cttee, 1984–90; Chm., Cathedrals and Churches Adv. Cttee, 1989–95); Cathedrals Adv. Commn for England, 1981–91; Cathedrals Fabric Commn for England, 1991–96; Manchester DAC for Care of Churches, 1973–79 and 1987–93; Manchester Cathedral Fabric Cttee, 1987–96; Blackburn Cathedral Fabric Cttee, 1989–96 (Chm.); Chester Cathedral Fabric Cttee, 1989–94 and 2004–09; Council, Soc. for Folk Life Studies, 1969–72 and 1980–83. Trustee, British Historic Buildings Trust, 1985–92. Hon. DArt De Montfort, 2001. Neale Bursar, RIBA, 1962; President's Award, Manchester Soc. of Architects, 1977; Henry Glessie Award, Vernacular Architecture Forum of USA and Canada, 2009. *Publications:* Illustrated Handbook of Vernacular Architecture, 1971, 3rd edn (enlarged) 1987; Vernacular Architecture of the Lake Counties, 1974; (with Alec Clifton-Taylor) English Brickwork, 1977; Traditional Buildings of Britain, 1981, 3rd edn (enlarged) 2004; Houses (in series, Collins Archaeology), 1982; Traditional Farm Buildings of Britain, 1982, 2nd edn (enlarged) 1987; Timber Building in Britain, 1985, 2nd edn (enlarged) 1994; Brick Building in Britain, 1990; Houses and Cottages of Britain, 1997; Traditional Farm Buildings and their Conservation, 1999; Vernacular Architecture: an illustrated handbook, 2000; Traditional Buildings of Cumbria, 2002; Brick and Clay Buildings of Britain, 2009; articles and reviews in archaeol and architectural jls. *Recreation:* enjoying the countryside. *Address:* 8 Overhill Road, Wilmslow SK9 2BE. *T:* (01625) 522099. *Died 9 Oct. 2015.*

BRYAN, Sir Arthur, Kt 1976; Lord-Lieutenant of Staffordshire, 1968–93; President, Waterford Wedgwood Holdings plc and a Director, Waterford Glass Group plc, 1986–88 (Managing Director, 1963–85, Chairman, 1968–86, Wedgwood); *b* 4 March 1923; *s* of William Woodall Bryan and Isobel Alan (*née* Tweedie); *m* 1947, Betty Ratford; one *s* one *d. Educ:* Longton High Sch., Stoke-on-Trent. Served with RAFVR, 1941–45. Joined Josiah Wedgwood & Sons Ltd, 1947; London Man., 1953–57; General Sales Man., 1959–60; Director and President, Josiah Wedgwood & Sons Inc. of America, 1960–62; Director: Josiah Wedgwood & Sons Ltd, Barlaston, 1962; Josiah Wedgwood & Sons (Canada) Ltd; Josiah Wedgwood & Sons (Australia) Pty Ltd; Phoenix Assurance Co., 1976–85; Friends' Provident Life Office, 1985–92; Rank Organisation, 1985–94; United Kingdom Fund Inc., 1987–2001. Member: BOTB, 1978–82 (Chm., N American Adv. Gp, 1973–82); British-American Associates, 1988–94; Marshall Aid Commem. Cttee, 1988–94. Pres., British Ceramic Manufacturers' Fedn, 1970–71; Mem., Design Council, 1977–82. Mem. Ct, Univ. of Keele. Fellow, Inst. of Marketing (grad. 1950); CCMI (FBIM 1968); Comp. Inst. Ceramics. KStJ 1972. Hon. MUniv Keele, 1978; Hon. DLitt Staffordshire, 1993. *Recreations:* walking, reading. *Address:* Parkfields Cottage, Tittensor, Stoke-on-Trent, Staffs ST12 9HQ. *T:* (01782) 372686. *Died 11 Feb. 2011.*

BRYAN, Dora May, (Mrs William Lawton), OBE 1996; actress; *b* 7 Feb. 1923; *d* of Albert Broadbent and Georgina (*née* Hill); *m* 1954, William Lawton (*d* 2008); one *s*, and one adopted *s* (one adopted *d* decd). *Educ:* Hathershaw Council Sch., Lancs. Pantomimes: London Hippodrome, 1936; Manchester Palace, 1937; Alhambra, Glasgow, 1938; Oldham Repertory, 1939–44; followed by Peterborough, Colchester, Westcliff-on-Sea. ENSA, Italy, during War of 1939–45. Came to London, 1945, and appeared in West End Theatres: Peace in our Time; Travellers' Joy; Accolade; Lyric Revue; Globe Revue; Simon and Laura; The Water Gypsies; Gentlemen Prefer Blondes; Six of One; Too True to be Good; Hello, Dolly!; They Don't Grow on Trees; Rookery Nook, Her Majesty's, 1979; The Merry Wives of Windsor, Regent's Park, 1984; She Stoops to Conquer, Nat. Theatre, 1985; The Apple Cart, Haymarket, 1986; Charlie Girl, Victoria Palace, 1986, Birmingham, 1988; Pygmalion, Plymouth, New York, 1987; 70, Girls, 70, Vaudeville, 1991; The Birthday Party, NT, 1994; Hello Dora (one-woman show), tour, 1996; Miss Prism, in The Importance of Being Earnest, tour, 1999; Talking Heads, tour, 2000; The Full Monty, Prince of Wales, 2002; Chichester Festival seasons, 1971–74 and 1995–97; London Palladium season, 1971; London Palladium Pantomime season, 1973–74. *Films include:* The Fallen Idol, 1949; A Taste of Honey, 1961 (British Acad. Award); Two a Penny, 1968; Great St Trinian's Train Robbery, 1970; Apartment Zero, 1989; Angel for May, 2002. *TV series:* appearances on A to Z; Sunday Night at the London Palladium; According to Dora, 1968; Both Ends Meet, 1972; Mother's Ruin, 1994; Last of the Summer Wine, 2001–05. Cabaret in Canada, Hong Kong and Britain. Made several recordings.

Publications: According to Dora (autobiog.), 1987, 2nd edn 1996. *Recreations:* reading, patchwork quilts, cooking, dog walking, tapestry. *Died 23 July 2014.*

BRYANT, (Alan) Christopher, OBE 1995; Life President, Bryant Group plc (formerly Bryant Holdings Ltd), since 1992 (Managing Director, 1960–88; Chairman, 1962–92); *b* 28 July 1923; *s* of Ebenezer John Bryant and Ivy Maud Bryant (*née* Seymour); *m* 1951, Jean Mary Nock (*d* 2002); four *d*. *Educ:* West House School, Birmingham; Malvern Coll.; Birmingham Univ. (BSc (Hons)). FCIOB 1958. Engineer Officer, Fleet Air Arm, 1944–47 (Sub-Lieut, RNVR); Project Manager, 1946–48, Director, 1948–86, C. Bryant & Son Ltd. Non-exec. Dir, BSG International plc, 1985–94. Chm., 1969–95, Pres., 1987–, Birmingham YMCA; Hon. Treas., Nat. Council of YMCAs, 1991–95. Hon. DEng Birmingham, 1992. *Recreations:* sailing, walking. *Club:* Naval. *Died 14 July 2012.*

BRYANT, Thomas, CMG 1995; HM Diplomatic Service, retired; Consul General, Zürich, 1991–95; *b* 1 Nov. 1938; *s* of George Edward Bryant and Ethel May Bryant (*née* Rogers); *m* 1st, 1961, Vivien Mary Theresa Hill (marr. diss. 2002); twin *s* one *d*; 2nd, 2002, Jean Hilary Todd (*née* Colbert). *Educ:* William Ellis Sch., London; Polytechnic of Central London (DMS). Nat. service, Army, 1957–59. Entered FO, 1957; Hong Kong, 1963; Peking, 1963–65; Vice Consul, Frankfurt, 1966–68; Second Sec., Tel Aviv, 1968–72; First Sec., FCO, 1973–76; Vienna, 1976–80; FCO, 1980–82, Counsellor, 1982; Hd of Finance Dept, 1982–84; Consul-Gen., Munich, 1984–88; Dep. High Comr, Nairobi, 1988–91. *Recreations:* cricket, soccer, tennis, classical music, laughter. *Address:* 36 Fulmar Drive, East Grinstead, W Sussex RH19 3NN. *Died 2 April 2013.*

BRYCE, Gabe Robb, OBE 1959; Sales Manager (Operations), British Aircraft Corporation, 1965–75; occupied in breeding dogs and boarding cats, until retirement from animal world, 1987; *b* 27 April 1921; *m* 1943, Agnes Lindsay; one *s* one *d*. *Educ:* Glasgow High School. Served in RAF, 1939–46. Vickers-Armstrongs (Aircraft) Ltd, 1946–60 (Chief Test Pilot, 1951–60). Participated as First or Second Pilot, in Maiden Flights of following British Aircraft: Varsity; Nene Viking; Viscount 630, 700 and 800; Tay Viscount; Valiant; Pathfinder; Vanguard; VC-10; BAC 1–11; Chief Test Pilot, British Aircraft Corporation, 1960–64. Fellow Soc. of Experimental Test Pilots (USA), 1967. Sir Barnes Wallis Meml Medal, GAPAN, 1980. *Recreations:* squash, tennis. *Address:* 8 Rowan Green, Rosslyn Park, Weybridge, Surrey KT13 9NF. *T:* (01932) 858996. *Died 7 May 2014.*

BRYCE-SMITH, Prof. Derek, PhD, DSc; CChem, FRSC; Professor of Organic Chemistry, University of Reading, 1965–89, part-time, 1989–91, then Emeritus; *b* 29 April 1926; *s* of Charles Philip and Amelia Smith; *m* 1st, 1956, Marjorie Mary Anne Stewart (*d* 1966); two *s* two *d*; 2nd, 1969, Pamela Joyce Morgan (*d* 2003); two step *d*. *Educ:* Bancroft's Sch., Woodford Wells; SW Essex Tech. Coll.; West Ham Municipal Coll.; Bedford Coll., London. Research Chemist: Powell Duffryn Res. Ltd, 1945–46; Dufay-Chromex Ltd, 1946–48; Inst. of Petroleum Student, Bedford Coll., 1948–51; ICI Post-doctoral Fellow, KCL, 1951–55; Asst Lectr in Chem., KCL, 1955–56; Lectr in Chem., 1956–63, Reader, 1963–65, Reading Univ. Founding Chm., European Photochem. Assoc., 1970–72; Founding Vice-Chm., UK Br., Internat. Solar Energy Soc., 1973–74; Chm., RSC Photochemistry Gp, 1981–92. John Jeyes Endowed Lectureship and Silver Medal, RSC, 1984–85. *Publications:* (with R. Stephens) Lead or Health, 1980, 2nd edn 1981; (with E. Hodgkinson) The Zinc Solution, 1986; (RSC Senior Reporter and contrib.) Photochemistry: a review of chemical literature, vols 1–25, 1970–94; contribs to learned jls in the fields of photochem., organometallic chem., environmental chem. and philosophy of sci. *Recreations:* gardening, making music. *Died 24 June 2011.*

BRYSON, Col (James) Graeme, OBE (mil.) 1954; TD 1949; JP; Vice Lord-Lieutenant of Merseyside, 1979–89; *b* 4 Feb. 1913; 3rd *s* of John Conway Bryson and Oletta Bryson; *m* Jean (*d* 1981), *d* of Walter Glendinning; two *s* four *d* (and one *s* decd). *Educ:* St Edward's Coll.; Liverpool Univ. (LLM 1935); Open Univ. (BSc 1994). Admitted solicitor, 1935. Commnd 89th Field Bde RA (TA), 1936; served War, RA, 1939–45 (Lt-Col 1944); comd 470 (3W/Lancs) HAA Regt, 1947–52, and 626 HAA Regt, 1952–55; Bt-Col 1955; Hon. Col 33 Signal Regt (V), 1975–81. Sen. Jt Dist Registrar and Liverpool Admiralty Registrar, High Court of Justice, Liverpool, and Registrar of Liverpool County Court, 1947–78; Dep. Circuit Judge, Northern Circuit, 1978–82. A Gen. Comr of Income Tax, 1968–88 (Chm., Merseyside Adv. Cttee, 1979–88). President: Assoc. of County Court Registrars, 1969; Liverpool Law Soc., 1969; W Lancs Co., 1959–79 (Hon. Life Pres., 1993), City of Liverpool, 1965–, NW Area, 1979–90, Royal British Legion; Merseyside Council of Ex-Service and Regtl Assocs, 1975–89 (Hon. Life Pres., 1989). Chm., Med. Appeal Tribunal, 1978–85; Member: Lord Chancellor's Cttee for enforcement of debts (Payne), 1965–69; IOM Commn to reform enforcement laws, 1972–74; Vice-Patron, Nat. Assoc. for Employment of Regular Sailors, Soldiers and Airmen, 1989– (Mem. Council, 1952–89); Life Vice President: RA Officers Assoc., 1996; RA Assoc., Liverpool, 1996. Kt, Hon. Soc. of Knights of the Round Table, 1987–. FRSA 1989. JP Liverpool, 1956; DL Lancs, 1965, later Merseyside. QCB 1961. KHS 1974; KCHS 1990; KCSG 1996. Hon. LLD Liverpool, 2011. Citizen of Honour, Liverpool City Council, 2009; Good Citizenship Award, John Moores Univ., 2009. *Publications:* (jtly) Execution, in Halsbury's Laws of England, 3rd edn 1976; Shakespeare in Lancashire, 1997; A Cathedral in My Time, 2000; (jtly) Liverpool Lawyers of the 20th Century, 2001; There's Poetry in my Veins, 2003; A Victorian Poet Policeman, 2009; Poppies and Pulpits, 2009; (contrib.) Oxford DNB. *Recreations:* local history, boating. *Address:* 36 Hillary Court, Freshfield Road, Formby, Merseyside L37 3PS. *T:* (01704) 834711. *Clubs:* Athenæum (Liverpool; Pres., 1969); Lancashire County Cricket. *Died 28 Sept. 2012.*

BUCHAN of Auchmacoy, Captain David William Sinclair; Chief of the Name of Buchan; *b* 18 Sept. 1929; *o s* of late Captain S. L. Trevor, late of Lathbury Park, Bucks, and Lady Olivia Trevor, *e d* of 18th Earl of Caithness; changed name from Trevor through Court of Lord Lyon King of Arms, 1949, succeeding 18th Earl of Caithness as Chief of Buchan Clan; *m* 1961, Susan Blanche Fionodbhar Scott-Ellis, *d* of 9th Baron Howard de Walden and 5th Baron Seaford, TD; three *s* one *d* (and one *s* decd). *Educ:* Eton; RMA Sandhurst. Commissioned 1949 into Gordon Highlanders; served Berlin, BAOR and Malaya; ADC to GOC, Singapore, 1951–53; retired 1955. Mem., London Stock Exchange. Sen. Partner, Messrs Gow and Parsons, 1963–72. Comr, Inland Revenue, 1974–76. Member: Queen's Body Guard for Scotland; The Pilgrims; Friends of Malta GC; Cook Soc., 1982–; Council, Royal Sch. of Needlework, 1987–96; Cons. Industrial Fund Cttee, 1988–97. Gov., London Clinic, 1988–95. Mem., Worshipful Company of Broderers (Master, 1992). Vice-President: Aberdeenshire CCC, 1962–; Bucks CCC, 1984–. JP Aberdeenshire, 1959–96; JP London, 1972–95. KStJ 1987 (OStJ 1981). *Recreations:* bridge, reading. *Address:* North Court, Clanfield, Oxon OX18 2RG. *Died 16 July 2015.*

BUCHAN, Janey, (Jane O'Neil Buchan); Member (Lab) Glasgow, European Parliament, 1979–94; *b* 30 April 1926; *d* of Joseph and Christina Kent; *m* 1945, Norman Findlay Buchan, MP (*d* 1990); one *s*. *Educ:* secondary sch.; commercial coll. Mem., Strathclyde Regl Council, 1974–79 (Vice-Chm., Educn Cttee). Former Chm., local consumer gp, Scottish Gas Consumers' Council. Trustee, Smith Art Gall. and Mus., Stirling, 1996–. Founder, Centre for Political Song, Glasgow Caledonian Univ. *Recreations:* books, music, theatre, watching television more carefully than ever especially after the Hutton enquiry. *Died 14 Jan. 2012.*

BUCHANAN, Rt Rev. (George) Duncan; Bishop of Johannesburg, 1986–2000; Priest-in-charge, St John's Parish, Houghton, 2001–11; *b* 23 April 1935; *s* of Wyndam Kelsey Fraser Buchanan and Phyllis Rhoda Dale Buchanan (*née* Nichols); *m* 1959, Diana Margaret Dacombe; two *d*. *Educ:* St John's Coll., Johannesburg; Rhodes Univ.,

Grahamstown (BA 1957); Ripon Hall, Oxford (GOE 1958); Gen. Theological Seminary (MDiv 1959). Curate, St Paul's Church, Durban, 1960; Rector, Parish of Kingsway, Natal, 1961–65; Diocesan Theol Tutor, Dio. Natal, 1963–65; Sub Warden, St Paul's Theol Coll., Grahamstown, 1966–76, Warden, 1976–86; Dean, St Mary's Cathedral, Johannesburg, May–Sept. 1986; Archdeacon of Albany, Diocese of Grahamstown, 1975–86. Chairman: Church Unity Commn, 1989–2000; Theol Educn by Extension Coll., 1993–2000; SA Anglican Theol Commn, 1995–2000; Co-ordinator, St Thomas Inst. for Leadership in Ministry, Dio. of Johannesburg, 2001–07. Hon. DD General Theological Seminary, 1987. *Publications:* The Counselling of Jesus, 1985; (ed) Meeting the Future: Christian leadership in South Africa, 1995. *Recreations:* carpentry, reading. *Address:* 35 East Street, East Town, Johannesburg 2195, South Africa. *T:* and *Fax:* (11) 7829201. *Died 8 Sept. 2012.*

BUCHANAN, Prof. James McGill; Holbert L. Harris University Professor, 1983–99, then Emeritus Professor, and Advisory General Director, Center for the Study of Public Choice, since 1988 (General Director, 1969–88), George Mason University; *b* 3 Oct. 1919; *s* of James Buchanan and Lila Scott; *m* 1945, Anne Bakke. *Educ:* Middle Tennessee State Coll. (BS 1940); Univ. of Tennessee (MA 1941); Univ. of Chicago (PhD 1948). Lieut, USNR, 1941–46. Professor of Economics: Univ. of Tennessee, 1950–51; Florida State Univ., 1951–56; Univ. of Virginia, 1956–62, 1962–68 (Paul G. McIntyre Prof.); UCLA, 1968–69; Virginia Polytechnic Inst., 1969–83 (Univ. Dist. Prof.). Fulbright Res. Scholar, Italy, 1955–56; Ford Faculty Res. Fellow, 1959–60; Fulbright Vis. Prof., Univ. of Cambridge, 1961–62. Fellow, Amer. Acad. of Arts and Scis; Dist. Fellow, Amer. Econ. Assoc. (Seidman Award, 1984). Hon. Dr, US and overseas Univs. Nobel Prize for Economics, 1986. *Publications:* Prices, Incomes and Public Policy (jtly), 1954; Public Principles of Public Debt, 1958; The Public Finances, 1960; Fiscal Theory and Political Economy, 1960; (with G. Tullock) The Calculus of Consent, 1962; Public Finance in Democratic Process, 1966; The Demand and Supply of Public Goods, 1968; Cost and Choice, 1969; (with N. Devletoglou) Academia in Anarchy, 1970; (ed jtly) Theory of Public Choice, 1972; (with G. F. Thirlby) LSE Essays on Cost, 1973; The Limits of Liberty, 1975; (with R. Wagner) Democracy in Deficit, 1977; Freedom in Constitutional Contract, 1978; What Should Economists Do?, 1979; (with G. Brennan) The Power to Tax, 1980; (ed jtly) Towards a Theory of the Rent-Seeking Society, 1980; (ed jtly) The Theory of Public Choice II, 1984; (with G. Brennan) The Reason of Rules, 1985; Liberty Market and State, 1985; (jtly) El Análisis Económico de lo Politico, 1985; (ed jtly) Deficits, 1987; Economics: between predictive science and moral philosophy, 1987; Economía y Política, 1987; Maktens Gränser, 1988; (ed) Explorations into Constitutional Economics, 1989; Essays on the Political Economy, 1989; Stato, mercato e libertà, 1989; The Economics and the Ethics of Constitutional Order, 1991; Constitutional Economics, 1991; Better than Plowing and Other Personal Essays, 1992; Ethics and Economic Progress, 1994; (ed jtly) Return to Increasing Returns, 1994; Post-Socialist Political Economy, 1997; (with R. Congleton) Politics by Principle, not Interest, 1998. *Address:* Center for the Study of Public Choice, Buchanan House, George Mason University, Fairfax, VA 22030, USA; PO Drawer G, Blacksburg, VA 24063–1021, USA. *Died 9 Jan. 2013.*

BUCHANAN, Sir John (Gordon St Clair), Kt 2012; PhD; Chairman: Smith & Nephew plc, 2006–14 (Deputy Chairman, 2005–06); ARM Holdings plc, 2012–14; *b* Auckland, NZ, 9 June 1943; *s* of Russell Penman Buchanan and Marguerite, (Ginette), St Clair Stuart (*née* Cabouret); *m* 1967, Rosemary June Johnston; one *s* one *d*. *Educ:* Auckland Grammar Sch.; Univ. of Auckland (MSc 1st cl. Hons, PhD Organic Chemistry); Harvard Business Sch. (PMD 1977). Post-Doctoral Res. Fellow, Wolfson Coll., Oxford, 1968–69; British Petroleum, 1970–2003: various operational, commercial, and marketing posts for BP Oil, 1970–76; seconded to Central Policy Rev. Staff, Cabinet Office, 1976–77; BP Switzerland, 1978–80; Manager, Mkting and Ops, BP NZ, 1980–82; Asst Gen. Manager, Supply Dept, 1982–85; Gen. Manager, Gp Corporate Planning, 1985–88; Chief Operating Officer and Dep. Chief Exec., BP Chemicals, 1988–95; Gp Treas. and Chief Exec., BP Finance, 1995–96; Exec. Dir and Chief Financial Officer, BP (formerly BP Amoco) plc, 1996–2002. Non-executive Director: Boots Co., 1997–2003; Astra Zeneca plc, 2002–10; Vodafone plc, 2003–12 (Dep. Chm., 2006–12); Sen. Ind. Dir, BHP Billiton plc, 2003–. Mem., Accounting Standards Bd, 1997–2001. Chm., Internat. Chamber of Commerce (UK), 2008–. Trustee: Univ. of Auckland UK Trust, 2001– (Chm., 2001–10); UK Friends of Auckland Grammar Sch., 2005–; Chm., UK Trustees, Christchurch Earthquake Appeal, 2010–. Fellow, Univ. of Auckland, 2008. Augusta Award, Auckland Grammar Sch., 2007. *Recreations:* golf, the arts, Polynesian culture. *Address:* c/o Smith & Nephew plc, 15 Adam Street, WC2N 6LA. *Clubs:* Tandridge Golf (Surrey); Parkstone Golf (Dorset); Royal Auckland Golf, Remuera Golf (Auckland, NZ). *Died 13 July 2015.*

BUCHANAN, John M.; *see* Macdonald-Buchanan.

BUCHANAN, Vice-Adm. Sir Peter (William), KBE 1980; *b* 14 May 1925; *s* of Lt-Col Francis Henry Theodore Buchanan and Gwendolen May Isobel (*née* Hunt); *m* 1953, Audrey Rowena Mary (*née* Edmondson); three *s* one *d*. *Educ:* Malvern Coll. Joined RN, 1943; served in HM Ships King George V, Birmingham, destroyers and frigates; comd HMS Scarborough 1961–63; Ops Officer, Far East Fleet, 1963–65 (despatches); HMS Victorious, 1965–67; British Antarctic Survey, 1967–68; comd HMS Endurance, 1968–70; MoD, 1970–72; comd HMS Devonshire, 1972–74; MoD, 1974–76; ADC to the Queen, 1975–76; Rear-Adm. 1976; Naval Sec., 1976–78; Vice-Adm., 1979; Chief of Staff, Allied Naval Forces Southern Europe, 1979–82. Mem., Lord Chancellor's Panel of Independent Inspectors, 1983–95. Younger Brother of Trinity House, 1963. Liveryman, Shipwrights' Co., 1984; Master, Guild of Freemen of City of London, 1996. MRIN; FNI. *Recreation:* sailing. *Clubs:* Caledonian; Royal Yacht Squadron. *Died 23 Nov. 2011.*

BUCHANAN, Sir Robert Wilson, (Sir Robin), Kt 1991; DL; CA; Chairman, NHS Supplies Authority, 1991–95; *b* 28 Sept. 1930; *s* of Robert Downie and Mary Hobson Buchanan; *m* Naomi Pauline (*née* Lewis) (*d* 2010); three *d* by a previous marriage. *Educ:* Dumbarton Acad.; Glasgow Acad. Mem., Inst. of Chartered Accts of Scotland, 1953. CA, Bath, 1965–. Chairman: Bath DHA, 1982–88; Wessex RHA, 1988–93; Vice-Chm., NHS Training Authy, 1983–88; Mem., Bath City Council, 1978–86. Mem. Council, Bath Internat. Fest., 1970–88 (Chm., 1982–86, 1988); Trustee, Robin Buchanan Charitable Trust, 1985–. Mem. Council, 1985–2001, Treasurer, 1995–2001, Bath Univ.; Mem. Council, Southampton Univ., 1990–93; Gov., Millfield Sch., 1992–2000 (Treas., 1963–92; Chm., 1997–2000). DL Avon, 1992, Somerset, 1996. *Recreations:* golf, beach walking. *Address:* Belmont Cottage, Belmont Road, Combe Down, Bath BA2 5JR. *T:* (01225) 833768; Cassia Heights, Royal Westmoreland, Barbados. *Died 19 Sept. 2013.*

BUCKLEY, Martin Christopher Burton; Chief Registrar in Bankruptcy, Companies Court, High Court of Justice, 1997–2001, and Clerk of Restrictive Practices Court, 1988–2001; *b* 5 Oct. 1936; *s* of late Hon. Dr Colin Burton Buckley and Evelyn Joyce Buckley (*née* Webster); *m* 1964, Victoria Gay, *d* of Dr Stanhope Furber; two *s* three *d*. *Educ:* Rugby School; Trinity College, Oxford (MA). Called to the Bar, Lincoln's Inn, 1961, Bencher, 1996; practised at Chancery Bar, 1962–88; Registrar in Bankruptcy, 1988–97. *Publications:* (ed jtly) Buckley on the Companies Acts, 14th edn 1981 (1st edn 1873–9th edn 1909 by grandfather, Henry Burton Buckley, later 1st Baron Wrenbury). *Recreations:* amateur theatre, choral singing. *Address:* Crouchers, Rudgwick, Horsham, W Sussex RH12 3DD. *Died 11 Dec. 2014.*

BUIST, John Latto Farquharson, (Ian), CB 1990; Under Secretary, Foreign and Commonwealth Office (Overseas Development Administration), 1976–90; *b* 30 May 1930; *s* of late Lt-Col Thomas Powrie Buist, RAMC, and Christian Mary (*née* Robertson); partner, 1981, J. E. Regensburg,

(Dennis Regensburg) (*d* 1988). *Educ:* Dalhousie Castle Sch.; Winchester Coll.; New Coll., Oxford (MA). Asst Principal, CO, 1952–54; seconded Kenya Govt, 1954–56; Principal, CO, 1956–61; Dept of Tech. Co-operation, 1961–62; Brit. High Commn, Dar-es-Salaam, 1962–64; Consultant, E African Common Services Org./Community, 1964–69; Sec., Commn on E African Co-operation and related bodies, 1966–69; Asst Sec., Min. of Overseas Develt, 1966–76. Director: PLAN International (UK), 1990–2012; PLAN Inc., 1991–2002; Interact Worldwide, 2009–12. Co-founder, Classical Assoc. of Kenya; Member: Thames Philharmonic (formerly John Bate) Choir; United Reformed Church; Lesbian and Gay Christian Movement. *Recreation:* choral singing. *Address:* 9 West Hill Road, SW18 1LH. *Died 19 Oct. 2012.*

BUKHT, Mirza Michael John, (Michael Barry), OBE 1996; food journalist; Programme Controller, Classic FM Radio, 1992–97; *b* 10 Sept. 1941; *s* of Mirza Jawan Bukht and Lilian Ray Bukht (*née* Oaten); *m* 1964, Jennie Mary Jones; one *s* three *d*. *Educ:* Haberdashers' Aske's Sch.; King's Coll. London (BA Hons). BBC general trainee, 1963; Producer, Tonight prog., 1965; Prog. Controller, JBC, Jamaica, 1967; Dep. Editor, 24 Hours, BBC TV, 1969; Editor, Special Projects, BBC TV, 1970; Prog. Controller, Capital Radio, 1972; Principal, Nat. Broadcasting Sch., 1979; Man. Dir, Invicta Radio, 1985; Gp Prog. Dir, GWR Gp, 1988. Chm., Kentish Fare Bd, 1994–2006. Mem. Cttee, Early Dance Circle, 1991–. Chairman: Canterbury Multi-Cultural Assoc., 2001–04; Ethnic and Minorities Council, 2005–. President: Canterbury Arts Council; Canterbury Music Club. Gov., St Edmund's Sch., Canterbury, 1997–2006. FRSA 1995; Fellow, Radio Acad., 1996. Hon. DCL Kent, 2002. *Publications:* (as Michael Barry) 5 Food and Drink books, 1984–89; Food Processor Cookery, 1985; Complete Crafty Cook Book, 1988; Exotic Food, 1989, 2nd edn 1996; Michael Barry's Cook Book, 1991; Big Food and Drink Book, 1993; Great House Cookery, 1993; Classic Recipes, 1993; The Radio Times Cookery Guide, 1994; Entertaining with Food and Drink, 1995; Crafty French Cooking, 1995; Italian Food, 1997; The Classic FM Recipes, 2000. *Recreations:* music, dance, sailing, military history, food. *Address:* 6 Chantry Hall, Dane John, Canterbury, Kent CT1 2QS. *Died 4 Aug. 2011.*

BULL, (Oliver) Richard (Silvester); Headmaster, Rugby School, 1985–90; *b* 30 June 1930; *s* of Walter Haverson Bull and Margaret Bridget Bull; *m* 1956, Anne Hay Fife; two *s* four *d*. *Educ:* Rugby Sch.; Brasenose Coll. Oxford (MA). Mil. Service (1st Beds and Herts), 1949–51. Asst Master, Eton Coll., 1955–77 (Housemaster, 1968–77); Headmaster, Oakham Sch., Rutland, 1977–84. *Recreations:* music, walking, reading, ball games. *Address:* 13 The Paddocks, Presteigne, Powys LD8 2NJ. *Died 11 Sept. 2015.*

BULLOCK, (Edward) Anthony (Watson); HM Diplomatic Service, retired; *b* 27 Aug. 1926; *yr s* of late Sir Christopher Bullock, KCB, CBE, and Lady Bullock (*née* Barbara May Lupton); *m* 1953, Jenifer Myrtle, *er d* of Sir Richmond Palmer, KCMG, and Lady Palmer (*née* Margaret Isabel Abel Smith); two *s* one *d*. *Educ:* Rugby Sch. (Scholar; Running VIII); Trinity Coll., Cambridge (Exhibitioner; MA). Chm., Cambridge Univ. Cons. Assoc. Served The Life Guards, 1944–47. Joined Foreign Service, 1950; served: FO, 1950–52; Bucharest, 1952–54; Brussels, 1955–58; FO, 1958–61; La Paz, 1961–65; ODM, 1965–67; FCO, 1967–69; Havana, 1969–72; HM Treasury, 1972–74; Head of Pacific Dependent Territories Dept, FCO, 1974–77; Consul-Gen., Marseilles, 1978–83; Counsellor, FCO, 1983–85. Chm., Buckhorn Weston and Kington Magna Parish Council, 1993–95; Founder, Buckhorn Weston Village Community Trust, 1993 (Chm., 1993–2014). *Recreations:* walking, gardening, National Gardens Scheme, tree-planting, reading, charity work. *Address:* Weston House, Buckhorn Weston, Gillingham, Dorset SP8 5HG. *T:* (01963) 371005. *Clubs:* Oxford and Cambridge; Union (Cambridge). *Died 21 Feb. 2015.*

BUNCE, Michael John, OBE 2001; Director, 1997–2008, and Chairman, 1999–2008, International Broadcasting Convention (Member, Management Committee, 1992–94); *b* 24 April 1935; *er s* of late Roland John Bunce, DipArch, ARIBA, and Dorrie Bunce (*née* Woods); *m* 1961, Tina Sims (*d* 2014); one *s* two *d* (and one *s* decd). *Educ:* St Paul's Sch.; Kingston Coll. Nat. Service, RAF. Joined BBC as engineer; subseq. Studio Manager; Tape Editor, European Enquiry, 6 Nations in Search of Their History (Italia Prize for Radio Documentary, 1961); Producer, People and Politics (World Service); Dir, Gallery; Producer: A Man Apart—The Murderer, 1965; Minorities in Britain; The Younger Generation; Italy and the Italians; Editor: The Money Programme, 1968–70; Nationwide, 1970–75; Chief Asst, TV Current Affairs and Editor, Tonight, 1975–78; Head: Information Services TV, 1978–82; Information Div., 1982–83; Controller, Information Services, 1983–91; Exec. Dir, RTS, 1991–2000. Member: Francis Cttee, 1977; EBU Working Party on Direct Elections, 1978; Adv. Bd, Univ. of Salford Media Centre, 1992–99; Comité d'Honneur, Internat. Television Symposium and Technical Exhibn, Montreux, 1995–98; Chm., Nat. Industries PR Officers Group, 1991–92. Trustee, Elizabeth R Broadcasting Fund, 2002–. Marshall Fund Vis. Fellow, USA, 1975. FRTS 1989. Shell Internat. Television Award, 1969; Gold Medal, RTS, 2009. *Recreations:* gardening, visiting fine buildings, fishing. *Address:* 51 Park Road, Hampton Hill, Middx TW12 1HX. *Club:* Century. *Died 31 Dec. 2014.*

BURCH, Maj.-Gen. Keith, CB 1985; CBE 1977 (MBE 1965); Director Personnel, Defence Staff, Ministry of Defence, 1985; Chapter Clerk, York Minster, 1985–95; *b* 31 May 1931; *s* of Christopher Burch and Gwendoline Ada (*née* James); *m* 1957, Sara Vivette Hales; one *s* two *d*. *Educ:* Bedford Modern Sch.; Royal Military Acad., Sandhurst. Commnd Essex Regt, 1951; DS Staff Coll., Camberley, 1968–69; Comd 3rd Bn Royal Anglian Regt, 1969–71; Asst Sec., Chiefs of Staff Cttee, MoD, 1972–75; Col GS HQ 2nd Armoured Div., 1975–78; Dir, Admin. Planning (Army), MoD, 1978–80; Indian National Defence Coll., New Delhi, 1981; Dep. Dir, Army Staff Duties, MoD, 1981–83; ACDS (Personnel and Logistics), 1984. Pres., N Yorks, RBL, 1999–2005. *Recreation:* retirement activities. *Address:* 11 Crowden Place, Harrowfield, Hamilton, New Zealand. *Died 27 March 2013.*

BURDEN, Derrick Frank; HM Diplomatic Service, retired; Counsellor and Head of Claims Department, Foreign and Commonwealth Office, 1973–78; *b* 4 June 1918; *s* of late Alfred Burden and Louisa Burden (*née* Dean); *m* 1942, Marjorie Adeline Beckley; two *d*. *Educ:* Bec Sch., London. Crown Agents, 1936. Served War, King's Royal Rifle Corps, 1939–41. Joined Foreign Office, 1945; Comr-Gen.'s Office, Singapore, 1950–53; 2nd Sec., Moscow, 1954–56; 2nd Sec., Tokyo, 1957–59; HM Consul, Lourenço Marques, 1959–61; FO, 1962–67 (Asst Head of Protocol Dept, 1965); HM Consul, Khorramshahr (Iran), 1967–69; 1st Sec., Nairobi, 1969–71; HM Consul, Luanda (Angola), 1972–73. *Recreations:* golf, gardening. *Address:* 12 Strathmore Drive, Charvil, Reading, Berks RG10 9QT. *T:* (0118) 934 0564. *Clubs:* Nairobi (Nairobi); Phyllis Court (Henley-on-Thames). *Died 8 April 2012.*

BURFORD, His Honour Jeremy Michael Joseph; QC 1987; a Circuit Judge, 1993–2010; *b* 3 June 1942; *s* of Alexander Joseph Burford and Arlene Burford. *Educ:* Rondebosch Boys' High Sch.; Diocesan Coll., Cape Town; BA Cape Town; MA, LLB Cantab; LLM Harvard. Called to the Bar, Inner Temple, 1968; a Recorder, 1991–93. *Died 10 March 2011.*

BURGES WATSON, Richard Eagleson Gordon; *see* Watson, R. E. G. B.

BURGESS, Gen. Sir Edward (Arthur), KCB 1982; OBE 1972; Deputy Supreme Allied Commander, Europe, 1984–87; Aide-de-Camp General to the Queen, 1985–87; *b* 30 Sept. 1927; *s* of Edward Burgess and Alice Burgess; *m* 1954, Jean Angelique Leslie Henderson; one *s* one *d*. *Educ:* All Saints Sch., Bloxham; Lincoln Coll., Oxford; RMA, Sandhurst. Commnd RA 1948; served Germany and ME, 1949–59; psc 1960; GSO 2 WO, 1961–63; served Germany and Far East, 1963–65; jssc 1966; Mil. Asst to C-in-C BAOR, 1966–67; GSO I (DS) Staff Coll., 1968–70; CO 25 Light Regt, RA, 1970–72; CRA 4th Div., 1972–74; Dir of

Army Recruiting, 1975–77; Dir, Combat Development (Army), 1977–79; GOC Artillery Div., 1979–82; Comdr, UK Field Army, and Inspector Gen. TA, 1982–84. Gentleman Usher to the Sword of State, 1988–97. Col Comdt, RA, 1982–92. Hon. Colonel: 6/7 (V) Bn Queen's Regt, 1991–92; 6/7 (V) Bn Princess of Wales's Royal Regt, 1992–97. Dep. Grand Pres., Royal (formerly British) Commonwealth Ex-Services League, 1996–2003; President: Royal British Legion, 1987–93; Army Football Assoc., 1982–88; Hon. Vice Pres., FA, 1982–88. Hon. Life Mem., RSL of Australia, 1991; Hon. Dominion Officer, Royal Canadian Legion, 2003. Freeman, City of London, 1988; Hon. Liveryman, Haberdashers' Co., 1990. *Publications:* articles in military jls. *Recreations:* fishing, music, reading, gardening. *Address:* c/o Lloyds, Haslemere, Surrey GU27 2JG. *Club:* Army and Navy. *Died 8 May 2015.*

BURGH, Sir John (Charles), KCMG 1982; CB 1975; President, Trinity College, University of Oxford, 1987–96 (Hon. Fellow, 1997); Chairman, Associated Board of the Royal Schools of Music, 1987–94; Director-General, British Council, 1980–87; *b* 9 Dec. 1925; *m* 1957, Ann Sturge; two *d*. *Educ:* Friends' Sch., Sibford; London Sch. of Economics (BSc Econ.; Leverhulme post-intermediate Schol.; Pres. of Union, 1949; Hon. Fellow, 1983). Asst Principal, BoT, 1950; Private Sec. to successive Ministers of State, BoT, 1954–57; Colonial Office, 1959–62; Mem., UK Delegation to UN Conf. on Trade and Develt, 1964; Asst Sec., DEA, 1964; Principal Private Sec. to successive First Secretaries of State and Secretaries of State for Econ. Affairs, 1965–68; Under-Sec., Dept of Employment, 1968–71; Dep.-Chm., Community Relations Commn, 1971–72; Deputy Secretary: Cabinet Office (Central Policy Rev. Staff), 1972–74; Dept of Prices and Consumer Protection, 1974–79; Dept of Trade, 1979–80. Member: Executive, PEP, 1972–78; Council, Policy Studies Inst., 1978–85; Council, RSA, 1982–85; Council, VSO, 1980–87; Acad. Council, Wilton Park, 1984–87; Exec. Cttee, Anglo-Austrian Soc., 1987–2000; Council, RIIA, 1993–95. Chairman: Nat. Opera Co-ordinating Cttee, 1991–2007 (Sec., 1972–91); Oxford Educnl Trust for Develt of the Arts, 1990–96; Dir, English Shakespeare Co., 1988–94. Chm. Ct of Governors, LSE, 1985–87 (Gov., 1980–2004); Vice-Chm., Yehudi Menuhin Sch., 1994–2009. Chm., New Berlioz Edition, 1993–. Patron, Dignity in Dying, 2011–. FRCM 1994. Hon. RNCM 1986. Hon. LLD Bath, 1987. *Recreations:* friends, music, the arts generally. *Address:* 2 Oak Hill Lodge, Oak Hill Park, NW3 7LN. *Club:* Royal Over-Seas League. *Died 12 April 2013.*

BURKE, Most Rev. Austin-Emile; Archbishop of Halifax (NS), (RC), 1991–98, then Emeritus; *b* 11 Jan. 1922; *s* of Arthur and Louise Burke. *Educ:* St Anne's Coll., Church Point (BA 1945); Holy Heart Seminary. Ordained priest, 1950; Suffragan Bishop of Yarmouth, 1968–91. *Address:* 215 Village Road, Herring Cove, NS B3V 1H2, Canada. *Died 12 Aug. 2011.*

BURKETT, Mary Elizabeth, OBE 1978; FRGS; FMA; Director of Abbot Hall Art Gallery, and Museum of Lakeland Life and Industry, 1967–86, and Borough Museum, Kendal, 1977–86; *b* 7 Oct. 1924; *d* of Ridley Burkett and Mary Alice Gaussen. *Educ:* Univ. of Durham (BA, Teachers' Cert.). FRGS 1978; FMA 1980. Taught art, craft, maths, etc, at Wroxall Abbey, 1948–54; Art and Craft Lectr, Charlotte Mason Coll., Ambleside, 1954–62; seven months in Turkey and Iran, 1962; Asst Dir, Abbot Hall, 1963–66. Formerly part-time Teacher of Art, Bela River Prison. Member: numerous cttees including National Trust (NW Region), 1978–85; Carlisle Diocesan Adv. Cttee, 1980–96; Carlisle Cathedral Fabric Cttee, 1991–2001. Dir, Border Television, 1982–93. Round the World trip, lecturing in Hong Kong, Perth (WA), NY as well as seeing the Great Wall of China, 1986. Pres. and Founding Mem., Internat. Feltmakers' Assoc. FRSA 1983; Fellow, Huguenot Soc., 1986. Hon. Fellow, Univ. of Cumbria, 2007 (Hon. Fellow, Cumbria Inst. of Arts, 2005). Hon. MA Lancaster, 1997. Leverhulme Award (to continue research on Lake District portraits), 1986–88. *Publications:* The Art of the Felt Maker, 1979; Kurt Schwitters (in the Lake District), 1979; (with David Sloss) William Green of Ambleside, 1984; (with David Sloss) Read's Point of View, 1995; (with Val Rickerby) Percy Kelly: a Cumbrian artist, 1997; Sutton and his Circle: the Cockermouth School of painting 1750–1880, 2001; Christopher Steele 1733–67 of Acre Walls, Egremont, George Romney's Teacher, 2003; (with G. Malet de Carteret) The Beckoning East: a journey through Persia and Turkey in 1962, 2006; (with V. M. Rickenby) A Softer Landscape: the life and work of Jenny Cowen, 2007; contrib. art and archaeol jls, and gall. and museum catalogues. *Recreations:* travel, bird watching, photography, writing, doing research into more Cumbrian artists, lecturing, picking up stones. *Address:* Isel Hall, Cockermouth, Cumbria CA13 0QG. *Died 12 Nov. 2014.*

BURNET, Sir James William Alexander, (Sir Alastair Burnet), Kt 1984; journalist; *b* 12 July 1928; *s* of late Alexander and Schonaid Burnet, Edinburgh; *m* 1958, Maureen Campbell Sinclair. *Educ:* The Leys Sch., Cambridge; Worcester Coll., Oxford. Sub-editor and leader writer, Glasgow Herald, 1951–58; Commonwealth Fund Fellow, 1956–57; Leader writer, The Economist, 1958–62; Political editor, Independent Television News, 1963–64; Editor, The Economist, 1965–74; Editor, Daily Express, 1974–76; broadcaster with ITN, 1976–91; Assoc. Editor, News at Ten, 1982–91. Ind. Dir, Times Newspapers Hldgs Ltd, 1982–2002; Dir, United Racecourses Hldgs Ltd, 1985–94. Member: Cttee of Award, Commonwealth Fund, 1969–76; Cttee on Reading and Other Uses of English Language, 1972–75; Monopolies Commn specialist panel on newspaper mergers, 1973–91; Council, Banking Ombudsman, 1985–96; Hon. Vice-Pres., Inst. of Journalists, 1990. Richard Dimbleby Award, BAFTA, 1966, 1970, 1979; Judges' Award, 1981, Hall of Fame, 1999, RTS. *Address:* 43 Hornton Court, Campden Hill Road, W8 7RU. *T:* (020) 7937 7563. *Died 20 July 2012.*

BURNETT, Air Chief Marshal Sir Brian (Kenyon), GCB 1970 (KCB 1965; CB 1961); DFC 1942; AFC 1939; Chairman, All England Lawn Tennis Club, Wimbledon, 1974–83; *b* 10 March 1913; *s* of late Kenneth Burnett and Anita Catherine Burnett (*née* Evans); *m* 1944, Valerie Mary (*née* St Ludger) (*d* 2003); two *s*. *Educ:* Charterhouse; Wadham Coll., Oxford (BA 1934; Hon. Fellow, 1974). Joined RAFO 1932; RAF 1934; Long Distance Record Flight of 7,158 miles from Egypt to Australia, Nov. 1938. Served War of 1939–45, in Bomber Command, incl. CO 51 Sqdn, 1942, and FTC; Co. 33 Air Navigation Sch., RAF Mount Hope, Canada, 1942–43; SASO 25 Gp, 1944; RAF Staff Coll. Course, 1944; Directing Staff, RAF Staff Coll., 1945–47; UN Military Staff Cttee, New York, 1947–48; Joint Planning Staff, 1949–50; SASO HQ No. 3 (Bomber) Group, 1951–53; CORAF Gaydon, 1954–55; ADC to the Queen, 1953–57; Director of Bomber and Reconnaissance Ops, Air Ministry, 1956–57; Imperial Defence Coll., 1958; Air Officer Administration, HQ Bomber Command, 1959–61; AOC No 3 Gp, Bomber Command, 1961–64; Vice-Chief of the Air Staff, 1964–67; Air Secretary, MoD, 1967–70; C-in-C, Far East Command, Singapore, 1970–71; retired 1972. Air ADC to the Queen, 1969–72. Pres., Squash Rackets Assoc., 1972–75. *Recreations:* tennis, squash rackets, golf, ski-ing. *Address:* Heather Hill, Littleworth Road, Sands, Farnham, Surrey GU10 1JN. *Clubs:* Royal Air Force; Vincent's (Oxford); All England Lawn Tennis (Vice-Pres., 1983–); Jesters Squash; International Lawn Tennis Clubs of Great Britain, USA, France, Australia, The Netherlands, Spain and Japan. *Died 16 Sept. 2011.*

BURNHAM, Peter Michael; Partner, 1970–93, Consultant, 1993–95, Coopers & Lybrand; *b* 13 May 1935; *s* of late Frank Burnham and Winifred Eileen Burnham (*née* Fyson); *m* 1963, Jill (*d* 2010), *d* of Comdr Langton Gowlland, RN; two *d*; partner, Helen, *widow* of Dr Tommie Allan. *Educ:* Eltham Coll.; Bristol Univ. (BA 1956). JDipMA. FCMA 1963; FCA 1969. With Sturges Fraser Cave & Co., 1956–59; served as Pilot Officer, RAF, 1959–61 (Sword of Honour); with Coopers & Lybrand, 1961–95: Dep. Man. Dir, Consulting Practice, 1981–88. Bd Mem., Historic Bldgs and Monuments Commn (English Heritage), 1984–88; Dir, UK Council for Computing Develt, 1984–88; Dir and Dep. Chm., E

London TEC, 1989–93; Dir, Satellite Observing Systems Ltd, 1993–95, 1998–2005; Mem., Adv. Cttee, HM Inspectorate of Pollution, 1994–95; Mem. Adv. Cttee, 1994–95, Bd Mem., 1995–97, Environment Agency. Member: Archbps' Commn on Cathedrals, 1992–94; Synod Follow-up Gp, 1995–96. *Publications:* various articles in professional jls. *Recreations:* sailing, travelling, music. *Address:* The Old Coach House, Sheep Lane, Midhurst, W Sussex GU29 9NT. *T:* and *Fax:* (01730) 812841; La Cumbre, Camino del Morro, 18697 La Herradura, Spain. *T:* and *Fax:* (958) 827426. *E:* pmburnham@waitrose.com. *Clubs:* Royal Air Force, Royal Thames Yacht. *Died 6 April 2012.*

BURNS, David Allan, CMG 1993; CBE 2003; HM Diplomatic Service, retired; Founder Chairman, Foreign and Commonwealth Office Association, 1999–2003; *b* 20 Sept. 1937; *s* of Allan Robert Desmond Burns, GM, and Gladys Frances Dine; *m* 1971, Inger Ellen Kristiansson; one *s* one *d*. *Educ:* Brentwood Sch., Essex. Served HM Forces, 1956–58. Language student and Third Secretary, British Embassy, Belgrade, 1962–65; Second Secretary, Bangkok, 1966–68; First Secretary, Washington, 1969–72; Head of Chancery, Belgrade, 1973–76; Asst Head of Arms Control Dept, FCO, 1976–79; Counsellor, Bangkok, 1979–83; Consul General, Boston, 1983–87; Hd of N America Dept, FCO, 1988–91; EU Monitor in Yugoslavia, 1991; Ambassador to Cambodia, 1991–94; Ambassador to Finland, 1995–97. Retirement Liaison Officer, FCO, 1998–99. *Recreations:* France, cinema. *Died 5 Oct. 2012.*

BURNS, James; JP; DL; Member, Strathclyde Regional Council, 1974–95 (Convener, 1982–86); *b* 8 Feb. 1931; *s* of late James Burns and of Mary Burns (*née* Magee); *m* 1959, Jean Ward; two *s*. *Educ:* St Patrick's Sch., Shotts; Coatbridge Tech. Coll. Engineer with NCB, 1966–71. Member: Lanark CC, 1967–75; Lanarks Health Bd, 1973–77; Strathclyde Regional Council: Chm., Gen. Purposes Cttee, 1975–82; Vice-Convener, 1978–82. Chm. Vis. Cttee, HM Prison, Shotts, 1980–; Member: Commonwealth Games Council for Scotland, 1982–86; Main Organising Cttee, Commonwealth Games 1986, 1982–86. Vice President: Glasgow Western St Andrew's Youth Club, 1982–86; St Andrew's Ambulance Assoc., 1984–86. Hon. President: Strathclyde CRC, 1982–86; Princess Louise Scottish Hosp. (Erskine Hosp.), 1982–86; Strathclyde Charities Band Assoc., 1982–86; Scottish Retirement Council, 1984–86; Hon. Vice Pres., SNO Chorus, 1982–86; Patron: Strathclyde Youth Club Assoc., 1982–86; YMCA Sports Centre, 1982–86; Scottish Pakistani Assoc., 1984–86. Trustee, The Pearce Institute, 1983–86. JP Motherwell, 1972. DL Monklands, Motherwell, Hamilton, E Kilbride and Clydesdale, 1989. *Recreations:* fishing, golf. *Address:* 57-59 Springhill Road, Shotts ML7 5JA. *T:* (01501) 820187. *Died 13 Oct. 2011.*

BURNS, Prof. James Henderson, FBA 1992; Professor of the History of Political Thought, University College London, 1966–86, then Emeritus; *b* 10 Nov. 1921; *yr s* of late William Burns and Helen Craig Tait Henderson; *m* 1947, Yvonne Mary Zéla Birnie (*d* 2010), *er d* of late Arthur Birnie, MA, and Yvonne Marie Aline Louis; two *s* (and one *d* decd). *Educ:* George Watson's Boys' Coll., Edinburgh; Univ. of Edinburgh (MA); Balliol Coll., Oxford (MA); PhD Aberdeen. Sub-Editor, Home News Dept, BBC, 1944–45; Lectr in Pol Theory, Univ. of Aberdeen, 1947–60; Head of Dept of Politics, 1952–60; University College London: Reader in the History of Political Thought, 1961–66; Head of History Dept, 1970–75; Hon. Fellow, 1999. John Hinkley Vis. Prof., Dept of History, Johns Hopkins Univ., Baltimore, 1987; Lectures: Creighton, London Univ., 1986; Carlyle, Oxford Univ., 1988; Gifford, Aberdeen Univ., 1994. Gen. Editor, The Collected Works of Jeremy Bentham, 1961–79; Vice-Chm., Bentham Cttee, 1983–92 (Sec., 1966–78); Pres., Internat. Bentham Soc., 1986–92. FRHistS 1962; Hon. Vice-Pres., RHistS, 1986– (Hon. Sec., 1965–70; Vice-Pres., 1978–82). *Publications:* Scottish University (with D. Sutherland Graeme), 1944; Scottish Churchmen and the Council of Basle, 1962; Lordship, Kingship and Empire: the idea of monarchy 1400–1525, 1992; The True Law of Kingship: concepts of monarchy in early-modern Scotland, 1996; *contributor to:* (with S. Rose) The British General Election of 1951, by D. E. Butler, 1952; Essays on the Scottish Reformation, ed D. McRoberts, 1962; Mill: a collection of critical essays, ed J. B. Schneewind, 1968; Bentham on Legal Theory, ed M. H. James, 1973; Jeremy Bentham: ten critical essays, ed B. Parekh, 1974; Absolutism in Seventeenth Century Europe, ed J. Miller, 1990; The Church and Sovereignty c. 590–1918, ed D. Wood, 1991; Political Discourse in Early Modern Britain, ed N. Phillipson and Q. Skinner, 1993; Politics, Ideology and the Law in Early Modern Europe, ed A. E. Bakos, 1994; Imperium/Empire/Reich, ed F. Bosbach and H. Hiery, 1999; The Medieval World, ed P. Lineham and J. Nelson, 2001; The Church, the Councils and Reform, ed G. Christiansen et al, 2008; Bentham et la France, ed E. de Champs and J.-P. Cléro, 2009; *edited* (with H. L. A. Hart): Jeremy Bentham, An Introduction in the Principles of Morals and Legislation, 1970; Jeremy Bentham, A Comment on the Commentaries and A Fragment on Government, 1977; (with F. Rosen) Jeremy Bentham, Constitutional Code, vol. I, 1983; The Cambridge History of Medieval Political Thought c. 350–c. 1450, 1988; The Cambridge History of Political Thought 1450–1700, 1991; (with T. M. Izbicki) Conciliarism and Papalism, 1997; articles and reviews in: English Historical Review, Scottish Historical Review, Innes Review, Political Studies, History, Trans of RHistSoc, Historical Jl, Jl of Eccles. History, Records of the Scottish Ch History Soc., British Jl for the History of Science, History of European Thought, Intellectual History Review, etc. *Address:* 6 Chiltern House, Hillcrest Road, Ealing, W5 1HL. *T:* (020) 8998 9515. *Died 4 Nov. 2012.*

BURRETT, (Frederick) Gordon, CB 1974; Deputy Secretary, Civil Service Department, 1972–81; *b* 31 Oct. 1921; *s* of Frederick Burrett and Marion Knowles; *m* 1943, (Margaret) Joan Giddins; one *s* two *d*. *Educ:* Emanuel Sch.; St Catharine's Coll., Cambridge. Served in Royal Engrs, N Africa, Italy, Yugoslavia, Greece, 1942–45 (despatches). HM Foreign, subseq. Diplomatic, Service, 1946; 3rd Sec., Budapest, 1946–49; FO, 1949–51; Vice-Consul, New York, 1951–54; FO, 1954–57; 1st Sec., Rome, 1957–60; transf. to HM Treasury, 1960; Private Sec. to Chief Sec., Treasury, 1963–64; Asst Secretary: HM Treasury, 1964; Cabinet Office, 1967–68; Secretary: Kindersley Review Body on Doctors' and Dentists' Remuneration; Plowden Cttee on Pay of Higher Civil Service, 1967–68; Civil Service Dept, 1968, Under-Sec. 1969. Mem., Civil Service Pay Res. Unit Bd, 1978–81; conducted govt scrutiny of V&A and Sci. Museums, 1982; Adviser to Govt of Oman on CS reorganisation, 1984; led govt review of policies and operations of Commonwealth Inst., 1986; leader of review team to examine responsibilities and grading of dirs of nat. museums and galls, 1987; conducted review of sen. posts of Arts Council and BFI, 1987–88; Chm., Cttee of Inquiry into CS Pay, Hong Kong, 1988–89. Chairman: Redundant Churches Fund, later Churches Conservation Trust, 1982–95; Wagner Soc., 1984–88. FSA 1985. Cross of St Augustine, 1995. *Publications:* article on the watercolours of John Massey Wright (1777–1866) in vol. 54 of the Old Water-Colour Society's Club Annual. *Recreations:* music, walking, reading. *Died 27 Oct. 2015.*

BURROUGHS, Prof. Andrew Kenneth, FRCP; FMedSci; Professor of Hepatology, University College London, since 2002; Consultant Physician and Hepatologist, Royal Free Hospital, since 1993; *b* Beckenham, Kent, 26 May 1953; *s* of late Kenneth Douglas Burroughs and Vidia Burroughs (*née* Stredda); *m* 1st, 1979, Rajesvarie Nulliah (marr. diss. 1991); one *d*; 2nd, 1993, Clare Constantine Davey; one *s* one *d*. *Educ:* Overseas Sch. of Rome; Kent Coll., Canterbury; Sch. of Medicine, Univ. of Liverpool (MB ChB Hons 1976). MRCP 1978, FRCP 1991. Registrar in Gen. Medicine and Gastroenterol., Royal Free Hosp., London, 1979–81; Hon. Clin. Lectr, Royal Free Hosp. Sch. of Medicine, 1981–83; Lectr in Medicine and Hon. Sen. Registrar, 1983–87, Sen. Lectr and Hon. Consultant Physician, 1988–93, Royal Free Hosp. and Royal Free Hosp. Sch. of Medicine, subseq. UCL Med. Sch. Mem. Council, RCP, 2007–10. British Society of Gastroenterology: Mem. Council, 1993–96 and 2004–07; Chm., Liver Section, 2004–06; Vice-Pres.

(Hepatol.), 2011–. Member: Cttee, Eur. Assoc. for Study of the Liver, 1996–2000 (Sec., 1997–99); Council, United Eur. Gastroenterol. Fedn, 1999–2002; Council, Internat. Assoc. for Study of the Liver, 1999–2002; Council, Internat. Liver Transplant Soc., 2003–06; Chm., Eur. Liver and Intestine Assoc., 2009–12. Fellow: Eur. Bd Gastroenterol., 1999; Eur. Bd Transplant Medicine, 2011; FMedSci 2010. Hon. DSc (Med) Athens, 2012. Bengt Ihre Medal, Swedish Med. Soc., 2003; NHS ACCEA Platinum Clinical Excellence Award, 2012; Arthur Hurst Medal, British Soc. Gastroenterol., 2013; Eur. Assoc. for Study of the Liver Recognition Award, 2013; British Assoc. for Study of the Liver Dist. Service Award, 2013. Cavaliere Ufficiale, Ordine del Merito (Italy), 1989. *Publications:* Evidence-based Gastroenterology and Hepatology, 1999, 3rd edn 2010; (ed jtly and contrib.) Sherlock's Liver and Biliary Diseases, 12th edn 2011; Thank You for Life, 2010; contribs to Medicine and over 500 peer reviewed papers. *Recreations:* philately, tourism, history, listening to choral music. *E:* andrew.burroughs@nhs.net.
Died 15 March 2014.

BURROWS, General Eva, AC 1994 (AO 1986); General of the Salvation Army, 1986–93; *b* 15 Sept. 1929; *d* of Robert John Burrows and Ella Maria Burrows (*née* Watson). *Educ:* Brisbane State High School; Queensland Univ. (BA); London Univ. (PGCE); Sydney Univ. (MEd). Salvation Army: Missionary Educator, Howard Inst., Zimbabwe, 1952–67; Principal, Usher Inst., Zimbabwe, 1967–69; Vice-Principal 1970–73, Principal 1974–75, Internat. Coll. for Officers, London; Leader, Women's Social Services in GB and Ireland, 1975–77; Territorial Commander: Sri Lanka, 1977–79; Scotland, 1979–82; Australia, 1982–86. Hon. Dr of Liberal Arts, Ehwa Woman's Univ., Seoul, S. Korea, 1988; Hon. LLD: Asbury Coll., USA, 1988; Univ. of NSW, 1996; Hon. DD Olivet Univ., USA, 1993; Hon. DPhil Queensland, 1993; DUniv Griffith, 1994; Hon. STD Melbourne Coll. of Divinity, 2000. *Recreations:* classical music, reading, travel. *Address:* Unit 102, 193 Domain Road, South Yarra, Melbourne, Vic 3141, Australia. *T:* (3) 98209701, 0409 906198. *Died 20 March 2015.*

BURROWS, Rt Rev. Simon Hedley; Bishop Suffragan of Buckingham, 1974–85, Area Bishop, 1985–94; an Honorary Assistant Bishop, Diocese of Winchester, 1994–2012; *b* 8 Nov. 1928; *s* of late Very Rev. H. R. Burrows, and Joan Lumsden, *d* of Rt Rev. E. N. Lovett, CBE; *m* 1960, Janet Woodd; two *s* three *d*. *Educ:* Eton; King's Coll., Cambridge (MA); Westcott House, Cambridge. Curate of St John's Wood, 1954–57; Chaplain of Jesus Coll., Cambridge, 1957–60; Vicar of Wyken, Coventry, 1960–67; Vicar of Holy Trinity, Fareham, 1967–74, and Rector of Team Ministry, 1971–74. Hon. DLitt Buckingham, 1992. Sub-Prelate, Order of St John, 1992–96. *Address:* 8 Quarry Road, Winchester, Hants SO23 0JF. *T:* (01962) 853332. *Died 5 Aug. 2015.*

BURSTON, Sir Samuel (Gerald Wood), Kt 1977; OBE 1966; Grazier at Noss Estate, Casterton, Victoria, 1945–85; President, Australian Woolgrowers and Graziers Council, 1976–79; *b* 24 April 1915; *s* of Maj.-Gen. Sir Samuel Burston, KBE, CB, DSO, VD, late RAAMC, and late Lady Burston; *m* 1st, 1940, Verna Helen Peebles (*d* 1980); one *s* one *d*; 2nd, 1995, Phyllis Elaine Irwin (*d* 2000). *Educ:* St Peter's Coll., Adelaide (Sch. Captain, 1933). Major, AIF, 1939–45 (despatches). Chm., Country Fire Authority, Vic, 1964–65; Pres., Graziers Assoc. of Vic, 1973–76; Councillor, Nat. Farmers Fedn, 1979–82; Vice-Pres., Confedn of Aust. Industry, 1978–82; Member: Nat. Employers Policy Cttee, 1970–78; Australian Wool Industry Policy Cttee, 1976–78; Aust. Sci. and Technol. Council, 1976–85 (acting Chm., 1982); Aust. Stats Adv. Council, 1976–80; Aust. Govt Econ. Consultative Gp, 1976–82; Nat. Labour Consultative Council, 1976–82; Reserve Bank Bd, 1977–87. Aust. Trade Develt Council, 1979–85; Trade Practices Cons. Council, 1979–82; Aust. Manufacturing Council, 1979–84; Chm., Perpetual Executors & Trustee Co. of Australia, 1981–87. Mem., Victorian Selection Cttee, Winston Churchill Meml Trust, 1967–81; Chm., Aust. Pastoral Res. Trust, 1988–92. *Recreations:* golf, swimming. *Address:* 31/52 Brougham Place, North Adelaide, SA 5006, Australia. *T:* (8) 82672152. *Clubs:* Adelaide, Naval, Military and Air Force of South Australia (Adelaide); Royal Adelaide Golf.
Died 14 July 2015.

BURT, Maurice Edward; Deputy Director, Building Research Establishment, 1975–81; *b* 17 Nov. 1921; *s* of Reginald Edward Burt and Bertha Winifred Burt; *m* 1947, Monica Evelyn Amy; one *s* three *d*. *Educ:* Victoria Coll., Jersey; Taunton's Sch., Southampton; BA Hons London, 1948. CEng, MICE; FRAeS. Aircraft industry, 1938–48; RAE, 1948–66 (Supt, Airworthiness, 1961–66); Head of Structures Dept, Transport and Road Res. Lab., 1966–73; Head of Res. Management, Dept of Environment, 1973–75. *Publications:* technical reports and articles. *Recreations:* walking, gardening, bridge.
Died 30 April 2012.

BURTON, 3rd Baron *cr* 1897; **Michael Evan Victor Baillie;** *b* 27 June 1924; *er s* of Brig. Hon. George Evan Michael Baillie, MC, TD (*d* 1941) and *g s* of Baroness Burton (2nd in line); *S* grandmother, 1962; *m* 1st, 1948, Elizabeth Ursula Forster (marr. diss. 1977; she *d* 1993), *er d* of late Capt. A. F. Wise; two *s* two *d* (and two *d* decd); 2nd, 1978, Coralie Denise, 2nd *d* of late Claud R. Cliffe. *Educ:* Eton. Lieut, Scots Guards, 1944. Mem., CC, 1948–75, JP 1961–75, DL 1963–65, Inverness-shire; Mem., Inverness Dist Council, 1984–92. Grand Master Mason, 1993–99. *Heir: s* Hon. Evan Michael Ronald Baillie [*b* 19 March 1949; *m* 1970, Lucinda (marr. diss. 1984), *e d* of Robert Law, Newmarket; two *s* one *d*; *m* 1998, June Gordon]. *Address:* Dochgarroch Lodge, Inverness IV3 8JG. *T:* (01463) 861252. *Died 30 May 2013.*

BURTON, Sir Carlisle (Archibald), Kt 1979; OBE 1968; Barbados High Commissioner to the Bahamas, 1978–93; *b* 29 July 1921; *m* 1946, Hyacinth Marjorie Adelle Barker. *Educ:* Harrison Coll., Barbados, WI; Univ. of London (BA); School of Librarianship, Leeds; Univ. of Pittsburgh (MS Hyg.). MCLIP. Assistant Master, Harrison Coll., Barbados, 1943–50; Sen. Asst Master, Bishop's High Sch., Tobago, 1950–51; Public Librarian, Barbados, 1953–58; Permanent Secretary: Min. of Educn, 1958–63; Min. of Health, 1963–71; Perm. Sec., Prime Minister's Office, and Head of Civil Service, 1972–81; Chm., Public Services Commn, Barbados, 1981–87, Turks and Caicos Islands, 1988–90. Member: Commonwealth Observer Gp at elections in Southern Rhodesia (Zimbabwe), 1980 and in Malaysia, 1990; Caribbean Community Review Team, 1989–91. Director: Barbados National Bank, 1978–86 (Dep. Chm., 1982–86); Insurance Corp. of Barbados, 1978–86 (Chm., 1981–86). Chm., Cave Hill Campus Council, Univ. of the WI, Barbados, 1984–94; Mem. Council, Barbados Mus. and Historical Soc., 1994–2005. Life Mem., Barbados Nat. Trust. Chm., Barbados Assoc. of Retired Persons, 1995–98. Hon. LLD Univ. of WI, 1995. FRSA 1953. *Recreations:* (active) swimming, bridge, reading; (spectator) cricket (Life Member, Barbados Cricket Assoc.), athletics (Life Member, Barbados Amateur Athletic Assoc.), soccer. *Address:* Caradelle, Mountjoy Avenue, Pine Gardens, St Michael, Barbados, West Indies. *T:* 4293724. *Died 18 Sept. 2012.*

BURTON, Sydney Harold; JP; FCIB; Director, Gateway Building Society, 1981–88 (Managing Director, 1975–81); *b* 6 April 1916; *s* of Sydney Collard Burton and Maud Burton; *m* 1st, 1941, Jean Cowling (*d* 1985); one *d*; 2nd, 1986, Irene Robertson (*d* 2008). *Educ:* Belle Vue High Sch., Bradford. Various appts with Bradford Equitable Building Soc. (excl. war years), 1932–63; joined Temperance Permanent Building Soc., 1963; Jt Gen. Manager, 1965; Gen. Man. and Sec., 1972; following merger of Temperance Permanent and Bedfordshire Bldg Socs became Chief Gen. Man. and Sec. of Gateway Bldg Soc., 1974. Pres., Building Societies Inst., 1976–77; Mem. Council, Building Societies Assoc., 1971–81. JP Worthing, 1974. *Recreations:* music and theatre, social and religious work. *Address:* Cherry Trees, 52 Beehive Lane, Ferring, Sussex BN12 5NR. *T:* (01903) 244704.
Died 27 Sept. 2013.

BURY, Michael Oswell, OBE 1968; Consultant, Education and Training, Confederation of British Industry, 1986–87; *b* 20 Dec. 1922; *o s* of Lt-Col Thomas Oswell Bury, TD, and Constance Evelyn Bury; *m* 1954, Jean Threlkeld Wood, *d* of late William Threlkeld Wood; two *s* one *d*. *Educ:* Charterhouse; London Sch. of Economics. Served War of 1939–45: The Rifle Brigade (ranks of Rifleman to Captain), 1941–47. Steel Company of Wales, 1947–49; British Iron and Steel Fedn, 1949–64 (Dep. Dir, Labour and Trng, 1962–64); Dir, Iron and Steel Industry Trng Bd, 1964–70; Confederation of British Industry: Director, Educn, Trng and Technol., 1970–81; Dir, Corporate Affairs, 1981–84; Dir, Educn, Trng and Technol., 1985–86. Mem., Manpower Services Commn, 1974–81, 1985–87. *Recreations:* gardening, fishing, travel. *Died 1 June 2011.*

BUSH, His Honour Bryan; a Circuit Judge, 1983–2005; *b* 28 Nov. 1936; *s* of Maurice and Hetty Bush; *m* 1963, Jacqueline (*née* Rayman); two *s* one *d*. *Educ:* Leeds Grammar Sch.; Keble Coll., Oxford (MA). Called to the Bar, Gray's Inn, 1961; practising on NE Circuit, 1961–83; a Recorder of the Crown Court, 1978–83. *Recreation:* theatre. *Address:* c/o Leeds Crown Court, Leeds LS1 3BE. *Died 18 Aug. 2014.*

BUSH, Adm. Sir John (Fitzroy Duyland), GCB 1970 (KCB 1965 CB 1963); DSC 1941, and Bars, 1941, 1944; Vice-Admiral of the United Kingdom and Lieutenant of the Admiralty, 1979–84; *b* 1 Nov. 1914; *s* of late Fitzroy Bush, Beach, Glos; *m* 1938, Ruth Kennedy Horsey (*d* 2013); three *s* two *d*. *Educ:* Clifton Coll. Entered Navy, 1933; served in Destroyers throughout War. Commanded HM Ships: Belvoir, 1942–44; Zephyr, 1944; Chevron, 1945–46. Comdr Dec. 1946; Plans Div., Admiralty, 1946–48; graduated Armed Forces Staff Coll., USA, 1949; Comd, HMS Cadiz, 1950–51; Capt. June 1952; Dep. Sec. Chiefs of Staff Cttee, 1953–55; Capt. (F) Sixth Frigate Sqdn, 1955–56; Cdre, RN Barracks, Chatham, 1957–59; Dir of Plans, Admiralty, 1959–60; Rear-Adm. 1961; Flag Officer Flotillas (Mediterranean), 1961–62; Vice-Adm. 1963; Comdr, British Naval Staff and Naval Attaché, Washington, 1963–65; Vice-Chief of the Naval Staff, Ministry of Defence, 1965–67; C-in-C Western Fleet, C-in-C Eastern Atlantic, and C-in-C Channel (NATO), 1967–70; Admiral 1968; retd, 1970. Rear-Admiral of the UK, 1976–79. Dir, Gordon A. Friesen International Inc., Washington, DC, 1970–73. Adm., Texas (USA) Navy. Governor, Clifton Coll., 1973– (Chm. Council, 1978–81; Pres., 1982–87). Pres., Old Cliftonians Soc., 1967–69; Vice-Pres., Eighth Army Veterans Assoc., 1984–. Mem., E Hants District Council, 1974–76. *Recreation:* gardening. *Died 10 May 2013.*

BUTCHER, Willard Carlisle; Chairman and Chief Executive Officer, 1981–90, Chairman, Executive Committee, 1990–91, Chase Manhattan Bank (formerly Chase National Bank), New York City; *b* Bronxville, NY, 25 Oct. 1926; *s* of Willard F. Butcher and Helen Calhoun; *m* 1st, 1949, Sarah C. Payne (*d* 1955); two *d*; 2nd, 1956, Elizabeth Allen (*d* 1978); one *s* one *d*; 3rd, 1979, Carole E. McMahon; one *s*. *Educ:* Scarsdale High School, New York; Middlebury Coll., Vermont; Brown Univ., Rhode Island (BA; Fellow, 1981, then Emeritus). Served with USNR, 1944–45. Joined Chase National Bank, 1947; Asst Vice-Pres., 1956; Vice-Pres., 1958; Sen. Vice-Pres., 1961; assigned Internat. Dept, 1968; Exec. Vice-Pres. in charge of Dept, 1969; Vice-Chm. 1972; Pres. 1972–81; Chief Exec. Officer, 1979. Trustee, Amer. Enterprise Inst. (Chm., 1986–90). Director: Texaco Inc., 1981–98; Asarco Inc., 1974–98; International Paper Co., 1989–98. Hon. LLD: Brown; Pepperdine; Tulane; Hon. HLD Pace. *Died 25 Aug. 2012.*

BUTLER, Allan Geoffrey Roy; HM Diplomatic Service, retired; *b* 25 Aug. 1933; *s* of Frederick William Butler and Florence May Butler; *m* 1965, Pauline Rosalind Birch, SRN; three *d*. *Educ:* Chatham House School, Ramsgate. RAF, 1952–54. Colonial Office, 1954–66; served in Aden and Washington; Asst Private Sec. to Colonial Sec., 1965–66; HM Diplomatic Service, 1966; Birmingham University, 1966; Consul, Athens, 1967; First Sec., Athens, 1969, Georgetown, 1972, FCO, 1975; Head of Chancery, Dakar, 1977; Nat. Defence Coll., Latimer, 1981; Head of Parly Relations, FCO, 1981; Ambassador to Mongolian People's Republic, 1984; Dep. Perm. Rep., UK Delegn to the Council of Europe, 1987–89. Director: Strategy, subseq. Saatchi & Saatchi Govt Communications, 1989–92; Park South Management, 1991–99; Hexagon Communications, 1991–93; Park South Ltd, 1996–2006. Chm., Anglo-Mongolian Soc., 1990–93. Chairman: Age Concern Diss, 1999–2003; Age Concern St Albans, 2004–07. *Recreation:* listening to music. *Address:* 23 Farringford Close, Chiswell Green, St Albans AL2 3HS. *Died 1 May 2011.*

BUTLER, Prof. John Nicholas, (Nick), OBE 1988; RDI 1981; FCSD; industrial designer; Chairman and Joint Managing Director, BIB Design Consultants, 1989–2003; *b* 21 March 1942; *s* of William and Mabel Butler; *m* 1st, 1967, Kari Ann Morrison (marr. diss. 1999); two *s*; 2nd, 2001, Mary Thompson. *Educ:* Leeds Coll. of Art (NDD); Royal Coll. of Art (DesRCA, 1st Cl. Hons). FCSD (FSIAD 1975). Founded BIB Design Consultants, 1967; Sen. Partner, 1967–89. Prof. of Industrial Design, RCA, 1987–90; Vis. Prof., Massey Univ., 1993–; Vis. Prof. and Chm., Industrial Adv. Bd, Univ. of Central Lancs, 2002– (Sen. Fellow, 2003); Chm., Faculty Adv. Bd, Cardiff Sch. of Creative and Cultural Industries, Glamorgan Univ., 2008–. Chm., British Design Export Gp, 1980–81; Member: Design Bd, RSA, 1987–; Design Council, 1988–93 (Mem., Chairman's Review Team, 1993–); Chairman's Design Bd, BAA, 1992–; Royal Fine Art Commn, 1998–99. Master, RDI, 1995–97. Chm., Creative Lancs Partnership, 2005–. Hon. Sec., SIAD, 1978–81, Treasurer 1981–84. FRSA 1983 (Vice Pres., 1995–). Sen. FRCA 1997. *Recreations:* reading, music, country pursuits, watching Rugby, drawing, watching cricket. *Died 17 Feb. 2012.*

BUTLER, Prof. Marilyn Speers, (Lady Butler), DPhil; FBA 2002; Rector, Exeter College, 1993–2004, and Titular Professor of English Language and Literature, 1998–2004, University of Oxford; *b* 11 Feb. 1937; *d* of Sir Trevor Evans, CBE and Margaret (*née* Gribbin); *m* 1962, David Edgeworth Butler (Sir David Butler, CBE, FBA); two *s* (and one *s* decd). *Educ:* Wimbledon High Sch.; St Hilda's Coll., Oxford (MA; DPhil). Trainee and talks producer, BBC, 1960–62; Oxford University: full-time res. and teaching, 1962–70, Jun. Res. Fellow, 1970–73, St Hilda's Coll.; Fellow and Tutor, St Hugh's Coll., 1973–85; Lectr, 1985–86; King Edward VII Prof. of English Lit., 1986–93, and Fellow of King's Coll., 1988–93, Univ. of Cambridge. Pt-time Lectr, ANU, 1967; British Academy Reader, 1982–85. Mem., HEFCE, 1997–2000. *Publications:* Maria Edgeworth: a literary biography, 1972; Jane Austen and the War of Ideas, 1975; Peacock Displayed, 1979; Romantics, Rebels and Reactionaries, 1981, 2nd edn 1985; (ed) Burke, Paine, Godwin and the Revolution Controversy, 1984; (ed with J. Todd) Works of Mary Wollstonecraft, 1989; (ed) Maria Edgeworth, Castle Rackrent, and Ennui, 1992; (ed) Frankenstein, the 1818 edition, 1993; (ed) Northanger Abbey, 1995; (ed) Works of Maria Edgeworth, 1999–2003. *Address:* 38 Ritchie Court, 380 Banbury Road, Oxford OX2 7PW. *Died 11 March 2014.*

BUTLER, Sir Michael; *see* Butler, Sir R. M. T.

BUTLER, Sir Michael (Dacres), GCMG 1984 (KCMG 1980 CMG 1975); HM Diplomatic Service, retired; Ambassador and Permanent UK Representative to European Communities, Brussels, 1979–85; *b* 27 Feb. 1927; *s* of T. D. Butler, Almer, Blandford, and Beryl May (*née* Lambert); *m* 1951, Ann, *d* of Rt Hon. Lord Clyde; two *s* two *d*. *Educ:* Winchester; Trinity Coll., Oxford. Joined HM Foreign Service, 1950; served in: UK Mission to UN, New York, 1952–56; Baghdad, 1956–58; FO, 1958–61 and 1965–68; Paris, 1961–65; Counsellor, UK Mission in Geneva, 1968–70; Fellow, Center for Internat. Affairs, Harvard, 1970–71; Counsellor, Washington, 1971–72; Head of European Integration Dept, FCO, 1972–74; Asst Under-Sec. in charge of European Community Affairs, FCO, 1974–76; Dep. Under-Sec. of State, FCO, 1976–79. Hambros PLC and Hambros Bank Ltd: Dir, 1986–94; non-executive Dir, 1994–97; Consultant, 1997–98; Chm., Internat. Adv. (formerly European Strategy) Bd, ICL, 1988–2001; Director: Eurosynergies (France), 1990–98; Homeport (UK and France), 2000–. Lab. Party's Special Envoy on EU Enlargement, 1996–97; Advr to Sec. of State for Foreign and Commonwealth Affairs, 1997–98. Advr,

Govt of Ukraine, 1991–94. Chairman: City European Cttee, British Invisibles (formerly BIEC), 1988–93; Oriental Art Magazine, 1988–95; European Unification Bd, Hercules Europe, 1989–94; Honda Eur. Communication and Consultation Gp, 1994–2009; Business Link-Dorset, 1994–2000; Halo Ltd, 1994–96; Pathway Gp Ltd, 1995–2000; Guidephone Ltd, 1997–2002; Treasury Mgt Internat. Editl Adv. Panel, 1992–2006; Member: Standing Cttee on Internat. Relations, ACOST, 1987–90; Panel of Conciliators, Internat. Centre for the Settlement of Investment Disputes, 1987–94; Bank of Montreal Internat. Adv. Council, 1992–98; Adv. Council, Foreign Policy Centre, 1997–; Bd, Britain in Europe, 2001–06; Chm., European Senior Experts Gp, 2003–. Dir, Wellcome Foundn, 1986–95; Pro-Provost and Chm. Council, RCA, 1991–96 (Sen. Fellow, 1997); Mem. Council, Oriental Ceramic Soc., 1977–80, 1985–88 and 1995–98; Dep. Chm., Bd of Trustees, V&A Museum, 1985–97. Hon. DBA Bournemouth, 1998. Knight Grand Cross, Order of Merit (Portugal), 1998. *Publications:* Chinese Porcelain, The Transitional Period 1620–82: a selection from the Michael Butler Collection, 1986; Europe: More than a Continent, 1986; The Butler Family Collection, 17th Century Chinese Porcelain, 1990; Treasures from an Unknown Reign: the Shunzhi period, 2002; Seventeenth Century Jingdezhen Porcelain from the Shanghai Museum and the Butler Collections, 2006; Late Ming Chinese Porcelain from the Butler Collections, National Museum of Luxembourg, 2008; contribs to Trans Oriental Ceramic Soc. *Recreation:* collecting Chinese porcelain. *Club:* Brooks's. *Died 24 Dec. 2013.*

BUTLER, Nick; *see* Butler, J. N.

BUTLER, Sir (Reginald) Michael (Thomas), 3rd Bt *cr* 1922, of Old Park, Devizes; QC (Ont); barrister and solicitor; sometime Partner of Butler, Angus, Victoria, BC; Hon. Director, Teck Resources Ltd (formerly Teck Cominco Ltd); *b* 22 April 1928; *s* of Sir Reginald Thomas, 2nd Bt, and Marjorie Brown Butler; *S* father, 1959; *m* 1st, 1952, Marja Margaret Elizabeth McLean (marr. diss. 1967); three *s*; 2nd, 1968, Barbara Anne Hogan (*née* Cahill) (marr. diss. 1974); one step *s* (whom he adopted); 3rd, 1975, Judith Ann Blackwell, LLB, *d* of Harold Blackwell. *Educ:* Brentwood Coll., Victoria, BC; Univ. of British Columbia (BA). Called to Bar (Hons) from Osgoode Hall Sch. of Law, Toronto, Canada, 1954. *Publications:* Milk Chronicles, 2007; Onward Chronicles, 2008; Balancing Act, 2010. *Heir: s* (Reginald) Richard (Michael) Butler [*b* 3 Oct. 1953; *m* 1st, 1982, Dale Karen Piner (marr. diss. 1998); three *s*; 2nd, 1999, Penelope Joy Lipsack]. *Address:* Old Park Cottage, 634 Avalon Road, Victoria, BC V8V 1N7, Canada. *E:* blackbart@telus.net. *Died 1 July 2012.*

BUTLER, Hon. Sir Richard (Clive), Kt 1981; DL; Chairman, County Natwest Investment Management, 1989–96; Life Member, Council, National Farmers' Union, since 1962 (President, 1979–86); farmer since 1953; *b* 12 Jan. 1929; *e s* of late Baron Butler of Saffron Walden, KG, CH, PC and Sydney, *oc* of late Samuel Courtauld; *m* 1952, Susan Anne Maud Walker; twin *s* one *d*. *Educ:* Eton Coll.; Pembroke Coll., Cambridge (MA). 2nd Lieut, Royal Horse Guards, 1947–49. Vice-Pres. 1970–71, Dep. Pres., 1971–79, NFU. Member: Agricultural Adv. Council, 1968–72; Central Council for Agricultural and Horticultural Co-operation, 1970–79. Director: NFU Mutual Insce Soc. Ltd, 1985–96; National Westminster Bank, 1986–96; Agroceres & Co. (formerly Ferruzzi Trading (UK)), 1986–98; Agricola (UK), 1986–92; Barton Bendish Farms, 1986–92; County Natwest Group (formerly Natwest Investment Bank), 1989–92; Avon Insurance, 1990–96. Chm., Kennedy Inst. for Rheumatology Trust, 1995–2009; Trustee, Arthritis Res. Campaign (formerly Arthritis and Rheumatism Council for Research), 1986–2005. Member, Court of Assistants: Farmers' Co. (Master, 1997–98); Skinners' Co. (Master, 1994–95). DL Essex, 1972. *Recreations:* hunting, shooting, DIY. *Address:* Gladfen Hall, Halstead, Essex CO9 1RN. *T:* (01787) 472828. *Club:* Farmers. *Died 28 Jan. 2012.*

BUTLER, Richard Edmund, AM 1988; telecommunication policy adviser; Secretary-General, International Telecommunication Union, United Nations, Specialised Agency, Geneva, 1983–89 (Deputy Secretary-General, 1968–82); *b* 25 March 1926; *m* 1951, Patricia Carmel Kelly; three *s* two *d*. *Educ:* A, DPA; CPA; FIPA. Posts in Australian Post Office, incl. Chief Industrial Officer, 1955–60; Exec. Officer, Dep. Asst Dir-Gen., 1960–68 (Ministerial and External Relations), 1960–68; apptd (in absentia) Sec., Aust. Telecommunications Commn, 1975 and later Dir, Corporate Planning Directorate. Formerly Member Australian delegations: for Internat. Telecommunication Satellite Consortium, Plenipotentiary Conf. 1965 (Dep. Leader; Mem. Administrative Council and Plan Cttees, 1962–68); to UN Conf. on Peaceful Uses of Outer Space, Vienna, 1968 (Dep. Leader). Mem., Admin. Cttee of Co-ordination for UN and Heads of Specialized Agencies; Chairman: Ad-Hoc UN Common System subsid. gps; ITU (Tripartite) Staff Pension Cttee, 1968–83; Member: Ministerial Adv. Cttee, Implementation of Australian Telecommns Reform decisions, 1990–91; Adv. Bd, Centre for Internat. Res. on Communication and ITs, Melbourne, 1991–2002; Associate Mem., Austr. Telecommn Authy), 1990–91. Chairman: Asiaspace Pty Ltd, 1999– (Mem. Bd, 1995–); Sky Station Australia Pty Ltd, 1999– (Mem. Bd, 1996–). Mem., Adv. Bd, Pacific Telecommns Council, Hawaii, 1993–; Mem. Bd, Volunteers in Technical Assistance, 1993–2005. Governor, Internat. Computer Commns Conf., 1975–85; UN System Co-ordinator, Develt of Commns Infrastructure prog., world commns year, 1983. Hon. Mem., Greek Soc. of Air and Space Law, 1984. FRIPA; Hon. Fellow, Instn of Electronic and Telecommunications Engrs, India, 1988. Fellow, Telecommns Soc. of Aust., 1995. Philipp Reis Medal, Germany, 1987. Grand Insignia, Order of Merit for Telecommunications, Spain, 1983. *Publications:* papers on changing telecommunication environment and on multi-dimensional consequences of telecommunications for economic development of nations. *Recreations:* golf, reading. *Address:* 40 Barrington Avenue, Kew, Vic 3101, Australia. *Clubs:* Royal Over-Seas League; CTA NSW (Sydney); Melbourne Cricket; Greenacres Golf (Kew). *Died 23 June 2012.*

BUTTERFIELD, (John) Michael; Chief Executive, National Association of Youth Clubs, 1975–86; *b* 2 July 1926; *s* of late John Leslie Butterfield and Hilda Mary Butterfield (*née* Judson); *m* 1955, Mary Maureen (*d* 1998), *d* of John Martin; one *s* twin *d* (and one *s* decd). *Educ:* Leeds Modern Sch.; Leeds Univ. John Butterfield & Son, Leeds, 1949–60; John Atkinson & Sons (Sowerby Bridge) Ltd, 1960–61. Youth Officer, Coventry Cathedral, 1961–68; Liverpool Council of Social Service: Head of Youth and Community Dept, 1968–72; Operations Dir, 1972–75. Mem., BCC, 1954–73 (Mem., 1952–68; Chm., Exec. Cttee, 1962–67, Youth Dept); Vice-Chairman: Nat. Council for Voluntary Youth Services, 1977–83; UK Adv. Cttee, SCF, 1990–93; Chairman: Leics Council of Voluntary Youth Services, 1985–98; Youthaid, 1986–90; Youth Club Leics, 1987–99; UK Grants Cttee, Charity Projects later Comic Relief, 1992–98; Voluntary Action Hinckley and Bosworth (formerly Hinckley and Bosworth CVS), 1997–2005; Dark Horse Venture, 2001–09. Merseyside Advr, Baring Foundn, 1987–96; UK Rep., Amer. Youth Work Center, 1987–98. *Recreations:* music, reading, walking, railways. *Address:* 20 The Leys, Hinckley Road, Burbage, Hinckley, Leics LE10 2AJ. *T:* (01455) 611027. *Died 17 Feb. 2013.*

BUTTERWORTH, Prof. Ian, CBE 1984; FRS 1981; Distinguished (formerly Senior) Research Fellow, Imperial College London, since 1991; Professor of Physics, University of London, 1971–91, then Emeritus; *b* 3 Dec. 1930; *s* of Harry and Beatrice Butterworth; *m* 1964, Mary Therese (*née* Gough) (*d* 2007); one *d*. *Educ:* Bolton County Grammar Sch.; Univ. of Manchester. BSc 1951; PhD 1954. Sen. Scientific Officer, UK Atomic Energy Authority, 1954–58; Lectr, Imperial Coll., 1958–64; Vis. Physicist, Lawrence Radiation Laboratory, Univ. of California, 1964–65; Sen. Lectr, Imperial Coll., 1965–68; Group Leader, Bubble Chamber Research Gp, Rutherford High Energy Laboratory, 1968–71; Professor, 1971–86, Head of Dept, 1980–83, Dept of Physics, Imperial Coll.; on leave of absence as Res. Dir, CERN, 1983–86; Principal, QMC, then QMW, 1986–91; Pro Vice-Chancellor for Eur. Affairs, London Univ., 1989–91. Science and Engineering Research Council (formerly Science Research Council): Mem., 1979–83 (Mem., Nuclear Physics Bd, 1972–75 and 1978–83, Chm., 1979–83; Mem., Particle Physics Cttee, 1978–79; Chm., Film Analysis Grants Cttee, 1972–75); UK deleg. on Council, CERN, 1979–82 (Mem., Research Bd, 1976–82; Chm., Super Proton Synchroton Cttee, 1976–79). Member: Physics Res. Cttee, Deutsches Elektronen Synchroton, Hamburg, 1981–85; Sci. Policy Cttee, Stanford Linear Accelerator Center, Calif, 1984–88; Sci. Adv. Cttee, British Council, 1986–91; Science Cttee, 2000–03, Natural Sci. Cttee, 2005–06, UK Nat. Commn for UNESCO; Physical Scis and Engrg Standing Cttee, ESF, 2000–06; IUPAP deleg. to Internat. Council for Scientific and Technical Inf., 1999–2006. Council Member: Royal Soc., 1989–90; Inst. of Physics, 1989–92 (Vice Pres., 1993–97; Chm., IOP Publishing Ltd, 1993–97); MAE 1989 (Vice Pres., 1997–2003). Hon. Mem., Manchester Lit. and Phil. Soc., 1987. Fellow, Imperial Coll., 1988. Dr *hc* Soka Univ., 1989. Glazebrook Prize and Medal, Inst. of Physics, 1993. *Publications:* numerous papers in learned jls (on experimental particle physics). *Recreations:* reading, history of art. *Address:* Blackett Laboratory, Imperial College London, Prince Consort Road, SW7 2AZ; 1 Paramount Court, University Street, WC1E 6JP. *Died 29 Nov. 2013.*

BUXTON, Sir Jocelyn (Charles Roden), 7th Bt *cr* 1840, of Belfield, Dorset; VRD 1975; *b* 8 Aug. 1924; *er s* of Captain Roden H. V. Buxton, CBE, RN (*d* 1970) and Dorothy Alina St John Buxton (*d* 1956); *S* cousin, 1996; *m* 1960, Ann Frances, *d* of late Frank Smitherman, MBE; three *d. Educ:* Eton. Served RNVR, 1942–45 (despatches); Korea, 1952. *Heir: nephew* Crispin Charles Gerard Buxton [*b* 29 March 1958; *m* 2006, Diana Nafula; one *s*]. *Address:* Rodwell House, Loddon, Norfolk. *Died 25 April 2014.*

BUXTON, Hon. Margaret Evelyn; *see* Aston, M. E.

BUXTON, Prof. Neil Keith; Vice-Chancellor, University of Hertfordshire, 1992–2003; *b* 2 May 1940; *s* of William F. A. Buxton and Janet A. Buxton; *m* 1962, Margaret G. Buxton (*née* Miller); two *s* one *d. Educ:* Aberdeen Univ. (MA Hons Political Econs); PhD Heriot-Watt. Asst Lectr, Dept of Political Econ., Aberdeen Univ., 1962–64; Lectr, Dept of Econ., Univ. of Hull, 1964–69; Lectr and Sen. Lectr, 1969–78, Prof., 1979–83, Heriot-Watt Univ.; Depute Dir, Glasgow Coll. of Technology, 1983–87; Dir, Hatfield Poly., 1987–92. Vis. Prof. in Econs and Public Admin, Lewis and Clark Coll., Oregon, 1982. Dir, Herts TEC, 1989–2001; Member: Board: Herts Business Centre (Businesslink), 1993; Herts Learning and Skills Council, 2001; Herts Prosperity Forum, 1998. Hon. DLaws Herts, 2009. *Publications:* (with T. L. Johnston and D. Mair) Structure and Growth of the Scottish Economy, 1971; (with D. I. Mackay) British Employment Statistics, 1977; Economic Development of the British Coal Industry, 1978; (ed) British Industry Between the Wars, 1979; articles in professional jls. *Recreations:* sport, bridge, overseas travel, pipe smoking. *Address:* 74 Marbuk Avenue, Port Macquarie, NSW 2444, Australia. *Died 11 Nov. 2015.*

BYATT, Sir Hugh Campbell, KCVO 1985; CMG 1979; HM Diplomatic Service, retired; Director, EFM Japan Trust PLC, 1992–97; Chairman: EFM Java Trust, 1990–98; EFM Dragon Trust, 1992–98 (Director, 1987–98); *b* 27 Aug. 1927; *e s* of late Sir Horace Byatt, GCMG, and Lady Byatt (*née* Olga Margaret Campbell), MBE; *m* 1954, Fiona, *d* of Ian P. Coats, DL, and May Coats, MBE; two *s* one *d. Educ:* Gordonstoun; New College, Oxford (MA 1951). Served in Royal Navy, 1945–48 (Sub-Lieut RNVR); HMOCS Nigeria, 1952–57; Commonwealth Relations Office, 1958; Bombay, 1961–63; CRO, 1964–65; seconded to Cabinet Office, 1965–67; Head of Chancery, Lisbon, 1967–70; Asst Head, South Asian Dept, FCO, 1970–71; Consul-General, Mozambique, 1971–73; Inspector, HM Diplomatic Service, 1973–75; RCDS, 1976; Dep. High Comr, Nairobi, 1977–78; Ambassador to Angola, 1978–81, to São Tomé, 1980–81, to Portugal, 1981–86. Advr, RTZ, 1986–96; Special Advr, Scottish Financial Enterprise, 1986–92. Mem., Parole Bd for Scotland, 1990–92. Chm., Cttee for Scotland, Malcolm Sargent Cancer Fund for Children, 1991–96. Chm. of Govs, Centre for Inf. on Lang. Teaching and Res., 1986–90. FSAScot 1989. Hon. Sheriff, Campbeltown, 1994. Knight Grand Cross, Mil. Order of Christ (Portugal), 1985. *Recreation:* life in Argyll. *Address:* Leargnahension, Tarbert, Argyll PA29 6YB. *T:* (01880) 820644. *Clubs:* Royal Ocean Racing; New (Edinburgh). *Died 16 Feb. 2011.*

BYERS, Dr Paul Duncan; Reader Emeritus in Morbid Anatomy, University of London; Head of Department of Morbid Anatomy, Institute of Orthopaedics, University of London, 1980–87 (Dean of Institute, 1971–79); *b* Montreal, 3 July 1922; *s* of A. F. Byers and Marion Taber; *m* 1959, Valery Garden (*d* 1999); *m* 1999, M. E. A. Brown. *Educ:* Bishop's College Sch., PQ, Canada; McGill Univ. (BSc, MD, CM); Univ. of London (DCP, PhD). FRCPath. Alan Blair Memorial Fellow, Canadian Cancer Soc., 1955–57. Asst Morbid Anatomist, Inst. of Orthopaedics, 1960; Reader in Morbid Anatomy, Univ. of London, 1974. Hon. Consultant, Royal National Orthopaedic Hosp., 1965; Hon. Senior Lectr, Royal Postgrad. Med. Sch., 1969. Chm., Osteosarcoma Histopathol. Panel, MRC/EORTC, 1983–86; Member: Osteosarcoma Wkg Party, MRC, 1982–86; Soft Tissue Sarcoma Wkg Party, MRC, 1983–84. Mem., Management Cttee, Courtauld Inst. of Art, Univ. of London, 1979–82. *Publications:* (jtly) Diseases of Bones and Joints, 1994; articles in medical press on arthritis, metabolic bone disease, bone tumours, medical education. *Recreation:* arts. *Address:* 2 Manorside, Barnet, Herts EN5 2LD. *T:* (020) 8440 3376. *Died 8 Oct. 2012.*

BYGRAVES, Max Walter, OBE 1983; entertainer; *b* 16 Oct. 1922; *s* of Henry and Lilian Bygraves, Rotherhithe, SE16; *m* 1942, Gladys Blossom Murray (*d* 2011); one *s* two *d. Educ:* St Joseph's, Rotherhithe. Began in advertising agency, carrying copy to Fleet Street, 1936. Volunteered for RAF, 1940; served 5 years as fitter. Performed many shows for troops; became professional, 1946; appeared in venues all over English-speaking world, incl. 19 Royal Command Performances; best selling record artist (31 Gold Discs). Host, Family Fortunes, TV, 1983–85. Freeman, City of London, 1994. *Publications:* I Wanna Tell You a Story (autobiog.), 1976; The Milkman's on his Way (novel), 1977; After Thoughts (autobiog.), 1988; I Wanna Tell You a Funny Story, 1992; In His Own Words (autobiog.), 1997; The Golden Years, 2004. *Recreations:* golf, painting, reading, writing. *Address:* c/o Johnny Mans Productions Ltd, PO Box 196, Hoddesdon, Herts EN10 7WG. *T:* (01992) 470907, *Fax:* (01992) 470516. *E:* johnnymansagent@aol.com. *Clubs:* St James's, East India. *Died 1 Sept. 2012.*

BYNOE, Dame Hilda Louisa, DBE 1969; in General Medical Practice, Port of Spain, Trinidad, 1974–89; *b* Grenada, 18 Nov. 1921; *d* of late Thomas Joseph Gibbs, CBE, JP, Estate Proprietor, and Louisa Gibbs (*née* La Touche); *m* 1947, Peter Cecil Alexander Bynoe, ARIBA, Dip. Arch., former RAF Flying Officer (*d* 2003); two *s. Educ:* St Joseph's Convent, St George's, Grenada; Royal Free Hospital Medical Sch., Univ. of London. MB, BS (London), 1951, MRCS, LRCP, 1951. Teacher, St Joseph's Convents, Trinidad and Grenada, 1939–44; hospital and private practice, London, 1951–53; public service with Govt of Trinidad and Tobago, 1954–55, with Govt of Guyana (later British Guiana), 1955–58, with Govt of Trinidad and Tobago, 1958–65; private practice, Trinidad, 1961–68; Governor of Associated State of Grenada, WI, 1968–74. Mem., Academic Bd, Sch. of Medicine, St George's Univ., Grenada. Mem. YWCA. Patron: Caribbean Women's Assoc., 1970–; John Hayes Meml Kidney Foundn, 1979–; Music Foundn of Trinidad and Tobago, 1986–; African Assoc. of Trinidad and Tobago. *Publications:* I Woke at Dawn, 1996. *Recreations:* swimming, music, reading, poetry-writing. *Club:* Soroptimist (Port of Spain). *Died 6 April 2013.*

BYRNE, Douglas Norman; Head of Marine Directorate, Department of Transport (formerly Marine Division, Department of Trade), 1980–84; *b* 30 Jan. 1924; *s* of Leonard William Byrne and Clarice Evelyn Byrne; *m* 1949, Noreen Thurlby Giles; one *s* one *d. Educ:* Portsmouth Grammar Sch.; St John's Coll., Cambridge (MA). RAF,

1942–46. Asst Principal, Min. of Supply, 1949; BoT, 1956; Cabinet Office, 1961–64; Asst Sec., 1964; on staff of Monopolies Commn, 1966–68; Under-Sec., Dept of Industry, 1974–77; Hd of Fair Trading Div., Dept of Prices and Consumer Protection, 1977–79; Under-Sec., Dept of Trade, 1979–83, Dept of Transport, 1983–84. *Recreations:* hill walking, natural history. *Deceased.*

BYWATER, Air Cdre David Llewellyn, FRAeS; aviation consultant; Commandant, Aeroplane and Armament Experimental Establishment, Boscombe Down, 1988–92; *b* 16 July 1937; *s* of Stanley and Gertrude Bywater; *m* 1960, Shelagh May Gowling; one *s* one *d*. *Educ:* Liverpool Inst. High Sch.; RAF Coll., Cranwell. No XV Sqdn, 1958–63; Empire Test Pilots Sch., 1964; Test Pilot, A&AEE, Boscombe Down, 1965–68; RAF Staff Coll., 1969; HQ RAF Germany, 1970–73; Wing Comdr Flying, RAE Farnborough, 1974–78; MoD Operational Requirements, 1979–81; Gp Captain, Superintendent of Flying, A&AEE, 1982–85; Gp Dir, RAF Staff Coll., Bracknell, 1985–88; Dir, Airport and Flight Ops, Marshall Aerospace, 1993–2002. Director: RAF Charitable Trust Enterprises, 2002–; Royal Internat. Air Tattoo, 2005– (Vice-Pres., 1992); British Light Aircraft Centre, 2006–; Aircraft Owners and Pilots Assoc., 2006– (Vice Pres., 2004–); Mem., Air League, 1994–. Hon. Mem., Airport Operators' Assoc., 2006. Liveryman, Hon. Co. of Air Pilots (formerly GAPAN), 2006. *Recreations:* sailing, ski-ing. *Club:* Royal Air Force. *Died 24 Sept. 2015.*

C

CACOYANNIS, Michael; director, stage and screen, since 1954; *b* 11 June 1922; *s* of late Sir Panayotis Cacoyannis and Angeliki, *d* of George M. Efthyvoulos and Zoe Constantinides, Limassol, Cyprus. *Educ:* Greek Gymnasium; Gray's Inn and Old Vic Sch., London. Radio Producer, BBC, Greek Service, 1941–50. Actor on English stage, 1946–51; parts included: Herod, in Salome, 1946; Caligula, in Caligula, 1949, etc. *Directed films:* Windfall in Athens, 1953; Stella, 1954; Girl in Black, 1956; A Matter of Dignity, 1958; Our Last Spring, 1960; The Wastrel, 1961; Electra, 1962; Zorba the Greek, 1964; The Day the Fish Came Out, 1967; The Trojan Women, 1971; The Story of Jacob and Joseph, 1974; Attila '74, 1975; Iphigenia, 1977; Sweet Country, 1986; Up, Down and Sideways, 1992; The Cherry Orchard, 1999; directed *plays:* produced several of these in Athens for Ellie Lambetti's Company, 1955–61; The Trojan Women, New York, 1963–65, Paris, 1965; Things That Go Bump in the Night, and The Devils, New York, 1965; Iphigenia in Aulis, New York, 1968; King Oedipus, Abbey Theatre, Dublin, 1973; Miss Margarita, Athens, 1975; The Bacchae, Comédie Française, 1977, New York, 1980; The Glass Menagerie, Nat. Theatre, Athens, 1978; Antony and Cleopatra, Athens, 1979; Zorba (musical), USA, 1983; Electra, Epidaurus, 1984; Naked, Athens, 1989; Henceforward, Athens, 1990; The Trojan Women, Epidaurus, 1995; Master Class, Athens, 1997; Medea, Epidaurus, 2001; Hamlet, Athens, 2003; Lysistrata, Delphi, Athens, 2005–06; Coriolanus, Athens, 2005; directed *operas:* Mourning Becomes Electra, Metropolitan Opera, NY, 1967; La Bohème, Juilliard, NY, 1972; La Traviata, Athens, 1983; Iphigenia in Aulis and in Tauris, Frankfurt State Opera, 1987; La Clemenza di Tito, Aix-en-Provence, 1988; Medea, Athens, 1995. Founder and Chm., Michael Cacoyannis Foundn, 2010–. Hon. DH Columbia Coll., Chicago, 1981; Hon. DLitt: Athens, 2002; Cyprus, 2003; Aristotelio Univ. of Thessaloniki, 2005. Silver Medal for Life Achievement, Greek Acad., 1995; Lifetime Achievement Awards: Fest. des Films du Monde, Montréal, 1999; Jerusalem Film Fest., 2000; Damascus Film Fest., 2004. Order of the Phœnix (Greece), 1965; Commandeur des Arts et des Lettres, 1987. *Publications:* In Other Words: a collection of essays, 1990; Stella: a screenplay, 1990; Collected Writings, 1990; *translations:* (into English) The Trojan Women, 1971; (into English) The Bacchae, 1982; (into Greek) Antony and Cleopatra, 1980; Hamlet, 1985; Coriolanus, 1990; Othello, 2001; (into modern Greek) The Trojan Women, 1995. *Recreations:* walking, swimming. *Address:* 15 Mouson Street, Athens 117–41, Greece. *Died 25 July 2011.*

CADBURY, Sir (George) Adrian (Hayhurst), CH 2015; Kt 1977; DL; a Director of the Bank of England, 1970–94; *b* 15 April 1929; *s* of late Laurence John Cadbury, OBE and Joyce Cadbury, OBE, *d* of Lewis O. Mathews, Birmingham; *m* 1st, 1956, Gillian Mary (*d* 1992), *d* of late E. D. Skepper, Neuilly-sur-Seine; two *s* one *d*; 2nd, 1994, Susan Jacqueline, *d* of late D. B. Sinclair. *Educ:* Eton Coll.; King's Coll., Cambridge (MA Economics). Coldstream Guards, 1948–49; Cambridge, 1949–52. Cadbury Schweppes: Dep. Chm. and Man. Dir, 1969–74; Chm., 1975–89; Director: Cadbury Bros Ltd, 1958; IBM UK Ltd, 1975–94; Nat. Exhibition Centre, 1989–2001. Mem., Panel on Takeovers and Mergers, 1990–94. Chancellor, Univ. of Aston, 1979–2004. Chairman: West Midlands Economic Planning Council, 1967–70; CBI Econ. & Financial Policy Cttee, 1974–80; Food & Drink Industries Council, 1981–83; Promotion of Non-Exec. Dirs, 1984–95; Cttee on Financial Aspects of Corporate Governance, 1991–95; Pres., Birmingham Chamber of Industry and Commerce, 1988–89. High Sheriff, 1994–95, DL 1995, W Midlands. Freeman, City of Birmingham, 1982. Hon. DSc: Aston, 1973; Cranfield, 1985; Birmingham, 1996; Hon. LLD: Bristol, 1986; Birmingham, 1989; Lancaster, 1993; Cambridge, 1994; Hon. Dr Leuven and Gent, 2003; DUniv UCE, 2004; Hon. DLitt Aston, 2005. Albert Medal, RSA, 1995; Internat. Corporate Governance Network Award, 2001; Laureate Medal for Corporate Governance, Global Center for Leadership and Business Ethics, 2005. *Publications:* The Company Chairman, 1990, 2nd edn 1995; Corporate Governance and Chairmanship, 2002. *Clubs:* Boodle's; Hawks (Cambridge); Leander (Henley). *Died 3 Sept. 2015.*

CADDICK, His Honour David William; a Circuit Judge, 2004–14; *b* 24 Dec. 1945; *s* of late William Caddick and Phyllis Caddick (*née* Brown, later Medhurst); *m* 1971, Susan Anne Wyton; two *s* two *d*. *Educ:* Simon Langton Grammar Sch., Canterbury; St John's Coll., Durham (BA 1967). Articled to D. L. Gulland, Solicitor, 1967–70; admitted solicitor, 1970; Partner, Gulland & Gulland, Solicitors, Maidstone, 1971–87; Dep. County Court Registrar, 1983–87; Registrar, then Dist Judge, 1987–2004; Nominated Dist Care Judge, Medway Care Centre, 1991–2004; a Recorder, Crown Court, 1998–2004. Chm. SE Circuit, Dist Judges' Assoc., 1995–98. *Recreations:* gardening, walking, all things connected with France. *Died 9 Dec. 2015.*

CAIN, John Clifford; broadcasting research historian; Controller, Public Affairs, BBC, 1981–84; Hon. Vice-President, Broadcasting Support Services, since 1989 (Chairman, 1980–85; Trustee, 1985–89); *b* 2 April 1924; *s* of William John Cain and Florence Jessie (*née* Wood); *m* 1954, Shirley Jean Roberts; two *d*. *Educ:* Emanuel Sch.; Imperial Coll., Borough Road Coll., London Univ. (BSc); University Coll., London Univ. (MSc); Open Univ. (BA (Hons) 1988; PhD 1996). Served RAF (aircrew), 1944–47. Maths and science teacher in grammar, secondary modern and comprehensive schs and in polytechnic, 1950–59; Lectr, Science Museum, 1959–61; Asst Head of Sch. Broadcasting, Associated-Rediffusion, 1961–63; BBC Television: Producer, 1963–71; Asst Head of Further Educn Dept, 1971–72, Head, 1972–77; Asst Controller, Educn Br., BBC, 1977–80. Dir, Broadcasters' Audience Res. Bd, 1982–84. Mem., Health Educn Council, 1978–83. FRSA 1990. *Publications:* Talking Machines, 1961; (jtly) Mathematics Miscellany, 1966; (contrib.) Culture, Education and the State, 1988; The BBC: 70 years of broadcasting, 1992; (jtly) In a Class of its Own: BBC Education 1924–1994, 1994; articles in EBU Review, Adult Educn, etc. *Recreations:* reading, gardening, music, theatre. *Died 12 April 2013.*

CAIRNCROSS, Neil Francis, CB 1971; Deputy Under-Secretary of State, Home Office, 1972–80; *b* 29 July 1920; *s* of late James and Olive Hunter Cairncross; *m* 1947, Eleanor Elizabeth Leisten; two *s* one *d*. *Educ:* Charterhouse; Oriel Coll., Oxford. Royal Sussex Regt, 1940–45. Called to the Bar, 1948. Home Office, 1948; a Private Sec. to the Prime Minister, 1955–58; Sec., Royal Commn on the Press, 1961–62; Dep. Sec., Cabinet Office, 1970–72; Dep. Sec., NI Office, March–Nov. 1972. Member: Parole Bd, 1982–85; Home Grown Timber Adv. Cttee, 1981–90; (co-opted) Avon Probation Cttee, 1983–89. *Recreation:* painting. *Address:* Little Grange, The Green, Olveston, Bristol BS35 4EJ. *T:* (01454) 613060. *Died 26 Feb. 2015.*

CAIRNS, David; MP (Lab) Inverclyde, since 2005 (Greenock and Inverclyde, 2001–05); *b* 7 Aug. 1966; *s* of John Cairns and Teresa Cairns (*née* Harkins). *Educ:* Gregorian Univ., Rome; Franciscan Study Centre, Canterbury. Priest, 1991–94; Dir, Christian Socialist Movement, 1994–97; Researcher to Siobhain McDonagh, MP, 1997–2001. Parly Under-Sec. of State: Scotland Office, 2005–07; NI Office, 2006–07; Minister of State, Scotland Office, 2007–08. *Recreations:* cinema, reading (US history). *Address:* House of Commons, SW1A 0AA. *Died 9 May 2011.*

CALDER, Nigel David Ritchie, MA; science writer; *b* 2 Dec. 1931; *e s* of Baron Ritchie-Calder, CBE; *m* 1954, Elisabeth Palmer; two *s* three *d*. *Educ:* Merchant Taylors' Sch.; Sidney Sussex Coll., Cambridge. Physicist, Mullard Research Laboratories, 1954–56; Editorial staff, New

Scientist, 1956–66; Science Editor, 1960–62; Editor, 1962–66. Science Correspondent, New Statesman, 1959–62 and 1966–71; Chairman, Assoc. of British Science Writers, 1962–64. Mem., Initiative Group, Foundn Scientific Europe, 1987–90; Consultant on public inf., ESA, 1994–2006. Vice-Pres., Cruising Assoc., 1981–84. FRAS. (Jtly) UNESCO Kalinga Prize for popularisation of science, 1972. *Publications:* Electricity Grows Up, 1958; Robots, 1958; Radio Astronomy, 1958; (ed) The World in 1984, 1965; The Environment Game, 1967; (ed) Unless Peace Comes, 1968; Technopolis: Social Control of the Uses of Science, 1969; Living Tomorrow, 1970; (ed) Nature in the Round: a Guide to Environmental Science, 1973; Timescale, 1983; 1984 and After, 1983; The English Channel, 1986; The Green Machines, 1986; (ed) Future Earth, 1988; (ed) Scientific Europe, 1990; Giotto to the Comets, 1992; Hubble Space Telescope, 1993; Beyond this World, 1995; The Manic Sun, 1997; Magic Universe: The Oxford Guide to Modern Science, 2003; (ed) Einstein, Relativity, 2006; (jtly) The Chilling Stars: a new theory of climate change, 2007, 2nd edn 2008; Supernova: how exploding stars rule the world, 2015; *books of own TV programmes:* The Violent Universe, 1969; The Mind of Man, 1970; The Restless Earth, 1972; The Life Game, 1973; The Weather Machine, 1974; The Human Conspiracy, 1975–76; The Key to the Universe, 1977; Spaceships of the Mind (TV series), 1978; Einstein's Universe, 1979, 2nd edn, 2005; Nuclear Nightmares, 1979; The Comet is Coming!, 1980; Spaceship Earth, 1991 (TV series). *Recreation:* painting. *Address:* 26 Boundary Road, Northgate, Crawley, W Sussex RH10 8BT. *T:* (01293) 549969. *Died 25 June 2014.*

CALDWELL, Maj.-Gen. Frank Griffiths, OBE 1953 (MBE 1945); MC 1941 and Bar 1942; Assistant Chief of General Staff (Operational Requirements), 1972–74; *b* 26 Feb. 1921; *s* of William Charles Francis and Violet Marjorie Kathleen Caldwell; *m* 1945, Betty (*d* 2012), *d* of Captain Charles Palmer Buesden; one *s* one *d*. *Educ:* Elizabeth Coll., Guernsey. Commnd Royal Engrs, 1940; served Western Desert RE, 1940–43 (MC and Bar; dispatches); Special Air Service NW Europe, 1944–45 (MBE); Malaya, 1951–53 (OBE); Comdr RE, 2 Div. BAOR, 1961–63; Corps Comdr RE, 1 (BR) Corps, 1967–68; Dir Defence Operational Plans, MoD, 1970; Engineer in Chief (Army), 1970–72. Col Comdt, RE, 1975–80. Director: Mabey and Johnson Ltd, 1974–78; Scout Insurance (Guernsey) Ltd, 1990–2000; Guernsey Envmtl Services, 2001–04 (Man. Dir, 2004–07). Chm., Mines Awareness Trust Ltd, 2001–10. President: RBL, Guernsey, 1986–2004; La Société Guernesiaise, 1994–96; Chm., Guernsey Scout Council, 1987–99. Belgian Croix de Guerre, 1940, and Croix Militaire, 1945. *Recreation:* ornithology. *Address:* 2 Fishermans Cottage, Route de la Lague, St Peters, Guernsey GY7 9BU. *Died 22 Nov. 2014.*

CALDWELL, Philip; Chief Executive Officer, 1979–85, and Chairman of Board, 1980–85, Ford Motor Company; *b* Bourneville, Ohio, 27 Jan. 1920; *s* of Robert Clyde Caldwell and Wilhelmina (*née* Hemphill); *m* 1945, Betsey Chinn Clark; one *s* two *d*. *Educ:* Muskingum Coll. (BA Econs 1940); Harvard Univ. Graduate Sch. of Business (MBA Indust. Management, 1942). Served to Lieut, USNR, 1942–46. With Navy Dept, 1946–53, as civilian (Dep. Dir, Procurement Policy Div., 1948–53); joined Ford Motor Co., 1953: Vice Pres. and Gen. Man. Truck Ops, 1968–70; Pres. and Dir, Philco-Ford Corp. (subsid. of Ford Motor Co.), 1970–71; Vice Pres. Manufg Gp, N Amer. Automotive Ops, 1971–72; Chm. and Chief Exec. Officer, Ford of Europe, Inc., 1972–73; Dir, Ford Motor Co., 1973–90; Exec. Vice Pres., Internat. Automotive Ops, 1973–77; Vice Chm. of Bd, 1977–79; Dep. Chief Exec. Officer, 1978–79; Pres., 1978–79; Director: Ford of Europe, 1972–85; Ford Latin America, 1973–85; Ford Mid-East and Africa, 1973–85; Ford Asia-Pacific, 1973–85; Ford Motor Credit Co., 1977–85; Ford of Canada, 1977–85; Mem., Eur. Adv. Council, 1976–88 (Chm., 1987–88). Sen. Man. Dir, Lehman Brothers Inc., 1985–98. Director: Digital Equipment Corp., 1980–95; Chase Manhattan Corp., and Chase Manhattan Bank, NA, 1982–85 (Mem., Chase Manhattan Bank Internat. Adv. Cttee, 1979–85); Federated Dept Stores, 1984–88; Russell Reynolds Associates, Inc., 1984–2005; Kellogg Co., 1985–92; Shearson Lehman Brothers Hldgs Inc., 1985–93; Amer. Guarantee and Liability Insce Co., 1986–99; Zurich Reinsurance Co. of New York, 1987–90; Zurich-American Insurance Gp, 1989–99; Mexico Fund, 1991–2006; Specialty Coatings Internat., 1991–93; Zurich Reinsurance Centre Holdings, 1993–97; Waters Corp., 1994–; Castech Aluminium Gp, 1994–96; Mettler-Toledo Inc., 1996–2005 (Chm., 1996–98); Detroit Symphony Orch., 1974–85; Harvard Business Sch. Associates, 1977–93. Vice Chairperson, New Detroit, Inc., 1977–85; Vice Chm., Japan Soc., 1987–89 (Mem., 1983–89; Chm. Exec. Cttee, 1987–89); Member: US Chamber of Commerce Transportation Cttee, 1968–77; US Council, Internat. Chamber of Commerce, 1973–77; US Council for Internat. Business, 1977–85; Soc. of Automotive Engrs, 1969–85; Engrg Soc. of Detroit, 1970–85; Motor Vehicle Manufrs Assoc. of US, 1978–85 (Chm., 1978 and 1983; Mem., Motor Truck Cttee, 1964–70); Econ. Club of Detroit, 1977–86; Highway Users Fedn, 1977–85; INSEAD, 1978–81 (Chm., US Adv. Bd, 1979–84; Mem., Internat. Council, 1983–2002); Conf. Bd, 1979–; Cttee for Econ. Develt, 1979–; (Charter Mem.) Business Higher Educn Forum, 1979–83; Business Council, 1980–2001; Policy Cttee, Business Roundtable, 1980–85; Trilateral Commn, 1980–86; Citizens Res. Council of Mich, 1980–85; Adv. Council on Japan-US Econ. Relations, 1981–85; US Trade Representative Adv. Cttee for Trade Negotiations, 1983–85; President's Export Council, 1985–89; Council on Foreign Relations, 1985–2009; Mexico-US Bus. Com., 1985–. Bd of Advrs, Jerome Levy Econs Inst., 1988–2001. Trustee: Muskingum Coll., 1967–; Winterthur Mus. and Gdns, 1986–2000. Philip Caldwell Professorship of Business Admin, Harvard Business Sch., established 1989. Hon. HHD Muskingum, 1974; Hon. DBA Upper Iowa Univ., 1978; Hon. LLD: Boston Univ. and Eastern Mich Univ., 1979; Miami Univ., 1980; Davidson Coll., 1982; Univ. of Mich, 1984; Ohio Univ., 1984; Lawrence Inst. of Technol., 1984. 1st William A. Jump Meml Award, 1950; Meritorious Civilian Service Award, US Navy, 1953; Muskingum Coll. Alumni Dist. Service Award, 1978; Brigham Young Univ. Sch. of Management Internat. Exec. of the Year Award, 1983; Automotive Industry Leader of the Year, 1984; Club of Greater NY Business Statesman Award, 1984; Alumni Achievement Award, Harvard Business Sch., 1985; Club of Columbus Businessman of the Year, Columbus, Ohio, 1984; Automotive Hall of Fame, 1990; Statesman of the Year, Detroit, 1991. *Address:* Ford Motor Co., 225 High Ridge Road, West Building, Stamford, CT 06905-3000, USA. *T:* (203) 3578880, *Fax:* (203) 3578241. *Clubs:* Links, River (New York). *Died 10 July 2013.*

CALDWELL-MOORE, Sir Patrick Alfred; *see* Moore, Sir P. A. C.

CALLAGHAN, Sir Paul (Terence), GNZM 2009 (PCNZM 2006); DPhil, DSc; FRS 2001; FRSNZ; Alan MacDiarmid Professor of Physical Sciences, Victoria University of Wellington, New Zealand, since 2001; *b* 19 Aug. 1947; *s* of Ernest Edward Callaghan and Mavis Eileen Callaghan; *m* 1st, 1969, Susan Audrey Roberts (marr. diss. 2005); one *s* one *d*; 2nd, 2006, Miang Hoong Lim. *Educ:* Victoria Univ. of Wellington (BSc Hons); Wolfson Coll., Oxford (DPhil 1974); DSc Oxon 1995. Massey University, NZ: Lectr in Physics, 1974–84; Prof. of Physics, 1984–2001; Sir Neil Waters Dist. Prof., 2001–. FRSNZ 1991; James Cook Fellow, Royal Soc. of NZ, 2008. Cooper Medal, 1991, Hector Medal, 1998, Rutherford Medal, 2005, Royal Soc. of NZ; Mechaelis Medal, Otago Univ., 1995; Ampere Prize, Groupement AMPERE, 2004; Blake Medal, Sir Peter Blake Trust, 2007; Günther Laukien Prize, Experimental Nuclear Magnetic Resonance Conf., 2010; NZ Prime Minister's Sci. Prize, 2010; Kiwibank New Zealander of the Year, 2011. *Publications:* Principles of Nuclear Magnetic Resonance Microscopy, 1991; As Far as We Know: conversations about science, life and the universe, 2007; Wool to Weta: transforming New Zealand's culture and economy, 2009; Translational Dynamics and Magnetic Resonance, 2011; contrib. numerous articles to learned jls. *Recreations:* music, walking. *Address:* School of Chemical and Physical Sciences, Victoria University of Wellington, Wellington, New Zealand. *T:* (4) 4721000. *Died 24 March 2012.*

CALLAWAY-FITTALL, Betty Daphne, (Betty Callaway), MBE 1984; trainer of skaters; skating consultant to Ice Arena, Slough, since 1986; *b* 22 March 1928; *d* of William A. Roberts and Elizabeth T. Roberts; *m* 1st, 1949, E. Roy Callaway (marr. diss. 1976; remarried 2003); 2nd, 1980, Captain W. Fittall (*d* 1990), British Airways, retd. *Educ:* Greycoat Sch., and St Paul's Convent, Westminster. Started teaching, Richmond Ice Rink, 1952; Nat. Trainer, W Germany, 1969–72; retired from full-time teaching, 1972. Commentator, ITV, 1984–. Pupils include: Angelika and Erich Buck (European Champions and 2nd in World Championship, 1972); Chrisztine Regoczy and Andras Sally (Hungarian and World Champions and Olympic silver medallists, 1980); Jayne Torvill and Christopher Dean (World Champions, 1981, 1982, 1983, 1984, European Champions, 1981, 1982, and Olympic gold medallists, 1984). Pres., British Ice Teachers Assoc., 1985–. Hon. Citizen, Ravensburg, Germany, 1972. Gold Medal, Nat. Skating Assoc., 1955; Hungarian Olympic Medal, 1980; Coach of the Year Award, Nat. Coaching Foundn, 1995. *Recreations:* music, water ski-ing, gardening. *Address:* 35 Long Grove, Seer Green, Beaconsfield, Bucks HP9 2YN. *Died 27 June 2011.*

CALNAN, Prof. Charles Dermod, MA, MB, BChir Cantab; FRCP; Director, Department of Occupational Dermatoses, St John's Hospital for Diseases of the Skin, 1974–82; Honorary Consultant Dermatologist: Royal Free Hospital, 1958–82; St John's Hospital for Diseases of the Skin, London, 1958–82; *b* 14 Dec. 1917; *s* of James Calnan, Eastbourne, Sussex; *m* 1950, Josephine Gerard Keane, *d* of late Lt-Col Michael Keane, RAMC; three *s* one *d*. *Educ:* Stonyhurst Coll.; Corpus Christi Coll., Cambridge (BA 1939, MA 1943; MB BChir 1942); London Hospital. RAMC Specialist in Dermatology, Major, 1942–46; Marsden Prof., Royal Free Hosp., 1958; Visiting Research Associate, Univ. of Pennsylvania, 1959; Prof. of Dermatology, Inst. of Dermatology, 1960–74. WHO Cons. Adviser to Nat. Inst. of Dermatology of Thailand, 1971–82. Editor: Transactions of the St John's Hosp. Dermatological Soc., 1958–75; Contact Dermatitis, 1975–87. Hon. Fellow, Brit. Assoc. of Dermatology; Hon. FRSocMed (Mem. Dermatological Section). Order of the White Elephant (Thailand), 1986. *Publications:* Atlas of Dermatology, 1974; The Life and Times of Geoffrey Barrow Dowling, 1992; various papers in med. and dermatological jls. *Address:* 8 The Croft, Lewis Lane, Cirencester, Glos GL7 1EE. *Died 7 March 2012.*

CALVERT, Barbara Adamson, (Lady Lowry); QC 1975; barrister-at-law; a Recorder of the Crown Court, 1980–98; *b* 30 April 1926; *d* of late Albert Parker, CBE; *m* 1st, 1948, John Thornton Calvert, CBE (*d* 1987); one *d* (one *s* decd); 2nd, 1994, Baron Lowry, PC (*d* 1999). *Educ:* St Helen's, Northwood; London Sch. of Economics (BScEcon). Called to Bar: Middle Temple, 1959 (Bencher 1982); NI, 1978 (QC 1978; Hon. Bencher, 1995). Admin. Officer, City and Guilds of London Inst., 1961; practice at Bar, 1962–. Full-time Chm., Industrial Tribunals, London, 1986–96 (part-time Chm., 1974–86); Mem., Matrimonial Causes Rules Cttee, 1983–85. Freeman, City of London, 1989; Liveryman: Arbitrators' Co.; Water Conservators' Co. *Recreations:* crosswords, swimming, poetry. *Address:* (home) 32 Ashgrove House, 28 Lindsay Square, Bessborough Gardens, Pimlico, SW1V 2HW; (chambers) 9–11 Fulwood Place, High Holborn, WC1V 6HG. *Clubs:* Royal Over-Seas League; Royal Fowey Yacht. *Died 22 July 2015.*

CALVERT, Norman Hilton; Deputy Secretary, Departments of the Environment and of Transport, 1978–80; *b* 27 July 1925; *s* of Clifford and Doris Calvert; *m* 1st, 1949, May Yates (*d* 1968); one *s* one *d*; 2nd, 1971, Vera Baker (*d* 1996). *Educ:* Leeds Modern Sch.; Leeds Univ.; King's Coll., Durham Univ. BA Hons 1st cl. Geography, 1950. Served Royal Signals, 1943–47: 81 (W African) Div., India, 1945–47. Min. of Housing and Local Govt: Asst Principal, 1950–55; Principal, 1956–64; Asst Sec., 1964–71; Sec., Water Resources Bd, 1964–68; Principal Regional Officer, Northern Region, 1969–71; Regional Dir, Northern Region, and Chm., Northern Econ. Planning Bd, 1971–73; Under Sec., DoE, 1971–78. *Recreations:* fell walking, listening to music, motoring. *Address:* 6 Monmouth Gardens, Beaminster, Dorset DT8 3BT. *T:* (01308) 863366. *Died 1 May 2014.*

CAMBRIDGE, Alan John; HM Diplomatic Service, retired; *b* 1 July 1925; *s* of Thomas David Cambridge and Winifred Elizabeth (*née* Jarrett); *m* 1947, Thelma Elliot; three *s* one *d*. *Educ:* Beckenham Grammar Sch. Served War, FAA and RAFVR, 1943–47 (Air Gunner, Bomber Comd). War Pensions Office and MPNI, 1948–55; entered CRO, 1955; Chief Clerk: Madras, 1956–58; Kuala Lumpur, 1959–62; 2nd Sec., Salisbury, Fedn of Rhodesia and Nyasaland, 1962–65; 1st Sec. (Political), Freetown, 1965–66; UN Dept, FCO, 1966–68; 1st Sec., Prague, 1969; 1st Sec. (Consular/Aid), Suva, 1970–72; HM Consul, Milan, 1972–74; Asst Head of Inf. Dept, FCO, 1974–78; 1st Sec., Ankara, 1978–81; Asst Head, 1981–82, Head and Counsellor, 1983–85, Migration and Visa Dept, FCO; Assessor, FCO, 1985–90. *Recreations:* photography, swimming. *Address:* 9 The Ferns, Carlton Road, Tunbridge Wells TN1 2JT. *T:* (01892) 531223. *Club:* Civil Service. *Died 3 June 2015.*

CAMBRIDGE, Sydney John Guy, CMG 1979; CVO 1979; HM Diplomatic Service, retired; *b* 5 Nov. 1928; *o s* of late Jack and Mona Cambridge; unmarried. *Educ:* Marlborough; King's Coll., Cambridge. Entered HM Diplomatic Service, Sept. 1952; Oriental Sec., British Embassy, Jedda, 1953–56; Foreign Office, 1956–60; First Sec., UK Delegn to United Nations, at New York, 1960–64; Head of Chancery, British Embassy, Djakarta, 1964–66; FO, 1966–70; Counsellor, British Embassy, Rome, 1970–73; Head of Financial Relations Dept, FCO, 1973–75; Counsellor, British High Commn, Nicosia, 1975–77; Ambassador: to Kuwait, 1977–82; to Morocco, 1982–84. *Address:* Saint Peter's House, Filkins, Lechlade, Glos GL7 3JQ. *Died Dec. 2014.*

CAME, Nicholas John Gard, FICS; Director, Australian, New Zealand and Papua New Guinea Chambers of Commerce (UK), 1993–96; *b* Swansea, 10 March 1937; *s* of Victor Henry Thomas Came and Dorothy Edith Came (*née* Prestidge); *m* 1961, Edelgard Elise Irma Meyer; two *d*. *Educ:* Bromsgrove Sch. FICS 1964; MCIT 1988. Officer Cadet Trng Vessel, Rakaia, 1954–57; Bethell Gwyn & Co., 1958–59; Nat. Service, commnd RA, 1959–61; Exec., Dowie & Marwood Ltd, 1961–66; Manager: NZ Shipping Co. Ltd, London, 1967–71; P&OSN Co., 1971–78; Dir, Shipping Corp. of NZ (UK) Ltd, 1978–91. Director: Internat. Shipping Fedn, 1983–91; Shipowners Refrigerated Cargo Res. Assoc., 1984–91; Mem. Council, Internat. Chamber of Shipping, 1983–92. Dir, Aust. and NZ Trade Adv. Cttee, 1993–96; Leader, British Trade Missions to Australasia, 1992, 1993, 1994 and 1996. Pres., NZ Soc., 1990–91. Mem., Exec. Cttee, City of London Br., RNLI, 1996–99. Associate Mem., Master Mariners' Co., 2006. *Recreations:* walking, music, languages, travel. *Clubs:* Royal Over-Seas League, Little Ship; Bristol Channel Yacht (Mumbles). *Died 29 March 2013.*

CAMERON, Major Allan John, MBE 1988; JP; Vice Lord-Lieutenant, Highland Region (Ross and Cromarty), 1977–92; *b* 25 March 1917; *s* of Col Sir Donald Cameron of Lochiel, KT, CMG (*d* 1951), and Lady Hermione Cameron (*d* 1978), *d* of 5th Duke of Montrose; *m* 1945, Mary Elizabeth Vaughan-Lee, Dillington, Somerset (*d* 2008); two *s* two *d* (and one *s* decd). *Educ:* Harrow; RMC Sandhurst. Served QO Cameron Highlanders, 1936–48; Major, Retd (POW Middle East, 1942). County Councillor, Ross-shire, 1955–75 (Chm. Educn Cttee, 1962–75); Councillor, 1975–96, Convener, 1991–96, Ross and Cromarty DC. Former Member: Red Deer Commn; Countryside Commn for Scotland; Broadcasting Council for Scotland. *Recreations:* curling (Past Pres. Royal Caledonian Curling Club), gardening, golf. *Address:* Quarryfield Farmhouse, Munlochy, Ross-shire IV8 8NZ. *T:* (01463) 811249. *Club:* Naval and Military. *Died 4 Dec. 2011.*

CAMERON, John Bell, CBE 1982; Chairman, World Meats Group, International Federation of Agricultural Producers, since 1984; Director, Argent Energy, since 2010; *b* 14 June 1939; *s* of John and Margaret Cameron; *m* 1964, Margaret (*née* Clapperton). *Educ:* Dollar Academy.

AIAgrE; FRAgS. Studied agriculture in various countries, Scandinavia, S America and Europe, 1956–61; farmed in Scotland, 1961–64. National Farmers' Union of Scotland: Mem. National Council, 1964; Vice-Pres., 1976; Pres., 1979–84 (first long-term Pres.). Mem., Agricultural Praesidium of EEC, 1979–89; Chairman: EEC Adv. Cttee for Sheep Meat, 1982–89; UK Sheep Consultative Cttee, 1986–87; Scottish Beef Council, 1997–2000; Standards Cttee, Quality Meat Scotland, 2005–. President: British Hereford Cattle Soc., 2003–05; Scottish Beef Cattle Assoc., 2005–; Scottish Nat. Sheep Assoc., 2005–. Chm., BR (Scotland) and Scottish Mem., BRB, 1988–93; Dir, SW Trains and Island Line, 1996–2007. Chm. Governors, Dollar Acad., 1984–. Hon. DTech Napier, 1998. Winner: George Headley Award to the UK Sheep Industry, 1986; Sir William Young Award to the Scottish Livestock Industry, 1986; NFU Scotland Ambassador Award, 2013. *Recreations:* flying, shooting, travelling. *Address:* Balbuthie Farm, By Leven, Fife, Scotland KY9 1EX. *T:* (01333) 730210. *Died 16 Dec. 2014.*

CAMERON, John Charles Finlay; Member, London Transport Executive, 1975–84; *b* 8 Feb. 1928; *s* of Robert John and Nancy Angela Cameron; *m* 1st, 1955, Ruth Thompson, Sydney, Australia; two *s* two *d*; 2nd, 1987, Nancy Foy (*d* 2010), author, Redlands, Calif. *Educ:* privately; University Coll., Southampton. CEng, MICE, FCILT, CCMI. Royal Marines, 1946–48. British Railways, Southern Region, Civil Engineering, 1948; BR Transport Commn, 1957; BR Rlys Workshops, 1962; Rank Organisation, 1968–75. Dir-Gen. and Sec., CIT, 1984–88 (Hon. Vice Pres., 1988–91; Chm., Scot. Sect., 1995–96); Dir, BURA, 1989–93; Chm., Highland Perthshire Develt Co., 1990–94. Member: Management Cttee, Abbotstone, Agricl Prop. Unit Trust, 1982–91; Westminster Br., IMgt (Chm., 1985–88; Vice-Pres., 1988–91). Gov., Pitlochry Fest. Theatre, 1991–98. Major, Engr and Transport Staff Corps, RE (TA), 1985–98. Liveryman, Carmen's Co., 1984–2001. *Recreation:* book binding and restoration. *Address:* Rivendell House, Oak Road, Birnam, Dunkeld, Perthshire PH8 0BL. *T:* (01350) 728647. *Club:* Oriental. *Died 28 March 2012.*

CAMERON WATT, Prof. Donald, FBA 1990; Stevenson Professor of International History in the University of London, 1981–93, then Professor Emeritus; *b* 17 May 1928; *s* of late Robert Cameron Watt and Barbara, *d* of late Rt Rev. E. J. Bidwell, former Bishop of Ontario; *m* 1st, 1951, Marianne Ruth Grau (*d* 1962); one *s*; 2nd, 1962, Felicia Cobb Stanley (*d* 1997); one step *d*. *Educ:* Rugby Sch.; Oriel Coll., Oxford (BA 1951; MA 1954; DLitt 1991; Hon. Fellow, 1998). FRHistS. Asst Editor, Documents on German Foreign Policy, 1918–1945, Foreign Office, 1951–54; Asst Lectr, Lectr, Sen. Lectr in Internat. History, LSE, 1954–66; Reader in Internat. History in Univ. of London, 1966; Titular Prof. of Internat. History, 1972–81. Editor, Survey of Internat. Affairs, Royal Inst. of Internat. Affairs, 1962–71; Rockefeller Research Fellow in Social Sciences, Inst. of Advanced Internat. Studies, Washington, 1960–61; Official Historian, Cabinet Office Historical Section, 1978–. Sec., 1967, Chm., 1970–77, Assoc. of Contemporary Historians; Mem. Bd, Inst. of Contemporary British History, 1987–2001; Chm., Greenwich Forum, 1974–84; Sec.-Treasurer, Internat. Commn for the Hist. of Internat. Relations, 1982–95 (Hon. Vice-Pres., 1995–). Member Editorial Board: Political Quarterly, 1969–2000; Marine Policy, 1978–94; Internat. History Rev., 1984–94; Intelligence and National Security, 1986–; Review of Internat. Studies, 1989–95; Gen. Ed. British Documents on Foreign Affairs, 1985–97; Ed., Amer. Studies in Europe newsletter, 1962–65. FRSA 1990. Foreign Mem., Polish Acad. of Arts and Scis, Krakow, 1993. *Publications:* (ed jtly) Oxford Poetry, 1950; Britain and the Suez Canal, 1956; (ed) Documents on the Suez Crisis, 1957; Britain looks to Germany, 1965; Personalities and Policies, 1965; (ed) Survey of International Affairs 1961, 1964; (ed) Documents on International Affairs 1961, 1966; (ed, with K. Bourne) Studies in International History, 1967; A History of the World in the Twentieth Century, Pt I, 1967; (ed) Contemporary History in Europe, 1969; (ed) Hitler's Mein Kampf, 1969, 2nd edn 1992; (ed) Survey of International Affairs 1962, 1969; (ed, with James Mayall): Current British Foreign Policy 1970, 1971; Current British Foreign Policy 1971, 1972; Current British Foreign Policy 1972, 1973; Too Serious a Business, 1975, 2nd edn 1993; (ed) Survey of International Affairs 1963, 1977; Succeeding John Bull: America in Britain's place 1900–1975, 1984; How War Came, 1989; (ed with Guido Di Tella) Argentina between the Great Powers, 1990. *Recreations:* exploring London, cats. *Address:* c/o London School of Economics and Political Science, Houghton Street, WC2A 2AE. *Died 30 Oct. 2014.*

CAMPBELL OF ALLOWAY, Baron *cr* 1981 (Life Peer), of Ayr in the District of Kyle and Carrick; **Alan Robertson Campbell,** ERD 1996; QC 1965; a Recorder of the Crown Court, 1976–89; *b* 24 May 1917; *s* of late J. K. Campbell; *m* 1st, 1945, Diana Watson-Smyth (marr. diss. 1953); one *d*; 2nd, 1957, Vivien (*d* 2010), *y d* of late Comdr A. H. de Kantzow, DSO, RN; 3rd, 2011, Dorothea, *d* of late Col Edward and Lady Elizabeth Berwick. *Educ:* Aldenham; Ecole des Sciences Politiques, Paris; Trinity Hall, Cambridge. Called to Bar, Inner Temple, 1939, Bencher, 1972; Western Circuit. Commissioned RA (Suppl. Res.), 1939; served France and Belgium, 1939–40; POW, 1940–45. Consultant to sub-cttee of Legal Cttee of Council of Europe on Industrial Espionage, 1965–74; Chm., Legal Res. Cttee, Soc. of Conservative Lawyers, 1968–80. Member: H of L Cttee for Privileges, 1982–2000; H of L Select Cttee on Murder and Life Imprisonment, 1988–89; Ecclesiastical Cttee, 2000–05; Jt Cttee on Human Rights, 2001–07; Jt Cttee on Statutory Instruments, 2008–. Member: Law Adv. Cttee, British Council, 1974–82; Management Cttee, UK Assoc. for European Law, 1975–90. Vice Pres., Assoc. de Juristes Franco-Britanniques, 1989–90. Pres., Colditz Assoc., 1998–2004. Patron, Inns of Court Sch. of Law Conservatives, 1996–2000. *Publications:* (with Lord Wilberforce) Restrictive Trade Practices and Monopolies, 1956, 2nd edn, 1966, Supplements 1 and 2, 1973; Restrictive Trading Agreements in the Common Market, 1964, Supplement, 1965; Common Market Law, vols 1 and 2, 1969, vol. 3, 1973 and Supplement, 1975; Industrial Relations Act, 1971; EC Competition Law, 1980; Trade Unions and the Individual, 1980. *Address:* House of Lords, SW1A 0PW. *Clubs:* Carlton (Mem., Political Cttee, 1967–79), Pratt's, Beefsteak. *Died 30 June 2013.*

CAMPBELL, Caroline Jane; *see* Harry Thomas, C. J.

CAMPBELL, Maj.-Gen. (Charles) Peter, CBE 1977; Director, Quicks (formerly H. & J. Quick) Group Plc, 1982–91; *b* 25 Aug. 1926; *s* of late Charles Alfred Campbell and Blanche Campbell; *m* 1st, 1949, Lucy Kitching (*d* 1986); two *s*; 2nd, 1986, Elizabeth Tristram. *Educ:* Gillingham Grammar Sch.; Emmanuel Coll., Cambridge. Commnd RE, 1945 (despatches, Palestine, 1948); psc 1957; DAA&QMG Trng Bde, RE, 1958–60; OC 11 Ind. Field Sqdn, RE, 1960–62; Jt Services Staff Coll., 1963; DAAG WO, 1963–65; Co. Comd, RMA Sandhurst, 1965–67; CO 21 Engr Regt, 1967–70; GSOI MoD, 1970–71; CRE 3 Div., 1971; Comd 12 Engr Bde, 1972–73; RCDS, 1974; COS HQ NI, 1975–77; Engineer-in-Chief (Army), 1977–80. Col Comdt, RE, 1981–86, Rep. Col Comdt, 1982; Hon. Colonel: RE (Vol.) (Explosive Ordnance Disposal), 1986–88; 101 (London) Engr Regt (Explosive Ordnance Disposal) (V), 1988–91. Chm., RE Assoc., 1983–89. Gov., Gordon's Sch., 1993–96; Mem., Foundn of Gordon's Sch., 1991–2001 (Vice-Chm., 1996–99). FCMI. *Recreation:* painting and collecting militaria. *Died 31 Aug. 2012.*

CAMPBELL, Donald le Strange, MC 1944; *b* 16 June 1919; *s* of late Donald Fraser Campbell and Caroline Campbell; *m* 1952, Hon. Shona Catherine Greig Macpherson (*d* 2004), *y d* of 1st Baron Macpherson of Drumochter; one *s* one *d*. *Educ:* Winchester Coll.; Clare Coll., Cambridge. Served War, 1939–45, Major RA (MC). EFCO Ltd, 1947–55; MEECO Ltd, 1955–61; Davy-Ashmore Ltd, 1961–67; Dep. Chm. and Man. Dir, Davy-Ashmore Internat., 1965–69; Dir, Hovair Ltd, 1970–78; farming, Berks and Devon, 1979–96. Chm., BNEC Latin America, 1967. *Recreations:* farming, sailing, field sports, music. *Address:* Flat 6, New Court, Sutton Manor, Sutton Scotney, Hants SO21 3JB. *Clubs:* Boodle's; Royal Yacht Squadron. *Died 10 March 2011.*

CAMPBELL, Gordon Arden, CBE 2006; FREng, FIChemE; Chairman: Jupiter Second Split Trust plc, since 2004; Accsys Technologies plc, since 2010 (non-executive Director, since 2005); *b* 16 Oct. 1946; *s* of late Hugh Eric Campbell and Jessie Campbell; *m* 1970, Jennifer Vaughan; two *d*. *Educ:* Churchill Coll., Cambridge (MA). FIChemE 1987. Joined Courtaulds Research, 1968; Dir, British Celanese, 1976; Managing Director: Courtaulds Chemicals, 1980–85; SAICCOR, S Africa, 1985–87; Dir, 1987, Dep. Chief Exec., 1995, Chief Exec., 1996–98, Courtaulds. Chairman: ITI Scotland, 2003–05; BNF plc, 2004–08 (Dir, 2000–08). Mem., UKAEA, 1994–96; non-executive Director: AEA Technol., 1996–97; Argos plc, 1997–98; HSS Ltd, 2005–07; non-executive Chairman: International Process Technologies, 1999–2001; Wade-Allied Hldgs, 1999–2003; Babcock International Gp, 2001–08. Consultant: Ineos plc, 2007–; Rolls Royce plc, 2009–. President: Comité Internat. de Rayon et Fibres Synthétiques, 1995–98; IChemE, 1998–99. Member: President's Council, CBI, 1995–2000, 2004–08; Council, British Heart Foundn, 1999–2005. Vis. Prof., Univ. of Strathclyde, 2003–. Mem. Court, Cranfield Univ., 1999–2006. FREng (FEng 1993; Vice-Pres., 2001–04). CCMI (CBIM 1990). *Recreations:* Rugby, golf, ski-ing. *Died 26 April 2014.*

CAMPBELL, Graham Gordon, CB 1984; Under-Secretary, Department of Energy, 1974–84; *b* 12 Dec. 1924; *s* of late Lt-Col and Mrs P. H. Campbell; *m* 1955, Margaret Rosamond Busby; one *d*. *Educ:* Cheltenham Coll.; Caius Coll., Cambridge (BA Hist.). Served War, Royal Artillery, 1943–46. Asst Principal, Min. of Fuel and Power, 1949; Private Sec. to Parly Sec., Min. of Fuel and Power, 1953–54; Principal, 1954; Asst Sec., Min. of Power, 1965; Under-Sec., DTI, 1973. *Recreations:* watching birds, music, hill-walking, clearing scrub. *Address:* 3 Clovelly Avenue, Warlingham, Surrey CR6 9HZ. *T:* (01883) 624671. *Died 24 July 2011.*

CAMPBELL, Prof. Iain (Donald), PhD; FRS 1995; Professor of Structural Biology, University of Oxford, 1992–2009, then Emeritus; Tutorial Fellow in Biochemistry, St John's College, Oxford, 1989–2009, then Emeritus Research Fellow; *b* 24 April 1941; *s* of Daniel Campbell and Catherine Campbell (*née* Lauder); *m* 1967, Karin C. Wehle; one *s* two *d*. *Educ:* Perth Acad.; St Andrews Univ. (BSc 1963; PhD 1967); MA Oxon 1987. University Lectr, Dept of Biochem., Oxford, 1976–92. Croonian Lectr, Royal Soc., 2006. Member: Molecular and Cellular Medicine Bd, MRC, 1992–96; Wellcome Trust Molecular Cell Bd, 1997–2002. Mem., EMBO, 1990. Delegate, OUP, 1996–2006. Mem., various editl bds of scientific jls. Trustee: Edward P. Abraham Cephalosporin Fund, 2004–; EMF Biol Res. Trust, 2007–. Fellow, Internat. Soc. for Magnetic Resonance in Medicine, 2011. Hon. DTech Lund, 2000; Hon. DSc: Portsmouth, 2000; St Andrews, 2012. Education in Partnership with Industry Award, DTI, 1982; BDH Medal, 1990, Novartis Medal, 2003, Biochem. Soc.; Croonian Medal, Royal Soc., 2006. *Publications:* Biophysical Techniques, 2012; numerous scientific papers and reviews. *Address:* Department of Biochemistry, Oxford University, South Parks Road, Oxford OX1 3QU. *T:* (01865) 613298, (St John's College) (01865) 277380, *Fax:* (01865) 613201. *Died 5 March 2014.*

CAMPBELL, Ian James, FRAS; Director General Research Maritime, Ministry of Defence, 1978–81; *b* 9 June 1923; *s* of Allan and Elizabeth Campbell; *m* 1946, Stella Margaret Smith (*d* 2001). *Educ:* George Heriot's Sch.; Edinburgh Univ. (MA Hons, Maths and Natural Phil.). FRAS 2004. Op. Res. Sect., HQ Bomber Comd, 1943–46; Asst Lectr in Astronomy, St Andrews Univ., 1946–48; joined Royal Naval Scientific Service, 1948; Dept of Aeronaut. and Eng Res., Admiralty, 1948–49; Admiralty Res. Lab., 1949–59; Admiralty Underwater Weapons Estab., 1959–68 (leader of res. team which established concept and technol. base for Stingray torpedo, 1962–68); Chief Scientist, Naval Construction Res. Estab., 1969–73; Head of Weapons Dept, Admiralty Underwater Weapons Estab., 1973–76; Ministry of Defence: Dir of Res. (Ships), 1976–78; Scientific Advr to Ship Dept, 1976–81. Defence sci. consultant, 1982–92; Technical Dir, CAP Scientific, 1983–87; Dir of Studies, Centre for Operational Res. and Defence Analysis, 1987–88. Chm., Res. Adv. Cttee, Electronic Engrg Assoc., 1989–91. *Publications:* papers on fluid mechanics in scientific proceedings and jls. *Recreations:* astronomy, Scottish country dancing. *Address:* 6 Queens Avenue, Dorchester, Dorset DT1 2EW. *T:* (01305) 264270. *Club:* Sloane. *Died 6 May 2012.*

CAMPBELL, John Davies, CVO 1980; CBE 1981 (MBE 1957); MC 1945, and bar 1945; HM Diplomatic Service, retired; Consul-General, Naples, 1977–81; *b* 11 Nov. 1921; *s* of late William Hastings Campbell and Hon. Mrs Campbell (Eugenie Anne Westenra, subsequently Harbord), *d* of 14th Baron Louth; *m* 1959, Shirley Bouch; one *s* two *d*. *Educ:* Cheltenham Coll.; St Andrews Univ. Served War, HM Forces, Argyll and Sutherland Highlanders and Popski's Private Army, 1940–46. HM Colonial Service (subseq. HMOCS), 1949–61 (despatches, 1957); HM Foreign (subseq. HM Diplomatic) Service, 1961; First Secretary, 1961; Counsellor, 1972; Counsellor (Information) Ottawa, 1972–77. Commendatore dell'ordine al merito della Repubblica Italiana, 1980. *Recreations:* travel, music, theatre. *Address:* Townsend House, Luston, Leominster, Herefordshire HR6 0DZ. *T:* (01568) 612446. *Clubs:* Victory Services, Special Forces. *Died 30 July 2015.*

CAMPBELL, Rev. Laurence Jamieson; Methodist Minister, Trinity Church, Newport, Gwent Circuit, 1987–94; Headmaster, Kingswood School, Bath, 1970–87; *b* 10 June 1927; *er s* of George S. Campbell and Mary P. Paterson; *m* 1954, Sheena E. Macdonald; two *s* one *d*. *Educ:* Hillhead High Sch., Glasgow; Aberdeen Univ.; Edinburgh Univ. (MA). Lieut RA, 1945–48. Housemaster, Alliance High Sch., Kenya, 1952–56; Presbyterian Church of E Africa, 1957–61: Tumutumu Coll., 1957–60; Supervisor of Schs, 1960–61; Educn Sec., Christian Council of Kenya, 1962; Headmaster, Alliance High Sch., Kenya, 1963–70. Methodist minister, ordained 1988. Contested North Kenya Constituency, Kenya General Election, 1961. Mem. Council, Univ. of East Africa, 1963–69; Chm., Heads Assoc. of Kenya, 1965–69; Official of Kenya Commonwealth Games Team, 1970. Schoolmaster Fellow, Balliol Coll., Oxford, 1970. Chairman: Christians Abroad, 1977–81; Bloxham Project, 1981–84. *Recreations:* golf, travel, church. *Address:* 1A Edward VII Avenue, Newport, Gwent NP20 4NF. *Died 17 July 2011.*

CAMPBELL, Maj.-Gen. Peter; *see* Campbell, Maj.-Gen. C. P.

CANDLIN, Prof. Christopher Noel, AO 2015; Senior Research Professor in Linguistics, Macquarie University, Sydney, part-time 2002–06, full-time, 2006–10, then Emeritus; *b* 31 March 1940; *s* of late Edwin Frank Candlin, OBE and of Nora Candlin (*née* Letts); *m* 1964, Sally (*née* Carter); one *s* three *d*. *Educ:* Jesus Coll., Oxford (MA); Univ. of London (PGCE); Yale Univ. (MPhil). Research Associate, Univ. of Leeds, 1967–68; University of Lancaster: Lectr, 1968, later Sen. Lectr; Prof. of Linguistics and Modern English Language, 1981–87; Macquarie University, Sydney: Prof. and Chm., Linguistics Dept, 1987–98; Exec. Dir, Nat. Centre for Eng. Lang. Teaching and Res., 1988–98; Dir, Centre for Lang. in Social Life, 1993–98; Adjunct Prof. of Linguistics, 1998; Chair Prof. of Applied Linguistics and Dir, Centre for English Lang. Educn and Communication Res., City Univ. of Hong Kong, 1998–2002; Prof. of Applied Linguistics (pt-time), Open Univ., 2002–05. Visiting Professor: Univ. of Giessen, 1975; East-West Centre, Honolulu, 1978; Ontario Inst. for Studies in Educn, Toronto, 1983; Univ. of Hawaii at Manoa, 1984; Univ. of Melbourne, 1985; Jyväskylä Univ., Finland, 1993; Univ. of Wales, Cardiff, 1995 (Hon. Prof., 1995); Adjunct Prof., Univ. of Technol., Sydney, 1998. General Editor: Applied Linguistics and Language Study; Language in Social Life; Language Teacher Educn Scheme; Language Teaching Methodology Series; Applied Linguistics in Action; Advances in Applied Linguistics. Pres., Internat. Assoc. of Applied Linguistics, 1996–2002. FRSA. Hon. PhD Jyväskylä, 1996. *Publications:* Challenges, 1978; The Communicative Teaching of English, 1981; Computers in English Language Teaching and Research, 1985; Language Learning Tasks, 1986; Language, Learning and Community, 1989; English at Work, vol. 1, 1991, vol. 2, 1992; (ed jtly) Australian Learners' Dictionary, 1997;

Writing: texts, processes and practices, 1999. *Recreations:* theatre, concerts, sailing, cooking. *Address:* Department of Linguistics, Macquarie University, Sydney, NSW 2109, Australia. *Died 9 May 2015.*

CANDY, Elizabeth Mary; Head Mistress, The Lady Eleanor Holles School, Hampton, 1981–2004; *b* 12 Oct. 1942; *d* of late Donald Glen Candy and Phyllis Mary Candy (*née* Denbury). *Educ:* Merrywood Grammar Sch., Bristol; Westfield Coll., London (BSc 1965). Chemistry Mistress then Jt Head of Science, Bromley High Sch., 1965–71; Head of Science then Second Mistress, Putney High Sch., 1971–81. Mem. Council, Royal Holloway, London Univ., 1995–2003. FRSA 1994. Gov., Old Vicarage Sch., Richmond, 2005–. Dame Chevalier, Ordre des Coteaux de Champagne, 1998. *Recreations:* opera, reading, France and French wine, photography, cycling, tennis, golf. *Address:* Miranda Cottage, 5 St John's Road, East Molesey, Surrey KT8 9JH. *T:* (020) 8941 3066. *Club:* Cripplegate Ward. *Died 9 Nov. 2015.*

CANNAN, Denis; dramatist and script writer; *b* 14 May 1919; *s* of late Captain H. J. Pullein-Thompson, MC, and Joanna Pullein-Thompson (*née* Cannan); he changed name to Denis Cannan, by deed poll, 1964; *m* 1st, 1946, Joan Ross (marr. diss.); two *s* one *d*; 2nd, 1965, Rose Evansky. *Educ:* Eton. A Repertory factotum, 1937–39. Served War of 1939–45, Queen's Royal Regt, Captain (despatches). Actor at Citizens' Theatre, Glasgow, 1946–48. *Publications: plays:* Max (prod. Malvern Festival), 1949; Captain Carvallo (Bristol Old Vic and St James's Theatres), 1950; Colombe (trans. from Anouilh), New Theatre, 1951; Misery Me!, Duchess, 1955; You and Your Wife, Bristol Old Vic, 1955; The Power and The Glory (adaptation from Graham Greene), Phoenix Theatre, 1956, and Phœnix Theatre, New York, 1958; Who's Your Father?, Cambridge Theatre, 1958; US (original text), Aldwych, 1966; adapted Ibsen's Ghosts, Aldwych, 1966; One at Night, Royal Court, 1971; The Ik (adaptation and collaboration), 1975; Dear Daddy, Oxford Festival and Ambassadors, 1976 (Play of the Year award, 1976); the screenplays of several films; plays for TV and radio, adaptations for TV series. *Address:* 30 Park Gate, Somerhill Road, Hove, Sussex BN3 1RL. *Died 25 Sept. 2011.*

CANNON, Prof. John Ashton, CBE 1985; PhD; Professor of Modern History, University of Newcastle upon Tyne, 1976–92, then Professor Emeritus; Pro-Vice Chancellor, 1983–86; *b* 8 Oct. 1926; *s* of George and Gladys Cannon; *m* 1st, 1948, Audrey Elizabeth, *d* of G. R. Caple (marr. diss. 1953); one *s* one *d*; 2nd, 1953, Minna, *d* of Frederick Pedersen, Denmark; one *s* two *d*. *Educ:* Hertford Grammar Sch.; Peterhouse, Cambridge (MA 1955). PhD Bristol, 1958. Served RAF, 1947–49 and 1952–55. History of Parlt Trust, 1960–61; Univ. of Bristol: Lectr, 1961; Sen. Lectr, 1967; Reader, 1970; Dean, Faculty of Arts, Univ. of Newcastle upon Tyne, 1979–82. Member: UGC, 1983–89 (Vice-Chm., 1986–89; Chm., Arts Sub-Cttee, 1983–89); Open Univ. Vis. Cttee, 1988–92. Lectures: Wiles, Queen's Univ. Belfast, 1982; Raleigh, British Acad., 1982; Prothero, RHistS, 1985; Stenton, Reading Univ., 1986; James Ford Special, Oxford, 1996. Chm., Radio Bristol, 1970–74. FRHistS 1980; FRSA 1990. *Publications:* The Fox-North Coalition: crisis of the constitution, 1970; Parliamentary Reform, 1640–1832, 1973; (ed with P. V. McGrath) Essays in Bristol and Gloucestershire History, 1976; (ed) The Letters of Junius, 1978; (ed) The Historian at Work, 1980; (ed) The Whig Ascendancy, 1981; Aristocratic Century, 1984; (ed jtly) The Blackwell Dictionary of Historians, 1988; (with R. Griffiths) The Oxford Illustrated History of the British Monarchy, 1988; Samuel Johnson and the politics of Hanoverian England, 1994; (ed) The Oxford Companion to British History, 1997; (ed) The Oxford Dictionary of British History, 2001; (with A. Hargreaves) The Kings and Queens of Britain, 2001. *Recreations:* music, losing at tennis. *Address:* 29 Lily Avenue, Jesmond, Newcastle upon Tyne NE2 2SQ. *T:* (0191) 281 4096. *Died 25 Oct. 2012.*

CAPE, Donald Paul Montagu Stewart, CMG 1977; CBE 1998; HM Diplomatic Service, retired; Ambassador and UK Permanent Representative to the Council of Europe, Strasbourg, 1978–83; *b* 6 Jan. 1923; *s* of late John Scarvell and Olivia Millicent Cape; *m* 1948, Cathune Johnston; three *s* one *d* (and one *s* decd). *Educ:* Ampleforth Coll.; Brasenose Coll., Oxford. Scots Guards, 1942–45. Entered Foreign Service, 1946. Served: Belgrade, 1946–49; FO, 1949–51; Lisbon, 1951–55; Singapore, 1955–57; FO, 1957–60; Bogota, 1960–61; Holy See, 1962–67; Head of Information Administration Dept, FCO, 1968–70; Counsellor, Washington, 1970–73; Counsellor, Brasilia, 1973–75; Ambassador to Laos, 1976–78. Administrator, Anglo-Irish Encounter, 1983–98; Chm., Anglo-Portuguese Soc., 1988–91. *Publications:* A Lucky Life (autobiog.), 1983. *Recreations:* golf, walking, swimming. *Address:* Hilltop, Wonersh, Guildford, Surrey GU5 0QT. *Died 16 June 2014.*

CARBERY, 11th Baron *cr* 1715; **Peter Ralfe Harrington Evans-Freke;** Bt 1768; *b* 20 March 1920; *o s* of Major the Hon. Ralfe Evans-Freke, MBE (*yr s* of 9th Baron) (*d* 1969), and Vera (*d* 1984), *d* of late C. Harrington Moore; *S* uncle, 1970; *m* 1st, 1941, Joyzelle Mary (*d* 2006), *o d* of late Herbert Binnie; three *s* two *d*; 2nd, 2007, Mary Elisabeth Carew Hunt (*née* Kober), *widow* of Basil Carew Hunt. *Educ:* Downside School. MICE. Served War of 1939–45, Captain RE, India, Burmah. Member of London Stock Exchange, 1955–68. *Recreations:* hunting, tennis, winter sports. *Heir: e s* Hon. Michael Peter Evans-Freke [*b* 11 Oct. 1942; *m* 1967, Claudia Janet Elizabeth, *o d* of Captain P. L. C. Gurney; one *s* three *d*]. *Died 28 July 2012.*

CARBERY, Prof. Thomas Francis, OBE 1983; Emeritus Professor, University of Strathclyde, since 1990; Consultant, Energy Action Scotland, 2005–14 (Member of Board, 1996–2005; Deputy Chairman, 2002–03); *b* 18 Jan. 1925; *oc* of Thomas Albert Carbery and Jane Morrison; *m* 1954, Ellen Donnelly (*d* 2013); one *s* two *d*. *Educ:* St Aloysius Coll., Glasgow; Univ. of Glasgow and Scottish Coll. of Commerce. Cadet Navigator, 1943–45, Meteorologist, 1945–47, RAFVR; Min. of Labour, 1947–61; Lectr, then Sen. Lectr, in Govt and Econs, Scottish College of Commerce, Glasgow, 1961–64; University of Strathclyde: Sen. Lectr in Govt-Business Relations, 1964–75; Head of Dept of Office Organisation, 1975–79, and Prof., 1979–85; Prof., Dept of Inf. Science, 1985–88, and Chm. of Dept, 1985–86; Prof. (part-time), Dept of Marketing, 1988–90. Chm., 1995–2005, Mem., Bd of Studies, 2005–07, Huron Univ. in London. Member: IBA (formerly ITA), 1970–79 (Chm., Scottish Cttee, 1970–79); Royal Commn on Gambling, 1976–78; Central Transport Users' Consultative Cttee, 1976–80 (Chm., Scottish Transport Users' Consultative Cttee, 1976–80); European (later International) Adv. Council, Salzburg Seminar, 1980–91; Broadcasting Complaints Commn, 1981–86; Data Protection Tribunal, 1984–98; Scottish Legal Aid Bd, 1986–92; Press Council, 1987–90. Dep. Chm., Scottish Consumer Council, 1980–84 (Mem., 1977–80); Chairman: S of Scotland Electricity Consumers' Cttee, 1990–95; Scottish Cttee, Information Technology, 1982–85; Ombudsman to Mirror Gp Newspapers Scottish titles, 1990–91; Special Adviser, H of C Select Cttee on Scottish Affairs, 1982. Academic Governor, Richmond Coll., 1983–95; Governor, 1984–2000, Trustee, 1991–2013, St Aloysius' Coll., Glasgow. Editor, Approaches to Information Technology (Plenum Press series), 1984–90. Hon. DBA Huron in London, 2007. KSG 1995. *Publications:* Consumers in Politics, 1969; (jtly) An Introduction to Office Management and Automation, 1991; *short stories:* Fifty Tales for a Wet Weekend in Tighnabruaich, 2010; Fifty Tales for a Grey Windy Weekend in Ardnamurchan, 2012. *Recreations:* conversation, spectating at Association football, listening to Radio 4, watching television. *Address:* 24 Fairfax Avenue, Glasgow G44 5AL. *T:* (0141) 637 0514. *Died 22 Feb. 2015.*

CAREY, Hugh Leo; Partner, Harris Beach LLP; *b* Brooklyn, NY, 11 April 1919; *s* of Denis Carey and Margaret (*née* Collins); *m* 1947, Helen Owen Twohy (*d* 1974); six *s* four *d* (and three *s* decd), and one step *d*. *Educ:* St Augustine's Academy and High School, Brooklyn; St John's Coll.; St John's Law School. JD 1951. Served War of 1939–45 (Bronze Star, Croix de Guerre with Silver Star); with US Army in Europe, 1939–46, rank of Lt-Col. Joined family business (petrochemicals), 1947. Called to Bar, 1951. Member US House of Reps, rep. 12th District of Brooklyn,

1960–75 (Democrat); Deputy Whip; Governor of New York State, 1974–83. Exec. Vice-Pres., W. R. Grace and Co., 1987–95. Dir, Triarc, 1994–. *Died 7 Aug. 2011.*

CAREY, Sir Peter (Willoughby), GCB 1982 (KCB 1976; CB 1972); Senior Adviser, Morgan Grenfell Group, 1990–96; Chairman, Dalgety PLC, 1986–92 (Director, 1983–92); Director: BPB Industries PLC, 1983–95; NV Philips Electronics, 1984–95; *b* 26 July 1923; *s* of Jack Delves Carey and Sophie Carey; *m* 1946, Thelma Young; three *d*. *Educ:* Portsmouth Grammar Sch.; Oriel Coll., Oxford; Sch. of Slavonic Studies. Served War of 1939–45: Capt., Gen. List, 1943–45. Information Officer, British Embassy, Belgrade, 1945–46; FO (German Section), 1948–51; Bd of Trade, 1953; Prin. Private Sec. to successive Presidents, 1960–64; IDC, 1965; Asst Sec., 1963–67, Under-Sec., 1967–69, Bd of Trade; Under-Sec., Min. of Technology, 1969–71; Dep. Sec., Cabinet Office, 1971–72; Dep. Sec., 1972–73, Second Permanent Sec., 1973–74, DTI; Second Permanent Sec., 1974–76, Permanent Sec., 1976–83, DoI. Director: Morgan Grenfell Hldgs, later Morgan Grenfell Gp, 1983–90 (Chm., 1987–89); Cable and Wireless, 1984–94; Westland Gp, 1986–88. Hon. LLD Birmingham, 1983; Hon. DSc Cranfield Inst. of Tech., 1984; Hon. DCL City, 1991. *Recreations:* music, theatre, travel. *Address:* Knowle Park Nursing Home, Cranleigh, Surrey GU6 8JL. *Died 4 Feb. 2011.*

CARLESS, Hugh Michael, CMG 1976; HM Diplomatic Service, retired; *b* 22 April 1925; *s* of late Henry Alfred Carless, CIE, and Gwendolen Pattullo; *m* 1956, Rosa Maria, *e d* of Martino and Ada Frontini, São Paulo; one *s* (and one *s* decd). *Educ:* Sherborne; Sch. of Oriental Studies, London; Trinity Hall, Cambridge. Served in Paiforce and BAOR, 1943–47; entered Foreign (subseq. Diplomatic) Service, 1950; 3rd Sec., Kabul, 1951; 2nd Sec., Rio de Janeiro, 1953; Tehran, 1956; 1st Sec., 1957; FO, 1958; Private Sec. to Minister of State, 1961; Budapest, 1963; Civil Service Fellow, Dept of Politics, Glasgow Univ., 1966; Counsellor and Consul-Gen., Luanda, 1967–70; Counsellor, Bonn, 1970–73; Head of Latin America Dept, FCO, 1973–77; Minister and Chargé d'Affaires, Buenos Aires, 1977–80; on secondment to Northern Engineering Industries International Ltd, 1980–82; Ambassador to Venezuela, 1982–85. Exec. Vice Pres., Hinduja Foundn (UK), 1986–97; Vice Chm., S Atlantic Council, 1987–97. Chm. British Cttee, Argentine-British Confs, 1994–96. Chm., GEECO International, 1997–2001. Cruise ship lectr, 2002–03. An Hon. Vice Pres., RSAA, 1992–95. *Recreations:* golf, history. *Address:* 15 Bryanston Square, W1H 2DN. *Clubs:* Travellers; Royal Mid Surrey Golf. *Died 20 Dec. 2011.*

CARLILE, Thomas, CBE 1975; FREng; Chairman, Burnett and Hallamshire Holdings, 1985–88; *b* 9 Feb. 1924; *s* of late James Love Carlile and Isobel Scott Carlile; *m* 1955, Jessie Davidson Clarkson; three *d*. *Educ:* Minchenden County Sch.; City & Guilds Coll., London. Joined Babcock & Wilcox Ltd, 1944; Man. Dir, 1968–84, Dep. Chm., 1978–84, Babcock Internat. plc. Chm., Shipbuilding Industry Training Board, 1967–70; Dep. Chm., Police Negotiating Bd, 1987–95. Mem., Energy Commn, 1977–79. Pres., Engineering Employers' Fedn, 1972–74, a Vice-Pres., 1979–84. Director: Chubb & Son plc, 1976–84; French Kier Hldgs Plc, 1985–86. Chm., British Soc. of Master Glass Painters, 1995–2000. FCGI 1978; FREng (FEng 1979). *Address:* 8 Aldenham Grove, Radlett, Herts WD7 7BW. *T:* (01923) 857033. *Died 29 Sept. 2014.*

CARLILL, Rear Adm. John Hildred, OBE 1969; DL; Royal Navy, retired 1982; *b* 24 Oct. 1925; *o s* of late Dr and Mrs H. B. Carlill; *m* 1955, (Elizabeth) Ann, *yr d* of late Lt Col and Mrs W. Southern; three *d*. *Educ:* RNC Dartmouth. psc 1961; jssc 1967. Served War 1939–45. Joined RN as Exec. Cadet 1939, transferred to Accountant Branch 1943; HMS Mauritius 1943–45. Comdr 1963, Captain 1972 (Sec. to FO Naval Air Comd, Dir Naval Manning and Training (S), Sec. to Second Sea Lord, Admty Interview Board, Cdre HMS Drake); Rear Admiral 1980; Adm. President, RNC Greenwich, 1980–82. Sec., Engineering Council, 1983–87. Chm., ABTA Appeal Bd, 1996–2010. President: Guildford Br., RN Assoc., 1989–2010; Guildford Sea Cadets, 1998–2007. Freeman, City of London, 1980; Freeman, 1983, Liveryman, 2009, Drapers' Co. DL Surrey, 1994. Chevalier de la Légion d'Honneur (France), 2004. *Address:* 1 Wonersh Court, The Street, Wonersh, Guildford, Surrey GU5 0PG. *T:* (01483) 893077. *Died 10 Nov. 2015.*

CARMICHAEL, Prof. Ian Stuart Edward, PhD; FRS 1999; Professor of Geology, University of California, Berkeley, 1967–2004, then Emeritus; *b* 29 March 1930; *s* of Edward Arnold Carmichael and Jeanette Carmichael; one *s* two *d* (and one *s* decd) from former marriages. *Educ:* Trinity Hall, Cambridge (BA 1954); Imperial Coll., London Univ. (PhD 1958). Lectr in Geology, Imperial Coll., London Univ., 1958–63; NSF Fellow, Univ. of Chicago, 1964; University of California, Berkeley: Mem. Faculty, 1964–; Chm., Dept of Geology, 1972–76, 1980–82; Associate Dean, 1976–78, 1985–2000; Associate Provost for Res., 1986–2000; Director: Lawrence Hall of Sci., 1996–2003; Botanic Garden, 1997–99. Day Medal, Geol Soc. Amer., 1991; Schlumberger Medal, Mineralol Soc., 1992; Murchison Medal, Geol Soc., 1995; Roebling Medal, Mineralol Soc. Amer., 1997. *Publications:* Igneous Petrology, 1974; contribs to jls. *Address:* Department of Earth and Planetary Science, University of California, Berkeley, CA 94720, USA. *E:* ian@eps.berkeley.edu. *Died 26 Aug. 2011.*

CARNEGIE, Lt-Gen. Sir Robin (Macdonald), KCB 1979; OBE 1968; DL; Director General of Army Training, 1981–82; *b* 22 June 1926; *yr s* of late Sir Francis Carnegie, CBE; *m* 1955, Iona, *yr d* of late Maj.-Gen. Sir John Sinclair, KCMG, CB, OBE; one *s* two *d*. *Educ:* Rugby. Commnd 7th Queen's Own Hussars, 1946; comd The Queen's Own Hussars, 1967–69; Comdr 11th Armd Bde, 1971–72; Student, Royal Coll. of Defence Studies, 1973; GOC 3rd Div., 1974–76; Chief of Staff, BAOR, 1976–78; Military Secretary, 1978–80. Col, The Queen's Own Hussars, 1981–87. Non-Service Mem., Police, Prison and Fire Service Selection Bds, 1987–96. DL Wilts, 1990. *Died 1 Jan. 2011.*

CARNELL, Rev. Canon Geoffrey Gordon; Chaplain to the Queen, 1981–88; Non-Residentiary Canon of Peterborough Cathedral, 1965–85, then Canon Emeritus; *b* 5 July 1918; *m* 1945, Mary Elizabeth Boucher Smith (*d* 2008); two *s*. *Educ:* City of Norwich Sch.; St John's Coll., Cambridge (Scholar, 1937; BA 1940; Naden Divinity Student, 1940; Lightfoot Scholar, 1940; MA 1944); Cuddesdon Coll., Oxford. Ordained deacon, Peterborough Cathedral, 1942; priest, 1943. Asst Curate, Abington, Northampton, 1942–49; Chaplain and Lectr in Divinity, St Gabriel's Coll., Camberwell, 1949–53; Rector of Isham with Great and Little Harrowden, Northants, 1953–71; Rector of Boughton, Northampton, 1971–85. Examining Chaplain to Bishop of Peterborough, 1962–86; Dir, Post-Ordination Trng and Ordinands, 1962–86; Peterborough Diocesan Librarian, Ecton House Diocesan Centre, 1967–93. Chaplain: to High Sheriff of Northants, 1972–73; to Mayor of Kettering, 1988–89. Member: Ecclesiastical History Soc., 1979–; Church of England Record Soc., 1992–; Acting Vice-Chm., Northants Record Soc., 1982–89 (Hon. Life Mem., 2012). *Publications:* The Bishops of Peterborough 1541–1991, 1993. *Recreations:* walking, music, art history, local history. *Died 14 Nov. 2015.*

CARO, Sir Anthony (Alfred), OM 2000; Kt 1987; CBE 1969; RA 2004; sculptor; *b* 8 March 1924; *s* of late Alfred and Mary Caro; *m* 1949, Sheila May Girling; two *s*. *Educ:* Charterhouse; Christ's Coll., Cambridge (Hon. Fellow, 1981); Regent Street Polytechnic; Royal Acad. Schs, London (Landseer Schol., 1st Landseer Award). Served FAA, 1944–46. Asst to Henry Moore, 1951–53; taught part-time, St Martin's Sch. of Art, 1953–79; taught sculpture at Bennington Coll., Vermont, 1963–65. Initiated and taught at Triangle Workshop, Pine Plains, NY, 1982–89. Visiting Artist, 1989: Univ. of Alberta; Red Deer Coll., Alberta. *One-man exhibitions include:* Galleria del Naviglio, Milan, 1956; Gimpel Fils, London, 1957; Whitechapel Art Gall., 1963; Andre Emmerich Gall., NY, 1964, 1966, 1968, 1970, 1972, 1973, 1974, 1977, 1978, 1979, 1982, 1984, 1986, 1988, 1989; Washington Gall. of Modern Art, Washington, DC, 1965; Kasmin Ltd, London, 1965, 1967, 1971, 1972; David Mirvish Gall., Toronto, 1966, 1971, 1974; Galerie Bischofberger, Zürich, 1966; Rijksmuseum, Kröller-Müller, Holland, 1967;

Hayward Gall., 1969; Norfolk and Norwich Triennial Fest., 1973; Kenwood House, Hampstead, 1974, 1981, 1994, 2004 (toured to Scripps Coll., Calif, Bentley Projects, Phoenix, and Garth Clark Gall., NY); Galleria dell'Ariete, Milan, 1974; Galerie Andre Emmerich, Zürich, 1974, 1978, 1985; Mus. of Modern Art, NY, 1975 (toured to Walker Art Center, Minn, Mus. of Fine Arts, Houston, Mus. of Fine Arts, Boston); Richard Gray Gall., Chicago, 1976, 1978, 1986, 1989; Watson/de Nagy Gall., Houston, 1976; Lefevre Gall., London, 1976; Galerie Wentzel, Hamburg, 1976, 1978, Cologne, 1982, 1984, 1985, 1988; Galerie Piltzer-Rheims, Paris, 1977; Waddington & Tooth Galls, London, 1977; Waddington Galls, London, 1983, 1986; Harkus Krakow Gall., Boston, 1978, 1981, 1985; Knoedler Gall., London, 1978, 1982, 1983, 1984, 1986, 1989, 1991; Ace Gall., Venice, Calif, 1978, Vancouver, 1979; Kunsthalle Mannheim, 1979; Kunstverein Braunschweig, 1979; Kunstverein Frankfurt, 1979; Städtische Galerie im Lenbachhaus, Munich, 1979; Gall. Kasahara, Osaka, Japan, 1979, 1990; York Sculptures, Christian Science Center, Boston, 1980; Acquavella Galls, NY, 1980, 1984, 1986; Galerie Andre, Berlin, 1980; Downstairs Gall., Edmonton, Alta, 1981; Storm King Art Center, Mountainville, NY, 1981; Städtische Galerie im Städel, Frankfurt, 1981; Saarland Mus., Saarbrücken, 1982; Gallery One, Toronto, 1982, 1985, 1987–88, 1990; Galerie de France, Paris, 1983; Martin Gerard Gall., Edmonton, 1984; Serpentine Gall., 1984; Whitworth Art Gall., Manchester, 1984; Leeds City Art Gall., 1984; Ordrupgaard Samlingen, Copenhagen, 1984; Kunstmuseum Düsseldorf, 1985; Joan Miró Foundn, Barcelona, 1985; C. Grimaldis Gall., Baltimore, 1985, 1987, 1989, 1994, 2004; Galerie Blanche, Stockholm, 1985; Galleri Lang, Malmö, 1985; Galerie Artek, Helsinki, 1985; Galleria Stendhal, Milan, 1985; Norrköpings Kunstmuseum, Sweden, 1985; Galerie Joan Prats, Barcelona, 1986, 2003; Comune di Bogliasco, Genoa, 1986; Iglesia de San Esteban, Spain, 1986; La Lonja, Spain, 1987; Soledad Lorenzo Galerie, Madrid, 1987; Northern Centre for Contemp. Art, Sunderland, 1987; Sylvia Cordish Fine Art, Baltimore, 1988; Elisabeth Franck Gall., Belgium, 1988; Galerie Renée Ziegler, Zürich, 1988; Annely Juda Fine Art, 1989, 1991, 1994 (retrospective), 1998, 2003, 2007, 2010; Walker Hill Art Center, Seoul, 1989; Galeria Fluxus, Porto, 1989; Galerie Lelong, Paris, 1990, 1996; Musée des Beaux Arts et de la Dentelle, Calais, 1990, 2008; Banque Paribas, Antwerp, 1990; Tate Gall., 1991, 2005; Yorkshire Sculpture Park, Wakefield, 1994, 2001; Kukje Gall., Seoul, 1994, 1998; Mus. of Contemp. Art, Tokyo, 1995; Galerie Josine Bokhoven, Amsterdam, 1995, 1998, 2004, 2009; Marlborough Gall., NY, 1997, 1998, 2001; Boca Raton, 1999; Nat. Gall., 1998; Garth Clark Gall., NY, 1998, 2004; Perimeter Gall., Chicago, 1998; Centrum Beeldende Kunst, Nijmegen, 1999; Museo des Bellas Artes, Bilbao, 2000; Galleri Weinberger, Copenhagen, 2000, 2007; Venice Design, Venice, 2000, 2007; Château-Musée, Dieppe, 2001; Kunsthalle Würth, Schwäbisch Hall, 2001, 2004; Centro Cultural Caixa Cataluña, Barcelona, 2002; Galeria Metta, Madrid, 2002, 2005; Galeria Altair, Palma, 2002, 2006, 2009; Galerie Besson, 2002; Mitchell Innes & Nash, NY, 2002, 2005, 2007, 2010; Frederik Meijer Sculpture Park, Grand Rapids, 2003; Meadows Mus., Dallas, 2003; Hubert Gall., NY, 2003; Artemis Greenberg van Doren, NY, 2003; Seoul Mus. of Art, 2004; Galerie Daniel Templon, Paris, 2005, 2008, 2010; Marc Selwyn/Daniel Weinberg, LA, 2005; Portland Art Mus., 2005; IVAM, Valencia, 2005, 2006; Joyas Grassy, 2006, 2008; Roche Ct, Salisbury, 2007; Mus. of Contemp. Art, Cleveland, 2007; NPG, 2008; LAAC, Dunkirk, 2008; Musée du dessin et de l'estampe, Gravelines, 2008; Musée des Beaux Arts, Angers, 2008; Centre de l'art sacrée contemporain, Lille, 2008; Hillsboro Fine Art, Dublin, 2008; Galería Álvaro Alcázar, 2008; Lightbox, Woking, 2008; Chatsworth, 2012. British Council touring exhibitions: 1977–79, Tel Aviv, NZ and Australia; 1993–95, Hungary, Romania, Turkey, Greece, Holland and Germany. *Group shows:* exhibited in over 200, many widely toured, in UK, USA, Canada, Europe, Australia and Far East, incl. Biennale in Venice, 1958, 1966, 1968, 1972, 1986, 1988 and 1999, Carrara, 1959, Paris, 1959 and 1977, Antwerp, 1959 and 1983, São Paolo, 1969, Arese, 1980, and Monte Carlo, 1989. Sculpture commnd by Nat. Gall. of Art, Washington, 1978. Co-Designer, Millennium Bridge, London, 1996–2000. Member: Council, RCA, 1981–83 (Hon. Fellow 1986); Council, Slade Sch. of Art, 1982–92; Trustee, Tate Gall., 1982–89. Sen. Academician, RA, 2004. Hon. Mem., Amer. Acad. and Inst. of Arts and Letters, 1979; For. Hon. Mem., Amer. Acad. of Arts and Sciences, 1988; Accademia di Belle Arte di Brera, 1992. Hon. FRIBA 1997; Hon. RBS 1997; Hon. Fellow: Alberta Univ., 1990; Wolfson Coll., Oxford, 1992; Southampton Univ., 1993; Glasgow Sch. of Art, 1998; Bretton Hall Coll., 1998; Univ. of the Arts London, 2004. Hon. DLitt: East Anglia, 1968; York Univ., Toronto, 1979; Brandeis Univ., Mass, 1981; Durham, 1997; Westminster, 1999; Hon. LittD Cambridge, 1985; DUniv Surrey, 1987; Hon. DFA: Yale, 1989; Florida, 1997; Hon. Dr RCA, 1994; Dr *hc* Charles de Gaulle, Lille, 1996, etc. Given key to City of New York, 1974. Henry Moore Grand Prize, 1991; Praemium Imperiale, 1992; Internat. Sculpture Centre Lifetime Achievement Award, 1997; Internat. Award for Visual Arts, Cristobal Gabarrón Foundn, 2004; Julio Gonzales Award, Generalitat Valenciana, 2005. Chevalier des Arts et Lettres (France), 1996. *Relevant publications:* Anthony Caro, by R. Whelan *et al*, 1974; Anthony Caro, by W. S. Rubin, 1975; Anthony Caro, by D. Waldman, 1982; Anthony Caro, by Terry Fenton, 1986; Caro, by Karen Wilkin, 1991; Anthony Caro, by Giovanni Carandente, 1992; Caro, by Anzai, 1992; Anthony Caro and Twentieth Century Sculpture, by Giovanni Carandente, 1999; Anthony Caro, by Ian Barker, 2004; Anthony Caro, by Julius Bryant, 2004; Anthony Caro, by Paul Moorhouse, 2005; Interpreting Anthony Caro, by Paul Moorhouse, 2005; Anthony Caro, 5 vols, ed Karen Wilkin, 2010. *Recreation:* his grandchildren. *Died 24 Oct. 2013.*

CARO, Prof. David Edmund, AO 1986; OBE 1977; MSc, PhD; FInstP, FAIP, FACE; Chancellor, University of Ballarat, 1998–2004; Vice-Chancellor: University of Melbourne, 1982–87; (interim), Northern Territory University, 1988–89; *b* 29 June 1922; *s* of George Alfred Caro and Alice Lillian Caro; *m* 1954, Fiona Macleod; one *s* one *d*. *Educ:* Geelong Grammar Sch.; Univ. of Melbourne (MSc); Univ. of Birmingham (PhD). FInstP 1960, FAIP 1963, FACE 1982. Served War, RAAF, 1941–45. Demonstrator, Univ. of Melbourne, 1947–49; 1851 Overseas Res. Scholar, Birmingham, 1949–51; University of Melbourne: Lectr, 1952; Sen. Lectr, 1954; Reader, 1958; Foundn Prof. of Exper. Physics, 1961; Dean, Faculty of Science, 1970; Dep. Vice-Chancellor, 1972–77; Vice-Chancellor, Univ. of Tasmania, 1978–82. Chairman: Antarctic Res. Policy Adv. Cttee, 1979–85; Aust. Vice-Chancellors Cttee, 1982–83; Melbourne Theatre Co., 1982–87; Pres., Victorian Coll. of the Arts, 1989–91. Chairman: SSAU Nominees Ltd, 1984–89; UniSuper Ltd, 1990–94; Sarou Pty Ltd, 1991–. Member: Management Cttee, Royal Melbourne Hosp., 1982–92; Council, Univ. of South Australia, 1990–94; Council, Univ. of Ballarat, 1994–2004. Hon. LLD: Melbourne, 1978; Tasmania, 1982; Hon. DSc: Melbourne, 1987; Ballarat, 2004. *Publications:* (jtly) Modern Physics, 1961, 3rd edn 1978. *Recreations:* gardening, theatre. *Address:* 17 Fairbairn Road, Toorak, Vic 3142, Australia. *Clubs:* Melbourne (Melbourne); Peninsula Golf (Vic). *Died 15 Aug. 2011.*

CARR OF HADLEY, Baron *cr* 1975 (Life Peer), of Monken Hadley; **(Leonard) Robert Carr;** PC 1963; FIC; *b* 11 Nov. 1916; *s* of late Ralph Edward and of Katie Elizabeth Carr; *m* 1943, Joan Kathleen, *d* of Dr E. W. Twining; two *d* (and one *s* decd). *Educ:* Westminster Sch. (Hon. Fellow, 1991); Gonville and Caius Coll., Cambridge (BA Nat. Sci Hons, 1938; MA 1942; Hon. Fellow, 2001). FIMMM (FIM 1957). Joined John Dale Ltd, 1938 (Dir, 1948–55; Chm., 1958–63); Director: Metal Closures Group Ltd, 1964–70 (Dep. Chm., 1960–63 and Jt Man. Dir, 1960–63); Carr, Day & Martin Ltd, 1947–55; Isotope Developments Ltd, 1950–55; Metal Closures Ltd, 1959–63; Scottish Union & National Insurance Co. (London Bd), 1958–63; S. Hoffnung & Co., 1963, 1965–70, 1974–80; Securicor Ltd and Security Services PLC, 1961–63, 1965–70, 1974–85; SGB Gp PLC, 1974–86; Prudential Assurance Co., 1976–85 (Dep. Chm., 1979–80, Chm., 1980–85); Prudential Corporation PLC, 1978–89 (Dep. Chm., 1979–80, Chm., 1980–85); Cadbury Schweppes PLC,

1979–87; Chm., Strategy Ventures, 1988–; Mem., London Adv. Bd, Norwich Union Insurance Gp, 1965–70, 1974–76; Member, Advisory Board: PA Strategy Partners, 1985–87; LEK Partnership, 1987–95. Mem. Council, CBI, 1976–87 (Chm., Educn and Trng Cttee, 1977–82); Chm., Business in the Community, 1984–87. MP (C) Mitcham, 1950–74, Sutton, Carshalton, 1974–76; PPS to Sec. of State for Foreign Affairs, Nov. 1951–April 1955, to Prime Minister, April–Dec. 1955; Parly Sec., Min. of Labour and Nat. Service, Dec. 1955–April 1958; Sec. for Technical Co-operation, 1963–64; Sec. of State for Employment, 1970–72; Lord President of the Council and Leader of the House of Commons, April–Nov. 1972; Home Secretary, 1972–74. Governor: St Mary's Hosp., Paddington, 1958–63; Imperial Coll. of Science and Technology, 1959–63 and 1976–87 (Fellow 1985); St Mary's Medical Sch. Council, 1958–63; Hon. Treas., Wright Fleming Inst. of Microbiology, 1960–63. Duke of Edinburgh Lectr, Inst. of Building, 1976. Pres., Surrey CCC, 1985–86. CCMI (CBIM 1982); CIPD (CIPM 1975). *Publications:* (jt) One Nation, 1950; (jt) Change is our Ally, 1954; (jt) The Responsible Society, 1958; (jt) One Europe, 1965; articles in technical jls. *Recreations:* lawn tennis, music, gardening. *Club:* Brooks's. *Died 17 Feb. 2012.*

CARR, Sir (Albert) Raymond (Maillard), Kt 1987; DLitt (Oxon); FRHistS; FRSL; FBA 1978; Warden, 1968–87, Fellow, since 1964, St Antony's College, Oxford (Hon. Fellow, 1988); *b* Bath, 11 April 1919; *s* of Reginald and Marion Maillard Carr; *m* 1950, Sara Ann Strickland (*d* 2004); two *s* one *d* (and one *s* decd). *Educ:* Brockenhurst Sch.; Christ Church, Oxford (Hon. Student, 1986). Gladstone Research Exhibnr, Christ Church, Oxford, 1941; Lectr, UCL, 1945–46; Oxford University: Fellow of All Souls Coll., 1946–53; Fellow of New Coll., 1953–64; Director, Latin American Centre, 1964–68; Prof. of History of Latin America, 1967–68; Sub-Warden, St Antony's Coll., 1966–68. Distinguished Prof., Boston Univ., 1980; King Juan Carlos Prof. of Spanish History, NY Univ., 1992. Mem., Nat. Theatre Bd, 1968–77. Chm., Soc. for Latin American Studies, 1966–68. Corresp. Mem., Royal Acad. of History, Madrid. Hon. DLitt Madrid, 1999. Award of Merit, Soc. for Spanish Hist. Studies of the US, 1987; Leimer Award for Spanish Studies, Univ. of Augsburg, 1990; Prince of Asturias Award in Social Scis, Prince of Asturias Foundn, 1999. Grand Cross of the Order of Alfonso el Sabio (Spain), 1983; Order of Infante Dom Henrique (Portugal), 1989. *Publications:* Spain 1808–1939, 1966; Latin America (St Antony's Papers), 1969; (ed) The Republic and the Civil War in Spain, 1971; English Fox Hunting, 1976; The Spanish Tragedy: the Civil War in Perspective, 1977; (jtly) Spain: Dictatorship to Democracy, 1979; Modern Spain, 1980; (with Sara Carr) Fox-Hunting, 1982; Puerto Rico: a colonial experiment, 1984; (ed) The Spanish Civil War, 1986; (ed) The Chances of Death: a diary of the Spanish Civil War, 1995; Visiones de fin de siglio, 1999; (ed) Spain: a history, 2000; articles on Swedish, Spanish and Latin American history. *Recreation:* fox hunting. *Address:* 58 Fitzgeorge Avenue, W14 0SW. *T:* (020) 7603 6975. *Clubs:* Beefsteak, Oxford and Cambridge. *Died 19 April 2015.*

CARR, Edward Arthur John, CBE 1995; heritage and tourism consultant, 1995–2008; Chief Executive, CADW, Welsh Historic Monuments Executive Agency, 1991–95 (Director, 1985–91); *b* 31 Aug. 1938; *s* of Edward Arthur Carr, CMG and Margaret Alys Carr (*née* Willson); *m* 1st, 1960, Verity Martin (marr. diss.); two *d*; 2nd, 1980, Patrice Metro; one *s* one *d*. *Educ:* Leys Sch., Cambridge; Christ's Coll., Cambridge (BA 1960; MA 1963). Journalist: Thomson Regional Newspapers, 1960–65; Financial Times, 1965–67; Sunday Times, 1967–70; Manager, Times Newspapers, 1970–81; Chief Executive, Waterlow & Sons, 1981; Dir, Neath Develt Partnership, 1982–84. Vice-Chm., Bro Morgannwg NHS Trust, 1999–2005; Chairman: Swansea NHS Trust, 2005–07; NHS Wales Governance in Health Project, 2007–09. Trustee, UK Buildings Preservation Trust, 1996–2007; Chm., Wales Cttee, Assoc. of Preservation Trusts, 1999–2007. *Recreations:* family, heritage, Rugby. *T:* (USA) (781) 3781291. *E:* eajcarr@gmail.com. *Died 17 Nov. 2012.*

CARR, (John) Roger, CBE 1991; Chairman, Countryside Commission for Scotland, 1986–92 (Member, 1979–84; Vice-Chairman, 1984–85); *b* 18 Jan. 1927; *s* of James Stanley Carr and Edith Carr (*née* Robinson); *m* 1951, Catherine Elise Dickson Smith (decd); two *s*. *Educ:* Ackworth and Ayton (Quaker Schools). FRICS. Royal Marines, 1944–47; Gordon Highlanders (TA), 1950–54. Factor, Walker Scottish Estates Co., 1950–54; Factor, 1954–67, Dir and Gen. Man., 1967–88, Dir, 1988–90, Moray Estates Develt Co. Dir, Strathearn Tourism Develt Co., 1959–98. Mem., Wkg Party, Management Training for Leisure and Recreation in Scotland, 1986; Chm., Countryside around Towns Forum, 1991–95; Vice Pres., Farming and Wildlife Adv. Gp for Scotland, 1992–98; Director: Macaulay Land Use Res. Inst., 1987–97; UK 2000 Scotland, 1991–93. Mem., Moray DC, 1974–80. JP Moray, 1975–2007. *Recreations:* growing old as gracefully as possible, reading, photography. *Address:* Kincarrathie House, Pitcullen Crescent, Perth PH2 7HX. *Died 19 March 2014.*

CARR, Sir Raymond; *see* Carr, Sir A. R. M.

CARR, Roger; *see* Carr, J. R.

CARR-ELLISON, Sir Ralph (Harry), KCVO 1999; Kt 1973; TD 1962; ED 1974; DL; Lord-Lieutenant of Tyne and Wear, 1984–2000; *b* 8 Dec. 1925; *s* of late Major John Campbell Carr-Ellison; *m* 1st, 1951, Mary Clare (*d* 1996), *d* of late Major Arthur McMorrough Kavanagh, MC; three *s* one *d*; 2nd, 1998, Louise Gay Dyer (*née* Walsh), *widow* of Simon Dyer, CBE. *Educ:* Eton. Served Royal Glos Hussars and 1st Royal Dragoons, 1944–49; Northumberland Hussars (TA), (Lt-Col Comdg), 1949–69; TAVR Col, Northumbrian Dist, 1969–72; Col, Dep. Comdr (TAVR), NE Dist, 1973; Chm., N of England TA&VRA, 1976–80 (Pres. 1987–90; Vice-Pres., 1990–2000); ADC (TAVR) to HM the Queen, 1970–75; Hon. Colonel: Northumbrian Univs OTC, 1982–86; QOY, 1988–90 (Northumberland Hussars Sqn, 1986–88); Col Comdt, Yeomanry RAC TA, 1990–94. Chairman: Northumbrian Water Authy, 1973–82; Tyne Tees Television Ltd, 1974–97 (Dir, 1966–97); Director: Newcastle & Gateshead Water Co., 1964–73; Trident Television, 1972–81 (Dep. Chm., 1976–81); Yorkshire-Tyne Tees Television Hldgs, 1992–97. Co. Comr, Northumberland Scouts, 1958–68; Mem. Cttee of Council, 1960–67, Mem. Council, 1982–2000, Scout Assoc. Chm., Berwick-on-Tweed Constituency Cons. Assoc., 1959–62, Pres., 1973–77; Northern Area Cons. Assocs: Treas., 1961–66, Chm., 1966–69; Pres., 1974–78; Vice-Chm., Nat Union of Cons. and Unionist Assocs, 1969–71. Chm., North Tyne Area, Manpower Bd, MSC, 1983–84. Vice Pres., Automobile Assoc., 1995–99 (Vice-Chm., 1985–86; Chm., 1986–95). Mem. Council, The Wildfowl Trust, 1981–88. Chm., Newcastle Univ. Develt Trust, 1978–81 (Mem., 1992–98); Mem. Ct, Newcastle Univ., 1979–2002; Governor, Swinton Conservative College, 1967–81. FRSA 1983. High Sheriff, 1972, JP 1953–75, DL 1981–85, Vice Lord-Lieut, 1984, Northumberland; DL Tyne and Wear, 2001. Hon. DCL Newcastle, 1989; Hon. LLD Sunderland, 1998. KStJ 1984. *Recreations:* Jt Master, West Percy Foxhounds, 1950–90. *Address:* Beanley Hall, Beanley, Alnwick, Northumberland NE66 2DX. *T:* (01665) 578273. *Clubs:* Cavalry and Guards, MCC; Northern Counties (Newcastle upon Tyne). *Died 26 Aug. 2014.*

CARRINGTON, Prof. Alan, CBE 1999; FRS 1971; Royal Society Research Professor, Southampton University, 1979–84 and 1987–99, Oxford University, 1984–87; *b* 6 Jan. 1934; *o s* of Albert Carrington and Constance (*née* Nelson); *m* 1959, (Noreen) Hilary Taylor; one *s* two *d*. *Educ:* Colfe's Grammar Sch.; Univ. of Southampton. BSc, PhD; MA Cantab, MA Oxon. FRSC 1989; FInstP 1993. University of Cambridge: Asst in Research, 1960; Fellow of Downing Coll., 1960, Hon. Fellow, 1999; Asst Dir of Res., 1963; Prof. of Chemistry, Univ. of Southampton, 1967; Fellow, Jesus Coll., Oxford, 1984–87. Sen. Fellowship, SRC, 1976. Tilden Lectr, Chem. Soc., 1972; George Pimentel Meml Lectr, Univ. of Calif at Berkeley, 1996. Pres., Faraday Div., RSC, 1997–99. FRSA 1999. Foreign Hon. Mem., Amer. Acad. of Arts and Scis, 1987; Foreign Associate, Nat. Acad. of Scis, USA, 1994. Hon. DSc Southampton, 1985. Harrison

Meml Prize, Chem. Soc., 1962; Meldola Medal, Royal Inst. of Chemistry, 1963; Marlow Medal, Faraday Soc., 1966; Corday Morgan Medal, Chem. Soc., 1967; Chem. Soc. Award in Structural Chemistry, 1970; Faraday Medal, 1985, Longstaff Medal, 2005, RSC; Davy Medal, Royal Soc., 1992. *Publications:* (with A. D. McLachlan) Introduction to Magnetic Resonance, 1967; Microwave Spectroscopy of Free Radicals, 1974; (with J. M. Brown) Rotational Spectroscopy of Diatomic Molecules, 2003; numerous papers on topics in chemical physics in various learned jls. *Recreations:* family, music, fishing. *Address:* 46 Lakewood Road, Chandler's Ford, Hants SO53 1EX. *T:* (023) 8026 5092. *Died 31 Aug. 2013.*

CARROL, Charles Gordon; Director, Commonwealth Institute, Scotland, 1971–97; *b* 21 March 1935; *s* of Charles Muir Carrol and Catherine Gray Napier; *m* 1970, Frances Anne, *o d* of John A. and Flora McL. Sinclair; three *s*. *Educ:* Melville Coll., Edinburgh; Edinburgh Univ. (MA); Moray House Coll. (DipEd). Education Officer: Govt of Nigeria, 1959–65; Commonwealth Inst., Scotland, 1965–71. Lay Member, Press Council, 1978–82. *Recreations:* walking, reading, cooking. *Address:* 11 Dukehaugh, Peebles, Scotland EH45 9DN. *T:* (01721) 721296. *Died 16 March 2013.*

CARROLL, Ven. Charles William Desmond; Archdeacon of Blackburn, 1973–86, then Archdeacon Emeritus; Vicar of Balderstone, 1973–86; *b* 27 Jan. 1919; *s* of Rev. William and Mrs L. Mary Carroll; *m* 1945, Doreen Daisy Ruskell; three *s* one *d*. *Educ:* St Columba Coll.; Trinity Coll., Dublin (BA 1943; Dip. Ed. Hons 1945; MA 1946). Asst Master: Kingstown Grammar Sch., 1943–45; Rickerby House Sch., 1945–50; Vicar of Stanwix, Carlisle, 1950–59; Hon. Canon of Blackburn, 1959; Dir of Religious Education, 1959; Hon. Chaplain to Bishop of Blackburn, 1961; Canon Residentiary of Blackburn Cathedral, 1964. *Publications:* Management for Managers, 1968. *Address:* 11 Assheton Road, Blackburn BB2 6SF. *T:* (01254) 51915. *Club:* Rotary (Blackburn). *Died 14 Feb. 2012.*

CARRUTHERS, Alwyn Guy; Director of Statistics, Department of Employment, 1981–83 (Deputy Director, 1972–80); *b* 6 May 1925; *yr s* of late John Sendall and of Lily Eden Carruthers, Grimsby; *m* 1950, Edith Eileen (*d* 2007), *o d* of late William and Edith Addison Lumb; no *c*. *Educ:* Wintringham Grammar Sch., Grimsby; King's Coll., London Univ. BA First Cl. Hons in Mathematics, Drew Gold Medal and Prize, 1945. RAE, Farnborough, 1945–46; Instructor Lieut, RN, 1946–49; Rothamsted Experimental Station, 1949. Postgraduate Diploma in Mathematical Statistics, Christ's Coll., Cambridge, 1951. Bd of Trade and DTI Statistics Divisions, 1951–72. Lay Reader, Church of England, 1994–. *Publications:* articles in official publications and learned jls. *Recreations:* gardening, music. *Address:* 24 Red House Lane, Bexleyheath, Kent DA6 8JD. *T:* (020) 8303 4898. *Died 26 July 2014.*

CARRUTHERS, William Buttrick; part-time Chairman, Industrial Tribunals, then Employment Tribunals, 1995–99; *b* 1 Aug. 1929; *s* of Alexander Norman and Olive Carruthers; *m* 1961, Jennifer Stevens; one *s* two *d*. *Educ:* Middlesex School, Concord, Mass; Radley College; Clare College, Cambridge (BA Hons, LLB). Called to the Bar, Lincoln's Inn, 1954; practised in N Rhodesia (later Zambia), 1956–70; part-time Chm., Industrial Tribunals, 1970; Chm., 1975, Regl Chm., 1990–95, Industrial Tribunals, Bedford. *Recreation:* bridge. *Address:* Worndtich Hall, Kimbolton, Huntingdon, Cambs PE28 0LB. *T:* (01480) 860203. *Died 16 Aug. 2011.*

CARTER, Bernard Thomas, Hon. RE 1975; full-time artist (painter and etcher), since 1977; *b* 6 April 1920; *s* of Cecil Carter and Ethel Carter (*née* Darby); *m* Eugenie Alexander, artist and writer; one *s*. *Educ:* Haberdashers' Aske's; Goldsmiths' College of Art, London Univ. NDD, ATD. RAF, 1939–46. Art lectr, critic and book reviewer, 1952–68; National Maritime Museum: Asst Keeper (prints and drawings), 1968; Dep. Keeper (Head of Picture Dept), 1970; Keeper (Head of Dept of Pictures and Conservation), 1972–77. One-man exhibns in London: Arthur Jeffress Gall., 1955; Portal Gall., 1963, 1965, 1967, 1969, 1974, 1978, 1979, 1981, 1984, 1987, 1990 and 1993; mixed exhibns: Royal Academy, Arts Council, British Council and galleries in Europe and USA; works in public collections, galleries abroad and British educn authorities, etc. TV and radio include: Thames at Six, Pebble Mill at One, Kaleidoscope, London Radio, etc. *Publications:* Art for Young People (with Eugenie Alexander), 1958. *Recreations:* reading, listening to music, gardening, theatre. *Died 2 April 2014.*

CARTER, Elliott (Cook), DrMus; composer; *b* New York City, 11 Dec. 1908; *m* 1939, Helen Frost-Jones (*d* 2003); one *s*. *Educ:* Harvard Univ. (MA); Ecole Normale, Paris (DrMus). Professor of Greek and Maths, St John's Coll., Annapolis, 1940–42; Professor of Music: Columbia Univ., 1948–50; Yale Univ., 1960–61; Juilliard Sch., 1967–84. *Compositions include:* First Symphony, 1942–43; Quartet for Four Saxophones, 1943; Holiday Overture, 1944; Piano Sonata, 1945; Ballet, The Minotaur, 1946–47; Woodwind Quintet, 1947; Sonata for Cello and Piano, 1948; First String Quartet, 1950–51; Sonata for Flute, Oboe, Cello and Harpsichord, 1952; Variations for Orchestra, 1953; Second String Quartet, 1960 (New York Critics' Circle Award; Pulitzer Prize; Unesco 1st Prize); Double Concerto for Harpsichord and Piano, 1961 (New York Critics' Circle Award); Piano Concerto, 1967; Concerto for Orchestra, 1970; Third String Quartet, 1971 (Pulitzer Prize); Duo for Violin and Piano, 1973–74; Brass Quintet, 1974; A Mirror on which to Dwell (song cycle), 1976; A Symphony of Three Orchestras, 1977; Syringa, 1979; Night Fantasies (for piano), 1980; In Sleep in Thunder, 1982; Triple Duo, 1983; Penthode, 1985; Fourth String Quartet, 1986; Oboe Concerto, 1988; Three Occasions for Orchestra, 1989; Violin Concerto, 1991; Partita, 1992; Adagio Tenebroso, 1993; Fifth String Quartet, 1995; Figment, 1996; Allegro Scorrevole, 1996; Clarinet Concerto, 1996; Luimen, 1997; What Next? (opera), 1998; Tempo e tempi, 1999; Statement, 1999; Fantasy, 1999; Asko Concerto, 2000; Cello Concerto, 2000; Oboe Quartet, 2001; Boston Concerto, 2002; Of Rewaking, 2002; Micomicon, 2003; Dialogue, 2003; Réflexions, 2004; Mosaic, 2004; Horn Concerto, 2007; Poems of Louis Zukofsky, 2008; What are Years, 2009; Concertino for Bass Clarinet and Chamber Orch., 2010; String Trio, 2011; A Sunbeam's Architecture (song cycle), 2011; Two Controversies and a Conversation (orchestral triptych), 2012; Dialogues II, 2012; Instances (chamber orch. work), 2012; 12 Short Epigrams, 2012. Member: Nat. Inst. of Arts and Letters, 1956 (Gold Medal for Music, 1971); Amer. Acad. of Arts and Sciences (Boston), 1962; Amer. Acad. of Arts and Letters, 1971; Akad. der Kunste, Berlin, 1971. Hon. degrees incl. MusD Cantab, 1983. Sibelius Medal (Harriet Cohen Foundation), London, 1961; Premio delle Muse, City of Florence, 1969; Handel Medallion, New York City, 1978; Mayor of Los Angeles declared Elliott Carter Day, 27 April 1979; Ernst Von Siemens Prize, Munich, 1981; Gold Medal, MacDowell Colony, 1983; National Medal of Arts, USA, 1985. Commandeur, Ordre des Arts et des Lettres (France) 1987; Commander, Order of Merit (Italy), 1991. *Publications:* The Writings of Elliott Carter, 1977; Collected Essays and Lectures 1937–1995, 1997; *relevant publications:* The Music of Elliott Carter, by David Schiff, 1983; Elliott Carter ou le temps fertile, by Max Noubel, 2001. *Address:* c/o Boosey & Hawkes, Aldwych House, 71–91 Aldwych, WC2B 4HN. *Died 5 Nov. 2012.*

CARTER, Sir John (Alexander), Kt 1989; Chairman, Stock Land & Estates Ltd, 1987–2000; *b* 2 Nov. 1921; *s* of Allan Randolph Carter and Beatrice Alice Carter; *m* 1954, Margaret; two *d*. *Educ:* Duke of York's Royal Military Sch., Dover, Kent. Served Territorial Army, 1939–45: Warwicks Yeo., RA and Loyal N Lancs Regt. Founder Chm., Carter Holdings PLC, 1964–89. Co-opted Mem., Conservative Central Bd of Finance, 1983–87; Conservative Party, East of England: Chm., Industrial Council, 1983–87; Chm., Property Adv. Bd, 1986–87. KStJ 1992; Chm. Council, Order of St John for Essex, 1988–94. *Recreations:* golf, swimming, reading. *Address:* Cobblers, Mill Road, Stock, near Ingatestone, Essex CM4 9RG. *T:* (01277) 840580. *Club:* Carlton. *Died 7 July 2015.*

CARTER, Peter Leslie; HM Diplomatic Service; Deputy High Commissioner, Lagos, since 2013; *b* 19 Nov. 1956; *s* of late Leonard Arthur Carter and of Evelyn Joyce Carter;

m 1st, 1985, Rachelle Rain Hays (marr. diss. 2009); one *d*; 2nd, 2012, Tami Johnson. *Educ:* Skinners' Sch., Tunbridge Wells; New Coll., Oxford (BA Modern Langs). Trainee mgt consultant, Arthur Andersen, 1979–80; freelance lang. consultant, Italy, 1980–84; joined HM Diplomatic Service, 1984: Maritime, Aviation and Envmt Dept, FCO, 1984–85; Hindi language trng, 1985–86; Second, later First Sec., New Delhi, 1986–89; Hd of Indo-China Section, SE Asia Dept, FCO, 1989–92; Hd of Recruitment, Personnel Policy Dept, FCO, 1992–94; Principal Adminr, Common Foreign and Security Policy Unit, Gen. Secretariat, Council of EU, 1994–98; Hd, NE Asia and Pacific Dept, FCO, 1998–2001; Dep. Hd of Mission and Consul Gen., Tel Aviv, 2001–05; Consul Gen., Milan, 2006–07; Ambassador to Estonia, 2007–12. *Recreations:* travel, reading, cinema, theatre. *Address:* c/o Foreign and Commonwealth Office, King Charles Street, SW1A 2AH. *T:* (020) 7008 1500. *Died 2 Sept. 2014.*

CARTER, Sir Philip (David), Kt 1991; CBE 1982; Managing Director, Littlewoods Organisation, 1976–83; *b* 8 May 1927; *s* of Percival Carter and Isobell (*née* Stirrup); *m* 1946, Harriet Rita (*née* Evans); one *s* two *d*. *Educ:* Waterloo Grammar Sch., Liverpool. Volunteered for Fleet Air Arm, 1945. Professional career in Littlewoods Organisation, 1948–83. Chm., Forminster plc, 1995–. Chm., Mail Order Traders Assoc. of GB, 1979–83; Pres., European Mail Order Traders Assoc., 1983; Chm., Man Made Fibres Sector Wkg Party, 1980–82; Member: Jt Textile Cttee, NEDO, 1979–82; Distributive Trades EDC, 1980–83; Merseyside Develt Corp., 1981–91 (Chm., 1987–91); Merseyside Residuary Body, 1986–89. Chm., Merseyside Tourism Bd, 1986–93. Chairman: Empire Theatre Trust, Liverpool, 1986–; Liverpool John Moores Univ. Trust, 1993–; Pro-Chancellor, 1994–, and Chm. Bd of Govs, 1997–, Liverpool John Moores Univ. Chm., Liverpool Conservative Assoc., 1985–95. Dir, Everton FC, 1975–2006, 2008– (Chm., 1978–91, 1998–2006; Life Pres., 2006–); Pres., Football League, 1986–88. Chm., Roy Castle Lung Cancer Foundn, 1998–. *Recreations:* football, private flying, music, theatre. *Address:* Oak Cottage, Noctorum Road, Noctorum, Wirral, Cheshire CH43 9UQ. *T:* (0151) 652 4053. *Died 23 April 2015.*

CARTER, Sir Richard (Henry Alwyn), Kt 1992; Chairman: Ports of Auckland Ltd, 1993–2000; Carter Holt Harvey Ltd, 1984–92; *b* 24 April 1935; *s* of Kenneth Clifford Alwyn Carter, OBE and Stella Grace (*née* Dedman); *m* 1960, June Doreen White; one *d*. *Educ:* Waitaki Boys' High Sch.; Auckland Univ. FCA. With Carter Consolidated, subseq. Carter Holt Hldgs, later Carter Holt Harvey Ltd, 1953–92: Gen. Manager, Admin, 1960; Associate Dir, 1961; Dir, 1966; Jt Man. Dir, 1974. Chm., Council, NZ Timber Industry, 1976–78; Member: NZ Timber Merchants Fedn Inc., 1960–78 (Pres., 1976–78); NZ Business Roundtable, 1974–92. *Recreations:* field shooting, farming. *Address:* Waytemore Farm, Ararimu Road, Drury RD 3, S Auckland, New Zealand. *T:* (9) 2925892. *Died 6 Jan. 2011.*

CARTER, Air Cdre Robert Alfred Copsey, CB 1956; DSO 1942; DFC 1943; Royal Air Force, retired; *b* 15 Sept. 1910; *s* of S. H. Carter and S. Copsey; *m* 1947, Sally Ann Peters (*d* 2007), Va, USA; two *s* one *d*. *Educ:* Portsmouth Grammar Sch.; RAF Coll., Cranwell. Cranwell Cadet, 1930–32; commissioned in RAF, 1932; served in India, 1933–36; grad. RAF School of Aeronautical Engineering, 1938; served in Bomber Command, 1940–45; commanded 103 and 150 Sqdns; Station Comdr, RAF, Grimsby; grad. RAF Staff Coll., 1945; attended US Armed Forces Staff Coll., Norfolk, Va, USA, 1947; attached to RNZAF, 1950–53; comd. RAF Station, Upwood, 1953–55; SASO, RAF Transport Command, 1956–58; Director of Personal Services, Air Ministry, 1958–61; AO i/c Admin, HQ, RAF Germany, 1961–64; retired 1964. MRAeS 1960; CEng, 1966. *Club:* Royal Air Force. *Died 10 Nov. 2012.*

CARTER, Ronald Louis, OBE 1999; DesRCA; RDI 1971; FCSD (FSIAD 1961); furniture designer; private consultancy design practice, 1974–96, then formed Ron Carter Design Ltd, 1996; *b* 3 June 1926; *s* of Harry Victor Carter and Ruth Allensen; *m* 1st, Marilyn Adel Clement (marr. diss.); three *d*; 2nd, 1985, Ann McNab (decd); one step *s* two step *d*. *Educ:* Birmingham Central College of Art: studied Industrial and Interior Design (NDD; Louisa Anne Ryland Schol. for Silver Design), 1946–49; Royal College of Art: studied Furniture Design (1st Cl. Dip.; Silver Medal for work of special distinction; Travelling Schol. to USA), 1949–52; DesRCA 1952; Fellow, RCA, 1966; Hon. Fellow, 1974; Sen. Fellow, 1994. Staff Designer with Corning Glass, 5th Avenue, NY City, 1952–53; freelance design practice, Birmingham and London, 1954; Tutor, School of Furniture, RCA, 1956–74; Partner: Design Partners, 1960–68; Carter Freeman Associates, 1968–74; Dir, Miles-Carter, 1980–92. Furniture designed for: V&A Cafe; Heathrow; Inst. of Dirs; Reading Room, British Library; British Mus.; Ashmolean Mus.; Hinxton Hall, Cambridge. FRSA. *Recreation:* painting and silversmithing. *Address:* 19 Denman Road, SE15 5NS. *T:* (020) 7708 1666. *Died 22 May 2013.*

CARTWRIGHT, David Edgar, DSc; FRS 1984; Assistant Director, Institute of Oceanographic Sciences, Bidston Observatory, Birkenhead, 1973–86; *b* 21 Oct. 1926; *s* of Edgar A. Cartwright and Lucienne Cartwright (*née* Tartanson); *m* 1952, Anne-Marie Guerin; one *s* two *d* (and one *s* decd). *Educ:* St John's Coll., Cambridge (BA); King's Coll., London (BSc, DSc). Dept of Naval Construction, Admiralty, Bath, 1951–54; Nat. Inst. of Oceanography (later Inst. of Oceanographic Sciences), Wormley, Surrey: Sci. Officer, rising to Individual Merit SPSO, 1954–73; Research Associate, Univ. of California, La Jolla, 1964–65, 1993, 1994; Sen. Res. Associate, NASA-Goddard Space Flight Center, Greenbelt, Md, 1987–89; Consultant, NASA, 1990–92. Vis. Res. Fellow, Nat. Oceanographic Centre, Southampton, 1992–. Fellow: Royal Astronomical Soc., 1975; Amer. Geophysical Union, 1991. Dr (*hc*) Toulouse, 1992. *Publications:* Tides—a Scientific History, 1999; over 80 papers on marine sci. research; reviews, etc, in various learned jls. *Recreations:* music, walking. *Address:* 3 Borough House West, Borough Road, Petersfield, Hants GU32 3LF. *T:* (01730) 267195. *Died 2 Dec. 2015.*

CARUS, Louis Revell, Hon. RAM, FRSAMD, FRCM, FBSM; Consultant to Benslow Musical Instrument Loan Scheme, Benslow Music Trust, since 1987; Principal, Birmingham School of Music, 1975–87; *b* Kasauli, India, 22 Oct. 1927; *s* of Lt-Col Martin and Enid Carus-Wilson; *m* 1951, Nancy Reade Noell (*d* 2005); two *s* one *d*. *Educ:* Rugby Sch.; Brussels Conservatoire; Peabody Conservatory, USA; Leeds Univ. (PGCA 2000). LRAM. Scottish National Orchestra, 1950; solo violinist and chamber music specialist, 1951–; Head of Strings, Royal Scottish Academy of Music, 1956; Scottish Trio and Piano Quartet, New Music Group of Scotland, 1956–75; Northern Sinfonia, Monteverdi Orchestras, 1963–73; Orchestra Da Camera, 1975; Artistic Dir, Internat. String Quartet Week, 1985–90. Adjudicator, 1960–; Examr, Associated Bd of Royal Schs of Music, 1976–96. Pres., ISM, 1986–87; FRSAMD 1976; Hon. RAM 1977; FRCM 1983; FBSM 1988. FUCEB. *Publications:* various musical journalism, e.g. Strad Magazine, ISM Jl, Gulbenkian Report. *Recreations:* painting, gardening, travel. *Clubs:* Royal Society of Musicians, Incorporated Society of Musicians, European String Teachers Association; Rotary (Glasgow). *Died 19 Aug. 2012.*

CARY, Sir Roger Hugh, 2nd Bt *cr* 1955; a consultant to BBC's Director-General, 1986–2002; *b* 8 Jan. 1926; *o s* of Sir Robert (Archibald) Cary, 1st Bt, and Hon. Rosamond Mary Curzon (*d* 1985), *d* of late Col Hon. Alfred Nathaniel Curzon; *S* father, 1979; *m* 1st, 1948, Marilda (marr. diss. 1951), *d* of Major Pearson-Gregory, MC; one *d*; 2nd, 1953, Ann Helen Katharine, *e d* of Hugh Blair Brenan, OBE (formerly Sec., Royal Hosp., Chelsea); two *s* one *d*. *Educ:* Ludgrove; Eton; New Coll., Oxford (BA Mod. Hist. 1949). Enlisted Grenadier Guards, 1943; Lieut 1945; Staff Captain and Instr, Sch. of Signals, Catterick, 1946; Signals Officer, Guards Trng Bn, 1946–47; R of O 1947. Sub-editor and Leader-writer, The Times, 1949–50; Archivist, St Paul's Cathedral, 1950; joined BBC, 1950: attached Home Talks, 1951; Producer, Overseas Talks, 1951–56; Asst, European Talks, 1956–58; Dep. Editor, The Listener, 1958–61; Mgt Trng Organiser, 1961–66; Asst, Secretariat, 1966–72, Sen. Asst, 1972–74; Sec., Central Music Adv. Cttee, 1966–77, 1982–83; Special Asst (Public Affairs), 1974–77; Special Asst to Alasdair Milne, when Man. Dir, BBC TV, 1977–82;

Chief Asst to Sec., BBC, 1982–83; Chief Asst to Dir of Progs, BBC TV, 1983–86; Research, Richard Cawston's documentary film, Royal Family, 1969; Secretary: Sims Cttee on portrayal of violence on TV, 1979, Wyatt Cttee revision 1983; Wenham Cttee on Subscription Television, 1980–81; Cotton Cttee on Sponsorship and BBC TV, 1981; British Deleg., Internat. Art-Historical Conf., Amsterdam, 1952; Salzburg Scholar in Amer. Studies, 1956. Associate, RHistS. Trustee, Kedleston, 1988–2002. *Recreation:* looking at pictures. *Heir:* *s* Nicolas Robert Hugh Cary [*b* 17 April 1955; *m* 1st, 1979, Pauline Jean (marr. diss. 1991), *d* of Dr Thomas Ian Boyd; three *s*; 2nd, 1994, Lesley Anne Gilham; one *s* one *d*]. *Address:* 36 Magnolia Road, Chiswick, W4 3QW. *Clubs:* Pratt's, First Guards. *Died 29 Dec. 2011.*

CASEY, Rt Hon. Sir Maurice (Eugene), Kt 1991; PC 1986; Judge of Court of Appeal of New Zealand, 1986–95; Judge of the Court of Appeal: Samoa and Cook Islands, 1995–2003; Fiji, 1995–2001; Niue, 1996–2001; Solomon Islands, 1996–98; *b* 28 Aug. 1923; *s* of Eugene Casey and Beatrice (*née* Nolan); *m* 1948, Stella Katherine Wright (Dame Stella Casey, DBE; she *d* 2000); three *s* six *d*. *Educ:* St Patrick's Coll., Wellington; Victoria Univ. (LLM Hons). Served War, Naval Officer, 1943–45. Barrister and Solicitor, 1946; Vice Pres., Auckland Dist Law Soc., 1974; Judge, Supreme (later High) Court, 1974. Chm., Penal Policy Review Cttee, 1981. Hon. CF (Fiji), 2003; Hon. CS (Samoa), 2005. *Publications:* Hire Purchase Law in New Zealand, 1961; Garrow and Casey's Principles of the Law of Evidence, 8th edn 1996; (contrib.) Laws of New Zealand, 1999. *Address:* 3A/5 The Promenade, Takapuna, Auckland, New Zealand. *T:* (9) 4864547. *Club:* Northern (Auckland). *Died 19 Jan. 2012.*

CASEY, Michael Vince, OBE 1990; BSc(Eng); FREng, FIMechE; Chief Engineer, Channel Tunnel Rail Link, British Rail, 1989–90; *b* 25 May 1927; *s* of Charles John Casey and May Louise Casey; *m* 1954, Elinor Jane (*née* Harris) (*d* 1987); two *s* two *d*. *Educ:* Glossop Grammar Sch.; The College, Swindon. BSc(Eng) Hons London. Premium Apprentice, GWR Locomotive Works, Swindon, 1944–49; Univ. of London External Degree Course, 1949–52; British Rail Western Region: Locomotive Testing and Experimental Office, Swindon, 1952–58; Supplies and Contracts Dept, Swindon, 1958–61; Chief Mechanical and Electrical Engr's Dept, Paddington, 1961–63; Area Maintenance Engr, Old Oak Common, 1963–66; Chief Mech. and Elec. Engr's Dept, Paddington, 1966–71; Chief Mech. and Elec. Engineer: Scottish Region, Glasgow, 1971–76; Eastern Region, York, 1976–78; Engrg Dir, British Rail Engrg Ltd, 1978–82; Dir, Mechanical and Electrical Engrg, BRB, 1982–87; Project Dir (BR Engrg), 1987–89. FREng (FEng 1985). *Recreations:* gardening, philately. *Died 18 Oct. 2012.*

CASHMAN, John Prescott; Under-Secretary, Department of Health (formerly of Health and Social Security), 1973–88; *b* 19 May 1930; *s* of late John Patrick Cashman and Mary Cashman (*née* Prescott). *Educ:* Balliol Coll., Oxford (MA (English Lang. and Lit.)). Army (Intell. Corps), 1948–49. Entered Min. of Health, 1951; Principal 1957; Private Sec. to Minister, 1962–65; Asst Sec. 1965; Nuffield Foundn Trav. Fellow, 1968–69; Private Sec. to Sec. of State, 1969. Trustee, Macfarlane Trust, 1989–97; Dir, Bd, Hospital Saving Assoc., 1999–2000 (Mem. Exec. Council, 1989–99). *Address:* 3 Paul Gardens, Croydon, Surrey CR0 5QL. *T:* (020) 8681 6578. *Died 5 March 2012.*

CASSAR, Francis Felix Anthony; Director, Omnirace Ltd, 1990–2000; *b* 10 May 1934; *s* of Carmelo and Filomena Cassar; *m* 1st, Anne; one *s*; 2nd, 1969, Doreen Marjorie; one *s*. *Educ:* Primary Sch., Malta; Lyceum, Malta. Emigrated to UK, 1953. Studied mech. engrg, 1953–58; Man. Dir of own motor engrg co., 1959–74; Co. Sec., Malta Drydocks (UK) Ltd, 1975–80. Represented Malta Labour Party in the UK, also at meetings of the Bureau of the Socialist International, 1960–80; Acting High Comr for Malta in London and Cyprus, 1981–85, High Comr, 1985–87; Chargé d'Affaires, Baghdad, 1988–90. Administrator, St Mark's Res. Foundn, 1991–2000; Financial Controller, St Mark's Educnl Trust, 1995–2000. Mem., Inst. of Management, 1977. JP: Brentford and Ealing, Tottenham, 1972–80; Enfield, 1990. *Recreations:* music, football, DIY, cooking. *Died 16 Feb. 2012.*

CASSELL, Frank, CB 1987; Chairman, Crown Agents Pension Scheme, 1997–2006 (Member, Board of Crown Agents, 1991–97); Economic Minister, Washington, and UK Executive Director, International Monetary Fund and World Bank, 1988–90; *b* 21 Aug. 1930; *s* of Francis Joseph Cassell and Ellen Blanche Cassell (*née* Adams); *m* 1957, Jean Seabrook; two *s* one *d*. *Educ:* Borden Grammar School; LSE (BSc Econ). Asst City Editor, News Chronicle, 1953–58; Dep. Editor, The Banker, 1958–65; HM Treasury: Economic Adviser, 1965; Senior Economic Adviser, 1968; Under Sec., 1974; Deputy Sec., 1983–88. Chm., Stats Cttee, Internat. Financial Services, London (formerly British Invisibles), 1994–2002. Vis. Scholar, Federal Reserve Bank of Minneapolis, 1970. *Publications:* Gold or Credit?, 1965; articles on economic policy, 1953–65. *Recreations:* walking, watching cricket, reading history. *Died 14 Oct. 2011.*

CASSELS, Prof. John William Scott, MA, PhD; FRS 1963; FRSE 1981; Sadleirian Professor of Pure Mathematics, Cambridge University, 1967–84; Head of Department of Pure Mathematics and Mathematical Statistics, 1969–84; *b* 11 July 1922; *s* of late J. W. Cassels (latterly Dir of Agriculture in Co. Durham) and late Mrs M. S. Cassels (*née* Lobjoit); *m* 1949, Constance Mabel Merritt (*née* Senior) (*d* 2000); one *s* one *d*. *Educ:* Neville's Cross Council Sch., Durham; George Heriot's Sch., Edinburgh; Edinburgh and Cambridge Univs. MA Edinburgh, 1943; PhD Cantab, 1949. Fellow, Trinity, 1949–; Lecturer, Manchester Univ., 1949; Lecturer, Cambridge Univ., 1950; Reader in Arithmetic, 1963–67. Mem. Council, Royal Society, 1970, 1971 (Sylvester Medal, 1973); Vice Pres., 1974–78, Mem. Exec., 1978–82, Internat. Mathematical Union; Pres., London Mathematical Soc., 1976–78. Dr (*hc*) Lille Univ., 1965; Hon. ScD Edinburgh, 1977. De Morgan Medal, London Mathematical Soc., 1986. *Publications:* An Introduction to Diophantine Approximation, 1957; An Introduction to the Geometry of Numbers, 1959; Rational Quadratic Forms, 1978; Economics for Mathematicians, 1981; Local Fields, 1986; Lectures on Elliptic Curves, 1991; (with E. V. Flynn) Prolegomena to a Middlebrow Arithmetic of Curves of Genus 2, 1996; papers in diverse mathematical journals on arithmetical topics. *Recreations:* arithmetic (higher only), gardening (especially common vegetables). *Address:* 3 Luard Close, Cambridge CB2 8PL. *T:* (01223) 246108. *Died 27 July 2015.*

CASSELTON, Prof. Lorna Ann, (Mrs W. J. D. Tollett), CBE 2012; PhD, DSc; FRS 1999; Professor of Fungal Genetics, University of Oxford, 1997–2003, then Emeritus; Fellow, St Cross College, Oxford, 1993–2003; *b* 18 July 1938; *d* of William Charles Henry Smith and Cecille Smith (*née* Bowman); *m* 1st, 1961, Peter John Casselton (marr. diss. 1978); 2nd, 1981, William Joseph Dennis Tollett. *Educ:* Southend High Sch. for Girls; University Coll. London (BSc; PhD 1964; DSc 1993); MA Oxon. Royal Commn for Exhibn of 1851 Sen. Student, 1963–65; Asst Lectr, RHC, 1966–67; Lectr, 1967–76, Reader, 1976–89, QMC; Prof. of Genetics, QMW, 1989–91; AFRC/BBSRC Postdoctoral Fellow, 1991–95, BBSRC Sen. Res. Fellow, 1995–2001, Univ. of Oxford. Vis. Prof. of Genetics, QMW, 1997–. Leverhulme Emeritus Fellow, 2003–05. Foreign Sec. and Vice-Pres., Royal Soc., 2006–11. Mem., Commonwealth Scholarships Commn, 2011–. MAE 2008. Hon. Fellow, St Hilda's Coll., Oxford, 2000. Hon. Mem., British Mycological Soc., 2003–. Hon DSc: QMUL, 2009; UCL, 2010. *Publications:* numerous res. and rev. articles. *Recreations:* reading, classical music, walking. *Address:* 83 St Bernard's Road, Oxford OX2 6EJ. *T:* (01865) 559997. *Died 14 Feb. 2014.*

CASSIDY, Very Rev. Herbert; Dean of Armagh and Keeper of the Library, 1989–2006; *b* 25 July 1935; *s* of Herbert Cassidy and Frederica Jane Somerville; *m* 1961, Elizabeth Ann Egerton; one *s* two *d*. *Educ:* Cork Grammar Sch.; Trinity Coll., Dublin (BA 1957; MA 1965). Curate Assistant: Holy Trinity, Belfast, 1958–60; Christ Church, Londonderry, 1960–62; Rector: Aghavilly and Derrynoose, 1962–65; St Columba's, Portadown, 1965–85; Dean of

Kilmore, 1985–89. Hon. Sec., Gen. Synod, Ch. of Ireland, 1990–2004. *Publications:* various pamphlets. *Recreations:* music, travel. *Address:* 2 Kilmore Meadows, Kilmore Road, Armagh BT61 8PA. *Died 10 April 2013.*

CASSIDY, Most Rev. Joseph; Archbishop of Tuam, 1987–95, then Archbishop Emeritus; pastor, Moore, 1995–2009; *b* 29 Oct. 1933; *s* of John Cassidy and Mary Gallagher. *Educ:* St Nathy's College, Maynooth; University College, Galway. Professor, Garbally College, Ballinasloe, 1959–77, President 1977–79; Coadjutor Bishop of Clonfert, 1979–82; Bishop of Clonfert, 1982–87; Spokesman for Irish Bishops' Conference, 1980–88. *Publications:* plays, articles and homilies. *Died 31 Jan. 2013.*

CASSIRER, Nadine, (Mrs Reinhold Cassirer); *see* Gordimer, N.

CASTRO, Rev. Emilio Enrique; Pastor, Methodist Church, Montevideo; *b* Uruguay, 2 May 1927; *s* of Ignacio Castro and Maria Pombo; *m* 1951, Gladys Nieves (*d* 2005); one *s* one *d*. *Educ:* Union Theol Seminary, Buenos Aires (ThL); University of Basel (post graduate work, 1953–54); University of Lausanne (ThD 1984). Ordained, 1948; Pastor: Durazno and Trinidad (Uruguay), 1951–53; Central Methodist Church, La Paz, 1954–56; Central Methodist Church, Montevideo, 1957–65; concurrently Prof. of Contemp. Theol. Thought, Mennonite Seminary, Montevideo; Coordinator, Commn for Evangelical Unity in Latin America, 1965–72; Exec. Sec., S American Assoc. of Theol. Schools, 1966–69; Pres., Methodist Church in Uruguay, 1970–72; Dir, WCC Commn on World Mission and Evangelism, 1973–83; Gen. Sec., WCC, 1985–92. Chm., Fellowship of Christians and Jews in Uruguay, 1962–66; Moderator, Conf. on future of CCIA, Netherlands, 1967; Chm., WCC's Agency for Christian Literature Develt, 1970–72. Hon. DHL: Westmar Coll., USA, 1984; Holy Cross, Boston, 1988; Hon. DTh Geneva, 1992. *Publications:* Jesus the Conqueror, 1956; When Conscience Disturbs, 1959; Mission, Presence and Dialogue, 1963; A Pilgrim People, 1965; Reality and Faith, 1966; Amidst Evolution, 1975; Towards a Latin American Pastoral Perspective, 1973; Sent Free: Mission and Unity in the Perspective of the Kingdom, 1985; When we pray together, 1989; (ed and contrib.) Christian Century, 1971–75; (ed and contrib.) International Review of Mission, 1973–83; (ed) To the Wind of God's Spirit: Reflections on the Canberra Theme, 1990; A Passion for Unity, 1992; numerous articles in several languages. *Recreation:* basketball. *Died 6 April 2013.*

CATER, Antony John E.; *see* Essex-Cater.

CATHERWOOD, Sir (Henry) Frederick (Ross), Kt 1971; Vice President, Evangelical Alliance, since 2001 (President, 1992–2001); President, International Fellowship of Evangelical Students, 1995–2003 (Vice President, 2003); Member (C) Cambridge and North Bedfordshire, European Parliament, 1984–94 (Cambridgeshire, 1979–84); *b* 30 Jan. 1925; *s* of late Stuart and of Jean Catherwood, Co. Londonderry; *m* 1954, Elizabeth, *er d* of late Rev. Dr D. M. Lloyd Jones, Westminster Chapel, London; two *s* one *d*. *Educ:* Shrewsbury; Clare Coll., Cambridge (Hon. Fellow, 1992). Articled Price, Waterhouse & Co.; qualified as Chartered Accountant, 1951; Secretary, Laws Stores Ltd, Gateshead, 1952–54; Secretary and Controller, Richard Costain Ltd, 1954–55; Chief Executive, 1955–60; Asst Managing Director, British Aluminium Co. Ltd, 1960–62; Managing Director, 1962–64; Chief Industrial Adviser, DEA, 1964–66; Dir-Gen., NEDC, 1966–71; Managing Dir and Chief Executive, John Laing & Son Ltd, 1972–74. European Parliament: Chm., Cttee for External Economic Relations, 1979–84; a Vice-Pres., 1989–91; Vice Pres., Foreign Affairs Cttee, 1992–94. British Institute of Management, subseq. Institute of Management: Mem. Council, 1961–66, 1969–79; Vice-Chm., 1972; Chm., 1974–76. Member of Council: NI Development Council, 1963–64; RIIA, 1964–77; BNEC, 1965–71; NEDC, 1964–71; Chm., BOTB, 1975–79. Pres., Fellowship of Independent Evangelical Churches, 1977; Chm. of Council, 1971–77, Pres., 1983–84, Univs and Colls Christian Fellowship (formerly Inter-Varsity Fellowship); Mem., Central Religious Adv. Cttee to BBC and IBA, 1975–79. Hon. DSc Aston, 1972; Hon. DSc (Econ.) QUB, 1973; Hon. DUniv Surrey, 1979. *Publications:* The Christian in Industrial Society, 1964, rev. edn 1980 (On the Job, USA, 1983); Britain with the Brakes Off, 1966; The Christian Citizen, 1969; A Better Way, 1976; First Things First, 1979; God's Time God's Money, 1987; Pro Europe?, 1991; David: Poet, Warrior, King, 1993; At the Cutting Edge (memoirs), 1995; Jobs & Justice, Homes & Hope, 1997; It Can be Done, 2000; The Creation of Wealth, 2002. *Recreations:* music, gardening, reading. *Club:* Oxford and Cambridge. *Died 30 Nov. 2014.*

CATHERWOOD, Herbert Sidney Elliott, CBE 1979; Chairman of Ulsterbus and Citybus, 1967–89; *b* 8 March 1929; *s* of Herbert Alexander Courtney Catherwood and Doreen Mary Catherwood (*née* Elliott); *m* 1956, Patricia, *d* of William Hall; one *s* two *d*. *Educ:* Belfast Royal Academy, N Ireland. Chairman, Ulsterbus Ltd, from inception, 1967; Member, NI Transport Holding Co., 1968–73; Director of Merger of Belfast Corporation Transport with Ulsterbus, 1972. Director: Sea Ferry Parcels, 1972–99; RMC Catherwood, 1974–96; Chm., Lombard Ulster Bank Ltd, 1989–97. *Address:* Boulderstone House, 912 Antrim Road, Templepatrick, Co. Antrim, N Ireland BT39 0AT. *Died 24 Aug. 2013.*

CATLING, Hector William, CBE 1989 (OBE 1980); MA, DPhil, FSA; Director of the British School at Athens, 1971–89; *b* 26 June 1924; *s* of late Arthur William Catling and Phyllis Norah Catling (*née* Vyvyan); *m* 1948, Elizabeth Anne (*née* Salter) (*d* 2000); two *s* one *d*. *Educ:* The Grammar Sch., Bristol; St John's Coll., Oxford (Hon. Fellow 1986). Casberd Exhibnr, 1948, BA 1950, MA 1954, DPhil 1957. Served War, RNVR, 1942–46. At Univ.: undergrad. 1946–50, postgrad. 1950–54. Goldsmiths' Travelling Schol., 1951–53. Archaeological Survey Officer, Dept of Antiquities, Cyprus, 1955–59; Asst Keeper, Dept of Antiquities, Ashmolean Museum, Univ. of Oxford, 1959–64, Sen. Asst Keeper, 1964–71. Fellow, 1967–71, Supernumerary Fellow, 1991–, Linacre Coll., Oxford. Founder, Friends of the British Sch. at Athens; Hon. Sec., British Sch. at Athens (UK), 1991–2011. Sanders Meml Lectr, Sheffield, 1979; Myres Meml Lectr, Oxford, 1987; Mitford Meml Lectr, St Andrews, 1989. Corresp. Mem., German Archaeological Inst., 1961; Hon. Mem., Greek Archaeological Soc., 1975 (Vice-Pres., 1998–). Hon. Dr Athens, 1987. *Publications:* Cypriot Bronzework in the Mycenaean World, 1964; (with J. N. Coldstream) Knossos, the North Cemetery: early Greek tombs, 4 vols, 1996; Sparta, Menelaion I: the Bronze Age, 2009; (with T. M. Mannack) Corpus Vasorum Antiquorum Oxford 4: Greek Geometric Pottery, 2010; contribs to jls concerned with prehistoric and classical antiquity in Greek lands. *Recreation:* ornithology. *Address:* Dunford House, Langford, Lechlade, Glos GL7 3LN. *Died 15 Feb. 2013.*

CATOVSKY, Dame Julia Margaret; *see* Polak, Dame J. M.

CATTERMOLE, Joan Eileen, (Mrs James Cattermole); *see* Mitchell, J. E.

CATTO, Gay; *see* Catto, P. G. W.

CATTO, Henry Edward; Chairman, Atlantic Council of the United States, 1999–2007; Partner, Catto & Catto, San Antonio, 1955–2003; Vice-Chairman, Aspen Institute; *b* 6 Dec. 1930; *s* of Henry E. Catto and Maurine H. Catto; *m* 1958, Jessica Hobby (*d* 2009); two *s* two *d*. *Educ:* Williams Coll. (BA). Businessman, San Antonio, Texas, 1952–69; Dep. US Rep., Orgn of American States, 1969–71; US Ambassador to El Salvador, 1971–73; US Chief of Protocol, 1974–76; Consultant, Washington DC, 1977–81; Asst Sec. of Defense, 1981–83; Vice-Chm., H & C Communications, 1983–89; US Ambassador to UK, 1989–91; Dir, US Inf. Agency, 1991–93. Diplomat-in-Residence, Univ. of Texas (San Antonio), 1993–. *Publications:* Ambassadors at Sea: the high and low adventures of a diplomat (memoirs), 1999. *Recreations:* tennis, hiking, running, ski-ing, golf. *Died 18 Dec. 2011.*

CATTO, (Patricia) Gay (Warren), CVO 2005; Ceremonial Officer, Cabinet Office, 2000–05; *b* 16 Nov. 1940; *d* of late Rt Rev. (William) Warren Hunt and Mollie Hunt (*née* Green); *m* 1971, Alistair William Gillespie Catto (*d* 2006); one *s* one *d*. *Educ:* Sherborne Sch. for Girls; St Hugh's Coll., Oxford (BA). Asst Principal, Min. of Pensions and Nat. Insce, 1963–66; Private Sec. to Perm. Sec., Home Office, 1966–67; Principal: Home Office, 1967–73; Dept of Employment, 1978–83; Assistant Secretary: Resources and Planning Div., HSE, 1983–88; Police Dept, 1988–96, Constitutional Unit, 1996–2000, Home Office. *Address:* 7 Canonbury Lane, N1 2AS. *T:* (020) 7359 7232. *Died 30 May 2014.*

CAVE-BROWNE-CAVE, Sir Robert, 16th Bt *cr* 1641; *b* 8 June 1929; *s* of 15th Bt, and Dorothea Plewman, *d* of Robert Greene Dwen, Chicago, Ill; *S* father, 1945; *m* 1st, 1954, Lois Shirley (marr. diss. 1975), *d* of John Chalmers Huggard, Winnipeg, Manitoba; one *s* one *d*; 2nd, 1977, Joan Shirley, *d* of Dr Kenneth Ash Peacock, West Vancouver, BC. *Educ:* University of BC (BA 1951). KSJ 1986. *Heir: s* John Robert Charles Cave-Browne-Cave [*b* 22 June 1957; *m* 2001, Jennifer Angelica Fong]. *Address:* 7126–199 Street, Langley, BC V2Y 3H8, Canada. *Died 30 Sept. 2011.*

CAVENDISH, Maj.-Gen. Peter Boucher, CB 1981; OBE 1969; DL; Chairman, Military Agency for Standardisation and Director, Armaments Standardisation and Interoperability Division, International Military Staff, HQ NATO, 1978–81; *b* 26 Aug. 1925; *s* of late Brig. R. V. C. Cavendish, OBE, MC (killed in action, 1943) and Helen Cavendish (*née* Boucher); *m* 1952, Marion Loudon (*née* Constantine) (decd); three *s*. *Educ:* Abberley Hall, Worcester; Winchester Coll.; New Coll., Oxford. Enlisted 1943; commnd The Royal Dragoons, 1945; transf. 3rd The King's Own Hussars, 1946; Staff Coll., Camberley, 1955; served Palestine, BAOR, Canada and N Africa to 1966; CO 14th/20th King's Hussars, 1966–69; HQ 1st British Corps, 1969–71; Comdt RAC Centre, 1971–74; Canadian Defence Coll., 1975; Sec. to Mil. Cttee and Internat. Mil. Staff, HQ NATO, 1975–78. Colonel, 14th/20th King's Hussars, 1976–81; Hon. Col, The Queen's Own Mercian Yeomanry, TAVR, 1982–87; Col Comdt, Yeomanry RAC TA, 1986–90. Mem., Peak Park Jt Planning Bd, 1982–91 (Vice-Chm., 1987–91). Chairman: SSAFA/FHS Derbyshire, 1987–96; Derbys Forces Link, 1990–2004. FCMI (FBIM 1979). High Sheriff, 1986–87, DL 1989, Derbys. *Recreations:* shooting, country pursuits, computers, DIY. *Address:* The Rakes End, Middleton-by-Youlgrave, Bakewell, Derbys DE45 1LS. *T:* and *Fax:* (01629) 636225. *E:* PBCav@aol.com. *Died 24 Oct. 2011.*

CAYZER, Sir James Arthur, 5th Bt *cr* 1904; *b* 15 Nov. 1931; *s* of Sir Charles William Cayzer, 3rd Bt, MP (*d* 1940), and Beatrice Eileen (*d* 1981), *d* of late James Meakin and Emma Beatrice (later wife of 3rd Earl Sondes); *S* brother, 1943. *Educ:* Eton. Director: Caledonia Investments, 1958–88; Cayzer Trust Co., 1988–2001. *Heir: cousin* Baron Rotherwick, *b* 12 March 1954. *Address:* Kinpurnie Castle, Newtyle, Angus PH12 8TW. *T:* (01828) 650207. *Club:* Carlton. *Died 27 Feb. 2012.*

CECIL, Sir Henry (Richard Amherst), Kt 2011; trainer of racehorses; *b* 11 Jan. 1943; *s* of late Hon. Henry Kerr Auchmuty Cecil and of Elizabeth Rohays Mary (who *m* 2nd, Sir Cecil Boyd-Rochfort, KCVO), *d* of Sir James Burnett, 13th Bt, CB, CMG, DSO; *m* 1st, 1966, Julia (marr. diss. 1990), *d* of Sir Noel Murless; one *s* one *d*; 2nd, 1992, Natalie Payne (marr. diss. 2002); one *s*; 3rd, 2008, Jane McKeown, *d* of Charles Guest. *Educ:* Canford School. Commenced training under flat race rules, 1969; previously Assistant to Sir Cecil Boyd-Rochfort. Leading Trainer, 1976, 1978, 1979, 1982, 1984, 1985, 1987, 1988, 1990, 1993. Sir Peter O'Sullevan Award, 2012. *Publications:* On the Level (autobiog.), 1983. *Recreation:* gardening. *Address:* Warren Place, Newmarket, Suffolk CB8 8QQ. *T:* (01638) 662387. *Died 11 June 2013.*

CESARANI, Prof. David, OBE 2006; DPhil; Research Professor of History, Royal Holloway, University of London, since 2004; *b* 13 Nov. 1956; *s* of late Henry Cesarani and Sylvia Cesarani (*née* Packman); *m* 1991, Dawn Waterman; one *s* one *d*. *Educ:* Latymer Upper Sch.; Queens' Coll., Cambridge (BA Hist.); Columbia Univ., NY (MA Jewish Hist.); St Antony's Coll., Oxford (DPhil 1986). Montague Burton Fellow in Modern Jewish Hist., Univ. of Leeds, 1983–86; part-time Lectr, Oxford Centre for Postgrad. Hebrew Studies, 1986–87; Barnett Shine Sen. Res. Fellow and Lectr in Politics, Dept of Political Studies, QMC, 1986–89; Dir of Studies and Educnl Activities, 1989–92, Dir, 1992–95 and 1996–2000, Inst. of Contemporary Hist. and Wiener Liby, London; Adjunct Lectr, Dept of Hebrew and Jewish Studies, UCL, 1990–95; Alliance Family Prof. of Modern Jewish Studies, Dept of Religions and Theol., Univ. of Manchester, 1995–96; Parkes-Wiener Prof. of Twentieth Century European Jewish Hist. and Culture, 1996–2000, Dir, AHRB Parkes Centre for the Study of Jewish/non-Jewish Relations and Prof. of Modern Jewish Hist., 2000–04, Southampton Univ. Trustee, Holocaust Meml Day, 2006–12. *Publications:* (ed) The Making of Modern Anglo-Jewry, 1990; Justice Delayed: how Britain became a refuge for Nazi war criminals, 1992; (ed with T. Kushner) The Internment of Aliens in Twentieth Century Britain, 1993; (ed) The Final Solution: origins and implementation, 1994; The Jewish Chronicle and Anglo-Jewry 1841–1991, 1994; (ed with M. Fulbrook) Citizenship, Nationality and Migration in Europe, 1996; (ed) Genocide and Rescue: the Holocaust in Hungary 1944, 1997; (ed jtly) Belsen in History and Memory, 1997; Arthur Koestler: the homeless mind, 1998; (ed with Paul Levine) Bystanders to the Holocaust: a re-evaluation, 2002; (ed) Port Jews: Jewish communities in cosmopolitan maritime trading centres 1650–1950, 2002; Eichmann: his life and crimes, 2004; (ed) After Eichmann: collective memory and the Holocaust since 1961, 2005; (ed with G. Romain) Jews and Port Cities 1590–1990: commerce, community and cosmopolitanism, 2006; (ed jtly) Place and Displacement in Jewish History, 2009; Major Farran's Hat: murder, scandal and Britain's war against Jewish terrorism 1945–1948, 2009; (with E. Sundquist) After the Holocaust: challenging the myth of silence, 2012; Final Solution: the fate of the Jews 1933–49, 2016 (posthumous). *Recreations:* running, cycling, films, friends and family. *Address:* Department of History, Royal Holloway, University of London, Egham, Surrey TW20 0EX. *Died 25 Oct. 2015.*

CHADWICK, Rev. Prof. (William) Owen, OM 1983; KBE 1982; FBA 1962; Chancellor, University of East Anglia, 1985–94; *b* 20 May 1916; 2nd *s* of John Chadwick, barrister and Edith (*née* Horrocks); *m* 1949, Ruth Romaine (*d* 2015), *e d* of late Bertrand Leslie Hallward and Catherine Margaret Hallward; two *s* two *d*. *Educ:* Tonbridge; St John's Coll., Cambridge; Cuddesdon Coll. Ordained deacon, 1940, priest, 1941; Curate, Huddersfield, 1940–42; Sch. Chaplain, Wellington Coll., Berks, 1942–46; Fellow of Trinity Hall, Cambridge, 1947–56; Master of Selwyn Coll., Cambridge, 1956–83; Dixie Professor of Ecclesiastical History, 1958–68; Regius Prof. of Modern History, 1968–83; Vice-Chancellor, Cambridge Univ., 1969–71. Pres., British Academy, 1981–85. Chm., Archbishops' Commn on Church and State, 1966–70; Mem., Royal Commn on Historical MSS, 1984–91. Trustee, Nat. Portrait Gall., 1978–94 (Chm., 1988–94). Hon. Mem., American Acad. of Arts and Scis, 1977. Hon. Freeman, Skinners' Co., 2000. Hon. FRSE. Hon. DD: St Andrews; Oxford; Wales; Hon. DLitt: Kent; Bristol; London; Leeds; Hon. LittD: UEA; Cambridge; Hon. Dr of Letters, Columbia; Hon. LLD Aberdeen. Wolfson Prize, 1982. *Publications:* John Cassian, 1950; The Founding of Cuddesdon, 1954; From Bossuet to Newman, 1957; Western Asceticism, 1958; Creighton on Luther, 1959; Mackenzie's Grave, 1959; Victorian Miniature, 1960; The Reformation, 1964; The Victorian Church, 1966, 1971; Freedom and the Historian, 1969; The Secularization of the European Mind in the 19th Century, 1976; Acton and Gladstone, 1976; Catholicism and History, 1978; The Popes and European Revolution, 1981; The Making of the Benedictine Ideal, 1981; Newman, 1983; Hensley Henson, 1983; Britain and the Vatican during the Second World War, 1986; Michael Ramsey, 1990; The Spirit of the Oxford Movement, 1990; The Christian Church in the Cold War, 1992; A History of Christianity, 1995; A History of the Popes 1830–1914, 1998; The Early Reformation on the Continent, 2002. *Address:* 67 Grantchester Street, Cambridge CB3 9HZ. *Died 17 July 2015.*

CHALMERS, Ian Pender, CMG 1993; OBE 1980; HM Diplomatic Service, retired; Counsellor, Foreign and Commonwealth Office, 1987–94; *b* 30 Jan. 1939; *s* of John

William Pender Chalmers and Beatrice Miriam Emery; *m* 1962, Lisa Christine Hay; two *s* two *d* (and one *d* decd). *Educ:* Harrow; Trinity College Dublin. Joined HM Diplomatic Service, 1963; Second Sec., Beirut, 1966–68; FCO, 1968–70; First Sec., Warsaw, 1970–72; FCO, 1972–76; First Sec., Paris, 1976–80; FCO, 1980–84; Counsellor, UK Mission to UN, Geneva, 1984–87; FCO, 1994–2006. *Recreations:* family, golf, watching sport (particularly Chelsea FC), reading, dogs. *Address:* Field End, Remenham Hill, Henley-on-Thames RG9 3EG. *Clubs:* Phyllis Court (Henley); Huntercombe Golf. *Died 10 Dec. 2014.*

CHAMBERLAIN, Prof. Geoffrey Victor Price, RD 1974; MD; FRCS, FRCOG; Apothecaries' Lecturer in History of Medicine, School of Medicine, Swansea University (formerly Clinical Medical School, University of Wales, Swansea), 2000–08; Professor and Chairman, Obstetrics and Gynaecology, St George's Hospital Medical School, 1982–95, then Emeritus Professor; *b* 21 April 1930; *s* of late Albert Chamberlain and Irene Chamberlain (*née* Price); *m* 1956, Jocelyn Olivia Kerley, *d* of late Sir Peter Kerley, KCVO, CBE; three *s* two *d*. *Educ:* Llandaff Cathedral Sch.; Cowbridge; University Coll. and UCH, London (Goldsmith Schol. 1948; MB 1954; Fellow, UCL, 1987); MD 1968; FRCS 1960; FRCOG 1978. Residencies at RPMS, Gt Ormond St, Queen Charlotte's and Chelsea Hosps, KCH, 1955–69; Tutor, George Washington Med. Sch., Washington DC, 1965–66; Consultant Obstetrician and Gynaecologist, Queen Charlotte's and Chelsea Hosps, 1970–82. RNR, 1955–74, Surgeon Comdr. Member: Council, RSocMed, 1977–84 (Council, Obst. Sect., 1970–93; Council, Open Sect., 1987–95); Council, RCOG, 1971–77, 1982–87, 1990–94 (Vice-Pres., 1984–87; Pres., 1993–94); Chairman: Med. Cttee, Nat. Birthday Trust, 1982–95; Blair Bell Res. Soc., 1977–80; Assoc. of Profs of Obstetrics and Gynaecology, 1989–92. Fulbright Fellow, 1966; Thomas Eden Fellow, RCOG, 1966; Visiting Professor: Beckman, USA, 1984; Daphne Chung, Hong Kong, 1985; Edwin Tooth, Brisbane, 1987; Peshawar, Pakistan, 1993; Chicago Univ., 1996. S African Representative Cttee, 1988. Hon. FACOG 1990; Hon. FSLCOG 1994; Hon. FFSRH (Hon. FFFP 1996); Hon. FMCOG, 2005. Hon. Mem., Polish Acad. of Medicine, 1992. Freeman, City of London, 1982; Liveryman, Apothecaries' Soc., 1981–. Foundn Prize, Amer. Assoc. of Obstetricians, 1967; James Simpson Gold Medal, RCSEd, 1993. Editor: Contemporary Reviews in Obstetrics and Gynaecology, 1987–2000; British Jl of Obstetrics and Gynaecology, 1992–95. *Publications:* Safety of the Unborn Child, 1969; Lecture Notes in Obstetrics, 1975, 8th edn 1999; British Births, 1970; Placental Transfer, 1979; Clinical Physiology in Obstetrics, 1980, 4th edn 1997; Tubal Infertility, 1982; Pregnant Women at Work, 1984; Prepregnancy Care, 1985; (ed) Obstetrics by Ten Teachers, 14th edn, 1985, to 16th edn, 1994; (ed) Gynaecology by Ten Teachers, 14th edn, 1985, to 16th edn, 1994; Birthplace, 1987; Lecture Notes in Gynaecology, 6th edn 1988 to 8th edn 1999; Manual of Obstetrics, 1988; Obstetrics, 1989, 3rd edn 1999; ABC of Antenatal Care, 1991, 4th edn 2002; Pregnancy in the 1990s, 1992; Relief of Pain in Labour, 1993; Homebirth, 1997; ABC of Labour Care, 1999; A Practice of Obstetrics and Gynaecology, 1999; The Life of Victor Bonney, 2000; Life of W. C. W. Nixon, 2004; The History of British Obstetrics and Gynaecology, 2007; contribs to BMJ, Lancet, UK and overseas Jls of Obst. and Gyn. *Recreations:* music, 20th century history. *Address:* 11 Hadley Heights, Hadley Road, Barnet EN5 5QH. *Died 30 Oct. 2014.*

CHAMIER, Anthony Edward Deschamps; Under Secretary, Department of Education and Science, 1980–92; *b* 16 Aug. 1935; *s* of Brig. George Chamier, OBE and Marion (*née* Gascoigne); *m* 1962, Anne-Carole Tweeddale Dalling, *d* of William and Kathleen Dalling, Transvaal, S Africa; one *s* one *d*. *Educ:* Stowe, Buckingham; Trinity Hall, Cambridge; Yale Univ. (Henry Fellow). Military service, 1st Bn Seaforth Highlanders, 1953–55. HM Foreign (later Diplomatic) Service, 1960; Third Secretary, Foreign Office, 1960–62; Second Sec., Rome, 1962–64; Asst Political Adviser, HQ Middle East Comd, Aden, 1964–66; First Sec., FCO, 1966–71; Head of Chancery, Helsinki, 1971–72; seconded, later transf. to Dept of Educn and Science; Principal, 1972–73; Principal Private Sec. to Sec. of State for Educn and Science, 1973–74; Asst Sec., 1974–79; Prin. Estabt Officer, 1980–84. Director, Clan Munro Heritage Ltd, 1994–. *Recreations:* shooting, gardening, family history. *Address:* Achandunie House, Ardross, by Alness, Ross-shire IV17 0YB. *Died 11 May 2014.*

CHANDLER, Sir Geoffrey, Kt 1983; CBE 1976; Chairman Emeritus, Business Group, Amnesty International UK (Founder Chairman, 1991–2001); *b* 15 Nov. 1922; *s* of Frederick George Chandler, MD, FRCP, and Marjorie Chandler; *m* 1955, Lucy Bertha Buxton; four *d*. *Educ:* Sherborne; Trinity Coll., Cambridge (MA History). Military Service, 1942–46: Captain 60th Rifles; Political Warfare Exec., Cairo; Special Ops Exec. (Force 133), Greece; Anglo-Greek Information Service, W Macedonia, 1945; Press Officer, Volos and Salonika, 1946. Cambridge Univ., 1947–49; Captain, Univ. Lawn Tennis, 1949. BBC Foreign News Service, 1949–51; Leader Writer and Features Editor, Financial Times, 1951–56; Commonwealth Fund Fellow, Columbia Univ., New York, 1953–54; Shell Internat. Petroleum Co.: Manager, Econs Div., 1957–61; Area Co-ordinator, W Africa, 1961–64; Chm. and Man. Dir, Shell Trinidad Ltd, 1964–69; Shell Internat. Petroleum Co.: Public Affairs Co-ordinator, 1969–78; Dir, 1971–78; Dir, Shell Petroleum Co., and Shell Petroleum NV, 1976–78; initiator, Shell's first Statement of Gen. Business Principles, 1976; Dir Gen., NEDO, and Mem., NEDC, 1978–83; Dir, Industry Year 1986, 1984–86; Leader, RSA Industry Matters team, 1987–89; Industry Advr, RSA, 1987–92. Pres., Inst. of Petroleum, 1972–74. Member: Council and Exec. Cttee, Overseas Develt Inst., 1969–78; British Overseas Trade Adv. Council, 1978–82; Council and Exec. Cttee, VSO, 1980–96; Chm., NCVO, 1989–96. Chm., BBC Consultative Group on Industrial and Business Affairs, and Mem. BBC Gen. Adv. Council, 1983–88; Chm., Consultative Council, Soc. of Educn Officers Schools Curriculum Award, 1984–96; Member: Wilton Park Academic Council, 1983–87; Council for Charitable Support, 1990–96; Council, SustainAbility Ltd, 2000–10; Associate, Ashridge Management Coll., 1983–89; Pres., Assoc. for Management & Business Educn, 1986–90. Trustee: Charities Aid Foundn, 1990–96; The Environment Foundation, 2001–09; UK Trustee, Council on Economic Priorities (Europe), 1997–99. FRSA. Hon. Mem., CGLI, 1988. Hon. Fellow: Sheffield City Polytechnic, 1981; Girton Coll., Cambridge, 1986; Hon. FInstPet 1982. Hon. DBA Internat. Management Centre from Buckingham, 1986; Hon. DSc: CNAA, 1986; Bradford, 1987; Aston, 1987; Hon. CGIA 1987. *Publications:* The Divided Land: an Anglo-Greek Tragedy, 1959, 2nd edn 1994; (jtly) The State of the Nation: Trinidad & Tobago in the later 1960s, 1969; Industry Year 1986: an attempt to change a culture, its allies and obstacles, 2003; contributed to: Britain's Economic Performance, 1994, 2nd edn 1998; Corporate Citizenship, 1998; Human Rights Standards and the Responsibility of Transnational Corporations, 1999; Human Rights and the Oil Industry, 2000; Business and Human Rights: dilemmas and solutions, 2003; Business Ethics and the 21st Century Organisation, 2006; articles on oil, energy, trans-national corporations, human rights and corporate responsibility; numerous speeches and articles, urging employee participation, coherent British indust. policy and the need for clearly articulated business principles. *Recreations:* gardening, music, observing butterflies. *Address:* Chevin House, Woodpecker Lane, Newdigate, Dorking, Surrey RH5 5DT. *T:* (01306) 631612. *Club:* Hawks (Cambridge). *Died 7 April 2011.*

CHAPMAN, Leslie Charles; Founder and Chairman, Campaign to Stop Waste in Public Expenditure, since 1981; *b* 14 Sept. 1919; *e s* of Charles Richard Chapman and Lilian Elizabeth Chapman; *m* 1947, Beryl Edith England; (one *s* decd). *Educ:* Bishopshalt Sch. Served War, Army, 1939–45. Civil Service, 1939 and 1945–74; Regional Dir, Southern Region, MPBW and PSA, 1967–74. Chm. and mem., various cttees; Mem. (pt-time), LTE, 1979–80. *Publications:* Your Disobedient Servant, 1978, 2nd revised edn 1979; Waste Away, 1982. *Recreations:* reading, music, spoiling our granddaughter Siobhan. *Address:* 3 Berrow Court, Gardens Walk, Upton-upon-Severn, Worcs WR8 0JP. *T:* (01684) 593942. *Died 24 Aug. 2013.*

CHAPMAN, Roy John, FCA; Chairman: Royal Mail (formerly Post Office, then Consignia) Pension Fund, 1995–2004; AEA Technology Pension Fund, 1996–2004; Director, Eurotunnel plc, 1995–2004; *b* 30 Nov. 1936; *s* of William George Chapman and Frances Harriet (*née* Yeomans); *m* 1961, Janet Gibbeson Taylor; two *s* one *d*. *Educ:* Kettering Grammar Sch.; St Catharine's Coll., Cambridge (Athletics Blue; MA). Joined Arthur Andersen & Co., Chartered Accountants, 1958; consulting, UK and abroad, incl. France, USA, Algeria, Greece, Turkey, Thailand and Switzerland, 1964–84; admitted to Partnership, 1970; Hd of Financial Services Practice, 1970–84; Man. Partner, London, 1984–89; Sen. Partner, 1989–93; Mem., Internat. Bd, 1988–93. Director: Halifax Bldg Soc., then Halifax plc, 1994–2001; Westminster Forum Ltd, 1989–99. Member: Adv. Council, London Enterprise Agency, 1985–88; Jt Disciplinary Scheme for Accounting Profession, 1994–2011. Mem. Governing Body, SOAS, London, 1990–2000. Council Mem., BITC, 1991–93. London Marathon, 1983 (Save the Children). St Catharine's College, Cambridge: Pres., St Catharine's Coll. Cambridge Soc., 1994–95; Chm., Develt Campaign, 1994–2000; Fellow Commoner, 2006–. Liveryman, Farriers' Co., 1992–. CCMI; FRSA. *Publications:* contribs to professional jls. *Recreations:* walking, reading, travel. *Address:* 9 Chislehurst Road, Bickley, Kent BR1 2NN. *T:* (020) 8467 3749. *Clubs:* Athenæum, Oxford and Cambridge, MCC; Hawks (Cambridge); Chislehurst Golf. *Died 22 Nov. 2015.*

CHAPMAN, Sir Sydney (Brookes), Kt 1995; RIBA; FRTPI; chartered architect and chartered town and country planner; Chairman, Wellington Street Partners, since 2011; private planning consultant (non-practising); freelance writer; *b* 17 Oct. 1935; *m* 1st, 1976, Claire Lesley McNab (*née* Davies) (marr. diss. 1987); two *s* one *d*; 2nd, 2005, Teresa Munoz Ernest. *Educ:* Rugby Sch.; Manchester University. DipArch 1958; ARIBA 1960; DipTP 1961; AMTPI 1962; FFB 1980. Nat. Chm., Young Conservatives, 1964–66 (Chm. and Vice-Chm. at every level of Movt); Sen. Elected Vice-Chm., NW Area of Nat. Union of C and U Assocs, 1966–70. Contested (C) Stalybridge and Hyde, 1964; MP (C): Birmingham, Handsworth, 1970–Feb. 1974; Chipping Barnet, 1979–2005; PPS to Sec. of State for Transport, 1979–81, to Sec. of State for Social Services, 1981–83; an Asst Govt Whip, 1988–90; a Lord Comr of HM Treasury (Govt Whip), 1990–92; Vice-Chamberlain of HM Household, 1992–95; PPS to Shadow Foreign and Commonwealth Sec., and Dep. Leader, Cons. Party, 2004–05. Member, Select Committee: on Environment, 1983–87; on Public Service, 1995–97; on Accommodation and Works, 1995–2001 (Chm., 1997–2001); on Public Admin, 2002–05; Member: House of Commons Services Cttee, 1983–87; Jt Cttee on Private Bill Procedure, 1987–88; Co-Chairman: Parly Road Transport Study Gp, 1997–2005; All Party Built Envmt Gp, 1997–2005. Chm., Parly Consultants Gp, British Consultants Bureau, 1980–88. Mem., Council of Europe and WEU Assembly, 1997–2005; Chm., Council of Europe Sustainable Develt Cttee, 2001–04. Lectr in Arch. and Planning at tech. coll., 1964–70; Dir (Information), British Property Fedn, 1976–79; Dir (non-exec.), Capital and Counties plc, 1980–88; consultant to YJ Lovell (Holdings) plc, 1982–88. Originator of nat. tree planting year, 1973; President: Arboricultural Assoc., 1983–89; London Green Belt Council, 1985–89; Chm., Queen's Silver Jubilee London Tree Group, 1977; Vice-Chm., Wildlife Link, 1985–89; Patron, Tree Council. Royal Institute of British Architects: Vice-Pres., 1974–75; Chm., Public Affairs Bd, 1974–75; Mem. Council, 1972–77 and 2009–; Mem., Conservation Gp, 2011–; Mem., Library Cttee, 2012–. President: Friends of Barnet Hosps, 1981–2006; Friends of Tamarisk Trust (formerly Peter Pan Homes), 1981–2005; Barnet Soc., 1990–2006. Trustee, Council of Christians and Jews, 2005–. Hon. Life Pres., Chipping Barnet Cons. Assoc., 2005. Hon. Mem. BVA, 2006– (Hon. Assoc. Mem., 1983–2005); Hon. ALI; FRSA; Hon. FBEng (Hon. FIAAS 1987); Hon. FFB 1989 (Pres., 1999–2000); Hon. FSVA 1997; Hon. RICS 2000. *Publications:* Town and Countryside: future planning policies for Britain, 1978; Back to the Drawing Board: memoirs of a Backbencher, 2010; regular contributor to bldg and property jls and to political booklets. *Recreation:* tree spotting. *Address:* 88 Lexham Gardens, Kensington, W8 5JB. *Clubs:* United & Cecil (Vice-Pres., 2005–); Clarendon (Oxford). *Died 9 Oct. 2014.*

CHARLES, Rt Rev. Adrian Owen, AM 1994; RFD 1983; ED 1976; Bishop of Western Region (Assistant Bishop of Diocese of Brisbane), 1984–92; Bishop to Australian Defence Force, 1989–94; *b* 31 July 1926; *s* of Robert Charles and Alice (*née* Donovan); *m* 1955, Leonie Olive (*née* Robinson) (*d* 2002); one *s* one *d*. *Educ:* Slade Sch., Warwick, Qld; St Francis Coll., Univ. of Qld; Anglican Central Coll., Canterbury (ThL, Diploma in Divinity). Ordained priest, 1952; Royal Australian Army Chaplains Dept, 1955–83; Rector: Christ Church, St Lucia, Brisbane, 1958–66; St Paul's, Ipswich, 1966–71; Dir, Religious Studies, Christ Church Grammar Sch., Perth, 1971–72; Dean, St James' Cathedral, Townsville, 1972–77; Rector, St David's, Chelmer, Brisbane, 1977–83; Sen. Chaplain, 1st Mil. Dist, 1981–83; Archdeacon and Chaplain to Archbishop of Brisbane, 1981–83; Bishop of Southern Region, 1983–84. Mem., Brisbane Cricket Ground Trust. *Recreations:* reading, cricket, golf, theatre. *Address:* 16 Sandalwood Street, Sinnamon Park, Qld 4073, Australia. *Club:* Brisbane Golf. *Died 10 April 2013.*

CHARLES, His Honour (Bernard) Leopold; QC 1980; a Circuit Judge, 1990–2002; a Senior Circuit Judge, 1998–2002; a Deputy Circuit Judge, 2002–04; *b* 16 May 1929; *s* of Chaskiel Charles and Mary Harris; *m* 1st, 1958, Margaret Daphne Abel (marr. diss. 1993); one *s* two *d*; 2nd, 1994, Judith Lynda Orus. *Educ:* King's Coll., Taunton. Called to the Bar, Gray's Inn, 1955. Practised in London and on South Eastern Circuit, 1956–90; a Recorder, 1985–90. Legal Assessor to GMC and GDC, 1985–90. *Recreations:* music, politics. *Address:* Lamb Building, Temple, EC4Y 7AS. *T:* (020) 7797 8300. *Died 2013.*

CHARLES, Hampton; *see* Martin, R. P.

CHARLES, Leopold; *see* Charles, His Honour B. L.

CHARLES, Air Vice-Marshal Richard Anthony, CB 2005; Director of Legal Services (Royal Air Force), 2002–09; *b* 24 Feb. 1954; *s* of James Anthony Charles, FREng and late Valerie E. Charles (*née* King); *m* 1979, Anne Moreland; two *s*. *Educ:* Perse Sch., Cambridge; Nottingham Univ. (LLB); Coll. of Law. Admitted solicitor, 1978; commnd Legal Branch, RAF, 1978; Legal Services: RAF Germany, 1979–83; MoD, 1983–85; RAF Hong Kong, 1985–87; MoD, 1987–89; Dep. Dir, Legal Services, RAF Germany, 1989–92; Legal Services: MoD, 1993–94; PTC, 1994–97; Dep. Dir, Legal Services, 1997–2002; Dir of Legal Services, RAF Prosecuting Authy, 2002–08. Adjudicator, Traffic Penalty Tribunal, 2001–. FRAeS 2008. *Recreations:* watching Rugby Union, walking the Cotswold Way, the Avro Lancaster. *Club:* Royal Air Force. *Died 21 July 2013.*

CHARLTON, Philip, OBE 1987; FCIB; Co-Founder, and Chairman, 1991–96, Charlton Associates; *b* 31 July 1930; *s* of George and Lottie Charlton; *m* 1953, Jessie Boulton (*d* 2008); one *s* one *d*. *Educ:* Chester Grammar School. Entered service of Chester Savings Bank, 1947; Gen. Manager, Chester, Wrexham and N Wales Savings Bank, 1966–75; Gen. Manager, TSB Wales & Border Counties, 1975–81; TSB Group Central Executive: Dep. Chief Gen. Manager, 1981–82; Chief Gen. Manager, 1982–85; Gp Man. Dir, 1986–88; Chief Exec., 1988–89; Dep. Chm., 1990–91; Mem., TSB Central Bd, 1976–77, 1981–90; Director: TSB Computer Services (Wythenshawe) Ltd, 1976–81; TSB Trust Co. Ltd, 1979–82; TSB Gp Computer Services Ltd, 1981–86; Central Trustee Savings Bank, later TSB Bank, 1982–89; TSB (Holdings) Ltd, 1982–86; Hill Samuel Gp, 1987–89. Council Mem., 1968–71, Hon. Treasurer, 1975–77, Savings Bank Inst.; Vice Pres., Internat. Savings Banks Inst. (Geneva), 1988–91; Mem., Bd of Admin, European Savings Banks Gp, Brussels, 1989–91. Chm., TSB Nat. Sports Council, 1979–82. FCIB (FIB 1977; Mem. Council, 1982–; Dep. Chm., 1989–91; Pres.,

1990–92); CCMI (CBIM 1983). *Recreations:* music, swimming, sport. *Address:* 48 Boughton Hall, Filkins Lane, Chester CH3 5BG. *T:* (01244) 341389. *Clubs:* Royal Automobile; City (Chester). *Died 28 March 2015.*

CHARTER, Joseph Stephen; High Commissioner for Grenada to the Court of St James's, 2005–08; *b* 26 Dec. 1943; *s* of late Vivian Charter and Daphne (later Mrs Daphne Johnson); *m* 1968, Aileen Valerie Cox; three *s* one *d*. *Educ:* Avery Hill Coll., Univ. of London (BEd Hons). Perm. Sec., Min. of Educn, Grenada, 1981; Ambassador, Libya, 1982–84; Permanent Secretary: Min. of Communication and Works, 1996–2001; Min. of Health and Envmt, 2001–04. Vice Pres., Chamber of Commerce, 1992–95; Chairman: Grenada Broadcasting Corp., 1998–2001; Nat. Water and Sewerage Authy, 1999–2002; Hosp. Governance Bd, 2003–05; Nat. Insce Bd, 2003–05. *Recreations:* music, theatre, sport. *Club:* Royal Over-Seas League. *Died 8 Dec. 2015.*

CHARVET, Richard Christopher Larkins, RD 1972; Consultant: Tyser & Co., 1999; Johnson Stevens Agencies, 1999–2000; General Manager, Morline Ltd (formerly Associate Director, Anglo Soviet Shipping Co. Ltd), 1988–94; *b* 12 Dec. 1936; *s* of late Patrice and Eleanor Charvet; *m* 1990; two *s* one *d* by a previous marriage. *Educ:* Rugby. FITT, ACIArb; FCIS; FCMI; MIFF; MIEx. FRSA 1985. National Service, Royal Navy, 1955–57; Mem., London Div., RNR, 1955–. Union Castle Line, 1957–58; Killick Martin & Co. Ltd, Shipbrokers, 1958–81; Vogt and Maguire Ltd, Shipbrokers, 1981–88. Consultant, Howden Marine Ltd, then AON Gp, 1994–99. Mem., Court of Common Council for Aldgate Ward, City of London, 1970–76; Alderman, Aldgate Ward, 1976–85; Sheriff, 1983–84. Prime Warden, Worshipful Co. of Shipwrights, 1985–86 (Renter Warden, 1984–85); Master, Guild of World Traders, 1991. Pres., City of London Sea Cadet Unit, 1994; Area Pres., N and E London, 1994–2000, New Forest, 2000, St John Ambulance, POW Dist; Chairman: City Br., St John Ambulance Appeal, 1985–92; City Br., RNLI, 1986–98. JP 1976–2001. KStJ 2001 (CStJ 1989). Hon. JSM, Malaysia, 1974. *Publications:* Peter and Tom in the Lord Mayor's Show, 1982. *Recreations:* gardening, travel, sailing. *Clubs:* Aldgate Ward, Lime Street Ward. *Died 8 Nov. 2013.*

CHASKALSON, Hon. Arthur, SCOB 2002; Chief Justice of South Africa and of the Constitutional Court of South Africa, 2001–05 (President, Constitutional Court of South Africa, 1994–2001); *b* Johannesburg, 24 Nov. 1931; *s* of Harry and Mary Chaskalson; *m* 1961, Lorraine Dianne Ginsberg; two *s*. *Educ:* Hilton Coll., Natal; Univ. of Witwatersrand (BCom 1952; LLB *cum laude* 1955). Called to Johannesburg Bar, 1956; SC 1971; in practice as barrister, 1956–94: defence counsel for mems of liberation movements at several major political trials, incl. that of Nelson Mandela, 1963–64. Jt Founder, 1978, and Dir, 1978–93, Legal Resources Centre. Member: Legal Aid Bd, 1992–2000; Judicial Service Commn, 1994–2005; Comr, Internat. Commn of Jurists, 1995– (Pres., 2002–08). Consultant to Namibian Constituent Assembly on drafting of Constitution of Namibia, 1989–90. Mem., Johannesburg Bar Council, 1967–71 and 1973–84 (Chm., 1976, 1982); Vice-Chm., Gen. Council of Bar of S Africa, 1982–87 (Jt Hon. Pres., 1994–); Vice-Chm., Internat. Legal Aid Div., Internat. Bar Assoc., 1983–93. Mem., Nat. Council of Lawyers for Human Rights, 1980–91. Hon. Prof. of Law, Univ. of Witwatersrand, 1981–95. Hon. LLD: Natal, 1986; Witwatersrand, 1990; Rhodes, 1997; Amsterdam, 2002; Port Elizabeth, 2002. Numerous awards, incl. (jtly) Human Rights Award, Foundn for Freedom and Human Rights, Berne, 1990. *Address:* c/o Constitutional Court, Private Bag X32, Braamfontein 2017, S Africa. *Died 1 Dec. 2012.*

CHATAWAY, Rt Hon. Sir Christopher (John), Kt 1995; PC 1970; Chairman, Bletchley Park Trust, 2000–07; *b* 31 Jan. 1931; *m* 1st, 1959, Anna Lett (marr. diss. 1975); two *s* one *d*; 2nd, 1976, Carola Walker; two *s*. *Educ:* Sherborne Sch.; Magdalen Coll., Oxford (BA Hons PPE). Rep. Great Britain, Olympic Games, 1952 and 1956; briefly held world 5,000 metres track record in 1954. Arthur Guinness Son & Co., 1953–55; Independent Television News, 1955–56; BBC Television, 1956–59. Elected for N Lewisham to LCC, 1958–61; Leader, Educn Cttee, ILEA, 1967–69. MP (C): Lewisham North, 1959–66; Chichester, May 1969–Sept. 1974; PPS to Minister of Power, 1961–62; Joint Parly Under-Secretary of State, Dept of Education and Science, 1962–64; Minister of Posts and Telecommunications, 1970–72; Minister for Industrial Develt, DTI, 1972–74. Chairman: LBC, 1981–93; CAA, 1991–96. Man. Dir, Orion Royal Bank, 1974–88; Director: BET, 1974–96; Credito Italiano Internat., 1992–96; Macquarie Securities Ltd, 1994–2001; 1975–92: Chm., United Med. Enterprises, Isola 2000, Kitcat & Aitken, RBC CI, Crown Communications; Dir, Fisons, Plessey Telecommunications, Dorchester Hotel, UK subsids of Honeywell, GE of America and Petrofina. Treasurer, Nat. Cttee for Electoral Reform, 1976–84. Chairman: Groundwork Foundn, 1985–90; UK Athletics, 1998–2000. Pres., Commonwealth Games Council for England, 1986–2009; Treas., 1976–86, Chm., 1986–92, Action Aid. Trustee, Foundn for Sport and the Arts, 1993–. Hon. DLitt: Loughborough, 1985; Macquarie, 2000; Hon. DSc Cranfield, 1994. Nansen Medal, 1960. *Club:* Garrick. *Died 19 Jan. 2014.*

CHATFIELD, Sir John (Freeman), Kt 1993; CBE 1982; DL; Chairman, Association of County Councils, 1989–92; Consultant Solicitor in private practice, 1989–95; *b* 28 Oct. 1929; *s* of Cecil Freeman Chatfield and Florence Dorothy Chatfield; *m* 1954, Barbara Elizabeth Trickett. *Educ:* Southdown Coll., Eastbourne; Roborough Sch., Eastbourne; Lawrence Sheriff Sch., Rugby; Lewes Grammar Sch.; Law Soc. Sch. (Final, 1951). Solicitor, 1952; Sen. Partner, Hart Reade & Co., Eastbourne, 1976–89; Dep. Registrar, County Court, 1965–78. Mem., E Sussex CC, 1972–93 (Leader, 1981–85; Chm., 1985–87); Chairman: Sussex Police Authy, 1982–85; Police Cttee, ACC, 1982–85; Official Side, Police Negotiating Bd, 1982–85; Mem., Police Adv. Bd, England and Wales, 1980–85; Vice-Chm., ACC, 1986–89; Chm., UK Local Authorities Internat. Bureau, 1989–92; first Chm., Internat. Council for Local Envmt Initiatives, 1990–93; Pres., Consultative Council of Local and Regional Authorities in Europe, 1990–93; a Vice-President: CEMR, 1989–93; British Section, IULA/CEMR, 1993–97; Leader, UK Delegn, 1989–92, Mem., Standing Cttee, 1990–93, CLRAE. Mem. Ct and Council, Sussex Univ., 1981–85 and 1991–2001 (Vice-Chm. Council, 1996–99); Gov., Ravensbourne Coll. of Design and Communication, 1999–2004. President: Eastbourne Law Soc., 1972–73; Eastbourne Symphony Orch., 2002–08 (Patron, 2008–). Freeman, City of London, 1994; Liveryman, Co. of Basketmakers, 1995–2005. DL E Sussex, 1986. *Recreations:* music, theatre, travel, watercolour painting. *Address:* 74 Linkswood, Compton Place Road, Eastbourne, E Sussex BN21 1EF. *T:* (01323) 638733. *Died 26 March 2011.*

CHATTERJEE, Dr Satya Saran, OBE 1971; JP; FRCP, FRCPE; Consultant Chest Physician and Physician in Charge, Department of Respiratory Physiology, Wythenshawe Hospital, Manchester, 1959–88; *b* 16 July 1922; *m* 1948, Enid May (*née* Adlington); one *s* two *d*. *Educ:* India, UK, Sweden and USA. MB, BS; FCCP (USA). Asst Lectr, Dept of Medicine, Albany Med. Coll. Hosp., NY, 1953–54; Med. Registrar, Sen. Registrar, Dept of Thoracic Medicine, Wythenshawe Hosp., Manchester, 1954–59. Mem., NW RHA, 1976–. Chairman: NW Conciliation Cttee, Race Relations Board, 1972–77; Overseas Doctors Assoc., 1975–81 (Pres., 1981–87); Manchester Area Cttee on Ethnic Minority Health, 1993–94; Member: Standing Adv. Council on Race Relations, 1977–86; GMC, 1979–92; NW Adv. Council, BBC, 1987–92; Vice-Pres., Manchester Council for Community Relations, 1974–. Chm., ODA News Review, 1986–99. President: Rotary Club, Wythenshawe, 1975–76; Indian Assoc., Manchester, 1962–71. Mem. Bd and Trustee, Community Technical Aid Centre, Manchester, 1998–99 (Dir, 1992–97). *Publications:* All My Yesterdays (memoir), 2006; research papers in various projects related to cardio/pulmonary disorders. *Address:* 15 Hunters Mews, Macclesfield Road, Wilmslow, Cheshire SK9 2AR. *T:* (01625) 522559. *Died 29 Oct. 2012.*

CHAUVIN, Yves; Research Director, Institut Français du Pétrole, 1991–95, then Honorary; *b* Menin, Belgium, 10 Oct. 1930; *m* 1960 (*d* 2004); two *s*. *Educ:* Ecole supérieure de chimie industrielle de Lyon. Research Engineer: Société Progil, 1958–60; Inst Français du Pétrole, 1960–95. Emeritus Dir of Res., Lab. de Chimie Organométallique de Surface, Ecole supérieure de chimie physique electronique de Lyon. Mem., Acad. des Scis, France, 2005. (Jtly) Nobel Prize for Chemistry, 2005. *Publications:* articles in jls. *Address:* c/o Institut Français du Pétrole, 1 & 4 avenue de Bois-Préau, 92852 Rueil-Malmaison Cedex, France. *Died 27 Jan. 2015.*

CHAVASSE, Christopher Patrick Grant; *b* 14 March 1928; *s* of late Grant Chavasse and Maureen Shingler (*née* Whalley); *m* 1st, 1955, Audrey Mary Leonard (*d* 2003); two *s* one *d*; 2nd, 2004, Rosamund Ann Viney, *widow* of Elliott Viney. *Educ:* Bedford Sch.; Clare Coll., Cambridge (Exhibitioner; MA). Commissioned The Rifle Brigade, 1947; served in Palestine (despatches), 1948; RAFVR 1949. Admitted Solicitor, 1955; Partner: Jacobs & Greenwood, 1960–70; Woodham Smith, 1970–80; President, Holborn Law Soc., 1977–78. Hon. Liveryman, Worshipful Co. of Grocers, 1988– (Clerk, 1981–88). Chairman: NADFAS Tours Ltd, 1986–92; Totnes DFAS, 1993–96; Vice-President: NADFAS, 1992–97 (Hon. Mem., 1997–); Chiltern DFAS, 1986–2009. Hon. Steward of Westminster Abbey, 1950–; Treasurer, St Mary-le-Bow Church, 1981–88. Secretary: Governing Body of Oundle and Laxton Schs, 1981–88; The Grocers' Charity, 1981–88. Mem. Ct, Corp. of Sons of the Clergy, 1985–2003. *Publications:* Conveyancing Costs, 1971; Non-Contentious Costs, 1975; The Discretionary Items in Contentious Costs, 1980; various articles in Law Society's Gazette, New Law Jl, Solicitors Jl, and others. *Address:* Whistler's View, 5 Oving Road, Whitchurch, Bucks HP22 4JF. *Clubs:* Royal Air Force; Leander. *Died 21 April 2013.*

CHÁVEZ FRÍAS, Hugo Rafael; President of Venezuela, since 1999; *b* 28 July 1954; *s* of Hugo de los Reyes Chávez and Elena de Chávez; *m* 1st, Nancy Colmenares (marr. diss.); one *s* two *d*; 2nd, Marisabel Rodriguez (marr. diss.); one *d*. *Educ:* Liceo O'Leary, Barinas State; Venezuelan Military Acad., Caracas (grad. 1975); Univ. Simón Bolívar, Caracas. Paratrooper, Venezuelan Army (Lt-Col). Jt Founder, Movimiento Revolucionario Bolivariano 200, 1982; led failed mil. coup against Pres. Carlos Pérez, 1992 (imprisoned); Founder, Movimiento Quinta República, 1997. *Address:* Central Information Office of the Presidency, Torre Oeste 18°, Parque Central, Caracas 1010, Venezuela. *Died 5 March 2013.*

CHEESEMAN, Prof. Ian Clifford, PhD; ARCS; CEng, FRAeS; Professor of Helicopter Engineering, University of Southampton, 1970–82, then Emeritus; consultant in aeronautical, acoustic and general engineering matters; *b* 12 June 1926; *s* of Richard Charles Cheeseman and Emily Ethel Clifford; *m* 1957, Margaret Edith Pither (*d* 2011); one *s* two *d*. *Educ:* Andover Grammar Sch.; Imperial Coll. of Science and Technology. Vickers Supermarine Ltd, 1951–53; Aeroplane and Armament Estab., 1953–56; Atomic Weapons Res. Estab., 1956–58; Nat. Gas Turbine Estab., 1958–70. Res. Dir, 1983–87, Dir and Consultant, 1987–88, Stewart Hughes Ltd, Southampton. Pres., Airship Assoc., 1986–94. *Publications:* (contrib.) Airship Technology, 1999; contribs to Jl RAeS, Jl CIT, Jl Sound and Vibration, Procs Phys. Soc. 'A', Vertica. *Recreations:* gardening, photography, historical research. *Address:* Abbey View, Tarrant Keynston, Blandford Forum, Dorset DT11 9JE. *T:* (01258) 456877. *Died 24 Dec. 2011.*

CHERRY, Colin; Director of Operations, Inland Revenue, 1985–90; *b* 20 Nov. 1931; *s* of late Reginald Cherry and Dorothy (*née* Brooks); *m* 1958, Marjorie Rose Harman; two *d*. *Educ:* Hymers Coll., Hull. Joined Inland Revenue, 1950; HM Inspector of Taxes, 1960; Under Sec., 1985. Fiscal Advr, IMF, 1994–99. Chm., CS Retirement Fellowship, 1992–94. *Recreations:* music, chrysanthemums, photography. *Died 20 Feb. 2011.*

CHESTER, Maj.-Gen. John Shane, OBE 1982; Chief Executive (formerly Secretary), Chartered Institute of Management Accountants, 1995–2001; *b* 21 April 1944; *s* of late Hugh Chester and Stella Florence Mary Chester (*née* Turner); *m* 1970, Amanda Gay, *d* of late Wing Comdr Stanley Graham Pritchard; two *s*. *Educ:* St Joseph's Coll., Ipswich; Southampton Solent Univ. (BA Hons 2007). 2nd Lieut, RM, 1963; served 40, 41, 43 and 45 Commandos RM (Borneo, Norway, NI), 1964–88 (despatches 1981); BM, 3 Commando Brigade, 1981–83 (incl. Falklands Campaign); CO 40 Commando RM, 1987–89 (despatches 1988); COS, HQ Special Forces, 1989–91; Brig. Comdg Training and Reserve Forces, RM, 1991–92; Sen. Directing Staff (Navy), RCDS, 1993–95. Gov., Royal Naval Scholarship Fund, 1996–2002. Lay Member: Special Immigration Appeals Commn, 2002–11 (Lay Advr, 2011–); Hants CC Standards Cttee, 2002–06. FCIPD (FIPD 1992). *Recreations:* sailing, golf, ski-ing, military history. *Address:* c/o Lloyds, Budleigh Salterton, Devon EX9 6NQ. *Clubs:* Army and Navy; Royal Marines Sailing. *Died 10 Sept. 2015.*

CHETWYN, Robert; *b* Sept. 1930; *né* Robert Frederick Suckling; *s* of Frederick Reuben Suckling and Eleanor Lavinia (*née* Boffee). *Educ:* Rutlish, Merton, SW; Central Sch. of Speech and Drama. First appeared as actor with Dundee Repertory Co., 1952; subseq. in repertory at Hull, Alexandra Theatre, Birmingham, 1954; Birmingham Repertory Theatre, 1954–56; various TV plays, 1956–59; 1st prodn, Five Finger Exercise, Salisbury Playhouse, 1960; Dir of Prodns, Opera Hse, Harrogate, 1961–62; Artistic Dir, Ipswich Arts, 1962–64; Midsummer Night's Dream, transf. Comedy (London), 1964; Resident Dir, Belgrade (Coventry), 1964–66; Assoc. Dir, Mermaid, 1966, The Beaver Coat, three one-act plays by Shaw; There's a Girl in My Soup, Globe, 1966 and Music Box (NY), 1967; A Present for the Past, Edinburgh Fest., 1966; The Flip Side, Apollo, 1967; The Importance of Being Earnest, Haymarket, 1968; The Real Inspector Hound, Criterion, 1968; What the Butler Saw, Queens, 1968; The Country Wife, Chichester Fest., 1968; The Bandwagon, Mermaid, 1968 and Sydney, 1970; Cannibal Crackers, Hampstead, 1969; When We are Married, Strand, 1970; Hamlet, in Rome, Zurich, Vienna, Antwerp, Cologne, then Cambridge (London), 1971; Parents Day, Globe, 1972; Restez Donc Jusqu'au Petit Déjeuner, Belgium, 1973; Who's Who, Fortune, 1973; At the End of the Day, Savoy, 1973; Chez Nous, Globe, 1974; Qui est Qui, Belgium, 1974; The Doctor's Dilemma, Mermaid, 1975; Getting Away with Murder, Comedy, 1976; Private Lives, Melbourne, 1976; It's All Right If I Do It, Mermaid, 1977; A Murder is Announced, Vaudeville, 1977; Arms and The Man, Greenwich, 1978; LUV, Amsterdam, 1978; Brimstone and Treacle, Open Space, 1979; Bent, Royal Court and Criterion, 1979; Pygmalion, National Theatre of Belgium, 1979; Moving, Queen's, 1980; Eastward Ho!, Mermaid, 1981; Beethoven's 10th, Vaudeville, 1983 (also Broadway, New York); Number One, Queen's, 1984; Why Me?, Strand, 1985; Selling The Sizzle, Hampstead, 1988; Independent State, Sydney Opera House, 1995. Produced and directed for BBC (incl. series Private Shultz, by Jack Pullman, film, That Uncertain Feeling, Born In the Gardens) and ITV (Irish RM first series, Small World, Case of the Late Pig). Trustee, Dirs' Guild of GB, 1984. *Publications:* (jtly) Theatre on Merseyside (Arts Council report), 1973. *Recreations:* tennis, films, gardening. *Address:* 1 Wilton Court, Eccleston Square, SW1V 1PH. *Died 8 Nov. 2015.*

CHETWYND, 10th Viscount *cr* 1717 (Ireland); **Adam Richard John Casson Chetwynd;** Baron Rathdown, 1717 (Ireland); Executive Consultant, Liberty Life Group, since 1986; *b* 2 Feb. 1935; *o s* of 9th Viscount and Joan Gilbert (*d* 1979), *oc* of late Herbert Alexander Casson, CSI, Ty'n-y-coed, Arthog, Merioneth; *S* father, 1965; *m* 1st, 1966, Celia Grace (marr. diss. 1974), *er d* of Comdr Alexander Robert Ramsay, DSC, RNVR, Fasque, Borrowdale, Salisbury, Rhodesia; twin *s* one *d*; 2nd, 1975, Angela May (*d* 2010), *o d* of late Jack Payne McCarthy, 21 Llanberis Grove, Nottingham. *Educ:* Eton. Fellow, Inst. of Life and Pension Advrs, 1982. 2nd Lieut Cameron Highlanders, 1954–56. With Colonial Mutual Life Assurance Soc. Ltd, Salisbury, Rhodesia, then Johannesburg, 1968–78; Liberty Life Group (formerly Prudential Assurance Co. of South Africa, later Liberty Life Assoc. of Africa), 1978–. Liveryman, Hon. Co. of Air Pilots (formerly GAPAN). Qualifying Mem., Million Dollar Round Table, 1979–; qualified Top of the Table, 1984–; Holder, Internat. Quality Award, 1979–. *Recreations:* astronomy, travel. *Heir: s* Hon. Adam Douglas

Chetwynd [*b* 26 Feb. 1969; *m* 2000, Johanna Marie Karatau; two *s* one *d*]. *Address:* PO Box 69062, Bryanston 2021, Republic of South Africa. *Club:* Rotary (Morningside). *Died 20 Aug. 2015.*

CHETWYND, Sir Robin John Talbot, 9th Bt *cr* 1795, of Brocton Hall, Staffordshire; Business Agent, Directors Guild of Canada, Alberta District Council, 2006–11; *b* 21 Aug. 1941; *s* of Sir Arthur Chetwynd, 8th Bt and Marjory May McDonald Chetwynd (*née* Lang); *S* father, 2004, but his name does not appear on the Official Roll of the Baronetage; *m* 1st, 1967, Heather Helen (marr. diss. 1986), *d* of George Bayliss Lothian; one *s* one *d*; 2nd, 1986, Donna Davey. *Heir: s* Peter James Talbot Chetwynd, *b* 21 Sept. 1973. *Died 18 May 2012.*

CHEYSSON, Claude; Commander Legion of Honour; Croix de Guerre (5 times); Hon. GCMG 1984; Member, European Parliament, 1989–94; Town Councillor, Bargemon, 1983–89 and since 1995; *b* 13 April 1920; *s* of Pierre Cheysson and Sophie Funck-Brentano; *m* 1969, Danièle Schwarz; one *s* two *d* (and two *s* one *d* by former marrs). *Educ:* Coll. Stanislas, Paris; Ecole Polytechnique; Ecole Nationale d'Administration. Escaped from occupied France, 1943; Tank Officer, Free French Forces, France and Germany, 1943–45. Liaison Officer with German authorities, Bonn, 1948–52; Political Adviser to Viet Nam Govt, Saigon, 1952–53; Personal Adviser: to Prime Minister of France, Paris, 1954–55; to French Minister of Moroccan and Tunisian Affairs, 1956; Sec.-Gen., Commn for Techn. Cooperation in Africa, Lagos, Nairobi, 1957–62; Dir-Gen., Sahara Authority, Algiers, 1962–66; French Ambassador in Indonesia, 1966–69; Pres., Entreprise Minière et Chimique, 1970–73; European Comr (relations with Third World), 1973–81, 1985–89; Minister for External Relations, 1981–84. Bd Mem., Le Monde, 1970–81, 1985–92. President: Institut Pierre Mendès-France, 1987–89; Arche de la Fraternité, 1989–93. Grand Cross, Grand Officer and Comdr of many national orders; US Presidential Citation. Dr *hc* Univ. of Louvain; Joseph Bech Prize, 1978; Luderitz Prize, 1983. *Publications:* Une idée qui s'incarne, 1978; articles on Europe, and develt policies. *Address:* 52 rue de Vaugirard, 75006 Paris, France. *T:* and *Fax:* 143264665. *Died 15 Oct. 2012.*

CHIBNALL, Marjorie McCallum, OBE 2004; MA, DPhil; FSA; FBA 1978; Fellow of Clare Hall, Cambridge, since 1975; *b* 27 Sept. 1915; *d* of J. C. Morgan, MBE; *m* 1947, Prof. Albert Charles Chibnall, FRS (*d* 1988); one *s* one *d* and two step *d*. *Educ:* Shrewsbury Priory County Girls' Sch.; Lady Margaret Hall, Oxford; Sorbonne, Paris. BLitt, MA, DPhil (Oxon); PhD (Cantab). Amy Mary Preston Read Scholar, Oxford, 1937–38; Goldsmiths' Sen. Student, 1937–39; Nursing Auxiliary, 1939; Susette Taylor Research Fellow, Lady Margaret Hall, Oxford, 1940–41; Asst Lectr, University Coll., Southampton, 1941–43; Asst Lectr, 1943–45, Lectr, 1945–47, in Medieval History, Univ. of Aberdeen; Lectr in History, later Fellow of Girton Coll., Cambridge, 1947–65; Research Fellow, Clare Hall, Cambridge, 1969–75; Leverhulme Emeritus Fellowship, 1982. Dir, Battle Conf. on Anglo-Norman Studies, 1989–93. Prothero Lectr, RHistS, 1987. Vice-Pres., Selden Soc., 1987–90. Corresp. Fellow, Medieval Acad. of America, 1983. Hon. Fellow, Girton Coll., Cambridge, 1988. Hon. DLitt Birmingham, 1979; Hon. LittD Cambridge, 2002. *Publications:* The English Lands of the Abbey of Bec, 1946; Select Documents of the English Lands of the Abbey of Bec, 1951; The *Historia Pontificalis* of John of Salisbury, 1956; The Ecclesiastical History of Orderic Vitalis, 6 vols, 1969–80; Charters and Custumals of the Abbey of Holy Trinity Caen, 1982; The World of Orderic Vitalis, 1984; Anglo-Norman England 1066–1166, 1986; (ed) Anglo-Norman Studies, XII, 1990, XIII, 1991, XIV, 1992, XV, 1993, XVI, 1994; The Empress Matilda, 1991; (ed with Leslie Watkiss) The Waltham Chronicle, 1994; (ed with R. H. C. Davis) The *Gesta Guillelmi* of William of Poitiers, 1998; The Debate on the Norman Conquest, 1999; Piety, Power and History in Medieval England and Normandy, 2000; The Normans, 2000; numerous articles and reviews, principally in English and French historical jls. *Club:* University Women's. *Died 23 June 2012.*

CHILVER, Baron *cr* 1987 (Life Peer), of Cranfield in the County of Bedfordshire; **(Amos) Henry Chilver,** Kt 1978; FRS 1982; FREng; Chairman, Chiroscience Group plc, 1995–98; *b* 30 Oct. 1926; *e s* of Amos H. Chilver and Annie E. Mack; *m* 1959, Claudia M. B. Grigson, MA, MB, BCh, *o d* of Sir Wilfrid Grigson; three *s* two *d*. *Educ:* Southend High Sch.; Bristol Univ. (Albert Fry Prize 1947). Structural Engineering Asst, British Railways, 1947; Asst Lecturer, 1950, Lecturer, 1952, in Civil Engineering, Bristol Univ.; Demonstrator, 1954, Lectr, 1956, in Engineering, Cambridge Univ.; Fellow of Corpus Christi Coll., Cambridge, 1958–61 (Hon. Fellow, 1981); Chadwick Prof. of Civil Engineering, UCL, 1961–69; Vice-Chancellor, Cranfield Inst. of Technology, 1970–89; Director: Centre for Environmental Studies, 1967–69; Node Course (for civil service and industry), 1974–75. Chairman: English China Clays, 1989–95 (Dir, 1973–95); RJB Mining plc, 1993–97; Director: SKF (UK), 1972–80; De La Rue Co., 1973–81; SE Reg., Nat. Westminster Bank, 1975–83; Delta Gp, 1977–84; Powell Duffryn, 1979–89; TR Technology Investment Trust, 1982–88; Hill Samuel Gp, 1983–87; Britoil, 1986–88; ICI, 1990–93; Zeneca Group, 1993–95. Chairman: Milton Keynes Develt Corp., 1983–92; Plymouth Develt Corp., 1996–98. Chairman: PO, 1980–81; Higher Educn Review Body, NI, 1978–81; Univs' Computer Bd, 1975–78; RAF Trng and Educn Adv. Cttee, 1976–80; Adv. Council, RMCS, Shrivenham, 1978–83; Working Gp on Advanced Ground Transport, 1978–81; Electronics EDC, 1980–85; ACARD, 1982–85; Interim Adv. Cttee on Teachers' Pay, 1987–91; UFC, 1988–91; Innovation Adv. Bd, DTI, 1989–93. Member: Ferrybridge Enquiry Cttee, 1965; Management Cttee, Inst. of Child Health, 1965–69; ARC, 1967–70 and 1972–75; SRC, 1970–74; Beds Educn Cttee, 1970–74; Planning and Transport Res. Adv. Council, 1972–79; Cttee for Ind. Technologies, 1972–76; ICE Special Cttee on Educn and Trng, 1973 (Chm.); CNAA, 1973–76; Royal Commn on Environmental Pollution, 1976–81; Standing Commn on Energy and the Envmt, 1978–81; Adv. Bd for Res. Councils, 1982–85; Bd, Nat. Adv. Body for Local Authority Higher Educn, 1983–85. Dep. Pres., Standing Conf. on Schools Sci. and Technol.; Assessor, Inquiry on Lorries, People and the Envmt, 1979–80. President: Inst. of Management Services, 1982–2000; Inst. of Logistics, 1993–95; Vice-Pres., ICE, 1981–83; Mem., Smeatonian Soc. of Civil Engrs (Pres., 1997). Member Council: Birkbeck Coll., 1980–82; Cheltenham Coll., 1980–88. Lectures: STC Communications, 1981; O'Sullivan, Imperial Coll., 1984; Lady Margaret Beaufort, Bedford, 1985; Fawley, Southampton Univ., 1985; Lubbock, Oxford, 1990. Telford Gold Medal, ICE, 1962; Coopers Hill War Meml Prize, ICE, 1977. FREng (FEng 1977). CCMI. Hon. DSc: Leeds, 1982; Bristol, 1983; Salford, 1983; Strathclyde, 1986; Bath, 1986; Cranfield, 1989; Buckingham, 1990; Compiègne, 1990. *Publications:* Problems in Engineering Structures (with R. J. Ashby), 1958; Strength of Materials (with J. Case), 1959, 3rd edn as Strength of Materials and Structures (with J. Case and C. T. Ross), 1993, 4th edn 1999; Thin-walled Structures (ed), 1967; papers on structural theory in engineering journals. *Clubs:* Athenæum, Oxford and Cambridge. *Died 8 July 2012.*

CHILVER, Elizabeth Millicent, (Mrs R. C. Chilver); Principal of Lady Margaret Hall, Oxford, 1971–79, Honorary Fellow, 1979; *b* 3 Aug. 1914; *o d* of late Philip Perceval Graves and Millicent Graves (*née* Gilchrist); *m* 1937, Richard Clementson Chilver, CB (*d* 1985). *Educ:* Benenden Sch., Cranbrook; Somerville Coll., Oxford (Hon. Fellow, 1977). Journalist, 1937–39; temp. Civil Servant, 1939–45; Daily News Ltd, 1945–47; temp. Principal and Secretary, Colonial Social Science Research Council and Colonial Economic Research Cttee, Colonial Office, 1948–57; Director, Univ. of Oxford Inst. of Commonwealth Studies, 1957–61; Senior Research Fellow, Univ. of London Inst. of Commonwealth Studies, 1961–64; Principal, Bedford Coll., Univ. of London, 1964–71, Fellow, 1974. Mem. Royal Commn on Medical Education, 1965–68. Trustee, British Museum, 1970–75; Mem. Governing Body, SOAS, Univ. of London, 1975–80. Médaille de la Reconnaissance française, 1945. *Publications:* (with U. Röshenthaler) Cameroon's Tycoon,

2001; articles on African historical subjects. *Address:* 47 Kingston Road, Oxford OX2 6RH. *T:* (01865) 553082. *Died 3 July 2014.*

CHILWELL, Hon. Sir Muir Fitzherbert, Kt 1989; Judge of the Court of Appeal, Cook Islands, 1990–2005; Judge of the High Court, Cook Islands, 1991–94; *b* 12 April 1924; *s* of Benjamin Charles Chilwell and Loris Madeleine Chilwell; *m* 1947, Lynette Erica Frances Cox; two *d* (one *s* decd). *Educ:* Auckland University Coll., Univ. of New Zealand (LLB 1949; LLM Hons 1950). Law Clerk, 1941–49; admitted Barrister and Solicitor, 1949; Partner, Haddow, Haddow & Chilwell, later Haddow Chilwell Pain & Palmer, 1949–65; QC 1965; admitted Victorian Bar (Aust.) and QC Vict. 1970; Judge of the Supreme, later High, Court of NZ, 1973–91; Admin. Div., High Court, 1982–91. Lectr, Univ. of Auckland, 1950 and 1953–60. Member: Contracts and Commercial Law Reform Cttee, 1966–68 (Chm., 1968–73); Law Revision Commn, 1968–73; Disciplinary Cttee, NZ Law Soc., 1971–73; Council, Legal Educn, NZ, 1985–91 (Assessor in Law of Contract, 1964–67); Chm., Legal Res. Foundn, 1977–81; Mem. Council, Auckland Dist Law Soc., 1960–67, Pres., 1967–68; Pres., Auckland Medico-Legal Soc., 1969–70, Life Mem., 1989. Silver Jubilee Medal, 1977; Commemoration Medal, NZ, 1990. *Recreation:* bowling. *Address:* 29A The Parade, St Heliers, Auckland 1071, New Zealand. *T:* (9) 5757999. *Clubs:* Royal New Zealand Yacht Squadron; St Heliers Bowling. *Died 10 June 2014.*

CHINNERY, (Charles) Derek; Controller, Radio 1, BBC, 1978–85; *b* 27 April 1925; *s* of Percy Herbert and Frances Dorothy Chinnery; *m* 1953, Doreen Grace Clarke. *Educ:* Gosforth Grammar School. Youth in training, BBC, 1941; RAF Cadet Pilot, 1943. BBC: Technical Asst, 1947; Programme Engineer, 1948; Studio Manager, 1950; Producer, 1952; Executive Producer, 1967; Head of Radio 1, 1972. *Recreations:* DIY, travelling. *Address:* 19 South Ridge, Brunton Park, Newcastle upon Tyne NE3 2EJ. *Died 22 March 2015.*

CHIPIMO, Elias Marko Chisha; Ambassador of Zambia to Japan, also accredited to Indonesia, Korea and the Philippines, and as High Commissioner, Australia and New Zealand, 2000; *b* 23 Feb. 1931; *s* of Marko Chipimo, Zambia (then Northern Rhodesia); *m* 1959, Anna Joyce Nkole Konie (*d* 2008); four *s* three *d*. *Educ:* St Canisius, Chikuni, Zambia; Munali; Fort Hare Univ. Coll., SA; University Coll. of Rhodesia and Nyasaland; Univ. of Zambia (LLB 1985). Schoolmaster, 1959–63; Sen. Govt Administrator, 1964–67; High Comr for Zambia in London, and Zambian Ambassador to the Holy See, 1968–69; Perm. Sec., Min. of Foreign Affairs, 1969; Hon. Minister, Lusaka Province, 1991–96; MP (MMD) Kantanshi, 1991–96; Nat. Chm., 1991–96, and Mem., Nat. Exec. Cttee, until 1996, MMD; Ambassador to Germany, 1997–2000. Chairman: Zambia Stock Exchange Council, 1970–72; Zambia Nat. Bldg Soc., 1970–71; Dep. Chm., Development Bank of Zambia Ltd, 1973–75; Dep. Chm., 1975, Chm., 1976–80, Standard Bank Zambia Ltd; Director: Zambia Airways Corp., 1975–81; Zambia Bata Shoe Co. Ltd, 1977–92. Mem., Nat Council for Sci. Res., 1977–80. Pres., Zambia Red Cross, 1990–95 (Vice-Pres., 1976–90; Life Mem., 1995; Pres., Lusaka Br., 1970–75); Mem., Zambia Univ. Council, 1970–76; Dir, Internat. Sch. of Lusaka, 1970–76. Cllr, Lusaka City Council, 1974–80. Rep., Commonwealth Soc., 1979–88. *Publications:* Our Land and People, 1966; Tied Loans and the Role of Banks (vol. 2 of International Financing of Economic Development), 1978; articles in Univ. of Zambia Jl. *Recreations:* gardening, reading, general literature, linguistics, philosophy, politics, economics, discussions, chess. *Address:* c/o Ministry of Foreign Affairs, PO Box 50069, Lusaka, Zambia. *Died 18 Jan. 2015.*

CHISHOLM, Prof. Alexander William John; Professor Emeritus, University of Salford, since 1994; *b* 18 April 1922; *s* of Thomas Alexander Chisholm and Maude Mary Chisholm (*née* Robinson); *m* 1945, Aline Mary (*née* Eastwood) (*d* 1995); one *s* (one *d* decd). *Educ:* Brentwood Sch., Essex; Northampton Polytechnic; Manchester Coll. of Science and Technology; Royal Technical Coll., Salford (BSc(Eng) London). CEng, FIMechE, FIET. Section Leader, Res. Dept, Metropolitan Vickers Electrical Co. Ltd, 1944–49; Sen. Scientific Officer, then Principal Scientific Officer, Nat. Engrg Lab., 1949–57; UK Scientific Mission, British Embassy, USA, 1952–54; Head of Dept of Mechanical Engrg, then Prof. of Mechanical Engrg, Royal Coll. of Advanced Technology, Salford, 1957–67; University of Salford: Prof. of Mech. Engineering, 1967–82; Research Prof. in Engrg, 1982–87; Professorial Fellow, 1987–94; Chm., Salford Univ. Industrial Centre, subseq. Salford Univ. Industrial Centre Ltd, 1968–82. Visitor, Cambridge Univ. Engrg Dept and Vis. Fellow, Wolfson Coll., 1973–74. Chm., Engrg Profs' Conf., 1976–80; Dir, Prog. for Improvement of Quality of Engrg Educn, 1990–95 (Hon. Chm., 1995–96). Chm., Industrial Admin and Engrg Prodn Gp, IMechE, 1960–62. Nat. Council for Technological Awards: Chm., Mechanical/Prodn Engrg Cttee, 1960–63; Vice-Chm., Bd of Studies in Engrg and Governor, 1963–65. Member: Technology Cttee, UGC, 1969–74; Engrg Processes Cttee, SERC, 1980–83. Pres., CIRP, 1983–84 (Hon. Life Mem. 1987; Chm., UK Bd, 1977–88). Mem., Court, Cranfield Inst. of Technology, 1974–91. Whitworth Prize, IMechE, 1965. *Publications:* numerous on production process technology, manufacturing systems, industrial research, educn and training of engineers, human factors in manufacturing. *Recreations:* hill walking, reading, writing. *Address:* 12 Legh Road, Prestbury, Macclesfield, Cheshire SK10 4HX. *T:* (01625) 829412. *Died 26 July 2014.*

CHISHOLM, Prof. Malcolm Harold, FRS 1990; Distinguished University Professor and Chair, Department of Chemistry, Ohio State University, since 2000; *b* 15 Oct. 1945; *s* of Angus and Gweneth Chisholm; *m* 1st, 1969, Susan Sage (marr. diss.); one *s*; 2nd, 1982, Cynthia Brown; two *s*. *Educ:* London Univ. (BSc 1966; PhD 1969). Sessional Lectr, Univ. of W Ontario, 1970–72; Asst Prof. of Chemistry, Princeton Univ., 1972–78; Indiana University: Associate Prof., 1978–80; Prof., 1980–85; Distinguished Prof. of Chemistry, 1985–99. Guggenheim Fellow, 1985–86. Editor, Polyhedron, 1983–98; Associate Editor: Dalton Trans., 1988–2003; Chemical Communications, 1995–99. FAAAS 1987; FRSE 2005; Fellow: Amer. Acad. Arts and Scis, 2004; German Acad. of Scis Leopoldina, 2005; Amer. Chem. Soc., 2009; MNAS, 2005. Hon. DSc: London, 1980; Western Ontario, 2008. RSC Award for Chem. and Electrochem. of Transition Elements, 1987; Alexander von Humboldt Sen. Scientist Award, 1988; (jtly) ACS Nobel Laureate Signature Award, 1988; ACS Award in Inorganic Chm., 1989; Centenary Medal and Lectr, RSC, 1995; ACS Distinguished Service to Inorganic Chemistry, 1999; Davy Medal, Royal Soc., 1999; Ludwig Mond Medal and Lectr, RSC, 2000; Basolo Medal, Northwestern Univ., Chicago, 2004; Bailar Medal, 2006; Nyholm Prize, RSC, 2010. *Publications:* Reactivity of Metal-Metal Bonds, 1982; Inorganic Chemistry: towards the 21st century, 1983; Early Transition Metal Clusters with π-Donor Ligands, 1995; numerous articles, mostly in chem. jls. *Recreations:* squash, gardening. *Address:* 100 Kenyon Brook Drive, Worthington, OH 43085, USA. *T:* (614) 9850942; 38 Norwich Street, Cambridge CB2 1NE. *T:* (01223) 312824. *Died 20 Nov. 2015.*

CHISWELL, Rt Rev. Peter; Bishop of Armidale, 1976–99; *b* 18 Feb. 1934; *s* of Ernest and Florence Ruth Chiswell; *m* 1960, Betty Marie Craik; two *s* one *d*. *Educ:* Univ. of New South Wales (BE); Moore Theological College (BD London, Th. Schol.). Vicar of Bingara, 1961–68; Vicar of Gunnedah, 1968–76; Archdeacon of Tamworth, 1971–76. Chm., Fed. Exec., CMS, Australia, 1999–2003. *Address:* 1/212 Markham Street, Armidale, NSW 2350, Australia. *T:* (2) 67713919. *Died 6 Dec. 2013.*

CHITNIS, Baron *cr* 1977 (Life Peer), of Ryedale, N Yorks; **Pratap Chidamber Chitnis;** Chairman, British Refugee Council, 1986–89; *b* 1 May 1936; *s* of late Chidamber N. Chitnis and Lucia Mallik; *m* 1964, Anne Brand; (one *s* decd). *Educ:* Penryn Sch.; Stonyhurst Coll.; Univs of Birmingham (BA) and Kansas (MA). Admin. Asst, Nat. Coal Board, 1958–59; Liberal Party Organisation: Local Govt Officer, 1960–62; Agent, Orpington Liberal Campaign, 1962; Trng Officer, 1962–64; Press Officer, 1964–66; Head of Liberal Party Organisation, 1966–69. Sec., 1969–75, Chief Exec. and Dir, 1975–88, Joseph Rowntree Social Service Trust. Mem., Community

Relations Commn, 1970–77; Chm., BBC Immigrants Programme Adv. Cttee, 1979–83 (Mem., 1972–77). Chm., Refugee Action, 1981–86. Reported on elections in: Zimbabwe, 1979; (jtly) Guyana, 1980; El Salvador, 1982, 1984, 1988 and 1989; Nicaragua, 1984. *Address:* Quartier des Trois Fontaines, 84490 Vaucluse, France. *Died 12 July 2013.*

CHITTY, Sir Thomas Willes, 3rd Bt *cr* 1924; author (as Thomas Hinde); *b* 2 March 1926; *e s* of Sir (Thomas) Henry Willes Chitty, 2nd Bt, and Ethel Constance (*d* 1971), *d* of S. H. Gladstone, Darley Ash, Bovingdon, Herts; *S* father, 1955; *m* 1951, Susan Elspeth Glossop, author (as Susan Chitty); one *s* three *d*. *Educ:* Winchester; University Coll., Oxford. Royal Navy, 1944–47. Shell Petroleum Co., 1953–60. Granada Arts Fellow, Univ. of York, 1964–65; Visiting Lectr, Univ. of Illinois, 1965–67; Vis. Prof., Boston Univ., 1969–70. *Publications: novels:* Mr Nicholas, 1952; Happy as Larry, 1957; For the Good of the Company, 1961; A Place Like Home, 1962; The Cage, 1962; Ninety Double Martinis, 1963; The Day the Call Came, 1964; Games of Chance, 1965; The Village, 1966; High, 1968; Bird, 1970; Generally a Virgin, 1972; Agent, 1974; Our Father, 1975; Daymare, 1980; In Time of Plague, 2006; *non-fiction:* (with wife, as Susan Hinde) On Next to Nothing, 1976; (with Susan Chitty) The Great Donkey Walk, 1977; The Cottage Book, 1979; Stately Gardens of Britain, 1983; Forests of Britain, 1985; (ed) The Domesday Book: England's heritage, then and now, 1986; Courtiers: 900 years of court life, 1986; Tales from the Pumproom: an informal history of Bath, 1988; Imps of Promise: a history of the King's School, Canterbury, 1990; Looking Glass Letters, 1991; Paths of Progress: a history of Marlborough College, 1993; A History of Highgate School, 1993; A History of King's College School, 1994; Carpenter's Children: a history of the City of London School, 1995; The University of Greenwich, 1996; The Martlet and the Griffen: a history of Abingdon School, 1997; *autobiography:* Sir Henry and Sons, 1980; *biography:* A Field Guide to the English Country Parson, 1983; Capability Brown, 1986; *anthology:* Spain, 1963. *Heir: s* Andrew Edward Willes Chitty, *b* 20 Nov. 1953. *Address:* Bow Cottage, West Hoathly, Sussex RH19 4QF. *T:* (01342) 810269. *Died 7 March 2014.*

CHRISTIE, Campbell, CBE 1997; General Secretary, Scottish Trades Union Congress, 1986–98; *b* 23 Aug. 1937; *s* of Thomas Christie and Johnina Rolling; *m* 1962, Elizabeth Brown Cameron; one *s* (and one *s* decd). *Educ:* Albert Sen. Secondary Sch., Glasgow; Woolwich Poly.; Langside Coll., Glasgow. Civil Service, 1954–72: Admiralty, 1954–59; DHSS, 1959–72; Society of Civil and Public Servants, 1972–85: Asst Sec., 1972–73; Asst Gen. Sec., 1973–75; Dep. Gen. Sec., 1975–85. Mem., EU Economic and Social Cttee, 1986–2002. Alternate Mem., Takeover Panel, 2006–. Board Member: Scottish Enterprise, 1998–2004; British Waterways, 1998–2008; South West Trains Ltd, 1998–2007. Mem., Scotland's Futures Forum, 2005–. Chm., Commn on Delivery of Public Services in Scotland, 2010–11. Trustee, Forth Valley Acute Hosps NHS Trust, 1993–2001; Mem. Bd, NHS Forth Valley, 2001–09. Chairman: Falkirk FC, 1993–94, 2002–09 (Mem. Bd, 1996–2002, 2009–); Raploch Urban Regeneration Co., 2008–. FEIS; FSQA. Hon. DLitt: Napier, 1992; Stirling, 2000; St Andrews, 2001; Hon. DLit: Queen Margaret Coll., Edinburgh, 1998; Glasgow Caledonian, 1999. *Address:* 20 Gowkhill Place, Larbert, Stirlingshire FK5 4US. *T:* (01324) 562213. *Died 28 Oct. 2011.*

CHRISTIE, Sir George (William Langham), CH 2002; Kt 1984; DL; Director, Glyndebourne Productions Ltd (Chairman, 1956–99); *b* 31 Dec. 1934; *o s* of John Christie, CH, MC, and Audrey Christie (*née* Mildmay); *m* 1958, Patricia Mary Nicholson; three *s* one *d*. *Educ:* Eton. Asst to Sec. of Calouste Gulbenkian Foundation, 1957–62. Chm. of various family companies. Mem., Arts Council of GB, 1988–92 (Chm., Adv. Panel on Music, 1988–92). Founder Chm., The London Sinfonietta, 1968–88. DL E Sussex, 1983. Hon. FRCM 1986; Hon. FRNCM 1986; Hon. GSM 1991. DUniv Sussex, 1990; Hon. DMus: Keele, 1993; Exeter, 1994. Cavaliere al Merito della Repubblica Italiana, 1977; Commandeur, l'Ordre des Arts et des Lettres (France), 2006. *Address:* Old House, Moor Lane, Ringmer, E Sussex BN8 5UR. *T:* (01273) 813706. *Died 7 May 2014.*

CHRISTMAS, Timothy John, MD; FRCS; Consultant Urological Surgeon, Royal Marsden Hospital, since 2000 and Charing Cross Hospital, since 1992; *b* 2 Feb. 1956; *s* of late Leslie George Christmas and of Lydia Valerie (*née* Brown); *m* 2003, Dr Ethna Mannion; one *s*. *Educ:* Bournemouth Sch.; Middlesex Hosp. Med. Sch., London Univ. (Simmonds' Scholar; MB BS 1980, MD 1992). FRCS 1984, FRCS (Urol) 1991. Surgical Registrar, London Hosp., 1986–88; Res. Fellow, UCL, 1988–91; Sen. Registrar, St Bartholomew's Hosp., 1991–92; Res. Fellow, Univ. of S California, LA, 1992; Consultant Urological Surgeon, Chelsea and Westminster Hosp., 1993–99. Fellow, European Bd of Urology, 1992. *Publications:* Benign Prostatic Hyperplasia, 1993, 2nd edn 1997; Prostate Cancer, 1996, 2nd edn 2001; Diseases of the Testis, 1997; Clinical Progress in Renal Cancer, 2006; numerous articles on genito-urinary cancer surgery. *Recreations:* travel, ornithology, photography. *Address:* Department of Urology, Royal Marsden Hospital, Fulham Road, SW3 6JJ. *T:* (020) 7808 2076. *E:* tim.christmas@rmh.nhs.uk. *Died 19 June 2011.*

CHRISTOPHER, John; *see* Youd, S.

CHRISTOPHER, Warren; lawyer; Senior Partner, O'Melveny and Myers, since 1997; Secretary of State, United States of America, 1993–97; *b* 27 Oct. 1925; *s* of Ernest and Catharine Christopher; *m* 1956, Marie Wyllis; two *s* one *d*; one *d* from former marriage. *Educ:* Univ. of Southern California; Stanford Law Sch. USNR, 1943–45. Joined O'Melveny and Myers, LA, 1950, partner, 1958–67, 1969–76, 1981–92. Dep. Attorney-Gen., USA, 1967–69; Dep. Sec. of State, 1977–81. US Medal of Freedom, 1981. *Publications:* In the Stream of History: shaping foreign policy for a new era, 1998; Chances of a Lifetime (memoirs), 2001. *Address:* (office) Suite 700, 1999 Avenue of the Stars, Los Angeles, CA 90067–6035, USA. *Died 18 March 2011.*

CHYNOWETH, David Boyd; Chief Executive, Universities Superannuation Scheme Ltd, 1994–2003; *b* 26 Dec. 1940; *s* of Ernest and Blodwen Chynoweth; *m* 1968, Margaret Slater; one *s* two *d*. *Educ:* Simon Langton Sch., Canterbury; Univ. of Nottingham (BA). CPFA (IPFA 1966); FCCA 1983. Public Finance posts with Derbs CC, 1962 and London Borough of Ealing, 1965; Asst County Treas., Flints CC, 1968; Dep. County Treas., West Suffolk CC, 1970; County Treasurer, S Yorks CC, 1973; Dir of Finance, Lothian Regl Council, 1985–94. Non-exec. Dir, Cartrefi Conwy Ltd, 2008–10. Vice-Chairman: UK-American Properties Inc., 1980–86; American Properties Unit Trust, 1980–86; Mem. Bd, Lazards Small Cos Exempt Unit Trust, 1979–97. Mem. Council, CIPFA, 1983–99 (Vice Pres., 1991–92; Pres., 1992–93); Mem. Investment Protection Cttee, 1976–80, 1982–86 and 1999–2004, Council Mem., 1998–2004, Nat. Assoc. of Pension Funds; Mem. Bd, Foundn for Regulation of Accountancy Profession, 1999–2004. Pres., Assoc. of Public Service Finance Officers, 1981–82. *Recreations:* walking, photography. *Address:* Rathowan, Main Road, Dirleton, Noth Berwick, East Lothian EH39 5DN. *T:* (01620) 850362. *Club:* Royal Over-Seas League. *Died 9 May 2013.*

CHYNOWETH, Rt Rev. Neville James, AM 1996; ED 1966; *b* 3 Oct. 1922; *s* of Percy James and Lilian Chynoweth; *m* 1951, Joan Laurice Wilson; two *s* two *d*. *Educ:* Manly High School; Sydney Univ. (MA); Melbourne Coll. of Divinity (BD); Moore Theological Coll. (ThL). ARSCM 1993. Assistant, St Michael's, Sydney, 1950; Rector, Kangaroo Valley, 1951–52; Chaplain, Royal Prince Alfred Hospital, 1952–54; Rector: St John's, Deewhy, 1954–63; St Anne's, Strathfield, 1963–66; All Saints, Canberra, 1966–71; St Paul's, Canberra, 1971–74; Archdeacon of Canberra, 1973–74; Assistant Bishop of Canberra and Goulburn, 1974–80; Bishop of Gippsland, 1980–87. *Recreations:* music, biography. *Address:* 10 Fortitude Street, Red Hill, Canberra, ACT 2603, Australia. *T:* (2) 62397056. *Died 11 Aug. 2011.*

CLANCY, His Eminence Cardinal Edward Bede, AC 1992 (AO 1984); Archbishop of Sydney, (RC), 1983–2001, then Emeritus; *b* 13 Dec. 1923; *s* of John Bede Clancy and Ellen Lucy Clancy (*née* Edwards). *Educ:* Marist Brothers Coll., Parramatta, NSW; St Patrick's Coll., Manly, NSW; Biblical Inst., Rome (LSS); Propaganda Fide Univ., Rome (DD). Ordained to priesthood, 1949; parish ministry, 1950–51; studies in Rome, 1952–54; parish ministry, 1955–57; seminary staff, 1958–61; studies in Rome, 1962–64; seminary staff, Manly, 1966–73; Auxiliary Bishop, Sydney, 1974–78; Archbishop of Canberra and Goulburn, 1979–83. Cardinal, 1988. Chancellor, Aust. Catholic Univ., 1990–2001. Hon. DHum Ateneo de Manila, Philippines, 2001; DUniv Aust. Catholic Univ., 2002. *Publications:* The Bible—The Church's Book, 1974; Come Back—the Church Loves You, 2002; Walk Worthy of Your Vocation—a Spiritual Journey with St Paul, 2004; God's Early Trailblazers—Great Figures in the Early Church, 2005; contribs to Australian Catholic Record. *Recreation:* golf. *Died 3 Aug. 2014.*

CLANCY, Thomas Leo, Jr, (Tom); writer; *b* 12 March 1947; *m* 1969, Wanda Thomas (marr. diss. 1998); one *s* three *d*; *m* 1999, Alexandra Maria Llewellyn. *Educ:* Loyola Coll., Baltimore, Md. Served USAR OTC. Former insurance agent, Baltimore, Md and Hartford, Conn; joined O. F. Bowen Agency, insurance firm, Owings, Md, 1973, owner (with wife), 1980; co-owner and Vice-Chm., Community Projects and Public Affairs, Baltimore Orioles. Co-founder, Red Storm Entertainment, 1996. *Publications:* (as Tom Clancy): *novels:* The Hunt for Red October, 1984 (filmed); Red Storm Rising, 1986; Patriot Games, 1987 (filmed); Cardinal of the Kremlin, 1988; Clear and Present Danger, 1989 (filmed); The Sum of all Fears, 1991 (filmed); Without Remorse, 1993; Debt of Honor, 1994; Reality Check, 1995; Executive Orders, 1996; Rainbow Six, 1998; The Bear and the Dragon, 2000; Red Rabbit, 2002; The Teeth of the Tiger, 2003; Dead or Alive, 2010; (with Mark Greaney) Locked On, 2011; (with Peter Telep) Against All Enemies, 2012; Net Force series (with Steve Pieczevik): Net Force; The Deadliest Game; End Game; The Great Race; One is the Loneliest Number; The Ultimate Escape; Cyberspy; Hidden Agendas; Gameprey; Deathworld; Night Moves; Breaking Point; Private Lives; Virtual Vandals; Springboard; Op Centre series (with Steve Pieczevik): Op Centre, 1995; Mirror Image, 1995; Games of State, 1996; Acts of War, 1997; State of Siege; Balance of Power, 1998; Divide and Conquer; Line of Control, 2003; Call to Treason, 2004; War of Eagles, 2005; Power Plays series (with M. H. Greenberg): Politika; Ruthless.com; Shadow Watch; Bio-Strike, 2000; Cutting Edge; Wild Card; *non-fiction:* Submarine, 1993; Fighter Wing, 1995; Armored Warfare, 1996; Marine, 1996; Airborne, 1997; Carrier, 1999; (with Fred Franks Jr) Into the Storm, 1997; (with J. B. Alexander) Future War; War in the Boats; Every Man a Tiger, 1999; (jtly) Battle Ready, 2004. *Died 1 Oct. 2013.*

CLARK, Alastair; *see* Clark, T. A.

CLARK, Alistair Campbell; Consultant, Blackadder Reid Johnston (formerly Reid Johnston Bell & Henderson), Solicitors, Dundee, 1995–99 (Partner, 1961–95); *b* 4 March 1933; *s* of Peter Campbell Clark and Janet Mitchell Scott or Clark; *m* 1960, Evelyn M. Johnston; three *s*. *Educ:* St Andrews Univ. Admitted solicitor, 1957. WS 1991. Hon. Sheriff, Tayside Central and Fife, 1986–. Mem. Council, Law Soc. of Scotland, 1982–91 (Pres., 1989–90); Dean, Faculty of Procurators and Solicitors, Dundee, 1979–81 (Hon. Mem., 1991). Chm., Scottish Conveyancing and Executry Services Bd, 1996–2003. Chm., Dovetail Enterprises. Founder Chm., Broughty Ferry Round Table; Founder Pres., Claverhouse Rotary Club, Dundee (Paul Harris Fellow, 2001; Hon. Mem., 2008). *Recreations:* family, travel, erratic golf, gardening, conversing. *Address:* Blythe Lodge, 85a Dundee Road, West Ferry, Dundee DD5 1LZ. *T:* (01382) 477989. *E:* alistair@blythelodge.co.uk. *Club:* Royal and Ancient (St Andrews). *Died 26 Jan. 2015.*

CLARK, Derek John, FCIS; Principal, DJC Services, since 1994; *b* 17 June 1929; *s* of Robert Clark and Florence Mary (*née* Wise); *m* 1949, Edna Doris Coome; one *s* one *d*. *Educ:* Selhurst Grammar Sch., Croydon; SE London Technical Coll. FCIS 1982 (ACIS 1961). National Service, RAF, 1948–49. Corp. of Trinity House, 1949–66; RICS, 1966–71; ICMA, 1971–82; Sec., IStructE, 1982–94. Secretary and Director: Detecnicks (Property) Ltd, 1999–; Detecnicks (Finance) Ltd, 2000–; Sec., Detecnicks Ltd, 1999. Hon. FIStructE 1994. *Recreations:* athletics (until 1961), squash (until 1994). *Address:* 24 North Way, Felpham, Bognor Regis, W Sussex PO22 7BT. *T:* (01243) 822585. *Died 25 May 2013.*

CLARK, Henry Maitland; journalist with Avon Advertiser, 1989–97; *b* 11 April 1929; *s* of Major H. F. Clark, Rockwood, Upperlands, Co. Londonderry; *m* 1972, Penelope Winifred Tindal (*d* 1994); one *s* two *d*. *Educ:* Shrewsbury Sch.; Trinity Coll., Dublin; Trinity Hall, Cambridge. Entered Colonial Service and appointed District Officer, Tanganyika, 1951; served in various Districts of Tanganyika, 1951–59; resigned from Colonial Service, 1959 (to stand for Parlt). Wine merchant, IDV Ltd and Cock Russell Vintners, 1972–76; Hd of Information, CoSIRA, 1977–89. MP (UU) Antrim North (UK Parliament), Oct. 1959–1970; Chm. Conservative Trade and Overseas Devel Sub-Cttee; Member: British Delegation to Council of Europe and WEU, 1962–65; Select Cttee on Overseas Aid and Devel, 1969–70. Grand Jury, Co. Londonderry, 1970. A Commonwealth Observer, Mauritius General Election, 1967. Mem., Exec. Cttee, Lepra (British Leprosy Relief Assoc.). Vice-Pres., Dublin Univ. Boat Club. *Recreations:* rowing coach, sailing, shooting, golf, collecting old furniture. *Address:* Staddles, Hindon Lane, Tisbury, Wilts SP3 6PU. *T:* (01747) 870330. *Club:* Royal Portrush Golf. *Died 24 March 2012.*

CLARK, (Henry) Wallace (Stuart), MBE 1970; DL; Vice Lord-Lieutenant of County Londonderry, 1993–2001; Director, Wm Clark & Sons, Linen Manufacturers, 1972–87 (non-executive Director, 1987–2002); *b* 20 Nov. 1926; *s* of Major H. F. Clark, MBE, JP, RA, Rockwood, Upperlands, and Sybil Emily (*née* Stuart); *m* 1957, June Elisabeth Lester Deane; one *s* (and one *s* decd). *Educ:* Shrewsbury School. Lieut, RNVR, 1945–47 (bomb and mine disposal); Cattleman, Merchant Navy, 1947–48. District Comdt, Ulster Special Constabulary, 1955–70; Major, Ulster Defence Regt, 1970–81. Foyle's Lectr, USA tour, 1964. Led Church of Ireland St Columba commemorative curragh voyage, Derry to Iona, 1963; Dir and Skipper, Lord of the Isles Voyage, Galway to Stornaway in 16th century galley, 1991. FRSAI 2005. DL 1962, High Sheriff 1969, Co. Londonderry. *Publications:* (jtly) North and East Coasts of Ireland, 1957; (jtly) South and West Coasts of Ireland, 1962, 2nd edn 1970; Guns in Ulster, 1967; Rathlin Disputed Island, 1972; Sailing Round Ireland, 1976; Linen on the Green, 1982; Lord of the Isles Voyage, 1993; Upperlands History and Visitors Guide, 1998; Sailing Round Russia: the story of Miles Clark's unique voyage, 1999; Brave Men and True: early days in the Ulster Defence Regiment, 2002; Sailing the Donegal Islands, 2003; Sailing the Connaught Islands, 2005; Five Years on Full Alert: diaries of Ulster anti-aircraft gunners, 2007; Growing up in Upperlands, 2007. *Recreation:* yacht cruising. *Address:* Gorteade Cottage, Upperlands, Co. Londonderry, N Ireland BT46 5SB. *T:* (028) 7964 2737. *Clubs:* Royal Cruising, Irish Cruising (Cdre 1962). *Died 8 May 2011.*

CLARK, James Leonard; Under Secretary, Establishment Personnel Division, Departments of Industry and Trade Common Services, 1980–83 (Under Secretary, Department of Trade, 1978–80); *b* 8 Jan. 1923; *s* of James Alfred and Grace Clark; *m* 1st, 1954, Joan Pauline Richards (*d* 1992); 2nd, 1997, Helga Thomas. *Educ:* Mercers' School. Lieut (A), Fleet Air Arm, 1942–46. Clerical Officer, HM Treasury, 1939; Private Sec. to successive First Secs of State, 1964–67; Cabinet Office, 1969–71; Asst Sec., Price Commn, 1973–75; Dept of Industry, 1975–78. CBI, 1983–85; Hd of Administration, SIB, 1985–89. *Address:* 4 Westcott Way, Cheam, Surrey SM2 7JY. *T:* (020) 8393 2622. *Died 1 Nov. 2012.*

CLARK, Prof. John Benjamin; Professor of Neurochemistry, Institute of Neurology, University of London, at University College London (formerly at British Postgraduate Medical Federation), 1990–2006, then Emeritus (Academic Vice Dean, 1996–2002); Hon. Consultant Neurochemist, National Hospital of Neurology and Neurosurgery, 1990–2006; *b* 30 Jan. 1941; *e s* of P. B.

Clark and J. E. Clark (*née* Smith); *m* 1965, Joan Gibbons; one *s* one *d* (and one *s* decd). *Educ:* Southend High Sch. for Boys; University College London (BSc 1962; PhD 1964; DSc 1982). St Bartholomew's Hospital Medical College, University of London: Lectr, Sen. Lectr and Reader in Biochemistry, 1965–86; Prof. of Cell Biochemistry, 1986–90. MRC Travelling Fellow, Johnson Res. Foundn, Univ. of Pennsylvania, 1969–70; Vis. Prof., Dept of Biochem. and Molecular Biol., UCL, 1991–2006. *Publications:* numerous contribs to sci. jls on mitochondrial metabolism and brain development. *Recreations:* walking, fine wines, reading. *Address:* c/o Miriam Marks Department of Neurochemistry, Institute of Neurology, Queen Square, WC1N 3BG. *T:* (020) 7829 8722. *Died 25 Feb. 2013.*

CLARK, Ven. Kenneth James, DSC 1944; Archdeacon of Swindon, 1982–92; *b* 31 May 1922; *er s* of Francis James Clark and Winifred Adelaide Clark (*née* Martin); *m* 1948, Elisabeth Mary Monica Helen Huggett (*d* 2005); three *s* three *d*. *Educ:* Watford Grammar School; St Catherine's Coll., Oxford (MA); Cuddesdon Theological Coll. Midshipman RN, 1940; Lieutenant RN, 1942; served in submarines, 1942–46. Baptist Minister, Forest Row, Sussex, 1950–52; Curate of Brinkworth, 1952–53; Curate of Cricklade with Latton, 1953–56; Priest-in-Charge, later Vicar (1959), of Holy Cross, Inns Court, Bristol, 1956–61; Vicar: Westbury-on-Trym, 1961–72; St Mary Redcliffe, Bristol, 1972–82; Hon. Canon of Bristol Cathedral, 1974. Member, Gen. Synod of C of E, 1980–92. *Recreations:* music, travel. *Address:* 1 The Sundials, Garden House, St Monica Trust, Cote Lane, Westbury-on-Trym, Bristol BS9 3UN. *Died 29 Jan. 2013.*

CLARK, Sir Robert (Anthony), Kt 1976; DSC 1944; Chairman, RP & C International (formerly Rauscher Pierce & Clark), since 1992; *b* 6 Jan. 1924; *yr s* of John Clark and Gladys Clark (*née* Dyer); *m* 1949, Andolyn Marjorie Lewis; two *s* one *d*. *Educ:* Highgate Sch.; King's Coll., Cambridge. Served War, Royal Navy, 1942–46. Partner with Slaughter and May, Solicitors, 1953–61; Director: Alfred McAlpine plc (formerly Marchwiel plc), 1957–96; Hill Samuel Bank Ltd, merchant bankers (formerly Philip Hill, Higginson, Erlangers Ltd, later Hill Samuel & Co. Ltd), 1961–91 (Chm., 1974–87); Bank of England, 1976–85; Eagle Star Holdings Ltd, 1976–87; BL, subseq. Rover Gp plc, 1977–88; Shell Transport and Trading Co., plc, 1982–94; SmithKline Beecham plc, 1987–95 (Vice-Chm.); Vodafone Group plc (formerly Racal Telecom PLC), 1988–98; Chairman: Hill Samuel Gp plc, 1980–88 (Chief Exec., 1976–80); IMI plc, 1981–89; Marley plc, 1985–89; Mirror Group (formerly Mirror Group Newspapers) plc, 1992–98; Lambert Fenchurch Gp (formerly Lowndes Lambert Group Hldgs) plc, 1995–98 (Dep. Chm., 1992–95); Dep. Chm., TSB Gp, 1989–91 (Dir, 1987–91). Chairman: Industrial Development Adv. Bd, 1973–80; Review Body on Doctors' and Dentists' Remuneration, 1979–86; Council, Charing Cross and Westminster Med. Sch., 1982–96; Dir, ENO, 1983–87. Hon. DSc Cranfield Inst. of Technol., 1982. *Recreations:* reading, collecting antiquarian books, music, the garden at Munstead Wood. *Address:* Munstead Wood, Godalming, Surrey GU7 1UN. *T:* (01483) 417867; RP & C International, 31A St James's Square, SW1Y 4JR. *Clubs:* Pratt's, Special Forces. *Died 3 Jan. 2013.*

CLARK, Prof. Robert Bernard, DSc, PhD; FRSE; Professor of Zoology, University of Newcastle upon Tyne, 1966–89, then Emeritus; *b* 13 Oct. 1923; *s* of Joseph Lawrence Clark and Dorothy (*née* Halden); *m* 1st, 1956, Mary Eleanor (*née* Laurence) (marr. diss.); 2nd, 1970, Susan Diana (*née* Smith); one *s* one *d*. *Educ:* St Marylebone Grammar Sch.; Chelsea Polytechnic (BSc London 1944); University Coll., Exeter (BSc 1950); Univ. of Glasgow (PhD 1956); DSc London 1965. FSB (FIBiol 1966); FLS 1969; FRSE 1970. Asst Experimental Officer, DSIR Road Research Laboratory, 1944; Asst to Prof. of Zoology, Univ. of Glasgow, 1950; Asst Prof., Univ. of California (Berkeley), 1953; Lectr in Zoology, Univ. of Bristol, 1956; Head of Dept of Zoology and Dir of Dove Marine Laboratory, Univ. of Newcastle upon Tyne, 1966–77, Dir of Research Unit on Rehabilitation of Oiled Seabirds, 1967–76; Dir of NERC Research Unit on Rocky Shore Biology, 1981–87. Member: NERC, 1971–77 and 1983–86; Royal Commn on Environmental Pollution, 1979–83; Adv. Cttee on Pesticides, 1986–90; Mem. Council, Nature Conservancy, 1975. *Publications:* Neurosecretion (ed jtly), 1962; Dynamics in Metazoan Evolution, 1964, corrected repr. 1967; Practical Course in Experimental Zoology, 1966; (jtly) Invertebrate Panorama, 1971; (jtly) Synopsis of Animal Classification, 1971; (ed jtly) Essays in Hydrobiology, 1972; (ed) The Long-Term Effects of Oil Pollution on Marine Populations, Communities and Ecosystems, 1982; Marine Pollution, 1986, 5th edn 2001; The Waters Around the British Isles: their conflicting uses, 1987; (ed jtly) Environmental Effects of North Sea Oil and Gas Development, 1987; Founder, 1968, and ed, Marine Pollution Bulletin; numerous papers in learned jls. *Recreations:* architecture, music, unambitious gardening, cooking. *Address:* Highbury House, 53 Highbury, Newcastle upon Tyne NE2 3LN. *T:* (0191) 281 4672. *Died 28 Sept. 2013.*

CLARK, Robert Joseph, CBE 2000; international court management consultant, British Council, European Union and others, since 2001; Circuit Administrator, South Eastern Circuit, Lord Chancellor's Department, 1997–2001; *b* 29 March 1942; *s* of late Edward Clark and Elsie Clark (*née* Bush); *m* 1970, Elke Agnes, *d* of late Hans Schmidt and Herma Schmidt; two *d*. *Educ:* state schools in London. Lord Chancellor's Department: Official Solicitor's Dept, 1960–70; Nat. Industrial Relns Court, 1970–74; HQ, 1974–77; Trng Centre, 1977–79; Chief Clerk, Court of Protection, 1979–83; S Eastern Circuit Office, 1983–88; Head: Civil Business Div., 1988–91; Judicial Appointments Div. II, 1991–93; Circuit Administrator, Western Circuit, 1993–97. *Recreations:* theatre, walking. *Address:* 36 Kayemoor Road, Sutton, Surrey SM2 5HT. *Club:* Civil Service. *Died 23 Sept. 2012.*

CLARK, (Thomas) Alastair, CBE 2009; Senior Adviser, HM Treasury, 2009–12; *b* 27 Feb. 1949; *s* of late Andrew Evans Clark and Freda (*née* Seal); *m* 1986, Shirley Anne Barker; one *s* (one *d* decd). *Educ:* Stockport Grammar Sch.; Emmanuel Coll., Cambridge (MA Maths); London Sch. of Econs (MSc Econs); Stanford Business Sch. (SEP). Bank of England, 1971–2008: PA to Dep. Governor, 1980–81; UK Alternate Exec. Dir, IMF, 1983–85; UK Alternate Dir, EIB, 1986–88; Head: Financial Markets and Instns Div., 1987–93; European Div., 1993–94; Dep. Dir, 1994–97; Exec. Dir, 1997–2003; Advr to Gov., 2003–07 and 2007–08. Mem., Interim Financial Policy Cttee, Bank of England, 2011–13. Director: Crestco, 1998–2002; LIFFE, 2007–13; Euronext, 2008–09. Mem. Bd, Jersey Financial Services Commn, 2009. Hon. Vis. Prof., Cass Business Sch., City Univ., 2007–. Gov., King's Coll. Sch., Wimbledon, 2007–. Hon. Fellow, ACT, 2007–. *Recreations:* joinery, hill-walking. *Address:* 54 Forest Road, Richmond, Surrey TW9 3BZ. *Died 11 Feb. 2015.*

CLARK, Wallace; *see* Clark, H. W. S.

CLARK, William P.; Senior Counsel, Clark, Cali and Negranti, since 1997; *b* 23 Oct. 1931; *s* of William and Bernice Clark; *m* 1955, Joan Brauner (*d* 2009); three *s* two *d*. *Educ:* Stanford Univ., California; Loyola Law Sch., Los Angeles, California. Admitted to practice of law, California, 1958; Sen. Member, law firm, Clark, Cole & Fairfield, Oxnard, Calif, 1958–67. Served on Cabinet of California, Governor Ronald Reagan, first as Cabinet Secretary, later as Executive Secretary, 1967–69; Judge, Superior Court, State of California, County of San Luis Obispo, 1969–71; Associate Justice: California Court of Appeal, Second District, Los Angeles, 1971–73; California Supreme Court, San Francisco, 1973–81; Dep. Secretary, Dept of State, Washington, DC, 1981–82; Assistant to Pres. of USA for Nat. Security Affairs, 1982–83; Sec. of the Interior, 1983–85. Chairman: Presidential Task Force on Nuclear Weapons Program Management, 1985; USA-ROC (Taiwan) Business Council; Member: Commn on Defense Management, 1985–86; Commn on Integrated Long-Term Strategy, 1987. Counselor, Standing Cttee on Law and Nat. Security, American Bar Assoc. Dir, Mus. of Flying, Santa Monica, California. *Publications:* judicial opinions in California Reports, 9 Cal. 3d through 29 Cal. 3d. *Recreations:* ranching, horseback riding, outdoor sports, flying. *Address:* Clark Company, Clark Building, 1031 Pine Street, Paso Robles, CA 93446–2537, USA. *Clubs:*

Bohemia (San Francisco); California Cattlemen's Association; Rancheros Visitadores (California). *Died 10 Aug. 2013.*

CLARKE, Prof. Alan Douglas Benson, CBE 1974; Professor of Psychology, University of Hull, 1962–84, then Emeritus; *b* 21 March 1922; *s* of late Robert Benson Clarke and Mary Lizars Clarke; *m* 1950, Prof. Ann Margaret (*née* Gravely); two *s*. *Educ:* Lancing Coll.; Univ. of Reading (BA Hons 1st cl. 1948); Univ. of London (PhD 1950). FBPsS. Reading Univ., 1940–41 and 1946–48. Sen. Psychol., 1951–57 and Cons. Psychol., 1957–62, Manor Hosp., Epsom. Dean of Faculty of Science, 1966–68, and Pro-Vice-Chancellor 1968–71, Univ. of Hull. Vis. Prof., Univ. of Hertfordshire, 1992–98. Rapporteur, WHO Expert Cttee on Organization of Services for Mentally Retarded, 1967; Mem. WHO Expert Adv. Panel on Mental Health, 1968–85; Chm., Trng Council for Teachers of Mentally Handicapped, 1969–74; Hon. Vice-Pres., Nat. Assoc. for Mental Health, 1970–; President: Internat. Assoc. for Sci. Study of Mental Deficiency, 1973–76 (Hon. Past-Pres., 1976–88; Hon. Life Pres., 1988–); BPsS, 1977–78. Member: Personal Social Services Council, 1973–77; DHSS/SSRC Organizing Gp Transmitted Deprivation, 1974–83 (Chm. 1978–83); Cons., OECD/NZ Conf. on Early Childhood Care and Educn, 1978; Chairman: Sec. of State's Adv. Cttee on Top Grade Clinical Psychologist Posts and Appts, NHS, 1981–82; Adv. Cttee, Thomas Coram Res. Unit, Univ. of London Inst. of Educn, 1981–98. Lectures: Maudsley, RMPA, 1967; Stolz, Guy's Hosp., 1972; Tizard Meml, Assoc. for Child Psychol. and Psychiatry, 1983. Hon. Life Mem., Amer. Assoc. on Mental Deficiency, 1975 (Research award, 1977, with Ann M. Clarke); Hon. Mem., Assoc. for Child and Adolescent Mental Health, 2009. Hon. FRCPsych 1989; Hon. FBPsS 2007. Hon. DSc Hull, 1986. (With Ann M. Clarke) Distinguished Achievement Award for Scientific Lit., Internat. Assoc. for Scientific Study of Mental Deficiency, 1982. Editor, Brit. Jl Psychol., 1973–79; Mem., Editorial Bds of other jls. *Publications:* with Ann M. Clarke: Mental Deficiency: the Changing Outlook, 1958, 4th edn 1985; Mental Retardation and Behavioural Research, 1973; Early Experience: myth and evidence, 1976; Early Experience and the Life Path, 2000; Human Resilience: a fifty year quest, 2003; (with B. Tizard) Child Development and Social Policy: the life and work of Jack Tizard, 1983; (with P. Evans) Combating Mental Handicap, 1991; numerous in psychol and med. jls. *Address:* 109 Meadway, Barnet, Herts EN5 5JZ. *T:* (020) 8441 9690. *Died 10 Dec. 2011.*

CLARKE, Dr Arthur S.; Keeper, Department of Natural History, Royal Scottish Museum, 1980–83; *b* 11 Feb. 1923; *yr s* of late Albert Clarke and Doris Clarke (*née* Elliott); *m* 1951, Joan, *er d* of Walter Andrassy; one *s* one *d*. *Educ:* Leeds Boys' Modern School; Aireborough Grammar School; Leeds Univ. (BSc 1948, PhD 1951). Pilot, RAF, 1943–46. Asst Lecturer, Glasgow Univ., 1951; Asst Keeper, Royal Scottish Museum, 1954; Deputy Keeper, 1973. *Address:* Knapdale, Princes Street, Innerleithen EH44 6JT. *Died 24 May 2012.*

CLARKE, Prof. Bryan Campbell, DPhil; FRS 1982; Foundation Professor of Genetics, 1971–93, Research Professor, 1993–97, University of Nottingham, then Professor Emeritus; *b* 24 June 1932; *s* of Robert Campbell Clarke and Gladys Mary (*née* Carter); *m* 1960, Ann Gillian, *d* of late Prof. John Jewkes, CBE; one *s* one *d*. *Educ:* Fay Sch., Southborough, Mass, USA; Magdalen Coll. Sch., Oxford; Magdalen Coll., Oxford (MA, DPhil). FLS 1980. National Service, 1950–52 (Pilot Officer, RAF). Asst 1959, Lectr 1963, Reader 1969, Dept of Zoology, Univ. of Edinburgh. Res. Fellow, Stanford Univ., 1973; SRC Sen. Res. Fellow, 1976–81; Hon. Res. Fellow, Natural Hist. Mus., 1993–2009. Joint Founder, Population Genetics Gp, 1967; Pres., Section D (Biology), BAAS, 1989; Vice-President: Genetical Soc., 1981; Linnean Soc., 1985–87; Soc. for Study of Evolution, USA, 1990–91; Zool Soc. of London, 1998–99; Chairman: Terrestrial Life Sciences Cttee, NERC, 1984–87; Biol Scis Sub-Cttee, HEFCE, 1992–97. Mem., Council, Royal Soc., 1994–96. Chm. Trustees, Charles Darwin Trust, 2000–04; Co-Founder and Trustee, Frozen Ark Project, 2004–. Scientific expeditions to: Morocco, 1955; Polynesia, 1962, 1967, 1968, 1980, 1982, 1986, 1991, 1994, 2000. Editor: Heredity, 1978–85; Proceedings of the Royal Society, Series B, 1989–93. Internat. Mem. (formerly Foreign Mem.), Amer. Philosophical Soc., 2003; Foreign Hon. Mem., Amer. Acad. of Arts and Scis, 2004. Linnean Medal for Zoology, 2003; Darwin-Wallace Medal, Linnean Soc., 2008; Darwin Medal, Royal Soc., 2010. *Publications:* Berber Village, 1959; contrib. scientific jls, mostly on ecological genetics and evolution. *Recreations:* sporadic painting, archaeology, computing. *Address:* Linden Cottage, School Lane, Colston Bassett, Nottingham NG12 3FD. *T:* (01949) 81243. *Club:* Royal Air Force. *Died 27 Feb. 2014.*

CLARKE, David Stuart, AO 1992; Chairman, Macquarie Group (formerly Macquarie Bank) Ltd, since 2007 (Executive Chairman, 1985–2007); *b* 3 Jan. 1942; *s* of Stuart Richardson Clarke and Ailsie Jean Talbot Clarke; *m* 1st, 1964, Margaret Maclean Partridge (marr. diss. 1994); two *s*; 2nd, 1995, Jane Graves. *Educ:* Knox Grammar Sch.; Sydney Univ. (BEcon Hons); Harvard Univ. (MBA). Hill Samuel Australia Ltd: Jt Man. Dir, 1971–77; Man. Dir, 1977–84; Exec. Chm., 1984–85; Director: Darling & Co. Ltd (later Schroder Australia Ltd), 1966–71; Babcock Aust. Holdings Ltd, 1972–81; Chairman: Accepting Houses Assoc. of Aust., 1974–76; Sceggs Darlinghurst Ltd, 1976–78; Barlile Corp. Ltd, 1986–93; Australian Vintage (formerly Brian McGuigan Wines, then McGuigan Simeon Wines) Ltd, 1991–2009; Goodman Fielder Ltd, 1995–2000; Goodman Internat. Ltd (formerly Macquarie Goodman Gp), 2000–09; Director: Hill Samuel & Co. Ltd (London), 1978–84; Hooker Corp. Ltd, 1984–86; Reil Corp. Ltd, 1986–87. Member: Lloyds of London, 1983–97; Fed. Govt Cttee under Financial Corporations Act, 1975–85; Exec. Cttee, Cttee for Econ. Develt of Australia, 1982–98; Affiliate, Aust. Stock Exch. Ltd, 1987–2004. Mem. Adv. Bd, Bloomberg Asia Pacific, 2006–. Chairman: Australian Opera, 1986–95; Aust. Wool Realisation Commn, 1991–93. Member: Council, Royal Agricl Soc. of NSW, 1986– (Chm., Wine Cttee, 1990–); Harvard Business Sch. Alumni Council, 1986–89; Investment Adv. Cttee, Australian Olympic Foundn, 1996–; Stage II Project, Nat. Inst. for Dramatic Art, 1996–2003; Asia Adv. Cttee, Harvard Business Sch., 1997–2009; Seoul Internat. Business Adv. Council, 2003–; Corporate Governance Cttee, Aust. Inst. of Co. Dirs, 2005–09. Hon. Fed. Treas., Liberal Party of Aust., 1987–89. Member: Bd Trustees, Financial Markets Foundn for Children, 1989–2000 (Hon. Life Mem.); Sydney Adv. Bd, Salvation Army, 1990–2006 (Chm., 1999–2006); Corporate Citizens Cttee, Children's Cancer Inst. of Australia, 1992–; Bd, Centre for Social Impact, 2008–09; Chairman: Salvation Army Red Shield Appeal, 1990–92 (Cttee Mem., 1985–88; Dep. Chm., 1989–90); Menzies Res. Centre, 1994–97; George Gregan Foundn, 2005–09; Nat. Leadership Council, Social Ventures Australia, 2007–; Campaign Chm., (NSW), Salvation Army Educn Foundn, 1996–98; Dir, Clayton Utz Foundn Pty Ltd, 2003–08; Advocate, Macfarlane Burnet Centre for Med. Res., 1999–. Gov., Aust. Ireland Fund, 1998–. Mem., Cook Soc., 1979– (Co-Convener, 1988–97). President: Nat. Council, Opera Australia, 1996–2000 (Chm., Opera Australia Capital Fund, 1996–); Winemakers' Fedn of Australia, 2007–08. Chairman: NSW Rugby Union, 1989–95 (Treas., 1989); Australian Rugby Union, 1998–2001 (Dir, 1990–97; Dep. Chm., 1997–98); Council Rep., Mem. Games Regulation Cttee and Mem. Bd Policy Cttee, Internat. Rugby Bd, 1998–2001; Vice-Pres., Sydney Univ. CC, 2000–; Chm., Sydney Univ. FC Foundn, 2003–. Chm., Business Club Australia Beijing 2008, Australian Trade Commn, 2007–08. Confrère des Chevaliers du Tastevin. Hon. DScEcon Sydney, 2000. Centenary Medal, Aust., 2001; Richard Pratt Business Leadership Award, Australia Business Arts Foundn, 2006. *Recreations:* opera, ski-ing, golf, bridge, philately, ballet, wine. *Clubs:* Australian, Harvard of Australia (Pres. 1977–79), Royal Sydney Golf, Elanora Country, Cabbage Tree, Vintage Golf (Sydney). *Died 8 April 2011.*

CLARKE, Geoffrey Petts, RA 1976 (ARA 1970); ARCA; artist and sculptor; *b* 28 Nov. 1924; *s* of John Moulding Clarke and Janet Petts; *m* 1947, Ethelwynne Tyrer (*d* 2007); two *s*. *Educ:* Royal College of Art (Hons). Exhibitions: Gimpel Fils Gallery, 1952, 1955; Redfern Gallery, 1965; Taranman Gallery, 1975, 1976, 1982; Yorkshire Sculpture

Park, Chappel Gall., Colchester, and Friends Room, Royal Acad., 1994; Fine Art Soc., 2000, 2006; Linton Ct Gall., Settle, 2011; Pangolin London, 2013; touring exhibitions: Christchurch Mansions, Ipswich, 1994; Herbert Art Gall., Coventry, and Pallant House, Chichester, 1995; Bury St Edmunds Art Gall., 2003; Derby Mus. and Art Gall., 2004. Works in public collections: Victoria and Albert Museum; Tate Gallery; Arts Council; Museum of Modern Art, NY; BM; Leeds Art Gall.; etc. Prizes for engraving: Triennial, 1951; London, 1953, Tokyo, 1957. Commissioned work includes: mosaics, Liverpool Univ. Physics Block; stained glass windows for Treasury, Lincoln Cathedral; bronze sculpture, Thorn Electric Building, Upper St Martin's Lane; 3 stained glass windows, high altar, cross and candlesticks, the flying cross and crown of thorns, all in Coventry Cathedral; sculpture, Nottingham Civic Theatre; UKAEA Culham; Univs of Liverpool, Exeter, Cambridge, Manchester, Loughborough and Warwick; screens in Royal Military Chapel, Birdcage Walk. Further work at Chichester, Newcastle, Manchester, Plymouth, Ipswich, Taunton, Winchester, St Paul, Minnesota, Lincoln, Nebraska, Newcastle Civic Centre, Leicester, Churchill Coll., Aldershot, Suffolk Police HQ, All Souls, W1, The Majlis, Abu Dhabi, York House, N1. *Died 30 Oct. 2014.*

CLARKE, Prof. John Frederick, FRS 1987; Professor of Theoretical Gas Dynamics, Cranfield Institute of Technology, 1972–91, Professor Emeritus, 1992; *b* 1 May 1927; *s* of Frederick William Clarke and Clara Auguste Antonie (*née* Nauen); *m* 1953, Jean Ruth Gentle; two *d*. *Educ:* Warwick School; Queen Mary Coll., Univ. of London (BSc Eng 1st Cl. Hons, David Allan Low Prize, PhD; Hon. Fellow, 1992). FIMA 1965; FRAeS 1969; FInstP 1999. Qualified Service Pilot, RN, 1946–48; Aerodynamicist, English Electric Co., 1956–57; Lectr, Coll. of Aeronautics, 1958–65 (Vis. Associate Prof. and Fulbright Scholar, Stanford Univ., 1961–62); Reader, Cranfield Inst. of Technology, 1965–72. Vis. Prof. at univs in USA, Australia and Europe; Vis. Res. Fellow, Centre for Non-linear Studies, Univ. of Leeds, 1987–; Benjamin Meaker Vis. Prof., Univ. of Bristol, 1988–89; first G. C. Steward Vis. Fellow, Gonville and Caius Coll., Cambridge, 1992. Member: NATO Collaborative Research Grants Panel, 1987–90; Esso Energy Award Cttee, 1988–93; Maths Cttee, SERC, 1990–91. Member, Editorial Board: Qly Jl Mech. Appl. Math., 1982–2003; Combustion Theory & Modelling, 1997–2003; Philosophical Trans A, Royal Soc., 1997–2002. *Publications:* (with M. McChesney) The Dynamics of Real Gases, 1964; (with M. McChesney) Dynamics of Relaxing Gases, 1976; contribs to professional jls on gas dynamics and combustion theory. *Recreation:* Sunday painter. *Address:* Field House, Green Lane, Aspley Guise MK17 8EN. *T:* (01908) 582234. *Died 11 June 2013.*

CLARKE, (John) Neil; Chairman, British Coal, 1991–97; *b* 7 Aug. 1934; *s* of late George Philip Clarke and Norah Marie Clarke (*née* Bailey); *m* 1958, Sonia Heather Beckett; three *s*. *Educ:* Rugby School; King's College London (LLB). FICA 1959. Partner, Rowley, Pemberton, Roberts & Co., 1960–69; Charter Consolidated, 1969–88: Dir, 1973; Exec. Dir, 1974; Man. Dir, 1979; Chief Exec., 1980; Dep. Chm. and Chief Exec., 1982–88; Chairman: Johnson Matthey, 1984–89; Molins, 1989–91 (Dir, 1987–91); Genchem Holdings, 1989–2006; Director: Anglo American Corp. of SA, 1976–90; Consolidated Gold Fields, 1982–89; Travis Perkins, 1990–2002. Chm., ESCP-EAP, London, 1986–2006. Trustee, King George VI and Queen Elizabeth Foundn of St Catharine's, 1974–. Chevalier, Ordre Nat. du Mérite (France), 2002. *Recreations:* music, tennis, golf. *Address:* High Willows, 18 Park Avenue, Farnborough Park, Orpington, Kent BR6 8LL. *T:* (01689) 851651. *Clubs:* MCC; Royal West Norfolk Golf, Addington Golf. *Died 27 Nov. 2011.*

CLARKE, Malcolm Roy, PhD, DSc; FRS 1981; Senior Principal Scientific Officer, Marine Biological Association of the UK, 1978–87; *b* 24 Oct. 1930; *s* of Cecil Dutfield Clarke and Edith Ellen Woodward; *m* 1958, Dorothy Clara Knight; three *s* one *d*. *Educ:* eleven schools and finally Wallingford County Grammar Sch.; Hull Univ. BSc 1955, PhD 1958, DSc 1978. National Service, Private, RAMC, 1949–50. Teacher, 1951; Hull Univ., 1951–58; Whaling Inspector in Antarctic, 1955–56; Scientific Officer, later PSO, Nat. Inst. of Oceanography, 1958–71; led Oceanographic Expedns on RRS Discovery, RRS Challenger, RRS Frederick Russell and RV Sarsia; PSO, Marine Biol Assoc. of UK, 1972–78. Visiting Professor: in Zoology, Liverpool Univ., 1987–2003; in Marine Biol., Azores Univ., 1994–. Involved in construction and curation of Cachalotes and Lulas mus. (private museum on sperm whales and squids), São João, 2003–11. *Publications:* (ed jtly) Deep Oceans, 1971; Identification of Cephalopod Beaks, 1986; (ed jtly) Evolution, vol. 10, The Mollusca, 1986, vol. 11, Form and Function, 1987, vol. 12, Palaeontology and Neontology of the Cephalopoda, 1987; (ed jtly) Identification of "Larval" Cephalopods, 1987; (ed jtly) Cephalopod Diversity, Ecology and Evolution, 1998; papers on squids and whales in Jl of Marine Biol Assoc., Nature etc, and a Discovery Report, 1980. *Recreations:* painting, writing. *Address:* Rua do Porto 18, São João, 9930-430 Lajes do Pico, Azores, Portugal. *Died 10 May 2013.*

CLARKE, Mary; Editor, Dancing Times, 1963–2008, then Emeritus; *b* 23 Aug. 1923; *d* of Frederick Clarke and Ethel Kate (*née* Reynolds); unmarried. *Educ:* Mary Datchelor Girls' School. London Corresp., Dance Magazine, NY, 1943–55; London Editor, Dance News, NY, 1955–70; Asst Editor and Contributor, Ballet Annual, 1952–63; joined Dancing Times as Asst Editor, 1954. Dance critic, The Guardian, 1977–94. FRSA. Queen Elizabeth II Coronation Award, Royal Acad. of Dancing, 1990; Nijinsky Medal, Poland, 1996. Kt, Order of Dannebrog (Denmark), 1992. *Publications:* The Sadler's Wells Ballet: a history and an appreciation, 1955; Six Great Dancers, 1957; Dancers of Mercury: the story of Ballet Rambert, 1962; ed (with David Vaughan) Encyclopedia of Dance and Ballet, 1977; (with Clement Crisp): Ballet, an Illustrated History, 1973, 2nd edn 1992; Making a Ballet, 1974, repr. 2010; Introducing Ballet, 1976; Design for Ballet, 1978; Ballet in Art, 1978; The History of Dance, 1981; The Balletgoer's Guide, 1981; Dancer, Men in Dance, 1984; Ballerina, 1987; contrib. Encycl. Britannica, Oxford DNB. *Recreation:* theatre - especially Shakespeare's Globe. *Address:* 54 Ripplevale Grove, N1 1HT. *T:* (020) 7607 3422. *Club:* Gautier. *Died 20 March 2015.*

CLARKE, Neil; *see* Clarke, J. N.

CLARKE, Peter, CBE 1983; PhD; CChem, FRSC; Principal, Robert Gordon's Institute of Technology, Aberdeen, 1970–85; Chairman, Scottish Vocational Education Council, 1985–91; *b* 18 March 1922; *s* of Frederick John and Gladys May Clarke; *m* 1st, 1947, Ethel Jones (*d* 1999); two *s*; 2nd, 2010, Marguerite Andrew. *Educ:* Queen Elizabeth's Grammar Sch., Mansfield; University Coll., Nottingham (BSc). Industrial Chemist, 1942; Sen. Chemistry Master, Buxton Coll., 1947; Lectr, Huddersfield Tech. Coll., 1949; British Enka Ltd, Liverpool, 1956; Sen. Lectr, Royal Coll. of Advanced Tech., Salford, 1962; Head of Dept of Chemistry and Biology, Nottingham Regional Coll. of Technology, 1963; Vice-Principal, Huddersfield Coll. of Technology, 1965–70. Member: SERC (formerly SRC), 1978–82; Council for Professions Supplementary to Medicine, 1977–85; Scottish Technical Educn Council, 1982–85; CNAA, 1982–87 (Chm., Cttee for Scotland, 1983). Chm., Assoc. of Principals of Colleges (Scotland), 1976–78; President: Assoc. of Principals of Colleges, 1980–81; Assoc. for Educnl and Trng Technol., 1993–95. Chairman: Aberdeen Enterprise Trust, 1984–92; Industrial Trng Centre Aberdeen Ltd, 1989–95; Gordon Cook Foundn, 1997–99 (Trustee, 1989–2005). Burgess of Guild, City of Aberdeen, 1973. Hon. LLD Aberdeen, 1985; Hon. DEd: CNAA, 1992; Robert Gordon, 1998. *Address:* 31 Whinhill Gate, Aberdeen AB11 7WF. *Died 26 Oct. 2012.*

CLARKE, William Malpas, CBE 1976; Chairman, Central Banking Publications Ltd, 1990–2007; *b* 5 June 1922; *o s* of late Ernest and Florence Clarke; *m* 1st, 1946, Margaret Braithwaite (marr. diss.); two *d*; 2nd, 1973, Faith Elizabeth Dawson. *Educ:* Audenshaw Grammar Sch.; Univ. of Manchester (BA Hons Econ). Served Royal Air Force, 1941–46; Flying Instructor, Canada, 1942–44; Flight-Lieut, 1945. Editorial Staff, Manchester Guardian, 1948–55; The Times, 1955–66: City Editor, 1957–62; Financial and Industrial Editor, 1962–66; Editor, The Banker, March–Sept. 1966, Consultant 1966–76. Dir, 1968–76,

Dep. Chm. and Dir Gen., 1976–87, British Invisible Exports Council (formerly Cttee on Invisible Exports); Deputy Chairman: City Communications Centre, 1976–87; Trade Indemnity Co. Ltd, 1980–86; Chairman: Grindlays Bank (Jersey), 1981–92; ANZ Merchant Bank, 1987–91 (Dir, 1985–91); Transatlantic Capital (Biosciences) Ltd, 1989–92; Director: ANZ Grindlays Bank (formerly Grindlays Bank), 1966–85, 1987–92; Euromoney Ltd, 1969–84; Trade Indemnity plc, 1971–87; Swiss Reinsurance Co. (UK) plc, 1977–93; ANZ Holdings, 1985–87. Chm., Harold Wincott Financial Journalist Press Award Panel, 1971–92. Governor, The Hospitals for Sick Children, 1984–90; Chm., Great Ormond Street Wishing Well Redevelt Appeal Trust, 1985–94. Hon. DLitt London Guildhall Univ., 1992. *Publications:* The City's Invisible Earnings, 1958; The City in the World Economy, 1965; Private Enterprise in Developing Countries, 1966; (ed, as Director of Studies) Britain's Invisible Earnings, 1967; (with George Pulay) The World's Money, 1970; Inside the City, 1979, rev. edn 1983; How the City of London Works, 1986, 6th edn 2004; The Secret Life of Wilkie Collins, 1988, rev. edn 2004; Planning for Europe: 1992, 1989; The Lost Fortune of the Tsars, 1994 (US and German edns, 1995; Argentine edn, 1996; Polish and Romanian edns, 1998), 4th edn as Romanoff Gold 2007; (ed) Letters of Wilkie Collins, 1999; The Golden Thread, 2001; Hidden Treasures of the Romanovs: saving the Royal Jewels, 2009. *Recreations:* books, theatre. *Address:* 37 Park Vista, Greenwich, SE10 9LZ. *T:* (020) 8858 0979. *Club:* Reform. *Died 23 April 2011.*

CLATWORTHY, Robert Ernest, RA 1973 (ARA 1968); sculptor; *b* Bridgwater, Somerset, 31 Jan. 1928; *s* of E. W. and G. Clatworthy; *m* 1952, Pamela Gordon (marr. diss.); two *s* one *d*. *Educ:* Dr Morgan's Grammar Sch., Bridgwater. Studied West of England Coll. of Art, Chelsea Sch. of Art, The Slade. Teacher, West of England Coll. of Art, 1967–71. Visiting Tutor, RCA, 1960–72; Mem., Fine Art Panel of Nat. Council for Diplomas in Art and Design, 1961–72; Governor, St Martin's Sch. of Art, 1970–71; Head of Dept of Fine Art, Central Sch. of Art and Design, 1971–75. Exhibited: Hanover Gall., 1954, 1956; Waddington Galls, 1965; Holland Park Open Air Sculpture, 1957; Battersea Park Open Air Sculpture, 1960, 1963; Tate Gallery, British Sculpture in the Sixties, 1965; British Sculptors 1972, Burlington House; Basil Jacobs Fine Art Ltd, 1972; Diploma Galls, Burlington House, 1977; Photographers Gall., 1980; Quinton Green Fine Art, London, 1986; British Sculpture 1950–65, New Art Centre, 1986; Chapman Gall., 1988, 1989; Keith H. Chapman Gall., 1988, 1992, 1994, 1996, 2010; Keith Chapman Fine Art, 2008; Austin Desmond Fine Art, 1991, 1998. Work in Collections: Arts Council, Contemporary Art Soc., Tate Gallery, Victoria and Albert Museum, Greater London Council, Nat. Portrait Gall. (portrait of Dame Elisabeth Frink, 1985). Public sculptures include: Large Bull, Roehampton, SW15, 1956; Monumental Horse and Rider, Finsbury Avenue, London, 1984, subseq. moved to Charing Cross Hosp., London. *Address:* Moelfre, Cynghordy, Llandovery, Carms SA20 0UW. *T:* (01550) 720201. *Clubs:* Chelsea Arts, Arts. *Died 16 March 2015.*

CLAUSEN, Alden Winship, (Tom); Chairman, and Chief Executive Officer, Bank of America, 1986–90; *b* 17 Feb. 1923; *s* of Morton and Elsie Clausen; *m* 1st, 1950, Mary Margaret Crassweller (*d* 2001); two *s*; 2nd, 2002, Helen T. Higgins. *Educ:* Carthage Coll. (BA 1944); Univ. of Minnesota (LLB 1949); Grad. Harvard Advanced Management Program, 1966. Admitted to Minnesota Bar, 1949, to California Bar, 1950. Joined Bank of America, 1949: Vice-Pres., 1961–65; Sen. Vice-Pres., 1965–68; Exec. Vice-Pres., 1968–69; Vice-Chm. of Bd, 1969; Pres. and Chief Exec. Officer, 1970–81; Pres., The World Bank, 1981–86. President: Fed. Adv. Council, 1972; Internat. Monetary Conf., Amer. Bankers' Assoc., 1977. Former Director: US-USSR Trade and Econ. Council, 1974–81; Nat. Council for US-China Trade, 1974–81; Co-Chm., Japan-California Assoc., 1973–80; Chm., World Affairs Council of Northern California, 1995–98. Hon. LLD: Carthage, 1970; Lewis and Clark, 1978; Gonzaga Univ., 1978; Univ. of Notre Dame, 1981; Univ. of the Pacific, 1987; Hon. DPS Univ. Santa Clara, 1981. *Address:* c/o Bank of America, 555 California Street, San Francisco, CA 94104, USA. *Died 22 Jan. 2013.*

CLAYMAN, David, CEng, FIChemE; Managing Director, Esso UK plc, 1986–95; *b* 28 May 1934; *s* of Maurice and Nancy Clayman; *m* 1956, Patricia Moore; two *s*. *Educ:* Purley Grammar Sch.; University College London (BSc Chem. Engrg). Joined Esso Petroleum Co., 1956; Supply Manager, London, 1966–67, Esso Europe Inc., 1970–71; Marketing Div. Dir, 1971–79; Exec. Asst to Chm., Exxon Corp., 1979–80; Dir, Esso Petroleum Co., 1982–83; Pres., Esso Africa Inc., 1983–86; Director: Esso Europe Inc., 1983–86; Esso Exploration and Production UK, 1986–95; Esso Pension Trust, 1986–95; Chm., Mainline Pipeline, 1986–95. Mem., Sen. Salaries Review Body, 1997–2006 (Chm., Judicial Sub-cttee, 2002–06). Council Member: GCBS, 1986–87; Foundn for Management Educn, 1986–95; Pres., UKPIA, 1988–90 and 1992–94 (Vice Pres., 1986–88); Vice-Pres., Oil Industries Club, 1988–95. *Clubs:* Royal Automobile; Burhill Golf. *Died 15 July 2015.*

CLAYTON, Prof. Dame Barbara (Evelyn), (Dame Barbara Klyne), DBE 1988 (CBE 1983); MD, PhD; FRCP, FRCPath; CBiol; Hon. Research Professor in Metabolism, Faculty of Medicine, University of Southampton, since 1987 (Professor of Chemical Pathology and Human Metabolism, 1979–87, and Dean of the Faculty of Medicine, 1983–86); *b* 2 Sept. 1922; *m* 1949, William Klyne (*d* 1977); one *s* one *d*. *Educ:* Univ. of Edinburgh (MD, PhD). FRCP 1972; FRCPath 1971; FRCPE 1985; CBiol 2000. Consultant in Chem. Pathology, Hosp. for Sick Children, London, 1959–70; Prof. of Chem. Pathology, Inst. of Child Health, Univ. of London, 1970–78. Leverhulme Emeritus Fellow, 1988–90. Hon. Consultant, 1979–92, Mem., 1983–87, Southampton and SW Hants HA. Member: Commonwealth Scholarship Commn, 1977–93; Royal Commn on Environmental Pollution, 1981–96. Chm., Task Force on Nutrition, DoH, 1992–95; Member: Study Gp on Long Term Toxicity, Royal Soc., 1976–78; Standing Med. Adv. Cttee (DHSS), 1981–87; Cttee on Toxicity of Chemicals in Food, Consumer Products and the Environment, DoH (formerly DHSS), 1977–93; Systems Bd, MRC, 1974–77; British Nat. Cttees on Chemistry and Biochemistry, 1977–78; British Nat. Cttee on Problems of the Environment, 1988–89; COMA Panel on Dietary Reference Values, 1987–91; WHO Expert Adv. Panel on Nutrition, 1989–97; DoH Steering Gp on Undergrad. Med. and Dental Educn and Res., 1989–; Adv. Gp on Medical Educn, Trng and Service, DoH, 1995–2003; Chairman: Adv. Cttee on Borderline Substances, 1971–83; MRC Adv. Gp on Lead and Neuropsychol Effects in Children, 1983–88; Cttee on Med. Aspects of Contaminants in Air, Soil and Water, 1984–90; Standing Cttee on Postgrad. Med. and Dental (formerly Med.) Educn, 1988–99; Med. and Scientific Panel, Leukaemia Res. Fund, 1989–2003; MRC Cttee on Toxic Hazards in the Workplace and the Environment, 1989–95. Council, RCPath, 1974–77 and 1982– (Pres., 1984–87); GMC, 1983–87. President: Assoc. of Clinical Biochemists, 1977, 1978; Soc. for Study of Inborn Errors of Metabolism, 1981–82; Biomedical Scis Sect., BAAS, 1989–90; British Dietetic Assoc., 1989–; Nat. Soc. for Clean Air and Envmtl Protection, 1995–97 (Vice Pres., 1999–); Hon. President: British Dietetic Assoc., 1989–; British Nutrition Foundn, 1999– (Gov., 1987–99). Member: Bd of Govs, Hosps for Sick Children, London, 1968–78; Scientific Adv. Cttee, Assoc. of Med. Res. Charities, 1990–97. Lectures: Stanley Davidson, RCPE, 1973; Harben, RIPH&H, 1988; Wellcome, Assoc. of Clinical Biochemists, 1988; Osler, 1989; Ireland, Liverpool, 1990; Hartley, Southampton Univ., 1990; G. H. Foote Meml, Southampton Med. Soc., 1991; Wilfred Fish Meml, GDC, 1993; British Nutrition Foundn Annual, 1997; Osler Annual Oration, 1997. Sen. Mem., Soc. for Endocrinol., 1951. Hon. Member: Soc. for Study of Inborn Errors of Metabolism, 1988; Assoc. of Clinical Biochemists, 1990; Corresponding Member: Société Française Pédiatric, 1975; Gesellschaft für Laboratoriumsmedizin, 1990. Member, Editorial Board: Archives of Diseases in Childhood; Clin. Sci.; Jl Endocrinol.; Clin. Endocrinol. Hon. Mem., British Dietetic Assoc., 1976; Hon. Fellow: Faculty of Pathology, RCPI, 1986; Amer. Soc. of Clin. Pathologists, 1987; Hon.

FIBiol 2000; Hon. FRCPCH 1997 (Hon. Mem., BPA, 1963); FMedSci 2000. Hon. DSc: Edinburgh, 1985; Southampton, 1989; Hon. DSc (Med) London, 2000. Jessie MacGregor Prize for Med. Sci., RCPE, 1955 and 1985; Wellcome Prize, Assoc. of Clin. Biochemists, 1988; BMA Gold Medal for Distinguished Merit, 1999. *Publications:* contrib. learned jls, incl. Jl Endocrinol., Arch. Dis. Childhood, and BMJ. *Recreations:* natural history, walking. *Address:* Bay View, The Glebe, Studland, Dorset BH19 3AS. *Died 11 Jan. 2011.*

CLAYTON, Prof. Keith Martin, CBE 1984; Professor of Environmental Sciences, University of East Anglia, 1967–93, then Emeritus; *b* 25 Sept. 1928; *s* of Edgar Francis Clayton and Constance Annie (*née* Clark); *m* 1st, 1950, Jean Mary Wilkinson (marr. diss. 1976); three *s* one *d*; 2nd, 1976, Jennifer Nan; one step *s*. *Educ:* Bedales Sch.; Univ. of Sheffield (MSc). PhD London. Demonstrator, Univ. of Nottingham, 1949–51. Served RE, 1951–53. Lectr, 1953–63, Reader in Geography, 1963–67, LSE; University of East Anglia: Founding Dean, Sch. of Environmental Scis, 1967–71 and 1987–93; Pro-Vice-Chancellor, 1971–73; Dir, Centre of E Anglian Studies, 1974–81. Vis. Prof., State Univ. of New York at Binghamton, 1960–62. Chm., Adv. Cttee, Document Supply Centre, British Library, 1986–93; Member: NERC, 1970–73; UGC, 1973–84; Nat. Radiological Protection Bd, 1980–85; Nat. Adv. Bd for Local Authority Higher Educn, 1982–84; Cttee on Med. Aspects of Radiation in Environment, DHSS, 1985–2001; Ministerial Adv. Cttee on Envmt and Energy, MoD, 1990–; Broads Authy, 1994–98; Dounreay Particles Adv. Gp, SEPA, 2000–06. Chm., Broadland Housing Assoc., 1995–2001. Councillor, Broadland DC, 1994–98. Pres., IBG, 1984. Hon. DSc Lancaster, 1995. Patron's Medal, RGS, 1989. *Publications:* Editor and publisher, Geo Abstracts, 1960–85. *Recreation:* gardening. *Address:* Well Close, Pound Lane, Thorpe St Andrew, Norwich NR7 0UA. *T:* (01603) 433780. *Died 12 Feb. 2013.*

CLEALL, Charles; author; *b* 1 June 1927; *s* of Sydney Cleal and Dorothy (*née* Bound); *m* 1953, Mary (*d* 2005), *yr d* of G. L. Turner, Archery Lodge, Ashford, Middx; two *d*. *Educ:* Hampton Sch.; Univ. of London (BMus); Univ. of Wales (MA); Jordanhill Coll. of Educn, Glasgow (Scottish Teacher's Cert.). ADCM, GTCL, FRCO(CHM), LRAM. Organist and Choirmaster, St Luke's, Chelsea, 1945–46; Command Music Adviser, RN, Plymouth Command, 1946–48; Prof. of Solo Singing and Voice Production, TCL, 1949–52; Conductor, Morley Coll. Orch., 1949–51; Choral Scholar, Westminster Abbey, 1949–52; Organist and Choirmaster, Wesley's Chapel, City Road, EC4, 1950–52; Conductor, Glasgow Choral Union, 1952–54; BBC Music Asst, Midland Region, 1954–55; Music Master, Glyn County Sch., Ewell, 1955–66; Conductor, Aldeburgh Festival Choir, 1957–60; Organist and Choirmaster: St Paul's, Portman Sq., W1, 1957–61; Holy Trinity, Guildford, 1961–65; Lectr in Music, Froebel Inst., 1967–68; Adviser in Music, London Borough of Harrow, 1968–72; Warden, Education Section, ISM, 1971–72; music specialist, N Div., HM Inspectorate of Schs in Scotland, 1972–87; Tutor in Speech-Training, Scottish Congregational Coll. and Scottish Churches' Open Coll., Napier Univ., 1996–2000. Regd Teacher, Sch. of Sinus Tone, 1985–; Hon. Mem., Tonic Sol-fa Coll., John Curwen Inst., 1960 Lay Minister (formerly Reader), Salisbury Dio., 2000–. Editor: Jl of Ernest George White Soc., 1983–88; Shaston Key-Ring, 2001–07. Presented papers at: study-conf. of teachers of singing, The Maltings, Snape, 1976; Nat. Course on Develt of Young Children's Musical Skills, Univ. of Reading Sch. of Educn, 1979; annual conf., Scottish Fedn of Organists, 1980; Nat. Conf., Assoc. of Music Advisers in Scotland, 1987; Edinburgh Centre of ISM, 1993. Internat. Composition Prizeman of Cathedral of St John the Divine, NY; Limpus Fellowship Prizeman of RCO. *Publications:* Voice Production in Choral Technique, 1955, rev. edn 1970; The Selection and Training of Mixed Choirs in Churches, 1960; Sixty Songs from Sankey, 1960; (ed) John Merbecke's Music for the Congregation at Holy Communion, 1963; Music and Holiness, 1964; Plainsong for Pleasure, 1969; Authentic Chanting, 1969; Guide to Vanity Fair, 1982; Walking round the Church of St James the Great, Stonehaven, 1993; A Jewel of a Church: Laleham-All Saints', 2001. *Recreations:* reading, writing, walking. *Address:* 14 Heathfields Way, Shaftesbury SP7 9JZ. *Died 11 Jan. 2015.*

CLEGG, Prof. Edward John, MD, PhD; FSB; Regius Professor of Anatomy, University of Aberdeen, 1976–89; Professor of Biological Anthropology, University of Aberdeen, 1990–91, then Emeritus; *b* 29 Oct. 1925; *s* of Edward Clegg and Emily Armistead; *m* 1958, Sheila Douglas Walls; two *d* (and one *d* decd). *Educ:* High Storrs Grammar Sch., Sheffield; Univ. of Sheffield (MB, ChB Hons 1948, MD 1964). PhD Liverpool, 1957; FSB (FIBiol 1974). RAMC, 1948–50 and RAMC (TA), 1950–61; late Major, RAMC (RARO). Demonstr, Asst Lectr and Lectr in Anatomy, Univ. of Liverpool, 1952–63; Lectr, Sen. Lectr and Reader in Human Biology and Anatomy, Univ. of Sheffield, 1963–77. MO, British Kangchenjunga Expedn, 1955; Sci. Mem., Chogolungma Glacier Expedn, 1959; Leader, WHO/IBP Expedn, Simien Mountains, Ethiopia, 1967. Pres., Anat. Soc. of GB and Ire., 1988–89; Chm., Soc. for the Study of Human Biology, 1988–92. *Publications:* The Study of Man: an introduction to human biology, 1968, 2nd edn 1978; papers on anatomy, endocrinology and human biology. *Recreations:* mountaineering, music. *Address:* 22 Woodburn Avenue, Aberdeen AB15 8JQ. *Clubs:* Alpine; Wayfarers (Liverpool). *Died 1 March 2015.*

CLEMENS, Clive Carruthers, CMG 1983; MC 1946; HM Diplomatic Service, retired; High Commissioner in Lesotho, 1981–84; *b* 22 Jan. 1924; British; *s* of late M. B. Clemens, Imperial Bank of India, and late Margaret Jane (*née* Carruthers); *m* 1947, Philippa Jane Bailey (*d* 2009); two *s* (and one *s* decd). *Educ:* Blundell's Sch.; St Catharine's Coll., Cambridge. War Service 1943–46: commissioned in Duke of Cornwall's Light Infantry; served in India and Burma, 1944–45. Entered HM Foreign Service and apptd to FO, 1947; Third Sec., Rangoon, 1948; Third (later Second) Sec., Lisbon, 1950; FO, 1953; First Sec., Budapest, 1954; Brussels, 1956; Seoul, 1959; FO, 1961; Strasbourg (UK Delegn to Council of Europe), 1964; Counsellor, Paris, 1967; Principal British Trade Comr, Vancouver, 1970–74; Dep. Consul-Gen., Johannesburg, 1974–78; Consul-Gen., Istanbul, 1978–81. *Recreations:* birdwatching, photography. *Address:* 22 St Ann Place, St Ann Street, Salisbury, Wilts SP1 2SU. *Died 2 Aug. 2013.*

CLERIDES, Glafcos John; President of Cyprus, 1993–2003; *b* Nicosia, 24 April 1919; *s* of Yiannis Clerides, CBE, QC and Elli Clerides; *m* 1946, Lilla Erulkar (*d* 2007); one *d*. *Educ:* Pancyprium Gymnasium, Nicosia; King's Coll., London (LLB 1948). Served in RAF, 1939–45; shot down and taken prisoner, 1942–45 (mentioned in despatches). Called to the Bar, Gray's Inn, 1951; practised in Cyprus, 1951–60; Head, Greek Cypriot Delegn, Jt Constitutional Cttee, 1959–60; Minister of Justice, 1959–60; Mem. for Nicosia, House of Representatives, 1960–76, 1981–93; First Pres. of House, 1960–76; Leader, Greek Cypriot Delegn to London Conf., 1964; Rep. of Greek Cypriots to intercommunal talks, 1968–76; Actg Pres., July–Dec. 1974 (after Turkish invasion of Cyprus). Founder and Leader: Unified Party, 1969–76; Democratic Rally Party, 1976–93. Cert. of Honour and Life Mem., Cyprus Red Cross (Pres., 1961–63). Gold Medal, Order of the Holy Sepulchre, 1961. Grand Cross of the Redeemer (Greece), 1993. *Publications:* My Deposition, 4 vols; Negotiating for Cyprus, 1993–2003, 2008. *Address:* 5 Ioannis Clerides Street, Nicosia, Cyprus. *Died 15 Nov. 2013.*

CLIBURN, Van, (Harvey Lavan Cliburn Jr); pianist; Artistic Adviser, Van Cliburn International Piano Competition, since 1962; *b* Shreveport, La, 12 July 1934; *oc* of late Harvey Lavan Cliburn and Rildia Bee (*née* O'Bryan). *Educ:* Kilgore High Sch., Texas; Juilliard Sch. of Music, New York. Made début in Houston, Texas, 1947; toured extensively in N and S America, Europe and Asia. Awards include first International Tchaikovsky Piano Competition, Moscow, 1958, and every US prize, for pianistic ability. US Presidential Medal of Freedom, 2003; Order of Friendship, Russian Fedn, 2004; Nat. Medal of Arts, USA, 2010. *Recreation:* swimming. *Address:* c/o Van Cliburn Foundation, 2525 Ridgmar Boulevard, Suite 307, Fort Worth, TX 76116, USA. *Died 27 Feb. 2013.*

CLOAKE, John Cecil, CMG 1977; FSA; HM Diplomatic Service, retired; *b* 2 Dec. 1924; *s* of late Dr Cecil Stedman Cloake, Wimbledon, and Maude Osborne Newling; *m* 1956, Margaret Thomure Morris (*d* 2008), Washington, DC, USA; one *s*. *Educ:* King's Coll. Sch., Wimbledon; Peterhouse, Cambridge. Served in Army, 1943–46 (Lieut RE). Foreign Office, 1948; 3rd Sec., Baghdad, 1949, and Saigon, 1951; 2nd Sec., 1952; FO, 1954; Private Sec. to Permanent Under-Sec., 1956, and to Parly Under-Sec., 1957; 1st Sec., 1957; Consul (Commercial), New York, 1958; 1st Sec., Moscow, 1962; FO, 1963; DSAO, 1965; Counsellor, 1966; Head of Accommodation Dept, 1967; Counsellor (Commercial), Tehran, 1968–72; Fellow, Centre for International Studies, LSE, 1972–73; Head of Trade Relations and Exports Dept, FCO, 1973–76; Ambassador to Bulgaria, 1976–80. Member: Council, British Inst. of Persian Studies, 1981–95 (Hon. Treas., 1982–90); Cttee of Honour for Bulgarian 1300th Anniv., 1981. Chairman: Richmond Soc. History Section, 1975–76, 1984–85; Richmond Local Hist. Soc., 1985–90 (Pres., 1990–); Richmond Museum Project, 1983–86; Mus. of Richmond, 1986–95; Pres., Richmond upon Thames Soc. of Voluntary Guides, 1997–2007. FSA 1998. Hon. DLitt Kingston, 2004. *Publications:* Templer: Tiger of Malaya, 1985; Richmond Past, 1991; Royal Bounty, 1992; Palaces and Parks of Richmond and Kew, Vol. 1, 1995, Vol. 2, 1996; Richmond Past and Present, 1999; Cottages and Common Fields of Richmond and Kew, 2001; monographs and articles on local history. *Recreations:* gardening, painting, architecture, local history, genealogy. *Address:* 4 The Terrace, Richmond Hill, Richmond, Surrey TW10 6RN. *Died 9 July 2014.*

CLOUDSLEY-THOMPSON, Prof. John Leonard, MA, PhD (Cantab), DSc (London); FRES, FLS, FZS, CBiol, FSB, FWAAS; Professor of Zoology, Birkbeck College, University of London, 1972–86, then Emeritus (Reader 1971–72); *b* Murree, India, 23 May 1921; *s* of Dr Ashley George Gyton Thompson, MA, MD (Cantab), DPH, and Muriel Elaine (*née* Griffiths); *m* 1944, Jessie Anne Cloudsley, MCSP, DipBS, LCAD (*d* 2012); three *s*. *Educ:* Marlborough Coll.; Pembroke Coll., Univ. of Cambridge. War of 1939–45: commissioned into 4th Queen's Own Hussars, 1941; transf. 4th Co. of Lond. Yeo. (Sharpshooters); N Africa, 7th Armoured Div., 1941–42 (severely wounded); Instructor (Capt.), Sandhurst, 1943; rejoined regt for D Day (escaped from Villers-Bocage), Caen Offensive, etc, 1944 (Hon. rank of Capt. on resignation). Lectr in Zoology, King's Coll., Univ. of London, 1950–60; Prof. of Zoology, Univ. of Khartoum, and Keeper, Sudan Nat. Hist. Museum, 1960–71. Nat. Science Foundn Sen. Res. Fellow, Univ. of New Mexico, Albuquerque, USA, 1969; Visiting Professor: Arizona State Univ., 1969; Univ. of Kuwait, 1978 and 1983; Univ. of Nigeria, Nsukka, 1981; Univ. of Qatar, 1986; Sultan Qaboos Univ., Muscat, 1988; Leverhulme Emeritus Fellow at UCL, 1987–89; Visiting Research Fellow: ANU, 1987; Desert Ecol. Res. Unit of Namibia, 1989. Hon. Consultant: Univ. of Malaya, 1969; Arabian Gulf Univ., Bahrain, 1986; Univ. of Kuwait, 1990; Indo-British Workshop on Biodiversity, 1993. Took part in: Cambridge Iceland Expedn, 1947; Expedn to Southern Tunisia, 1954; univ. expedns with his wife to various parts of Africa, 1960–73, incl. trans-Sahara crossing, 1967. Chairman: British Naturalists' Assoc., 1974–83 (Vice-Pres., 1985–; Hon. FBNA 2007); Biological Council, 1977–82 (Medal, 1985). President: British Arachnological Soc., 1982–85 (Vice-Pres., 1985–86); British Soc. for Chronobiology, 1985–87; Vice-President: Linnean Soc., 1975–76 and 1977–78; 1st World Congress of Herpetology, 1989. Hon. Mem., British Herpetological Soc., 1983 (Pres., 1991–96; Fellow 2009); Hon. FLS 1997; Hon. Member: Royal African Soc., 1969 (Medal, 1969); Internat. Soc. of Arachnology (formerly Centre Internat. de Documentation Arachnologique, Paris), 1995. Numerous TV and radio appearances. Liveryman, Worshipful Co. of Skinners, 1952. Silver Jubilee Gold Medal and Hon. DSc, Khartoum, 1981. Inst. of Biology K. S. S. Charter Award, 1981; J. H. Grundy Meml Medal, Royal Army Med. Coll., 1987; Foundn for Envmtl Conservation Prize, Geneva, 1989; Peter Scott Meml Award, British Naturalists' Assoc., 1993. Editor-in-Chief (formerly Founding Editor) (assisted by wife), Jl of Arid Environments Vol. 1, 1978–Vol. 37, 1997, later Editor Emeritus; Editor: (with wife) Natural History of the Arabian Gulf (book series), 1981–82; Adaptations of Desert Organisms (book series), 1989–2000 (25 vols). *Publications:* Biology of Deserts (ed), 1954; Spiders, Scorpions, Centipedes and Mites, 1958, 2nd edn 1968; Animal Behaviour, 1960; Rhythmic Activity in Animal Physiology and Behaviour, 1961; Land Invertebrates (with John Sankey), 1961; Life in Deserts (with M. J. Chadwick), 1964; Desert Life, 1965; Animal Conflict and Adaptation, 1965; Animal Twilight: man and game in eastern Africa, 1967; Microecology, 1967; Zoology of Tropical Africa, 1969; The Temperature and Water Relations of Reptiles, 1971; Desert Life, 1974; Terrestrial Environments, 1975; Insects and History, 1976; Evolutionary Trends in the Mating of Arthropoda, 1976; (ed jtly) Environmental Physiology of Animals, 1976; Man and the Biology of Arid Zones, 1977; The Water and Temperature Relations of Woodlice, 1977; The Desert, 1977; Animal Migration, 1978; Why the Dinosaurs Became Extinct, 1978; Wildlife of the Desert, 1979; Biological Clocks: their functions in nature, 1980; Tooth and Claw: defensive strategies in the animal world, 1980; (ed) Sahara Desert, 1984; Guide to Woodlands, 1985; Evolution and Adaptation of Terrestrial Arthropods, 1988; Ecophysiology of Desert Arthropods and Reptiles, 1991; The Diversity of Desert Life, 1993; (novel) The Nile Quest, 1994; Predation and Defence Amongst Reptiles, 1994; Biotic Interactions in Arid Lands, 1996; Teach Yourself Ecology, 1998; The Diversity of Amphibians and Reptiles: an introduction, 1999; Ecology and Behaviour of Mesozoic Reptiles, 2005; Sharpshooter: memories of armoured warfare 1939–45, 2006; contribs to Encyclopædia Britannica, Encyclopedia Americana; shorter monographs and eleven children's books; many scientific articles in learned jls, etc. *Recreations:* music (especially opera), photography, travel. *Address:* 44 Alconbury Road, E5 8RH. *Died 4 Oct. 2013.*

CLOUGH, Philip Gerard; Justice of Appeal: Hong Kong, 1986–92; Bermuda, 1998–2004; Gibraltar, 1998–2004; *b* 11 March 1924; *s* of Gerard Duncombe Clough and Grace Margaret (*née* Phillips); *m* 1st, Mary Elizabeth Carter (marr. diss.); one *s*; 2nd, Margaret Joy Davies; one *s* one *d*. *Educ:* Dauntsey's Sch.; King's Coll., Cambridge (Exhibnr; MA). War service, Sub Lieut (A) RNVR, 1942–46. Called to the Bar, Inner Temple, 1949; Colonial Legal Service: Federal Counsel, Malaya, 1951–58; Chancery Bar, Lincoln's Inn, 1958–78; Legal Affairs Advr, Brunei, 1978–81; Dist Judge, 1981–83, High Court Judge, 1983–86, Hong Kong. Non permanent Mem., Court of Final Appeal, Hong Kong, 1997–2006. *Clubs:* Garrick; Hong Kong. *Died 16 Feb. 2015.*

COASE, Prof. Ronald Harry, DSc; Professor Emeritus and Senior Fellow in Law and Economics, University of Chicago, since 1982; *b* 29 Dec. 1910; *s* of Henry Joseph Coase and Rosalie Elizabeth (*née* Giles); *m* 1937, Marian Ruth Hartung (*d* 2012). *Educ:* Kilburn Grammar Sch.; LSE (BCom 1932; DSc Econ 1951). Assistant Lecturer: Dundee Sch. of Econs, 1932–34; Univ. of Liverpool, 1934–35; later Lectr, then Reader, LSE, 1935–40, 1946–51; War service: Hd of Statistical Div., Forestry Commn, 1940–41; Statistician, later Chief Statistician, Central Statistical Office, Offices of War Cabinet, 1941–46; Professor: Univ. of Buffalo, 1951–58; Univ. of Virginia, 1958–64; Clifford R. Musser Prof., Univ. of Chicago Law Sch., 1964–82. Fellow, Amer. Acad. of Arts and Scis, 1978; Dist. Fellow, Amer. Econ. Assoc., 1980; Membre Titulaire, European Acad., 1992; Corresp. Fellow, British Acad., 1985; Hon. Fellow, LSE. Hon. doctorates: Dr rer. pol. Cologne, 1988; DSocSc Yale, 1989; LLD Washington, St Louis, 1991; LLD Dundee, 1992; DSc Buckingham, 1995; DHL Beloit Coll., 1996; Dr *hc* Paris, 1996; DHum Clemson, 2003. Nobel Prize for Economics, 1991; Innovations Award, The Economist, 2003. *Publications:* British Broadcasting: a study in monopoly, 1950; The Firm, the Market and the Law, 1988; Essays on Economics and Economists, 1994. *Address:* University of Chicago Law School, 1111 East 60th Street, Chicago, IL 60637, USA; The Hallmark, 2960 N Lake Shore Drive, Chicago, IL 60657, USA. *Died 2 Sept. 2013.*

COATES, Prof. Geoffrey Edward, MA, DSc; Professor of Chemistry, University of Wyoming, 1968–79, then Emeritus; *b* 14 May 1917; *er s* of Prof. Joseph Edward Coates, OBE; *m* 1951, (Winifred) Jean Hobbs; one *s* one *d*. *Educ:* Clifton Coll.; Queen's Coll., Oxford. Research Chemist, Magnesium Metal Corp., 1940–45; Univ. of Bristol: Lecturer in Chemistry, 1945–53; Sub-Warden of Wills Hall, 1946–51; Prof. of Chemistry, Univ. of Durham, 1953–68. *Publications:* Organo-metallic Compounds (monograph), 1956, 3rd edn (2 vols), 1967–68; Principles of Organometallic Chemistry, 1968; papers in scientific journals. *Club:* Royal Commonwealth Society. *Died 10 Jan. 2013.*

COATS, Sir Alastair Francis Stuart, 4th Bt *cr* 1905; *b* 18 Nov. 1921; *s* of Lieut-Col Sir James Stuart Coats, MC, 3rd Bt and Lady Amy Coats (*d* 1975), *er d* of 8th Duke of Richmond and Gordon; *S* father, 1966; *m* 1947, Lukyn (*d* 2006), *d* of Capt. Charles Gordon; one *s* one *d*. *Educ:* Eton. Served War of 1939–45, Coldstream Guards (Capt.). *Heir: s* Alexander James Coats [*b* 6 July 1951; *m* 1999, Clara, *d* of Ernesto Abril de Vivero]. *Address:* 122 Pelham Road, Wimbledon, SW19 1PA. *T:* (020) 8540 8349. *Died 13 Oct. 2015.*

COCHRANE, (Alexander John) Cameron, MBE 1987; MA; National Education Officer, Atlantic Council of UK, 2001–03; *b* 19 July 1933; *s* of late Dr Alexander Younger Cochrane and Jenny Johnstone Cochrane; *m* 1958, Rosemary Aline (*d* 2014), *d* of late Robert Alexander Ogg and Aline Mary Ogg; one *s* two *d*. *Educ:* The Edinburgh Academy; University Coll., Oxford. National Service in RA, 1952–54. Asst Master, St Edward's Sch., Oxford, 1957–66; Warden, Brathay Hall, Ambleside, Cumbria, 1966–70; Asst Dir of Educn, City of Edinburgh, 1970–74; Headmaster, Arnold Sch., Blackpool, 1974–79; Headmaster, Fettes Coll., Edinburgh, 1979–88; first Principal, Prince Willem-Alexander Coll., Holland, 1988–91; Principal, British Internat. Sch., Cairo, 1992–95. Consultant, Dutch and Internat. Educn Services, 1996–2006. Member: Lancashire CC Educn Cttee, 1976–79; Council, Outward Bound Trust, 1979–88; Admiralty Interview Bd, 1979–88; Scottish Cttee, Duke of Edinburgh's Award, 1981–86; Chairman: Outward Bound Ullswater, 1979–84; Outward Bound Loch Eil, 1984–88; Lothian Fedn of Boys' Clubs, 1981–84; HMC Services Cttee, 1982–88. Commandant, XIII Commonwealth Games Village, Edinburgh, 1986. Governor: Aiglon Coll., 1985–94; Pocklington Sch., 1985–2002. Session Clerk, Auchtertool Kirk, 1998–2004. CFM 1988. *Recreations:* games, the countryside, photography, friends, family, France. *Address:* 4/6 Spylaw Road, Edinburgh EH10 5BH. *T:* (0131) 445 1437. *Clubs:* East India, MCC; Vincent's (Oxford). *Died 18 Dec. 2015.*

COCKBURN, Sir John (Elliot), 12th Bt of that Ilk, *cr* 1671; *b* 7 Dec. 1925; *s* of Lieut-Col Sir John Brydges Cockburn, 11th Bt of that Ilk, DSO and Isabel Hunter (*d* 1978), *y d* of late James McQueen, Crofts, Kirkcudbrightshire; *S* father, 1949; *m* 1949, Glory Patricia (*d* 2011), *er d* of Nigel Tudway Mullings; three *s* two *d* (of whom one *s* one *d* are twins). *Educ:* RNC Dartmouth; Royal Agricultural Coll., Cirencester. Served War of 1939–45, joined RAFVR, July 1943. *Recreation:* reading. *Heir: s* Charles Christopher Cockburn [*b* 19 Nov. 1950; *m* 1985, Ruth, *d* of Samuel Bell; two *s* one *d* (of whom one *s* one *d* are twins)]. *Address:* 48 Frewin Road, SW18 3LP. *Died 12 June 2015.*

COCKERTON, Rev. Canon John Clifford Penn; Rector of Wheldrake with Thorganby, 1985–92 (Rector of Wheldrake, 1978–85); Canon of York (Prebend of Dunnington), 1987–92, Canon Emeritus 1992; *b* 27 June 1927; *s* of late William Penn Cockerton and Eleanor Cockerton; *m* 1974, Diana Margaret Smith (*d* 1987), *d* of Mr and Mrs W. Smith, Upper Poppleton, York. *Educ:* Wirral Grammar Sch.; Univ. of Liverpool; St Catherine's Society, Oxford; Wycliffe Hall, Oxford. Deacon 1954; Priest 1955; Asst Curate, St Helens Parish Church, 1954–58; Tutor, 1958–60, Chaplain, 1960–63, Cranmer Hall, Durham; Vice-Principal, St John's Coll., Durham, 1963–70; Principal, St John's College and Cranmer Hall, Durham, 1970–78. Examining Chaplain to Bishop of Durham, 1971–73; Proctor in Convocation, 1980–85. *Recreation:* music. *Died 9 Dec. 2015.*

COCKETT, Frank Bernard, MS, FRCS; Consulting Surgeon to: St Thomas' Hospital; King Edward VII Hospital for Officers, London; *b* Rockhampton, Australia, 22 April 1916; *s* of late Rev. Charles Bernard Cockett, MA, DD; *m* 1945, Felicity Ann (*d* 1958), *d* of Col James Thackeray Fisher, DSO, Frieston, near Grantham, Lincs; one *s* two *d*; *m* 1960, Dorothea Anne Newman (MBE 1999); twin *s*. *Educ:* Bedford Sch.; St Thomas's Hosp. Med. Sch. BSc (1st Cl. Hons), 1936; MRCS, LRCP 1939; MB, BS (London) 1940; FRCS Eng 1947; MS (London) 1953. Sqdn Ldr (Surgical Specialist) RAFVR, 1942–46; Surgical Registrar, St Thomas' Hosp., 1947–48; Resident Asst Surg., St Thomas' Hosp., 1948–50, Consultant, 1954–81; Senior Lecturer in Surgery, St Thomas' Hosp. Med. Sch., 1950–54; Consultant, King Edward VII Hosp. for Officers, 1974–81. Fellow Assoc. of Surgs of Gt Brit.; Mem. European Soc. of Cardiovascular Surgery; Pres., Vascular Surgical Soc. of GB and Ireland, 1980; Chm., Venous Forum, RSM, 1986–87. *Publications:* The Pathology and Surgery of the Veins of the Lower Limb, 1956, 2nd edn 1976; several contribs to Operative Surgery (ed C. G. Rob and Rodney Smith), 1956; The War Diary of St Thomas' Hospital 1939–1945, 1991; Early Sea Painters, 1995; Peter Monamy, 2000; various papers in medical and surgical journals. *Recreations:* sailing, tennis, gardening, marine paintings. *Address:* 14 Essex Villas, Kensington, W8 7BN. *T:* (020) 7937 9883. *Died 17 Jan. 2014.*

COCKETT, Geoffrey Howard; consultant; Chief Scientific Officer, Ministry of Defence, and Deputy Director, Royal Armament Research and Development Establishment, 1983–86; *b* 18 March 1926; *s* of late William Cockett and Edith (*née* Dinham); *m* 1951, Elizabeth Bagshaw; two *d*. *Educ:* King Edward VI Sch., Southampton; Univ. of Southampton (BSc, Hons Maths, and Hons Physics). MRI; FInstP; CPhys. Royal Aircraft Establishment, 1948–52; Armament Research Estabt, Woolwich, 1952–62; RARDE, 1962–68; ASC 1965; Supt of Physics Div., Chemical Defence Estabt, 1968–71; RARDE: Supt, Optics and Surveillance Systems Div., 1971–76; Head, Applied Physics Group, 1976–83. Chm., Sci. Recruitment Bds, CS Commn, 1985–94; Consultant, Directorate of Sci. (Land), MoD, 1986–98. FLS 2012. (Jtly) Gold Medal, Congrès des Matériaux Résistants à Chaud, Paris, 1951. *Publications:* official reports; scientific and technical papers in various learned jls. *Recreations:* computing, photography, supporting activities at Charles Darwin's home and laboratory. *E:* ghc1uk@yahoo.co.uk. *Club:* Civil Service. *Died 28 Sept. 2015.*

COCKRILL, Prof. Maurice, RA 1999; PRCA (RCA 2001); artist; Keeper of the Royal Academy of Arts, 2004–11; *b* Hartlepool, 8 Oct. 1935; *s* of William and Edith Cockrill; *m* 1st, 1957, Pauline Hinds (marr. diss. 1963); one *s*; 2nd, 1963, Elizabeth Ashworth (marr. diss. 1968); one *s*; partner 1974, Helen Moslin; one *s*. *Educ:* Wrexham Sch. of Art (NDD 1960); Univ. of Reading (ATD 1964). Numerous exhibns in UK, Paris, Düsseldorf, Frankfurt, Stavelot, NY, Sydney 1960–, including: Edward Totah Gall., London, annually 1982–86; Kunstmus., Düsseldorf, 1985; Bernard Jacobson Gall., annually 1986–96; Retrospectives, Walker Art Gall., Liverpool, 1994; RWA, 1998; work in many collections, including: BM; Arts Council; Contemporary Arts Soc.; Walker Art Gall.; Kunstmus., Düsseldorf; Deutsche Bank; Unilever; RA. Pres., Royal Cambrian Acad., 2006. Hon. Prof. of Contemporary Fine Art, Liverpool John Moores Univ., 2005–. *Publications:* Paintings and Drawings, 2002; various exhibn catalogues and bibliography. *Recreations:* walking esp. in Snowdonia (small studio there), reading esp. modern poetry, contemporary classical music, jazz, nature. *Address:* 78B Park Hall Road, SE21 8BW. *E:* admin@cockrill.co.uk. *Clubs:* Chelsea Arts, Arts, Lansdowne. *Died 1 Dec. 2013.*

COE, Denis Walter; Founder, 1987 and Executive Chairman, 1987–97, British Youth Opera; *b* 5 June 1929; *s* of James and Lily Coe, Whitley Bay, Northumberland; *m* 1953, Margaret Rae Chambers (marr. diss. 1979); three *s* one *d*; *m* 1979, Diana Rosemary (*d* 2014), *d* of Maxwell and Flora Barr. *Educ:* Bede Trng Coll., Durham; London Sch. of Economics. Teacher's Certificate, 1952; BSc (Econ.) 1960; MSc (Econ.) 1966. National Service in RAF, 1947–50; Junior and Secondary Schoolmaster, 1952–59; Dep. Headmaster, Secondary Sch., 1959–61; Lectr in Govt, Manchester Coll. of Commerce, 1961–66. Contested (Lab) Macclesfield, 1964; MP (Lab) Middleton, Prestwich and Whitefield, 1966–70; Parly deleg. to Council of Europe and WEU, 1968–70. Dean of Students, NE London Polytechnic, 1970–74; Asst Dir, Middx Polytechnic, 1974–82; Dir of Cleveland Arts, 1986–89; Founder/Dir, Cleveland Music Fest., 1985–89. Member: Archbishops Cttee, Church and State, 1966–69; Warnock Cttee of Enquiry on Special Educational Needs, 1974–78; Planning Cttee, Arts Council, 1987–90. Vice Pres., NYT, 1989– (Mem., Governing Council, 1968–89); Founder Chm., Nat. Bureau for Handicapped Students, 1975–83. FRSA 1992; Hon. Fellow, South Bank Univ., 1993; Hon. FGS (Hon. GSM 1993); Hon. FRAM 1998. DUniv Middlesex, 1994. *Publications:* Variety Certainly Adds Spice: a memoir of my life in education, politics and the arts, 2008. *Recreations:* music, drama, walking, painting. *Died 3 March 2015.*

COHEN, Sir Edward, Kt 1970; company director; solicitor; *b* 9 Nov. 1912; *s* of Brig. Hon. H. E. Cohen; *m* 1939, Meryl D. (*d* 2010), *d* of D. G. Fink; one *s*. *Educ:* Scotch Coll., Melbourne (Exhibnr in Greek and Roman History); Ormond Coll., Univ. of Melbourne (LLB; Aust. Blue Athletics, Hockey). Served, 1940–45: AIF, 2/12 Fd Regt, 9th Div. Artillery, Captain 1942. Partner, Pavey, Wilson, Cohen & Carter, 1945–76, later, following amalgamation, Consultant, Corrs Chambers Westgarth, solicitors, Melbourne, 1976–98; Director: Carlton and United Breweries, 1947–84 (Chm., 1967–84); Swan Brewery, 1947–57; Associated Pulp & Paper Mills Ltd, 1951–83 (Dep. Chm. 1981–83); Electrolytic Zinc Co., A'asia, 1951–84 (Chm., 1960–84); Glazebrooks Paints and Chemicals Ltd, 1951–61; Standard Mutual Bldg Soc., 1951–64; E. Z. Industries, 1956–84 (Chm., 1960–84, Pres., 1984–); Pelaco Ltd, 1959–68; Commercial Union Assurance, 1960–82 (Chm., 1964–82); Union Assce Soc. of Aust., 1960–75 (Local Advisor, 1951–60); Michaelis Bayley Ltd, 1964–80; Qld Brewery (later CUB Qld), 1968–84; Herald and Weekly Times Ltd, 1974–77 (Vice-Chm., 1976–77); Chairman: Derwent Metals, 1957–84; CUB Fibre Containers, 1963–84; Emu Bay Railway Co., 1967–84; Manufrs Bottle Co., Vic, 1967–84; Northern Aust. Breweries (CUB (N Qld)), 1967–84; Nat. Commercial Union, 1982–84. Past Member: Faculty of Law of Melbourne Univ.; Internat. Hse Council, Melbourne Univ.; Council of Legal Education and Bd of Examiners. Mem. Council Law Inst. of Victoria, 1959–68, Pres. 1965–66. Chairman: Pensions Cttee, Melbourne Legacy, 1961–84 (Mem., 1955–84); Royal Women's Hosp. 1968 Million Dollar Bldg Appeal; Eileen Patricia Goulding Meml Fund Appeal, 1983; Life Governor: Austin, Prince Henry's, Royal Children's, Royal Melbourne, Royal Women's Hosps; Corps of Commissionaires; Adult Deaf and Dumb Soc. of Victoria. Hon. Solicitor, Queens Fund, 1951–94. Twelfth Leonard Ball Orator, Victorian Foundn on Alcoholism and Drug Dependence, 1980. *Address:* 1/722 Orrong Road, Toorak, Victoria 3142, Australia. *Clubs:* Naval and Military, Victoria Racing, Royal Automobile, Melbourne Cricket, Kooyong Lawn Tennis (Melbourne). *Died 22 June 2011.*

COHEN, Prof. Robert Donald, CBE 1997; MD; FRCP, FMedSci; Professor of Medicine and Director, Academic Medical Unit (Whitechapel), St Bartholomew's and the Royal London School of Medicine and Dentistry, Queen Mary and Westfield College, (formerly London Hospital Medical College), University of London, 1981–99, then Professor Emeritus; *b* 11 Oct. 1933; *s* of Dr Harry H. and Ruby Cohen; *m* 1961, Dr Barbara Joan Boucher; one *s* one *d*. *Educ:* Clifton Coll.; Trinity Coll., Cambridge (MA); MD (Cantab); London Hosp. Med. Coll. Hon. Cons. Physician, London Hosp., 1967–99; Dir, Academic Unit of Metabolism and Endocrinology, 1974, Prof. of Metabolic Medicine, 1974–81, London Hosp. Med. Coll. Chairman: Adv. Cttee on the Application of Computing Science to Medicine and the Nat. Health Service, 1976–77; DHSS Computer R&D Cttee, 1977–80; DHSS/MRC Monitoring Cttee on Magnetic Resonance Imaging, 1986–89; Review Body, British Diabetic Assoc., 1990–95; Member: Jt Cttee on Higher Med. Trng, 1983–90, 1996–97 (Chm., Special Adv. Cttee on Gen. Internal Medicine, 1983–90); GMC, 1988–96; Physiological Systems Bd, MRC, 1990–92; Health Services Res. Cttee, MRC, 1990–92; Physiological Medicine and Infections Bd, MRC, 1992–94; Health Services and Public Health Bd, MRC, 1992–94; Innovation Grants Cttee, MRC, 1998–2000; Cttee, Nat. Kidney Res. Fund, 1992–98; Council, King Edward VII Hosp., Midhurst, 1997–2000. Chm., ICRF, 1994–2003 (Mem. Council, 1989–2002; Vice-Chm., 1991–94); Mem. Council, Cancer Res. UK, 2002–03. Sen. Censor and First Vice-Pres., RCP, 1991–93. Founder FMedSci 1998. Hon. Fellow, QMW, 2001. Chm., Editorial Bd, Clinical Science and Molecular Medicine, 1973–74. External Reviewer, Canada Foundn for Innovation, 2000–. *Publications:* Clinical and Biochemical Aspects of Lactic Acidosis (with H. F. Woods), 1976; (jtly) The Metabolic and Molecular Basis of Acquired Disease, 1990; papers in Clin. Sci. and Molecular Med., Jl of Clin. Investigation, Lancet, Biochemical Jl, Diabetes, Qly Jl Medicine, Computational and Mathematical Methods in Medicine. *Address:* Long Meadow, East Dean, Chichester, W Sussex PO18 0JB. *T:* (01243) 811230. *E:* rcohen@doctors.org.uk. *Died 17 Oct. 2014.*

COHEN, Prof. Stanley, PhD; FBA 1997; Martin White Professor of Sociology, London School of Economics, 1995–2005, then Professor Emeritus; *b* 23 Feb. 1942; *s* of Ray and Sie Cohen; *m* 1963, Ruth Kretzmer; two *d*. *Educ:* Univ. of Witwatersrand, Johannesburg (BA); LSE, Univ. of London (PhD; Hon. Fellow 2010). Psychiatric social worker, 1963–64; Lectr in Sociology: Enfield Coll., 1965–67; Univ. of Durham, 1967–72; Sen. Lectr in Sociol., 1972–74, Prof. of Sociol., 1974–81, Univ. of Essex; Prof. of Criminology, Hebrew Univ., Jerusalem, 1981–95. Vis. Centennial Prof., LSE, 1994–95. DU Essex, 2003; Hon. Dr Middlesex, 2008. Sellin-Glueck Award, Amer. Soc. of Criminology, 1985; Award for Outstanding Achievement, British Soc. of Criminology, 2009. *Publications:* Images of Deviance, 1971; Folk Devils and Moral Panics, 1972; Psychological Survival, 1972; The Manufacture of News, 1973; Escape Attempts, 1976; Prison Secrets, 1978; Social Control and the State, 1984; Visions of Social Control: crime, punishment and classification, 1985; Against Criminology, 1988; States of Denial: knowing about atrocities and suffering, 2000 (British Acad. Book Prize, 2002). *Address:* Department of Sociology, London School of Economics, Houghton Street, WC2A 2AE. *Died 7 Jan. 2013.*

COKER, Naaz; Chair, St George's Healthcare NHS Trust, 2003–11; independent management consultant (part-time), since 2002; *b* 14 Oct. 1948; *d* of Rahemtula and Shirin Suleman; *m* 1973, Raymond Coker. *Educ:* Portsmouth Univ. (BSc Pharm.); Chelsea Coll., London Univ. (MSc); Open Univ. (MBA). Chief Pharmacist, Royal Marsden Hosp., Sutton, 1973–76; Principal Pharmacist, Bromley & Beckenham Hosps, 1976–79; Dist Pharmaceutical Officer, Lewisham Health Dist, 1979–87; Guy's and Lewisham NHS Trust: Dir, Pharmacy and Med. Supplies, 1988–90; Clinical Dir, Clinical Support Services, 1990–92; Actg Unit Gen. Manager, 1992; King's Fund: Fellow, Leadership Develt, 1992–2002; Dir, Race and Diversity, 1998–2002. Hon. Clinical Lectr, Dept of Pharmacy, Univ. of Brighton, 1992–96. Chair: British Refugee Council, 1998–2005; Shelter, 2007–08; Mem., Race Equality Adv. Panel, Home Office, 2003–06. Non-exec. Dir, Nat. Audit Office, 2012–. Chm., Aga Khan Health Bd UK (for Ismaili Muslim community), 1990–93; Mem., Ismaili Council for EU, 1999–2005. Mem. Council, St George's, Univ. of London, 2006–11. Chm., First Steps Nursery Sch., Streatham and London, 1985–87; Mem., Mgt Cttee, St Cecilia's Leonard Cheshire Foundn Home, Bromley, 1996–2000. Non-exec. Dir, Ethical Property Co., 2009–13. Trustee: Media Trust, 2001–05; Ashoka Trust, 2002–03; RSA, 2004–11 (Vice Chm., 2009–10); Clore Social Leadership Prog., 2010–; RCOG, 2013–. Hon. DSc Leeds Metropolitan, 2005; DUniv UCE, 2007. Asian Woman of Year: Asia Mktg Gp, 2000; Asian Guild, 2003; Asian Women of Achievement Award, 2004; Lifetime Achievement Award, Lloyds TSB/KPMG Jewel Awards, 2009. *Publications:* (ed) Racism in

Medicine, 2001; interviews and book reviews; numerous articles, chapters and reports in med., pharmaceutical and mgt jls. *Recreations:* reading, gardening, walking, cooking. *Died 2015.*

COLE, Frank; *see* Cole, G. F.

COLE, George Edward, OBE 1992; actor on stage, screen, radio and television; *b* Tooting, 22 April 1925; *m* 1st, 1954, Eileen Moore (marr. diss. 1966); one *s* one *d*; 2nd, 1967, Penelope Morrell; one *s* one *d*. *Educ:* Surrey County Council Secondary Sch., Morden. Made first stage appearance in White Horse Inn, tour and London Coliseum, 1939; Cottage to Let, Birmingham, 1940; West End and on tour, 1940–41; subseq. West End plays included Goodnight Children, New, 1942; Mr Bolfry, Playhouse, 1943. Served in RAF, 1943–47. Returned to stage in Dr Angelus, Phoenix, 1947; The Anatomist, Westminster, 1948; Mr Gillie, Garrick, 1950; A Phoenix too Frequent and Thor with Angels, Lyric, Hammersmith, 1951; Misery Me, Duchess, 1955; Mr Bolfry, Aldwych, 1956; Brass Butterfly, Strand, 1958; The Bargain, St Martin's, 1961; The Sponge Room and Squat Betty, Royal Court, 1962; Meet Me on the Fence (tour), 1963; Hedda Gabler, St Martin's, 1964; A Public Mischief, St Martin's, 1965; Too True To Be Good, Strand, 1965; The Waiting Game, Arts, 1966; The Three Sisters, Royal Court, 1967; Doubtful Haunts, Hampstead, 1968; The Passionate Husband, 1969; The Philanthropist, Mayfair, 1971; Country Life, Hampstead, 1973; Déjà Revue, New London, 1974; Motive (tour), 1976; Banana Ridge, Savoy, 1976; The Case of the Oily Levantine, Guildford, 1977; Something Afoot, Hong Kong, 1978; Brimstone and Treacle, Open Space, 1979; Liberty Hall, Greenwich, 1980; The Pirates of Penzance, Drury Lane, 1982; A Month of Sundays, Duchess, 1986; A Piece of My Mind, Apollo, 1987; Peter Pan, Cambridge, 1987; The Breadwinner (tour), 1989; Natural Causes (tour), 1993; Theft (tour), 1995; Lock Up Your Daughters, Chichester, 1996; Heritage, Hampstead, 1997; The Play What I Wrote, Wyndhams, 2001; Party Piece (tour), 2004–05. *Films include:* Cottage to Let, 1941; Morning Departure, Laughter in Paradise, Scrooge, Top Secret, 1949–51; Will Any Gentleman?, The Intruder, 1952; Happy Ever After, Our Girl Friday, 1953; Belles of St Trinian's, 1954; Quentin Durward, 1955; The Weapon, It's a Wonderful World, The Green Man, 1956; Blue Murder at St Trinian's, Too Many Crooks, Don't Panic Chaps, The Bridal Path, 1957–59; The Pure Hell of St Trinian's, Cleopatra, Dr Syn, 1961–62; One Way Pendulum, Legend of Dick Turpin, 1964; Great St Trinian's Train Robbery, 1965; The Green Shoes, 1969; Vampire Lovers, 1970; Girl in the Dark, 1971; The Blue Bird, 1975; Minder on the Orient Express (TV film), 1985; Mary Reilly, 1996; The Ghost of Greville Lodge, 2000. *Television:* appearances in The Sleeper, Station Jim, Life after Life, Single Voices, Bodily Harm, A Class Apart, Diamond Geezer, Miss Marple, New Tricks, The Dinner Party, Midsomer Murders, Heartbeat; series include Life of Bliss (also radio), A Man of our Times, Don't Forget to Write, Minder (9 series), The Bounder (2 series), Blott on the Landscape, Comrade Dad, My Good Friend (2 series), An Independent Man, Dad (2 series), Family Business. *Address:* c/o Spotlight, Cranbourn Street, WC2H 7AL. *Died 5 Aug. 2015.*

COLE, George Francis, (Frank); Founder Director, Frank Cole (Consultancy) Ltd, since 1979; *b* 3 Nov. 1918; *m* 1940, Gwendoline Mary Laver (decd); two *s* one *d*; *m* Barbara Mary Booth (*née* Gornall). *Educ:* Manchester Grammar Sch. Dir and Gen. Manager, Clarkson Engineers Ltd, 1944–53; Gen. Man., Ariel Motors Ltd (BSA Group), 1953–55; Dir, later Man. Dir, Vono Ltd, 1955–67. Past Chairman: Grovewood Products Ltd; Portways Ltd; R. & W. H. Symington Holdings Ltd; National Exhibition Centre Ltd; Crane's Screw (Hldgs); Stokes Bomford (Holdings) Ltd; Debenholt Ltd; Stokes Bomford (Foods) Ltd; James Cooke (Birmingham) Ltd; Franklin Medical Ltd; Aero Needles Gp plc; Needle Industries Gp Ltd; F. J. Neve & Co. Ltd; Wild Barnsley Engrg Gp Ltd; Past Director: Duport Ltd; Shipping Industrial Holdings Ltd; G. Clancey Ltd; Armstrong Equipment PLC (retd as Dep. Chm., 1989); William Mitchell (Sinkers) Ltd (Chm., 1982–89); Director: Alexander Stenhouse (formerly Reed Stenhouse) UK Ltd, 1981–91; Mitchell-Grieve Ltd, 1989–91. Pres., Birmingham Chamber of Commerce and Industry, 1968–69. Leader of Trade Missions to West Germany, Yugoslavia, Romania and Hungary. Life Governor, Birmingham Univ.; Liveryman of City of London. Radio and Television appearances. *Publications:* press articles on economics, exports, etc. *Recreations:* tennis (regular competitor in Nat. Veteran Championships of GB), oil painting, snooker, gardening. *Address:* 2 Woodcote Drive, Dorridge, Solihull, West Midlands B93 8JR. *T:* (01564) 777795. *Died 15 Sept. 2011.*

COLE, John Morrison; Political Editor, BBC, 1981–92; *b* 23 Nov. 1927; *s* of George Cole and Alice Jane Cole, Belfast; *m* 1956, Margaret Isobel, *d* of Mr and Mrs John S. Williamson, Belfast; four *s*. *Educ:* Fortwilliam and Skegoneill Primary Schs, Belfast; Belfast Royal Acad.; London Univ. (BA External). Belfast Telegraph, 1945–56: successively reporter, industrial, municipal and political correspondent; The Guardian: reporter, 1956–57; Labour Correspondent, 1957–63; News Editor, 1963–69; Dep. Editor, 1969–75; The Observer: Asst Editor, 1975; Dep. Editor, 1976–81. DUniv Open, 1992; Hon. DSSc QUB, 1992; Hon. DLitt Ulster, 1992; Hon. LLD St Andrews, 1993. Granada TV Scoop of the Year Award, 1960; Television Journalist of the Year, RTS, 1990; Richard Dimbleby Award, BAFTA, 1992. *Publications:* The Poor of the Earth, 1976; The Thatcher Years: a decade of revolution in British politics, 1987; As It Seemed To Me: political memoirs, 1995; A Clouded Peace (novel), 2001; contrib. to books on British and Irish politics. *Recreations:* reading, travel. *Address:* c/o BBC Office, House of Commons, Westminster, SW1A 0AA. *T:* (020) 7219 4765. *Club:* Athenæum. *Died 7 Nov. 2013.*

COLE, Robert Templeman, CBE 1981; DL; FREng; Chairman, Conder Group plc, 1979–87; *b* 14 Dec. 1918; *s* of Percival P. Cole and Amy Gladys Cole (*née* Templeman); *m* 1947, Elspeth Lawson (*d* 2007); one *s* one *d*. *Educ:* Harrow; Cambridge Univ. (MA). FIStructE; FREng (FEng 1982). Served RAF, 1940–46. Hampshire County Council, 1946–47; Founder Partner, Conder Engineering, 1947; Chairman: Conder Engineering Co. Ltd, 1950; Conder International Ltd, 1964. DL Hants 1988. Hon. DSc Southampton, 1980. *Recreations:* contemplation, travel. *Died 15 Oct. 2013.*

COLEBROOK, Philip Victor Charles, CEng; Managing Director, Imperial Continental Gas Association, 1973–84 (Director, 1971; Director, CompAir Ltd, 1980–84); Director: Calor Group Ltd, 1969–84; Century Power & Light Ltd, 1980–84; Contibel SA (Belgium), 1978–84; *b* 8 March 1924; *s* of Frederick Charles Colebrook and Florence Margaret (*née* Cooper); *m* 1946, Dorothy Ursula Kemp; one *s* three *d*. *Educ:* Andover Grammar Sch.; Guildford Technical Coll.; Battersea Polytechnic, London. Served War of 1939–45, RNVR. Joined Pfizer as Works and Production Manager, 1952; Dir, 1956, Man. Dir, 1958–69, Pfizer Ltd; Chm. and Man. Dir, Pfizer Gp, 1961–69; Vice-Pres., Pfizer Internat., 1967–69; Man. Dir, Calor Gas Holding Co., 1969–80. Member: NHS Affairs Cttee, Assoc. of the British Pharmaceutical Industry, 1963–67; CBI Cttee on State Intervention in Private Business, 1975–78. Trustee and Mem. of Steering Cttee, Univ. of Kent at Canterbury, 1964–65. *Publications:* Going International, 1972. *Recreations:* sailing, ski-ing, golf, painting (exhib. RA, 2001). *Died 5 Feb. 2012.*

COLEMAN, Dr Dena; Headteacher, Yavneh College, 2005–13; *b* 7 Sept. 1952; *d* of Norman and Muriel Friedman; *m* 1974, Gordon David Coleman; one *s* one *d*. *Educ:* Copthall Co. Grammar Sch.; Manchester Univ. (BSc Hons Botany and Zool.; PGCE); Chelsea Coll., London (MA); King's Coll. London (PhD 1991). Sci. teacher, various London schools, 1974–86; Head of Sci., Queenswood Sch., 1986–90; Dep. Headteacher, 1990–95, Headteacher, 1995–98, Hasmonean High Sch.; Headteacher, Bushey Meads Sch., 1998–2005. Mem., Teaching Agency Professional Conduct Panel, 2012–. Member: Exec. Cttee, Foundn and Aided Schs Nat. Assoc. (formerly Grant Maintained and Aided Schs, then Assoc. Foundn and Vol. Aided Schs), 1997–2010; Herts Sch. Orgn Cttee, 1999–2005; Salters' Inst. Teachers' Prize Cttee, 2001–05; Adv. Gp, Nat. Network of Science Learning

Centres, 2003–05; Bd, Herts Learning and Skills Council, 2003–09; Exec., Herts Assoc. of Secondary Sch. Heads, 2010–13; Partnership Steering Gp for Initial Teacher Trng, Middlesex Univ., 2012–; Pikuach Adv. Gp, 2011–. Consultant, York Univ. Nat. Curriculum Sci. QCA Proj., 2000–01. *Publications:* (with R. Gold) Running a School, 2002; contrib. to Hist. of Educn Jl. *Recreations:* foreign travel, piano, clothes shopping. *Died 18 June 2013.*

COLEMAN, John Ennis, CB 1990; Legal Adviser, Department of Education and Science, 1983–90; *b* 12 Nov. 1930; *o s* of late Donald Stafford Coleman and Dorothy Jean Balieff (*née* Ennis); *m* 1958, Doreen Gwendoline Hellinger; one *s* one *d*. *Educ:* Dean Close Sch., Cheltenham; Dulwich Coll.; Worcester Coll., Oxford (MA). Solicitor (Hons), 1957. Legal Asst, Treasury Solicitor's Dept, 1958; Senior Legal Asst, 1964; Asst Solicitor, 1971; Under Sec. (Legal), Depts of Industry and Trade, 1980–83. Jt Editor, The Law of Education, 1993–2008. *Publications:* (jtly) Butterworth's Education Law, 1997. *Died 10 Nov. 2014.*

COLFOX, Sir (William) John, 2nd Bt *cr* 1939; JP, DL; *b* 25 April 1924; *yr* and *o* surv. *s* of Sir (William) Philip Colfox, 1st Bt, MC, and Mary (Frances) Lady Colfox (*d* 1973); *S* father, 1966; *m* 1962, Frederica Loveday, *d* of Adm. Sir Victor Crutchley, VC, KCB, DSC; two *s* three *d*. *Educ:* Eton. Served in RNVR, 1942–46 (Battle of North Cape, 1943), leaving as Lieut. Qualified Land Agent, 1950. Chm., Land Settlement Assoc., 1979–81. Vice-Chm., TSW plc, 1979–92. Mem. Council, Royal Bath and West Show, 1950– (Chm., Sheep Shearing Cttee); Chairman: Dorset Agricl Exec. Cttee, 1960–73; Golden Shears World Championship Cttee, 1977–2005; Jt Founder, World Fedn of Golden Shears; President: W Dorset Scouts, 1960–80; Dorset Young Farmers, 1964. Mem., Bridport RDC, 1953–74. JP Dorset, 1962, High Sheriff of Dorset, 1969, DL Dorset, 1977. Chm. Govs, Colfox Comp. Sch., later Sir John Colfox Sch., 1970–97, Gov. Emeritus, 1997. *Heir: s* Philip John Colfox [*b* 27 Dec. 1962; *m* 1993, Julia, *yr d* of G. St G. Schomberg; one *s* three *d* (incl. twins)]. *Address:* Symondsbury House, Bridport, Dorset DT6 6HB. *T:* (01308) 422956. *Died 12 July 2014.*

COLLEE, Prof. (John) Gerald, CBE 1991; MD; FRCPath; FRCPE; FRSE; Robert Irvine Professor of Bacteriology and Head of Department of Medical Microbiology (formerly Department of Bacteriology), University of Edinburgh, 1979–91, then Emeritus Professor; Chief Bacteriologist to Edinburgh Royal Infirmary and Consultant Bacteriologist, Lothian Health Board, 1979–91; Consultant Adviser in Microbiology to Scottish Home and Health Department, 1986–91; *b* 10 May 1929; *s* of John Gerald Collee and Mary Hay Wilson Kirsopp Cassels; *m* 1st, 1952, Isobel McNay Galbraith (marr. diss. 1995); two *s* one *d*; 2nd, 1995, Anne Ferguson (*d* 1998). *Educ:* Bo'ness Acad.; Edinburgh Acad.; Edinburgh Univ. MB ChB, MD (Gold Medal). Ho. Phys., 1951–52. AMS (Captain RAMC), 1952–54. Lectr in Bacteriology, Edinburgh, 1955–63; WHO Vis. Prof. of Bacteriol., Baroda, 1963–64; Sen. Lectr, Edinburgh, and Hon. Cons. Bacteriologist, 1964–70; Reader in Bacteriol. 1970–74, Personal Prof. of Bacteriol. 1974–79, Edinburgh. Member: Scottish Health Service Planning Council Adv. Gp on Infection, 1981–90; Jt Cttee on Vaccination and Immunisation, 1982–95; Cttee on Safety of Medicines, 1987–92; Cttee on Vaccination and Immunisation Procedures, MRC, 1988–95; Medicines Commn, 1992–95. *Publications:* Applied Medical Microbiology, 1976, 2nd edn 1981; contrib. and ed several textbooks, incl. Mackie and McCartney's Practical Medical Microbiology, 1996; many sci. papers on aspects of infection, anaerobes of clin. importance, antimicrobial drugs and immunization, BSE and VCJD. *Recreations:* woodwork, poetry, fishing, music, painting. *Address:* 45 Grange Road, Edinburgh EH9 1UF. *T:* (0131) 667 4198. *Clubs:* Scottish Arts, New (Edinburgh). *Died 10 Sept. 2013.*

COLLETT, Sir Christopher, GBE 1988; JP; Partner in Ernst & Young, Chartered Accountants, London, retired 1993; Lord Mayor of London, 1988–89; *b* 10 June 1931; 2nd *s* of Sir Henry Seymour Collett, 2nd Bt, and Lady (Ruth Mildred) Collett (*née* Hatch) (*d* 1994); *m* 1959, Christine Anne, *d* of Oswald Hardy Griffiths, Nunthorpe, Yorks; two *s* one *d*. *Educ:* Harrow; Emmanuel Coll., Cambridge. MA; FCA. Nat. Service, RA and Surrey Yeomanry; Captain TA (RA). Articled with Cassleton Elliott & Co., Chartered Accountants, 1954; qualified, 1958; Partner, Ghana 1960, London 1963; firm merged to become Josolyne Miles and Cassleton Elliott, Josolyne Layton Bennett & Co., Arthur Young, and then Ernst & Young. Mem., Court of Common Council (Broad Street Ward), City of London, 1973–79; Alderman, 1979–2001; Sheriff, City of London, 1985–86; HM Lieut, 1988–2001; Trustee, Temple Bar Trust, 1992– (Chm., 1993–); Chm., Lord Mayor's 800th Anniversary Awards Trust, 1989–. Liveryman: Glovers' Co., 1965 (Master, 1981); Chartered Accts in Eng. and Wales' Co., 1984 (Asst, 1986–93); Haberdashers' Company: Hon. Liveryman, 1990; Asst, 1991; Third Warden, 1993; Hon. Asst, 1994–2006; Member: Guild of Freemen, 1983–2000; City of London TAVR Cttee, 1980–92. Non-exec. Mem., Dumfries and Galloway Health Bd, 1997–2001. Council Mem., Action Research for the Crippled Child, 1984–93; Mem., Scottish Appeals Cttee, Police Dependants' Trust, 2001–04 (Mem., 1996, Chm., 2001–04, Dumfries & Galloway Appeals Cttee); Chm., South of Scotland Youth Awards Trust, 1999–. Governor: Haberdashers' Aske's Schs, Elstree, 1982–94; King Edward's Sch., Witley, 1983–94; Music Therapy Gp Ltd, 1986–94; Bridewell Royal Hosp., 1987–94; Hon. Treas., Lee House, Wimbledon, 1980–2002; Trustee, Morden Coll., 1993–2004; Chm., Eskdale Foundn, 1996–2006. Pres., Broad Street Ward Club, 1979–2001. JP City of London, 1979. Hon. DSc City, 1988. KStJ 1988. Order of Merit (cl. II), State of Qatar, 1985; Orden del Merito Civil (cl. II), Spain, 1986; Commander, Order of Merit, Federal Republic of Germany, 1986; CON, 1st cl. (Nigeria), 1989. *Recreations:* gardening, fishing. *Address:* Altnaharrie, Lodsworth, Petworth, West Sussex GU28 9DG. *T:* (01798) 861792. *Died 2 Dec. 2012.*

COLLEY, Surg. Rear-Adm. Ian Harris, OBE 1963; Member, Committee of Management, Royal National Lifeboat Institution, since 1982; *b* 14 Oct. 1922; *s* of Aubrey James Colley and Violet Fulford Colley; *m* 1952, Joy Kathleen (*née* Goodacre). *Educ:* Hanley Castle Grammar Sch.; King's Coll., London and King's Coll. Hosp. MB, BS 1948; DPH; MFOM; FFCM. Royal Naval Medical Service, 1948–80: MO HMS Cardigan Bay and HMS Consort, 1949–52; service with Fleet Air Arm, 1955–78: as PMO HMS Centaur; MO i/c Air Med. Sch.; Pres., Central Air Med. Bd; Comd MO to Flag Officer, Naval Air Comd; Surg. Rear Adm. (Ships and Estabs), 1978–80. QHP 1978–80. Consultant in Aviation Medicine; former Examr to Conjoint Bd, Royal College of Surgeons and Royal College of Physicians for DAvMed. Life Vice-Pres., RNLI, 1997 (Vice-Pres., 1989–97; Chm., Med. and Survival Cttee, 1984–88). CStJ 1980. *Publications:* papers in field of aviation medicine. *Address:* c/o Royal Bank of Scotland, Inveraray, Argyll PA32 8TY. *Died 12 July 2014.*

COLLIER, Prof. Leslie Harold, MD, DSc; FRCP, FRCPath; Professor of Virology, University of London, 1966–86, then Emeritus; Consulting Pathologist, Royal London Hospital (formerly London Hospital), since 1987; *b* 9 Feb. 1921; *s* of late Maurice Leonard Collier and Ruth (*née* Phillips); *m* 1942, Adeline Barnett; one *s*. *Educ:* Brighton Coll.; UCH Med. Sch. MD London 1953; DSc London 1968; MRCP 1969; FRCPath 1975; FRCP 1980. House Phys., UCH, 1943; served RAMC, 1944–47; Asst Pathologist, St Helier Hosp., Carshalton, 1947; Lister Inst. of Preventive Medicine, 1948–78: Head, Dept of Virology, 1955–74; Dep. Dir, 1968–74; Dir, Vaccines and Sera Laboratories, 1974–78; Hon. Dir, MRC Trachoma Unit, 1957–73; Prof. of Virology and Sen. Lectr, Jt Dept of Virology, London Hosp. Med. Coll. and St Bartholomew's Hosp. Med. Coll., 1978–86; Hd, Dept of Virology, London Hosp. Med. Coll., 1982–86. Hon. Consultant in Virology, Tower Hamlets HA, 1978–86. Pres., Sect. of Pathology, RSM, 1986–88, Hon. Mem., 1994. Chibret Gold Medal, Ligue contre le Trachome, 1959; Luys Prize, Soc. de Médecine de Paris, 1963. *Publications:* (ed jtly) Topley and Wilson's Principles of Bacteriology, Virology and Immunity, 8th edn, 1990, 9th edn, as Topley and Wilson's Microbiology and Microbial Infections (Editor in Chief), 1997 (Soc. of Authors and Med. Soc. of London award, 1998); (jtly) Human Virology, 1993, 3rd edn 2006; papers in med. and scientific jls. *Recreation:* various. *Address:* 8 Peto Place, Regent's Park, NW1 4DT. *T:* (020) 7487 4848. *Died 14 March 2011.*

COLLING, Rev. Canon James Oliver, MBE 1995; Rector of Warrington, 1973–97; Canon Diocesan of Liverpool Cathedral, 1976–97, then Canon Emeritus; Chaplain to The Queen, 1990–2000; *b* 3 Jan. 1930; *e s* of late Leonard Colling and Dorothy Colling (*née* Atherton); *m* 1957, Jean Wright; one *s* one *d* (one twin *s* decd). *Educ:* Leigh Grammar Sch.; Univ. of Manchester (BA 1950); Cuddesdon Coll., Oxford. Commissioned RAF, 1950–52 (Nat. Service). Ordained deacon 1954; priest 1955; Asst Curate, Wigan Parish Church, 1954–59; Vicar of Padgate, 1959–71, Rector, 1971–73; Rural Dean of Warrington, 1970–82 and 1987–89, Area Dean, 1989–95. Chairman: Warrington CHC, 1974–82; Warrington Community Council, 1974–87; Warrington Jt Consultative Cttee, 1987–89; Vice-Chm., Warrington HA, 1982–89; Member: Cheshire Family Practitioner Cttee, 1983–85; Cheshire FHSA, 1990–94 (Chm., Pharmaceutical Develt Gp). Chairman: Warrington C of E Educnl Trust, 1973–97; Warrington and Dist Soc. for the Deaf, 1974–93 (Vice-Pres., 1993–); Warrington Charities Trust, 1989–91 (Patron, 1992–); Vice-Pres., Cheshire Deaf Soc. (operating as Deafness Support Network), 1980–. Chairman: Governors, Sir Thomas Boteler High Sch., Warrington, 1988–97; Boteler Educnl Trust, 1995–97. *Recreations:* looking at buildings and places, local history. *Address:* 19 King Street, Chester CH1 2AH. *T:* (01244) 317557. *Died 7 Nov. 2011.*

COLLINS, Jacqueline Jill, (Jackie), OBE 2013; writer; *b* London, 4 Oct. 1937; *d* of late Joseph Collins and Elsa (*née* Bessant); *m* 1960, Wallace Austin (marr. diss.; he *d* 1966); one *d*; *m* 1966, Oscar Lerman (*d* 1992); two *d*. Formerly TV and film actress. *Publications:* The World is Full of Married Men, 1968; The Stud, 1969 (filmed, 1978); Sunday Simmons and Charlie Brick, 1971 (new edn as Sinners, 1984); Lovehead, 1974; The World is Full of Divorced Women, 1975; Lovers and Gamblers, 1977; The Bitch, 1979 (filmed, 1979); Chances, 1981 (televised, 1990); Hollywood Wives, 1983 (televised); Lucky, 1985 (televised); Hollywood Husbands, 1986; Rock Star, 1988; Love Killers, 1989; Lady Boss, 1990 (televised); American Star, 1993; Hollywood Kids, 1994; Vendetta: Lucky's revenge, 1996; Thrill, 1998; LA Connections (four parts), 1998; Dangerous Kiss, 1999; Lethal Seduction, 2000; Hollywood Wives: the new generation, 2001; Hollywood Divorces, 2003; Lovers and Players, 2005; Drop Dead Beautiful, 2007; Married Lovers, 2008; Poor Little Bitch Girl, 2009; Goddess of Vengeance, 2011; The Power Trip, 2012; Confessions of a Wild Child, 2013; The Santangelos, 2015. *Address:* c/o Simon and Schuster, 1st Floor, 222 Gray's Inn Road, WC1X 8HB. *Died 19 Sept. 2015.*

COLLINS, Prof. Jeffrey Hamilton, FRSE; FREng; Professor and Specialist Advisor to Vice-Chancellor, Napier University, 1994–97; *b* 22 April 1930; *s* of Ernest Frederick and Dora Gladys Collins; *m* 1956, Sally Parfitt; two *s*. *Educ:* Royal Grammar Sch., Guildford; London Univ. (BSc, MSc, DSc). FIET (FIEE 1973), CPhys 1974, FInstP 1974, FIEEE 1980; CEng 1973, FREng (FEng 1981), FRSE 1983. GEC Research Laboratories, London, 1951–56; Ferranti Ltd, Edinburgh, 1956–57; Univ. of Glasgow, 1957–66; Research Engr, Stanford Univ., Calif, 1966–68; Dir of Physical Electronics, Rockwell International, Calif, 1968–70; University of Edinburgh: Research Prof., 1970–73; Prof. of Industrial Electronics, 1973–77; Prof. of Electrical Engrg and Hd of Dept, 1977–84; Emeritus Prof., 1984; Chm., Parallel Computing Centre, 1991–94. Dir, Automation and Robotics Res. Inst., and Prof. of Electrical Engrg, Univ. of Texas at Arlington, 1976–77 and 1987–90; Sen. Technical Specialist, Lothian Regl Council, 1991–93. Member: Electronics Res. Council, 1979; Computer Bd for Univs and Res. Councils, 1985–86; Information Systems Cttee, UFC, 1992–93; Jt Information Systems Cttee, HEFCs, 1993–94. Director: MESL, 1970–79; Racal-MESL, 1979–81; Advent Technology, 1981–86; Filtronics Components, 1981–85; Burr-Brown Ltd, 1985; River Bend Bank, Fort Worth, 1987–90. Member Honour Societies: Eta Kappa Nu; Tau Beta Pi; Upsilon Pi Epsilon; Phi Beta Delta. Hon. DEng Napier, 1997. *Publications:* Computer-Aided Design of Surface Acoustic Wave Devices, 1976; 197 articles in learned soc. electrical engrg jls. *Recreations:* music, DIY, tennis. *Died 23 Sept. 2015.*

COLLINS, John Ernest Harley, MBE 1944; DSC 1945 and Bar 1945; Chairman: Morgan Grenfell Holdings Ltd, 1974–80; Guardian Royal Exchange Assurance, 1974–88; *b* 24 April 1923; *o s* of late G. W. Collins, Taynton, Glos; *m* 1st, 1946, Gillian (*d* 1981), *e d* of 2nd Baron Bicester; one *s* one *d*; 2nd, 1986, Jennifer Faith, *widow* of Capt. A. J. A. Cubitt, and *yr d* of Lt Gen. W. H. E. Gott, CB, CBE, DSO, MC. *Educ:* King Edward's Sch., Birmingham; Birmingham Univ. Royal Navy, 1941–46. Morgan Grenfell & Co. Ltd, 1946, Dir 1957. Director: Royal Exchange Assce, 1957; Rank Hovis McDougall Ltd, 1965–91; Charter Consolidated Ltd, 1966–83; Hudson's Bay Co., 1957–74. Chm. United Services Trustee, 1968–76. DL Oxon, 1975–96; High Sheriff, Oxon, 1975. KStJ 1983. *Address:* Chetwode Manor, Buckingham MK18 4BB. *T:* (01280) 848333. *Died 4 Sept. 2012.*

COLLINS, (John) Martin; QC 1972; Commissioner, Royal Court, Jersey, 2000–02; a Judge of the Courts of Appeal of Jersey, 1984–99, and of Guernsey, 1984–2000; *b* 24 Jan. 1929; *s* of John Lissant Collins and Marjorie Mary Collins; *m* 1957, Daphne Mary, *d* of George Martyn Swindells, Prestbury; two *s* one *d*. *Educ:* Uppingham Sch.; Manchester Univ. (LLB). Called to Bar, Gray's Inn, 1952 (Bencher, 1981; Chm., Mgt Cttee, 1990; Vice-Treas., 1998; Treas., 1999); called to the Bar of Gibraltar, 1990. Dep. Chm., Cumberland QS, 1969–72; a Recorder, 1972–88. Member: Senate of Inns of Court and Bar, 1981–84; Gen. Council of the Bar, 1991. *Address:* Les Grandes Masses, 50580 Denneville, France. *Club:* Athenæum. *Died 30 Dec. 2011.*

COLLINSON, Prof. Patrick, CBE 1993; PhD; FBA 1982; FRHistS, FAHA; Regius Professor of Modern History, University of Cambridge, 1988–96, then Emeritus; Fellow of Trinity College, Cambridge, since 1988; *b* 10 Aug. 1929; *s* of William Cecil Collinson and Belle Hay (*née* Patrick); *m* 1960, Elizabeth Albinia Susan Selwyn; two *s* two *d*. *Educ:* King's Sch., Ely; Pembroke Coll., Cambridge (Exhibnr 1949, Foundn Scholar 1952; BA 1952, 1st Cl. Hons Hist. Tripos Pt II; Hadley Prize for Hist., 1952; Hon. Fellow); PhD London, 1957. University of London: Postgrad. Student, Royal Holloway Coll., 1952–54; Res. Fellow, Inst. of Hist. Res., 1954–55; Res. Asst, UCL, 1955–56; Lectr in Hist., Univ. of Khartoum, 1956–61; Asst Lectr in Eccles. Hist., King's Coll., Univ. of London, 1961–62, Lectr, 1962–69 (Fellow 1976); Professor of History: Univ. of Sydney, 1969–75; Univ. of Kent at Canterbury, 1976–84; Prof. of Modern Hist., Sheffield Univ., 1984–88. Vis. Fellow, All Souls Coll., Oxford, 1981; Andrew W. Mellon Fellow, Huntington Library, California, 1984; Douglas S. Freeman Vis. Prof., Richmond Univ., Va, 1999; Vis. Hon. Prof., Univ. of Warwick, 2000–03. Lectures: Ford's, in Eng. Hist., Univ. of Oxford, 1978–79; Birkbeck, Univ. of Cambridge, 1981; Stenton Meml, Univ. of Reading, 1985; Neale Meml, Univ. of Manchester, 1986; Anstey Meml, Univ. of Kent, 1986; Neale Meml, UCL, 1987; F. D. Maurice, KCL, 1990; Homer J. Crotty, Huntington Liby, 1990; Sir D. Owen Evans Meml, UCW Aberystwyth, 1992; A. H. Dodd Meml, UCNW Bangor, 1992; Raleigh, British Academy, 1993; S. T. Bindoff Meml, QMW, 1995; Douglas S. Freeman, Richmond Univ., Va, 1999; Eberhard L. Faber, Princeton Univ., 1999; Creighton, Univ. of London, 2002; St Robert Southwell, Fordham, 2007. Chm., Adv. Editorial Bd, Jl of Ecclesiastical History, 1982–93. President: Ecclesiastical Hist. Soc., 1985–86; C of E Record Soc., 1991–2001 (Vice-Pres., 2001–); Mem. Council, British Acad., 1986–89. FRHistS 1967 (Mem. Council, 1977–81, Vice-Pres., 1983–87 and 1994–98, Hon. Vice-Pres., 2001–); FAHA 1974. MAE 1989; Corresp. Mem., Massachusetts Historical Soc., 1990. DUniv York, 1988; Hon. DLitt: Kent at Canterbury, 1989; Oxford, 1997; Essex, 2000; Warwick, 2003; Hon. LittD: TCD, 1992; Sheffield, 1995. Medlicott Medal, Histl Assoc., 1998. *Publications:* The Elizabethan Puritan Movement, 1967 (USA 1967; repr. 1982); Archbishop Grindal 1519–1583: the struggle for a Reformed Church, 1979 (USA 1979); The Religion of Protestants: the Church in English Society 1559–1625 (Ford Lectures, 1979), 1982;

Godly People: essays on English Protestantism and Puritanism, 1983; English Puritanism, 1983; The Birthpangs of Protestant England: religious and cultural change in the 16th and 17th centuries, 1988; Elizabethan Essays, 1994; (jtly) A History of Canterbury Cathedral, 1995; (ed jtly) The Reformation in English Towns 1500–1640, 1998; (jtly) A History of Emmanuel College, Cambridge, 1999; (ed) Short Oxford History of the British Isles: The Sixteenth Century, 2002; Elizabethans, 2002; The Reformation, 2003 (Portuguese edn 2004; Slovak edn 2005; Brazilian edn 2006); (jtly) Conferences and Combination Lectures in the Elizabethan Church: Dedham and Bury St Edmunds, 1582–1590, 2003; From Cranmer to Sancroft, 2005; Elizabeth I, 2007; The History of a History Man: or, the Twentieth Century viewed from a safe distance, the memoirs of Patrick Collinson, 2011; This England: essays on the English nation and Commonwealth in the sixteenth century, 2011; articles and revs in Bull. Inst. Hist. Res., Eng. Hist. Rev., Jl of Eccles. Hist., Studies in Church Hist., London Rev. of Books. *Recreations:* hills, music, grandchildren. *Address:* New House, Crown Square, Shaldon, Teignmouth, Devon TQ14 0DS; Trinity College, Cambridge CB2 1TQ. *Died 28 Sept. 2011.*

COLOMBO, Emilio; Minister of Foreign Affairs, Italy, 1980–83 and 1992–93; Life Senator, Italy, since 2003; *b* Potenza, Italy, 11 April 1920. *Educ:* Rome Univ. Deputy: Constituent Assembly, 1946–48; (Christian Democrat), Italian Parlt, 1948–94; Under-Secretary: of Agriculture, 1948–51; of Public Works, 1953–55; Minister: of Agriculture, 1955–58; of Foreign Trade, 1958–59; of Industry and Commerce, 1959–60, March–April 1960, July 1960–63; of the Treasury, 1963–70, Feb.–May 1972, 1974–76; Prime Minister, 1970–72; Minister of State for UN Affairs, 1972–73; Minister of Finance, 1973–74. European Parliament: Mem., 1976–80, 1989–92; Chm., Political Affairs Cttee, 1976–77; Pres., 1977–79. Pres., Italian Atlantic Cttee, 1990; Formerly Vice-Pres., Italian Catholic Youth Assoc. Charlemagne Prize, 1979. *Address:* Via Vittorio Veneto 146, Rome, Italy. *Died 24 June 2013.*

COLQUHOUN, Prof. Alan Harold; architect; Professor, School of Architecture, Princeton University, 1981–91, then Emeritus; *b* 27 June 1921; *s* of John Sydney Plumptree Colquhoun and Clariss Thelma Colquhoun (*née* Soden). *Educ:* Edinburgh Coll. of Art; AA Dip 1949. Architects' Dept, LCC, 1949–55; Candilis and Woods, Paris, 1955–56; Lyons Israel and Ellis, London, 1956–61; own practice, Colquhoun & Miller, Architects, 1961–88. Lectr, PCL, 1974–78; many short-term or part-time teaching posts in UK, Switzerland, Ireland and USA, 1957–; lectures and seminars in UK, France, Germany, Spain, Holland, Switzerland, Portugal, USA, Canada, Brazil, Argentina, Chile, India and Singapore, 1960–. Guggenheim Fellowship, 1996; Centre for Advanced Study in the Visual Arts Fellowship, Nat. Gall. of Art, Washington, 1996. *Publications:* Modern Architecture and Historical Change, 1982 (trans. French, Italian, Spanish and Turkish); Modernity and the Classical Tradition, 1987 (trans. Spanish and Portuguese); Modern Architecture 1890–1965, 2002 (trans. French and Spanish); Collected Essays in Architectural Criticism, 2009; contrib. learned jls in UK, USA and Europe. *Recreations:* music (as listener), painting (as occasional practitioner and enjoyer), literature. *Address:* 96 Regent's Park Road, NW1 8UG. *Died 13 Dec. 2012.*

COLYER, Peter John, DPhil; Research Fellow, Centre for Christianity and Culture, Regent's Park College, Oxford, 2006–12; *b* 24 March 1943; *s* of Sydney Colyer and Beryl Colyer; *m* 1968, Kay Holloway; three *s*. *Educ:* Hertford Coll., Oxford (MA 1969); Regent's Park Coll., Oxford (MSt 2003; DPhil 2007). Research Scientist, Hydraulics Res., Wallingford, Oxon, 1966–83; Scientific Advr, Laboratorio de Hidraulica Aplicada, Buenos Aires, 1972–74; Science Policy Unit, Dept of Transport, 1983–86 and 1990; Sen. Principal, Sci. and Technol. Secretariat, Cabinet Office, 1986–90; Co-ordinator of Scientific Networks, ESF, Strasbourg, 1991–95; Exec. Sec., Academia Europaea, 1995–2001; Sec., UK Sci. and Religion Forum, 2007–10. Erasmus Medal, Erasmus Univ., Rotterdam, 2001. *Publications:* The Prescientific Bible, 2013; The Self-Emptying God, 2013; numerous scientific reports and papers. *Recreations:* cricket, painting, walking the SW Coast Path. *Address:* Regent's Park College, Oxford OX1 2LB. *Died 10 Dec. 2014.*

COMBER, Dr Elizabeth; *see* Han Suyin.

COMFORT, Anthony Francis; HM Diplomatic Service, retired; *b* Plymouth, 12 Oct. 1920; *s* of Francis Harold Comfort and Elsie Grace (*née* Martin); *m* 1948, Joy Margaret Midson (*d* 2003); two *s* one *d*. *Educ:* Bristol Grammar Sch.; Oriel Coll., Oxford. Entered Foreign Service, 1947; 2nd Sec. (Commercial), Athens, 1948–51; Consul, Alexandria, 1951–53; 1st Sec. (Commercial), Amman, 1953–54; Foreign Office, 1954–57; seconded to Colonial Office, 1957–59; 1st Sec. (Commercial), Belgrade, 1959–60; 1st Sec. and Consul, Reykjavik, 1961–65; Inspector, 1965–68, retired 1969. *Recreations:* walking, looking at churches. *Address:* 4 Charles Ponsonby House, Osberton Road, Oxford OX2 7PQ. *T:* (01865) 552677. *Died 1 Jan. 2014.*

COMPTON, Michael Graeme, CBE 1987; Keeper of Museum Services, Tate Gallery, 1970–87; *b* 29 Sept. 1927; *s* of Joseph Neild Compton, OBE, and Dorothy Margaret Townsend Compton; *m* 1952, Susan Paschal, *d* of Sir John Andrews Benn, 3rd Bt; two *d*. *Educ:* Courtauld Institute, London (BA Hons History of Art). Asst to Director, Leeds City Art Gallery and Templenewsam, 1954–57; Keeper of Foreign Schools, Walker Art Gallery, Liverpool, 1957–59; Dir, Ferens Art Gall., Hull, 1960–65; Asst Keeper, Modern Collection, Tate Gall., 1965–70. Frederick R. Weisman Art Foundn Award, 1991. *Publications:* Optical and Kinetic Art, 1967; Pop Art, 1970; (jtly) Catalogue of Foreign Schools, Walker Art Gallery, 1963; Marcel Broodthaers, 1989; articles in art jls, exhibn catalogues. *Died 12 July 2013.*

COMRIE, Rear-Adm. (Alexander) Peter, CB 1982; Director, A. Comrie & Sons Ltd, 1983–2009; *b* 27 March 1924; *s* of Robert Duncan Comrie and Phyllis Dorothy Comrie; *m* 1945, Madeleine Irene (*née* Bullock) (*d* 1983); one *s* one *d*. *Educ:* Sutton Valence Sch., Kent; County Technical Coll., Wednesbury, Staffs, and in the Royal Navy. Joined Royal Navy, 1945; served in cruisers, frigates, minesweepers and RN air stations; RCDS 1973; Captain HMS Daedalus, 1974; Director of Weapons Coordination and Acceptance (Naval), 1975; Deputy Controller Aircraft, MoD, 1978–81; Dir-Gen. Aircraft (Navy), 1981–83, retired. Vice Pres., IEE, 1988–91 (Mem. Council, 1981–84); Member: IEE Electronics Divisional Bd, 1976–77; IEE Qualifications Bd, 1981–88; Chairman: IEE International (formerly Overseas) Bd, 1988–91; Executive Gp Cttee 3, Engrg Council, 1986–94. FIET (FIEE 1975); FRAeS 1978; Eur Ing 1987. *Recreations:* sailing, swimming, DIY. *Club:* Royal Commonwealth Society. *Died 13 April 2011.*

CONGLETON, 8th Baron *cr* 1841; **Christopher Patrick Parnell;** Bt 1766; *b* 11 March 1930; 3rd *s* of 6th Baron Congleton (*d* 1932) and Hon. Edith Mary Palmer Howard (MBE 1941) (she *m* 2nd, 1946, Flight Lieut A. E. R. Aldridge, who died 1950), *d* of late R. J. B. Howard and late Lady Strathcona and Mount Royal; *S* brother, 1967; *m* 1955, Anna Hedvig, *d* of G. A. Sommerfelt, Oslo, Norway; two *s* three *d*. *Educ:* Eton; New Coll., Oxford (MA). Mem., Salisbury and Wilton RDC, 1964–74; Vice-President: RDCA, 1973–74; Assoc. of District Councils, 1974–79. Chm., Salisbury and S Wilts Museum, 1972–77; Mem., Adv. Bd for Redundant Churches, 1981–87. President: Nat. Ski Fedn of GB, 1976–81; Ski Club of GB, 1991–97; Mem., Eligibility Cttee, Internat. Ski Fedn, 1976–88. Trustee: Sandroyd Sch. Trust, 1975–92 (Chm., 1980–84); Wessex Med. Trust, 1984–90 (Chm., 1996–2000); Southampton Univ. Develt Trust, 1986–95. Hon. LLD Southampton, 1990. *Recreations:* music, fishing. *Heir:* *s* Hon. John Patrick Christian Parnell [*b* 17 March 1959; *m* 1985, Marjorie-Anne, *o d* of John Hobdell, Cobham, Surrey; two *s* one *d*]. *Address:* West End Lodge, Ebbesbourne Wake, Salisbury, Wilts SP5 5JR. *Died 11 Dec. 2015.*

CONGREVE, Ambrose, CBE 1965; *b* London, 4 April 1907; *s* of John Congreve, DL, JP, and Lady (Helena Blanche) Irene Ponsonby, *d* of 8th Earl of Bessborough; *m* 1935, Marjorie (*d* 1995), *d* of Dr Arthur Graham Glasgow,

London, and Richmond, Virginia, and Margaret, *d* of John P. Branch, President of Virginia's Merchants National Bank. *Educ:* Lockers Park; Eton; Trinity Coll., Cambridge. Employed by Unilever Ltd, in England and China, 1927–36; joined Humphreys & Glasgow Ltd (London), as Director, 1936; responsible for the company, 1939–83, in succession to Dr Glasgow who founded the firm in 1892. Served War of 1939–45: Air Intelligence, working for Plans and Bomber Command, then Min. of Supply under Sir Vyvyan Board. A Vice-Pres., RHS; First Patron, RHS Ireland; Patron, Tree Council of Southern Ireland. Hon. FIChemE 1967; Hon. Fellow, Royal Dublin Soc., 2003; Hon. Mem., An Taisce, Ireland, 2007. Hon. Dr Iur Dublin, 2002. Veitch Meml Medal, RHS, 1987; Gold Medal (for A Great Garden of the World), Botanic Gardens, Boston, Mass, 2001; Special Award, City of Waterford, 2006. *Recreations:* large-scale outdoor cultivation in Ireland of plant species and hybrids from all over the world, incl. Asiatic magnolias and camellias. *Address:* Mount Congreve, Waterford, Ireland; Warwick House, Stable Yard, St James's, SW1A 1BD. *Club:* Beefsteak. *Died 24 May 2011.*

CONLAN, Bernard; engineer; *b* 24 Oct. 1923; *m* Irene (decd); one *d*. *Educ:* Manchester Primary and Secondary Schs. Mem., AEU (later AEEU), 1940–, Officer, 1943–87. City Councillor, Manchester, 1954–66. Joined Labour Party, 1942; contested (Lab) High Peak, 1959. MP (Lab) Gateshead East, 1964–87. A Vice-Chm., Parly Lab. Party Trade Union Gp, 1974–. Member: House of Commons Expenditure Cttee (from inception), 1971–79; Trade and Industry Select Cttee, 1983–86; Select Cttee on Defence, 1979–83. *Address:* 33 Beccles Road, Sale, Cheshire M33 3RP. *T:* (0161) 973 3991. *Died 12 Dec. 2013.*

CONN, Edward, CBE 1979; FRCVS; Technical Consultant, Norbrook Laboratories Ltd, Newry, Northern Ireland, 1983–90; *b* 25 March 1918; *s* of late Edward and Elizabeth Conn; *m* 1st, 1943, Kathleen E. Victoria, (Betty), Sandford (*d* 1974); three *d*; 2nd, 1975, Lilian Frances Miley. *Educ:* Coleraine Academical Instn; Royal (Dick) Veterinary Sch., Edinburgh Univ. Qual. Vet. Surgeon, 1940; Diploma; MRCVS 1940; FRCVS 1984. Gen. practice, Coleraine, 1940–43; Chief Vet. Officer, Hampshire Cattle Breeders, 1943–47; Dept of Agriculture, NI, 1947–83, Chief Vet. Officer, 1958–83. Pres., Coleraine Old Boys Assoc., 1979–80 (Pres., Belfast Br., 1991–92). Governor, Coleraine Academical Instn, 1972. *Recreations:* golf, walking; watching all sports, particularly Rugby and athletics. *Address:* Ardeena, 23 The Brae, Groomsport, Co. Down BT19 6JQ. *Clubs:* Clandeboye Golf; Bangor Rugby and Athletic (Pres., 1974–75). *Died 25 Oct. 2011.*

CONNELL, George Edward, OC 1987; PhD; FCIC; FRSC; President, University of Toronto, 1984–90; *b* 20 June 1930; *s* of Dr J. Lorne Connell and Dr Mabel Killins Connell; *m* 1955, Sheila Horan; two *s* two *d*. *Educ:* Univ. of Toronto (BA, PhD Biochemistry). FCIC 1971; FRSC 1975. Post-doctoral Fellow, Div. of Applied Biol., National Res. Council, Ottawa, Ont, 1955–56; Fellow, National Science Foundn (US), Dept of Biochem., New York University Coll. of Medicine, 1956–57; University of Toronto: Asst Prof. of Biochem., 1957–62; Associate Prof. of Biochem., 1962–65; Prof. and Chm. Dept of Biochem., 1965–70; Associate Dean, Faculty of Med., 1972–74; Vice-Pres., Res. and Planning, 1974–77; Pres. and Vice-Chancellor, Univ. of Western Ontario, 1977–84. Prin. Advr, Commn of Enquiry on Blood System of Canada, 1993–95; Sen. Policy Advr, Canada Foundn for Innovation, 1997; Mem., Res. Adv. Panel, Walkerton Inquiry, 2000–01. Chairman: Exec. Cttee, Internat. Congress of Biochem., 1979; Nat. Round Table on the Envmt and Economy, 1991–95; Technical Cttee 207 (Envmtl Management), ISO, 1993–96; Task Force on Funding and Delivery of Med. Care in Ontario, 1995–96; Canadian Prostate Cancer Res. Initiative, 2000–; Vice-Chairman: Envmtl Assessment Bd, Ontario, 1990–93; Sustainable Cities Foundn, 1993–98; Protein Engrg Nat. Centre of Excellence, 1995–97; Mem. Bd of Dirs, Lake Simcoe Region Conservation Foundn, 2001–. Member: MRC of Canada, 1966–70; Ont Council of Health, 1978–84; Bd of Dirs and Nat. Exec. Cttee, Canadian Arthritis and Rheumatism Soc., 1965–75; Bd of Dirs, Nat. Inst. of Nutrition, 1984–91; Bd of Res. Inst., Toronto Hosp., 1994–96; Council, Ont Univs, 1977–90 (Chm., 1981–83); Bd of Governors, Upper Canada Coll., 1982–90; Bd of Trustees, Royal Ont Mus., 1984–90; Trustee, R. Samuel McLaughlin Foundn, 1996–2001. Mem., Ontario Press Council, 1996–. Member, Board of Directors: Southam Inc., 1985–93; Allelix Biopharmaceuticals Inc., 1995–99. Hon. LLD: Trent, 1984; Univ. of Western Ont, 1985; McGill, 1987; Hon. DSc Toronto, 1993. *Publications:* scientific papers in jls incl. Canadian Jl of Biochem., Biochemical Jl (UK), and Jl of Immunol. *Recreations:* ski-ing, tennis, wilderness canoe trips. *Address:* 904–130 Carlton Street, Toronto, ON M5A 4K3, Canada. *E:* george.connell@sympatico.ca. *Club:* Badminton and Racquet (Toronto). *Died 13 March 2015.*

CONNELL, John MacFarlane; Chairman, The Distillers Company plc, 1983–86; *b* 29 Dec. 1924; *s* of late John Maclean Connell and Mollie Isobel MacFarlane; *m* 1949, Jean Matheson Sutherland Mackay, *d* of late Major George Sutherland Mackay and Christine Bourne; two *s*. *Educ:* Stowe; Christ Church, Oxford. Joined Tanqueray, Gordon & Co. Ltd, 1946, Export Dir 1954, Man. Dir 1962–70; Dir, Distillers Co. Ltd, 1965, Mem., Management Cttee, 1971–86; Chm., United Glass Holdings plc, 1979–83. Chm., Gin Rectifiers and Distillers Assoc., 1968–71. Pres., Royal Warrant Holders Assoc., 1975. *Recreations:* golf, shooting, fishing. *Club:* Royal and Ancient (St Andrews). *Died 18 March 2014.*

CONNELL, Hon. Sir Michael (Bryan), Kt 1991; a Judge of the High Court of Justice, Family Division, 1991–2002; *b* 6 Aug. 1939; *s* of late Lorraine Connell and Joan Connell; *m* 1965, Anne Joan Pulham; three *s* one *d*. *Educ:* Harrow; Brasenose Coll., Oxford (MA Jurisprudence). Called to the Bar, Inner Temple, 1962, Bencher, 1988; QC 1981; a Recorder, 1980–91. Governor, Harrow Sch., 1983–2002 (Chm., 1997–2002). Mem., 1988–, Dep. Sen. Steward, 2004–08, Jockey Club; Dir, Horseracing Regulatory Authy, 2006–07; Mem. Regulatory Cttee, British Horseracing Authy, 2007–. *Recreations:* steeplechasing, cricket, foxhunting. *Clubs:* Garrick, Buck's; MCC. *Died 30 Jan. 2013.*

CONQUEST, (George) Robert (Acworth), CMG 1996; OBE 1955; writer; *b* Malvern, Worcs, 15 July 1917; *s* of late Robert Folger Westcott Conquest and Rosamund, *d* of H. A. Acworth, CIE; *m* 1st, 1942, Joan Watkins (marr. diss. 1948); two *s*; 2nd, 1948, Tatiana Mihailova (marr. diss. 1962); 3rd, 1964, Caroleen Macfarlane (marr. diss. 1978); 4th, 1979, Elizabeth, *d* of late Col Richard D. Neece, USAF. *Educ:* Winchester; Magdalen Coll., Oxford. MA Oxon 1972; DLitt 1975. Oxf. and Bucks LI, 1939–46; Foreign Service, 1946–56; Fellow, LSE, 1956–58; Vis. Poet, Univ. of Buffalo, 1959–60; Literary Editor, The Spectator, 1962–63; Fellow: Columbia Univ., 1964–65; Woodrow Wilson International Center, 1976–77; Hoover Instn, 1977–79 and 1981–; Distinguished Vis. Scholar, Heritage Foundn, 1980–81; Research Associate, Harvard Univ., 1982–83; Adjunct Fellow, Center for Strategic and Internat. Studies, 1983–. Jefferson Lecture in Humanities, 1993. FRSL 1972; Corresp. FBA 1994. Presidential Medal of Freedom (USA), 2005. *Publications:* Poems, 1955; A World of Difference, 1955; (ed) New Lines, 1956; Where Do Marxists Go From Here?, 1958; (ed) Back to Life: poems from behind the Iron Curtain, 1958; Common Sense About Russia, 1960; Power and Policy in the USSR, 1961; Courage of Genius, 1962; Between Mars and Venus, 1962; (ed) New Lines II, 1963; (with Kingsley Amis) The Egyptologists, 1965; Russia after Khrushchev, 1965; The Great Terror, 1968; Arias from a Love Opera, 1969; The Nation Killers, 1970; Lenin, 1972; Kolyma, 1978; The Abomination of Moab, 1979; Present Danger, 1979; Forays, 1979; We and They, 1980; (with Jon Manchip White) What to do when the Russians Come, 1984; Inside Stalin's Secret Police, 1985; The Harvest of Sorrow, 1986; New and Collected Poems, 1988; Tyrants and Typewriters, 1989; Stalin and the Kirov Murder, 1989; The Great Terror Reassessed, 1990; Stalin: breaker of nations, 1991; Demons Don't, 1998; Reflections on a Ravaged Century, 1999; The Dragons of Expectation: reality and delusion in the course of history, 2005; Penultima (poems), 2009. *Address:* 52 Peter Coutts Circle, Stanford, CA 94305–2506, USA. *Club:* Travellers. *Died 3 Aug. 2015.*

CONSTABLE, (Charles) John, DBA; management educator and consultant; Director-General, British Institute of Management, 1985–86; *b* 20 Jan. 1936; *s* of late Charles and Gladys Constable; *m* 1960, Elisabeth Mary Light; three *s* one *d*. *Educ:* Durham Sch.; St John's Coll., Cambridge (MA); Royal Sch. of Mines, Imperial Coll. London (BSc); Harvard Grad. Sch. of Bus. Admin. (DBA). NCB, 1959–60; Wallis & Linnel Ltd, 1960–63; Arthur Young & Co., 1963–64; Lectr and Sen. Lectr, Durham Univ. Business Sch., 1964–71; Prof. of Operations Management, Business Policy, 1971–82, Dir 1982–85, Cranfield Sch. of Management. Chairman: Bright Tech Develts, 1989–98; LTB Ltd, 2001–03; Internetcamerasdirect Ltd, 2001–04; Riversimple LLP, 2007–; non-executive Director: IMS Ltd, 1984–91; Lloyds Abbey Life (formerly Abbey Life), 1987–97; Sage Gp plc, 1996–2005; NMBZ Holdings Ltd, 1997–03. Member: Heavy Electrical EDC, NEDO, 1977–87; N Beds HA, 1987–90; Res. Grants Bd, ESRC, 1989–90. Chm. of Govs, Harpur Trust, 1995–2003 (Governor, 1979–2003); Trustee, Pensions Trust, 1996–2003. *Publications:* (jtly) Group Assessment Programmes, 1966; (jtly) Operations Management Text and Cases, 1976; (jtly) Cases in Strategic Management, 1980; The Making of British Managers (BIM/CBI report), 1987. *Recreations:* golf, family. *Address:* 12 Mount Street, Taunton TA1 3QB. *Died 17 Jan. 2011.*

COOK, Francis; *b* 3 Nov. 1935; *s* of James Cook and Elizabeth May Cook; *m* 1959, Patricia (marr. diss. 1998), *d* of Thomas and Evelyn Lundrigan; one *s* three *d*; *m* Princess Somsangouane Baldinger. *Educ:* Corby School, Sunderland; De La Salle College, Manchester; Institute of Education, Leeds. Schoolmaster, 9½ years; Construction Project Manager with Capper-Neill International. MP (Lab) Stockton N, 1983–2010; contested (Ind) same seat, 2010. Vice-Pres., NATO Parly Assembly, 1998–2010; a Dep. Speaker in Westminster Hall, 1999–2010. *Recreations:* climbing, fell walking, singing, swimming. *Address:* 128 Oxbridge Lane, Stockton-on-Tees TS18 4HW. *Died 11 Jan. 2012.*

COOKE, Rear-Adm. David John, CB 2009; MBE 1989; Clerk and Chief Executive, Christ's Hospital, Horsham, 2009–13; *b* 15 Aug. 1955; *s* of Rear-Adm. Anthony John Cooke, CB, and late Margaret Anne Cooke; *m* 1980, Sarah Jane Keeble; two *s* one *d*. *Educ:* Tonbridge Sch. Entered RN, 1973; specialised in submarines and navigation; served HM Ships: Lowestoft, 1975; Oberon, 1976–80; Warspite, 1980–84; Trafalgar, 1984–86; CO, HMS Onslaught, 1986–88; SWO to Captain Submarine Sea Trng, 1989; Comdr 1989; CNOCS, 1990–91; USS Cincinnati, 1991; CO, HMS Torbay, 1992–94; Navy Plans, MoD, 1994–96; Captain 1995; DOR (Sea), 1996–98; Cdre, Strategic Defence Review Implementation Team, 1999; HCSC 2000; CO, HMS Cumberland, 2000–01; Dir, Equipment Plan, MoD, 2001–04; Rear-Adm., 2004; Dep. Comdr, Strike Force NATO, 2004–06; Comdr (Ops) to C-in-C Fleet, Comdr Allied Submarines N and Rear Admiral Submarines, 2006–09. Younger Brother, Trinity House, 1988. Freeman, City of London, 2008; Liveryman, Shipwrights' Co., 2008. *Recreations:* heritage, military history, maintaining an old house, philately. *Address:* 2 Crescent Road, Alverstoke, Hampshire PO12 2DH. *Died 1 Dec. 2014.*

COOKE, Sir Howard (Felix Hanlan), ON 1991; GCMG 1991; GCVO 1994; CD 1978; Governor-General of Jamaica, 1991–2006; Chancellor, International University of the Caribbean, 2006; *b* 13 Nov. 1915; *s* of David Brown Cooke and Mary Jane Minto; *m* 1939, Ivy Sylvia Lucille Tai; two *s* one *d*. Teacher, Mico Trng Coll., 1936–38; Headmaster, Belle Castle All-Age Sch., 1939–50; Teacher: Port Antonio Upper Sch., 1951; Montego Bay Boys' Sch., 1952–58; Br. Manager, Standard Life Insce Co., 1960–71; Unit Manager, Jamaica Mutual Life Assce Co., 1971–81; Br. Manager, Alico Jamaica, 1982–91. Member: WI Federal Parlt, 1958–62; Senate, 1962–67; House of Representatives, 1967–80; Govt Minister, 1972–80. Sen. Elder, United Church of Jamaica and Grand Cayman; lay pastor and former Chm., Cornwall Council of Churches. Mem., Ancient and Accepted Order of Masons. Special Plaque for Distinguished Service, CPA, 1980. *Recreations:* cricket, football, gardening, reading. *Address:* c/o Office of Governor General, King's House, Hope Road, Kingston 6, Jamaica, WI. *Died 11 July 2014.*

COOKE, Air Vice-Marshal John Nigel Carlyle, CB 1984; OBE 1954; Consultant Physician: Civil Aviation Authority, 1985–2003; King Edward VII Hospital, Midhurst, 1988–93; *b* 16 Jan. 1922; *s* of Air Marshal Sir Cyril Bertram Cooke, KCB, CBE and Phyllis Amelia Elizabeth Cooke; *m* 1958, Elizabeth Helena Murray Johnstone; two *s* one *d*. *Educ:* Felsted Sch.; St Mary's Hosp., Paddington (MD, BS (London)). FRCP, FRCPEd, MRCS, MFOM. House Physician, St Mary's, Paddington, 1945; RAF medical Br., 1945–85; Sen. Registrar, St George's, London, 1956–58; Consultant Physician, RAF, 1958–85; overseas service in Germany, Singapore, Aden; Prof. of Aviation Medicine, 1974–79; Dean of Air Force Medicine, 1979–83; Senior Consultant, RAF, 1983–85. UK Mem., Medical Adv. Bd, European Space Agency, 1978–84; Consultant to CAA, UK, 1972–; Consultant Advr to Sultan of Oman's Air Force, 1985–91. Chairman: Defence Med. Services Postgrad. Council, 1980–82; Ethics Cttee, RAF Inst. of Aviation Medicine, 1987–89; Pres., Assoc. of Aviation Med. Examiners, 1986–94. QHP 1979–85. *Publications:* articles on metabolic and aviation medicine subjects in numerous medical jls. *Recreations:* gliding, fly fishing. *Address:* 4 Lincoln Close, Stoke Mandeville, Bucks HP22 5YS. *Club:* Royal Air Force. *Died 25 April 2011.*

COOMBS, Derek Michael; *b* 12 Aug. 1937; *s* of Clifford and Mary Coombs; *m* 1st, 1959, Patricia O'Toole (marr. diss.); one *s* one *d*; 2nd, 1986, Jennifer Lonsdale; one *s* (and one *s* decd). *Educ:* Rydal Prep. Sch.; Bromsgrove. Dir, Metalrax Gp plc, 1975–2002; Chairman: S & U plc, 1976–2008; Co-Founder, Chm., 1995–2007, Chief Exec., 1999–2007, President, 2007–, Prospect Magazine. Political journalist. MP (C) Yardley, 1970–Feb. 1974. Successfully introduced unsupported Private Member's Bill for relaxation of Earnings Rule, 1972, establishing parly record for a measure of its kind; specialist on economic affairs. Lectured on foreign affairs at Cons. weekend confs. Active pro-European. Governor, Royal Hosp. and Home for Incurables. *Publications:* numerous articles on home, economic and European affairs. *Recreations:* friends, reading, painting. *Address:* Cheyne Row, SW3. *T:* (020) 7352 6709. *Died 30 Dec. 2014.*

COOMBS, Douglas Stafford, PhD; Controller, Books Division, British Council, 1980–83; *b* 23 Aug. 1924; *s* of Alexander John Coombs and Rosina May (*née* Stafford); *m* 1950, Valerie Nyman; one *s* three *d*. *Educ:* Royal Liberty Sch., Romford; University College of Southampton; University College London (BA Hons, PhD). Served Royal Air Force, 1943–47. Lecturer in History, University College of the Gold Coast (subseq. Univ. of Ghana), 1952–60; British Council, 1960–83: Nigeria, 1960–62; Overseas Student Centre, London, 1962–67; Bombay, 1967–73; Representative: Zambia, 1973–76; Yugoslavia, 1976–79; Visiting Fellow, Postgrad. School of Librarianship and Information Science, Univ. of Sheffield, 1979–80. Consultant, Byways and Bridleways Trust, 1984–2011; Chm., Wootton Rivers Village Soc., 1985–88. Election Agent, Devizes CLP, 1996–97. Jt Editor, Rights of Way Law Review, 1998–2001. *Publications:* The Conduct of the Dutch, 1958; The Gold Coast, Britain and The Netherlands, 1963; Spreading the Word: the library work of the British Council, 1988; articles in historical jls. *Recreations:* travel, walking, watching cricket. *Address:* 33 Whiteledges, Ealing, W13 8JB. *T:* (020) 8998 6311. *Died 19 Sept. 2014.*

COOPER, Beryl Phyllis; QC 1977; a Recorder of the Crown Court, 1977–98; Deputy High Court Judge, 1980–98; *b* 24 Nov. 1927; *oc* of late Charles Augustus Cooper and Phyllis Lillie Cooper (*née* Burrows). *Educ:* Surbiton High Sch. (Head Girl, 1945–46); Univ. of Birmingham (BCom 1950; Hon. Sec., Guild of Undergrads, 1949–50). Called to the Bar, Gray's Inn, 1960, Bencher, 1988; barrister, 1960–98; Dep. Circuit Judge, 1972–77. Hosp. Sec., Gray's Inn Rd and Liverpool Rd branches, Royal Free Hosp., 1951–57. Councillor, St Pancras MBC, 1959–62. Formerly: Mem., Homeopathic Hosp. Cttee; Mem., Bd of Visitors, Wandsworth Prison.

Conservative Parly Candidate, Stepney, 1966; Founder Mem., Bow Gp (former Sec. and Council Mem.); Mem. Exec. Cttee, Soc. of Cons. Lawyers, 1981–87. Chm., Justice Report on Fraud Trials, 1985–86. Formerly Member: Cripps Cttee, Women and the Law; Home Office Cttee on Criminal Statistics (Perks Cttee); Member: Housing Corp., 1976–79; Lambeth, Southwark and Lewisham AHA (Teaching), 1980–82; Criminal Injuries Compensation Bd, 1978–98; Review Body for Nursing Staff, Midwives, Health Visitors, and Professions Allied to Medicine, 1983–90; Council of Justice, 1986–96; Family Law Bar Assoc. Cttee, 1986–88. FRHS 1951; FRSA 1992. *Publications:* pamphlets for CPC, Justice, Bow Gp, etc.; articles on social, legal, criminal and local govt matters. *Recreations:* travel, swimming. *Address:* 8d South Cliff Tower, Bolsover Road, Eastbourne, Sussex BN20 7JN. *T:* (01323) 732884. *Clubs:* English-Speaking Union; Devonshire (Eastbourne); Royal Eastbourne Golf. *Died 23 Feb. 2012.*

COOPER, Derek Macdonald, OBE 1997; author, broadcaster and journalist; *b* 25 May 1925; *s* of George Stephen Cooper and Jessie Margaret Macdonald; *m* 1953, Janet Marian Feaster (*d* 2010); one *s* one *d*. *Educ:* Raynes Park Grammar Sch.; Portree High Sch.; University Coll., Cardiff; Wadham Coll., Oxford (MA Hons). Served RN, 1943–47. Joined Radio Malaya as producer, 1950, retired as Controller of Progs, 1960; Producer, Roving Report, ITN, 1960–61; worked widely as presenter, interviewer and writer in both television and radio. Columnist: The Listener; Guardian; Observer magazine; Sunday Standard (House of Fraser Press Award, 1984); Homes & Gardens; Saga magazine; Woman's Journal; Scotland on Sunday. Founder Mem. and first Chm., 1985–88, Pres., 1988–95, Guild of Food Writers. Hon. DLitt Queen Margaret UC, Edinburgh, 1999. Glenfiddich Trophy as Wine and Food Writer, 1973, 1980; Broadcaster of the Year, 1984. *Publications:* The Bad Food Guide, 1967; Skye, 1970, 4th edn 1995; The Beverage Report, 1970; The Gullibility Gap, 1974; Hebridean Connection, 1977, 2nd edn 1991; Guide to the Whiskies of Scotland, 1978; Road to the Isles, 1979 (Scottish Arts Council Award, 1980), 4th edn 2002; (with Dione Pattullo) Enjoying Scotch, 1980; Wine With Food, 1982, 2nd edn 1986; (with Fay Godwin) The Whisky Roads of Scotland, 1982; The Century Companion to Whiskies, 1983; Skye Remembered, 1983, 2nd edn 1993; The World Of Cooking, 1983; The Road to Mingulay, 1985, 2nd edn 1989; The Gunge File, 1986; A Taste of Scotch, 1989; The Little Book of Malt Whiskies, 1992; The Balvenie, 1993; Snail Eggs and Samphire, 2000, 2nd edn 2002. *Address:* c/o 23 Charleville Road, W14 9JJ. *T:* (020) 7386 7476. *Died 18 April 2014.*

COOPER, Emmanuel, OBE 2002; PhD; artist potter; Editor, Ceramic Review, 1997–2010; Art Critic, Tribune, since 1990; *b* 12 Dec. 1938; *s* of Fred Cooper and Kate Elizabeth (*née* Cooke); civil partnership 2006, David Horbury. *Educ:* Dudley Trng Coll.; Bournemouth Coll. of Art; Hornsey Coll. of Art; PhD Middlesex 1996. Art teacher, Downs View Central Sch., 1961–63; asst art master (pt-time), Harrow Sch., 1963–65; art teacher (pt-time), Central Foundn Girls' Sch., Spitalfields, 1965–70; Lectr (pt-time), Hornsey Sch. of Art, 1971–75; Sen. Lectr (pt-time), Middx Poly., later Middx Univ., 1975–96. Vis. Prof. of Ceramics and Glass, RCA, 2000–; Visiting Lecturer: Camberwell Sch. of Art, 1976–80; Goldsmiths' Coll., 1995–. Co-Ed. and publisher, Ceramic Rev., 1970–97; Series Ed., The Complete Potter, 1985–95. External Assessor: Glasgow Sch. of Art, 1988–92; Buckingham Coll. of Higher Educn, 1990–94; Cardiff Sch. of Art, UWIC, 1992–96; Bath Spa UC, 1997–2002; Univ. of Westminster, 2005–. Numerous one-man exhibns in UK and Germany; work in mixed exhibns and in public collections in UK and USA. Arts Council England (formerly Arts Council of England): Mem., 2000–02; Mem., London Regl Council, 2002–08. Fellow: Craft Potters' Assoc.; Soc. of Designer Craftsmen; FRSA 1998. Mem., Internat. Acad. Ceramics, 2006. Trustee, Craft Potters Charitable Trust, 1995–. Writers' Guild Award, 1997; Crafts Council Award, 1997; Silver Medal, Soc. of Designer Craftsmen, 2002. Hon. MA, Surrey Inst. of Art and Design UC, 2003. *Publications:* Handbook of Pottery, 1970; History of Pottery, 1972; (with E. Lewenstein) Potters, 1972, 8th edn 1989; (with E. Lewenstein) New Ceramics, 1974; Taking Up Pottery, 1974; Pottery, 1976; Ceramic Review Book of Glaze Recipes, 1977, 7th edn 1995; (with D. Royle) Glazes for the Studio Potter, 1978; World History of Pottery, 1982; Electric Kiln Pottery, 1982; Baron Von Gloeden: photographer (monograph), 1982; Interiors: paintings by Cornelius McCarthy, 1984; The Sexual Perspective: homosexuality and art in the last 100 years in the West, 1986, 2nd edn 1994; Cooper's Book of Glaze Recipes, 1987; The Life and Work of Henry Scott Tuke, 1987; Machinations: photographs by Arthur Tress, 1989; Fully Exposed: the male nude in photography, 1990, 2nd edn 1995; People's Art: working class art from 1750 to the present day, 1994; Ten Thousand Years of Pottery, 2000; (ed) Lucie Rie, 2002; David Leach, 2003; Bernard Leach, Life and Work, 2003; Male Bodies: male nude in photography, 2004; Janet Leach: a potter's life, 2006; Contemporary Ceramics: international trends, 2009; contribs to numerous books and catalogues; *posthumous publication:* Lucie Rie: modernist potter, 2012. *Recreations:* theatre, fine craft, the South coast, modern dance. *Address:* 38 Chalcot Road, NW1 8LP. *T:* (020) 7722 9090. *E:* emmanuelcooper@lineone.net. *Died 21 Jan. 2012.*

COOPER, George Alfred; marketing and business consultant; Chairman, Independent Television Publications Ltd, 1971–89; *b* 9 Oct. 1915; *s* of late Joseph Cooper; *m* 1944, Irene Burns; one *d*. Exec. with internat. publishing gp; served War of 1939–45, Royal Artillery (Captain); Exec., Hulton Press, 1949–55; Director: ABC Television Ltd, 1955–77; Thames Television Ltd, 1968 (Man. Dir, 1974–77); Independent Television News, 1976–77; Chm., Network Programme Cttee of Independent Television, 1975–77. FRTS 1987. *Address:* 43 Rivermill, 151 Grosvenor Road, SW1V 3JN. *T:* (020) 7821 9305. *Club:* Royal Automobile. *Died 21 April 2015.*

COOPER, Sir Henry, Kt 2000; OBE 1969; professional boxer, 1954–71; *b* 3 May 1934; *s* of late Henry William Cooper and Lily Nutkins; *m* 1960, Albina Genepri (*d* 2008); two *s*. *Educ:* Athelney Street Sch., Bellingham. Presenter, Be Your Own Boss (series), Channel 4, 1983. KSG 1978. *Film:* Royal Flash, 1975. *Publications:* Henry Cooper: an autobiography, 1972; The Great Heavyweights, 1978; Henry Cooper's Book of Boxing, 1982; Henry Cooper's 100 Greatest Boxers, 1990. *Recreation:* golf. *Address:* 15 Barley House, Hildenbrook Farm, Riding Lane, Hildenborough, Kent TN11 9JN. *Died 1 May 2011.*

COOPER, Prof. John Philip, CBE 1983; DSc; FRS 1977; FSB; Emeritus Professor of Agricultural Botany, University of Wales, 1984; *b* Buxton, Derbyshire, 16 Dec. 1923; *o s* of Frank Edward and Nora Goodwin Cooper; *m* 1951, Christine Mary Palmer; one *s* three *d*. *Educ:* Stockport Grammar Sch.; Univ. of Reading (BSc 1945, PhD 1953, DSc 1964); FitzWilliam House, Cambridge (DipAgrSc 1946). Scientific Officer, Welsh Plant Breeding Station, 1946–50; Lectr, Univ. of Reading, 1950–54; Welsh Plant Breeding Station, University College of Wales, Aberystwyth: Plant Geneticist, 1950–59; Head, Dept of Develtl Genetics, 1959–75; Dir, and Prof. of Agricl Botany, 1975–83. Consultant, FAO Headquarters, Rome, 1956; Nuffield Royal Society Bursary, CSIRO, Canberra, 1962; Visiting Professor: Univ. of Kentucky, 1965; Univ. of Khartoum, 1975; Univ. of Reading, 1984–89; Hon. Fellow, BBSRC (formerly AFRC) Inst. for Grassland and Envmtl Res., 1992–. Member: UK Seeds Exec., 1979–86; Internat. Bd for Plant Genetics Resources, 1981–86. *Publications:* (ed with P. F. Wareing) Potential Crop Production, 1971; (ed) Photosynthesis and Productivity in Different Environments, 1975; various papers on crop physiology and genetics in sci. jls. *Recreation:* gentle gardening. *Address:* The Steppes Residential Care Home, Cossack Square, Nailsworth GL6 0DB. *T:* (01453) 833375. *Died 18 Nov. 2011.*

COOPER, Margaret Jean Drummond, OBE 1980; Chief Education Officer, General Nursing Council for England and Wales, 1974–82; *b* 24 March 1922; *d* of Canon Bernard R. Cooper and A. Jean Cooper (*née* Drackley). *Educ:* School of St Mary and St Anne, Abbots Bromley; Royal College of Nursing; Open Univ. (BA 1987). SRN, SCM, RNT. Nursing trng and early posts, Leicester Royal Infirmary, 1941–45; Midwifery trng, General Lying-in

Hosp., SW1 and Coventry and Warwicks Hosp.; Nurse Tutor, Middlesex Hosp., 1953–55; Principal Tutor: General Hosp., Northampton, 1956–63; Addenbrooke's Hosp., Cambridge, 1963–68; Principal, Queen Elizabeth Sch. of Nursing, Birmingham, 1968–74. Chm., General Nursing Council for England and Wales, 1971–74 (Mem., 1965–74). *Recreations:* birds, books, buildings. *Address:* Howard House, 8 Vicarage Way, Gerrards Cross, Bucks SL9 8AT. *Died 15 Sept. 2013.*

COOPER, Ronald Cecil Macleod, CB 1981; Deputy Secretary, Department of Transport, 1986–90; *b* 8 May 1931; *s* of Cecil Redvers Cooper and Norah Agnes Louise Cooper (*née* Macleod); *m* 1st, 1953, June Bicknell (marr. diss. 1967); 2nd, 1967, Christine Savage; one *s* two *d. Educ:* Royal Grammar Sch., Newcastle upon Tyne; St Edmund Hall, Oxford (MA). Asst Principal, Min. of Supply, 1954–59; Principal, Min. of Aviation, 1959–62; on loan to European Launcher Develt Org., Paris, 1962–67; Asst Sec., Min. of Technology, 1968–70, DTI, 1970–73; Under Sec., Dept of Trade, 1973–78; Sec., Price Commn, 1979; Dep. Sec. and Principal Estabt and Finance Officer, DTI, 1979–85. *Recreations:* music, reading. *Address:* 18 Rignall Road, Great Missenden, Bucks HP16 9AN. *Died 2 Aug. 2014.*

COPLEY, His Honour Peter Edward; a Circuit Judge, 1995–2013; *b* 15 Feb. 1943; *s* of Edward Thomas Copley and Florence Hilda Copley; *m* 1st; one *s* one *d*; 2nd, 1986, Janice Patricia Webster; one *d. Educ:* College of Law. Qualified Solicitor, 1966; Asst Recorder, 1989–93; Recorder, 1993–95. Part-time Legal Mem., Immigration Appeals Tribunal, 1998. *Recreation:* sailing. *Address:* c/o Circuit Administrator, 2nd Floor, Rose Court, 2 Southwark Bridge, SE1 9HS. *Died 8 Aug. 2013.*

COPPOCK, Surgeon Rear-Adm. (D) David Arthur, CB 1990; Director, Defence Dental Services, 1988–90; *b* 19 April 1931; *s* of Oswald John Coppock and Ada Katherine Beaven; *m* 1st, 1956, Maria Averil Ferreira (*d* 1985); two *d*; 2nd, 1990, Sally Annette Arnold. *Educ:* Bishop Wordsworth School; Guy's Hosp. (BDS); George Washington Univ. (MSc). Entered RN 1955; HM Ships Eagle, 1956, Tamar, Hong Kong, 1959, Hermes, 1963, Rooke, Gibraltar, 1965; US Navy exchange, 1972; Dep. Dir, Naval Dental Services, 1980; Comd Dental Surgeon to C-in-C Naval Home Command, 1983; Dir, Naval Dental Services, 1985–88. QHDS, 1983–90. Mem., Assoc. of Professional Game Angling Instructors, 1991–. OStJ 1983. *Recreation:* fishing. *Address:* 12 Fitzhamon House, Idsworth Down, Petersfield, Hants GU31 4EB. *T:* (01730) 710618. *Died 1 Dec. 2014.*

CORBETT OF CASTLE VALE, Baron *cr* 2001 (Life Peer), of Erdington in the County of West Midlands; **Robin Corbett;** journalist; *b* 22 Dec. 1933; *s* of Thomas Corbett and Marguerite Adele Mainwaring; *m* 1970, Val Hudson; one *d*, and one *s* one *d* from former marriage. *Educ:* Holly Lodge Grammar Sch., Smethwick. Newspaper and magazine journalist, 1950–69; Editorial Staff Develt Exec., IPC Magazines, 1969–72; Sen. Lab. Adviser, IPC Magazines, 1972–74. Mem. Nat. Union of Journalists Nat. Exec. Council, 1965–69. MP (Lab): Hemel Hempstead, Oct. 1974–1979; Birmingham, Erdington, 1983–2001. Opposition front bench spokesman on home affairs, 1985–92, on broadcasting, the media and nat. heritage, 1992–94, on disabled people's rights, 1994–95. Member of Select Committee: on Agriculture, 1996–97; on Home Affairs, 1997–2001 (Chm., 1999–2001); on Communications, 2006–; Member: Expenditure Cttee, 1976–79; Commons Home Affairs Cttee, 1984–86; Vice Chm., All Party Animal Welfare Gp, 1976–79; Jt Vice-Chm., All Party Motor Gp, 1987–; Treas., All Party Anzac Gp, 1992– (Chm., 1997–2001; Jt Sec., 1985); Chm., All Party MS Gp, 1997–2001; Vice-Chm., Indo-British Parly Gp, 1997–2001; Chairman: PLP Agric. Gp, 1977–78; PLP Home Affairs Cttee, 1984–86; Sec., PLP Civil Liberties Gp, 1974–79; Mem., PLP Campaign Unit, 1985–86. Mem., Sub-cttee F, EU Select Cttee, H of L, 2002–07. Chm., Lab Peers Gp, 2005–. Chm., Friends of Cyprus, 2001– (Jt Vice-Chm., 1987). Mem., Food and Agriculture Sub-Cttee, Labour Party Nat. Exec. Cttee, 1974–79; Chm., farm animal welfare co-ordinating exec., 1977–92. Member, Council: RCVS, 1989–92; SCF, 1987–90; Mem. Bd, Rehab UK, 1996–; sponsor, Terrence Higgins Trust, 1987–99. Mem., Wilton Park Acad. Council, 1995–2006. Chm., Mgt Bd, Castle Vale HAT, 2002–04, Partnership Bd, Castle Vale Neighbourhood, 2004–. Pres., Josiah Mason Sixth Form Coll., Erdington, 2002–. Fellow, 1979, Trustee, 2010, Industry and Parlt Trust. Hon. Vice-Pres., Birchfield Harriers, 2009. *Publications:* (jtly) Can I Count on your Support?, 1986; On the Campaign Trail, 1987. *Recreations:* walking, reading, pottering. *Address:* House of Lords, SW1A 0PW. *Clubs:* Castle Vale Residents Association; Forget-Me-Not (Erdington). *Died 19 Feb. 2012.*

CORBETT, Captain Hugh Askew, CBE 1968; DSO 1945; DSC 1943; RN (retired); Warden of the University Centre, University of Cambridge, 1967–83; *b* 25 June 1916; *s* of late Rev. F. St John Corbett, MA, FRSL, FRHistS and Elsie L. V. (*née* Askew); *m* 1945, Patricia Nancy, *d* of late Thomas Patrick Spens, OBE, MC, LLD; three *s. Educ:* St Edmund's Sch., Canterbury. Joined Royal Navy, 1933; HMS Cæsar as Capt. (D), 8th Destroyer Sqdn, 1961–63; HMS Fearless, 1965–67 (Capt.). *Address:* Holly Cottage, 3 Clare Road, Cambridge CB3 9HN. *T:* (01223) 357735. *Died 19 April 2012.*

CORDINER, William Lawson, OBE 1995; HM Diplomatic Service, retired; High Commissioner, Kingdom of Tonga, and Consul for Pacific Islands under American sovereignty South of the Equator, 1990–94; *b* 9 March 1935; *s* of late Alexander Lamb Cordiner and Jessie Cordiner; *m* 1958, Anne Milton; one *s. Educ:* Peterhead Acad.; Boroughmuir, Edinburgh. Inland Revenue, 1952–60; E African Common Services Orgn, 1960–67; HM Diplomatic Service: London, 1967–68; Saigon, 1968–70; Addis Ababa, 1971–74; Kuwait, 1974–75; Baghdad, 1975–77; on secondment to Export Div., DHSS, 1977–79; Rhodesia Dept, FCO, 1979–80; Govt Rep., Antigua and Barbuda, and St Kitts Nevis, 1980–83; Consul for Pacific NW of USA, Seattle, 1983–87; Asst, Commonwealth Co-ordination Dept, FCO, 1988–90. British Delegn Sec., Commonwealth Heads of Govt Meeting, Kuala Lumpur, 1989. Hon. Citizen of Washington State, 1987; Hon. Ambassador of Goodwill, Washington State, 1987. *Publications:* Diplomatic Wanderings: from Saigon to the South Seas, 2003. *Recreations:* golf, gardening, writing, oil painting, travel, music. *Address:* L'Ancien Chai, 24240 Saussignac, France. *T:* and *Fax:* (33) 553272383. *E:* bill.cordiner@wanadoo.fr. *Clubs:* St Francis Bay Golf (South Africa); Château des Vigiers (Monestier, France). *Died 21 June 2012.*

CORDINGLEY, Maj.-Gen. John Edward, OBE 1959; *b* 1 Sept. 1916; *s* of Air Vice-Marshal Sir John Cordingley, KCB, KCVO, CBE, and late Elizabeth Ruth Carpenter; *m* 1st, 1940, Ruth Pamela (marr. diss. 1961; she *d* 2007), *d* of late Major S. A. Boddam-Whetham; two *s*; 2nd, 1961, Audrey Helen Anne (*d* 2009), *d* of late Maj-Gen. F. G. Beaumont-Nesbitt, CVO, CBE, MC; two step *d. Educ:* Sherborne; RMA, Woolwich. 2nd Lieut RA, 1936; served War of 1939–45, Europe and India. Brigade Comdr, 1961–62; Imperial Defence Coll., 1963; Dir of Work Study, Min. of Defence (Army), 1964–66; Dep. Dir, RA, 1967–68; Maj.-Gen., RA, BAOR, 1968–71. Controller, Royal Artillery Instn, 1975–82; Chm. Bd of Management, RA Charitable Fund, 1977–82. Col Comdt, RA, 1973–82. Bursar, Sherborne Sch., 1971–74; Chm., J. W. Carpenter Ltd, 1984–87. Fellow, Inst. of Work Study Practitioners, 1965; MCMI (MBIM 1966); FInstD 1985. *Recreation:* golf and gardening. *Address:* 15 High Street, Ramsbury, Marlborough, Wilts SN8 2PA. *T:* (01672) 520056. *Clubs:* Army and Navy; Senior Golfers. *Died 14 Oct. 2011.*

CORNER, Frank Henry, CMG 1980; Permanent Secretary of Foreign Affairs, New Zealand, 1973–80; *b* 17 May 1920; *y s* of Charles William Corner, Napier, NZ, and Sybil Corner (*née* Smith); *m* 1943, Lynette Robinson; two *d. Educ:* Napier Boys' High Sch.; Victoria Univ. of Wellington. MA, 1st cl. History; James Macintosh and Post-graduate Scholar. External Affairs Dept, NZ, and War Cabinet Secretariat, 1943; 1st Sec., NZ Embassy, Washington, 1948–51; Sen. Counsellor, NZ High Commn, London, 1952–58; Dep. Sec. NZ Dept of External Affairs, 1958–62; Perm. Rep. (Ambassador) to

UN, 1962–67; Ambassador of NZ to USA, 1967–72; Permanent Head of Prime Minister's Dept, 1973–75; Administrator of Tokelau, 1976–85. Chm., NZ Defence Cttee of Enquiry, 1985–86. Mem., NZ Delegn to Commonwealth Prime Ministers' Meetings, 1944, 1946, 1951–57, 1973, 1975, 1977, 1979; Deleg. to UN Gen. Assembly, 1949–52, 1955, 1960–68, 1973, 1974; NZ Rep. on UN Trusteeship Council, 1962–66 (Pres., 1965–66; Chm., UN Vis. Mission to Micronesia, 1964); NZ Rep. on UN Security Council, 1966; Adviser, NZ Delegn: Paris Peace Conf., 1946; Geneva Conf. on Korea, 1954; numerous other internat. confs as adviser or delegate. Mem., Bd of NZ-US Educnl Foundn, 1980–88 (Chm., 1983–88); Patron, Assoc. of NZ Art Socs, 1973–88; Mem. Council, Victoria Univ. of Wellington, 1981–87. FRSA. Hon. LLD Victoria Univ. of Wellington, 2005. *Publications:* contrib. to: New Zealand's External Relations, 1962; The Feel of Truth, 1969; An Eye, an Ear and a Voice, 1993; Unofficial Channels, 1999; Three Labour Leaders, 2001; Celebrating New Zealand's Emergence, 2005. *Address:* 26 Burnell Avenue, Wellington 6011, New Zealand. *T:* (4) 4737022; 29 Kakariki Grove, Waikanae 5036, New Zealand. *T:* (4) 2936235. *Died 27 Aug. 2014.*

CORNFORD, James Peters; *b* 25 Jan. 1935; *s* of John Cornford and Rachel Peters; *m* 1960, Avery Amanda Goodfellow; one *s* three *d*. *Educ:* Winchester Coll.; Trinity Coll., Cambridge (MA). Fellow, Trinity Coll., Cambridge, 1960–64; Harkness Fellow, 1961–62; Univ. of Edinburgh: Lectr in Politics, 1964–68; Prof. of Politics, 1968–76; Dir, Outer Circle Policy Unit, 1976–80; Director: Nuffield Foundn, 1980–88; Inst. for Public Policy Res., 1989–94; Paul Hamlyn Foundn, 1994–97; Special Adviser to Chancellor of Duchy of Lancaster, 1997–98; Dep. Dir, Inst. of Community Studies, 1998–2000. Chm., Constitution Unit, UCL, 1995–97. Vis. Fellow, All Souls Coll., Oxford, 1975–76; Vis. Prof., Birkbeck Coll., Univ. of London, 1977–80. Mem., Cttee of Inquiry into Educn of Children from Ethnic Minority Gps (DES), 1981–85. Dir, 1979–97, Chm., 1999–2002, Job Ownership Ltd. Mem. Bd, Co-op. Develt Agency, 1987–90. Chairman of Council: RIPA, 1984–85; Campaign for Freedom of Information, 1984–97, 1998–. Chm. of Trustees, Southern African Advanced Educn Project, 1990–99; Trustee: Elm Farm Res. Centre, 1997–2005; Dartington Hall Trust, 1998– (Chm., 2002–07); Sch. for Social Entrepreneurs, 2000– (Chm., 2000); Foundn for Social Entrepreneurs, 2001–05; Inst. of Community Studies, 2001–05; The Young Foundn, 2005–. Chm., The Political Quarterly, 1993–99 (Lit. Ed., 1976–93). *Publications:* contribs to books and jls. *Address:* Osborne House, High Street, Stoke Ferry, King's Lynn, Norfolk PE33 9SF. *T:* (01366) 500808. *Died 26 Sept. 2011.*

CORNFORTH, Sir John (Warcup), AC 1991; Kt 1977; CBE 1972; DPhil; FRS 1953; Royal Society Research Professor, University of Sussex, 1975–82, then Emeritus; *b* 7 Sept. 1917; *er s* of J. W. Cornforth, Sydney, Aust.; *m* 1941, Rita (*d* 2012), *d* of W. C. Harradence; one *s* two *d*. *Educ:* Sydney High Sch.; Univ. of Sydney (BSc 1937; MSc 1938); 1851 Exhibition Overseas Scholarship, 1939–42; Univ. of Oxford (DPhil 1941). Scientific staff of MRC, 1946–62; Dir, Shell Research, Milstead Lab. of Chem. Enzymology, 1962–75. Assoc. Prof. in Molecular Sciences, Univ. of Warwick, 1965–71; Vis. Prof., Univ. of Sussex, 1971–75; Hon. Prof., Beijing Med. Univ., 1986–. Lectures: Pedler, Chem. Soc., 1968–69; Max Tishler, Harvard Univ., 1970; Robert Robinson, Chem. Soc., 1971–72; Sandin, Univ. of Alberta, 1977. For. Hon. Mem., Amer. Acad., 1973; Corresp. Mem., Aust. Acad., 1977; For. Associate, US Nat. Acad. of Scis, 1978; For. Mem., Royal Netherlands Acad. of Scis, 1978. Hon. Fellow, St Catherine's Coll., Oxford, 1976; Hon. DSc: ETH Zürich, 1975; Oxford, Warwick, Dublin, Liverpool, 1976; Aberdeen, Hull, Sussex, Sydney, 1977; Kent, 1995. Corday-Morgan Medal and Prize, Chem. Soc., 1953; (with G. J. Popjak) CIBA Medal, Biochem. Soc., 1965; Flintoff Medal, Chem. Soc., 1966; Stouffer Prize, 1967; Ernest Guenther Award, Amer. Chem. Soc., 1969; (with G. J. Popjak) Davy Medal, Royal Soc., 1968; Prix Roussel, 1972; (jtly) Nobel Prize for Chemistry, 1975; Royal Medal, Royal Soc., 1976; Copley Medal, Royal Soc., 1982. Deaf since boyhood. *Publications:* numerous papers on organic chemical and biochemical subjects. *Recreations:* chess, gardening. *Died 8 Dec. 2013.*

CORREA, Charles Mark; Padma Vibhushan, 2006 (Padma Shri, 1972); architect and planner; *b* 1 Sept. 1930; *s* of Carlos M. Correa and Ana Florinda de Heredia; *m* 1961, Monika Sequeira; one *s* one *d*. *Educ:* Univ. of Michigan (BArch); MIT (MArch). Private practice, Bombay, 1958–; work includes: Mahatma Gandhi Memorial, Sabarmati Ashram; State Assembly for Madhya Pradesh; low cost housing projects in Delhi, Bombay, Ahmedabad and other cities in India; Jawahar Kala Kendra, Jaipur; Nat. Crafts Mus., and British Council HQ, Delhi; Brain and Cognitive Scis Center, MIT; Champalimaud Centre for the Unknown, Lisbon; Chief Architect for planning of New Bombay. Jawaharlal Nehru Vis. Prof. and Fellow of Churchill Coll., Cambridge, 1985–86. Chm., Nat. Commn on Urbanisation, 1985–88. Founder Mem., Steering Cttee, Aga Khan Award for Architecture, 1977–86; Jury Mem., Pritzker Prize, 1993–98. Hon. Vis. Prof., Tonji Univ., Shanghai. Member: French Acad., 1985; Internat. Acad. of Architects, Bulgaria, 1987; Finnish Assoc. of Architects, 1992; Foreign Hon. Mem., Amer. Acad. of Arts and Scis, 1993; Hon. MRIAI, 1997; Amer. Acad. of Arts and Letters, 1998. Hon. Fellow: United Architects of Philippines, 1990; RIBA 1993. Hon. FAIA 1979. Hon. Dr Michigan, 1980. Royal Gold Medal for Architecture, RIBA, 1984; Gold Medal, Indian Inst. of Architects, 1987; Gold Medal, IUA, 1990; Praemium Imperiale Prize, Japan Art Assoc., 1994; Aga Khan Award for Architecture, 1998; Charles Jencks Award, RIBA, 2009; Gomant Vibhushan Award, Govt of Goa, 2011. *Publications:* The New Landscape, 1984; Housing and Urbanisation, 1999; A Place in the Shade, 2010; The Champalimaud Centre & Other Works, 2013; *relevant publications:* S. Cantacuzino, Charles Correa, 1984; Kenneth Frampton, Charles Correa, 1996. *Recreations:* tennis, model trains, chess, films. *Address:* Sonmarg, Nepean Sea Road, Mumbai 400.006, India. *T:* (22) 23633306. *Clubs:* Bombay Gymkhana, Willingdon Sports, Royal Bombay Yacht (Bombay). *Died 16 June 2015.*

CORSAR, Col Charles Herbert Kenneth, LVO 1989; OBE 1981; TD 1960; Vice Lord-Lieutenant, Lothian Region (District of Midlothian), 1993–97; *b* 13 May 1926; *s* of Kenneth Charles Corsar and Winifred Paton (*née* Herdman); *m* 1953, Mary Drummond Buchanan Smith (Hon. Dame Mary Corsar, DBE); two *s* two *d* (and one *d* decd). *Educ:* Merchiston Castle Sch.; King's Coll., Cambridge (MA). Farmer, 1953–89. Commnd Royal Scots TA, 1948; comd 8/9 Royal Scots, 1964–67; Edinburgh and Heriot-Watt Univs OTC, 1967–72; TA Col, 1972–75; Hon. ADC to the Queen, 1977–81; Chm., Lowland TAVRA, 1984–87; Hon. Col, 1/52 Lowland Vols, 1975–87. Zone Comr, Home Defence, E of Scotland, 1972–74. County Cllr, Midlothian, 1958–67. Vice-Pres., Boys' Brigade, 1970–91; Chairman: Scottish Standing Conf. of Voluntary Youth Orgns, 1973–78; Earl Haig Fund (Scotland), 1984–90; Mem., Scottish Sports Council, 1972–75; Secretary: Prince's Trust (Lothian & Borders), 1982–93; (for Scotland) Duke of Edinburgh's Award, 1966–87. JP Midlothian, 1964; DL Midlothian, 1975. *Recreation:* gardening. *Address:* Flat 4, 85 South Oswald Road, Edinburgh EH9 2HH. *T:* (0131) 662 0194. *Club:* New (Edinburgh). *Died 9 April 2012.*

CORSAR, Kenneth; Chairman, Lanarkshire NHS Board, since 2006 (non-executive Director, 2003–06); *b* 16 July 1946; *s* of Peter and Ruby Corsar; *m* 1972, Mary Massie; two *s*. *Educ:* Alloa Acad.; St Andrews Univ. (MA Hons 1968); Aberdeen Univ. (DipEd 1970); Aberdeen Coll. of Education (PGCE 1970); Glasgow Univ. (MEd Hons 1976). Teacher of Classics, Dumbarton Acad., 1970–71; Principal Teacher: Kirkintilloch High Sch., 1971–72; Uddingston Grammar Sch., 1972–75; Strathclyde Regional Council: Educn Officer, 1975–86; Sen. Educn Officer, 1986–88; Divl Educn Officer, 1988–93; Depute Dir of Educn, 1993–95; Dir of Educn, Glasgow CC, 1995–2002; Scottish Dir, Nat. Deaf Children's Soc., 2003–06. Advr, Scottish Exec. Educn Dept/COSLA, 2003. Vice-Pres., 1992–93, Pres., 1993–94, Assoc. of Dirs of Educn in Scotland. DUniv Glasgow, 2001. *Publications:* Discovering the Greeks, 1975; Discovering Greek Mythology, 1977;

articles in educn press on educn and local govt. *Recreations:* golf, calligraphy, gardening. *Address:* 9 Eaglesfield Crescent, Strathaven, S Lanarks ML10 6HY. *T:* (01357) 520817. *Club:* Strathaven Golf. *Died 7 May 2012.*

COSTANZI, Edwin J. B.; *see* Borg Costanzi.

COSTELLO, Declan; President, High Court of the Republic of Ireland, 1995–98; *b* 1 Aug. 1926; *s* of John A. Costello and Ida (*née* O'Malley); *m* 1953, Joan Fitzsimms; three *s* two *d. Educ:* Xavier Sch., Dublin; University Coll., Dublin. King's Inns, Dublin; Called to the Bar, 1948; Inner Bar, 1965. TD (FG): Dublin NW, 1951–69; Dublin SW, 1973–77; Attorney-Gen., 1973–77; Judge of the High Court, 1977–95. Mem., Consultative Assembly, Council of Europe, 1957–63. Chairman: Nat. Youth Policy Cttee, Ireland, 1983; Cttee on Fund-raising for Charitable Purposes, Ireland, 1989. *Recreations:* tennis, reading, film-going. *Address:* 8 Eglinton Park, Dublin 4, Republic of Ireland. *T:* (1) 2697963. *Clubs:* St Stephen's Green (Dublin); Fitzwilliam Lawn Tennis (Dublin). *Died 6 June 2011.*

COSTELOE, Prof. Michael Peter, PhD; FRHistS; Professor of Hispanic and Latin American Studies, University of Bristol, 1981–98, then Emeritus; *b* 12 March 1939; *s* of late John Myles Costeloe and of Etheleen Winifred Costeloe, Bishop Auckland; *m* 1962, Eleanor, *d* of late William and Margaret Bonney; one *d. Educ:* King James I Grammar Sch., Bishop Auckland; Univ. of Durham (BA 1961); Univ. of Newcastle (DipEd 1962; PhD 1965). FRHistS 1976. University of Bristol: Asst Lectr and Lectr in Latin American Studies, 1965–76; Reader, 1976–81; Dean of Arts, 1993–96. Vis. Prof., Univ. of Texas, 1967. Corresp. Fellow, Acad. Mexicana de la Historia, 1995. *Publications:* Church Wealth in Mexico, 1967; (ed and trans.) Alienation of Church Wealth in Mexico, by J. Bazant, 1971; (with C. Steele) Independent Mexico, 1973; La primera república federal de Mexico, 1975; Mexico State Papers, 1976; Response to Revolution: Imperial Spain and the Spanish American Revolutions, 1986; The Central Republic in Mexico 1835–1846, 1993; Bonds and Bondholders: British investors and Mexico's foreign debt 1824–1888, 2003; William Bullock - Connoisseur and Virtuoso of the Egyptian Hall: Piccadilly to Mexico (1773–1849), 2008. *Recreations:* Anthony Trollope, golf. *Address:* Department of Hispanic Studies, University of Bristol, 15 Woodland Road, Bristol BS8 1TE. *Club:* Henbury Golf. *Died 24 Aug. 2011.*

COTILL, John Atrill T.; *see* Templeton-Cotill.

COTRAN, His Honour Eugene, LLD; a Circuit Judge, 1992–2007; *b* Jerusalem, Palestine, 6 Aug. 1938; *s* of Michael Cotran and Hassiba (*née* Khoury); *m* 1963, Christiane Avierino; three *s* one *d. Educ:* Victoria Coll., Alexandria, Egypt; Univ. of Leeds (LLB, LLM 1958); Trinity Hall, Univ. of Cambridge (Dip. Internat. Law 1959); LLD London, 1971. FCIArb. Called to the Bar, Lincoln's Inn, 1959. Res. Officer in African Law, SOAS, Univ. of London, 1960–63, Lectr, 1963–77; practised at the Bar, 1963–92; Law Comr, Kenya, 1967–68; High Court Judge, Kenya, 1977–82; a Recorder, 1989–92. Mem., 5 Bell Yard Chambers. Vis. Prof. of Law and Chm., Centre for Islamic and ME Law, SOAS, 1987–. Internat. and Chartered Arbitrator, Internat. Court of Arbitration, Paris and London, 1985–92; Legal Mem., Immigration Appeal Tribunal, 1997–2003. Consultant: on laws of the Middle East; to Civil and Commercial Ct, Qatar. Vice Pres., Med. Aid for Palestinians, 1996–; Mem. Bd, Palestinian Ind. Commn for Citizens Rights, 1994–. Gen. Editor, Yearbook of Islamic and Middle Eastern Law, 1994–; Jt Editor, CIMEL Book Series, 1994–. *Publications:* Restatement of African Law, Kenya: Vol. I, Marriage and Divorce, Vol. II, Succession, 1968; Casebook on Kenya Customary Law, 1987; Butterworth's Immigration Law Service, 1991; edited jointly: The Role of the Judiciary in the Protection of Human Rights, 1997; Democracy, the Rule of Law and Islam, 1999; The Palestinian Exodus 1948–1998, 1999; The Rule of Law in the Middle East and the Islamic World: human rights and the judicial process, 2000; articles in internat. law jls and African law jls. *Recreations:* horse-racing, swimming, bridge. *Address:* 32 Gloucester Road, Acton, W3 8PD. *T:* (020) 8992 0432, *Fax:* (020) 8992 7228. *Died 7 June 2014.*

COTTELL, Michael Norman Tizard, OBE 1988; FREng; FICE, FCIHT; Chairman and Executive Director, Aspen Consultancy Group, 1996–2001; President, Institution of Civil Engineers, 1992–93; *b* 25 July 1931; *s* of late Norman James Cottell and Eileen Clare Cottell (*née* Tizard); *m* 1957, Joan Florence Dolton (*d* 2011); two *s. Educ:* Peter Symonds Sch., Winchester; University Coll., Southampton. CEng, FREng (FEng 1990); FCIHT (FIHT 1954); MICE 1958, FICE 1976. Trainee Civil Engr, Hants CC, 1949–51; Nat. Service, RE, Malaya and Suez, 1951–53, 1956; Engineering Assistant: Glos CC, 1954–57; Northants CC, 1957–58; Resident Engr, Oxford Western Bypass, 1958–61; Project Engr, M4 Motorway, Glos, 1961–67; Asst County Surveyor, Suffolk CC, 1967–73; Dep. County Surveyor, E Sussex CC, 1973–76; County Surveyor: Northants CC, 1976–84; Kent CC, 1984–91. Exec. Consultant, Travers Morgan, 1991–95. Trustee: Rees Jeffries Road Fund, 1991–; ICE Pensions Funds, 1995–. Lt-Col, RE & Logistics Staff Corps (TA), 1992–. MCMI 1971. *Recreations:* golf, swimming, walking, theatre, jazz, travel, viewing historic buildings, as a spectator keen on most sports. *Address:* Salcey Lawn, Harrow Court, Stockbury, Kent ME9 7UQ. *Clubs:* Athenæum, Royal Automobile. *Died 10 Feb. 2014.*

COTTRELL, Sir Alan (Howard), Kt 1971; FRS 1955; FREng; Master of Jesus College, Cambridge, 1974–86 (Hon. Fellow 1986); Vice-Chancellor, University of Cambridge, 1977–79; *b* 17 July 1919; *s* of Albert and Elizabeth Cottrell; *m* 1944, Jean Elizabeth Harber (*d* 1999); one *s. Educ:* Moseley Grammar Sch.; University of Birmingham (BSc 1939; PhD 1942); ScD(Cantab) 1976. Lectr in Metallurgy, University of Birmingham, 1943–49; Prof. of Physical Metallurgy, University of Birmingham, 1949–55; Deputy Head of Metallurgy Division, Atomic Energy Research Establishment, Harwell, Berks, 1955–58; Goldsmiths' Prof. of Metallurgy, Cambridge Univ., 1958–65; Fellow of Christ's Coll., Cambridge, 1958–70, Hon. Fellow, 1970; Dep. Chief Scientific Adviser (Studies), Min. of Defence, 1965–67, Chief Adviser, 1967; Dep. Chief Scientific Advr to HM Govt, 1968–71, Chief Scientific Advr, 1971–74. Part-time Mem., UKAEA, 1962–65, 1983–87; Member: Adv. Council on Scientific Policy, 1963–64; Central Adv. Council for Science and Technology, 1967–; Exec. Cttee, British Council, 1974–87; Adv. Council, Science Policy Foundn, 1976–; Security Commn, 1981–92. Dir, Fisons plc, 1979–90. A Vice-Pres., Royal Society, 1964, 1976, 1977. Foreign Hon. Mem., American Academy of Arts and Sciences, 1960; Foreign Associate: Nat. Acad. of Sciences, USA, 1972; Nat. Acad. of Engrg, USA, 1976; Mem., Academia Europaea, 1991–; Hon. Member: Amer. Soc. for Metals, 1972 (Fellow, 1974); Metals Soc., 1977 (Hon. FIM 1989, Hon. FIMMM); Japan Inst. of Metals, 1981. FIC 1991; FREng (FEng 1979); Fellow, Royal Swedish Acad. of Scis; Hon. Fellow, Internat. Congress on Fracture, 1985–. Hon. DSc: Columbia Univ., 1965; Newcastle Univ., 1967; Liverpool Univ., 1969; Manchester, 1970; Warwick, 1971; Sussex, 1972; Bath, 1973; Strathclyde, 1975; Cranfield, 1975; Aston, 1975; Oxford, 1979; Birmingham, 1983; DUniv Essex, 1982; Hon. DEng Tech. Univ. of Nova Scotia, 1984; Hon. LLD Cantab, 1996. Rosenhain Medallist of the Inst. of Metals; Hughes Medal, 1961, Rumford Medal, 1974, Copley Medal, 1996, Royal Society; Inst. of Metals (Platinum) Medal, 1965; Réaumur Medal, Société Française de Métallurgie, 1964; James Alfred Ewing Medal, ICE, 1967; Holweck Medal, Société Française de Physique, 1969; Albert Sauveur Achievement Award, Amer. Soc. for Metals, 1969; James Douglas Gold Medal, Amer. Inst. of Mining, Metallurgy and Petroleum Engrs, 1974; Harvey Science Prize, Technion Israel Inst., 1974; Acta Metallurgica Gold Medal, 1976; Guthrie Medal and Prize, Inst. of Physics, 1977; Gold Medal, Amer. Soc. for Metals, 1980; Brinell Medal, Royal Swedish Acad. of Engrg Sciences, 1980; Kelvin Medal, ICE, 1986; Hollomon Award, Acta Metallurgica, 1991; Von Hippel Award, Materials Res. Soc., 1996. *Publications:* Theoretical Structural Metallurgy, 1948, 2nd edn 1955;

Dislocations and Plastic Flow in Crystals, 1953; The Mechanical Properties of Matter, 1964; Theory of Crystal Dislocations, 1964; An Introduction to Metallurgy, 1967; Portrait of Nature, 1975; Environmental Economics, 1978; How Safe is Nuclear Energy?, 1981; Introduction to the Modern Theory of Metals, 1988; Chemical Bonding in Transition Metal Carbides, 1995; Concepts in the Electron Theory of Alloys, 1998; scientific papers to various learned journals. *Recreations:* music, reading. *Address:* 40 Maids Causeway, Cambridge CB5 8DD. *T:* (01223) 363806. *Died 15 Feb. 2012.*

COULTASS, (George Thomas) Clive; historian; Keeper of Audio-Visual Records, Imperial War Museum, 1983–91; *b* 5 July 1931; *m* 1962, Norma Morris (*d* 2004). *Educ:* Tadcaster Grammar Sch.; Univ. of Sheffield (BA Hons). Teacher in various London schools, 1955–62; Lectr/Sen. Lectr in History, James Graham Coll., Leeds, 1962–69; Imperial War Museum: Keeper of Film Programming, 1969–70; Keeper, Dept of Film, 1970–83. Vice-Pres., Internat. Assoc. for Audio-Visual Media in Hist. Res. and Educn, 1978–85. Organiser: various film historical confs, 1973–90; exhibn on British film and World War II, 1982. *Publications:* Images for Battle, 1989; sections in: The Historian and Film, 1976; Britain and the Cinema in the Second World War, 1988; articles in various historical jls. *Recreations:* travel, music, including opera, reading, cinema. *Address:* 39 Fairfield Grove, SE7 8UA. *Died 24 April 2015.*

COURTAULD, Rev. (Augustine) Christopher (Caradoc); Vicar of St Paul's, Knightsbridge, 1978–99; *b* 12 Sept. 1934; *s* of late Augustine Courtauld and Mollie Courtauld (*née* Montgomerie; she later *m* Baron Butler of Saffron Walden, KG, CH, PC); *m* 1978, Dr Elizabeth Ann Molland, MD, FRCPath, *d* of late Rev. Preb. John W. G. Molland; two *d*. *Educ:* Eton; Trinity College, Cambridge (BA 1958, MA 1961); Westcott House, Cambridge. Ordained deacon, 1960, priest 1961, Manchester; Curate of Oldham Parish Ch, 1960–63; Chaplain: Trinity College, Cambridge, 1963–68; The London Hospital, 1968–78. Area Dean, Westminster (St Margaret), 1992–97. *Recreation:* sailing. *Address:* Broke House, The Drift, Levington, Ipswich, Suffolk IP10 0LF. *Died 11 Jan. 2014.*

COUSINS, Philip, CB 1982; Deputy Comptroller and Auditor General, National Audit Office (formerly Secretary, Exchequer and Audit Department), 1979–84; *b* 28 Feb. 1923; *s* of Herbert and Ella Cousins; *m* 1948, Ruby Laura Morris (*d* 2010); two *d*. *Educ:* Royal Liberty School, Romford. Served in Royal Air Force, 1943–47. Joined Treasury, 1949; Under Secretary, 1974–79. *Address:* 102 Philbeach Gardens, SW5 9ET. *T:* (020) 7373 6164. *Died 22 March 2012.*

COUTTS, Ian Dewar, CBE 1982; in practice as chartered accountant, 1950–95; Member, Forestry Commission, 1984–93; Director, Eastern Electricity plc, 1990–95 (Member, Eastern Electricity Board, 1982–90); *b* 15 May 1927; *s* of David Dewar Coutts and Dorothy Helen Coutts; *m* 1st, 1950, Sheila Margaret Cargill (marr. diss. 1983); one *s* two *d*; 2nd, 1983, Hilary Ballard; one *s* one *d*. *Educ:* Ipswich Sch.; Culford Sch.; UEA (BA History, 2000). Chartered Accountant, 1949. Served 1st Essex Regt, 1946–48. Norfolk County Councillor, 1970–89; Leader, Norfolk CC, 1973–79. Chm., ACC Finance Cttee, 1977–83; Mem., Consultative Council on Local Govt Finance, 1977–83. Mem., Local Govt Audit Commn, 1983–90. Chm., S Norfolk Conservative Assoc., 1970–73; Parly Cand., Norwich S, 1979. Mem., Council, Univ. of East Anglia, 1974–86. *Recreation:* sailing. *Died 17 Nov. 2011.*

COUZENS, Brian William; classical recording producer; Chairman, Chandos Records Ltd, since 2004; Managing Director, Chandos Music, since 1961; *b* 17 Jan. 1933; *s* of William and Vera Couzens; *m* 1st, 1956, Ilse Elizabeth Hauguth (*d* 2005); three *s* one *d*; 2nd, 2006, Deborah Jill Frogel. Self educated. Musician, 1948–51; Nat. Service, 1951–53; composer and arranger for BBC and publishers, 1954–59; orchestration for films incl. Where Eagles Dare, Magnificent Men in their Flying Machines, 633 Squadron, and 34 films working for Ron Goodwin, John Williams, Dimitri Tiomkin, and others, 1959–69; formed Chandos Music Ltd, 1961; independent sound engr and record producer of classical music, 1969–78; formed Chandos Records Ltd, 1979. DUniv Anglia Ruskin, 2007. Numerous internat. awards incl. Grammy, and Gramophone. *Recreations:* photography, video, nature and wildlife. *Address:* Chandos Records Ltd, Chandos House, 1 Commerce Park, Commerce Way, Colchester CO2 8HX. *T:* (01206) 225200. *Died 17 April 2015.*

COVENEY, Prof. James; Professor of French, University of Bath, 1969–85, then Professor Emeritus; *b* 4 April 1920; *s* of James and Mary Coveney; *m* 1955, Patricia Yvonne Townsend; two *s*. *Educ:* St Ignatius Coll., Stamford Hill, London; Univ. of Reading (BA 1st Cl. Hons French, 1950); Univ. of Strasbourg (Dr Univ. 1953). Served War of 1939–45: Welch Regt, 1940; Royal West Kent Regt, 1941; RAF (Flt-Lt 1945 (Pilot)). French Govt Res. Scholar, 1950–51, Lectr, 1951–53, Univ. of Strasbourg; Lectr in Medieval French, Univ. of Hull, 1953–58; Asst Dir, Civil Service Commn, 1958–59; UN Secretariat, New York, 1959–61; NATO Secretariat, 1961–64; University of Bath: Head of Mod. Langs Gp, 1964–68; Jt Dir, Centre for European Industrial Studies, 1969–75; Head of Sch. of Mod. Langs, 1969–77 and 1980–83. Visiting Professor: Ecole Nat. d'Administration, Paris, 1974–85; Univ. of Buckingham, 1974–86 (Mem., Acad. Adv. Council, 1974–83); Bethlehem Univ., 1985. Consultant: Univ. of Macau, 1988; Internat. Communications Inc., Tokyo, 1991–94. Lang. Trng Advr, McKinsey & Co., 1967–73. Member: British-French Cultural Commn, 1973–79; Bd of Govs, British Inst. in Paris, 1975–79; European League for Econ. Co-operation, 1997. Trustee, Friends of Birzeit Univ., 1991–2004. Corresp. Mem., Académie des Sciences, Agriculture, Arts et Belles-Lettres, Aix-en-Provence, 1975; Confrère de Saint-Etienne, Alsace, 1998. Officier, Ordre des Palmes Académiques (France), 2007 (Chevalier, 1978); Officier, Ordre National du Mérite (France), 1986. *Publications:* La Légende de l'Empereur Constant, 1955; (with S. Moore) Glossary of French and English Management Terms, 1972; (with J. Grosjean) Le français pour l'ingénieur, 1974; (with S. Kempa) Guide to French Institutions, 1978; (with S. Moore) French Business Management Dictionary, 1993. *Address:* 2 Campions Court, Graemesdyke Road, Berkhamsted, Herts HP4 3PD. *T:* (01442) 865657. *Club:* Travellers. *Died 12 June 2013.*

COWAN, Prof. Charles Donald, (Jeremy), CBE 1988; MA Cantab, PhD London; FRAS; Chairman, External System, University of London, 1993–97; *b* London, 18 Nov. 1923; *s* of W. C. Cowan and Minnie Ethel (*née* Farrow); *m* 1st, 1945, Mary Evelyn (marr. diss. 1960), *d* of Otto Vetter, Perth, WA; two *d*; 2nd, 1962, Daphne Eleanor (*d* 2004), *d* of Walter Rishworth Whittam, Rangoon. *Educ:* Kilburn Grammar Sch.; Peterhouse, Cambridge. Served Royal Navy, 1941–45. Lectr in History, Raffles Coll., Singapore, 1947–48, and University of Malaya, 1948–50; School of Oriental and African Studies, University of London: Lectr in the History of South-East Asia, 1950–60; Prof., 1961–80, Prof. of Oriental History, 1980–89; Dir, 1976–89; London University: Pro-Vice-Chancellor, 1985–86; Dep. Vice-Chancellor, 1988–90; Chm. of Convocation, 1990–94. Visiting Prof. of Southeast Asian Hist., Cornell Univ., 1960–61. Chm., Cttee for SE Asian Studies, British Acad., 1990–97. Governor: James Allen's Girls School, 1977–89; Alleyn's Sch., 1980–98; Dulwich Coll., 1980–98; Richmond Coll., 1988–92. Trustee, Dulwich Estate, 1985–98. Hon. DSc London, 2008. *Publications:* Nineteenth Century Malaya, 1961; (ed) The Economic Development of South-East Asia, 1964; (ed) The Economic Development of China and Japan, 1964; (with P. L. Burns) Sir Frank Swettenham's Malayan Journals, 1975; (with O. L. Wolters) Southeast Asian History and Historiography, 1976. *Address:* 34 Great Brownings, College Road, SE21 7HP. *Died 3 Sept. 2013.*

COWAN, Brig. Colin Hunter, CBE 1984; Chief Executive, Cumbernauld Development Corporation, 1970–85; *b* 16 Oct. 1920; *s* of late Lt-Col S. Hunter Cowan, DSO and Mrs Jean Hunter Cowan; *m* 1st, 1949, Elizabeth Williamson, MD (*d* 1985); one *s* one *d* (and one *s* decd); 2nd, 1988, Mrs Jen Burnett, *widow* of A. H. Burnett. *Educ:* Wellington Coll.; RMA Woolwich; Trinity Coll., Cambridge (MA). MICE. Comd Engineer Regt, 1960–63; Defence Adviser, UK Mission to the UN, 1964–66;

Brigadier Engineer Plans, MoD (Army), 1968–70. DL Dunbartonshire, 1973–88. *Recreations:* music, photography. *Address:* Flat 11, Varrich House, 7 Church Hill, Edinburgh EH10 4BG. *T:* (0131) 447 9768. *Died 21 Feb. 2014.*

COWAN, Jeremy; *see* Cowan, C. D.

COWARD, David John, CMG 1965; OBE 1962; Registrar General, Kenya, 1955–82; *b* 21 March 1917; *s* of late Robert J. Coward, Exmouth, Devon; *m* 1954, Joan, *d* of late Reginald Frank, Doncaster; three *d. Educ:* Exmouth Grammar Sch. and Law Society's Sch. of Law. FCIS 1961; ACIArb 1984. Admitted a solicitor, 1938. Joined RN as a rating at outbreak of war, 1939; commissioned, 1941; demobilized as Lieut-Comdr (S) RNVR, 1947. ADC to Governor of Trinidad, 1947. Joined Colonial Legal Service, 1948, Asst Registrar Gen., Kenya; Dep. Registrar Gen., 1952; Registrar Gen., Official Receiver and Public Trustee, 1955–82. Acted as Permanent Sec. for Justice and Constitutional Affairs, 1963–64. Served in Kenya Police Reserve, 1949–63, latterly as Senior Superintendent i/c Nairobi Area. Chm., Working Party on future of Company Secretarial Profession in Kenya; Mem. Accountants' Registration Bd, 1978–82; Trustee, Nat. Museums of Kenya, 1979–82. Pres., Storrington Br., Royal British Legion, 2002–11 (Chm., 1993–97). Liveryman, 1985 and Hon. Archivist, 1995–2002, Chartered Secretaries' and Administrators' Co. Silver Medal, Internat. Olympic Cttee, 1981. *Recreations:* golf, genealogy. *Address:* North Perretts, Spinney Lane, West Chiltington, W Sussex RH20 2NX. *T:* (01903) 742521. *Clubs:* Naval; Nairobi and Limuru Country (Kenya). *Died 5 Dec. 2011.*

COWARD, (John) Stephen; QC 1984; barrister-at-law; a Recorder of the Crown Court, 1980–2003; *b* 15 Nov. 1937; *s* of Frank and Kathleen Coward; *m* 1967, Ann Lesley Pye; four *d. Educ:* King James' Grammar Sch., Almondbury, Huddersfield; University Coll. London (LLB). Lecturer in Law and Constitutional History, University Coll. London and Police Staff Coll., 1962–64; called to the Bar, Inner Temple, 1964, Bencher, 2002; in practice on Midland and Oxford Circuit, 1964–2007. *Recreation:* trying to grow calceolarias and a decent row of peas. *Address:* 3 Chalmore Gardens, Wallingford OX10 9EP. *Died 19 Oct. 2014.*

COWDEROY, Brenda; General Secretary, Girls' Friendly Society, 1978–85; *b* 27 June 1925; *oc* of Frederick and Evelyn Cowderoy (*née* Land). *Educ:* Surbiton High Sch.; St Hugh's Coll., Oxford (MA). Called to Bar, Gray's Inn, 1949. John Lewis Partnership: Asst Legal Adviser, 1954–56; Head of Legal Dept, 1956–70; Nat. Gen. Sec., YWCA, 1971–77. *Address:* 26 Rossetti Road, Birchington, Kent CT7 9ER. *Died 21 July 2015.*

COWEN, Rt Hon. Sir Zelman, AK 1977; GCMG 1977 (CMG 1968); GCVO 1980; Kt 1976; PC 1981; QC; Provost of Oriel College, Oxford, 1982–90; Pro-Vice-Chancellor, University of Oxford, 1988–90; Director, John Fairfax Holdings Ltd, 1992–96 (Chairman, 1992–94); *b* 7 Oct. 1919; *s* of late Bernard and of Sara Cowen; *m* 1945, Anna Wittner; three *s* one *d. Educ:* Scotch Coll., Melbourne; Univ. of Melbourne (BA 1939; LLB 1941; LLM 1942); New and Oriel Colls, Oxford (BCL, MA 1947, DCL 1968). Lieut, RANVR, 1941–45. Called to Bar, Gray's Inn, 1947; Hon. Bencher, 1978; called to Vic (Aust.) Bar, 1951, Queensland Bar, 1971; QC 1972. Victorian Rhodes Schol., 1941; Vinerian Schol., Oxford Univ., 1947. Fellow and Tutor, Oriel Coll., Oxford, 1947–50, Hon. Fellow 1977; Prof. of Public Law and Dean of Faculty of Law, Univ. of Melbourne, 1951–66; Dominion Liaison Officer to Colonial Office (UK), 1951–66; Prof. Emer., Univ. of Melbourne, 1967; Vice-Chancellor and Professor, Univ. of New England, Armidale, NSW, 1967–70; Vice-Chancellor, Qld Univ., 1970–77; Governor-General of Australia, 1977–82. Visiting Professor: Univ. of Chicago, 1949; Harvard Law Sch. and Fletcher Sch. of Law and Diplomacy, 1953–54 and 1963–64; Univ. of Utah, 1954; Univ. of Illinois, 1957–58; Washington Univ., St Louis, 1959; Tagore Law Prof., Univ. of Calcutta, 1975; Menzies Schol. in Res., Univ. of Va, 1983; Lee Kuan Yew Dist. Vis. Fellow, Singapore, 1986; Dist. Vis. Prof., Victoria Univ. of Technol., 1994–. Broadcaster on radio and TV on nat. and internat. affairs; Mem. and Chm., Victorian State Adv. Cttee of Australian Broadcasting Commn (at various times during 1950s and 1960s); Mem., Chief Justice's Law Reform Cttee, 1951–66; President: Asthma Foundn of Victoria, 1963–66; Adult Educn Assoc. of Australia, 1968–70; Aust. Inst. of Urban Studies, 1973–77; Mem., Law Reform Commn, Australia, 1976–77; Chairman: Aust. Vice-Chancellors' Cttee, 1977; Aust. Studies Centre Cttee, London, 1982–90; Nat Council, Australian Opera, 1983–95; Press Council, 1983–88; Trustees, Visnews Ltd, 1986–91; Victoria League for Commonwealth Friendship, 1987–89; Australian Nat. Acad. of Music, 1995–2000. Mem., Club of Rome, 1974–77. National President: Order of Australia Assoc. Ltd, 1992–95; Australia-Britain Soc., 1993–95. Academic Governor, Bd of Governors, Hebrew Univ. of Jerusalem, 1969–77, 1982–; Mem., Academic Bd of Govs, Tel Aviv Univ., 1983–; Weizmann Inst., 1988–. Trustee: Van Leer Inst. of Jerusalem, 1985– (Chm. Trustees, 1988–95); Winston Churchill Meml Trust, 1987–89; Sir Robert Menzies Meml Trust, 1987–; Dir, Sir Robert Menzies Meml Foundn Ltd, 1990–97. For. Hon. Mem., Amer. Acad. of Arts and Scis, 1965. Fellow, Australian Nat. Acad. of Music, 2000; Hon. FASSA 1977; Hon. FACE 1978; Hon. FRAIA 1978; Hon. FTS 1979; Hon. FRACP 1979; Hon. FAHA 1980; Hon. FASA 1980; Hon. FRACMA 1981; Hon. FRACOG 1981; Hon. FCA 1981; Hon. FACRM 1982; Hon. Fellow: New Coll. Oxford 1978; University House, ANU, 1978; ANZAAS 1983; TCD, 1985; St John's Coll., Univ. of Qld, 1985; Australian Council of Educnl Admin, 1991. Hon. Law Prof., Griffith Univ., Qld, 1992. Hon. LLD: Hong Kong, 1967; Queensland, 1972; Melbourne, 1973; Western Australia, 1981; Turin, 1981; ANU, 1985; Tasmania, 1990; Victoria Univ. of Technol., 1998; Deakin, 2003; Monash, 2004; Hon. DLitt: New England, 1979; Sydney, 1980; James Cook Univ. of N Qld, 1982; Oxford, 1983; Hon. DHL: Hebrew Union Coll., Cincinnati, 1980; Redlands Univ., Calif., 1986; DUniv: Newcastle, 1980; Griffith, 1981; Sunshine Coast, 1999; Hon. DPhil: Hebrew Univ. of Jerusalem, 1982; Tel Aviv, 1985. KStJ (A) 1977. Kt Grand Cross, Order of Merit (Italy), 1990. *Publications:* (ed jtly) Dicey's Conflict of Laws, 1949; Australia and the United States: Some Legal Comparisons, 1954; (with P. B. Carter) Essays on the Law of Evidence, 1956; American-Australian Private International Law, 1957; Federal Jurisdiction in Australia, 1959, 3rd edn 2002; (with D. M. da Costa) Matrimonial Causes Jurisdiction, 1961; Sir John Latham and other papers, 1965; British Commonwealth of Nations in a Changing World, 1964; Isaac Isaacs, 1967, 2nd edn 1993; The Private Man, 1969; Individual Liberty and the Law, 1977; The Virginia Lectures, 1984; Reflections on Medicine, Biotechnology, and the Law, 1986; A Touch of Healing, 1986; The Memoirs of Sir Zelman Cowen: a public life, 2006; articles and chapters in legal works in UK, US, Canada, Germany, Australia. *Recreations:* swimming, music, performing and visual arts. *Address:* Commonwealth Offices, 4 Treasury Place, East Melbourne, Vic 3002, Australia. *Clubs:* Oxford and Cambridge; Queensland (Brisbane); Pioneer (Sydney). *Died 8 Dec. 2011.*

COWEY, Prof. Alan, PhD; FMedSci; FRS 1988; Professor of Physiological Psychology, University of Oxford, 1981–2002, then Emeritus; Fellow of Lincoln College, Oxford, 1981–2002, then Supernumerary Fellow; MRC Research Professor, 1997–2002; *b* 28 April 1935; *s* of Harry and Mary Cowey; *m* 1959, Patricia Leckonby; three *d. Educ:* Bede Grammar Sch., Sunderland; Emmanuel Coll., Cambridge (MA, PhD). Rockefeller Foundn Fellow, Center for Brain Research, Univ. of Rochester, New York, 1961–62; Univ. Demonstrator in Experimental Psychology, Cambridge, 1962–67; Fellow and Coll. Tutor, Emmanuel Coll., Cambridge, 1964–67; Vis. Sen. Fulbright Fellow, Psychology Dept, Harvard Univ., 1967; Sen. Res. Officer, Inst. of Experimental Psychology, Univ. of Oxford, 1967–68; Nuffield Sen. Res. Fellow, Lincoln Coll., Oxford, 1968–81; Henry Head Res. Fellow of Royal Society, 1968–73; Reader in Physiolog. Psychology, Oxford Univ., 1973–81; Dir, Oxford Res. Centre in Brain and Behaviour, 1991–96. Member: MRC Neurosciences Grants Cttee, 1974–77 (Chm., 1979–81); MRC Neurosciences Board, 1979–83 (Chm., 1981–83); Mem. Council, MRC, 1981–85. President: European Brain and Behaviour Soc., 1986–88; Experimental Psychology Soc.,

1990–92; Assoc. for Scientific Study of Consciousness, 2008–. Mem., Hungarian Acad. Sci., 2010. Founder FMedSci 1998. Hon. DSc Durham, 2000. Spearman Medal, 1967, Lifetime Achievement Award, 2011, BPsS. *Publications:* numerous articles in psychological and physiological jls. *Recreations:* gardening, swimming, reading, walking. *Address:* Department of Experimental Psychology, South Parks Road, Oxford OX1 3UD. *T:* (01865) 271352. *Died 19 Dec. 2012.*

COWIE, Sir Thomas, (Sir Tom), Kt 1992; OBE 1982; Life President, T. Cowie Ltd, subseq. T. Cowie PLC, later Arriva, motor vehicle distribution and finance, 1993–2010 (Chairman, 1948–93); *b* 9 Sept. 1922; *s* of late Thomas Stephenson Knowles Cowie and Florence Cowie; *m* 1st, 1948, Lillas Roberts Hunnam (marr. diss.; she *d* 1994); one *s* four *d*; 2nd, 1975, Diana Carole Wentworth Kenyon; three *d*, and one step *s* one step *d*. *Educ:* Bede Grammar School, Sunderland. *Relevant publications:* The Tom Cowie Story, by Phil Martin, 1988; Sir Tom Cowie: a true entrepreneur, by Denise Robertson, 2004. *Recreations:* game shooting, walking, music. *Address:* Broadwood Hall, Lanchester, Co. Durham DH7 0TD. *T:* (01207) 520464. *Died 18 Jan. 2012.*

COWLEY, Prof. Roger Arthur, FRS 1978; FRSE; FRSC; Dr Lee's Professor of Experimental Philosophy, University of Oxford, 1988–2007, then Emeritus Professor of Physics; Fellow of Wadham College, Oxford, 1988–2007, then Emeritus; *b* 24 Feb. 1939; *s* of Cecil A. Cowley and Mildred S. Cowley; *m* 1964, Sheila J. Wells; one *s* one *d*. *Educ:* Brentwood Sch., Essex; Cambridge Univ. (MA, PhD). FRSE 1972; FRSC 2001. Fellow, Trinity Hall, Cambridge, 1962–64; Research Officer, Atomic Energy of Canada Ltd, 1964–70; Prof. of Physics, Edinburgh Univ., 1970–88; Chm. of Physics, Univ. of Oxford, 1993–96, 1999–2002. Max Born Medal, Inst. of Physics and German Physical Soc., 1973; Holweck Medal and Prize, Inst. of Physics and French Physical Soc., 1990; W. Hälg Medal and Prize, Eur. Neutron Scattering Soc., 2003; Faraday Medal and Prize, Inst. of Physics, 2008. *Publications:* Structural Phase Transitions, 1981; over 350 articles. *Address:* Oxford Physics, Clarendon Laboratory, Parks Road, Oxford OX1 3PU. *T:* (01865) 272224; Tredinnock, Harcourt Hill, Oxford OX2 9AS. *T:* (01865) 247570. *Died 27 Jan. 2015.*

COX, Graham Loudon; QC (Scot.) 1993; Sheriff Principal of South Strathclyde, Dumfries and Galloway, 1993–2000; *b* 22 Dec. 1933; *s* of Rev. Thomas Loudon Cox and Leonainie Violet Rose (*née* Watson); *m* 1st, 1959, June Mary Constance Gunner (marr. diss. 1975); three *d*; 2nd, 1977, Jean Nelson. *Educ:* Hamilton Acad.; Grove Acad.; Univ. of Edinburgh (MA 1954; LLB 1956). Commnd RASC, 1957; transferred to Directorate Army Legal Services, 1958–61 (Temp. Major). Called to Scottish Bar, 1962; Advocate Depute, 1967; Sheriff, Tayside Central and Fife, at Dundee, 1968–93. Mem., Scottish Criminal Justice Forum, 1996–2000; Chm., Scottish Adoption Policy Review Gp, 2001–05. Hon. Vice Pres., Scottish Assoc. for Study of Delinquency, 1996–2002; Pres., Sheriffs' Assoc., 1992–93; Mem. Council, Commonwealth Magistrates and Judges Assoc., 1991–94, 1997–2000. Comr, Northern Lighthouse Bd, 1993–2000 (Vice-Chm., 1997–2000). *Recreations:* golf, gardening, travelling. *Address:* Crail House, Crail, Fife KY10 3SJ. *T:* (01333) 450270. *E:* coxcrail@btinternet.com. *Club:* Royal & Ancient Golf (St Andrews). *Died 27 Dec. 2014.*

COX, Philip (Joseph), DSC 1943; QC 1967; Honorary Recorder of Northampton, since 1972; *b* 28 Sept. 1922; *s* of Joseph Parriss Cox, Rugby; *m* 1951, Margaret Jocelyn Cox, *d* of R. C. H. Cox, Purley, Surrey; one *s* one *d*. *Educ:* Rugby Sch.; Queens' Coll., Cambridge. Lance-Corp., LDV and HG, 1940–42; RNVR, 1942–46 (Lieut): Radar Officer, Gp B3, N Atlantic Convoy Close Escort Gp, 1943–44; Application Officer for S and X band Radar, Admiralty Signal Establishment, 1944–45; orgn of Radar Section, Royal Hellenic Navy, 1945–46. Called to Bar, Gray's Inn, 1949; Bencher, 1972 (Vice-Treas., 1990; Treas., 1991); practised at Bar, Birmingham, 1949–67, London, 1967–91. Deputy Chairman: Northants QS, 1963–71; Warwicks QS, 1966–71; a Recorder, 1972–94; Leader, Midland and Oxford Circuit, 1975–79; a Dep. High Court Judge, 1977–92. Member: County Court Rules Cttee, 1962–68; Senate, Inns of Court and Bar, 1974–80. Legal Assessor to Disciplinary Cttee, RCVS, 1969–2000; Chm., Cttee of Enquiry into London Smallpox Outbreak, 1973; Chairman: Code of Practice Appeal Bd, Prescription Medicines Code of Practice Authy, 1993–2000; Code of Practice Cttee, Assoc. of British Pharmaceut. Industries, 1978–92; Code of Practice Cttee, Internat. Fedn of Pharmaceut. Manufacturers Assocs, 1985–2000; Gen. Optical Council, 1985–88; Code of Practice Cttee, Nat. Office of Animal Health, 1987–92; WHO Internat. Gp of Experts on Ethical Criteria for Drug Promotion, 1987. Pres., Mental Health Review Tribunals, 1984–95. Chm., Birmingham Forward Br., RBL, 2003–05. Pres., Edgbaston Liberal Assoc., 1974–86. *Recreations:* sailing, golf, gardening, reading, woodwork. *Address:* 9 Sir Harry's Road, Edgbaston, Birmingham B15 2UY. *T:* (0121) 440 0278. *Club:* Bar Yacht. *Died 14 Nov. 2014.*

COX, Richard Charles, MBE 1961; HM Diplomatic Service, retired; *b* 27 May 1920; *s* of Charles Victor Cox and Marjorie Eleanor Cox (*née* Fox); *m* 1941, Constance (*née* Goddard) (*d* 2011); one *s*. *Educ:* Gravesend Grammar Sch.; BA Open Univ., 1985. Served War of 1939–45, RAF; released with rank of Sqdn Leader, 1946. Entered Colonial Office, 1937; Dominions Office, 1946; High Commn, Colombo, 1949–52; Second Sec., Calcutta, 1953–54; CRO, 1954–56; First Sec., Bombay, 1956–59; CRO, 1960–63; First Sec., Valletta, 1964–68; FCO, 1968–72; NI Office, 1972–74; Dep. Sec. Gen., Cento, 1975–77. *Recreations:* swimming, gardening, watching Rugby football. *Address:* 31 Lotfield Street, Orwell, near Royston, Herts SG8 5QT. *T:* (01223) 207969. *Died 5 Jan. 2014.*

COXWELL-ROGERS, Col Richard Annesley; Vice Lord-Lieutenant of Gloucestershire, 1993–2007; *b* 26 April 1932; *s* of Maj.-Gen. Norman Annesley Coxwell-Rogers, CB, CBE, DSO and Diana Coxwell-Rogers (*née* Coston); *m* 1st, 1965, Martha Felicity Hurrell (*d* 1998); two *s*; 2nd, 2003, Louisa, *widow* of David Wagg. *Educ:* Eton Coll.; RMA Sandhurst. Commissioned 15th/19th Hussars, 1952; served Germany, UK, Malaya, Cyprus; Comd 15th/19th Hussars, 1973–75; Col, 15th/19th Hussars, 1988–92. Area Appeals Organiser, CRC, 1982–93. DL Glos 1990; High Sheriff of Glos, 1994. *Recreation:* country sports. *Address:* Hookash, Foxcote, Andoversford, Cheltenham, Glos GL54 4LP. *T:* (01242) 821410. *Club:* Cavalry and Guards. *Died 3 April 2013.*

COYNE, James Elliott; Canadian banker and financial consultant; *b* Winnipeg, 17 July 1910; *s* of James Bowes Coyne and Edna Margaret Coyne (*née* Elliott); *m* 1957, Meribeth Stobie; one *s* one *d*. *Educ:* University of Manitoba (BA); University of Oxford (BCL). RCAF (Flying Officer), 1942–44. Admitted to the Bar, Manitoba, 1934; solicitor and barrister in Manitoba, 1934–38; Financial Attaché, Canadian Embassy, Washington, DC, 1941; Mem. Wartime Prices and Trade Board, Ottawa, 1942 (Dep.-Chm.). Bank of Canada, Ottawa: Asst to the Governors, 1944–49; Deputy-Governor, 1950–54; Governor, 1955–61. *Address:* 404–160 Tuxedo Avenue, Winnipeg, MB R3P 1B2, Canada. *Died 12 Oct. 2012.*

CRACKNELL, (William) Martin; Chief Executive, Glenrothes Development Corporation, 1976–93; *b* 24 June 1929; *s* of John Sidney Cracknell and Sybil Marian (*née* Wood); *m* 1962, Gillian Goatcher; two *s* two *d*. *Educ:* St Edward's School, Oxford; RMA Sandhurst. Regular Army Officer, Royal Green Jackets, 1949–69; British Printing Industries Fedn, 1969–76. Mem. Exec., Scottish Council (Develt and Industry), 1984–90; Chm., Scottish Cttee, German Chamber of Industry and Commerce in UK, 1987–92. Director: Glenrothes Enterprise Trust, 1983–89; New Enterprise Develt, 1987–90. FRSA 1993. Cross of Order of Merit (Germany), 1992. *Address:* West End Cottage, Freuchie, Fife KY15 7EZ. *T:* (01337) 857849. *Club:* Royal Green Jackets. *Died 16 Dec. 2011.*

CRAGG, Rt Rev. (Albert) Kenneth, DPhil; an Honorary Assistant Bishop, Diocese of Oxford, 1982–2012; *b* 8 March 1913; *yr s* of Albert and Emily Cragg; *m* 1940, Theodora Melita (*d* 1989), *yr d* of John Wesley Arnold; three *s* (one *d* decd). *Educ:* Blackpool Grammar Sch.; Jesus Coll., Oxford (Hon. Fellow, 1999); Tyndale Hall, Bristol. BA Oxon 2nd

Cl. Hons Mod. Hist., 1934; MA Oxon 1938; DPhil 1950. Ellerton Theol. Essay Prize, Oxford, 1937; Green Moral Philos. Prize, Oxford, 1947. Deacon, 1936; Priest, 1937; Curate, Higher Tranmere Parish Church, Birkenhead, 1936–39; Chaplain, All Saints', Beirut, Lebanon, 1939–47; Warden, St Justin's House, Beirut, 1942–47; Asst Prof. of Philos., Amer. University of Beirut, 1942–47; Rector of Longworth, Berks, 1947–51; Sheriff's Chap., Berks, 1948; Prof. of Arabic and Islamics, Hartford Seminary, Conn, USA, 1951–56; Rockefeller Travelling Schol., 1954; Res. Canon, St George's Collegiate Church, Jerusalem, 1956–61; Fellow, St Augustine's Coll., Canterbury, 1959–60, Sub-Warden, 1960–61, Warden, 1961–67; Examng Chaplain to Archbishop of Canterbury, 1961–67; Hon. Canon of Canterbury, 1961–80; Asst Bishop to Archbishop in Jerusalem, 1970–74; Reader in Religious Studies, Sussex Univ., and Hon. Asst Bishop, Dio. of Chichester, 1973–78; Vicar of Helme, W Yorks, and Hon. Asst Bishop, Dio. of Wakefield, 1978–81. Select Preacher: Cambridge, 1961; Dublin, 1962; Oxford, 1974. Proctor in Convocation, Canterbury, 1965–68; Vis. Prof., Union Theological Seminary, New York, 1965–66; Lectr, Faculty of Divinity, Cambridge, 1966; Jordan Lectr, Sch. of Oriental and African Studies, University of London, 1967; Vis. Prof., University of Ibadan, Nigeria, 1968; Bye-Fellow, Gonville and Caius Coll., Cambridge, 1968–74; Vis. Prof., Virginia Theol Seminary, 1984, 1985. Hon. DD: Leeds, 1993; Toronto, 2001; DD Lambeth, 2002. Editor, The Muslim World Quarterly, 1952–60. *Publications:* The Call of the Minaret, 1956, 2nd edn 1986; Sandals at the Mosque, 1959; The Dome and the Rock, 1964; Counsels in Contemporary Islam, 1965; Christianity in World Perspective, 1968; The Privilege of Man, 1968; The House of Islam, 1969; Alive to God, 1970; The Event of the Qur'ān, 1971; The Mind of the Qur'ān, 1973; The Wisdom of the Sufis, 1976; The Christian and Other Religion, 1977; Islam from Within, 1979; This Year in Jerusalem, 1982; Muhammad and the Christian, 1983; The Pen and the Faith, 1985; Jesus and the Muslim, 1985; The Christ and the Faiths, 1986; Readings in the Qur'ān, 1988; What Decided Christianity, 1989; The Arab Christian, 1991; Troubled by Truth, 1992; To Meet and to Greet, 1992; Faith and Life Negotiate (autobiog.), 1994; The Lively Credentials of God, 1996; Defending (the) Faith, 1997; Palestine: the prize and price of Zion, 1997; With God in Human Trust, 1999; The Weight in the Word, 1999; The Education of Christian Faith, 2000; Islam Among the Spires, 2000; Muhammad in the Qur'ān, 2002; Am I Not Your Lord?, 2002; Faiths in their Pronouns, 2003; The Christian Jesus, 2003; The Tragic in Islam, 2004; A Certain Sympathy of Scriptures: Biblical and Quranic, 2004; Semitism: the whence and whither, 2005; Faith at Suicide, 2005; God's Wrong is Most of All, 2006; The Qur'an and the West, 2006; The Order of the Wounded Hands, 2007; A Christian/Muslim Inter-Text Now, 2007; Mosque Sermons, 2008; The Iron in the Soul, 2008; The Compass of the Globe, 2009; Trans Action in Biblical Society, 2009; School for Souls, 2011; Bent to Literary Event: masters in their masterpieces, 2011; translated: City of Wrong, 1959; The Theology of Unity, 1965; A Passage to France, 1976; The Hallowed Valley, 1977; contributor: Journal of World History, 1957; Religion in the Middle East, 1969. *Address:* 3 Goring Lodge, White House Road, Oxford OX1 4QE. *Died 13 Nov. 2012.*

CRAIG, Prof. David Parker, AO 1985; FRS 1968; FAA 1969; FRSC; FRSN; University Fellow and Emeritus Professor, Australian National University, since 1985; *b* 23 Dec. 1919; *s* of Andrew Hunter Craig, Manchester and Sydney, and Mary Jane (*née* Parker); *m* 1948, Veronica, *d* of Cyril Bryden-Brown, Market Harborough and Sydney; three *s* one *d*. *Educ:* Sydney Church of England Grammar Sch.; University of Sydney; University Coll., London. MSc (Sydney) 1941, PhD (London) 1950, DSc (London) 1956. Commonwealth Science Scholar, 1940. War Service: Capt., Australian Imperial Force, 1941–44. Lectr in Chemistry, University of Sydney, 1944–46; Turner and Newall Research Fellow, 1946–49, and Lectr in Chemistry, University Coll., London, 1949–52; Prof. of Physical Chemistry, Univ. of Sydney, 1952–56; Prof. of Chemistry, University Coll., London, 1956–67; Prof. of Chemistry, 1967–85, Dean, Research Sch. of Chemistry, 1970–73 and 1977–81, ANU. Vis. Prof., UCL, 1968–90; Firth Vis. Prof., Univ. of Sheffield, 1973; Vis. Prof., University Coll., Cardiff, 1975–89. Part-time Mem., CSIRO Exec., 1980–85. Chm., Adv. Cttee, Aust. Nat. Botanic Gdns, 1986–89. Pres., Australian Acad. of Sci., 1990–94. Fellow of University Coll., London, 1964–. FRSN 2010; Hon. FRSC 1987. Hon. Dr Chem. Bologna, 1985; Hon. DSc Sydney, 1985. *Publications:* books and original papers on chemistry in scientific periodicals. *Address:* 216 Dryandra Street, O'Connor, ACT 2602, Australia. *Club:* Athenæum. *Died 1 July 2015.*

CRAIG, John Egwin, CBE 1998 (OBE 1990); with N. M. Rothschild & Sons, 1964–91, Director, 1970–91; *b* 16 Aug. 1932; *s* of late Thomas Joseph Alexander Craig, CIE, and Mabel Frances (*née* Quinnell); *m* 1959, Patricia Costa Lopes; three *s*. *Educ:* Charterhouse. FCA 1961–2000. Cooper Bros (later Coopers & Lybrands), 1958–61; Council of Stock Exchange, 1961–64; Man. Dir, N. M. Rothschild, 1981–89; Chm., Jupiter European Investment Trust, 1990–2000; Director: New Star Investment Trust, 2001–05 (Chm., 2005); New Star Asset Management plc, 2005–08. Chairman: Powerscreen Internat. plc, 1989–99; Belfast Internat. Airport Hldgs, 1994–96; Director: Standard Chartered, 1989–94; Jupiter Tyndall Gp, then Jupiter Internat. Gp, 1991–2000 (Vice Chm., 1991–94). Govt Dir, Internat. Fund for Ireland, 1989–96. Member: Exec. Cttee, BBA, 1981–89 (Chm., 1987–89); Deposit Protection Bd, 1986–89. Mem. Council, LPO, 1983–87. Trustee, Restoration of Appearance and Function Trust, 2000–07. FRSA 1988. *Address:* 143 Forest Road, Tunbridge Wells, Kent TN2 5EX. *Died 23 Sept. 2012.*

CRAIG, Rt Hon. William; PC (N Ire.) 1963; solicitor and company director; *b* 2 Dec. 1924; *s* of late John Craig and Mary Kathleen Craig (*née* Lamont); *m* 1960, Doris Hilgendorff; two *s*. *Educ:* Dungannon Royal Sch.; Larne Grammar Sch.; Queen's Univ., Belfast. Served War of 1939–45, Royal Air Force, 1943–46. Qualified as solicitor, 1952. MP (U) Larne Div. of Antrim, NI Parliament, 1960–73; Mem. (Vanguard Unionist Progressive), N Antrim, NI Assembly, 1973–75; Mem. (UUC), E Belfast, NI Constitutional Convention, 1975–76; MP (UU) Belfast East, Feb. 1974–1979. Chief Whip, Parliament of Northern Ireland, 1962–63; Minister of Home Affairs, 1963–64, and 1966–68; Minister of Health and Local Government, 1964; Minister of Development, 1965–66. Founder: Ulster Vanguard, 1972 (Leader, 1972–77); Vanguard Unionist Party, 1973 (Leader, 1973–77). Member: Council of Europe, 1976–79; WEU, 1976–79. *Recreations:* travel, motoring, shooting. *Died 25 April 2011.*

CRAMPTON, Peter Duncan; *b* 10 June 1932; *s* of Edmund Crampton and Louisa Crampton (*née* Thurman); *m* 1955, Margaret Eva McMillan; two *s*. *Educ:* Blackpool Grammar School; Nottingham Univ. (BA Hons Geography); Birmingham Univ. (MA African Studies); Hull Univ. (Dip. W European Studies); London Univ. (PGCE). Casual work, mainly as farm worker, 1954–55; Statistician, Plessey Co., 1955–56; Geography Teacher, Coventry, 1957–61; Educn Officer, Uganda, 1961–64; Lectr i/c Geography, Technical Coll., Birmingham, 1964–70; Lectr in Geography, Hull Coll. of Educn, later Humberside Coll. of HE, 1970–85; part-time work as lectr, writer, parly assistant, 1985–89. Chairman: European Nuclear Disarmament Campaign, 1984–86; Internat. Cttee, CND, 1988–90. MEP (Lab) Humberside, 1989–99. European Parliament: First Vice-Pres., Political Affairs Cttee, 1989–94, For. Affairs Cttee, 1989–94; Member: Regl Policy Cttee, 1994–99; Fishing Cttee, 1994–99; Vice Pres., Delegn to Mongolia and Central Asia, 1994–96. *Publications:* (contrib.) Voices for One World, 1988; articles in jls on population geography in Africa, electoral behaviour and nuclear disarmament. *Recreations:* travel, hill-walking, music. *Address:* 135 Westbourne Avenue, Hull HU5 3HU. *T:* (01482) 494796. *Died 12 July 2011.*

CRANE, Sir Peter (Francis), Kt 2000; a Judge of the High Court of Justice, Queen's Bench Division, 2000–07; *b* 14 Jan. 1940; *s* of late Prof. Francis Roger Crane and Jean Berenice Crane (*née* Hadfield); *m* 1967, Elizabeth Mary Pittman (*d* 2012); four *d*. *Educ:* Nottingham High Sch.; Highgate Sch.; Gonville and Caius Coll., Cambridge (MA, LLM); Tulane Univ., New Orleans (LLM). Called to the

Bar, Gray's Inn, 1964 (Barstow Scholar, 1963); in practice on Midland and Oxford Circuit, 1965–87; Recorder, 1982–87; a Circuit Judge, 1987–2000; Resident Judge, Peterborough Crown and County Court, 1992–2000. Mem., Senate of Inns of Court and the Bar, 1983–86 (Member: Professional Conduct Cttee, 1984–86; Bar Cttee, 1985–86). Mem., Judicial Studies Bd, 1993–96, 2001–06 (Chm., Criminal Cttee, 2001–06). Mem., Sentencing Guidelines Council, 2004–06. Chairman: Kettering Constituency Liberal Assoc., 1981–84; Pytchley Parish Council, 1985–86, 2008–. *Publications:* (co-ed) Phipson on Evidence, 14th edn 1990, 15th edn 2000. *Recreations:* walking, gardening, reading, wine, travel. *Address:* Royal Courts of Justice, Strand, WC2A 2LL. *Died 22 Feb. 2013.*

CRANFIELD, Rev. Prof. Charles Ernest Burland, FBA 1982; Emeritus Professor of Theology, University of Durham, since 1980; *b* 13 Sept. 1915; *s* of Charles Ernest Cranfield and Beatrice Mary Cranfield (*née* Tubbs); *m* 1953, Ruth Elizabeth Gertrude, *d* of Rev. T. Bole; two *d*. *Educ:* Mill Hill Sch.; Jesus Coll., Cambridge; Wesley House, Cambridge. MA Cantab. Research in Basel, cut short before it properly began by outbreak of war. Probationer in Methodist Church, 1939; ordained 1941; Minister, Shoeburyness; Chaplain to the Forces, 1942–46; from end of hostilities worked with German prisoners-of-war and was first staff chaplain to POW Directorate, War Office; Minister, Cleethorpes, 1946–50; admitted to Presbyterian Church of England (later United Reformed Church) as a minister, 1954. Lecturer in Theology, Durham Univ., 1950–62; Sen. Lectr, 1962–66; Reader, 1966–78; Prof. of Theology (personal), 1978–80. Joint general editor, new series of International Critical Commentary, 1966–2005. Hon. DD Aberdeen, 1980. Burkitt Medal for Biblical Studies, 1989. *Publications:* The First Epistle of Peter, 1950, 4th imp. 1958; The Gospel according to Saint Mark, 1959, supplemented and somewhat revised over the years, 13th imp. 2000; I and II Peter and Jude, 1960; A Ransom for Many, 1963; The Service of God, 1965; A Commentary on Romans 12–13, 1965; A Critical and Exegetical Commentary on the Epistle to the Romans, vol. 1 1975, 16th imp. 2010, vol. 2 1979, 10th imp. 2006; Romans: a shorter commentary, 1985, 6th imp. 2001; If God Be For Us: a collection of sermons, 1985; The Bible and Christian Life: a collection of essays, 1985; The Apostles' Creed: a faith to live by, 1993, 3rd imp. 2004; On Romans and Other New Testament Essays, 1998; contribs to composite works and to various theological periodicals. *Address:* 30 Albert Street, Western Hill, Durham City DH1 4RL. *T:* (0191) 384 3096. *Died 27 Feb. 2015.*

CRAWFORD, John Michael; Director of Education (formerly Chief Education Officer), Birmingham, 1977–88; *b* 6 Dec. 1938; *s* of James and Emily Crawford; *m* 1962, Geraldine Kay Weaver; two *d*. *Educ:* Ipswich Sch.; University Coll., London (BA); Fitzwilliam House, Cambridge. Asst Master, Merchant Taylor's, Crosby, 1961–63; Admin. Asst, E Suffolk CC, 1963–66; Sen. Admin. Asst, Lancs CC, 1966–68; Asst Educn Officer, W Riding CC, 1968–73; Dep. Educn Officer, Birmingham, 1973–77. *Died 26 March 2012.*

CRAWFORD, Robert Gammie, CBE 1990; Chairman, Highlands and Islands Airports Ltd, 1986–93; *b* 20 March 1924; *s* of William and Janet Beveridge Crawford; *m* 1st, 1947, Rita Veiss (*d* 2004); one *d*; 2nd, 2010, Margaret Grace Robson. *Educ:* Robert Gordon's Coll., Aberdeen. Solicitor of the Supreme Court, England. Navigator, RAF, 1942–47. Practised as Solicitor, 1950–73, Partner, Ince and Co. (Internat. Shipping Lawyers); Director: UK Freight Demurrage and Defence Assoc. Ltd, 1976–2010 (Chm., 1987–90); UK Mutual Steamship Assurance Assoc. Ltd, 1980–94 (Chm., 1983–90); AVDEL plc, 1983–94; Sturge Aviation Syndicates Management Ltd, 1994–96; L. R. Integrity Management Ltd, 1994–96; Ockham Sturge Aviation Agency, 1996–97; Chairman: Silver Line Ltd, 1974–83; Silver Line Pension Fund, 1983–2008; UK Mutual War Risk Assoc. Ltd, 1982–2010 (Dir, 1980–2010); Independent Claims Services Ltd, 1995–99. Mem., Lloyd's, 1975–95; Mem. Bd, 1982–94, Gen. Cttee, 1982–2009, Lloyd's Register of Shipping; Trustee, Lloyd's Register Superannuation Fund, 1982–2006. Member: Bd, CAA, 1984–93; Bd, PLA, 1985–92 (Vice Chm., 1986–92). Freeman: City of London, 1988; Co. of Watermen and Lightermen, 1985. *Recreations:* shooting, reading, conversation. *Address:* 9 London House, Avenue Road, NW8 7PX. *T:* and *Fax:* (020) 7483 2754. *E:* r.g.crawford@btinternet.com. *Club:* Royal Northern and University (Aberdeen). *Died 2 May 2015.*

CRAWLEY, Frederick William, CBE 1998; FCIB; FRAeS; Chairman: Alliance & Leicester Building Society, 1991–94 (Director, since 1988; Deputy Chairman, 1990–91); Girobank PLC, 1992–94 (Director, since 1990; Deputy Chairman, 1990–92); *b* 10 June 1926; *s* of William Clement Crawley and Elsie Florence Crawley; *m* 1951, Ruth Eva Jungman (*d* 2003); two *d*. Joined Lloyds Bank, 1942; Chief Accountant, 1969–72; Asst Chief Gen. Man., 1977–78; Dep. Chief Gen. Man., 1978–82; Chief Exec., Lloyds Bank, Calif, 1982–83; Dep. Chief Gen. Man., 1983–84, Chief Gen. Man., 1984–85, Dep. Chief Exec., 1985–87, Lloyds Bank plc. Chairman: Black Horse Agencies Ltd, 1985–88; Betta Stores, 1990–92; Legal & General Recovery Investment Trust, 1994–98; Director: Black Horse Life Assce Co., 1977–82; Lloyds Bank Unit Trust Managers, 1977–82; Lloyds Leasing, 1977–82; Lloyds Development Capital, 1981–82; Lloyds Bank International, 1982–83; Internat. Commodities Clearing House Hldgs, 1984–87; Lloyds Bank, 1984–88; Lloyds Bank Export Finance, 1985–87; Lloyds Bowmaker Finance, 1985–87; FS Assurance, 1988–90; Barratt Developments, 1988–96; Lloyds Development Capital, 1988–92; Legal & General Bank Ltd, 1997–2001; Aeroclub Ltd, 1987–2004; Chm., The Property Jungle Ltd, 2000. RAF Benevolent Fund: Hon. Treas., 1988–2004, and Dep. Chm., 1988–2004, RAF Benevolent Fund Enterprises (formerly Internat. Air Tattoo); Dir, Air Shows Europe (formerly Battle of Britain Appeal), 1988–2004; Chm., RAF Charitable Trust Enterprises, 2005–11; Trustee, RAF Charitable Trust, 2005–12; Hon. Vice Patron, Royal Internat. Air Tattoo, 2011–. Develt Trustee, Mus. of Army Flying, 1993–2001. Fellow, St Andrews Strategic Management Ltd, 1995–96. FCIB (FIB 1971); FRAeS 2006 (ARAeS 1984). Freeman, City of London, 2006; Freeman, 1992, Liveryman, 2006, Hon. Co. of Air Pilots (formerly GAPAN). Hon. Citizen, Texas, 1983. *Recreations:* aviation, shooting, photography. *Address:* 4 The Hexagon, Fitzroy Park, N6 6HR. *T:* (020) 8341 2279. *Club:* Royal Air Force. *Died 9 Sept. 2014.*

CRAWSHAY, Elisabeth Mary Boyd, (Lady Crawshay), CBE 1986; Chairman, Local Government Boundary Commission, Wales, 1981–94; Deputy Chief Commissioner, St John's Ambulance Brigade, Wales, 1979–84; *b* 2 July 1927; *d* of Lt-Col Guy Franklin Reynolds, late 9th Lancers, and Katherine Isobel (*née* Macdonell); *m* 1950, Col Sir William (Robert) Crawshay, DSO, ERD, TD. *Educ:* Convent of Sacred Heart, Roehampton; St Anne's Coll., Oxford (MA). Mem., Mental Health Act Commn, 1983–88. DL Gwent 1978–90; JP Abergavenny, 1972–96 (Chm., Juvenile Bench, 1980–95; Mem., Borstal Board of Visitors, 1975–84). DJStJ 1970. *Address:* Ty Carreg, Govilon, Abergavenny, Mon NP7 9PT. *T:* (01873) 832220. *Died 6 Oct. 2015.*

CRESSWELL, Jeremy Michael, CVO 1996; HM Diplomatic Service, retired; Director, Foreign Service Programme, University of Oxford, since 2010; Fellow, Kellogg College, Oxford, since 2010; *b* 1 Oct. 1949; *s* of late John Cresswell and of Jean Cresswell; *m* 1st, 1974, Petra Forwick (marr. diss. 2006); one *s* one *d*; 2nd, 2009, Dr Barbara Munske. *Educ:* Eton Coll. Choir Sch.; Sir William Borlase's Sch., Marlow; Exeter Coll., Oxford (BA Hons); Johannes-Gutenberg Univ., Mainz, Germany. Entered FCO, 1972: Brussels, 1973–77; Kuala Lumpur, 1977–78; FCO, 1978–82 (Private Sec. to Minister of State, 1980–82); Dep. Pol Advr, BMG, Berlin, 1982–86; Dep. Head, News Dept, 1986–88, Asst Head, S America Dept, 1988–90, FCO; Counsellor (Political), UK Delegn to NATO, 1990–94; Dep. Head of Mission, Prague, 1995–98; Sen. Directing Staff, RCDS, 1998; Hd of EU Dept (Bilateral), FCO, 1999–2001; Minister and Dep. Hd of Mission, Berlin, 2001–05; High Comr to Jamaica and the Commonwealth of the Bahamas, 2005–09. *Recreations:* tennis, music. *Address:* Foreign Service Programme,

Department for Continuing Education, Rewley House, 1 Wellington Square, Oxford OX1 2JA. *T:* (01865) 270366. *E:* jeremy.cresswell@conted.ox.ac.uk. *Died 19 June 2015.*

CRIBB, Air Cdre Peter Henry, CBE 1957; DSO 1942, and Bar, 1944; DFC 1941; JP; *b* 28 Sept. 1918; *s* of late Charles B. Cribb and Mrs Ethel Cribb; *m* 1949, Vivienne Janet, *yr d* of late Col S. T. J. Perry, MC, TD, DL, Oxton, Birkenhead, Cheshire; three *s. Educ:* Bradford Grammar Sch.; Prince Henry's Sch., Otley. Flt Cadet, RAF Coll., 1936–38; Flying duties in Bomber Comd, 1938–45 (Comd No. 582 Sqdn, RAF Little Staughton); Comdg RAF Salbani, RAF Peshawar, India and Staff No. 1 Indian Gp, 1945–47; OC 203 Sqdn, 1947, and HQ Staff, 1950, Coastal Comd; RAF Staff Coll., Bracknell, 1951; Asst Dir Tech. Intell., Air Min., 1951–53; Gp Capt. Plans and Policy, HQ Bomber Comd, 1953–57; 2nd TAF, Germany (OC Oldenburg, Ahlhorn and Gutersloh), 1957–60; Air Min., Dep. Dir Air Staff Briefing, 1959–61, Dir, 1961–62; SASO, Air Forces, Middle East, 1962–63; IDC, 1964; Deputy to Asst Chief of Defence Staff (Joint Warfare), MoD 1965–66; retired, 1966. Administrative Manager, Goldsworthy Mining Ltd, 1966–68. Associate Fellow, Australian Inst. of Management, 1969; Past State Pres., Ryder-Cheshire Foundn of WA, Inc.; Patron, Pathfinder Assoc. of WA. Foundn Chm. Council, Univ. of Third Age (Univ. of Western Australia) Inc., 1986–88. Patron (RAF), UK Combined Services Fedn, WA, 1990–. JP Western Australia, 1968. *Recreation:* mainly cerebral. *Address:* Unit 183, RAAFA Estate, 19 Hughie Edwards Drive, Merriwa, WA 6030, Australia. *Died 20 June 2011.*

CRICHTON-BROWN, Sir Robert, KCMG 1980; Kt 1972; CBE 1970; TD; Executive Chairman, Rothmans International plc, 1985–88; *b* Melbourne, 23 Aug. 1919; *s* of late L. Crichton-Brown, Sydney; *m* 1941, Norah Isabelle (*d* 2011), *d* of late A. E. Turnbull; one *s* one *d. Educ:* Sydney Grammar Sch. Served War, 1939–45, BEF; Major, Royal Artillery and Gen. Staff, France, Iceland, India, Burma (despatches twice). Chairman: Lumley Corp. Ltd (formerly Edward Lumley Ltd), 1974–89 (Man. Dir, 1952–82); Lumley Life Ltd, 1961–87 (Dir, 1961–89); Lumley Gen. Insce Ltd, 1974–88 (Dir, 1952–88); NEI Pacific Ltd, 1961–85; Rothmans of Pall Mall (Australia) Ltd, 1981–85 (Dir, 1971–85 and 1987–88); Commercial Banking Co. of Sydney Ltd, 1976–82 (Dir, 1970–82); Commercial & General Acceptance Ltd, 1977–82; Westham Dredging Co. Pty Ltd, 1975–85; Vice Chairman: Nat. Australia Bank Ltd, 1982–85; Custom Credit Corp., 1982–85; Director: Daily Mail and General Trust Ltd (UK), 1979–95; Edward Lumley Hldgs, 1989–2003. Fed. Pres., Inst. of Dirs in Aust., 1967–80 (Chm., NSW Branch, 1965–80; Councillor, 1980–89; Hon. Life Mem.). Mem. Federal Exec. and Federal Hon. Treas., Liberal Party of Australia, 1973–85. Pres., Med. Foundn, Sydney Univ., 1962–87; Dir, Royal Prince Alfred Hosp., 1970–84; Hon. Life Governor, Aust. Postgraduate Fedn in Medicine; Member: Cttee, RACP, 1973–85; Adv. Bd, Girl Guides Assoc. of Australia, 1973–85; Adv. Bd, Salvation Army, 1973–85; Internat. Forum and Panel, Duke of Edinburgh's Award, 1979–84 (Nat. Co-ordinator, Duke of Edinburgh's Award Scheme in Aust., 1979–84); Council, Imperial Soc. of Knights Bachelor, 1983–97 (Vice-Chm., Pacific Reg.); Nat. Councillor, Scout Assoc. of Aust., 1980–85; Mem. Council, Maritime Trust (formerly Cutty Sark Maritime Trust), 1987–99; Gov., Cutty Sark Soc., 1987–89. Underwriting Mem. of Lloyd's, 1946–97. Hon. Fellow, Sydney Univ., 1987. Mem., Australia's winning Admiral's Cup Team (Balandra), UK, 1967; winner, Sydney-Hobart Yacht Race (Pacha), 1970. *Clubs:* White's, Royal Cruising; Royal Yacht Squadron; Australian, Union (Sydney); Cruising Yacht Club of Australia, Royal Sydney Yacht Squadron, Royal Prince Alfred Yacht. *Died 11 July 2013.*

CRITCHLEY, Tom; international business adviser, since 1990; *b* 17 Aug. 1928; *s* of late Leonard and Jessie Critchley; *m* 1951, Margaret Bland; one *s. Educ:* Sheffield Coll. of Commerce and Technology (Freshgate Trust Award, 1958). Davy-Ashmore Group, 1951–66; Cammell Laird and Upper Clyde Groups, 1966–69; J. C. B. Group, 1969–70; EMI Group, 1970–80; Head, Investment Casting Mission to Canada; UN Adviser to Tanzanian Govt; Adviser to UN High Commn for Refugees; Chm., MATC Ltd; Senior Partner, internat. consultancy practice, 1980–85; Under Sec., DHSS, subseq. Dept of Health, and NHS Management Bd Mem., 1986–90; Head, healthcare missions to Japan, Philippines, Indonesia, USSR and Poland, 1989–90; UK Chm., Anglo-Soviet Health-care Gp, 1989–91; Managing Director: Bio-Flo Ltd, 1991–95; Eurosep, Poland, 1992–95. Chairman: UK Trade Assoc., 1990–92; European Timeshare Fedn, 1991–92; Mem. Board, Nat. Inst. of Govt Purchasing, USA, 1977–78; Sen. UK Deleg., Internat. Fedn of Purchasing & Materials Management, 1980–85; Dir, Internat. Management Inst., Paris, 1980–88; Faculty Mem., Management Centre Europe, Brussels, 1980–85; Mem., Business in the Community, 1989–92. Institute of Purchasing & Supply, later Chartered Inst. of Purchasing and Supply: Mem., 1959–; FCIPS (Fellow, 1967); Chm. Council, 1974–75; Pres., 1977–78; Chm., Ext. Affairs, 1978–82; Mem., Internat. Council, 1979–82. Pres., Internat. Cttee of Friendship for Internat. Students, Imperial Coll., London, 1996–97. Millennium Adviser: The Children's Soc., 1996–98; Friends of the Elderly, 1998–2000; Business Develt Advr, SE Regl Arts Centre, 2000–02. Chm., Huntleigh Foundn, 1997–2003; Capital Appeal Co-ordinator, Harlington Hospice, 2003–05. Vice-Patron, British Assoc. for Services to Elderly, 2006–. *Recreations:* competitive sports, live theatre, North American history. *Address:* 3 Laurel Court, Chesham Bois, Amersham, Bucks HP6 5LP. *T:* (01494) 723249. *Died 14 April 2014.*

CROCKETT, Sir Andrew (Duncan), Kt 2003; President, JP Morgan Chase International, since 2003; *b* 23 March 1943; *s* of late Dr Andrew Stuart Crockett and of Sheilah Crockett (*née* Stewart); *m* 1966, Marjorie Frances Hlavacek; two *s* one *d. Educ:* Queens' College, Cambridge (MA Econ.); Yale Univ. (MA). Bank of England, 1966–72; International Monetary Fund, 1972–89; Exec. Dir, Bank of England, 1989–93; Gen. Manager, BIS, 1994–2003. *Publications:* Money: theory, policy, institutions, 1973; International Money: issues and analysis, 1977; contribs to professional jls. *Recreations:* reading, golf, tennis. *Address:* JP Morgan Chase, 560 Mission Street, 20th Floor, San Francisco, CA 94105, USA. *Died 3 Sept. 2012.*

CROFT, Roy Henry Francis, CB 1983; Member, Competition (formerly Monopolies and Mergers) Commission, 1995–2001; *b* 4 March 1936; *s* of late William Henry Croft and Dorothy Croft; *m* 1961, Patricia Ainley; one *s* two *d. Educ:* Isleworth Grammar Sch.; Christ's Coll., Cambridge (MA). BoT, 1959; Treasury, 1961–62; DEA, 1964–67; Private Sec. to Pres. Bd of Trade, 1968–70; Cabinet Office, 1970–72; Civil Aviation Div., Dept of Trade, 1973–76; Finance and Economic Appraisal Div., DoI, 1976–79; Posts and Telecommunications Div., DoI, 1979–80; Dep. Sec. DTI, 1980–85; Exec. Dir and Chief Operating Officer, SIB, 1985–93. Dir (non-exec.), Morgan Stanley Bank Internat. Ltd, 1999–2005. *Died 6 Sept. 2012.*

CROHAM, Baron *cr* 1978 (Life Peer), of the London Borough of Croydon; **Douglas Albert Vivian Allen,** GCB 1973 (KCB 1967; CB 1963); Chairman, Guinness Peat Group, 1983–87; Head of the Home Civil Service and Permanent Secretary, Civil Service Department, 1974–77; *b* 15 Dec. 1917; *s* of late Albert Allen; *m* 1941, Sybil Eileen Allegro (*d* 1994), *d* of late John Marco Allegro; one *s* one *d* (and one *s* decd). *Educ:* Wallington County Grammar Sch.; London School of Economics. BSc (Econ.) First Class Hons, 1938. Entered Board of Trade, 1939; Royal Artillery, 1940–45; Cabinet Office, 1947; Treasury, 1948–58; Under-Secretary, Ministry of Health, 1958–60; Under-Secretary, Treasury, 1960–62, Third Secretary, 1962–64; Dept of Economic Affairs: Dep. Under-Sec. of State, 1964–66; Second Permanent Under-Sec. of State, May–Oct. 1966; Permanent Under-Sec. of State, 1966–68; Permanent Sec., HM Treasury, 1968–74. Director: Pilkington plc (formerly Pilkington Bros), 1978–92; Guinness Mahon & Co., 1989–92; Dep. Chm., 1978–82, Chm., 1982–85, BNOC; Chm., Trinity Insurance, 1988–92. An Industrial Adviser to the Governor, Bank of England, 1978–83. President: Inst. for Fiscal Studies, 1979–92; British Inst. of Energy Economies, 1985–94. A Trustee, Anglo-German Foundn, 1977–2009 (Chm., 1982–97). CCMI; FRSA 1975. Hon. Fellow, LSE, 1969; Hon. DSc (Social Sciences)

Southampton, 1977. *Recreation:* bridge. *Address:* 9 Manor Way, South Croydon, Surrey CR2 7BT. *T:* (020) 8688 0496. *Club:* Reform. *Died 11 Sept. 2011.*

CRONIN, Vincent Archibald Patrick; author; *b* 24 May 1924; *s* of late Archibald Joseph Cronin, MD, MRCP, DPH and of Agnes Mary Gibson, MB, ChB; *m* 1949, Chantal, *d* of Comte Jean de Rolland; two *s* three *d. Educ:* Ampleforth; Harvard; Trinity Coll., Oxford. Rifle Bde, 1943–45. *Publications:* The Golden Honeycomb, 1954; The Wise Man from the West, 1955; The Last Migration, 1957; A Pearl to India, 1959; The Letter after Z, 1960; Louis XIV, 1964; Four Women in Pursuit of an Ideal, 1965; The Florentine Renaissance, 1967; The Flowering of the Renaissance, 1970; Napoleon, 1971; Louis and Antoinette, 1974; trans., Giscard d'Estaing, Towards a New Democracy, 1977; Catherine, Empress of all the Russias, 1978; The View from Planet Earth, 1981; Paris on the Eve, 1989; Paris: City of Light 1919–1939, 1995; Chile Discovered, 2009. *Address:* Manoir de Brion, Dragey 50530, France. *Died 25 Jan. 2011.*

CROOK, Kenneth Roy, CMG 1978; HM Diplomatic Service, retired; Ambassador to Afghanistan, 1976–79; *b* 30 July 1920; *s* of Alexander Crook, Prescot, Lancs, and Margaret Kay Crook; *m* 1943, Freda Joan Vidler; two *d. Educ:* Prescot Grammar Sch., Lancs; Skerry's Coll., Liverpool. Appointed to: Board of Trade, 1937; Min. of War Transport, 1939. Royal Navy, 1941–46. Board of Trade, 1946–49; Commonwealth Relations Office, 1949; Second Sec., Canberra, 1951–54; First Sec., Madras, 1956–59; Deputy High Commissioner: Peshawar, W Pakistan, 1962–64; Dacca, E Pakistan, 1964–67; Counsellor, FCO, 1967; Head of Information Research Dept, FCO, 1969–71; Governor, Cayman Is, 1971–74; Canadian Nat. Defence Coll., 1974–75; Head of Science and Technology Dept, FCO, 1975–76. *Recreations:* walking, gardening, music appreciation. *Address:* 16 Burntwood Road, Sevenoaks, Kent TN13 1PT. *Died 24 July 2012.*

CROSFIELD, Rev. Canon (George) Philip (Chorley), OBE 1990; Provost of St Mary's Cathedral, Edinburgh, 1970–90, Hon. Canon, since 1991; *b* 9 Sept. 1924; *s* of James Chorley Crosfield and Marjorie Louise Crosfield; *m* 1956, Susan Mary Jullion (*née* Martin); one *s* two *d. Educ:* George Watson's Coll., Edinburgh; Selwyn Coll., Cambridge (BA 1950; MA 1955). Royal Artillery, 1942–46 (Captain). Priest, 1952; Asst Curate: St David's, Pilton, Edinburgh, 1951–53; St Andrew's, St Andrews, 1953–55; Rector, St Cuthbert's, Hawick, 1955–60; Chaplain, Gordonstoun School, 1960–68; Canon and Vice Provost, St Mary's Cathedral, Edinburgh, 1968–70. *Recreations:* walking, reading. *Address:* 21 Biggar Road, Silverburn, Penicuik EH26 9LQ. *T:* (01968) 676607. *Died 13 March 2013.*

CROSLAND, Susan Barnes; writer; *b* Baltimore, Maryland, 23 Jan. 1927; *y d* of Susan Owens and Mark Skinner Watson; *m* 1st, Patrick Skene Catling (marr. diss.); two *d*; 2nd, Rt Hon. (Charles) Anthony (Raven) Crosland, PC, MP (*d* 1977). Journalism: Sunday Express, 1960–64; freelance, 1964–; profile-writer and columnist, Sunday Times and various jls. Trustee, Nat. Portrait Gallery, 1978–92. *Publications:* Behind the Image, 1974; Tony Crosland, 1982; Looking Out, Looking In, 1987; Great Sexual Scandals, 2002; *novels:* Ruling Passions, 1989; Dangerous Games, 1991; The Magnates, 1994; The Prime Minister's Wife, 2001. *Recreation:* freedom. *Address:* 16 Stanford Court, 45 Cornwall Gardens, SW7 4AB. *Club:* Academy. *Died 26 Feb. 2011.*

CROSSLAND, Sir Bernard, Kt 1990; CBE 1980; MSc (London); PhD (Bristol); DSc (Nottingham); FRS 1979; FREng; FIAE; MRIA; Emeritus Professor, The Queen's University, Belfast, since 1984 (Professor and Head of Department of Mechanical and Industrial Engineering, 1959–82, Research Professor, 1982–84; Dean, 1964–67; Pro-Vice-Chancellor, 1978–82); *b* 20 Oct. 1923; *s* of R. F. Crossland and K. M. Rudduck; *m* 1946, Audrey Elliott Birks; two *d. Educ:* Simon Langton's, Canterbury. Apprentice, Rolls Royce Ltd, 1940–44; Nottingham Univ., 1941–43; Technical Asst, Rolls Royce, 1943–45; Asst Lectr, Lectr and later Senior Lectr in Mechanical Engineering, Univ. of Bristol, 1946–59. Member: AFRC, 1981–87; Engrg Council, 1983–88; Chairman: Bd for Engineers' Registration, 1983–86; Youth Careers Guidance Cttee, NI, 1975–79, 1979–81; NI Manpower Council, 1981–86; Adv. Bd for Postgrad. Awards, NI Dept of Educn, 1982–95; Member: NI Training Council, 1964–76, 1977–81; NI Economic Council, 1981–85; NI Industrial Develt Bd, 1982–87. Dir, Gilbert Associates (Europe) Ltd, 1991–94. Assessor, King's Cross Fire Investigation, 1988; Chm., Public Hearing into Bilsthorpe Colliery Accident, 1994; Expert Witness for HSE in prosecution arising from Port of Ramsgate walkway disaster, 1997. Mem. Council and a Vice-Pres., Royal Soc., 1984–86; Mem. Council, Fellowship of Engrg, 1985–88; Pres., Section 6, British Assoc., 1987; Institution of Mechanical Engineers: Chm., Engineering Sciences Div., 1980–84; Vice-Pres., 1983–84; Dep. Pres., 1984–86; Pres., 1986–87; Past Pres., 1987–91; Leonardo da Vinci Lectr, 1970; George Stephenson Lectr, 1989; Thomas Lowe Gray Lectr, 1999; George Stephenson and Thomas Hawksley Medals; Hon. Fellow, 1997; James Watt Internat. Medal, 1999. Lectures: Richard Weck, Welding Inst., 1992; Seamus Timoney, NUI, 1993; McLaughlin, Instn of Engrs of Ireland, 1998. Trustee, Mackie Foundn, 1983–94. Freeman, City of London, 1987; Liveryman, Worshipful Co. of Engrs, 1988. FREng (FEng 1979); Founder FIAE 1998. Hon. MASME 1987; Hon. FWeldI 1990 (Pres., 1995–98); Hon. FIEI 1993; Hon. FIStructE 2001. Hon. Fellow, Univ. of Luton, 1994. Hon. DSc: NUI, 1984; Dublin, 1985; Edinburgh, 1987; QUB 1988; Aston, 1988; Cranfield Inst. of Technology, 1989; Hon. DEng: Bristol, 1992; Limerick, 1993; Liverpool, 1993. Kelvin Medal, ICE, 1992; Cunningham Medal, RIA, 2001; Lifetime Achievement Award, Instn of Engrs of Ireland, 2007; Sustained Achievement Award, RAEng, 2009. *Publications:* An Introduction to the Mechanics of Machines, 1964; Explosive Welding and its Application, 1982; The Lives of Great Engineers of Ulster, vol. 1, 2003, vols 2 and 3, 2008; The Anatomy of an Engineer - an autobiography, 2006; various papers on fatigue of metals and effect of very high fluid pressures on properties of materials; strength of thick-walled vessels, explosive welding, friction welding, design and history of engineering, engineering disasters. *Recreation:* hobbling. *Address:* The Queen's University, Belfast BT7 1NN. *T:* (028) 9097 4238; 16 Malone Court, Belfast BT9 6PA. *T:* (028) 9066 7495. *Club:* Athenæum. *Died 17 Jan. 2011.*

CROSSLEY, Maj.-Gen. Ralph John, CB 1987; CBE 1981; *b* 11 Oct. 1933; *s* of Edward Crossley and Eva Mary Crossley (*née* Farnworth); *m* 1957, Marion Hilary Crossley (*née* Bacon); one *s* one *d. Educ:* Quainton Sch., Harrow; Felsted School. Commnd 1952 (Nat. Service); Air Observation Post Pilots course, 1953; Regimental Duty: Canal Zone, 1954–56; BAOR, 1956–59; Instructor in Gunnery, Larkhill, 1959–63; Technical Staff Course, 1963–65; Regtl Duty, BAOR, 1965–67, 1969–71; Weapons Staff, UK, 1967–69; Gen. Staff, UK, 1971–72; Instructor, RMCS, 1972–74; CO, 94 Locating Regt, 1974–77; Project Manager, 155 Systems, 1977–81; Dep. Comdt, RMCS, 1981–84; Dir Gen. of Weapons (Army), 1984–86; retired 1986. Defence Advr, Avon Rubber, 1987–91. Chairman: Salisbury HA, 1990–93; Salisbury Healthcare NHS Trust, 1993–97. Chm. Govs, Redlynch Primary Sch., 1998–2005. *Recreations:* golf, walking, gardening, grandchildren. *Died 16 May 2011.*

CROW, Robert; General Secretary, National Union of Rail, Maritime and Transport Workers, since 2002; *b* 13 June 1961; *s* of George William Crow and Lillian (*née* Hutton); partner, Nicola Hoarau; one *d* and one step *s* one step *d*; one *d* from a former marriage. *Educ:* Hainault High Sch. Joined London Underground as railway worker, 1977. Mem. Nat. Exec., 1994–, Asst Gen. Sec., 1994–2002, RMT. Contested (No2EU) London Region, European Parly elections, 2009. *Recreations:* football, boxing, darts. *Address:* National Union of Rail, Maritime and Transport Workers, Unity House, 39 Chalton Street, NW1 1JD. *Club:* Millwall Football. *Died 11 March 2014.*

CROWDER, Ven. Norman Harry; Archdeacon of Portsmouth, 1985–93, then Archdeacon Emeritus; *b* 20 Oct. 1926; *s* of Laurence Smethurst Crowder and Frances Annie (*née* Hicks); *m* 1971, Pauleen Florence Alison (*née*

Styles); one *s*. *Educ:* Nottingham High School; St John's Coll., Cambridge (MA); Westcott House, Cambridge. Nat. Service, Flying Officer, RAF Educn Branch, 1948–50. Curate, St Mary's, Radcliffe-on-Trent, 1952–55; Residential Chaplain to Bishop of Portsmouth, 1955–59; Asst Chaplain, Canford School, 1959–64, Chaplain 1964–72; Vicar, St John's, Oakfield, Ryde, IoW, 1972–75; Dir of Religious Educn, Portsmouth Dio., and Res. Canon of Portsmouth Cathedral, 1975–85. *Recreations:* water colours of J. M. W. Turner, poetry of T. S. Eliot, conservation of elephants. *Address:* 37 Rectory Road, Salisbury SP2 7SD. *T:* (01722) 320052. *Club:* MCC. *Died 10 Feb. 2013.*

CROWE, His Honour Gerald Patrick; QC 1973; a Circuit Judge, 1980–95; *b* 3 April 1930; *y s* of Patrick Crowe and Ethel Maud Crowe (*née* Tooth); *m* 1st, 1954, Catherine Mary (*d* 2000), *d* of Joseph and Rose Murphy, Newry, N Ireland; 2nd, 2004, Marie Therese Murphy. *Educ:* St Francis Xavier's Coll.; Liverpool Univ. (LLB). Called to Bar, Gray's Inn, 1952; practised Northern Circuit. A Recorder of the Crown Court, 1976–80. Mem., Lord Chancellor's Adv. Cttee on Legal Aid, 1984–91. *Recreations:* golf, fishing. *Address:* The Spinney, Long Hey Road, Caldy, Cheshire CH48 1LY. *T:* (0151) 625 8848. *Died 4 Nov. 2014.*

CROWLEY-MILLING, Michael Crowley, CMG 1982; CEng, FIET; consultant on computer control systems; *b* 7 May 1917; *s* of Thomas William Crowley-Milling and Gillian May (*née* Chinnery); *m* 1958, Gladys Jessie, (Gee), Dickson (*d* 2005). *Educ:* Radley Coll.; St John's Coll., Cambridge (MA 1943). CEng, FIET (FIEE 1956). R&D on radar systems, Metropolitan-Vickers Electrical Co. Ltd, Manchester, 1938–46; design and develt of electron linear accelerators for physics, medical and irradiation purposes, 1946–63; contrib. to construction of electron synchrotron, Daresbury Nuclear Physics Lab., Warrington, 1963–71; CERN, Geneva: resp. for control system for Super Proton Synchrotron (SPS), 1971–75; SPS Div. Leader, 1977–78; Dir, Accelerator Prog., 1979–80; Consultant, 1982–83; Consultant to: SLAC, Stanford Univ., Calif., 1984–85; Los Alamos Nat. Lab., New Mexico, 1986–94; SSC Lab., Dallas, 1991–93; Dir, Crowley Consultants, 1984–. Crompton Premium, IEE, 1959; Glazebrook Medal, Inst. of Physics, 1980. Captain LMBC, 1938. Patents for improvements in radar systems and particle accelerators, 1940–60. *Publications:* (ed) Accelerator Control Systems, 1986; (ed) Accelerator and Large Experimental Control Systems, 1990, 1994; John Bertram Adams, Engineer Extraordinary, 1993; articles and chapters in books on particle accelerators and computer control systems. *Recreations:* vintage cars, sailing. *Address:* 5 West Court, Hollins Hall, Harrogate HG3 2WY. *Clubs:* Vintage Sports Car, Royal Yacht. *Died 24 Dec. 2012.*

CROWTHER, (Joseph) Stanley; freelance journalist, since 1951; *b* 30 May 1925; *s* of Cyril Joseph Crowther and Florence Mildred (*née* Beckett); *m* 1948, Margaret Royston; two *s*. *Educ:* Rotherham Grammar Sch.; Rotherham Coll. of Technology. Royal Signals, 1943–47. Journalist: Rotherham Advertiser, 1941–43 and 1947–50; Yorkshire Evening Post, 1950–51. Mem., Rotherham Borough Council, 1958–59, 1961–76; Mayor of Rotherham, 1971–72, 1975–76; Chm., Yorkshire and Humberside Develt Assoc., 1972–76. MP (Lab) Rotherham, June 1976–1992. Vice-Pres., Town and Country Planning Assoc., 1990–2000. Freedom of Bor. of Rotherham, 2009. *Publications:* One Thing After Another (memoirs), 2005. *Recreations:* singing, listening to jazz. *Died 10 March 2013.*

CROXON, Raymond Patrick Austen; QC 1983; *b* 31 July 1928; *s* of late Randolph Croxon, bandmaster, Salvation Army, and Rose Harvey, Home League Sec., Salvation Army; *m* 1952, Monica Howard (marr. diss. 1992); two *s* two *d*; *m* 2001, Hara Marinou. *Educ:* Strand College; King's College London. LLB. Served in RAMC, 1946–49. Called to the Bar, Gray's Inn, 1960; Hd of Regency Chambers, 1995–2003. *Recreations:* travel, walking, swimming, reading, music, theatre, modern Greek language. *Club:* Savage. *Died 30 Nov. 2014.*

CROZIER, Brian Rossiter; writer and consultant on international affairs; Distinguished Visiting Fellow, Hoover Institution on War, Revolution and Peace, Stanford University, California, 1996–2002; contributor, National Review, New York, since 1982; *b* 4 Aug. 1918; *s* of R. H. Crozier and Elsa (*née* McGillivray); *m* 1st, 1940, Mary Lillian Samuel (*d* 1993); one *s* three *d*; 2nd, 1999, Jacqueline Marie Mitchell. *Educ:* Lycée, Montpellier; Peterborough Coll., Harrow; Trinity Coll. of Music, London. Music and art critic, London, 1936–39; reporter-sub-editor, Stoke-on-Trent, Stockport, London, 1940–41; aeronautical inspection, 1941–43; sub-editor: Reuters, 1943–44; News Chronicle, 1944–48; and writer, Sydney Morning Herald, 1948–51; corresp., Reuters-AAP, 1951–52; features editor, Straits Times, 1952–53; leader writer, corresp. and editor, Foreign Report, Economist, 1954–64; commentator, BBC English, French and Spanish overseas services, 1954–66; Chm., Forum World Features, 1965–74; Columnist: Nat. Review, NY, 1978–95; Now!, 1979–81; The Times, 1982–83; Freedom Today (formerly The Free Nation), 1982–89. Co-founder, Inst. for the Study of Conflict, 1970 (Dir, 1970–79). Adjunct Scholar, Heritage Foundn, Washington, 1984–95. *Publications:* The Rebels, 1960; The Morning After, 1963; Neo-Colonialism, 1964; South-East Asia in Turmoil, 1965, 3rd edn 1968; The Struggle for the Third World, 1966; Franco, 1967; The Masters of Power, 1969; The Future of Communist Power (in USA: Since Stalin), 1970; De Gaulle, vol. 1 1973, vol. 2 1974; A Theory of Conflict, 1974; The Man Who Lost China (Chiang Kai-shek), 1976; Strategy of Survival, 1978; The Minimum State, 1979; Franco: crepúsculo de un hombre (Spanish orig.), 1980; The Price of Peace, 1980, new edn 1983; (jtly) Socialism Explained, 1984; (jtly) This War Called Peace, 1984; (as John Rossiter) The Andropov Deception (novel), 1984 (pubd under own name, NY, 1986); Socialism: dream and reality, 1987; (ed) The Grenada Documents, 1987; The Gorbachev Phenomenon, 1990; Communism: why prolong its death-throes?, 1990; Free Agent, 1993; The KGB Lawsuits, 1995; (jtly) Le Phénix rouge, 1995; The Rise and Fall of the Soviet Empire, 1999; The Other Brian Croziers, 2003; Political Victory: the elusive prize of military wars, 2005; contrib. to jls in various countries. *Recreations:* piano, films. *Address:* 18 Wickliffe Avenue, N3 3EJ. *T:* (020) 8346 8124. *Club:* Royal Automobile. *Died 4 Aug. 2012.*

CRUTHERS, Sir James (Winter), Kt 1980; AO 2008; Vice-Chairman and Executive Vice-President, News America Publishing Inc., 1984–90 (Director, 1983); Vice-Chairman, News America Holdings Inc., 1984–90 (Director, 1984); *b* 20 Dec. 1924; *s* of James William and Kate Cruthers; *m* 1950, Alwyn Sheila Della (*d* 2011); one *s* one *d*. *Educ:* Claremont Central State Sch.; Perth Technical College. Started as junior in Perth Daily News, 1939; war service, AIF and RAAF (Pilot), 1942; Journalist, Perth Daily News, 1946; Editor, Weekly Publications, West Australian Newspapers Ltd, 1953; TVW Enterprises Ltd: General Manager, 1958; Managing Director, 1969; Dep. Chm., 1974; Chm., 1976–81; Chm., Australian Film Commn, 1982–83. Director: News Corp. Ltd, 1981–92; Satellite Television plc, 1984–90 (Chm., 1985–88). Western Australian Citizen Of The Year, Industry and Commerce, 1980. *Recreations:* golf, jogging. *Clubs:* Weld, Lake Karrinyup Country (Perth). *Died 13 Oct. 2015.*

CRUTTWELL, Geraldine, (Mrs Hugh Cruttwell); *see* McEwan, G.

CUBBON, Sir Brian (Crossland), GCB 1984 (KCB 1977; CB 1974); Permanent Under Secretary of State, Home Office, 1979–88; *b* 9 April 1928; *m* 1956, Elizabeth Lorin Richardson; three *s* one *d*. *Educ:* Bury Grammar Sch.; Trinity Coll., Cambridge. Entered Home Office, 1951; Cabinet Office, 1961–63, 1971–75; Private Sec. to Home Sec., 1968–69; Permanent Under-Sec. of State, Northern Ireland Office, 1976–79. Mem., 1995–2002, Charter Comr, 2004–09, Press Complaints Commn. Vice-Pres., Hakluyt Foundn, 1995–2002. *Address:* Brook Farm House, Capel, Tonbridge, Kent TN12 6TT. *T:* (01892) 832534. *Club:* Oxford and Cambridge. *Died 20 May 2015.*

CULLEN, Prof. Alexander Lamb, OBE 1960; DSc(Eng); FRS 1977; FREng, FIET, FIEEE, FInstP, FCGI; Emeritus Professor, University of London; Hon. Research Fellow,

Department of Electronic and Electrical Engineering, University College London, since 1984 (SERC Senior Research Fellow, 1980–84); *b* 30 April 1920; *s* of Richard and Jessie Cullen, Lincoln; *m* 1940, Margaret (*d* 2008), *er d* of late Andrew Lamb, OBE; two *s* one *d*. *Educ:* Lincoln Sch.; City and Guilds Coll., London. Staff of Radio Dept, RAE Farnborough, working on development of radar, 1940–46; Lectr in Electrical Engineering, University Coll., London, 1946–55 (title of Reader conferred 1955); Prof. of Electrical Engineering, University of Sheffield, 1955–67; Pender Prof. of Electrical Engineering, University College London, 1967–80. Hon. Prof., Northwestern Polytechnical Univ., Xian, China, 1981. Mem., IBA, 1982–89. Institution of Electrical Engineers: Kelvin premium, 1952; Ambrose Fleming premium, 1956 (with J. C. Parr), 1975 (with Dr J. R. Forrest), 1988 (with S. P. Yeo); Duddell premium, 1957 (with Dr H. A. French); Faraday Medal, 1984; Electronics Letters premium, 1985; Maxwell premium, 1996 (jtly). Microwave Career Award, IEEE, 1989. Chm., Brit. Nat. Cttee, URSI, 1981–85; Vice-Pres., Internat. URSI, 1981–87, Pres., 1987–90; Mem. Council, Royal Soc., 1984–86. Clifford Paterson Lecture, Royal Soc., 1984; Clerk Maxwell Lecture, IERE, 1986. FREng (FEng 1977). Hon. FIERE 1987; Hon. Fellow, UCL, 1993. Hon. DSc: Chinese Univ. of Hong Kong, 1981; Kent, 1986. Hon. DEng Sheffield, 1985. Royal Medal, Royal Soc., 1984. *Publications:* Microwave Measurements (jointly with Prof. H. M. Barlow), 1950; a number of papers on electromagnetic waves and microwave measurement techniques in IEE proceedings and elsewhere. *Recreations:* music, reading. *Address:* 3 Felden Drive, Felden, Hemel Hempstead, Herts HP3 0BD. *E:* alex.304@btinternet.com. *Died 27 Dec. 2013.*

CULLIMORE, Colin Stuart, CBE 1978; DL; Chairman, Lincoln Cathedral Council, 2000–07 (Member, Transitional Council, 1998–2000); *b* 13 July 1931; *s* of Reginald Victor Cullimore and May Maria Cullimore; *m* 1952, Kathleen Anyta Lamming; one *s*. *Educ:* Westminster Sch.; Grenoble Univ.; National Coll. of Food Technol. Commnd Royal Scots Fusiliers, 1951; seconded Parachute Regt; transf. when perm. officer cadre formed; Major 1956; 10th Bn Parachute Regt TA, 1960. Gen. Man., Payne & Son (Butchers) Ltd, 1960; Asst Gen. Man., J. H. Dewhurst Ltd, 1965, Gen. Man., 1969, Man. Dir, 1976–90; Dir of External Affairs, Vestey Gp, 1990–92; Dir, Airborne Initiative Holdings Ltd, 1991–93; Chm., NAAFI, 1993–96 (non-exec. Dir, 1984–96); Director: Longhurst Housing Assoc., 1996–2001; Longhurst Gp, 2000–02 (Chm., Audit Cttee, 2000–02). Trustee, Western United Gp Pension Scheme, 1986–2010. Chairman: Retail Consortium Food Cttee, 1973–74; Multiple Shops Fedn, 1977–78; Vice-Chairman: Multiple Food Retailers Assoc., 1972–74; Retail Consortium, 1982–88 (Vice-Pres., 1990–92); Pres., British Retailers Assoc., 1984–89 (Vice Pres., 1978–84); Dep. Chm., Meat Promotion Exec., 1975–78; Vice Pres., Bd of Admin, CECD (European Retailers), 1986–88 (Mem., 1981–85); Gov., Coll. for Distributive Trades, 1976–79 (Vice Chm.), 1984–88. Member: EDC for Distribn Trades, 1972–80; Council and Management Cttee, Inst. of Meat (Vice-Chm., 1981–83); Cttee of Commerce and Distribn, EEC, 1984–93; Council, Industry & Parlt Trust, 1987–93. Chm. Council, Westminster Sch. Soc., 1999–2007 (Mem., 1990–2008). Vice Pres., Royal Smithfield Club, 1991– (Mem. Council, 1993–95). Gov., Court of London Inst., 1984–87 and 1989–90; Exec. Trustee, Airborne Assault Normandy Trust, 1983–2004; Chm., Reserve Forces Ulysses Trust, 1992–96; Member: Regtl Council, Parachute Regt, 1991–97; Lincoln Diocese Trust and Bd of Finances, 1993–2001 (Chm. Resources Cttee, 1994–96). FInstD 1979; CCMI (CBIM 1984); FRSA 1987. Liveryman, Butchers' Co. (Mem. Court, 1992–2007; Warden, 1998–2003; Providitor, 2002–03; Master, 2004–05). DL Lincs, 1998. Gold Medal: Inst. of Meat, 1956; Butchers' Co., 1956. OStJ 1988. *Address:* 20 Minster Yard, Lincoln LN2 1PY. *T:* (01522) 569581, *Fax:* (01522) 524205. *E:* colincullimore@yahoo.co.uk. *Clubs:* Naval and Military, Farmers. *Died 22 Dec. 2015.*

CULSHAW, John Douglas; Assistant Chief Scientific Adviser (Capabilities), Ministry of Defence, 1985–87; *b* 22 Oct. 1927; *s* of Alfred Henry Douglas Culshaw and Dorothy Yeats Culshaw (*née* Hogarth); *m* 1951, Hazel Speirs Alexander (*d* 1998); one *s* one *d*. *Educ:* Washington Alderman Smith Grammar Sch., Co. Durham; University Coll., Nottingham. BSc London 1949; MSc Nottingham 1950. Joined Weapons Dept, Royal Aircraft Estabt, Min. of Supply, Farnborough, 1950; OC (Scientific) 6 Joint Services Trials Unit RAF (UK), 1956; OC (Sci.) 16 JSTU RA Weapons Research Estabt, Salisbury, S Australia, 1961; Co-ordinating Research and Development Authority Technical Project Officer, RAE, 1964; Supt Mine Warfare Br., Royal Armament R&D Estabt, MoD, Sevenoaks, 1967; Director, Scientific Adv. Br., Home Office, 1970; Dept of Chief Scientific Adviser (Army), 1972; Head of Mathematics and Assessment Dept, RARDE, MoD, Sevenoaks, 1974; Head of Defence Science II, MoD, 1975; RCDS 1976; Dep. Dir, Scientific and Technical Intelligence, 1977; Dir, Defence Operational Analysis Estabt and Asst Chief Scientific Advr (Studies), MoD, 1979–84. *Recreation:* historical research. *Club:* Civil Service. *Died 21 July 2013.*

CUNLIFFE, Stella Vivian, MBE 1993; consultant statistician; *b* 12 Jan. 1917; *d* of Percy Cunliffe and Edith Blanche Wellwood Cunliffe. *Educ:* privately, then Parsons Mead, Ashtead; London School of Economics (BScEcon). Danish Bacon Co., 1939–44; Voluntary Relief Work in Europe, 1945–47; Arthur Guinness Son and Co. Ltd, 1947–70; Head of Research Unit, Home Office, 1970–72; Dir of Statistics, Home Office, 1972–77. Statistical Adviser to Cttee of Enquiry into Engineering Profession, 1978–80. Pres., Royal Statistical Soc., 1975–77. *Recreations:* work with youth organisations; gardening; prison after-care. *Died 20 Jan. 2012.*

CUNNINGHAM-JARDINE, Ronald Charles, CVO 2007; Lord-Lieutenant, Dumfries and Galloway Region, districts of Nithsdale, Annandale and Eskdale, 1991–2006 (Vice Lord-Lieutenant, 1988–91); *b* 19 Sept. 1931; *s* of Charles Frederick Cunningham and Dorothy Agnes Jessie Jardine; *m* 1959, Constance Mary Teresa Inglis; one *s* one *d*. *Educ:* Ludgrove; Eton College; RMA Sandhurst. Royal Scots Greys, 1950–58; Edinburgh Agricultural College, 1959–60; farming, 1960–95. *Recreation:* all country sports. *Address:* Fourmerkland, Lockerbie, Dumfriesshire DG11 1EH. *T:* (01387) 810226. *Clubs:* White's; Muthaiga (Nairobi). *Died 25 May 2015.*

CUOMO, Mario Matthew; lawyer; Democrat; Partner, Willkie Farr & Gallagher LLP, since 1995; *b* 15 June 1932; *s* of late Andrea and Immaculata Cuomo; *m* 1954, Matilda M. Raffa; two *s* three *d*. *Educ:* St John's Coll., NY (Latin Amer. Studies, English, Philosophy; BA 1953); St John's Univ. (LLB 1956). Admitted to NY Bar, 1956, US Supreme Court, 1960; Asst to Judge A. P. Burke, NY State Court of Appeals, 1956–58; joined Corner, Weisbrod, Froeb & Charles (later Corner, Finn, Cuomo & Charles), 1958, Partner, 1963–75; Prof., St John's Univ. Law Sch., 1963–73; Sec. of State for NY, 1975–78 (Chm., NY Urban & Rural Affairs, Adv. Council on Disabled; 1st NY Ombudsman); Lt-Governor, NY, 1979–82; Governor, NY State, 1983–95. *Publications:* The Forest Hills Controversy: a report and comment, 1972; Forest Hills Diary: the crisis of low income housing, 1974; Diaries of Mario M. Cuomo: the campaign for Governor, 1984; (ed jtly) Lincoln on Democracy, 1990; More than Words: the speeches of Mario Cuomo, 1993; New York Idea: an experiment in democracy, 1994; Reason to Believe, 1995; (for children) The Blue Spruce, 1999; Why Lincoln Matters: today more than ever, 2004; articles in legal jls. *Died 1 Jan. 2015.*

CURLEY, Carlo James; international concert organist; *b* 24 Aug. 1952; *s* of James Dennis Curley and Gladys Maynard Curley. *Educ:* N Carolina Sch. of Arts; privately with Virgil Fox, Robert Elmore and Sir George Thalben Ball. Organist/choirmaster, Druid Hills Baptist Ch, Atlanta, Ga, 1968–71; Artist-in-Residence, Fountain St Ch, Grand Rapids, Mich, 1970–71; Summer Organist-in-Residence, Alexandra Palace, London, 1977–78; numerous community and civic concerts, N America, 1979–88; played first solo classic organ recital at the White House, by invitation of the Pres., 1989; various Royal Comd performances; performances world-wide, both solo and orchestral, 1989–; numerous radio, TV and media appearances world-wide, 1989–; numerous recordings. Hon. Fellow, Guild of Musicians and Singers, 1996. *Publications:* In the Pipeline

(autobiog.), 1997. *Recreations:* reading, walking, swimming, fine food and wines. *Address:* c/o PV Media Ltd, County House, St Mary's Street, Worcester WR1 1HB. *T:* (01905) 616100, *Fax:* (01905) 641842. *E:* maggie@pva.co.uk.
Died 11 Aug. 2012.

CURNOW, (Elizabeth) Ann (Marguerite); QC 1985; a Recorder of the Crown Court, 1980–2000; *b* 5 June 1935; *d* of Cecil Curnow and Doris Curnow (*née* Behr); *m* 1981, (William) Neil Denison (His Honour W. N. Denison, QC). *Educ:* St Hilda's Sch., Whitby, Yorks; King's Coll., London (LLB). Called to the Bar, Gray's Inn, 1957, Bencher, 1985. Treasury Counsel, Middx Crown Court, 1972–77; Central Criminal Court: Jun. Treasury Counsel, 1977–81; Sen. Prosecuting Counsel to the Crown, 1981–85. Member: Parole Bd, 1992–94; Criminal Injuries Compensation Bd, 1996–2002; Mental Health Rev. Tribunal, 2000–04. Chm., Victim Support, Lambeth, 1987–2003. *Recreations:* Burmese cats, listening to music, especially opera, tapestry, gardens. *Address:* 6 King's Bench Walk, Temple, EC4Y 7DR. *T:* (020) 7583 0410, *Fax:* (020) 7353 8791. *Died 11 May 2011.*

CURRIE, Sir Donald Scott, 7th Bt *cr* 1847; Chief of Maintenance, National Park Service, Department of the Interior, 1976; *b* 16 Jan. 1930; *s* of George Donald Currie (*d* 1980) (*ggs* of 1st Bt) and Janet K. (*d* 1990), *d* of late James Scott; *S* cousin, 1987, but his name does not appear on the Official Roll of the Baronetage; *m* 1st, 1948, Charlotte (marr. diss. 1951), *d* of Charles Johnstone; twin *d* (and one *s* decd); 2nd, 1952, Barbara Lee (*d* 1993), *d* of A. P. Garnier; one *s* two *d*; 3rd, 1994, Barbara Lou Lebsack, *d* of Joshua Fenn. Rancher and farmer, 1949–75. *Clubs:* American Legion (Colorado, USA); National Rifle Association (USA); North American Hunting. *Died 9 Feb. 2014.*

CURTIS, John Henry, CB 1981; FTSE; Chairman, Nortel Australia Pty Ltd, 1989–92, retired; *b* 20 March 1920; *s* of K. H. and E. M. Curtis; *m* 1943, Patricia Foote (*d* 1989); one *s* one *d*. *Educ:* Ipswich Grammar Sch.; Queensland Univ. (BE Hons 1950, BSc 1951, BA 1957). FIEAust 1981; FAIM 1970; FTSE (FTS 1979). Dir of Posts and Telegraphs, Qld, 1971–73; Dep. Dir Gen., Postmaster-Gen.'s Dept, 1973–75; Man. Dir, Australian Telecommunications Commn, 1975–81; Chairman: D. Richardson & Sons, later Richardson Pacific, 1982–90; A. W. A. Nortel, 1986–89. Comr, Overseas Telecommunications Commn (Australia), 1974–87. Pres., Victorian Div., Aust. Inst. of Management, 1979–81; Dir, Cttee for Econ. Develt of Aust., 1981–93 (Hon. Life Mem., 1993). Mem., Bd of Management, Defence Aerospace, 1984–86. Gov., Internat. Council for Computer Communication, 1982–94. Hon. Life Mem., IREE, 1982. Centenary Medal, 2004. *Died 10 July 2013.*

CURTIS, Sir William (Peter), 7th Bt *cr* 1802; *b* 9 April 1935; *s* of Sir Peter Curtis, 6th Bt, and Joan Margaret, *d* of late Reginald Nicholson; *S* father, 1976. *Educ:* Winchester College; Trinity College, Oxford (MA); Royal Agricultural College, Cirencester. *Heir: cousin* Major Edward Philip Curtis, 16th/5th The Queen's Royal Lancers (retd) [*b* 25 June 1940; *m* 1978, Catherine, *d* of H. J. Armstrong, Christchurch, NZ; two *s* two *d*. *Educ:* Bradfield; RMA Sandhurst]. *Address:* Oak Lodge, Bank Street, Bishop's Waltham, Hants SO32 1AN. *Died 25 April 2014.*

CURTISS, Air Marshal Sir John (Bagot), KCB 1981 (CB 1979); KBE 1982; FRAeS; Chairman, Oakhaven Hospice Trust, 2001–04; *b* 6 Dec. 1924; *s* of Major E. F. B. Curtiss, RFC; *m* 1946, Peggy Drughorn Bowie; three *s* one *d*. *Educ:* Radley Coll.; Wanganui Collegiate Sch., NZ; Worcester Coll., Oxford. Served War: Oxford Univ. Air Sqdn, 1942–43; Bomber Comd, 578 and 158 sqdns, 1944–45; Transport Comd, 51 and 59 sqdn, 1945–49; Training Comd, 1950–53; Fighter Comd, 29 and 5 sqdns, 1953–64; Dir, RAF Staff Coll., 1967–69; Stn Comdr RAF Bruggen, RAFG, 1970–72; Gp Capt. Ops, HQ Strike Comd, 1972–74; SASO, HQ 11 Gp, 1974–75; Dir-Gen. Organisation, RAF, 1975–77; Comdt, RAF Staff Coll., 1977–80; Air Comdr, Falklands Operations, 1982; AOC No 18 Gp, 1980–83, retd. Dir and Chief Exec., SBAC, 1984–89; Sec., Defence Inds Council, 1985–89. Mem. Exec. Cttee, Air League, 1982–93; President: Aircrew Assoc., 1987–93; Berlin Airlift Assoc., 1998–2010; RAF Oxford and Cambridge Soc., 1998–2005, then Pres. Emeritus; Milford-on-Sea Br., RBL, 2002–. Chm., Pathfinders Disaster Relief, 1995–2000; Chief Exec., Assoc. of Pathfinders, 1996–2000. Trustee, Buskaid, 1995–2004 (Chm., 1999–2004). Chm., Governors, Canford Sch., 1990–95. FRAeS 1984. *Recreations:* family, fishing, sailing, reading, bicycling. *Address:* Normandy House, Barnes Lane, Milford-on-Sea, Hants SO41 0RQ. *Clubs:* MCC, Pilgrims; Colonels (Pres. and Founder Mem.); Keyhaven Yacht.
Died 14 Sept. 2013.

CURWEN, Sir Christopher (Keith), KCMG 1986 (CMG 1982); HM Diplomatic Service, retired; *b* 9 April 1929; *s* of late Rev. R. M. Curwen and Mrs M. E. Curwen; *m* 1st, 1956, Noom Tai (marr. diss. 1977; she *d* 2002); one *s* two *d*; 2nd, 1977, Helen Anne Stirling; one *s* one *d*. *Educ:* Sherborne Sch.; Sidney Sussex Coll., Cambridge (BA). Served HM Forces, 4th Queen's Own Hussars, 1948–49 (despatches). Joined FO, 1952; Bangkok, 1954; Vientiane, 1956; FO, 1958; Bangkok, 1961; Kuala Lumpur, 1963; FO, 1965; Washington, 1968; FCO, 1971; Geneva, 1977; FCO, 1980–85; Hd, Secret Intelligence Service, 1985–88; Dep. Sec., Cabinet Office, 1989–91. Mem., Security Commn, 1991–98. Chm., Century Benevolent Fund, 1993–99; Trustee, Bath Preservation Trust, 1992–2004. *Recreations:* books, gardening, motoring. *Died 18 Dec. 2013.*

CUTT, Rev. Canon Samuel Robert; Canon Residentiary, 1979–93, and Treasurer, 1985–93, Wells Cathedral (Chancellor, 1979–85); *b* 28 Nov. 1925; *er s* of Robert Bush Cutt and Lilian Elizabeth Cutt (*née* Saint); *m* 1972, Margaret Eva (*d* 1975), *yr d* of Norman and Eva McIntyre. *Educ:* Skegness Grammar Sch.; Selwyn Coll., Cambridge; Cuddesdon Coll., Oxford. BA Cantab 1950, MA 1954. Ordained deacon, 1953, priest, 1954. Asst Curate, St Aidan, West Hartlepool, 1953–56; Tutor for King's Coll. London at St Boniface Coll., Warminster, 1956–59; Sub-Warden for KCL at St Boniface Coll., 1959–65; Lectr and Tutor of Chichester Theol Coll., 1965–71; Priest Vicar of Chichester Cath., 1966–71; Minor Canon, 1971–79, and Succentor, 1974–79, St Paul's Cathedral, and Warden, Coll. of Minor Canons, 1974–79; part-time Lectr, Theological Dept, KCL, 1973–79; Priest in Ordinary to the Queen, 1975–79; Dio. Dir of Ordinands, Bath and Wells, 1979–86; Examining Chaplain to Bishop of Bath and Wells, 1980–93; Warden, Community of St Denys, Warminster, 1987–91. OStJ 1981. *Recreations:* walking, music, biographical studies, heraldry, cooking. *Died 10 Sept. 2011.*

CUTTS, Adrian Clive Tylden; Executive Director of Resources, Lancashire County Council, 2006–09; *b* Wingerworth, Derbys, 16 Oct. 1949; *s* of Geoffrey Wilson Cutts and Noel Deidre Cutts; *m* 1979, Lynda Keegan; three *d*. *Educ:* Wade Deacon Grammar Sch., Widnes; Liverpool Coll. of Commerce. CIPFA 1973. Audit Clerk, Widnes BC, 1968; various posts from Audit Asst to Principal Accountant, St Helens CBC, subseq. MBC, 1971–84; Lancashire County Council: Principal Accountant (Educn), 1984–89; Chief Accountant, 1989–2001; Dir of Finance, 2001–06; Treas. to Lancs Fire Authy, 2001–05. *Recreations:* keen fell walker, playing contract bridge at Preston Bridge Club, reading, foreign travel (preferably to mountain regions; Himalayan treks 2009 and 2011). *Address:* 6 Forest Way, Fulwood, Preston PR2 8PR. *T:* (01772) 774206, *Fax:* (01772) 264705. *E:* cuttsfamily@blueyonder.co.uk.
Died 16 Jan. 2015.

D

DACRE, Baroness (27th in line), *cr* 1321; **Rachel Leila Douglas-Home;** *b* 24 Oct. 1929; *er* surv. *d* of 4th Viscount Hampden, CMG (*d* 1965) (whose Barony of Dacre was called out of abeyance in her favour, 1970) and Leila Emily (*d* 1996), *o d* of late Lt-Col Frank Evelyn Seely; *m* 1951, Hon. William Douglas-Home (*d* 1992), author and playwright; one *s* three *d*. *Heir: s* Hon. James Thomas Archibald Douglas-Home [*b* 16 May 1952; *m* 1979, Christine (*née* Stephenson) (*d* 2008); one *d*]. *Died 25 Dec. 2012.*

DACRE, 28th Baron *cr* 1321; **James Thomas Archibald Douglas-Home;** journalist and writer, since 1989; *b* 16 May 1952; *o s* of Baroness Dacre (27th in line) and Hon. William Douglas-Home (*d* 1992), author and playwright; *S* mother, 2012; *m* 1979, Christine Stephenson (*d* 2008); one *d*. *Educ:* Eton Coll.; Univ. of Bristol (BA Combined Hons). Race-horse trainer, 1979–89. Gov., Emanuel Sch., 2005–. *Publications:* Horse Racing in Berkshire, 1992; Horse Racing, 2000; (with J. Henderson) Watching Monty, 2005; Stately Passions: the scandals of Britain's great houses, 2006. *Recreations:* shooting, racing, walking. *Heir: d* Hon. Emily Douglas-Home, *b* 7 Feb. 1983. *Died 8 May 2014.*

DALBY, Ven. (John) Mark (Meredith); Chaplain, The Beauchamp Community, Newland, 2000–07; Archdeacon of Rochdale, 1991–2000, then Emeritus; *b* 3 Jan. 1938; *s* of William and Sheila Mary Dalby (*née* Arkell). *Educ:* King George V Sch., Southport; Exeter Coll., Oxford, (MA 1965); Ripon Hall, Oxford; Univ. of Nottingham (PhD 1977). Ordained deacon 1963, priest 1964; Curate: Hambleden, Bucks, 1963–68; Fawley, Fingest, Medmenham and Turville, Bucks, 1965–68; Vicar of St Peter, Spring Hill, Birmingham, 1968–75; Rural Dean of Birmingham City, 1973–75; Sec., Cttee for Theol Educn, and Selection Sec., ACCM, 1975–80; Hon. Curate of All Hallows, Tottenham, 1975–80; Vicar of St Mark, Worsley, 1980–84; Team Rector of Worsley, 1984–91; Rural Dean of Eccles, 1987–91. Examining Chaplain to the Bp of Manchester, 1980–2000. Member: Gen. Synod of C of E, 1985–95; Liturgical Commn, 1986–95. *Publications:* Open Communion in the Church of England, 1959; The Gospel and the Priest, 1975; Tottenham Church and Parish, 1979; The Cocker Connection, 1989; Open Baptism, 1989; Anglican Missals and their Canons, 1998; Infant Communion: the New Testament to the Reformation, 2003; Infant Communion: post-Reformation to present-day, 2009; (ed) Victorian Wesleyan Sermons, 2010. *Recreations:* travel, family history, philately, freemasonry, liturgy. *Address:* St Christopher's, Beauchamp Community, Newland, Malvern, Worcestershire WR13 5AX. *T:* (01684) 899198. *Died 11 Feb. 2013.*

DALGARNO, Prof. Alexander, PhD; FRS 1972; Phillips Professor of Astronomy, Harvard University, since 1977; Member of Smithsonian Astrophysical Observatory, since 1967; *b* 5 Jan. 1928; *s* of William Dalgarno; *m* 1st, 1957, Barbara Kane (marr. diss. 1972); two *s* two *d*; 2nd, 1972, Emily Izsák (marr. diss. 1987). *Educ:* Southgate Grammar Sch.; University Coll., London (Fellow 1976). BSc Maths, 1st Cl. Hons London, 1947; PhD Theoretical Physics London, 1951; AM Harvard, 1967. The Queen's University of Belfast: Lectr in Applied Maths, 1952; Reader in Maths, 1956; Dir of Computing Lab., 1960; Prof. of Quantum Mechanics, 1961; Prof. of Mathematical Physics, 1966–67; Harvard University: Prof. of Astronomy, 1967–; Acting Dir, Harvard Coll. Observatory, 1971–73; Chm., Dept of Astronomy, 1971–76; Associate Dir, Centre for Astrophysics, 1973–80. Chief Scientist, Geophysics Corp. of America, 1962–63. Vikram A. Sarabhai Prof., Physical Res. Lab., Ahmedabad, 2002; Oort Prof., Leiden Univ., 2003; Charles M. and Martha Hitchcock Prof., Univ. of Calif, Berkeley, 2003. Spiers Meml Lectr and Medal, Faraday Div., RSC, 1992. Editor, Astrophysical Journal Letters, 1973–2002. Fellow: Amer. Acad. of Arts and Sciences, 1968; Amer. Geophysical Union, 1972; Amer. Physical Soc., 1980; FInstP 2000; Member: Internat. Acad. Astronautics, 1972; US Nat. Acad. of Scis, 2001. MRIA 1989. FUMIST 1992. Hon. DSc: QUB, 1980; York, Canada, 2000. Prize of Internat. Acad. of Quantum Molecular Sci., 1969; Hodgkins Medal, Smithsonian Instn, 1977; Davisson-Germer Prize, Amer. Physical Soc., 1980; Gold Medal, Royal Astronomical Soc., 1986; Meggers Prize, Optical Soc. of America, 1986; Fleming Medal, Amer. Geophys. Union, 1995; Hughes Medal, Royal Soc., 2002. *Publications:* numerous papers in scientific journals. *Recreations:* squash, books. *Address:* c/o Harvard-Smithsonian Center for Astrophysics, 60 Garden Street, Cambridge, MA 02138, USA. *Died 9 April 2015.*

DALRYMPLE-HAMILTON of Bargany, Captain North Edward Frederick, CVO 1961; MBE 1953; DSC 1943; JP; Royal Navy; *b* 17 Feb. 1922; *s* of Admiral Sir Frederick Dalrymple-Hamilton of Bargany, KCB; *m* 1st, 1949, Hon. Mary Colville (*d* 1981), *d* of 1st Baron Clydesmuir, PC, GCIE, TD; two *s*; 2nd, 1983, Antoinette (*d* 2009), *widow* of Major Rowland Beech, MC. *Educ:* Eton. Entered Royal Navy, 1940; Comdr 1954; Captain 1960. Comdg Officer HMS Scarborough, 1958; Executive Officer, HM Yacht Britannia, 1959; Captain (F) 17th Frigate Squadron, 1963; Dir of Naval Signals, 1965; Dir, Weapons Equipment Surface, 1967; retd, 1970. Lieut, Royal Company of Archers, Queen's Body Guard for Scotland. DL 1973, JP 1980, Ayrshire. *Address:* Malin Court, Turnberry, Ayrshire KA26 9PB. *T:* (01655) 334317. *Clubs:* Pratt's, MCC. *Died 8 July 2014.*

DALTON, Alfred Hyam, CB 1976; Deputy Chairman, Board of Inland Revenue, 1973–82 (Commissioner of Inland Revenue, 1970–82); *b* 29 March 1922; *m* 1946, Elizabeth Stalker (*d* 1992); three *d*; *m* 1995, Sylvia Winifred West (*née* Boyce). *Educ:* Merchant Taylors' Sch., Northwood; Aberdeen Univ. Served War, REME, 1942–45 (despatches). Entered Inland Revenue, 1947; Asst Sec., 1958; Sec. to Board, 1969. *Address:* 22 Clifton Avenue, Eaglescliffe TS16 9BA. *T:* (01642) 648850. *Died 7 Dec. 2012.*

DALTON, Irwin, CBE 1986; Executive Vice-Chairman, 1985–88, and Chief Executive (Operations), 1986–88, National Bus Company; *b* 25 July 1932; *s* of Harry Farr Dalton and Bessie Dalton; *m* 1954, Marie Davies (decd); two *d*. *Educ:* Cockburn High Sch., Leeds. FCA 1973; FCIT 1978. Accountancy profession, 1947–62; Asst Company Sec., 1962–67, Company Sec., 1968–70, West Riding Automobile, Wakefield; Company Sec., Crosville Motor Services, 1971–74; Dir and Gen. Manager, Ribble Motor Services, 1974–76; National Bus Company: Regional Dir, 1977–81; Mem. for Personnel Services, 1981–83; Exec. Bd Mem., 1983–84. Dir, Leyland Bus Gp, 1987–88. A Vice-Pres., Bus and Coach Council, 1983–87, Pres., 1987–88. *Recreations:* golf, other sporting activities. *Address:* 7 Aultmore Court, Kingswood Road, Tunbridge Wells, Kent TN2 4UF. *T:* (01892) 533459. *Club:* Tunbridge Wells Golf. *Died 10 Aug. 2013.*

DANCE, Brian David, MA; Headmaster, St Dunstan's College, Catford, 1973–93; *b* 22 Nov. 1929; *s* of late L. H. Dance and Mrs M. G. Swain (*née* Shrivelle); *m* 1955, Chloe Elizabeth, *o d* of late J. F. A. Baker, CB, FEng; two *s* two *d*. *Educ:* Kingston Grammar Sch.; Wadham Coll., Oxford (BA 1952; MA 1956). Asst Master, Kingston Grammar Sch., 1953–59; Sen. History Master: Faversham Grammar Sch., 1959–62; Westminster City Sch., 1962–65; Headmaster, Cirencester Grammar Sch., 1965–66; Principal, Luton Sixth Form Coll., 1966–73. Member: Cambridge Local Examination Syndicate, 1968–73; Headmasters' Assoc. Council, 1968–76 (Exec. Cttee, 1972–76, Hon. Legal Sec. 1975–76); Chm., London Area, SHA, 1984–85. Chm., Lewisham Environment Trust, 1987–88. Gov., Bromley High Sch., 1985–2005 (Chm., 2002–05). Hon. Assoc. for Life, GDST, 2005. Vice-Pres., Rugby Fives Assoc., 1993–. *Publications:* articles in: Times Educnl Supp.; Headmasters' Assoc. 'Review'. *Recreations:* watching most ball games (especially cricket and Rugby football), music, philately, theatre. *Address:* 5 Sycamore, Richmond Letcombe Regis, South Street, Letcombe Regis, Oxon OX12 9RG. *T:* (01235) 774769. *Died 2 July 2011.*

DANIEL, William Wentworth, CBE 1997; independent social scientist; Director, Policy Studies Institute, 1986–93; *b* 19 Nov. 1938; *s* of late George Taylor Daniel and Margaret Elizabeth Daniel; *m* 1st, 1961, Lynda Mary Coles Garrett (marr. diss.); one *s* two *d*; 2nd, 1990, Eileen Mary Reid (*née* Loudfoot) (*d* 1996). *Educ:* Shebbear Coll., Devon; Victoria Univ. of Manchester (BA Hons); Univ. of Manchester Inst. of Science and Technology (MSc Tech). Directing Staff, Ashorne Hill Management Coll., 1963–65; Sen. Res. Officer, Research Services Ltd, 1965–67; Senior Research Fellow: Bath Univ., 1967–69; PSI (formerly PEP), 1969–81; Dep. Dir, PSI, 1981–86. Member: ESRC, 1992–96; Eur. Foundn for Improvement of Living and Wkg Conditions, Dublin, 1992–96. Dir, Holsworthy Biogas Ltd, 1999. Mem. Bd of Govs, Plymouth Univ., 2001. *Publications:* Racial Discrimination in England, 1968; Whatever Happened to the Workers in Woolwich?, 1972; The Right to Manage?, 1972; A National Survey of the Unemployed, 1974; Sandwich Courses in Higher Education, 1975; Pay Determination in Manufacturing Industry, 1976; Where Are They Now?: a follow-up survey of the unemployed, 1977; The Impact of Employment Protection Laws, 1978; Maternity Rights: the experience of women, 1980; Maternity Rights: the experience of employers, 1981; Workplace Industrial Relations in Britain, 1983; Workplace Industrial Relations and Technical Change, 1987; The Unemployed Flow, 1989; (with Terence Hogarth) Britain's New Industrial Gypsies, 1989. *Recreations:* golf, lawn tennis. *Address:* Bryn-Mor, 7 Maer Down Road, Bude, Cornwall EX23 8NG. *T:* (01288) 356678. *Clubs:* National Liberal; Bude & N Cornwall Golf; David Lloyd Slazenger Racquet (Heston). *Died 19 Nov. 2015.*

DANIELS, George, CBE 2010 (MBE 1982); FSA, FBHI; author, watchmaker; horological consultant to Sotheby's, since 1970; *b* 19 Aug. 1926; *s* of George Daniels and Beatrice (*née* Cadou); *m* 1964, Juliet Anne (*née* Marryat) (marr. diss.); one *d. Educ:* elementary. 2nd Bn E Yorks Regt, 1944–47. Started professional horology, 1947; restoration of historical watches, 1956–; hand watch making to own designs, 1969–; invented co-Axial escapement, 1975, developed and patented, 1980, industrialised by Swiss makers, 1997; invented Daniels' independent double wheel chronometer, 1975, industrialised by Messrs Frodsham, London; designed IOM Millennium postage stamps, commemorating English chronometer inventors, 1999. Horological lectures, both antiquarian and modern technical, to RSA, Royal Instn, Antiquarian Horol Soc., Harvard Univ., Cambridge Phil Soc., British Horol Inst., Amer. Watchmakers' Inst., Swedish Watchmakers' Inst., RAS, RCA. President: British Horological Inst., 1980 (Fellow, 1951); British Clock and Watchmakers' Benevolent Soc., 1980; Chm. and Founder, BHI Educn Trust, 1998. One man exhibition, Goldsmiths' Hall, 1992; retrospective exhibition, 50 yrs of Daniels of London, Sotheby's, 2006. Worshipful Co. of Clockmakers: Liveryman, 1968; Warden, 1977; Master, 1980; Tompion Gold Medal, 1981; Asst Hon. Surveyor, 1972–81; Founding Chm., Horological Industries Cttee, 1985–. Freeman, Goldsmiths' Co., 1979; FSA 1976. Hon. DSc City, 1994. Arts, Sciences and Learning Award, City Corporation, London, 1974; Victor Kullberg Medal, Stockholm Watch Guild, 1977; Gold Medal, British Horol Inst., 1981; Gold Badge and Hon. Fellow, Amer. Watchmakers Inst., 1985; Hon. FCGI 1986; City and Guilds Gold Medal for Craftsmanship, 1991; Gaïa Award, Mus. Internat. d'Horlogerie, 2002. *Publications:* Watches (jtly), 1965, 3rd edn 1978 (trans. German 1982); English and American Watches, 1967; The Art of Breguet, 1975, 3rd edn 1985 (trans. French 1985, Italian 1990); (jtly) Clocks and Watches of the Worshipful Company of Clockmakers, 1975; Sir David Salomons Collection, 1978; Watchmaking, 1981, 2nd edn 1985 (trans. French 1993); The Practical Watch Escapement, 1995, 2nd edn 1997; All in Good Time: reflections of a watchmaker (autobiog.), 2000, rev. edn 2001. *Recreations:* vintage cars, fast motorcycles, opera. *Address:* c/o 34 New Bond Street, W1A 2AA. *Died 21 Oct. 2011.*

DANSON, Hon. Barnett Jerome; PC (Can.) 1974; CC 2007 (OC 1996); author; company director; *b* 8 Feb. 1921; *s* of Joseph B. Danson and Saidie W. Danson, Toronto; *m* 1943, Isobel, *d* of Robert John Bull, London, England; three *s* (one *s* decd). *Educ:* Toronto public and high schs. Served War: enlisted Queen's Own Rifles as Rifleman, 1939; commnd, 1943; wounded in France, 1944; retd 1945, Lieut. Manager, Jos. B. Danson & Sons Ltd, Toronto, 1945–50; Sales Man., Maple Leaf Plastics Ltd, 1950–53; Principal (Pres.), Danson Corp. Ltd, Scarborough, 1953–74; Chairman: CSPG Consultants, 1980–84; de Havilland Aircraft of Canada Ltd, 1981–84; Canadian Consul General, Boston, Mass, 1984–86. Active in Liberal Party, 1946–: MP (L) for York North, 1968–79; Parly Sec. to Prime Minister Trudeau, 1970–72; Minister of State for Urban Affairs, 1974–76; Minister of Nat. Defence, Canada, 1976–79; former Mem., Standing Cttee on Finance, Trade and Econ. Affairs, and Ext. Affairs and National Defence. Chm., GSW Thermoplastics Co.; Dir, Algoma Central Railway Ltd. Dir Emeritus, Canadian Council of Native Business; Director: Atlantic Council of Canada; Canadian Inst. of Strategic Studies; Canadian Centre for Global Security; Canadian Exec. Services Orgn, Toronto; Royal Conservatory of Music, Canada; Scholarship Foundn, F. J. L. Woodcock/Sir Arthur Pearson Assoc. of War Blinded; Mem. Council, Canadian Nat. Inst. for Blind. Chm. Bd, No Price Too High Foundn; former Pres. and first Chm. Bd, Soc. of Plastics Industry Inc. Dir, Canadian Council of Christians and Jews. Hon. Dir, Empire Club, Canada. Chm., Adv. Cttee, Canadian War Mus., 1998–. Trustee, Canadian Mus. of Civilisation, 1998–. Former Hon. Lt-Col, Queen's Own Rifles of Canada. Dr of Laws (*hc*) Royal Military Coll. of Canada, 1993; Hon. LLD York Univ., Toronto, 2006. Award for Excellence in the cause of parly democracy, Churchill Soc., 1995; Vimy Award, Conf. of Defence Assocs, 2000. Officer, Order of Merit (France), 1994; Chevalier, Legion of Honour (France), 2007. *Publications:* Not Bad for a Sergeant (memoirs), 2002. *Recreations:* fishing, reading, music. *Address:* 1132 Bay Street, Apt 1501, Toronto, ON M5S 2Z4, Canada. *Died 17 Oct. 2011.*

DARELL, Brig. Sir Jeffrey (Lionel), 8th Bt *cr* 1795; MC 1945; *b* 2 Oct. 1919; *s* of late Lt-Col Guy Marsland Darell, MC (3rd *s* of 5th Bt); *S* cousin, 1959; *m* 1953, Bridget Mary, *e d* of Maj.-Gen. Sir Allan Adair, 6th Bt, GCVO, CB, DSO, MC; one *s* two *d. Educ:* Eton; RMC, Sandhurst. Commissioned Coldstream Guards, July 1939; served War of 1939–45: Coats Mission, 1940–41 (to guard Royal Family in case of invasion); ADC to GOC-in-C, Southern Comd, 1942; Bde Major, Guards Bde, 1953–55; Officer Comdg 1st Bn Coldstream Guards, 1957–59; GSO1, PS12, War Office, 1959; College Comdr RMA Sandhurst, 1961–64; Comdg Coldstream Guards, 1964–65; Comdr, 56 Inf. Brigade (TA), 1965–67; Vice-Pres., Regular Commns Bd, 1968–70; Comdt, Mons OCS, 1970–72; MoD, 1972–74; retd 1974. ADC to HM the Queen, 1973–74. Trustee and Mem., London Law Trust, 1981–99. High Sheriff, Norfolk, 1985. *Recreation:* normal. *Heir: s* Guy Jeffrey Adair Darell [*b* 8 June 1961; *m* 1988, Justine Samantha, *d* of Mr Justice T. Reynolds, Quambi Place, Sydney, Australia; one *s* two *d*]. *Address:* Denton Lodge, Harleston, Norfolk IP20 0AD. *T:* (01986) 788206. *Clubs:* Army and Navy, MCC. *Died 27 Feb. 2013.*

DARKE, Geoffrey James, RIBA; Principal, Geoffrey Darke Associates, Architects and Planners, since 1987; *b* 1 Sept. 1929; *s* of late Harry James Darke and Edith Anne (*née* Rose); *m* 1959, Jean Yvonne Rose, BA, ARCM; one *s* two *d. Educ:* Prince Henry's Grammar Sch., Evesham, Worcs; Birmingham School of Architecture (DipArch); ARIBA 1956. National Service, Malaya, commnd RE, 1954–56. Asst Architect, Stevenage Development Corp., 1952–58; private practice, 1958–61; Partner, Darbourne and Darke, Architects and Landscape Planners, 1961–87. Work includes many large commissions, particularly public buildings. Success in national and internat. housing competitions, in Stuttgart, 1977, Hanover, 1979 and 1980, and in Bolzano, Italy, 1980; numerous medals and awards for architectural work; co-recipient of Fritz Schumacher Award, Hamburg, 1978, for services to architecture and town planning. Mem. Council, RIBA, 1977–83; Chm., RIBA Competitions Cttee, 1979–84; served on many professional committees; Mem., Access Cttee for England, 1992–98. Mem., Aldeburgh Foundn, 1979–98. FRSA 1981. *Recreation:* music. *Address:* 2 Murray Court, 80 Banbury Road, Oxford OX2 6LQ. *Died 8 Nov. 2011.*

DARLING, Sir Clifford, GCVO 1994; Kt 1977; Governor-General, Bahamas, 1992–94; *b* Acklins Island, 6 Feb. 1922; *s* of Charles and Aremelia Darling; *m* Igrid Smith; two *s* five *d. Educ:* Acklins Public Sch.; several public schs in Nassau. Became taxi-driver (Gen. Sec. Bahamas Taxicab Union for 8 yrs, Pres. for 10 yrs). An early Mem., Progressive Liberal Party; MHA for Englerston; Senator, 1964–67; Dep. Speaker, House of Assembly, 1967–69; Minister of State, Oct. 1969; Minister of Labour and Welfare, Dec. 1971; Minister of Labour and Nat. Insurance, 1974–77; Speaker, House of Assembly, 1977–92. Past Chm., Tourist Advisory Bd; instrumental in introd. of a comprehensive Nat. Insce Scheme in the Bahamas, Oct. 1974. Member: Masonic Lodge; Elks Lodge; Acklins, Crooked Is and Long Cays Assoc. *Publications:* A Bahamian Life Story (autobiog.), vol. 1, 1922–1958, 2002. *Address:* PO Box N-1050, Nassau, Bahamas. *Died 27 Dec. 2011.*

DARWEN, 3rd Baron *cr* 1946, of Heys-in-Bowland; **Roger Michael Davies;** *b* 28 June 1938; *s* of 2nd Baron Darwen and of Kathleen Dora, *d* of George Sharples Walker; *S* father, 1988; *m* 1961, Gillian Irene, *d* of Eric G. Hardy, Bristol; two *s* three *d. Educ:* Bootham School, York. *Heir: s* Hon. Paul Davies, *b* 20 Feb. 1962. *Address:* Labourer's Rest, Green Street, Pleshey, Chelmsford CM3 1HT. *Died 26 May 2011.*

DASHWOOD, Sir Richard (James), 9th Bt *cr* 1684, of Kirtlington Park; TD 1987; Senior Director, EFG Harris Allday (formerly Partner, Harris Allday Lea & Brooks, then Harris Allday), stockbrokers; *b* 14 Feb. 1950; *s* of Sir Henry George Massy Dashwood, 8th Bt, and Susan Mary (*d* 1985), *er d* of late Major V. R. Montgomerie-Charrington, Hunsdon House, Herts; *S* father, 1972; *m* 1984, Kathryn Ann (marr. diss. 1993), *er d* of Frank Mahon, Eastbury, Berks; one *s. Educ:* Maidwell Hall Preparatory Sch.; Eton College. Commissioned 14th/20th King's Hussars, 1969, later King's Royal Hussars; T&AVR, 1973– (Major 1992). *Heir: s* Frederick George Mahon Dashwood, *b* 29 Jan. 1988. *Address:* Ledwell Cottage, Sandford St Martin, Oxfordshire OX7 7AN. *T:* (01608) 683267. *Died 14 April 2013.*

DAUNT, Patrick Eldon; Head of Bureau for Action in favour of Disabled People, EEC, 1982–87; international consultant on education and disability; *b* 19 Feb. 1925; *s* of Dr Francis Eldon Daunt and Winifred Doggett Daunt (*née* Wells); *m* 1958, Jean Patricia, *d* of Lt-Col Percy Wentworth Hargreaves and of Joan (*née* Holford); three *s* one *d. Educ:* Rugby Sch.; Wadham Coll., Oxford (BA, 1st Cl. Hons Lit. Hum., 1949, MA 1954). Housemaster, Christ's Hosp., 1959; Headmaster, Thomas Bennett Comprehensive Sch., Crawley, 1965. Chm., Campaign for Comprehensive Educn, 1971–73; Principal Administrator, EEC, 1974–82. Vis. Fellow, London Inst. of Educn, 1988–94. Chm., ASBAH, 1990–95. UNESCO consultant, special educn in Romania, 1992–97; ILO consultant, 1998–99. Ravenswood Foundn Internat. Award, 1992. *Publications:* Comprehensive Values, 1975; Meeting Disability, a European Response, 1991; (ed) Teacher Education for Special Needs in Europe, 1995; Good Gospel, Good God, 2010. *Recreations:* books, botany. *Address:* 4 Bourn Bridge Road, Little Abington, Cambridge CB21 6BJ. *T:* (01223) 891485. *Club:* Oxford and Cambridge. *Died 6 Nov. 2013.*

DAVENPORT, (Arthur) Nigel; President, British Actors' Equity Association, 1986–92; *b* 23 May 1928; *s* of Arthur Henry Davenport and Katherine Lucy (*née* Meiklejohn); *m* 1st, 1951, Helena White (marr. diss. 1960; she *d* 1978); one *s* one *d*; 2nd, 1972, Maria Penelope Katharine Aitken (marr. diss. 1981); one *s. Educ:* Cheltenham Coll.; Trinity Coll., Oxford (MA). Entered acting profession, 1951; for first ten years worked almost exclusively in theatre; original mem. English Stage Co. at Royal Court Th., 1956; A Taste of Honey, on Broadway, 1960; television and films, 1961–; Murder is Easy, Duke of York's, 1993; Our Betters, Chichester, 1997; toured England: King Lear (title rôle), 1986; The Old Country, 1989; Sleuth, 1990; The Constant Wife, 1994–95; Brideshead Revisited, 1995; On That Day, 1996; *films:* Look Back in Anger, 1958; Peeping Tom, 1960; In the Cool of the Day, 1963; The Third Secret, 1964; A High Wind in Jamaica, Life at the Top, Sands of the Kalahari, Where the Spies Are, 1965; A Man for All Seasons, 1966; Play Dirty, Sebastian/Mr Sebastian, The Strange Affair, 1968; Royal Hunt of the Sun, Sinful Davey, The Virgin Soldiers, 1969; The Last Valley, The Mind of Mr Soames, No Blade of Grass, 1970; Mary, Queen of Scots, Villain, 1971; Living Free, 1972; Charlie One-Eye, 1973; La Regenta, Phase IV, 1974; The Island of Dr Moreau, Stand Up Virgin Soldiers, 1977; The Omega Connection, Zulu Dawn, 1979; Chariots of Fire, Den Tüchtigen gehört die Welt, Nighthawks, 1981; Strata, 1982; Greystoke, 1984; Caravaggio, 1986; Without a Clue, 1988; The Cutter, 1992; Hotel Shanghai, 1995; La Revuelta de El Coyote, 1997; David Copperfield, 1999; *television:* South Riding; George III in The Prince Regent; Howard's Way, 1987–88, 1990; Trainer, 1991; The Treasure Seekers, The Opium Wars, 1996; Longitude, 1999. Mem. Council, British Actors' Equity, 1976 (Vice Pres., 1978–82, 1985–86). *Recreations:* gardening, horse racing. *Died 25 Oct. 2013.*

DAVENPORT-HANDLEY, Sir David (John), Kt 1980; OBE 1962; JP; DL; Chairman, Clipsham Quarry Co., since 1947; *b* 2 Sept. 1919; *s* of John Davenport-Handley, JP; *m* 1943, Leslie Mary Goldsmith (*d* 2010); one *d* (one *s* decd). *Educ:* RNC Dartmouth. RN retd 1947. Chm., Rutland and Stamford Conservative Assoc., 1952–65; Treasurer, East Midlands Area Conservative Assoc., 1965–71, Chm. 1971–77; Vice-Chm., Nat. Union of Conservative & Unionist Assocs, 1977–79, Chm., 1979–80. Member: Consumers' Cttees for GB and for England and Wales, 1956–65; Parole Bd, 1981–84. Chm., Rutland Historic Churches Preservation Trust, 1987–2005. President: E Midlands Area Cons. Assoc., 1987–94; Nat. Union of Cons. and Unionist Assocs, 1990–91. Governor, Swinton Conservative Coll., 1973–77; Chairman: Board of Visitors, Ashwell Prison, 1955–73; Governors, Casterton Community Coll., 1960–78; Trustee, Oakham Sch., 1970–86. JP 1948, High Sheriff 1954, DL 1962, Vice-Lieutenant 1972, Rutland; Chm., Rutland Petty Sessional Div., 1957–84; DL Leicestershire 1974. *Recreations:* gardening, music. *Address:* Clipsham Hall, Oakham, Rutland, Leics LE15 7SE. *T:* (01780) 410204. *Died 10 Jan. 2014.*

DAVEY, Hon. Sir David Herbert P.; *see* Penry-Davey.

DAVEY, Prof. William, CBE 1978; PhD; FRSC; President, Portsmouth Polytechnic, 1969–82; Honorary Professor, University of Westminster (formerly Polytechnic of Central London), since 1979; *b* Chesterfield, Derbyshire, 15 June 1917; *m* 1941, Eunice Battye (*d* 2011); two *s. Educ:* University Coll., Nottingham; Technical Coll., Huddersfield. BSc, PhD (London, ext.). Chemist: ICI Scottish Dyes, 1940; Boots, 1941; Shell, 1942–44. Lectr and Sen. Lectr in Organic Chemistry, Acton Techn. Coll., 1944–53; Head of Dept of Chemistry and Biology, The Polytechnic, Regent Street, London, W1, 1953–59; Principal, Coll. of Technology, Portsmouth, 1960–69. FRSA, FRSC, CCMI. DUniv Portsmouth, 1993. *Publications:* Industrial Chemistry, 1961; numerous original papers in: Jl Chem. Soc., Inst. Petroleum, Jl Applied Chem. *Recreations:* motoring, foreign travel. *Address:* 67 Ferndale, Waterlooville, Portsmouth PO7 7PH. *T:* (023) 9226 3014. *Died 7 Jan. 2015.*

DAVID, Sir (Jean) Marc, Kt 1986; CBE 1982; QC (Mauritius) 1969; Barrister, in private practice 1964–2005, and consultant, 2005; Hon. Professor of Law, University of Mauritius, since 1990; *b* 22 Sept. 1925; *s* of late Joseph Claudius David and Marie Lucresia David (*née* Henrisson); *m* 1948, Mary Doreen Mahoney (*d* 2009); three *s* three *d. Educ:* Royal Coll., Port Louis; Royal Coll., Curepipe, Mauritius (Laureate (classical side) of English Scholarship, 1945); LSE (LLB Hons). Called to the Bar, Middle Temple, 1949. Barrister in private practice, 1950–54; Dist Magistrate, then Crown Law Officer (Crown Counsel, Sen. Crown Counsel and Actg AAG), 1954–64. Chm.,

Mauritius Bar Assoc., 1968, 1979, 2000. Chairman: various arbitration tribunals, commns of enquiry and cttees apptd by govt, 1958–; Electoral Supervisory and Boundaries Commns, 1973–82 (Mem., 1968–73); Mem., Panel of Conciliators and Arbitrators, Internat. Centre for Settlement of Investment Disputes, 1969–. Visitor, Univ. of Mauritius, 1980–81. *Recreations:* reading, listening to music, horse racing. *Address:* Le Flamboyant, Bonne Terre, Vacoas, Mauritius. *T:* 6961667. *Clubs:* Turf, Racing (Mauritius). *Died 24 Jan. 2013.*

DAVID, Timothy James; HM Diplomatic Service, retired; High Commissioner, Zambia, 2002–05; *b* 3 June 1947; *s* of late Herman Francis David and Mavis Jeanne David (*née* Evans); *m* 1996, Rosemary (*née* Kunzel); one *s* one *d*. *Educ:* Stonyhurst Coll.; New Coll., Oxford (BA Hons 1969; MA Hons 1978); Univ. of Rhodesia (Grad. Cert. in Educn 1972); Univ. of London. Volunteer Teacher, Southern Rhodesia, 1965–66; Headmaster, St Peter's Community Secondary Sch., Salisbury (later Harare, Zimbabwe), 1970–71; British Council, 1973; Educn Dir, Help the Aged, 1974; FCO by open competition, 1974; 2nd, later 1st, Sec., Dar es Salaam, and, non-resident, Antananarivo, 1977–80; Commonwealth Co-ordination Dept, 1980–82; Sec. to UK Delegn to Commonwealth Heads of Govt Meeting, Melbourne, 1981; UKMIS to UN, NY, 1982; Central and Southern Africa Dept, ODA, 1983–84; UKMIS to UN, Geneva, 1985–88; Head of Internat. and Planning Section and Dep. Head, Aid Policy Dept, ODA/FCO, 1988–89; Counsellor and Head, Narcotics Control and Aids Dept, FCO, 1989–91; Ambassador to Fiji and High Comr to Nauru and Tuvalu, 1992–95, and to Kiribati, 1994–95; Counsellor, Middle East Dept, FCO, 1995; Dep. High Comr, Harare, 1996–98; High Comr, Belize, 1998–2001; Dean, Diplomatic Corps in Belize, 2001. UK Dir, Tuvalu Trust Fund, 1992–95. Member: Council, Univ. of S Pacific, 1993–95; Rhodes Scholarship Selection Cttee, Zambia, 2002–05; Chm., Marlborough Brandt Gp, 2007–11. Mem., Royal African Soc., 2004–08. Patron, SCF (Fiji), 1993–95. Chm., Bd of Trustees, AbleChildAfrica, 2008–10. Governor: Oaksey Village Primary Sch., 2006–; Emmaus (Gloucester), 2007–; Trustee, Oaksey Playing Field Trust, 2006–. Hon. Citizen, Gunjur, The Gambia, 2007. *Recreations:* friends, reading, music, tennis, walking, writing, local history. *Address:* The Old House, The Street, Oaksey, near Malmesbury, Wilts SN16 9TD. *Club:* All England Lawn Tennis and Croquet. *Died 12 May 2014.*

DAVIDSON, 2nd Viscount *cr* 1937, of Little Gaddesden; **John Andrew Davidson;** Captain of the Yeomen of the Guard (Deputy Government Chief Whip), 1986–91; *b* 22 Dec. 1928; *er s* of 1st Viscount Davidson, GCVO, CH, CB, PC, and Frances Joan, Viscountess Davidson (Baroness Northchurch), DBE (*d* 1985), *y d* of 1st Baron Dickinson, KBE, PC; *S* father, 1970; *m* 1st, 1956, Margaret Birgitta Norton (marr. diss. 1974); three *d* (including twin *d*) (and one *d* decd); 2nd, 1975, Mrs Pamela Dobb (*née* Vergette) (*d* 2006). *Educ:* Westminster School; Pembroke College, Cambridge (BA). Served in The Black Watch and 5th Bn KAR, 1947–49. Pres., CU Footlights Club, 1951. A Lord in Waiting (Govt Whip), 1985–86. Director: Strutt & Parker (Farms) Ltd, 1960–75; Lord Rayleigh's Farms Inc., 1960–75; Member of Council: CLA, 1965–75; RASE, 1973; Chm., Management Committee, Royal Eastern Counties Hospital, 1966–72; Mem., East Anglia Economic Planning Council, 1971–75. *Recreation:* music. *Heir: b* Hon. Malcolm William Mackenzie Davidson [*b* 28 Aug. 1934; *m* 1970, Mrs Evelyn Ann Carew Perfect (*d* 2011), *yr d* of William Blackmore Storey; one *s* one *d*]. *Address:* c/o Gibson, Collyers, The Street, Slinfold, Horsham, W Sussex RH13 0RR. *Died 20 July 2012.*

DAVIDSON, Very Rev. Prof. Robert, FRSE; Professor of Old Testament Language and Literature, University of Glasgow, 1972–91; Principal, Trinity College, Glasgow, 1982–91; *b* 30 March 1927; *s* of George Braid Davidson and Gertrude May Ward; *m* 1952, Elizabeth May Robertson; four *s* four *d*. *Educ:* Univ. of St Andrews (MA 1st Cl Hons Classics, 1949; BD, Distinction in Old Testament, 1952). FRSE 1989. Asst Lectr, then Lectr in Biblical Studies, Univ. of Aberdeen, 1953–60; Lectr in Hebrew and Old Testament, Univ. of St Andrews, 1960–66; Lectr in Old Testament Studies, Univ. of Edinburgh, 1966–69, Sen. Lectr, 1969–72. Edward Cadbury Lectr, Birmingham Univ., 1988–89. Moderator, Gen. Assembly, Church of Scotland, 1990–91. Hon. DD: Aberdeen, 1985; Glasgow, 1993. *Publications:* The Bible Speaks, 1959; The Old Testament, 1964; (with A. R. C. Leaney) Biblical Criticism (Vol. 3 of Pelican Guide to Modern Theology), 1970; Genesis 1–11 (Cambridge Bible Commentary), 1973; Genesis 12–50 (Cambridge Bible Commentary), 1979; The Bible in Religious Education, 1979; The Courage to Doubt, 1983; Jeremiah 1–20 (Daily Study Bible), 1983; Jeremiah II, Lamentations (Daily Study Bible), 1986; Ecclesiastes and Song of Songs (Daily Study Bible), 1986; Wisdom and Worship, 1990; A Beginner's Guide to the Old Testament, 1992; Go By the Book, 1996; The Vitality of Worship, 1998; articles in Vetus Testamentum, Annual Swedish Theol Inst., Expository Times, Scottish Jl of Theol., Epworth Review and The Furrow. *Recreations:* music, gardening. *Address:* 30 Dumgoyne Drive, Bearsden, Glasgow G61 3AP. *T:* (0141) 942 1810. *Died 22 Sept. 2012.*

DAVIE, (James) Alan, CBE 1972; RA 2012; RWA 1991; HRSA 1977; painter, poet, musician, silversmith and jeweller; *b* 28 Sept. 1920; *m* 1947, Janet Gaul (*d* 2007); one *d*. *Educ:* Edinburgh Coll. of Art. DA. Gregory Fellowship, Leeds Univ., 1956–59. Teaching, Central Sch. of Arts and Crafts, London, 1953–56 and 1959–60, and Emily Carr Coll. of Art, Vancouver, 1982. *One-man exhibitions:* Gimpel Fils Galleries in London, Zürich and New York, 1946–; Edinburgh Fest., 1972; Brussels, Paris, Athens and London, 1977; London, Florida, Stuttgart, Zürich, Amsterdam, St Andrews and Edinburgh, 1978; Florida, Edinburgh Fest., Belgium, Sydney and Perth, Australia, 1979; New York, Australia, Colchester and Philadelphia, 1980; London, Frankfurt, NY and Toronto, 1981; Toronto, Edinburgh, Basle, Harrogate, Hong Kong, Paris (Foire Internat. d'Art Contemporain) and Vancouver, 1982; Amsterdam, FIAC Paris, Basel, Madrid, Glasgow and London, 1983; New York, Frankfurt, Cologne, Edinburgh, Windsor, Hertford and Bath, 1984; London (Art Fair, Olympia), Edinburgh and Bonn, 1985; London, Arizona and NY, 1986; Gal. Carre and FIAC, Paris, London, Edinburgh, 1987; Paintings 1956–88, touring Scotland, Helsingborg, 1988; Edinburgh (Scottish Art Gall., and Nat. Gall. of Modern Art), and galleries and museums in Scotland and Sweden, 1989; Madrid, Paris, Helsingford, New York, 1990; Bath, Cracow, Penzance, Copenhagen, 1991; Edinburgh, Vienna, and British Council Travelling Exhibn, 1992; Brighton, Hastings, Ramsgate, Newcastle upon Tyne, Nottingham, Stirling, 1993; Porto, Lisbon, 1994; Brighton, Chichester, 1996; Edinburgh, Brighton, London, Chichester, NY, Inverness, 1997; Pier Arts Centre, Stromness, 1998; Milan, 2001; Tate St Ives, 2003; *retrospective exhibitions:* Sheffield and Lincoln, 1965; Texas, Montreal and Oakland, 1970; Edinburgh, 1972; Germany, 1973; Edinburgh, and Glasgow, 1992; S America, 1993; Barbican, NY and Ireland, 1993; Chicago, 1994; Edinburgh (Scottish Nat. Gall. of Modern Art), 2000; (small paintings) Brighton and Edinburgh Univs, London (Gimpel Fils), Holland, 2001. Work represented in exhibitions: 4th Internat. Art Exhibn, Japan; Pittsburgh Internat.; Documenta II & III, Kassel, Germany; British Painting 1700–1960, Moscow; Salon de Mai, Paris; Peggy Guggenheim Collection; ROSC Dublin; Peter Stuyvesant Collection; British Painting and Sculpture 1960–1970, Washington; III Bienal de Arte Coltejer, Colombia; Hannover, 1973; British Paintings, 1974; Hayward Gall., 1974; Paris, 1975; Lausanne, 1975; 25 years of British Art, RA, 1977; South America, 1977; Kassell, 1977; Sydney, 1979; Works on paper, Gimpel Fils, 1989; SW Arts Touring Exhibn, 1989; Glasgow and Edinburgh, and Royal W of England Acad., 1992. Works in Public Collections: Tate Gall., Gulbenkian Foundn London, Belfast, Bristol, Durham, Edinburgh, Hull, Leeds, Manchester, Newcastle, Wakefield; Boston, Buffalo, Dallas, Detroit, Yale New Haven, Phoenix, Pittsburgh, Rhode Island, San Francisco, NY (MOMA); Ottawa, Adelaide, Sydney, Auckland, São Paulo, Tel Aviv, Venice, Vienna, Baden-Baden, Bochum, Munich, Amsterdam, Eindhoven, The Hague, Rotterdam, Oslo, Basle, Stockholm, Gothenburg, St Paul de Vence and Paris. Created mural, Tarot Sculpture Gdn, Garavicchio,

Tuscany, 1987; commnd to design tapestry, Edinburgh Hosp., 2001. First public recital of music, Gimpel Fils Gall., 1971; music and lecture tour, Sydney, Melbourne, Canberra, 1979. Vis. Prof., Brighton Univ., 1993–. Hon. DLitt: Heriot-Watt, 1994; Hertfordshire, 1995; Hon. Dr Edinburgh, 2003. Prize for Best Foreign Painter, VII Bienal de São Paulo, 1963; Saltire Award, 1977. *Publications:* Magic Reader: eighteen original lithographs, 1992; Alan Davie Drawings, 1997; *relevant publications:* Alan Davie (ed Alan Bowness), 1967; Alan Davie, by D. Hall and M. Tucker, 1992; Alan Davie: the quest for the miraculous (ed Michael Tucker), 1993. *Address:* Gamels Studio, Rush Green, Hertford SG13 7SB. *Died 5 April 2014.*

DAVIES, Prof. Anna Elbina, (A. Morpurgo Davies), Hon. DBE 2000; FBA 1985; Diebold Professor of Comparative Philology, Oxford University, 2003–04 (Professor of Comparative Philology, 1971–2003), then Emeritus; Fellow of Somerville College, Oxford, 1971–2004, then Emeritus; *b* Milan, 21 June 1937; *d* of Augusto Morpurgo and Maria (*née* Castelnuovo); *m* 1962, Prof. John Kenyon Davies, FBA (marr. diss. 1978). *Educ:* Liceo-Ginnasio Giulio Cesare, Rome; Univ. of Rome (Dott.lett. 1959; Libera docente 1963); MA Oxford, 1964. Asst in Classical Philology, Univ. of Rome, 1959–61; Junior Research Fellow, Center for Hellenic Studies, Harvard Univ., 1961–62; Univ. Lectr in Classical Philology, Oxford, 1964–71; Fellow of St Hilda's Coll., Oxford, 1966–71, Hon. Fellow, 1972–. Visiting Professor: Univ. of Pennsylvania, 1971; Yale Univ., 1977; Pavia, 2005; Berkeley, 2006, 2007; Collitz Prof. of Ling. Soc. of America, Univ. of South Florida, 1975; Webster Vis. Prof., Stanford Univ., 1988; Sather Prof. of Classics, Univ. of Calif at Berkeley, 2000. Lectures: Semple, Univ. of Cincinnati, 1983; Jackson, Harvard Univ., 1990; Sather, Berkeley, 2000. Pres., Philological Soc., 1976–80, Hon. Vice-Pres., 1980–. Delegate, Oxford University Press, 1992–2004. FSA 1974; Internat. Mem. (formerly Foreign Mem.), Amer. Philosophical Soc., 1991; Foreign Hon. Mem., Amer. Acad. of Arts and Sciences, 1986; Corresponding Member: Österreichische Akademie der Wissenschaften, Vienna, 1988; Inst. de France (Acad. des inscriptions et belles-lettres), 1992; Bayerische Akademie der Wissenschaften, 1998; Mem., Academia Europaea, 1989; Hon. Mem., Linguistic Soc. of America, 1993. Hon. DLitt St Andrews, 1981; dr *hc* Nancy, 2009. Premio linceo per la linguistica, 1996, Socio straniero, 2010, Accademia dei Lincei. *Publications:* (as A. Morpurgo) Mycenaeae Graecitatis Lexicon, 1963; (ed with W. Meid) Studies in Greek, Italic and Indo-European Linguistics, festschrift for L. R. Palmer, 1976; (ed with Y. Duhoux) Linear B: a 1984 survey, 1985; La linguistica dell'Ottocento, 1996; Nineteenth-Century Linguistics, 1998; (ed with Y. Duhoux) A Companion to Linear B: Mycenaean Greek texts and their world, vol. 1, 2008, vol. 2, 2011; *festschrift:* Indo-European Perspectives, ed by J. H. W. Penney, 2004; articles and reviews on comparative and classical philology in learned jls. *Address:* Somerville College, Oxford OX2 6HD; 22 Yarnells Hill, Oxford OX2 9BD. *T:* (01865) 247099. *Died 27 Sept. 2014.*

DAVIES, Brian Meredith; *see* Davies, J. B. M.

DAVIES, Sir (Charles) Noel, Kt 1996; CEng; Chairman, Ricardo PLC (formerly Ricardo Group plc), 1997–2003; *b* 2 Dec. 1933; *s* of Henry Norman Davies and Vena Mary Bebb; *m* 1958, Sheila Rigby; two *s* one *d*. *Educ:* Ellesmere Coll., Shropshire; Imperial Coll., London (BSc). CEng 1956; FCGI 1980. Dir, Vickers PLC, 1980–84; Chief Executive: 600 Gp, 1984–89; VSEL PLC, 1989–95; Dep. Chm., British Energy PLC, 1995–99; Chairman: Nuclear Electric Ltd, 1995–98; Powell Duffryn PLC, 1996–2000. Mem., Sec. of State's Industrial Develt Adv. Bd, 1987–94. Pres., EEF, 1994–96. *Recreations:* vintage cars, motor-cycles, gardening. *Died 10 Feb. 2015.*

DAVIES, Hon. Sir (David Herbert) Mervyn, Kt 1982; MC 1944; TD 1946; a Judge of the High Court of Justice, Chancery Division, 1982–93; *b* Swansea, 17 Jan. 1918; *s* of Herbert Bowen Davies and Esther Davies, Llangunnor, Carms; *m* 1951, Zita Yollanne Angelique Blanche Antoinette (*d* 2014), 2nd *d* of Rev. E. A. Phillips, Bale, Norfolk. *Educ:* Swansea Gram. Sch. Solicitor, 1939 (Travers Smith Scholar and Daniel Reardon Prize, Law Soc., 1939). 18th Bn Welch Regt and 2nd London Irish Rifles, Africa, Italy and Austria, 1939–45. Called to Bar, Lincoln's Inn, 1947; Bencher, 1974; QC 1967; a Circuit Judge, 1978–82. Mem., Bar Council, 1972; Mem., Senate of Inns of Court, 1975. *Address:* 3 Stone Buildings, Lincoln's Inn, WC2A 3XL. *Club:* Army and Navy. *Died 12 May 2015.*

DAVIES, Douglas; *see* Davies, Percy D.

DAVIES, (James) Brian Meredith, MD, DPH, FFPH; Director of Social Services, City of Liverpool, 1971–81; *b* 27 Jan. 1920; *s* of late Dr G. Meredith Davies and Caroline Meredith Davies; *m* 1944, Charlotte (*née* Pillar); three *s*. *Educ:* Bedford Sch.; Medical Sch., St Mary's Hosp., London Univ. MB, BS (London) 1943, MD (London) 1948; DPH 1948; FFPH (MFCM 1972, FFCM 1974). Various hosp. appts. Served War, RAMC, Captain, 1944–47. Asst MOH, Lancashire CC, 1948–50; Dep. MOH, City of Oxford, 1950–53; Clin. Asst (infectious Diseases), United Oxford Hosps, 1950–53; Dep. MOH, 1953–69, Dir of Personal Health and Social Services, 1969–71, City of Liverpool; pt-time Lectr in Public Health, 1953–71, and Hon. Lectr in Preventive Paediatrics, 1964–85, Liverpool Univ. Chm., Liverpool div., BMA, 1958–59; Council of Europe Fellowship, to study Elderly: in Finland, Sweden, Norway and Denmark, 1964 (report awarded special prize); Mem. Public Health Laboratory Service Bd, 1966–71. Teaching Gp of Soc. of Community Med. (Sec. of Gp, 1958–72, Pres. Gp, 1972–73). Member: Personal Social Services Council, 1978–80; Mental Health Review Tribunal, Mersey Area, 1982–. Governor, Occupational Therapy Coll., Huyton, Liverpool, 1969–85; Dir of MERIT (Merseyside Industrial Therapy Services Ltd), 1970–75; Mem. Council, Queen's Inst. of District Nursing, 1971–78; Assoc. of Dirs of Social Services: Chm., NW Br., 1971–73; Mem. Exec. Council, 1973–78; Pres. 1976–77; Mem. Exec. Cttee of Central Council for the Disabled, 1972–76; Adviser to Social Services Cttee of Assoc. of Metropolitan Authorities, 1974–81; Member: RCP Cttee on Rheumatism and Rehabilitation, 1974–83; DES Cttee of Enquiry into Special Educn for Disabled Children, 1975–78; Exec. Cttee, Liverpool Personal Services Soc., 1973–81; Adv. Panel Inf. Service, Disabled Living Foundn, 1979–81; UK Steering Cttee, Internat. Year for the Disabled, 1979–80; Jt Cttee on Mobility of Blind and Partially Sighted People, 1980–81; Exec. Cttee, N Regional Assoc. for the Blind, 1980–81. Vice Pres., MIND Appeal, 1978–79. Christopher Kershaw Meml Lectr, London, 1984. Pres., Merseyside Ski Club, 1970–77. Mem. Council, Prospect Hall Coll., 1973–77; Chm., Bd of Governors, William Rathbone Staff Coll., Liverpool, 1961–75. Duncan Medal, 1998 (for services to public health in Liverpool, 1953–71). *Publications:* Community Health and Social Services, 1965, 6th edn as Public Health, Preventive Medicine and Social Services, 1995; Community Health, Preventive Medicine and Social Services, 1966, 6th edn 1993; (contrib.) Going Home (a Guide for helping the patient on leaving hospital), 1981; The Disabled Child and Adult, 1982; (contrib.) Rehabilitation: a practical guide to the management of physical disability in adults, 1988; numerous papers on Public Health, Physically and Mentally Handicapped and various social services, in scientific and other jls. *Recreations:* ski-ing, golf, fishing, gardening, music. *Address:* Tree Tops, Church Road, Thornton Hough, Wirral, Merseyside CH63 1JN. *T:* (0151) 336 3435. *Club:* Bromborough Golf. *Died 30 June 2013.*

DAVIES, Lewis Mervyn, CMG 1966; CBE 1984 (OBE 1962); HM Overseas Civil Service, retired; *b* 5 Dec. 1922; *s* of late Rev. Canon L. C. Davies; *m* 1st, 1950, Ione Podger (*d* 1973); one *s*; 2nd, 1975, Mona A. Birley; two step *s*. *Educ:* St Edward's Sch., Oxford. Served with Fleet Air Arm, 1941–46: Lieut A, RNVR. Administrative Officer, Gold Coast, 1948; Western Pacific: Senior Asst Secretary, 1956–62; Financial Secretary, 1962–65; Chief Secretary, 1965–70; Deputy Governor, Bahamas, 1970–73; Secretary for Security, 1973–82, Secretary (Gen. Duties), 1983–85, Hong Kong. Commandeur de l'Ordre National du Mérite, 1966. *Address:* Carrer Cals Julians 16, 07141 Sa Cabaneta-Marratxi, Mallorca, Spain. *T:* and *Fax:* (971) 602519. *Club:* Oriental. *Died 10 Aug. 2011.*

DAVIES, Hon. Sir Mervyn; *see* Davies, Hon. Sir D. H. M.

DAVIES, Sir Noel; *see* Davies, Sir C. N.

DAVIES, (Percy) Douglas, CB 1981; *b* 17 Sept. 1921; *s* of late Thomas Davies; *m* 1947, Renée Margaret Billings (*d* 2001); one *s* one *d*. *Educ:* Liverpool Collegiate School; Open Univ. (BA 1989). Clerical Officer, Ministry of Transport, 1938; served Royal Armoured Corps, 1941–46; Chief Executive Officer, Min. of Transport, 1963; Asst Secretary, 1966; Principal Establishment Officer, Under Secretary, Property Services Agency, Dept of the Environment, 1972–81. Chm., Council of Management, London Hostels Assoc., 1983–2000. *Recreations:* gardening, making things work. *Address:* Hill House Nursing Home, 48–50 Park Road, Kenley, Surrey CR8 4AR. *T:* (020) 8645 8985. *Died 24 Nov. 2011.*

DAVIES, Prof. Rodney Deane, CBE 1995; DSc, PhD; FRS 1992; CPhys, FInstP; FRAS; Professor of Radio Astronomy, University of Manchester, 1976–97, then Professor Emeritus; Director, Nuffield Radio Astronomy Laboratories, Jodrell Bank, 1988–97; *b* 8 Jan. 1930; *s* of Holbin James Davies and Rena Irene (*née* March), Mallala, S Australia; *m* 1953, Valda Beth Treasure; one *s* two *d* (and one *s* decd). *Educ:* Adelaide High Sch.; Univ. of Adelaide (BSc Hons, MSc); Univ. of Manchester (PhD, DSc). Research Officer, Radiophysics Div., CSIRO, Sydney, 1951–53; Univ. of Manchester: Asst Lectr, 1953–56; Lectr, 1956–67; Reader, 1967–76. Visiting Astronomer, Radiophysics Div., CSIRO, Australia, 1963. Member: Internat. Astronomical Union, 1958; Org. Cttee and Working Gps of various Commns; Bd and various panels and cttees of Astronomy Space and Radio Bd and Science Bd of Science Research Council; British Nat. Cttee for Astronomy, 1974–77. Royal Astronomical Society: Mem. Council, 1972–75 and 1978–89; Sec., 1978–86; Vice-Pres., 1973–75 and 1986–87; Pres., 1987–89. *Publications:* Radio Studies of the Universe (with H. P. Palmer), 1959; Radio Astronomy Today (with H. P. Palmer and M. I. Large), 1963; The Crab Nebula (co-ed with F. G. Smith), 1971; numerous contribs to Monthly Notices of RAS and internat. jls on the galactic and extragalactic magnetic fields, structure and dynamics of the Galaxy and nearby external galaxies, use of radio spectral lines, the early Universe and studies of the Cosmic Microwave Background. *Recreations:* gardening, fell-walking. *Address:* University of Manchester, Jodrell Bank Observatory, Macclesfield, Cheshire SK11 9DL. *T:* (01477) 571321. *Died 8 Nov. 2015.*

DAVIES, Rt Rev. Roy Thomas; Bishop of Llandaff, 1985–99; *b* 31 Jan. 1934; *s* of Hubert and Dilys Davies; unmarried. *Educ:* St David's Coll., Lampeter (BA); Jesus Coll., Oxford (BLitt); St Stephen's House, Oxford. Asst Curate, St Paul's, Llanelli, 1959–64; Vicar of Llanafan, 1964–67; Chaplain to Anglican Students, University Coll. of Wales, Aberystwyth, 1967–73; Sec., Provincial Council for Mission and Unity of Church in Wales, 1973–79; Vicar of St David's, Carmarthen, 1979–83; Vicar of Llanegwad, 1983–85; Archdeacon of Carmarthen, 1982–85; Clerical Sec., Governing Body of Church in Wales, 1983–85. ChStJ 1986–2000. *Recreations:* walking, reading. *Address:* 25 Awel Tywi, Llangunnor, Carmarthen SA31 2NL. *Died 7 Aug. 2013.*

DAVIS, Christine Agnes Murison, CBE 1997; Chairman: Scottish Legal Aid Board, 1991–98 (Member, 1986–89, 1990–91); Scottish Power Green Energy Trust, since 2008; *b* Salisbury, Wilts, 5 March 1944; *d* of William Russell Aitken and Betsy Mary Murison or Aitken; *m* 1968, Robin John Davis; one *d* (and one *d* decd) (twins). *Educ:* Perth Acad.; Ayr Acad.; St Andrews Univ. (MA Hons Modern History 1966); Aberdeen Univ. (DipEd 1967). Teacher of History and Modern Studies: Cumbernauld High Sch., 1967–68; High Sch. of Stirling, 1968–69; HM Instn, Cornton Vale, 1979–87. Member: Dunblane Town Council (non-political), 1972–75; (ex-officio) Perth and Kinross Jt County Council, 1972–75. Mem., 1974–77, Vice Chm., 1978–79, Chm., 1980–90, Electricity Consultative Council for N of Scotland Dist; Member: N Scotland Hydro Electric Bd, 1980–90; Legal Aid Central Cttee, 1980–87; Scottish Econ. Council, 1987–95; Scottish Cttee, Council on Tribunals, 1989–95; Rail Users' Consultative Cttee for Scotland, subseq. Rail Passengers' Cttee Scotland, 1997–2005; Vice Chm., IT82 Scottish Cttee, 1981–83; Chm., Scottish Agricl Wages Bd, 1995–2004 (Mem., 1991–95); Ind. Advr on Public Appts, 1998–2002. Trustee: Nat. Energy Foundn, 1991–2002; Energy Action Scotland, 1991–2002, 2003–08 (Convener, 2004–08); Joseph Rowntree Charitable Trust, 1996–. Co-opted Mem. Court, Univ. of St Andrews, 2004–08 (Gen. Council Assessor, 2000–03). A Quaker; a Pres., CCBI, 1990–92. Swarthmore Lectr, Soc. of Friends, 2008. *Recreations:* gardening, walking, sewing. *T:* (01786) 823226. *E:* christine.davis@jrct.org.uk. *Club:* Penn. *Died 17 Feb. 2015.*

DAVIS, Sir Colin (Rex), CH 2001; Kt 1980; CBE 1965; Principal Conductor, 1995–2007, President, since 2007, London Symphony Orchestra; *b* 25 Sept. 1927; *s* of Reginald George and Lillian Davis; *m* 1949, April Cantelo (marr. diss. 1964); one *s* one *d*; *m* 1964, Ashraf Naini, (Shamsi) (*d* 2010); three *s* two *d*. *Educ:* Christ's Hospital; Royal College of Music. Orchestral Conductor, Freelance wilderness, 1949–57; Asst Conductor, BBC Scottish Orchestra, 1957–59. Conductor, Sadler's Wells, 1959, Principal Conductor, 1960–65, Musical Director, 1961–65; Chief Conductor, BBC Symphony Orchestra, 1967–71, Chief Guest Conductor, 1971–75; Musical Dir, Royal Opera House, Covent Garden, 1971–86; Chief Conductor, Bavarian Radio Symphony Orch., 1983–92; Principal Guest Conductor: Boston SO, 1972–84; LSO, 1975–95; NY Philharmonic, 1998–2003; Hon. Conductor, Dresden Staatskapelle, 1990. Conducted at: Metropolitan Opera House, New York, 1969, 1970, 1972; Bayreuth Fest., 1977; Vienna State Opera, 1986; Bavarian State Opera, 1994. Hon. DMus: RAM 2002; Keele, 2002; Dr *hc* La Sorbonne, 2006. Freedom, City of London, 1992; Hon. Freedom, Co. of Musicians, 2005. Sibelius Medal, Finland Sibelius Soc., 1977; Grosse Schallplattenpreis, 1978; Gold Medal, Royal Philharmonic Soc., 1995; Distinguished Musician Award, ISM, 1996; Sibelius Birthplace Medal, 1998; Best Opera Performance (for Falstaff), Grammy Awards, 2006; Best Male Artist, Classical Brit Awards, 2008; Queen's Medal for Music, 2009; Annual Award, Assoc. of British Orchs, 2010; Theodore Thomas Award, Conductors Guild, 2012; Critics' Circle Award, 2013; Berlioz Soc. Medal, 2013. Commendatore of Republic of Italy, 1976; Commander's Cross, Order of Merit (FRG), 1987; Commandeur, l'Ordre des Arts et des Lettres (France), 1990; Commander, Order of Lion (Finland), 1992; Order of Merit (Bavaria), 1993; Officier, Légion d'Honneur (France), 1999 (Chevalier, 1982); Order of Maximilian (Bavaria), 2000; Commander, Order of Dannebrog (Denmark), 2012. *Recreations:* reading, cooking, gardening, knitting. *Address:* c/o Alison Glaister, 39 Huntingdon Street, N1 1BP. *Club:* Athenæum. *Died 14 April 2013.*

DAVIS, Derek Alan, CEng; Director, World Energy Council Commission, 1990–93; *b* 5 Oct. 1929; *s* of Irene Davis (*née* Longstaff) and Sydney George Davis; *m* 1954, Ann Margery Willett; three *s*. *Educ:* private schools; Battersea Polytechnic; London University. BScEng (First Hons) 1950; MIMechE; CCMI. De Havilland Engine Co. Ltd: post-graduate apprentice, 1950–52; develt engineer, Gas Turbine Div., 1952–53, Rocket Div., 1953–56; Central Electricity Generating Board: Research Labs, 1956–60; Manager, Mech. and Civil Engineering, 1960–65; Group Head Fuel, 1965, System Econ. Engineer, 1970, System Planning Engineer, 1973–75, Planning Dept; Dir, Resource Planning, later Dir Production, NE Region, 1975–81; Dir Corporate Strategy Dept, 1981–84; Bd Mem., 1984–90. Member: SERC, 1989–94; Meteorology Cttee, MoD, 1986–99; ACORD, Dept of Energy, 1990–92. *Publications:* articles in tech. and engineering jls. *Recreations:* playing, now watching, sport; gardening, DIY, reading. *Died 6 Dec. 2015.*

DAVIS, Rear-Adm. Graham Noel, CB 1993; Director-General, Fleet Support for Operations and Plans, 1991–93; software development consultant, 1993–2010; *b* 24 Dec. 1937; *s* of Edward Davis and Ruth (*née* Bullen); *m* 1964, Mary Jenkins; one *s* one *d*. *Educ:* Eltham Coll.; London Univ. (BSc Hons Physics). Joined RN 1963: Comdr, 1973; Capt., 1981; Dean, RNC, Greenwich, 1981–83; rcds 1983; Dir, various depts, MoD, 1984–90; Rear-Adm.,

1991. Chm., Sussex Ouse Restoration Soc., 2000–03. *Recreations:* cooking, pottery, exploring UK and European canals by boat. *E:* davis5@which.net. *Died 1 Sept. 2013.*

DAVIS, Madeline; *see* Gibson, Madeline.

DAVIS, Dr Michael; Hon. Director General, European Commission, Brussels, since 1989; *b* 9 June 1923; *s* of William James Davis and Rosaline Sarah (*née* May); *m* 1951, Helena Hobbs Campbell, *e d* of Roland and Catherine Campbell, Toronto. *Educ:* Exeter Univ. (BSc); Bristol Univ. (PhD). CEng, FIMMM; CPhys, FInstP. Radar Officer, Flagship, 4th Cruiser Sqdn, British Pacific Fleet, Lieut (Sp. Br.) RNVR, 1943–46 (despatches). Res. Fellow, Canadian Atomic Energy Project, Toronto Univ., 1949–51; Sen. Sci. Officer, Services Electronics Res. Lab., 1951–55; UKAEA: Commercial Dir and Techn. Adviser, 1956–73; Dir of Nuclear Energy, Other Primary Sources and Electricity, EC, 1973–81; Dir for Energy Saving, Alternative Sources of Energy, Electricity and Heat, EC, 1981–88. Chm., OECD Cttee on World Uranium Resources, 1965–73; Dir, NATO Advanced Study Inst., 1971; advised NZ Govt on Atomic Energy, 1967. Mem., Ecumenical Commn, Westminster Dio., 1966–73. McLaughlin Meml Lectr, Instn of Engineers of Ireland, 1977. *Publications:* (ed jtly) Uranium Prospecting Handbook, 1972; papers in various sci. jls. *Recreations:* sculpture, writing. *Club:* Oxford and Cambridge. *Died 7 April 2011.*

DAVISON, Prof. Alan, PhD; FRS 2000; Professor of Inorganic Chemistry, Massachusetts Institute of Technology, 1974–2005, then Emeritus; *b* 24 March 1936; *s* of John W. Davison and Ellen J. Davison (*née* Woodley); *m* Lynne Penney; three *s* four *d*. *Educ:* UC, Swansea (BSc 1959); Imperial Coll. (PhD 1962; DIC). Lectr in Chemistry, Harvard Univ., 1962–64; Asst Prof., 1964–67, Associate Prof., 1967–74, MIT. Alfred P. Sloan Foundn Fellow, 1967–69. Amer. Chem. Soc. Award, 2006. *Publications:* articles in learned jls. *Address:* Department of Chemistry, Massachusetts Institute of Technology, 77 Massachusetts Avenue, Cambridge, MA 02139–4307, USA. *Died 14 Nov. 2015.*

DAWKINS, Douglas Alfred; Associate Director, Bank of England, 1985–87; *b* 17 Sept. 1927; *s* of Arthur Dawkins and Edith Annie Dawkins; *m* 1953, Diana Pauline (*née* Ormes); one *s* one *d*. *Educ:* Edmonton County Secondary Sch.; University Coll. London (Rosa Morison Scholar; BA Hons). Entered Bank of England, 1950; Bank for Internat. Settlements, 1953–54; Adviser to Governors, Bank of Libya, 1964–65; Asst Chief of Overseas Dept, 1970; First Dep. Chief of Exchange Control, 1972; Chief of Exchange Control, 1979; Asst Dir, 1980. *Address:* c/o Bank of England, Threadneedle Street, EC2R 8AH. *Died 30 Nov. 2015.*

DAWOOD, Nessim Joseph; Arabist and Middle East Consultant; Chairman, The Arabic Advertising and Publishing Co. (Aradco) Ltd, London, since 2000 (Managing Director, 1958–2000); *b* Baghdad, 27 Aug. 1927; 4th *s* of late Yousef Dawood, merchant, and Muzli (*née* Twaig); *m* 1949, Juliet, 2nd *d* of late M. and N. Abraham, Baghdad and New York; three *s*. *Educ:* The American Sch. and Shamash Sch., Baghdad; Iraq State Scholar in England, UC Exeter, 1945–49; Univ. of London, BA (Hons). FCIL (FIL 1959). Dir, Bradbury Wilkinson (Graphics) Ltd, 1975–86. Written and spoken radio and film commentaries. *Publications:* The Muqaddimah of Ibn Khaldun, 1967 (US, 1969); Penguin Classics: The Thousand and One Nights, 1954; The Koran, 1956, 68th edn 2013, rev. edn, 2014, parallel Arabic/English edn, 1990; Aladdin and Other Tales, 1957; Tales from The Thousand and One Nights, 1973, 46th edn 2014; Arabian Nights (illus. children's edn), 1978; Puffin Classics: Aladdin & Other Tales, 1989; Sindbad the Sailor & other Tales, 1989; contribs to specialised and technical English-Arabic dictionaries; translated numerous technical publications into Arabic; occasional book reviews. *Recreation:* going to the theatre. *Address:* (office) Aradco House, 132 Cleveland Street, W1T 6AB. *T:* (020) 7692 7700. *Club:* Hurlingham. *Died 20 Nov. 2014.*

DAWSON, Ven. Peter; Archdeacon of Norfolk, 1977–93, then Emeritus; *b* 31 March 1929; *s* of late Leonard Smith and Cicely Alice Dawson; *m* 1955, Kathleen Mary Sansome; one *s* three *d*. *Educ:* Manchester Grammar School; Keble Coll., Oxford (MA); Ridley Hall, Cambridge. Nat. service, Army, 1947–49; University, 1949–52; Theological College, 1952–54. Asst Curate, St Lawrence, Morden, Dio. of Southwark, 1954–59; Vicar of Barston, Warwicks, Dio. of Birmingham, 1959–63; Rector of St Clement, Higher Openshaw, Dio. of Manchester, 1963–68; Rector of Morden, Dio. of Southwark, 1968–77, and Rural Dean of Merton, 1975–77. *Recreations:* gardening, politics, the rural community, historical studies. *Address:* The Coach House, Harmony Hill, Milnthorpe LA7 7QA. *T:* (015395) 62020. *Died 6 Jan. 2013.*

DAY, Sir Derek (Malcolm), KCMG 1984 (CMG 1973); HM Diplomatic Service, retired; High Commissioner to Canada, 1984–87; *b* 29 Nov. 1927; *s* of late Mr and Mrs Alan W. Day; *m* 1955, Sheila Nott; three *s* one *d*. *Educ:* Hurstpierpoint Coll.; St Catharine's Coll., Cambridge. Royal Artillery, 1946–48. Entered HM Foreign Service, Sept. 1951; Third Sec., British Embassy, Tel Aviv, 1953–56; Private Sec. to HM Ambassador, Rome, 1956–59; Second, then First Sec., FO, 1959–62; First Sec., British Embassy, Washington, 1962–66; First Sec., FO, 1966–67; Asst Private Sec. to Sec. of State for Foreign Affairs, 1967–68; Head of Personnel Operations Dept, FCO, 1969–72; Counsellor, British High Commn, Nicosia, 1972–75; Ambassador to Ethiopia, 1975–78; Asst Under-Sec. of State, 1979, Dep. Under-Sec. of State, 1980, and Chief Clerk, 1982–84, FCO. Dir, Monenco Ltd (Canada), 1988–92; Chm., Crystal Palace Sports and Leisure Ltd, 1992–97. Mem., Commonwealth War Graves Commn, 1987–92; Vice-Chm. of Council, British Red Cross, 1988–94. Chm. Governors, Hurstpierpoint Coll., 1987–97; Gov., Bethany Sch., 1987–2000. GB Hockey XI, Olympic Games, 1952 (Bronze Medal). *Address:* Pedlars End, The Plain, Goudhurst, Kent TN17 1AD. *Club:* Hawks. *Died 7 March 2015.*

DAY, Lance Reginald; Keeper, Science Museum Library, 1976–87; *b* 2 Nov. 1927; *s* of late Reginald and Eileen Day; *m* 1959, Mary Ann Sheahan; one *s* two *d*. *Educ:* Sherrardswood Sch., Welwyn Garden City; Alleyne's Grammar Sch., Stevenage; Northern Polytechnic (BSc London); University Coll., London (MSc Hist. and Philos. of Sci.). Res. Asst, Science Museum Library, 1951–64, Asst Keeper 1964–70; Asst Keeper, Science Museum, Dept of Chemistry, 1970–74; Keeper, Science Museum, Dept of Communications and Electrical Engrg, 1974–76. Sec., Nat. Railway Museum Cttee, 1973–75; Newcomen Society: Hon. Sec., 1973–82; Hon. Mem., 1996; Ed., Trans of Newcomen Soc., 1990–2000 (Chm., Editl Bd, 1992–2000); Newcomen Fellow, 2010. *Publications:* Broad Gauge, 1985; (contrib.) Encyclopaedia of the History of Technology, 1990; (ed jtly and contrib.) Biographical Dictionary of the History of Technology, 1996; reviews and articles. *Recreation:* music. *Address:* 12 Rhinefield Close, Brockenhurst, Hants SO42 7SU. *T:* (01590) 622079. *Died 6 May 2015.*

DEAN, Winton (Basil), FBA 1975; author and musical scholar; *b* Birkenhead, 18 March 1916; *e s* of late Basil Dean, CBE, and Esther, *d* of A. H. Van Gruisen; *m* 1939, Hon. Thalia Mary Shaw (*d* 2000), 2nd *d* of 2nd Baron Craigmyle; one *s* one adopted *d* (and two *d* decd). *Educ:* Harrow; King's Coll., Cambridge (MA). Translated libretto of Weber's opera Abu Hassan (Arts Theatre, Cambridge) 1938. Served War of 1939–45: in Admiralty (Naval Intelligence Div.), 1944–45. Member: Music Panel, Arts Council, 1957–60, Cttee of Handel Opera Society (London), 1955–60; Council, Royal Musical Assoc., 1965–98 (Vice-Pres., 1970–98; Hon. Mem., 1998–). Ernest Bloch Prof. of Music, 1965–66, Regent's Lectr, 1977, Univ. of California (Berkeley); Matthew Vassar Lectr, Vassar Coll., Poughkeepsie, NY, 1979. Member: Management Cttee, Halle Handel Soc., 1979– (Vice-Pres., 1991–99; Hon. Mem., 1999); Kuratorium, Göttingen Handel Fest., 1981–97 (Hon. Mem., 1997–); Corresp. Mem., Amer. Musicological Soc., 1989–. Ed, with Sarah Fuller, Handel's opera Julius Caesar (Barber Inst. of Fine Arts, Birmingham), performed 1977. Hon. RAM 1971.

Hon. MusD Cambridge, 1996. City of Halle Handel Prize, 1995. *Publications:* The Frogs of Aristophanes (trans. of choruses to music by Walter Leigh), 1937; Bizet (Master Musicians), 1948 (3rd rev. edn, 1975); Carmen, 1949; Introduction to the Music of Bizet, 1950; Franck, 1950; Hambledon *v* Feathercombe, the Story of a Village Cricket Match, 1951; Handel's Dramatic Oratorios and Masques, 1959; Shakespeare and Opera (Shakespeare in Music), 1964; Georges Bizet, His Life and Work, 1965; Handel and the Opera Seria, 1969, Japanese rev. edn 2005; Beethoven and Opera (in The Beethoven Companion), 1971; ed, Handel, Three Ornamented Arias, 1976; (ed) E. J. Dent, The Rise of Romantic Opera, 1976; The New Grove Handel, 1982; (with J. M. Knapp) Handel's Operas 1704–1726, 1987 (Yorkshire Post Lit. Prize, 1988), 2nd edn 1995; Essays on Opera, 1990; (ed jtly) Handel, Julius Caesar, 1999; Handel's Operas 1726–1741, 2006; contributed to Grove's Dictionary of Music and Musicians (5th and 6th edns), New Oxford History of Music and to musical periodicals and learned journals. *Recreations:* cricket, shooting, salmon fishing, naval history. *Address:* Hambledon Hurst, Godalming, Surrey GU8 4HF. *T:* (01428) 682644. *Died 19 Dec. 2013.*

DEANE, Prof. Phyllis Mary, FBA 1980; Professor of Economic History, University of Cambridge, 1981–83; Fellow of Newnham College, 1961–83, Hon. Fellow, 1983; *b* 13 Oct. 1918; *d* of John Edward Deane and Elizabeth Jane Brooks; single. *Educ:* Chatham County Sch.; Hutchesons' Girls' Grammar Sch., Glasgow; Univ. of Glasgow (MA Hons Econ. Science 1940); MA Cantab. Carnegie Research Scholar, 1940–41; Research Officer, Nat. Inst. of Econ. and Social Research, 1941–45; Colonial Research Officer, 1946–48; Research Officer: HM Colonial Office, 1948–49; Cambridge University: Dept of Applied Econs, 1950–61; Lectr, Faculty of Econs and Politics, 1961–71; Reader in Economic History, 1971–81. Vis. Prof., Univ. of Pittsburgh, 1969. Editor, Economic Jl, 1968–75. Pres., Royal Economic Soc., 1980–82. Hon. DLitt Glasgow, 1989. *Publications:* (with Julian Huxley) The Future of the Colonies, 1945; The Measurement of Colonial National Incomes, 1948; Colonial Social Accounting, 1953; (with W. A. Cole) British Economic Growth 1688–1959, 1962; The First Industrial Revolution, 1965; The Evolution of Economic Ideas, 1978; The State and the Economic System, 1989; The Life and Times of Neville Keynes, 2001; papers and reviews in econ. jls. *Died 28 July 2012.*

DEANE-DRUMMOND, Maj.-Gen. Anthony John, CB 1970; DSO 1960; MC 1942 and Bar, 1945; Assistant Chief of Defence Staff (Operations), 1968–70; *b* 23 June 1917; *s* of late Col J. D. Deane-Drummond, DSO and Bar, OBE, MC; *m* 1944, Mary Evangeline Boyd (*d* 2002); four *d.* *Educ:* Marlborough Coll.; RMA, Woolwich. Commissioned Royal Signals, 1937. War Service in Europe and N Africa; POW, Italy, 1941 (escaped, 1942); Staff Coll., 1945; Bde Major, 3rd Parachute Bde, 1946–47; Instructor, Sandhurst, 1949–51 and Staff Coll., 1952–55; CO, 22 Special Air Service Regt, 1957–60; Bde Comdr, 44 Parachute Bde, 1961–63; Asst Comdt, RMA, Sandhurst, 1963–66; GOC 3rd Division, 1966–68; retired 1971. Col Comdt, Royal Corps of Signals, 1966–71. Director: Paper and Paper Products Industry Trng Bd, 1971–79; Wood Burning Centre, 1980–83. British Gliding Champion, 1957; Pilot, British Gliding Team, 1958, 1960, 1963, 1965. *Publications:* Return Ticket, 1951; Riot Control, 1975; Arrows of Fortune (autobiog.), 1991; (contrib.) The Imperial War Museum Book of Modern Warfare, 2002. *Recreations:* carpentry and carving, antique furniture restoration, shooting. *Address:* c/o Royal Bank of Scotland, PO Box 412, 62–63 Threadneedle Street, EC2R 8LA. *Died 4 Dec. 2012.*

de BELLAIGUE, Sir Geoffrey, GCVO 1996 (KCVO 1986; CVO 1976; LVO 1968); FSA; FBA 1992; Director of the Royal Collection, 1988–96; Surveyor of the Queen's Works of Art, 1972–96, then Surveyor Emeritus; *b* 12 March 1931; *s* of late Vicomte Pierre de Bellaigue and Marie-Antoinette Ladd; *m* 1971, Sheila (LVO 2000), 2nd *d* of late Rt Rev. J. K. Russell; two *d.* *Educ:* Wellington Coll.; Trinity Coll., Cambridge (BA 1954, MA 1959); Ecole du Louvre. With J. Henry Schroeder & Co., 1954–59; with the National Trust, Waddesdon Manor, 1960–63 (Keeper of the Collection, 1962–63); Dep. Surveyor, the Queen's Work's of Art, 1963–72. Mem., Exec. Cttee, NACF, 1977–2005. Trustee, Wallace Collection, 1998–2006. Hon. Pres., French Porcelain Soc., 1985–99. Officier de l'Ordre des Arts et des Lettres (France), 1987; Officier, Légion d'Honneur, 1999. *Publications:* The James A. de Rothschild Collection at Waddesdon Manor: furniture, clocks and gilt bronzes, 1974; (jtly) Buckingham Palace, 1986; Sèvres Porcelain in the Collection of HM the Queen, Vol. I, 1986; (with S. Eriksen) Sèvres Porcelain, 1987; French Porcelain in the Collection of HM the Queen, 2009; articles in art historical jls and exhibn catalogues, principally for The Queen's Gallery. *Address:* 85 Tantallon Road, SW12 8DQ. *Died 4 Jan. 2013.*

de BLANK, Justin Robert; Chairman, The Justin de Blank Co. Ltd, 2002 (Vice-Chairman, 1996–2002); *b* 25 Feb. 1927; *s* of William de Blank and Agnes Frances de Blank (*née* Crossley); *m* 1st, 1972, Mary Jacqueline Christina du Bois Godet (Molly); 2nd, 1977, Melanie Alexandra Margaret Irwin; three *d.* *Educ:* Grenham House School, Birchington-on-Sea; Marlborough College; Corpus Christi College, Cambridge (BA); Royal Acad. Sch. of Architecture. Unilever, 1953–58; J. Walter Thompson, London and Paris, 1958–66; Conran Design Group, 1967; formed own company, 1968; Chm. and Man. Dir, Justin de Blank Provisions Ltd, 1968–93; Chm., de Blank Restaurants, 1986–95; Pres., Justin de Blank Foods Ltd, 1993–95. Director: Kitchen Range Foods Ltd, 1976–96; Millers Damsels Ltd, 1989–96; The Original Porter's Provisions Co. Ltd, 1993–96; Chm., Chantdene, 1999–2002. *Recreations:* reading, television. *Died 17 Dec. 2012.*

DE CLERCQ, Willy; Member (L) European Parliament, 1979–81, and 1989–2004; Minister of State, Belgium, since 1985; *b* 8 July 1927; *s* of Frans De Clercq; *m* 1953, Fernande Fazzi; two *s* one *d.* *Educ:* Ghent Univ. (Dr in Law 1950); Univ. of Syracuse, USA (MA SocSci 1951). Called to Belgian Bar, 1951; Municipal Councillor, Ghent, 1952–79; Dep. Sec.-Gen., Belgian Liberal Party, 1957; MP Ghent-Eeklo, 1958–85; Dep. State Sec., Min. of Budget, 1960; Leader, Parly Gp of Belgian Liberal Party, 1965; Dep. Prime Minister, 1966–68; created Flemish Liberal Party (PVV) (Chm., 1972–73 and 1977–81); Dep. Prime Minister, 1973; Minister of Finance, 1974–77 (Chm., Interim Cttee, IMF; Mem., Bd of Governors, EIB; Governor, World Bank); Dep. Prime Minister and Minister of Finance and Foreign Trade, 1981–85; Mem., Commn of European Communities, 1985–88. European Parliament: Chairman: External Econ. Relations Cttee, 1989–97; Cttee on Legal Affairs and Citizens' Rights, 1997–2004. Pres., European Liberal Democrat and Reform Party (formerly Fedn of Eur. Liberal Democratic and Reform Parties), 1981–85 and 1991–95 (Hon. Pres., 1995). President: Eur. Movt, Belgium, 1992 (Hon. Pres.); Eur. Federalist Movt, Belgium, 1992 (Hon. Pres.). Comdr, Order of Leopold; Grand Cross, Order of Leopold II; numerous foreign decorations. *Address:* Cyriel Buyssestraat 12, 9000 Ghent, Belgium. *T:* (9) 2211813. *Died 28 Oct. 2011.*

de DENEY, Sir Geoffrey Ivor, KCVO 1992 (CVO 1986); Clerk of the Privy Council, 1984–92; Chief Executive, Royal College of Anaesthetists, 1993–97; *b* 8 Oct. 1931; *s* of late Thomas Douglas and Violet Ivy de Deney; *m* 1959, Diana Elizabeth Winrow; two *s.* *Educ:* William Ellis Sch.; St Edmund Hall, Oxford (MA, BCL); Univ. of Michigan. Home Office: joined, 1956; Asst Principal, 1956–61 (Private Sec. to Parly Under Sec. of State, 1959–61); Principal, 1961–69; Sec. to Graham Hall Cttee on maintenance limits in magistrates' courts; Sec. to Brodrick Cttee on Death Certification and Coroners; Private Sec. to Sec. of State, 1968; Asst Sec., 1969–78; seconded to Cabinet Office, 1975; Asst Under Sec. of State, 1978–84; Community Programmes and Equal Opportunities Dept, 1978–80; General Dept (and Registrar of the Baronetage), 1980–84. Trustee, Gordon House Assoc., later Gordon Moody Assoc., 1990 (Chm., 2002–12). Hon. FRCA 1997. *Recreations:* books, walking. *Address:* 17 Ladbroke Terrace, W11 3PG. *Died 2015.*

de DUVE, Prof. Christian René Marie Joseph, Viscount 1989; Grand Cross Order of Leopold II 1975; Professor of Biochemistry, Catholic University of Louvain, 1951–85, then Emeritus; Founding Member, and President 1974–91, International Institute of Cellular and Molecular Pathology, later re-named de Duve Institute, Brussels; Andrew W. Mellon Professor at Rockefeller University, New York, 1962–88, then Emeritus; *b* England, 2 Oct. 1917; *s* of Alphonse de Duve and Madeleine Pungs; *m* 1943, Janine Herman (*d* 2008); two *s* two *d*. *Educ:* Jesuit Coll., Antwerp; Catholic Univ. of Louvain; Med. Nobel Inst., Stockholm; Washington Univ., St Louis. MD 1941, MSc 1946, Agrégé de l'Enseignement Supérieur 1945, Louvain. Lectr, Med. Faculty, Catholic Univ. of Louvain, 1947–51. Vis. Prof. at various univs. Mem. editorial and other bds and cttees; mem. or hon. mem. various learned socs, incl. For. Assoc. Nat. Acad. of Scis (US) 1975, and For. Mem of Royal Soc., 1988. Holder of hon. degrees. Awards incl. (jtly) Nobel Prize in Physiol. or Med., 1974. *Publications:* A Guided Tour of the Living Cell, 1985; Blueprint for a Cell, 1991; Vital Dust, 1995; Constraints on the Origin and Evolution of Life, 1998; Life Evolving: molecules, mind and meaning, 2002; Singularities: landmarks on the pathways of life, 2005; Genetics of Original Sin: the impact of natural selection on the future of humanity, 2010; numerous scientific. *Recreations:* walking, swimming. *Address:* Le Pré St Jean, 239 rue de Weert, 1390 Nethen (Grez-Doiceau), Belgium. *T:* (10) 866628; de Duve Institute, Avenue Hippocrate 75, 1200 Brussels, Belgium; Rockefeller University, 1230 York Avenue, New York, NY 10021, USA. *E:* deduve_private@icp.ucl.ac.be. *Died 4 May 2013.*

de FERRANTI, Sebastian (Basil Joseph) Ziani; DL; Chairman, Ferranti plc, 1963–82 (Managing Director, 1958–75; Director 1954); Director, GEC plc, 1982–97; *b* 5 Oct. 1927; *er s* of Sir Vincent de Ferranti, MC, and late Dorothy H. C. Wilson; *m* 1st, 1953, Mona Helen (*d* 2008), *d* of T. E. Cunningham; one *s* two *d*; 2nd, 1983, Naomi Angela Rae, DL (*d* 2001); 3rd, 2011, Gillian Nadine Brown, *d* of John William France. *Educ:* Ampleforth. 4th/7th Dragoon Guards, 1947–49; Cheshire Yeo. Brown Boveri, Switzerland, and Alsthom, France, 1949–50. Director: British Airways Helicopters, 1982–84; Nat. Nuclear Corp., 1984–88. President: Electrical Research Assoc., 1968–69; BEAMA, 1969–70; Centre for Educn in Science, Educn and Technology, Manchester and region, 1972–82. Chm., Internat. Electrical Assoc., 1970–72. Member: Nat. Defence Industries Council, 1969–77; Council, IEE, 1970–73. Trustee, Tate Gallery, 1971–78; Chm., Civic Trust for the North-West, 1978–83; Comr, Royal Commn for Exhibn of 1851, 1984–97. Pres., Hallé Concerts Soc., 1997– (Chm., 1988–96). Mem. Bd of Govs, RNCM, 1988–2000 (Hon. RNCM 1997). Chm. assessors, architect for Manchester City Art Gall extn, 1995–. FRSA 1972 (Vice-Pres., 1980–84). Lectures: Granada, Guildhall, 1966; Royal Instn, 1969; Louis Blériot, Paris, 1970; Faraday, 1970–71. High Sheriff of Cheshire, 1988–89; DL Cheshire, 1995. Hon. Fellow, UMIST. Hon. DSc: Salford Univ., 1967; Cranfield Inst. of Technology, 1973; Hon. LLD Manchester, 1998. *Address:* Henbury Hall, Macclesfield, Cheshire SK11 9PJ. *Clubs:* Cavalry and Guards, Pratt's. *Died 15 Oct. 2015.*

de FRANCIA, Prof. Peter Laurent; artist; Professor, School of Painting, Royal College of Art, London, 1972–86; *b* 25 Jan. 1921; *s* of Fernand de Francia and Alice Groom; *m* 1943 (marr. diss.); *m* 1980 (marr. diss. 1988); *m* 2004, Alix MacSweeney. *Educ:* Academy of Brussels; Slade Sch., Univ. of London. Canadian Exhibition Commn, Ottawa, 1949–50; American Museum, Central Park West, NY, 1950–51; Talks Producer, BBC, Television, 1951–52; Tutor: St Martin's Sch. of Art, London, 1953–68; Royal College of Art, 1963–69; Principal, Dept of Fine Art, Goldsmiths Coll., 1969–72. DAAD Fellow, Berlin, 1990; Vis. Prof., Univ. of Baroda, 1991; Vis. Tutor: Sch. of Fine Art, Nicosia, 1991; New York Studio Sch., 1992; Vermont Studio Center, 1994. *Solo exhibitions:* Waddington Galls, London, 1958; Colonna Gall., Milan, 1958, 1959; Galerie d'Endt, Amsterdam, 1961; Gall. of Union of Czech Writers, Prague, 1962; Forum Gall., NY, 1962, 1983; New 57 Gall., Edinburgh, 1969, 1977; New Art Centre, London, 1976, 1980; Camden Arts Centre, 1977, 1987; Gall. of Inst. of Cultural Relns, Budapest, 1978; Graves Art Gall., Sheffield, 1987; Frith St Gall., London, 1989; Centre for Contemporary Art, New Delhi, 1990; Pomeroy Purdy Gall., London, 1990; Gloria Gall., Nicosia, 1995; Austin/Desmond Fine Art, London, 1996; The Place, London, 1999; Ruskin Sch., Oxford, 1999; Queen's Gall., British Council, New Delhi, 2002; Tate Modern, 2003–06; The Gall., Wimbledon Sch. of Art, 2004; James Hyman Fine Art, 2005, 2009, 2011; Tate Britain, 2006; Pallant House, Chichester, 2007–08; NY Studio Sch., 2008; Charleston, Sussex, 2008. Work represented in public collections: Tate Gall.; Nat. Portrait Gall.; V&A Mus.; Mus. of Modern Art, NY; Arts Council of GB; British Mus.; Ashmolean Mus., Oxford; Graves Art Gall., Sheffield; Mus. of Modern Art, Prague; Scottish Nat. Gall. of Modern Art, Edinburgh; Imperial War Mus.; Ulster Mus., Belfast. *Publications:* Impressionism, 1950; (trans. with Anna Bostock) Le Corbusier, The Modulor and The Modulor 2, 1954; Léger: the great parade, 1969; Fernand Léger, 1983; "Untitled", 1990; Fables, 2002. *Address:* c/o James Hyman Fine Art, 5 Savile Row, W1S 3PD. *T:* (020) 7494 3857. *Died 19 Jan. 2012.*

DEHAENE, Jean-Luc; Member (PPE-DE), European Parliament, since 2004; *b* Montpellier, 7 Aug. 1940; *s* of late Albert Dehaene and of Andrée Verstraete; *m* 1965, Celie Verbeke; two *s* two *d*. *Educ:* Univ. of Namur; Univ. of Kul. Comr, Flemish Assoc. of Catholic Scouts, 1963–67; Christian Social Party (CVP): Nat. Vice Pres., CVP Youth, 1967–71; Mem., Nat. Cttee; Councillor: for Public Works, 1972–73; for Public Health, 1973–74; then Leader of Cabinet for Econ. Affairs, 1974–77; Leader of Cabinet for Flemish Affairs, 1977–78; Pres., CVP, Bruxelles-Hal-Vivorde, 1977–81; Leader of Cabinet, 1979–81; Leader of Cabinet for Instnl Reforms, 1981; co-opted Senator, 1982–87; Deputy, 1987–99; Minister of Social Affairs and Instnl Reforms, 1981–88; Dep. Prime Minister and Minister of Communications and Instnl Reforms, 1988–92; Prime Minister of Belgium, 1992–99. A Vice-Chm., Eur. Convention, 2002–03. Mayor of Vilvoorde, 2001–07. *Address:* Berkendallaan 52, 1800 Vilvoorde, Belgium. *Died 15 May 2014.*

DEJOUANY, Guy Georges André; Commandeur, Légion d'Honneur; Hon. Chairman, Vivendi (Chairman and Managing Director, Compagnie Générale des Eaux, 1976–96); *b* 15 Dec. 1920; *s* of André Dejouany and Jeanne (*née* Imbard); *m* 1958, Véronique Honoré (decd); two *s* (and one *d* decd); *m* 1996, Renée Marnet. *Educ:* Ecole Polytechnique, Paris; Ponts et Chaussées, Paris. Civil Engineer: Metz, 1945–49; Paris, 1949–50; joined Compagnie Générale des Eaux, 1950: Manager, 1961–65; Dep. Man. Dir, 1965–72; Man. Dir, 1972–73; Dir, 1973–, co. name later Vivendi. Chm. and Man. Dir, Cie des Eaux et de l'Ozone, 1970–96; Man. Dir, Soc. Monégasque des Eaux, 1970–96. *Address:* (office) 52 rue d'Anjou, 75008 Paris, France; 26 rue de Franqueville, 75116 Paris, France. *Died 14 Nov. 2011.*

de la LANNE-MIRRLEES, Robin Ian Evelyn Stuart; *see* Mirrlees.

de la MADRID HURTADO, Miguel; President of Mexico, 1982–88; Director General, Fondo de Cultura Económica, 1990–2000; *b* 12 Dec. 1934; *m* 1959, Paloma Cordero de la Madrid; four *s* one *d*. *Educ:* Nat. Autonomous Univ., Mexico (Law degree with hon. mention for thesis; with master); Harvard Univ. (MPA). Legal Dept, Nat. Bank of Foreign Trade, 1953–57; Asst Gen. Man., Bank of Mexico, 1960–64; Asst Dir Gen., Credit Mexican, Min. of Treasury, 1965–70; Dir of Finance, Pemex, 1970–72; Gen. Dir, Credit, 1972–75, Under Sec., 1975–79, Min. of Treasury; Minister, Nat. Planning and Budget, Govt of Mexico, 1979–81. Pres., Nat. Assoc. of Lawyers, 1989–. Pres., Mexican Inst. of Culture, 1989–. Mem., InterAction Council, 1989–. *Publications:* economic and legal essays. *Address:* (office) Parras #46, Barrio Sta Catarina, Deleg. Coyoacán, 04010, México DF. *T:* (525) 6584459. *Died 1 April 2012.*

DELANEY, Shelagh; playwright; *b* Salford, Lancs, 25 Nov. 1939; one *d*. *Educ:* Broughton Secondary Sch. *Plays:* A Taste of Honey, Theatre Royal, Stratford, 1958 and 1959, Wyndhams, 1959, New York, 1960 and 1961, off-Broadway revival, trans. to Broadway, 1981 (Charles Henry

Foyle New Play Award, Arts Council Bursary, New York Drama Critics' Award); The Lion in Love, Royal Court 1960, New York 1962. *Films:* A Taste of Honey, 1961 (British Film Academy Award, Robert Flaherty Award); The White Bus, 1966; Charlie Bubbles, 1968 (Writers Guild Award for best original film writing); Dance with a Stranger, 1985 (Prix Film Jeunesse-Etranger, Cannes, 1985). *TV plays:* St Martin's Summer, LWT, 1974; Find Me First, BBC TV, 1979; The Railway Station Man, BBC, 1993; *TV series:* The House that Jack Built, BBC TV, 1977 (stage adaptation, NY, 1979). *Radio plays:* So Does the Nightingale, BBC, 1980; Don't Worry About Matilda, 1983; Tell Me a Film, 2003; Country Life, 2004. FRSL 1985. *Publications:* A Taste of Honey, 1959 (London and New York); The Lion in Love, 1961 (London and New York); Sweetly Sings the Donkey, 1963 (New York), 1964 (London). *Address:* c/o Sayle Literary Agency, 1 Petersfield, Cambridge CB1 1BB. *Died 20 Nov. 2011.*

DELBRIDGE, Richard; Director: Standard Chartered plc, 2010–13; University College London Hospitals NHS Foundation Trust, 2010–13; *b* 21 May 1942; *s* of late Tom Delbridge and Vera Kate Delbridge (*née* Lancashire); *m* 1966, Diana Genevra Rose Bowers-Broadbent; one *s* two *d*. *Educ:* Copleston Sch., Ipswich; LSE (BSc Econ); Univ. of California at Berkeley (MBA). FCA. Arthur Andersen & Co., subseq. Andersen Consulting, 1963–66 and 1968–76, Partner 1974–76; Morgan Guaranty Trust Co., NY: Vice-Pres., 1976–79; Sen. Vice-Pres. and Comptroller of Morgan Guaranty Trust Co. and J. P. Morgan Inc., 1979–85; Sen. Vice-Pres. and Asst Gen. Manager, 1985–87, Man. Dir and Gen. Manager, 1987–89, London offices, J. P. Morgan Inc.; Dir, Group Finance, Midland Bank, 1990–92; Gp Finance Dir, HSBC Hldgs, 1993–95; Dir and Chief Financial Officer, NatWest Gp, 1996–2000. Director: Innogy plc, 2000–02; Egg plc, 2000–03; Tate & Lyle PLC, 2000–10; Cazenove Gp, 2002–05; Balfour Beatty plc, 2002–05; Gallaher Gp Plc, 2002–07; Fortis Gp, 2004–09; JP Morgan Cazenove Hldgs, 2005–10. Member: Bd, Securities Assoc., 1988–89; UK Council, INSEAD, 1993–99; Financial Reporting Review Panel, 1998–2007. Dir, City Arts Trust, 1998–2001. Trustee, Wordsworth Trust, 2000–07. Mem. Council and Treas., Open Univ., 2001–09. FRSA. *Recreations:* hill walking, books. *Died 23 July 2015.*

DELIGHT, Ven. John David; Archdeacon of Stoke, 1982–90, Archdeacon Emeritus, 1990; *b* 24 Aug. 1925; *s* of Rev. Sidney John Delight and Elizabeth Ethel (*née* Tuckett); *m* 1952, Eileen Elsie Braden; four *s* two *d*. *Educ:* Christ's Hospital, Horsham; Liverpool Univ.; Oak Hill Theol Coll.; Open Univ. RNVR (Fleet Air Arm), 1942–46. Curate: Tooting Graveney, 1952–55; Wallington, 1955–58; Travelling Sec., Inter-Varsity Fellowship, 1958–61; Vicar, St Christopher's, Leicester, 1961–69; Chaplain, Leicester Prison, 1965–67; Rector of Aldridge, 1969–82; RD, Walsall, 1981–82; Prebendary of Lichfield Cathedral, 1980–82; volunteer associate of Crosslinks (formerly BCMS) and CMS, to develop theol educn by extension in Dio. of Machakos, Kenya, 1990–94; retired 1994 and licensed to officiate, Dio. of Chester. Hon. Canon, All Souls Cathedral, Machakos, 1990–94. *Publications:* (contrib.) Families, Facts and Frictions, 1976. *Recreations:* travel, music, gardening, reading. *Died 16 Feb. 2013.*

DELLAL, Jack; Chairman, Allied Commercial Holdings Ltd; *b* 2 Oct. 1923; *s* of Sulman and Charlotte Dellal; *m* 1st, 1952, Zehava Helmer (marr. diss. 1975; she *d* 2011); one *s* three *d* (and one *d* decd); 2nd, 1997, Ruanne Louw; one *s* one *d*; two *d* from a previous relationship. *Educ:* Heaton Moor Coll., Manchester. Chm., Dalton, Barton & Co. Ltd, 1962–72; Dep. Chm., Keyser Ullman Ltd, 1972–74; Chm., Highland Electronics Group Ltd, 1971–76; Director: Anglo African Finance PLC, 1983–; General Tire & Rubber (SA) Ltd, 1983–87; Williams, Hunt South Africa Ltd, 1983–87. Vice-Pres., Anglo-Polish Conservative Society, 1970–. Officer, Order of Polonia Restituta, 1970. Freeman Citizen of Glasgow, 1971. *Recreations:* lawn tennis, squash, music, art. *Clubs:* Royal Thames Yacht, Queen's, Hurlingham. *Died 28 Oct. 2012.*

DENHOLM, (James) Allan, CBE 1992; Chairman, East Kilbride Development Corporation, 1983–94 (Member, 1979–94); Director, William Grant & Sons Ltd, 1975–96 (Secretary, 1966–96); President, Institute of Chartered Accountants of Scotland, 1992–93; *b* 27 Sept. 1936; *s* of James Denholm and Florence Lily Keith (*née* Kennedy); *m* 1964, Elizabeth Avril McLachlan, CA; one *s* one *d*. *Educ:* Hutchesons' Boys' Sch., Glasgow. CA. Apprentice with McFarlane Hutton & Patrick, 1954–60; Chief Accountant, A. & W. Smith & Co. Ltd, 1960–66. Councillor, Eastwood DC, 1962–64. Mem., Council, Inst. of Chartered Accountants, Scotland, 1978–83 (Sen. Vice-Pres., 1991–92). Chm., Glasgow Jun. Chamber of Commerce, 1972–73. Director: Scottish Cremation Soc. Ltd, 1980–; Scottish Mutual Assurance PLC, 1987–2003 (Dep. Chm., 1992–2003); Abbey National PLC, 1992–97; Deputy Chairman: Abbey National Life PLC, 1997–2003; Scottish Provident Instn PLC, 2001–03 (Mem., Adv. Cttee, 2001–06). Visitor, Incorporation of Maltmen, Glasgow, 1980–81. Trustee: Scottish Cot Death Trust, 1985–96; Neurosciences Foundn, Glasgow, 2003–14; Dir, Assoc. for the Relief of Incurables in Glasgow and W of Scotland, 1999–. Mem., W of Scotland Adv. Bd, Salvation Army, 1996–. Elder, New Kilpatrick Parish Church, Bearsden, 1971–. Preses, Weavers' Soc., Anderston, 1994–95; President: 49 Wine & Spirit Club of Scotland, 1983–84; Assoc. of Deacons of the Fourteen Incorporated Trades, Glasgow, 1994–95; Deacon Convener, The Trades House, Glasgow, 1998–99; Deacon, Soc. of Deacons and Free Preseses, Glasgow, 1999–2000. Patron, Royal Incorp. of Hutchesons' Hosp., 1998–2009. FSAScot 1987. FRSA 1992. *Recreations:* golf, shooting. *Address:* Greencroft, 19 Colquhoun Drive, Bearsden, Glasgow G61 4NQ. *Club:* Western (Glasgow) (Chm., 2004–05). *Died 16 Aug. 2015.*

DENISON, Ann, (Mrs W. N. Denison); *see* Curnow, E. A. M.

DENISON, Dulcie Winifred Catherine, (Dulcie Gray), CBE 1983; actress, playwright, authoress; *b* 20 Nov. 1915; *d* of late Arnold Savage Bailey, CBE, and Kate Edith (*née* Clulow Gray); *m* 1939, Michael Denison, CBE (*d* 1998). *Educ:* England and Malaya. In Repertory in Aberdeen, 1st part Sorrel in Hay Fever, 1939; Repertory in Edinburgh, Glasgow and Harrogate, 1940; BBC Serial, Front Line Family, 1941; Shakespeare, Regents Park; Alexandra in The Little Foxes, Piccadilly; Midsummer Night's Dream, Westminster, 1942; Brighton Rock, Garrick; Landslide, Westminster, 1943; Lady from Edinburgh, Playhouse, 1945; Dear Ruth, St James's; Wind is 90, Apollo, 1946; on tour in Fools Rush In, 1946; Rain on the Just, Aldwych, 1948; Queen Elizabeth Slept Here, Strand, 1949; The Four-poster, Ambassadors, 1950 (tour of S Africa, 1954–55); See You Later (Revue), Watergate, 1951; Dragon's Mouth, Winter Garden, 1952; Sweet Peril, St James's, 1952; We Must Kill Toni, Westminster; The Diary of a Nobody, Arts, 1954; Alice Through the Looking Glass, Chelsea Palace, 1955, Ashcroft Theatre, Croydon, 1972; appeared in own play, Love Affair, Lyric Hammersmith, 1956; South Sea Bubble, Cape Town, 1956; Tea and Sympathy, Melbourne and Sydney, 1956; South Sea Bubble, Johannesburg, 1957; Double Cross, Duchess, 1958; Let Them Eat Cake, Cambridge, 1959; Candida, Piccadilly and Wyndham's, 1960; Heartbreak House, Wyndham's, 1961; A Marriage Has Been Arranged, and A Village Wooing (Hong Kong); Shakespeare Recital (Berlin Festival); Royal Gambit for opening of Ashcroft Theatre, Croydon, 1962; Where Angels Fear to Tread, Arts and St Martin's, 1963; An Ideal Husband, Strand, 1965; On Approval, St Martin's, 1966; Happy Family, St Martin's, 1967; Number 10, Strand, 1967; Out of the Question, St Martin's, 1968; Three, Fortune, 1970; The Wild Duck, Criterion, 1970; Clandestine Marriage (tour), 1971; Ghosts, York; Hay Fever (tour), 1972; Dragon Variation (tour), 1973; At the End of the Day, Savoy, 1973; The Sack Race, Ambassadors, 1974; The Pay Off, Comedy, 1974, Westminster, 1975; Time and the Conways (tour), 1976; Ladies in Retirement (tour), 1976; Façade, QEH, 1976; The Cabinet Minister (tour), 1977; A Murder is Announced, Vaudeville, 1977; Bedroom Farce, Prince of Wales, 1979; The Cherry Orchard, Exeter, 1980; Lloyd George Knew my Father (tour), 1980; The Kingfisher, Windsor, 1980, Worthing and on tour, 1981; Relatively

Speaking (Dinner Theatre Tour, Near and Far East), 1981; A Coat of Varnish, Haymarket, 1982; Cavell, Chichester Fest., 1982; School for Scandal, Haymarket, transf. to Duke of York's, and British Council 50th Anniversary European Tour, 1983; There Goes the Bride (Dinner Theatre tour, Near and Far East), 1985; The Living Room, Royalty, 1987; The Chalk Garden, Windsor and tour, 1989; The Best of Friends (tour) 1990, 1991; The Importance of Being Earnest (tour), 1991; Tartuffe, Playhouse, 1991–92; Bedroom Farce (tour), 1992; An Ideal Husband, Globe, 1992, tour, 1993, Haymarket and NY, 1996, Haymarket, transf. Gielgud, 1997; Pygmalion, and The Schoolmistress, Chichester Fest., 1994; Two of a Kind (tour), 1995; The Importance of Being Earnest, Leatherhead, 1995; The Ladykillers (tour), 1999; Les Liaisons Dangereuses (tour), 2000; The Lady Vanishes (tour), 2000; Three Sisters (tour), 2002. *Films include:* They were Sisters, 1944; Wanted for Murder, 1945; A Man about the House, 1946; Mine Own Executioner, 1947; My Brother Jonathan, 1947; The Glass Mountain, 1948; The Franchise Affair, 1951; Angels One Five, 1952; There was a Young Lady, 1953; A Man Could Get Killed, 1965; The Black Crow, 1994. Has appeared in television plays and radio serials; *television series:* Howard's Way, 1985–90. Fellow, Linnean Soc., 1984. FRSA. Queen's Silver Jubilee Medal, 1977. *Publications: play:* Love Affair; *books:* Murder on the Stairs; Murder in Melbourne; Baby Face; Epitaph for a Dead Actor; Murder on a Saturday; Murder in Mind; The Devil Wore Scarlet; No Quarter for a Star; The Murder of Love; Died in the Red; The Actor and His World (with Michael Denison); Murder on Honeymoon; For Richer, For Richer; Deadly Lampshade; Understudy to Murder; Dead Give Away; Ride on a Tiger; Stage-Door Fright; Death in Denims; Butterflies on my Mind (TES Senior Information Book Prize, 1978); Dark Calypso; The Glanville Women; Anna Starr; Mirror Image; Looking Forward, Looking Back (autobiog.); J. B. Priestley (biog.). *Recreations:* swimming, butterflies. *Address:* Shardeloes, Amersham, Bucks HP7 0RL; c/o Burnett Granger Crowther, 3 Clifford Street, W1S 2LF. *T:* (020) 7437 8008. *Died 16 Nov. 2011.*

DENISON, His Honour (William) Neil; QC 1980; a Circuit Judge, 1985–2001; Common Serjeant in the City of London, 1993–2001; *b* 10 March 1929; *s* of William George Denison and Jean Brodie; *m* 1955, Philippa Jean Wilkinson; three *s*; *m* 1981, Elizabeth Ann Marguerite Curnow, QC (*d* 2011). *Educ:* Queen Mary's Sch., Walsall; Univ. of Birmingham (LLB); Hertford Coll., Univ. of Oxford (BCL). Called to the Bar, Lincoln's Inn, 1952, Bencher, 1993. A Recorder of the Crown Court, 1979–85. Hon. Bencher, Gray's Inn, 2011. Liveryman, Wax Chandlers' Co., 1988 (Master, 2001–02). *Recreations:* walking, reading rubbish. *Club:* Garrick. *Died 21 Dec. 2014.*

DENMAN, 5th Baron *cr* 1834; **Charles Spencer Denman,** CBE 1976; MC 1942; TD; Bt 1945; Senior Advisor, Al Farida Investments; *b* 7 July 1916; *e s* of Hon. Sir Richard Douglas Denman, 1st Bt; *S* father, 1957 and to barony of cousin, 1971; *m* 1943, Sheila Anne (*d* 1987), *d* of late Lt-Col Algernon Bingham Anstruther Stewart, DSO, Seaforth Highlanders, of Ornockenoch, Gatehouse of Fleet; three *s* (and one *d* decd). *Educ:* Shrewsbury. Served War of 1939–45 with Duke of Cornwall's Light Infantry (TA), India, Middle East, Western Desert and Dodecanese Islands; Major, 1943. Contested (C) Leeds Central, 1945. Director: Close Brothers Group Plc; British Water & Wastewater Ltd; Albaraka Internat. Bank Ltd; Arab-British Centre Ltd; New Zealand Holdings (UK) Ltd; formerly Chairman: Marine and General Mutual Life Assurance Soc.; Tennant Guaranty Ltd; Gold Fields Mahd adh Dhahab Ltd; Arundell House Plc; formerly Director: C. Tennant Sons & Co. Ltd; Consolidated Gold Fields Plc; British Bank of the Middle East; Saudi British Bank; British Arabian Corp.; Fletcher Challenge Corp.; MGM Life Assurance Soc. Member: Cttee for ME Trade, 1963 (Chm., 1971–75); Advisory Council of Export Credits Guarantee Department, 1963–68; British National Export Council, 1965; Cttee on Invisible Exports, 1965–67; British Invisible Exports Council; Res. Inst. for Study of Conflict and Terrorism; UK/Saudi Jt Cultural Cttee; Lord Kitchener Nat. Meml Fund. President: RSAA, 1984–; NZ-UK Chamber of Commerce and Industry; Vice President: ME Assoc.; Saudi-British Soc.; Chm., Arab British Chamber Charitable Foundn; formerly Chm., Governors of Windlesham House Sch. Liveryman, World Traders' Co. *Heir: s* Hon. Richard Thomas Stewart Denman [*b* 4 Oct. 1946; *m* 1984, (Lesley) Jane, *d* of John Stevens; one *s* three *d*]. *Club:* Brooks's. *Died 21 Nov. 2012.*

DENNE, Christopher James Alured, CMG 1991; HM Diplomatic Service, 1967–78 and 1983–98; *b* 20 Aug. 1945; *s* of late Lt Comdr John Richard Alured Denne, DSC, RN and Alison Patricia Denne; *m* 1968, Sarah Longman; two *s* one *d*. *Educ:* Wellington Coll.; Southampton Univ. (BSc Soc. Sci. 1967). Entered Diplomatic Service, 1967; New Delhi, 1969–72; Second Sec., FCO, 1972–74; First Sec. (Information), Lagos, 1974–77; FCO, 1977; resigned, 1978; BBC External Services, 1979–80; reinstated FCO, 1983; First Sec. and Dep. Permanent Rep., UK Mission to UN, Vienna, 1985–89; Head of Consular Dept, FCO, 1989–92; Dep. Hd of Mission, Athens, 1993–97. Mem., Nat. Council, European Movt, 2009–13 (Chm., Tamar Br., 2007–15). *Address:* 15 Plymouth Road, Tavistock, Devon PL19 8AU. *Died 21 Oct. 2015.*

DENNIS, Felix; poet, author and magazine publisher; Founder and Chairman, Dennis Publishing Ltd, since 1973; *b* Kingston-upon-Thames, 27 May 1947; *s* of late Reginald Dennis and Dorothy Grace Dennis (*née* Coller). *Educ:* Surbiton Grammar Sch.; St Nicholas Grammar Sch.; Harrow Coll. of Art. Publisher of magazines in Britain, USA, India and elsewhere, including: The Week; Auto Express; Viz; Computer Shopper; PC Pro; Evo; Octane; Mac User; Men's Fitness; Maxim. Dir, Butler, Tanner & Dennis, 2010– (Chm., 2008–10). Founder, Heart of England Forest (formerly Forest of Dennis) (charity), 2001–. Fellow: Nat. Liby of the Blind, 2002; Wordsworth Trust, 2004. Marcus Morris Award, PPA, 1991; Belsky Award, Soc. of Portrait Sculptors, 2009; Lifetime Achievement Award, British Media Awards, 2013; Peter Savill Award, Woodland Heritage, 2014. *Publications:* Mohammad Ali: the glory years, 2002; How to Get Rich, 2006; 88 The Narrow Road, 2010; *poetry:* A Glass Half Full, 2002; Lone Wolf, 2004; When Jack Sued Jill: nursery rhymes for modern times, 2006; Island of Dreams, 2007; Homeless in My Heart, 2008; Tales From the Woods, 2010; Love of a Kind, 2013; Do What the F**k I Say, 2013. *Recreations:* writing poetry, planting trees, breeding rare pigs (and eating them), drinking French wine, commissioning bronze sculpture. *Address:* The Old Manor, Dorsington, Warwicks CV37 8AR. *T:* (office) (020) 7636 1305, *Fax:* (020) 7436 0350; Dennis Publishing Ltd, 30 Cleveland Street, W1T 4JD. *Clubs:* Groucho, Soho Strangers, Lunar. *Died 22 June 2014.*

DENNISTON, Rev. Robin Alastair, PhD; Oxford Publisher and Senior Deputy Secretary to the Delegates, Oxford University Press, 1984–88 (Academic and General Publisher, 1980–84); Priest-in-charge of Great with Little Tew and Over Worton with Nether Worton, 1995–2002; *b* 25 Dec. 1926; *s* of late Alexander Guthrie Denniston, CMG, CBE, head of Govt code and cipher school, and Dorothy Mary Gilliat; *m* 1st, 1950, Anne Alice Kyffin Evans (*d* 1985), *y d* of late Dr Geoffrey Evans, MD, FRCP, consulting Physician at St Bartholomew's Hosp., and Hon. E. M. K. Evans; one *s* two *d*; 2nd, 1987, Dr Rosa Susan Penelope Beddington, FRS (*d* 2001). *Educ:* Westminster Sch. (King's Schol.; Captain of School, 1945); Christ Church, Oxford (Classical Schol.; 2nd cl. Hons Lit. Hum.); MSc Edinburgh 1992; PhD London 1997. National Service: commnd into Airborne Artillery, 1948. Editor at Collins, 1950–59; Man. Dir, Faith Press, 1959–60; Editor, Prism, 1959–61; Promotion Man., Hodder & Stoughton Ltd, 1960–64, Editorial Dir, 1966, Man. Dir, 1968–72; Dir, Matthew Hodder Ltd (and subsid. cos), 1968–72; Dep. Chm., George Weidenfeld & Nicolson (and subsid. cos), 1973–75; non-exec. Chm., A. R. Mowbray & Co., 1974–88; Dir, Thomson Publications Ltd, 1975–77; also Chm. of Michael Joseph Ltd, Thomas Nelson & Sons (and subsid. cos), George Rainbird Ltd, 1975–77 and Sphere Books, 1975–76; Academic Publisher, OUP, 1978; non-exec. Dir, W. W. Norton, 1989–2008. Student of Christ Church, 1978–88. Ordained Deacon, 1978, Priest, 1979; Hon. Curate: Clifton-on-Teme, 1978; New with South Hinksey, 1985; Non-Stipendiary Minister: Great with Little

Tew, 1987–90 and 1995–2001; West Fife Team Ministry, 1990–93. A Church Comr, 1989–90. *Publications:* The Young Musicians, 1956; Partly Living, 1967; (ed) Part Time Priests?, 1960; (co-ed) Anatomy of Scotland, 1992; Churchill's Secret War, 1997; Trevor Huddleston: a life, 1999; Thirty Secret Years: A. G. Denniston's work in signals in intelligence 1914–44, 2007; contrib. Oxford DNB. *Recreations:* reading, contemplation, music. *Address:* Davenham, 148 Graham Road, Malvern, Worcs WR14 2HY. *Died 6 April 2012.*

DENNY, Sir Anthony Coningham de Waltham, 8th Bt *cr* 1782, of Tralee Castle, Co. Kerry, Ireland; designer; Consultant, Verity and Beverley, Architects and Designers (offices in Tetbury, Lisbon and New York), since 2002 (Partner, 1959–2001); *b* 22 April 1925; *s* of Rev. Sir Henry Lyttleton Lyster Denny, 7th Bt, and Joan Lucy Dorothy, *er d* of Major William A. C. Denny, OBE; *S* father, 1953; *m* 1949, Anne Catherine, *e d* of S. Beverley, FRIBA; two *s* one adopted *d*. *Educ:* Clayesmore Sch. Served War of 1939–45: Middle East, RAF (Aircrew), 1943–47. Anglo-French Art Centre, 1947–50; Mural Painter and Theatrical Designer, 1950–54. Trustee, Waltham Abbey. Hereditary Freeman of City of Cork. FRSA; MCSD. *Recreations:* architecture, painting. *Heir: s* Piers Anthony de Waltham Denny [*b* 14 March 1954; *m* 1987, Ella Jane, *o d* of Peter P. Huhne; two *d*]. *Address:* Almonry Cottage, Muchelney, Langport, Somerset TA10 0DG. *T:* (01458) 252621. *Club:* Chelsea Arts. *Died 13 Sept. 2013.*

DENNY, Barry Lyttelton, LVO 1979; HM Diplomatic Service, retired; *b* 6 June 1928; *s* of Rev. Sir Henry Lyttelton Lyster Denny, 7th Bt, and Joan Lucy Dorothy, *er d* of Major William A. C. Denny, OBE; *m* 1st, 1951 (marr. diss. 1968); one *s* one *d*; 2nd, 1969, Anne Rosemary Jordon, *o d* of late Col James F. White, MC; one *d*. *Educ:* Clayesmore Sch.; RMA, Sandhurst. Indian Army Cadet, 1946–47; commnd RA, 1949; retd from HM Forces as Captain (Temp. Major), 1960. Joined Foreign Office, 1962; First Sec., Nicosia, 1964; FO, later FCO, 1966; Kaduna, 1969; FCO, 1972; Vientiane, 1973; FCO, 1975; Kuwait, 1977; Counsellor, Oslo, 1980; seconded to MoD, 1984–89. Comdr, Order of St Olav (Norway), 1981. *Recreations:* collecting, my family. *Died 4 Feb. 2011.*

DENTON-THOMPSON, Aubrey Gordon, OBE 1958; MC 1942; *b* 6 June 1920; *s* of late M. A. B. Denton-Thompson; *m* 1944, Ruth Cecily Isaac (*d* 1959); two *s* (one *d* decd); *m* 1961, Barbara Mary Wells. *Educ:* Malvern Coll. Served in RA 1940–44; seconded to Basutoland Administration, 1944; apptd to HM Colonial Service, 1945; transferred to Tanganyika as Asst District Officer, 1947; seconded to Colonial Office, 1948–50, District Officer; seconded to Secretariat, Dar es Salaam, as Asst Sec., 1950; Colonial Sec., Falkland Islands, 1955–60; Dep. Permanent Sec., Ministry of Agriculture, Tanganyika, 1960–62; retired from Tanganyika Civil Service, 1963. Man. Dir, Tanganyika Sisal Marketing Assoc. Ltd, 1966–68 (Sec. 1963); Sen. Agricl Advr, UNDP, 1968–78, and FAO Country Rep.: Korea, 1970–73, Indonesia, 1973–76, Turkey, 1976–78; Sen. Advr to Director General, FAO, Rome, July–Dec. 1978; retd Jan. 1979. Chm., New Forest Conservative Assoc., 1985–88 (Dep. Chm., 1983–85). *Address:* Octave Cottage, 43 Ramley Road, Pennington, Lymington, Hants SO41 8GZ. *T:* (01590) 676626. *Died 8 Nov. 2012.*

de PAULA, (Frederic) Clive, CBE 1970; TD 1950 and Clasp 1951; FCA, JDipMA; Chairman, Dennys Sanders & Greene Ltd, 1987–2008; *b* 17 Nov. 1916; 2nd *s* of late F. R. M. de Paula, CBE, FCA, and Agnes Smithson de Paula (*née* Clark) (American Medal of Freedom, 1947). *Educ:* Rugby Sch.; Spain and France. ACA 1940, FCA 1951; JDipMA 1966. Articled to de Paula, Turner, Lake & Co., chartered accountants, London, 1934–39. 2nd Lieut, TA, 1939; Liaison Officer, Free French Forces in London and French Equatorial Africa, 1940; Specially employed Middle East and E Africa, 1941; SOE Madagascar, 1942; comd special forces unit with 11th E African Div., Ceylon and Burma, 1943; Finance Div., Control Commn, Germany, 1945; demobilised as Major, 1946; Captain 21st Special Air Service Regt (Artists) TA, 1947–56. Joined Robson, Morrow & Co., management consultants, 1946; Partner, 1951; seconded to DEA then to Min. of Technology as an Industrial Adviser, 1967; Co-ordinator of Industrial Advisers to Govt, 1969; returned as Sen. Partner, Robson, Morrow & Co., 1970–71; Man. Dir, Agricultural Mortgage Corp. Ltd, 1971–81; Dir, 1972–83, Dep. Chm., 1978–80, Chm., 1980–83, Tecalemit plc; non-exec. Dir, Green's Economiser Group plc, 1972–83; Dep. Chm., C. & J. Clark Ltd, 1985–86. Mem., EDC for Agric., 1972–81. Member: ICAEW, 1940–; Inst. of Cost & Works Accountants, 1947–72; British Computer Soc., 1964–74 (Mem. Council, 1965–68); Management Consultants Assoc., 1964–72 (Mem. Council, 1970–71); BIM, 1970–84 (Mem. Council, 1971–76; CIMgt 1970). Gen. Comr of Income Tax, Winslow Div., Bucks, 1965–82. Vice Pres., Schoolmistresses and Governesses Benevolent Instn, 1982–2003 (Hon. Treas., 1947–81); Chm., Internat. Wine and Food Soc., 1980–83 (Silver Medal, 1996). *Publications:* first published paper in world to forecast coming impact of electronic computers on accountancy, 1952; Accounts for Management, 1954; (ed) P. Tovey, Balance Sheets: how to read and understand them, 4th edn, 1954; (ed) F. R. M. de Paula, The Principles of Auditing, 12th edn 1957 (trans. Sinhalese, 1967), (with F. A. Attwood) 15th edn as Auditing: Principles and Practice, 1976, (with F. A. Attwood and N. D. Stein) 17th edn as de Paula's Auditing, 1986; Management Accounting in Practice, 1959 (trans. Japanese 1960); (ed with A. G Russell) A. C. Smith, Internal Control and Audit, 2nd edn, 1968; (with A. W. Willsmore) The Techniques of Business Control, 1973; (with F. A. Attwood) Auditing Standards, 1978. *Address:* c/o National Westminster Bank, 60 High Street, Esher, Surrey KT10 9QY. *Died 27 Oct. 2013.*

DERRETT, Prof. (John) Duncan (Martin), MA, PhD, DCL, LLD, DD; Professor of Oriental Laws in the University of London, 1965–82, then Emeritus; *b* 30 Aug. 1922; *s* of John West Derrett and Fay Frances Ethel Kate (*née* Martin); *m* 1950, Margaret Esmé Griffiths; four *s* one *d*. *Educ:* Emanuel Sch., London; Jesus Coll., Oxford; Sch. of Oriental and Afr. Studies, London; Inns of Court School of Law. MA 1947, DCL 1966 (Oxon); PhD 1949, LLD 1971, DD 1983 (London). Served RA and RAMC, 1940–45. Called to the Bar, Gray's Inn, 1953. Lectr in Hindu Law, SOAS, 1949; Reader in Oriental Laws, 1956, Prof. of Oriental Laws, 1965, Univ. of London; Tagore Prof. of Law, Univ. of Calcutta, 1953 (lectures delivered, 1955); Vis. Professor: Univ. of Chicago, 1963; Univ. of Michigan, 1970; Wilde Lectr in Natural and Compar. Religion, Univ. of Oxford, 1978–81; Japan Soc. Prom. Sci. Fellow and Vis. Prof., Oriental Inst., Univ. of Tokyo, 1982. Fellow, Indian Law Inst., Delhi, 1988. Mem., Editorial Bd, Zeitschrift für vergleichende Rechtswissenschaft, 1954–85, subseq. of Kannada Studies, Bharata Manisha, Kerala Law Times. Mem., Stud. Novi Test. Soc., 1971–2001. Barcelona Prize in Comparative Law, 1954; N. C. Sen-Gupta Gold Medal, Asiatic Soc. (Calcutta), 1977. *Publications:* The Hoysalas, 1957; Hindu Law Past and Present, 1957; Introduction to Modern Hindu Law, 1963; Religion, Law and the State in India, 1968, repr. 1999; Critique of Modern Hindu Law, 1970; Law in the New Testament, 1970, repr. 2005; Jesus's Audience, 1973; Dharmaśāstra and Juridical Literature, 1973; History of Indian Law (Dharmaśāstra), 1973; Henry Swinburne (?1551–1624) Civil Lawyer of York, 1973; trans. R. Lingat, Classical Law of India, 1973, repr. 1998; Bhāruci's Commentary on the Manusmrti, 1975; Essays in Classical and Modern Hindu Law, vols I-IV, 1976–79; Studies in the New Testament, vols I-VI, 1977–96; The Death of a Marriage Law, 1978; Beiträge zu Indischem Rechtsdenken, 1979; The Anastasis: the Resurrection of Jesus as an Historical Event, 1982; A Textbook for Novices: Jayarakshita's Perspicuous Commentary on the 'Compendium of Conduct', 1983; The Making of Mark, 1985; New Resolutions of Old Conundrums: a fresh insight into Luke's Gospel, 1986; The Ascetic Discourse: an explanation of the Sermon on the Mount, 1989; The Victim: the Johannine passion narrative reexamined, 1993; The Sermon on the Mount, 1994; Prophecy in the Cotswolds 1804–1947, 1994; Studies in Hindu Law, 1994; Two Masters: the Buddha and Jesus, 1995; Some Telltale Words in the New Testament, 1997; Law and Morality, 1998; The Bible and the Buddhists, 2000; The Blockley Deanery in the Fifteenth Century, 2009; *edited:* Studies in the Laws of Succession in Nigeria, 1965; Introduction to Legal Systems, 1968; (with W. D. O'Flaherty) The Concept of Duty in South Asia, 1978; A Second Blockley Miscellany, 1994; collab. with Yale Edn, Works of St Thomas More, Société Jean Bodin, Brussels, Max Planck Inst., Hamburg, Fritz Thyssen Stiftung, Cologne, Institut für Soziologie, Heidelberg, Aufstieg und Niedergang der Römischen Welt, Tübingen, and Sekai Kyusei Kyo, Atami; *Festschriften:* Indology and Law, 1982; Novum Testamentum, 24, 1982, fasc. 3 and foll. *Address:* Half Way House, High Street, Blockley, Moreton-in-Marsh, Glos GL56 9EX. *T:* (01386) 700828. *Died 21 Oct. 2012.*

DERVAIRD, Hon. Lord; John Murray; Dickson Minto Professor of Company Law, Edinburgh University, 1990–99, then Professor Emeritus; a Senator of the College of Justice in Scotland, 1988–89; *b* 8 July 1935; *o s* of J. H. Murray, farmer, Stranraer; *m* 1960, Bridget Jane, *d* of Sir William Godfrey, 7th Bt, and of Lady Godfrey; three *s*. *Educ:* Stranraer schs; Edinburgh Academy; Corpus Christi Coll., Oxford (BA 1st cl. Lit. Hum., 1959); Edinburgh Univ. (LLB 1962). FCIArb 1991. Advocate, 1962; QC (Scot.) 1974. Dean, Faculty of Law, Edinburgh Univ., 1994–96. Mem., Scottish Law Commn, 1979–88. Chairman: Scottish Lawyers' European Gp, 1975–78; Scottish Council of Law Reporting, 1978–88; Scottish Cttee on Law of Arbitration, 1986–96; Scottish Council for Internat. Arbitration, 1989–2003; Panel of Professional Adjudicators, 2004–; Member: City Disputes Panel, 1994–; Panel of Arbitrators, Internat. Centre for Investment Disputes, 1998–2004; Adv. Bd, Internat. Arbitration Inst., Paris, 2000–; Academic Council, SICA-FICA, 2002–; Internat. Arbitration Club, 2009–; Vice-President: Centre of Conciliation and Arbitration for Advanced Techniques, Paris, 2000–; Scottish Arbitration Centre, 2011–. Vice-President: Agricultural Law Assoc., 1985–91 (Chm., 1979–85); Comité Européen de Droit Rural, 1989–91, 1995–96. Hon. Pres., Advocates' Business Law Group, 1988–. Dir and Chm., BT Scottish Ensemble, 1988–2000. Corresp. Mem., ICC Cttee on Business Law, Paris, 1994–. Trustee, David Hume Inst., 1994–2007. Grand Chaplain, Von Poser Soc. of Scotland, 1995; Knight, Order of Von Poser, 1996. *Publications:* contributed to: Festschrift für Dr Pikalo, 1979; Mélanges offerts à Jean Megret, 1985; Stair Encyclopedia of Scots Law, 1987, 1992, 1998, 2001; Scottish Legal Tradition, 1991; Corporate Law—the European Dimension, 1991; European Company Law, 1992; International Handbook on Commercial Arbitration, 1995; Essays in Honour of Lord Mackenzie-Stuart of Dean, 1996; Science and Law, 2000; The International Arbitration Review, 3rd edn 2013; articles in legal and ornithological jls. *Recreations:* farming, gardening, birdwatching, music, curling, field sports. *Address:* Auchenmalg House, Auchenmalg, Glenluce, Wigtownshire DG8 0JS. *T:* (01581) 500205, *Fax:* (0131) 220 0644; Wood of Dervaird Farm, Glenluce DG8 9JT. *T:* (01581) 300222. *E:* murraydervaird@talk21.com. *Clubs:* New (Edinburgh); Aberlady Curlers. *Died 23 Dec. 2015.*

DEVENPORT, Rt Rev. Eric Nash; an Honorary Assistant Bishop: Diocese of Europe, since 1992; Diocese of Norwich, since 2000; *b* 3 May 1926; *s* of Joseph and Emma Devenport; *m* 1954, Jean Margaret Richardson; two *d*. *Educ:* Kelham Theological Coll. BA (Open Univ.). Curate, St Mark, Leicester, 1951–54; St Matthew, Barrow-in-Furness, 1954–56; Succentor, Leicester Cathedral, 1956–59; Vicar of Shepshed, 1959–64; Oadby, 1964–73; Proctor in Convocation, 1964–80; Hon. Canon of Leicester Cathedral, 1973–80; Leader of Mission, Diocese of Leicester, 1973–80; Bishop Suffragan of Dunwich, 1980–92; Archdeacon of Italy and Chaplain of St Mark's, Florence, 1992–97. Chairman: Diocesan Communication Officers Cttee, 1986–92; C of E Hospital Chaplaincies Council, 1986–91; Jt Hosp. Chaplaincies Cttee, 1988–91; E Anglian Ministerial Trng Course, 1990–92. Chaplain, Worshipful Company of Framework Knitters, 1964–80; Area Chaplain, Actors' Church Union, 1980–92. Chm., Local Radio Adv. Council for Radio Suffolk, 1990–92. *Publications:* Preaching at the Parish Communion: ASB Gospels-Sundays: Year One, Vol. 2, 1989. *Recreation:* theatre. *Address:* 6 Damocles Court, Pottergate, Norwich NR2 1HN. *T:* (01603) 664121. *Died 10 Nov. 2012.*

DEVESI, Sir Baddeley, GCMG 1980; GCVO 1982; Deputy Prime Minister and Minister for Transport, Works, Communication and Aviation, Solomon Islands, 1996–2000; *b* 16 Oct. 1941; *s* of late Mostyn Tagabasoe Norua and Laisa Otu; *m* 1969, June Marie Barley; six *s* three *d* (and one *d* decd). *Educ:* St Stephen's Sch., Auckland, NZ; Ardmore Teachers' Coll., Auckland, NZ; Univ. of Western Aust.; Univ. of S Pacific. MLC and Mem. Exec. Council, 1967–69. Headmaster, St Nicholas Sch., Honiara, 1968; Educn Officer and Lectr, Solomon Is Teachers' Coll., 1970–71; Sen. Asst Sec., Solomon Is, 1972; Dist Officer, 1973; Dist Comr, Dist Magistrate and Clerk to Malaita Council, 1974–75; Permanent Sec., Ministry of Transport and Communications, 1976; Governor-Gen. of the Solomon Islands, 1978–88; Minister for Home Affairs and Dep. Prime Minister, 1989; Minister for For. Affairs and Trade Relations and Dep. Prime Minister, 1990–92; Minister for Health and Med. Services and Dep. Prime Minister, 1993; Leader of the Opposition, 1994. Dep. Chm., Solomon Islands Broadcasting Corp., 1976; Chm., AcP, 1990–91. Chancellor, Univ. of S Pacific, 1980–83. Captain, Solomon Islands team, 2nd South Pacific Games, 1966. Comr, Boy Scouts Assoc., 1968; Chief Scout, 1980–88. Hon. DU Univ. of the South Pacific, 1981. KStJ 1984. *Recreations:* reading, snooker, golf. *Address:* PO Box 227, Honiara, Solomon Islands. *Died 16 Feb. 2012.*

DEVLIN, Alexander, OBE 1977; JP; Member, Glenrothes New Town Development Corporation, 1958–78; *b* 22 Dec. 1927; *s* of Thomas Devlin and Jean Gibson; *m* 1949, Annie Scott Gordon. *Educ:* Cowdenbeath St Columba's High Sch.; National Council of Labour Colls (Local Govt and Public Speaking). Member: Fife CC, 1956–74; Fife Regional Council, 1974–78; Chm., Fife Educn Cttee, 1963–78; Vice-Chm., Educn Cttee of Convention of Scottish Local Authorities, 1974–78. Member: Dunning Cttee on Scottish System for Assessment of Pupils after 4 years Secondary Educn, 1974–77; Scottish Sports Council, 1964–74; Manpower Services Commn, 1978–79. Mem. Bd, 1992, Fellow, 1996–, Glenrothes Coll. Pres., Glenrothes & Dist Burns Club, 1995–97. JP Fife, 1963. *Died 30 July 2012.*

DEVLIN, His Honour Keith Michael, PhD; a Circuit Judge, 1984–95; a Deputy Circuit Judge, 1995–99; *b* 21 Oct. 1933; *e s* of late Francis Michael Devlin and of Norah Devlin (*née* Gregory); *m* 1958, Pamela Gwendoline Phillips; two *s* one *d*. *Educ:* Price's Sch., Fareham; Eaton Hall OCS; King's Coll., London Univ. (LLB 1960, MPhil 1968); PhD Brunel 1976. Commnd RAOC, 1953. Called to the Bar, Gray's Inn, 1964; Dep. Chief Clerk, Metropolitan Magistrates' Courts Service, 1964–66; various appts as Dep. Metropolitan Stipendiary Magistrate, 1975–79; Asst Recorder, 1980–83; a Recorder, 1983–84; Liaison Judge, Bedfordshire, 1990–93; Resident Judge, Luton Crown Court, 1991–93. Brunel University: Lectr in Law, 1966–71; Reader in Law, 1971–84; Associate Prof. of Law, 1984–96; Professorial Res. Fellow, 1996–; Mem., Court, 1985–88. Fellow, Netherlands Inst. for Advanced Study in the Humanities and Social Sciences, Wassenaar, 1975–76. Chm., Mental Health Review Tribunals, 1991–93, 1995–98. Mem., Consumer Protection Adv. Cttee, 1976–81. MRI (Member: Finance Cttee, 1988–97; Council, 1994–97). Magistrates' Association: Mem., 1974–, Vice-Chm., 1984–89, Legal Cttee; co-opted Mem. Council, 1980–88; a Vice-Pres., Bucks Br., 1993–. Mem. Court, Luton Univ., 1994–98. Mem., Inst. of Cancer Res., 1999– (Mem. Council, 1999–2001; Chm., Ethics Cttee, 2000–03). JP Inner London (Juvenile Court Panel), 1968–84 (Chm., 1973–84). Liveryman, Feltmakers' Co. (Mem., Ct of Assts, 1991–; Master, 1998–99). FRSA 1989. Jt Founder and Editor, Anglo-Amer. Law Rev., 1972–84. *Publications:* Sentencing Offenders in Magistrates' Courts, 1970; (with Eric Stockdale) Sentencing, 1987; articles in legal jls. *Recreations:* watching cricket, fly-fishing, Roman Britain. *Clubs:* Athenæum, MCC; Hampshire County Cricket. *Died 4 Nov. 2012.*

DEVON, 18th Earl of, *cr* 1553; **Hugh Rupert Courtenay;** Bt 1644; landowner, farmer; Vice Lord-Lieutenant of Devon, 2002–07; *b* 5 May 1942; *o s* of 17th Earl of Devon, and Venetia, former wife of 6th Earl of Cottenham and *d* of Captain J. V. Taylor; *S* father, 1998; *m* 1967, Diana Frances, *er d* of J. G. Watherston, Jedburgh, Roxburghshire; one *s* three *d*. *Educ:* Winchester; Magdalene Coll., Cambridge (BA). MRICS. Captain, Wessex Yeomanry, retd. Chm., Devon Br., CLA, 1987–89. DL Devon, 1991. *Recreations:* riding, hunting, shooting. *Heir: s* Lord Courtenay, *b* 14 Aug. 1975. *Address:* Powderham Castle, near Exeter, Devon EX6 8JQ. *T:* (01626) 890370. *Died 18 Aug. 2015.*

DEVONSHIRE, Dowager Duchess of; Deborah Vivien Cavendish, DCVO 1999; housewife; Trustee, Royal Collections Trust, 1993–99; *b* 31 March 1920; 6th *d* of 2nd Baron Redesdale and Sydney (*née* Bowles); *m* 1941, Lord Andrew Cavendish (later 11th Duke of Devonshire, KG, MC, PC) (*d* 2004); one *s* two *d*. *Educ:* private. Director: Peacock Hotel (Baslow) Ltd, 1975–; Elm Tree Farm Ltd, 1975–; Chatsworth House Trust, 1981–2006; Devonshire Arms Hotel (Bolton Abbey) Ltd, 1981–2006; non-executive Director: Tarmac plc, 1984–92; W. & F. C. Bonhams & Sons Ltd, 1988–95. President: Royal Smithfield Show, 1972–74 and 1985; Royal Smithfield Club, 1975 (Vice-Pres., 1974–); RASE, 1995; Vice-Pres., Derbys Br., BRCS; Pres. or Patron, local charitable orgns, Derbys. Hon. Fellow, Sheffield City Poly., 1990. DUniv Middlesex, 1996; Hon. LittD Sheffield, 1998; Hon. Dr Derby, Buxton, 2006. *Publications:* The House: a portrait of Chatsworth, 1982; The Estate: a view from Chatsworth, 1990; Farm Animals, 1991; Treasures of Chatsworth: a private view, 1991; The Garden at Chatsworth, 1999; Counting My Chickens…and Other Home Thoughts, 2001; Chatsworth: the house, 2002; The Duchess of Devonshire's Chatsworth Cookery Book, 2003; Round about Chatsworth, 2005; Memories of Andrew Devonshire, 2007; (contrib.) The Mitfords: letters between six sisters, 2007; (contrib.) In Tearing Haste: letters between Deborah Devonshire and Patrick Leigh Fermor, 2008; Home to Roost…and other Peckings, 2009; Wait for Me!, 2010; All in One Basket, 2011; contribs to Spectator, Daily Telegraph. *Address:* 1 Old Vicarage, Edensor, Bakewell, Derbyshire DE45 1PH. *T:* (01246) 584020, *Fax:* (01246) 584021. *Died 24 Sept. 2014.*

DEWAR, Robert James, CMG 1969; CBE 1964; Chief of Agricultural Division, Regional Mission for Eastern Africa, World Bank, 1974–84; *b* 13 Jan. 1923; *s* of late Dr Robert Scott Dewar, MA, MB, ChB, and Mrs Roubaix Dewar, Dumbreck, Glasgow; *m* 1947, Christina Marianne, *d* of late Olof August Ljungberger, Stockholm, Sweden; two *s* one *d*. *Educ:* High Sch. of Glasgow; Edinburgh Univ. (BSc, Forestry); Wadham Coll., Oxford. Asst Conservator of Forests, Colonial Forest Service, Nigeria and Nyasaland, 1944–55; Dep. Chief Conservator of Forests, Nyasaland, 1955–61; Chief Conservator of Forests, Dir of Forestry and Game, Nyasaland (later Malawi), 1961–64; Mem. Nyasaland Legislative Council, 1960. Permanent Secretary, Malawi: Min. of Natural Resources, 1964–67 and 1968–69; Min. of Economic Affairs, 1967–68; retd from Malawi CS, 1969; Sen. Agriculturalist, World Bank, 1969–74. Mem. Nat. Development Council, Malawi, 1966–69. Chm. of Trustees, Zimbiala Trust, 2002–09. Chm., Friends of Malawi Assoc., 1996–2008. *Recreations:* gardening, golf, angling. *Address:* Dundurn, 5 Knock Road, Crieff, Perthshire PH7 4AH. *T:* (01764) 654830. *Club:* Royal Commonwealth Society. *Died 4 Dec. 2013.*

de WARDENER, Prof. Hugh Edward, CBE 1982 (MBE (mil.) 1946); MD, FRCP; Professor of Medicine, University of London, Charing Cross Hospital, 1960–81, then Emeritus; Honorary Consultant Physician to the Army, 1975–80; *b* 8 Oct. 1915; *s* of Edouard de Wardener and Becky (*née* Pearce); *m* 1st, 1939, Janet Lavinia Bellis Simon (marr. diss. 1947; later decd); one *s*; 2nd, 1947, Diana Rosamund Crawshay (marr. diss. 1954); 3rd, 1954, Jill Mary Foxworthy (marr. diss. 1969); one *d*; 4th, 1969, Josephine Margaret Storey, MBE; two *s*. *Educ:* Malvern Coll. St Thomas's Hosp., 1933–39; RAMC, 1939–45; St Thomas's Hosp., 1945–60, Registrar, Senior Lecturer, Reader. MRCP 1946, MD 1949, FRCP 1958. Hon. MD: Univ. Pierre et Marie Curie, Paris, 1980; Univ. Paul Sabatier, Toulouse, 1996. President: Internat. Soc. of Nephrology, 1969–72; Renal Assoc., 1973–76; Mem. Council, Imp. Cancer Res. Fund, 1981–88. *Publications:* The Kidney: An Outline of Normal and Abnormal Structure and Function, 1958, 5th edn 1986; (with G. A. MacGregor) Salt, Diet and Health, 1998; papers in various scientific journals. *Recreations:* writing, walking. *Address:* 9 Dungarvan Avenue, Putney, SW15 5QU. *T:* (020) 8878 3130. *Died 29 Sept. 2013.*

de WINTER, Carl; Secretary General, Federation of British Artists, 1978–84 (Deputy Secretary General, 1968–78); *b* 18 June 1934; *s* of Alfred de Winter; *m* 1958, Lyndall Bradshaw; one *s* one *d*. *Educ:* Pangbourne. Purser, Orient Line, 1951–60. Art Exhibitions Bureau: PA to Man. Dir, 1961–66; Director, 1967–84; Royal Soc. of Portrait Painters: Asst Sec., 1962–78; Sec., 1978–84; Royal Soc. of Miniature Painters, Sculptors and Gravers: Asst Sec., 1964–67; Sec., 1968–84; Hon. Mem., 1984; Royal Soc. of Marine Artists: Asst Sec., 1964–70; Sec., 1971–78; Royal Soc. of British Artists: Asst Keeper, 1969–73; Keeper, 1974–84; Royal Inst. of Oil Painters: Sec., 1973–84; Royal Inst. of Painters in Watercolours: Sec., 1979–84; National Soc. of Painters, Sculptors and Printmakers: Sec., 1973–84; New English Art Club: Sec., 1973–84; United Soc. of Artists: Sec., 1975–81. *Died 2 Aug. 2012.*

DHENIN, Air Marshal Sir Geoffrey (Howard), KBE 1975; AFC 1953 and Bar, 1957; GM 1943; MA, MD, DPH; FFCM 1975; FRAeS 1971; Director-General, Medical Services (RAF), 1974–78; *b* 2 April 1918; *s* of Louis Richard Dhenin and Lucy Ellen Dagg; *m* 1st, 1946, Claude Andree Evelyn Rabut (*d* 1996); one *s* two *d* (and one *s* decd); 2nd, 2002, Syvia Howard. *Educ:* Hereford Cathedral Sch.; St John's Coll., Cambridge; Guy's Hosp., London. Joined RAF; various sqdn and other med. appts, Bomber Comd, 2nd TAF, 1943–45 (despatches 1945); pilot trng, 1945–46; various med. officer pilot appts, 1946–58; Staff Coll., Bracknell, 1958–59; comd Princess Mary's RAF Hosp. Akrotiri, Cyprus, 1960–63; comd RAF Hosp. Ely, 1963–66; PMO Air Support Comd, 1966–68; Dir of Health and Research, RAF, 1968–70; Dep. DGMS, RAF, 1970–71; PMO Strike Comd, 1971–73. Fellow, Internat. Acad. of Aerospace Medicine, 1972. CStJ 1974. QHP 1970–78. Adviser to Saudi Arabian Nat. Guard, 1978–79. *Publications:* (ed) Textbook of Aviation Medicine, 1978. *Recreations:* golf, ski-ing, sub-aqua. *Address:* Virginia Water. *T:* (01344) 844943. *Clubs:* Royal Air Force; Wentworth. *Died 6 March 2011.*

DIAMOND, Prof. Derek Robin; Professor of Geography with special reference to Urban and Regional Planning, London School of Economics and Political Science, 1982–95, then Emeritus Professor; *b* 18 May 1933; *s* of John Diamond (Baron Diamond, PC) and Sadie Diamond; *m* 1957, Esme Grace Passmore; one *s* one *d*. *Educ:* Oxford Univ. (MA); Northwestern Univ., Illinois (MSc). Lecturer: in Geography, 1957–65, in Town and Regional Planning, 1965–68, Glasgow Univ.; Reader in Geography, London School of Economics, 1968–82. Pres., IBG, 1994–95. Hon. MRTPI, 1989. Hon. Fellow LSE, 2006. Hon. Prof. of Human Geography, Inst. of Geography, Beijing, 1990. Editor: Progress in Planning, 1973–2003; Geoforum, 1974–93. *Publications:* Regional Policy Evaluation, 1983; Infrastructure and Industrial Costs in British Industry, 1989; Evaluating the Effectiveness of Land Use Planning, 1992; Metropolitan Governance: its contemporary transition, 1997; Managing the Metropolis in the Global Village, 2002; The 1898 Pictorial Issue of New Zealand, 2014. *Recreation:* philately. *Address:* 9 Ashley Drive, Walton-on-Thames, Surrey KT12 1JL. *T:* (01932) 223280. *Club:* Geographical. *Died 6 May 2015.*

DICK, James Brownlee, CB 1977; MA, BSc, FInstP, FCIBS, FIOB; retired consultant; *b* 19 July 1919; *s* of James Brownlee Dick and Matilda Forrest; *m* 1944, Audrey Moira Shinn (*d* 2007); two *s*. *Educ:* Wishaw High Sch.; Glasgow Univ. Royal Naval Scientific Service, 1940. Building Research Station, later Building Research Establishment: Physics Div., 1947; Head of User Requirements Div., 1960; Head of Production Div., 1963; Asst Dir, 1964; Dep. Dir, 1969; Dir, 1969–79. Pres., Internat. Council for Building Res., 1974–77. *Publications:* papers in professional and scientific journals. *Address:* Abbeyfield North Downs Society, David Gresham House, 2 Oak Close, Oxted RH8 0BA. *Died 6 Aug. 2013.*

DICKENS, James McCulloch York, OBE 1991; Chief Personnel Officer, Agricultural and Food Research Council, 1983–91; *b* 4 April 1931; *e s* of A. Y. Dickens and I. Dickens (*née* McCulloch); *m* 1st, 1955, M. J. Grieve (marr. diss. 1965); 2nd, 1969, Mrs Carolyn Casey. *Educ:* Shawlands Academy, Glasgow; Newbattle Abbey Coll., Dalkeith, Midlothian; Ruskin Coll. and St Catherine's Coll., Oxford. Administrative Asst, National Coal Board, 1956–58; Industrial Relations Officer, National Coal Board, 1958–65; Management Consultant, 1965–66; MP (Lab) West Lewisham, 1966–70; Asst Dir of Manpower, Nat. Freight Corp., 1970–76; National Water Council: Asst Dir (Ind. Rel.), Manpower Services Div., 1976–80; Dir of Manpower, 1980–82; Dir of Manpower and Trng, 1982–83. Mem. (Lab), Westminster CC, 1962–65. Chm., Governing Body, Anerley Primary Sch., 2001–03. *Recreations:* music, theatre, the countryside. *Address:* 64 Woodbastwick Road, Sydenham, SE26 5LH. *Died 5 April 2013.*

DICKINSON, Brian Henry Baron; Under Secretary, Animal Health Group, Ministry of Agriculture, Fisheries and Food, 1996–2000; *b* 2 May 1940; *s* of Alan Edgar Frederic Dickinson and Ethel Mary Dickinson (*née* McWilliam); *m* 1971, Sheila Minto Lloyd (*d* 2006). *Educ:* Leighton Park School, Reading; Balliol College, Oxford (BA). Ministry of Agriculture, Fisheries and Food, 1964; Dept of Prices and Consumer Protection, 1975; MAFF, 1978; Under Sec., 1984; Principal Finance Officer, 1986; Under Sec. (Food Safety), 1989. FRSA 1995. *Recreations:* bird-watching, bridge, island living. *Died 11 May 2014.*

DICKINSON, Prof. (Christopher) John, DM, FRCP; ARCO; Professor of Medicine and Chairman, Department of Medicine, St Bartholomew's Hospital Medical College, 1975–92, then Professor Emeritus; *b* 1 Feb. 1927; *s* of Reginald Ernest Dickinson and Margaret Dickinson (*née* Petty); *m* 1953, Elizabeth Patricia Farrell; two *s* two *d*. *Educ:* Berkhamsted School; Oxford University (MA, MSc, DM); University College Hospital Medical Sch. FRCP 1968. Junior med. posts, UCH, 1953–54; RAMC (Junior Med. Specialist), 1955–56; Registrar and Research Fellow, Middlesex Hosp., 1957–60; Rockefeller Travelling Fellow, Cleveland Clinic, USA, 1960–61; Lectr, then Sen. Lectr and Consultant, UCH and Med. Sch., 1961–75. R. Samuel McLoughlin Vis. Prof., McMaster Univ., Canada, 1970; King Edward Fund Vis. Fellow, NZ, 1972. Examr in Medicine, UC Dublin and Univs of Oxford, Cambridge, London, Sheffield, Leeds, Southampton, Hong Kong, Singapore, Kuwait. Sec., European Soc. for Clinical Investigation, 1969–72; Censor, 1978–80, Senior Censor and Vice-Pres., 1982–83, Croonian Lectr, 1986, RCP; Pres., Sect. of Medicine, RSM, 1975–76. Chairman: Med. Research Soc., 1983–87; Assoc. of Professors of Medicine, 1983–87; Vice Chm. Council, BHF, 1995–2000; Mem., MRC, 1986–90. Medical Adviser: Jules Thorn Charitable Trust, 1994–98; St Thomas'/Guy's Hosps' Special Trustees, 1996–98; Trustee: St Bartholomew's Hosp. Foundn for Res., 1983–; BHF, 1995–2000; Chronic Disease Res. Foundn, 1996– (Chm., 1996–). ARCO 1987. FRSA 1995. *Publications:* Electrophysiological Technique, 1950; Clinical Pathology Data, 1951, 2nd edn 1957; (jtly) Clinical Physiology, 1959, 5th edn 1984; Neurogenic Hypertension, 1965, 2nd edn 1991; A Computer Model of Human Respiration, 1977; (jtly) Software for Educational Computing, 1980; 21 Medical Mysteries, 2000; Motorcycling in Towns and Cities, 2002; Medical Mysteries: the testament of a clinical scientist, 2005; Cardiovascular Hypertension, 2012; papers on hypertension, respiratory physiology, and general medicine. *Recreations:* theatre, opera, playing the organ, squash. *Address:* Wolfson Institute of Preventive Medicine, Charterhouse Square, EC1M 6BQ. *T:* (020) 7882 6219; Griffin Cottage, 57 Belsize Lane, NW3 5AU. *T:* (020) 7431 1845. *Club:* Garrick. *Died 30 Sept. 2015.*

DICKINSON, Hon. Peter Malcolm de Brissac, OBE 2009; FRSL; author; *b* 16 Dec. 1927; *s* of late Hon. Richard Sebastian Willoughby Dickinson and of May Southey (Nancy) Lovemore; *m* 1st, 1953, Mary Rose Barnard (*d* 1988); two *d* two *s*; 2nd, 1992, Robin McKinley. *Educ:* Eton; King's Coll., Cambridge (BA). Asst Editor, Punch, 1952–69. Chm., Management Cttee, Soc. of Authors, 1978–80. FRSL 1999. *Publications: children's books:* The Weathermonger, 1968; Heartsease, 1969; The Devil's Children, 1970 (trilogy republished 1975 as The Changes); Emma Tupper's Diary, 1970; The Dancing Bear, 1972; The Gift, 1973; The Iron Lion, 1973; Chance, Luck and Destiny, 1975; The Blue Hawk, 1976 (Guardian Award); Annerton Pit, 1977; Hepzibah, 1978; Tulku, 1979 (Whitbread Prize; Carnegie Medal); The Flight of Dragons, 1979; City of Gold, 1980 (Carnegie Medal); The Seventh Raven, 1981; Healer, 1983; Giant Cold, 1984; (ed) Hundreds and Hundreds, 1984; A Box of Nothing, 1985; Mole Hole, 1987; Merlin Dreams, 1988; Eva, 1988; AK, 1990 (Whitbread Children's Award); A Bone from a Dry Sea, 1992; Time and the Clockmice etcetera, 1993; Shadow of a Hero, 1994; Chuck and Danielle, 1996; The Kin, 1998; Touch and Go, 1999; The Lion Tamer's Daughter, 1999; The Ropemaker, 2001; (with Robin McKinley) Elementals: Water, 2002; The Tears of the Salamander, 2003; The Gift Boat, 2004; Angel Isle, 2006; (with Robin McKinley) Fire: tales of elemental spirits, 2009; Tales of Elemental Creatures: Earth and Air, 2012; In the Palace of the Khans, 2012; *TV series,* Mandog (Mandog, by Lois Lamplugh, 1972, is based on the Changes series); *novels:* Skin Deep, 1968; A Pride of Heroes, 1969; The Seals, 1970; Sleep and His Brother, 1971; The Lizard in the Cup, 1972; The Green Gene, 1973; The Poison Oracle, 1974; The Lively Dead, 1975; King and Joker, 1976; Walking Dead, 1977; One Foot in the Grave, 1979; A Summer in the Twenties, 1981; The Last House-party, 1982; Hindsight, 1983; Death of a Unicorn, 1984; Tefuga, 1986; Perfect Gallows, 1988; Skeleton-in-Waiting, 1989; Play Dead, 1991; The Yellow Room Conspiracy, 1994; Some Deaths Before Dying, 2000; *poetry:* The Weir, 2008. *Recreation:* bridge. *Address:* 1 Arlebury Park Mews, Alresford, Hants SO24 9ER. *Died 16 Dec. 2015.*

DICKSON, Arthur Richard Franklin, CBE 1974; QC (Belize), 1979; Commissioner for Law Revision, Belize, 1978; *b* 13 Jan. 1913; *m* 1949, Joanna Maria Margaretha van Baardwyk (*d* 1998); four *s*. *Educ:* Rusea's Secondary Sch. and Cornwall Coll., Jamaica. Called to the Bar, Lincoln's Inn, 1938. Judicial Service. HM Overseas Judiciary: Jamaica, 1941; Magistrate, Turks and Caicos Islands, 1944–47; Asst to Attorney-Gen., and Legal Draftsman, Barbados, 1947–49; Magistrate, British Guiana, 1949–52; Nigeria, 1952–62: Magistrate, 1952–54; Chief Magistrate, 1954–56; Chief Registrar, High Court, Lagos, 1956–58; Judge of the High Court, Lagos, 1958–62; retired. Temp. appointment, Solicitors Dept, GPO London, 1962–63; served Northern Rhodesia (latterly Zambia), 1964–67; Judge of the High Court, Uganda, 1967–71; Deputy Chm., Middlesex QS, July-Aug., 1971; Chief Justice, Belize, 1973–74; Judge of the Supreme Court, Anguilla (part-time), 1972–76; part-time Chm., Industrial Tribunals, England and Wales, 1972–85. *Publications:* Revised Ordinances (1909–1941) Turks and Caicos Islands, 1944; (ed) Revised Laws of Belize, 1980. *Recreations:* gardening, walking, swimming. *Died 21 May 2011.*

DICKSON, David John Scott; consultant; Editor, SciDev.Net (Science and Development Network), 2011–12 (Director, 2001–11); *b* 30 Aug. 1947; *s* of David and Rachel Mary Dickson; *m* 1973, Prudence Mary Richardson (marr. diss. 1999); one *s* one *d*. *Educ:* Westminster Sch.; Trinity Coll., Cambridge. Medical News, 1968–70; Sec., Brit. Soc. for Social Responsibility in Science, 1970–72; science corresp., 1973–75, features editor, 1975–77, THES; Washington corresp., Nature, 1977–82; European corresp., Science, 1982–89; news editor, 1989–90, Editor, 1990–92, New Scientist; News Editor, Nature, 1993–2001. Lectures organiser, ICA, 1976–77. Recorder, Gen. Section, 2001–, Mem. Council, 2008–, British Sci. Assoc. (formerly BAAS). Visiting Research Fellow: Univ. of Linköping, Sweden, 1981; Open Univ., 1989; Hon. Res. Fellow, UCL, 2002. Award for Meritorious Achievement, Council of Sci. Editors, 2006; Writers Award (jtly), 2006, Lifetime Achievement Award, 2012, Assoc. of British Sci. *Publications:* Alternative Technology, 1974; The New Politics of Science, 1984; Het verval van de Geest (The Death of the Spirit), 1990; contribs to various jls on science, technology and society. *Recreations:* music, photography, painting. *Died 31 July 2013.*

DICKSON WRIGHT, Clarissa Teresa; cook; TV presenter and countryside campaigner; *b* 24 June 1947; *d* of Arthur Dickson Wright and Molly Bath. *Educ:* Sacred Heart Convent, Hove; University Coll. London (LLB). Called to the Bar, Gray's Inn, 1968; barrister; pheasant plucker; Proprietor, The Cooks' Bookshop, Edinburgh. Lord Rector, Aberdeen Univ., 1999–2005. Mem., Gen. Council, NT, 2002–03. Pres., Farmers' Markets Assoc., Scotland; Patron, Farmers' Markets Assoc., England. Co-Pres., Union Country Sports Workers. Presenter, TV series: with Jennifer Paterson, Two Fat Ladies, 1996–99; with Sir John Scott, Clarissa and the Countryman, 2000–03; Breakfast, Lunch and Dinner, 2012. Member: Butchers' Co., 2000; Yorks Guild of Butchers, 2007. *Publications:* The Haggis: a history, 1996; Heiland Foodie, 1997; Spilling the Beans (autobiog.), 2007; Clarissa's Comfort Food, 2008; Rifling Through My Drawers, 2009; Potty! Clarissa's One Pot Cookbook, 2010; A History of English Food, 2011; Clarissa's England: A Gamely Gallop Through the English Counties, 2012; (with Jennifer Paterson): Two Fat Ladies, 1996; Two Fat Ladies Ride Again, 1997; Two Fat Ladies Full Throttle, 1998; Two Fat Ladies Obsessions, 1999; (with Sir John Scott): Clarissa and the Countryman, 2000; Clarissa and the Countryman Sally Forth, 2001; A Sunday Roast, 2002; The Game Cookbook, 2004; A Greener Life, 2005. *Recreations:* hunting, shooting, fishing, food, Rugby, men. *Died 15 March 2014.*

DIESKAU, Dietrich F.; *see* Fischer-Dieskau.

DIGNAN, Maj.-Gen. (Albert) Patrick, CB 1978; MBE 1952; FRCS, FRCSI; Director of Army Surgery and Consulting Surgeon to the Army, 1973–78; Hon. Consultant Surgeon, Royal Hospital, Chelsea, 1973–78; Hon. Consultant in Radiotherapy and Oncology, Westminster Hospital, 1974–78; *b* 25 July 1920; *s* of Joseph Dignan; *m* 1952, Eileen Helena White (*d* 2001); two *s* one *d*. *Educ:* Trinity Coll., Dublin (Med. Schol.). MB, BCh, BAO, BA 1943, MA, MD 1968, FRCSI 1947, FRCS 1976. Prof. of Physiol. Prize, TCD. Posts in Dublin, Belfast and Wigan; subseq. NS Sen. Specialist in Surgery, Major RAMC Malaya; Sen. Registrar in Surgery, Bristol Royal Infirmary and Wanstead Hosp.; Sen. Specialist in Surgery, BAOR Mil. Hosps and Consultant Surg., Brit. Mil. Hosps Singapore and Tidworth, 1953–68; Brig., and Consulting Surg., Farelf, 1969–70; Consultant Surg., Mil. Hosp. Tidworth, 1971–72; Consultant Surgeon, Queen Alexandra Mil. Hosp. Millbank, 1972–73; Consultant in Accident and Emergency, Ealing Dist, DHSS, 1978–79. Pres., Army Med. Bds, 1980–90. Fellow, Association of Surgeons of GB and Ireland; FRSocMed. Mem., Acad. of Medicine, Singapore, 1969–71. QHS, 1974–78. *Publications:* A Doctor's Experiences of Life (autobiog.), 1994; papers in Brit. Jl Surgery, BMJ, Jl of RAMC, Postgrad. Med. Jl, Univ. Singapore Med. Soc. Med. Gazette. *Recreations:* gardening, golf. *Died 11 Oct. 2012.*

DIMMOCK, Peter, CVO 1968; OBE 1961; Chairman, Zenith Entertainment (formerly Television Enterprise and Asset Management) plc, 1991–2000; *b* 6 Dec. 1920; *e s* of late Frederick Dimmock, OBE, and Paula Dimmock (*née* Hudd); *m* 1960, Mary Freya, (Polly) (*d* 1987), *e d* of late Hon. Mr Justice Elwes, OBE, TD; three *d*; *m* 1990, Christabel Rosamund, *e d* of Sir John Bagge, 6th Bt, ED, DL and *widow* of James Hinton Scott. *Educ:* Dulwich Coll.; France. TA; RAF pilot, instr, and Air Ministry Staff Officer, 1939–45. After demobilisation became Press Association correspondent; joined BBC as Television Outside Broadcasts Producer and commentator, 1946; produced both studio and outside broadcasts, ranging from documentaries to sporting, theatrical and public events; produced or commentated on more than 500 television relays, including Olympic Games 1948, Boat Race 1949, first international television relay, from Calais, 1950, King George VI's Funeral, Windsor, 1952. Produced and directed television outside broadcast of the Coronation Service from Westminster Abbey, 1953; first TV State Opening of Parliament, 1958; first TV Grand National, 1960; TV for Princess Margaret's Wedding, 1960. Created BBC Sportsview Unit and introduced new television programme Sportsview, 1954, regular presenter of this live weekly network programme, 1954–64; Gen. Manager and Head of Outside Broadcasts, BBC TV, 1954–72; responsible for Liaison between BBC and Royal Family, 1963–77; Gen. Manager, BBC Enterprises, 1972–77; Vice-Pres., ABC Worldwide Sales and Marketing TV Sports, 1978–86; Vice-Pres. and Consultant, ABC Video Enterprises Div., Capital Cities/ABC Inc., NY, 1984–91; Dir, Entertainment and Sports Cable Network, 1984–90. Chm. Sports Cttee and Adviser, European Broadcasting Union, 1959–72. Mem., Greater London and SE Sports Council, 1972–77; Chm., Sports Develt Panel, 1976–77. FRTS 1978 (Hall of Fame, 1996). Freeman, City of London, 1977. *Publications:* Sportsview Annuals, 1954–65; Sports in View, 1964; (contrib.) The BBC Book of Royal Memories, 1990. *Recreations:* flying, winter sports, golf. *Address:* Exbury House, Upton Grey, Hants RG25 2SG. *Clubs:* Garrick, Boodle's, Royal Air Force; Berkshire Golf; St Enedoc Golf; New York Athletic. *Died 20 Nov. 2015.*

DIMMOCK, Rear-Adm. Roger Charles, CB 1988; Chairman, Archer Mullins Ltd, 1989–2004; *b* 27 May 1935; *s* of late Frank Dimmock and Ivy Dimmock (*née* Archer); *m* 1958, Lesley Patricia Reid; two *d* (and one *d* decd). *Educ:* Price's School. Entered Royal Navy, 1953; pilot's wings FAA, 1954, USN, 1955; qualified Flying Instructor, 1959; Master Mariner Foreign Going Cert. of Service, 1979. Served RN Air Sqdns and HM Ships Bulwark, Albion, Ark Royal, Eagle, Hermes, Anzio, Messina, Murray, Berwick (i/c), Naiad (i/c), to 1978; CSO to FO Carriers and Amphibious Ships, 1978–80; Comd RNAS Culdrose, 1980–82; Comd HMS Hermes, 1982–83; Dir, Naval Air Warfare, MoD, 1983–84; Naval Sec., 1985–87; FONAC, 1987–88. Dir, Charnauds (formerly Manufg and Marketing Services) Ltd, 1993–98. Mem. Cttee of Management, RNLI, 1987 (Pres., Denmead and Hambledon Br., 1981). Chm. Trustees, Fleet Air Arm Museum, 1987–88. President: RN Hockey Assoc., 1985–89; CS Hockey Assoc., 1987–93; Vice Pres., Hockey Assoc., 1997. Mem., Royal Aero Club, 1988–. *Recreations:* hockey (player and umpire), cricket, squash, golf, family, home and garden, RNLI. *Address:* Beverley House, 19 Beverley Grove, Farlington, Portsmouth PO6 1BP. *T:* (023) 9261 7224. *Club:* Royal Navy of 1765 and 1785. *Died 6 May 2014.*

DINGEMANS, Rear-Adm. Peter George Valentin, CB 1990; DSO 1982; Director, Sussex Innovation Centre Management Ltd, 2004–10; Governor, Queen Victoria Hospital Foundation Trust, 2005–10; *b* 31 July 1935; *s* of late Dr George Albert and Marjorie Dingemans; *m* 1961, Faith Vivien Bristow; three *s*. *Educ:* Brighton College. Entered RN 1953; served HM Ships Vanguard, Superb, Ark Royal, 1953–57; qualified Torpedo Anti Submarine specialist, 1961; Comd, HMS Maxton, 1967; RAF Staff Course, 1968; Directorate of Naval Plans, 1971–73; Comd, HMS Berwick, HMS Lowestoft, 1973–74; Staff Asst, Chief of Defence Staff, 1974–76; Captain, Fishery Protection, 1977–78; rcds, 1979; Comd HMS Intrepid, 1980–83 (incl. service South Atlantic, 1982); Commodore, Amphibious Warfare, 1983–85; Flag Officer Gibraltar, 1985–87; COS to C-in-C Fleet, 1987–90, retd. Director: Administration, Argosy Asset Management PLC, 1990–91; Ivory and Sime, 1991–92; Hd, Benefits Payroll and Insurances, Slaughter and May, 1992–2001; Strategic Advr, St Dunstan's, 2001–05. President: Royal Naval Assoc., Horsham, 1994–2011; British Legion, Cowfold, 1994–2011; Assoc. of Old Brightonians, 1995–97. Mem. Council, Sussex Univ., 1999–2005; Mem. Bd, Brighton Coll., 2001–06 (Mem. Council, 1998–2001). Trustee, Brighton Coll. Scholarship Trust Fund, 1999–2009. FCMI (FBIM 1990). Freeman, City of London, 1984; Liveryman, Coach Makers and Coach Harness Makers Co., 1984. *Recreation:* family and friends. *Address:* c/o Lloyds Bank, Steyning, Sussex BN44 3ZA. *Club:* Royal Naval of 1765 and 1785 (Trustee, 1995–2006, Chm. Trustees, 1996–2006). *Died 6 Dec. 2015.*

DI PALMA, Vera June, (Mrs Ernest Jones), OBE 1986; FCCA, FTII; Chairman, Mobile Training Ltd, 1978–2003; *b* 14 July 1931; *d* of late William Di Palma and Violet Di Palma; *m* 1972, Ernest Jones (*d* 1995). *Educ:* Haverstock Central Sch., London. Accountant in public practice, 1947–64; Taxation Accountant, Dunlop Co., 1964–67; Sen. Lectr in Taxation, City of London Polytechnic, 1967–71; taxation consultant, 1971–80. Pres., Assoc. of Certified Accountants, 1980–81 (Dep. Pres., 1979–80);

Public Works Loan Comr, 1978–2002 (Dep. Chm., 1997–2002); Dep. Chm., Air Travel Trust Cttee, 1986–2000; Mem., VAT Tribunals, 1977–2000; non-exec. Mem., S Warwicks HA, 1991–93. *Publications:* Capital Gains Tax, 1972, 5th edn 1981; Your Fringe Benefits, 1978. *Recreations:* dog-walking, bridge, tennis, dancing, gardening. *Address:* Hogsbottom, North Aston Road, Middle Aston, Oxon OX25 5RH. *T:* (01869) 349242. *Died 7 June 2015.*

DIX, Geoffrey Herbert, OBE 1979; Secretary-General, The Institute of Bankers, 1971–82; *b* 1 March 1922; *o s* of late Herbert Walter and Winifred Ada Dix; *m* 1945, Margaret Sybil Outhwaite, MA (Cantab) (*d* 1981); one *s*. *Educ:* Watford Grammar Sch.; Gonville and Caius Coll., Cambridge (MA (Mod. langs)). Served War, 1942–45: commissioned into Royal Devon Yeomanry; later served with HQ 1st Airborne Corps. Inst. of Export, 1946–51; with Inst. of Bankers, 1951–82: Asst Sec., 1956; Under-Sec. 1962; Dep. Sec. 1968. Mem., Jt Cttee for National Awards in Business Studies, 1960–76. *Recreations:* Mozart, theatre. *Address:* 2 Kirklands, Old Costessey, Norwich NR8 5BW. *T:* (01603) 745181. *Club:* Caterham Players. *Died 21 July 2013.*

DIXON, John Watts; His Honour Judge Dixon; a Circuit Judge, since 2004; *b* 27 Sept. 1951; *e s* of late John David Dixon and Carol Emmie Lucinda Dixon (*née* Watts); *m* 1980, Catherine Barbara Borton; one *s* four *d*. *Educ:* Harrow Sch.; Queen's Coll., Oxford (MA Jurisprudence). Called to the Bar, Middle Temple, 1975; in practice as barrister, 1975–2004; Legal Reader, Associated Newspapers, 1981–2004; Asst Recorder, 1998–2000, Recorder, 2000–04. Chm., British-Ukrainian Law Assoc., 2000–. Freeman, City of London, 1977. *Publications:* (jtly) Crown Court Index, 2011–. *Recreations:* joys of family life, gardening, cycling, the stage. *Address:* The Law Courts, Winchester, Hants SO23 9EL. *T:* (01962) 814100. *Died 12 Aug. 2014.*

DOBBIN, James; MP (Lab and Co-op) Heywood and Middleton, since 1997; *b* 26 May 1941; *s* of William Dobbin and Catherine McCabe; *m* 1964, Pat Russell; two *s* two *d*. *Educ:* St Columba's High Sch., Cowdenbeath; St Andrew's High Sch., Kirkcaldy; Napier Coll., Edinburgh. Microbiologist, NHS, 1966–94. Mem., Rochdale MBC, 1983–97 (Leader, 1996–97). Contested (Lab) Bury N, 1992. Mem., Transport Select Cttee, 2010–. Chairman: All-Pty Pro Life Gp, 2002–; All-Pty Tranquiliser Addiction Gp, 2008–; Co-Chm., All-Pty Health and Vaccine Preventable Diseases Gp, 2011–; Mem., Chairmen's Panel/ Panel of Chairs, 2010–; Mem., Parly Assembly, Council of Europe, 2010–. KCSG 2008. *Address:* House of Commons, SW1A 0AA; 43 Stonehill Drive, Rochdale, Lancs OL12 7JN. *Died 7 Sept. 2014.*

DOBBS, Mattiwilda; Order of North Star (Sweden), 1954; opera singer (coloratura soprano); *b* Atlanta, Ga, USA, 11 July 1925; *d* of John Wesley and Irene Dobbs; *m* 1957, Bengt Janzon (*d* 1997), Dir of Information, Nat. Ministry of Health and Welfare, Sweden; no *c*. *Educ:* Spelman Coll., USA (BA 1946); Columbia Univ., USA (MA 1948). Studied voice in NY with Lotte Leonard, 1946–50; special coaching Paris with Pierre Bernac, 1950–52. Marian Anderson Schol., 1948; John Hay Whitney Schol., 1950; 1st prize in singing, Internat. Comp., Geneva Conservatory of Music, 1951. Appeared Royal Dutch Opera, Holland Festival, 1952. Recitals, Sweden, Paris, Holland, 1952; appeared in opera at La Scala, Milan, 1953; Concerts, England and Continent, 1953; Glyndebourne Opera, 1953–54, 1956, 1961; Covent Garden Opera, 1953, 1954, 1956, 1958; command performance, Covent Garden, 1954. Annual concert tours: US, 1954–90; Australia, New Zealand, 1955, 1959, 1968; Australia, 1972, 1977; Israel, 1957 and 1959; USSR concerts and opera (Bolshoi Theater), 1959; San Francisco Opera, 1955; début Metropolitan Opera, 1956; there annually, 1956–64. Appearances Hamburg State Opera, 1961–63; Royal Swedish Opera, 1957 and there annually, 1957–73; Norwegian and Finnish Operas, 1957–64. Vis. Prof., Univ. of Texas at Austin, 1973–74; Professor: Univ. of Illinois, 1975–76; Univ. of Georgia, 1976–77; Howard Univ., Washington, 1977–91. Hon. Dr of Music: Spelman Coll., Atlanta, 1979; Emory Univ., Atlanta, 1980. *Died 8 Dec. 2015.*

DOBSON, Prof. (Richard) Barrie, FSA; FRHistS; FBA 1988; Professor of Medieval History, and Fellow of Christ's College, University of Cambridge, 1988–99; Hon. Professor of History, University of York, since 1999; *b* 3 Nov. 1931; *s* of Richard Henry Dobson and Mary Victoria Dobson (*née* Kidd); *m* 1959, Narda Leon; one *s* one *d*. *Educ:* Barnard Castle Sch.; Wadham Coll., Oxford (BA 1st cl. Modern Hist.; MA 1958; DPhil 1963; Hon. Fellow, 1989). Senior demy, Magdalen Coll., Oxford, 1957–58; Lectr in Medieval History, Univ. of St Andrews, 1958–64; University of York: Lectr, Sen. Lectr, Reader, Prof. of History, 1964–88; Dep. Vice-Chancellor, 1984–87. British Acad. Fellow, Folger Shakespeare Liby, Washington, 1974; Cornell Vis. Prof., Swarthmore Coll., USA, 1987; Vis. Fellow, Trinity Coll., Toronto, 1994. FRHistS 1972 (Vice-Pres., 1985–89); FSA 1979; President: Surtees Soc., 1987–2002; Jewish Historical Soc. of England, 1990–91; Ecclesiastical History Soc., 1991–92; Chairman: York Archaeol Trust, 1990–96; Friends of the PRO, 1994–98. Trustee, York Glaziers Trust, 2004–. Life Mem., Merchant Taylors' Co., York (Master, 2003–04). Gen. Editor, Yorks Archaeol. Soc., Record Series, 1981–86. *Publications:* The Peasants' Revolt of 1381, 1971, 2nd edn 1983; Durham Priory 1400–1450, 1973; The Jews of Medieval York and the Massacre of March 1190, 1974; (with J. Taylor) Rymes of Robyn Hood, 1977; (ed) York City Chamberlains' Accounts 1396–1500, 1980; (ed) The Church, Politics and Patronage in the Fifteenth Century, 1984; (contrib.) A History of York Minster, 1977; (contrib.) History of the University of Oxford, Vol. II, 1993; Church and Society in the Medieval North of England, 1996; (ed with D. Smith) The Merchant Taylors of York: a history, 2006; The Jewish Communities of Medieval England: collected essays of R. B. Dobson, 2010; articles in learned jls. *Recreations:* hill walking, cinema, chess, modern jazz. *Address:* Centre for Medieval Studies, University of York, The King's Manor, York YO1 7EP. *T:* (01904) 433910. *Died 29 March 2013.*

DOCKER, Rt Rev. (Ivor) Colin; Bishop Suffragan of Horsham, 1975–91; an Honorary Assistant Bishop, Diocese of Exeter, since 1991; *b* 3 Dec. 1925; *s* of Colonel Philip Docker, OBE, TD, DL, and Doris Gwendoline Docker (*née* Whitehill); *m* 1950, Thelma Mary, *d* of John William and Gladys Upton; one *s* one *d*. *Educ:* King Edward's High Sch., Birmingham; Univ. of Birmingham (BA); St Catherine's Coll., Oxford (MA). Curate of Normanton, Yorks, 1949–52; Lecturer of Halifax Parish Church, 1952–54; CMS Area Sec., 1954–59; Vicar of Midhurst, Sussex, 1959–64; RD of Midhurst and Rector, All Hallows, Woolbeding, 1961–64; Vicar and RD of Seaford, 1964–71; Canon and Prebendary of Colworth in Chichester Cathedral, 1966–81; Vicar and RD of Eastbourne, 1971–75; Proctor in Convocation, 1970–75. Chm., Nat. Council for Social Concern (formerly C of E Nat. Council for Social Aid), 1987–2001 and 2003–12 (Vice-Chm., 2002–03); Chm., CARA (Caring and Resource for People with HIV/AIDS), 1995–97 (Patron, 2001–). *Recreations:* photography, travel, reading. *Address:* Braemar, Bradley Road, Bovey Tracey, Newton Abbot, Devon TQ13 9EU. *T:* (01626) 832468. *Died 3 Nov. 2014.*

DOCTOROW, Edgar Lawrence; Glucksman Professor of American and English Letters, New York University, since 1987; *b* 6 Jan. 1931; *s* of David R. Doctorow and Rose Doctorow Buck; *m* 1954, Helen Setzer; one *s* two *d*. *Educ:* Kenyon College (AB 1952); Columbia Univ. (graduate study). Script-reader, Columbia Pictures, NY, 1956–59; sen. editor, New American Library, 1959–64; editor-in-chief, 1964–69, publisher, 1968–69, Dial Press; writer-in-residence, Univ. of California, Irvine, 1969–70; Mem., Faculty, Sarah Lawrence Coll., NY, 1971–78; Creative Writing Fellow, Yale Sch. of Drama, 1974–75; Vis. Sen. Fellow, Council on Humanities, Princeton, 1980–81. Member: AAAL; Amer. Acad. of Arts and Scis; Amer. Philosophical Soc. Hon. degrees from Brandeis Univ., Kenyon, Hobart and William Smith Colls. Guggenheim Fellowship, 1972; Creative Arts Service Fellow, 1973–74. Nat. Humanities Medal, USA, 1998; Saul Bellow Award, PEN, 2012; Medal for Dist. Contrib. to American Letters,

Nat. Book Foundn, 2013; Library of Congress Prize for American Fiction, 2014. *Publications:* Welcome to Hard Times, 1960; Big as Life, 1966; The Book of Daniel, 1971; Ragtime, 1975 (Amer. Acad. Award, Nat. Book Critics Circle Award); Drinks Before Dinner, 1979 (play, 1978); Loon Lake, 1980; Lives of the Poets (stories), 1984; World's Fair, 1985 (Nat. Book Award); Billy Bathgate, 1989 (Howells Medal, Amer. Acad.; PEN/Faulkner and Nat. Books Critics Awards; Premio Letterario Internazionale, 1991); The Waterworks, 1994; City of God, 2000; Sweet Land Stories, 2004; The March, 2006 (PEN/Faulkner and Nat. Book Critics Circle Awards); Homer and Langley, 2010; All the Time in the World (stories), 2011; Andrew's Brain, 2014; *essays:* Jack London, Hemingway and the Constitution, 1993; Reporting the Universe, 2003; Creationists, 2006. *Address:* c/o Random House Publishers, 1745 Broadway, New York, NY 10019, USA. *Club:* Century Association (NY). *Died 21 July 2015.*

DODDS, Sir Ralph (Jordan), 2nd Bt *cr* 1964, of West Chiltington, Co. Sussex; *b* 25 March 1928; *o s* of Sir (Edward) Charles Dodds, 1st Bt, MVO, FRS, and Constance Elizabeth (*d* 1969), *o d* of late J. T. Jordan, Darlington; *S* father, 1973; *m* 1954, Marion, *er d* of late Sir Daniel Thomas Davies, KCVO; two *d. Educ:* Winchester; RMA, Sandhurst. Regular commission, 13/18th Royal Hussars, 1948; served UK and abroad; Malaya, 1953 (despatches); resigned, 1958. Underwriting Member of Lloyd's, 1964–97. *Address:* 49 Sussex Square, W2 2SP. *Clubs:* Cavalry and Guards, Hurlingham. *Died 24 May 2015 (ext).*

DODSON, Prof. (George) Guy, PhD; FRS 1994; Professor of Biochemistry, University of York, 1985–2004, then Emeritus; Head, Division of Protein Structure, MRC National Institute for Medical Research, London, 1993–2004, then visiting worker; *b* 13 Jan. 1937; *m* 1965, Eleanor Joy McPherson (Prof. E. J. Dodson, FRS); three *s* one *d. Educ:* New Zealand Univ. (MSc, PhD). Rockefeller res. award, Oxford Univ., 1962; Res. Fellow, Wolfson Coll., Oxford, 1973; Lectr, 1976, Reader, 1983, York Univ. Mem., EMBO 1997. FMedSci 2002; FIASc 2004; Fellow, INSA, 2004. *Publications:* (ed jtly) Structural Studies on Molecules of Biological Interest, 1981; articles in learned jls on protein structure and function, particularly insulin and proteins of medical interest. *Recreations:* reading, music, wife's gardening, cricket. *Address:* Department of Chemistry, York Structural Biology Laboratory, University of York, York YO10 5YW. *T:* (01904) 328264, (Sec.) 328259, *Fax:* (01904) 328266; MRC National Institute for Medical Research, Mill Hill, NW7 1AA. *T:* (Sec.) (020) 8816 2136, *Fax:* (020) 8816 4477. *Died 24 Dec. 2012.*

DODSWORTH, Sir John Christopher S.; *see* Smith-Dodsworth.

DOHA, Aminur Rahman S.; *see* Shams-Ud Doha, A. R.

DOLBY, Ray Milton, Hon. OBE 1986; PhD; engineering company executive; electrical engineer; Founder and Chairman, Dolby Laboratories Inc., San Francisco and London, 1965–2009, then Director Emeritus; *b* Portland, Ore, 18 Jan. 1933; *s* of Earl Milton Dolby and Esther Eufemia (*née* Strand); *m* 1966, Dagmar Baumert; two *s. Educ:* San Jose State Coll.; Washington Univ.; Stanford Univ. (Beach Thompson award, BS Elec. Engrg); Pembroke Coll., Cambridge (Marshall schol., 1957–60, Draper's studentship, 1959–61, NSF Fellow, 1960–61; PhD Physics 1961; Fellow, 1961–63; research in long-wave length x-rays, 1957–63; Hon. Fellow 1983). Electronic technician/jun. engr, Ampex Corp., Redwood City, Calif, 1949–53. Served US Army 1953–54. Engr, 1955–57; Sen. Engr, 1957; UNESCO Advr, Central Sci. Instruments Org., Punjab, 1963–65; Cons., UKAEA, 1962–63. Inventions, research, pubns in video tape rec., x-ray microanalysis, noise reduction and quality improvements in audio and video systems; 50 UK patents. Trustee, Univ. High Sch., San Francisco, 1978–84; Mem., Marshall Scholarships Selection Cttee, 1979–85; Dir, San Francisco Opera; Governor, San Francisco Symphony. Mem., Acad. of Motion Picture Arts and Scis, 2001. Fellow: Audio Engrg Soc. (Silver Medal, 1971; Gold Medal, 1992; Governor, 1972–74, 1979–84; Pres., 1980–81); Brit. Kinematograph, Sound and Television Soc. (Outstanding Technical and Scientific Award, 1995); Soc. Motion Picture, TV Engrs (S. L. Warner award, 1978; Alexander M. Poniatoff Gold Medal, 1982; Progress Medal, 1983; Hon. Mem., 1992); Inst. of Broadcast Sound, 1987; Amer. Acad. of Arts and Scis, 2003; Hon. Fellow, Assoc. of Motion Picture Sound, 1999; Hon. FREng 2004. MIEEE (Ibuka Award, 1997); Tau Beta Pi. Hon. ScD Cambridge, 1997; DUniv York, 1999. Other Awards: Emmy, for contrib. to Ampex video recorder, 1957, and for noise reduction systems on video recorder sound tracks, 1989; Trendsetter, Billboard, 1971; Lyre, Inst. High Fidelity, 1972; Emile Berliner Assoc. Maker of Microphone award, 1972; Top 200 Execs Bi-Centennial, 1976; Sci. and Engrg, 1979, Oscar, 1989, Acad. of Motion Picture Arts and Scis; Man of the Yr, Internat. Tape Assoc., 1987; Pioneer Award, Internat. Teleproduction Soc., 1988; Eduard Rhein Ring, Eduard Rhein Foundn, 1988; Life Achievement Award, Cinema Audio Soc., 1989; Grammy, Nat. Acad. of Recording Arts and Scis, 1995; Medal of Achievement, Amer. Electronics Assoc., 1997; Nat. Medal of Technol., US Dept of Commerce, 1997; inductee, Hall of Fame, Consumer Electronics Assoc., 2000; Internat. Honour for Excellence (John Tucker Award), Internat. Broadcasting Convention, 2000; Lifetime Achievement Award, Acad. of TV Arts and Scis, USA, 2005. *Recreations:* yachting, ski-ing, flying. *Address:* (home) 3340 Jackson Street, San Francisco, CA 94118, USA. *T:* (415) 5636947; (office) 100 Potrero Avenue, San Francisco, CA 94103, USA. *T:* (415) 5580200. *Died 12 Sept. 2013.*

D'OLIVEIRA, Basil Lewis, CBE 2005 (OBE 1969); cricketer; *b* 4 Oct. 1931; *s* of Lewis and Moira D'Oliveira; *m* 1960, Naomi Brache; two *s.* Cricketer: played for: Middleton CC, Central Lancs League, 1960–63; Worcs CCC, 1964–80; MCC, 1964–71; England, 1966–72 (44 caps); coach, Worcs CCC, 1980–90. Order of Ikhamanga for excellence in sports (SA), 2003. *Publications:* Time to Declare: an autobiography, 1980; *relevant publication:* Basil D'Oliveira: cricket and controversy, by Peter Oborne, 2004. *Address:* c/o Worcestershire County Cricket Club, County Ground, New Road, Worcester WR2 4QQ. *Died 19 Nov. 2011.*

DOMB, Prof. Cyril, PhD; FRS 1977; Professor of Physics, Bar-Ilan University, 1981–89, then Emeritus; *b* 1920; *m* 1957, Shirley Galinsky; three *s* three *d. Educ:* Hackney Downs Sch.; Pembroke Coll., Cambridge. Major Open Schol., Pembroke Coll., 1938–41; Radar Research, Admiralty, 1941–46; MA Cambridge, 1945; Nahum Schol., Pembroke Coll., 1946; PhD Cambridge, 1949; ICI Fellowship, Clarendon Laboratory, Oxford, 1949–52; MA Oxon, 1952; University Lecturer in Mathematics, Cambridge, 1952–54; Prof. of Theoretical Physics, KCL, 1954–81; FKC 1978. Max Born Prize, Inst. of Physics and German Physical Soc., 1981. *Publications:* (ed) Clerk Maxwell and Modern Science, 1963; (ed) Memories of Kopul Rosen, 1970; Phase Transitions and Critical Phenomena, (ed with M. S. Green) vols 1 and 2, 1972, vol. 3, 1974, vols 5a, 5b, 6, 1976, (ed with J. L. Lebowitz) vols 7 and 8, 1983, vol. 9, 1984, vol. 10, 1986, vol. 11, 1987, vol. 12, 1988, vol. 13, 1989, vol. 14, 1991, vol. 15, 1992, vol. 16, 1994, vol. 17, 1995, vols 18–20, 2001; (ed with A. Carmell) Challenge, 1976; The Critical Point, 1996; articles in scientific journals. *Recreation:* swimming. *Address:* Department of Physics, Bar-Ilan University, 52900 Ramat-Gan, Israel; 32 Cumberland Gardens, NW4 1LD. *Died 15 Feb. 2012.*

DOMINIAN, Dr Jacobus, (Jack), MBE 1994; FRCPEd, FRCPsych; DPM; Hon. Consultant, Central Middlesex Hospital, since 1988 (Senior Consultant Psychiatrist, 1965–88); *b* 25 Aug. 1929; *s* of late Charles Joseph Dominian and Mary Dominian (*née* Scarlatou); *m* 1955, Edith Mary Smith (*d* 2006); four *d. Educ:* Lycée Leonin, Athens; St Mary's High Sch., Bombay; Stamford Grammar Sch., Lincs; Cambridge Univ.; Oxford Univ. MA, MB BChir (Cantab). Postgraduate work in medicine, various Oxford hosps, 1955–58, Maudsley Hosp. (Inst. of Psychiatry), 1958–64; training as psychiatrist at Maudsley Hosp.; Dir, One Plus One: Marriage and Partnership Research, 1971–86. Hon. DSc Lancaster, 1976. *Publications:* Psychiatry and the Christian, 1961; Christian Marriage, 1967; Marital Breakdown, 1968; The Church and the

Sexual Revolution, 1971; Cycles of Affirmation, 1975; Depression, 1976; Authority, 1976; (with A. R. Peacocke) From Cosmos to Love, 1976; Proposals for a New Sexual Ethic, 1977; Marriage, Faith and Love, 1981; Make or Break, 1984; The Capacity to Love, 1985; Sexual Integrity: the answer to AIDS, 1987; Passionate and Compassionate Love, 1991; (with Edmund Flood) The Everyday God, 1993; Marriage, 1995; One Like Us, 1998; Let's Make Love, 2001; Living Love, 2004; A Guide to Loving, 2005; Being Jack Dominian: reflections on marriage, sex and love, 2007; contribs to Lancet, BMJ, the Tablet, TLS. *Recreations:* enjoyment of the theatre, music, reading and writing. *Address:* Pefka, 19 Clements Road, Chorleywood, Herts WD3 5JS. *T:* (01923) 283115. *Died 10 Aug. 2014.*

DOMINIC, Zoë Denise, OBE 2007; FBIPP, FRPS; professional photographer; *b* 4 July 1920; *d* of Lionel J. Levi and Dora Jane Macdonald; name changed to Dominic by Deed Poll, 1960. *Educ:* Francis Holland Sch., Regent's Park. FRPS 1972 (Hood Medal, 1986); FBIPP 1993. Photographer, stage, opera and ballet: English Stage Co. at Royal Court Theatre, 1957–67; National Theatre, 1963–70; Royal Shakespeare Co., 1958; Royal Ballet; Royal Opera Co.; ENO; English Music Theatre; WNO; Stratford, Ontario, 1975. Chm., Avenue Productions, 1987– (Dir, 1986); produced: A Private Treason, Watford, 1986; Blithe Spirit, Vaudeville, 1987; Noël and Gertie, Donmar Warehouse 1987, Comedy, 1989; specialist photographer on films: Dr Zhivago, Nijinsky, Reds, Travels With My Aunt, Victor Victoria; exhibns of ballet photographs, Photographers' Gallery, 1971, Riverside Studios, 1979. Mem. Council, LAMDA, 1989– (Mem., Finance Cttee (Chm., 1991–94)). Trustee, Theatre Projects Trust, 1970 (Chm., 1983–92). *Publications:* Frederick Ashton, 1971; (jtly) John Cranko and the Stuttgart Ballet, 1973; Theatre at Work (text Jim Hiley), 1981; Full Circle (text Dame Janet Baker), 1982; The Best of Plays and Players 1953–68, 1987. *Recreation:* gardening. *Address:* 3 Lexham Walk, W8 5JD. *T:* (020) 7373 6461. *Died 11 Jan. 2011.*

DONALD, Air Marshal Sir John (George), KBE 1985 (OBE 1972); Medical Adviser, AMI Middle East Services Ltd, 1989–95; *b* 7 Nov. 1927; *s* of John Shirran Donald and Janet Knox (*née* Napier); *m* 1954, Margaret Jean Walton; one *s* two *d*. *Educ:* Inverurie Acad.; Aberdeen Univ. (MB, ChB 1951); DTM&H Edin 1964; MRCGP 1971, FRCGP 1977; MFCM 1972, FFCM 1985; MFOM 1982 (AFOM 1980); FRCPE 1986. Commnd RAF, 1953; Senior Medical Officer: Colombo, Ceylon, 1954–57; RAF Stafford, 1957–60; RAF Waddington, 1960–63; student, RAF Staff Coll., 1965; SMO, HQ AFCENT, France and Holland, 1966–68; Dep. Dir, Medical Personnel (RAF), 1969–72; OC, The Princess Mary's RAF Hosp., Akrotiri, Cyprus, 1972–76; OC, RAF Hosp., Ely, 1976–78; PMO, RAF Germany, 1978–81; PMO, RAF Strike Comd, 1981–84; Dir-Gen., RAF Med. Services, 1984–85; Dep. Surg. Gen. (Ops), MoD, and Dir Gen., RAF Med. Services, 1985–86; Med. Dir, Security Forces Hosp., 1986–89. QHS, 1983–86. CStJ 1984. *Recreations:* golf, skiing, camping, ornithology. *Address:* 8 Oratory Gardens, Canford Cliffs, Poole, Dorset BH13 7HJ. *Club:* Royal Society of Medicine. *Died 6 Nov. 2014.*

DONNE, David Lucas; Director, Marathon Asset Management, since 1989; *b* 17 Aug. 1925; *s* of late Dr Cecil Lucas Donne, Wellington, NZ; *m* 1st, 1957, Jennifer Margaret Duncan (*d* 1975); two *s* one *d*; 2nd, 1978, Clare, *d* of Maj. F. J. Yates. *Educ:* Stowe; Christ Church, Oxford (MA Nat. Science). Called to the Bar, Middle Temple, 1949. Studied Business Admin, Syracuse Univ., 1952–53; Charterhouse Group, 1953–64; William Baird, 1964–67. Chairman: Crest Nicholson, 1973–92; Dalgety, 1977–86 (Dep. Chm., 1975–77); Steetley, 1983–92 (Dep. Chm., 1979–83); ASDA–MFI, 1986–87; Argos, 1990–95; Director: Royal Trust Bank, 1972–93 (Dep. Chm., 1989–93); Sphere Investment Trust, 1982–95 (Chm., 1989–95). Member: Nat. Water Council, 1980–83; Bd, British Coal (formerly NCB), 1984–87; Stock Exchange Listed Cos Adv. Cttee, 1987–91. Chm., Calibre Cassette Liby for the Blind, 1997–2004. Fellow, Game Conservancy, 1987. *Recreations:* shooting, opera, sailing. *Address:* 8 Montagu Mews North, W1H 2JU. *Club:* Royal Thames Yacht. *Died 11 April 2011.*

DOREY, Sir Graham (Martyn), Kt 1993; Bailiff of Guernsey, 1992–99 (Deputy Bailiff, 1982–92); a Judge of the Court of Appeal of Jersey, 1992–99; President, Guernsey Court of Appeal, 1992–99; *b* 15 Dec. 1932; *s* of late Martyn Dorey and Muriel (*née* Pickard); *m* 1st, 1962, Penelope Cecile (*d* 1996), *d* of Maj. E. A. Wheadon, ED; two *s* two *d*; 2nd, 1998, Mrs Cicely Ruth Lummis. *Educ:* Kingswood Sch., Bath; Ecole des Roches, Verneuil; Univs of Bristol and Caen. Admitted Solicitor, 1959; Advocate, Royal Court of Guernsey, 1960; called to the Bar, Gray's Inn, 1992; People's Deputy, States of Guernsey, 1970; Solicitor Gen., 1973, Attorney Gen., 1977, Guernsey. KStJ 1996 (CStJ 1992). *Recreations:* sailing, maritime history, music. *Address:* Les Marchez Farm, La Rue des Reines, St Pierre du Bois, Guernsey GY7 9AE. *T:* (01481) 266186, *Fax:* (01481) 266289. *Clubs:* Royal Ocean Racing; Royal Yacht Squadron. *Died 25 June 2015.*

DOUGHTY, Nigel Edward; Joint Founder, 1985, and Executive Co-Chairman, since 2009, Doughty Hanson & Co. (Co-Chief Executive, 1985–2009); *b* 10 June 1957; *s* of Francis Edward Doughty and late Mercia Mary Doughty (*née* Lambert); *m* 1st, 1985, Carol Elizabeth Green (marr. diss. 1997); one *s* one *d*; 2nd, 2004, Lucy Vasquez; two *s*. *Educ:* Magnus Sch., Newark; Cranfield Univ. (MBA 1984). American Express/Shearson Lehman, 1979–83; Standard Chartered Bank, 1984–89 (Anglo-American Banking Schol., 1985). Chairman: Tarkett AG, 1994–98; Geberit AG, 1997–99; Dunlop Standard Aerospace, 1998–2004; Umbro plc, 2000–08; Nottingham Forest FC, 2002–11; Tumi Inc., 2005–09; Dir, Tag Heuer, SA, 1995–97. Mem., World Econ. Forum, Davos, 1998. Asst Treas., Labour Party, 2009–. Mem., Adv. Bd, Cranfield Sch. of Mgt, 2009–. Dir, Bridges Community Ventures, 2003–. Trustee: Doughty Hanson Charitable Foundn, 1998–; Doughty Family Foundn, 2008–; Founder, Doughty Centre for Corporate Responsibility, 2007. Pres., Cranfield Trust, 2011. Dist. Alumni Award, Cranfield Sch. of Mgt, 2004. *Recreations:* Nottingham Forest FC, gardening. *Address:* c/o Doughty Hanson & Co., 45 Pall Mall, SW1Y 5JG. *T:* (020) 7663 9300, *Fax:* (020) 7663 9371. *E:* nigel.doughty@doughtyhanson.com. *Club:* Metropolitan (New York). *Died 4 Feb. 2012.*

DOUGHTY, Sir William (Roland), Kt 1990; Chairman, North West Thames Regional Health Authority, 1984–94; Deputy Chairman, Britannia Refined Metals Ltd, later MIM UK Ltd, 1982–94 (Director, 1978–94); *b* 18 July 1925; *s* of Roland Gill Doughty and Gladys Maud Doughty (*née* Peto); *m* 1952, Patricia Lorna Cooke; three *s*. *Educ:* Headstone Sch.; Acton Technical Coll.; Trinity Coll., Dublin (MA); Harvard Business Sch. (AMP). Metal Box Co. Ltd, 1953–66; Molins Ltd, 1966–69, Dir, 1967; Cape Industries, 1969–84, Dir, 1972, Man. Dir, 1980–84; Chairman: Surgicare Ltd, 1995–2001; The Next Challenge Ltd, 1998–2001. Member: SE Economic Planning Council, 1966–79 (Chm., Industry and Employment Cttee, 1972–79); CBI Council, 1975–86 (Chm., London Region, 1981–83). Founder and Chm., Assoc. for Conservation of Energy, 1981–85 (Pres., 1985–). Gov., SE Tech. Coll., 1967–69; Trustee, Gt Ormond St Hosp. for Sick Children, 1978–90; Mem., Gen. Council, King Edward VII's Hosp. Fund for London, 1984– (Mem., Management Cttee, 1987–95); Chairman: King's Fund Centre Cttee, 1991–95; Adv. Cttee on Distinction Awards, NHS, 1994–97. Chairman: Cord Blood Charity, 1998–2004; Headway, The Brain Injury Assoc., 1999–2004; Inventure Trust, 2001–03. Life Mem., Sickle Cell Soc. (Patron, 2007–). Chm., Thorpe House Sch. Trust, 1995–2005. LHSM 1986. CCMI; FRSA. *Recreations:* cricket, theatre, golf, horse racing. *Club:* MCC. *Died 21 March 2015.*

DOUGLAS, Kenneth, CBE 1991; CEng; Managing Director, Austin and Pickersgill Ltd, 1958–69, and 1979–83; Chairman, Kenton Shipping Services, Darlington, 1968–83; *b* 28 Oct. 1920; British; *m* 1942, Doris Lewer; one *s* two *d*. *Educ:* Sunderland Technical Coll. (Dip. Naval Architecture). CEng. Dep. Shipyard Manager, Vickers Armstrong Naval Yard, Newcastle-upon-Tyne,

1946–53; Dir and Gen. Manager, Wm Gray & Co. Ltd, West Hartlepool, 1954–58; Man. Dir, Upper Clyde Shipbuilders Ltd, Chm., Simons Lobnitz Ltd and Chm., UCS Trng Co., 1969–73; Dep. Chm., Govan Shipbuilders, 1971–73; Chm., Douglas (Kilbride) Ltd, 1972–77; Chm. and Man. Dir, Steel Structures Ltd, 1974–76; Shiprepair Marketing Dir, British Shipbuilders, 1978–79; Mem. Bd, PCEF, 1988–91. Mem., Tyne and Wear Residuary Body, DoE, 1985–89. Hon. Fellow, Sunderland Univ., 1993 (Fellow, 1980 and 1992–93, Chm. of Govs, 1982–93, Sunderland Poly., subseq. Univ.). Formerly: FRINA, MBIM, MInstD. *Recreations:* fishing, golf. *Address:* 2 Abbots Lea, Dalton Piercy, Hartlepool, Cleveland TS27 3JS. *T:* (01429) 279284. *Died 10 July 2014.*

DOUGLAS, Richard Giles; *b* 4 Jan. 1932; *m* 1954, Jean Gray, *d* of Andrew Arnott; two *d. Educ:* Co-operative College, Stanford Hall, Loughborough; Univ. of Strathclyde; LSE; Univ. of St Andrews (MA 2003). Engineer (Marine). Tutor organiser in Adult Educn, Co-operative movement, 1957; Sectional Educn Officer, Scotland, 1958–61; Lectr in Economics, Dundee Coll. of Technol., 1964–70. Contested (Lab): South Angus, 1964, Edinburgh West, 1966, Glasgow Pollok, March 1967; (Lab and Co-op) Clackmannan and E Stirlingshire, Oct. 1974; MP (Lab and Co-op) Clackmannan and E Stirlingshire, 1970–Feb. 1974; MP Dunfermline, 1979–83, Dunfermline West, 1983–92 (Lab and Co-op, 1979–90, SNP, 1990–92); contested (SNP) Glasgow, Garscadden, 1992. Contested (SNP) Scotland Mid and Fife, Euro. Parly elecns, 1994. Chm., Scottish Water and Sewerage Customers' Council, 1995–98. *Address:* 11 Seymour Gate, Chipping Campden, Glos GL55 6BP. *Died 13 May 2014.*

DOUGLAS-WILSON, Ian, MD; FRCPE; Editor of the Lancet, 1965–76; *b* 12 May 1912; *o s* of late Dr H. Douglas-Wilson; *m* 1939, Beatrice May (*d* 1999), *e d* of late R. P. Bevan; one *s* two *d. Educ:* Marlborough Coll.; Edinburgh Univ. MB ChB 1936; MD (commended) Edinburgh 1938; FRCP Edinburgh 1945. Served with RAMC, 1940–45. House-physician, Royal Infirmary, Edinburgh, 1937; joined the Lancet staff, 1946; Asst Ed., 1952–62; Dep. Ed., 1962–64. Corresp. Mem., Danish Soc. of Internal Med., 1965. Dr (*hc*) Edinburgh, 1974. *Died 15 Oct. 2013.*

DOW, Andrew Richard George; railway and aviation historian and writer; *b* 1 Dec. 1943; *s* of late George Dow and Doris Mary Dow (*née* Soundy); *m* 1973, Stephanie Brenda Murphy; one *s* one *d. Educ:* The Hall, Hampstead; Brighton Coll. Chartered Secretary; ACIS. Commercial Apprentice, Bristol Siddeley Engines, 1962–67; appts in Bristol Siddeley and Rolls-Royce Commercial Depts, Bristol, Coventry and New Jersey, 1962–75; Commercial Manager, later Business Manager, Pegasus, 1975–91; Commercial Exec., 1989; Head of Business (Mil.), 1990; Head, Nat. Railway Mus., 1992–94; Contracts Manager, BR Special Trains Unit, and Commercial Man., BR Infrastructure Services, 1994–95; Dir, 1995–97, and Commercial Dir, 1996–97, Fastline Track Renewals Ltd. Director: Fastline Group Ltd, 1996–97; Fastline Hldgs Ltd, 1996–97; Lynton and Barnstaple Light Railway Co., 1995–2001 (Chm., 2000–01); Locomotive Construction Co., 1997–99; Fastline Photographic Ltd, 2000–05; Tornado Steam Traction Ltd, 2001–04; Fastline Films Ltd, 2005–; Mem., Lexington Gp (USA), 2008–. Director: York Visitor and Conf. Bureau, 1992–94; FNRM Enterprises Ltd, 1992–94, 1999–2006; A1 Steam Locomotive Trust, 1994–2004; Gresley Soc. Trust Ltd, 1999–. President: Leighton Buzzard Narrow Gauge Rly Soc., 1994–99; Lynton and Barnstaple Rly Assoc., 1994–2002. Pres., Stephenson Locomotive Soc., 2000–13 (Vice-Pres., 1992–2000); Vice-President: Great Central Rly Soc., 1994–; British Overseas Rly Historical Trust, 1994–; Vice-Chm., Gresley Soc., 1997–2015; Trustee, Darlington Rly Mus. Trust, 2002–. Fellow, Permanent Way Instn, 1994. Editor and writer, Behind the Scenes (series of archive DVDs, 2004–07); Producer, Fastline Films (series of DVDs on maintenance of signalling, level crossings and permanent way, 2006–08). *Publications:* Norfolk and Western Coal Cars, 1998 (US); Telling the Passenger Where to Get Off, 2005; Dow's Dictionary of Railway Quotations, 2006; Pegasus: the heart of the Harrier, 2009; Memories of a Railway Childhood, 2010; The Railway: British track since 1804, 2014; book reviews and articles in British and American railway jls. *Recreations:* family life, railways, aviation history, travel, photography, collecting. *Address:* Wyverns, Newton-on-Ouse, York YO30 2BR. *T:* (01347) 848808. *Died 24 April 2015.*

DOW, Harold Peter Bourner; QC 1971; *b* 28 April 1921; *s* of late Col H. P. Dow and P. I. Dow; *m* 1943, Rosemary Merewether (*d* 2002), *d* of late Dr E. R. A. Merewether, CB, CBE, FRCP; two *s* one *d. Educ:* Charterhouse; Trinity Hall, Cambridge (MA). Served RAF (Air Crew), 1941–42. Min. of Supply, 1943–45. Barrister, Middle Temple, 1946. *Publications:* Restatement of Town and Country Planning, 1947; National Assistance, 1948; (with Q. Edwards) Rights of Way, 1951; (ed) Hobsons Local Government, 1951 and 1957 edns. *Recreations:* music, painting. *Address:* Mustow House, Mustow Street, Bury St Edmunds, Suffolk IP33 1XL. *T:* (01284) 725093. *Died 9 Dec. 2011.*

DOWNS, Sir Diarmuid, Kt 1985; CBE 1979; FRS 1985; FREng, FIMechE; Managing Director, 1967–84, Chairman, 1976–87, Ricardo Consulting Engineers plc; *b* 23 April 1922; *s* of John Downs and Ellen McMahon; *m* 1951, Mary Carmel Chillman; one *s* three *d. Educ:* Gunnersbury Catholic Grammar Sch.; Northampton Poly. (BScEng London Univ., 1942). CEng, FIMechE 1961. Ricardo Consulting Engineers Ltd, 1942–87: Head, Petrol Engine Dept, 1947; Dir, 1957. Mem., Adv. Council for Applied R&D, 1976–80; Member: SERC, 1981–85 (Chm., Engineering Bd); Design Council, 1981–89; Bd of Dirs, Soc. of Automotive Engineers Inc., 1983–86; Bd of British Council, 1987–93; Council, Motor Industry Res. Assoc., 1987–89. President: Assoc. of Ind. Contract Res. Organisations, 1975–77; Fédération Internationale des Sociétés d'Ingénieurs des Techniques de L'Automobile, 1978 (Vice-Pres., 1975); IMechE, 1978–79 (Vice-Pres., 1971–78); Section G, British Assoc. for Advancement of Science, 1984; Royal Commn for Exhibn of 1851, 1985–96. Chm., Technology Activities Cttee, Royal Soc., 1989–95; Mem., Adv. Bd, Parly Office of Science and Technology, 1988–93. Dir, Gabriel Communications (formerly Universe Publications) Ltd, 1986–93. Vis. Fellow, Lincoln Coll. Oxford, 1987–88. Hinton Lecture, Fellowship of Engrg, 1987. Pres., Smeatonian Soc. of Civil Engrs, 2003. Foreign Associate, Nat. Acad. of Engrg, USA, 1987; Hon. Mem., Hungarian Acad. of Scis, 1988. Liveryman, Co. of Engineers, 1984–. Pro Chancellor, Surrey Univ., 1992–94 (Mem. Council, 1983–94, Chm., 1989–92); Mem. Council, City Univ., 1980–82. Hon. Fellow, St Mary's UC, Strawberry Hill, 1995. Hon. DSc: City, 1978; Cranfield Inst. of Technol., 1981; DUniv Surrey, 1995. George Stephenson Research Prize, 1951, Crompton Lanchester Medal, 1951 and Dugald Clerk Prize, 1952, IMechE; James Alfred Ewing Medal, ICE, 1985; Medal, Internat. Fedn of Automobile Engrs' and Technicians' Assocs, 1986. KSG 1993. *Publications:* papers on internal combustion engines in British and internat. engrg jls and conf. proc. *Recreation:* theatre. *Address:* The Downs, 143 New Church Road, Hove, East Sussex BN3 4DB. *T:* (01273) 419357. *Club:* Hove (Hove). *Died 12 Feb. 2014.*

DOWNWARD, Maj.-Gen. Sir Peter (Aldcroft), KCVO 1999; CB 1979; DSO 1967; DFC 1952; Governor, Military Knights of Windsor, 1989–2000; *b* 10 April 1924; *s* of late Aldcroft Leonard and Mary Downward; *m* 1st, 1953, Hilda Hinckley Wood (*d* 1976); two *s*; 2nd, 1980, Mrs Mary Boykett Procter (*née* Allwork) (*d* 2008). *Educ:* King William's Coll., Isle of Man. Enlisted 1942; 2nd Lieut, The South Lancashire Regt (Prince of Wales's Volunteers), 1943; served with 13th Bn (Lancs) Parachute Regt, NW Europe, India, Far East, 1944–46, Greece and Palestine, 1947; transf. to Glider Pilot Regt, 1948; Berlin Airlift, 1949, Korea, 1951–53; 1st Bn The South Lancs Regt (PWV) in Egypt and UK, 1953–54; instructor at Light Aircraft Sch., 1955–56; RAF Staff Coll., 1958; War Office, 1959–60; BAOR, 1961–63; Brigade Major 127 Bde, 1964; Comd 4th Bn The East Lancs Regt, 1965–66; Comd 1st Bn The Lancs Regt (PWV), Aden, 1966–67; Allied Forces N Europe, Oslo, 1968–69; instructor, Sch. of Infantry, 1970–71; Comd Berlin Inf. Bde, 1971–74; Comdt, Sch. of Infantry, 1974–76; GOC West Midland District, 1976–78; Lt-Governor and Sec., The Royal Hosp., Chelsea,

1979–84. Col, The Queen's Lancashire Regt, 1978–83; Col Comdt, The King's Division, 1979–83; Hon. Col, Liverpool Univ. OTC, 1980–89. Dir, Oxley Develts Co. Ltd, 1984–89. Chm., Museum of Army Flying, 1984–88; President: British Korean Veterans Assoc., 1986–97; Assoc. of Service Journals (formerly of Service Newspapers), 1986–2003; Trustee, Princess Christian Hosp., Windsor, 1989–94. *Address:* 71 Kings Road, Windsor, Berks SL4 2AD. *Died 18 Oct. 2014.*

DOWSON, Sir Philip (Manning), Kt 1980; CBE 1969; MA; PPRA (RA 1986; ARA 1979); RIBA, FCSD; a Senior Partner, Ove Arup Partnership, 1969–90 (Founding Trustee, 1995); Architectural Founder Partner, Arup Associates, architects and engineers; President, Royal Academy of Arts, 1993–99; *b* 16 Aug. 1924; *s* of Robert Dowson and Ina Cowen Dowson; *m* 1950, Sarah Crewdson (MBE 1998); one *s* two *d*. *Educ:* Gresham's Sch.; University Coll., Oxford; Clare Coll., Cambridge (Hon. Fellow, 1991); Architectural Association. AA Dip. Lieut, RNVR, 1943–47. Award-winning work includes: university and college buildings in Oxford, Cambridge, Birmingham and Leicester; headquarter buildings; buildings for music and the arts; urban and landscape projects. Member: Royal Fine Art Commn, 1971–97; Craft Adv. Cttee, 1972–75. Governor, St Martin's Sch. of Art, 1975–82. Trustee: The Thomas Cubitt Trust, 1978–98; Royal Botanic Gdns, Kew, 1983–95; Royal Armouries, 1984–89; Nat. Portrait Gall., 1993–99; Coram Foundn, 1993–99. Foundn Fellow, Birmingham Univ., 2007. Hon. Fellow, Duncan of Jordanstone Coll. of Arts, 1985; Hon. FAIA; Hon. FRCA, 1989; Hon. FRIAS. Hon. DArt De Montfort, 2000. Royal Gold Medal for Architecture, RIBA, 1981. *Recreation:* sailing. *Clubs:* Garrick, MCC. *Died 22 Aug. 2014.*

DRAKE, Sir (Frederick) Maurice, Kt 1978; DFC 1944; a Judge of the High Court of Justice, Queen's Bench Division, 1978–95; *b* 15 Feb. 1923; *o s* of late Walter Charles Drake and Elizabeth Drake; *m* 1954, (Alison) May, *d* of late W. D. Waterfall, CB; two *s* three *d*. *Educ:* St George's Sch., Harpenden; Exeter Coll., Oxford. MA Hons 1948. Served War of 1939–45 as Navigator, RAF 96 and 255 Nightfighter Squadrons. Called to Bar, Lincoln's Inn, 1950, QC 1968, Bencher, 1976. Dep. Chm., Beds QS, 1966–71; a Recorder of the Crown Court, 1972–78; Dep. Leader, Midland and Oxford Circuit, 1975–78, Presiding Judge, 1979–83. Standing Senior Counsel to RCP, 1972–78. Nominated Judge for appeals from Pensions Appeal Tribunal, 1985–95. Vice-Chm., Parole Bd, England and Wales, 1985–86 (Mem., 1984–86). Treas., Lincoln's Inn, 1997. Chm. Governors, Aldwickbury Prep. Sch. (Trust), 1969–80; Governor, St George's Sch., Harpenden, 1975–79. Hon. Alderman, St Albans DC, 1976–. *Recreations:* listening to music, opera and audio books, looking back on life. *Address:* The White House, West Common Way, Harpenden, Herts AL5 2LH. *T:* (01582) 712329. *Died 6 April 2014.*

DRAKE, Jack Thomas Arthur H.; *see* Howard-Drake.

DRAKE, Sir Maurice; *see* Drake, Sir F. M.

DRAYCOTT, Simon Douglas; QC 2002; a Recorder, since 2000; *b* 29 Sept. 1950; *s* of Douglas and Elizabeth Draycott; *m* 1st, 1979, Rukhsana (*née* Shah) (marr. diss. 2002); three *d*; 2nd, 2010, Simone (*née* Colwell). *Educ:* Uppingham; Coll. of Law. Called to the Bar, Middle Temple, 1977; Hd of Chambers, 5 St Andrew's Hill, 2006–. Specialist fraud advocate. *Recreation:* sailing. *Address:* 5 St Andrews Hill Chambers, EC4V 5BZ. *Died 22 Aug. 2015.*

DREW, David Ernest, MBE 2006; Character Principal Dancer, Royal Ballet, since 1974; choreographer; Founder, Ballet Scenarios, 2007; *b* London, 12 March 1938; *s* of Thomas Ernest Drew and Phyllis Adelaide (*née* Talbot-Tindale); *m* 1st, 1962, Avril Bergen (marr. diss. 1973); one *s*; 2nd, 1985, June Ritchie; one step *d*. *Educ:* Bristol Grammar Sch.; Westbury Sch. of Dancing, Bristol; Royal Ballet Upper Sch. Nat. Service, commnd RCS, 1958–60. Joined Royal Ballet at Royal Opera House, Covent Gdn, 1955: Soloist, 1961; Prin. Dancer, 1974; *created rôles* with Royal Ballet include: Bay Middleton, Mayerling; Demetrius, The Dream; Max Merx, Isadora; Celestial, Shadow-Play; Gaoler, Manon; The Master, Rituals; The Captain, Different Drummer; Leading Baboon, Prince of the Pagodas; G. B. Shaw, Grand Tour; Giles, The Crucible; *major rôles* include: Von Rothbart, Swan Lake; Monsieur G. M., Manon; Hilarion and Duke of Courtland, Giselle; Thomas, La Fille Mal Gardée; Catalabutte and King, Sleeping Beauty; Mercutio, Lord Capulet and Tybalt, Romeo and Juliet; Step Sister, Cinderella; Ivan and Kostchei, The Firebird; Mrs Pettitoes, Tales of Beatrix Potter; Armand's Father, Marguerite and Armand; Rajah and Brahmin, La Bayadère; *choreographic work* includes: five ballets for Sadler's Wells Royal Ballet: Intrusion, 1969; From Waking Sleep, 1970; St Thomas' Wake, 1971; Sacred Circles, 1972; Sword of Alsace, 1973; *musicals* include: Canterbury Tales, 1968; His Monkey Wife, 1970; *operas* include: Dido and Aeneas; Macbeth; Die Fledermaus; writer of scenario, The Three Musketeers, Northern Ballet Th., 2006, Estonian Nat. Ballet, 2009; also contribs to theatre and TV. Teacher, Royal Ballet Upper Sch., Pas de Deux at all levels, incl. Grad. Class, 1976–99; assisted in Direction of Choreographic Composition Course, 1986–99. Founder Pres., Ballet Assoc., 1975. Gold Medal, Royal Acad. of Dancing, 1954. *Recreations:* writing, theatre, inventing non-computer games and composing brainteasers. *Address:* c/o Royal Opera House, Covent Garden, WC2E 9DD. *Died 16 Oct. 2015.*

DRING, Richard Paddison; Editor of Official Report (Hansard), House of Commons, 1972–79; *b* 6 Nov. 1913; *s* of late Fred Dring and Florence Hasleham Dring, East Sheen; *m* 1939, Joan Wilson (*d* 1999); one *s*; *m* 2000, Margaret Foorde (*d* 2007). *Educ:* St Paul's School. Captain, RAOC during the War, serving in Europe and later in India with IA. Herts Advertiser, 1932; Press Association, 1936; Official Report (Hansard), House of Commons, 1940: Asst Editor, 1954; Dep. Editor, 1970. *Address:* 28 Vicarage Drive, SW14 8RX. *T:* (020) 8878 6604. *Club:* Richmond Golf. *Died 22 April 2014.*

DRINKALL, John Kenneth, CMG 1973; HM Diplomatic Service, retired; High Commissioner to Jamaica, and Ambassador (non-resident) to Haiti, 1976–81; *b* 1 Jan. 1922; *s* of J. H. Drinkall; *m* 1961, Patricia Ellis; two *s* two *d*. *Educ:* Haileybury Coll.; Brasenose Coll., Oxford. Indian Army, 1942–45. Entered HM Foreign Service, 1947; 3rd Sec., Nanking, 1948; Vice-Consul, Tamsui, Formosa, 1949–51; Acting Consul, 1951; Foreign Office, 1951–53; 1st Sec., Cairo, 1953–56; Foreign Office, 1957–60; 1st Sec., Brasilia, 1960–62; Foreign Office, 1962–65. Appointed Counsellor, 1964; Counsellor: Nicosia, Cyprus, 1965–67; British Embassy, Brussels, 1967–70; FCO, 1970–71; Canadian Nat. Defence Coll., 1971–72; Ambassador to Afghanistan, 1972–76. *Recreations:* lawn tennis, golf, racquets and squash. *Address:* 68 Rivermead Court, Ranelagh Gardens, SW6 3RZ. *Clubs:* Hurlingham, All England Lawn Tennis. *Died 30 May 2015.*

DRISCOLL, James; Senior Partner, Woodcote Consultancy Services, 1990–96; *b* 24 April 1925; *s* of Henry James Driscoll and Honorah Driscoll; *m* 1955, Jeanne Lawrence Williams, BA, CertEd; one *s* one *d*. *Educ:* Coleg Sant Illtyd, Cardiff; University Coll., Cardiff (BA 1st Cl. Hons). Chm., Welsh Young Conservatives, 1948–49; Nat. Dep. Chm., Young Conservatives, 1950; Dep. Chm., Univ. Cons. Fedn, 1949–50; Dep. Chm., NUS, 1951–53. Vice-Chm., European Youth Campaign, 1951–53. Contested (C) Rhondda West, 1950. Asst Lectr, UC Cardiff, 1950–53; Council of Europe Res. Fellowship, 1953. Joined British Iron and Steel Fedn, 1953; various econ. and internat. posts; Econ. Dir and Dep. Dir-Gen., 1963–67; various posts, British Steel Corporation, 1967–80; Man. Dir, Corporate Strategy, 1971–76, Board Adviser, 1976–80; Dir, 1976–90, Policy Advr, 1990–96, NICG; Chm. and Man. Dir, Woodcote Consultants Ltd, 1980–90; Chm., Webb Estate Ltd, 2001–03. Chm., Lifecare NHS Trust, 1990–94. Member: Grand Council, FBI, 1957–65; CBI Council, 1970–93; Observer, NEDC, 1977–91; Lay Mem., Investigation Cttee, ICA, 1991–96. Chm., Econ. Studies Cttee, Internat. Iron and Steel Inst., 1972–74. Vice-Chm., Croydon Mencap Ltd, 1997–2002. Mem., Court of Governors, Cardiff Univ. (formerly UC, Cardiff, later Univ. of Wales Coll. of Cardiff), 1970–2005 (Fellow,

1986). FREconS; FRSA. *Publications:* various articles and pamphlets on econ. and internat. affairs, esp. steel affairs, European integration, wages policy and financing of world steel investment. *Recreations:* travel, bridge, reading. *Address:* Foxley Hatch, 10A Upper Woodcote Village, Purley, Surrey CR8 3HE. *Died 20 Aug. 2011.*

DRIVER, Prof. Jonathon Stevens, DPhil; FMedSci; FBA 2008; Professor of Cognitive Neuroscience, since 1998, and Royal Society Anniversary Research Professor, since 2009, University College London (Director, Institute of Cognitive Neuroscience, 2004–09); *b* 4 July 1962; *s* of Dennis and Jane Driver; *m* 1995, Nilli Lavie; two *s*. *Educ:* Queen's Coll., Oxford (MA Exptl Psychol. 1984; DPhil Exptl Psychol. 1988). Jun. Res. Fellow, Christ Church, Oxford, 1988–90; Lectr in Exptl Psychol., 1991–96, and Fellow, Gonville and Caius Coll., 1994–96, Univ. of Cambridge; Prof. of Psychol., Birkbeck Coll., London, 1997–98. FMedSci 2005. *Publications:* Control of Cognitive Processes, 2000; Crossmodal Space and Crossmodal Attention, 2004; Mental Processes and the Human Brain, 2008; over 250 papers in learned jls. *Recreations:* the three Fs (family, fishing, football), science, guitar. *Address:* UCL Institute of Cognitive Neuroscience, 17 Queen Square, WC1N 3AR. *Clubs:* Piscatorial Society, Red Spinners Angling Society. *Died 28 Nov. 2011.*

DRUMMOND, Maj.-Gen. Anthony John D.; *see* Deane-Drummond.

DRURY, Sir (Victor William) Michael, Kt 1989; OBE 1978; FRCP; FRCGP; FRACGP; Professor of General Practice, University of Birmingham, 1980–91, then Emeritus; Vice President, Age UK (formerly Age Concern England), since 1995 (Chairman, 1992–95); *b* 5 Aug. 1926; *s* of Leslie and Beatrice Drury; *m* 1950, Joan (*née* Williamson); three *s* one *d*. *Educ:* Bromsgrove Sch.; Univ. of Birmingham (MB ChB Hons; Foundn Fellow 2006); MRCS LRCP 1949; FRCGP 1970 (MRCGP 1963); FRCP 1988; FRACGP 1988. Ho. Surg., Birmingham Gen., 1949–50; RSO, Kidderminster, 1950–51; Major, RAMC, 1951–53; Principal in Gen. Practice, Bromsgrove, 1953–91; Nuffield Trav. Fellow, 1965; Clarkson Sen. Clin. Tutor, Univ. of Birmingham, 1973–80. Lectures: James MacKenzie, 1983, Eli Lilley, 1984; Sir David Bruce, 1985; Gale, 1986; Fulton, 1996. Royal College of General Practitioners: Mem. Council, 1971–85 (Vice-Chm., 1980); Chm., Practice Org., 1966–71, Cttee and Res. Div., 1983–85; Pres., 1985–88. Member: Cttee on Safety of Medicines (Adverse Drug Reaction), 1975–79; Prescription Pricing Authy, 1981–86; DHA, 1981–85; Res. Cttee, RHA, 1982–86; GMC, 1984–94; Standing Cttee, Post Grad. Med. Educn, 1988–93. Chairman: Med. and Social Services Cttee, Muscular Dystrophy Gp, 1992–99; UK Centre for Advancement of Interprofessional Educn, 1994–97; Trustee, Nat. Asthma Trng Centre, 1991–2002. Civilian Advr in Gen. Practice to Army, 1984–91. Mem. Ct, Liverpool Univ., 1980–87; Vice-Pres., Bromsgrove Sch., 2004– (Gov. and Trustee, 1990–2003). Mem., Lunar Soc., 1993–. Hon. FRCPCH 1996. *Publications:* Introduction to General Practice, 1974; (ed) Treatment, 1978–; Medical Secretaries Handbook, 6th edn 1992; Treatment and Prognosis, 1990; The New Practice Manager, 1990, 3rd edn 1994; Teaching and Training Techniques for Hospital Doctors, 1998; General Practice and Clinical Negligence, 2000; various chapters in books on Drug Safety, Gen. Practice, etc; res. articles in Lancet, BMJ, Brit. Jl of Surgery, Jl RCGP. *Recreations:* gardening, reading, bridge, talking and listening. *Address:* Magellan House, Bourton Road, Moreton-in-Marsh, Glos GL56 0BD. *T:* (01608) 812325. *Died 11 June 2014.*

DRYSDALE WILSON, John Veitch, Eur Ing, CEng, FIMechE, FCIArb; Deputy Secretary, Institution of Mechanical Engineers, 1979–90; *b* 8 April 1929; *s* of Alexander Drysdale Wilson and Winifred Rose (*née* Frazier); *m* 1954, Joan Lily, *e d* of Mr and Mrs John Cooke, Guildford; one *s* one *d*. *Educ:* Solihull School; Guildford Technical Coll. Dennis Bros Ltd, Guildford: Engineer Apprentice, 1946–50; MIRA Research Trainee, 1949–50; Jun. Designer, 1950–51. National Service Officer, REME, 1951–53, Captain on Staff of CREME, 6th Armd Div. Management Trainee, BET Fedn, 1953–55; Technical Sales Engr, subseq. Head of Mechanical Laboratories, Esso Petroleum Co. Ltd, 1955–66; Chief Engr, R&D, Castrol Ltd, subseq. Burmah Oil Trading Ltd and Edwin Cooper Ltd, 1966–77; Projects and Res. Officer, Instn of Mechanical Engineers, 1977–79. Director: Mechanical Engineering Publications Ltd, 1979–90; Professional Engineers Insurance Bureau Ltd, 1989–90. Freeman, City of London, 1986; Liveryman: Co. of Engineers, 1987; Co. of Arbitrators, 1987. Mem., Casterbridge Probus Club. *Publications:* numerous papers to learned societies in USA and Europe on subjects related to engine lubrication. *Recreations:* travel, genealogy, horology, ink sketching, water colour painting. *Club:* Caravan. *Died 10 April 2011.*

DU CANE, John; *see* Wilkinson, J. A. D. C.

DU CANE, John Peter, OBE 1964; Director, Amax Inc., 1966–91; *b* 16 April 1921; *s* of Charles and Mathilde Du Cane; *m* 1945, Patricia Wallace (*née* Desmond) (*d* 2012); two *s*. *Educ:* Canford Sch., Wimborne. Pilot, Fleet Air Arm, RN, 1941–46. De Beers Consolidated Mines, 1946–54; Sierra Leone Selection Trust, 1955–63; Director: Consolidated African Selection Trust, 1963–81; Selection Trust Ltd, 1966–81 (Man. Dir, 1975–80; Chm., 1978–81); BP International Ltd, 1981; Chief Exec., BP Minerals Internat. Ltd, 1980–81; Director: Australian Consolidated Minerals Pty, 1981–86 (Dep. Chm., 1983–86); Ultramar Plc, 1983–87; Austamax Resources Ltd, 1984–86 (Dep. Chm., 1984–86). *Recreation:* photography. *Died 1 Nov. 2012.*

DUCKWORTH, His Honour Brian Roy; DL; a Circuit Judge, 1983–2004; Deputy Senior Judge, Cyprus Sovereign Base Areas Court, 1998–2007; *b* 26 July 1934; *s* of late Roy and Kathleen Duckworth; *m* 1964, Nancy Carolyn Duckworth, JP, *d* of late Chris and Annie Holden; three *s* one *d*. *Educ:* Sedbergh Sch.; Worcester Coll., Oxford (MA). Called to Bar, Lincoln's Inn, 1958; a Recorder of the Crown Court, 1972–83; Member: Northern Circuit; Bar Council, 1979–82. Councillor, Blackburn RDC, 1960–74 (Chm. 1970–72); Mem., Blackburn HMC, 1966–74. Liaison Judge and Hon. Pres., South Cumbria Magistracy, 1987–92; Liaison Judge, SW Lancs Magistracy, 1993–2004. Member: Lord-Lieut's Magistracy Adv. Cttee, 1993–2004; Lancs Probation Cttee, 1991–2001; Cttee, Council of Circuit Judges, 1995–2004. Gov., Lancs Teaching Hosps NHS Trust, 2008–. Chm., Samlesbury Hall Charitable Trust, 1993–2010 (Vice-Chm., 2010–). Vice-Pres., 2003–06, Pres., 2006–, Blackburn Br., Prayer Book Soc. Mem. Court, Lancaster Univ., 2003–10. Pres., Old Sedberghian Club, 1996–99. DL Lancs 1995. *Recreations:* golf, sailing, gardening, motor sport. *Address:* c/o The Crown Court, Ringway, Preston PR1 2LL. *T:* (01772) 844700. *Club:* Pleasington Golf. *Died 23 March 2014.*

DUCKWORTH, Eric; *see* Duckworth, W. E.

DUCKWORTH, John Clifford, FREng; FIET, FInstP; Managing Director, National Research Development Corporation, 1959–70; *b* 27 Dec. 1916; *s* of late H. Duckworth, Wimbledon, and of Mrs A. H. Duckworth (*née* Woods); *m* 1942, Dorothy Nancy Wills; three *s*. *Educ:* KCS, Wimbledon; Wadham Coll., Oxford (MA). FIET (FIEE 1957); FInstP 1957; Sen. FEI (Sen. FInstE 1957); FREng (FEng 1976). Radar Research and Development, Telecommunications Research Establishment, Malvern, 1939–46; National Research Council, Chalk River, Ont, 1946–47; Atomic Energy Research Establishment, Harwell, 1947–50; Chief Engineer, Wythenshawe Laboratories, Ferranti Ltd, 1950–54; Nuclear Power Engineer, Brit. Electricity Authority, 1954–58; Central Electricity Authority, 1957–58; Chief Research and Development Officer, Central Electricity Generating Board, 1958–59. Mem. Bd, AEA, 1963–68. Mem., Defence Res. Adv. Council, 1955–65. Chm., IDJ Investment Services Ltd, 1970–82; Chm. or non-exec. dir of various public cos, 1970–83. Pres., Institute of Fuel, 1963–64; Vice-Pres., Parliamentary and Scientific Cttee, 1964–67. Chairman: MacRobert Award Cttee, 1970–76; Science Mus. Adv. Council, 1972–84; Trustee, Science Mus., 1984–90. Vice-Pres., IEE, 1974–77. *Publications:* Weighty Matters, Worthy People, 2007. *Address:* Pengilly, Little-in-Sight, Mawnan Smith, Falmouth TR11 5EY. *Club:* Athenæum. *Died 8 Jan. 2015.*

DUCKWORTH, (Walter) Eric, OBE 1991; PhD; FREng; FIMMM, FInstP; Managing Director, Fulmer Ltd (formerly Fulmer Research Institute), 1969–90; Chairman: Bournville Consultants Ltd, since 1994; Digital Doctor Ltd, since 2006; *b* 2 Aug. 1925; *s* of Albert Duckworth and Rosamund (*née* Biddle); *m* 1949, Emma Evans (*d* 2009); one *s*. *Educ:* Cambridge Univ. (MA, PhD). Research Manager, Glacier Metal Co., 1955; Asst Director, BISRA, 1966; Chm., Yarsley Technical Centre, 1973–89; Director: Ricardo Consulting Engineers plc, 1978–85; H. Darnell Ltd, 1982–94; Fleming Technol. Investment Trust plc, 1984–90. Chm., Council of Science and Technology Insts, 1977–78; first Charter Pres., Instn of Metallurgists, 1974–75; Pres., Assoc. of Independent Res. and Technol. Organisations (formerly Assoc. of Ind. Contract Res. Organs), 1978–79, 1988–89; Hon. Treas., Metals Soc., 1981–84; Chm., Professional Affairs Bd, Inst. of Metals, 1985–88. Member: Parly and Scientific Cttee, 1968–94; Res. and Technol. Cttee, 1979–88, and Indust. Policy Cttee, 1983–88, Council, 1988–89, CBI; Nominations Cttee, 1983–88, Standing Cttee on Industry, 1988–94, Engrg Council; Engrg Bd, SERC, 1985–87; Council, Assoc. for Schools' Sci., Engrg and Technol. (formerly Standing Conf. on Schools' Sci. and Technol.), 1994–99. Chm., Christian Nationals Evangelism Commn, 1974–93; Trustee: Comino Foundn, 1981–; FMI, 1995–99 (Mem. Council, 1995–99); Vice-Pres., St Mary's Hosp. Med. Sch., 1976–97; Mem. Court, Brunel Univ., 1978–85, and 1991–. Liveryman: Worshipful Co. of Scientific Instrument Makers; Co. of Engineers; Freeman, City of London. First Edwin Liddiard Meml Lectr, London Metallurgical Soc. of Inst. of Metals, 1982. FREng (FEng 1980). Hon. DTech Brunel, 1976; DUniv Surrey, 1980. Editor, 1978–85, Chm., Editorial Bd, 1985–92, Materials and Design. *Publications:* A Guide to Operational Research, 1962, 3rd edn 1977; Statistical Techniques in Technological Research, 1968; Electroslag Refining, 1969; Manganese in Ferrous Metallurgy, 1976; Contract Research, 1991; *circa* 100 contribs to learned and other jls on many topics. *Recreation:* changing other people's attitudes. *Address:* Orinda, Church Lane, Stoke Poges, Bucks SL2 4PB. *T:* (01753) 645778. *Died 4 Feb. 2012.*

du CROS, Sir Claude Philip Arthur Mallet, 3rd Bt *cr* 1916; *b* 22 Dec. 1922; *s* of Sir (Harvey) Philip du Cros, 2nd Bt, and Dita, *d* of late Sir Claude Coventry Mallet, CMG; *S* father, 1975; *m* 1st, 1953, Mrs Christine Nancy Tordoff (marr. diss. 1974; she *d* 1988), *d* of late F. R. Bennett, Spilsby, Lincs; one *s*; 2nd, 1974, Mrs Margaret Roy Cutler (marr. diss. 1982), *d* of late R. J. Frater, Gosforth, Northumberland. *Heir: s* Julian Claude Arthur Mallet du Cros [*b* 23 April 1955; *m* 1984, Patricia (marr. diss. 2003), *o d* of Gerald Wyatt, Littlefield School, Liphook; one *s* two *d*]. *Died 24 July 2014.*

DUDLEY, 4th Earl of, *cr* 1860; **William Humble David Ward;** Baron Ward, 1644; Viscount Ednam, 1860; *b* 5 Jan. 1920; *e s* of 3rd Earl of Dudley, MC, TD, and Rosemary Millicent, RRC (*d* 1930), *o d* of 4th Duke of Sutherland; *S* father, 1969; *m* 1st, 1946, Stella (marr. diss., 1961), *d* of M. A. Carcano, KCMG, KBE; one *s* twin *d*; 2nd, 1961, Maureen Swanson (*d* 2011); one *s* five *d*. *Educ:* Eton; Christ Church, Oxford. Joined 10th Hussars, 1941, Adjt, 1944–45; ADC to Viceroy of India, 1942–43. Served War of 1939–45 (wounded). *Heir: s* Viscount Ednam, *b* 27 March 1947. *Clubs:* White's, Pratt's. *Died 16 Nov. 2013.*

DUDLEY, Prof. Hugh Arnold Freeman, CBE 1988; FRCSE, FRCS, FRACS; Professor of Surgery, St Mary's Hospital, London University, 1973–88, then Emeritus; *b* 1 July 1925; *s* of W. L. and Ethel Dudley; *m* 1947, Jean Bruce Lindsay Johnston; one *s* one *d* (and one *s* decd). *Educ:* Heath Grammar Sch., Halifax; Edinburgh and Harvard Univs. MB, ChB Edin. 1947; ChM (Gold Medal and Chiene Medal) Edin. 1958; FRCSE 1951; FRACS 1965; FRCS 1974. Research Fell., Harvard Univ., 1953–54; Lecturer in Surgery, Edinburgh Univ., 1954–58; Sen. Lectr, Aberdeen Univ., 1958–63; Foundation Prof. of Surgery, Monash Univ., Melbourne, 1963–72. President: Surgical Res. Soc. of Australasia, 1968; Biol. Engrg Soc. of GB, 1978–80; Surgical Res. Soc. of GB, 1981. Regl Research Co-ordinator, NW Thames RHA, 1989–92. Chairman, Independent Ethics Committee: Army Personnel Res. Estabt, Farnborough, 1989–94; Chemical and Biological Defence Estabt, Porton Down, 1988–96 (Mem. Council, 1992–94). Chm., Med. Writers Gp, 1980–83, Mem. Cttee, 1984–87, Soc. of Authors. Corresponding Member: Surgical Res. Soc., Australia; Surgical Res. Soc. of SA; Vascular Soc. of SA; Hon. Member: Hellenic Soc. of Experimental Medicine; Aberdeen Medico-Chirurgical Soc.; Hon. Fellow: Amer. Surgical Assoc.; Amer. Assoc. for the Surgery of Trauma; S African Coll. of Surgeons. Chm. Editorial Board of Br. Jl of Surgery and of Br. Jl Surgery Soc. Ltd, 1980–88; Associate Editor, BMJ, 1988–91. *Publications:* Principles of General Surgical Management, 1958; (jtly); Access and Exposure in Abdominal Surgery, 1963; (jtly) Guide for House Surgeons in the Surgical Unit, 5th edn 1974, to 8th edn 1988; (ed) Rob and Smith's Operative Surgery, 3rd edn 1976, 4th edn 1988; Hamilton Bailey's Emergency Surgery, 10th edn 1977, 11th edn 1986; Communication in Medicine and Biology, 1977; (ed) Aid to Clinical Surgery, 2nd edn 1978 to 4th edn 1988; (jtly) Practical Procedures for House Officers, 1988; (jtly) The People's Hospital of North East Scotland, 1992; (ed jtly) Scientific Foundations of Trauma, 1996; papers in med. and sci. jls. *Recreations:* missing pheasants; annoying others; surgical history. *Address:* Glebe Cottage, Glass, Huntly, Aberdeenshire AB54 4XH. *T:* (01466) 700376. *Died 28 June 2011.*

DUFFY, Peter Clarke, QPM 1979; Director General, Federation Against Copyright Theft, 1985–89; *b* Hamilton, Scotland, 10 May 1927; *s* of Hugh Duffy and Margaret Archibald; *m* 1958, S. M. Joyce (marr. diss.); one *s* two *d*. *Educ:* Our Lady's High Sch., Motherwell. MInstAM 1983. Served Army, Western Arab Corps, Sudan Defence Force, 1945–48 (War Medal). Joined Metropolitan Police, 1949; Criminal Investigation Dept, 1954; Comdr, New Scotland Yard, 1976–83; Dir, Investigations, Fedn Against Copyright Theft, 1983–85. *Recreations:* golf, living. *Club:* Royal Automobile. *Died 18 May 2012.*

DUGDALE, Sir William (Stratford), 2nd Bt *cr* 1936, of Merevale and Blyth, Co. Warwick; CBE 1982; MC 1943; DL; Director and Chairman, General Utilities PLC, 1988–99; *b* 29 March 1922; *er s* of Sir William Francis Stratford Dugdale, 1st Bt, and Margaret, 2nd *d* of Sir Robert Gordon Gilmour, 1st Bt, of Liberton and Craigmillar; *S* father, 1965; *m* 1st, 1952, Lady Belinda Pleydell-Bouverie (*d* 1961), 2nd *d* of 6th Earl of Radnor; one *s* three *d*; 2nd, 1967, Cecilia Mary, *e d* of Sir William Malcolm Mount, 2nd Bt; one *s* one *d*. *Educ:* Eton; Balliol Coll., Oxford. Served War of 1939–45, Grenadier Guards (Captain), Admitted as solicitor, 1949. Director: Phoenix Assurance Co., 1968–85; Lee Valley Water Co., 1989–90; North Surrey Water Co., 1989–98; Chairman: Severn Trent Water Authority, 1974–83; National Water Council, 1982–83; Birmingham Diocesan Board of Finance, 1979–92. Steward, Jockey Club, 1985–87. Chm., Wolverhampton Racecourse PLC, 1965–91. Governor, Lady Katherine Leveson's Hosp., Temple Balsall, 1956–99. Mem., Warwicks CC, 1964–76; High Steward, Stratford upon Avon, 1977. JP 1951–97, DL 1955, High Sheriff 1971, Warwicks. *Publications:* Settling the Bill, 2011; contrib. DNB. *Heir: s* William Matthew Stratford Dugdale [*b* 22 Feb. 1959; *m* 1990, Paige Sullivan; two *s* two *d*]. *Address:* Blyth Hall, Coleshill, Birmingham B46 2AD. *T:* (01675) 462203; Merevale Hall, Atherstone CV9 2HG. *T:* (01827) 713143; 24 Bryanston Mews West, W1H 7FR. *T:* (020) 7262 2510. *Clubs:* Brooks's, White's, MCC; Jockey (Newmarket). *Died 13 Nov. 2014.*

DUGUID, Prof. James Paris, CBE 1979; MD, BSc; FRCPath; Professor of Bacteriology, University of Dundee, 1967–84; Consultant, Tayside Health Board, 1963–84; *b* 10 July 1919; *s* of late Maj.-Gen. David Robertson Duguid, CB, and Mary Paris; *m* 1944, Isobel Duff (decd); one *s* two *d* (and one *d* decd). *Educ:* Edinburgh Academy; Univ. of Edinburgh (MB ChB Hons 1942; BSc 1st Cl. Hons 1943; MD (Gold Medal) 1949); FRCPath 1966. Lectr, Sen. Lectr and Reader, Univ. of Edinburgh, 1944–62; Prof. of Bacteriology, Univ. of St Andrews, 1963–67; Director of Postgrad. Medical Educn, Univ. of Dundee, 1968–71, Dean of Faculty of Medicine, 1971–74, Mem. Univ. Court, 1977–81. Cons. Adviser in Microbiology, Scottish Home and Health Dept, 1967–85, Mem. Adv. Cttee on Medical

Research, 1967–71; Member: Eastern Regional and Tayside Health Bds, 1967–77; Adv. Cttee on Laboratory Services, Scottish Health Serv. Council, 1967–74 (Chm., Epidemiology Sub-cttee, 1966–71); Scottish Health Services Planning Council, 1974–77 (Member: Adv. Cttee on New Developments in Health Care, 1976–84; Scientific Services Adv. Gp, 1975–79; Chm., Microbiology and Clin. Immunology Cttees, 1975–77); Jt Cttee on Vaccination and Immunisation, Health Services Councils, 1967–74; GMC, 1975–81; Council for Professions Supp. to Medicine, 1978–86; Independent Adv. Gp on Gruinard Island, 1986–87; Optimum Population Trust, 1993–; Migration Watch UK, 2002–. Hon. Member: Pathol Soc. of GB and Ireland, 1985; Soc. for General Microbiology, 2001. Co-Editor: Jl of Pathology and Bacteriology, 1959–68; Jl of Medical Microbiology, 1968–71. *Publications:* (co-ed) Mackie and McCartney, Medical Microbiology, 11th edn 1969, 12th edn 1973, 13th edn 1978; (ed) Mackie and McCartney, Practical Medical Microbiology, 1989; scientific papers on bacterial fimbriae, adhesins, biotyping and phylogeny, airborne infection, and the action of penicillin. *Recreations:* grandchildren and great grandchildren, gardening, presbyterian atheism, population studies. *Address:* Glenside, Merlewood Road, Inverness IV2 4NL. *T:* (01463) 220118. *Died 9 March 2012.*

DUKE, Rt Rev. Michael Geoffrey H.; *see* Hare Duke.

DULBECCO, Dr Renato; Senior Clayton Foundation Investigator, since 1979, and President Emeritus, since 1993, The Salk Institute for Biological Studies (President, 1989–93); *b* Italy, 22 Feb. 1914; USA citizen; *s* of late Leonardo Dulbecco and Maria Virdia; *m* 1st, 1940, Giuseppina Salvo (marr. diss.); one *d* (one *s* decd); 2nd, 1963, Maureen R. Muir; one *d*. *Educ:* Univ. of Turin Medical Sch. (MD). Assistente, Univ. of Turin: Inst. Pathology, 1940–46; Anatomical Inst., 1946–47; Res. Assoc., Indiana Univ., 1947–49; Sen. Res. Fellow, 1949–52, Assoc. Prof., 1952–54, Prof. 1954–63, California Inst. Technology; Vis. Prof., Rockefeller Inst., 1962; Royal Soc. Vis. Prof. at Univ. of Glasgow, 1963–64; Salk Institute: Resident Fellow, 1963–72, Fellow, 1972–77; Distinguished Res. Prof., 1977–82; Imperial Cancer Research Fund: Asst Dir of Res., 1972–74; Dep. Dir of Res., 1974–77; Prof. of Pathology and Medicine, Univ. of Calif San Diego Med. Sch., 1977–81. MNAS; Member: Fedn of Amer. Scientists; Amer. Assoc. for Cancer Research; Cancer Center, Univ. of Calif at San Diego; Bd of Scientific Counselors, Dept of Cancer Etiology, NCI; Amer. Acad. of Arts and Scis; Internat. Physicians for Prevention of Nuclear War, Inc.; Pres., Amer.-Ital. Foundn for Cancer Res. Trustee: Amer.-Italian Foundn for Cancer Res.; La Jolla Country Day School. Foreign Member: Academia dei Lincei, 1969; Royal Society, 1974; Hon. Member: Accademia Ligure di Scienze e Lettere, 1982; Società Medico-Chirurgica di Modena, 1985; Tissue Culture Assoc., 1988. Many lectures to learned instns. Hon. DSc Yale, 1968; Hon. LLD Glasgow, 1970; *hc* Dr Med., Vrije Universiteit Brussel, Brussels, 1978; Hon. DSc Indiana, 1984. (Jtly) Nobel Prize for Physiology or Medicine, 1975; Premio Fregene, Italy, 1988; numerous other prizes and awards. *Publications:* (jtly) Microbiology, 1967; numerous in sci. jls. *Recreation:* music. *Address:* The Salk Institute, PO Box 85800, San Diego, CA 92186–5800, USA. *Died 19 Feb. 2012.*

DUMMETT, (Agnes Margaret) Ann, (Lady Dummett); writer; *b* 4 Sept. 1930; *d* of Arthur William Chesney and late Kitty Mary Chesney; *m* 1951, Sir Michael Anthony Eardley Dummett, FBA (*d* 2011); three *s* two *d* (and one *s* one *d* decd). *Educ:* Guildhouse Sch., Pimlico; Ware Grammar Sch. for Girls; Somerville Coll., Oxford (MA). Pres., Oxford Univ. Liberal Club, 1949. Community Relations Officer, Oxford, 1966–69; teaching in further education, 1969–71; Research Worker: Inst. of Race Relations, 1971–73; Runnymede Trust, 1975, 1977; Jt Council for the Welfare of Immigrants, 1978–84; Dir, Runnymede Trust, 1984–87. Consultant (pt-time) on Eur. policies, CRE, 1990–98. *Publications:* A Portrait of English Racism, 1973; Citizenship and Nationality, 1976; A New Immigration Policy, 1978; (with Ian Martin) British Nationality: a guide to the new law, 1982; (ed) Towards a Just Immigration Policy, 1986; chapters in: Justice First (with Michael Dummett), 1969; Colloque de la Société Française pour le Droit International, 1979; Moral Philosophy, 1979; (with Andrew Nicol) Subjects, Citizens, Aliens and Others, 1990; Free Movement, 1992; Individual Rights and the Law in Britain, 1994; (ed) Racially Motivated Crime, 1997; numerous articles and pamphlets. *Recreations:* walking about cities, theatre going, popular music. *Address:* 54 Park Town, Oxford OX2 6SJ. *T:* (01865) 558698. *Died 7 Feb. 2012.*

DUMMETT, Sir Michael (Anthony Eardley), Kt 1999; FBA; Wykeham Professor of Logic, University of Oxford, 1979–92, Professor Emeritus 1992; Emeritus Fellow, All Souls College, Oxford, 1979; *b* 27 June 1925; *s* of George Herbert Dummett and Iris Dummett (*née* Eardley-Wilmot); *m* 1951, (Agnes Margaret) Ann Chesney (Ann Dummett, writer); three *s* two *d* (and one *s* one *d* decd). *Educ:* Sandroyd Sch.; Winchester Coll. (1st Schol.); Christ Church, Oxford (major hist. schol., 1942; First Class Hons, PPE 1950); DLitt Oxford, 1989. Served in Army, 1943–47: in RA and Intell. Corps (India, 1945, Malaya, 1946–47, Sgt). Asst Lectr in Philosophy, Birmingham Univ., 1950–51; Commonwealth Fund Fellow, Univ. of California, Berkeley, 1955–56; Reader in the Philosophy of Mathematics, Univ. of Oxford, 1962–74; All Souls College, Oxford: Fellow, 1950–79, Senior Research Fellow, 1974–79; Sub-Warden, 1974–76; Fellow, 1979–92, Emer. Fellow, 1992–98. Hon. Fellow, New Coll., Oxford, 1998. Vis. Lectr, Univ. of Ghana, 1958; Vis. Professor: Stanford Univ., several occasions, 1960–66; Univ. of Minnesota, 1968; Princeton Univ., 1970; Rockefeller Univ., 1973; William James Lectr in Philosophy, Harvard Univ., 1976; Alex. von Humboldt-Stiftung Vis. Res. Fellow, Münster Univ., 1981; Gifford Lectr, St Andrews Univ., 1996–97; Dewey Lectr, Columbia Univ., 2002. Founder Mem., Oxford Cttee for Racial Integration, 1965 (Chm., Jan.–May 1966); Member: Exec. Cttee, Campaign Against Racial Discrimination, 1966–67; Legal and Civil Affairs Panel, Nat. Cttee for Commonwealth Immigrants, 1966–68; Chairman: Jt Council for the Welfare of Immigrants, 1970–71 (Vice-Chm., 1967–69, 1973–75); unofficial cttee of enquiry into events in Southall 23 April 1979, 1979–80; shadow board, Barclays Bank, 1981–82. FBA 1968–84, re-elected 1995. For. Hon. Mem., Amer. Acad. of Arts and Scis, 1985. Hon. PhD Nijmegen, 1983; Hon. DLitt: Caen, 1993; Aberdeen, 1993; Athens, 2005; DUniv Stirling, 2002. Lakatos Award in Phil. of Sci., LSE, 1994; Rolf Schock Prize for Logic and Philosophy, Royal Swedish Acad. of Scis, 1995. *Publications:* Frege: philosophy of language, 1973, 2nd edn 1981; The Justification of Deduction, 1973; Elements of Intuitionism, 1977, rev. edn 2000; Truth and other Enigmas, 1978; Immigration: where the debate goes wrong, 1978; Catholicism and the World Order, 1979; The Game of Tarot, 1980; Twelve Tarot Games, 1980; The Interpretation of Frege's Philosophy, 1981; Voting Procedures, 1984; The Visconti-Sforza Tarot Cards, 1986; Ursprünge der analytischen Philosophie, 1988, 2nd edn as Origins of Analytical Philosophy, 1993; Frege and Other Philosophers, 1991; The Logical Basis of Metaphysics, 1991; Frege: Philosophy of Mathematics, 1991; Grammar and Style for Examination Candidates and Others, 1993; The Seas of Language, 1993; Il Mondo e l'Angelo, 1993; I Tarocchi Siciliani, 1995, 2nd edn 2002; (jtly) A Wicked Pack of Cards, 1996; Principles of Electoral Reform, 1997; On Immigration and Refugees, 2001; La Natura e il futuro della filosofia, 2001; (jtly) A History of the Occult Tarot 1870–1970, 2002; Truth and the Past, 2004; (jtly) A History of Games Played with the Tarot Pack, 2004; Thought and Reality, 2006; *contributions to:* Mind and Language, 1975; Truth and Meaning, 1976; Studies on Frege, 1976; Contemporary British Philosophy, 1976; Meaning and Use, 1979; Perception and Identity, 1979; Perspectives on the Philosophy of Wittgenstein, 1981; Approaches to Language, 1983; Frege: tradition and influence, 1984; Reflections on Chomsky, 1989; Meaning and Method, 1990; What is a Philosophical Question?, 2002; contrib. entry on Frege, to Encyclopedia of Philosophy (ed P. Edwards), 1967; (with Ann Dummett) chapter on Rôle of the Government, in Justice First (ed L. Donnelly), 1969; preface to R. C. Zaehner, The City Within the Heart, 1980; articles in: Aristotelian Soc. Proceedings, Philos. Review, Bull. of London Math. Soc., Synthese, Inquiry, Econometrica, Jl of Symbolic Logic,

Zeitschrift für mathematische Logik, Dublin Review, New Blackfriars, Clergy Review, Jl of Warburg and Courtauld Insts, Jl of Playing-Card Soc., Artibus et Historiae. *Recreations:* listening to the blues, investigating the history of card games. *Address:* 54 Park Town, Oxford OX2 6SJ. *T:* (01865) 558698. *Died 27 Dec. 2011.*

DUMPER, Rt Rev. Anthony Charles; Hon. Assistant Bishop, Diocese of Birmingham, since 1993; *b* 4 Oct. 1923; *s* of Charles Frederick and Edith Mildred Dumper; *m* 1948, Sibylle Anna Emilie Hellwig (*d* 2001); two *s* one *d*. *Educ:* Surbiton Grammar School; Christ's Coll., Cambridge (MA); Westcott House, Cambridge. Relief Worker, Germany, 1946–47; ordained, 1947; Curate, East Greenwich, 1947–49; Vicar of South Perak, Malaya, 1949–57; Archdeacon of North Malaya, 1955–64; Vicar of Penang, Malaya, 1957–64; Dean of St Andrew's Cathedral, Singapore, 1964–70; Vicar of St Peter's, Stockton on Tees, and Rural Dean of Stockton, 1970–77; Bishop Suffragan of Dudley, 1977–93. *Publications:* Vortex of the East, 1963. *Recreations:* walking, gardening. *Address:* 117 Berberry Close, Bournville, Birmingham B30 1TB. *Died 27 Aug. 2012.*

DUNBAR, Alexander Arbuthnott; *b* 14 March 1929; *yr s* of Sir Edward Dunbar, 9th (by some reckonings 10th) Bt (*d* 1969); *m* 1965, Elizabeth Susannah, *d* of Rev. Denzil Wright; one *s* one *d*. *Educ:* Wellington Coll., Berks; Pembroke Coll., Cambridge (MA); Edinburgh Sch. of Agriculture, 1980–81. Mil. Service, Lieut QO Cameron Highlanders, 1947–49. Called to the Bar, Inner Temple, 1953. Joined ICI, 1954: Asst Sec., Wilton Works, 1959–63. Joined North Eastern Assoc. for the Arts, 1963, Sec. 1964, Dir 1967; Director: Northern Arts, 1967–69; UK and British Commonwealth Branch, Calouste Gulbenkian Foundn, 1970–71; Scottish Arts Council, 1971–80. Chm., Northern Adv. Cttee, Scottish Wildlife Trust, 1986–93; Member: Arts and Disability Enquiry, Carnegie UK Trust, 1982–85; Museums and Galleries Commn Wkg Party on Museums in Scotland, 1984–86. DL Moray, 1987–2004. *Recreations:* art, theatre, conservation, history. *Address:* Pitgaveny, Elgin, Moray IV30 5PQ. *Died 2 Feb. 2012.*

DUNBAR of Northfield, Sir Archibald (Ranulph), 11th Bt *cr* 1700; *b* 8 Aug. 1927; *er s* of Sir (Archibald) Edward Dunbar, 9th Bt (by some reckonings 10th Bt) and Olivia Douglas Sinclair (*d* 1964), *d* of Maj.-Gen. Sir Edward May, KCB, CMG; *S* father, 1969; *m* 1974, Amelia Millar Sommerville, *d* of Horace Davidson; one *s* two *d*. *Educ:* Wellington Coll.; Pembroke Coll., Cambridge; Imperial Coll. of Tropical Agriculture, Trinidad. Mil. Service, 2nd Lt, Cameron (att. Gordon) Highlanders, 1945–48. Entered Colonial Agricultural Service, Uganda, as Agricultural Officer, 1953; retired, 1970. Hon. Sheriff, Sheriff Court District of Moray, 1989–. Kt of Honour and Devotion, SMO Malta, 1989. *Publications:* A History of Bunyoro-Kitara, 1965; Omukama Chwa II Kabarega, 1965; The Annual Crops of Uganda, 1969; various articles in Uganda Jl. *Heir: s* Edward Horace Dunbar, Younger of Northfield [*b* 18 March 1977; *m* 2005, Caroline Mary Oliver; one *s* one *d*]. *Address:* The Old Manse, Duffus, Elgin, Scotland IV30 5QD. *T:* (01343) 830270. *Died 30 Nov. 2015.*

DUNBOYNE, 29th Baron by Prescription, 1324, 19th Baron by Patent, *cr* 1541 (Ire.); **John Fitzwalter Butler;** *b* 31 July 1951; *o s* of 28th/18th Baron Dunboyne and Anne Marie, *d* of Sir Victor Mallet, GCMG, CVO; *S* father, 2004; *m* 1975, Diana Caroline, *yr d* of Sir Michael Sanigear Williams, KCMG; one *s* two *d* (and one *d* decd). *Educ:* Winchester; Trinity Coll., Cambridge (BA 1973; MA 1977); London Business Sch. (Sloan Fellow, 1979). Hill Samuel Gp, 1974–75; Stolt Nielsen Inc., 1977–78; Lazard Brothers & Co. Ltd, 1979–80; mgt consultant, 1980–; Dir, Fitzwalter & Co. Ltd, 1985– (projects include: EU consortium for privatisation in Kazakstan, 1994; EU Tacis Enterprise Support Centres for Large and Medium-sized Enterprises in Western Siberia, 1998–99; ISCRA investment support centres to Russia, 2000–02; EU Tacis Assistance to Kabardino-Balkarian Republic, 2004). Transatlantic voyage in small sailing boat, 1975–76. *Recreations:* international relations, sailing, country pursuits, quixotic causes. *Heir: s* Hon. Richard Pierce Theobald Butler [*b* 5 July 1983; *m* 2012, Anneka Eileen, *d* of A. Anketell-Jones]. *Address:* Argos Hill House, Rotherfield, East Sussex TN6 3QG. *Clubs:* Butler Society (Vice-Pres.), Irish Peers Association; Cruising Association. *Died 11 July 2013.*

DUNCAN, Rev. Denis Macdonald, MA, BD; *b* 10 Jan. 1920; *s* of late Rev. Reginald Duncan, BD, BLitt and Clarice Ethel (*née* Hodgkinson); *m* 1942, Henrietta Watson McKenzie (*née* Houston) (*d* 1993); one *s* (one *d* decd). *Educ:* George Watson's Boys' Coll., Edinburgh; Edinburgh Univ.; New Coll., Edinburgh. Ordained, 1943; Minister of: St Margaret's, Juniper Green, Edinburgh, 1943–49; Trinity Duke Street Parish Church, Glasgow, 1949–57; Founder-editor, Rally, 1956–67; Managing Editor, British Weekly, 1957–70 (Man. Dir, 1967–70); Managing Director: DPS Publicity Services Ltd, 1967–74; Arthur James Ltd (Publishers), 1983–94; broadcaster and scriptwriter, Scottish Television, 1963–68; concert promotion at Edinburgh Festival and elsewhere, 1966–; Concert series "Communication through the Arts" poetry/music anthologies (with Benita Kyle), 1970–80. Dir, Highgate Counselling Centre, 1969–86; Associate Dir and Trng Supervisor, Westminster Pastoral Foundn, 1971–79; Chm., Internat. Cttee of World Assoc. of Pastoral Care and Counselling, 1977–79; Dir, Churches' Council for Health and Healing, 1982–88; Moderator of the Presbytery of England, Church of Scotland, 1984. PhD Somerset Univ., 1989. *Publications:* (ed) Through the Year with William Barclay, 1971; (ed) Through the Year with Cardinal Heenan, 1972; (ed) Daily Celebration, vol. 1, 1972, vol. 2, 1974; Marching Orders, 1973; (ed) Every Day with William Barclay, 1973; (ed) Through the Year with J. B. Phillips, 1974; Marching On, 1974; Here is my Hand, 1977; Creative Silence, 1980; A Day at a Time, 1980; Love, the Word that Heals, 1981; The Way of Love, 1982; Victorious Living, 1982; Health and Healing: a ministry to wholeness, 1988; Be Still and Know…: 100 Daily Telegraph meditations, 1994; Solitude, stillness, serenity…: a further 75 Daily Telegraph meditations, 1997; The Road Taken: autobiographical reflections on communication, 1997; Rainbows Through the Rain: a third collection of 75 Daily Telegraph Meditations, 2000; Meditations through the Year: 367 Daily Telegraph meditations, 2003; (ed) Morning and Evening: William Barclay's meditations, 2003; Towards the Light: through depression to healing, 2009. *Recreation:* cricket. *Died 7 Jan. 2014.*

DUNCAN, Prof. James Playford, DSc Manchester; CEng; FIMechE, FIET; Professor of Mechanical Engineering, University of British Columbia, 1966–84, then Emeritus; Adjunct Professor, University of Victoria, 1985–87; *b* 10 Nov. 1919; *s* of late Hugh Sinclair Duncan and Nellie Gladys Duncan; *m* 1942, Jean Marie Booth; three *s* one *d*. *Educ:* Scotch Coll., Adelaide; University of Adelaide, S Australia (ME). MInstP. Executive Engineer, Richards Industries Ltd, Keswick, S Australia, 1941–46; Senior Physics Master, Scotch Coll., Adelaide, 1946–47; Lecturer in Mechanical Engineering, University of Adelaide, 1948–49, Senior Lecturer, 1950–51 and 1953–54; Turbine Engineer, Metropolitan Vickers Electrical Co., Trafford Park, Manchester, 1952; Turner and Newall Research Fellow, University of Manchester, 1955; Lecturer in Mechanical Engineering, University of Manchester, 1956; Prof. of Mechanical Engineering, University of Sheffield, 1956–66. *Publications:* Sculptured Surfaces in Engineering and Medicine, 1983; Computer Aided Sculpture, 1989. *Recreations:* sailing, flautist. *Died 7 Feb. 2011.*

DUNCOMBE, Sir Philip (Digby) Pauncefort-, 4th Bt *cr* 1859; DL; one of HM Body Guard, Honourable Corps of Gentlemen-at-Arms, since 1979 (Harbinger, 1993–97); *b* 18 May 1927; *o s* of Sir Everard Pauncefort-Duncombe, 3rd Bt, DSO, and Evelyn Elvira (*d* 1986), *d* of Frederick Anthony Denny; *S* father, 1971; *m* 1951, Rachel Moyra, *d* of Major H. G. Aylmer; one *s* two *d*. *Educ:* Stowe. 2nd Lieut, Grenadier Guards, 1946; served in Palestine, 1947–48; Malaya, 1948–49; Cyprus, 1957–59; Hon. Major, retired 1960, Regular Army Reserve. County Comdt, Buckinghamshire Army Cadet Force, 1967–70. DL Bucks 1971, High Sheriff, 1987–88. CStJ 1992. *Heir: s* David Philip Henry Pauncefort-Duncombe [*b* 21 May 1956; *m* 1987, Sarah, *d* of late Reginald Battrum and of Mrs Reginald Battrum; one *s* one *d*]. *Address:* Church

Close, Church Lane, Great Brickhill, Bucks MK17 9AE. *T:* (01525) 261205. *Club:* Cavalry and Guards. *Died 22 Dec. 2011.*

DUNCOMBE, Roy, VRD 1957; Chairman, Nationwide Building Society, 1989–91; *b* 7 June 1925; *s* of Joseph William Duncombe and Gladys May Duncombe (*née* Reece); *m* 1946, Joan Thornley Pickering; one *s* one *d* (and one *d* decd). *Educ:* Hinckley Grammar School. RNR, 1943–68 (Lt-Comdr (A); Pilot, Fleet Air Arm). Financial Dir, Ferry Pickering Gp, 1965–87; Chm., Anglia Building Soc., 1985–87; following merger with Nationwide Bldg Soc., Vice Chm., Nationwide Anglia Bldg Soc., 1987–89; name changed to Nationwide Bldg Soc., 1989. *Recreations:* walking, swimming, photography, ornithology. *Address:* Westways, Market Bosworth, Nuneaton, Warwickshire CV13 0LQ. *T:* (01455) 291728; 3 The Old Grammar School, Chipping Campden, Glos GL55 6HB. *T:* (01386) 841455. *Club:* Naval and Military. *Died 16 March 2013.*

DUNLOP, Rev. Canon Ian Geoffrey David, FSA; Canon and Chancellor of Salisbury Cathedral, 1972–92, Canon Emeritus, since 1992; *b* 19 Aug. 1925; *s* of late Walter N. U. Dunlop and Marguerite Irene (*née* Shakerley); *m* 1957, Deirdre Marcia, *d* of late Dr Marcus Jamieson; one *s* one *d*. *Educ:* Winchester Coll.; New Coll., Oxford (MA); Strasbourg Univ. (Diploma); Lincoln Theol Coll. FSA 1965. Served Irish Guards, 1944–46 (Lieut). Curate, Hatfield, 1956–60; Chaplain, Westminster Sch., 1960–62; Vicar of Bures, Suffolk, 1962–72. Member: Gen. Synod, 1975–85; Cathedrals' Adv. Commn, 1981–86. Trustee, Nat. Churches Trust (formerly Historic Churches Preservation Trust), 1969–. *Publications:* Versailles, 1956, 2nd edn 1970; Palaces and Progresses of Elizabeth I, 1962; Châteaux of the Loire, 1969; Companion Guide to the Ile de France, 1979, 2nd edn 1985; Cathedrals Crusade, 1981; Royal Palaces of France, 1985; Thinking It Out, 1986; (contrib.) Oxford Companion to Gardens, 1986; Burgundy, 1990; Marie-Antoinette: a portrait, 1993; Louis XIV, 1999 (Enid McLeod Prize, Franco-British Soc., 2000); Edward VII and the Entente Cordiale, 2004; weekly column in Church Times, 1970–90. *Recreations:* painting, bird watching. *Address:* Gowanbrae, The Glebe, Selkirk TD7 5AB. *T:* (01750) 20706; Hill Cottages, Marsh Lane, Felixstowe, Suffolk IP11 9RP. *T:* (01394) 286118. *Died 10 Sept. 2011.*

DUNN, Rt Hon. Sir Robin Horace Walford, Kt 1969; MC 1944; PC 1980; a Lord Justice of Appeal, 1980–84; *b* 16 Jan. 1918; *s* of late Brig. K. F. W. Dunn, CBE, and of Ava, *d* of Brig.-Gen. H. F. Kays, CB; *m* 1941, Judith (*d* 1995), *d* of late Sir Gonne Pilcher, MC; one *d* (one *s* and one *d* decd); *m* 1997, Joan, *e d* of Sir Cecil Stafford-King-Harman, 2nd Bt and *widow* of Captain George Dennehy. *Educ:* Wellington; Royal Military Academy, Woolwich (Sword of Honour). First Commissioned, RA, 1938; RHA, 1941; Staff Coll., 1946; retired (hon. Major), 1948. Served War of 1939–45; France and Belgium, 1939–40; Western Desert and Libya, 1941–42; Normandy and NW Europe, 1944–45 (wounded thrice, despatches twice, MC); Hon. Col Comdt, RA, 1980–84, Hon. Col 1984–. Called to Bar (Inner Temple), 1948; Master of the Bench, Inner Temple, 1969. Western Circuit, Junior Counsel to Registrar of Restrictive Trading Agreements, 1959–62; QC 1962; Judge of the High Court of Justice, Family Division (formerly Probate, Divorce and Admiralty Division), 1969–80; Presiding Judge, Western Circuit, 1974–78. Treas., Gen. Council of the Bar, 1967–69 (Mem., 1959–63); Chm. Betting Levy Appeal Tribunal, 1964–69; Dep. Chm., Somerset QS, 1965–71; Mem., Lord Chancellor's Cttee on Legal Educn, 1968–69. *Publications:* Sword and Wig: memoirs of a Lord Justice, 1994. *Recreation:* hunting. *Address:* Lynch Mead, Allerford, Somerset TA24 8HJ. *T:* (01643) 862509. *Club:* Cavalry and Guards. *Died 5 March 2014.*

DUNNING, Joseph, CBE 1977; Chairman, Lothian Health Board, 1983–84; Principal, Napier College of Commerce and Technology, Edinburgh, 1963–81; *b* 9 Oct. 1920; *s* of Joseph and Elizabeth Ellen Dunning; *m* 1st, 1948, Edith Mary Barlow (*d* 1972); one *s* one *d*; 2nd, 1992, Eileen Murdoch, OBE. *Educ:* London University (BSc Hons); Durham University (MEd); Manchester College of Technology (AMCT). Metallurgical Industry and lecturing, 1936–56; Principal, Cleveland Technical College, 1956–63. MA Open Univ.; FEIS. Hon. Fellow, Napier Polytech. of Edinburgh, 1989. Hon. DEd CNAA, 1983. *Recreations:* silversmithing, photography. *Address:* 3 Barnes Green, Great Salkeld, Penrith, Cumbria CA11 9LU. *Club:* New (Edinburgh). *Died 18 June 2012.*

DUNNINGTON-JEFFERSON, Sir Mervyn (Stewart), 2nd Bt *cr* 1958; Company Director, since 1968; *b* 5 Aug. 1943; *s* of Sir John Alexander Dunnington-Jefferson, 1st Bt, DSO, and Frances Isobel, *d* of Col H. A. Cape, DSO; *S* father, 1979; *m* 1971, Caroline Anna, *o d* of J. M. Bayley; one *s* two *d*. *Educ:* Eton College. Joined Charrington & Co. Ltd (Brewers), 1961; left in 1968 to become self-employed. *Recreations:* sport—cricket, ski-ing, golf, etc. *Heir:* *s* John Alexander Dunnington-Jefferson [*b* 23 March 1980; *m* Joanna Lee; one *d*]. *Address:* 7 Bolingbroke Grove, SW11 6ES. *T:* (020) 8675 3395. *Clubs:* MCC, Queen's, Turf. *Died 9 Jan. 2014.*

DUNRAVEN and MOUNT-EARL, 7th Earl of, *cr* 1822; **Thady Windham Thomas Wyndham-Quin;** Baron Adare, 1800; Viscount Mountearl, 1816; Viscount Adare, 1822; Bt 1871; *b* 27 Oct. 1939; *s* of 6th Earl of Dunraven and Mount-Earl, CB, CBE, MC, and Nancy (*d* 1994), *d* of Thomas B. Yuille, Halifax County, Va; *S* father, 1965; *m* 1969, Geraldine, *d* of Air Commodore Gerard W. McAleer, CBE, MB, BCh, DTM&H, Wokingham; one *d*. *Educ:* Ludgrove; Le Rosey. *Heir:* none. *Address:* Kilgobbin House, Adare, Co. Limerick, Ireland. *Club:* Kildare Street and University (Dublin). *Died 25 March 2011* (*ext*).

DUNSANY, 20th Baron of, *cr* 1439; **Edward John Carlos Plunkett;** painter and designer; *b* 10 Sept. 1939; *o s* of 19th Baron of Dunsany and Vera Plunkett, *d* of G. de Sà Sottomaior; *S* father, 1999; *m* 1982, Maria Alice Villela de Carvalho; two *s*. *Educ:* Eton; Slade Sch. of Fine Art; Ecole des Beaux Arts, Paris. *Heir:* *s* Hon. Randal Plunkett, *b* 9 March 1983. *Address:* Dunsany Castle, Co. Meath, Eire. *Died 24 May 2011.*

DUNSTAN, Lt-Gen. Sir Donald (Beaumont), AC 1991; KBE 1980 (CBE 1969; MBE 1954); CB 1972; Governor of South Australia, 1982–91; *b* 18 Feb. 1923; *s* of late Oscar Reginald Dunstan and Eileen Dunstan; *m* 1948, Beryl June Dunningham; two *s*. *Educ:* Prince Alfred Coll., South Australia; RMC, Duntroon. Served War of 1939–45: Regimental and Staff appts in SW Pacific Area, 1942–45. Served in Korea, 1954; Instructor: RMC Duntroon, 1955–56, 1963; Staff Coll., Queenscliff, 1958; Staff Coll., Camberley, 1959–60; Dep. Comdr 1 Task Force, Vietnam, 1968–69; Comdr, 10th Task Force, Holsworthy, NSW, 1969; idc 1970; Commander Aust. Force, Vietnam, 1971; Chief of Materiel, 1972–74; GOC Field Force Comd, 1974–77; CGS, 1977–82. KStJ 1982. *Address:* 52 Martin Court, West Lakes, SA 5021, Australia. *Clubs:* Australian (Sydney); Royal Sydney Golf, Royal Adelaide Golf. *Died 15 Oct. 2011.*

DUNSTAN, Ivan, PhD; CChem, FRSC; FCQI; Director-General International, British Standards Institution, 1991–93; *b* 27 Aug. 1930; *s* of Edward Ernest and Sarah Kathleen Dunstan; *m* 1955, Monica Jane (*née* Phillips); two *s* one *d*. *Educ:* Falmouth Grammar Sch.; Bristol Univ. (BSc). Joined Scientific Civil Service, working at Explosives Research and Development Estabt, Waltham Abbey, 1954; became Supt of Gen. Chemistry Div., 1967; Warren Spring Laboratory (DTI) as Dep. Dir (Resources), 1972–74; Dir, Materials Quality Assurance, MoD (PE), 1974–79; Dir, Bldg Res. Estabt, DoE, 1979–83; Standards Dir, 1983–86, Dir-Gen., 1986–91, BSI. Chm., UK Nat. Forum for Quality Policy and Conformity Assessment, 1993–2001. President: RILEM, 1988; European Standards Organ, 1990; European Orgn for Testing and Certification, 1990–92; Inst. of Quality Assurance, 1997–2002 (Vice-Pres., 1986–97); Mem., British Bd of Agrément, 1987. CCMI (CBIM 1986). *Recreations:* golf, opera, gardening. *Address:* 6 High Oaks Road, Welwyn Garden City, Herts AL8 7BH. *T:* (01707) 322272. *Died 12 June 2013.*

DUPREE, Sir (Thomas William James) David, 6th Bt *cr* 1921, of Craneswater, Portsmouth; *b* 5 Feb. 1930; *s* of James Dupree, 5th *s* of 1st Bt and Mary Ethel Gillott (*née* Reid); *S* cousin, 2006. *Heir:* none. *Died 29 June 2013* (*ext*).

DURBIN, Prof. James, FBA 2001; Professor of Statistics, University of London (London School of Economics), 1961–88, then Emeritus; *b* 30 June 1923; *m* 1958, Anne Dearnley Outhwaite; two *s* one *d*. *Educ:* Wade Deacon GS, Widnes; St John's Coll., Cambridge. Army Operational Research Group, 1943–45. Boot and Shoe Trade Research Assoc., 1945–47; Dept of Applied Economics, Cambridge, 1948–49; Asst Lectr, then Lectr in Statistics, London Sch. of Economics, 1950–53; Reader in Statistics, 1953–61. Visiting Professor: Indian Statistical Inst., 1953; Univ. of North Carolina, 1959–60; Stanford Univ., 1960; Univ. of Wisconsin, 1965; Johns Hopkins Univ., 1965–66; Univ. of Washington, 1966; ANU, 1970–71; Univ. of Calif, Berkeley, 1971; Univ. of Cape Town, 1978; UCLA, 1984; Univ. of Calif, Santa Barbara, 1989; Nat. Univ. of Singapore, 1989–90; Univ. of Trento, Italy, 1991; Ohio State Univ., 1993; Moscow Acad. of Scis, 1995; Hon. Prof., UCL, 2007–. Research Fellow: US Bureau of the Census, 1992; Statistics Canada, 1994; Statistics NZ, 1997. Member: Home Office Data Protection Cttee, 1976–78; Dept of Transport Adv. Cttee on Trunk Rd Assessment, 1977–81. Member: ESRC, 1983–86 (Chm., Res. Resources and Methods Cttee, 1982–85); Internat. Statistical Inst., 1955 (Pres., 1983–85; Hon. Mem., 1999); Bd of Dirs, Amer. Statistical Assoc., 1980–82 (Fellow, 1960); Fellow, Inst. of Mathematical Statistics, 1958; Fellow, Econometric Soc., 1967; Royal Statistical Society: Vice Pres., 1969–70 and 1972–73; Pres. 1986–87; Guy Medal in Bronze, 1966, in Silver, 1976, in Gold, 2008. Dr *hc* Tucuman, Argentina, 2001. *Publications:* Distribution Theory for Tests based on the Sample Distribution Function, 1973; (with S. J. Koopman) Time Series Analysis by State Space Methods, 2001; articles in statistical journals, incl. Biometrika, Jl of Royal Statistical Society, etc. *Recreations:* travel, opera, theatre, visiting Suffolk. *Address:* 31 Southway, NW11 6RX. *T:* (020) 8458 3037. *E:* durbinja@aol.com. *Died 23 June 2012.*

DURWARD, (Alan) Scott; Director, 1985–91, and Group Chief Executive, 1989–91, Alliance & Leicester Building Society; Chairman, Girobank Plc, 1990–91; *b* 30 Aug. 1935; *oc* of late Prof. Archibald Durward, MD and Dorothy Durward; *m* 1962, Helen Gourlay; two *s*. *Educ:* Stowe; St John's Coll., Cambridge (MA). Imperial Tobacco Co. Ltd, 1958–65; Rowntree & Co. Ltd, 1965–67; Cheltenham & Gloucester Bldg Soc., 1967–75; Leicester Building Society: Dep. Gen. Man., 1975–77; Gen. Man., 1977–81; Dir and Chief Gen. Man., 1981–85; merger with Alliance Bldg Soc. to form Alliance & Leicester Bldg Soc., 1985; Jt Chief Gen. Manager, 1985–86; Chief Gen. Manager, 1986–89. Chm., Midland Assoc. of Bldg Socs, 1984–85; Member: Council, Bldg Socs Assoc., 1981–85 and 1987–91; Council, Eur. Fedn of Bldg Socs, 1987–91. Director: Gourlay Properties, 1985–99; John Laing plc, 1987–89; Mem. Bd, BR (London Midland), 1990–92. Dir, Leics Ambulance and Paramedic Service NHS Trust, 1993–99. General Comr for Income Tax, 1994–. Chm., Peterborough Diocesan Bd of Finance, 1993–2003. Mem. Council, Loughborough Univ. of Technology, 1984–97 (Treas., 1991–97). JP Leicester, 1999–2004. *Recreations:* tennis, fishing. *Club:* Oxford and Cambridge. *Died 26 Aug. 2014.*

DUTHIE, Prof. Sir Herbert Livingston, Kt 1987; MD; FRCS, FRCSEd; Provost of the University of Wales College of Medicine (formerly the Welsh National School of Medicine, University of Wales), 1979–94; *b* 9 Oct. 1929; *s* of Herbert William Duthie and Margaret McFarlane Livingston; *m* 1959, Maureen McCann; three *s* one *d*. *Educ:* Whitehill Sch., Glasgow; Univ. of Glasgow (MB, ChB 1952; MD Hons 1962; ChM Hons 1959). FRCSEd 1956; FRCS 1957. Served RAMC, 1954–56. Sen. House Officer, Registrar, and Lectr in Surgery, Western Infirmary, Glasgow, 1956–59; Rockefeller Travelling Fellow, Mayo Clinic, Rochester, Minn, USA, 1959–60; Lectr in Surg., Univ. of Glasgow, 1960–61; Sen. Lectr in Surg., Univ. of Leeds, 1961–63, Reader, 1964; Prof. of Surg., Univ. of Sheffield, 1964–79 (Dean, Faculty of Medicine, 1976–78). Mem., S Glam HA, 1980–94. Chm., Med. Adv. Cttee, CVCP, 1992–93. President: Surgical Res. Soc., 1978–80; Assoc. of Surgeons of GB and Ireland, 1989–90; Member: GMC, 1976–99 (Treas., 1981–94); Welsh Med. Cttee, 1980–94. Hon. LLD: Sheffield, 1990; Wales, 1995. *Publications:* articles on gastroenterological topics. *Address:* 1 The Malverns, Malvern Place, Cheltenham GL50 2JL. *T:* (01242) 583938. *Club:* Army and Navy. *Died 24 April 2015.*

DUXBURY, Philip Thomas; Chairman, Bradford and Bingley Building Society, 1988–91; *b* 4 Sept. 1928; *s* of Tom Duxbury and Ellen Duxbury (*née* Hargreaves); *m* 1952, Katherine Mary Hagley; three *s*. *Educ:* Bradford Grammar School. Magnet and Southerns plc, 1944–84 (Dir, 1963; Man. Dir, 1975); Dir, Bradford and Bingley Building Soc., 1980–91. *Recreations:* DIY, travel. *Address:* Highfield House, East Morton, Keighley BD20 5SE. *T:* (01274) 564894. *Died 28 Jan. 2011.*

DWORKIN, Paul David, FSS; an Assistant Director, Central Statistical Office, 1989–91; *b* 7 April 1937; *s* of Louis and Rose Dworkin; *m* 1959, Carole Barbara Burke; two *s*. *Educ:* Hackney Downs Grammar Sch., London; LSE (BScEcon 1958). FSS 1969. E Africa High Commn, Dar es Salaam, Tanganyika, 1959; E African Common Services Org., Nairobi, Kenya, 1961; Asst Statistician, BoT, 1962, Stat. 1965; Chief Statistician: DTI, 1972; Dept of Employment, 1977; Under Secretary: Depts of Trade and Industry, 1977–81; Central Statistical Office, 1982–83; Dir of Stats, Dept of Employment, 1983–89. *Club:* Civil Service. *Died 11 April 2014.*

DWORKIN, Prof. Ronald Myles, FBA 1979; Bentham Professor of Jurisprudence, University College London, 2004–08, then Emeritus (Quain Professor of Jurisprudence, 1998–2004); *b* 11 Dec. 1931; *s* of David Dworkin and Madeline Talamo; *m* 1st, 1958, Betsy Celia Ross (*d* 2000); one *s* one *d* (twins); 2nd, Irene Brendel. *Educ:* Harvard Coll.; Oxford Univ.; Harvard Law Sch. Legal Sec. to Judge Learned Hand, 1957–58; Associate, Sullivan & Cromwell, New York, 1958–62; Yale Law School: Associate Prof. of Law, 1962–65; Prof. of Law, 1965–68; Wesley N. Hohfeld Prof. of Jurisprudence, 1968–69; Prof. of Jurisprudence, Oxford Univ., 1969–98, then Emeritus; Fellow of UC, Oxford, 1969–98, then Emeritus. Vis. Prof. of Philosophy, Princeton Univ., 1974–75; Prof. of Law, 1975–, Sommer Prof. of Law and Philosophy, 1984–, NY Univ. Law Sch.; Prof.-at-Large, Cornell Univ., 1976–80; Vis. Prof. of Philosophy and Law, Harvard Univ., 1977, Vis. Prof. of Philosophy, 1979–82. Member: Council, Writers & Scholars Educnl Trust, 1982–; Programme Cttee, Ditchley Foundn, 1982–. Co-Chm., US Democratic Party Abroad, 1972–76. Fellow, Amer. Acad. of Arts and Scis, 1979. Hon. QC 1998; Hon. Fellow, UCL, 2004. Hon. Bencher, Middle Temple, 1999. *Publications:* Taking Rights Seriously, 1977; (ed) The Philosophy of Law, 1977; A Matter of Principle, 1985; Law's Empire, 1986; Philosophical Issues in Senile Dementia, 1987; A Bill of Rights for Britain, 1990; Life's Dominion, 1993; Freedom's Law, 1996; Sovereign Virtue, 2000; Justice in Robes, 2005; Is Democracy Possible Here?, 2006; Justice for Hedgehogs, 2011; several articles in legal and philosophical jls. *Address:* 17 Chester Row, SW1W 9JF. *Club:* Oxford American Democrats (Oxford). *Died 14 Feb. 2013.*

DYE, Maj.-Gen. Jack Bertie, CBE 1968 (OBE 1965); MC 1945; Vice Lord-Lieutenant of Suffolk, 1983–94; Director, Volunteers, Territorials and Cadets, 1971–74; Major-General late Royal Norfolk Regiment; *b* 13 Dec. 1919; *m* 1942, Jean Prall; two *d*. Served War of 1939–45 (MC). Brigadier, 1966; idc, psc. Commanded South Arabian Army, 1966–68; GOC Eastern District, 1969–71. Col Comdt, The Queen's Division, 1970–74; Col, Royal Anglian Regt, 1976–82 (Dep. Col, 1974–76). DL Suffolk, 1979. *Died 10 June 2013.*

DYER, His Honour Mark; a Circuit Judge, 1977–96; a Senior Circuit Judge, 1996–2001; *b* 20 Nov. 1928; *er s* of late Maj.-Gen. G. M. Dyer, CBE, DSO, and Evelyn Mary (*née* List); *m* 1953, Diana, *d* of Sir Percy Lancelot Orde, CIE; two *d*. *Educ:* Ampleforth Coll.; Christ Church, Oxford (MA). 2nd Lieut, Royal Scots Greys, 1948–49; The Westminster Dragoons (2nd CLY) TA, 1950–58, Captain.

Called to the Bar: Middle Temple, 1953; Inner Temple, 1972, Bencher, 1998; part-time Lectr in Law, Univ. of Southampton, 1957–67; Dep. Chm., Isle of Wight QS, 1971; a Recorder of the Crown Court, 1972–77; Liaison Judge for Wiltshire, 1981; Hon. Recorder: Devizes, 1988; Bristol, 1996–2001. Mem., Parole Bd, 1992–96, 2002–05. Member: Gen. Council of the Bar, 1965–69; Judicial Studies Bd, 1986–91. Pres., Council of HM Circuit Judges, 1992 (Hon. Sec., 1989–91). FRSA 1994. Hon. LLD UWE, 2001. *Recreation:* enjoying retirement. *Address:* The Court Service, 2nd Floor, Southside Offices, Law Courts, Winchester, Hants SO23 9DL. *Club:* Cavalry and Guards. *Died 19 April 2013.*

DYMOKE, Lt-Col John Lindley Marmion, MBE 1960; Vice Lord-Lieutenant of Lincolnshire, 1991–2001; 34th Hereditary Queen's Champion, 1946; *b* 1 Sept. 1926; *s* of late Lionel Marmion Dymoke and Rachel, *d* of Hon. Lennox Lindley; *m* 1953, Susan Cicely Fane; three *s*. *Educ:* Christ's Hosp. Commnd Royal Lincs Regt, 1946; Staff Coll., 1957; Armed Forces Staff Coll., USA, 1964; Coll. Chief Instructor, RMA Sandhurst, 1961–64; Comd 3rd Bn, Royal Anglian Regt, 1966–69; military service included: India, Sumatra, Malaya, Egypt, Jordan, Aden, France, Germany, USA and UK; retired 1972. Farmer and landowner, 1972–. Mem., E Lindsey DC, 1973–99. President: Lincs Br., CLA, 1995–2002 (Chm., 1982–85); Lincs Agricl Soc., 1995. Chm., Horncastle Grammar Sch., 1979–91. Master, Grocers' Co., 1977–78. DL 1976, High Sheriff 1979, Lincs. *Recreation:* care of Scrivelsby Estate. *Address:* Scrivelsby Court, near Horncastle, Lincolnshire LN9 6JA. *T:* (01507) 523325. *Died 21 March 2015.*

DYSART, Countess of (12th in line) *cr* 1643; **Katherine Grant of Rothiemurchus;** Lady Huntingtower, 1643; *b* 1 June 1918; *yr d* of Owain Greaves and Wenefryde Agatha Greaves (*née* Scott), Countess of Dysart (10th in line); *S* sister, 2003; *m* 1941, Colonel John Peter Grant of Rothiemurchus, MBE (*d* 1987); one *s* one *d*. *Educ:* Oxenfoord Castle, Ford, Midlothian. Wartime ambulance driver, 1939–41. WRVS; Red Cross Rep.; SSAFA Rep. *Heir: s* Lord Huntingtower, *b* 22 Oct. 1946. *Address:* Rothiemurchus, Aviemore PH22 1QH. *Clubs:* Royal Over-Seas League; Royal Overseas (Edinburgh). *Died 8 Nov. 2011.*

DYSON, John Alva, MVO 1995; HM Diplomatic Service, retired; Ambassador to Montenegro, 2006–07; *b* 15 April 1949; *s* of Louis and Myrtle Dyson; *m* 1971, Deirdre Anne George; two *s*. *Educ:* Devonport High Sch., Plymouth. Entered HM Diplomatic Service, 1966; served Port of Spain, Geneva, Yaoundé, Tehran, Nuku'alofa, Kathmandu, Jedda, Cape Town, Havana, and Damascus; Chargé d'Affaires, Asmara, 2001–02; Deputy High Commissioner: Suva, 2002–03; Bandar Seri Begawan, 2003; Dep. COS, CPA (S) Basra, 2003–04; FCO, 2004–06. *Recreations:* archery, diving, tennis. *Address:* 28 Harrogate Road, Caversham, Reading RG4 7PN. *T:* (0118) 946 4873. *E:* dysonfam@gmail.com. *Club:* Civil Service. *Died 14 Oct. 2011.*

E

EADIE, Alexander, BEM 1960; JP; *b* 23 June 1920; *m* 1st, 1941, Jemima Ritchie (*d* 1981); one *s*; 2nd, 1983, Janice Murdoch. *Educ:* Buckhaven Senior Secondary Sch. Coalminer from 1934. Chm., Fife County Housing Cttee, 9 yrs; Chm., Fife County Educn Cttee, 18 mths; Governor, Moray House Teachers' Training Coll., Edinburgh, 5 years; Exec. Committee: Scottish Council of Labour Party, 9 yrs; NUM Scottish Area, 2 yrs; Mem., Eastern Regional Hosp. Bd (Scotland), 14 yrs. Contested Ayr, 1959 and 1964; MP (Lab) Midlothian, 1966–92. Former PPS to Miss M. Herbison, MP, Minister of Social Security, and Mem. of Parly Select Cttee on Scottish Affairs; Opposition Front Bench Spokesman on Energy (incl. N Sea Oil), 1973–74; Parly Under-Sec. of State, Dept of Energy, 1974–79; Shadow Front Bench Spokesman on Energy, 1979–92. Chm., All Party Energy Studies Gp, 1991–92; Chm., Parly Labour Party Power and Steel Gp, 1972–74; Sec., Miners' Parly Gp, 1983–92; Vice-Chm., Parly Trade Union Group, 1972–74. JP Fife, 1951. *Recreations:* bowling, gardening. *Address:* Balkerack, The Haugh, East Wemyss, Fife KY1 4SB. *T:* (01592) 713636. *Died 25 Jan. 2012.*

EADIE, Helen Stirling; Member (Lab) Cowdenbeath, Scottish Parliament, since 2011 (Dunfermline East, 1999–2011); *b* Stenhousemuir, 7 March 1947; *d* of James Jack Miller and Elizabeth Reid Stirling Miller; *m* 1967, Robert William Eadie, *s* of late Alexander Eadie, BEM; two *d*. *Educ:* Larbert High Sch.; Falkirk Tech. Coll.; London Sch. of Econs and Pol Sci. Political researcher for Harry Ewing, MP and Alex Eadie, MP; Equal Opportunities and Political Officer, GMB. Mem. (Lab) Fife Regl Council, 1986–99 (Dep. Leader, 1992–96). Contested (Lab) Roxburgh and Berwickshire, 1997. Substitute Mem., Conf. of Local and Regl Authorities in Europe (Convenor, Cross Pty Gps on heart and stroke disease, on musculo-skeletal conditions, on industrial communities alliance; Mem., Cancer Cross Pty Gp). Former Vice-Pres., N Sea Commn. Past Bureau Mem., Conf. of Peripheral and Maritime Regions. *Address:* Scottish Parliament, Edinburgh EH99 1SP; (office) 25 Church Street, Inverkeithing, Fife KY11 1LG. *T:* (0131) 348 5749; 3 Hopeward Mews, Dalgety Bay, Fife KY11 9TB. *T:* (01383) 412856, *Fax:* (01383) 412855. *W:* www.heleneadie.com. *Died 9 Nov. 2013.*

EAGLES, Lt-Col (Charles Edward) James, LVO 1988; Member, HM Body Guard of the Honourable Corps of Gentlemen-at-Arms, 1967–88 (Harbinger, 1981–86; Standard Bearer, 1986–88); *b* 14 May 1918; *o s* of late Major C. E. C. Eagles, DSO, RMLI and Esmé Field; *m* 1941, Priscilla May Nicolette, *d* of late Brig. A. F. B. Cottrell, DSO, OBE; one *s* three *d*. *Educ:* Marlborough Coll. 2nd Lieut RM, 1936; served: HMS Sussex, Mediterranean and S Atlantic, 1938–40; Mobile Naval Base Def. Orgn, UK, ME, Ceylon and India, 1940–43; 1 HAA Regt RM, India, UK and NW Europe, 1943–45; Asst Mil. Sec., 1945; Amphibious Trng Wing, 1945–47; Staff of Maj.-Gen. RM, Portsmouth, 1947–50; HMS Devonshire, 1951–52; RN Staff Course, 1952; DS, Amphibious Warfare Sch., 1952–55; HMS Afrikander, SO (Intell.), S Atlantic, 1955–57; Dep. Dir, PRORM, 1957–59; CSO, Plymouth Gp, 1960; AAG, Staff of CGRM, 1960–62; Dir, PRORM, 1962–65; retd 1965; Civil Service, MoD, 1965–83. Pres., T. S. Churchill Sea Cadet Corps, 1988–99. *Recreation:* genealogy. *Address:* 2 The Old Brewery, Northleach, Glos GL54 3HB. *Died 26 Aug. 2013.*

EARDLEY-WILMOT, Sir Michael (John Assheton), 6th Bt *cr* 1821, of Berkswell Hall, Warwickshire; *b* 13 Jan. 1941; *o s* of Sir John Eardley-Wilmot, 5th Bt, LVO, DSC and Diana Elizabeth (*née* Moore); *S* father, 1995; *m* 1st, 1971, Wendy Wolstenholme (marr. diss. 1987); two *s* one *d*; 2nd, 1987, Diana Wallis; one *d*. *Educ:* Clifton. FRSA. *Recreations:* days in Barbados, nights in New York. *Heir: s* Benjamin John Eardley-Wilmot [*b* 24 Jan. 1974; *m* 2009, Clementine Daisy Langton; one *s*]. *Address:* c/o Coutts Bank, 440 Strand, WC2R 0QS. *Died 15 Nov. 2014.*

EARL, Christopher Joseph, MD; FRCP, FRCOphth; Hon. Consultant Physician to: Neurological Department, Middlesex Hospital, 1988 (Physician, 1971–88); National Hospital, Queen Square, 1988 (Physician, 1958–88); Moorfields Eye Hospital, 1988 (Physician, 1959–88); *b* 20 Nov. 1925; *s* of Christopher and Winifred Earl, Ashbourne, Derbyshire; *m* 1951, Alma Patience Hopkins, Reading; two *s* three *d*. *Educ:* Cotton Coll.; Guy's Hosp. (MB BS 1948). MRCP 1951, FRCP 1964; FRCOphth 1993. House phys. and house surg., Guy's Hosp., and MO, RAF, 1948–50. Lecturer in Chemical Pathology, Guy's Hosp., 1950–52; Research Fellow, Harvard Med. Sch., and Neurological Unit, Boston City Hosp., 1952–54; Resident MO, Nat. Hosp., Queen Square, 1954–56; Chief Asst, Neurological Dept, Guy's Hosp., 1956–58; Physician, Neurological Dept, London Hosp., 1961–71; Consultant Neurologist: King Edward VII Hosp. for Officers, 1966–95; Hosp. of St John and St Elizabeth, 1967–96. Civil Consultant in Neurol., RAF, 1976–88; Consultant Advr in Neurology to CMO, DoH, 1983–88. Director: Medical Sickness Annuity & Life Assce Soc. Ltd, 1981–95 (Chm., 1993–95); Permanent Insurance Co., 1985–95. Hon. Dir of Photography, Royal Society of Medicine, 1967–73. Hon. Sec., 1968–74, Pres., 1989–90, Assoc. British Neurologists; Mem. Council, 1967–91, Vice Chm. Bd of Management, 1993–96, Med. Defence Union; Censor, 1983–85, Chm., Cttee on Neurology, 1975–85, RCP. Corresp. Mem., Amer. Neurological Assoc., 1978. *Publications:* (ed jtly) Medical Negligence: the cranium, spine and nervous system, 1999; papers in learned jls on biochemistry and neurology. *Recreation:* reading history. *Address:* 23 Audley Road, Ealing, W5 3ES. *T:* (020) 8997 0380. *Club:* Garrick. *Died 4 March 2012.*

EARLE, John Nicholas Francis, (Nick); Headmaster, Bromsgrove School, 1971–85; *b* 14 Nov. 1926; *s* of John William Arthur Earle and Vivien Constance Fenton (*née* Davies); *m* 1959, Ann Veronica Lester; one *s* two *d*. *Educ:* Winchester Coll.; Trinity Coll., Cambridge. 1st cl. Maths Tripos pt 2, 1st cl. Theol Tripos pt 1; MA. Ordained deacon, 1952, priest, 1953; relinquished Holy Orders, 1994. Curate, St Matthew, Moorfields, 1952–57; PARS Fellow, Union Theol Seminary, New York, 1957–58; Lectr, St Botolph, Aldgate, 1958–61; Asst Master, Dulwich Coll., 1961–71. *Publications:* What's Wrong With the Church?, 1961; Culture and Creed, 1967; Logic, 1973; Does God Make Sense?, 1998. *Recreation:* reading. *Address:* 1 Red Post Hill, Pond Mead, SE21 7BX. *Died 3 Jan. 2014.*

EAST, Kenneth Arthur, CMG 1971; HM Diplomatic Service, retired; Ambassador to Iceland, 1975–81; *b* 9 May 1921; *s* of H. F. East; *m* 1946, Katherine Blackley; two *s* three *d*. *Educ:* Taunton's Sch.; Southampton Univ. Served HM Forces, 1942–46. India Office/ Commonwealth Relations Office, 1946–50; Asst Private Sec. to Sec. of State; First Secretary: Ottawa, 1950–53; Colombo, 1956–60; Head of East and General Africa Dept, CRO, 1961–63; Head of Personnel Dept, CRO, 1963–64; Counsellor, Diplomatic Service Administration, 1965; Counsellor and Head of Chancery, Oslo, 1965–70; Minister, Lagos, 1970–74. *Club:* Hants CC. *Died 20 June 2014.*

EASTWOOD, Dr Wilfred, PhD; FREng, FICE, FIStructE, FIMechE; Senior Partner, Eastwood and Partners, Consulting Engineers, 1972–2000; *b* 15 Aug. 1923; *s* of Wilfred Andrew Eastwood and Annice Gertrude Eastwood; *m* 1947, Dorothy Jean Gover; one *s* one *d*. *Educ:* PhD Aberdeen 1949. Road Research Laboratory, 1945–46; University of Manchester, 1946–47; University of Aberdeen, 1947–53; University of Sheffield, 1954–70: Head, Dept of Civil Engrg, 1964–70; Dean, Faculty of Engrg, 1967–70. Pres., IStructE, 1976–77; Chairman: CEI, 1983–84; Commonwealth Engrg Council, 1981–85. Hon. DEng Sheffield, 1980. Médaille de la Ville de Paris, 1983.

Publications: papers in Proc. ICE and Jl IStructE, etc. *Address:* 45 Whirlow Park Road, Sheffield S11 9NN. *T:* (0114) 236 4645. *Died 2 Sept. 2014.*

EATES, Edward Caston, CMG 1968; LVO 1961; QPM 1961; CPM 1956; Commissioner, The Royal Hong Kong Police, 1967–69, retired; re-employed at Foreign and Commonwealth Office, 1971–76; *b* London, 8 April 1916; *o s* of late Edward Eates and Elizabeth Lavinia Issac Eates (*née* Caston); *m* 1941, Maureen Teresa McGee (*d* 1987); no *c. Educ:* Highgate Sch.; King's Coll., London (LLB). Asst Examr, Estate Duty Office, 1935. Army, 1939–46 (RAC): Western Desert and NW Europe; Adjt 2nd Derby Yeo., 1943; Temp. Maj. 1944; Staff Coll. Quetta (sc), 1945. Apptd to Colonial Police Service, Nigeria, 1946; Sen. Supt, Sierra Leone, 1954; Comr, The Gambia, 1957; Asst Comr, 1963, Dep. Comr, 1966, Hong Kong. *Recreations:* cricket and association football, travel, motoring. *Address:* 2 Riverside Court, Colleton Crescent, Exeter EX2 4BZ. *T:* (01392) 436434. *Clubs:* Royal Commonwealth Society, East India; Surrey County Cricket. *Died 29 March 2012.*

EBERT, Peter; producer; *b* 6 April 1918; *s* of Carl Ebert, CBE, and Lucie Oppenheim; *m* 1st, 1944, Kathleen Havinden; two *d*; 2nd, 1951, Silvia Ashmole; five *s* three *d. Educ:* Salem Sch., Germany; Gordonstoun, Scotland. BBC Producer, 1948–51; 1st opera production, Mefistofele, Glasgow, 1951; Mozart and Rossini guest productions: Rome, Naples, Venice, 1951, 1952, 1954, 1955: Wexford Festival: 12 prods, 1952–65; 1st Glyndebourne Fest. prod., Ariecchino, 1954, followed by Seraglio, Don Giovanni, etc.; 1st Edinburgh Fest. prod., Forza del Destino, 1955; Chief producer: Hannover State Opera, 1954–60; Düsseldorf Opera, 1960–62; directed opera class, Hannover State Conservatory, 1954–60; Head of Opera studio, Düsseldorf, 1960–62. Guest productions in Europe, USA, Canada. TV productions of Glyndebourne operas, 1955–64; 1st TV studio prod., 1963; Opera Adviser to BBC TV, 1964–65; Dir of Productions, 1965–77, Gen. Administrator, 1977–80, Scottish Opera Co. First drama prod., The Devils, Johannesburg, 1966; first musical, Houdini, London, 1966. Dir, Opera Sch., University of Toronto, 1967–68; Intendant: Stadttheater, Augsburg, 1968–73; Stadttheater Bielefeld, 1973–75; Staatstheater Wiesbaden, 1975–77. Hon. DMus St Andrews, 1979. *Publications:* In This Theatre of Man's Life: a biography of Carl Ebert, 1999. *Recreation:* family. *Address:* 12 Greater Paddock, Ringmer, East Sussex BN8 5LH. *Died 31 Dec. 2012.*

EBERTS, John David, (Jake), OC 1992; Founder, and Chief Executive, since 1985, Allied Productions (formerly Allied Filmmakers); *b* 10 July 1941; *s* of Edmond Howard Eberts and Elizabeth Evelyn MacDougall; *m* 1968, Fiona Louise Leckie; two *s* one *d. Educ:* McGill Univ. (BChemEng 1962); Harvard Univ. (MBA 1966). Project Engr, L'Air Liquide, Paris, 1962–64; Marketing Manager, Cummins Engine Co., Brussels, 1966–68; Vice Pres., Laird Inc., NY, 1968–71; Man. Dir, Oppenheimer and Co. Ltd, London, 1971–76; Founder, 1976, and Chief Exec., 1976–83 and 1985–86, Goldcrest Films and Television Ltd; Pres., Embassy Communications International, 1984–85. Dir, Sundance Inst., 1993, then Emeritus; Chm., National Geographic Films, 2002–. Involved in prodn of many BAFTA and Amer. Acad. award-winning films, including: Chariots of Fire; Gandhi; The Dresser; The Killing Fields; The Name of the Rose; Hope and Glory; Driving Miss Daisy; Dances with Wolves; A River Runs Through It; James and the Giant Peach; Chicken Run; The Legend of Bagger Vance; Open Range; March of the Penguins; Oceans; The Illusionist. Film Producers' Award of Merit, 1986; Evening Standard Special Award, 1987. Hon. DLitt McGill, 1998; Hon. DCL Bishop's Univ., 1999; Hon. LLD Trent, 2005. *Publications:* (with Terry Ilott) My Indecision is Final, 1990. *Recreations:* golf, tennis, ski-ing, photography. *Clubs:* Memphremagog; Mt Bruno. *Died 6 Sept. 2012.*

EBSWORTH, Prof. Evelyn Algernon Valentine, CBE 1996; PhD, ScD; FRSC, FRSE; Chairman, Council for the Registration of Forensic Practitioners, 1998–2005; *b* 14 Feb. 1933; *s* of Brig. Wilfred Algernon Ebsworth, CB, CBE and late Cynthia (*née* Blech); *m* 1st, 1955, Mary Salter (*d* 1987); one *s* three *d*; 2nd, 1990, Rose Zuckerman. *Educ:* King's Coll., Cambridge (BA 1st Cl., 1954; PhD 1957; MA 1958; ScD 1967). FRSE 1969. Fellow, King's Coll., Cambridge, 1957–59; Res. Associate, Princeton Univ., 1958–59; Cambridge University: Demonstrator, 1959–63; Lectr, 1963–67; Fellow, 1959–67, Tutor, 1963–67, Christ's Coll.; Crum Brown Prof. of Chemistry, Edinburgh, 1967–90; Vice-Chancellor, Durham Univ., 1990–98. Chairman of Governors: The Leys Sch., Cambridge, 2002–10; St Faith's Sch., Cambridge, 2002–10. Corresp. Mem., Acad. of Scis, Göttingen. Hon. DCL Durham, 2002; Hon. DSc Edinburgh, 2013. *Publications:* Volatile Silicon Compounds, 1963; (with S. Cradock and D. W. H. Rankin) Structural Methods in Inorganic Chemistry, 1988; papers in learned jls. *Recreations:* opera, gardening. *Address:* 16 Conduit Head Road, Cambridge CB3 0EY. *Died 16 July 2015.*

ECCLES-WILLIAMS, Hilary a'Beckett, CBE 1970; *b* 5 Oct. 1917; *s* of late Rev. Cyril Eccles-Williams and Hermione (*née* Terrell); *m* 1941, Jeanne, *d* of W. J. Goodwin; two *s* four *d. Educ:* Eton; Brasenose Coll., Oxford (MA). Served War of 1939–45, Major RA (anti-tank), Dunkirk and Normandy (wounded). Consul: for Nicaragua, 1951–59; for Cuba, 1952–60; for Costa Rica, 1964–93; for Bolivia, 1965–82. Chairman of companies; Chm., 1978–82, non-exec. Dir, 1982–87, Rabone Petersen; travelled 900,000 miles on export business. Chairman: Brit. Export Houses Assoc., 1958–59; Guardians of Birmingham Assay Office, 1979–88 (Guardian, 1970–); President: Birmingham Chamber of Commerce, 1965–66; Assoc. of Brit. Ch. of Commerce (93 Chambers), 1970–72. Comr of Income Tax, 1966–70. Chairman: Birmingham Cons. Assoc., 1976–79 (Pres., 1979–84); W Midlands Metropolitan Co. Co-ordinating Cttee, Cons. Party, 1980–86; European Parlt constituency of Birmingham S Cons. Assoc., 1978–82 (Pres., 1982–84); Latin Amer. Gp, Cons. Foreign and Overseas Council, 1986–89; President: Eur. Parlt constituency of Birmingham E Cons. Assoc., 1984–95; Sparkbrook Constituency Cons. Assoc., 1988–92; Anglo-Asian Cons. Soc., 1984–87; Cons. Party One Nation Forum, 1990–; Mem., National Union Exec. Cttee, Cons. Party, 1975–85. Mem., Brit. Hallmarking Council, 1976–88; Pres., Birmingham Consular Assoc., 1973–74; Chairman: Asian Christian Colls Assoc., 1960–66; Brit. Heart Foundn, Midland Counties, 1973–74; Golden Jubilee Appeal Cttee, Queen Elizabeth Hosp., Birmingham, 1987–90; W Midlands Macmillan Nurse Appeal, 1991–94; Mem., Nat. Council, Cancer Relief Macmillan Fund, 1992–94. Life Governor, Birmingham Univ., 1966; Trustee, Birmingham Centre for Drama, 1994–97. Liveryman, Worshipful Co. of Glaziers, 1974; Freeman, Goldsmiths' Co., 1988. Hon. Captain, Bolivian Navy, 1969. Numerous TV appearances. *Recreations:* walking, golf. *Address:* 49 Second Avenue, Frinton-on-Sea, Essex CO13 9LY. *Clubs:* Frinton Golf; Frinton Lawn Tennis. *Died 29 Dec. 2013.*

EDDERY, Patrick James John, Hon. OBE 2005; trainer; founder, Pat Eddery Racing, 2003; *b* 18 March 1952; *s* of Jimmy and Josephine Eddery; *m* (marr. diss.); one *s* two *d.* Rode for Peter Walwyn, 1972–80; Champion Jockey, 1974, 1975, 1976, 1977, 1986, 1988, 1989, 1990, 1991, 1993, 1996; Champion Jockey in Ireland, 1982; retired as jockey, 2003. Winner: Oaks, on Polygamy, 1974, on Scintillate, 1979, on Lady Carla, 1996; Derby, on Grundy, 1975, on Golden Fleece, 1982, on Quest for Fame, 1990; Prix de l'Arc de Triomphe, on Detroit, 1980, on Rainbow Quest, 1985, on Dancing Brave, 1986, on Trempolino, 1987; St Leger, on Moon Madness, 1986, on Toulon, 1991, on Moonax, 1994, on Silver Patriarch, 1997 (his 4,000th win in GB). *Recreations:* watching tennis, snooker. *Address:* Musk Hill Farm, Nether Winchendon, Aylesbury, Bucks HP18 0EB. *T:* (01844) 296153, *Fax:* (01844) 290282. *Died 10 Nov. 2015.*

EDELMAN, Prof. Gerald Maurice, MD, PhD; Director, Neurosciences Institute, La Jolla, since 1981; Chairman, Department of Neurobiology, Scripps Research Institute, 1992–2013; *b* NYC, 1 July 1929; *s* of Edward Edelman and Anna Freedman; *m* 1950, Maxine Morrison; two *s* one *d. Educ:* Ursinus Coll. (BS); University of Pennsylvania (MD); The Rockefeller University (PhD). Med. Hse Officer, Massachusetts Gen. Hosp., 1954–55; Asst Physician, Hosp.

of The Rockefeller Univ., 1957–60; The Rockefeller University, NY: Asst Prof. and Asst Dean of Grad. Studies, 1960–63; Associate Prof. and Associate Dean of Grad. Studies, 1963–66; Prof., 1966–74; Vincent Astor Distinguished Prof. of Biochem., 1974–92. Trustee, Rockefeller Brothers Fund, 1972–82; Associate, Neurosciences Res. Program, 1965– (Scientific Chm., 1980–). Mem., Adv. Bd, Basel Inst. Immunology, 1970–77 (Chm., 1975–77); Member Emeritus, Weizmann Inst. of Science, 1987 (Mem., Bd of Governors, 1971–87); non-resident Fellow and Mem. Bd Trustees, Salk Inst. for Biol. Studies, 1973–85; Member: Biophysics and Biophys. Chem. Study Section, Nat. Insts of Health, 1964–67; Sci. Council, Center for Theoretical Studies, 1970–72; Bd of Overseers, Faculty Arts and Scis, Univ. of Pa, 1976–83; Board of Trustees, Carnegie Inst. of Washington (Mem., Adv. Cttee). Member: Nat. Acad. Scis; Amer. Acad. Arts Scis; Amer. Philosophical Soc.; Fellow: AAAS; NY Acad. Scis; NY Acad. of Medicine; Member: Amer. Soc. Biol Chemists; Amer. Assoc. Immunologists; Genetics Soc. of America; Harvey Soc. (Pres., 1975–76); Amer. Chem. Soc.; Amer. Soc. Cell Biol.; Soc. for Developmental Biol.; Sigma XI; Alpha Omega Alpha; Council of Foreign Relations. Hon. Member: Pharmaceutical Soc. of Japan; Japanese Biochem. Soc.; Foreign Mem., Académie des Sciences, Institut de France. Hon. DSc: Pennsylvania, 1973; Gustavus Adolphus Coll., Minn., 1975; Paris, Cagliari, Georgetown Univ. Sch. of Med., 1989; Univ. degli Studi di Napoli Federico II, 1990; Tulane, 1991; Adelphi, NY, 1995; Miami, 1995; Hon. ScD: Ursinus Coll., 1974; Williams Coll., 1976; Hon. MD Univ. Siena, 1974; Hon. Dr Bologna, 1998. Spencer Morris Award, Univ. of Pennsylvania, 1954; Eli Lilly Award in Biol Chem., Amer. Chem. Soc., 1965; Annual Alumni Award, Ursinus College, 1969; (jtly) Nobel Prize in Physiology or Medicine, 1972; Albert Einstein Commemorative Award, Yeshiva Univ., 1974; Buchman Meml Award, Caltech, 1975; Rabbi Shai Shacknai Meml Prize in Immunology and Cancer Res., Hebrew Univ. Hadassah Med. Sch., 1977; Regents Medal of Excellence, New York State, 1984; Hans Neurath prize, Washington Univ., 1986; Sesquicentennial Commem. Award, Nat. Liby of Medicine, 1986; Cécile and Oskar Vogt award, Dusseldorf Univ., 1988; Dist. Grad. Award, Pennsylvania Univ., 1990; Personnalité de l'année, Paris, 1990; Warren Triennial Prize, Massachusetts Gen. Hosp., Boston, 1992; Jiménez Diaz Meml Prize, Fundación Conchita Rábago de Jiménez Diaz, Madrid, 1999; C. U. Ariëns-Kappers Medal, Netherlands Inst. for Brain Res., 1999; Medal of Presidency of Italian Republic, 1999; Médaille de la Ville de Paris, 2002; Santiago Grisolía Chair Prize, Cátedra Santiago Grisolía, Valencia, 2003; Caianiello Meml Internat. Award, INNS and Calabria Award, Calabria, 2003; Navigator Lifetime Achievement Award, Potomac Inst. Policy Studies, Washington, 2010. *Publications:* Neural Darwinism, 1987; Topobiology, 1988; The Remembered Present, 1989; Bright Air, Brilliant Fire, 1992; (with Giulio Tononi) Consciousness: how matter becomes imagination, 2000; Wider Than the Sky: the phenomenal gift of consciousness, 2004; Second Nature: brain science and human knowledge, 2006. *Address:* Neurosciences Institute, 10640 John Jay Hopkins Drive, San Diego, CA 92121, USA. *Died 17 May 2014.*

EDMONDS, John Christopher, CMG 1978; CVO 1971; HM Diplomatic Service, retired; *b* 23 June 1921; *s* of late Captain A. C. M. Edmonds, OBE, RN, and Mrs Edmonds; *m* 1st, 1948, Elena Tornow (marr. diss., 1965); two *s*; 2nd, 1966, Armine Williams (*d* 2005). *Educ:* Kelly College. Entered Royal Navy, 1939; psc, 1946. Staff: of NATO Defence Coll., Paris, 1953–55; of C-in-C Home Fleet, 1956–57 (Comdr, 1957); of Chief of Defence Staff, 1958–59. Entered Diplomatic Service, 1959; Foreign Office, 1959–60; 1st Secretary (Commercial), Tokyo, 1960–62; FO, 1963–67; 1st Secretary and Head of Chancery, Ankara, 1967–68; Counsellor: Ankara, 1968–71; Paris, 1972–74; Head of Arms Control and Disarmament Dept, FCO, 1974–77; Leader, UK Delegn to Comprehensive Test Ban Treaty Negotiations, Geneva, with personal rank of Ambassador, 1978–81. Chm., Jt SDP-Liberal Alliance Commn on Defence and Disarmament, 1984–86. Vis. Fellow in Internat. Relations, Reading Univ., 1981–2000. Chm., Sonning Parish Council, 1984–90. Pres., Sonning & Sonning Eye Soc., 2007–. *Address:* North Lodge, Sonning, Berks RG4 6ST. *Died 17 Aug. 2015.*

EDWARDS, Barrie; *see* Edwards, Gwilym B.

EDWARDS, David; Director, John Laing plc, 1982–99; Chairman, Londondome Ltd, 1988–93; *b* 27 Oct. 1929; *s* of Col Cyril Edwards, DSO, MC, DL and Jessie Edwards; *m* 1966, Gay Clothier; two *s* one *d.* *Educ:* Felsted Sch.; Trinity Hall, Cambridge (MA, LLM). Called to the Bar, Middle Temple, 1952; Harmsworth Scholar, Middle Temple, 1955; admitted Solicitor, 1958. Partner, E. Edwards Son & Noice, 1959–75; Sec., Legal Aid, 1976–86, and Dep. Sec.-Gen., 1982–86, Law Soc. Dir, Laing Properties, 1988–90. Chm., Offshore Racing Council, 1970–78; Dep. Chm., Royal Yachting Assoc., 1976–81. *Recreations:* sailing, forestry, conservation. *Address:* Olivers, Colchester, Essex CO2 0HJ. *Clubs:* Royal Ocean Racing; Royal Yacht Squadron (Cowes). *Died 8 June 2012.*

EDWARDS, Very Rev. Erwyd; *see* Edwards, Very Rev. T. E. P.

EDWARDS, Griffith; *see* Edwards, J. G.

EDWARDS, Prof. (Gwilym) Barrie, CBE 2004; FRCVS; DVetMed; Professor of Equine Studies, 1987–2005, then Emeritus, and Head, Department of Veterinary Clinical Sciences, 2000–06, University of Liverpool; *b* 20 May 1938; *s* of William Idris and Glenys Edwards; *m* 1967, Nina Susan Kemble; one *s* one *d.* *Educ:* Grove Park Grammar Sch., Wrexham; Univ. of Liverpool (BVSc 1961); RVC, London Univ. (DVetMed 1991). FRCVS 1993. Lectr, Large Animal Surgery, Univ. of Liverpool, 1961–70; Sen. Lectr, RVC, London Univ., 1970–87. *Publications:* (jtly) An Atlas of Veterinary Surgery, 3rd edn 1995; (jtly) Handbook of Equine Colic, 1999; numerous contribs to textbooks and more than 120 articles in scientific jls. *Recreations:* classical music, photographing and drawing African wildlife, watching sport, playing golf. *Address:* The Hollies, 17 Tower Road North, Heswall, Wirral CH60 6RS. *T:* (0151) 342 4683. *E:* g.b.edwards@liv.ac.uk. *Club:* Caldy Golf. *Died 16 May 2011.*

EDWARDS, Prof. (James) Griffith, CBE 1989; DM, DSc; FRCP, FRCPsych, FMedSci; Professor of Addiction Behaviour, Institute of Psychiatry, University of London, 1979–94, Professor Emeritus since 1994; Hon. Director, Addiction Research Unit, 1970–94 (Principal Investigator, 1967–70); Hon. Consultant, Bethlem and Maudsley Hospitals, since 1967; *b* 3 Oct. 1928; *yr s* of late Dr J. T. Edwards and Constance Amy (*née* McFadyean); *m* 1st, 1969, Evelyn Morrison (marr. diss. 1981); one *s* one *d* (and one *d* decd); 2nd, 1981, Frances Susan Stables. *Educ:* Andover Grammar Sch.; Balliol Coll., Oxford (BA Physiology 1952; MA; Theodore Williams Schol. in Anatomy); St Bartholomew's Hosp. (Kirkes Schol. and Gold Medal); DM Oxford, 1966; DPM London, 1962; DSc London, 1990; FRCP 1976; FRCPsych 1976 (Hon. FRCPsych 1998). Served RA, 1948–49 (2nd Lieut). Jun. hosp. appts, King George, Ilford, St Bartholomew's, Hammersmith and Maudsley Hosps, 1956–62; Inst. of Psychiatry: res. worker, 1962; Lectr, 1966; Sen. Lectr, 1967; Reader, 1973. Chm., RC Psych. Special Cttee on Drug Dependence, 1983–87 (on Alcohol and Alcoholism, 1975–78); Member: Home Office Working Party on Drunkenness Offenders, 1967–70; WHO Expert Adv. Cttee on Drug Dependence, 1969–2002; DoE Cttee on Drinking and Driving, 1974–75; Home Office Adv. Council on Misuse of Drugs, 1972–2000; DHSS Adv. Cttee on Alcoholism, 1975–78; ESRC (formerly SSRC), 1981–89; S African Adv. Cttee on Drug Abuse, 1995; Cabinet Office Adv. Gp on Alcohol Policy, 2002–03; Expert Advr, H of C Public Health Cttee, 2005. Consultant Advr on Alcoholism, DHSS, subseq. DoH, 1986–94; ODA Consultant in Bolivia, 1987. Chm., Nat. Addiction Centre, 1991–94; Med. Advr, Phoenix House, 1990–94; Patron, Clouds House, 1996. Jt contrib. report, Calling Time, Acad. Med. Scis, 2004. Editor, 1978–96, Editor-in-Chief, 1996–2004, Editl Advr, 2005–, Addiction (formerly British Jl of Addiction); Editor-in-Chief, Internat. Research Monographs on the Addictions, 1995–. Roche Vis. Prof., Aust. and NZ, 1982; Hon. Prof., Univ.

of Chile, 1992–; Vis. Prof., Amer. Coll. of Neuropsychopharmacology, 1993. Steven's Lectr and Gold Medallist, RSM, 1971; Lectures: Dent, KCL, 1980; Pollak, 1988, Okey, 1995, Inst. of Psychiatry; Maudsley, RCPsych, 2001. FMedSci 1999; Dist. Fellow, Soc. for Study of Addiction, 2004. Jellinek Meml Award, 1980; Evian Award, 1986; Prize, Assoc. for Med. Educn and Res. on Substance Abuse, USA, 1990; Nathan B. Eddy Gold Medal, Coll. on Problems of Drug Dependence, USA, 1996; Auguste Forel Prize, Internat. Order of Good Templars, 1998; Biennial Award, European Fedn of Therapeutic Communities, 2011. *Publications:* Unreason in an Age of Reason, 1971; (jtly) Alcohol Control Policies, 1975; (ed jtly) Drugs in Socio-Cultural Perspective, 1980; (jtly) Opium and the People, 1981; Treatment of Drinking Problems, 1982 (trans. into 6 langs), 4th edn 2003; (ed) Drug Scenes, 1987; (ed jtly) Nature of Dependence, 1990; (ed) Personal Influences and Scientific Movements, 1991; (ed) Nature of Alcohol and Drug Problems, 1992; (ed jtly) Drugs, Alcohol and Tobacco: strengthening the science and policy connections, 1993; (ed jtly) Addiction: processes of change, 1994; (ed jtly) Alcohol and Alcohol Problems, 1994; (jtly) Alcohol Policy and the Public Good, 1994 (trans. 8 langs); (jtly) Alcohol and Public Policy, Evidence and Issues, 1995; (jtly) Psychotherapy, Psychological Treatments and the Addictions, 1996; Alcohol: the ambiguous molecule, 2000 (US edn as Alcohol: the world's favorite drug, 2002); (ed) Addiction: evolution of a specialist field, 2002; (jtly) Alcohol: no ordinary commodity, 2003; Matters of Substance, 2004; (ed jtly) Drug Policy and the Public Good, 2010; (jtly) Physician to the Fleet: the life and times of Thomas Trotter, 1760–1832, 2011; (ed jtly) Addiction and the making of International Careers, 2012; The Heroin Trial (novel), 2012; articles in jls on scientific, historical and policy aspects of alcohol and drug dependence. *Recreations:* frequenting junk shops, putting the drink down, smoking the devils out. *Address:* 32 Crooms Hill, SE10 8ER. *T:* (020) 8858 5631. *E:* (home) grifsu@crooms.freeserve.co.uk, (office) gill@addictionjournal.org. *Club:* Athenæum. *Died 13 Sept. 2012.*

EDWARDS, James Valentine, CVO 1978; MA; *b* 4 Feb. 1925; *s* of late Captain Alfred Harold Edwards, OBE, and Mrs Eleanor Edwards; *m* 1965, Barbara (*d* 2010), Princess Cantacuzene, Countess Speransky, *d* of late Sir John Hanbury-Williams, CVO, and Lady Hanbury-Williams; two *d*, and one step *s* one step *d*. *Educ:* St Edmund's, Hindhead; Radley; Magdalen Coll., Oxford (MA). Served RN, 1943–47. Oxford, 1943 and 1947–49. *Address:* Wyndhams, Camel Street, Marston Magna, Yeovil, Somerset BA22 8DB. *T:* (01935) 851538. *Clubs:* MCC, Free Foresters; Vincent's (Oxford). *Died 28 May 2012.*

EDWARDS, Rear Adm. (John) Phillip, CB 1984; LVO 1972; CEng, FIMechE 1982; Fellow, Wadham College, Oxford, 1984–94, then Emeritus (Domestic Bursar, 1984–94; Development Director, 1994–99); *b* 13 Feb. 1927; *s* of Robert Edwards and Dilys (*née* Phillips); *m* 1951, Gwen Lloyd Bonner; two *d* (and one *d* decd). *Educ:* Brynhyfryd Sch., Ruthin, Clwyd; HMS Conway; Royal Naval Engrg Colls, Keyham and Manadon (King's Sword, 1947). MA 1984. Served, 1944–72: HMS King George V, Vengeance, Mauritius, Caledonia, Torquay, Lion, Diamond, Defender, HMCS Stadacona, and HMY Britannia; Mechanical Trng Estab., Portsmouth; Personnel Panel; Staff of C-in-C Fleet; SOWC; Dep. Dir, RN Staff Coll., 1972–74; Asst Dir, Dir Gen. Ships, 1974–76; RCDS, 1977; Captain of Portland Naval Base, 1978–80; Dir Gen., Fleet Support Policy and Services, 1980–83; ADC to the Queen, 1980. Comdr 1964, Captain 1971, Rear Adm. 1980. Mem. (non-exec.), Welsh Office Health Policy Bd, 1985–90. President: Oxford Sea Cadets, 1984–; Oxford Royal Naval Assoc., 1984–90; Oxford Royal Naval and Royal Marine Assoc., 1994–; Midland Naval Officers Assoc., 1985–95 (Vice-Pres., 1995–); Vice-Pres., Oxfordshire SSAFA, 1984–. Vice-Pres., Oxford Preservation Trust, 2006– (Trustee, 1994–2006). Freeman, City of London, 1984; Liveryman, Co. of Engineers, 1984. FCMI (FBIM 1980). Hon. FISTC 1976. *Recreation:* golf. *Address:* Wadham College, Oxford OX1 3PN. *Club:* Frilford Heath Golf. *Died 12 Dec. 2014.*

EDWARDS, Prof. Philip Walter, PhD; FBA 1986; King Alfred Professor of English Literature, University of Liverpool, 1974–90, then Emeritus; *b* 7 Feb. 1923; *er s* of late R. H. Edwards, MC, and late Mrs B. Edwards; *m* 1st, 1947, Hazel Margaret (*d* 1950), *d* of late Prof. C. W. and late Mrs E. R. Valentine; 2nd, 1952, Sheila Mary, *d* of late R. S. and late Mrs A. M. Wilkes, Bloxwich, Staffs; three *s* one *d*. *Educ:* King Edward's High Sch., Birmingham; Univ. of Birmingham. MA, PhD Birmingham; MA Dublin. Royal Navy, 1942–45 (Sub-Lieut RNVR). Lectr in English, Univ. of Birmingham, 1946–60; Commonwealth Fund Fellow, Harvard Univ., 1954–55; Prof. of English Lit., TCD, 1960–66; Fellow of TCD, 1962–66; Prof. of Lit., Univ. of Essex, 1966–74; Pro-Vice-Chancellor, Liverpool Univ., 1980–83. Visiting Professor: Univ. of Michigan, 1964–65; Williams Coll., Mass, 1969; Otago Univ., NZ, 1980; Internat. Christian Univ., Tokyo, 1989; Visiting Fellow: All Souls Coll., Oxford, 1970–71; Huntington Liby, Calif., 1977, 1983. *Publications:* Sir Walter Ralegh, 1953; (ed) Kyd, The Spanish Tragedy, 1959; Shakespeare and the Confines of Art, 1968; (ed) Pericles Prince of Tyre, 1976; (ed with C. Gibson) Massinger, Plays and Poems, 1976; Threshold of a Nation, 1979; (ed jtly) Shakespeare's Styles, 1980; (ed) Hamlet Prince of Denmark, 1985; Shakespeare: a writer's progress, 1986; Last Voyages, 1988; The Story of the Voyage, 1994; Sea-Mark, 1997; Pilgrimage and Literary Tradition, 2005; numerous articles on Shakespeare and literature of his time in Shakespeare Survey, Proc. British Acad., etc. *Recreations:* gardening, calligraphy. *Address:* High Gillinggrove, Gillinggate, Kendal, Cumbria LA9 4JB. *Died 27 Nov. 2015.*

EDWARDS, Rear Adm. Phillip; *see* Edwards, Rear Adm. J. P.

EDWARDS, Sir Robert (Geoffrey), Kt 2011; CBE 1988; FRS 1984; Professor of Human Reproduction, Cambridge University, 1985–89, then Emeritus; Extraordinary Fellow, Churchill College, Cambridge; *b* 27 Sept. 1925; *s* of Samuel and Margaret Edwards; *m* 1956, Ruth Eileen Fowler; five *d*. *Educ:* Manchester Central High Sch.; Univs of Wales and Edinburgh. PhD (Edin) 1955; DSc (Wales) 1962; MA (Cantab). Service in British Army, 1944–48; commnd 1946. UC North Wales, Bangor, 1948–51; Univ. of Edinburgh, 1951–57; Res. Fellow at California Inst. of Tech., 1957–58; Scientist at Nat. Inst. of Medical Research, Mill Hill, NW7, 1958–62; Glasgow Univ. 1962–63; in Dept of Physiology, Cambridge Univ., 1963–89; Ford Foundation Reader in Physiology, 1969–85. Scientific Dir, Bourn Hallam Clinics, Cambridgeshire and London, 1988–91. Founder Chm., European Soc. of Human Reproduction and Embryology, 1984–86. Visiting Scientist: in Johns Hopkins Hosp., Baltimore, 1965; Univ. of N Carolina, 1966; Visiting Professor: Free Univ., Brussels, 1984; Univ. of Hong Kong, 1998. Hon. Pres., British Fertility Soc., 1988–; Patron, UK Nat. Gamete Donation Trust, 1999. Hon. FRCOG 1985; Hon. MRCP 1986; Hon. FIBiol 2007. Hon. Member: Assoc. of UK Clinical Embryologists, 1998; French Soc. for Infertility, 1983; Greek Fertility Soc., 1998; Middle East Fertility Soc., 1999. Life Fellow, Australian Fertility Soc., 1985; Hon. Fellow, Internat. Fedn of Fertility Socs, 1998. Hon. Citizen of Bordeaux, 1985. Hon. DSc: Hull, 1983; York; Dr *hc* Vrije Univ., Brussels. Spanish Fertility Soc. Gold Medal, 1985; King Faisal Award, 1989; Nobel Prize in Physiology or Medicine, 2010. Chief Ed., Human Reproduction, 1986–2000; Founding Ed., Reproductive Biomedicine Online, 2000 (Ed. Emeritus, 2009). *Publications:* A Matter of Life (with P. C. Steptoe), 1980; Conception in the Human Female, 1980; (with C. R. Austin) Mechanisms of Sex Differentiation in Animals and Man; (with J. M. Purdy) Human Conception in Vitro, 1982; (with J. M. Purdy and P. C. Steptoe) Implantation of the Human Embryo, 1985; (with M. Seppälä) In Vitro Fertilisation and Embryo Transfer, 1985; Life Before Birth, 1989; editor of several scientific textbooks on reproduction; numerous articles in scientific and medical jls, organiser of conferences, etc. *Recreations:* farming, politics, music. *Address:* Duck End Farm, Dry Drayton, Cambridge CB23 8DB. *T:* (01954) 780602. *Died 10 April 2013.*

EDWARDS, Robert John, CBE 1986; Deputy Chairman, Mirror Group Newspapers, 1985–86 (Senior Group Editor, 1984–85); *b* 26 Oct. 1925; *m* 1st, 1952, Laura Ellwood (marr. diss. 1972); two *s* two *d*; 2nd, 1977, Brigid Segrave. *Educ:* Ranelagh Sch., Bracknell. Editor, Tribune, 1951–54; feature writer, London Evening Standard, 1954–57; Dep. Editor, Sunday Express, 1957–59; Man. Editor, Daily Express, 1959–61; Editor: Daily Express, 1961, 1963–65; Evening Citizen, Glasgow, 1962–63; Sunday People, 1966–72; Sunday Mirror, 1972–84; Dir, Mirror Group Newspapers, 1976–88. Ombudsman to Today newspaper, 1990–95. Chm., Scoop of the Year Awards Panel, London Press Club, 1988–2003. *Publications:* Goodbye Fleet Street (autobiog.), 1988. *E:* edwardsrj@aol.com. *Clubs:* Garrick, Reform. *Died 28 May 2012.*

EDWARDS, Robert Septimus Friar, CVO 1964; CBE 1963; *b* 21 Oct. 1910; *y s* of late Augustus C. Edwards and Amy Edwards; *m* 1946, Janet Mabel Wrigley; one *s* two *d*. *Educ:* Hereford Cathedral Sch. Chief Engineering Asst, Hereford, until 1936; Min. of Transport, Highway Engineering, 1936–43; Principal, Min. of War Transport, 1943; Mem. British Merchant Shipping Mission, Washington, DC, 1944–46. Sec. Gen. Internat. Conf. on Safety of Life at Sea, 1948; Principal Private Sec. to Minister of Transport, 1949–51; Shipping Attaché, British Embassy, Washington, DC, 1951–54; Dir of Sea Transport, 1954–57; Gen. Manager, London Airports, 1957–63; Gen. Manager, 1967–69, Dir-Gen., 1969–71, Mersey Docks and Harbour Board. Chm., Morris & David Jones Ltd, 1973–74. Called to the Bar, Middle Temple, 1941. *Address:* Robins Cottage, Upottery, Honiton, Devon EX14 9PL. *Died 28 Sept. 2011.*

EDWARDS, Prof. Sir Samuel Frederick, (Sir Sam Edwards), Kt 1975; FRS 1966; Cavendish Professor of Physics, 1984–95, Professor Emeritus, since 1995 (John Humphrey Plummer Professor, 1972–84), and Pro-Vice-Chancellor, 1992–95, Cambridge University; Fellow, Gonville and Caius College, Cambridge, since 1972 (President, 1992–97); *b* 1 Feb. 1928; *s* of Richard and Mary Jane Edwards, Manselton, Swansea; *m* 1953, Merriell E. M. Bland; one *s* three *d*. *Educ:* Swansea Grammar Sch.; Gonville and Caius Coll., Cambridge (MA, PhD); Harvard University. Inst. for Advanced Study, Princeton, 1952; Univ. of Birmingham, 1953; Univ. of Manchester, 1958, Prof. of Theoretical Physics, 1963–72. Chief Scientific Adviser, Department of Energy, 1983–88. Chm., SRC, 1973–77. UK Deleg. to NATO Science Cttee, 1974–79; Mem., Planning Cttee, Max-Planck Gesellschaft, 1974–77. Vice-Pres., Institute of Physics, 1970–73 (Mem. Council, 1967–73); Mem. Council, Inst. of Mathematics and its Applications, 1976– (Vice-Pres., 1979, Pres., 1980–81). Member: Physics Cttee, SRC, 1968–73 (Chm. 1970–73); Polymer Cttee, SRC, 1968–73; Science Bd, SRC, 1970–73; Council, European Physical Soc., 1969–71 (Chm., Condensed Matter Div., 1969–71); UGC, 1971–73; Defence Scientific Adv. Council, 1973– (Chm., 1977–80); Metrology and Standards Req. Bd, Dept of Industry, 1974–77; AFRC, 1990–94; HEFCW, 1992–95. Chm., Adv. Council on R&D, Dept of Energy, 1983–88 (Mem., 1974–77); Member Council: European R&D (EEC), 1976–80; Royal Soc., 1982–83 (a Vice-Pres., 1982–83); Pres., BAAS, 1988–89 (Chm. Council, 1977–82). Non-exec. Director: Lucas Industries, 1981–93; Steetley plc, 1985–93; Chm., Sen. Adv. Gp, Unilever, 1992–95; Mem., Adv. Gp, BP, 1992–98. Hon. Mem., European Physical Soc., 1996; Foreign Member: Acad. des Scis, France, 1989; Nat. Acad. of Scis, USA, 1996; Russian Acad. of Sci., 2007. FIMA; FRSC. Hon. FInstP 1996; Hon. Fellow, French Physical Soc. Hon. DTech Loughborough, 1975; Hon. DSc: Salford, Edinburgh, 1976; Bath, 1978; Birmingham, 1986; Wales, 1987; Sheffield, 1989; Dublin, 1991; Leeds, 1994; UEA, 1995; Mainz, 2002; Tel Aviv, 2006; Hon. ScD Cambridge, 2001; DUniv Strasbourg, 1986. Hon. Fellow, UC Swansea, 1994. Maxwell Medal and Prize, Inst. of Physics, 1974; High Polymer Physics Prize, Amer. Phys. Soc., 1982; Davy Medal, Royal Soc., 1984; Gold Medal, Inst. of Maths, 1986; Guthrie Medal and Prize, Inst. of Physics, 1987; Gold Medal, Rheological Soc., 1990; Louis Vaillon Moët Hennessy Prize (Science pour l'Art), 1993; Boltzmann Medal, IUPAP, 1995; Founders Polymer Prize, Inst. of Physics, 2001; Royal Medal, Royal Soc., 2001; Dirac Medal, Internat. Centre for Theoretical Physics, 2006. *Publications:* Technological Risk, 1980; (with M. Doi) Theory of Polymer Dynamics, 1986; (with S. M. Aharoni) Networks of Liquid Crystal Polymers, 1994; contribs to learned jls. *Address:* 7 Penarth Place, Cambridge CB3 9LU. *T:* (01223) 366610. *Club:* Athenæum. *Died 7 May 2015.*

EDWARDS, Very Rev. (Thomas) Erwyd (Pryse); Dean of Bangor, 1988–98, then Emeritus; *b* 26 Jan. 1933; *s* of Richard and Gwladys Edwards; *m* 1961, Mair (*née* Roberts); two *s*. *Educ:* St David's University College, Lampeter (BA 1956); St Michael's College, Llandaff. Curate of Caernarfon, 1958–63; Asst Chaplain, St George's Hosp., London, 1963–66; Chaplain, King's College Hosp., London, 1966–72; Vicar: Penmon, Anglesey, 1972–75; Menai Bridge, 1975–61; St David's, Bangor, 1981–85; St David's and St James's, Bangor, 1985–88; Canon of Bangor Cathedral, 1988. *Address:* 61 Ffriddoedd Road, Bangor, Gwynedd LL57 2TT. *T:* (01248) 362108. *E:* erwyd@erwyd.wanadoo.co.uk. *Died 11 March 2011.*

EGMONT, 12th Earl of, *cr* 1733 (Ire.); **Thomas Frederick Gerald Perceval;** Bt 1661; Baron Perceval 1715; Viscount Perceval 1722; Baron Lovel and Holland (GB) 1762; Baron Arden 1770; Baron Arden (UK) 1802; *b* 17 Aug. 1934; *e s* of 11th Earl of Egmont and Ann Geraldine (*née* Moodie); *S* father, 2001. *Heir:* none. *Died 6 Nov. 2011 (ext).*

EHRMAN, John Patrick William, FBA 1970; historian; *b* 17 March 1920; *o s* of late Albert and Rina Ehrman; *m* 1948, Elizabeth Susan Anne, *d* of late Vice-Adm. Sir Geoffrey Blake, KCB, DSO; four *s*. *Educ:* Charterhouse; Trinity Coll., Cambridge (MA). Served Royal Navy, 1940–45. Fellow of Trinity Coll., Cambridge, 1947–52; Historian, Cabinet Office, 1948–56; Lees Knowles Lectr, Cambridge, 1957–58; James Ford Special Lectr, Oxford, 1976–77. Hon. Treas., Friends of the National Libraries, 1960–77; Trustee of the Nat. Portrait Gall., 1971–85; Member: Reviewing Cttee on Export of Works of Art, 1970–76; Royal Commn on Historical Manuscripts, 1973–94; Chairman: Adv. Cttee to British Library Reference Div., 1975–84; Nat. Manuscripts Conservation Trust, 1989–94; Vice-Pres., Navy Records Soc., 1968–70, 1974–76. FSA 1958; FRHistS. *Publications:* The Navy in the War of William III, 1953; Grand Strategy, 1943–5 (2 vols, UK Official Military Histories of the Second World War), 1956; Cabinet Government and War, 1890–1940, 1958; The British Government and Commercial Negotiations with Europe, 1783–1793, 1962; The Younger Pitt, vol. 1, The Years of Acclaim, 1969, vol. 2, The Reluctant Transition, 1983, vol. 3, The Consuming Struggle (Yorkshire Post Book of the Year Award), 1996; contrib. Oxford DNB. *Address:* The Mead Barns, Taynton, near Burford, Oxfordshire OX18 4UH. *Clubs:* Army and Navy, Garrick. *Died 15 June 2011.*

ELEY, Prof. Daniel Douglas, OBE 1961; ScD, PhD Cantab; MSc, PhD Manchester; FRS 1964; CChem, FRSC; Professor of Physical Chemistry, University of Nottingham, 1954–80, then Emeritus; Dean of Faculty of Pure Science, 1959–62; *b* 1 Oct. 1914; *s* of Daniel Eley and Fanny Allen Eley (*née* Ross); *m* 1942, Brenda May Williams, MA, MB, BChir (Cantab) (*d* 1992), 2nd *d* of Benjamin and Sarah Williams, Skewen, Glam; one *s*. *Educ:* Christ's Coll., Finchley; Manchester Univ.; St John's Coll., Cambridge; Manchester Univ. (Woodiwiss Schol. 1933, Mercer Schol. 1934, Darbishire Fellow 1936, DSIR Sen. Award 1937; PhD 1937); PhD 1940, ScD 1954, Cambridge. Bristol University: Lectr in Colloid Chemistry, 1945; Reader in Biophysical Chemistry, 1951. Leverhulme Emeritus Fellow, 1981. Lectures: Reilly, Univ. of Notre Dame (USA), 1950; Royal Aust. Chem. Inst., 1967; Sir Jesse Boot Foundn, Nottingham Univ., 1955, 1981; Sir Eric Rideal, Soc. of Chem. Industry, 1975. Mem. Council of Faraday Soc., 1951–54, 1960–63; Vice-Pres., 1963–66. Corresp. Mem., Bavarian Acad. of Sciences, 1971. Meetings Sec., British Biophysical Soc., 1961–63, Hon. Sec., 1963–65, Hon. Mem., 1983. Scientific Assessor to Sub-Cttee on Coastal Pollutions, House of Commons Select Cttee on Science and Technology, 1967–68. Medal of Liège Univ., 1950. *Publications:* (ed) Adhesion, 1961; papers in Trans Faraday Soc., Proc. Royal Soc., Jl Chem.

Soc., Biochem. Jl, etc. *Recreations:* hill walking, gardening, reading. *Address:* Brooklands, 35 Brookland Drive, Chilwell, Nottingham NG9 4BD; Chemistry Department, Nottingham University, University Park, Nottingham NG7 2RD. *Died 3 Sept. 2015.*

ELIOTT of Stobs, Sir Charles (Joseph Alexander), 12th Bt *cr* 1666 (NS); *b* 9 Jan. 1937; *s* of Charles Rawdon Heathfield Eliott (*d* 1972) and Emma Elizabeth Harris (*d* 1999); *S* cousin, 1989; *m* 1959 (marr. diss. 1996); one *s* four *d* (and one *s* decd). *Educ:* St Joseph's Christian Brothers' College, Rockhampton. *Heir: s* Rodney Gilbert Charles Eliott [*b* 15 July 1966; *m* 1988 (marr. diss. 1998); one *s* two *d*]. *Address:* PO Box 402, Longreach, Qld 4730, Australia. *Died 8 July 2014.*

ELKES, Prof. Joel, MD, ChB; FACP, FAPA; psychiatrist and pharmacologist; Distinguished Service Professor Emeritus, The Johns Hopkins University, since 1975; Distinguished University Professor Emeritus, University of Louisville; Founding Fellow, 1989 and Senior Scholar-in-Residence, since 1993, Fetzer Institute, Kalamazoo; *b* Konigsberg, 12 Nov. 1913; *s* of Dr Elchanan Elkes and Miriam (*née* Malbin); *m* 1st, 1943, Dr Charmian Bourne (marr. diss.); one *d*; 2nd, 1975, Josephine Rhodes (*d* 1999), MA; 3rd, 2001, Sally Ruth Lucke. *Educ:* private schools; Lithuania and Switzerland; St Mary's Hosp., London; Univ. of Birmingham Med. Sch. (MB, ChB 1947; MD Hons 1949). University of Birmingham: Sir Halley Stewart Research Fellow, 1942–45; Lectr, Dept of Pharmacology, 1945–48; Senior Lectr and Actg Head of Dept, 1948–50; Prof. and Chm., Dept of Experimental Psychiatry, 1951–57 (first dept of its kind in the world); Clinical Professor of Psychiatry, George Washington Univ. Med. Sch., Washington, 1957–63; Chief of Clinical Neuropharmacology Research Center, Nat. Inst. of Mental Health, Washington, 1957–63; Dir, Behavioral and Clinical Studies Center St Elizabeth's Hosp., Washington, 1957–63; Henry Phipps Prof. and Dir, Dept of Psychiatry and Behavioural Scis, Johns Hopkins Univ. Sch. of Medicine, and Psychiatrist-in-Chief, Johns Hopkins Hosp., 1963–74; Samuel McLaughlin Prof.-in-residence, McMaster Univ., 1975; Professor of Psychiatry: McMaster Univ., 1976–80; Univ. of Louisville, 1980–84 (Director: Div. of Behavioral Medicine, 1982; Arts in Medicine Prog.). Dir, Foundns Fund for Research in Psychiatry, 1964–68; Consultant, WHO, 1957. Vis. Fellow, New York Univ. and New England Med. Center, Boston, 1950; Benjamin Franklin Fellow, RSA, 1974. Lectures: Harvey, 1962; Salmon, 1963; Jacob Bronowski Meml, 1978, etc. President: (first) Amer. Coll. of Neuropsychopharmacology, 1962; Amer. Psychopathological Assoc., 1968; Chairman: Bd, Israel Inst. of Psychobiol., 1961–2004; Foundns Fund Prize Bd for Res. in Psychiatry, 1977–81; Board Member: Inst. for Advancement of Health, 1982; Govs, Hebrew Univ. of Jerusalem; Govs, Haifa Univ. Formerly Member: Council, Collegium Internationale Neuro-psychopharmacologicum; Central Council, Internat. Brain Research Organisation, UNESCO (Chm., Sub-Cttee on Educn); RSM. Life Fellow, Amer. Psych. Assoc.; Charter Fellow, RCPsych, GB; Fellow: Amer. Acad. of Arts and Scis; Amer. Coll. of Psychiatry; Amer. Coll. of Neuropsychopharmacol. (Joel Elkes Internat. Award estab. 1986); Amer. Acad. of Behavioral Medicine Res. and Soc. of Behavioral Medicine; Fetzer Inst., 1990; Fellow and Mem. Exec. Cttee, World Acad. of Art and Sci., 1985; Former Member: Physiological Soc., GB; Pharmacological Soc., GB; Amer. Soc. for Pharmacology and Experimental Therapeutics; Sigma Xi; Scientific Assoc.; Acad. of Psychoanalysis. Hon. DPhil Hebrew Univ. of Jerusalem, 1989. Hans Selye Internat. Award, 1994; (jtly) First Internat. Pioneer Award in Psychopharmacology, Glasgow Congress, 1998; Lifetime-Achievement Award, Louisville Cathedral Heritage Foundn, 2000. Two internat. symposia in his honour, 1984, 1985; Joel Elkes Res. Labs, Dept of Psychiatry, Johns Hopkins Univ., dedicated 1989; Elkes Cottage, Fetzer Inst., dedicated 1998. One man show, In Praise of Trees, Selby Gardens, Sarasota, 2008. *Publications:* papers to various jls and symposia. *Recreation:* painting. *Address:* Fetzer Institute, 9292 WKL Avenue, Kalamazoo, MI 49009, USA. *Club:* Cosmos (Washington). *Died 30 Oct. 2015.*

ELKINGTON, Prof. Andrew Robert, CBE 1996; FRCS; FRCOphth; Professor of Ophthalmology, University of Southampton, 1990–98, then Emeritus; Consultant Ophthalmic Surgeon, Southampton General Hospital, 1974–98; *b* 12 Dec. 1935; *s* of late Dr George Ernest Elkington, MC, FRCS, Newport, Salop and Kathleen Mary Elkington (*née* Budgen); *m* 1964, Patricia Kathleen Wright, *er d* of late R. M. Wright, MC and Bar and Joan Wright; four *s*. *Educ:* Repton Sch., Derbys; Clare Coll., Cambridge (MA); St Thomas' Hosp. (BChir, MB). FRCS 1969; FRCOphth 1988 (Hon. FRCOphth 1999); DRCOG 1965; DO 1968. Moorfields Eye Hospital: Hse Surgeon and Sen. Resident Officer, 1967–70; Chief Clinical Asst, 1970–74; Sen. Registrar in Ophthalmol., Westminster Hosp., 1970–74. European Vis. Prof., RSocMed, 1992–93. Examr, DO, 1977–83 (Chm., Examng Bd, 1981–83); Mem., Ct of Examrs (Ophthalmol.), RCS, 1984–89 (Chm., 1988–89); Ext. Examr, RCPSG (Ophthalmol.), 1984–89; Examr in ophthalmol., Univs of Bristol, 1987, London, 1988, Glasgow, 1991, Leicester, 1992, Nottingham, 1993; Examr to Ophthalmic Nursing Bd, 1980–98. Section of Ophthalmology, Royal Society of Medicine: Mem. Council, 1980–92; Hon. Sec., 1980–83; Vice Pres., 1983–86; Pres., 1990–92; Faculty of Ophthalmologists, subseq. Royal College of Ophthalmologists: Mem. Council, 1985–88; Hon. Sec., 1986–91; Vice-Pres., 1991–94; Pres., 1994–97; Ophthalmological Society of UK: Mem. Council, 1979–82; Vice Pres., 1987–88; Pres., British and Irish Orthoptic Soc., 2002–09. Member: Council, RCS, 1994–96; GMC, 1994–98 (Mem., Educn Cttee, 1994–98). Chm., British Council for Prevention of Blindness, 2000–09; Member: Council, Oxford Ophthalmol. Congress, 1982–98; Senate, Royal Surgical Colls, 1994–96; Conf. and Scottish Conf. of Med. Royal Colls and their Faculties, 1994–96; Standing Med. Adv. Cttee, 1994–97. Govt of Hong Kong Commnd Trainer in ophthalmol., 1991. Mem., Bd of Govs, Moorfields Eye Hosp., 1988–94. *Publications:* (jtly) Clinical Optics, 1984, 3rd edn 1999; Ophthalmology for Nurses, 1986; ABC of Eyes, 1988, 4th edn 2004; Aids to Ophthalmology, 1989; contribs on trauma, glaucoma and retinal detachment to ophthalmic jls. *Recreations:* wildlife, tending vegetables. *Club:* Travellers. *Died 11 Sept. 2014.*

ELLACOMBE, Air Cdre John Lawrence Wemyss, CB 1970; DFC 1942 (Bar 1944); FCMI; *b* Livingstone, N Rhodesia, 28 Feb. 1920; *s* of Dr Gilbert H. W. Ellacombe; *m* 1951, Wing Officer Mary Hibbert, OBE, WRAF (*d* 2007); one *s* two *d*. *Educ:* Diocesan Coll., Rondebosch, Cape. War of 1939–45: RAF, 1939; Fighter Comd and Two ATA Force, 1940–45 (Pilot, Battle of Britain). Aden, 1946–48; RAF Staff Coll., 1948–49; Fighter Command, 1949–57; BJSM, Washington, 1959. JSSC, 1959–60; Gp Captain, CO RAF Linton on Ouse, to Nov. 1962; CFE, to Aug. 1965; Defence Operational Analysis Estabt, West Byfleet, 1965–68; Air Cdre, Commander Air Forces Gulf, 1968–70; Dir of Ops (Air Defence and Overseas), MoD (Air), 1970–73; St Thomas' Hospital: Dir, Scientific Services, 1973–80; Administrator to Special Trustees, 1980–85. *Recreations:* photography, golf, cricket. *Club:* Royal Air Force. *Died 11 May 2014.*

ELLENBOROUGH, 8th Baron *cr* 1802; **Richard Edward Cecil Law;** *b* 14 Jan. 1926; *s* of 7th Baron and Helen Dorothy, *o d* of late H. W. Lovatt; *S* father, 1945; *m* 1st, 1953, Rachel Mary (*d* 1986), *o d* of late Major Ivor Hedley; three *s*; 2nd, 1994, Mrs Frances Kimberley (*d* 2004). *Educ:* Eton Coll.; Magdalene Coll., Cambridge. Partner, McAnally Montgomery, stockbrokers, 1969–78. Director: Towry Law & Co., 1958–96; Towry Law Gp, 1958–96. Pres., Nat. Union of Ratepayers' Associations, 1960–90. *Heir: s* Major the Hon. Rupert Edward Henry Law, Coldstream Guards, retd [*b* 28 March 1955; *m* 1981, Hon. Grania, *d* of Baron Boardman, MC, TD; two *s* one *d*]. *Address:* High Broom Residential Home, Stone Cross, Crowborough, East Sussex TN6 3SL. *T:* (01892) 663139. *Club:* Turf. *Died 7 June 2013.*

ELLINGWORTH, Richard Henry; HM Diplomatic Service, retired; *b* 9 March 1926; *e s* of Vincent Ellingworth and Dora Ellingworth (*née* Church); *m* 1952, Joan Mary, *e d* of Sir Percival Waterfield, KBE, CB and Lady Waterfield;

one *s* three *d*. *Educ:* Uppingham; Aberdeen Univ.; Magdalen Coll., Oxford (Demy); Exeter Univ. (certificates in French, 1989, Theology, 1991, and Russian, 1993). Served War of 1939–45: RA, and Intelligence Corps, 1944–47. Oxford, 1947–50 (first Lit. Hum.); HM Embassy, Japan, 1951–55; FO, 1955–59; HM Embassy: Belgrade, 1959–63; Japan, 1963–68 (Olympic Attaché, 1964); Head of Oil Dept, FCO, 1969–71; Research Associate, Internat. Inst. for Strategic Studies, 1971–72; Counsellor, Tehran, 1972–75; seconded to Dept of Energy, 1975–77. Course Dir (European Training), Civil Service Coll., 1978–83. Mem., Farningham Parish Council, 1979–83; pt-time Agent, Sevenoaks Liberal Assoc., 1983–84; Hon. Organiser, Farningham, Royal British Legion, 1982–87. *Publications:* (with A. N. Gilkes) An Anthology of Oratory, 1946; Japanese Economic Policy and Security, 1972. *Recreations:* gardening, music. *Address:* c/o Marian Ellingworth, 12 Lloyd Square, WC1X 9BA. *E:* ellingworthm@tuckerssolicitors.com. *Died 31 March 2015.*

ELLIOTT OF MORPETH, Baron *cr* 1985 (Life Peer), of Morpeth in the County of Northumberland and of the City of Newcastle-upon-Tyne; **Robert William Elliott,** Kt 1974; DL; Vice-Chairman, Conservative Party Organisation, 1970–74; *b* 11 Dec. 1920; *s* of Richard Elliott; *m* 1956, Jane Morpeth; one *s* four *d* (of whom two are twin *d*). *Educ:* Morpeth Grammar Sch. Farmer, 1939–, at Low Heighley, Morpeth, Northumberland. MP (C) Newcastle-upon-Tyne North, March 1957–1983; Parliamentary Private Secretary: to joint Parliamentary Secs, Ministry of Transport and Civil Aviation, April 1958–Oct. 1959; to Under-Sec., Home Office, Nov. 1959–60; to Minister of State, Home Office, Nov. 1960–61; to Sec. for Technical Co-operation, 1961–63; Asst Govt Whip (unpaid), 1963–64; Opposition Whip, 1964–70; Comptroller of the Household, June–Sept. 1970. Chm., Select Cttee on Agric., Fisheries and Food, 1980–83. DL Northumberland, 1985. *Address:* Crown House, Kings Cliffe, Peterborough PE8 6XQ. *T:* (01780) 470888. *Clubs:* Carlton; Northern Counties (Newcastle upon Tyne). *Died 20 May 2011.*

ELLIOTT, Frank Alan, CB 1991; Permanent Secretary, Department of Health and Social Services, Northern Ireland, 1987–97; *b* 28 March 1937; *s* of Frank Elliott and Doreen Allen; *m* 1964, Olive Lucy O'Brien; one *s* two *d*. *Educ:* Royal Belfast Academical Instn; Trinity Coll., Dublin (BA (Mod.) 1st cl.). Entered NI Civil Service, 1959; Principal, Min. of Health, 1966, Asst Sec., 1971; Sen. Asst Sec., Dept of Health and Social Services, 1975, Under Sec., 1981. Chm., Chief Execs' Forum, 1997–2001. Trustee, Leonard Cheshire Disability (formerly Leonard Cheshire Foundn), 2002–08 (Vice-Chm., 2005–08). DUniv Ulster, 1998. *Publications:* Curing and Caring: 50 years of health and personal social services in NI, 1998. *Recreations:* music and the arts, travel. *Died 17 Feb. 2014.*

ELLIS, Carol Jacqueline, (Mrs Ralph Gilmore), CBE 1995; QC 1980; Consultant Editor, Road Traffic Reports, since 1970; *b* 6 May 1929; *d* of Ellis W. Ellis and Flora Bernstein; *m* 1957, Ralph Gilmore (*d* 1996); two *s*. *Educ:* Abbey Sch., Reading; La Ramée, Lausanne; Univ. of Lausanne; University Coll. London (LLB 1950; MA Renaissance Studies, 2005). Called to the Bar, Gray's Inn, 1951; supernumerary law reporter for The Law Reports, The Times, and other legal jls, 1952; law reporter to The Law Reports and Weekly Law Reports, 1954; Asst Editor, Weekly Law Reports, 1969; Managing Editor, The Law Reports and Weekly Law Reports, 1970; Editor, 1976–90, Consultant Editor, 1990–99, Weekly Law Reports; Editor, 1976–96, Consultant Editor, 1996–99, The Law Reports. Mem., Inner London Probation Cttee, 1989–95. JP W Central Div. Inner London, 1972–98. *Recreations:* travel, music, theatre. *Address:* 11 Old Square, Lincoln's Inn, WC2A 3TS. *T:* (020) 7403 0341. *Died 12 July 2015.*

ELLIS, Herbert; *see* Ellis, W. H. B.

ELLIS, John, CB 1985; Head of Royal Armament Research and Development Establishment, Chertsey, 1984–85; *b* 9 Jan. 1925; *s* of Frank William and Alice Ellis; *m* 1958, Susan Doris (*née* Puttock). *Educ:* Leeds Univ. BSc, 1st cl. hons. Mech. Eng; CEng, MIMechE. Hydro-Ballistic Research Estabt, Admty, 1945–47; David Brown & Sons Ltd, Huddersfield, 1948; RAE, Min. of Supply (Structures Dept, Armament Dept, Weapons Dept), 1948–68; MVEE (formerly FVRDE), MoD, 1968–84; Dir, MVEE, Chertsey, 1978–84, when MVEE and RARDE amalgamated. Ind. technical consultant, 1985–2001. *Recreations:* motoring, golf. *Address:* Foresters, 1 Kitchers Close, Sway, Lymington, Hants SO41 6DS. *T:* (01590) 682410. *Died 17 Jan. 2014.*

ELLIS, John Norman, OBE 1995; industrial relations consultant, since 1995, Chairman, 2000–07, Talking People Ltd; Chairman, Tandridge Leisure Ltd, since 2008 (Vice-Chairman, 2000–08); *b* 22 Feb. 1939; *s* of Margaret and Albert Ellis; *m* 1st; one *s* one *d*; 2nd, Diane Anderson; two step *s*. *Educ:* Osmondthorpe; Leeds Secondary Modern; Leeds College of Commerce. Post Office Messenger and Postman, 1954–58; Clerical Officer and Executive Officer, MPBW, 1958–67; Civil and Public Services Association: Asst Sec., 1968–82; Dep. Gen. Sec., 1982–86; Gen. Sec., 1986–92; Sec., CCSU, 1992–95. Member: Gen. Council, TUC, 1988–92 (Mem. Economic, Social Services, Industrial Welfare, Public Services and Pensions Specialists Cttees, 1988–92); Inst. of Employment Rights, 1989–; Industrial Tribunal Panel, 1992–2009; Exec. Cttee, Civil Service Pensioners' Alliance, 1996–2004; Exec. Cttee, London (South) Tribunal Members Assoc., 2001–. Chm., Caterham Br., Lab. Party, 1997–2004 (Vice-Chm., 1996). Vice-Chm., Caterham Valley Parish Council, 2002–04. *Recreations:* reading, watching sport, gardening, listening to music, dog walking, computer building. *Address:* 26 Harestone Valley Road, Caterham, Surrey CR3 6HD. *Died 28 Feb. 2011.*

ELLIS, Prof. John Romaine; Professor of Automobile Engineering, 1960–82 and Director, 1960–76, School of Automotive Studies, Cranfield; *b* 30 Sept. 1922; *m* 1947, Madelaine Della Blaker; one *s* one *d*. *Educ:* Tiffin Sch., Kingston-on-Thames; Univ. of London (ext.) (BSc 1947; MSc 1954; PhD 1960; DSc 1983). Royal Aircraft Establishment, 1944–56; Fairey Aviation Company, 1946–48; Royal Military Coll. of Science, Shrivenham, near Swindon, Wilts, 1949–60. *Publications:* Vehicle Dynamics, 1969; Vehicle Handling Dynamics, 1993. *Recreations:* golf, music. *Died 11 Feb. 2014.*

ELLIS, Richard Peter; Principal Assistant Treasury Solicitor, Legal Advisory Division, Ministry of Defence, 1988–91; *b* 25 Oct. 1931; *s* of late Comdr Thomas Ellis, RN and Kathleen Mary Ellis (*nee* Lewis); *m* 1963, Penelope Jane, *yr d* of late Captain J. B. Hall, RN; two *s* two *d*. *Educ:* Sherborne; RMA Sandhurst. Commissioned Royal Irish Fusiliers, 1952; served 1st Bn, BAOR, Berlin, Korea, Kenya; resigned commission 1957. Called to the Bar, Lincoln's Inn, 1960; Practised Common Law Bar, 1960–65, Oxford Circuit; Treasury Solicitor's Dept, 1965–91. *Recreations:* country pursuits, travel, reading. *Address:* c/o TSB, Somerton, Somerset TA11 7NB. *Died 10 Feb. 2015.*

ELLIS, Dr (William) Herbert (Baxter), AFC 1954; MD; Medical Adviser, Department of Health and Social Security, 1972–92; Underwriting Member of Lloyd's; *b* Newcastle upon Tyne, 2 July 1921; *er s* of William Baxter Ellis and Georgina Isabella Ellis (*née* Waller); *m* 1st, 1948, Margaret Mary Limb (marr. diss.); one *s* one *d*; 2nd, 1977, Mollie Marguerite Clarke (marr. diss.); 3rd, 1994, Jean Stanley Stawell Gross (*d* 2013), *widow* of Ken Gross. *Educ:* Oundle Sch.; Durham Univ. (BS, MD). Royal Navy, 1945–59: Surg. Comdr, Fleet Air Arm Pilot. Developed audio airspeed device to aid aircraft deck-landing, later used as car parking aid. Motor industry, 1960–71; research into human aspects of road traffic accidents, 1960–71; Dir-Gen., Dr Barnardo's, 1971–73; dir of various companies. Industrial Medical Consultant: Wellworthy, 1979–87; Telephone Manufacturing Co., 1980–87; Plessey Co., 1981–87. Part-time Mem., Employment Medical Adv. Service, 1973–81. Freeman, City of London, 1994; Liveryman, Apothecaries' Soc., 1997. St John Ambulance: Chief Comdr, 1989–91; County Surgeon, 1979–87, Comdr, 1987–89, Glos Br.; Chm., St John Fellowship, 2001–04, then Chm. Emeritus. KStJ 1989 (CStJ 1988). Gilbert Blane Medal, RCP, 1954. *Publications:* Physiological and Psychological Aspects of Deck Landings, 1954; Hippocrates, RN—memoirs of a naval flying doctor (autobiog.), 1988; Why Not Live a

Little Longer?, 1997; various on the human factor in industrial management. *Recreations:* memories of walking, observing humanity, mending fences. *Address:* Littlecroft, 21 Buckswood Grange, Rocks Road, Uckfield, East Sussex TN22 3PU. *T:* (01825) 767876. *Clubs:* Army and Navy, Naval and Military. *Died 4 Oct. 2014.*

ELLISON, Sir Ralph Harry C.; *see* Carr-Ellison, Sir R. H.

ELLSWORTH, Robert; Partner, Hamilton Bio Ventures LP, since 2000; *b* 11 June 1926; *s* of Willoughby Fred Ellsworth and Lucile Rarig Ellsworth; *m* 2002, Rev. Eleanor Bradford Lynch; one *s* one *d* from former marriage. *Educ:* Univs of Kansas (BSME) and Michigan (JD). Active service, US Navy, 1944–46, 1950–53 (Lt-Comdr). Mem. United States Congress, 1961–67; Asst to President of US, 1969; Ambassador and Permanent Representative of US on N Atlantic Council, 1969–71; Asst Sec. of Defense (Internat. Security Affairs), 1974–75; Dep. Sec. of Defense, 1975–77. Vice Pres., IISS, 1998– (Mem., 1973–; Chm. Council, 1990–96). Licensed Lay Reader, Episcopal Dio. of Washington. Hon. LLD: Ottawa, 1969; Boston, 1970. Knight of Honour, Johanniter Orden, Berlin, 1996. *Recreations:* single sculling, swimming, music. *Address:* 2205 Caminito del Barco, Del Mar, CA 92014, USA. *Clubs:* Brook (New York); Cosmos (Washington). *Died 9 May 2011.*

ELPHINSTON of Glack, Sir John, 11th Bt *cr* 1701, of Logie Elphinstone and Nova Scotia; land agent; *b* 12 Aug. 1924; *s* of Thomas George Elphinston (*d* 1967), and of Gladys Mary Elphinston, *d* of late Ernest Charles Lambert Congdon; *S* uncle, 1970; *m* 1953, Margaret Doreen, *d* of Edric Tasker; four *s*. *Educ:* Eagle House, Sandhurst, Berks; Repton; Emmanuel College, Cambridge (BA). Lieut, Royal Marines, 1942–48. Chartered Surveyor; Land Agent with ICI plc, 1956–83; Consultant, Gandy & Son, Northwich, 1983–88. Past Pres., Cheshire Agricultural Valuers' Assoc.; Past Chm., Land Agency and Agric. Div., Lancs, Cheshire and IoM Branch, RICS; Mem., Lancs River Authority, 1970–74. *Heir: s* Alexander Elphinston [*b* 6 June 1955; *m* 1986, Ruth, *er d* of Rev. Robert Dunnett; three *s* one *d*]. *Died 28 May 2015.*

ELTON, Sir Leslie (Norman), Kt 2004; DL; Chief Executive, Gateshead Council, 1984–2004; *b* 27 Feb. 1947; *s* of Harry Elton and Marjorie Elton; *m* 1969, Christine Mary Price; one *s* one *d*. *Educ:* Hulme Grammar Sch., Oldham; Univ. of Manchester (LLB 1968). Admitted solicitor, 1971; various posts with Salford, Nottingham, Stockport and Newcastle upon Tyne Councils, 1969–84; Clerk to Northumbria Police Authy, 1984–2004. Vis. Prof., Business Sch., 2004–08, Mem. Council, 2004–07, Univ. of Newcastle upon Tyne. Chairman: Northern Film and Media, 2007–; Port of Tyne Authy, 2012– (Dep. Chm., 2004). Gov., Northumbria Univ., 2007–12 (Chm., 2009–12). DL: Tyne and Wear, 2005–09; Northumberland, 2010. *Recreations:* gardening, golf, family, good food. *Address:* The Hayway, Ovingham, Northumberland NE42 6DE. *T:* (01661) 836541. *E:* les.elton@btinternet.com. *Died 12 July 2014.*

EMERTON, Rev. Prof. John Adney, FBA 1979; Regius Professor of Hebrew, Cambridge, 1968–95, then Emeritus Professor; Fellow of St John's College, since 1970; Honorary Canon, St George's Cathedral, Jerusalem, since 1984; *b* 5 June 1928; *s* of Adney Spencer Emerton and Helena Mary Emerton; *m* 1954, Norma Elizabeth Bennington; one *s* two *d*. *Educ:* Minchenden Grammar Sch., Southgate; Corpus Christi Coll., Oxford; Wycliffe Hall, Oxford. BA (1st class hons Theology), 1950; 1st class hons Oriental Studies, 1952; MA 1954. Canon Hall Jun. Greek Testament Prize, 1950; Hall-Houghton Jun. Septuagint Prize, 1951, Senior Prize, 1954; Houghton Syriac Prize, 1953; Liddon Student, 1950; Kennicott Hebrew Fellow, 1952. Corpus Christi Coll., Cambridge, MA (by incorporation), 1955; BD 1960; DD 1973. Ordained deacon, 1952, priest, 1953. Curate of Birmingham Cathedral, 1952–53; Asst Lecturer in Theology, Birmingham Univ., 1952–53; Lecturer in Hebrew and Aramaic, Durham Univ., 1953–55; Lecturer in Divinity, Cambridge Univ., 1955–62; Reader in Semitic Philology and Fellow of St Peter's Coll., Oxford, 1962–68. Visiting Professor: of Old Testament and Near Eastern Studies, Trinity Coll., Toronto Univ., 1960; of Old Testament, Utd Theol Coll., Bangalore, 1986; Fellow, Inst. for Advanced Studies, Hebrew Univ. of Jerusalem, 1982–83. Select Preacher before Univ. of Cambridge, 1962, 1971, 1986. President: Internat. Orgn for the Study of the Old Testament, 1992–95 (Sec., 1971–89); SOTS, 1979. Mem. Editorial Bd, Vetus Testamentum, 1971–97. Corresp. Mem., Akademie der Wissenschaften, Göttingen, 1990. Hon. DD Edinburgh, 1977. Burkitt Medal for Biblical Studies, British Acad., 1991. *Publications:* The Peshitta of the Wisdom of Solomon, 1959; The Old Testament in Syriac: Song of Songs, 1966; (ed) Studies in the Historical Books of the Old Testament, 1979; (ed) Prophecy: essays presented to Georg Fohrer, 1980; (ed) Studies in the Pentateuch, 1990; Editor, Congress Volumes (International Organization for Study of the Old Testament): Edinburgh 1973, 1974; Göttingen 1977, 1978; Vienna 1980, 1981; Salamanca 1983, 1985; Jerusalem 1986, 1988; Leuven 1989, 1991; Paris 1992, 1995; Cambridge 1995, 1997; articles in Journal of Semitic Studies, Journal of Theological Studies, Palestine Exploration Qly, Theology, Vetus Testamentum, Zeitschrift für die Alttestamentliche Wissenschaft. *Address:* 34 Gough Way, Cambridge CB3 9LN. *Died 12 Sept. 2015.*

EMERY, Lina, (Mrs Ralph Emery); *see* Lalandi-Emery, L.

EMLYN JONES, John Hubert, CBE 1986 (MBE (mil.) 1941); FRICS; JP; Member of the Lands Tribunal, 1968–86; *b* 6 Aug. 1915; *s* of late Ernest Pearson Jones and Katharine Cole Jones (*née* Nicholas); *m* 1954, Louise Anne Montague, *d* of late Raymond Ralph Horwood Hazell; two *s* one *d*. *Educ:* Dulwich. FRICS 1939. Served War, RE, 1939–46: Major 1943. Partner, Rees-Reynolds and Hunt, and Alfred Savill & Sons, Chartered Surveyors, 1950–68. President: Rating Surveyors Assoc., 1965–66 (Hon. Mem. 1968); Climbers' Club, 1966–69 (Hon. Mem. 1970); Alpine Club, 1980–82 (Hon. Mem. 2006). Mem. Council, RICS, 1964–69. Mem. Bureau, 1964–72, Treasurer 1967–69, Fédération Internationale des Géomètres. Mem., expedns to Himalayas: Annapurna, 1950; Ama Dablam, 1959 (Leader). High Sheriff, Bucks, 1967–68, JP 1968. *Publications:* articles and revs in mountaineering jls. *Recreations:* mountaineering, music. *Address:* Ivinghoe Manor, Leighton Buzzard, Beds LU7 9EH. *T:* (01296) 668202. *Clubs:* Garrick, Alpine. *Died 4 Feb. 2014.*

EMMS, David Acfield, OBE 1995; MA; Director, The London Goodenough Trust (formerly London House) for Overseas Graduates, 1987–95; *b* 16 Feb. 1925; *s* of late Archibald George Emms and Winifred Gladys (*née* Richards); *m* 1950, Pamela Baker Speed; two *s* one *d* (and one *s* decd). *Educ:* Tonbridge Sch.; Brasenose Coll., Oxford. BA Hons Mod. Langs Oxford, 1950, Diploma in Education, 1951; MA 1954. Served War of 1939–45, RA, 1943–47. Undergraduate, 1947–50; Asst Master, Uppingham Sch. (Head of Mod. Languages Dept, CO, CCF Contingent), 1951–60; Headmaster of: Cranleigh School, 1960–70; Sherborne School, 1970–74; Master, Dulwich Coll., 1975–86. Chm., HMC, 1984; Pres., ISCO, 2001–06. Dep. Chm., E-SU, 1984–89; Chm., Jt Educnl Trust, 1987–90; Mem. Cttee, GBA, 1989–92. Vice-Chm. Council and Dep. Pro-Chancellor, City Univ., 1989–91; Governor: Bickley Park, 1978–81; Feltonfleet, 1967–86; Brambletye, 1982–88; St Felix Sch., Southwold, 1981–88; Portsmouth Grammar Sch., 1987–98; Tonbridge, 1988–2000; St George's, Montreux, 1989–2000; St Dunstan's Coll., 1992–97. President: Alleyn Club, 1985; Brasenose Soc., 1987. Mem. Council, Fairbridge Soc., 1984–96. FRSA 1988. Freeman, City of London; Master, Skinners' Co., 1987–88. Hon. Col, 39th (City of London) Signal Regt (Special Communications) (Volunteers), 1988–91. Chm., RNLI, Chichester, 1997–2005. Cdre, Alleynian Sailing Soc., 2008–14. Played Rugby football: Oxford *v* Cambridge, 1949, 1950; Northampton, 1951–56; Eastern Counties, 1951–57 (Capt. 1957); Barbarians, 1953. *Publications:* HMC Schools and British Industry, 1981. *Recreation:* putting names to faces. *Clubs:* East India, Devonshire, Sports and Public Schools, Pilgrims; Vincent's (Oxford). *Died 21 Dec. 2015.*

ENGLAND, Glyn, BSc(Eng); FREng, FIET, FIMechE; Chairman: RSA Sustainability Action Group Exchange, 1998–2003; Bayswater Institute, since 2011; *b* 19 April 1921; *m* 1942, Tania Reichenbach (*d* 2009); two *d*. *Educ:* Penarth County Sch.; Queen Mary Coll., London Univ. (BSc (Eng)); London School of Economics. Department of Scientific and Industrial Research, 1939. War service, 1942–47. Chief Ops Engr, CEGB, 1966–71; Dir-Gen., SW Region, 1971–73; Chm., SW Electricity Bd, 1973–77; part-time Mem., 1975–77, Chm., 1977–82, CEGB. Director: F. H. Lloyd (Hldgs), 1982–87; Triplex Lloyd, 1987–90; The Wind Fund plc, 1994–2000; Chm., Windcluster Ltd, 1991–96. Consultant, World Bank, 1983–89. Mem., British Nat. Cttee, World Energy Conf., 1977–82; Vice-Pres., Internat. Union of Producers and Distributors of Electrical Energy, 1981–82. Mem., Bd of Dirs, UK CEED, 1984–96. Chairman: Council for Envmtl Conservation, 1983–88; Bd of Trustees, Silvanus Trust (formerly Dartington Action Res. Trust), 1985–94; Woodlands Initiatives, later Silvanus Services Ltd, 1988–96. Pres., Mendip Soc., 1999–2001. Sometime Labour Mem., Herts CC; Mem. Council, Magistrates' Assoc. JP Welwyn, Herts, 1962–71. Freeman, City of London, 1979. FRSA 1965; CCMI (FBIM 1976). Hon. DSc Bath, 1981. *Publications:* (with Rex Savidge) Landscape in the Making; papers on: Economic Growth and the Electricity Supply Industry, Security of Electricity Supplies, Planning for Uncertainty, Railways and Power (IMechE Tritton Lecture), Efficiency Audits, Industrial Ecology. *Recreation:* actively enjoying the countryside. *Address:* Woodbridge Farm Cottage, Ubley, Bristol BS40 6PX. *T:* (01761) 462886. *Died 20 June 2013.*

ENSOM, Donald, FRICS; Chartered Surveyor; Consultant, Debenham Tewson & Chinnocks, 1986–92 (Partner, 1962–86); *b* 8 April 1926; *s* of Charles R. A. W. Ensom and Edith (*née* Young); *m* 1951, Sonia (*née* Sherrard); one *s* one *d*. *Educ:* Norbury Manor Sch., Croydon. Qualified as Chartered Surveyor, 1951; FRICS 1958; FCIArb 1970. Served RA, 1943–47. Partner, Nightingale, Page & Bennett/Debenham Tewson & Chinnocks (after merger), 1958–86. Chm., Bldg Conservation Trust, 1981–83; Royal Institution of Chartered Surveyors: Pres., Bldg Surveyors Div., 1975–76; Chm., Professional Practice Cttee, 1978–83; Hon. Sec., 1983–90; Vice-Pres., 1988–90. Pres., Land Economy Soc., Univ. of Cambridge, 1990–91. Member: Pyramus and Thisbe Club (Chm. 1987–89); 1913 Wilderness Club (formerly Chartered Surveyors (1913) Club). *Publications:* (jtly) Party Walls, 1993; (jtly) The Party Wall Act Explained, 1997; numerous professional papers. *Recreations:* reading, opera and music, transport history, crossword puzzles, freemasonry. *Address:* 8 The Oast House, Grange Road, Cambridge CB3 9AP. *Club:* East India. *Died 18 Aug. 2013.*

ENSOR, Michael de Normann, CMG 1980; OBE 1958; Head, East Africa Development Division, Overseas Development Administration, 1975–80; *b* 11 June 1919; *s* of Robert Weld Ensor and Dr Beatrice Ensor; *m* 1945, Mona Irene Blackburn (*d* 2002); two *s*. *Educ:* Bryanston School; St John's Coll., Oxford. Military service, 1940; Colonial Service, Gold Coast/Ghana Civil Service, 1940–58; Secretary, Foundation for Mutual Assistance in Africa South of the Sahara, 1958–64; Dept of Technical Cooperation/Min. of Overseas Development/Overseas Development Administration, 1964–80. Chairman: Paragon Management Co., 1983–86; Overseas Service Pensioners' Benevolent Soc., 1986–91. *Address:* Flat 1, 12 The Paragon, Blackheath, SE3 0NZ. *T:* (020) 8852 5345. *Club:* Travellers. *Died 13 Feb. 2015.*

ENTWISTLE, Prof. Kenneth Mercer; Professor of Metallurgy and Materials Science, University of Manchester Institute of Science and Technology, 1962–90, then Emeritus; *b* 3 Jan. 1925; *s* of William Charles and Maude Elizabeth Entwistle; *m* 1949, Alice Patricia Mary Johnson; two *s* two *d*. *Educ:* Urmston Grammar Sch.; Univ. of Manchester (BSc Elect. Eng. 1945, MSc 1946, PhD 1948). FIMMM, CEng. University of Manchester: Lectr in Metallurgy, 1948; Sen. Lectr, 1954; Reader, 1960; Dean, Faculty of Technology, 1976–77; Pro-Vice-Chancellor, 1982–85; Vice-Principal, UMIST, 1972–74. Adjunct Prof., Univ. of Canterbury, NZ, 2001–. Chairman: Materials Cttee, CNAA, 1972–74; Educn Cttee, Instn of Metallurgists, 1977–79; Metallics Sub-Cttee, SRC, 1979–81; Mem., UGC, 1985–89 (Chm., Technology Sub-Cttee, 1985–89); Engrg Advr to Chief Exec. of UFC, 1989–92. Comp. UMIST, 1991. Hon. Fellow, Sheffield Polytechnic, 1971. *Publications:* numerous papers in scientific jls. *Recreations:* Scottish dancing, choral singing. *Address:* Heronswood, 22 Castlegate, Prestbury, Macclesfield, Cheshire SK10 4AZ. *T:* (01625) 829269. *E:* ken.entwistle@manchester.ac.uk. *Club:* Athenæum. *Died 10 April 2015.*

ERNE, 6th Earl of, *cr* 1789; **Henry George Victor John Crichton,** KCVO 2012; JP; Baron Erne 1768; Viscount Erne (Ireland), 1781; Baron Fermanagh (UK), 1876; Lord Lieutenant of Co. Fermanagh, Northern Ireland, 1986–2012; *b* 9 July 1937; *s* of 5th Earl and Lady Katharine Cynthia Mary Millicent (Davina) Lytton (who *m* 1945, Hon. C. M. Woodhouse, later 5th Baron Terrington, DSO, OBE; she *d* 1995), *yr d* of 2nd Earl of Lytton, KG, PC, GCSI, GCIE; *S* father, 1940; *m* 1958, Camilla Marguerite (marr. diss. 1980), *er d* of late Wing-Comdr Owen G. E. Roberts and Mrs Roberts; one *s* four *d*; *m* 1980, Mrs Anna Carin Hitchcock (*née* Bjork). *Educ:* Eton. Page of Honour to the Queen, 1952–54 (to King George VI, 1952). Lieut, North Irish Horse, 1959–66. Member: Royal Ulster Agricultural Society; Royal Forestry Society. JP Co. Fermanagh. *Recreations:* sailing, fishing, shooting. *Heir: s* Viscount Crichton, *b* 19 June 1971. *Address:* Crom Castle, Newtownbutler, Co. Fermanagh BT92 8AP. *T:* (028) 6773 8208. *Clubs:* White's; Lough Erne Yacht. *Died 23 Dec. 2015.*

ERRINGTON, Col Sir Geoffrey (Frederick), 2nd Bt *cr* 1963; OBE 1998; Chairman, Harefield Hospital NHS Trust, 1991–98; *b* 15 Feb. 1926; *er s* of Sir Eric Errington, 1st Bt, JP, and Marjorie (*d* 1973), *d* of A. Grant Bennett; *S* father, 1973; *m* 1955, Diana Kathleen Forbes, *o d* of late E. Barry Davenport, Edgbaston, Birmingham; three *s*. *Educ:* Rugby Sch.; New Coll., Oxford. GSO 3 (Int.), HQ 11 Armd Div., 1950–52; GSO 3, MI3 (b), War Office, 1955–57; psc 1958; Bde Major 146 Inf. Bde, 1959–61; Coy Comdr, RMA Sandhurst, 1963–65; Military Assistant to Adjutant-General, 1965–67; CO 1st Bn, The King's Regt, 1967–69; GSO 1, HQ 1st British Corps, 1969–71; Col. GS, HQ NW District, 1971–74; AAG MI (Army), MoD, 1974–75; retired 1975. Col, The King's Regt, 1975–86; Chm., The King's and Manchester Regts Assoc., 1971–86. Director: Personnel Services, British Shipbuilders, 1977–78; Executive Appointments, 1979–90 (Chm., 1982–90). Employer Bd Mem., Shipbuilding ITB, 1977–78. Chm., Assoc. for Prevention of Addiction, Community Drug and Alcohol Initiatives, 1994–98 (Vice-Chm., 1991–94); Mem. Gen. Cttee, Not Forgotten Assoc., 1991–. Chm., Standing Council of the Baronetage, 2001–06 (Vice-Pres., 2006–). Vice-Pres., Britain-Australia Soc., 2009– (Hon. Dir, 1998–2006; Dir-Gen., 2006–09). Chm., Woodroffe's Club, 1988–94. Freeman, City of London, 1980; Liveryman: Broderers' Co.; Coachmakers' and Coach Harness Makers' Co. FRSA 1994. *Recreations:* music, travelling, gardening. *Heir: s* Robin Davenport Errington [*b* 1 July 1957; *m* 2001, Margerita Dudek; two *s*]. *Address:* Stone Hill Farm, Sellindge, Ashford, Kent TN25 6AJ; 203A Gloucester Place, NW1 6BU. *Clubs:* Boodle's, Oxford and Cambridge. *Died 3 Oct. 2015.*

ERRINGTON, Sir Lancelot, KCB 1976 (CB 1962); Second Permanent Secretary, Department of Health and Social Security, 1973–76; *b* 14 Jan. 1917; *e s* of late Major L. Errington; *m* 1939, Katharine Reine (*d* 2009), *o d* of late T. C. Macaulay; two *s* two *d*. *Educ:* Wellington Coll.; Trinity Coll., Cambridge. Entered Home Office, 1939. Served RNVR, 1939–45. Transferred to Ministry of National Insurance, 1945; Principal Private Sec. to Minister of National Insurance, 1951; Asst Sec., 1953; Under-Sec., 1957–65; Cabinet Office, 1965–68; Min. of Social Security, 1968; Asst Under-Sec. of State, DHSS, 1968–71, Dep. Under-Sec. of State, 1971–73. *Recreation:* sailing. *Address:* Forthside, Liberty, Elie, Fife KY9 1AU. *T:* (01333) 330227. *Died 18 Oct. 2011.*

ERSKINE-HILL, Prof. (Henry) Howard, PhD, LittD; FBA 1985; Professor of Literary History, 1994–2003, then Emeritus, and Fellow of Pembroke College, 1980–2003, then Emeritus, Cambridge University; *b* 19 June 1936; *s* of late Henry Erskine-Hill and Hannah Lilian Poppleton. *Educ:* Ashville Coll.; Nottingham Univ. (BA, PhD); MA Cantab; LittD Cantab 1988. University of Wales, Swansea: Tutor, 1960; Asst Lectr, 1961; Lectr in Eng. Lit., 1962; Sen. Fellow, 1964–65; University of Cambridge: Lectr in English, 1969–84; Reader in Literary Hist., 1984–94; Fellow, 1969–80, Tutor, 1970–76, Jesus Coll.; Tutor for Graduates, Pembroke Coll., 1983–84. Olin Fellow, Nat. Humanities Center, NC, USA, 1988–89. Taught at British Council seminars in Britain, 1962–69; invited lectr, univs of Alberta, Adelaide, Berkeley (Calif), Bristol, Davis (Calif), Essex, Flinders (S Australia), Liverpool, London, Monash, Nantes, Oxford, Saskatchewan, Stanford, Singapore, Wales (Swansea), Victoria (BC), Warwick, W Australia and York; also at David Nichol Smith Seminar, Canberra, Inter-Univ. Centre, Dubrovnik, Inst. of Hist. Res., London, and Herzog-August Library, Wolfenbüttel. *Publications:* (ed) Alexander Pope: Horatian Satires and Epistles, 1964; Pope: The Dunciad, 1972; The Social Milieu of Alexander Pope, 1975; (ed with Anne Smith) The Art of Alexander Pope, 1978; (ed with Graham Storey) Revolutionary Prose of the English Civil War, 1983; The Augustan Idea, 1983; (ed with Alexander Lindsay) William Congreve: the critical heritage, 1989; Gulliver's Travels, 1993; (ed with Richard A. McCabe) Presenting Poetry, 1995; Poetry and the Realm of Politics, 1996; Poetry of Opposition and Revolution, 1996; (introd and ed) Alexander Pope: world and word, 1998; (ed) Alexander Pope, Selected Letters, 2000; (ed with Jonathan Clark) Samuel Johnson in Historical Context, 2002; (with Eveline Cruickshanks) The Atterbury Plot, 2004; (with Jonathan Clark) The Politics of Samuel Johnson, 2012; (ed with Jonathan Clark) The Interpretations of Samuel Johnson, 2012; contributions to: Renaissance and Modern Essays, ed G. R. Hibbard, 1966; English Drama: forms and development, ed Marie Axton and Raymond Williams, 1977; Ideology and Conspiracy, ed Eveline Cruickshanks, 1982; Samuel Johnson: new critical essays, ed Isobel Grundy, 1984; English Satire and the Satiric Tradition, ed Claude Rawson, 1984; The Enduring Legacy: Alexander Pope tercentenary essays, ed G. S. Rousseau and Pat Rogers, 1988; Lord Burlington: architect, art and life, ed Toby Barnard and Jane Clark, 1995; The Stuart Court in Exile and the Jacobites, ed Eveline Cruickshanks and Edward Corp, 1995; Enlightened Groves: essays in honour of Zenzo Suzuki, ed Eiichi Hara, Hiroshi Ozawa and Peter Robinson, 1996; Imagined Commonwealths, ed T. J. Cribb, 1999; John Dryden: tercentary essays, ed Paul Hammond and David Hopkins, 2000; That Second Bottle: essays on John Wilmot, Earl of Rochester, ed Nicholas Fisher, 2000; A Court in Exile, ed Edward Corp, 2004; John Dryden: his politics, his plays and his poets, ed Claude Rawson, 2004; Sustaining Literature, ed Greg Clingham, 2007; The Cambridge Companion to Alexander Pope, ed Pat Rogers, 2007; jls incl. Agenda, Age of Johnson, English Literary History, Essays in Criticism, Eighteenth-Century Studies, Jl of the Warburg and Courtauld Insts, Modern Language Review, Rev. of English Studies, Renaissance and Modern Studies, Yearbook of English Studies. *Recreation:* collecting. *Address:* Pembroke College, Cambridge CB2 1RF. *T:* (01223) 338100. *Club:* Oxford and Cambridge. *Died 26 Feb. 2014.*

ESSAYAN, Michael; QC 1976; *b* 7 May 1927; *s* of late Kevork Loris Essayan and Rita Sirvarte (*née* Gulbenkian); *m* 1956, Geraldine St Lawrence Lee Guinness, *d* of K. E. L. Guinness, MBE; one *s* one *d*. *Educ:* France; Harrow; Balliol Coll., Oxford (1st Cl. Class. Hon. Mods 1949, 1st Cl. Lit. Hum. 1951, MA). Served with RA, 1945–48 (Palestine, 1947–48). Iraq Petroleum Co., London and ME, 1951–56. Called to the Bar, Middle Temple 1957 (Bencher 1983), joined Lincoln's Inn *ad eundem* 1958. Mem., Gen. Council of the Bar, 1987–88. Mem., Bd of Administration, Calouste Gulbenkian Foundn, Lisbon, 1981–2005, Hon. Pres., 1992–. Hon. FKC 2008. Comdr, Order of Merit (Portugal), 1993; Grand Cross, Order of Prince Henry the Navigator (Portugal), 2005. *Publications:* The New Supreme Court Costs (with M. J. Albery, QC), 1960; (ed with Hon. Mr Justice Walton) Adkin's Landlord and Tenant, 15th, 16th, 17th and 18th edns. *Recreation:* wine and wife. *Address:* 6 Chelsea Square, SW3 6LF. *T:* (020) 7352 6786. *Club:* Brooks's. *Died 23 Oct. 2012.*

ESSEX-CATER, Dr Antony John, LRCP, MRCS; FFPH; FRAI; Medical Officer of Health, States of Jersey, Channel Islands, 1974–88; Venereologist, General Hospital, Jersey, 1974–88; Vice President, National Association for Maternal and Child Welfare, since 1988 (Chairman, 1975–88); *b* 28 Sept. 1923; *s* of Herbert Stanley Cater and Helen Marjorie Essex; *m* 1947, Jane Mary Binning; two *s* one *d* (and one *s* decd). *Educ:* Solihull Sch.; King's Coll., Univ. of London; Charing Cross Hosp.; School of Hyg. and Trop. Med., Univ. of London. Bygott Postgrad. Schol., Univ. of London, 1952–53. DPH, DIH, DCH; FRSPH; AFOM. Medical Br., RAF, 1948–50. Dep. MOH, Swansea, 1953–58; Admin. MOH, Birmingham, 1958–61; Dep. MOH, Manchester, 1961–68; County MOH, Monmouthshire, 1968–74. Part-time Lectr in Child Health, Univ. of Birmingham, 1958–61; Council of Europe Medical Fellow, 1968. Short-term Consultant, WHO, 1988–89. Mem. Exec. Cttee 1958, Vice-Chm. 1969, Nat. Assoc. for Maternal and Child Welfare; Member: Public Health Lab. Services Bd, 1969–75; Steering Cttee, Nat. Health Service Reorganization (Wales), 1971–72; Founder Fellow and Mem. First Bd, Fac. of Community Med., Royal Colls of Physicians of UK, 1972–73. Member: BMA; Med. Soc. for Study of Venereal Diseases. *Publications:* Synopsis of Public Health and Social Medicine, 1960, 2nd edn 1967; Manual of Public Health and Community Medicine, 3rd edn 1979; numerous papers on medical and allied subjects. *Recreations:* literary, music, sport. *Address:* Honfleur, La Vallette, Mont Cambrai, St Lawrence, Jersey, CI JE3 1JP. *T:* (01534) 872438. *Club:* Society of Authors. *Died 5 Jan. 2012.*

ETCHELLS, Dr (Dorothea) Ruth, MA, BD; Principal, St John's College with Cranmer Hall, University of Durham, 1979–88 (Hon. Fellow, St John's College, Durham, 1991); *b* 17 April 1931; *d* of late Walter and Ada Etchells. *Educ:* Merchant Taylors' School for Girls, Crosby, Liverpool; Universities of Liverpool (MA) and London (BD). Head of English Dept, Aigburth Vale High Sch., Liverpool, 1959; Lectr in English, 1963, Sen. Lectr in English and Resident Tutor, 1965, Chester College of Education; Trevelyan College, Univ. of Durham: Resident Tutor and part-time Lectr in English, 1968; Vice Principal, 1972; Sen. Lectr, 1973; Mem. Council, Durham Univ., 1985–88. Examining Chaplain to Bishop of Bath and Wells, 1984–88. Member: Gen. Synod, 1985–95; Doctrine Commn, 1986–91; Crown Appointments Commn, 1987–96; Bishop's Council and Standing Cttee of Durham Diocesan Synod, 1975–97 (Chm., House of Laity, 1988–94); Council, Durham Cathedral, 2002–08. Vice-Chm., Durham FHSA, 1990–96 (Chm., Med. Services Cttee, 1990–96). Mem., Governing Council, Ridley Coll., Cambridge, 1988–2003; Mem., Governing Body, Durham High Sch., 1995–2002. Trustee, Anvil, 1983–92; Mem. Trustees, Hosp. of God, Greatham, 1995–99. Hon. Vice-Pres., CMS, 1992–. DD Lambeth, 1992; Hon. DLitt Liverpool, 2003. Chancellor's Medal, Univ. of Durham, 2010. *Publications:* Unafraid To Be, 1969; The Man with the Trumpet, 1970; A Model of Making, 1983; (ed) Poets and Prophets, 1988; Praying with the English Poets, 1990; Just as I am: personal prayers for every day, 1994, rev. edn 2008; Set My People Free: a lay challenge to the Churches, 1996; A Reading of the Parables of Jesus, 1998; Safer than a Known Way: personal prayers for every day, vol. 1, 2006, The Rainbow-coloured Cross: personal prayers for every day, vol. 2, 2007. *Recreations:* friends, quiet, country walking, painting and work in stained glass. *Address:* Flat 6, Ferens House, Christ's Hospital in Sherburn, Durham DH1 2SE. *T:* (0191) 3720067. *Died 8 Aug. 2012.*

EVANS, Rev. Prof. Christopher Francis, FBA 1991; MA; Professor of New Testament Studies, King's College, London, 1962–77, then Emeritus Professor, University of London; *b* 7 Nov. 1909; 2nd *s* of Frank and Beatrice Evans; *m* 1941, Elna Mary Pasco (*d* 1980), *d* of Walter and Elizabeth Burt; one *s*, and one step *d* (one step *s* decd). *Educ:* King Edward's Sch., Birmingham; Corpus Christi Coll., Cambridge. Asst Curate, St Barnabas, Southampton, 1934–38; Tutor Schol. Canc. Linc., 1938–44; Chaplain and

Divinity Lecturer, Lincoln Training Coll., 1944–48; Chaplain, Fellow and Lecturer in Divinity, Corpus Christi Coll., Oxford, 1948–58, Emeritus Fellow, 1977; Lightfoot Prof. of Divinity in the University of Durham and Canon of Durham Cathedral, 1959–62; Vis. Fellow, Trevelyan Coll., Durham, 1982–83. Select Preacher, University of Oxford, 1955–57; Proctor in Convocation for University of Oxford, 1955–58; Exam. Chaplain: to Bishop of Bristol, 1948–58; to Bishop of Durham, 1958–62; to Archbishop of Canterbury, 1962–74; to Bishop of Lichfield, 1969–75. FKC, 1970. Hon. Fellow, Ripon Coll., Cuddesdon, 2005. Hon. DLitt Southampton, 1977; Hon. DD Glasgow, 1987. *Publications:* Christology and Theology, 1961; The Lord's Prayer, 1963; The Beginning of the Gospel, 1968; Resurrection and the New Testament, 1970; (ed jtly) The Cambridge History of the Bible: vol. I, From the Beginnings to Jerome, 1970; Is 'Holy Scripture' Christian?, 1971; Explorations in Theology 2, 1977; The Theology of Rhetoric, 1988; Saint Luke, 1990; contribs to Journal of Theological Studies, Theology and Religious Studies, to Studies in the Gospels and to Christian Faith and Communist Faith. *Address:* Flat 23, The Foundation of Lady Katherine Leveson, Temple Balsall, Knowle, Solihull B93 0AN. *T:* (01564) 776233. *Died 30 July 2012.*

EVANS, Prof. (David) Ellis, DPhil; FBA 1983; Jesus Professor of Celtic, University of Oxford, 1978–96, then Emeritus, and Fellow of Jesus College, 1978–96, then Emeritus; *b* Llanfynydd, 23 Sept. 1930; *yr s* of David Evans and Sarah Jane (*née* Lewis); *m* 1957, Sheila Mary, *er d* of David and Evelyn Jeremy; two *d. Educ:* Llandeilo Grammar Sch.; University Coll. of Wales, Aberystwyth (Hon. Fellow, 1992), and University Coll., Swansea (Hon. Fellow, 1985) (BA Wales, 1952; MA Wales, 1954); Jesus Coll., Oxford (Meyricke Grad. Scholar, 1952–54; DPhil 1962, MA 1978; Hon. Fellow, 1997). Hosp. porter, Swansea, 1954–56; University College of Swansea: Asst Lectr in Welsh, 1957; Lectr, 1960; Reader, 1968; Prof. of Welsh Lang. and Lit. and Head of Dept of Welsh, 1974; Hon. Prof., 1990; Chm., Faculty of Medieval and Modern Langs, Oxford Univ., 1985–86. Lectures: Sir John Rhys Meml, British Acad., 1977; Rudolf Thurneysen Meml, Univ. of Bonn, 1979, 1994; O'Donnell, Univ. of Wales, 1980; G. J. Williams Meml, UC Cardiff, 1986; Sir Thomas Parry-Williams Meml, UCW, Aberystwyth, 1990. Pres. and Organizing Sec., Seventh Internat. Congress of Celtic Studies, Oxford, 1983; President: Cymdeithas Dafydd ap Gwilym, 1978–96; Irish Texts Soc., 1983–92 (Mem. Council, 1978–); Cambrian Archaeol Assoc., 1990–91; Vice President: N Amer. Congress of Celtic Studies, Ottawa, 1986; Nat. Liby of Wales, 1987–91 (Mem. Court and Council, 1974–91); Hon. Soc. of Cymmrodorion, 1999– (Mem. Council, 1984–98). Chairman: Welsh Dialect Studies Group, 1977–80; Council for Name Studies of GB and Ireland, 1980–84 (Mem. Council, 1962–); Member: Bd of Celtic Studies, Univ. of Wales, 1968–96; Internat. Cttee of Onomastic Sciences, 1975–; Welsh Arts Council, 1981–87; Royal Commn on Ancient and Hist. Monuments in Wales, 1984–96; Court, University of Wales, 1978–; Court, UC Swansea, 1980–; Court, Univ. of Wales Coll. of Cardiff, 1983–; UNESCO Internat. Cttee for the Study of Celtic Cultures, 1984– (Provisional Cttee, 1981–83); Celtic Commn, Austrian Acad. of Scis, 1987–98; Welsh Cttee, UFC, 1989–92. Editor, Lang. and Lit. Section, Bull. of Bd of Celtic Studies, 1972– (Editor-in-Chief, 1988–93); Editor-in-Chief, Studia Celtica, 1994–96; Mem. Editorial Bd: Geiriadur Prifysgol Cymru/A Dictionary of the Welsh Language, 1973–; Nomina, 1980–85; Welsh Acad. English-Welsh Dictionary, 1981–95. Hon. Mem., Druidic Order of Gorsedd of Bards, 1976–; Correspondant étranger, Etudes celtiques, 1982; For. Hon. Mem., Amer. Acad. of Arts and Scis, 1992; Hon. MRIA 2000. Hon. DLitt Wales, 1993. *Publications:* Gaulish Personal Names: a study of some continental Celtic formations, 1967; Gorchest y Celtiaid yn yr Hen Fyd, 1975; (ed) Cofiant Agricola, Rheolwr Prydain, 1975; Termau Gwleidyddiaeth, 1976; (ed) Proc. 7th Internat. Congress of Celtic Studies, Oxford (1983), 1986; (ed with R. Brinley Jones) Cofio'r Dafydd, 1987; (consultant ed.) Dictionary of Celtic Mythology, ed James MacKillop, 1998; *contributed:* Swansea and its Region, ed W. G. V. Balchin, 1971; Homenaje a Antonio Tovar, 1972; (contrib.) The Anatomy of Wales, ed R. Brinley Jones, 1972; Indogermanisch und Keltisch, ed K. H. Schmidt, 1977; Aufstieg und Niedergang der römischen Welt, ed H. Temporini and W. Haase, 1983; Proc. 6th Internat. Congress of Celtic Studies, Galway (1979), 1983; Geschichte und Kultur der Kelten, ed K. H. Schmidt, 1986; Y Gwareiddiad Celtaidd, ed Geraint Bowen, 1987; Cell Gymysg o'r Genedlaethol, 1989; Britain 400–600: Language and History, 1990; Cof Cenedl, 1992; Lengua y Cultura en la Hispania Prerromana, 1993; (jtly) The Celtic Languages, ed M. J. Ball, 1993; Indogermanica et Caucasica, ed R. Bielmeier, 1994; The World of the Celts, ed M. Aldhouse Green, 1995; Die grosseren altkeltischen Sprachdenkmäler, 1996; Irish Texts Society: the first hundred years, 1998; contrib. Proc. British Acad., colloquia and Festschriften; articles and revs in learned journals. *Recreations:* music, flowers. *Died 26 Sept. 2013.*

EVANS, Sir Haydn T.; *see* Tudor Evans.

EVANS, Prof. John Davies, OBE 1996; FBA 1973; Director, UCL Institute of Archæology (formerly University of London Institute of Archæology), and Professor of Archæology in the University of London, 1973–89, then Professor Emeritus; *b* 22 Jan. 1925; *o s* of Harry Evans and Edith Haycocks; *m* 1957, Evelyn Sladdin. *Educ:* Liverpool Institute High Sch. (open schol. in English to Pemb. Coll.); Pembroke Coll., Cambridge. War Service, 1943–47. BA 1948, MA 1950, PhD 1956, LittD 1979; Dr *hc* Lyon 2, 1983. Fellow of British Institute of Archæology at Ankara, 1951–52; Research Fellow of Pembroke Coll., Cambridge, 1953–56; Prof. of Prehistoric Archæology, London Univ., 1956–73. President: Prehistoric Soc., 1974–78; Council for British Archæology, 1979–82; Member: Permanent Council, Internat. Union of Prehistoric and Protohistoric Scis, 1975– (Pres., 1982–86); Royal Commn on Historical Monuments (England), 1985–92; Chairman: Area Archaeol Adv. Cttee for SE England, 1975–79; Treasure Trove Reviewing Cttee, Dept of Nat. Heritage, 1988–96. FSA 1955 (Dir, 1975–80, 1983–84, Pres., 1984–87); Member: German Archaeological Inst., 1979– (Corresp. Mem., 1968–79); Instituto Italiano di Preistoria e Protostoria, 1983–. *Publications:* Malta (Ancient Peoples and Places Series), 1959; (with Dr A. C. Renfrew) Excavations at Saliagos, near Antiparos, 1968; The Prehistoric Antiquities of the Maltese Islands, 1971; papers and reports in archæological journals. *Recreations:* walking, listening to music. *Address:* Melbury Cottage, 5 Love Lane, Shaftesbury, Dorset SP7 8BG. *Died 4 July 2011.*

EVANS, His Honour John Field; QC 1972; a Circuit Judge, 1978–93; *b* 27 Sept. 1928; 2nd *s* of late John David Evans, Llandaff, and Lucy May Evans (*née* Field). *Educ:* Cardiff High Sch.; Exeter Coll., Oxford (MA). Pilot Officer, RAF, 1948–49. Called to Bar, Inner Temple, 1953; Dep. Chm., Worcestershire QS, 1964–71; a Recorder of the Crown Court, 1972–78. *Died 11 March 2014.*

EVANS, John Robert, CC 1978; OOnt 1991; MD, DPhil; FRCP, FRCPC, FRSC; Vice Chairman, NPS-Allelix Inc. (formerly Allelix Inc. Biotechnology), 1999–2006; Chairman: Torstar Corporation, 1993–2006; Alcan Aluminium Ltd, 1995–2002; *b* 1 Oct. 1929; *s* of William Watson Evans and Mary Thompson; *m* 1954, Gay Glassco; four *s* two *d. Educ:* Univ. of Toronto (MD); University Coll., Oxford (Rhodes Schol.; DPhil; Hon. Fellow, 1990). MACP; FRCP 1980. Jun. interne, Toronto Gen. Hosp., 1952–53; Hon. Registrar, Nat. Heart Hosp., London, 1955; Asst Res.: Sunnybrook Hosp., Toronto, 1956; Toronto Gen. Hosp., 1957; Ontario Heart Foundn Fellow, Hosp. for Sick Children, Toronto, 1958; Chief Res. Physician, Toronto Gen. Hosp., 1959; Research Fellow, Baker Clinic Research Lab., Harvard Med. Sch., 1960; Markle Schol. in Acad. Med., Univ. of Toronto, 1960–65; Associate, Dept of Med., Faculty of Med., Univ. of Toronto, 1961–65; Asst Prof., 1965–66; Dean, Faculty of Med., McMaster Univ., 1965–72, Vice-Pres., Health Sciences, 1967–72; Pres., Univ. of Toronto, 1972–78 (Pres. Emeritus, 1995); Dir, Dept of Population, Health and Nutrition, IBRD, Washington, 1979–83; CEO, Allelix Inc. (Biotechnology), 1983–89. Member: Council RCP (Can.), 1972–78; Inst. of Medicine, Nat. Acad. Sci., USA,

1972 (Mem. Council, 1976–80); Adv. Cttee Med. Res., WHO, 1976–80. Chairman: Trustees, Rockefeller Foundn, 1987–95; Canada Foundn for Innovation, 1997–2006; Walter & Duncan Gordon Charitable Foundn, Toronto, 1997–2000; MaRS Discovery District, 2000–09, then Emeritus. Dir, MDS Health Gp Ltd, Toronto. Fellow, LSHTM, 1988. Hon. LLD: McGill, 1972; Dalhousie, 1972; McMaster, 1972; Queen's, 1974; Wilfred Laurier, 1975; York, 1977; Yale, 1978; Toronto, 1980; Calgary, 1996; Hon. DSc: Meml Univ. of Newfoundland, 1973; Montreal, 1977; Royal Mil Coll., Kingston, 1989; DU: Ottawa, 1978; Limbourg, 1980; Hon. DHL Johns Hopkins, 1978. *Recreations:* ski-ing, fishing, farming. *Address:* 58 Highland Avenue, Toronto, ON M4W 2A3, Canada. *Died 13 Feb. 2015.*

EVANS, John Yorath Gwynne; Deputy Director (Air), Royal Aircraft Establishment, 1972–76; medical engineering consultant, 1980–88; *b* 10 Feb. 1922; *s* of Randell and Florence Evans, Carms; *m* 1948, Paula Lewis (*d* 2008), *d* of late Roland Ford Lewis; two *s* one *d*. *Educ:* UCW Aberystwyth. Royal Aircraft Estabt, 1942; attached to RAF, Germany, 1945–46; Supt Wind Tunnels, RAE Bedford, 1958; Head of Aerodynamics Dept, RAE, 1971. *Publications:* contrib. various sci. and tech. jls. *Recreation:* reading. *Died 1 March 2012.*

EVANS, Lloyd Thomas, AO 1979; DSc, DPhil; FRS 1976; FAA; Hon. Research Fellow, Commonwealth Scientific and Industrial Research Organization Division of Plant Industry, Canberra, Australia, since 1992; *b* 6 Aug. 1927; *s* of C. D. Evans and G. M. Fraser; *m* 1954, Margaret Honor Newell (decd); two *s* one *d* (and one *d* decd). *Educ:* Wanganui Collegiate Sch., NZ; Univ. of NZ (BSc, MAgrSc, DSc); Univ. of Oxford (DPhil). FAA 1971. Rhodes Scholar, Brasenose Coll., Oxford, 1950–54; Commonwealth Fund Fellow, Calif Inst. of Technol., 1954–56; res. scientist, CSIRO Div. of Plant Industry, Canberra, 1956–92 (Chief, Div. of Plant Industry, 1971–78). National Acad. of Sciences (USA) Pioneer Fellow, 1963; Overseas Fellow, Churchill Coll., Cambridge, 1969–70; Vis. Fellow, Wolfson Coll., Cambridge, 1978. President: ANZAAS, 1976–77; Aust. Acad. of Science, 1978–82. Member, Board of Trustees: Internat. Foundn for Sci., Stockholm, 1982–87; Internat. Rice Res. Inst., Philippines, 1984–89; Internat. Center for Improvement of Wheat and Maize, 1990–95. Mem., Norwegian Acad. of Sci. and Letters, 1990; Foreign Fellow, Nat. Acad. of Agricl Scis, India, 1992. Hon. Member: Royal Soc., NZ, 1986; RASE, 1987. Hon. LLD Canterbury, 1978. Adolph E. Gude Award, Amer. Soc. of Plant Biol., 2004. *Publications:* Environmental Control of Plant Growth, 1963; The Induction of Flowering, 1969; Crop Physiology, 1975; Daylength and the Flowering of Plants, 1976; Wheat Science: today and tomorrow, 1981; Policy and Practice, 1987; Crop Evolution, Adaptation and Yield, 1993; Feeding the Ten Billion: plants and population growth, 1998; more than 200 scientific papers in jls. *Recreations:* tennis, chopping wood, Charles Darwin. *Address:* 3 Elliott Street, Canberra, ACT 2612, Australia. *T:* (2) 62477815. *Died 23 March 2015.*

EVANS, Rt Rev. Michael; Bishop of East Anglia, (RC), since 2003; *b* 10 Aug. 1951; *s* of Ralph and Jeannette Evans. *Educ:* St John's Seminary, Wonersh; Heythrop Coll., Univ. of London (MTh 1979). Ordained priest, 1975; Asst Priest, Richmond, Surrey, 1975–77; St John's Seminary, Wonersh: Lectr in Christian Doctrine, 1979–87, 1993–95; Vice-Rector, 1985–87, 1993–95; Chaplain to S London Univs, 1987–93; Parish Priest, Tunbridge Wells, 1995–2003. Member: Catholic Bps' Conf. Cttee for Ministerial Formation, 1989–2003; British Methodist/Catholic Cttee, 1991–; Internat. Jt Commn for Dialogue between the RC Church and the World Methodist Council, 1996–; Chm., Cttee for Christian Unity, 2005–. Jt Pres., Christian-Muslim Forum, 2006–09. *Publications:* Let My People Go, 1979; A Catholic Priest Today and Tomorrow, 1993; numerous booklets and articles. *Recreations:* listening to music, supporting Leeds United FC. *Address:* The White House, 21 Upgate, Poringland, Norwich NR14 7SH. *T:* (01508) 492202. *E:* office@east-angliadiocese.org.uk. *Died 11 July 2011.*

EVANS, Sir Richard (Mark), KCMG 1984 (CMG 1978); KCVO 1986; HM Diplomatic Service, retired; Emeritus Fellow, Wolfson College, Oxford (Senior Research Fellow, 1988–95); *b* 15 April 1928; *s* of late Edward Walter Evans, CMG; *m* 1960, Margaret Elizabeth Sessinger (marr. diss. 1970); *m* 1973, Rosemary Grania Glen Birkett; two *s*. *Educ:* Dragon Sch., Oxford; Repton Sch.; Magdalen Coll., Oxford (BA 1949; MA 1992). Joined HM Foreign (later Diplomatic) Service: Third Sec., London, 1952–55; Third Sec., Peking, 1955–57; Second Sec., London, 1957–62; First Sec.: Peking, 1962–64; Berne, 1964–68; London, 1968–70; Head of Near Eastern Dept, FCO, 1970–72, Head of Far Eastern Dept, 1972–74; Fellow, Centre for Internat. Affairs, Harvard Univ., 1974–75; Commercial Counsellor, Stockholm, 1975–77; Minister (Economic), Paris, 1977–79; Asst Under-Sec. of State, 1979–82, Dep. Under-Sec. of State, 1982–83, FCO; Ambassador to People's Republic of China, 1984–88. Master, Ironmongers' Co., 1999–2000. *Publications:* Deng Xiaoping and the Making of Modern China, 1993. *Recreations:* travel, reading, music. *Address:* Sevenhampton House, Sevenhampton, near Highworth, Wilts SN6 7QA. *Club:* Oxford and Cambridge. *Died 24 Aug. 2012.*

EVANS, Roy Lyon, OBE 1993; General Secretary, Iron and Steel Trades Confederation, 1985–93; *b* 13 Aug. 1931; *s* of David Evans and Sarah (*née* Lyon); *m* 1960, Brenda Jones; one *s* two *d*. *Educ:* Gowerton Grammar Sch., Swansea. Employed in Tinplate Section of Steel Industry, 1948. Iron and Steel Trades Confederation: Divl Organiser, NW Area, 1964–69; Divl Organiser, W Wales Area, 1969–73; Asst Gen. Sec., 1973–85. Mem., Gen. Council, TUC, 1985–93. Jt Sec., Jt Industrial Council for the Slag Industry, 1975–85; Mem., ECSC Consultative Cttee, 1985–93 (Pres., 1986–88); Hon. Sec., British Section, IMF, 1985–93 (Pres., Iron and Steel Dept (World), 1986). Member: Jt Accident Prevention Adv. Cttee, 1974–93 (Chm., 1983); NEC of Labour Party, 1981–84. Bd Mem., British Steel (Industry) Ltd, 1986–94. *Recreations:* reading, walking. *Died 3 Dec. 2015.*

EVANS, Valerie Jean, CBE 1991; FRSB; Chair, Gender Statistics Users Group, since 2000; human rights activist; *b* 26 July 1930; *d* of Connie and Wilfred Evans. *Educ:* Wales; Bedford Coll., London Univ. (BSc). Science teacher, 1952–67; HM Inspectorate of Schools, 1967–90: specialist in science and develt of secondary school curriculum; Divl Staff Inspector, E and W Midlands Div., Birmingham, 1977–90. Soroptimist Internat. UK rep. on Women's Nat. Commn, 1994–97; Co-Chair, 1997–98, Chair, 1998–99, Women's Nat. Commn; Soroptimist Internat. Rep. to Econ. Commn of Europe reg. of UN, 1999–2002. Trustee or member, numerous educnl advisory bodies. *Recreations:* reading, music, china, paintings, cooking, gardens, wine. *Address:* Coombe, 84 Salisbury Road, Moseley, Birmingham B13 8JY. *Died 26 July 2015.*

EVELEIGH, Rt Hon. Sir Edward Walter; PC 1977; Kt 1968; ERD; MA; a Lord Justice of Appeal, 1977–85; *b* 8 Oct. 1917; *s* of Walter William and Daisy Emily Eveleigh; *m* 1940, Vilma Bodnar; *m* 1953, Patricia Helen Margaret Bury (*d* 1990); two *s* (and one *s* decd); *m* 1996, Nell A. Cox. *Educ:* Peter Symonds; Brasenose Coll., Oxford (Hon. Fellow 1977). Commissioned in the Royal Artillery (Supplementary Reserve), 1936; served War of 1939–45 (despatches, 1940). Called to Bar, Lincoln's Inn, 1945, Bencher 1968, Treas., 1988; QC 1961. Recorder of Burton-on-Trent, 1961–64, of Gloucester, 1964–68; Chm., QS, County of Oxford, 1968–71 (Dep. Chm., 1963–68); a Judge of the High Court of Justice, Queen's Bench Div., 1968–77; Presiding Judge, SE Circuit, 1971–76. Mem., General Council of the Bar, 1965–67. Mem., Royal Commn on Criminal Procedure, 1978–80; Chm., Statute Law Soc., 1985–89; President: British-German Jurists' Assoc., 1974–85; Bar Musical Soc., 1980–89. Hon. Citizen: Texas, 1980; Austin, 1985; Dallas, 1985. *Died 24 Sept. 2014.*

EVERITT, Caroline Mary; *see* Ludlow, C. M.

EVERTON, Timothy Charles; Dean of Educational Studies, 2001–06, and Head, Faculty of Education, 2002–06, University of Cambridge; Fellow, Homerton College, Cambridge, 2001–07, then Emeritus; owner and licencee, Phoenix Inn, York, since 2009; *b* 28 March 1951; *s* of Charles John Everton and Patricia Anne Everton (*née* Sharpe); *m* 1974, Valerie Bates; three *d*. *Educ:* Queen Mary's Grammar Sch., Walsall; Keble Coll., Oxford (MA); Univ. of Keele (MSc). Teacher of maths in secondary schs in Walsall and Shrewsbury, 1974–81; Lectr in Maths Educn, NUU, 1981–83; Lectr, later Sen. Lectr in Educn, Univ. of Leicester, 1983–92; Homerton College, Cambridge: Dep. Principal, 1992–2001; Vice-Principal, 2001–05; Sen. Tutor, 1995–2001. Treasurer: British Curriculum Foundn, 1991–2007; UCET, 1999–2005. *Publications:* jointly: IT-INSET: partnership in training, 1989; Effective Learning: into a new ERA, 1990; 16–19 Mathematics: problem solving, 1991; 16–19: changes in education and training, 1992; 16–19 Mathematics: handbook for teachers, 1993; Mathematics for A and AS Level: Pure Mathematics, 1997. *Recreations:* watching sport, walking, reading, listening to jazz. *Died 23 March 2011.*

EWANS, Sir Martin Kenneth, KCMG 1987 (CMG 1980); HM Diplomatic Service, retired; Chairman, Children's Aid Direct, 1996–2002; *b* 14 Nov. 1928; *s* of late John Ewans; *m* 1953, Mary Tooke; one *s* one *d*. *Educ:* St Paul's; Corpus Christi Coll., Cambridge (major scholar, MA). Royal Artillery, 1947–49, 2nd Lt. Joined Commonwealth Relations Office, 1952; Second Sec., Karachi, 1954–55; First Sec.: Ottawa, 1958–61; Lagos, 1962–64; Kabul, 1967–69. Counsellor, Dar-es-Salaam, 1969–73; Head of East African Dept, FCO, 1973–77; Minister, New Delhi, 1978–82; Sen. Civilian Instructor, RCDS, 1982–83; High Commissioner: Zimbabwe, 1983–85; Nigeria, 1986–88. Chm., CSSB, 1989–95. Dir, Casalee SA, 1989–94. *Publications:* Bharatpur, Bird Paradise, 1989; The Battle for the Broads, 1992; Afghanistan: a new history, 2001; Afghanistan: a short history of its people and politics, 2002; European Atrocity, African Catastrophe, 2002; The Great Game: Britain and Russia in Central Asia, 2003; Conflict in Afghanistan, 2005; Great Power Rivalry in Central Asia 1842–1880, 2005; Britain and Russia in Central Asia, 1880–1907, 2008; (ed) George Nathaniel Curzon: collected writings: travels in Asia, 2008; Securing the Indian Frontier in Central Asia: confrontation and negotiation, 1865–1895, 2010. *Recreations:* bird watching, writing. *Address:* 48 Gretton Court, Girton, Cambridge CB3 0QN. *Died 5 April 2012.*

EWBANK, Sir Anthony (Bruce), Kt 1980; Judge of the High Court of Justice, Family Division, 1980–95; *b* 30 July 1925; *s* of late Rev. Harold Ewbank and Gwendolen Ewbank (*née* Bruce); *m* 1958, Moya McGinn (*d* 2009); four *s* one *d*. *Educ:* St John's Sch., Leatherhead; Trinity Coll., Cambridge, Natural Sciences Tripos (MA). Sub Lieut RNVR, 1945–47. Maths Master, Stamford School, 1947–50; Physics Master, Epsom Coll., 1950–53. Permanent RNVR, 1951–56. Called to Bar, Gray's Inn, 1954; Bencher, 1980. Junior Counsel to Treasury in Probate matters, 1969; QC 1972; a Recorder of the Crown Court, 1975–80. Chm., Family Law Bar Assoc., 1978–80. *Address:* Beech Down, Elmhurst Road, Goring on Thames, Oxon RG8 9BN. *Died 25 June 2011.*

EWBANK, Ven. Walter Frederick; Archdeacon of Carlisle, 1977–84, then Archdeacon Emeritus; Canon Residentiary, Carlisle Cathedral, 1977–82, then Canon Emeritus (Honorary Canon, 1966–77); *b* Poona, India, 29 Jan. 1918; *er s* of late Sir Robert Benson Ewbank, CSI, CIE, and Frances Helen, *d* of Rev. W. F. Simpson; *m* 1st, 1941, Ida Margaret (*d* 1976), 3rd *d* of late John Haworth Whitworth, DSO, MC, Inner Temple; three *d*; 2nd, 1976, Mrs Josephine Alice Williamson (*née* Cartwright), MD, ChB, FRCOG (*d* 2003). *Educ:* Shrewsbury Sch.; Balliol Coll., Oxford (Classical Scholar, 1936; 1st, Classical Hon. Mods, 1938; 2nd, Hon. Sch. of Theology, 1946; BA and MA 1946); Bishops' Coll., Cheshunt, 1946; BD Oxon 1952. Friends' Ambulance Unit, 1939–42; agricl labourer, 1942–45; ordained deacon, 1946, priest, 1947; Asst Curate, St Martin's, Windermere, 1946–49; Dio. Youth Chaplain and Vicar of Ings, 1949–52; Chap. to Casterton Sch. and Vicar of Casterton, 1952–62; Domestic Chap. to Bp of Carlisle, and Vicar of Raughtonhead, 1962–66; Vicar of St Cuthbert's, Carlisle, and Chap. to Corporation, 1966–71; Rural Dean of Carlisle, 1970–71; Archdeacon of Westmorland and Furness, and Vicar of Winster, 1971–77; Administrator of Church House, Carlisle and Chm., Diocesan Glebe Cttee, 1977–84. Proctor in Convocation and Mem. Ch Assembly, 1957–70; Member: Canon Law Standing Commn, 1968–70; Faculty Jurisdiction Commn, 1979–83; Diocesan Director: of Ordinands, 1962–70; of Post Ordination Trng, 1962–66; Vice-Chm., Diocesan Synod, 1970–79; Chm., Diocesan Board of Finance, 1977–82. Chm., Carlisle Tithe Barn Restoration Cttee, 1968–70. Winter War Remembrance Medal (Finland), 1940. *Publications:* Salopian Diaries, 1961; Morality without Law, 1969; Charles Euston Nurse—A Memoir, 1982; Thomas Bloomer—A Memoir, 1984; Poems of Cumbria and of the Cumbrian Church, 1985; Ellen Margaret Cartwright—A Memoir, 1991; Memories of the Border Regiment in the First World War, 1991; Faith of Our Fathers, 1992; Characters and Occasions, 2002; articles in Church Quarterly Review. *Recreation:* classical studies. *Address:* 10 Castle Court, Castle Street, Carlisle CA3 8TP. *Died 23 March 2014.*

EWING, Hamish O.; *see* Orr-Ewing, H.

EWINGTON, John, OBE 1996; General Secretary, Guild of Church Musicians, 1979–2013, then General Secretary Emeritus, and Administrative Secretary, 2014; Consultant, Carroll & Partners Ltd, 2001–03; *b* 14 May 1936; *s* of William and Beatrice Ewington; *m* 1967, Hélène Mary Leach; two *s*. *Educ:* South East Essex County Technical Sch., Dagenham; ACertCM 1968; Dip Church Music, Goldsmiths' Coll., 1988. Nat. Service, RN, 1954–56. Admin. Assistant, Inst. of London Underwriters, 1953–67; Underwriting Asst, P. C. W. Agencies, Lloyd's, 1967–86; Sen. Broker, 1986–97, Consultant, 1997–2000, HSBC Gibbs. Director of Music and Organist: Blechingley Parish Church, 1966–97; St Mary Woolnoth, 1970–93 (also Sen. Ch Warden, 1973–93); St Katharine Cree, 1998–; Dir, City Singers, 1976–. Freeman, City of London, 1980; Liveryman, Musicians' Co., 2002–. Hon. Associate and Conjoint Sen. Lectr, Conservatorium of Music and Drama, Faculty of Music and Arts, Univ. of Newcastle, NSW, 2004–. Governor: de Stafford Sch., Caterham, 1980–85; Oxted Sch., 1985–2005 (Vice Chm. of Govs, 1993–2005). FGCM 1988. Hon. FCSM 1990; Hon. FFCM, Central Sch. of Religion, Indiana, 1998; Hon. RSCM 2002. MA Lambeth, 2003. KLJ 2007 (CLJ 2005). *Publications:* (with Canon A. Dobb) Landmarks in Christian Worship and Church Music, 2001; Now What (autobiog.), 2013; articles on church music in jls. *Recreations:* church music, cooking, eating out. *Address:* Hillbrow, Godstone Road, Bletchingley, Surrey RH1 4PJ. *T:* (01883) 743168. *E:* JohnMusicsure@orbixmail.co.uk. *Club:* Friday (Bletchingley). *Died 15 Aug. 2015.*

EWUSIE, Prof. Joseph Yanney; Chairman, Promotion of the Study, Research and Application of Mathematics, Science and Technology, since 2007; *b* 18 April 1927; *s* of Samuel Mainsa Wilson Ewusie and Elizabeth Dickson; *m* 1st, 1959, Stella Turkson (*d* 1989); five *s*, and one adopted *d*; 2nd, 1992, Emma (*née* Ghampson) (marr. diss. 1997); 3rd, 1998, Ruth (*née* Ohene Parry). *Educ:* Winneba Anglican Sch.; Mfantsipim Sch.; University Coll. of the Gold Coast; Univ. of Cambridge. BSc (London), PhD (Cantab). Lectr in Botany, Univ. of Ghana, 1957–62; Gen. Sec. (Chief Exec.), Ghana Academy of Sciences (highest learned and res. org. in Ghana), 1963–68; University of Cape Coast: Associate Prof. of Botany, 1969–72, Prof., 1973–79; Head, Dept of Botany, 1969–73; Dean, Faculty of Science, 1971–74; Pro-Vice Chancellor, 1971–73; Vice Chancellor, 1973–78. Vis. Prof./Prof., Univs of Nairobi and Ahmadu Bello, Nigeria, 1979–80; Sec.-Gen., Pan African Inst. for Development, 1980–83; Professor of Biology: Univ. of Swaziland, 1984–90; Univ. of Bophuthatswana, 1989–92. Mem. Exec. Cttee, ICSU, 1964–67. Founder and First Pres., Ghana Inst. of Biology, 1994 (Fellow 1995). Member: Bimillennium Foundn, Washington DC, 1984–; NY Acad. of Sciences, 1984–. FWA 1963. Co-Founder and First Editor, Swaziland Jl of Sci. and Technol. Hon. DSc Cape Coast, 1994. Medal (Govt of Hungary) for internat. understanding between Ghana and Hungary, 1964; Dip. of Merit, Internat. Acad. of Science, Letters and Arts, Rome, 1968; Dip. of Honour, Internat. Inst. of Community Service, 1975; Ghana Scientist of the Year, Ghana Science Assoc., 1985. *Publications:* School Certificate

Biology for Tropical Schools, 1964, 4th edn 1974; Tropical Biological Drawings, 1973; Elements of Tropical Ecology, 1980; Phenology in Tropical Ecology, 1992. *Address:* PO Box LG 696, Legon-Accra, Ghana. *Died 14 June 2012.*

EYRE, Brian Leonard, CBE 1993; DSc; FRS 2001; FREng; CPhys; Senior Visiting Fellow, University of Oxford, since 2006 (Visiting Professor, 1996–2006); Chairman, Council for the Central Laboratory of the Research Councils, 2000–01 (Member, 1998–2001); *b* 29 Nov. 1933; *s* of Leonard George and Mabel Eyre; *m* 1965, Elizabeth Caroline (*née* Rackham); two *s. Educ:* Greenford Grammar Sch.; Univ. of Surrey (BSc, DSc). FREng (FEng 1992); FIMMM; FInstP. Research Officer, CEGB, 1959–62; Gp Leader, UKAEA, Harwell, 1962–79; Prof., Materials Science, Univ. of Liverpool, 1979–84; United Kingdom Atomic Energy Authority: Dir, Fuel and Engrg Technology, Risley, 1984–87; Mem. Bd, 1987–96; Dep. Chm., 1989–96; Chief Exec., 1990–94; Dep. Chm., AEA Technology plc, 1996–97. Mem., PPARC, 1996–2000. Visiting Professor: Univ. of Illinois, 1969–70; Univ. of Wisconsin, 1976; Univ. of Liverpool, 1984–; UCL, 1995–; Vis. Fellow, Wolfson Coll., Oxford, 1996–2001. Mem. Council, Foundn of Sci. and Technology, 1994–2001. For. Associate, US NAE, 2009–. *Publications:* over 150 papers in Procs Royal Soc., Philosophical Magazine, Acta Metallurgica, etc. *Recreations:* sailing, walking, mountaineering. *Address:* Materials Department, University of Oxford, Parks Road, Oxford OX1 3PH. *Died 28 July 2014.*

EYRE, Very Rev. Richard Montague Stephens; Dean of Exeter, 1981–95; *b* 16 May 1929; *s* of Montague Henry and Ethel Mary Eyre; *m* 1963, Anne Mary Bentley; two *d. Educ:* Charterhouse; Oriel Coll., Oxford (MA); St Stephen's House, Oxford. Deacon 1956, priest 1957; Curate, St Mark's Church, Portsea, 1956–59; Tutor and Chaplain, Chichester Theological Coll., 1959–62; Chaplain, Eastbourne Coll., 1962–65; Vicar of Arundel, 1965–73; Vicar of Good Shepherd, Brighton, 1973–75; Archdeacon of Chichester, 1975–81; Treasurer of Chichester Cathedral, 1978–81; Priest i/c, St Andrew's, Pau, France, 2001–03. Mem., Gen. Synod of C of E, 1985–95. *Publications:* Faith in God?, 1990. *Recreations:* golf, music, travel, gardening. *Address:* 32 Exe Vale Road, Exeter EX2 6LF. *Club:* Oxford and Cambridge. *Died 12 Dec. 2012.*

EZRA, Baron *cr* 1983 (Life Peer), of Horsham in the County of West Sussex; **Derek Ezra,** Kt 1974; MBE 1945; President, National Home Improvement Council, 1986–2005 (Hon. Vice-President, since 2005); *b* 23 Feb. 1919; *s* of David and Lillie Ezra; *m* 1950, Julia Elizabeth Wilkins (*d* 2011). *Educ:* Monmouth Sch.; Magdalene Coll., Cambridge (MA, Hon. Fellow, 1977). Army, 1939–47. Joined NCB, 1947; representative of NCB at Cttees of OEEC and ECE, 1948–52; Mem. of UK Delegn to High Authority of European Coal and Steel Community, 1952–56; Dep. Regional Sales Manager, NCB, 1956–58; Regional Sales Manager, 1958–60; Dir-Gen. of Marketing, NCB, 1960–65; NCB Bd Mem., 1965–67; Dep. Chm., 1967–71; Chm., 1971–82. Chairman: Associated Heat Services plc, 1966–99; J. H. Sankey & Son Ltd, 1977–82; Petrolex PLC, 1982–85; Throgmorton Trust PLC, 1984–91; Sheffield Heat and Power Ltd, 1985–2000; Associated Gas Supplies Ltd, 1987–95; Energy and Technical Services Gp plc, 1990–99; Micropower Ltd, 2000–05 (Patron, Micropower Council, 2005–); Director: British Fuel Co., 1966–82; Solvay SA, 1979–90; Redland PLC, 1982–89; Supervisory Bd, Royal Boskalis Westminster NV, 1982–85. Industrial Advr, Morgan Grenfell & Co. Ltd, 1982–88. Chm., NICG, 1972 and 1980–81; President: Nat. Materials Handling Centre, 1979; Coal Industry Soc., 1981–86 (Chm., 1961); W European Coal Producers' Assoc., 1976–79; BSI, 1983–86; Economic Res. Council, 1985–2000; Inst. of Trading Standards Admin, 1987–92; Vice-Pres., BIM, 1978 (Chm., 1976–78); Chm., British Iron and Steel Consumers' Council, 1983–86; Member: BOTB, 1972–82 (Chm., European Trade Cttee); Cons. Cttee, ECSC, 1973–82 (Pres., 1978–79); Adv. Council for Energy Conservation, 1974–79; Adv. Bd, Petrofina SA, 1982–90; Internat. Adv. Bd, Creditanstalt Bankverein, 1982–90; Energy Commn, 1977–79; Ct of Governors, Administrative Staff Coll., 1971–82; Internat. Adv. Bd, Banca Nazionale del Lavoro, 1984–94; Governor, London Business Sch., 1973–82. Pres., Keep Britain Tidy Gp, 1985–89 (Chm., 1979–85). Hon. Liveryman, Haberdashers' Co., 1982; Liveryman, Fuellers' Co., 1987. Hon. DSc Cranfield, 1979; Hon. LLD Leeds, 1982. Bronze Star (USA), 1945; Grand Officer, Italian Order of Merit, 1979; Comdr, Luxembourg Order of Merit, 1981; Officer of Légion d'Honneur, 1981. *Publications:* Coal and Energy, 1978; The Energy Debate, 1983. *Address:* House of Lords, Westminster, SW1A 0PW. *T:* (020) 7219 3180. *Died 22 Dec. 2015.*

PARLIAMENTARY
ARCHIVES

F

FABER, Michael Leslie Ogilvie; Professor Emeritus, Institute of Development Studies, Sussex University (Director, 1982–87; Professorial Fellow, 1982–94); *b* 12 Aug. 1929; *s* of George and Kathleen Faber; *m* 1956, Diana Catriona Howard (*d* 2004); two *s* twin *d*. *Educ:* Avon Old Farms, USA; Eton; Magdalen Coll., Oxford (MA); Univ. of Michigan. MA Cantab. Served 11th Hussars, PAO, Germany, 1948–49. Merchant Seaman, 1953–54. Claims Adjuster, Amer. Internat. Underwriters, Japan and Korea, 1954; Foreign Correspondent for Sunday Times, Observer, and Economist in FE, ME, N and Central Africa, 1954–60; Lectr in Econs, UCRN, 1958–60; community develt worker with Danilo Dolci in Sicily, 1961; Lectr in Econs, UWI, 1962–63; Sen. Economist and Under-Sec., Govt of Zambia, 1964–67; Dept of Applied Econs, Cambridge, 1968; Overseas Develt Gp, UEA, 1969–78; Dir, Tech. Assistance Gp, Commonwealth Secretariat, 1972–75 and 1978–82. Member: Council, Overseas Develt Inst., 1982–2001; Bd, Commonwealth Develt Corp., 1988–97. Pres., UK Chapter, Soc. for Internat. Develt, 1986–91. Leader, UNDP/IBRD Mission to PNG, 1972; specialist negotiator of debt and resource agreements. *Publications:* Economic Structuralism and its Relevance, 1965; (with J. Potter) Towards Economic Independence, 1971; (ed with Dudley Seers) The Crisis in Economic Planning, 1972; (with R. Brown) Mining Agreements: law and policy, 1977; (with R. Brown) Changing the Rules of the Game, 1980; Conciliatory Debt Reduction: why it must come and how it could come, 1988; Beware of Debtspeak, 1988. *Address:* Rodmell Hill Cottage, Mill Lane, Rodmell, E Sussex BN7 3HS. *Club:* Brooks's. *Died 26 Feb. 2015.*

FAGAN, Maj.-Gen. Patrick Feltrim, CB 1990; MBE (mil.) 1966; FRICS 1971; FRGS 1966; *b* 8 Dec. 1935; *s* of late Air Cdre Thomas Patrick Feltrim Fagan and Hon. Isabel Mairi, *yr d* of 15th Baron Arundell of Wardour; *m* 1967, Veronica Thompson (*née* Lorant) (*d* 2003), *widow* of Captain C. J. C. Thompson, RE; two *s*. *Educ:* Stonyhurst Coll.; RMA, Sandhurst; University Coll. London (MSc (Hons) 1969). Commnd RE, 1955; served in Gibraltar, Germany, Aden and Oman. Internat. Scientific Expedn to Karakoram, 1961–62; UAE-Oman Border Survey, 1964; Jt Services Expedn to S Georgia, 1964–65; Ordnance Survey, 1969–73; Geographic Advr, AFCENT, 1979–83; Chief Geographic Officer, SHAPE, 1983–85; Dir, Survey Operations and Prodn, 1985–87; Dir Gen. of Military Survey, 1987–90. Member: Council, RGS, 1987–92 and 1993–95 (Vice-Pres., 1990–92); Council, BSES, 1987–90; Cttee of Management, Mt Everest Foundn, 1989–95 (Chm., 1992–94); Nat. Cttee for Photogrammetry and Remote Sensing, 1987–91; Adv. Bd, Inst. of Engrg, Surveying and Space Geodesy, Nottingham Univ., 1987–91; Council, RICS Land Surveyors, 1988–91; RICS Pres.'s Disciplinary and Appeals Tribunal, 1989–95; Pres., Defence Surveyors' Assoc., 2004–12. Dep. Pres., Army RU, 1989–91. Col Comdt, RE, 1991–96, Rep. Col Comdt, 1992. Chm., James Caird Soc., 2000–06. FCMI (FBIM 1971). *Publications:* articles on surveying and mapping in Geographical Jl, Photogrammetric Record, Survey Rev., Chartered Surveyor, and on ski mountaineering in subject jls. *Recreations:* mountain sports, cricket, reading, photography, opera, travel. *Clubs:* Royal Over-Seas League, Alpine (Vice Pres., 1999–2001), Alpine Ski (Pres., 1995–98), Eagle Ski (Pres., 1988–90), MCC, Geographical. *Died 28 June 2013.*

FAIRCLOUGH, Anthony John, CMG 1990; Hon. Director General, European Commission (formerly Commission of the European Communities), since 1989; *b* 30 Aug. 1924; *m* 1957, Patricia Monks; two *s*. *Educ:* St Philip's Grammar Sch., Birmingham; St Catharine's Coll., Cambridge (Scholar 1944, BA Cantab 1945, MA 1950). Ministry of Aircraft Production and Ministry of Supply, 1944–48; Colonial Office, 1948–65; Secretary, Nyasaland Commn of Inquiry, 1959; Private Secretary to Minister of State for Commonwealth Relations and for the Colonies, 1963–64; Assistant Secretary, 1964; Head of Pacific and Indian Ocean Dept, Colonial Office, subseq. Commonwealth Office, 1964–68; Head of W Indian Dept, FCO, 1968–70; Head of New Towns 1 Div., DoE, 1970–72; Under-Sec., 1973; Head of Planning, Minerals and Countryside Directorate, 1973, of Planning, Sport and Countryside Directorate, 1973–74; Dir, Central Unit on Environmental Pollution, 1974–78; Dir, Internat. Transport, Dept of Transport, 1978–81; Dir for the Environment, CEC, 1981–85; Actg Dir Gen. for the Environment, Consumer Protection and Nuclear Safety, CEC, 1985–86; Dep. Dir-Gen. for Develt, CEC, 1986–89. Senior UK Commissioner at Sessions of South Pacific Commn, 1965–67; Minister's Deputy, European Conf. of Ministers of Transport, 1978–81; Chairman: Environment Cttee, OECD, 1976–79; British Channel Tunnel Co., 1978–81; British Co-Chm., Jt UK/USSR Cttee established under UK/USSR Agreement on cooperation in field of Environmental Protection, 1974–78; Special Advr, EC, 1989–94; Capacity 21 Advr, UNDP, 1993–95; Sen. Adviser, Envmtl Resources Mgt, 1989–99; Chm., Network for Envmtl Technology Transfer, asbl, Belgium, 1989–; Dir, Groundwork Foundn, 1989–95. Consultant to European Orgn for Res. and Treatment of Cancer, 1989–95. Member: Royal Soc.'s British Nat. Cttee on Problems of Environment, 1974–78; EDC for Internat. Freight Movement, 1978–80; Governing Body, Chiswick Sch., 1973–79. CompICE, 1989–93. FRSA. *Address:* 6 Cumberland Road, Kew, Richmond, Surrey TW9 3HQ. *Died 9 Feb. 2014.*

FAIRWEATHER, Clive Bruce, CBE 2003 (OBE 1990); HM Chief Inspector of Prisons for Scotland, 1994–2002; *b* 21 May 1944; *s* of George Fairweather and Helen Fairweather (*née* Henderson); *m* 1980, Ann Beatrice Dexter (marr. diss. 2003); one *s* two *d*. *Educ:* George Heriot's Sch.; RMA Sandhurst. Army Staff Coll., 1975–76; CO, Scottish Infantry Depot, 1984–87; Instr, RAF Staff Coll., 1987; CO, 1st Bn King's Own Scottish Borderers, 1987–89; Divl Col, Scottish Div., 1991–94. *Publications:* (jtly) Women Offenders: a safer way, 1998; Punishment First - Verdict Later, 2000. *Recreation:* piano. *Address:* c/o Cox's & King's, 7 Pall Mall, SW1Y 5NA. *E:* clive.fairweather@combatstress.org.uk. *Club:* Special Forces. *Died 13 Oct. 2012.*

FAITH, (Irene) Sheila; JP; dental surgeon; *b* 3 June 1928; *yr d* of late I. Book; *m* 1950, Dennis Faith. *Educ:* Central High School, Newcastle upon Tyne; Durham Univ. LDS 1950. Practised as schools dental surgeon, Northumberland. Member: Northumberland CC, 1970–74 (Mem., Health and Social Services Cttees; Rep., S Northumberland Youth Employment Bd); Newcastle City Council, 1975–77 (Mem., Educn Cttee). Vice-Chm., Jt Consultative Cttee on Educn for District of Newcastle during local govt reorganisation, 1973–74. Mem., Parole Bd, 1991–94. Contested (C) Newcastle Central, Oct. 1974; MP (C) Belper, 1979–83. Mem., Select Cttee on Health and Social Services, 1979–83; Sec., Conservative backbench Health and Social Services Cttee, 1982–83. MEP (C) Cumbria and Lancs N, 1984–89; Member: Transport Cttee, 1984–87; Cttee on Energy, Res. and Technol., 1987–89. Mem., Exec. Cttee, Cons. Medical Soc., 1981–84; Pres., Cumbria and Lancs N Cons. Euro Constituency Council, 1989–95; Dep. Chm., Hampstead and Highgate Cons. Assoc., 1991–92. Served as Chm. or Mem. several school governing bodies and Manager of Community Homes and with CAB, Newcastle upon Tyne. JP: Northumberland County, 1972–74; Newcastle upon Tyne, 1974–78; Inner London, 1978–. *Recreations:* reading, music. *Address:* 52 Moor Court, Westfield, Gosforth, Newcastle upon Tyne NE3 4YD. *T:* (0191) 285 4438. *Club:* Royal Society of Medicine. *Died 28 Sept. 2014.*

FALCON, Michael Gascoigne, CBE 1979; JP, DL; Chairman: Norwich Union Insurance Group, 1981–94 (Director, 1963–94; Vice Chairman, 1979–81); Norwich

Winterthur Holdings Ltd, 1984–94; *b* 28 Jan. 1928; *s* of late Michael Falcon and Kathleen Isabel Frances Gascoigne; *m* 1954, April Daphne Claire Lambert; two *s* one *d*. *Educ:* Stowe Sch., Bucks; Heriot-Watt Coll., Edinburgh. National Service, Grenadier Gds and Royal Norfolk Regt, 1946–48. Head Brewer and Jt Man. Dir, E. Lacon & Co. Ltd, Great Yarmouth, 1952–68; Exec. Dir, Edgar Watts, Willow Merchants, 1968–73; Chairman: National Seed Develt Orgn Ltd, 1972–82; Pauls & Whites PLC, 1976–85 (Dir, 1973–85); Eastern Counties Regional Bd, Lloyds Bank Plc, 1979–91 (Dir, 1972–91); Director: Securicor (East) Ltd, 1969–72; Lloyds Bank UK Management Ltd, 1979–85; Matthew Brown plc, 1981–87; National Bus Properties Ltd, 1983–86; Greene King & Sons PLC, 1988–96; British Railways (Anglia) Bd, 1988–92. Chairman: Norwich HA, 1988–94; Norfolk and Norwich Health Care NHS Trust, 1994–97. Trustee, E Anglian Trustee Savings Bank, 1963–75. Chm., Trustees, John Innes Foundn, 1990–98. Mem., Norwich Prison Bd of Visitors, 1969–82. Chm., St John Council for Norfolk, 1980–89. JP 1967, High Sheriff 1979, DL 1981, Co. of Norfolk; High Steward, Great Yarmouth, 1984–. Hon. Freeman, Bor. of Great Yarmouth, 2009. CStJ 1986. Hon. LLD Nottingham, 1988. *Recreation:* country pursuits. *Address:* Keswick Old Hall, Norwich, Norfolk NR4 6TZ. *T:* (01603) 454348. *Clubs:* Norfolk (Norwich); Royal Norfolk and Suffolk Yacht (Lowestoft). *Died 18 Feb. 2013.*

FALCONER, Alexander, (Alex); Secretary, Dunfermline and Coast Association of Community Councils, 2000–10; *b* Dundee, 1 April 1940; *s* of John Falconer, labourer, and Margaret McFarlane Falconer, canteen assistant; *m* Margaret Cavell Falconer, chef; one *s* one *d*. Former foundry worker; served with RN, 1959–68; insulator, Rosyth dockyard, 1969–84. Shop Steward, TGWU, 1970–84; Chm., Fife Fedn of Trades Councils. MEP (Lab) Mid Scotland and Fife, 1984–99. Mem., CND. *Address:* Forthview, 2 Greenacres, Kingseat, Fife KY12 0RW. *Died 12 Aug. 2012.*

FALLE, Sir Sam, KCMG 1979 (CMG 1964); KCVO 1972; DSC 1945; HM Diplomatic Service, retired; *b* 19 Feb. 1919; *s* of Theodore and Hilda Falle; *m* 1945, Merete Rosen; one *s* three *d*. *Educ:* Victoria Coll., Jersey, CI. Served Royal Navy, 1937–48; joined Foreign (subseq. Diplomatic) Service, 1948; British Consulate, Shiraz, Iran, 1949–51; British Embassy, Tehran, 1952; British Embassy, Beirut, 1952–55; FO, 1955–57; British Embassy, Baghdad, 1957–61; Consul-Gen., Gothenburg, 1961–63; Head of UN Dept, FO, 1963–67; with Lord Shackleton's mission to Aden, 1967; Deputy High Comr, Kuala Lumpur, 1967–69; Ambassador to Kuwait, 1969–70; High Comr, Singapore, 1970–74; Ambassador to Sweden, 1974–77; High Comr in Nigeria, 1977–78; Delegate, Commn of the European Communities, Algiers, 1979–82; carried out evaluation of EEC aid to Zambia, 1983–84, and Swedish aid to Swaziland, 1986. Hon. Fellow, Univ. of St Andrews, 1997. Kt Grand Cross, Order of Polar Star, Sweden, 1975. *Publications:* My Lucky Life (memoirs), 1996. *Recreations:* swimming, ski-ing. *Address:* c/o Harris, 26 High Street, Frome, Somerset BA11 1ER. *T:* (01373) 462263. *Died 20 Feb. 2014.*

FALLON, Padraic Matthew; Chairman, Euromoney Institutional Investor (formerly Euromoney Publications) PLC, since 1992; *b* 21 Sept. 1946; *s* of Padraic Fallon, poet and Dorothea (Don) (*née* Maher); *m* 1972, Gillian Elizabeth Hellyer; one *s* three *d*. *Educ:* St Peter's Coll., Wexford; Blackrock Coll., Co. Dublin; Trinity Coll., Dublin (BBS, MA). Reporter: Thomson Newspapers City office, 1969–70; Daily Mirror, 1970–72; Daily Mail City pages, 1972–74; Managing Editor, Middle East Money, Beirut, 1974; Editor, Euromoney, 1974–85; Euromoney Publications, subseq. Euromoney Instnl Investor, PLC: Dir, 1975–; Man. Dir, 1985–89; Chief Exec., 1989–92. Director: Allied Irish Banks plc, 1988–2007; Daily Mail & General Trust plc, 1999–. ORBIS Internat. Ambassador, 2011–. *Publications:* A Hymn of the Dawn, 2003; The Circles of Archimedes, 2009. *Recreation:* country sports. *Address:* Euromoney Institutional Investor PLC, Nestor House, Playhouse Yard, EC4V 5EX. *T:* (020) 7779 8888; 34 Abbotsbury Close, W14 8EQ. *T:* (020) 7602 1253. *Clubs:* Garrick; Kildare Street and University (Overseas Member) (Dublin). *Died 13 Oct. 2012.*

FANSHAWE, Col David Valentine, LVO 2003; OBE 1977; Lieutenant, HM Body Guard of the Honourable Corps of Gentlemen-at-Arms, 2000–03; *b* 1 Nov. 1933; *s* of late Major Richard Gennys Fanshawe and Ruth Violet Mary, later Ruth, Baroness Dulverton, *o d* of Sir Walter Farquhar, 5th Bt; *m* 1963, Sheila McNeill; three *s*. *Educ:* Stowe; RMA Sandhurst. Commnd Grenadier Guards, 1954: served Europe, USA, Africa, Far East, and Middle East; Comdr, Guards Independent Parachute Co., 1967–70; Adjutant, RMA Sandhurst, 1970–73; CO 2nd Bn Grenadier Guards, 1974–76; Regtl Comdr, Grenadier Guards, 1978–80; Defence Attaché, Sudan and Somalia, 1981–83. Mem., HM Body Guard of Hon. Corps of Gentlemen-at-Arms, 1986–2003. Dir, Hedley Foundn, 1983–98; Chm., Dulverton Trust, 2000–07. *Recreations:* sailing, ornithology. *Address:* Upper Mill, Sydling St Nicholas, Dorchester, Dorset DT2 9PD. *T:* (01300) 341230. *Club:* Cavalry and Guards. *Died 3 June 2012.*

FARMBROUGH, Rt Rev. David John; Bishop Suffragan of Bedford, 1981–93; Hon. Assistant Bishop, Diocese of St Albans, since 1994; *b* 4 May 1929; 2nd *s* of late Charles Septimus and Ida Mabel Farmbrough; *m* 1955, Angela Priscilla Hill, DL; one *s* three *d*. *Educ:* Bedford Sch.; Lincoln Coll., Oxford (BA 1951, MA 1953); Westcott House, Cambridge, 1951–53. Deacon, 1953, priest, 1954; Curate of Bishop's Hatfield, 1953–57; Priest-in-charge, St John's, Hatfield, 1957–63; Vicar of Bishop's Stortford, 1963–74; Rural Dean of Bishop's Stortford, 1973–74; Archdeacon of St Albans, 1974–81. Mem., Gen. Synod, 1972–81; Chm., and Treas., Clergy Orphan Corp., 1995–97. Chm. Govs, St Margaret's Sch., Bushey, 1999–2001. *Publications:* In Wonder, Love and Praise, 1966; Belonging, Believing, Doing, 1971. *Recreation:* gardening. *Address:* St Michael Mead, 110 Village Road, Bromham, Beds MK43 8HU. *T:* (01234) 825042. *Died 9 March 2013.*

FARMER, Michael; *see* Farmer, P. M.

FARMER, Paul Roy; a District Judge (Magistrates' Courts), Devon and Cornwall, 2002–11; *b* 4 Dec. 1946; *s* of Charles Harry Farmer and Joan Farmer (*née* Mead); *m* 2nd, 1997, Christine Gillian Jago (*née* Pearce); one *d* from previous marriage. *Educ:* St Austell County Grammar Sch.; UWIST (LLB (ext.) London). Admitted Solicitor, 1971; articled Clerk, 1969–71, Asst Solicitor, 1971–74, Partner, 1974–78, Stephens and Scown, Solicitors; Dep. Justices' Clerk, 1978–86, Justices' Clerk, 1986–98, PSDs (Falmouth and Kerrier, Pydar, Truro, S Powder, 1986–98, E Penwith, Isles of Scilly, Penwith, 1991–98); acting Stipendiary Magistrate for Hampshire and Devon, 1994–98; Provincial Stipendiary Magistrate, subseq. a Dist Judge (Magistrates' Courts), Dorset, 1998–2002. Pres., Devon and Cornwall Justices' Clerks Soc., 1993–94. *Recreations:* golf, Rugby Union, cricket, music. *Address:* 4 The Grove, Love Lane, Bodmin, Cornwall PL31 2BJ. *Club:* Carlyon Bay Golf. *Died 4 June 2014.*

FARMER, (Pryce) Michael; QC 1995; **His Honour Judge Farmer;** DL; a Circuit Judge, since 2001; *b* 20 May 1944; *er s* of Sarah Jane Farmer; *m* 1975, Olwen Mary, *d* of late Rev. Griffith John Roberts, MA, and of Margaret Morris Roberts; one *s* one *d*. *Educ:* Ysgol Dyffryn Nantlle, Penygroes; King's Coll., London (BA Hons); Inns of Court Sch. of Law. Schoolmaster, St David's Coll., Llandudno, 1968–71; called to the Bar, Gray's Inn, 1972, Bencher, 2005; practice, Wales and Chester Circuit, 1973–; Junior, Wales and Chester Circuit, 1992; Head of Chambers, Sedan House, Chester, 1995. Asst Recorder, 1993–95; a Recorder, 1995–2001; part-time Pres., Mental Health Review Tribunal, 2001–08; Designated Family Judge, N Wales, 2004–; Dep. Liaison Judge for Welsh lang., Wales and Chester Circuit, 2004–; Dep. Sen. Judge, Sov. Base areas of Dhekelia and Akrotiri, Cyprus, 2004–. Wales and Chester Circuit Rep., Public Affairs Cttee, Bar Council, 1997–2001. Chm., Special Review Cttee, Ynys Môn CC, 1998–99. Contested (Plaid Cymru) Conwy, Feb. and Oct. 1974. Admitted to Gorsedd of Bards, Nat. Eisteddfod, 2009. DL Clwyd, 2010. *Recreations:* listening to classical music, reading, gardening, watching Rugby football.

Address: Rhyl County Court, Clwyd Street, Rhyl LL18 3LA. *T:* (01745) 352940. *Clubs:* Reform; Rygbi yr Wyddgrug (Mold) (Pres., 2001–05). *Died 9 April 2011.*

FARQUHAR MUNRO, John; *see* Munro.

FARQUHARSON, Rt Hon. Sir Donald (Henry), Kt 1981; PC 1989; DL; a Lord Justice of Appeal, 1989–95; *b* 1928; *yr s* of Charles Anderson Farquharson, Logie Coldstone, Aberdeenshire, and Florence Ellen Fox; *m* 1960, Helen Mary (*d* 2008), *er d* of Comdr H. M. Simpson, RN (retd), Abbots Brow, Kirkby Lonsdale, Westmorland; three *s* (one *d* decd). *Educ:* Royal Commercial Travellers Sch.; Keble Coll., Oxford (MA; Hon. Fellow, 1989). Called to Bar, Inner Temple, 1952; Bencher, 1979. Dep. Chm., Essex QS, 1970; a Recorder of the Crown Court, 1972–81; QC 1972; Judge, High Court of Justice, QBD, 1981–89; Presiding Judge, SE Circuit, 1985–88. A Legal Assessor to GMC and GDC, 1978–81; Chairman: Disciplinary Cttee of Bar, 1983–85; Judicial Studies Bd, 1992–94 (Mem., 1984–85); Criminal Justice Consultative Council, 1992–94. DL Essex, 1990. *Recreations:* opera, walking. *Address:* Bay Tree House, Bures, Suffolk CO8 5JG. *Died 21 Aug. 2011.*

FARRER, (Arthur) Mark; DL; Partner, Farrer & Co., 1968–99; *b* 25 March 1941; *s* of Hugh Frederick Francis Farrer and Elizabeth Mary Cross; *m* 1969, Zara Jane Thesiger; one *d*. *Educ:* Eton. Served with Queen Victoria's Rifles, KRRC, 1959–65, subseq. transferred to TARO. Admitted solicitor, 1966. Chairman: Essex Water Co., 1992–96 (Dir, 1986–96; Dep. Chm., 1987); Suffolk Water Co., 1992–96 (Dir, 1990–96); Dir, Lyonnaise Europe, 1989–96. Mem. Council, Lloyd's, 1988–91; Chm., Assoc. of Lloyd's Members Ltd, 1991–92. Chm., N and W Salmon Fishery Dist Bd, 1999–2005. Pres., Old Etonian Assoc., 2005–06. DL Essex, 1996. *Publications:* articles in learned jls. *Recreations:* gardening, salmon fishing, the steam railway. *Address:* The Brick House, The Pightle, Finchingfield, Essex CM7 4LB. *T:* (01371) 810283; 56 Sangomore, Durness by Lairg, Sutherland IV27 4PZ. *Clubs:* Brooks's; Celer et Audax (Winchester). *Died 18 Aug. 2011.*

FARRIMOND, Herbert Leonard, CBE 1977; Adviser, The Associated Octel Company Ltd, 1982–88; Chairman, H. L. Farrimond & Associates Ltd, 1978–88; *b* 4 Oct. 1924; *s* of late George and Jane Farrimond, Newcastle upon Tyne; *m* 1951, Patricia Sara (*née* McGrath); one *s*. *Educ:* St Cuthbert's Grammar Sch., Newcastle upon Tyne; Durham Univ. BA (Hons) Politics and Economics. Lieut RM, 1943–46. Australian Dept of Labour and Nat. Service, 1948–50; Imperial Chemical Industries Ltd, and Imperial Metal Industries Ltd, 1950–68; Upper Clyde Shipbuilders Ltd, 1968–69; Dir of Personnel, Dunlop Ltd, 1970–72; Mem., British Railways Bd, 1972–77. Director: British Rail Engineering Ltd; British Rail Shipping and Internat. Services Div.; Transmark Ltd (Chm.); Portsmouth and Sunderland Newspapers Ltd, 1978–80; Chm., British Transport Hotels, 1976–78. Adviser to industrial and commercial cos, 1978–88. Mem. Council, Advisory, Conciliation and Arbitration Service, 1974–78. Part-time Mem., British Waterways Bd, 1980–82. Governor, British Transport Staff Coll. Ltd, 1972–77. FCILT. *Recreations:* golf, gardening, music. *Address:* 9 Ardgare, Shandon, Helensburgh, Argyle and Bute G84 8NW. *T:* (01436) 820803. *Died 4 Feb. 2012.*

FATT, Prof. Paul, FRS 1969; Emeritus Professor, University of London, since 1989; *b* 13 Jan. 1924; *s* of David Fatt and Annie Fatt (*née* Arkin); *m* 1st, 1953, Ione Copplestone (marr. diss. 1960); one *s* two *d*; 2nd, 1961, Gertrude Falk; one *d*. *Educ:* Los Angeles City Coll.; Univ. of Calif, Berkeley. Served US Army, 1943–46. University Coll., London, 1948–52; ANU, 1952–55; Reader, 1956–76, Prof. of Biophysics, 1976–89, University College, London; Fellow, UCL, 1973. *Publications:* papers in various scientific jls. *Address:* 25 Tanza Road, NW3 2UA. *T:* (020) 7435 9802. *Died 28 Sept. 2014.*

FAUCONBERG, Baroness, 9th in line, *cr* 1295, **AND CONYERS**, 15th in line, *cr* 1509; **Diana Mary Miller;** *b* 5 July 1920; *er d* of 5th Earl of Yarborough and Nancye (*née* Brocklehurst); *S* to Baronies of father (in abeyance since 1948), 2012, on the death without issue of her co-heiress; *m* 1952, Robert Miller (*d* 1990); two *d*. *Co-heiresses:* *d* Marcia Anne, *b* 21 June 1954 (adopted by Major Michael Lycett, CBE and renamed Anthea Theresa Lycett but retains her right to the succession); *d* Beatrix Diana [*b* 23 Aug. 1955; *m* 1991, Simon William Jones Armstrong (*d* 2012); two *s*]. *Address:* c/o C. David Harrison, Glan y Mor, Criccieth, Gwynedd LL52 0LA. *Died 2 March 2013.*

FAULKNER OF DOWNPATRICK, Lady; Lucy (Barbara Ethel) Faulkner, CBE 1985; *b* 1 July 1925; *d* of William John Forsythe and Jane Ethel Sewell; *m* 1951, Arthur Brian Deane Faulkner (MP (NI) 1949–73; PC 1959; *cr* Baron Faulkner of Downpatrick, 1977) (killed in a hunting accident, 1977); two *s* one *d*. *Educ:* Aubrey House; Bangor Collegiate Sch.; Trinity College Dublin. BA (Hons History). Journalist, Belfast Telegraph, 1947; Personal Secretary to Sir Basil Brooke, Prime Minister of N Ireland, 1949. Nat. Governor for NI, BBC, 1978–85; Chm., Broadcasting Council for NI, 1981–85; Researcher, 1977, Trustee 1980, Ulster Historical Foundation; Mem., NI Tourist Bd, 1985–91. Governor, Linen Hall Library, 1982. Hon. LLD QUB, 1994. *Recreations:* hunting and dressage, genealogy, book collecting. *Address:* Toberdoney, Farranfad, Downpatrick BT30 8NH. *T:* (028) 4481 1712. *Died 20 Jan. 2012.*

FAULKNER, Prof. Douglas, WhSch, BSc, PhD; FREng, FRINA, FIStructE, FSNAME; RCNC; consulting structural engineer and naval architect, specialising in ship casualty investigations, since 1995; Head of Department of Naval Architecture and Ocean Engineering, University of Glasgow, 1973–95, then Emeritus Professor; *b* 29 Dec. 1929; *s* of Vincent and Florence Faulkner; *m* 1st, 1954, Jenifer Ann Cole-Adams (marr. diss. 1986); three *d*; 2nd, 1987, Isobel Parker Campbell. *Educ:* Sutton High Sch., Plymouth; HM Dockyard Technical Coll., Devonport; RNC, Greenwich. Aircraft Carrier Design, 1955–57; Production Engrg, 1957–59; Structural Research at NCRE, Dunfermline, 1959–63; Asst Prof. of Naval Construction, RNC, Greenwich, 1963–66; Structural Adviser to Ship Dept, Bath, 1966–68; Constructor Comdr attd British Embassy, Washington DC, 1968–70, and Mem. Ship Research Cttee, Nat. Acad. of Scis, 1968–71; Res. Associate and Defence Fellow, MIT, 1970–71; Structural Adviser to Ship Dept, Bath, and to the Merrison Box Girder Bridge Cttee, 1971–73. UK Rep., Standing Cttee, Internat. Ship Structures Congress, 1973–85. Chm., Conoco-ABS cttee producing a design code for Tension Leg Platforms offshore, 1981–83; Dir, Veritec Ltd, 1985–88; Mem. Bd of Govs, BMT Quality Assessors Ltd, 1990–93. Technical Assessor, Lord Donaldson of Lymington's Assessment, MV Derbyshire, Dept of Transport, 1995–97; Ind. Expert Witness, re-opened formal investigation into loss of MV Derbyshire, 2000. President: Instn of Engrs and Shipbuilders in Scotland, 1995–97; Whitworth Soc., 1997–98. FREng (FEng 1981). FRSA 1983–99. Consulting Editor, Jl of Marine Structures, 1990–99 (Editor, 1987–90). Hon. DSc: Technical Univ. of Gdansk, 1993; Technical Univ. of Lisbon, 2001. David W. Taylor Medal, SNAME, 1991; William Froude Medal, RINA, 1993; Peter the Great Medal, St Petersburg Univ. of Ocean Technology, 1993. *Publications:* (ed jtly) Integrity of Offshore Structures, 1981; Integrity of Offshore Structures—3, 1987; Integrity of Offshore Structures—4, 1990; Integrity of Offshore Structures—5, 1993; chapters in Ship Structural Design Concepts (Cornell Maritime Press), 1975; papers related to structural design of ships, in Trans RINA, Jl of Ship Res., Behaviour of Offshore Structures, etc. *Recreations:* walking, music. *Address:* 4 Murdoch Drive, Milngavie, Glasgow G62 6QZ. *T:* (0141) 956 5071. *Died 13 Feb. 2011.*

FAWCUS, His Honour Simon James David; a Circuit Judge, 1985–2003; *b* 12 July 1938; *s* of late Ernest Augustus Fawcus and of Jill Shaw; *m* 1966, Joan Mary (*née* Oliphant); one *s* four *d*. *Educ:* Aldenham Sch.; Trinity Hall, Cambridge (MA). Called to the Bar, Gray's Inn, 1961; in practice on Northern Circuit, 1962–85; a Recorder, 1980–85. Pres., Council of Circuit Judges, 1996. *Recreations:* real tennis and other lesser sporting activities, music (listening). *Address:* Marton Oak House, Oak Lane, Marton, Macclesfield SK11 9HE. *Clubs:* MCC; Manchester Tennis and Racquet, Big Four (Manchester); Circuit Judges Golfing Soc. *Died 12 June 2012.*

FEARN, John Martin, CB 1976; Secretary, Scottish Education Department, 1973–76; *b* Dundee, 24 June 1916; *s* of William Laing Fearn and Margaret Kerr Fearn; *m* 1947, Isobel Mary Begbie, MA, MB, ChB (*d* 2006); one *d*. *Educ:* High Sch. of Dundee; Univ. of St Andrews; Worcester Coll., Oxford. Indian Civil Service, Punjab, 1940–47; District Magistrate, Lahore, 1946; Scottish Home Dept, 1947; Under-Sec., 1966; Under-Sec., Scottish Educn Dept, 1968. Chairmen's Panel, CSSB, 1977–85. *Recreation:* golf. *Address:* 10/8 St Margaret's Place, Edinburgh EH9 1AY. *T:* (0131) 447 5301. *Died 18 Oct. 2014.*

FEARNLEY, David; Vice Lord-Lieutenant, West Yorkshire, 1992–2001; *b* 20 Dec. 1924; *s* of late Wilfred Fearnley and Elizabeth (*née* Walker); *m* 1947, Patricia Bentley; one *s* one *d*. *Educ:* Pocklington Sch., York; Univs of Bradford and Leeds. Served RN, War of 1939–45. Joined family firm, Walter Walker & Sons Ltd, 1945; Dir, 1955; Man. Dir, 1960; co. purchased by Allied Textiles, 1971; Dir, Allied Textiles plc, 1971–99. Chm., Louis Latour Ltd, 1990–; Director: WW Gp Ltd, 1990–99; Sharrow Bay Hotel, 1999–2004. Gen. Comr of Inland Revenue, Wakefield Div., 1973–2000 (Chm., 1987–99). Mem. Bd, Wakefield Prison, 1979–94. Fellow, Woodard Corp., 1989–95. High Sheriff, W Yorks, 1982–83. *Recreations:* fell walking, wine, tennis (playing), Rugby football (watching). *Address:* The Grange, Hopton, Mirfield, W Yorks WF14 8EL. *Club:* Garrick. *Died 23 Dec. 2014.*

FEATHERSTONE, Simon Mark, CMG 2011; HM Diplomatic Service; High Commissioner to Malaysia, 2010–14; *b* 24 July 1958; *s* of David and Nora Featherstone; *m* 1981, Gail Teresa Salisbury; one *s* two *d*. *Educ:* Whitgift Sch., Croydon; Lincoln Coll., Oxford (BA Hons Law, MA). FCO, 1980; Chinese lang. trng, SOAS and Hong Kong, 1981–83; Second Sec., Peking, 1984; First Sec., FCO, 1987; on loan to Cabinet Office, 1988; First Sec. (Envmt), UK Perm. Rep. to EC, Brussels, 1990; Consul-Gen., Shanghai, 1994; Counsellor (Political), Peking, 1996; Hd, EU Dept (External), FCO, 1998–2003; Ambassador to Switzerland and to Liechtenstein, 2004–08; Prime Minister's Internat. Rep. on Energy Issues, 2008–09; Dir, Shanghai Expo 2010, 2009–10. *Recreations:* golf, running, church activities. *Address:* c/o Foreign and Commonwealth Office, King Charles Street, SW1A 2AH. *Died 26 Aug. 2014.*

FEAVER, (Mary Frances) Clare; *see* Harvey, M. F. C.

FEDDEN, (Adye) Mary, (Mrs J. O. Trevelyan), OBE 1997; RA 1992; RWA; painter; *b* 14 Aug. 1915; *d* of Harry Vincent Fedden and Ida Margaret Fedden; *m* 1951, Julian Otto Trevelyan, Sen. Hon. RA (*d* 1988); one step *s*. *Educ:* Badminton Sch., Bristol; Slade Sch. of Art (Schol). Exhibns yearly in London and provinces, 1948–; paintings in collections of the Queen, Prince Hassan of Jordan, Tate Gall., city art galls in UK, NZ, Malta, USA, and in private collections in England and overseas. Tutor: Royal College of Art, 1956–64; Yehudi Menuhin Sch., 1964–74. Pres., Royal West of England Acad., 1984–88. Hon. DLitt Bath, 1996. *Publications:* books illustrated: The Green Man, by Jane Gardam, 1998; Birds, introd. Mel Gooding, 1999; *relevant publication:* Mel Gooding, Mary Fedden, 1995. *Recreation:* reading. *Address:* Durham Wharf, Hammersmith Terrace, W6 9TS. *Died 22 June 2012.*

FELL, Robert, CB 1972; CBE 1966; Commissioner of Banking, Hong Kong, 1984–87; *b* 6 May 1921; *s* of Robert and Mary Ann Fell, Cumberland; *m* 1946, Eileen Wicks (*d* 2001); two *s* one *d*; *m* Roslyn Junor. *Educ:* Whitehaven Grammar School. War Office, 1939; military service, 1940–46 (despatches); BoT, 1947; Trade Comr, Qld, 1954–59; Asst Sec., Tariff Div., 1961; Commercial Counsellor, Delhi, 1961–66; Under-Sec. i/c export promotion, 1967–71; Sec., ECGD, 1971–74; Chief Exec., The Stock Exchange, 1975–82; Comr for Securities, Hong Kong, 1981–84. Mem., British Overseas Trade Board, 1972–75; Pres., City Branch, BIM, 1976–82. FRSA. *Recreations:* Rugby football (watching), gardening. *Club:* Travellers. *Died 19 Jan. 2015.*

FELLOWS, Edward Frank; Editorial Consultant, Fellows Media Ltd (formerly Fellows Associates), publishers, since 1999 (Managing Director, 1992–99); *b* 25 Sept. 1930; *s* of Edward Fellows and Gladys Nora Fellows; *m* 1962, Christine Woolmore; three *s*. *Educ:* Ewell primary and secondary schs; Epsom Sch. of Art (schol.); Merrist Wood Agricl Inst. Nat. Service, CRMP, 1949. Joined editorial staff of Farmer and Stockbreeder, 1957; Editor, Power Farming, 1974; Dep. Editor, Farmers Weekly, 1982; Editor, Crops, 1984; Editor, Farmers Weekly, 1987–90; Editor-in-Chief, Reed Farmers Publishing Group, 1990–91; Features Editor, Shell Agriculture, 1993–94; Editor, Farming OPUS, 1995–97. Hon. Mem., Falkland Islands Assoc., 1983–. *Publications:* Tim Chooses Farming, 1962. *Recreations:* Labrador dogs, walking, photography, gardening, reading. *Address:* Manzanas, Orchard Mead, Painswick, Glos GL6 6YD. *T:* (01452) 814072. *E:* tedfellows@waitrose.com. *Died 23 Feb. 2011.*

FENDALL, Prof. Neville Rex Edwards, MD; Professor of International Community Health, School of Tropical Medicine, University of Liverpool, 1971–81, then Emeritus Professor; Visiting Professor of Public Health, Boston University, since 1982; *b* 9 July 1917; *s* of Francis Alan Fendall and Ruby Inez Matthews; *m* 1942, Margaret Doreen (*née* Beynon). *Educ:* University College Hosp. (MD, BSc); London Sch. of Hygiene and Tropical Med. (DPH); FFPH. Colonial Medical Service, 1944–64, Nigeria, Malaya, Singapore, Kenya; Brit. Mil. Admin, 1945–46; Dir of Med. Services, Kenya; Staff Mem., Rockefeller Foundn, 1964–66; Regional Dir, Population Council Inc., New York, 1966–71. Mem., Panel of Experts, WHO, 1957–83; Consultant: World Bank; UN Fund for Population Activities; ODM; Cento; Internat. Develt Res. Centre, Canada; APHA; USAID; Overseas govts; Vis. Consultant, Univ. of Hawaii. Adjunct Prof. of Community Health, Univ. of Calgary, 1983–88; Visiting Lecturer: Harvard, 1966–83; Inst. of Tropical Medicine, Marseilles; Univ. of Glasgow; Univ. of Bradford; Commonwealth Foundn Travelling Lectr, 1976; Dist. Fellow, Boston Univ. Center for Internat. Health, 1992. Mem., Acad. of Med., Physical and Nat. Scis, Guatemala, 1986–. Patron, Commonwealth Human Ecology Council, 1994–. Langley Meml Prize, UNCAST, 1963; Gold Medal, Mrigendra Medical Trust, Nepal, 1983; Fendall Prize, Center for Internat. Health, Boston, USA, 1996. *Publications:* Auxiliaries in Health Care, 1972 (English, French, Spanish edns); (with J. M. Paxman and F. M. Shattock) Use of Paramedicals for Primary Health Care in the Commonwealth, 1979; (with F. M. Shattock) Restraints and Constraints to Development, 1983; contribs on primary health care, epidemiology, population dynamics, in various books and jls. *Recreations:* gardening, travel. *Address:* The Coach House, Mill Street, Ludlow, Shropshire SY8 1BB. *Died 25 May 2014.*

FENN, Peter John; His Honour Judge Fenn; a Circuit Judge, since 2005; *b* 31 Oct. 1956; *s* of Eric Arthur William Fenn and Beryl Marjorie Fenn; *m* 2000, Maxine Helen Adams (*d* 2013). *Educ:* Hertford Coll., Oxford (MA). Called to the Bar, Middle Temple, 1979; in practice as a barrister, Colchester, 1980–97, London, 1997–2005; a Recorder, 2003–05. Dir of Music, Stowmarket URC, 1995–2007. *Recreations:* travel, music, horse riding. *Address:* The Courthouse, 1 Russell Road, Ipswich, Suffolk IP1 2AG. *T:* (01473) 228585, *Fax:* (01473) 228560. *Died 15 March 2013.*

FENNELL, Hon. Sir (John) Desmond (Augustine), Kt 1990; OBE 1982; a Judge of the High Court of Justice, Queen's Bench Division, 1990–92; *b* 17 Sept. 1933; *s* of late Dr A. J. Fennell, Lincoln; *m* 1966, Susan Primrose, *d* of late J. M. Trusted; one *s* two *d*. *Educ:* Ampleforth; Corpus Christi Coll., Cambridge. Served with Grenadier Guards, 1956–58. Called to the Bar, Inner Temple, 1959, Bencher, 1983; Dep. Chm., Bedfordshire QS, 1971; a Recorder of the Crown Court, 1972–89; QC 1974; Leader, Midland and Oxford Circuit, 1983–88; a Judge of the Court of Appeal of Jersey and Court of Appeal of Guernsey, 1984–89; a Judge of the Employment Appeal Tribunal, 1991–92. Vice-Chm., 1988, Chm., 1989, Gen. Council of the Bar. Inspector, King's Cross Underground fire, 1988. Pres., Stoke Mandeville Burns and Reconstructive Surgery

Res. Trust, 2002– (Chm., 1994–2002). Chm., Buckingham Div. Cons. Assoc., 1976–79 (Pres., 1983–89). Hon. positions various local orgns. *Clubs:* Boodle's, Pilgrims. *Died 29 June 2011.*

FENNER, Dame Peggy (Edith), DBE 1986; DL; *b* 12 Nov. 1922; *m* 1940, Bernard Fenner (*d* 2001); (one *d* decd). *Educ:* LCC School, Brockley; Ide Hill, Sevenoaks. Contested (C) Newcastle-under-Lyme, 1966. MP (C) Rochester and Chatham, 1970–Sept. 1974 and 1979–83, Medway, 1983–97; contested (C) Medway, 1997. Parly Sec., MAFF, 1972–74 and 1981–86. Mem., British Delegn to European Parlt, Strasbourg, 1974; UK rep. to Council of Europe and WEU, 1987–97. Member: West Kent Divisional Exec. Educn Cttee, 1963–72; Sevenoaks Urban District Council, 1957–71 (Chairman, 1962 and 1963); Exec. of Kent Borough and Urban District Councils Assoc., 1967–71; a Vice-Pres., Urban District Councils Assoc., 1971. DL Kent, 1992. *Recreations:* reading, travel, theatre, gardening. *Died 15 Sept. 2014.*

FENTON, Prof. Alexander, CBE 1986; DLitt; Professor of Scottish Ethnology and Director, School of Scottish Studies, University of Edinburgh, 1990–94, then Professor Emeritus; Consultant, Scotland Inheritance Fund, since 2007; *b* 26 June 1929; *s* of Alexander Fenton and Annie Stirling Stronach; *m* 1956, Evelyn Elizabeth Hunter; two *d*. *Educ:* Turriff Academy; Aberdeen Univ. (MA); Cambridge Univ. (BA); Edinburgh Univ. (DLitt). Senior Asst Editor, Scottish National Dictionary, 1955–59; Asst Keeper, Nat. Museum of Antiquities of Scotland, 1959–75, Dep. Keeper, 1975–78, Director, 1978–85; Res. Dir, Nat. Museums of Scotland, 1985–89; Dir, European Ethnological Res. Centre, 1989–2007 (Trustee, 2007–). Mem., Ancient Monuments Bd for Scotland, 1979–94. Hon. Prof. of Antiquities to Royal Scottish Acad., 1996–. Member: Royal Gustav Adolf Acad., Uppsala, Sweden, 1978; Royal Danish Acad. of Scis and Letters, 1979; Soc. Royale des Lettres de Lund, Sweden, 1998; Jury, Europa Preis für Volkskunst (FVS Foundation, Hamburg), 1975–96. Hon. DLitt Aberdeen, 1989. Co-editor, Tools and Tillage (Copenhagen), 1968–2004; Editor: Review of Scottish Culture, 1984–2005; Scottish Studies, 1992–99; Gen. Ed., Scottish Life and Society: a compendium of Scottish ethnology, 14 vols, 2000–11. *Publications:* The Various Names of Shetland, 1973, 2nd edn 1977; Scottish Country Life, 1976, 3rd edn 1999; (trans.) S. Steensen Blicher, En Landsbydegns Dagbog (The Diary of a Parish Clerk, 1976); The Island Blackhouse, 1978; The Northern Isles: Orkney and Shetland, 1978, 2nd edn 1997; (with B. Walker) The Rural Architecture of Scotland, 1981; The Shape of the Past, 2 vols, 1985; (trans.) S. Weöres, Ha a Világ Rigó Lenne (If All the World were a Blackbird), 1985; Wird's an' Wark 'e Seasons Roon, 1987; Country Life in Scotland, 1987; The Turra Coo: a legal episode in the popular culture of NE Scotland, 1989; Scottish Country Life, 1989; Craiters—or Twenty Buchan Tales, 1995; Buchan Words and Ways, 2005; Scottish Life and Society: a compendium of Scottish ethnology, vol. 5: The Food of the Scots, 2007; (ed) A Swedish Field Trip to the Outer Hebrides, 1934, 2012; numerous articles in learned jls. *Address:* 132 Blackford Avenue, Edinburgh EH9 3HH. *T:* (0131) 667 5456. *Died 9 May 2012.*

FENWICK, Very Rev. Jeffery Robert; Dean of Guernsey, 1989–95; *b* 8 April 1930; *s* of Stanley Robert and Dorothy Fenwick; *m* 1955, Pamela Frances (*née* Galley); one *s* two *d*. *Educ:* Torquay and Selhurst Grammar Schools; Pembroke Coll., Cambridge (MA); Lincoln Theol Coll. Deacon 1955, priest 1956, Liverpool; Curate, St Thomas the Martyr, UpHolland, 1955; Priest-in-charge, Christ the King, Daramombe, Mashonaland, 1958; Secretary, USPG, Oxford, 1964; Rector, Gatooma 1965, Salisbury East 1967, Mashonaland; Dean, Bulawayo, Matabeleland, 1975; Canon Residentiary, Worcester Cathedral, 1978; Librarian and Treasurer, 1978–89. Examining Chaplain, Mashonaland and Matabeleland, 1966–78; Archdeacon of Charter, 1970–75, of Bulawayo, 1975–78. Hon. Canon of Winchester Cathedral, 1989–95, then Emeritus. Chm., Cathedrals Finance Conf. for England, 1983–89. Chm., Britain-Zimbabwe Soc., 1996–. *Publications:* Chosen People, 1971; (contrib.) The Pattern of History, 1973. *Recreations:* painting, music, gardening, walking. *Address:* 3 Suid Street, Alexandria 6185, S Africa. *Died 14 Sept. 2014.*

FERGUSON, Sir Ian Edward J.; *see* Johnson-Ferguson.

FERGUSON, John Alexander; HM Senior Chief Inspector of Schools in Scotland, 1981–87; *b* 16 Oct. 1927; *s* of George Ferguson and Martha Crichton Dykes; *m* 1953, Jean Stewart; two *s* one *d*. *Educ:* Royal Coll. of Science and Technology, Univ. of Glasgow (BSc Hons, Diploma). Teacher, Airdrie Central Sch., 1950–51; Lectr, 1951–55, Head of Dept of Engrg, 1955–61, Coatbridge Technical Coll.; HM Inspector of Schs, 1961–72, Asst Sec., 1972–75, Scottish Educn Dept; HM Depute Sen. Chief Inspector of Schs, 1975–81. *Recreations:* golf, bridge. *Club:* Craigmillar Park Lawn Tennis (Edinburgh). *Died 20 Dec. 2014.*

FERGUSON FLATT, Very Rev. Roy Francis; *see* Flatt.

FERMOR, Sir Patrick (Michael) Leigh, Kt 2004; DSO 1944; OBE (mil.) 1943; CLit 1991; author; Hon. Citizen of Herakleion, Crete, 1947, Gytheion, Laconia, 1966, and of Kardamyli, Messenia, 1967; *b* 11 Feb. 1915; *s* of late Sir Lewis Leigh Fermor, OBE, FRS, DSc, and Eileen, *d* of Charles Taaffe Ambler; *m* 1968, Hon. Joan Eyres-Monsell (*d* 2003), *d* of 1st Viscount Monsell, PC, GBE. *Educ:* King's Sch., Canterbury. After travelling for four years in Central Europe, Balkans and Greece, enlisted in Irish Guards, 1939; "I" Corps, 1940; Lieut, British Mil. Mission, Greece, 1940; Liaison Officer, Greek GHQ, Albania; campaigns of Greece and Crete; joined SOE, 1941; 2 years in German occupied Crete with Resistance, commanded some minor guerilla operations; team-commander in Special Allied Airborne Reconnaissance Force, N Germany, 1945. Dep.-Dir British Institute, Athens, till middle 1946; travelled in Caribbean and Central American republics, 1947–48. Corresp. Mem., Athens Acad., 1980. Hon. DLitt: Kent, 1991; Amer. Sch. of Greece, 1993; Warwick Univ., 1996. Municipality of Athens Gold Medal of Honour, 1988; Prix Jacques Audiberti, Ville d'Antibes, 1992. Officier, l'Ordre des Arts et des Lettres (France), 1995; Commander, Order of the Phoenix (Greece), 2007. *Publications:* The Traveller's Tree (Heinemann Foundation Prize for Literature, 1950, and Kemsley Prize, 1951); trans. Colette, Chance Acquaintances, 1952; A Time to Keep Silence, 1953; The Violins of Saint Jacques, 1953; Mani, 1958 (Duff Cooper Meml Prize; Book Society's Choice); (trans.) The Cretan Runner (George Psychoundakis), 1955; Roumeli, 1966; A Time of Gifts, 1977 (W. H. Smith & Son Literary Award, 1978); Between the Woods and the Water, 1986 (Thomas Cook Travel Book Award, 1986; Internat. PEN/Time Life Silver Pen Award, 1986); Three Letters from the Andes, 1991; Words of Mercury, 2004. *Recreation:* travel. *Address:* c/o John R. Murray, 50 Albemarle Street, W1S 4BD. *Clubs:* White's, Travellers, Pratt's, Beefsteak, Special Forces, Puffin's. *Died 10 June 2011.*

FERRANTI, Sebastian Basil Joseph Ziani de; *see* de Ferranti.

FERRERS, 13th Earl *cr* 1711; **Robert Washington Shirley;** PC 1982; DL; Viscount Tamworth 1711; Bt 1611; High Steward of Norwich Cathedral, 1979–2007, then Emeritus; *b* 8 June 1929; *o s* of 12th Earl Ferrers and Hermione Morley (*d* 1969); *S* father, 1954; *m* 1951, Annabel Mary, *d* of late Brig. W. G. Carr, CVO, DSO; two *s* one *d* (and two *d* decd). *Educ:* Winchester Coll.; Magdalene Coll., Cambridge (MA (Agric.)). Lieut Coldstream Guards, 1949 (as National Service). A Lord-in-waiting, 1962–64, 1971–74; Parly Sec., MAFF, 1974; Jt Dep. Leader of the Opposition, House of Lords, 1976–79; Dep. Leader of House of Lords, 1979–83, 1988–97; Minister of State: MAFF, 1979–83; Home Office, 1988–94; DTI, 1994–95; DoE (Minister for the Envmt and Countryside), 1995–97; elected Mem., H of L, 1999. Mem., Armitage Cttee on political activities of civil servants, 1976. Chm., TSB of Eastern England, 1977–79; Mem., TSB Central Bd, 1977–79; Director: Central TSB, 1978–79; TSB Trustcard Ltd, 1978–79; Norwich Union Insurance Group, 1975–79 and 1983–88. Chairman: RCHM(Eng.), 1984–88; British Agricl Export Council, 1984–88; Mem. Council, Food From Britain, 1984–88; Director: Economic Forestry Gp, 1985–88; Chatham

Historic Dockyard Trust, 1984–88. Pres., Assoc. of Cons. Peers, 2006–. Mem. Council, Hurstpierpoint Coll., 1959–68; Sub-Warden, Winchester Coll., 1998–2003 (Fellow, 1988–2003). DL Norfolk, 1983. Liveryman, Farriers' Co., 2004. Grand Prior, Order of St Lazarus of Jerusalem, 2002–11. *Publications:* Whatever Next?, 2011. *Heir: s* Viscount Tamworth, *b* 29 Dec. 1952. *Address:* Park Lodge, Hedenham, Norfolk NR35 2LE. *Club:* Beefsteak. *Died 13 Nov. 2012.*

FERRIER, Prof. Robert Patton, FRSE 1977; Professor of Natural Philosophy, University of Glasgow, 1973–2002, then Emeritus, and Hon. Senior Research Fellow, since 2002; *b* 4 Jan. 1934; *s* of William McFarlane Ferrier and Gwendoline Melita Edwards; *m* 1961, Valerie Jane Duncan (*d* 2008); two *s* one *d*. *Educ:* Glebelands Sch. and Morgan Academy, Dundee; Univ. of St Andrews (BSc, PhD). MA Cantab. FInstP. Scientific Officer, AERE Harwell, 1959–61; Res. Assoc., MIT, 1961–62; Sen. Asst in Res., Cavendish Lab., Cambridge, 1962–66; Fellow of Fitzwilliam Coll., Cambridge, 1965–73; Asst Dir of Res., Cavendish Lab. 1966–71; Lectr in Physics, Univ. of Cambridge, 1971–73; Guest Scientist, IBM Res. Labs San José, Calif, 1972–73. Chm., SERC Semiconductor and Surface Physics Sub-Cttee, 1979–. *Publications:* numerous papers in Phil. Mag., Jl Appl. Physics, Jl Physics, etc. *Recreations:* do-it-yourself, tennis, gardening, reading novels. *Address:* Glencoe, 31 Thorn Road, Bearsden, Glasgow G61 4BS. *T:* (0141) 570 0769, *T:* (office) (0141) 330 5388. *E:* Robert.Ferrier@glasgow.ac.uk. *Died 30 Sept. 2012.*

FIELD, Brig. Anne, CB 1980; CBE 1996; Deputy Controller Commandant, Women's Royal Army Corps, 1984–92 (Director, 1977–82); Chairman of Council, 1991–97, and Life Vice President, 1999, WRAC Association (Vice President, 1984–97); *b* 4 April 1926; *d* of Captain Harold Derwent and Annie Helena Hodgson. *Educ:* Keswick Sch.; St George's, Harpenden; London Sch. of Economics. Joined ATS, 1947; commissioned: ATS, 1948; WRAC, 1949; Lt-Col, 1968; Col, 1971. Hon. ADC to the Queen, 1977–82. Dep. Col Comdt, AGC, 1992–94. Dir, London Regl Bd, Lloyds Bank, 1982–91 (Dep. Chm., 1990–91). Special Comr, Duke of York's Royal Mil. Sch., 1989–. Chm., ATS and WRAC Benevolent Fund, 1984–97. Patron, ATS Dinner Club, 1996–. Freeman, City of London, 1981; Liveryman, Spectacle Makers' Co., 1990. CCMI (FBIM 1978). *Address:* c/o Lloyds TSB, PO Box 1190, 7 Pall Mall, SW1Y 5NA. *Club:* Army and Navy. *Died 25 June 2011.*

FIELD, Dr Ian Trevor, CBE 1994; Secretary General, World Medical Association, 1994–97; *b* 31 Oct. 1933; *s* of late Major George Edward Field, MBE, IA, and Bertha Cecilia Field; *m* 1960, Christine Mary Osman, OBE, JP; three *s*. *Educ:* Shri Shivaji School, Poona; Bournemouth School; Guy's Hosp. Med. School. MB, BS; FFPH; FFOM. Royal Engineers, 1952–54; Med. Sch., 1954–60; house posts, 1960–62; general practice, 1962–64; Asst Sec., later Under Sec., BMA, 1964–75; SMO, 1975–78, SPMO/Under Sec., 1978–85, DHSS, (Internat. Health and Communicable Disease Control, later NHS Regional Orgn); Chief Med. and Health Services Advr, ODA, 1978–83; Dep. Sec., 1985–89, Sec., 1989–93, BMA. Member: Council, Liverpool Sch. of Trop. Med., 1979–83, 1993–96; Bd of Management, London Sch. of Hygiene and Trop. Med., 1979–83; Council, Royal Vet. Coll., 1982–88; WHO Global Adv. Cttee on Malaria Control, 1979–82 (Chm., 1981). Liveryman, Soc. of Apothecaries, 1971– (Ct of Assistants, 1986–2009; Master, 1998–99). *Publications:* contribs to medical jls. *Recreations:* military history, opera, watching cricket and rugby. *Address:* Flat 2, Sturges Court, 70 Sturges Road, Wokingham, Berks RG40 2HE. *Died 23 Dec. 2012.*

FIENNES, Very Rev. Hon. Oliver William Twisleton-Wykeham-; Dean of Lincoln, 1969–89, Dean Emeritus, since 1989; *b* 17 May 1926; *yr s* of 20th Baron Saye and Sele, OBE, MC, and Hersey Cecilia Hester, *d* of late Captain Sir Thomas Dacres Butler, KCVO; *m* 1956, Juliet (*d* 2005), *d* of late Dr Trevor Braby Heaton, OBE; two *s* two *d*. *Educ:* Eton; New College, Oxford; Cuddesdon College. Asst Curate, New Milton, Hants, 1954; Chaplain, Clifton College, Bristol, 1958; Rector of Lambeth, 1963. Church Comr, 1977–88. Chairman: Pilgrims Assoc., 1986–89; St Matthew Housing (formerly St Matthew Soc.), 1994–2001 (Vice Pres., 2001). World Fellow, Thanksgiving Square, Dallas, 1980; Vice Pres., Lincoln Br., Inst. of Advanced Motorists, 2002– (Pres., 1973–2002); Chm., Radio Lincolnshire Adv. Cttee, 1992–95. Governor, Marlborough Coll., 1970–89. Nat Patron, E-SU in USA, 1987. ChStJ 1971; KStJ 1996. *Recreations:* cricket, travel, country activities. *Address:* 3A Vicars Court, Lincoln LN2 1PT. *T:* (01522) 526036. *Died 8 June 2011.*

FIFE, 3rd Duke of, *cr* 1899; **James George Alexander Bannerman Carnegie;** Lord Carnegie of Kinnaird (Scot.), 1616; Earl of Southesk and Lord Carnegie of Kinnaird and Leuchars (Scot.), 1633; Bt (NS), 1663; Baron Balinhard, 1869; Earl of Macduff, 1899; *b* 23 Sept. 1929; *o s* of 11th Earl of Southesk (*d* 1992), and Princess Maud (*d* 1945); *S* aunt, HRH Princess Arthur of Connaught (Dukedom of Fife), 1959; *m* 1956, Hon. Caroline Cicely Dewar (marr. diss. 1966; she *m* 1980, Gen. Sir Richard Worsley), *er d* of 3rd Baron Forteviot, MBE; one *s* one *d*. *Educ:* Gordonstoun. Nat. Service, Scots Guards (Malayan Campaign), 1948–50. Royal Agricultural College. Clothworkers' Company, and Freeman City of London. Pres. of ABA, 1959–73, Vice-Patron, 1973–94; Ship's Pres., HMS Fife, 1967–87; a Vice-Patron, Braemar Royal Highland Soc.; a Vice-Pres., British Olympic Assoc., 1973–2000. *Heir: s* Earl of Southesk, *b* 3 March 1961. *Address:* Kinnaird Castle, Brechin, Angus DD9 6TZ. *Died 22 June 2015.*

FIGG, Sir Leonard (Clifford William), KCMG 1981 (CMG 1974); HM Diplomatic Service, retired; *b* 17 Aug. 1923; *s* of late Sir Clifford Figg and Lady (Eileen) Figg (*née* Crabb); *m* 1955, Jane Brown (*d* 2004), *d* of late Judge Harold Brown; three *s*. *Educ:* Charterhouse; Trinity Coll., Oxford. RAF, 1942–46 (Flt-Lt). HM Diplomatic Service, 1947; served in: Addis Ababa, 1949–52; FO, 1952–58; Amman, 1958–61; FO, 1961–67; Counsellor, 1965; Deputy Consul-General, Chicago, 1967–69; DTI, 1970–73; Consul General and Minister, Milan, 1973–77; Asst Under Sec. of State, FCO, 1977–80; Ambassador to Ireland, 1980–83. Mem. Council, Cooperation Ireland, 1985–95. A Vice-Chm., British Red Cross Soc., 1983–88; a Vice-Pres., Bucks Red Cross, 1988–96. President: Aylesbury Divl Conservative Assoc., 1985–95; Bucks Assoc. of Youth Clubs, 1987–2001; Chiltern Soc., 1990–2003; Bucks and Oxfordshire East Euro Constituency Cons. Assoc., 1998; Chm., Bucks Farming and Wildlife Adv. Gp, 1991–2000. *Recreations:* forestry, listening to tapes. *Address:* Little Hampden Farm, Great Missenden, Bucks HP16 9PS. *Died 11 Aug. 2014.*

FINKELSTEIN, Prof. Ludwik, OBE 1990; DSc, PhD; FREng; FIET; CPhys, FInstP; Professor of Measurement and Instrumentation, City University, 1980–97, then Emeritus; *b* 6 Dec. 1929; *s* of Adolf and Amalia Finkelstein; *m* 1957, Mirjam Emma, *d* of Dr Alfred and Dr Margarethe Wiener; two *s* one *d*. *Educ:* Univ. of London (BSc, MSc). DSc City Univ., 1989; Leo Baeck Coll. (MA 1996, PhD 2006, Open Univ.). Physicist, Technical Staff, Electronic Tubes Ltd, 1951–52; Scientist, Instrument Br., NCB Mining Res. Estabt, 1952–59; Northampton Coll., London, and City University, London: Lectr, 1959–61; Sen. Lectr, 1961–63; Principal Lectr, 1963–67; Reader, 1967–70; Prof. of Instrument and Control Engineering, 1970–80; Head of Dept of Systems Science, 1974–79; Head of Dept of Physics, 1980–88; Dean, Sch. of Electrical Engrg and Applied Physics, 1983–88; Dean, Sch. of Engrg, 1988–93; Pro-Vice-Chancellor, 1991–94. Visiting Prof., Delft Univ. of Technology, 1973–74. Pres., Inst. of Measurement and Control, 1980 (Vice-Pres., 1972–75, 1977–79; Hartley Silver Medal, 1980); Chm., Management and Design Div., IEE, 1984–85 (Management and Design Divl Premium (jtly), 1984). FREng (FEng 1986). Hon. FInstMC 1991. Hon. Dr St Petersburg Technical Univ., 1994; Hon. DCL City, 1999. *Publications:* papers in learned jls and conference procs. *Recreations:* books, conversation, Jewish studies. *Address:* City University, Northampton Square, EC1V 0HB; 9 Cheyne Walk, Hendon, NW4 3QH. *T:* (020) 8202 6966. *Died 27 Aug. 2011.*

FINLAY-MAXWELL, David Campbell, MBE 1994; PhD; CEng, MIET; FTI, FSDC; Director, D. F. Maxwell Co., since 1991; *b* 2 March 1923; *s* of Luke Greenwood Maxwell and of Lillias Maule Finlay; *m* 1954, Constance Shirley Hood; one *s* one *d*. *Educ:* St Paul's; Heriot-Watt Coll. (Edinburgh Univ.) (Electronic and Control Engrg). CEng 1950; MIET (MIEE 1950); FTI 1974; FSDC 1985. PhD Leeds, 1983. Major Royal Signals and SOE, 1945. Harvard Univ. Advanced Management Programme, 1968. Man. Dir, 1946–86, Chm., 1960–89, Dir, 1993–98, John Gladstone & Co.; Chm. and Man. Dir, John Gladstone & Co. (Engrg), 1948–89. Chairman: Manpower Working Party, NEDO, 1970–73; Wool Industries Res. Assoc., 1974–77; Textile Res. Council, 1977–82; Wool Textile EDC, 1977–79, UK Rep., Consultative Cttee for R&D, Brussels, 1979–84. EEC Reviewer, ESPRIT Prog., 1986–2001. Dir, Wool Foundn (Internat. Wool Secretariat), 1985–. Member: Council, Textile Inst., 1972–74; British Textile Council, 1977–85; Textile Industry and Dyeing Adv. Cttee, Leeds Univ. Council, 1974–95; Soc. of Dyers and Colourists, 1950–. *Recreations:* radio propagation, satellite tracking. *Address:* D. F. Maxwell Co., Tarrens, The Green, Pirbright, Surrey GU24 0JT. *Club:* Special Forces. *Died 1 July 2014.*

FINNEY, Sir Thomas, Kt 1998; CBE 1992 (OBE 1961); *b* Preston, 5 April 1922; *s* of late Alf and Margaret Finney; *m* 1945, Elsie Noblett (*d* 2004); one *s* one *d*. *Educ:* Deepdale County Primary Sch.; Deepdale Modern Sch. Joined plumbing firm of Pilkington's as apprentice, 1936. Professional footballer with Preston North End, 1940–42, 1946–60, for whom he played 433 league games and scored 187 goals; 76 appearances for England, 1946–58; Pres., Preston North End FC, 1975–76. Chm., Preston HA, 1985–88. Freeman, Borough of Preston, 1979. Hon. Fellow, Lancashire Poly., 1988. Hon. LLD Lancaster Univ., 1988. Footballer of the Year, Football Writers' Assoc., 1954, 1957. *Publications:* My Autobiography, 2003. *Died 14 Feb. 2014.*

FIRNBERG, David; Principal, DFA Ltd, since 1989; *b* 1 May 1930; *s* of L. B. Firnberg and K. L. E. Firnberg; *m* 1957, Sylvia Elizabeth du Cros; one *s* three *d*. *Educ:* Merchant Taylors' Sch., Northwood. Went West, 1953–56; Television Audience Measurement Ltd, 1956–59; ICT/ICL, 1959–72; David Firnberg Associates Ltd, 1972–74; Dir, Nat. Computing Centre Ltd, 1974–79; Eosys Ltd: Man. Dir, 1980–88; Chm., 1989–91; Chm., The Networking Centre Ltd, 1985–91; Chief Exec., Strategic Planning Soc., 1985–87. President: UK Assoc. of Project Managers, 1978–84 (Hon. Fellow 1984); British Computer Soc., 1983–84 (Chm., IT Support for Disabled People project, 1989–91); Chairman: UK Council for Computing Develt, 1990–91; Steering Cttee, RSA Design Bursaries for Communications and Computing, 1989–94; Member: Foundn for Sci. and Technology, 1987–; Council, PITCOM, 1989–2002; Quality Audit Steering Council, Higher Educn Quality Council, 1992–97. Chm., Buckingham DFAS, 2004–08. Freeman, City of London, 1987. FBCS 1973; FInstD 1982; FRSA 1978. *Publications:* Computers Management and Information, 1973; Cassell's New Spelling Dictionary, 1976; Cassell's Spelling Dictionary, 1984; (ed) The Blooding of Bourton, 2003; historical vignettes. *Address:* Mastings, Main Street, Preston Bissett, Buckingham MK18 4JR. *T:* (01280) 848772. *E:* david@firnberg.com. *Died 23 July 2013.*

FIRTH, (David) Colin; Headmaster, Cheadle Hulme School, 1977–89; *b* 29 Jan. 1930; *s* of Jack and Muriel Firth; *m* 1954, Edith Scanlan; three *s* one *d*. *Educ:* Rothwell Grammar Sch.; Sheffield Univ. (BSc, DipEd). Royal Signals, 1952–54; Stand Grammar Sch., 1954–57; East Barnet Grammar Sch., 1957–61; Bristol Grammar Sch., 1961–73; The Gilberd Sch., 1973–77. Treasurer: Penrith and Dist Probus Club; Watermillock Painting Gp, 2006–. *Publications:* A Practical Organic Chemistry, 1966; Elementary Thermodynamics, 1969; (jtly) Introductory Physical Science, 1971. *Recreations:* golf, fell walking, talking about gardening, singing. *Address:* Hill House, Fell Lane, Penrith, Cumbria CA11 8BJ. *Died 9 May 2011.*

FISCHER-DIESKAU, Dietrich; baritone; *b* Berlin, 28 May 1925; *s* of Dr Albert Fischer-Dieskau; *m* 1949, Irmgard Poppen (*d* 1963); three *s*; *m* 1965, Ruth Leuwerik (marr. diss. 1967); *m* 1968, Christina Pugall-Schule (marr. diss. 1975); *m* 1977, Julia Varady. *Educ:* High Sch., Berlin; Music Academy, Berlin. First Baritone, Städtische Oper, Berlin, 1948–78, Hon. Mem., 1978–; Mem., Vienna State Opera, 1957–63. Extensive Concert Tours of Europe and USA; soloist in Festivals at Edinburgh, Salzburg, Bayreuth, Vienna, Berlin, Munich, Holland, Luzern, Prades, etc. Opera roles include: Wolfram, Jochanaan, Almaviva, Marquis Posa, Don Giovanni, Falstaff, Mandryka, Wozzeck, Danton, Macbeth, Hans Sachs. Many recordings. Prof., Music Acad., Berlin, 1983; Member: Acad. of Arts, Berlin; Acad. of Fine Arts, Munich; Hon. RAM, 1972; Honorary Member: Wiener Konzerthausgesellschaft, 1962; Königlich-Schwedische Akad., 1972; Acad. Santa Cecilia, Rome; Royal Philharmonic Soc., 1985. Hon. DMus Oxford, 1978; Dr *hc*: Sorbonne, 1980; Yale, 1980. Kunstpreis der Stadt Berlin, 1950; Internationaler Schallplattenpreis, from 1955 nearly every year; Orfeo d'oro, 1955 and 1966; Bayerischer Kammersänger, 1959; Edison Prize, 1961, 1964, 1966, 1970; Naras Award, USA, 1962; Mozart-Medaille, Wien, 1962; Berliner Kammersänger, 1963; Electrola Award, 1970; Léonie Sonning Music Prize, Copenhagen, 1975; Golden Gramophone Award, Germany, 1975; Ruckert-Preis, Schweinfurt, 1979; President's Prize, Charles Gros Acad., Paris, 1980; Ernst Von Siemens Prize, 1980; Artist of the Year, Phonoakademie, Germany, 1980; Gold Medal, Royal Philharmonic Soc., 1988. Bundesverdienstkreuz (1st class), 1958, Grosses Verdienstkreuz, 1974, Stern zum Grossen Bundesverdienstkreuz, 1986; Pour le mérite, Deutschland (FRG), 1984; Chevalier de la Légion d'Honneur (France), 1990. *Publications:* Texte Deutscher Lieder, 1968 (The Fischer-Dieskau Book of Lieder, 1976); Auf den Spuren der Schubert-Lieder, 1971; Wagner und Nietzsche, 1974; Robert Schumann—Wort und Musik, 1981; Töne sprechen, Worte klingen, 1985; Nachklang, 1987; Wenn Musik der Liebe Nahrung ist: Künstlerschicksale im 19 Jahrhundert, 1990; Weil nicht alle Blütenträume reifen (Reichardt), 1991; Johann Friedrich Reichardt: Kapellmeister dreier Preussenkönige, 1992; Fern die Klage des Fauns (Debussy), 1993; Carl Friedrich Zelter (biog.), 1997. *Died 18 May 2012.*

FISH, Prof. Francis, OBE 1989; BPharm, PhD; Dean, School of Pharmacy, 1978–88 (Hon. Fellow, 1992), Professor of Pharmacy, 1988, Professor Emeritus, 1989, University of London; *b* 20 April 1924; *s* of William Fish and Phyllis (*née* Griffiths); *m* 1949, Hilda Mary Brown (*d* 2003); two *s*. *Educ:* Houghton-le-Spring Grammar Sch.; Technical Coll., Sunderland (later Univ. of Sunderland). BPharm (London) 1946; PhD (Glasgow) 1955. Asst Lectr, 1946–48, Lectr, 1948–62, Royal Coll. of Science and Technology, Glasgow; University of Strathclyde: Sen. Lectr, 1962–69; Reader in Pharmacognosy and Forensic Science, 1969–76; Personal Prof., 1976–78; Dean, Sch. of Pharmaceutical Sciences, 1977–78; Supervisor, MSc course in Forensic Science, 1966–78. Mem. Editorial Bd, Jl Pharm. Pharmacol., 1964–70 and 1975–78. Member: Pharm. Soc. Cttee on Pharmacognosy, 1963–74; British Pharm. Codex Pharmacognosy Sub-Cttee A, 1968–73; Brit. Pharm. Conf. Sci. Cttee, 1973–78 (Science Chm., 1977); Brit. Pharmacopoeia Pharmacognosy Panel, 1974–77; Council, Forensic Science Soc., 1974–77 (Vice-Pres., 1981–82); Professional and Gen. Services Cttee, Scottish Council on Alcoholism, 1976–78; British Pharmacopœia Commn, 1980–91; Cttee on Safety of Medicines, 1980–83 (Mem., Herbal Sub-Cttee, 1978–80; Mem., Chemistry, Pharmacy and Standards Sub-Cttee, 1980–92); Univ. of London Senate, 1981–88; DHSS Standing Pharmaceutical Adv. Cttee, 1982–88; UGC Panel on Studies Allied to Medicine, 1982–89 (Chm., 1984–89); Nuffield Foundn Cttee of Inquiry into Pharmacy, 1983–86; Cttee on Review of Medicines, 1984–91; UGC Medical Subcttee, 1984–89. Chm., Post Qualification Educn Bd for NHS Pharmacists in Scotland, 1989–92. Mem., Governing Body, Wye College, 1985–88. Harrison Meml Medal, 1982; Charter Gold Medal, RPSGB, 1987. *Publications:* (with J. Owen Dawson) Surgical Dressings, Ligatures and Sutures, 1967;

research pubns and review articles in Pharmaceut., Phytochem. and Forensic Sci. jls. *Address:* Wardside House, Muthill, Perthshire PH5 2AS. *Died 26 April 2011.*

FISHER, 3rd Baron *cr* 1909, of Kilverstone; **John Vavasseur Fisher,** DSC 1944; JP; Director, Kilverstone Latin-American Zoo and Wild Life Park, 1973–91; *b* 24 July 1921; *s* of 2nd Baron and Jane (*d* 1955), *d* of Randal Morgan, Philadelphia, USA; *S* father, 1955; *m* 1st, 1949, Elizabeth Ann Penelope (marr. diss. 1969), *yr d* of late Herbert P. Holt, MC; two *s* two *d*; 2nd, 1970, Hon. Mrs Rosamund Anne Fairbairn, *d* of 12th Baron Clifford of Chudleigh. *Educ:* Stowe; Trinity Coll., Cambridge. Member: Eastern Gas Bd, 1962–71; East Anglia Economic Planning Council, 1971–77. DL Norfolk, 1968–82; JP Norfolk, 1970. *Heir: s* Hon. Patrick Vavasseur Fisher [*b* 14 June 1953; *m* 1977, Lady Karen Carnegie, *d* of 13th Earl of Northesk; three *s* four *d* (of whom one *s* one *d* are twins)]. *Address:* Marklye, Rushlake Green, Heathfield, Sussex TN21 9PN. *T:* (01435) 830270. *Died 31 Oct. 2012.*

FISHER, Dr David Richard; Teaching Fellow, Department of War Studies, King's College London, since 2010; *b* 13 May 1947; *s* of William Horace and Margaret Catherine Fisher; *m* 1970, Sophia Josephine Hibbard; two *d. Educ:* Reading Sch.; St John's Coll., Oxford (BA 1969, 1st cl. LitHum, 1st cl. Hon. Mods); King's Coll. London (PhD 2010). Ministry of Defence, 1970–2007: Private Sec. to successive RAF Ministers, 1973–74; naval programme and budget, 1976–79; Defence Budget, 1981–83; Vis. Res. Fellow, Nuffield Coll., Oxford, 1983–84; Head, Resources and Progs (Air), 1984–88; Defence Counsellor, UK Delegn to NATO, Brussels (on loan to FCO), 1988–92; Asst Under-Sec. of State (Systems), MoD, 1992–97; Dep. Hd, Defence and Overseas Secretariat, Cabinet Office, 1997–99 (on secondment); Dir, Defence Trng Review, MoD, 1999–2001; Strategy Dir, EDS, 2001–07 (on secondment). Co-Chm., Council on Christian Approaches to Defence and Disarmament, 2010–. *Publications:* Morality and the Bomb, 1985; (contrib.) Ethics and European Security, 1986; (contrib.) Just Deterrence, 1990; (contrib.) Some Corner of a Foreign Field, 1998; (contrib.) The Crescent and the Cross, 1998; (contrib.) Britain's Bomb—What Next?, 2006; (contrib.) The Price of Peace, 2007; (ed) Just War on Terror?, 2010; Morality and War: can war be just in the twenty-first century?, 2011; (contrib.) Military Chaplaincy in Contention, 2013; (contrib.) When Soldiers Say No, 2014; contribs to jls on defence and ethical issues. *Recreations:* philosophy, gardening. *Address:* Department of War Studies, King's College London, Strand, WC2R 2LS. *Club:* Royal Over-Seas League. *Died 28 Feb. 2014.*

FISHER, Desmond (Michael); Vice-Chairman, Provincial Publishers Ltd, 2002–04; *b* 9 Sept. 1920; *e s* of Michael Louis Fisher and Evelyn Kate Shier; *m* 1948, Margaret Elizabeth Smyth; three *s* one *d. Educ:* St Columb's Coll., Derry; Good Counsel Coll., New Ross, Co. Wexford; University Coll., Dublin (BA (NUI)). Asst Editor, Nationalist and Leinster Times, Carlow, 1945–48; Foreign Editor, Irish Press, Dublin, 1948–51; Economic Correspondent, Irish News Agency, Dublin, 1951–54; London Editor, Irish Press, 1954–62; Editor, Catholic Herald, 1962–66; Radio Telefis Eireann: Dep. Head of News, 1967–73; Head of Current Affairs, 1973–75; Dir of Broadcasting Develt, 1975–83; Nationalist and Leinster Times, Carlow: Ed. and Man. Dir, 1984–89; Exec. Dir, 1989–92; Chm., 1992–2001. Columnist, Church Times, 1966–74. *Publications:* The Church in Transition, 1967; Pope Pius XII and the Jews: an answer to Hochhuth's play 'Der Stellvertreter' (The Deputy) by Desmond Fisher, 1975; Broadcasting in Ireland, 1978; The Right to Communicate: a status report, 1981; The Right to Communicate: a new human right, 1983; contributor to The Economist, The Furrow, Irish Digest and to various Irish, US and foreign magazines. *Address:* Louvain 22, Dublin 14, Ireland. *T:* (1) 2884608. *Died 30 Dec. 2014.*

FISHER, Donald, CBE 1987; County Education Officer, Hertfordshire, 1974–90; *b* 20 Jan. 1931; *s* of John Wilfred and Mabel Fisher; *m* 1953, Mavis Doreen (*née* Sutcliffe); one *s* two *d. Educ:* Heckmondwike Grammar Sch.; Christ Church, Oxford (MA). Teacher, Hull GS, 1954–59; Admin. Asst, Cornwall LEA, 1959–61; Asst Educn Officer, W Sussex LEA, 1961–64; Headmaster: Helston GS, 1964–67; Midhurst GS, 1967–72; Dep. Educn Officer, W Sussex LEA, 1972–74. Chm., Assoc. of Educn Officers, 1982; Pres., Soc. of Educn Officers, 1984. Hon. DEd Hatfield Polytechnic, 1989. *Publications:* (contrib.) Educational Administration, 1980, 3rd edn 1989; articles and book reviews in Education. *Recreations:* playing with grandchildren, reading. *Address:* 3 Scotchel Green, Pewsey, Wilts SN9 5AU. *T:* (01672) 562982. *Died 5 Sept. 2011.*

FISHER, Dudley Henry, CBE 1990; DL; CPFA; Chairman, Wales Region, British Gas Corporation, 1974–87; *b* 22 Aug. 1922; *s* of Arthur and Mary Fisher; *m* 1st, 1946, Barbara Lilian Sexton (*d* 1984); one *s* two *d*; 2nd, 1985, Jean Mary Livingstone Miller, *d* of late Dr and Mrs Robert Brown Miller, Cowbridge, S Glam. *Educ:* City of Norwich Sch. Various accountancy positions in Local Govt and Eastern Electricity Bd, 1938–53. War service, RAF, 1942–46 (pilot; Flt Lt). Northern Gas Bd, 1953–56; Wales Gas Board: Asst Chief Accountant, Dep. Chief Accountant, Chief Accountant, Dir of Finance, 1956–69; Dep. Chm., 1970. Member: Adv. Cttee on Local Govt Audit, 1979–82; Audit Commn for Local Authorities in England and Wales, 1983–88; Broadcasting Council for Wales, 1986–90; Hon. Treasurer, British National Cttee, 1980–89, and Chm., Admin. Cttee, 1986–89, World Energy Conf. Chm., Welsh Council, CBI, 1987–89; Mem., Wales Festival of Remembrance Cttee, 1996–2007; Dep. Chm., Inst. of Welsh Affairs, 1991–95. Mem. Council, 1983–88, Treas., 1987–88, UC Cardiff; Member of Council: Univ. of Wales Cardiff (formerly Univ. of Wales Coll. of Cardiff), 1988–2002; Univ. of Wales Coll. of Medicine, 1992–2003; Chm., Audit Cttee, Univ. of Wales, 1994–96. Governor, United World Coll. of the Atlantic, 1988–96. Trustee, Help the Aged, 1987–97; Vice Chm., HelpAge Internat., 1993–97. Liveryman, Welsh Livery Guild, 1996–2007. High Sheriff, 1988–89, DL 1991, S Glam. *Recreations:* golf, gardening, reading. *Address:* Norwood Edge, 8 Cyncoed Avenue, Cardiff CF23 6SU. *T:* (029) 2075 7958. *Club:* Royal Air Force. *Died 4 Sept. 2012.*

FISHWICK, Avril, OBE 1997; Vice Lord-Lieutenant of Greater Manchester, 1988–98; *b* 30 March 1924; *yr d* of Frank Platt and Charlotte Winifred Young; *m* 1950, Thomas William Fishwick (decd); two *d. Educ:* Woodfield; High Sch. for Girls, Wigan; Liverpool Univ. (LLB 1946; LLM 1947). Admitted Solicitor 1949. War service, Foreign Office, Bletchley Park, 1942–45; Partner, Frank Platt & Fishwick, 1958–94. Chm., Envmtl Res. and Consultancy Unit (ERCU Ltd) Tidy Britain (formerly Tidy Britain Enterprises Ltd), 1990–2000; Dir, Northern Adv. Bd, National Westminster Bank, 1984–92. Member: Wigan and Leigh HMC, 1960–73 (Mem., Exec. Council, 1966–73); NW RHA, 1985–88; Chm., Wigan AHA, 1973–82. Local President: Civic Trust, 1976–91; RSPCA, 1974–99; Little Theatre, 1985–91; Drumcroon Arts Centre, 1995–2007; Hon. Mem., Soroptimists Internat., 1973–; Mem., Groundwork Trust, 1986–93. Trustee: Skelton Bounty, 1985–2003; Gtr Manchester Police Community Charity, 1986–98; Friends of Rosie, 1995–2009. Hon. Associate Mem., Manchester Naval Officers Assoc., 2004–. Mem. Court, Manchester Univ., 1984–2001. DL 1982, High Sheriff 1983–84, Gtr Manchester. Hon. MA Manchester, 1993. Paul Harris Fellow, Rotary Internat., 1995; Queen Mother's Birthday Award for Envmtl Improvement, 1996. *Recreations:* family, natural history. *Address:* 6 Southfields, Richmond Road, Bowdon, Altrincham, Cheshire WA14 2TY. *T:* (0161) 941 6660. *Died 28 Oct. 2014.*

FITCH, Rodney Arthur, CBE 1990; PPCSD (FSIAD 1976); Professor and Chair of Retail Design, Delft University of Technology, Netherlands, since 2010; *b* 19 Aug. 1938; *s* of late Arthur and Ivy Fitch; *m* 1965, Janet Elizabeth, *d* of Sir Walter Stansfield, CBE, MC, QPM; one *s* four *d. Educ:* Willesden Polytechnic, Sch. of Building and Architecture; Central School of Arts and Crafts (Theatre, TV Design, Interior and Furniture Design); Hornsey Sch. of Art (Typography). Trainee designer, Hickman Ltd, 1956–58; National Service, RAPC, 1958–60; Charles Kenrick Associates, 1960–62; Conran Design Gp Ltd, 1962–69; C.D.G. (Design Consultants) Ltd, 1969–71; Founder, 1972 (resigned 1994), Fitch and Company, subseq. Fitch-RS and Fitch, a multi-discipline design practice; Founder and Chief Exec., Rodney Fitch, specialist design consultancy, 1994–2003; Chm. and Chief Exec., Fitch (Design Consultants), 2003–09; Founder, Rodney Fitch Associates, 2011. Mem., Design Council, 1988–94. Dir Bd, City of London Fest. of Arts, 1996–99. Member: Court of Govs, Univ. of the Arts, London (formerly London Inst.), 1989–2008 (Dep. Chm., 1989–2005); Council, RCA, 1989–94; Trustee, V&A Museum, 1991–2001; Chm., V&A Enterprises, 2003–13. CSD (formerly SIAD): Pres., 1985–87; Vice-Pres., 1982–84; Hon. Treas., 1984–87; Past Pres., DAAD, 1983. Hon. FRCA 1990; Hon. Fellow, Univ. of the Arts, 2008. FRSA 1976. Hon. DHumLit Virginia Commonwealth Univ., 2009. Legion of Honor, Inst. of Store Planners, USA, 2006. *Publications:* (with L. Knobel) Fitch on Retail Design, 1990; regular contributor to design publications. *Recreations:* cricket, opera, theatre, his family. *Address:* The Court House, Aldbourne, Marlborough, Wilts SN8 2EJ. *Died 20 Oct. 2014.*

FITCHEW, Geoffrey Edward, CMG 1993; Chairman, Insolvency Practices Council, since 2005; *b* 22 Dec. 1939; *s* of Stanley Edward Fitchew and Elizabeth Scott; *m* 1966, Mary Theresa Spillane; two *s*. *Educ:* Uppingham School; Magdalen Coll., Oxford (MA); London Sch. of Economics (MScEcon). Asst Principal, HM Treasury, 1964; Private Sec. to Minister of State, 1968–69; Principal, 1969; Gwilym Gibbon Research Fellow, Nuffield Coll., Oxford, 1973–74; Asst Sec., Internat. Finance Div., HM Treasury, 1975–77; Counsellor (Economics and Finance), UK Perm. Rep. to EEC, 1977–80; Asst Sec., HM Treasury, 1980–83; Under Sec., HM Treasury, 1983–86; Dir-Gen. (for Banking, Financial Services and Company Law), Directorate Gen. XV, EC, Brussels, 1986–93; Dep. Sec., Cabinet Office, 1993–94. Chm. and First Comr, Building Socs Commn, and Chief Registrar of Friendly Socs, 1994–2001. Vice-Chm., Internat. Commn on Holocaust Era Insurance Claims, 1999–2003; Mem., Determinations Panel, Pensions Regulator, 2005–. *Recreations:* golf, theatre, opera, reading, armchair supporter of Manchester United. *Address:* (office) PO Box 698, Godalming, Surrey GU7 9AR. *Died 20 April 2011.*

FITTALL, Betty Daphne C.; *see* Callaway-Fittall.

FITZ-GERALD, Desmond John Villiers, (29th Knight of Glin); Consultant, Christie, Manson & Woods Ltd, since 2003 (Irish Agent, 1975–2003); *b* 13 July 1937; *s* of Desmond Windham Otho Fitz-Gerald, 28th Knight of Glin (*d* 1949), and Veronica (who *m* 2nd, 1954, Ray Milner, CC (Canada), QC, Edmonton, Alta, and Qualicum Beach, Vancouver Island, BC), 2nd *d* of late Ernest Amherst Villiers, MP, and of Hon. Elaine Augusta Guest, *d* of 1st Baron Wimborne; *m* 1st, 1966, Louise Vava Lucia Henriette (marr. diss. 1970), *d* of the Marquis de la Falaise, Paris; 2nd, 1970, Olda Ann, *o d* of T. V. W. Willes, 39 Brompton Sq., SW3; three *d*. *Educ:* Stowe Sch.; University of British Columbia (BA 1959); Harvard Univ. (MA 1961). FSA 1970; MRIAI 1996. Asst Keeper, 1965–72, Dep. Keeper, 1972–75, Dept of Furniture and Woodwork, V&A. Pres., Irish Georgian Soc., 1991–; Chm., Irish Georgian Foundn, 1990– (Dir, 1974–); Dir, Castletown Foundn, 1979–. MRIA 2009. Hon. RHA 2003. Hon. DLitt TCD, 2002. *Publications:* (ed) Georgian Furniture, 1969; (with Maurice Craig) Ireland Observed, a handbook to the buildings and antiquities, 1970; The Music Room from Norfolk House, 1972; (with Edward Malins) Lost Demesnes: Irish Landscape Gardening 1660–1845, 1976; (with Anne Crookshank) The Painters of Ireland, 1978; Irish Furniture, 1978; (jtly) Vanishing Country Houses of Ireland, 1988; (jtly) The Watercolours of Ireland, 1994; (with Anne Crookshank) Ireland's Painters, 2002; (with J. Peill) Irish Furniture, 2007; *catalogues*, all jointly: Irish Houses and Landscapes, 1963; Irish Architectural Drawings, 1965; Irish Portraits 1660–1860, 1969; Mildred Anne Butler, 1981; articles and reviews on architecture and the decorative arts in many Art periodicals. *Address:* Glin Castle, Glin, Co. Limerick, Ireland. *T:* (068) 34077 and 34173, *Fax:* (068) 34364; 52 Waterloo Road, Dublin 4, Ireland. *T:* (1) 680765, *Fax:* (1) 680271. *Clubs:* Beefsteak, Brooks's, Society of the Dilettanti; Kildare Street and University (Dublin). *Died 15 Sept. 2011.*

FitzGERALD, Garret, PhD; Barrister-at-Law; Member of the Dáil (TD) (FG) for Dublin South East, 1969–92; Taoiseach (Prime Minister of Ireland), June 1981–March 1982 and 1982–87; *b* Dublin, 9 Feb. 1926; *s* of late Desmond FitzGerald (Minister for External Affairs, Irish Free State, 1922–27, and Minister for Defence, 1927–32) and Mabel FitzGerald (*née* McConnell); *m* 1947, Joan (*d* 1999), *d* of late Charles O'Farrell; two *s* one *d*. *Educ:* St Brigid's Sch., Bray; Coláiste na Rinne, Waterford; Belvedere Coll., University Coll., and King's Inns (Hon. Bencher, 1993), Dublin. Called to the Bar, 1947. Aer Lingus (Irish Air Lines), 1947–58; Rockefeller Research Asst, Trinity Coll., Dublin, 1958–59; College Lectr, Dept of Political Economy, University Coll., Dublin, 1959–87. Member: Seanad Eireann (Irish Senate), 1965–69; Dáil Cttee on Public Accounts, 1969–73; Minister for Foreign Affairs, Ireland, 1973–77; Leader and President, Fine Gael Party, 1977–87; Leader of the Opposition, 1977–June 1981, and March–Dec. 1982. President: Council of Ministers, EEC, Jan.–June 1975; European Council, July–Dec. 1984; Irish Council of Eur. Movement, 1977–81 and March–Dec. 1982; Mem., Internat. Exec. Cttee of Eur. Movement, 1972–73; Vice-Pres., Eur. People's Party, 1979–87; Member: Trilateral Commission, 1977–81, 1987–; Adv. Bd, Centre for Economic Policy Res., 1992–97; Internat. Adv. Bd, RILA Inc., 1999–. Mem., Oireachtas Library Cttee, 1965–69; Governor, Atlantic Inst. of Internat. Relations, Paris, 1972–73; Mem. Bd, Internat. Peace Acad., NY, 1990–; Chm., Council of Patrons, Saferworld, 1992–; Member: Senate of National Univ. of Ireland, 1973– (Chancellor, 1997–2009); Authy, Radio Telefis Eireann, 1995–2000. Formerly: Irish Correspondent of BBC, Financial Times, Economist and other overseas papers; Economic Correspondent, Irish Times; also Managing Dir, Economist Intelligence Unit of Ireland; Economic Consultant to Fedn of Irish Industries and Construction Industry Fedn, and Rep. Body for Guards. Past Member: Exec. Cttee and Council, Inst. of Public Admin; Council, Statistical and Social Inquiry, Soc. of Ireland; Senate Electoral Law Commn; Workmen's Compensation Commn; Transport Advisory Cttee for Second Programme; Cttee on Industrial Organisation; Gen. Purposes Cttee of Nat. Industrial Economic Council. Director: Trade Develt Inst., Dublin, 1987; Point Holdings Ltd, 1996; Election.com, 1999–. Weekly columnist, Irish Times, 1991–. Lectures: Radcliffe, Warwick Univ., 1980; Richard Dimbleby, BBC, 1982; Heinz, Pittsburgh Univ., 1980; Dunbar, Tulane Univ., 1987; Bass, Univ. of Ulster, 1988; Gaitskell, Nottingham Univ., 1988; Centenary Reckitt, London, 1988; Boston Coll., 1988, 1989; Schumann, UC, Cork, 1989; Morrell, Univ. of York, 1989; Mackintosh, Edinburgh Univ., 1990; Williamson, Univ. of Stirling, 1990; White, QUB, 1990; 2500 Anniv. of Democracy, Manchester Univ., 1993; Lloyd George, Criccieth, 1996. Hon. LLD: New York, 1974; St Louis, 1974; St Mary's, Halifax, NS, 1985; Keele, 1986; Boston Coll., 1987; Westfield Coll., Mass, 1990; Hon. DCL: Oxon, 1987; NUI, 1991; Dublin, 1998; QUB, 2000. Grand Cordon, Order of Al-Kaubar Al-Undari (Jordan), 1975; Grand Officier, Ordre de la République (Tunisia), 1976; Grand Cross (1st Cl.), Order of Merit (FRG), 1986; Order of Christ (Portugal), 1986; Grand Cordon, Order of Rising Sun (Japan), 1989; Comdr, Légion d'Honneur (France), 1995. *Publications:* State-sponsored Bodies, 1959; Planning in Ireland, 1968; Towards a New Ireland, 1972; Unequal Partners (UNCTAD), 1979; Estimates for Baronies of Minimum Level of Irish Speaking Amongst Successive Decennial Cohorts 1771–1781 to 1861–1871, 1984; All in a Life: an autobiography, 1991; Reflections on the Irish State, 2002; Ireland in the World, 2005; Just Garret: tales from the political front line, 2010. *Address:* 37 Annavilla, Dublin 6, Ireland. *T:* 4962600, *Fax:* (1) 4962126. *E:* garretfg@iol.ie. *Clubs:* Reform; Royal Irish Yacht (Dun Laoghaire). *Died 19 May 2011.*

FitzGERALD, Rowanne; *see* Pasco, R.

FLANAGAN, Sir Maurice, KBE 2010 (CBE 2000); Executive Vice Chairman, Emirates Airline and Group, United Arab Emirates, 2006–13; *b* Leigh, Lancs, 17 Nov. 1928; *s* of Patrick and Theresa Flanagan; *m* 1955, Audrey Bolton; one *s* two *d*. *Educ:* Liverpool Univ. (BA 1950). Nat. Service, Navigation Officer, RAF, 1951–52. With

BOAC, later British Airways, 1953–80: grad. trainee, 1953–55; overseas posts, Station Manager to Area Manager, 1956–70; Regl Manager, Midlands and Northern England, 1970–74; British Airways Regl Sales Manager, UK South and Dep. Gen. Sales Manager, 1974–78; on secondment to Dubai Govt as Dir and Gen. Manager, Dubai Nat. Air Transport Assoc., 1978–80; Managing Director: Dubai Nat. Air Transport Assoc., 1980–90; Emirates Airline, 1985–90; Gp Man. Dir, 1990–2003, Vice Chm. and Gp Pres., 2003–06, Emirates Gp. Hon. FRAeS 2005 (FRAeS 1998). Freeman, City of London, 2008; Liveryman, Hon. Co. of Air Pilots (formerly GAPAN), 2008. Hon. LLD Liverpool, 2008; Hon. DLitt Bradford, 2008. *Recreations:* omnivorous reader, aspiring boogie woogie pianist, classical music and pre-1940 jazz, watching cricket and soccer, aspiring Arabist. *Address:* 53 Drayton Gardens, SW10 9RX. *T:* (020) 7244 7177. *Clubs:* Royal Air Force; Capital (Dubai). *Died 7 May 2015.*

FLATT, Rev. Roy Francis Ferguson; Dean of Argyll and the Isles, 1999–2005 (Hon. Canon, since 2006); Rector of Christ Church, Lochgilphead, with St Columba's, Poltalloch (Kilmartin), and All Saints, Inveraray, since 1983; *b* 4 Sept. 1947; *s* of Ray and Trixie Flatt; *m* 1978, Andrina Ferguson; two *s*. *Educ:* King Edward VI Grammar Sch., Bury St Edmunds; Scottish Sch. of Librarianship, Univ. of Strathclyde; Coates Hall, Edinburgh. Ordained deacon, 1980, priest 1981; Curate, St Andrews, Elie and Earlsferry and Pittenweem, Dio. of St Andrews, 1980–82; Diocesan Supernumerary, 1982–83. *Recreations:* reading, sketching, playing solitaire on the PC, adding to the family semiopathy collection. *Address:* Bishopton House, Lochgilphead, Argyll PA31 8PY. *T:* (01546) 602315. *Died 13 March 2011.*

FLEISCHMANN, Prof. Martin, FRS 1986; FRSC 1980; Research Professor: Department of Chemistry, University of Southampton, since 1983; University of Utah, since 1988; *b* 29 March 1927; *s* of Hans Fleischmann and Margarethe Fleischmann (*née* Srb); *m* 1950, Sheila Flinn; one *s* two *d*. *Educ:* Worthing High School; Imperial College of Science and Technology. ARCS 1947; BSc 1948; PhD 1951. ICI Fellow, King's College, Univ. of Durham, 1952–57; Lectr, then Reader, Univ. of Newcastle upon Tyne, 1957–67; Electricity Council Faraday Prof. of Electrochemistry, Univ. of Southampton, 1967–77; Senior Fellowship, SERC, 1977–82. Pres., Internat. Soc. of Electrochemistry, 1970–72. Palladium Medal, US Electrochemical Soc., 1985. *Publications:* numerous papers and chapters in books. *Recreations:* ski-ing, walking, music, cooking. *Address:* Bury Lodge, Duck Street, Tisbury, Wilts SP3 6LJ. *T:* (01747) 870384. *Died 3 Aug. 2012.*

FLEMING, John Bryden; Secretary, Scottish Special Housing Association, 1978–83; *b* 23 June 1918; *s* of W. A. Fleming, advocate, and Maria MacLeod Bryden; *m* 1st, 1942, Janet Louise Guthrie (*d* 1981); one *s* three *d*; 2nd, 1998, Valerie Howard (*née* Forbes). *Educ:* Edinburgh Academy; Univ. of Edinburgh (MA Hons Geog.); Univ. of London (BScEcon). Army, 1940–46, RASC and REME. Planning Officer, Dept of Health for Scotland, 1946; Principal, 1956; Asst Sec., Scottish Develt Dept, 1963, Under Sec., 1974–78. *Recreations:* gardening, hill walking. *Address:* The Old Parsonage, Cambridge Street, Alyth, Perthshire PH11 8AW. *T:* (01828) 632027. *Died 11 April 2011.*

FLOOD, Prof. John Edward, OBE 1986; DSc, PhD; CEng, FIET; FInstP; Professor of Electrical Engineering, 1965–90, then Emeritus, and Head of Department of Electrical and Electronic Engineering, 1967–81 and 1983–89, University of Aston in Birmingham; *b* 2 June 1925; *s* of Sydney E. Flood and Elsie G. Flood; *m* 1949, Phyllis Mary Groocock; two *s*. *Educ:* City of London Sch.; Queen Mary Coll., Univ. of London (BSc 1945; PhD 1951; DSc 1965). CEng, FIET (FIEE 1959); FInstP 1987. Admiralty Signals Estab., 1944–46; Standard Telephone and Cables Ltd, 1946–47; PO Res. Stn, 1947–52; Siemens Brothers Ltd, 1952–57; Chief Engr, Advanced Develt Labs, AEI Telecommunications Div., 1957–65; Dean, Faculty of Engrg, 1971–74, and Sen. Pro-Vice-Chancellor, 1981–83, Univ. of Aston in Birmingham. Chairman: IEE Professional Gp on Telecommunications, 1974–77; IEE S Midland Centre, 1978–79; Univs Cttee on Integrated Sandwich Courses, 1981–82; BSI Cttee on Telecommunications, 1981–92; Member: British Electrotechnical Council, 1981–86; Monopolies and Mergers Commn, 1985–98. FCGI 1991 (CGIA 1962). Freeman, City of London, 1957. *Publications:* Telecommunication Networks, 1975, 2nd edn 1997; Transmission Systems, 1991; Telecommunications Switching, Traffic and Networks, 1995; papers in scientific and technical jls; patents. *Recreations:* swimming, wine-making. *Address:* 60 Widney Manor Road, Solihull, West Midlands B91 3JQ. *T:* (0121) 705 3604. *Club:* Royal Over-Seas League. *Died 17 Jan. 2011.*

FLOUD, Mrs Jean Esther, CBE 1976; MA, BSc(Econ); Principal, Newnham College, Cambridge, 1972–83, Hon. Fellow, 1983; *b* 3 Nov. 1915; *d* of Annie Louisa and Ernest Walter McDonald; *m* 1938, Peter Castle Floud, CBE (*d* 1960), formerly Keeper of Circulation, Victoria and Albert Museum, *s* of late Sir Francis Floud, KCB, KCSI, KCMG; two *d* (one *s* decd). *Educ:* public elementary and selective secondary schools; London School of Economics (BScEcon 1936), Hon. Fellow, 1972. Asst Dir of Educn, City of Oxford, 1940–46; Teacher of Sociology in the University of London (London School of Economics and Inst. of Educn), 1947–62; Official Fellow of Nuffield College, Oxford, 1963–72, Hon. Fellow, 1983; Hon. Fellow, Darwin Coll., Cambridge, 1986. Member: Franks Commission of Inquiry into the University of Oxford, 1964–66; University Grants Cttee, 1969–74; Social Science Research Council, 1970–73; Exec. Cttee, PEP, 1975–77; Adv. Bd for the Res. Councils, 1976–81; Council, Policy Studies Inst., 1979–83. Hon. LittD Leeds, 1973; Hon. DLitt: City, 1978; London, 2003. *Publications:* (with A. H. Halsey and F. M. Martin) Social Class and Educational Opportunity, 1956; (with Warren Young) Dangerousness and Criminal Justice, 1981; papers and reviews in sociological and educational jls. *Recreations:* books, music. *Address:* Elderwick House, The Ridings, Shotover, Oxford OX3 8TB. *Died 28 March 2013.*

FLYNN, Prof. Frederick Valentine, MD (Lond), FRCP, FRCPath; Professor of Chemical Pathology in University of London at University College School of Medicine, 1970–89, then Professor Emeritus; Civil Consultant in Chemical Pathology to Royal Navy, 1978–92; *b* 6 Oct. 1924; *e s* of Frederick Walter Flynn and Jane Laing Flynn (*née* Valentine); *m* 1955, Catherine Ann, *o d* of Dr Robert Walter Warrick and Dorothy Ann Warrick (*née* Dimock); one *s* one *d*. *Educ:* University Coll. London; University Coll. Hosp. Med. Sch. (Fellow, UCL, 1974). Obstetric Ho. Surg. and various posts, incl. Research Asst and Registrar, Dept of Clin. Pathology, UCH, 1947–60; Associate in Clin. Path., Pepper Laboratory of Clin. Medicine, Univ. of Pennsylvania, and British Postgrad. Med. Fedn Travelling Fellow, 1954–55; Consultant Chemical Pathologist, UCH, 1960–70. Chairman: Assoc. of Clin. Biochemists Sci. and Technical Cttee, 1968–70; Dept of Health's Adv. Gp on Scientific and Clinical Applications of Computers, 1971–76; Organising Cttee for 1st, 2nd and 3rd Internat. Confs on Computing in Clinical Labs, 1972–80; Research Cttee, NE Thames RHA, 1984–88; Member: Min. of Health Lab. Equipment and Methods Adv. Gp, 1966–71; Min. of Technol. Working Party on Lab. Instrumentation, 1966–67; BMA Working Party on Computers in Medicine, 1968–69; Dept of Health's Adv. Cttee on Med. Computing, 1969–76, and Laboratory Develts Adv. Gp, 1972–75; MRC Working Party on Hypogammaglobulinaemia, 1959–70; MRC Adv. Panel on Applications for Computing Facilities, 1973–77; NW Thames RHA Sci. Cttee, 1973–74; Med. Lab. Techns Bd, Council for Professions Supplementary to Medicine, 1984–88; NHS Supraregional Assay Services Bd, 1990–92; Sir Jules Thorn Charitable Trust: Mem. Med. Adv. Cttee, 1983–97; Trustee, 1988–2006; Section of Pathology, RSM: Mem. Council, 1968–72, 1986–93; Vice-Pres., 1971–72, 1989–91; Royal Coll. of Pathologists: Chm., Panel of Examrs in Chem. Path., 1972–82; Mem. Council, 1973–83 and 1984–87; Vice-Pres., 1975–78; Treas., 1978–83; Dir of Continuing Med. Educn, 1992–97; College Medal, 1995; Association of Clinical Pathologists: Chm., Working Party on Data Processing in Labs, 1964–67; Mem. Council, 1988–90; Pres.-elect, 1988–89; Pres., 1989–90. Mem. Editl

Bd, Jl of Clin. Pathol., 1995–96. *Publications:* numerous contribs to med. and sci. books and jls. *Recreations:* photography, genealogy, gardening. *Died 4 July 2011.*

FLYNN, Most Rev. Thomas, DD; Bishop of Achonry, (RC), 1977–2007, then Bishop Emeritus; *b* 8 July 1931; *s* of Robert and Margaret Flynn. *Educ:* St Nathy's, Ballaghaderreen; Maynooth College. BD, LPh, MA. Diocesan Religious Inspector of Schools, 1957–64; teaching in St Nathy's College, Ballaghaderreen, 1964–73; President and Headmaster of St Nathy's Coll., 1973–77. DD 1977. *Recreations:* gardening, fishing, golf. *Address:* St Michael's, Cathedral Grounds, Ballaghaderreen, Co. Roscommon, Eire. *Died 2 June 2015.*

FOAKES, Prof. Reginald Anthony; Professor of English, University of California at Los Angeles, 1983–93, then Emeritus; *b* 18 Oct. 1923; 2nd *s* of William Warren Foakes and Frances (*née* Poate); *m* 1st, 1951, Barbara (*d* 1988), *d* of Harry Garratt, OBE; two *s* two *d*; 2nd, 1993, Mary (*d* 1996), *d* of Albert White. *Educ:* West Bromwich Grammar Sch.; Birmingham Univ. (MA, PhD). Fellow of the Shakespeare Inst., 1951–54; Lectr in English, Durham Univ., 1954–62; Sen. Lectr, 1963–64; University of Kent at Canterbury: Prof. of Eng. Lit., 1964–82, then Emeritus Prof. of Eng. and Amer. Lit.; Dean, Faculty of Humanities, 1974–77. Commonwealth Fund (Harkness) Fellow, Yale Univ., 1955–56; Visiting Professor: University Coll., Toronto, 1960–62; Univ. of California, Santa Barbara, 1968–69; UCLA, 1981. *Publications:* (ed) Shakespeare's King Henry VIII, 1957; The Romantic Assertion, 1958; (ed with R. T. Rickert) Henslowe's Diary, 1961, 2nd edn 2002; (ed) The Comedy of Errors, 1962; (ed) The Revenger's Tragedy, 1966; (ed) Macbeth and Much Ado About Nothing, 1968; Romantic Criticism, 1968; Coleridge on Shakespeare, 1971; Shakespeare, the Dark Comedies to the Last Plays, 1971; (ed) The Henslowe Papers, 2 vols, 1977; Marston and Tourneur, 1978; (ed) A Midsummer Night's Dream, 1984; Illustrations of the English Stage 1580–1642, and Visitor's Guide, 1985; (ed) S. T. Coleridge, Lectures 1808–19: On Literature, 2 vols, 1987; (ed) Troilus and Cressida, 1987; (ed) Coleridge's Criticism of Shakespeare, 1989; Hamlet versus King Lear: cultural politics and Shakespeare's art, 1993; (ed) King Lear, 1997; (with Mary Foakes) The Columbia Dictionary of Quotations from Shakespeare, 1998; Shakespeare and Violence, 2003; Inventing Parents, 2003; Imagined Places, 2005; Just Watch Your Step, 2010. *Address:* 34 Bridgetown Road, Stratford-upon-Avon, Warwicks CV37 7JA. *Died 22 Dec. 2013.*

FOALE, Air Cdre Colin Henry; *b* 10 June 1930; *s* of late William Henry Foale and Frances M. (*née* Muse); *m* 1954, Mary Katherine Harding, Minneapolis, USA; one *s* one *d* (and one *s* decd). *Educ:* Wolverton Grammar Sch.; RAF Coll., Cranwell. 1951–74: 13 Sqdn Pilot, Egypt; 32 Sqdn Flt Comdr; Fighter Flt, RAF Flying Coll., Manby; Officer and Aircrew Selection, Hornchurch; OC 73 Sqdn, Cyprus (Sqdn Ldr); Staff Coll., Bracknell; Air Staff, HQ RAF Germany (Wing Comdr); Jt Services Staff Coll., Latimer; OC 39 Sqdn, Malta; SO Flying, MoD (PE) (Gp Captain); Stn Comdr, Luqa, Malta, 1974–76; RCDS, 1977 (Air Cdre); Dir of Public Relations (RAF), 1977–79; retired at own request, 1979. Trng Advr to Chm., Conservative Party, 1980–81; Pilot to Cttee for Aerial Photography, Univ. of Cambridge, 1981–90. Member: St Catharine's Coll., Cambridge; Selwyn Coll., Cambridge; Univ. Air Sqdn, Cambridge; RAF Histl Soc.; Anglo Zulu War Histl Soc. FCMI; FIWM. *Publications:* Waystation to the Stars, 1999. *Recreations:* drama, writing. *Address:* 37 Pretoria Road, Cambridge CB4 1HD; St Catharine's College, Cambridge CB2 1RL. *Club:* Royal Air Force. *Died 14 Feb. 2012.*

FOGEL, Prof. Robert William; Charles R. Walgreen Distinguished Service Professor of American Institutions, University of Chicago, since 1981; *b* 1 July 1926; *s* of Harry G. Fogel and Elizabeth (*née* Mitnik); *m* 1949, Enid Cassandra Morgan (*d* 2007); two *s*. *Educ:* Cornell Univ. (AB 1948); Columbia Univ. (AM 1960); Johns Hopkins Univ. (PhD 1963). Instructor, Johns Hopkins Univ., 1958–59; Asst Prof., Univ. of Rochester, 1960–64; Assoc. Prof., Univ. of Chicago, 1964–65; Prof., Econs and History, Univ. of Chicago, 1965–75, Univ. of Rochester, 1968–75. Taussig Research Prof., Harvard Univ., 1973–74; Pitt Prof. of Amer. History and Instns, Cambridge Univ., 1975–76; Harold Hitchings Burbank Prof. of Econs and Prof. of History, Harvard Univ., 1975–81. President: Economic History Assoc., 1977–78; Social Sci. Hist. Assoc., 1980–81; American Econ. Assoc., 1998–99; Mem., Eur. Acad. of Sci., 1994. Fellow: Econometric Soc., 1971; Amer. Acad. of Arts and Scis, 1972; Nat. Acad. of Scis, 1973; Amer. Philosophical Soc., 2000; FAAAS, 1978; FRHistS 1975; Corresponding FBA, 1991. Hon. DSc: Rochester, 1987; Palermo, 1994; Brigham Young, 1995; SUNY Binghamton, 1999; Torino, 2000. Phi Beta Kappa, 1963; Arthur H. Cole Prize, Economic History Assoc., 1968; Schumpeter Prize, Harvard Univ., 1971; Bancroft Prize, Columbia Univ., 1975; Gustavus Myers Prize, 1990; (jtly) Nobel Prize for Economics, 1993; Distinguished Alumnus Prize, Johns Hopkins, 2001. *Publications:* The Union Pacific Railroad: a case in premature enterprise, 1960; Railroads and American Economic Growth: essays in econometric history, 1964 (Spanish edn 1972); (jtly) The Reinterpretation of American Economic History, 1971 (Italian edn 1975); (jtly) The Dimension of Quantitative Research in History, 1972; (jtly) Time on the Cross: the economics of American Negro slavery, 1974 (Japanese edn 1977, Spanish edn 1981); Ten Lectures on the New Economic History, 1977; (jtly) Which Road to the Past? Two Views of History, 1983; Without Consent or Contract: the rise and fall of American slavery, vol. 1, 1989, vols 2–4 (jtly), 1992; The Fourth Great Awakening and the Future of Egalitarianism, 2000; The Slavery Debates 1952–1990: a retrospective, 2003; The Escape from Hunger and Premature Death 1700–2100: Europe, America and the Third World, 2004; (jtly) The Changing Body: health, nutrition and development in the Western world since 1700, 2011; numerous papers in learned jls. *Address:* (office) University of Chicago, Booth School of Business, 5807 S Woodlawn Avenue, Chicago, IL 60637–1610, USA. *Died 11 June 2013.*

FOGG, Cyril Percival, CB 1973; Director, Admiralty Surface Weapons Establishment, Ministry of Defence (Procurement Executive), 1973–75; *b* 28 Nov. 1914; *s* of Henry Fogg and Mabel Mary (*née* Orton); *m* 1st, 1939, Margaret Amie Millican (*d* 1982); two *d*; 2nd, 1983, June Adele McCoy. *Educ:* Herbert Strutt Sch., Belper; Gonville and Caius Coll., Cambridge (MA, 1st cl. Mechanical Sciences Tripos). Research Staff, General Electric Co., 1936–37; various positions in Scientific Civil Service from 1937 with Air Ministry, Ministries of Aircraft Production, Supply, Aviation and Technology. Head of Ground Radar Dept, RRE Malvern, 1956–58; Dir Electronics R&D (Ground), 1959–63; Imperial Defence Coll., 1961; Dir of Guided Weapons Research, 1963–64; Dir-Gen. of Electronics R&D, Min. of Aviation, 1964–67; Dep. Controller of Electronics, Min. of Technology, later MoD (Procurement Executive), 1967–72. *Address:* 10 Miles Cottages, Taylors Lane, Bosham, Chichester, West Sussex PO18 8QG. *Died 8 April 2011.*

FOLEY, 8th Baron *cr* 1776; **Adrian Gerald Foley;** *b* 9 Aug. 1923; *s* of 7th Baron and Minoru (*d* 1968), *d* of late H. Greenstone, South Africa; *S* father, 1927; *m* 1st, 1958, Patricia Meek (marr. diss. 1971); one *s* one *d*; 2nd, 1972, Ghislaine Lady Ashcombe (*d* 2000); *m* 2003, Hannah, (Bebe), Steinberg. *Heir: s* Hon. Thomas Henry Foley, *b* 1 April 1961. *Club:* White's. *Died 12 Feb. 2012.*

FOLEY, Thomas Stephen, Hon. KBE 1995; Partner, Akin, Gump, Strauss, Hauer & Feld, 1995–97 and 2001–08; Chairman, North American Trilateral Commission, 2001–08; *b* 6 March 1929; *s* of Ralph E. Foley and Helen Marie (*née* Higgins); *m* 1968, Heather Strachan. *Educ:* Gonzaga High Sch.; Gonzaga Univ.; Washington Univ. (BA 1951; LLB 1957). Partner, Higgins and Foley, 1957–58; Lectr in Law, Gonzaga Univ., 1958–60; Dep. Prosecuting Attorney, Spokane County, 1958–60; Asst Attorney Gen., Washington State, 1960–61; Special Counsel, Senate Interior and Insular Affairs Cttee, 1961–64; Mem. of 89th–101st Congresses from 5th Dist Washington (Democrat), 1964–95. Chm., 1975–80, Vice-Chm., 1981–86, Agriculture Cttee. Chm., House Democratic Caucus, 1976–80; House Majority Whip, 1981–87;

Majority Leader, 1987–89; Speaker, US House of Representatives, 1989–95; American Ambassador to Japan, 1997–2001. Dir, Council on Foreign Relations, 1988–94. *Died 18 Oct. 2013.*

FONTAINE, André Lucien Georges; Managing Editor and Publisher, le Monde, 1985–91; *b* 30 March 1921; *s* of Georges Fontaine and Blanche Rochon Duvigneaud; *m* 1943, Belita Cavaillé; two *s* one *d*. *Educ:* Paris Univ. (diplômes études supérieures, droit public et économie politique, lic.lettres). Joined Temps Présent, 1946; le Monde, 1947: Foreign Editor, 1951; Chief Editor, 1969. Editorialist, Radio Luxemburg, 1980–91. Chm. Adv. Gp, Internat. Strategy for the 9th Plan, 1982–84; Mem. Bd, Institut Français des Relations Internationales, 1982–92; Vice-Chm., French section, Franco-British Council, 2000–02. Mem. Bd, Bank Indosuez, 1983–85. Grand Officer, Order of Dom Enrique (Portugal); Commander: German Merit; Italian Merit; Greek Phoenix; Officer, Orders of Vasa (Sweden), Leopold (Belgium) and Lion (Finland); Kt, Dannebrog (Denmark) and Crown of Belgium; Order of Tudor Vladimirescu (Romania). Atlas' Internat. Editor of the Year, 1976. *Publications:* L'Alliance atlantique à l'heure du dégel, 1960; Histoire de la guerre froide, vol. 1 1965, vol. 2 1966 (English trans., History of the Cold War, 1966 and 1967); La Guerre civile froide, 1969; Le dernier quart du siècle, 1976; La France au bois dormant, 1978; Un seul lit pour deux rêves, 1981; (with Pierre Li) Sortir de l'Hexagonie, 1984; L'un sans l'autre, 1991; Après eux, le déluge, 1995; La tache rouge, 2004. *Address:* 80 Boulevard Auguste Blanqui, 75707 Paris Cedex 13, France. *Died 17 March 2013.*

FOOT, Michael Colin, OBE 1984; Director, Australia, British Council, 1989–93; *b* 3 Feb. 1935; *s* of William Reginald Foot and Elsie (*née* Collins); *m* 1964, Heather Pearl Foot (*née* Beaton); two *s* one *d* (and one *d* decd). *Educ:* Taunton's Sch., Southampton; University Coll., Leicester (BA London); Leicester Univ. (PGCE); Univ. of Essex (MA 1994). Lycée Champollion, Grenoble, 1959–60; Ashlyn's Sch., Berkhamsted, 1960–63. Served RAF, 1963–66. British Council: Asst Rep., Chile, 1966–71; Hd of Overseas Recruitment, Personnel Div., 1971–75; Dep. Rep., Nigeria, 1975–78; Dep. Dir, Personnel, 1978–81; Rep., Bangladesh, 1981–83; Dir, Personnel, 1984–85; Controller, Personnel, 1986–89. Pt-time Tutor, Internat. Acad., Univ. of Essex, 1994–2012. *Recreations:* reading, theatre, music, botany, swimming. *Address:* c/o HSBC, Bitterne, Southampton SO18 1DB. *Club:* Royal Air Force. *Died 24 Jan. 2015.*

FOOT, Michael Richard Daniell, CBE 2001; TD 1945; historian; *b* 14 Dec. 1919; *s* of late R. C. Foot and Nina (*née* Raymond); *m* twice; one *s* one *d*; 3rd, 1972, Mirjam Michaela Romme (Prof. M. M. Foot). *Educ:* Winchester (scholar); New Coll., Oxford (scholar). Served in Army, 1939–45 (Major RA, parachutist, wounded). Taught at Oxford, 1947–59; research, 1959–67; Prof. of Modern Hist., Manchester, 1967–73; Dir of Studies, European Discussion Centre, 1973–75. Fellow, St Deiniol's Liby, Hawarden, 2001. Hon. Vice-Pres., RHistS, 2004–. French Croix de Guerre, 1945; Officer, Order of Orange Nassau (Netherlands), 1989; Chevalier, Legion of Honour (France), 2005. *Publications:* Gladstone and Liberalism (with J. L. Hammond), 1952; British Foreign Policy since 1898, 1956; Men in Uniform, 1961; SOE in France, 1966, new edn 2004; (ed) The Gladstone Diaries: vols I and II, 1825–1839, 1968; (ed) War and Society, 1973; (ed with Dr H. C. G. Matthew) The Gladstone Diaries: vols III and IV, 1840–1854, 1974; Resistance, 1976; Six Faces of Courage, 1978, 2nd edn 2003; (with J. M. Langley) MI9, 1979; SOE: an outline history, 1984, 4th edn 2008; Art and War, 1990; (ed) Holland at war against Hitler, 1990; (ed with I. C. B. Dear) Oxford Companion to World War II, 2001, 2nd edn 2005; SOE in the Low Countries, 2001; Memoirs of an SOE Historian, 2008; *festschrift:* (ed. K. G. Robertson) War, Resistance and Intelligence: collected essays in honour of M. R. D. Foot, 1999. *Recreations:* reading, talking. *Address:* Martins Cottage, Nuthampstead, Royston, Herts SG8 8ND. *Clubs:* Savile, Special Forces. *Died 18 Feb. 2012.*

FORBES, 22nd Lord *cr* 1445 or before; **Nigel Ivan Forbes,** KBE 1960; JP, DL; Premier Lord of Scotland; Representative Peer of Scotland, 1955–63; Major (retired) Grenadier Guards; Chairman, Rolawn Ltd, 1975–98; *b* 19 Feb. 1918; *o s* of 21st Lord and Lady Mabel Anson (*d* 1972), *d* of 3rd Earl of Lichfield; *S* father, 1953; *m* 1942, Hon. Rosemary Katharine Hamilton-Russell, *o d* of 9th Viscount Boyne; two *s* one *d*. *Educ:* Harrow; RMC Sandhurst. Served War of 1939–45 (wounded); Adjt, Grenadier Guards, Staff Coll. Military Asst to High Comr for Palestine, 1947–48. Minister of State, Scottish Office, 1958–59. Member: Inter-Parly Union Delegn to Denmark, 1956; Commonwealth Parly Assoc. Delegn to Canada, 1961; Parly Delegn to Pakistan, 1962; Inter-Parly Union Delegn to Hungary, 1965; Inter-Parly Union Delegn to Ethiopia, 1971. Director: Grampian Television PLC, 1960–88; Blenheim Travel Ltd, 1981–88; Dep. Chm., Tenant Caledonian Breweries Ltd, 1964–74. Mem., Aberdeen and District Milk Marketing Bd, 1962–72; Mem. Alford District Council, 1955–58; Chm., River Don District Bd, 1962–73. Pres., Royal Highland and Agricultural Society of Scotland, 1958–59; Member: Sports Council for Scotland, 1966–71; Scottish Cttee, Nature Conservancy, 1961–67; Chm., Scottish Br., Nat. Playing Fields Assoc., 1965–80; Pres., Scottish Scout Assoc., 1970–88. Pres., Books Abroad, 1982–; Chm., Alford Car Transport Service, 2000–09. Patron, Friends of Insch Hosp., 1992–2011. JP 1955, DL 1958, Aberdeenshire. *Recreations:* wildlife, travel, photography. *Heir: s* Master of Forbes, *b* 6 May 1946. *Address:* Balforbes, Alford, Aberdeenshire AB33 8DR. *T:* (01975) 562516. *Died 5 March 2013.*

FORBES, Bryan, CBE 2004; film director and author; *b* 22 July 1926; *né* John Theobald Clarke; *m* 1955, Nanette Newman; two *d*. *Educ:* West Ham Secondary Sch. Studied at RADA, 1941; entered acting profession, 1942, and (apart from war service) was on West End stage, then in films in the UK and in Hollywood, 1948–60. Formed Beaver Films with Richard Attenborough, 1959; wrote and co-produced The Angry Silence, 1960. Subseq. wrote, dir. and prod. numerous films; *films include:* The League of Gentlemen, Only Two Can Play, Whistle Down the Wind, 1961; The L-Shaped Room, 1962; Séance on a Wet Afternoon, 1963; King Rat (in Hollywood), 1964; The Wrong Box, 1965; The Whisperers, 1966; Deadfall, 1967; The Madwoman of Chaillot, 1968; The Raging Moon, 1970; The Tales of Beatrix Potter, 1971; The Stepford Wives, 1974 (USA); The Slipper and the Rose, 1975 (Royal Film Perf., 1976); International Velvet, 1978; (British segment) The Sunday Lovers, 1980; Better Late Than Never, 1981; The Naked Face, 1983; (narrator and co-dir) I am a Dancer, 1971. *Stage:* directed: Macbeth, Old Vic, 1980; Killing Jessica, Savoy, 1986; The Living Room, Royalty, 1987; One Helluva Life, Dublin Fest., 2002, (renamed Barrymore) Th. Royal, Windsor, 2004; directed and acted in Star Quality, Th. Royal, Bath, 1983. *Television:* produced and directed: Edith Evans, I Caught Acting Like the Measles, Yorkshire TV, 1973; Elton John, Goodbye Norma Jean and Other Things, ATV 1973; Jessie, BBC, 1980; The Endless Game, C4, 1989; acted in: December Flower, Granada, 1984; First Among Equals, Granada, 1986. Man. Dir and Head of Production, ABPC Studios, 1969–71; Man. Dir and Chief Exec., EMI-MGM, Elstree Studios, 1970–71; Dir, Capital Radio Ltd, 1973–97. Member: BBC Gen. Adv. Council, 1966–69; BBC Schs Council, 1971–73; President: Beatrix Potter Soc., 1982–96; Nat. Youth Theatre, 1984–2005; Writers' Guild of GB, 1988–91. Hon. DLit London, 1992; Hon. DLitt Sussex, 1999. Won British Acad. Award, 1960; Writers' Guild Award (twice); London Film Critics' Circle Award for Excellence in Film, 2005; Lifetime Achievement Award, BAFTA, 2007; numerous internat. awards. *Publications:* Truth Lies Sleeping, 1950; The Distant Laughter, 1972; Notes for a Life, 1974; The Slipper and the Rose, 1976; Ned's Girl: biography of Dame Edith Evans, 1977; International Velvet, 1978; Familiar Strangers, 1979; That Despicable Race, 1980; The Rewrite Man, 1983; The Endless Game, 1986; A Song at Twilight, 1989; A Divided Life, 1992; The Twisted Playground, 1993; Partly Cloudy, 1995; Quicksand, 1996; The Memory of All That, 1999; The Fatal Trinity, 2002; The Choice, 2007; The Soldier's Story, 2010; contribs to: The Spectator, and other periodicals. *Recreations:* reading, landscape gardening, photography. *Address:* Pinewood Studio, Iver Heath, Bucks SL0 0NH. *Died 8 May 2013.*

FORBES, James, FCA; Chairman, Tate & Lyle Group Pension Fund, 1978–85; Forestry Commissioner, 1982–88; *b* 2 Jan. 1923; *s* of Donald Forbes and Rona Ritchie Forbes (*née* Yeats); *m* 1948, Alison Mary Fletcher Moffat; two *s*. *Educ:* Christ's Hospital; Officers' Training School, Bangalore. APMI. Commissioned Indian Army, 1942; 15 Punjab Regt, 1943–44, Capt. CO Mobile Army Inspection Unit; Maj. DADOS AHQ, 1945–46; released 1947, Hon. Major. Peat Marwick Mitchell Co., 1952–58; Chief Accountant, L. Rose, 1958; Group Operational Research Manager, Schweppes, 1960, Group Chief Accountant, 1963 (Dir, subsid. cos); Sec. and Financial Adviser, Cadbury Schweppes (on formation), 1969, Main Board Dir, 1971, Group Finance Dir to April 1978; Senior Exec. Dir, Tate & Lyle, 1978, Vice-Chm., 1980–84. Non-executive Director: British Transport Hotels, 1978–83; British Rail Investments, 1980–84; Steetley plc, 1984–89; Compass Hotels, 1984–99; Lautro Ltd, 1986–90. Mem. Council, Inst. of Chartered Accountants, 1971–88 (Treasurer, 1984–86). Gov., Christ's Hosp., 1983– (Chm. and Treas., Council of Almoners, 1987–96). Mem., Highland Society. *Recreation:* golf. *Address:* 31 Rosemary Court, Church Road, Haslemere, Surrey GU27 1BH. *Clubs:* Caledonian, Royal Commonwealth Society. *Died 26 Feb. 2011.*

FORD, Sir Colin Anson St C.; *see* St Clair-Ford.

FORD, (Martin) Geoffrey; Librarian, 1990–2002, and Director of Information Services, 1999–2002, University of Bristol; *b* 24 Jan. 1942; *s* of George Frederick Ford and Muriel (*née* Dowding); *m* 1974, Elizabeth Jill Barker. *Educ:* Sir Joseph Williamson's Mathematical Sch., Rochester; Leicester Univ. (BSc 1963); Sheffield Univ. (DipLib 1965; MSc 1973). MCLIP (ALA 1967). Liby Asst, Leicester Univ., 1963–64; Durham University: Asst Librarian, 1965–67; Sen. Res. Asst, 1968–69; Res. Associate, Bristol Univ., 1969–72; Asst Dir, Liby Res. Unit, Lancaster Univ., 1972–75; Sen. Res. Officer and Dir, Centre for Res. on User Studies, Sheffield Univ., 1976–78; Southampton University: Sub-librarian, 1978–87; Dep. Librarian, 1987–89. Member: Adv. Council, British Library, 1995–2000 (Member: Res. Cttee, 1990–94; Adv. Cttee on Bibliographic Services, 1991–94); SCONUL Council, 1992–2001 (Vice Chm., 1996–98; Chm., 1998–2000); Vice-Chm., SW Regl Liby System, 1999–2002 (Chm., 1998–99). (Jtly) Robinson Medal, LA, 1972. *Publications:* Review of Methods for Determining the Use of Library Stock, 1990; (contrib.) A Boyhood Library, 2009; Lansdown Poets' Anthology 2010: electric leap, 2010; res. reports, articles and reviews in learned jls. *Recreations:* travelling on trains, gentle walking, listening to jazz, naval and transport history, writing. *Address:* 21 Redland Grove, Bristol BS6 6PT. *Died 6 Aug. 2011.*

FORD, Prof. Philip John, PhD; FBA 2009; Professor of French and Neo-Latin Literature, University of Cambridge, since 2004; Fellow, Clare College, Cambridge, since 1982; *b* Ilford, 28 March 1949; *s* of Peter Ford and Leah Ford (*née* Alvarez); *m* 1982, Lenore Muskett; one *s*. *Educ:* Ilford Co. High Sch. for Boys; King's Coll., Cambridge (BA 1971, MA 1975; PhD 1977); Univ. de Bordeaux III (Maîtrise ès lettres modernes 1977). Res. Fellow, Girton Coll., Cambridge, 1977–78; Lectr in French, Univ. of Aberdeen, 1978–81; University of Cambridge: Asst Lectr in French, 1981–86; Lectr in French, 1986–99; Reader in French and Neo-Latin Lit., 1999–2004. Associate Mem., Belgian Royal Acad., 2004–. Officier, Ordre des Palmes Académiques (France), 2004 (Chevalier, 2001). *Publications:* George Buchanan, Prince of Poets, 1982; Ronsard's Hymnes: a literary and iconographical study, 1997; Jean Dorat, Mythologicum, 2000; De Troie à Ithaque: réception des épopées homériques à la Renaissance, 2007; The Montaigne Library of Gilbert de Botton at Cambridge University Library, 2008; The Judgment of Palaemon: the contest between neo-Latin and vernacular poetry in Renaissance France, 2013. *Recreations:* cooking, travel, learning new languages, classical music, walking. *Address:* Clare College, Cambridge CB2 1TL. *T:* (01223) 333271, *Fax:* (01223) 333219. *E:* pjf2@cam.ac.uk. *Died 8 April 2013.*

FORD, Gen. Sir Robert (Cyril), GCB 1981 (KCB 1977; CB 1973); CBE 1971 (MBE 1958); Vice-Chairman, Commonwealth War Graves Commission, 1989–93 (Commissioner, 1981–93); *b* 29 Dec. 1923; *s* of late John Stranger Ford and Gladys Gertrude Ford, Yealmpton, Devon; *m* 1st, 1949, Jean Claudia Pendlebury (*d* 2002), *d* of late Gp Capt. Claude Pendlebury, MC, TD; one *s*; 2nd, 2003, Caroline Margaret Peerless (*née* Leather) (*d* 2013). *Educ:* Musgrave's Coll. War of 1939–45: commissioned into 4th/7th Royal Dragoon Guards, from Sandhurst, 1943; served with Regt throughout NW European campaign, 1944–45 (despatches) and in Egypt and Palestine, 1947–48 (despatches). Instructor, Mons OCS, 1949–50; Training Officer, Scottish Horse (TA), 1952–54; Staff Coll., Camberley, 1955; GSO 2 Mil. Ops, War Office, 1956–57; Sqdn Ldr 4/7 RDG, 1958–59; Bde Major, 20th Armoured Bde, 1960–61; Brevet Lt-Col, 1962; Sqdn Ldr, 4/7 RDG, 1962–63; GSO1 to Chief of Defence Staff, 1964–65; commanded 4/7 RDG in S Arabia and N Ireland, 1966–67; Comdr, 7th Armd Bde, 1968–69; Principal Staff Officer to Chief of Defence Staff, 1970–71; Comdr Land Forces, N Ireland, 1971–73; Comdt, RMA Sandhurst, 1973–76; Military Secretary, 1976–78; Adjutant-General, 1978–81; ADC General to the Queen, 1980–81; Governor, Royal Hosp., Chelsea, 1981–87. Colonel Commandant: RAC, 1980–82; SAS Regt, 1980–85; Col 4th/7th Royal Dragoon Gds, 1984–88. President: Services Kinema Corp., 1978–81; Army Boxing Assoc., 1978–81. Chm., 1981–87, and Pres., 1986–97, Army Benevolent Fund; Chm., Royal Cambridge Home for Soldiers' Widows, 1981–87; Nat. Pres., Forces Help Soc. and Lord Roberts Workshops, 1981–91. Governor, Corps of Commissionaires, 1981–94. Freeman, City of London, 1981. CCMI. *Recreations:* watching cricket, tennis, war studies, theatre. *Clubs:* Cavalry and Guards, MCC. *Died 24 Nov. 2015.*

FORD, Robert Webster, CBE 1982; HM Diplomatic Service, retired; *b* 27 March 1923; *s* of late Robert Ford; *m* 1956, Monica Florence Tebbett (*d* 2012); two *s*. *Educ:* Alleyne's Sch. Served RAF, 1939–45. Served with British Mission, Lhasa, Tibet and Political Agency in Sikkim and Bhutan, 1945–47; joined Tibetan Govt Service, 1947; advised on and installed Tibet's first radio communication system and broadcasting stn; travelled extensively in Northern and Eastern Tibet, 1947–50; taken prisoner during Chinese Occupation of Tibet, 1950; imprisoned in China, 1950–55; freelance writer and broadcaster on Chinese and Tibetan affairs, 1955; entered Foreign Service, 1956; 2nd Sec., Saigon, 1957–58; 1st Sec. (Information), Djakarta, 1959; Washington, 1960–62; FO, 1962–67; Consul-Gen., Tangier, 1967–70; Counsellor, 1970; Consul-General: Luanda, 1970–74; Bordeaux, 1974–78; Gothenburg, 1978–80; Geneva, 1980–83. *Publications:* Captured in Tibet, 1956, repr. 1990. *Recreations:* ski-ing, gardening, travelling. *Address:* Cedar Garth, Latimer Road, Monken Hadley, Barnet, Herts EN5 5NU. *Clubs:* Royal Commonwealth Society, Royal Geographical Society. *Died 20 Sept. 2013.*

FORD, Roy Arthur, MA; Director of Visits, Canterbury Cathedral, 1986–90; *b* 10 May 1925; *s* of Arthur Ford and Minnie Elizabeth Ford; *m* 1965, Christine Margaret Moore; two *s*. *Educ:* Collyer's Sch., Horsham; Corpus Christi Coll., Cambridge (Scholar; 1st Cl. Pts I and II, History Tripos; BA 1949, MA 1971). Asst Master: Uppingham Sch., 1951–54; Tonbridge Sch., 1954–66; Uppingham Sch., (also Head of History and Sixth Form Master), 1966–71; Headmaster: Southwell Minster Grammar Sch., 1971–75; King's Sch., Rochester, 1975–86. *Recreations:* walking, travel, music. *Address:* North Street Farmhouse, Sheldwich, Kent ME13 0LN. *T:* (01795) 537614. *Died 24 April 2011.*

FOREMAN, Sir Philip (Frank), Kt 1981; CBE 1972; DL; FREng, FIMechE; Member Council, 1986–98, Chairman, 1988–91, and President, 1994–98, British Standards Institution; *b* 16 March 1923; *s* of late Frank and Mary Foreman; *m* 1971, Margaret Cooke; one *s*. *Educ:* Soham Grammar Sch., Cambs; Loughborough Coll., Leics. (DLC (Hons)). Royal Naval Scientific Service, 1943–58. Short

Bros, 1958–88: Man. Dir, 1967–88; Chm., 1983–88. Director: Simon Engrg Ltd, 1987–94 (Dep. Chm., 1992; Chm., 1993); Progressive Bldg Soc., 1987–2000 (Chm., 1990–2000); Ricardo Group (formerly Ricardo International) plc, 1988–97 (Chm., 1992–97); Consultant, Foreman Associates, 1988–2001. Member: Design Council, 1986–92; NI Economic Council, 1972–88; Chm., Teaching Co. Management Cttee, 1987–90; Trustee, Scotch-Irish Trust, 1980–2008. Mem. Senate, QUB, 1993–2002. Pres., IMechE, 1985–86. FREng (FEng 1982); Hon. FIAE 2008 (FIAE 1997); Fellow: Irish Management Inst., 1986; Irish Inst. of Engrs, 1987; MInstD 1987; CCMI. FRSA 1978. A Freeman, City of London, 1980; Liveryman, Engineers' Co., 1992–. DL Belfast, 1975. Hon. FRAeS 1983. Hon. DSc QUB, 1976; Hon. DTech Loughborough, 1983; DUniv Open, 1985. *Publications:* papers to: Royal Aeronautical Soc.; Instn of Mechanical Engineers. *Recreation:* gardening. *Address:* Ashtree House, 26 Ballymenoch Road, Holywood, Co. Down BT18 0HH. *T:* (028) 9042 5673. *Died 23 Feb. 2013.*

FORFAR, Prof. John Oldroyd, MC; Professor of Child Life and Health, University of Edinburgh, 1964–82, then Professor Emeritus; *b* 16 Nov. 1916; *s* of Rev. David Forfar, MA and Elizabeth Edith Campbell; *m* 1942, Isobel Mary Langlands Fernback (*d* 2012), MB, ChB, DPH, AFOM; two *s* one *d*. *Educ:* Perth Acad.; St Andrews Univ. BSc 1938, MB, ChB 1941, St Andrews; DCH (London) 1948; FRCPE 1953 (MRCPE 1948); MD (Commendation) St Andrews, 1958; FRCP 1964 (MRCP 1947); FRSE 1975; FRCPGlas 1979 (MRCPGlas 1978). House Officer, Perth Royal Infirmary, 1941; RAMC, 1942–46: Med. Off., 47 Royal Marine Commando, 1943–45 (MC 1944; despatches, 1945); Registrar and Sen. Registrar, Dundee Royal Infirmary, 1946–48; Sen. Lectr in Child Health, St Andrews Univ., 1948–50; Sen. Paediatric Phys., Edinburgh Northern Gp of Hosps, and Sen. Lectr in Child Life and Health, Edinburgh Univ., 1950–64; Consultant Paediatrician, Royal Hosp. for Sick Children and Royal Infirm., Edinburgh, 1964–82. Chairman: Scottish Assoc. of Voluntary Child Care Organisations, 1965–69; Medical Gp, Assoc. of British Adoption Agencies, 1966–76; Jt Paediatric Cttee of Royal Colls of Physicians and British Paediatric Assoc., 1979–85; President: Scottish Paediatric Soc., 1972–74; Assoc. of Clinical Professors and Heads of Departments of Paediatrics, 1980–83; Pres., BPA, 1985–88. Vice-President: Gt Ormond St Wishing Well Appeal, 1987–89; Royal Hosp. for Sick Children Appeal, 1992–95; Trustee, Malcolm Sargent Cancer Fund for Children, 1975–84. Fellow, Amer. Coll. of Nutrition, 1977; Hon. Member: Australian Coll. of Paediatrics, 1986; Faculty of Paediatrics, RCPI, 1986. Hon. FRCPCH 1997. James Spence Medallist, BPA, 1983. *Publications:* (ed) Textbook of Paediatrics, 1973, 7th edn 2009; Child Health in a Changing Society, 1988; The British Paediatric Association 1928–1988, 1989; From Omaha to the Scheldt: the story of 47 Royal Marine Commando, 2001 (Royal Marine Histl Soc. Award, 2005); From Gold to Omaha, 2005; contribs to general medical and to paediatric jls and books. *Recreations:* walking, writing. *Died 14 Aug. 2013.*

FORMAN, Sir Denis, Kt 1976; OBE 1956; Chairman, Granada Television, 1974–87; Deputy Chairman, Granada Group, 1984–90 (Director, 1964–90); *b* 13 Oct. 1917; *s* of late Rev. Adam Forman, CBE, and Flora Smith; *m* 1st, 1948, Helen de Mouilpied (*d* 1987); two *s*; 2nd, 1990, Moni, *widow* of James Cameron, CBE; one step *s* one step *d*. *Educ:* at home; Loretto; Pembroke Coll., Cambridge. Served War, 1940–45: Argyll and Sutherland Highlanders; Commandant, Orkney and Shetland Defences Battle Sch., 1942 (wounded, Cassino, 1944). Chief Production Officer, Central Office of Information Films, 1947; Dir, British Film Inst., 1948–55 (Chm., Bd of Governors, 1971–73); Granada TV Ltd, 1955–87: Dir, 1959; Jt Man. Dir, 1965–81; Chm., Novello & Co., 1971–88. Dep. Chm., Royal Opera Hse, Covent Gdn, 1983–91 (Dir, 1981–91); Chm., Scottish Film Production Fund, 1990–93; Mem. Council, RNCM, 1975–84 (Hon. Mem., RNCM, 1981; Hon. FRNCM 1993). Fellow, BAFTA, 1977. DUniv: Stirling, 1982; Keele, 1990; DU Essex, 1986; Hon. LLD: Manchester, 1983; Lancaster, 1989; Hon. Dr Manchester Metropolitan, 1990. Ufficiale dell'ordine Al Merito della Repubblica Italiana. *Publications:* Mozart's Piano Concertos, 1971; Son of Adam (autobiog.), 1990; To Reason Why (autobiog.), 1991; (ed) The Good Opera Guide, 1994; Persona Granada: some memories of Sidney Bernstein and the early days of Independent Television (autobiog.), 1997; The Good Wagner Guide, 2000. *Recreation:* music. *Address:* Flat 2, 15 Lyndhurst Gardens, NW3 5NT. *Clubs:* Garrick, Savile, Oriental; New (Edinburgh). *Died 24 Feb. 2013.*

FORMAN, Sir John Denis; *see* Forman, Sir Denis.

FORT, Jean; Headmistress of Roedean School, Brighton, 1961–70; *b* 4 Jan. 1915; *d* of G. B. Rae; *m* 1943, Richard Fort (*d* 1959), MP Clitheroe Division of Lancs; four *s* one *d*. *Educ:* Benenden Sch.; Lady Margaret Hall, Oxford (MA, DipEd). Asst Mistress, Dartford County Sch. for Girls, 1937–39; WVS Headquarters staff, 1939–40; Junior Civil Asst, War Office, 1940–41; Personal Asst to Sir Ernest Gowers, Sen. Regional Comr for Civil Def., London, 1941–44. *Address:* Lashbrook House, Mill Road, Shiplake, Henley-on-Thames, Oxon RG9 3LP. *Died 19 Jan. 2012.*

FORTUNE, John; scriptwriter and actor; *b* 30 June 1939; *s* of Hubert William George Wood and Edna Maude Fortune; *m* 1st, 1962, Susannah Waldo (marr. diss. 1976); one *s* one *d*; 2nd, 1995, Emma Burge. *Educ:* Cathedral Sch., Bristol; King's Coll., Cambridge (MA). Work in theatre and television, 1961–; *television* includes: writer and performer: Not So Much a Programme, More a Way of Life; BBC3; The Late Show; Rory Bremner; Rory Bremner… Who Else?; Bremner, Bird and Fortune; writer: Roger Doesn't Live Here Anymore; Round and Round. *Publications:* (with John Wells) A Melon for Ecstasy, 1971; (with Eleanor Bron) Is Your Marriage Really Necessary?, 1972; (with John Bird) The Long Johns, 1996; (with John Bird and Rory Bremner) You Are Here, 2004. *Recreation:* lounging about. *Address:* c/o Richard Stone Partnership, Suite 3, De Walden Court, 85 New Cavendish Street, W1W 6XD. *T:* (020) 7497 0849. *Died 31 Dec. 2013.*

FOSTER, Samuel, CBE 2002; Member (UU) Fermanagh and South Tyrone, Northern Ireland Assembly, 1998–2003; *b* 7 Dec. 1931; *s* of late Samuel and Margaret Foster; *m* 1952, Dorothy Claire Brown; two *s* one *d*. *Educ:* Enniskillen Tech. Coll.; Ulster Poly., Belfast (CQSW). Compositor and proof reader, 1946–66; Sen. Educn Welfare Officer, Western Educn and Liby Bd, 1967–78; Social Worker: Wirral Social Services, 1979; Western Health and Social Services, 1980–96. Co. Comdr, UDR, 1970–78 (Major). Mem. (UU), Fermanagh DC, 1981–2001 (Chm., 1995–97). Mem. for Fermanagh and S Tyrone, NI Forum for Political Dialogue, 1996–98. Minister for the Envmt, NI Assembly, 1999–2002. Member: Police Authy for NI, 1982–85; NI Policing Bd, 2002–06. Hon. Fellow, Inst. of Road Safety Officers, 2002. Hon. Pres., Fermanagh and S Tyrone, UU Assoc. *Publications:* Recall: a little history of Orangeism and Protestantism in Fermanagh—King William Prince of Orange and all that … (booklet), 1990. *Recreations:* sport, especially soccer, table tennis, historical aspects, debate. *Address:* 35 Derrychara Road, Enniskillen, Co. Fermanagh BT74 6JF. *T:* (028) 6632 3594. *Club:* Fermanagh Unionist (Enniskillen). *Died 19 Aug. 2014.*

FOULKES, Sir Nigel (Gordon), Kt 1980; Chairman: ECI International Management Ltd, 1987–91; ECI Management (Jersey) Ltd, 1986–91; Equity Capital Trustee Ltd, 1983–90; *b* 29 Aug. 1919; *s* of Louis Augustine and Winifred Foulkes; *m* 1948, Elisabeth Walker (*d* 1995), *d* of Ewart B. Walker, Toronto; one *s* one *d* of former marr. *Educ:* Gresham's Sch., Holt; Balliol Coll., Oxford (Schol., MA). RAF, 1940–45. Subsequently executive, consulting and boardroom posts with: H. P. Bulmer; P. E. Consulting Gp; Birfield; Greaves & Thomas; International Nickel; Rank Xerox (Asst Man. Dir 1964–67, Man. Dir 1967–70); Charterhouse Group Ltd (Dir, 1972–83); Dir, Charterhouse J. Rothschild plc, 1984–85; Chm., Equity Capital for Industry, 1983–86 (Vice-Chm., 1982); Dir, Bekaert Gp (Belgium), 1973–85. Chairman: British Airports Authority, 1972–77; Civil Aviation Authority, 1977–82. CCMI; FRSA. *Club:* Royal Air Force. *Died 16 Aug. 2013.*

FOWLER, Dennis Houston, OBE 1979 (MBE 1963); HM Diplomatic Service, retired; *b* 15 March 1924; *s* of Joseph Fowler and Daisy Lilian Wraith Fowler (*née* Houston); *m* 1944, Lilias Wright Nairn Burnett (*d* 2014); two *s* one *d*. *Educ:* Alleyn's Sch., Dulwich. Colonial Office, 1940; RAF, 1942–46; India Office (subseq. CRO), 1947; Colombo, 1951; Second Secretary, Karachi, 1955; CRO, 1959; First Secretary, Dar es Salaam, 1961; Diplomatic Service Administration (subseq. FCO), 1965; First Sec. and Head of Chancery, Reykjavik, 1969; FCO, 1973; First Sec., Head of Chancery and Consul, Kathmandu, 1977; Counsellor and Hd of Claims Dept, FCO, 1980–83. *Recreations:* music, do-it-yourself. *Address:* 25 Dartnell Park Road, West Byfleet, Surrey KT14 6PN. *T:* (01932) 341583. *Clubs:* West Byfleet Golf; Royal Nepal Golf (Kathmandu). *Died 20 April 2015.*

FOX, Roy, CMG 1980; OBE 1967; HM Diplomatic Service, retired; consultant with various companies; *b* 1 Sept. 1920; *s* of J. S. and A. Fox; *m* 1st, 1943, Sybil Verity; two *s* one *d*; 2nd, 1975, Susan Rogers Turner. *Educ:* Wheelwright Grammar Sch., Dewsbury; Bradford Technical Coll. Served in RNVR, 1940–46. Bd of Trade, 1947–58; British Trade Commissioner: Nairobi, 1958–60; Montreal, 1960–62; Winnipeg, 1962–64; Dep. Controller, Bd of Trade Office for Scotland, 1964–65. First Sec. Commercial, Karachi, 1965–68; Deputy High Comr, E Pakistan, 1968–70; Consul-Gen. and Commercial Counsellor, Helsinki, 1970–74; promoted to Minister, 1977; Consul-Gen., Houston, 1974–80. *Recreations:* reading, walking. *Address:* 18 Calgarth Park, Troutbeck Bridge, Windermere LA23 1LF. *Died 20 Dec. 2013.*

FOX, Winifred Marjorie, (Mrs E. Gray Debros); Under-Secretary, Department of the Environment, 1970–76; *d* of Frederick Charles Fox and Charlotte Marion Ogborn; *m* 1953, Eustachy Gray Debros (*d* 1954); one *d*. *Educ:* Streatham County Sch.; St Hugh's Coll., Oxford. Unemployment Assistance Board, 1937; Cabinet Office, 1942; Ministry of Town and Country Planning, 1944; Ministry of Housing and Local Govt, 1952 (Under-Sec., 1963); Dept of the Environment, 1970; seconded to CSD as Chm., CS Selection Bd, 1971–72. *Address:* West Dalling, Rock's Lane, High Hurstwood, Uckfield, E Sussex TN22 4BN. *Died 21 Feb. 2012.*

FRAGA-IRIBARNE, Manuel; President, Government of Galicia, 1989–2005; Member for Galicia, Senate of Spain, since 2006; *b* 23 Nov. 1922; *m* 1948, María del Carmen Estévez (*d* 1996); two *s* three *d*. *Educ:* Insts of Coruña, Villalba and Lugo; Univs of Santiago de Compostela and Madrid. Joined Legal Corps, Spanish Parlt, 1945, Diplomatic Sch., 1947; Prof. of Pol Law, Univ. of Valencia, 1948; Prof. of Pol Sci. and Constit. Law, Univ. of Madrid, 1953–87; Sec.-Gen., Instituto de Cultura Hispánica, 1951; Sec.-Gen. in Min. of Educn, 1953; Head, Inst. of Pol Studies, 1961; Minister of Information and Tourism, 1962–69; Ambassador to UK, 1973–75; Govt Vice-Pres. and Interior Minister, Spain, 1975–76; Mem., Cortés, 1977–87; Leader of the Opposition, 1982–86; MEP (EDG), 1987–89. Founder Mem., 1976, Pres., 1979–86 and 1989, Popular Alliance, subseq. Popular Party, Spain. Hon. Dr of 19 nat. and internat. univs. Numerous foreign orders. *Publications:* more than 90 books on law, pol sci., history and sociology, incl. one on British Parlt. *Recreations:* shooting, fishing. *Address:* Palacio del Senado, Plaza de la Marina Española No 8, 28013 Madrid, Spain. *Died 15 Jan. 2012.*

FRANCE, Sir Christopher (Walter), GCB 1994 (KCB 1989; CB 1984); Permanent Secretary, Ministry of Defence, 1992–95; *b* 2 April 1934; *s* of W. J. and E. M. France; *m* 1961, Valerie Edith Larman (Valerie Edith France, OBE); one *s* one *d*. *Educ:* East Ham Grammar Sch.; New College, Oxford (MA (PPE), DipEd). CDipAF. HM Treasury, 1959–84: Principal Private Secretary to the Chancellor of the Exchequer, 1973–76; Principal Establishment Officer, 1977–80; on secondment to Electricity Council, 1980–81; Dep. Sec., 1981; on secondment to MoD, 1981–84; Dep. Sec., 1984–86, Second Perm. Sec., 1986, Perm. Sec., 1987–92, DHSS, subseq. DoH. Staff Counsellor for Security and Intelligence Services, 1995–99. Bd Mem., Macmillan Cancer Relief, 1995–2004 (Vice-Pres., 2004–); Trustee, Nuffield (formerly Nuffield Provincial Hosps) Trust, 1998–2004. Chm. Council, QMW, 1995–2003. Founder FMedSci 1998. Liveryman, Drapers' Co., 2003–. Hon. Col, RMR (City of London), 1996–99. Hon. DMSc London, 2004. *Died 21 Oct. 2014.*

FRANCE, Rev. Richard Thomas; Rector, Wentnor with Ratlinghope, Myndtown, Norbury, More, Lydham and Snead, Diocese of Hereford, 1995–99; *b* 2 April 1938; *s* of Edgar and Doris Woosnam France; *m* 1965, Barbara Wilding; one *s* one *d*. *Educ:* Bradford Grammar School; Balliol Coll., Oxford (MA); BD London; PhD Bristol. Asst Curate, St Matthew's Church, Cambridge, 1966–69; Lectr in Biblical Studies, Univ. of Ife, Nigeria, 1969–73; Librarian, Tyndale House, Cambridge, 1973–76; Sen. Lectr in Religious Studies, Ahmadu Bello Univ., Nigeria, 1976–77; Warden, Tyndale House, Cambridge, 1978–81; London Bible College: Senior Lectr, 1981–88; Vice-Principal, 1983–88; Principal, Wycliffe Hall, Oxford, 1989–95. Hon. Canon Theologian, Ibadan Cathedral, 1994–. Hon. Res. Fellow, Dept of Theol. and Religious Studies, Bangor Univ. (formerly Univ. of Wales, Bangor), 2004–. *Publications:* Jesus and the Old Testament, 1971; (ed with D. Wenham) Gospel Perspectives, vols 1–3, 1980–83; The Gospel According to Matthew: an introduction and commentary, 1985; The Evidence for Jesus, 1986; Matthew: evangelist and teacher, 1989; Divine Government, 1990; (ed with A. E. McGrath) Evangelical Anglicans, 1993; Women in the Church's Ministry, 1995; The Gospel of Mark: a commentary on the Greek text, 2002; The Gospel of Matthew (New International Commentary on the New Testament), 2007. *Recreations:* mountains, wildlife, travel, music. *Address:* Ty'n-y-Twll, Llangelynin, Llwyngwril, Gwynedd LL37 2QL. *T:* (01341) 250596. *Died 10 Feb. 2012.*

FRANCIS, Prof. (Edward) Howel, DSc; FRSE; CGeol; FGS; Professor of Earth Sciences, University of Leeds, 1977–89; *b* 31 May 1924; *s* of Thomas Howel Francis and Gwendoline Amelia (*née* Richards); *m* 1952, Cynthia Mary (*née* Williams) (*d* 1997); one *d*. *Educ:* Port Talbot County Sch.; Univ. of Wales, Swansea (BSc, DSc; Hon. Fellow 1989). FGS 1948; FRSE 1962. Served Army, 1944–47. Geological Survey of Great Britain (later incorporated in British Geol Survey): Field Geologist, Scotland, 1949–62; Dist Geologist, NE England, 1962–67, N Wales, 1967–70; Asst Dir, Northern England and Wales, 1971–77. Geological Society of London: Murchison Fund, 1963; Mem. Council, 1972–74; Pres., 1980–82; Pres., Section C (Geol.), BAAS, 1976; Mem., Inst. of Geol., 1978. Clough Medal, Edinburgh Geol Soc., 1983; Sorby Medal, Yorks Geol Soc., 1983; Major John Sacheverell A'Deane Coke Medal, Geol Soc. of London, 1989. *Publications:* memoirs, book chapters and papers on coalfields, palaeovolcanic rocks and general stratigraphy, mainly of Britain. *Recreations:* opera, golf. *Address:* 3 Manor Farm Barn, Newton, Porthcawl, Bridgend, Glam CF36 5SP. *Died 22 May 2014.*

FRANCIS, Gwyn Jones, CB 1990; Director-General and Deputy Chairman, Forestry Commission, 1986–90, retired; *b* 17 Sept. 1930; *s* of Daniel Brynmor Francis and Margaret Jane Francis (*née* Jones); *m* 1st, 1954, Margaretta Meryl Jeremy (*d* 1985); one *s* one *d* (and one *s* decd); 2nd, 1986, Audrey Gertrude (*née* Gill). *Educ:* Llanelli Grammar Sch.; University Coll. of N Wales, Bangor (BSc Hons 1952); Univ. of Toronto (MSc 1965). Served RE, 1952–54. Forestry Commission: Dist Officer, 1954; Principal, Forester Training Sch., 1962; Asst Conservator, 1969; Dir, Harvesting and Marketing Div., 1976; Comr, 1983–86. Mem. Council, 1992–98, and Chm., Scottish Cttee, 1992–98, RSPB. FICFor 1982; FIWSc 1984. Hon. Fellow, Univ. of Wales, 1991. *Recreations:* bird-watching, painting. *Address:* 2/16 Succoth Court, Succoth Park, Edinburgh EH12 6BZ. *T:* (0131) 337 5037. *Club:* New (Edinburgh). *Died 27 Nov. 2015.*

FRANÇOIS-PONCET, Jean André; Member of the French Senate (Lot-et-Garonne), 1983–2011 (Chairman of the Economic Committee, 1986–2001); *b* 8 Dec. 1928; *s* of André François-Poncet, Grand'Croix de la Légion d'Honneur, and Jacqueline (*née* Dillais); *m* 1959, Marie-Thérèse de Mitry; two *s* one *d*. *Educ:* Paris Law Sch.; Ecole Nationale d'Administration; Wesleyan Univ.; Fletcher Sch.

of Law and Diplomacy. Joined Ministry of Foreign Affairs, 1955; Office of Sec. of State, 1956–58; Sec. Gen. of French delegn to Treaty negotiations for EEC and Euratom, 1956–58; Dep. Head, European Orgns, Ministry of Foreign Affairs, 1958–60; Head of Assistance Mission, Morocco, 1961–63; Dep. Head, African Affairs, 1963–65; Counsellor, Tehran, 1969–71. Professor, Institut d'Etudes Politiques, Paris, 1960–. Chm. 1971, Vice-Pres. 1972, Pres. and Chief Exec. 1973–75, Carnaud SA. Sec. of State for Foreign Affairs, Jan.–July 1976; Sec.-Gen. to Presidency of France, 1976–78; Minister for Foreign Affairs, 1978–81. Vice-Chm., Foreign Relns Cttee, French Senate, 2004–11. *Publications:* The Economic Policy of Western Germany, 1970; 37 Quai d'Orsay: mémoires pour aujourd'hui et pour demain, 2008. *Address:* 53 rue de Varenne, 75007 Paris, France; (office) Palais du Luxembourg, 15 rue de Vaugirard, 75291 Paris cedex 06, France; (office) Préfecture de Lot-et-Garonne, Place de Verdun, 47920 Agen cedex 9, France. *Died 18 July 2012.*

FRANKLIN, George Henry; Consultant, Third World planning and development; *b* 15 June 1923; *s* of late George Edward Franklin, RN, and Annie Franklin; *m* 1950, Sylvia D. Franklin (*née* Allen); three *s* one *d.* *Educ:* Hastings Grammar Sch.; Hastings Sch. of Art; Architectural Assoc. Sch. of Arch. (AADipl); Sch. of Planning and Research for Regional Develt, London (SPDip); RIBA, FRTPI. Served War of 1939–45: Parachute Sqdn; RE, Europe; Bengal Sappers and Miners, RIE, SE Asia. Finchley Bor. Council, 1952–54; Architect, Christian Med. Coll., Ludhiana, Punjab, India, 1954–57; Physical Planning Adviser (Colombo Plan) to Republic of Indonesia, 1958–62, and Govt of Malaysia, 1963–64; Physical Planning Adviser, Min. of Overseas Develt, later Overseas Develt Admin, FCO, 1966–83 (Overseas Div., Building Research Station, 1966–73, ODM, later ODA, 1973–83). Hon. Prof., Dept of Town Planning, UWIST, 1982–88; Sen. Advr, Develt Planning Unit, UCL, 1983–. Chm., Overseas Sch., Town and Country Planning Summer Sch., 1970–75. Commonwealth Assoc. of Planners: Mem. Exec. Cttee, 1970–80; Pres., 1980–84; Hon. Sec., 1984–88; Member: Exec. Cttee, Commonwealth Human Ecology Council, 1970–90; Internat. Adv. Bd, Centre for Develt and Environmental Planning, Oxford Polytechnic, 1985–92; World Service Cttee, United Bible Socs, 1968–77. Chm., Warminster Bible Soc. Action Gp, 1991–; Vice Chm., W Wilts, Leonard Cheshire Care-at-Home (formerly Family Support) Service, 1994–96 (Chm., Warminster and Westbury Dist, 1990–94). Co-ordinator, Christian Aid, Warminster Dist, 1991–2006. Member Editorial Board: Third World Planning Review, 1979–91; Cities, 1983–91. FRSA; AIIA, 1955; AITP India, 1956. *Publications:* papers to internat. confs and professional jls concerning planning, building and housing in the Third World. *Recreations:* family, Christian, Third World, human rights and environmental issues and interests, fly-fishing. *Address:* The Manse, Sutton Veny, Warminster, Wilts BA12 7AW. *T:* (01985) 840072. *Club:* Victory Services. *Died 7 Dec. 2012.*

FRANKLIN, Gordon Herbert, CVO 1989 (LVO 1976; MVO 1965); a Serjeant-at-Arms to HM the Queen, 1990–93; Personnel Officer, Royal Household, 1988–93; *b* 1 Sept. 1933; *s* of late Herbert and Elsie Franklin; *m* 1959, Gillian Moffett; three *d.* *Educ:* Windsor County Boys' Sch. Barclays Bank, 1950. 2nd ATAF, Germany, 1952–54. Royal Household, 1956–93: Chief Clerk, Master of the Household's Dept, 1975; Chief Accountant of Privy Purse, 1982. Member: Central Finance Board and Council of Methodist Church, 1984–96; Methodist Council Exec., 1993–97. Vice-Pres., Friends of Wesley's Chapel, 1989–. Foundn Gov., Royal Sch., Great Park, Windsor, 1997–2007; Gov., Brigidine Sch., Windsor, 1999–2003. Chm., Windsor and Eton Soc., 1998–2004. Methodist local preacher, 1955–. Freeman, City of London, 1982; Liveryman, Painter Stainers' Co., 1983–. *Recreations:* theatre, walking, travel. *Address:* 10 Cumberland Lodge Mews, The Great Park, Windsor, Berks SL4 2JD. *Died 17 July 2014.*

FRANKS, Cecil Simon; solicitor; company director; Chairman, Pryde Investments Ltd, residential property, since 1960; *b* 1 July 1935; *m* (marr. diss. 1978); (one adopted *s* decd); partner, 1990, Anne. *Educ:* Manchester Grammar Sch.; Manchester Univ. (LLB). Admitted solicitor, 1958. Member: Salford City Council, 1960–74 (Leader, Cons. Gp); Manchester City Council, 1975–84 (Leader, Cons. Gp). Mem., North West RHA, 1973–75. MP (C) Barrow and Furness, 1983–92; contested (C) Barrow and Furness, 1992. Ind. Mem., Parole Bd, 1994–96. *Recreations:* theatre, literature. *Address:* Oak Cottage, 3 Church Brow, Bowdon, Cheshire WA14 2SF. *T:* (0161) 928 7561. *Died 2 Feb. 2014.*

FRASER OF CARMYLLIE, Baron *cr* 1989 (Life Peer), of Carmyllie in the District of Angus; **Peter Lovat Fraser;** PC 1989; *b* 29 May 1945; *s* of Rev. George Robson Fraser and Helen Jean Meiklejohn or Fraser; *m* 1969, Fiona Macdonald Mair; one *s* two *d.* *Educ:* St Andrews Prep. Sch., Grahamstown, S Africa; Loretto Sch., Musselburgh; Gonville and Caius Coll., Cambridge (BA Hons; LLM Hons); Edinburgh Univ. Called to Scottish Bar, 1969; QC (Scot.) 1982. Lectr in Constitutional Law, Heriot-Watt Univ., 1972–74; Standing Jun. Counsel in Scotland to FCO, 1979. Director: Total Exploration and Production (UK), 1997–; Carnoustie Golf Course Hotel, 1998–2006; Alkane Energy, 2001–09; Chairman: JKX Oil and Gas plc, 1997–2011; Ram Energy, 2002–. Director: ICE Futures Europe (formerly Internat. Petroleum Exchange), 1997– (Chm., 1999); London Metal Exchange, 1997–2009; ICE Clear, 2007–. Contested (C): N Aberdeen, Oct. 1974; Angus E, 1987; MP (C): S Angus, 1979–83; Angus E, 1983–87. PPS to Sec. of State for Scotland, 1981–82; Solicitor Gen. for Scotland, 1982–89; Lord Advocate, 1989–92; Minister of State: Scottish Office, 1992–95; DTI, 1995–97 (Minister for Energy, 1996–97); Dep. Leader of the Opposition, H of L, 1997–98. Chm., Scottish Conservative Lawyers Law Reform Group, 1976. Chm., Statutory Cttee, RPSGB, 2000–07. Hon. Vis. Prof. of Law, Dundee Univ., 1986. Hon. Bencher, Lincoln's Inn, 1989. Hon. President: Attend (formerly Nat. Assoc. of Leagues of Hosp. Friends, then Nat. Assoc. of Hosp. and Community Friends), 1983–; CIArb, 2003–06. Patron, Queen Margaret Univ. (formerly Queen Margaret UC), 1999–. *Recreations:* ski-ing, golf. *Address:* Slade House, Carmyllie, by Arbroath, Angus DD11 2RE. *T:* (01241) 860215. *Clubs:* Pratt's; New (Edinburgh); Hon. Co. of Edinburgh Golfers (Muirfield). *Died 22 June 2013.*

FRASER, Sir Alasdair (MacLeod), Kt 2001; CB 1992; QC 1989; Director of Public Prosecutions for Northern Ireland, 1989–2010; *b* 29 Sept. 1946; *s* of late Rev. Dr Donald Fraser and Ellen Hart McAllister; *m* 1975, Margaret Mary Glancy; two *s* one *d.* *Educ:* Sullivan Upper School, Holywood; Trinity College Dublin (BA (Mod.); LLB); Queen's Univ., Belfast (Dip. Laws). Called to the Bar of Northern Ireland, 1970, Bencher, 1999. Director of Public Prosecutions for Northern Ireland: Court Prosecutor, 1973; Asst Dir, 1974; Senior Asst Dir, 1982; Dep. Dir, 1988. *Address:* c/o Belfast Chambers, 93 Chichester Street, Belfast BT1 3JR. *Died 16 June 2012.*

FRASER, Gen. Sir David (William), GCB 1980 (KCB 1973); OBE 1962; Vice Lord-Lieutenant of Hampshire, 1988–96; *b* 30 Dec. 1920; *s* of Brig. Hon. William Fraser, DSO, MC, *y s* of 18th Lord Saltoun and Pamela, *d* of Cyril Maude and *widow* of Major W. La T. Congreve, VC, DSO, MC; *m* 1st, 1947, Anne Balfour (marr. diss. 1952); one *d*; 2nd, 1957, Julia de la Hey; two *s* two *d.* *Educ:* Eton; Christ Church, Oxford. Commnd into Grenadier Guards, 1941; served NW Europe; comd 1st Bn Grenadier Guards, 1960–62; comd 19th Inf. Bde, 1963–65; Dir, Defence Policy, MoD, 1966–69; GOC 4 Div., 1969–71; Asst Chief of Defence Staff (Policy), MoD, 1971–73; Vice-Chief of the General Staff, 1973–75; UK Mil. Rep. to NATO, 1975–77; Commandant, RCDS, 1978–80; ADC General to the Queen, 1977–80. Col, The Royal Hampshire Regt, 1981–87. DL Hants, 1982. Hon. DLitt Reading, 1992. *Publications:* Alanbrooke, 1982; And We Shall Shock Them, 1983; The Christian Watt Papers, 1983; August 1988, 1983; A Kiss for the Enemy, 1985; The Killing Times, 1986; The Dragon's Teeth, 1987; The Seizure, 1988; A Candle for Judas, 1989; In Good Company, 1990; Adam Hardrow, 1990; Codename Mercury, 1991; Adam in the Breach, 1993; The Pain of Winning, 1993; Knight's Cross: a life of Field Marshal Erwin Rommel, 1993; Will: a portrait of William Douglas Home, 1995; Frederick the Great, 2000;

Wars and Shadows, 2002. *Address:* Vallenders, Isington, Alton, Hants GU34 4PP. *T:* (01420) 23166. *Clubs:* Turf, Pratt's. *Died 15 July 2012.*

FRASER, Dame Dorothy (Rita), DBE 1987; QSO 1978; JP; Australasian Chairman, Community Systems Foundation Australasia, 1991–94 (New Zealand Director, 1975–91); *b* 3 May 1926; *d* of Ernest and Kate Tucker; *m* 1947, Hon. William Alex Fraser; one *s* one *d*. *Educ:* Gisborne High Sch. Chm., Otago Hosp. Bd, 1974–86 (Mem., 1953–56, 1962–86); Member: Nursing Council of NZ, 1981–87; Grading Review Cttee (Health Service Personnel Commn), 1984–87; Hosps Adv. Council, 1984–86; NZ Health Service Personnel Commn, 1987–88; Otago Plunket-Karitane Hosp. Bd, 1979–87; NZ Lottery Bd, 1985–90; Vice-Pres., NZ Hosp. Bds Assoc., 1981–86; Chairman: Southern Region Health Services Assoc., 1984–86; Hosp. and Specialist Services Cttee, NZ Bd of Health, 1985–88. Consultant, ADT Ltd Australasia, later Command Pacific Group, 1988–91. Chm., Otago Jt Tertiary Educn Liaison Cttee, 1988–99; Panel Chm., NZ Colls of Educn Accreditation Cttee, 1996–2004; Member: Council, Univ. of Otago, 1974–86; Otago High Schs Bd of Governors, 1964–85. Chm., Dunedin Airport Cttee, 1971–74; Member: Dunedin CC, 1970–74; NZ Exec. Marr. Guidance, 1969–75. Chairman: Montecillo Trust, 2001–08; Montecillo Veterans' Home and Hospital Ltd, 2001–08. Life Mem., NZ Labour Party; Gold Badge for Service to Labour Party. JP 1959. Hon. LLD Otago, 1994. Silver Jubilee Medal, 1977. *Recreations:* gardening, golf, reading. *Address:* 21 Ings Avenue, St Clair, Dunedin, New Zealand. *T:* (3) 4558663. *Died 24 May 2015.*

FRASER, Rt Hon. (John) Malcolm, AC 1988; CH 1977; PC 1976; MA Oxon; Prime Minister of Australia, 1975–83; *b* 21 May 1930; *s* of late J. Neville Fraser; *m* 1956, Tamara, *d* of S. R. Beggs; two *s* two *d*. *Educ:* Melbourne C of E Grammar Sch.; Magdalen Coll., Oxford (MA 1952; Hon. Fellow, 1982). MHR (L) for Wannon, Vic, 1955–83; Mem. Jt Party Cttee on Foreign Affairs, 1962–66; Minister: for the Army, 1966–68; for Educn and Science, 1968–69, 1971–72; for Defence, 1969–71; Leader of Parly Liberal Party, 1975–83; Leader of the Opposition, 1975. Sen. Adjunct Fellow, Center for Strategic and Internat. Studies, Georgetown Univ., Washington, 1983–86. Chairman: UN Sec. Gen's Expert Gp on African Commodity Problems, 1989–90; CARE Australia, 1987–2001; Vice-Pres., CARE Internat., 1995–99 (Pres., 1990–95). Co-Chm., Commonwealth Eminent Persons Gp on S Africa, 1986. Member: InterAction Council for Former Heads of Govt (Chm., 1996–); ANZ Internat. Bd of Advice, 1987–93. Distinguished Internat. Fellow, Amer. Enterprise Inst. for Public Policy Res., 1984–86; Fellow, Center for Internat. Affairs, Harvard Univ., 1985. Mem. Council, Aust. Nat. Univ., 1964–66. Hon. Vice President: Oxford Soc., 1983; Royal Commonwealth Soc., 1983. Hon. LLD: Univ. of SC, 1981; UTS, 2002; Murdoch Univ., 2002; Univ. of NSW, 2003; Hon. DLitt: Deakin Univ., 1989; Macquarie Univ., 2014. Grand Cordon, Order of the Rising Sun (Japan), 2006; Grand Companion, Order of Logohu (Papua New Guinea), 2011; Medal of Gratitude (Poland), 2011. *Publications:* Common Ground: issues that bind and divide us, 2002; (with M. Simons) Malcolm Fraser – The Political Memoirs, 2010; (with C. Roberts) Dangerous Allies, 2014. *Recreations:* fishing, photography, vintage cars, golf. *Address:* Level 32, 101 Collins Street, Melbourne, Vic 3000, Australia. *Club:* Melbourne. *Died 20 March 2015.*

FRASER, William James; JP; Lord Provost of Aberdeen, 1977–80; Member, City of Aberdeen District Council, 1974–96; *b* 31 Dec. 1921; *s* of late William and Jessie Fraser; *m* 1961, Mary Ann; three *s* one *d*. *Educ:* York Street Sch., Aberdeen; Frederick Street Sch., Aberdeen. Joined Aberdeen Post Office, 1936. War service with RAF air traffic control. Mem., Scottish Exec., Labour Party, 1949–74 (Chm., 1962–63). Pres., Aberdeen Trades Council, 1952. JP Aberdeen, 1950. Hon. LLD Aberdeen, 1995. *Address:* Thorngrove House, 500 Great Western Road, Aberdeen AB10 6PF. *Died 1 Oct. 2013.*

FRAZER, Prof. Malcolm John, CBE 1992; PhD, FRSC; education consultant; *b* 7 Feb. 1931; *m* 1st, 1957, Gwenyth Ida Biggs (marr. diss. 1990), JP, MA; three *s*; 2nd, 1991, Aleksandra Kornhauser. *Educ:* Univ. of London (BSc 1952, PhD 1955). Royal Military Coll. of Science, 1956–57; Lecturer and Head of Dept of Chemistry, Northern Polytechnic, London, 1965–72; Prof. of Chemical Educn, 1972–86, and Pro-Vice Chancellor, 1976–81, Univ. of East Anglia, Norwich; Chief Executive: CNAA, 1986–93; HEQC, 1992–93; Chm., CATE, 1993–94. Vis. Prof., Open Univ., 1993–. Vice-President: RSC, 1973–74; Royal Instn, 1988–91; SHRE, 1993–; Gen. Sec./Vice-Pres., Chm. Council, BAAS, 1978–91. Hon. Fellow: N London Poly., 1988; SCOTVEC, 1990; Poly. South West, 1991; Brighton Poly., 1992; Manchester Metropolitan Univ., 1993; Bolton Inst., 1994; Cardiff Inst. of Higher Educn, 1994. Hon. FCollP, 1988. Hon. Dr Leuven, 1985; Hon. DSc: Leicester, 1993; Luton, 1993; Hon. DEd: CNAA, 1992; Heriot-Watt, 1993; Bath, 2002; Hon. DLitt Glasgow Caledonian, 1993; DUniv Open, 1994. Nyholm Medal, RSC, 1982. *Publications:* textbooks on chemistry, chemical educn, and problem solving; contribs to Jl Chem. Soc., etc. *Address:* Sora, Abingdon Road, Tubney, Oxon OX13 5QQ. *Died 20 April 2014.*

FREELAND, Sir John Redvers, KCMG 1984 (CMG 1973); QC 1987; HM Diplomatic Service, retired; Judge, Arbitral Tribunal and Mixed Commission for Agreement on German External Debts, since 1988; Judge, European Court of Human Rights, 1991–98; *b* 16 July 1927; *o s* of C. Redvers Freeland and Freda Freeland (*née* Walker); *m* 1952, Sarah Mary, *er d* of late S. Pascoe Hayward, QC; one *s* one *d*. *Educ:* Stowe; Corpus Christi Coll., Cambridge. Royal Navy, 1945 and 1948–51. Called to Bar, Lincoln's Inn, 1952, Bencher, 1985; Mem. *ad eundem*, Middle Temple. Asst Legal Adviser, FO, 1954–63, and 1965–67; Legal Adviser, HM Embassy, Bonn, 1963–65; Legal Counsellor, FCO (formerly FO), 1967–70; Counsellor (Legal Advr), UK Mission to UN, NY, 1970–73; Legal Counsellor, FCO, 1973–76; Second Legal Advr, 1976–84, Legal Advr, 1984–87, FCO. Agent of UK govt, cases before European Commn of Human Rights, 1966–70. Mem., US-Chile Internat. Commn of Investigation, 1989–. Member: Exec. Cttee, David Davies Meml Inst. of Internat. Studies, 1974–2001; Council of Management, British Inst. of Internat. and Comparative Law, 1984–87; Cttee of Management, Inst. of Advanced Legal Studies, 1984–87; Bd of Govs, British Inst. of Human Rights, 1992–2004. *Died 29 June 2014.*

FREEMAN, David John; Founder, 1952, Senior Partner, 1952–92, Consultant, 1992–2003, D. J. Freeman, Solicitors (name changed to Kendall Freeman, 2003, then Edwards Angell Palmer and Dodge UK LLP, 2008, later Edwards Wildman Palmer UK LLP 2011); *b* Cardiff, 25 Feb. 1928; *s* of late Meyer Henry and Rebecca Freeman; *m* 1st, 1950, Iris Margaret Alberge (*d* 1997); two *s* one *d*; 2nd, 2001, Connie Levy. *Educ:* Christ's Coll., Finchley. Lieut, Army, 1946–48. Admitted Solicitor, 1952. Dept of Trade Inspector into the affairs of AEG Telefunken (UK) Ltd, and Credit Collections Ltd, 1977. Chairman: Trustees and Exec. Cttee, Holocaust Conference, Remembering for the Future, Oxford, 2000; UCL Inquiry into the provenance of 654 Aramaic incantation bowls, 2005–06; UCL Inquiry to recommend sound principles for the future treatment of cultural objects, 2005–08. Governor, Royal Shakespeare Theatre, 1979–96. *Recreations:* reading, theatre, gardening, golf. *Address:* 6 Hyde Park Gardens, W2 2LT. *Clubs:* Athenæum; Huntercombe Golf. *Died 23 Feb. 2015.*

FREEMAN, Dr Ernest Allan, CEng, FIET; CMath, FIMA; Director, Trent Polytechnic, 1981–83; *b* 16 Jan. 1932; *s* of William Freeman and Margaret Sinclair; *m* 1954, Mary Jane Peterson; two *d*. *Educ:* Sunderland Technical Coll.; King's Coll., Univ. of Durham (Mather Scholarship, 1955–57). BSc, PhD, Durham; DSc Newcastle upon Tyne; MA (Oxon) 1972. Sunderland Forge & Engineering Co. Ltd, 1949–55; English Electric Co., 1957–58; Ferranti Ltd (Edinburgh), 1958–59; Sunderland Polytechnic: Dir of Research, 1959–65; Head of Control Engrg Dept, 1965–72; Rector, 1976–80; Tutor and Fellow in Engrg, St Edmund Hall, Oxford Univ., 1972–76. FRSA. *Publications:* contribs mainly in the fields of control engrg, systems theory and computing, to Wireless Engr, Proc. IEE (Heaviside Prize, 1974), Jl of Electronics and Control, Trans AIEE, Electronic Technol., Control, Jl of

Optimisation Theory and Application, Trans Soc. of Instrument Technol., Proc. Internat. Fedn for Analogue Computation, Internat. Jl of Control. *Recreations:* swimming, browsing around antique shops, playing bridge. *Address:* 12 Rolfe Place, Headington, Oxford OX3 0DS. *Died 10 Jan. 2015.*

FREEMAN, Frank Gerard, FRAD; international freelance classical ballet teacher, lecturer, examiner, adjudicator, writer and choreographer; *b* Bangalore, India, 16 July 1945; *s* of Frank James and Amber Theresa Freeman. *Educ:* Royal Ballet Sch., White Lodge; Royal Ballet Upper Sch.; Royal Acad. of Dance (Professional Dancers' Teaching Dip. (Dist.) 1976). FRAD 2000. With Royal Ballet, 1963–71; Royal Ballet Educnl Unit, Ballet for All, 1971; soloist, Festival Ballet, 1971–72; teacher: Hirofumi Inoue Ballet Co., 1977, Bangkok, 1978 (under auspices of British Council); Kobayashi Ballet Theatre and Sch., Tokyo, 1978–80; at major British vocational schs, 1976–, incl. Royal Ballet Schs, English Nat. Ballet Sch., Arts Educnl Schs, Rambert Sch. of Ballet and Contemp. Dance, Central Sch. of Ballet, Elmhurst Sch. for Dance, Northern Ballet Sch., Ballet West, Doreen Bird Coll., Bush Davies Sch., Performers Coll., Laine Th. Arts and Guildford Sch. of Acting Conservatoire; Lectr on Professional Dancers' Teaching Dip. for RAD, 1977–2007; introduced RAD syllabus in Japan, 1978. Vocational Grades Examr, RAD, 1976–; trained Vocational Grades Examrs for RAD, 2001–05; interviewer for Voices of British Ballet Sound Archive, 2006–. Member: Artistic Cttee, RAD, 2001– (Trustee, 2008–); Dance Panel, Laurence Olivier Awards, 2001 and 2002; Judging Panel, Young British Dancer of Year, 2007 and 2008. Founder Patron, Nat. Youth Ballet of GB, 1988–. Gov., Royal Ballet Cos, 2007–. Choreographer: Puccini's opera, Le Villi for London Univ. Opera, 1982; Massenet's opera, Cendrillon for RNCM, 1984; Set Dances for GCSE O Level dance syllabus, 1984. *Publications:* (jtly) The Foundations of Classical Ballet Technique, 1997; (jtly) The Progressions of Classical Ballet Technique, 2002; contrib. articles on ballet to Dancing Times, Dance Now, Dance Expression and Dance Gazette. *Recreations:* music, opera, ballet, reading, collecting antique glass and 19th century watercolours. *Address:* c/o Royal Academy of Dance, 36 Battersea Square, SW11 3RA. *Died 24 Feb. 2011.*

FREEMAN, Hugh Lionel, FRCPsych; FFPH; Hon. Consultant Psychiatrist, Salford Mental Health Trust (formerly Health Authority), University of Manchester School of Medicine, since 1988 (Consultant Psychiatrist, 1961–88); *b* Salford, 4 Aug. 1929; *s* of late Bernard Freeman, FBOA and Dora Doris Freeman (*née* Kahn); *m* 1957, Sally Joan Casket (Dr S. J. Freeman); three *s* one *d.* *Educ:* Altrincham Grammar Sch.; St John's Coll., Oxford (open schol.; BM BCh 1954; MA; DM 1988); MSc Salford 1980. DPM 1958; FFPH (FFCM 1989). Captain, RAMC, 1956–58. House Surg., Manchester Royal Inf., 1955; Registrar, Bethlem Royal and Maudsley Hosps, 1958–60; Consultant Psychiatrist, Salford Royal Hosp., 1961–70; Hon. Consultant Psychiatrist: Salford Health Dept, 1961–74; Salford Social Services Dept, 1974–88. Hon. Med. Consultant, NAMH, 1963–74. Med. Advisor, NW Fellowship for Schizophrenia, 1980–88; Professional Advr, SANE, 1998–. Chairman: Psychiatric Sub-Cttee, NW Reg. Med. Adv. Cttee, 1978–83; Area Med. Cttee and Med. Exec. Cttee, Salford AHA, 1974–78. University of Manchester: Hon. Lectr, 1973–99; Mem., Univ. Court, 1989–94; Hon. Res. Fellow, UC and Middlesex Sch. of Medicine, 1989; Centre for Psychoanalytic Studies, Kent Univ., 1993. Visiting Professor: Univ. of WI, 1970; Univ. of WA, 1990; Univ. of Bern, 1995; Hungarian Medical Schools, 1996; Rockefeller Foundn Vis. Fellow, Italy, 1980; Vis. Fellow, 1986–97, Hon. Vis. Fellow, 1997, Green Coll., Oxford. Delta Omega Lectr, Tulane Univ., 1977; Linacre Lectr, Linacre Coll., Oxford, 1996. Examiner: Univ. of Manchester, United Examg Bd, 1993–2001; RCPsych. Med. Mem., Mental Health Rev. Tribunal, 1982–93. Member: Sex Educn Panel, Health Educn Council, 1968–72; Working Party on Behaviour Control, Council for Sci. and Society, 1973–76; Minister of State's Panel on Private Practice, DHSS, 1974–75; UK Delegn to EC Conf. on Mental Health in Cities, Milan, 1980; Mental Health Act Commn, 1983–84; Home Sec's Wking Party on Fear of Crime, 1989; Historic Building Panel, City of Manchester, 1981–89. WHO Consultant: Grenada, 1970; Chile, 1978; Philippines, 1979; Bangladesh, 1981; Greece, 1985; Rapporteur: WHO Conf. on Mental Health Services in Pilot Study Areas, Trieste, 1984; WHO Workshop on Nat. Mental Health Progs, Rwanda, 1985. Editor, British Jl of Clin. and Social Psych., 1982–84; Dep. Editor, Internat. Jl of Social Psych., 1980–83; Editor: British Jl of Psych., 1983–93 (Asst Editor, 1978–83); Current Opinion in Psychiatry, 1988–93; Co-Editor, Psychiatric Bulletin, 1983; Associate Editor, Internat. Jl of Mental Health, 1981–; Asst Editor, History of Psychiatry, 1993–. Mem. Internat. Res. Seminars, US National Inst. of Mental Health: Washington, 1966; Pisa, 1977; lectured to and addressed univs, confs and hosps worldwide; advr on and participant in radio and TV progs. Mem. Exec. Cttees, Royal Medico-Psychol Assoc., 1965–69. Royal College of Psychiatrists: Foundn Mem., 1971; Fellow 1971, Hon. Fellow 1998; Mem. Council, 1983–93; Chm., Journal Cttee; Vice-Chm., Social and Community Gp; Maudsley Lectr, 1993. FRSH (Hon. Sec., Mental Health Gp, 1973–76); Vice-Chm., 1983–87, Mem., Council, 1987–91, MIND. Corresp. Fellow, Amer. Psychiatric Assoc., 1993; Corresp. Member: US Assoc. for Clinical Psychosociol Res.; US Assoc. for Behavioral Therapies; Hon. Member: Chilean Soc. of Psych., Neurol. and Neurosurgery; Egyptian Psychiatric Assoc.; Polish Psychiatric Assoc., 1986; Hungarian Psychiatric Soc., 1991; Bulgarian Soc. for Neuroscis, 1991; Sen. Common Room, Pembroke Coll., Oxford, 1981. Mem., Hon. Cttee, European Assoc. for History of Psychiatry, 2003–. Vice-Chm., Manchester Heritage Trust, 1983–89; Mem., Mercian Regional Cttee, NT, 1986–92. Hon. Professorial Fellow, Salford Univ., 1986. Freeman, City of London; Liveryman, Soc. of Apothecaries, 1984 (Mem., Livery Cttee, 1987). Hon. Editor, The Apothecary, 2007. Distinguished Service Commendation, US Nat. Council of Community Mental Health Centers, 1982; 650 Anniversary Medal of Merit, Charles Univ., Prague, 1999. *Publications:* (ed jtly) Trends in the Mental Health Services, 1963; (ed) Psychiatric Hospital Care, 1965; (ed jtly) New Aspects of the Mental Health Service, 1968; (ed) Progress in Behaviour Therapy, 1969; (ed) Progress in Mental Health, 1970; (ed) Pavlovian Approach to Psychopathology, 1971; (ed jtly) Dangerousness, 1982; Mental Health and the Environment, 1985; (jtly) Mental Health Services in Europe, 1985; (ed jtly) Mental Health Services in Britain: the way ahead, 1985; (ed jtly) Interaction between Mental and Physical Illness, 1989; (ed jtly) Community Psychiatry, 1991; (ed jtly) 150 Years of British Psychiatry, 1991; La Malattie del Potere, 1994; (ed jtly) 150 Years of British Psychiatry: the aftermath, 1996; (ed jtly) Quality of Life in Mental Disorders, 1997, 2nd edn 2005; (ed) A Century of Psychiatry, 1999; (ed jtly) Psychiatric Cultures Compared, 2006; (ed jtly) Impact of the Environment on Psychiatric Disorders, 2008; contribs to national press and learned jls. *Recreations:* architecture, travel, music. *Address:* 21 Montagu Square, W1H 2LF. *Club:* Oxford and Cambridge. *Died 4 May 2011.*

FREEMAN, Rt Hon. John, MBE 1943; PC 1966; *b* 19 Feb. 1915; *m* 1st, 1938, Elizabeth Allen Johnston (marr. diss. 1948); 2nd, 1948, Margaret Ista Mabel Kerr (*d* 1957); one adopted *d*; 3rd, 1962, Catherine Wheeler (*née* Dove) (marr. diss. 1976); two *s* one *d*; 4th, 1976, Judith Mitchell; two *d.* *Educ:* Westminster Sch.; Brasenose College, Oxford (Hon. Fellow, 1968). Active service, 1940–45. MP (Lab) Watford Div. of Herts, 1945–50; Borough of Watford, 1950–55; PPS to Sec. of State for War, 1945–46; Financial Sec., War Office, 1946; Parly Under Sec. of State for War, April 1947; Leader, UK Defence Mission to Burma, 1947; Parly Sec., Min. of Supply, 1947–51, resigned. Asst Editor, New Statesman, 1951–58; Deputy Editor, 1958–60; Editor, 1961–65. British High Commissioner in India, 1965–68; British Ambassador in Washington, 1969–71. Chairman: London Weekend Television Ltd, 1971–84; LWT (Holdings) plc, 1976–84; Page & Moy (Holdings) Ltd, 1976–84; Hutchinson Ltd, 1978–82 (Director, until 1984); ITN, 1976–81. Vis. Prof. of Internat. Relns, Univ. of California, Davis, 1985–90. Governor, BFI, 1976–82. Vice-Pres., Royal Television Soc., 1975–85 (Gold Medal, 1981). *Died 20 Dec. 2014.*

FREER, Air Chief Marshal Sir Robert (William George), GBE 1981 (CBE 1966); KCB 1977; Commandant, Royal College of Defence Studies, 1980–82; *b* Darjeeling, 1 Sept. 1923; *s* of late William Freer, Stretton, Cirencester, Glos; *m* 1950, Margaret, 2nd *d* of late J. W. Elkington and Mrs M. Elkington, Ruskington Manor, near Sleaford, Lincs; one *s* one *d*. *Educ:* Gosport Grammar Sch. Flying Instructor, S Africa and UK, 1944–47; RAF Coll., Cranwell, 1947–50; served 54 and 614 Fighter Sqdns, 1950–52; Central Fighter Estabt, 1952–54; commanded 92 Fighter Sqdn, 1955–57 (Queen's Commendation, 1955); psa 1957; Directing Staff, USAF Acad., 1958–60; pfc 1960; Staff of Chief of Defence Staff, 1961–63; Station Comdr, RAF Seletar, 1963–66; DD Defence Plans (Air), MoD, 1966–67; IDC, 1968; Air ADC to the Queen, 1969–71; Dep. Comdt, RAF Staff Coll., 1969–71; SASO, HQ Near East Air Force, 1971–72; AOC 11 Group, 1972–75; Dir-Gen., Organisation (RAF), April–Sept. 1975; AOC No 18 Group, RAF, 1975–78; Dep. C-in-C, Strike Command, 1978–79. Director: Rediffusion, 1982–88; British Manufg & Res. Co., 1984–88; Rediffusion Simulation, 1985–88; Pilatus Britten-Norman Ltd, 1988–96. Mem. Council, RAF Benevolent Fund and Chm. Mgt Bd, Princess Marina House, Rustington, 1993–96. Pres., RAF LTA, 1975–81; Mem., Sports Council, 1980–82. CCMI (FBIM 1977); FRSA 1988–94; FRAeS 1995. *Recreations:* golf, tennis, hill-walking. *Address:* Cotterstock House, Clumps Road, Lower Bourne, Farnham, Surrey GU10 3HF. *Clubs:* Royal Air Force; All England Lawn Tennis and Croquet; Hankley Common Golf. *Died 15 Jan. 2012.*

FRENCH, Philip Neville, OBE 2013; writer and broadcaster; Film Critic, The Observer, 1978–2013; *b* Liverpool, 28 Aug. 1933; *s* of late John and Bessie French; *m* 1957, Kersti Elisabet Molin; three *s*. *Educ:* Bristol Grammar Sch.; Exeter Coll., Oxford (BA Law) (editor, The Isis, 1956); Indiana Univ. Nat. Service, 2nd Lieut Parachute Regt, 1952–54. Reporter, Bristol Evening Post, 1958–59; Producer, BBC N Amer. Service, 1959–61; Talks Producer, BBC Radio, 1961–67; New Statesman: Theatre Critic, 1967–68; Arts Columnist, 1967–72; Sen. Producer, BBC Radio, 1968–90: editor of The Arts This Week, Critics' Forum and other series, writer-presenter of arts documentaries, Radio 3. Vis. Prof., Univ. of Texas, 1972. Mem., BFI Prodn Bd, 1968–74; Jury Mem., Cannes Film Fest., 1986. Fellow, BFI, 2013. Hon. Life Mem., BAFTA, 2008; Hon. Associate, London Film Sch., 2011. Hon. DLitt Lancaster, 2006. Critic of the Year, Nat. Press Awards, 2009. *Publications:* Age of Austerity 1945–51 (ed with Michael Sissons), 1963; The Movie Moguls, 1969; Westerns: aspects of a movie genre, 1974, 3rd expanded edn as Westerns and Westerns Revisited, 2005; Three Honest Men: Edmund Wilson, F. R. Leavis, Lionel Trilling, 1980; (ed) The Third Dimension: voices from Radio Three, 1983; (ed with Deac Rossell) The Press: observed and projected, 1991; (ed) Malle on Malle, 1992; (ed with Ken Wlaschin) The Faber Book of Movie Verse, 1993; (with Kersti French) Wild Strawberries, 1995; (with Karl French) Cult Movies, 1999; (with Julian Petley) Censoring the Moving Image, 2007; I Found It At the Movies: reflections of a cinephile, 2011; numerous articles and essays in magazines, newspapers and anthologies. *Recreations:* woolgathering in England, picking wild strawberries in Sweden. *Address:* 62 Dartmouth Park Road, NW5 1SN. *T:* (020) 7485 1711. *Died 27 Oct. 2015.*

FRERE, Prof. Sheppard Sunderland, CBE 1976; FBA 1971; Professor of the Archæology of the Roman Empire, and Fellow of All Souls College, Oxford University, 1966–83, then Professor Emeritus and Emeritus Fellow; *b* Graffham, W Sussex, 23 Aug. 1916; *e s* of Noel Gray Frere, CMG; *m* 1961, Janet Cecily Hoare; one *s* one *d*. *Educ:* Lancing Coll.; Magdalene Coll., Cambridge. BA 1938, MA 1944, LittD 1976, DLitt 1977. FSA 1944. Master, Epsom Coll., 1938–40. National Fire Service, 1940–45. Master, Lancing Coll., 1945–54; Lecturer in Archæology, Manchester Univ., 1954–55; Reader in Archæology of the Roman Provinces, London Univ. Inst. of Archæology, 1955–62; Prof. of the Archæology of the Roman Provinces, London Univ., 1963–66. Dir, Canterbury Excavations, 1946–60; Dir, Verulamium Excavations, 1955–61. Vice-Pres., Soc. of Antiquaries, 1962–66; President: Oxford Architectural and Historical Soc., 1972–80; Royal Archæological Inst., 1978–81; Soc. for Promotion of Roman Studies, 1983–86. Hon. Corresp. Mem. German Archæological Inst., 1964, Fellow, 1967; Member: Royal Commn on Hist. Monuments (England), 1966–83; Ancient Monuments Board (England), 1966–82. Hon. LittD: Leeds, 1977; Leicester, 1983; Kent, 1985. Gold Medal, Soc. of Antiquaries, 1989. Editor, Britannia, 1969–79. *Publications:* (ed) Problems of the Iron Age in Southern Britain, 1961; Britannia, a history of Roman Britain, 1967, 4th edn 1999; Verulamium Excavations, vol. I, 1972, vol. II, 1983, vol. III, 1984; Excavations on the Roman and Medieval Defences of Canterbury, 1982; Excavations at Canterbury, vol. VII, 1983; (with J. K. St Joseph) Roman Britain from the Air, 1983; (with F. A. Lepper) Trajan's Column, 1988; (with J. J. Wilkes) Strageath: excavations within the Roman fort, 1989; (ed with R. Tomlin) The Roman Inscriptions of Britain, vol. II, fasc. 1, 1990, fascs 2–3, 1991, fasc. 4, 1992, fasc. 5, 1993, fasc. 6, 1994, fascs 7–8, and Epigraphic Indexes, 1995; Excavations at the Roman Fort at Bowes, 2009; papers in learned jls. *Recreation:* gardening. *Address:* Netherfield House, Marcham, Abingdon, Oxon OX13 6NP. *Died 26 Feb. 2015.*

FREUD, Lucian, OM 1993; CH 1983; painter; *b* 8 Dec. 1922; *s* of late Ernst and Lucie Freud; *m* 1st, 1948, Kathleen Garman (marr. diss. 1952; she *d* 2011), *d* of Jacob Epstein; two *d*; 2nd, 1953, Lady Caroline Maureen Blackwood (marr. diss. 1957; she *d* 1996), *d* of 4th Marquess of Dufferin and Ava. *Educ:* Central Sch. of Art; East Anglian Sch. of Painting and Drawing. Worked on merchant ship SS Baltrover as ordinary seaman, 1942. Teacher, Slade Sch. of Art, 1948–58; Vis. Asst, Norwich Sch. of Art, 1964–65. Painted mostly in France and Greece, 1946–48; Cyclamen bathroom, 1959, Thornhill bedroom, Chatsworth House, Derbyshire. Hon. Mem., Amer. Acad. and Inst. of Arts and Letters, 1988. Hon. DLitt Glasgow, 2003. Jerg-Ratgeb Prize, Reutlingen, 2002. *Exhibitions:* Lefevre Gall., 1944, 1946; London Gall., 1947, 1948; British Council and Galérie René Drouin, Paris, 1948; Hanover Gall., 1950, 1952; British Council and Vancouver Art Gall., 1951; British Council, Venice Biennale, 1954; Marlborough Fine Art, 1958, 1963, 1968, 2005; Anthony d'Offay, 1972, 1978 (subseq. Davis & Long, NY), 1982; Nishimura Gall., Tokyo, 1979, 1991; Thos Agnew & Sons, 1983; Scottish Nat. Gall. of Modern Art, 1988; Berggruen Gall., Paris, 1990; Saatchi Collection, 1990; Thomas Gibson Fine Art Ltd, 1991; Palazzo Ruspoli, Rome, 1991; Castello Sforzesca, Milan, 1991; Art Gall. of NSW, 1992; Tochigi Prefectural Mus. of Fine Arts, Otani Meml Art Mus., Nishinomiya, and Setagaya Art Museum, Tokyo, Japan, 1992; Whitechapel Art Gall., 1993; Metropolitan Mus. of Art, New York, 1993; Museo Nacional Centro de Arte Reina Sofia, Madrid, 1994; Astrup Fearnley Museet for Moderne Kunst, Oslo, 1994; Dulwich Picture Gall., 1994; Fondation Maeght, St Paul de Vence, 1995; Abbot Hall Art Gall., Kendal, 1996; Acquavella Contemp. Art, NY, 1996; Tel Aviv Mus. of Art, 1996; Nat. Gall. of Scotland, 1997; Tate Gall., 1998; Yale Center for British Art, 1999; Nat. Gall., 2000; Timothy Taylor Gall., 2003; Hunterian Gall., Glasgow, 2003; Wallace Collection, 2004; Aquavella Gall., NY, 2004, 2006; *retrospectives:* Hayward Gall., 1974 (subseq. Bristol, Birmingham and Leeds), 1988 (also Washington, Paris and Berlin, 1987–88); Works on Paper, Ashmolean Mus., Oxford, 1988 (subseq. other towns in provinces and in USA); Tate Gall., Liverpool, 1992; Tate Britain, 2002; Fundacion la Caixa, Barcelona, 2002; Mus. of Contemp. Art, LA, 2003; Scottish Nat. Gall. of Modern Art, 2004; Museo Correr, Venice, 2005; Irish Mus. of Modern Art, Dublin, 2007; Louisiana Mus., Copenhagen, 2007; Mus. of Modern Art, NY, 2007–08; Gemeente Mus., The Hague, 2008; Pompidou Centre, Paris, 2010. *Works included in public collections:* London: Tate Gall.; Nat. Portrait Gall.; V & A Museum; Arts Council of GB; British Council; British Mus.; DoE; provinces: Cecil Higgins Museum, Bedford; Fitzwilliam Mus., Cambridge; Nat. Mus. of Wales, Cardiff; Scottish Nat. Gall. of Mod. Art, Edinburgh; Hartlepool Art Gall.; Walker Art Gall., Liverpool; Liverpool Univ.; City Art Gall. and Whitworth Gall., Manchester; Ashmolean Mus. of Art, Oxford; Harris Mus. and Art Gall., Preston; Rochdale Art Gall.; Southampton Art Gall.; Australia: Queensland Art Gall., Brisbane; Art Gall. of S Australia, Adelaide; Art Gall. of WA, Perth; France: Musée National d'Art Moderne, Centre Georges Pompidou, Paris; Beaverbrook Foundn, Fredericton, New Brunswick; USA: Art Inst. of Chicago; Mus. of Mod. Art, NY; Cleveland Mus. of Art, Ohio; Mus. of Art, Carnegie Inst., Pittsburgh; Achenbach Foundn for Graphic Arts and Fine Arts Mus. of San Francisco; Art Mus., St Louis; Hirshhorn Mus. and Sculpture Garden, Smithsonian Instn, Washington. Rubenspreis, City of Siegen, 1997. *Relevant publications:* Lucian Freud, by Lawrence Gowing, 1982; Lucian Freud, Paintings, by Robert Hughes, 1987; Lucian Freud, works on paper, by Nicholas Penney and Robert Flynn Johnson, 1988; The Etchings of Lucian Freud: a catalogue raisonné, by Craig Hartley, 1995; Lucian Freud, introd. by Bruce Bernard, 1996; Lucian Freud 1996–2005, introd. by Sebastian Smee, 2005; Lucian Freud, by William Feaver, 2007; Lucian Freud on Paper, by Sebastian Smee and Richard Calvocoressi, 2008. *Address:* c/o Diana Rawstron, Goodman Derrick LLP, 90 Fetter Lane, EC4A 1PT. *E:* drawstron@gdlaw.co.uk. *Died 21 July 2011.*

FRIEL, Brian; writer; *b* 9 Jan. 1929; *s* of Patrick Friel and Christina Friel (*née* MacLoone); *m* 1954, Anne Morrison; one *s* three *d* (and one *d* decd). *Educ:* St Columb's Coll., Derry; St Patrick's Coll., Maynooth; St Joseph's Trng Coll., Belfast. Taught in various schools, 1950–60; writing full-time from 1960. Lived in Minnesota during first season of Tyrone Guthrie Theater, Minneapolis. Member: Irish Acad. of Letters, 1972; Aosdána, 1983–; Amer. Acad. of Arts and Letters. FRSL 1998. Hon. DLitt: Chicago, 1979; NUI, 1983; NUU, 1986. Hon. DLit: QUB, 2004; TCS, 2006; UCD, 2008. Ulysses Medal, UCD, 2010. *Publications: collected stories:* The Saucer of Larks, 1962; The Gold in the Sea, 1966; *plays:* Philadelphia, Here I Come!, 1965; The Loves of Cass McGuire, 1967; Lovers, 1968; The Mundy Scheme, 1969; Crystal and Fox, 1970; The Gentle Island, 1971; The Freedom of the City, 1973; Volunteers, 1975; Living Quarters, 1976; Aristocrats, 1979; Faith Healer, 1979; Translations, 1981 (Ewart-Biggs Meml Prize, British Theatre Assoc. Award); (trans.) Three Sisters, 1981; The Communication Cord, 1983; (trans.) Fathers and Sons, 1987; Making History, 1988; London Vertigo, 1989; Dancing at Lughnasa, 1990; A Month in the Country, 1990; Wonderful Tennessee, 1993; Molly Sweeney, 1995; Give Me Your Answer, Do!, 1997; (trans.) Uncle Vanya, 1998; (trans.) The Bear, 2002; The Yalta Game, 2002; Afterplay, 2002; Performances, 2003; The Home Place, 2005 (Best Play, Evening Standard Th. Awards, 2005); (trans.) Hedda Gabler, 2008. *Address:* Drumaweir House, Greencastle, Co. Donegal, Ireland. *Died 2 Oct. 2015.*

FRIEND, Rev. Frederick James; Hon. Director, Scholarly Communication, University College London, since 2002 (Librarian, 1982–97; Director, 1997–2002); *b* 7 April 1941; *s* of James Frederick Friend and Emily Mary Friend (*née* Giddens); *m* 1969, Margaret Rusholme; one *s* one *d*. *Educ:* Dover Grammar Sch. for Boys; King's Coll., London (BA 1963); University Coll. London (DipLib 1965); Oak Hill Coll. Asst Librarian, Manchester Univ. Library, 1965–71; Sub-Librarian, Leeds Univ., 1971–76; Dep. Librarian, Nottingham Univ., 1976–78; Librarian, Essex Univ., 1978–82. Mem. Council, 1985–88, Chm. Scholarly Communication Cttee, 1996–2000, Sec., 2000–04, SCONUL; Treas., Consortium of Univ. Res. Libraries, 1996–98. Scholarly Commn Consultant, JISC, 2003–11; Open Access Advocate, Open Soc. Inst., 2003–05; ind. expert EC, 2006–. Ordained deacon 1982, priest 1983. Permission to officiate, Hughenden, Dio. of Oxford, 2011– (NSM, 1982–2011). *Publications:* various articles in learned jls. *Recreations:* walking the dog, prayer. *Address:* The Chimes, Cryers Hill Road, High Wycombe, Bucks HP15 6JS. *Died 23 April 2014.*

FRIEND, Dame Phyllis (Muriel), DBE 1980 (CBE 1972); Chief Nursing Officer, Department of Health and Social Security, 1972–82; *b* 28 Sept. 1922; *d* of late Richard Edward Friend. *Educ:* Herts and Essex High Sch., Bishop's Stortford; The London Hospital (SRN); Royal College of Nursing (RNT). Dep. Matron, St George's Hospital, 1956–59; Dep. Matron, 1959–61, Matron, 1961–68, Chief Nursing Officer 1969–72, The London Hospital. *Address:* Barnmead, Start Hill, Bishop's Stortford, Herts CM22 7TA. *T:* (01279) 654873. *Died 24 June 2013.*

FRITH, Air Vice-Marshal Edward Leslie, CB 1973; *b* 18 March 1919; *s* of late Charles Edward Frith, ISO. *Educ:* Haberdashers' Aske's School. Gp Captain, 1961; Air Cdre, 1968; Dir of Personal Services (2) RAF, MoD, 1969–71; Air Vice-Marshal, 1971; Air Officer Administration, Maintenance Comd, later Support Comd, 1971–74, retd. *Recreations:* lawn tennis, bridge. *Clubs:* All England Lawn Tennis and Croquet, Veterans' Lawn Tennis of GB. *Died 30 Aug. 2012.*

FROSSARD, Sir Charles (Keith), KBE 1992; Kt 1983; Bailiff of Guernsey, 1982–92; Judge of the Court of Appeal, Jersey, 1983–92; a Judge of the Courts of Appeal of Jersey and Guernsey, 1992–95; *b* 18 Feb. 1922; *s* of late Edward Louis Frossard, CBE, MA, Hon. CF, Dean of Guernsey, 1947–67, and Margery Smith Latta; *m* 1950, Elizabeth Marguerite, *d* of late J. E. L. Martel, OBE; two *d*. *Educ:* Elizabeth Coll., Guernsey; Univ. de Caen (Bachelier en Droit; D*hc* 1990). Enlisted Gordon Highlanders, 1940; commnd 1941, 17 Dogra Regt, Indian Army; seconded to Tochi Scouts and Chitral Scouts; served India and NW Frontier, 1941–46. Called to Bar, Gray's Inn, 1949, Hon. Bencher, 2000; Advocate of Royal Court of Guernsey, 1949; People's Deputy, States of Guernsey, 1958–67; Conseiller, States of Guernsey, 1967–69; HM Solicitor General, Guernsey, 1969–73; HM Attorney General, Guernsey, 1973–76; Dep. Bailiff of Guernsey, 1977–82. Member, Church Assembly and General Synod, Church of England, 1960–82. Pres., Indian Army Assoc., 1993–; Member Council: British Assoc. of Cemeteries in SE Asia, 1998–; Royal (formerly British) Commonwealth Ex-Services League, 1999–. KStJ 1985. Médaille de Vermeil, Paris, 1984. *Recreations:* hill walking, fishing. *Address:* Les Lierres, Rohais, St Peter Port, Guernsey GY1 1YW. *T:* (01481) 722076. *Clubs:* Naval and Military; United (Guernsey). *Died 15 July 2012.*

FROST, Abraham Edward Hardy, CBE 1972; Counsellor, Foreign and Commonwealth Office, 1972–78; *b* 4 July 1918; *s* of Abraham William Frost and Margaret Anna Frost; *m* 1972, Gillian (*née* Crossley); two *d*. *Educ:* Royal Grammar Sch., Colchester King's Coll., Cambridge (MA); London Univ. (BScEcon). FCIS. RNVR, 1940–46 (Lieut). ILO, Geneva, 1947–48; HM Treasury, 1948–49; Manchester Guardian, City Staff, 1949–51; FO (later FCO), 1951–78. *Publications:* In Dorset Of Course (poems), 1976. *Died 4 Dec. 2012.*

FROST, Sir David (Paradine), Kt 1993; OBE 1970; interviewer, author, producer, columnist, and television presenter; Chairman and Chief Executive, David Paradine Ltd, since 1966; *b* 7 April 1939; *s* of late Rev. W. J. Paradine Frost, Tenterden, Kent; *m* 1st, 1981, Lynne Frederick (marr. diss. 1982; she *d* 1994), *widow* of Peter Richard Henry Sellers; 2nd, 1983, Lady Carina Fitzalan-Howard, 2nd *d* of 17th Duke of Norfolk, KG, GCVO, CB, CBE, MC; three *s*. *Educ:* Gillingham Grammar Sch.; Wellingborough Grammar Sch.; Gonville and Caius Coll., Cambridge (MA). Sec., The Footlights; Editor, Granta. Jt Founder, LWT, 1967–68; Jt Founder and Dir, TV-am, 1981–93. BBC Television series: That Was the Week That Was, 1962–63 (in USA, 1964–65); A Degree of Frost, 1963, 1973; Not So Much a Programme, More a Way of Life, 1964–65; The Frost Report, 1966–67; Frost Over England, 1967; Frost Over America, 1970; Frost's Weekly, 1973; The Frost Interview, 1974; We British, 1975–76; Forty Years of Television, 1976; The Frost Programme, 1977; The Guinness Book of Records Hall of Fame, 1986, 1987, 1988; Breakfast with Frost, 1993–2005; Through the Keyhole, 1997–; The Frost Interviews, 2005–06; single programmes: Margaret Thatcher: the path to power and beyond, 1995; Nick Leeson: the man who broke the bank, 1995; Norma Major Behind Closed Doors, 1996; Prince Charles, Why it Matters to Me, 1997; Forty Years with Frost, 2000; The Frost Report is Back!, 2007; Frost on Sketch Shows, 2013; BBC Radio: David Frost at the Phonograph, 1966, 1972; Frost on Thursday, 1974; The Frost Years, 2006; The Frost Collection, 2010; Frost on Satire, 2010; series, Pull the Other One, 1987, 1988, 1990; ITV series and programmes: The Frost Programme, 1966–67, 1967–68, 1972, 1973, 1993–95; Frost on Friday, 1968–69, 1969–70; The Sir Harold Wilson Interviews, 1976; A Prime Minister on Prime Ministers, 1977–78; Are

We Really Going to be Rich?, 1978; David Frost's Global Village, 1979, 1980, 1982; The 25th Anniversary of ITV, The Begin Interview, and Elvis—He Touched Their Lives, 1980; The BAFTA Awards, and Onward Christian Soldiers, 1981; A Night of Knights: a Royal Gala, 1982; The End of the Year Show, 1982, 1983; Frost on Sunday (TV-am), 1983–92; David Frost Presents Ultra Quiz, 1984; Twenty Years On, 1985, 1986; Through the Keyhole, 1987–96; Beyond Belief, 1995, 1996, 1997; Live for Peace, 1995; A Royal Gala, 1996; A Gala Comedy Hour, 1996; The Easter Enigma, 1996; Masters of Talk, 1996–97; Frost's Century, 1997–98; The Alpha Series, 2001; Hitler and Hess, 2001; Muhammad Ali—Then and Now, 2003; Inside Elton's World, 2005; Frost Tonight, 2006; series, The World's Greatest Sporting Legends (Sky One), 2005. Al Jazeera English TV series, Frost Over the World, 2006–. US programmes include: That Was The Week That Was, 1964–65; David Frost's Night Out in London, 1966–67; The Next President, 1968; Robert Kennedy the Man, 1968; The David Frost Show, 1969–70, 1970–71, 1971–72; The David Frost Revue, 1971–72, 1972–73; That Was the Year That Was, 1973, 1985; David Frost Presents the Guinness Book of Records, 1973–76; Frost over Australia, 1972, 1973, 1974, 1977; Frost over New Zealand, 1973, 1974; The Unspeakable Crime, 1975; Abortion—Merciful or Murder?, 1975; The Beatles—Once Upon a Time, 1975; David Frost Presents the Best, 1975; The Nixon Interviews with David Frost, 1976–77; The Crossroads of Civilization, 1977–78; Headliners with David Frost, 1978; A Gift of Song—MUSIC FOR UNICEF Concert, The Bee Gees Special, and The Kissinger Interview, 1979; The Shah Speaks, and The American Movie Awards, 1980; Show Business, This Is Your Life 30th Anniversary Special, The Royal Wedding (CBS), 1981; David Frost Presents The Internat. Guinness Book of World Records, annually 1981–86; The American Movie Awards, Rubinstein at 95, and Pierre Elliott Trudeau, 1982; Frost over Canada, 1982, 1983; David Frost Live by Satellite from London, 1983; The Search for Josef Mengele, 1985; Spitting Image: Down and Out in the White House, 1986; The Spitting Image Movie Awards, 1987; The Spectacular World of Guinness Records, 1987–88; Entertainment Tonight, 1987, 1988; The Next President with David Frost, 1987–88; ABC Presents a Royal Gala, 1988; The President and Mrs Bush Talking with David Frost, 1989; Talking with David Frost (USA), 1991–98; Interviews I'll Never Forget, 1998; David Frost, One-on-One, 1999–; The Complete Nixon, 2002; In Their Own Words, 2003; The Strategic Humor Initiative, 2003; President George W. Bush Talking with David Frost, 2003; Decisive Battles of the Ancient World, 2004–05; Frost/Nixon: the original Watergate interview, 2009. Stage: An Evening with David Frost (Edinburgh Fest.), 1966; An Audience with David Frost, 2004–. Produced films: The Rise and Rise of Michael Rimmer, 1970; Charley One-Eye, 1972; Leadbelly, 1974; The Slipper and the Rose, 1975; James A. Michener's Dynasty, 1975; The Ordeal of Patty Hearst, 1978; The Remarkable Mrs Sanger, 1979; Rogue Trader, 1999. Mem., British/USA Bicentennial Liaison Cttee, 1973–76; Pres., Lord's Taverners, 1985, 1986. Companion, TRIC, 1992. Hon. Prof., Thames Valley Univ., 1994. Golden Rose, Montreux, for Frost Over England, 1967; Royal Television Society's Silver Medal, 1967; Richard Dimbleby Award, 1967; Emmy Award (USA), 1970, 1971; Religious Heritage of America Award, 1970; Albert Einstein Award, Communication Arts, 1971; MOMI Award, NY, 1998; Mus. of TV and Radio Salute, 1999; Bernard Delfont Award, Variety Club, 2005; Man of the Year Award, Media Soc., 2005; BAFTA Fellowship, 2005; Internat. Emmy Founders Award, 2009. LLD Emerson Coll., USA; Hon. DLitt: Sussex, 1994; Kent, 2008; Winchester, 2009. *Publications:* That Was the Week That Was, 1963; How to Live under Labour, 1964; Talking with Frost, 1967; To England With Love, 1967; The Presidential Debate 1968, 1968; The Americans, 1970; Whitlam and Frost, 1974; I Gave Them a Sword, 1978; I Could Have Kicked Myself, (David Frost's Book of the World's Worst Decisions), 1982; Who Wants to be a Millionaire?, 1983; (jtly) The Mid-Atlantic Companion, 1986; (jtly) The Rich Tide, 1986; (jtly) If You'll Believe That; The World's Shortest Books, 1987; David Frost: an autobiography: part one: From Congregations to Audiences, 1993; Billy Graham: thirty years of conversations with David Frost, 1997; Frost/Nixon, 2007. *Address:* David Paradine Productions Ltd, The Penthouse, 346 Kensington High Street, W14 8NS. *T:* (020) 7371 3111, *Fax:* (020) 7602 0411. *Died 31 Aug. 2013.*

FROUDE, Andrew Christopher Haysom; Chairman, Jackson-Stops & Staff Consortium, 1992–2013; *b* 17 Oct. 1936; *s* of Robert and Dorothy Froude; *m* 1998, Patricia Elizabeth Roberts; two *s*. *Educ:* Leighton Park Sch., Reading; Coll. of Estate Management, London. FRICS 1969. Dir, Jackson-Stops & Staff Ltd, 1982–92; Chm., Jackson-Stops & Staff (North West) Ltd, 1992–2008. *Recreations:* golf, gardening, country pursuits. *Address:* The Riddings, Clotton Common, Tarporley, Cheshire CW6 0HQ. *Clubs:* Chester City; Chartered Surveyors Golfing Society (Capt., 1990). *Died 19 Dec. 2014.*

FRUTIGER, Adrian; typeface designer; *b* 24 May 1928; *m* 1956, Simone Bickel (*d* 2008); one *s*. *Educ:* compositor at Schlaefli Printer's, Interlaken; School of Applied Art, Zurich (Dip. in Type Design 1951). Typeface Designer and Artistic Manager, Deberny & Peignot, Paris, 1952–60; typeface designer and Studio Manager, Arcueil, Paris, 1960–92; Lecturer in type design, hist. of type and type drawing, Ecole Estienne, Paris, 1952–60; Ecole Nat. Supérieure des Arts Décoratifs, Paris, 1954–68; designed more than 40 alphabets, incl. Univers, Frutiger, Centennial, OCR-B, Meridien, and Indian alphabet, Devanagari. Gutenberg Preis, City of Mainz, 1986; Medal, Type Dirs Club, NY, 1987; Grand Prix Nat. des Arts Graphiques, France, 1993; Aficionados Award, Soc. of Typography, 2006; Prix Designer, Switzerland, 2007. Officier de l'Ordre des Arts et des Lettres (France), 1993. *Publications:* Der Mensch und seine Zeichen, 1978; Signs and Symbols, 1998; Forms and Counterforms, 1998; Life Cycle, 1999; Ein Leben für die Schrift, 2003; Typefaces: the complete work, 2009. *Recreations:* walking through forest, drawing, wood cutting. *Address:* Altersheim Chalchacker, 3047 Bremgarten, Switzerland. *T:* and *Fax:* (31) 3026666; c/o Erich Alb, Duggelistrasse 31, 6330 Cham, Switzerland. *E:* erich.alb@bluewin.ch. *Died 10 Sept. 2015.*

FRY, Sir Peter (Derek), Kt 1994; *b* 26 May 1931; *s* of Harry Walter Fry and late Edith Fry; *m* 1st, 1958, Edna Roberts (marr. diss. 1982); one *s* one *d*; 2nd, 1982, Helen Claire Mitchell. *Educ:* Royal Grammar School, High Wycombe; Worcester College, Oxford (MA). Tillotsons (Liverpool) Ltd, 1954–56; Northern Assurance Co., 1956–61; Political Education Officer, Conservative Central Office, 1961–63. Member, Bucks County Council, 1961–67. Consultant to Parly Monitoring Services Ltd, 1992–. Contested (C) North Nottingham, 1964, East Willesden, 1966. MP (C) Wellingborough, 1969–97; contested (C) same seat, 1997. Mem., Select Cttee on Transport, 1979–92; Joint Chairman: All-Party Roads Study Gp, 1974–97; Parly Road Passenger Gp, 1992–97; All-Party Aviation Gp, 1992–97; Parly Transport Forum, 1992–97; Vice. Chm., Cons. Aviation Cttee, 1994–97; Chairman: All-Party Footwear and Leather Gp, 1979–87; Anglo-Bahamas Parly Gp, 1980–97; British Slovenia Gp, 1993–97; British Macedonia Gp, 1993–97; formerly Chm., British Yugoslav Parly Gp; Vice-Chairman: British Bosnia Gp, 1993–95; British Croatia Gp, 1993–95; All-Party CSA Monitoring Gp, 1995–97; Jt Chm., All-Party Recreation and Leisure Gp, 1994–97. Formerly Mem., Delegn to Council of Europe/WEU. Vice Pres., British Southern Slav Soc.; Pres., Wellingborough Anglo-Polish Soc., 2009–. Non-exec. Chm., Bingo Assoc., 1999–2009; Pres., EUBingo, 2006–. Pres., Rushden and Higham Arthritis Care, 2000–. Chm., Cranford PC, 2007–11. Played Rugby for Bucks County, 1956–58, Hon. Secretary, 1958–61. *Recreations:* watching Rugby football, reading history and biographies. *Address:* Glebe Farm House, Church Lane, Cranford, Kettering, Northants NN14 4AE. *Died 12 May 2015.*

FRY, William Norman H.; *see* Hillier-Fry.

FRYE, Michael John Ernest, CBE 1997; President and Director-General, Swiss Digital Technologies, 1999–2006; Executive Chairman: WaterCarrier Ltd, since 2007; WaterCarrier Investments, since 2010; *b* 2 June 1945; *s* of late Jack Frye, CBE and Daphne Page-Croft; *m* 1st, 1970, Geraldine Elizabeth Kendall; one *s*; 2nd, 1989, Valerie Patricia Harfield-Simpson; one *d*. *Educ:* Marlborough Coll.; MIT (SB Business Management, Mech. Eng. Minor). B. Elliott and subsidiaries, 1967–99; Dir, Goldfields Industrial, 1973–76; Overseas Dir, B. Elliott, 1974–76, non-exec. Dir, 1976–87, Chm., 1987–92, Chief Exec., 1988–99; Chm. and Chief Exec., Rotaflex Gp of Cos, 1975–87; Chm., Concord Lighting, 1976–87; non-exec. Dir, Thorn Lighting Group, 1993–99. Chairman: Deltadot, 2000–04; Water & Waste plc, 2001–04; Classical Renaissance, 2008–. Chm. and Founder, Light and Health Res. Council, 1978; Member: NEDC Sub-Cttee, exports for luminaire manufrs, 1980–81; Council, Lighting Industry Fedn, 1980–87 (Vice-Pres., 1987); Illuminating Eng. Soc. of N America, 1979–; Chairman: Cttee to establish nat. lighting award, 1984–87; Lighting Div., CIBSE, 1987–88. Chairman: West London Leadership, 1990–2002; Business Link London, 1995–96; Creative London, 2003–06; London Sci. and Industry Council, 2003–05; Dep. Chm., Park Royal Partnership, 1993–95 (Chm., 1991–92); Director: London First, 1992–2002 (a Dep. Chm., 1996–2002); London Develt Partnership, 1998–2001 (Chm., Skills Taskforce, 1998–2001); Member Board: London Develt Agency, 2001–08; London Climate Change Agency, 2005–08. Chm., CBI London Reg., 1997–99 (Vice-Chm., 1996–97). Mem., Public Services Productivity Panel, 2000–08, Public Services and Public Expenditure Cttee, 2001–08, HM Treasury; Ministerial Cttee on E-commerce, 2001–08. Chm. and Mem., numerous technical and arts organisations. Hon. Prof., Thames Valley Univ., 1995. Liveryman, Turners' Co. and Lightmongers' Co. FRAeS 1994; Fellow, RSPB, 1987; FRSA 1978 (Vice Pres., 1990–; Chm., 1991–93; Dep. Chm., 1993–94). Hon. Fellow, RCA, 1987. DUniv Brunel, 2001; Hon. DEng London Metropolitan, 2004. *Recreations:* golf, tennis, chess, bird watching, collecting old or rare bird books, writing books on mind, body and spirit. *Address:* Lynara (Management) Ltd, Crown House, 72 Hammersmith Road, W14 8TH. *Clubs:* Boodle's, City Livery, Royal Automobile; Royal Worlington and Newmarket Golf. *Died 21 Oct. 2012.*

FUAD, Kutlu Tekin, CBE 1993; SPMB 1999; President, Court of Appeal, Negara Brunei Darussalam, 1993–2000; a non-permanent Judge, Court of Final Appeal, Hong Kong, 1997–2009; *b* 23 April 1926; *s* of Mustafa Fuad Bey, CMG, and Belkis Hilmi; *m* 1952, Inci Izzet; two *s* one *d*. *Educ:* Temple Grove; Marlborough Coll.; St John's Coll., Cambridge (MA). Called to the Bar, Inner Temple, 1952, Hon. Bencher, 1993. Mil. Service, Lieut KRRC, 1944–48 (Palestine 1946–48). Colonial Legal Service, 1953–62: Magistrate, Cyprus; Resident Magistrate, Sen. Crown Counsel, Legal Draftsman, and Dir of Public Prosecutions, Uganda; Judge of the High Court, Uganda, 1963–72 (Pres., Industrial Court; Chm., Law Reform Cttee); Dir, Legal Div., Commonwealth Secretariat, 1972–80; Judge, High Court of Hong Kong, 1980–82; Justice of Appeal, 1982–88, Vice-Pres., 1988–93, Court of Appeal, Hong Kong. Comr, Supreme Ct of Negara Brunei Darussalam, 1983–86, 1988–92. Nominated by Turkey as *ad hoc* judge for case brought to ECHR, 2000. Mem., Law Reform Commn, Hong Kong, 1983–89. Pres., Hong Kong Family Law Assoc., 1986–93. Formerly Chm., Visitation Cttee, Makerere University Coll. *Recreations:* music, Rugby football, gardening. *Address:* PO Box 415, Lefkoşa, Mersin 10, Turkey. *T:* (392) 2283299. *Died 25 July 2013.*

FUENTES, Prof. Carlos; Professor at Large, Brown University, since 1995; *b* 11 Nov. 1928; *s* of Ambassador Rafael Fuentes and Berta Fuentes; *m* 1st, 1957, Rita Macedo (marr. diss.); one *d*; 2nd, 1973, Sylvia Lemus; (one *s* one *d* decd). *Educ:* Law School, Nat. Univ., Mexico; Inst. des Hautes Etudes Internationales, Geneva. Sec., Mexican Deleg. to ILO, Geneva, 1950; Under Director of Culture, Nat. Univ., Mexico, 1952–54; Head, Cultural Relations Dept, Min. of Foreign Affairs, Mexico, 1955–58; Ambassador to France, 1975–77; Prof. of English and Romance Languages, Univ. of Pennsylvania, 1978–83; Prof. of Comparative Literature, Harvard, 1984–86; Simón Bolivar Prof., Cambridge, 1986–87; Robert F. Kennedy Prof. of Latin American Studies, Harvard, 1987–90. Member: El Colegio Nacional, Mexico, 1974–; Mexican Nat. Commn on Human Rights, 1989–; Fellow, Wilson Center, Washington DC, 1974; Mem., Amer. Acad. and Inst. of Arts and Letters, 1986; Trustee, NY Public Library, 1987. Hon. DLitt: Wesleyan, 1982; Warwick, 1992; Hon. LLD Harvard, 1983; Hon. LittD Cambridge, 1987; DUniv Essex, 1987; Dr *hc*: Tufts, 1993; UCLA, 1993; Salamanca, 2002. Nat. Prize for Literature, Mexico, 1985; Miguel de Cervantes Prize, 1987; Menéndez Pelayo Prize, Univ. of Santander, 1992; Delaware Commonwealth Award, 2002. Légion d'Honneur (France), 1992; Order Cruzeiro do Sul (Brazil), 1997. *Publications:* Where the Air is Clear, 1958; The Good Conscience, 1959; The Death of Artemio Cruz, 1962; Aura, 1962; A Change of Skin, 1967 (Biblioteca Breve Prize, Barcelona); Terra Nostra, 1975 (Rómulo Gallegos Prize); Distant Relations, 1980; Burnt Water, 1982; The Old Gringo, 1984 (filmed, 1989); Cristóbal Nonato, 1987; Myself with Others: selected essays, 1988; The Campaign, 1991; Valiente Mundo Nuevo: essays, 1991; Constancia and other stories for virgins, 1991; The Buried Mirror, 1992 (televised); El Naranjo (The Orange Tree) (novellas), 1993; Geography of the Novel: essays, 1993; A New Time for Mexico, 1997; Diana, 1997; Por un Progreso Incluyente, 1997; The Crystal Frontier: a novel in nine stories, 1997; Portraits in Time (photo essay), 1998; The Years with Laura Diaz, 1999; (ed jtly) The Picador Book of Latin American Stories, 1999; Los Cinco Solesda México, 2000; Inez, 2003; The Eagle's Throne, 2003; This I Believe, 2004; Happy Families, 2008. *Address:* c/o Brandt & Brandt, 1501 Broadway, New York, NY 10036, USA. *Died 15 May 2012.*

FULLER, Geoffrey Herbert, CEng, FRINA, FIMarEST; RCNC; defence and maritime consultant; Director, British Maritime Technology Ltd, Teddington, 1985–2000 (Deputy Chairman, 1985–95); *b* 16 Jan. 1927; *s* of late Major Herbert Thomas Fuller and Clarice Christine Fuller; *m* 1952, Pamela-Maria Quarrell (*d* 2008); one *d*. *Educ:* Merchant Taylors', Northwood, Middx; Royal Naval Engrg Coll., Keyham; Royal Naval Coll., Greenwich. FRINA 1965; FIMarEST (FIMarE 1974). Constructor Commander: Staff of Flag Officer (Submarines), 1958; British Navy Staff, Washington, 1960; RCDS, 1973; Support Manager Submarines, 1976; Dep. Dir, Submarines/Polaris, Ship Dept, MoD, 1979; Dir of Naval Ship Production, 1981–82; Dir, Manpower and Productivity, HM Dockyards, 1982–83; Mem. Bd, and Man. Dir, Warship Div., British Shipbuilders, 1983–85; Exec. Chm., 1984–86, Technical Adviser, 1986–87, Vickers Shipbuilding and Engrg Ltd, Barrow. Vice-Pres., RINA, 2004–07 (Chm. Council, 1994–96; Treas., 1999–2004). FRSA 1995. *Address:* Room 15, Oakfield, Weston Park, Bath BA1 4AS. *T:* (01225) 466054. *E:* casafuller@btinternet.com. *Died 17 Sept. 2015.*

FYFE OF FAIRFIELD, Baron *cr* 2000 (Life Peer), of Sauchie in Clackmannanshire; **George Lennox Fyfe;** Chairman, Unity Trust Bank, 2000–09; Chief Executive, Midlands Co-operative Society, 1995–2000 (Leicestershire Co-operative Society, 1975–95); *b* 10 April 1941; *s* of late George L. and Elizabeth S. Fyfe; *m* 1965, Ann Clark Asquith (*d* 1999); one *d* (one *s* decd). *Educ:* Alloa Acad.; Co-operative Coll., Loughborough. Gen. Manager, Kirriemuir Co-operative Soc., 1966–68; Regl Manager, Scottish Co-operative Soc., 1968–72; Gp Gen. Manager, CWS, 1972–75. Director: Shoefayre Ltd, 1981–2000 (Chm., 1984–2000); CWS, 1981–2000 (Vice-Chm., 1986–89; Chm., 1989–2000); Co-operative Insce Soc. Ltd, 1982–2000; Central TV-East, 1983–92; Co-operative Bank plc, 1986–2000 (Dep. Chm., 1996–2000). Mem. Central Cttee, Internat. Co-op. Alliance, 1989–2000; Pres., Co-op. Congress, 2001. Mem., E Midlands Econ. Planning Council, 1976–79. Member: EU Sub-Cttee D, Envmt, Agric., Public Health and Consumer Protection, H of L, 2000–03; EU Sub-Cttee B, Internal Mkt, H of L, 2005–. Mem. Court, Leicester Univ. JP Perthshire, 1972–75. CCMI. *Recreation:* observing human nature. *Address:* House of Lords, SW1A 0PW. *Clubs:* Reform, Farmers, Royal Automobile. *Died 1 Feb. 2011.*

FYFE, Prof. William Sefton, CC (Canada) 1989; FRS 1969; Professor of Geology, University of Western Ontario, 1972–92, then Emeritus (Dean of Science, 1986–90); *b* 4 June 1927; *s* of Colin and Isabella Fyfe; *m* 1st,

1968, Elisabeth Stumpfl; two *s* (one *d* decd); 2nd, 1972, Marie-Louise Dedouvre; 3rd, 1981, Patricia. *Educ:* Otago Univ., New Zealand. BSc 1948, MSc 1949, PhD 1952; FRS(Can) 1980; FRSNZ 1970. Univ. of California, Berkeley: Lecturer in Chemistry, 1952, Reader, 1958; Prof. of Geology, 1959; Royal Soc. Res. Prof. (Geochemistry), Univ. of Manchester, 1967–72. Guggenheim Fellow, 1983. Pres., IUGS, 1992–96. Hon. Fellow, Geol Soc. Amer.; Corresponding Member: Brazilian Acad. of Science; Russian Acad. of Scis; Indian Acad. of Scis. Hon. DSc: Meml Univ. of Newfoundland, 1989; Lisbon, 1990; Lakehead, 1990; Guelph, 1991; Otago, 1995; Western Ontario, 1996. Mineralogical Soc. of Amer. Award, 1964; Logan Medal, Geol Assoc. of Canada, 1982; Willet G. Miller Medal, Royal Soc. of Canada, 1985; Arthur Holmes Medal, European Union of Geoscientists, 1989; Day Medal, Geol Soc. of America, 1990; Canada Gold Medal for Science and Engineering, 1992; Roebling Medal, Mineralogical Soc. of America. Commemoration Medal, New Zealand, 1990, Canada, 1992; Ordem Nacional do Mérito Científico (Brazil), 1996; Wollaston Medal, Geol Soc., London, 2000. *Publications:* Metamorphic Reactions and Metamorphic Facies, 1958; The Geochemistry of Solids, 1964; Fluids in the Earth's Crust, 1978; also numerous scientific papers. *Address:* Department of Earth Sciences, University of Western Ontario, London, ON N6A 5B7, Canada. *E:* wsfyfe@uwo.ca.

Died 11 Nov. 2013.

FYFE, William Stevenson, CBE 1992 (OBE 1987); FIIM; Chairman, Greater Glasgow Health Board, 1993; *b* Glasgow, 10 June 1935; *s* of Dr Andrew Fyfe and Janet Isabella Fyfe (*née* Soutar), New Cumnock; *m* 1986, Margaret H. H. Auld; one *s* one *d*. *Educ:* Dollar Acad.; Scottish Coll. of Commerce. FIIM 1985. Town Councillor (C), Prestwick, 1967–73; Co. Councillor (C), Ayrshire, 1970–73; Ayrshire and Arran Health Board: Financial Convener, 1973–81; Chm., 1981–93. Exec. Officer, Minerva Housing Assoc., Prestwick, 1997–2004. Chm., Scottish Health Services Adv. Council, 1989–93; Mem., General Whitley Council, 1989–93. *Recreation:* gardening. *Address:* 30 Kilbrandon Crescent, Doonfoot, Ayr KA7 4JX.

Died 22 Oct. 2015.

FYJIS-WALKER, Richard Alwyne, CMG 1980; CVO 1976; HM Diplomatic Service, retired; Chairman, Commonwealth Institute, 1988–93; *b* 19 June 1927; *s* of Harold and Marion Fyjis-Walker; *m* 1st, 1951, Barbara Graham-Watson (marr. diss.); one *s*; 2nd, 1972, Gabrielle Josefi; one *s*. *Educ:* Bradfield Coll.; Magdalene Coll., Cambridge (MA). Army (KRRC), 1945–48. Joined Foreign (subseq. Diplomatic) Service, 1955; served: Amman, 1956; FO, 1957–61; Paris, 1961–63; Cairo, 1963–65; FCO, 1966–71; Counsellor, 1970; Ankara, 1971–74; Counsellor (Information), Washington, 1974–78; Counsellor, UK Mission to UN, NY, 1978–79; Ambassador to the Sudan, 1979–84; Ambassador to Pakistan, 1984–87. *Address:* 17 Stonefield Street, N1 0HW.

Died 17 Sept. 2013.

G

GAGGERO, Joseph James, CBE 1989; President, Bland Group of Shipping, Aviation and Travel Companies; *b* 20 Nov. 1927; *s* of Sir George Gaggero, OBE, JP and Mabel Andrews-Speed; *m* 1st, 1958, Marilys Healing (marr. diss. 1987); one *s* one *d*; 2nd, 1994, Christina Russo (marr. diss. 2008). *Educ:* Downside Sch. Dir, Gibraltar Chamber of Commerce, 1951–56; Head, Gibraltar Govt Tourist Dept, 1955–59; served on or led other Gibraltar Govt Cttees and Gibraltar Trading Assocs, 1948–. Hon. Consul Gen. for Sweden in Gibraltar, 1971–95. Director: Hovertravel; Cadogan Holidays; President: Rock Hotel; Gibraltar Airways. Dep. Pres., Moroccan-British Business Council, 2008–. Pres., British Moroccan Soc., 2005–; Vice Pres., Gibraltar Soc. Freeman, City of London, 1997; Liveryman, GAPAN, 1997–. Patron and Vice President: Hispanic British Foundn, Madrid; Gibraltar Philharmonic Orch. Air League Founders' Medal, 2007. KHS. Comdr, Royal Order of the Polar Star (Sweden), 1991; Comdr, Royal Order Al Alaoui (Morocco), 2006. *Publications:* Running with the Baton (autobiog.), 2005. *Recreations:* travel, painting. *Address:* Cloister Building, Gibraltar. *T:* 78456. *Clubs:* Travellers; Valderrama Golf. *Died 10 Feb. 2012.*

GAINFORD, 3rd Baron *cr* 1917; **Joseph Edward Pease;** *b* 25 Dec. 1921; *s* of 2nd Baron Gainford, TD, and Veronica Margaret (*d* 1995), *d* of Sir George Noble, 2nd Bt; *S* father, 1971; *m* 1953, Margaret Theophila Radcliffe (*d* 2010), *d* of late Henry Edmund Guise Tyndale; two *d*. *Educ:* Eton; Gordonstoun; Open Univ. (Dip. in Eur. Humanities, 1995; BA Hons, 1997). RAFVR, 1941–46. Hunting Aerosurveys Ltd, 1947–49; Directorate of Colonial Surveys, 1951–53; Soil Mechanics Ltd, 1953–58; London County Council, 1958–65; Greater London Council, 1965–78. UK Delegate to UN, 1973. Mem., Coll. of Guardians, Nat. Shrine of Our Lady of Walsingham, 1979–. Mem., Plaisterers' Co., 1976. *Recreations:* Association football, music, veteran and vintage aviation. *Heir: b* Hon. George Pease [*b* 20 April 1926; *m* 1958, Flora Daphne (*d* 2010), *d* of late Dr N. A. Dyce Sharp; two *s* two *d*]. *Address:* 1 Dedmere Court, Marlow, Bucks SL7 1PL. *T:* (01628) 484679. *Died 4 April 2013.*

GALBRAITH, Samuel Laird; *b* 18 Oct. 1945; *m* 1987, Nicola Tennant; three *d*. *Educ:* Glasgow Univ. (BSc Hons 1968; MB ChB Hons 1971; MD 1977); FRCSGlas 1975. Consultant in Neurosurgery, Gtr Glasgow Health Bd, 1978–87. MP (Lab) Strathkelvin and Bearsden, 1987–2001. Opposition spokesman on Scottish affairs and health, 1988–92, on employment, 1992–93; Parly Under-Sec. of State, Scottish Office, 1997–99. Scottish Parliament: Mem. (Lab) Strathkelvin and Bearsden, 1999–2001; Minister: for Children and Educn, Culture and the Arts and Sport, 1999–2000; for the Envmt, 2000–01. *Publications:* An Introduction to Neurosurgery, 1983. *Died 18 Aug. 2014.*

GALLACHER, John; HM Diplomatic Service, retired; *b* 16 July 1931; *s* of John Gallacher and Catherine Gallacher (*née* Crilly); *m* 1956, Eileen Agnes (*née* McGuire); one *s*. *Educ:* Our Lady's High School, Motherwell. Nat. Service, RAF, 1950–52. Kenya Police, 1953–65 (retired as Supt of Police, 1965); Libyan Govt (attached to Min. of Interior), 1965–67; FCO, 1967–70; Lagos, 1970–73; FCO, 1973–74; Kuwait, 1974–77; FCO 1977; Counsellor, FCO, 1983–84. Gp Security Advr, Gallaher Ltd, 1985–91; Rep. (Scotland), Control Risks Gp, 1992–98. *Recreations:* reading, golf, travel, gardening. *Died 17 June 2015.*

GALLAGHER, (Francis George) Kenna, CMG 1963; HM Diplomatic Service, retired; *b* 25 May 1917; *er s* of late George and Johanna Gallagher. *Educ:* St Joseph's Coll.; King's Coll., University of London (LLB (Hons)). Served in HM Forces, 1941–45; apptd a Mem., HM Foreign (subseq. Diplomatic) Service, 1945; Vice-Consul Marseilles, 1946–48; HM Embassy, Paris, 1948–50; FO, 1950–53; First Sec., HM Embassy, Damascus, 1953–55; FO, 1955; appointed Counsellor and Head of European Economic Organisations Dept, 1960; Counsellor (Commercial), HM Embassy, Berne, 1963–65; Head of Western Economic Dept, CO, 1965–67, of Common Market Dept, 1967–68; Asst Under-Sec. of State, FCO, 1968–71; Ambassador and Head of UK Delegn to OECD, 1971–77. Consultant on Internat. Trade Policy, CBI, 1978–80. *Recreations:* music, reading. *Address:* 37 Howard Terrace, Morpeth, Northumberland NE61 1HT. *T:* (01670) 504384. *Died 19 April 2011.*

GALLAGHER, Dame Monica (Josephine), DBE 1976; *b* 5 April 1923; *m* 1946, Dr John Paul Gallagher, OAM, KCSG, KM (decd); two *s* two *d*. Mem., Friends of St Mary's Cathedral, Sydney, 1994–2001 (Chm., 1984–87 and 1998–2001; Dep. Chm., 1988–93); Pres., Flower Festival Cttee, 1987–95, Dir, Flower Fest., 1996–97, St Mary's Cathedral; Mem. Cttee, Order of British Empire Assoc., NSW, 1976– (Vice-Pres., 1985–89; Pres., 1989–92); Vice-Pres., SCF, NSW, 1992–94; Member: Dr Horace Nowland Travelling Scholarship; Adv. Bd, Fest. of Light; former Mem., Nursing Adv. Cttee, Australian Catholic Univ. (formerly Catholic Coll. of Educn), Sydney. Tour Guide, St Mary's Cathedral. State Pres., NSW, and Gen. Pres., Sydney Archdiocese, Catholic Women's League, Aust., 1972–80 (Nat. Pres., 1972–74); Past President: Catholic Central Cttee for Care of Aged; Catholic Women's Club, Sydney; Associated Catholic Cttee; Catholic Inst. of Nursing Studies. Former Member: Austcare; NSW Div., UNA; UN Status of Women Cttee; Exec. Bd, Mater Misericordiae Hosp., N Sydney; Bd, Gertrude Abbott Nursing Home; Selection Cttee, Queen Elizabeth II Silver Jubilee Trust; Australian Church Women, NSW Div.; former Chm., YWCA Appeal Cttee, Sydney. Patron, Flower Club of NSW, 1999–. Good Citizen Award, Festival of Light, 1979; Papal Honour, Augustae Crucis Insigne pro Ecclesia et Pontifice, 1981; DCSG 2001. *Address:* Unit 92/2 Artarmon Road, Willoughby, NSW 2068, Australia. *Died 18 Sept. 2013.*

GALLEN, Hon. Sir Rodney (Gerald), KNZM 2000; QC 1976; High Court Judge, New Zealand, 1983–99; *b* 12 Aug. 1933; *s* of Gerald Collins Gallen and Eva Susan Ann Gallen. *Educ:* Victoria UC, Wellington (LLB). *Recreations:* gardening, music, reading. *Address:* Birchwood RD2, Hastings 4172, New Zealand. *T:* (6) 8778499. *Clubs:* Wellington, Hawkes Bay. *Died 3 March 2012.*

GALLIE, Philip Roy; Member (C) Scotland South, Scottish Parliament, 1999–2007; Managing Consultant, PG Business Advice, 1998–2007; *b* 3 June 1939; *s* of George Albert Gallie and Ivy Edith Gallie (*née* Williams); *m* 1964, Marion Wands Whyte (*d* 2006); one *s* one *d*. *Educ:* Dunfermline High Sch.; Kirkcaldy Tech. Coll. MIPlantE; TE. Apprentice elect. fitter, HM Dockyard, Rosyth, 1955–60; Elect. Engineer, Ben Line Steamers, 1960–64; Electricity Supply Industry; Kincardine, Ironbridge and Inverkip Power Stations; SSEB Central Maint. Orgn; Galloway and Lanark Hydros and Inverkip Power Station (Manager, 1989–92). Dist Councillor, Cunninghame, 1980–84. Contested (C): Cunninghame South, 1983; Dunfermline West, 1987. MP (C) Ayr, 1992–97; contested (C) same seat, 1997, 2001. Vice-Chm., Scottish Cons. and Unionist Party, 1995–97; party spokesman on industry and economy, 1997–99, on justice and home affairs, 1999–2001, on constitutional and European affairs, 2001–07. Mem. Bd, Ayr Coll., 2007–. Assoc. Mem., Prestwick Br., RAFA. *Recreations:* politics, sports. *E:* philgallie@btinternet.com. *Clubs:* Rotary (Alloway); Ayr Rugby Football. *Died 24 Jan. 2011.*

GALLOWAY, Maj.-Gen. Kenneth Gardiner, CB 1978; OBE 1960; Director, Army Dental Service, 1974–78; *b* 3 Nov. 1917; *s* of David and Helen Galloway, Dundee and Oban; *m* 1949, Sheila Frances (*née* Dunsmor); two *d* (one *s* decd). *Educ:* Oban High Sch.; St Andrews Univ. LDS 1939, BDS 1940. Lieut Army Dental Corps, 1940; Captain 1941; Major 1948; Lt-Col 1955; Col 1963; Brig. 1972; Maj.-Gen. 1974. Served in Egypt, Palestine, Syria and Iraq, 1942–46;

Chief Instructor and 2nd in comd, Depot and Training Establishment, RADC, 1956–60; Malta and BAOR, 1960–67; Asst Dir Dental Service, MoD, 1967–71; Dep. Dir Dental Service: Southern Comd, 1971–72; BAOR, 1972–74. QHDS 1971–78. Col Comdt, RADC, 1980–83. OStJ 1960. *Recreations:* tennis, golf, gardening. *Address:* Berwyn Court, 63 Avenue Road, Farnborough, Hants GU14 7BH. *T:* (01252) 544948. *Died 27 Feb. 2013.*

GALPIN, Rodney Desmond; Chairman, Alpha Airports Group PLC, 1994–2002; *b* 5 Feb. 1932; *s* of Sir Albert James Galpin, KCVO, CBE; *m* 1956, Sylvia Craven; one *s* one *d. Educ:* Haileybury and Imperial Service Coll. Joined Bank of England, 1952; Sec. to Governor (Lord Cromer), 1962–66; Dep. Principal, Discount Office, 1970–74; Dep. Chief Cashier, Banking and Money Markets Supervision, 1974–78; Chief of Establishments, 1978–80; Chief of Corporate Services, 1980–82; Associate Dir, 1982–84; Exec. Dir, Bank of England, 1984–88; Chairman and Group Chief Executive: Standard Chartered plc, 1988–93; Standard Chartered Bank, 1988–93. Director: Cater Allen Holdings PLC, 1993–97; Capital Shopping Centres PLC, 1994–2000; Ascot (formerly Ascot Holdings) PLC, 1995–2001; P&O, 1996–2005; Abbey National Treasury Services PLC, 1997–2002. Chm., Independent Review Body (formerly Code of Banking Practice Review Cttee), 1994–99. Mem. Council, Foundn for Management Educn, 1984–86. Chm., Look Ahead Housing Assoc. Ltd, 1994–2003. Life Gov., 1973, and Council Mem., 1973–2004, Haileybury; Member, Council: Scout Assoc., 1972–; St George's House, Windsor, 1995–2001. CCMI (FBIM 1979); FCIB 1988. Freeman, City of London, 1981. OStJ. *Recreations:* tennis, gardening, music. *E:* Rdgalpin@aol.com. *Club:* Bankers' (Pres., 1992–93). *Died 6 Oct. 2011.*

GALVIN, John Rogers; General, United States Army; Supreme Allied Commander, Europe, and Commander-in-Chief, US European Command, Stuttgart, 1987–92; Dean, Fletcher School of Law and Diplomacy, Tufts University, 1995–2000, then Emeritus; *b* 13 May 1929; *s* of John J. Galvin and Mary Josephine Logan; *m* 1961, Virginia Lee Brennan; four *d. Educ:* US Mil. Acad. (BS); Columbia Univ. (MA); US Army Command and General Staff Coll.; Univ. of Pennsylvania; US Army War Coll.; Fletcher Sch. of Law and Diplomacy (US Army War Coll. Fellowship). Platoon Leader, I Co., 65 Inf. Regt, Puerto Rico, 1955–56; Instructor, Ranger Sch., Colombia, 1956–58; Co. Comdr, 501 Airborne Battle Group, 101 Airborne Div., 1958–60; Instructor, US Mil. Acad., 1962–65; DACOS, Plans, 1st Cavalry Div., Vietnam, 1966–67; MA and Aide to Sec. of US Army, 1967–69; Comdr, 1st Bn, 8th Cavalry, 1st Cavalry Div., Vietnam, 1969–70; Dep. Sec., Jt Staff, US European Comd, Stuttgart, 1973–74; MA to SACEUR, 1974–75; Comdr, Div. Support Comd, 1975–77; COS, 3rd Inf. Div. (Mechanized), Würzburg, 1977–78; Asst Div. Comdr, 8th Inf. Div. (Mechanized), Mainz, 1978–80; Asst DCOS for Training, US Army Training and Doctrine Comd, 1980–81; Comdg Gen., 24 Inf. Div. (Mechanized), and Fort Stewart, 1981–83; Comdg Gen., VII Corps, Stuttgart, 1983–85; C-in-C, US Southern Comd, Panama, 1985–87. Olin Dist. Prof. of Nat. Security, W Point, 1992–94; Dist. Policy Analyst, Mershon Center, Ohio State Univ., 1994–95. Defense DSM, Army DSM, Navy DSM, Air Force DSM, Silver Star, Legion of Merit (with 2 Oak Leaf Clusters), DFC, Soldier's Medal, Bronze Star (with 2 Oak Leaf Clusters), Combat Infantryman Badge, Ranger Tab, foreign decorations. *Publications:* The Minute Men, 1967; Air Assault: the development of airmobility, 1969; Three Men of Boston, 1975; Fighting the Cold War: A Soldier's Memoir, 2015. *Recreations:* walking, jogging. *Address:* 2714 Lake Jodeco Circle, Jonesboro, GA 30236–5326, USA. *Died 25 Sept. 2015.*

GARCÍA MÁRQUEZ, Gabriel; *see* Márquez.

GARDNER, Antony John; Registrar, Central Council for Education and Training in Social Work, 1988–92 (Principal Registration Officer, 1970–88); *b* 27 Dec. 1927; *s* of David Gardner, head gardener, and Lillian Gardner; *m* 1956, Eveline A. Burden (*d* 2003). *Educ:* elem. school; Co-operative Coll.; Southampton Univ. (Pres. Union, Southampton, 1958–59; BSc (Econ) 1959). Apprentice toolmaker, 1941–45; National Service, RASC, 1946–48; building trade, 1948–53. Tutor Organiser, Co-operative Union, 1959–60; Member and Education Officer, Co-operative Union, 1961–66. Contested (Lab): SW Wolverhampton, 1964; Beeston, Feb. and Oct. 1974; MP (Lab) Rushcliffe, 1966–70. Contested (Lab) Dorset and E Devon, Eur. Parly elecns, 1994. *Recreations:* angling, gardening and the countryside generally. *Address:* 12 Heath Avenue, Poole, Dorset BH15 3EJ. *T:* (01202) 676683. *Club:* Parkstone Trades and Labour (Poole). *Died 16 Oct. 2011.*

GARDNER, John Linton, CBE 1976; composer; *b* 2 March 1917; *s* of late Dr Alfred Gardner, Ilfracombe, and Muriel (*née* Pullein-Thompson); *m* 1955, Jane (*d* 1998), *d* of late N. J. Abercrombie; one *s* two *d. Educ:* Eagle House, Sandhurst; Wellington Coll.; Exeter Coll., Oxford (BMus). Served War of 1939–45: RAF, 1940–46. Chief Music Master, Repton Sch., 1939–40. Staff, Covent Garden Opera, 1946–52; Tutor: Morley Coll., 1952–76 (Dir of Music, 1965–69); Bagot Stack Coll., 1955–62; London Univ. (extra-mural) 1959–60; Dir of Music, St Paul's Girls' Sch., 1962–75; Prof. of Harmony and Composition, Royal Acad. of Music, 1956–86. Conductor: Haslemere Musical Soc., 1953–62; Dorian Singers, 1961–62; European Summer Sch. for Young Musicians, 1966–75; Bromley YSO, 1970–76. Brit. Council Lecturer: Levant, 1954; Belgium, 1960; Iberia, 1963; Yugoslavia, 1967. Adjudicator, Canadian Festivals, 1974, 1980. Chm., Composers' Guild, 1963; Member: Arts Council Music Panel, 1958–62; Cttee of Management, Royal Philharmonic Soc., 1965–72; Brit. Council Music Cttee, 1968. Dir, Performing Right Soc., 1965–92 (Dep. Chm., 1983–88). Worshipful Co. of Musicians: Collard Fellow, 1962–64; elected to Freedom and Livery, 1965. Hon. RAM 1959; Hon. Mem., Royal Philharmonic Soc., 1998. Bax Society's Prize, 1958. *Works include: orchestral:* Symphony no 1, 1947; Variations on a Waltz of Carl Nielsen, 1952; Piano Concerto no 1, 1957; Sinfonia Piccola (strings), 1960; Occasional Suite, Aldeburgh Festival, 1968; An English Ballad, 1969; Three Ridings, 1970; Sonatina for Strings, 1974; Divertimento, 1977; Symphony no 2, 1984; Symphony no 3, 1989; Concerto for Oboe and Strings, 1990; Concerto for Flute and Strings, 1995; Irish Suite, 1996; Concerto for Bassoon and Strings, 2004; *chamber:* Concerto da Camera (4 insts), 1968; Partita (solo 'cello), 1968; Chamber Concerto (organ and 11 insts), 1969; English Suite (harpsichord), 1971; Sonata Secolare for organ and brass, 1973; Sonata da Chiesa for two trumpets and organ, 1976; String Quartet no 2, 1979; Hebdomade, 1980; Sonatina Lirica for brass, 1983; Triad, 1984; Quartet for Saxes, 1985; Oboe Sonata no 2, French Suite for Sax. 4tet, 1986; String Quartet no 3, 1987; Octad, 1987; Piano Sonata no 3, 1988; Larkin Songs, 1990; Organ Sonata, 1992; Sextet for piano and wind, 1995; Easter Fantasy for organ and brass, 1997; *ballet:* Reflection, 1952; *opera:* A Nativity Opera, 1950; The Moon and Sixpence, 1957; The Visitors, 1972; Bel and the Dragon, 1973; The Entertainment of the Senses, 1974; Tobermory, 1976; *musical:* Vile Bodies, 1961; *choral:* Cantiones Sacrae 1973; (sop., chor. and orch.), 1952; Jubilate Deo (unacc. chor.), 1957; The Ballad of the White Horse (bar., chor. and orch.), 1959; Herrick Cantata (ten. solo, chor. and orch.), 1961; A Latter-Day Athenian Speaks, 1962; The Noble Heart (sop., bass, chor. and orch.), Shakespeare Quatercentenary Festival, 1964; Cantor popularis vocis, 18th Schütz Festival Berlin, 1964; Mass in C (unacc. chor.), 1965; Cantata for Christmas (chor. and chamb. orch.), 1966; Proverbs of Hell (unacc. chor.), 1967; Cantata for Easter (soli, chor., organ and percussion), 1970; Open Air (chor. and brass band), 1976; Te Deum for Pigotts, 1981; Mass in D, 1983; Cantata for St Cecilia, 1991; Stabat Mater (sop., chor., organ and timpani), A Burns Sequence (chor. and orch.), 1993; Seven Last Words, 1996; many smaller pieces and music for films, Old Vic and Royal Shakespeare Theatres, BBC. *Publications:* Robert Schumann, the man and his music, 1972; The Musical Companion, 1978; contributor to: Dublin Review, Musical Times, Tempo, Composer, Listener, Music in Education, DNB. *Recreations:* jazz, bore-watching. *Address:* Forest Brow, Liss Forest, Hants GU33 7BL. *W:* www.johnlintongardner.co.uk. *Died 12 Dec. 2011.*

GARDNER, Norman Keith Ayliffe; *b* 2 July 1925; *s* of late Charles Ayliffe Gardner and Winifred Gardner; *m* 1951, Margaret Patricia Vinson; one *s* one *d*. *Educ:* Cardiff High Sch.; University Coll., Cardiff (BScEng); College of Aeronautics, Cranfield; Univ. of London Commerce Degree Bureau (BScEcon Hons). CEng. Flight Test Observer, RAE, 1944; Test Engr, Westland Aircraft Ltd, 1946; Development Engr, Handley Page Ltd, 1950; Engr, Min. of Aviation, 1964; Economic Adviser, Min. of Technology, 1970; Asst Dir (Engrg), DTI, 1973; Sen. Economic Adviser, 1974, Under Secretary: DoI, 1977; Dept of Employment, 1979; DTI, 1984–85. *Publications:* The Economics of Launching Aid, in The Economics of Industrial Subsidies (HMSO), 1976; Decade of Discontent: the changing British economy, 1987; A Guide to United Kingdom and European Community Competition Policy, 1990, 2nd edn as A Guide to United Kingdom and European Union Competition Policy, 1996, 3rd edn 2000; Mistakes: how they have happened and how some might be avoided, 2007; papers in Jl Instn Prodn Engrs and other engrg jls; articles for Citizendium. *Recreation:* music. *Address:* 15 Chanctonbury Way, N12 7JB. *T:* (020) 8922 0847. *Died 10 May 2013.*

GARDOM, Hon. Garde Basil; QC (Canada) 1975; Lieutenant-Governor of British Columbia, 1995–2001; *b* 17 July 1924; *s* of Basil Gardom and Gabrielle Gwladys (*née* Bell); *m* 1956, Theresa Helen Eileen Mackenzie; one *s* four *d*. *Educ:* Univ. of British Columbia (BA, LLB). Called to Bar of British Columbia, 1949; elected to BC Legislature as Mem. for Vancouver-Point Grey, 1966; re-elected, 1969, 1972, 1975, 1979, 1983; Govt House Leader, 1977–86; Attorney Gen. of BC, 1975–79; Minister of Intergovtl Relns, 1979–86; Chairman: Constitution Cttee, 1975–86; Legislation Cttee, 1975–86; Mem., Treasury Bd and Planning and Priorities Cttee, 1983–86; Minister responsible, Official Visits to Expo '86; Policy Cons., Office of the Premier, 1986–87; Agent General for BC in the UK and Europe, 1987–92; Director: Crown Life Insurance Co., 1993–95; Brouwer Claims Canada Ltd, 2001–. Member: Canadian Bar Assoc., 1949–; Vancouver Bar Assoc., 1949–; British Columbia Sports Hall of Fame, 1995; Phi Delta Theta Fraternity, 1943. Director: Canadian Club, BC, 2003; Justice Inst. of BC, 2004. Hon. Patron: Nature Conservancy Canada, 2001; BC Alcohol and Drug Educn Services, 2002; BCAA Traffic Foundn, 2004; Heraldry Soc. of Canada; RUSI Vancouver Is.; Pacific Alzheimer Res. Foundn, 2007. Hon. Col, BC Regt (Duke of Connaught's Own), 1997. Freeman, City of London, 1992. Hon. LLD: Vancouver, 2002; Victoria, 2003. Lifetime Achievement Award, Univ. of British Columbia, 2002. KStJ 1996. *Recreation:* fishing. *Address:* 2122 SW Marine Drive, Vancouver, BC V6P 6B5, Canada. *Clubs:* Royal Over-Seas League, Royal Commonwealth Society; Vancouver, Union Club of BC, Vancouver Lawn Tennis and Badminton (British Columbia). *Died 18 June 2013.*

GARLAND, Patrick Ewart; director and producer of plays, films, television; writer; Artistic Director, Chichester Festival Theatre, 1980–84 and 1991–94; *b* 10 April 1935; *s* of late Ewart Garland and Rosalind, *d* of Herbert Granville Fell, editor of The Connoisseur; *m* 1980, Alexandra Bastedo. *Educ:* St Mary's Coll., Southampton; St Edmund Hall, Oxford (MA; Hon. Fellow, 1997). Actor, Bristol Old Vic, 1959; Age of Kings, BBC TV, 1961; lived in Montparnasse, 1961–62; writing—two plays for ITV, 1962; Research Asst, Monitor, BBC, 1963; Television interviews with: Stevie Smith, Philip Larkin, Sir Noel Coward, Sir John Gielgud, Sir Ralph Richardson, Dame Ninette de Valois, Claire Bloom, Tito Gobbi, Marcel Marceau, 1964–78. Director and Producer, BBC Arts Dept, 1962–74; Stage Director: *West End:* 40 Years On, 1968, 1984; Brief Lives, 1968; Getting On, 1970; Cyrano, 1971; The Doll's House (New York and London), 1975; Billy, the Musical, 1976; Under the Greenwood Tree, 1978; Look After Lulu, 1978; Beecham, 1980; Hair (Israel), 1972; York Mystery Plays, 1980; My Fair Lady (US), 1980; Kipling (Mermaid and New York), 1984; Canaries Sometimes Sing, Albery, 1987; The Secret of Sherlock Holmes, Wyndham's, 1988; A Room of One's Own, Hampstead, 1989, 2002, New York, 1991; Song in the Night, Lyric, Hammersmith, 1989; The Dressmaker, Windsor and tour, 1990; Tovarich, Piccadilly, 1991; Vita and Virginia, Ambassadors, 1993; The Tempest, Regent's Park Open Air, 1996; The Importance of Being Oscar, Savoy, 1997; The Mystery of Charles Dickens, Comedy, 2000, Albery and NY, 2002; The Woman in Black, San Diego and NY, 2001; Full Circle, UK tour, 2004; Visiting Mr Green, UK tour, 2007–08, Trafalgar Studio, 2008; (and adapted) Doctor Marigold and Mr Chops, Edinburgh Fest., 2008, transf. to Riverside Studios, 2009–10, UK tour, 2012–13; Brief Lives, UK tour, 2008; co-author, Underneath the Arches, Chichester, and Prince of Wales, 1982–83; Director, *Chichester Festival Theatre:* The Cherry Orchard, 1981; The Mitford Girls, 1981 (also London, 1981); On the Rocks, 1982; Cavell, 1982; Goodbye, Mr Chips, 1982; As You Like It, 1983; Forty Years On, Merchant of Venice, 1984; Victory (adapted from The Dynasts by Thomas Hardy), 1989; Tovarich, 1991; Pickwick, 1993; Pygmalion, 1994; Beatrix, 1996; Chimes at Midnight, 1998; produced: Fanfare for Elizabeth, the Queen's 60th birthday gala, Covent Garden, 1986; Celebration of a Broadcaster, for Richard Dimbleby Cancer Fund at Westminster Abbey, 1986; Thanksgiving service for Lord Olivier, 1989; *television:* prod Christmas Glory, ITV, annually 1997–; Director: Talking Heads, 1998; Telling Tales, 2000. *Films:* The Snow Goose, 1974; The Doll's House, 1976. Creative Writing Fellowship, Bishop Otter Coll., Chichester, 1984–85. Hon. DLitt Southampton, 1994. *Publications:* Brief Lives, 1967; The Wings of the Morning (novel), 1989; Oswald the Owl (for children), 1990; Angels in the Sussex Air: an anthology of Sussex poems, 1995; The Incomparable Rex: a memoir of Rex Harrison in the 1980s, 1998; poetry in: London Magazine, 1954; New Poems, 1956; Sussex Seams, 1996; Poetry West; Encounter; short stories in: Transatlantic Review, 1976; England Erzählt, Gemini, Light Blue Dark Blue. *Recreations:* reading Victorian novels, walking in Corsica. *Club:* Garrick. *Died 20 April 2013.*

GARNER, Sir Anthony (Stuart), Kt 1984; parliamentary and public affairs consultant, since 1988; Director of Organisation, Conservative Central Office, 1976–88; *b* 28 Jan. 1927; *s* of Edward Henry Garner, MC, FIAS, and Dorothy May Garner; *m* 1967, Shirley Taylor; two *s*. *Educ:* Liverpool Coll. Grenadier Guards, 1945–48. Young Conservative Organiser, Yorks Area, 1948–51; Conservative Agent, Halifax, 1951–56; Nat. Organising Sec., Young Conservative Org., 1956–61; Conservative Central Office Agent for: London Area, 1961–64; Western Area, 1964–66; North West Area, 1966–76. Chm., Conservative Agents' Examination Bd, 1976–88. Pres., Conservative Agents' Benevolent Assoc., 1976–88. Director: Carroll Anglo-American Corp., 1989–94; Clifton Court Residents Ltd, 1990–2009 (Chm., 1996–2009); Farnborough Aerospace Develt Corp., 1994–95; Carroll Aircraft Corp., 1994–95; Co-Founder, British-Iranian Chamber of Commerce, 1996–2000 (Vice Chm., 1996–2000). Trustee, Old Sessions Hse Charitable Trust, 2004–09. Life Governor, Liverpool Coll., 1980. Pres., Old Lerpoolian Soc., 1995–97. *Recreations:* travelling, theatre. *Address:* The Beeches, Bottom Lane, Seer Green, Beaconsfield, Bucks HP9 2UH. *Club:* Carlton. *Died 22 March 2015.*

GARNER, Maurice Richard; formerly specialist in the structure and governmental control of public enterprises; *b* 31 May 1915; *o s* of Jesse H. Garner; *m* 1943, Joyce W. Chapman (*d* 2009); one *s* one *d*. *Educ:* Glendale County Sch.; London Sch. of Economics and Political Science. Royal Armoured Corps, 1942–45 (despatches). Inland Revenue (Tax Inspectorate), 1938–46; BoT, Asst Principal and Principal, 1947; Commercial Sec. and UK Trade Comr in Ottawa, 1948–55; transf. to Min. of Power, 1957; Asst Sec. 1960; Under-Sec., Electricity Div., Min. of Technology, 1969, later DTI, retired 1973. Vis. Prof., Dept of Govt, LSE, 1981–85. *Recreations:* reading, oenology. *Address:* 52 Brook Court, Burcot Lane, Bromsgrove, Worcs B60 1AD. *T:* (01527) 870242. *Club:* Army and Navy. *Died 5 Jan. 2013.*

GARVAGH, 5th Baron *cr* 1818; **Alexander Leopold Ivor George Canning;** Accredited Representative, Trade and Industry, The Cayman Islands, 1981; *b* 6 Oct. 1920; *s* of 4th Baron and Gladys Dora May (*d* 1982), *d* of William Bayley Parker; *S* father, 1956; *m* 1st, 1947, Christine Edith (marr.

diss. 1974; she *d* 2013), *d* of Jack Cooper; one *s* two *d*; 2nd, 1974, Cynthia Valerie Mary, *d* of Eric E. F. Pretty, CMG, Kingswood, Surrey. *Educ:* Eton; Christ Church, Oxford. Commissioned Corps of Guides Cavalry, Indian Army, 1940; served Burma (despatches). Founder Dir, Internat. Business Services Ltd, 1947; Director: Stonehaven Tankers Ltd; Campden Research & Sales Ltd; Independent Chartering Ltd; AODC (UK) Ltd; Camco Machinery Ltd; Telomex (New York) Inc. Founder Mem., Instituto de Propietarios Extranjeros (Spain), 1985. Mem., Baltic Exchange, 1978. Mem., British Inst. of Exports, 1957; MCMI (MBIM 1962); FInstD 1964. Past Mem. Court, Painter Stainers Co. Consultant and contributor, Spanish Property Gazette, 1987–88. *Publications:* contrib. to The Manufacturing Optician, 1949. *Recreations:* travel, motoring, and motor sport; writing articles, short stories, etc. *Heir:* *s* Hon. Spencer George Stratford de Redcliffe Canning [*b* 12 Feb. 1953; *m* 1979, Julia Margery Morison Bye (*d* 2009), *er d* of Col F. C. E. Bye, Twickenham; one *s* two *d*]. *Address:* The Courtyard, Water Street, Deal, Kent CT14 6DJ. *Died 31 Oct. 2013.*

GASKELL, Sir Richard (Kennedy Harvey), Kt 1989; Consultant, TLT Solicitors (formerly Lawrence Tucketts), 1997–2009 (Partner, 1963–89; Senior Partner, 1989–97); President of the Law Society, 1988–89; *b* 17 Sept. 1936; *o s* of late Dr Kenneth Harvey Gaskell, MRCS, LRCP, DMRD and Jean Winsome Gaskell; *m* 1965, Judith Poland; one *s* (one *d* decd). *Educ:* Marlborough Coll. Admitted solicitor, 1960. Chm., Nat. Cttee, Young Solicitors' Gp, 1964–65; Law Society: Mem. Council, 1969–92; Dep. Vice-Pres., 1986–87; Vice Pres., 1987–88; President: Bristol Law Soc., 1978–79; Assoc. of South Western Law Socs, 1980–81. Member: Crown Court Rules Cttee, 1977–83; Security Service Tribunal, 1989–2000; Intelligence Services Tribunal, 1994–2000; Criminal Justice Consultative Council, 1991–94; Criminal Injuries Compensation Bd, 1992–2000; Criminal Injuries Compensation Appeals Panel, 1997–2004; Investigatory Powers Tribunal, 2000–11; Professional Conduct Cttee, GMC, 2001–06. Director: Law Society Trustees Ltd, 1974–92; Bristol Waterworks Co., 1989–91; Bristol Water Gp plc, 1991–2005 (Dep. Chm., 1998–2005). Mem., Adv. Council, PYBT, 1988–2000. Dir, Wildfowl Trust (Hldgs) Ltd, 1980–2005; Mem. Council, Wildfowl and Wetlands (formerly Wildfowl) Trust, 1980–92 (Chm., 1983–87; Vice-Pres., 1992–); Vice-Pres., SS Great Britain Project Ltd, 2000– (Chm., 1992–2000; Chm. Exec. Cttee and Council, SS Great Britain, 1992–2000). Trustee: Frenchay and Southmead Med. Trust, 1968–99; Laura Ashley Foundn, 1990–97; CLIC (UK), 1991–95. Kt Vice-Pres., Imperial Soc. of Kts Bachelor, 2012– (Mem. Council, 1995–2006; Chm., 1999–2000; Kt Principal, 2000–06; Kt Pres., 2007–12). Mem. Court, Bristol Univ., 1973–2000. Liveryman, Farmers' Co., 2002–; Hon. Freeman, Butchers' Co., 2002. Hon. LLD Bristol, 1989; Hon. LLM Bristol Polytechnic, 1989. *Address:* Grove Farm, Yatton Keynell, Chippenham, Wilts SN14 7BS. *T:* (01249) 782289. *Club:* Farmers. *Died 17 July 2015.*

GASKIN, Prof. Maxwell, DFC 1944 (and Bar 1945); Jaffrey Professor of Political Economy, Aberdeen University, 1965–85, then Professor Emeritus; *b* 18 Nov. 1921; *s* of late Albert and Beatrice Gaskin; *m* 1952, Brenda Patricia, *yr d* of late Rev. William D. Stewart; one *s* three *d*. *Educ:* Quarry Bank Sch., Liverpool; Liverpool Univ. (MA). Lever Bros Ltd, 1939–41. Served War, RAF Bomber Comd, 1941–46. Economist, Raw Cotton Commn, 1949–50; Asst Lectr, Liverpool Univ., 1950–51; Lectr and Sen. Lectr, Glasgow Univ., 1951–65; Visiting Sen. Lectr, Nairobi Univ., 1964–65. Consultant to Sec. of State for Scotland, 1965–87. Member, Committee of Inquiry: into Bank Interest Rates (N Ire.), 1965–66; into Trawler Safety, 1967–68; Member and Chairman: Wages Councils, 1967–93; Bd of Management for Foresterhill and Associated Hosps, 1971–74; Independent Member: Scottish Agricl Wages Bd, 1972–90; EDC for Civil Engineering, 1978–84; Chm., Industry Strategy Cttee for Scotland (Building and Civil Engrg EDCs), 1974–76. Director: Offshore Med. Support Ltd, 1978–85; Aberdeen Univ. Research & Industrial Services, 1981–85. President: Section F, British Assoc., 1978–79; Scottish Economic Soc., 1981–84. *Publications:* The Scottish Banks, 1965; (co-author and ed) North East Scotland: a survey of its development potential, 1969; (jtly) The Economic Impact of North Sea oil on Scotland, 1978; (ed) The Political Economy of Tolerable Survival, 1981; articles in economic and banking jls; reports on the international coal trade. *Recreation:* music and country life. *Address:* 22 North Mill Place, Halstead, Essex CO9 2FA. *T:* (01787) 478062. *Died 7 April 2012.*

GASSON, John Gustav Haycraft, CB 1990; Head of Policy and Legal Services Group, Lord Chancellor's Department, 1987–91; *b* 2 Aug. 1931; *s* of late Dr and Mrs S. G. H. Gasson; *m* 1964, Lesley, *d* of L. L. Thomas, Nyamandhlovu, Zimbabwe; two *s* one *d*. *Educ:* Diocesan Coll., Rondebosch, Cape Town; Cape Town Univ. (BA); Pembroke Coll., Oxford (Rhodes Schol. Rhodesia 1953; MA, BCL). Called to the Bar, Gray's Inn, 1957; Advocate of High Court of S Rhodesia, 1959; Lord Chancellor's Dept, 1964; Sec., Law Commn, 1982–87. *Recreations:* cycling, gardening. *Address:* The White House, Candys Lane, Blandford Road, Shillingstone, Dorset DT11 0SF. *Club:* Bulawayo (Zimbabwe). *Died 9 Feb. 2012.*

GAUTREY, Peter, CMG 1972; CVO 1961; DK (Brunei) 1972; HM Diplomatic Service, retired; High Commissioner in Guyana, 1975–78, concurrently Ambassador (non-resident) to Surinam, 1976–78; *b* 17 Sept. 1918; *s* of late Robert Harry Gautrey, Hindhead, Surrey, and Hilda Morris; *m* 1947, Marguerite Etta Uncles; one *s* one *d*. *Educ:* Abbotsholme Sch., Derbys. Joined Home Office, 1936. Served in Royal Artillery, (Capt.), Sept. 1939–March 1946. Re-joined Home Office; Commonwealth Relations Office, 1948; served in British Embassy, Dublin, 1950–53; UK High Commission, New Delhi, 1955–57 and 1960–63; British Deputy High Commissioner, Bombay, 1963–65; Corps of Diplomatic Service Inspectors, 1965–68; High Commissioner: Swaziland, 1968–71; Brunei, 1972–75. FRSA 1972. *Recreations:* walking, music, art. *Address:* 24 Fort Road, Guildford, Surrey GU1 3TE. *Died 7 Feb. 2014.*

GAVRON, Baron *cr* 1999 (Life Peer), of Highgate in the London Borough of Camden; **Robert Gavron,** CBE 1990; Chairman: Folio Society Ltd, since 1982; St Ives plc, 1964–93; Proprietor, Carcanet Press Ltd, since 1983; *b* 13 Sept. 1930; *s* of Nathaniel and Leah Gavron; *m* 1955, Hannah Fyvel (*d* 1965); one *s* (and one *s* decd); *m* 1967, Felicia Nicolette Coates (marr. diss. 1987); two *d*; *m* 1989, Katharine Gardiner (*née* Macnair). *Educ:* Leighton Park Sch.; St Peter's Coll., Oxford (MA; Hon. Fellow, 1992). Called to the Bar, Middle Temple, 1955. Entered printing industry, 1955; founded St Ives Gp, 1964 (public co., 1985). Director: Octopus Publishing plc, 1975–87; Electra Management Plc, 1981–91; Chm., Guardian Media Group plc, 1997–2000; Dir, National Gallery Company (formerly National Gallery Publications) Ltd, 1996–2001 (Chm., 1996–98). Chm., Open Coll. of the Arts, 1991–96 (Trustee, 1987–96); Dir, Royal Opera House, 1992–98. Trustee: Nat. Gall., 1994–2001; Scott Trust, 1997–2000; IPPR, 1991–2010 (Treas., 1994–2000). Gov., LSE, 1997–2002. Hon. Fellow: RCA, 1990; RSL 1996. Hon. Mem., Poetry Soc.; Hon. Life Mem., Barbados Cricket Assoc., 2010. *Publications:* (jtly) The Entrepreneurial Society, 1998. *Recreations:* books, music. *Address:* 44 Eagle Street, WC1R 4FS. *T:* (020) 7400 4300. *Club:* MCC. *Died 7 Feb. 2015.*

GAZE, Dr (Raymond) Michael, FRS 1972; FRSE 1964; Head, Medical Research Council Neural Development and Regeneration Group, Edinburgh University, 1984–92, Hon. Professor, since 1986; *b* 22 June 1927; *s* of late William Mercer Gaze and Kathleen Grace Gaze (*née* Bowhill); *m* 1957, Robinetta Mary Armfelt; one *s* two *d*. *Educ:* at home; Sch. of Medicine, Royal Colleges, Edinburgh; Oxford Univ. (MA, DPhil). LRCPE, LRCSE, LRFPSG. House Physician, Chelmsford and Essex Hosp., 1949; National Service, RAMC, 1953–55; Lectr, later Reader, Dept of Physiology, Edinburgh Univ., 1955–70; Alan Johnston, Lawrence and Moseley Research Fellow, Royal Soc., 1962–66; Head, Div. of Developmental Biol., 1970–83, Dep. Dir 1977–83, Nat. Inst. for Med. Research. Visiting Professor: of Theoretical Biology, Univ. of Chicago, 1972; of Biology, Middlesex Hosp. Med. Sch., 1972–74. *Publications:* The Formation of Nerve

Connections, 1970; Editor, 1975–88, and contrib., Development (formerly Jl Embryology and Exper. Morphology); various papers on neurobiology in Jl Physiology, Qly Jl Exper. Physiology, Proc. Royal Soc., etc. *Recreations:* drawing, hill-walking, music. *Address:* 37 Sciennes Road, Edinburgh EH9 1NS. *T:* (0131) 667 6915. *Died 11 Sept. 2012.*

GEACH, Prof. Peter Thomas, FBA 1965; Professor of Logic, University of Leeds, 1966–81; *b* 29 March 1916; *o s* of Prof. George Hender Geach, IES, and Eleonora Frederyka Adolfina Sgonina; *m* 1941, Gertrude Elizabeth Margaret Anscombe, FBA (*d* 2001); three *s* four *d*. *Educ:* Balliol Coll., Oxford (Domus Schol.; Hon. Fellow, 1979). 2nd cl. Class, Hon. Mods, 1936; 1st cl. Lit. Hum., 1938. Gladstone Research Student, St Deiniol's Library, Hawarden, 1938–39; philosophical research, Cambridge, 1945–51; University of Birmingham: Asst Lectr in Philosophy, 1951; Lectr, 1952; Sen. Lectr, 1959; Reader in Logic, 1961. Vis. Prof., Univ. of Warsaw, 1985. Lectures: Stanton, in the Philosophy of Religion, Cambridge, 1971–74; Hägerström, Univ. of Uppsala, 1975; O'Hara, Univ. of Notre Dame, 1978. Forschungspreis, A. Von Humboldt Stiftung, 1983; Aquinas Medal, Amer. Catholic Philosophical Assoc., 2000. Papal medal, Pro Ecclesia et Pontifice, 1999. *Publications:* Mental Acts, 1957; Reference and Generality, 1962, 4th edn 2006; (with G. E. M. Anscombe) Three Philosophers, 1961; God and the Soul, 1969; Logic Matters, 1972; Reason and Argument, 1976; Providence and Evil, 1977; The Virtues, 1977; Truth, Love, and Immortality: an introduction to McTaggart's philosophy, 1979; Truth and Hope, 2001; articles in Mind, Philosophical Review, Analysis, Ratio, etc. *Recreations:* reading stories of detection, mystery and horror; collecting and annotating old bad logic texts. *Address:* 3 Richmond Road, Cambridge CB4 3PP. *T:* (01223) 353950. *Club:* Union Society (Oxford). *Died 21 Dec. 2013.*

GEDLING, Raymond, CB 1969; Deputy Secretary, Department of Health and Social Security, 1971–77; *b* 3 Sept. 1917; *s* of late John and Mary Gedling; *m* 1956, Joan Evelyn Chapple (*d* 2000); one *s*. *Educ:* Grangefield Grammar Sch., Stockton-on-Tees. Entered Civil Service as Executive Officer, Min. of Health, 1936; Asst Principal, 1942, Principal, 1947. Cabinet Office, 1951–52; Principal Private Sec. to Minister of Health, 1952–55; Asst Sec., 1955; Under-Sec., 1961; Asst Under-Sec. of State, Dept of Educn and Science, 1966–68; Dep. Sec., Treasury, 1968–71. *Recreations:* walking, chess. *Address:* 27 Wallace Fields, Epsom, Surrey KT17 3AX. *T:* (020) 8393 9060. *Died 5 Feb. 2011.*

GEE, Anthony Hall; QC 1990; **His Honour Judge Anthony Gee;** a Circuit Judge, since 2004; *b* 4 Nov. 1948; *s* of late Harold Stephenson Gee and Marjorie Gee (*née* Hall); *m* 1975, Gillian Pauline Glover, St Annes-on-Sea; one *s* two *d*. *Educ:* Cambs High School for Boys; Chester City Grammar Sch.; Inns of Court School of Law. Called to the Bar, Gray's Inn, 1972; Mem., Northern Circuit, 1972–; a Recorder, 1985–2004. Mem., Probation Bd, 2004–. *Recreations:* golf, cricket, tennis, fly-fishing, fell walking. *Address:* Manchester Crown Court, Crown Square, Manchester M3 3FL. *Clubs:* Bramhall Golf; Lancashire County Cricket; Northern Lawn Tennis (Didsbury). *Died 25 Aug. 2013.*

GEFFEN, Dr Terence John; Medical Adviser, Capsticks Solicitors, 1990–99; *b* 17 Sept. 1921; *s* of late Maximilian W. Geffen and Maia Geffen (later Reid); *m* 1965, Judith Anne Steward; two *s*. *Educ:* St Paul's Sch.; University Coll., London; UCH. MD, FRCP. House Phys., UCH, 1943; RAMC, 1944–47; hosp. posts, Edgware Gen. Hosp., Hampstead Gen. Hosp., UCH, 1947–55; Min. of Health (later DHSS), 1956–82, SPMO, 1972–82; Consultant in Public Health Medicine, NW Thames RHA, 1982–90. FRSocMed 1991. *Publications:* various in BMJ, Lancet, Clinical Science, etc. *Recreations:* music, reading, bridge. *Address:* 2 Stonehill Close, SW14 8RP. *T:* (020) 8878 0516. *Died 28 Oct. 2015.*

GEMMILL, Moira Elizabeth; Director of Capital Programmes, Royal Collection Trust, since 2015; *b* Campbeltown, Argyll, 18 Sept. 1959; *d* of John A. and Helen C. Gemmill. *Educ:* Campbeltown Grammar Sch.; Glasgow Sch. of Art (BA Hons 1981). Magazine design for various pubns, 1981–88; publisher, CityGirl mag., 1983–88; Head: of Exhibns, Aberdeen Art Gall., 1988–98; of Design and Exhibns, Mus. of London, 1998–2002; Dir, Design, Exhibns and FuturePlan, V&A Mus., 2002–15; Board Director: V&A Dundee (Design Dundee Ltd), 2011–; Soc. for Envmtl Graphic Design, 2011–. FRSA 2003. Hon. FRIBA 2011. *Recreations:* architecture, design, film, music, friends, family, golf. *Address:* c/o Royal Collection Trust, York House, St James's Palace, SW1A 1BQ. *E:* moira.gemmill@royalcollection.org.uk, megemmill@gmail.com. *Died 9 April 2015.*

GEMS, Iris Pamela, (Pam); playwright; *b* 1 Aug. 1925; *d* of late James Price and Elsie Mabel Price; *m* 1949, Keith Leopold Gems; two *s* two *d*. *Educ:* Brockenhurst Grammar Sch.; Manchester Univ. *Plays* include: Betty's Wonderful Christmas, 1972; The Project, 1974; Dusa, Fish, Stas and Vi, 1976; Queen Christina, 1977; Piaf, 1978, revival, 2008; Franz into April, 1978; Ladybird Ladybird, 1979; The Treat, 1979; Pasionaria, 1981; Aunt Mary, 1982; Camille, 1985; The Danton Affair, 1986; The Blue Angel, 1991; Deborah's Daughter, 1994; I Wish You Love, 1995; Stanley, 1995 (Evening Standard Award, Best Play; Olivier award for best play, 1997); Marlene, 1997; The Snow Palace, 1998; Natalya Ivanovna, 1998; Nelson, 2005; Mrs Pat, 2006; plays performed RSC, RNT, Hampstead, West End and Broadway; (adapted): Uncle Vanya, Royal Court, 1978; The Cherry Orchard, RNT, 1984; The Seagull, RNT, 1991; Yerma, Royal Exchange, Manchester, 2003; The Lady from the Sea, Almeida, 2003; The Little Mermaid, Greenwich, 2004; The Cherry Orchard, Crucible, Sheffield, 2007. *Publications:* (novels) Mrs Frampton, 1986; Bon Voyage, Mrs Frampton, 1988. *Recreation:* working. *Address:* c/o Rose Cobbe, United Agents, 12–26 Lexington Street, W1F 0LE. *Died 13 May 2011.*

GEORGALA, Prof. Douglas Lindley, CBE 1986; PhD; FIFST; Director of Food Research, Agricultural and Food Research Council, 1988–94; External Professor, University of Leeds, 1993–2008; independent scientific consultant, 1994–2002; *b* 2 Feb. 1934; *s* of late John Michael Georgala and of Izetta Iris Georgala; *m* 1959, Eulalia Catherina Lochner; one *s* one *d*. *Educ:* South African College Sch., Cape Town; Univ. of Stellenbosch (BScAgric); Univ. of Aberdeen (PhD). FIFST 1987. Research Officer, Fishing Research Inst., Univ. of Cape Town, 1957–60; Research Microbiologist, 1960–69, Division Manager, 1969–72, Head of Laboratory, 1977–86, Unilever Colworth Laboratory; Technical Member, Unilever Meat Products Co-ordination, 1973–77; Mem., Unilever Res. Div., 1987–88; Indust. Consultant, Biotechnology Unit, DTI, 1987–88. Chairman: Fisheries Res. Bd, 1980–84; Adv. Cttee of Food Science Dept, Leeds Univ., 1984–88; Scientific and Technical Cttee, Food and Drink Fedn, 1986–88; Adv. Cttee on Microbiological Safety of Food, 1996–2004 (Mem., 1991–; Acting Chm., 1994–95); Member: ACARD, 1980–83; Food Cttee, 1984–88, Strategy Bd, 1991–93, AFRC; Co-ordinating Cttee for Marine Science and Technol., 1988–89; Food Adv. Cttee, 1989–94; Council, Inst. of Food Science and Technology, 1992–94; Ownership Bd, Centre for Envmt, Fisheries and Agric. Sci., 1997–2001. Vis. Prof., UEA, Leeds and Reading Univs, 1988–94. Scientific Governor, British Nutrition Foundn, 1992–2002. Trustee, World Humanity Action Trust, 1999–2000. FRSA 1984. *Publications:* papers in jls of general microbiology, applied bacteriology, hygiene, etc. *Recreations:* gardening, recorded music. *Died 30 May 2013.*

GEORGE, Sir Arthur (Thomas), AO 1987; Kt 1972; solicitor and company director; *b* 17 Jan. 1915; *s* of late Thomas George; *m* 1939, Renee (AM 1998) (*d* 2010), *d* of Anthony Freeleagus; one *d*. *Educ:* Sydney High Sch., NSW. Chm. and Man. Dir, George Investment Pty Ltd Group, 1943; Chm., Australia Solenoid Holdings Ltd, 1967. Chm., Assoc. for Classical Archæology, Sydney Univ., 1966–2002. Chm., Australian Soccer Fedn, 1969–88; Comr, Australian Sports Commn, 1986–89; Member: Exec., FIFA, 1981–94; Organising Cttee, 1983 World Youth Championship. Founder, The Arthur T. George Foundation Ltd, 1972.

Fellow, Confedn of Australian Sport, 1985; Hon. Fellow, Senate of Univ. of Sydney, 1985. Gold Order of Merit, FIFA, 1994. Coronation Medal; Silver Jubilee Medal, 1977; Centenary Medal, Australia, 2003. Grand Commander (Keeper of the Laws), Cross of St Marks, and Gold Cross of Mount Athos, Greek Orthodox Church; Order of Phoenix (Greece). *Recreations:* sport, especially Association football, etc. *Address:* Unit 15, 47 William Street, Double Bay, NSW 2028, Australia. *Died 4 Sept. 2013.*

GEORGE, Prof. Donald William, AO 1979; Vice-Chancellor and Principal, University of Newcastle, New South Wales, 1975–86; *b* 22 Nov. 1926; *s* of late H. W. George, Sydney; *m* 1950, Lorna M. Davey, Parkes, NSW; one *s* one *d*. *Educ:* Univ. of Sydney (BSc, BE, PhD). FTSE, FIET, FIMechE, FIEAust, FAIP. Lectr, Elec. Engrg, NSW Univ. of Technology, 1949–53; Exper. Officer, UKAEA, Harwell, 1954–55; Res. Officer, Sen. Res. Officer, AAEC, Harwell and Lucas Heights, 1956–59; Sen. Lectr, Elec. Engrg, Univ. of Sydney, 1960–66; Associate Prof., Elec. Engrg, Univ. of Sydney, 1967–68; P. N. Russell Prof. of Mech. Engrg, Univ. of Sydney, 1969–74. Chairman: Australian-American Educational Foundn, 1977–84; Australian Atomic Energy Commn, 1976–83. Hon. Life Trustee, Asian Inst. of Technology, 1998 (Trustee, 1978–98). Hon. DEng Newcastle, NSW, 1986; Hon. DTech Asian Inst. of Technol., Bangkok, 1999. *Publications:* numerous sci. papers and techn. reports. *Address:* 150 Maidens Brush Road, Wyoming, NSW 2250, Australia. *T:* (2) 43255079. *Died 1 Jan. 2014.*

GEORGE, Henry Ridyard, CBE 1979; Director of Petroleum Engineering, Department of Energy, 1973–81; *b* 14 May 1921; *s* of Charles Herbert George and Mary Ridyard; *m* 1st, 1948, Irene May Myers (*d* 1981); one *s*; 2nd, 1985, Gwen (*née* Gooderham) (*d* 2004), *widow* of Prof. E. O'Farrell Walsh. *Educ:* George Dixon's Secondary Sch., Birmingham; Univ. of Birmingham (1st Cl. Hons degree, Oil Engrg and Refining and Petroleum Technol., 1941). Served War, REME/IEME, 1941–46 (2nd Lieut, later Captain). Pet. Engr with Royal Dutch/Shell Gp, 1947–68: service in USA, Holland, Brunei, Nigeria and Venezuela in a variety of positions, incl. Chief Pet. Engr in last 3 countries; Dept of Energy, 1968–81. *Recreations:* gardening, bridge. *Address:* Flat 3, 269 Dyke Road, Hove, E Sussex BN3 6PB. *T:* (01273) 540297. *Died 13 Sept. 2012.*

GERARD, Ronald, OBE 1987; philanthropist; *b* 30 Oct. 1925; *s* of Samuel and Caroline Gerard; *m* 1952, Patricia Krieger; one *s* one *d*. *Educ:* Regent Street Polytechnic; College of Estate Management. FRICS 2000 (FSVA 1968). Royal Engineers, 1943–47, Italy and Egypt; articled to a City Chartered Surveyor, 1947–50; Principal, R. P. Gerard & Co., Surveyors and Valuers, 1952–59; Jt Man. Dir, 1959–87, Chm., 1982–87, London & Provincial Shop Centres Plc. Chm., Ronald Gerard Charitable Trust, 1983–95; also funded many charitable enterprises, several of them eponymous, incl. student accommodation at Pembroke Coll., Oxford, Ronald Gerard Renal Res. Fund, Royal Free Hosp., 1987, medical research, facilities for the handicapped and the general public. Funded: restoration of works of art incl. Barry murals at RSA and Verrio mural at Royal Hosp., Chelsea; restoration of Tavern Room Adam ceiling and redesign of Gerard Bar, RSA. Special interest in mil. charitable orgns, incl. Army Benevolent Fund, and Not Forgotten Assoc.; donated Sovereign's Mace, 2002 and Carved Crest of Coat of Arms, by Sarah Berry, 2005 to Royal Hosp., Chelsea. Hon. Benefactor, William Shipley Gp for RSA Hist., 2005 (Barry Medal, 2005). Work in youth cricket includes: President: London Community Cricket Assoc., 1992–94; London Cricket Coll., 1992–94; Middlesex Cricket Union, 1992–95; Middlesex Colts Assoc., 1995–97; Middlesex CCC, 1999–2001 (Life Vice-Pres., 1992; Trustee, Youth Centenary Trust, 1984–94); Vice-President: English Schools Cricket Assoc., 1981–; Seaxe Club, 2001–; Patron, Wilf Slack Young Cricketers Develt Trust, 1999; Hon. Mem., Middlesex Cricket Bd, 2002; Mem. Council, Lord's Taverners, 1984–90 (Hon. Benefactor). Patron, Brooklands Club, Brooklands Motor Mus., 1991. Liveryman, Glass Sellers' Co., 1990; Freeman, City of London, 1990. FRSA (Hon. Benefactor). KStJ 1992. Granted Arms, 1989. *Clubs:* Carlton, MCC (Life Mem.). *Died 10 Jan. 2015.*

GERRARD, Ronald Tilbrook, FREng, FICE, FCIWEM; Senior Partner, Binnie & Partners, Consulting Engineers, 1974–83; *b* 23 April 1918; *s* of Henry Thomas Gerrard and Edith Elizabeth Tilbrook; *m* 1950, Cecilia Margaret Bremner; three *s* (one *d* decd). *Educ:* Imperial Coll. of Science and Technology, Univ. of London. BSc(Eng). FCGI; FICE 1957; FIWE 1965; FREng (FEng 1979); MEIC. Served War, RE, 1939–45. Resident Engr, sea defence and hydro-electric works, 1947–50; Asst Engr, design of hydro-power schemes in Scotland and Canada, 1951–54; Binnie & Partners: Sen. Engr, 1954; Partner, 1959; resp. for hydro-power, water supply, river engrg, coast protection and indust. works in UK and overseas. Chm., Assoc. of Cons. Engrs, 1969–70; Mem. Council, ICE, 1974–77. Telford Silver Medal, ICE, 1968. *Publications:* (jtly) 4 papers to ICE. *Address:* 6 Ashdown Road, Epsom, Surrey KT17 3PL. *T:* (01372) 724834. *Club:* Athenæum. *Died 10 Feb. 2013.*

GERRARD-WRIGHT, Maj.-Gen. Richard Eustace John, CB 1985; CBE 1977 (OBE 1971; MBE 1963); DL; Director, Territorial Army and Cadets, 1982–85; *b* 9 May 1930; 2nd *s* of Rev. Robert Lancelot Gerrard-Wright; *m* 1960, Susan Kathleen, *d* of Lt-Col Frederick Walter Young, MBE, Royal Lincolnshire Regt; two *s* one *d* (and one *d* decd). *Educ:* Christ's Hospital; RMA Sandhurst. Commnd Royal Lincolnshire Regt, 1949; served Egypt, Germany and UK, 1950–55; Malaya, 1955–58 (despatches, 1958); Instructor, RMA Sandhurst, 1958–62 (2nd E Anglian Regt, 1960); Staff Coll., India, 1962–63; served Kenya, Aden, Malta, Malaya, 1963–70 (Royal Anglian Regt, 1964); Bn Comdr, UK, Germany, NI, 1970–73 (despatches 1973); Comdr, 39 Inf. Bde, Belfast, 1975–77; Nat. Defence Coll., Canada, 1977–78; Chief of Staff, 1 (Br) Corps, 1978–79; GOC Eastern District, 1980–82. Dep. Col, Royal Anglian Regt, 1975–80; Col Comdt, Queen's Div., 1981–84. Pres., SSAFA Forces Help, Lincs, 1998–2010. Chief Exec. and Sec., Hurlingham Club, 1985–87. DL Cambs, 1993–97; DL Lincs 1997–. *Address:* 21 Market Place, Folkingham, Sleaford, Lincs NG34 0SE. *Clubs:* Army and Navy, MCC; Free Foresters. *Died 12 May 2012.*

GHODSE, Prof. (Abdol) Hamid, Hon. CBE 1999; MD, PhD, DSc; FRCP, FRCPsych; Professor of Psychiatry and Addictive Behaviour, 1987–2003, then Professor Emeritus of International Drug Policy, and Director, International Centre for Drug Policy (formerly Centre for Addiction Studies), since 1992, St George's, University of London (formerly University of London at St George's Hospital Medical School); Hon. Consultant Psychiatrist: St George's Hospital, since 1978; Springfield University Hospital, since 1978; *b* 30 April 1938; *s* of Abdol Rahim Ghods and Batool Daneshmand; *m* 1973, Barbara Bailin; two *s* one *d*. *Educ:* Esfehan, Tabriz and Tehran; American Univ., Beirut (Schol. 1958); MD Iran 1965; DPM 1974; PhD 1976, DSc 2002, London. FRCPsych 1985; FRCP 1992; MFPHM 1996, FFPH (FFPHM 1997); FRCPE 1997. Lieut, Iranian Health Corps, 1965–67. Postgrad. trng, Morgannwg Hosp., Wales, and St Bartholomew's and Maudsley Hosps, London, 1968–74; res. psychiatrist, Inst. of Psychiatry, Univ. of London, 1974–78; Consultant Psychiatrist, St Thomas' Hosp., 1978–88; Hon. Consultant, Public Health, Wandsworth PCT (formerly Merton, Sutton and Wandsworth HA), 1987–. Vis. Prof., Keele Univ., 2002–05. Mem. Council, St George's Hosp. Med. Sch., 1993–96. Co-ordinator, Higher Degrees in Psychiatry, Univ. of London, 1993–2009 (Chm., Subject Panel in Psychiatry, 2003–09; Mem., Medical Studies Cttee, 2003–09). Director: Regl Drug and Alcohol Team, SW Thames RHA, 1991–97; Medical Council on Alcoholism, 1996–2006 (Patron, 2011–); Addiction Resource Agency for Comrs, 1997–2004; Nat. Clinical Assessment Authy, 2001–05; Nat. Patient Safety Agency, 2005–. Member: WHO Adv. Panel, 1979–; WHO Prog. Planning Wkg Gp, 1986–89; Scientific Cttee on Tobacco and Health, 2000–; Vice-Chm., London S Sub-Cttee, NHS Clinical Excellence Awards, 2004–06; Med. Dir, Adv. Cttee on Clin. Excellence Awards, DoH, 2006–09; Convenor, Mem., Rapporteur and Chm. of various WHO Expert Cttees and Wkg Gps on Drug Dependence, 1980–; Chm., CMO's Internat. Health Adv. Bd, 2009–10. Advr, BNF, 1984–; Clinical Advr, Parly and Health Service Ombudsman, 2004–06. Editor: Internat. Jl Social

Psychiatry, 1982–2000; Substance Misuse Section, Current Opinion in Psychiatry, 1994–2001; Internat. Psychiatry, 2003–. Royal College of Psychiatrists: Mem., Exec. Cttee, Substance Misuse Faculty, 1981–95; Chm., Substance Misuse Sect., 1990–94; Mem. Council, 1990–94, 2000–01; Mem., Court of Electors, 1993–99; Vice-Pres., 2000–02; Dir, Bd of Internat. Affairs, 2001–07; Chm., Honours Cttee, RCPsych, 2004–; President: Assoc. for Prevention of Addiction, 1984–90; Internat. Narcotics Control Bd, 1993–95, 1997–99, 2000–02, 2004–06, 2008, 2010–12 (Mem., 1992–); European Collaborating Centres for Addiction Studies, 1995–. Hon. Sec., Assoc. of Profs of Psychiatry, 1990–2002 (Chm., 2002–); Convenor, Assoc. of European Profs of Psychiatry, 1996–; Mem., Fedn of Assocs of Clinical Profs. McLeod Prof., SA, 1990; Hon. Professor: Beijing Med. Univ., 1997; Peking Univ., 2000. Devised Ghodse Opiate Addiction Test (US, German, French and UK patents); invented pupillometer for measuring anisocoria (European, Canadian and US patents). Hon. Fellow: World Psychiatric Assoc., 2008; St George's Univ. of London, 2011; FHEA 2007; Internat. FAPA 2010. Lifetime Achievement Award, RCPsych, 2011. *Publications:* (jtly) Misuse of Drugs, 1986, 3rd edn 1996; (jtly) Psychoactive Drugs: improving prescribing practices, 1988 (trans. 8 langs); Drugs and Addictive Behaviour: a guide to treatment, 1989, 4th edn as Ghodse's Drugs and Addictive Behaviour: a guide to treatment, 2010; (ed jtly) Substance Abuse and Dependence, 1990; (ed jtly) Drug Misuse and Dependence, 1990; (ed jtly) Doctors and their Health, 2000; (ed jtly) Young People and Substance Misuse, 2004; Addiction at Work, 2005; International Drug Control into the 21st Century, 2008; (ed jtly) Substance Abuse Disorders, 2011; International Perspectives on Mental Health, 2011; numerous articles on self-poisoning, substance misuse and med. educn. *Recreations:* reading, cycling. *Address:* St George's, University of London, International Centre for Drug Policy, Cranmer Terrace, SW17 0RE. *T:* (020) 8725 2624. *Club:* Athenæum. *Died 27 Dec. 2012.*

GIBB, Sir Francis Ross, (Sir Frank), Kt 1987; CBE 1982; BSc; FREng; FICE; Chairman and Chief Executive, Taylor Woodrow Group, 1985–89 (Joint Managing Director, 1979–85, and a Joint Deputy Chairman, 1983–85); President, Taylor Woodrow Construction, since 1985 (Chairman, 1978–85); *b* 29 June 1927; *s* of Robert Gibb and Violet Mary Gibb; *m* 1st, 1950, Wendy Marjorie Fowler (*d* 1997); one *s* two *d*; 2nd, 2000, Kirsten Harwood. *Educ:* Loughborough Coll. BSc(Eng); CEng. Dir, 1963–70, Man. Dir, then Jt Man. Dir, 1970–84, Taylor Woodrow Construction; Director: Taylor Woodrow Internat., 1969–85; Taylor Woodrow plc, 1972–89; Chm., Taywood Santa Fe, 1975–85. Jt Dep. Chm., Seaforth Maritime Ltd, 1986–89; Director: Seaforth Maritime Hldgs, 1978–89; (ind.) Energy Saving Trust Ltd, 1992–99 (Chm., 1995–98); non-executive: Eurotunnel plc, 1986–87; Babcock Internat. Group, 1989–97; Steetley plc, 1990–92; Nuclear Electric plc, 1990–94; H. R. Wallingford, 1995–2008; AMCO Corporation plc, 1995–99. Member: Construction Industry Adv. Cttee, HSE, 1978–81; Gp of Eight, 1979–81; Board, British Nuclear Associates, 1980–88 (Chm., Agrément Bd, 1980–82); Chm., Nat. Nuclear Corp., 1981–88. Mem. Council, CBI, 1979–80, 1985–90. Dir, Holiday Pay Scheme, 1980–84 and Trustee, Benefits Scheme, 1980–84, Building and Civil Engrg Trustees. Federation of Civil Engineering Contractors: Vice-Chm., 1978–79; Chm., 1979–80; Vice Pres., 1980–84; Pres., 1984–87; Vice-Pres., ICE, 1988–90. Freeman, City of London, 1978. Hon. FINucE 1984; Hon. FCGI 1990. Hon. DTech Loughborough, 1989. *Recreations:* ornithology, gardening, walking, music. *Address:* Ross Gibb Consultants, 11 Latchmoor Avenue, Gerrards Cross, Bucks SL9 8LJ. *Club:* Arts. *Died 30 May 2013.*

GIBBENS, Barnaby John, OBE 1989; Chairman, Skin Treatment and Research Trust, 1991–2000; *b* 17 April 1935; *s* of late Dr Gerald Gibbens and Deirdre Gibbens; *m* 1st, 1960, Sally Mary Stephenson (marr. diss. 1990); one *s* two *d*; 2nd, 1990, Kristina de Zabala. *Educ:* Winchester College. FCA 1972. Founder, 1962, Dep. Chm., 1962–81, Chm., 1981–90, Computer Analysts & Programmers (later CAP Group, then SEMA Group); Chairman: Enterprise Systems Group Ltd, 1989–96; The Royal Tennis Court, Hampton Court Palace, 1995–2001; Mercator Systems Ltd, 2000–02. Chairman: Computing Services Industry Trng Council, 1984–93; IT Industry Lead Body, 1987–93; IT Trng Accreditation Council, 1991–94; IT Industry Trng Orgn, 1992–95; a Director: National Computing Centre, 1987–90; UK Skills, 1990–2001; Member: Nat. Cttee on Computer Networks, 1978; NCVQ, 1989–92; NCET, 1991–94. Pres., Computing Services Assoc., 1975. Chm., Young IT Technician of the Year, 1993–2000. Founding Master, Co. of Information Technologists, 1987. Hon. Mem., C & G, 1993. FRSA 1993. *Recreations:* golf, Real tennis, music, gardening. *Address:* 12 Kings Road, Wimbledon, SW19 8QN. *T:* (020) 8542 3878. *Clubs:* MCC; Wisley Golf. *Died 4 June 2012.*

GIBBINS, Rev. Dr Ronald Charles; Methodist Minister; Superintendent Minister, Wesley's Chapel, London, 1978–88; *b* 19 Sept. 1922; *s* of Charles and Anne Gibbins; *m* 1949, Olive Ruth (*née* Patchett); one *s* two *d*. *Educ:* London Univ. (BScSociol); Wesley Theological Coll., Bristol; Eden Theological Seminary, US (DMin). Methodist Minister: Bradford, 1948–49; Spennymoor, 1949–50; Middlesbrough, 1950–57; Basildon, 1957–64; East End Mission, London, 1964–78. *Publications:* Mission for the Secular City, 1976; The Lumpen Proletariat, 1979; The Stations of the Resurrection, 1987. *Recreations:* travel, journalism. *Died 26 Aug. 2015.*

GIBBON, His Honour Michael; QC 1974; a Senior Circuit Judge, 1993–99 (a Circuit Judge, 1979–99); *b* 15 Sept. 1930; 2nd *s* of late Frank and Jenny Gibbon; *m* 1956, Malveen Elliot Seager (*d* 2007); two *s* one *d*. *Educ:* Brightlands; Charterhouse; Pembroke Coll., Oxford (MA). Commnd in Royal Artillery, 1949. Called to the Bar, Lincoln's Inn, 1954. A Recorder of the Crown Court, 1972–79; Hon. Recorder, City of Cardiff, 1986–99; Resident Judge, Cardiff Crown Court, 1993–99. Chairman: Electoral Adv. Cttee to Home Sec., 1972; Local Govt Boundary Commn for Wales, 1978–79 (Dep. Chm., 1974–78); Lord Chancellor's Adv. Cttee for S Glam, 1990–2000; Criminal Justice Area Liaison Cttee for S and SW Wales, 1992–99; Mem., Parole Bd, 1986–88. A Chm., Bar Disciplinary Tribunal, 1988. *Recreations:* music, golf. *Clubs:* Cardiff and County (Cardiff); Cardiff Golf. *Died 2 May 2012.*

GIBBONS, Hon. Sir (John) David, KBE 1985; JP; Chairman, Colonial Insurance Co. Ltd, Bermuda, since 1986; *b* 15 June 1927; *s* of late Edmund G. Gibbons, CBE, and Winifred G. Gibbons, MBE; *m* 1958, Lully Lorentzen; three *s* (and one *d* by former *m*). *Educ:* Saltus Grammar Sch., Bermuda; Hotchkiss Sch., Lakeville, Conn; Harvard Univ., Cambridge, Mass (BA). Mem. Govt Boards: Social Welfare Bd, 1949–58; Bd of Civil Aviation, 1958–60; Bd of Educn, 1956–59 (Chm., 1973–74); Trade Develt Bd, 1960–74. MP Bermuda, 1972–84; Minister of Health and Welfare, 1974–75, of Finance, 1975–84; Premier of Bermuda, 1977–82. Chm., Bank of N. T. Butterfield & Son Ltd, Bermuda, 1986–97. Chairman: Bermuda Monetary Authy, 1984–86; Economic Council, Bermuda, 1984–86. Mem., Law Reform Cttee, 1969–72. Mem. Governing Body, subseq. Chm., Bermuda Technical Inst., 1956–70. Trustee, Massachusetts Financial Services, 1988–2002. CCMI. JP Bermuda, 1974. *Recreations:* tennis, golf, ski-ing, swimming. *Address:* Leeward, 5 Leeside Drive, Pembroke HM 05, Bermuda. *T:* (441) 2952396. *Clubs:* Phoenix (Cambridge, Mass); Harvard (New York); Royal Bermuda Yacht, Royal Hamilton Amateur Dinghy, Mid-Ocean, Riddell's Bay Golf, Spanish Point Boat (Bermuda); Lyford Cay (Bahamas). *Died 30 March 2014.*

GIBSON, Joseph, CBE 1980; PhD; CChem, FRSC; FREng, FEI; Coal Science Adviser, National Coal Board, 1981–83 (Member for Science, 1977–81); *b* 10 May 1916; *m* 1944, Lily McFarlane Brown; one *s* one *d*. *Educ:* King's Coll. (now Univ. of Newcastle upon Tyne; MSc, PhD). Res., Northern Coke Res. Lab. 1938; Head of Chemistry Dept, Sunderland Technical Coll., and Lectr, Durham Univ., 1948; Chief Scientist, Northern Div., 1958, and Yorks Div., 1964, NCB; Director: Coal Res. Estab., 1968; Coal Utilisation Res., 1975. President: Inst. of Fuel, 1975–76; BCURA, 1977–81 and 1992– (Chm. 1972–77). Lectures: Cadman Meml, 1980, 1983; Prof. Moore Meml,

1981; Brian H. Morgans Meml, 1983. Coal Science Lecture Medal, 1977; Carbonisation Sci. Medal, 1979. Hon. FIChemE. Hon. DCL Newcastle, 1981. *Publications:* jointly: Carbonisation of Coal, 1971; Coal and Modern Coal Processing, 1979; Coal Utilisation: technology, economics and policy, 1981; papers on coal conversion and utilisation. *Recreations:* bridge, gardening. *Address:* 31 Charlton Close, Charlton Kings, Cheltenham, Glos GL53 8DH. *T:* (01242) 517832. *Died 27 Jan. 2012.*

GIBSON, Madeline; Regional Nursing Officer, Oxford Regional Health Authority, 1973–83; *b* 12 March 1925; *d* of late James William Henry Davis, JP, and Mrs Edith Maude Davis; *m* 1977, Comdr William Milburn Gibson, RN (*d* 1991). *Educ:* Haberdashers' Aske's Hatcham Girls' Sch.; Guy's Hosp. (SRN); British Hosp. for Mothers and Babies, Woolwich; Bristol Maternity Hosp. (SCM). Ward Sister, then Dep. Night Supt, Guy's Hosp., 1949–53; Asst Matron, Guy's Hosp., 1953–57; Admin. Sister then Dep. Matron, St Charles' Hosp., London, 1957–61; Asst Nursing Officer, 1962–68, Chief Regional Nursing Officer, 1968–73, Oxford Regional Hosp. Bd. Formerly Mem., Central Midwives Board. *Recreations:* village community work, theatre. *Address:* Cherry Holt, Middle Street, Islip, Oxon OX5 2SF. *Died 28 Oct. 2014.*

GIBSON, Prof. Quentin Howieson, FRS 1969; Professor of Biochemistry and Molecular Biology, Cornell University, Ithaca, NY, 1966–90, then Emeritus; *b* 9 Dec. 1918; *s* of William Howieson Gibson, OBE, DSc; *m* 1951, Audrey Jane (*d* 2008), *yr d* of G. H. S. Pinsent, CB, CMG, and Katharine Kentisbeare, *d* of Sir George Radford, MP; one *s* three *d*. *Educ:* Repton. MB, ChB, BAO, Belfast, 1941, MD 1944, PhD 1946, DSc 1951. Demonstrator in Physiology, Belfast, 1941–44; Lecturer in Physiology: Belfast, 1944–46; Sheffield Univ., 1946–55; Professor of Biochem., Sheffield Univ., 1955–63; Prof. of Biophys. Chem., Johnson Research Foundn, University of Pennsylvania, 1963–66. Dist. Faculty Fellow, Rice Univ., Houston, 1996–. Fellow, Amer. Acad. of Arts and Sciences, 1971; MNAS 1982. *Recreation:* sailing. *Address:* QHG: Box 58, 80 Lyme Road, Hanover, NH 03755, USA. *Died 16 March 2011.*

GIBSON, Ven. Terence Allen; Archdeacon of Ipswich, 1987–2005, then Archdeacon Emeritus; *b* 23 Oct. 1937; *s* of Fred William Allen and Joan Hazel Gibson. *Educ:* Jesus Coll., Cambridge (MA); Cuddesdon Coll., Oxford. Curate of St Chad, Kirkby, 1963–66; Warden of Centre 63, Kirkby C of E Youth Centre, 1966–75; Rector of Kirkby, Liverpool, 1975–84; RD of Walton, Liverpool, 1979–84; Archdeacon of Suffolk, 1984–87. *Address:* 5 Berry Close, Purdis Farm, Ipswich IP3 8SP. *T:* (01473) 714756. *Died 26 Sept. 2015.*

GIFFORD, Joshua Thomas, (Josh), MBE 1989; racehorse trainer, 1970–2003; *b* 3 Aug. 1941; *s* of late Thomas Gifford and Dinah Florence Gifford (*née* Newman); *m* 1969, Althea Meryl Roger-Smith; one *s* one *d*. Flat racing jockey, 1951–58; National Hunt jockey, 1958–70; rode 700 winners; champion jockey, 1962, 1963, 1967, 1968; National Hunt trainer, 1970–2003; trained 1586 winners, incl. Aldaniti, Grand National, 1981. *Recreations:* cricket, shooting, golf. *Address:* The Downs, Findon, Worthing, Sussex BN14 0RR. *T:* (01903) 872226, *Fax:* (01903) 8777232. *Died 9 Feb. 2011.*

GILBERT, Baron *cr* 1997 (Life Peer), of Dudley, in the co. of West Midlands; **John William Gilbert;** PC 1978; PhD; *b* 5 April 1927; *m* 1st, 1950, Hilary Kenworthy (marr. diss. 1954); one *d* (and one *d* decd); 2nd, 1963, Jean Olive Ross Skinner. *Educ:* Merchant Taylors' Sch.; St John's Coll., Oxford; New York Univ. (PhD in Internat. Economics, Graduate Sch. of Business Administration). Chartered Accountant, Canada. Contested (Lab): Ludlow, 1966; Dudley, March 1968; MP (Lab) Dudley, 1970–74; Dudley E, Feb. 1974–1997. Opposition front-bench spokesman on Treasury affairs, 1972–74; Financial Secretary to the Treasury, 1974–75; Minister for Transport, DoE, 1975–76; Minister of State, MoD, 1976–79 and 1997–99. Member: Select Cttee on Expenditure, 1970–74; Select Cttee on Corporation Tax, 1973; Select Cttee on Defence, 1979–87; Select Cttee on Trade and Industry, 1987–92; Cttee on Intelligence and Security, 1994–97; Chm., PLP Defence Gp, 1981–83; Vice-Chm., Lab. Finance and Industry Group, 1983–92. Member: Fabian Soc.; RUSI; RIIA; IISS; GMB; WWF. FRGS 1993. Hon. LLD Wake Forest, S Carolina, 1983. *Address:* House of Lords, SW1A 0PW. *Club:* Reform. *Died 2 June 2013.*

GILBERT, Rt Hon. Sir Martin (John), Kt 1995; CBE 1990; PC 2009; DLitt; FRSL; historian; Hon. Fellow of Merton College, Oxford, since 1994 (Fellow, 1962–94); Distinguished Fellow, Hillsdale College, Michigan, since 2002; Official Biographer of Sir Winston Churchill, since 1968; *b* 25 Oct. 1936; *s* of late Peter and Miriam Gilbert; *m* 1st, 1963, Helen Constance, *yr d* of late Joseph Robinson, CBE; one *d*; 2nd, 1974, Susan, *d* of late Michael Sacher; two *s*; 3rd, 2005, Esther Poznansky, *d* of late Ben Goldberg. *Educ:* Highgate Sch.; Magdalen Coll., Oxford (MA); DLitt Oxon 1999. Nat. Service (Army), 1955–57; Sen. Research Scholar, St Antony's Coll., Oxford, 1960–62; Vis. Lectr, Budapest Univ., 1961; Res. Asst (sometime Sen. Res. Asst) to Hon. Randolph S. Churchill, 1962–67; Vis. Prof., Univ. of S Carolina, 1965; Recent Hist. Correspt for Sunday Times, 1967; Res. Asst (Brit. Empire) for BBC, 1968; Historical Adviser (Palestine) for Thames Television, 1977–78. Visiting Professor: Tel-Aviv Univ., 1979; Hebrew Univ. of Jerusalem, 1980–82 (Vis. Lectr 1975); UCL, 1995–96; UCSD, 2002; Georgetown Univ., 2003; Visiting Lecturer: Univ. of Cape Town (Caplan Centre), 1984; MoD and Acad. of Sciences, Moscow, 1985; White House, Washington, 2002; India Internat. Centre, Delhi, 2002. Non-Govtl Rep., UN Commn on Human Rights (43rd Session), Geneva, 1987, (44th Session), Geneva, 1988. Mem., Prime Minister's delegns to Israel and Jordan, and to Washington, 1995. Script designer and co-author, Genocide (Acad. Award winner, best doc. feature film), 1981; Historical Consultant to Southern Pictures TV series, Winston Churchill: The Wilderness Years, 1980–81; Historical Adviser, BBC TV, for Auschwitz and the Allies, 1981–82; historical consultant, Yalta 1945, for BBC TV, 1982–83; writer and narrator, Churchill, BBC TV, 1989–91. Governor, Hebrew Univ. of Jerusalem, 1978–. Hon. Fellow, Univ. of Wales Lampeter, 1997. Hon. DLitt: Westminster Coll., Fulton, 1981; Buckingham, 1992; Gratz Coll., Penn, 2000; George Washington Univ., Washington, 2000; Western Ontario, 2003; Hebrew Univ. of Jerusalem, 2004; Ben Gurion, 2011. *Publications:* The Appeasers, 1963 (with Richard Gott), 3rd edn 2001 (trans. German, Polish, Romanian); (ed) Britain and Germany Between the Wars, 1964; The European Powers 1900–1945, 1965, 2nd edn 2002 (trans. Italian, Spanish); Plough My Own Furrow: The Life of Lord Allen of Hurtwood, 1965; (ed) Servant of India: A Study of Imperial Rule 1905–1910, 1966; The Roots of Appeasement, 1966; Recent History Atlas 1860–1960, 1966; Winston Churchill (Clarendon Biogs for young people), 1966; British History Atlas, 1968, 5th edn 2011; American History Atlas, 1968, 6th edn 2009 (trans. Japanese); Jewish History Atlas, 1969, 8th edn 2010 (trans. Spanish, Dutch, Hebrew, Polish, Russian, Hungarian, Italian, Japanese, Chinese); First World War Atlas, 1970, 3rd edn 2008 (trans. Spanish); Winston S. Churchill, vol. iii, 1914–1916, 1971, companion volume (in two parts) 1973; Russian History Atlas, 1972, 4th edn 2007 (trans. Japanese); Sir Horace Rumbold: portrait of a diplomat, 1973; Churchill: a photographic portrait, 1974, 3rd edn 2000; The Arab-Israeli Conflict: its history in maps, 1974, 10th edn 2012 (trans. Spanish, Hebrew); Churchill and Zionism (pamphlet), 1974; Winston S. Churchill, vol. iv, 1917–1922, 1975, companion volume (in three parts), 1977; The Jews in Arab Lands: their history in maps, 1975, illustr. edn, 1976 (trans. Hebrew, Arabic, French, German); Winston S. Churchill, vol. v, 1922–1939, 1976, companion volume, part one, The Exchequer Years 1922–1929, 1980, part two, The Wilderness Years 1929–1935, 1981, part three, The Coming of War 1936–1939, 1982; The Jews of Russia: Illustrated History Atlas, 1976 (trans. Spanish); Jerusalem Illustrated History Atlas, 1977, 4th edn 2008 (trans. Hebrew, Spanish); Exile and Return: The Emergence of Jewish Statehood, 1978; Children's Illustrated Bible Atlas, 1979; Final Journey, the Fate of the Jews of Nazi Europe, 1979 (trans. Dutch, Hebrew); Auschwitz and the Allies, 1981, 3rd edn 2001 (trans. German, Hebrew); Churchill's Political Philosophy,

1981; The Origin of the 'Iron Curtain' speech, 1981 (pamphlet); Atlas of the Holocaust, 1982, 4th edn 2009 (trans. German, Hebrew, French, Polish, Japanese); Winston S. Churchill, vol. vi, Finest Hour, 1939–41, 1983 (Wolfson History Prize, 1983); The Jews of Hope: the plight of Soviet Jewry today, 1984 (trans. Hebrew, Japanese); Jerusalem: rebirth of a city, 1985; The Holocaust: the Jewish tragedy, 1986 (trans. Bulgarian, Macedonian, Portuguese); Winston S. Churchill, vol vii, Road to Victory, 1986; Shcharansky: hero of our time, 1986 (trans. Dutch, Hebrew); Winston S. Churchill, vol. viii, 'Never Despair', 1945–65, 1988; Second World War, 1989, 4th edn 2009 (trans. German, Italian, Portuguese, Japanese, Polish, Spanish, Czech); Churchill, A Life, 1991 (trans. Czech, Italian, Polish, Spanish, Danish, Turkish); Atlas of British Charities, 1993; The Churchill War Papers, vol. 1, At the Admiralty, September 1939–May 1940, 1993; In Search of Churchill, 1994; First World War, a History, 1994, 2nd edn 2008 (trans. Polish, Italian, Spanish, Portuguese, Czech); The Day the War Ended: VE-Day 1945, 1995 (trans. Czech); The Churchill War Papers, vol. 2, Never Surrender, May–December 1940, 1995; Jerusalem in the Twentieth Century, 1996; The Boys: triumph over adversity, 1996 (trans. German); A History of the Twentieth Century, vol. 1, 1900–1933, 1997, vol. 2, 1933–1951, 1998, vol. 3, 1952–1999, 1999 (trans. German, Danish, Polish, Russian, Czech, Chinese); Holocaust Journey, Travelling in Search of the Past, 1997 (trans. Croatian); Israel: a history, 1998, 2nd edn 2008 (trans. Hungarian, Czech, Portuguese); Never Again: an illustrated history of the Holocaust, 2000 (trans. Italian, French, German, Polish, Dutch, Lithuanian); The Churchill War Papers, vol. 3, The Ever-Widening War, 1941, 2000; The Jews in the Twentieth Century: an illustrated history, 2001 (trans. Russian, Italian, Dutch, Danish, French, German, Czech); Letters to Auntie Fori: the 5000 year history of the Jewish people and their faith, 2002 (trans. Italian, German, Polish, Bulgarian, Portuguese, Chinese); The Righteous: the unsung heroes of the Holocaust, 2003 (trans. French, Italian, Bulgarian); D-Day, 2004 (trans. Spanish); Winston Churchill's War Leadership, 2004 (trans. Portuguese, Greek, Czech); Churchill and America, 2005 (trans. Czech); Kristallnacht, Prelude to Destruction, 2006 (trans. Czech, Italian, Korean, Polish, Portuguese); Somme, the Heroism and the Horror of War, 2006 (trans. Dutch, Spanish); The Will of the People, Churchill and Parliamentary Democracy, 2006; Churchill and the Jews, 2007 (trans. Czech, Hebrew); The Story of Israel, 2008 (trans. French); Atlas of the Second World War, 2008, 2nd edn 2009; In Ishmael's House: a history of the Jews in Muslim lands, 2010 (trans. Hebrew); (ed) Churchill: the power of words, 2012; The Churchill Documents, Testing Times, 1942, 2014; Editor: A Century of Conflict: Essays Presented to A. J. P. Taylor, 1966; Churchill, 1967, and Lloyd George, 1968 (Spectrum Books); compiled Jackdaws: Winston Churchill, 1970; The Coming of War in 1939, 1973; contribs historical articles and reviews to jls (incl. Purnell's History of the Twentieth Century, Reader's Digest, New York Rev. of Books, History Today, The Listener). *Recreation:* drawing maps. *Address:* Merton College, Oxford OX1 4JD. *Club:* Athenæum. *Died 3 Feb. 2015.*

GILES, Ann, (Mrs Keith Giles); *see* Howard, A.

GILES, Rear-Adm. Sir Morgan Charles M.; *see* Morgan-Giles.

GILL, Sir Arthur Benjamin Norman, (Sir Ben), Kt 2003; CBE 1996; Managing Director, Hawk Creative Business Park Ltd, since 2007 (Director, since 2007); Director, Hawkhills Consultancy Ltd, since 2004; *b* 1 Jan. 1950; *o s* of William Norman Gill and Annie (Nancy) Gill (*née* Almack); *m* 1973, Carolyn Davis; four *s*. *Educ:* Easingwold Primary Sch.; Barnard Castle Sch.; St John's Coll., Cambridge (MA Agric. 1971). Various posts at Namasagali Coll., Jinja, Uganda, 1972–75; i/c pig unit, Holderness, Humberside, 1975–77; running family farm, Vale of York, 1978–2007. National Farmers' Union: Mem. Council, 1985–2004; Vice-Chm., 1986–87, Chm., 1987–91, Livestock and Wool Cttee; Vice-Pres., 1991–92; Dep. Pres., 1992–98; Pres., 1998–2004. Chairman: Westbury Dairies Ltd, 2004–06; English Apples and Pears Ltd, 2007–; Eden Research plc, 2009– (non-exec. Dir, 2007–); Visit Herefordshire Ltd, 2010–; Meritas Develts Ltd, 2011–; Cawood Scientific, 2011–; Dir, Countrywide Farmers plc, 2004–. Member: AFRC, 1991–94; BBSRC, 1994–97 (Chm., Agricl Systems Directorate, 1994–97; Mem., Biosci. for Industry Panel, 2007–); Mem. Panel, Agric., Natural Resources and Envmt, 1994–95, Agric., Horticulture and Forestry, 1995–99, Technology Foresight, OST. Chairman: Alternative Crops Technology Interaction Network, 1995–2004; Govt Biomass Task Force, 2004–05. Dir, FARM Africa, 1991–98. Mem. Council, Food from Britain, 1999–2005; Mem., Carnegie Commn on Rural Community Develt, 2004–07; Vice-Pres., COPA, 1999–2003; Mem., Governing Council, John Innes Centre, Norwich, 2002–; Mem., Governing Bd, Univ. of Lincoln, 2004–10. President: Confedn of European Agriculture, 2000–04; Potato Growers Res. Assoc., Univ. of Cambridge, 2004–. Vis. Prof., Leeds Univ., 1996–. Patron: Farmers Overseas Action Gp, 1998–; Rural Stress Inf. Network, 2000–07; St John Ambulance Bricks and Wheels Appeal, 2001; Pentalk, 2005–; Trustee: Plants & Us campaign, 2004–; John Innes Foundn, 2010–. FRAgS 1995; FIGD 1998. Hon. DSc: Leeds, 1997; Cranfield, 2000; UWE, 2002; Hon. DCL UEA, 2003. *Recreation:* rowing (Founder Mem., Guy Fawkes Boat Club, York). *Address:* Prospect Farm, Upper Dormington, Hereford HR1 4ED. *Club:* Farmers. *Died 8 May 2014.*

GILL, Rt Rev. Kenneth Edward; Assistant Bishop of Newcastle (full time), 1980–98, an Honorary Assistant Bishop, since 1999; *b* 22 May 1932; *s* of Fred and Elsie Gill; *m* 1957, Edna Hammond; one *s* two *d*. *Educ:* Harrogate Grammar School; Hartley Victoria Coll., Manchester. Ordained in Church of South India, deacon, 1958, presbyter, 1960; Mysore Diocese, 1958–72; Bishop of Karnataka Central Diocese, Church of S India, 1972–80. MA Lambeth, 2004; Hon. DD Serampore, 2006. *Publications:* Meditations on the Holy Spirit, 1979; Count us Equal, 1990; Roots to Fruits, 2001; Darkness to Light, 2004; A Multi-faceted Ministry, 2008. *Recreation:* gardening. *Address:* Kingfisher Lodge, 41 Long Cram, Haddington EH41 4NS. *T:* (01620) 822113. *Died 16 Feb. 2013.*

GILLES, Prof. Dennis Cyril; Professor of Computing Science, University of Glasgow, 1966–90; *b* 7 April 1925; *s* of George Cyril Gilles and Gladys Alice Gilles (*née* Batchelor); *m* 1955, Valerie Mary Gardiner; two *s* two *d*. *Educ:* Sidcup Gram. Sch.; Imperial Coll., University of London. Demonstrator, Asst Lectr, Imperial Coll., 1945–47; Asst Lectr, University of Liverpool, 1947–49; Mathematician, Scientific Computing Service, 1949–55; Research Asst, University of Manchester, 1955–57; Dir of Computing Lab., University of Glasgow, 1957–66. *Publications:* contribs to Proc. Royal Society and other scientific jls. *Address:* Elmtree, Lochard Road, Aberfoyle, Stirlingshire FK8 3SZ. *T:* (01877) 389070. *Died 5 Oct. 2013.*

GILLES, Prof. Chevalier Herbert Michael Joseph, CMG 2005; MD; FRCP, FFPH; Alfred Jones and Warrington Yorke Professor of Tropical Medicine, University of Liverpool, 1972–86, then Emeritus; *b* 10 Sept. 1921; *s* of Joseph and Clementine Gilles; *m* 1955, Wilhelmina Caruana (*d* 1972); three *s* one *d*; *m* 1979, Dr Mejra Kačić-Dimitri. *Educ:* St Edward's Coll., Malta; Royal Univ. of Malta (MD). Rhodes Schol. 1943. MSc Oxon; FMCPH (Nig.), DTM&H. Served War of 1939–45 (1939–45 Star, Africa Star, VM). Mem., Scientific Staff, MRC Lab., Gambia, 1954–58; University of Ibadan: Lectr, Tropical Med., 1958–63; Prof. of Preventive and Social Med., 1963–65; Liverpool University: Sen. Lectr, Tropical Med., 1965–70; Prof. of Tropical Med. (Personal Chair), 1970; Dean, Liverpool Sch. of Tropical Medicine, 1978–83. Vis. Prof., Tropical Medicine, Univ. of Lagos, 1965–68; Royal Society Overseas Vis. Prof., Univ. of Khartoum, Sudan, 1979–80; Hon. Prof. of Tropical Medicine, Sun-Yat-Sen Med. Coll., Guangzhou, People's Republic of China, 1984; Visiting Professor: Public Health, Univ. of Malta, 1989–; Internat. Health, Royal Colls of Surgeons, Ireland, 1994–; Tropical Medicine, Mahidol Univ., Bangkok, 1994–. Consultant Physician in Tropical Medicine, Liverpool AHA(T) and Mersey RHA, 1965–86; Consultant in

Malariology to the Army, 1974–86; Consultant in Tropical Medicine to the RAF, 1978–86, to the DHSS, 1980–86. Pres., RSTM&H, 1985–87; Vice President: Internat. Fedn of Tropical Medicine, 1988–92; Liverpool Sch. of Tropical Medicine, 1991; Hon. Pres., Malta Assoc. of Public Health Physicians, 2001. Hon. MD Karolinska Inst., 1979; Hon. DSc Malta, 1984. Darling Foundn Medal and Prize, WHO, 1990; Mary Kingsley Medal, Liverpool Sch. of Tropical Medicine, 1994; Manson Medal, RSTM&H, 2007. KJSJ 2006. Title of Chevalier awarded for medical work in the tropics. Officer, Nat. Order of Merit (Malta), 2003; Companion, Order of White Elephant (Thailand), 2008. *Publications:* Tropical Medicine for Nurses, 1955, 4th edn 1975; Pathology in the Tropics, 1969, 2nd edn 1976; Management and Treatment of Tropical Diseases, 1971; (jtly) A Short Textbook of Preventive Medicine for the Tropics, 1973, 4th edn, as A Short Textbook of Public Health Medicine for the Tropics, 2003; Atlas of Tropical Medicine and Parasitology, 1976, 4th edn 1995 (BMA Book Prize, 1996); Recent Advances in Tropical Medicine, 1984; Human Antiparasitic Drugs, Pharmacology and Usage, 1985; The Epidemiology and Control of Tropical Diseases, 1987; Management of Severe and Complicated Malaria, 1991; Hookworm Infections, 1991; *edited:* Protozoal Diseases, 1999; Tropical Medicine—a clinical text, 4th edn 2006; Essential Malariology, 4th edn 2002. *Recreations:* swimming, music. *Died 20 Oct. 2015.*

GILMORE, Carol Jacqueline; *see* Ellis, C. J.

GILMOUR, Sir John, 4th Bt *cr* 1897, of Lundin and Montrave, co. Fife; farmer; Vice Lord-Lieutenant of Fife, since 2008; *b* 15 July 1944; *er s* of Col Sir John (Edward) Gilmour, 3rd Bt, DSO, TD and Ursula Mabyn (*née* Wills); *S* father, 2007; *m* 1967, Valerie Jardine Russell; two *s* two *d*. *Educ:* Eton; Aberdeen Coll. of Agriculture. Director: MFH (Fife), 1973–2003; Greenside Engineering Ltd, 1978–; Moredun Foundn, 1994–; Perth Race Course, 1999–; Pentland Science Parks Ltd, 2004–. Hon. Col, Fife and Forfar Yeomanry/Scottish Horse, 1997. DL Fife, 1988. *Recreations:* fishing, reading, horse racing. *Heir:* *s* John Nicholas Gilmour [*b* 15 Dec. 1970; *m* 1996, Airin Thamrin; two *s*]. *Address:* Wester Balcormo, Leven, Fife KY8 5QF. *T:* (01333) 320252. *E:* john@johngilmour.co.uk. *Died 10 Feb. 2013.*

GILSON, Rev. Nigel Langley, DFC 1944; Methodist minister; President of the Methodist Conference, 1986–87; *b* 11 April 1922; *s* of Clifford Edric and Cassandra Jeanette Gilson; *m* 1951, Mary Doreen (*née* Brown); four *d*. *Educ:* Holcombe Methodist Elementary; Midsomer Norton Co. Secondary; St Catherine's Soc., Oxford Univ. (MA Hons); Wesley House and Fitzwilliam House, Cambridge Univ. (BA Hons). Served RAF, 1941–45 (Navigator (Wireless) 107 Sqdn, 1944–45), Flying Officer. Methodist Minister: Tintagel, Cornwall, 1950–52; Newark-upon-Trent, 1952–58; Rhodesia Dist, 1958–67; Chaplain, Hunmanby Hall Sch., Filey, Yorks, 1967–71; Supt Minister of Oxford Methodist Circuit, 1971–75 and 1988–89; Chm., Wolverhampton and Shrewsbury Dist, 1975–88. *Recreations:* gardening, theatre, family, community and multi-cultural activities. *Died 29 Dec. 2013.*

GLAMANN, Prof. Kristof, OBE 1985; Hon. FBA 1985; author; President, Carlsberg Foundation, 1976–93 (Director, since 1969); Chairman, Carlsberg Ltd, 1977–93 (Director, since 1969); *b* 26 Aug. 1923; *s* of Kai Kristof Glamann, bank manager, and Ebba Henriette Louise (*née* Madsen); *m* 1954, Kirsten Lise (*née* Jantzen), MA, lecturer; two *s*. *Educ:* Odense Katedralskole; Univ. of Copenhagen (MA Hist. 1948, PhD Econ. Hist., 1958). University of Copenhagen: Research Fellow, 1948–56; Associated Prof., 1956–60; Prof. of History, 1960–80. Visiting Professor: Pennsylvania, 1960; Wisconsin, 1961; LSE 1964; Vis. Overseas Fellow, Churchill Coll., Cambridge, 1971–72, 1993; Toho Gakkai, Japan, 1977; Master, 4th May and Hassager Coll., Copenhagen, 1961–81. Chm., Scand. Inst. of Asian Studies, 1967–71; Hon. Pres., Internat. Econ. Hist. Assoc., 1974 (Pres., 1970–74; Vice-Pres., 1968–70). Director: Carlsberg Brewery Ltd, UK, 1977–93; Fredericia Brewery Ltd, 1975–93; Royal Copenhagen (Holmegaard) Ltd, 1975–93; Politiken Foundn, 1990–2009. Chm., Danish State Research Council of Humanities, 1968–70; Mem. Bd, HM Queen Ingrid's Roman Foundn, 1980–2005; Vice-Pres., Scandinavia-Japan Sasakawa Foundn, 1985–2006; Member: Royal Danish Acad. of Science and Letters, 1969; Royal Danish Hist. Soc., 1961; Swedish Acad., Lund, 1963; Hist. Soc. of Calcutta, 1962; Corresp. FRHistS 1972; Founding Mem., Acad. Europaea, 1988; Fellow, Royal Belgian Acad., 1989. Editor, Scand. Econ. History Review, 1961–70. Hon. LittD Gothenburg, 1974. Erasmus Medal, Acad. Europaea, 2000. Comdr (I), Order of the Dannebrog, 1990 (Kt 1984); Comdr, Northern Star of Sweden, 1984; Order of Orange-Nassau, Netherlands, 1984; Comdr, Falcon of Iceland, 1987; Das Grosse Verdienstkreuz, FRG, 1989; Order of Gorkha Dakshina Bahu, 3rd Cl., Nepal, 1989; Grand Comdr, Ordem do Mérito Agricola e Industrial, Portugal, 1992. *Publications:* History of Tobacco Industry in Denmark 1875–1950, 1950; Dutch-Asiatic Trade 1620–1740, 1958, 2nd edn 1981; (with Astrid Friis) A History of Prices and Wages in Denmark 1660–1800, vol. I, 1958; A History of Brewing in Denmark, 1962, rev. edn 2005; Studies in Mercantilism, 1966, 2nd edn 1984; European Trade 1500–1750, 1971; Carlsbergfondet, 1976; Cambridge Econ. Hist. of Europe, vol. V, 1977; J. C. Jacobsen of Carlsberg, Brewer and Philanthropist, 1991; The Carlsberg Foundation since 1970, 1993; Carl Jacobsen of New Carlsberg, 1995; The Carlsberg Group since 1970, 1997; Time Out: an essay, 1998; En Blandet Landhandel (memoirs), 2002; The Carlsberg Foundation: origin and first hundred years, 2003; (with Kirsten Glamann) The Scandinavian Pasteur: a biography of the scientist Emil Christian Hansen, 2004, English edn as The Story of Emil Christian Hansen, 2009. *Recreations:* painting, walking. *Address:* Høeghsmindeparken 10, 2900 Hellerup, Denmark. *T:* 39403977. *Died 8 Oct. 2013.*

GLASER, Prof. Donald Arthur; Professor of Physics and of Neurobiology (formerly of Molecular and Cell Biology), University of California, 1960–94, then Emeritus; *b* 21 Sept. 1926; *s* of William Joseph and Lena Glaser; *m* 1st, 1960, Ruth Louise Thompson (marr. diss. 1969); one *s* one *d*; 2nd, 1975, Lynn Bercovitz. *Educ:* Case Institute of Technology (BS 1946); California Inst. of Technology (PhD 1950). University of Michigan: Instr of Physics, 1949–53; Asst Prof., 1953–55; Associate Prof., 1955–57; Prof. of Physics, 1957–59; University of California, Berkeley: Vis. Prof., 1959–60; Prof. of Physics, 1960–; Miller Res. Biophysicist, 1962–64; Prof. of Molecular Biol., 1964–89. National Science Foundation Fellow, 1961; Guggenheim Fellow, 1961–62. Grass Award Lectr, Soc. for Neurosci., 2002. Member: National Academy of Sciences (USA), 1962; NY Acad. of Science; Fellow Amer. Physical Soc.; FAAAS. Hon. ScD: Case Inst., 1959; Michigan, 2002. Henry Russel Award, 1955; Charles Vernon Boys Prize, 1958; Amer. Phys. Soc. Prize, 1959; Nobel Prize for Physics, 1960. *Publications:* chapters in: Topics in the Biology of Aging, 1965; Biology and the Exploration of Mars, 1966; Frontiers of Pattern Recognition, 1972; New Approaches to the Identification of Microorganisms, 1975; articles in Physical Review, Handbuch der Physik, Jl Molecular Biol., Pattern Recognition and Image Processing, Somatic Cell Genetics, Cell Tissue Kinetics, Computers and Biomed. Res., Proc. Nat. Acad. of Scis (USA), Suppl. to Investigative Ophthalmol & Visual Sci., Jl Opt. Soc. of Amer. A, Vision Res., Visual Neurosci., Cell Biophys, Perception, Computational Neuroscience, Neurocomputing, etc. *Address:* Glaser Laboratory, Department of Molecular and Cell Biology, University of California, 16 Barker Hall #3206, Berkeley, CA 94720–3206, USA; 41 Hill Road, Berkeley, CA 94708, USA. *Died 28 Feb. 2013.*

GLAUERT, Audrey Marion, ScD; Fellow of Clare Hall, University of Cambridge, 1966, then Emeritus; Head of Electron Microscopy Department, Strangeways Research Laboratory, Cambridge, 1956–89 (Associate Director, 1979–85); *b* 21 Dec. 1925; *d* of late Hermann Glauert, FRS and Muriel Glauert (*née* Barker); *m* 1959, David Franks (marr. diss. 1979). *Educ:* Perse Sch. for Girls, Cambridge; Bedford Coll., Univ. of London (BSc 1946; MSc 1947). MA Cantab 1967, ScD Cantab 1970. Asst Lectr in Physics, Royal Holloway Coll., Univ. of London, 1947–50; Mem. Scientific Staff, Strangeways Res. Lab., Cambridge, Sir Halley Stewart Research Fellow, 1950–89. Chairman:

British Joint Cttee for Electron Microscopy, 1968–72; Fifth European Congress on Electron Microscopy, 1972; Pres., Royal Microscopical Soc., 1970–72, Hon. Fellow, 1973. Hon. Member: French Soc. for Electron Microscopy, 1967; Microscopy (formerly Electron Microscopy) Soc. of America, 1990 (Dist. Scientist Award for Biol. Scis, 1990). JP Cambridge, 1975–88. Editor: Practical Methods in Electron Microscopy, 1972–99; Jl of Microscopy, Royal Microscopical Soc., 1986–88. *Publications:* Fixation Dehydration and Embedding of Biological Specimens, 1974; (ed) The Control of Tissue Damage, 1988; Biological Specimen Preparation for Transmission Electron Microscopy, 1998; papers on cell and molecular biology in scientific jls. *Recreations:* sailing, gardening, working for prison reform. *Address:* 29 Cow Lane, Fulbourn, Cambridge CB21 5HB. *T:* (01223) 880463; Clare Hall, Herschel Road, Cambridge CB3 9AL. *E:* amg44@cam.ac.uk. *Died 29 July 2014.*

GLAZIER, John Francis, PhD; Principal, King Edward VI College, Stourbridge, 2001–08; *b* 18 July 1950; *s* of late Derrick Robert Glazier and Joan Agnes Glazier; *m* 1st, 1971, Marianne Frances Iszatt (marr. diss. 1992); three *d*; one *d* by former relationship; 2nd, 1992, Janet Eileen Parnell (*née* Sykes); one step *s* one step *d*. *Educ:* Univ. of Leicester (BSc 1971); Nottingham Univ. (PhD 1978). Physics Lectr, Boston Coll., 1975–93; Hd of Dept, Telford Coll. of Arts and Technol., 1993–96; Rutland College: Vice Principal, 1996–97; Principal, 1997–2001. *Publications:* contrib. Qly Jl of RMetS. *Recreations:* hill walking, listening to music (international concert season subscriber at Birmingham Symphony Hall), foreign holidays, visiting art galleries, attendee at local jazz club, renewed retirement interest in philately, armchair supporter of Hull City. *Address:* 27 Stourton Crescent, Stourbridge, West Midlands DY7 6RR. *T:* (01384) 878868. *E:* jfglazier@yahoo.co.uk. *Died 23 Oct. 2012.*

GLEN HAIG, Dame Mary (Alison), DBE 1993 (CBE 1977; MBE 1971); *b* 12 July 1918; *e d* of late Captain William James and Mary (*née* Bannochie); *m* 1943, Andrew Glen Haig (decd). *Educ:* Dame Alice Owen's Girls' School. Mem., Sports Council, 1966–82; Vice Pres., CCPR, 1982 (Chm., 1974–80); Mem., Internat. Olympic Cttee, 1982–93 (Hon. Mem., 1993). Vice Pres., Sports Aid Foundn, 1987; Life Pres., Disability Sport England (formerly British Sports Assoc. for the Disabled), 1991 (Pres., 1981–90); Hon. Pres., British Fencing Assoc. (formerly Amateur Fencing Assoc.), 1986 (Pres., 1974–86); Patron, Women's Sports Foundn, 1998. British Ladies' Foil Champion, 1948–50; Olympic Games, 1948, 1952, 1956, 1960; Commonwealth Games Gold Medal, 1950, 1954, Bronze Medal, 1958; Captain, Ladies' Foil Team, 1950–57. Asst Dist Administrator, S Hammersmith Health District, 1975–82. Member: Adv. Council Women's Transport Service (FANY), 1980–2004 (Vice Pres., 2005); Exec. Cttee, Arthritis and Rheumatism Council, 1992. Chm. of Trustees, HRH The Princess Christian Hosp., Windsor, 1981–94; Trustee: Wishbone Trust, 1991–2003; Kennedy Inst., 1998. *Recreations:* fencing, gardening. *Club:* Lansdowne. *Died 15 Nov. 2014.*

GLENAMARA, Baron *cr* 1977 (Life Peer), of Glenridding, Cumbria; **Edward Watson Short;** CH 1976; PC 1964; Chairman, Cable and Wireless Ltd, 1976–80; *b* 17 Dec. 1912; *s* of Charles and Mary Short, Warcop, Westmorland; *m* 1941, Jennie (*d* 2008), *d* of Thomas Sewell, Newcastle upon Tyne; one *s* one *d*. *Educ:* Bede College, Durham; LLB London. Served War of 1939–45 and became Capt. in DLI. Headmaster of Princess Louise County Secondary School, Blyth, Northumberland, 1947; Leader of Labour Group on Newcastle City Council, 1950; MP (Lab) Newcastle upon Tyne Central, 1951–76; Opposition Whip (Northern Area), 1955–62; Dep. Chief Opposition Whip, 1962–64; Parly Sec. to the Treasury and Govt Chief Whip, 1964–66; Postmaster General, 1966–68; Sec. of State for Educn and Science, 1968–70; Lord Pres. of the Council and Leader, House of Commons, 1974–76. Dep. Leader, Labour Party, 1972–76. Mem. Council, WWF, 1983–92. President: Finchale Abbey Training Coll. for the Disabled (Durham), 1985–; North East People to People, 1989–. Chancellor, Polytechnic of Newcastle upon Tyne, 1984–92, Univ. of Northumbria at Newcastle, 1992–2005. Freeman, City of Newcastle upon Tyne, 2001. Hon. FCP, 1965. Hon. DCL: Dunelm, 1989; Newcastle, 1998; DUniv Open, 1989; Hon. DLitt CNAA, 1990. *Publications:* The Story of The Durham Light Infantry, 1944; The Infantry Instructor, 1946; Education in a Changing World, 1971; Birth to Five, 1974; I Knew My Place, 1983; Whip to Wilson, 1989. *Recreation:* painting. *Address:* 21 Priory Gardens, Corbridge, Northumberland NE45 5HZ. *T:* (01434) 632880. *Died 4 May 2012.*

GLENN, Sir (Joseph Robert) Archibald, Kt 1966; OBE 1965; BCE; FIChemE, FIE (Aust.); Managing Director, 1953–73, Chairman, 1963–73, ICI Australia; *b* 24 May 1911; *s* of late J. R. Glenn, Sale, Vic., Aust.; *m* 1st, 1939, Elizabeth M. M. (*d* 1988), *d* of late J. S. Balderstone; one *s* two *d* (and one *d* decd); 2nd, 1992, Mrs Sue Debenham (*née* Hennesey). *Educ:* Scotch Coll. (Melbourne); University of Melbourne; Harvard (USA). Joined ICI Australia Ltd, 1935; Design and Construction Engr, 1935–44; Explosives Dept, ICI (UK), 1945–46; Chief Engineer, ICI Australia Ltd, 1947–48; Controller, Nobel Group, 1948–50; General Manager, 1950–52, ICI Australia Ltd; Director: Westpac Banking Corp. (formerly Bank of NSW), 1967–84; ICI, London, 1970–75; Hill Samuel Australia Ltd, 1973–83; Westralian Sands Ltd, 1977–85; Alcoa of Australia Ltd, 1973–86; Tioxide Australia Ltd, 1973–86; Newmont Pty Ltd, 1977–88; Chairman: Fibremakers Ltd, 1963–73; Rocky Dam Pty Ltd, 1968–; IMI Australia Ltd, 1970–78; Collins Wales Pty Ltd, 1973–84; I. C. Insurance Australia Ltd, 1973–85. Chancellor, La Trobe Univ., 1967–72 (Hon. DUniv 1981); Chairman: Council of Scotch Coll., 1960–81. Ormond Coll. Council, 1976–81; Member: Manufacturing Industry Advisory Council, 1960–77; Industrial Design Council, 1958–70; Australia/Japan Business Co-operation Cttee, 1965–75; Royal Melbourne Hospital Bd of Management, 1960–70; Melbourne Univ. Appointments Bd; Bd of Management, Melbourne Univ. Engrg Sch. Foundn, 1982–88; Council, Inst. of Pacific Affairs, 1976–; Governor, Atlantic Inst. of Internat. Affairs, 1970–88. Mem., Nat. Finance Cttee, Aust. Red Cross, 1982–98. J. N. Kirby Medal, 1970. *Recreations:* golf, tennis, collecting rare books. *Address:* 8 Freemans Road, Mount Eliza, Vic 3930, Australia. *T:* (3) 97875850. *Clubs:* Australian (Life Mem.), Melbourne (Life Mem.), Frankston Golf, Melbourne Univ. Boat (Melbourne). *Died 4 Jan. 2012.*

GLIN, Knight of; *see* Fitz-Gerald, D. J. V.

GLOAK, Graeme Frank, CB 1980; Solicitor for the Customs and Excise, 1978–82; *b* 9 Nov. 1921; *s* of late Frank and Lilian Gloak; *m* 1944, Mary, *d* of Stanley and Jane Thorne; one *s* one *d* (and one *s* decd). *Educ:* Brentwood School. Royal Navy, 1941–46; Solicitor, 1947; Customs and Excise: Legal Asst, 1947; Sen. Legal Asst, 1953; Asst Solicitor, 1967; Principal Asst Solicitor, 1971. Sec., Civil Service Legal Soc., 1954–62. Member: Dairy Produce Quota Tribunal, 1984–85; Agricl Wages Cttee for Essex and Herts, 1984–90 (Vice-Chm., 1987–90); Chm., Agricl Dwelling House Adv. Cttee, Essex and Herts, 1984–93. Member: Barking and Havering FPC, 1986–90; Barking and Havering FHSA, 1990–96; Barking and Havering HA, 1996–97. *Publications:* (with G. Krikorian and R. K. F. Hutchings) Customs and Excise, in Halsbury's Laws of England, 4th edn, 1973. *Recreations:* badminton, walking, watching cricket. *Address:* 31 Burses Way, Hutton, Brentwood, Essex CM13 2PL. *T:* (01277) 212748. *Clubs:* MCC; Essex County Cricket (Chelmsford). *Died 1 Feb. 2011.*

GLOSTER, Prof. John, MD; Hon. Consulting Ophthalmologist, Moorfields Eye Hospital; Emeritus Professor of Experimental Ophthalmology, University of London; *b* 23 March 1922; *m* 1947, Margery (*née* Williams); two *s*. *Educ:* Jesus Coll., Cambridge; St Bartholomew's Hosp. MB, BChir 1946; MRCS, LRCP 1946; DOMS 1950; MD Cantab 1953; PhD London 1959. Registrar, Research Dept, Birmingham and Midland Eye Hosp., 1950–54; Mem. Staff, Ophth. Research Unit, MRC, 1954–63; Prof. of Experimental Ophthalmology, Inst. of Ophth., Univ. of London, 1975–82; Dean of the Inst. of Ophthalmology, 1975–80. Mem. Ophth. Soc. UK; Hon.

Mem., Assoc. for Eye Res. *Publications:* Tonometry and Tonography, 1966; (jtly) Physiology of the Eye, System of Ophthalmology IV, ed Duke-Elder, 1968; contribs to jls. *Address:* 14 Church Place, Ickenham, Middlesex UB10 8XB. *Died 28 May 2011.*

GLOVER, Myles Howard; Clerk, Worshipful Company of Skinners, 1959–90; *b* 18 Dec. 1928; *yr s* of Cedric Howard Glover and Winifred Mary (*née* Crewdson); *m* 1969, Wendy Gillian, *er d* of C. M. Coleman; one *s* two *d*. *Educ:* Rugby; Balliol Coll., Oxford (MA). Called to the Bar, Lincoln's Inn, 1954. Sec., CIFE, 1991–98. Chm., Cttee of Clerks to Twelve Chief Livery Cos of City of London, 1975–81. Hon. Sec., GBA, 1967–91. Member: City & Guilds Art Sch. Cttee, 1960–71; Adv. Cttee, Gresham Coll., 1985–86; Governing Council: St Paul's Cathedral Choir Sch., 1986–90; Cambridge Tutors' Coll., 1993–94, 2000–04; Governing Body, St Leonards-Mayfield Sch., 1988–93; Hon. Addnl Mem., GBA Cttee, 1991–2003. Hon. Member: Old Tonbridgian Soc., 1986; Old Skinners' Soc., 1990 (Leopard of the Year Trophy, 1990); CIFE, 1999. Liveryman, Musicians' Co., 1954; Hon. Freeman: Fellmongers' Co., Richmond, N Yorks, 1991; Skinners' Co., 1993. *Recreation:* music. *Address:* Wisteria Cottage, 31 The Green, Woodchurch, Ashford, Kent TN26 3PF. *T:* (01233) 860288. *Died 29 Sept. 2014.*

GLUE, George Thomas; Director-General of Supplies and Transport (Naval), Ministry of Defence, 1973–77; *b* 3 May 1917; *s* of Percy Albert Glue and Alice Harriet Glue (*née* Stoner); *m* 1947, Eileen Marion Hitchcock; one *d*. *Educ:* Portsmouth Southern Secondary School. Admiralty: Asst Naval Store Officer, 1937; Dep. Naval Store Officer, Mediterranean, 1940; Naval Store Officer, Mediterranean, 1943; Asst Dir of Stores, 1955; Suptg Naval Store Officer, Devonport, 1960; Dep. Dir of Stores, 1963; Dir of Stores, 1970; Dir, Supplies and Transport (Naval), 1971. *Recreation:* reading. *Address:* 18 Late Broads, Winsley, near Bradford-on-Avon, Wilts BA15 2NW. *T:* (01225) 722717. *Died 17 Dec. 2012.*

GLYNN, Prof. Alan Anthony, MD; FRCP, FRCPath; Director, Central Public Health Laboratory, Colindale, London, 1980–88; Visiting Professor of Bacteriology, London School of Hygiene and Tropical Medicine, 1983–88; *b* 29 May 1923; *s* of late Hyman and Charlotte Glynn; *m* 1962, Nicole Benhamou; two *d*. *Educ:* City of London Sch.; University Coll. London (Fellow, 1982) and UCH Med. Sch., London (MB, BS 1946, MD 1959). MRCP 1954, FRCP 1974; MRCPath 1963, FRCPath 1973. House Physician, UCH, 1946; Asst Lectr in Physiol., Sheffield Univ., 1947–49; National Service, RAMC, 1950–51; Registrar, Canadian Red Cross Meml Hosp., Taplow, 1955–57; St Mary's Hospital Medical School: Lectr in Bacteriology, 1958–61; Sen. Lectr, 1961–67; Reader, 1967–71; Prof., 1971–80; Hon. Consultant Bacteriologist, 1961–83; Visiting Prof. of Bacteriology, St Mary's Hosp., 1980–83. Examr in Pathol., Univs of Edinburgh, 1974–76, 1983–85, Glasgow, 1975–78, and London, 1979–80. Member: DHSS Jt Cttee on Vaccination and Immunization, 1979–85; Adv. Gp, ARC Inst. for Res. in Animal Diseases. Almroth Wright Lectr, Wright-Fleming Inst., 1972; Erasmus Wilson Demonstrator, RCS, 1973. Mem. Editorial Board: Immunology, 1969–79; Parasite Immunity, 1979–87. *Publications:* papers on bacterial infection, genetics and immunity and hospital acquired infections. *Recreations:* theatre, walking. *Club:* Athenæum. *Died 2 April 2014.*

GOBLE, John Frederick; solicitor; *b* 1 April 1925; *o s* of John and Evileen Goble; *m* 1953, Moira Murphy O'Connor; one *s* three *d*. *Educ:* Finchley Catholic GS; Highgate Sch.; Brasenose Coll., Oxford (MA). Sub-Lieut, RNVR, 1944–46. Admitted solicitor, 1951; Herbert Smith: Partner, 1953–88; Hong Kong office, 1982–83; Sen. Partner, 1983–88. Crown Agents, 1974–82 (Dep. Chm., 1975–82); Director: British Telecommunications, 1983–91; Wren Underwriting Agencies, 1988–91. A Dep. Chm., City Panel on Takeovers and Mergers, 1989–97. Chm., St Barnabas Soc., 1992–95. Governor, Highgate Sch., 1976–96. Chm., The Friends of Highgate Sch. Soc., 1978–87; Pres., Old Cholmeleian Soc., 1983–84. KCSG 1994. *Recreations:* music, golf. *Address:* 114 Rivermead Court, Ranelagh Gardens, SW6 3SB. *Clubs:* Garrick, MCC, Hurlingham; New Zealand Golf (West Byfleet). *Died 11 Feb. 2012.*

GODDARD, Her Honour Ann Felicity; QC; a Circuit Judge, 1993–2008 (a Senior Circuit Judge, 1997–2008); *b* 22 Jan. 1936; *oc* of late Graham Elliott Goddard and Margaret Louise Hambrook Goddard (*née* Clark). *Educ:* Grey Coat Hosp., Westminster; Birmingham Univ. (LLB); Newnham Coll., Cambridge (LLM and Dip. in Comparative Legal Studies). Called to the Bar, Gray's Inn, 1960; Bencher, 1990; a Recorder, 1979–93. Member: Gen. Council of the Bar, 1988–93; Criminal Justice Consultative Council, 1992–93. Pres., British Acad. of Forensic Scis, 1995–96. Freeman, 1994, Liveryman, 1996–, Clockmakers' Co.; Liveryman, Gardeners' Co., 2003–. *Recreations:* travel, my Burmese cat. *Club:* Athenæum. *Died 23 March 2011.*

GODDARD, David Rodney, MBE 1985; Director, International Sailing Craft Association, 1966–96; *b* 16 March 1927; *s* of Air Marshal Sir Victor Goddard, KCB, CBE, and Mildred Catherine Jane, *d* of Alfred Markham Inglis; *m* 1951, Susan Ashton; three *s* one *d*. *Educ:* Bryanston School; Wanganui Collegiate Sch., New Zealand; Peterhouse, Cambridge. MA Hons Geography. Joined Royal Marines, 1944, hostilities only commn, 1946, demob. 1948. Whaling, United Whalers, 1949; Schoolmaster, 1950–52. Joined Somerset Light Infantry, 1952; active service, Malaya (mentioned in despatches, 1954); served: Germany, Kenya (King's African Rifles), Bahrein, N Ireland; retired at own request, as Major, 1968, to found and direct Internat. Sailing Craft Assoc. and Exeter Maritime Museum; Dir, Exeter Maritime Mus., 1968–88, 1991–96. Chief Leader, British Schs Exploring Soc. to Arctic Norway, 1965. *Recreations:* shooting, fishing, sailing, bird watching, photography. *Address:* The Mill, Lympstone, Exmouth, Devon EX8 5HD. *T:* (01395) 265575. *Died 30 June 2015.*

GODFREY, John Arthur Cadas, CBE 1998; DL; FCA; farmer, since 1972; Chairman, Agriculture and Horticulture Development Board, 2011–14; *b* Caistor, 1948; *s* of Arthur Eric Godfrey and Ethelreda Godfrey (*née* Cadas); *m* 1979, Phoebe Ingleson. *Educ:* Epsom Coll.; St Mary's, Melrose. FCA 1971; FRAgS 2004. Chm., Nat. Pig Assoc., 1999–2001. President: Lincs Agricl Soc., 2007 (Treas., 2015–); Scunthorpe United FC, 2005–. Chm., Bd of Govs, Univ. of Lincoln, 2005–09. High Sheriff, 2010–11, DL, 2014, Lincs. DUniv Lincoln, 2009. *Recreations:* bridge, football, walking, wine. *Address:* Wootton Road, Elsham Top, Brigg DN20 0NU. *E:* john.godfrey@godfrey.uk.com. *Died 1 Dec. 2015.*

GODWIN, William Henry; *b* 29 Nov. 1923; *s* of George Godwin and Dorothy (*née* Purdon); *m* 1961, Lela Milosevic; one *s* one *d*. *Educ:* Colet Court; Lycée Français de Londres; St John's Coll., Cambridge. Called to the Bar, Middle Temple, 1948. Treasury Solicitor's Office, 1948–90; Under Sec., 1977; UK Agent before Europ. Ct of Justice, 1973–85; Legal Advr to Cabinet Office, European Secretariat, 1982–85. Consultant, 1985–98. *Died 24 Oct. 2012.*

GOFF, Martyn, CBE 2005 (OBE 1977); Hon. President, Henry Sotheran Ltd, since 2007 (Director and Executive Chairman, 1988–2007); *b* 7 June 1923; *s* of Jacob and Janey Goff. *Educ:* Clifton College. Served in Royal Air Force, 1941–46. Film business, 1946–48; bookseller, 1948–70; National Book League, then Book Trust: Dir, later Chief Exec., 1970–88; Dep. Chm., 1991–92 and 1996–97; Chm., 1992–96; Vice Pres., 2000–; Administrator, Booker, subseq. Man Booker, Prize, 1970–2006 (Chm., Adv. Cttee, 2002–06). Lectured on: music; English fiction; teenager morality; the book trade, 1946–70; fiction reviewer, 1975–88, non-fiction, 1988–, Daily Telegraph. Founder and Chm., Bedford Square Bookbang, 1971. Member: Arts Council Literature Panel, 1970–78; Arts Council Trng Cttee, 1973–78; Greater London Arts Assoc. Literature Panel, 1973–81; British Nat. Bibliography Res. Fund, 1976–88; British Library Adv. Council, 1977–82; PEN Exec. Cttee, 1978–2003; Exec. Cttee, Gtr London Arts Council, 1982–88; Library and Information Services Council, 1984–86; Bd, British Theatre Assoc., 1983–85; Chairman: Paternosters '73 Library Adv. Council, 1972–74;

New Fiction Soc., 1975–88; School Bookshop Assoc., 1977–; Soc. of Bookmen, 1982–84 (Pres., 1997–); 1890s Soc., 1990–99; Nat. Life Story Collections, 1996–2003; Poetry Book Soc., 1996–99 (Mem. Bd, 1992–99); Wingate Scholarships, H. H. Wingate Foundn, 1988–2003; Vice-Pres., Royal Over-Seas League, 1996–; Dir, Battersea Arts Centre, 1992–97 (Trustee, 1981–85); Trustee: Cadmean Trust, 1981–99; Nat. Literacy Trust, 1993–2003; Booker Prize Foundn, 2006–. Judge, Glenfiddich Awards, 1993. FIAL 1958, FRSA 1979. Hon. FRSL 2003. Hon. DLitt Oxford Brookes, 2003. *Publications: fiction:* The Plaster Fabric, 1957, new edn 2014; A Season with Mammon, 1958; A Sort of Peace, 1960; The Youngest Director, 1961, new edn 2013; Red on the Door, 1962; The Flint Inheritance, 1965; Indecent Assault, 1967, new edn 2014; The Liberation of Rupert Bannister, 1978; Tar and Cement, 1988; *non-fiction:* A Short Guide to Long Play, 1957; A Further Guide to Long Play, 1958; LP Collecting, 1960; Why Conform?, 1968; Victorian and Edwardian Surrey, 1972; Record Choice, 1974; Royal Pavilion, 1976; Organising Book Exhibitions, 1982; Publishing, 1988; Prize Writing, 1989. *Recreations:* travel, collecting paintings and sculptures, music. *Address:* 95 Sisters Avenue, SW11 5SW. *T:* (020) 7228 8164. *Clubs:* Athenæum, Savile, Groucho. *Died 25 March 2015.*

GOGGINS, Rt Hon. Paul (Gerard), PC 2009; MP (Lab) Wythenshawe and Sale East, since 1997; *b* 16 June 1953; *s* of John Goggins and late Rita Goggins; *m* 1977, Wyn, *d* of Tom and Mary Bartley; two *s* one *d*. *Educ:* St Bede's Sch., Manchester; Birmingham Poly.; Manchester Poly. Child care worker, Liverpool Catholic Social Services, 1974–75; Officer-in-Charge, local authy children's home, Wigan, 1976–84; Project Dir, NCH Action for Children, Salford, 1984–89; Nat. Dir, Church Action on Poverty, 1989–97. Mem. (Lab) Salford MBC, 1990–98. PPS to Minister of State for Health, 1998–2000, to Sec. of State for Educn and Employment, 2000–01, to Home Sec., 2001–03; Parliamentary Under-Secretary of State: Home Office, 2003–06; NI Office, 2006–07; Minister of State, NI Office, 2007–10. Mem., Intelligence and Security Cttee, 2010–. *Address:* House of Commons, SW1A 0AA. *T:* (constituency) (0161) 499 7900. *Died 7 Jan. 2014.*

GOLD, Jack; film director; *b* 28 June 1930; British; *m* 1957, Denyse (*née* Macpherson); two *s* one *d*. *Educ:* London Univ. (BSc (Econs), LLB). Asst Studio Manager, BBC radio, 1954–55; Editor, Film Dept, BBC, 1955–60; Dir, TV and film documentaries and fiction, 1960–. Desmond Davies Award for services to television, BAFTA, 1976. *TV films:* Tonight; Death in the Morning (BAFTA Award, 1964); Modern Millionairess; Famine; Dispute; 90 Days; Dowager in Hot Pants; World of Coppard (BAFTA Award, 1968); Mad Jack (Grand Prix, and Monte Carlo Catholic Award, 1971); Stocker's Copper (BAFTA Award, 1972); Arturo Ui; The Lump; Catholics (Peabody Award, 1974); The Naked Civil Servant (Italia Prize, 1976, Internat. Emmy, and Critics Award, 1976); Thank You Comrades; Marya; Charlie Muffin; A Walk in the Forest; Merchant of Venice; Bavarian Night; A Lot of Happiness (Kenneth Macmillan), 1981 (Internat. Emmy Award); Praying Mantis, Macbeth, L'Elegance, 1982; The Red Monarch, 1983; Good and Bad at Games, 1983; Sakharov, 1984 (Assoc. Cable Enterprises Award); Murrow, 1986 (Assoc. Cable Enterprises Award); Me and the Girls, 1985; Escape from Sobibor, 1987 (Golden Globe Award); Stones for Ibarra, 1988; The Tenth Man, 1989; Masterclass, 1989; Ball-trap on the Côte Sauvage, 1989; The Rose and the Jackal, 1990; She Stood Alone, 1991 (Christopher Award); The Last Romantics, 1992; Heavy Weather, 1995; Mute of Malice, 1997; Blood Money, 1997; Into the Blue, 1997; Kavanagh QC, 1998; Goodnight Mr Tom, 1998 (Silver Hugo Award, Chicago, 1998, BAFTA Award, 1999); The Remorseful Day, 2000 (BAFTA Award, 2001); End of Law, 2001; The John Thaw Story, 2002; The Brief, 2004; *cinema:* The Bofors Gun, 1968; The Reckoning, 1969; The National Health, 1973 (Evening News Best Comedy Award); Who?, 1974; Man Friday, 1974; Aces High, 1976 (Evening News Best Film Award); The Medusa Touch, 1977; The Sailor's Return, 1978 (jt winner, Martin Luther King Meml Prize, 1980; Monte Carlo Catholic Award, and Monte Carlo Critics Award, 1981; Karoly Vary Award, 1978), 1978; Little Lord Fauntleroy, 1981 (Christopher Award); The Chain, 1985; The Lucona Affair, 1993; Return of the Native, 1994; Spring Awakening, 1994; *theatre:* Council of Love, 1971; The Devil's Disciple, Aldwych, 1976; This Story of Yours, 1987, Danger! Memory, 1988, Hampstead; Three Hotels, 1993, Crossing Jerusalem, 2003, Tricycle Th. *Recreations:* music, reading, tennis. *Address:* 24 Wood Vale, N10 3DP. *Died 9 Aug. 2015.*

GOLDBERGER, Prof. Marvin Leonard, PhD; Professor of Physics, 1993–2000, then Emeritus, and Dean of Natural Sciences, 1994–99, University of California, San Diego; *b* 22 Oct. 1922; *s* of Joseph Goldberger and Mildred (*née* Sedwitz); *m* 1945, Mildred Ginsburg (*d* 2006); two *s*. *Educ:* Carnegie Inst. of Technology (BS); Univ. of Chicago (PhD). Asst to Associate Prof., Univ. of Chicago, 1950–55; Prof., Univ. of Chicago, 1955–57; Princeton University: Higgins Prof. of Mathematical Physics, 1957–77; Chm., Dept of Physics, 1970–76; Joseph Henry Prof. of Physics, 1977–78; Pres., California Inst. of Technology, 1978–87; Dir, Inst. for Advanced Study, Princeton, NJ, 1987–91; Prof. of Physics, UCLA, 1991–93. Hon. ScD: Carnegie-Mellon, 1979; Notre Dame, Indiana, 1979; Brandeis, 1991; Hon. DHL: Hebrew Union Coll., 1980; Univ. of Judaism, 1982; Hon. LLD Occidental Coll., 1980. *Publications:* (jtly) Collision Theory, 1964; professional papers in Physical Rev. *Recreations:* jogging, cooking. *E:* mgoldberger@ucsd.edu. *Died 26 Nov. 2014.*

GOLDEN, Surgeon Rear-Adm. Francis St Clair, OBE 1981; Consultant in Applied Physiology, and Hon. Lecturer, Portsmouth University, since 1998; *b* 5 June 1936; *s* of Harry Golden and Nora Golden (*née* Murphy); *m* 1964, Jennifer (*née* Beard); two *s* one *d*. *Educ:* Presentation Coll., Cork; University Coll., Cork (MB BCh, BAO); London Univ. (Diploma in Aviation Medicine); Leeds Univ. (PhD Physiol). GP, Kingston on Thames, 1961–63; HMS Jaguar, 1963–64; RNAS Culdrose, 1964–67; RN Air Med. Sch., 1967–73; Inst. of Naval Medicine, 1973–85; MoD, 1985–86; Fleet MO, 1986–88; MO i/c Haslar, 1988–90; Surg. Rear-Adm., Support Med. Services, 1990–93, retd. QHP 1990–93. Consultant in Applied Physiol., Robens Inst., Surrey Univ., 1994–98. Chm., Med. and Survival Cttee, RNLI, 1994–2006. Hon. FNI 1982. OStJ. *Publications:* (with M. J. Tipton) Essentials of Sea Survival, 2002; papers in sci. jls and chapters in medical textbooks on immersion, drowning, hypothermia. *Recreations:* born again golfer, armchair Rugby. *Address:* 15 Beech Grove, Gosport, Hants PO12 2JE. *Clubs:* Royal Society of Medicine; Lee-on-the-Solent Golf (Capt., 1998–99). *Died 5 Jan. 2014.*

GOLDIE, Prof. Peter Lawrence, DPhil; Samuel Hall Professor of Philosophy, University of Manchester, since 2005; *b* 5 Nov. 1946; *s* of Kenneth and Norah Goldie; *m* 1st, Jennie (marr. diss. 1989); two *s*; 2nd, 1990, Sophie Hamilton. *Educ:* Felsted Sch., Essex; UCL (BA 1993); Balliol Coll., Oxford (BPhil 1995; DPhil 1997). Chief Executive: Abaco Investments PLC, 1983–86; British & Commonwealth Hldgs, 1987–89; Dir, Guinness Mahon, 1973–83. Lectr in Philosophy Magdalen Coll., Oxford, 1996–98; Lectr, 1998–2004, Reader in Philosophy, 2004–05, KCL. *Publications:* The Emotions, 2000; On Personality, 2004; Who's Afraid of Conceptual Art?, 2009; articles in philosophical jls. *Recreation:* physical and mental exercise. *Died 22 Oct. 2011.*

GOLDING, Francis Nelson; architecture, planning and conservation consultant, since 2000; *b* 28 Jan. 1944; *s* of late Frank Edwards Golding and Ella Golding (*née* Morris); civil partnership 2006, Dr Satish Padiyar. *Educ:* King's Sch., Macclesfield; Clare Coll., Cambridge (Exhibnr; BA 1966; MA 2000). Min. of Public Building and Works, 1967; DoE, 1972; Royal Commn on the Press, 1975–77; Asst Sec., DoE, 1978; English Heritage: Head of Secretariat, 1984; Head of Properties, 1986–90; Sec., ICOMOS, 1992–94; Sec., Royal Fine Art Commn, 1995–99; Chief Exec., Commn for Architecture and the Built Envmt, 1999. Hon. FRIBA 2000. *Publications:* Building in Context, 2002. *Recreations:* Chinese pots and jade, going to India. *Address:* 3 Stonefield Street, N1 0HP. *T:* (020) 7278 1558. *Died 8 Nov. 2013.*

GOLDING, (Harold) John, CBE 1992; PhD; FBA 1994; painter; Senior Tutor in the School of Painting, Royal College of Art, 1981–86 (Tutor, 1973); *b* 10 Sept. 1929; *s* of Harold S. Golding and Dorothy Hamer. *Educ:* Ridley Coll. (St Catherine's, Ontario); Univ. of Toronto (BA 1951); Courtauld Inst. of Art, Univ. of London (MA 1953; PhD 1957). Lectr, 1962–77, and Reader in History of Art, 1977–81, Courtauld Inst., Univ. of London; Slade Prof. of Fine Art, Cambridge Univ., 1976–77; Andrew W. Mellon Lectr in the Fine Arts, Nat. Gall. of Art, Washington, 1997. Co-Curator, Matisse Picasso exhibn, NY, London and Paris, 2002. Solo exhibn of paintings, Tate Britain, 2010. Trustee, Tate Gallery, 1984–91. Hon. Fellow, RCA, 1987. *Publications:* Cubism 1907–14, 1959, 3rd edn 1988; (with Christopher Green) Leger & Purist Paris, 1970; Duchamp: The Bride Stripped Bare by her Bachelors, Even, 1972; (ed with Roland Penrose) Picasso 1881–1973, 1973; Visions of the Modern, 1994; (with Elizabeth Cowling) Picasso: sculptor/painter, 1994; Paths to the Absolute, 2000. *Address:* 24 Ashchurch Park Villas, W12 9SP. *T:* (020) 8749 5221. *Died 9 April 2012.*

GOLDING, John Anthony, CVO 1966; Queen's Messenger, 1967–80; *b* 25 July 1920; *s* of George Golding, Plaxtol, Kent; *m* 1950, Patricia May, *d* of Thomas Archibald Bickel; two *s*. *Educ:* Bedford Sch.; King's Coll., Auckland. Served with King's African Rifles and Military Administration, Somalia, 1939–46 (Captain). Entered Colonial Service, 1946; Dep. Provincial Comr, Tanganyika, 1961; Administrator, Turks and Caicos Is, 1965–67. *Publications:* Colonialism: the golden years, 1987. *Recreations:* gardening, fishing. *Address:* c/o Barclays Bank, 11 High Street, Hythe, Kent CT21 5AE. *Died 18 April 2012.*

GOLDMAN, Prof. John Michael, DM; FRCP, FRCPath, FMedSci; Professor of Leukaemia Biology and Therapy, Imperial College School of Medicine, 1987–2004, then Emeritus; Chairman, Department of Haematology, Imperial College London/Hammersmith Hospital, 1994–2004; Director, Leukaemia Research Fund Centre for Adult Leukaemia, 1992–2004; *b* 30 Nov. 1938; *s* of Carl Heinz Goldman and Berthe Goldman (*née* Brandt); *m* 1st, 1967, Jeannine Fuller (marr. diss.); one *d*; 2nd, 1972, Constance Wilson; one *s* one *d*. *Educ:* Westminster Sch. (Schol.); Magdalen Coll., Oxford (Ann Shaw Schol.; BM BCh 1963; DM 1981); St Bartholomew's Hosp., London. FRCP 1979; FRCPath 1986. Fellow in Hematology, Univ. of Miami, 1967–68; Fellow in Oncology, Massachusetts Gen. Hosp./Harvard Univ., 1968–70; mem. staff, MRC Leukaemia Unit, 1970–92, Cons. Haematologist, 1976–2004, Hammersmith Hosp. Ham-Wasserman Lectr, Amer. Soc. Hematology, 1997; McCredie Lectr, Leukemia Soc. Amer., 2000; Fogarty Schol., Hematology Br., Nat. Heart, Lung and Blood Inst., NIH, Bethesda, MD, 2005–06. Ed., Bone Marrow Transplantation, 1985–. Med. Dir, Anthony Nolan Bone Marrow Trust, 1987–2010; Scientific Advr, Kay Kendall Leukaemia Fund, 1991–2004; Chairman: Adv. Cttee, Internat. Bone Marrow Transplant Registry, 1998–2001; Internat. Chronic Myeloid Leukaemia Foundn, 1999–. President: Internat. Soc. for Exptl Hematology, 1984–85; Eur. Gp for Blood and Marrow Transplantation, 1990–94; Eur. Hematology Assoc., 1996–98. FMedSci 1999. Hon. MD: Louvain, 1993; Poitiers, 1995. *Publications:* contrib. scientific papers on haematology, leukaemia, lymphoma, stem cell transplantation and molecular biol. *Recreations:* reading, skiing, riding. *Address:* 33 Northumberland Place, W2 5AS. *T:* (020) 7727 6092. *Died 24 Dec. 2013.*

GOLDSTEIN, His Honour Simon Alfred; a Circuit Judge, 1987–2003; *b* 6 June 1935; *s* of Harry and Constance Goldstein; *m* 1973, Zoë Philippa, *yr d* of late Basil Gerrard Smith, TD. *Educ:* East Ham Grammar Sch.; Fitzwilliam Coll., Cambridge (BA 1956). Educn Officer, RAF, 1957–60. Called to the Bar, Middle Temple, 1961; Dep. Circuit Judge, 1975; a Recorder, 1980–87. *Recreation:* bridge. *Address:* The Garden Flat, 15 Montagu Place, W1H 2ET. *Died 18 Dec. 2014.*

GOLDSTONE, His Honour Peter Walter; a Circuit Judge, 1978–97; *b* 1 Nov. 1926; *y s* of late Adolph Lionel Goldstone and Ivy Gwendoline Goldstone; *m* 1955, Patricia (*née* Alexander), JP; one *s* two *d*. *Educ:* Manchester Grammar Sch.; Manchester Univ. Solicitor, 1951. Fleet Air Arm, 1944–47. Partner in private practice with brother Julian S. Goldstone, 1951–71. Manchester City Councillor (L), 1962–65; Chm., Manchester Rent Assessment Panel, 1967–71; Reserve Chm., Manchester Rent Tribunal, 1969–71; Dep. Chm., Inner London QS, Nov. 1971; a Metropolitan Stipendiary Magistrate, 1971–78; a Recorder of the Crown Court, 1972–78. Designated Care Judge, Watford Care Centre, 1994–97. *Recreations:* walking, gardening, reading. *Address:* c/o Watford County Court, Cassiobury House, 11/19 Station Road, Watford WD1 1EZ. *T:* (01923) 249666. *Club:* MCC. *Died 2 Aug. 2013.*

GOMME, Robert Anthony, CB 1990; Under Secretary, Department of the Environment, 1981–90, retired; *b* 19 Nov. 1930; *s* of Harold Kenelm Gomme and Alice Grace (*née* Jacques); *m* 1960, Helen Perris (*née* Moore); one *s* one *d*. *Educ:* Colfe's Grammar Sch., Lewisham; London School of Economics, Univ. of London (BScEcon 1955). National Service, Korean War, Corporal with Royal Norfolk Regt, 1951–52; Pirelli Ltd, 1955–66; NEDO, 1966–68; direct entrant Principal, Min. of Public Building and Works, 1968; Asst Sec., DoE, 1972–74, 1979–81; RCDS 1975; Cabinet Office, 1976–79; Department of the Environment: Dir of Defence Services, PSA, 1981–86; Prin. Finance Officer, 1987–90; Chief Exec., Crown Suppliers, 1990. Mem., Commonwealth War Graves Commn, 1981–86. Trustee: Friends of the National Libraries, 1991–97, 1999–2003; London Library, 1992–95, 1996–2000, 2001–05. Hon. Treas., Friends of Greenwich Park, 1992–95. *Publications:* George Herbert Perris: 1866–1920, the life and times of a radical, 2003; contrib. Oxford DNB and to learned jls. *Recreations:* historical research, music, theatre, travel. *Address:* 14 Vanbrugh Fields, Blackheath, SE3 7TZ. *T:* (020) 8858 5148. *Died 2015.*

GOMMIER, Marie-Claire Geneviève; *see* Alain, M.-C. G.

GÖNCZ, Árpád, Hon. GCB 1999; Hon. KCMG 1991; President, Republic of Hungary, 1990–2000; *b* 10 Feb. 1922; *s* of Lajos Göncz and Ilona Heimann; *m* 1947, Mária Zsuzsanna Göntér; two *s* two *d*. *Educ:* Pázmány Péter Univ. (DJ 1944); Univ. of Agric. Scis. Nat. Land Bank, 1942–45; Independent Smallholders' Party: Sec. to Gen. Sec.; Leader, Independent Youth; Editor in Chief, Generation (weekly), 1947–48; jobless from 1948, worked as welder and metalsmith; sentenced to life imprisonment for political activity, 1957; released under general amnesty, 1963; freelance writer and literary translator, esp. of English works, 1963–; Pres., Hungarian Writers' Union, 1989–90; founding mem., Free Initiatives Network, Free Democratic Fedn, Historic Justice Cttee; MP, regional list, 1990; Speaker of Parliament and President *ai*, Republic of Hungary, May–Aug. 1990. József Attila Literary Prize, 1983; Wheatland Prize, 1989; Premio Mediterraneo, 1991. *Publications:* Men of God (novel), 1974; Hungarian Medea (play), Iron Bars (play), 1979; Encounters (short stories), 1980; Balance (6 plays, incl. A Pessimistic Comedy, and Persephone), 1990; Homecoming (short stories), 1991; Shavings (essays), 1991. *Recreations:* reading, walking. *Address:* Kossuth tér 4, 1055 Budapest, Hungary. *T:* 4413550. *Died 6 Oct. 2015.*

GOODBOURN, Dr David Robin; President, Partnership for Theological Education, Manchester, 2005–11, then President Emeritus; *b* 1 Aug. 1948; *s* of Albert Lewis Goodbourn and Olive Mary Goodbourn (*née* Pring); *m* 1972, Evlynn Ann Cassie; one *s* one *d*. *Educ:* Sir Roger Manwood's Sch., Sandwich; Univ. of Durham (BA 1969); Univ. of Manchester (MEd 1980; PhD 1989). Sec. for Student Work, Baptist Union of GB, 1969–71; Dir, Baptist World Poverty Educn Prog., 1971–73; Tutor, Northern Baptist Coll., and Lectr, Northern Coll. (URC and Congregational), 1973–85; Adult Educn Advr, Church of Scotland, 1985–94; Asst Dir, 1994–98, then Depute Dir, 1998–99, Ch of Scotland Bd of Parish Educn, and Dean, Scottish Churches Open Coll., 1996–99; Gen. Sec., CTBI, 1999–2006. Member: Bd and Exec., Christian Aid, 1999–2006; Central Cttee, WCC, 2006–13; Governing Body, SPCK, 2006–09; Council, 2009–14, Bd of Trustees, 2011–14, Baptist Union of GB; Chairman: Roots for Churches Ltd, 2002–05; Feed the

Minds, 2006–13. *Recreations:* walking, reading, and a moderately educated taste for malt whisky. *Address:* 38 St Werburgh's Road, Chorlton cum Hardy, Manchester M21 0TJ. *Died 9 Nov. 2014.*

GOODHART, Rear-Adm. (Hilary Charles) Nicholas, CB 1972; FRAeS; Managing Director, Goodhart Ltd, since 1999; *b* 28 Sept. 1919; *s* of G. C. Goodhart; *m* 1975, Molly Copsey. *Educ:* RNC Dartmouth; RNEC Keyham. Joined RN, 1933; served in Mediterranean in HM Ships Formidable and Dido, 1941–43; trained as pilot, 1944; served as fighter pilot in Burma Campaign, 1945; trained as test pilot, 1946; invented mirror deck-landing system for aircraft carriers, 1952; served on British Naval Staff, Washington, 1953–55; idc 1965; Rear-Adm. 1970; Mil. Dep. to Head of Defence Sales, MoD, 1970–73, retired. World Gliding Champion, 2-seaters, 1956; British Gliding Champion, 1962, 1967 and 1971. Freedom of London, 1945; Mem. Ct of Grocers' Co., 1975, Master, 1981. US Legion of Merit, 1958. *Recreation:* staying alive. *Address:* Cable House, Lindridge Park, Teignmouth, Devon TQ14 9TF. *T:* (01626) 779790. *Died 9 April 2011.*

GOODHART, Sir Philip (Carter), Kt 1981; *b* 3 Nov. 1925; *s* of late Prof. Arthur Lehman Goodhart, Hon. KBE, QC, FBA, and Cecily (*née* Carter); *m* 1950, Valerie Winant (*d* 2014); three *s* four *d. Educ:* Hotchkiss Sch., USA; Trinity Coll., Cambridge. Served KRRC and Parachute Regt (an Elder), 1943–47. Editorial staff, Daily Telegraph, 1950–54; Ed., Time and Tide, 1955; Editorial staff, Sunday Times, 1955–57. Mem., LCC Educn Cttee, 1956–57. Contested (C) Consett, Co. Durham, Gen. Election, 1950; MP (C) Beckenham, March 1957–1992. Parly Under-Sec. of State, Northern Ireland Office, and Minister responsible for Dept of the Environment (NI), 1979–81; Parly Under Sec. of State, MoD, 1981. Joint Hon. Sec., 1922 Cttee, 1960–79; Mem., Cons. Adv. Cttee on Policy, 1973–79; Chairman: Cons. Parly Defence Cttee, 1972–74 (Vice-Chm., 1974–79); Cons. Parly NI Cttee, 1976–79; Parly Select Cttee on Sound Broadcasting, 1983–87; Anglo-Taiwan Parly Gp, 1987–92. Member: British Delegation to Council of Europe and WEU, 1961–63; British Delegation to UN Gen. Assembly, 1963; North Atlantic Assembly, 1964–79 and 1983–92; Leader, CPA Delegns to Australia, 1984, Sri Lanka, 1989. Member: Council, Consumers' Assoc., 1959–68, 1970–79 (Vice-Pres., 1983–); Adv. Council on Public Records, 1970–79; Exec. Cttee, British Council, 1974–79; Council, RUSI, 1973–76. Chairman: Bd of Sulgrave Manor, 1982–2002; Warship Preservation Trust, 1987–2006; Warrior Preservation Trust, 1993–97; Dir, Flagship Portsmouth, 1993–97. Chm. and Capt., Lords and Commons Ski Club, 1971–73. Order of the Brilliant Star (China), 1992. *Publications:* (with Ian Henderson, GM) The Hunt for Kimathi, 1958; Shadow of the Sword, 1964; Fifty Ships that Saved the World, 1965; (with Christopher Chataway) War without Weapons, 1968; Referendum, 1970; The 1922: the history of the 1922 Committee, 1973; Full-Hearted Consent, 1975; various pamphlets including: Stand on Your Own Four Feet: a study of work sharing and job splitting, 1982; Jobs Ahead, 1984; Colonel George Washington: soldier of the King, 1993; The Royal Americans, 2005; A Stab in the Front: the Suez conflict, 2006. *Address:* 25 Abbotsbury Road, W14 8EJ. *T:* (020) 7602 8237. *Clubs:* Beefsteak, Carlton, Garrick. *Died 5 July 2015.*

GOODMAN, Dame Barbara; *see* Goodman, Dame P. B.

GOODMAN, Geoffrey George, CBE 1998; Founding Editor, British Journalism Review, 1989–2002, then Chairman Emeritus; broadcaster and commentator, BBC and commercial television and radio, since 1986; *b* 2 July 1922; *s* of Michael Goodman and Edythe (*née* Bowman); *m* 1947, Margit (*née* Freudenbergova); one *s* one *d. Educ:* elementary schs, Stockport and Manchester; grammar schs, London; LSE (BScEcon). RAF, 1940–46. Manchester Guardian, 1946–47; Daily Mirror, 1947–48; News Chronicle, 1949–59; Daily Herald, 1959–64; The Sun (IPC), 1964–69; Daily Mirror, 1969–86 (Industrial Editor, 1969–86; Asst Editor, 1976–86). Fellow, Nuffield Coll., Oxford, 1974–76. Broadcaster, BBC Current Affairs, and LBC/IRN, later London News Radio, 1986–97. Head of Govt's Counter-inflation Publicity Unit, 1975–76; Member: Labour Party Cttee on Industrial Democracy, 1966–67; Royal Commn on the Press, 1974–77; TGWU; NUJ. Chm., Hugh Cudlipp Trust, 2004–. Hon. MA Oxon; Hon. DA Bedfordshire, 2010. Descriptive Writer of the Year, Nat. Press Awards, 1971; Gerald Barry Award for Journalism, Granada TV Press Awards, 1984. *Publications:* General Strike of 1926, 1951; Brother Frank, 1969; The Awkward Warrior, 1979; The Miners' Strike, 1985; The State of the Nation, 1997; From Bevan to Blair, 2003; Lord Bill Morris (biog.), 2010; contrib. London Inst. of World Affairs, 1948. *Recreations:* pottering, poetry, supporting Tottenham Hotspur FC, and climbing—but not social. *Club:* Savile. *Died 5 Sept. 2013.*

GOODMAN, Dame (Pearl) Barbara, DBE 1989; QSO 1981; JP; Member, Auckland City Council, 1989–2001; *b* 5 Oct. 1932; *d* of late Horace Robinson and Lillie Robinson (*née* Shieff); *m* 1954, Harold Goodman (*d* 1988); two *s* one *d. Educ:* Parnell Sch.; St Cuthbert's Coll. Mayoress, City of Auckland, 1968–80; founding Trustee, HELP Foundn, 1980–85; Chm., Auckland Spastic Soc., 1980–84; Chm., Odyssey House Trust, 1981–92; former Mem. Exec. Cttee, NZ Fedn of Voluntary Welfare Organisations. Mem., NZ Internat. Trade Fair Cttee, 1985–89; Chm., Auckland 1990 Trust Board, 1989–91; Mem., Telethon Trust Bd, 1981. Guardian, NZ Women's Refuge Foundn; former Patron and Mem., Aotearoa NZ Peace Foundn; Patron: Child Safety Foundn; (Regional) Internat. Year of Disabled Persons, 1981. Member: Cttee, Shalom Court; Women's Internat. Zionist Orgn. Vice Patron, Auckland Cricket Assoc. *Publications:* For Flying Kiwis, 1990; Mayoress and Councillor, 2012. *Recreations:* meeting people, travel, reading, cooking, embroidery. *Address:* Unit 62, Remuera Gardens, 57 Richard Farrell Avenue, Remuera, Auckland 1050, New Zealand. *T:* (9) 5201233, *Fax:* (9) 5200690. *E:* barbara@goodman.co.nz. *Died 21 June 2013.*

GOODSON, Sir Mark (Weston Lassam), 3rd Bt *cr* 1922, of Waddeton Court, Co. Devon; *b* 12 Dec. 1925; *s* of Major Alan Richard Lassam Goodson (*d* 1941) (2nd *s* of 1st Bt) and Clarisse Muriel Weston (*d* 1982), *d* of John Weston Adamson; *S* uncle, 1986; *m* 1949, Barbara Mary Constantine, *d* of Surg.-Capt. Reginald Joseph McAuliffe Andrews, RN; one *s* three *d. Educ:* Radley; Jesus College, Cambridge. *Heir: s* Alan Reginald Goodson [*b* 15 May 1960; *m* 1990, Melanie Lodder; one *s* one *d*]. *Address:* Bowmont Way, Yew Tree Road, Town Yetholm, Kelso, Roxburghshire TD5 8RY. *T:* (01573) 420322. *Died 1 Feb. 2015.*

GOODWIN, Sir Matthew (Dean), Kt 1989; CBE 1981; CA; Chairman: CrestaCare plc, 1995–2000 (Director 1994–2000); Murray Enterprise plc, 1988–2001; *b* 12 June 1929; *s* of Matthew Dean Goodwin and Mary Gertrude Barrie; *m* 1st, 1955, Margaret Eileen Colvil (marr. diss. 1982); two *d*; 2nd, 1996, Margaret Adamson. *Educ:* Hamilton Acad.; Glasgow Acad. FO, RAF, 1952–54. Raeburn & Verel, Shipowners, 1954–56; Partner, Davidson Downe McGowan, CA, 1956–68; Exec. Dir, 1960–79, Chm., 1979–95, Hewden Stuart. Director: Irvine Develt Corp., 1980–90; F/S Assurance, 1980–89; Murray Ventures PLC, 1981–; Eastpark Children's Home, 1989–2002; Chm., Scotcare Ltd, 1988–2000. Mem., Scottish Econ. Council, 1991–97. Jt Dep. Chm., Scottish Conservative Party, 1991–97 (Hon. Treas., 1982–90). DUniv Glasgow, 2001. *Recreations:* bridge, fishing, shooting, farming. *Address:* 87 Kelvin Court, Anniesland, Glasgow G12 0AH. *T:* (0141) 221 7331. *Club:* Western (Glasgow). *Died 10 Oct. 2012.*

GOODWIN, (Trevor) Noël; freelance critic, writer and broadcaster, specialising in music and dance; *b* 25 Dec. 1927; *s* of Arthur Daniel Goodwin and Blanche Goodwin (*née* Stephens); *m* 1st, 1954, Gladys Marshall Clapham (marr. diss. 1960); 2nd, Anne Myers (*née* Mason); one step *s. Educ:* mainly in France. BA (London). Assistant Music Critic: News Chronicle, 1952–54; Manchester Guardian, 1954–55; Music and Dance Critic, Daily Express, 1956–78; Exec. Editor, Music and Musicians, 1963–71; regular reviewer for: The Times, 1978–98; Internat. Herald Tribune, 1978–84; Opera News, 1975–90; Ballet News, 1979–86; Dance and Dancers, 1957– (Associate Editor, 1972–); Opera, 1984– (Overseas News Editor,

1985–91; Mem. Editl Bd, 1991–99). Member: Arts Council of GB, 1979–81 (Mem., 1973–81, Chm., 1979–81, Dance Adv. Panel; Mem., 1974–81, Dep. Chm., 1979–81, Music Adv. Panel; Council's rep. on Visiting Arts Unit of GB, 1979–81); Dance Adv. Panel, UK Branch, Calouste Gulbenkian Foundn, 1972–76; Nat. Enquiry into Dance Educn and Trng in Britain, 1975–80; Drama and Dance Adv. Cttee, British Council, 1973–88; HRH The Duke of Kent's UK Cttee for European Music Year 1985, 1982–84 (Chm., sub-cttee for Writers and Critics); Trustee-dir, Internat. Course for Professional Choreographers and Composers, 1975–2005. Pres., The Critics' Circle, 1977 (Jt Trustee, 1984–2009). Planned and presented numerous radio programmes of music and records for BBC Home and World Services, and contributed frequently to music and arts programmes on Radios 3 and 4. *Publications:* London Symphony: portrait of an orchestra, 1954; A Ballet for Scotland, 1979; (with Sir Geraint Evans) A Knight at the Opera, 1984; editor, Royal Opera and Royal Ballet Yearbooks, 1978, 1979, 1980; area editor and writer, New Grove Dictionary of Music and Musicians, 1981; (ed) A Portrait of the Royal Ballet, 1988; contribs to: Encyclopaedia Britannica, 15th edn, 1974; Encyclopaedia of Opera, 1976; Britannica Books of the Year, annually 1980–93; Cambridge Encyclopaedia of Russia and the Soviet Union, 1982, 2nd edn 1994; New Oxford Companion to Music, 1983; Pipers Enzyklopädie des Musiktheaters, 1986; New Grove Dictionary of Opera, 1992; Viking Opera Guide, 1993; International Dictionary of Ballet, 1993; Metropolitan Opera Guide to Recorded Opera, 1993; Penguin Opera Guide, 1995; International Encyclopedia of Dance, 1998; Larousse Dictionnaire de la danse, 2000; Oxford DNB. *Recreation:* philately. *Address:* 76 Skeena Hill, SW18 5PN. *T:* (020) 8788 8794. *Died 27 March 2013.*

GOODWYN, Charles Wyndham, LVO 2002; FRICS; FRPSL; Keeper, Royal Philatelic Collection, 1995–2002; *b* 11 March 1934; *s* of Charles Colin Goodwyn and Phylis Goodwyn; *m* 1962, Judith Elisabeth Ann Riley; two *s* two *d*. *Educ:* Wellington Coll.; London Univ. (LLB Hons). FRICS 1964; FCIArb 1976. Joined Wilks Head & Eve, Chartered Surveyors, 1956, Sen. Partner, 1990–95. Royal Philatelic Society: Mem., 1965–; Fellow, 1975, Hon. Fellow, 2000; Hon. Treas., 1981–82; Hon. Sec., 1982–90; Vice Pres., 1990–92; Pres., 1992–94. Medal, Royal Philatelic Soc., 1994; Signatory, Roll of Distinguished Philatelists, 1995; Award for Philatelic Achievement, Smithsonian Mus., 2003. *Publications:* The Crown Colony of Wei Hai Wei, 1985; Royal Reform, 1999; contrib. articles to London Philatelist, etc. *Recreations:* tennis, golf, cricket. *Address:* Wyndham, 30 Mill Lane, Amersham, Bucks HP7 0EH. *T:* (01494) 726291. *Club:* MCC. *Died 10 June 2015.*

GOODY, Sir John (Rankine), (Sir Jack), Kt 2005; FBA 1976; William Wyse Professor of Social Anthropology, University of Cambridge, 1973–84, then Professor Emeritus; Fellow, St John's College, Cambridge, since 1960; *b* 27 July 1919; *m* 1946, Joan Wright (marr. diss. 1956; she *d* 2008); one *s* two *d*; *m* 1956, Esther Robinson Newcomb (marr. diss. 1996); two *d*; *m* 2000, Prof. Juliet Constance Wyatt Mitchell, FBA. *Educ:* St Albans Sch.; St John's Coll., Cambridge; Balliol Coll., Oxford. BA 1946, Dip. Anthrop. 1947, PhD 1954, ScD 1969, Cantab; BLitt Oxon 1952. HM Forces, 1939–46. Educnl admin, 1947–49; Cambridge Univ.: Asst Lectr, 1954–59; Lectr, 1959–71; Dir, African Studies Centre, 1966–73; Smuts Reader in Commonwealth Studies, 1972. Mem., Academia Europaea, 1991; Foreign Hon. Member: Amer. Acad. of Arts and Scis, 1980; NAS, 2005. Hon. DLit Kent, 1996; Hon. LLD Toronto, 2002; D*hc* Bordeaux, 2004; Hon. Dr: Paul Verlaine-Metz, 2006; Nanterre, Paris X, 2006; Malta, 2011; Lisbon, 2012. International Prize, Fondation Fyssen, 1991. Mem., Ordre des Palmes Académiques, 1993; Commandeur dans l'Ordre des Arts et des Lettres (France), 2006 (Chevalier, 1996; Officier, 2001). *Publications:* The Social Organisation of the LoWiili, 1956; (ed) The Developmental Cycle in Domestic Groups, 1958; Death, Property and the Ancestors, 1962; (ed) Succession to High Office, 1966; (with J. A. Braimah) Salaga: the struggle for power, 1967; (ed) Literacy in Traditional Societies, 1968; Comparative Studies in Kinship, 1969; Technology, Tradition and the State in Africa, 1971; The Myth of the Bagre, 1972; (with S. J. Tambiah) Bridewealth and Dowry, 1973; (ed) The Character of Kinship, 1973; (ed) Changing Social Structure in Ghana, 1975; Production and Reproduction, 1977; The Domestication of the Savage Mind, 1977; (with S. W. D. K. Gandah) Une Recitation du Bagré, 1981; Cooking, Cuisine and Class, 1982; The Development of the Family and Marriage in Europe, 1983; The Logic of Writing and the Organization of Society, 1986; The Interface between the Oral and the Written, 1987; The Oriental, the Ancient and the Primitive, 1990; The Culture of Flowers, 1993; The Expansive Moment, 1995; The East in the West, 1996; Jack Goody: l'homme, l'écriture et la mort, 1996; Representations and Contradictions, 1997; Oltre i Muri: la mia prigionia in Italia, 1997, French rev. edn 2004; Food and Love: a cultural history of East and West, 1999; The European Family, 2000; The Power of the Written Tradition, 2000; (with S. W. D. K. Gandah) A Myth Revisited: the third Bagre, 2003; Islam in Europe, 2003; Capitalism and Modernisation: the great debate, 2004; The Theft of History, 2007; Ghana Revisited, 2008; Renaissances?: the one or the many?, 2009; The Eurasian Miracle, 2009; Myth, Ritual and the Oral, 2010; Metals, Capitalism and the Near East, 2012; contrib. learned jls. *Address:* St John's College, Cambridge CB2 1TP. *T:* (01223) 338638. *Died 16 July 2015.*

GORDIMER, Nadine, FRSL; author; *b* 20 Nov. 1923; *d* of Isidore Gordimer and Nan Gordimer (*née* Myers); *m* 1st, 1949, Gerald Gavron (marr. diss. 1952); one *d*; 2nd, 1954, Reinhold Cassirer (*d* 2001); one *s*. *Educ:* Convent Sch.; Witwatersrand Univ. Neil Gunn Fellowship, Scottish Arts Council, 1981. Vice-Pres., PEN Internat. Goodwill Ambassador, UNDP. Hon. Member: Amer. Acad. of Art and Literature, 1979; Amer. Acad. of Arts and Sciences, 1980. DLit *hc* Leuven, Belgium, 1980; DLitt *hc*: City Coll. of NY, 1985; Smith Coll., 1985; Harvard, 1986; Yale, 1986; Columbia, 1987; New Sch. for Social Res., 1987; York, 1987; Oxford, 1994. MLA Award, USA, 1981; Malaparte Prize, Italy, 1985; Nelly Sachs Prize, W Germany, 1985; Bennett Award, USA, 1986; Nobel Prize for Literature, 1991; Grinzane Cavour Prize, 2007. Comdr, Ordre des Arts et des Lettres (France); Order of the Southern Cross (S Africa); Order of Friendship (Cuba); Presidential Medal of Honour (Chile); Légion d'Honneur (France), 2007. *Publications: novels:* The Lying Days, 1953; A World of Strangers, 1958; Occasion for Loving, 1963; The Late Bourgeois World, 1966; A Guest of Honour, 1971 (James Tait Black Meml Prize, 1971); The Conservationist, 1974 (jtly, Booker Prize 1974; Grand Aigle d'Or, France, 1975); Burger's Daughter, 1979; July's People, 1981; A Sport of Nature, 1987; My Son's Story, 1990; None to Accompany Me, 1994; The House Gun, 1997; The Pickup, 2001; Get a Life, 2005; No Time Like the Present, 2012; *stories:* The Soft Voice of the Serpent, 1953; Six Feet of the Country, 1956; Friday's Footprint, 1960 (W. H. Smith Lit. Award, 1961); Not for Publication, 1965; Livingstone's Companions, 1972; Selected Stories, 1975; Some Monday for Sure, 1976; A Soldier's Embrace, 1980; Something Out There, 1984; Jump, 1991; Loot, 2003; Beethoven was One-sixteenth Black, 2007; Life Times: stories, 1952–2007, 2010; *non-fiction:* South African Writing Today (jt editor), 1967; The Essential Gesture: writing, politics and places, 1988; Writing and Being (Charles Eliot Norton Lectures), 1995; Living in Hope and History: notes from our century (essays), 1999; (ed and contrib.) Telling Tales, 2004; Telling Times: writing and living, 1950–2008, 2010. *Address:* c/o A. P. Watt, United Agents, 12–26 Lexington Street, W1F 0LE. *Died 13 July 2014.*

GORDON, Rt Rev. (Archibald) Ronald (McDonald); Canon and Sub-Dean of Christ Church, Oxford, 1991–96; an Assistant Bishop, Diocese of Oxford, since 1991; *b* 19 March 1927; *s* of Sir Archibald Gordon, CMG, and Dorothy Katharine Gordon, Bridge House, Gerrards Cross, Bucks. *Educ:* Rugby Sch.; Balliol Coll., Oxford (Organ Schol., MA 1950); Cuddesdon Theol Coll. Deacon 1952; priest 1953; Curate of Stepney, 1952–55; Chaplain, Cuddesdon Coll., 1955–59; Vicar of St Peter, Birmingham, 1959–67; Res. Canon, Birmingham Cathedral, 1967–71; Vicar of University Church of St Mary the Virgin with St

Cross and St Peter in the East, Oxford, 1971–75; Bishop of Portsmouth, 1975–84; Bishop at Lambeth (Hd of Archbp's Staff), 1984–91; an Asst Bishop, Dio. of Southwark, 1984–91; Bishop to the Forces, 1985–90. Mem., H of L, 1981–84. Fellow of St Cross Coll., Oxford, 1975; Select Preacher, Univ. of Oxford, 1985, 1993, 1997. Mem., Church Assembly and General Synod and Proctor in Convocation, 1965–71; Chm., ACCM, 1976–83. Member: Court of Ecclesiastical Causes Reserved, 1991–2004; Archbishops' Commn on Cathedrals, 1992–94; Adv. Bd for Redundant Churches, 1992–98. Chm., Malaŵi Church Trust, 1993–95; Pres., Oxford Mission, 1992–2001. *Recreations:* piano playing, refraining from giving advice. *Address:* St Katharine's House, Ormond Road, Wantage OX12 8EA. *Died 8 Aug. 2015.*

GORDON-SMITH, David Gerard, CMG 1971; Director-General in Legal Service, Council of Ministers, European Communities, 1976–87; *b* 6 Oct. 1925; *s* of late Frederic Gordon-Smith, QC, and Elsie Gordon-Smith (*née* Foster); *m* 1952, Angela Kirkpatrick Pile; one *d* (and one *s* decd). *Educ:* Rugby Sch.; Trinity Coll., Oxford. Served in RNVR, 1944–46. BA (Oxford) 1948; called to the Bar, Inner Temple, 1949; Legal Asst, Colonial Office, 1950; Sen. Legal Asst, 1954; CRO, 1963–65; Asst Legal Adviser, CO, 1965–66; Legal Counsellor, CO, later FCO, 1966–72; Dep. Legal Advr, FCO, 1973–76. *Address:* Kingscote, Westcott, Surrey RH4 3NX. *Died 15 Oct. 2015.*

GORE, Paul Annesley, CMG 1964; CVO 1961; *b* 28 Feb. 1921; *o s* of late Charles Henry Gore, OBE and Hon. Violet Kathleen (*née* Annesley); *m* 1946, Gillian Mary (*d* 2010), *d* of T. E. Allen-Stevens; two *s* (and one *s* decd). *Educ:* Winchester Coll.; Christ Church, Oxford. Military Service, 1941–46: 16/5 Lancers. Colonial Service, 1948–65; Dep. Governor, The Gambia, 1962–65. *Address:* 16 Brookside, Watlington, Oxon OX49 5AQ. *Died 11 Sept. 2012.*

GORMAN, Sir John Reginald, Kt 1998; CVO 1961; CBE 1974 (MBE 1959); MC 1944; DL; Member (UU) Down North, 1998–2003, and Deputy Speaker, 1999–2002, Northern Ireland Assembly; *b* 1 Feb. 1923; *s* of Major J. K. Gorman, MC; *m* 1948, Heather, *d* of George Caruth, solicitor, Ballymena; one *s* two *d* (and one *s* decd). *Educ:* Rockport, Haileybury and ISC; Portora; Glasgow Univ.; Harvard Business Sch. FCIT, FIPM; MIH. Irish Guards, 1941–46, Normandy, France, Belgium, Holland, Germany (Captain, 1944–46). Royal Ulster Constabulary, 1946–60; Chief of Security, BOAC, 1960–63 (incl. Royal Tour of India, 1961); Personnel Dir and Mem. Bd of Management, BOAC, 1964–69; British Airways: Regional Man., Canada, 1969–75; Regional Man., India, Bangladesh, Sri Lanka, 1975–79; Vice-Chm. and Chief Exec., NI Housing Exec., 1979–85; Dir, Inst. of Dirs, NI, 1986–95. Dir, NI Airports Bd, 1985–92. Pres., British Canadian Trade Assoc., 1972–74; Vice-Chm., Federated Appeal of Montreal, 1973–74. Chm., Bd of Airline Representatives, India, 1977–79; Chm., Inst. of Housing (NI), 1984. Chm., NI Forum for Political Dialogue, 1996–98. DL, 1982, High Sheriff, 1987–88, Co. Down. Kt Hospitaller, SMO of St John of Malta, NI, 1997. Chevalier, Légion d'Honneur, 2005. *Publications:* The Times of My Life: an autobiography, 2002. *Recreations:* gardening, bee keeping, country pursuits. *Address:* 10 Strangford Avenue, Killyleagh, Co. Down BT30 9UJ. *T:* (028) 4482 8400. *Clubs:* Cavalry and Guards; Ulster Reform (Belfast). *Died 26 May 2014.*

GORMAN, Teresa Ellen; *b* Sept. 1931; *m* 1952, Jim Gorman (*d* 2007); *m* 2010, Peter Clarke. *Educ:* Fulham Co. Sch.; London Univ. (BSc 1st cl. Hons). Founder and manager of own company, Banta Ltd. Mem., Westminster City Council, 1982–86. MP (C) Billericay, 1987–2001. Contested (Ind.) Streatham, Oct. 1974. Founder and Chairman: Alliance of Small Firms & Self Employed People Ltd, 1974; Amarant Trust, 1986. Mem., Cons. Women's Nat. Cttee, 1983. *Publications:* The Bastards: dirty tricks and the challenge to Europe, 1993; The Amarant Book of HRT, 1989; No, Prime Minister!, 2001; research papers for IEA, Adam Smith Inst., CPS. *Died 28 Aug. 2015.*

GORRIE, Donald Cameron Easterbrook, OBE 1984; DL; Member (Lib Dem) Central Scotland, Scottish Parliament, 1999–2007; *b* 2 April 1933; *s* of Robert Maclagan Gorrie and Sydney Grace Gorrie (*née* Easterbrook); *m* 1957, Astrid Margaret Salvesen; two *s*. *Educ:* Hurst Grange Sch., Stirling; Oundle Sch.; Corpus Christi Coll., Oxford (MA Classical Mods and Modern History). Schoolmaster, Gordonstoun Sch., 1957–60; School Master and Dir of Phys. Educn, Marlborough Coll., 1960–66; Researcher and Adult Educn Lectr in Scottish History, 1966–68; Dir of Res., 1968–71, Dir of Admin, 1971–75, Scottish Liberal Party; Founder, Edinburgh Translations Ltd, 1976 (Dir, 1976–2009); Jt Founder, Scoted Ltd, 1978 (Dir, 1978–84). Member (L, subseq. Lib Dem): Edinburgh Town Council, 1971–75; also Group Leader: Lothian Regl Council, 1974–96; City of Edinburgh DC, 1980–96, City of Edinburgh Council, 1995–97. MP (Lib Dem) Edinburgh West, 1997–2001. Scottish Parliament: Committee Member: Procedures, 1999–2003 (Convener, 2005–07); Local Govt, 1999–2001; Transport and Envmt, 2000–01; Finance, 2001–02; Justice, 2001–03; Communities, 2003–05; Standards, 2003–07; Lib Dem spokesman on culture, sport, voluntary sector, older people. Member of Board/Committee: Edinburgh Fest., 1975–80, 1988–97; Royal Lyceum Theatre, 1975–97; Scottish Chamber Orch., 1988–96; Lothian Assoc. of Youth Clubs, 1975–97; Castle Rock Housing Assoc., 1973–97; Queen's Hall, Edinburgh, 1980–; Corstorphine Dementia Project, 2007– (Chm., 2007–); Youth Scotland, 2008–, and other local orgns; Chm., Edinburgh Youth Orch., 2000–03; Convener: Diverse Attractions, 1984–99; Edinburgh City Youth Café, 1990–97 (Hon. Pres., 1997–); Sec., Friends of Corstorphine Hill, 2007–. Trustee, Nancy Ovens Trust, 2004–. Hon. President: Lothian Assoc. Youth Clubs; Edinburgh Athletic Club; Corstorphine AAC; Vice Pres., Achilles Club. DL City of Edinburgh, 1996. *Recreations:* former Scottish native record holder for 880 yards, reading, music, opera, drama, visiting ruins. *Address:* 9 Garscube Terrace, Edinburgh EH12 6BW. *Clubs:* Achilles (Vice Pres., 2006–); Royal Scots. *Died 25 Aug. 2012.*

GOSS, Wayne Keith; Chair, Deloitte Touche Tohmatsu, Australia, since 2005 (Managing Partner, 1999–2003); Member, National Board, Deloitte Touche Tohmatsu, since 2003; *b* 26 Feb. 1951; *s* of Allan James Goss and Norma Josephine Goss; *m* 1981, Roisin Anne Hirschfeld; one *s* one *d*. *Educ:* Univ. of Queensland (LLB 1975; MBA 1997). Admitted solicitor, 1973; Partner, Goss and Downey, 1977–83. MLA (ALP) Salisbury, 1983–86 and Logan, Queensland, 1986–98; Opposition Minister for Lands, Forestry and Police, 1983–86, for Justice, 1986–88; Leader of Opposition, 1988–89; Premier of Queensland, 1989–96; Minister for the Arts, 1989–92, for Economic and Trade Develt, 1989–96. Chairman: Lincolne Scott Pty Ltd, 2000–05; Ausenco Ltd, 2003–; Free TV Australia Ltd, 2008–; Director: Peplin Ltd, 2000–05; Ingeus Ltd, 2003–07. Chairman: Qld Art Gall., 2001–08; Goodwill Games Brisbane Ltd, 1998–2002; Adv. Council, Graduate Sch. of Govt, Univ. of Sydney, 2003–06. FAICD 2000. Hon. Dr: Queensland Univ. of Technol., 2001; Griffith, 2003; Univ. of Queensland, 2007. *Address:* Unit 21, One Macquarie, 1 Macquarie Street, Teneriffe, Qld 4005, Australia. *Died 10 Nov. 2014.*

GOSWELL, Sir Brian (Lawrence), Kt 1991; FRICS; Chairman: ISS Group Ltd, 2000–07; ISS Safe Havens Ltd, 2002–07; Intelligence and Security Solutions Ltd, 2002–07; *b* 26 Nov. 1935; *s* of late Albert George Goswell and Florence Emily (*née* Barnett); *m* 1961, Deirdre Gillian Stones; two *s*. FRICS 2000 (FSVA 1968). Mil. service, Oxford and Bucks Light Infantry, 1954–57. Joined Healey & Baker, Surveyors, 1957; Partner, 1969; Managing Partner, 1977; Dep. Sen. Partner, 1988–97; Dep. Chm., 1997–2000; Consultant, 2000–02. Chairman: Roux Restaurants Ltd, 1988–96; Avon City Ltd, 1989–98; Sunley Secure II PLC, 1993–99; Brent Walker Gp PLC, 1993–97; William Hill Gp Ltd, 1994–97; Pubmaster Ltd, 1994–96; Internat. Security Mgt Gp Ltd, 1998–2002. Member: Adv. Bd, Sir Alexander Gibb & Partners Ltd, 1990–96; Adv. Panel, AAIM Gp Plc (formerly AAIM Property Fund Ltd), 2005–07. Pres., 1993–94, and Mem. Bd of Mgt, British Council for Offices; Pres., Amer. Chamber of Commerce (UK), 1994–98; Member: Adv. Bd, Fulbright Commn, 1997–2004; Duke of Edinburgh's Award Internat. Fellowship, 1997–. President: ISVA, 1986–87; Land Inst., 1997–2009. Trustee, Conservative and Unionist Agents' Superannuation Fund, 1993–98. FRSA 1993. *Recreations:*

cricket, horse-racing, shooting, fishing. *Address:* Pipers, Camley Park Drive, Pinkneys Green, Maidenhead, Berks SL6 6QF. *T:* (01628) 630768. *Clubs:* Carlton, United & Cecil, City Livery, Rifles London Officers, MCC; Leander (Henley-on-Thames). *Died 23 March 2014.*

GOUGH, Sir (Charles) Brandon, Kt 2002; DL; FCA; Chancellor, University of East Anglia, since 2003; *b* 8 Oct. 1937; *s* of late Charles Richard Gough and Mary Evaline (*née* Goff); *m* 1961, Sarah Smith; one *s* two *d*. *Educ:* Douai Sch.; Jesus Coll., Cambridge (MA); BA Open Univ., 2005. FCA 1974. Joined Cooper Brothers & Co. subseq. Coopers & Lybrand, 1964, Partner 1968; Chm., 1983–94; Mem., Exec. Cttee, Coopers & Lybrand (Internat.), 1982–94 (Chm., 1985 and 1991–92); Chm., Coopers & Lybrand Europe, 1989, and 1992–94. Chairman: Yorkshire Water, then Kelda Gp, 1996–2000; De La Rue plc, 1997–2004 (Dir, 1994–2004); Locate in Kent Ltd, 2006–; Govt Dir, BAe plc, 1987–88; Director: British Invisibles, 1990–94; S. G. Warburg Gp, 1994–95 (Dep. Chm., 1995); National Power, 1995–2000; George Wimpey, 1995–99; Montanaro UK Smaller Cos Investment Trust plc, 1998–2005 (Chm., 1999–2005); Singer & Friedlander Gp, 1999–2005; Innogy Hldgs, 2000–02; Partnership Council, Freshfields, 1996–2000; Chm., Montanaro European Smaller Cos, 2000–04. Mem. Council, Inst. of Chartered Accountants in England and Wales, 1981–84; Chm., CCAB Auditing Practices Cttee, 1981–84 (Mem., 1976–84); Member: Accounting Standards Review (Dearing) Cttee, 1987–88; Financial Reporting Council, 1990–96. City University Business School: Chm., City Adv. Panel, 1986–91 (Mem., 1980–91); Mem. Council, 1986–93 (Chm., 1992–93); Chm., Finance Cttee, 1988–91; Member: Council of Lloyd's, 1983–86; Cambridge Univ. Careers Service Syndicate, 1983–86; Governing Council, 1984–88, Council, 1988–94, President's Cttee, 1992–94, Business in the Community; Council for Industry and Higher Educn, 1985–93; Management Council, GB-Sasakawa Foundn, 1985–96; UK Nat. Cttee, Japan-European Community Assoc., 1989–94; CBI Task Force, Vocational Educn and Trng, 1989; CBI Educn & Trng Affairs Cttee, 1990–94; Council, Foundn for Educn Business Partnerships, 1990–91; Council, City Univ., 1991–93; Council, Prince of Wales Business Leaders Forum of Internat. Business in the Community, 1992–94. Chairman: Common Purpose Trust, 1991–97 (Trustee, 1989–97); Nat. Trng Task Force working gp on role of TECs in local econ. develt, 1991–92; Doctors' and Dentists' Pay Review Body, 1993–2001; HEFCE, 1993–97. Mem., Council of Management, Royal Shakespeare Theatre Trust, 1991–97; Trustee: GSMD Foundn, 1989–95; Hospice in the Weald, 2003–10; Canterbury Cathedral Trust Fund, 2006–12; Leeds Castle Foundn, 2006– (Chm., 2007–). DL Kent, 2005. Hon. DSc City, 1994; Hon. DCL: UEA, 2003; Kent, 2009. Lloyd's Silver Medal, 1986. *Recreation:* music. *Address:* University of East Anglia, Norwich NR4 7TJ. *Died 26 April 2012.*

GOULD OF BROOKWOOD, Baron *cr* 2004 (Life Peer), of Brookwood in the County of Surrey; **Philip Gould;** Founder, Philip Gould Associates, polling and political strategy, 1985; Deputy Chairman, freud communications, since 2008; *b* 30 March 1950; *s* of Wilfred Caleb Gould and Fennigien Anna Gould (*née* de-Jager); *m* 1985, Gail Ruth Rebuck (Dame Gail Rebuck, DBE); two *d*. *Educ:* Knaphill Secondary Modern Sch., Woking; E London Coll.; Univ. of Sussex (BA Politics); LSE (MA with Dist. Hist. of Political Thought); London Business Sch. (Sloan Fellow (Dist.)). Account Dir, Wasey, Campbell-Ewald, 1975–79; Dir, Tinker and Partners, 1979–81; Founder, Brignull LeBas Gould, 1981–83; Mgt Dir, Doyle Dane Bernbach, 1984–85. Vis. Prof., LSE. *Publications:* The Unfinished Revolution, 1998; *posthumous publication*: When I Die: lessons from the death zone, 2012. *Recreations:* friends, family, QPR, tennis, reading, travel. *Address:* House of Lords, SW1A 0PW. *T:* (home) (020) 7486 5255. *Died 6 Nov. 2011.*

GOULSTONE, Very Rev. (Thomas Richard) Kerry; Dean of St Asaph Cathedral, 1993–2001; *b* 5 June 1936; *s* of Thomas Louis and Elizabeth Goulstone; *m* 1963, Lyneth Ann Harris; one *s* one *d*. *Educ:* Llanelli Boys' Grammar Sch.; St David's University Coll., Lampeter (BA); St Michael's Theol Coll., Llandaff. Deacon 1959, priest 1960, St David's; Curate: Llanbadarn Fawr, 1959–61; St Peter's, Carmarthen, 1961–64; Vicar: Whitchurch with Solva, 1964–67; Gorslas, 1967–76; Burry Port with Pwll, 1976–84; St Peter's, Carmarthen, 1984–93; Canon, St David's Cathedral, 1986–91; RD of Carmarthen, 1988–91; Archdeacon of Carmarthen, 1991–93. Chaplain, West Wales Hosp., 1984–93. *Recreations:* music, sport, collecting porcelain. *Address:* 25 Parc Tyisha, Burry Port SA16 0RR. *T:* (01554) 832090. *Died 29 Jan. 2013.*

GOURLAY, Gen. Sir (Basil) Ian (Spencer), KCB 1973; CVO 1990; OBE 1956 (MBE 1948); MC 1944; Vice President, United World Colleges, since 1990 (Director General, 1975–90); *b* 13 Nov. 1920; *er s* of late Brig. K. I. Gourlay, DSO, OBE, MC and Victoria May Gourlay (*née* Oldrini); *m* 1948, Natasha, *d* of Col Dimitri Zinovieff and Princess Elisaveta Galitzine; one *s* one *d*. *Educ:* Eastbourne Coll. Commissioned RM, 1940; HMS Formidable, Arctic, Indian Ocean, Mediterranean, 1941–44; 43 Commando, Yugoslavia, Italy, 1944–45; 45 Commando, Hong Kong, 1946–48; Instructor, RNC Greenwich, 1948–50; Adjt RMFVR, City of London, 1950–52; Instructor, RM Officers' Sch., 1952–54; psc 1954; Bde Major, 3rd Commando Bde, Malta, Cyprus, Suez landings, 1955–57 (despatches); OC RM Officers' Trng Wing, Infantry Training Centre RM, 1957–59; 2nd in Comd, 42 Commando, Singapore, 1959–61; GSO1, HQ Plymouth Gp, 1961–63; CO 42 Commando, Singapore, Borneo, 1963–65; Col GS, Dept of CGRM, Min. of Defence, 1965–66; Col 1965; Comdr, 3rd Commando Bde, Singapore, 1966–68; Maj.-Gen. Royal Marines, Portsmouth, 1968–71; Commandant-General, Royal Marines, 1971–75; Lt-Gen., 1971; Gen., 1973. Vice Patron, RM Museum. *Clubs:* Army and Navy; Royal Navy Cricket (Vice-Pres.). *Died 17 July 2013.*

GOW, Gen. Sir (James) Michael, GCB 1983 (KCB 1979); DL; Commandant, Royal College of Defence Studies, 1984–86; *b* 3 June 1924; *s* of late J. C. Gow and Mrs Alastair Sanderson; *m* 1946, Jane Emily Scott, *e d* of late Capt. and Hon. Mrs Mason Scott; one *s* four *d*. *Educ:* Winchester College. Enlisted Scots Guards, 1942; commnd 1943; served NW Europe, 1944–45; Mil. Div., Quadripartite Control Commn, Berlin, 1945–46; Malayan Emergency, 1949; Equerry to HRH the Duke of Gloucester, 1952–53; psc 1954; Bde Major 1955–57; Regimental Adjt Scots Guards, 1957–60; Instructor Army Staff Coll., 1962–64; comd 2nd Bn Scots Guards, Kenya and England, 1964–66; GSO1, HQ London District, 1966–67; comd 4th Guards Bde, 1968–69; idc 1970; BGS (Int) HQ BAOR and ACOS G2 HQ Northag, 1971–73; GOC 4th Div. BAOR, 1973–75; Dir of Army Training, 1975–78; GOC Scotland and Governor of Edinburgh Castle, 1979–80; C-in-C BAOR and Comdr, Northern Army Gp, 1980–83 (awarded die Plakette des deutschen Heeres); ADC Gen. to the Queen, 1981–84. Colonel Commandant: Intelligence Corps, 1973–86; Scottish Division, 1979–80. Mem., Queen's Body Guard for Scotland, Royal Company of Archers, 1963– (Capt., 2003; non active list, 2005). UK Mem., Eurogroup US Tour, 1983. UK Kermit Roosevelt Lectr, USA, 1984. President: Royal British Legion, Scotland, 1986–96; Earl Haig Fund Scotland, 1986–96 (Vice Pres., 1996–); Nat. Assoc. of Supported Employment, 1993–96; Officers' Assoc. Scotland, 1995–96 (Vice Pres., 1996–); Chairman: Scottish Ex-Services' Charitable Orgn, 1989–96; Scots at War Trust, 1992–; Patron, Disablement Income Group Scotland, 1993–. Vice-President: Royal Patriotic Fund Corp., 1983–88; Scottish Nat. Instn for War Blinded, 1995–; Mem. Council, Erskine Hosp., 1990– (Hon. Pres., 1979–80); Mem., Thistle Foundn, 2000–. Chm., Queen Victoria Sch., Dunblane, 1979–80; Vice-President: Royal Caledonian Schs, Bushey, 1980–96; Royal Caledonian Schs Educnl Trust, 1996–. Trustee Emeritus, Ludus Baroque (Chm., 1999–2005). County Comr, British Scouts W Europe, 1980–83 (Silver Acorn). Freeman: City of London, 1980; State of Kansas, USA, 1984; Freeman and Liveryman, Painters' and Stainers' Co., 1980. Elder of Church of Scotland, Canongate Kirk, 1988–. FSAScot 1991–2002. DL Edinburgh, 1994. *Publications:* Trooping the Colour: a history of the Sovereign's Birthday Parade by the Household troops, 1989; Jottings in a General's Notebook, 1989; General Reflections: a military man at large, 1991; articles in mil. and hist. jls. *Recreations:* sailing, music, travel, reading. *Address:* 18 Ann Street, Edinburgh EH4 1PJ. *T:* (0131) 332 4752. *Clubs:* Pratt's, Highland Society of London, Third Guards, Blue Seal. *Died 26 March 2013.*

GOWANS, Gen. John; General of The Salvation Army, 1999–2002; *b* 13 Nov. 1934; *s* of John and Elizabeth Gowans; *m* 1957, Gisèle Marie Bonhotal; two *s*. *Educ:* Halesowen Grammar Sch.; William Booth Meml Trng Coll. Served with Salvation Army, 1955–2002; commnd officer, in Liverpool, N Wales, London, Manchester, Yorkshire, Nottingham, 1955–77; Chief Sec., Paris, 1977–81; Leader for Southern California, LA, 1981–86; Territorial Commander in: France, 1986–93; Australia E and PNG, 1993–97; UK and Republic of Ireland, 1997–99. Freeman, City of London, 2000. Hon. DLitt Yonsei, Korea, 2000. Paul Harris Fellow, Rotary Internat., 1999. *Publications:* O Lord!, 1977, 3rd edn 1996; There's a boy here… (autobiog.), 2002; libretto for ten Salvation Army musicals. *Recreations:* reading, gardening, English literature, drama. *Address:* c/o The Salvation Army, 101 Queen Victoria Street, EC4V 4EH. *T:* (020) 7332 0101. *Died 8 Dec. 2012.*

GRAAFF, Sir David (de Villiers), 3rd Bt *cr* 1911, of Cape Town; farmer, since 1964; wine farmer and producer of De Grendel wines, since 2000; *b* 3 May 1940; *er s* of Sir de Villiers Graaff, 2nd Bt and of Helena Le Roux Graaff (*née* Voigt); *S* father, 1999; *m* 1969, Sally Williams; three *s* one *d*. *Educ:* Diocesan Coll.; Stellenbosch Univ. (BSc Agric.); Grenoble Univ. (Premier Degré); Magdalen Coll., Oxford (BA Hons; MA). MP (Nat. Party), Wynberg, 1987–98; Dep. Minister, Trade and Industry, 1991–94. Mem., Audit Commn, 1992–94. Dir, Deciduous Fruit Bd, 1983–87. Director: Graaff's Trust, 1969–; Milnerton Estates, 1969–. Hon. Col, Cape Garrison Artillery, 2000–. *Recreation:* golf. *Heir: s* De Villiers Graaff [*b* 16 July 1970; *m* 2000, Gaedry Kriel; three *s* one *d*]. *Address:* De Grendel, PO Box 15192, Panorama 7506, Cape Town, South Africa. *T:* (21) 5587030. *Clubs:* Cape Town, Royal Cape Golf. *Died 24 Jan. 2015.*

GRABHAM, Sir Anthony (Herbert), Kt 1988; FRCS; Chairman, British Medical Journal Group, 1993–2004; *b* 19 July 1930; *s* of John and Lily Grabham; *m* 1960, Eileen Pamela Rudd; two *s* two *d*. *Educ:* St Cuthbert's Grammar School, Newcastle upon Tyne. MB BS Durham. RSO, Royal Victoria Infirmary, Newcastle upon Tyne; Consultant Surgeon, Kettering and District Gen. Hosp., 1965–95. Chm., BMA Services, 1982–2002; Dir, PPP, 1984–96, Vice-Chm., PPP Healthcare Gp plc, 1996–99. British Medical Association: Chairman: Central Cttee for Hosp. Med. Services, 1975–79; Council, 1979–84; Pres., 2002–03. Chairman: Jt Consultants Cttee, 1984–90; Cttee, BMJ, 1993–2004; Member: GMC, 1979–99; Council, World Med. Assoc., 1979–84; Hon. Sec. and Treasurer, Commonwealth Med. Assoc., 1982–86 (Vice-Pres., 1980–84). *Address:* Rothesay House, 56 Headlands, Kettering, Northants NN15 6DG. *T:* (01536) 513299. *Club:* Army and Navy. *Died 22 Feb. 2015.*

GRACE, John Oliver Bowman; QC 1994; Consultant, Leigh Day & Co., Solicitors, since 2010; *b* 13 June 1948; *s* of late Oliver Grace, MBE, TD and Marjorie (*née* Bowman); *m* 1973, Carol S. Roundhill; two *s* one *d*. *Educ:* Marlborough; Southampton Univ. (LLB Hons). Called to the Bar, Middle Temple, 1973, Bencher, 2001. Founder Mem., 3 Serjeants' Inn Chambers, Hd of Chambers, 2000–07. Chm., Mental Health Research UK, 2008–. *Recreations:* gardening, modern art, reading, music, cricket, church, brick-laying, sailing. *Address:* Leigh Day & Co., Priory House, 25 St John's Lane, EC1M 4LB. *Clubs:* 4W's (Wandsworth); Whitstable Yacht. *Died 16 July 2011.*

GRACEY, John Halliday, CB 1984; Director General (Deputy Secretary), Board of Inland Revenue, 1981–85; Commissioner of Inland Revenue, 1973–85; *b* 20 May 1925; *s* of Halliday Gracey and Florence Jane (*née* Cudlipp); *m* 1950, Margaret Procter; three *s*. *Educ:* City of London Sch.; Brasenose Coll., Oxford (MA). Army, 1943–47. Entered Inland Revenue, 1950; HM Treasury, 1970–73. Hon. Treas., NACRO, 1987–98. *Recreations:* walking, reading, music. *Address:* 3 Woodberry Down, Epping, Essex CM16 6RJ. *T:* (01992) 572167. *Club:* Reform. *Died 7 Oct. 2011.*

GRADY, Terence, MBE 1967; HM Diplomatic Service, retired; Ambassador at Libreville, 1980–82; *b* 23 March 1924; *s* of Patrick Grady and Catherine (*née* Fowles); *m* 1960, Jean Fischer; one *s* four *d*. *Educ:* St Michael's Coll., Leeds. HM Forces, 1942–47; Foreign Office, 1949; HM Embassy: Baghdad, 1950; Paris, 1951; Asst Private Secretary to Secretary of State for Foreign Affairs, 1952–55; HM Legation, Budapest, 1955–58; HM Embassy, Kabul, 1958–60; FO, 1960–63; Vice Consul, Elisabethville, 1963; Consul, Philadelphia, 1964–69; UK High Commission, Sydney, 1969–72; FCO, 1972–75; Head of Chancery, Dakar, 1975–77; Consul, Istanbul, 1977–80. *Recreations:* tennis, walking. *Address:* 207 Orchard Place, Sewickley, PA 15143, USA. *Died 27 Oct. 2014.*

GRAFTON, 11th Duke of, *cr* 1675; **Hugh Denis Charles FitzRoy,** KG 1976; DL; Earl of Euston, Viscount Ipswich; Captain Grenadier Guards; *b* 3 April 1919; *e s* of 10th Duke of Grafton, and Lady Doreen Maria Josepha Sydney Buxton (*d* 1923), *d* of 1st Earl Buxton; *S* father, 1970; *m* 1946, Fortune (GCVO 1980); one *s* three *d* (and one *s* decd). *Educ:* Eton; Magdalene Coll., Cambridge. ADC to the Viceroy of India, 1943–46. Vice-Chm. of Trustees, Nat. Portrait Gall., 1967–92; Mem., Royal Fine Art Commn, 1971–94. Chairman: Architectural Heritage Fund, 1976–94; Cathedrals Adv. Commn, 1981–91; Member: Hist. Bldgs Council for England, 1953–84; Hist. Bldgs Adv. Cttee, 1984–2001, Cathedrals and Churches Adv. Cttee, 1984–2001, English Heritage; Properties Cttee, Nat. Trust, 1981–94; President: Suffolk Preservation Soc., 1957–; SPAB, 1989–; Trustee: Sir John Soane's Mus. (Chm., 1975–97); Hist. Churches Preservation Trust (Chm., 1980–97); Tradescant Trust, 1976–99; Buildings at Risk Trust, 1986–2000; Patron, Historic Houses Assoc. President: Internat. Students House, 1972–; East Anglia Tourist Bd, 1973–93; British Soc. of Master Glass Painters. Patron, Hereford Herd Book Soc. DL Suffolk, 1973. Hon. DCL East Anglia, 1990. *Heir: g s* Viscount Ipswich, *b* 6 April 1978. *Address:* Euston Hall, Thetford, Norfolk IP24 2QW. *T:* (01842) 753282. *Club:* Boodle's. *Died 7 April 2011.*

GRAFTON, Peter Witheridge, CBE 1972; Senior Partner, G. D. Walford & Partners, Chartered Quantity Surveyors, 1978–82 (Partner 1949–78); *b* 19 May 1916; *s* of James Hawkins Grafton and Ethel Marion (*née* Brannan); *m* 1st, 1939, Joan Bleackley (*d* 1969); two *d* (and one *s* one *d* decd); 2nd, 1971, Margaret Ruth Ward; two *s*. *Educ:* Westminster City Sch.; Sutton Valence Sch.; Coll. of Estate Management. FRICS. Served War of 1939–45, Queen's Westminster Rifles, Dorsetshire Regt and RE, UK and Far East (Captain). Pres., RICS, 1978–79 (Vice-Pres., 1974–78); Mem. and Past Chm., Quantity Surveyors Council; Mem. Council, Construction Industries Research and Information Assoc., 1963–69; Member: Research Adv. Council to Minister of Housing and Construction, 1967–71; Nat. Cons. Council for Building and Civil Engrg Industries, 1968–76; British Bd of Agrément, 1973–88; Chm., Nat. Jt Consultative Cttee for Building Industry, 1974–75 (Mem., 1970–77). Master, Worshipful Co. of Chartered Surveyors, 1983–84. Trustee, United Westminster Schs; Governor, Sutton Valence Sch., 1971–96 (Chm., 1976–91); Chm., Old Suttonians Assoc., 1971–75 (Pres., 1996–2005). Contested (L) Bromley, 1950. *Publications:* numerous articles on techn. and other professional subjects. *Recreation:* golf (founder, Chm., 1962–94, Pres., 1994–, Public Schs Old Boys Golf Assoc., Co-donor Grafton Morrish Trophy; past Captain and past Pres. of Chartered Surveyors Golfing Soc.). *Died 20 May 2012.*

GRAHAM, Douglas; *see* Graham, M. G. D.

GRAHAM, Gordon; *see* Graham, W. G.

GRAHAM, Maj.-Gen. John David Carew, CB 1978; CBE 1973 (OBE 1966); Secretary to the Administrative Trustees of the Chevening Estate, 1978–86; *b* 18 Jan. 1923; *s* of late Col J. A. Graham, late RE, and Constance Mary Graham (*née* Carew-Hunt); *m* 1956, Rosemary Elaine

Adamson; one *s* one *d*. *Educ:* Cheltenham Coll. psc 1955; jssc 1962. Commissioned into Argyll and Sutherland Highlanders, 1942 (despatches, 1945); served with 5th (Scottish) Bn, The Parachute Regt, 1946–49; British Embassy, Prague, 1949–50; HQ Scottish Comd, 1956–58; Mil. Asst to CINCENT, Fontainebleau, 1960–62; comd 1st Bn, The Parachute Regt, 1964–66; Instr at Staff Coll., Camberley, 1967; Regtl Col, The Parachute Regt, 1968–69; Comdr, Sultan's Armed Forces, Oman, 1970–72; Indian Nat. Defence Coll., New Delhi, 1973; Asst Chief of Staff, HQ AFCENT, 1974–76; GOC Wales, 1976–78. Hon. Col, Kent ACF, 1981–88 (Chm., Kent ACF Cttee, 1979–86); Hon. Col, 203 (Welsh) Gen. Hosp., RAMC, TA, 1983–88. Freeman, City of London, 1992. OStJ 1978, and Chm., St John Council for Kent, 1978–86; CStJ 1983. Order of Oman, 1972. *Publications:* Ponder Anew: reflections on the twentieth century, 1999; (with Humphrey Metzgen) Caribbean Wars Untold: a salute to the British West Indies, 2007. *Address:* Montrose, 58 Rendez-Vous Ridge East, Christ Church BB15 110, Barbados, WI. *Died 14 Dec. 2012.*

GRAHAM, Rev. John Galbraith, MBE 2005; crossword setter as Araucaria, since 1958; *b* 16 Feb. 1921; *s* of Rt Rev. Eric and Phyllis Norton Graham; *m* 1st, 1952, Ernesta Mary Davies (marr. diss.); 2nd, 1983, Margaret Crawshaw Entwistle (*d* 1993). *Educ:* St Edward's Sch., Oxford; King's Coll., Cambridge (Schol.; MA); Ely Theol Coll. Served RAF, 1942–45, navigator/bomb-aimer (mentioned in dispatches, 1945). Ordained deacon, 1948, priest, 1949; Curate, St John, E Dulwich, 1948–49; Chaplain, St Chad's Coll., Durham, 1949–52; Curate: Aldershot, 1952–55; Beaconsfield, 1955–62; Chaplain, Reading Univ., 1962–72; Curate, St Peter, Eaton Sq., London, 1972–74; Rector, Houghton with Wyton, Dio. of Ely, 1974–78. *Publications:* Monkey Puzzles, Vol. 1, 2002, Vol. 2, 2004; Chambers Book of Araucaria Crosswords, 2003; Chambers 2nd Book of Araucaria Crosswords, 2005; Chambers 3rd Book of Araucaria Crosswords, 2006; Chambers 4th Book of Araucaria Crosswords, 2008. *Recreations:* quizzes, bridge, friends. *Address:* 31 Rectory Lane, Somersham, Huntingdon PE28 3EL. *Died 26 Nov. 2013.*

GRAHAM, (Malcolm Gray) Douglas; DL; Chairman: The Midland News Association Ltd, since 1984 (Deputy Chairman, 1978–84); Claverley Co., since 1993; Deputy Chairman, Guiton Group Ltd, since 2003; *b* 18 Feb. 1930; *s* of late Malcolm Graham and Annie Jeanette Robinson; *m* 1980, Sara Anne Elwell (*née* Anderson). *Educ:* Shrewsbury Sch. National Service, RM, 1948–50. Newspaper trng, UK and Australia, 1950–53; Dir, Express & Star (Wolverhampton) Ltd, 1957. President: Young Newspapermen's Assoc., 1969; W Midlands Newspaper Soc., 1973–74; Chm., Evening Newspaper Advertising Bureau, 1978–79. DL Shropshire, 1997. *Recreation:* shooting. *Address:* Roughton Manor, Bridgnorth, Shropshire WV15 5HE. *T:* (01746) 716209. *Died 21 March 2015.*

GRAHAM, His Honour Martin; QC 1976; a Circuit Judge, 1986–2000; *b* 10 Feb. 1929; *m* 1962, Jane Filby; one *d*. *Educ:* Emanuel School; Trinity College, Oxford (Scholar; MA, PPE). Called to the Bar, Middle Temple, 1952; a Recorder, 1986. Nat. Service, Officer BAOR, 1953–55. *Recreations:* swimming, tennis. *Address:* 7 Oakeshott Avenue, Highgate, N6 6NT. *Clubs:* Reform, Royal Automobile, Hurlingham. *Died 16 Sept. 2014.*

GRAHAM, Stuart Twentyman, CBE 1981; DFC 1943; FCIS, FCIB; Chairman, Aitken Hume Bank (formerly Aitken Hume) Ltd, 1985–93; *b* 26 Aug. 1921; *s* of late Twentyman Graham; *m* 1948, Betty June Cox (*d* 1999); one *s*. *Educ:* Kilburn Grammar Sch. Served War, 1940–46: commissioned, RAF, 1942. Entered Midland Bank, 1938; Jt Gen. Manager, 1966–70; Asst Chief Gen. Manager, 1970–74; Chief Gen. Manager, 1974–81; Gp Chief Exec., 1981–82; Dir, 1974–85. Chairman: Northern Bank Ltd, 1982–85; International Commodities Clearing House Ltd, 1982–86; Director: Allied Lyons plc, 1981–92; Sheffield Forgemasters Holdings, 1983–85; Aitken Hume International, 1985–93; Scotia (formerly Efamol) Hldgs, 1985–95. *Recreations:* music, reading. *Club:* Royal Air Force. *Died 2 Oct. 2015.*

GRAHAM, (William) Gordon, MC 1944 (Bar 1945); Editor, LOGOS, 1990–2005, Editor Emeritus, 2006–09; Group Chairman, Butterworth Publishers, 1975–90 (Chief Executive, 1974–87); *b* 17 July 1920; *s* of Thomas Graham and Marion Hutcheson; US citizen, 1963; *m* 1st, 1943, Margaret Milne, Bombay (*d* 1946); one *d*; 2nd, 1948, Friedel Gramm, Zürich (*d* 1992); one *d*; 3rd, 1994, Betty Cottrell, USA. *Educ:* Hutchesons' Grammar Sch.; Glasgow Univ. (MA 1940). Commissioned, Queen's Own Cameron Highlanders, 1941; served in India and Burma, 1942–46: Captain 1944, Major 1945; GSO II India Office, 1946. Newspaper correspondent and publishers' representative in India, 1946–55; Internat. Sales Manager, 1956–63, Vice-Pres., 1961–63, McGraw-Hill Book Co., New York; Man. Dir, McGraw-Hill Publishing Co., UK, 1963–74; Director: W & R Chambers, Edinburgh, 1974–83; International Publishing Corp., 1975–82; Reed Publishing Gp, 1982–90; Chairman: Internat. Electronic Publishing Res. Centre Ltd, 1981–84; Publishers Database Ltd, 1982–84; Bd, R. R. Bowker Co., 1986–90; Mem. Bd, Polish Scientific Publishers, 1994–99. Chm., Soc. of Bookmen, 1972–75; Publishers Association: Mem. Council, 1972–87; Chm., Electronic Publishing Panel, 1980–83; Vice Pres., 1984–85, 1987–88; Pres., 1985–87. Member Board: British Liby, 1980–86; Eur. Foundn for Liby Co-operation, 1991–95. Hon. Mem., Soc. of Young Publishers, 2007. Trustee, Kraszna-Krausz Foundn, 1987–97 (Chm. Trustees, 1990–95); Pres., Kohima Educnl Trust, 2006– (Trustee, 2002–06). Correspondent, Christian Science Monitor, 1946–56. FRSA 1978. DUniv Stirling, 1993. *Publications:* As I Was Saying: essays on the international book business, 1994; Butterworths: history of a publishing house, 1997; The Trees are all Young on Garrison Hill, 2005; From Trust to Takeover: an intimate history of Butterworths 1943–67, 2006; articles in US and British trade press. *Recreations:* writing, fostering transatlantic understanding, landscape gardening, singing sentimental songs. *Address:* White Lodge, Beechwood Drive, Marlow, Bucks SL7 2DH. *T:* (01628) 483371; Juniper Acres, 1039 Hurricane Road, Keene, NY 12942, USA. *Died 24 April 2015.*

GRAHAM-DIXON, Anthony Philip; QC 1973; *b* 5 Nov. 1929; *s* of late Leslie Charles Graham-Dixon, QC; *m* 1956, Margaret Suzanne Villar (*d* 2010); one *s* one *d*. *Educ:* Westminster Sch.; Christ Church, Oxford. MA (1st Cl. Hon. Mods, 1st Cl. Lit. Hum.). RNVR, 1953–55, Lieut (SP). Called to the Bar, Inner Temple, 1956, Bencher 1982; Member of Gray's Inn, 1965–. Mem. Council, Charing Cross Hosp. Medical School, 1976–83. Chm., London Concertino Ltd, 1982–. Dep. Chm., PHLS, 1988–96 (Mem. Bd, 1987–96). Gov., Bedales Sch., 1988–96. Trustee, SPNM, 1988–97 (Chm. Trustees, 1994–97). Chm., London Jupiter Orch. Trust Ltd, 2001–. Chm., External Adv. Panel, Faculty of Music, Univ. of Oxford, 2008–. Liveryman, Goldsmiths' Co., 1980–. *Publications:* (mem. adv. bd) Competition Law in Western Europe and the USA, 1976. *Recreations:* music (especially opera), gardening. *Address:* 46A Courtfield Gardens, SW5 0NA. *T:* (020) 7373 1461; Masketts Manor, Nutley, Uckfield, East Sussex TN22 3HD. *T:* (01825) 712010. *Died 6 March 2012.*

GRAHAME-SMITH, Prof. David Grahame, CBE 1993; Rhodes Professor of Clinical Pharmacology, University of Oxford, 1972–2000; Hon. Director, Smith Kline Beecham Centre of Applied Neuropsychobiology, Oxford University, 1990–99; Fellow of Corpus Christi College, Oxford, 1972–2000, then Emeritus (Vice-President, 1998–99); *b* 10 May 1933; *s* of George E. and C. A. Smith; *m* 1957, Kathryn Frances, *d* of Dr F. R. Beetham; two *s*. *Educ:* Wyggeston Grammar Sch., Leicester; St Mary's Hosp. Medical Sch., Univ. of London. MB BS (London) 1956; MRCS, LRCP 1956; MRCP 1958; PhD (London) 1966; FRCP 1972. House Phys., Paddington Gen. Hosp., London, 1956; House Surg., Battle Hosp., Reading, 1956–57. Captain, RAMC, 1957–60. Registrar and Sen. Registrar in Medicine, St Mary's Hosp., Paddington, 1960–61; H. A. M. Thompson Research Scholar, RCP, 1961–62; Saltwell Research Scholar, RCP, 1962–65; Wellcome Trust Research Fellow, 1965–66; Hon. Med. Registrar to Med. Unit, St Mary's Hosp., 1961–66; MRC Travelling Fellow, Dept of Endocrinology, Vanderbilt Univ., Nashville, Tennessee, USA, 1966–67; Sen. Lectr in

Clinical Pharmacology and Therapeutics, St Mary's Hosp. Med. Sch., Univ. of London, 1967–71; Hon. Cons. Physician, St Mary's Hosp., Paddington, 1967–71; Hon. Dir, MRC Unit of Clin. Pharm., Radcliffe Infirmary, Oxford, 1972–93. Vis. Prof., Peking Union Medical Coll., Beijing, China, 1985–. Non-exec. Mem., Oxfordshire HA, 1992–98. Member: Cttee on Safety of Medicines, 1975–86; Jt Cttee on Vaccination and Immunisation, 1987–89; Chairman: Adv. Gp on Hepatitis, 1987–89; Adv. Council on Misuse of Drugs, 1988–98. Lilly Prize, Clinical Sect., British Pharmacol Soc., 1995 (Hon. Fellow, 2007); Lifetime Achievement Award, British Assoc. of Psycho-pharmacology, 2002. *Publications:* (with J. K. Aronson) Oxford Textbook of Clinical Pharmacology and Drug Therapy, 1984, 3rd edn 2002; papers on biochemical, therapeutic and med. matters in scientific jls. *Recreation:* jazz. *Address:* Romney, Lincombe Lane, Boars Hill, Oxford OX1 5DY. *Died 17 June 2011.*

GRANT, Alexander (Marshall), CBE 1965; Artistic Director, National Ballet of Canada, 1976–83; *b* Wellington, New Zealand, 22 Feb. 1925; *s* of Alexander and Eleather Grant. *Educ:* Wellington Coll., NZ. Arrived in London, Feb. 1946, to study with Sadler's Wells School on Scholarship given in New Zealand by Royal Academy of Dancing, London; Sadler's Wells Ballet (later Royal Ballet Company), Aug. 1946–76. Dir, Ballet for All (touring ballet company), 1971–76 (Co-Director, 1970–71). Senior Principal, London Fest. Ballet, later English National Ballet, 1985–91; Guest Artist: Royal Ballet, 1985–89; Joffrey Ballet, USA, 1987–89. Frequent judge at internat. ballet competitions, notably Varna (Bulgaria), Paris, Budapest, Jackson, Mississippi and Moscow. Danced leading rôles in following: Mam'zelle Angot, Clock Symphony, Boutique Fantasque, Donald of the Burthens, Rake's Progress, Job, Three Cornered Hat, Ballabile, Cinderella, Sylvia, Madame Chrysanthème, Façade, Daphnis and Chloé, Coppélia, Petrushka, Ondine, La Fille Mal Gardée, Jabez and the Devil, Perséphone, The Dream, Jazz Calendar, Enigma Variations, Sleeping Beauty (Carabosse), A Month in the Country, La Sylphide, The Nutcracker, Napoli, Shéhérazade, Variations on a Theme of Purcell, Don Quixote; *films:* Tales of Beatrix Potter (Peter Rabbit and Pigling Bland); Steps of the Ballet. Icon Award, NZ Arts Foundn, 2005; Queen Elizabeth II Coronation Award, RAD, 2007; De Valois Award for outstanding achievement in ballet, Critics' Circle, 2010. *Recreations:* gardening, cinema and theatre going, cuisine. *Died 30 Sept. 2011.*

GRANT, Sir Clifford (Harry), Kt 1977; Chief Stipendiary Magistrate, Western Australia, 1982–90; *b* England, 12 April 1929; *m* 1962, Karen Ann Ferguson. *Educ:* Montclair, NJ, USA; Harrison Coll., Barbados; Liverpool Coll.; Liverpool Univ. (LLB (Hons) 1949). Solicitor, Supreme Court of Judicature, 1951; Comr for Oaths, 1958; in private practice, London; apptd to HM Overseas Judiciary, 1958; Magistrate, Kenya, 1958, Sen. Magistrate, 1962; transf. to Hong Kong, Crown Solicitor, 1963, Principal Magistrate, 1965; transf. to Fiji, Sen. Magistrate, 1967; admitted Barrister and Solicitor, Supreme Court of Fiji, 1969; Chief Magistrate, 1971; Judge of Supreme Court, 1972; Chief Justice of Fiji, 1974–80. Pres., Fiji Court of Appeal, and Chm., Judicial and Legal Services Commn, 1974–80; sole Comr, Royal Commn on Crime, 1975 (report published 1976). Sometime Actg Governor-General, 1973–79. Fellow, Flinders Univ. Foundn, 1992. Fiji Independence Medal, 1970. *Publications:* articles for legal jls. *Recreations:* evolutionary biology and psychology, mythology, literature, music. *Address:* Sir Clifford Grant Chambers, 16 Irwin Street, Perth, WA 6000, Australia. *Died 11 Feb. 2014.*

GRANT, Donald Blane, CBE 1989; TD 1964; Partner, KMG Thomson McLintock, CA (formerly Moody Stuart & Robertson, then Thomson McLintock & Co.), 1950–86; *b* 8 Oct. 1921; *s* of Quintin Blane Grant and Euphemia Phyllis Grant; *m* 1944, Lavinia Margaret Ruth Ritchie (*d* 2013); three *d. Educ:* High Sch. of Dundee. CA 1948. Served War, RA, 1939–46: TA Officer, retd as Major. Director: Dundee & London Investment Trust PLC, 1969–93; HAT Group PLC, 1969–86; Don Brothers Buist PLC, 1984–87. Institute of Chartered Accountants of Scotland: Mem. Council, 1971–76; Vice Pres., 1977–79, Pres., 1979–80. Chairman: Tayside Health Bd, 1984–91; Scottish Legal Aid Bd, 1986–91. Mem. Court, Univ. of Dundee, 1992–2002. Hon. LLD Dundee, 1989. *Recreations:* shooting, fishing, golf, bridge, gardening. *Clubs:* Institute of Directors; Royal and Ancient Golf (St Andrews); Panmure Golf (Carnoustie). *Died 21 Sept. 2014.*

GRANT, Donald David, CB 1985; Director General, Central Office of Information, 1982–85; *b* 1 Aug. 1924; *s* of Donald Herbert Grant and Florence Emily Grant; *m* 1954, Beatrice Mary Varney; two *d. Educ:* Wandsworth Sch. Served War, RNVR, Sub-Lt (A), 1942–46. Journalist, Evening Standard, Reuters, 1946–51; Dir, Sidney Barton Ltd, PR Consultants, 1951–61; Chief Information Officer, Min. of Aviation and Technology, 1961–67; Dir, Public Relations, STC Ltd, 1967–70; Director of Information: GLC, 1971–72; DTI, 1972–74; Home Office, 1974–82. Vis. Prof., Graduate Centre for Journalism, City Univ., 1986–90. *Recreation:* sailing. *Address:* Bayards House, Bayards Cove, Dartmouth, Devon TQ6 9AT. *T:* (01803) 833095. *Club:* Dartmouth Yacht. *Died 13 Oct. 2012.*

GRANT, John Donald; Consultant, Grant & Fairgrieve, 1988–96; *b* 31 Oct. 1926; *s* of Ian and Eleanor Grant; *m* 1951, Helen Bain Fairgrieve Wilson (*d* 2003), *d* of late James Wilson and Clara Wilson; two *s. Educ:* various schs; King's Coll., Cambridge (Exhibnr; MA Natural Scis). National Service, REME, 1947–49; TA, London Rifle Bde, 1949–56. N Thames Gas Bd, 1949–60; Imperial Chemical Industries: Plastics Div., 1960–71; Head Office, 1971–82; Chief Exec., FIMBRA (formerly NASDIM), 1983–88. Dir, Cadogan Management Ltd, 1991–95. Chairman: Strategic Planning Soc., 1989–91; Fedn of Software Systems, 1989–91. Mem., Money Management Council, 1989–2001. Chm., Henley Alumni Assoc., 1996–98; Mem. Ct of Govs, Henley Mgt Coll., 1996–99. *Recreations:* opera, music. *Died 11 June 2011.*

GRANT, Peter James, CBE 1997; Deputy Chairman, London Merchant Securities, 1994–2007 (Director, 1985–2007); *b* 5 Dec. 1929; 2nd *s* of late Lt-Col P. C. H. Grant, Scots Guards, and Mrs Grant (*née* Gooch); *m* 1st, 1953, Ann (marr. diss. 1964), *d* of late Christopher Pleydell-Bouverie; one *s* one *d*; 2nd, Paula, *d* of late E. J. P. Eugster; one *s* two *d. Educ:* Winchester; Magdalen Coll., Oxford. Lieut, Queen's Own Cameron Highlanders. Edward de Stein & Co., 1952, merged with Lazard Brothers & Co. Ltd, 1960; Vice-Chm., 1983–85, Dep. Chm., 1985–88, Lazard Bros & Co.; Dir, 1973–95, Vice-Chm., 1976, Chm., 1983–95, Sun Life Assurance Soc. Chairman: Highlands and Islands Airports, 1993–2001; Egypt Investment Co., 1996–; CDP-Concord Egyptian Direct Investment Fund Ltd, subseq. Egyptian Direct Investment Fund Ltd, 2000–; Concord Coral Fund Ltd, 2006–; Director: Walter Runciman plc, 1973–90; Standard Industrial Gp, 1966–72; Charrington, Gardner, Lockett & Co. Ltd, 1970–74; Scottish Hydro, 1990–94; Union des Assurances de Paris International, 1989–91 (Internat. Adv. Bd, 1991–95); BNP (UK) plc, subseq. BNP Paribas UK Hldgs Ltd, 1991–2005; Transatlantic Hldgs, 1992–95. Member: Industrial Develt Adv. Bd, 1985–92; CAA, 1993–95; Cromarty Firth Port Authority, 1994–2000 (Chm., 2000). Mem. Council and Chm., Finance Cttee, British Red Cross Soc., 1972–85; Mem. Council, Inst. of Dirs, 1989–99. *Recreations:* shooting, golf, gardening. *Address:* Mountgerald, near Dingwall, Ross-shire IV15 9TT. *T:* (01349) 62244; 2 Windsor Court, Jubilee Place, SW3 3TB. *T:* (020) 7349 9099. *Clubs:* Boodle's, Caledonian, Flyfishers'. *Died 21 Dec. 2012.*

GRANTHAM, Roy Aubrey, CBE 1990; National Secretary, APEX Partnership (white collar section of GMB), 1989–91; *b* 12 Dec. 1926; *m* 1964, Maura Teresa Walsh (marr. diss. 1988; remarried 2005); two *d. Educ:* King Edward Grammar Sch., Aston, Birmingham. Association of Professional, Executive, Clerical & Computer Staff: Midland area Organiser, 1949; Midland area Sec., 1959; Asst Sec., 1963; Gen. Sec., 1970–89, when APEX merged with GMB. Mem., TUC Gen. Council, 1983–92. Exec. Mem., Labour Cttee for Europe. Member: Royal Commn on Environmental Pollution, 1976–79; CNAA, 1976–79; IBA, 1984–90; former Mem., MSC, subseq. Training Commn. Director: Chrysler UK Ltd, 1977–79, Talbot UK

Ltd, 1979–81; Ansvar Insce Co. Ltd, 1990–97. Governor, Henley Management Coll., 1979–91; Mem., Ditchley Foundn, 1982–97. Chm., UK Temperance Alliance, 1989–2001. Councillor (Lab), London Bor. of Croydon, 1994–2002. *Publications:* Guide to Grading of Clerical and Administrative Work, 1968. *Recreations:* walking, reading, chess. *Address:* 76 Arden Road, Henley in Arden, Warwicks B95 5LN. *Died 25 Oct. 2013.*

GRASS, Günter Wilhelm; German writer and artist; *b* Danzig, 16 Oct. 1927; *m* 1st, 1954, Anna Schwarz; three *s* (inc. twin *s*) one *d*; 2nd, 1979, Ute Grunert. *Educ:* Volksschule and Gymnasium, Danzig; Düsseldorf Kunstakademie; Hochschule für Bildende Künste, Berlin. Lecture Tour of US, 1964, and many other foreign tours. Member: Deutscher PEN, Zentrum der Bundesrepublik; Verband Deutscher Schriftsteller; Amer. Academy of Arts and Sciences. Prizes: Lyric, Süddeutscher Rundfunk, 1955; Gruppe 47, 1958; Bremen Literary, 1959 (prize money withheld); Literary, Assoc. of German Critics, 1960; Meilleur livre étranger, 1962; Georg-Büchner, 1965; Fontane, Berlin, 1968; Theodor-Heuss, 1969; Internat., Mondello, 1978; Antonio-Feltrinelli, 1982; Grinzane Cavour, 1992; Chodowiecki, 1992; Hidalgo, 1993; Bayerischen Akad. der Schönen Künste, 1994; (with Philip Roth) Karel Capek, 1994; Hans Fallada, 1995; Sonning, 1995; Thomas Mann, 1996; Asturias, 1999; Nobel Prize for Literature, 1999; medals: Ossietzky, 1968; Hermann Kesten, 1995. *Publications: novels:* Die Blechtrommel, 1959 (The Tin Drum, 1962; filmed 1979); Katz und Maus, 1961 (Cat and Mouse, 1963); Hundejahre, 1963 (Dog Years, 1965); Örtlich betäubt, 1969 (Local Anaesthetic, 1970); Aus dem Tagebuch einer Schnecke, 1972 (From the Diary of a Snail, 1974); Der Butt, 1977 (The Flounder, 1978); Das Treffen in Telgte, 1979 (The Meeting at Telgte, 1981); Kopfgeburten, 1980 (Headbirths, 1982); Die Rättin, 1986 (The Rat, 1987); Unkenrufe (The Call of the Toad), 1992; Ein weites Feld (A Wide Field), 1995; Im Krebsgang (Crabwalk), 2002; *poetry:* (also drawings) Die Vorzüge der Windhühner, 1956; (also drawings) Gleisdreieck, 1960; Ausgefragt, 1967; Ach Butt, dein Märchen geht böse aus, 1983; Novemberland, 1994; (also paintings) Fundsachen für Nichtleser, 1997; Letzte Tänze, 2003; Lyrische Beute, 2004; *poetry in translation:* Selected Poems, 1966; Poems of Günter Grass, 1969; In the Egg and other poems, 1978; Novemberland: selected poems 1956–1993, 1996; *drama:* Hochwasser, 1957 (Flood, 1968); Noch zehn Minuten bis Buffalo, 1958 (Only Ten Minutes to Buffalo, 1968); Onkel, Onkel, 1958 (Onkel, Onkel, 1968); Die bösen Köche, 1961 (The Wicked Cooks, 1968); Die Plebejer proben den Aufstand, 1966 (The Plebeians rehearse the Uprising, 1967); Davor, 1969; *prose:* Über das Selbstverständlische, 1968 (Speak Out!, 1969); Dokumente zur politischen Wirkung, 1971; Der Bürger und seine Stimme, 1974; Denkzettel, 1978; Aufsätze zur Literatur, 1980; Zeichnen und Schreiben, Band I, 1982, Band II, 1984; Widerstand lernen, 1984; On Writing and Politics 1967–83, 1985; Zunge Zeigen, 1988 (Show Your Tongue, 1989); Two States - One Nation?, 1990; Schreiben nach Auschwitz, 1990; Deutscher Lastenausgleich, 1990; Ein Schnäppchen namens DDR, 1990; Deutschland, einig Vaterland, 1990; Alptraum und Hoffnung, 1990; Gegen die verstreichende Zeit, 1991; Rede vom Verlust, 1992; Angestiftet, Partei zu ergreifen, 1994; Die Deutschen und ihre Dichter, 1995; Gestern, vor 50 Jahren (correspondence with Kenzaburo Öe), 1995; Beim Häuten der Zwiebel (memoir), 2006 (Peeling the Onion, 2007); Die Box (memoir), 2008 (The Box, 2010); Grimms Wörter: eine Liebeserklärung (memoir), 2010; *graphic work:* Mit Sophie in die Pilze gegangen, 1987; Totes Holz, 1990; Brief aus Altdöbern, 1991; Vier Jahrzehnte, 1991; In Kupfer, auf Stein, 1994; Der Schatten: Hans Christian Andersens Märchen gesehen von Günter Grass (The Shadow: Hans Christian Andersen's stories, seen by Günter Grass), 2004. *Address:* Glockengiesserstrasse 21, 23552 Lübeck, Germany. *Died 13 April 2015.*

GRATWICK, Stephen; QC 1968; *b* 19 Aug. 1924; *s* of late Percival John Gratwick and Kathleen Mary Gratwick, Fawkham, Kent; *m* 1954, Jocelyn Chaplin, Horton Kirby, Kent; four *d*. *Educ:* Charterhouse; Balliol Coll., Oxford. Oxford 1942–44; Signals Research and Develt Estabt, 1944–47. BA (Physics) 1946; MA 1950. Called to the Bar, Lincoln's Inn, 1949, Bencher, 1976. *Publications:* What Does God Do?, 2009. *Recreation:* the study of secular theology. *Address:* Haymist, 14a Kippington Road, Sevenoaks TN13 2LH. *Died 21 March 2014.*

GRAY, Dulcie; *see* Denison, D. W. C.

GRAY, (Edna) Eileen (Mary), CBE 1997 (OBE 1978); President, London Youth Games, since 2008 (Chairman, 1990–2007); *b* 25 April 1920; *d* of late William Thomas Greenaway and Alice Evelyn Mary (*née* Jenkins); *m* 1946, Walter Herbert Gray (*d* 2001); one *s*. *Educ:* St Saviour's and St Olave's Grammar Sch. for Girls, London. Inspectorate for Fighting Vehicles, 1940–45. Invited to ride for women's cycling team, in Copenhagen, 1946; campaigner for internat. recognition of women in cycling; Team Manager, GB team, inaugural World Championship for Women, Paris, 1958. Mem., Exec. Cttee, British Cycling Fedn, 1958–87 (Pres., 1973–86); Pres., Women's Cycle Racing Assoc., 1963–76; Mem., British Cycling Nat. Council. Vice-Pres., British Olympic Assoc., 1992– (Vice-Chm., 1988–92). Internat. Official, Commonwealth Games, Edmonton, 1978, and Brisbane, 1982. Mem., Kingston upon Thames BC, 1982–98 (Mayor of Kingston, 1990–91). Trustee, London Marathon Trust. Freeman, City of London, 1987. Olympic Order, IOC, 1993. *Address:* 129 Grand Avenue, Surbiton, Surrey KT5 9HY. *T:* (020) 8399 0068. *Died 20 May 2015.*

GRAY, Prof. George William, CBE 1991; PhD; FRS 1983; FRSE; CChem, FRSC; Research Consultant; Emeritus Professor, University of Hull, since 1992; *b* 4 Sept. 1926; *s* of John William Gray and Jessie Colville (*née* Hunter); *m* 1953, Marjorie Mary (*née* Canavan) (*d* 2013); two *d* (and one *d* decd). *Educ:* Univ. of Glasgow (BSc); Univ. of London (PhD). CChem, FRSC 1972; FRSE 1989. Joined staff of Chem. Dept, Univ. of Hull, 1946; Sen. Lectr, 1960; Reader, 1964; Prof. of Organic Chem., 1978; G. F. Grant Prof. of Chem., 1984–90. Res. Co-ordinator, Merck Ltd (formerly BDH Ltd), 1990–93. Vis. Prof., Univ. of Southampton, 1990–2002; Vis. Sen. Fellow, DERA, 1999. For. Associate, Engrg Acad. of Japan, 1995; Hon. Mem., Internat. Liquid Crystal Soc., 1998. Hon. MRIA 2001. Hon. DSc: Hull, 1991; Nottingham Trent, 1994; Southampton, 1996; East Anglia, 1997; Aberdeen, 2001; Exeter, 2002. Clifford Paterson Prize Lectr, Royal Soc., 1985. Queen's Award for Technol Achievement, 1979; Rank Prize for Optoelectronics, 1980; Leverhulme Medal, Royal Soc., 1987; SCI Medallist, 1993; Kyoto Laureate, Inamori Foundn, 1995; Karl Ferdinand Braun Medal, Soc. for Inf. Display, 1996; Fréedericksz Medal, Russian Liquid Crystal Soc., 1997. Editor, Liquid Crystals, 1992–2002. *Publications:* Molecular Structure and the Properties of Liquid Crystals, 1962; (ed and jtly with P. A. Winsor) Liquid Crystals and Plastic Crystals, 1974; (ed jtly with G. R. Luckhurst) The Molecular Physics of Liquid Crystals, 1979; (with J. W. Goodby) Smectic Liquid Crystals – textures and structures, 1984; (ed) Thermotropic Liquid Crystals, 1987; (ed jtly) Handbook of Liquid Crystals, Vols 1–3, 1998; 360 pubns on liquid crystals in Jl Chem. Soc., Trans Faraday Soc., Phys. Rev., Molecular Cryst. and Liquid Cryst., Jl Chem. Phys., and Proc. IEEE. *Recreations:* gardening, philately. *Address:* Juniper House, Furzehill, Wimborne, Dorset BH21 4HD. *T:* (01202) 880164. *E:* ggray83828@aol.com. *Died 12 May 2013.*

GRAY, Gilbert; QC 1971; a Recorder of the Crown Court, 1972–98; *b* 25 April 1928; *s* of late Robert Gray, JP, Scarborough, and of Mrs Elizabeth Gray; *m* 1954, Olga Dilys Gray (*née* Thomas), BA, JP; two *s* two *d*. *Educ:* Scarborough Boys' High Sch.; Leeds Univ. (LLB). Pres., Leeds Univ. Union. Called to the Bar, Gray's Inn, 1953; Bencher, 1979. Leader of NE Circuit, 1984–87. *Recreation:* sailing. *Address:* 3 Raymond Buildings, Gray's Inn, WC1R 5BH; Park Court Chambers, 16 Park Place, Leeds LS1 1SJ; Treasurer's House, York. *Died 7 April 2011.*

GRAY, Rt Hon. Herb(ert Eser), CC 2003; PC (Can.) 1969; Chairman, Canadian Section, International Joint Commission, 2002–10; *b* 25 May 1931; *s* of Harry and Fannie Gray; *m* 1967, Sharon Sholzberg; one *s* one *d*. *Educ:* McGill Univ., Montreal; Osgoode Hall Law Sch., Toronto. Mem., Ontario Bar. MP (L) Windsor West, Canada, 1962–2002; Minister: without Portfolio (Finance),

1969–70; of Nat. Revenue, 1970–72; of Consumer and Corporate Affairs, 1972–74; of Industry, Trade and Commerce, 1980–82; of Regl Econ. Expansion, 1982; Pres., Treasury Bd, 1982–84; Opposition House Leader, 1984–90; Dep. Leader of the Opposition, 1989–90, Leader, 1990–91; Finance Critic for Official Opposition, 1991–93; Solicitor Gen. and Leader of the Govt in H of C, 1993–97; Dep. Prime Minister of Canada, 1997–2002. Chancellor, Carleton Univ., Ottawa, 2008–11. *Died 21 April 2014.*

GRAY, Sir John (Archibald Browne), Kt 1973; MA, MB, ScD; FRS 1972; Member, External Scientific Staff, MRC, 1977–83: working at Marine Biological Association Laboratory, Plymouth, 1977–93; *b* 30 March 1918; *s* of late Sir Archibald Gray, KCVO, CBE; *m* 1946, Vera Kathleen Mares (*d* 2010); one *s* one *d*. *Educ:* Cheltenham Coll.; Clare Coll., Cambridge (Hon. Fellow, 1976); University Coll. Hospital. BA 1939; MA 1942; MB, BChir 1942; ScD 1962. Service Research for MRC, 1943–45; Surg. Lieut, RNVR, 1945–46; Scientific Staff of MRC at Nat. Inst. for Med. Research, 1946–52; Reader in Physiology, University Coll., London, 1952–58; Prof. of Physiology, University Coll., London, 1959–66; Medical Research Council: Second Sec., 1966–68; Sec., 1968–77; Dep. Chm., 1975–77. Chm., EC Cttee for Medical Res., 1972–76; Member of Council: Marine Biol Assoc., 1969–88 (Vice-Pres., 1988–); Freshwater Biol Assoc., 1981–88 (Pres., 1983–88; Chm. of Council, 1985–88; Vice-Pres., 1988–). QHP 1968–71. FSB; FRCP 1974. Hon. DSc Exeter, 1985. *Publications:* papers, mostly on sensory receptors and sensory nervous system, in Jl of Physiology, Procs of Royal Soc. series B, Jl of Marine Biol Assoc., etc. *Recreation:* painting. *Address:* Seaways, Kingsway, Kingsand, near Torpoint, Cornwall PL10 1NG. *T:* (01752) 822745. *Died 4 Jan. 2011.*

GRAY, Lt-Gen. Sir Michael Stuart, KCB 1986; OBE 1970; DL; Lieutenant of the Tower of London, 1995–98; Chairman, MS&P (Rosedale) Ltd, incorporating Milburn Arms Hotel, Rosedale Abbey, N Yorkshire, 2003–08; *b* Beverley, E Yorkshire, 3 May 1932; *e s* of Lieut Frank Gray, RNVR (killed in action 1940), and Joan Gray (*née* Gibson); *m* 1958, Juliette Antonia Noon, Northampton; two *s* one *d*. *Educ:* Beverley Grammar Sch.; Christ's Hosp., Horsham; RMA Sandhurst. FCMI; FInstD; FICFM. Enlisted RA, 1950; commissioned E Yorkshire Regt, 1952; served Malaya; transf. to Parachute Regt, 1955; served Cyprus, Suez, Jordan, Greece, Bahrain, Aden, N Ireland; sc Camberley, 1963; BM HQ 44 Para Bde Gp TA, 1964–65; Co. Comd 2 Para, 1965–66; MoD (MOI), 1967–69; commanded 1st Bn Parachute Regt, 1969–71; DS Staff Coll., Camberley, 1971–73; Col GS 1 Div. BAOR, 1973–75; RCDS 1976; last Comdr 16 Para Bde, 1977; Comdr 6 Field Force and COMUKMF, 1977–79; Comdr British Army Staff and Mil. Attaché, Washington, 1979–81 (Mil. Advr to Gov. of Bermuda; Mem., UN Mil. Cttee, NY), and Head of British Def. Staff and Def. Attaché, Washington, 1981; GOC SW Dist, and Maj.-Gen., UKMF(L), 1981–83; COS, HQ BAOR, 1984–85; GOC SE Dist and Comdr Jt Force HQ, 1985–88, retd. Dep. Col Comdt, Parachute Regt, 1986–90, Col Comdt, 1990–93. Hon. Colonel: 10 Para (V), 1984–88; 250 (Hull) Field Amb. RAMC (V), 1991–99. Consultant, Brittany Ferries (wrote Battlefield Tours audio tapes of Pegasus Trail, 1989 and British D-Day Trail, 1994), 1988–96; Defence Industries Advr, Airborne Systems, IRVIN-GQ Ltd (formerly Wardle Storeys plc), 1989–2007; Chm., IRVIN-GQ Parachute Museum Ltd, 2007–. Dir and Co. Sec., Chesterford Wealth Mgt Gp, 2000–. Chm., Airborne Assault Normandy Trust (AAN), to preserve the history of 6 AB Division in Normandy, 1972–; Pres. d'Honneur, Assoc. Franco Britannique de gestion de la Batterie de Merville, 1986–; Citoyen d'honneur, Merville-Franceville Plage, 2007; Trustee: AB Forces Security Fund, 1986–2007; AB Forces Charities (formerly AB Forces Charities Develt Trust), 1990–2000 (Chm., 1990–94); Pres., York Br., 1991–, Vice Pres., NI Br. and Tyneside Br., 2000–, Parachute Regt Assoc.; Vice Pres., Army Parachute Assoc. (Free Fall), 1987– (Pres., 1981–87); Normandy Veterans Association: Vice-Pres., Goole Br., 1988–2008; Pres., Leeds Br., 1991–; Pres., Grimsby Br., 1995–; Pres., E Yorks Cttee, Seafarers Charity (formerly King George's Fund for Sailors), 2000– (Chm., 1988–2000); Mem., Amicable Soc. of Blues, 1989– (Pres., 2007); Patron: Combined Ex-Service Assoc., Bridlington, 1988–2008; Yorks Air Mus., Elvington, 1999–; Normandy MN Meml Fund, 2002–05; Pres., Dover & Dist MN Meml Fund, 2007–08. Mem. Council, 2001–04, Dep. Patron, 2004–05, BESO. Chairman: Thelma Turner Homes Ltd, 1996–2001; Thelma Turner Charitable Trust, 1998–2002. Hon. Brother, Trinity House, Hull, 2000–. Freeman, City of London, 1983. DL ER of Yorks, 1997. Officier, Légion d'Honneur (France), 1994. *Recreations:* military history, gardening, DIY, photography, painting. *Address:* The Old Forge, Canal Head, Pocklington, York YO42 1NW. *Club:* Army and Navy. *Died 13 March 2011.*

GRAY, Prof. Peter, MA, PhD, ScD (Cantab); FRS 1977; CChem, FRSC; Master, 1988–96, then Life Fellow, Gonville and Caius College, Cambridge; *b* Newport, 25 Aug. 1926; *er s* of late Ivor Hicks Gray and Rose Ethel Gray; *m* 1st, 1952, Barbara Joan Hume, PhD (*d* 1992), 2nd *d* of J. B. Hume, London; two *s* two *d*; 2nd, 1996, Rachel Katharine, *d* of late P. A. Buxton, FRS, and *widow* of C. Herzig, CBE. *Educ:* Newport High Sch.; Gonville and Caius Coll., Cambridge (Major Schol., 1943; Prizeman, 1944, 1945 and 1946; BA 1st cl. hons Nat. Sci. Tripos, 1946; Dunlop Res. Student, 1946; PhD 1949; ScD 1963). Ramsay Meml Fellow, 1949–51; Fellow, Gonville and Caius Coll., 1949–53; ICI Fellow, 1951; University Demonstrator in Chem. Engrg, University of Cambridge, 1951–55; Physical Chemistry Dept, University of Leeds: Lectr, 1955; Reader, 1959; Prof., 1962; Head of Dept, 1965–88; Chm., Bd of Combined Faculties of Science and Applied Science, 1972–74; Hon. Vis. Prof., 1988–2001; University of Cambridge: Chm., Faculty of Engrg, 1989–94; Mem., Council of Senate, 1990–96; Mem., Financial Bd, 1991–94. Gauss Prof., Univ. of Göttingen, 1979, 1986; Visiting Professor: Univ. of BC, 1958–59; Univ. of W Ont., 1969; Macquarie Univ., 1980; Beijing Univ. of Technol., 1984; Univ. of Paris, 1986; Calabria Univ., 1988; Lectures: H. C. Hottel, Orléans, 1990; Pierre Bruylants, Louvain, 1994; Larmor, Cambridge, 1995; Visitor, Fire Res. Orgn, 1984–90 (G. R. Nice Lectr, 1989). Mem. Council: Faraday Soc., 1965 (Vice-Pres., 1970–83, 1985–95; Treasurer, 1973; Pres., 1983–85); Chemical Soc., 1969. Pres., Cambridge Phil Soc., 1992–93. Chairman: Schiff Foundn, 1989–95; Oppenheimer Fund, 1988–95; Trustee, Edward Boyle Meml Trust, 1989–98; Mem. Adv. Council, Ramsay Meml Fellowship Trust, 1982–2002. Hon. DSc Leeds, 1997. Meldola Medal, Royal Inst. Chem., 1956; Marlow Medal, Faraday Soc., 1959; B. Lewis Gold Medal, Combustion Inst., 1978; Award for Combustion, Royal Soc. of Chemistry, 1986; Italgas Prize for Chemistry, 1988. Associate Editor, Royal Society, 1983–97; Member, Editorial Board: Combustion and Flame, 1976–82; Dynamics and Stability of Systems, 1986–; Jl of Non equilibrium Thermodynamics, 1990–95; Discrete Dynamics in Nature & Soc., 1995–; Internat. Jl of Discrete Chaotic Dynamics, 1995–. *Publications:* (with S. K. Scott) Chemical Oscillations and Instabilities, 1990; (ed with S. K. Scott and G. Nicolis) Spatial Inhomogeneities and Transient Behaviour in Chemical Kinetics, 1990; (with J. M. T Thompson) Chaos and Dynamical Complexity, 1990; (with J. E. Field) Energetic Materials, 1992; numerous papers on phys. chem. subjects in scientific jls. *Recreations:* hill walking, reading large print books. *Address:* Gonville and Caius College, Cambridge CB2 1TA. *T:* (01223) 332478, *Fax:* (01223) 332456. *E:* pg263@cai.cam.ac.uk; 2 Fendon Close, Cambridge CB1 7RU. *T:* (01223) 212660. *Died 7 June 2012.*

GRAY, Richard Paul; QC 1993; *b* 1 Nov. 1945; *s* of John Montgomery Gray and Margaret Elizabeth Gray (*née* Welsh); *m* 1977, Emma Serena Halpin; one *s*. *Educ:* Tonbridge Sch.; St Andrews Univ. (LLB). MCIArb 2004. Called to the Bar, Inner Temple, 1970. *Recreations:* family, gardens, games. *Died 14 Oct. 2014.*

GRAY DEBROS, Winifred Marjorie, (Mrs E. Gray Debros); *see* Fox, W. M.

GREEN, Rev. Bernard; General Secretary, Baptist Union of Great Britain, 1982–91; Moderator of the Free Church Federal Council, 1988–89; *b* 11 Nov. 1925; *s* of

George Samuel Green and Laura Annie Agnes (*née* Holliday); *m* 1952, Joan Viccars (*d* 2006); two *s* one *d*. *Educ:* Wellingborough Sch.; Bristol Baptist Coll.; Bristol Univ. (BA); Regent's Park Coll., Oxford, and St Catherine's Coll., Oxford (MA); London Univ. BD taken externally. Served War as coal-miner, 1944–47. Ordained as Baptist Minister, 1952; pastorates at: Yardley, Birmingham, 1952–61; Mansfield Road, Nottingham, 1961–76; Horfield, Bristol, 1976–82. Dir, Baptist Insce Co., 1982–93. Vice Pres., Churches' Council for Health and Healing, 1988–99. Regular broadcaster on BBC Radio Nottingham until 1976 and on BBC Radio Bristol until 1982. *Publications:* (jtly) Patterns and Prayers for Christian Worship, 1991; (ed jtly) Baptist Praise and Worship, 1991; Tomorrow's Man: a biography of James Henry Rushbrooke, 1997; Crossing the Boundaries: a history of the European Baptist Federation 1949–1999, 1999; European Baptists and the Third Reich, 2009. *Died 20 March 2013.*

GREEN, Candida L.; *see* Lycett Green.

GREEN, John Michael, CB 1976; Commissioner, 1971–85, Deputy Chairman, 1973–85, Board of Inland Revenue; *b* 5 Dec. 1924; *s* of late George and Faith Green; *m* 1951, Sylvia (*née* Crabb) (*d* 1999); one *s* one *d*. *Educ:* Merchant Taylors' Sch., Rickmansworth; Jesus Coll., Oxford (MA (Hons)). Served War, Army, RAC, 1943–46. Entered Inland Revenue as Asst Principal, 1948; served in HM Treasury, as Principal, 1956–57; Asst Sec., 1962; Under Sec., Bd of Inland Revenue, 1971. Mem., NW Surrey HA, 1989–95. *Recreation:* reading. *Address:* 36 Copper Beech House, Heathside Crescent, Woking, Surrey GU22 7BB. *T:* (01483) 772599. *Died 25 Jan. 2015.*

GREENAWAY, Frank, PhD; CChem, FRSC, FSA, FMA; Research Fellow, The Science Museum, 1980–91 (Hon. Fellow, 1992); Reader in the History of Science, Davy-Faraday Research Laboratory of the Royal Institution, 1970–85; *b* 9 July 1917; 3rd *s* of late Henry James Greenaway; *m* 1942, Margaret, (Miranda) (*d* 2008), 2nd *d* of late R. G. Heegaard Warner and *widow* of John Raymond Brumfit; three *d* (one *s* and one step *s* decd). *Educ:* Cardiff High Sch.; Jesus Coll., Oxford (Meyricke Exhibitioner; MA); University Coll. London (PhD). Served War of 1939–45, RAOC, as Inspecting Ordnance Officer, 1940–41 (invalided). Science Master: Bournemouth Sch., 1941–42; Epsom GS, 1942–43; Passport Control, 1943–44; Research Labs, Kodak Ltd, 1944–49; Asst Keeper, Science Museum, 1949; Dep. Keeper, 1959; Keeper, Dept of Chemistry, 1967–80. Regents' Fellow, Smithsonian Instn, Washington, DC, 1985. Member Council: Brit. Soc. for the Hist. of Science, 1958–68, 1974–78 (Vice-Pres. 1962–65); Museums Assoc., 1961–70, 1973–76 (Hon. Editor, 1965–70); Mem. Brit. Nat. Cttee, ICOM, 1956–58, 1962–71, 1977–83; Royal Institution: Mem., 1990–93, Vice-Pres., 1992–93, Council; Chm., Cttee of Visitors, 1964–65. Membre Correspondant de l'Académie Internationale d'Histoire des Sciences, 1963; Member: Council, Soc. for History of Alchemy and Chemistry, 1967–74 (Sec., 1967–74); History of Medicine Adv. Panel, The Wellcome Trust, 1968–74; Higher Educn Adv. Cttee, The Open Univ., 1970–73; British Nat. Cttee for Hist. of Sci., 1972–81; British Nat. Cttee, ICSU, 1972–77; Council, Internat. Union of the Hist. and Philos. of Science, 1972–81 (Sec., 1972–77); Council of Management, Royal Philharmonic Soc., 1980–84, 1986–89; President: Commonwealth Assoc. of Museums, 1979–83; Nonsuch Antiquarian Soc., 1990–97. Boerhaave Medal, Leyden Univ., 1968. *Publications:* Science Museums in Developing Countries, 1962; John Dalton and the Atom, 1966; (ed) Lavoisier's Essays Physical and Chemical, 1971; (ed with Roger French) Science in the Early Roman Empire, 1986; Science International: the history of the International Council of Scientific Unions, 1996; Chymica Acta (autobiog.), 2007; Editor, Royal Institution Archives, 1971; Official Publications of the Science Museum; papers on history of chemistry and on museology. *Recreations:* music, travel. *Address:* St Luke's Residential Home, Marshland Square, Emmer Green, Reading RG4 8RP. *T:* (0118) 947 9952. *Club:* Athenæum. *Died 16 June 2013.*

GREENAWAY, Sir John (Michael Burdick), 3rd Bt *cr* 1933, of Coombe, Surrey; DL; farmer, since 1980; *b* 9 Aug. 1944; *o s* of Sir Derek Burdick Greenaway, 2nd Bt, CBE, and Sheila Beatrice Greenaway (*née* Lockett); *S* father, 1994; *m* 1982, Susan Margaret (*née* Birch); one *s* one *d*. *Educ:* Harrow Sch.; Grenoble Univ. The Life Guards, 1965–70. Dir, Daniel Greenaway & Sons Ltd, 1970–79. DL Northants, 2005. *Recreations:* ski-ing, tennis, riding. *Heir:* *s* Thomas Edward Burdick Greenaway, *b* 3 April 1985. *Address:* Lois Weedon House, Weedon Lois, Towcester, Northants NN12 8PJ. *T:* (01327) 860472. *Died 16 March 2015.*

GREENFIELD, Edward Harry, OBE 1994; Chief Music Critic, The Guardian, 1977–93; *b* 30 July 1928; *s* of Percy Greenfield and Mabel (*née* Hall). *Educ:* Westcliff High Sch.; Trinity Hall, Univ. of Cambridge (MA). Joined staff of Manchester Guardian, 1953: Record Critic, 1955; Music Critic, 1964; succeeded Sir Neville Cardus as Chief Music Critic, 1977. Broadcaster on music and records for BBC radio. Mem., critics' panel, Gramophone, 1960–. Pres., Fedn of Recorded Music Socs, 1997–2009. Master, Art Workers Guild, 2002. Hon. GSM 1991. Goldenes Verdienstzeichen, Salzburg, 1981. *Publications:* Puccini: keeper of the seal, 1958; monographs on Joan Sutherland, 1972, and André Previn, 1973; (with Robert Layton, Ivan March and initially Denis Stevens) Stereo Record Guide, 9 vols, 1960–74; Penguin Stereo Record Guide, 5th edn 1986; (jtly) Penguin Guide to Compact Discs, Cassettes and LPs, 1986, 4th edn as Penguin Guide to Compact Discs, 1992, 23rd edn 2011; Penguin Guide to Opera on Compact Discs, 1993; Portrait Gallery: a life in classical music, 2014. *Recreations:* work, living in Spitalfields. *Address:* 16 Folgate Street, E1 6BX. *T:* (020) 7377 7555. *Club:* Critics' Circle. *Died 1 July 2015.*

GREENLAND, Dennis James, DPhil; FRS 1994; FSB; Scientific Dir, CAB International, 1987–92; *b* 13 June 1930; *s* of James John and Lily Florence Greenland; *m* 1955, Edith Mary Johnston; one *s* two *d*. *Educ:* Portsmouth Grammar Sch.; Christ Church, Oxford (MA, DPhil). Lecturer: Univ. of Ghana, 1955–59; Waite Agricl Res. Inst., Adelaide, 1959–63; Reader and Head of Soil Science, Waite Agricl Res. Inst., 1963–70; Professor and Head of Dept of Soil Science, Univ. of Reading, 1970–79; Director of Research, Internat. Inst. of Tropical Agriculture, Nigeria, 1974–76 (on secondment from Univ. of Reading); Dep. Dir Gen., Internat. Rice Res. Inst., Los Baños, Philippines, 1979–87. Vis. Prof., Univ. of Reading, 1987–2007. Chm., Scientific Adv. Panel, Commonwealth Develt Corp., 1992–96. FSB (FIBiol 1974); FWA 1987. Hon. Member: Amer. Soc. of Soil Science, 1993; Amer. Soc. of Agronomy, 1993. Hon. DAgSc Ghent, 1982; Hon. DSc Ohio State, 2003. *Publications:* contributions: (jtly) The Soil Under Shifting Cultivation, 1960; (ed jtly) Soil Conservation and Management in the Humid Tropics, 1977; (ed jtly) Chemistry of Soil Constituents, 1978; (ed jtly) Soil Physical Properties and Crop Production in the Tropics, 1979; (ed) Characterisation of Soils in Relation to Their Classification and Management for Crop Production: some examples from the humid tropics, 1981; (ed jtly) The Chemistry of Soil Processes, 1981; (ed jtly) Soil Resilience and Sustainable Land Use, 1994; The Sustainability of Rice Farming, 1997; (ed jtly) Land Resources: on the edge of the Malthusian precipice, 1997; numerous scientific articles in learned jls. *Recreations:* walking, watching cricket. *Address:* Berrylands, Riverside Gardens, Romsey SO51 8HN. *Died 23 Dec. 2012.*

GREENWOOD, Prof. Norman Neill, DSc Melbourne; PhD, ScD Cambridge; FRS 1987; CChem, FRSC; Professor of Inorganic and Structural Chemistry, University of Leeds, 1971–90, then Emeritus; *b* Melbourne, Vic, 19 Jan. 1925; *er s* of Prof. J. Neill Greenwood, DSc and Gladys, *d* of late Moritz and Bertha Uhland; *m* 1951, Kirsten Marie Rydland, Bergen, Norway; three *d*. *Educ:* University High School, Melbourne; University of Melbourne; Sidney Sussex Coll., Cambridge. Laboratory Cadet, CSIRO Div. of Tribophysics, Melbourne, 1942–44; BSc Melbourne 1945, MSc Melbourne 1948; DSc Melbourne 1966. Masson Memorial Medal, Royal Australian Chem. Institute, 1945. Resident Tutor and Lecturer in Chemistry, Trinity Coll., Melbourne, 1946–48. Exhibn of 1851,

Overseas Student, 1948–51; PhD Cambridge 1951; ScD Cambridge 1961. Senior Harwell Research Fellow, 1951–53; Lectr, 1953–60, Senior Lectr, 1960–61, in Inorganic Chemistry, Univ. of Nottingham; Prof. of Inorganic Chemistry, Univ. of Newcastle upon Tyne, 1961–71. Visiting Professor: Univ. of Melbourne, 1966; Univ. of Western Australia, 1969; Univ. of Western Ontario, 1973; Univ. of Copenhagen, 1979; La Trobe Univ., Melbourne, 1985; Wuhan Univ., People's Republic of China, 1985; Toho Univ., Tokyo, 1991–93; National Science Foundation Distinguished Vis. Prof., Michigan State Univ., USA, 1967. International Union of Pure and Applied Chemistry: Mem., 1963–83; Vice-Pres., 1975–77, Pres., 1977–81, Inorganic Chemistry Div.; Chm., Internat. Commn on Atomic Weights, 1969–75. Chemical Society: Vice Pres., 1979–80; Pres., Dalton Div., 1979–81; Award in Main Group Chemistry, 1975. Vice-Pres., 1989–90, Pres., 1990–91, Section B, Chemistry, BAAS. Lectures: Tilden, Chemical Soc., 1966–67; Hofmann, Ges. Deutscher Chemiker, 1983; Liversidge, RSC, 1983; first Egon Wiberg, Munich Univ., 1989; Ludwig Mond, RSC, 1991; Humphry Davy, Royal Soc., 2000. MRI 1998. For. Associate, Académie des Sciences, Institut de France, 1992. Dr *hc* de l'Université de Nancy I, 1977; DSc *hc* Toho Univ., Tokyo, 2000. *Publications:* Principles of Atomic Orbitals, 1964 (rev. edns 1968, 1973, 1980); Ionic Crystals, Lattice Defects, and Nonstoichiometry, 1968; (jointly) Spectroscopic Properties of Inorganic and Organometallic Compounds, vols I–IX, 1968–76; (with W. A. Campbell) Contemporary British Chemists, 1971; (with T. C. Gibb) Mössbauer Spectroscopy, 1971; Periodicity and Atomic Structure, 1971; (with B. P. Straughan and E. J. F. Ross) Index of Vibrational Spectra, vol. I, 1972, (with E. J. F. Ross) vol. II, 1975, vol. III, 1977; The Chemistry of Boron, 1973, rev. edn 1975; (with A. Earnshaw) Chemistry of the Elements, 1984, rev. edn 1997; numerous original papers and reviews in chemical jls and chapters in scientific monographs. *Recreations:* music, travel. *Address:* Department of Chemistry, University of Leeds, Leeds LS2 9JT. *E:* n.n.greenwood@chem.leeds.ac.uk. *Died 14 Nov. 2012.*

GREER, Ian Bramwell; Chairman, Corporate and Government Relations International Ltd, 1998–2012; *b* 5 June 1933; *s* of Bramwell and Janet Greer; *m* 2013, Clive Ferreira. *Educ:* Cranbrook Coll., Essex; Victoria Sch., Glasgow. Conservative Central Office and Party Agent, 1956–67; Nat. Dir, Mental Health Trust, 1967–70; Man. Dir, Russell Greer & Associates, 1970–82; Chairman: Ian Greer Associates, 1982–96; Internat. Govt Relations, 1997–2004. Chm., Helderberg Street People's Centre, 2000–; Mem., Bd of Visitors, HMP Wormwood Scrubs, 1992–98. *Publications:* Right to be Heard, 1985; One Man's Word, 1997. *Recreations:* antiques, walking, gardening, dogs. *Address:* The Long House, PO Box 213, Stellenbosch, Western Cape 7599, South Africa. *Club:* Royal Automobile. *Died 4 Nov. 2015.*

GREET, Rev. Dr Kenneth Gerald; Secretary of the Methodist Conference, 1971–84; President of the Methodist Conference, 1980–81; Moderator, Free Church Federal Council, 1982–83; Vice-President, World Disarmament Campaign, since 1994; *b* 17 Nov. 1918; *e s* of Walter and Renée Greet, Bristol; *m* 1947, Mary Eileen Edbrooke (*d* 2013); two *d* (and one *s* decd). *Educ:* Cotham Grammar Sch., Bristol; Handsworth Coll., Birmingham. Minister: Cwm and Kingstone Methodist Church, 1940–42; Ogmore Vale Methodist Church, 1942–45; Tonypandy Central Hall, 1947–54; Sec., Dept of Christian Citizenship of Methodist Church, 1954–71; Member: BCC, 1955–84 (Chm. of Exec., 1977–81); World Methodist Council, 1957–2001 (Chm., Exec. Cttee, 1976–81); Chairman: Exec., Temperance Council of Christian Churches, 1961–71; World Christian Temperance Fedn, 1962–72. Pres., Methodist Peace Fellowship, 1999–2010, then Emeritus. Rep. to Central Cttee, WCC, Addis Ababa, 1971, Nairobi, 1975. Beckly Lectr, 1962; Willson Lectr, Kansas City, 1966; Cato Lectr, Sydney, 1975. Chm. Govs, Southlands Coll., Wimbledon, 1987–97. Hon. DD Ohio, USA, 1968; DUniv Surrey, 1998. *Publications:* The Mutual Society, 1962; Man and Wife Together, 1962; Large Petitions, 1964; Guide to Loving, 1965; The Debate about Drink, 1969; The Sunday Question, 1970; The Art of Moral Judgement, 1970; When the Spirit Moves, 1975; A Lion from a Thicket, 1978; The Big Sin: Christianity and the arms race, 1983; What Shall I Cry?, 1986; Life of Jabez Bunting, 1995; Fully Connected (autobiog.), 1997. *Recreations:* reading, photography. *Address:* 89 Broadmark Lane, Rustington, Sussex BN16 2JA. *T:* (01903) 773326. *E:* kgreet@talktalk.net. *Died 11 Feb. 2014.*

GREGSON, Sir Peter (Lewis), GCB 1996 (KCB 1988; CB 1983); Permanent Secretary, Department of Trade and Industry, 1989–96; *b* 28 June 1936; *s* of late Walter Henry Gregson and Lillian Margaret Gregson. *Educ:* Nottingham High Sch.; Balliol Coll., Oxford. Classical Hon. Mods, class I; Lit. Hum. class I; BA 1959; MA 1962. Nat Service, 1959–61; 2nd Lieut RAEC, attached to Sherwood Foresters. Board of Trade: Asst Principal, 1961; Private Sec. to Minister of State, 1963–65; Principal, 1965; Resident Observer, CS Selection Bd, 1966; London Business Sch., 1967; Private Sec. to the Prime Minister, 1968–72 (Parly Affairs, 1968–70; Econ. and Home Affairs, 1970–72); Asst Sec., DTI, and Sec., Industrial Development Adv. Bd, 1972–74; Under Sec., DoI, and Sec., NEB, 1975–77; Under Sec., Dept of Trade, 1977–80, Dep. Sec. (Civil Aviation and Shipping), 1980–81; Dep. Sec., Cabinet Office, 1981–85; Perm. Under-Sec. of State, Dept of Energy, 1985–89. Sen. Ind. Dir, Scottish Power plc, 1996–2004; Dir, Woolwich plc, 1998–2000; Chm., Woolwich Pension Fund Trust Co. Ltd, 1999–2000. Chairman: Beckenham and Bromley NT Centre, 2003–06; Beckenham Decorative and Fine Arts Soc., 2009–12. CCMI (CBIM 1988; Mem., Bd of Companions, 1996–2002 (Dep. Chm., 1999–2002)); FRSA 1999. *Recreations:* gardening, listening to music. *Address:* 9 Lavender Court, 10 Greenways, Beckenham, Kent BR3 3NG. *T:* (020) 8650 5925. *Died 12 Dec. 2015.*

GREIG, Sir (Henry Louis) Carron, KCVO 1995 (CVO 1973); CBE 1986; DL; Chairman, Horace Clarkson PLC (formerly H. Clarkson (Holdings) plc), 1976–93; Director, James Purdey & Sons Ltd, 1972–2000; an Extra Gentleman Usher to the Queen, since 1995 (Gentleman Usher, 1961–95); *b* 21 Feb. 1925; *s* of late Group Captain Sir Louis Greig, KBE, CVO, DL; *m* 1955, Monica Kathleen, *d* of late Hon. J. J. Stourton, TD; three *s* one *d*. *Educ:* Eton. Scots Guards, 1943–47, Captain. Joined H. Clarkson & Co. Ltd, 1948; Dir, 1954; Man. Dir, 1962; Chairman: H. Clarkson & Co. Ltd, 1973–85; Baltic Exchange (formerly Baltic Mercantile and Shipping Exchange), 1983–85 (Dir, 1978–85); Director: Williams & Glyn's Bank, 1983–85; Royal Bank of Scotland, 1985–95; Charterhouse, 1990–93. Vice-Chm., Not Forgotten Assoc., 1979–96. Chm., Schoolmistresses and Governesses Benevolent Instn, 1992–2003 (Dep. Chm., 1966–92). Governor, United World Coll. of the Atlantic, 1985–96. DL Hants, 1992. *Address:* Brook House, Fleet, Hants GU51 2RF; Binsness, Forres, Moray. *Clubs:* White's; Royal Findhorn Yacht. *Died 11 July 2012.*

GRENVILLE, Prof. John Ashley Soames; Professor of Modern History, University of Birmingham, 1969–94, then Emeritus; *b* Berlin, 11 Jan. 1928; *m* 1st, 1960, Betty Anne Rosenberg (*d* 1974), New York; three *s*; 2nd, 1975, Patricia Carnie; one *d* one step *d*. *Educ:* Mistley Place and Orwell Park Prep. Sch.; Cambridge Techn. Sch.; corresp. courses; Birkbeck Coll.; LSE; Yale Univ. BA, PhD London; FRHistS. Postgrad. Schol., London Univ., 1951–53; Asst Lectr, subseq. Lectr, Nottingham Univ., 1953–64; Commonwealth Fund Fellow, 1958–59; Postdoctoral Fellow, Yale Univ., 1960–63; Reader in Modern History, Nottingham Univ., 1964–65; Prof. of Internat. History, Leeds Univ., 1965–69. Vis. Prof., Queen's Coll., NY City Univ., 1964, etc; Guest Professor, Univ. of Hamburg, 1980, 1994. Chm., British Univs History Film Consortium, 1968–71; Mem. Council: RHistS, 1971–73; List and Index Soc., 1966–71; Baeck Inst., London, 1981–. Consultant, American and European Bibliographical Centre, Oxford and California and Clio Press, 1960–88; Dir of Film for the Historical Assoc., 1975–78; Historical Adviser, World History, ZDF, German Television, 1982–98. Editor: Fontana History of War and Society, 1969–78; Leo Baeck Year Book, 1992–. *Publications:* (with J. G. Fuller) The Coming of the Europeans, 1962; Lord Salisbury and Foreign Policy, 1964, 2nd edn 1970; (with G. B. Young)

Politics, Strategy and American Diplomacy: studies in foreign policy 1873–1917, 1966, 2nd edn 1971; Documentary Films (with N. Pronay), The Munich Crisis, 1968; The End of Illusions: from Munich to Dunkirk, 1970; The Major International Treaties 1914–1973: a history and guide, 1974, 4th edn (jtly) 1900–2004; Europe Reshaped 1848–78, 1975, enlarged edn, 2000; Nazi Germany, 1976; World History of the Twentieth Century I, 1900–1945, 1980; Collins World History of the Twentieth Century, 1994, 2nd edn 1998 (trans. Russian and Chinese), 4th edn as World History from the Twentieth to the Twenty-first Century, 2010; (jtly) The Major Laws and Decrees of the Third Reich, 2011; The Jews of Hamburg: the death of a civilization, from 1790 to the Holocaust, 2011; contrib. various learned jls. *Recreations:* listening to music, travel, tutoring students. *Address:* University of Birmingham, School of History, Birmingham B15 2TT. *Club:* Athenæum. *Died 7 March 2011.*

GREVILLE, Brig. Phillip Jamieson, CBE 1972; freelance writer on defence, foreign affairs and Australian history; Australian Director, International Institute for Prisoners of War, since 1992; *b* 12 Sept. 1925; *s* of Col S. J. Greville, OBE and Mrs D. M. Greville; *m* 1948, June Patricia Anne Martin; two *s* one *d* (and one *s* one *d* decd). *Educ:* RMC Duntroon; Sydney Univ. (BEng). 2/8 Field Co., 2nd AIF, New Guinea, 1945; 1 RAR Korea (POW), 1951–53; Senior Instructor SME Casula, 1953–55; CRE, RMC Duntroon, 1955–58; Staff Coll., Camberley and Transportation Trng UK, 1959–61; Dir of Transportation AHQ, 1962–65; GSO1 1st Div., 1966; CE Eastern Comd, 1969–71; Comdr 1st Australian Logistic Support Group, Vietnam, 1971; Actg Comdr 1st Australian Task Force, Vietnam, 1971–72 (CBE); Dir of Transport, 1973–74; Dir Gen., Logistics, 1975–76; Comdr, Fourth Mil. District, 1977–80, retired. Adelaide Advertiser: Defence Writer, 1980–86; Pacific Defence Reporter, 1987–92. Dir, Dominant Australia Pty, 1982–86. Nat. Pres., RUSI of Aust., 1983–84. FIE(Aust), FCILT. *Publications:* A Short History of Victoria Barracks Paddington, 1969; The Central Organisation for War and its Application to Movements, 1975, Sapper series (RE Officers in Australia); The Army Portion of the National Estate, 1977; Why Australia Should Not Ratify the New Law of War, 1989; vol. 4, History of the Royal Australian Engineers, 1999. *Recreation:* golf. *Address:* 3 River Downs Crescent, River Downs, Qld 4212, Australia. *Club:* United Services (Brisbane). *Died 10 March 2011.*

GREY, 6th Earl *cr* 1806; **Richard Fleming George Charles Grey;** Bt 1746; Baron Grey, 1801; Viscount Howick, 1806; *b* 5 March 1939; *s* of late Albert Harry George Campbell Grey (Trooper, Canadian Army Tanks, who *d* on active service, 1942) and Vera Helen Louise Harding; *S* cousin, 1963; *m* 1st, 1966, Margaret Ann (marr. diss. 1974), *e d* of Henry Bradford, Ashburton; 2nd, 1974, Stephanie Caroline, *o d* of Donald Gaskell-Brown and formerly wife of Surg.-Comdr Neil Leicester Denham, RN. *Educ:* Hounslow Coll.; Hammersmith Coll. of Bldg (Quantity Surveying). Public relations consultant. Chm., London Cremation Co., 1992–; Dir, Covent Garden Quality, 1993–. President: Assoc. of Cost and Executive Accountants, 1978; Cremation Soc. of GB, 1992–. Mem., Liberal Party. *Recreation:* sailing. *Heir:* *b* Philip Kent Grey [*b* 11 May 1940; *m* 1968, Ann Catherine, *y d* of Cecil Applegate, Kingsbridge, Devon; one *s* one *d*]. *Died 10 Sept. 2013.*

GRIERSON, Sir Ronald (Hugh), Kt 1990; Vice-Chairman, General Electric Co., 1968–91; Chairman, Louis Dreyfus Foundation, since 2012; Senior Advisor, Roland Berger, since 2009; *b* Nürnberg, Bavaria, 6 Aug. 1921; *s* of Mr and Mrs E. J. Griessmann (name changed by Deed Poll in 1943); *m* 1966, (Elizabeth) Heather, Viscountess Bearsted (*d* 1993), *er d* of Mr and Mrs G. Firmston-Williams; one *s*, and one step *d*. *Educ:* Realgymnasium, Nürnberg; Lycée Pasteur, Paris; Highgate Sch., London; Balliol Coll., Oxford. Served HM Forces 1940–47 (despatches); TA, 1948–54. Staff Mem., The Economist, 1947–48; S. G. Warburg & Co., 1948–86 (Dir, 1958–68 and 1980–86); Dep. Chm. and Man. Dir, IRC, 1966–67; Chm., Orion Bank, 1971–73; Dir-Gen., Industrial and Technological Affairs, EEC, 1973–74; Sen. Partner, Panmure Gordon & Co., 1974–76. Board Member: BAC, 1970–71; Internat. Computers, 1974–76; Davy Internat., 1969–73; Nat. Bus Co., 1984–86; RJR Nabisco Inc. (formerly R. J. Reynolds), 1977–89; Chrysler Corp., 1983–91; W. R. Grace & Co., 1987–94; Daily Mail & Gen. Trust, 1994–2001; Chime Communications, 1998–2003. Chairman: European Orgn for Cancer Treatment Res., 1976–2000; South Bank Bd, 1984–90; Bain & Co. Internat., 1988–2009; Adv. Bd, Blackstone Gp, 1989–2013; GEC Internat., 1991–95. Mem., Bd of Trustees, Phillips Collection, Washington, 1980–98. Member: Atlantic Coll. Council, 1960–70; Harvard Coll. Faculty, 1964–65; CNAA, 1978–84; Arts Council of GB, 1984–88; Ernst von Siemens Foundn, 1977–98; Bd of Visitors, N Carolina Sch. of the Arts, 1984–90; European Arts Foundn, 1987–88; Trustee: Prince of Liechtenstein Foundn, 1991–; European Studies Foundn, Oxford Univ., 1991–; Royal Acad., 2003–. Hon. Dr of Law, Grove City Coll., USA, 1986. Commander: Order of Merit (Italy), 1980; Légion d'honneur (France), 1994; Order of Merit (Austria), 2002; SMO (Malta), 2006; Comdr's Cross, Order of Merit (Germany), 1993. *Address:* 40 Berkeley Square, W1J 5AL. *Clubs:* White's, Pratt's, Beefsteak; Brook (New York). *Died 23 Oct. 2014.*

GRIFFIN, Paul, MBE 1961; MA Cantab; writer; *b* 2 March 1922; *s* of late John Edwin Herman Griffin; *m* 1946, Felicity Grace, *d* of late Canon Howard Dobson; one *s* one *d*. *Educ:* Framlingham Coll.; St Catharine's Coll., Cambridge. Served War in Gurkhas, India, Burma, Malaya, 1940–46; North-West Frontier, 1941–43; Chindits, 1943–44. Asst Master and Senior English Master, Uppingham Sch., 1949–55; Principal, English Sch. in Cyprus, 1956–60; Headmaster, Aldenham Sch., 1962–74; Principal, Anglo-World Language Centre, Cambridge, 1976–82; Treasurer, Corp. of Sons of the Clergy, 1978–86. Cambridge University Seatonian Prize, 2001, 2007 and 2010. *Publications:* Sing Jubilee, 1996; Nearly Funny Poems, 1996; Songs About Suffolk, 1997; Going Away, 1999; Lighthearted Lines, 2000; The Sound of Violins, 2003; Diamonds for Aphrodite, 2006; collaborated in: How to Become Ridiculously Well-Read in One Evening, 1985; How to Become Absurdly Well-Informed about the Famous and Infamous, 1987; The Dogsbody Papers, 1988; How to Be Tremendously Tuned-in to Opera, 1989; How to Be Well-Versed in Poetry, 1990; How to Be European, 1991; poems, humour, articles, broadcasts. *Recreation:* literary competitions. *Address:* 1 Crombie House, The Common, Southwold, Suffolk IP18 6AL. *T:* (01502) 723709. *Died 29 Jan. 2012.*

GRIFFITH EDWARDS, James; *see* Edwards.

GRIFFITHS, Baron *cr* 1985 (Life Peer), of Govilon in the County of Gwent; **William Hugh Griffiths,** Kt 1971; MC 1944; PC 1980; a Lord of Appeal in Ordinary, 1985–93; *b* 26 Sept. 1923; *s* of late Sir Hugh Griffiths, CBE, MS, FRCS; *m* 1949, Evelyn (*d* 1998), *d* of Col K. A. Krefting; one *s* three *d*; *m* 2000, Baroness Brigstocke, CBE (*d* 2004); *m* 2009, Mrs Greta Fenston. *Educ:* Charterhouse; St John's Coll., Cambridge (Hon. Fellow, 1985). Commissioned in Welsh Guards, 1942; demobilised after war service, 1946. Cambridge, 1946–48. BA 1948. Called to the Bar, Inner Temple, 1949, Bencher, 1971; QC 1964; Treasurer of the Bar Council, 1968–69. Recorder of Margate, 1962–64, of Cambridge, 1964–70; a Judge of the High Court of Justice, Queen's Bench Division, 1971–80; a Lord Justice of Appeal, 1980–85. A Judge, National Industrial Relations Court, 1973–74. Chm., Security Commn, 1985–92; Mem., Adv. Council on Penal Reform, 1967–70; Chm., Tribunal of Inquiry on Ronan Point, 1968; Vice-Chm., Parole Bd, 1976–77; Mem., Chancellor's Law Reform Cttee, 1976–93; Pres., Senate of the Inns of Court and the Bar, 1982–84; Chm., Lord Chancellor's Adv. Cttee on Legal Educn and Conduct, 1991–93. Hon. Mem., Canadian Bar Assoc., 1981; Hon. Fellow: Amer. Inst. of Judicial Admin, 1985; Amer. Coll. of Trial Lawyers, 1988. Hon. LLD: Wales, 1987; De Montfort, 1993. *Recreations:* cricket, golf, fishing. *Address:* c/o House of Lords, SW1A 0PW. *Clubs:* Garrick, MCC (Pres., 1990–91); Hawks (Cambridge); Royal and Ancient (St Andrews) (Captain, 1993–94); Sunningdale Golf. *Died 30 May 2015.*

GRIFFITHS, Rt Rev. Ambrose; *see* Griffiths, Rt Rev. M. A.

GRIFFITHS, Ven. Dr David Nigel, FSA; Archdeacon of Berkshire, 1987–92, then Archdeacon Emeritus; Chaplain to The Queen, 1977–97; *b* 29 Oct. 1927; *o s* of late William Cross Griffiths, LDS, and Doris May (*née* Rhodes); *m* 1953, Joan Fillingham; two *s* one *d*. *Educ:* King Edward's Sch., Bath; Cranbrook; Worcester Coll., Oxford (MA; Gladstone Meml Prize, Arnold Historical Essay Prize); Lincoln Theol Coll.; PhD Reading, 1991. An economist before ordination; Consultant at FAO, Rome, 1952–53. Curate, St Matthew, Northampton, 1958–61; Headquarters Staff, SPCK, 1961–67; Rector of Minster Parishes, Lincoln, 1967–73; Vice-Chancellor and Librarian, Lincoln Cathedral, 1967–73; Rector of Windsor, 1973–87; Rural Dean of Maidenhead, 1977–82 and 1985–87; Hon. Canon of Christ Church, Oxford, 1983–88, then Emeritus. Warden, St Anne's Bede Houses, Lincoln, 1993–98. Trustee: Lincolnshire Old Churches Trust, 1995–2008; Jews' Court, Lincoln and Bardney Abbey, 1999–. Served TARO and RMFVR, 1946–50; Chaplain, RNR, 1963–77 (Reserve Decoration, 1977); OCF, Household Cavalry, 1973–87, 1st Bn Irish Guards, 1977–80. FSA 1973. Fredson Bowers Award, Bibliographical Soc. of America, 1996; Bibliographical Soc. Award (UK), 1997. *Publications:* The Bibliography of the Book of Common Prayer, 2002; articles on bibliography and church history. *Recreations:* walking, bibliomania. *Address:* 2 Middleton's Field, Lincoln LN2 1QP. *T:* (01522) 525753. *E:* david27.g@mac.com. *Died 13 Feb. 2012.*

GRIFFITHS, Sir Eldon (Wylie), Kt 1985; Patron, World Affairs Councils of America, since 2004 (National Chairman, 2001, then Chairman Emeritus); *b* 25 May 1925; *s* of Thomas H. W. Griffiths and Edith May; *m* 1st, 1949, Sigrid Gante (marr. diss. 1985); one *s* one *d*; 2nd, 1985, Betty Stannard (*d* 2010); 3rd, 2013, Susan Donnell. *Educ:* Ashton Grammar Sch.; Emmanuel Coll., Cambridge (MA); MA Yale. Fellow, Saybrook Coll., Yale, 1948–49; Correspondent, Time and Life magazines, 1949–55; Foreign Editor, Newsweek, 1956–63; Columnist, Washington Post, 1962–63; Conservative Research Department, 1963–64. MP (C) Bury St Edmunds, May 1964–1992; Parly Sec., Min. of Housing and Local Govt, June–Oct. 1970; Parly Under-Sec. of State, DoE, and Minister for Sport, 1970–74; opposition spokesman on trade and industry, and Europe, 1974–76. Former Chairman: Anglo-Iranian Parly Gp; Anglo-Polish Parly Gp. Pres., Special Olympics (UK). Consultant/Adviser, Nat. Police Federation, to 1988; President: Assoc. of Public Health Inspectors, 1969–70; Friends of Gibraltar; World Affairs Council, Orange County, California. Regents' Prof., Univ. of California, Irvine. Dir, Center for Internat. Business, Chapman Univ., Orange, Calif. Dir, US and UK cos. Hon. Freeman, City of London; Hon. Citizen, Orange County, California. Medal of Honour, Republic of China, Taiwan. *Publications:* The Hutton Story, 1998; Walter: a German immigrant, 2001; Turbulent Iran, 2006; TransAtlantic Man (memoirs), 2011; Global Citizen (memoirs), 2011; Iranian Imbroglio, 2013. *Recreations:* reading, swimming. *Address:* (Nov.–May) 29091 Ridgeview, Laguna Niguel, CA 92677, USA; (June–Oct.) The Coach House, West Courtyard, Great Church Yard, Bury St Edmunds IP33 1RS. *Club:* Carlton. *Died 3 June 2014.*

GRIFFITHS, Howard Barton; Editor-in-Chief, Pulse, 2003–05 (Editor, 1979–2003); Group Editor, The Practitioner, 1994–2005 (Editor, 1988–94); *b* 6 Aug. 1947; *m* 1977, Lynda Smith; three *d*. *Educ:* Cowbridge Grammar School; Merton College, Oxford (BA). Feature writer, Pulse, 1973. *Recreation:* family. *Died 7 June 2015.*

GRIFFITHS, Rt Rev. (Michael) Ambrose, OSB; Bishop of Hexham and Newcastle, (RC), 1992–2004, then Emeritus; Assistant Priest, St Mary's, Leyland, since 2004; *b* 4 Dec. 1928; *s* of Henry and Hilda Griffiths. *Educ:* Ampleforth Coll.; Balliol Coll., Oxford (MA, BSc Chemistry). Entered monastery at Ampleforth, 1950; theological studies at S Anselmo, Rome, 1953–56; ordained priest, 1957; Prof. of Theology at Ampleforth, 1963; Sen. Science Master, Ampleforth Coll., 1967; Inspector of Accounts for English Benedictine Congregation, 1971 and 1985–92; Procurator (Bursar) at Ampleforth, 1972; Abbot of Ampleforth, 1976–84; Parish Priest, St Mary's, Leyland, Preston, 1984–92. Mem. Public School Bursars' Assoc. Cttee, 1975. *Recreation:* walking. *Address:* St Mary's, Broadfield Walk, Leyland PR25 1PD. *Died 14 June 2011.*

GRIFFITHS, Peter Harry Steve; *b* 24 May 1928; *s* of W. L. Griffiths, West Bromwich; *m* 1962, Jeannette Christine (*née* Rubery); one *s* one *d*. *Educ:* City of Leeds Training Coll. BSc (Econ.) Hons London, 1956; MEd Birmingham, 1963. Headmaster, Hall Green Road Sch., West Bromwich, 1962–64. Senior Lectr in Economic Hist., The Polytechnic, Portsmouth (formerly Portsmouth Coll. of Technology), 1967–79. Fulbright Exchange Prof. of Economics, Pierce Coll., Los Angeles, Calif, 1968–69. Councillor, Smethwick, 1955–64 (Chm., Education Cttee; Leader, Conservative Group of Councillors, 1960–64). MP (C): Smethwick, 1964–66; Portsmouth N, 1979–97; contested (C) Portsmouth N, Feb. 1974, and 1997. *Publications:* A Question of Colour?, 1966. *Recreations:* motoring, writing, computing. *Club:* Sloane. *Died 20 Nov. 2013.*

GRIFFITHS, Richard, OBE 2008; actor; *b* Thornaby-on-Tees, 31 July 1947; *s* of Thomas Griffiths, steelworker, and Jane Griffiths (*née* Denmark); *m* Heather. *Educ:* St Bede's RC Boys' Secondary Modern Sch.; Stockton/Billingham Tech. Coll.; Northern Sch. of Music (Drama Dept); RCA, Manchester; Sch. of Theatre, Manchester Poly. (Dip. Speech and Drama (Hons); Dip. Associateship). *Stage* includes: Royal Shakespeare Company: Henry VIII, 1983; Once in a Lifetime; Volpone, 1983; Red Star, 1984; After Aida, 1988, Verdi's Messiah, Old Vic; Rules of the Game, 1992, The Life of Galileo, 1994, Almeida; Art, 1997, 2001, Heroes, 2005, Wyndham's; Katherine Howard, 1998, The Man Who Came to Dinner, 1999, Chichester Fest. Th.; Luther, NT, 2001; The History Boys, NT, 2004, NY, 2006 (Evening Standard and Critics' Circle Awards, 2004, Olivier Award, 2005, Tony Award, 2006, for best actor); Equus, Gielgud, 2007, Broadhurst, NY, 2008–09; The Habit of Art, NT, 2009; The Sunshine Boys, Savoy Th., 2012; *films* include: Gandhi, 1982; Gorky Park, 1983; A Private Function, 1984; Greystoke, 1984; Withnail and I, 1988; King Ralph, 1991; Naked Gun 2½, 1991; Funny Bones, 1995; Sleepy Hollow, 2000; Vatel, 2000; Harry Potter and the Philosopher's Stone, 2001; Harry Potter and the Chamber of Secrets, 2002; Harry Potter and the Prisoner of Azkaban, 2004; The History Boys, 2006; Bedtime Stories, 2008; Harry Potter and the Deathly Hallows, Pt 1, 2010; Pirates of the Caribbean: On Stranger Tides, 2011; The Invention of Hugo Cabret, 2011; *television* includes: Bird of Prey, 1982; The Cleopatras, 1983; Merry Wives of Windsor, 1983; Whoops Apocalypse, 1986; The Marksman, 1987; Ffizz, 1987; A Kind of Living, 1988; Pie in the Sky, 1994; In the Red, 1998; Gormenghast, 2000; Hope and Glory, 2000; tlc, 2002; Ballet Shoes, 2007; Henry V, 2012; numerous radio appearances. Awards include: Carleton Hobbs, BBC, 1970; Best Supporting Actor, Clarence Derwent, 1979; Best Newcomer, and Best Supporting Actor, Plays and Players, 1979; Gold (Best Actor), 1994, Silver, 1996, Sony Radio Awards; Gold, Assoc. of Colls, 2000. Hon. DLitt: Durham, 1998; Teesside, 2006. *Address:* c/o Dalzell & Beresford, 26 Astwood Mews, SW7 4DE. *Died 28 March 2013.*

GRIGGS, Norman Edward, CBE 1976; Vice-President, The Building Societies Association, since 1981 (Secretary-General, 1963–81); *b* 27 May 1916; *s* of late Archibald Griggs and Maud Griggs (*née* Hewing); *m* 1947, Livia Lavinia Jandolo; one *s* (one step *s* decd). *Educ:* Newport Grammar Sch.; London Sch. of Econs and Pol Science (BScEcon). FCIS. Accountancy Dept, County of London Electric Supply Co. Ltd, 1933–40; service in RE and RAPC, Middle East, 1940–46; Asst Sec., Glass Manufrs' Fedn, 1946–52; Sec., Plastics Inst., 1952–56; Asst Sec., Building Socs Assoc., 1956–61, Dep. Sec. 1961–63. Sec.-Gen., Internat. Union of Building Socs and Savings Assocs, 1972–77. *Publications:* poetry: Life in the Withered Shell, 1990; Sharp-Eyed and Wary, 1991; The Solitary Watcher, 1995; Life on the Brink, 1999. *Recreation:* print addict. *Address:* 5 Gledhow Gardens, SW5 0BL. *T:* (020) 7373 5128. *Died 21 May 2011.*

GRIMWADE, Rev. Canon John Girling; Chaplain to the Queen, 1980–90; permission to officiate, Dioceses of Gloucester and Oxford, since 1989; *b* 13 March 1920; *s* of Herbert Alfred and Edith Grimwade; *m* 1951, Adini Anne Carus-Wilson (*d* 2011); one *s* one *d*. *Educ:* Colet Court; St Paul's Sch.; Keble Coll., Oxford; Cuddesdon Coll. MA Oxon. Friends' Ambulance Unit, 1940–45. Curate of Kingston-upon-Thames, 1950–53; Curate, University Church of St Mary-the-Virgin, Oxford, and Secretary of Oxford Univ. Student Christian Movement, 1953–56; Vicar of St Mark's, Smethwick, 1956–62; Rector of Caversham, 1962–81, and Priest-in-Charge of Mapledurham, 1968–81; Rector of Caversham and Mapledurham, 1981–83; Priest-in-Charge, Stonesfield, Oxford, 1983–89. Chm., House of Clergy, Oxford Diocesan Synod, 1976–82; Agenda Sec., Oxford Dio. Synod, 1983–88; Diocesan Press Officer, Oxford, 1983–89. Hon. Canon of Christ Church, Oxford, 1974–90, Hon. Canon Emeritus, 1990–. *Recreation:* reading. *Address:* 88 Alexander Drive, Cirencester, Glos GL7 1UJ. *Died 30 July 2012.*

GROSBERG, Prof. Percy, PhD; CEng, MIMechE, FTI; Research Professor of Textile Engineering, 1961–90, and Head of Department of Textile Industries, 1975–83 and 1987–89, University of Leeds, then Emeritus Professor; Marcus Sieff Professor of Textile Technology, Shenkar College of Engineering and Design (formerly of Textile Technology and Fashion), Ramat Gan, Israel, 1991–2008; *b* 5 April 1925; *s* of late Rev. and Mrs Gershon Grosberg, Tel-Aviv; *m* 1951, Queenie Fisch; one *s* one *d* (and one *s* decd). *Educ:* Parktown Boys' High Sch., Johannesburg; Univ. of the Witwatersrand; University of Leeds. BScEng, MScEng, PhD Witwatersrand. CEng, MIMechE 1965; FTI 1966 (Hon. FTI 1988). Sen. Res. Officer S African Wool Textile Res. Inst., 1949–55; University of Leeds: ICI Res. Fellow, 1955; Lectr in Textile Engrg, 1955–61. Hon. Fellow, Shenkar Coll. of Textile Technology and Fashion, Israel, 1993. Warner Memorial Medal, 1968; Textile Inst. Medal, 1972; Distinguished Service Award, Indian Inst. of Technol., Delhi, 1985. *Publications:* An Introduction to Textile Mechanisms, 1968; Structural Mechanics of Fibres, Yarns and Fabrics, 1969; Yarn Production: theoretical aspects, 1999; papers on rheology of fibrous assemblies, mechan. processing of fibres, and other res. topics in Jl of Textile Inst., Textile Res. Jl, and other sci. jls. *Recreations:* music, travel. *Address:* Apartment 25, 55 Shlomo Hamelech Street, Netanya 42267, Israel. *Died 10 Dec. 2012.*

GROSS, John Jacob; writer and editor; *b* 12 March 1935; *s* of late Abraham Gross and Muriel Gross; *m* 1965, Miriam Marianna May (marr. diss. 1988); one *s* one *d*. *Educ:* City of London Sch.; Wadham Coll., Oxford. Editor, Victor Gollancz Ltd, 1956–58; Asst Lectr, Queen Mary Coll., Univ. of London, 1959–62; Fellow, King's Coll., Cambridge, 1962–65; Literary Editor, New Statesman, 1973; Editor, TLS, 1974–81; editorial consultant, Weidenfeld (Publishers) Ltd, 1982; on staff of New York Times, 1983–88; Dir, Times Newspapers Holdings, 1982; theatre critic, Sunday Telegraph, 1989–2005. A Trustee, National Portrait Gall., 1977–84. Hon. DHL Adelphi Univ., 1995. *Publications:* The Rise and Fall of the Man of Letters (1969 Duff Cooper Memorial Prize), 1969; Joyce, 1971; (ed) The Oxford Book of Aphorisms, 1983; (ed) The Oxford Book of Essays, 1991; Shylock, 1992; (ed) The Modern Movement, 1992; (ed) The Oxford Book of Comic Verse, 1994; (ed) The New Oxford Book of English Prose, 1998; A Double Thread (memoir), 2001; (ed) After Shakespeare: an anthology, 2002; (ed) The New Oxford Book of Literary Anecdotes, 2006; (ed) The Oxford Book of Parodies, 2010. *Address:* Flat 16, 2 Porchester Gardens, W2 6JL. *Club:* Beefsteak. *Died 10 Jan. 2011.*

GROSS, Solomon Joseph, CMG 1966; *b* 3 Sept. 1920; *s* of late Abraham Gross; *m* 1948, Doris Evelyn Barker (*d* 2000); two *d*. *Educ:* Hackney Downs Sch.; University Coll., London. RAF, Burma, India. Ministry of Supply, 1947; OEEC, Paris, 1948–51; British Embassy, Washington, 1951–53; Board of Trade, 1954–57; British Trade Comr, Pretoria, SA, 1958–62; Principal British Trade Comr, Ghana, 1963–66; British Deputy High Comr, Ghana, 1966–67; Board of Trade, 1967–69; Minister, British Embassy, Pretoria, 1969–73; Chargé d'Affaires at various times in Ghana and S Africa; Under-Sec., Dept of Industry, 1974–80; Dir for Regional Affairs, British Technology Gp, 1983–84. Bd Mem., BSC, later British Steel plc, 1978–90; Dir, Technical Audit Group Ltd, 1986–90. Mem., Overseas Cttee, CBI, 1987–90; Mem., External Relations Cttee and Chm., USA Wkg Pty, UNICE, Brussels, 1987–90. *Recreations:* gardening, history, do-it-yourself. *Address:* 38 Barnes Court, Station Road, New Barnet, Herts EN5 1QY. *T:* (020) 8449 2710. *Died 16 March 2012.*

GROUND, Sir Richard (William), Kt 2012; OBE 1991; a Justice of the Court of Appeal: Turks and Caicos Islands, since 2005; Cayman Islands, since 2012; Bermuda, since 2013; *b* Stamford, Lincs, 17 Dec. 1949; *s* of William James Ground and Billie Ground (*née* Glen); *m* 1986, Margarita, (Dace) McCoy. *Educ:* Oakham Sch., Rutland; Lincoln Coll., Oxford (Open Schol.; BA English Lang. and Lit. 1970). Called to the Bar, Gray's Inn, 1975, Bencher, 2011; in practice as barrister, London, 1976–83; QC (Cayman Is) 1987; Crown Counsel, 1983–87, Attorney Gen., 1987–92, Cayman Is; Puisne Judge, Bermuda, 1992–98; Chief Justice: Turks and Caicos Is, 1998–2004; Bermuda, 2004–12. *Publications:* Birds of the Turks and Caicos Islands, 2001. *Recreations:* wildlife photography, fly-fishing, numismatics. *Club:* Cressbrook and Litton Flyfishers. *Died 22 Feb. 2014.*

GROVE, Rear-Adm. John Scott, CB 1984; OBE 1964; RN retired, 1985; nuclear engineering consultant to Ministry of Defence, 1985–99; *b* 7 July 1927; *s* of late William George Grove and Frances Margaret Scott Grove; *m* 1950, Betty Anne (*née* Robinson) (*d* 2013); one *s* (one *d* decd). *Educ:* Dundee High Sch.; St Andrews Univ. University Coll., 1944–47 (BScEng 1st Cl. Hons). National Service, Royal Engineers, 1947–48; Instructor Br., Royal Navy, 1948–50; Electrical Engrg Br., RN, 1950, qualified in Submarines, 1953; post graduate trng in Nuclear Engrg, Imperial Coll., London, 1958–59; sea service in HMS Forth and HM Submarines Tally-Ho, Turpin (FO Subs' Commendation, special op., 1955), Porpoise, Dreadnought (1st Sen. Engrg Officer, RN first nuclear sub., 1960–64); service in Ship Dept, 1964–67; staff of Flag Officer Submarines, 1967–70; Naval Asst to Controller of the Navy, 1970–73; staff of Flag Officer Submarines, 1975–77; commanded HMS Fisgard, 1977–79; Chief Strategic Systems Exec. (formerly Chief Polaris Exec.), 1980–85; Chief Naval Engr Officer, 1983–85. Comdr 1963; Captain 1970; Rear-Adm. 1980. Dir, Devonport Mgt Ltd, Devonport Royal Dockyard, 1987–91; engrg consultant, 1991–98. Gov., British Maritime Technol. (Quality Assurance), 1990–94. Chm., Friends of RN Mus. and HMS Victory, 1995–99. Master, Engineers' Co., 1994–95 (Sen. Warden, 1993–94). *Recreations:* walking, gardening. *Died 29 Sept. 2013.*

GRUFFYDD, Prof. (Robert) Geraint, FBA 1991; Director, University of Wales Centre for Advanced Welsh and Celtic Studies, Aberystwyth, 1985–93; *b* Tal-y-bont, Merioneth, 9 June 1928; *s* of Moses and Ceridwen Griffith; *m* 1953, Elizabeth Eluned Roberts; two *s* one *d*. *Educ:* University Coll. of N Wales, Bangor (BA; Hon. Fellow, 1993); Jesus Coll., Oxford (DPhil; Hon. Fellow, 1992). Asst Editor, Geiriadur Prifysgol Cymru, 1953–55; Lectr, Dept of Welsh, UCNW, 1955–70; Prof. of Welsh Language and Literature, UCW, Aberystwyth, 1970–79; Librarian, Nat. Library of Wales, 1980–85. Vice-Pres., Univ. of Wales, Aberystwyth, 1996–2001. Chairman: Welsh Books Council, 1980–85; Welsh Language Section, Welsh Acad., 1986–90; Bd of Celtic Studies, Univ. of Wales, 1991–93. President: Cambrian Archæol Assoc., 1991–92; Internat. Congress of Celtic Studies, 1995–2003. Consulting Ed., Geiriadur Prifysgol Cymru (A Dictionary of the Welsh Language), 1999–. Hon. Fellow, Univ. of Wales, Aberystwyth, 2004. Hon. DLitt Wales, 1997. *Publications:* (ed) Meistri'r Canrifoedd, 1973; (ed) Cerddi '73, 1973; (ed) Bardos, 1982; (ed) Cerddi Saunders Lewis, 1986; Dafydd ap Gwilym, 1987; (ed) Y Gair ar Waith, 1988; Llenyddiaeth y Cymry, ii, 1989; (gen. editor) Cyfres Beirdd y Tywysogion (Poets of the Princes series), 7 vols, 1991–96; (consulting ed.) Cyfres Beirdd yr Uchelwyr (Poets of the Nobility series), 40 vols, 1994–; (co-ed) Hispano-Gallo-Brittonica, 1995; (ed) A Guide to Welsh Literature, Vol. 3, 1997; (co-ed) Gwaith Einion Offeiriad a Dafydd Ddu o Hiraddug, 1997; Y Ffordd Gadarn, 2008; articles, etc, on Welsh literary and religious history in various collaborative vols and learned jls. *Recreations:* reading, walking, travel. *Address:* Eirianfa, Caradog Road, Aberystwyth, Ceredigion SY23 2JY. *T:* (01970) 623396. *Died 24 March 2015.*

GUILD, Ivor Reginald, CBE 1985; FRSE; Partner in Shepherd and Wedderburn, WS, 1951–94; *b* 2 April 1924; 2nd *s* of Col Arthur Marjoribanks Guild, DSO, TD, DL, and Phyllis Eliza Cox. *Educ:* Cargilfield; Rugby; New Coll., Oxford (MA); Edinburgh Univ. (LLB). FRSE 1990. WS 1950. Procurator Fiscal of the Lyon Court, 1960–94; Bailie of Holyrood House, 1980–95; Registrar, Episcopal Synod of Episc. Church in Scotland, 1967–2007; Chancellor, Diocese of: Edinburgh, 1985–95; St Andrews, 1985–98. Chairman: Edinburgh Investment Trust Ltd, 1974–94 (Dir, 1972–94); Dunedin Income Growth Investment Trust plc (formerly First Scottish American Investment Trust plc), 1973–94 (Dir, 1964–94); Dunedin Worldwide Investment Trust plc (formerly Northern American Investment Trust plc), 1973–94 (Dir, 1964–94); Scottish Oriental Smaller Companies Trust PLC, 1995–2004; Dir, New Fulcrum Investment Trust, 1986–2005. Member: Council on Tribunals, 1976–85; Interception of Communications Tribunal, 1985–96; Immigration Appeal Adjudicator, 1988–95. Chm., Nat. Mus. of Antiquities of Scotland, 1981–85. Editor, Scottish Genealogist, 1959–94. *Recreations:* genealogy, golf. *Club:* New (Edinburgh). *Died 3 Jan. 2015.*

GUINNESS, Sir Kenelm (Ernest Lee), 4th Bt *cr* 1867; formerly independent engineering consultant; *b* 13 Dec. 1928; *s* of late Kenelm Edward Lee Guinness and Mrs Josephine Lee Guinness; *S* uncle, 1954; *m* 1961, Mrs Jane Nevin Dickson; two *s*. *Educ:* Eton Coll.; Massachusetts Institute of Technology, USA. Late Lieut, Royal Horse Guards. With IBRD, Washington, 1954–75. *Heir: s* Kenelm Edward Lee Guinness, *b* 30 Jan. 1962. *Address:* (home) Rich Neck, Claiborne, MD 21624, USA. *T:* (410) 7455079. *Club:* Cruising of America. *Died 6 May 2011.*

GUNN, Sir Robert (Norman), Kt 1995; DL; Chairman, Further Education Funding Council for England, 1992–97; Chairman, 1985–90, Chief Executive, 1983–87 and Director, 1976–90, The Boots Company PLC; *b* 16 Dec. 1925; *s* of late Donald Macfie Gunn and Margaret (*née* Pallister); *m* 1956, Joan Parry, JP (*d* 2008); one *d*. *Educ:* Royal High Sch., Edinburgh; Worcester Coll., Oxford (MA). Served RAC, 1944–47 (Lieut). Joined Boots, 1951; Merchandise Buyer, 1962–70; Head of Warehousing and Distribn, 1971–73; Dir of Property, 1973–78; Dir, Industrial Div., 1979–83 (Man. Dir 1980–83); Vice-Chm., 1983–85. Director: Foseco plc (formerly Foseco Minsep), 1984–91; East Midlands Electricity, 1990–95; Nottingham Building Soc., 1990–97. Member: Bd of Management, Assoc. of British Pharmaceutical Industry, 1981–84 (Vice-Pres., 1983–84); Council, CBI, 1985–90; PCFC, 1989–93; HEFCE, 1992–94. CCMI (CBIM 1983); FInstD 1985; FRSA. DL Notts, 1995. Hon. LLD Nottingham, 1993. *Recreations:* gardening, travel. *Address:* Tor House, Pinfold Lane, Elston, near Newark, Notts NG23 5PD. *Died 29 March 2015.*

GUTHRIE, (Garth) Michael, OBE 2007; Deputy Chairman, Welcome Break Holdings Ltd, 2002–07 (Director, 1997–2007; Chairman, 2000–02); *b* 30 April 1941; *s* of Harry and Ann Guthrie; *m* 1963, Joyce Fox; one *s* two *d*. *Educ:* Blackpool Catering Coll. (FHCIMA). Joined Mecca Leisure, 1961; Man. Dir, 1980; Chm., 1981–90; Chief Exec., 1985–90; Founder Dir, 1990, Chm. and Chief Exec., 1991–96, BrightReasons Gp; Chm. and CEO, Pavilion Services Gp, 1991–94; Jt Dep. Chm., Queensborough Hldgs, 1997–2000. Non-exec. Dir, Mission Capital plc, 2005–08. Chm., 1996–98, Dep. Chm., 1998–2000, Tomorrow's People Trust (Mem., Ambassadors' Gp, 2008–). FBHA 2010; FInstD. Hon. Fellow, Oxford Brookes Univ. 1995. DUniv Middlesex, 2010. *Recreations:* ski-ing, swimming, gardening. *Address:* Hyde Heath Farm, Bullbaiters Lane, Hyde Heath, Amersham, Bucks HP6 5RW. *Died 11 Jan. 2014.*

GUTHRIE, Roy David, (Gus), AM 1996; PhD, DSc; FTSE, FRSC, FRACI; higher education consultant; *b* 29 March 1934; *s* of David Ephraim Guthrie and Ethel (*née* Kimmins); *m* 1st, 1956, Ann Hoad (marr. diss. 1981); three *s*; 2nd, 1982, Lyn Fielding (separated 2010). *Educ:* Dorking Grammar Sch.; King's Coll., Univ. of London (BSc, PhD, DSc). Shirley Inst., Manchester, 1958–60; Asst Lectr, then Lectr, Univ. of Leicester, 1960–63; Lectr, then Reader, Univ. of Sussex, 1963–73; Griffith University, Brisbane: Foundation Prof. of Chemistry, 1973–81; Inaugural Chm., School of Science, 1973–78; Pro-Vice-Chancellor, 1980–81; Professor Emeritus, 1982; Sec. Gen., Royal Soc. of Chemistry, 1982–85; Pres., NSW Inst. of Technol., 1986–87, Vice-Chancellor and Pres., Univ. of Technol., Sydney, 1988–96. Chm., Qld Innovation Council, 1999–2002. Mem. Council, Univ. of Sunshine Coast, 1999–2005. Chm., Buderim Foundn, 2003–04. DUniv: Griffith, 1981; UTS, 1996; Hon. LLD Humberside, 1995. *Publications:* An Introduction to the Chemistry of Carbohydrates (with J. Honeyman), 2nd edn 1964, 3rd edn 1968, 4th edn 1974; over 130 scientific papers. *Recreations:* theatre, music, tai chi, croquet, caring clowning, playing the ukulele. *Address:* PO Box 285, Bli Bli, Qld 4560, Australia. *Died 12 Jan. 2013.*

GUZ, Prof. Abraham, MD; FRCP; Professor of Medicine, Charing Cross and Westminster Medical School, University of London, 1981–94; Emeritus Professor, Imperial College School of Medicine, since 1998; *b* 12 Aug. 1929; *s* of Akiwa Guz and Esther Guz; *m* 1957, Nita (*née* Florenz); three *d*. *Educ:* Grocers' Co. Sch.; Charing Cross Hosp. Med. Sch., Univ. of London (MB BS 1952; MD 1967). MRCP 1954, FRCP 1969. Hosp. appts, Charing Cross Hosp., 1952–53; Asst Lectr in Pharmacol., Charing Cross Hosp. Med. Sch., 1953–54; RAMC 1954–56; Hosp. appts, RPMS, Hammersmith Hosp., 1956–57; Research Fellow: Harvard Med. Sch., 1957–59; Cardiovascular Res. Inst., Univ. of California, 1959–61; Lectr in Medicine, 1961, later Sen. Lectr and Reader, Charing Cross Hosp. Med. Sch. Pro-Censor and Censor, RCP, 1979–87. Visiting Scientist, Univ. Lab. of Physiology, Oxford, 1994–. Treas., Med. Res. Soc., 2004–08. Fellow, Imperial Coll. Sch. of Medicine, 2000–. *Publications:* Dyspnoea, 1984; articles on mechanisms underlying breathlessness, mechanisms resp. for ventilatory response to exercise, measurement of performance of left ventricle. *Recreations:* family, violin in quartet, Jewish culture study. *Address:* 3 Littleton Road, Harrow, Middx HA1 3SY. *T:* (020) 8422 2786; (office) Charing Cross Hospital, Fulham Palace Road, W6 8RF. *T:* (020) 8846 7337, *Fax:* (020) 8846 7326. *E:* a.guz@imperial.ac.uk. *Died 11 April 2014.*

H

HACKER, Alan Ray, OBE 1988; clarinettist and conductor; *b* 30 Sept. 1938; *s* of Kenneth and Sybil Hacker; *m* 1st, 1959, Anna Maria Sroka; two *d*; 2nd, 1977, Karen Evans (marr. diss. 1994); one *s*; 3rd, 1995, Margaret Lee. *Educ:* Dulwich Coll.; Royal Academy of Music. FRAM. Joined LPO, 1958; Prof., RAM, 1960–76; Lectr, 1976–84, Sen. Lectr in Music, 1984–87, Univ. of York. Founded: Pierrot Players (with S. Pruslin and H. Birtwistle), 1965; Matrix, 1971; Music Party for authentic performance of classical music, 1972; Classical Orch., 1977; Guest Cond., Orchestra la Fenice, Venice, 1981–; operatic cond. début, Den Bergtagna, Sweden, 1986, York Fest., 1988; conducted 1st major British prodn of Mozart's La Finta Giardiniera, 1989; German operatic début, Don Giovanni, Così fan Tutte, Stuttgart, 1991, Julius Caesar, Halle, Ulisse, Stuttgart, 1992; La Cenerentola, Barcelona, 1993; King Arthur, Stuttgart, 1995; Xerxes, Cologne, 1996; Alcina, Stuttgart, 1998; Saul, Berlin, 1999. Orchestral work with: Südwestfunk and Berlin Radio Orch., 1992; Orchestre Nat. de Lille, 1996; Gürzenich Orchester, Cologne, 1996. First modern "authentic" perfs, 1977–, incl: Mozart's Symphonies 39, 40; Beethoven's Symphonies 2, 3, 7, 9 and Egmont; Haydn's Harmonie and Creation Masses, Symphony 104 and Trumpet Concerto. Revived basset clarinet and restored orig. text, Mozart's concerto and quintet, 1967; revived baroque clarinet (hitherto unplayed), 1975. Solo clarinettist, premieres of music by Birtwistle, Boulez, Morton Feldman, Goehr, Maxwell Davies, Stockhausen, Blake, Mellers and Salvatore Sciarrino; conductor, premiere of opera by Judith Weir; cond 5 staged perfs of Bach's St John Passion for European Music Year, 1984; basset clarinettist and saxophonist, Birtwistle's The Bacchai, 2002; conductor and basset clarinettist, Birtwistle's The Io Passion, 2004. Sir Robert Mayer Lectr, Leeds Univ., 1972–73. Mem. Fires of London, 1970–76; Dir, York Early Music Festival. Teacher, lectr and conductor, Banff Centre, Canada, 1986–. Many recordings. *Publications:* Scores of Mozart Concerto and Quintet, 1972; 1st edn of reconstructed Mozart Concerto, 1973; Schumann's Soiréestucke, 1985. *Recreation:* cookery. *Address:* Hindlea, Broughton, Malton, N Yorks YO17 6QJ. *Died 16 April 2012.*

HADFIELD, Sir Ronald, Kt 1995; QPM 1989; DL; Police Advisor to North Wales Tribunal into Child Abuse, 1996–98; Chief Constable, West Midlands, 1990–96; *b* 15 July 1939; *s* of George and Phyllis Marjorie Hadfield; *m* 1961, Anne Phyllisia Worrall; one *s* one *d*. *Educ:* Chadderton Grammar School. Joined Oldham Borough Police Force, 1958; served in Lancashire and Greater Manchester Police Forces; Asst Chief Constable, Derbyshire Constabulary, 1981; Dep. Chief Constable, 1986, Chief Constable, 1987, Nottinghamshire Constabulary. Advr in communications and law to cos in Midlands. DL W Midlands, 1994. *Recreations:* golf, fishing. *Died 31 Jan. 2013.*

HAGUE, Prof. Sir Douglas (Chalmers), Kt 1982; CBE 1978; Hon. Fellow, Green Templeton College (formerly Templeton College), Oxford, since 2005 (Associate Fellow, 1983–2005); Emeritus Fellow, Saïd Business School, Oxford, since 2008; *b* Leeds, 20 Oct. 1926; *s* of Laurence and Marion Hague; *m* 1947, Brenda Elizabeth Fereday (marr. diss. 1986); two *d*; *m* 1986, Janet Mary Leach. *Educ:* Moseley Grammar Sch.; King Edward VI High Sch., Birmingham; University of Birmingham. Assistant Tutor, Faculty of Commerce, Birmingham Univ., 1946; Assistant Lecturer, University College, London, 1947–50, Lecturer, 1950–57; Reader in Political Economy in University of London, 1957; Newton Chambers Professor of Economics, University of Sheffield, 1957–63. Visiting Professor of Economics, Duke Univ., USA, 1960–61; Head of Department of Business Studies, University of Sheffield, 1962–63; Professor of Applied Economics, University of Manchester, 1963–65; Prof. of Managerial Economics, Manchester Business Sch., 1965–81, Dep. Dir, 1978–81, Vis. Prof., 1981–; Vis. Prof., Imperial Coll. of Science and Technol., London, 1988–92. Chairman: Metapraxis Ltd, 1984–90; Doctus Consulting Europe, 1991–94; Wire Ltd, 1999–2000; Oxford Strategy Network, 1984–2000. Director: Economic Models Ltd, 1970–78; The Laird Gp, 1976–79; CRT Gp, 1990–96 (Chm., 1992–93). Rapporteur to International Economic Association, 1953–78, Editor General, 1981–86; Chm., ESRC, 1983–87; Member Working Party of National Advisory Council on Education for Industry and Commerce, 1962–63; Consultant to Secretariat of NEDC, 1962–63; Member: Treasury Working Party on Management Training in the Civil Service, 1965–67; EDC for Paper and Board, 1967–70; (part-time) N Western Gas Board, 1966–72; Working Party, Local Govt Training Bd, 1969–70; Price Commn, 1973–78 (Dep. Chm., 1977); Director: Manchester School of Management and Administration, 1964–65; Centre for Business Research, Manchester, 1964–66. Member Council, Manchester Business School, 1964–81; Chairman, Manchester Industrial Relations Society, 1964–66; President, NW Operational Research Group, 1967–69; British Chm., Carnegie Project on Accountability, 1968–72; Jt Chm., Conf. of Univ. Management Schools, 1971–73; Chairman: DoI Working Party, Kirkby Manufacturing and Engineering Co., 1978; Professional Develt Cttee, Inst. of Dirs, 1993–96; Planning Cttee, Oxford Risk Inst., 1998–99. Trustee, Demos, 1996–. Economic adviser to Mrs Thatcher, Gen. Election campaign, 1979; Adviser to PM's Policy Unit, 10 Downing St, 1979–83. Industrial Consultant. Hon. LittD Sheffield, 1987. *Publications:* Costs in Alternative Locations: The Clothing Industry (with P. K. Newman), 1952; (with A. W. Stonier) A Textbook of Economic Theory, 1953, 4th edn 1973; (with A. W. Stonier) The Essentials of Economics, 1955; The Economics of Man-Made Fibres, 1957; (ed) Stability and Progress in the World Economy, 1958; (ed) The Theory of Capital, 1961; (ed) Inflation, 1962; (ed with Sir Roy Harrod) International Trade Theory in a Developing World, 1965; (ed) Price Formation in Various Economies, 1967; Managerial Economics, 1969; (ed with Bruce L. R. Smith) The Dilemma of Accountability in Modern Government, 1970; Pricing in Business, 1971; (with M. E. Beesley) Britain in the Common Market: a new business opportunity, 1973; (with W. E. F. Oakeshott and A. A. Strain) Devaluation and Pricing Decisions: a case study approach, 1974; (with W. J. M. Mackenzie and A. Barker) Public Policy and Private Interests: the institutions of compromise, 1975; (with Geoffrey Wilkinson) The IRC: an experiment in industrial intervention, 1983; (with Peter Hennessy) How Adolf Hitler reformed Whitehall, 1985; (ed) The Management of Science, 1991; Beyond Universities: a new republic of the intellect, 1991; Transforming the Dinosaurs, 1993; (with Kate Oakley) Spin-offs and Start-ups in UK Universities, 2000; (with Christine Holmes) Oxford Entrepreneurs, 2006; (with Anthea Milnes) From Bright Sparks to Brilliant Businesses, 2010; articles in economic, financial and management journals. *Recreations:* church organs, watching Manchester United. *Address:* Green Templeton College, Oxford OX2 6HG. *T:* (01865) 274775. *Club:* Athenæum. *Died 1 Feb. 2015.*

HAHN, Prof. Frank Horace, FBA 1975; Professor of Economics, University of Cambridge, 1972–92, then Emeritus; Fellow of Churchill College, Cambridge, since 1960; *b* 26 April 1925; *s* of Dr Arnold Hahn and Maria Hahn; *m* 1946, Dorothy Salter; no *c*. *Educ:* Bournemouth Grammar School; London School of Economics (Hon. Fellow, 1989). PhD London, MA Cantab. Univ. of Birmingham, 1948–60, Reader in Mathematical Economics, 1958–60; Univ. Lectr in Econs, Cambridge, 1960–67; Prof. of Economics, LSE, 1967–72; Frank W. Taussig Res. Prof., Harvard, 1974–75. Visiting Professor:

MIT, 1956–57; Univ. of California, Berkeley, 1959–60; Schumpeter Prof., Vienna Univ. of Econs and Business Admin, 1984; Prof. Ordinario, Univ. of Siena, 1992–2000. Fellow, Inst. of Advanced Studies in Behavioural Sciences, Stanford, 1966–67. Mem. Council for Scientific Policy, later Adv. Bd of Res. Councils, 1972–75. Fellow, Econometric Soc., 1962; Vice-Pres., 1967–68; Pres., 1968–69; Pres., Royal Economic Soc., 1986–89. Managing Editor, Review of Economic Studies, 1965–68. Foreign Hon. Mem., Amer. Acad. of Arts and Sciences, 1971; Hon. Mem., Amer. Economic Assoc., 1986; For. Associate, US Nat. Acad. of Scis, 1988; Mem., Academia Europaea, 1989. Hon. DSocSci Birmingham, 1981; Hon. DLitt: East Anglia, 1984; Leicester, 1993; Dr Econ *hc* Strasbourg, 1984; Hon. DSc(Econ) London, 1985; DUniv York, 1991; Hon. PhD Athens, 1993; Dr *hc* Paris X (Nanterre), 1999. Palacky Gold Medal, Czechoslovak Acad. of Scis, 1991. *Publications:* (with K. J. Arrow) General Competitive Analysis, 1971; The Share of Wages in the National Income, 1972; Money and Inflation, 1982; Equilibrium and Macro-Economics, 1984; Money, Growth and Stability, 1985; (ed and contrib.) The Economics of Missing Markets, Information and Games, 1989; (with Robert Solow) A Critical Essay on Modern Macroeconomic Theory, 1995; (ed jtly and contrib.) General Equilibrium: problems and prospects, 2003; articles in learned journals. *Address:* 16 Adams Road, Cambridge CB3 9AD. *T:* (01223) 352560. *Died 29 Jan. 2013.*

HAIG, Ian Maurice, AM 1988; International Affairs Adviser, The Global Foundation, 1996–2005, then Honorary Member; *b* 13 Dec. 1936; *s* of P. K. Haig; *m* 1959, Beverley, *d* of J. A. Dunning, OBE; two *s* one *d*. *Educ:* Pulteney Grammar School, Adelaide; University of Adelaide. Private Sec. to Pres. of Senate, Canberra, 1958–59; Asst Sec., Commonwealth Parly Conf., London, 1960; Public Relations Officer, Shell Co. of Australia, 1962; British Foreign Office School of Middle East Studies, 1963; Asst Trade Comr and Trade Comr, Los Angeles, 1966–68; Trade Comr, Beirut, 1969–73; Ambassador at large, Middle East, 1973; Ambassador to Saudi Arabia, Kuwait and United Arab Emirates, 1974–76; Australian Comr, Hong Kong, 1976–79; Dir of Administration, A.C.I. Ltd, 1979–81; Man. Dir, A.C.I. Fibreglass (Aust.), 1982; Agent Gen. for Victoria in London, 1983–85 and 1988–90; Chm., Immigration Panel, 1987; Dir, Aust. Wheat Bd, 1985–88; Chief Exec., Monash-ANZ Centre for Internat. Briefing, 1990–96. *Publications:* Arab Oil Politics, 1978; Oil and Alternative Sources of Energy, 1978; Australia and the Middle East, 1983. *Recreations:* reading, watching cricket. *Address:* 11/546 Toorak Road, Toorak, Vic 3142, Australia. *Clubs:* MCC; Australian (Melbourne). *Died 10 March 2014.*

HAIG, Dame Mary Alison G.; *see* Glen Haig.

HAIGH, Brian Roger; Lecturer for Hawksmere plc, 1993–2001; *b* 19 Feb. 1931; *s* of Herbert Haigh and Ruth Haigh (*née* Lockwood); *m* 1953, Sheila Carter; one *d* (one *s* decd). *Educ:* Hillhouse Central School, Huddersfield. Min. of Supply, 1949; National Service, RAF, 1949–51. Min. of Supply/Min. of Aviation, 1951–62; NATO Bullpup Production Orgn, 1962–67 (Head of Contracts, Finance and Admin, 1965–67); Min. of Technology, Aviation Supply, Defence (Defence Sales Orgn), 1968–73 (Asst Dir, Sales, 1971–73); Nat. Defence Coll., 1973–74; Ministry of Defence: Asst Dir, Contracts, 1974; Dir of Contracts (Weapons), Dec. 1974; Principal Dir of Navy Contracts, 1978; Under Secretary, 1980; Dir-Gen., Defence Contracts, 1980–86. Dir of Professional Educn and Trng, Lion Worldwide Div., Keiser Enterprises Inc., 1986–91. *Recreations:* family, music, opera, bridge. *Address:* c/o Barclays Bank plc, Kingston Business Centre, 9 Clarence Road, Kingston-upon-Thames KT1 1NY. *Died 3 Aug. 2015.*

HAIGH, Maurice Francis; a Recorder of the Crown Court, 1981–96; a Chairman of Tribunals, 1984–2001; *b* 6 Sept. 1929; *s* of William and Ceridwen Francis Haigh. *Educ:* Repton. Asst cameraman in film production; worked for Leslie Laurence Productions Ltd, London, Manchester Film Studios, and finally for Anglo-Scottish Pictures Ltd at London Film Studios, Shepperton, 1946–49; in commerce, 1950–52. Called to the Bar, Gray's Inn, 1955. *Recreations:* reading, walking. *Died 29 March 2012.*

HALL, Prof. Alan, PhD; FRS 1999; Alfred P. Sloan Professor and Chairman, Cell Biology Program, Sloan-Kettering Institute, since 2006; *b* 19 May 1952. *Educ:* Wadham Coll., Oxford (BA 1974); Harvard Univ. (PhD 1977). Post-doctoral Fellow, Univ. of Edinburgh, 1977–79, Zürich Univ., 1979–80; Senior Scientist: Inst. for Cancer Res., 1980–92; UCL, 1992–93; Prof. of Cell and Molecular Biol., Dept of Biochem. and Molecular Biol., 1993–2006, and Dir, MRC Cell Biol. Unit and Lab. for Molecular Cell Biol., 2001–06, UCL. FMedSci 2004. Gairdner Internat. Award, Gairdner Foundn, 2006. *Publications:* contribs to jls. *Address:* Cell Biology Program, Memorial Sloan-Kettering Cancer Center, 1275 York Avenue, New York, NY 10065, USA. *Died 3 May 2015.*

HALL, Rt Rev. (Albert) Peter; Bishop Suffragan, then Area Bishop, of Woolwich, 1984–96; Hon. Assistant Bishop, Diocese of Birmingham, since 1997; *b* 2 Sept. 1930; *s* of William Conrad Hall and Bertha Gladys Hall; *m* 1957, Valerie Jill Page; one *s* (and one *s* decd). *Educ:* Queen Elizabeth Grammar School, Blackburn; St John's Coll., Cambridge (MA Mod. Langs); Ridley College, Cambridge. Ordained deacon 1955, priest 1956; Curate: St Martin, Birmingham, 1955–60; St Mary Magdalene, Avondale, Zimbabwe, 1960; Rector of Avondale, Zimbabwe, 1963–70; Rector of St Martin-in-the-Bull-Ring, Birmingham, 1970–84. Chair: Unlock (formerly Evangelical Urban Training Project), 1981–2003; Archbishops' Commn on Urban Priority Areas, 1990–96. *Recreation:* mountain walking. *Address:* 27 Jacey Road, Birmingham B16 0LL. *Died 28 Dec. 2013.*

HALL, Sir Basil (Brodribb), KCB 1977 (CB 1974); MC 1945; TD 1952; Member, European Commission of Human Rights, 1985–93; Legal Adviser, Broadcasting Complaints Commission, 1981–93; *b* 2 Jan. 1918; *s* of late Alfred Brodribb Hall and of Elsie Hilda Hall, Woking, Surrey; *m* 1955, Jean Stafford Gowland; two *s* one *d*. *Educ:* Merchant Taylors' Sch. Articled Clerk with Gibson & Weldon, Solicitors, 1935–39; admitted Solicitor, 1942. Served War of 1939–45: Trooper, Inns of Court Regt, 1939; 2nd Lieut, 12th Royal Lancers, 1940; Captain, 27th Lancers, 1941; Major, 27th Lancers, 1942. Legal Asst, Treasury Solicitor's Dept, 1946; Sen. Legal Asst, 1951; Asst Treasury Solicitor, 1958; Principal Asst Solicitor, 1968; Dep. Treasury Solicitor, 1972; HM Procurator Gen. and Treasury Solicitor, 1975–80. Chm., Civil Service Appeal Bd, 1981–84 (Dep. Chm., 1980–81). Mem. Council, Nat. Army Museum, 1981–92. *Recreations:* military history, travel. *Address:* Woodlands, 16 Danes Way, Oxshott, Surrey KT22 0LX. *T:* (01372) 842032. *Clubs:* Athenæum, Cavalry and Guards. *Died 2 May 2011.*

HALL, Sir (Frederick) John (Frank), 3rd Bt *cr* 1923; *b* 14 Aug. 1931; *er s* of Sir Frederick Henry Hall, 2nd Bt, and Olwen Irene (*d* 1993), *yr d* of late Alderman Frank Collis, Stokeville, Stoke-on-Trent, and Deganwy, Llandudno; *S* father, 1949; *m* 1st, 1956, Felicity Anne (marr. diss. 1960), *d* of late Edward Rivers-Fletcher, Norwich, and Mrs L. R. Galloway; 2nd, 1961, Patricia Ann Atkinson (marr. diss. 1967); two *d*; re-married, 1967, 1st wife, Felicity Anne Hall (*d* 2011); two *d*. *Educ:* Bryanston Sch. Personnel Manager, Universal Pattern & Precision Engineering Co. Ltd, 1955–59; Personnel Officer, The Nestlé Co. Ltd, 1959–63; Personnel Man., SC Johnson & Sons Ltd, 1963–65; UK Head Office Trng and Mgt Develt Man., The Nestlé Co. Ltd, 1965–67; Gp Personnel Man., Findus Ltd, 1967–69; Sen. Man., McLintock Mann & Whinney Murray, 1969–76; Dir, Thomson McLintock Associates, 1976–87; founder Chm., KPMG Career Consultancy Services, 1983–93; Partner, KPMG Peat Marwick, 1987–93, retd. Dir, Roffey Park Inst., 1978–90 (Vice Chm., 1983–85; Chm., 1985–87). *Recreations:* music, collecting antique gramophone records, magic (Mem., The Magic Circle). *Heir:* *b* David Christopher Hall [*b* 30 Dec. 1937; *m* 1st, 1962, Irene (marr. diss. 1987), *d* of William Duncan, Aberdeen; one *s* one *d*; 2nd, 1991, Annie Madelaine Renée

Olivier, adopted *d* of late Bottemanne Raould]. *Address:* Carradale, 29 Embercourt Road, Thames Ditton, Surrey KT7 0LH. *T:* (020) 8398 2801. *Died 1 Sept. 2013.*

HALL, Prof. Henry Edgar, FRS 1982; Emeritus Professor of Physics, University of Manchester, since 1995; *b* 1928; *s* of John Ainger Hall; *m* 1962, Patricia Anne Broadbent; two *s* one *d*. *Educ:* Latymer Upper Sch., Hammersmith; Emmanuel Coll., Cambridge. BA 1952; PhD 1956. At Royal Society Mond Laboratory, Cambridge, 1952–58; Senior Student, Royal Commission for the Exhibition of 1851, 1955–57; Research Fellow of Emmanuel Coll., 1955–58; Lecturer in Physics, 1958–61, Prof. of Physics, 1961–95, Univ. of Manchester. Visiting Professor: Univ. of Western Australia, 1964; Univ. of Oregon, 1967–68; Cornell Univ., 1974, 1982–83; Univ. of Tokyo, 1985. Simon Memorial Prize (with W. F. Vinen), 1963; Guthrie Medal and Prize, 2004. *Publications:* Solid State Physics, 1974; papers in scientific journals. *Recreation:* mountain walking. *Address:* The Schuster Laboratory, The University, Manchester M13 9PL. *Died 4 Dec. 2015.*

HALL, Sir John; *see* Hall, Sir F. J. F.

HALL, Prof. Michael Robert Pritchard, FRCP, FRCPE; Professor of Geriatric Medicine, University of Southampton, 1970–87, then Emeritus; Hon. Consultant Physician, Southampton University Hospitals, 1970–87; *b* 13 May 1922; *s* of Augustus Henry Hall, MC and Elizabeth Jane Lord; *m* 1947, Joan Jardine, (Eileen), *d* of Dr John McCartney; two *d*. *Educ:* Shrewsbury Sch.; Worcester Coll., Oxford (MA, BM, BCh). FRCP 1970; FRCPE 1971. Served War, Indian Army, 1941–46 (Temp. Captain). Consultant Physician, Newcastle upon Tyne Gen. Hosp., 1962–70; Hon. Lecturer in Medicine: Univ. of Durham, 1962–63; Univ. of Newcastle upon Tyne, 1963–70. Auckland Savings Bank Vis. Prof., Univ. of Auckland, NZ, 1974; Vis. Lecturer: Dalhousie Univ., NS, 1979; (Tayside Health Bd), Univ. of Dundee, 1981; Examr, Dip. of Geriatric Medicine, RCP, 1985–91. Chairman: British Soc. for Res. on Ageing, 1976–79; Assoc. of Professors of Geriatric Medicine, 1985–86; European Cttee, Sandoz Foundn of Gerontological Research, 1986–90 (Mem., 1990–92); Member: DHSS Cttee for Review of Medicines, 1976–82; Fitness and Health Adv. Gp to Sports Council, 1977–90; Southampton and SW Hants CHC, 1997–2001 (Chm., 1999–2001); Governing Body and Exec. Cttee, Age Concern (England), 1975–77 and 1980–83; Council, Internat. Assoc. of Gerontology, 1981–85; President: Tissue Viability Soc., 1983–84; Bath Res. Inst. for Care of the Elderly, 1987–94; Chm., Age Concern (Hants), 1992–95; Life Vice-Pres., Northumberland Cheshire Home, 1970; Vice-Pres., Research into Ageing (formerly British Foundn for Age Res.), 1998– (Trustee and Gov., 1979–97); Member: NEC, Abbeyfield Soc., 1989–93 (Chm., Extra Care Cttee, 1989–90; Chm., Care and Develt Cttee, 1990–93); Council, RSAS, 1989–96; BMA, 1953–; British Geriatrics Soc., 1963– (President's Medal, 1992); Trustee: Brendoncare Foundn, 1984–2006 (Vice-Chm., 1986–99); McCarthy Foundn, 1987–96. FRSocMed 1991. *Publications:* Medical Care of the Elderly, 1978, 3rd edn 1993; chapters and contribs to various books on aspects of ageing and geriatric medicine; articles and papers in med. jls. *Recreations:* fly-fishing, golf, gardening. *Address:* Peartree Cottage, Emery Down, Lyndhurst, Hants SO43 7FH. *T:* (023) 8028 2541. *Club:* MCC. *Died 23 June 2012.*

HALL, Rt Rev. Peter; *see* Hall, Rt Rev. A. P.

HALL, Peter Dalton, CB 1986; Under Secretary, Solicitor's Office, Board of Inland Revenue, 1979–86; *b* 1 Aug. 1924; *s* of Edward and Kathleen Hall; *m* 1952, Stella Iris Breen (*d* 2007); four *s* two *d*. *Educ:* Rishworth Sch.; St Catharine's Coll., Cambridge (exhibnr; MA, LLB). Served War of 1939–46, Intelligence Corps; seconded to AIF and served with US Forces in New Guinea and Philippines; SEALF, 1946–47 (GOC-in-C Commendation); Major. Called to the Bar, Middle Temple, 1951; Inland Revenue Solicitor's Office, 1952–88. Mem., Bar Council 1967–70; Clerk to City of London Comrs, 1988–99. Chm., N Bucks Dist, and Trustee, Bucks Co. Br., CPRE. Parish Councillor, 1967–2011. Non-exec. Dir, Milton Keynes HA, 1992–93. Freeman, City of London, 1993. *Publications:* contrib. legal works. *Recreations:* grandchildren (19), great grandchildren (2), gardening, music, conservation. *Address:* Apple Tree Cottage, 6 The Green, Woughton-on-the-Green, Bucks MK6 3BE. *T:* and *Fax:* (01908) 679504. *Died 8 Nov. 2013.*

HALL, Sir Peter (Geoffrey), Kt 1998; FBA 1983; Professor of Planning and Regeneration (formerly of Planning), University College London, since 1992; Director, Institute of Community Studies, 2001–04; *b* 19 March 1932; *s* of Arthur Vickers Hall and Bertha Hall (*née* Keefe); *m* 1st, 1962, Carla Maria Wartenberg (marr. diss. 1966); 2nd, 1967, Magdalena Mróz; no *c*. *Educ:* Blackpool Grammar Sch.; St Catharine's Coll., Cambridge Univ. (MA, PhD; Hon. Fellow, 1988). Asst Lectr, 1957, Lectr, 1960, Birkbeck Coll., Univ. of London; Reader in Geography with ref. to Regional Planning, London Sch. of Economics and Political Science, 1966; University of Reading: Prof. of Geography, 1968–89, then Prof. Emeritus; Head, Dept of Geog., 1968–80; Chm., Sch. of Planning Studies, 1971–77 and 1983–86; Dean of Urban and Regional Studies, 1975–78; Prof. of City and Regl Planning, 1980–92, and Dir, Inst. of Urban and Regl Develt, 1989–92, Univ. of Calif, Berkeley, then Prof. Emeritus; Dir, Sch. of Public Policy, UCL, 1995–99. Member: SE Regional Planning Council, 1966–79; Nature Conservancy, 1968–72; Transport and Road Research Laboratory Adv. Cttee on Transport, 1973–78; Environmental Bd, 1975–79; SSRC, 1975–80 (Chm., Planning Cttee); EEC Expert Gp on New Tendencies of Social and Economic Develt, 1975–77; Standing Adv. Cttee on Trunk Road Assessment, 1978–80; DETR Urban Task Force, 1998–99; Exec. Cttee, Fabian Soc., 1964–80 (Chm. 1971–72). President: TCPA, 2003– (Chm., 1995–99); Regional Studies Assoc., 2006– (Mem. Exec. Cttee, 1967–78; Hon. Jl Editor, 1967–78). Special Advr, Sec. of State for Environment, 1991–94. Chm., Blackpool Urban Regeneration Co., 2005–08. Editor, Built Environment, 1977–. Governor, Centre for Environmental Studies, 1975–80. Chm., Tawney Soc., 1983–85 (Vice-Chm., 1982–83). FRGS; Hon. RTPI 1975; Hon. RIBA 2000. Hon. DSS: Birmingham, 1989; London, 2004; Hon. PhD Lund Univ., Sweden, 1992; Hon. LittD: Sheffield, 1995; Newcastle, 1995; London Guildhall, 2002; Hon. DEng Technical Univ. of Nova Scotia, 1996; Hon. DArts Oxford Brookes, 1997; Hon. LLD: Reading, 1999; Manchester, 2001; Hon. DSc: West of England, 2000; Loughborough, 2005; Hon. DTech Greenwich, 2004. Ebenezer Howard Meml Medal, TCPA, 1999; Prix Vautrin Lud, Internat. Fest. of Geography, 2001; Gold Medal, RTPI, 2003; Dep. Prime Minister's Lifetime Achievement Award, 2005; Balzan Prize, Internat. Balzan Foundn, 2005; Sir Patrick Abercrombie Prize, IUA, 2008. *Publications:* The Industries of London, 1962; London 2000, 1963 (reprint, 1969); Labour's New Frontiers, 1964; (ed) Land Values, 1965; The World Cities, 1966, 3rd edn 1984; Containment of Urban England, 1973; Urban and Regional Planning, 1974, 2nd edn 1982; Europe 2000, 1977; Great Planning Disasters, 1980; Growth Centres in the European Urban System, 1980; The Inner City in Context, 1981; Silicon Landscapes, 1985; Can Rail Save the City?, 1985; High Tech America, 1986; Cities of Tomorrow, 1988; London 2001, 1989; The Rise of the Gunbelt, 1991; Technopoles of the World, 1994; Sociable Cities, 1998, 2nd edn 2014; Cities in Civilization, 1998; Urban Future 21, 2000; Working Capital, 2002; To-morrow: a peaceful path to real reform, 2003; The Polycentric Metropolis, 2006; London Voices London Lives, 2007; Good Cities, Better Lives, 2013. *Recreations:* writing, reading, talking. *Address:* Bartlett School, University College London, Wates House, 22 Gordon Street, WC1H 0QB; 12 Queens Road, W5 2SA. *Club:* Athenæum. *Died 30 July 2014.*

HALL, Peter George; (part-time) Chairman, Snamprogetti Ltd, 1988–97; *b* 10 Dec. 1924; *s* of Charles and Rosina Hall; *m* 1949, Margaret Gladys (*née* Adams); two *s* two *d*. *Educ:* Sandown, IoW, Grammar Sch.; Southampton Univ. (BScEng). Anglo-Iranian Oil Co., 1946–51; Esso Petroleum Co. Ltd: various positions at Fawley Refinery, 1951–63; Manager, Milford Haven Refinery, 1963–66; Employee Relations Manager, 1966–70; Vice-Pres., General Sekiyu Seisei, Tokyo, 1971–74; Asst Gen. Man., Refining, Imperial Oil Ltd, Toronto, 1974–76; Refining Man., Exxon Corp., New York, 1976–77; Director, Esso

Petroleum Co. Ltd, London, 1977–78; Vice-Pres., Esso Europe Inc. London, 1979–81; Man. Dir, Esso Petroleum Co., 1982–84; Pres., Esso Norge, 1984–87. *Recreations:* opera, classical music, walking, gardening. *Address:* Oakley, Mill Lane, Burley, Ringwood, Hants BH24 4HP. *Died 11 Nov. 2012.*

HALL, Prof. Stuart McPhail, FBA 2005; Professor of Sociology, The Open University, 1979–98, then Emeritus; Visiting Professor, Goldsmiths College, London University; *b* 3 Feb. 1932; *s* of Herman and Jessie Hall; *m* 1964, Catherine Mary Barrett; one *s* one *d*. *Educ:* Jamaica Coll.; Merton Coll., Oxford (MA; Rhodes Scholar, 1951; Hon. Fellow, 2001). Editor, New Left Review, 1957–61; Lectr, Film and Mass Media Studies, Chelsea Coll., London Univ., 1961–64; Centre for Cultural Studies, Univ. of Birmingham: Res. Fellow, 1964–68; Actg Dir, 1968–72; Dir, 1972–79. Vis. Prof., Tavistock Inst., 2001. Hon. Fellow, Portsmouth Polytechnic, 1988; Centenary Fellow, Thames Polytechnic, 1990. Hon. DLitt: Massachusetts, 1989; City, Kingston, Oxford Brookes, 1993; Sussex, 1994; Leeds, Middlesex, Keele, 1995; East London, London, 1998; W Indies, 1999; Birmingham, Tampere, Teesside, 2000; RCA, 2003; Hon. DCL Durham, 2001. *Publications:* (jtly) The Popular Arts, 1964; (ed jtly) Resistance Through Rituals, 1974; (jtly) Policing The Crisis, 1978; Culture, Media, Language, 1980; (ed jtly) The Politics of Thatcherism, 1983; State and Society in Contemporary Britain, 1984; Politics and Ideology, 1986; The Hard Road to Renewal, 1988; (jtly) Questions of Cultural Identity, 1996; Critical Dialogues in Cultural Studies, 1996; Representations, 1997; *festschrift:* Without Guarantees, 2000. *Address:* 21 Ulysses Road, NW6 1ED. *Died 10 Feb. 2014.*

HALL, William, CBE 1991; DFC 1944; FRICS; Member of the Lands Tribunal for Scotland, 1971–91, and for England and Wales, 1979–91; *b* 25 July 1919; *s* of Archibald and Helen Hall; *m* 1945, Margaret Semple (*née* Gibson) (*d* 2010); one *s* three *d*. *Educ:* Paisley Grammar Sch. FRICS 1948. Served War, RAF (pilot) 1939–45 (despatches, 1945). Sen. Partner, R. & W. Hall, Chartered Surveyors, 1949–79. Chm., Scottish Br., RICS, 1971; Member: Valuation Adv. Council, 1970–80; Erskine Hosp. Exec., 1976–99. Hon. Sheriff, Paisley, 1974–. *Recreation:* golf. *Address:* Windyridge, Brediland Road, Paisley, Renfrewshire PA2 9HF. *T:* (01505) 813614. *Died 25 July 2012.*

HALLETT, Victor George Henry; Deputy Social Security Commissioner and Deputy Child Support Commissioner, 1993–95; *b* 11 Feb. 1921; *s* of Dr Denys Bouhier Imbert Hallett; *m* 1947, Margaret Hamlyn (*d* 2003). *Educ:* Westminster; Queen's Coll., Oxford (exhibitioner; MA). Served War, 1939–45 (wounded 1945, despatches 1946). Called to the Bar, Inner Temple, 1949. Mem., Land Registration Rules Cttee, 1971–76; Conveyancing Counsel of the Court, 1971–76; Nat. Insce, subseq. Social Security, Comr, 1976–93. *Publications:* Key and Elphinstone's Conveyancing Precedents (ed jtly), 15th edn, 1952; Prideaux's Precedents in Conveyancing (ed jtly), 25th edn, 1953; Hallett's Conveyancing Precedents, 1965; (with Nicholas Warren) Settlements, Wills and Capital Transfer Tax, 1979. *Address:* c/o Leigholt Farm, Somerton Road, Street, Somerset BA16 0SU. *T:* (01458) 841281. *Club:* Travellers. *Died 18 Nov. 2014.*

HALLIGAN, Prof. Aidan William Francis, MD; FRCP, FRCOG; Director, Well North, since 2014; Principal, NHS Staff College, since 2007; *b* Dublin, 17 Sept. 1957; *s* of Michael and Maureen Halligan; *m* 1985, Dr Carol Mary Sarah Furlong; three *d*. *Educ:* Templeogue Coll., Dublin; Trinity Coll., Dublin (MB BCh BAO, MA); MD. MRCOG 1991, FRCOG 2004; MRCPI 1996; FFPH (FFPHM 2003); FRCP 2004. SHO, Royal City of Dublin Hosp., St James's and Rotunda Hosps, Dublin, 1986–88; Registrar, Rotunda Hosp., then Mater Misericordiae Hosp., Dublin, 1989–90; Res. Registrar, Rotunda Hosp., Dublin, 1991–93; Lectr, 1993–94, Sen. Lectr, 1994–97, in Obstetrics and Gynaecology, Leicester Univ.; Consultant Obstetrician and Gynaecol., Leicester Royal Infirmary, 1994–97; Prof. of Fetal Maternal Medicine, Leicester Univ. and Univ. Hosps of Leicester NHS Trust, 1997–99; Postgrad. Dir, Training, Obstetrics and Gynaecol., 1995–99, Hd, Obstetric Service, 1998–99, Univ. Hosps of Leicester NHS Trust; Prog. Trng Dir, Obstetrics and Gynaecol., S Trent, 1995–99; Hd, NHS Clinical Governance Support Team, 1999–2002; Dep. CMO, DoH, 2003–05; Dir of Clinical Governance for NHS, 1999–2006; Chief Exec., Elision Health Ltd, 2006–08; Dir, Educn, UCL Hosp., 2007–13; Chief of Safety, Brighton and Sussex Univ. Hosps NHS Trust, 2008–13. Visiting Professor: Dept of Surgical Oncology and Technol., Imperial Coll. London, 2005–10; Postgrad. Med. Sch., Univ. of Surrey, 2007–09. Chm., London Pathway Homeless Health Service, 2009–. *Publications:* articles in Br. Jl of Obstetrics and Gynaecol., BMJ, Lancet, Jl of Hypertension, Obstetrics and Gynecol., Hypertension in Pregnancy, Amer. Jl of Obstetrics and Gynecol., Br. Jl of Clinical Governance, Jl of RSocMed, and other learned jls. *Recreations:* reading, walking. *Address:* Well North, Manchester Academic Science Centre, University of Manchester, Core Technology Facility, Grafton Street, Manchester M13 9NT. *T:* (0161) 275 0180. *E:* aidan.halligan@manchester.ac.uk. *Died 27 April 2015.*

HALNAN, His Honour Patrick John; a Circuit Judge, 1986–97; *b* 7 March 1925; *s* of E. T. and A. B. Halnan; *m* 1955, Judith Mary (*née* Humberstone) (*d* 2003); one *s* three *d*. *Educ:* Perse Sch., Cambridge; Trinity Coll., Cambridge (MA). Army, 1943–47 (incl. RA in Burma); TA, 1951–58 (incl. 23 SAS). Solicitor. Asst Solicitor, Hants CC, 1954–58; Clerk to the Justices, Cambs, 1958–78; Metropolitan Stipendiary Magistrate, 1978–86; a Recorder, 1983–86; SE Circuit. Sec., Justices' Clerks' Soc., 1972–76, Pres., 1978. Chm., Road Traffic Cttee, Magistrates' Assoc., 1981–87. A Vice Pres., Cambs Girl Guides, 2009–. *Publications:* (ed with Prof. R. M. Jackson) Leo Page, Justice of the Peace, 3rd edn 1967; (ed) Wilkinson's Road Traffic Offences, 7th edn 1973 to 14th edn 1989; (with David Latham) Drink/Driving Offences, 1979; Road Traffic, 1981; Drink/Drive: the new law, 1984. *Recreations:* Freemasonry, travelling, bridge, postal history. *Address:* Room 56, Cornwallis Court, Hospital Road, Bury St Edmunds, Suffolk IP33 3NH. *Died 14 Dec. 2014.*

HALSEY, Prof. Albert Henry, FBA 1995; Professor of Social and Administrative Studies, University of Oxford, 1978–90, then Emeritus; Professorial Fellow of Nuffield College, Oxford, 1962–90, then Emeritus; *b* 13 April 1923; *m* 1949, Gertrude Margaret Littler (*d* 2004); three *s* two *d*. *Educ:* Kettering Grammar Sch.; London Sch. of Econs (BSc (Econ); PhD; Hon. Fellow, 1993); MA Oxon. RAF, 1942–47; student LSE, 1947–52; Research Worker, Liverpool Univ., 1952–54; Lectr in Sociology, Birmingham Univ., 1954–62; Dir, Dept of Social and Admin. Studies, Oxford Univ., 1962–78. Fellow, Center for Advanced Study of Behavioral Sciences, Palo Alto, Calif, 1956–57; Vis. Prof. of Sociology, Univ. of Chicago, 1959–60. Adviser to Sec. of State for Educn, 1965–68; Chm. of CERI at OECD, Paris, 1968–70. Reith Lectr, 1977. MAE 1992; Foreign Associate, Amer. Acad. of Educn; Foreign Mem., Amer. Acad. of Arts and Scis, 1988. Hon. Fellow: Goldsmiths' Coll., 1992; Westminster Coll., 1996; Royal Statistical Soc., 1999. Hon. DSocSc Birmingham, 1987; DUniv Open, 1990; Hon. DLitt: Glamorgan, 1994; Leicester, 1995; Warwick, 1995. *Publications:* (jtly) Social Class and Educational Opportunity, 1956; (jtly) Technical Change and Industrial Relations, 1956; (with J. E. Floud) The Sociology of Education, Current Sociology VII, 1958; (jtly) Education, Economy and Society, 1961; Ability and Educational Opportunity, 1962; (with G. N. Ostergaard) Power in Co-operatives, 1965; (with Ivor Crewe) Social Survey of the Civil Service, 1969; (with Martin Trow) The British Academics, 1971; (ed) Trends in British Society since 1900, 1972; (ed) Educational Priority, 1972; Traditions of Social Policy, 1976; Heredity and Environment, 1977; Change in British Society, 1978, 4th edn 1995; (jtly) Origins and Destinations, 1980; (with Norman Dennis) English Ethical Socialism, 1988; Decline of Donnish Dominion, 1992, 2nd edn 1995; No Discouragement, 1996; (jtly) Education, Culture, Economy, Society, 1997; (ed) British Social Trends: the twentieth century, 2000; A History of Sociology in Britain, 2004; (with R. G. Runciman) British Sociology from Within and Without, 2005; Democracy in Crisis?, 2007;

Changing Childhood, 2009; Essays on the Evolution of Oxford and Nuffield College, 2012; numerous articles and reviews. *Address:* 49 Home Close, Wolvercote, Oxford OX2 8PT. *T:* (01865) 558625. *Died 14 Oct. 2014.*

HAMBLEDEN, 4th Viscount *cr* 1891; **William Herbert Smith;** *b* 2 April 1930; *e s* of 3rd Viscount and Patricia, GCVO (*d* 1994), *d* of 15th Earl of Pembroke, MVO; *S* father, 1948; *m* 1st, 1955, Donna Maria Carmela Attolico di Adelfia (marr. diss. 1988), *d* of late Count Bernardo Attolico and of Contessa Eleonora Attolico di Adelfia, Via Porta Latina, Rome; five *s*; 2nd, 1988, Mrs Lesley Watson. *Educ:* Eton. *Heir:* *s* Hon. William Henry Bernard Smith [*b* 18 Nov. 1955; *m* 1983, Sarah Suzanne, *d* of Joseph F. Anlauf and Mrs Suzanne K. Anlauf; two *d*]. *Address:* The Estate Office, Hambleden, Henley-on-Thames, Oxon RG9 6SG. *T:* (01491) 571252. *Died 2 Aug. 2012.*

HAMILTON; *see* Dalrymple Hamilton.

HAMILTON, Alexander Macdonald, CBE 1979; Senior Partner, 1977–90, Consultant, 1990–94, McGrigor Donald, Solicitors, Glasgow; *b* 11 May 1925; *s* of John Archibald Hamilton and Thomasina Macdonald or Hamilton; *m* 1953, Catherine Gray (*d* 2005); two *s* one *d*. *Educ:* Hamilton Acad. (Dux, 1943); Glasgow Univ. (MA 1948, LLB 1951). Solicitor. Served War, RNVR, 1943–46. Dir, Royal Bank of Scotland, 1978–96 (Vice Chm., 1990–96). Law Soc. of Scotland: Mem. Council, 1970–82; Vice-Pres., 1975–76; Pres., 1977–78. Pres., Glasgow Juridical Soc., 1955–56. Vice-Pres. and Chm., 1978–85, Pres., 2002–08, Greater Glasgow Scout Council; Pres., Clyde Regl Scout Council, 2008–; Cttee Chm., Scottish Council, Scout Assoc., 1986–92. Sec., Cambuslang Old Parish Church, 1991– (Session Clerk, 1969–91); Vice-Chm., Cambuslang Community Council, 1978–94. *Recreations:* golf, sailing. *Address:* 30 Wellshot Drive, Cambuslang, Glasgow G72 8BT. *T:* (0141) 641 1445. *Club:* Pollok (Glasgow). *Died 25 May 2012.*

HAMILTON, David Stewart, MBE 2006; Director of Legal Services for Metropolitan Police Service (formerly Solicitor to Commissioner of Police of the Metropolis), 1995–2006; *b* 1 April 1946; *s* of late Ralph James Hamilton and of Jean Isabel Hamilton; *m* 1975, Maureen Underwood; two *d*. *Educ:* Highgate Sch.; Coll. of Law, Lancaster Gate. Articled Clerk, 1965–70, Asst Solicitor, 1970–71, Partner, 1971–78, D. Miles Griffiths Piercy & Co.; Asst Solicitor, 1978–79, Partner, 1979–80, Gaitskell Dodgson & Bleasdale; joined Solicitor's Dept, Metropolitan Police, 1980: Sen. Legal Asst, 1981–85; Asst Solicitor, 1985–95. Mem., Law Soc., 1970–; Life Member: Assoc. of Police Lawyers, 2006; ACPO, 2006. *Recreations:* walking the dog, volunteer with N Norfolk Railway. *Address:* c/o Directorate of Legal Services, Metropolitan Police, New Scotland Yard, Broadway, Victoria, SW1H 0BG. *T:* (020) 7230 7353. *Died 30 June 2013.*

HAMILTON, Sir James (Arnot), KCB 1978 (CB 1972); MBE 1952; FRSE; FREng; Permanent Under-Secretary of State, Department of Education and Science, 1976–83; *b* 2 May 1923; *m* 1947, Christine Mary McKean (marr. diss.); three *s*; partner, Marcia Cunningham. *Educ:* University of Edinburgh (BSc). Marine Aircraft Experimental Estab., 1943: Head of Flight Research, 1948; Royal Aircraft Estab., 1952; Head of Projects Div., 1964; Dir, Anglo-French Combat Aircraft, Min. of Aviation, 1965; Dir-Gen. Concorde, Min. of Technology, 1966–70; Deputy Secretary: (Aerospace), DTI, 1971–73; Cabinet Office, 1973–76. Dir, Hawker Siddeley Gp, 1983–91; Mem. Adv. Bd, Brown & Root (UK) Ltd, 1983–97; Chm., Brown & Root (UK) Ltd (later Brown & Root Ltd), 1998–2000; Director: Smiths Industries plc, 1984–93; Devonport Royal Dockyard, 1987–97. Trustee, British Museum (Natural Hist.), 1984–88. President: Assoc. for Science Educn, 1984–85; NFER in England and Wales, 1984–98. Vice-Pres., Council, Reading Univ., 1983–95; Vice-Chm. Council, UCL, 1985–98. FREng (FEng 1981); FRAeS 1983. Hon. FIMechE 1980. DUniv Heriot-Watt, 1983; Hon. LLD CNAA, 1983. *Publications:* papers in Reports and Memoranda series of Aeronautical Research Council, Jl RAeS, and technical press. *Address:* 32 Alison Way, Winchester, Hants SO22 5BT. *T:* (01962) 842001. *Club:* Athenæum. *Died 24 May 2012.*

HAMILTON, Martha, (Mrs R. R. Steedman), OBE 1988; Headmistress, St Leonards School, St Andrews, 1970–88; *b* Edinburgh, 12 May 1929; *d* of Rev. John Edmund Hamilton and Hon. Lilias Maclay; *m* 1977, Robert Russell Steedman, OBE. *Educ:* Roedean Sch.; St Andrews Univ. (MA Hons Hist.); Cambridge Univ. (DipEd); Edinburgh Univ. (Dip. Adult Educn). Principal, Paljor Namgyal Girls' High School, Gangtok, Sikkim, 1959–66. Mem., Task Force to examine under-achievement in schs in Scotland, 1996. Member: Assoc. for Protection of Rural Scotland Award Panel, 1989–92; Fife Health Bd, 1991–98 (Vice Chm., 1994–98); Court of Dirs, Edinburgh Acad., 1992–2000. Convenor, Assoc. for Applied Arts, 1992–98. Gov., New Sch., Butterstone, 1997–2003. Awarded Pema Dorji (for services to education), Sikkim, 1966. *Recreations:* travel, bird-watching. *Address:* Muir of Blebo, Blebo Craigs, by Cupar, Fife KY15 5UG. *Died 3 March 2015.*

HAMILTON, Richard, CH 2000; painter; *b* 24 Feb. 1922; *s* of Peter and Constance Hamilton; *m* 1st, 1947, Terry O'Reilly (*d* 1962); one *s* one *d*; 2nd, 1991, Rita Donagh. *Educ:* elementary; Royal Academy Schs; Slade Sch. of Art. Jig and Tool draughtsman, 1940–45. Lectr, Fine Art Dept, King's Coll., Univ. of Durham (later Univ. of Newcastle upon Tyne), 1953–66. *Devised exhibitions:* Growth and Form, 1951; Man, Machine and Motion, 1955. *Collaborated on:* This is Tomorrow, 1956; 'an Exhibit', 1957; exhibn with D. Roth, ICA New Gall., 1977. *One man art exhibitions:* Gimpel Fils, 1951; Hanover Gall., 1955, 1964; Robert Fraser Gall., 1966, 1967, 1969; Whitworth Gall., 1972; Nigel Greenwood Inc., 1972; Serpentine Gall., 1975; Stedelijk Mus., Amsterdam, 1976; Waddington Gall., 1980, 1982, 1984; Anthony d'Offay Gall., 1980, 1991, 1995; Charles Cowles Gall., NY, 1980; Galérie Maeght, Paris, 1981; Tate Gall., 1983–84; Thorden and Wetterling, Stockholm, 1984; DAAD Gall., Berlin, 1985; Fruitmarket Gall., Edinburgh, 1988; Moderna Museet, Stockholm, 1989; Venice Biennale, 1993; San Francisco Mus. of Modern Art, 1996; Imaging James Joyce's Ulysses, British Mus., 2002; A Host of Angels, Venice Biennale, 2007; Modern Moral Matters, Serpentine Gall., 2010; Picasso's Meninas, Museo Nacional del Prado, 2010; other exhibitions abroad include: Kassel, 1967, 1997 (Arnold Bode Prize); New York, 1967; Milan, 1967, 1968, 1969, 1971, 1972, 1974, 1990; Hamburg, 1969; Berlin, 1970, 1971, 1973; Bremen, 1998; *retrospective exhibitions:* Tate Gallery, 1970 (also shown in Eindhoven and Bern), 1992; Guggenheim Museum, New York, 1973 (also shown in Cincinnati, Munich, Tübingen, Berlin); Musée Grenoble, 1977; Kunsthalle Bielefeld, 1978; Kunstmus., Winterthur, 1990 (also shown in Hannover and Valencia); Tate Gall., 1992; Irish Mus. of Modern Art, Dublin, 1992; MACBA, Barcelona, 2003. William and Noma Copley award, 1960; John Moores prize, 1969; Talens Prize International, 1970; Golden Lion of Venice, 1993; Gold Medal, Ljubljana Print Trianalle, 1999; Beckman Prize, Frankfurt, 2007. *Publications:* Collected Words 1953–1982, 1982. *Address:* c/o Tate Gallery, Millbank, SW1P 4RG. *Died 13 Sept. 2011.*

HAMLEY, Donald Alfred, CBE 1985; HM Diplomatic Service, retired; *b* 19 Aug. 1931; *s* of Alfred Hamley and Amy (*née* Brimacombe); *m* 1958, Daphne Griffith; two *d*. *Educ:* Devonport High Sch., Plymouth. Joined HM Foreign (subseq. Diplomatic) Service, 1949; Nat. Service, 1950–52; returned to FO; served in: Kuwait, 1955–57; Libya, 1958–61; FO, 1961–63; Jedda, 1963–65 and 1969–72; Rome, 1965–69; seconded to DTI, 1972–73; Commercial Counsellor, Caracas, 1973–77; seconded to Dept of Trade, 1977–80; Consul-Gen., Jerusalem, 1980–84; retired, 1984. *Address:* 1 Forge Close, Hayes, Bromley BR2 7LP. *T:* (020) 8462 6696. *Club:* Royal Automobile. *Died 4 March 2013.*

HAMLISCH, Marvin; composer, conductor, pianist, entertainer; *b* 2 June 1944; *s* of Max and Lilly Hamlisch; *m* 1989, Terre Blair. *Educ:* Professional Children's Sch.; Queen's Coll., NY; Juilliard Sch., NY. Début as a pianist, Minnesota Orch., 1975; solo concert tours; conductor of various orchestras throughout USA; Musical Dir and Conductor, Barbra Streisand tour, 1994 (Emmy Awards for Outstanding Individual Achievement in Music and Lyrics and in Music Direction, 1995); Principal Pops Conductor: Pittsburgh SO, 1995–; Baltimore SO, 1996–2000; National SO, Washington, 2000–; Milwaukee SO; San Diego Symphony. Mem., ASCAP. *Compositions* include: *film scores:* The Swimmer, 1968; Bananas, 1971; The Way We Were (Acad. and Grammy Awards for Best Original Score, and for Best Song of the Year for title song), 1974; Starting Over, 1979; Ordinary People, 1980; Sophie's Choice, 1982; The Informant!, 2009; *film themes:* Three Men and a Baby, 1987; January Man, 1988; The Experts, 1989; *songs:* Sunshine Lollipops and Rainbows; Good Morning America; Nobody Does it Better; One Song (for Barcelona Olympics), 1992; *musicals:* A Chorus Line, 1975 (Pulitzer Prize); They're Playing Our Song, 1979; The Goodbye Girl, 1993; Sweet Smell of Success, 2000; *symphony in one movement,* Anatomy of Peace, 1991. Acad. Award for best adaptation, for The Sting, 1974; Grammy Awards: Best New Artist, 1974; Best Pop Instrumental, for The Entertainer, 1974. *Publications:* The Way I Was (autobiog.), 1992. *Recreation:* loves to travel. *Address:* c/o Seton Ijams, Columbia Artists Management LLC, 1790 Broadway, New York, NY 10019, USA. *Died 6 Aug. 2012.*

HAMLYN, Prof. David Walter; Professor of Philosophy and Head of Philosophy Department, Birkbeck College, University of London, 1964–88, then Professor Emeritus (Head of Classics Department, 1981–86); Vice-Master, Birkbeck College, 1983–88, Fellow, 1988; *b* 1 Oct. 1924; *s* of late Hugh Parker Hamlyn and Gertrude Isabel Hamlyn; *m* 1949, Eileen Carlyle Litt; one *s* one *d*. *Educ:* Plymouth Coll.; Exeter Coll., Oxford. BA (Oxon) 1948, MA 1949 (1st cl. Lit. Hum., 1st cl. Philosophy and Psychology, 1950). War Service, RAC and IAC, Hodson's Horse (Lieutenant), 1943–46. Research Fellow, Corpus Christi Coll., Oxford, 1950–53; Lecturer: Jesus Coll., Oxford, 1953–54; Birkbeck Coll., London, 1954–63, Reader, 1963–64. Pres., Aristotelian Soc., 1977–78. Member: Council, Royal Inst. of Philosophy, 1968– (Vice-Chm., 1991–95; Mem. Exec., 1971–97); Nat. Cttee for Philosophy, 1986–92 (Hon. Vice-Pres., 1992–2003). Mem., London Univ. Senate, 1981–87 (Mem. several cttees; Chm., Academic Council Standing Sub-cttee in Theology, Arts and Music, 1984–87); Governor: Birkbeck Coll., 1965–69; City Lit., 1982–86 (Vice-Chm., 1985–86); Central London Adult Educn Inst., 1987–90; Chm. Governors, Heythrop Coll., 1971–78, Mem., 1984–95, Fellow, 1978. Mem., Wissenschaftliche Leitung der Schopenhauerges., 1992–. Editor of Mind, 1972–84; Consulting Editor, Jl of Medical Ethics, 1981–90. *Publications:* The Psychology of Perception, 1957 (repr. with additional material, 1969); Sensation and Perception, 1961; Aristotle's *De Anima*, Books II and III, 1968; The Theory of Knowledge, 1970 (USA), 1971 (GB); Experience and the Growth of Understanding, 1978, repr. 2010 (trans. Spanish, 1981; trans. Korean, 1990); Schopenhauer, 1980; Perception, Learning and the Self, 1983; Metaphysics, 1984 (trans. Korean, 2000); History of Western Philosophy, 1987 (trans. Dutch, 1988; trans. Portuguese, 1990; trans. Swedish, 1995); In and Out of the Black Box, 1990; Being a Philosopher, 1992; Understanding Perception, 1996; contrib. to several other books and to many philosophical, psychological and classical jls. *Recreations:* playing and listening to music, reading, gardening. *Address:* 38 Smithy Knoll Road, Calver, Hope Valley, Derbyshire S32 3XW. *T:* (01433) 631326. *Died 15 July 2012.*

HAMMARSKJÖLD, Knut (Olof Hjalmar Åkesson); Director, 1948, and Chairman, 1987–94, then Emeritus Chairman, Sydsvenska Dagbladet AB, Newspaper Group, Malmö; Minister Plenipotentiary, since 1966; *b* Geneva, 16 Jan. 1922; Swedish; *m* Inga-Lill; four *s* from former marriages. *Educ:* Stockholm Univ. Entered Swedish Foreign Service, 1946; served in Paris, Vienna, Moscow, Bucharest, Kabul, Sofia, 1947–55; 1st Sec., Foreign Office, 1955–57; Head of Foreign Relations Dept, Royal Bd of Civil Aviation, Stockholm, 1957–59; Dep. Head of Swedish Delegn to OEEC, Paris, 1959–60; Dep. Sec.-Gen., EFTA, Geneva, 1960–66; International Air Transport Association (IATA): Dir Gen., 1966–84; Chm. Exec. Cttee, 1981–84; Internat. Affairs Counsel, 1985–86; Mem., Inst. of Transport, London; Dir, Inst. of Air Transport, Paris, 1974–; Dir-Gen., Atwater Inst. Inf./Communications, Montreal, 1985–98; Mem., Internat. Aviation Management Training Inst., Montreal; Director: Prisma Transport Consultants Ltd, Geneva/Brussels, 1987–; Blenheim Aviation Services Ltd, 1992–. Chm., I-L Consult Baltic, Suders/Hamra, Gotland, 1994–. Chm., Ind. Commn for Reform of UNESCO, 1989–93; Sen. Special Advr to Dir Gen. of UNESCO, 1993–; Hon. Ambassador, UNESCO, 1991. Hon. Fellow, Canadian Aeronautics and Space Inst., Ottawa; Hon. Academician, Mexican Acad. of Internat. Law; Hon. FCIT (London). Edward Warner Award, ICAO, 1983. Comdr (1st cl.), Order of North Star (Sweden); NOR (Sweden); Légion d'Honneur (France); Grand Cross Order of Civil Merit (Spain); Grand Officer, Order of Al-Istiqlal (Jordan); Commander: Order of Lion (Finland); Oranje Nassau (Netherlands); Order of Falcon (1st cl.) (Iceland); Order of Black Star (Benin). *Publications:* articles on political, economic and aviation topics. *Recreations:* music, painting, ski-ing. *Died 3 Jan. 2012.*

HAMMERTON, His Honour Rolf Eric; a Circuit Judge, 1972–94; *b* 18 June 1926; *s* of Eric Maurice Hammerton and Dora Alice Hammerton (*née* Zander); *m* 1953, Thelma Celestine Hammerton (*née* Appleyard); one *s* three *d*. *Educ:* Brighton, Hove and Sussex Grammar Sch.; Peterhouse, Cambridge (MA, LLB). Served Army, 1944–47; commnd Royal Sussex Regt, 1945; attached 2nd Bn Nigeria Regt, 1946, 5th Bn Nigeria Regt, 1946–47. Philip Teichman Prize, 1952; called to the Bar, Inner Temple, 1952; Sussex County Courts: Designated Judge, Children's Cases, 1990–94; Principal Judge, Civil Matters, 1992–94. Contributing Editor, Butterworth's County Court Precedents and Pleadings, 1985–2000. Liveryman, Cooks' Co., 1979– (Master, 2002–03). *Recreation:* cooking. *Died 18 Jan. 2014.*

HAMMICK, Sir Stephen (George), 5th Bt *cr* 1834; OBE 2004; DL; *b* 27 Dec. 1926; *s* of Sir George Hammick, 4th Bt; *S* father, 1964; *m* 1953, Gillian Elizabeth Inchbald; one *s* one *d* (and one *s* decd). *Educ:* Stowe. Royal Navy as Rating (hostilities only), 1944–48; RAC Coll., Cirencester, 1949–50; MFH Cattistock Hunt, 1961 and 1962. Mem. (C), Dorset CC, 1958–96 (Vice-Chm., 1985–88; Chm., 1988–93). High Sheriff, Dorset, 1981–82, DL Dorset, 1989. Farmer, with 450 acres. *Recreations:* hunting, fishing, sailing. *Heir: s* Jeremy Charles Hammick [*b* 3 Feb. 1956; *m* 1997, Melanie Louise Stock]. *Address:* Badgers, Wraxall, Dorchester DT2 0HN. *T:* (01935) 83343. *Died 15 Feb. 2014.*

HAMMOND-STROUD, Derek, OBE 1987; concert and opera baritone; Professor of Singing, Royal Academy of Music, 1974–90; *b* 10 Jan. 1926; *s* of Herbert William Stroud and Ethel Louise Elliott. *Educ:* Salvatorian Coll., Harrow, Middx; Trinity Coll. of Music, London; in Vienna and Munich with Elena Gerhardt and Gerhard Hüsch. Glyndebourne Festival Opera, 1959; Sadler's Wells Opera (later ENO), 1961; Royal Opera, Covent Garden, 1971; Houston Grand Opera, USA, 1975; Netherlands Opera, 1976; Metropolitan Opera, NY, 1977; Teatro Colón, Buenos Aires, 1981; Munich State Opera, 1983. Concerts and Lieder recitals at Edinburgh, Aldeburgh, Munich and Vienna Festivals, and in Spain, Iceland and Denmark. BBC Promenade Concerts, 1968–. Pres., Univ. of London Opera Gp, 1971. Freeman, City of London, 1952; Hon. RAM 1976; Hon. FTCL, 1982. Sir Charles Santley Meml Gift, Worshipful Co. of Musicians, 1988. Recordings include: The Ring (Goodall); Der Rosenkavalier (de Waart). *Recreations:* chess, study of philosophy. *Address:* 18 Sutton Road, Muswell Hill, N10 1HE. *T:* (020) 8883 2120. *Died 14 May 2012.*

HAMNETT, Thomas Orlando; Chairman, Greater Manchester Council, 1975–76, Vice-Chairman, 1976; *b* 28 Sept. 1930; *s* of John and Elizabeth Hamnett; *m* 1954, Kathleen Ridgway; one *s* five *d*. *Educ:* Stockport Jun. Techn. Sch. Sheetmetal craftsman, 1946. Member, Manchester City Council, 1963 until re-organisation (Vice-Chm., Health Cttee, Chm. sub cttee on Staff on Cleansing Cttee, Mem. Policy and Finance Cttees), and 1978–92 (Member: Direct works, Markets, and Personnel Cttees; Transportation, Education, and Recreation and Arts Cttees, Greater Manchester Council; Chm., Environmental Services Cttee, City Council, Manchester, 1982). *Recreations:* football, cricket, table tennis. *Address:* 22

Harris Avenue, Denton, Manchester M34 2PX. *T:* (0161) 320 1069. *Club:* Gorton Trades and Labour (Chm.). *Died 16 Feb. 2013.*

HAMPSON, Prof. Norman, FBA 1980; Professor of History, University of York, 1974–89; *b* 8 April 1922; *s* of Frank Hampson and Elizabeth Jane Fazackerley; *m* 1948, Jacqueline Gardin (*d* 2007); two *d*. *Educ:* Manchester Grammar Sch.; University Coll., Oxford (MA); Dr de l'Univ. Paris. Service in Royal Navy, 1941–45. Manchester Univ., 1948–67: Lectr and Sen. Lectr; Prof. of Modern History, Univ. of Newcastle, 1967–74. Hon. DLitt Edinburgh, 1989. *Publications:* La Marine de l'an II, 1959; A Social History of the French Revolution, 1963; The Enlightenment, 1968; The First European Revolution, 1969; The Life and Opinions of Maximilien Robespierre, 1974; A Concise History of the French Revolution, 1975; Danton, 1978; Will and Circumstance: Montesquieu, Rousseau and the French Revolution, 1983; Prelude to Terror, 1988; Saint-Just, 1991; The Perfidy of Albion, 1998; Not Really What You'd Call a War, 2001. *Address:* 305 Hull Road, York YO10 3LU. *T:* (01904) 412661. *Died 8 July 2011.*

HAMPTON, Bryan; Head of Exports to the Americas, Department of Trade and Industry, 1992–95; *b* 4 Dec. 1938; *s* of William Douglas Hampton and Elizabeth Cardwell; *m* 1964, Marilyn Joseph; five *d*. *Educ:* Harrow County Grammar Sch. for Boys. Board of Trade: Exec. Officer, 1957; Asst Private Sec. to Parly Sec., 1961; Private Sec. to Minister of State (Lords), 1963; Asst Principal, 1965; Second Sec., UK Delegn to EFTA/GATT, Geneva, 1966; Principal, DTI, 1969; Asst Sec., Dept of Energy, 1974; Counsellor (Energy), Washington, 1981–86; Head, Br. 1, Atomic Energy Div., 1986–89, Dir, Personnel, 1989–92, Dept of Energy. Gov., Chenies Sch., 1996–2000. *Recreations:* music, golf. *Address:* Byfields, 15 Greenbury Close, Chorleywood, Herts WD3 5QT. *T:* (01923) 282311. *Club:* Northwood Golf. *Died 29 March 2015.*

HAMPTON, Surgeon Rear-Adm. Trevor Richard Walker, CB 1988; FRCPE; Surgeon Rear-Admiral (Operational Medical Services), 1987–89; *b* 6 June 1930; *s* of Violet and Percy Hampton; *m* 1st, 1952, Rosemary (*née* Day); three *d*; 2nd, 1976, Jennifer (*née* Bootle) (*d* 2002); 3rd, 2004, Kate Wilson. *Educ:* King Edward VII Grammar School, King's Lynn; Edinburgh University. MB ChB 1954; MRCPE 1964. Resident House Officer, Edinburgh Royal Infirmary, 1954–55; joined RN as Surgeon Lieut, 1955; served in HM Ships Ganges, Harrier and Victorious, 1955–62; Clinical Asst, Dept of Medicine, Edinburgh Univ., 1964; RN Hosp., Gibraltar, 1965–68; Consultant Physician, RN Hospitals, Plymouth, 1969–74, Haslar, 1975–79; MO i/c, RN Hosp., Gibraltar, 1980–82, RN Hosp., Plymouth, 1982–84; Surgeon Rear-Adm., Support Medical Services, 1984–87. QHP 1983–89. OStJ 1983. *Publications:* contribs to Jl of RN Med. Service. *Recreations:* reading, writing, resting. *Died 7 Oct. 2012.*

HAN Suyin, (Dr Elizabeth Comber); doctor and author; *b* 12 Sept. 1917; *née* Elizabeth Kuanghu Chow; *d* of Y. T. Chow (Zhou) (Chinese) and M. Denis (Belgian); *m* 1st, 1938, General P. H. Tang (*d* 1947); one adopted *d*; 2nd, 1952, L. F. Comber (marr. diss. 1968); 3rd, 1971, Vincent Ruthnaswamy (*d* 2003). *Educ:* Yenching Univ., Peking, China; Brussels Univ., Brussels, Belgium; London Univ., London, England. Graduated MB BS, London (Hons) in 1948, a practising doctor until 1964. *Publications: as Han Suyin:* Destination Chungking, 1942; A Many Splendoured Thing, 1952 (filmed 1955); And the Rain My Drink, 1956; The Mountain Is Young, 1958; Cast but One Shadow and Winter Love, 1962; The Four Faces, 1963; China in the Year 2001, 1967; The Morning Deluge, 1972; Wind in the Tower, 1976; Lhasa, the Open City, 1977; Les Cent Fleurs: La Peinture Chinoise, 1978; La Chine aux Mille Visages, 1980; Chine: Terre Eau et Hommes, 1981; Till Morning Comes, 1982; The Enchantress, 1985; A Share of Loving, 1987; Han Suyin's China, 1988; Fleur de Soleil, 1988; Tigers and Butterflies, 1990; Les Yeux de Demain, 1992; Eldest Son: Zhou Enlai and the making of modern China (1898–1976), 1994; *autobiography:* China: autobiography, biography, history (6 vols): The Crippled Tree, 1965; A Mortal Flower, 1966; Birdless Summer, 1968; My House Has Two Doors, 1980; Phoenix Harvest, 1980; Wind in my Sleeve, 1992. *Recreations:* economics studies, lecturing, founding exchanges in science. *Address:* avenue de Montoie 37, 1007 Lausanne, Switzerland. *Died 2 Nov. 2012.*

HANCOCK, Sir David (John Stowell), KCB 1985; civil servant and investment banker; *b* 27 March 1934; *s* of late Alfred George Hancock and Florence Hancock (*née* Barrow); *m* 1966, Sheila Gillian Finlay; one *s* one *d*. *Educ:* Whitgift Sch.; Balliol Coll., Oxford. 2nd Lieut, RTR, 1953–54. Asst Principal, Bd of Trade, 1957; transf. to HM Treasury, 1959; Principal, 1962; Harkness Fellow, 1965–66; Private Sec. to Chancellor of the Exchequer, 1968–70; Asst Sec., 1970; Financial and Economic Counsellor, Office of UK Permanent Rep. to European Communities, 1972–74; Under Sec., 1975–80, Dep. Sec., 1980–82, HM Treasury; Dep. Sec., Cabinet Office, 1982–83; Perm. Sec., DES, 1983–89; Exec. Dir, Hambros Bank Ltd, 1989–98; Dir, Hambros PLC, 1989–98; Sen. Advr, S. G. Hambros, 1998–99. Dir, European Investment Bank, 1980–82. Chairman: Dyvell (Hldgs) Ltd, 1990–94; MRC Pension Trust Ltd, 1991–2004; Combined Landfill Projects Ltd, 1993–2001; Director: AXA Equity & Law plc, 1992–95; Royal National Theatre Enterprises Ltd, 2003–05. Sen. Advr, Newcourt, subseq. Tyco, Capital, 1999–2002. Chm., NFHA Inquiry into Governance of Housing Assocs, 1994–95. Chairman: British Selection Cttee of Harkness Fellowships, 1988–92 (Mem., 1984–92); Foundn for Young Musicians, 1990–99; Member: E London Partnership, 1991–98; Royal Nat. Theatre Bd, 1996–2002; South Bank Bd, 2000–02; Court, Luton Univ., 1998–2001; British American Drama Acad. Bd, 2003–08; Governor: City Lit. Inst., 2000–01; Whitgift Sch., 2000–08. Trustee: St Catharine's Foundn, Cumberland Lodge, 1989–2008; Société Gén. UK Defined Benefit Pension Scheme, 2003–07; Chm., St Katharine and Shadwell Trust, 1990–99. Pres., Old Whitgiftian Assoc., 2000–01. Freeman, City of London, 1989. FRSA 1986; CCMI (CBIM 1987). Hon. LLD Poly. of E London, 1990. *Recreations:* reading, theatre, opera. *Clubs:* Athenæum, Civil Service. *Died 5 Sept. 2013.*

HANCOCK, Geoffrey Francis, CMG 1977; HM Diplomatic Service, retired; Foreign and Commonwealth Office, 1979–82; *b* 20 June 1926; *s* of Lt-Col Sir Cyril Hancock, KCIE, OBE, MC; *m* 1960, Amelia Juana Aragon; one *s* one *d*. *Educ:* Wellington; Trinity Coll., Oxford. MA 1951. Third Sec., Mexico City, 1953; Second Sec., Montevideo, 1956; Foreign Office, 1958; Madrid, 1958; FO, 1960; MECAS, 1962; First Sec., Baghdad, 1964–67 and 1968–69; FCO, 1969–73; Counsellor, Beirut, 1973–78. Founder, Middle East Consultants, 1983. *Recreations:* music, sailing. *Address:* c/o Lloyds TSB, 8/10 Waterloo Place, SW1Y 4BE. *Clubs:* Athenæum, Royal Air Force. *Died 2 July 2011.*

HANCOCK, Ronald John; business consultant; *b* 11 Feb. 1934; *s* of George and Elsie Hancock; *m* 1970, Valerie Hancock; two *d*. *Educ:* Dudley Grammar Sch., Dudley. FCMA. Served HM Forces, 1952–61. Schweppes Ltd, 1962–63; Mullard Ltd, 1963–66; Valor Group, 1966–68; BL Ltd, 1968–85. Chairman: Leyland Vehicles, 1981–85; Leyland Vehicles Exports Ltd, 1981–85; Bus Manufacturers Limited, 1981–85; Bus Manufacturers (Holdings) Ltd, 1981–85; Eastern Coachworks Ltd, 1981–85; Bristol Commercial Vehicles Ltd, 1981–85; Self-Changing Gears Ltd, 1981–85; Bedfordshire Chamber of Training Ltd, 1990–92; Director: BL Staff Trustees Ltd, 1981–85; Leyland Nigeria Ltd, 1981–85; BL International Ltd, 1981–85; Land Rover-Leyland International Holdings Ltd (formerly BLIH), 1982–85; Land Rover-Leyland Ltd, 1983–85; Chloride Gp plc, 1985–87; Man. Dir, AWD Ltd, 1987–90. Director: Insituform Ltd, 1987–94; Travelines, 1991–94; Permaline, 1991–94. *Recreations:* travel, reading. *Address:* 61 Bath Hill Court, Bath Road, Bournemouth BH1 2HS. *Died 22 Feb. 2015.*

HANDLEY, Sir David John D.; *see* Davenport-Handley.

HANDLEY, Prof. Eric Walter, CBE 1983; FBA 1969; Professor of Ancient Literature, Royal Academy, since 1990; Fellow, Trinity College, Cambridge, since 1984; *b* 12 Nov. 1926; *s* of late Alfred W. Handley and A. Doris Cox; *m* 1952, Carol Margaret Taylor. *Educ:* King Edward's

Sch., Birmingham; Trinity Coll., Cambridge. Stewart of Rannoch Schol. and Browne Medal, 1945. University College London: Asst Lectr in Latin and Greek, 1946; Lectr, 1949; Reader, 1961; Prof. of Latin and Greek, 1967–68; Prof. and Head of Dept of Greek, 1968–84; Hon. Fellow, 1989; Dir, 1967–84, Sen. Res. Fellow, 1995–, Inst. of Classical Studies, Univ. of London; Regius Prof. of Greek, Cambridge Univ., 1984–94. Vis. Lectr on the Classics, Harvard, 1966; Vis. Mem., Inst. for Advanced Study, Princeton, 1971; Visiting Professor: Stanford Univ., 1977; Melbourne Univ., 1978; Vis. Senior Fellow, Council of the Humanities, Princeton, 1981. Sec. Council Univ. Classical Depts, 1969–70, Chm., 1975–78. President: Classical Assoc., 1984–85; Hellenic Soc., 1993–96; Foreign Sec., British Academy, 1979–88. Union Académique Internationale: Mem., Commn des Affaires Internes, 1984–91; Mem. du Bureau, 1991–2000; Vice-Pres., 1995–97, 1999–2000; Mem., Comité Scientifique, Fondation Hardt, Geneva, 1978–99 (Conseil, 1995–99). Member: Academia Europaea, 1988; Norwegian Acad. of Science and Letters, 1996. Foreign Mem., Societas Scientiarum Fennica, 1984; Hon. Mem., Hungarian Acad. of Scis, 1993; Corresp. Mem., Acad. of Athens, 1995. Chm., Gilbert Murray Trust, 1988–2006 (Hon. Pres., 2006–). Hon. RA 1990. Dr *hc* Athens, 1995. (Jtly) Cromer Greek Prize, 1958. *Publications:* (with John Rea) The Telephus of Euripides, 1957; The Dyskolos of Menander, 1965; (contrib.) Cambridge History of Classical Literature, 1985; (with André Hurst) Relire Ménandre, 1990; (jtly) The Oxyrhynchus Papyri LIX, 1992; (with J.-M. Bremer) Aristophane, 1993; (with J. R. Green) Images of the Greek Theatre, 1995; (jtly) The Oxyrhynchus Papyri LXIV, 1997; papers in class. jls, etc. *Address:* Trinity College, Cambridge CB2 1TQ. *Club:* Oxford and Cambridge. *Died 17 Jan. 2013.*

HANDLIN, Prof. Oscar; Carl M. Loeb University Professor, Harvard University, since 1984; Director, Harvard University Library, 1979–84; *b* 29 Sept. 1915; *m* 1st, 1937, Mary Flug; one *s* two *d*; 2nd, 1977, Lilian Bombach. *Educ:* Brooklyn Coll. (AB); Harvard (MA, PhD). Instructor, Brooklyn Coll., 1938–39; Harvard Univ.: Instructor, 1939–44; Asst Prof., 1944–48; Associate Prof., 1948–54; Prof. of History, 1954–65; Charles Warren Prof. of Amer. Hist., and Dir, Charles Warren Center for Studies in Amer. Hist., 1965–72; Carl H. Pforzheimer Univ. Prof., 1972–84; Harmsworth Prof. of Amer. History, Oxford Univ., 1972–73. Dir, Center for Study of History of Liberty in America, 1958–67; Chm., US Bd of Foreign Scholarships, 1965–66 (Vice-Chm. 1962–65). Hon. Fellow, Brandeis Univ., 1965. Hon. LLD: Colby Coll., 1962; Harvard, 1993; Hon. LHD: Hebrew Union Coll., 1967; Northern Michigan, 1969; Seton Hall Univ., 1972; Hon. HumD Oakland, 1968; Hon. LittD Brooklyn Coll., 1972; Hon. DHL: Boston Coll., 1975; Lowell, 1980; Cincinnati, 1981; Massachusetts, 1982; Clark Univ., Mass, 1989. *Publications:* Boston's Immigrants 1790–1865, 1941; (with M. F. Handlin) Commonwealth, 1947; Danger in Discord, 1948; (ed) This Was America, 1949; Uprooted, 1951, 2nd edn 1972; Adventure in Freedom, 1954; American People in the Twentieth Century, 1954 (rev. edn 1963); (ed jtly) Harvard Guide to American History, 1954; Chance or Destiny, 1955; (ed) Readings in American History, 1957; Race and Nationality in American Life, 1957; Al Smith and his America, 1958; (ed) Immigration as a Factor in American History, 1959; John Dewey's Challenge to Education, 1959; (ed) G. M. Capers, Stephen A. Douglas, Defender of the Union, 1959; Newcomers, 1960; (ed jtly) G. Mittleberger, Journey to Pennsylvania, 1960; (ed) American Principles and Issues, 1961; (with M. F. Handlin) The Dimensions of Liberty, 1961; The Americans, 1963; (with J. E. Burchard) The Historian and the City, 1963; Firebell in the Night, 1964; A Continuing Task, 1964; (ed) Children of the Uprooted, 1966; The History of the United States, vol. 1, 1967, vol. 2, 1968; America: a History, 1968; (with M. F. Handlin) The Popular Sourçes of Political Authority, 1967; The American College and American Culture, 1970; Facing Life: Youth and the Family in American History, 1971; A Pictorial History of Immigration, 1972; (with M. F. Handlin) The Wealth of the American People, 1975; Truth in History, 1979, 2nd edn 1997; The Distortion of America, 1981, 2nd edn 1997; with L. Handlin: Abraham Lincoln and the Union, 1980; A Restless People, 1982; Liberty and Power, 1986; Liberty in Expansion, 1989; Liberty in Peril, 1992; Liberty and Equality, 1994; From the Outer World, 1997. *Address:* 18 Agassiz Street, Cambridge, MA 02140, USA. *Club:* Faculty (Cambridge, Mass). *Died 20 Sept. 2011.*

HANDY, Prof. Nicholas Charles, ScD; FRS 1990; Professor of Quantum Chemistry, Cambridge University, 1991–2004, then Professor Emeritus; Fellow, St Catharine's College, Cambridge, 1965–2004, then Fellow Emeritus; *b* 17 June 1941; *s* of late Kenneth George Edwards Handy and of Ada Mary Handy (*née* Rumming); *m* 1967, Elizabeth Carole Gates; two *s*. *Educ:* Clayesmore Sch., Dorset; St Catharine's College, Cambridge (MA, PhD); ScD Cantab 1996. Cambridge University: Salters' Fellow, 1967–68; Demonstrator, 1972–77; Lectr, 1977–89; Reader in Quantum Chemistry, 1989–91; Steward, 1971–88, Pres., 1994–97, St Catharine's Coll. Harkness Fellow, Johns Hopkins Univ., 1968–69; Vis. Prof., Berkeley, Bologna, Sydney, Georgia. Lennard-Jones Lectr, 1983, Boys-Rahman Lectr, 2004, RSC. Mem., Internat. Acad. of Quantum Molecular Science, 1988–. Dr *hc* Univ. de Marne-la-Vallée, France, 2000. Prize in Theoretical Chem., RSC, 1987; Schrödinger Medal, World Assoc. of Theoretically Oriented Chemists, 1997; Leverhulme Medal, Royal Soc., 2002. *Publications:* papers in learned jls of chem. phys. *Recreations:* gardening, bridge, philately, travel. *Address:* Department of Chemistry, Lensfield Road, Cambridge CB2 1EW. *T:* (01223) 336373. *Died 2 Oct. 2012.*

HANSON, Derrick George; financial consultant; writer, director of companies; Chairman: Moneyguide Ltd, 1978–2009; Albany Investment Trust plc, 2000–04 (Director, 1980–2004); barrister; *b* 9 Feb. 1927; *s* of late John Henry Hanson and of Frances Elsie Hanson; *m* 1st, 1951, Daphne Elizabeth (*née* Marks) (*d* 1971); one *s* two *d*; 2nd, 1974, Hazel Mary (*née* Buckley) (*d* 1984); 3rd, 1986, Patricia (*née* Skillicorn). *Educ:* Waterloo Grammar Sch.; London Univ. (LLB (Hons)); Liverpool Univ. (LLM); Lancaster Univ. (MPhil). Called to the Bar, Lincoln's Inn, 1952. Joined Martins Bank Ltd, 1943; Chief Trustee Manager, Martins Bank Ltd, 1963; Dir and Gen. Manager, Martins Bank Trust Co. Ltd, 1968; Dir and Gen. Manager, Barclays Bank Trust Co. Ltd, 1969–76; Chairman: Barclays Unicorn Ltd, 1972–76; Barclays Life Assce Co. Ltd, 1972–76; City of London & European Property Co. Ltd, 1980–86; Key Fund Managers Ltd, 1984–87; Birmingham Midshires Bldg Soc., 1988–90 (Dir, 1982–90); British Leather Co. Ltd, 1993–94 (Dir, 1983–94); A. C. Morrell Employees' Trust, 1983–95; Director: Barclaytrust Property Management Ltd, 1971–76; Barclays Bank plc, Manchester Bd, 1976–77; Toye & Co. plc, 1981–92; James Beattie PLC, 1984–97; Sen. Adviser (UK), Manufacturers Hanover Trust Co., 1977–79; Adviser, Phillips Gp, Fine Art Auctioneers, 1977–82. Assessor, Cameron Tribunal, 1962; Dir, Oxford Univ. Business Summer Sch., 1971. Chm., Southport and Formby DHA, 1986–89; Member: NW Industrialists' Council, 1977–83; South Sefton Health Authority, 1979–82; Mersey RHA, 1982–86. Pres., Assoc. of Banking Teachers, 1979–88. Mem. Council, Liverpool Univ., 1980–84; Chm., Christian Arts Trust, 1980–86, 1996–2004. Mem., NW Regl Cttee, NT, 1990–96. Hon. FCIB 1987. Hon. Fellow, City Univ., 1977–86. *Publications:* Within These Walls: a century of Methodism in Formby, 1974; Service Banking, 1979; Moneyguide: The Handbook of Personal Finance, 1981; Dictionary of Banking and Finance, 1985; God and the Profits, 1998; Favourite Hymns: their stories and their meaning, vols I–XII, 2003–09. *Recreations:* gardening, writing. *Address:* Fell Dale, Deepdale, Patterdale, Penrith, Cumbria CA11 0NR. *Club:* Royal Automobile. *Died 12 March 2012.*

HANSON, James Donald; Chairman, Georgica plc, 2000–09; *b* 4 Jan. 1935; *s* of late Mary and Leslie Hanson; *m* 1st, 1959, Patricia Margaret Talent (marr. diss. 1977); two *s*; 2nd, 1978, Anne Barbara Asquith. *Educ:* Heath Grammar School, Halifax. ACA 1956, FCA 1966. Joined Arthur Andersen & Co., Chartered Accountants, 1958; established north west practice, 1966, Managing Partner, North West, 1968–82; Sen. Partner, UK, 1982–89; Man.

Partner, Strategic Affairs and Communications, Andersen Worldwide, 1989–97. Chm., Northern Leisure plc, 1999–2000. Member: Internat. Operating Cttee, 1982–97; Internat. Board of Partners, 1985–97; Manchester Soc. of Chartered Accountants, 1967–81 (Pres., 1979); Council, CBI, 1982–97. Mem., Council and Court, Manchester Univ., 1982–; Chm., Manchester Univ. Superannuation Scheme, 1996–. *Recreations:* skiing, tennis. *Died 29 Oct. 2014.*

HANSON, Neil; Under Secretary, and Controller, Newcastle upon Tyne Central Office, Department of Health and Social Security, 1981–83; *b* 21 March 1923; *s* of late Reginald William Hanson and Lillian Hanson (*née* Benson); *m* 1st, 1950, Eileen Ashworth (*d* 1976); two *s*; 2nd, 1977, Margaret Brown-Smelt. *Educ:* City of Leeds Sch. Served War, 1942–46, N Africa, Sicily, Italy. Jun. Clerk, Leeds Social Welfare Cttee, 1939; Clerical Officer, 1948–50, Exec. Officer, 1950–56, Nat. Assistance Bd; Manager, Suez and Hungarian Refugee Hostels, 1956–59; Higher Exec. Officer, 1959–62, Sen. Exec. Officer, 1963–66, Nat. Assistance Bd; Principal, Min. of Social Security, 1967–73; Sen. Principal, 1973–76, Asst Sec., 1976–80, Asst Under Sec., 1980–83, DHSS. *Recreations:* bowls, bridge, music, walking. *Address:* 7 Woodville Court, Leeds LS8 1JA. *T:* (0113) 266 7870. *Died 16 Feb. 2015.*

HARBOTTLE, (George) Laurence; Consultant, Harbottle & Lewis, Solicitors (Senior Partner, 1955–95); *b* 11 April 1924; *s* of George Harbottle, MC, Croix de Guerre and Winifred Ellen Benson Harbottle. *Educ:* The Leys Sch., Cambridge; Emmanuel Coll., Cambridge (MA). Solicitor 1952. Served War: commnd RA, 1942; Burma and India; Temp. Captain; Adjt 9th Fd Regt, 1945–47. Theatre Companies: Chairman: Theatre Centre, 1959–88; Prospect, 1966–77; Royal Exchange (69), 1968–83; Cambridge, 1969–92; Director: The Watermill, 1970–75; The Bush (Alternative), 1975–77. Arts Council: Mem., 1976–77–78; Mem., Drama Panel, 1974–78; Chairman: Housing the Arts, 1977–78; Trng Cttee, 1977–78; Chm. of Govs, Central Sch. of Speech and Drama, 1982–99 (Vice Chm., 1977–82); Chm., ICA, 1986–90 (Dep. Chm., 1977–86). Hon. Solicitor: Soc. for Theatre Res. Pres., Theatrical Management Assoc., 1979–85 (Hon. Vice-Pres., 1992–); Vice-President: Music Users Council, 1985–91; Theatres Adv. Council, 1986–88; Theatres Nat. Cttee, 1986–91. Member: Justice Cttee on Privacy, 1970; Theatres Trust, 1980–99 (Chm., 1992–99); Equity Trust Fund, 2006– (Trustee, 1989–94). Gov., City Literary Inst., 1990–94; Trustee: Olivier Foundn, 1990–2009; Peggy Ramsay Foundn, 1992–. Hon. Fellow, Birkbeck Coll., Univ. of London, 2006. Award for theatrical achievement, TMA, 1996; award for services to drama trng, Conf. of Drama Schs, 2004. *Recreations:* works of art, gardening. *Address:* c/o Harbottle & Lewis, Hanover House, 14 Hanover Square, W1S 1HP. *Died 1 May 2015.*

HARDING, Derek William; Executive Secretary, Royal Statistical Society, 1986–92; *b* 16 Dec. 1930; *o s* of late William Arthur Harding; *m* 1954, Daphne Sheila, *yr d* of late Reginald Ernest Cooke; one *s* one *d*. *Educ:* Glendale Grammar Sch., London; Univ. of Bristol (BSc). FInstP, CPhys, CEng. Develt Engr, Pye Ltd, 1954–56; Sen. Physics Master, Thornbury Grammar Sch., Bristol, 1956–60; Sen. Lectr in Physical Science, St Paul's Coll., Cheltenham, 1960–64; Asst Organiser, Nuffield Foundn Science Teaching Project, 1964–67; joined staff of Instn Metallurgists, 1967, Registrar-Sec., 1969–76; Sec.-Gen., British Computer Soc., 1976–86. Pres., Rotary Club of Enfield, 2000–01. *Recreations:* theatre, music. *Address:* 29 The Mansions, Compton Street, Eastbourne, E Sussex BN21 4AP. *T:* (01323) 411942. *Died 3 July 2012.*

HARDING, Air Vice-Marshal Peter John, CB 1993; CVO 1998; CBE 1985; AFC 1974; FRAeS; Defence Services Secretary to the Queen, Director General of Reserve Forces and Cadets, and Assistant Chief of Defence Staff (Personnel), 1994–98; *b* 1 June 1940; *s* of John Fitz Harding and Marjorie Clare; *m* 1966, Morwenna Jacquiline St John Grey; two *s*. *Educ:* Solihull School. Joined RAF, 1960; Pilot, 249 Sqn, Cyprus, 1962–65; RAF Coll., 1965–70; Cyprus, 1971–72; Waddington, 1972–74; RNC, 1974; RAF Germany, 1974–76; OC Pilot Buccaneers Sqns, 1977–80; Directing Staff, RAF Staff Coll., 1981; Station Comdr, Honington, 1982–84; RCDS 1985; Dir Nuclear Systems, MoD, 1986–88; Dep. C-in-C, RAF Germany, 1989–91; Dep. COS (Ops), HQ AAFCE, 1991–94. ADC to the Queen, 1982–84. Dep. Chm. Govs, Taunton Sch., 2001–08 (Gov., 2000–08). Legion of Merit (USA), 1998. *Recreations:* cricket, golf, gardening, family, philately, hobby farming, classic cars. *Clubs:* Royal Air Force, Innominate, Pilgrims. *Died 27 Dec. 2013.*

HARDING, Sir Roy (Pollard), Kt 1985; CBE 1978; *b* 3 Jan. 1924; *s* of W. F. N. Harding, BEM and P. E. Harding; *m* 1948, Audrey Beryl Larkin, JP; two *s* one *d*. *Educ:* Liskeard Grammar Sch.; King's Coll., Univ. of London (BSc, AKC, DPA). CMath, FIMA; FZS. Ballistics research, schools and college teaching, to 1950; Educn Admin, Wilts, Bucks, Herts, Leics, to 1960; Dep. Chief Educn Officer, 1960–66, Chief Educn Officer, 1966–84, Bucks. Adviser: County Councils Assoc., 1972–74; Assoc. of County Councils, 1973–84 (incl. Finance, 1978–81, Policy, 1981–84); Council of Local Educn Authorities, 1975–84. Member: Printing and Publishing Ind. Trng Bd, 1970–72; BBC Further Educn Adv. Council, 1970–75; Burnham Cttee, 1972–77; Sec. of State's Vis. Cttee, Cranfield Inst. of Technology, 1976–81; DES/Local Authority Expenditure Steering Gp, Educn, 1976–84; Councils and Educnl Press (Longmans) Editorial Adv. Panel, 1977–86; Teaching of Mathematics in Schools (Cockcroft) Cttee, 1978–82; Educn Management Inf. Exchange, 1981–89; Board, Nat. Adv. Body for Higher Educn, 1982–84; A Level (Higginson) Cttee, 1987–88; Assoc. of Educn Cttees Trust, 1989–; CBI Educn Foundn, 1990–94; Educn Cttee, Royal Soc., 1991–96 (Vice-Chm., 1995–96); various univ. cttees, incl. Open Univ. Council, 1985–96; Chairman: County Educn Officers' Soc., 1978–79 (Sec., 1973–76); Educn Policy Interchange Cttee, 1979–89; Open Univ. INSET Sector Programme Bd, 1983–87; Governing Body, Staff Coll. (formerly Further Educn Staff Coll.), 1986–95; EMIS Ltd, 1988–91; FEFCE Tariff Adv. Cttee, 1993–98; Vice-Chm., Secondary Exams Council, 1983–86. President: Soc. of Educn Officers, 1977–78 (Mem. Exec., 1974–79; Chm. Internat. Cttee, 1980–83; Gen. Sec., 1984–89); British Educnl Equipment Assoc., 1980–83; Educn Sect., BAAS, 1986–87; Nat. Inst. Adult Continuing Educn, 1988–94; IMA, 1990, 1991 (Council, 1983–88, 1990–97). Centenary Fellow, Thames Polytechnic, 1990. DUniv Open, 1985; Hon. LLD Leicester, 1995. Wappenteller, Rheinland/Pfalz, Germany, 1978. Gold Cross of Merit, Polish Govt in Exile, 1984. *Recreations:* travel, music. *Address:* 27 King Edward Avenue, Aylesbury, Bucks HP21 7JE. *T:* (01296) 423006. *Died 31 Oct. 2011.*

HARDINGE, 7th Viscount *cr* 1846, of Lahore and of King's Newton, Derbyshire; **Andrew Hartland Hardinge;** Bt 1801; *b* 7 Jan. 1960; *s* of 5th Viscount Hardinge and of Zoë Anne, *d* of Hon. Hartland de Montarville Molson, OBE, Montreal; *S* brother, 2004; *m* 1990, Sophia Mary (*née* Bagnell); two *s* one *d*. *Educ:* The Gow Sch.; Trinity Coll. Sch. Gallery owner. *Recreations:* shooting, fishing. *Heir: s* Hon. Thomas Henry de Montarville Hardinge, *b* 19 June 1993. *Address:* 20 Niton Street, SW6 6NJ. *T:* (020) 7385 8678. *Club:* White's. *Died 11 Feb. 2014.*

HARDY, His Honour Robert James; a Circuit Judge, 1979–94; *b* 12 July 1924; *s* of James Frederick and Ann Hardy; *m* 1951, Maureen Scott; one *s* one *d*. *Educ:* Mostyn House Sch.; Wrekin Coll.; University Coll., London (LLB). Served, 1942–46, Royal Navy, as Pilot, Fleet Air Arm. Called to the Bar, 1950; a Recorder of the Crown Court, 1972–79. *Recreation:* reading. *Address:* 12 Bollin Mews, Prestbury, Cheshire SK10 4DP. *T:* (01625) 820026; Betlem, Mallorca. *Died 9 Nov. 2015.*

HARE, Prof. Lisa Anne; *see* Jardine, L. A.

HARE DUKE, Rt Rev. Michael Geoffrey; Bishop of St Andrews, Dunkeld and Dunblane, 1969–94; *b* Calcutta, 28 Nov. 1925; *s* of late A. R. A. Hare Duke, Civil Engineer; *m* 1949, Grace Lydia Frances McKean Dodd (*d* 2012); one *s* three *d*. *Educ:* Bradfield Coll.; Trinity Coll., Oxford. BA 1949, MA 1951. Sub-Lt, RNVR, 1944–46. Deacon 1952, priest 1953; Curate, St John's Wood Church, 1952–56; Vicar, St Mark's, Bury, 1956–62; Pastoral Dir, Clin. Theol. Assoc., Nottingham, 1962–64; Vicar, St Paul's, Daybrook, and Pastoral Consultant to Clin. Theol. Assoc., 1964–69; OCF, E Midland Dist HQ, 1968–69. Chairman: Scottish Pastoral Assoc., 1970–74; Scottish Assoc. for Mental Health, 1978–85; Age Concern Scotland, 1994–2000; Nat. Forum on Older Volunteering, 2001–04. Mem. Editorial Bd, Contact Magazine, 1962–79. Hon. DD St Andrews, 1994. *Publications:* (jtly) The Caring Church, 1963; (jtly) First Aid in Counselling, 1968; Understanding the Adolescent, 1969; The Break of Glory, 1970; Freud, 1972; Good News, 1976; Stories, Signs and Sacraments in the Emerging Church, 1982; (ed) Praying for Peace, 1991; Hearing the Stranger, 1994; One Foot in Heaven, 2001; contributor to: Expository Times, Blackfriars, New Christian, Church Quarterly Review, Church Times, Contact. *Address:* 2 Balhousie Avenue, Perth PH1 5HN. *T:* and *Fax:* (01738) 622642. *E:* bishmick@btinternet.com. *Died 15 Dec. 2014.*

HAREWOOD, 7th Earl of, *cr* 1812; **George Henry Hubert Lascelles,** KBE 1986; Hon. AM 2010; Baron Harewood, 1796; Viscount Lascelles, 1812; President, British Board of Film Classification, 1985–97; *b* 7 Feb. 1923; *er s* of 6th Earl of Harewood, KG, GCVO, DSO, and HRH Princess Mary (Princess Royal; who *d* 28 March 1965); *S* father, 1947; *m* 1st, 1949, Maria Donata (marr. diss. 1967; she *m* 1973, Rt Hon. (John) Jeremy Thorpe), *d* of late Erwin Stein; three *s*; 2nd, 1967, Patricia Elizabeth, *d* of Charles Tuckwell, Australia; one *s* and one step *s*. *Educ:* Eton; King's Coll., Cambridge (MA; Hon. Fellow, 1984). Served War of 1939–45, Capt. Grenadier Guards (wounded and prisoner, 1944, released May 1945); ADC to Earl of Athlone, 1945–46, Canada. Editor of magazine "Opera" 1950–53; Royal Opera House, Covent Garden: a Dir, 1951–53; on staff, 1953–60; a Dir, 1969–72; Chm. Bd, ENO (formerly Sadler's Wells Opera), 1986–95 (Man. Dir, 1972–85); Artistic Director: Edinburgh Internat. Festival, 1961–65; Leeds Festival, 1958–74; Adelaide Festival 1988; Artistic Adviser: New Philharmonia Orch., London, 1966–76; Buxton Fest., 1993–98; Man. Dir, English Nat. Opera North, 1978–81. Governor of BBC, 1985–87. Chm., Music Advisory Cttee of British Council, 1956–66; Chancellor of the Univ. of York, 1963–67; Member: Arts Council, 1966–72; Gen. Adv. Council of BBC, 1969–77. President: English Football Assoc., 1963–72; Leeds United Football Club, 1962–. Hon. RAM 1983; Hon. LLD: Leeds, 1959; Aberdeen, 1966; Hon. DMus Hull, 1962; DUniv York, 1982. Janáček Medal, 1978. *Publications:* (ed) Kobbé's Complete Opera Book, 1953, 4th edn 1997; The Tongs and the Bones (autobiog.), 1981; Kobbé's Illustrated Opera Book, 1989; Pocket Kobbé, 1994. *Heir: s* Viscount Lascelles, *b* 21 Oct. 1950. *Address:* Harewood House, Leeds LS17 9LG. *Died 11 July 2011.*

HARGREAVES, Prof. John Desmond; Professor of History, University of Aberdeen, 1962–85; *b* Colne, Lancs, 25 Jan. 1924; *s* of Arthur Swire Hargreaves and Margaret Hilda (*née* Duckworth); *m* 1950, Sheila Elizabeth (*née* Wilks); one *s* two *d*. *Educ:* Skipton Grammar Sch.; Bootham; Manchester Univ. War service, 1943–46. Asst Principal, War Office, 1948; Lectr in History: Manchester Univ., 1948–52; Fourah Bay Coll., Sierra Leone, 1952–54; Aberdeen Univ., 1954–62. Vis. Prof., Union Coll. Schenectady, New York, 1960–61; Univ. of Ibadan, 1970–71. Pres., African Studies Assoc. (UK), 1972–73. Hon. DLitt Sierra Leone, 1984. *Publications:* Life of Sir Samuel Lewis, 1958; Prelude to the Partition of West Africa, 1963; West Africa: the Former French States, 1967; France and West Africa, 1969; West Africa Partitioned: Vol. I, The Loaded Pause, 1974, Vol. II, The Elephants and the Grass, 1985; The End of Colonial Rule in West Africa, 1979; Aberdeenshire to Africa, 1981; Decolonization in Africa, 1988, 2nd edn 1996; (ed) Aberdeen University 1945–81, 1989; Academe and Empire, 1994; Adrian Adams in Kounghani, 2005. *Recreations:* theatre, community arts. *Address:* Balcluain, Raemoir Road, Banchory, Kincardine AB31 5UJ. *T:* (01330) 825588. *Died 14 Feb. 2015.*

HARGREAVES, (Joseph) Kenneth, MBE 2007; Secretary, Association of Conservative Clubs, 1995–99; *b* 1 March 1939; *s* of James and Mary Hargreaves. *Educ:* St Mary's Coll., Blackburn; Manchester Coll. of Commerce. ACIS. Standard Cost/Wages Clerk, NCB, 1957–61; Audit Asst, Treasurer's Dept, Lancs CC, 1961–63; Office Manager, Shopfitters (Lancashire) Ltd, Oswaldtwistle, 1963–83. MP (C) Hyndburn, 1983–92; contested (C) Hyndburn, 1992. Nat. Chm., Right to Life, 2000–; Pres., Accrington and Dist Blind Soc., 1999–. ACIS, 1962; FFA, 1989. Fellow, Inst. of Financial Accountants. *Recreations:* Gilbert and Sullivan, classical music, travel. *Address:* 9 Hippings Vale, Oswaldtwistle, Accrington, Lancs BB5 3LH. *T:* (01254) 230401. *Died 23 June 2012.*

HARKER, (Ronald) David, CBE 2011 (OBE 2003); Chief Executive, Citizens Advice (formerly National Association of Citizens Advice Bureaux), 1997–2010; *b* 2 March 1951; *s* of Stanley Harker and Mary Harker (*née* Macaulay); *m* 1980, Diane Summers; one *s*. *Educ:* Queen Elizabeth Grammar Sch., Darlington; Univ. of E Anglia (BA Social Studies 1972); Univ. of Essex (MA Sociol. 1973); Univ. of South Bank (Dip Finance 1982); London Business Sch. (MBA 1986). Dep. Gen. Sec., Voluntary Action Lewisham, 1974–78; Res. and Press Asst, COHSE, 1978–79; Policy Analyst, London Borough of Camden, 1979–80; Dir, Lady Margaret Hall Settlement, 1980–84; Director: CAG Consultants, 1985–89; Nat. Deafblind and Rubella Assoc. (Sense), 1989–97. Mem., Lewisham LBC, 1982–86. Non-executive Director: PIRC Ltd, 1985–2002; Gas and Electricity Markets Authy, 2009–; Financial Conduct Authy, 2013–. Member: NHS Modernisation Bd, 2000–04; Council, Advertising Standards Authority, 2007–14; Financial Services Consumer Panel, 2011–13; Chm., Pensions Adv. Service, 2014–. Trustee, Alcohol Recovery Project, 1994–97. Associate, Civil Exchange, 2011–. CCMI 2009. *Recreations:* cycling, ski-ing, walking. *E:* rdharker@btinternet.com. *Died 2 March 2015.*

HARLAND, Air Marshal Sir Reginald (Edward Wynyard), KBE 1974; CB 1972; AE 1945; engineering and management consultant; *b* 30 May 1920; *s* of Charles Cecil Harland and Ida Maud (*née* Bellhouse); *m* 1942, Doreen Rosalind (*d* 2011), *d* of late W. H. C. Romanis; two *s* one *d* (and one *s* one *d* decd). *Educ:* Summer Fields, Oxford; Stowe; Trinity Coll., Cambridge (MA). Served War of 1939–45: RAE Farnborough, 1941–42; N Africa, Italy and S France, 1942–45. Techn. trng, techn. plans and manning depts, Air Min., 1946–49; pilot trng, 1949–50; Chief Engrg Instructor, RAF Coll., Cranwell, 1950–52; Guided Weapon trng, RMCS Shrivenham, 1952–53; Thunderbird Project Officer: RAE Farnborough, 1953–55; Min. of Supply, 1955–56; psa 1957; Ballistic Missile Liaison Officer, (BJSM) Los Angeles, 1958–60; CO, Central Servicing Develt Estab., Swanton Morley, 1960–62; STSO, HQ No 3 (Bomber) Gp, Mildenhall, 1962–64; AO i/c Engrg, HQ Far East Air Force, Singapore, 1964–66; Harrier Project Dir, HQ Min. of Technology, 1967–68; idc 1969; AOC No 24 Group, RAF, 1970–72; AO Engineering, Air Support Command, 1972; AOC-in-C, RAF Support Command, 1973–77. Technical Dir, W. S. Atkins & Partners, 1977–82; Consultant to Short Brothers Ltd, 1983–88. Mem. Council, IMgt (formerly BIM), 1973–78, 1980–86, 1987–90, 1992–98; President: Soc. of Environmental Engrs, 1974–77 (Fellow, 1977); IIExE, 1997–99 (Fellow, 1997); Vice-Chm., CEI, 1983–84. Chairman: Suffolk Preservation Soc., 1988–91; Suffolk Professional Engrs, 1991–97; Suffolk Br., Cambridge Soc., 1998–2005; Gov., ESU, 1993–2000; President: East Reg., ESU, 1992–2007; Old Stoic Soc., 1999–2000; Bury St Edmunds Soc., 2004– (Chm., 1993–94). Contested Bury St Edmunds, (SDP) 1983, (SDP/Alliance) 1987. Sen. Academic Fellow, Leicester Poly. (then De Montfort Univ.), 1989. CEng 1966; FIMechE 1967; FIET (FIEE 1964); FRAeS 1967; CCMI (FBIM 1974; Verulam Medal, 1991); Hon. FAPM 2003 (FAPM 1988). FRSA 1993. *Publications:* (ed) Singapore and Thailand Burma Railway, by Lt Col Alfred Knights, DSO, MC, MM, 2013; occasional articles in engrg and management jls. *Recreations:* better management, better government. *E:* rewharland@aol.com. *Club:* Royal Air Force. *Died 30 July 2013.*

HARPER, Malcolm Charles, CMG 2000; international consultant, since 2004; Joint President, United Nations Association, since 2004 (Director, 1982–2004); *b* 21 June 1939; *s* of Leonard Robert Harper and Enid Harper (*née* Redman); *m* 1966, Ann Patricia Broad; one *s* two *d*. *Educ:* Marlborough Coll.; Trinity Hall, Cambridge (MA Hons Hist. and Theol.). Lay Personal Asst to Anglican Archbp of

Cape Town, 1961–62; with OXFAM, 1963–81: served in E Africa, 1968–71; Emergencies Officer, 1972–75; Communications Dir, 1975–81; in Cambodia, 1979–80. Mem. Exec. Cttee, World Fedn of UNAs, Geneva, 1981–2004 (Chm., 1995–2000). Mem. Bd, Internat. Broadcasting Trust, 1978–2012. Gov., Burford Sch., Oxon, 1987– (Chm., 1993–2008); Mem. Bd of Govs, Internat. Students House, 1994–2009 (Fellow 2009–). Trustee: Afghanaid, 2005–12; Commonwealth Soc. for the Deaf, 2005–12 (Chm., 2011–12; Mem., Projects Cttee, 2005–); Action on Armed Violence (formerly Landmine Action Trust), 2007–12. Sec., Friends of N Uganda, 2004–. Mem., RIIA, 1999–2010. Albert Einstein Gold Medal, UNESCO, 1995; Soka Gakkai Internat. Medal (Japan), 1999. *Publications:* contrib. chapters to several UN-orientated books. *Recreations:* cricket, long-distance walking, jogging, photography, theatre. *Address:* The Cottages, Church Lane, Charlbury, Oxon OX7 3PX. *T:* (01608) 810464, 07778 450515. *Clubs:* Royal Commonwealth Society, MCC; Charlbury Cricket (Oxon), Nonnunquam Cricket. *Died 9 May 2013.*

HARRINGTON, Dr Albert Blair, CB 1979; Head of Civil Service Department Medical Advisory Service, 1976–79; *b* 26 April 1914; *s* of late Albert Timothy Harrington and Lily Harrington; *m* 1939, Valerie White (*d* 1996); one *d*. *Educ:* Brisbane Grammar Sch., Qld; Aberdeen Univ. MB, ChB 1938, MD 1944. House Phys., Woodend Hosp., Aberdeen, 1938–39; service in RAMC (Field Amb., Blood Transfusion Phys., Neurologist), 1940–45; MO (Head Injuries) and Dep. Supt, Stoke Mandeville Hosp., 1946–48; Med. Supt, Dunston Hill Hosp., Gateshead, 1948–50; SMO (Pensions), Cleveleys, 1950–53; Med. Supt, Queen Mary's Hosp., Roehampton, 1954–56; SMO, Dept of Health (Hosp. Bldg and later Regional Liaison Duties), 1956–68; PMO (Hosp. Bldg), 1968–73; SPMO (Under-Sec.), DHSS, 1973–76. Chm., CS Med. Appts Bds, 1979–86. FFCM (Foundn Fellow) 1972. *Publications:* articles on Sjögren's Disease, paralytic poliomyelitis, and hospital planning, medical care and the work of the Medical Advisory Service. *Recreations:* gardening, country life; formerly tennis. *Address:* 59 Lauderdale Drive, Petersham, Richmond, Surrey TW10 7BS. *T:* (020) 8940 1345. *Club:* Athenæum. *Died 3 Aug. 2013.*

HARRINGTON, Illtyd; JP; DL; *b* 14 July 1931; *s* of Timothy Harrington and Sarah (*née* Burchell); unmarried. *Educ:* St Illtyd's RC Sch., Dowlais; Merthyr County Sch.; Trinity Coll., Caermarthen. Member: Paddington Borough Council, 1959–64; Westminster City Council, 1964–68 and 1971–78, Leader, Lab. Gp, 1972–74; GLC, 1964–67 and for Brent S, 1973–86: Alderman, 1970–73; Chairman, Policy and Resources Cttee, 1973–77, Special Cttee, 1985–86; Dep. Leader, 1973–77, 1981–84; Dep. Leader of the Opposition, 1977–81; Chm. of the Council, 1984–85. Special Advr to Chm. and Leader of ILEA, 1988–90; Waterways Advr to Mayor of London, 2001–. JP Willesden 1968. First Chairman, Inland Waterways Amenity Adv. Council, 1968–71; Chm., London Canals Consultative Cttee, 1965–67, 1981–; Vice Pres., IWA, 1990–; Member: British Waterways Bd, 1974–82; BTA, 1976–80. Member: Bd, Theatre Royal, Stratford E, 1978–; Bd, Wiltons Music Hall, 1979–; Nat. Theatre Bd, 1975–77; Bd, National Youth Theatre, 1976–; Globe Theatre Trust, 1986–2001; Chm., Half Moon Theatre, 1978–90; Director: Soho Poly Theatre, 1981–2001; The Young Vic, 1981–2001. Chm., Nat. Millennium Maritime Fest., 1997–2000; Mem., London Dockland Mgt Adv. Gp, 1997–. President: Grand Union Canal Soc., 1974–; Islington Boat Club, 1985–; SE Region, IWA, 1986–; Immunity (Legal aid facility for AIDS victims), 1986–; Chairman: Kilburn Skills, 1977–2001; Battersea Park Peace Pagoda, 1984–; Limehouse Basin Users Gp, 1986–; Vice Pres., Coventry Canal Soc., 1970–. Gov., London Marathon, 1980–91. Trustee: Kew Bridge Pumping Mus., 1976–; Queen's Jubilee Walkway, 1977–; Chiswick Family Rescue, 1978–2001; Arthur Koestler Awards for Prisoners, 1987–; CARE, 1987–; Dominica Overseas Student Fund, 1987–; Mem., Montgomery Canal Trust, 1988–; Managing Trustee, Mutual Municipal Insurance Co., 1985–96. Governor, Brunel Univ., 1981–87. Patron: Westminster Cathedral Appeal, 1977–; Abandoned and Destitute Children Appeal (India), 2006–. DL Greater London, 1986. Contributor, The Guardian, 1982–; Literary Ed., Camden Jl gp of papers, 1995–. *Recreations:* defender of local government; laughing, singing and incredulity. *Address:* 44 Belbourne Court, Bread Street, Brighton BN1 1TT. *T:* (01273) 732693. *Club:* Savile. *Died 1 Oct. 2015.*

HARRIS, Prof. David Russell, FBA 2004; FSA; Professor of Human Environment, Institute of Archaeology, University College London, 1979–98, then Professor Emeritus (Director, 1989–96); *b* 14 Dec. 1930; *s* of Dr Herbert Melville Harris and Norah Mary Harris; *m* 1957, Helen Margaret Wilson; four *d*. *Educ:* St Christopher Sch., Letchworth; Oxford Univ. (MA, BLitt); Univ. of California, Berkeley (PhD). Nat. Service, RAF, 1949–50. Teaching Asst and Instructor, Univ. of California, 1956–58; Lectr, QMC, London, 1958–64; Lectr and Reader, UCL, 1964–79. Member: Mus. of London Archaeol. Cttee, 1984–91; English Heritage Sci. and Conservation Panel, 1985–99; Chm., Sci.-based Archaeol. Cttee, SERC, 1989–92. President: Prehistoric Soc., 1990–94; UK Chapter, Soc. for Economic Botany, 1995–97; Anthropol. and Archaeol. Sect., BAAS, 2000. Hon. Fellow, UCL, 2000. *Publications:* Plants, Animals and Man in the Outer Leeward Islands, 1965; (with B. W. Hodder) Africa in Transition, 1967; Human Ecology in Savanna Environments, 1980; (with G. C. Hillman) Foraging and Farming, 1989; Settling Down and Breaking Ground: rethinking the neolithic revolution, 1990; (with K. D. Thomas) Modelling Ecological Change, 1991; The Archaeology of V. Gordon Childe, 1994; The Origins and Spread of Agriculture and Pastoralism in Eurasia, 1996; (jtly) Plants for Food and Medicine, 1998; Origins of Agriculture in Western Central Asia, 2010; contrib. to collected works; papers in learned jls. *Recreations:* mountain walking, archaeological-ecological travel. *Address:* Institute of Archaeology, University College London, 31–34 Gordon Square, WC1H 0PY. *T:* (020) 7679 7495. *Club:* Athenæum. *Died 25 Dec. 2013.*

HARRIS, Sir Henry, Kt 1993; FRCP; FRCPath; FRS 1968; Regius Professor of Medicine, University of Oxford, 1979–92; Head of the Sir William Dunn School of Pathology, 1963–94; Hon. Director, Cancer Research Campaign, Cell Biology Unit, 1963–92; Fellow of Lincoln College, Oxford, 1963–79, Hon. Fellow 1980; Student of Christ Church, Oxford, 1979–92, Emeritus Student, 1992, Hon. Student, 2007; *b* 28 Jan. 1925; *s* of late Sam and Ann Harris; *m* 1950, Alexandra Fanny Brodsky; one *s* two *d*. *Educ:* Sydney Boys' High Sch. and University of Sydney, Australia; Lincoln Coll., Oxford. Public Exhibnr, University of Sydney, 1942; BA Mod. Langs, 1944; MB BS 1950; Travelling Schol. of Austr. Nat. Univ. at Univ. of Oxford, 1952; MA; DPhil (Oxon), 1954, DM 1979. Dir of Research, Brit. Empire Cancer Campaign, at Sir William Dunn Sch. of Pathology, Oxford, 1954–59; Visiting Scientist, Nat. Institutes of Health, USA, 1959–60; Head of Dept of Cell Biology, John Innes Inst., 1960–63; Prof. of Pathology, Univ. of Oxford, 1963–79. Vis. Prof., Vanderbilt Univ., 1968; Walker-Ames Prof., University of Washington, 1968; Foreign Prof., Collège de France, 1974. Non-exec. Mem., Oxford RHA, 1990–92; Hon. Consulting Pathologist, Oxford HA, 1992. Member: ARC, 1968–78 (Chm., Animals Res. Bd, 1976–78); Council, European Molecular Biology Organization, 1974–76; Council, Royal Society, 1971–72; Scientific Adv. Cttee, CRC, 1961–85; Governor, European Cell Biology Organization, 1973–75. Lectures: Almroth Wright, 1968; Harvey, Harvey Soc. NY, 1969; Dunham, Harvard, 1969; Jenner Meml, 1970; Croonian, Royal Soc., 1971; Nat. Insts of Health, USA, 1971; Foundation, RCPath, 1973; Woodhull, Royal Instn, 1975; Rotherham, Lincoln Coll., Oxford, 1979; Herbert Spencer, Oxford Univ., 1979, 1992; Opening Plenary, Internat. Congress of Cell Biology, 1980; First Distinguished, in Experimental Pathology, Pittsburgh Univ., 1982; Louis Gross Meml, NY, 1983; Claude Bernard, Acad. des Sciences, Paris, 1984; Jean Brachet Meml, Vancouver, 1990; Kettle, RCPath, 1991; Romanes, Oxford Univ., 1993. Foreign Hon. Mem., Amer. Acad. Arts and Sciences; Foreign Mem., Max-Planck Soc.; Hon. Member: Amer. Assoc. of Pathologists; German Soc. of Cell Biology; Corresp. Member: Amer. Assoc. for Cancer Res.; Aust. Acad. of Science. Foreign Correspondent, Waterford Striped Bass Derby Assoc.; Hon. Fellow,

Cambridge Philosophical Soc. Hon. FRCPA. Hon. DSc Edinburgh, 1976; Hon. MD: Geneva, 1982; Sydney, 1983. Feldberg Foundn Award, Ivison Macadam Meml Prize, RCSE; Prix de la Fondation Isabelle Decazes de Noüe for cancer research; Madonnina Prize for medical scis (City of Milan), 1979; Royal Medal, Royal Soc., 1980; Osler Medal, RCP, 1984; Katherine Berkan Judd Award, Sloan-Kettering Inst., NY, 1991; Medal of Honour, Univ. of Pavia, 2000. *Publications:* Nucleus and Cytoplasm, 1968, 3rd edn, 1974; Cell Fusion, 1970; La Fusion cellulaire, 1974; The Balance of Improbabilities, 1987; The Cells of the Body: a history of somatic cell genetics, 1995; The Birth of the Cell, 1999; Things Come to Life, 2002; Remnants of a Quiet Life, 2006; Boveri Concerning the Origin of Malignant Tumours, 2008; papers on cellular physiology and biochemistry, in scientific books and jls, and some fiction. *Recreation:* history. *Address:* c/o Sir William Dunn School of Pathology, South Parks Road, Oxford OX1 3RE. *T:* (01865) 275500. *Died 31 Oct. 2014.*

HARRIS, Joanne Olga Charlotte; Her Honour Judge Harris; a Circuit Judge, since 2007; *b* London, 13 July 1958; *d* of Dennis Harris and Marguerite, (Peggy), Harris; partner, Michael O'Donnell (*d* 2006); two *s*. *Educ:* Liverpool Univ. (BA Hons); London Sch. of Econs and Pol Sci. (MSc); Inns of Court Sch. of Law. Called to the Bar, Gray's Inn, 1991; Dep. Dist Judge, 2002; Recorder, 2004–07. *Recreation:* ski-ing and other holidays. *Address:* Watford County Court, Cassiobury House, 11–19 Station Road, Watford, Herts WD17 1EZ. *T:* (01923) 699400, *Fax:* (01923) 699404. *Died 17 April 2014.*

HARRIS, Prof. Roy, MA, DPhil, PhD; Professor of General Linguistics, University of Oxford, 1978–88, then Emeritus; Fellow of Worcester College, Oxford, 1978–88; *b* 24 Feb. 1931; *s* of Harry and Emmie J. Harris; *m* 1955, Rita Doreen Shulman; one *d*. *Educ:* Queen Elizabeth's Hospital, Bristol; St Edmund Hall, Oxford (MA, DPhil; Hon. Fellow 1987); SOAS, London (PhD). Lecteur, Ecole Normale Supérieure, Paris, 1956–57; Asst Lectr, 1957–58, Lectr, 1958–60, Univ. of Leicester; Exeter Coll., Oxford, 1960–76; Keble Coll., Oxford, 1960–67; Magdalen Coll., Oxford, 1960–76; New Coll., Oxford, 1960–67; Faculty of Medieval and Modern Languages, Oxford, 1961–76; Fellow and Tutor in Romance Philology, Keble Coll., Oxford, 1967–76; Prof. of the Romance Langs, Oxford Univ., and Fellow of Trinity Coll., 1976–77; Prof. of English Language, Univ. of Hong Kong, 1988–91; Dir d'études associé, Ecole Pratique des Hautes Etudes, Paris, 1991–92; Fellow, Univ. Professors, Boston, 1993–95. Visiting Professor: Jawaharlal Nehru Univ., New Delhi, 1986; State Univ. of NY, 1987; Overseas Res. Fellow, Univ. of Cape Town, 1996; Dist. Vis. Schol., Univ. of Adelaide, 1997, 1999. Council Member, Philological Soc., 1978–82. Editor, Language & Communication, 1980–2010. FRSA. Scott Moncrieff prize, Translators' Assoc. (Soc. of Authors), 1984. *Publications:* Synonymy and Linguistic Analysis, 1973; Communication and Language, 1978; The Language-Makers, 1980; The Language Myth, 1981; (trans.) F. de Saussure: Course in General Linguistics, 1983; (ed) Approaches to Language, 1983; (ed) Developmental Mechanisms of Language, 1985; The Origin of Writing, 1986; Reading Saussure, 1987; Language, Saussure and Wittgenstein, 1988; (ed) Linguistic Thought in England 1914–1945, 1988; (with T. J. Taylor) Landmarks in Linguistic Thought: the Western tradition from Socrates to Saussure, 1989, 2nd edn 1997; La sémiologie de l'écriture, 1993; Signs of Writing, 1995; The Language Connection, 1996; Signs, Language and Communication, 1996; Introduction to Integrational Linguistics, 1998; Rethinking Writing, 2000; Saussure and his Interpreters, 2001, 2nd edn 2003; The Necessity of Artspeak, 2003; The Linguistics of History, 2004; The Semantics of Science, 2005; Integrationist Notes and Papers, 2006; (with C. M. Hutton) Definition in Theory and Practice, 2007; Mindboggling, 2008; Rationality and the Literate Mind, 2009; After Epistemology, 2009; The Great Debate about Art, 2010; Integrating Reality, 2012; contribs to Analysis, Behavioral and Brain Sciences, Encounter, Essays in Criticism, French Studies, History and Philosophy of Logic, International Jl of Moral and Social Studies, Jl of Linguistics, Language Sciences, Linguistics, Medium Ævum, Mind, Revue de linguistique romane, Semiotica, Studies in Eighteenth-Century Culture, Theoria, Times Higher Educn, TLS, Zeitschrift für romanische Philologie. *Recreations:* cricket, modern art and design. *Address:* 2 Paddox Close, Oxford OX2 7LR. *T:* (01865) 554256. *Died 9 Feb. 2015.*

HARRISON, (Alastair) Brian (Clarke); DL; *b* 3 Oct. 1921; *s* of late Brig. E. F. Harrison, Melbourne; *m* 1952, Elizabeth Hood Hardie, Oaklands, NSW, Aust.; one *s* one *d*. *Educ:* Geelong Grammar Sch.; Trinity Coll., Cambridge. Capt. AIF. MP (C) Maldon, Essex, 1955–Feb. 1974; Parliamentary Private Secretary to: Minister of State, Colonial Office, 1955–56; Sec. of State for War, 1956–58; Minister of Agriculture, Fisheries and Food, 1958–60. Mem. Victoria Promotion Cttee (London); Mem. One Nation Gp which published The Responsible Society, and One Europe; toured USA on ESU Ford Foundation Fellowship, 1959; Commonwealth Parliamentary Assoc. Delegations: Kenya and Horn of Africa, 1960; Gilbert and Ellice Islands, New Hebrides and British Solomon Islands Protectorate. Chm., Standing Conf. of Eastern Sport and Physical Recreation, 1974–. Organizer (with Univ. of WA), expedns to Nepal studying human physiol., 1979–87. High Sheriff, 1979, DL 1980, Essex. *Publications:* (jtly) The cumulative effect of High Altitude on Motor Performance: a comparison between caucasian visitors and native highlanders, 1985; (jtly) Entrainment of respiratory frequency to exercise rhythm during hypoxia, 1987. *Recreations:* photography, gardening. *Address:* Green Farm House, Copford, Colchester, Essex CO6 1DA. *Clubs:* Carlton, Pratt's; Melbourne (Melbourne); Weld (Perth). *Died 21 Aug. 2011.*

HARRISON, (Fred) Brian, CBE 1982; FCA; *b* 6 March 1927; *s* of Fred Harrison and Annie Harrison; *m* 1950, Margaret Owen (*d* 1995); two *s*. *Educ:* Burnley Grammar Sch. FCA 1960 (ACA 1950). East Midlands Div., NCB, 1953–67 (Chief Accountant, No 1 Area, 1962–67); Chief Accountant, N Derbyshire Area, NCB, 1967–68; Finance Dir, Coal Products Div., NCB, 1968–71; Dep. Man. Dir, Coal Products Div., NCB, subseq. Dep. Chief Exec., NCB (Coal Products) Ltd, 1971–76, Chm., 1978–83. Mem., NCB, 1976–85. Chm., British Investment Trust, 1978–85. Master, Chartered Accountants' Co., 1994–95; Mem., Ct of Assistants, Fuellers' Co., 1996– (Master, 2000–01). Mem., Governing Body, United Wards Club, 2009–. *Recreations:* music, theatre. *Address:* 11 Hillcrest, King Harry Lane, St Albans, Herts AL3 4AT. *T:* (01727) 46938. *Died 16 Jan. 2014.*

HARRISON, Jessel Anidjah; President, Slimma Group Holdings Ltd, retired 1989; *b* 28 May 1923; *s* of Samuel Harrison and Esta (*née* Romain); *m* 1st, 1943, Irene (*née* Olsberg) (marr. diss. 1956); one *s* one *d*; 2nd, 1961, Doreen Leigh. *Educ:* Vernon House Preparatory Sch.; Brondesbury Coll.; Macauley Coll., Cuckfield, Sussex. Chairman: Slimma Ltd, 1964; Slimma (Wales) Ltd, 1971; Emu Wool Industries, later Slimma Gp Hldgs, 1973; Dir, Tootals Clothing Div., 1977–89. Member: European Trade Cttee, 1975–98; Clothing Industry Productivity Resources Agency, 1978–85; British Overseas Trade Adv. Council, 1978–85. Vice Pres., Clothing Export Council of Great Britain, 1977 (Chm., 1973); Chm., British Overseas Trade Group for Israel, 1978–83, Vice-Pres., 1987–98. Pres., Clothing Institute, 1978. *Recreations:* golf, walking. *Address:* 113 Abbotsbury Road, W14 8EP. *T:* (020) 7603 7468. *Club:* Royal Automobile. *Died 18 Dec. 2013.*

HARRISON, Michael Anthony; Director, Kettle's Yard, University of Cambridge, 1992–2011; *b* 30 April 1947; *s* of late William Harrison and Gweneth Harrison (*née* Cooke); *m* 1973, Marie-Claude Bouquet; three *s* one *d*. *Educ:* Newcastle Royal GS; Aylesbury GS; Oxford Coll. of Technol.; Univ. of Nottingham (BA Hons Fine Art/Art Hist.). Arts Council: Regl Art Officer, 1971–73; Exhibn Organiser, 1973–77; Asst Dir for Regl Exhibns, Arts Council, 1977–88, South Bank Centre, 1988–90; Head of Fine Art, Winchester Sch. of Art, 1990–92. *Publications:* Alan Reynolds: the making of a concretist artist, 2011; numerous exhibn catalogues. *Recreations:* art, places, books, cinema, music, more art. *Address:* c/o Kettle's Yard, Castle Street, Cambridge CB3 0AQ. *Died 25 April 2013.*

HARRISON, Peter John; QC 2006; a Recorder, since 2007; *b* 14 Feb. 1965; *s* of Robin Harrison and Paddy Harrison (*née* Smith); *m* 2000, Kate Belinda Tucker. *Educ:* Warden Park Comprehensive Sch., Cuckfield; Haywards Heath VIth Form Coll.; St John's Coll., Durham Univ. (BA Hons). Called to the Bar, Inner Temple, 1987, Bencher, 2009. Member: SE Circuit Planning and Envmt Bar Assoc., 1990–; Criminal Bar Assoc., 1992–; Admin. Law Bar Assoc., 1994–; Ecclesiastical Law Assoc., 2010–. Mem. Faculty, SE Circuit Keble Internat. Advocacy trng course, 2003–. Church Comr, 2008–. Lectures in field of regulatory and envmtl crime. *Publications:* (with F. Darroch) Environmental Crime, 1999. *Recreations:* ceroc dancing, English cookery. *Address:* 6 Pump Court, Temple, EC4Y 7AR. *T:* (020) 7797 8400. *E:* peterharrison@6pumpcourt.co.uk. *Died 22 Jan. 2013.*

HARRISON, Rt Hon. Walter; PC 1977; JP; *b* 2 Jan. 1921; *s* of Henry and Ada Harrison; *m* 1948, Enid Mary (*née* Coleman) (*d* 1990); one *s* one *d*; *m* 1991, Jane Marguerite Richards (*d* 2000). *Educ:* Dewsbury Technical and Art Coll. Served RAF, 1940–45. Electrical Inspector and Electrical Foreman, Electricity Supply Industry, 1937–64; Welfare Personnel Officer, Civil and Engrg Industry, 1945–48. MP (Lab) Wakefield, 1964–87. Asst Govt Whip, 1966–68; a Lord Comr of the Treasury, 1968–70; Dep. Chief Opposition Whip, 1970–74 and 1979–83; Treasurer of HM Household and Dep. Chief Govt Whip, 1974–79. Held several positions in the Trade Union and Labour movements. West Riding CC, 1958–64; Alderman, Castleford Borough Council, 1959–66 (Councillor, 1952–59); JP West Riding Yorks, 1962. Hon. Freeman, City of Wakefield, 2003. *Address:* 1 Milnthorpe Drive, Sandal, Wakefield WF2 7HU. *T:* (01924) 255550. *Died 19 Oct. 2012.*

HARRISS, Gerald Leslie, DPhil; FBA 1986; Fellow and Tutor, Magdalen College, Oxford, 1967–92, then Emeritus Fellow; Reader in Modern History, Oxford University, 1990–92; *b* 22 May 1925; *s* of Walter and Mabel Harriss; *m* 1959, Margaret Anne Sidaway; two *s* three *d*. *Educ:* Chigwell Sch.; Magdalen Coll., Oxford (BA 1st Cl. History, MA, DPhil). Service in RNVR, 1944–46. Research Fellow, Durham Univ., 1953–55; Asst Lectr, Manchester Univ., 1955–56; Lectr 1956, Sen. Lectr 1965, Reader 1965–67, Durham Univ. *Publications:* King, Parliament and Public Finance in Medieval England, 1975; (ed) Henry V: the practice of kingship, 1985; Cardinal Beaufort, 1988; (ed) K. B. McFarlane, Letters to Friends, 1997; Shaping the Nation: England 1360–1461, 2005; numerous articles on late medieval English history. *Address:* Fairings, 2 Queen Street, Yetminster, Dorset DT9 6LL. *Died 2 Nov. 2014.*

HARROD, Dominick Roy; journalist and broadcaster; Programme Director, St George's House, Windsor Castle, 1994–98; President, Institute of Journalists, 1994–95; *b* 21 Aug. 1940; *s* of Sir Roy Forbes Harrod, FBA and Wilhelmine Harrod (*née* Cresswell), OBE; *m* 1974, Christina Hobhouse (*d* 1996); one *s*. *Educ:* Dragon Sch., Oxford; Westminster Sch.; Christ Church, Oxford (MA Modern Greats). Sunday Telegraph, 1962–66; Daily Telegraph: Washington corresp., 1966–69; Economics corresp., 1969–71; BBC Economics corresp., 1971–78; Dir of Information, Dunlop Ltd, 1979; Economics Editor, BBC Radio, 1979–93; City Editor, The Yorkshire Post, 1993–94. Member: Council, SCF, 1988–96; Bd for Social Responsibility, C of E, 1996–2000. Founder Mem., Norfolk Churches Trust, 1973; Chm., Friends of Morston Church, 2003–. FJI 1990; FRSA 1992. *Publications:* The Politics of Economics, 1978; Making Sense of the Economy, 1983; War, Ice and Piracy, 2000; (contrib.) The Turn of the Tide, 2005. *Recreations:* reading, sailing. *Address:* 4 Duke's Avenue, W4 2AE. *Club:* Garrick. *Died 4 Aug. 2013.*

HARRY THOMAS, Caroline Jane; QC 2008; a Recorder, since 2003; *b* 23 March 1957; *d* of David and Elizabeth Harry Thomas; *m* 1985, Mark Campbell (*d* 2009); one *s* two *d*. *Educ:* Ellerslie Sch., Malvern, Worcs; Exeter Univ. (LLB Hons). Called to the Bar, Middle Temple, 1981, Bencher, 2010; in practice as barrister, specialising in medical law. Vice Chm. Council, Malvern Coll., Worcs, 2007–. *Publications:* (contrib.) Heywood & Massey Court of Protection Practice, 2007–. *Recreations:* theatre, opera, travel. *Address:* Littleton Chambers, 3 King's Bench Walk North, Temple, EC4Y 7HR. *T:* (020) 7797 8600. *Club:* The Scarlets Rugby (Llanelli). *Died 21 Dec. 2011.*

HART, Anthony John, OBE 1995; DSC 1945; JP; Chairman, Cunningham Hart & Co. Ltd, 1985–87 (Senior Partner, 1972–85); *b* 27 Dec. 1923; *s* of Cecil Victor Hart and Kate Winifred Hart (*née* Boncey); *m* 1st, 1947, E. Penelope Morris (*d* 2001); one *s* one *d*; 2nd, 2003, Mrs Mary Eggleton (*d* 2012). *Educ:* King's College Sch., Wimbledon; Dauntsey's Sch. ACII, FCILA. RN, 1942–46 (Ordinary Seaman to Lieut). Joined Hart & Co., 1946, Partner 1952, Senior Partner 1969; on merger name changed to Cunningham Hart & Co. Mem. Council, CILA, 1964, Pres., 1970–71. Chm., Medic Alert Foundn in UK, 1971–83; Governor, Dauntsey's Sch., 1982–93; Mem. Council, Mansfield House University Settlement, 1975–90. Liveryman, 1960, Master, 1976–77, Broderers' Co.; Liveryman, 1979, Mem. Court, 1986, Insurers' Co. Alderman, Ward of Cheap, City of London, 1977–84. FRSA. JP City of London, 1977 (Vice-Chm. of Bench, 1991–93). *Recreation:* golf. *Address:* Dove Barn, Chapel Lane, Minchinhampton, Stroud, Glos GL6 9DL. *T:* (01453) 882154. *Club:* Minchinhampton Golf. *Died 16 Nov. 2015.*

HART, Sir David (Michael), Kt 2006; OBE 1988; General Secretary, National Association of Head Teachers, 1978–2005; *b* 27 Aug. 1940; *s* of Edwin Henry Hart and Freda Muriel Hart; *m* 1st, 1963, Mary Chalmers (marr. diss.); two *s*; 2nd, 1996, Frances Katrina Morton. *Educ:* Hurstpierpoint Coll., Sussex. Solicitor 1963, Herbert Ruse Prizeman. Editor, Heads' Legal Guide, 1984. Hon. FCollP 1986; FRSA 1990. Hon. Dr UCE, 1999. *Recreations:* tennis, walking, riding. *Address:* Whinby Cottage, Haltcliffe, Hesket Newmarket, Wigton, Cumbria CA7 8JT. *T:* (01697) 478318. *Died 14 March 2013.*

HARTE, Dr Michael John; consultant in information technology, 1995–2010; Director General Information Technology Systems, Ministry of Defence, 1994–95; *b* 15 Aug. 1936; *s* of late Harold Edward Harte and Marjorie Irene Harte; *m* 1st, 1962, Diana Hayes (marr. diss. 1971); 2nd, 1975, Mary Claire Preston; four step *d*. *Educ:* Charterhouse; Trinity Coll., Cambridge (BA); University Coll., London (PhD; Dip. in Biochem. Engrg). Sen. Scientific Officer, Micro-biol Res. Estab., MoD, 1963; Principal, MoD, 1967; Private Sec. to Minister of State for Def., 1972; Asst Sec., Central Policy Rev. Staff, 1973; Asst Sec., MoD, 1975–77; Counsellor, Budget and Infrastructure, UK Delegn to NATO, 1977–81; Chm., NATO Civil and Mil. Budget Cttees, 1981–83; Asst Sec., MoD, 1983–85; Assistant Under Secretary of State: (Dockyard Planning Team), MoD, 1985–87; (Personnel) (Air), MoD, 1987–90; (Resources), MoD, 1990–93. Non-exec. Dir, GlaxoChem., 1988–91. Founder, 2003, and Chm., Wadhurst History Soc., 2003–; Pres., Wealden Bldgs Study Gp, 2009–11. Webmaster, www.wadhurst.info. *Publications:* Wadhurst Then and Now, 2003; The Day Wadhurst Changed, 2006; Wadhurst in the Second World War, 2008; Wadhurst Back in Time 1900–1936, 2011. *Recreations:* local history, local information website design and maintenance, local choral singing. *Address:* Greenman Farm, Wadhurst, E Sussex TN5 6LE. *T:* (01892) 783292. *Died 24 July 2012.*

HARTLEY, His Honour Gilbert Hillard; a Circuit Judge (formerly Judge of County Courts), 1967–82; *b* 11 Aug. 1917; *s* of late Percy Neave Hartley and Nellie Bond Hartley (*née* Hillard); *m* 1948, Jeanne (*d* 2000), *d* of late C. W. Gall, Leeds; one *s* two *d*. *Educ:* Ashville, Harrogate; Exeter Coll., Oxford. Called to the Bar, Middle Temple, 1939. Served with Army, 1940–46. Recorder of Rotherham, 1965–67; Dep. Chm., WR of Yorkshire QS, 1965–71. *Address:* 3 Rossett Beck, Harrogate HG2 9NT. *Died 4 Feb. 2012.*

HARVEY, Arthur Douglas; Assistant Under-Secretary of State, Ministry of Defence, 1969–76; *b* 16 July 1916; *o s* of late William Arthur Harvey and Edith Alice; *m* 1940, Doris Irene Lodge (*d* 1997); one *s* (and one *s* decd). *Educ:* Westcliff High Sch.; St Catharine's Coll., Cambridge.

Wrangler, Maths Tripos, 1938. Entered War Office, 1938; served in Army, 1940–45; Princ. 1945; Registrar, Royal Military College of Science, 1951–54; Asst Sec. 1954; Under-Sec. 1969. *Address:* 36b Lovelace Road, Long Ditton, Surrey KT6 6ND. *T:* (020) 8399 0587. *Died 12 March 2013.*

HARVEY, Prof. Brian Wilberforce; Professor of Law, University of Birmingham, 1973–98, then Emeritus; *b* 17 March 1936; *s* of Gerald and Noelle Harvey; *m* 1962, Rosemary Jane Brown; two *s* two *d. Educ:* Clifton Coll., Bristol; St John's Coll., Cambridge (Choral Schol., MA, LLM). Solicitor, 1961. Lectr, Birmingham Univ., 1962–63; Sen. Lectr, Nigerian Law Sch., 1965–67; Lectr, Sen. Lectr and Prof. of Law, QUB, 1967–73; University of Birmingham: Dir, Legal Studies, 1973–76; Dean, Faculty of Law, 1982–85; Pro-Vice-Chancellor, 1986–91; Founding Dir, Legal Office, 1990–98. Vis. Prof., Univ. of Singapore, 1985–86. Chairman: Gtr Birmingham Social Security Appeal Tribunals, 1982–99; Medical Appeals Tribunals, 1985–99; Disability Appeal Tribunals, 1992–99. Member: Statute Law Cttee (NI), 1972–73; Cttee on Legal Educn (NI), 1972–73; Adviser, Council of Legal Educn (NI), 1976–79. Mem., British Hallmarking Council, 1989–91. *Publications:* Law of Probate Wills and Succession in Nigeria, 1968; (jtly) Survey of Northern Ireland Land Law, 1970; Settlements of Land, 1973; (ed) Vocational Legal Training in UK and Commonwealth, 1975; (ed) The Lawyer and Justice, 1978; The Law of Consumer Protection and Fair Trading, 1978, 6th edn 2000; (jtly) Consumer and Trading Law Cases and Materials, 1985, 2nd edn 1998; (jtly) Law and Practice of Auctions, 1985, 3rd edn 2006; (jtly) The Law and Practice of Marketing Goods and Services, 1990; Violin Fraud: deception, forgery, theft and the law, 1992, 2nd edn (jtly) 1997; The Violin Family and its Makers in the British Isles: an illustrated history and directory, 1995; Buying and Selling Art and Antiques—The Law, 1998; (ed jtly) Edward Heron-Allen's Journal of the Great War, 2002; (jtly) Elgar, Vicat Cole and the Ghosts of Brinkwells, 2007. *Recreation:* performing and listening to music. *Address:* Pear Tree Cottage, Evesham Road, Cookhill, Alcester, Warwicks B49 5LJ. *T:* (01789) 400132. *Died 23 March 2014.*

HARVEY, Clare; *see* Harvey, M. F. C.

HARVEY, Prof. Jonathan Dean; composer; Professor of Music, Stanford University, 1995–2000; *b* 3 May 1939; *s* of Gerald and Noelle Harvey; *m* 1960, Rosaleen Marie Barry; one *s* one *d. Educ:* St Michael's Coll., Tenbury; Repton; St John's Coll., Cambridge (MA, DMus; Hon. Fellow, 2002); Glasgow Univ. (PhD). Lectr, Southampton Univ., 1964–77; Sussex University: Reader, 1977–80; Prof. of Music, 1980–95; Hon. Prof., 1995. Bloch Prof., Univ. of California, Berkeley, 1995; Vis. Prof., Imperial Coll., London, 1999–2002. Harkness Fellow, Princeton Univ., 1969–70; Fellow, Wissenschaftskolleg, Berlin, 2009. Composer in association with: Sinfonia 21, 1996–; Ictus Ensemble, 1997–; BBC Scottish SO, 2004–08. Works performed at most festivals and international centres. Member: Academia Europaea, 1989; Royal Acad. of Belgium, 2011. FRCM 1995; FRSCM 2000. Hon. RAM 2002. Hon. DMus: Southampton, 1990; Bristol, 1994; Sussex, 2000; Huddersfield, 2008; Birmingham City, 2009. Composer Award, British Acad., 2003; Giga-Hertz Prize, 2007; Gramophone Award, 2008; Composition Prize, Prince Pierre de Monaco Foundn, 2009; Académie Charles Cros Grand Prix du Président de la République for a life's work, 2009; Prix Caecilia (Belgium), 2010, 2011. *Publications:* The Music of Stockhausen, 1975; Music and Inspiration, 1999; In Quest of Spirit, 1999; *compositions:* Persephone Dream, for orch., 1972; Inner Light (trilogy), for performers and tape, 1973–77; Smiling Immortal, for chamber orch., 1977; String Quartet, 1977; Magnificat and Nunc Dimittis, for choir and organ, 1978; Album, for wind quintet, 1978; Hymn, for choir and orch., 1979; Be(com)ing, for clarinet and piano, 1979; Concelebration, instrumental, 1979, rev. 1981; Mortuos Plango, Vivos Voco, for tape, 1980; Passion and Resurrection, church opera, 1981; Resurrection, for double chorus and organ, 1981; Bhakti, for 15 insts and tape, 1982; Easter Orisons, for chamber orch., 1983; The Path of Devotion, for choir and orch., 1983; Nachtlied, for soprano, piano and tape, 1984; Gong-Ring, for ensemble with electronics, 1984; Song Offerings, for soprano and players, 1985 (Britten Award for Composition, 1993); Madonna of Winter and Spring, for orch., synthesizers and electronics, 1986; Lightness and Weight, for tuba and orch., 1986; Forms of Emptiness, for choir, 1986; Tendril, for ensemble, 1987; Timepieces, for orch., 1987; From Silence, for soprano and players with electronics, 1988; Valley of Aosta for 13 players, 1988; String Quartet No 2, 1989; Ritual Melodies, for tape, 1990; Cello Concerto, 1990; Serenade in Homage to Mozart, for wind, 1991; Inquest of Love (opera), 1992; Lotuses, 1992; Scena, 1992; The Riot, for trio, 1993; One Evening, for 2 singers, instruments and electronics, 1994; String Quartet No 3, 1996; Percussion Concerto, 1997; Ashes Dance Back, for choir with electronics, 1997; Wheel of Emptiness, for ensemble, 1997; Calling Across Time, for chamber orch., 1998; Tranquil Abiding, for orch., 1998; White as Jasmine, for soprano and orch., 1999; Mothers Shall Not Cry, for voices, orch. and electronics, 2000; Bird Concerto with Pianosong, 2001; The Summer Cloud's Awakening, for choir and instruments with electronics, 2001; Songs of Li Po, for voice and chamber orch., 2002; Chu, for soprano and two instruments, 2002; String Quartet No 4 (with electronics), 2003; Jubilus, for viola and ensemble, 2003; Two Interludes for an Opera, 2004; String Trio, 2004; Towards a Pure Land, for orch., 2005 (Royal Philharmonic Soc. Award, 2007); Wagner Dream (opera), 2006; Body Mandala, for orch., 2007; Messages, for orch. and chorus, 2007; Cello Octet, 2008; Speakings, for orch. and electronics, 2008; Sringara Chaconne, for ensemble, 2009; 80 Breaths for Tokyo, for orch., 2010; Weltethos, for speaker, choirs and orch., 2011. *Recreation:* meditation. *Address:* c/o Faber Music, Bloomsbury House, 74–77 Great Russell Street, WC1B 3DA. *T:* (020) 7908 5310. *Died 4 Dec. 2012.*

HARVEY, (Mary Frances) Clare, (Mrs D. R. Feaver), MA; Headmistress, St Mary's Hall, Brighton, 1981–88; *b* 24 Aug. 1927; *e d* of late Rev. Oliver Douglas Harvey and Frances Hilda Harvey (*née* Howes); *m* 1988, Rt Rev. Douglas Russell Feaver (*d* 1997). *Educ:* St Mary's Sch., Colchester; St Hugh's Coll., Oxford (BA, Final Honour Sch. of Mod. Hist., 1950; Diploma in Educn, 1951; MA 1954). History Mistress, St Albans High Sch., 1951; Head of History Dept, Portsmouth High Sch., GPDST, 1956; Headmistress: Sch. of St Clare, Penzance, 1962–69; Badminton Sch., Westbury on Trym, Bristol, 1969–81. Governor, Bristol Cathedral Sch., 1978–81; Foundn Gov. and Trustee, Sexey's Sch., Bruton, 1994–95. *Recreations:* music, travel, reading, needlework. *Address:* Blackman House, Canon Lane, Chichester, West Sussex PO19 1PX. *Died 17 Dec. 2015.*

HARVEY, Michael, MBE 2001; freelance lettering designer, since 1955; *b* 11 Nov. 1931; *s* of Leslie Arthur Harvey and Betty Eileen Harvey; *m* 1956, Patricia Evelyn Hills; three *d. Educ:* Ewell Castle Sch. Engrg draughtsman, 1947–55; Asst to Reynolds Stone, inscription carving, 1955–61. Pt-time Lectr, Bournemouth & Poole Coll. of Art & Design, 1961–80; Vis. Lectr, Dept of Typography & Graphic Communication, Univ. of Reading, 1993–2001. Co-Founder, Fine Fonts, 2000; est. 47Editions to publish photographic bks, 2008. *Work* includes: inscription carving, book jacket design, type design (Monotype, Adobe, Dutch Type Library); collaboration with Ian Hamilton Finlay on carved poetry, sundials, graphic works; design and carving of inscriptions, Sainsbury Wing, Nat. Gall., London, 1990. Mem., Royal Mint Adv. Cttee, 1991–2005. Gov., Arts Inst. at Bournemouth, 1998–2001 (Hon. Fellow, 2001). Mem., Wynkyn de Worde Soc. *Publications:* Lettering Design, 1975; Creative Lettering: drawing & design, 1985; Carving Letters in Stone & Wood, 1987; Calligraphy in the Graphic Arts, 1988; Reynolds Stone: engraved lettering in wood, 1992; Creative Lettering Today, 1996; Adventures with Letters, 2012. *Recreations:* reading, listening to jazz, photography. *Address:* 4 Valley Road, Bridport, Dorset DT6 4JR. *T:* (01308) 422777. *E:* perdido@dircon.co.uk. *Club:* Double Crown. *Died 18 Oct. 2013.*

HARVEY, Neil; Head of Business Statistics Division, Central Statistical Office, 1989–93; *b* 10 Feb. 1938; *s* of Edward Felters and Lucy Felters (*née* Graves; she *m* 2nd, Frederick Harvey); *m* 1963, Clare Elizabeth Joscelyne; two *s. Educ:* Eton House Sch., Essex; LSE. BSc(Econ). Economist/Statistician, Kuwait Oil Co., 1959–62; Statistician, Midland Bank Economics Dept, 1962–65; Asst Statistician/Statistician, DEA, 1965–69; Statistician, HM Treasury, 1969–73; Chief Statistician, Inland Revenue, 1973–77; Controller, Statistical Office, HM Customs and Excise, 1977–84; Under Sec., Statistics Div. 1, DTI, 1984–89. *Recreation:* reading. *Died 12 Oct. 2012.*

HARVEY, Peter, CB 1980; Consultant, Solicitor's Office, Department of Trade and Industry, 1994–96 and 1997–99; *b* 23 April 1922; *o s* of Rev. George Leonard Hunton Harvey and Helen Mary (*née* Williams); *m* 1st, 1950, Mary Vivienne (*d* 2006), *d* of John Osborne Goss and Elsie Lilian (*née* Bishop); one *s* one *d*; 2nd, 2011, Judith, *o d* of Walter Edward Jensen and Judith Jensen (*née* Skinner) and *widow* of John Harry Bray. *Educ:* King Edward VI High Sch., Birmingham; St John's Coll., Oxford (MA, BCL). RAF, 1942–45. Called to the Bar, Lincoln's Inn, 1948. Entered the Home Office as a Legal Assistant, 1948; Principal Asst Legal Advr, 1971–77; Legal Advr, DES, 1977–83; Consultant, Legal Advr's Br., Home Office, 1983–86; Asst Counsel to the Speaker, H of C, 1986–94. Mem., Legal Affairs Cttee, Inst. for Citizenship Studies, 1992–94. *Publications:* contributor to Halsbury's Laws of England (3rd and 4th edns). *Recreations:* history, genealogy, travel. *Address:* 1 George Street, Cromarty, Ross-shire IV11 8YJ. *Died 26 Aug. 2014.*

HASKELL, (Donald) Keith, CMG 1991; CVO 1979; international affairs consultant and lecturer; HM Diplomatic Service, retired; *b* 9 May 1939; *s* of Donald Eric Haskell and Beatrice Mary Haskell (*née* Blair); *m* 1966, Maria Luisa Soeiro Tito de Morais; two *s* two *d* (and one *s* one *d* decd). *Educ:* Portsmouth Grammar Sch.; St Catharine's Coll., Cambridge (BA 1961, MA 1964). Joined HM Foreign Service, 1961; served in: London, Lebanon, Iraq, Libya; HM Consul, Benghazi, 1969–70; First Sec., Tripoli, 1970–72; Foreign and Commonwealth Office, 1972–75; Chargé d'Affaires and Consul-Gen., Santiago, 1975–78; Counsellor and Consul-Gen., Dubai, 1978–81; Hd, Nuclear Energy Dept, FCO, 1981–83; Hd, Middle East Dept, FCO, 1983–84; Hd of Chancery, Bonn, 1985–88; on secondment as an advr to industry, 1988–89; Ambassador: to Peru, 1990–95; to Brazil, 1995–99. Dr *hc* Nat. Univ. of Peruvian Amazonia, Iquitos, 1992. Foundation Medal, Soka Univ. of Japan, 1975. Grand Cross, Order of Rio Branco (Brazil), 1997. *Recreations:* rifle shooting (captained Cambridge Univ. Rifle Assoc., 1960–61; represented England and GB in shooting competitions on various occasions), ski-ing, wine and food. *Address:* Barn Cottage, Brightstone Lane, Farringdon, Alton, Hants GU34 3DP. *Club:* Hawks (Cambridge). *Died 28 Nov. 2012.*

HASKELL, Peter Thomas, CMG 1975; PhD, CBiol, FSB; Research Consultant, School of Pure and Applied Biology, University of Wales College of Cardiff, 1992–94, Fellow, 1994; *b* 21 Feb. 1923; *s* of late Herbert James and Mary Anne Haskell; *m* 1st, 1946, Betty Jackson; one *s*; 2nd, 1979, Aileen Kirkley. *Educ:* Portsmouth Grammar Sch.; Imperial Coll., London. BSc, ARCS, PhD. Asst Lectr, Zoology Dept, Imperial Coll., London, 1951–53; Lectr, 1953–55; Sen. Sci. Officer, Anti-Locust Research Centre, Colonial Office, 1955–57; Principal Sci. Officer, 1957–59; Dep. Dir, 1959–62; Dir, Anti-Locust Research Centre, ODM, 1962–71; Dir, Centre for Overseas Pest Res. and Chief Advr on Pest Control, ODA, 1971–83; Dir, Cleppa Park Field Res. Stn, UC Cardiff, later Univ. of Wales Coll. of Cardiff, 1984–91. Consultant: FAO, UN, 1962–; UNDP, 1970–; WHO, 1973–91; OECD, 1975–; UNEP, 1976–91; Agricl and Vet. Adv. Cttee, British Council, 1976–90; Plants and Soils Res. Cttee, AFRC, later Plants and Envmt Res. Cttee, 1988–91; IFAD, 1995–; Mem., UNDP/FAO Special Adv. Cttee on Desert Locust, 1990–. Vice-Pres., Inst. of Biology, 1982. Professorial Res. Fellow, University Coll. Cardiff, 1971–83. Mem., Bd of Governors, Internat. Centre for Insect Physiology and Ecology, Kenya, 1972– (Vice-Chm., 1978; Chm., 1979–). Vis. Prof., Univ. of Newcastle, 1977. Thamisk Lectr, Royal Swedish Acad. of Scis, 1979. Van Den Brande Internat. Prize, 1982. Chief Editor, Tropical Pest Management, 1985–92; Mem., Editorial Bd, Review of Applied Entomol., 1988–91. *Publications:* Insect Sounds, 1962; The Language of Insects, 1962; Pesticide Application: principles and practice, 1985; Ecotoxicology: pesticides and beneficial organisms, 1998; many papers and articles in scientific and literary jls. *Recreations:* gardening, reading. *Address:* 14 Maddox Drive, Worth, W Sussex RH10 7PQ. *Died 26 Sept. 2012.*

HASTINGS, Michael Gerald; playwright; *b* 2 Sept. 1938; *s* of Max Emmanuel Gerald and Marie Catherine Hastings; *m* 1975, Victoria Hardie; two *s*, and one *d* by a previous marriage. *Educ:* various South London comprehensive schools. Bespoke tailoring apprentice, London, 1953–56. FRGS. *Plays:* Don't Destroy Me, 1956; Yes and After, 1957; The World's Baby, 1962; Lee Harvey Oswald: 'a far mean streak of indepence brought on by neglect', 1966; The Cutting of the Cloth (unperformed autobiographical play), 1969; The Silence of Saint-Just, 1971; For the West (Uganda), 1977; Gloo Joo, 1978; Full Frontal, 1979; Carnival War a Go Hot, 1980; Midnite at the Starlite, 1980; Molière's The Miser (adaptation), 1982; Tom and Viv, 1984, new version, 2006; Stars of the Roller State Disco (Brixton community play), 1985; The Emperor (adapted with Jonathan Miller), 1987; A Dream of People, 1990; Roberto Cossa's La Nona (translation), 1991; Unfinished Business, 1994; Calico, 2004; *for film and television:* For the West (Congo), 1963; Blue as his Eyes the Tin Helmet He Wore, 1966; The Search for the Nile (6 parts, with Derek Marlowe), 1972; The Nightcomers, 1972; Auntie Kathleen's Old Clothes, 1977; Murder Rap, 1980; Midnight at the Starlight, 1980; Michael Hastings in Brixton, 1980; Stars of the Roller State Disco, 1984; The Emperor (dir. by Jonathan Miller), 1988; Tom and Viv, 1994; adaptations for television: Absolute Hell, 1991; La Nona (also trans.), 1992; Six Characters in Search of an Author (also trans.), 1994. *Publications: plays include:* Three Plays, 1965; Three Plays, 1968; Two Plays, 1972; Tom and Viv, 1985; Three Political Plays, 1990; Unfinished Business and Other Plays, 1994; Dance of the Mexican Rattlesnake, 2003; Calico, 2004; *novels:* The Game, 1957; The Frauds, 1960; Tussy is Me, 1968; The Nightcomers, 1971; And in the Forest the Indians, 1975; *stories:* Bart's Mornings and other Tales of Modern Brazil, 1975; *libretti:* Man and Boy: Dada (opera by Michael Nyman), 2003; Love Counts (opera by Michael Nyman), 2006; *poems:* Love me Lambeth, 1959; *criticism:* Rupert Brooke, The Handsomest Young Man in England, 1967; Sir Richard Burton: a biography, 1978. *Address:* 2 Helix Gardens, Brixton Hill, SW2 2JP. *E:* 113132.624@compuserve.com. *Died 19 Nov. 2011.*

HAUPTMAN, Prof. Herbert Aaron, PhD; President, Hauptman-Woodward Medical Research Institute, Inc. (formerly Medical Foundation of Buffalo), since 1986; *b* 14 Feb. 1917; *s* of Israel Hauptman and Leah Hauptman (*née* Rosenfeld); *m* 1940, Edith Citrynell; two *d*. *Educ:* City Coll., NY (BS 1937); Columbia Univ. (MA 1939); Univ. of Maryland (PhD 1955). Census Bureau, 1940–42; Electronics Instructor, USAF, 1942–43, 1946–47; Aerology Officer, USNR, 1943–46; Naval Research Laboratory: Physicist-Mathematician, 1947–70; Rep. of Univ. of Maryland Math. Dept, 1956–70, and part-time Prof., Univ. of Maryland; Head, Mathematical Physics Br., 1965–67; Acting Supt, Math. and Inf. Scis. Div., 1967–68; Head, Applied Math. Br., Math. Div., 1968–69; Head, Math. Staff, Optical Scis Div., 1969–70; Medical Foundation of Buffalo: Head, Math. Biophysics Lab., 1970–72; Dep. Res. Dir, 1972; Exec. Vice-Pres., and Res. Dir, 1972–85; Res. Prof. of Biophysical Scis, State Univ. of NY at Buffalo, 1970–. Mem., US scientific instns. Numerous honours and awards; Hon. DSc: Maryland, 1985; City Coll. of NY, 1986; D'Youville Coll., 1989; Bar-Ilan Univ., Israel, and Columbia Univ., NY, 1990; Technical Univ. of Lodz, Poland, 1992; Queen's Univ., Kingston, Ont, 1993; Niagara Univ., 1996; Univ. of Toledo, 1999; Hon. Dr Chem., Univ. of Parma, 1989. Nobel Prize in Chemistry (with Jerome Karle), 1985. *Publications:* Solution of the Phase Problem (with J. Karle), 1953; Crystal Structure Determination, 1972; (ed) Direct Methods in Crystallography (procs 1976 Intercongress Symposium), 1978; 101 Great Ideas for Introducing Key Concepts in Mathematics, 2001; On the Beauty of Science, 2008; numerous articles on crystallography in learned jls. *Recreations:* stained glass art, swimming, hiking. *Address:* Hauptman Woodward Medical Research

Institute, 700 Ellicott Street, Buffalo, NY 14203–1196, USA. *Clubs:* Cosmos (Washington); Saturn (Buffalo). *Died 23 Oct. 2011.*

HAVEL, Václav; writer; President of Czech Republic, 1993–2003; *b* Prague, 5 Oct. 1936; *s* of Václav M. Havel and Božena Havel (*née* Vavrečková); *m* 1st, 1964, Olga Šplíchalová (*d* 1996); 2nd, 1997, Dagmar Veskrnova. *Educ:* Faculty of Economy, 1955–57 (unfinished); Drama Dept, Acad. of Arts, Prague, 1966. Chemical Lab. Technician, 1951–55; in Czechoslovak army, 1957–59; stagehand, ABC Theatre, Prague, 1959–60; Theatre on the Balustrade, Prague: stagehand, 1960–61; Asst to Artistic Dir, 1961–63; Literary Manager, 1963–68 (play, Zahradní slavnost (The Garden Party), 1963); Resident Playwright, 1968; Editl Bd, Tvář, 1965; freelance work, 1969–74; labourer, Trutnov Brewery, N Bohemia, 1974; freelance work, 1975–89; Co-Founder, Charter 77 (human rights movement), 1977, and one of its first three spokesmen; Co-Founder, Cttee for Defence of Unjustly Prosecuted (VONS), 1978; under house arrest, 1978–79; imprisoned, Oct. 1979–March 1983; Editl Bd and regular contributor, Lidové noviny, 1987–89; imprisoned, Jan.–May 1989; Co-Founder, Civic Forum, 1989; Pres. of Czech and Slovak Federal Republic, 1989–92. Chm., Young Writers, Czechoslovak Writers Assoc., 1965–69; Member: Czechoslovak Helsinki Cttee, 1989–; Czech Pen Club, 1989–. Hon. degrees from many institutions. Awards received include: Austrian State Prize for European Literature, 1969; Erasmus Prize, 1986; Olof Palme Prize, 1989; Simon Bolivar Prize, UNESCO, 1990. *Publications: plays in translation:* The Garden Party, 1969; The Increased Difficulty of Concentration, 1972; The Memorandum, 1980; Selected Plays by Václav Havel, 1991; Leaving, 2008; *others in translation:* Letters to Olga, 1988; Disturbing the Peace, 1990; Open Letters: selected writings 1965–1990, 1991; Summer Meditations, 1992; Toward a Civil Society, 1994; The Art of the Impossible, 1997; To the Castle and Back, 2008; essays in New York Rev. of Books, Granta, Index on Censorship, Independent, etc. *Died 18 Dec. 2011.*

HAWLEY, Henry Nicholas, (8th Bt *cr* 1795); *S* father, 1988, but does not use the title and his name does not appear on the Official Roll of the Baronetage. *Died 10 Jan. 2015.*

HAWORTH, His Honour Richard James; a Circuit Judge, 1993–2008; *b* 1 Dec. 1943; *s* of late Richard Arthur Haworth and Lily Haworth; *m* 1974, Jane Seren, *y d* of His Honour John Glyn Burrell, QC and of Dorothy Burrell. *Educ:* Ampleforth. Called to the Bar, Inner Temple, 1970; practised on SE Circuit, 1970–93; a Recorder, 1990–93. Mem., Inner Temple Bar Liaison Cttee, 1987–93. *Recreations:* music (modern jazz), English naive paintings, lunch. *Address:* c/o 2 Bedford Row, WC1R 4BU. *Clubs:* Ronnie Scott's; Thames Ditton Cricket. *Died 6 July 2015.*

HAWTHORN, Prof. Geoffrey Patrick; Professor of International Politics, University of Cambridge, 1998–2007, then Emeritus; Fellow, Clare Hall, Cambridge, 1982–2007, then Emeritus; *b* 28 Feb. 1941; *s* of Kathleen Mary Hawthorn (*née* Candy); *m* 1st, 1969, Ruth Legg (marr. diss. 1986); two *s*; 2nd, 1987, Gloria Carnevali; one *s*. *Educ:* Jesus Coll., Oxford (BA); London Sch. of Economics. Lectr in Sociology, Univ. of Essex, 1964–70; University of Cambridge: Lectr in Sociology, 1970–85; Reader in Sociology and Politics, 1985–98; Fellow, Churchill Coll., 1970–76. Vis. Prof. of Sociology, Harvard Univ., 1973–74, 1989–90; Vis. Mem., IAS, Princeton, 1979–80. *Publications:* The Sociology of Fertility, 1970; Enlightenment and Despair, 1976, 2nd edn 1987; (ed) Population and Development, 1977; (ed) The Standard of Living, 1987; Plausible Worlds, 1991; The Future of Asia and the Pacific, 1998; Thucydides on Politics, 2014; articles and reviews in learned jls and other periodicals. *Recreations:* ornithology, music. *Address:* 19 St Luke's Street, Cambridge CB4 3DA. *Died 31 Dec. 2015.*

HAWTHORNE, Prof. Sir William (Rede), Kt 1970; CBE 1959; MA; ScD; FRS 1955; FREng, FIMechE; Master of Churchill College, Cambridge, 1968–83; Hopkinson and ICI Professor of Applied Thermodynamics, University of Cambridge, 1951–80; Head of Department of Engineering, 1968–73; *b* 22 May 1913; *s* of William Hawthorne, MInstCE, and Elizabeth C. Hawthorne; *m* 1939, Barbara Runkle (*d* 1992), Cambridge, Massachusetts, USA; one *s* two *d*. *Educ:* Westminster Sch.; Trinity Coll., Cambridge (Hon. Fellow, 1995); Massachusetts Institute of Technology, USA. Development Engineer, Babcock & Wilcox Ltd, 1937–39; Scientific Officer, Royal Aircraft Establishment, 1940–44; seconded to Sir Frank Whittle, Power Jets, 1940–41; British Air Commission, Washington, 1944; Dep. Dir Engine Research, Min. of Supply, 1945; Massachusetts Institute of Technology: Associate Prof. of Mechanical Engineering, 1946; George Westinghouse Prof. of Mechanical Engineering, 1948–51; Jerome C. Hunsaker Prof. of Aeronautical Engineering, 1955–56; Vis. Inst. Prof., 1962–69; Mem. Corporation, 1969–74. Chairman: Home Office Scientific Adv. Council, 1967–76; Defence Scientific Adv. Council, 1969–71; Adv. Council for Energy Conservation, 1974–79; Member: Energy Commn, 1977–79; Standing Commn on Energy and the Environment, 1978–81. Director: Dracone Developments Ltd, 1958–87; Cummins Engine Co. Inc., 1974–86. Governor, Westminster Sch., 1956–76. A Vice-Pres., Royal Soc., 1969–70 and 1979–81; Mem. Council, 1968–70, 1979–81 (Royal Medal, 1982). Foreign Associate: US Nat. Acad. of Sciences, 1965; US Nat. Acad. of Engrg, 1976. Fellow, Imperial Coll., London Univ., 1983. Hon. FAIAA; Hon. FRAeS; Hon. FASME; Hon. FRSE 1983. Hon. DEng: Sheffield, 1976; Liverpool 1982; Hon. DSc: Salford, 1980; Strathclyde, 1981; Bath, 1981; Oxon, 1982; Sussex, 1984. Medal of Freedom (US), 1947. *Publications:* papers in mechanical and aeronautical journals. *Address:* Churchill College, Cambridge CB3 0DS. *Club:* Athenæum. *Died 16 Sept. 2011.*

HAYHOE, Baron *cr* 1992 (Life Peer), of Isleworth in the London Borough of Hounslow; **Bernard John Hayhoe, (Barney),** Kt 1987; PC 1985; CEng, FIMechE; Chairman, Guy's and St Thomas' NHS Trust, 1993–95; *b* 8 Aug. 1925; *s* of late Frank Stanley and Catherine Hayhoe; *m* 1962, Anne Gascoigne Thornton (*d* 2012), *o d* of Bernard William and Hilda Thornton; two *s* one *d*. *Educ:* State schools; Borough Polytechnic. Tool Room Apprentice, 1941–44; Armaments Design Dept, Ministry of Supply, 1944–54; Inspectorate of Armaments, 1954–63; Conservative Research Dept, 1965–70. Heston and Isleworth, 1970–74, MP (C) Brentford and Isleworth, 1974–92; PPS to Lord President and Leader of House of Commons, 1972–74; an additional Opposition Spokesman on Employment, 1974–79; Parly Under Sec. of State for Defence for the Army, 1979–81; Minister of State: CSD, 1981; HM Treasury, 1981–85; (Minister for Health) DHSS, 1985–86. Member: Select Cttee on Race Relations and Immigration, 1971–73; Select Cttee on Defence, 1987–92; H of C Commn, 1987–92; Public Accounts Commn, 1987–92; H of L Select Cttee on Public Service, 1997–98; Hon. Sec., 1970–71, Vice-Chm., 1974, Cons. Parly Employment Cttee; Jt Hon. Sec., 1970–73, Vice-Chm., 1973–76, Cons. Gp for Europe; Vice-Chm., Cons. Party Internat. Office, 1973–79. Mem., Trilateral Commn, 1977–79. Chm., Hansard Soc., 1990–94. Governor, Birkbeck Coll., 1976–79. Pres., Help the Hospices, 1992–98; Trustee: British Brain and Spine Foundn, 1992–2001; Foundn for Liver Res. (formerly Liver Res. Trust), 1994–2006. *Address:* 20 Wool Road, SW20 0HW. *T:* (020) 8947 0037. *Club:* Garrick. *Died 7 Sept. 2013.*

HAYWARD, Sir Anthony (William Byrd), Kt 1978; *b* 29 June 1927; *s* of Eric and Barbara Hayward; *m* 1955, Jenifer Susan McCay; two *s* two *d*. *Educ:* Stowe Sch., Buckingham; Christ Church, Oxford. Served RNVR, 1945–48. With family business in Calcutta, 1948–57; Shaw Wallace & Co. Ltd, India, 1957–78; Man. Dir, Guthrie Berhad, Singapore, 1978–81; Pres. and Chief Exec. Officer, Private Investment Co. for Asia (PICA) SA, 1982–84. Pres., Associated Chambers of Commerce and Industry of India, 1977–78. *Recreations:* golf, photography, reading. *Address:* Manwood House, Sandwich, Kent CT13 9HX. *T:* (01304) 612244. *Clubs:* Oriental; Royal St George's Golf. *Died 4 March 2011.*

HAYWARD, Sir Jack (Arnold), Kt 1986; OBE 1968; Chairman, Grand Bahama Development Co. Ltd and Freeport Commercial and Industrial Ltd, since 1976; *b* Wolverhampton, 14 June 1923; *s* of late Sir Charles

Hayward, CBE and Hilda, *d* of John and Alexandra Arnold; *m* 1948, Jean Mary Forder; two *s* one *d*. *Educ:* Northaw Prep Sch.; Stowe Sch., Buckingham. Volunteered RAF, 1941; flying training in Clewiston, Florida, USA; active service as officer pilot in SE Asia Comd, demobilised as Flt-Lt, 1946. Joined Rotary Hoes Ltd, 1947; served S Africa branch until 1950. Founded USA operations Firth Cleveland Gp of Companies, 1951; joined Grand Bahama Port Authority Ltd, Freeport, Grand Bahama Island, 1956. President: Lundy Field Soc.; Wolverhampton Wanderers FC; Vice-Pres., SS Great Britain project; Hon. Life Vice-Pres., Maritime Trust, 1971. FRGS 1989. Freeman, City of Wolverhampton, 2003; Hon. Freeman, City of Bristol, 2003. Hon. LLD Exeter, 1971; Hon. DBA Wolverhampton, 1994. Paul Harris Fellow (Rotary), 1983; William Booth Award, Salvation Army, 1987. *Recreations:* promoting British endeavours, mainly in sport; watching cricket; amateur dramatics; preserving the British landscape, keeping all things bright, beautiful and British. *Address:* Seashell Lane (PO Box F-40099), Freeport, Grand Bahama Island, Bahamas. *T:* (242) 3525165. *Clubs:* MCC (Hon. Life Mem.), Pratt's, Royal Air Force, Royal Automobile (Sen. One Hundred); Surrey CC (Hon. Life Mem.). *Died 13 Jan. 2015.*

HEAD, His Honour Adrian Herbert; a Circuit Judge, 1972–96; *b* 4 Dec. 1923; *s* of late Judge Head and Mrs Geraldine Head (*née* Pipon); *m* 1947, Ann Pamela, *d* of late John Stanning and Mrs A. C. Lewin, of Leyland and Njoro, Kenya; three *s*. *Educ:* RNC Dartmouth (invalided, polio); privately; Magdalen Coll., Oxford (BA; MA). Arden Scholar, Gray's Inn, 1947. Called to Bar, Gray's Inn, 1947 (subseq. *ad eundem* Inner Temple). Chm., Agricultural Land Tribunals (SE Region), 1971; Dep. Chm., Middlesex QS, 1971. Chm., Norfolk Lavender Ltd, and Chilvers & Son Ltd, 1958–71 (Dir, 1953–71). Mem., Law Adv. Bd, UEA, 1979–98. Tredegar Memorial Lectr, RSL, 1948. Licensed Reader, C of E, 1961. Co-founder and subseq. Sen. Trustee, Norfolk Family Conciliation Service, 1983–96; Pres., W Norfolk and Fenland, Marriage Guidance Council, then Relate, 1984–95. Hon. DCL UEA, 1987. *Publications:* (contrib.) Oxford Poetry 1942–1943, 1943; The Seven Words and The Civilian, 1946; contrib. Essays by Divers Hands, 1953; Safety Afloat (trans. from Dutch of W. Zantvoort), 1965; Consumer Credit Act Supplement to McCleary's County Court Precedents, 1979; Poems in Praise, 1982, 2nd edn 1987; Freundschaft und Andenken (Dichtung), 1989; (devised and general ed., 1985–87, consulting ed., 1987–, and contrib.) Butterworths County Court Precedents and Pleadings, 1985, later Butterworths Civil Court Precedents. *Recreations:* painting, writing, trees. *Address:* Overy Staithe, King's Lynn, Norfolk PE31 8TG. *T:* (01328) 738312; 5 Raymond Buildings, Gray's Inn, WC1R 5BP. *T:* (020) 7405 7146. *Clubs:* Jersey Soc.; Norfolk (Norwich) (Pres., 1995–96); Royal Naval Sailing Association, Cruising Association. *Died 22 Feb. 2012.*

HEALD, His Honour Thomas Routledge; a Circuit Judge (formerly County Court Judge), 1970–95; *b* 19 Aug. 1923; *s* of late John Arthur Heald and Nora Marion Heald; *m* 1950, Jean, *d* of James Campbell Henderson; two *s* one *d* (and one *d* decd). *Educ:* Merchant Taylors' Sch.; St John's Coll., Oxford (Fish Schol., 1941; BA (Jurisprudence) 1947; MA 1949). Lieut, RAC, 1943–45. Called to Bar, Middle Temple, 1948; Midland Circuit; Prosecuting Counsel to Inland Revenue (Midland Circuit), 1965–70; Deputy Chairman, QS: Lindsey, 1965–71; Notts, 1969–71; Notts designated Family Judge, 1991–96. Council of HM Circuit Judges: Asst Sec., 1980–83; Sec., 1984–85; Vice-Pres., 1986–87; Pres., 1988–89; Member: Matrimonial Rules Cttee, 1980–83; President's Cttee on Adoption, 1983–95; President's Family Cttee, 1984–93. Mem., Senate of Inns of Court, 1984–86. Chairman: Notts Children's and Families Mediation Service, 1995–2000; Notts Guardian *Ad Litem*/ Reporting Officers Panel, 1995–98. Mem. Council, Nottingham Univ., 1974–93 (Chm., Physical Recreation Adv. Cttee, 1979–85; Chm., Law Adv. Cttee, 1976–84; Chm., Estates and Buildings Cttee, 1985–89); Chm., Law Adv. Cttee, Trent Polytechnic, 1979–84. *Recreations:* golf, local history, family history. *Club:* Notts Golf. *Died 12 Oct. 2015.*

HEALEY, Baron *cr* 1992 (Life Peer), of Riddlesden in the County of West Yorkshire; **Denis Winston Healey,** CH 1979; MBE 1945; PC 1964; *b* 30 Aug. 1917; *s* of late William Healey, Keighley, Yorks; *m* 1945, Edna May Edmunds (Lady Healey, writer, *d* 2010); one *s* two *d*. *Educ:* Bradford Grammar Sch.; Balliol Coll., Oxford (Hon. Fellow, 1979). First Cl. Hons Mods 1938; Jenkyns Exhib. 1939; Harmsworth Sen. Schol., First Cl. Lit. Hum., BA 1940; MA 1945. War of 1939–45; entered Army, 1940; served N Africa, Italy. Major RE 1944 (despatches). Contested (Lab) Pudsey and Otley Div., 1945; Sec., International Dept, Labour Party, 1945–52. MP (Lab) SE Leeds, Feb. 1952–1955, Leeds E, 1955–92; Shadow Cabinet, 1959–64, 1970–74, 1979–87; Secretary of State for Defence, 1964–70; Chancellor of the Exchequer, 1974–79; opposition spokesman on Foreign and Commonwealth Affairs, 1980–87; Dep. Leader of Labour Party, 1980–83. Mem. Brit. Delegn to Commonwealth Relations Conf., Canada, 1949; British Delegate to: Consultative Assembly, Council of Europe, 1952–54; Inter Parly Union Conf., Washington, 1953; Western European Union and Council of Europe, 1953–55. Chm., IMF Interim Cttee, 1977–79. Mem. Exec. Fabian Soc., 1954–61. Mem., Labour Party Nat. Exec. Cttee, 1970–75. Councillor: RIIA, 1948–60; Inst. of Strategic Studies, 1958–61. Pres., Birkbeck Coll., 1993–99. Pres., Corelli Ensemble, 2011–. Freeman, City of Leeds, 1992. FRSL 1993. Hon. Fellow, Leeds Polytechnic, 1987. Hon. DLitt Bradford, 1983; Hon. LLD Sussex, 1991. Grand Cross of Order of Merit, Germany, 1979. *Publications:* The Curtain Falls, 1951; New Fabian Essays, 1952; Neutralism, 1955; Fabian International Essays, 1956; A Neutral Belt in Europe, 1958; NATO and American Security, 1959; The Race Against the H Bomb, 1960; Labour Britain and the World, 1963; Healey's Eye, 1980; Labour and a World Society, 1985; Beyond Nuclear Deterrence, 1986; The Time of My Life (autobiog.), 1989; When Shrimps Learn to Whistle (essays), 1990; My Secret Planet, 1992; Denis Healey's Yorkshire Dales, 1995; Healey's World, 2002. *Recreations:* travel, photography, music, painting. *Address:* Pingles Place, Alfriston, East Sussex BN26 5TT. *Died 3 Oct. 2015.*

HEALY, Bernadine P., (Mrs Floyd Loop), MD; Member, President's Council of Advisors on Science and Technology, USA, 2001–09; medical and health columnist, US News and World Report, since 2002; *b* 2 Aug. 1944; *d* of Michael J. Healy and Violet (*née* McGrath); *m* Dr George Bulkley (marr. diss. 1981); one *d*; *m* 1985, Dr Floyd Loop; one *d*. *Educ:* Vassar Coll. (AB *summa cum laude* 1965); Harvard Med. Sch. (MD *cum laude* 1970). Intern in medicine, 1970–71, asst resident, 1971–72, Johns Hopkins Hosp., Balt.; Staff Fellow, Sect. Pathology, Nat. Heart, Lung and Blood Inst., NIH, 1972–74; Johns Hopkins University School of Medicine: Fellow, Cardiovascular Div., Dept of Medicine, 1974–76; Fellow, Dept of Pathology, 1975–76; Asst Prof. of Medicine and Pathology, 1976–81; Associate Prof. of Medicine, 1977–82; Asst Dean for Postdoctoral Programs and Faculty Develt, 1979–84; Associate Prof. of Pathology, 1981–84; Prof. of Medicine, 1982–84; Active Staff, Medicine and Pathology, 1976, Dir, Coronary Care Unit, 1977–84, Johns Hopkins Hosp.; Dep. Dir, Office of Sci. and Technol. Policy, Exec. Office of Pres., White House, Washington, 1984–85; Chm., Res. Inst., Cleveland Clinic Foundn, 1985–91; Dir, NIH, 1991–93; Sen. Policy Advr, Page Center for Health and Science Policy, Cleveland Clinic Foundn, 1993–95; Dean, Coll. of Medicine, Ohio State Univ., 1995–99; Pres. and CEO, American Red Cross, 1999–2001. *Publications:* A New Prescription for Women's Health, 1996; Living Time: faith and facts to transform your cancer journey, 2007. *Died 6 Aug. 2011.*

HEALY, Prof. John Francis, MA, PhD; Professor of Classics, London University, 1966–90, then Professor Emeritus; Chairman of Department, Royal Holloway and Bedford New College, 1985–88 (Head of Department, Royal Holloway College, 1966–85); *b* 27 Aug. 1926; *s* of late John Healy and Iris Maud (*née* Cutland); *m* 1st, 1957, Carol Ann McEvoy; one *s*; 2nd, 1985, Barbara Edith Henshall. *Educ:* Trinity Coll., Cambridge (Open Exhibn in Classics 1943; Classical Prelim. Cl. 1 1944; Classical Tripos: 1st Cl. Pt I 1949, 1st Cl. Pt II 1950 (dist. Cl. Archaeol.);

Sen. Schol. 1950; BA 1950, MA 1952, PhD 1955). War service, 1944–48; Captain, Intelligence Corps, 1946–48. Walston student, Brit. Sch. of Archaeol., Athens, 1950; G. C. Winter Warr Schol., Cambridge, 1951; Manchester University: Asst Lectr in Classics, 1953–56; Lectr in Classics and Class. Archaeol., 1956–61; London University: Reader in Greek, Bedford Coll., 1961–66; Chm., Bd of Studies in Classics, 1979–81; Dean of Faculty of Arts, Royal Holloway Coll., 1978–81. Chm. Finance Cttee, Inst. of Classical Studies, London, 1967–88. FRNS 1950; FRSA 1971; MRI 1979. *Publications:* contrib. (A. Rowe) Cyrenaican Expeditions of the University of Manchester, 1955–57; Mining and Metallurgy in the Greek and Roman World, 1978, rev. and trans. edn, Miniere e Metallurgia nel Mondo Greco e Romano, 1993; Sylloge Nummorum Graecorum, vol. VII, The Raby and Güterbock collections in Manchester University Museum, 1986; Pliny the Elder, Natural History, 1991; Pliny the Elder, On Science and Technology, 1999; articles and reviews in Jl of Hellenic Studies, Numismatic Chron., Nature, Amer. Num. Soc.'s Mus. Notes, Jl of Metals, Class. Rev., Gnomon. *Recreations:* travel, music, creative gardening. *Club:* Cambridge Union Society. *Died 25 April 2012.*

HEANEY, Seamus Justin, FBA; MRIA; Professor of Poetry, Oxford University, 1989–94; Boylston Professor of Rhetoric and Oratory at Harvard University (formerly Visiting Professor), 1985–97; Ralph Waldo Emerson Poet in Residence, Harvard University, 1998–2007; *b* 13 April 1939; *s* of Patrick and Margaret Heaney; *m* 1965, Marie Devlin; two *s* one *d*. *Educ:* St Columb's College, Derry; Queen's University, Belfast (BA first cl. 1961). Teacher, St Thomas's Secondary Sch., Belfast, 1962–63; Lectr, St Joseph's Coll. of Educn, Belfast, 1963–66; Lectr, Queen's Univ., Belfast, 1966–72; free-lance writer, 1972–75; Lectr, Carysfort Coll., 1975–81. Corresp. FBA, 1999. Hon. DLitt Oxon, 1997; Hon. DLit London, 2003. Bennett Award, 1982; Nobel Prize in Literature, 1995; David Cohen Prize, Arts Council, 2009. *Publications:* Preoccupations: Selected Prose 1968–1978, 1980; The Government of the Tongue, 1988; The Cure at Troy (a version of Sophocles' Philoctetes), 1990; The Redress of Poetry, 1995; (jtly) Homage to Robert Frost, 1998; Finders Keepers: selected prose 1971–2001, 2002; *poetry:* Eleven Poems, 1965; Death of a Naturalist, 1966 (Somerset Maugham Award, 1967; Cholmondeley Award, 1968); Door into the Dark, 1969; Wintering Out, 1972; North, 1975 (W. H. Smith Award; Duff Cooper Prize); Field Work, 1979; Selected Poems, 1965–1975, 1980; (ed with Ted Hughes) The Rattle Bag, 1982; Sweeney Astray, 1984, rev. edn as Sweeney's Flight, (with photographs by Rachel Giese), 1992; Station Island, 1984; The Haw Lantern, 1987 (Whitbread Award, 1987); New Selected Poems 1966–1987, 1990; Seeing Things, 1991; The Spirit Level (Whitbread Book of the Year), 1996; (ed with Ted Hughes) The School Bag, 1997; Opened Ground: poems 1966–1996, 1998; trans., Beowulf (Whitbread Book of the Year), 1999; Electric Light, 2001; trans., The Burial at Thebes, 2004; District and Circle, 2006 (T. S. Eliot Prize, 2007); trans. The Testament of Cresseid and Seven Fables, 2009 (David Cohen Prize, John S. Cohen Foundn); Human Chain, 2010 (Forward Poetry Prize). *Address:* c/o Faber & Faber, Bloomsbury House, 74–77 Great Russell Street, WC1B 3DA. *Died 30 Aug. 2013.*

HEARNE, Peter Ambrose, FREng; Chairman, GEC Avionics, 1992–94; *b* 14 Nov. 1927; *e s* of late Arthur Ambrose Hearne, MD, and Helen Mackay Hearne; *m* 1952, Georgina Gordon Guthrie; three *s*. *Educ:* Sherborne Sch., Dorset; Loughborough Coll. of Technol. (DLC); Cranfield Inst. of Technol. (MSc); MIT. Design Engr, Saunders Roe, 1946–47; Ops Develt Engr, BOAC, 1949–54; Helicopter Proj. Engr, BEA, 1954–58; Marketing Manager, British Oxygen, 1958–59; Divl Man., Guided Weapons, Elliott Flt Automation, 1959; Asst Gen. Man., 1960, Dir and Gen. Man., 1966–87, Marconi (later GEC) Avionics; Asst Man. Dir, 1987–90, Pres., US Ops, 1990–92, GEC Marconi. Vis. Prof., Cranfield Inst. of Technol., 1981–82. Chm., Cranfield Soc., 1965–67, Pres., 1981–85; Pres., Royal Aeronautical Society, 1980–81 (Vice-Pres., 1976–79; Hon. FRAeS 1990; Wright Bros Lectr, 1991); Vice Chm., 1997–99, Vice Pres., 1999–, British Gliding Assoc. FREng (FEng 1984); FRIN 1999. John Curtis Sword, Aviation Week, 1982; Diamond C badge, 1988. *Publications:* (ed) Pilot's Summer, 2nd edn 2000; papers in Jl of RAeS and NATO Agard series. *Recreations:* flying sailplanes, model railways. *Address:* The Limes, Wateringbury, Kent ME18 5NY. *Clubs:* Royal Air Force; Surrey and Hants Gliding; Aero Alpin (Gap). *Died 24 Jan. 2014.*

HEARTH, John Dennis Miles, CBE 1983; Chief Executive, Royal Agricultural Society of England, 1972–89 and 1991–92; *b* 8 April 1929; *s* of late Cyril Howard Hearth, MC, and Dr Pauline Kathleen Hearth, MB, BCh; *m* 1959, Pamela Anne (*née* Bryant); two *s* (one *d* decd). *Educ:* The King's Sch., Canterbury; Brasenose Coll., Oxford (MA). Called to the Bar, Gray's Inn, 1962. Administrative Officer, HM Overseas Civil Service, 1953–61; Editor, Fairplay Shipping Journal, Fairplay Publications Ltd, 1961–66; Cunard Steam-Ship Co. Ltd, 1966–71 (various appts and Main Board Joint Ventures Director, 1969–71). Mem., Gen. Adv. Council, BBC, 1990–95; Chairman: Rural and Agricl Affairs Cttee, BBC, 1990–96; Nat. Rural Enterprise Centre, RASE, 1988–94; British Food and Farming Ltd, 1989–2004; Management Cttee, Nat. Fedn of Young Farmers' Clubs, 1989–95. Pres., British Pig Assoc., 1990–93. Mem. Council, Conservation Foundn, 1987–94; Dep. Chm., Rural Housing Trust (formerly NAC Rural Trust), 1992–2004 (Trustee, 1987–2004); Chm., English Villages Housing Assoc., 1995–97 (Mem., 1990–2004; Chm. Finance Cttee, 1990–97); Chm., English Rural Housing Assoc., 1999–2003 (Mem. Cttee, 1993–2003); Mem., Rural Adv. Gp, Housing Corp., 1999–2004. Governor, RAC, Cirencester, 1975–92; Mem., 1985–98, Treasurer, 1989–98, Warwick Univ. Council; Director: Univ. of Warwick Science Park Ltd, 1990–98; Warwick Univ. Trng Ltd, 1998–2004; Warwick Univ. Services Ltd, 1998–2004; Trustee, Univ. of Warwick Foundn, 2001–04. CCMI (CBIM 1980); FRSA 1989. Hon. FRASE 1989. Hon. LLD Warwick, 1999. *Recreations:* travel, history, theatre, photography, golf. *Address:* Sheen Farmhouse, Temple End, Harbury, Leamington Spa, Warwicks CV33 9NE. *T:* (01926) 612238. *Died 1 Sept. 2014.*

HEATH, Bernard Oliver, OBE 1980; CEng, FRAeS; Professor of Aeronautical Engineering (British Aerospace Integrated Chair), Salford University, 1983–89; *b* 8 March 1925; *s* of Bernard Ernest Heath and Ethel May Heath; *m* 1948, Ethel Riley; one *s*. *Educ:* Derby Sch.; Bemrose Sch., Derby; University Coll. of Nottingham (BSc Univ. of London 1944); Imperial Coll. of Science and Technology (DIC 1945). CEng 1966; FRAeS 1978. English Electric Co.: Stressman (loading and stressing of Canberra), 1945; Aerodynamicist, Lightning, 1948; Aerostructures Gp Leader (Lightning loading and aeroelasticity), 1951; Chief Proj. Engr, 1957; Asst Chief Engr, Canberra and TSR2, 1959; British Aircraft Corporation: TSR2 Proj. Manager (Develt), 1963; Special Dir, 1965; Leader, Jaguar Technical Team, 1965; Proj. Manager, AFVG, 1966; Panavia: Dir, Systems Engrg (Warton), 1969–81; Dir, MRCA, 1970; Dir of Engrg, 1974; British Aerospace: Technical Dir, Warton Div., 1978–81; Divisional Dir of Advanced Engrg, 1981–84. Chm., SBAC Technical Bd, 1980–82. Hon. MIED 1975. RAeS Silver Medal (for outstanding work over many yrs on design and develt of mil. aircraft), 1977; (jtly) Internat. Council of Aeronautical Sciences Von Karman Award (for successful internat. co-operation on Tornado), 1982; Corresp. Mem., Deutsche Ges. für Luft und Raumfahrt, 1993. *Publications:* papers to AGARD, Internat. Council of Aeronautical Sciences Congresses, RAF Histl Soc.; contrib. RAeS Jl, Flight, The Times, R & D Mgt and Aircraft Engrg. *Recreation:* history of transport. *Address:* c/o Company Secretary, BAE Systems, Warton Aerodrome, Preston, Lancs PR4 1AX. *Died 11 Aug. 2014.*

HEATHCOTE, Brig. Sir Gilbert (Simon), 9th Bt *cr* 1733; CBE 1964 (MBE 1945); *b* 21 Sept. 1913; *s* of Col R. E. M. Heathcote, DSO (*d* 1970), Manton Hall, Rutland, and Millicent Heathcote (*d* 1977), *d* of William Walton, Horsley Priory, Nailsworth, Glos; *S* to baronetcy of 3rd Earl of Ancaster, KCVO, 1983; *m* lst, 1939, Patricia Margaret (*née* Leslie) (marr. diss. 1984); one *s* one *d*; 2nd, 1984, Ann, *widow* of Brig. J. F. C. Mellor, DSO, OBE. *Educ:* Eton; RMA Woolwich. Commnd RA, 1933, War Service in Europe, 1939–44; Comdr RA, 1960–62; Chief of Staff, Middle East Comd, 1962–64; retd. *Recreations:* writing, travel. *Heir: s* Mark Simon Robert Heathcote, OBE [*b* 1 March 1941; *m* 1975, Susan, *d* of late Lt-Col George Ashley; two *s*]. *Address:* The Coach House, Tillington, near Petworth, Sussex GU28 0RA. *Clubs:* Garrick, Army and Navy. *Died 15 April 2014.*

HEATHER, Stanley Frank, CBE 1980; Comptroller and City Solicitor, City of London Corporation, 1974–80; Attorney and General Counsel, City of London (Arizona) Corporation, 1974–81; *b* 8 Jan. 1917; *s* of Charles and Jessie Heather; *m* 1946, Janet Roxburgh Adams (*d* 1989), Perth; one *s* one *d*. *Educ:* Downhills Sch.; London Univ. Commnd Reconnaissance Corps, RAC, 1941; India/Burma Campaign, 1942–45. Admitted Solicitor, 1959. Asst Solicitor, City of London, 1963; Dep. Comptroller and City Solicitor, 1968. Captain, Sussex Professional Golfers' Union, 1985–86; Patron, Southern Reg., PGA. Freeman, City of London, 1964; Liveryman, Solicitors' Co., 1965–; Hon. Liveryman: Clothworkers' Co., Engineers' Co., 1983; Scriveners' Co., 1993; Hon. Freeman, Water Conservators' Co., 1995. FRSA 1981. *Recreations:* golf, fishing. *Clubs:* City Livery, Guildhall. *Died 28 Aug. 2015.*

HEATLY, Sir Peter, Kt 1990; CBE 1971; DL; Chairman, Commonwealth Games Federation, 1982–90; *b* Leith, 9 June 1924; *s* of Robert Heatly and Margaret Ann Heatly; *m* 1st, 1948, Jean Robertha Hermiston (*d* 1979); one *s* two *d* (and one *s* decd); 2nd, 1984, Mae Calder Cochrane (*d* 2003). *Educ:* Leith Academy; Edinburgh Univ. (BSc). CEng, FICE. Civil Engr, Naval Dockyard, Rosyth. Scottish Diving Champion, 1946–58; Mem., GB team, Olympic Games, London, 1948; British Empire Games, later British Empire and Commonwealth Games: Gold Medal, 10m high board, Silver Medal, 3m springboard, Auckland, 1950; Gold Medal, 3m springboard, Bronze Medal, 10m highboard, Vancouver, 1954; Gold Medal, 10m highboard, Cardiff, 1958. Dir, Peter Heatly & Co. Ltd, 1958–96. Chm., Scottish Sports Council, 1975–87. DL City of Edinburgh, 1984. Dr *hc* Edinburgh, 1992; Hon. DLitt Queen Margaret Coll., 1994; DUniv Stirling, 1998. *Recreation:* swimming. *Died 17 Sept. 2015.*

HEATON-WARD, Dr (William) Alan, FRCPsych; Lord Chancellor's Medical Visitor, 1978–89; *b* 19 Dec. 1919; *s* of Ralph Heaton-Ward, MA, and Mabel Orton; *m* 1st, 1945, Christine Edith Fraser (marr. diss. 2005; she *d* 2010); two *d*; 2nd, 2006, Betty Edgar. *Educ:* Sefton Park Jun. Sch.; Queen Elizabeth's Hosp., Bristol; Univ. of Bristol Med. Sch. MB, ChB, 1944; DPM 1948; Foundn FRCPsych 1971. Jun. Clerk, Messrs W. D. & H. O. Wills, 1936–38; House Phys., Bristol Royal Inf., 1944–45; MO, Littlemore Mental Hosp., 1945–46; served RNVR, 1946–48: Surg. Lt-Comdr; Neuropsychiatrist, Nore Comd; Sen. Registrar, St James Hosp., Portsmouth, 1948–50; Dep. Med. Supt, Hortham Brentry Gp, 1950–54; Stoke Park Hosp. Group: Consultant Psych., 1954–78, Hon. Consultant Psych., 1978–; Med. Supt, 1954–61; Cons. Psych. i/c, 1963–74; Clinical Teacher in Mental Health, Univ. of Bristol, 1954–78; Cons. Psych., Glos Royal Hosp., 1962–67. Mem., SW Mental Health Review Tribunal, 1960–78, 1985–92. Hon. Cons. Adviser: NAMH, 1966–73; CARE, 1970–78; British Council Vis. Lectr, Portugal, 1971. Royal Coll. of Psychiatrists: Vice Pres., 1976–78; Blake Marsh Lectr, 1976; Burden Res. Gold Medal and Prize Winner, 1978; José Jancar Meml Lectr, 2003. Pres., Brit. Soc. for Study of Mental Subnormality, 1978–79; Vice-President: Fortune Centre of Riding Therapy, 1980–; RESCARE, Nat. Soc. for Mentally Handicapped People in Residential Care, 1995–2005; Avon Riding Centre for the Disabled, 1997–; Mem. Council, Inst. of Mental Subnormality, 1972–76; Hon. Mem., Amer. Assoc. of Physician Analysts, 1976–. Mem., Adv. Council, Radio Bristol, 1985–88. *Publications:* Notes on Mental Deficiency (jtly), 1952, 3rd edn 1955; Mental Subnormality, 1960, 5th edn, (jtly) as Mental Handicap, 1984; Left Behind, 1977; papers on all aspects of care and treatment of mentally handicapped people and on gen. psychiatric topics; book revs. *Recreations:* following all forms of outdoor sport, gardening, seeking the sun, philately, asking Why? *Address:* Bala Netty, 27 Withey Close West, Westbury on Trym, Bristol BS9 3SX. *T:* (0117) 968 1940. *Died 2 June 2011.*

HECK, Prof. Richard Fred, PhD; Willis F. Harrington Professor, University of Delaware, until 1989, then Professor Emeritus; *b* Springfield, Mass, 15 Aug. 1931; *m* 1979, Socorro (*d* 2012). *Educ:* Univ. of Calif, Los Angeles (BS Chem. 1952; PhD 1954). Nat. Sci. Foundn Postdoctoral Fellow, Federal Inst. of Technol., Zurich, 1954–55; UCLA, 1955–56; Hercules Powder Co., Wilmington, Delaware, 1956–71; Univ. of Delaware, 1971–89. Vis. Prof., Queen's Univ., Canada, 2006. Hon. Dr Uppsala, 2010. Wallace H. Carothers Award, 2005, Herbert C. Brown Award, 2006, Amer. Chemical Soc.; (jtly) Nobel Prize in Chemistry, 2010. *Publications:* over 200 scientific papers. *Address:* c/o Department of Chemistry and Biochemistry, University of Delaware, Newark, DE 19716, USA. *Died 10 Oct. 2015.*

HEDGER, Eric Frank, CB 1979; OBE 1960; Under Secretary, Director General of Defence Contracts, Ministry of Defence, 1969–80; *b* 15 Sept. 1919; *s* of late Albert Frank Hedger and Ellen Agnes Hedger (*née* Laffey); *m* 1945, Joan Kathleen Bernas (*d* 2005); two *s* one *d*. *Educ:* St Luke's, Southsea. War Service, 1939–46 (despatches 1945): Adjutant, 10 Air Formation Signals; Adjutant, then 2nd i/c, 7 Indian Air Formation Signals. Secretary, Admiralty Awards Council, 1946–49; Admin. Staff Coll., 1958; Dir of Navy Contracts, 1968. Mem. of Council and Bd of Management, Inst. of Purchasing and Supply, 1974–75. Advr, Defence Manufacturers Assoc., 1983–88. FInstPS. *Recreations:* music, reading. *Address:* Helere House, Ridgeway Mead, Sidmouth, Devon EX10 9DT. *T:* (01395) 577741. *Died 4 June 2012.*

HEDLEY, Prof. Ronald; Director, Trent Polytechnic, Nottingham, 1970–80, Emeritus Professor, 1980; *b* 12 Sept. 1917; *s* of Francis Hedley, Hebburn, Co. Durham; *m* 1942, Audrey (*d* 2008); one *s* one *d*. *Educ:* Jarrow Grammar Sch.; Durham Univ. (MA, DipEd); Ecole Normale d'Instituteurs, Evreux. Various appts in teaching and educational administration, 1947–64; Dep. Dir of Education, Nottingham, 1964–70. Chm., Regional Acad. Bd, Regional Adv. Council for Further Educn in E Midlands, 1972–76; Member: Central Council for Educn and Trng in Social Work, 1971–77; Nat. Adv. Council for Educn for Ind. and Commerce, 1973–77; Central Council for Educn and Trng of Health Visitors, 1972–77; Cttee for Arts and Social Studies, CNAA, 1974–76; Personal Social Services Council, 1974–78; Cttee on Recreation Management Training, 1977–80; Local Govt Trng Bd, 1978–81; Adv. Cttee for Supply and Educn of Teachers, 1980–81, Chm., Local Cttee for Teacher Educn, King Alfred's Coll., Winchester, 1986–89. FRSA 1970. Hon. Fellow: Trent Polytechnic, 1980; Nottingham Trent, 1992. Hon. Senator, Fachhochschule, Karlsruhe, Germany, 1980. Hon. LLD Nottingham, 1981; DUniv Nottingham Trent, 1993. *Address:* The Cedar House, Avington, Winchester, Hants SO21 1DE. *T:* (01962) 791177. *Died 27 April 2013.*

HELE, James Warwick, CBE 1986; High Master of St Paul's School 1973–86; *b* 24 July 1926; *s* of John Warwick Hele, Carlisle; *m* 1948, Audrey Whalley; four *d*. *Educ:* Sedbergh Sch.; Hertford Coll., Oxford; Trinity Hall, Cambridge (Schol., MA). 1st cl. hons History Tripos 1951. 5th Royal Inniskilling Dragoon Guards, 1946–48. Asst Master, Kings College Sch., Wimbledon, 1951–55; Rugby School: Asst Master, 1955–73; Housemaster, Kilbracken, 1965–73; 2nd Master, 1970–73. Chairman: Headmasters' Conference, 1982 (Chm., Acad. Cttee, 1979–81); Ind. Schs Adv. Cttee, 1983–88; Member: Secondary Exams Council, 1986–88; Exec. Cttee, GBA, 1988–97. Chairman: Westminster Centre for Educn, 1991–97; Combined Trusts Scholarship Trust, 1986–2003. Mem., Dorset FHSA, 1990–92. Trustee, Brathay Hall, 1977–91. Governor: Rossall Sch., 1985–90; Uppingham Sch., 1986–92; Port Regis Sch., Shaftesbury, 1986–2001; Sherborne Sch., 1986–96 (Chm. Govs, 1990–96); Chm., Clouds House, East Knoyle, 1992–2000. *Recreations:* Rugby football (Oxford Univ. XV 1944), hill walking. *Address:* 2 John Wood House, Cathedral Views, Crane Bridge Road, Salisbury, Wilts SP2 7TW. *T:* (01722) 322690. *Clubs:* East India, Devonshire, Sports and Public Schools. *Died 4 Aug. 2011.*

HELLIER, Maj.-Gen. Eric James, CBE 1977 (OBE 1970; MBE 1967); Regional Manager, International Military Services, 1981–92; *b* 23 July 1927; *s* of Harry and Elizabeth Hellier; *m* 1952, Margaret Elizabeth Leadeham; one *s* one *d* (and one *s* decd). *Educ:* Hugh Saxons Sch.; Cardiff Univ. Served, 1945–66: Exec. Officer, RNVR; regtl duty, Royal Signals; Staff Coll. and Jt Services Staff Coll.; GSO2 WO; DAA&QMG 39 Inf. Bde; CO, 24 Signals Regt, 1967–69; GSO1 Plans (Operational Requirements) MoD, 1970; Col A/Q HQ 4 Div., 1971–72; Comd Bde Royal Signals and Catterick Garrison, 1973–74; RCDS, 1975; Brig A/Q HQ 1(BR), Corps, 1976–79; Maj. Gen. Admin, UKLF, 1979–81. Col Comdt, 1981–87, Rep. Col Comdt, 1983, Royal Corps of Signals. Chairman: Gen. Purposes Cttee, Regular Forces Employment Assoc., 1983–91; Royal Signals Instn, 1984–89; Fund Raising Cttee, Nat. Mus. of Army Communications, 1991–97; Trustee, Royal Signals Mus., 1998–2005. *Recreations:* golf, gardening. *Address:* Goddards, 27 Church Street, Wherwell, Hants SP11 7JJ. *T:* (01264) 860710. *Died 31 Oct. 2011.*

HEMINGWAY, Peter, FCA; Director and Chief General Manager, Leeds Permanent Building Society, 1982–87; *b* 19 Jan. 1926; *s* of William Edward and Florence Hemingway; *m* 1952, June Maureen, *d* of Maurice and Lilian A. Senior. *Educ:* Leeds College of Commerce. With John Gordon, Walton & Co., Chartered Accountants, Leeds, 1941–62, Partner 1959–62; Director, Provincial Registrars Ltd, 1955–62; joined Leeds Permanent Bldg Soc. as Secretary, 1962. Local Dir (Leeds), Royal Insurance (UK) Ltd, 1983–93; Dir, Homeowners Friendly Soc., 1983–86. Hon. Sec. 1970–82, Vice-Chm. 1982–84, Chm. 1984–86, Yorkshire and North Western Assoc. of Building Societies; Vice Pres., Northern Assoc. of Building Socs, 1988–96; Mem. Council: Building Societies Assoc., 1981–87; Chartered Building Societies Inst., 1982–87. *Recreations:* travel, motor racing, music, gardening. *Address:* Old Barn Cottage, Kearby, near Wetherby, Yorks LS22 4BU. *T:* (0113) 288 6380. *Died 21 Aug. 2013.*

HEMPHILL, 5th Baron *cr* 1906, of Rathkenny and Cashel; **Peter Patrick Fitzroy Martyn Martyn-Hemphill;** *b* 5 Sept. 1928; *o s* of 4th Baron Hemphill and Emily, *d* of F. Irving Sears, Webster, Mass; *S* father, 1957; *m* 1952, Olivia Anne, *er d* of Major Robert Francis Ruttledge, MC, Cloonee, Ballinrobe, County Mayo; one *s* two *d*; assumed surname of Martyn in addition to Hemphill, 1959. *Educ:* Downside; Brasenose Coll., Oxford (MA Jurisp.). Sen. Steward, Irish Turf Club, 1985–88; Steward, Irish Nat. Hunt Steeplechase Cttee, 1973–76 and 1978–81. Chm., Galway Race Cttee, 1991–97. Jt Master, County Galway Hunt, 1957–60, 1967–69, 1972–85. *Heir: s* Hon. Charles Andrew Martyn Martyn-Hemphill [*b* 8 Oct. 1954; *m* 1985, Sarah J. F., *e d* of Richard Lumley; two *s* three *d*]. *Address:* Dunkellin, Kiltulla, Co. Galway, Eire. *E:* hemphill@eircom.net. *Died 6 April 2012.*

HEMSLEY, Thomas Jeffrey, CBE 2000; free-lance opera and concert singer; Professor: Guildhall School of Music and Drama, 1987–2004; Trinity College of Music, 1988–93; *b* 12 April 1927; *s* of Sydney William Hemsley and Kathleen Annie Hemsley (*née* Deacon); *m* 1960, Hon. Gwenllian Ellen James, *d* of 4th Baron Northbourne; three *s*. *Educ:* Ashby de la Zouch Grammar Sch.; Brasenose Coll., Oxford (MA). Vicar Choral, St Paul's Cathedral, 1950–51; Prin. Baritone, Stadttheater, Aachen, 1953–56; Deutsche Oper am Rhein, 1957–63; Opernhaus, Zurich, 1963–67; Glyndebourne, Bayreuth, Edinburgh Festivals, etc. Dir of Opera, Dartington Internat. Summer Sch., 1988–. Vis. Prof., RCM, 1986; Guest Prof., Royal Danish Acad. of Music, 1990–91. Mem., Roy. Philharmonic Soc., 1968–. Recordings of operas, lieder and melodies. FGS (FGSM 1996); Hon. RAM 1974; Hon. FTCL 1988. FRSA 1991. *Publications:* Singing & Imagination, 1998. *Address:* 10 Denewood Road, N6 4AJ. *T:* (020) 8348 3397. *Club:* Garrick. *Died 11 April 2013.*

HENDERSON, Derek, FDSRCS; Senior Consultant Oral and Maxillo-facial Surgeon, St Thomas' Hospital, 1975–93; Consultant, St George's Hospital, 1975–86; Emeritus Consultant in Oral and Maxillo-facial Surgery, Guy's and St Thomas' Hospital NHS Trust, since 1993; *b* 9 April 1935; *s* of Robert Henderson and Dorothy Edith Henderson; *m* 1961, Jennifer Jill Anderson; one *s* one *d*. *Educ:* Dulwich Coll.; London Univ. (BDS Hons 1956, MB, BS Hons 1963). FDSRCS (Eng) 1960 (LDS 1956); MRCS, LRCP 1963. Dental and med. trng, KCH, London, 1952–56 and 1959–63 (Prizeman); house surg. appts, KCH and Royal Dental Hosp., 1956–59; King's Coll. Hospital: Lectr in Dental Materials, 1958–65; ENT House Officer, and Casualty Off., 1964; Registrar in Oral Surg., Queen Mary's Hosp., Roehampton, and Westminster Hosp., 1965; Sen. Registrar in Oral Surg., United Cardiff Hosps, 1965–67; Consultant Oral Surgeon to Eastern Reg. Hosp. Bd, Scotland, and Dundee Dental Hosp., 1967–69 (Hon. Sen. Lectr, Univ. of Dundee); Consultant i/c Reg. Maxillo-facial Service to Glasgow and West of Scotland, based on Canniesburn Plastic and Oral Surg. Unit, Glasgow, 1969–75 (Hon. Clinical Teacher, Glasgow Univ.); Consultant, Royal Dental Hosp., 1975–85. Recognised Teacher, London Univ., 1977–93; Hon. Consultant, Charing Cross Hosp., 1977–93; Hon. Civilian Consultant: Queen Elizabeth Mil. Hosp., Woolwich (formerly Queen Alexandra Mil. Hosp., Millbank), 1976–81; in Oral Surgery, RN, 1971–93, Army, 1981–93; Hon. Sen. Lectr in Oral Surg., Royal Dental Sch., London, 1977–85. Vis. Prof. and Lectr, Brazil, Argentina, Chile, USA, Spain, Venezuela, Australia, Holland, Saudi Arabia, Uruguay, Italy, SA, NZ. Mem. Senate, Royal Surgical Colls of GB and Ire., 1993–96; Royal College of Surgeons: Hunterian Prof., 1975–76; Mem. Council, 1984–86 (Collyer Gold Medal, 1995); Kelsey Fry Adviser in Postgraduate Educnl Trng, 1975–80, Mem. Bd, 1978–86, Mem. Exec. Cttee, 1983–86, and Vice-Dean, 1984–85, Faculty of Dental Surgery (also Examr, FDSRCS). Member: Central Cttee for Hospital Dental Services, 1978–85 (Mem. Exec. Cttee, 1980–85); Central Cttee for Univ. Dental Teachers and Research Workers, 1978–81; Negotiating Subcttee, CCHMS, 1980–85; European Assoc. for Maxillo-Facial Surg.; BMA; Craniofacial Soc. (Mem. Council, 1973–77); Oral Surgery Club GB (Pres., 1992–93). Fellow: BAOMS (Pres., 1994–95; Mem. Council, 1974–76, 1977–80, 1984–86; Downs Prize, 1992). Internat. Assoc. of Oral Surgeons. Hon. Mem., Amer. Assoc. of Oral Surgeons in Europe; Hon. Associate Life Mem., Soc. of Maxillo-facial and Oral Surgeons of SA; Hon. Pres., Inst. of Maxillo-Facial Technol., 1977–78. *Publications:* An Atlas and Textbook of Orthognathic Surgery, 1985 (Astra Prize, Soc. of Authors, 1986); contribs on general oral surgery to British Jl of Oral Surgery and British Dental Jl, and especially on surgery of facial and jaw deformity to Brit. Jl of Oral Surg. and Brit. Jl of Plastic Surg. *Recreation:* fly fishing. *Address:* La Soleille, Route de Beaulieu, Beynat 19190, France. *Club:* Royal Navy Medical. *Died 9 March 2013.*

HENDERSON, Robert Ewart; QC (Scot.) 1982; *b* 29 March 1937; *s* of William Ewart Henderson and Agnes Ker Henderson; *m* 1st, 1958, Olga Sunter (marr. diss. 1978); one *s* two *d*; 2nd, 1982, Carol Black (marr. diss. 1988); one *s*; 3rd, 1995, Carolyn Gell. *Educ:* Larchfield Sch., Helensburgh; Morrison's Acad., Crieff; Glasgow Univ. (BL 1962). Admitted to Faculty of Advocates, 1963. National Service, 2nd Lieut RA, 1956–58. Hon. Sheriff-Substitute, Stirling, Dunbarton and Clackmannan, 1968; Standing Jun. Counsel in Scotland, DTI, 1970–74, Dept of Trade, 1974–77; Temp. Sheriff, 1978. Pres., Glasgow Univ. Law Soc., 1961–62; Chairman: NHS Appeal Tribunal, 1972; Medical Appeal Tribunal (Scotland), 1985–93; War Pensions Appeal Tribunal, 1986–2004. Contested (C) Inverness-shire, Feb. and Oct. 1974. *Recreations:* golf, sailing. *Address:* Chateau de Surimeau, Le Logis de Surimeau, 79000 Niort, France. *T:* (549) 793821. *E:* roberthqc@gmail.com. *Clubs:* New (Edinburgh); Hon. Company of Edinburgh Golfers (Muirfield); Royal St George's Golf (Sandwich). *Died 9 Dec. 2012.*

HENDRY, Prof. Arnold William; Professor of Civil Engineering, University of Edinburgh, 1964–88, then Emeritus; *b* 10 Sept. 1921; *s* of late Dr George Hendry, MB, ChB, Buckie, Scotland; *m* 1st, 1946, Sheila Mary Cameron Roberts (*d* 1966), Glasgow; one *d* (two *s* decd); 2nd, 1968, Elizabeth Lois Alice Inglis (*d* 2003), Edinburgh. *Educ:* Buckie High Sch.; Aberdeen Univ. Civil engineer with Sir William Arrol & Co. Ltd, Bridge builders and Engineers, Glasgow, 1941–43; Asst in Engineering, University of

Aberdeen, 1943–46; Lecturer in Civil Engineering, 1946–49; Reader in Civil Engineering, Univ. of London, King's Coll., 1949–51; Prof. of Civil Engrg and Dean of Fac. of Engrg, Univ. of Khartoum, 1951–57; Prof. of Building Science, University of Liverpool, 1957–63. *Publications:* An Introduction to Photo-Elastic Analysis, 1948; (with L. G. Jaeger) The Analysis of Grid Frameworks, 1958; The Elements of Experimental Stress Analysis, 1964, 2nd edn 1977; Structural Brickwork, 1981; An Introduction to the Design of Load Bearing Brickwork, 1981; Structural Masonry, 1990, 2nd edn 1998; (ed) Reinforced and Prestressed Masonry, 1991; (with B. P. Sinha and S. R. Davies) Design of Masonry Structures, 1997; (with F. M. Khalaf) Masonry Wall Construction, 2000; A Career in Ivory Towers, 2001; The Edinburgh Transport Saga, 2002; over 150 papers and articles in professional and technical jls. *Recreations:* walking, reading. *Address:* Apartment 44 Regents Court, 29 Park Road West, Southport, Merseyside PR9 0JU. *Died 14 Dec. 2013.*

HENLEY, Rt Rev. Michael Harry George, CB 1991; Bishop of St Andrews, Dunkeld and Dunblane, 1995–2004; *b* 16 Jan. 1938; *s* of Eric Edward Henley and Evelyn Agnes Henley (*née* Lilly); *m* 1965, Rachel Jean (*née* Allen) (*d* 2013); two *d. Educ:* St Marylebone Grammar Sch.; St John's Hall, London (LTh). Ordained deacon, 1961, priest, 1962; Curate, St Marylebone Parish Ch, 1961–64; Chaplain: RN, 1964–68; St Andrews Univ., 1968–72; Royal Hosp. Sch., 1972–74; RN, 1974–93 (Chaplain of the Fleet, Archdeacon for RN and Dir Gen. Naval Chaplaincy Services, 1989–93; Archdeacon Emeritus of the Fleet); Priest i/c, Holy Trinity, Pitlochry, 1994–95. Hon. Canon, Holy Trinity Cathedral, Gibraltar, 1989–93. QHC 1989–93. *Recreations:* golf, fishing. *Address:* West Chattan, Mavis Haugh, 108 Hepburn Gardens, St Andrews, Fife KY16 9LT. *Clubs:* Army and Navy; Royal and Ancient Golf (St Andrews) (Hon. Chaplain, 2006–). *Died 21 March 2014.*

HENRY, Sir Geoffrey (Arama), KBE 1992; Deputy Prime Minister, Cook Islands, 2002 and 2004–05 (Prime Minister, 1983, and 1989–99); President, Cook Islands Sports and National Olympic Committee, since 2009; *b* Aitutaki, Cook Is, 16 Nov. 1940; *s* of Arama Henry and Mata Uritaua; *m* 1965, Louisa Olga Hoff; three *s* two *d* (and one *s* decd). *Educ:* St George's Prep. Sch., Wanganui, NZ; Wanganui Collegiate Sch.; Victoria Univ., Wellington, NZ (BA English and Educn). School Teacher, 1965–67; entered politics, 1965–68; public service, 1970–72; returned to politics, and Cabinet Minister, 1972–78; Leader of Opposition, 1978–83, 1983–84; Dep. Prime Minister in Coalition Govt, 1984; Leader of Opposition, 1985–89, 1999–2002, 2003–04. Chm., Standing Cttee, Pacific Is Develt Prog. (EWC), 1989; Organiser, Jt Commercial Commn, USA and Pacific Is, 1990; Chm., Econ. Summit of Small Island States, 1992. Chancellor, Univ. of S Pacific, 1992. Chambellan de l'Ordre des Coteaux de Champagne, 1991. Silver Jubilee Medal, 1977; NZ Commemoration Medal, 1990. *Recreations:* golf, Rugby, Rugby league, other sports, reading, music. *Address:* PO Box 281, Rarotonga, Cook Islands. *Clubs:* Rarotonga Golf, Rarotonga Bowling, Rarotonga Fishing, Lions, Rarotonga (Cook Islands). *Died 9 May 2012.*

HENZE, Hans Werner; composer; Professor of Composition, Royal Academy of Music, 1987–91; *b* 1 July 1926; *s* of Franz Gebhard Henze and Margarete Geldmacher. *Educ:* Bünde i/W; Bielefeld i/W; Braunschweig. Studied music in Heidelberg, 1945; first work performed (Chamber Concerto), at Darmstadt-Kranichstein, 1946; Artistic Dir of Ballet, Hessian States Theatre, Wiesbaden, 1950; Prof. of Composition, Acad. Mozarteum, Salzburg, 1962–67. Definite departure for Italy; Artistic Director: Internat. Art Workshop, Montepulciano, Tuscany, 1976–80, 1989–; Philharmonic Acad., Rome, 1981–82; Munich Biennale, Internat. Fest. of New Music Theatre, 1988, 1990, 1992, 1994, 1996; Prof. of Composition, Hochschule für Musik, Cologne, 1980–91; Composer-in-Residence, Berlin Philharmonic Orchestra, 1991–92. Member: German Acad. of Arts, Berlin; Philharmonic Acad., Rome; Acad. Scientiarum et Artium Europaea, Salzburg, 1992. Hon. Member: Deutsche Oper, Berlin, 1982; AAIL, 1982; Internat. Soc. for New Music, 1991; Nat. Acad. of Santa Cecilia, Rome, 1995. Hon. FRNCM 1998. Hon. DMus: Edinburgh, 1970; Univ. of Osnabrück, 1996; RCM, 2010. Robert Schumann Prize, 1951; Prix d'Italia, 1953; Nordrhein-Westfalen Award, 1957; Berlin Prize of Artists, 1959; Great Prize for Artists, Hanover, 1961; Louis Spohr Prize, Brunswick, 1976; Bach Prize, Hamburg, 1983; Siemens Prize, 1990; Duisburg Music Award, Köhler Osbahr Foundn, 1995; Special Cultural Award, Munich, 1996; Annette von Droste Hülshoff Prize, Landschaftsverband Westfalen-Lippe, 1996; Hans von Bülow Medal, Berlin Philharmonic Orch., 1997; Bavarian Order of Maximilian for Science and Art, 1998. Grand Cross, Order of Merit (Germany), 1991. *Compositions:* 10 symphonies; 14 full length operas, 3 one-act operas, 1 children's opera, 2 radio-operas; ballets; chamber music; choral works; concerti for piano, violin, viola, violoncello, double bass, oboe, clarinet, trumpet, guitar and harp; various symphonic works; song cycle; music theatre works incl. The Magic Theatre, Boulevard Solitude, The Prince of Homburg, Elegy for Young Lovers, The Bassarids, The Young Lord, Natascha Ungeheuer, Moralities, La Cubana, Das Verratene Meer, Venus and Adonis; L'Upopa and the Triumph of Filial Love (opera), 2003; Phaedre (opera), 2007. *Publications:* Undine, Diary of a Ballet, 1959; Essays, 1964; (with H. Enzenberger) El Cimarrón: ein Werkstattbericht, 1971; Musik und Politik, 1975, 1984; Neue Aspekte der musikalischen Ästhetik: vol. I, Zwischen den Kulturen, 1979; vol. II, Die Zeichen, 1981; vol. III, Lehrgänge, 1986; vol. IV, Chiffren, 1990; vol. V, Musik und Mythos, 1997; The English Cat, 1983; Reiselieder mit böhmischen Quinten (autobiog.), 1996 (trans. English as Bohemian Fifths, 1998); Komponieren in der Schule, 1998. *Address:* Schott Musik International, Weihergarten 5, 55116 Mainz, Germany; Chester Music, 14–15 Berners Street, W1T 3LJ. *Died 27 Oct. 2012.*

HEPBURN, John William; Director of Establishments, Ministry of Agriculture, Fisheries and Food, 1996–98; *b* 8 Sept. 1938; *s* of late Dugald S. Hepburn and Margarita R. Hepburn; *m* 1972, Isla Marchbank (*d* 2006); one *s. Educ:* Hutchesons' Grammar Sch.; Glasgow Univ. (MA); Brasenose Coll., Oxford. Assistant Principal, 1961, Principal, 1966, MAFF; First Secretary, UK Delegn to European Communities, Brussels, 1969–71; Private Sec. to Minister of Agriculture, Fisheries and Food, 1971–73; Asst Sec., 1973–81, Under Sec., 1982–96, MAFF. *Recreation:* golf. *Died 10 Dec. 2014.*

HEPPLE, Prof. Sir Bob Alexander, Kt 2004; FBA 2003; Master of Clare College, Cambridge, 1993–2003, then Emeritus; Professor of Law, University of Cambridge, 1995–2001, then Emeritus; Judge, UN Administrative Tribunal, 2007–09 (Senior Vice-President, 2009); *b* 11 Aug. 1934; *s* of late Alexander Hepple and Josephine Zwarenstein; *m* 1st, 1960, Shirley Goldsmith (marr. diss. 1993); one *s* one *d*; 2nd, 1994, Mary Winifred Coussey (CBE 2007). *Educ:* Univ. of Witwatersrand (BA 1954, LLB *cum laude* 1957); Univ. of Cambridge (LLB 1966; MA 1969; LLD 1993). Attorney, S Africa, 1958; Lectr in Law, Univ. of Witwatersrand, 1959–62; Advocate, S Africa, 1962–63. Left S Africa after detention without trial for anti-apartheid activities, 1963. Called to Bar, Gray's Inn, 1966, Bencher, 1996; Lectr in Law, Nottingham Univ., 1966–68; Fellow of Clare Coll., Cambridge and Univ. Lectr in Law, 1968–76; Prof. of Comparative Social and Labour Law, Univ. of Kent, 1976–77 (Hon. Prof., 1978–83); Prof. of English Law, 1982–93, Dean of Faculty of Laws and Head of Dept of Laws, 1989–93, UCL; Chm., Cttee of Heads of Univ. Law Schs, 1992–93. Chairman: Industrial Tribunals (England and Wales), pt-time 1975–77 and 1982–93, full-time 1977–82; Cttee, Justice Report on Industrial Tribunals, 1987. Member: Judicial Studies Bd (Tribunals Cttee), 1988–93; Lord Chancellor's Adv. Cttee on Legal Educn and Conduct, 1994–99; Commn on Future of Multi-Ethnic Britain, 1998–2000; Legal Services Consultative Panel, 2000–01; Mem., Nuffield Council on Bioethics, 2000–07 (Chm., 2003–07); Chm., Appointing Authy for Phase 1 Ethics Cttees, 2007–09. Mem., CRE, 1986–90. Chairman: Univ. of Cambridge Local Exams Syndicate, 1994–98; Septemviri, Univ. of Cambridge, 1995–98; Managers, Smuts Fund, Cambridge, 1995–2003. Expert consultant to EC Commn, 1974–, and to ILO, 1990–; Advr to Russian Fedn, 1992, to S African Govt, 1994–96. Trustee, Canon Collins Educnl Trust for SA,

1990–2007. Chairman: European Roma Rights Centre, 2001–07; Equal Rights Trust, 2006–14 (Hon. Pres., 2014–); Mem. Bd, Internat. Centre for Protection of Human Rights, 2005–07. Hon. Pres., Industrial Law Soc., 2012–. Leverhulme Emeritus Fellow, 2003–05; Nuffield Foundn New Career Develt Fellow, 2003–06; Fellow, Stellenbosch Inst. for Advanced Study, 2011. Hon. QC 1996. Hon. Prof., Univ. of Cape Town, 1999–2005. Hon. LLD: Witwatersrand, 1996; UCL, 2005; Cape Town, 2006; Bari, 2009; Kent, 2015. Lifetime Achievement Award, Labour Law Res. Network, 2013; Order of Luthuli (Gold) for exceptional contribn to struggle for democracy and human rights (S Africa), 2014. *Publications:* The Making of Labour Law in Europe, 1986; (with M. Coussey) Independent Review of Enforcement of UK Anti-Discrimination Legislation, 2000; Labour Laws and Global Trade, 2005; Rights at Work (Hamlyn Lectures), 2005; The Transformation of Labour Law in Europe, 2009; Equality: the new legal framework, 2011, 2nd edn 2014; Young Man with a Red Tie: a memoir of Mandela and the failed revolution 1960–63, 2013; various books and articles on labour law, race relations, law of tort, etc; Founding Ed., Industrial Law Jl, 1972–77; Gen. Ed. (jtly), Encyclopedia of Labour Relations Law, 1972–90; Chief Ed., Internat. Encyclopedia of Comparative Law, Vol. XV, Labour Law, 1979–2011. *Address:* c/o Clare College, Cambridge CB3 9AJ. *Died 21 Aug. 2015.*

HEPWORTH, Rear-Adm. David, CB 1976; retired from RN, 1976; *b* 6 June 1923; *s* of Alfred Ernest Hepworth and Minnie Louisa Catherine Bennet Tanner (*née* Bowden); *m* 1st, 1946, Brenda June Case (marr. diss. 1974); one *s* one *d*; 2nd, 1975, Eileen Mary Macgillivray (*née* Robson). *Educ:* Banbury Grammar School. Boy Telegraphist, RN, 1939; HMS Ganges, 1939–40; served in Atlantic, Mediterranean and E Indies Fleets; commnd 1944; submarines and midget submarines, 1945–50; CO HMS Tudor, 1951–52; CO HMS Thorough, 1954–55; CO HMS Truncheon, 1956–58; Sen. Officer Submarines Londonderry and CO HMS Stalker, 1959–61; CO HMS Ashanti, 1961–64; jssc 1964; Dep. Dir Undersea Warfare, MoD, 1964–66; idc 1967; CO HMS Ajax and Captain (D) 2nd Far East Destroyer Sqdn, 1968–69; Dir RN Tactical Sch. and Maritime Tactical Sch., 1969–71; Dir Naval Warfare, MoD, 1971–73; Staff of Vice-Chief of Naval Staff, 1973–76. Lt-Comdr 1952; Comdr 1958; Captain 1964; Rear-Adm. 1974. Naval Advr to Imperial Iranian Navy, 1974–76. Naval Advr to Internat. Military Services Ltd, 1977–83. *Recreation:* home and garden. *Address:* Garden House, Lower Heyford, Oxon OX25 5PD. *T:* (01869) 347460. *Died 11 June 2012.*

HERBERT, James, OBE 2010; author; *b* 8 April 1943; *s* of Herbert Herbert and Catherine (*née* Riley); *m* 1967, Eileen O'Donnell; three *d*. *Educ:* Our Lady of Assumption Sch., Bethnal Green; St Aloysius Coll., Highgate; Hornsey Coll. of Art. Typographer, paste-up artist, general dogsbody for John Collings Advertising, 1962–65; Art director, later group head and associate dir, Charles Barker Advertising, 1965–77. Mem., Lloyd's, 1983–89. Avoriaz Grand Prize for Literature Fantastique, 1977; Grand Master of Horror, Worldwide Horror Convention, 2010. *Publications:* The Rats, 1974 (filmed, 1982); The Fog, 1975; The Survivor, 1976 (filmed, 1986); Fluke, 1977 (filmed, 1995); The Spear, 1978; Lair, 1979; The Dark, 1980; The Jonah, 1981; Shrine, 1983; Domain, 1984; Moon, 1985; The Magic Cottage, 1986; Sepulchre, 1987; Haunted, 1988 (filmed, 1995); Creed, 1990; Portent, 1992; James Herbert: haunted by horror (ed S. Jones), 1992; James Herbert's Dark Places, 1993; The City, 1993; The Ghosts of Sleath, 1993; '48, 1996; Others, 1999; Once, 2001; Nobody True, 2003; The Secret of Crickley Hall, 2006; Ash, 2011; *relevant publication:* James Herbert: devil in the dark (biog.), by Craig Cabell, 2003. *Recreations:* playing guitar, piano, painting, sketching, photography, study of unnatural phenomena and the paranormal, swimming, reading, films, people. *Address:* c/o Bruce Hunter, David Higham Associates, 5–8 Lower John Street, Golden Square, W1R 4HA. *T:* (020) 7437 7888. *Died 20 March 2013.*

HERBERT-JONES, Hugh Jarrett, (Hugo), CMG 1973; OBE 1963; HM Diplomatic Service, retired; company director; *b* 11 March 1922; *s* of late Dora Herbert-Jones (*née* Rowlands), MBE and Captain H. Herbert-Jones, RWF; *m* 1954, Margaret (*d* 1996), *d* of Rev. J. P. Veall; one *s* two *d*. *Educ:* Bryanston; Worcester Coll., Oxford. History Scholar. Commnd Welsh Guards, 1941; served NW Europe and Middle East; wounded 1944; demobilised 1946 (Major). Entered Foreign (later Diplomatic) Service, 1947; served: Hamburg, 1947; Berlin, 1949; Hong Kong, 1951; Phnom Penh, 1955; Saigon, 1956; Nairobi, 1959; Pretoria/Cape Town, 1963; FCO, 1966; Paris, 1973; FCO, 1975–79; Internat. Affairs Dir, CBI, 1979–87. Pres., Aldeburgh Soc., 1997–99; Chairman: Aldeburgh United Charities, 1996–2000; Aldeburgh Community & Sports Trust, 2000–07. Mayor of Aldeburgh, 2007–08. *Recreations:* music, spectator sports, formerly golf, shooting and sailing. *Address:* Prior's Hill, 48 Park Road, Aldeburgh, Suffolk IP15 5ET. *T:* (01728) 453335. *E:* hugoherbertjones@gmail.com. *Clubs:* Garrick, MCC; London Welsh Rugby Football; Aldeburgh Yacht. *Died 19 Nov. 2014.*

HERD, Frederick Charles; Assistant Under-Secretary of State (Civilian Management, General), Ministry of Defence, 1970–75; *b* 27 April 1915. *Educ:* Strode's Sch., Egham; Sidney Sussex Coll., Cambridge. Asst Principal, Admiralty, 1937; Principal, 1941; Asst Sec., 1950; Asst Under-Sec. of State, 1964. *Recreations:* music, country walking, bridge. *Address:* Room 15, Chestnut House, Sunrise, Frognal House, Frognal Avenue, Sidcup, Kent DA14 6LF. *Died 7 Jan. 2012.*

HERDMAN, (John) Mark (Ambrose), CBE 1990; LVO 1979; HM Diplomatic Service, retired; *b* 26 April 1932; *s* of late Comdr Claudius Alexander Herdman, DL, RN, and Joan Dalrymple Herdman (*née* Tennant); *m* 1963, Elizabeth Anne Dillon; one *s* two *d*. *Educ:* St Edward's Sch., Oxford; Trinity Coll., Dublin (BA, MA); Queen's Coll., Oxford (postgrad.). HMOCS, Kenya, 1954–64; joined HM Diplomatic Service, 1964; Second, later First Sec., CRO, 1964–65; ODM, 1965; MECAS, 1965–66; Amman, 1966–68; FCO, 1969–71; Lusaka, 1971–74; Hd of Chancery, Jedda, 1974–76; FCO, 1976–78; Lilongwe, 1978–81; FCO, 1981–83; Dep. Governor, Bermuda, 1983–86; Gov., British Virgin Is, 1986–91; Hd of British Delegn to EC Monitoring Mission in Yugoslavia, 1991–92. *Recreations:* fishing, watching cricket, philately. *Address:* Tullywhisker House, Berry Lane, Fox Corner, Worplesdon, Surrey GU3 3PU. *T:* (01483) 232900. *Clubs:* Ebury Court; Surrey CC. *Died 5 Aug. 2015.*

HERMER, Julius; solicitor; Consultant with: Howard Palser Grossman Hermer & Partners, 1996–99; Robertsons, since 1999; Lord Mayor of Cardiff, 1987–88; *b* 18 Nov. 1933; *s* of Saul and Cissie Hermer; *m* 1960, Gloria Cohen; three *s* one *d*. *Educ:* St Illtyd's Coll., Cardiff; Peterhouse, Cambridge (BA, MA). Partner, 1959–95, Grossman & Hermer, subseq. Crowley, Grossman & Hermer, Grossman, Hermer & McCarthy, and Grossman, Hermer Seligman. Member: Cardiff City Council, 1964–88, 1991–96 (Chm., Planning Cttee, 1980–84; Dep. Lord Mayor of Cardiff, 1979–80, 1986–87); S Glam CC, 1974–96 (Vice-Chm. of Council and Dep. Leader of Cons. Party, 1977–78). Pres., Cardiff W Cons. Assoc., 1999–2002 (Dep. Chm., 1985). Chm., S Glam Appeal, Sir Geraint Evans Wales Heart Res. Inst., 1991–97. Pres., Cardiff Independent Citizens, 2005–. Chm., Cardiff Masonic Hall Co. Ltd, 1989–. *Recreations:* Freemasonry, sport, wine, food, travel, politics. *Address:* 28 Palace Road, Llandaff, Cardiff CF5 2AF. *T:* (029) 2056 6198. *Died 18 Sept. 2011.*

HERON, Sir Michael (Gilbert), Kt 1996; Chairman, Post Office, 1993–97; *b* 22 Oct. 1934; *s* of Gilbert Thwaites Heron and Olive Lilian (*née* Steele); *m* 1958, Celia Veronica Mary Hunter; two *s* one *d* (and one *d* decd). *Educ:* St Joseph's Acad., Blackheath; New Coll., Oxford (MA Hist.). Lieut RA, 1953–55. Dir, BOCM Silcock, 1971–76; Chm., Batchelors Foods, 1976–82; Dep. Co-ordinator, Food & Drinks Co-ordination, Unilever, 1982–86; Dir, Unilever, 1986–92. Food and Drink Federation: Mem. Cttee, 1986–92; Mem. Council, 1986–92; Chm., Food Policy Res. Cttee, 1987–92. Mem., Armed Forces Pay Rev. Bd, 1981–82. Dep. Chm. and Mem. Bd, BITC, 1991–95; Member: Policy Steering Bd, BESO, 1992–93; CBI Council, 1992–95; Dep. Chm., NACETT, 1993–95; Chairman: NCVQ, 1994–97; Council for Industry and

Higher Educn, 1999–2004. Chm., N London, Prince's Trust Business Div. formerly PYBT), 1999–2004. Chm. Council, St George's Hosp. Med. Sch., 1992–98; Mem., Governing Body, Douai Abbey, 1991–97. *Recreation:* avid Rugby football watcher. *Died 7 May 2014.*

HERRIES OF TERREGLES, Lady (14th in line, of the Lordship *cr* 1490); **Anne Elizabeth Fitzalan-Howard;** *b* 12 June 1938; *e d* of 16th Duke of Norfolk, KG, GCVO, GBE, TD, PC, and Lavinia Duchess of Norfolk, LG, CBE (*d* 1995); *S* to lordship upon death of father, 1975; *m* 1985, Colin Cowdrey (Baron Cowdrey of Tonbridge, CBE; *d* 2000). Racehorse trainer. *Recreations:* riding, golf, breeding spaniels. *Heir: sister* Lady Mary Katharine Mumford, DCVO, *b* 14 Aug. 1940. *Address:* Angmering Park, Littlehampton, West Sussex BN16 4EX. *T:* (01903) 871421. *Died 23 Nov. 2014.*

HERVEY-BATHURST, Sir Frederick John Charles Gordon; *see* Bathurst.

HETZEL, Phyllis Bertha Mabel, (Mrs R. D. Hetzel, Jr); Registrar of the Roll, and Bye-Fellow, Newnham College, Cambridge, 1993–98; President, Lucy Cavendish College, Cambridge, 1979–84; *b* 10 June 1918; *d* of Stanley Ernest and Bertha Myson; *m* 1st, 1941, John Henry Lewis James (*d* 1962); one *d*; 2nd, 1974, Baron Bowden (marr. diss. 1983, he *d* 1989); 3rd, 1985, Ralph Dorn Hetzel (*d* 1994). *Educ:* Wimbledon High Sch.; Newnham Coll., Cambridge (MA). Commonwealth (later Harkness) Fellow, 1957–58. BoT, 1941; Principal 1947; Asst Sec., 1960; DEA, 1964–69; Min. of Technology, 1969–70; Dept of Trade and Industry, 1970–75; Asst Under-Sec. of State 1972; Regional Dir, NW Region, DTI, subseq. DoI, 1972–75. Member: Monopolies and Mergers Commn, 1975–78; Local Govt Boundary Commn for England, 1977–81; W Midlands Cttee, National Trust, 1976–81. Chm., Manchester, Marriage Guidance Council, 1976–79. Member: Court, Manchester Univ., 1976–83; Court and Council, UMIST, 1978–80; Council of Senate, Cambridge Univ., 1983–84; Bd, American Friends of Cambridge University Inc., 1985–98. Vice-Pres., Oxford and Cambridge Club of Los Angeles, 1986–92. *Publications:* The Concept of Growth Centres, 1968; Gardens through the Ages, 1971; Regional Policy in Action, 1980; contrib. Public Administration, Cambridge Review, Encycl. Britannica, Oxford DNB. *Recreations:* landscape painting, conservation, writing, piano, family. *Address:* 18 Trafalgar Road, Cambridge CB4 1EU. *T:* (01223) 369878; Newnham College, Cambridge CB3 9DF. *Died 6 Jan. 2011.*

HEWITT, Harry Ronald, FREng; Chairman, Johnson Matthey PLC, 1983–84; *b* 12 April 1920; *s* of Charles William Hewitt and Florence Hewitt; *m* 1954, Rosemary Olive, *d* of Walter George Hiscock and Olive Mary Hiscock; two *s* one *d*. *Educ:* City of Leeds High Sch.; Leeds Coll. of Technol. (BSc London 1941). FREng (FEng 1982); MIChemE 1949; MRSC 1944; CBIM 1983 (MBIM 1947). Jun. Chemist, Joseph Watson & Sons, soap manufrs, Leeds, 1936–41; Chemist, Royal Ordnance Factories (explosive manuf.), 1941–45; Control Officer, Chemical Br., Control Commn, Germany, 1945–47; Works Manager, Consolidated Zinc Corp., Avonmouth and Widnes, 1947–58; Johnson Matthey: Gen. Man., 1958–62; Exec. Dir, 1962–76; Gp Man. Dir, 1976–83. Freeman, City of London, 1979; Liveryman, Worshipful Co. of Clockmakers, 1979. FRSA. *Recreations:* golf, tennis, ski-ing, music. *Address:* 6 Loom Lane, Radlett, Herts WD7 8AD. *T:* (01923) 5243. *Died 10 March 2011.*

HEYWOOD, Geoffrey, MBE (mil.) 1945; JP; Consulting Actuary; *b* 7 April 1916; *s* of Edgar Heywood and Annie (*née* Dawson), Blackpool; *m* 1941, Joan Corinna Lumley (*d* 2014); one *s* one *d*. *Educ:* Arnold Sch., Blackpool; Open Univ. (BA Hons). Served War, 1940–46: Royal Artillery, N Africa, Italy, Greece; commissioned, 1941, Major, 1944; despatches, 1945. Refuge Assce Co. Ltd, 1933–40; Duncan C. Fraser & Co. (Consulting Actuaries), 1946–86 (Sen. Partner, 1952–86). Pres., Manchester Actuarial Soc., 1951–53; Chm., Assoc. of Consulting Actuaries, 1959–62; Founder Chm., Internat. Assoc. of Consulting Actuaries, 1968–72; Pres., Inst. of Actuaries, 1972–74 (Vice-Pres., 1964–67). Mem. Page Cttee to Review National Savings. Dep. Chm., Mersey Docks & Harbour Co., 1975–85; Mem., Nat. Bus Co., 1978–85. Chm., Merseyside Cable Vision, 1982–90; Director: Barclays Bank Trust Co., 1967–86; Liverpool Bd Barclays Bank, 1972–86; Barclays Unicorn Gp, 1977–85; Universities Superannuation Scheme, 1974–86. Hon. Vice-Pres., Royal Patriotic Corp., 2004. Corresp. Mem., Assoc. des Actuaires Suisses, 1973. FFA 1939; FIA 1946; FRAS 1982; FRSA 1986. Founder Master, Actuaries Co., 1979; Liveryman, Clockmakers' Co. JP Liverpool 1962. *Publications:* contribs to Jl Inst. Actuaries. *Recreation:* antiquarian horology. *Address:* Drayton, 46 Croft Drive East, Caldy, Wirral, Merseyside CH48 1LS. *T:* (0151) 625 6707. *Club:* Army and Navy. *Died 25 May 2014.*

HICK, Prof. John Harwood; Danforth Professor, 1979–92, and Director of Blaisdell Programs in World Religions and Cultures, 1983–92, Claremont Graduate School, California, then Professor Emeritus, Claremont Graduate University; *b* 20 Jan. 1922; *s* of Mark Day Hick and Mary Aileen (Hirst); *m* 1953, (Joan) Hazel (*d* 1997), *d* of F. G. Bowers, CB, CBE, and Frances Bowers; two *s* one *d* (and one *s* decd). *Educ:* Bootham Sch., York; Edinburgh Univ. (MA 1948 (1st cl. hons Philos); DLitt 1974); Oriel Coll., Oxford (Campbell-Fraser schol.; DPhil 1950); Westminster Coll., Cambridge. Friends' Ambulance Unit, 1942–45. Ordained, Presb. C of E, 1953; Minister, Belford Presb. Church, Northumberland, 1953–56; Asst Prof. of Philosophy, Cornell Univ., 1956–59; Stuart Prof. of Christian Philosophy, Princeton Theolog. Seminary, 1959–64; S. A. Cook Bye-Fellow, Gonville and Caius Coll., Cambridge, 1963–64; PhD by incorporation; Lectr in Divinity, Cambridge Univ., 1964–67; H. G. Wood Prof. of Theology, Univ. of Birmingham, 1967–82, then Emeritus. Guggenheim Fellow, 1963–64, and 1985–86; Leverhulme Res. Fellow, 1976; Scholar-in-residence, Rockefeller Foundn Research Center, Bellagio, Italy, 1986; Fellow, Inst. for Advanced Res. in Arts and Social Scis (formerly the Humanities), Birmingham Univ., 1988–; Hon. Prof., Univ. of Wales, Lampeter, 1995–2003. Lectures: Mead-Swing, Oberlin Coll., USA, 1962–63; Mary Farnum Brown, Haverford Coll., USA 1964–65; James W. Richard, Univ. of Virginia, 1969; Distinguished Vis., Univ. of Oregon, 1969; Arthur Stanley Eddington Meml, 1972; Stanton, Cambridge Univ., 1974–77; Teape, Delhi, Calcutta and Madras, 1975; Ingersoll, Harvard, 1977; Hope, Stirling, 1977; Younghusband, London, 1977; Mackintosh, East Anglia, 1978; Riddell, Newcastle, 1978–79; Berkeley, TCD, 1979; Greenhoe, Louisville Pres. Sem., 1979; Potter, Washington State Univ., 1980; Montefiore, London, 1980; Brooks, Univ. of S California, 1982; Mars and Shaffer, Northwestern Univ., 1983; Niebuhr, Elmhurst Coll., 1986; Gifford, Edinburgh, 1986–87; Kegley, Calif State Univ.; Bakersfield, 1988; Suarez, Spring Hill Coll., 1988; Gates, Grinnell Coll., 1989; Birks, McGill Univ., 1989; Fritz Marti, Univ. of Southern Illinois, 1989; Brooke Anderson, Brown Univ., 1990; Eliot, Reed Coll., 1990; Resler, Ohio State Univ., 1991; Showers, Univ. of Indianapolis, 1993; McMartin, Ottawa Univ., 1993; Auburn, Union Theol Seminary, NY, 1994; Lily Montagu, London Soc. of Jews and Christians, London, 1994; Killeen, St Norbert Coll., Wis, 1995; Anne Spencer, Bristol Univ., 1996; Whyte, Oxford, 1998; Alister Hardy, World Congress of Faiths, 2005. Visiting Professor: Banares Hindu Univ., 1971; Visva Bharati Univ., 1971; Punjabi Univ., Patiala, 1971; Goa Univ., 1990; Visiting Fellow: British Acad. Overseas, 1974 and 1990; Univ. of Sri Lanka, 1974. Hulsean Preacher, Cambridge Univ., 1969; Select Preacher, Oxford Univ., 1970. Chairman: Religious and Cultural Panel, Birmingham Community Relations Cttee, 1969–74; Co-ordinating Working Party, Statutory Conf. for Revision of Agreed Syllabus of Religious Educn, Birmingham, 1971–74; Birmingham Inter-Faiths Council, 1975; President: Soc. for the Study of Theology, 1975–76; All Faiths for One Race, 1980–85 (Chm., 1972–73, 1978–80); Vice-President: World Congress of Faiths, 1993–; British Soc. for Philosophy of Religion, 1994– (Mem., 1990–); Member: Amer. Acad. of Religion, 1980–94; Adv. Bd, Inst. for Philosophy and Religion, Boston Univ., 1984–; Internat. Bd, Global Ethics and Religion Forum, Calif, 1998–; Member Emeritus: Amer. Soc. for the Study of Religion, 1992 (Mem., 1983); Amer.

Philosophical Assoc., 1992 (Mem., 1980). Internat. Consultant, Internat. Interfaith Centre, Oxford, 1996–. Mem. Council, Selly Oak Colls, 1967–80; Governor, Queen's Coll., Birmingham, 1972–80. Mem. Editl Bd, The Encyclopedia of Philosophy. Hon. Teol. Dr Uppsala, 1977; Hon. DD: Glasgow, 2002; Birmingham, 2011. Louisville Grawemeyer Award in Religion, Univ. of Louisville and Louisville Theol Seminary, 1991. *Publications:* Faith and Knowledge, 1957, 2nd edn 1966; Philosophy of Religion, 1963, 4th edn 1990 (also Spanish, Portuguese, Chinese, Japanese, Korean, Finnish, Polish, Farsi, Hindi and Swedish edns); (ed) Faith and the Philosophers, 1963; (ed) The Existence of God, 1963; (ed) Classical and Contemporary Readings in the Philosophy of Religion, 1963, 3rd edn 1990; Evil and the God of Love, 1966, 3rd edn 2007 (trans. Korean); (ed) The Many-Faced Argument, 1967; Christianity at the Centre, 1968, 2nd edn as The Centre of Christianity, 1977 (trans. Dutch, Korean and Chinese); Arguments for the Existence of God, 1971 (trans. German, Polish); Biology and the Soul, 1972; God and the Universe of Faiths, 1973; (ed) Truth and Dialogue, 1974; Death and Eternal Life, 1976 (trans. Dutch); (ed) The Myth of God Incarnate, 1977 (trans. German, Arabic, Farsi); God has Many Names, 1980 (trans. German, Japanese, Korean); (ed with Brian Hebblethwaite) Christianity and Other Religions, 1980; The Second Christianity, 1983 (trans. Japanese); (with Michael Goulder) Why Believe in God?, 1983; Problems of Religious Pluralism, 1985 (trans. Japanese, Chinese, Farsi); (ed with Hasan Askari) The Experience of Religious Diversity, 1985; An Interpretation of Religion, 1989, 2nd edn 2004 (trans. German, Chinese, Farsi); (ed with Edmund Meltzer) Three Faiths—One God, 1989; (ed with Lamont Hempel) Gandhi's Significance for Today, 1989; (ed with Paul Knitter) The Myth of Christian Uniqueness, 1992 (trans. Japanese, Italian); Disputed Questions in Theology and the Philosophy of Religion, 1993; The Metaphor of God Incarnate, 1993 (trans. Japanese, Chinese, Portuguese, Spanish, Korean); The Rainbow of Faiths, 1995 (trans. Japanese, Chinese, Portuguese, Turkish); The Fifth Dimension, 1999, 2nd edn 2004 (trans. Chinese, Japanese, Russian, Danish, Polish, Farsi, Indonesian, Italian); Dialogues in the Philosophy of Religion, 2001; John Hick: an autobiography, 2003 (trans. Japanese); The New Frontier of Religion and Science, 2006; Who or What is God?, 2008 (trans. Chinese); Between Faith and Doubt, 2010. *Address:* 144 Oak Tree Lane, Selly Oak, Birmingham B29 6HU. *Died 9 Feb. 2012.*

HICKS, Group Captain (Harry) David, MBE 1967; Director General, English-Speaking Union, 1990–91 (Deputy Director General, 1985–90); *b* 13 July 1923; *s* of Walter Hicks and Clara Ann (*née* Jagger); *m* 1948, Jane Irene Mary Tibbs; one *s* one *d*. *Educ:* Grange Grammar Sch., Bradford; London Univ. (BA Hons 1947); Nottingham Univ. (PGCE 1948). Served War, 1942–45, as Pilot, 149 Sqdn, Bomber Comd. Schoolmaster, Surbiton Grammar Sch., 1948–49; Royal Air Force: Educn Br., 1950–54; Admin. Br., 1954–76, finally as Dep. Dir, Recruiting; Dir of Educn, E-SU, 1976–85; Gen. Dir, Internat. Shakespeare Globe Centre, 1991–92. Special Consultant to BBC English, 1991–95; German Language Consultant to Callon Sch., 1992. *Recreations:* golf, tennis, playing piano. *Died 16 Feb. 2012.*

HIGGINBOTHAM, Prof. James Taylor, PhD; FBA 1995; Linda MacDonald Hilf Professor of Philosophy, since 2004, Distinguished Professor of Philosophy and Linguistics, since 2006, and Chair, Department of Linguistics, since 2006, University of Southern California; *b* 17 Aug. 1941; *s* of William Rufus Higginbotham and Eunice Taylor Higginbotham; *m* 1st, 1972, Jenni W. Caldwell (marr. diss. 1988); two *s*; 2nd, 1988, Nancy L. Roberts (marr. diss. 2009); two *s* two *d*. *Educ:* Columbia Univ., NY (BS 1967; PhD 1973). Columbia University, New York: Instructor in Philosophy, 1970–73; Asst Prof., 1973–80; Fellow in Humanities, 1975–77 and 1979–80; Massachusetts Institute of Technology: Vis. Associate Prof. of Philosophy, 1980–82; Associate Prof., 1982–87; Prof. of Philosophy and Linguistics, 1987–93; Prof. of Gen. Linguistics, Univ. of Oxford, 1993–2000; Fellow, Somerville Coll., Oxford, 1993–2000; University of Southern California: Prof. of Philosophy and Linguistics, 2000–04; Prof. of Linguistics, 2004–06; Dir, Sch. of Philosophy, 2000–06. Vis. Prof. of Philosophy, Univ. of Oxford, 2009–11. Fellow, Amer. Acad. Arts and Scis, 2011. *Publications:* Tense, Aspect, and Indexicality, 2009; articles in Jl Philosophy, Linguistic Inquiry, Mind and Language, Linguistics and Philosophy; contribs to several collections in linguistics and in philosophy. *Recreations:* chess, music. *Address:* School of Philosophy, University of Southern California, 3709 Trousdale Parkway, Los Angeles, CA 90089–0451, USA. *T:* (213) 8212308, (mobile) (213) 2803309. *Died 25 April 2014.*

HIGGINSON, Sir Gordon (Robert), Kt 1992; DL; PhD; FREng; Vice-Chancellor, 1985–94, Emeritus Professor of Engineering, 1994, University of Southampton; *b* 8 Nov. 1929; *s* of Frederick John and Letitia Higginson; *m* 1954, Marjorie Forbes Rannie (*d* 1996); three *s* two *d*. *Educ:* Leeds Univ. (BSc, PhD). FICE; FIMechE; FREng (FEng 1991). Scientific Officer, then Sen. Scientific Officer, Min. of Supply, 1953–56; Lectr, Leeds Univ., 1956–62; Associate Prof., RMCS, Shrivenham, 1962–65; Durham University: Prof. of Engrg, 1965–85; Dean of Faculty of Science, 1972–75. Non-executive Director: Rolls-Royce, 1988–99; Pirelli General, 1995–2002; Pirelli UK Tyres, 1997–2002. DL Hants, 1994. Hon. FRCP 1992. Hon. DSc: Durham, 1991; Southampton, 1995; Bournemouth, 1997; Loughborough, 2002; Hon. DSc (Eng) London, 1997; Hon. DEng Portsmouth, 1993; Hon. LLD Leeds, 1994. IMechE James Clayton Fund Prize, 1963 and 1979; Gold Medal, Brit. Soc. of Rheology, 1969. *Publications:* Elastohydrodynamic Lubrication (with D. Dowson), 1966, 2nd edn 1977; Foundations of Engineering Mechanics, 1974; papers on mechanics in various jls. *Address:* 61 Albany Park Court, Westwood Road, Southampton SO17 1LA. *Died 5 Nov. 2011.*

HIGHAM, Norman, OBE 1984; Librarian, University of Bristol, 1966–89; *b* 14 June 1924; *s* of John Henry Higham, MM, and Edith Fanny (*née* Hubbard); *m* 1954, Jean Elizabeth (MBE 2006), *d* of Frederick William and Isabel Traylen; one *s* one *d*. *Educ:* Firth Park Grammar Sch., Sheffield; Univ. of Sheffield (BA 1st Cl. Hons English, Philos., Spanish); MA Leeds 1961. Served RNVR, 1942–46 (Lieut Coastal Forces). Assistant Librarian: Univ. of Sheffield, 1953–57; Univ. of Leeds, 1957–62; Librarian, Loughborough Coll. of Advanced Technology, 1962–63; Dep. Librarian, Univ. of Leeds, 1963–66. Mem. Council, Standing Conf. on Nat. and Univ. Libraries, 1972–75 and 1979–86 (Chm., 1976–79); Pres., LA, 1983 (Mem. Council, 1975–86, Chm., 1978–81 and 1985–87); Member: UGC Steering Gp on Liby Res., 1977–83; Brit. Liby Bd, 1986–89 (Adv. Council, 1976–79, and 1990–94); Liby and Inf. Services Council (England), 1977–83; Sci. Inf. Cttee, Royal Soc., 1982–91; Standing Cttee on Libraries, CVCP, 1982–89; Nat. Cttee on Regl Liby Co-operation, 1985–89; Council, Liby and Inf. Co-operation Council, 1989–94 (Chm., 1989–92). Mem. Council and Trustee, Oxfam, 1973–79 and 1980–86. Hon. DLitt Bristol, 1989. *Publications:* A Very Scientific Gentleman: the major achievements of Henry Clifton Sorby, 1963; Computer Needs for University Library Operations, 1973; The Library in the University: observations on a service, 1980; articles and reviews in librarianship and history of science. *Recreations:* literature and the arts, music. *Address:* 30 York Gardens, Clifton, Bristol BS8 4LN. *T:* (0117) 973 6264. *Died 2 July 2014.*

HIGNETT, John Mulock, FCA; Chairman, Schroder Income Growth Fund plc, 1995–2005; *b* 9 March 1934; *s* of late Reginald and Marjorie Hignett; *m* 1961, Marijke Inge de Boer; one *s* one *d*. *Educ:* Harrow Sch.; Magdalene Coll., Cambridge (MA). Kemp Chatteris & Co., 1958–61; Deloitte & Co., 1961–63; joined Lazard Brothers & Co. Ltd, 1963; Manager, Issues Dept, 1971; Dir, 1972; Head of Corporate Finance Div., 1980; Man. Dir, 1984–88; Glaxo Holdings plc: Finance Dir, 1988–92; Man. Dir, Corporate Funds, 1992–94. Non-executive Director: TI Group plc, 1989–2000; Sedgwick Group plc, 1993–99; Alfred McAlpine plc, 1994–98; Smiths Gp plc, 2000; Camper & Nicholsons Marina Investments Ltd; World Trust Fund. Director-General: Panel on Take-Overs and Mergers, 1981–83; Council for the Securities Industry, 1983. Dep.

Chm., Internat. Shakespeare Globe Centre Ltd, 1990–. *Clubs:* Royal Thames Yacht, MCC; Hawks (Cambridge). *Died 23 Oct. 2013.*

HIGNETT, Peter George; Regional Veterinary Officer, People's Dispensary for Sick Animals, 1982–90; *b* 3 June 1925; *s* of Harry Sutton Hignett and Annie Hignett; *m* 1st, 1948, Patricia Bishop (marr. diss. 1988); two *s* one *d*; 2nd, 1997, Janet McCully. *Educ:* Pontesbury C of E Sch.; King Edward VI Sch., Birmingham; Univ. of Liverpool (MRCVS). General practice, 1947–49; Wellcome Veterinary Res. Station, 1949–54; Reader in Veterinary Reproduction, Univ. of Glasgow, 1954–76; Gen. Man., Hampshire Cattle Breeders' Soc., 1976–82. Mem. Council, RCVS, 1972–96, Pres., 1981–82; President: Soc. for Study of Animal Breeding, 1966–68; Southern Counties Veterinary Soc., 1983–84; Secretary: Associated AI Centres, 1977–82; Edgar Meml Trust, 1977–82; Member: Trehane Cttee, 1979–82; Scientific Adv. Cttee, Animal Health Trust, 1983–85; Banner Cttee on Ethics of Emerging Technologies in Animal Breeding, 1993–95. Gov., Berks Coll. of Agric., 1990–93. Hon. FRCVS 1998. *Publications:* scientific papers on fertility in domestic animals. *Recreations:* gardening, sailing, music. *Address:* 70 Stonerock Cottages, Chilgrove Park Road, Chichester, W Sussex PO18 9NA. *T:* (01243) 535330. *Died 14 Aug. 2013.*

HIGTON, Dennis John, CEng, FIMechE, FRAeS; aeronautical mechanical engineer; *b* 15 July 1921; *s* of John William and Lillian Harriett Higton; *m* 1945, Joy Merrifield Pickett; one *s* one *d*. *Educ:* Guildford Technical Sch.; RAE Farnborough Technical Sch. Mid-Wessex Water Co., 1937–38. RAE Engineering Apprentice, 1938–42; RAE Aerodynamics Dept (Aero Flight), 1942–52; learned to fly at No 1 EFTS RAF Panshanger, 1946; A&AEE Boscombe Down, Head of Naval Test and Supt of Performance, 1953–66; British Defence Staff, Washington DC, USA, 1966–70; MoD(PE) Anglo-French Helicopter Production, 1970–72; Director Aircraft Production, 1972–75; Under-Sec. and Dir-Gen. of Mil. Aircraft Projects, MoD, 1976–79, of Aircraft 4, 1979–80, of Aircraft 3, 1980–81; Hd, Engrg Profession, Air Systems Controllerate, MoD, 1976–81; aeronautical consultant and company dir, 1981–93. Chm., Technology Div., CS Commn, 1984–89. Mem., Fleet Air Arm Officers Assoc., 1960–. Chm., S Wilts and Salisbury Br., NSPCC, 1982–96; Vice Pres., Boscombe Down Br., RAeS, 2002–. Mem., Exec. Cttee, Salisbury Gp of Artists, 1987–92. Associate, Empire Test Pilots' Sch., 2003–. *Publications:* research and memoranda papers mainly on aerodynamic flight testing, early jet propulsion and attitude control of jet borne VSTOL flight. *Recreations:* sailing, gardening, enjoying Salisbury Plain, painting (Diploma in Fine Art, Southampton Inst. of Higher Educn, 1994). *Address:* Jasmine Cottage, Rollestone Road, Shrewton, Salisbury, Wiltshire SP3 4HG. *T:* (01980) 620276. *Died 18 May 2012.*

HILDREW, Bryan, CBE 1977; FREng; Managing Director, Lloyds Register of Shipping, 1977–85; *b* 19 March 1920; *s* of Alexander William Hildrew and Sarah Jane (*née* Clark); *m* 1950, Megan Kathleen Lewis (*d* 2009); two *s* one *d*. *Educ:* Bede Collegiate Sch., Sunderland; Technical Coll., Sunderland; City and Guilds, Imperial Coll., London (MSc, DIC). FIMechE, FIMarEST; FREng (FEng 1976). Engineer Officer, RN, 1941–46. Lloyds Register of Shipping: Research Surveyor, 1948–67 (Admiralty Nuclear Submarine Project, 1956–61); Chief Engineer Surveyor, 1967–70; Technical Dir, 1970–77. Chm., Abbeyfield, Orpington, 1985–2004. President: IMechE, 1980–81; IMarE, 1983–85; Chm., CEI, 1981–82. FCGI 1990. Hon. DEng Newcastle, 1987; DUniv Surrey, 1994. *Recreations:* orienteering, walking. *Address:* 8 Westholme, Orpington, Kent BR6 0AN. *T:* (01689) 825451. *Died 11 Jan. 2012.*

HILL, Prof. Alan Geoffrey, MA; FBA 1994; Professor of English Language and Literature in the University of London at Royal Holloway and Bedford New College (formerly Royal Holloway College), 1980–96, then Emeritus; *b* 12 Dec. 1931; *yr s* of Thomas Murton Hill and Alice Marion Hill (*née* Nunn); *m* 1960, Margaret Vincent Rutherford, MA; three *d*. *Educ:* Dulwich Coll. (Sen. Foundn Schol.); St Andrews Univ. (MA 1st Cl. Hons English Lang. and Lit.); Merton Coll., Oxford (BLitt). Asst Lectr/Lectr in English, Exeter Univ., 1958–62; Lectr in English, St Andrews Univ., 1962–68; Sen. Lectr in English, Dundee Univ., 1968–80. Vis. Professor of English, Univ. of Saskatchewan, 1973–74; British Acad./Royal Soc. of Canada Vis. Lectr, Canadian univs, 1997; Hon. Fellow, Inst. for Advanced Res. in Humanities, Birmingham Univ., 1996–2012. External Examiner in English: Univ. of Buckingham, 1986–90; Nat. Univ. of Singapore, 1996–98. Lectures: Crowsley, Charles Lamb Soc., 1981; Warton, British Acad., 1986; Newman Centenary, Univ. of Malta, 1990; Lambeth Palace Library, 1992; Tewkesbury Abbey, 2000. Founded Centre for Study of Victorian Art, RHC, 1981. Trustee, Dove Cottage, subseq. Wordsworth Trust, 1969–2001, then Life Fellow; General Editor, The Letters of William and Dorothy Wordsworth, 1979–. Mem. Council, Friends of Tewkesbury Abbey, 1999–2010. Member: Editl Bd, Forum for Modern Language Studies, 1964–69; Publications Bd, Tennyson Res. Bulletin, 1993–2001. *Publications:* The Letters of William and Dorothy Wordsworth, vol. III, The Middle Years, Part 2, 1812–1820, 2nd edn (rev. and ed with Mary Moorman), 1970; vol. IV, The Later Years, Part 1, 1821–1828, 2nd edn (rev. and ed), 1978; vol. V, The Later Years, Part 2, 1829–1834, 2nd edn (rev. and ed), 1979; vol. VI, The Later Years, Part 3, 1835–1839, 2nd edn (rev. and ed), 1982; vol. VII, The Later Years, Part 4, 1840–1853, 2nd edn (rev. and ed), 1988; vol. VIII, A Supplement of New Letters, 1993; (ed) Selected Letters of Dorothy Wordsworth, 1981; (ed) Selected Letters of William Wordsworth, 1984; (ed) John Henry Newman, Loss and Gain, 1986; Wordsworth's Grand Design, 1987; (ed with Ian Ker) Newman After A Hundred Years, 1990; (ed) Ford Madox Ford, The Soul of London, 1995; Tennyson, Wordsworth, and the 'Forms' of Religion, 1997; Newman's Idea of a University, Revisited, 1998; Lyrical Ballads (1800), a Bicentenary Celebration, 2000; (ed) Newman, Callista, 2001; contrib. DNB, Oxford DNB, articles and reviews in literary, historical and theological jls. *Recreations:* music, fine arts, ecclesiology, travel. *Address:* 4 Lawnside House, Albert Road South, Malvern, Worcs WR14 3AH. *Club:* Savile. *Died 14 April 2015.*

HILL, Sir Arthur (Alfred), Kt 1989, CBE 1980; Chairman, Walsall District Health Authority, 1982–92; *b* 14 May 1920; *s* of Arthur James Hill and Phoebe Mary Hill (*née* Prees); *m* 1947, Alma M. E. Bate (CBE 1981); one *s* two *d*. *Educ:* Langley High Sch.; Halesowen Technical Coll. Served RAFVR, 1939–45. Joint Company Director: Arthur Brook Cars Ltd, 1948–68; Abro Finance Ltd, 1950–65; Cradley Heath Motor Co. Ltd, 1956–65. Trainer/Man., Dudley Council Voluntary Services, 1980–82. Chm., CPC, 1969–72; Treas., 1973–76, Chm., 1976–79, Pres., 1985–88, W Midlands Area Cons. Council; Mem., Cons. Nat. Union, 1966–80; Chairman: Kidderminster Cons. Assoc., 1964–67; Walsall S Cons. Assoc., 1981–84. Mem., Rowley Regis BC, 1948–57. Chm., Bd of Govs, Rowley Regis Grammar Sch., 1961–64. *Recreations:* travelling, golf. *Address:* 1 Mellish Road, Walsall, West Midlands WS4 2DQ. *T:* (01922) 634949. *Died 8 Feb. 2013.*

HILL, His Honour (Ian) Starforth; QC 1969; a Circuit Judge, 1974–94; Resident Judge, Winchester Combined Court Centre, 1992–94; *b* 30 Sept. 1921; *s* of late Harold Victor John Hill; *m* 1st, 1950, Bridget Mary Footner; one *s* two *d*; 2nd, 1982, Greta Grimshaw; 3rd, 1986, Wendy Elizabeth Stavert. *Educ:* Shrewsbury Sch.; Brasenose Coll., Oxford (MA). 11th Sikh Regt, Indian Army, 1940–45, India, Africa, Italy (despatches). Called to Bar, Gray's Inn, 1949; Dep. Chm., Isle of Wight QS, 1968–71; Western Circuit; a Recorder of the Crown Court, 1972–74. Mem., Parole Bd, 1983–84. *Address:* Amberley House, Haig Road, Alresford, Hants SO24 9LX. *T:* (01962) 732131. *Died 8 July 2011.*

HILL, James William Thomas, (Jimmy), OBE 1995; Chairman, Jimmy Hill & Co. (formerly Jimmy Hill Ltd), 1972–2008; Presenter, Jimmy Hill's Sunday Supplement, Sky Sports, 2001–07; *b* 22 July 1928; *s* of William Hill and Alice Hill (*née* Wyatt); *m* 1st, 1949, Gloria Mary Flude (marr. diss. 1961); two *s* one *d*; 2nd, 1962, Heather Christine (marr. diss. 1982); one *s* one *d*; 3rd, 1991, Bryony

Ruth Jarvis. *Educ:* Henry Thornton School, Clapham. Player, Brentford FC, 1949–52, Fulham FC, 1952–61; Gen. Manager, Coventry City FC, 1961–67, Managing Director, 1975–83, Chm., 1980–83; Chm., Fulham Football Club (1987) Ltd, 1987–97. London Weekend Television: Head of Sport, 1967–72; Controller of Press, Promotion and Publicity, 1971–72; Deputy Controller, Programmes, 1972–73; Soccer analyst, BBC, 1973–98; Presenter, The Last Word, Sky Sports, 1998–2001. Mem., Sports Council, 1971–76. Hon. Chm., The Professional Footballers Assoc., 1957–61. *Publications:* Striking for Soccer, 1961; Improve your Soccer, 1964; Football Crazy, 1985; The Jimmy Hill Story (autobiog.), 1998. *Recreations:* keeping in touch with the world of sport in general, football in particular, but from his armchair. *Address:* Goldbridge House, Langton Lane, Hurstpierpoint, West Sussex BN6 9HA. *Club:* All England Lawn Tennis and Croquet. *Died 19 Dec. 2015.*

HILL, Len; *see* Hill, R. K. L.

HILL, Rodney, FRS 1961; PhD; ScD; Professor of Mechanics of Solids, University of Cambridge, 1972–79 (Reader, 1969–72); Fellow, Gonville and Caius College, since 1972; *b* 11 June 1921; *o s* of Harold Harrison Hill, Leeds; *m* 1946, Jeanne Kathlyn (*d* 2003), *yr d* of C. P. Wickens, Gidea Park; one *d*. *Educ:* Leeds Grammar Sch.; Pembroke Coll., Cambridge. MA, PhD, ScD Cambridge. Armament Research Dept, 1943–46; Cavendish Laboratory, Cambridge, 1946–48; British Iron and Steel Research Assoc., 1948–50; University of Bristol: Research Fellow, 1950–53, Reader, 1953; Univ. of Nottingham: Prof. of Applied Mathematics, 1953–62; Professorial Research Fellow, 1962–63; Berkeley Bye-Fellow, Gonville and Caius Coll., Cambridge, 1963–69. Hon. DSc: Manchester, 1976; Bath, 1978. Von Karman Medal, ASCE, 1978; Gold Medal and Internat. Modesto Panetti Prize, Accademia delle Scienze di Torino, 1988; Royal Medal, Royal Soc., 1993. Editor, Jl of Mechanics and Physics of Solids, 1952–68. *Publications:* Mathematical Theory of Plasticity, 1950; Principles of Dynamics, 1964; papers on mechanics of solid continua, esp. metals. *Died 2 Feb. 2011.*

HILL, Roy Kenneth Leonard, (Len), CBE 1983; Chairman, South West Water Authority, 1977–87; *b* 28 May 1924; *m* 1944, Barbara May Kendall (*d* 2005). Mem., ASLEF; Plymouth City Councillor, 1961–68, 1970–74 (formerly Dep. Lord Mayor); County Councillor, Devon, 1974 (formerly Leader of Labour Gp). Chm., Water Authorities Assoc., 1983–86. Mem., SW Econ. Planning Council. Formerly: Chm. Council, Coll. of St Mark and St John, Plymouth; Governor, Plymouth Polytechnic; Mem. Bd of Visitors, Dartmoor Prison. JP Plymouth, 1968. *Address:* 5 Revell Park Road, Plympton, Plymouth PL7 4EH. *T:* (01752) 339125. *Died 11 July 2012.*

HILL, Starforth; *see* Hill, His Honour I. S.

HILLIER-FRY, (William) Norman, CMG 1982; HM Diplomatic Service, retired; High Commissioner in Uganda, 1980–83; *b* 12 Aug. 1923; *o s* of William Henry and Emily Hillier Fry; *m* 1948, Elizabeth Adèle Misbah; two *s* two *d*. *Educ:* Colfe's Grammar School, Lewisham; St Edmund Hall, Oxford (BA 1946). Served Army, 1942–45; commissioned, Loyal Regt, 1942. HM Foreign Service, 1946; served: Iran, 1947–52; Strasbourg (Delegation to Council of Europe), 1955–56; Turkey, 1956–59; Czechoslovakia, 1961–63; Counsellor, UK Disarmament Delegn, Geneva, 1968–71; Hd of ME Dept, ODA, 1971–74; Consul-Gen., Hamburg, 1974–79; Ambassador to Afghanistan, 1979–80. *Recreations:* music, theatre. *Address:* 127 Coombe Lane West, Kingston-upon-Thames, Surrey KT2 7HF. *Died 11 Jan. 2015.*

HILLS, Air Vice-Marshal David Graeme Muspratt, CB 1985; OBE 1965; Director, Medical Policy and Plans, Ministry of Defence, 1983–85; *b* 28 Feb. 1925; *s* of late Arthur Ernest Hills and Muriel Steinman Hills (*née* Fisher); *m* 1960, Hilary Enid Mary, *d* of Rev. Raymond Morgan Jones and Mary Jones (*née* Ritson); two *s* one *d*. *Educ:* Salisbury Cathedral School; Epsom College; Middlesex Hosp. Medical School. MB BS 1949; MFCM, DPH, AFOM. Commissioned RAF Med. Branch, 1950; served UK, Korea (Casualty Evacuation and MO to 77 Sqn, RAAF; despatches), A&AEE, RAF Stanmore Park, RAF Tengah and MoD, 1951–68; OC RAF Hosp., Muharraq Bahrain, 1968–70; SMO RAF Cranwell, 1970–72; Dep. Dir Medical Personnel, RAF, 1972–75; PMO RAF Germany, 1975–78; Dep. Dir Gen., RAF Medical Services, 1979–83. QHS, 1980–85. Chm. of Council, Coll. of St Barnabas, Lingfield, 1996–2000. CStJ. *Recreations:* music, painting, gardening, golf. *Club:* Royal Air Force. *Died 4 July 2011.*

HILLS, Air Vice-Marshal (Eric) Donald, CB 1973; CBE 1968 (MBE 1941); SASO Maintenance Command, 1971–73; *b* 26 Jan. 1917; *s* of late Henry James Hills; *m* 1st, 1945, Pamela Mary (*d* 1989), *d* of late Col A. P. Sandeman, Cape Town; one *s* one *d*; 2nd, 1991, Lady Cynthia Way (*d* 2001). *Educ:* Maidstone Grammar Sch. Joined RAF 1939; Group Captain 1962; Dir of Equipment 3 (RAF), 1968–69; Air Cdre 1969; Dir of Equipment (Policy) (RAF), MoD, 1969–71; Air Vice-Marshal 1971. *Recreations:* gardening, sport as spectator. *Club:* Royal Air Force. *Died 27 Jan. 2012.*

HILLS, Sir Graham (John), Kt 1988; PhD, DSc; FRSE, CChem, FRSC; Principal and Vice-Chancellor of the University of Strathclyde, 1980–91; Scottish Governor of the BBC, 1989–94; *b* 9 April 1926; *s* of Albert Victor Hills and Marjorie Hills (*née* Harper); *m* 1st, 1950, Brenda Stubbington (*d* 1974); one *s* three *d*; 2nd, 1980, Mary Jane McNaughton (*d* 2013). *Educ:* Birkbeck Coll., London Univ. (BSc 1946, PhD 1950, DSc 1962; Hon. Fellow 1984). Lecturer in Physical Chemistry, Imperial College, 1949–62; Professor of Physical Chemistry, Univ. of Southampton, 1962–80; Visiting Professor: Univ. of Western Ontario, 1968; Case Western Reserve Univ., 1969; Univ. of Buenos Aires, 1977. Chm., Ness (formerly Highland Psychiatric Res.) Foundn, 1998–2003. President: Internat. Soc. of Electrochemistry, 1983–85; Soc. of Chemical Industry, 1991–93; Design Industries Assoc., 1992–96. Member: ACOST, 1987–93; Council, RSC, 1983–86; Council, CNAA, 1988–93; Design Council, 1989–90; Scottish Enterprise, 1991–93. Non-executive Director: Scottish Post Office Bd, 1986–99; Scottish Develt Agency, 1988–90; Glasgow Action, 1986–90; Britoil, 1988–90. Chm. Council, Quarriers' Homes, 1992–97. FRSA 1978. Hon. FRSAMD 1988; Hon. Fellow, Polytechnic of E London, 1991; Hon. FRCPSGlas 1992; Hon. FCSD 1996. Hon. ScD Technical Univ. of Łodz, Poland, 1984; Hon. DSc: Southampton, 1984; Lisbon, 1994; Hon. LLD: Glasgow, 1985; Waterloo, Canada, 1991; Strathclyde, 1991; DUniv Paisley, 1993; Hon. DEd Abertay Dundee, 1999. Hon. Medal, Univ. of Pavia, 1988. Commander: Polish Order of Merit, 1984; Royal Norwegian Order of Merit, 1986. *Publications:* Reference Electrodes, 1961; Polarography, 1964; UHI: the making of a university, 2003; contrib. Faraday Transactions, on physical chemistry, espec. electrochemistry. *Recreations:* music, European political history, rocking the boat. *Died 9 Feb. 2014.*

HINDE, Thomas; *see* Chitty, Sir Thomas Willes.

HINTON, Michael Herbert, FCA; FFA; *b* 10 Nov. 1934; *s* of late Walter Leonard Hinton and Freda Millicent Lillian Hinton; *m* 1st, 1955, Sarah Sunderland (marr. diss. 1982); one *s* two *d*; 2nd, 1984, Jane Margaret Manley, *d* of Arthur Crichton Howell. *Educ:* Ardingly Coll. Liveryman: Farmers' Co., 1964 (Master, 1981–82); Wheelwrights' Co.; Arbitrators' Co. (Master, 1998–99); Mem. Court of Common Council, 1970–71, Alderman, 1971–79, Ward of Billingsgate; Clerk to Wheelwrights' Co., 1965–71; Sheriff, City of London, 1977–78. JP City of London, 1971. FRSA. *Recreations:* cricket, Association football, theatre, travel. *Address:* 37 Westgate Road, Beckenham, Kent BR3 5DT. *T:* (020) 8650 1996. *Clubs:* Farmers, MCC, City Livery (Pres., 1976–77). *Died 5 Dec. 2012.*

HIRST, Rt Hon. Sir David (Cozens-Hardy), Kt 1982; PC 1992; a Lord Justice of Appeal, 1992–99; *b* 31 July 1925; *er s* of late Thomas William Hirst and Margaret Joy Hirst, Aylsham, Norfolk; *m* 1951, Pamela Elizabeth Molesworth Bevan, *d* of Col T. P. M. Bevan, MC; three *s* two *d*. *Educ:* Eton (Fellow, 1976–96); Trinity Coll., Cambridge. MA. Served 1943–47; RA and Intelligence Corps, Capt. 1946. Barrister, Inner Temple, 1951, Bencher, 1974, Reader,

1994, Treas., 1995; QC 1965; a Judge of the High Court, QBD, 1982–92. Vice-Chm. of the Bar, 1977–78, Chm., 1978–79. Member: Lord Chancellor's Law Reform Cttee; Council on Tribunals, 1966–80; Cttee to review Defamation Act, 1952, 1971–74; Chm., Spoliation Adv. Panel, 1999–; Hon. Life Mem., Amer. Bar Assoc. *Recreations:* theatre and opera, growing vegetables. *Address:* c/o Royal Courts of Justice, Strand, WC2A 2LL. *Clubs:* Boodle's, Royal Automobile (Chm. Stewards, 2000–05), MCC. *Died 31 Dec. 2011.*

HISLOP, George Steedman, CBE 1976; PhD; FREng, FIMechE; FRSE; Director, Aviall Airline Services (Caledonian), 1978–94; *b* 11 Feb. 1914; *s* of George Alexander Hislop and Marthesa Maria Hay; *m* 1942, Joan Daphne (*d* 2009), *d* of William Beer and Gwendoline Fincken; two *s* one *d*. *Educ:* Clydebank High Sch.; Royal Technical Coll., Glasgow (ARTC); Cambridge Univ. (PhD). BScEng London. CEng, FIMechE 1949; FRAeS 1955; FREng (FEng 1976); FRSE 1976. A&AEE, RAF Boscombe Down, 1939–45; RAE, Farnborough, 1945–46; BEA, 1947–53; Chief Engr/Dir, Fairey Aviation Ltd, 1953–60; Westland Aircraft Ltd, 1960–79: Technical Dir (Develt), 1962–66; Dep. Man. Dir, 1966–68; Man. Dir, 1968–72; Vice-Chm., 1972–76. Chm., CEI, 1979–80 (Vice-Chm., 1978–79); Mem., Airworthiness Requirements Bd, CAA, 1976–83 (Chm., 1982–83). Vis. Prof., Univ. of Strathclyde, 1978–84. Mem. Council, RAeS, 1960–83 (Pres., 1973–74; Hon. FRAeS, 1983); Gov., Inveresk Res. Foundn, 1980–90. FRSA 1959; LRPS 1992. Hon. DSc Strathclyde, 1976. *Publications:* contrib. R & M series and RAeS Jl. *Recreations:* hill walking, photography, bird watching. *Address:* Hadley, St John's Hill, Old Coulsdon, Surrey CR5 1HD. *T:* (020) 8660 1008. *Clubs:* MCC, Royal Air Force. *Died 24 July 2013.*

HITCHCOCK, Dr Anthony John Michael; Head of Safety and Transportation Department, Transport and Road Research Laboratory, 1978–89; *b* 26 June 1929; *s* of Dr Ronald W. Hitchcock and Hilda (*née* Gould); *m* 1st, 1953, Audrey Ellen Ashworth (*d* 1990); one *s* two *d*; 2nd, 1992, Louise Nickel (*d* 1999). *Educ:* Bedales; Manchester Grammar Sch.; Trinity Coll., Cambridge; Univ. of Chicago. PhD, BA; MInstP. Asst, Univ. of Chicago, 1951–52; AEA, 1953–67; Department of Transport: Head of Traffic Dept, 1967–71, Head of Transport Ops Dept, 1971–75, TRRL; Head, Res. Policy (Transport) Div., DoE/DoT, 1975–78. Vis. Researcher, Program for Advanced Technol. on the Highway, Univ. of Calif at Berkeley, 1990–94. Vis. Prof., Transport Studies, Cranfield Inst. of Technology, 1978–81. Health and Safety Volunteer, WRVS, 2002–07. *Publications:* Nuclear Reactor Control, 1960; research reports and articles in learned jls. *Recreation:* bridge. *Address:* Seal Point, 2 Oakfield Place, Witney, Oxon OX28 4NH. *Died 29 Sept. 2013.*

HITCHEN, Brian, CBE 1990; Chairman, Brian Hitchen Communications Ltd, since 1996; Chairman and Publisher, Kerry Life Ltd, since 1996; *b* 8 July 1936; *s* of Fred and Alice Hitchen, Lancs; *m* 1962, Ellen Josephine O'Hanlon (*d* 2013), Kildare, Eire; one *s* one *d*. *Educ:* Hegginbottom Sch., Ashton-under-Lyne, Lancs, and elsewhere. Served Army, WO, Whitehall, 1954–56. Copy Boy, Daily Despatch, 1951; Gen. Reporter, Bury Times, 1952–54; Reporter, Manchester Evening News, 1957; Reporter, 1958–63, Foreign Correspondent, Paris Bureau, 1963–64, Daily Mirror; For. Corresp., Mirror US Bureaux, New York and Washington, 1964–72; Dep. News Editor, Daily Mirror, 1972; News Editor, Daily Express, 1973–76; Asst Editor, National Enquirer, USA, 1976, European Bureau Chief, 1977; Asst Editor, Now! magazine, 1978–80; London Editor, The Daily Star, 1981–86; Dep. Editor, Sunday Express, 1986–87; Ed., Daily Star, 1987–94; Ed., Sunday Express, Classic mag. and Sunday Express Magazine, 1994–95; Chm. and Publisher, Irish Country Life Ltd, 1996–2000. Director: Airspeed Internat. Corp., 1973–93; Express Newspapers, 1988–96; Independent Star, Eire, 1988–95. Member: Press Complaints Commn, 1991–95; Defence, Press and Broadcasting Adv. Cttee, 1993–96; NPA Code of Conduct Cttee, 1994–95; Honours Cttee, Media and Broadcasting, 1997–2004. Internat. Media Consultant to Saudi Arabian Amb. to UK and Ireland, 1996–2009; Press Officer, Lifeboat, Shoreham-by-Sea, W Sussex, 1994–2010. Member, Committee: Friends of Airborne Forces Charity, 1996–2010; Saudi-British Jt Cultural Cttee, 2001–. *Publications:* Everything off the Mantlepiece, 1997; Eye of the Storm, 2000; Mischief Maker, 2004. *Recreations:* golf, shooting, writing. *Address:* 32 Palmeira Square, Hove, East Sussex BN3 2JP. *Club:* Reform. *Died 2 Dec. 2013.*

HITCHENS, Christopher Eric; author and journalist; *b* 13 April 1949; *s* of late Comdr Eric Ernest Hitchens and Yvonne Jean Hitchens (*née* Hickman); *m* 1st, 1981, Eleni Meleagrou; one *s* one *d*; 2nd, 1991, Carol Blue; one *d*. *Educ:* Leys Sch., Cambridge; Balliol Coll., Oxford (BA PPE 1970). Social sci. corresp., THES, 1971–73; writer and Asst Editor, New Statesman, 1973–81; columnist and corresp. in Washington, 1982–; Columnist: The Nation (NY), 1982–2002; Vanity Fair (NY), 1982–; Atlantic Monthly, 2002–. Mellon Prof. of English, Univ. of Pittsburgh, 1997; Prof. of Liberal Studies, New Sch., NY, 2000–; Media Fellow, Hoover Instn, Stanford, 2008–. Lannan Literary Award for Non-Fiction, 1992; Nat. Mag. Award, 2007. *Publications:* Karl Marx and the Paris Commune, 1971; James Callaghan, 1976; Hostage to History: Cyprus from the Ottomans to Kissinger, 1984; Imperial Spoils: the curious case of the Elgin Marbles, 1986; Prepared for the Worst: selected essays, 1989; Blood, Class and Nostalgia: Anglo-American ironies, 1990; For the Sake of Argument: selected essays, 1993; When the Borders Bleed: the struggle of the Kurds, 1994; The Missionary Position: Mother Teresa in theory and practice, 1995; No One Left to Lie To, 1999; Unacknowledged Legislation, 2001; The Trial of Henry Kissinger, 2001; Letters to a Young Contrarian: the art of mentoring, 2001; Orwell's Victory, 2002; A Long Short War: the postponed liberation of Iraq, 2003; Blood, Class and Empire: the enduring Anglo-American relationship, 2004; Love, Poverty and War: journeys and essays, 2005; Thomas Jefferson: author of America, 2005; Thomas Paine's Rights of Man, 2006; God Is Not Great: the case against religion, 2007; (ed) The Portable Atheist, 2007; Hitch-22: a memoir, 2010; Arguably, 2011; *posthumous publications:* Mortality, 2012; And Yet, 2016. *Recreations:* reading, travel, disputation. *Address:* 2022 Columbia Road NW, Washington, DC 20009–1352, USA. *T:* (202) 3874842. *Died 15 Dec. 2011.*

HO, Eric Peter, CBE 1981; Chairman, Public Service Commission, Hong Kong, 1987–91; *b* 30 Dec. 1927; *s* of Sai-Ki Ho and Doris (*née* Lo); *m* 1956, Grace Irene, OBE (*d* 2007), *d* of Mr and Mrs A. V. Young; two *s* one *d*. *Educ:* Univ. of Hong Kong (BA 1950). Inspector of Taxes (under training), London, 1950–53; Hong Kong Civil Service, 1954–87: Sec. for Social Services, 1977–83; Sec. for Trade and Industry, 1983–87. RCDS, London, 1976. *Publications:* Times of Change: a memoir of Hong Kong's governance 1950–1991, 2005; Tracing My Children's Lineage, 2010. *Address:* London, SW15. *Died 25 March 2015.*

HOAD, Air Vice-Marshal Norman Edward, CVO 1972; CBE 1969; AFC 1951 and Bar, 1956; artist; *b* 28 July 1923; *s* of Hubert Ronald Hoad and Florence Marie (*née* Johnson); *m* 1945, Olive Coe; two *s*. *Educ:* Brighton. Joined RAF, 1941, pilot trng, S Rhodesia; Lancaster pilot until shot down and taken prisoner in Germany, 1944; various flying and instructional duties, 1945–51; Sqdn Ldr 1951; OC No 192 Sqdn, 1953–55; psc 1956; Wing Comdr, HQ 2 ATAF, 1957–59; pfc 1960; OC No 216 Sqdn, 1960–62; jssc 1963; Gp Capt., MoD, 1963–65; idc 1966; Stn Comdr: RAF Lyneham, 1967, RAF Abingdon, 1968; Defence and Air Attaché, British Embassy, Paris, 1969–72; Dir, Defence Policy (A), 1972–74; Chief of Staff, 46 Gp, RAF Strike Comd, April–Oct. 1974; AOC No 46 Group, and Comdr, UK Jt Airborne Task Force, 1974–75; Senior RAF Mem., RCDS, 1976–78. Director, Air League, 1978–82. Founder Mem., Guild of Aviation Artists; Chm., Soc. of Equestrian Artists. MCMI (MBIM 1970). *Address:* Flowerknot, Starr Lane, All Stretton, Shropshire SY6 6HS. *T:* (01694) 723309. *Club:* Royal Air Force. *Died 29 Nov. 2014.*

HOBAN, Russell Conwell, FRSL 1988; writer; *b* 4 Feb. 1925; *s* of Abram Hoban and Jenny Dimmerman; *m* 1st, 1944, Lillian Aberman (marr. diss. 1975; she *d* 1998); one *s* three *d*; 2nd, 1975, Gundula Ahl; three *s*. *Educ:* Lansdale High Sch.; Philadelphia Museum Sch. of Industrial Art.

Served US Army, 1943–45: 339th Inf., 85th Div., Italy (Bronze Star Medal, 1945). Various jobs, 1945–56; free-lance illustration, 1956–65; copywriter with Doyle, Dane, Bernbach, New York, 1965–67; resident in London, 1969–. Drama: (television) Come and Find Me, 1980; (stage) The Carrier Frequency, 1984; (radio) Perfect and Endless Circles, Radio 3, 1995; By a River in the Mind, Radio 4, 1999; opera: The Second Mrs Kong (music by Sir Harrison Birtwistle), Glyndebourne, 1994; stories for BBC Radio 4. *Publications: children's books:* What Does It Do and How Does It Work?, 1959; The Atomic Submarine, 1960; Bedtime for Frances, 1960, 2nd edn 1995; Herman the Loser, 1961; The Song in My Drum, 1962; London Men and English Men, 1963; Some Snow Said Hello, 1963; A Baby Sister for Frances, 1964, 2nd edn 1993; Nothing To Do, 1964; Bread and Jam for Frances, 1964, 2nd edn 1993; The Sorely Trying Day, 1964; Tom and the Two Handles, 1965; The Story of Hester Mouse, 1965; What Happened When Jack and Daisy Tried To Fool the Tooth Fairies, 1965; Goodnight, 1966; Henry and the Monstrous Din, 1966; Charlie the Tramp, 1966; The Little Brute Family, 1966; Save My Place, 1967; The Mouse and His Child, 1967 (filmed, 1977); The Stone Doll of Sister Brute, 1968; A Birthday for Frances, 1968, 2nd edn 1995; Ugly Bird, 1969; Best Friends for Frances, 1969, 2nd edn 1994; Harvey's Hideout, 1969; The Mole Family's Christmas, 1969; A Bargain for Frances, 1970, 2nd edn 1992; Emmet Otter's Jug-Band Christmas, 1971 (filmed for TV, 1977); The Sea-Thing Child, 1972, rev. edn 1999; Letitia Rabbit's String Song, 1973; How Tom Beat Captain Najork and His Hired Sportsmen, 1974 (Whitbread Literary Award); Ten What?, 1974; Dinner at Alberta's, 1975; Crocodile and Pierrot, 1975; A Near Thing for Captain Najork, 1975; The Twenty-Elephant Restaurant, 1977; Arthur's New Power, 1978; The Dancing Tigers, 1979; La Corona and Other Tin Tales, 1979; Ace Dragon Ltd, 1980; Flat Cat, 1980; The Serpent Tower, 1981; The Great Fruit Gum Robbery, 1981; They Came from Aargh!, 1981; The Flight of Bembel Rudzuk, 1982; The Battle of Zormla, 1982; Jim Frog, 1983; Big John Turkle, 1983; Charlie Meadows, 1984; Lavinia Bat, 1984; The Rain Door, 1986; The Marzipan Pig, 1986; Ponders, 1988; Monsters, 1989; Jim Hedgehog's Supernatural Christmas, 1989; Jim Hedgehog and the Lonesome Tower, 1990; M.O.L.E. (Much Overworked Little Earthmover), 1993; The Court of the Winged Serpent, 1994; Monster Film, 1995; Trouble on Thunder Mountain, 1998; Jim's Lion, 2001; Soonchild, 2011; *novels:* The Lion of Boaz-Jachin and Jachin-Boaz, 1973; Kleinzeit, 1974; Turtle Diary, 1975 (filmed, 1985); Riddley Walker, 1980 (John W. Campbell Meml Award, 1981, Best Internat. Fiction, Aust. Sci. Fiction Achievement Award, 1983; adapted for stage, 1986); Pilgermann, 1983; The Medusa Frequency, 1987; Fremder, 1996; The Trokeville Way, 1996; Mr Rinyo-Clacton's Offer, 1998; Angelica's Grotto, 1999; Amaryllis Night and Day, 2001; The Bat Tattoo, 2002; Her Name Was Lola, 2003; Come Dance With Me, 2005; Linger Awhile, 2006; My Tango with Barbara Strozzi, 2007; Angelica Lost and Found, 2010; *verse:* The Pedalling Man and Other Poems, 1968, 2nd edn 1991; Egg Thoughts and Other Frances Songs, 1972, 2nd edn 1994; (contrib.) Six of the Best (ed A. Harvey), 1989; The Last of the Wallendas and Other Poems, 1997; *anthology:* The Moment Under the Moment, 1992; stories and essays in Fiction Magazine and Granta; *films:* (also narrated): Deadsy, 1989; Door, 1989. *Recreation:* rewriting yesterday's pages. *Address:* David Higham Associates Ltd, 5–8 Lower John Street, Golden Square, W1R 4HA. *T:* (020) 7434 5900, *Fax:* (020) 7437 1072. *Died 13 Dec. 2011.*

HOBDAY, Sir Gordon (Ivan), Kt 1979; Lord Lieutenant and Keeper of the Rolls for Nottinghamshire, 1983–91; Chancellor, Nottingham University, 1979–92 (President of the Council, 1973–82); *b* 1 Feb. 1916; *e s* of late Alexander Thomas Hobday and Frances Cassandra (*née* Meads); *m* 1st, 1940, Margaret Jean Joule (*d* 1995); one *d*; 2nd, 2002, Patricia Birge. *Educ:* Long Eaton Grammar Sch.; UC Nottingham. BSc, PhD London; FRSC. Joined Boots Co., 1939; Dir of Research, 1952–68; Man. Dir, 1970–72; Chm., 1973–81; Chm., Central Independent Television, 1981–85; Dir, Lloyds Bank, 1981–86. A Dep. Chm., Price Commn, 1977–78. Pres., Portland Coll., 1990–93. DL Notts, 1981. KStJ 1983. Hon. LLD Nottingham, 1977. *Recreations:* handicrafts, gardening. *Address:* Ravenshead, Nottingham NG15 9FD. *Died 27 May 2015.*

HOBHOUSE, (Mary) Hermione, MBE 1981; FSA; writer and conservationist; General Editor, Survey of London, 1983–94; *b* 2 Feb. 1934; *d* of late Sir Arthur Lawrence Hobhouse and Konradin, *d* of Rt Hon. Frederick Huth Jackson; *m* 1958, Henry Trevenen Davidson Graham (marr. diss. 1988); one *s* one *d*. *Educ:* Ladies' Coll., Cheltenham; Lady Margaret Hall, Oxford (Hons Mod. Hist.). Researcher/Writer, Associated-Rediffusion TV and Granada TV, 1957–65; Tutor in Architectural History, Architectural Assoc. Sch., London, 1973–78; Sec., Victorian Soc., 1977–82. Member: Royal Commn for Exhibn of 1851, 1983–98; Council, Nat. Trust, 1983–2001; Council, Soc. of Antiquaries, 1984–87; London DAC, 1988–92; Council, Royal Albert Hall, 1988–2004. *Publications:* Thomas Cubitt: Master Builder, 1971 (Hitchcock Medal, 1972), reprinted 1995; Lost London, 1971; History of Regent Street, 1975, 2nd edn 2008; Oxford and Cambridge, 1980; Prince Albert: his life and work, 1983; (ed) Survey of London, vol. 42, Southern Kensington: Kensington Square to Earls Court, 1986, vol. 17, County Hall, 1991, vols 42 and 43, Poplar, Blackwall and the Isle of Dogs, 1994; London Survey'd: the work of the Survey of London 1894–1994, 1994; The Crystal Palace and the Great Exhibition: Art, Science and Productive Industry: the history of the Royal Commission for the Great Exhibition of 1851, 2002; contrib. Architectural Jl, Architectural Review. *Recreations:* gardening, looking at buildings of all periods. *Address:* Westcombe Stables, Evercreech, Shepton Mallet, Somerset BA4 6ES. *T:* (01749) 830465. *Club:* Reform. *Died 17 Oct. 2014.*

HOBSBAWM, Prof. Eric John Ernest, CH 1998; FBA 1976; Emeritus Professor of Economic and Social History, University of London, since 1982; Emeritus Professor, New School for Social Research, New York, since 1991; *b* 9 June 1917; *s* of Leopold Percy Hobsbawm and Nelly Grün; *m* 1962, Marlene Schwarz; one *s* one *d*. *Educ:* Vienna; Berlin; St Marylebone Grammar Sch.; Univ. of Cambridge (BA, PhD). Lectr, Birkbeck Coll., 1947; Fellow, King's Coll., Cambridge, 1949–55, Hon. Fellow, 1973; Birkbeck College, London University: Reader, 1959; Prof., 1970–82; Pres., 2002–; Prof. of Politics and Society, Graduate Faculty, New Sch. for Social Res., New York, 1984–97. Hon. DPhil Univ. of Stockholm, 1970; Hon. DHL: Univ. of Chicago, 1976; New Sch. of Social Res., 1982; Bard Coll., 1986; Hon. LittD: UEA, 1982; York Univ., Canada, 1986; Columbia, 1997; Oxon, 2001; Hon. DLit London, 1993; DU Essex, 1996; D*hc*: Pisa, 1987; Buenos Aires, 1998; Univ. de Artes e Ciencias Sociales, Santiago de Chile, 1998; Univ. of the Republic, Montevideo, 1999; Turin, 2000; Pennsylvania, 2002; Thessaloniki, 2004; Vienna, 2008; Girona, 2008. Foreign Hon. Mem., American Academy of Arts and Sciences, 1971; Hon. Mem., Hungarian Acad. of Sciences, 1979; Foreign Member: Accademia delle Scienze di Torino, 1998; Japan Acad., 2005. Palmes Académiques (France), 1993; Comdr, Order of Southern Cross (Brazil), 1996; Ehrenkreuz für Wissenschaft und Kunst (Austria), 2007. *Publications:* Labour's Turning Point, 1948; Primitive Rebels, 1959; (*pseud.* F. Newton) The Jazz Scene, 1959; The Age of Revolution, 1962; Labouring Men, 1964; (ed) Karl Marx, Precapitalist Formations, 1964; Industry and Empire, 1968; (with G. Rudé) Captain Swing, 1969; Bandits, 1969; Revolutionaries, 1973; The Age of Capital, 1975; (with T. Ranger) The Invention of Tradition, 1983; Worlds of Labour, 1984; The Age of Empire, 1987; Politics for a Rational Left, 1989; Nations and Nationalism since 1780, 1990; Echoes of the Marseillaise, 1990; Age of Extremes: the short Twentieth Century, 1994; On History, 1997; Uncommon People: resistance, rebellion and jazz, 1998; (with A. Polito) The New Century, 2000; Interesting Times: a twentieth-century life, 2002; Globalisation, Democracy and Terrorism, 2007; How to Change the World: tales of Marx and Marxism, 2011; Fractured Times: culture and society in the 20th Century, 2013; contribs to jls. *Recreation:* travel. *Address:* Birkbeck College, Malet Street, WC1E 7HX. *T:* (020) 7631 6299. *Died 1 Oct. 2012.*

HOBSON, Anthony Robert Alwyn, DLitt; FBA 1992; book historian; *b* 5 Sept. 1921; *s* of Geoffrey Dudley Hobson, MVO and Gertrude Adelaide, *d* of Rev. Thomas Vaughan, Rector of Rhuddlan, Flintshire; *m* 1959, Elena Pauline Tanya (*d* 1988), *d* of Igor Vinogradoff; one *s* two *d*. *Educ:* Eton Coll. (Oppidan Scholar); New Coll., Oxford (MA); DLitt Oxon, 1992. Served Scots Guards, 1941–46, Captain; Italy, 1943–46 (mentioned in despatches). Joined Sotheby & Co., 1947: Dir, 1949–71, Associate, 1971–77. Sandars Reader in Bibliography, Univ. of Cambridge, 1974–75; Franklin Jasper Walls Lectr, Pierpont Morgan Library, NY, 1979; Vis. Fellow, All Souls Coll., Oxford, 1982–83; Rosenbach Fellow, Univ. of Pennsylvania, 1990; Lyell Reader in Bibliography, Univ. of Oxford, 1990–91. President: Bibliographical Soc., 1977–79; Association internationale de Bibliophilie, 1985–99; Hon. Pres., Edinburgh Bibliographical Soc., 1971–; Trustee: Eton Coll. Collections Trust, 1977–97; Lambeth Palace Library, 1984–90. Hon. Fellow, Pierpont Morgan Library, 1983–; For. Associate, Ateneo Veneto, 1987–. Cavaliere Ufficiale, Al Merito della Repubblica Italiana, 1979. *Publications:* French and Italian Collectors and their Bindings, 1953; Great Libraries, 1970; Apollo and Pegasus, 1975; Humanists and Bookbinders, 1989 (Premio Felice Feliciano, Verona, 1991; Triennial Prize, Internat. League of Antiquarian Booksellers, 1991); (with Paul Culot) Italian and French Sixteenth-century Bookbindings, 1990; Renaissance Book Collecting: Jean Grolier and Diego Hurtado de Mendoza, their books and bindings, 1999; (ed) Ronald Firbank: letters to his mother 1920–1924, 2001; (ed jtly) Bartolomeo Sanvito: the life and work of a Renaissance scribe, by A. de la Mare and L. Nuvolini, 2009; Some Memories of Congresses and Colloquia of the Association internationale de Bibliophilie, 2011; contrib. The Library, TLS, etc. *Recreations:* travel, opera, visiting libraries founded before 1800. *Address:* The Glebe House, Whitsbury, near Fordingbridge, Hants SP6 3QB. *T:* (01725) 518221. *Clubs:* Brooks's, Beefsteak, Roxburghe; Grolier (New York); Société des Bibliophiles François (Paris). *Died 12 July 2014.*

HOCKLEY, Rev. Canon Raymond Alan; Canon Residentiary, Precentor, Succentor Canonicorum and Chamberlain of York Minster, 1976–95, Canon Emeritus, since 1995; *b* 18 Sept. 1929; 2nd *s* of late Henry Hockley and Doris (*née* Stonehouse); unmarried. *Educ:* Firth Park School, Sheffield; Royal Academy of Music, London; Westcott House, Cambridge. MA, LRAM. Macfarren Schol., Royal Acad. of Music, 1951–54; Charles Lucas Medal, William Corder Prize, Cuthbert Nunn Prize, etc; Theodore Holland Award, 1955. Clements Memorial Prize for Chamber Music by a British subject, 1954. Curate of St Augustine's, Sheffield, 1958–61; Priest-in-charge of Holy Trinity, Wicker, with St Michael and All Angels, Neepsend, 1961–63; Chaplain of Westcott House, Cambridge, 1963–68; Fellow, Chaplain and Dir of Studies in Music, Emmanuel Coll., Cambridge, 1968–76. Compositions performed include: Songs for Tenor, Soprano; String Quartet; Divertimento for piano duet; Cantata for Easter and the Ascension; Symphony; Suite for Orchestra; Mass for Choir and Organ; various anthems and motets; incidental music for plays. Other works include: two more Symphonies, A Woman's Last Word for three sopranos; Mysterium Dei, oratorio; twelve Suites for piano; Canticles for Men's Voices. *Publications:* Six Songs of Faith; New Songs for the Church; Intercessions at Holy Communion; contribs to theological and musical jls. *Address:* 26 Buckingham Mews, Sutton Coldfield B73 5PR. *T:* (0121) 354 7083. *Died 11 Sept. 2012.*

HODGETTS, Robert Bartley; Clerk to Worshipful Company of Glaziers, 1979–85; *b* 10 Nov. 1918; *s* of late Captain Bartley Hodgetts, MN and Florence Hodgetts (*née* Stagg); *m* 1st, 1945, A. K. Jeffreys; one *d*; 2nd, 1949, Frances Grace (*d* 2007), *d* of late A. J. Pepper, Worcester; two *d*. *Educ:* Merchant Taylors' Sch., Crosby; St John's Coll., Cambridge (Scholar, MA). Served RNVR (A), 1940–45. Asst Principal, Min. of Nat. Insce, 1947; Principal 1951; Asst Sec. 1964; Under-Sec., DHSS, 1973–78. *Recreation:* watching cricket and Rugby football. *Address:* 10 The Close, Winchester, Hants SO23 9LS. *T:* (01962) 890987. *Died 15 Nov. 2015.*

HODGSON, Gordon Hewett; Master of the Supreme Court, Queen's Bench Division, 1983–2000; *b* 21 Jan. 1929; *s* of late John Lawrence Hodgson and Alice Joan Hodgson (*née* Wickham); *m* 1958, Pauline Audrey Gray (*d* 2010); two *s*. *Educ:* Oundle School; University College London. LLB (Hons). National Service, RAEC, 1947–49; called to the Bar, Middle Temple, 1953; private practice, South Eastern Circuit, 1954–83; Asst Boundary Commissioner, 1976; Asst Recorder, 1979. Mem. Cttee, Bentham Club, 1987– (Chm., 1990–95). Sec., Dacorum Heritage Trust Ltd, 2003–09. FZS 1990. *Publications:* (ed jtly) Supreme Court Practice, 1991, 1995 and 1999. *Recreations:* gardening, enjoying Tuscany. *Address:* Tenterden Nursing Home, Lye Lane, Bricket Wood, Herts AL2 3AN. *T:* (01923) 672894. *Clubs:* East India; Bar Yacht. *Died 18 July 2013.*

HODGSON, Sir Maurice (Arthur Eric), Kt 1979; Chief Executive, 1982–85, and Chairman, 1982–87, British Home Stores plc; *b* 21 Oct. 1919; *s* of late Walter Hodgson and of Amy Hodgson (*née* Walker); *m* 1945, Norma Fawcett (*d* 2002); one *s* one *d*. *Educ:* Bradford Grammar Sch.; Merton Coll., Oxford (Hon. Fellow, 1979). MA, BSc; FREng, FIChemE; CChem, FRSC. Joined ICI Ltd Fertilizer & Synthetic Products Gp, 1942; seconded to ICI (New York) Ltd, 1955–58; Head of ICI Ltd Technical Dept, 1958; Develt Dir, ICI Ltd Heavy Organic Chemicals Div., 1960, Dep. Chm., 1964; Gen. Man., Company Planning, ICI Ltd, 1966; Commercial Dir and Planning Dir, ICI Ltd, 1970; Dep. Chm., ICI Ltd, 1972–78, Chm., 1978–82; Director: Carrington Viyella Ltd, 1970–74; Imperial Chemicals Insce Ltd, 1970–78 (Chm. 1972); Dunlop Holdings plc, 1982–84 (Chm. 1984); Storehouse, 1985–89; Member: Internat. Adv. Bd, AMAX Inc., 1982–85; European Adv. Council, Air Products and Chemicals Inc., 1982–84; Council, Lloyd's of London, 1987–94. Chm., Civil Justice Review Adv. Cttee, 1985–88; Member: Court, British Shippers' Council, 1978–82; Council, CBI, 1978–82; Internat. Council, Salk Inst., 1978–97; Court, Univ. of Bradford, 1979–90. Vis. Fellow, Sch. of Business and Organizational Studies, Univ. of Lancaster, 1970–80. Governor, London Grad. Sch. of Business Studies, 1978–87. DUniv Heriot-Watt, 1979; Hon. DTech Bradford, 1979; Hon. DSc Loughborough, 1981; Hon. FUMIST, 1979. Messel Medal, Soc. of Chemical Industry, 1980; George E. Davis Medal, IChemE, 1982. *Recreations:* horse-racing, swimming, fishing. *Died 1 Oct. 2014.*

HODSON, Denys Fraser, CBE 1981; Director, Arts and Recreation, Thamesdown Borough Council, 1974–92; *b* 23 May 1928; *s* of late Rev. Harold Victor Hodson, MC and Marguerite Edmée Ritchie; *m* 1954, Julie Compton Goodwin (*d* 2009); one *s* one *d*. *Educ:* Marlborough Coll.; Trinity Coll., Oxford (MA). After a career in commerce and industry, apptd first Controller of Arts and Recreation, Swindon Bor. Council, 1970. Chairman: Southern Arts Assoc., 1974–80 and 1985–87; Council, Regional Arts Assocs, 1975–80; Chief Leisure Officers' Assoc., 1974 and 1982–84; Chm., Public Arts Commns Agency, 1993–2000; Vice-Chm., Arts Council of GB, 1989–94 (Mem., 1987–94); a Director: Oxford Playhouse Co., 1974–86; Oxford Stage Co., 1988–89; Chairman: Brewery Arts, 1994–98; Arts Research Ltd, 1999–2006 (Trustee, 1995–); Vice-Pres., Voluntary Arts Network, 1998– (Vice-Chm., 1992–94; Chm., 1994–98); a Governor: BFI, 1976–87 (Dep. Chm., 1985–87); Wyvern Arts Trust, 1984–95. Chairman: Friends of Fairford Church, 1998–2012; Friends of Lydiard Park, 2005–10. *Publications:* (contrib.) Arts Centres, 1981; (contrib.) The Future of Leisure Services, 1988; conf. papers and articles. *Recreations:* bird-watching, fishing, the arts. *Address:* Manor Farm House, Fairford, Glos GL7 4AR. *T:* (01285) 712462. *Died 13 Jan. 2013.*

HOGBEN, Ven. Peter Graham; Archdeacon of Dorking, 1982–90, then Archdeacon Emeritus; *b* 5 July 1925; *s* of Harold Henry and Winifred Minnie Hogben; *m* 1948, Audree Sayers; two *s*. *Educ:* Harvey Grammar School, Folkestone; Bishops' College, Cheshunt. Served Royal Engineers, 1943–47 (three years in Far East). Office Manager for two firms of Agricultural Auctioneers in Kent and Herts, 1948–59; theological college, 1960–61; ordained, 1961; Asst Curate of Hale, 1961–64; Vicar of

Westborough, Guildford, 1964–71; Chaplain to WRAC, 1964–71; Vicar of Ewell, 1971–82; Rural Dean, Epsom, 1980–82. Editor, Guildford Diocesan Leaflet, 1978–82; Hon. Canon of Guildford, 1979–90, Canon Emeritus, 1990. *Recreations:* walking, gardening, water colour painting. *Address:* 3 School Road, Rowledge, Farnham, Surrey GU10 4EJ. *T:* (01252) 793533. *Died 26 Nov. 2011.*

HOGGART, Richard (Herbert), LittD; Warden, Goldsmiths' College, University of London, 1976–84; *b* 24 Sept. 1918; 2nd *s* of Tom Longfellow Hoggart and Adeline Emma Hoggart; *m* 1942, Mary Holt France; one *s* one *d* (and one *s* decd). *Educ:* elementary and secondary schs, Leeds; Leeds Univ. (MA, LittD 1978). Served 1940–46, RA; demobilised as Staff Capt. Staff Tutor and Sen. Staff Tutor, University Coll. of Hull and University of Hull, 1946–59; Sen. Lectr in English, University of Leicester, 1959–62; Prof. of English, Birmingham Univ., 1962–73, and Dir, Centre for Contemporary Cultural Studies, 1964–73; an Asst Dir-Gen., Unesco, 1970–75. Vis. Fellow, Inst. of Development Studies, Univ. of Sussex, 1975. Visiting Prof., University of Rochester (NY), USA, 1956–57; Chichele Lectr, All Souls Coll., Oxford 1961; Reith Lectr, 1971. Member: Albemarle Cttee on Youth Services, 1958–60; (Pilkington) Cttee on Broadcasting, 1960–62; Arts Council, 1976–81 (Chm., Drama Panel, 1977–80; Vice-Chm., 1980–82); Statesman and Nation Publishing Co. Ltd, 1977–81 (Chm., 1978–81); Chairman: Adv. Council for Adult and Continuing Educn, 1977–83; European Museum of the Year Award, 1977–95; Broadcasting Research Unit, 1981–91; Book Trust, 1995–97 (Vice-Chm., 1997–); Vice-Chm., Unesco Forum, 1997–. Patron, Nat. Book Cttee, 1998–. Governor, Royal Shakespeare Theatre, 1962–88. Pres., British Assoc. of Former UN Civil Servants, 1979–86. Hon. Professor: UEA, 1984; Univ. of Surrey, 1985; Hon. Fellow: Sheffield Polytechnic, 1983; Goldsmiths' Coll., 1987; DUniv: Open, 1973; Surrey, 1981; Hon DèsL: Univ. of Bordeaux, 1975; Paris, 1987; Hon. LLD: CNAA, 1982; York (Toronto), 1988; Sheffield, 1999; Hon. LittD East Anglia, 1986; Hon. DLitt: Leicester, 1988; Hull, 1988; Keele, 1995; Leeds Metropolitan, 1995; Westminster, 1996; East London, 1998; London Metropolitan, 2003; Hon. DLit London, 2000. *Publications:* Auden, 1951; The Uses of Literacy, 1957; W. H. Auden, 1957; W. H. Auden—A Selection, 1961; chap. in Conviction, 1958; chapter in Pelican Guide to English Literature, 1961; Teaching Literature, 1963; chapter in Of Books and Humankind, 1964; The Critical Moment, 1964; How and Why Do We Learn, 1965; The World in 1984, 1965; Essays by Divers Hands XXXIII; Guide to the Social Sciences, 1966; Technology and Society, 1966; Essays on Reform, 1967; Your Sunday Paper (ed), 1967; Speaking to Each Other: vol. I, About Society; vol. II, About Literature, 1970; Only Connect (Reith Lectures), 1972; An Idea and Its Servants, 1978; (ed with Janet Morgan) The Future of Broadcasting, 1982; An English Temper, 1982; (ed) The Public Service Idea in British Broadcasting: main principles, 1986; Writers on Writing, 1986; (jtly) The British Council and The Arts, 1986; (with Douglas Johnson) An Idea of Europe, 1987; A Local Habitation (autobiog.), 1988; (ed) Liberty and Legislation, 1989; (ed) Quality in Television: programmes, programme makers, systems, 1989; A Sort of Clowning: life and times 1940–59 (autobiog.), 1990; An Imagined Life: life and times 1959–91 (autobiog.), 1992; Townscape with Figures, 1994; The Way We Live Now, 1995; First and Last Things, 1999; Richard Hoggart en France (essays), ed J.-C. Passeron, 1999; Between Two Worlds, 2001; Everyday Language and Everyday Life, 2003; Mass Media in a Mass Society: myth and reality, 2004; Promises to Keep: thoughts in old age, 2005; numerous introductions, articles, pamphlets and reviews. *Recreation:* pottering. *Died 10 April 2014.*

HOGGART, Simon David; Parliamentary Reporter, The Guardian, since 1993; *b* 26 May 1946; *s* of late Richard Herbert Hoggart, LittD; *m* 1983, Alyson Clare Corner; one *s* one *d*. *Educ:* Hymers College, Hull; Wyggeston Grammar Sch., Leicester; King's College, Cambridge. MA. Reporter, The Guardian, 1968–71, N Ireland corresp., 1971–73, political corresp., 1973–81; feature writer, The Observer, 1981–85; political columnist, Punch, 1979–85; US correspondent, 1985–89, columnist, 1989–92, Political Editor, 1992–93, The Observer; television critic, 2000–, wine corresp., 2001–, The Spectator. Chairman, The News Quiz, Radio 4, 1996–2006. *Publications:* (with Alistair Michie) The Pact, 1978; (with David Leigh) Michael Foot: a portrait, 1981; On the House, 1981; Back on the House, 1982; House of Ill Fame, 1985; (ed) House of Cards, 1988; America: a user's guide, 1990; House of Correction, 1994; (with Michael Hutchinson) Bizarre Beliefs, 1995; (with Steve Bell) Live Briefs, 1996; Playing to the Gallery, 2002; Punch Lines, 2003; The Cat That Could Open the Fridge, 2004; The Hamster That Loved Puccini, 2005; (with Emily Monk) Dear Mum, 2006; The Hands of History, 2007; The Christmas Letters, 2007; Life's Too Short to Drink Bad Wine, 2009; A Long Lunch, 2010; Send Up The Clowns, 2011; House of Fun, 2012. *Recreations:* reading, writing, wine. *Address:* Parliamentary Press Gallery, House of Commons, SW1A 0AA. *T:* (020) 7219 4700. *E:* simon.hoggart@guardian.co.uk. *Died 5 Jan. 2014.*

HOGWOOD, Christopher Jarvis Haley, CBE 1989; harpsichordist, conductor, musicologist, writer, editor and broadcaster; Founder and Director, Academy of Ancient Music, 1973–2006, then Emeritus Director; *b* 10 Sept. 1941; *s* of Haley Evelyn Hogwood and Marion Constance Higgott. *Educ:* Pembroke Coll., Cambridge (MA; Hon. Fellow, 1992); Charles Univ., Prague. With Acad. of St Martin-in-the-Fields, 1965–76; Founder Mem., Early Music Consort of London, 1965–76; Artistic Director: King's Lynn Festival, 1976–80; Handel & Haydn Soc., Boston, USA, 1986–2001 (Conductor Laureate, 2001–); Summer Mozart Fest., Nat. Symphony Orch., USA, 1993–2001; Dir of Music, St Paul Chamber Orchestra, USA, 1987–92, Prin. Guest Conductor, 1992–98; Associate Dir, Beethoven Academie, Antwerp, 1998–2002; Principal Guest Conductor: Kammerorchester Basel, 2000–06; Orquesta Ciudad de Granada, 2001–04; Orch. Sinfonica di Milano Giuseppe Verdi, 2003–06. Internat. Prof. of Early Music Performance, RAM, 1992–; Vis. Prof., KCL, 1992–96; Hon. Professor of Music: Keele Univ., 1986–90; Univ. of Cambridge; RAM; Gresham Prof. of Music, Gresham Coll., 2010–. Keyboard and orchestral recordings. Mem. Editl Bd, Early Music, 1993–97; Chm., Adv. Bd, C. P. E. Bach Complete Works, 1999–; Chm., Adv. Cttee and Gen. Ed., Francesco Geminiani Opera Omnia, 2008–. Freeman, Co. of Musicians, 1989. FRSA 1982. Hon. RAM 1995; Hon. Fellow, Jesus Coll., Cambridge, 1989. Hon. DMus: Keele, 1991; Cambridge, 2008; RCM, 2013. Walter Willson Cobbett Medal, Co. of Musicians, 1986; Distinguished Musician Award, ISM, 1997; Martinu Medal, Bohuslav Martinu Foundn, Prague, 1999; Handel Prize, Halle, Germany, 2008. *Publications:* Music at Court (Folio Society), 1977; The Trio Sonata, 1979; Haydn's Visits to England (Folio Society), 1980; (ed with R. Luckett) Music in Eighteenth-Century England, 1983; Handel, 1984, rev. edn 2007; (ed) Holmes' Life of Mozart (Folio Society), 1991; (ed) The Keyboard in Baroque Europe, 2003; Handel: Water Music and Music for the Royal Fireworks, 2005. *Address:* 10 Brookside, Cambridge CB2 1JE. *T:* (01223) 363975. *E:* christopher@hogwood.org. *Died 24 Sept. 2014.*

HOLBROOK, David Kenneth, FEA; author; *b* 9 Jan. 1923; *o s* of late Kenneth Redvers and Elsie Eleanor Holbrook; *m* 1949, Margot Davies-Jones; two *s* two *d*. *Educ:* City of Norwich Sch.; Downing Coll., Cambridge (Exhibr). Intell., mines and explosives officer, ER Yorks Yeo., Armd Corps, 1942–45. Asst Editor, Our Time, 1948; Asst Editor, Bureau of Current Affairs, 1949; Tutor organiser, WEA, 1952–53; Tutor, Bassingbourn Village Coll., Cambs, 1954–61; Fellow, King's Coll., Cambridge, 1961–65; Sen. Leverhulme Res. Fellow, 1965; College Lectr in English, Jesus Coll., Cambridge, 1968–70; Compton Poetry Lectr, Hull Univ., 1969 (resigned); Writer in Residence, Dartington Hall, 1970–73 (grant from Elmgrant Trust); Downing Coll., Cambridge: Asst Dir, English Studies, 1973–75; Fellow and Dir of English Studies, 1981–88, Emeritus Fellow, 1988–; Leverhulme Emeritus Res. Fellow, 1988–90. Hooker Distinguished Vis. Prof., McMaster Univ., Ontario, 1984. Founding FEA 2000. Arts Council Writers Grants, 1970, 1976, 1979. Mem. Editorial Bd, New Universities Qly, 1976–86. *Publications: poetry:* Imaginings, 1961; Against the Cruel Frost, 1963; Object Relations, 1967; Old World, New

World, 1969; Moments in Italy, 1976; Chance of a Lifetime, 1978; Selected Poems, 1980; Bringing Everything Home, 1999; Collected Poems, 2009; *fiction:* Lights in the Sky Country, 1963; Flesh Wounds, 1966; A Play of Passion, 1978; Nothing Larger than Life, 1987; Worlds Apart, 1988; A Little Athens, 1990; Jennifer, 1991; The Gold in Father's Heart, 1992; Even If They Fail, 1994; Getting it Wrong with Uncle Tom, 1998; Going Off the Rails, 2003; *on education:* English for Maturity, 1961; English for the Rejected, 1964; The Secret Places, 1964; The Exploring Word, 1967; Children's Writing, 1967; English in Australia Now, 1972; Education, Nihilism and Survival, 1977; English for Meaning, 1980; Education and Philosophical Anthropology, 1987; Further Studies in Philosophical Anthropology, 1988; English in a University Education, 2006; *literary criticism:* Llareggub Revisited, 1962; The Quest for Love, 1965; The Masks of Hate, 1972; Dylan Thomas: the code of night, 1972; Sylvia Plath: poetry and existence, 1976; Lost Bearings in English Poetry, 1977; The Novel and Authenticity, 1987; Images of Woman in Literature, 1989; The Skeleton in the Wardrobe: the fantasies of C. S. Lewis, 1991; Edith Wharton and the Unsatisfactory Man, 1991; Where D. H. Lawrence was Wrong about Woman, 1991; Charles Dickens and The Image of Woman, 1993; Tolstoy, Women and Death, 1997; Wuthering Heights: a drama of being, 1997; A Study of George MacDonald and the Image of Woman, 2000; Lewis Carroll: nonsense against sorrow, 2001; Jane Austen and the Authentic Choice, 2009; The Literature of Childhood, 2009; Henry James' Sexual Ambiguity, 2011; *music criticism:* Gustav Mahler and the Courage to Be, 1975; *general:* Children's Games, 1957; Human Hope and the Death Instinct, 1971; Sex and Dehumanization, 1972; The Pseudo-revolution, 1972; (ed) The Case Against Pornography, 1972; Evolution and the Humanities, 1987; (ed) What is it to be Human?: report on a philosophy conference, 1990; Creativity and Popular Culture, 1994; *anthologies:* edited: Iron, Honey, Gold, 1961; People and Diamonds, 1962; Thieves and Angels, 1963; Visions of Life, 1964; (with Elizabeth Poston) The Cambridge Hymnal, 1967; Plucking the Rushes, 1968; (with Christine Mackenzie) The Honey of Man, 1975; *opera libretti:* (with Wilfrid Mellers) Mary Easter, 1957 and The Borderline, 1958, published as Two Scripts for Plays in Music, 2004; (with John Joubert) The Quarry, 1967; *festschrift:* Powers of Being: David Holbrook and his work, ed E. Webb, 1996. *Recreations:* painting, cooking. *Address:* 1 Tennis Court Terrace, Cambridge CB2 1QX. *Died 11 Aug. 2011.*

HOLLAND, Hon. Sir Alan (Douglas), Kt 1995; Judge, High Court (formerly Supreme Court) of New Zealand, 1978–94, retired; *b* 20 June 1929; *s* of Clarence Cyril Holland and Marjorie Evelyn Holland; *m* 1961, Felicity Ann Ower; one *s*. *Educ:* Waitaki Boys' High Sch.; Canterbury Coll., Univ. of New Zealand (LLB). Part-time Lectr in Law and Commerce Faculties of Canterbury Univ., 1953–63; Partner, Wynn Williams & Co., Solicitors, Christchurch, 1956–78. Pres., Canterbury Dist Law Soc., 1973 (Mem. Council, 1963–73); Mem. Council and associated cttees, NZ Law Soc., 1970–74. *Recreation:* general. *Address:* Villa 18, 60 Browns Road, Merivale, Christchurch 8014, New Zealand. *T:* (3) 3557102. *Club:* Christchurch. *Died 3 June 2014.*

HOLLAND, Sir Philip (Welsby), Kt 1983; *b* 14 March 1917; *s* of late John Holland, Middlewich, Cheshire; *m* 1943, Josephine Alma Hudson (*d* 1999); one *s*. *Educ:* Sir John Deane's Grammar Sch., Northwich. Enlisted RAF 1936; commissioned 1943. Factory Manager, Jantzen Knitting Mills, 1946–47; Management Research, 1948–49; Manufacturers' Agent in Engineering and Refractories Products, 1949–60. Contested (C) Yardley Div. of Birmingham, Gen. Election, 1955; MP (C): Acton, 1959–64; Carlton, 1966–83; Gedling, 1983–87. PPS: to Minister of Pensions and Nat. Insurance, 1961–62; to Chief Sec. to Treasury and Paymaster-Gen., 1962–64; to Minister of Aviation Supply, 1970; to Minister for Aerospace, 1971; to Minister for Trade, 1972. Pres., Cons. Trade Union Nat. Adv. Cttee, 1972–74. Personnel Manager, The Ultra Electronics Group of Companies, 1964–66; Personnel Consultant to Standard Telephones and Cables Ltd, 1969–81. Chm., Cttee of Selection, H of C, 1979–84; Standing Cttee Chm., 1983–87. Councillor, Royal Borough of Kensington, 1955–59. Rector's Warden, St Margaret's Church, Westminster, 1990–95. *Publications:* The Quango Explosion (jtly), 1978; Quango, Quango, Quango, 1979; Costing the Quango, 1979; The Quango Death List, 1980; The Governance of Quangos, 1981; Quelling the Quango, 1982; (jtly) A–Z Guide to Parliament, 1988; Lobby Fodder?, 1988; St Margaret's Westminster, 1993; The Hunting of the Quango, 1994. *Recreations:* travel, writing. *Address:* 53 Pymers Mead, West Dulwich, SE21 8NH. *Died 2 June 2011.*

HOLLIDAY, Dr Robin, FRS 1976; Chief Research Scientist, Commonwealth Scientific and Industrial Research Organisation (Australia), 1988–97; *b* 6 Nov. 1932; *s* of Clifford and Eunice Holliday; *m* 1st, 1957, Diana Collet (*née* Parsons) (marr. diss. 1983); one *s* three *d*; 2nd, 1986, Lily Irene (*née* Huschtscha); one *d*. *Educ:* Hitchin Grammar Sch.; Univ. of Cambridge (BA, PhD); Fulbright Scholar, 1962. Member, Scientific Staff: Dept of Genetics, John Innes Inst., Bayfordbury, Herts, 1958–65; Division of Microbiology, Nat. Inst. for Med. Research, Mill Hill, 1965–70; Head, Div. of Genetics, Nat. Inst. for Med. Research, 1970–88. Mem., EMBO, 1976. FAA 2005. For. Fellow, INSA, 1995. Lord Cohen Medal, 1987; Royal Medal, Royal Society, 2011. *Publications:* The Science of Human Progress, 1981; Genes, Proteins and Cellular Aging, 1986; Understanding Ageing, 1995; Slaves and Saviours, 2000; Aging: the paradox of life, 2007; Origins and Outcomes: an autobiography, 2008; over 250 scientific papers on genetic recombination, repair, epigenetics and cellular ageing. *Recreations:* sculpture, writing. *Address:* 12 Roma Court, West Pennant Hills, NSW 2125, Australia. *T:* (2) 98733476. *E:* randl.holliday@bigpond.com. *W:* www.robinholliday.com. *Died 9 April 2014.*

HOLLINS, Rear-Adm. Hubert Walter Elphinstone, CB 1974; marine consultant; *b* 8 June 1923; *s* of Lt-Col W. T. Hollins; *m* 1963, Jillian Mary McAlpin; one *s* one *d*. *Educ:* Stubbington House; Britannia RNC Dartmouth. Cadet RN, 1937; Comdr 1957; Captain 1963; Rear-Adm. 1972; comd HM Ships Petard, Dundas, Caesar and Antrim; Flag Officer, Gibraltar, 1972–74; Admiral Commanding Reserves, 1974–77; Gen. Man., ME Navigation Aids Service, Bahrain, 1977–84. Younger Brother of Trinity House; Mem., Trinity House Lighthouse Bd, 1985–91. Commodore, Bahrain Yacht Club, 1981–83. Master Mariner. Trustee, Royal Merchant Navy Sch., Bearwood, 1985–92; President: Newbury RN Assoc., 1985–90; Newbury Sea Cadet Corps, 1985–91 (Patron, 1991); Milford Haven Sea Cadet Corps, 2006–11. Vice Patron, Gallantry Medallists' League, 1995–2003. *Recreation:* fishing. *Address:* Waunllan, Llandyfriog, Newcastle Emlyn, Cardiganshire SA38 9HB. *T:* (01239) 710456. *E:* jillieandhugo@hotmail.co.uk. *Died 31 Jan. 2014.*

HOLLMAN, Arthur, MD; FRCP; FLS; Hon. Consultant Cardiologist, East Sussex Hospitals NHS Trust, since 2002; Consultant Cardiologist, University College Hospital, London, 1962–87, then Consulting Cardiologist; Consultant Cardiologist, Hospital for Sick Children, London, 1978–88, then Consulting Cardiologist; Hon. Senior Lecturer, University College London Medical School (formerly University College and Middlesex School of Medicine), since 1962; *b* 7 Dec. 1923; *s* of W. J. and I. R. Hollman; *m* 1949, Catharine Elizabeth Large (*d* 2006); three *d* (and one *d* decd). *Educ:* Tiffin Boys' Sch., Kingston upon Thames; University Coll. London (Fellow, 1978); UCH Med. Sch. (MD). FRCP 1967. FLS 1983. Jun. hosp. appts, London, Banbury and Taplow, 1946–57; Bilton Pollard Fellow of UCH Med. Sch. at Children's Meml Hosp., Montreal, 1951–52; Clinical Asst, National Heart Hosp., 1954–56; Sen. Registrar and Asst Lectr, Royal Postgraduate Med. Sch., 1957–62; Hon. Consultant Cardiologist, Kingston Hosp., 1964–87. Advisor in Cardiology: to Mauritius Govt, 1966–86; to Republic of Seychelles, 1974–94. Coll. Gardener, 1975–85, Councillor, 1976–79, RCP. Thomas Lewis Lectr, British Cardiac Soc., 1981; Fitzpatrick Lectr, RCP, 1982; Lectr, Soc. of Apothecaries, 1991–2012; President's Lect., Duchy Health Charity, 2011. Member: Adv. Cttee, Chelsea Physic Garden, 1971–98; Council, British Heart Foundn, 1975–80; British Cardiac Soc. (Mem. Council, Asst Sec., and Sec., 1971–76; Archivist, 1993–2013); Assoc. of

Physicians of GB and Ireland. Member: Pett Parish Council, 2003–11; Probus Club, Rye, 2005–12. Pres., Osler Club, 1983–84. Curator of Physic Garden, Barbers' Co., 1995–2013 (Liveryman, 2000; Barber Emeritus, 2011). President's Medal, RCP, 1998. *Publications:* Plants in Medicine, 1989, 3rd edn 1996; Plants in Cardiology, 1992; Sir Thomas Lewis: pioneer cardiologist and clinical scientist, 1997; (ed jtly) British Cardiology in the 20th Century, 2000; scientific papers on cardiology, and articles and chapters on the history of cardiology and medicinal plants. *Recreations:* gardening, especially medicinal plants, medical history, lectures to medical and local organisations, Glyndebourne opera, collecting hatpins and hatpin holders. *Address:* Sea Bank, Chick Hill, Pett, Hastings, East Sussex TN35 4EQ. *T:* (01424) 813228. *E:* arthur@hollman.co.uk. *Club:* Athenæum. *Died 13 Aug. 2014.*

HOLLOM, Sir Jasper (Quintus), KBE 1975; Chairman: Eagle Star Holdings PLC, 1985–87; Eagle Star Insurance Co. Ltd, 1985–87; *b* 16 Dec. 1917; *s* of Arthur and Kate Louisa Hollom; *m* 1954, Patricia Elizabeth Mary Ellis (*d* 2013). *Educ:* King's Sch., Bruton. Entered Bank of England, 1936; appointed Deputy Chief Cashier, 1956; Chief Cashier, 1962–66; Director, 1966–70, 1980–84; Deputy Governor, 1970–80. Director: BAT Industries plc, 1980–87; Portals Hldgs plc, 1980–88. Chairman: Panel on Take-overs and Mergers, 1980–87; Council for the Securities Industry, 1985–86; Commonwealth Develt Finance Co. Ltd, 1980–86; Pres., Council of Foreign Bondholders, 1983–89. *Address:* The Long Barn, Alexanders Lane, Privett, Alton, Hants GU34 3PW. *T:* (01730) 828417. *Died 29 Aug. 2014.*

HOLLOWAY, Hon. Sir Barry (Blyth), KBE 1984 (CBE 1974); *b* 26 Sept. 1934; *s* of Archibald and Betty Holloway; *m* 1990, Fua Evelin; one *s* four *d*, and three *s* four *d* by previous marriage. *Educ:* Launceston Church Grammar Sch., Tasmania; Sch. of Pacific Administration, Sydney, 1957; Univ. of Papua New Guinea. Dip., Pacific Admin. District Officer in Papua New Guinea, 1953–64. Elected to first PNG Parliament, 1964; Foundn Mem., Pangu Pati, 1966; MP Eastern Highlands Province. Member of various parliamentary cttees, incl. Public Accounts; Speaker of Parliament, 1972–77; Finance Minister, 1977–80; Minister for Educn, 1982–85. Policy Co-ordinator, Planning, Prime Minister's Dept, 1995–96. Chairman of Constituent Assembly responsible for the formation of Constitution of the Independent State of Papua New Guinea, 1974–75. Consultant, World Bank, to establish Anti-Corruption Commn, PNG, 1997–98; Alternate Exec. Dir, Asian Develt Bank, Manila, Philippines, 1999–. Director of various companies. *Recreations:* reading, agriculture. *Address:* PO Box 6361, Boroko, Papua New Guinea. *T:* 3231611. *Died 16 Jan. 2013.*

HOLLOWAY, Frank, FCA; Managing Director, Supplies and Transport, 1980–83 and Board Member, 1978–83, British Steel Corporation; *b* 20 Oct. 1924; *s* of Frank and Elizabeth Holloway; *m* 1949, Elizabeth Beattie; two *d*. *Educ:* Burnage High Sch., Manchester. Served War, Royal Navy, 1943–46. Various senior finance appts in The United Steel Companies Ltd and later in British Steel Corp., 1949–72. Managing Director: Supplies and Production Control, 1973–76, Finance and Supplies, 1976–80, British Steel Corp. *Recreations:* cricket, collecting books. *Died 22 May 2012.*

HOLMES, Anthony, CBE 1982; Head of Passport Department, Home Office (formerly Chief Passport Officer, Foreign and Commonwealth Office), 1980–88; *b* 4 Sept. 1931; *s* of Herbert and Jessie Holmes; *m* 1954, Sheila Frances Povall. *Educ:* Calday Grange Grammar School. Joined HM Customs and Excise, 1949; served HM Forces, 1950–52; Passport Office, 1955; Dep. Chief Passport Officer, 1977. *Recreations:* golf, sailing. *Address:* Hilbre, Mill Road, West Chiltington, Pulborough, West Sussex RH20 2PZ. *Clubs:* West Sussex Golf (Pulborough); El Paraiso Golf (Estepona, Spain). *Died 29 June 2012.*

HOLMES, Christopher John, CBE 1998; Director, Shelter, 1995–2002; *b* Otley, W Yorks, 13 July 1942; *s* of Gordon Holmes and Doris Holmes (*née* Waite); *m* 1st, 1969, Ann Warden (marr. diss. 1989); one *s* one *d*; 2nd, 2003, Hattie Llewelyn-Davies; one *s* one *d*. *Educ:* Clare Coll., Cambridge (MA Hons Econs 1964); Univ. of Bradford (Dip. in Industrial Admin 1966). Asst Gen. Sec., Student Christian Movement, 1964–65; John Laing Construction, 1966–68; NE Islington Community Project, then N Islington Housing Rights Project, 1969–74; Dep. Dir, Shelter, 1974–76; Director: Soc. for Co-operative Dwellings, 1976–79; E London Housing Assoc., 1979–82; CHAR, 1982–87; Consultant, Priority Estates Project, 1988–89; Dir of Housing, London Borough of Camden, 1990–95. Member: Nat. Consumer Council, 1975–80; Youth Justice Bd, 2002–10; Housing Corporation Bd, 2004–10. *Publications:* The Other Notting Hill, 2004; A New Vision for Housing, 2006. *Recreations:* my family, reading, theatre. *Address:* c/o Hattie Llewelyn-Davies, 1 Carpenters Yard, Park Street, Tring, Herts HP23 6AR. *Died 2 Dec. 2014.*

HOLMES, Prof. (Edward) Richard, CBE (mil.) 1998 (OBE (mil.) 1988); TD 1979 (Bar 1985, 2nd Bar 1996); PhD; JP; Professor of Military and Security Studies, 1995–2009, then Emeritus, and Co-Director, Security Studies Institute, 1989–2009, Cranfield University; *b* 29 March 1946; *s* of Edward William Holmes and Helen Holmes; *m* 1975, Katharine Elizabeth Saxton; two *d*. *Educ:* Forest Sch.; Emmanuel Coll., Cambridge (MA; Hon. Fellow 2007); Northern Illinois Univ.; Reading Univ. (PhD 1975). Royal Military Academy, Sandhurst: Lectr, Dept of War Studies, 1969–73; Sen. Lectr, 1973–84; Dep. Hd of Dept, 1984–86; Lt Col (non-Regular Perm. Staff), CO 2nd Bn, Wessex Regt (Vols), 1986–88. Writer and presenter, various TV documentaries, including: War Walks, 1996; War Walks 2, 1997; The Western Front, 1999; Battlefields, 2001; Wellington: the Iron Duke, 2002; Rebels and Redcoats, 2003; In the Footsteps of Churchill, 2005. Wellington Archive Vis. Prof., Southampton Univ., 2009–. Territorial Army: enlisted Essex Yeo., 1964; commnd 1966; Brig., 1994–2001; Dir, Reserve Forces and Cadets, 1997–2000; Col, The Princess of Wales's Royal Regt, 1999–2007. Trustee, Royal Armouries, 2005–. President: Corps of Drums Soc., 2003–; Battlefields Trust, 2004–; British Commn for Military History, 2006–; Chm., Project Hougoumont, 2007–. Hon. President: Battle of Cheriton Project; Napoleonic Assoc.; Vice-Pres., Sealed Knot, 2006–. Patron, Guild of Battlefields Guides, 2003–. JP Hants, 1989. Hon. DLitt: Leicester, 2006; Kent, 2007. Comdr 1st cl., Order of the Dannebrog (Denmark), 2000; Officier, Ordre des Palmes Académiques (France), 2009. *Publications:* (with P. Young) The English Civil War, 1974; The Little Field Marshal: Sir John French, 1984; Firing Line, 1985 (US edn as Acts of War, 1986), 4th edn 1994; (with J. Keegan) Soldiers, 1985; Riding the Retreat, 1995; War Walks, 1996; War Walks 2, 1997; The Western Front, 1999; Battlefields, 2001; (Gen. Ed.) The Oxford Companion to Military History, 2001; Redcoat, 2001; Wellington: the Iron Duke, 2002; Tommy, 2004; The D-Day Experience, 2004; In the Footsteps of Churchill, 2005; Sahib: the British soldier in India, 2005; Dusty Warriors: modern soldiers at war, 2006; The World at War, 2007; Marlborough: England's fragile genius, 2008; Shots From the Front, 2008; Churchill's Bunker, 2009; *posthumous publication*: Soldiers: army lives and loyalties from redcoats to dusty warriors, 2011. *Recreation:* riding. *Address:* c/o Sheil Land Associates, 52 Doughty Street, WC1N 2LF. *T:* (020) 7831 2127. *Club:* Naval and Military. *Died 30 April 2011.*

HOLMES, Sir Frank (Wakefield), Kt 1975; JP; Emeritus Professor, since 1985, and Deputy Chairman, 1984–89, Chairman, 1989–91, Institute of Policy Studies, Victoria University of Wellington; *b* 8 Sept. 1924; *s* of James Francis Wakefield and Marie Esme Babette Holmes; *m* 1947, Nola Ruth Ross; two *s*. *Educ:* Waitaki Boys' Jun. High Sch. (Dux 1936); King's High Sch. (Dux 1941); Otago Univ.; Auckland University Coll. (Sen. Schol. 1948); Victoria University Coll. MA (1st Cl. Hons) 1949. Flying Officer, Royal NZ Air Force, 1942–45 (despatches). Economic Div., Prime Minister's and External Affairs Depts 1949–52; Lectr to Prof., Victoria Univ. of Wellington, 1952–67; Macarthy Prof. of Economics, 1959–67; Dean, Faculty of Commerce, 1961–63; Economics Manager, Tasman Pulp & Paper Co. Ltd, 1967–70; Victoria Univ. of Wellington: Prof. of Money and Finance, 1970–77; Vis. Prof. and Convener, Master of Public Policy Programme, 1982–85. Adviser, Royal Commn on Monetary, Banking and Credit

Systems, 1955; Consultant, Bank of New Zealand, 1956–58 and 1964–67; Chm., Monetary and Economic Council, 1961–64 and 1970–72; Jt Sec., Cttee on Universities, 1959; Mem., NZ Council Educnl Research, 1965–77 (Chm. 1970–74); Chairman: Adv. Council on Educnl Planning and Steering Cttee, Educnl Develt Conf., 1973–74; NZ Govt Task Force on Economic and Social Planning, 1976; NZ Planning Council, 1977–82; Asia 2000 Foundn, NZ, 1994–96 (Hon. Advr, 1996–2008); Cttee Advising on Professional Educn, 1995–98. President: NZ Assoc. of Economists, 1961–63 (Distinguished Fellow 2004; Life Mem. 2009); Economic Section, ANZAAS, 1967, Education Section, 1979; Central Council, Economic Soc. of Australia and NZ, 1967–68; NZ Inst. of Internat. Affairs, 1998–2000 (Life Mem. 2009). Chairman: South Pacific Merchant Finance Ltd, 1985–89 (Dir, 1984–89); Hugo Group Ltd, 1989–2007 (Exec. Dir, 1986–2007); State Insurance Ltd, 1990–94; Norwich Holdings Ltd, 1990–94; Norwich Union Life Insce (NZ) Ltd, 1993–94; Director: National Bank of NZ Ltd, 1982–95; Norwich Union Life Insce Soc. 1983–92; Lloyds Bank NZA Ltd, Sydney, 1992–95. Mem., Internat. Organising Cttee, Pacific Trade and Develt Confs, 1982. FRSA; FNZIM 1986; Fellow, NZ Inst. of Dirs, 1995 (Distinguished Fellow, 1999). Life Member: Otago Univ. Students' Assoc., 1947; VUW Students' Assoc., 1967; Australia-NZ Business Council, 1998. JP 1960. Hon. LLD Otago, 1997; Hon. DCom Victoria, Wellington, 2004. *Publications:* Money, Finance and the Economy, 1972; Government in the New Zealand Economy, 1977, 2nd edn 1980; Closer Economic Relations with Australia, 1986; Partners in the Pacific, 1988; (ed) Stepping Stones to Freer Trade, 1989; (jtly) Meeting the East Asia Challenge, 1989; Meeting the European Challenge, 1991; NAFTA, CER and a Pacific Basin Initiative, 1992; A New Approach to Central Banking, 1994; CER: Trends and Linkages, 1994; New Zealand and ASEAN, 1995; Trans-Tasman Co-operation, 1996; The Thoroughbred Among Banks in New Zealand, 1999; An Anzac Dollar?, 2000; Banking in New Territory, 2003; Jungle Bomber, 2004; pamphlets and articles on econs, finance, educn and internat. affairs. *Recreations:* walking, dining, music, theatre. *Address:* 2 Millwood Place, Silverstream, Upper Hutt 5019, New Zealand. *T:* (4) 5285751. *Club:* Wellington (Wellington). *Died 23 Oct. 2011.*

HOLMES, Richard; *see* Holmes, E. R.

HOLROYD, Air Marshal Sir Frank (Martyn), KBE 1989; CB 1985; FREng; Chairman, Military Asset Services Ltd, since 2007; *b* 30 Aug. 1935; *s* of George L. Holroyd and Winifred H. Holroyd; *m* 1958, Veronica Christine (*d* 2001), *d* of Arthur G. Booth; two *s* one *d*. *Educ:* Southend-on-Sea Grammar Sch.; Cranfield Inst. of Technology (MSc). FIET; CEng, FREng (FEng 1992). Joined RAF, 1956; Fighter Comd units, 1957–60; Blind Landing Development RAE Bedford, 1960–63; Cranfield Inst. of Tech., 1963–65; HQ Fighter Comd, 1965–67; Far East, 1967–69; Wing Comdr, MoD, 1970–72; RAF Brize Norton, 1972–74; Gp Captain Commandant No 1 Radio School, 1974–76; SO Eng. HQ 38 Gp, 1976–77; Air Cdre Director Aircraft Engrg, MoD, 1977–80; RCDS 1981; Dir Weapons and Support Engrg, MoD, 1982, Air Vice-Marshal 1982; DG Strategic Electronics Systems, MoD (Procurement Exec.), 1982–86; AO Engrg, Strike Comd, 1986–88; Chief Engr, 1988–91, and Chief of Logistics Support, 1989–91, RAF. Chairman: AVR Communications Ltd, 1992–95; Elettronica (UK) Ltd, 1992–95; Composite Technology Ltd, 1992–2004; Troy Court Mgt Ltd, 2003–07; Military Aircraft Spares Ltd, 2004–06 (Dep. Chm., 1999–2003); Director: Admiral plc, 1992–2000; Ultra Electronics Hldgs, 1995–2003; REW Communications Ltd, 1995–96; Airinmar Ltd, 1996–2000. Engineering Council: Mem., 1990–2000; Chm. of Trustees, Pension Fund, 2000–09. Pres., RAeS, 1992–93. Member: Court, 1988–, and Council, 1990–97 (Dep. Chm., 1997–2005), Inst. of Technology, later Univ., Cranfield; Adv. Council, RMCS, Shrivenham, 1988–91; BBC Engrg Adv. Bd, 1984–90. Trustee, Macrobert Award Trust, Royal Acad. of Engrg, 1993–98; Mem., Tribology Trust Awards Cttee, IMechE, 1997–. Life Vice-Pres., Chelmsford Br., RAFA, 1990–. Patron: Victim Support Somerset, 2004–07; Southend-on-Sea High Sch. Develt Project, 2004–. CCMI (Mem., 1991–98, Chm., 1998–99, Companions Bd). Hon. DSc Cranfield, 2006. *Recreations:* travel, gardening, maintaining 14th century house, shooting (game birds). *Club:* Royal Air Force. *Died 18 Jan. 2014.*

HOLROYD, John Hepworth, CB 1993; CVO 1999; DL; Secretary for Appointments to the Prime Minister, and Ecclesiastical Secretary to the Lord Chancellor, 1993–99; *b* 10 April 1935; *s* of late Rev. Harry Holroyd and Annie Dodgshun Holroyd; *m* 1963, Judith Mary Hudson; one *s* one *d*. *Educ:* Kingswood Sch., Bath; Worcester Coll., Oxford (Open Schol.; BA(Hist.); MA 1987). Joined MAFF, 1959; Asst Sec., 1969–78; Under Secretary, 1978; Resident Chm., Civil Service Selection Bd, 1978–80; Dir of Establishments, MAFF, 1981–85; Cabinet Office: Under Sec., European Secretariat, 1985–89; First CS Comr and Dep. Sec., 1989–93. Advr to Assoc. of Lord-Lieutenants, 1999–2007. UK Gov., Eur. Inst. of Public Admin, 1987–93. Governor: Kingswood Sch., 1985–2005; King's Sch., Gloucester, 2001– (Chm. of Govs, 2009–12). Lay Reader: St Albans Cathedral, 1975–2001; Gloucester Cathedral, 2001–. Chm., Wells Cathedral Council, 2000–07. Trustee: St Albans Cathedral Trust, 1980–2001; Gloucester Cathedral Trust, 2002–08; Dementia Care Trust, 2002–06. Hon. Minor Canon, Gloucester Cathedral, 2004–. Mem., Exec. Cttee, Three Choirs Festival, 2007–. DL Herts, 1999–2001, Glos, 2002. *Recreations:* music, carpentry, managing 4 acres of Cornish woodland, travel. *Address:* The Miller's House, 2 Miller's Green, Gloucester GL1 2BN. *Died 29 Nov. 2014.*

HOLT, Sir James (Clarke), Kt 1990; FSA 1967; FBA 1978; Professor of Medieval History, Cambridge University, 1978–88; Master of Fitzwilliam College, Cambridge, 1981–88 (Hon. Fellow, 1988; Life Fellow, 2000); *b* 26 April 1922; *s* of late Herbert Holt and Eunice Holt, BEM; *m* 1950, Alice Catherine Elizabeth Suley (*d* 1998); one *s*. *Educ:* Bradford Grammar Sch.; Queen's Coll., Oxford (Hastings Schol.; BA 1st cl. Modern Hist.; MA 1947; Hon. Fellow, 1996); Merton Coll., Oxford (Harmsworth Sen. Schol., 1947; DPhil 1952; Hon. Fellow, 2001). University of Nottingham: Asst Lectr, 1949; Lectr, 1951; Sen. Lectr, 1961; Prof. of Medieval History, 1962; Reading University: Prof. of History, 1966–78; Dean, Faculty of Letters and Soc. Scis, 1972–76; Professorial Fellow, Emmanuel Coll., Cambridge, 1978–81 (Hon. Fellow, 1985). Vis. Prof., Univ. of Calif, Santa Barbara, 1977; Vis. Hinkley Prof., Johns Hopkins Univ., 1983; Vis. JSPS Fellow, Japan, 1986. Raleigh Lectr, British Acad., 1975. Mem., Adv. Council on Public Records, 1974–81. President: Royal Historical Soc., 1980–84; Selden Soc., 2003–06; Life Pres., Pipe Roll Soc., 1999; Vice-Pres., British Academy, 1987–89. Corresp. Fellow, Medieval Acad. of America, 1983. Hon. DLitt: Reading, 1984; Nottingham, 1996. Comdr, Order of Civil Merit (Spain), 1988. *Publications:* The Northerners: a study in the reign of King John, 1961, 2nd edn 1992; Praestita Roll 14–18 John, 1964; Magna Carta, 1965, 2nd edn 1992; The Making of Magna Carta, 1966; Magna Carta and the Idea of Liberty, 1972; The University of Reading: the first fifty years, 1977; Robin Hood, 1982, 2nd edn 1989; (ed with J. Gillingham) War and Government in the Middle Ages, 1984; Magna Carta and Medieval Government, 1985; (with R. Mortimer) Acta of Henry II and Richard I, 1986; (ed) Domesday Studies, 1987; Colonial England 1066–1215, 1997; (with J. Everard) Jersey 1204: the forging of an island community, 2004; papers in English Historical Review, Past and Present, Economic History Review, Trans Royal Hist. Soc. *Recreations:* mountaineering, cricket, fly-fishing, music. *Address:* 5 Holben Close, Barton, Cambridge CB23 7AQ. *T:* (01223) 264923. *Clubs:* Oxford and Cambridge, National Liberal, MCC; Wayfarers' (Liverpool). *Died 9 April 2014.*

HOLT, (James) Richard (Trist); President, Pensions Appeal Tribunals (England & Wales), 1993–98; *b* 17 Aug. 1924; *s* of George Richard Holt and Gladys Floyd Holt (*née* Bennetts); *m* 1st, 1952, Helen Worswick (marr. diss); one *s* one *d*; 2nd, 1977, Patricia Mary Hartley. *Educ:* Giggleswick Sch.; Queen's Coll., Oxford (MA 1950); London Univ. (ext. LLB 1952). Served Royal Signals, 1942–47, commnd 1945. Articled clerk, 1941; admitted solicitor, 1951; called to the Bar, Gray's Inn, 1973. Part-time Chairman: Med. Appeal Tribunals, 1979–96;

Vaccine Damage Tribunals, 1982–96; Pensions Appeal Tribunals, 1985–98; Disability Appeal Tribunals, 1992–96; Immigration Appeals Adjudicator, 1982–90; Mem., Mental Health Act Commn, 1985–86. Contested (C) Rossendale, 1959. *Publications:* contrib. Law Soc. Gazette. *Recreation:* reading history. *Address:* The Hey Farm, Newton-in-Bowland, near Clitheroe, Lancs BB7 3EE. *T:* (01200) 446213. *Died 22 Oct. 2014.*

HOLT, Sir Michael, Kt 1995; CBE 1981; FCA; Chairman, Eastern Area Conservative Provincial Council, 1992–96; *b* 23 Dec. 1927; *s* of Frank Holt, MM, FCA and Helen Gertrude Holt (*née* Wheeler); *m* 1955, Janet Michelle Simon; two *s* one *d*. *Educ:* Epsom Coll.; Downing Coll., Cambridge (MA, LLM). Called to the Bar, Inner Temple, 1953; qualified as Chartered Accountant, 1958; Sen. Partner, Arthur Goddard & Co., Chartered Accountants, 1966–83. Dir, Lay and Wheeler Gp Ltd, 1983–2002, and other cos. External Mem., Lloyds, 1983–96. Member: NE Essex HA, 1982–89, 1990–93; Bd of Govs, St John's Hosp. for Diseases of the Skin, 1980–82. Conservative Party: Hon. Treas., Colchester Assoc., 1965–76; Chm., 1983–85, Vice Pres., 1985–95, N Colchester Assoc.; Vice Pres., N Essex Assoc., 1995–; Hon. Treas., 1975–80, Vice Chm., then Dep. Chm., 1986–92, Eastern Area Provincial Council; Pres., N Essex and S Suffolk Eur. Constituency Council, 1994–99; Vice Chm., 1985–86, Chm., 1986–90, Pres., 1991–94, NE Essex European Cons. Council; Mem. Exec. Cttee, Nat. Union of Cons. and Unionist Assocs, 1975–83, 1986–98. *Address:* The Tower House, Bildeston, Suffolk IP7 7ER. *T:* (01449) 741313. *Died 5 Sept. 2011.*

HOLT, Richard; *see* Holt, J. R. T.

HONEYCOMBE, (Ronald) Gordon; author, playwright, television presenter, actor and narrator; *b* Karachi, British India, 27 Sept. 1936; *s* of Gordon Samuel Honeycombe and Dorothy Louise Reid Fraser. *Educ:* Edinburgh Acad.; University Coll., Oxford (MA English). National Service, RA, mainly in Hong Kong, 1955–57. Announcer: Radio Hong Kong, 1956–57; BBC Scottish Home Service, 1958; actor: with Tomorrow's Audience, 1961–62; with RSC, Stratford-on-Avon and London, 1962–63; Newscaster with ITN, 1965–77; Newscaster, TV-am, 1984–89. Acted in TV plays, series and shows including: That Was the Week that Was, 1964; The Brack Report, 1982; CQ, 1984; Numbats, 1994; appearances as TV presenter include: (also writer) A Family Tree and Brass Rubbing (documentaries), 1973; The Late Late Show (series), and Something Special (series), 1978; (also ed and jt writer) Family History (series), 1979; appearances as TV narrator include: Arthur C. Clarke's Mysterious World (series), 1980; A Shred of Evidence, 1984; stage appearances include: Play-back 625, Royal Court, 1970; Paradise Lost, York and Old Vic, 1975; Suspects, Swansea, 1989; Aladdin, Wimbledon, 1989–90, Bournemouth, 1990–91; Run For Your Wife!, tour, 1990; The Taming of the Shrew, Perth, WA, 1998; film appearances include: The Medusa Touch; The Fourth Protocol; Let's Get Skase; The Sculptor; Short Film Maker. Author of stage productions: The Miracles, Oxford, 1960 and (perf. by RSC), Southwark Cath., 1963 and Consett, 1970; The Princess and the Goblins (musical), Great Ayton, 1976; Paradise Lost, York, Old Vic and Edinburgh Fest., 1975–77; Waltz of my Heart, Bournemouth, 1980; Lancelot and Guinevere, Old Vic, 1980; author of TV plays: The Golden Vision, 1968; Time and Again, 1974 (Silver Medal, Film and TV Fest., NY, 1975); The Thirteenth Day of Christmas, 1986; radio dramatisations (all Radio 4): Paradise Lost, 1975; Lancelot and Guinevere, 1976; A King shall have a Kingdom, 1977; devised Royal Gala performances: God save the Queen!, Chichester, 1977; A King shall have a Kingdom, York, 1977. Directed and prod, The Redemption, Fest. of Perth, 1990. *Publications: non-fiction:* Nagasaki 1945, 1981; Royal Wedding, 1981; The Murders of the Black Museum, 1982; The Year of the Princess, 1982; Selfridges, 1984; TV-am's Official Celebration of the Royal Wedding, 1986; More Murders of the Black Museum, 1993; The Complete Murders of the Black Museum, 1995; Australia For Me, 1996; Murders of the Black Museum, 2009; *documentary novels:* Adam's Tale, 1974; Red Watch, 1976; Siren Song, 1992; *fiction:* The Redemption (play), 1964; Neither the Sea nor the Sand, 1969; Dragon under the Hill, 1972; The Edge of Heaven, 1981; Beach, 2005; contrib. national newspapers and magazines. *Recreations:* bridge, crosswords, genealogy. *Address:* c/o RGM WA, 649 Beaufort Street, Mt Lawley, Perth, WA 6050, Australia. *T:* (8) 93285788. *Died 9 Oct. 2015.*

HONEYMAN, Gitta; *see* Sereny, G.

HONEYSETT, Martin; cartoonist and illustrator, since 1969; *b* 20 May 1943; *s* of Donovan Honeysett and Kathleen Ethel Ivy Probert; *m* 1970, Maureen Elizabeth Lonergan (marr. diss. 1988); one *s* one *d* (and one *s* decd). *Educ:* Selhurst Grammar Sch.; Croydon Art Coll. (for one year). After leaving Art Coll., 1961, spent several years in NZ and Canada doing variety of jobs; returned to England, 1968; started drawing cartoons part-time, 1969; became full-time freelance, working for Punch, Private Eye and other magazines and newspapers, 1972; illustrator of series of books by the author/poet, Ivor Cutler. Vis. Prof., Faculty of Art, Kyoto Seika Univ., Japan, 2005–07. *Publications:* Private Eye Cartoonists No 4, 1974; Honeysett at Home, 1976; The Motor Show Book of Humour, 1978; The Not Another Book of Old Photographs Book, 1981; Microphobia, 1982; The Joy of Headaches, 1983; Fit for Nothing, 1984; Animal Nonsense Rhymes, 1984; The Best of Honeysett, 1985; (with Ivor Cutler): Gruts, 1961, repr. 1986; Life in a Scotch Sitting Room, vol. 2, 1984, 2nd edn 1998; Fremsley, 1987; Glasgow Dreamer, 1990, 2nd edn 1998. *Recreations:* walking, swimming. *Died 21 Jan. 2015.*

HONIGMANN, Prof. Ernst Anselm Joachim, DLitt; FBA 1989; Joseph Cowen Professor of English Literature, University of Newcastle upon Tyne, 1970–89, then Professor Emeritus; *b* Breslau, Germany, 29 Nov. 1927; *s* of Dr H. D. S. Honigmann and U. M. Honigmann (*née* Heilborn); *m* 1958, Dr Elsie M. Packman (*d* 1994); two *s* one *d*. *Educ:* Glasgow Univ. (MA 1948; DLitt 1966); Merton Coll., Oxford (BLitt 1950). Asst Lectr, 1951, Lectr, Sen. Lectr and Reader, 1954–67, Glasgow Univ.; Fellow, Shakespeare Inst., Birmingham Univ., 1951–54; Reader, Univ. of Newcastle upon Tyne, 1968–70. Jt Gen. Ed., The Revels Plays, 1976–2000. *Publications:* The Stability of Shakespeare's Text, 1965; Shakespeare: Seven Tragedies, the dramatist's manipulation of response, 1976, 2nd edn 2002; Shakespeare's Impact on his Contemporaries, 1982; Shakespeare: the lost years, 1985, 2nd edn 1998; John Weever: a biography, 1987; Myriad-minded Shakespeare, 1989, 2nd edn 1998; The Texts of Othello, 1996; Harold Jenkins 1909–2000, 2001; *editor:* King John, 1954; Milton's Sonnets, 1966; The Masque of Flowers, 1967; Richard III, 1968; Twelfth Night, 1971; Paradise Lost, Book 10 (with C. A. Patrides), 1972; Shakespeare and his Contemporaries: essays in comparison, 1986; (with Susan Brock) Playhouse Wills 1558–1642, 1993; British Academy Shakespeare Lectures 1980–1989, 1993; Othello, 1996; Harold Jenkins, Structural Problems in Shakespeare, 2001; Togetherness: episodes from the life of a refugee, 2006. *Recreations:* grandchildren, gardening, travel. *Address:* 18 Wilson Gardens, Newcastle upon Tyne NE3 4JA. *Died 18 July 2011.*

HOOKWAY, Sir Harry (Thurston), Kt 1978; Pro-Chancellor, Loughborough University of Technology, 1987–93; *b* 23 July 1921; *s* of William and Bertha Hookway; *m* 1956, Barbara Olive (*d* 1991), *o d* of late Oliver and Olive Butler; one *s* one *d*. *Educ:* Trinity Sch. of John Whitgift; London Univ. (BSc, PhD). Various posts in industry, 1941–49; DSIR, 1949–65; Asst Dir, National Chemical Laboratory, 1959; Dir, UK Scientific Mission (North America), Scientific Attaché, Washington, DC, and Scientific Adviser to UK High Comr, Ottawa, 1960–64; Head of Information Div., DSIR, 1964–65; CSO, DES, 1966–69; Asst Under-Sec. of State, DES, 1969–73; Dep. Chm. and Chief Exec., The British Library Bd, 1973–84; Chairman: Publishers Databases Ltd, 1984–87; LA Publishing Ltd, 1986–89. Chairman: UNESCO Internat. Adv. Cttee for Documentation, Libraries and Archives, 1975–79; British Council Libraries Adv. Cttee, 1982–86; President: Inst. of Information Scientists, 1973–76; Library Assoc., 1985. Mem., Royal Commn on Historical Monuments (England), 1981–89. Governor, British Inst. for Recorded Sound, 1981–86. Dir, Arundel Castle Trustees Ltd, 1976–. Hon. FCLIP

(Hon. FLA, 1982); Hon. FIInfSc. Hon. LLD Sheffield, 1976; Hon. DLitt Loughborough, 1980. Gold Medal, Internat. Assoc. of Library Assocs, 1985. *Publications:* various contribs to jls of learned societies. *Recreations:* music, travel. *Address:* 3 St James Green, Thirsk, N Yorks YO7 1AF. *Club:* Athenæum. *Died 21 June 2014.*

HOOLEY, Frank Oswald; *b* 30 Nov. 1923; *m* 1945, Doris Irene Snook; two *d*. *Educ:* King Edward's High Sch., Birmingham; Birmingham Univ. Admin. Asst, Birmingham Univ., 1948–52; Sheffield Univ.: Asst Registrar, 1952–65; Sen. Asst Registrar, 1965–66; Registrar, Fourah Bay Coll., Sierra Leone, 1960–62 (secondment from Sheffield); Sen. Admin. Asst, Manchester Poly., 1970–71; Chief Admin. Officer, Sheffield City Coll. of Educn, 1971–74. Res. Asst to John Tomlinson, MEP, 1984–88. MP (Lab) Sheffield, Heeley, 1966–70 and Feb. 1974–1983. Chm., Parly Liaison Gp for Alternative Energy Strategies, 1978; formerly Member, Select Committees on Public Accounts, Estimates, Sci. and Technol., Overseas Aid, Foreign Affairs, and Procedure. Contested (Lab) Stratford-on-Avon, 1983. Vice-Chairman: Sutton Coldfield Lab. Party, 1988–98; Brecon and Radnorshire Lab. Party, 2001–03 (Chm., 2000–01, 2003–04). Chairman: Co-ordinating Cttee, Internat. Anti-Apartheid Year, 1978; Central Reg., UNA, 1994–98; Mem., UK Commn, UNESCO, 1999–2000; Pres., 2002–07, Vice-Pres., 2007–, UNA Wales. Governor: Bishop Vesey Sch., 1985–98; Banners Gate Jun. Sch., 1993–98. Trustee: Sutton Coldfield Municipal Charities, 1986–98; Presteigne and Norton Community Support, 2010–. Methodist Local Preacher, 1985–. *Address:* 50 Caenbrook Meadow, Presteigne, Powys LD8 2NE. *T:* (01544) 260790. *Died 21 Jan. 2015.*

HOOPER, Noel Barrie; Judge of the High Court, Hong Kong, 1981–93; *b* 9 Nov. 1931; twin *s* of late Alfred Edward Hooper and Constance Violet Hooper; *m* 1959, Pauline Mary (*née* Irwin); two *d*. *Educ:* Prince of Wales Sch., Kenya; St Peter's Hall, Oxford (BA 1954). Called to the Bar, Gray's Inn, 1956. Advocate of High Court, Uganda, 1956–61; Magistrate, Basutoland, 1961–64 and Hong Kong, 1964–68; Sen. Magistrate, Hong Kong, 1968–73; Principal Magistrate, 1973–76; Dist Judge, 1976–81; Comr of the Supreme Court of Brunei, 1983–86, 1986–89, 1990–93, 1994–. *Recreations:* tennis, cricket, golf, reading. *Clubs:* MCC; Corhampton Golf; Forty. *Died 30 Jan. 2012.*

HOOSON, Baron *cr* 1979 (Life Peer), of Montgomery in the County of Powys and of Colomendy in the County of Clwyd; **Hugh Emlyn Hooson;** QC 1960; a Recorder of the Crown Court, 1972–93 (Recorder of Swansea, 1971); *b* 26 March 1925; *s* of late Hugh and Elsie Hooson, Colomendy, Denbigh; *m* 1950, Shirley Margaret Wynne, *d* of late Sir George Hamer, CBE; two *d*. *Educ:* Denbigh Grammar Sch.; University Coll. of Wales, Aberystwyth. Called to Bar, Gray's Inn, 1949 (Bencher, 1968; Vice-Treasurer, 1985; Treasurer, 1986); Wales and Chester Circuit (Junior, 1954–55; Leader, 1971–74); Dep. Chm., Flint QS, 1960–71; Dep. Chm., Merioneth QS, 1960–67, Chm., 1967–71; Recorder of Merthyr Tydfil, 1971. MP (L) Montgomery, 1962–79. Leader, 1966–79, Pres., 1983–86, Welsh Liberal Party. Vice-Chm. Political Cttee, North Atlantic Assembly, 1975–79. Dir (non-exec.), Laura Ashley (Holdings), 1985–96 (Chm., 1995–96); Chm., Severn River Crossing, 1991–2000. President: Royal Nat. Eisteddfod of Wales, Newtown, 1965, Denbigh, 2001; Llangollen Internat. Eisteddfod, 1987–93; Wales International, 1995–98. Gov., Inst. of Grassland and Envmtl Res., 1989–92. Hon. Professorial Fellow, Univ. of Wales Aberystwyth (formerly UCW), 1971–. Hon. LLD Wales, 2003. White Bard, Royal Nat. Eisteddfod of Wales, Gorsedd Circle, 1966. *Address:* Summerfield Park, Llanidloes, Powys SY18 6AQ. *T:* (01686) 412298. *Died 21 Feb. 2012.*

HOPE, Sir Colin (Frederick Newton), Kt 1996; MA; FREng, FIMechE, FIMI; Executive Chairman, T & N plc, 1995–98; *b* 17 May 1932; *s* of Frederick and Mildred Hope; *m* 1959, Gillian Carden; two *s*. *Educ:* Stowe Sch.; St Catharine's College, Cambridge (MA). CEng, FREng (FEng 1995). Glacier Metal Co., 1963–70; Managing Dir, 1970–73, Exec. Chm., 1973–75, Covrad; Director: Engineering Group, Dunlop, 1975–79; Tyres UK Dunlop, 1979–82; Tyres Europe Dunlop Holdings, 1982–84; Chief Exec., Dunlop Engineering International, 1984–85; Gp Man. Dir, 1985–89, Chm. and Chief Exec., 1989–95, Turner & Newall, subseq. T & N plc. Chairman: Bryant Gp, 1992–2001; Ibstock Johnsen, 1993–97 (Dir, 1989–98). Pres., SMMT, 1991–93. Trustee, Nat. Motor Mus., 1991–2002; Patron, Armstrong Siddeley Heritage Trust, 2011–. Hon. DSc Cranfield, 1998. *Recreations:* theatre, music, vintage motor cars. *Address:* 16 Castle Walk, Doonfoot, Ayr KA7 4HH. *T:* (01292) 441560. *Club:* Royal Automobile. *Died 31 Aug. 2015.*

HOPE-WALLACE, (Dorothy) Jaqueline, CBE 1958; *b* 1909; 2nd *d* of Charles Nugent Hope-Wallace and Mabel Chaplin. *Educ:* Lady Margaret Hall, Oxford. Entered Ministry of Labour, 1932; transferred to National Assistance Board, 1934; Under-Sec., 1958–65; Under-Sec., Min. of Housing and Local Govt, 1965–69. Commonwealth Fellow, 1952–53. Comr, Public Works Loan Bd, 1974–78; Member Board: Corby Develt Corp., 1969–80; Inst. for Recorded Sound, 1971–74, 1979–83 (Chm. 1975–76); Nat. Corp. for Care of Old People (then Centre for Policy on Ageing), 1973–81 (Chm., 1978–80); Mem., Nat. Sound Archive Adv. Cttee, 1983–84. Mem. Bd of Govs, UCH, 1970–74; Pres., Friends of UCH, 1999–2005 (Chm., 1973–85). *Recreations:* arts, travel. *Address:* 17 Ashley Court, Morpeth Terrace, SW1P 1EN. *Died 23 Oct. 2011.*

HOPEWELL, John Prince; Consultant Surgeon, Royal Free Hospital, 1957–86 (Hon. Consulting Surgeon (Urology), since 1986); *b* 1 Dec. 1920; *s* of Samuel Prince and Wilhelmina Hopewell; *m* 1st, 1959, Dr Natalie Bogdan (*d* 1975); one *d* (one *s* decd); 2nd, 1984, Dr Rosemary Radley-Smith. *Educ:* Bradfield Coll., Berks; King's Coll. Hosp., London. RAMC, 1945–48. Postgrad. education at King's Coll. Hosp. and Brighton, Sussex, and Hosp. for Sick Children, Gt Ormond Street. Formerly Consultant Surgeon, Putney Hosp. and Frimley Hosp., Surrey. Mem., Hampstead DHA, 1982–85; Chm., Camden Div., BMA, 1985–93; Past Chm., Med. Cttee, Royal Free Hosp.; Chm., Hon. Med. Staff Cttee, Hosp. of St John and St Elizabeth, 1984–86; Past Mem., N Camden Dist Med. Cttee. Founder Mem., British Transplantation Soc., 1972; Member: Internat. Soc. of Urology; British Assoc. Urol. Surgeons; Past President: Chelsea Clinical Soc.; Section of Urology, RSM, 1982–83; Fellowship of Postgrad. Medicine. Founder Mem., Assoc. of Univ. Hospitals. Hon. Mem., NY Section, AUA. Hunterian Prof., RCS, 1958. Mem. Court of Examiners, RCSE, 1969–75. Member: Friends of St Helena; Soc. of Ornamental Woodturners. Ed., www.renhist.co.uk, 2011–. *Publications:* Can You Ever Tell (autobiog.), 2012; St Helena and the Hopewells, 2012; Three Clinical Cases of Renal Transplantation, British Medical Jl, 1964, Early History of Haemodialysis and Transplantation in the United Kingdom, and contribs to various medical journals. *Address:* Old Vicarage, Langrish, Petersfield, Hants GU32 1QY. *T:* (01730) 261354. *Died 14 Jan. 2015.*

HOPKINS, Alan Cripps Nind; *b* 27 Oct. 1926; *s* of late Rt Hon. Sir Richard V. N. Hopkins, GCB and Lady Hopkins; *m* 1st, 1954, Margaret Cameron (from whom divorced, 1962), *d* of E. C. Bolton, Waco, Texas, USA; one *s*; 2nd, 1962, Venetia, *d* of Sir Edward Wills, 4th Bt; twin *s*. *Educ:* Winchester Coll.; King's Coll., Cambridge (BA 1947; MA 1950); Yale University Law Sch., USA (LLB 1952). Barrister, Inner Temple, 1948. MP (C and Nat L) Bristol North-East, 1959–66; PPS to Financial Sec. to Treasury, 1960–62. Chm., Wellman Engrg Corp., 1972–83. *Recreation:* travelling. *Address:* Apt 502, Place du Village 6, 1972 Anzere, Valais, Switzerland. *T:* (27) 3981651. *Club:* Brooks's. *Died 12 Nov. 2012.*

HOPKINS, Antony, CBE 1976; composer and conductor; *b* 21 March 1921; *s* of late Hugh and of Marjorie Reynolds; adopted *c* of Major and Mrs T. H. C. Hopkins since 1925; *m* 1st, 1947, Alison Purves (*d* 1991); 2nd, 2012, Beatrix Taylor. *Educ:* Berkhamsted Sch.; Royal Coll. of Music. Won Chappell Gold Medal and Cobbett Prize at RCM, 1942; shortly became known as composer of incidental music for radio; numerous scores composed for BBC (2 for programmes winning Italia prize for best European programme of the year, 1952 and 1957). Composed music for many productions at Stratford and in West End. Dir, Intimate Opera Co., 1952–, and wrote a number of chamber operas for this group; *ballets:* Etude and Café des Sports, for Sadler's Wells; *films* (*music*) *include:* Pickwick Papers, Decameron Nights, Cast a Dark Shadow, Billy Budd; John and the Magic Music Man (narr. and orch.; Grand Prix, Besançon Film Festival, 1976). Regular broadcaster with a series of programmes entitled Talking about Music. Recording, Antony Hopkins: a portrait, 2012. Hon. FRCM 1964; Hon. RAM 1979; Hon. Fellow, Robinson Coll., Cambridge, 1980. DUniv Stirling, 1980. *Publications:* Talking about Symphonies, 1961; Talking about Concertos, 1964; Music All Around Me, 1968; Lucy and Peterkin, 1968; Talking about Sonatas, 1971; Downbeat Guide, 1977; Understanding Music, 1979; The Nine Symphonies of Beethoven, 1980; Songs for Swinging Golfers, 1981; Sounds of Music, 1982; Beating Time (autobiog.), 1982; Pathway to Music, 1983; Musicamusings, 1983; The Concertgoer's Companion: Vol. I, 1984, Vol. II, 1985, one vol. edn, 1993; The Seven Concertos of Beethoven, 1996. *Address:* Woodyard Cottage, Ashridge, Berkhamsted, Herts HP4 1PS. *T:* (01442) 842257. *Died 6 May 2014.*

HOPKINS, Elizabeth Ann; Clerk, House of Lords, 1998–2000; *b* 25 Sept. 1941; *d* of Philip G. H. Hopkins and Edith A. I. (Nessie) Hopkins (*née* Holmes). *Educ:* Parkstone Grammar Sch.; King Edward VI High Sch., Birmingham; Lady Margaret Hall, Oxford (BA Hons); Univ. of Ibadan (MSc); Univ. of Sussex (DPhil). Asst Lectr, Univ. of Sussex, 1965–68; Res. Officer, Inst. of Develt Studies, Sussex, 1968–72; Economist, Govt of Zambia, 1972–76; DoE, 1977–86; Dept of Transport (Channel Tunnel; Internat. Aviation), 1986–90; Regl Dir (SW), Depts of the Envmt and of Transport, 1990–93; Dir of Finance, Dept of Transport, 1993–95; Financial Mgt Advr, Dept of Transport, S Africa, 1995–96; Clerk/Advr, H of C Select Cttee on Eur. Legislation, 1997–98. Dep. Chm., FARM-Africa, 2001–07. *Recreation:* travel. *Address:* 33 Barkston Gardens, SW5 0ER. *T:* (020) 7370 7981. *E:* elizabeth.hopkins@btinternet.com. *Died 7 Sept. 2014.*

HOPKINSON, John Edmund; Judge of the High Court, Hong Kong, 1985–89; *b* 25 Oct. 1924; *s* of Captain E. H. Hopkinson, OBE, RN and Mrs E. H. Hopkinson; *m* 1961, Inge Gansel; one *s* one *d*. *Educ:* Marlborough Coll., Wilts; Pembroke Coll., Cambridge (MA). Called to the Bar, Lincoln's Inn, 1949. Served War, RN, 1943–46: Ordinary Seaman, Midshipman RNVR, 1943; Sub-Lt RNVR, 1944–46. Prudential Assurance Co., 1949–50; Legal Asst, Colonial Office, 1950–55; Resident Magistrate and Crown Counsel, Uganda, 1955–62; Hong Kong, 1962–89: Crown Counsel, 1962; Principal Crown Counsel, 1972; Dist Judge, 1974. *Recreations:* golf, tennis, music. *Address:* 41 Clavering Avenue, SW13 8DX. *Clubs:* Roehampton; Royal Cinque Ports Golf. *Died 3 Nov. 2012.*

HOPKIRK, Peter; author and traveller; *b* 15 Dec. 1930; *s* of Rev. Frank Stuart Hopkirk and Mary Hopkirk; *m* 1970, Kathleen Partridge; one *s* one *d*, and one *s* one *d* from previous marriages. *Educ:* Dragon Sch., Oxford; Marlborough. Military service, 1949–51: Subaltern, 4th (Uganda) Bn, KAR; served ex-Italian Somaliland and Kenya. Reporter, Sunday Express, London, 1954–56 (Algerian War, 1956); Ed., Drum (W African news mag.), 1956–57; ITN reporter and newscaster, London, 1958–59; foreign corresp., Daily Express, 1959–62: NY Bureau, 1960–61 (imprisoned Havana, 1961, Bay of Pigs invasion); Beirut corresp., 1962 (expelled); various writing assignments abroad, 1962–64, incl. China, Africa (visiting Albert Schweitzer at Lambaréné leper hosp.), and resident corresp., Istanbul; joined IPC newspapers, London, 1964; assigned to open group's first Moscow bureau, but visa blocked by Soviets; staff reporter, The Times, London, 1966–85: (June 1967 War, Cairo); Chief Reporter, later ME and FE specialist (hijacked by Arab terrorists, 1974). Sir Percy Sykes Meml Medal, RSAA, 1999. *Publications:* Foreign Devils on the Silk Road, 1980; Trespassers on the Roof of the World, 1982; Setting the East Ablaze, 1984; The Great Game, 1990; On Secret Service East of Constantinople, 1994; Quest for Kim, 1996; trans of books in 17 langs incl. Russian, Chinese, Turkish and Japanese. *Recreation:* collecting early picture postcards of Middle East and Central Asia. *Address:* c/o John Murray, 50 Albemarle Street, W1S 4BD. *Died 22 Aug. 2014.*

HORD, Brian Howard, CBE 1989; FRICS; company director; chartered surveyor; Director General, Bureau of European Building Consultants and Experts, 1991–95; *b* 20 June 1934; *s* of late Edwin Charles and Winifred Hannah Hord; *m* 1960, Christine Marian Lucas; two *s*. *Educ:* Reedham Orphanage; Purley Co. Grammar Sch. County Planning Dept, Middx CC, 1950–51; Surveyor, G. L. Hearn & Partners, 1951–57; National Service, RAF, 1957–59; Estates Surveyor, United Drapery Stores, 1959–66; Richard Costain Ltd, 1966–70; Director, Capcount UK Ltd, principal subsid. of Capital & Counties Property Co. Ltd, 1970–75; Partner, Howard Hord & Palmer, Chartered Surveyors, 1975–84. Chm., Bexley HA, 1986–92. Member: London Rent Assessment Panel, 1985–2005; London Regl Passengers' Cttee, 1997–2000; Chairman: Sevenoaks Rail Travellers' Assoc., 2001–02; Bexhill Rail Action Gp, 2005–. Contested (C) Darlington, Feb. and Oct. 1974. MEP (C) London West, 1979–84; Whip of European Democratic Gp, 1982–83; Mem., Agric. and Budgets Cttees, EP. Vice-Pres., Sevenoaks Cons. Assoc., 1997–. *Publications:* (jtly) Rates-Realism or Rebellion. *Recreations:* photography, music, theatre, swimming, gardening, walking the S Downs. *Died 30 Aug. 2015.*

HORDER, Dr John Plaistowe, CBE 1981 (OBE 1971); FRCP, FRCPE, FRCGP, FRCPsych; general practitioner of medicine, 1951–81; Founder, National Centre for the Advancement of Interprofessional Education, 1987 (Chairman, 1987–94); *b* 9 Dec. 1919; *s* of Gerald Morley Horder and Emma Ruth Horder; *m* 1940, Elizabeth June Wilson; two *s* two *d*. *Educ:* Lancing Coll.; University Coll., Oxford (BA 1945); London Hosp. (BM BCh 1948). FRCP 1972 (MRCP 1951); FRCGP 1970 (MRCGP 1957); FRCPsych 1980 (MRCPsych 1975); FRCPE 1982. Consultant, 1959, Travelling Fellow, 1964, WHO; Vis. Lectr, London School of Economics and Pol Sci., 1964–69; Sir Harry Jeffcott Vis. Prof., Univ. of Nottingham, 1975; Visiting Professor: Royal Free Hosp. Med. Sch., 1982–91; Zagreb Univ., 1990–. Samuel Gee Lectr, RCP, 1991. Consultant Adviser, DHSS, 1978–84. Pres., Medical Art Soc., 1990–93. Pres., RCGP, 1979–82 (John Hunt Fellow, 1974–77; Wolfson Travelling Prof., 1978); Hon. FRSocMed 1983 (Vice-Pres., 1987–89; Pres., Sect. of Gen. Practice, 1970). Hon. Fellow: Green Coll., Oxford, 1988; QMW, 1997. Hon. MD Free Univ. Amsterdam, 1985; Hon. DSc: Westminster, 2000; Kingston, 2001. Hon. Mem., Coll. of Family Physicians of Canada, 1982. *Publications:* ed and co-author: The Future General Practitioner—learning and teaching, 1972; General Practice under the National Health Service 1948–1997, 1998. *Recreations:* painting, music. *Address:* 98 Regent's Park Road, NW1 8UG. *T:* (020) 7722 3804. *Died 31 May 2012.*

HORLOCK, Sir John (Harold), Kt 1996; FRS 1976; FREng; Vice-Chancellor, 1981–90, and Fellow, since 1991, Open University; *b* 19 April 1928; *s* of Harold Edgar and Olive Margaret Horlock; *m* 1953, Sheila Joy Stutely; one *s* two *d*. *Educ:* Edmonton Latymer Sch.; (Scholar) St John's Coll., Cambridge (Hon. Fellow 1989). 1st Class Hons Mech. Sci. Tripos, Pt I, 1948, Rex Moir Prize; Pt II, 1949; MA 1952; PhD 1955; ScD 1975. Design and Development Engineer, Rolls Royce Ltd, Derby, 1949–51; Fellow, St John's Coll., Cambridge, 1954–57 and 1967–74; Univ. Demonstrator, 1952–56; University Lecturer, 1956–58, at Cambridge Univ. Engineering Lab.; Harrison Prof. of Mechanical Engineering, Liverpool Univ., 1958–66; Prof. of Engineering, and Dir of Whittle Lab., Cambridge Univ., 1967–74; Vice-Chancellor, Univ. of Salford, 1974–80. Visiting Asst Prof. in Mech. Engineering, Massachusetts Inst. of Technology, USA, 1956–57; Vis. Prof. of Aero-Space Engineering, Pennsylvania State Univ., USA, 1966. Chm., ARC, 1979–80 (Mem., 1960–63, 1969–72); Member: SRC, 1974–77; Cttee of Inquiry into Engineering Profession, 1977–80; Engineering Council, 1981–83; Chm., Adv. Cttee on Safety in Nuclear Installations, 1984–93. Director: BICERA Ltd, 1964–65; Cambridge Water Co., 1971–74; British Engine Insurance

Ltd, 1979–84; Gaydon Technology Ltd, 1978–88; Open University Educational Enterprises Ltd, 1981–88; National Grid Co., 1989–94. Chm., Electro-magnetic Field Biol Res. Trust, 1997–2005. A Vice-Pres., 1981–83, 1992–97, Treas., 1992–97, Royal Soc. Calvin Rice Lectr, ASME, 1994. FREng (FEng 1977); FIMechE; Fellow ASME; Hon. FRAeS 2003. Foreign Associate, US Nat. Acad. of Engrg. Hon. Fellow, UMIST, 1991 (a Pro-Chancellor, 1995–2001). Hon. DSc: Heriot-Watt, 1980; Salford, 1981; CNAA, 1991; de Montfort, 1995; Cranfield, 1997; Hon. ScD East Asia, 1987; Hon. DEng Liverpool, 1987; DUniv Open, 1991. Clayton Prize, 1962, Thomas Hawksley Gold Medal, 1969, Arthur Charles Main Prize, 1997, IMechE; R. Tom Sawyer Award, ASME, 1997; Sir James Ewing Medal, ICE, 2001; Achievement Award, ISABE, 2003. *Publications:* The Fluid Mechanics and Thermodynamics of Axial Flow Compressors, 1958; The Fluid Mechanics and Thermodynamics of Axial Flow Turbines, 1966; Actuator Disc Theory, 1978; (ed) Thermodynamics and Gas Dynamics of Internal Combustion Engines, vol. I, 1982, vol. II, 1986; Cogeneration—Combined Heat and Power, 1987; Combined Power Plants, 1992; (ed) Energy for the Future, 1995; Advanced Gas Turbine Cycles, 2003; An Open Book, 2006; Energy—Resources, Utilisation and Policies, 2009; contribs to mech. and aero. engineering jls and to Proc. Royal Society. *Recreations:* music, watching sport. *Address:* 2 The Avenue, Ampthill, Bedford MK45 2NR. *T:* (01525) 841307. *Died 22 May 2015.*

HORN, Prof. Sir Gabriel, Kt 2002; MA, MD, ScD; FRS 1986; Professor of Zoology, University of Cambridge, 1978–95, then Emeritus; Master of Sidney Sussex College, Cambridge, 1992–99, Emeritus Fellow, since 1999; Fellow of King's College, Cambridge, 1962–74, 1978–92 and since 1999; *b* 9 Dec. 1927; *s* of late Abraham and Annie Horn; *m* 1st, 1952, Ann Loveday Dean Soper (marr. diss. 1979); two *s* two *d*; 2nd, 1980, Priscilla Barrett. *Educ:* Handsworth Technical Sch. and Coll., Birmingham (Nat. Cert. in Mech. Engrg); Univ. of Birmingham (BSc Anatomy and Physiology; MD, ChB). MA, ScD Cantab. Served in RAF (Educn Br.), 1947–49. House appts, Birmingham Children's and Birmingham and Midland Eye Hosps, 1955–56; University of Cambridge: Univ. Demonstrator in Anat., 1956–62; Lectr in Anat., 1962–72; Reader in Neurobiology, 1972–74; Prof. and Head of Dept of Anat., Univ. of Bristol, 1974–77; University of Cambridge: Hd of Dept, 1979–94; Dep. Vice-Chancellor, 1994–98; Chairman: Core Cttee, Govt Policy Prog., 1998–2009; Review Cttee on Origin of BSE, 2001. Sen. Res. Fellow in Neurophysiol., Montreal Neurol Inst., McGill Univ., 1957–58; Leverhulme Res. Fellow, Laboratoire de Neurophysiologie Cellulaire, France, 1970–71; Leverhulme Emeritus Fellow, 2002–04. Vis. Prof. of Physiol Optics, Univ. of Calif, Berkeley, 1963; Vis. Res. Prof., Ohio State Univ., 1965; Vis. Prof. of Zool., Makerere University Coll., Uganda, 1966; Dist. Vis. Prof., Univ. of Alberta, Edmonton, Canada, 1988; Vis. Miller Prof., Univ. of Calif, Berkeley, USA, 1989. Charnock Bradley Lectr, Edinburgh Univ., 1988; Crisp Lectr, Univ. of Leeds, 1990. Dir, Cambridge Consultants Ltd, 1966–69; Sen. Consultant, PA Technology, 1976–86; Mem., Scientific Adv. Bd, Parke-Davis, 1988–99 (Chm., 1996). Member: Biol Sciences Cttee, SRC, 1973–75; Jt MRC and SRC Adv. Panel on Neurobiol., 1971–72; Res. Cttee, Mental Health Foundn, 1973–78; Council, Anatomical Soc., 1976–78; Adv. Gp, ARC Inst. of Animal Physiology, Babraham, 1981–87; AFRC, 1991–94; Chairman: Mgt Cttee, Wellcome Trust and CRC Inst. of Cancer and Develtl Biol., 1990–97; BBSRC Wkg Party on Biol. of Spongiform Encephalopathies, 1991–95; Animal Scis and Psychol. Res. Grants Cttee, BBSRC, 1994–96; Wkg Party on Brain Scis, Addiction and Drugs, Acad. of Med. Scis, 2005–08. Dir, Co. of Biologists, 1980–93. Hon. FRCP, 2007. Foreign Fellow, Acad. of Scis, Republic of Georgia, 1997; Hon. Member: Anatomical Soc. of GB and Ireland, 1997; Eur. Brain and Behaviour Soc., 2004. Hon. DSc: Birmingham, 1999; Bristol, 2003; Georgian Acad. of Scis, 2004. Kenneth Craik Award in Physiol Psychol., 1962; Royal Medal, Royal Soc., 2001; British Neuroscience Assoc. Award for contribns to Neurosci., 2011. *Publications:* (ed with R. A. Hinde) Short-Term Changes in Neural Activity and Behaviour, 1970; Memory, Imprinting and the Brain, 1985; (ed with J. R. Krebs) Behavioural and Neural Aspects of Learning and Memory, 1991; (jtly) Brain Sciences: addiction and drugs, 2008; contrib. scientific jls, mainly on topics in neurosciences. *Recreations:* walking, cycling, music, reading, poetry. *Address:* Sub-Department of Zoology, University of Cambridge, Madingley, Cambridge CB23 8AA. *Died 2 Aug. 2012.*

HORN, Gyula, PhD; Prime Minister of Hungary, 1994–98; *b* 5 July 1932; *s* of Geza Horn and Anna Csornyei; *m* 1956, Anna Király; one *s* one *d*. *Educ:* Rostow Inst. Econs, USSR; Polit. Acad., Budapest (PhD 1976). Official, Min. of Finance, Budapest, 1954–59; desk officer, Min. of Foreign Affairs, 1959–61; Embassy Secretary, Diplomatic Mission: Sofia, 1961–63; Belgrade, 1963–69; Staff Mem., then Hd, Internat. Dept, Hungarian Socialist Workers Party (MSZMP), Budapest, 1969–85; State Sec., Min. of Foreign Affairs, 1985–89; Minister of Foreign Affairs, 1989–90; Chm., Foreign Affairs Cttee, Hungarian Parlt, 1990–93. MP (MSzP) Republic of Hungary, 1990–2010. Founder, Hungarian Socialist Party (MSzP), 1989 (Pres., 1990–98). Mem., Hungarian Soc. of Political Scis. Mem., European Hon. Senate, 1991–. Glass of Understanding, Kassel; Karl Prize for work towards European unification, Aachen, 1991. Golden Labour Award of Merit (Hungary); Grand Cross (FRG). *Publications:* Development of East-West Relations in the 70s, 1970; Yugoslavia: our neighbour, 1971; Social and Political Changes in Albania since World War II, 1973; Pikes (autobiog.), 1991; Cölöpök, 1991; Freiheit die ich meine, 1991; Those Were the 90s, 1999; books on E-W relations in the Seventies, European security and co-operation and develt of internat. contacts; contrib. numerous articles to professional jls. *Died 19 June 2013.*

HORN, Dr Pamela Lucy Ray; author; freelance lecturer, since 1991; *b* 2 May 1936; *d* of Gilbert L. Jones and Marjorie H. Jones; *m* 1963, Clifford Alfred Horn (*d* 2008). *Educ:* Girls' High Sch., Burton on Trent; Leicester Univ. (BSc Econ. 1964; PhD 1968). Sec., Derbys CC, 1954–58; Assistant Lecturer: Burton on Trent Tech. Coll., 1958–59; Derby & Dist Coll. of Technol., 1959–63; part-time Lectr in Econ. and Social Hist., Oxford Poly., 1967–91. *Publications:* Joseph Arch, 1971; (ed) Agricultural Trade Unionism in Oxfordshire, 1974; The Victorian Country Child, 1974, 3rd edn 1997; The Rise and Fall of the Victorian Servant, 1975, 3rd edn 2004; Labouring Life in the Victorian Countryside, 1976, 2nd edn 1995; Education in Rural England, 1978; (ed) Village Education in 19th Century Oxfordshire, 1979; The Rural World 1780–1850, 1980; The Changing Countryside, 1984; Rural Life in England in the First World War, 1984; Life and Labour in Rural England 1780–1850, 1987; Around Abingdon in Old Photographs, 1987; The Victorian and Edwardian Schoolchild, 1989, 2nd edn 2010; Victorian Countrywomen, 1991; Ladies of the Manor, 1991, 2nd edn 1997; High Society, 1992; Children's Work and Welfare 1780–1890, 1994; Women in the 1920s, 1995, 2nd edn 2010; The Victorian Town Child, 1997; Pleasures and Pastimes in Victorian Britain, 1999, 2nd edn 2011; Life Below Stairs in the Twentieth Century, 2001, 2nd edn 2010; Flunkeys and Scullions, 2004; Behind the Counter, 2006; Life as a Victorian Lady, 2007; Life in a Victorian Household, 2007; My Ancestor was in Service, 2009; Abingdon Through Time, 2009; The Victorian Country House, 2010; Young Offenders: juvenile delinquency 1700–2000, 2010; The Real Lark Rise to Candleford, 2012; The Real Life Women of Downton Abbey, 2012; Life in a Victorian School, 2013; contributor to several books. *Recreations:* walking, gardening, foreign travel. *Address:* 11 Harwell Road, Sutton Courtenay, Abingdon, Oxon OX14 4BN. *T:* (01235) 847424. *Died 17 July 2013.*

HORNBY, Sir Derek (Peter), Kt 1990; *b* 10 Jan. 1930; *s* of F. N. Hornby and V. M. Pardy; *m* 1st, 1953, Margaret Withers (marr. diss.); one *s* one *d*; 2nd, 1971, Sonia Margaret Beesley; one *s* one *d*. *Educ:* Canford School. With Mobil Oil, Mars Industries and Texas Instruments; Xerox Corp., 1973 (Dir, Internat. Ops); Exec. Dir, Rank Xerox, 1980–84; Chm., Rank-Xerox (UK), 1984–90. Mem. Bd, British Rail, 1985–90; Civil Service Comr, 1986–90; Chairman: BOTB, 1990–95 (Mem., 1987–95; Chm., N Amer. Gp, 1987); NACCB, 1980–84. Chairman: Video Arts, 1993–96; Partnership Sourcing Ltd, 1993–98; London

& Continental Railways, 1994–98; IRG, 1997–2000; Director: Cogent Elliott, 1988–2011; London and Edinburgh Insurance Gp, 1989–96; Kode International, 1989–97; Dixons, 1990–97; Sedgwick Group, 1993–98; Pillar Properties plc, 1994–2005; Morgan Sindall Ltd, 1995–2002 (Chm., 1995–2000). Mem. Bd, Savills, 1988–95. Pres., Shaw Trust, 1995–2002. Chm. Govs, Priors Court Sch. for Autism, 1999–2002. CCMI (Chm., 1990–93). FRSA. Hon. DSc Aston, 1993. *Recreations:* Real tennis, theatre, cricket. *Address:* Badgers Farm, Idlicote, Shipston-on-Stour, Warwicks CV36 5DR. *Clubs:* Garrick, MCC; Leamington Real Tennis. *Died 16 Dec. 2013.*

HORNE, Dr Nigel William, FREng, FIET; company director; *b* 13 Sept. 1940; *s* of late Eric Charles Henry and Edith Margaret Horne; *m* 1965, Jennifer Ann Holton; one *s* two *d.* *Educ:* John Lyon Sch., Harrow; Univ. of Bristol (BScEng 1962); Univ. of Cambridge (PhD 1968). FREng (FEng 1982); FIET (FIEE 1984). GEC Telecommunications, 1958–82: Management Systems Manager, 1970–72; Manufg Gen. Manager, 1972–75; Dir and Gen. Manager, Switching, 1976–82; Managing Dir, GEC Inf. Systems, 1982–83; Director: Technical and Corporate Develt, STC, 1983–90; Abingworth, 1985–90; LSI Logic, 1986–90; FI Gp, 1992–98; Xansa (formerly FI Gp) Employees Trust, 1998–2004; Wireless Systems Internat. Ltd, 1995–2001; Foresight Technology VCT Plc, 1997–2008; Onyvax Ltd, 1997–2002; Parc Technologies Ltd, 1999–2000; Sarantel Ltd, 2000–02; Aspex Semiconductor (formerly Aspex Technol.), 2002–08; Jersey Telecom Gp, 2002–11; Intergence Systems Ltd, 2006–08; Chm., Alcatel UK Ltd, 1992–2001. IT Partner, KPMG Peat Marwick, 1990–92; Interim Chief Technol. Officer, NATS, 2005. Vis. Prof., Univ. of Bristol, 1990–98. Member: Nat. Electronics Council, 1985–90; EC Esprit Adv. Bd, 1988–93; ACOST, Cabinet Office, 1989–93; EC Strategy Bd, DGIII, 1994–98; Ind. Review, Higher Educn Pay and Conditions, 1998; British N American Cttee, 1998–; Chairman: Computing and Control Div., IEE, 1988–89; DTI/SERC IT Adv. Bd, 1988–91. Freeman, City of London; Liveryman, Inf. Technologists' Co. Hon. DEng Bristol, 1992; Hon. DSc: Hull, 1992; City, 1995. Caballeros del Monasterio de Yuste (Spain), 1992. *Publications:* papers in learned jls. *Recreations:* piano, walking, gardening. *Club:* Athenæum. *Died 15 Jan. 2013.*

HORROCKS, Raymond, CBE 1983; Chairman: Owenbell Ltd, 1987–2000; Chloride Group, 1988–99 (Director, 1986–99; Chief Executive, 1989–91); *b* 9 Jan. 1930; *s* of Elsie and Cecil Horrocks; *m* 1953, Pamela Florence Russell; three *d.* *Educ:* Bolton Municipal Secondary School. Textile Industry, 1944–48 and 1950–51; HM Forces, Army, Intelligence Corps, 1948–50; Sales Rep., Proctor & Gamble, 1951–52; Merchandiser, Marks & Spencer, 1953–58; Sub Gp Buying Controller, Littlewoods Mail Order Stores, 1958–63; various plant, departmental and divisional management positions, Ford Motor Co., 1963–72; Regional Dir, Europe and Middle East, Materials Handling Gp, Eaton Corp., 1972–77; Chm. and Man. Dir, Austin Morris Ltd, 1978–80; Man. Dir, BL Cars, 1980–81; Chm. and Chief Exec., BL Cars Gp, 1981–82; Exec. Dir and Bd Mem., BL, 1981–86; Gp Chief Exec., Cars, 1982–86; Chairman: Unipart Group Ltd, 1981–86; Austin Rover Gp Hldgs, 1981–86; Jaguar Cars Holdings Ltd, 1982–84; Kay Consultancy Group, 1989–91; Dir, Nuffield Services, 1982–86; non-executive Director: Jaguar plc, 1984–85; The Caravan Club, 1983–87; Electrocomponents, 1986–99; Lookers, 1986–99; WOL Hldgs Ltd, 1988–89; Burtree Caravans, 1988–96; Applied Hldgs (UK) Pty, 1988–96; Smith Millington Motor Co. Ltd (formerly SMAC Gp), 1988–96 (Chm., 1988–89); Applied Chemicals, 1988–96 (Dep. Chm., 1988–94); Jabiru UK, 1989–96. Member: Council, CBI, 1981–86; Europe Cttee, CBI, 1985–86. FIMI; CCMI. *Recreations:* fly fishing, gardening, walking. *Address:* Far End, Riverview Road, Pangbourne, Reading, Berks RG8 7AU. *Died 15 July 2011.*

HORSBRUGH-PORTER, Sir John (Simon), 4th Bt *cr* 1902; *b* 18 Dec. 1938; *s* of Col Sir Andrew Marshall Horsbrugh-Porter, 3rd Bt, DSO and Bar, and Annette Mary (*d* 1992), *d* of Brig.-Gen. R. C. Browne-Clayton, DSO; *S* father, 1986; *m* 1964, Lavinia Rose, *d* of Ralph Turton; one *s* two *d.* *Educ:* Winchester College; Trinity Coll., Cambridge (BA Hons History). Formerly, School Master. *Recreations:* literature, music. *Heir:* *s* Andrew Alexander Marshall Horsbrugh-Porter [*b* 19 Jan. 1971; *m* 2005, Jennie, *d* of Keith Downing; one *s* one *d*]. *Address:* Bowers Croft, Coleshill, Amersham, Bucks HP7 0LS. *T:* (01494) 724596. *Died 10 March 2013.*

HORSFIELD, Peter Muir Francis; QC 1978; *b* 15 Feb. 1932; *s* of Henry Taylor Horsfield, AFC, and Florence Lily (*née* Muir); *m* 1962, Anne Charlotte, *d* of late Sir Piers Debenham, 2nd Bt, and Lady (Angela) Debenham; three *s.* *Educ:* Beaumont; Trinity Coll., Oxford (BA 1st Cl. Hons Mods and Greats). Served RNR, 1955–57; Lieut RNR, 1960. Called to the Bar, Middle Temple, 1958, Bencher, 1984; in practice at Chancery Bar, 1958–94. Pt-time Chm., VAT Tribunals and Special Comr of Income Tax, 1993–2003. *Recreation:* painting (one-man shows, Cassian de Vere Cole Fine Arts, 1997, Abbott & Holden, 2004). *Club:* Garrick. *Died 15 April 2013.*

HORSHAM, Jean, CBE 1979; Deputy Parliamentary Commissioner for Administration, 1981–82; Chairman, Solicitors Complaints Bureau, 1986–89; *b* 25 June 1922; *d* of Albert John James Horsham and Janet Horsham (*née* Henderson). *Educ:* Keith Grammar Sch. Forestry Commn, 1939–64, seconded to Min. of Supply, 1940–45; Min. of Land and Natural Resources, 1964–66; Min. of Housing and Local Govt, 1966; Office of Parly Comr for Administration, 1967–82. Member: Subsidence Compensation Review Cttee, 1983–84; Law Soc. Professional Purposes Cttee, 1984–86; Council on Tribunals, 1986–92; Chorus Enquiry at Royal Opera House, 1988–89; Tribunals Cttee, Judicial Studies Bd, 1990–92. *Died 24 Oct. 2011.*

HORSLEY, Colin Robert, OBE 1963; FRCM 1973; Hon. RAM 1977; pianist; Professor, Royal College of Music, London, 1953–90; *b* Wanganui, New Zealand, 23 April 1920. *Educ:* Royal College of Music. Debut at invitation of Sir John Barbirolli at Hallé Concerts, Manchester, 1943. Soloist with all leading orchestras of Great Britain, the Royal Philharmonic Soc. (1953, 1959), Promenade Concerts, etc. Toured Belgium, Holland, Spain, France, Scandinavia, Malta, Ceylon, Malaya, Australia and New Zealand. Festival appearances include Aix-en-Provence, International Contemporary Music Festival, Palermo, British Music Festivals in Belgium, Holland and Finland. Vis. Prof., Royal Manchester Coll., later RNCM, 1964–80. Frequent broadcasts; many recordings. *Recreation:* gardening. *Address:* Belmont, Dreemskerry, Maughold, Isle of Man IM7 1BF. *T:* (01624) 813095. *Died 28 July 2012.*

HORTON, Sir Robert (Baynes), Kt 1997; Director, 1987–2011, and Member of European Advisory Council, since 1999, Emerson Electric Co.; *b* 18 Aug. 1939; *s* of late William Harold Horton and Dorothy Joan Horton (*née* Baynes); *m* 1962, Sally Doreen (*née* Wells); one *s* one *d.* *Educ:* King's School, Canterbury; University of St Andrews (BSc); Massachusetts Inst. of Technology (SM; Sloan Fellow, 1970–71). British Petroleum, 1957–92: General Manager, BP Tankers, 1975–76; Gen. Manager, Corporate Planning, 1976–79; Chief Exec. Officer, BP Chemicals, 1980–83; a Man. Dir, 1983–86 and 1988–92; Chm. and Chief Exec. Officer, 1990–92; Chm., Standard Oil, 1986–88; Vice-Chm., BRB, 1992–93; Chairman: Railtrack, 1993–99; Chubb plc, 2002–03; Sporting Exchange Ltd, 2004–06. Director: ICL plc, 1982–84; Pilkington Brothers plc, 1985–86; National City Corp., 1986–88; Partner Re, 1993–2003; Premier Farnell plc, 1995–2004; Estate Incomes Ltd, 1998–2005. Pres., Chemicals Industry Assoc., 1982–84; Vice-Chm., BIM, 1985–91 (CCMI (CBIM 1982)); Member: SERC, 1985–86; UFC, 1989–92; Bd and Management Cttee, Amer. Petroleum Inst., 1986–88; US Business Roundtable, 1986–88; Nat. Petroleum Council, USA, 1986–88. Pres., BESO, 1993–97. Trustee: Cleveland Orchestra, 1986–93; MIT Corp., 1987–97; Case Western Reserve Univ., 1987–93; Oxford Philomusica, 2008–; Chairman: Tate Foundation, 1988–92; Business in the Arts, 1988–96. Chancellor, Univ. of Kent at Canterbury, 1990–95. Gov., King's Sch., Canterbury, 1984–2005 (Gov. Emeritus, 2005–). FCIT 1994; FRSA. Hon.

FIChemE 1990; Hon. FCGI 1992. Hon. LLD: Dundee, 1988; Aberdeen, 1992; Hon. DCL Kent, 1990; Hon. DBA N London Poly., 1991; Hon. DSc Cranfield, 1992; DUniv Open, 1993; Hon. DCL Kingston, 1994. Corporate Leadership Award, MIT, 1987; Civic Award, Cleveland, 1988; SCI Gold Medal, 1990. *Recreations:* rare books, music, country activities. *Address:* Stoke Abbas, South Stoke, Oxon RG8 0JT. *Clubs:* Athenæum; Leander; Huntercombe Golf. *Died 30 Dec. 2011.*

HOSKINS, Robert William, (Bob); actor; *b* 26 Oct. 1942; *s* of Robert Hoskins and Elsie Lilian Hoskins; *m* 1st, 1970, Jane Livesey; one *s* one *d*; 2nd, 1982, Linda Banwell; one *s* one *d*. *Educ:* Stroud Green Sch. *Stage:* Intimate Theatre, Palmers Green, 1966; Victoria, Stoke on Trent, 1967; Century Travelling Theatre, 1969; Royal Court, 1972; Doolittle in Pygmalion, Albery, 1974; RSC season, Aldwych, 1976; The World Turned Upside Down, Has Washington Legs?, 1978, True West, Guys and Dolls, 1981, NT; Old Wicked Songs, Gielgud, 1996; As You Desire Me, Playhouse, 2005; *television:* On the Move, 1976; Pennies from Heaven, 1978; Flickers, 1980; The Dunera Boys, 1985; The Changeling, 1993; World War II: When Lions Roared, 1993; David Copperfield, 1999; The Lost World, 2001; The Street, 2009 (Best Actor, Internat. Emmy Awards, 2010); Neverland, 2011; *films:* Zulu Dawn, 1980; The Long Good Friday, 1981; The Honorary Consul, 1982; Lassiter, 1984; Cotton Club, 1984; Sweet Liberty, 1986; Mona Lisa, 1986 (Best Actor award, Cannes Fest.; Golden Globe Award); A Prayer for the Dying, 1988; The Raggedy Rawney (writer, dir, actor), 1988; Who Framed Roger Rabbit, 1988; The Lonely Passion of Judith Hearne, 1989; Heart Condition, 1990; Mermaids, 1991; The Favour, the Watch and the Very Big Fish, 1992; Hook, 1992; The Inner Circle, 1992; Super Mario Brothers, 1993; Nixon, 1996; The Rainbow (dir, actor), 1996; Michael, 1996; Cousin Bette, 1996; TwentyFourSeven, 1997; The Secret Agent (producer, actor), 1998; Captain Jack, Parting Shots, Felicia's Journey, 1999; Enemy at the Gates, 2001; Last Orders, 2002; Beyond the Sea, 2004; Vanity Fair, Mrs Henderson Presents, Unleashed, 2005; Hollywoodland, 2006; Sparkle, 2007; Made in Dagenham, 2010; Outside Bet, 2011; Snow White and The Huntsman, 2012. *Recreations:* photography, gardening, playgoing. *Address:* c/o United Agents, 12–26 Lexington Street, W1F 0LE. *Died 29 April 2014.*

HOSKYNS, Sir (Edwyn) Wren, 17th Bt *cr* 1676, of Harewood, Herefordshire; FRCPCH; Consultant Paediatrician, Leicester General Hospital, since 1993; *b* 4 Feb. 1956; *er s* of Sir Benedict Leigh Hoskyns, 16th Bt and of Ann (*née* Wilkinson); *S* father, 2010, but his name does not appear on the Official Roll of the Baronetage; *m* 1981, Jane Sellers; one *s* one *d*. *Educ:* Nottingham Univ. (BM BS 1979). MRCP 1984; FRCPCH 1996. *Heir: s* Robin Chevallier Hoskyns, *b* 5 July 1989. *Died 19 Feb. 2015.*

HOSKYNS, Sir John (Austin Hungerford Leigh), Kt 1982; Director-General, Institute of Directors, 1984–89; Chairman: The Burton Group plc, 1990–98; Arcadia Group plc, 1998; *b* 23 Aug. 1927; *s* of Lt-Colonel Chandos Benedict Arden Hoskyns and Joyce Austin Hoskyns; *m* 1956, Miranda Jane Marie Mott; two *s* one *d*. *Educ:* Winchester College. Served in The Rifle Brigade, 1945–57 (Captain); IBM United Kingdom Ltd, 1957–64; founded John Hoskyns & Co. Ltd, later part of Hoskyns Group plc (Chm. and Man. Dir), 1964–75; Director: Martin Marietta Data Systems Inc., 1975–79; ICL plc, 1982–84; AGB Research plc, later Pergamon AGB plc, 1983–89; Clerical Medical & General Life Assurance Soc., 1983–98; McKechnie plc, 1983–93; Ferranti Internat. plc, 1986–94; EMAP plc, 1993–98 (Chm., 1994–98). Hd of PM's Policy Unit, 1979–82. Hon. DSc Salford, 1985; DU Essex, 1987. *Publications:* Just In Time: inside the Thatcher revolution, 2000. *Recreations:* opera, shooting. *Address:* c/o Child & Co., 1 Fleet Street, EC4Y 1BD. *Clubs:* Travellers, Green Jackets. *Died 20 Oct. 2014.*

HOSKYNS, Sir Wren; *see* Hoskyns, Sir E. W.

HOUGH, John Patrick; Secretary, Institute of Chartered Accountants in England and Wales, 1972–82; *b* 6 July 1928; *s* of William Patrick Hough, MBE, Lt-Comdr RN and Eva Harriet Hough; *m* 1956, (Dorothy) Nadine Akerman; four *s* one *d*. *Educ:* Purbrook High School. FCA, MIMC, FBCS. Articled M. R. Cobbett & Co., Portsmouth, 1950–53; Derbyshire & Co., 1953–54; Turquand Youngs & Co., 1954–57; Computer Specialist, IBM United Kingdom Ltd, 1957–61; Consultant 1961–62, Partner 1962–69, Robson Morrow & Co.; Dep. Sec., Inst. of Chartered Accountants in England and Wales, 1969–71. *Recreations:* music, food. *Address:* 5 South Row, Blackheath, SE3 0RY; Coastguard Cottage, Newtown, Newport, Isle of Wight PO30 4PA. *Club:* London Rowing. *Died 15 June 2011.*

HOUGHTON, Maj.-Gen. Robert Dyer, CB 1963; OBE 1947; MC 1942; DL; *b* 7 March 1912; *s* of late J. M. Houghton, Dawlish, Devon; *m* 1940, Dorothy Uladh (*d* 1995), *y d* of late Maj.-Gen. R. W. S. Lyons, IMS; two *s* one *d*. *Educ:* Haileybury Coll. Royal Marines Officer, 1930–64; Col Comdt, Royal Marines, 1973–76. Gen. Sec., Royal UK Beneficent Assoc., 1968–78. DL East Sussex, 1977. *Recreations:* gardening, model engineering. *Address:* Vert House, Whitesmith, near Lewes, East Sussex BN8 6JQ. *Club:* Army and Navy. *Died 17 Jan. 2011.*

HOULDER, John Maurice, CBE 1977 (MBE (mil.) 1941); Lessee and Operator, Elstree Aerodrome, since 1951; *b* 20 Feb. 1916; *m* 1981, Rody, *d* of late Major Luke White; two *s* one *d* by former marriages. Private Pilot's Licence, 1938–; instrument rating, 1949–. Chm., Houlder Diving Research Facility Ltd, 1978–; Pres., Houlder (formerly Houlder Offshore Engrg) Ltd, 2002– (Chm., 1984–2002). Vis. Prof., Dept of Naval Architecture (formerly Dept of Ship and Marine Technol.), Univ. of Strathclyde, 1982–. Chm., London Ocean Shipowners Joint Dock Labour Piecework Cttee, 1950–60; first Chm., River Plate Europe Freight Conf., 1961–70; Chm., Bulk Cargo Cttee, Continental River Plate Conf., 1954–70. Member: Gen. Cttee, 1970–, Exec. Board, 1970–93, and Technical Cttee, 1970–95, Lloyds Register of Shipping; Light Aircraft Requirements Cttee, CAA, 1955–84; Adv. Cttee on R&D to Sec. of State for Energy, 1987–90. Member, Council: RSPB, 1974–79; RINA, 1981–87; Pres., Soc. for Underwater Technology, 1978–80 (President's Award, 1987). Hon. DSc Strathclyde, 1986. Stanley Gray Award, Inst. of Marine Engrs, 1982; Master Air Pilot, GAPAN, 2006. *Recreations:* ski-ing, flying, bird-watching, computer programming. *Address:* 59 Warwick Square, SW1V 2AL. *T:* (020) 7834 2856, *Fax:* (020) 7834 1647. *Clubs:* Air Squadron; Kandahar Ski, 1001. *Died 2 Feb. 2012.*

HOUSE, Lt-Gen. Sir David (George), GCB 1977 (KCB 1975); KCVO 1985; CBE 1967; MC 1944; Gentleman Usher of the Black Rod, House of Lords, 1978–85; Serjeant-at-Arms, House of Lords, and Secretary to the Lord Great Chamberlain, 1978–85; *b* 8 Aug. 1922; *s* of A. G. House; *m* 1947, Sheila Betty Darwin (*d* 2006); two *d*. *Educ:* Regents Park Sch., London. War service in Italy; and thereafter in variety of regimental (KRRC and 1st Bn The Royal Green Jackets) and staff appts. Comd 51 Gurkha Bde in Borneo, 1965–67; Chief BRIXMIS, 1967–69; Dep. Mil. Sec., 1969–71; Chief of Staff, HQ BAOR, 1971–73; Dir of Infantry, 1973–75; GOC Northern Ireland, 1975–77. Colonel Commandant: The Light Division, 1974–77; Small Arms School Corps, 1974–77. Dir, Yorks and Humberside, Lloyds Bank, 1985–91. *Address:* Dormer Lodge, Aldborough, near Boroughbridge, N Yorks YO51 9EY. *Died 14 July 2012.*

HOUSE, Prof. John Peter Humphry, PhD; Walter H. Annenberg Professor, Courtauld Institute of Art, University of London, 2002–10, then Emeritus; *b* 19 April 1945; *s* of Madeline Edith Church and Arthur Humphry House; *m* 1968, Jill Elaine Turner (marr. diss. 2009); two *s*. *Educ:* Westminster Sch.; New Coll., Oxford (BA); Courtauld Inst. of Art (MA, PhD). Lecturer: UEA, 1969–76; UCL, 1976–80; Lectr, 1980–87, Reader, 1987–95, Prof., 1995–2010, Dep. Dir, 1996–99, Courtauld Inst., London Univ. Slade Prof. of Fine Art, Univ. of Oxford, 1986–87; British Acad. Res. Reader, 1988–90; Samuel H. Kress Prof., Nat. Gall. of Art, Washington DC, 2008–09. Organiser: Impressionism Exhibn, RA, 1974; Landscapes of France exhibn, Hayward Gall., 1995; Impressionists by the Sea exhibn, RA, 2007; Co-organiser: Post Impressionism exhibn, RA, 1979–80; Renoir exhibn, Arts Council, 1985. *Publications:* Monet, 1977, 2nd edn 1981; Monet: nature

into art, 1986; (jtly) Impressionist and Post-Impressionist Masterpieces from the Courtauld Collection, 1987; (jtly) Impressionism for England: Samuel Courtauld as Patron and Collector, 1994; Renoir: la promenade, 1997; Impressionism: paint and politics, 2004; author/co-author, exhibition catalogues; articles in Burlington Magazine, Art History, Art in America. *Recreations:* second hand bookshops, early music. *E:* john.house@courtauld.ac.uk.
Died 7 Feb. 2012.

HOUSTON, Maj.-Gen. David, CVO 2005; CBE 1975 (OBE 1972); Lord-Lieutenant of Sutherland, 1991–2004; *b* 24 Feb. 1929; *s* of late David Houston and Christina Charleson Houston (*née* Dunnett); *m* 1959, Jancis Veronica Burn; two *s. Educ:* Latymer Upper Sch. Commissioned, Royal Irish Fusiliers, 1949; served Korea, Kenya, BAOR, N Africa; Staff Coll., Camberley, 1961; commanded 1 Loyals and newly amalgamated 1st QLR, 1969–71; in comd 8th Inf. Bde, Londonderry, N Ireland, 1974–75; Mem. RCDS, 1976; Military Attaché and Commander, British Army Staff, Washington, 1977–79; HQ UKLF, 1979–80; Pres., Regular Commissions Bd, 1980–83; retd 1984. Hon. Col, Manchester and Salford Univs OTC (TA), 1985–90; Col, The Queen's Lancashire Regt, 1983–92. DL Sutherland, 1991; JP Sutherland, 1991–2007. *Recreation:* fishing. *Address:* Fas-na-cloiche, Linsidemore, Lairg, Sutherland IV27 4EU. *Died 10 Nov. 2014.*

HOUSTON, James Caldwell, CBE 1982; MD, FRCP; Physician to Guy's Hospital, 1953–82, then Emeritus Physician; Dean, United Medical and Dental Schools, Guys and St Thomas's Hospitals, 1982–84 (Hon. Fellow, 1993; Dean, Medical and Dental Schools, Guy's Hospital, 1965–82); *b* 18 Feb. 1917; *yr s* of late David Houston and Minnie Walker Houston; *m* 1946, Thelma Cromarty Cruickshank, MB, ChB (*d* 2009), 2nd *d* of late John Cruickshank, CBE; four *s. Educ:* Mill Hill Sch.; Guy's Hosp. Medical Sch. MRCS, LRCP 1939; MB, BS (London) 1940; MRCP 1944; MD 1946; FRCP 1956. Late Major RAMC; Medical Registrar, Guy's Hospital, 1946. Asst Ed., 1954, Jt Ed., 1958–67, Guy's Hosp. Reports. Member: Bd of Governors, Guy's Hosp., 1965–74; SE Metropolitan Regional Hosp. Bd, 1966–71; Lambeth, Lewisham and Southwark AHA (Teaching), 1974–78; Court of Governors, London Sch. of Hygiene and Tropical Med., 1969–84; Senate, Univ. of London, 1970–84; Bd of Faculty of Clinical Medicine, Cambridge Univ., 1975–81; Cttee of Vice-Chancellors and Principals, 1977–80; Chm., Collegiate Council, Univ. of London, 1976–79; Special Trustee, Guy's Hosp., 1974–82; Trustee, Hayward Foundn, 1978–2001. Dir, Clerical, Medical & Gen. Life Assurance Soc., 1965–87; Vice-Pres., Medical Defence Union, 1970–92. *Publications:* Principles of Medicine and Medical Nursing (jtly), 1956, 5th edn 1978; A Short Text-book of Medicine (jtly), 1962, 8th edn 1984; articles in Quart. Jl Med., Brit. Med. Bull., Lancet, etc. *Recreations:* golf, gardening. *Address:* Discovery Cottage, 1 Mews Street, E1W 1UG. *T:* (020) 7481 8912. *Died 8 May 2013.*

HOWARD, Alan (Mackenzie), CBE 1998; actor; Associate Artist, Royal Shakespeare Company, since 1967; *b* 5 Aug. 1937; *s* of late Arthur John Howard and of Jean Compton Mackenzie; *m* 1st, Stephanie Hinchcliffe Davies (marr. diss. 1976); 2nd, 2004, Sally Beauman; one *s. Educ:* Ardingly Coll. Belgrade Theatre, Coventry, 1958–60; parts incl. Frankie Bryant in Roots (also at Royal Court and Duke of York's); Wesker Trilogy, Royal Court, 1960; A Loss of Roses, Pembroke, Croydon, 1961; The Changeling, Royal Court, 1961; The Chances, and The Broken Heart, inaugural season, Chichester Festival, 1962; Virtue in Danger, Mermaid and Strand, 1963; Bassanio in The Merchant of Venice, Lysander in A Midsummer Night's Dream, in tour of S America and Europe, 1964; Simon in A Heritage and its History, Phoenix, 1965; Angelo in Measure for Measure, Bolingbroke in Richard II, Nottingham, 1965–66; Cyril Jackson in The Black and White Minstrels, Traverse, Edinburgh, 1972, Hampstead, 1973; A Ride Across Lake Constance, Hampstead and Mayfair, 1973; The Silver King, Chichester, 1990; Scenes from a Marriage, Chichester, transf. Wyndhams, 1990; Kings, 1991; Vladimir in Waiting for Godot, Old Vic, 1997; title rôle in King Lear, Old Vic, 1997; the Man in Play about the Baby, Almeida, 1998; Schon in Lulu, Almeida and Washington, 2001; Gabriel in Gates of Gold, Gate Th., Dublin, 2002; *Royal Shakespeare Company:* joined company, 1966, playing Orsino in Twelfth Night, Lussurioso in The Revenger's Tragedy; 1967: Jaques in As You Like It (also LA, 1968), Young Fashion in The Relapse; 1968: Edgar in King Lear, Achilles in Troilus and Cressida, Benedick in Much Ado about Nothing; 1969: Benedick (also in LA and San Francisco), Achilles, Lussurioso, and Bartholomew Cokes in Bartholomew Fair; 1970: Mephistophilis in Dr Faustus, Hamlet, Theseus/Oberon in A Midsummer Night's Dream, Ceres in The Tempest; 1971: Theseus/Oberon (NY debut); 1971–72: Theseus/Oberon, Nikolai in Enemies, Dorimant in The Man of Mode, The Envoy in The Balcony; 1972–73: Theseus/Oberon, in tour of E and W Europe, USA, Japan, Australia; 1974: Carlos II in The Bewitched; 1975: Henry V, Prince Hal in Henry IV parts I and II; 1976: Prince Hal (SWET Award for Best Actor in revival), Henry V in tour of Europe and USA, Jack Rover in Wild Oats (also Piccadilly); 1977: Henry V, Henry VI parts I, II and III, Coriolanus (Plays and Players London Critics Award, SWET Award for Best Actor in revival, Evening Standard Best Actor Award, 1978); 1978: Antony in Antony and Cleopatra; 1979: Coriolanus in tour of Europe, The Children of the Sun; 1980: title rôles in Richard II and Richard III (Variety Club Best Actor Award); 1981–82: Neschastlivsev in The Forest; Good (Standard Best Actor Award, 1981); 1985: Nikolai in Breaking the Silence; 2011: The School for Scandal; *Royal National Theatre:* Prof. Higgins in Pygmalion, 1992; title rôle in Macbeth, 1993; George in Les Enfants Terribles, 1994; Calogero in La Grande Magia, 1995; Player in Rosencrantz and Guildenstern are Dead, 1995; title rôle, Oedipus Plays, 1996; Khludov in Flight, 1998; Sloper in The Heiress, 2000; Teiresias in Oedipus, 2008. Best Actor (jt), 1981, Drama (British Theatre Assoc.) awards for Richard II, Good and The Forest. *Films include:* The Heroes of Telemark; Work is a Four Letter Word; The Return of the Musketeers; Secret Rapture; The Cook, The Thief, his Wife and her Lover; The Lord of the Rings: The Fellowship of the Ring; The Lord of the Rings: The Return of the King. *Television appearances include:* The Way of the World; Comet Among the Stars; Coriolanus; The Holy Experiment; Poppyland; Sherlock Holmes, Evensong, Life Story, 1986; A Perfect Spy, 1987; The Dog it Was That Died, 1988; Death in Holy Orders, 2003; Parade's End, 2012. *Radio includes:* Soames in Forsyte Chronicles, 1990–91. *Address:* c/o Julian Belfrage Associates, 3rd Floor, 9 Argyll Street, W1F 7TG. *T:* (020) 7287 8544. *Died 14 Feb. 2015.*

HOWARD, Ann Pauline; freelance opera singer (mezzo-soprano), 1971–99, then teaching privately; *b* 22 July 1936; *d* of William Alfred and Gladys Winifred Swadling; *m* 1954, Keith Giles (*d* 2004); one *d. Educ:* privately; with Topliss Green, Rodolfa Lhombino (London) and Dominic Modesti (Paris) via scholarship from Royal Opera House, Covent Garden. Principal Mezzo-Soprano, Sadler's Wells Opera, 1964–73. Main rôles: Carmen, Dalila (Samson et Dalila), Azucena (Il Trovatore), Amneris (Aida), Fricka (Das Rheingold and Die Walküre), La Grande Duchesse de Gerolstein, Brangäne (Tristan und Isolde), Kabanicha (Kátya Kabanová), Gingerbread Witch (Hansel and Gretel), Eboli (Don Carlos), Katisha (Mikado), La Belle Hélène, Babulenka (The Gambler), Fairy Queen (Iolanthe), Dulcinée (Don Quichotte), Hérodiade, Klytemnestra (Electra), Isabella (Italian Girl in Algiers), Old Lady (Candide), Prince Orlofsky (Die Fledermaus), Hostess and Marina (Boris Godunov), Step-Mother (Into the Woods), Auntie (Peter Grimes), Baba (Rake's Progress), Emma Jones (Street Scene), Jezi Baba (Rusalka), Lilli Vanessi (Kiss Me Kate), Marcellina (Marriage of Figaro), Ortrud (Lohengrin); world premières: Madam Leda (The Mines of Sulphur), Sadler's Wells, 1965; Mrs Danvers (Rebecca), Opera North, 1983; Caliban (The Tempest), Santa Fé Festival Opera, USA, 1985; Mrs Worthing (The Plumber's Gift), ENO, 1989; 2nd Official (The Doctor of Myddfai), WNO, 1996; British premières: Cassandra (The Trojans, Pts 1 and 2), Scottish Opera, 1969; Mescalina (Le Grand Macabre), ENO, 1982; début Metropolitan Opera, NY, 1994 (Auntie); also performances in France, Italy, Belgium, Austria, Germany, USA (incl. series of Gilbert and Sullivan operas at Performing Arts Center, NY State Univ., 1993–98), Canada, Mexico, Chile, Portugal; many recordings and videos. Sir Charles Santley Meml Award, Musicians' Co., 2002. *Recreations:* gardening, cooking. *Died 26 March 2014.*

HOWARD, Elizabeth Jane, CBE 2000; FRSL; novelist; *b* 26 March 1923; *d* of David Liddon and Katharine M. Howard; *m* 1st, 1942, Peter M. Scott (marr. diss. 1951; later Sir Peter Scott, CH, CBE, FRS (*d* 1989)); one *d*; 2nd, 1959, James Douglas-Henry; 3rd, 1965, Kingsley Amis (later Sir Kingsley Amis, CBE) (marr. diss. 1983; he *d* 1995). *Educ:* home. FRSL 1994. Trained at London Mask Theatre Sch. Played at Stratford-on-Avon, and in repertory theatre in Devon; BBC, Television, modelling, 1939–46; Sec. to Inland Waterways Assoc., 1947; subsequently writing, editing, reviewing, journalism and writing plays for television, incl. serials of After Julius in three plays and Something in Disguise in six plays. John Llewellyn Rhys Memorial Prize for The Beautiful Visit, 1950. Hon. Artistic Dir, Cheltenham Literary Festival, 1962; Artistic co-Dir, Salisbury Festival of Arts, 1973. Film script, The Attachment, 1986. *Publications:* The Beautiful Visit, 1950; The Long View, 1956; The Sea Change, 1959; After Julius, 1965; Something in Disguise, 1969 (TV series, 1982); Odd Girl Out, 1972; Mr Wrong, 1975; (ed) A Companion for Lovers, 1978; Getting It Right, 1982 (Yorkshire Post Prize) (film script, 1985); (jtly) Howard and Maschler on Food: cooking for occasions, 1987; The Light Years, 1990; Green Shades (anthology), 1991; Marking Time, 1991; Confusion, 1993; Casting Off, 1995; Anthology on Marriage, 1997; Falling, 1999; Slipstream (autobiog.), 2002; Love All, 2008; All Change, 2013. *Recreations:* music, gardening, enjoying all the arts, natural history. *Address:* c/o Jonathan Clowes, Iron Bridge House, Bridge Approach, NW1 8BD. *Died 2 Jan. 2014.*

HOWARD, Philip Nicholas Charles, FRSL; leader writer, columnist, modern manners and word watching, The Times, since 1992; *b* 2 Nov. 1933; *s* of late Peter Dunsmore Howard and Doris Emily Metaxa; *m* 1959, Myrtle (*d* 2014), *d* of Sir Reginald Houldsworth, 4th Bt, OBE, TD; two *s* one *d*. *Educ:* Eton Coll. (King's Scholar); Trinity Coll., Oxford (Major Scholar; first cl. Lit. Hum; MA). Glasgow Herald, 1959–64; The Times, 1964–: reporter, writer, columnist; Literary Ed., 1978–92. Member: Classical Assoc. (Pres., 2002); Horatian Soc.; Soc. of Bookmen; Literary Soc.; Flaccidae. Founder Patron, Friends of Classics, 1991. FRSL 1987. Liveryman, Wheelwrights' Co. London Editor, Verbatim, 1977–. *Publications:* The Black Watch, 1968; The Royal Palaces, 1970; London's River, 1975; New Words for Old, 1977; The British Monarchy, 1977; Weasel Words, 1978; Words Fail Me, 1980; A Word in Your Ear, 1983; The State of the Language, English Observed, 1984; (jtly) The Times Bicentenary Stamp Book, 1985; We Thundered Out, 200 Years of The Times 1785–1985, 1985; Winged Words, 1988; Word-Watching, 1988; (jtly) London, The Evolution of a Great City, 1989; A Word in Time, 1990; (ed) The Times Bedside Book, 1991; Reading a Poem, 1992; (ed) The Times Bedside Book, 1992; The British Library: a treasure house of knowledge, 2008; Lost Words: a feast of forgotten words, their origins and their meanings, 2012; Modern Manners, 2013. *Recreations:* walking, reading, talking, music, the classics, beagles not beagling, Jack Russells, stand at Twickenham. *Address:* Flat 1, 47 Ladbroke Grove, W11 3AR. *T:* (020) 7727 1077. *Clubs:* Garrick; Ad Eundem (Oxford and Cambridge); Eton Ramblers; International PEN. *Died 5 Oct. 2014.*

HOWARD-DRAKE, Jack Thomas Arthur; Assistant Under-Secretary of State, Home Office, 1974–78; *b* 7 Jan. 1919; *o s* of Arthur Howard and Ruby (*née* Cherry); *m* 1947, Joan Mary, *o d* of Hubert and Winifred Crook; one *s* two *d*. *Educ:* Hele's Sch., Exeter. Asst Inspector, Ministry of Health Insurance Dept, 1937–39 and 1946–47. Served War, RA, 1939–46 (Major, despatches). Colonial Office: Asst Principal, 1947; Principal, 1949; Private Sec. to Sec. of State, 1956–62; Asst Sec., 1962; Asst Sec., Cabinet Office, 1963–65; Asst Sec., Home Office, 1965–72; Asst Under-Sec. of State, NI Office, 1972–74. Chairman: Oxfordshire Local History Assoc., 1984–91; Wychwoods Local History Soc., 1984–92. *Publications:* Oxford Church Courts: Depositions 1542–1550, 1991, 1570–1574, 1993, 1581–1586, 1994, 1589–1593, 1997, 1592–1596, 1998, 1603–1606, 1999, 1609–1616, 2003, 1616–1622, 2005, 1629–1634, 2007, 1634–1639, 2008. *Recreations:* gardening, local history. *Address:* 26 Sinnels Field, Shipton-under-Wychwood, Chipping Norton, Oxon OX7 6EJ. *T:* (01993) 830792. *Died 7 May 2013.*

HOWARTH, Peter James, CBE 1995; Managing Director, Royal Mail, 1992–96, and Board Member, 1991–96, Post Office; *b* 27 July 1935; *s* of late Sidney and Margaret Howarth; *m* 1964, Susan Mary Briggs; one *s* one *d*. *Educ:* St Joseph's Coll., Blackpool. Entered Post Office, 1953; held junior and middle management positions; Head Postmaster, Manchester, 1979–85; Chm., NW Postal Bd, 1985–86; Gen. Manager, West and London Letters Territories, 1986–88; Dir Ops, Royal Mail, 1988–91; Asst Man. Dir, Royal Mail, 1991; Man. Dir, Parcelforce, 1991–92. Mem., Billericay Mayflower Rotary Club; Paul Harris Fellow, Rotary Club. *Recreations:* golf, fishing, reading. *Address:* 5 Swallowfield Gardens, Appleton, Warrington WA4 5QY. *Died 5 Jan. 2012.*

HOWE OF ABERAVON, Baron *cr* 1992 (Life Peer), of Tandridge, in the County of Surrey; **Richard Edward Geoffrey Howe,** CH 1996; Kt 1970; PC 1972; QC 1965; *b* 20 Dec. 1926; *er s* of late B. E. Howe and Mrs E. F. Howe, JP (*née* Thomson), Port Talbot, Glamorgan; *m* 1953, Elspeth Rosamund Morton Shand (Baroness Howe of Idlicote, CBE); one *s* two *d*. *Educ:* Winchester Coll. (Exhibitioner); Trinity Hall, Cambridge (Scholar, MA, LLB; Hon. Fellow, 1992); Pres., Trinity Hall Assoc., 1977–78. Lieut Royal Signals 1945–48. Chm. Cambridge Univ. Conservative Assoc., 1951; Chm. Bow Group, 1955; Managing Dir, Crossbow, 1957–60, Editor 1960–62. Called to the Bar, Middle Temple, 1952, Bencher, 1969, Reader, 1993; Mem. General Council of the Bar, 1957–61; Mem. Council of Justice, 1963–70. Dep. Chm., Glamorgan QS, 1966–70. Contested (C) Aberavon, 1955, 1959; MP (C): Bebington, 1964–66; Reigate, 1970–74; Surrey East, 1974–92. Sec. Conservative Parliamentary Health and Social Security Cttee, 1964–65; an Opposition Front Bench spokesman on labour and social services, 1965–66; Solicitor-General, 1970–72; Minister for Trade and Consumer Affairs, DTI, 1972–74; opposition front bench spokesman on social services, 1974–75, on Treasury and economic affairs, 1975–79; Chancellor of the Exchequer, 1979–83; Sec. of State for Foreign and Commonwealth Affairs, 1983–89; Lord Pres. of the Council, Leader of H of C, and Dep. Prime Minister, 1989–90. Mem., H of L, 1992–2015. Chm., Interim Cttee, IMF, 1982–83. Chm., Framlington Russian Investment Fund, 1994–2003; Director: Sun Alliance & London Insce Co. Ltd, 1974–79; AGB Research Ltd, 1974–79; EMI Ltd, 1976–79; BICC plc, 1991–97; Glaxo Hldgs, 1991–95; Glaxo Wellcome plc, 1995–96. Special Advr, Internat. Affairs, Jones, Day, Reavis and Pogue, 1991–2000; Member: J. P. Morgan Internat. Adv. Council, 1992–2001; Adv. Council, Bertelsmann Foundn, 1992–97; Fuji Wolfensohn Internat. European Adv. Bd, 1996–98; Carlyle Gp Eur. Adv. Bd, 1997–2001; Fuji Bank Internat. Adv. Council, 1999–2002. Member: (Latey) Interdeptl Cttee on Age of Majority, 1965–67; (Street) Cttee on Racial Discrimination, 1967; (Cripps) Cons. Cttee on Discrimination against Women, 1968–69; Chm. Ely Hospital, Cardiff, Inquiry, 1969. Chm. Steering Cttee, Tax Law Rewrite Project, Inland Revenue, 1996–2005. Visitor, SOAS, Univ. of London, 1991–2001; Vis. Fellow, John F. Kennedy Sch. of Govt, Harvard Univ., 1991–92; Herman Phleger Vis. Prof., Stanford Law Sch., Calif, 1993. Member, International Advisory Council: Inst. of Internat. Studies, Stanford Univ., Calif, 1990–2005; Centre for Eur. Policy Studies, 1992–2005; Chm., Adv. Bd, English Centre for Legal Studies, Warsaw Univ., 1992–99; Pres., Acad. of Experts, 1996–2005; Vice-President: RUSI, 1991–; English Coll. Foundn in Prague, 1992–. President: Cons. Political Centre Nat. Adv. Cttee, 1977–79; Nat. Union of Cons. and Unionist Assocs, 1983–84; GB China Centre, 1992–; Russian/European Trust, 1997–; Jt Pres., Wealth of Nations Foundn, 1991–2004; Chm., Thomson Foundn, 2004–07 (Trustee, 1995–2007); Trustee: Cambridge Commonwealth Trust, 1993–2010; Cambridge Overseas Trust, 1993–2010. Mem., Adv. Council, Presidium of Supreme Rada of Ukraine, 1991–97. Mem.

Council of Management, Private Patients' Plan, 1969–70; Mem., Steering Cttee, Project Liberty, 1991–97; Patron: Enterprise Europe, 1990–2004; UK Metric Assoc., 2003– (Pres., 2005–); McKechnie Foundn, 2005–. Pres., Which? (formerly Assoc. for Consumer Res.), 1992–2010 (an Hon. Vice-Pres., 1974–92). Freeman, City of London, 2004; Hon. Freeman, Co. of Tax Advisors, 2004. Hon. Fellow: UCW, Swansea, 1996; UCW, Cardiff, 1999; Amer. Bar Foundn, 2000; Chartered Inst. of Taxation, 2000; SOAS, 2003. Hon. Freeman, Port Talbot, 1992. Hon. LLD: Wales, 1988; LSE, 2004; Glamorgan, 2004; Hon. DCL City, 1993. Joseph Bech Prize, FVS Stiftung, Hamburg, 1993; Paul Harris Fellow, Rotary Internat., 1995. Grand Cross, Order of Merit (Portugal), 1987; Grand Cross, Order of Merit (Germany), 1992; Order of Public Service (Ukraine), 2001. *Publications:* Principles in Practice, 1960; Conservative Opportunity, 1965; Conflict of Loyalty (memoirs), 1994; *contributed:* The Chancellors' Tales: managing the British economy, 2006; British Diplomacy: foreign secretaries reflect, 2007; World Crisis: the way forward after Iraq, 2008; various political pamphlets for Bow Group and Conservative Political Centre. *Clubs:* Athenæum, Garrick.
Died 9 Oct. 2015.

HOWE, Prof. Geoffrey Leslie, TD 1962 (Bars 1969 and 1974); Professor of Oral Surgery and Oral Medicine, 1987–96, and Dean, 1988–96, Jordan University of Science and Technology; *b* 22 April 1924; *e s* of late Leo Leslie John Howe, Maidenhead, Berks; *m* 1st, 1948, Heather Patricia Joan Hambly (*d* 1997); (one *s* decd); 2nd, 2003, Mrs Margaret Samuel (*née* Hall) (*d* 2010). *Educ:* Royal Dental and Middlesex Hospitals. LDS RCS 1946; LRCP, MRCS 1954; FDS RCS 1955; MDS Dunelm, 1961; FFD RCSI 1964; FICD 1981. Dental and Medical Sch. Prizeman; Begley Prize, RCS, 1951; Cartwright Prize, RCS, 1961. Dental Officer, Royal Army Dental Corps, 1946–49. House appointments, etc., Royal Dental and Middlesex Hospitals, 1949–55. Registrar in Oral Surgery, Eastman Dental Hosp. (Institute of Dental Surgery), 1955–56; Senior Registrar in Oral Surgery, Plastic and Oral Surgery Centre, Chepstow, Mon, 1956; Senior Registrar in Oral Surgery, Eastman Dental Hospital, 1956–59; Professor of Oral Surgery, University of Newcastle upon Tyne (formerly King's Coll., University of Durham), 1959–67; Prof. of Oral Surgery, Royal Dental Hosp., London Sch. of Dental Surgery, 1967–78 (Dean of School, 1974–78); Prof. of Oral Surgery and Oral Medicine, and Dean of Dental Studies, Univ. of Hong Kong, 1978–83; Dir, Prince Philip Dental Hosp., 1981–83. Cons. Oral Surgeon, United Newcastle upon Tyne Hosps, 1959–67; Chm., Central Cttee for Hosp. Dental Services, 1971–73; Vice-Pres., BDA, 1979– (Vice-Chm., 1971–73; Chm., 1973–78); Pres., Internat. Assoc. of Oral Surgeons, 1980–83. Hon. Col Comdt, RADC, 1975–89. OStJ. *Publications:* The Extraction of Teeth, 1961, 2nd edn 1970; Minor Oral Surgery, 1966, 3rd edn 1985; (with F. I. H. Whitehead) Local Anaesthesia in Dentistry, 1972, 3rd edn 1990; Reflections of a Fortunate Fellow (autobiog.), 2002; contribs to: Medical Treatment Yearbook, 1959; Modern Trends in Dental Surgery, 1962, and to numerous medical and dental journals. *Recreations:* sailing; Territorial Army Volunteer Reserve (lately Col, OC 217 (L) Gen. Hosp. RAMC (V), graded Cons. Dental Surgeon RADC, TAVR). *Address:* 24 Amberley Drive, Woodham, Addlestone, Surrey KT15 3SL. *Clubs:* Travellers, Gents, Oral Surgery; Hong Kong; Hong Kong Yacht. *Died 17 July 2014.*

HOWE, Prof. G(eorge) Melvyn, PhD, DSc; FRSE, FRGS, FRSGS, FRMetS; Professor of Geography, University of Strathclyde, 1967–85, then Emeritus; *b* Abercynon, 7 April 1920; *s* of Reuben and Edith Howe, Abercynon; *m* 1947, Patricia Graham Fennell, Pontypridd; three *d*. *Educ:* Caerphilly Boys' Grammar Sch.; UCW Aberystwyth (BSc 1940; BSc 1st cl. hons Geog. and Anthrop., 1947; MSc 1949; PhD 1957); DSc Strathclyde 1974. Served with RAF, 1940–46: Meteorological Br., 1940–42; commnd Intell. (Air Photographic Interpretation) Br., 1942–46, in Middle East Comd. Lectr, later Sen. Lectr, in Geography, UCW Aberystwyth, 1948; Reader in Geog., Univ. of Wales, 1964. Vis. Prof. (Health and Welfare, Canada), 1977. Mem. Council, Inst. of British Geographers (Pres., 1985); Mem. Medical Geography Cttee, RGS, 1960–; British Rep. on Medical Geog. Commn of IGU, 1970–; Mem., British Nat. Cttee for Geography, RGS, 1978–83. Gill Memorial Award, RGS, 1964. *Publications:* Wales from the Air, 1957, 2nd edn 1966; (with P. Thomas) Welsh Landforms and Scenery, 1963; National Atlas of Disease Mortality in the United Kingdom, 1963, 2nd edn 1970; The Soviet Union, 1968, 2nd edn 1983; The USSR, 1971; Man, Environment and Disease in Britain, 1972, 2nd edn 1976; (ed and contrib.) Atlas of Glasgow and the West of Scotland, 1972; (contrib.) Wales (ed E. G. Bowen), 1958; (contrib.) Modern Methods in the History of Medicine (ed E. Clarke), 1970; (ed with J. A. Loraine, and contrib.) Environmental Medicine, 1973, 2nd edn 1980; (contrib.) Environment and Man (ed J. Lenihan and W. W. Fletcher), 1976; (ed and contrib.) A World Geography of Human Diseases, 1977; (ed and contrib.) Global Geocancerology, 1986; People, Environment, Disease and Death in Britain, 1997; articles in geographical, meteorological, hydrological and medical jls. *Recreation:* travel. *Address:* Hendre, 50 Heol Croes Faen, Nottage, Porthcawl CF36 3SW. *T:* (01656) 772377. *Club:* Royal Air Force. *Died 27 Aug. 2012.*

HOWELL, Prof. John Bernard Lloyd, CBE 1991; Chairman, Southampton and SW Hampshire District Health Authority, 1983–98; Foundation Professor of Medicine, University of Southampton, 1969–91, then Emeritus (Dean of the Faculty of Medicine, 1978–83); Hon. Consultant Physician, Southampton General Hospital, 1969–91, then Emeritus; *b* 1 Aug. 1926; *s* of late David John Howells and Hilda Mary Hill, Ynystawe, Swansea; *m* 1952, Heather Joan Rolfe; two *s* one *d*. *Educ:* Swansea Grammar Sch.; Middx Hosp. Med. Sch. (Meyerstein Scholar 1946). BSc, MB, BS, PhD; FRCP. House Officer posts, Middx and Brompton Hosps; MO RAMC, 1952–54; Lectr in Physiol Medicine, 1954–56, in Pharmacol Medicine, 1958–60, Middlesex Hosp. Med. Sch.; Manchester Royal Infirmary: Sen. Lectr in Medicine and Hon. Consultant Physician, 1960–66; Consultant Physician, 1966–69. Eli Lilly Travelling Fellow, Johns Hopkins Hospital, 1957–58; Goulstonian Lectr, RCP, 1966. Member: Physiol Soc., 1956–; Med. Res. Soc., 1956–; Assoc. of Physicians of GB and Ire., 1964–; GMC, 1978–83. President: British Thoracic Soc., 1988–89; BMA, 1989–90 (Chm., Bd of Sci. and Educn, 1991–98). Mem. Soc. of Scholars, Johns Hopkins Univ., 1998–. Hon. Life Mem., Canadian Thoracic Soc., 1978; Hon. FACP 1982. Hon. DSc Southampton, 1994. *Publications:* (ed jtly) Breathlessness, 1966; chapters in: Cecil and Loeb's Textbook of Medicine, 13th edn 1970, 14th edn 1974; Recent Advances in Chest Medicine, 1976; Thoracic Medicine, 1981; Oxford Textbook of Medicine, 1982; Respiratory Medicine, 1995; Asthma and Rhinitis, 1995; papers on respiratory physiology and medicine and health care. *Recreations:* France, DIY, wine. *Address:* The Coach House, Bassett Wood Drive, Southampton SO16 3PT. *T:* (023) 8076 8878. *Died 1 Jan. 2015.*

HOWELL, Maj.-Gen. Lloyd, CBE 1972; Consultant, Technical Education Development, University College, Cardiff, 1980–86 (Fellow, 1981); *b* 28 Dec. 1923; *s* of Thomas Idris Howell and Anne Howell; *m* 1st, 1945, Hazel Barker (*d* 1974); four *s* three *d* (and one *s* decd); 2nd, 1975, Elizabeth June Buchanan Husband (*née* Atkinson); two step *s*. *Educ:* Barry Grammar Sch.; University Coll. of S Wales and Monmouthshire (BSc); Royal Military Coll. of Science. CEng, MRAeS. Commissioned RA, 1944; Field Regt, RA, E Africa, 1945–46; Staff, Divl HQ, Palestine, 1946–47; RAEC 1949; Instr, RMA Sandhurst, 1949–53; TSO II Trials Estabt, 1954–57; SO II (Educn), Divl HQ, BAOR, 1957–59; DS, Royal Mil. Coll. of Science, 1960–64; SEO, Army Apprentices Coll., 1964–67; Headmaster/Comdg, Duke of York's Royal Mil. Sch., 1967–72; Col (Ed), MoD (Army), 1972–74; Chief Educn Officer, HQ UKLF, 1974–76; Dir, Army Educn, 1976–80. Col Comdt, RAEC, 1982–86. Dir (non-exec.), Building Trades Exhibitions Ltd, 1980–93. Mem. Council, CGLI, 1977–90; Mem., Ct of Governors, Cardiff Univ. (formerly UWCC), 1980–. Hon. MA Open Univ., 1980. *Recreations:* gardening, golf, reading. *Address:* c/o HSBC, The Forum, Old Town, Swindon, Wilts SN3 1QT. *Died 25 Oct. 2011.*

HOWIE, Prof. John Mackintosh, CBE 1993; Regius Professor of Mathematics, University of St Andrews, 1970–97; Dean, Faculty of Science, 1976–79; *b* 23 May 1936; *s* of Rev. David Y. Howie and Janet McD. Howie (*née* Mackintosh); *m* 1960, Dorothy Joyce Mitchell Miller; two *d*. *Educ:* Robert Gordon's Coll., Aberdeen; Univ. of Aberdeen; Balliol Coll., Oxford. MA, DPhil, DSc; FRSE 1971. Asst in Mathematics: Aberdeen Univ., 1958–59; Glasgow Univ., 1961–63; Lectr in Mathematics, Glasgow Univ., 1963–67; Visiting Asst Prof., Tulane Univ., 1964–65; Sen. Lectr in Mathematics, Stirling Univ., 1967–70; Visiting Professor: Monash Univ., 1979; N Illinois Univ., 1988; Univ. of Lisbon, 1996. Mem., Cttee to Review Examination Arrangements (Dunning Cttee), 1975–77; Chairman: Scottish Central Cttee on Mathematics, 1975–82; Cttee to Review Curriculum and Exams in Fifth and Sixth Years (Howie Cttee), Scottish Office Educn Dept, 1990–92. Vice-Pres., London Mathematical Soc., 1984–86. Chm., Bd of Governors, Dundee Coll. of Educn, 1983–87. DUniv Open, 2000. Keith Prize for 1979–81, RSE, 1982. *Publications:* An Introduction to Semigroup Theory, 1976; Automata and Languages, 1991; Fundamentals of Semigroup Theory, 1995; Real Analysis, 2001; Complex Analysis, 2003; Fields and Galois Theory, 2006; articles in British and foreign mathematical jls. *Recreations:* music, gardening. *Address:* Longacre, 19 Strathkinness High Road, St Andrews, Fife KY16 9UA. *T:* (01334) 474103. *Died 26 Dec. 2011.*

HOWIE, Prof. Robert Andrew, PhD, ScD; FGS; FKC; Lyell Professor of Geology, Royal Holloway and Bedford New College, University of London, 1985–87, then Emeritus Professor of Mineralogy; *b* 4 June 1923; *s* of Robert Howie; *m* 1st, 1952, Honor Eugenie (marr. diss. 1998; she *d* 2010), *d* of Robert Taylor; two *s*; 2nd, 1998, Irene, *d* of G. R. Ancliff. *Educ:* Bedford Sch.; Trinity Coll., Cambridge (MA, PhD, ScD). FGS 1950. Served War, RAF, 1941–46. Research, Dept of Mineralogy and Petrology, Univ. of Cambridge, 1950–53; Lectr in Geology, Manchester Univ., 1953–62; King's College, London: Reader in Geol., 1962–72; Prof. of Mineralogy, 1972–85; Fellow 1980; Dean, Faculty of Science, Univ. of London, 1979–83; Chairman: Academic Council, Univ. of London, 1983–86; Computer Policy Cttee, Univ. of London, 1987–93; Vice-Chm., Bd of Management, Univ. of London Computer Centre, 1989–93. Mem., Commonwealth Scholarships Commn, 1988–96. Geological Society: Mem. Council, 1968–71, 1972–76; Vice-Pres., 1973–75. Mineralogical Society: Mem. Council, 1958–61, 1963–2003; Gen. Sec., 1965; Ed., Mineralogical Abstracts, 1966–2003 (designated Principal Ed., 1971–2003); Vice-Pres., 1975–77; Pres., 1978–80; Managing Trustee, 1978–87; Hon. Life Fellow, 1994. Fellow, Mineral Soc. of America, 1962 (Dist. Public Service Award, 1999). Member: Gemmological Assoc. and Gem Testing Lab. of GB, 1968– (Pres., 1996–2000; Hon. FGA 1996); Council, Internat. Mineral Assoc., 1974–82; Senate, Univ. of London, 1974–78, 1980–90; Court, Univ. of London, 1984–89. Hon. Mem., Mineralogical Soc. of India, 1973, of USSR, 1982, of France, 1986, of Bulgaria, 1991; For. Mem., Accad. Naz. dei Lincei, Rome, 2003. Hon. DSc Derby, 2009. Murchison Medal, Geol Soc., 1976. *Publications:* Rock-forming Minerals (with Prof. W. A. Deer and Prof. J. Zussman), 5 vols, 1962–63 (2nd edn in 10 vols, 1978–); An Introduction to the Rock-forming Minerals, 1966, 2nd edn 1992; scientific papers dealing with charnockites and with silicate mineralogy. *Recreation:* mineral collecting. *Address:* Ashcroft, Glebe Close, Church Street, Bonsall, Matlock, Derbyshire DE4 2AE. *Club:* Geological. *Died 10 March 2012.*

HOWITT, Anthony Wentworth; Senior Consultancy Partner, Peat, Marwick, Mitchell & Co., Management Consultants, 1957–84; *b* 7 Feb. 1920; *o s* of late Sir Harold Gibson Howitt, GBE, DSO, MC, and Dorothy Radford; *m* 1951, June Mary Brent. *Educ:* Uppingham; Trinity Coll., Cambridge (MA). FCA, FCMA, JDipMA, FIMC. Commissioned RA; served in UK, ME and Italy, 1940–46 (Major). With Peat, Marwick, Mitchell & Co., Chartered Accountants, 1946–57. British Consultants Bureau: Vice-Chm., 1981–83; Mem. Council, 1968–75 and 1979–84; led mission to Far East, 1969. Member Council: Inst. of Management Consultants, 1964–77 (Pres., 1967–68); Inst. of Cost and Management Accountants, 1966–76 (Pres., 1972–73; Gold Medal, 1991); Management Consultants Assoc., 1966–84 (Chm., 1976); Mem., Devlin Commn of Inquiry into Industrial Representation, 1971–72. Member: Bd of Fellows of BIM, 1973–76; Adv. Panel to Overseas Projects Gp, 1973–76; Price Commn, 1973–77; Domestic Promotions Cttee, British Invisible Exports Council, 1984. Member Council: Anglo-Jordanian Soc., 1983–96; Anglo-Indonesian Soc., 1991–2000; Anglo-Arab Assoc., 1993–2004. CCMI. Mem., Court of Assistants, Merchant Taylors' Co., 1971– (Master, 1980–81). *Publications:* papers and addresses on professional and management subjects. *Recreations:* fox-hunting, tennis, golf. *Address:* Wimbledon Beaumont, 35 Arterberry Road, SW20 8AG. *Clubs:* Army and Navy; MCC; Harlequins. *Died 3 Sept. 2013.*

HOWLAND JACKSON, Anthony Geoffrey Clive; Chairman, General Insurance Standards Council, 1999–2005; Director, Hiscox PLC, 1997–2006; *b* 25 May 1941; *s* of late Arthur Geoffrey Howland Jackson and of Pamela (*née* Wauton); *m* 1963, Susan Ellen Hickson; one *s* two *d*. *Educ:* Sherborne Sch. Chief Executive: H. Clarkson Insurance Hldgs, 1979–81; Clarkson Puckle, 1981–83; Dir, Gill & Duffus plc, 1983–87; Man. Dir, Bain Clarkson Ltd, 1987; Dep. Chm. and Chief Exec., 1987–93, Chm., 1993–94, Hogg Group plc; Chm., Bain Hogg plc, 1994–97. Dir, AON UK Hldgs, 1997–99. Lloyd's: Mem., 1976–97; Mem., Regulatory Bd, 1993–2002; Chm., Lloyd's Insurance Brokers' Cttee, 1996, 1998, 1999. Mem., Worshipful Co. of Insurers, 1981. *Recreations:* shooting, cricket, racing, golf. *Club:* Turf. *Died 26 Aug. 2013.*

HOYLAND, John, RA 1991 (ARA 1983); Professor of Painting, Royal Academy Schools, since 2000; *b* 12 Oct. 1934; *s* of John Kenneth and Kathleen Hoyland; *m* 1958, Airi Karkainen (marr. diss. 1968); one *s*; *m* 2008, Beverley Heath. *Educ:* Sheffield Coll. of Art (NDD 1956); Royal Academy Schs (RA Cert. 1960). Taught at: Hornsey Coll. of Art, 1960–62; Chelsea Sch. of Art, 1962–69, Principal Lectr, 1965–69; St Martin's Sch. of Art, 1974–77; Slade Sch. of Art, 1974–77, 1980, 1983, resigned 1989; Charles A. Dana Prof. of Fine Arts, Colgate Univ., NY, 1972. Artist in residence: Studio Sch., NY, 1978; Melbourne Univ., 1979. Selector: Hayward Annual, 1979; RA Silver Jubilee exhibn, 1979; organized and curated Hans Hofman exhibn, Lateworks, Tate Gall., 1988. *One-man exhibitions* include: Marlborough New London Gall., 1964; Whitechapel Gall., 1967; Waddington Galls, 1967, annually 1969–71 and 1973–76, 1978, 1981, 1983, 1985, 1987, 1990, 1995; Carlow Arts Fest., Ireland, 1996; Galerie Fine, London, 1999; Nevill Keating Pictures Ltd, London, 2001, 2008; Beaux Art Gall., London, 2001, 2003, 2006, 2008, 2009; Tate St Ives, 2006; also in USA, Australia, Netherlands, Canada, Norway, Ireland, France and Austria; retrospectives: Serpentine Gall., 1979; RA, 1999; Graves Art Gall., Sheffield, 2001 and in Canada, USA, Brazil, Italy, Portugal, W Germany and Australia. *Group exhibitions* include: Tate Gall., 1964; Hayward Gall., 1974; Walker Art Gall., Liverpool (in every John Moores exhibn, 1963–); British Art in the 20th Century, Royal Acad., 1987; Waddington Gall., 1987; Tate Gall. of Liverpool, 1993; Barbican Gall., 1993; also in Belgium, France, Japan and Norway. Work in public collections incl. RA, Tate Gall., V&A Mus. and other galls and instns in UK, Europe, USA and Australia. *TV appearances:* 6 Days in September, BBC TV, 1979; Signals, Channel 4, 1989. Designs for Zansa, Ballet Rambert, 1986; designed Mural Mosaic for Metro, Rome, 2001; designed Don Restaurant, London, 2001. Hon. Dr Sheffield Hallam, 2001. Gulbenkian Foundn purchase award, 1963; Peter Stuyvesant travel bursary, 1964; John Moores Liverpool exhibn prize, 1965, 1st prize, 1983; Open Paintings exhibn prize, Belfast, 1966; (jtly) 1st prize, Edinburgh Open 100 exhibn, 1969; 1st prize, Chichester Nat. Art exhibn, 1975; Arts Council purchase award, 1979; Athena Art Award, 1987. Order of the Southern Cross (Brazil), 1986. *Relevant publications:* John Hoyland, by Mel Gooding, 1990; Scatter the Devils, by Andrew Lambirth, 2009. *Address:* 41 Charterhouse Square, EC1M 6EA. *Died 31 July 2011.*

HUANG, Rayson Lisung, Hon. CBE 1976; DSc, DPhil; FRCPE; Vice-Chancellor, University of Hong Kong, 1972–86; *b* 1 Sept. 1920; *s* of Rufus Huang; *m* 1949, Grace

Wei Li; two *s. Educ:* Munsang Coll., Hong Kong; Univ. of Hong Kong (BSc); Univ. of Oxford (DPhil, DSc); Univ. of Chicago. DSc (Malaya) 1956. FRCPE 1984. Demonstrator in Chemistry, Nat. Kwangsi Univ., Kweilin, China, 1943; Post-doctoral Fellow and Research Associate, Univ. of Chicago, 1947–50; Univ. of Malaya, Singapore: Lecturer in Chemistry, 1951–54; Reader, 1955–59; Univ. of Malaya, Kuala Lumpur: Prof. of Chemistry, 1959–69, and Dean of Science, 1962–65; Vice-Chancellor, Nanyang Univ., Singapore, 1969–72. Chm. Council, ACU, 1980–81; Pres., Assoc. of SE Asian Instns of Higher Learning, 1970–72, 1981–83. MLC Hong Kong, 1977–83. Mem. Drafting Cttee (Beijing) and Vice Chm. Consulting Cttee (Hong Kong), for the Basic Law for Special Administrative Region of Hong Kong, 1985–90. Mem. Adv. Bd, IBM China/Hong Kong Corp., 1989–93. Vice Chm. Council, Shantou Univ., China, 1987–94; Life Member: Court, Univ. of Hong Kong; Bd of Trustees, Croucher Foundn, Hong Kong; Life Trustee, Rayson Huang Foundn, Kuala Lumpur, 2001. JP. Hon. DSc Hong Kong, 1968; Hon. LLD East Asia, Macao, 1987. Order of the Rising Sun (Japan), 1986. *Publications:* Organic Chemistry of Free Radicals, 1974 (London); A Lifetime in Academia (autobiog.), 2000; about 50 research papers on chemistry of free radicals, molecular rearrangements, etc, mainly in Jl of Chem. Soc. (London). *Recreations:* music, violin playing. *Address:* Raycrest II, 10 The Stables, Selly Park, Birmingham B29 7JW. *Died 8 April 2015.*

HUBBARD, Michael Joseph; QC 1985; a Recorder of the Crown Court, since 1984; *b* 16 June 1942; *s* of Joseph Thomas Hubbard and Gwendoline Hubbard; *m* 1967, Ruth Ann; five *s. Educ:* Lancing College. Admitted Solicitor, 1966; called to the Bar, Gray's Inn, 1972; Western Circuit; Prosecuting Counsel to Inland Revenue, 1983–85; Head of Chambers, 1 Paper Buildings, Temple, 2004–. Freeman, City of London, 1995. *Recreation:* sailing and messing about in boats in Cornwall and South of France (yacht Wild Confusion). *Died 17 July 2014.*

HUBEL, Prof. David Hunter, MD; Research Professor of Neurobiology, Harvard Medical School, since 2000; *b* Canada, 27 Feb. 1926; US citizen; *s* of Jesse H. Hubel and Elsie M. Hunter; *m* 1953, S. Ruth Izzard (*d* 2013); three *s. Educ:* McGill Univ. (BSc Hons Maths and Physics, 1947); McGill Univ. Med. Sch. (MD 1951). Rotating Intern, Montreal Gen. Hosp., 1951–52; Asst Resident in Neurology, Montreal Neurol Inst., 1952–53, and Fellow in Electroencephalography, 1953–54; Asst Resident in Neurol., Johns Hopkins Hosp., 1954–55; Res. Fellow, Walter Reed Army Inst. of Res., 1955–58; Res. Fellow, Wilmer Inst., Johns Hopkins Univ. Med. Sch., 1958–59; Harvard Medical School: Associate in Neurophysiology and Neuropharmacology, 1959–60; Asst Prof. of Neurophys. and Neuropharm., 1960–62; Associate Prof. of Neurophys. and Neuropharm., 1962–65; Prof. of Neurophys., 1965–67; George Packer Berry Prof. of Physiol. and Chm., Dept of Physiol., 1967–68; George Packer Berry Prof. of Neurobiol., 1968–82; John Franklin Enders Univ. Prof., 1982–2000, Emeritus, 2002–. George Eastman Vis. Prof., Univ. of Oxford, and Fellow, Balliol Coll., 1990–91. Sen. Fellow, Harvard Soc. of Fellows, 1971–; Mem., Bd of Syndics, Harvard Univ. Press, 1979–83. Associate, Neurosciences Res. Program, 1974. Fellow, Amer. Acad. of Arts and Sciences, 1965; Member: Amer. Physiol Soc., 1959; National Acad. of Sciences, USA, 1971; Deutsche Akademie der Naturforscher Leopoldina, DDR, 1971; Soc. for Neuroscience, 1970; Assoc. for Res. in Vision and Ophthalmology, 1970; Amer. Philosophical Soc., 1982; Sigma Xi-Scientific Res. Soc., 1995; Foreign Mem., Royal Soc., 1982; Foreign MAE, 1995; Hon. Member: Physiol Soc., 1983; Amer. Neurol Assoc.; Spanish Soc. of Ophth., 1997. Lectures: George H. Bishop, Washington Univ., St Louis, 1964; Bowditch, Amer. Physiol Soc., 1966; Jessup, Columbia Univ., 1970; Ferrier, Royal Soc., 1972; James Arthur, Amer. Mus. of Nat. Hist., 1972; Harvey, Rockefeller Univ., 1976; Grass Foundn, Soc. for Neuroscience, 1976; Weizmann Meml, Weizmann Inst. of Science, Israel, 1979; Vanuxem, Princeton Univ., 1981; Hughlings Jackson, Montreal Neurol Inst., 1982; first David Marr, Cambridge Univ., 1982; first James S. McDonnell, Washington Univ. Sch. of Medicine, 1982; James A. F. Stevenson Meml, Univ. of W Ont, 1982; Keys Meml, Trinity Coll., Toronto, 1983; Nelson, Univ. of Calif. Davis, 1983; Deane, Wellesley Coll., 1983; first James M. Sprague, Univ. of Pa, 1984; Vancouver Inst., Univ. of BC, 1985; Wilder Penfield, Montreal Neurol Inst., 1998; inaugural Frederick Hughes Scott, Univ. of Toronto, 2000; Case Western Reserve Univ., 2000; Corpus Christi Coll., Oxford, 2001. Hon. DSc: McGill, 1978; Manitoba, 1983; Oxford, 1994; Ohio State, 1995; Hon. DHL Johns Hopkins, 1990; Dr *hc*: Madrid, 1997; Miguel Hernandez, 1998; Toronto, 2002; Optometry, SUNY, 2004; McMaster, 2005; Hon. LLD Dalhousie, 1998. Awards: Res. to Prevent Blindness Trustees, 1971; Lewis S. Rosenstiel for Basic Med. Res., Brandeis Univ., 1972; Friedenwald, Assoc. for Res. in Vision and Ophthalmol., 1975; New England Ophthalmol Soc. Annual, 1983; Paul Kayser Internat. Award of Merit for Retina Res., 1989. Prizes: Karl Spencer Lashley, Amer. Phil Soc., 1977; Louisa Gross Horwitz, Columbia Univ., 1978; Dickson in Medicine, Univ. of Pittsburgh, 1979; Ledlie, Harvard Univ., 1980; Nobel in Medicine or Physiol., 1981; Helen Keller, Hellen Keller Eye Res. Foundn, 1995. *Publications:* Eye, Brain and Vision, 1987; (with Torsten N. Wiesel) Brain and Visual Perception: the story of a 25 year collaboration, 2004; articles in scientific jls. *Recreations:* music, photography, astronomy, amateur radio, Japanese. *Address:* Harvard Medical School, Department of Neurobiology, 220 Longwood Avenue, Boston, MA 02115, USA. *T:* (617) 4321655. *Died 22 Sept. 2013.*

HUCKSTEP, Prof. Ronald Lawrie, CMG 1971; MD; FRCS, FRCSE, FRACS, FTSE; Professor of Traumatic and Orthopaedic Surgery, University of New South Wales, 1972–92, then Emeritus Professor and Emeritus Orthopaedic Consultant, Prince of Wales/Prince Henry Hospital Group; Chairman of Departments of Orthopaedic Surgery and Director of Accident Services, Prince of Wales and Prince Henry Hospitals, Sydney, Australia, 1972–92; Consultant Orthopaedic Surgeon, Royal South Sydney and Sutherland Hospitals, 1972–92; *b* 22 July 1926; *er s* of late Herbert George Huckstep and Agnes Huckstep (*née* Lawrie-Smith); *m* 1960, Margaret Ann, *e d* of late Ronald Græme Macbeth, DM, FRCS; two *s* one *d. Educ:* Cathedral Sch., Shanghai, China; Queens' Coll., Cambridge; Middx Hosp. Med. Sch., London. MA, MB, BChir (Cantab) 1952; MD (Cantab) 1957; FRCSE 1957; FRCS 1958; FAOrthA 1972; FRACS 1973. Registrar and Chief Asst, Orthopaedic Dept, St Bartholomew's Hosp., and various surgical appts Middx and Royal Nat. Orthopaedic Hosps, London, 1952–60; Hunterian Prof., RCS, 1959–60; Makerere Univ. Coll., Kampala, Uganda: Lectr, 1960–62, Sen. Lectr, 1962–65 and Reader, 1965–67, in Orthopaedic Surgery, with responsibility for starting orthopaedic dept in Uganda; Prof. of Orthopaedic Surgery, Makerere Univ., Kampala, 1967–72. Became Hon. Cons. Orthopaedic Surgeon, Mulago and Mengo Hosps, and Round Table Polio Clinic, Kampala; Adviser on Orthopaedic Surgery, Ministry of Health, Uganda, 1960–72. Vis. Prof. of Surgery, Univ. of Sydney, 1995–. Corresp. Editor: Brit. and Amer. jls of Bone and Joint Surgery, 1965–72; Jl Western Pacific Orthopædic Assoc.; British Jl of Accident Surgery. Fellow, British Orthopaedic Assoc., 1967; Hon. Fellow: Western Pacific Orthopaedic Assoc., 1968; Assoc. of Surgeons of Uganda, 1993. Commonwealth Foundn Travelling Lectr, 1970, 1978–79 and 1982. FRSocMed; FTSE (FTS 1982). Patron Med. Soc., Univ. of NSW; Founder, World Orthopaedic Concern, 1973 (Hon. Mem. 1978); Vice-Pres., Australian Orthopaedic Assoc., 1982–83 (Betts Medal, 1983); Pres., Coast Med. Assoc., Sydney, 1985–86; Chairman, Fellow or Mem. various med. socs and of assocs, councils and cttees concerned with orthopaedic and traumatic surgery, accident services and rehabilitation of physically disabled. Inventions incl. Huckstep femoral fracture nail, hip, knee, shoulder, shoulder staple and circlip. Hon. Mem., Mark Twain Soc., 1978. Hon. MD NSW, 1988. Irving Geist Award, 11th World Congress, Internat. Soc. for Rehabilitation of the Disabled, 1969; James Cook Medal, Royal Soc. of NSW, 1984; Sutherland Medal, Australian Acad. of Technological Scis, 1986; Paul Harris Fellow and Medal, Rotary Internat., 1987; Humanitarian Award, Orthopaedics Overseas, 1991. Rotary Vocational Service Award, 1994; Centenary Medal, Australia, 2003; Eyre-Brook Medal, World Orthopaedic Concern, 2009.

Publications: Typhoid Fever and Other Salmonella Infections, 1962; A Simple Guide to Trauma, 1970, 5th edn 1995 (trans. Italian 1978, Japanese 1982); Poliomyelitis, A Guide for Developing Countries, Including Appliances and Rehabilitation, 1975 (ELBS and repr. edns 1979, 1983, French edn 1983); A Simple Guide to Orthopaedics, 1993; Colour Test in Orthopaedics and Trauma, 1994; various booklets, chapters in books, papers and films on injuries, orthopaedic diseases, typhoid fever, appliances and implants. *Recreations:* photography, designing orthopaedic appliances and implants for cripples in developing and developed countries, swimming, travel. *Address:* 108 Sugarloaf Crescent, Castlecrag, Sydney, NSW 2068, Australia. *T:* (612) 99581786, *Fax:* (612) 99672971. *Club:* Australian (Sydney). *Died 10 April 2015.*

HUDSON, Prof. Anthony Hugh, PhD; Professor of Common Law, Liverpool University, 1977–92, then Emeritus (Dean of Faculty of Law, 1971–78 and 1984–91); *b* 21 Jan. 1928; *s* of late Dr Thomas A. G. Hudson and Bridget Hudson; *m* 1962, Joan O'Malley; one *s* three *d.* *Educ:* St Joseph's Coll., Blackpool; Pembroke Coll., Cambridge (LLB 1950, MA 1953); PhD Manchester 1966. Called to Bar, Lincoln's Inn, 1954. Lecturer in Law: Hull Univ., 1951–57; Birmingham Univ., 1957–62; Manchester Univ., 1962–64; Liverpool University: Sen. Lectr, 1964–71; Professor of Law, 1971–77. *Publications:* (jtly) Hood Phillips: A First Book of English Law, 7th edn 1977, 8th edn 1988; (jtly) Pennington Commercial Banking Law, 1978; (jtly) Stevens and Borrie Mercantile Law, 17th edn 1978; Halsbury's Laws of England, 4th edn (contrib. or ed with N. E. Palmer and others) vol. 8 (i) Confidence, 1996, 2003, vol. 12 (i) Damages, 1998, vol. 45 (i) Tort, 1999, vol. 5 (i) Carriers, 2004; Encyclopaedia of Forms and Precedents, 5th edn, vol. 34 Sale of Goods, 2002; contribs on common and commercial law to various legal books and periodicals. *Recreations:* gardening, history. *Address:* 18 Dowhills Road, Blundellsands, Liverpool L23 8SW. *T:* (0151) 924 5830. *Died 17 Feb. 2011.*

HUDSON, (Eleanor) Erlund, RE 1946 (ARE 1938); RWS 1949 (ARWS 1939); ARCA 1937; artist; *b* 18 Feb. 1912; *d* of Helen Ingeborg Olsen, Brookline, Boston, USA, and Harold Hudson. *Educ:* Torquay; Dorking; Royal College of Art (Diploma 1937, Travelling Scholarship 1938). Former Mem. Chicago Print Soc. and Soc. of Artist Print-Makers. Studied and travelled in Italy, summer 1939. Interrupted by war. Exhibited in London, Provinces, Scandinavia, Canada, USA, etc; works purchased by War Artists Advisory Council, 1942–43. Gp exhibn, Witness: Women War Artists, Imperial War Mus. North, 2009. Formerly Artistic Dir and designer, Brooking Ballet Sch., W1. *Recreations:* music, country life. *Address:* 81 Campden Street, W8 7EN. *Died 9 March 2011.*

HUDSON, Peter Geoffrey; Member, Panel of Chairmen, Civil Service Selection Board, 1987–94; *b* 26 July 1926; *s* of late Thomas Albert Hudson and Gertrude Hudson; *m* 1954, Valerie Mary, *yr d* of late Lewis Alfred Hart and Eva Mary Hart; two *s.* *Educ:* King Edward VII Sch., Sheffield; Queen's Coll., Oxford (Hastings Scholar, MA). Gold Medallist, Royal Schs of Music, 1940. Sub-Lt RNVR, 1944–46 (Bletchley Park, 1944–45). Min. of Transport, 1949; Private Sec. to Minister of Transport and Civil Aviation, 1951–53; Principal, Min. of Transport and Civil Aviation, 1953–57; Admin. Staff Coll., Henley, 1957; British Civil Air Attaché, SE Asia and Far East, 1958–61; Asst Sec., Overseas Policy Div. and Estabt Div., Min. of Aviation and BoT, 1963–68; Counsellor (Civil Aviation), British Embassy, Washington, 1968–71; Under-Sec., DTI, 1971–84; Dir of Resources, British Tourist Authority and English Tourist Bd, 1984–86. Ind. Advr to Lady Marre Cttee on Future of Legal Profession, 1987–88. Vice Chm., Bromley CAB, 1989–95. Governor, Coll. of Air Trng, Hamble, 1974–75. *Recreation:* music. *Address:* Candle Hill, Raggleswood, Chislehurst, Kent BR7 5NH. *T:* (020) 8467 1761. *Died 3 July 2012.*

HUDSON, Peter John, CB 1978; Deputy Under-Secretary of State (Finance and Budget), Ministry of Defence, 1976–79; *b* 29 Sept. 1919; *o s* of late A. J. Hudson; *m* 1954, Joan Howard FitzGerald (*d* 1998); one *s* one *d.* *Educ:* Tollington Sch.; Birkbeck Coll., London. Exchequer and Audit Dept, 1938; RNVR, 1940–46 (Lieut); Asst Principal, Air Min., 1947; Private Sec. to Perm. Under Sec. of State for Air, 1948–51; Asst Sec., 1958; Head of Air Staff Secretariat, 1958–61; Imperial Defence Coll., 1962; Head of Programme and Budget Div., MoD, 1966–69; Under-Sec., Cabinet Office, 1969–72; Asst Under-Sec. of State, MoD, 1972–75; Dep. Under-Sec. of State (Air), MoD, 1975–76. *Address:* Folly Hill, Haslemere, Surrey GU27 2EY. *T:* (01428) 642078. *Club:* Royal Air Force. *Died 15 June 2012.*

HUDSON, Prof. Robert Francis, PhD; FRS 1982; Professor of Organic Chemistry, University of Kent at Canterbury, 1967–85 (part-time, 1981–85), then Emeritus; *b* 15 Dec. 1922; *s* of late John Frederick Hudson and Ethel Hudson; *m* 1945, Monica Ashton Stray (*d* 2000); one *s* twin *d.* *Educ:* Brigg Grammar Sch.; Imperial Coll. of Science and Technol., London (BSc, ARCS, PhD, DIC). Asst Lectr, Imperial Coll., London, 1945–47; Consultant, Wolsey Ltd, Leicester, 1945–50; Lectr, Queen Mary Coll., London, 1947–59; Res. Fellow, Purdue Univ., 1954; Gp Dir, Cyanamid European Res. Inst., Geneva, 1960–66. Vis. Professor: Rochester, USA, 1970; Bergen, 1971; CNRS, Thiais, Paris, 1973; Calgary, 1975; Mainz, 1979; Queen's, Kingston, Ont, 1983. Lectures: Frontiers, Case-Western Reserve Univ., USA, 1970; Nuffield, Canada, 1975; Quest, Queen's, Ont, 1983. Vice-Pres., Inst. of Science Technol., 1970–76; Member: Council, Chemical Soc., 1967–70 (Foundn Chm., Organic Reaction Mechanism Gp, 1973); Dalton Council, 1973–76; Perkin Council, 1980–83. *Publications:* (with P. Alexander) Wool—its physics and chemistry, 1954, 2nd edn 1960; Structure and Mechanism in Organophosphorus Chemistry, 1965; papers mainly in Jl of Chem. Soc., Helvetica Chimica Acta and Angewandte Chemie. *Address:* 37 Puckle Lane, Canterbury, Kent CT1 3LA. *T:* (01227) 761340. *Club:* Athenæum. *Died 19 Aug. 2012.*

HUGH SMITH, Sir Andrew (Colin), Kt 1992; Chairman, London Stock Exchange (formerly International Stock Exchange), 1988–94 (Member, 1970, Member of Council, 1981–91); Chairman, Barloworld (formerly Barlow International) Plc, 2000–02; *b* 6 Sept. 1931; *s* of late Lt-Comdr Colin Hugh Smith and Hon. Mrs C. Hugh Smith; *m* 1964, Venetia, *d* of Lt-Col Peter Flower; two *s.* *Educ:* Ampleforth; Trinity Coll., Cambridge (BA). Called to Bar, Inner Temple, 1956; Hon. Bencher, 1995. Courtaulds Ltd, 1960–68; with Capel-Cure Carden (later Capel-Cure Myers), 1968–85; ANZ Merchant Bank, 1985–88. Chairman: Holland & Holland, 1987–95; Penna plc, then Penna Consulting Plc, 1995–2001; Eur. Adv. Bd, Accenture (formerly Andersen Consulting), 1995–2001; Director: Matheson Lloyds Investment Trust, 1994–97; Barloworld (formerly J. Bibby & Sons, then Barlow Internat.), 1997–2002; Barlow Ltd, 1998–2002. Vice-Chm., GBDA, 1990–2001; Hon. Treas., Malcolm Sargent Cancer Fund for Children, 1992–2002. *Recreations:* gardening, shooting, fishing, reading. *Clubs:* Brooks's, Pratt's. *Died 3 Oct. 2012.*

HUGHES, Catherine Eva, CMG 1984; HM Diplomatic Service, retired; Principal, Somerville College, Oxford, 1989–96; *b* 24 Sept. 1933; *d* of late Edmund Ernest Pestell and Isabella Cummine Sangster; *m* 1991, Dr (John) Trevor Hughes. *Educ:* Leeds Girls' High Sch.; St Hilda's Coll., Oxford (MA). FO, 1956; Third Sec., The Hague, 1958; Second Sec., Bangkok, 1961; FO, 1964; First Sec., UK Delegn to OECD, Paris, 1969; FCO, 1971; St Antony's Coll., Oxford, 1974; Counsellor, East Berlin, 1975–78; Cabinet Office, 1978–80; Diplomatic Service Inspector, 1980–82; Minister (Economic), Bonn, 1983–87; Asst Under-Sec. (Public Depts), FCO, 1987–89. *Address:* 2 Bishop Kirk Place, Oxford OX2 7HJ. *Club:* Reform. *Died 10 Dec. 2014.*

HUGHES, Prof. George Morgan; Professor of Zoology, Bristol University, 1965–85, then Emeritus; *b* 17 March 1925; *s* of James Williams Hughes and Edith May Hughes; *m* 1954, Jean Rosemary, *d* of Rowland Wynne Frazier and Jessie Frazier; two *s* one *d.* *Educ:* Liverpool Collegiate Sch.; King's Coll., Cambridge (Scholar; Martin Thackeray Studentship, 1946–48; MA, PhD, ScD); Frank Smart Prize, Cambridge Univ., 1946. Cambridge Univ. Demonstr,

1950–55, Lectr, 1955–65; successively Bye-Fellow, Research Fellow and Fellow of Magdalene Coll., Cambridge, 1949–65; University of Bristol: Head of Dept of Zoology, 1965–70; Head of Res. Unit for Comparative Animal Respiration, 1970–90. Research Fellow, California Inst. of Technology, 1958–59; Visiting Lectr in Physiology, State Univ. of New York, at Buffalo, 1964; Visiting Professor: Duke Univ., 1969; Japan Society for the Promotion of Science, Kochi, Kyoto, Kyushu and Hokkaido Univs, 1974; Univ. of Regensburg, 1977; Univs of Bhagalpur and Bretagne Occidentale, 1979; Kuwait, 1983; Nairobi, 1985. Invited Prof., Nat. Inst. of Physiolog. Sciences, Okazaki, 1980; Hon. Prof., Univ. of Wales Coll. of Cardiff, 1991–99. Mem., Internat. Cœlacanth Expedn, 1972. *Publications:* Comparative Physiology of Vertebrate Respiration, 1963; (jtly) Physiology of Mammals and other Vertebrates, 1965; (jtly) Air-breathing Fishes of India, 1992; (ed) several symposium vols; papers in Jl of Experimental Biology and other scientific jls, mainly on respiration of fishes. *Recreations:* travel, Welsh genealogy, photography; hockey (played for Cambridge Univ., 1945, and Wales, 1952–53). *Address:* 11 Lodge Drive, Long Ashton, Bristol BS41 9JF. *T:* (01275) 393402. *Died 30 Jan. 2011.*

HUGHES, Prof. Leslie Ernest, FRCS, FRACS; Professor of Surgery, University of Wales College of Medicine (formerly Welsh National School of Medicine), 1971–92; *b* 12 Aug. 1932; *s* of Charles Joseph and Vera Hughes; *m* 1955, Marian Castle; two *s* two *d*. *Educ:* Parramatta High Sch.; Sydney Univ. MB, BS (Sydney); DS (Queensland), 1975. FRCS, 1959; FRACS, 1959. Reader in Surgery, Univ. of Queensland, 1965–71. Hunterian Prof., RCS, 1986. Eleanor Roosevelt Internat. Cancer Fellow, 1970. President: Welsh Surgical Soc., 1991–93; Surgical Res. Soc., 1992–94; Hist. of Medicine Soc. of Wales, 2000. Audio-visual Aid Merit Award, Assoc. of Surgeons of GB and Ireland, 1983, 1986. Educn Editor and Chm., Editl Bd, European Jl of Surgical Oncology, 1992–97. *Publications:* (jtly) Benign Disorders of the Breast, 1988, 3rd edn 2008; numerous papers in medical jls, chiefly on immune aspects of cancer, and diseases of the colon. *Recreations:* music, travel. *Address:* Sunrise Senior Living, Stockbridge Road, Winchester SO22 5JH. *Died 3 March 2011.*

HUGHES, Robert Studley Forrest; Senior Writer (Art Critic), Time Magazine, New York, 1970; *b* Sydney, Australia, 28 July 1938; *s* of Geoffrey E. F. Hughes and Margaret Sealey Vidal; *m* 2001, Doris Downes, artist; (one *s* decd from a previous marriage). *Educ:* St Ignatius Coll., Riverview, Sydney; Sydney Univ. (architecture course, unfinished). Contributed articles on art to The Nation and The Observer, Sydney, 1958–62; to Europe, 1964, living in Italy until 1966, when moved to London; freelancing for Sunday Times, BBC and other publications/instns, 1966–70. TV credits include: Landscape with Figures, ten-part series on Australian art for ABC, Australia; Caravaggio, Rubens and Bernini, for BBC, 1976–77; The Shock of the New, eight-part series for BBC, 1980, 2004; American Visions, BBC, 1996; Visions of Space: Antoni Gaudi, BBC, 2003; The Mona Lisa Curse, Channel 4, 2009. Mem., Amer. Acad. of Arts and Scis, 1993. Hon. Dr Fine Arts, Sch. of Visual Arts, NY, 1982; Hon. DLitt Melbourne, 1997. Frank Jewett Mather Award, Coll. Art Assoc. of America, 1982, 1985; Golden Plate Award, Amer. Acad. of Achievement, 1988; El Brusi Prize, Barcelona Olympiad, 1992; Dimbleby Award for lifetime achievement in broadcasting, 1997. *Publications:* The Art of Australia, 1966; Heaven and Hell in Western Art, 1969; The Shock of the New (BBC publication), 1980, rev. edn 1991; The Fatal Shore, 1987; Frank Auerbach, 1990; Nothing If Not Critical, 1991; Barcelona, 1992; Culture of Complaint: the fraying of America, 1993; American Visions, 1997; A Jerk on One End, 1999; Goya, 2003; Things I Didn't Know: a memoir, 2006; Rome, 2010. *Recreations:* gardening, woodworking, river and sea fishing, cooking. *Address:* Knopf Publishing/Random House Inc., 1745 Broadway, New York, NY 10019, USA. *Died 7 Aug. 2012.*

HUGHES, Ronald Frederick, CEng, FICE; quality management consultant, since 1992; Systems Consultant, London Underground Ltd, 1992; *b* 21 Oct. 1927; *s* of Harry Frederick and Kate Hughes; *m* 1957, Cecilia Patricia, *d* of Maurice Nunis, MCS, State Treasurer, Malaya, and Scholastica Nunis; two *s* one *d*. *Educ:* Birmingham Central Technical College; Bradford College of Technology. Articled pupil, Cyril Boucher and Partners, 1943; Royal Engineers Engineering Cadet, 1946; commissioned RE, 1950; service in Malaya, 1950–53. Res. Asst, BISRA, 1954; Civil Engineer, H. W. Evans & Co. Ltd, Malaya, 1955, Man. Dir, 1958; War Office, 1959; Head of War Office Works Group, Singapore, 1963; Works Adviser to C-in-C, FARELF, 1964; District Civil Engineer, Malaya, 1966; Property Services Agency: Regional Site Control Officer, Midland Region, 1969; Principal Engineer, Post Office Services, 1970; Area Works Officer, Birmingham, 1977; Asst Dir, 1979, Dir, 1983–87, Civil Engineering Services; Dir and Quality Systems Manager, Mott MacDonald Consultants, 1987–92. Dir, Construction Industry Computing Assoc., 1982–86; Member: Standing Cttee for Structural Safety, 1985–88; Maritime Bd, ICE, 1985–90; Nat. Jt Consultative Cttee for Building, 1986–88; Member Council: Construction Industry Res. and Inf. Assoc., 1984–88; BSI, 1985; Perm. Internat. Assoc. of Navigation Congresses, 1983–94; Parly Maritime Gp, 1988–96; Vice Pres., Concrete Soc., 1989–95. *Recreations:* photography, music. *Address:* 9A The Street, West Horsley, Surrey KT24 6AY. *T:* (01483) 282182. *Clubs:* Naval; Effingham (Surrey). *Died 4 June 2011.*

HUGHESDON, Charles Frederick, AFC 1944; FRAeS; *b* 10 Dec. 1909; *m* 1st, 1937, Florence Elizabeth (actress, as Florence Desmond) (*d* 1993), *widow* of Captain Tom Campbell Black; one *s*; 2nd, 1993, Carol Elizabeth, *widow* of Baron Havers, PC; two step *s*. *Educ:* Raine's Foundation School. Entered insurance industry, 1927; learned to fly, 1932; Flying Instructor's Licence, 1934; commnd RAFO, 1934; Commercial Pilot's Licence, 1936. Joined Stewart, Smith & Co. Ltd, 1936; RAF Instructor at outbreak of war; seconded to General Aircraft as Chief Test Pilot, 1939–43; rejoined RAF, 1943–45 (AFC). Rejoined Stewart, Smith & Co. Ltd, 1946; retired as Chm. of Stewart Wrightson 1976. Dir, Aeronautical Trusts Ltd; Chm., The Charles Street Co. Hon. Treas., RAeS, 1969–85. Upper Freeman, City of London; Member: GAPAN; Gunmakers' Guild. Order of the Cedar, Lebanon, 1972. *Recreations:* shooting, horseracing, riding (dressage). *Clubs:* Royal Air Force, Royal Thames Yacht. *Died 11 April 2014.*

HUGILL, John; QC 1976; a Recorder of the Crown Court, 1972–96; *b* 11 Aug. 1930; *s* of late John A. and Alice Hugill; *m* 1956, Patricia Elizabeth Hugill (*née* Welton); two *d*. *Educ:* Sydney C of E Grammar Sch., NSW; Fettes Coll.; Trinity Hall, Cambridge (MA). 2nd Lieut RA, 1948–49; Capt., RA (T), 1954. Called to the Bar, Middle Temple, 1954 (Bencher, 1984); Northern Circuit, 1954; Assistant Recorder, Bolton, 1971; a Dep. High Court Judge, 1985–96. Chairman: Darryn Clarke Inquiry, 1979; Stanley Royd Inquiry, 1985. Member: Criminal Injuries Compensation Bd, 1998–2000; Criminal Injuries Compensation Appeals Panel, 2000–02. Member: Senate of the Inns of Court and the Bar, 1984–86; Gen. Council of the Bar, 1987–89. Hon. Legal Advr, Clay Pigeon Shooting Assoc., 1992–2009. *Recreation:* talking and reading about yachting. *Address:* Boundary House, Hodgehill Lane, Lower Withington, Macclesfield, Cheshire SK11 9LU. *Died 23 Sept. 2012.*

HUGILL, Michael James; Assistant Master, Westminster School, 1972–86; *b* 13 July 1918; 2nd *s* of late Rear-Adm. R. C. Hugill, CB, MVO, OBE, and Winifred (*née* Backwell). *Educ:* Oundle; King's Coll., Cambridge (Exhibitioner; BA 1939; MA 1943). War Service in the RN; Mediterranean, Home and Pacific Fleets, 1939–46; rank on demobilisation, Lt-Comdr. Mathematics Master, Stratford Grammar Sch., 1947–51; Senior Mathematics Master, Bedford Modern Sch., 1951–57; Headmaster, Preston Grammar Sch., 1957–61; Headmaster, Whitgift School, Croydon, 1961–70; Lectr, Inst. of Education, Keele Univ., 1971–72. *Publications:* Advanced Statistics, 1985. *Address:* 4 Glenmore, Kersfield Road, SW15 3HL. *Died 28 Aug. 2013.*

HULL, His Honour John Grove; QC 1983; a Circuit Judge, 1991–2003; *b* 21 Aug. 1931; *s* of Tom Edward Orridge Hull and Marjory Ethel Hull; *m* 1961, Gillian Ann, *d* of Leslie Fawcett Stemp; two *d*. *Educ:* Rugby School;

King's College, Cambridge. BA (1st cl. in Mech. Scis Tripos) 1953, MA 1957; LLB 1954. National Service, commissioned RE, 1954–56; called to the Bar, Middle Temple, 1958 (Cert. of Honour, Bar Final), Bencher, 1989; in practice, common law Bar, 1958–91; a Recorder, 1984–91. *Recreations:* gardening, English literature. *Died 19 Nov. 2015.*

HUMMEL, Frederick Cornelius, MA, DPhil, BSc; Head of Forestry Division, Commission of the European Communities, 1973–80; *b* 28 April 1915; *s* of Cornelius Hummel, OBE, and Caroline Hummel (*née* Riefler); *m* 1st, 1941, Agnes Kathleen Rushforth (marr. diss. 1961); one *s* (and one *s* decd); 2nd, 1961, Floriana Rosemary Hollyer; three *d. Educ:* St Stephan, Augsburg, Germany; Wadham Coll., Oxford. District Forest Officer, Uganda Forest Service, 1938–46; Forestry Commn, 1946–73; Mensuration Officer, 1946; Chief, Management Sect., 1956; released for service with FAO as Co-Dir, Mexican Nat. Forest Inventory, 1961–66; Controller, Management Services, Forestry Commn, 1966–68, Comr for Harvesting and Marketing, 1968–73. Hon. Member: Société Royale Forestière de Belgique; Asociación para el Progreso Forestal, Spain; Corresponding Member: Mexican Acad. of Forest Scis; Italian Acad. of Forest Scis; Soc. of Forestry, Finland. Dr *hc* Munich, 1978. Bernard Eduard Fernow Plaquette, (jtly) Amer. Forestry Assoc. and Deutscher Forstverein, 1986; Alexander von Humboldt Gold Medal, 1995. *Publications:* Forest Policy, 1984; Biomass Forestry in Europe, 1988; Forestry Policies in Europe: an analysis, 1989; Memories of Forestry and Travel, 2001. *Address:* Ridgemount, 8 The Ridgeway, Guildford, Surrey GU1 2DG. *T:* (01483) 572383. *Died 21 Oct. 2012.*

HUNSWORTH, John Alfred; Director, Banking Information Service, 1954–81; *b* 23 Dec. 1921; *s* of late Fred Sheard Hunsworth and Lillian Margaret (*née* Wetmon); *m* 1972, Phyllis Sparshatt (*d* 1994). *Educ:* Selhurst Grammar Sch.; LSE (BCom). Served War, 1941–46: commnd E Surrey Regt; served 2nd Punjab Regt, Indian Army, 1942–45. Dep. Editor, Bankers' Magazine, 1948–54. Freeman, City of London. *Publications:* contrib. prof. jls. *Recreations:* gardening, world travel, philately; formerly lawn tennis and Rugby football. *Address:* 29 West Hill, Sanderstead, Surrey CR2 0SB. *T:* (020) 8657 2585. *Clubs:* Reform, Royal Over-Seas League; Surrey County Cricket. *Died 3 Feb. 2011.*

HUNT, Bernard John, MBE 1977; Professional Golfer, Foxhills Golf and Country Club, since 1975; *b* 2 Feb. 1930; *s* of John and Lilian Hunt; *m* 1955, Margaret Ellen Clark; one *s* two *d. Educ:* Atherstone Grammar Sch. Mem., Ryder Cup team, 1953, 1957–69 (Captain, 1973, 1975); Winner: H. Vardon Trophy, 1958, 1960, 1965; over 30 major tournaments, incl. Dunlop Masters, 1963, 1965, and German, French, Brazilian and Belgian Opens. Captain, PGA, 1966, 1995, 1996. *Recreations:* golf, badminton. *Address:* Foxhills Golf and Country Club, Stonehill Road, Ottershaw, Surrey KT16 0EL. *Died 21 June 2013.*

HUNT, Derek Simpson; Chairman: MFI Furniture Group Plc, 1987–2000 (Chief Executive, 1987–94); MFI Furniture Centres Ltd, 1987–2000 (Managing Director, 1987–90); *b* 9 June 1939; *s* of late John William Hunt and of Elizabeth (*née* Simpson); *m* 1967, Sandra Phyllis Jones; two *s. Educ:* Queen Elizabeth Grammar Sch., Darlington, Co. Durham. Joined MFI as Retail Area Controller, 1972; Branch Ops Controller, 1973; Dir, MFI Furniture Centres, 1974; MFI Furniture Group: Dir, 1976; Man. Dir, 1981; Chm., 1984; during merger with Asda, also Chief Exec. and Dep. Chm., Asda-MFI, 1985–87; returned to MFI and effected management buy-out, 1987. Gov., Ashridge Management Coll., 1986–95. Vice Pres., NCH Action for Children (formerly Nat. Children's Home), 1989–2000. Founding Fellow, Nat. Children's Home George Thomas Soc., 1989. Hon. Fellow, Manchester Polytechnic, 1988. *Recreations:* sailing, Rugby Union, golf. *Died 19 Jan. 2012.*

HUNT, (Henry) Holman, CBE 1988; Deputy Chairman, 1985–91, Member, 1980–91, Monopolies and Mergers Commission; *b* 13 May 1924; *s* of Henry Hunt and Jessie Brenda Beale; *m* 1954, Sonja Blom; one *s* two *d. Educ:* Queen's Park Sch., Glasgow; Glasgow Univ. (MA). FCMA, FIMC, FBCS, FInstAM. Caledonian Insce Co., 1940–43; RAF, 1943–46; Glasgow Univ., 1946–50; Cadbury Bros, 1950–51; PA Management Consultants: Consultant, 1952–57; Manager, Office Organisation, 1958–63; Dir, Computer Div., 1964–69; Bd Dir, 1970–83; Man. Dir, PA Computers and Telecommunications, 1976–83. Pres., Inst. of Management Consultants, 1974–75. *Recreations:* music, reading, walking, travel, photography. *Address:* 28 The Ridings, Epsom, Surrey KT18 5JJ. *T:* (01372) 720974. *Club:* Caledonian. *Died 6 Dec. 2015.*

HUNT, Prof. John David, PhD; FRS 2001; Professor of Materials, University of Oxford, 1996–2002, then Emeritus; Fellow and Tutor in Metallurgy, St Edmund Hall, Oxford, 1968–2002, then Emeritus Fellow; *b* 12 Dec. 1936; *s* of Frederick John Hunt and Eleanor Hunt; *m* 1961, Ann Mercy Carroll; one *s* one *d* (and one *s* decd). *Educ:* Wellington Sch., Som; Christ's Coll., Cambridge (BA 1960; PhD 1963). Sen. Scientist, Bell Telephone Labs, Murray Hill, NJ, 1963–65; SSO, UKAEA, Harwell, 1965–66; Lectr, Dept of Metallurgy, 1966–90, Reader in Physical Metallurgy, 1990–96, Univ. of Oxford. Hon. Prof., Key Solidification Lab. of China, N Western Poly. Univ., Xian, China, 1996. Mathewson Gold Medal, 1967, Bruce Chalmers Award, 1996, Amer. Inst. Metallurgical Engrs; Rosenhain Medal and Prize, Inst. Metals, 1981; Armourers' and Brasiers' Award, Royal Soc., 2001. *Publications:* numerous contribs on solidification theory and experiment to learned jls. *Recreations:* keeping livestock, growing ferns, walking. *Address:* Church Farm House, Church Road, Northleigh, Witney, Oxon OX29 6TX. *Died 10 Dec. 2012.*

HUNT, John Maitland, MA, BLitt; Headmaster of Roedean, 1971–84; *b* 4 March 1932; *s* of Richard Herbert Alexander Hunt and Eileen Mary Isabelle Hunt (*née* Witt); *m* 1969, Sarah, *d* of Lt-Gen. Sir Derek Lang, KCB, DSO, MC; two *s. Educ:* Radley College; Wadham College, Oxford. BA 1956; BLitt 1959; MA 1960. Assistant Master, Stowe School, 1958–70 (Sixth Form tutor in Geography). Chm., Bd of Managers, Common Entrance Exam. for Girls' Schs, 1974–81. *Publications:* Dutch South Africa, 2005; various articles on fine arts and architecture. *Recreations:* estate management, fine arts, writing, travel. *Address:* Logie, Dunfermline, Fife KY12 8QN. *Club:* Royal Commonwealth Society. *Died 16 Jan. 2014.*

HUNT, Adm. Sir Nicholas (John Streynsham), GCB 1987 (KCB 1985); LVO 1961; DL; Chairman, Ferrero UK Ltd, since 2005; *b* 7 Nov. 1930; *s* of Brig. and Mrs J. M. Hunt; *m* 1966, Meriel Eve Givan; two *s* one *d. Educ:* BRNC, Dartmouth. CO HMS Burnaston, HMS Palliser, HMS Troubridge, HMS Intrepid, and BRNC, Dartmouth; Asst Private Sec. to Princess Marina, Duchess of Kent, 1959–62; Executive Officer, HMS Ark Royal, 1969–71; RCDS 1974; Dir of Naval Plans, 1976–78; Flag Officer, Second Flotilla, 1980–81; Dir-Gen., Naval Manpower and Training, 1981–83; Flag Officer, Scotland and NI, and Port Admiral Rosyth, 1983–85; C-in-C, Fleet, and Allied C-in-C, Channel and Eastern Atlantic, 1985–87, retd. Rear-Adm. of the UK, 1994–97, Vice Adm. of the UK and Lt of the Admiralty, 1997–2001. Dep. Man. Dir (Orgn and Develt), Eurotunnel, 1987–89; Dir-Gen., Chamber of Shipping, 1991–97; Chm., Chatham Historic Dockyard Trust, 1998–2005. Chairman: SW Surrey DHA, 1990–95; Nuffield Hosps, 1996–2001. Comr, CWGC, 1988–92. Freeman, City of London, 1988. DL Surrey, 1996. Gov., Sutton's Hosp. in Charterhouse, 2002–06. *Recreation:* family. *Clubs:* Boodle's, Royal Navy of 1765 and 1785; Surrey. *Died 25 Oct. 2013.*

HUNT, Philip Bodley; Director, Welsh Office Industry Department, 1975–76; *b* 28 July 1916; *s* of Bernard and Janet Hunt; *m* 1940, Eleanor Margaret Parnell (*d* 1989); three *s* one *d. Educ:* Sedbergh Sch.; Christ Church, Oxford (Boulter Exhibnr; 1st cl. PPE; MA). Joined Board of Trade, 1946; Trade Commissioner, Montreal, 1952; Principal Trade Commissioner, Vancouver, 1955; Commercial Counsellor, Canberra, 1957; returned Board of Trade, 1962; Dept of Economic Affairs, 1964–65; Director, London & SE Region, BoT, 1968; Dir, DTI Office for Wales, 1972–75. Chm., S Wales Marriage Guidance Council, 1974–83; Mem. Nat. Exec., Nat. Marriage Guidance Council, 1977–83; Dept Mem. of Panel, County

Structure Plans of S and W Glamorgan, 1978, of Gwent and Mid Glamorgan, 1979; Vice-Pres., Develt Corporation for Wales, 1980–83. Chm., John Macmurray Fellowship, 1993–2002. Silver Jubilee Medal, 1977. *Publications:* John Macmurray and the BBC: 1930–1941, 1995. *Recreation:* life and works of John Macmurray. *Address:* 3 Allen Gardens, Ecclesfield, Sheffield S35 9TT. *T:* (0114) 245 7758. *Died 11 Dec. 2011.*

HUNT, Sir Rex (Masterman), Kt 1982; CMG 1980; HM Diplomatic Service, retired; Civil Commissioner, Falkland Islands, 1982–Sept. 1985, and High Commissioner, British Antarctic Territory, 1980–85 (Governor and Commander-in-Chief, Falkland Islands, 1980–82; Governor, Oct. 1985); *b* 29 June 1926; *s* of H. W. Hunt and Ivy Masterman; *m* 1951, Mavis Amanda Buckland; one *s* one *d*. *Educ:* Coatham Sch.; St Peter's Coll., Oxford (BA). Served with RAF, 1944–48; Flt Lt RAFO. Entered HM Overseas Civil Service, 1951; District Comr, Uganda, 1962; CRO, 1963–64; 1st Sec., Kuching, 1964–65; Jesselton, 1965–67; Brunei, 1967; 1st Sec. (Econ.), Ankara, 1968–70; 1st Sec. and Head of Chancery, Jakarta, 1970–72; Asst, ME Dept, FCO, 1972–74; Counsellor, Saigon, 1974–75, Kuala Lumpur, 1976–77; Dep. High Comr, Kuala Lumpur, 1977–79. Mem., RAFA. Hon. Air Cdre, City of Lincoln Sqn, RAuxAF, 1987–97. Hon. Freeman: City of London, 1981; Stanley, Falkland Is, 1985. *Publications:* My Falkland Days, 1992. *Recreations:* golf, gardening. *Address:* The Grooms House, Elton, Stockton-on-Tees TS21 1AG. *Died 11 Nov. 2012.*

HUNT, Robert Alan, OBE 1984; QPM 1992; Assistant Commissioner, Territorial Operations Department, Metropolitan Police, 1990–95; *b* 6 July 1935; *s* of Peter and Minnie Hunt; *m* 1956, Jean White; one *s* three *d*. *Educ:* Dulwich Coll.; London Univ. (LLB external 1970). Served in RA. Joined Metropolitan Police, 1955: Chief Superintendent, 1973; Comdr, 1976; Dep. Asst Comr, 1981. *Recreations:* music—traditional and light classical, reading, the family. *Died 15 May 2013.*

HUNTER JOHNSTON, David Alan; *b* 16 Jan. 1915; *s* of James Ernest Johnston and Florence Edith Johnston (*née* Hunter); *m* 1949, Philippa Frances Ray (*d* 2008); three *s* one *d*. *Educ:* Christ's Hospital; King's Coll., London. FKC 1970. Royal Ordnance Factories, Woolwich, 1936–39; S Metropolitan Gas Co., 1939–44; Min. of Economic Warfare (Economic and Industrial Planning Staff), 1944–45; Control Office for Germany and Austria, 1945–47; Sec. to Scientific Cttee for Germany, 1946; FO (German Section), Asst Head, German Gen. Economic Dept, 1947–49; HM Treasury, Supply, Estabt and Home Finance Divs, 1949–53. Central Bd of Finance of Church of England: Sec. (and Fin. Sec. to Church Assembly), 1953–59, and Investment Manager, 1959–65; concurrently, Dir, Local Authorities Mutual Investment Trust, 1961–65, and Investment Man. to Charities Official Investment Fund, 1963–65; a Man. Dir, J. Henry Schroder Wagg & Co. Ltd, 1965–74; Chairman: Schroder Executor & Trustee Co. Ltd, 1966–74; Reserve Pension Bd, 1974–75; Assoc. of Investment Trust Cos, 1975–77; Director: Trans-Oceanic Trust, subseq. Schroder Global Trust plc, 1965–88; Clerical, Medical & General Life Assurance Soc., 1970–74; Lindustries Ltd, 1970–79 and of other investment trust cos for many years. Mem., Monopolies Commn, 1969–73. Lay Reader, 1959–85, licensed in Dio. of St Albans, Dio. of Bath and Wells. *Publications:* The Christian Stewardship of Money, 1959; Money in Christian Life, 1960; Stewardship and the Gospel, 1995; Church Synod State and Crown, 1997; Theodicy and the Gospel, 2000. *Address:* The Close, Hewelsfield Common, Lydney, Glos GL15 6UU. *E:* james@hunterjohnston.co.uk. *Died 28 March 2011.*

HUNTINGTON-WHITELEY, Sir Hugo (Baldwin), 3rd Bt *cr* 1918; DL; *b* 31 March 1924; *e* surv. *s* of Captain Sir Maurice Huntington-Whiteley, 2nd Bt, RN, and Lady (Pamela) Margaret Huntington-Whiteley (*d* 1976), 3rd *d* of 1st Earl Baldwin of Bewdley, KG, PC; *S* father, 1975; *m* 1959, Jean Marie Ramsay, JP 1973, DStJ; two *d*. *Educ:* Eton. Royal Navy, 1942–47 (despatches). Chartered Accountant; Partner, Price Waterhouse, 1963–83. Mem. Ct of Assts, Goldsmiths' Co., 1982– (Prime Warden, 1989–90). Worcs: High Sheriff 1971; DL 1972. *Recreations:* music, travel. *Heir:* *b* (John) Miles Huntington-Whiteley, VRD, Lieut-Comdr RNR [*b* 18 July 1929; *m* 1960, Countess Victoria Adelheid Clementine Louise, *d* of late Count Friedrich Wolfgang zu Castell-Rudenhausen; one *s* two *d*]. *Address:* Ripple Hall, Tewkesbury, Glos GL20 6EY. *T:* (01684) 592431; 22 Park Close, Ilchester Place, W14 8ND. *T:* (020) 7603 3029. *Club:* Brooks's. *Died 17 June 2014.*

HURST, George; conductor; *b* 20 May 1926; Romanian father and Russian mother; *m* 2007, Denise Ham; one *d* from a previous marriage. *Educ:* various preparatory and public schs in the UK and Canada; Royal Conservatory, Toronto, Canada. First prize for Composition, Canadian Assoc. of Publishers, Authors and Composers, 1945. Asst Conductor, Opera Dept, Royal Conservatory of Music, Toronto, 1946; Lectr in Harmony, Counterpoint, Composition etc, Peabody Conservatory of Music, Baltimore, Md, 1947; Conductor of York, Pa, Symph. Orch., 1950–55, and concurrently of Peabody Conservatory Orch., 1952–55; Asst Conductor, LPO, 1955–57, with which toured USSR 1956; Associate Conductor, BBC Northern Symphony Orchestra, 1957; Principal Conductor, BBC Northern Symphony Orchestra (previously BBC Northern Orchestra), 1958–68; Artistic Adviser, 1968–73, Staff Conductor, 1968–88, Vice-Pres., 1979, Western Orchestral Soc. (Bournemouth SO and Bournemouth Sinfonietta); Prin. Conductor, Nat. SO of Ireland, 1990–91. Consultant, Nat. Centre of Orchestral Studies, 1980–87; RAM conducting studies consultant, 1983–; Principal Guest Conductor, BBC Scottish Symphony Orchestra, 1986–89. Frequent guest conductor in Europe, Israel, Canada, 1956–. Founder, Conductors' Course, Canford Summer Sch. of Music, 1959. *Publications:* piano and vocal music (Canada). *Recreations:* yachting, horse-riding. *Died 15 Sept. 2012.*

HURST, Henry Ronald Grimshaw; Overseas Labour Adviser, Foreign and Commonwealth Office, 1976–81; *b* 24 April 1919; *s* of Frederick George Hurst and Elizabeth Ellen (*née* Grimshaw); *m* 1st, 1942, Norah Joyce (*d* 1984), *d* of John Stanley Rothwell; one *s* one *d*; 2nd, 1986, Joy Oldroyde (*d* 1991). *Educ:* Darwen and Blackpool Grammar Schs; St Catharine's Coll., Cambridge (MA). Served War, Army, 1940–46. Colonial Service, 1946–70: Permanent Sec., Min. of Labour, Tanzania, 1962–64; Labour Adviser, Tanzania, 1965–68, and Malaŵi, 1969–70; Dep. Overseas Labour Adviser, FCO, 1970–76. *Recreations:* cricket, gardening. *Address:* Woodside Nursing Home, Bathwick Hill, Bath BA2 6EN. *Club:* Civil Service. *Died 24 Aug. 2013.*

HURWITZ, His Honour Vivian Ronald; a Circuit Judge, 1974–91; *b* 7 Sept. 1926; *s* of Alter Max and Dora Rebecca Hurwitz; *m* 1963, Dr Ruth Cohen, Middlesbrough; one *s* two *d*. *Educ:* Roundhay Sch., Leeds; Hertford Coll., Oxford (MA). Served RNVR: Univ. Naval Short Course, Oct. 1944–March 1945, followed by service until March 1947. Called to Bar, Lincoln's Inn, 1952, practised NE Circuit. A Recorder of Crown Court, 1972–74. *Recreations:* bowls, bridge, music (listening), art (looking at), sport—various (watching). *Died 16 Aug. 2011.*

HUSSAIN, Karamat, SQA 1983; Councillor (Lab) Mapesbury Ward, London Borough of Brent, 1971–86; Chairman, National Standing Conference of Afro-Caribbean and Asian Councillors, 1980–86 (Founder Member); *b* Rawalpindi, 1926; *m* Shamim. *Educ:* Aligarh Muslim Univ., India (BA Hons Humanities, MPhil). Political Educn Officer, Brent E, 1967–70. Brent Council: Chm., Planning Cttee, 1978–86; Vice Chm., Develt Cttee, 1978–86; Mem., Housing and Finance Cttees, 1978–86; Mayor of Brent, 1981–82 (Dep. Mayor, 1980–81); formerly Mem. and Vice-Chm., Brent Community Relations Council. Former Member: Regl Adv. Council on Higher Technical Educn, London and Home Counties; ASTMS. Gov., Willesden Coll. of Technology, 1971–86. *Recreation:* research in political philosophy. *Address:* 14 Tregwilym Road, Rogerstone, Newport, Gwent NP10 9DW. *T:* (01633) 892187. *Died 24 Aug. 2014.*

HUTCHINSON, His Honour Arthur Edward; QC 1979; a Circuit Judge, 1984–2000; *b* 31 Aug. 1934; *s* of late George Edward Hutchinson and Kathleen Hutchinson; *m*

1967, Wendy Pauline Cordingley; one *s* two *d*. *Educ:* Silcoates Sch.; Emmanuel Coll., Cambridge (MA). Commissioned, West Yorkshire Regt, 1953; served in Kenya with 5th Fusiliers, 1953–54. Called to Bar, Middle Temple, 1958; joined NE Circuit, 1959; a Recorder, 1974–84. *Recreation:* day-dreaming. *Died 21 May 2011.*

HUTCHISON, Robert Edward, (Robin); Keeper, Scottish National Portrait Gallery, 1953–82; *b* 4 Aug. 1922; *y s* of late Sir William Hutchison; *m* 1946, Heather (decd), *d* of late Major A. G. Bird; one *d* (and one *s* decd). *Educ:* Gresham's Sch., Holt. Served War, 1940–46, Infantry and RA; Asst Keeper, Scottish National Portrait Gallery, 1949. Hon. MA Edinburgh, 1972. *Publications:* (with Stuart Maxwell) Scottish Costume 1550–1850, 1958. *Died 7 Jan. 2013.*

HUXLEY, Sir Andrew Fielding, OM 1983; Kt 1974; FRS 1955; MA, Hon. ScD Cantab; Master, 1984–90, Fellow, 1941–60 and since 1990, Trinity College, Cambridge (Hon. Fellow, 1967–90); *b* 22 Nov. 1917; *s* of late Leonard Huxley and Rosalind Bruce; *m* 1947, Jocelyn Richenda Gammell Pease (*d* 2003); one *s* five *d*. *Educ:* University College Sch.; Westminster Sch. (Hon. Fellow, 1991); Trinity Coll., Cambridge (MA). Operational research for Anti-Aircraft Command, 1940–42, for Admiralty, 1942–45. Demonstrator, 1946–50, Asst Dir of Research, 1951–59, and Reader in Experimental Biophysics, 1959–60, in Dept of Physiology, Cambridge Univ.; Dir of Studies, Trinity Coll., Cambridge, 1952–60; Jodrell Prof., 1960–69 (then Emeritus), Royal Soc. Research Prof., 1969–83, UCL (Hon. Fellow, 1980). Lectures: Herter, Johns Hopkins Univ., 1959; Jesup, Columbia Univ., 1964; Alexander Forbes, Grass Foundation, 1966; Croonian, Royal Society, 1967; Review Lectr on Muscular Contraction, Physiological Soc., 1973; Hans Hecht, Univ. of Chicago, 1975; Sherrington, Liverpool, 1977; Florey, ANU, 1982; John C. Krantz Jr, Maryland Univ. Sch. of Medicine, 1982; Darwin, Darwin Coll., Cambridge, 1982; Romanes, Oxford, 1983; Fenn, IUPS XXIX Internat. Congress, Sydney, 1983; Blackett, Delhi, 1984; Green Coll., Oxford, 1986; Tarner, Trinity Coll., Cambridge, 1988; Maulana Abul Kalam Azad Meml, Delhi, 1991; C. G. Bernhard, Stockholm, 1993; Davson Meml, Amer. Physiol. Soc., 1998. Fullerian Prof. of Physiology and Comparative Anatomy, Royal Institution, 1967–73; Cecil H. and Ida Green Vis. Prof., Univ. of British Columbia, 1980. President: BAAS, 1976–77; Royal Soc., 1980–85 (Mem. Council, 1960–62, 1977–79, 1980–85); Internat. Union of Physiological Scis, 1986–93; Vice-Pres., Muscular Dystrophy Gp of GB, 1980–. Member: ARC, 1977–81; Nature Conservancy Council, 1985–87. Trustee: BM (Nat. Hist.), 1981–91; Science Museum, 1984–88. Hon. Member: Physiolog. Soc., 1979; Amer. Soc. of Zoologists, 1985; Japan Acad., 1988; Hon. MRIA, 1986; Foreign Associate, Nat. Acad. of Scis, USA, 1979; Internat. Mem. (formerly Foreign Mem.), Amer. Philosophical Soc., 1975; Foreign Hon. Member: Amer. Acad. of Arts and Sciences, 1961; Royal Acad. of Medicine, Belgium, 1978; Foreign Fellow, Indian Nat. Science Acad., 1985; Hon. MRI, 1981; Associate Mem., Royal Acad. of Scis, Letters and Fine Arts, Belgium, 1978; Mem., Leopoldina Academy, 1964; Foreign Member: Danish Acad. of Sciences, 1964; Dutch Soc. of Sciences, 1984. Hon. Fellow: Imperial Coll., London, 1980; Darwin Coll., Cambridge, 1981; QMW, London, 1987; RHBNC, London, 1994. Hon. FIBiol 1981; Hon. FRSC (Canada) 1982; Hon. FRSE 1983; Hon. FREng (Hon. FEng 1986); Hon. FMedSci 1999. Hon. MD: University of the Saar, 1964; Humboldt, E Berlin, 1985; Ulm, 1993; Charles Univ., Prague, 1998; Hon. DSc: Sheffield, 1964; Leicester, 1967; London, 1973; St Andrews, 1974; Aston, 1977; Western Australia, 1982; Oxford, 1983; Pennsylvania, 1984; Harvard, 1984; Keele, 1985; East Anglia, 1985; Maryland, 1987; Brunel, 1988; Hyderabad, 1991; Glasgow, 1993; Witwatersrand, 1998; Hon. LLD: Birmingham, 1979; Dundee, 1984; DUniv York, 1981; Hon. DHL New York, 1982; Hon. Dr: Marseille Fac. of Medicine, 1979; Toyama Med. and Pharm. Univ., Japan, 1995. Nobel Prize for Physiology or Medicine (jtly), 1963; Copley Medal, Royal Soc., 1973; Swammerdam Medal, Soc. for Natural Sci., Medicine and Surgery, Amsterdam, 1997. Grand Cordon, Order of Sacred Treasure (Japan), 1995. *Publications:* Reflections on Muscle (Sherrington Lectures XIV), 1980; (contrib.) The Pursuit of Nature, 1977; papers in the Journal of Physiology, etc. *Recreations:* walking, designing scientific instruments. *Address:* Manor Field, 1 Vicarage Drive, Grantchester, Cambridge CB3 9NG. *T:* and *Fax:* (01223) 840207; Trinity College, Cambridge CB2 1TQ. *T:* (01223) 338586. *Died 30 May 2012.*

HUXLEY, Hugh Esmor, MBE 1948; MA, PhD, ScD; FRS 1960; Professor of Biology, 1987–97, then Emeritus and Director, 1988–94, Rosenstiel Basic Medical Sciences Research Center, Brandeis University, Boston, Mass; *b* 25 Feb. 1924; *s* of late Thomas Hugh Huxley and Olwen Roberts, Birkenhead, Cheshire; *m* 1966, Frances Fripp, *d* of G. Maxon, Milwaukee; one *d*, and two step *s* one step *d*. *Educ:* Park High Sch., Birkenhead; Christ's Coll., Cambridge (Exhibitioner and Scholar; Hon. Fellow 1981). Natural Science Tripos, Cambridge, 1941–43 and 1947–48 (Pt II Physics); BA 1948, MA 1950, PhD 1952, ScD 1964. Served War of 1939–45, Radar Officer, RAF Bomber Command and Telecommunications Research Establishment, Malvern, 1943–47; Mem. Empire Air Armaments Sch. Mission to Australia and NZ, 1946. Research Student, MRC Unit for Molecular Biology, Cavendish Lab., Cambridge, 1948–52; Commonwealth Fund Fellow, Biology Dept, MIT, 1952–54; Research Fellow, Christ's Coll., Cambridge, 1953–56; Mem. of External Staff of MRC, and Hon. Res. Associate, Biophysics Dept, UCL, 1956–62; Fellow: King's Coll., Cambridge, 1962–67; Churchill Coll., Cambridge, 1967–87; Scientific Staff, MRC Lab. of Molecular Biol., Cambridge, 1962–87 (Dep. Dir, 1977–87; Jt Head, Structural Studies Div., 1975–87). Ziskind Vis. Prof., Brandeis Univ., 1971; Lectures: Harvey Soc., New York, 1964–65; Hooke, Univ. of Texas, 1968; Dunham, Harvard Med. Sch., 1969; Croonian, Royal Soc., 1970; Mayer, MIT, 1971; Penn, Pennsylvania Univ., 1971; Carter-Wallace, Princeton Univ., 1973; Adam Muller, State Univ. of NY, 1973; Pauling, Stanford, 1980; Jesse Beams, Virginia, 1980; Ida Beam, Iowa, 1981; Staples, Univ. of Maine, 1994; Davson, Amer. Physiol. Soc., 1994. Member: Council, Royal Soc., 1973–75, 1984–85; President's Adv. Bd, Rosentiel Basic Med. Scis Center, Brandeis Univ., 1971–77; Scientific Adv. Council, European Molecular Biol. Lab., 1976–81. Mem., German Acad. of Sci., Leopoldina, 1964; Hon. Member: Amer. Soc. of Biol Chem., 1976; Amer. Assoc. of Anatomy, 1981; Amer. Physiol. Soc., 1981; Amer. Soc. of Zoologists, 1986; Foreign Hon. Member: Amer. Acad. of Arts and Scis, 1965; Danish Acad. of Scis, 1971; Foreign Associate, US Nat. Acad. of Scis, 1978. Member, Editorial Board: Jl Ultrastructure Res., 1958–67; Jl Cell Biol., 1961–64; Jl Molecular Biol., 1962–70, 1978–87, 1990–93; Jl Cell Sci., 1966–70. Hon. ScD: Harvard, 1969; Leicester, 1989; Hon. DSc: Chicago, 1974; Pennsylvania, 1976. Feldberg Foundation Award for Experimental Medical Research, 1963; William Bate Hardy Prize (Camb. Phil. Soc.) 1965; Louisa Gross Horwitz Prize, 1971; Internat. Feltrinelli Prize, 1974; Gairdner Foundn Award, 1975; Baly Medal, RCP, 1975; Royal Medal, 1977, Copley Medal, 1997, Royal Soc.; E. B. Wilson Award, Amer. Soc. Cell Biology, 1983; Albert Einstein Award, World Cultural Council, 1987; Franklin Medal, Franklin Inst., Philadelphia, 1990; Distinguished Scientist Award, Electron Microscope Soc. of America, 1991. *Publications:* contrib. to learned jls. *Recreation:* sailing. *Address:* Rosenstiel Basic Medical Sciences Research Center, Brandeis University, Waltham, MA 02454, USA. *T:* (781) 7362490. *Died 25 July 2013.*

HYLAND, (James) Graham (Keith); QC 1998; a Recorder, since 1996; *b* 11 Jan. 1955; *s* of Reginald Keith Hyland and Evelyn (*née* Graham); *m* 1st, 1979, Angela Lancaster (marr. diss. 1993); one *s*; 2nd, 1995, Jane Alison Davies; one *d*. *Educ:* Heath Grammar Sch., Halifax; Newcastle upon Tyne Poly. (BA Law 1977). Called to the Bar, Inner Temple, 1978, Bencher, 2007. *Recreations:* walking, music, reading, wine, cricket. *Address:* Broadway House, 9 Bank Street, Bradford BD1 1TW. *T:* (01274) 722560; 9 Lincoln's Inn Fields, WC2A 3BP. *Clubs:* Bradford; South Caernarvonshire Yacht. *Died 25 Feb. 2014.*

HYSLOP, Kathleen Rachel M.; *see* Maxwell-Hyslop.

I

IBBS, Sir (John) Robin, KBE 1988; Kt 1982; Chairman: Lloyds TSB Group PLC, 1995–97; Lloyds Bank, 1993–97 (Director, 1985–97; Deputy Chairman, 1988–93); *b* 21 April 1926; *o s* of late Prof. T. L. Ibbs, MC, DSc, FInstP and of Marjorie Ibbs (*née* Bell); *m* 1st, 1952, Iris Barbara (*d* 2005), *d* of late S. Hall; one *d*; 2nd, 2006, Penelope Ann, *d* of late Capt. H. C. Buckland. *Educ:* West House Sch.; Gresham's Sch.; Upper Canada Coll., Toronto; Univ. of Toronto; Trinity Coll., Cambridge (MA Mech. Scis). Instr Lieut, RN, 1947–49. Called to the Bar, Lincoln's Inn, 1952 (Hon. Bencher 1999). C. A. Parsons & Co. Ltd, 1949–51; joined ICI, 1952; Dir, 1976–80 and 1982–88; on secondment as Head, Central Policy Review Staff, Cabinet Office, 1980–82; Advr (pt-time) to Prime Minister on Efficiency and Effectiveness in Govt, 1983–88; Chm., Lloyds Merchant Bank Hldgs, 1989–92; Dep. Chm., Lloyds Bank Canada, 1989–90. Dir, IMI, 1972–76. Chm., Adv. Council, PA Search and Selection, 1997–98. Member: Governing Body and Council, British Nat. Cttee of ICC, 1976–80; Industrial Develt Adv. Bd, DoI, 1978–80; Council, CBI, 1982–87 (Mem. Companies Cttee, 1978–80); Council, CIA, 1976–79, 1982–87 (Vice Pres., 1983–87; Hon. Mem., 1987); Chemicals EDC, NEDO, 1982–88; Council, RIIA, Chatham House, 1983–89; Top Salaries Review Body, 1983–89; Adv. Cttee on Business Appts, 1991–98; second Mem., Sierra Leone Arms Investigation, 1998; Leader, Review of H of C Services, 1990. Pres., Bankers Club, 1994–95. Vice Pres., CIB, 1993–97 (FCIB 1993). Trustee and Dep. Chm., Isaac Newton Trust, 1988–99. Mem. Court, Cranfield Inst. of Technology, 1983–88; Chm. of Council, UCL, 1989–95; Mem. Council, Foundn for Sci. and Technol., 1997–2002. CCMI (CBIM 1985). Hon. Fellow UCL, 1993. Hon. DSc Bradford, 1986; Hon. LLD Bath, 1993. BIM Special Award, 1989. *Address:* c/o Lloyds Banking Group, 25 Gresham Street, EC2V 7HN. *Clubs:* Oxford and Cambridge (Trustee, 1989–2002), Royal Society of Medicine. *Died 27 July 2014.*

IGGO, Prof. Ainsley, PhD, DSc; FRCPE; FRS 1978; FRSE; Professor of Veterinary Physiology, University of Edinburgh, 1962–90, then Emeritus; *b* 2 Aug. 1924; *s* of late Lancelot George Iggo and Catherine Josefine Fraser; *m* 1952, Betty Joan McCurdy, PhD, *d* of late Donald A. McCurdy, OBE; three *s*. *Educ:* Gladstone Sch., NZ; Southland Technical High Sch., NZ; Lincoln Coll., NZ (Sen. Scholar; MAgrSc 1947); Univ. of Otago (BSc 1949). PhD Aberdeen, 1954; DSc Edinburgh, 1962. FRSE 1962; FRCPE 1985. Asst Lectr in Physiology, Otago Univ. Med. Sch., 1948–50; NZ McMillan Brown Trav. Fellow, Rowett Inst., 1950–51; Lectr in Physiol., Univ. of Edinburgh Med. Sch., 1952–60; Nuffield Royal Soc. Commonwealth Fellow, ANU, 1959; Royal Soc. Locke Res. Fellow, 1960–62; Dean, Faculty of Veterinary Med., Univ. of Edinburgh, 1974–77 and 1985–90. Vis. Professor: Univ. of Ibadan, Nigeria, 1968; (also Leverhulme Res. Fellow) Univ. of Kyoto, 1970; Univ. of Heidelberg, 1972. Chm., IUPS Somatosensory Commn, 1974–84. Mem. Council: RCVS, 1975–78 and 1985–90; Royal Soc., 1982–83; Pres., Internat. Assoc. for Study of Pain, 1980–83. Governor, E of Scotland Coll. of Agriculture, 1968–77. Hon. DSc Pennsylvania; Hon. DVM&S Edinburgh, 1993. *Publications:* (ed) Sensory Physiology: Vol. II, Somatosensory System, 1973; articles on neurophysiol topics in Jl Physiol., etc. *Recreation:* gardening. *Address:* 5 Relugas Road, Edinburgh EH9 2NE. *T:* (0131) 667 4879. *Died 25 March 2012.*

ILERSIC, Prof. Alfred Roman; Emeritus Professor of Social Studies, Bedford College, University of London, since 1984 (Professor, 1965–84); *b* 14 Jan. 1920; *s* of late Roman Ilersic and Mary (*née* Moss); *m* 1st, 1944, Patricia Florence Bertram Liddle (marr. diss. 1976); one *s* one *d*; 2nd, 1976, June Elaine Browning. *Educ:* Polytechnic Sec. Sch., London; London Sch. of Economics. Lectr in Econs, University Coll. of S West, Exeter, 1947–53; Lectr in Social Statistics, Bedford Coll., 1953; Reader in Economic and Social Statistics, Bedford Coll., London, 1963. Vis. Prof., Univ. of Bath, 1983–87. Mem., Cost of Living Adv. Cttee, 1970–88. Chm., Inst. of Statisticians, 1968–70. Mem., Wilts CC, 1989–93. Hon. Mem., Rating and Valuation Assoc., 1968. *Publications:* Statistics, 1953; Government Finance and Fiscal Policy in Post-War Britain, 1956; (with P. F. B. Liddle) Parliament of Commerce 1860–1960, 1960; Taxation of Capital Gains, 1962; Rate Equalisation in London, 1968; Local Government Finance in Northern Ireland, 1969. *Recreations:* listening to music, walking. *Died 18 Feb. 2012.*

ILLMAN, John, CMG 1999; HM Diplomatic Service, retired; Ambassador to Peru, 1995–99; *b* 26 Oct. 1940; *s* of Reginald Thomas Illman and Hilda Kathleen Illman (*née* Targett); *m* 1962, Elizabeth Hunter Frame; one *s* two *d*. *Educ:* Reading Sch.; St Andrews Univ. Joined Foreign Office, 1961: Leopoldville, later Kinshasa, 1963–66; Dublin, 1967–71; Paris, 1971–73; First Sec., FCO, 1973–75; Buenos Aires, 1975–79; Lagos, 1979–82; Commonwealth Co-ordination Dept, FCO, 1982–86; Dep. Head of Mission and Consul-Gen., Algiers, 1986–90; Consul-Gen., Marseilles and for Principality of Monaco, 1990–94. Member: Anglo-Peruvian Trade and Investment Gp, 1997–; Anglo-Peruvian Soc., 1999– (Chm., 2003–04). Freeman, City of London, 2000. Chairman: BCT Peru, 1998–; MS Yavari Trust, 2006– (Trustee, 2002–). Pres., Old Redingensians Assoc., 2003. *Recreations:* squash, tennis, Rugby, cricket, amateur dramatics. *Clubs:* Royal Commonwealth Society, Candlewick Ward. *Died 4 Aug. 2011.*

ILLSLEY, Prof. Raymond, CBE 1979; PhD; Professorial Fellow in Social Policy, University of Bath, 1984–2003; *b* 6 July 1919; *s* of James and Harriet Illsley; *m* 1948, Jean Mary Harrison; two *s* one *d*. *Educ:* St Edmund Hall, Oxford (BA 1948); PhD Aberdeen 1956. Served War, 1939–45: active service in GB and ME, 1939–42; PoW, Italy and Germany, 1942–45. Econ. Asst, Commonwealth Econ. Cttee, London, 1948; Social Res. Officer, New Town Develt Corp., Crawley, Sussex, 1948–50; Sociologist, MRC, working with Dept of Midwifery, Univ. of Aberdeen, as Mem., Social Med. Res. Unit and later Mem., Obstetric Med. Res. Unit, 1951–64; Prof. of Sociology, Univ. of Aberdeen, 1964–75, Prof. of Medical Sociology, 1975–84. Dir, MRC Medical Sociology Unit, 1965–83. Vis. Prof., Cornell Univ., NY, 1963–64; Vis. Scientist, Harvard Univ., 1968; Sen. Foreign Scientist, National Sci. Foundn, Boston Univ., 1971–72; Vis. Prof., Dept of Sociology, Boston Univ., 1971–72, Adjunct Prof., 1972–76. Chairman: Scottish TUC Inquiry on Upper Clyde Shipbuilders Ltd, 1971; Social Sciences Adv. Panel, Action for the Crippled Child, 1971–76; Health Services Res. Cttee, Chief Scientist's Org., SHHD, 1976–84. Member: Sec. of State's Scottish Council on Crime, 1972–76; Exec. Cttee, Nat. Fund for Res. into Crippling Diseases, 1972–76; Chief Scientist's Cttee, SHHD, 1973–85; EEC Cttee on Med. Res., 1974–77; SSRC, 1976–78 (Chairman: Sociol. and Soc. Admin Cttee, 1976–79; Social Affairs Cttee, 1982–85); Chief Scientist's Adv. Cttee, DHSS, 1980–81; European Adv. Cttee for Med. Res., WHO, 1981–85. Rock Carling Fellow, Nuffield Prov. Hosps Trust, 1980. Hon. DSc Univ. of Hull, 1984; DUniv Stirling, 1987; Hon. dr med. Copenhagen, 1992. *Publications:* Mental Subnormality in the Community: a clinical and epidemiological study (with H. Birch, S. Richardson, D. Baird et al), 1970; Professional or Public Health, 1980; (with R. G. Mitchell) Low Birth Weight, 1984; articles in learned jls on reproduction, migration, social mobility, mental subnormality. *Recreation:* rough husbandry. *Address:* Tisbut House, Box Hill, Wilts SN13 8HG. *T:* (01225) 742313. *Died May 2013.*

INCHBALD, Michael John Chantrey, FCSD; architectural and interior designer; design consultant; *b* 8 March 1920; *s* of late Geoffrey H. E. Inchbald and

Rosemary, *d* of Arthur Ilbert and *niece* of Sir Courtenay Ilbert, GCB, KCSI, CIE; *m* 1955, Jacqueline Ann Bromley (OBE 2013) (marr. diss. 1964); one *s* one *d*; *m* 1964, Eunice Haymes (marr. diss. 1970). *Educ:* Sherborne; Architect. Assoc. Sch. of Architecture. FCSD (MSIA 1947). Director, Michael Inchbald Ltd, 1953–83. Work exhibited: Triennale, Milan; V & A Mus.; Design Centres London, New York, Helsinki. Design projects for: Bank of America; Crown Estate Comrs; Cunard; Dunhill worldwide; Ferragamo; Imperial Group; Justerini & Brooks; Law Soc.; John Lewis; Manufacturers Hanover Bank; Manufacturers Hanover Trust Bank; John Player; Plessey Co.; Pratt Burnard Engineering; Savoy Group—Berkeley, Claridges and Savoy hotels, and the restaurant complex Stones Chop House; Scottish Highland Industries; Trust House Forte—Post House, London Airport and several restaurants; Wolsey; ships, QE2, Carmania, Franconia and Windsor Castle; royal and private yachts and houses. Consultant to furniture and carpet manufacturers. Consulted *re* changes at Buckingham Palace; other projects, for the Duc de la Rochefoucauld, 13th Duke of St Albans, 8th Marquess of Ailesbury, 6th Marquess of Bristol, 17th Earl of Perth, 9th Earl of Dartmouth, 2nd Earl St Aldwyn, 3rd Baron Gisborough, 6th Baron Kilmarnock, 7th Baron Latymer, and 4th Baron St Levan. Inchbald schs founded under his auspices, 1960. Winner of four out of four nat. design competitions entered, including: Shapes of Things to Come, 1946; Nat. Chair Design Competition, 1955. Freeman, Clockmakers' Co., 1985. Award for outstanding contribution to design, idFX/BIDA, 2005. *Publications:* contrib. Arch. Rev., Arch. Digest, Connaissance des Arts, Connoisseur, Country Life, Harpers/Queen, House & Garden, Internat. Lighting Rev., Tatler, and Vogue. *Recreations:* arts, travel, antiques. *Address:* Stanley House, 10 Milner Street, SW3 2PU. *T:* (020) 7584 8832. *Died 23 Feb. 2013.*

INCHYRA, 2nd Baron *cr* 1962, of St Madoes, Co. Perth; **Robert Charles Reneke Hoyer Millar;** Treasurer, Multiple Sclerosis International Federation, 2000–08; *b* 4 April 1935; *er s* of 1st Baron Inchyra, GCMG, CVO and Elizabeth de Marees van Swinderen; *S* father, 1989; *m* 1961, Fiona Mary, *d* of Major E. C. R. Sheffield; one *s* two *d*. *Educ:* Eton; New Coll., Oxford. J. Henry Schroder Wagg & Co., 1958–64; Barclays Bank, 1964–88: Local Dir, Newcastle upon Tyne, 1967–75; Reg. Gen. Man., 1976–81; Dep. Chm., Barclays Bank Trust Co., 1982–85; Gen. Man. and Dir, UK Financial Services, 1985–88; Sec. (later Dir) Gen., BBA, 1988–94. Chm., European Utilities Trust plc (formerly Johnson Fry, later Legg Mason Investors), 1994–2005; Dir, Witan Investment Co., 1979–2002. Chm., NABC-CYP, subseq. Nat. Assoc. of Clubs for Young People, 1994–2003. *Heir:* *s* Hon. Christian James Charles Hoyer Millar [*b* 12 Aug. 1962; *m* 1992, Caroline, *d* of Robin Swan; one *s* two *d*]. *Address:* Rookley Manor, Kings Somborne, Stockbridge, Hants SO20 6QX. *T:* (01794) 388319. *Clubs:* White's, Pratt's. *Died 27 June 2011.*

INGAMELLS, John Anderson Stuart; Senior Fellow, Paul Mellon Centre for Studies in British Art, since 1992; *b* 12 Nov. 1934; *s* of late George Harry Ingamells and Gladys Lucy (*née* Rollett); *m* 1964, Hazel Wilson (*d* 2012); two *d*. *Educ:* Hastings Grammar School; Eastbourne Grammar School; Fitzwilliam House, Cambridge. National Service, Army (Cyprus), 1956–58; Art Asst, York Art Gallery, 1959–63; Asst Keeper, Dept of Art, National Museum of Wales, 1963–67; Curator, York Art Gallery, 1967–77; Asst to the Director, 1977–78, Director, 1978–92, Wallace Collection. Mem. Exec. Cttee, NACF, 1992–97. *Publications:* The Davies Collection of French Art, 1967; The English Episcopal Portrait, 1981; (ed) Dictionary of British and Irish Travellers in Italy 1701–1800, 1997; (ed jtly) The Letters of Sir Joshua Reynolds, 2001; numerous catalogues, including: Philip Mercier (with Robert Raines), 1969; Portraits at Bishopthorpe Palace, 1972; Paintings by Allan Ramsay (ed), 1999; museum catalogues at York, Cardiff, Wallace Collection, Dulwich Picture Gall. and Nat. Portrait Gall.; articles in Apollo, Connoisseur, Burlington Magazine, Walpole Soc., etc. *Address:* 39 Benson Road, SE23 3RL. *Died 10 Nov. 2013.*

INGLIS, Sir Brian Scott, AC 1988; Kt 1977; FTSE; Chairman: Optus Communications, 1992–96; Scalzo Automotive Research Ltd, 1986–95; *b* Adelaide, 3 Jan. 1924; *s* of late E. S. Inglis, Albany, WA; *m* 1953, Leila, *d* of E. V. Butler; three *d*. *Educ:* Geelong Church of England Grammar School; Trinity Coll., Univ. of Melbourne (BSc; Mem. Council, 1985). Served War of 1939–45; Flying Officer, RAAF, 453 Sqdn, 1942–45. Director and Gen. Manufacturing Manager, 1963–70, first Australian Man. Dir, Ford Motor Co. of Australia Ltd, 1970–81, Vice-Pres., 1981–83, Chm. 1981–85; Chm., Ford Asia-Pacific Inc., 1983–84. Chairman: Newcrest Mining (formerly Newmont Holdings), 1985–94; Aerospace Technologies of Aust. Pty Ltd, 1987–94; Amcor, 1989–94 (Dep. Chm., 1988–89; Dir, 1984–94); non-exec. Dir, Australian Paper, 1994–98. Chm., Defence Industry Cttee, 1984–87 (Mem., 1982–87). Chm., Centre for Molecular Biology and Medicine, Monash Univ. Hon. LLD Monash. James N. Kirby Medal, IProdE, 1979; Kernot Medal, Faculty of Engrg, Univ. of Melbourne, 1979. Légion d'Honneur (France), 2005. *Address:* 10 Bowley Avenue, Balwyn, Victoria 3103, Australia. *Clubs:* Australian (Melbourne); Barwon Heads Golf. *Died 24 Sept. 2014.*

INGRAM, Sir John (Henderson), Kt 1994; CBE 1984; FIMechE, Dist. FIPENZ; company director; *b* 3 Sept. 1924; *s* of John Garden Ingram and Irene Caro Ingram (*née* Simpson); *m* 1952, Rosemary Clara Cuningham; three *d*. *Educ:* Nelson Coll., NZ; Canterbury Univ., Christchurch, NZ (BE; Dist. Alumnus, 1999). FIPENZ (FNZIE 1969; Dist. FIPENZ 1997); FAusIMM 1975; FIMechE 1991. Served RNZAF, NZ and Pacific, 1943–45. Man. Dir, NZ Steel Ltd, 1969–86; Dir, Nat Bank of NZ, 1983–95; Chm., Auckland Uniservices Ltd, 1988–99. Chm., Youth Skills NZ, 1989–97; Mem., Auckland HA, 1990–91. President: Inst. of Professional Engrs, NZ, 1976–77; Auckland Manufacturers' Assoc., 1989–91. Mem., Waitangi Tribunal, 1993–98. Mem. Council, 1979–96, Pro Chancellor, 1982–83 and 1995–96, Fellow, 1997, Univ. of Auckland. Dist. FInstD (NZ) 2003. Commemoration Medal, NZ, 1990. *Publications:* contrib. papers in Inst. of Professional Engrs, NZ Jl, Conf. papers IISI, Inst. of Engrs, Australia, Aust. Inst. of Metals. *Recreations:* garden, ski-ing. *Address:* 6 Glenbrook Street, Remuera, Auckland 1050, New Zealand. *T:* (9) 5200167. *Club:* Northern (Auckland). *Died 1 April 2015.*

INKIN, Sir Geoffrey (David), Kt 1993; OBE 1974 (MBE 1971); Chairman, Cardiff Bay Development Corporation, 1987–2000; *b* 2 Oct. 1934; *e s* of late Noel D. Inkin and Evelyn Margaret Inkin; *m* 1st, 1961, Susan Elizabeth Sheldon (marr. diss. 1998); three *s*; 2nd, 1998, Mrs Susan Inglefield (*née* Turcan). *Educ:* Dean Close Sch.; RMA, Sandhurst; Staff Coll., Camberley; Royal Agricl Coll., Cirencester. Commnd The Royal Welch Fusiliers, 1955; served Malaya, 1955–57 and Cyprus, 1958–59 (despatches); commanded 1st Bn The Royal Welch Fusiliers, 1972–74. Member: Gwent CC, 1977–83; Gwent Police Authority, 1979–83; Mem. Bd, 1980–83, Chm., 1983–87, Cwmbran Develt Corp.; Chm., Land Authy for Wales, 1986–98; Mem. Bd, Welsh Develt Agency, 1984–87. Judicial Appts Comr, 2006–11. Gov., Haberdashers' Monmouth Schs, 1977–90; Mem. Bd, WNO, 1987–91, 1993–95; Member Council: UWIST, 1987–88; Cardiff Univ., 1988–2002. Patron, Butler Trust, 1996–2005. Parly Cand. (C) Ebbw Vale, 1977–79. Hon. MRICS 2002. Gwent: DL, 1983–91; High Sheriff, 1987–88. Hon. Consul for Hungary, 2000–09. Hon. Dr Univ. of Glamorgan, 1996. *Address:* Castle Upon Alun, St Brides Major, Bridgend CF32 0TN. *T:* (01656) 880298. *Clubs:* Cardiff and County (Cardiff); Royal Porthcawl Golf. *Died 22 Aug. 2013.*

INMAN, Roger, OBE (mil.) 1945 (MBE (mil.) 1944); TD 1945; Vice Lord-Lieutenant of South Yorkshire, 1981–90; Joint Managing Director, since 1951, and Chairman, since 1997, Harrison Fisher Group; *b* 18 April 1915; *y s* of S. M. Inman, Sheffield; *m* 1939, Christine Lucas (decd), *e d* of Lt-Col J. Rodgers, Sheffield; two *s*. *Educ:* King Edward VII Sch., Sheffield. Commissioned into 71st (WR) Field Bde, RA TA, 1935; served War, with RA and General Staff, Western Desert, Middle East, Italy, 1939–46; released, 1946, with rank of Lt-Col; reformed and commanded 271 (WR) Fd Regt, RA TA, 1947–51; Brevet Col 1953; Hon.

Col, Sheffield Artillery Volunteers, 1964–70; Member, W Riding T&AFA, 1947–; Vice-Chm., Yorkshire and Humberside TA&VRA, 1973–80. JP 1954 (Chm. Sheffield City Bench, 1974–80), DL 1967, West Riding. General Commissioner of Income Tax, 1969–90; Chm. of Comrs, Don Div. of Sheffield, 1975–90. Chm., Guardians of Standard of Wrought Plate within the Town of Sheffield, 1988–98. *Recreation:* golf. *Address:* Flat 1, Mayfield View, 15 Whitworth Road, Sheffield S10 3HD. *Club:* Hallamshire Golf (Sheffield). *Died 3 March 2013.*

INNES, William James Alexander; Assistant Under Secretary of State, 1985–94, Head of Fire and Emergency Planning Department, 1992–94, Home Office; *b* 11 Oct. 1934; *s* of late William Johnstone Innes and Helen Margaret Meldrum Porter; *m* 1st, 1959, Carol Isabel Bruce (marr. diss. 1983); one *s* one *d*; 2nd, 1992, Mrs Ann Harrold. *Educ:* Robert Gordon's Coll., Aberdeen; Aberdeen Univ. (MA). Served Royal Air Force, 1956, Officer Commanding 45 Sqdn, 1967–70. Principal, Home Office, 1972; Private Sec. to Home Sec., 1974–76; Asst Sec., 1977; Asst Under Sec. of State, seconded to NI Office, 1985–88; Dir of Operational Policy, Prison Dept, Home Office, 1988–90; Dir of Custody, Prison Service HQ, Home Office, 1990–92. *Recreations:* opera, theatre. *Address:* Nightingales, Nightingale Lane, Maidenhead, Berks SL6 7QL. *Club:* Royal Air Force. *Died 18 July 2015.*

IRBY, Charles Leonard Anthony, FCA; Director: North Atlantic Smaller Companies Investment Trust, since 2002; Gabelli Value Plus + Trust, since 2015; *b* 5 June 1945; *s* of Hon. Anthony P. Irby and Mary Irby (*née* Apponyi); *m* 1971, Sarah Jane Sutherland; one *s* one *d*. *Educ:* Eton Coll. FCA 1979. Binder Hamlyn & Co., Chartered Accountants, 1965–69; Joseph Sebag & Co., Stockbrokers, 1971–74; Baring Brothers & Co. Ltd, 1974–95 (Dir, 1985–95); Baring Brothers Asia Ltd, 1976–79; Dir, Baring Brothers Internat. Ltd, 1995–99 (Dep. Chm., 1997–99); Man. Dir, 1995–99, Sen. UK Advr, 1999–2001, ING Barings; Dir, 1999–2009, Chm., 2000–09, Aberdeen Asset Mgt plc. Director: E. C. Harris, 2001–05; QBE Insce Gp Ltd, 2001–13; Great Portland Estates plc, 2004–14; Mem., Adv. Bd, Nardello and Co. LLP, 2011–12. Mem., Panel on Takeovers and Mergers, 1998–99. Chm., Corporate Finance Cttee, London Investment Bankers' Assoc., 1998–99. Mem. Council, King Edward VII's Hosp. Sister Agnes, 2000–13. FRSA. *Recreations:* travel, photography. *Address:* 125 Blenheim Crescent, W11 2EQ. *T:* (020) 7221 2979. *Clubs:* Boodle's, City of London. *Died 15 Sept. 2015.*

IRELAND, Norman Charles; Chairman, BTR, 1993–96 (Director, 1969–96); *b* 28 May 1927; *s* of Charles and Winifred Ireland; *m* 1953, Gillian Margaret (*née* Harrison) (*d* 2001); one *s* one *d*. *Educ:* England, USA, India. CA (Scot.); Chartered Management Accountant. With Richard Brown & Co., Edinburgh, 1944–50; Brown Fleming & Murray, London, 1950–54; Avon Rubber Co., Melksham, 1955–64; Chief Accountant, United Glass, 1964–66; Finance Dir, BTR, 1967–87; Chm., Bowater plc, 1987–93. Chairman: The Housing Finance Corp., 1988–93; Intermediate Capital Gp, 1989–93; Dir, Meggitt, 1987–93. *Recreations:* gardening, ballet, opera, music. *Died 5 Oct. 2011.*

IRVIN, Albert, OBE 2013; RA 1998; painter; *b* 21 Aug. 1922; *s* of Albert Henry Jesse Irvin and Nina Lucy Irvin; *m* 1947, Beatrice Olive Nicolson; two *d*. *Educ:* Northampton Sch. of Art; Goldsmiths' Coll. Sch. of Art (NDD (Painting); Hon. Fellow, 2002). Navigator, RAF, 1941–46. Lectr, Goldsmiths' Coll. Sch. of Art, 1962–83; visitor at art schs, Britain and abroad. Hon. Fellow, Plymouth Coll. of Art, 2012. *Solo exhibitions* include: New Art Centre, London, 1961, 1963, 1965, 1971, 1973; Acme Gall., London, 1980; Gimpel Fils, London, 1982, 1984, 1986, 1990, 1992, 1994, 1996, 1998, 2002, 2004, 2007, 2010, 2012, 2014; Aberdeen Art Gall., 1976, 1983; Third Eye Centre, Glasgow, 1983; Ikon Gall., Birmingham, 1983; Talbot Rice Gall., Edinburgh, 1989; Serpentine Gall., London, 1990; Oriel and Chapter, Cardiff, 1990; RHA, Dublin, 1995; RWA, Bristol, 1999; Stühler Galerie, Berlin, 2002; Lancaster Univ. and Storey Galls, Lancaster, 2003; Peppercanister Gall., Dublin, 2003, 2006, 2008, 2011; Advanced Graphics, London 2005, 2010; Tate Britain, 2008; King's Place, London, 2008, 2010; Northumbria Univ. Gall., Newcastle upon Tyne, 2009, 2011; Gimpel Müller Gall., Paris, 2009; Churchill Coll., Cambridge, 2010; Prints, RA, 2011; Clifford Chance, 2012; Barrow River Arts Fest., Carlow, 2012; Møller Centre, Churchill Coll., Cambridge, 2013; prints, Atkinson Gall., Millfield, 2013; gouaches, Univ. of Northumbria Gall., 2013; Crosstown, Advanced Graphics London, 2013; Plimsoll, Plymouth Coll. of Art Gall., 2013; also at galls and museums in USA, Australia, Austria, Germany, France, Belgium, Spain, Saudi Arabia, etc; *group exhibitions* include: British Art, Hayward, 1974; British Art, Royal Acad., 1977; Hayward, 1980; Presence of Painting, Mappin Gall., Sheffield and tour, 1988; Experience of Painting, Laing Art Gall., Newcastle and tour, 1989; Great British Art Show, Glasgow, 1990; Here and Now, Serpentine, 1994; "1979", Bloomberg SPACE, London, 2005; Réalités Nouvelles, Paris, 2006; Dreischritt, Galerie Parterre, Berlin, 2006; Royal Acad. Summer Show, 1949, 1950, 1951 and annually, 1987–; 10 Royal Academicians, Dubai, 2006; Encounter: the Royal Acad. in Asia and ME, 2012; London Gp Centenary Exhibn, 2013; Riff/T, Baltic Gall., Newcastle, 2013; *work in public collections* including: Tate Gall.; Royal Acad.; V&A; British Council; Arts Council; also in other British and internat. collections; *commissions* include: painting for Homerton Hosp., Hackney, 1987; design for Diversions Dance Co., 1994; painting for Chelsea and Westminster Hosp., 1996. *Television:* A Feeling for Paint, 1983; Off the Wall: the Byker Show, 1994; Albert Irvin: artist at work, 2000; Albert Irvin: portrait (France), 2003; radio interviews. Arts Council Awards, 1968, 1975, 1980; Prizewinner, John Moores Liverpool Exhibn, 1982; Gulbenkian Award for Printmaking, 1983; Giles Bequest Prize, V&A and British Mus., 1986; Korn/Ferry Internat. Premier Award, Royal Acad., 1989. *Relevant publications:* Albert Irvin: life to painting, by Paul Moorhouse, 1998; Albert Irvin: the complete prints, by Mary Rose Beaumont, 2010. *Recreation:* music. *Address:* 19 Gorst Road, SW11 6JB. *T:* (020) 7228 2929; 71 Stepney Green, E1 3LE. *Clubs:* Chelsea Arts, Arts. *Died 26 March 2015.*

IRVINE, James Montgomery, RDI 2004; industrial designer; Founder: Studio James Irvine, 1988; James Irvine Srl, 2003; *b* London, 29 Dec. 1958; *s* of Alan Montgomery Irvine, RDI and Betty Middleton-Sandford; *m* 2005, Marialaura Rossiello; two *s*. *Educ:* Kingston Poly. (BA Hons 1981); Royal Coll. of Art (DesRCA 1984). Moved to Milan, 1984; Consultant for industrial products with Olivetti Design Studio, Milan, 1984–92; exchange designer with Toshiba Design Studio, Tokyo, 1987–88; returned to Milan and opened own design office specialising in product design, 1988; Partner, Sottsass Associati, with resp. for industrial design gp, Milan, 1993–97. Work includes city bus for Hanover transport system, 2000 (131 built by Mercedes Benz); other clients include: Alias, Arper, Artemide, B&B Italia, Canon Japan, Muji, Olivetti, Thonet, WMF, Olivetti and Zumtobel. Hon. DDes Kingston Univ., 2007. *Recreations:* travel, Italian food, classic British motorcycles. *Address:* James Irvine Srl, Via Vigevano 8, 20144 Milan, Italy. *T:* (02) 89059980. *E:* info@james-irvine.com. *Club:* BSA Owners. *Died 18 Feb. 2013.*

IRVINE, John Ferguson, CB 1983; financial consultant to local charities, 1995–2002; Chief Executive, Industrial Therapy Organisation (Ulster), 1984–94; *b* 13 Nov. 1920; *s* of Joseph Ferguson Irvine and Helen Gardner; *m* 1st, 1945, Doris Partridge (*d* 1973); one *s* one *d*; 2nd, 1980, Christine Margot Tudor; two *s* and two step *s*. *Educ:* Ardrossan Acad.; Glasgow Univ. (MA); Sorbonne Univ. RAF, 1941–46; Scottish Home Dept, 1946–48; NI Civil Service, 1948–66; Chief Exec., Ulster Transport Authority, 1966–68; Chief Exec., NI Transport Holding Co., 1968; NI Civil Service, 1969–83; Dep. Sec., DoE, NI, 1971–76; Permanent Secretary: attached NI Office, 1977–80; Dept of Manpower Services, 1980–81; DoE for NI, 1981–83. Chm. Management Cttee, 1974–75, and Vice-Chm. General Council, 1975, Action Cancer; Chm., Down Care and Aftercare Cttee, 1992–2000 (Mem. Cttee, 2000–07); Member: NI Marriage Guidance Council (Chm., 1976–78); Council, PHAB (NI), 1984–86; Council, PHAB

(UK), 1984–86; Trustee, Heart Fund, Royal Victoria Hosp., Belfast, 1986–88. Mem., Downpatrick Inter-Church Caring Project, 1996–2002. *Recreations:* yoga, Majorca, football. *Address:* 11 Quarry Hill, Strawberry Fields, Strangford, Co. Down BT30 7GZ. *T:* (028) 4488 1613. *Died 25 Sept. 2013.*

IRVINE, Prof. (John) Maxwell, PhD; CPhys, FInstP; FRAS; FRSE; Professor of Physics, University of Manchester, since 2001; *b* 28 Feb. 1939; *s* of John MacDonald Irvine and Joan Paterson (*née* Adamson); *m* 1962, Grace Ritchie; one *s*. *Educ:* George Heriot's Sch., Edinburgh; Edinburgh Univ. (BSc Math. Phys. 1961); Univ. of Michigan (MSc 1962); Univ. of Manchester (PhD 1964). FInstP 1971; CPhys 1985; FRAS 1986; FRSE 1993. English-Speaking Union Fellow, Univ. of Michigan, 1961–62; Asst Lectr, Univ. of Manchester, 1964–66; Res. Associate, Cornell Univ., 1966–68; University of Manchester: Lectr, 1968–73; Sen. Lectr, 1973–76; Reader, 1976–83; Prof. of Theoretical Physics, 1983–91; Dean of Science, 1989–91; Principal and Vice-Chancellor, Aberdeen Univ., 1991–96; Vice-Chancellor and Principal, Univ. of Birmingham, 1996–2001. Chairman: CVCP Information Systems Sector Gp, 1996–98; Cttee of Scottish Univ. Principals, 1994–96; W Midlands Regl Innovation Strategy Gp, 1996–2001; Jt Information Systems Cttee, 1998–2003; RSE Inquiry into Energy Issues for Scotland, 2005–. Advr to Cttee on Radioactive Waste Mgt, 2005–06. Director: Grampian Enterprise Ltd, 1992–96; Rowett Res. Inst., 1992–96. Member: Nuclear Physics Bd, SERC, 1983–88 (Chm., Nuclear Structure Cttee, 1984–88); Bd, Scottish Council for Develt and Industry, 1992–96; Scottish Econ. Council, 1993–96; Scottish Cttee, British Council, 1994–96; BT Scottish Forum, 1994–96; Bd, HEQC, 1994–97; Univ. and Colls Employers Assoc., 1995–2001; UCAS, 1995–2001; Bd, PHLS, 1998–2005; Quality Mgt Panel, European Univs Assoc., 1999–; Commonwealth Scholarship Commn, 2002–06; Educnl Consultancy Service, 2002–03; NMC, 2005–06; Energy Steering Gp, Eur. Acads Sci. Adv. Cttee, 2005–. Member Council: ACU, 1994–2004 (Chm., 1995; Treas., 1998–2004); CVCP, 1996–2001; NERC, 1998–2001. Vice-Pres., 1982–87, Mem. Council, 1981–87, 1988–94, Inst. of Physics. Gov., ESU, 1999–2005. Sen. Advr, Oxford Round Table, 2001–. FRSA 1993; CCMI (CIMgt 1996). DL West Midlands, 1999–2001. Hon. FRCSEd 1995. Hon. DSc: Coll. of William and Mary in Va, 1995; Aston, 2002; Hon. DEd Robert Gordon Univ., 1995; DUniv: Edin., 1995; Birmingham, 2001; Hon. LLD Aberdeen, 1997. *Publications:* The Basis of Modern Physics, 1967 (trans. Dutch and French 1969); Nuclear Structure Theory, 1972; Heavy Nuclei, Superheavy Nuclei and Neutron Stars, 1975; Neutron Stars, 1978; Nuclear Power, 2011; research articles on nuclear physics, astrophysics and condensed matter physics. *Recreations:* hill walking, tennis, bridge, staying alive. *Address:* 27 Belfield Road, Manchester M20 6BJ. *Died 24 March 2012.*

IRVING, Edward, CM 2002; ScD; FRS 1979; FRSC 1973; Research Scientist, Pacific Geoscience Centre, Sidney, BC, 1981–92, Emeritus since 1992; *b* 27 May 1927; *s* of George Edward and Nellie Irving; *m* 1957, Sheila Ann Irwin; two *s* two *d*. *Educ:* Colne Grammar Sch.; Cambridge Univ., 1948–54 (BA, MA, MSc, ScD). Served Army, 1945–48. Research Fellow, Fellow and Sen. Fellow, ANU, 1954–64; Dominion Observatory, Canada, 1964–66; Prof. of Geophysics, Univ. of Leeds, 1966–67; Res. Scientist, Dominion Observatory, later Earth Physics Br., Dept of Energy, Mines and Resources, Ottawa, 1967–81; Adjunct Professor: Carleton Univ., Ottawa, 1975–81; Univ. of Victoria, 1985–94. FRAS 1958; Fellow: Amer. Geophysical Union, 1976 (Walter H. Bucher Medal, 1979); Geological Soc. of America, 1979 (Arthur L. Day Medal, 1997); For. Associate, NAS, US, 1998. Hon. FGS 1989. Hon. DSc: Carleton, 1979; Memorial Univ. of Newfoundland, 1986; Victoria, 1999. Gondwanaland Medal, Mining, Geological and Metallurgical Soc. of India, 1962; Logan Medal, Geol Assoc. of Canada, 1975; J. T. Wilson Medal, Canadian Geophys. Union, 1984; Alfred Wegener Medal, European Geoscience Union, 1995; Wollaston Medal, Geol Soc. of London, 2005. Golden Jubilee Medal, 2002; Diamond Jubilee Medal, 2013. *Publications:* Paleomagnetism, 1964; numerous contribs to learned jls. *Recreations:* gardening, carpentry, choral singing. *Address:* Pacific Geoscience Centre, 9860 West Saanich Road, Box 6000, North Saanich, BC V8L 4B2, Canada. *T:* (250) 3636508; 9363 Carnoustie Crescent, North Saanich, BC V8L 5G7, Canada. *T:* (250) 6569645. *E:* stirving@telus.net. *Died 25 Feb. 2014.*

ISAAC, Maurice Laurence Reginald, MA; Headmaster, Latymer Upper School, Hammersmith, W6, 1971–88; *b* 26 April 1928; *s* of late Frank and Lilian Isaac; *m* 1954, Anne Fielden (*d* 2003); three *d*. *Educ:* Selhurst Grammar Sch., Croydon; Magdalene Coll., Cambridge. BA Hist. Tripos, 1950; MA 1955, Cambridge; Certif. in Educn, 1952. Asst Master: Liverpool Collegiate Sch., 1952–56; Bristol Grammar Sch., 1956–62; Head of History, Colchester Royal Grammar Sch., 1962–65; Headmaster, Yeovil Sch., 1966–71. Mem. Council, Francis Holland Schools Trust, 1982–95. *Publications:* A History of Europe, 1870–1950, 1960; contributor to The Teaching of History, 1965. *Died 11 Jan. 2015.*

ISEPP, Martin Johannes Sebastian; Head of Music, Opera Akademie, Royal Danish Opera, Copenhagen, 2006–08; Head of Music Studies, National Opera Studio, 1979–95; *b* Vienna, 30 Sept. 1930; *s* of Sebastian and Helene Isepp; *m* 1966, Rose Henrietta Harris; two *s*. *Educ:* St Paul's Sch.; Lincoln Coll., Oxford; Royal Coll. of Music, London (ARCM 1952). Studied piano with Prof. Leonie Gombrich, 1939–52. English Opera Gp, 1954–57; Glyndebourne Fest. Opera, 1957–2007 (Head of Music Staff, 1973–93; Chief Guest Coach, 1994–2007); Head of Opera Trng Dept, Juilliard Sch. of Music, New York, 1973–78; Hd, Acad. of Singing, Banff Sch. of Fine Arts, Alberta, Canada, 1982–93. As accompanist, began career accompanying mother, Helene Isepp (the singer and voice teacher); accompanied many of the world's leading singers and instrumentalists, notably Elisabeth Schwarzkopf, Elisabeth Söderström, Janet Baker and John Shirley-Quirk; harpsichordist with Handel Opera Soc. of New York in most of their Handel Festivals, 1966–; master classes in opera and song: at Amer. univs, incl. Southern Calif, Ann Arbor, Maryland, Minnesota and Colorado, 1975–; Pacific Music Fest., Sapporo, Japan, 1995–98; lieder courses, Britten-Pears Sch. for Advanced Musical Studies, Aldeburgh, 1988–; coached Peking Opera and Peking Conservatory in Mozart operas, 1983; opera prodns, Centre de la Voix, Fondation Royaumont, France, 1992–; annual opera course (Music Dir), Walton Foundn, Ischia, Italy, 1992–95; classes at New Nat. Opera, Tokyo, 2001–04; Mentor, Vocal Prog., Marlboro Music Fest., Vt, 2005–. As conductor: Le Nozze di Figaro, Glyndebourne Touring Op., 1984; Don Giovanni, Glyndebourne Touring Op., 1986; Abduction from the Seraglio, Washington Op., 1986–87; Così fan Tutte, Canadian Opera Co. Ensemble, Toronto, 2009; Asst Conductor, Met. Op., NY, 1994–. Hon. DMus Wake Forest, NC, 2001; Hon. DFA Colorado, 2009. Carroll Donner Stuchell Medal for Accompanists, Harriet Cohen Internat. Musical Foundn, 1965. *Recreations:* photography, walking. *Address:* 55 Parliament Hill, NW3 2TB. *T:* (020) 7722 3085. *Died 25 Dec. 2011.*

ISTEAD, Maj.-Gen. Peter Walter Ernest, CB 1989; OBE 1978; GM 1966; DL; Chief Executive, Institute of Brewing, 1990–96; *b* 7 Aug. 1935; *s* of Walter and Marie Istead; *m* 1961, Jennifer Mary Swinson; one *s* one *d*. *Educ:* Whitgift Trinity Sch., Croydon. Enlisted as boy soldier into Scots Guards, 1952; commnd Queen's Royal Regt, 1954; seconded to KAR, 1954–56; transf. RAOC, 1957; HQ 16 Parachute Bde, 1958–62; sc 1968; Directing Staff, Staff Coll., Camberley, 1971–73; DCS, 4 Armd Div., 1978–81; RCDS, 1982; Dir, Admin. Planning (Army), 1983–86; Comdr Supply, BAOR, 1986–87; Dir Gen., Logistic Policy (Army), 1987–90. Hon. Col Comdt, RAOC, 1989–92. Freeman, City of London, 1986. DL Greater London, 1997. *Recreation:* angling. *Died 30 June 2014.*

J

JACK, Sir David, Kt 1993; CBE 1982; PhD; FRS 1992; FRSE; pharmacologist; *b* 22 Feb. 1924; *s* of Andrew Jack and Mary McDougal Jack (*née* Maiden); *m* 1952, Lydia Downie Brown; two *d. Educ:* Markinch and Buckhaven Schools, Fife; Univ. of Glasgow (BSc); Univ. of London (PhD); Royal Technical Coll., Glasgow. FRSC, FSB, FRPharmS; FRSE 1978. Lectr in Pharmacology, Glasgow Univ. and RTC Glasgow, 1948–51; Scientist, Glaxo Labs, 1951–53; Head of Product Develt, Smith Kline and French, 1953–61; Res. Dir, Allen & Hanburys, 1961–78; R&D Dir, Glaxo Holdings, 1978–87; associated with new medicines for the treatment of asthma (salbutamol, salmeterol, beclomethasone dipropionate, fluticasone propionate), peptic ulcer (ranitidine), migraine (sumatriptan), and controlling side-effects of cancer chemotherapy (ondansetron). Hon. DL Dundee, 1991. Hon. DSc: Strathclyde, 1982; Bath, 1987; CNAA, 1987; Liverpool, 1998; London, 1999; Glasgow, 2001. Medicinal Chem. Medal, RSC, 1980; Award for Drug Discovery, Soc. for Drug Research, 1985; Lilly Prize Medal, British Pharm. Soc., 1989; Mullard Medal, Royal Soc., 1991; Galen Medal, Soc. of Apothecaries, 1995; Host-Madsen Medal, Internat. Pharmaceutical Fedn, 1995; Royal Medal, RSE, 2006; Hanbury Meml Award, RPSGB, 2006. *Publications:* papers in Br. Jl Pharmacology etc. *Recreations:* theatre, gardening, golf. *Address:* 6 The Slype, Gustard Wood, Wheathampstead, Herts AL4 8RY. *T:* (01582) 832241. *Died 8 Nov. 2011.*

JACK, Prof. Kenneth Henderson, OBE 1997; PhD, ScD; FRS 1980; CChem, FRSC; Professor of Applied Crystal Chemistry, University of Newcastle upon Tyne, 1964–84, then Emeritus Professor, and Director of Wolfson Research Group for High-Strength Materials, 1970–84; Leverhulme Emeritus Fellow, 1985–87; *b* 12 Oct. 1918; *e s* of late John Henderson Jack, DSC, and Emily (*née* Cozens), North Shields, Northumberland; *m* 1942, Alfreda Hughes (*d* 1974); two *s. Educ:* Tynemouth Municipal High Sch.; King's Coll., Univ. of Durham, Newcastle upon Tyne (BSc 1939, DThPT 1940, MSc 1944); Fitzwilliam Coll., Univ. of Cambridge (PhD 1950, ScD 1978). Experimental Officer, Min. of Supply, 1940–41; Lectr in Chemistry, King's Coll., Univ. of Durham, 1941–45, 1949–52, 1953–57; Sen. Scientific Officer, Brit. Iron and Steel Res. Assoc., 1945–49; research at Crystallographic Lab., Cavendish Laboratory, Cambridge, 1947–49; Research Engr, Westinghouse Elec. Corp., Pittsburgh, Pa, 1952–53; Research Dir, Thermal Syndicate Ltd, Wallsend, 1957–64. Consultant, Cookson Group, 1986–94. Hon. Prof. of Materials Engrg, Univ. of Wales Swansea, 1996–2011. Lectures: J. W. Mellor Meml, Brit. Ceramic Soc., 1973; Harold Moore Meml, Metals Soc., 1984; W. Hume-Rothery Meml, Oxford Metallurgical Soc., 1986; Sosman Meml, Amer. Ceramic Soc., 1989. Fellow, Amer. Ceramic Soc., 1984 (Dist. Life Mem., 2007); Membre d'Honneur, Société Française de Métallurgie, 1984; Mem., Internat. Acad. of Ceramics, 1990; Hon. Member: Materials Res. Soc. of India, 1991; Ceramic Soc. of Japan, 1991. Saville-Shaw Medal, Soc. of Chem. Industry, 1944; Sir George Beilby Meml Award, Inst. of Metals, RIC and Soc. of Chem. Industry, 1951; Kroll Medal and Prize, Metals Soc., 1979; (with Dr R. J. Lumby) Prince of Wales Award for Industrial Innovation and Production, 1984; Armourers & Brasiers' Co. Award, Royal Soc., 1988; World Materials Congress Award, ASM Internat., 1988; A. A. Griffith Silver Medal and Prize, Inst. of Metals, 1989; Centennial Award, Ceramic Soc. of Japan, 1991. *Publications:* papers in scientific jls and conf. proc. *Address:* 147 Broadway, Cullercoats, North Shields, Tyne and Wear NE30 3TA. *T:* (0191) 257 3664. *Died 28 Jan. 2013.*

JACKSON, Anthony Geoffrey Clive H.; *see* Howland Jackson.

JACKSON, Michael Walter; Under Secretary and Head of Marine Directorate, Department of Transport, 1993–94; *b* 5 April 1934; *s* of late William Henry Jackson and Nellie Jackson; *m* 1963, Mary Bruce Hope Sinclair; one *s* one *d. Educ:* Queen Elizabeth Grammar Sch., Wakefield; Queen's Coll., Oxford (MA Lit.Hum.). UKAEA, 1959–68; joined MoT, 1968; Assistant Secretary: MoT, 1973–76; PSA, 1976–80; Dept of Transport, 1980–93. *Recreations:* hill-walking, opera. *Address:* 4 Hobbs Way, Welwyn Garden City, Herts AL8 6HX. *T:* (01707) 323925. *Died 31 March 2012.*

JACKSON, (Walter) Patrick, CB 1987; FRHistS; Under-Secretary, Department of Transport, 1981–89; *b* 10 Feb. 1929; *m* 1952, Kathleen Roper; one *s* one *d. Educ:* University Coll., Oxford. John Lewis Partnership, 1952–66; Principal, Min. of Transport and DoE, 1966–72; Asst Sec., DoE, 1972–78; Under Sec. and Regional Dir (E Midlands), DoE and Dept of Transport, 1978–81. FRHistS 2001. *Publications:* The Last of the Whigs, 1994; Education Act Forster, 1997; Harcourt and Son, 2004; Enigma Variation, 2004; Loulou, 2006; Morley of Blackburn, 2012. *Recreation:* historical research. *Died 7 Nov. 2014.*

JACKSON-LIPKIN, Miles Henry, (Li Pak-Kim); QC (Hong Kong) 1974; SC 1997; JP; a Judge of the High Court of Hong Kong, 1981–87; *b* Liverpool, 24 May 1924; *s* of late I. J. Jackson-Lipkin, MD and F. A. Patley; *m* Lucille Yun-Shim Fung, DCLJ, barrister; one *s. Educ:* Harrow; Trinity Coll., Oxford. FCIArb 1986; Mem., HKIArb; Chartered Arbitrator, Canada, Hong Kong and UK. Called to the Bar, Middle Temple, 1951; admitted Hong Kong Bar, 1963, NSW Bar, 1980. Comr, Supreme Court of Negara Brunei Darussalam, 1984–87. Panel Member: Inland Revenue Bd of Review, Hong Kong, 1975; London Court of Internat. Arbitration, 1994; WIPO, 1995; British Columbia Arbitration Mediation Inst., 1995; Hong Kong Internat. Arbitration Centre Mediation Gp, 1996. Chief Legal Advr, Hope and Lee (Consultants) Ltd, 1988. Chm. Exec. Cttee, and Man. Dir, Hong Kong Children and Youth Services, 1978. Member: Medico-Legal Soc., 1952; Justice, 1956; Council of Honour, Monarchist League, 1969; Council, Constitutional Monarchy Assoc., 1995; Founder Member: Hong Kong Br., Justice, 1963; Hong Kong Medico-Legal Soc., 1974 (Mem. Cttee, 1976). Hon. Advr, China North-West Coll. of Law. Vice-Chm., Hong Kong Island Br., Internat. Wine and Food Soc. Hon. Mem., Chinese Soc. for Wind Engrg. Delegate, HKSAR, Order of St Lazarus of Jerusalem, 1999. Liveryman: Meadmakers' Co. (Edinburgh), 1984; Arbitrators' Co., 1986; Freeman, City of London, 1986. JP Hong Kong, 1977. GLJ 1998 ((Grand Priory of Lochore); KCLJ 1983; KLJ 1977; CLJ 1973). *Publications:* The Beaufort Legitimation, 1957; Scales of Justice, 1958; Israel Naval Forces, 1959. *Recreations:* gardening, heraldry, classical music, philately, walking. *Address:* 309 The Capilano, 2024 Fullerton Avenue, West Vancouver, BC V7P 3G4, Canada. *Clubs:* Naval and Military, MCC; Hong Kong, Hong Kong Cricket, Hong Kong Golf, Hong Kong Jockey, American, Arts, Classic Car, (Hon.) Shanghai Fraternity Assoc. (Hong Kong). *Died 18 Feb. 2012.*

JACOB, Prof. François; Croix de la Libération; Grand-Croix de la Légion d'Honneur; biologist; Head of Cellular Genetics Unit, Pasteur Institute, 1960–91; Professor of Cellular Genetics, at the College of France, 1964–91; *b* Nancy (Meurthe & Moselle), 17 June 1920; *m* 1st, 1947, Lysiane Bloch (*d* 1984); three *s* one *d*; 2nd, 1999, Geneviève Barrier. *Educ:* Lycée Carnot, France. DenM 1947; DèsS 1954. Pasteur Institute: Asst, 1950–56; Head of Laboratory, 1956–60; Prof., 1960–; Pres., 1982–88. Member: Acad. of Scis, Paris, 1977; Acad. Française, Paris, 1996. Charles Léopold Mayer Prize, Acad. des Sciences, Paris, 1962; Nobel Prize for Medicine, 1965. Foreign Member: Royal Danish Acad. of Letters and Sciences, 1962; Amer. Acad. of Arts and Sciences, 1964; Nat. Acad. of Scis, USA, 1969; Royal Soc., 1973; Acad. Royale de Médecine, Belgique, 1973; Acad. of Sci., Hungary, 1986; Royal Acad. of Sci., Madrid, 1987. Hon. doctorates from several univs, incl. Chicago, 1965. *Publications:* La Logique du Vivant, 1970 (The Logic of Life, 1974); Le Jeu des Possibles, 1981 (The Possible and the Actual, 1982); La Statue Intérieure, 1987 (The Statue Within, 1988); La Souris, la Mouche et l'Homme, 1997 (Of Flies, Mice and Men, 1998); various scientific papers. *Recreation:* painting. *Address:* Institut Pasteur, 28 rue du Dr Roux, 75724 Paris, Cedex 15, France. *Died 19 April 2013.*

JACOBS, Baron *cr* 1997 (Life Peer), of Belgravia in the City of Westminster; **David Anthony Jacobs,** Kt 1988; FCA; *b* 13 Nov. 1931; *s* of Ridley and Ella Jacobs; *m* 1954, Evelyn Felicity Patchett; one *s* one *d*. *Educ:* Clifton Coll.; London Univ. (BCom). Chairman: Nig Securities Gp, 1957–72; Tricoville Gp, 1961–90, 1992–94; British Sch. of Motoring, 1973–90. Contested (L) Watford, Feb. and Oct. 1974. Jt Treas., Liberal Party, 1984–87; Vice-Pres., Soc. & Lib Dem, 1988; Chm., Federal Exec., Soc. & Lib Dem, 1988. *Recreations:* golf, reading, theatre, opera, travel. *Address:* 9 Nottingham Terrace, NW1 4QB. *T:* (020) 7486 6323. *Club:* Palm Beach Country (USA). *Died 21 June 2014.*

JACOBS, David Lewis, CBE 1996; DL; radio and television broadcaster; *b* 19 May 1926; *s* of David Jacobs and Jeanette Victoria Jacobs; *m* 1st, 1949, Patricia Bradlaw (marr. diss. 1972); three *d* (one *s* decd); 2nd, 1975, Caroline Munro (*d* 1975); 3rd, 1979, Mrs Lindsay Stuart-Hutcheson. *Educ:* Belmont Coll.; Strand Sch. RN, 1944–47. First broadcast, Navy Mixture, 1944; Announcer, Forces Broadcasting Service, 1944–45; Chief Announcer, Radio SEAC, Ceylon, 1945–47; Asst Stn Dir, Radio SEAC, 1947; News Reader, BBC Gen. Overseas Service, 1947, subseq. freelance. Major radio credits include: Book of Verse, Housewives' Choice, Journey into Space, Dateline London, Grande Gingold, Curioser and Curioser, Puffney Post Office, Follow that Man, Man about Town, Jazz Club, Midday Spin, Music Through Midnight, Scarlet Pimpernel, Radio 2 DJ Show, Pick of the Pops, Saturday Show Band Show, Melodies for You (12 years), Saturday Star Sounds, Any Questions (Chm. for 17 years), Any Answers; Internat. Fest. of Light Music. TV credits incl.: Focus on Hocus, Vera Lynn Show, Make up your Mind, Tell the Truth, Juke Box Jury, Top of the Pops, Hot Line, Miss World, Top Town, David Jacobs' Words and Music, Sunday Night with David Jacobs, Little Women, There Goes that Song Again, Make a Note, Where are they Now, What's My Line, Who What or Where, Frank Sinatra Show, Mario Lanza Show, Walt Disney Christmas Show, Wednesday Show, Wednesday Magazine, Eurovision Song Contest, TV Ice Time, Twist, A Song for Europe, Ivor Novello Awards, Aladdin, Airs and Graces, Tell Me Another, Those Wonderful TV Times, Blankety Blank, Come Dancing, Questions (TVS), Primetime, Countdown, Holiday Destinations (Sky). Numerous film performances incl. Golden Disc, You Must Be Joking, It's Trad Dad, Stardust; former commentator, British Movietone News. 6 Royal Command Performances; 6 yrs Britain's Top Disc Jockey on both BBC and Radio Luxembourg; Variety Club of Gt Brit., BBC TV Personality of Year, 1960, and BBC Radio Personality of the Year, 1975; Sony Gold Award for Outstanding Contribution to Radio over the Years, 1984; RSPCA Richard Martin Award, 1978. Chairman: Kingston FM, 1994–95; Thames FM, 1995–. Director: Duke of York's Theatre, 1979–85; Man in the Moon (UK) Ltd, 1986–; Video Travel Guides, 1990–91; Tom Smith Crackers, 1997–98; private banking section, Guinness Mahon, 1997–98. Dir, Kingston Th. Trust, 1991–2008 (Chm., 1990–2008); Pres., Kingston Th. Appeal, 1992–2008; Life Pres., Rose Th., Kingston, 2008; Dir, College of Driver Educn, 1991–96. Vice-President: Stars Organisation for Spastics (Past Chm.); Soc. of Stars, 1996–; Mem. Council, RSPCA, 1969–77, Vice-Chm. 1975–76; Vice-Pres., The St John Ambulance London (Prince of Wales's), 1985–97. Past Pres., Nat. Children's Orch.; Vice-Pres., Wimbledon Girls Choir. Chm., Think British Council, 1985–89 (Dep. Chm., 1983–85); Vice-Pres., Invest in Britain Campaign, 1992– (Chm., 1989–92). President: Kingston upon Thames Royal British Legion, 1984–2008; SW London Area, SSAFA 1995–2008; Jt Pres., SW London Community Foundn, 1994–; Vice-President: Royal Star and Garter Home, Richmond, 1988–; Friends of Chelsea and Westminster Hosp., 1993–; Patron: Age Resource, 1990–; Kingston Wel-Care Assoc., 1995; Queen Alexandra Hosp. Home, 2007–. Pres., Kingston Alcohol Adv. Service, 1993–; Vice Pres., Kingston Arts Council; Trustee, Dine-a-Mite, 1994–. Life Gov., ICRF, 1995. DL Greater London, 1983, Kingston upon Thames, 1984–2001 (representative); High Steward, Kingston upon Thames, 2001. DUniv Kingston, 1994. *Publications:* (autobiog.) Jacobs' Ladder, 1963; Caroline, 1978; (with Michael Bowen) Any Questions?, 1981. *Recreations:* talking and listening, hotels. *Address:* Wyncombe Hill Cottage, The Fleet, Fittleworth, Pulborough, W Sussex RH20 1HN. *Clubs:* St James', Chelsea Arts, Sloane. *Died 2 Sept. 2013.*

JACOBS, Hon. Sir Kenneth (Sydney), KBE 1976; Justice of High Court of Australia, 1974–79; *b* 5 Oct. 1917; *s* of Albert Sydney Jacobs and Sarah Grace Jacobs (*née* Aggs); *m* 1952, Eleanor Mary Neal (*d* 2002); one *d*. *Educ:* Knox Grammar Sch., NSW; Univ. of Sydney (BA, LLB); University Coll. London (MA Ancient History 2006). Admitted to NSW Bar, 1947; QC 1958; Supreme Court of NSW: Judge, 1960; Judge of Appeal, 1966; Pres., Court of Appeal, 1972. *Publications:* Law of Trusts, 1958. *Address:* 18A Bath Street, Brighton BN1 3TB. *Died 24 May 2015.*

JACOBSON, Prof. Dan; novelist, critic; Professor Emeritus, University College London, since 1994; *b* 7 March 1929; *s* of Michael Hyman Jacobson and Liebe Jacobson (*née* Melamed); *m* 1954, Margaret Dunipace Pye; two *s* one *d*. *Educ:* Kimberley Boys' High Sch., SA; Univ. of Witwatersrand, Johannesburg (BA 1949). Fellow in Creative Writing, Stanford Univ., Calif, 1956–57; University College London: Reader in English, 1979–86; Prof. of English, 1986–94. Vis. Prof., Syracuse Univ., NY, 1965–66; Visiting Fellow: State Univ. of NY, 1972; Humanities Research Centre, ANU, 1981. Lectures: Ernest Jones Meml, British Inst. of Psycho-Analysis, 1988; Ethel M. Wood, Univ. of London, 1990; Bernard Krikler Meml, Wiener Liby, 1995; Lord Northcliffe, UCL, 2001. FRSL 1974–99, 2007–. Hon. DLitt Witwatersrand, 1997. Llewellyn Rhys Award, Book Trust, 1958; W. Somerset Maugham Award, Soc. of Authors, 1962. Mary Elinore Smith Poetry Prize, Amer. Scholar, 1992. *Publications: fiction:* The Trap, 1955; A Dance in the Sun, 1956; The Price of Diamonds, 1957; The Evidence of Love, 1960; The Beginners, 1966; The Rape of Tamar, 1970; Inklings: selected stories, 1973; The Wonder-Worker, 1973; The Confessions of Josef Baisz, 1977 (H. H. Wingate Award, Jewish Chronicle, 1979); Her Story, 1987; Hidden in the Heart, 1991; The God-Fearer, 1992; All For Love, 2005; *criticism:* The Story of the Stories, 1982; Adult Pleasures, 1988; *autobiography:* Time and Time Again, 1985 (J. R. Ackerley Prize, PEN, 1986); *travel:* The Electronic Elephant, 1994; *memoir:* Heshel's Kingdom, 1998; *translation:* H. van Woerden, A Mouthful of Glass, 2000; *interviews:* Ian Hamilton, New Review, 1977; Michael Freeman, PN Review, 1989; Richard Lansdown, Critical Review, 1999; Gareth Cornwall, S African Review of Bks, 1999; Ian Hamilton, London Review of Bks, 1999; Ian Hamilton in Conversation with Dan Jacobson, 2002. *Recreations:* tennis, walking, reading, talking. *Address:* c/o A. M. Heath & Co., 6 Warwick Court, WC1R 5DJ. *T:* (020) 7242 2811. *Died 12 June 2014.*

JAEGER, Prof. Leslie Gordon, CM 2002; FRSE 1966; Research Professor of Civil Engineering and Applied Mathematics, Technical University of Nova Scotia, 1988–92, then Emeritus; *b* 28 Jan. 1926; *s* of Henry Jaeger; *m* 1st, 1948, Annie Sylvia Dyson (decd); two *d*; 2nd, 1981, Kathleen Grant. *Educ:* King George V Sch., Southport; Gonville and Caius Coll., Cambridge. PhD, DSc (Eng) London. Royal Corps of Naval Constructors, 1945–48; Industry, 1948–52; University College, Khartoum, 1952–56; Univ. Lectr, Cambridge, 1956–62; Fellow and Dir of Studies, Magdalene Coll., Cambridge, 1959–62; Prof. of Applied Mechanics, McGill Univ., Montreal, 1962–65; Regius Prof. of Engineering, Edinburgh Univ., 1965–66; Prof. of Civil Engineering, McGill Univ., 1966–70; Dean, Faculty of Engineering, Univ. of New Brunswick, 1970–75; Academic Vice-Pres., Acadia Univ., NS, 1975–80; Vice-Pres. (Res.), Technical Univ. of NS, 1980–88. Pres., Canadian Soc. for Civil Engrg, 1992–93. Hon. Prof. of Civil Engrg, Tong Ji Univ., Shanghai, 1987; Hon. Rector, Usman Inst. of Technol., Karachi, 1993. DEng *hc*: Carleton Univ., Ottawa, 1991; Meml Univ.,

Newfoundland, 1994; Technical Univ. of NS, 1995; LLD *hc* Dalhousie, 2005. Telford Premium, ICE, 1959; A. B. Sanderson Award, 1983, P. L. Pratley Award, 1994, Horst Leipholz Medal, 2007, Canadian Soc. for Civil Engrg; Gzowski Medal, 1985, Julian C. Smith Medal, 1996, Engrg Inst. of Canada. *Publications:* The Analysis of Grid Frameworks and Related Structures (with A. W. Hendry), 1958; Elementary Theory of Elastic Plates, 1964; Cartesian Tensors in Engineering Science, 1965; (with B. Bakht) Bridge Analysis Simplified, 1985; (with B. Bakht) Bridge Analysis by Microcomputer, 1989; various papers on grillage analysis in British, European and American Journals. *Recreations:* golf, curling, contract bridge. *Address:* PO Box 1000, Halifax, NS B3J 2X4, Canada. *T:* (902) 4779571. *Died 20 Aug. 2013.*

JAFFREY, Saeed, OBE 1995; actor and writer; *b* Malerkotla, Punjab, 8 Jan. 1929; *s* of late Dr Hamid Hussain Joffrey and Hadia Begum Joffrey; *m* 1st, 1958, Madhur Bahadur (marr. diss. 1966); three *d*; 2nd, 1980, Jennifer Irene Sorrell. *Educ:* Allahabad Univ. (MA Medieval Hist. 1950); Catholic Univ., Washington DC (MFA Drama 1958). First Indian actor to tour USA in Shakespeare, 1958, and to appear on Broadway, in A Passage to India, 1962; *films* include: The Wilby Conspiracy, 1974; The Man Who Would Be King, 1975; The Chess Players, 1977 (Best Actor Awards, Filmfare, and Filmworld, 1978); Touch Wood, 1981; Masoom, 1982; Gandhi, 1982; My Beautiful Laundrette, 1985 (BAFTA award, 1986); A Passage to India, 1985; Ram Teri Ganga Maili, 1985; Henna, 1989; Masala (Canadian Acad. Award), 1992; *television* includes: Gangsters, 1975–77; Jewel in the Crown, Staying On, 1980–82; Far Pavilions, 1985; Partition, Tandoori Nights, 1985–87; Love Match, 1986; Killing on the Exchange, 1986; Rumpole, 1990; Little Napoleons, 1994–95; Common as Muck, 1996–97; Ravi Desai in Coronation Street, 1998–99; *theatre* includes: Captain Brassbound's Conversion, 1972; Midsummer Night's Dream, 1989; White Chameleon, 1991; My Fair Lady, 1997; The King & I, 2001; *radio* includes: wrote and presented first programme on India in America, Reflections of India, 1961–63; numerous plays incl. Art of Love (Kama Sutra), The Pump, Shakuntala, Savitri, A Suitable Boy, and The Silver Castle. *Publications:* Saeed: an actor's journey, 1998. *Recreations:* snooker, cartooning and caricatures, watching cricket and tennis. *Died 15 Nov. 2015.*

JAMES OF HOLLAND PARK, Baroness *cr* 1991 (Life Peer), of Southwold in the County of Suffolk; **Phyllis Dorothy White, (P. D. James),** OBE 1983; JP; FRSL; author; *b* 3 Aug. 1920; *d* of Sidney Victor James and Dorothy Amelia James (*née* Hone); *m* 1941, Connor Bantry White (*d* 1964); two *d*. *Educ:* Cambridge Girls' High Sch. Administrator, National Health Service, 1949–68; Civil Service: apptd Principal, Home Office, 1968; Police Dept, 1968–72; Criminal Policy Dept, 1972–79. Associate Fellow, Downing Coll., Cambridge, 1986. A Gov., BBC, 1988–93; Member: BBC Gen. Adv. Council, 1987–88; Arts Council, 1988–92 (Chm., Literature Adv. Panel, 1988–92); Bd, British Council, 1988–93 (Mem., Literature Cttee, 1988–93). Chm., Booker Prize Panel of Judges, 1987. Pres., Soc. of Authors, 1997– (Chm., 1984–86); Mem., Detection Club. JP: Willesden, 1979–82; Inner London, 1984. FRSL 1987; FRSA. Hon. Fellow: St Hilda's Coll., Oxford, 1996; Downing Coll., Cambridge, 2000; Girton Coll., Cambridge, 2000; Lucy Cavendish Coll., Cambridge, 2012; Hon. Bencher, Inner Temple, 2009. Hon. DLitt: Buckingham, 1992; Hertfordshire, 1994; Glasgow, 1995; Durham, 1998; Portsmouth, 1999; Hon. DLit London, 1993; DU Essex, 1996. Awarded many major prizes for crime writing in GB, America, Italy and Scandinavia; Grand Master award, Mystery Writers of America, 1999. *Publications:* Cover Her Face, 1962 (televised 1985); A Mind to Murder, 1963 (televised 1995); Unnatural Causes, 1967 (televised 1993); Shroud for a Nightingale, 1971 (televised 1984); (with T. A. Critchley) The Maul and the Pear Tree, 1971; An Unsuitable Job for a Woman, 1972 (filmed 1982; televised 1998); The Black Tower, 1975 (televised 1986); Death of an Expert Witness, 1977 (televised 1983); Innocent Blood, 1980; The Skull beneath the Skin, 1982; A Taste for Death, 1986 (televised 1988); Devices and Desires, 1989 (televised 1991); The Children of Men, 1992; Original Sin, 1994 (televised 1997); A Certain Justice, 1997 (televised 1998); A Time to be in Earnest: a fragment of autobiography, 1999; Death in Holy Orders, 2001 (televised 2003); (ed with Harriet Harvey Wood) Sightlines, 2001; The Murder Room, 2003; The Lighthouse, 2005; The Private Patient, 2008; Talking About Detective Fiction, 2009; Death Comes to Pemberley, 2011 (televised 2013). *Recreations:* exploring churches, walking by the sea. *Address:* c/o Greene & Heaton Ltd, 37 Goldhawk Road, W12 8QQ. *Died 27 Nov. 2014.*

JAMES, (Arthur) Walter; Principal, St Catharine's, Windsor, 1974–82 (Hon. Fellow, 2006); *b* 30 June 1912; *s* of late W. J. James, OBE; *m* 1st, 1939, Elisabeth (marr. diss. 1956), *e d* of Richard Rylands Howroyd; one *d*; 2nd, 1957, Ann Jocelyn (*d* 2004), *y d* of late C. A. Leavy Burton; one *d* and one adopted *s* two adopted *d*. *Educ:* Uckfield Grammar Sch.; Keble Coll., Oxford (Scholar); 1st Cl. Mod. Hist.; Liddon Student; Arnold Essay Prizeman. Senior Demy of Magdalen Coll., 1935; Scholar in Mediæval Studies, British School at Rome, 1935; Editorial staff, Manchester Guardian, 1937–46. NFS 1939–45. Contested (L) Bury, Lancs, 1945. Dep. Editor, The Times Educational Supplement, 1947–51, Editor, 1952–69; Special Advisor on Educn, Times Newspapers, 1969–71; also Editor, Technology, 1957–60. Reader in Journalism, Univ. of Canterbury, NZ, 1971–74. Member: BBC Gen. Advisory Council, 1956–64; Council of Industrial Design, 1961–66; Council, Royal Society of Arts, 1964; Cttee, British-American Associates, 1964; Governor, Central School of Art and Design, 1966. Woodard Lecturer, 1965. *Publications:* (Ed.) Temples and Faiths 1958; The Christian in Politics, 1962; The Teacher and his World, 1962; A Middle-class Parent's Guide to Education, 1964; (contrib.) Looking Forward to the Seventies, 1967. *Recreation:* gardening. *Club:* National Liberal. *Died 5 Aug. 2015.*

JAMES, Cecil; *see* James, T. C. G.

JAMES, His Honour Charles Edwin Frederic; a Circuit Judge, 1993–2011; *b* 17 April 1943; *s* of Frederic Crockett Gwilym James and Marjorie Peggy James (*née* Peace); *m* 1968, Diana Mary Francis (*née* Thornton); two *s*. *Educ:* Trent College, Long Eaton, Derbyshire; Selwyn College, Cambridge. MA 1968. Called to the Bar, Inner Temple, 1965; practised on Northern Circuit, 1965–93; Jun. of Northern Circuit, 1966. A Recorder, 1982–93. *Recreation:* family pursuits. *Clubs:* Cambridge University Cricket; Royal Liverpool Golf, Royal Mersey Yacht. *Died 20 Sept. 2013.*

JAMES, Sir Cynlais Morgan, (Sir Kenneth), KCMG 1985 (CMG 1976); HM Diplomatic Service, retired; Director General, Canning House, 1987–92; *b* 29 April 1926; *s* of Thomas James and Lydia Ann James (*née* Morgan); *m* 1953, Mary Teresa (*d* 2009), *d* of R. D. Girouard and Lady Blanche Girouard; two *d*. *Educ:* Trinity Coll., Cambridge (MA). Service in RAF, 1944–47. Cambridge 1948–51. Entered Senior Branch of Foreign Service, 1951; Foreign Office, 1951–53; Third Sec., Tokyo, 1953–56; Second Sec., Rio de Janeiro, 1956–59; First Sec. and Cultural Attaché, Moscow, 1959–62; FO, 1962–65; Paris, 1965–69; promoted Counsellor, 1968; Counsellor and Consul-General, Saigon, 1969–71; Head of W European Dept, FCO, 1971–75; NATO Defence Coll., Rome, 1975–76; Minister, Paris, 1976–81; Ambassador to Poland, 1981–83; Asst Under Sec. of State, FCO, 1983; Ambassador to Mexico, 1983–86. Director: Thomas Cook, 1986–91; Latin American Investment Trust, 1990–96; Foreign and Colonial Emerging Markets, 1993–96; Polish Investment Trust, 1996–2002; Consultant, Darwin Instruments, 1986; Advr, Amerada Hess Ltd, 1997. Chairman: British-Mexican Soc., 1987–90; British Inst. in Paris, 1988–2000; Bd, Inst. of Latin American Studies, 1992–98; Mem., Franco-British Council, 1986–99. Hon. Dr Mexican Acad. of Internat. Law, 1984. Order of the Aztec, 1st cl. (Mexico), 1985; Order of Andres Bello, 1st cl. (Venezuela), 1990; Order of Merit (Chile), 1991; Chevalier, Legion of Honour (France), 1995. *Recreation:* tennis. *Clubs:* Brooks's, Beefsteak, Pratt's, MCC; Travellers (Paris). *Died 19 July 2013.*

JAMES, Dr David Gwynfor; Head of Meteorological Research Flight, Royal Aircraft Establishment, Farnborough, 1971–82; *b* 16 April 1925; *s* of William James and Margaret May Jones; *m* 1953, Margaret Vida Gower; two *d*. *Educ:* Univ. of Wales, Cardiff (BSc, PhD). Joined Meteorological Office, 1950; Met. Res. Flight, Farnborough, 1951; Forecasting Res., Dunstable, 1953; Christmas Island, Pacific, 1958; Satellite Lab., US Weather Bureau, 1961; Cloud Physics Res., Bracknell, 1966; Met. Res. Flight, RAE, 1971. Fellow, UC Cardiff, 1987. *Publications:* papers in Qly Jl Royal Met. Soc., Jl Atmospheric Sciences, Met. Res. Papers, and Nature. *Recreations:* golf, choral singing. *Died 4 Dec. 2013.*

JAMES, Eleanor Mary; Lecturer in Mathematics, University College of Wales, Aberystwyth, 1957–92; *b* 31 Aug. 1935; *d* of Morris and Violet Mary Jones; *m* 1958, David Bryan James. *Educ:* Ardwyn Grammar Sch., Aberystwyth; University College of Wales, Aberystwyth (BSc 1955; PhD 1972). Member: Welsh Consumer Council, 1981–90; CECG, 1982–84; Consumer Develt Sub-Cttee, Nat. Consumer Council, 1983–85; Layfield Cttee of Enquiry, Local Govt Finance, 1974–76; Audit Commn for Local Authorities and NHS, 1988–91; Dyfed-Powys Police Authy, 1994–99. Member: N Wales Area Cttee, NACAB (formerly CAB), 1987–90, 1991–99 (Chm., Aberystwyth, 1988–93, 1998–2000); POUNC, 1991–97 (Chm., Council for Wales, 1991–97); Radioactive Waste Management Adv. Cttee, 1991–94; Wkg Pty, Churches' Enquiry into Unemployment and Future of Work, 1995–97; Chm., Wales Rural Forum, 1994–97; Campaign for the Protection of Rural Wales: Chm., Ceredigion Br., 1992–2000; Mem., Exec. Cttee, 1996–2004; Vice-Chm., 2001–04. National Federation of Women's Institutes: Mem., Envmt and Public Affairs Sub-Cttee, 1981–84; Vice Chm., Fedn of Wales Sub-Cttee, 1991–94; Chm., Dyfed Ceredigion Fedn of WIs, 1993–96 (Treas., 1989–92). University College of Wales: Mem. Council, 1982–86; Mem., Court of Governors, 1982–2011; Treas., Old Students' Assoc., 1975–2010. *Publications:* (with T. V. Davies) Nonlinear Differential Equations, 1966. *Recreations:* walking, the WI. *Address:* Dolhuan, Llandre, Bowstreet, Ceredigion SY24 5AB. *T:* (01970) 828362. *Died 15 June 2011.*

JAMES, Rev. Canon Eric Arthur; an Extra Chaplain to HM the Queen, since 1995 (Chaplain, 1984–95); Hon. Director, Christian Action, 1990–96 (Director, 1979–90); *b* 14 April 1925; *s* of John Morgan James and Alice Amelia James. *Educ:* Dagenham County High School; King's Coll. London (MA, BD; FKC 1986). Asst Curate, St Stephen with St John, Westminster, 1951–55; Chaplain Trinity Coll., Cambridge, 1955–59; Select Preacher to Univ. of Cambridge, 1959–60; Vicar of St George, Camberwell and Warden of Trinity College Mission, 1959–64; Director of Parish and People, 1964–69; Proctor in Convocation, 1964–72; Canon Precentor of Southwark Cathedral, 1964–73; Canon Residentiary and Missioner, Diocese of St Albans, 1973–83; Hon. Canon, 1983–90; Canon Emeritus, 1990. Preacher to Gray's Inn, 1978–97; Select Preacher to Univ. of Oxford, 1991–92. Commissary to Bishop of Kimberley, 1965–67, to Archbishop of Melanesia, 1969–93. Examining Chaplain to Bishop of St Albans, 1973–83, to Bishop of Truro, 1983–93. Hon. Bencher Gray's Inn, 1997. FRSA 1992. DD Lambeth, 1993. *Publications:* The Double Cure, 1957, 2nd edn 1980; Odd Man Out, 1962; (ed) Spirituality for Today, 1968; (ed) Stewards of the Mysteries of God, 1979; A Life of Bishop John A. T. Robinson: Scholar, Pastor, Prophet, 1987; (ed) God's Truth, 1988; Judge Not: a selection of sermons preached in Gray's Inn Chapel, 1989; Collected Thoughts: fifty scripts for BBC's Thought for The Day, 1990; (ed) A Last Eccentric: a symposium concerning the Rev. Canon F. A. Simpson: historian, preacher and eccentric, 1991; Word Over All: forty sermons 1985–1991, 1992; The Voice Said, Cry: forty sermons 1990–1993, 1994; A Time to Speak: forty sermons 1993–95, 1997; In Season, Out of Season: sermons 1996–97, 1999; Who Is This?: Holy Week meditations and other sermons 1998–2000, 2001; Collected Thoughts: BBC Radio 4 Thought for the Day broadcasts, 2002; The House of My Friends: memories and reflections, 2003; The Voice of This Calling: twenty-five sermons, 2005; Old Men Ought to be Explorers: the journal of a journey, 2006. *Address:* Queen Elizabeth II Infirmary, Charterhouse, Charterhouse Square, EC1M 6AN. *T:* (020) 7608 0313. *Clubs:* Reform, Royal Commonwealth Society. *Died 1 May 2012.*

JAMES, Sir Kenneth; *see* James, Sir C. M.

JAMES, P. D.; *see* Baroness James of Holland Park.

JAMES, Patrick Leonard, FRCS, FDS RCS; Hon. Consulting Oral and Maxillo-facial Surgeon: Royal London (formerly London) Hospital, Whitechapel (Senior Consultant Surgeon, 1963–91); North East Thames Regional Hospital Board Hospitals (Consultant Surgeon, 1963–91); Recognized Teacher in Oral Surgery, London University, since 1965; *b* 7 Jan. 1926; *s* of late John Vincent James and Priscilla Elsie James; *m* 1951, Jean Margaret, *er d* of Leslie and Ruth Hatcher; one *s* two *d*. *Educ:* King's Coll., London; London Hosp. FDSRCS 1958; FRCS 1985 (MRCS 1956); LRCP 1956. Served RAF, Flt Lieut, ME Comd, 1949–51. Sen. Registrar, Queen Victoria Hosp., E Grinstead, 1959–63; Hon. Consulting Oral and Maxillo-facial Surgeon: to London Hosp., Honey Lane Hosp., Waltham Abbey, Herts and Essex Hosp., Bishop's Stortford (Consultant Surgeon, 1963); to King George Hosp. (Consultant Surgeon, 1967); St Margaret's Hosp., Epping (Consultant Surgeon, 1966); Black Notley Hosp. (Consultant Surgeon, 1969); Hon. Civil Consultant (Oral and Maxillo-facial Surgery), RAF, 1989 (Civil Consultant in Oral Surgery, 1979–89). Exchange Fellow, Henry Ford Hosp., Detroit, Mich., 1962; Hunterian Prof., RCS, 1970–71. Member: Academic Bd, London Hosp. Med. Coll., 1968–71; Adv. Cttee in Plastic Surgery, NE Met. Reg. Hosp. Bd, 1969–77; NE Thames Reg. Manpower Cttee, 1975–78. Fellow: BAOS, 1963– (Mem. Council, 1971–74); Internat. Assoc. of Oral Surgs (BAOS Rep. on Council, 1974–78); Chm., Sci. Session, 6th Internat. Congress of Oral Surgs, Sydney, 1977; Associate Mem., Brit. Assoc. of Plastic Surgs, 1958–77. FRSocMed; Mem., Acad. of Expert Witnesses. Member: Council, Chelsea Clin. Soc.; Bd of Governors, Eastman Hosp., 1983–84. Liveryman, Soc. of Apothecaries, 1969; Freeman, City of London, 1978. *Publications:* (chapter in Oral Surgery) Malignancies in Odontogenic Cysts, 1967; (chapter in Oral Surgery) Correction of Apertognathia with Osteotomies and Bone Graft, 1970; (chapter in Oral Surgery, vol. 7) Surgical Treatment of Mandibular Joint Disorders, 1978; numerous articles on surgical treatment of mandibular joint disorders, surgery of salivary glands and maxillo facial surgery in med. and surg. jls. *Recreations:* reading, sailing (Cdre, United Hosps Sailing Club, 1968–75). *Address:* Meesden Hall, Meesden, Buntingford, Herts SG9 0AZ. *E:* patrickjames@btconnect.com. *Club:* Boodle's. *Died 14 April 2012.*

JAMES, Sir Stanislaus (Anthony), GCSL 1992; GCMG 1992 (CMG 1990); OBE 1985; Governor General of Saint Lucia, West Indies, 1988–96; *b* 13 Nov. 1919; *s* of Raymond and Theresa James; *m* 1952, Lucille MacDonald; two *s* two *d*. *Educ:* St Mary's Coll., St Lucia; Govt Training Coll., Trinidad; Univ. of Wales, Swansea; Carleton Univ., Ottawa. Educn Dept, St Lucia, 1944–46; Head, Public Relations and Social Welfare Dept, Probation Officer, 1948–50; Chief Clerk, Govt Office, 1954–56; PR and Social Welfare Officer, 1956–65; Perm. Sec., Min. of Trade, Industry, Agric. and Tourism, Min. of Housing, Community, Social Affairs and Labour, Min. of Educn and Health, 1965–74; National Co-ordinator: for Non-Govt Orgns, 1974–88; for Emergency Services, 1979–88. *Recreation:* horticulture. *Address:* Sunny Acres, Choc, Castries, St Lucia, West Indies. *T:* 4519562. *Died 26 May 2011.*

JAMES, (Thomas) Cecil (Garside), CMG 1966; Assistant Under-Secretary of State, Ministry of Defence, 1968–77; *b* 8 Jan. 1918; *s* of Joshua James, MBE, Ashton-under-Lyne; *m* 1941, Elsie Williams (*d* 2002), Ashton-under-Lyne; one *s* two *d*. *Educ:* Manchester Grammar Sch.; St John's Coll., Cambridge. Prin. Priv. Sec. to Sec. of State for Air, 1951–55; Asst Sec., Air Min., 1955; Civil Sec., FEAF, 1963–66; Chief of Public Relations, MoD, 1966–68. RAF historian. Order of Merit (Poland), 1998. *Publications:* The Battle of Britain, The Official Narrative, 2000; The Growth of Fighter Command 1936–40, 2002. *Address:* 4 The Granary, Wilson Road, Hadleigh, Suffolk IP7 5TJ. *Club:* Royal Air Force. *Died 1 Nov. 2011.*

JAMES, Walter; *see* James, A. W.

JAMESON, Derek; news, TV and radio commentator; Co-Presenter, Jamesons, Radio 2, 1992–97; *b* 29 Nov. 1929; *e s* of Mrs Elsie Jameson; *m* 1st, 1948, Jacqueline Sinclair (marr. diss. 1966); one *s* one *d*; 2nd, 1971, Pauline Tomlin (marr. diss. 1978); two *s*; 3rd, 1988, Ellen Petrie. *Educ:* elementary schools, Hackney. Office boy rising to Chief Sub-editor, Reuters, 1944–60; Editor, London American, 1960–61; features staff, Daily Express, 1961–63; Picture Editor, Sunday Mirror, 1963–65; Asst Editor, Sunday Mirror, 1965–72; Northern Editor, Sunday and Daily Mirror, 1972–76; Managing Editor, Daily Mirror, 1976–77; Editor, Daily Express, 1977–79; Editor-in-Chief, The Daily Star, 1978–80; Editor, News of the World, 1981–84. Presenter: Radio 2 Jameson Show, 1986–91; Jameson Tonight, Sky TV, 1989–90. *Publications:* Touched by Angels (autobiog.), 1988; Last of the Hot Metal Men (autobiog.), 1990. *Recreations:* opera, music, reading. *Address:* The Lodge, Broadwater Road, Worthing, Sussex BN14 8HU. *E:* derekjameson333@hotmail.com. *Died 12 Sept. 2012.*

JAMIESON, Air Marshal Sir (David) Ewan, KBE 1986 (OBE 1967); CB 1981; Chief of Defence Staff, New Zealand, 1983–86; *b* Christchurch, 19 April 1930; *s* of Judge R. D. Jamieson, CMG; *m* 1957, Margaret Elaine, *d* of L. J. Bridge; three *s* one *d*. *Educ:* Christchurch and New Plymouth Boys' High Sch. Joined RNZAF, 1949; OC Flying, Ohakea, 1964; CO Malaysia, 1965–66; Jt Services Staff Coll., 1969; CO Auckland, 1971–72; AOC Ops Group, 1974–76; RCDS 1977; Chief of Air Staff, RNZAF, 1979–83. *Address:* 14 Hinerau Grove, Taupo 3330, New Zealand. *Died 21 March 2013.*

JAMIESON, Susan Mary; *see* Ward, S. M.

JANNER OF BRAUNSTONE, Baron *cr* 1997 (Life Peer), of Leicester in the co. of Leicestershire; **Greville Ewan Janner;** QC 1971; barrister, author, lecturer, journalist and broadcaster; *b* 11 July 1928; *s* of Baron Janner and Lady Janner; *m* 1955, Myra Louise Sheink (*d* 1996), Melbourne; one *s* two *d*. *Educ:* Bishop's Coll. Sch., Canada; St Paul's Sch. (Foundn Schol.); Trinity Hall, Cambridge (Exhibnr; MA); Harvard Post Graduate Law School (Fulbright and Smith-Mundt Schol.); Harmsworth Scholar, Middle Temple, 1955. Nat. Service: Sgt RA, BAOR, War Crimes Investigator. Pres., Cambridge Union, 1952; Chm., Cambridge Univ. Labour Club, 1952; Internat. Sec., Nat. Assoc. of Labour Students, 1952; Pres., Trinity Hall Athletic Club, 1952. Contested (Lab) Wimbledon, 1955. MP (Lab) Leicester NW, 1970–74, Leicester W, 1974–97. Mem., Select Cttee on Employment, 1982–96 (Chm., 1992–96); Co-Chm., All Party Employment Gp, 1996–97; Chairman: All-Party Industrial Safety Gp, 1975–97; All-Party Magic Group, 1991–97; Founder, 1973, and former Chm., All-Party Cttee for Homeless and Rootless People; Founder, 1990, and Vice-Chm., 1990–92, All Party Race and Community Gp; Vice-Chairman: All-Party Parly Cttee for Jews in the Former Soviet Union (formerly Cttee for Release of Soviet Jewry), 1971–97; (Jt), British-Israel Parly Gp, 1983–2008 (Chm., 2008–); British-India Parly Gp, 1991–97 (Jt Vice-Chm., 1987–91); British-Spanish Parly Gp, 1987–97 (Sec., 1986); All-Party British-Romanian Gp, 1990–92; All-Party Parly Cttee for E Eur. Jewry, 1990–97; Sec., All-Party War Crimes Gp, 1987–97, 2000–; Founder and Pres. of World Exec., Inter-Parly Council Against Anti-Semitism, 1990–97. President: National Council for Soviet Jewry, 1979–85; Bd of Deputies of British Jews, 1979–85; Commonwealth Jewish Council, 1983–2012 (Founder Pres., 2012–); Assoc. of Jewish Ex-Servicemen and Women, 2009–12; Vice-President: Assoc. for Jewish Youth, 1970–; IVS, 1983–; World Jewish Congress: European Vice-Pres., 1984–86; Mem. World Exec., 1986–; Vice-Pres., 1990–2009; Hon. Vice-Pres., 2009–; Jt Pres., Coexistence Trust (formerly Political Council for Co-existence), 2005–12; Mem., Adv. Bd, Community Security Trust, 2006–. Partner, JSB Associates, 1984–88; Chm., JSB Gp Ltd, 1988–97 (Hon. Pres., 1997); non-exec. Dir, Ladbroke Plc, 1986–95. Member: Nat. Union of Journalists (Life Mem.); Soc. of Labour Lawyers; Magic Circle; Internat. Brotherhood of Magicians; Pres., REACH, 1982–; Pres., Jewish Museum, 1985–2001; Mem. Bd of Dirs, Jt Israel Appeal, 1985–; Vice-Pres., Guideposts Trust, 1983–; Founder and Pres., Maimonides Foundn, 1992–2002; Chairman: Holocaust Educnl Trust, 1987–2012 (Founding Patron, 2012–); Lord Forte Charitable Foundn, 1995–. Formerly Dir, Jewish Chronicle Newspaper Ltd; Trustee, Jewish Chronicle Trust. Hon. Mem., Leics NUM, 1986–. FIPD (FIPM 1976). Hon. PhD Haifa Univ., 1984; Hon. LLD: De Montfort, 1998; Leicester, 2008. Comdr, Order of Grand Duke Gediminas (Lithuania), 2002; Freedom of City of Gibraltar, and Gibraltar Medallion of Honour, 2012. *Publications:* 66 books, mainly on employment and industrial relations law, presentational skills, and on public speaking, including: Complete Speechmaker; Janner on Presentation; One Hand Alone Cannot Clap; To Life! (memoirs). *Recreations:* family, magic, languages—speaks nine. *Died 19 Dec. 2015.*

JANZON, Mrs Bengt; *see* Dobbs, M.

JARDINE, Prof. Lisa Anne, CBE 2005; FRS 2015; PhD; Director, Centre for Editing Lives and Letters, since 2002; Professor of Renaissance Studies, and Director, UCL Centre for Humanities Interdisciplinary Research Projects, University College London, since 2012; *b* 12 April 1944; *d* of Jacob Bronowski and Rita (*née* Coblenz); *m* 1st, 1969, Nicholas Jardine, FBA (marr. diss. 1979); one *s* one *d*; 2nd, 1982, John Robert Hare; one *s*. *Educ:* Cheltenham Ladies' Coll.; Newnham Coll., Cambridge (BA Maths and English 1966; MA 1968; PhD 1973); Univ. of Essex (MA 1967). Res. Fellow, Warburg Inst., Univ. of London, 1971–74; Lectr in Renaissance Literature, Univ. of Essex, 1974; Res. Fellow, Cornell Univ., 1974–75; University of Cambridge: Res. Fellow, Girton Coll., 1974–75; Fellow: King's Coll., 1975–76 (Hon. Fellow, 1995); Jesus Coll., 1976–89 (Hon. Fellow, 2006); Lectr in English, 1976–89; Reader in Renaissance English, 1989; Associate, Newnham Coll., 1992–2002; Prof. of Renaissance Studies, 1989–2005, Centenary Prof. of Renaissance Studies, 2005–12, QMW, later QMUL. Davis Center Fellow, Princeton Univ., 1987–88; Francis Bacon Vis. Prof. of Hist., Calif Inst. of Technol., 2014. Chm., AHRB Wkg Party on public understanding of the arts and humanities, 2002; Mem., AHRC (formerly AHRB), 2003–07 (Chm., Mus and Collections Cttee, 2004–07). Trustee: V & A Mus., 2003–11 (Chm., Collections Cttee, 2004–11; Chm., Bethnal Green Mus. Cttee, 2007–09); Artangel, 2006–08; Sir Joseph Banks Archive Proj., 2007; Chelsea Physic Garden 2011–; Mem. Council, Royal Instn, 2004–09; Patron: Nat. Council on Archives, 2007–09; Archives and Records Assoc., 2009–; non-exec. Dir, National Archives, 2011–. Chair, Human Fertilisation and Embryology Authy, 2008–14. Presenter: Night Waves, BBC Radio 3, 1992–96; author and presenter: A Point of View, 2006–; Seven Ages of Science, BBC Radio 4, 2013. Chair of Govs, Westminster City Sch., 1999–2006; London Dio. Bd for Schs Foundn Gov., St Marylebone Secondary Sch., 2006–11. Tanner Lectures, Yale Univ., 2012. Chair of Judges: Baileys Women's Prize for Fiction (formerly Orange Prize for Fiction), 1997 (Patron, 2010–); Booker Prize for Fiction, 2002; Mem., Michael Faraday Prize Cttee, Royal Soc., 2003–06. Mem., Apeldoorn British Dutch Conf. Steering Bd, 2009–12. President: British Sci. Assoc., 2013–14 (Hon. Fellow, 2012); Antiquarian Horology Assoc., 2014–. MAE 2013. FRHistS 1992; FRSA 1992. Hon. Bencher, Middle Temple, 2012. Hon. Dr: Sheffield Hallam, 2004; York, 2015; Hon. DLitt: St Andrews, 2005; Keele, 2014; DUniv Open, 2006; Hon. DSc Aberdeen, 2011. President's Medal, British Acad., 2012; Bacon Medal for History of Sci., CIT, 2012. *Publications:* Francis Bacon: discovery and the art of discourse, 1974; Still Harping on Daughters: women and drama in the age of Shakespeare, 1983; (jtly) From Humanism to the Humanities: education and the liberal arts in fifteenth- and sixteenth-century Europe, 1986; (jtly) What's Left? Women In Culture and the Labour Movement, 1989; Erasmus, Man of Letters, 1993; Reading Shakespeare Historically, 1996; Wordly Goods: a new history of the Renaissance, 1996; Erasmus, the Education of a Christian Prince, 1997; (jtly) Hostage to Fortune: the troubled life of Francis Bacon, 1998; Ingenious Pursuits:

building the scientific revolution, 1999; Francis Bacon, A New Organon and Other Writings, 1999; (jtly) Global Interests: Renaissance art between East and West, 2000; On a Grander Scale: the outstanding career of Sir Christopher Wren, 2002; The Curious Life of Robert Hooke: the man who measured London, 2003; (jtly) London's Leonardo, 2003; The Awful End of Prince William the Silent, 2005; Going Dutch: how England plundered Holland's glory, 2008 (Cundill Internat. History Prize, 2009); A Point of View, 2008; Another Point of View, 2009; Temptation in the Archives: essays in Golden Age Dutch culture, 2015; contribs to newspapers, numerous articles in learned jls. *Recreations:* conversation, cookery, contemporary art. *Address:* 51 Bedford Court Mansions, Bedford Avenue, WC1B 3AA. *Died 25 Oct. 2015.*

JARDINE, Ronald Charles C.; *see* Cunningham-Jardine.

JARMAN, Nicholas Francis Barnaby; QC 1985; barrister; a Recorder of the Crown Court, since 1982; *b* 19 June 1938; *s* of late A. S. Jarman and Helene Jarman; *m* 1st, 1973, Jennifer Michelle Lawrence-Smith (marr. diss. 1978); one *d*; 2nd, 1989, Julia Elizabeth MacDougall (*née* Owen-John). *Educ:* Harrow; Christ Church, Oxford (MA Jurisprudence). Commnd RA, 1956–58 (JUO Mons, 1957). Called to the Bar, Inner Temple, 1965 (Duke of Edinburgh Scholar). Bar Chm., Bucks, Berks and Oxon Jt Liaison Cttee, 1986–96. Pres., Mental Health Appeals Tribunal, 2000–05. *Recreations:* France, fly-fishing. *Address:* Le Domaine de Vallagrand, 30700 Flaux, France. *T:* (4) 66030308; 12 Chatsworth Court, W8 6DG. *Club:* Garrick. *Died 17 Feb. 2015.*

JARRETT, Prof. William Fleming Hoggan, FRS 1980; FRSE 1965; Professor of Veterinary Pathology, 1968–91, Senior Research Fellow, 1991, University of Glasgow; *b* 2 Jan. 1928; *s* of James and Jessie Jarrett; *m* 1952, Anna Fraser Sharp (*d* 2010); two *d*. *Educ:* Lenzie Academy; Glasgow Veterinary Coll.; Univ. of Glasgow; PhD, FRCVS, FRCPath. Gold Medal, 1949; John Henry Steele Meml Medal, 1961; Steele Bodger Meml Schol. 1955. ARC Research Student, 1949–52; Lectr, Dept of Veterinary Pathology, Univ. of Glasgow Vet. Sch., 1952–53; Head of Hospital Path. Dept of Vet. Hosp., Univ. of Glasgow, 1953–61; Reader in Pathology, Univ. of Glasgow, 1962–65; seconded to Univ. of E Africa, 1963–64; Titular Prof. of Experimental Vet. Medicine, Univ. of Glasgow, 1965. Lectures: Leeuwenhoek, Royal Soc., 1986; McFadyean Meml, RVC, 1986. Fogarty Scholar, NIH, 1985. Hon. FRCPSGlas 1988. Dr *hc* Liège Univ., 1986; DUniv Stirling, 1988; Hon. DSc: East Anglia, 1989; Edinburgh, 1989; Hon. DVSc RVC, London, 1991. Centennial Award, Univ. of Pennsylvania, 1984; Makdougall Brisbane Prize, RSE, 1984; J. T. Edwards Meml Medal, RCVS, 1984; Feldberg Prize, 1987; Tenovus-Scotland Margaret McLellan Award, 1989; Saltire Award, 1989; WSAVA Waltham Internat. Award, 1991. *Publications:* various, on tumour viruses, leukaemia and immunology. *Recreations:* sailing, ski-ing, mountaineering, music. *Clubs:* Clyde Cruising; Glencoe Ski. *Died 27 Aug. 2011.*

JEBB, Dom (Anthony) Philip, MA; Prior, Downside Abbey, 1991–2001; Cathedral Prior, Bath, since 2002; Parish Priest, Radstock, 1998–2002; *b* 14 Aug. 1932; 2nd *s* of late Reginald Jebb and Eleanor, *d* of Hilaire Belloc. *Educ:* Downside; Christ's Coll., Cambridge, 1957–60 (MA Classics). Professed at Downside, 1951; priest, 1956; Curate, Midsomer Norton, 1960–62; teaching at Downside, 1960–97; House master, 1962–75; Dep. Head Master, 1975–80; Headmaster, 1980–91; Dir of Sch. Appeal, 1996–98; Guest Master, 2003–07. Archivist and Annalist, English Benedictine Congregation, 1972–2009; Mem., EBC Theological Commn, 1969–82 (Chm., 1979–82); Delegate to General Chapter, EBC, 1981–2001; Mem., Central Cttee, 1987–88, Chm., SW Div., 1988, HMC; Member: Council, Somerset Records Soc., 1975–97; Cttee, Area 7, SHA, 1984–91; Court, Bath Univ., 1983–85. Trustee, Somerset Archaeol and Natural Hist. Soc., 1989–97 (Pres., 1993–94). Vice-Pres., SW Amateur Fencing Assoc., 1970–. Chaplain of Magistral Obedience, British Assoc., Sovereign Mil. Order of Malta, 1978–; Asst Chaplain, Shepton Mallet Prison, 1995–2001. Gov., St Antony's-Leweston Sch., 1980–97. *Publications:* Missale de Lesnes, 1964; Religious Education, 1968; Widowed, 1973, 2nd edn 1976; contrib. Consider Your Call, 1978, 2nd edn 1979; A Touch of God, 1982; (ed) By Death Parted, 1986; In a Quiet Garden, 1999; contribs to Downside Review, The Way, The Sword. *Recreations:* fencing, archaeology, astronomy, canoeing. *Address:* Downside Abbey, Stratton-on-the-Fosse, Radstock BA3 4RH. *T:* (01761) 235148. *Died 8 June 2014.*

JEFFERIES, Sheelagh, CBE 1987; Deputy Director General, 1983–87, Acting Director General, Jan.–June 1987, Central Office of Information; *b* 25 Aug. 1926; *d* of late Norman and Vera Jefferies. *Educ:* Harrogate Grammar Sch.; Girton Coll., Cambridge (MA); Smith Coll., Northampton, Mass, USA (MA). FCIPR; FCAM. Archivist, RIIA, 1947–50, 1951–52; COI, 1953–60; Office of Chancellor of Duchy of Lancaster, 1960–61; Press Officer, Prime Minister's Office, 1961–67; Principal Inf. Officer, Privy Council Office, 1967–69; Chief Press Officer, Min. of Housing and Local Govt, 1969–71; Head of Parly Liaison Unit and later Head of News, DoE, 1971–74; Chief Inf. Officer, Dept of Prices and Consumer Protection, 1974–77; Central Office of Information: Dir, Overseas Press and Radio, 1977–78; Controller (Home), 1978–83. Press Consultant, WRVS, 1988–92. *Recreations:* reading, conversation. *Died 22 May 2014.*

JEFFERS, John Norman Richard, CStat; CBiol, FSB; FICFor; consultant; Visiting Professor: Mechanical, Materials and Manufacturing, University of Newcastle, since 1994; Mathematical Institute, University of Kent, since 1993; School of Mathematics, Statistics and Computing, University of Greenwich, since 1994; *b* 10 Sept. 1926; *s* of late Lt-Col John Harold Jeffers, OBE, and Emily Matilda Alice (*née* Robinson); *m* 1951, Edna May (*née* Parratt); one *d*. *Educ:* Portsmouth Grammar Sch.; Forestry Commission Forester Trng Sch., 1944–46. Forester in Forestry Commn Research Br., 1946–55; joined Min. of Agriculture, 1955, as Asst Statistician, after succeeding in limited competition to Statistician Class; rejoined Forestry Commn as Head of Statistics Section of Forestry Commn Research Br., 1956; Dir, Nature Conservancy's Merlewood Research Station, 1968; Dep. Dir, Inst. of Terrestrial Ecology, NERC, 1973, Dir, 1976–86. Editor, Internat. Jl of Sustainable Develt and World Ecology, 1994–. Hon. DSc Lancaster, 1988. *Publications:* Experimental Design and Analysis in Forest Research, 1959; Mathematical Models in Ecology, 1972; Introduction to Systems Analysis: with ecological applications, 1978; Modelling, 1982; Practitioner's Manual on the Modelling of Dynamic Change in Ecosystems, 1988; Microcomputers in Environmental Biology, 1990; Research, Ecology and Environment, 2003; numerous papers in stat., forestry and ecol. jls. *Recreations:* military history and wargaming, amateur dramatics. *Address:* Little Thatch, Arrowsmith Road, Wimborne, Dorset BH21 3BE. *T:* (01202) 697696. *Died 28 Nov. 2011.*

JEFFERSON, Bryan; *see* Jefferson, J. B.

JEFFERSON, Sir George Rowland, Kt 1981; CBE 1969; BSc Hons (London); FREng, Hon. FIMechE, FIET, FRAeS; FCGI; Chairman, 1981–87 and Chief Executive, 1981–86, British Telecommunications plc; *b* 26 March 1921; *s* of Harold Jefferson and Eva Elizabeth Ellen; *m* 1943, Irene Watson-Browne (*d* 1998); three *s*. *Educ:* Grammar Sch., Dartford, Kent. Engrg Apprentice, Royal Ordnance Factory, Woolwich, 1937–42; commnd RAOC, 1942; transf. REME, 1942; served 1942–45, Anti-Aircraft Comd on heavy anti-aircraft power control systems and later Armament Design Dept, Fort Halstead, on anti-aircraft gun mounting development; subseq. Mem. Min. of Supply staff, Fort Halstead, until 1952; joined Guided Weapons Div., English Electric Co. Ltd, 1952; Chief Research Engr, 1953; Dep. Chief Engr, 1958; Dir, English Electric Aviation Ltd, 1961 (on formation of co.); British Aircraft Corporation: Dir and Chief Exec., BAC (Guided Weapons) Ltd, 1963 (on formation of Corp.), Dep. Man. Dir, 1964, Mem. Board, 1965–77, Man. Dir, 1966–68, Chm. and Man. Dir, 1968–77; a Dir, British Aerospace, and Chm. and Chief Exec., Dynamics Gp, British Aerospace, 1977–80 (Mem., Organizing Cttee, 1976–77); Chm., Stevenage/Bristol and

Hatfield/Lostock Divs, Dynamics Gp, 1978–80; Chm., BAC (Anti-Tank), 1968–78; Dep. Chm., Post Office, 1980; Chm., 1981–87, Chief Exec., 1981–86, British Telecommunications plc. Chairman: Matthew Hall, 1987–88; City Centre Communications, 1988–90; Videotron Corp., 1990–97. Director: British Aerospace (Australia) Ltd, 1968–80; British Scandinavian Aviation AB, 1968–80; Hawker Siddeley Dynamics, 1977–80; Engineering Sciences Data Unit Ltd, 1975–80; Babcock International, 1980–87; Lloyds Bank, 1986–89; AMEC, 1988–91. Member: NEB, 1979–80; NEDC, 1981–84; NICG, 1980–84; Member Council: SBAC, 1965–80; Electronic Engineering Assoc., 1968–72; RAeS, 1977–79 (Vice-Pres., 1979). Freeman of the City of London. FRSA; CCMI. Hon. DSc Bristol, 1984; DUniv Essex, 1985. *Address:* Suncroft, Bracklin, Edgeworthstown, Near Longford, County Longford, Republic of Ireland. *Died 1 Sept. 2012.*

JEFFERSON, (John) Bryan, CB 1989; CBE 1983; PPRIBA; Architectural Adviser to Department for Culture, Media and Sport (formerly National Heritage), 1993–2001; Visiting Professor, School of Architecture, Sheffield University, 1992–2000; *b* 26 April 1928; *s* of John Jefferson and Marjorie Jefferson (*née* Oxley); *m* 1st, 1954, Alison Gray (marr. diss. 1965); two *s* (and one *s* decd); 2nd, 1999, Jean Marsden. *Educ:* Lady Manners Sch., Bakewell; Sheffield Univ. DipArch 1954. ARIBA 1954. Morrison and Partners, Derby, 1955–57; established practice in Sheffield and London with Gerald F. Sheard, 1957; Sen. Partner, Jefferson Sheard and Partners, 1957–84; Dir-Gen. of Design, PSA, DoE, 1984–89; Chm., PSA Projects, DoE, 1989–92; Mem., Standing Cttee on Structl Safety, 1991–99. President: Sheffield Soc. of Architects, 1973–74; Concrete Soc., 1977–78; RIBA, 1979–81; Chm., RIBA Yorks Region, 1974–75. Trustee, Civic Trust, 1998–2003. Hon. FRAIC 1980; Hon. Mem., RICS 1987. Hon. DEng Bradford, 1986; Hon. LittD Sheffield, 1992. *Publications:* broadcasts; articles in lay and professional jls. *Recreation:* music. *Address:* 6 St Andrews Mansions, Dorset Street, W1U 4EQ. *Club:* Royal Automobile. *Died 19 Oct. 2014.*

JEFFERSON, Sir Mervyn Stewart D.; *see* Dunnington-Jefferson.

JEFFRIES, Prof. Donald James, CBE 2007; FRCP, FRCPath; Professor of Virology, Barts and the London, Queen Mary's School of Medicine and Dentistry (formerly St Bartholomew's Hospital Medical College), University of London, 1990–2006, then Professor Emeritus; Hon. Consultant in Virology, Barts and the London NHS Trust (formerly St Bartholomew's Hospital), 1990–2006; *b* 29 Aug. 1941; *s* of late Edmond Frederick Jeffries and Eileen Elizabeth (*née* Elton); *m* 1966, Mary Millicent Bray; two *s* one *d*. *Educ:* William Ellis Grammar Sch., Highgate; Royal Free Hosp. Sch. of Medicine (BSc Hons Physiol. 1963; MB BS 1966). MRCPath 1974, FRCPath 1986; FRCP 2001. St Mary's Hospital Medical School: Sen. Registrar in Microbiol., 1970–72; Lectr in Virol., 1972–74; Sen. Lectr in Virol., 1974–87; Reader, 1987–90; Hd, Div. of Virol., 1982–90; Dir, Clinical Studies, 1985–90; Hd, Microbiol. and Virol. Clinical Service, Barts and the London NHS Trust, 1998–2006. Vis. Prof., Univ. of Riyadh, 1988; C. T. Huang Lectr, Hong Kong Univ., 1991; Wellcome Vis. Prof., Coll. of Medicine of S Africa, 1993. Consultant in Virol., St John Ambulance, 1994–. Sen. Examr, Univ. of London, 1993–2000. Chairman: Transmissible Spongiform Encephalopathies Wkg Gp, Adv. Cttee on Dangerous Pathogens, 1999–; Decontamination Res. Gp, DoH, 2000–; Expert Adv. Gp on AIDS, DoH, 2003–05 (Mem., 1992–2002); Steering Gp on Health Care Associated Infections, HPA, 2004–07; Assoc. of British Insurers Expert Wkg Gp on HIV, 2005–08; Expert Adv. Gp on Health and Insurance, 2008–; Member: Adv. Cttee on Genetic Modification, HSE, 1988–99; UK Adv. Panel for Health Care Workers infected with blood-borne viruses, 1992–2002; Adv. Cttee on Dangerous Pathogens, 1993–2002; Diagnostics and Imaging Panel, NHS Health Technol. Assessment, 1993–98; CJD Incidents Panel (Dep. Chm., 2000–; Actg Chm., 2003–05); Cttee on Safety of Medicines, 2001–05 (Mem., Biologicals Sub-cttee, 1999–2005, Chm., 2003–05); Nat. Expert Panel on New and Emerging Infections, 2003–07; Adv. Cttee on Decontamination Sci. and Technol., DoH, 2009–. Royal College of Pathologists: Mem. Council, 1996–2002; Vice-Pres., 1999–2002; Chairman: Virol. Examrs' Panel, 1995–2000; Exams Cttee, 1999–2002; Special Adv. Cttee in Microbiol., 1999–2002; Chm., Jt Cttee on Infection and Tropical Medicine, RCP/RCPath, 1999–2002. Member: Soc. Gen. Microbiol., 1970–; Hosp. Infection Soc., 1980– (Mem. Council, 1980–83 and 1990–93). Ellison Nash Prize, Barts and the London, 2001. *Publications:* Lecture Notes on Medical Virology, 1987; (ed jtly) Current Topics in AIDS, Vol. I 1987, Vol. II 1989: (ed with E. de Clercq) Antiviral Chemotherapy, 1995; (ed with C. N. Hudson) Viral Infections in Obstetrics and Gynaecology, 1999; papers and reviews on aspects of medical virology, especially HIV/AIDS, antiviral drugs, herpes viruses. *Recreations:* hill walking, fly fishing, gardening. *Address:* 63 Manor Park Avenue, Princes Risborough, Bucks HP27 9AS. *T:* (01844) 343821. *E:* d.j.jeffries@qmul.ac.uk. *Died 7 Dec. 2011.*

JENKINS, Christopher Dennis Alexander M.; *see* Martin-Jenkins.

JENKINS, Ven. David Thomas Ivor; Archdeacon of Westmorland and Furness, 1995–99, then Emeritus; *b* 3 June 1929; *s* of Edward Evan and Edith Olwen Jenkins; *m* 1st, 1953, Rosemary German (*d* 1990); one *d*; 2nd, 1992, Kathleen Theresa Sidey. *Educ:* King's Coll. London (BD, AKC); Birmingham Univ. (MA (Theol.)). Ordained deacon, 1953, priest, 1954; Asst Curate, St Mark's Bilton, Rugby, 1953–56; Vicar, St Margaret's, Wolston, Coventry, 1956–61; Asst Dir, Religious Educn, Dio. of Carlisle, 1961–63; Vicar: St Barnabas, Carlisle, 1963–72; St Cuthbert's, Carlisle, 1972–91; Canon Residentiary, Carlisle Cathedral, 1991–95, Canon Emeritus, 2000. Sec., Carlisle Diocesan Synod and Bishop's Council, 1972–95; Diocesan Synod Sec., 1984–95; Sec., Synod of Convocation of York, 1985–2005. *Recreations:* golf, reading, good food and wine with friends, foreign travel. *Address:* Irvings House, Sleagill, Penrith, Cumbria CA10 3HD. *T:* (01931) 714400. *Died 16 Sept. 2014.*

JENKINS, Very Rev. Frank Graham; Dean of Monmouth and Vicar of St Woolos, 1976–90; *b* 24 Feb. 1923; *s* of Edward and Miriam M. Jenkins; *m* 1950, Ena Doraine Parry; two *s* one *d*. *Educ:* Cyfarthfa Sec. Sch., Merthyr Tydfil; Port Talbot Sec. Sch.; St David's Coll., Lampeter (BA Hist); Jesus Coll., Oxford (BA Theol., MA); St Michael's Coll., Llandaff. HM Forces, 1942–46. Deacon 1950, priest 1951, Llandaff; Asst Curate, Llangeinor, 1950–53; Minor Canon, Llandaff Cathedral, 1953–60; CF (TA), 1956–61; Vicar of Abertillery, 1960–64; Vicar of Risca, 1964–75; Canon of Monmouth, 1967–76; Vicar of Caerleon, 1975–76. *Address:* Gravelly Close, Bottom Road, Radnage, High Wycombe, Bucks HP14 4EQ. *T:* (01494) 485258. *Died 22 Oct. 2011.*

JENKINS, Sir Michael (Romilly Heald), KCMG 1990 (CMG 1984); CRAeS; Senior Adviser, since 2010, and Chairman, Advisory Board, since 2011, Kleinwort Benson; *b* 9 Jan. 1936; *s* of late Prof. Romilly Jenkins and Juliette Celine Haeglar; *m* 1968, Maxine Louise Hodson; one *s* one *d*. *Educ:* St Christopher Sch., Letchworth; privately; King's Coll., Cambridge (Exhibr, BA). Entered Foreign (subseq. Diplomatic) Service, 1959; served in Paris, Moscow and Bonn; Deputy Chef de Cabinet, 1973–75, Chef de Cabinet, 1975–76, to Rt Hon. George Thomson, EEC; Principal Advr to Mr Roy Jenkins, Pres. EEC, Jan.–Aug. 1977; Head of European Integration Dept (External), FCO, 1977–79; Hd of Central Adv. Gp, EEC, 1979–81; Dep. Sec. Gen., Commn of the Eur. Communities, 1981–83; Asst Under Sec. of State (Europe), FCO, 1983–85; Minister, Washington, 1985–87; Ambassador to the Netherlands, 1988–93; Exec. Dir, 1993–96, Vice-Chm., 1996–2003, Kleinwort Benson Gp, then Dresdner Kleinwort Benson, subseq. Dresdner Kleinwort Wasserstein. Director: Aegon NV, 1995–2001; EO plc, 2000–02; Frontiers Capital, 2006– (Chm., 2008–); GeoPark Hldgs Ltd, 2006–; Chm., Matra Petroleum plc, 2007–; Pres., Boeing UK, 2003–05. Member: European Exec. Cttee, Trilateral Commn, 1994–99; President's Adv. Council, Atlantic Council, 1994–. Comr, Royal Hospital Chelsea, 2007–13 (Dep. Chm., 2011–13). Chairman, Action Centre for Europe, 1995–2004. Advr, Prince's

Trust, 2002–. CRAeS 2004. *Publications:* Arakcheev, Grand Vizier of the Russian Empire, 1969; A House in Flanders, 1992; (ed) The View from Downshire Hill (memoir), by Elizabeth Jenkins, 2004; contrib. History Today. *Address:* c/o Kleinwort Benson, 14 St George Street, W1S 1FE. *Clubs:* Brooks's, Pilgrims, MCC (Treas., 1999–2000; Chm., 2000–01; Trustee 2001–07). *Died 31 March 2013.*

JENKINS, Thomas Harris, (Tom), CBE 1981; General Secretary, Transport Salaried Staffs' Association, 1977–82; *b* 29 Aug. 1920; *s* of David Samuel Jenkins and Miriam Hughes (*née* Harris); *m* 1946, Joyce Smith; two *d. Educ:* Port Talbot Central Boys' Sch.; Port Talbot County Sch.; Shrewsbury Technical Coll. (evenings); Pitman's Coll., London (evenings). Served War, RAMC, 1941–46 (Certif. for Good Service, Army, Western Comd, 1946). Railway clerk, 1937–41; railway/docks clerk, 1946–49. Full-time service with Railway Clerks' Assoc., subseq. re-named Transport Salaried Staffs' Assoc., 1949–82: Southern Reg. Divl Sec., 1959; Western Reg. Divl Sec., 1963; LMR Divl Sec., 1966; Sen. Asst Sec., 1968; Asst Gen. Sec., 1970, also Dep. to Gen. Sec., 1973. Member: Cttee of Transport Workers in European Community, 1976–82; Transport Industry, Nationalised Industries, and Hotel and Catering Industry Cttees of TUC, 1977–82; Management and Indus. Relns Cttee, SSRC, 1979–81; Air Transport and Travel Industry Trng Bd, 1976–82; Hotel and Catering Industry Trng Bd, 1978–82; Employment Appeal Tribunal, 1982–91; British Railways Midland and NW Reg. Bd, 1982–86; Police Complaints Bd, 1983–85; Central Arbitration Cttee, 1983–90; ACAS Arbitration Bd, 1983–90. Mem. Labour Party, 1946–; Mem., Lab. Party Transport Sub-Cttee, 1970–82. *Recreations:* watching cricket, athletics and Rugby football. *Address:* 23 The Chase, Edgware, Middx HA8 5DW. *T:* (020) 8952 5314. *Died 18 July 2012.*

JENKINSON, Dr David Stewart, FRS 1991; Lawes Trust Senior Fellow, Rothamsted Research (formerly Rothamsted Experimental Station), since 1990; *b* 25 Feb. 1928; *s* of Hugh McLoughlin Jenkinson and Isabel Frances (*née* Glass); *m* 1958, Moira O'Brien; three *s* one *d. Educ:* Armagh Royal Sch.; Trinity Coll., Dublin (BA 1950; BSc 1950; PhD 1954). MRSC 1955. Asst Lectr, Univ. of Reading, 1955–57; on scientific staff, Rothamsted Exptl Station, 1957–88. Hannaford Res. Fellow, Univ. of Adelaide, 1976–77; Vis. Scientist, CSIRO, 1977. Vis. Prof., Univ. of Reading, 1992–2009. Lectures: Hannaford, Univ. of Adelaide, 1977; Distinguished Scholars, QUB, 1989; Univ. of Kent, 1992; Massey Ferguson Nat. Agricl Award, 1993. Hon. Member: Soil Science Soc. of Amer., 1995; British Soc. of Soil Science, 2007. *Publications:* Nitrogen Efficiency in Agricultural Soils, 1988; numerous papers in jls of soil science, soil biochemistry and agronomy. *Recreations:* Irish history and literature, low input gardening. *Address:* 15 Topstreet Way, Harpenden, Herts AL5 5TU. *T:* (01582) 715744. *Died 16 Feb. 2011.*

JENNINGS, James, OBE 1998; JP; Convener, Strathclyde Regional Council, 1986–90; *b* 18 Feb. 1925; *s* of late Mark Jennings and Janet McGrath; *m* 1st, 1943, Margaret Cook Barclay (decd); three *s* two *d*; 2nd, 1974, Margaret Mary Hughes, JP (decd); two *d. Educ:* St Palladius School, Dalry; St Michael's College, Irvine. In steel industry, 1946–79. Member: Ayr County Council, 1958 (Chairman: Police and Law Cttee, 1964–70; Ayrshire Jt Police Cttee, 1970–75; N Ayrshire Crime Prevention Panel, 1970–82); Strathclyde Regional Council, 1974–96 (Chm., Police and Fire Cttee, 1978–82, 1990–96; Vice-Convener, 1982–86); N Ayrshire Unitary Council, 1995– (Chm., Social Work Cttee, 1995–). Convention of Scottish Local Authorities: Rep. for Strathclyde, 1974–96; Chm., Protective Services Cttee, 1977–82; Mem., Exec. Policy Cttee, 1982–96. Chm., Official Side, Police Negotiating Bd, 1986–88, 1992–94 (Vice-Chm., 1984–86). Chm., Garnock Valley Develt Exec., 1988–. Contested (Lab) Perth and East Perthshire, 1966. Hon. Sheriff, Kilmarnock, 1991–. Hon. Vice-President: Royal British Legion Scotland (Dalry and District Branch); Scottish Junior FA, 1994. JP Cunninghame, 1969 (Chm., Cunninghame Justices Cttee, 1974–). Freeman, N Ayrshire, 1997. *Recreation:* local community involvement. *Address:* 4 Place View, Kilbirnie, Ayrshire KA25 6BG. *T:* (01505) 683339. *Clubs:* Garnock Labour (Chairman), Garnock Community. *Died 25 Jan. 2013.*

JEPHCOTT, Sir Neil (Welbourn), 3rd Bt *cr* 1962, of East Portlemouth, Devon; engineer; *b* 3 June 1929; *yr s* of Sir Harry Jephcott, 1st Bt and Doris Jephcott (*née* Gregory); *S* brother, 2003; *m* 1st, 1951, Mary Denise Muddiman (*d* 1977); two *s* one *d*; 2nd, 1978, Mary Florence Daly. *Educ:* Emmanuel Coll., Cambridge (MA). MIMarEST 1955, CEng 1960, MIMechE 1960. Engine Repair Manager, J. I. Thornycroft & Co., 1956–61; Asst Gen. Manager, Silley Cox & Co., 1961–69; Managing Director: Ocean Aids, 1969–71; W. Visick & Sons, 1972–82; Surveyor to Amer. Bureau of Shipping & Bureau Veritas, 1982–90. *Recreations:* yachting, bell ringing. *Heir: s* David Welbourn Jephcott [*b* 9 Aug. 1952; *m* 1977, Madeleine Ann, *d* of Maurice Arthur Burridge; one *d*]. *Address:* Thalassa, East Portlemouth, Salcombe, Devon TQ8 8PU. *Clubs:* Royal Society of Medicine, Royal Ocean Racing. *Died 12 Aug. 2012.*

JEVONS, Prof. Frederic Raphael, AO 1986; Hon. Professorial Associate, Department of History and Philosophy of Science, University of Melbourne, Australia, 1996–2005; *b* 19 Sept. 1929; *s* of Fritz and Hedwig Bettelheim; *m* 1956, Grete; two *s. Educ:* Langley Sch., Norwich; King's Coll., Cambridge (Major Schol.). 1st Cl. Hons Nat. Scis Pt II (Biochem.) Cantab 1950; PhD Cantab 1953; DSc Manchester 1966. Postdoctoral Fellow, Univ. of Washington, Seattle, 1953–54; Fellow, King's Coll., Cambridge, 1953–59; Univ. Demonstrator in Biochem., Cambridge, 1956–59; Lectr in Biol Chem., Manchester Univ., 1959–66; Prof. of Liberal Studies in Science, Manchester Univ., 1966–75; Vice-Chancellor, Deakin Univ., Australia, 1976–85, subseq. Emeritus Prof.; consultant on distance educn in southern Africa, 1986–87; Prof. of Science and Technology Policy, Murdoch Univ., Australia, 1988–92. Simon Sen. Res. Fellow, Univ. of Manchester, 1992; Hon. Professorial Fellow, Dept of Mgt, Monash Univ., 1994–96. Chairman: Gen. Studies Cttee, Schools Council, 1974–75; Grad. Careers Council of Aust., 1976–80; Policy Cttee, Victorian Technical and Further Educn Off-Campus Network, 1985–88; Member: Jt Matriculation Bd, Manchester, 1969–75; Jt Cttee, SRC and SSRC, 1974–75; Educn Res. and Develt Cttee, Aust., 1980–81; Council, Sci. Mus. of Vic., 1980–83; Council, Mus. of Vic., 1983–87; Aust. Vice-Chancellors' Exec. Cttee, 1981–82; Standing Cttee on External Studies, Commonwealth Tertiary Educn Commn, Canberra, 1985–87; Aust. Sci. and Technol. Council, 1986–89. Interviewer for Civil Service Commn on Final Selection Bds, 1970–75; Adviser to Leverhulme project on educnl objectives in applied science, Strathclyde Univ., 1972–75; British Council tours in India, E Africa, Nigeria, 1972–75. Mem., Editorial Advisory Boards: R and D Management, 1972–76; Studies in Science Educn, 1974–84; Scientometrics, 1978–; Australasian Studies in History and Philosophy of Science, 1980–86. Life Gov., Geelong Hosp., 1986. DUniv Open, 1985; Hon. DLitt Deakin, 1986; Hon. DSc Manchester, 1986. Inaugural winner, UNESCO prize for science and technology policy, 1992. *Publications:* The Biochemical Approach to Life, 1964, 2nd edn 1968 (trans. Italian, Spanish, Japanese, German); The Teaching of Science: education, science and society, 1969; (ed jtly) University Perspectives, 1970; (jtly) Wealth from Knowledge: studies of innovation in industry, 1972; (ed jtly) What Kinds of Graduates do we Need?, 1972; Science Observed: science as a social and intellectual activity, 1973; Knowledge and Power, 1976; numerous papers on biochem., history of science, science educn and science policy. *Recreations:* music, theatre, reading. *Address:* 21 Goodwin Street, Glen Iris, Vic 3146, Australia. *T:* (3) 98892441. *E:* colin.jevons@gmail.com; 162 B Solomon Street, South Fremantle, WA 6162, Australia. *Died 30 Sept. 2012.*

JHABVALA, Mrs Ruth Prawer, CBE 1998; author; *b* in Germany, of Polish parents, 7 May 1927; *d* of Marcus Prawer and Eleonora Prawer (*née* Cohn); came to England as refugee, 1939; *m* 1951, C. S. H. Jhabvala; three *d. Educ:* Hendon County Sch.; Queen Mary Coll., London Univ. Started writing after graduation and marriage, alternating between novels and short stories; occasional original filmscripts (with James Ivory and Ismail Merchant), including: Shakespeare-wallah, 1965; The Guru, 1969; Bombay Talkie, 1971; Autobiography of a Princess, 1975; Roseland, 1977; Hullabaloo over Georgie and Bonnie's Pictures, 1978; The Europeans (based on Henry James' novel), 1979; Jane Austen in Manhattan, 1980; Quartet (based on Jean Rhys' novel), 1981; Heat and Dust (based on own novel), 1983; The Bostonians (based on Henry James' novel), 1984; A Room with a View (based on E. M. Forster's novel), 1986 (Academy Award, 1987); Mr and Mrs Bridge (based on Evan Connell's novels), 1991; Howards End (based on E. M. Forster's novel), 1992 (Academy Award, 1993); Remains of the Day (based on Kazuo Ishiguro's novel), 1993; Jefferson in Paris, 1995; Surviving Picasso, 1996; A Soldier's Daughter Never Cries, 1998; The Golden Bowl (based on Henry James' novel), 2000; City of Your Final Destination, 2010; film script (with John Schlesinger), Madame Sousatzka, 1988. *Publications: novels:* To Whom She Will, 1955; The Nature of Passion, 1956; Esmond in India, 1958; The Householder, 1960; Get Ready for Battle, 1962; A Backward Place, 1965; A New Dominion, 1973; Heat and Dust, 1975 (Booker Prize, 1975); In Search of Love and Beauty, 1983; Three Continents, 1987; Poet and Dancer, 1993; Shards of Memory, 1995; My Nine Lives: chapters of a possible past, 2004; *short story collections:* Like Birds, like Fishes, 1964; A Stronger Climate, 1968; An Experience of India, 1971; How I became a Holy Mother and other Stories, 1976; Out of India: selected stories, 1986; East into Upper East, 1998; A Lovesong for India, 2011. *Address:* 400 East 52nd Street, New York, NY 10022, USA. *Died 3 April 2013.*

JOBS, Steven Paul; Joint Founder, 1975, and Chairman, since 2011, Apple Inc. (formerly Apple Computer Inc.) (Chief Executive Officer, 2000–11); *b* 1955; adopted *s* of Paul and Clara Jobs; one *d*; *m* 1991, Laurene Powell; one *s* two *d*. *Educ:* Homestead High Sch.; Reed Coll. Electronics engr; Video Game Designer, Atari Inc., 1974; Apple Computer Inc., later Apple Inc.: Jt Designer, Apple I computer, 1976; Chm., 1975–77, 1981–84; Dir, 1995–; Consultant, 1995; Pres., NeXT Inc., 1985–96 (CEO); Chm. and CEO, Pixar Animation Studios, 1986–2006. *Address:* c/o Apple Inc., 1 Infinite Loop, Cupertino, CA 95014–2084, USA. *Died 5 Oct. 2011.*

JOHN-CHARLES, Most Rev. Brother; *see* Vockler, Most Rev. J. C.

JOHNSON, Anne Montgomrey; Market Research, Harris Research Centre, 1983–92; *b* 12 June 1922; *y c* of late Frederick Harold Johnson and Gertrude Le Quesne (*née* Martin). *Educ:* St John's, Bexhill-on-Sea; Queen Elizabeth Hosp. (SRN); Royal Brompton Hosp. (BTA Hons); Simpson Memorial Maternity Pavilion, Edinburgh (SCM). Asst Matron, Harefield Hosp., 1956–59; Dep. Matron, St Mary's Hosp., Paddington, 1959–62; Matron, Guy's Hosp., 1962–68; Mem. Directing and Tutorial Staff, King Edward's Hosp. Fund for London, 1968–71; Regional Dir, Help the Aged, 1971–73; Matron, The Royal Star and Garter Home for Disabled Sailors, Soldiers and Airmen, 1975–82. Sec., King's Fund Working Party, 'The Shape of Hospital Management 1980', 1966–67 (report pub. 1967); Member: Jt Cttee of Gen. Synod Working Party 'The Hospital Chaplain' (report pub. 1974); Hosp. Chaplaincies Council, 1963–81; Nursing Cttee, Assoc. of Ind. Hosps, 1978–83. Gov., Orleans Park Sch., Twickenham, 1988–97. *Recreations:* straight theatre, travel. *Address:* Flat 5, 6 Cardigan Road, Richmond-on-Thames, Surrey TW10 6BJ. *Died 25 Sept. 2011.*

JOHNSON, David Bryan; Chief Executive, North and East Yorkshire and Northern Lincolnshire Strategic Health Authority, 2002–06; Provider Development, Department of Health, 2006–07; *b* 27 Feb. 1957; *s* of Audrey and Bernard Johnson; *m* 1980, Gillian Pobgee; one *s*. *Educ:* Sheffield Univ. (BA Hons Politics 1978). Nat. Management Trainee, NHS, 1980–83; Asst, then Dep. Administrator, Manchester Royal Infirmary, 1983–85; Unit Gen. Manager, Pontefract HA Acute and Maternity Services, 1985–90; Dir of Ops, 1990–92, Acting Chief Exec., Feb.–May 1992, St James's Univ. Hosp.; Chief Executive: St James's and Seacroft Univ. Hosps NHS Trust, 1992–98; Leeds Teaching Hosps NHS Trust, 1998–2002. Trustee, Martin Hse Children's Hospice, Boston Spa, W Yorks, 2008– (Chm., 2011–). *Recreations:* cycling, guitar, travel, current affairs. *Died 27 Oct. 2013.*

JOHNSON, David Burnham; QC 1978; commercial arbitrator; a Recorder, 1984–98; *b* 6 Aug. 1930; *s* of late Thomas Burnham Johnson and of Elsie May Johnson; *m* 1968, Julia Clare Addison Hopkinson, *o d* of late Col H. S. P. Hopkinson, OBE; one *s* three *d*. *Educ:* Truro Sch.; Univ. of Wales. Solicitor and Notary Public, Oct. 1952. Commissioned, National Service, with Royal Artillery, 1952–54. Private practice as solicitor, Cardiff and Plymouth, 1954–67; called to Bar, Inner Temple, 1967, Bencher, 1985. *Recreations:* sailing, walking, shooting, reading, music. *Address:* 25 Murray Road, Wimbledon, SW19 4PD. *T:* (020) 8947 9188; (chambers) 20 Essex Street, WC2R 3AL. *T:* (020) 7583 9294. *Clubs:* Lansdowne; Royal Western Yacht (Plymouth). *Died 21 June 2011.*

JOHNSON, His Honour John Robin; a Circuit Judge, 1973–93; *b* 5 Nov. 1927; *s* of Sir Philip Bulmer Johnson, Hexham, Northumberland; *m* 1958, Meriel Jean (*d* 2009), *d* of H. B. Speke, Aydon, Corbridge; one *s* one *d*. *Educ:* Winchester; Trinity Coll., Cambridge. Called to Bar, Middle Temple, 1950. Dep. Chm., Northumberland QS, 1966–71; a Recorder of the Crown Court, 1972–73. *Address:* Kirk Fenwick, Cambo, Morpeth NE61 4BN. *Died 17 July 2013.*

JOHNSON, Prof. Kenneth Langstreth, PhD; FRS 1982; FREng; Professor of Engineering, Cambridge University, 1977–92, then Emeritus; Fellow of Jesus College, Cambridge, 1957–92, then Emeritus; *b* 19 March 1925; *s* of Frank Herbert Johnson and Ellen Howorth Langstreth; *m* 1954, Dorothy Rosemary Watkins; one *s* two *d*. *Educ:* Barrow Grammar Sch.; Manchester Univ. (MScTech, MA, PhD). FIMechE; FREng (FEng 1987). Engr, Messrs Rotol Ltd, Gloucester, 1944–49; Asst Lectr, Coll. of Technology, Manchester, 1949–54; Lectr, then Reader in Engrg, Cambridge Univ., 1954–77. Hon. FUMIST, 1993. Tribology Trust Gold Medal, IMechE, 1985; Mayo Hersey Award, ASME, 1991; William Prager Medal, Amer. Soc. Engrg Sci., 1999; Royal Medal, Royal Soc., 2003; Timoshenko Medal, ASME, 2006. *Publications:* Contact Mechanics, 1985; contrib. scientific and engrg jls, and Proc. IMechE. *Recreations:* mountain walking, swimming. *Address:* 1 New Square, Cambridge CB1 1EY. *T:* (01223) 355287. *Died 21 Sept. 2015.*

JOHNSON, Dame Louise (Napier), DBE 2003; FRS 1990; David Phillips Professor of Molecular Biophysics, and Professorial Fellow, Corpus Christi College, Oxford, 1990–2007; Diamond Fellow, Diamond Light Source, since 2008 (Director of Life Sciences, 2003–08); *b* 26 Sept. 1940; *m*; one *s* one *d*. *Educ:* Wimbledon High Sch. for Girls; University College London (BSc 1962; Fellow, 1993); Royal Institution, London (PhD 1965). Research Asst, Yale Univ., 1966; University of Oxford: Demonstrator, Zoology Dept, 1967–73; Lectr in Molecular Biophysics, 1973–90; Reader, 1990; Additional Fellow, Somerville College, 1973–90, Hon. Fellow, 1991. Member: Council, Royal Soc., 1998–2001; CCLRC, 1998–2001; Scientific Adv. Council, EMBL, 1994–2001 (Chm., 1998–2001). Mem., EMBO, 1991. Trustee, Cambridge Crystallographic Data Base, 1996–2003. Gov., Westminster Sch., 1993–2001. Associate Fellow, Third World Acad. of Scis, 2000; MAE, 2001; Foreign Fellow: Bangladesh Acad. of Scis, 2005; Amer. Acad. of Arts and Scis, 2007. Hon. DSc: St Andrews, 1992; Bath, 2004; Imperial Coll. London, 2009; Cambridge, 2010. Kaj Linderström-Lang Prize, 1989; Charmian Medal, Royal Soc. Chem., 1997; Datta Medal, FEBS, 1998; Novartis Prize, Biochem. Soc., 2008. *Publications:* Protein Crystallography (jtly with T. L. Blundell), 1976; papers on lysozyme, glycogen phosphorylase, kinases and cell cycle proteins, protein crystallography, enzyme mechanism and allosteric mechanisms. *Recreations:* family, horses. *Address:* Laboratory of Molecular Biophysics, New Biochemistry Building, University of Oxford, South Parks Road, Oxford OX1 3QU; Diamond Light Source Ltd, Harwell Science and Innovation Campus, Diamond House, Chilton, Didcot, Oxon OX11 0DE. *Died 25 Sept. 2012.*

JOHNSON, Richard Keith; actor and producer; *b* Upminster, Essex, 30 July 1927; *s* of Keith Holcombe and Frances Louisa Olive Johnson; *m* 1st, 1957, Sheila Sweet (marr. diss); one *s* one *d*; 2nd, 1965, Kim Novak (marr. diss.); 3rd, 1982, Marie-Louise Norlund (marr. diss.); one *s* one *d*; 4th, 2004, Lynne Gurney; one step *s*. *Educ:* Parkfield School; Felsted School; RADA. RN, 1945–48. 1st stage appearance, Opera House, Manchester, 1944; repertory, Haymarket, 1944–45; *stage:* contract, Royal Shakespeare Theatre, 1957–62; Antony in Antony and Cleopatra, RSC, 1972–73, and 1992–93; NT, 1976–78; The War That Still Goes On, Young Vic, 1991; King, in All's Well that Ends Well, RSC, 1992–93; An Inspector Calls, Aldwych, 1994; The Rivals, Albery, 1994–95; Freddie in Gangster No 1, Almeida, 1995; Tyrone in Long Day's Journey into Night, Young Vic, 1996; Serebyakov in Uncle Vanya, Albery, 1996; Tusker in Staying On, nat. tour, 1997; Atticus in To Kill a Mockingbird, nat. tour, 1997; Sir Leonard Darwin in Plenty, Albery, 1999; Dr Dorn in The Seagull, RSC, 2000; Heinrich Mann in Tales from Hollywood, Donmar, 2001; Mrs Warren's Profession, Strand, 2002; The Hollow Crown, RSC, 2003, 2005; And Then There Were None, Gielgud, 2005; Victory, Th. Royal, Bath, 2007; On Golden Pond, UK tour, 2012; *films:* MGM contract, 1959–65; acted in: The Haunting; Moll Flanders; Operation Crossbow; Khartoum; The Pumpkin Eater; Danger Route; Deadlier than the Male; Oedipus the King; Hennessy (also wrote original story); Aces High; The Four Feathers; Happy Days, 2000; Tomb Raider, 2001; The Boy in the Striped Pyjamas, 2008; produced: Turtle Diary; Castaway (Exec. Producer); The Lonely Passion of Judith Hearne; *television:* Rembrandt (title rôle); Hamlet (King); Antony and Cleopatra (Antony); The Member for Chelsea (title rôle); The Camomile Lawn (Oliver); Anglo-Saxon Attitudes (Gerald); Breaking the Code (Knox); The Robinsons (Hector Robinson); Wallis and Edward (Stanley Baldwin); *radio:* Bleak Expectations (series), Radio 4, 2006–. Jt Founder, United British Artists, 1982; Founder, It's a Green Green World; The Shakespeare Masterclass. Member, Council: BAFTA, 1977–79; RADA, 2000–12. *Recreations:* reading, gardening, travelling. *Died 6 June 2015.*

JOHNSON-FERGUSON, Sir Ian (Edward), 4th Bt *cr* 1906, of Springkell, Dumfries, of Kenyon, Newchurch-in-Culceth, Lancaster, and of Wiston, Lanark; *b* 1 Feb. 1932; *s* of Sir Neil Edward Johnson-Ferguson, 3rd Bt, TD and Sheila Marion (*d* 1985), *er d* of Col H. S. Jervis, MC; *S* father, 1992; *m* 1964, Rosemary Teresa, *yr d* of late C. J. Whitehead; three *s*. *Educ:* Ampleforth Coll.; Trinity Coll., Cambridge (BA 1953); Imperial Coll., London (DIC Geophysics 1954). Royal Dutch Shell, 1954–62; IBM UK Ltd, 1963–90. *Heir:* *s* Lt-Col Mark Edward Johnson-Ferguson, RE [*b* 14 Aug. 1965; *m* 1995, Dr Julia Catherine, *d* of T. D. Getley; three *d*]. *Died 6 Dec. 2015.*

JOHNSTON, David Alan H.; *see* Hunter Johnston.

JOHNSTON, William James; Secretary, Association of Local Authorities of Northern Ireland, 1979–82; Chairman, National House Building Council, Northern Ireland, 1989–95; *b* 3 April 1919; *s* of late Thomas Hamilton Johnston and of Mary Kathleen Johnston; *m* 1943, Joan Elizabeth Nancye (*née* Young) (*d* 2008); two *d*. *Educ:* Portora Royal Sch., Enniskillen. FCA(Ire.). Professional accountancy, 1937–44; Antrim CC, 1944–68, Dep. Sec., 1951–68; Dep. Town Clerk, Belfast, 1968–73, Town Clerk, 1973–79. Dir, NI Adv. Bd, Abbey Nat. Bldg Soc., 1982–89. Member: NI Adv. Council, BBC, 1965–69; Council, ICAI, 1967–71; NI Tourist Bd, 1980–85; Local Govt Staff Commn, 1974–85; Public Service Trng Council (formerly Public Service Trng Cttee), 1974–83 (Chm., 1974–83); Arts Council of NI, 1974–81. Chm., Extra Care for Elderly People (NI) Ltd, 1999–2004. NI Rep., Duke of Edinburgh's Commonwealth Study Conf., Canada, 1962. *Recreations:* golf, live theatre. *Address:* Apt 3, 35 Newforge Lane, Belfast BT9 5NW. *T:* (028) 9066 9373; 4 Riverside Close, Cushendall, Ballymena BT44 0NR. *T:* (028) 2177 2013. *Club:* Ulster Reform (Belfast). *Died 9 March 2011.*

JOLLIFFE, William Orlando, CPFA, FCA; County Treasurer of Lancashire, 1973–85; *b* 16 Oct. 1925; *s* of late William Dibble Jolliffe and Laura Beatrice Jolliffe; *m* 1st (marr. diss.); one *d* (one *s* decd); 2nd, 1975, Audrey (*née* Dale); one step *d*. *Educ:* Bude County Grammar Sch. Chartered Accountant (first place in final exam. of (former) Soc. of Incorporated Accountants, 1956). Joined Barclays Bank Ltd, 1941. Served War of 1939–45 (HM Forces, 1944–48). Subseq. held various appts in Treasurers' depts of Devon CC, Winchester City Council, Doncaster CB Council, Bury CB Council (Dep. Borough Treas.), and Blackpool CB Council (Dep. 1959, Borough Treas., 1962). Mem. Council, Chartered Inst. of Public Finance and Accountancy, 1969–85 (Pres., 1979–80); Financial Adviser, ACC, 1976–85; Mem. Council (Pres. 1974–75), Assoc. of Public Service Finance Officers, 1963–76; Chm., Officers' Side, JNC for Chief Officers of Local Authorities in England and Wales, 1971–76; Mem. Exec. Cttee (Pres. 1970–71), NW Soc. of Chartered Accountants, 1966–76; Chm., NW and N Wales Region of CIPFA, 1974–76; Mem., Soc. of County Treasurers (Mem. Exec. Cttee, 1977–85); Hon. Treas., Lancashire Playing Fields Assoc., 1974–85. Financial Adviser to Assoc. of Municipal Corporations, 1969–74; Mem. (Govt) Working Party on Collab. between Local Authorities and the National Health Service, 1971–74. *Publications:* articles for Public Finance and Accountancy and other local govt jls. *Address:* 12 The Leylands, Lytham St Annes, Lancs FY8 5QS. *T:* (01253) 739358. *Club:* St Annes Old Links Golf. *Died 16 Feb. 2015.*

JOLOWICZ, Prof. John Anthony; QC 1990; Professor of Comparative Law, University of Cambridge, 1976–93; Fellow, Trinity College, Cambridge, since 1952; *b* 11 April 1926; *e s* of late Prof. Herbert Felix Jolowicz and Ruby Victoria Wagner; *m* 1957, Poppy Stanley; two *d* (one *s* decd). *Educ:* Oundle Sch.; Trinity Coll., Cambridge (Scholar; MA; 1st Cl. Hons Law Tripos 1950). Served HM Forces (commnd RASC), 1944–48. Called to the Bar, Inner Temple and Gray's Inn, 1952; Bencher, Gray's Inn, 1978. Univ. of Cambridge: Asst Lectr in Law, 1955, Lectr, 1959; Reader in Common and Comparative Law, 1972. Professeur associé, Université de Paris 2, 1976; Lionel Cohen Lectr, Hebrew Univ. of Jerusalem, 1983. Pres., SPTL, 1986–87. Vice-Pres., Internat. Acad. of Comparative Law, 1994–2006 (Pres., Common Law Gp, 1990–98). Editor, Jl of Soc. of Public Teachers of Law, 1962–80. Corresp., Institut de France, Acad. des Sciences morales et politiques, 1989; MAE 1988. Hon. Dr Universidad Nacional Autónoma de México, 1985; Hon. LLD Buckingham, 2000. Chevalier de la Légion d'Honneur (France), 2002. *Publications:* (ed) H. F. Jolowicz's Lectures on Jurisprudence, 1963; Winfield and Jolowicz on Tort, 1971, 16th edn (ed W. V. H. Rogers) 2002; (with M. Cappelletti) Public Interest Parties and the Active Role of the Judge, 1975; (jtly) Droit Anglais, 1986, 2nd edn 1992; (jtly) Recourse against Judgments in the European Union, 1999; On Civil Procedure, 2000; contrib. to Internat. Encyc. of Comparative Law and to legal jls. *Address:* Trinity College, Cambridge CB2 1TQ. *T:* (01223) 338400; West Green House, Barrington, Cambridge CB22 7SA. *T:* (01223) 870495. *Clubs:* Royal Automobile; Leander (Henley-on-Thames). *Died 17 Jan. 2012.*

JONES, Alan; *see* Jones, David A.

JONES, Alan Wingate, FREng, FIET; Chairman, Manchester Airports Group, 2004–08; *b* 15 Oct. 1939; *s* of Gilbert Victor Jones and Isobel Nairn Jones; *m* 1974, Judi Ann Curtis; one *s* one *d*. *Educ:* Sutton Valence Sch.; King's Coll., Cambridge (MA MechScis). GEC, 1961–73; Plessey Co. Plc, 1973–89: Man. Dir, Plessey Marine, 1975–79; Divl Man. Dir, Plessey Displays and Sensors, 1979–85; Internat. Dir, 1985–87; Man. Dir, Plessey Electronic Systems, 1987–89; Dir, Plessey Plc, 1985–89; Chief Exec., Westland Gp, 1989–95; Dir, GKN, 1994–95; Chief Exec., BICC plc, 1995–99. Chm., Britax Internat., 2001–04; Director: Witan Investment Trust, 1996–2009; AgustaWestland, 2005–. Mem., Financial Reporting Council, 1998–2001. FREng (FEng 1989); FIET (FIEE 1990); FRAeS 1993; CCMI (CIMgt 1995). *Recreations:* opera, shooting, sailing. *Address:* Sherborne House, Sherborne Street, Lechlade, Glos GL7 3AH. *Died 22 March 2014.*

JONES, (David) Alan; HM Diplomatic Service, retired; High Commissioner to Belize, 2004–07; *b* 26 Oct. 1953; *m* 1st, 1975, Jennifer Anne Wright (marr. diss. 1992); 2nd, 1994, Daphne Patricia Foley; one *d.* Joined LCD, 1970; FCO, 1971–2007; served Tehran, 1975–78, Islamabad, 1978–81; MoD, 1981–83 (on loan); First Sec. (Commercial), Cairo, 1986–89; Dep. Head of Mission and Consul, Luanda, 1993–96; Dep. High Comr, Dar es Salaam, 1996–2000; High Comr, Sierra Leone, and non-resident Ambassador to Guinea, 2000–03. *Address:* c/o Foreign and Commonwealth Office, SW1A 2AH. *Died 19 Dec. 2014.*

JONES, David Evan Alun, CBE 1985; DL; Commissioner for Local Administration in Wales, 1980–85; *b* 9 Aug. 1925; *s* of David Jacob Jones, OBE, Master Mariner, and Margaret Jane Jones; *m* 1952, Joan Margaret Erica (*née* Davies); two *s*. *Educ:* Aberaeron County Sch.; University Coll. of Wales, Aberystwyth (LLB; Sir Samuel Evans Prize, 1949). Solicitor. Served War, RAF, 1943–47 (Flt Lieut). Articled service, Exeter, 1949–52; asst solicitor posts with Ilford Bor., Southampton County Bor., Berks County and Surrey County Councils, 1952–61; Dep. Clerk, Denbighshire CC, subseq. Clerk of CC and Clerk of the Peace, 1961–74; Chief Exec., Gwynedd CC, 1974–80. Chm., All Wales Adv. Panel on Develt of Services for Mentally Handicapped People, 1985–90; Member: Broadcasting Council for Wales, 1980–85; Local Govt Boundary Commn for Wales, 1985–89; Prince of Wales's Cttee, 1985–92 (Chm., Gwynedd County Gp, 1990–92); Gwynedd HA, 1986–88. Pres., Gwynedd Voluntary Services, 1994–96; Chm., N Wales Masonic Benevolent Assoc., 1996–99. Dir, Nat. Welsh-Amer. Foundn, 1992–2004. Treasurer, Univ. of Wales, Bangor (formerly UCNW), 1988–2000. Asst Provincial Grand Master, N Wales, 1987–94. Mem., Gorsedd of Bards, 1974. Freeman, City of Bangor, 1999. DL Gwynedd, 1988. *Recreations:* gardening, travel, a little golf. *Address:* Min-y-Don, West End, Beaumaris, Anglesey LL58 8BG. *T:* (01248) 810225. *Club:* Baron Hill Golf (Beaumaris). *Died 16 March 2015.*

JONES, Derek R.; *see* Rudd-Jones.

JONES, Prof. Douglas Samuel, MBE 1945; FRS 1968; Ivory Professor of Mathematics, University of Dundee, 1965–92, then Emeritus Professor; *b* 10 Jan. 1922; *s* of late J. D. Jones and B. Jones (*née* Streather); *m* 1950, Ivy Styles; one *s* one *d*. *Educ:* Wolverhampton Grammar Sch.; Corpus Christi Coll., Oxford (MA 1947; Hon. Fellow, 1980); DSc Manchester 1957. FIMA 1964, CMath 1992; FRSE 1967; CEng, FIET (FIEE 1989); CSci 2005. Flt-Lt, RAFVR, 1941–45. Commonwealth Fund Fellow, MIT, 1947–48; Asst Lectr in Maths, University of Manchester, 1948–51; Lectr 1951–54, Research Prof. 1955, New York Univ.; Sen. Lectr in Maths, Univ. of Manchester, 1955–57; Prof. of Maths, Univ. of Keele, 1957–64. Vis. Prof., Courant Inst., 1962–63. Member: UGC, 1976–86 (Mem., 1971–86, Chm., 1976–86, Mathematical Scis Sub-Cttee); Computer Bd, 1977–82; Open Univ. Vis. Cttee, 1982–87. Member Council: Royal Soc., 1973–74; IMA, 1982–85, 1986–97 (Pres., 1988–89). Hon. DSc Strathclyde, 1975. Keith Prize, RSE, 1974; Marconi Prize, IEE, 1974; van der Pol Gold Medal, Internat. Union of Radio Sci., 1981; Naylor Prize, London Mathematical Soc., 1987. Trustee, Quarterly Jl of Mechanics and Applied Maths, 1980–92; Associate Editor: Jl IMA, 1964–2003; RSE, 1969–82; SIAM Jl on Applied Maths, 1975–92; Applicable Analysis, 1976–92; Mathematical Methods in the Applied Sciences, 1977–2002; Royal Soc., 1978–83; Methods and Applications of Analysis, 1992–2012; Jl of Engrg Maths, 1992–2011; Communications in Applied Analysis, 1997–2008; International Jl of Pure and Applied Mathematics, 2008–12. *Publications:* Electrical and Mechanical Oscillations, 1961; Theory of Electromagnetism, 1964; Generalised Functions, 1966; Introductory Analysis, vol. 1, 1969, vol 2, 1970; Methods in Electromagnetic Wave Propagation, 1979, 2nd edn 1994; Elementary Information Theory, 1979; The Theory of Generalised Functions, 1982; Differential Equations and Mathematical Biology, 1983, 3rd edn 2010; Acoustic and Electromagnetic Waves, 1986; Assembly Programming and the 8086 Microprocessor, 1988; 80×86 Assembly Programming, 1991; Introduction to Asymptotics, 1997; articles in mathematical and physical jls. *Recreations:* golf, walking, photography. *Address:* 1 The Nurseries, St Madoes, Glencarse, Perth PH2 7NX. *T:* (01738) 860544. *Died 27 Nov. 2013.*

JONES, Elizabeth A.; *see* Blandino, E. A.

JONES, Prof. Emrys Lloyd, FBA 1982; Goldsmiths' Professor of English Literature, Oxford University, and Fellow, New College, Oxford, 1984–98; *b* 30 March 1931; *s* of Peter Jones and Elizabeth Jane (*née* Evans); *m* 1965, Barbara Maud Everett; one *d*. *Educ:* Neath Grammar Sch.; Magdalen Coll., Oxford (BA, MA). Tutor in English, Magdalen Coll., 1955–77; Reader in Eng. Lit., Oxford Univ., 1977–84; Fellow, Magdalen Coll., Oxford, 1955–84. Hon. DPhil Lund, 1994. *Publications:* (ed) Poems of Henry Howard, Earl of Surrey, 1964; Pope and Dulness, 1972; Scenic Form in Shakespeare, 1971; The Origins of Shakespeare, 1977; (ed) Antony and Cleopatra, 1977; (ed) The New Oxford Book of Sixteenth Century Verse, 1991; contribs to jls and books. *Recreations:* looking at buildings, opera. *Address:* New College, Oxford OX1 3BN. *T:* (01865) 279555. *Died 20 June 2012.*

JONES, Fred, CB 1978; CBE 1966; Deputy Secretary, HM Treasury, 1975–80; *b* 5 May 1920; *s* of late Fred Jones and of Harriet (*née* Nuttall); *m* 1954, Joy (*née* Field) (decd); two *s*. *Educ:* Preston Grammar Sch.; St Catherine's Coll., Oxford. Economist, Trades Union Congress, 1951–59; Tutor in Economics and Industrial Relations, Ruskin Coll., Oxford, 1960–62; Economist, National Economic Development Office, 1962–64; Dept of Economic Affairs: Senior Economic Adviser, 1964–66; Asst Sec., 1966–68; Asst Under-Sec. of State, 1968–69; HM Treasury, Asst Under-Sec. of State, 1969–75. *Recreations:* walking, gardening, reading. *Died 10 July 2012.*

JONES, Geoffrey; *see* Jones, His Honour John G.

JONES, Hugh Jarrett, (Hugo), H.; *see* Herbert-Jones.

JONES, Hon. Jeffrey Richard, CBE 1978; MA; Chief Justice and President of the Court of Appeal, Kiribati, 1980–85; Member, Appeal Courts of Solomon Islands and of Vanuatu, 1983; *b* 18 Nov. 1921; *s* of Rev. Thomas Jones and Winifred (*née* Williams); *m* 1955, Anna Rosaleen Carberry (*d* 2001); one *s* one *d*. *Educ:* Grove Park Sch., Wrexham; Denstone Coll., Staffs; Keble Coll., Oxford, 1940, 1946–49 (MA). Council of Legal Educn, 1950–52. Served RAFVR, Flt Lieut (Pilot), 1940–46. Schoolmaster, Mountgrace Comprehensive, Potters Bar, 1953–55. Called to the Bar, Middle Temple, 1954; private practice, Zaria, Nigeria, 1955–57; Magistrate, 1957, High Court Judge, 1965, Sen. Puisne Judge, 1970, Northern Nigeria; Chief Justice, Kano State, N Nigeria, 1975, Chief Judge (change of title, decree 41 of 1976), 1976–80. President, Rotary Club, Kano, 1977. Editor, Northern Nigeria Law Reports, 1966–74. *Publications:* Some Cases on Criminal Procedure and Evidence in Northern Nigeria, 1968; Some Cases on Criminal Procedure and Evidence in Northern Nigeria, 1969, 2nd edn combining 1968–69, 1970; Criminal Procedure in the Northern States of Nigeria (annotated), 1975, repr. 1978, 2nd edn 1979; Criminal Procedure in the Native Courts of Northern Nigeria, 1975. *Recreations:* painting, gardening, bridge, golf. *Address:* Bradley Cottage, Bradley Lane, Holt, near Trowbridge, Wilts BA14 6QE. *T:* (01225) 782004. *Died 29 Aug. 2012.*

JONES, John Ernest P.; *see* Powell-Jones.

JONES, His Honour (John) Geoffrey; a Circuit Judge, 1975–96, a Deputy Circuit Judge, 1996–2001; *b* 14 Sept. 1928; *s* of Wyndham and Lilias Jones; *m* 1954, Sheila (*née* Gregory); three *s*. *Educ:* Brighton and Hove Grammar Sch.; St Michael's Sch., Llanelli; St David's Coll., Lampeter; University Coll., London. LLB London 1955; LLM London 1985. Army service, 1946–48, commnd into RASC, 1947. Electrical wholesale business, 1948–52. Called to Bar, Gray's Inn, 1956; practised Leicester, 1958–70 and London, 1970–75. Pres., Mental Health Review Tribunals, 1985–2000; Chm., Mental Health Rev. Tribunal for Wales, 1996–99. Hon. Sen. Academic Fellow, Leicester Polytechnic, 1989. Hon. LLD De

Montfort, 1996. *Recreation:* golf. *Address:* 6 Llewellyn Court, Elmsleigh Avenue, Leicester LE2 2DH. *Died 14 June 2014.*

JONES, John Hubert E.; *see* Emlyn Jones.

JONES, Sir Keith (Stephen), Kt 1980; FRCSE; FRACS; *b* 7 July 1911; *s* of Stephen William and Muriel Elsy Jones; *m* 1936, Kathleen Mary Abbott; three *s.* *Educ:* Newington Coll.; Univ. of Sydney (MB, BS). General practitioner, Army MO, Surgeon; President, Aust. Medical Assoc., 1973–76; Chief MO, NSW State Emergency Service, 1966–74; Mem., NSW Medical Bd, 1971–81. Mem., Newington Coll. Council, 1951–72; Mem., Nat. Specialist Recognition Appeals Cttee, 1970–83 (Chm., 1980–83; Chm., Nat. Spec. Qualifications Cttee, 1980–83). Chairman: Australasian Medical Publishing Co., 1976–82; Manly Art Gall., 1982–85; President: Medical Benefits Fund of Aust., 1983–85; Blue Cross Assoc. of Aust., 1983–85. Acting Editor, Medical Jl of Aust., 1981. Fellow, Australian Coll. of Emergency Medicine, 1984; Hon. FRACGP 1975. Gold Medal, AMA, 1976. *Publications:* One Man's Story (autobiog.), 2004. *Recreation:* swimming. *Died 2 March 2012.*

JONES, Peter Eldon, FRIBA, FRTPI; architect sole trader, since 1996; *b* 11 Oct. 1927; *s* of Wilfrid Eldon Jones and Jessie Meikle (*née* Buchanan); *m* 1st, 1954, Gisela Marie von Arnswaldt; two *s* one *d*; 2nd, 1985, Claudia Milner-Brown (*née* Laurence). *Educ:* privately and Surbiton County Grammar Sch.; Kingston Sch. of Art; University College London. DipTP. Private practice, 1950–54; joined LCC Architects Dept, 1954; Dep. Schools Architect, LCC, 1960–65; Town Development Architect/Planner, 1965–71; Technical Policy Architect, GLC, 1971–74; Education Architect, ILEA, 1974–82; Acting Director of Architecture, 1980–82, Dir of Architecture and Superintending Architect of Metrop. Bldgs, 1982–86, GLC. Consultant, DES, subseq. DFE, 1988–92. Dir, Assoc. of Small Historic Towns and Villages of the UK, 1993–95. Director: Interior Transformation Ltd, 1985–87; Watkins Gray Peter Jones, 1986–91. Part-time Lectr in Architectl Design, Kingston Poly., 1986–90. Mem., EC Adv. Cttee on Educn and Training in Architecture, 1987–92. Pres., Soc. of Chief Architects of Local Authorities, 1984–85; Mem. Council, Chm. Membership Cttee, and Vice-Pres., RIBA, 1985–87. *Publications:* articles and papers on town development, educn building, housing design and planning. *Recreations:* bridge, travel, golf. *Club:* Woking Golf. *Died 26 Sept. 2013.*

JONES, Peter Trevor S.; *see* Simpson-Jones.

JONES, Rhona Mary; Chief Nursing Officer, St Bartholomew's Hospital, 1969–74; *b* 7 July 1921; *d* of late Thomas Henry Jones and Margaret Evelyn King; single. *Educ:* Liverpool; Alder Hey Children's Hosp.; St Mary's Hosp., Paddington. RSCN 1943; SRN 1945; SCM 1948. Post-Registration Training, and Staff Nurse, Queen Charlotte's Hosp., 1946–48; Ward Sister, 1948–50, Departmental Sister, 1950–52, St Mary's Hosp., Paddington; General Duty Nurse, Canada, 1952–53; Asst Matron, Gen. Infirmary, Leeds, 1953–57; Dep. Matron, Royal Free Hosp., London, 1957–59; Matron, Bristol Royal Hosp., 1959–67; Matron and Superintendent of Nursing, St Bartholomew's Hosp., 1968–69. Chm., Bristol Branch, Royal Coll. of Nursing, 1962–65; Member: Standing Nursing Adv. Cttee, Central Health Services Council, 1963–74; Exec. Cttee, Assoc. Nurse Administrators (formerly Assoc. Hosp. Matrons for England and Wales), 1963–74; Area Nurse Trng Cttee, SW Region, 1965–67; NE Metropolitan Area Nurse Training Cttee, 1969–74; E London Group Hosp. Management Cttee, 1969–74. Vice-Pres., Bristol Royal Hosp. Nurses League. *Recreations:* reading, travel, listening to music. *Address:* Bedford Citizens Charter House, 1A Kimbolton Road, Bedford MK40 2PU. *Died 17 Dec. 2011.*

JONES, Robyn Anne, OBE 2011; Co-Founder, CH&Co Catering Ltd (formerly Charlton House Catering), since 1991; *b* Sutton Coldfield, 20 Aug. 1961; *d* of David and Patricia Lardge; *m* 1986, Timothy John Jones; one *s* one *d.* *Educ:* Buxton Coll. (OND Hotel Catering and Instnl Mgt). Asst Cook, Compass Catering, 1981–83; Catering Manager, Gardner Merchant, 1983–85; Catering Adv. Officer, Potato Mktg Bd, 1985–87; Ops Manager, High Table Ltd, 1987–88; Ops Manager, Compass Catering, 1988–90; Business Develt Manager, Gazeway Catering, 1990–91. FIH (FHCIMA 1992; MHCIMA 1985). *Address:* Bryants Farm, Kiln Road, Dunsden, Reading, Berks RG4 9PB. *E:* Robyn.jones@chandco.net. *Club:* Phyllis Court (Henley on Thames). *Died 21 Sept. 2015.*

JONES, Vera June, (Mrs Ernest Jones); *see* Di Palma, V. J.

JONKMAN, (Pieter Jan) Hans, Hon. GCVO 1982; Commander, Order of Orange Nassau; Cross of Honour, Order of House of Orange Nassau; Secretary-General of the Permanent Court of Arbitration, The Hague, 1990–99; *b* 2 June 1925; *s* of Jan A. Jonkman and Johanna L. M. de Bruïne; *m* 1959, Maria Elisabeth te Winkel; one *s* two *d.* *Educ:* Univ. of Leyden (law degree). Entered Min. of Foreign Affairs, 1955; served Paris, Pretoria, Leopoldville, Buenos Aires; Min. of Foreign Affairs, 1962–66; Brussels, Beirut, Jakarta; Min. of Foreign Affairs, 1975–80; Grand-Officer for Special Services of HM Queen of the Netherlands, 1980–82; Grand-Master, House of The Queen, 1982–87; Ambassador of the Netherlands to UK and concurrently to Iceland, 1987–90. Various foreign decorations. *Died 4 Nov. 2012.*

JOWELL, Sir Roger Mark, Kt 2008; CBE 2001; AcSS; Director, European Social Survey, Centre for Comparative Social Surveys, City University, since 2003; *b* 26 March 1942; *s* of Jack and Emily Jowell, Cape Town, SA; *m* 1st, 1970, Tessa Jane Helen Douglas Palmer (Rt Hon. Dame Tessa Jowell, DBE) (marr. diss. 1977); 2nd, 1979, Nighat Gilani (marr. diss. 1995); two *s*; 3rd, 1996, Sharon Witherspoon. *Educ:* Cape Town Univ. (BA 1963). Researcher, Res. Services Ltd, 1964–68; Founder and Co-Dir, 1969–84, sole Dir, 1984–2001, Dir, European Social Survey, 2001–03, Social and Community Planning Res., later Nat. Centre for Social Res.; Co-dir, ESRC Centre for Res. into Elecns and Social Trends, 1994–2002; Fellow: Centre for Mgt and Policy Studies, Cabinet Office, 2001–03; Prime Minister's Strategy Unit, 2002–05. Mem., Commn on Taxation and Citizenship, 1999–2001; Chm., Cabinet Office Review of Govt 'Pilots', 2002–03; Dep. Chm., UK Statistics Authy, 2008–. Visiting Professor: City Univ., 1980–88 and 2001–; LSE, 1993–2005. Founder Dir, British Social Attitudes Survey series, 1983–2001; Co-dir, British Election Studies, 1983–2000. Member, Editorial Boards: Jl Royal Statistical Soc., 1990–92; Electoral Studies, 1997–; Internat. Jl Mkt Res., 2001–. Formulated Internat. Code of Ethics for Statisticians, 1980–85. Founder Chm., Internat. Social Survey Prog., 1984–90; Chm., Assoc. Res. Centres in Social Scis, 1999–2001; Board Mem., Inf. Centre on Asylum and Refugees, 2001–06; Trustee, IPPR, 2001–. Alderman, Camden BC, 1970–77; Mem., Internat. Statistical Inst., 1985; FSS 1978. AcSS 1999. Hon. LLD Oxford Brookes, 1999; Hon. DSc: City, 2003; Umeå, Sweden, 2006. Descartes Prize Laureate, 2005; Helen Dinerman Award, 2005; Robert Kitchin Prize, 2006. *Publications:* (jtly) Britain into Europe, 1976; (jtly) Survey Research Practice, 1978; (jtly) How Britain Votes, 1985; (jtly) Understanding Political Change, 1991; (jtly) Labour's Last Chance?, 1994; (jtly) The Quality of Life in London, 1995; (jtly) The Rise of New Labour, 2001; (ed and contrib.) British Social Attitudes, annually 1984–2000; contribs to Jl Royal Stat. Soc., Public Opinion Qly, Amer. Behavioral Scientist, Parly Affairs, Eur. Sociol Rev., Jl Official Stats, British Jl of Pol Science, 21st Century. *Recreations:* tennis, cricket. *Address:* Centre for Comparative Social Surveys, School of Social Sciences, City University, Northampton Square, EC1V 0HB. *T:* (020) 7040 4904. *Died 25 Dec. 2011.*

JOYNT, Rt Rev. Michael Charles S.; *see* Scott-Joynt.

JUKES, Rt Rev. John, OFMConv; STL; Auxiliary Bishop of Southwark, 1980–2000, then Emeritus Auxiliary Bishop; Titular Bishop of Strathearn, since 1980; *b* 7 Aug. 1923; *s* of Francis Bernard Jukes and Florence Jukes (*née* Stampton). *Educ:* Blackheath; Rome. Professed in Order of Friars Minor Conventual, 1948; priest, 1952; Lectr in Canon Law, Franciscan Internat. Study Centre, Univ. of Kent at Canterbury, Rector, 1999–; Minister Provincial, English Province, 1979. Formerly: Episcopal Vicar for Religious,

Southwark, Area Bishop with special responsibility for Deaneries of Canterbury, Chatham, Dover, Gravesend, Maidstone, Ramsgate and Tunbridge Wells; Parish Priest, Huntly, RC Dio. of Aberdeen, 2000–09. Mem., RC Bishops' Conf. of England and Wales (Chm., World of Work Cttee, 1983–2000; Mem., Internat. Bio-Ethics Cttee, 1996–); Vice Pres., Christian Council on Defence and Disarmament. Chm. Governors, St Mary's UC, Surrey Univ., 1991–99. DUniv Surrey. *Publications:* contribs to Misc. Francescana, Studia Canonica, New Life, Clergy Rev., etc. *Recreation:* mountain walking and climbing. *Address:* Huntly AB54 8BD. *Died 21 Nov. 2011.*

JUKES, Very Rev. Keith Michael; Dean of Ripon, since 2007; *b* 18 Feb. 1954; *s* of George Jukes and Agnes Ethel Jukes (*née* Dobbs); *m* 1978, Susanne Weatherhogg, (Rev. Susanne Jukes); one *s* one *d*. *Educ:* Leeds Univ. (BA 1976); Lincoln Theol Coll. Ordained deacon, 1978, priest, 1979; Assistant Curate: Holy Trinity, Wordsley, 1978–81; St Chad's with St Peter's, Wolverhampton, 1981–83; Curate-in-charge, St Martin in the Delph, Stoneydelph, 1983–88; Team Rector, Glascote and Stoneydelph Team Ministry, 1988–91; Rural Dean, Tamworth, 1989–91; Team Rector, Cannock and Vicar, Hatherton, 1991–97; Priest-in-charge, 1997–99, Vicar, 1999–2007, Selby Abbey. Prebendary, Lichfield Cathedral, 1996–97. Vis. Lectr in Liturgy, W Midlands Ordination Trng Course, Queen's Coll., Birmingham, 1984–91. Non-exec. Dir, York Hosps NHS Trust, 1998–2006. Chaplain to Chm., N Yorks CC, 1999–2000, 2006–07. *Recreations:* photography, graphic design, architecture. *Address:* The Minster House, Bedern Road, Ripon, N Yorks HG4 1PE. *T:* (01765) 602609. *E:* deankeith@riponcathedral.org.uk. *Died 21 May 2013.*

JURINAC, (Srebrenka) Sena; opera singer; Member of Vienna State Opera, 1944–82, then Honorary; retired from stage, 1982; *b* Travnik, Yugoslavia, 24 Oct. 1921; *d* of Ludwig Jurinac, MD, and Christine Cerv; *m* 1953, Sesto Bruscantini (marr. diss. 1956); *m* 1965, Josef Lederle. *Educ:* High Sch.; Musical Academy. Made first appearance on stage as Mimi with Zagreb Opera, 1942. Frequent appearances at Glyndebourne Festivals, 1949–56, as well as at the Salzburg Festivals, 1947–67. Guest appearances at La Scala, Covent Garden, San Francisco, Teatro Colón, Munich, Stuttgart, Hamburg, Berlin. Principal parts include: Cherubino and Countess in Nozze di Figaro; Donna Anna and Donna Elvira in Don Giovanni; Dorabella and Fiordiligi in Così fan tutte; Pamina in Die Zauberflöte; Marzelline and Leonore in Fidelio; Elisabeth in Tannhäuser; Eva in Meistersinger; Madame Butterfly; Tosca; Jenufa; Marie in Wozzeck; Marschallin in Der Rosenkavalier; Composer in Ariadne auf Naxos; Elisabeth in Don Carlos; Desdemona in Othello. *Films:* Der Rosenkavalier, 1960; Otello, 1965; Wozzeck, 1970; Hänsel und Gretel, 1981. Singing teacher; frequent appearances as mem. of jury in singing competitions. Kammersängerin award, 1951; Ehrenkreuz für Wissenschaft und Kunst, 1961; Grosses Ehrenzeichen für Verdienste um die Republik Oesterreich, 1967; Ehrenring, Wiener Staatsoper, 1968; Ehrenmitglied, Wiener Staatsoper, 1971; Fidelio Medaille, 1982; Silberne Rose, Wiener Philharmoniker; Goldenes Ehrenzeichen, Stadt Wien, 2001. *Relevant publication:* Sena Jurinac: der jahrhundert-Rosenkavalier, by Ursula Tamussino, 2001. *Address:* Lerchenweg 10, 86356 Neusäss-Hainhofen, Germany. *Died 22 Nov. 2011.*

K

KAFITY, Rt Rev. Samir; Presidential Consultant, Palestinian Presidency Office, since 1998; Anglican Bishop in Jerusalem, 1984–98; Bishop-in-Residence, St Bartholomew's Episcopal Church, Poway, since 1998; *b* 21 Sept. 1933; *s* of Hanna and Nazha Kafity; *m* 1963, Najat Abed; two *d*. *Educ:* American Univ., Beirut (BA); Near East Sch. of Theol. (DipTh). Ordained deacon, 1957, priest, 1958; Parish priest: to the Arab congregation at St George's Cathedral, Jerusalem, 1957–59; St Andrew's Ramallah, 1959–64; St Peter's, Beir Zeit, then All Saints, Beirut, 1964–77; Lectr, Beir Zeit Univ.; Archdeacon of Jerusalem, 1977–82; Coadjutor Bp in Jerusalem, 1982; Pres. Bishop, Episcopal Church in Jerusalem and the ME, 1986–96, Former Pres. Bishop, 1997–. Member: Standing Cttee, ACC, 1965; Bd of Managers and Exec. Cttee, Near East Sch. of Theol., 1965; Council of Evangelical Community in Syria and Lebanon, 1965–77. Hon. Life Pres., ME Council of Churches (Sec., 1974–94, Pres., 1985). Hon. Canon, Cathedral Church of St John the Divine, NY, 1988. Member: Royal Hashemite Commn on Jerusalem; Moslem-Christian Council, Palestine. President: Supreme Council, Jerusalem YMCA (Chm., Jerusalem); Jerusalem Crippled Children's Instn. Hon. STD Dickenson Coll., Pa, 1985; Hon. DD: Virginia Theol Seminary, 1986; Kent at Canterbury, 1998. KHS; KCLJ 1998; ChStJ. First recipient, Palestinian Jerusalem Medal, 1997. *Publications:* articles in Anglican and ecumenical jls. *Recreation:* travel. *Address:* St Bartholomew's Episcopal Church, 11964 Callado Road, San Diego, CA 92128, USA. *Died 21 Aug. 2015.*

KALAM, Dr (Avul Pakir Jainulabdeen) Abdul; President of India, 2002–07; *b* 15 Oct. 1931. *Educ:* Madras Inst. of Technol. Joined Defence, R&D Orgn, India, 1958; Indian Space Res. Orgn, 1963 (posts incl. Project Dir, Satellite Launch Vehicle-III); rejoined Defence R&D Orgn, 1982 (conceived Integrated Guided Missile Develt Prog.); Scientific Advr to Minister of Defence and Sec., Dept of Defence R&D, 1992–99; Principal Scientific Advr, Indian govt, 1999–2001. Formerly Chm., Technol. Inf., Forecasting and Assessment Council. Prof. of Technol. and Societal Transformation, Anna Univ., Chennai. Indira Gandhi Award for Nat. Integration, 1997. Padma Bhushan, 1981; Padma Vibhushan, 1990; Bharat Ratna, 1997. *Address:* c/o Rashtrapati Bhavan, New Delhi 110004, India. *Died 27 July 2015.*

KAN Yuet-Keung, Sir, GBE 1979 (CBE 1967; OBE 1959); Kt 1972; JP; Chairman, Hong Kong Trade Development Council, 1979–83; Chairman, Bank of East Asia Ltd, 1963–83; *b* 27 July 1913; *s* of late Kan Tong Po, JP; *m* 1940, Ida (*d* 1999); two *s* one *d*. *Educ:* Hong Kong Univ.; London Univ. BA Hong Kong 1934. Solicitor and Notary Public. Sen. Unofficial MLC 1968–72, Sen. Unofficial MEC 1974–80, Hong Kong. Pro-Chancellor, Chinese Univ. of Hong Kong, 1983–96 (Chm., Council, 1973–83). Hon. Fellow, LSE, 1980. Hon. LLD: Chinese Univ. of Hong Kong, 1968; Univ. of Hong Kong, 1973. Order of Sacred Treasure, 3rd Class, Japan; Officier de l'Ordre National du Mérite (France), 1978; Officer's Cross, Order of Merit 1st class (Germany), 1983; Grand Decoration of Honour in Gold with Star (Austria), 1983; Order of Sacred Treasure, 2nd class (Japan), 1983; Knight Grand Cross, Royal Order of Northern Pole Star (Sweden), 1983. *Recreations:* tennis, swimming, golf. *Died 19 Sept. 2012.*

KARK, Nina Mary, (Mrs A. S. Kark); *see* Bawden, N. M.

KARLE, Jerome, PhD; Chief Scientist, Laboratory for the Structure of Matter, 1968–2009; *b* NY, 18 June 1918; *s* of Louis Karfunkle and Sadie Helen Kun; *m* 1942, Isabella, *d* of Zygmunt and Elizabeth Lugoski; three *d*. *Educ:* Abraham Lincoln High Sch.; City Coll. of NY (BS 1937); Harvard Univ. (AM 1938); Univ. of Michigan (MS 1942; PhD 1943). Research Associate, Manhattan Project, Chicago, 1943–44; US Navy Project, Michigan, 1944–46; Head, Electron Diffraction Section, Naval Res. Lab., 1946–58, Head of Diffraction Branch, 1958–68. Prof. (part-time), Univ. of Maryland, 1951–70. Pres., Amer. Crystallographic Assoc., 1972; Chm., US Nat. Cttee for Crystallography, NAS and Nat. Res. Council, 1973–75; Pres., Internat. Union of Crystallography, 1981–84. Fellow, Amer. Phys. Soc., 1960; Member: NAS, 1976; Amer. Phil. Soc., 1990. (Jtly) Nobel Prize for Chemistry, 1985; (jtly) US Dept of Navy Distinguished Civilian Service Award, 2009. *Publications:* articles in learned jls on study of atoms, molecules, crystals and solid surfaces by diffraction methods. *Recreations:* stereo-photography, swimming, ice skating. *Died 6 June 2013.*

KATIN, Peter Roy; concert pianist; *b* 14 Nov. 1930; *m* 1954, Eva Zweig (marr. diss. 1988); two *s*. *Educ:* Henry Thornton Sch.; Westminster Abbey; Royal Academy of Music. First London appearance at Wigmore Hall, 1948. Leading Chopin interpreter. Performances abroad include most European countries, West and East, S and E Africa, Japan, Canada, USA, Hong Kong, India, New Zealand, Singapore, Malaysia. Many recordings, incl. complete sonatas of Mozart, complete nocturnes and impromptus of Chopin, complete preludes of Rachmaninov, complete lyric pieces of Grieg, fortepiano works of Clementi, Chopin and Schubert, and major works by Brahms, Mendelssohn, Scarlatti, Schubert, Schumann and Tchaikovsky. Professor: Royal Acad. of Music, 1956–59; RCM, 1992–2001; London Coll. of Music and Media, Univ. of W London (formerly Thames Valley Univ.), 2001–04. Vis. Prof. in piano, Univ. of Western Ontario, 1978–84. Founder: Katin Centre for Advanced Piano Studies, 1991; Katin Trio, 1997. Mem. Incorporated Soc. of Musicians (ISM). FRAM, ARCM. Hon. DMus De Montfort, 1994. Chopin Arts Award, NY, 1977. *Recreations:* reading, writing, theatre, tape recording, photography. *Address:* 41 First Avenue, Bexhill-on-Sea, E Sussex TN40 2PL. *T:* (01424) 211167. *E:* peter.katin@btinternet.com. *W:* www.peterkatin.com. *Died 19 March 2015.*

KATRITZKY, Prof. Alan Roy, DPhil, PhD, ScD; FRS 1980; FRSC; Kenan Professor of Chemistry, since 1980, and Director, Center for Heterocyclic Compounds, since 1986, University of Florida; *b* 18 Aug. 1928; *s* of Frederick Charles Katritzky and Emily Catherine (*née* Lane); *m* 1952, Agnes Juliane Dietlinde Kilian; one *s* three *d*. *Educ:* St Catherine's Coll., Oxford (BA, BSc 1953, MA; DPhil 1954; Hon. Fellow, 2005); Trinity Hall, Cambridge (PhD 1963); Churchill Coll., Cambridge (ScD 1963). FRIC 1963. Sen. Demy, Magdalen Coll., Oxford, 1954–57; Lecturer: Pembroke Coll., Oxford, 1956–58; Trinity Hall, Cambridge, 1958–63; Founder Fellow of Churchill Coll., Cambridge, 1960–63; Prof. of Chemistry, Univ. of E Anglia, 1963–80, Dean, Sch. of Chem. Sciences, UEA, 1963–70 and 1976–80. Foreign Member: Polish Acad. of Sci., 1991; Real Acad. Catalonia, Barcelona, 1995; Slovenian Acad., 2001; Russian Acad. of Sci., Siberian Section, 2003; Indian Nat. Acad. of Sci., 2003; Eur. Acad. of Arts and Scis, Salzburg, 2008. Foreign Fellow, RACI, 1983; FAAAS 2000; Fellow, World Innovation Foundn, 2003; Hon. Fellow: Italian Chem. Soc., 1978; Polish Chem. Soc., 1985; Internat. Soc. of Heterocyclic Chem., 1995; Chem. Res. Foundn of India, 2003. Hon. Prof., Beijing Inst. of Tech., China, 1995. Dr *hc*: Univ. Nacional, Madrid, 1986; Univ. Poznan, Poland, 1990; Medical Acad., Gdansk, 1994; Univ. of E Anglia, 1995; Univ. of Toulouse, 1996; Univ. of St Petersburg, 1997; Technical Univ., Bucharest, 1998; Rostov Univ., 2000; Univ. Ghent, 2001; Bundelkhand Univ., 2001; Univ. of Timişoara, Romania, 2003; Univ. of Wrotzlaw, Poland, 2005; Univ. of Jena, Germany, 2006; Univ. of Tartu, Estonia, 2006. Tilden Medal, Chem. Soc., 1975–76. Heterocyclic Award, 1983, Robinson Award, 2009, RSC; Medals of Tartu State Univ., subseq. Univ. of Tartu, Estonia, 1986, 1992; Golden Tiger award, Exxon Corp., 1989; Internat. Soc. of Heterocyclic Chemistry Award, 1993; Medal of Univ. of Thessaloniki, 1993; Florida Award, 1995, Cope Sen.

Scholar Award, 2001, ACS; Heyrovský Medal, Czech Acad., 1997; Kametani Prize, Japan, 1999; Gold Medal, Scientific Partnership Foundn, Moscow, 2001; Curie Medal, Polish Chem. Soc., 2003; Globe Award, Scientific Partnership Foundn, Moscow, 2003; Lifetime Achievement Award, Indian Chem. Soc., 2003. Cavaliere ufficiale, Order Al Merito Della Repubblica Italiana, 1975. *Publications:* (ed) Advances in Heterocyclic Chemistry, Vols 1–101, 1963–; (ed) Physical Methods in Heterocyclic Chemistry, Vols 1–6, 1963–72; Principles of Heterocyclic Chemistry, 1968 (trans. into French, German, Italian, Japanese, Russian, Polish and Spanish); Chemistry of Heterocyclic N-Oxides (monograph), 1970; Heteroaromatic Tautomerism (monograph), 1975; Handbook of Heterocyclic Chemistry, 1985, 3rd edn 2010; Heterocycles in Life and Society, 1998; Chm. Editorial Bd, Comprehensive Heterocyclic Chemistry (8 vols), 1985, 2nd edn (10 vols) 1996; 3rd edn (17 vols) 2008; Chm. Editorial Bd, Comprehensive Organic Functional Group Transformations (7 vols), 1995, 2nd edn (7 vols) 2003; scientific papers in Heterocyclic Chem. *Recreations:* walking, travel, windsurfing. *Address:* Department of Chemistry, University of Florida, Gainesville, FL 32611, USA. *T:* (352) 3920554, *Fax:* (352) 3929199. *Club:* Oxford and Cambridge. *Died 10 Feb. 2014.*

KAUFMAN, Prof. Matthew Howard, PhD, DSc; FRCPE, FRCSE, FRSE; Professor of Anatomy, University of Edinburgh, 1985–2007, then Emeritus (Head of Department of Anatomy, 1985–95); *b* 29 Sept. 1942; *s* of Benjamin and Dora Kaufman; *m* 1973, Claire Lesley Kaufman (*née* Farrow); two *s*. *Educ:* Westminster City Sch.; Univ. of Edinburgh (MB ChB 1967; DSc 1984); Univ. of Cambridge (PhD 1973; MA 1975; ScD 1993). FRCPE 1996; FRCSE 2000; FRSE 2008. Pre- and post-registration clinical posts, 1967–69; Research Associate, Inst. of Animal Genetics, Edinburgh, 1970; MRC Jun. Research Fellow, Physiol Lab., Cambridge, 1970–73; Royal Soc./Israel Acad. of Scis Research Fellow, and MRC Travelling Fellow, Weizmann Inst. of Science, 1973–75; University of Cambridge: Univ. Demonstrator, 1975–77; Lectr in Anatomy, 1977–85; Fellow and College Lectr in Anatomy, King's Coll., 1980–85. Chm., W. R. Henderson Trust, 1988–2007. Symington Meml Prize in Anatomy, Anatomical Soc., 1979; Evian Health Award, 1988. *Publications:* Early Mammalian Development: parthenogenetic studies, 1983; The Atlas of Mouse Development, 1992; (with J. B. L. Bard) The Anatomical Basis of Mouse Development, 1999; Surgeons at War, 2000; The Regius Chair of Military Surgery in the University of Edinburgh, 2003; Musket-ball and Sabre Injuries, 2003; Medical Teaching in Edinburgh during the 18th and 19th centuries, 2003; Edinburgh Phrenological Society: a history, 2005; Dr John Barclay (1758–1826): extra-mural teacher of anatomy in Edinburgh, 2007; Robert Liston: surgery's hero, 2009; (with A. Y. Nikitin and J. P. Sundberg) Histologic Basis of Mouse Endocrine Development, 2009; Sir John Struthers (1823–99), 2011; research papers in the fields of experimental and descriptive embryology (co-author, first paper pub. on embryonic stem cells, 1981), cytogenetics, developmental biology and teratology, medical history. *Recreations:* history of medicine, particularly of anatomy; the artefacts of phrenology, military surgery. *E:* professor.kaufman@yahoo.co.uk. *Died 11 Aug. 2013.*

KAVANAGH, P. J., (Patrick Joseph Gregory Kavanagh), FRSL; writer; columnist: Times Literary Supplement, 1997–2002; The Spectator, 1983–97; *b* 6 Jan. 1931; *s* of H. E. (Ted) Kavanagh and Agnes O'Keefe; *m* 1st, 1956, Sally Philipps (*d* 1958); 2nd, 1965, Catherine Ward; two *s*. *Educ:* Douai Sch.; Lycée Jaccard, Lausanne; Merton Coll., Oxford (MA). British Council, 1957–59. Actor, 1959–70. Mem., Kingman Cttee of Inquiry into English Lang., 1986–88. *Publications: poems:* One and One, 1960; On the Way to the Depot, 1967; About Time, 1970; Edward Thomas in Heaven, 1974; Life before Death, 1979; Selected Poems, 1982; Presences (new and selected poems), 1987; An Enchantment, 1991; Collected Poems, 1992 (Cholmondeley Prize, 1992); Something About, 2004; New Selected Poems, 2014; *novels:* A Song and Dance, 1968 (Guardian Fiction Prize, 1968); A Happy Man, 1972; People and Weather, 1979; Only by Mistake, 1986; *essays:* People and Places, 1988; A Kind of Journal, 2003; *autobiography:* The Perfect Stranger, 1966 (Richard Hillary Prize, 1966); *travel autobiography:* Finding Connections, 1990; *for children:* Scarf Jack, 1978; Rebel for Good, 1980; *edited:* Collected Poems of Ivor Gurney, 1982; (with James Michie) Oxford Book of Short Poems, 1985; The Bodley Head G. K. Chesterton, 1985; Selected Poems of Ivor Gurney, 1990; A Book of Consolations, 1992; Voices in Ireland: a traveller's literary companion, 1994. *Recreation:* walking. *Address:* c/o Peters, Fraser, Dunlop, Drury House, 34–43 Russell Street, WC2B 5HA. *Died 26 Aug. 2015.*

KAVANAGH, Patrick Bernard, CBE 1977; QPM 1974; Deputy Commissioner, Metropolitan Police, 1977–83; *b* 18 March 1923; *s* of late Michael Kavanagh and Violet Kavanagh (*née* Duncan); *m* Beryl (*d* 1984), *er d* of late Lt-Comdr Richard Owen Williams, RNR and Annie (*née* McShiells); one *s* two *d*. *Educ:* St Aloysius Coll., Glasgow. Rifle Bde, 1941–43; Para. Regt, 1943–46 (Lieut). Manchester City Police (Constable to Supt), 1946–64; Asst Chief Constable, Cardiff City Police, 1964–69; Asst and Dep. Chief Constable, S Wales Constabulary, 1969–73; Asst Comr (Traffic), Metropolitan Police, 1974–77. Attended Administrative Staff Coll., Henley-on-Thames, 1961. Mem., Gaming Bd for GB, 1983–91. *Recreations:* walking, bird watching, music, crosswords. *Address:* c/o Metropolitan Police, 2 Bessborough Street, SW1V 2JF. *Club:* Royal Automobile. *Died 11 Dec. 2013.*

KAY, Sir Andrew Watt, Kt 1973; Regius Professor of Surgery, University of Glasgow, 1964–81; part-time Chief Scientist, Scottish Home and Health Department, 1973–81; *b* 14 Aug. 1916; of Scottish parentage; *m* 1st, 1943, Janetta M. Roxburgh (*d* 1990); two *s* two *d*; 2nd, 1992, Phyllis Gillies. *Educ:* Ayr Academy; Glasgow Univ. MB, ChB (Hons) with Brunton Memorial Prize, 1939; FRCSEd 1942; FRFPSG 1956 (Pres. 1972–); FRCS 1960; FRCSGlas 1967; FRSE 1971; MD (Hons) with Bellahouston Gold Medal, 1944. Major Royal Army Medical Corps i/c Surgical Div., Millbank Military Hospital, 1946–48; ChM (Hons) 1949; Consultant Surgeon in charge of Wards, Western Infirmary, Glasgow, 1956–58; Asst to Regius Prof. of Surgery, Glasgow Univ., 1942–56; Prof. of Surgery, University of Sheffield, 1958–64. Sims Travelling Prof., Australasia, 1969; McLaughlin Foundn Edward Gallie Vis. Prof., Canada, 1970. Rock Carling Fellowship, 1977. Pres., Surgical Research Soc., 1969–71. Member: Royal Commission on Medical Education, 1965–68; MRC, 1967–71; Chm., Scottish Hosps Endowment Research Trust, 1983–89; Hon. Mem., The N Pacific Surgical Assoc. FRACS 1970; FRCSCan 1972; FCS(SoAf) 1972; Hon. Fellow: Norwegian Surgical Assoc., Belgian Surgical Soc.; Amer. Surg. Assoc., 1972; Hon. FACS, 1973; Hon. FRCSI, 1979. Hon. DSc: Leicester, 1973; Sheffield, 1975; Manchester, 1981; Nebraska, 1981; Hon. MD Edinburgh, 1981. Cecil Joll Prize, RCS, 1969; Gordon-Taylor Lectureship and Medal, 1970. *Publications:* (with R. A. Jamieson, FRCS) Textbook of Surgical Physiology, 1959, 2nd edn 1964; Research in Medicine: problems and prospects, 1977; several papers in medical and surgical jls on gastroenterological subjects. *Recreation:* gardening. *Address:* 5 Loch Road, Milngavie, Glasgow G62 8BB. *Died 1 Feb. 2011.*

KAY, Maj.-Gen. Patrick Richard, CB 1972; MBE 1945; RM; *b* 1 Aug. 1921; *y s* of late Dr and Mrs A. R. Kay, Blakeney, Norfolk; *m* 1944, Muriel Austen Smith (*d* 2013); three *s* one *d*. *Educ:* Eastbourne Coll. Commissioned in Royal Marines, 1940; HMS Renown, 1941–43; 4 Commando Bde, 1944–45; Combined Ops HQ, 1945–48; Staff of Commandant-Gen., Royal Marines, 1948–50 and 1952–54; Staff Coll., Camberley, 1951; 40 Commando, RM, 1954–57; Joint Services Amphibious Warfare Centre, 1957–59; Plans Div., Naval Staff, 1959–62; CO, 43 Commando, RM, 1963–65; CO, Amphibious Training Unit, RM, 1965–66; Asst Dir (Jt Warfare) Naval Staff, 1966–67; Asst Chief of Staff to Comdt-Gen. RM, 1968; IDC, 1969; C of S to Comdt-Gen., RM, 1970–74, retired 1974. Dir of Naval Security, 1974–81. Sec., Defence, Press and Broadcasting Cttee, 1984–86. *Recreations:* gardening, golf. *Address:* c/o Barclays Bank, Fleet, Hants GU51 3BN. *Died 19 Sept. 2013.*

KEAL, Dr Edwin Ernest Frederick, FRCP; Honorary Consulting Physician, St Mary's and Brompton Hospitals, London; *b* 21 Aug. 1921; *s* of Frederick Archibald Keal and Mabel Orange Keal; *m* 1945, Constance Mary Gilliams (*d* 2008); one *s*. *Educ:* Kingston High Sch., Hull; London Hospital Med. Coll. MB BS London 1952, DCH 1954, MD London 1971; FRCP 1973 (MRCP 1957). Service in RNVR (Exec. Lieut), 1939–46. Junior hosp. posts, London Hosp., 1952–59; Sen. Medical Registrar, Brompton Hosp., 1959–63; Consultant Physician: St Charles Hosp., London, 1963–77; Kensington Chest Clinic, 1963–86; Brompton Hosp., 1966–86; St Mary's Hosp., London, 1977–86; Cardiothoracic Institute: Sen. Lectr, 1972–77; Hon. Sen. Lectr, 1978–86; Dean, 1979–84. Hon. Consultant in Chest Diseases to the Army, 1979–86. Member: Bd of Governors, National Heart and Chest Hosps, 1975–85; Cttee of Management, Cardiothoracic Inst., 1978–84. *Publications:* chapters in various books, and articles, mainly related to diseases of the chest. *Recreations:* gardening, travel. *Address:* Blackberry Cottage, 2 Huntsmans Drive, Oakham, Rutland LE15 6RP. *T:* (01572) 755603. *Died 24 March 2011.*

KEARNS, David Todd; Deputy Secretary of Education, US Department of Education, 1991–93; *b* 11 Aug. 1930; *m* 1954, Shirley Cox; two *s* four *d*. *Educ:* Univ. of Rochester (BS). Served US Navy; IBM, 1954–71; Xerox Corp.: Corporate Vice Pres., 1971; Group Vice Pres. and Board of Dirs, 1976; Pres. and Chief Operating Officer, 1977; Chief Exec., 1982–90; Chm., 1985–91. Mem. Boards of Directors: Chase Manhattan Corp.; Time Inc.; Dayton Hudson Corp.; Ryder System. Member: Council on Foreign Relations; Business Roundtable; Business Council; President's Commn on Executive Exchange. Trustee, Cttee for Economic Develt; Chairman: Nat. Urban League; New American Sch.; Univ. of Rochester (Mem. Exec. Adv. Commn, William E. Simon Sch. of Business); Member: Bd of Dirs, Junior Achievement; Bd of Visitors, Fuqua Sch. of Business Administration, Duke Univ. *Publications:* (with D. P. Doyle) Winning the Brain Race, 1988; (with David Nadler) Profits in the Dark, 1992; (with James Harvey) A Legacy of Learning, 2000. *Died 25 Feb. 2011.*

KEATING, Frank; Sports Columnist, The Guardian, since 1976; *b* 4 Oct. 1937; *s* of Bryan Keating and Monica Marsh; *m* 1st, Sally Head; 2nd, 1987, Jane Sinclair; one *s* one *d*. *Educ:* Belmont Abbey; Douai. Local newspapers, Stroud, Hereford, Guildford, Bristol, Southern Rhodesia, Gloucester and Slough, 1956–63; Editor, Outside Broadcasts, Rediffusion Television, 1963–67; Editor, Features, and Head of Special Projs, Thames Television, 1968–72; columnist: The Guardian, 1972–; Punch, 1979–90; The Spectator, 1990–96, 2004–08; The Oldie, 1997–. Astroturf Sportswriter of the Year, 1978; 'What the Papers Say' Sportswriter of the Year, 1979; Sports Council Magazine Writer of the Year, 1987; Specialist Writer of Year, Magazine Publishers Awards, 1988; Sports Journalist of the Year, British Press Awards, 1988. *Television series:* Maestro, BBC, 1981–85. *Publications:* Caught by Keating, 1979; Bowled Over, 1980; Another Bloody Day in Paradise, 1981; Up and Under, 1983; Long Days, Late Nights, 1984; High, Wide and Handsome, 1986; Gents and Players, 1986; Passing Shots, 1988; Sportswriter's Eye, 1989; Half-Time Whistle (autobiog.), 1992; The Great Number Tens, 1994; (with Graham Gooch) Gooch: My Autobiography, 1995; Band of Brothers, 1996; Frank Keating's Sporting Century, 1998; contrib. New Statesman, BBC. *Recreation:* roses. *Address:* Church House, Marden, near Hereford HR1 3EN. *T:* (01432) 880213. *Club:* Chelsea Arts. *Died 25 Jan. 2013.*

KEATING, Henry Reymond Fitzwalter; author; *b* 31 Oct. 1926; *s* of John Hervey Keating and Muriel Marguerita Keating (*née* Clews); *m* 1953, Sheila Mary Mitchell; three *s* one *d*. *Educ:* Merchant Taylors' Sch.; Trinity Coll., Dublin. Journalism, 1952–60; Crime Reviewer for The Times, 1967–83. Chairman: Crime Writers' Assoc., 1970–71; Society of Authors, 1983–84; Pres., Detection Club, 1985–2001. FRSL 1990. Diamond Dagger, British Crime Writers' Assoc., 2006. *Publications:* Death and the Visiting Firemen, 1959; Zen there was Murder, 1960; A Rush on the Ultimate, 1961; The Dog it was that Died, 1962; Death of a Fat God, 1963; The Perfect Murder, 1964 (filmed 1988); Is Skin-Deep, Is Fatal, 1965; Inspector Ghote's Good Crusade, 1966; Inspector Ghote Caught in Meshes, 1967; Inspector Ghote Hunts the Peacock, 1968; Inspector Ghote Plays a Joker, 1969; Inspector Ghote Breaks an Egg, 1970; Inspector Ghote goes by Train, 1971; The Strong Man, 1971; (ed) Blood on My Mind, 1972; Inspector Ghote Trusts the Heart, 1972; The Underside, 1974; Bats Fly Up for Inspector Ghote, 1974; A Remarkable Case of Burglary, 1975; Filmi, Filmi, Inspector Ghote, 1976; Murder Must Appetize, 1976; (ed) Agatha Christie: First Lady of Crime, 1977; A Long Walk to Wimbledon, 1978; Inspector Ghote Draws a Line, 1979; Sherlock Holmes: the man and his world, 1979; The Murder of the Maharajah, 1980; Go West, Inspector Ghote, 1981; (ed) Whodunit, 1982; The Lucky Alphonse, 1982; The Sheriff of Bombay, 1984; Mrs Craggs, Crimes Cleaned Up, 1985; Under a Monsoon Cloud, 1986; Writing Crime Fiction, 1986; The Body in the Billiard Room, 1987; Crime and Mystery: the 100 best books, 1987; Dead on Time, 1988; Inspector Ghote, His Life and Crimes, 1989; (ed) Bedside Companion to Crime, 1989; The Iciest Sin, 1990; (ed) Crime Wave 1, 1991; Cheating Death, 1992; (ed) The Man Who, 1992; The Rich Detective, 1993; Doing Wrong, 1994; The Good Detective, 1995; The Bad Detective, 1996; Asking Questions, 1996; The Soft Detective, 1997; In Kensington Gardens Once, 1997; Bribery, Corruption Also, 1999; Jack, the Lady Killer (verse), 1999; The Hard Detective, 2000; Breaking and Entering, 2000; A Detective in Love, 2001; A Detective Under Fire, 2002; The Dreaming Detective, 2003; Detective at Death's Door, 2004; One Man and his Bomb, 2006; Rules, Regs and Rotten Eggs, 2007; Inspector Ghote's First Case, 2008; A Small Case for Inspector Ghote?, 2009. *Recreation:* popping round to the post. *Address:* 35 Northumberland Place, W2 5AS. *T:* (020) 7229 1100. *Died 27 March 2011.*

KEE, Robert, CBE 1998; author and broadcaster; *b* 5 Oct. 1919; *s* of late Robert and Dorothy Kee; *m* 1st, 1948, Janetta (marr. diss. 1950), *d* of Rev. G. H. Woolley, VC, OBE, MC; one *d*; 2nd, 1960, Cynthia (marr. diss. 1989), *d* of Edward Judah; one *s* one *d* (and one *s* decd); 3rd, 1990, Hon. Catherine Mary, *yr d* of Rt Hon. Lord Trevelyan, KG, GCMG, CIE, OBE and Violet Margaret Trevelyan. *Educ:* Stowe Sch. (Schol.); Magdalen Coll., Oxford (Exhibr, MA). RAF, 1940–46. Atlantic Award for Literature, 1946. Picture Post, 1948–51; Picture Editor, WHO, 1953; Special Corresp., Observer, 1956–57; Literary Editor, Spectator, 1957; Special Corresp., Sunday Times, 1957–58; BBC TV (Panorama, etc), 1958–62; Television Reporters International, 1963–64; ITV (Rediffusion, Thames, London Week-End, ITN, Yorkshire (documentary series, Faces of Communism)), 1964–78, Presenter, First Report, ITN's first lunch-time news prog., 1972–74; BBC, 1978–82; Presenter: Ireland: a television history (13 part television series), 1980; Panorama, BBC1, 1982; TV-am, 1983; Channel 4's Seven Days, 1984–88; miscellaneous BBC radio broadcasts, 1946–. Alistair Horne Research Fellow, St Antony's Coll., Oxford, 1972–73. Hon. DLitt London Metropolitan, 2003. BAFTA Richard Dimbleby Award, 1976. *Publications:* A Crowd Is Not Company, 1947, repr. 2000; The Impossible Shore, 1949; A Sign of the Times, 1955; Broadstrop In Season, 1959; Refugee World, 1961; The Green Flag, 1972, repr. 2000; Ireland: a history, 1980, new edn 2003; The World We Left Behind, 1984; The World We Fought For, 1985; Trial and Error, 1986; Munich: the eleventh hour, 1988; The Picture Post Album, 1989; The Laurel and the Ivy: Parnell and Irish nationalism, 1993; many translations from German. *Recreations:* swimming, listening to music. *Address:* c/o Rogers, Coleridge and White, 20 Powis Mews, W11 1JN. *Club:* Reform. *Died 11 Jan. 2013.*

KEEGAN, Sir John (Desmond Patrick), Kt 2000; OBE 1991; FRSL; FRHistS; military historian; Defence Editor, The Daily Telegraph, 1986–2009; *b* 15 May 1934; *e s* of Francis Joseph Keegan and Eileen Mary Keegan (*née* Bridgman); *m* 1960, Susanne Ingeborg Everett; two *s* two *d*. *Educ:* King's Coll., Taunton; Wimbledon Coll.; Balliol Coll., Oxford (BA 1957; MA 1962; Hon. Fellow, 1999). Political Analyst, US Embassy, London, 1958–60; Sen. Lectr in Mil. Hist., RMA Sandhurst, 1960–86; corresp. from numerous countries, incl. Gulf, 1991. Delmas Vis.

Dist. Prof. of Hist., Vassar Coll., 1997–98; Vis. Fellow, Princeton, 1984; Lectures: Lees Knowles, Cambridge, 1986; Eisenhower Meml, Kansas State, 1986; Brown Meml, Brown Univ., 1989; Whidden Meml, McMaster, 1990; Frum Meml, Toronto, 1994; Reith, BBC, 1998. Visitor, Hugh Sexey's Hosp., 1986–; Dir, E Somerset NHS Trust, 1991–97. Trustee: Nat. Heritage Meml Fund, 1994–2000; Heritage Lottery Fund, 1994–2000; Comr, Commonwealth War Graves Commn, 2001–06. Contributing Editor: The New Republic, 1980–90; US News and World Report, 1986–. Hon. LLD New Brunswick, 1997; Hon. DLit QUB, 2000; Hon. DLitt Bath, 2002. Samuel Eliot Morison Prize, US Soc. for Mil. Hist., 1996. KM 1999. *Publications:* The Face of Battle, 1976; World Armies, 1978; Six Armies in Normandy, 1982; The Mask of Command, 1987; The Price of Admiralty, 1988, reissued as Battle at Sea, 1993; The Second World War, 1989; (ed) The Times Atlas of the Second World War, 1989; (ed) Churchill's Generals, 1991; A History of Warfare, 1993 (Duff Cooper Prize, 1994); Warpaths: travels of a military historian in North America, 1995; The Battle for History, 1996; The First World War, 1998 (Westminster Medal, 1999); War and Our World: the Reith Lectures, 1998; (ed) The Penguin Book of War: great military writings, 1999; Churchill, 2002; Intelligence in War, 2003; The Iraq War, 2004; The American Civil War, 2009; contribs to DNB, Encyclopaedia Britannica. *Address:* The Manor House, Kilmington, near Warminster, Wilts BA12 6RD. *T:* (01985) 844856. *Clubs:* Garrick; Brook (NY). *Died 2 Aug. 2012.*

KEEN, (David) Alan; MP (Lab and Co-op) Feltham and Heston, since 1992; *b* 25 Nov. 1937; one *s* one *d*; *m* 1980, Ann Lloyd; one step *s*. *Educ:* Sir William Turner's Sch., Redcar. Various posts as systems analyst, accountant and manager, 1963–92. Mem. (Lab) Hounslow BC, 1986–90. Mem., Select Cttee on Culture, Media and Sport, 1997–; Chm., All Party Football Gp, 2001–. *Address:* House of Commons, SW1A 0AA. *Died 10 Nov. 2011.*

KEEN, Maurice Hugh, OBE 2004; FSA; FBA 1990; Fellow of Balliol College, Oxford, 1961–2000, then Emeritus; *b* 30 Oct. 1933; *e s* of Harold Hugh Keen and Catherine Eleanor Lyle Keen (*née* Cummins); *m* 1968, Mary Agnes Keegan; three *d*. *Educ:* Winchester College; Balliol College, Oxford (BA 1st Cl. Mod. Hist. 1957). FSA 1987. Nat. Service 1952–54, commissioned Royal Ulster Rifles. Oxford University: Junior Res. Fellow, The Queen's Coll., 1957–61; Tutor in Medieval History, Balliol Coll., 1961–2000; Clerk of the Market, 2002–06. External examr, Nat. Univ. of Ireland, 1971–78. Fellow, Winchester Coll., 1989–2002. Alexander Prize, RHistS, 1962. *Publications:* The Outlaws of Medieval Legend, 1961; The Laws of War in the Later Middle Ages, 1965; A History of Medieval Europe, 1968; England in the Later Middle Ages, 1973; Chivalry, 1984 (Wolfson History Prize, 1985); English Society in the later Middle Ages, 1990; Origins of the English Gentleman, 2002. *Recreations:* fishing, shooting. *Address:* 4 Walton Street, Oxford OX1 2HG. *Club:* Oxford and Cambridge. *Died 11 Sept. 2012.*

KEENE, John Robert R.; *see* Ruck-Keene.

KELLER, Prof. Rudolf Ernst, MA Manchester; DrPhil Zürich; Professor of German Language and Medieval German Literature, University of Manchester, 1960–82, then Emeritus; *b* 3 Feb. 1920; *m* 1947, Ivy Sparrow; two *d*. *Educ:* Kantonsschule Winterthur, Switzerland; University of Zürich. Teacher at Kantonsschule Winterthur, 1944–46; Asst, 1946–47, Asst Lecturer, 1947–49, University of Manchester; Lecturer in German, Royal Holloway College, University of London, 1949–52; Sen. Lecturer, 1952–59, Reader in German, 1959–60, Dean of Faculty of Arts, 1968–70, Pro-Vice-Chancellor, 1976–79, University of Manchester. Corresp. Mem., Inst. für deutsche Sprache, 1969; Goethe Medal, 1981. *Publications:* Die Ellipse in der neuenglischen Sprache als semantisch-syntaktisches Problem, 1944; Die Sprachen der Welt, 1955 (trans. Bodmer: The Loom of Language); German Dialects, Phonology and Morphology with Selected Texts, 1961; The German Language, 1978; articles in learned periodicals. *Recreations:* reading, travel. *Address:* 8 Wadham Way, Hale, Altrincham, Cheshire WA15 9LJ. *T:* (0161) 980 5237. *Died 19 Oct. 2014.*

KELLETT-BOWMAN, Dame (Mary) Elaine, DBE 1988; MA; *b* 8 July 1923; *d* of late Walter Kay; *m* 1st, 1945, Charles Norman Kellett (*d* 1959); three *s* one *d*; 2nd, 1971, Edward Thomas Kellett-Bowman. *Educ:* Queen Mary Sch., Lytham; The Mount, York; St Anne's Coll., Oxford; Barnett House, Oxford (post-graduate distinction in welfare diploma). Called to Bar, Middle Temple, 1964. Mem., Denbigh BC, 1952–55; Camden Borough Council: Alderman, 1968–74; Vice-Chm., Housing Cttee, 1968; Chm., Welfare Cttee, 1969. Contested (C): Nelson and Colne, 1955; South-West Norfolk, March and Oct. 1959; Buckingham, 1964, 1966. MP (C) Lancaster, 1970–97. Mem. (C) European Parlt, 1975–84 (Mem. for Cumbria, 1979–84); Mem. Social Affairs, Regional Policy and Development Cttees, Eur. Parlt, 1975–84. Lay Mem., Press Council, 1964–68. Pres., Nat. Assoc. of Widows, 1999–2001. Governor, Culford Sch., 1963–2003; Mem. Union European Women, 1956; Delegate to Luxemburg, 1958. No 1 Country Housewife, 1960; Christal MacMillan Law Prize, 1963. *Recreation:* gardening. *Address:* Endymion, Ampfield, Romsey, Hants SO51 9BD. *Died 4 March 2014.*

KELLOCK, Jane Ursula; JP; Member, Council on Tribunals, 1987–93; *b* 21 Oct. 1925; *d* of late Arthur George Symonds and Gertrude Frances Symonds; *m* 1967, His Honour Thomas Oslaf Kellock (*d* 1993). *Educ:* Prior's Field Sch., Godalming. WRNS, 1943–45. Sec., Africa Bureau, London, 1957–67; Editor, Africa Digest, 1957–75; Member: Bd, Commonwealth Development Corporation, 1965–73; Police Complaints Board, 1977–85. Former Mem., S Metropolitan Conciliation Cttee, Race Relations Bd. JP: Inner London, 1968–77; Nottingham City Bench, 1977–91; Inner London (N Westminster), 1992–95. Editor, Commonwealth Judicial Jl, 1985–89. *Died 16 Feb. 2012.*

KELLY, Andrew; *see* Kelly, T. A.

KELLY, Prof. Anthony, CBE 1988; DL; FRS 1973; FREng; Life Fellow, Churchill College, Cambridge, 1985; *b* 25 Jan. 1929; *s* of late Group Captain Vincent Gerald French and Mrs Violet Kelly; *m* 1956, Christina Margaret Dunleavie, BA (*d* 1997); three *s* one *d*. *Educ:* Presentation Coll., Reading; Univ. of Reading (Schol.; BSc 1949); Trinity Coll., Cambridge (PhD 1953, ScD 1968). Research Assoc., Univ. of Illinois, 1953–55; ICI Fellow, Univ. of Birmingham, 1955; Asst, Associate Prof., Northwestern Univ., 1956–59; Univ. Lectr, Cambridge, 1959–67; Founding Fellow, Churchill Coll., 1960; Dir of Studies, Churchill Coll., 1960–67; Supt, Div. of Inorganic and Metallic Structure, 1967–69, Dep. Dir, 1969–75, Nat. Physical Lab. (seconded to ICI, 1973–75); Vice-Chancellor, Univ. of Surrey, 1975–94. Univ. Prof., Univ. of Surrey, 1987. Director: Johnson Wax Ltd, 1981–96; QUO-TEC Ltd, 1984–2000; NPL Management Ltd, 1995–2001; Chm., Surrey Satellite Technology, 1985–95. Vis. Fellow, Univ. of Göttingen, 1960; Vis. Prof., Carnegie Inst. of Technol., 1967; Prof. invité, Ecole Polytechnique Fédérale de Lausanne, 1977. Chm., Jt Standing Cttee on Structural Safety, Instns of Civil and Structural Engrs, 1988–98; Member: SRC Cttee, 1967–72; Council, Inst. of Metals, 1969–74; Council, British Non-Ferrous Metals Res. Assoc., 1970–73; Engrg Materials Requirements Bd, DoI, 1973–75 (Chm., 1976–80); Adv. Cttee, Community Ref. Bureau of EEC, 1973–75. Pres., Inst. of Materials, 1996–97. Mem., Academia Europaea, 1990; Foreign Associate, Nat. Acad. of Engrg of USA, 1986. Lee Kuan Yew Dist. Visitor to Commonwealth of Singapore, 1999. Eminent Speaker, Engineers Australia, 2008. FRSA 1992. DL Surrey, 1993. Hon. FIL 1988; Hon. FIStructE 1996; Hon. FICE 1997. DUniv Surrey, 1994; Hon. DSc: Birmingham, 1997; Reading, 2002; Hon. DEng Hanyang, S Korea, 2001; Dr *hc* Navarra, Spain, 2003. William Hopkins Prize, Cambridge Philosophical Soc., 1967; Beilby Medal, RIC, 1967; A. A. Griffith Medal, 1974, Platinum Medal, 1992, Inst. of Materials; Medal of Excellence, Univ. of Delaware, 1984; Internat. Gold Medal, Amer. Soc. for Materials, 1991; Acta Metallurgica Gold Medal, 2000; Alfred Ewing Medal, ICE, 2003; President's Medal, RAEng, 2011. KSG 1992. *Publications:* Strong Solids, 1966,

3rd edn (with N. H. Macmillan) 1986; (with G. W. Groves) Crystallography and Crystal Defects, 1970, 2nd edn (with K. M. Knowles) 2011; many papers in jls of physical sciences. *Recreations:* science of materials, sailing. *Address:* 29 Madingley Road, Cambridge CB3 0EG. *Club:* Oxford and Cambridge. *Died 4 June 2014.*

KELLY, Brian; *see* Kelly, Air Vice-Marshal H. B.

KELLY, Charles Henry, CBE 1986; QPM 1978; DL; Chief Constable of Staffordshire, 1977–96; *b* 15 July 1930; *s* of Charles Henry Kelly and Phoebe Jane Kelly; *m* 1952, Doris (*née* Kewley) (*d* 1999); one *s* one *d.* *Educ:* Douglas High Sch. for Boys, IOM; London Univ. LLB (Hons). Asst Chief Constable of Essex, 1972; Dep. Chief Constable of Staffordshire, 1976. Associate Prof., Criminal Justice Dept, Michigan State Univ., 1990–2000. Pres., Staffordshire Small Bore Rifle Assoc., 1977–96; Chairman: Staffordshire Police St John Special Centre, 1978–96; ACPO Communications Cttee, 1982–92; No 3 Region, ACPO Cttee, 1985–93. Pres., Staffordshire Soc., 1997–99. Mem. Court, Keele Univ., 1990–2011. MUniv Keele, 1991; Hon. LLD Staffordshire Univ., 1996. DL Stafford, 1979. KStJ 1991 (County Pres., Staffordshire, 1996–). *Recreations:* cricket, reading, walking. *Address:* Milford Lodge, 174 Main Road, Milford, Stafford ST17 0UN. *T:* (01785) 614301. *Club:* Special Forces. *Died 31 Dec. 2014.*

KELLY, Air Vice-Marshal (Herbert) Brian, CB 1983; LVO 1960; MD, FRCP; Consultant Adviser in Medicine to RAF, 1974, Senior Consultant, 1979–83; *b* 12 Aug. 1921; *s* of late Surg. Captain James Cecil Kelly and of Meta Matheson (*née* Fraser). *Educ:* Epsom Coll.; St Thomas' Hosp. (MB, BS 1943, MD 1948). MRCP 1945, FRCP 1968; DCH 1966; MFOM 1982. House appts, St Thomas' Hosp., and St Luke's Hosp., Guildford, 1943–45; RNVR, Med. Specialist, RNH Hong Kong, 1945–48; Med. Registrar and Lectr in Medicine, St Thomas' Hosp., 1948–53; joined RAF Medical Br., 1953; Consultant in Medicine at RAF Hosps, Aden, Ely, Nocton Hall, Singapore, Cyprus, Germany, 1953–83. QHS 1978–83. Consultant, CAA, 1974–93. FRSocMed. Liveryman, Worshipful Soc. of Apothecaries, 1978; Freeman, City of London, 1978. *Publications:* papers in BMJ, Lancet, Brit. Heart Jl, and Internat. Jl of Epidemiology. *Recreation:* choir singing. *Address:* 32 Chiswick Quay, Hartington Road, W4 3UR. *T:* (020) 8995 5042. *E:* bkelly32@me.com. *Club:* Royal Air Force. *Died 27 June 2012.*

KELLY, Rosaline; publishing and industrial relations consultant; Visiting Lecturer in Journalism, London College of Printing, 1981–85; *b* 27 Nov. 1922; *d* of Laurence Kelly and Ellen (*née* Fogarty), Drogheda, Co. Louth, Eire. *Educ:* St Louis Convent, Carrickmacross; University Coll., Dublin, NUI. Journalist with Woman magazine, 1958–77; local management, IPC Magazines Ltd, 1977–80. Active in NUJ, 1958–: Mem., National Exec. Council, 1972–78; first woman Pres., 1975–77; Membership of Honour, 1979; Member: NUJ Appeals Tribunal, 1978–; NUJ Standing Orders Cttee, 1978–2000; Trustee, NUJ Provident Fund Management Cttee, 1977– (Chairperson, 1980–82). Mem., Press Council, 1977–80 (first woman to represent Press side). Rejected as a catalogue holder by Empire Stores. *Recreations:* language and languages, music, compulsive reader. *Address:* c/o National Union of Journalists, 2nd Floor, Spencer House, Spencer Row, off Store Street, Dublin 1, Eire; Arash Areesh, 7 Lakeview Road, Wicklow, Eire. *T:* (404) 69596. *Died 11 April 2013.*

KELLY, (Thomas) Andrew; QC 2000; *b* Oakville, Ontario, 18 July 1955; *s* of John Kelly and Mary Rea Kelly (*née* McKelvey). *Educ:* Bangor Grammar Sch., NI; Christ Church, Oxford (MA). Called to the Bar: Lincoln's Inn, 1978; NI, 1982; in practice at the Bar, 1981–; Res. Asst, H of C, 1981–84. Cross of Royal House of Romania, 2008. *Recreations:* sports, arts, travel, gardening, Bristol cars, Irish silver. *Address:* Francis Taylor Building, Temple, EC4Y 7BY. *T:* (020) 7353 8415. *Clubs:* Royal Automobile; Royal Ulster Yacht; Clandeboye Golf. *Died 3 April 2011.*

KEMBALL, Brig. Humphrey Gurdon, CBE 1971 (OBE 1966); MC 1940; *b* 6 Nov. 1919; *s* of late Brig.-Gen. Alick Gurdon Kemball (late IA) and Evelyn Mary (*née* Synge); *m* 1945, Ella Margery Emmeline (*née* Bickham) (*d* 1997); no *c.* *Educ:* Trinity Coll., Glenalmond; RMC, Sandhurst. Commissioned 1939, 1st Bn The Prince of Wales's Volunteers. Served War of 1939–45 (MC); Staff Coll., 1943. JSSC, 1956; commanded 1st Bn The Lancashire Regt (PWV), 1961–63; i/c Administration, HQ Federal Regular Army, Aden, 1964–66; Asst Dir, MoD, 1966–68; Mil. Attaché, Moscow, 1968–71; HQ British Forces, Near East, 1971–73; Dep. Comdr, SW District, 1973–74. *Recreations:* fishing, travelling. *Address:* 28 Windsor End, Beaconsfield, Bucks HP9 2JW. *T:* (01494) 671698. *Club:* Naval and Military. *Died 6 May 2014.*

KEMP, Robert Thayer; export credit consultant; *b* 18 June 1928; *s* of Robert Kemp and Ada Kemp (*née* Thayer); *m* 1951, Gwendolyn Mabel Minty; three *s.* *Educ:* Bromley Grammar Sch.; London Univ. (BA (Hons) Medieval and Mod. History). Export Credits Guarantee Department: Asst Sec., 1970; Under-Sec., 1975; Head of Project Underwriting Gp, 1981–85; Director: Internat. Gp, 1985–88; Sedgwick Credit, 1989–95. *Publications:* Review of Future Status Options (ECGD), 1989. *Recreations:* cricket, music, theatre. *Address:* 18 Stowell Crescent, Wareham, Dorset BH20 4PY. *T:* (01929) 551919. *Died 24 June 2014.*

KENNEDY, A(lfred) James, CBE 1979; DSc (London), PhD (London); FREng, MIET, FIMMM, FInstP; physicist; *b* 6 Nov. 1921; *m* 1950, Anna Jordan (*d* 1986); no *c.* *Educ:* Haberdashers' Aske's Hatcham Sch.; University Coll., London (BSc (Physics) 1943; Fellow 1976). Commissioned R Signals, 1944; Staff Major (Telecommunications) Central Comd, Agra, India, 1945–46 and at Northern Comd, Rawalpindi, 1946–47; Asst Lectr in Physics, UCL 1947–50; Res. Fellow, Davy-Faraday Lab. of Royal Institution, London, 1950–51; Royal Society, Armourers' and Brasiers' Research Fellow in Metallurgy (at Royal Institution), 1951–54; Head of Metal Physics Sect., BISRA, 1954–57; Prof. of Materials and Head of Dept of Materials, Coll. of Aeronautics, Cranfield, 1957–66; Dir, British Non-Ferrous Metals Res. Assoc., later BNF Metals Technol. Centre, Wantage, 1966–78; Dir of Research, Delta Metal Co., and Man. Dir, Delta Materials Research Ltd, 1978–81; Dep. Dir, Technical Change Centre, 1981–86; Dir, BL Technology Ltd, 1979–83. Vis. Prof. in Metallurgy, Imperial Coll. of Science and Technol., London, 1981–86. Institution of Metallurgists: Pres., 1976–77; a Vice Pres., 1971–74, 1975–76; Mem. Council, 1968–76. President: Inst. of Metals, 1970–71 (Mem. Council, 1968–73; Fellow, 1973); Engrg Section, BAAS, 1983; Member: Metallurgy Cttee, CNAA, 1965–71; ARC, 1967–70, 1971–74, 1977–80 (also Mem., ARC cttees); Adv. Council on Materials, 1970–71; Council, The Metals Soc., 1974–84 (Platinum Medallist, 1977); Inst. of Physics, 1968–71; SRC, 1974–78; Metall. and Mat. Cttee, SRC, 1970–75 (Chm. 1973–74); Engrg Bd, 1973–78; Council of Envmtl Sci. and Engrg, 1973–78; Adv. Council for Applied R&D, 1976–80; Mat. and Chem. Res. Requirements Bd, DoI, 1981–83 (Chm., Non-Ferrous Metals Cttee); Chm., Council of Sci. and Tech. Insts, 1983–84. Fellow, Amer. Soc. Met., 1972. Pres., Brit. Soc. of Rheology, 1964–66; a Governor, Nat. Inst. for Agric. Engrg, 1966–74. Hon. DSc Aston, 1980. *Publications:* Processes of Creep and Fatigue in Metals, 1962; The Materials Background to Space Technology, 1964; Creep and Stress Relaxation in Metals (English edn), 1965; (ed) High Temperature Materials, 1968; research papers and articles, mainly on physical aspects of deformation and fracture in crystalline materials, particularly metals. *Recreations:* music, painting. *Address:* Woodhill, Milton under Wychwood, Chipping Norton, Oxford OX7 6EP. *T:* (01993) 830334. *Club:* Athenæum. *Died 6 Jan. 2011.*

KENNEDY, Rt Hon. Charles (Peter); PC 1999; *b* Inverness, 25 Nov. 1959; *yr s* of late Ian Kennedy, crofter, and Mary McVarish MacEachen; *m* 2002, Sarah Gurling (marr. diss. 2010); one *s.* *Educ:* Lochaber High Sch., Fort William; Univ. of Glasgow (joint MA Hons Philosophy and Politics). President, Glasgow Univ. Union, 1980–81; winner, British Observer Mace for Univ. Debating, 1982. Journalist, BBC Highland, Inverness, 1982; Fulbright Schol. and Associate Instructor in Dept of Speech Communication, Indiana Univ., Bloomington Campus, 1982–83. MP Cromarty and Skye, 1983–97, Ross, Skye and Inverness W, 1997–2005 (SDP, 1983–88, Lib Dem, 1988–2005); MP (Lib Dem) Ross, Skye and Lochaber, 2005–15; contested (Lib Dem) same seat, 2015. SDP spokesman on health, social services, social security and Scottish issues, 1983–87; SDP-Liberal Alliance spokesman on social security, 1987; Lib Dem spokesman on trade and industry, 1988–89, on health, 1989–92, on Europe and East-West relations, 1992–97, on agriculture and rural affairs, 1997–99; Leader, Liberal Democrats, 1999–2006. Member, Select Committee: on Social Services, 1986–87; on Televising of H of C, 1988–90; on Standards and Privileges, 1997–99. Chm., SDP Council for Scotland, 1986–88; Pres., Lib Dems, 1990–94. Rector, Univ. of Glasgow, 2008–14. Occasional journalist, broadcaster and lecturer. *Publications:* The Future of Politics, 2000. *Club:* National Liberal. *Died 2 June 2015.*

KENNEDY, Hon. Geoffrey Alexander, AO 1994; Judge of the Supreme Court of Western Australia, 1981–2001; *b* 6 Sept. 1931; *s* of Alexander Patrick Kennedy and Dorothy Kennedy (*née* Everington); *m* 1964, Alison King; one *s* two *d*. *Educ:* Scotch College, WA; Univ. of Western Australia (BA, LLB); Wadham Coll., Oxford (Rhodes Scholar, 1955; BCL). Partner, Robinson Cox & Co., Solicitors, 1958–75; Mem., Independent Bar, 1976–80; QC (WA) 1977. Mem., Judicial System Adv. Cttee, Constitutional Commn, Australia, 1986–88; Chm., Royal Commn on Commercial Activities of WA Govt, 1991–92; Royal Comr into WA Police Service, 2001–04. Member: Bd, Princess Margaret Hosp. for Children, 1970–88; WA Medical Bd, 1976–81. Chancellor, Univ. of Western Australia, 1990–98; Chairman: Council, Scotch Coll., WA, 1974–83; Nat. Council of Ind. Schs, 1979–81; WA Mus., 1984–91. Hon. LLD Univ. of WA, 1999. *Address:* 32 Keane Street, Peppermint Grove, WA 6011, Australia. *T:* (8) 93845635. *Club:* Weld (Perth). *Died 16 July 2012.*

KENNEDY, (George) Michael (Sinclair), CBE 1997 (OBE 1981); Music Critic, The Sunday Telegraph, 1989–2005; Staff Music Critic, The Daily Telegraph, 1950–89 (Joint Chief Critic, 1987–89); *b* 19 Feb. 1926; *s* of Hew Gilbert Kennedy and Marian Florence Sinclair; *m* 1st, 1947, Eslyn Durdle (*d* 1999); no *c*; 2nd, 1999, Dr Joyce Bourne. *Educ:* Berkhamsted School. Joined Daily Telegraph, Manchester, 1941; served Royal Navy (BPF), 1943–46; rejoined Daily Telegraph, Manchester, serving in various capacities on editorial staff; Asst Northern Editor, 1958; Northern Ed., 1960–86. Mem. Cttee, Vaughan Williams Trust, 1965– (Chm., 1977–2009); Chm., Vaughan Williams Charitable Trust, 2007–; Vice-President: Elgar Foundn and Elgar Soc.; Hallé Concerts Soc., 2014. Hon. Mem., Royal Manchester Coll. of Music, 1971. Hon. Mem., Royal Philharmonic Soc., 2005. FJI 1967; FRNCM 1981; CRNCM 1999. Hon. MA 1975, Hon. DMus 2003, Manchester. Gold Medal, Elgar Soc., 2011. *Publications:* The Hallé Tradition, 1960; The Works of Ralph Vaughan Williams, 1964, 2nd edn 1980; Portrait of Elgar, 1968, 4th edn 1993; Portrait of Manchester, 1970; Elgar Orchestral Works, 1970; History of Royal Manchester College of Music, 1971; Barbirolli: Conductor Laureate, 1971, revd edn 2003; (ed) The Autobiography of Charles Hallé, 1973; Mahler, 1974, 3rd edn 2000 (Japanese edn 1978); Richard Strauss, 1976, 2nd edn 1995; (ed) Concise Oxford Dictionary of Music, 3rd edn, 1980, 5th edn 2006; Britten, 1981, 3rd edn 2000; The Hallé, 1858–1983, 1983; Strauss Tone Poems, 1984; Oxford Dictionary of Music, 1985, 3rd edn 2006; Adrian Boult, 1987; Portrait of Walton, 1989, 2nd edn 1997; Music Enriches All: 21 years of the Royal Northern College of Music, 1994; Richard Strauss: man, musician, enigma, 1999; The Life of Elgar, 2004; Buxton: an English festival, 2004; Glyndebourne: a short history, 2010; scripts for BBC, contrib. musical jls. *Recreations:* listening to music, watching cricket. *Address:* The Bungalow, 62 Edilom Road, Manchester M8 4HZ. *T:* (0161) 740 4528. *E:* majkennedy@bungalow62.fsnet.co.uk. *Clubs:* Athenæum; Lancashire CC, Middlesex CC. *Died 31 Dec. 2014.*

KENNEDY, James; *see* Kennedy, A. J.

KENNEDY, Sir Jock; *see* Kennedy, Air Chief Marshal Sir T. L.

KENNEDY, John Maxwell; Senior Partner, Allen & Overy, 1986–94; *b* 9 July 1934; *s* of George and Betty Gertrude Kennedy; *m* 1958, Margaret Joan (*née* Davies); four *s*. *Educ:* University Coll., London (LLB). Admitted Solicitor, 1957; Partner, Allen & Overy, 1962. Chm., Law Debenture Corp., 1994–2000; Dir, Amlin (formerly Angerstein Underwriting Trust) plc, 1993–2004 (Chm., 1996–98). Mem., FSA (formerly SIB), 1993–98. Dir, Nuclear Liabilities (formerly Nuclear Generation Decommissioning) Fund Ltd, 1996–2008. Chm., Lloyd's Corporate Capital Assoc., 1995–97. *Recreations:* sport, music, reading. *Address:* 16 Kensington Park Road, W11 3BU. *T:* (020) 7727 6929. *Clubs:* City of London, City Law, Hurlingham; Royal Wimbledon Golf. *Died 24 Sept. 2012.*

KENNEDY, Michael; *see* Kennedy, G. M. S.

KENNEDY, Sir Michael Edward, 8th Bt *cr* 1836, of Johnstown Kennedy, Co. Dublin; *b* 12 April 1956; *s* of Sir (George) Ronald Derrick Kennedy, 7th Bt and of Noelle Mona, *d* of Charles Henry Green; *S* father, 1988, but his name does not appear on the Official Roll of the Baronetage; *m* 1984, Helen Christine Jennifer (marr. diss. 2005), *d* of Patrick Lancelot Rae; one *s* three *d*. *Heir:* *s* George Mathew Rae Kennedy, *b* 9 Dec. 1993. *Died 6 May 2012.*

KENNEDY, Thomas Alexander; economist; *b* 11 July 1920; *s* of late Rt Hon. Thomas Kennedy, PC, and Annie S. Kennedy (*née* Michie); *m* 1947, Audrey (*née* Plunkett) (*d* 1991); one *s* two *d*. *Educ:* Alleyn's Sch., Dulwich; Durham Univ. (BA). Economist: Bd of Trade, 1950–52; Colonial Office, 1952–55; Lectr in Econs, Makerere Coll., Uganda, 1955–61; Economist: HM Treasury, Foreign Office, DEA, 1961–67; Economic Dir, NEDO, 1967–70; Under-Secretary: DTI, 1970–74; Dept of Energy, 1974–80, resigned. Chief Tech. Adviser (Economist Planner), Min. of Petroleum and Mineral Resources, Bangladesh, 1980–81. Vis. Fellow, Clare Hall, Cambridge, 1981–82. Consultant, World Bank: Uganda, Zambia, Swaziland, 1983–86, retired 1987. *Publications:* Harry Hyndman: an uncommon socialist, 1995. *Address:* 1 Beckside Mews, Staindrop, Darlington, Co. Durham DL2 3PG. *T:* (01833) 660616. *Died 11 Feb. 2013.*

KENNEDY, Air Chief Marshal Sir Thomas Lawrie, (Sir Jock), GCB 1985 (KCB 1980 CB 1978); AFC 1953 and Bar 1960; Lord-Lieutenant of Rutland, 1997–2003; Controller, RAF Benevolent Fund, 1988–93; *b* 19 May 1928; *s* of James Domoné Kennedy and Margaret Henderson Lawrie; *m* 1959, Margaret Ann Parker; one *s* two *d*. *Educ:* Hawick High Sch. RAF Coll., Cranwell, 1946–49; commissioned, 1949. Sqdn service, 1949–53; exchange service, RAAF, 1953–55; returned to UK, 1955; 27 Sqdn (Canberra), 1955–57; Radar Research Estabt, 1957–60; RAF Coll. Selection Bd, 1960–62; RN Staff Coll., Greenwich, 1962; HQ Middle East, 1962–64; CO, No 99 (Britannia) Sqdn, 1965–67; HQ Air Support Comd, 1967–69; CO, RAF Brize Norton, 1970–71; Dep. Comdt, RAF Staff Coll., 1971–73; Dir of Ops (AS) MoD, 1973–75; Royal Coll. of Defence Studies, 1976; Comdr, Northern Maritime Air Region, 1977–79; Deputy C-in-C, RAF Strike Command, 1979–81; C-in-C, RAF Germany, and Comdr, 2nd Allied Tactical Air Force, 1981–83; Air Mem. for Personnel, 1983–86; Air ADC to the Queen, 1983–86. Dir, Dowty Group, 1987–92. Freeman, City of London, 1987; Hon. Liveryman, Fruiterers' Co., 1987. DL Leics, 1989. *Recreations:* golf, sailing. *Address:* c/o Lloyds TSB, Cox's & King's Branch, PO Box 1190, SW1Y 5NA. *Club:* Royal Air Force. *Died 18 Nov. 2013.*

KENNY, David John, CBE 1991; Regional General Manager, North West Thames Regional Health Authority, 1984–91 (Regional Administrator, 1982–84); *b* 2 Dec. 1940; *s* of late Gerald Henry Kenny and Ellen Veronica (*née* Crosse); *m* 1964, Elisabeth Ann, *d* of late Robert and of Jean Ferris; three *s*. *Educ:* Royal Belfast Academical Instn; Queen's Univ., Belfast (LLB). FHSM. Dep. House Governor, Bd of Governors, London Hosp., 1972; Dist Administrator, Tower Hamlets Health Dist, 1974; Area Administrator, Kensington and Chelsea and Westminster AHA, 1978. Mem. Nat. Council, Inst. of Health Service Managers, 1975–86 and 1988–91 (Pres. 1981–82); Chm.,

Gen. Managers of RHAs, 1989–91. Chm., Data Protection Working Gp, Internat. Med. Informatics Assoc., 1979–87. *Publications:* (jtly) Data Protection in Health Information Systems, 1980; articles on management topics, data protection and ethics. *Recreations:* cinema, theatre, athletics, rugby football. *Address:* 131 Maze Hill, SE3 7UB. *T:* (020) 8858 1545. *Died 1 Sept. 2011.*

KENT, Pendarell Hugh, CBE 1997; Executive Director, Bank of England, 1994–97; *b* 18 Aug. 1937; *s* of Hugh and Ann Kent; *m* 1960, Jill George; one *s* one *d.* *Educ:* University College Sch.; Jesus Coll., Oxford (MA Hons). Intelligence Corps, 2nd Lieut, 1959–61. Bank of England, 1961–97: UK Alternate Exec. Dir, IMF, 1976–79; Head: of Inf. Div., 1984–85; of Internat. Div. (Internat. Financial Instns and Developing Countries), 1985–88; Associate Dir, Finance and Industry, 1988–94. Dir, Private Finance Panel, 1993–97. Chm., CRESTCo, 1994–96; Exec. Chm., European Securities Forum, 2000–02; Chm., Euroclear UK Mkt Adv. Cttee, 2002–11; non-executive Director: BR Southern Region, 1986–92 (Chm., 1989–92); NatWest Gp, 1997–2000; Strategic Rail Authy, 1999–2006 (Chm., 2006); Schroder & Co. Ltd, 2001–; F & C Capital and Income Investment Trust, 2003–12 (Chm., 2005–12); CDC (Mem., Commonwealth Develt Corp., 1995–2001); Punjab Nat. Bank Internat., 2007–. Dir, City of London Fest., 1996–2002 (Chm., 1997–2001); Dep. Chm., Heart of the City, 2000–10. Gov., NYO, 2000–08. Patron, Blind in Business, 2003– (Trustee, 1992–2002; Chm., 1996–2001). Property Award, Coll. of Estate Mgt, 1997. *Publications:* Nursery Schools for All (with Jill Kent), 1970. *Recreations:* art, jazz. *Died 30 Dec. 2013.*

KENWORTHY-BROWNE, (Bernard) Peter (Francis); a District Judge (formerly Registrar) of the High Court (Family Division), 1982–2002; *b* 11 May 1930; *s* of late Bernard Evelyn Kenworthy-Browne and Margaret Sibylla Kenworthy-Browne; *m* 1989, Elizabeth Anne, *o d* of late Dr J. A. Bowen-Jones. *Educ:* Ampleforth; Oriel Coll., Oxford. MA. 2nd Lieut, Irish Guards, 1949–50. Called to the Bar, Lincoln's Inn, 1955; Oxford, and Midland and Oxford Circuit, 1957–82; a Recorder of the Crown Court, 1981–82. *Recreations:* music, field sports, gardening. *Address:* The Old Vicarage, Staverton, Northants NN11 6JJ. *T:* (01327) 704667. *Club:* Cavalry and Guards. *Died 22 May 2014.*

KERMACK, Stuart Ogilvy; Sheriff of Tayside, Central and Fife: at Forfar, 1971–93; at Perth, 1971–75; at Arbroath, 1975–91; at Dundee, 1991–93; *b* 9 July 1934; *s* of late Stuart Grace Kermack, CBE and of Nell P., *y d* of Thomas White, SSC; *m* 1961, Barbara Mackenzie, BSc; three *s* one *d.* *Educ:* Glasgow Academy; Jesus Coll., Oxford; Glasgow Univ.; Edinburgh Univ. BA Oxon (Jurisprudence), 1956; LLB Glasgow, 1959. Called to Scots Bar, 1959. Sheriff Substitute of Inverness, Moray, Nairn and Ross, at Elgin and Nairn, 1965–71. *Publications:* The Pictish Symbols and the Vita Sancti Columbae, 2009; contrib. Pictish Arts Soc. Jl; articles in legal journals. *Address:* 23 South Learmonth Gardens, Edinburgh EH4 1EZ. *T:* (0131) 332 1898. *Died 8 Aug. 2012.*

KERMAN, Prof. Joseph Wilfred; Professor of Music, University of California at Berkeley, 1974–94, then Emeritus (Chambers Professor of Music, 1986–89); *b* 3 April 1924; *m* 1945, Vivian Shaviro (*d* 2007); one *s* one *d* (and one *s* decd). *Educ:* New York Univ. (AB); Princeton Univ. (PhD). Dir of Graduate Studies, Westminster Choir Coll., Princeton, NJ, USA, 1949–51; Music Faculty, Univ. of California at Berkeley, 1951–72, 1974– (Dep. Chm., 1960–63, 1991–93); Heather Prof. of Music, Oxford Univ., and Fellow of Wadham Coll., Oxford, 1972–74. Co-editor, 19th Century Music, 1977–88. Guggenheim, Fulbright and NEH Fellowships; Visiting Fellow: All Souls Coll., Oxford, 1966; Society for the Humanities, Cornell Univ., USA, 1970; Clare Hall, Cambridge, 1971; Walker-Ames Vis. Prof., Univ. of Washington, 1986; Valentine Vis. Prof., Amherst Coll., 1988; Gauss Lectr, Princeton Univ., 1988; Phi Beta Kappa Scholar, 1993; Charles Eliot Norton Prof. of Poetry, Harvard Univ., 1997–98. Fellow: American Academy of Arts and Sciences; Amer. Philos. Soc.; Corresp. FBA 1984. Hon. Mem., Amer. Musicol Soc., 1995. Hon. FRAM. Hon. DHL Fairfield Univ., 1970. *Publications:* Opera as Drama, 1956, rev. edn 1988; The Elizabethan Madrigal, 1962; The Beethoven Quartets, 1967; A History of Art and Music (with H. W. Janson), 1968; (ed) Ludwig van Beethoven: Autograph Miscellany, 1786–99 (Kafka Sketchbook), 2 vols, 1970 (Kinkeldey Award); Listen, 1972, 9th edn 2011; The Masses and Motets of William Byrd, 1981 (Kinkeldey Award; Deems Taylor Award); The New Grove Beethoven (with A. Tyson), 1983; (co-ed) Beethoven Studies, vol. 1 1973, vol. 2 1977, vol. 3 1982; Musicology, 1985; (ed) Music at the Turn of the Century, 1990; Write All These Down, 1994 (Deems Taylor Award); Concerto Conversations, 1999; The Art of Fugue, 2005; Opera and the Morbidity of Music, 2009; essays, in music criticism and musicology, in: Hudson Review, New York Review, San Francisco Chronicle, etc. *Address:* Music Department, University of California, Berkeley, CA 94720, USA; 107 Southampton Avenue, Berkeley, CA 94707–2036, USA. *Died 17 March 2014.*

KERR, Prof. David Nicol Sharp, CBE 1992; MSc; FRCP, FRCPE; Professor of Renal Medicine, 1987–91, Dean, 1984–91, Royal Postgraduate Medical School, University of London; Professor Emeritus of Renal Medicine, Imperial College London; *b* 27 Dec. 1927; *s* of William Kerr and Elsie (Ransted) Kerr; *m* 1960, Eleanor Jones; two *s* one *d.* *Educ:* George Watson's Boys' College; Edinburgh University (MB ChB); University of Wisconsin (MSc). FRCPE 1966; FRCP 1967. House Physician and Surgeon, Royal Infirmary, Edinburgh, 1951–52; Exchange scholar, Univ. of Wisconsin, 1952–53; Surgeon Lieut, RNVR, 1953–55; Asst Lectr, Univ. of Edinburgh, 1956–57; Registrar, Hammersmith Hosp., 1957–59; Lectr, Univ. of Durham, 1959–63; Consultant Physician, Royal Victoria Infirmary, Newcastle upon Tyne, 1962–83; Senior Lectr, 1963–68, Prof. of Medicine, 1968–83, Univ. of Newcastle upon Tyne. Postgrad. Med. Advr, NW Thames RHA, later N Thames Regl Office, NHS Executive, 1991–97. Med. Awards Administrator, Commonwealth Scholarships Commn, 1993–98. Member: Council, Internat. Soc. of Nephrology, 1984–93; Council, British Heart Foundn, 1989–97; NW Thames RHA, 1989–91; Hammersmith and Queen Charlotte's SHA, 1984–91; Ealing Hosp. NHS Trust, 1991–95; Standing Med. Adv. Cttee, DHSS, 1979–90. Sen. Censor and First Vice Pres., RCP, 1990–91. Eur. Dialysis Transplant Assoc., subseq. ERA EDTA: Founder Mem., 1964; Ed., 1964–70; Pres., 1983; Hon. Mem., 1987. Hon. Fellow, SA Coll. of Medicine, 1992; Hon. Mem., Spanish Soc. of Nephrology, 1992. Vice-Pres., Nat. Kidney Res. Fund, 2003– (Trustee, 1999–, Chm. Trustees, 2000–02). Hon. DSc Khartoum, 2005. Editor, Jl of RCP, 1994–98. *Publications:* Short Textbook of Renal Disease, 1968; (ed) Oxford Textbook of Clinical Nephrology, 1992, 2nd edn 1997; chapters in numerous books incl. Cecil-Loeb Textbook of Medicine and Oxford Textbook of Medicine; articles on renal disease in med. jls. *Recreations:* church, walking, theatre, opera. *Address:* 22 Carbery Avenue, W3 9AL. *T:* and *Fax:* (020) 8992 3231. *Died 20 April 2014.*

KERR, Dr Edwin, CBE 1986; Chairman, Student Employment Services Ltd, since 1995; *b* 1 July 1926; *e s* of late Robert John Kerr and Mary Elizabeth Kerr (*née* Ferguson); *m* 1949, Gertrude Elizabeth (*née* Turbitt); one *s* two *d.* *Educ:* Royal Belfast Academical Instn; Queen's Univ., Belfast (BSc, PhD). FIMA, FBCS. Asst Lectr in Maths, QUB, 1948–52; Lectr in Maths, Coll. of Technology, Birmingham (later Univ. of Aston in Birmingham), 1952–55; Lectr in Maths, Coll. of Science and Technology, Manchester (later Univ. of Manchester Inst. of Science and Technology), 1956–58; Head of Maths Dept, Royal Coll. of Advanced Technology, Salford (later Univ. of Salford), 1958–66; Principal, Paisley Coll. of Technology, 1966–72; Chief Officer, CNAA, 1972–86; Chm. and Chief Exec., Exam. Bd for Financial Planning, 1987–89; Chief Exec., Coll. for Financial Planning, 1988–96; Chm., Vocational and Academic Bd, Inst. of Health and Care Develts, 1996–99; Academic Dir, Regent's Business Sch., Regent's Coll., London, 1997–2001. Member: Adv. Cttee on Supply and Training of Teachers, 1973–78; Adv. Cttee on Supply and Educn of Teachers, 1980–85; Bd for Local Authority Higher Educn, 1982–85; Bd for Public Sector Higher Educn, 1985–86;

Mem. and Vice-Chm., Continuing Educn Standing Cttee, 1985–88. President: Soc. for Res. into Higher Educn, 1974–77; The Mathematical Assoc., 1976–77. Hon. FCP 1984; Hon. Fellow: Coventry Lanchester, Newcastle upon Tyne, Portsmouth and Sheffield Polytechnics, 1986; Huddersfield Polytechnic, and Paisley Coll. of Technol., 1987; Goldsmiths' Coll., London, 1991. DUniv: Open, 1977; Paisley, 1993; Hon. DSc Ulster, 1986; Hon. DEd CNAA, 1989. *Publications:* (with R. Butler) An Introduction to Numerical Methods, 1962; various mathematical and educational. *Recreation:* gardening. *Address:* 17 Old Galgorm Manor, Ballymena, Co. Antrim BT42 1RY. *Club:* Travellers. *Died 12 May 2012.*

KERR, William Francis Kennedy, OBE 1984; PhD, CEng, FIMechE; Principal, Belfast College of Technology, 1969–84; *b* 1 Aug. 1923; *m* 1953, H. Adams; two *s*. *Educ:* Portadown Technical Coll. and Queen's Univ., Belfast. BSc (Hons) in Mech. Engineering, MSc, PhD. Teacher of Mathematics, Portadown Techn. Coll., 1947–48; Teacher and Sen. Lectr in Mech. Engrg, Coll. of Techn., Belfast, 1948–55; Lectr and Adviser of Studies in Mech. Engrg, Queen's Univ. of Belfast, 1955–62; Head of Dept of Mech., Civil, and Prodn Engrg, Dundee Coll. of Techn., 1962–67; Vice-Principal, Coll. of Techn., Belfast, 1967–69. Chm., NI Cttee for Educnl Technology, 1973–79; Member: Mech. and Prodn Engrg Subject Panel, CNAA, 1964–67; Council for Educnl Technology, 1973–79; Belfast Educn and Library Bd, 1977–81; NI Council for Educnl Develt, 1980–84; NI Manpower Council, 1981–84; Chm., Assoc. of Principals of Colleges (NI Branch), 1982; Governor, Royal Belfast Academical Instn, 1969–84; Mem. Court, Ulster Univ., 1985–92. *Publications:* contribs on environmental testing of metals, etc. *Recreations:* golf, motoring, reading. *Address:* Apt 1, Avoca House, 83 Princetown Road, Bangor, Co. Down, Northern Ireland BT20 3TD. *Died 30 Sept. 2012.*

KERRY, Sir Michael (James), KCB 1983 (CB 1976); QC 1984; *b* 5 Aug. 1923; *s* of Russell Kerry and Marjorie (*née* Kensington); *m* 1951, Sidney Rosetta Elizabeth (*née* Foster) (*d* 2003); one *s* two *d*. *Educ:* Rugby Sch.; St John's Coll., Oxford (MA; Hon. Fellow 1986). Served with RAF, 1942–46. Called to Bar, Lincoln's Inn, 1949, Bencher 1984. Joined BoT as Legal Asst, 1951; Sen. Legal Asst, 1959; Asst Solicitor, 1964; Principal Asst Solicitor, Dept of Trade and Industry, 1972, Solicitor, 1973–80; HM Procurator Gen. and Treasury Solicitor, 1980–84. Dep. Chm., LAUTRO, 1988–91. *Recreations:* golf, gardening. *Address:* South Bedales, Lewes Road, Haywards Heath, W Sussex RH17 7TE. *T:* (01444) 831303. *Club:* Piltdown Golf. *Died 11 May 2012.*

KERSHAW, Jennifer Christine; QC 1998; **Her Honour Judge Kershaw;** a Circuit Judge, since 2005; *b* 1 May 1951; *m* 2010, Richard Peter Vellacott Jenkins, (His Honour Judge Richard Jenkins, QC); one step *s* one step *d*; one *s* two *d* by a former marriage. *Educ:* King's Coll., London (LLB 1973). Called to the Bar, Lincoln's Inn, 1974; a Recorder, 2000–05. *Recreations:* horses, gardening. *Died 3 Oct. 2012.*

KHORANA, Prof. Har Gobind; Sloan Professor of Chemistry and Biology, Massachusetts Institute of Technology, 1970–97, then Emeritus; *b* Raipur, India, 9 Jan. 1922; *s* of Shri Ganpat Rai and Shrimata Krishna (Devi); *m* 1952, Esther Elizabeth Sibler (*d* 2001); one *s* one *d* (and one *d* decd). *Educ:* Punjab Univ. (BSc 1943; MSc 1945); Liverpool Univ. (PhD 1948; Govt of India Student). Post-doctoral Fellow of Govt of India, Federal Inst. of Techn., Zurich, 1948–49; Nuffield Fellow, Cambridge Univ., 1950–52; Head, Organic Chemistry Group, BC Research Council, 1952–60. Univ. of Wisconsin: Prof. and Co-Dir, Inst. for Enzyme Research, 1960–70; Prof., Dept of Biochemistry, 1962–70; Conrad A. Elvehjem Prof. in the Life Sciences, 1964–70. Visiting Professor: Rockefeller Inst., NY, 1958–60; Stanford Univ., 1964; Harvard Med. Sch., 1966; Andrew D. White Prof.-at-large, Cornell Univ., 1974–80. Special or memorial lectures in USA, Poland, Canada, Switzerland, UK and Japan. Fellow: Chem. Inst. of Canada, 1959; Amer. Assoc. for Advancement of Science, 1966; Amer. Acad. of Arts and Sciences, 1967. Overseas Fellow, Churchill Coll., Cambridge, 1967. Member: Nat. Acad. of Sciences, 1966; Deutsche Akademie der Naturforscher Leopoldina, 1968; Pontifical Acad. of Scis, Rome, 1978; Foreign Member: Indian Acad. of Scis, 1976; Royal Society, 1978; RSE, 1982. Various hon. degrees. Merck Award, Chem. Inst. Canada, 1958; Gold Medal for 1960, Professional Inst. of Public Service of Canada; Dannie-Heineman Preis, Germany, 1967; Remsen Award, Johns Hopkins Univ., ACS Award for Creative Work in Synthetic Organic Chemistry, Louisa Gross Horwitz Award, Lasker Foundn Award for Basic Med. Research, Nobel Prize for Physiology or Medicine (jtly), 1968; Gairdner Foundn Award, 1980; US Nat. Medal of Science, 1987. Order of San Carlos (Columbia), 1986. *Publications:* Some Recent Developments in the Chemistry of Phosphate Esters of Biological Interest, 1961; numerous papers in Biochemistry, Jl Amer. Chem. Soc., Proc. Nat. Acad. Scis, etc. *Recreations:* hiking, swimming. *Address:* Department of Biology, Massachusetts Institute of Technology, Cambridge, MA 02139, USA. *Died 9 Nov. 2011.*

KIDD, Prof. Ian Gray, FBA 1993; Emeritus Professor of Greek, since 1987, Chancellor's Assessor, 1989–98, University of St Andrews; *b* 6 March 1922; *s* of A. H. Kidd and I. Gray; *m* 1949, Sheila Elizabeth Dow (*d* 2007); three *s*. *Educ:* Dundee High Sch.; Univ. of St Andrews (MA, Miller Prize 1947); Queen's Coll., Oxford (BA Greats, MA). Served War of 1939–45: commnd Argyll and Sutherland Highlanders; Sicily, Italy, 1943–44; POW, 1944–45. St Andrews University: Lectr in Greek, 1949–65; Sen. Lectr, 1965–73; Professor: of Ancient Philosophy, 1973–76; of Greek, 1976–87; Vice-Pres., Univ. Court, 1997–98; Provost, St Leonard's Coll., 1978–83 (Hon. Fellow, 1987). Vis. Prof. of Classics, Univ. of Texas at Austin, 1965–66; Mem., Inst. for Advanced Study, Princeton, 1971–72 and 1979–80. General Comr of Inland Revenue, 1982–97. Chm., E Fife Educnl Trust, 1977–89. Gov., Dollar Acad., 1982–91. Hon. Fellow, Inst. for Res. in Classical Philosophy and Sci., Princeton, 1989–. Hon. DLitt St Andrews, 2001. *Publications:* (ed) Posidonius, Works: vol. I, (with L. Edelstein) The Fragments, 1972, 2nd edn 1989; vol. II(i) and (ii), The Commentary, 1988; vol. III, The Translation of the Fragments, 1999; (with R. Waterfield) Plutarch, Essays, 1992; contributions to: Concise Encyclopedia of Western Philosophy and Philosophers, 1960; The Encyclopedia of Philosophy, ed P. Edwards, 1967; Problems in Stoicism, 1971; The Stoics, 1978; Les Stoiciens et leur Logique, 1978; Stoic and Peripatetic Ethics, 1983; Aspects de la Philosophie Hellénistique, 1986; The Criterion of Truth, 1989; Philosophia Togata, 1989; Owls to Athens, 1990; Handbook of Metaphysics and Ontology, 1991; Theophrastus, 1992; Socratic Questions, 1992; Philosophen der Antike, 1996; The Oxford Classical Dictionary, 1996; Polyhistor: studies in the history of ancient philosophy, 1996; Collecting Fragments, 1997; Fragmentsammlungen philosophischer Texte der Antike, 1998; The Philosophy of Zeno, 2002; articles in learned jls. *Recreations:* music, sea air, thinking, looking at pictures. *Address:* Craigmount Care Home, 32 The Scores, St Andrews, Fife KY16 9AS. *T:* (01334) 473608. *Died 20 March 2011.*

KIELY, Dr David George; Chief Naval Weapons Systems Engineer (Under Secretary), Ministry of Defence, Procurement Executive, 1983–84; consultant engineer; *b* 23 July 1925; *o s* of late George Thomas and Susan Kiely, Ballynahinch, Co. Down; *m* 1956, Dr Ann Wilhelmina (*née* Kilpatrick), MB, BCh, BAO, DCH, DPH, MFCM, Hillsborough, Co. Down; one *s* one *d*. *Educ:* Down High Sch., Downpatrick; Queen's Univ., Belfast (BSc, MSc); Sorbonne (DSci). CEng, FIET; CPhys, FInstP; psc 1961. Appts in RN Scientific Service from 1944; Naval Staff Coll., 1961–62; Head of Electronic Warfare Div., ASWE, 1965–68; Head of Communications and Sensor Dept, ASWE, 1968–72; Dir-Gen., Telecommunications, 1972–74, Dir-Gen., Strategic Electronic Systems, 1974–76, Dir-Gen., Electronics Res., 1976–78, Exec. Officer, Electronics Research Council, 1976–78, Dir, Naval Surface Weapons, ASWE, 1978–83, MoD, PE. Gp Chief Exec. and Dir, Chemring PLC, 1984–85. Chm., R&D Policy Cttee, Gen. Lights Authorities of UK and Eire, 1974–89. Governor: Portsmouth Coll. of Technology, 1965–69; Springfield Sch., Portsmouth, 1993–97. Mem., 1982–89,

Chm., 1985–89, Council, Chichester Cathedral. *Publications:* Dielectric Aerials, 1953; Marine Navigational Aids for Coastal Waters of the British Isles, 1987; Naval Electronic Warfare, 1988; Naval Surface Weapons, 1988; Defence Procurement, 1990; The Future for the Defence Industry, 1990; chapter: in Progress in Dielectrics, 1961; in Fundamentals of Microwave Electronics, 1963; in Naval Command and Control, 1989; papers in Proc. IEE and other learned jls, etc. *Recreations:* fly fishing, gardening. *Address:* Cranleigh, 107 Havant Road, Emsworth, Hants PO10 7LF. *T:* (01243) 372250. *Died 24 March 2012.*

KIERNAN, Prof. Christopher Charles; Professor of Behavioural Studies in Mental Handicap, University of Manchester, 1984–2001 (Director, Hester Adrian Research Centre, 1984–2000); *b* 3 June 1936; *s* of Christopher J. and Mary L. Kiernan; *m* 1962, Diana Elizabeth Maynard; two *s* one *d.* *Educ:* Nottingham Univ. (BA); London Univ. (PhD); ABPsS. Lecturer in Psychology, Birkbeck Coll., London Univ., 1961–70; Sen. Lectr, Child Development, Univ. of London Inst. of Education, 1970–74; Dep. Director, Thomas Coram Research Unit, Univ. of London Inst. of Education, 1975–84. *Publications:* Behaviour Assessment Battery, 1977, 2nd edn 1982; Starting Off, 1978; Behaviour Modification with the Severely Retarded, 1975; Analysis of Programmes for Teaching, 1981; Signs and Symbols, 1982; Research to Practice, 1993. *Recreation:* survival. *Died 23 April 2011.*

KILMAINE, 7th Baron *cr* 1789; **John David Henry Browne;** Bt 1636; Director: Whale Tankers Ltd, 1974–2001; Fusion (Bickenhill) Ltd, 1969–96; *b* 2 April 1948; *s* of 6th Baron Kilmaine, CBE, and Wilhelmina Phyllis, *o d* of Scott Arnott, Brasted, Kent; *S* father, 1978; *m* 1982, Linda, *yr d* of Dennis Robinson; one *s* one *d.* *Educ:* Eton. Chm., Irish Peers' Assoc., 1990–2011. Trustee: William Blake House (Northants) Ltd, 2001–; Glasallt Fawr Camphill Centre, 2008–. *Heir:* *s* Hon. John Francis Sandford Browne, *b* 4 April 1983. *Died 12 Jan. 2013.*

KILPATRICK OF KINCRAIG, Baron *cr* 1996 (Life Peer), of Dysart in the district of Kirkcaldy; **Robert Kilpatrick,** Kt 1986; CBE 1979; President, General Medical Council, 1989–95 (Member, 1972–76 and 1979–95); *b* 29 July 1926; *s* of Robert Kilpatrick and Catherine Sharp Glover; *m* 1950, Elizabeth Gibson Page Forbes; two *s* one *d.* *Educ:* Buckhaven High Sch.; Edinburgh Univ. MB, ChB (Hons) 1949; Ettles Schol.; Leslie Gold Medallist; MD 1960; FRCP(Ed) 1963; FRCP 1975; FRCPSGlas 1991; FRSE 1998. Med. Registrar, Edinburgh, 1951–54; Lectr, Univ. of Sheffield, 1955–66; Rockefeller Trav. Fellowship, MRC, Harvard Univ., 1961–62; Commonwealth Trav. Fellowship, 1962; Prof. of Clin. Pharmacology and Therapeutics, Univ. of Sheffield, 1966–75; Dean, Faculty of Medicine, Univ. of Sheffield, 1970–73; Univ. of Leicester: Prof. and Head of Dept of Clinical Pharmacology and Therapeutics, 1975–83; Dean, Faculty of Medicine, 1975–89; Prof. of Medicine, 1984–89. Chairman: Adv. Cttee on Pesticides, 1975–87; Soc. of Endocrinology, 1975–78; Scottish Hosp. Endowment Res. Trust, 1996–2000. Pres., BMA, 1997–98. Hon. FRCS 1995; Hon. FRCPI 1995; Hon. FRCPath 1996; Hon. FRCSE 1996; Hon. FRCPE 1996. Dr *hc* Edinburgh, 1987; Hon. LLD: Dundee, 1992; Sheffield, 1995; Hon. DSc: Hull, 1994; Leicester, 1994. *Publications:* articles in med. and sci. jls. *Recreation:* golf. *Address:* 12 Wester Coates Gardens, Edinburgh EH12 5LT. *Clubs:* New (Edinburgh); Royal and Ancient (St Andrews). *Died 16 Sept. 2015.*

KILPATRICK, Prof. (George) Stewart, OBE 1986; MD; FRCP, FRCPE; David Davies Chair of Tuberculosis and Chest Diseases and Head of Department, 1968–92, Vice-Provost, 1987–90, University of Wales College of Medicine, Cardiff; Senior Hon. Consultant Physician to South Glamorgan Health Authority, 1963–90; *b* 26 June 1925; *s* of Hugh Kilpatrick and Annie Merricks Johnstone Stewart; *m* 1954, Joan Askew. *Educ:* George Watson's Coll., Edinburgh; Edinburgh Univ. Med. Sch. (MB ChB 1947, MD 1954). MRCPE 1952, FRCPE 1966; MRCP 1971, FRCP 1975. Medical posts in Edinburgh; Captain RAMC, 1949–51; Mem., Scientific Staff, MRC Pneumoconiosis Research Unit, 1952–54; med. and res. posts, London, Edinburgh and Cardiff; Dean of Clin. Studies, Univ. of Wales Coll. of Medicine, 1970–87. Formerly Chm., Sci. Cttees, Internat. Union Against Tuberculosis (formerly Chm., Treatment Cttee); Chm. Council, Assoc. for Study of Med. Educn, 1981–86; Chm., Assoc. of Medical Deans in Europe, 1982–85. Ext. Examr in Medicine, Queen's Univ. Belfast, 1986–88. Marc Daniels Lectr, RCP 1987. Pres., Cardiff Medical Soc., 1990–91. FRSocMed. Silver Jubilee Medal, 1977. *Publications:* numerous papers to med. and sci. jls; chapters in books on chest diseases, tuberculosis, heart disease, anaemia and med. educn. *Recreations:* travel, reading, photography. *Address:* Millfield, 14 Millbrook Road, Dinas Powys, Vale of Glamorgan CF64 4DA. *T:* (029) 2051 3149. *Died 7 March 2013.*

KIM, Young Sam; President, Republic of Korea, 1993–98; *b* 20 Dec. 1927; *m* 1951, Sohn Myoung Soon; two *s* three *d.* *Educ:* Coll. of Liberal Arts and Science, Seoul Nat. Univ. (BA). Mem., Nat. Assembly, 1954–93; Member: Liberal Party, 1954–60; Democratic Party, 1960–63; Civil Rule Party, 1963–65; Minjung Party, 1965–67 (also spokesman and floor leader); New Democratic Party, 1967–86 (floor leader, 1967–71, Pres., 1974–76 and 1979); Advr to New Korea Democratic Party, 1986–87; Pres., Reunification Democratic Party, 1987–90; Exec. Chm., 1990–92, Pres., 1992–96, Democratic Liberal Party; Pres., New Korea Party, 1996–97. Candidate for Pres., Republic of Korea, 1987. Chm., Council for the Promotion of Democracy, 1984–86. Averell Harriman Democracy Award, Nat. Democratic Inst. for Internat. Affairs, USA, 1993; Global Leadership Award, UNA, USA, 1995. Grand Order of Mugunghwa (Republic of Korea). *Publications:* We Can Depend on No One but Ourselves, 1964; Why our Country needs Standard-Bearers who are in their 40s, 1971; Government Power is Short, Politics is Long; Hoisting the Flag of Democracy; The True Reality of My Fatherland, 1984; My Resolution, 1987; Democratization, the Way of Salvation of My Country, 1987; Society which wins Honesty and Truth, 1987; New Korea 2000, 1992. *Address:* 7–6 Sangdo 1-dong, Dongjak-gu, Seoul, Korea 156–031. *Died 22 Nov. 2015.*

KIMBALL, Baron *cr* 1985 (Life Peer), of Easton in the County of Leicestershire; **Marcus Richard Kimball,** Kt 1981; DL; *b* 18 Oct. 1928; *s* of late Major Lawrence Kimball; *m* 1956, June Mary Fenwick; two *d.* *Educ:* Eton; Trinity Coll., Cambridge. Dir, Royal Trust Co. of Canada, subseq. Royal Trust Bank, 1970–94. External Mem. Council, Lloyd's, 1982–90. Contested (C) Derby South, 1955; MP (C) Lincs, Gainsborough, Feb. 1956–1983. Privy Council Rep., Council of RCVS, 1969–82, Hon. ARCVS 1982. Jt Master and Huntsman: Fitzwilliam Hounds, 1950–51 and 1951–52; Cottesmore Hounds, 1952–53, 1953–54, 1955–56 (Jt Master, 1956–58). Chm., 1966–82, Pres., 1995–98, British Field Sports Soc.; Dep. Pres., Countryside Alliance, 1999–. Chairman: River Naver Fishing Bd, 1964–92; Firearms Consultative Cttee, 1989–94; British Greyhound Racing Fund, 1993–96. President: Hunters Improvement Soc., 1990; Olympia Internat. Showjumping, 1991–99; British Inst. of Innkeeping, 1992–97; Chm., Cambridge Univ. Vet. Sch. Trust, 1989–98. Lt Leics Yeo. (TA), 1947; Capt., 1951. Mem. Rutland CC, 1955. DL Leics, 1984. *Address:* Great Easton Manor, Market Harborough, Leics LE16 8TB. *T:* (01536) 770333. *Clubs:* White's, Pratt's. *Died 26 March 2014.*

KIMBER, Sir Timothy (Roy Henry), 4th Bt *cr* 1904, of Lansdowne Lodge, co. London; DL; Advisor, Border Asset Management, since 2011 (Director, 1988–2011; Chairman, 2005–11); *b* 3 June 1936; *s* of Sir Charles Dixon Kimber, 3rd Bt and Ursula Roy Nettie Kimber (*née* Bird); *S* father, 2008; *m* 1st, 1960, Antonia Kathleen Brenda Williams (marr. diss. 1974); two *s*; 2nd, 1979, Susan Hare (*née* Brooks), *widow* of Richard North. *Educ:* Eton Coll. Sub-Lt 2nd Submarine Sqdn, RNVR, 1955–57. English Electric Co., 1958–64; Dir, Algrey Holdings, 1965; Trainee, then Exec. Dir, Lazard Bros, 1966–89; Director: Lazard Securities, 1974–89; Romney Trust, 1982–88; Development Capital Group, 1983–86; Raeburn Investment Trust, 1983–88; Japan Ventures Ltd, 1984–91; Noble & Co., 1989–2006; Adam Investment Management, 1989–2005; Martin Currie Pacific Trust, 1988–2004 (Chm., 1992–2005); Jardine Fleming India Fund (Saffron

Trust), 1995–2004; Cumberland Building Soc., 1995–2004; Invesco Japan Discovery Investment Trust, 1994–2007 (Chm., 2003–07); Dep. Chm., New Zealand Investment Trust, 1988–2008; Chairman: Dartmoor Investment Trust, 1990–2005; Exeter Selective Investment Trust, 1991–2004; Taiwan Opportunities Fund, 1995–2009 (Dir); Taiwan Catalyst Partnership, 2006–10. Chairman: Lancs Assoc. of Clubs for Young People, 1999–2004; Friends of Eden, Lakeland and Lunesdale Scenery, 2003–. Pres., Wildlife Trust of Lancs, Greater Manchester and N Merseyside, 2005–. Mem. Council (Dep. Treas.), Lancaster Univ., 1990–96. High Sheriff, 1996–97, DL 1997, Lancs. *Recreations:* country activities, golf, football, travel, military history. *Heir: s* Rupert Edward Watkin Kimber [*b* 20 June 1962; *m* 1997, Lisa Cave; three *d*]. *Address:* Newton Hall, near Carnforth, Lancs LA6 2NZ. *T:* (015242) 71232, *Fax:* (015242) 71552. *E:* TK@TimothyKimber.com. *Clubs:* Boodle's; Royal Lytham & St Anne's Golf. *Died 4 Dec. 2012.*

KINDER, Eric; Chairman: Smith & Nephew, 1990–97; Brunner Mond plc, 1992–98; *b* 26 Dec. 1927; *s* of William and Amy Kinder; *m* 1954, Isobel Margaret Barnes (decd); one *s* one *d*. *Educ:* Ashton-under-Lyne and Accrington Grammar Schs. ATI. Joined Textile Div., Smith & Nephew plc, 1957: Divisional Man. Dir, 1969–72; Dir, 1972–97; Chief Exec., 1982–90. Chm., Merchant Retail plc, 1991–94; non-exec. Dir, Intermediate Capital Group plc, 1994–98. Non-exec. Dir, Christie Hosp. NHS Trust, Manchester, 1994–97. *Recreations:* tennis, angling, golf, music. *Died 30 Aug. 2011.*

KINDERSLEY, 3rd Baron *cr* 1941; **Robert Hugh Molesworth Kindersley;** DL; Chairman, Commonwealth Development Corporation, 1980–89; a Vice-Chairman, Lazard Brothers & Co. Ltd, 1981–85 (Director, 1960–90); *b* 18 Aug. 1929; *s* of 2nd Baron Kindersley, CBE, MC, and Nancy Farnsworth (*d* 1977), *d* of Dr Geoffrey Boyd, Toronto; *S* father, 1976; *m* 1st, 1954, Venice Marigold (Rosie) (marr. diss. 1989), *d* of late Captain Lord (Arthur) Francis Henry Hill; two *s* one *d* (and one *s* decd); 2nd, 1989, Patricia Margaret Crichton-Stuart, *d* of late Hugh Norman. *Educ:* Eton; Trinity Coll., Oxford; Harvard Business Sch., USA. Lt Scots Guards; served Malaya, 1948–49. Chairman: Siam Selective Growth Fund, 1990–2000; Brent Walker Gp, 1991–92; Director: London Assurance, 1957–96; Witan Investment Co. Ltd, 1958–85; Steel Company of Wales, 1959–67; Marconi Co. Ltd, 1963–68; Sun Alliance & London Insurance Gp, 1965–96; English Electric Co. Ltd, 1966–68; Gen. Electric Co. Ltd, 1968–70; British Match Corp. Ltd, 1969–73; Swedish Match Co., 1973–85; Maersk Co. Ltd, 1986–2001; Maersk India, 1988–2001. Financial Adviser to Export Gp for the Constructional Industries, 1961–86; Mem., Adv. Panel, Overseas Projects Gp, 1975–77; Dep. Chm., ECGD Adv. Council, 1975–80; Chm., Exec. Cttee, BBA, 1976–78; Pres., Anglo-Taiwan Trade Cttee, 1976–86. Hon. Treasurer, YWCA, 1965–76. Mem., Institut International d'Etudes Bancaires, 1971–85. Chm., Smith's Charity, 1990–97. Mem. Ct, Fishmongers' Co., 1973–, Prime Warden, 1989–90. DL Kent, 1986. *Recreations:* all country pursuits, including tennis and skiing. *Heir: s* Hon. Rupert John Molesworth Kindersley [*b* 11 March 1955; *m* 1975, Sarah, *d* of late John D. Warde; one *s* one *d*]. *Address:* West Green Farm, Shipbourne, Kent TN11 9QA. *T:* (01732) 810293. *Clubs:* Pratt's, MCC, All England Lawn Tennis and Croquet, Queen's; Vincent's (Oxford). *Died 9 Oct. 2013.*

KING OF WEST BROMWICH, Baron *cr* 1999 (Life Peer), of West Bromwich in the county of West Midlands; **Tarsem King;** JP; Managing Director, Sandwell Polybags Ltd, 1990–2007; *b* Kultham, Punjab, 24 April 1937; *s* of Ujagar Singh and Dalip Kaur; *m* 1957, Mohinder Kaur; one *s*. *Educ:* Punjab Univ. (BA); Nat. Foundry Coll., Wolverhampton (Dip. Foundry Technol. and Mgt); Aston Univ. (Dip. Mgt Studies); Teacher Trng Coll., Wolverhampton (CertEd); Essex Univ. (MSc Stats and Operational Res.). Lab. Asst, 1960–62; Foundry Trainee, 1964–65; Teacher, Churchfield Sch., W Bromwich, 1968–74; Dep. Hd, Maths Dept, Great Barr Sch., Birmingham, 1974–90. Formerly non-exec. Dir, Sandwell TEC; non-exec. Dir, Sandwell HA, 1990–98. Vice Pres., YMCA, 2006–; Mem., S Staffs Water Charitable Trust, 1997–2011. Member: (Lab) Sandwell MBC, 1979–2007 (Leader, 1997–2001); Sandwell CHC, 1982–83; Sandwell DHA, 1983–89. JP West Bromwich, 1987. Hon. Freeman, Bor. of Sandwell, 2009 (Hon. Alderman, 2008). Hon. PhD Wolverhampton, 2001. *Recreations:* reading, music. *Address:* House of Lords, SW1A 0PW; 27 Roebuck Lane, West Bromwich B70 6QP. *Died 9 Jan. 2013.*

KING, (Albert) Norman, CMG 2002; LVO 1983; OBE 1997; HM Diplomatic Service, retired; *b* 29 March 1943; *s* of late Albert King and Muriel Elizabeth King (*née* McBrien); *m* 1969, Dympna Mary Farren; one *s* two *d*. *Educ:* Strabane Grammar Sch., Co. Tyrone. Trng posts, Customs and Excise, then Govt Actuary's Dept, 1963; entered HM Diplomatic Service, 1964; CRO, 1964–67; Ibadan, 1967–70; BMG, Berlin, 1971–72; Second Secretary (Commercial): Singapore, 1972–76; Muscat, 1976–80; First Secretary: Dhaka, 1980–84; S Asia Dept, FCO, 1984–86; Personnel Services Dept, 1986–88; Vienna, 1988–93; Inf. Services Dept, FCO, 1993–94; Lagos, 1994–97; Resources Dept, FCO, 1997–99; Counsellor, New Delhi, 1999–2003. *Recreations:* Rugby, music, photography, reading, drinking French red wines. *Address:* Raj Bhavan, Glenevish Hill, Strabane, Co. Tyrone BT82 8LZ. *Died 27 June 2015.*

KING, Colin Sainthill W.; *see* Wallis-King.

KING, Francis Henry, CBE 1985 (OBE 1979); FRSL 1948; author; Drama Critic, Sunday Telegraph, 1978–88; *b* 4 March 1923; *o s* of late Eustace Arthur Cecil King and Faith Mina Read. *Educ:* Shrewsbury; Balliol Coll., Oxford. British Council, 1950–63 (Asst Rep., Helsinki, 1957–58; Regl Dir, Kyoto, 1958–63). Chm., Soc. of Authors, 1975–77; Internat. Vice-Pres., PEN, 1989– (Pres., English PEN, 1978–86; Vice-Pres., 1977; Internat. Pres., 1986–89). *Publications: novels:* To the Dark Tower, 1946; Never Again, 1947; An Air That Kills, 1948; The Dividing Stream, 1951 (Somerset Maugham Award, 1952); The Dark Glasses, 1954; The Widow, 1957; The Man on the Rock, 1957; The Custom House, 1961; The Last of the Pleasure Gardens, 1965; The Waves Behind the Boat, 1967; A Domestic Animal, 1970; Flights (two short novels), 1973; A Game of Patience, 1974; The Needle, 1975; Danny Hill, 1977; The Action, 1978; Act of Darkness, 1983; Voices in an Empty Room, 1984; Frozen Music, 1987; The Woman Who Was God, 1988; Punishments, 1989; Visiting Cards, 1990; The Ant Colony, 1991; (with Tom Wakefield and Patrick Gale) Secret Lives, 1991; The One and Only, 1994; Ash on an Old Man's Sleeve, 1996; Dead Letters, 1997; Prodigies, 2001; The Nick of Time, 2003; With My Little Eye, 2007; Cold Snap, 2010; *short stories:* So Hurt and Humiliated, 1959; The Japanese Umbrella, 1964 (Katherine Mansfield Short Story Prize, 1965); The Brighton Belle, 1968; Hard Feelings, 1976; Indirect Method, 1980; One is a Wanderer, 1985; A Hand at the Shutter, 1996; The Sunlight on the Garden, 2006; *poetry:* Rod of Incantation, 1952; *biography:* E. M. Forster and His World, 1978; (ed) My Sister and Myself: the diaries of J. R. Ackerley, 1982; Yesterday Came Suddenly (autobiog.), 1993; *general:* (ed) Introducing Greece, 1956; Japan, 1970; Florence, 1982; (ed) Lafcadio Hearn: Writings from Japan, 1984; Florence: A Literary Companion, 1991. *Address:* 19 Gordon Place, W8 4JE. *T:* (020) 7937 5715. *E:* fhk@dircon.co.uk. *Club:* PEN. *Died 3 July 2011.*

KING, Sir John (Christopher), 4th Bt *cr* 1888, of Campsie, Stirlingshire; *b* 31 March 1933; *s* of Sir James Granville Le Neve King, 3rd Bt, TD and of Penelope Charlotte, *d* of late Capt. E. Cooper-Key, CB, MVO, RN; *S* father, 1989; *m* 1st, 1958, Patricia Foster (marr. diss. 1972); one *s* one *d*; 2nd, 1984, Aline Jane Holley (marr. diss. 2000), *d* of Col D. A. Brett, GC, OBE, MC. *Educ:* Eton. Sub Lt, RNVR, 1952–54; Lt, Berks Yeomanry, 1955–60. Mem., Stock Exchange, 1961–73. *Recreations:* sailing, travelling. *Heir: s* James Henry Rupert King [*b* 24 May 1961; *m* 1995, Elizabeth, *y d* of Richard Henry Ellingworth; two *s* one *d*]. *Club:* Brooks's. *Died 5 Dec. 2014.*

KING, John Edward; Principal Establishment Officer and Under Secretary, Welsh Office, 1977–82; Chairman, 1990–92, President, 1992–2002, Friends of the Welsh College of Music and Drama; *b* 30 May 1922; *s* of late Albert Edward and Margaret King; *m* 1st, 1948, Pamela

White (marr. diss.); one *d*; 2nd, 1956, Mary Margaret Beaton (*d* 2004); two *d*. *Educ:* Penarth County Grammar Sch.; Sch. of Oriental and African Studies, London Univ. Served with Rifle Bde, RWF and Nigeria Regt, 1941–47; Captain, Chindit campaign, Burma (despatches). Cadet, Colonial Admin. Service, N Nigeria, 1947; Permanent Sec., Fed. Govt of Nigeria, 1960; retired from HMOCS, 1963. Principal, CRO, 1963; Navy Dept, MoD, 1966–69; Private Sec. to Sec. of State for Wales, 1969–71; Asst Sec., Welsh Office, 1971–77. CS Mem., 1977–82, External Mem., 1982–86, Final Selection Bd, CS Commn. Consultant, Dept of Educn and Dir, China Studies Centre, UC, Cardiff, 1984–87. *Recreations:* books, swimming, watercolour painting. *Address:* 46 Groveway, SW9 0AR. *Clubs:* Civil Service; Outer Hebrides Tennis. *Died 6 May 2013.*

KING, Hon. Leonard James, AC 1987; Chief Justice of South Australia, 1978–95; *b* 1 May 1925; *s* of Michael Owen and Mary Ann King; *m* 1953, Sheila Therese (*née* Keane); two *s* three *d*. *Educ:* Marist Brothers Sch., Norwood, S Aust; Univ. of Adelaide, S Aust (LLB). Admitted to Bar, 1950; QC 1967. Member, House of Assembly, Parlt of S Australia, 1970; Attorney-General and Minister of Community Welfare, 1970; additionally, Minister of Prices and Consumer Affairs, 1972. Judge of Supreme Court of S Aust., 1975. *Address:* 19 Wall Street, Norwood, SA 5067, Australia. *T:* (8) 83317220. *Died 23 June 2011.*

KING, Norman; *see* King, A. N.

KING, Vice-Adm. Sir Norman (Ross Dutton), KBE 1989; Chairman, Buckinghamshire Health Authority, 1993–96; President, Safety Centre (Milton Keynes) Ltd, since 1997 (Chairman, 1992–96); *b* 19 March 1933; *s* of Sir Norman King, KCMG and Lady (Mona) King (*née* Dutton); *m* 1967, Patricia Rosemary, *d* of Dr L. B. Furber; two *d*. *Educ:* Fonthill School; RNC Dartmouth; graduate, Naval Command College, Newport, USA, 1969; RCDS 1978. RN Cadet, 1946; served HM Ships Indefatigable, Tintagel Castle, Ceylon, Wild Goose, Hickleton, 1951–57, and Corunna, 1957–59; long TAS course, 1960; BRNC Dartmouth, 1961–63; CO HMS Fiskerton, 1963–64; Jun. Seaman Appointer, Naval Sec's Dept, 1965–66; CO HMS Leopard, 1967–68; Staff Officer (TAS) to CBNS (Washington), 1969–71; XO HMS Intrepid, 1972–73; Staff Warfare TAS Officer, to Dir Naval Warfare, 1974–75; Naval Asst to Second Sea Lord, 1975–77; CO HMS Newcastle and Capt. 3rd Destroyer Sqn, 1979–80; CSO to CBNS (Washington), 1981–82; Dir of Naval Officer Appts (Seaman Officers), 1983–84; Comdr, British Navy Staff and British Naval Attaché, Washington, and UK Nat. Liaison Rep. to SACLANT, 1984–86; Naval Sec., 1987–88; COS to Comdr Allied Naval Forces Southern Europe, 1988–91. Mem., Lord Chancellor's Panel of Independent Inspectors, 1992–2001. *Publications:* (jointly) All The Queen's Men, 1967, paperback edn as Strictly Personal, 1972. *Recreations:* tennis, golf, music, chess. *Address:* c/o Lloyd's Bank, Secklow Gate West, Milton Keynes MK9 3EH. *Died 6 March 2013.*

KING, Air Vice-Marshal Peter Francis, CB 1987; OBE (mil.) 1964; FRCSE; The Senior Consultant, RAF, 1985–87; Air Vice-Marshal, Princess Mary's RAF Hospital, Halton, 1983–87; Consultant Otorhinolaryngologist, King Edward VII Hospital, Midhurst, 1988–96; *b* 17 Sept. 1922; *s* of Sqn Ldr William George King, MBE, RAF, and Florence Margaret King (*née* Sell); *m* 1945, Doreen Maxwell Aaröe (*d* 2006), 2nd *d* of Jorgen Hansen-Aaröe; one *d* (one *s* decd). *Educ:* Framlingham Coll.; King's Coll. London, 1940–42; Charing Cross Hosp., 1942–45; Univ. of Edinburgh, 1947. DLO; MRCS, LRCP; MFOM. Kitchener Med. Services Schol. for RAF, 1941; Ho. Phys., Ho. Surg., Charing Cross Hosp., 1945; commnd RAF, 1945; specialist in Otorhinolaryngology, employed Cosford, Ely, Fayid, Halton, CME; Cons. in Otorhinolaryngology, 1955; Hunterian Prof., RCS, 1964; Cons. Adviser in Otorhinolaryngology, 1966; Air Cdre 1976; Reader in Aviation Med., Inst. of Aviation Med., 1977; Whittingham Prof. in Aviation Med., IAM and RCP, 1979; QHS 1979–87; Dean of Air Force Medicine, 1983. Cons. to Herts HA, 1963, and CAA, 1973; Examiner for Dip. in Aviation Med., RCP, 1980. Littler Meml Lectr, British Soc. of Audiology, 2001. Pres., Sect. of Otology, RSocMed, 1977–78 (Sec., 1972–74); Chm., Brit. Soc. of Audiology, 1979–81 (Hon. Life Mem., 1998); Vice-Pres., RNID, 1990–2004 (Vice-Chm., 1980–88); Member: BMA, 1945– (Life Mem., 1996); Scottish Otological Soc., 1955–90; Royal Aeronaut. Soc., 1976– (FRAeS 1998); Council, Brit. Assoc. of Otorhinolaryngologists, 1960–89 (Hon. Life Mem., 1996); Editorial Bd, British Jl of Audiology, 1980–88. Fellow, Inst. of Acoustics, 1977. FRSocMed. CStJ 1987. Lady Cade Medal, RCS, 1967; (jtly) Howells Meml Prize, Univ. of London, 1992; recognised as co-descriptor of King-Kopetzky Syndrome, 1992. *Publications:* Noise and Vibration in Aviation (with J. C. Guignard), 1972; (with John Ernsting) Aviation Medicine, 1988; (jtly) Assessment of Hearing Disability, 1992; Peter Pilgrim's Progress, 2011; numerous articles, chapters, lectures and papers, in books and relevant jls on aviation otolaryngology, noise deafness, hearing conservation, tympanoplasty, facial paralysis, otic barotrauma, etc. *Recreations:* sculpture, looking at prints. *Address:* 5 Churchill Gate, Oxford Road, Woodstock, Oxon OX20 1QW. *T:* (01993) 813115. *Club:* Royal Air Force. *Died 11 Nov. 2015.*

KING, Robert George Cecil; Chairman, Social Security Appeal Tribunals, 1987–98; Under Secretary (Legal), HM Customs and Excise, 1985–87; *b* 21 Jan. 1927; *s* of Stanley Cecil and Kathleen Mary King; *m* 1952, Mary Marshall. *Educ:* Nunthorpe Grammar School, York. Called to the Bar, Lincolns Inn, 1965. Army, 1945–48; British Rail, 1948–53; Judicial Dept, Kenya, 1954–61; East African Common Services Organisation, 1962–64; Solicitor's Office, HM Customs and Excise, 1965–87. *Recreations:* golf, bowls, gardening, watching cricket, watching television. *Address:* 181 Greenshaw Drive, Wigginton, York YO32 2SD. *T:* (01904) 765039. *Clubs:* York Golf, Royal Nairobi Golf. *Died 1 Jan. 2014.*

KING-SMITH, Ronald Gordon, (Dick), OBE 2010; author; *b* 27 March 1922; *s* of Ronald King-Smith and Grace King-Smith; *m* 1943, Myrle England (*d* 2000); one *s* two *d*; *m* 2001, Zona Bedding. *Educ:* Marlborough; Bristol Univ. (BEd 1975). Served Grenadier Guards, 1941–46. Farmer, 1947–67; teacher, Farmborough Primary Sch., 1975–82. *Publications:* over 110 titles include: The Fox Busters, 1978; Daggie Dogfoot, 1980; The Mouse Butcher, 1982; Magnus Powermouse, 1982; The Queen's Nose, 1983; The Sheep Pig, 1984 (filmed as Babe, 1995); Harry's Mad, 1984; Saddlebottom, 1985; Noah's Brother, 1986; The Hedgehog, 1987; George Speaks, 1988; Martin's Mice, 1988; Sophie's Snail, 1988; The Toby Man, 1989; Dodos are Forever, 1989; Ace, 1990; Paddy's Pot of Gold, 1990; The Water Horse, 1990; The Cuckoo Child, 1991; Sophie's Tom, 1991; Sophie Hits Six, 1991; The Guard Dog, 1991; Find the White Horse, 1991; Lady Daisy, 1992; Pretty Polly, 1992; Dragon Boy, 1993; The Merrythought, 1993; Sophie in the Saddle, 1993; The Schoolmouse, 1994; Harriet's Hare, 1994; Sophie is Seven, 1994; Bobby the Bad, 1994; King Max the Last, 1995; Sophie's Lucky, 1995; The Terrible Trins, 1995; Clever Duck, 1996; Godhanger, 1996; Dick King-Smith's Animal Friends, 1996; Treasure Trove, 1997; Puppy Love, 1997; What Sadie Saw, 1997; The Stray, 1997; The Merman, 1998; How Green Was My Mouse, 1998; A Mouse Called Wolf, 1998; The Crowstarver, 1998; Mr Ape, 1998; Poppet, 1999; The Magic Carpet Slippers, 2000; The Roundhill, 2000; Funny Frank, 2001; Chewing the Cud (autobiog.), 2001. *Recreations:* reading, enjoying the countryside, washing-up. *Died 4 Jan. 2011.*

KINGDON, Roger Taylor, CBE 1990; FIMechE, FIMMM; Chief Executive, Davy Corporation, 1987–90; *b* 27 June 1930; *s* of late Fletcher Munroe Kingdon and Laetitia May Kingdon (*née* Wissler); *m* 1956, Gaynor Mary Downs; two *s* one *d*. *Educ:* Christ's Hospital; Pembroke College, Cambridge (MA). CEng. Graduate trainee, Woodall Duckham Construction Co., 1954–58; Ashmore Benson Pease & Co., 1958–68 (Dir, 1964–68); Managing Director: Newell Dunford Group, 1968–80; Herbert Morris (Davy Group), 1980–83; Chm., Davy McKee (Stockton), 1983–87; Director: Dunford & Elliot, 1971–80;

Peugeot Talbot Motor Co., 1979–92; Davy Corp., 1986–90; Teesside Develt Corp., 1987–98; Carbo plc (formerly Hopkinson Group), 1992–2002. President: Process Plant Assoc., 1979–80; NE Engineering Employers' Assoc., 1986–89; Chairman: British Metallurgical Plant Constructors' Assoc., 1985–87; Latin American Trade Adv. Group, 1989–90. Vice Chm., South Tees Acute NHS Trust, 1992–95. Mem. Council, Durham Univ., 1995–2000. CCMI. *Address:* Borrowby Hill, The Green, Borrowby, Thirsk, North Yorks YO7 4QL. *T:* (01845) 537663. *Died 12 May 2015.*

KINGSDOWN, Baron *cr* 1993 (Life Peer), of Pemberton in the County of Lancashire; **Robert Leigh-Pemberton, (Robin),** KG 1994; PC 1987; Governor, Bank of England, 1983–93; Lord-Lieutenant of Kent, 1982–2002 (Vice Lord-Lieutenant, 1972–82); *b* 5 Jan. 1927; *e s* of late Robert Douglas Leigh-Pemberton, MBE, MC, Sittingbourne, Kent; *m* 1953, Rosemary Davina, OBE, *d* of late Lt-Col D. W. A. W. Forbes, MC, and late Dowager Marchioness of Exeter; four *s* (and one *s* decd). *Educ:* St Peter's Court, Broadstairs; Eton; Trinity Coll., Oxford (MA; Hon. Fellow, 1984). Grenadier Guards, 1945–48. Called to Bar, Inner Temple, 1954 (Hon. Bencher, 1983); practised in London and SE Circuit until 1960. National Westminster Bank: Dir, 1972–83; Dep. Chm., 1974; Chm., 1977–83. Director: Birmid Qualcast, 1966–83 (Dep. Chm., 1970; Chm., 1975–77); University Life Assce Soc., 1967–78; Redland Ltd, 1972–83, 1993–98; Equitable Life Assce Soc., 1979–83 (Vice-Pres., 1982–83); Glaxo-Wellcome (formerly Glaxo Holdings), 1993–96; Foreign and Colonial Investment Trust, 1993–98; Hambros, 1993–98. County Councillor (Chm. Council, 1972–75), 1961–77, CA 1965, Kent. Member: SE Econ. Planning Council, 1972–74; Medway Ports Authority, 1974–76; NEDC, 1982–92; Prime Minister's Cttee on Local Govt Rules of Conduct, 1973–74; Cttee of Enquiry into Teachers' Pay, 1974; Cttee on Police Pay, 1977–79. Chm., Cttee of London Clearing Bankers, 1982–83. Trustee: Glyndebourne Arts Trust, 1978–83; RA Trust, 1982–88 (Hon. Trustee Emeritus, 1988–). Pro-Chancellor, Univ. of Kent at Canterbury, 1977–83; Seneschal, Canterbury Cathedral, 1983–. Hon. Colonel: Kent and Sharpshooters Yeomanry Sqn, 1979–92; 265 (Kent and Co. of London Yeo.) Signal Sqn (V), 1979–92; 5th (Volunteer) Bn, The Queen's Regt, 1987–92. Gov., Ditchley Foundn, 1987–2002. Hon. DCL Kent, 1983; Hon. DLitt: City, 1988; Loughborough, 1990. FRSA 1977; FCMI (FBIM 1977). JP 1961–75, DL 1970, Kent. KStJ 1983. *Recreation:* country life. *Address:* Torry Hill, Sittingbourne, Kent ME9 0SP. *Clubs:* Brooks's, Cavalry and Guards. *Died 24 Nov. 2013.*

KINGSLAND, Sir Richard, Kt 1978; AO 1989; CBE 1967; DFC 1940; idc; psa; President, Barnardos Canberra, 1995–2003; *b* Moree, NSW, 19 Oct. 1916; *m* 1943, Kathleen Jewel, *d* of late R. B. Adams; one *s* two *d*. Served War: No 10 Sqdn, Eng., 1939–41; commanded: No 11 Sqdn, New Guinea, 1941–42; RAAF Stn, Rathmines, NSW, 1942–43; Gp Captain 1943; Dir, Intell., RAAF, 1944–45. Dir, Org. RAAF HQ, 1946–48; Manager, Sydney Airport, 1948–49; Airline Pilot, 1949–50; SA Reg. 1950–51, NT Reg. 1951–52, Dept of Civil Aviation; Chief Admin. Asst to CAS, RAAF, 1952–53; IDC 1955; Asst Sec., Dept of Air, Melb., 1954–58; First Asst Sec., Dept of Defence, 1958–63; Secretary: Dept of Interior, 1963–70; Dept of Repatriation, 1970–74; Repatriation and Compensation, 1974–76; Dept of Veterans' Affairs, Canberra, 1976–81. Chairman: Repatriation Commn, 1970–81; ACT Arts Develt Bd (first Chm.), 1981–83; Commonwealth Films Bd of Review, 1982–86; Uranium Adv. Council, 1982–84. Member-at-Large, Nat. Heart Foundn, 1990– (Hon. Nat. Sec., 1976–90); Chm., ACT Health Promotion Fund, 1990–94; a Dir, Sir Edward Dunlop Med. Res. Foundn, 1995–. A Dir, Arts Council of Aust., 1970–72; first Chairman Council: Canberra Sch. of Music, 1970–74; Canberra Sch. of Art, 1976–83; Mem. Original Council, Australian Conservation Foundn, 1967–69; Member: Canberra Theatre Trust, 1965–75; Aust. Opera Nat. Council, 1983–96; Canberra Festival Cttee, 1988–92; Mem. Bd of Trustees, Aust. War Meml, Canberra, 1966–76; Mem. Council, E. V. Llewellyn Meml Trust, 1982–; a Dir, Aust. Bicentennial Authority, 1983–89. Pres., Bd of Management, Goodwin Retirement Villages, 1984–88; Vice Pres., Australia Day in the Nat. Capital Cttee, 1987–91. Life Governor: Sir Moses Montefiore Homes, NSW, 1975; Nat. Gall. of Aust., 1982. *Address:* 36 Vasey Crescent, Campbell, ACT 2612, Australia. *Clubs:* Commonwealth, National Press (Canberra). *Died 27 Aug. 2012.*

KINGSLEY, David John, OBE 2006; consultant in management, marketing and communications, since 1975; Chairman, Kingsley and Kingsley, since 1974; *b* 10 July 1929; *s* of Walter John Kingsley and Margery Kingsley; *m* 1st, 1954, Enid Sophia Jones; two *d*; 2nd, 1968, Gillian Leech; two *s*; 3rd, 1988, Gisela Reichardt. *Educ:* Southend High Sch.; London School of Economics (BScEcon; Hon. Fellow, 1992). Pres., Students' Union, LSE, 1952; Vice-Pres., Nat. Union of Students, 1953. Served RAF, Personnel Selection, commnd 1948. Prospective Parly Candidate (Lab) E Grinstead, 1952–54; founded Kingsley, Manton and Palmer (KMP), advertising agency, 1964; Publicity Advisor to Labour Party and Govt, 1962–70; Publicity and Election advisor to President of Republic of Zambia, 1974–82; Election and Broadcasting advisor to Govt of Mauritius, 1976–81; Publicity advisor to SDP, 1981–87. Mem. Boards, CNAA, 1970–82; Mem., Central Religious Adv. Cttee for BBC and IBA, 1974–82; Governor, LSE, 1965–2005 (Gov. Emeritus, 2006). Chair, Worldaware, 1992–96; Dir, At-Bristol (formerly Bristol 2000) Millennium Project, 1993–2002; Chairman: Children 2000, 1994–; Children's Discovery Centre, 2003–06; Dir, Fun Radio UK (formerly Children's Radio UK), 2005–. Chairman: Inter-Action Trust, 1981–90; Design and Industries Assoc., 1994–96. Trustee, Royal Philharmonic Orch., 1993–99 (Vice-Chm., 1972–77); Dir, Wren Orch., 1990–98; Mem., Develt Cttee, RCM, 1985–2000. Vice-Pres., Schumacher Soc., 1999–2004; Vice-Chm., Media Soc., 2001–04. Hon. Pres., LSE Envmtl Network, 2000–; Founder Chm., LSE Alumni Assoc., 2005–07 (Chair Emeritus, 2008). Chairman: Cartoon Arts Trust, 1994–2001; Creative Summit, 1999; Member: Bd, Mediawise, 2003–06; Adv. Bd, Inst. for Global Ethics, 2003–; Advr, Greenhouse Project, 2003–06. FIPA; FRSA; MCSD. Hon. FRCM. Hon. Fellow, Soka Univ., Tokyo, 1990. *Publications:* Albion in China, 1979; How World War II Was Won on the Playing Fields of LSE, 2003; contribs to learned jls; various articles. *Recreations:* politics, creating happy national events, music, travel, art and books. *Address:* 81 Mortimer Road, N1 5AR. *Club:* Reform. *Died 13 April 2014.*

KINKEAD-WEEKES, Prof. Mark, FBA 1992; Professor of English and American Literature, University of Kent at Canterbury, 1974–84, then Professor Emeritus; *b* 26 April 1931; *s* of Lt-Col Alfred Bernard Kinkead-Weekes, MC and Vida May Kinkead-Weekes; *m* 1959, Margaret Joan Irvine; two *s*. *Educ:* Potchefstroom Boys' High Sch.; Univ. of Cape Town (BA); Brasenose Coll., Oxford (BA, MA). University of Edinburgh: Asst Lectr in English, 1956–58; Lectr, 1958–65; University of Kent at Canterbury: Lectr, 1965–66; Sen. Lectr, 1966–74; Pro-Vice-Chancellor, 1974–77. Rhodes Scholarship (Cape Province), 1951; Woodrow Wilson Fellow, Smithsonian Instn, 1993–94. Former Governor: Christ Church Coll., Canterbury; King's Coll., Rochester; Contemp. Dance Trust. Chm., Friends of St George, Ramsgate. *Publications:* William Golding, a Critical Study (with Ian Gregor), 1967, 2nd edn 1984; Samuel Richardson: dramatic novelist, 1973; (ed) D. H. Lawrence: The Rainbow, 1989; D. H. Lawrence: triumph to exile 1912–1922, 1996; William Golding: a critical study of the novels, 2002; articles, mainly on fiction. *Recreations:* walking, music, travel. *Died 7 March 2011.*

KINLOSS, Lady (12th in line, of the Lordship *cr* 1602); **Beatrice Mary Grenville Freeman-Grenville;** (surname changed by Lord Lyon King of Arms, 1950); *b* 18 Aug. 1922; *e d* of late Rev. Hon. Luis Chandos Francis Temple Morgan-Grenville, Master of Kinloss; *S* grandmother, 1944; *m* 1950, Dr Greville Stewart Parker Freeman-Grenville (*d* 2005), FSA, FRAS (name changed from Freeman by Lord Lyon King of Arms, 1950), Capt. late Royal Berks Regt, *er s* of late Rev. E. C. Freeman; two *d* (one *s* decd). Cross-bencher; Mem., EC Sub-Cttee C (Social and Consumer Affairs), H of L, 1993–95; served on numerous select cttees. FRAS 1997. *Heir: er d* Hon. Teresa

Mary Nugent Freeman-Grenville, Mistress of Kinloss, *b* 20 July 1957. *Address:* North View House, Sheriff Hutton, York YO60 6ST. *T:* (01347) 878447. *Died 30 Sept. 2012.*

KINLOSS, Master of; Hon. Bevil David Stewart Chandos Freeman-Grenville; *b* 20 June 1953; *s* of late Dr Greville Stewart Parker Freeman-Grenville, FSA, Capt. late Royal Berks Regt, and of Beatrice Mary Grenville Freeman-Grenville, Lady Kinloss; *m* 2001, Marie-Thérèse, *d* of late William Driscoll, and *widow* of Stuart Sturrock. *Educ:* Redrice Sch. *Address:* Orchard House, 6 Warwick Close, Sheriff Hutton, York YO60 6QW. *T:* (01347) 878346. *E:* bevilkinloss@aol.com. *Died 31 Jan. 2012.*

KINNOULL, 15th Earl of, *cr* 1633; **Arthur William George Patrick Hay;** Viscount Dupplin and Lord Hay, 1627, 1633, 1697; Baron Hay (Great Britain), 1711; *b* 26 March 1935; *o* surv. *s* of 14th Earl and Mary Ethel Isobel Meyrick (*d* 1938); *S* father, 1938; *m* 1961, Gay Ann, *er d* of Sir Denys Lowson, 1st Bt; one *s* three *d*. *Educ:* Eton. Chartered Land Agent, 1960; Mem., Agricultural Valuers' Assoc., 1962; Fellow, Chartered Land Agents' Soc., 1964; FRICS 1970. Pres., National Council on Inland Transport, 1964–76. Mem. of Queen's Body Guard for Scotland (Royal Company of Archers), 1965. Junior Cons. Whip, House of Lords, 1966–68; Cons. Opposition Spokesman on Aviation, House of Lords, 1968–70. Mem., British Delegn, Council of Europe, 1985–95. Chairman: Property Owners' Building Soc., 1976–87 (Dir, 1971–87); Woolwich Homes, 1994–97; Dir, Woolwich Equitable Building Soc., 1987–97. Mem., Air League Council, 1972; Council Mem., Deep Sea Fishermen's Mission, 1977 (Chm., 1997–2001). Vice-Pres., Nat. Assoc. of Local Councils (formerly Nat. Assoc. of Parish Councils), 1970–80. Vice-Chm., Bd of Regents, Harris Manchester Coll., Oxford, 2002 (Hon. Fellow, 2007). Gov., St John's Sch., Leatherhead, 1978–2005. *Heir: s* Viscount Dupplin, *b* 20 Dec. 1962. *Address:* 15 Carlyle Square, SW3 6EX; Pier House, Seaview, Isle of Wight PO34 5BN. *Clubs:* Turf, Pratt's, Lansdowne, MCC. *Died 7 June 2013.*

KIRBY, Dennis, MVO 1961; MBE 1955; Hon. Manager, European Investment Bank, Luxembourg; *b* 5 April 1923; *s* of William Ewart Kirby and Hannah Kirby; *m* 1st, 1943, Mary Elizabeth Kilby (*d* 1994); 2nd, 1994, Ava Robertson. *Educ:* Hull Grammar Sch.; Queens' Coll., Cambridge. Lt (A) RNVR (fighter pilot), 1940–46. Colonial Service, Sierra Leone, 1946–62 (District Comr, 1950; Perm. Sec., 1961–62); 1st Sec., UK Diplomatic Service, 1962; Managing Director: East Kilbride Development Corp., 1963–68; Irvine Development Corp., 1967–72; Industrial Dir, Scotland, DTI, 1972–74; European Investment Bank, 1974–87: Conseiller Principal, 1974; Dir Adjoint, 1976; Dir Associé, 1984; Dir, NM UK Ltd, 1988–93. *Recreation:* bridge. *Address:* Bottle Cottage, Almodington, Chichester, W Sussex PO20 7LD. *Died 7 Dec. 2013.*

KIRBY, Prof. Gordon William, ScD, PhD; FRSC; FRSE; FRAS; Regius Professor of Chemistry, 1972–96, Professor of Chemistry, 1997, then Emeritus, University of Glasgow; *b* 20 June 1934; *s* of William Admiral Kirby and Frances Teresa Kirby (*née* Townson); *m* 1964, Audrey Jean Rusbridge (marr. diss. 1983; remarried 2004), *d* of Col C. E. Rusbridge; two *s*. *Educ:* Liverpool Inst. High Sch.; Gonville and Caius Coll., Cambridge (Schuldham Plate 1956; MA, PhD, ScD). FRIC 1970; FRSE 1975; FRAS 2004. 1851 Exhibn Senior Student, 1958–60, Asst Lectr, 1960–61, Lectr, 1961–67, Imperial Coll. of Science and Technology; Prof. of Organic Chemistry, Univ. of Technology, Loughborough, 1967–72; Mem., Chem. Cttee, SRC, 1971–75. Chm., Jls Cttee, Royal Soc. of Chemistry, 1981–84. Corday-Morgan Medal, Chem. Soc., 1969; Tilden Lectr, Chem. Soc., 1974–75. *Publications:* Co-editor: Elucidation of Organic Structures by Physical and Chemical Methods, vol. IV, parts I, II, and III, 1972; Fortschritte der Chemie organischer Naturstoffe, subseq. entitled Progress in the Chemistry of Organic Natural Products, 1971–2003; (ed) Comprehensive Organic Functional Group Transformations, vol. IV, 1995; contributor to Jl Chem. Soc., etc. *Address:* Tugwell Farm, Halse, Taunton, Somerset TA4 3JL. *Died 6 May 2011.*

KIRCHNER, Peter James, MBE 1970; HM Diplomatic Service, retired; Consul General, Berlin, 1978–80; *b* 17 Sept. 1920; *s* of late William John Kirchner and Winifred Emily Homer (*née* Adams); *m* 1952, Barbro Sarah Margareta (*née* Klockhoff); one *s* two *d*. *Educ:* St Brendan's Coll., Clifton, Bristol; BA Open, 1991, BA Hons 1996. Served War, RA, 1939–41. Timber production, UK and Germany, 1941–48; FO, Germany, 1948; Home Office Immigration Dept, 1952–64; Head of UK Refugee Missions in Europe, 1960–63; FCO (formerly FO): Barbados, 1965; Nairobi, 1968; Ankara, 1970; Vienna, 1973; Jerusalem, 1976. Mem., Bd of Trustees, Retirement Trust (Chm., 1995–2001). Freeman, City of London, 1963. *Recreations:* golf, croquet, modern European history, northern baroque architecture, travel in Europe. *Address:* 86 York Mansions, Prince of Wales Drive, SW11 4BN. *T:* (020) 7622 7068. *Died 7 Oct. 2012.*

KIRKNESS, Donald James, CB 1980; Deputy Secretary, Overseas Development Administration, 1977–80; *b* 29 Sept. 1919; *s* of Charles Stephen and Elsie Winifred Kirkness; *m* 1947, Monica Mary Douch (*d* 2006); one *d*. *Educ:* Harvey Grammar Sch., Folkestone. Exchequer and Audit Dept, 1938. Served War: RA and Royal Berkshire Regt, 1939–46. Colonial Office, 1947 (Asst Principal); Financial and Economic Adviser, Windward I, 1955–57; Dept of Economic Affairs, 1966; Civil Service Dept, 1970–73; ODA/ODM, 1973. UK Governor, Internat. Fund for Agricultural Develt, 1977–81; Mem., Exec. Bd, UNESCO, 1978–83. *Died 30 Dec. 2013.*

KIRKWOOD, Sir Andrew (Tristram Hammett), Kt 1993; a Judge of the High Court of Justice, Family Division, 1993–2008; *b* 5 June 1944; *s* of Maj. T. G. H. Kirkwood, RE (killed in action, 1944) and late Lady Faulks; *m* 1968, Penelope Jane (*née* Eaton); two *s* one *d*. *Educ:* Radley Coll., Abingdon, Oxon; Christ Church, Oxford (MA). Called to the Bar, Inner Temple, 1966, Bencher, 1993; QC 1989; a Recorder, 1987–93; a Judge, Employment Appeal Tribunal, 1996–98; Liaison Judge, Family Div., Midland and Oxford Circuit, 1999–2001, Midland Circuit, 2001–06. Chm., Leics Inquiry, 1992. Mem., Judicial Studies Bd, 1994–99 (Co-Chm., Civil and Family Cttee, 1994–98; Chm., Family Cttee, 1998–99). *Address:* c/o Royal Courts of Justice, Strand, WC2A 2LL. *Club:* MCC. *Died 8 May 2014.*

KIRNER, Hon. Joan Elizabeth, AC 2012 (AM 1980); Chairman, Australian Centre for Equity through Education, 1996–2001; Co-Convenor, 1996–2006, Ambassador, since 2006, EMILY's List, Australia; *b* 20 June 1938; *d* of J. K. and B. E. Hood; *m* 1960, Ronald Kirner; two *s* one *d*. *Educ:* University High Sch.; Melbourne Univ. (BA, Dip. Educn). English and Social Studies Teacher, Ballarat Tech. Sch., 1959–60; positions with Vic. Fedn of State Schs Parents' Clubs, Aust. Council of State Schs Orgns, to 1982. Joined ALP 1976; MLC Melbourne West, 1982–88; MLA (ALP) Williamstown, Victoria, 1988–94; Minister for: Conservation, Forests and Lands, 1985–88; Education, 1988–90; Ethnic Affairs, 1990–91; Women's Affairs, 1990–92; Dep. Premier, 1989–90; Premier of Victoria, 1990–92; Leader of the Opposition, 1992–94; Shadow Minister for Ethnic Affairs, and for Women's Affairs, 1992–93. Chairman: Employment Services Regulatory Authy, 1994–97; Adv. Cttee, Centenary of Federation, 1994–96; Victorian Cttee on Federation, 2000–02; Ministerial Adv. Cttee on Social Inclusion and Social Inclusion Report, 2004–07. Board Member: Playbox Th., 1995–97; Aust. Children's Television Foundn, 2001–06; Mus. of Vic, 2003–12 (Life Mem.); Member: Victorian Women's Trust, 1983–; Australian Conservation Foundn; Adv. Cttee, Gardiner (Dairy) Foundn, 2010–. Patron: Women's Circus, 1985–; Living Mus. of the West, 1985–; Positive Women, 1993–2003; Victorian Women's Refuges and Domestic Violence Services, 2002–; Royal Dist Nursing Service, 2002–; Victorian Community Amb., 2007–. Participant, 2020 Summit, Australian Govt. Fellow, Aust. Coll. of Educn, 1983. *Publications:* (with Moira Rayner) Women's Power Handbook, 1999; (with Moira Rayner) Women's Power Pocket Book, 2001. *Recreations:* films, walking, music. *Address:* Old Treasury Building, Spring Street, Melbourne, Vic 3000, Australia. *T:* (3) 96516510. *Died 1 June 2015.*

KITCHENER OF KHARTOUM, 3rd Earl *cr* 1914, and of Broome, in the county of Kent; **Henry Herbert Kitchener,** TD; DL; Viscount Kitchener of Khartoum; and of the Vaal, Transvaal, and of Aspall, Suffolk, 1902; Viscount Broome, 1914; Baron Denton, 1914; late Major, Royal Corps of Signals; *b* 24 Feb. 1919; *er s* of Viscount Broome (*d* 1928) and Adela Mary Evelyn (*d* 1986), *e d* of late J. H. Monins, Ringwould House, near Dover; *S* grandfather, 1937. *Educ:* Sandroyd Sch.; Winchester Coll.; Trinity Coll., Cambridge. President: Lord Kitchener Nat. Meml Fund, 1950–2008; Henry Doubleday Res. Assoc., 1972–2008; Inst. for Food, Brain and Behaviour, 2010–. DL Cheshire, 1972. *Heir:* none. *Address:* Westergate Wood, Eastergate, Chichester, W Sussex PO20 3SB. *T:* (01243) 543061. *Club:* Brooks's. *Died 16 Dec. 2011* (*ext*).

KITZINGER, Sheila Helena Elizabeth, MBE 1982; author, social anthropologist, lecturer and birth educator; *b* 29 March 1929; *d* of Alec and Clare Webster; *m* 1952, Uwe Kitzinger, CBE; five *d* (incl. twins). *Educ:* Bishop Fox's Girls' Sch., Taunton; Ruskin Coll., Oxford; St Hugh's Coll., Oxford; motherhood. Res. Asst, Dept of Anthropology, Univ. of Edinburgh, 1952–53 (MLitt 1954; thesis on race relations in Britain). Course Team Chm., Open Univ., 1981–83. Mem. Editl Bd, Midwives Information and Resource Service; Chairperson, Foundation for Women's Health Res. and Develt, 1985–87; Consultant, Internat. Childbirth Educn Assoc.; Adviser: Baby Milk Coalition; Maternity Alliance. Founder and Dir, Birth Crisis Network, 1996–. Hon. Pres., Birth Companions (woman-to-woman help for pregnant women and mothers in prison), 1996–; Patron: Seattle Sch. of Midwifery; Doula UK. Co-founder (with Uwe Kitzinger), Lentils for Dubrovnik, 1991 (relief agency sending aid to women and children in Croatia). MRSocMed. Hon. Prof., Thames Valley Univ., 1994. Joost de Blank Award, to do research on problems facing West Indian mothers in Britain, 1971–73. *Publications:* The Experience of Childbirth, 1962, 6th edn 1987, updated and expanded edn as The New Experience of Childbirth, 2004; Giving Birth, 1971, rev. and expanded edn 1987; Education and Counselling for Childbirth, 1977; Women as Mothers, 1978; (ed with John Davis) The Place of Birth, 1978; Birth at Home, 1979; The Good Birth Guide, 1979; The Experience of Breastfeeding, 1979, 2nd edn 1987; Pregnancy and Childbirth, 1980, 4th edn as The New Pregnancy and Childbirth: choices and challenges, 2003, rev. edn, 2008; Sheila Kitzinger's Birth Book, 1981; (with Rhiannon Walters) Some Women's Experiences of Episiotomy, 1981; Episiotomy: physical and emotional aspects, 1981; Birth over Thirty, 1982; The New Good Birth Guide, 1983; Woman's Experience of Sex, 1983; (ed with Penny Simkin) Episiotomy and the Second Stage of Labor, 1984; Being Born, 1986; Celebration of Birth, 1987; Freedom and Choice in Childbirth (US edn Your Baby Your Way), 1987; Giving Birth: how it really feels, 1987; Some Women's Experiences of Epidurals, 1987; (ed) The Midwife Challenge, 1988; The Crying Baby, 1989; Breastfeeding Your Baby, 1989; (with Celia Kitzinger) Talking With Children About Things That Matter, 1989; (contrib.) Ethnography of Fertility and Birth, 1982; (contrib.) The Management of Labour, 1985; (contrib.) Effective Care in Pregnancy and Childbirth, 1989; (with Vicky Bailey) Pregnancy Day by Day, 1990; Homebirth, 1991; (contrib.) Women's Health Matters, 1991; Ourselves as Mothers, 1992; The Year After Childbirth, 1994; Birth Over Thirty-Five, 1994, 2nd edn 2011; Becoming a Grandmother, 1997; (contrib.) Childbirth and Authoritative Knowledge, 1997; Breastfeeding, 1998; Rediscovering Birth, 2000, 2nd edn 2011; Birth Your Way, 2002, 2nd edn 2011; The Politics of Birth, 2005; Understanding Your Crying Baby, 2005; Birth Crisis, 2006; Pregnancy and Childbirth: choices and challenges, 2011; Birth and Sex, 2012; *posthumous publication*: A Passion for Birth (autobiog.), 2015. *Recreations:* painting, vegetarian cooking. *Address:* The Manor, Standlake, Oxfordshire OX29 7RH. *T:* (01865) 300266, *Fax:* (01865) 300438. *W:* www.sheilakitzinger.com. *Died 11 April 2015.*

KLARE, Hugh John, CBE 1967; *b* Berndorf, Austria, 22 June 1916; *yr s* of F. A. Klare; *m* 1946, Eveline Alice Maria, *d* of Lieut-Col J. D. Rankin, MBE. *Educ:* privately. Came to England, 1932. Served war in Middle East and Europe; Major. Dep. Dir, Economic Organisation Br., Brit. Control Commn for Germany, 1946–48; Sec., Howard League for Penal Reform, 1950–71; seconded to Council of Europe as Dep. Head, Div. of Crime Problems, 1959–61; Head of Div., 1971–72; Member of Council: Internat. Soc. of Criminology, 1960–66; Inst. for Study and Treatment of Delinquency, 1964–66; Nat. Assoc. for Care and Resettlement of Offenders, 1966–71. Chm. Planning Cttee, Brit. Congress on Crime, 1966. Member: Bd of Visitors, Long Lartin Prison, 1972–76; Gloucestershire Probation and Aftercare Cttee, 1972–85; Parole Board, 1972–74. Founder and Trustee, Cheltenham and N Cotswold Eye Therapy Trust, 1976–; Chm. of Trustees, Gloucestershire Arthritis Trust, 1987–95 (Trustee, 1984). A Governor, British Inst. of Human Rights, 1974–80. *Publications:* Anatomy of Prison, 1960; (ed and introd) Changing Concepts of Crime and its Treatment, 1966; (ed jtly) Frontiers of Criminology, 1967; People in Prison, 1972; contribs on crime and penology to Justice of the Peace. *Address:* 34 Herriots Court, St George's Crescent, Droitwich, Worcs WR9 8HJ. *T:* (01905) 773332. *Died 14 May 2012.*

KLEIN, Bernat, CBE 1973; FCSD (FSIAD 1974); Chairman and Managing Director, Bernat Klein Ltd, 1973–93; *b* 6 Nov. 1922; *s* of Lipot Klein and Serena Weiner; *m* 1951, Margaret Soper (*d* 2008); one *s* two *d*. *Educ:* Senta, Yugoslavia; Bezalel Sch. of Arts and Crafts, Jerusalem; Leeds Univ. Designer to: Tootal, Broadhurst, Lee, 1948–49; Munrospun, Edinburgh, 1949–51; Chm. and Man. Dir, Colourcraft, 1952–62; Man. Dir of Bernat Klein Ltd, 1962–66; Chm. and Man. Dir, Bernat Klein Design Ltd, 1966–81. Member: Council of Industrial Design, Scottish Cttee, 1965–71; Royal Fine Art Commn for Scotland, 1980–87. Exhibitions of paintings: E-SU, 1965; Alwyn Gall., 1967; O'Hana Gall., 1969; Assoc. of Arts Gall., Cape Town, Goodman Gall., Johannesburg, and O'Hana Gall., 1972; Laing Art Gall., Newcastle upon Tyne, 1977; Manchester Polytechnic, 1977; Scott Gall., Hawick, 2005; Heriot-Watt Univ., 2006. Hon. FRIAS 1990. Hon. DLitt Heriot-Watt, 2003. *Publications:* Eye for Colour, 1965; Design Matters, 1976. *Recreations:* reading, tennis, walking. *Address:* High Sunderland, Galashiels, Selkirkshire TD1 3PL. *T:* (01750) 20730. *Died 17 April 2014.*

KLEIN, Prof. Lawrence Robert; economist; Benjamin Franklin Professor, University of Pennsylvania, 1968–91, Emeritus 1991; *b* Omaha, 14 Sept. 1920; *s* of Leo Byron Klein and Blanche Monheit; *m* 1947, Sonia Adelson; one *s* three *d*. *Educ:* Univ. of Calif at Berkeley (BA); MIT (PhD 1944); Lincoln Coll., Oxford (MA 1957; Hon. Fellow, 2005). Chicago Univ., 1944–47; Nat. Bureau of Econ. Res., NY, 1948–50; Michigan Univ., 1949–54; Oxford Inst. of Stats, 1954–58; Prof., 1958, University Prof., 1964, Univ. of Pennsylvania. Consultant: UNCTAD, 1966, 1967, 1975; UNIDO, 1973–75; Congressional Budget Office, 1977–82; Council of Econ. Advisers, 1977–80. Mem., Commn on Prices, Fed. Res. Bd, 1968–70. Member: Adv. Bd, Strategic Studies Center, Stanford Res. Inst., 1974–76; Adv. Council, Inst. for Advanced Studies, Vienna, 1977–; Director: Nat. Bureau of Econ. Res., Inc., 1989–; Inst. for East-West Security Studies, 1989–; W. P. Carey & Co. (later LLC), 1984– (Trustee, W. P. Carey Foundn). Corresp. FBA, 1991; Fellow: Econometric Soc. (past Pres.); Amer. Acad. of Arts and Scis; Member: Nat. Acad. of Scis; Amer. Philosophical Soc.; Amer. Economic Assoc. (Past Pres.; J. B. Clark Medal, 1959). Hon. DSc Pennsylvania, 2006. William F. Butler Award, NY Assoc. of Business Economists, 1975; Nobel Prize for Economics, 1980. *Publications:* The Keynesian Revolution, 1947; Textbook of Econometrics, 1953; An Econometric Model of the United States 1929–52, 1955; Wharton Econometric Forecasting Model, 1967; Essay on the Theory of Economic Prediction, 1968; (ed) Econometric Model Performance, 1976; (ed) Comparative Performance of US Econometric Models, 1991. *Address:* 1400 Waverly Road, Apt B035, Gladwyne, PA 19035–1260, USA. *Died 20 Oct. 2013.*

KLEIN, Ralph Phillip, OC 2012; AOE 2010; Premier of Alberta, Canada, 1992–2006; Senior Business Adviser, Borden, Ladner, Gervais, LLP, 2007–10; *b* Calgary, 1 Nov. 1942; *m* 1961, Hilda May Hepner (marr. diss.); two *c*; *m*

1972, Colleen Hamilton; one *d*. *Educ:* Calgary Business Coll. Teacher, later Principal, Calgary Business Coll.; PR with Alberta Div. of Red Cross and United Way of Calgary and Dist, 1963–69; Sen. Civic Affairs reporter, CFCN TV and Radio, 1969–80. Mayor of Calgary, 1980–89; Government of Alberta: MLA (Progressive C) for Calgary-Elbow, 1989–2007; Minister of Envmt, 1989–92; Leader, Progressive Cons. Party, 1992–2006. OStJ 1986. Officier, Légion d'Honneur (France), 2008. *Died 29 March 2013.*

KLYNE, Dame Barbara Evelyn; *see* Clayton, Dame B. E.

KNIGHT, Warburton Richard, CBE 1987; Director of Educational Services, Bradford Metropolitan District Council, 1974–91; *b* 2 July 1932; *s* of late Warburton Henry Johnston and Alice Gweneth Knight; *m* 1961, Pamela Ann (*née* Hearmon); two *s* one *d*. *Educ:* Trinity Coll., Cambridge (MA). Teaching in Secondary Modern and Grammar Schs in Middlesex and Huddersfield, 1956–62; joined West Riding Educn Authority, 1962; Asst Dir for Secondary Schs, Leics, 1967; Asst Educn Officer for Sec. Schs and later for Special and Social Educn in WR, 1970. Hon. DLitt Bradford, 1992. *Recreations:* walking, choral music, travel. *Address:* Thorner Grange, Sandhills, Thorner, Leeds LS14 3DE. *T:* (0113) 289 2356. *Club:* Royal Over-Seas League. *Died 15 Oct. 2015.*

KNIGHTS, Baron *cr* 1987 (Life Peer), of Edgbaston in the County of West Midlands; **Philip Douglas Knights,** Kt 1980; CBE 1976 (OBE 1971); QPM (Dist. Service) 1964; DL; Chief Constable, West Midlands Police, 1975–85; *b* 3 Oct. 1920; *s* of Thomas James Knights and Ethel Knights; *m* 1945, Jean Burman (*d* 2008). *Educ:* King's Sch., Grantham. Lincolnshire Constabulary: Police Cadet, 1938–40; Constable, 1940. Served War, RAF, 1943–45. Sergeant, Lincs Constab., 1946; seconded to Home Office, 1946–50; Inspector, Lincs Constab., 1953, Supt 1955, Chief Supt 1957. Asst Chief Constable, Birmingham City Police, 1959; seconded to Home Office, Dep. Comdt, Police Coll., 1962–66; Dep. Chief Constable, Birmingham City Police, 1970; Chief Constable, Sheffield and Rotherham Constab., 1972–74; Chief Constable, South Yorks Police, 1974–75. Winner of Queen's Police Gold Medal Essay Competition, 1965. Mem., Lord Devlin's Cttee on Identification Procedures, 1974–75. Pres., Assoc. of Chief Police Officers, 1978–79. Member: Council, Univ. of Aston, 1985–98; Adv. Council, Cambridge Univ. Inst. of Criminology, 1986–2002. CCMI. DL W Midlands, 1985. Hon. DSc Aston, 1996. *Recreations:* sport, gardening. *Address:* House of Lords, SW1A 0PW. *Club:* Royal Over-Seas League. *Died 11 Dec. 2014.*

KNOWLAND, Raymond Reginald, CBE 1992; Managing Director, British Petroleum, 1990–92; *b* 18 Aug. 1930; *s* of Reginald George Knowland and Marjorie Doris Knowland (*née* Alvis); *m* 1956, Valerie Mary Higgs; three *s*. *Educ:* Bristol Grammar Sch.; Sir John Cass College London. CChem, FRSC 1972. BP Chemicals: specialty plastics and PVC Plant Management, Barry Works, 1957–69; Works Gen. Manager, Barry Works, 1969–75, Baglan Bay Works, 1975–78; Man. Dir, Belgium, 1978–80; Dir, London, 1980–90; Chief Exec. Officer, London, 1983–90. Non-executive Director: BSI plc, 1992–99; Laporte plc, 1992–99; Sterling Chemicals Inc., 1992–96; BNFL, 1993–97; Sentrachem Internat. Holdings Ltd, 1992–96; Reaction Systems Engineering Ltd, 2006–08. President: British Plastics Fedn, 1983–84; Assoc. of Petrochemical Producers in Europe, 1985–88; CIA, 1990–92; Vice Pres., SCI, 1993–96. Chm., European Chemical Industry Ecology and Toxicology Centre, 1986–90. Liveryman, Horners' Co., 1987 (Master, 2000, Dep. Master, 2001). *Recreations:* sailing, photography, Rugby football (spectator). *Address:* Buoys, The Quay, Appledore, Bideford, N Devon EX39 1QS. *T:* (01237) 471489. *Clubs:* Athenæum, Savage. *Died 14 Oct. 2015.*

KNOWLTON, Richard James, CBE 1983; QFSM 1977; HM Chief Inspector of Fire Services (Scotland), 1984–89; *b* Southampton, 2 Jan. 1928; *s* of Richard John Knowlton, GC, RN and Florence May Humby; *m* 1949, Pamela Vera Horne; one *s*. *Educ:* Bishop Wordsworth's Sch., Salisbury. FIFireE. Served 42 Commando RM, 1945. Southampton Fire Bde, 1948; Station Officer, Worcester City and County Fire Bde, 1959; London Fire Brigade: Asst Divl Officer, 1963; Divl Officer, 1965; Divl Comdr, 1967; Winston Churchill Travelling Fellowship, 1969; Firemaster: SW Area (Scotland) Fire Bde, 1971; Strathclyde Fire Bde, 1975–84. Mem., later Chm., Bds, Fire Service Coll. Extended Interview, 1970–81; Mem., Fire Service Coll. Bd, 1978–82; Mem., later Chm., Scottish Fire Services Examinations Panel, 1971–75; Mem., Scottish Fire Service Examinations Bd, 1974–75; Fire Adviser: to Scottish Assoc. of CCs, 1974; to Convention of Scottish Local Authorities, 1975–81; Sec. to Appliances and Equipment Cttee of Chief and Asst Chief Fire Officers Assoc., 1974–81, Pres. of the Assoc., 1980; Chm., Scottish Dist Chief and Asst Chief Fire Officers Assoc., 1977–81; Zone Fire Comdr (Designate), CD for Scotland, 1975–84; Member: Scottish Central Fire Bdes Adv. Council, 1977–81 (Uniform and Personal Equipment Cttee, 1974–82); Jt Cttee on Design and Develt, 1978–82; England and Wales Central Fire Bdes Adv. Council, 1979–81; Chairman: London Branch, Instn of Fire Engineers, 1969; Scottish Assoc., Winston Churchill Fellows, 1979–81; Hazfile Cttee, 1979–81; Vice-Pres., Fire Services Nat. Benevolent Fund, 1981– (Chm. 1980). Mem., Nat. Jt Council for Chief Fire Officers, 1980–82; Mem., later Chm., Management Structures Working Gp of Nat. Jt Council for Local Authority Fire Bdes, 1980–83; British Mem., Admin. Council of European Assoc. of Professional Fire Bde Officers, 1981–85 (Vice Pres., 1984–85). *Died 19 Sept. 2014.*

KNOX, (Alexander) David, CMG 1988; Vice President, International Bank for Reconstruction and Development, 1980–87; *b* 15 Jan. 1925; *s* of James Knox and Elizabeth Maxwell Knox; *m* 1950, Beatrice Lily (*née* Dunell); one *s* two *d*. *Educ:* Univ. of Toronto (BA); London School of Economics and Political Science (Hon. Fellow, 1982). LSE, 1949–63, Reader in Economics, 1955–63; International Bank for Reconstruction and Development (World Bank), 1963–87: Vice President: W Africa, 1980–84; Latin America, 1984–87. Chm., Task Force on Project Quality, African Develt Bank, 1993–94. Member: Bd of Dirs, Liverpool Associates in Tropical Health, 1990–99; Prog. Adv. Panel, SCF, 1993–99; Council, Worldaware, 1994–2002. *Publications:* Latin American Debt: facing facts, 1990; articles in Economica, OECF Res. Qly (Japan), etc. *Recreations:* opera, walking. *Address:* Knights Barn, Manor Farm Lane, East Hagbourne, Oxon OX11 9ND. *T:* (01235) 817792. *Died 29 Nov. 2014.*

KNOX, Bryce Harry, CB 1986; a Deputy Chairman, and Director General, Internal Taxation Group, Board of Customs and Excise, 1983–88; *b* 21 Feb. 1929; *e s* of late Brice Henry Knox and Rose Hetty Knox; *m* 1957, Norma (*d* 2008), *d* of late George and Rose Thomas; one *s*. *Educ:* Stratford Grammar Sch.; Nottingham Univ. BA(Econ). Asst Principal, HM Customs and Excise, 1953; Principal, 1958; on loan to HM Treasury, 1963–65; Asst Sec., HM Customs and Excise, 1966; seconded to HM Diplomatic Service, Counsellor, Office of UK Perm. Rep. to European Communities, 1972–74; Under-Sec., 1974, Comr, 1975, HM Customs and Excise. *Clubs:* Reform, MCC. *Died 11 Dec. 2013.*

KNOX, David; *see* Knox, A. D.

KNOX, John, (Jack), RSA 1979 (ARSA 1972); RGI 1980; RSW 1987; Head of Painting Studios, Glasgow School of Art, 1981–92; *b* Kirkintilloch, 16 Dec. 1936; *s* of Alexander and Jean Knox; *m* 1960, Margaret Kyle Sutherland; one *s* one *d*. *Educ:* Lenzie Acad.; Glasgow Sch. of Art (DA). On the Drawing and Painting Staff at Duncan of Jordanstone Coll. of Art, Dundee, 1965–81. Work in permanent collections: Scottish Nat. Gallery of Modern Art; Arts Council; Contemporary Arts Soc.; Scottish Arts Council; Otis Art Inst., Los Angeles; Olinda Museum, São Paulo; Aberdeen, Dundee and Manchester art galleries; Hunterian Museum, Glasgow; Scottish Nat. Portrait Gall.; Kelvingrove Art Galls and Mus. Retrospective exhibn, Knox 1960–83, Scottish Arts Council, 1983. Member: Scottish Arts Council, 1974–79; Trustees Cttee, Scottish Nat. Gall. of Modern Art, 1975–81; Bd of Trustees, Nat. Galls of Scotland, 1982–87. Sec., Royal Scottish Acad., 1990–91. Member: Bd of Governors, Duncan of Jordanstone Coll. of Art, Dundee,

1980–82; Bd of Governors, Glasgow Sch. of Art, 1985–88. Hon. FRIAS 1997. Hon. DLitt Glasgow, 2005. *Address:* 66 Seafield Road, Broughty Ferry, Dundee DD5 3AQ. *Died 12 April 2015.*

KNOX, Sir John (Leonard), Kt 1985; a Judge of the High Court of Justice, Chancery Division, 1985–96; *b* 6 April 1925; *s* of Leonard Needham Knox and Berthe Hélène Knox; *m* 1st, 1953, Anne Jacqueline Mackintosh (*d* 1991); one *s* three *d*; 2nd, 1993, Benedicta Eugenie Cooksey. *Educ:* Radley Coll.; Worcester Coll., Oxford (Hon. Mods, 1st Cl.; Jurisprudence, 1st Cl.). Called to the Bar, Lincoln's Inn, 1953, Bencher, 1977; Member, Senate of the Inns of Court, 1975–78. QC 1979; Junior Treasury Counsel: in *bona vacantia*, 1971–79; in probate, 1978–79; Attorney-Gen., Duchy of Lancaster, 1984–85. Mem., Council of Legal Educn, 1975–79; Chm., Chancery Bar Assoc., 1985. Dep. Chm., Parly Boundary Commn, 1987–95. *Died 28 May 2015.*

KOCH, Edward Irving; Partner, Bryan Cave LLP (formerly Robinson, Silverman, Pearce, Aronsohn & Berman), New York, since 1990; Mayor, City of New York, 1978–89; *b* 12 Dec. 1924; *s* of Louis Koch and Joyce Silpe. *Educ:* Southside High School, Newark, NJ; City Coll. of NY; NY Univ. Law Sch. Served US Army, 1943–46, USA, France, Rhineland. Mem., NY State Bar, 1949; private law practice, 1949–64; Senior Partner, Koch, Lankenau, Schwartz & Kovner, 1965–69. Democratic dist. leader, Greenwich Village, 1963–65; Mem., NY City Council, 1967–68; NY Congressman, 1969–77. Mem., US Holocaust Meml Council. Regular broadcaster, columnist and lecturer. *Publications:* Mayor, 1983; Politics, 1985; (jtly) His Eminence and Hizzoner, 1989; All the Best, 1990; Citizen Koch (autobiog.), 1992; Ed Koch on Everything, 1994; Murder at City Hall, 1995; Murder on Broadway, 1996; Murder on 34th Street, 1997; The Senator Must Die, 1998; Giuliani: nasty man, 1999; I'm not done yet, 1999; (for children, with Pat Koch Thaler): Eddie, Harold's Little Brother, 2004; Eddie's Little Sister Makes a Splash, 2007. *Address:* (office) 1290 Avenue of the Americas, New York, NY 10104–3300, USA. *Died 1 Feb. 2013.*

KOENIGSBERGER, Prof. Helmut Georg, MA, PhD; FBA 1989; Professor of History, King's College London, 1973–84, then Emeritus; *b* 24 Oct. 1918; *s* of late Georg Felix Koenigsberger, chief architect, borough of Treptow, Berlin, Germany, and of late Käthe Koenigsberger (*née* Born); *m* 1961, Dorothy M. Romano; two *d* (twins). *Educ:* Adams' Grammar Sch., Newport, Shropshire; Gonville and Caius Coll., Cambridge. Asst Master: Brentwood Sch., Essex, 1941–42; Bedford Sch., 1942–44. Served War of 1939–45, Royal Navy, 1944–45. Lectr in Economic History, QUB, 1948–51; Sen. Lectr in Economic History, Univ. of Manchester, 1951–60; Prof. of Modern History, Univ. of Nottingham, 1960–66; Prof. of Early Modern European History, Cornell, 1966–73. Visiting Lecturer: Brooklyn Coll., New York, 1957; Univ. of Wisconsin, 1958; Columbia Univ., 1962; Cambridge Univ., 1963; Washington Univ., St Louis, 1964; Fellow, Historisches Kolleg, Munich, 1984–85. Sec., 1955–75, Vice-Pres., 1975–80, Pres., 1980–85, Internat. Commn for the History of Representative and Parliamentary Institutions; Vice-Pres., RHistS, 1982–85. Hon. FKC 1999. Encomienda, Order of Isabel the Catholic (Spain), 1997. *Publications:* The Government of Sicily under Philip II of Spain, 1951, new edn, as The Practice of Empire, 1969; The Empire of Charles V in Europe (in New Cambridge Modern History II), 1958; Western Europe and the Power of Spain (in New Cambridge Modern History III), 1968; Europe in the Sixteenth Century (with G. L. Mosse), 1968, 2nd edn (with G. L. Mosse and G. Q. Bowler) 1989; Estates and Revolutions, 1971; The Habsburgs and Europe, 1516–1660, 1971; (ed) Luther: a profile, 1972; Politicians and Virtuosi, 1986; Medieval Europe, 1987; Early Modern Europe, 1987; (ed) Republiken und Republikanismus im Europa der frühen Neuzeit, 1988; Monarchies, States Generals and Parliaments, 2001; contrib. to historical journals. *Recreations:* playing chamber music, sailing, travel. *Died 8 March 2014.*

KREISEL, Prof. Georg, FRS 1966; Professor Emeritus of Logic and the Foundations of Mathematics, Stanford University, Stanford, California, USA; *b* 15 Sept. 1923. *Address:* Institut für Wissenschaftstheorie, Linzergasse 16, 5020 Salzburg, Austria. *Died 1 March 2015.*

KRIKORIAN, Gregory, CB 1973; Solicitor for the Customs and Excise, 1971–78; *b* 23 Sept. 1913; *s* of late Kevork and Christine Krikorian; *m* 1943, Seta Mary (*d* 1995), *d* of Souren Djirdjirian; one *d*. *Educ:* Polytechnic Secondary Sch.; Lincoln Coll., Oxford (BA). Called to Bar, Middle Temple, 1939; practised at Bar, 1939; BBC Overseas Intell. Dept, 1940; served in RAF as Intell. Officer, Fighter Comd, 1940–45 (despatches); practised at Bar, 1945–51, Junior Oxford Circuit, 1947; joined Solicitor's Office, HM Customs and Excise, 1951. *Publications:* (jtly) Customs and Excise, in Halsbury's Laws of England, 1975; Through the Eye of an Armenian Needle, 2002. *Recreations:* gardening, bird-watching. *Address:* The Coach House, Hawkchurch, Axminster, Devon EX13 5TX. *T:* (01297) 678414. *Clubs:* Reform, Civil Service. *Died 29 July 2011.*

KUHN, Prof. Karl Heinz, FBA 1987; Professor of Coptic, Durham University, 1982–84, then Emeritus Professor; *b* 2 Aug. 1919; *s* of Max Kuhn and Gertrud Kuhn (*née* Hiller); *m* 1949, Rachel Mary Wilkinson; one *s* (one *d* decd). *Educ:* school in Germany; St John's Coll., Univ. of Durham (BA 1949, PhD 1952). Scarbrough Research Studentship, Durham Univ. and abroad, 1949–53; Univ. of Durham: Research Fellow in Arts, 1953–55; Lectr, later Sen. Lectr in Hebrew and Aramaic, 1955–77; Reader in Coptic, 1977–82; Prof. of Coptic, 1982–84. Mem., Editl Bd, Corpus Scriptorum Christianorum Orientalium, Louvain, 1970–2000. *Publications:* Letters and Sermons of Besa, 1956; Pseudo-Shenoute: on Christian behaviour, 1960; A Panegyric on John the Baptist attributed to Theodosius, Archbishop of Alexandria, 1966; A Panegyric on Apollo, Archimandrite of the Monastery of Isaac by Stephen, Bishop of Heracleopolis Magna, 1978; (contrib.) Sparks, The Apocryphal Old Testament, 1984; (with W. J. Tait) Thirteen Coptic Acrostic Hymns from Manuscript M574 of the Pierpont Morgan Library, 1996; (contrib.) English trans. of Foerster, Gnosis, 1974, and Rudolph, Gnosis, 1983; articles in Jl of Theol Studies, Le Muséon and other learned jls. *Recreation:* music. *Address:* 31 Burford Lodge, Pegasus Grange, Whitehouse Road, Oxford OX1 4QG. *T:* (01865) 241258. *Died 10 June 2013.*

KUME, Yutaka; President, 1985–92, Chairman, 1992, Nissan Motor Co.; *b* 20 May 1921; *s* of Kinzaburo Kume and Chiyo Kume; *m* 1947, Aya Yamamoto; one *s* one *d*. *Educ:* Univ. of Tokyo (BE aircraft engineering). Joined Nissan Motor Co., 1946; General Manager: Production control and Engineering Dept, Zama Plant, 1964; Yoshiwara Plant, 1971; Tochigi Plant, 1973–78; Dir and Mem. Bd, 1973; Managing Dir, 1977; Exec. Managing Dir, 1982; Exec. Vice-Pres. and Gen. Manager, Quality Admin Div., 1983. Blue Ribbon Medal from Emperor of Japan, 1986; Commander, Order of Orange Nassau (Holland), 1986; Order of Cruz de San Jordi (Catalonia, Spain), 1990; Commander, Order of the Crown (Belgium), 1991. *Recreations:* photography, haiku (Japanese short poems), reading. *Died 10 Sept. 2014.*

KUSTOW, Michael David; writer, producer and director; *b* 18 Nov. 1939; *m* 1973, Orna (marr. diss. 1998), *d* of Jacob and Rivka Spector, Haifa, Israel. *Educ:* Haberdashers' Aske's; Wadham Coll., Oxford (BA Hons English). Festivals Organiser, Centre 42, 1962–63; Royal Shakespeare Theatre Company: Dir, RSC Club, Founder of Theatregoround, Editor of Flourish, 1963–67; Dir, Inst. of Contemporary Arts, 1967–70; Associate Dir, National Theatre, 1973–81; Commissioning Ed. for Arts progs, Channel Four TV, 1981–89; Dir, Michael Kustow Productions, 1990–; Co-Dir, The Greek Collection, 1990–. Lectr in Dramatic Arts, Harvard Univ., 1980–82; Vis. Prof., Royal Holloway, London Univ., 2000–. Chevalier de l'Ordre des Arts et des Lettres, République Française, 1980. *Productions:* Punch and Judas, Trafalgar Square, 1963; I Wonder, ICA, 1968; Nicholas Tomalin Reporting, 1975; Brecht Poetry and Songs, 1976; Larkinland, Groucho Letters, Robert Lowell, Audience,

1977–78; Miss South Africa, Catullus, A Nosegay of Light Verse, The Voice of Babel, Anatol, 1979; Iris Murdoch's Art and Eros, Shakespeare's Sonnets, Stravinsky's Soldier's Tale, 1980; Charles Wood's Has Washington Legs, Harold Pinter's Family Voices, 1981; The Mahabharata, 1989; The War that Never Ends, 1991; The Last Bolshevik, 1993; ABC of Democracy, 1994; A Maybe Day in Kazakhstan, 1994; Fireworks, 1994; Shakespeare Workshops, 1994; Everybody's Shakespeare Festival, 1994; Hiroshima, 1995; Jerusalem, Between Heaven and Hell, 1996; Dionysus and the Mighty Mouse, 1998; *films:* Prometheus, 1998; Pandaemonium, 1999; Tantalus, 2000. *Exhibitions:* Tout Terriblement Guillaume Apollinaire, ICA, 1968; AAARGH! A Celebration of Comics, ICA, 1971. *Publications:* Punch and Judas, 1964; The Book of US, 1968; Tank: an autobiographical fiction, 1975; One in Four, 1987; theatre@risk, 2000; Peter Brook: and the way of theatre, 2005. *Recreations:* painting, jazz. *Address:* 17 Haslemere Road, N8 9QP. *T:* (020) 8347 6423. *Died 29 Aug. 2014.*

KWAPONG, Alexander Adum, MA, PhD Cantab; Director, African Programmes, Teacher Education, Research and Evaluation, The Commonwealth of Learning, Vancouver, 1991–93; *b* Akropong, Akwapim, 8 March 1927; *s* of E. A. Kwapong and Theophilia Kwapong; *m* 1956, Evelyn Teiko Caesar, Ada; six *d. Educ:* Presbyterian junior and middle schools, Akropong; Achimota Coll.; King's Coll., Cambridge (Exhibr, Minor Schol. and Foundn Schol.). BA 1951, MA 1954, PhD 1957, Cantab. 1st cl. prelims, Pts I and II, Classical Tripos, 1951; Sandys Res. Student, Cambridge Univ.; Richards Prize, Rann Kennedy Travel Fellowship, King's Coll., Cambridge. Lectr in Classics, UC Gold Coast, 1953, Sen. Lectr in Classics 1960; Vis. Prof., Princeton Univ., 1961–62; Prof. of Classics, Univ. of Ghana, 1962; Dean of Arts, Pro-Vice-Chancellor, Univ. of Ghana, 1962–65, Vice-Chancellor 1966–75; Vice-Rector for Instnl Planning and Resource Develt, UN Univ., 1976–88 (Sen. Advr to Rector, 1988–); Lester B. Pearson Prof. in Develt Studies, Dalhousie Univ., Halifax, Canada, 1988–91. Chairman: Educn Review Cttee, Ghana Govt, 1966–67; Smithsonian Instn 3rd Internat. Symposium, 1969; Assoc. of Commonwealth Univs, 1971. Sir Samuel Manuwa Meml Lectr, W African Coll. of Surgeons, 1990. Member: Admin. Bd, Internat. Assoc. Univs, Paris, 1970–80; Exec. Bd, Assoc. African Univs, 1967–74; Bd of Trustees, Internat. Council for Educnl Develt, NY; Aspen Inst. for Humanistic Studies, 1972–85; Board of Directors: Internat. Assoc. for Cultural Freedom, Paris, 1967–75; Internat. Cttee for the Study of Educnl Exchange; Aspen Berlin Inst., 1975–; IDRC; Harold Macmillan Trust, 1986–; Internat. Foundn for Educn and Self Help, Phoenix, Arizona, 1988–; African Leadership Forum. Consultant, World Bank, 1988–89. Fellow, Ghana Academy of Arts and Sciences. Hon. DLitt: Warwick; Ife; Ghana; Hon. LLD Princeton. Order of Volta, Ghana. *Publications:* The Role of Classical Studies in Africa Today, 1969; Higher Education and Development in Africa Today: a reappraisal, 1979; Underdevelopment and the Challenges of the 1980's: the role of knowledge, 1980; The Relevance of the African Universities to the Development Needs of Africa, 1980; What Kind of Human Beings for the 21st Century—a second look, 1981; The Humanities and National Development: a second look, 1984; The Crisis of Development: education and identity, 1985; Medical Education and National Development, 1987; Culture, Development and African Unity, 1988; African Scientific and Technical Institution—Building and the Role of International Co-operation, 1988; The Challenge of Education in Africa, 1988; (ed with B. Lesser) Capacity Building and Human Resource Development in Africa, 1990; (ed with B. Lesser) Meeting the Challenge: the African Capacity Building Initiative, 1992; *contribs to:* Grecs et Barbars, 1962; Dawn of African History (ed R. Oliver); Man and Beast: Comparative Social Behaviour (ed J. F. Eisenberg and W. S. Dillon), 1971; Pearson Notes, 1988–89; The Role of Service-Learning in International Education (procs of Wingspread conf.) (ed S. W. Showalter), 1989; Culture, Development and Democracy: role of intellectuals in Africa, 1991; Recent Trends in Governance in African Universities: the challenge of scientific and intellectual leadership, 1992; various articles in classical jls, especially on Ancient and Greco-Roman Africa; various addresses and lectures on internat. higher educn in ICED pubns. *Recreations:* tennis, billiards, music and piano-playing, learning Japanese. *Address:* 19 Highfield Avenue, Golders Green, NW11 9EU. *T:* (020) 8209 0878. *Club:* Athenæum. *Died 9 Aug. 2014.*

L

LACEY, George William Brian; Keeper, Department of Transport, Science Museum, London, 1971–86; *b* 15 Nov. 1926; *m* 1956, Lynette (*née* Hogg); two *s*. *Educ:* Brighton, Hove and Sussex Grammar Sch., 1938–44; Brighton Technical Coll., 1944–47; BSc(Eng) 2nd Cl. Hons (External, London). National Service, REME, 1947–49. Rolls-Royce Ltd, Derby: Grad. Apprentice, Tech. Asst, Mechanical Develt and Performance Analysis, 1949–54; Asst Keeper, Science Museum, London, SW7, 1954–71. Chm., Historical Gp, Royal Aeronautical Soc., 1971–78; Vice-Pres., Assoc. British Transport Museums, 1990– (Chm., 1973–83); Mem. Council, Transport Trust, 1978–89. *Recreations:* golf, genealogy. *Address:* Hurst Grange Cottage, Albourne Road, Hurstpierpoint, W Sussex BN6 9ES. *T:* (01273) 833914. *Died 8 Aug. 2012.*

LACOME, Myer; professional artist/designer; Principal, Duncan of Jordanstone College of Art, Dundee, 1978–87; *b* 13 Nov. 1927; *s* of Colman Lacome and Sara (*née* Sholl); *m* 1954, Jacci Edgar (*d* 2008); one *s* two *d*. *Educ:* Regional Coll. of Art, Liverpool. MSIAD, MSTD; FRSA. National Service, RAF, 1946–48. Post-grad. course, 1948–49; designer, New York, 1949–51; consultant designer, London, 1951–59; Head of Sch. of Design, Duncan of Jordanstone Coll. of Art, Dundee, 1962–77. Vis. Fellow, Royal Melbourne Inst. of Technol., 1979. Chm., Visual Art Cttee, Scottish Arts Council, 1986–93; Member: Council, CNAA, 1979–84; Higher Educn Cttee, Scottish Design Council, 1984–86; Governor, Scottish Film Council, 1982–. One-man exhibitions include: Paris: paintings and collages, French Cultural Inst., Edin., Paperpoint Gall., Covent Gdn, and Univ. of Dundee, 1992; Holocaust and After?, Chessel Gall., Edinburgh, 1995, Mackintosh Mus. Sch., Glasgow, 1996, Manchester Jewish Mus., 1997; Scottish Exec., 2000, 2001, 2003; Edinburgh Internat. Fest., 2007, 2008, 2009; works in permanent collections of nat. museums and galls in Europe and USA. *Publications:* papers on crafts in Scotland and on Scandinavian design and crafts. *Recreations:* enjoying: no longer sitting on committees or quangos, not wearing a tie, painting in my studio, listening to Bach, Glenn Gould, Miles Davis and Thelonius Monk. *Address:* 4 Campbells Close, off Royal Mile, Edinburgh EH8 8JJ. *Died 30 Sept. 2011.*

LACON, Sir Edmund (Vere), 8th Bt *cr* 1818; *b* 3 May 1936; *s* of Sir George Vere Francis Lacon, 7th Bt, and Hilary Blanche, *d* of late C. J. Scott, Adyar, Walberswick; *S* father, 1980; *m* 1963, Gillian, *d* of J. H. Middleditch, Wrentham, Suffolk; one *s* one *d*. *Educ:* Taverham Hall, Norfolk; Woodbridge School, Suffolk. RAF Regiment, 1955–59. *Recreations:* golf, water ski-ing, being politically incorrect. *Heir:* *s* (Edmund) Richard (Vere) Lacon [*b* 2 Oct. 1967; *m* 1997, Natalie, *o d* of Joginder Shinh; one *s*]. *Died 17 Oct. 2014.*

LAIGHT, Barry Pemberton, OBE 1970; Eur Ing; FREng, FIMechE, FRAeS; Consultant to: Design Council, since 1983; VAWT Ltd, since 1983; RES Ltd, since 1983; Production Engineering Research Association, since 1986; Department of Trade and Industry, 1988–90; *b* 12 July 1920; *s* of Donald Norman Laight and Nora (*née* Pemberton); *m* 1951, Ruth Murton; one *s* one *d*. *Educ:* Johnston Sch., Durham; Birmingham Central Tech. Coll.; Merchant Venturers' Tech. Coll., Bristol; Bristol Univ. (MSc). FREng (FEng 1981). SBAC Scholar, apprentice, Bristol Aeroplane Co., 1937; Chief Designer, 1952, Technical Dir, 1960, Blackburn & General Aircraft (develt of Beverley and design of Buccaneer, 1953, for RN service, 1960); Chief Engineer Kingston, 1963, Dir for Military Projects, 1968, Hawker Siddeley Aviation (Harrier develt to RAF service; introd. Hawk Trainer); Exec. Dir Engineering, Short Brothers, 1977–82 (develt SD360 and Blowpipe); Sec., RAeS, 1983–85. Mem. Council, RAeS, 1955–90 (Pres., 1974–75; British Silver Medal in Aeronautics, 1963); Chairman: Educn Cttee, SBAC, 1962–67; Tech. Board, SBAC, 1967–82; Member: Aircraft Res. Assoc. Board, 1972–77 (Chm., Tech. Cttee); ARC, 1973–76; Air Educn and Recreational Organisation Council, 1969–72; CBI: Mem., Res. and Tech. Cttee; Educn Cttee; Chm., Transport Technology Panel, SRC, 1969–73; Hon. Treasurer, Internat. Council of Aero. Scis, 1978–84; AGARD Nat. Delegate, 1968–73; Sec., Bristol Gliding Club, 1949–52. Mem., Mensa, 1945. AFAIAA; FInstD. *Publications:* papers in RAeS jls. *Recreations:* reading on any subject, house and car maintenance, music. *Address:* 5 Littlemead, Esher, Surrey KT10 9PE. *T:* (01372) 463216. *Died 6 Oct. 2012.*

LAING, Gerald O.; *see* Ogilvie-Laing.

LAINSON, Prof. Ralph, OBE 1996; FRS 1982; Director, Wellcome Parasitology Unit, Instituto Evandro Chagas, Belém, Pará, Brazil, 1965–92; *b* 21 Feb. 1927; *s* of Charles Harry Lainson and Anne (*née* Denyer); *m* 1st, 1957, Anne Patricia Russell; one *s* two *d*; 2nd, 1974, Zeá Constante Lins. *Educ:* Steyning Grammar Sch., Sussex; London Univ. (BSc, PhD, DSc). Lecturer in Medical Protozoology, London Sch. of Hygiene and Tropical Medicine, London Univ., 1955–59; Officer-in-Charge, Dermal Leishmaniasis Unit, Baking-Pot, Cayo Dist, Belize, 1959–62; Attached Investigator, Dept of Medical Protozoology, London Sch. of Hygiene and Tropical Medicine, 1962–65. Career devoted to research in Medical Protozoology in the Tropics. Hon. Fellow, LSHTM, 1982; Hon. Professor, Federal Univ. of Pará, Brazil, 1982; Associate Fellow, Third World Acad. of Scis, 1989; Hon. FRSTM&H 1997; Hon. Member: British Soc. of Parasitology, 1984; Soc. of Protozoologists, 1997; Amer. Soc. of Tropical Medicine and Hygiene, 2009. Chalmer's Medal, Royal Soc. of Tropical Medicine and Hygiene, 1971; Oswaldo Cruz Medal, Conselho Estadual de Cultura do Pará, 1973; Manson Medal, Royal Soc. of Tropical Medicine and Hygiene, 1983; Commemorative medals: 10th anniv., Health Council for State of Pará, Brazil, 1983; 30th anniv., Fed. Univ. of Pará, Brazil, 1988. *Publications:* author, or co-author, of approximately 300 pubns in current scientific jls and text-books, on protozoal parasites of man and animals. *Recreations:* fishing, swimming, collecting South American Lepidoptera, music, philately. *Address:* Avenida Visconde de Souza Franco, 1237 (Edificio 'Visconti'), Apartamento 902, 66053–000 Belém, Pará, Brazil. *T:* (91) 32232382. *Died 5 May 2015.*

LAIRD, Endell Johnston; Director and Editor in Chief, Scottish Daily Record and Sunday Mail, 1988–94; Editor in Chief, The Glaswegian, 1988–94; *b* Forfar, 6 Oct. 1933; *m* 1958, June Keenan; one *s* two *d*. *Educ:* Forfar Academy. Served RAF, 1952–54. Journalist: Dundee Courier, 1954–56; Scottish Daily Express, 1956–58; Evening Times, 1958–60; Sunday Mail, 1960–71; Daily Record, 1971–81; Editor, Sunday Mail, 1981–88. Editl Dir (SDR), Mirror Gp Newspapers, 1991–94. Chm., Scottish Editors Cttee, 1986–88; Mem., D-Notice Cttee, 1986–94. Mem. Bd, Children's Hospice Assoc. Scotland, 1994–. *Recreations:* walking, golf, bridge. *Clubs:* Bishopbriggs Golf; Bishopbriggs Bridge. *Died 8 July 2015.*

LAIRD, Margaret Heather, OBE 1999; Third Church Estates Commissioner, 1989–99; *b* 29 Jan. 1933; *d* of William Henry Polmear and Edith Polmear; *m* 1961, Rev. Canon John Charles Laird; two *s*. *Educ:* High Sch., Truro; Westfield College, London (BA Hons Mediaeval History, 1954); King's College London (Cert. in Religious Knowledge, 1955). Divinity Mistress: Grey Coat Hospital, SW1, 1955–59; Newquay Grammar Sch., 1959–60; St Albans High Sch., 1960–62; Head of Religious Studies, Dame Alice Harpur Sch., Bedford, 1969–89. Member: Gen. Synod of C of E, repr. Dio. St Albans, 1980–90, ex officio, 1990–99 (Mem., Standing Cttee, 1989–98); Panel of Assessors, Dio. St Albans, 1988–2000; C of E Pensions Bd, 1989–98. Vice Pres., English Clergy Assoc., 2001–; Mem., Exec. Cttee, Anglican Assoc., 2008–14. Vice-Pres., Soc. for Maintenance of the Faith, 1995–. Trustee:

Lambeth Palace Library, 1993–99; Oxford Movt Anniv. Appeal Trust, 1996–2010; Kentish's Educnl Foundn, 2001–06; Cleaver Ordination Candidates Foundn, 2001–14; Member: Allchurches Trust Ltd, 1994–; Exec., Open Churches Trust, 1995–2007; Exec. Cttee, Choose Life, 2001–10; Private Patrons' Gp, 2002–14. Mem., Royal Instn of Cornwall, 1997–2013. Governor, 1993–, Vice Pres., 2014–, Pusey House, Oxford. FRSA 1996–2010. *Publications:* Through A Glass Darkly (contrib.), 1993; From Now to Eternity, 2001; articles in The Times and various jls. *Recreations:* mediaeval art, architecture, pilgrims' routes. *Address:* 1–2 Prospect Place, Truro, Cornwall TR1 1HW. *Club:* Oxford and Cambridge. *Died 11 May 2014.*

LAITHWAITE, John, FIMechE, FInstPet; engineering consultant; Director, Capper Neill Ltd, 1965–83 (Vice-Chairman, 1972–82); *b* 29 Nov. 1920; *s* of Tom Prescott Laithwaite and Mary Anne Laithwaite; *m* 1943, Jean Chateris; one *s* two *d*. *Educ:* Manchester Univ. (BSc Hons Mech. Eng). FIMechE 1974; FInstPet 1960; MInstW 1950. Wm Neill & Son (St Helens) Ltd, 1942–43; Dartford Shipbuilding & Engineering Co., 1943–44; Dir, Wm Neill & Son (St Helens) Ltd, 1955–58, Man. Dir, 1958–64; Man. Dir, Capper Neill Ltd, 1968–72. Mem. Council, NW Regional Management Centre. Chm., Process Plant Assoc., 1975–77, Hon. Vice-Pres., 1980. *Publications:* articles on process plant industry and pressure vessel standardisation. *Recreations:* shooting, golf. *Address:* 44 Deganwy Beach, Deganwy, Conwy LL31 9YR. *T:* (01492) 582214. *Died 29 Sept. 2012.*

LAKE, Sir (Atwell) Graham, 10th Bt *cr* 1711; Senior Technical Adviser, Ministry of Defence, retired 1983; *b* 6 Oct. 1923; *s* of Captain Sir Atwell Henry Lake, 9th Bt, CB, OBE, RN, and Kathleen Marion, *d* of late Alfred Morrison Turner; *S* father, 1972; *m* 1983, Mrs Katharine Margaret Lister, *d* of late D. W. Last and M. M. Last. *Educ:* Eton. British High Commission, Wellington, NZ, 1942; Gilbert and Ellice Military Forces, 1944; Colonial Administrative Service, 1945 (Secretary to Govt of Tonga, 1950–53); Norris Oakley Bros, 1957; Min. of Defence, 1959; British High Commission, New Delhi, 1966; attached Foreign and Commonwealth Office, 1969–72. Chm., Abbeyfield Epping Soc., 1995–97 (Hon. Sec., 1987–96). *Recreations:* golf, bridge, chess. *Heir:* *b* Edward Geoffrey Lake [*b* 17 July 1928; *m* 1965, Judith Ann, *d* of John Fox; one *s* one *d*]. *Died 25 May 2013.*

LAKIN, Sir Michael, 4th Bt *cr* 1909; *b* 28 Oct. 1934; *s* of Sir Henry Lakin, 3rd Bt, and Bessie (*d* 1965), *d* of J. D. Anderson, Durban; *S* father, 1979; *m* 1st, 1956, Margaret Wallace (marr. diss. 1963); 2nd, 1965, Felicity Ann Murphy; one *s* one *d*. *Educ:* Stowe. *Heir:* *s* Richard Anthony Lakin [*b* 26 Nov. 1968; *m* 1997, Lara Maryanne Rose (marr. diss. 2009); one *s* one *d*]. *Address:* Little Sherwood, Tunley, near Cirencester, Glos GL7 6LW. *Died 13 Jan. 2014.*

LAL, Prof. Devendra, PhD; FRS 1979; Professor, Geological Research Division, Scripps Institution of Oceanography, University of California, La Jolla, since 1967; Fellow: Physical Research Laboratory, Ahmedabad, since 1990 (Director, 1972–83; Senior Professor, 1983–89); Tata Institute of Fundamental Research, Bombay, since 1996; *b* 14 Feb. 1929; *s* of Radhekrishna Lal and Sita Devi; *m* 1955, Aruna L. Damany (*d* 1993). *Educ:* Banaras Hindu Univ. (BSc; MSc); Univ. of Bombay (PhD). Fellow, Indian Acad. of Sciences, 1964. Tata Inst. of Fundamental Research, Bombay: Res. Student, 1949–50; Res. Asst, 1950–53; Res. Fellow, 1953–57; Fellow, 1957–60; Associate Prof., 1960–63; Prof., 1963–70; Sen. Prof., 1970–72. Res. Geophysicist, UCLA-IGPP, 1965–66. Vis. Prof., UCLA, 1983–84. K. S. Krishnan Meml Lect., INSA, 1981. Foreign Sec., Indian Nat. Sci. Acad., 1981–84 (Fellow, 1971); Founder Mem., Third World Acad. of Scis, Trieste, 1983; President: Internat. Assoc. of Physical Scis of the Ocean, 1979–83; Internat. Union of Geodesy & Geophysics, 1983–87. Fellow: Nat. Acad. of Scis, Allahabad, 1988; Physical Res. Lab., Ahmedabad, 1996; Tata Inst. of Fundamental Res., Bombay, 1996; Amer. Geophysical Union, 2005; FAAAS 1997; Foreign Associate, Nat. Acad. of Sciences, USA, 1975; For. Mem., Amer. Acad. of Arts and Scis, 1989; Associate, RAS, 1984; Mem., Internat. Acad. Astronautics, 1985. Mem., Sigma Xi, USA, 1984. Hon. Fellow, Geol Soc. of India, 1992. Hon. DSc Banaras Hindu Univ., 1981. Krishnan Medal for Geochemistry and Geophysics, Indian Geophysical Union, Hyderabad, 1965; Shanti Swarup Bhatnagar Award for Physical Sciences, CSIR, 1967; Outstanding Scientist Award, Fedn of Indian Chambers of Commerce and Industry, 1974; Pandit Jawaharlal Nehru Award for Scis, Madhya Pradesh Govt, 1986; C. V. Raman Birth Centenary Award, Indian Sci. Congress Assoc., 1996–97; V. M. Goldschmidt Medal, and Fellow, Geochem. Soc., USA, 1997. Padma Shri, 1971. *Publications:* (ed) Early Solar System Processes and the Present Solar System, 1980; (ed) Biogeochemistry of the Arabian Sea, 1994; *contributed:* Earth Science and Meteoritics, 1963; International Dictionary of Geophysics, 1968; The Encyclopedia of Earth Sciences: vol. IV, Geochemistry and Environmental Sciences, 1972; Further Advances in Lunar Research: Luna 16 and 20 samples, 1974; McGraw Hill Encyclopedia of Science and Technology, 1992; jt author of chapters in books; scientific papers to learned jls; proc. confs. *Recreations:* music, puzzles, painting, photography. *Address:* Scripps Institution of Oceanography, University of California at San Diego, La Jolla, CA 92093–0244, USA. *T:* (office) (858) 5342134, (home) (858) 5871535. *E:* dlal@ucsd.edu. *Died 1 Dec. 2012.*

LALANDI-EMERY, Lina, (Mrs Ralph Emery), OBE 1975; Director, English Bach Festival, since 1962; *b* Athens, 13 July 1920; *d* of late Nikolas Kaloyeropoulos (former Dir of Byzantine Museum, Athens, and Dir of Beaux Arts, Min. of Educn, Athens) and Toula Gelekis; *m* 1946, Cyprian Waller-Bridge (marr. diss. 1952); *m* Ralph Emery (*d* 2001). *Educ:* Athens Conservatoire (grad. with Hons in Music); privately, in England (harpsichord and singing studies). International career as harpsichordist in Concert, Radio and TV. Founded English Bach Festival Trust, 1962; later specialised in presentation of baroque opera perfs at Royal Opera House, Covent Gdn and numerous music fests. Officier, l'Ordre des Arts et des Lettres (France), 1978; Gold Cross of the Phoenix (Greece), 2004. *Recreations:* astrophysics, reading, knitting. *Address:* 15 South Eaton Place, SW1W 9ER. *T:* (020) 7730 5925, *Fax:* (020) 7730 1456. *E:* info@ebf.org.uk. *Died 8 June 2012.*

LAMB, Prof. Joseph Fairweather, PhD; FRCPE; FRSE; Chandos Professor of Physiology, St Leonard's College, University of St Andrews, 1969–93, then Professor Emeritus; *b* 18 July 1928; *s* of Joseph and Agnes May Lamb; *m* 1st, 1955, Olivia Janet Horne (marr. diss. 1989); three *s* one *d*; 2nd, 1989, Bridget Cecilia Cook; two *s*. *Educ:* Auldbar Public Sch.; Brechin High School (Dux, 1947); Edinburgh Univ. (MB ChB, BSc, PhD). FRCPE 1985. National Service, RAF, 1947–49. House Officer, Dumfries and Edinburgh, 1955–56; Hons Physiology Course, 1956–57; Univ. Junior Res. Fellow, 1957; Lectr in Physiology, Royal (Dick) Vet. Sch., 1958–61; Lectr, Sen. Lectr in Physiol., Glasgow, 1961–69. Sec., Physiol. Soc., 1982–85; Chm., Save British Science Soc., 1986–97; Chm./Organiser, Gas Greed Campaign, 1994–95. Gov., Rowett Res. Inst., Aberdeen, 1998–2004. Editor: Jl of Physiol., 1968–74; Amer. Jl of Physiol., 1985–88. FRSA; FRSE 1985. *Publications:* Essentials of Physiology, 1980, 3rd edn 1991; articles in learned jls. *Recreations:* reading, NHS voluntary work. *Died 18 Sept. 2015.*

LAMBERT, Henry Uvedale Antrobus; Chairman: Sun Alliance Insurance Group, 1985–93; Agricultural Mortgage Corporation PLC, 1985–93; *b* 9 Oct. 1925; *o s* of late Roger Uvedale Lambert and Muriel, *d* of Sir Reginald Antrobus, KCMG, CB; *m* 1951, Diana (*d* 2009), *y d* of Captain H. E. Dumbell, Royal Fusiliers; two *s* one *d*. *Educ:* Winchester College (Scholar); New College, Oxford (Exhibitioner; MA). Served War of 1939–45, Royal Navy, in HM Ships Stockham and St Austell Bay in Western Approaches and Mediterranean, subseq. RNR; Lt-Comdr (retired). Entered Barclays Bank 1948; a Local Dir at Lombard Street, 1957, Southampton, 1959, Birmingham, 1969; Vice-Chm., Barclays Bank UK Ltd, 1972; Vice-Chm., Barclays Bank Ltd, 1973; Chm., Barclays Bank Internat., 1979–83; Dep. Chm., 1979–85, Dir, 1966–91, Barclays Bank PLC; Agricultural Mortgage Corporation: Dir, 1966; Dep. Chm., 1977–85; Sun Alliance Insurance

Group: Dir, 1972; Vice-Chm., 1978–83; Dep. Chm., 1983–85. Dir, British Airways, 1985–89. Mem. Council, RASE, 1985–2000 (Vice Pres., 1994–96; Hon. Vice Pres., 1996–2000). Trustee: Imperial War Graves Endowment Fund, 1987–94 (Chm., 1989–94); Nat. Maritime Mus., 1990–95. Vice-Pres., Navy Records Soc., 1985–89, 1992–96, 2001– (Hon. Treas., 1974–85); Mem. Council, White Ensign Assoc., 1982–2002 (Chm., 1992–96). Fellow, Winchester Coll., 1979–91. Hon. Mem., RICS, 1993. *Recreations:* fishing, gardening, golf, naval history. *Address:* Lowton Manor, Taunton, Somerset TA3 7SX. *Clubs:* Brooks's, MCC. *Died 19 April 2011.*

LAMBERT, Sir John (Henry), KCVO 1980; CMG 1975; HM Diplomatic Service, retired; President, Heritage of London Trust, since 2005 (Director, 1981–96; Vice-President, 1996–2005); *b* Chelsea, 8 Jan. 1921; *s* of Col R. S. Lambert, MC, and Mrs H. J. F. Mills; *m* 1950, Jennifer Ann (*née* Urquhart) (*d* 2013); one *s* two *d*. *Educ:* Eton Coll.; Sorbonne; Trinity Coll., Cambridge. Grenadier Guards, 1940–45 (Captain). Appointed 3rd Secretary, HM Embassy, The Hague, 1945; Member of HM Foreign Service, 1947; FO, 1948; 2nd Secretary, Damascus, 1951; 1st Secretary, 1953; FO, 1954; Dep. to UK Representative on International Commn for Saar Referendum, 1955; Belgrade, 1956; Head of Chancery, Manila, 1958; UK Delegation to Disarmament Conference, Geneva, 1962; FO, 1963; Counsellor, Head of Chancery, Stockholm, 1964–67; Head of UN (Political) Dept, FCO, 1967–70; Commercial Counsellor and Consul-Gen. Vienna, 1971–74; Minister and Dep. Comdt, Berlin, 1974–77; Ambassador to Tunisia, 1977–81. Chm., Channel Tunnel Investments plc, 1986–92. *Recreations:* the arts, music, tennis, golf. *Address:* 103 Rivermead Court, SW6 3SB. *T:* (020) 7731 5007. *Clubs:* MCC; Hurlingham, Royal St George's Golf. *Died 6 July 2015.*

LAMFALUSSY, Baron Alexandre; President, European Monetary Institute, 1994–97; Professor, Institute of European Studies, Catholic University of Louvain, 1997; *b* 26 April 1929; *cr* Baron, 1993; *m* 1957, Anne-Marie Cochard; two *s* two *d*. *Educ:* Catholic Univ., Louvain (economics degree); Nuffield Coll., Oxford (PhD). Banque de Bruxelles: economist, 1955–61; Economic Advr, 1962; Exec. Dir, later Chm., Exec. Bd, 1965–76; Bank for International Settlements, Basle: Economic Advr, 1976–80; Asst Gen. Manager, 1981; Gen. Manager, 1985–93. Dir, Assoc. for the Monetary Union of Europe, 2000–. Vis Lectr, Yale, 1961–62. Hon. doctorates: Univ. Lumière-Lyon, 1987; Inst. d'Etudes Politiques, Paris, 1993. *Publications:* Investment and Growth in Mature Economies, 1961; The UK and the Six, 1963; Les marchés financiers en Europe, 1968; The Restructuring of the Financial Industry, 1992; The Per Jacobsson Lecture, 1994; Financial Crises in Emerging Markets: an essay on financial globalisation and fragility, 2000. *Recreations:* hiking, sailing. *Address:* c/o European Monetary Institute, Eurotower, Kaiserstrasse 29, 60311 Frankfurt, Germany. *T:* (69) 272270. *Died 9 May 2015.*

LAMFORD, (Thomas) Gerald, OBE 1979; ASVU Representative, Cyprus, 1985–88; Commandant, Police Staff College, Bramshill, 1976–79; *b* Carmarthen, 3 April 1928; *s* of late Albert and Sarah Lamford; *m* 1952, Eira Hale (*d* 2008); one *s* one *d*. *Educ:* Technical Coll., Swansea; London Univ. (LLB 1969); Police Coll. (Intermed. Comd Course, 1969; Sen. Comd Course, 1973). Radio Officer, Merchant Navy, 1945; Wireless Operator, RAF, 1946–48, Aden. Carmarthenshire Constab. (later Dyfed Powys Police), 1949; reached rank of Chief Inspector, CID, Crime Squad; Force Trng Officer, 1965–69; Supt, Haverfordwest, 1970; Chief Supt, Llanelli, 1971–74; Asst Chief Constable, Greater Manchester Police, 1974–79; Investigating Officer, FCO, 1981–84. Vis. Prof. of Police Science, John Jay Coll. of Criminal Justice, City Univ. of New York, 1972; sometime Vis. Lecturer: Southern Police Inst., Univ. of Louisville, Ky; N Eastern Univ., Boston; NY Univ. Sch. of Law; Rutgers Univ., NJ; Mercy Coll., Detroit. County Comr, St John Amb. Bde, Pembrokeshire, 1970; SBStJ. Mem., Probus Club, Ammanford (Pres., 1996). *Publications:* The Defence of Lucy Walter, 2001; articles in Police Studies, Internat. Rev. of Police Develt, Police Rev., Bramshill Jl, World Police. *Recreations:* photography, genealogy. *Address:* 2A Walter Road, Ammanford SA18 2NH. *Died 20 April 2011.*

LAMPL, Sir Frank (William), Kt 1990; Life President, Bovis Lend Lease Holding, since 2000 (Chairman, 1999–2000); Director, Mills Corporation, Washington, 2004–07; *b* Brno, Czechoslovakia, 6 April 1926; adopted British nationality, 1974; *s* of Dr Otto Lampl and Olga (*née* Jelinek); *m* 1st, 1948, Blanka (*née* Kratochvílová) (*d* 2001); one *s*; 2nd, 2002, Wenda (*née* Scarborough). *Educ:* Univ. of Brno, Czechoslovakia (Dip Eng, Faculty of Architecture and Engineering). Emigrated from Czechoslovakia to UK, 1968, after Russian invasion; Exec. Dir, Bovis Construction, 1974; Man. Dir, Bovis International, 1978; Dir, Bovis, 1979; Chm., Bovis Construction and Bovis International, 1985; Dep. Chm., Lehrer MacGovern-Bovis, NY, 1987; Chm., Bovis Construction Gp, 1989–2000; Exec. Dir, P&OSN Co., 1985–99. Mem., Adv. Bd, Intelligent Engrg, 2007–. Pres., Czech British Chamber of Commerce, 2009–. First Chancellor, Kingston Univ., 1994–2000. Mem., RSA. FCIOB 1973 (Pres.'s Gold Medal, 1993); FAPM 1973; CCMI. Hon. DEng Technical Univ., Brno, 1993; Dr *hc* Kingston, 1994; Hon. DSc: Reading, 1995; Middlesex, 1998. Building Lifetime Achievement Award, Building Magazine, 2002; Gratias Agit award, Foreign Ministry, Czech Republic, 2008. *Recreation:* reading. *Address:* Bovis Lend Lease, 142 Northolt Road, Harrow, Middx HA2 0EE. *Club:* Royal Automobile. *Died 23 March 2011.*

LANE, Dr Anthony John, FRCP, FFPH; Regional Medical Officer, North Western Regional Health Authority, 1974–86; *b* 6 Feb. 1926; *s* of John Gill Lane and Marian (*née* Brumfield); *m* 1948, Hannah Holečková (*d* 2008); one *s* two *d*. *Educ:* St Christopher's Sch., Letchworth; Emmanuel Coll., Cambridge. MA, MB, BChir. House posts in surgery, medicine, obstetrics, and paediatrics, London area, 1949–51; MO with Methodist Missionary Soc., Andhra State, India, 1951–57; Registrar: Tropical Diseases, UCH, 1958; Gen. Med., St James' Hosp., Balham, 1958–61; Infectious Diseases, Western Hosp., Fulham, 1961–63; MO (Trainee), Leeds RHB, 1963–64; Asst Sen. MO, Leeds RHB, 1964–66; Principal Asst Sen. MO, Leeds RHB, 1966–70; Dep. Sen. Admin. MO, SW Metrop. RHB, 1970–71; Sen. Admin. MO, Manchester RHB, 1971–74. Hon. MD Manchester, 1986. *Publications:* contrib. Positions, Movements and Directions in Health Services Research, 1974; contrib. Proc. Royal Soc. Med. *Recreations:* music, competitive indoor games, walking, gardening. *Address:* 5A Chapel Lane, Wilmslow, Cheshire SK9 5HZ. *T:* (01625) 532572. *Died 11 June 2014.*

LANE, Dr Anthony Milner, FRS 1975; Deputy Chief Scientific Officer, Atomic Energy Research Establishment, Harwell, 1976–89; *b* 27 July 1928; *s* of Herbert William Lane and Doris Ruby Lane (*née* Milner); *m* 1st, 1952, Anne Sophie Zissman (*d* 1980); one *s* one *d* (and one *s* decd); 2nd, 1983, Jill Valerie Parvin (*d* 2002); five step *d*. *Educ:* Trowbridge Boys' High Sch.; Selwyn Coll., Cambridge. BA Maths, PhD Theoretical Physics. Joined Harwell, 1953. *Publications:* Nuclear Theory, 1963; numerous research articles in Review of Modern Physics, Phys. Review, Nuclear Physics, etc. *Recreations:* gardening, bird-watching. *Address:* 21 Squitchey Lane, Oxford OX2 7LD. *T:* (01865) 556565. *Died 9 Feb. 2011.*

LANG, Very Rev. John Harley; Dean of Lichfield, 1980–93, then Emeritus; Chaplain to HM the Queen, 1976–80; Member, Broadcasting Standards Commission, 1997–98 (Broadcasting Standards Council, 1994–97); *b* 27 Oct. 1927; *e s* of Frederick Henry Lang and Eileen Annie Lang (*née* Harley); *m* 1972, Frances Rosemary Widdowson; three *d*. *Educ:* Merchant Taylors' Sch.; King's Coll., London (BD); MA Cantab; MST Oxon 1999; LRAM. Subaltern, XII Royal Lancers, 1951–52; Asst Curate, St Mary's Portsea, 1952–57; Priest Vicar, Southwark Cathedral, 1957–60; Chaplain, Emmanuel Coll., Cambridge, 1960–64; Asst Head of Religious Broadcasting, BBC, 1964–67; Head of Religious Programmes, Radio, 1967–71; Head of Religious Broadcasting, BBC, 1971–80. Mem., English Heritage

Cathedrals and Churches Adv. Cttee, 1994–99. Trustee, Historic Churches Preservation Trust, 1994–2000. President: Staffordshire Soc., 1993–95; Lichfield Festival, 1994–2006. Mem., Kellogg Coll., Oxford, 1997–. Freeman, Goldsmiths' Co., 1994. Hon. DLitt Keele, 1988. *Recreations:* books, music. *Died 3 June 2012.*

LANGDON, David, OBE 1988; FRSA; cartoonist, illustrator and caricaturist; contributor to Punch, 1937–92, The New Yorker, since 1952, and The Spectator, since 1997; *b* 24 Feb. 1914; *er s* of late Bennett and Bess Langdon; *m* 1955, April Sadler-Phillips; two *s* one *d. Educ:* Davenant Grammar Sch., London. Architect's Dept, LCC, 1931–39; Executive Officer, London Rescue Service, 1939–41; served in Royal Air Force, 1941–46; Squadron Leader, 1945. Editor, Royal Air Force Jl, 1945–46. Creator of Billy Brown of London Town for LPTB. Official Artist to Centre International Audio-Visuel d'Etudes et de Recherches, St Ghislain, Belgium, 1970–75. Cartoonist to Sunday Mirror, 1948–93. Caricatures: of High Court Judges for Sweet and Maxwell, 1956; of racing celebrities for Ladbrokes Racing Calendar, 1959–94. Exhibitions: Ottawa, Oxford, New York, Lille, London. Lifetime Achievement Award, Cartoon Art Trust, 2001. *Publications:* Home Front Lines, 1941; All Buttoned Up, 1944; Meet Me Inside, 1946; Slipstream (with R. B. Raymond), 1946; The Way I See It, 1947; Hold Tight There!, 1949; Let's Face It, 1951; Wake Up and Die (with David Clayton), 1952; Look at You, 1952; All in Fun, 1953; Laugh with Me, 1954; More in Fun, 1955; Funnier Still, 1956; A Banger for a Monkey, 1957; Langdon At Large, 1958; I'm Only Joking, 1960; Punch with Wings, 1961; How to Play Golf and Stay Happy, 1964; David Langdon's Casebook, 1969; How To Talk Golf, 1975; Punch in the Air, 1983; Soccer—It's a Funny Old Game, 1998. *Recreation:* golf. *Address:* 4 Oaklands Court, Chesham Road, Amersham, Bucks HP6 5ES. *T:* (01494) 432545. *Club:* Royal Air Force. *Died 18 Nov. 2011.*

LANGFORD, Prof. Paul, DPhil; FRHistS; FBA 1993; Professor of Modern History, University of Oxford, 1996–2012; Fellow, and Tutor in Modern History, 1970–2012, and Rector, 2000–12, Lincoln College, Oxford; *b* 20 Nov. 1945; *s* of Frederick Wade Langford and Olive Myrtle Langford (*née* Walters); *m* 1970, Margaret Veronica Edwards; one *s. Educ:* Monmouth Sch.; Hertford Coll., Oxford (MA, DPhil; Hon. Fellow, 2000). FRHistS 1979. Jun. Res. Fellow, Lincoln Coll., Oxford, 1969–70; Reader in Modern History, Oxford Univ., 1994–96. Ford's Lectr in English History, Oxford Univ., 1990; Raleigh Lectr, British Acad., 1996. Mem., Humanities Res. Bd, British Acad., 1995–98. Chm. and Chief Exec., AHRB, 1998–2000. Sen. Fellow, RCA, 2001. General Editor: The Writings and Speeches of Edmund Burke, 1974–; Oxford History of the British Isles, 1996–; Chm., Editl Bd, History of Parliament, 2009–12. Hon. DLitt Sheffield, 2002. *Publications:* The First Rockingham Administration 1765–66, 1973; The Excise Crisis: society and politics in the age of Walpole, 1975; (ed) Writings and Speeches of Edmund Burke, vol. II: Party, Parliament and The American Crisis 1766–74, 1981; A Polite and Commercial People 1727–83, 1989 (New Oxford History of England series); Public Life and the Propertied Englishman 1689–1789, 1991; Englishness Identified: manners and character 1650–1850, 2000. *Recreation:* gardening. *Club:* Athenæum. *Died 27 July 2015.*

LANGMAN, Prof. Michael John Stratton, MD; FRCP; William Withering Professor of Medicine, University of Birmingham, 1987–2000, then Emeritus (Dean, Faculty of Medicine and Dentistry, 1992–97); *b* 30 Jan. 1935; *s* of John A. H. and E. Margaret Langman; *m* 1960, Rosemary A. Hempton; two *s* two *d. Educ:* St Paul's Sch.; Guy's Hosp. Med. Sch., Univ. of London (BSc, MB (Hons), MD). FRCP 1973; FFPM (by distinction) 1989. House Physician and Surg., Guy's Hosp., 1958–59; House Physician, Brompton, Hammersmith and Queen Square Hosps, 1959–61; Registrar, Central Middlesex Hosp., 1961–63; Lectr in Medicine, Guy's Hosp., 1963–68; Mem., Scientific Staff, MRC Statistical Res. Unit, UCH, 1963–68; Consultant Physician and Sen. Lectr, 1968–70, Reader, 1970–74, in Medicine, Nottingham Hosps and Univ.; Boots Prof. of Therapeutics, Univ. of Nottingham, 1974–87. Non-exec. Dir, Birmingham HA, 1992–98. Hon. Sen. Res. Fellow, European Inst. of Oncology, Milan, 1996–2003; Hon. Consultant, WHO, 1996–99; Hon. Consultant, WHO Centre for Internat. Drug Monitoring, 2008–. Hon. Prof., Univ. of Warwick, 2005–09. Lectures: Avery Jones, Central Middx Hosp., 1977; Melrose, Caledonian Soc. of Gastroenterology, 1987; William Withering Prize, RCP, 1988; Honeyman Gillespie, Edinburgh Univ., 1989; Barany, Swedish Soc. of Gastroenterology, 1992. Chairman: Adv. Expert Gp on Vitamins and Minerals, Food Standards Authy (formerly MAFF), 1999–2003; Jt Cttee on Vaccination and Immunization UK, 2000–05; Birmingham and Black Country Br., NIHR, 2007–11; Member: Cttee on Review of Medicines, 1980–87; Cttee on Safety of Medicines, 1987–2005 (Chm., Subcttee on Pharmacovigilance, 1992–95). Chm., Coventry and Warwicks Ambulance NHS Trust, 2000–06. Pres., British Soc. of Gastroenterology, 1997–99. Gov., St Martin's Sch., Solihull, 1997–2003. Founder FMedSci 1998. *Publications:* Concise Textbook of Gastroenterology, 1973, 2nd edn 1982 (Spanish edn, 1976, Italian edn, 1985); The Epidemiology of Chronic Digestive Disease, 1979; (ed jtly) The Genetics and Epidemiology of Inflammatory Bowel Disease, 1986; various papers on chronic digestive disease. *Recreations:* croquet, cricket. *Address:* c/o Dean's Office, Medical School, University of Birmingham, Edgbaston, Birmingham B15 2TT. *T:* (0121) 627 2380. *Clubs:* Athenæum, MCC. *Died 8 April 2014.*

LANGSDALE, Philip Richard, FIET; Director General, Information Technology and Chief Information Officer, Department for Work and Pensions, since 2012; Chairman, Cornish Crabbers LLP, since 2009; *b* 23 Dec. 1955; *s* of Reginald Eric Langsdale and Dorothy May Langsdale; *m* 1984, Vanessa Gabrielle Marsland; two *d. Educ:* King's Coll., Cambridge (MA Maths); London Business Sch. (MSc 2004). CEng 1993; FIET (FIEE 2002). Systems Engr, IBM UK, 1979–82; IT Consultant, Nolan Norton & Co., 1982–85; Associate Dir, Coopers & Lybrand, 1985–88; Dir, IT Planning, Midland Bank, 1988–92; IT Director: Asda Gp, 1992–97; Cable & Wireless Communications, 1997–98; BBC: Dir, Technology, subseq. Distribution and Technology, 1998–2001; Chief Exec., BBC Technology, 2001–02; Mem., Exec. Cttee, 2000–02; Chief Exec., Langsdale Crook LLP (formerly Langsdale Associates), 2002–08; Chief Inf. Officer, BAA, 2008–12. Non-exec. Dir, UK Hydrographic Office, 2007–11. *Recreations:* opera, sailing, music. *Address:* 25 Highbury Place, N5 1QP. *Died 22 Dec. 2012.*

LAPPER, Maj.-Gen. John; Medical Director, International Hospitals Group, 1984–88; *b* 24 July 1921; *s* of late Col Wilfred Mark Lapper, OBE, Legion of Merit (USA), late RE, and Agnes Lapper (*née* Powner); *m* 1948, Dorothy, *d* of late Roland John and Margaret Simpson (*née* Critchlow); three *s. Educ:* Wolverhampton Grammar Sch.; King Edward VI Sch., Birmingham; Birmingham Univ. MB, ChB 1946; DLO 1952. House appts, Queen Elizabeth and Children's Hosp., Birmingham, and Ronkswood Hosp. and Royal Infirm., Worcester; Registrar, Royal Berks Hosp., Reading. Commnd RAMC, 1950; ENT specialist, Mil. Hosps in UK, Libya, Egypt, Germany, Singapore, Malaya; CO 14 Field Amb., BAOR, 1958; CO BMH Rinteln, BAOR, 1964; Asst Comdt, Royal Army Med. Coll., 1965–68; ADMS Hong Kong, 1969–71; CO Queen Alexandra's Mil. Hosp., Millbank, 1971–73; ADMS 3 Div., 1973; DDMS HQ UKLF, 1974–77; Dir, Med. Supply, MoD, 1977; Dir, Med. Policy and Plans, MoD, 1978–80; QHS 1977–80. Hospital and Medical Dir, Nat. Guard Saudi Arabia, 1981–83. Hudson-Evans Lectr, W Kent Medico-Chirurgical Soc., 1980; Mem. Sands Cox Med. Soc., Birmingham Univ. FFPH (FFCM 1980); FCMI (FBIM 1980); FRSocMed; FMedSoc London; Mem. BMA; Pres., Med. Soc., Hong Kong, 1970–71; Mem., RUSI; Chm. Council, Yateley Industries for the Disabled, 1983–95. OStJ 1959. *Publications:* articles in professional jls. *Recreations:* travel, militaria. *Address:* The Chimes, 4 Manor Fields, Alrewas, Burton-upon-Trent, Staffs DE13 7DA. *T:* (01283) 791628. *Died 23 July 2012.*

LAPPERT, Prof. Michael Franz, FRS 1979; Research Professor of Chemistry, University of Sussex, 1997–2008, then Emeritus (Professor of Chemistry, 1969–97); *b* 31 Dec. 1928; *s* of Julius Lappert and Kornelie Lappert (*née* Beran); *m* 1980, Lorna McKenzie. *Educ:* Wilson's Grammar School; Northern Polytechnic, London. BSc, PhD, DSc (London). FRSC. Northern Polytechnic, London: Asst Lecturer, 1952–53; Lecturer, 1953–55; Sen. Lectr, 1955–59. UMIST: Lectr, 1959–61; Sen. Lectr, 1961–64; Reader, Univ. of Sussex, 1964–69. SERC Sen. Res. Fellow, 1980–85. Pres., Dalton Div., RSC, 1989–91. Tilden Lectr, Chem. Soc., 1972–73; Nyholm Lectr, 1994, Frankland Lectr, 1999, RSC. Hon. Professor: Ondokuz Mayis Univ., Samsun, Turkey, 1996; Shanxi Univ., Taiyuan, China, 2000; Kimya Bolumu, Univ. of Malatya, Turkey, 2011. Hon. Dr rer. nat. München, 1989; Dr *hc* Murcia, 2013. First recipient of (London) Chemical Soc. Award in Main Group Metal Chemistry, 1970; Award in Organometallic Chemistry, 1978; F. S. Kipping Award of American Chem. Soc., 1976; Alfred Stock Meml Award, German Chem. Soc., 2008. *Publications:* (ed jtly) Developments in Inorganic Polymer Chemistry, 1962; (jtly) Metal and Metalloid Amides, 1980; (jtly) Organo-zirconium and -hafnium Compounds, 1986; (jtly) Metal Amides, 2009; more than 800 papers in Jl Chem. Soc., etc. *Recreations:* theatre, opera, tennis, walking. *Address:* Department of Chemistry, School of Life Sciences, University of Sussex, Brighton BN1 9QJ; 4 Varndean Gardens, Brighton BN1 6WL; John Dalton Cottage, Eaglesfield, Cockermouth, Cumbria CA13 0SD. *Died 28 March 2014.*

LAPSLEY, Peter Michael; Patient Editor, British Medical Journal, since 2005; *b* 19 June 1943; *s* of Air Marshal Sir John Hugh Lapsley, KBE, CB, DFC, AFC and Jean Margaret (*née* McIvor); *m* 1st, 1970, Jennifer Mary Blockley (marr. diss. 1985); one *s* one *d*; 2nd, 1986, Elizabeth Ann Wyatt. *Educ:* Aldenham Sch., Elstree; RMA, Sandhurst. Served Army, King's Own Royal Border Regt, 1962–73: served Germany, UK, British Guyana, Aden, Trucial States (UAE), NI; Principal, then Sen. Principal, MoD, 1973–80; Co-owner/Manager, Rockbourne Trout Fishery, 1980–84; Sen. Principal, MoD, 1984–87; Chief Exec., Nat. Back Pain Assoc., 1987–90; Dept of Transport, 1990–96 (HM Chief Inspector of Aviation Security, 1991–96); Chief Executive: Nat. Eczema Soc., 1997–2001; Skin Care Campaign, 2001–07. Chm., Adv. Gp (formerly Oversight Cttee), All Party Parly Gp on Skin, 2009–. Chm., Bd of Trustees, Primary Care Dermatology Soc., 2009–. Mem. Exec. Cttee, Falkland Is Assoc., 1996–2005. Pres., Wandle Piscators, 2012–. *Publications:* The Bankside Book of Stillwater Trout Flies, 1978, 2nd edn 1983; Trout From Stillwaters, 1981; River Trout Flyfishing, 1988; (ed) The Complete Fly Fisher, 1990; (jtly) Fly Fishing by J. R. Hartley, 1991; Fly Fishing for Trout, 1992; (jtly) J. R. Hartley Casts Again, 1992; Fishing for Falklands Sea Trout, 2000; River Fly-Fishing, 2003; Pocket Guide to Matching the Hatch, 2010. *Recreations:* fly fishing, writing, photography, travel, fly-tying. *Address:* 27 Lillian Avenue, W3 9AN. *T:* (020) 8993 7453. *Club:* Flyfishers'. *Died 3 Aug. 2013.*

LARSEN, Prof. Henning; architect; founder and owner, Henning Larsen Architects A/S, architectural practice; Professor of Architecture, Royal Academy of Fine Arts, Copenhagen, 1968–95; *b* 20 Aug. 1925; *s* of Erik Peter Larsen and Johanne Mary Gøbel; *m* Lone Backe; one *s* one *d* by a former marriage. *Educ:* Royal Acad. of Fine Arts, Copenhagen (Dip. 1952); Sch. of Architecture, London; MIT, USA. Major projects include: Trondheim Univ., 1978; Min. of Foreign Affairs, Riyadh, 1984; Copenhagen Business Sch., 1989; Nation Centre, Nairobi, 1992; Roskilde Univ. Centre, 1996–; NeuroSearch Co. HQ, 1999; Physics Res. Centre, Stockholm, 2001; Ferring Co. HQ, 2002; Copenhagen Opera House, 2004; housing and commercial develts in Denmark and Sweden. Founder: architectural magazine Skala; Gallery Skala, 1985–94. Guest Professor: Yale, 1964, Princeton, 1965. Member: Royal Danish Acad. of Fine Arts; Royal Swedish Acad. of Fine Arts, Hon. mem. of Arch. Insts in England, Scotland, Germany, USA. Awards in competitions include: Kammergericht, Berlin, 1979; Compton Verney Opera House, 1989; Conf. Centre, Cambridge, 1989; Extension of Ny Carlsberg Glyptotek, Copenhagen, 1992; New Concert Hall, Copenhagen, 1993; City Library, Malmö, 1993; Danish Design Centre, Copenhagen, 1994; Max Planck Inst., Rostock, 1996; Terminal 2, Copenhagen Airport, 1997; Kunsthalle Adolf Würth, Germany, 1997; Faculty of Arts, Univ. of Plymouth, 2004; Busan Opera House, S Korea, 2012. Hon. Dr Royal Inst. of Technol., Stockholm, 2001. Architectural prizes include: Internat. Design Award, UK, 1987; Domino's 30 Architects, USA, 1988; Aga Khan Award, 1989; Marble Architectural Award, Carrara, 1990 and 1999; Europa Nostra Diploma of EC, 1998; Praemium Imperiale Architecture Award, 2012. *Address:* (office) Vesterbrogade 76, 1620 Copenhagen V, Denmark. *T:* 8233 3000. *Died 26 June 2013.*

LATOUR-ADRIEN, Hon. Sir (Jean François) Maurice, Kt 1971; Chief Justice of Mauritius, 1970–77; Chairman, Mauritius Union Assurance Co. Ltd, 1982–2005 (Director, 1978–82); *b* 4 March 1915; 2nd *s* of late Louis Constant Emile Adrien and late Maria Ella Latour. *Educ:* Royal Coll., Mauritius; Univ. Coll., London; Middle Temple, London. LLB 1940. Called to the Bar, Middle Temple, 1940. Mauritius: Dist Magistrate, 1947; Crown Counsel, 1950; Addnl Subst. Procureur and Advocate-Gen., 1954; Sen. Crown Counsel, 1958; Asst Attorney-Gen., 1960; Solicitor-Gen., 1961; Dir of Public Prosecutions, 1964; Puisne Judge, 1966–70; Acting Governor-Gen., Feb. 1973, July–Aug. 1974, Jan.–Feb. and June–Aug. 1975, July–Sept. 1976. Vice-Pres., Inst. Internat. de Droit d'Expression Française (IDEF). Pres., Mauritius Commercial Bank Ltd, 1993–94 (Dir, 1980–83, 1984–87, 1988–91, 1992–95, 1996–99, 2000–02; Vice-Pres., 1992–93, 1996–97); Legal Consultant: Mauritius Commercial Bank Ltd, 1983–; Promotion and Development Ltd, 1985–; Mauritius Commercial Bank Finance Corp., 1991–94; Mauritius Commercial Bank Registry and Securities, 1991–; Caudan Development Co. Ltd, 1991–; Fincorp Investment Ltd, 1994–. President: Mental Health Assoc., 1985– (Vice-Pres., 1978–84); Mauritius Red Cross Soc., 1978–2007. Mem., War Meml Bd of Trustees, 1978–84 (Vice Pres., 1985–). KLJ 1969. *Address:* Vacoas, Mauritius. *Died 31 July 2014.*

LAUTI, Rt Hon. Sir Toaripi, GCMG 1990; PC 1979; Governor-General of Tuvalu, 1990–93; *b* Papua New Guinea, 28 Nov. 1928; *m*; three *s* two *d*. *Educ:* Tuvalu; Fiji; Wesley Coll., Paerata, NZ; St Andrew's Coll., Christchurch, NZ; Christchurch Teachers' Coll., NZ. Taught in KGV, Tarawa, Kiribati, 1953–62; Labour Relations and Trng Officer, Nauru and Ocean Islands, engaged by British Phosphate Comrs; returned to Tuvalu, 1974, and entered politics; MP, elected unopposed to House of Assembly, May 1975; elected Chief Minister, Tuvalu, upon separation of Ellice Islands (Tuvalu) from Kiribati, Oct. 1975, re-elected Chief Minister in Sept. 1977; First Prime Minister, Tuvalu, 1978–81; Leader of the Opposition, 1981–90. Chm., 18th South Pacific Conference, Noumea, Oct. 1978. *Address:* PO Box 84, Funafuti, Tuvalu, Central Pacific. *Died 25 May 2014.*

LAWRENCE, Dennis George Charles, OBE 1963; Director, 1978–82, Board Member, 1981–84, Cooperative Development Agency; *b* 15 Aug. 1918; *s* of George Herbert and Amy Frances Lawrence; *m* 1946, Alida Jantine, *d* of Willem van den Berg, The Netherlands. *Educ:* Haberdashers' Aske's Hatcham School. Entered Civil Service as Clerical Officer, Min. of Transport, 1936; served RA, 1939–46; Exec. Officer 1946; Asst Principal, Central Land Board, 1947; Principal, 1949; GPO, 1953; Asst Sec., 1960; Sec., Cttee on Broadcasting, 1960–62; Asst Sec., GPO, 1962; Under-Secretary: GPO, 1969; Min. of Posts and Telecommunications, 1969–74; Dept of Industry, 1974–78. Chm., Working Group on a Cooperative Develt Agency, 1977. *Publications:* Democracy and Broadcasting (pamphlet), 1986; The Third Way, 1988. *Recreations:* reading, gardening, remembrance of things past. *Address:* Little London Farmhouse, Cann, Shaftesbury, Dorset SP7 0PZ. *Died 17 Dec. 2011.*

LAWRENCE, Sir (John) Patrick (Grosvenor), Kt 1988; CBE 1983; DL; Chairman: Enterprise Venture Capital Trust plc, 1996–2004; The VCT Charitable Trust, since 2005; *b* 29 March 1928; *s* of Ernest Victor Lawrence and Norah Grosvenor Lawrence (*née* Hill); *m* 1954, Anne Patricia (*née* Auld); one *d* (one *s* decd). *Educ:* Denstone

Coll., Staffs. Served RNVR, 1945–48. Admitted Solicitor 1954; Partner, Wragge & Co., Solicitors, Birmingham, 1959–93 (Sen. Partner, 1982–93). Chm., Midland Rent Assessment Panels, 1971–98. Chm., Kidderminster Healthcare NHS Trust, 1993–96. Mem., Bromsgrove RDC, 1967–74. Chm., Nat. Union of Conservative and Unionist Assocs, 1986–87; Pres., W Midlands Conservative Council, 1988–91 (Chm., 1979–82). Pres., British Shooting Sports Council, 2005–08 (Vice-Chm., 1985–96; Chm., 1996–2002; Vice-Pres., 2002–05). Member of Council: Denstone Coll., Staffs, 1989–98; Birmingham Chamber of Industry and Commerce, 1989–93; ABCC, 1990–93; Aston Univ., 1990–2001 (Vice-Chm. Council, 1999–2001); White Ensign Assoc. Ltd, 1996–2005 (Vice Pres., 2005–). Chm., Birmingham Cathedral in Need Appeal, 1990; Mem., Admin. Chapter, Birmingham Cathedral, 1995–2002. Freeman, City of London, 1991; Liveryman, Gunmakers' Co., 1991. DL West Midlands, 1993. Hon. DSc Aston, 1996. *Address:* Cherwell, Oxford Close, Oxford Street, Cheltenham, Glos GL52 6EP. *Clubs:* Bean (Birmingham); Law Society's Yacht. *Died 29 Nov. 2011.*

LAWRENCE, Sir William (Fettiplace), 5th Bt *cr* 1867, of Ealing Park, Middlesex; OBE 2003; General Manager, Newdawn & Sun Ltd, 1981–98; *b* 23 Aug. 1954; *s* of Sir William Lawrence, 4th Bt and Pamela, *yr d* of J. E. Gordon; *S* father, 1986. *Educ:* King Edward VI School, Stratford-upon-Avon. Assistant Accountant, Wilmot Breeden Ltd/ W. B. Bumpers Ltd, 1973–81. Member: Stratford-on-Avon District Council, 1982– (Chm., 1990–91); S Warwickshire CHC, 1983–84; S Warwickshire HA, 1984–92; S Warwickshire Gen. Hosps NHS Trust, 1993–; Cttee, Employment of People with Disabilities, Coventry and Warwickshire, 1994–97; Rural Develt Commn, Warwickshire, 1995–; Dir, S Warwickshire Business Partnership, 1995–. Chm., Heart of England Tourist Bd, 1991– (Mem. Bd, 1989–); Mem., W Midlands Arts, 1989–91 (Mem., Management Council, 1984–89); Director: Unicorn Tourism Ltd, 1994–98; Stratford-upon-Avon and Dist Marketing Ltd, 1995–97; Midland Music Fests, 1996–98; Stratford-upon-Avon Crossroads Care Attendant Scheme Ltd, 1996–. President: Stratford and District Mencap, 1990–; Stratford-upon-Avon Chamber Music Soc., 1991–; Stratford Town FC, 1992–94; Pres., and Chm. of Trustees, Action Unlimited Trust, 1991– (Trustee, 1988–). Consultant Trainer, Insite Consultancy, Edinburgh, 1995–. Mem. Court, Univ. of Birmingham, 1990–. Mem., Corp. of Stratford-upon-Avon Coll., 1996–; Gov., King Edward VI GS, Stratford-upon-Avon, 1987. Hon. Gov., Royal Shakespeare Theatre, 2012 (Gov., 1991). *Heir: cousin* Aubrey Lyttelton Simon Lawrence [*b* 22 Sept. 1942; *m* 1984, Danielle de Froidmont; one *s*]. *Address:* The Knoll, Walcote, near Alcester, Warwickshire B49 6LZ. *T:* (01789) 488303. *Died 10 Feb. 2015.*

LAWS, Frederick Geoffrey; Vice-Chairman, Commission for Local Administration in England, 1984–94; *b* Blackpool, 1 Aug. 1928; *s* of Frederick and Annetta Laws; *m* 1955, Beryl Holt; two *d*; *m* 1998, Eleanor May Fettes (*née* Dick). *Educ:* Arnold School; Manchester Univ.; London Univ. (LLB). Admitted Solicitor 1952; Asst Solicitor, Blackpool Corp., 1952–54, Bournemouth Corp., 1954–59; Southend-on-Sea Corporation: Asst Solicitor, 1959–62; Dep. Town Clerk and Clerk of the Peace, 1962–71; Town Clerk, 1971–74; Chief Exec., Southend-on-Sea Borough Council, 1974–84. Pres., Southend-on-Sea Law Soc., 1981. Hon. Freeman, Southend-on-Sea Borough Council, 1985. *Died 15 June 2011.*

LAWS, Richard Maitland, CBE 1983; PhD, ScD; FRS 1980; Director, British Antarctic Survey, 1973–87; Master, St Edmund's College, Cambridge, 1985–96; *b* 23 April 1926; *s* of Percy Malcolm Laws and Florence May (*née* Heslop); *m* 1954, Maureen Isobel Winifred (*née* Holmes); three *s*. *Educ:* Dame Allan's Sch., Newcastle-on-Tyne; St Catharine's Coll., Cambridge (Open Scholar, 1944–47; BA 1st Cl. Hons 1947, MA 1952; Res. Scholar, 1952–53; PhD 1953; ScD 1994; Hon. Fellow, 1982). FSB (FIBiol 1973). Biologist, Base Leader, Magistrate and Postmaster, Falkland Is Dependencies Survey, 1947–53; Biologist and Whaling Inspector, F/F Balaena, 1953–54; Sen. and Principal Sci. Officer, Nat. Inst. of Oceanography, 1954–61; Dir, Nuffield Unit of Tropical Animal Ecology, Uganda, 1961–67; Dir, Tsavo Research Project, Kenya, 1967–68; University of Cambridge: Smuts Meml Fund Fellowship, 1968–69; Leverhulme Research Fellowship, 1969; Head, Life Sciences Div., British Antarctic Survey, 1969–73. Dir, NERC Sea Mammal Res. Unit, 1977–87; ICSU Scientific Committee for Antarctic Research: Member: Biology Working Gp, 1972–90 (Chm., 1980–86); Logistics Working Gp, 1974–80; Member Group of Specialists: on Seals, 1972–98 (Convener, 1972–88); on Marine Living Resources, 1972–90; on Envmtl Impact Assessment of Mineral Resource Exploitation and Exploitation in Antarctica, 1976–78; UK Delegate, 1984–93 and 1998; Pres., 1990–94; Hon. Mem., 1996; Member: UK Nat. Cttee on Antarctic Res., 1973–2005 (Chm., 1988–94); UK Nat. Cttee on Ocean Res., 1973–79. Food and Agriculture Organization: Mem., 1974–77, Chm., 1976–77, Working Party on Marine Mammals; Chm., Scientific Consultation on Conservation and Management of Marine Mammals and their Environment, 1976. Zoological Society of London: Mem. Council, 1982–84; Vice-Pres., 1983–84; Sec., 1984–88; Zoo Mgt Cttee, 1984–88. University of Cambridge: Mem., Financial Bd, 1988–91; Mem., Council of Senate, 1989–92; Chm., Local Examinations Syndicate, 1990–94. Vice-Pres., Inst. Biol., 1984–85. Mem., NERC Polar Scis Cttee, 1986–93; Chm. Ditchley Foundn Conf. on Antarctica, 1988; Trustee, UK Antarctic Heritage Trust, 1992–2000. Chm., Antarctic Science Ltd, 2001–06. Mem., Soc. of Wildlife Artists, 1963–75. Mem. Editl Bd, Applied Biology, 1976–84. Hon. Mem., Soc. for Marine Mammalogy, 1994. Foreign Mem., Norwegian Acad. of Sci. and Letters, 1998. Hon. Lectr, Makerere Univ., 1962–66. Lectures: 22nd annual, Univ. of Saskatchewan, 1969; 36th annual, CIBA Foundn, 1984; 2nd Cranbrook Meml, Mammal Soc., 1986; 4th DICE (Durrell Inst. Conservation and Ecol.), Univ. of Kent, 1997. Hon. Warden, Uganda Nat. Parks, 1996. Hon. Fellow, St Edmund's Coll., Cambridge, 1996. Hon. DSc Bath, 1991. Bruce Medal, RSE, 1954; Scientific Medal, Zool Soc. London, 1965; Polar Medal, 1976, and clasp, 2001; Jubilee Medal, 1977. *Publications:* (with I. S. C. Parker and R. C. B. Johnstone) Elephants and their Habitats, 1975; (ed) Scientific Research in Antarctica, 1977; (ed) Antarctic Ecology, 1984; (ed jtly) Antarctic Nutrient Cycles and Food Webs, 1985; Antarctica: the last frontier, 1989; (ed jtly) Life at Low Temperatures, 1990; (ed jtly) Antarctica and Environmental Change, 1992; (ed) Antarctic Seals: research methods and techniques, 1993; (ed jtly) Elephant Seals: aspects of population, ecology, behaviour and physiology, 1994; papers mainly on large mammals in their envmts in biol and other jls. *Recreations:* gardening, photography, painting. *Address:* 3 The Footpath, Coton, Cambridge CB23 7PX. *T:* (01954) 210567. *Died 7 Oct. 2014.*

LAWSON, Richard Henry, CBE 1994; Chairman: Greenwell Montagu, Stockbrokers, 1987–91; Securities and Futures Authority, 1991; *b* 16 Feb. 1932; *s* of Sir Henry Brailsford Lawson, MC, and Lady (Mona) Lawson; *m* 1958, Janet Elizabeth Govier; three *s* (one *d* decd). *Educ:* Lancing College. ICI, 1952–54; W. Greenwell & Co. (later Greenwell Montagu & Co.), 1954–91; Jt Sen. Partner, 1980–86. Deputy Chairman: Stock Exchange, 1985–86; Securities Assoc., 1986–91. Chm., Investors Compensation Scheme, 1993–96 (Dir, 1989–96); Dir, Securities Institute, 1992–93. *Recreations:* golf, tennis, walking, birdwatching, ski-ing. *Died 17 Feb. 2015.*

LEA, Vice-Adm. Sir John (Stuart Crosbie), KBE 1979; Director General, Naval Manpower and Training, 1977–80; *b* Simla, 4 June 1923; *m* 1947, Patricia Anne Thoseby (*d* 2010); one *s* two *d*. *Educ:* Boxgrove Sch., Guildford; Shrewsbury Sch.; RNEC, Keyham. Entered RN, 1941; Cruisers Sheffield and Glasgow, 1943; RNEC, 1942–45; HMS Birmingham, 1945; entered Submarines, 1946; HMS/Ms Talent, Tireless, Aurochs, Explorer; Sen. Engr, HMS Forth (Depot Ship), 1952–53; on Staff, RNEC, 1954–57; psc 1958; Sqdn Engr Officer, 2nd Destroyer Sqdn and HMS Daring, 1959–61; Staff of CinC Portsmouth, 1961–62; Naval Staff in Ops Div., 1963–65; Engr Officer, HMS Centaur, 1966; Staff of Flag Officer Submarines; Dep. Supt, Clyde Submarine Base, 1967–68; idc 1969; Dir of

Naval Admin. Planning, 1970–71; Cdre HMS Nelson, 1972–75; Asst Chief of Fleet Support, 1976–77. Comdr 1957; Captain 1966; Rear-Adm. 1976; Vice-Adm. 1978. Chm., 1980–86, Dir, 1986–88, GEC Marine & Industrial Gears Ltd. Chairman: Portsmouth Naval Heritage Trust, 1983–87; Regular Forces Employment Assoc., 1986–89; RN and RM Br. and Special Duties Officers Benevolent Fund, 1993–98. Chm., RN Athletics Assoc., 1972–80; Pres., RN Boxing Assoc., 1975–80. Mem., MCC, 1980–2013. President: Hayling Island Horticultural Soc., 1994–2006 (Chm., 1980–94); Hants Autistic Soc., 1988–95. Churchwarden, St Mary's Ch, Hayling Island, 1970–75. Trustee: Hayling Island Community Centre, 1981–2001; Plumbers Museum and Workshop, Singleton, 1993–2001; Patron: Friends of St Mary's, 2002; D Boat Assoc., 2003–. Master, Worshipful Co. of Plumbers, 1988–89. *Recreations:* watching cricket, writing unpublished letters to The Times, surviving. *Died 20 May 2015.*

LEACH, Admiral of the Fleet Sir Henry (Conyers), GCB 1978 (KCB 1977); DL; *b* 18 Nov. 1923; 3rd *s* of Captain John Catterall Leach, MVO, DSO, RN and Evelyn Burrell Leach (*née* Lee), Yarner, Bovey Tracey, Devon; *m* 1958, Mary Jean (*d* 1991), *yr d* of Adm. Sir Henry McCall, KCVO, KBE, CB, DSO; two *d. Educ:* St Peter's Court, Broadstairs; RNC Dartmouth. Cadet 1937; served in: cruiser Mauritius, S Atlantic and Indian Ocean, 1941–42; battleship Duke of York, incl. Scharnhorst action, 1943–45; destroyers in Mediterranean, 1945–46; spec. Gunnery, 1947; various gunnery appts, 1948–51; Gunnery Officer, cruiser Newcastle, Far East, 1953–55; staff appts, 1955–59; comd destroyer Dunkirk, 1959–61; comd frigate Galatea as Captain (D) 27th Sqdn and Mediterranean, 1965–67; Dir of Naval Plans, 1968–70; comd Commando Ship Albion, 1970; Asst Chief of Naval Staff (Policy), 1971–73; Flag Officer First Flotilla, 1974–75; Vice-Chief of Defence Staff, 1976–77; C-in-C, Fleet, and Allied C-in-C, Channel and Eastern Atlantic, 1977–79; Chief of Naval Staff and First Sea Lord, 1979–82. First and Principal Naval ADC to the Queen, 1979–82. psc 1952; jssc 1961. Chm., St Dunstan's, 1983–98 (Hon. Vice Pres., 1999–2010); President: RN Benevolent Soc., 1983–95; Sea Cadet Assoc., 1984–93; Royal Bath and West of England Soc., 1993 (Vice-Pres., 1994–); Patron, Hampshire RBL, 1994–2009. Chm. Council, King Edward VII Hosp., 1987–98. Gov., Cranleigh Sch., 1983–93. Freeman: City of London; Shipwrights' Co.; Hon. Freeman, Merchant Taylors' Co. DL Hampshire, 1992. *Publications:* Endure no Makeshifts (autobiog.), 1993; Anecdotage, 1996. *Recreations:* fishing, shooting, gardening, antique furniture repair. *Address:* Wonston Lea, Wonston, Winchester, Hants SO21 3LS. *Died 26 April 2011.*

LEACH, Rodney, PhD; CEng; FRINA; FCIM; company director; Chief Executive and Managing Director, VSEL Consortium plc, 1985–88; Chief Executive, 1985–88, and Chairman, 1986–88, Vickers Shipbuilding and Engineering Ltd; Chairman, Cammell Laird Shipbuilders Ltd, 1985–88; led successful privatisation of Vickers and Cammell Laird shipyards, 1986; *b* 3 March 1932; *s* of Edward and Alice Leach; *m* 1958, Eira Mary (*née* Tuck); three *s* one *d. Educ:* Baines Grammar Sch., Poulton-le-Fylde, Lancs; Birmingham Univ. (BSc, PhD). CEng, FRINA 1987; FCIM (FInstM 1972); FCMI (FIIM 1987). Radiation Physicist, Nuclear Power Plant Co. Ltd, 1957; Physicist, UKAEA, 1960; Sen. Physicist, South of Scotland Electricity Board, 1963; Associate, McKinsey & Co. Inc., 1965, Partner, 1970; Peninsular & Oriental Steam Navigation Co.: Hd of European and Air Transport Div., 1974; Dir, 1978–85; Chairman: P&O European Transport Services Ltd, 1979–83; P&O Cruises Ltd, 1980–85. Director: Jasmin plc, 1989–97; United Utilities (formerly North West Water Group) plc, 1989–99; Mem., NW Water Authority, 1989; Vice-Chm. and Dir, S Cumbria Community and Mental Health NHS Trust, 1993–97. Member: Gen. Council, Cumbria Tourist Bd, 1986–92; Northern Council for Sport and Recreation, 1991–95. Dir, 1989–93, Vice-Chm., 1991–94, Renaissance Arts Theatre Trust Ltd. Pres., Lakeland Sinfonia Concert Soc., 1998–2004. Conseiller Spécial, Chambre de Commerce et d'Industrie de Boulogne-sur-Mer et de Montreuil, 1989–94. Mem., RYA, 1977–. Gov., St Anne's Sch., Windermere, 1991–97. Liveryman: Worshipful Company of Carmen, 1976; Worshipful Company of Shipwrights, 1988–; Freeman, City of London, 1976. FRSA 1989. *Publications:* (jtly) Containerization: the key to low cost transport, 1965; frequent papers in scientific and technical jls, 1965–72. *Recreations:* fell-walking, sailing, gardening, literature. *Address:* April Cottage, Loughrigg Meadow, Ambleside, Cumbria LA22 0DZ. *T:* (01539) 431800. *Club:* Royal Automobile. *Died 23 March 2014.*

LEAHY, Sir John (Henry Gladstone), KCMG 1981 (CMG 1973); HM Diplomatic Service, retired; *b* 7 Feb. 1928; *s* of late William Henry Gladstone and late Ethel Leahy; *m* 1954, Elizabeth Anne, *d* of late J. H. Pitchford, CBE; two *s* two *d. Educ:* Tonbridge Sch.; Clare Coll., Cambridge; Yale University. RAF, 1950–52; FO, 1952–54 (Asst Private Sec. to Minister of State, 1953–54); 3rd, later 2nd Sec., Singapore, 1955–57; FO, 1957–58; 2nd, later 1st Sec., Paris, 1958–62; FO, 1962–65; Head of Chancery, Tehran, 1965–68; Counsellor, FCO, 1969; Head of Personnel Services Dept, 1969–70; Head of News Dept, FCO, 1971–73; Counsellor and Head of Chancery, Paris, 1973–75; seconded as Under Sec., NI Office, 1975–76; Asst Under-Sec. of State, FCO, 1977–79; Ambassador to South Africa, 1979–82; Dep. Under-Sec. of State, FCO, 1982–84; High Comr, Australia, 1984–88. Chm., Lonrho, 1994–97 (Dir, 1993–98; Vice-Chm., 1994); Dir, The Observer, 1989–93. Chm., Urban Foundn (London), 1991–94 (Exec. Dir, 1989–91). Pro-Chancellor, City Univ., 1991–97. Chm., British-Australia Soc., 1994–97. Mem., Franco-British Council (Chm., 1989–93). Master, Skinners' Co., 1993–94. Hon. DCL City, 1997. Officier, Légion d'Honneur (France), 1996. *Publications:* A Life of Spice, 2006. *Address:* 16 Ripley Chase, The Goffs, Eastbourne, East Sussex BN21 1HB. *T:* (01323) 725368. *Died 17 Nov. 2015.*

LEAKEY, Dr David Martin, FREng; Group Technical Adviser, British Telecom, 1990–92; independent consultant, David Leakey Consultancy in telecommunication services, systems and networks, since 1992; *b* 23 July 1932; *s* of Reginald Edward and Edith Doris Leakey; *m* 1st, 1957, Shirley May Webster (*d* 2003); one *s* one *d*; 2nd, 2006, Betty Ethel, *widow* of Cedric Walter Garland. *Educ:* Imperial College, Univ. of London (BScEng, PhD, DIC). FCGI 1976; FIET (FIEE 1969); FREng (FEng 1979). GEC Coventry, 1953–57; GEC Hirst Research Centre, 1957–63; Tech. Manager, Public Exchange Div., GEC Coventry, 1963–66; Head, Elect. Eng. Dept, Lanchester Polytechnic, 1966–67; Advanced Product Planning Manager, 1967–69, Technical Dir, 1969–84, GEC Coventry; Dep. E-in-C, 1984–86, Chief Scientist, 1986–90, British Telecom. Director: Fulcrum Ltd, 1985–92; Mitel Corp., 1986–92. Vis. Prof., Univ. of Bristol, 1987–. Vice-Pres., IEE, 1984–87. Freeman, City of London, 1985; Liveryman, Worshipful Co. of Engineers, 1985–. Hon. DEng Bristol, 1995. *Publications:* papers to professional journals. *Recreations:* horticulture, wine. *Address:* 33 MacDonald Close, Chesham Bois, Amersham, Bucks HP6 5LZ. *Died 26 Sept. 2013.*

LEANING, Very Rev. David; Dean (formerly Provost) and Rector of Southwell, 1991–2006, then Dean Emeritus; Priest-in-charge, Edingley with Halam, 2003–06; *b* 18 Aug. 1936. *Educ:* Keble Coll., Oxford, 1957–58; Lichfield Theological Coll. Deacon 1960, priest 1961, dio. Lincoln; Curate of Gainsborough, 1960–65; Rector of Warsop with Sookholme, 1965–76; Vicar of Kington and Rector of Huntington, Diocese of Hereford, 1976–80; RD of Kington and Weobley, 1976–80; Archdeacon of Newark, 1980–91; Priest-in-charge, Rolleston with Fiskerton, Morton and Upton, 1991–93; Warden, Community of St Laurence, Belper, then Southwell, 1984–96 and 2002–13. Mem., Bd of Selectors, ABM (formerly ACCM), 1988–96, 2000–06. MA Lambeth, 2001; Hon. MA Nottingham Trent, 2003. *Address:* 21 Mosse Gardens, Fishbourne, W Sussex PO19 3PQ. *Died 28 July 2015.*

LEAPER, Prof. Robert Anthony Bernard, CBE 1975; Professor of Social Administration, University of Exeter, 1970–86, Professor Emeritus 1987; *b* 7 June 1921; *s* of William Bambrick Leaper and Gertrude Elizabeth (*née* Taylor); *m* 1950, Elizabeth Arno; two *s* one *d. Educ:* Ratcliffe Coll., Leicester; St John's Coll., Cambridge (MA);

Balliol Coll., Oxford (MA). Dipl. Public and Social Admin (Oxon). Coal miner, 1942–45. Warden, St John Bosco Youth Centre, Stepney, 1945–47; Cadet officer, Civil Service, 1949–50; Co-operative Coll., Stanford Hall, 1950–56; Principal, Social Welfare Trng Centre, Zambia, 1956–59; Lectr, then Sen. Lectr, then Acting Dir, Social Admin, UC, Swansea, 1960–70. Vis. Lectr, Roehampton Inst., Univ. of Surrey, 1986–98; Vis. Prof., Post-grad. Med. Sch., Univ. of Exeter, 1996–2001. Exec., later Vice-Chm., Nat. Council of Social Service, 1964–80; Pres., European Region, Internat. Council on Social Welfare, 1971–79; Chm., Area Bd, MSC, 1975–86; Governor, Centre for Policy on Ageing, 1982–88; Trustee, Age Concern England, 1993–98; Chm., AGILE (Devon Action Gp on Later Life), 2000–03. Editor, Social Policy and Administration, 1973–93. DUniv Surrey, 1992; Dr *hc* Univ. de Rennes, 1987. Médaille de l'Ecole Nationale de la Santé, France, 1975; Certificat d'Honneur Marcinelle, Inst. Européen Interuniversitaire de l'Action Sociale, 2006. *Publications:* Communities and Social Change, 1966; Community Work, 1969, 2nd edn 1972; Health, Wealth and Housing, 1980; Change and Continuity, 1984, 2nd enlarged edn 2005; At Home in Devon, 1986; Age Speaks for Itself, 1988; Age Speaks for Itself in Europe, 1993; Employment Post 50, 1998. *Recreations:* walking, railways, wine. *Address:* Birchcote, New North Road, Exeter EX4 4AD. *T:* (01392) 272565. *Died 22 Dec. 2014.*

LEATHAM, Dr Aubrey (Gerald), FRCP; cardiologist; Hon. Consulting Physician: St George's Hospital, London; National Heart Hospital; King Edward VII Hospital, London; *b* 23 Aug. 1920; *s* of Dr H. W. Leatham (*d* 1973), Godalming and Kathleen Pelham Burn (*d* 1971), Nosely Hall, Leicester; *m* 1954, Judith Augustine Savile Freer; one *s* three *d*. *Educ:* Charterhouse; Trinity Hall, Cambridge; St Thomas' Hospital. BA Cambridge 1941; MB, BChir 1944; MRCP 1945; FRCP 1957. House Phys., St Thomas' Hosp., 1944; RMO, Nat. Heart Hosp., 1945; Phys., RAMC, 1946–47; Sherbrook Research Fellow, Cardiac Dept, and Sen. Registrar, London Hosp., 1948–50; Asst Dir, Inst. of Cardiology, 1951–54, Dean, 1962–69. Goulstonian Lectr, RCP, 1958. R. T. Hall Travelling Prof., Australia and NZ, 1963. Member: Brit. Cardiac Soc.; Sociedad Peruana de Cardiologia, 1966; Sociedad Colombiana de Cardiologia, 1966. Hon. FACC 1986. Royal Order of Bhutan, 1966. *Publications:* Auscultation of the Heart and Phonocardiography, 1970; (jtly) Lecture Notes in Cardiology, 1990; Hearts and Life and the Kingdom of Bhutan, 2011; articles in Lancet, British Heart Jl, etc, on auscultation of the heart and phonocardiography, artificial pacemakers, coronary artery disease, etc. *Recreations:* ski-ing and ski-touring, mountain walking, tennis, racquets, gardening, photography. *Address:* Rookwood Farmhouse, West Wittering, W Sussex PO20 8QH. *T:* (01243) 514649. *E:* aubreyleatham@googlemail.com. *Died 7 Aug. 2012.*

LEAVETT, Alan; Under-Secretary, Department of Environment, 1974–81; Chairman, Long Ashton Parish Council, 1997–99; *b* 4 May 1924; *s* of George and Mabel Dorothy Leavett; *m* 1948, Jean Mary Wanford; three *d*. *Educ:* Gosport County Sch.; UC, Southampton (BA Hons 1943). MAP (RAE), 1943; HM Customs and Excise, 1947; HM Foreign Service, 1949; Rio de Janeiro, 1950–53; Bangkok, 1955–59; UK Perm. Delegate to ECAFE, 1958; Cabinet Office, 1961; Min. of Housing and Local Govt, 1963; Sec., Noise Adv. Council, 1970; Under-Sec., Civil Service Selection Bd, 1973. Gen. Sec., Avon Wildlife Trust, 1981–84; Member: Rural Develt Commn, 1982–91; Council, World Wildlife Fund UK, 1983–86; Clifton Suspension Bridge Trust, 1991–95; Vice-Pres., ACRE, 1987–92; Vice-Chm., Avon Community Council, 1981–89. Mem., Woodspring DC, 1986–95. *Publications:* Historic Sevenoaks, 1969. *Recreations:* book-collecting, music. *Address:* Elm View Nursing Home, Moor Lane, Clevedon N Som BS21 6EU. *T:* (01275) 878670. *Died 26 Jan. 2013.*

le BROCQUY, Louis, FCSD (FSIAD 1960); HRHA 1983; painter, since 1939; *b* Dublin, 10 Nov. 1916; *s* of late Albert le Brocquy, MA, and Sybil Staunton; *m* 1st, 1938, Jean Stoney (marr. diss., 1948); one *d*; 2nd, 1958, Anne Madden Simpson; two *s*. *Educ:* St Gerard's Sch., Wicklow, Ireland. Self-taught. Founder-mem. of Irish Exhibn of Living Art, 1943; Visiting Instructor, Central Sch. of Arts and Crafts, London, 1947–54; Visiting Tutor, Royal Coll. of Art, London, 1955–58. Member: Irish Council of Design, 1963–65; Adv. Council, Guinness Peat Awards, 1980–85. Dir, Kilkenny Design Workshops, 1965–77; Founding Bd Mem., Irish Mus. of Modern Art, 1989–94. Represented Ireland, Venice Biennale (awarded internat. prize), 1956. Work exhibited in: "50 Ans d'Art Moderne", Brussels, 1958; Painting since World War II, Guggenheim Mus., New York, 1987–88; Olympiad of Art, Seoul, 1988; L'Europe des Grands Maîtres 1870–1970, Inst. de France, 1989; Internat. Art Fest., Seoul, 1991; Premiers Chefs d'Oeuvres des Grands Maîtres, Museums of Art, Tokyo, Osaka, Kyoto, 1992. One Man Shows: Leicester Galleries, London, 1948; Gimpel Fils, London, 1947, 1949, 1951, 1955, 1956, 1957, 1959, 1961, 1966, 1968, 1971, 1974, 1978, 1983, 1988, 1991, 1993, 1997, 2001, 2006; Waddington, Dublin, 1951; Robles Gallery, Los Angeles, 1960; Gallery Lienhard, Zürich, 1961; Dawson/Taylor Gallery, Dublin, 1962, 1966, 1969, 1971, 1973, 1974, 1975, 1981, 1985, 1986, 1988, 1991, 1992, 1993, 1994, 1995, 1996, 1998, 1999, 2000, 2006; Municipal Gallery of Modern Art, Dublin, 1966, 1978, 1992; Ulster Mus., Belfast, (retrospective) 1967, 1987, 1993; Gimpel-Hanover, Emmerich Zürich, 1969, 1978, 1983; Gimpel, NY, 1971, 1978, 1983; Fondation Maeght, 1973; Bussola, Turin, 1974; Arts Council, Belfast, 1975, 1978; Musée d'Art Moderne, Paris, 1976; Giustiniani, Genoa, 1977; Waddington, Montreal, Toronto, 1978; Maeght, Barcelona, Madrid, Granada, 1978–79; Jeanne Bucher, Paris, 1979, 1982, 2006; NY State Mus., 1981; Boston Coll. 1982; Westfield Coll., Mass, 1982; Palais des Beaux Arts, Charleroi, 1982; Art 13, Internat. Basel (Börjeson), 1982; Chicago Internat. Expo (Brownstone Gall.), 1986; Arts Council, Dublin, 1987; Nat. Gall. of Vic, Melbourne, Festival Centre, Adelaide, and Mus. of Contemp. Art, Brisbane, 1988; Musée Picasso, Antibes, 1989; Kerlin, Dublin, 1991; Mus. of Modern Art, Kamakura, 1991; Itami City Mus. of Art, Osaka, 1991; City Mus. of Contemp. Art, Hiroshima, 1991; Carré Davidson, Tours, 1995; Irish Mus. of Modern Art, 1996, 2006; Espace Ricard, Paris, 1996; Galerie Maeght, Paris, 1996; Château Musée de Tours, 1997; Municipal Gall. of Modern Art, Ljubljana, 1998; Museo de Arte Contemporáneo, Instituto de Artes Gráficas, Oaxaca, 2000; Agnew's, 2001; Hunt Mus., Limerick, 2006; Nat. Gall. of Ireland, 2007; Dublin City Gall. The Hugh Lane, 2007. Public Collections possessing work include: Albright Museum, Buffalo; Arts Council of Ireland; Arts Council, London; Carnegie Inst., Pittsburgh; Centre Georges Pompidou, Paris; Chicago Arts Club; l'Etat Français; Columbus Mus., Ohio; Detroit Inst. of Art; Dublin Municipal Gallery; Fort Worth Center, Texas; Foundation of Brazil Museum, Bahia; Gulbenkian Mus., Lisbon; Guggenheim Museum, NY; J. H. Hirshhorn Foundation, Washington; Ho-Am Mus., Seoul; Hugh Lane Municipal Gall. of Modern Art, Dublin; Irish Mus. of Modern Art, Dublin; Itami Mus., Osaka; Kunsthaus, Zürich; Fondation Maeght, St Paul; Leeds City Art Gallery; Musée d'Art Moderne, Paris; Musée Picasso, Antibes; Mus. of Contemp. Art, Hiroshima; Mus. of Modern Art, Kamakura; NY State Mus.; Nat. Gall. of Ireland; San Diego Mus., Calif.; Tate Gallery; Uffizi, Florence; Ulster Museum, Belfast; Vatican Mus.; V&A Museum. RHA 1950–69. *Films:* An Other Way of Knowing, RTE, 1986; The Inner Human Reality, RTE, 2006. Freeman, City of Dublin, 2007. Hon. Associate, Nat. Coll. of Art and Design, Dublin, 2006. Hon. DLitt Dublin, 1962; Hon. LLD NUI, 1988; Hon. DPh: Dublin City, 1999; Dublin Inst. of Technol., 2004; DUniv QUB, 2002. Saoi, Aosdána, Irish Arts Council, 1993. Commandeur du Bontemps de Médoc et des Graves, 1969. Chevalier de la Légion d'Honneur, 1975; Officier: Ordre des Arts et des Lettres (France), 1996; Ordre de la Couronne (Belgium), 2001. *Publications: Illustrated work:* The Táin, trans. Thomas Kinsella, 1969; The Playboy of the Western World, Synge, 1970; The Gododdin O'Grady, 1978; Dubliners, Joyce, 1986; Stirrings Still, Samuel Beckett, 1988. *Relevant publications:* Louis le Brocquy by D. Walker, introd. John Russell, Ireland 1981, UK 1982; The Irish Landscape, by G. Morgan, 1992; Seeing his Way, by A. Madden le

Brocquy, 1994; Procession, by G. Morgan, 1994; The Head Image: interviews by G. Morgan and M. Peppiatt, 1996. *Address:* c/o Gimpel Fils, 30 Davies Street, W1Y 1LG. *Died 25 April 2012.*

LECKY, (Arthur) Terence, CMG 1968; HM Diplomatic Service, retired; *b* 10 June 1919; *s* of late Lieut-Colonel M. D. Lecky, DSO, late RA, and Bertha Lecky (*née* Goss); *m* 1946, Jacqualine (*d* 1974), *d* of late Dr A. G. Element; three *s*. *Educ:* Winchester Coll.; Clare Coll., Cambridge (1938–39). Served RA, 1939–46. FO (Control Commission for Germany), 1946–49; FO, 1950–54; Vice-Consul, Zürich, 1954–56; FO, 1957–61; First Secretary, The Hague, 1962–64, FCO (formerly FO), 1964–70. Mem., Hants CC, 1981–89. Vice-Chm., Hants Police Authority, 1988–89. *Address:* c/o Green Farm Cottage, The Green, Fringford, Bicester, Oxon OX27 8DY. *Died 16 Nov. 2012.*

LEDGER, Sir Philip (Stevens), Kt 1999; CBE 1985; composer, conductor and pianist; *b* 12 Dec. 1937; *s* of Walter Stephen Ledger and Winifred Kathleen (*née* Stevens); *m* 1963, Mary Erryl (*née* Wells); one *s* one *d*. *Educ:* Bexhill Grammar Sch.; King's Coll., Cambridge (Maj. Schol.; John Stewart of Rannoch Schol. in Sacred Music; 1st Cl. Hons in Pt I and Pt II of Music Tripos; MA, MusB). FRCO (Limpus and Read prizes); FRCM 1983; FRNCM 1989. Master of the Music, Chelmsford Cathedral, 1962–65; Dir of Music, Univ. of East Anglia, 1965–73 (Dean of Sch. of Fine Arts and Music, 1968–71); Dir of Music and Organist, King's Coll., Cambridge, 1974–82; Conductor, CU Musical Soc., 1973–82; Principal, RSAMD, 1982–2001. Artistic Dir, 1968–89, Vice-Pres., 1989–, Aldeburgh Festival of Music and the Arts. Hon. Prof., Univ. of Glasgow, 1993–98. President: RCO, 1992–94; ISM, 1994–95; Chm., Cttee of Principals of Conservatoires, 1994–98. Hon. RAM 1984; Hon. FGS (Hon. GSM 1989). Hon. LLD Strathclyde, 1987; DUniv UCE, 1998; Hon. DMus: Glasgow, 2001; RSAMD, 2001; St Andrews, 2001. *Publications:* (ed) Anthems for Choirs 2 and 3, 1973; (ed) The Oxford Book of English Madrigals, 1978; other edns, compositions incl. Requiem (A Thanksgiving for Life), 2007; The Risen Christ, 2011, carols, anthems and arrangements. *Recreations:* swimming, theatre, Master of Music to The Sette of Odd Volumes. *Address:* 2 Lancaster Drive, Upper Rissington, Cheltenham, Glos GL54 2QZ. *W:* www.sirphilipledger.com. *Died 18 Nov. 2012.*

LEDWITH, Prof. Anthony, CBE 1995; FRS 1995; Professor and Head of Department of Chemistry, University of Sheffield, 1996–99, then Emeritus Professor; Chairman, Engineering and Physical Sciences Research Council, 1999–2003 (Member, 1994–97); *b* 14 Aug. 1933; *s* of Thomas Ledwith and Mary (*née* Coghlan); *m* 1960, Mary Clare Ryan; one *s* three *d*. *Educ:* BSc (external) London 1954; PhD 1957, DSc 1970, Liverpool Univ. FRSC 1986. Liverpool University: Lectr, 1959, Prof., 1976, Campbell Brown Prof. of Industrial Chem., 1980, Dept of Inorganic Physical and Industrial Chem.; Dean, Faculty of Sci., 1980–83; Dep. Dir, Group R&D, 1984–88, Dir, Group Res., 1988–96, Pilkington plc. Chm., DSAC, 2001– (Mem., 1988–91); Mem., SERC, 1990–94. Pres., RSC, 1998–2000. *Publications:* (with A. D. Jenkins) Reactivity, Mechanism and Structure in Polymer Chemistry, 1974; (with A. M. North) Molecular Behaviour and the Development of Polymeric Materials, 1975; (with S. J. Moss) The Chemistry of the Semiconductor Industry, 1987; (ed jtly) Comprehensive Polymer Science, 7 vols, 1989. *Address:* 193 Wigan Road, Standish, Wigan WN6 0AE. *Died 5 Jan. 2015.*

LEE, Alan Peter; racing correspondent, The Times, since 1999; *b* 13 June 1954; *s* of Peter Alexander Lee and Christina Carmichael; *m* 1980, Patricia Drury; one *s* one *d*. *Educ:* Cavendish Grammar Sch., Hemel Hempstead. With Watford Observer, 1970–74; Hayters Agency, 1974–78; freelance, 1978–82; cricket correspondent: Mail on Sunday, 1982–87; The Times, 1988–99. Racing Journalist of the Year, HWPA Derby Awards, 2001, 2004, 2014. *Publications:* A Pitch in Both Camps, 1979; Diary of a Cricket Season, 1980; Lambourn, Village of Racing, 1983; Raising the Stakes: the modern cricket revolution, 1996; The Course Inspector: racecourse guide to Britain, 2001; *biographies:* (with Tony Greig) My Story, 1978; (with David Gower) With Time to Spare, 1980; (with Graham Gooch) Out of the Wilderness, 1985; Fred (biog. of Fred Winter), 1991; (with Pat Eddery) To Be A Champion, 1992; Lord Ted: the Dexter enigma, 1995; (with David Lloyd) David Lloyd: the autobiography, 2000; (with Richard Johnson) Out of the Shadows: the Richard Johnson story, 2002. *Recreations:* National Hunt racing (has owned or part-owned ten horses), tennis, wine. *Address:* 8 The Courtyard, Montpellier Street, Cheltenham, Glos GL50 1SR. *T:* (01242) 572637. *Club:* Cricketers'. *Died 19 Dec. 2015.*

LEE, Sir Christopher (Frank Carandini), Kt 2009; CBE 2001; actor; entered film industry, 1947; *b* 27 May 1922; *s* of Geoffrey Trollope Lee (Lt-Col 60th KRRC) and Estelle Marie Carandini; *m* 1961, Birgit, *d* of Richard Emil Kroencke; one *d*. *Educ:* Wellington Coll. RAFVR and Special Forces, 1941–46 (Flt Lieut; mentioned in despatches, 1944). Films include: Moulin Rouge, 1952; Tale of Two Cities, Dracula, 1958; Rasputin, 1966; The Devil Rides Out, 1968; Private Life of Sherlock Holmes, 1970; The Wicker Man, The Three Musketeers, 1973; The Four Musketeers, The Man with the Golden Gun, 1974; To the Devil, a Daughter, 1976; Airport '77, 1977; The Passage, Bear Island, 1941, 1979; The Serial, 1980; An Eye for An Eye, The Salamander, 1981; The Last Unicorn, Safari 3000, 1982; The Return of Captain Invincible, The House of the Long Shadows, 1983; Mio Min Mio, 1987; The Return of the Musketeers, The French Revolution, 1989; Gremlins II, The Rainbow Thief, 1990; A Feast at Midnight, 1994; The Stupids, 1996; Jinnah, 1998; Sleepy Hollow, 1999; The Fellowship of the Ring, 2001; Star Wars, Episode II: Attack of the Clones, The Two Towers, 2002; The Return of the King, 2003; Star Wars, Episode III: Revenge of the Sith, Charlie and the Chocolate Factory, The Corpse Bride, 2005; The Adventures of Greyfriars Bobby, 2006; The Golden Compass, 2007; Triage, Glorious '39, 2009; Alice in Wonderland, Season of the Witch, Boogie Woogie, The Heavy, 2010; Hugo, The Wicker Tree, 2011; Dark Shadows, The Hobbit: An Unexpected Journey, 2012; The Hobbit: The Battle of the Five Armies, 2014; television includes: Charles and Diana: a royal love story, 1982; The Far Pavilions, 1984; The Disputation, 1986; Treasure Island, 1990; Sherlock Holmes - The Golden Years, 1991; Young Indy, 1992; Death Train, 1993; Tales of Mystery and Imagination, 1994; Moses 1995; Gormenghast, 2000. Fellow: BAFTA, 2011; BFI, 2013. CStJ 1997 (OStJ 1986). Comdr de l'Ordre des Arts et des Lettres (France), 2012 (Officier, 2002). *Publications:* Christopher Lee's 'X' Certificate, 1975, 2nd edn 1976; Christopher Lee's Archives of Evil, USA 1975, 2nd edn 1976; Tall, Dark and Gruesome (autobiog.), 1977, new edn 1997; Lord of Misrule, 2005. *Recreations:* opera, golf. *Address:* c/o 42 M&P Ltd, 8 Flitcroft Street, WC2H 8DL. *Clubs:* Buck's, Pugs; Honourable Company of Edinburgh Golfers; Travellers (Paris). *Died 7 June 2015.*

LEE KUAN YEW, Hon. CH 1970; Hon. GCMG 1972; Prime Minister, Singapore, 1959–90; Minister Mentor, Prime Minister's Office, 2004–11; Senior Advisor, Government of Singapore Investment Corporation, since 2011; *b* 16 Sept. 1923; *s* of Lee Chin Koon and Chua Jim Neo; *m* 1950, Kwa Geok Choo (*d* 2010); two *s* one *d*. *Educ:* Raffles Coll., Singapore; Fitzwilliam Coll., Cambridge (class 1 both parts of Law Tripos). Called to Bar, Middle Temple, 1950, Hon. Bencher, 1969. Advocate and Solicitor, Singapore, 1951. Formed People's Action Party, 1954, Sec.-Gen., 1954–92; People's Action Party won elections, 1959; became PM, 1959, re-elected 1963, 1968, 1972, 1976, 1980, 1984, 1988; MP Fed. Parlt of Malaysia, 1963–65; Sen. Minister, Prime Minister's Office, 1990–2004. Hon. Freeman, City of London, 1982. *Publications:* The Singapore Story (memoirs), 1998; From Third World to First: the Singapore Story 1965–2000 (memoirs), 2000; Grand Master's Insights on China, the United States and the World, 2013; One Man's View of the World, 2013. *Recreation:* swimming. *Address:* c/o Prime Minister's Office, Orchard Road, Istana, Singapore 238823. *Died 23 March 2015.*

LEE-STEERE, Sir Ernest (Henry), KBE 1977 (CBE 1963); JP; Lord Mayor of Perth, Western Australia, 1972–78; company director, pastoralist and grazier; *b* Perth, 22 Dec. 1912; *s* of Sir Ernest Lee-Steere, JP, KStJ; *m* 1942, Jessica Margaret, *d* of Frank Venn; two *s* three *d*. *Educ:* Hale Sch., Perth; St Peter's Coll., Adelaide. Served War: Captain Army/Air Liaison Group, AIF; SW Pacific Area, 1944–45 (Philippine Liberation Medal, 1996). President (for WA): Pastoralists and Graziers Assoc., 1959–72; Boy Scout Assoc., 1957–64; National Trust, 1969–72. Vice-Pres., Council of Royal Flying Doctor Service of WA, 1954–59 and 1962–74. Chairman: State Adv. Cttee, CSIRO, 1962–71 (Councillor, Fed. Adv. Council, 1960–71); WA Soil Conservation Adv. Cttee, 1955–72; Aust. Capital Cities Secretariat, 1975–76; WA Turf Club, 1963–84 (Vice-Chm., 1959–63). Member: Nat. Council of Aust. Boy Scouts Assoc., 1959–64; Exec. Cttee of WA State Cttee, Freedom from Hunger Campaign; WA State Adv. Cttee, Aust. Broadcasting Commn, 1961–64; Aust. Jubilee Cttee for the Queen's Silver Jubilee Appeal for Young Australians, 1977; Aust. Wool Industry Conf., 1971–74 (also Mem. Exec. Cttee). Councillor: Aust. Wool Growers and Graziers Council (Pres., 1972–73); St George's Coll., Univ. of WA, 1945–81. Chm. and dir of several cos. Leader, Trade Mission to India, 1962. JP Perth, 1965. *Publications:* Be Fair & Fear Not (autobiog.), 1995. *Recreation:* polo (played in WA Polo Team in Australasian Gold Cup). *Address:* Dardanup, 26 Odern Crescent, Swanbourne, WA 6010, Australia. *T:* (9) 3842929. *Club:* Weld (Perth). *Died 9 Jan. 2011.*

LEECH, Prof. Geoffrey Neil, FBA 1987; Research Professor of English Linguistics, University of Lancaster, 1996–2002, then Professor Emeritus; *b* 16 Jan. 1936; *s* of Charles Richard Leech and Dorothy Eileen Leech; *m* 1961, Frances Anne Berman; one *s* one *d*. *Educ:* Tewkesbury Grammar School; University College London (BA 1959; MA 1963; PhD 1968). Asst Lectr, UCL, 1962–64; Harkness Fellow, MIT, 1964–65; Lectr, UCL, 1965–69; University of Lancaster: Reader, 1969–74; Prof. of Linguistics and Modern English Lang., 1974–96. Visiting Professor: Brown Univ., 1972; Kobe Univ., 1984; Kyoto Univ., 1991; Meikai Univ., 1999, 2000. Hon. Fil Dr Lund, 1987; Hon. DLitt: Wolverhampton, 2002; Lancaster, 2002; UCL, 2014; Hon. PhD Charles Univ., Prague, 2012. *Publications:* English in Advertising, 1966; A Linguistic Guide to English Poetry, 1969; Towards a Semantic Description of English, 1969; Meaning and the English Verb, 1971, 3rd edn 2004; (with R. Quirk, S. Greenbaum and J. Svartvik) A Grammar of Contemporary English, 1972; Semantics, 1974, 2nd edn 1981; (with J. Svartvik) A Communicative Grammar of English, 1975, 3rd edn 2002; Explorations in Semantics and Pragmatics, 1980; (ed with S. Greenbaum and J. Svartvik) Studies in English Linguistics: for Randolph Quirk, 1980; (with M. Short) Style in Fiction, 1981, 2nd edn 2007; (with R. Hoogenraad and M. Deuchar) English Grammar for Today, 1982, 2nd edn 2005; Principles of Pragmatics, 1983; (with R. Quirk, S. Greenbaum, and J. Svartvik) A Comprehensive Grammar of the English Language, 1985; (ed with C. N. Candlin) Computers in English Language Teaching and Research, 1986; (ed with R. Garside and G. Sampson) The Computational Analysis of English: a corpus-based approach, 1987; An A-Z of English Grammar and Usage, 1989, 2nd edn (with B. Cruickshank and R. Ivanič) 2001; Introducing English Grammar, 1992; (ed with E. Black and R. Garside) Statistically-driven Computer Grammars of English, 1993; (ed with G. Myers and J. Thomas) Spoken English on Computer, 1995; (ed with R. Garside and T. McEnery) Corpus Annotation: linguistic information from computer text corpora, 1997; (jtly) Longman Grammar of Spoken and Written English, 1999; (with P. Rayson and A. Wilson) Word Frequencies in Written and Spoken English, 2001; (with D. Biber and S. Conrad) Student Grammar of Spoken and Written English, 2002; (with J. Svartvik) English: One Tongue - Many Voices, 2006; A Glossary of English Grammar, 2006; Language in Literature, 2008; (jtly) Change in Contemporary English: a grammatical study, 2009; Selected Works of Geoffrey Leech on Applied Linguistics, 2011; (ed jtly) The Verb Phrase in English: investigating recent language change with corpora, 2013; The Pragmatics of Politeness, 2014. *Recreations:* music, esp. playing the piano in chamber music groups and playing the church organ, walking. *Address:* Department of Linguistics and English Language, University of Lancaster, Bailrigg, Lancaster LA1 4YL. *Died 19 Aug. 2014.*

LEECH, Rev. Kenneth; M. B. Reckitt Urban Fellow, St Botolph's Church, Aldgate, 1991–2004; *b* 15 June 1939; *s* of late John and Annie Leech; *m* 1970, Rheta Wall (marr. diss. 1993); one *s*; *m* 2014, Julie Wood. *Educ:* King's College London (BA Hons Mod. History, AKC 1961); Trinity Coll., Oxford (BA Hons Theol. 1961, MA 1968); St Stephen's House, Oxford. Deacon 1964, priest 1965; Curate: Holy Trinity, Hoxton, N1, 1964–67; St Anne, Soho, W1, 1967–71; Sec., Soho Drugs Group, 1967–71; Dir, Centrepoint, Soho, 1969–71; Chaplain and Tutor, St Augustine's Coll., Canterbury, 1971–74; Rector of St Matthew, Bethnal Green, 1974–80; Field Work Sec., BCC, 1980; Race Relations Field Officer, C of E Bd for Social Responsibility, 1981–87; Hon. Assistant Curate: St Clement and St Mark, Notting Hill, 1982–85; St Clement and St Mark, Notting Dale, and St James's, Norland, 1985–88; Dir, Runnymede Trust, 1987–90. Visiting Lecturer: St Stephen's House, Chicago, 1978–90; Brent House, Chicago, 1990–2003. DD Lambeth, 1998. *Publications:* Pastoral Care and the Drug Scene, 1970; A Practical Guide to the Drug Scene, 1972; Keep the Faith, Baby, 1972; Youthquake, 1973; Soul Friend, 1977; True Prayer, 1980; The Social God, 1981; True God, 1984; Spirituality and Pastoral Care, 1986; Struggle in Babylon: Racism in the Cities and Churches of Britain, 1988; Care and Conflict, 1990; Subversive Orthodoxy, 1992; The Eye of the Storm, 1992 (HarperCollins Religious Book Award, 1993); We Preach Christ Crucified, 1994; The Sky is Red, 1997; Drugs and Pastoral Care, 1998; Through Our Long Exile, 2001; Race, 2005; Doing Theology in Altab Ali Park, 2006. *Recreations:* cartoon drawing, Lancashire dialect poetry, pubs. *Address:* Sandon House, Market Street, Mossley, Ashton-under-Lyne OL5 0JG. *T:* (01457) 838655. *E:* kenleech@aol.com. *Died 12 Sept. 2015.*

LEES, His Honour C(harles) Norman; a Circuit Judge, 1980–96; Designated Family Judge, Greater Manchester, 1991–96; *b* 4 Oct. 1929; *s* of late Charles Lees, Bramhall, Cheshire; *m* 1961, Stella (*d* 1987), *d* of late Hubert Swann, Stockport; one *d*. *Educ:* Stockport Sch.; Univ. of Leeds (LLB 1950). Called to Bar, Lincoln's Inn, 1951. Dep. Chm., Cumberland County QS, 1969–71; a Recorder of the Crown Court, 1972–80; Chm., Mental Health Review Tribunal, Manchester Region, 1977–80 (Mem., 1971–80; Pres. (restricted patients), 1983–98). *Recreations:* tennis, music, history. *Address:* 24 St John Street, Manchester M3 4ES. *T:* (0161) 214 6000. *Clubs:* Lansdowne; Northern Lawn Tennis. *Died 22 March 2012.*

LEES, Geoffrey William; Headmaster, St Bees School, 1963–80; *b* 1 July 1920; *o s* of late Mr and Mrs F. T. Lees, Manchester; *m* 1949, Joan Needham, *yr d* of late Mr and Mrs J. Needham, Moseley, Birmingham. *Educ:* King's Sch., Rochester; Downing Coll., Cambridge (BA 2nd Cl. Hons English Tripos, Pt I, 1947; History Tripos, Pt II, 1948). Royal Signals, 1940–46 (despatches): commissioned 1941; served in NW Europe and Middle East, Captain. Asst Master, Brighton Coll., 1948–63. Leave of absence in Australia, Asst Master, Melbourne Church of England GS, 1961–62. *Recreations:* reading, lepidoptera, walking. *Address:* 10 Merlin Close, Upper Drive, Hove, Sussex BN3 6NU. *Clubs:* Hawks, Union (Cambridge). *Died 17 Aug. 2012.*

LEES, Norman; *see* Lees, His Honour C. N.

LE FLEMING, Peter Henry John; health management consultant, since 1988; Regional General Manager, South East Thames Regional Health Authority, 1984–88; *b* 25 Oct. 1923; *s* of late Edward Ralph Le Fleming and Irene Louise Le Fleming (*née* Adams); *m* 1st, 1949, Gudrun Svendsen (marr. diss. 1981); two *s*; 2nd, 1987, Jean, *yr d* of Edgar and Alice Price, Llangenny, Wales. *Educ:* Addison Gardens Sch., Hammersmith; Pembroke Coll., Cambridge (MA). FHSM. Served 1942–47, RTR and Parachute Regt, MEF, CMF, Palestine; commnd 1943. Sudan Political Service, Equatoria, Kassala, Blue Nile Provinces, 1949–55; National Health Service: Redevelt Sec., St Thomas's Hosp., London, 1955–57; Hosp. Sec., The London Hosp., 1957–61; Dep. Clerk to the Governors, Guy's Hosp.,

1961–69; Gp Sec., Exeter and Mid Devon Hosp. Management Cttee, 1969–74; Area Administrator, Kent AHA, 1974–81; Regional Administrator, SE Thames RHA, 1981–84. Mem., Health Service Supply Council, 1982–86. Clerk to Special Trustees, Guy's Hosp., 1988–97; Chm., Evelina Family Trust, 1996–98. Freeman, City of London, 1992. *Recreations:* long distance fell walking, horse riding, trad jazz and serious music. *Address:* Lilacs, Leys Road, Tostock, near Bury St Edmunds, Suffolk IP30 9PN. *T:* (01359) 271015. *Died 16 Oct. 2014.*

LEGGATT, Sir Hugh (Frank John), Kt 1988; art dealer; *b* 27 Feb. 1925; 2nd *s* of late Henry and Beatrice Leggatt; *m* 1st, 1953, Jennifer Hepworth (marr. diss. 1990); two *s*; 2nd, 1991, Gaynor, *yr d* of late W. L. Tregoning, CBE and D. M. E. Tregoning. *Educ:* Eton; New Coll., Oxford. RAF, 1943–46. Joined Leggatt Bros, 1946; Partner, 1952; Sen. Partner, 1962–92. Hon. Rep., Nat. Portrait Galls of London and Edinburgh, 1946–92. Pres., Fine Art Provident Instn, 1960–63; Chm., Soc. of London Art Dealers, 1966–70; Mem., Museums and Galleries Commn, 1983–92. Hon. Sec., Heritage in Danger, 1974–. *Address:* 21 Rue du Lac, 1800 Vevey, Switzerland. *Club:* White's. *Died 8 March 2014.*

LE GOY, Raymond Edgar Michel, FCILT; a Director General, Commission of the European Communities, later European Union, 1981–84, then Emeritus; *b* 20 April 1919; *e s* of J. A. S. M. N. and May Le Goy; *m* 1960, Ernestine Burnett, Trelawny, Jamaica; one *s* (and one *s* decd). *Educ:* William Ellis Sch.; Gonville and Caius Coll., Cambridge (BA 1st cl. hons Hist. Tripos, 1939, 1940; MA). Sec. Cambridge Union; Chm., Union Univ. Liberal Socs. Served Army, 1940–46: Staff Captain, HQ E Africa, 1944; Actg Major, 1945. LPTB, 1947; Min. of Transport, 1947; UK Shipping Adviser, Japan, 1949–51; Far East and SE Asia, 1951; Dir, Goeland Co., 1952; Asst Secretary: MoT, 1958; Min. of Aviation, 1959; BoT and DEA, 1966; Under-Sec., 1968, BoT, later DTI; Dir Gen. for Transport, EEC, 1973–81. FCILT (FCIT 1974; FILT 1999). *Publications:* The Victorian Burletta, 1953. *Recreations:* theatre, music, race relations. *Address:* c/o Fortis Banque, Agence Schuman, Rond Point Schuman 10, 1040 Brussels, Belgium. *Died 30 Sept. 2011.*

LEICESTER, 7th Earl of, *cr* 1837; **Edward Douglas Coke,** CBE 2005; Viscount Coke 1837; *b* 6 May 1936; *er s* of 6th Earl of Leicester and his 1st wife, Moyra Joan (*d* 1987), *d* of Douglas Crossley; *S* father, 1994; *m* 1st, 1962, Valeria Phyllis (marr. diss. 1985), *e d* of late L. A. Potter; two *s* one *d*; 2nd, 1986, Mrs Sarah de Chair. *Educ:* St Andrew's, Grahamstown, CP, S Africa. Mem., King's Lynn and W Norfolk BC, 1973–91 (Leader, 1980–85; Chm. Planning Cttee, 1987–91). Comr, English Heritage, 2002–10. Pres., HHA, 1998–2003. President: Wells, Norfolk Br., RNLI; League of Friends, Wells Cottage Hosp.; Royal Norfolk Show, 1995; Ancient Monument Soc., 2009–. Mem. Council, Royal Norfolk Agricl Assoc. DL Norfolk, 1981–85, 2005–11. *Recreations:* history, conservation of the built heritage, wildlife matters, reading. *Heir: s* Viscount Coke, *b* 6 July 1965. *Address:* Model Farm, Holkham, Wells-next-the-Sea, Norfolk NR23 1RP. *Clubs:* Brooks's, White's, Farmers. *Died 25 April 2015.*

LEIGH, Peter William John, FRICS; chartered surveyor and property consultant; *b* 29 June 1929; *s* of John Charles Leigh and Dorothy Grace Leigh; *m* 1956, Mary Frances (*née* Smith); two *s* one *d*. *Educ:* Harrow Weald County Grammar Sch.; Coll. of Estate Management (ext.). National Service, Royal Signals, 1947–49. Private surveying practice, 1949–53; Valuation Asst, Middx CC, 1953–60; Commercial Estates Officer, Bracknell Develt Corp., 1960–66; sen. appts, Valuation and Estates Dept, GLC, 1966–81; Dir of Valuation and Estates, GLC, 1981–84; Dir of Property Services, Royal County of Berks, 1984–88. Member: Gen. Council, RICS, 1984–86; RICS Gen. Practice Divl Council, 1993–96; Govt Property Adv. Gp, 1984–88. Exec. Mem., Local Authority Valuers Assoc., 1981–88. *Recreations:* exploring Cornwall, drawing, gardening (therapy). *Address:* 41 Sandy Lane, Wokingham, Berks RG41 4SS. *T:* (0118) 978 2732. *Died 15 April 2011.*

LEIGH FERMOR, Sir Patrick; *see* Fermor.

LEIGHTON, Jane; Chair, Waveney Primary Care NHS Trust, 2003–06; Deputy Chair, Broadcasting Standards Commission, 1997–2001; *b* 17 March 1944; *d* of Robert and Doris Palmer; *m* Bernard Leighton (marr. diss.); one *s* one *d*. Administrator, British Pregnancy Adv. Service, 1971–74; Sec., Liverpool CHC, 1974–79; reporter, World in Action, Granada TV, 1979–85; Producer, Channel 4, 1985–88; Independent Consultancy, Littlewoods Orgn, 1985–88; Exec. Dir, Mersey TV, 1988–90; Hd of Public Affairs, Granada TV Ltd, 1990–92; Industrial Relns Consultant, Liverpool HAT, 1992–96; Hd of Organisational Develt, Tate Gall., 1995–97; Dir, London Mental Health Learning Partnership, subseq. Virtuall, 2000–05. Chair: Mental Health Services, Salford NHS Trust, 1993–95; Camden and Islington Area Mental Health Cttee, 1998–2000; non-exec. Dir, Camden and Islington NHS Community Trust, 1998–2001. Mem., Broadcasting Complaints Commn, 1993–96 (Chm., 1996–97). Non-executive Director: City of London Sinfonia, 1992–97; Hallé Concerts Soc., 1992–95; Royal Liverpool Philharmonic Orch., 1990–92. Mem., NW Arts Bd. Gov., UC, Salford, 1992–95. FRSA 1997. RTS Award for best internat. current affairs programme, 1981; BMA Award for medical progs, 1983; Equal Opportunities Award, Women in Mgt Award, 1987. *Address:* 94 London Road, Halesworth, Suffolk IP19 8LS. *E:* leightonjane@btinternet.com. *Died 4 July 2012.*

LELLO, Walter Barrington, (Barry); Deputy Director, North-West Region, Department of Trade and Industry, 1988–91; *b* 29 Sept. 1931; *o s* of Walter Joseph Lello and Louisa (*née* McGarrigle); *m* 1959, Margaret, *o d* of Alexander and Alice McGregor. *Educ:* Liverpool Institute High School. Nat. Service, RN, 1950–52. Open Exec. Comp. to Civil Service, 1949; Min. of Supply, later Aviation, 1952–64; Asst British Civil Aviation Rep., Far East, Hong Kong, 1964–67; BoT, later Dept of Trade, 1967–71; Civil Air Attaché, Middle East, Beirut, 1971–76; DTI, 1976–78; Dir Gen., Saudi-British Economic Co-operation Office, Riyadh, 1978–81; seconded to British Electricity International as Dir, Middle East Ops, 1981–83; DTI, 1983; Commercial Counsellor, Cairo, 1984–88. *Recreations:* walking, public rights of way and Wirral Green Belt protection, reading. *Address:* 15 Long Meadow, Gayton, Wirral CH60 8QQ. *Died 17 May 2012.*

LEORO-FRANCO, Dr Galo Alberto; Gran Cruz, National Order Al Mérito of Ecuador, 1970; Minister of Foreign Affairs, Ecuador, 1994–97; Member, Consultative Board, Ministry of Foreign Affairs, since 1997; *s* of José Miguel Leoro and Albertina Franco de Leoro; *m* 1957, Aglae Monroy de Leoro; one *s* two *d*. *Educ:* Central Univ., Quito. Licenciado in Political and Soc. Scis, 1949; Dr in Jurisprudence, Faculty of Law, 1951. Third Sec., Washington, 1955–56, Second Sec., 1956–58; First Sec., Ministry of Foreign Affairs, 1960; Counsellor, Mexico, 1961, Chargé d'Affaires, 1962; Counsellor, Alternate Rep. of Ecuador to OAS, Washington, DC, 1962–64, Minister, 1964–68; Ambassador, 1968–; Chief Legal Advisor to Ministry of Foreign Affairs, 1969–70; Under-Sec. Gen., Ministry of Foreign Affairs, 1970–71; Ambassador to the Dominican Republic, 1971–72; Perm. Rep. of Ecuador to OAS, 1972–79; Advisor on Internat. Orgns, Ministry of Foreign Affairs, 1979–81; Advisor on Nat. Sovereignty, Ministry of Foreign Affairs, and Rep. of the Ministry in Nat. Congress, 1981–83; Ambassador to UK, 1983–84; Ambassador and Permanent Rep. to Office of UN, Geneva, 1984–91; Chief Legal Advr, Ministry of Foreign Affairs, 1991–92; Ambassador to Holy See, 1993–94. Chairman: OAS Permanent Council, 1972–78 (Chm. of several Cttees of OAS Council and Gen. Assembly); Cttee II, Special Commn for Study of Interamerican System, Economic Co-operation problems, Washington, DC, 1973–75; INTELSAT Panel of Jurisexperts, Washington, DC, 1983–85; Rapporteur, Interamerican Conf. for Revision of TIAR; elected mem., Interamerican Juridical Cttee, Rio de Janeiro, 1981–84, Vice-Chm., 1982–83, Chm., 1985–96; Conciliator, Internat. Center for Settlement of Investment Disputes, IMF, Washington, DC, 1986–; Ecuadorian Mem., National Gp of Arbiters, Internat. Court of Arbitration, The Hague, 1987. Representative of Ecuador at over 100 internat. conferences and Chm. of the Delegation at various of them. Gran Cruz: Iron Cross, Fed.

Repub. of Germany, 1970; Order of Duarte, Sánchez and Mella, Dominican Repub., 1972; Order of the Sun, Perú, 1976; 1st Class, Order of Francisco de Miranda, Venezuela, 1976; Order of Piana, Holy See; Order of San Carlos, Colombia; Order of Bernardo O'Higgins, Chile; 1st Class, Al Merito, Korea. *Publications:* contrib. Interamerican Law Year Book and Courses of Internat. Law of the OAS, Washington; various papers for Ecuadorean Year Book of Internat. Law. *Recreations:* chess, tennis. *Address:* González Suárez Avenida, N33–12 Quito, Ecuador. *Club:* Quito Tennis and Golf. *Died 26 June 2014.*

LE PORTZ, Yves; Commandeur de la Légion d'Honneur 1978; Grand Officier de l'Ordre National du Mérite; French financial executive; Inspector-General of Finances, 1971–84; *b* Hennebont, 30 Aug. 1920; *m* 1946, Bernadette Champetier de Ribes; five *c. Educ:* Univ. de Paris à la Sorbonne; Ecole des Hautes Etudes Commerciales; Ecole Libre des Sciences Politiques. Attached to Inspection Générale des Finances, 1943; Directeur Adjoint du Cabinet, Président du Conseil, 1948–49; Sous-Directeur, then Chef de Service, Min. of Finance and Economic Affairs, 1949–51; Directeur du Cabinet: Sec. of State for Finance and Economic Affairs, 1951–52; Minister for Posts, Telegraphs and Telephones (PTT), 1952–55; Minister for Reconstruction and Housing, 1955–57; French Delegate to UN Economic and Social Council, 1957–58; Dir-Gén., Finance, Algeria, 1958–62; Administrateur-Gén., Development Bank of Algeria, 1959–62. European Investment Bank: Vice-Pres. and Vice-Chm., Bd of Dirs, 1962–70; Pres. and Chm. Bd of Dirs, 1970–84; Hon. Pres., 1984. Chairman: Commn des Opérations de Bourse, Paris, 1984–88; Investment Funds Supervisory Cttee, Principality of Monaco, 1988–2002; Statutory Auditors' Ethics Cttee, 1999–2003. *Address:* 127 avenue de Wagram, 75017 Paris, France. *Died 8 Dec. 2013.*

LEPPING, Sir George (Geria Dennis), GCMG 1988; MBE 1981; President, People's Alliance Party, Solomon Islands, 1996; Governor-General of the Solomon Islands, 1988–94; *b* 22 Nov. 1947; *e s* of Chief Dionisio Tanutanu, BEM and Regina Suluki; *m* 1972, Margaret Kwalea Teioli; two *s* four *d* (incl. twins) and one adopted *d. Educ:* St John's and St Peter's Primary Schs; King George VI Secondary Sch.; Agricl Coll., Vudal, PNG (Dip. Tropical Agric.); Reading Univ. (Dip. Agric.; MSc). Joined Solomon Is Public Service as Field Officer, Dept of Agric. and Rural Economy, 1968; Sen. Field Officer, then Under-Sec. (Agricl), Min. of Agric., 1979–80; Permanent Secretary: Min. of Home Affairs and Nat. Develt, 1981–84; Special Duties, as Project Dir, Rural Services Project (Develt), 1984–87; Min. of Finance, 1988; Policy Evaluation Unit, 2002. Sometime Dir, Chm. or Mem., various govt cos and authorities; Chairman: Nat. Disaster Council, 1981–84; Eminent Persons Adv. Gp, Constitutional Reform Unit, 2008–09; Nat. Organising Cttee, 11th Festival of Pacific Art, 2012. Pres., Solomon Is Amateur Athletics Union, 1970–73, 1981–82 (first Solomon Is athlete to win internat. sports medals). KStJ 1991. *Recreations:* reading, swimming, lawn tennis, snooker, snorkelling, high-speed boat driving, fishing. *Address:* PO Box 1431, Honiara, Solomon Islands. *Died 24 Dec. 2014.*

LE QUESNE, Sir (John) Godfray, Kt 1980; QC 1962; Judge of Courts of Appeal of Jersey, 1964–97, and Guernsey, 1964–95; a Recorder, 1972–97; *b* 18 Jan. 1924; 3rd *s* of late C. T. Le Quesne, QC; *m* 1963, Susan Mary Gill; two *s* one *d. Educ:* Shrewsbury Sch.; Exeter Coll., Oxford (MA). Pres. of Oxford Union, 1943. Called to Bar, Inner Temple, 1947; Master of the Bench, Inner Temple, 1969, Reader, 1988, Treasurer, 1989; admitted to bar of St Helena, 1959. Dep. Chm., Lincs (Kesteven) QS, 1963–71. Chm., Monopolies and Mergers Commn, 1975–87 (a part-time Mem., 1974–75). Chm. of Council, Regent's Park Coll., Oxford, 1958–87. *Publications:* Jersey and Whitehall in the Mid-Nineteenth Century, 1992. *Recreations:* music, railways. *Address:* c/o 3 Hare Court, Temple, EC4Y 7BJ. *Died 2 Oct. 2013.*

LE QUESNE, Prof. Leslie Philip, CBE 1984; DM, MCh, FRCS; Medical Administrator, Commonwealth Scholarship Commission, 1984–91; *b* 24 Aug. 1919; *s* of late C. T. Le Quesne, QC; *m* 1969, Pamela Margaret (*d* 1999), *o d* of late Dr A. Fullerton, Batley, Yorks; two *s. Educ:* Rugby; Exeter Coll., Oxford; Middlesex Hosp. Med. Sch. Jun. Demonstrator, Path. and Anat., 1943–45; House Surgeon, Southend Hosp. and St Mark's Hosp., 1945–47; Appointments at Middlesex Hospital: Asst, Surgical Professorial Unit, 1947–52; Asst Dir, Dept of Surgical Studies, 1952–63; Surgeon, 1960–63; Prof. of Surgery, Med. Sch., and Dir, Dept of Surgical Studies, 1963–84; Dep. Vice-Chancellor and Dean, Fac. of Medicine, Univ. of London, 1980–84. Sir Arthur Sims Commonwealth Travelling Prof., 1975. Mem. GMC, 1979–84. Arris and Gale Lectr, RCS, 1952; Baxter Lectr, Amer. Coll. Surgs, 1960. Mem., Ct of Examrs, RCS, 1971–77. Formerly Chm., Assoc. of Profs of Surgery; Pres., Surgical Res. Soc. Chm., The British Jl of Surgery. Hon. FRACS, 1975; Hon. FACS, 1982; Hon. Fellow Imperial Coll. (formerly RPMS), 1985. Moynihan Medal, 1953. *Publications:* medical articles and contribs to text books; Fluid Balance in Surgical Practice, 2nd edn, 1957. *Recreations:* fishing, reading. *Address:* The Charterhouse, Charterhouse Square, EC1M 8AN. *T:* (020) 7608 1722. *Died 5 Aug. 2011.*

LESLIE, James Bolton, AC 1993 (AO 1984); MC 1944; ED 1966; Chancellor, Deakin University, 1987–96; *b* 27 Nov. 1922; *s* of Stuart Deacon Leslie and Dorothy Clare (*née* Murphy); *m* 1955, Alison Baker three *s* (one *d* decd). *Educ:* Trinity Grammar Sch., Melbourne; Harvard Business Sch., Boston, USA. Served war, Australian Infantry, Pacific Theatre, 1941–46. Mobil Oil Australia Ltd: joined, 1946; Manager, Fiji, 1947–50; various postings, Australia, 1950–59; Mobil Corp., New York, 1959–61; Gen. Manager, New South Wales, 1961–66; Director, Mobil Australia, 1966–68; Chm. and Chief Exec., Mobil New Zealand, 1968–72; Chairman: Mobil Australia and Pacific, 1972–80; Qantas Airways, 1980–89; Christies Australia Ltd, 1990–95; Boral Ltd, 1991–94. Chm., Corps of Commissionaires Aust Ltd, 1991–; Dep. Chm., Equity Trustees, 1990–97. Hon. LLD Deakin, 1997. *Recreations:* golf, gardening, art collecting. *Address:* PO Box 73, East Melbourne, Victoria 8002, Australia. *T:* (3) 94196149. *Clubs:* Melbourne, Melbourne Cricket. *Died 28 May 2012.*

LESSING, Mrs Doris (May), CH 2000; CLit 2001; author; *b* Persia, 22 Oct. 1919; *d* of Captain Alfred Cook Tayler and Emily Maude McVeagh; lived in Southern Rhodesia, 1924–49; *m* 1st, 1939, Frank Charles Wisdom (marr. diss. 1943); one *d* (one *s* decd); 2nd, 1945, Gottfried Anton Nicholas Lessing (marr. diss. 1949); (one *s* decd). Associate Member: AAAL, 1974; Nat. Inst. of Arts and Letters (US), 1974. Mem., Inst. for Cultural Res., 1974. Hon. Fellow, MLA (Amer.), 1974. Hon. DLitt: Princeton, 1989; Durham, 1990; Warwick, 1994; Bard Coll., NY State, 1994; Harvard, 1995; London, 1999. Austrian State Prize for European Literature, 1981; Shakespeare Prize, Hamburg, 1982; Grinzane Cavour Award, Italy, 1989; Premio Internacional, Cataluña, 1999; David Cohen British Lit. Prize, 2001; Prince of Asturias Prize, 2001; Nobel Prize for Literature, 2007. *Publications:* The Grass is Singing, 1950 (filmed 1981); This Was the Old Chief's Country, 1951; Martha Quest, 1952; Five, 1953 (Somerset Maugham Award, Soc. of Authors, 1954); A Proper Marriage, 1954; Retreat to Innocence, 1956; The Habit of Loving (short stories), 1957; A Ripple from the Storm, 1958; Fourteen Poems, 1959; In Pursuit of the English, 1960 (adapted for stage, 1990); The Golden Notebook, 1962 (Prix Médicis 1976 for French trans., Carnet d'or); A Man and Two Women (short stories), 1963; African Stories, 1964; Landlocked, 1965; The Four-Gated City, 1969; Briefing for a Descent into Hell, 1971; The Story of a Non-Marrying Man (short stories), 1972; The Summer Before the Dark, 1973; The Memoirs of a Survivor, 1975 (filmed 1981); Collected Stories: Vol. I, To Room Nineteen, 1978; Vol. II, The Temptation of Jack Orkney, 1978; Canopus in Argos: Archives: Re Planet 5, Shikasta, 1979; The Marriages Between Zones Three, Four and Five, 1980; The Sirian Experiments, 1981; The Making of the Representative for Planet 8, 1982 (libretto, 1988); The Sentimental Agents in the Volyen Empire, 1983; The Diaries of Jane Somers, 1984 (Diary of a Good Neighbour, 1983; If the Old Could…, 1984; published under pseudonym Jane Somers); The Good Terrorist, 1985 (W. H. Smith Literary Award, 1986; Palermo Prize and Premio

Internazionale Mondello, 1987); The Fifth Child, 1988; Doris Lessing Reader, 1990; London Observed (short stories), 1992; Love, Again, 1996; Playing the Game, 1996; Mara and Dann: an adventure, 1999; Ben, in the World, 2000; The Sweetest Dream, 2001; The Grandmothers, 2003; The Story of General Dann and Mara's Daughter, Griot and the Snow Dog, 2005; The Cleft, 2006; Alfred and Emily, 2008; *non-fiction:* Going Home, 1957; Particularly Cats, 1966, rev. edn as Particularly Cats and More Cats, 1990; Prisons We Choose to Live Inside, 1986; The Wind Blows Away Our Words, 1987; African Laughter: four visits to Zimbabwe, 1992; Under My Skin: volume one of my autobiography to 1949, 1994 (James Tait Black Meml Prize, 1995; LA Times Book Prize, 1995); A Small Personal Voice, 1994; Walking in the Shade: volume two of my autobiography 1949–1962, 1997; Time Bites (essays), 2004; *play:* Play with a Tiger, 1962. *Address:* c/o Jonathan Clowes Ltd, 10 Iron Bridge House, Bridge Approach, NW1 8BD. *Died 17 Nov. 2013.*

LETWIN, Prof. William; Professor of Political Science, London School of Economics, 1976–88, then Emeritus; *b* 14 Dec. 1922; *s* of Lazar and Bessie Letwin; *m* 1944, Shirley Robin (*d* 1993); one *s*. *Educ:* Univ. of Chicago (BA 1943, PhD 1951); London Sch. of Economics (1948–50). Served US Army, 1943–46. Postdoctoral Fellow, Economics Dept, Univ. of Chicago, 1951–52; Research Associate, Law Sch., Univ. of Chicago, 1953–55; Asst Prof. of Industrial History, MIT, 1955–60; Associate Prof. of Economic History, MIT, 1960–67; Reader in Political Science, LSE, 1966–76. Senior Advisor: Putnam, Hayes & Bartlett, 1988–96; Spectrum Strategy Consultants, 1996–97. Chm., Bd of Studies in Economics, Univ. of London, 1971–73. *Publications:* (ed) Frank Knight, on The History and Method of Economics, 1956; Sir Josiah Child, 1959; Documentary History of American Economic Policy, 1961, 2nd edn 1972; Origins of Scientific Economics 1660–1776, 1963; Law and Economic Policy in America, 1965; (ed) Against Equality, 1983; Freeing the Phones, 1991; articles in learned jls. *Address:* c/o 255 Kennington Road, SE11 6BY. *Died 20 Feb. 2013.*

LEVEN, 14th Earl of, *cr* 1641, **AND MELVILLE,** 13th Earl of, *cr* 1690; **Alexander Robert Leslie Melville;** Baron Melville, 1616; Baron Balgonie, 1641; Viscount Kirkcaldie, 1690; Lord-Lieutenant of Nairn, 1969–99; *b* 13 May 1924; *e s* of 13th Earl of Leven and Lady Rosamond Sylvia Diana Mary Foljambe (*d* 1974), *d* of 1st Earl of Liverpool; *S* father, 1947; *m* 1953, Susan, *er d* of Lieut-Colonel R. Steuart-Menzies of Culdares, Arndilly House, Craigellachie, Banffshire; one *s* one *d* (and one *s* decd). *Educ:* Eton. ADC to Governor General of New Zealand, 1951–52. Formerly Capt. Coldstream Guards; retired, 1952. Vice-Pres., Highland Dist TA. Pres., British Ski Fedn, 1981–85. DL, County of Nairn, 1961; Convener, Nairn CC, 1970–74. Chm. Governors, Gordonstoun Sch., 1971–89. *Heir: g s* Hon. Alexander Ian Leslie Melville, *b* 29 Nov. 1984. *Address:* Raith, Old Spey Bridge, Grantown-on-Spey, Morayshire PH26 3NQ. *T:* (01479) 872908. *Club:* New (Edinburgh). *Died 7 April 2012.*

LEVI-MONTALCINI, Prof. Rita; research scientist; President, European Brain Research Institute, since 2002; *b* 22 April 1909; *d* of Adamo Levi and Adele Montalcini. *Educ:* Turin Univ. Med. Sch. Neurological research, Turin and Brussels, 1936–41, Piemonte, 1941–43; in hiding in Florence, 1943–44; worked among war refugees, Florence, 1944–45; Univ. of Turin, 1945; with Prof. Viktor Hamburger, St Louis, USA, at Washington Univ., 1947–77 (Associate Prof., 1956, Prof., 1958–77); Dir, Inst. of Cell Biology, Italian Nat. Council of Research, Rome, 1969–79, Guest Prof., 1979–. Life Senator, Republic of Italy, 2001. For. Mem., Royal Soc., 1995. (Jtly) Nobel Prize for Physiology or Medicine, 1986. *Publications:* In Praise of Imperfection: my life and work (autobiog.), 1988; articles in learned jls on chemical growth factors controlling growth and development of different cell lines. *Address:* European Brain Research Institute, Via del Fosso di Fiorano 64/65, 00143, Rome, Italy. *Died 30 Dec. 2012.*

LEVINE, Sir Montague (Bernard), Kt 1979; FRCGP, FRCP, FRCPI; general practitioner, 1956–87; HM Coroner, Inner South District, Greater London, 1987–97; Clinical Tutor in General Practice, St Thomas' Hospital, 1972–97; *b* 15 May 1922; *s* of late Philip Levine and of Bessie Levine; *m* 1959, Dr Rose Gold; one *s* one *d*. *Educ:* Royal Coll. of Surgeons in Ireland (LRCSI); Royal Coll. of Physicians in Ireland (MRCPI, LRCPI, LM). DMJ Clin.; FRCGP 1988; FRCPI 2000; FRCP 2002. Licentiate of Rubber Industry, 1944. Industrial physicist, rubber industry, 1939–45; House Surgeon: Royal Victoria Hosp., Bournemouth, 1955; Meath Hosp., Dublin, 1955; Metrop. Police Surg., 1960–66; Asst Dep. Coroner, Inner South London, 1974. Hon. Lectr in Coroners' Law, St Thomas' Hosp. and Guy's Hosp., 1987–97. President: British Acad. of Forensic Sciences, 1993–94; Hunterian Soc., 1997–98. Fellow, Hunterian Soc., 1990. Freeman, Borough of Southwark, 1997. Hon. DSc City, 1997. Royal College of Surgeons in Ireland: Stoney Meml Gold Medal in Anatomy, 1951; Silver Medallist, Medicine, 1953, Pathology, 1953, and Medical Jurisprudence, 1954; MacNaughton Gold Medal in Obs and Gyn., 1955; Lectr in Anat., 1956. *Publications:* Inter-parental Violence and its Effect on Children, 1975; Levine on Coroners' Courts, 1999. *Recreations:* fishing, photography, painting. *Address:* Gainsborough House, 120 Ferndene Road, Herne Hill, SE24 0AA. *T:* (020) 7274 9196. *Club:* Organon. *Died 14 Feb. 2013.*

LEVISON, Rev. Mary Irene; an Extra Chaplain to the Queen in Scotland, since 1993 (Chaplain, 1991–93); *b* 8 Jan. 1923; *d* of late Rev. David Colville Lusk and Mary Theodora Lusk (*née* Colville); *m* 1965, Rev. Frederick Levison (*d* 1999). *Educ:* St Leonard's Sch., St Andrews; Lady Margaret Hall, Oxford (BA); Univ. of Edinburgh (BD). Deaconess in the parish of Inveresk, Musselburgh, 1954–58; Tutor, St Colm's Coll., Edinburgh, 1958–61; Asst Chaplain, Univ. of Edinburgh, 1961–64; Asst Minister, St Andrew's and St George's Church, Edinburgh and Chaplain to the retail trade, 1978–83. Moderator of the Presbytery of Edinburgh, 1988. Vice-Pres., St Leonard's Sch., 1996–2005. Hon. DD Edinburgh, 1994. *Publications:* Wrestling with the Church, 1992. *Recreations:* music, gardening. *Died 12 Sept. 2011.*

LEVY, Prof. Philip Marcus, PhD; CPsychol, FBPsS; Professor of Psychology, University of Lancaster, 1972–94, then Professor Emeritus; *b* 4 Feb. 1934; *s* of late Rupert Hyam Levy and of Sarah Beatrice Levy; *m* 1958, Gillian Mary (*née* Harker) (*d* 2003); two *d*. *Educ:* Leeds Modern School; Univ. of Leeds (BA 1955); Univ. of Birmingham (PhD 1960). Res. Fellow, Birmingham Univ., 1955–59; Psychologist, RAF, 1959–62; Sen. Res. Fellow, Lectr, Sen. Lectr, Birmingham Univ., 1962–72. Economic and Social Research Council (formerly Social Science Research Council): Mem. Council, 1983–86; Mem., Psychol. Cttee, 1976–82 (Chm., 1979–82); Chm., Educn and Human Develt Cttee, 1982–87; Chm., Human Behaviour and Develt R&D Gp, 1987–89 (Mem. Council, 1987–89). British Psychological Society: Mem. Council, 1973–80; Pres., 1978–79. Editor, Brit. Jl of Mathematical and Statistical Psychology, 1975–80. *Publications:* (jtly) Tests in Education, 1984; (jtly) Cognition in Action, 1987; numerous in psychol jls. *Died 23 Jan. 2011.*

LEWERS, Very Rev. Benjamin Hugh; Provost of Derby, 1981–97; *b* 25 March 1932; *s* of late Hugh Bunnett Lewers, DSO, OBE and Coral Helen Lewers; *m* 1957, Sara Blagden; three *s*. *Educ:* Sherborne School; Selwyn Coll., Cambridge (MA); Lincoln Theological Coll. Employee, Dunlop Rubber Co., 1953–57. Curate, St Mary, Northampton, 1962–65; Priest-in-charge, Church of the Good Shepherd, Hounslow, 1965–68; Industrial Chaplain, Heathrow Airport, 1968–75; Vicar of Newark, 1975–80, Rector 1980–81. A Church Commissioner, 1985–97. *Recreations:* cricket, music, gardening, wine and rug making, photography. *Address:* Thimble Cottage, Marshwood, Bridport, Dorset DT6 5QF. *T:* (01297) 678515. *Died 25 March 2015.*

LEWIS OF NEWNHAM, Baron *cr* 1989 (Life Peer), of Newnham in the County of Cambridgeshire; **Jack Lewis,** Kt 1982; FRS 1973; FRSC; (first) Warden of Robinson College, Cambridge, 1975–2001; Professor of Chemistry, University of Cambridge, 1970–95; Hon. Fellow of Sidney Sussex College (Fellow, 1970–77); *b* 13 Feb. 1928; *m* 1951,

Elfreida Mabel (*née* Lamb); one *s* one *d*. *Educ:* Barrow Grammar Sch. BSc London 1949; PhD Nottingham 1952; DSc London 1961; MSc Manchester 1964; MA Cantab 1970; ScD Cantab 1977. Lecturer: Univ. of Sheffield, 1954–56; Imperial Coll., London, 1956–57; Lecturer-Reader, University Coll., London, 1957–61; Prof. of Chemistry: Univ. of Manchester, 1961–67; UCL, 1967–70. Firth Vis. Prof., Univ. of Sheffield, 1967; Vis. Prof., UCL, 1996–; Lectures: Frontiers of Science, Case/Western Reserve, 1963; Tilden, RIC, 1966; Miller, Univ. of Illinois, 1966; Shell, Stanford Univ., 1968; Venables, Univ. of N Carolina, 1968; A. D. Little, MIT, 1970; Boomer, Univ. of Alberta, 1971; AM, Princeton, 1974; Baker, Cornell, 1974; Nyholm, Chem. Soc., 1974; Chini, Italian Chem. Soc., 1980; Bailar, Illinois Univ., 1981; Dwyer, NSW Inst. of Tech., 1982; Power, Queensland Univ., 1982; Mond, Chem. Soc., 1984; Leeumaker, Wesleyan Univ., 1984; Pettit May, Texas, 1985; Nieuwland, Notre Dame, 1986; Wheeler, Dublin, 1987; Bakerian, Roy. Soc., 1989; Sir Jesse Boot Foundn, Nottingham, 1989; Garner, 1993; Gordon Stone, 1993; Shell, Edinburgh, 1994. Member: CNAA Cttee, 1964–70; Exec. Cttee, Standing Cttee on Univ. Entry, 1966–76; Schs Council, 1966–70; SERC (formerly SRC): Polytechnics Cttee, 1973–79; Chemistry Cttee (Chm., 1975–82); Science Bd, 1975–79; Council, 1979–84; SERC/SSRC Jt Cttee, 1979–84; UGC (Phys. Sci.), 1973–79; Council, Royal Soc., 1982–84 (a Vice-Pres., 1984); Vis. Cttee, Cranfield Inst. of Tech., 1982–92 (Chm., 1985–92); Royal Commn on Environmental Pollution, 1985–92 (Chm., 1986–92); Chairman: Standing Cttee on Structural Safety, 1998–2002; ESART Bd, 1998–. Mem., H of L European Communities Select Cttee, 1993–95, 1997–2001 (Chm. Sub-Cttee C, 1993–95). Pres., Royal Soc. of Chemistry, 1986–88 (Hon. Fellow, 1998); Sci. Rep. for UK on NATO Sci. Cttee, 1986–98. Trustee: Kennedy Meml Trust, 1989–99; Croucher Foundn, 1989–98. Dir, BOC Foundn, 1990–2003. Pres., Arthritis Res. UK (formerly Arthritis Res. Campaign), 1998–. Hon. Pres., Envmtl Industries Commn, 1996–2000. Patron, Student Community Action Develt Unit, 1985–. Hon. Mem., SCI, 1996. Chm. Govs, Leys Sch., 1997–2002. FNA 1980 (For. Fellow 1986); Foreign Member: Amer. Acad. of Arts and Science, 1983; Amer. Philos. Soc., 1994; Accademia Nazionale dei Lincei, Italy, 1995; Polish Acad. of Arts and Scis, 1996; Fellow, Indian Nat. Sci. Acad., 1985; For. Fellow, Bangladesh Acad. of Scis, 1992; For. Associate, Nat. Acad. of Sciences, USA, 1987; Hon. Fellow: Aust. Inst. of Chem., 1987; Inst. of Chem. of Ireland, 2011. Hon. Fellow: UCL, 1990; UMIST, 1990; Central Lancs, 1993. Dr *hc* Rennes, 1980; DUniv: Open, 1982; Kingston, 1993; Hon. DSc: East Anglia, 1983; Nottingham, 1983; Keele, 1984; Leicester, 1988; Birmingham, 1988; Waterloo, Canada, 1988; Manchester, 1990; Wales (Swansea), 1990; Sheffield, 1992; Cranfield, 1993; Edinburgh, 1994; Bath, 1995; Durham, 1996; Hong Kong, 1998; NUI, 1999; Anglia, 2004. American Chem. Soc. Award in Inorganic Chemistry, 1970; Transition Metal Award, Chem. Soc., 1973; Davy Medal, Royal Soc., 1985; Mallinckrodt Award in Inorganic Chemistry, American Chem. Soc., 1986; Gold Medal, Apothecaries Soc., 1993; Paracelsus Prize and Gold Medal, New Swiss Chemical Soc., 1996; Sir Geoffrey Wilkinson Prize, Elsevier Science SA, 1997; August Wilhelm von Hofmann Denkmünze Meml Medal, German Chemical Soc., 1999; Royal Medal, Royal Soc., 2004. Chevalier, Ordre des Palmes Académiques, 1993; Commander, Cross of the Order of Merit (Poland), 1996. *Publications:* papers, mainly in Jl of Chem. Soc. *Address:* Robinson College, Grange Road, Cambridge CB3 9AN. *Club:* Oxford and Cambridge. *Died 17 July 2014.*

LEWIS, (Alun) Kynric; QC 1978; QC (NI) 1988; a Recorder of the Crown Court, 1979–97; *b* Harlech, 23 May 1928; 3rd *s* of late Rev. Cadwaladr O. Lewis and Ursula Lewis; *m* 1955, Bethan, *er d* of late Prof. Edgar Thomas, CBE, and Eurwen Thomas; one *s* two *d*. *Educ:* The Grammar School, Beaumaris; University Coll. of N Wales (BSc); London School of Economics (LLB). Barrister, Middle Temple, 1954, Bencher, 1988; Gray's Inn, 1961; in practice in intellectual property law chambers, 1955–98. Asst Comr, Parly Boundary Commn for Wales, 1996–99. Member: Cttees of Investigation for GB and England and Wales under Agricl Marketing Act, 1979–88; Parole Bd, 1982–85; Welsh Arts Council, 1986–92. Hon. Counsel, Welsh Books Council, 1989–2002. *Recreations:* walking, fishing, gardening. *Address:* Penrallt, Llys-faen, Caerdydd CF14 0TG; 8 New Square, Lincoln's Inn, WC2A 3QP. *Died 4 June 2015.*

LEWIS, Anthony; *see* Lewis, Joseph A.

LEWIS, David Whitfield, RDI 1995; freelance design consultant, since 1967; *b* 19 Feb. 1939; *s* of John Whitfield Lewis and Joan Lewis; *m* 1964, Marianne Mygind; one *s* one *d*. *Educ:* Central Sch. of Design, London. Employed by Danish design consultancy, working on radio and television equipment designs, incl. designs for Beolab 5000 Series Hi-Fi music systems for Bang & Olufsen, and invented slide rule motif, 1960–68; collaborated with Henning Moldenhawer on television equipment for Bang & Olufsen, and industrial processing machinery and marine products, 1968–80; work included in Design Collection, Mus. of Modern Art, NY. Hon. FRIBA, 2007. ID Prize, Danish Design Centre, 1976 (marine folding propeller), 1982 (dental tools), 1986 (television set), 1990 (push button system), 1994 (audio system); Design Prize, EC, 1988; MITI, G-Mark Grand Prix, 1991 (audio hi-fi system); Internat. Design Prize, Baden-Württemberg, 1993 (audio hi-fi system); Annual Prize, Danish Design Council, 2003. Knight of the Order of Dannebrog (Denmark), 2003. *Address:* David Lewis Designers Aps, Blegdamsvej 28F, 2200 Copenhagen N, Denmark. *T:* 33139635; Piniehøj 2, 2960 Rungsted Kyst, Denmark. *Died 8 Nov. 2011.*

LEWIS, His Honour Esyr ap Gwilym; QC 1971; a Circuit Judge (Official Referee), 1984–98; Senior Official Referee, 1994–98; *b* 11 Jan. 1926; *s* of late Rev. T. W. Lewis, BA, and Mary Jane May Lewis (*née* Selway); *m* 1957, Elizabeth Anne Vidler Hoffmann, 2nd *d* of O. W. Hoffmann, Bassett, Southampton; four *d*. *Educ:* Salford Grammar Sch.; Mill Hill Sch.; Trinity Hall, Cambridge (MA, LLM). Served in Intelligence Corps, 1944–47. Exhibitioner, 1944, Scholar, 1948, at Trinity Hall (Dr Cooper's Law Studentship, 1950); 1st cl. hons, Law Tripos II, 1949, 1st cl. LLB, 1950, Cambridge. Holker Sen. Schol., Gray's Inn, 1950; Called to Bar, Gray's Inn, 1951 (Bencher, 1978; Treas., 1997). Law Supervisor, Trinity Hall, 1950–55; Law Lectr, Cambridgeshire Technical Coll., 1949–50. A Recorder, 1972–84; a Dep. High Court Judge, 1978–84; Leader, Wales and Chester Circuit, 1978–81. Member: Bar Council, 1965–68; Council of Legal Education, 1967–73; Criminal Injuries Compensation Bd, 1977–84. Contested (L) Llanelli, 1964. *Publications:* contributor to Newnes Family Lawyer, 1963. *Recreations:* reading, gardening, watching Rugby football. *Address:* 2 South Square, Gray's Inn, WC1R 5HP. *T:* (020) 7405 5918. *Clubs:* Garrick; Old Millhillians. *Died 25 March 2011.*

LEWIS, Prof. Gwynne, DPhil; Professor of History, University of Warwick, 1984–97, then Emeritus; *b* 4 Nov. 1933; *s* of Rev. Dewi Emlyn Lewis and Elizabeth May Lewis; *m* 1960, Madeline Ann Rosser (*d* 2006); two *s* one *d*. *Educ:* Pontypridd Grammar Sch.; UCW, Aberystwyth (BA); Univ. of Manchester (MA); DPhil Oxford. Asst Lectr, 1963–65, Lectr, 1965–68, UCW, Aberystwyth; University of Warwick: Lectr, 1968–74; Sen. Lectr, 1974–80; Reader, 1980–84; Dir, Centre for Social Hist., 1992–97. Hon. Vis. Fellow, Southampton Univ., 1997–2001. *Publications:* Life in Revolutionary France, 1971; The Second Vendee, 1978; The Advent of Modern Capitalism in France 1770–1840, 1993; The French Revolution: rethinking the debate, 1993; France 1715–1804: power and the people, 2004; Madame de Pompadour's Protégé: Henri Bertin and the collapse of Bourbon absolutism *c* 1750–1792, 2011. *Recreations:* music, Rugby, walking, Paris. *Address:* 9 Balmoral Quays, Penarth, Vale of Glamorgan CF64 3NS. *Died 10 Dec. 2014.*

LEWIS, Henry Nathan; company director; *b* 29 Jan. 1926; *m* 1953, Jenny Cohen (*d* 2014); one *s* two *d*. *Educ:* Hollywood Park Council Sch., Stockport; Stockport Sch.; Manchester Univ. (BA Com); LSE. Served RAF (Flt Lt), 1944–48. Joined Marks & Spencer, 1950; Dir, 1965; Jt Man. Dir responsible for textiles, 1973–76, 1983–85, for foods, 1976–83; retired 1985. Chm., Primrose Care Ltd, 1992–97; Dep. Chm., S&W Berisford, subseq. Berisford

Internat., 1987–90; Director: Dixons Group, 1985–95; Hunter Saphir, 1987–91; Porter Chadburn (formerly LDH Group), 1987–2000; Delta Galil, 1988–2000; Gabicci, 1992–93; Cupid, 1993–94; Oasis, 1994–2000; Value Retail, 1994–2005; Electronics Boutique plc (formerly Rhino), 1995–2000; Uno plc, 1996–99. *Address:* Flat 15, Pavilion Court, Frognal Rise, NW3 6PZ. *Died 31 Jan. 2015.*

LEWIS, Ian Talbot; Under Secretary (Legal), Treasury Solicitor's Office, 1982–90; *b* 7 July 1929; *s* of late Cyril Frederick Lewis, CBE and Marjorie (*née* Talbot); *m* 1st, 1962, Patricia Anne (*née* Hardy) (marr. diss. 1978); two *s*; 2nd, 1986, Susan Lydia Sargant (*d* 2011). *Educ:* Marlborough Coll. Admitted Solicitor, 1951. National Service, 3rd The King's Own Hussars, 1952–53. Solicitor, private practice, London, 1954–57; Treasury Solicitor's Office: Legal Asst, 1957; Sen. Legal Asst, 1963; Asst Treasury Solicitor, 1977. Chm., Penshurst Parish Council, 1994–96. Chm., Fordcombe Soc., 1990–94; Trustee, Fordcombe Village Hall, 1997–2007. Gov., Fordcombe C of E Primary Sch., 1991–93. Trustee, Penshurst Retreat Charity, 1993–2002. Liveryman, Merchant Taylors' Co., 1966–. *Recreations:* sport, natural history, modern first editions, theatre. *Address:* Gables, Fordcombe, near Tunbridge Wells, Kent TN3 0RY. *T:* (01892) 740413. *Clubs:* Cavalry and Guards, MCC; Blackheath Football (Rugby Union) (Past Pres.); Blackheath Cricket (Hon. Vice Pres.); Falconhurst Cricket (Vice-Pres.); Fordcombe Cricket (Pres., 2005–07). *Died 5 Sept. 2012.*

LEWIS, Prof. Ioan Myrddin, DPhil; FBA 1986; Professor of Anthropology, London School of Economics and Political Science, 1969–93, then Emeritus; Consultative Director, International African Institute, since 1988 (Hon. Director, 1981–88); *b* 30 Jan. 1930; *s* of John Daniel Lewis and Mary Stevenson Scott (*née* Brown); *m* 1954, Ann Elizabeth Keir; one *s* three *d*. *Educ:* Glasgow High Sch.; Glasgow Univ. (BSc 1951); Oxford Univ. (Dip. in Anthrop., 1952; BLitt 1953; DPhil 1957). Res. Asst to Lord Hailey, Chatham House, 1954–55; Colonial SSRC Fellow, 1955–57; Lectr in African Studies, University Coll. of Rhodesia and Nyasaland, 1957–60; Lectr in Social Anthrop., Glasgow Univ., 1960–63; Lectr, then Reader in Anthrop., UCL, 1963–69. Hitchcock Prof., Univ. of Calif at Berkeley, 1977; Vis. Professor: Univ. of Helsinki, Finland, 1982; Univ. of Rome, 1983; Univ. of Malaya, 1986; Univ. of Kyoto, 1986; Univ. of Naples, 1989; Univ. of Addis Ababa, 1992; CNRS, Marseille, 1993. Malinowski Meml Lectr, London, 1966; Blackwood Lectr, Oxford, 1994. Hon. Sec., Assoc. of Social Anthropologists of the Commonwealth, 1964–67; Member: Council and Standing Cttee of Council, Royal Anthropol Inst., 1965–67 and 1981–84 (Vice-Pres., 1992–96); Court of Governors and Standing Cttee, LSE, 1984–88; Internat. Cttee, Centro di Ricerca e Documentazione Febbraio '74, 1980–; Patron, Africa Educnl Trust (formerly African Educn Trust), 2010– (Trustee, 1992; Chm., 1993). Editor, Man (Jl of RAI), 1969–72. *Publications:* Peoples of the Horn of Africa, 1955, 3rd edn 1994; A Pastoral Democracy: pastoralism and politics among the Northern Somali of the Horn of Africa, 1961, 3rd edn 1999 (trans. Italian); (with B. W. Andrzejewski) Somali Poetry, 1964, 2nd edn 1968; The Modern History of Somaliland: from nation to state, 1965, 4th edn as A Modern History of the Somali: nation and state, 2002; Ecstatic Religion, 1971, 3rd edn 2002 (trans. Dutch, Italian, French, Portuguese and Japanese); Social Anthropology in Perspective, 1976, 4th edn 1990 (trans. Italian and Chinese); Religion in Context: cults and charisma, 1986 (trans. German and Italian), rev. edn 1996; (ed and introd): Islam in Tropical Africa, 1966, 3rd edn 1980; History and Anthropology, 1968 (trans. Spanish); Symbols and Sentiments: cross-cultural studies in symbolism, 1977; (co-ed with Fred Eggan and C. von Fürer-Haimendorf), Atlas of Mankind, 1982; Nationalism and Self-Determination in the Horn of Africa, 1983; (co-ed with Gustav Jahoda) Acquiring Culture: cross cultural studies in child development, 1988; (ed jtly) Women's Medicine: the Zar-Bori Cult in Africa and beyond, 1991; Understanding Somalia, 1993; Blood and Bone: the call of Kinship in Somali society, 1994; (co-ed with R. J. Hayward) Voice and Power: the culture of language in North-East Africa, 1996; Saints and Somalis: Islam in a clan-based society, 1998; Arguments with Ethnography: comparative approaches to history, politics and religion, 1999, 2nd edn 2004; Social and Cultural Anthropology, 2003; Understanding Somalia and Somaliland, 2008; Making and Breaking States in Africa: the Somali experience, 2010; contrib. learned jls. *Recreations:* travel, fishing. *Address:* 26 Bramshill Gardens, NW5 1JH. *T:* (020) 7272 1722. *Died 14 March 2014.*

LEWIS, (Joseph) Anthony; writer; Chief London Correspondent, New York Times, 1965–72, editorial columnist, 1969–2001; Lecturer in Law, Harvard Law School, 1974–89; James Madison Visiting Professor, Columbia University, 1983–2008; *b* 27 March 1927; *s* of Kassel Lewis and Sylvia Lewis (*née* Surut), NYC; *m* 1st, 1951, Linda (marr. diss. 1982), *d* of John Rannells, NYC; one *s* two *d*; 2nd, 1984, Margaret, *d* of Bernard Charles Marshall, Osterville, Mass. *Educ:* Horace Mann Sch., NY; Harvard Coll. (BA). Sunday Dept, New York Times, 1948–52; Reporter, Washington Daily News, 1952–55; Legal Corresp., Washington Bureau, NY Times, 1955–64; Nieman Fellow, Harvard Law Sch., 1956–57. Governor, Ditchley Foundation, 1965–72. Member: Amer. Acad. of Arts and Scis, 1991; Amer. Philosophical Soc., 2005. Pulitzer Prize for Nat. Correspondence, 1955 and 1963; Heywood Broun Award, 1955; Overseas Press Club Award, 1970. Hon. DLitt: Adelphi Univ., NY, 1964; Rutgers Univ., NJ, 1973; NY Med. Coll., 1976; Williams Coll., Mass, 1978; Clark Univ., Mass, 1982; Hon. LLD: Syracuse, 1979; Colby Coll., 1983; Northeastern Univ., Mass, 1987. Presidential Citizens Medal (US), 2001. *Publications:* Gideon's Trumpet, 1964; Portrait of a Decade: The Second American Revolution, 1964; Make No Law: the Sullivan case and the First Amendment, 1991; Freedom for the Thought That We Hate: a biography of the First Amendment, 2008; articles in American law reviews. *Recreation:* dinghy sailing. *Address:* 1010 Memorial Drive, Cambridge, MA 02138, USA. *Died 25 March 2013.*

LEWIS, Dr Julian Hart, FRS 2012; Group Leader, Vertebrate Development Laboratory, Cancer Research UK London Research Institute, 1996–2011, then Emeritus Scientist; *b* London, 12 Aug. 1946; *s* of Sir Aubrey Julian Lewis and Dr Hilda N. Lewis; *m* 1983, Sherry L. Granum; three *d*. *Educ:* St Paul's Sch., London; Balliol Coll., Oxford (BA 1967; DPhil 1971; MA 1987). Res. Fellow, Inst. for Physical Problems, Moscow, 1970–71; Res. Asst, Middx Hosp. Med. Sch., 1971–78; Lectr, 1978–86, Sen. Lectr, 1986, KCL; Sen. Scientist, ICRF Develt Biol. Unit, Oxford, 1986–96. Vis. Associate Prof., UCSF, 1987–88; Hon. Reader, 1997, Hon. Prof., 1999, UCL. Mem., EMBO, 2005–. Waddington Medal, British Soc. Develtl Biol., 2003. *Publications:* (jtly) Molecular Biology of the Cell, 1983, 5th edn 2008; (jtly) Essential Cell Biology, 1998, 3rd edn 2010; contrib. papers to scientific jls. *Recreations:* languages, Russian literature, films, books, woodwork, microscopes. *Address:* Cancer Research UK London Research Institute, 44 Lincoln's Inn Fields, WC2A 3LY. *E:* julian.lewis@cancer.org.uk. *Died 30 April 2014.*

LEWIS, Kynric; *see* Lewis, A. K.

LEWIS, Trevor Oswin, CBE 1983; DL; *b* 29 Nov. 1935; *s* of 3rd Baron Merthyr, KBE, TD, PC, and Violet, *y d* of Brig.-Gen. Sir Frederick Charlton Meyrick, 2nd Bt, CB, CMG; *S* father, 1977, as 4th Baron Merthyr, but disclaimed his peerage for life; also as 4th Bt (*cr* 1896) but does not use the title; *m* 1964, Susan Jane, *yr d* of A. J. Birt-Llewellin; one *s* three *d*. *Educ:* Downs Sch.; Eton; Magdalen Coll., Oxford; Magdalene Coll., Cambridge. Member: Landscape Adv. Cttee, Dept of Transport, 1968–92 (Chm., 1991–92); Countryside Commn, 1973–83 (Dep. Chm., 1980–83); Chm., Countryside Commn's Cttee for Wales, 1973–80. JP Pembs, then Dyfed, 1969–94; DL Dyfed, 1994. *Heir:* (*to disclaimed peerage*): *s* David Trevor Lewis, *b* 21 Feb. 1977. *Address:* Hean Castle, Saundersfoot SA69 9AL. *T:* (01834) 810347. *Died 5 Aug. 2015.*

LI, Fook Kow, CMG 1975; JP; Chairman, Public Service Commission, Hong Kong, 1980–87; *b* 15 June 1922; *s* of Tse Fong Li; *m* 1946, Edith Kwong Li (*d* 1992); two *s* two *d*. *Educ:* Massachusetts Inst. of Technology (BSc, MSc). Mem. Hong Kong Admin. Service; Teacher, 1948–54; various departmental posts and posts in the Government

Secretariat, 1955–60; Asst Financial Sec., Asst Estabt Officer, Dep. Financial Sec. and Estabt Officer, 1961–69; Dep. Dir of Commerce and Industry, 1970; Dep. Sec. for Home Affairs, 1971–72; Dir of Social Welfare, 1972; Sec. for Social Services, 1973; Sec. for Home Affairs, 1977–80. JP Hong Kong, 1959. *Address:* H22 Celeste Court, 12 Fung Fai Terrace, Hong Kong. *Clubs:* Hong Kong Jockey, Hong Kong Country. *Died 27 Oct. 2011.*

LI, Simon Fook Sean, GBM 1997; *b* 19 April 1922; 3rd *s* of late Koon Chun Li and Doy Hing Tam Li; *m* Marie Veronica Lillian Yang; four *s* one *d. Educ:* King's Coll., Hong Kong; Hong Kong Univ.; Nat. Kwangsi Univ.; University Coll., London Univ. (LLB 1950; Fellow, 1991). Barrister-at-Law, Lincoln's Inn, 1951. Crown Counsel, Attorney-General's Chambers, Hong Kong, 1953; Senior Crown Counsel, 1962; District Judge, 1966–71, Puisne Judge, 1971–80, Justice of Appeal, 1980–84, Vice-Pres., Court of Appeal, 1984–87, Hong Kong. Dir, Bank of East Asia Ltd, Hong Kong, 1987–2006. Chm., Insce Claims Complaints Bd, 1990–94; Mem., Hong Kong Special Admin. Region Basic Law Drafting Cttee, 1985–90. PR China: Hong Kong Affairs Advr, 1992–97; Dep. Dir, Preliminary Working Cttee, 1993–95, and HK Special Admin. Region Prep. Cttee, 1996–97. Hon. LLD 1986, Hon. Fellow 2002, Chinese Univ., Hong Kong. *Recreations:* hiking, swimming. *Address:* 3/F Shun Pont Comm. Bldg, 5–11 Thomson Road, Wanchai, Hong Kong. *T:* 28668680. *Clubs:* Royal Commonwealth Society; Hong Kong (Chm., 1995–96), Hong Kong Jockey (Hon. Steward) (Hong Kong). *Died 26 Feb. 2013.*

LIDDELL, Alasdair Donald MacDuff, CBE 1997; independent healthcare consultant; *b* 15 Jan. 1949; *s* of late Donald Liddell and Barbara Liddell (*née* Dixon); *m* 1976, Jennifer Gita Abramsky (Dame Jennifer Abramsky, DBE); one *s* one *d. Educ:* Balliol College, Oxford (BA Hons Jurisp. 1970); DMS Thames Polytechnic; LHA. King's College and Royal Free Hosps, 1972–77; Administrator (Planning and Policy), Tower Hamlets HA, 1977–79; Area Gen. Administrator, Kensington and Chelsea and Westminster AHA (T), 1979–82; District Administrator, Hammersmith and Fulham HA, 1982–84; District Administrator later District Gen. Manager, Bloomsbury HA, 1984–88; Regl Gen. Manager, E Anglian RHA, 1988–94; Dir of Planning, DoH, 1994–2000. Dir, HCL plc, 2005–11 (Dep. Chm., 2007–11). Sen. Associate, King's Fund, 2006–11 (Internat. Fellow, 1987–88). Trustee, Cambodia Trust, 1999–2004; Jt Chm. and Founder, Assoc. for Public Health, 1992–94. Fellow, Young Foundn, 2012–. FRSA 2012. *Publications:* (contrib.) In Dreams Begins Responsibility: a tribute to Tom Evans, 1987; (jtly) Towards an Effective NHS, 1993; (jtly) Windmill 2007: the future of health care reforms in England, 2007; (jtly) Making it Happen: next steps in NHS reform, 2008; (jtly) Technology in the NHS: transforming the patients' experience of care, 2008; (jtly) Windmill 2009: NHS response to the financial storm, 2009. *Recreations:* skiing, playing with computers, buying French wine. *Address:* 3 Brookfield Park, NW5 1ES. *T:* (020) 7485 7465. *E:* alasdair@aliddell.com. *Died 31 Dec. 2012.*

LIDDIARD, Ronald; aviation, management and public administration consultant, 1997–2014; *b* 26 July 1932; *s* of Tom and Gladys Liddiard; *m* 1957, June Alexandra (*née* Ford); two *d. Educ:* Canton High Sch., Cardiff; Colleges of Commerce and Technology, Cardiff; Inst. of Local Govt Studies, Birmingham Univ.; Oxford Air Training Sch. Dip. Municipal Admin; CSW; ATPL. Health Administrator, 1958–60; Social Worker, 1960–64; Sen. Welfare Administrator, 1964–70; Dir of Social Services: Bath, 1971–74; Birmingham, 1974–85; professional air transport pilot, 1987–97; commercial flying instructor. Hon. Kentucky Col, 1977. *Publications:* How to Become an Airline Pilot, 1989; chapters in: Innovations in the Care of the Elderly, 1984; Self-Care and Health in Old Age, 1986; articles in social work, aviation, management and health jls. *Died 6 July 2014.*

LIGHTBODY, Ian (Macdonald), CMG 1974; Chairman, Public Services Commission, Hong Kong, 1978–80; *b* 19 Aug. 1921; *s* of Thomas Paul Lightbody and Dorothy Marie Louise Lightbody (*née* Cooper); *m* 1954, Noreen, *d* of late Captain T. H. Wallace, Dromore, Co. Down; three *s* one *d. Educ:* Queen's Park Sch., Glasgow; Glasgow Univ. (MA). War service, Indian Army, India and Far East, 1942–46 (Captain); Colonial Admin. Service, Hong Kong, 1945; various admin. posts; District Comr, New Territories, 1967–68; Defence Sec., 1968–69; Coordinator, Festival of Hong Kong, 1969; Comr for Resettlement, 1971; Sec. for Housing and Chm., Hong Kong Housing Authority, 1973–77; Sec. for Admin, Hong Kong, 1977–78. MLC 1971; MEC 1977; retd from Hong Kong, 1980. Mem., Arun DC, 1983–91. *Recreation:* reading. *Address:* Flat 18, Providence Place, Chapel Street, Chichester, Sussex PO19 1BS. *Died 10 March 2015.*

LIGHTMAN, Ivor Harry, CB 1984; Chairman of Trustees, Autism Cymru, 2002–08; *b* 23 Aug. 1928; *s* of late Abraham Lightman, OBE and Mary Lightman (*née* Goldschneider); *m* 1950, Stella Doris Blend; one *s. Educ:* Abergele Grammar Sch. Clerical Officer, Min. of Food, 1946; Officer of Customs and Excise, 1949–56; Asst Principal, then Principal, Ministry of Works, 1957–65; HM Treasury, 1965–67; Assistant Secretary: MPBW, 1967–70; CSD, 1970–73; Under Secretary: Price Commn, 1973–76; Dept of Prices and Consumer Protection, 1976–78; Dept of Industry, 1978–81; Dep. Sec., Welsh Office, 1981–88, retd. Member: Parole Bd, 1990–94; Bd of Deputies of British Jews, 2006–08. Chm., First Choice Housing Assoc., 1989–94; Mem. Bd, United Welsh Housing Assoc., 1994–2003; Chm., All-Wales Adv. Panel on Services for Mentally Handicapped People, 1990–96. Chm., Cardiff Univ. of Third Age, 2000–05. *Address:* 6 Clos Coedydafarn, Lisvane, Cardiff CF14 0ER. *Died 4 Dec. 2013.*

LILLEY, Prof. Geoffrey Michael, OBE 1981; CEng, FRSA, FRAeS, MIMechE, FIMA; Professor of Aeronautics and Astronautics, University of Southampton, 1964–84, then Emeritus Professor; Vice President, INTECH (formerly Hampshire Technology Centre), since 2007 (Founder Member, 1985; Director, 1985–2007); *b* Isleworth, Middx, 16 Nov. 1919; *m* 1948, Leslie Marion Wheeler (*d* 1996); one *s* two *d. Educ:* Isleworth Grammar Sch.; Battersea and Northampton Polytechnics; Imperial Coll. BSc(Eng) 1944, MSc(Eng) 1945, DIC 1945. RAF, 1935–36. Gen. engrg trng, Benham and Kodak, 1936–40; Drawing Office and Wind Tunnel Dept, Vickers Armstrong Ltd, Weybridge, 1940–46; Coll. of Aeronautics: Lectr, 1946–51; Sen. Lectr, 1951–55; Dep. Head of Dept of Aerodynamics, 1955, and Prof. of Experimental Fluid Mechanics, 1962–64. Visiting Professor: Stanford Univ., 1977–78; ME Technical Univ., Ankara, Turkey, 1983–90; Univ. of the Witwatersrand, 1990; Visiting Scientist: Inst. of Computer Applications in Sci. and Engrg, NASA Langley Res. Center, 1992–94, 1997–2006 (Chief Scientist, 1998–2000); Center for Turbulence Res., Stanford Univ., 1995–96. Past Member: Aeronautical Res. Council (past Mem. Council and Chm. Aerodynamics, Applied Aerodynamics, Noise Res., Fluid Motion and Performance Cttees); Noise Advisory Council (Chm., Noise from Air Traffic Working Group); Past Chm., Aerodynamics Cttee, Engrg Sci. Data Unit. Consultant to: Rolls Royce, 1959–61, 1967–84; AGARD, 1959–63 and 1988–89; OECD, 1969–71. FAIAA 2009. Hon. DSc Southampton, 2004. Gold Medal for Aeronautics, RAeS, 1983; Aerodynamic Noise Medal, AIAA, 1985. *Publications:* (jt editor) Proc. Stanford Conf. on Complex Turbulent Flows; articles in reports and memoranda of: Aeronautical Research Council; Royal Aeronautical Soc., and other jls. *Recreations:* music, chess, walking. *Address:* Plovers, Station Road, Sway, Lymington, Hants SO41 6AA. *T:* (01590) 681018. *Club:* Athenæum. *Died 20 Sept. 2015.*

LIM FAT, Sir (Maxime) Edouard (Lim Man), Kt 1991; Professor Emeritus, University of Mauritius, since 1975; company director; *b* 5 Oct. 1921; *s* of V. Lim Fat and S. Lifo; *m* 1952, Y. H. Chan Wah Hak; two *s* one *d. Educ:* Univ. of London (BSc Chem. Eng.); Univ. of Newcastle (MSc Agric. Eng.). AEE Harwell, 1950–51; Engineer, Min. of Agriculture, Mauritius, 1951–63; Principal, Mauritius Coll. of Agriculture, 1963–68; Head, Sch. of Industrial Technology, Univ. of Mauritius, 1968–80; Director: Bank of Mauritius, 1980–92; NEDC, 1991–; two factories; Chm., Mauritius Freeport, 1992–. *Publications:* From Vision to Miracle (autobiog.), 2010; numerous articles, mainly on industrial develt and educn.

Recreations: golf, economics, music. *Address:* 19 Rev. Lebrun Street, Rose-hill, Mauritius. *T:* (home) 4547680, *T:* (office) 4548288, *Fax:* 4545656. *Club:* Gymkhana Golf (Vacoas). *Died 2 March 2015.*

LIMON, Sir Donald (William), KCB 1997 (CB 1993); Clerk of the House of Commons, 1994–97; *b* 29 Oct. 1932; *s* of late Arthur and Dora Limon; *m* 1987, Joyce Beatrice Clifton. *Educ:* Durham Cathedral Chorister Sch.; Durham Sch.; Lincoln Coll., Oxford (MA). A Clerk in the House of Commons, 1956–97: Sec. to House of Commons Commn, 1979–81; Clerk of Financial Cttees, 1981–84; Principal Clerk, Table Office, 1985–89; Clerk of Cttees, 1989–90; Clerk Asst, 1990–94. *Publications:* (ed jtly) Erskine May's Parliamentary Practice, 22nd edn 1997. *Recreations:* cricket, golf, singing. *Died 26 July 2012.*

LINACRE, Sir (John) Gordon (Seymour), Kt 1986; CBE 1979; AFC 1943; DFM 1941; Deputy Chairman, United Newspapers plc, 1981–91 (Director, 1969–91; Joint Managing Director, 1981–83; Chief Executive, 1983–88); President, Yorkshire Post Newspapers Ltd, since 1990 (Managing Director, 1965–83; Deputy Chairman, 1981–83; Chairman, 1983–90); *b* 23 Sept. 1920; *s* of John James Linacre and Beatrice Barber (*née* Seymour); *m* 1943, Irene Amy (*née* Gordon) (*d* 2013); two *d*. *Educ:* Firth Park Grammar Sch., Sheffield. Served War, RAF, 1939–46, Sqdn Ldr. Journalistic appts, Sheffield Telegraph/Star, 1937–47; Kemsley News Service, 1947–50; Dep. Editor: Newcastle Journal, 1950–56; Newcastle Evening Chronicle, 1956–57; Editor, Sheffield Star, 1958–61; Asst Gen. Man., Sheffield Newspapers Ltd, 1961–63; Exec. Dir, Thomson Regional Newspapers Ltd, London, 1963–65. Chairman: United Provincial Newspapers Ltd, 1983–88; Sheffield Newspapers Ltd, 1981–88; Lancashire Evening Post Ltd, 1982–88; Northampton Mercury Co. Ltd, 1983–88; The Reporter Ltd, 1970–88; Blackpool Gazette & Herald Ltd, 1984–88; Chameleon Television, 1992–2008; Dep. Chm., Express Newspapers, 1985–88; Director: United Newspapers (Publications) Ltd, 1969–88; Trident Television Ltd, 1970–84; Yorkshire Television Ltd, 1967–90. Dir, INCA/FIEJ Res. Assoc., Darmstadt, Germany, 1971–79 (Pres., 1974–77); Pres. FIEJ, 1984–88 (Mem. Bd, 1971–90). Dir, ASA, 1991–94; Member: Newspaper Soc. Council, 1966–90 (Pres., Newspaper Soc., 1978–79); Press Assoc., 1967–74 (Chm., 1970–71); Reuters Ltd, 1970–74 (Trustee, 1974–98); Evening Newspaper Advertising Bureau Ltd, 1966–78 (Chm., 1975–76); N Eastern Postal Bd, 1974–80; Adv. Bd, Yorks and Lincs, BIM, 1973–75; Health Educn Council, 1973–77; Leeds TEC, 1989–91 (Chm.). Mem., ENO, 1978–81; Chm., 1978–98, Pres., 1998–, Opera North (formerly English Nat. Opera North). Governor, Harrogate Festival of Arts and Sciences Ltd, 1973–2003 (Pres., 1992–2003). Trustee, Yorks and Lincs Trustee Savings Bank, 1972–78; Mem. Council, 1985–93, and Court, 1995–2000, Chm. Foundation, 1989–2000, Leeds Univ. CCMI (FBIM 1973). Kt, Order of White Rose (Finland), 1987; Grande Ufficiale al Merito della Repubblica Italiana, 1988 (Commendatore, 1973). *Recreations:* golf, fishing, walking. *Clubs:* Alwoodley Golf; Burnsall Angling. *Died 5 Feb. 2015.*

LIND, Per; Swedish Ambassador to the Court of St James's, 1979–82; *b* 8 Jan. 1916; *s* of Erik and Elisabeth Lind; *m* 1942, Eva Sandström; two *s* two *d*. *Educ:* Univ. of Uppsala. LLB 1939. Entered Swedish Foreign Service as Attaché, 1939; served in Helsinki, 1939–41; Berlin, 1942–44; Second Sec., Stockholm Foreign Ministry, 1944–47; First Sec., Swedish Embassy, Washington, 1947–51; Personal Asst to Sec.-General of UN, 1953–56; re-posted to Swedish Foreign Ministry: Chief of Div. of Internat. Organisations, 1956–59; Dep. Dir Political Affairs, 1959–64; Ambassador with special duties, 1964–66; Ambassador to Canada, 1966–69; Under-Sec. of State for Administration at Foreign Ministry, Stockholm, 1969–75; Chm. Special Political Cttee of 29th Session of Gen. Assembly of UN, 1974; Ambassador to Australia, 1975–79. *Recreation:* golf. *Address:* Gyllenstiernsgatan 7, 11526 Stockholm, Sweden. *Died 30 Nov. 2012.*

LINDLEY, Prof. Dennis Victor; Professor and Head of Department of Statistics and Computer Science, University College London, 1967–77; *b* 25 July 1923; *s* of Albert Edward and Florence Louisa Lindley; *m* 1947, Joan Armitage; one *s* two *d*. *Educ:* Tiffin Boys' Sch., Kingston-on-Thames; Trinity Coll., Cambridge. MA Cantab 1948. Min. of Supply, 1943–45; Nat. Physical Lab., 1945–46 and 1947–48; Statistical Lab., Cambridge Univ., 1948–60 (Dir, 1957–60); Prof. and Head of Dept of Statistics, UCW, Aberystwyth, 1960–67, Hon. Professorial Fellow, 1978–. Hon. Prof., Univ. of Warwick, 1978–96. Vis. Professor: Chicago and Stanford Univs, 1954–55; Harvard Business Sch., 1963; Univ. of Iowa, 1974–75; Univ. of Bath, 1978–81. Fellow, Inst. Math. Statistics; Fellow, American Statistical Assoc. Wald Lectr, Inst. Math. Statistics, 1988. Guy Medal (Gold), Royal Statistical Soc., 2002. *Publications:* (with J. C. P. Miller) Cambridge Elementary Statistical Tables, 1953; Introduction to Probability and Statistics (2 vols), 1965; Making Decisions, 1971, rev. edn 1985; Bayesian Statistics, 1971; (with W. F. Scott) New Cambridge Elementary Statistical Tables, 1985, rev. edn as New Cambridge Statistical Tables, 1995; Understanding Uncertainty, 2006; contribs to Royal Statistical Soc., Biometrika, Annals of Math. Statistics. *Address:* Woodstock, Quay Lane, Minehead, Somerset TA24 5QU. *T:* (01643) 705189. *Died 14 Dec. 2013.*

LINDOP, Sir Norman, Kt 1973; DL; MSc; CChem, FRSC; Director, Hatfield Polytechnic, 1969–82; Chairman, Hertfordshire County Council, 1997–99 (Member (Lab), 1993–2001); *b* 9 March 1921; *s* of Thomas Cox Lindop and May Lindop, Stockport, Cheshire; *m* 1974, Jenny C. Quass; one *s*. *Educ:* Northgate Sch., Ipswich; Queen Mary Coll., Univ. of London (BSc, MSc). Various industrial posts, 1942–46; Lectr in Chemistry, Queen Mary Coll., 1946; Asst Dir of Examinations, Civil Service Commn, 1951; Sen. Lectr in Chemistry, Kingston Coll. of Technology, 1953; Head of Dept of Chemistry and Geology, Kingston Coll. of Technology, 1957; Principal: SW Essex Technical Coll. and Sch. of Art, 1963; Hatfield Coll. of Technology, 1966; Principal, British Sch. of Osteopathy, 1982–90. Chairman: Cttee of Dirs of Polytechnics, 1972–74; Council for Professions Supplementary to Medicine, 1973–81; Home Office Data Protection Cttee, 1976–78; Cttee of Enquiry into Public Sector Validation, DES, 1984–85; British Library Adv. Council, 1986–94; Herts Area Manpower Bd, 1986–88; Res. Council for Complementary Medicine, 1989–90; Member: CNAA, 1974–81; US-UK Educn (Fulbright) Commn, 1971–81; SRC, 1974–78; GMC, 1979–84. Chm. Council, Westfield Coll., London Univ., 1983–89. FCP 1980; Fellow: QMC, 1976; Hatfield Polytechnic, 1983; Hon. Fellow, Brighton Polytechnic, 1990. FRSA. DL Hertford, 1989. Hon. DEd CNAA, 1982; Hon. DSc: Ulster, 1994; Hertfordshire, 1997; Kingston, 2002. *Recreations:* mountain walking, music (especially opera). *Address:* 36 Queens Road, Hertford, Herts SG13 8AZ. *Died 24 Jan. 2014.*

LIPKIN, Miles Henry J.; *see* Jackson-Lipkin.

LIPSCOMB, Prof. William Nunn; Abbott and James Lawrence Professor of Chemistry, Harvard University, 1971–90, then Emeritus; *b* 9 Dec. 1919; *s* of late William Nunn Lipscomb Sr, and of Edna Patterson Porter; *m* 1944, Mary Adele Sargent; one *s* one *d*; *m* 1983, Jean Craig Evans; one *d*. *Educ:* Univ. of Kentucky (BS 1941); California Inst. of Technology (PhD 1946). Univ. of Minnesota, Minneapolis: Asst Prof. of Physical Chem., 1946–50; Associate Prof., 1950–54; Actg Chief, Physical Chem. Div., 1952–54; Prof. and Chief of Physical Chem. Div., 1954–59; Harvard Univ.: Prof. of Chemistry, 1959–71 (Chm., Dept of Chem., 1962–65). Member: Bd of Dirs, Dow Chemical Co., USA, 1982–89; Scientific Adv. Bd, Robert A. Welch Foundn, 1982–. Member: Amer. Chemical Soc. (Chm., Minneapolis Section, 1949); Amer. Acad. of Arts and Sciences, 1959–; Nat. Acad. of Sciences, USA, 1961–; Internat. Acad. of Quantum Molecular Science, 1980; Académie Européenne des Scis, des Arts et des Lettres, Paris, 1980; Foreign Mem., Netherlands Acad. of Arts and Sciences, 1976; Hon. Member: Internat. Assoc. of Bioinorganic Scientists, 1979; RSC, 1983. Hon. MA Harvard, 1959; Hon. DSc: Kentucky, 1963; Long Island, 1977; Rutgers, 1979; Gustavus Adolphus, 1980; Marietta, 1981; Miami, 1983; Dr *hc* Munich, 1976. Nobel Prize in Chemistry, 1976. *Publications:* Boron Hydrides, 1963 (New

York); (with G. R. Eaton) Nuclear Magnetic Resonance Studies of Boron and Related Compounds, 1969 (New York); chapters in: The Aesthetic Dimensions of Science, ed D. W. Curtin, 1982; Crystallography in North America, ed D. McLachlan and J. Glusker, 1983; contribs to scientific jls concerning structure and function of enzymes and natural products in inorganic chem. and theoretical chem. *Recreations:* tennis, chamber music. *Address:* Department of Chemistry and Chemical Biology, Harvard University, 12 Oxford Street, Cambridge, MA 02138, USA. *T:* (617) 4954098. *Died 14 April 2011.*

LISBURNE, 8th Earl of, *cr* 1776; **John David Malet Vaughan;** Baron Fethard, 1695; Viscount Lisburne and Lord Vaughan, 1695; barrister-at-law; *b* 1 Sept. 1918; *o s* of 7th Earl of Lisburne; *S* father, 1965; *m* 1943, Shelagh, *er d* of late T. A. Macauley, 1266 Redpath Crescent, Montreal, Canada; three *s*. *Educ:* Eton; Magdalen Coll., Oxford (BA, MA). Captain, Welsh Guards, 1939–46. Called to Bar, Inner Temple, 1947. Director: British Home Stores Ltd, 1964–87; S Wales Regional Bd, Lloyds Bank Ltd, 1978–; Divisional Dir for Wales, Nationwide Building Soc., 1982–. Founder, and Chm., then Pres., Wales Council for Voluntary Action (formerly Council of Social Service for Wales), 1976–97; Dep. Chm., Westward Television, 1963–82; Hon. Life Mem., AA (Mem. Exec. Cttee, 1981–88). Gov., UCW, 1969. DL Dyfed, 1972. *Heir: s* Viscount Vaughan, *b* 15 June 1945. *Address:* Bringewood, Burway Lane, Ludlow SY8 1DT. *Clubs:* Beefsteak, Turf. *Died 2 Sept. 2014.*

LISTER, Tom, CBE 1978; QFSM 1977; Chief Fire Officer, West Midlands County Council, 1975–81; *b* 14 May 1924; *s* of late T. Lister and Mrs E. Lister; *m* 1954, Linda, *d* of late T. J. and Mrs H. Dodds; one *d*. *Educ:* Charter House, Hull. Hull Fire Service, 1947–53; sub officer, Halifax Fire Service, 1953–55; divisional officer: Croydon, 1955–61; Lancs, 1961–62; Assistant Chief Fire Officer: Warwicks, 1962–66; Lancs, 1966–68; Chief Fire Officer, Glos, 1968–71, Bristol and Avon, 1972–75. *Died 20 Aug. 2013.*

LITHERLAND, Robert Kenneth; former politician; *b* 23 June 1930; *s* of Robert Litherland and Mary (*née* Parry); *m* 1953, Edna Litherland; one *s* one *d*. *Educ:* North Manchester High Sch. for Boys. Formerly sales representative for printing firm. Mem., Manchester City Council, 1971 (Dep. Chm., Housing Cttee, 1979; Chm., Manchester Direct Works Cttee, 1974–78); Dep. Chm., Public Works Cttee, Assoc. of Municipal Authorities, 1977–78. MP (Lab) Manchester Central, Sept. 1979–1997. Member: Council of Europe, 1987–97; WEU, 1987–97. *Address:* 32 Darley Avenue, Didsbury, Manchester M20 8YD. *Died 13 May 2011.*

LITTLE, Ian Malcolm David, CBE 1997; AFC 1943; FBA 1973; Professor of Economics of Underdeveloped Countries, University of Oxford, 1971–76; *b* 18 Dec. 1918; *s* of Brig.-Gen. M. O. Little, CB, CBE, and Iris Hermione Little (*née* Brassey); *m* 1st, 1946, Doreen Hennessey (*d* 1984); one *s* one *d*; 2nd, 1991, Lydia Segrave. *Educ:* Eton; New Coll., Oxford (MA, DPhil; Hon. Fellow, 1999). RAF Officer, 1939–46. Fellow: All Souls Coll., Oxford, 1948–50; Trinity Coll., Oxford, 1950–52; Nuffield Coll., Oxford, 1952–76, Emeritus Fellow, 1976. Dep. Dir, Economic Section, Treasury, 1953–55; Mem., MIT Centre for Internat. Studies, India, 1958–59 and 1965; Vice-Pres., OECD Develt Centre, Paris, 1965–67. Dir, Investing in Success Ltd, 1960–65; Bd Mem., British Airports Authority, 1969–74. Dir, Gen. Funds Investment Trust, 1974–76; Special Adviser, IBRD, 1976–78. Hon. DSc (SocSci) Edinburgh, 1976. *Publications:* A Critique of Welfare Economics, 1950; The Price of Fuel, 1953; (jtly) Concentration in British Industry, 1960; Aid to Africa, 1964; (jtly) International Aid, 1965; (jtly) Higgledy-Piggledy Growth Again, 1966; (jtly) Manual of Industrial Project Analysis in Developing Countries, 1969; (jtly) Industry and Trade in Some Developing Countries, 1970; (jtly) Project Analysis and Planning, 1974; Economic Development: theory, policy and international relations, 1982; (jtly) Small Manufacturing Enterprises, 1987; (jtly) Boom, Crisis and Adjustment, 1993; (jtly) India: macroeconomics and political economy 1964–1991, 1994; (jtly) India's Economic Reforms 1991–2001, 1996; (ed jtly) India's Economic Reforms and Development: essays for Manmohan Singh, 1998; Ethics, Economics and Politics, 2002; many articles in learned jls. *Died 13 July 2012.*

LITTMAN, Mark; QC 1961; Director: Granada Group PLC, 1977–93; Burton Group plc, 1983–93; *b* 4 Sept. 1920; *s* of Jack and Lilian Littman; *m* 1965, Marguerite Lamkin, USA. *Educ:* Owen's Sch.; London Sch. of Economics (BScEcon (1st class hons) 1939); The Queen's Coll., Oxford (MA 1941). Served RN, Lieut, 1941–46. Called to Bar, Middle Temple, 1947 (Bencher, 1970, Treas., 1988); practised as Barrister-at-law, 1947–67 and 1979–2010; Head of Littman Chambers, 1979–2010. Member: General Council of the Bar, 1968–72; Senate of Inns of Court and the Bar, 1968. Dep. Chm., BSC, 1970–79. Mem. Royal Commn on Legal Services, 1976–79. Director: Rio Tinto-Zinc Corp. PLC, 1968–91; Commercial Union Assurance Co. Ltd, 1970–81; Amerada Hess Corp. (US), 1973–86; British Enkalon Ltd, 1976–80; Envirotech Corp. (US), 1974–78. Mem., Internat. Council for Commercial Arbitration, 1978–. Mem., Ct of Governors, LSE, 1980–. *Address:* 79 Chester Square, SW1W 9DU. *Clubs:* Garrick, Reform, Oxford and Cambridge, Royal Automobile; Century Association (New York). *Died 19 June 2015.*

LITTON, Peter Stafford; Under Secretary, Department of Education and Science, 1978–81; a General Commissioner of Income Tax, Epsom Division, 1983–96; *b* 26 Oct. 1921; *s* of late Leonard Litton and Louisa (*née* Horn); *m* 1942, Josephine Peggy Bale (*d* 2003); one *d*. *Educ:* Barnstaple Grammar School. Clerical Officer, Board of Education, 1938. Served in Royal Corps of Signals, 1941–46. Min. of Education, 1946; Principal Private Sec. to Secretary of State for Educn and Science, 1965–66. *Recreations:* reading, armchair astronomy. *Died 27 Oct. 2013.*

LIU, Tsz-Ming, Benjamin, GBS 1999; a Justice of Appeal, Court of Appeal of the High Court (formerly Supreme Court), Hong Kong, 1994–99; *b* 17 May 1931; *s* of late Dr Y. T. Liu and Dorothy Mei-Kow (*née* Kwok); *m* 1954, Annemarie Marent; one *s* one *d*. *Educ:* Wah Yan College. Called to the Bar, Lincoln's Inn, 1957, Hong Kong, 1959; QC (Hong Kong) 1973; Judge of the District Court, Hong Kong, 1973–79; Judicial Comr, Supreme Ct, State of Brunei, 1978–89; a Judge of the High Court, Hong Kong, 1980–94. Panel Mem., Inland Revenue Bd of Review, Hong Kong, 1972; Chairman: Sub-Cttee on Bail in Criminal Proceedings, Law Reform Commn, 1985–89; Working Party on appropriate safeguards for execution of Anton Piller Orders, 1992–94. Adjunct Prof., Law Faculty, Wu Nam Univ., 2003–09; Vis. Prof., Law Faculty, Chung Shan Univ., 2005–08; Ext. Acad. Advr, 2001–04, Vis. Fellow, 2008–10, Adjunct Prof., 2008–10, City Univ. of Hong Kong. Hon. Consultant, China Law Office, 2003–. Pres., 1992–99, Advr, 1999–, Hong Kong Local Judicial Officers' Assoc. Hong Kong Expert, China Foreign Experts Bureau, 2002; Hon. Pres., 2001–, Exec. Chm., 2005–, Hong Kong Soc. of Experts. Mem., Ethics Instnl Review Bd, Hong Kong Univ. Hosp. Authy, 2002–05; Mem. Council, UNA of China, 2002–; Hon. Advr, Hong Kong WTO Res. Inst., 2002–. Member: Council, 2004–09, Exec. Council, 2009–, China Law Soc.; Adv. Council, Trade Commercial Mediation Commn, Hong Kong Chinese Enterprises Assoc., 2010–. Director: China Overseas Friendship Assoc., 1999–2003 (Hon. Dir, 2003–); Shanghai Overseas Friendship Assoc., 2002–. *Publications:* How Are We Judged?, 2000; The Triad Societies Before and After the 1997 Change-over, 2001 (trans. Chinese 2003); Judiciary Agony—Judgment Writing, 2010; The Glory, Misconception and Future of the Common Law, 2010; (in Chinese) Judicial Ethics, 2010; (with Chinese trans.) Judicial Activism, 2011; articles in press and law jls. *Address:* 1B 22 Kennedy Road, Hong Kong SAR. *T:* 28495803, *Fax:* 28495817. *Clubs:* Hong Kong, Chinese, Hong Kong Country, Correctional Services Officers' (Hong Kong). *Died 16 Oct. 2013.*

LIVINGSTON, Air Vice-Marshal Graham; consultant occupational health physician; *b* 2 Aug. 1928; *s* of late Neil Livingston and Margaret Anderson (*née* Graham); *m* 1970, Carol Judith Palmer; one *s* one *d* (and one *s* one *d* (and one *d* decd) of former marriage). *Educ:* Bo'ness Academy; Edinburgh Univ. (MB ChB 1951, DPH 1963); DIH

(Conjoint) 1963; MFPHM (MFCM 1974); MFOM 1981. Joined RAF 1952; served N Ireland and Egypt, 1952–55; civilian GP and obst., 1956–57; rejoined RAF 1958; served Lindholme and Honington, 1958–62; post grad. study in public and indust. health, Edinburgh Univ., 1962–63; SMO, RAF Laarbruch, 1963–66; RAF Coll., Cranwell, 1966–70; served Cosford, Halton and Akrotiri, 1970–74; OC RAF Hosps, Cosford, 1974–76, Wegberg, 1976–79; Dep. Dir Med. Personnel and Dep. Dir Med. Orgn, MoD, 1979–80; Dep. PMO, Strike Command, 1981–83; Principal Medical Officer: RAF Germany, 1983–84; RAF Support Comd, 1984–89; QHS 1985–89. Consultant in community medicine, 1984; Consultant Occupational Health Physician: NW Herts HA, 1989–94; Wycombe HA, 1991–94. Freeman, City of London, 1982. FCMI (FBIM 1986). *Recreations:* golf, gardening, dog walking. *Address:* c/o Lloyds, Cox's and King's Branch, PO Box 1190, 7 Pall Mall, SW1Y 5NA. *Clubs:* Royal Air Force; Ashridge Golf. *Died 5 Oct. 2014.*

LLOYD, Air Vice-Marshal Darrell Clive Arthur, CB 1980; Commander, Northern Maritime Air Region, 1981–83; *b* 5 Nov. 1928; *s* of Cecil James Lloyd and Doris Frances Lloyd; *m* 1957, Pamela (*née* Woodside); two *s*. *Educ:* Stowe; RAF Coll., Cranwell. Commnd 1950; ADC to C-in-C, ME Air Force, 1955–57; Instr, Central Flying Sch., 1958–60; Personal Air Sec. to Sec. of State for Air, 1961–63; CO, RAF Bruggen, 1968–70; RCDS, 1972; Dir of Defence Policy, UK Strategy Div., 1973–75; Dep. Comdr, RAF Germany, 1976–78; ACAS (Ops), 1978–81. FCMI (FBIM 1972). *Recreations:* travel, golf, painting. *Address:* c/o Halifax, 63 High Street, Deal, Kent CT14 6EH. *Clubs:* Royal Air Force; Royal Cinque Ports Golf (Deal); Tandridge Golf (Oxted). *Died 18 Feb. 2015.*

LLOYD, Stephen Thomas; Consultant and Senior Counsel, Bates Wells & Braithwaite London LLP, since 2013 (Senior Partner, 2006–13); *b* Barnet, Herts, 17 July 1951; *s* of Thomas Henry Lloyd and Edith Ethel Lloyd (*née* Haggith); *m* 1972, Lorna Marion Frizzell; four *s*. *Educ:* Finchley Catholic Grammar Sch.; Univ. of Bristol (BA Hist. 1972); St Edmund Coll., Cambridge (1st pt Law Tripos 1973). Admitted solicitor, 1977; trng, then Solicitor, Freshfields, 1975–78; In-house Lawyer, Frizzell Gp, 1978–80; Solicitor, 1980–, Partner, 1984–2013, Bates Wells & Braithwaite London LLP. Chm., Charity and Social Enterprise Insce Mgt LLP, 2007–. Special Legal Advr to Lord Hodgson on operation of Charities Act 2006, 2011–12. Chairman: Centre for Innovation in Voluntary Action, 1995–; Charity Law Assoc., 2003–06; Trustees UnLimited, 2010–; Dir, Social Stock Exchange, 2011–; Trustee: Burney Street Garden Proj., 1980–84; Blackheath Soc., 1986–93; UK Envmtl Law Assoc., 1987–94; Transport 2000 Charitable Trust, 1990–95; Envmtl Law Foundn, 1992–95; Iran Aid Foundn, 1998–2004; Blackheath Halls, 1998–2006; Chelwood, 1999–2004; CAF Common Investment Fund, 2005–09; Global Cool Foundn, 2008–12; Rainmaker Foundn, 2011–13. Director: Natural Scientific Technologies Ltd, 2011–13; Buzzbank, 2011–. *Publications:* The Barclays Guide to Law for the Small Business, 1989; Charities: the new law, 1993, rev. edn 2007; Charities, Trading and the Law, 1995, 2nd edn 2010; (contrib.) The Fundraiser's Guide to the Law, 1998. *Recreations:* walking, cycling, classical music, reading, my family. *Address:* Bates Wells & Braithwaite London LLP, 2–6 Cannon Street, EC4M 6YH. *T:* (020) 7551 7777, *Fax:* (020) 7551 7800. *E:* s.lloyd@bwbllp.com. *Club:* Newport Boat. *Died 20 Aug. 2014.*

LOBO, Sir Rogerio Hyndman, (Sir Roger), Kt 1985; CBE 1978 (OBE 1972); JP; Chairman, P. J. Lobo & Co. Ltd, Hong Kong, 1946–2001; Chairman, Broadcasting Authority of Hong Kong, 1989–97; *b* 15 Sept. 1923; *s* of Dr P. J. Lobo and Branca Helena (*née* Hyndman); *m* 1947, Margaret Mary (*née* Choa); five *s* five *d*. *Educ:* Escola Central, Macao; Seminario de S Jose, Macao; Liceu Nacional Infante Dom Henrique, Macao; La Salle Coll., Hong Kong. Director: Kjeldsen & Co. (HK) (formerly Danish Fancy Food Gp), 1982–2013; Shun Tak Hldgs Ltd, 1994–; PCCW (formerly Pacific Century CyberWorks) Ltd, 1999–2011; HKT Ltd, 2011–; HKT Management Ltd, 2011–; dir of 3 other cos. Unofficial MLC, Hong Kong, 1972–85 (Sen. Mem., 1980–85); Unofficial MEC, 1978–85. Member: Urban Council, 1965–78; Housing Authority, 1967–83; Chm., Adv. Cttee on Post-Retirement Employment, 1987–98; Comr, Civil Aid Services, 1977–92 (Mem., 1955–). Hon. LLD Univ. of Hong Kong, 1982. JP Hong Kong, 1963. Silver Jubilee Medal, 1977; Civil Aid Services Long Service Medal, 1970; Civil Defence Long Service Clasp, 1982. Comdr, Order of St Gregory the Great, The Vatican, 1969. *Recreation:* golf. *Address:* Woodland Heights, E1, 2 Wongneichong Gap Road, Hong Kong. *T:* 25740779; (business) Level 10, Central Building, 1–3 Pedder Street, Central, Hong Kong. *T:* 25269418. *Clubs:* Dynasty, Hong Kong, Rotary, Hong Kong Jockey, Hong Kong Golf, Hong Kong Country (Hong Kong). *Died 18 April 2015.*

LOCK, John Arthur, QPM 1975; Deputy Assistant Commissioner, Metropolitan Police, and National Co-ordinator, Regional Crime Squads of England and Wales, 1976–79; *b* 20 Oct. 1922; *s* of Sidney George Lock and Minnie Louise Lock; *m* 1950, Patricia Joyce Lambert; two *d*. *Educ:* George Palmer Central School, Reading. Royal Air Force, 1941–46; Wireless Operator/Air Gunner; Flying Officer. Joined Metropolitan Police, 1946. *Recreation:* golf. *Club:* St Mellion Golf and Country. *Died 4 Feb. 2011.*

LOCKE, Patrick, CBE 1998; Secretary to Church Commissioners, 1992–98; *b* 17 March 1934; *s* of Roy Albert Locke and Nora Katherine Locke (*née* Taylor); *m* 1959, Iris Constance Cory; one *s* one *d*. *Educ:* Bristol Cathedral Sch.; Wadham Coll., Oxford (Schol.; MA). Nat. Service, 1952–54. Church Commissioners Office, 1957–98: Dep. Sec., 1985–92. Trustee, Pollen Estate, 1991–2008 (Chm., 2002–08). Gov., Pusey House, Oxford, 1999–2010. *Recreations:* 18th and 19th century literature, theatre. *Address:* Romans, Beggars Lane, Winchester, Hants SO23 0HE. *T:* (01962) 866386. *Club:* Athenæum. *Died 16 Oct. 2012.*

LOCKETT, His Honour Reginald; a Circuit Judge, 1981–99, a Senior Circuit Judge, 1997–99; *b* 24 June 1933; *s* of George Alfred Lockett and Emma (*née* Singleton); *m* 1959, Edna (*née* Lowe); one *s* one *d*. *Educ:* Ashton-in-Makerfield Grammar Sch.; Manchester Univ.; London Univ. (LLB 1954). Solicitor, 1955. Asst Coroner for Wigan, 1963–70; Dist Registrar and County Court Registrar, Manchester, 1970–81; a Recorder of the Crown Court, 1978–81. Hon. Recorder, Borough of Preston, 1996–99; Asst Deemster, IOM, 2000–03. Pres., Manchester Law Students' Soc., 1975–77. Pres., The Boys' Bde, 1999–2003 (Vice Pres., 1978–99; Dist Pres., NW Dist, 1973–90). Reader, Anglican Church, 1970–2013. Editor, Butterworths Family Law Service, 1983–90; Consultant Editor, Sweet-Maxwell's High Court Litigation Manual, 1990. *Recreations:* music, photography. *Address:* 7 Blandford Rise, Lostock, Bolton BL6 4JH. *T:* (01204) 699791. *Died 26 May 2013.*

LOCKWOOD, Prof. David, CBE 1998; FBA 1976; Professor of Sociology, University of Essex, 1968–2001 (Pro-Vice-Chancellor, 1989–92); *b* 9 April 1929; *s* of Herbert Lockwood and Edith A. (*née* Lockwood); *m* 1954, Leonore Davidoff; three *s*. *Educ:* Honley Grammar Sch.; London Sch. of Economics. BScEcon London, 1st Cl. Hons 1952; PhD London, 1957. Trainee, textile industry, 1944–47; Corp., Intell. Corps, Austria, 1947–49. Asst Lectr and Lectr, London Sch. of Economics, 1953–60; Rockefeller Fellow, Univ. of California, Berkeley, 1958–59; Univ. Lectr, Faculty of Economics, and Fellow, St John's Coll., Cambridge, 1960–68. Visiting Professor: Dept of Sociology, Columbia Univ., 1966–67; Delhi Univ., 1975; Stockholm Univ., 1989; Vis. Fellow, ANU, 1993. Mem., SSRC (Chm., Sociol. and Soc. Admin Cttee), 1973–76; Chm., ESRC Rev. of Govt Social Classifications, 1994–98. Mem., Academia Europaea, 1990. DU Essex, 2001; Hon. LittD Cantab, 2004. Lifetime Achievement Award, British Sociological Assoc., 2011. *Publications:* The Blackcoated Worker, 1958, 2nd edn 1989; (jtly) The Affluent Worker in the Class Structure, 3 vols, 1968–69; Solidarity and Schism, 1992; numerous articles in jls and symposia. *Address:* 82 High Street, Wivenhoe, Essex CO7 9AB. *T:* (01206) 823530. *Died 6 June 2014.*

LOEWE, Raphael James, MC 1943; Goldsmid Professor of Hebrew, University College, London, 1981–86; *b* Calcutta, 16 April 1919; *s* of Herbert Loewe and Ethel Loewe (*née* Hyamson); *m* 1952, Chloe Klatzkin; two *d*. *Educ:* Dragon Sch., Oxford; The Leys Sch., Cambridge; St John's Coll., Cambridge (Schol.; BA Classics 1942; Hon. Fellow, 2009). Served War, Suffolk Regt, RAC. Postgrad. res. at Balliol Coll., Oxford; Lectr in Hebrew, Leeds Univ., 1949–53; Bye Fellow, Gonville and Caius Coll., Cambridge, 1953; University College London: Dir, Inst. of Jewish Studies, 1973–86; Lectr in Hebrew, 1975–78; Reader, 1978–81. Vis. Prof. in Judaica, Brown Univ., 1962–63. President: Jewish Historical Soc. of England, 1973–75; SOTS, 1980–81; British Assoc. for Jewish Studies, 1998. Actively involved in admin and pubns of Spanish and Portuguese Jews' Congregation, London (formerly Elder). *Publications:* Position of Women in Judaism, 1966; (contrib.) Encyclopaedia Judaica, 1972; (ed) The Rylands Haggadah, 1988; Solomon Ibn Gabirol, 1989; Isaac Ibn Sahula's Meshal Haqadmoni, 2004; Hebrew Poems and Translations, 2010; articles on Judaism and (Anglo-) Jewish history, etc in specialist periodicals. *Recreations:* 3-way translation of poetry (English, Latin, Hebrew), walking, The Times crosswords. *Address:* 50 Gurney Drive, N2 0DE. *T:* (020) 8455 5379. *Died 27 May 2011.*

LOFTHOUSE OF PONTEFRACT, Baron *cr* 1997 (Life Peer), of Pontefract in the co. of West Yorkshire; **Geoffrey Lofthouse,** Kt 1995; JP; *b* 18 Dec. 1925; *s* of Ernest and Emma Lofthouse; *m* 1946, Sarah Lofthouse (*d* 1985); one *d*. *Educ:* Featherstone Primary and Secondary Schs; Leeds Univ. FIPD (MIPM 1984). Haulage hand in mining industry at age of 14. Personnel Manager, NCB Fryston, 1970–78. Member: Pontefract Borough Council, 1962–74 (Mayor, 1967–68); Wakefield Metropolitan District Council, 1974–79 (Chm., 1974–75; Chm., Housing Cttee, 1974–79). MP (Lab) Pontefract and Castleford, Oct. 1978–1997. Dep. Chm. of Ways and Means, and Dep. Speaker, H of C, 1992–97; Dep. Speaker, H of L, 1998–. Chairman: Wakefield HA, 1998–2002; Mid Yorks NHS Trust (formerly Mid Yorks Hosps NHS Trust), 2002–. Mem., NUM, 1939–64, APEX, 1970–. JP Pontefract, 1970. *Publications:* A Very Miner MP (autobiog.), 1986; Coal Sack to Woolsack (autobiog.), 1999. *Recreations:* Rugby League, cricket. *Address:* 67 Carleton Crest, Pontefract, West Yorkshire WF8 2QR. *Died 1 Nov. 2012.*

LOGAN, William Philip Dowie, MD, PhD, BSc; DPH, FRCP; epidemiological consultant to various national and international organisations, 1974–89; Director, Division of Health Statistics, WHO, 1961–74; *b* 2 Nov. 1914; *s* of late Frederick William Alexander Logan and late Elizabeth Jane Dowie; *m* 1st, 1941, Pearl (*née* Piper) (marr. diss.); four *s* two *d* (and one *s* decd); 2nd, Barbara (*née* Huneke). *Educ:* Queen's Park Sch., Glasgow; Univ. of Glasgow (BSc, DPH, MD); PhD London. RAF Med. Branch, 1940–46 (Squadron Leader). Hospital appointments in Glasgow, 1939–40 and 1946. Gen. practice in Barking, Essex, 1947–48; General Register Office, 1948–60 (Chief Medical Statistician, Adviser on Statistics to Ministry of Health, Head of WHO Centre for Classification of Diseases, and Member, WHO panel of experts on Health Statistics). *Publications:* contribs on epidemiology, vital and health statistics in official reports and medical jls. *Address:* 16 Southview Road, Bognor Regis, West Sussex PO22 7JA. *Died 11 Dec. 2012.*

LOGUE, Christopher, CBE 2007; writer and poet; *b* 23 Nov. 1926; *s* of John Logue and Molly Logue (*née* Chapman); *m* 1985, Rosemary Hill. *Educ:* Prior Park Coll., Bath; Portsmouth Grammar Sch. Mem., Equity. *Screen plays:* Savage Messiah (dir Ken Russell), 1972; (with Walon Green) Crusoe (based on Defoe's novel), 1989. *Broadcast:* The Arrival of the Poet in the City: a melodrama for narrator and seven musicians (music by George Nicholson), 1985; Strings (melodrama for voice and 14 musicians, with music by Jason Osborn), 1988. *Recordings:* (with Tony Kinsey and Bill Le Sage) Red Bird (poetry and jazz), 1960; Songs from The Establishment (singer Annie Ross), 1962; The Death of Patroclus (with Vanessa Redgrave, Alan Dobie and others), 1963; Audiologue (readings of own poetry set to music), 2001. *Film roles:* Swinburne, in Ken Russell's Dante's Inferno, 1966; John Ball, in John Irvin's The Peasants' Revolt, 1969; Cardinal Richelieu, in Ken Russell's The Devils, 1970; TV and stage roles. Wilfred Owen Award (first), for poetry concerning warfare, 1998. Trans. Baal, by Brecht, perf. 1985. Hon. DLitt Portsmouth, 2007. *Publications: verse:* Wand & Quadrant, 1953; Devil, Maggot & Son, 1956; Songs, 1959; Patrocleia, 1962; ABC, 1966; Pax, 1967; New Numbers, 1969; Twelve Cards, 1972; The Crocodile (illus. Binette Schroeder), 1976; Abecedary (illus. Bert Kitchen), 1977; Ode to the Dodo, 1981; War Music, 1981, Kings, 1991, The Husbands, 1995, collected into one vol. as War Music: an account of Homer's Iliad, 2001; Selected Poems, 1996; All Day Permanent Red: War Music continued, 2003; Cold Calls: War Music continued, 2005 (Whitbread Prize for Poetry, 2005); *prose:* Ratsmagic (illus. Wayne Anderson), 1976; The Magic Circus (illus. Wayne Anderson), 1979; The Bumper Book of True Stories (illus. Bert Kitchen), 1980; *plays:* The Trial of Cob & Leach, 1959; (with Harry Cookson) The Lilywhite Boys, 1959; trans. Hugo Claus, Friday, 1971; trans. Brecht and Weill, The Seven Deadly Sins, 1986; *anthologies:* The Children's Book of Comic Verse, 1979; London in Verse, 1982; Sweet & Sour, 1983; The Oxford Book of Pseuds, 1983; The Children's Book of Children's Rhymes, 1986; *autobiography:* Prince Charming: a memoir, 1999; contrib. Private Eye, The Times, The Sunday Times, etc; *as Count Palmiro Vicarion:* Lust, a pornographic novel, 1957; (ed) Count Palmiro Vicarion's Book of Limericks, 1957; (ed) Count Palmiro Vicarion's Book of Bawdy Ballads, 1957; *relevant publication:* Christopher Logue: a bibliography 1952–1997, by George Ramsden, 1998. *Address:* 41 Camberwell Grove, SE5 8JA. *Died 2 Dec. 2011.*

LOKOLOKO, Sir Tore, GCMG 1977; GCVO 1982; OBE; Chairman, Indosuez Niugini Bank, 1983–89; *b* 21 Sept. 1930; *s* of Loko Loko Tore and Kevau Sarufa; *m* 1950, Lalahaia Meakoro; four *s* six *d*. *Educ:* Sogeri High Sch., PNG. Dip. in Cooperative, India. Chm., PNG Cooperative Fedn, 1965–68; MP, 1968–77 (two terms); Minister for Health, and Dep. Chm. of National Exec. Council, 1968–72. Rep. PNG: Co-op. Conf., Australia, 1951; S Pacific Conf., Lae, 1964; attended UN Gen. Assembly, 1969, and Trusteeship Council, 1971. Governor-General of Papua New Guinea, 1977–82. KStJ 1979. *Address:* PO Box 5622, Boroko, NCD, Papua New Guinea. *Died 13 March 2013.*

LOMER, William Michael, PhD; Director, Culham Laboratory, United Kingdom Atomic Energy Authority, 1981–90; *b* 2 March 1926; *s* of Frederick John Lomer and Dorothy Lomer; *m* 1952, Pamela Anne Wakelin; one *s* two *d*. *Educ:* St Austell County School; University College of the South West, Exeter (MSc London); Queens' College, Cambridge (MA, PhD). Research Scientist, UKAEA, 1952; AERE Harwell: Division Head, Theory Div., 1958–62; Division Head, Solid State Physics, 1962–68; Research Director, 1968–81; Dep. Dir, Inst. Laue Langevin, Grenoble, 1973–74. Hon. Treasurer, Inst. of Physics, 1980–82. Chm., Oxford CAB, 1994–97. Trustee, Oxford Trust, 1991–2005. FInstP. *Publications:* papers in physics and metallurgical jls. *Recreations:* gardening, walking. *Address:* 7 Hids Copse Road, Cumnor Hill, Oxford OX2 9JJ. *T:* (01865) 862173. *Died 19 Oct. 2013.*

LONDONDERRY, 9th Marquess of, *cr* 1816; **Alexander Charles Robert Vane-Tempest-Stewart;** Baron Londonderry, 1789; Viscount Castlereagh, 1795; Earl of Londonderry, 1796; Baron Stewart, 1814; Earl Vane, Viscount Seaham, 1823; *b* 7 Sept. 1937; *s* of 8th Marquess of Londonderry and Romaine (*d* 1951), *er d* of Major Boyce Combe, Great Holt, Dockenfield, Surrey; *S* father, 1955; *m* 1st, 1958, Nicolette (marr. diss. 1971; she *d* 1993), *d* of Michael Harrison, Netherhampton, near Salisbury, Wilts; two *d*; 2nd, 1972, Doreen Patricia Wells, Royal Ballet dancer (marr. diss. 1989); two *s*. *Educ:* Eton. *Heir: s* Viscount Castlereagh, *b* 6 Sept. 1972. *Address:* PO Box No 8, Shaftesbury, Dorset SP7 0LR. *Died 20 June 2012.*

LONGBOTTOM, Charles Brooke, OBE 2012; company director; Chairman, Awareness Foundation (formerly Trinity Foundation for Christianity and Culture), since 2003; *b* 22 July 1930; *s* of late William Ewart Longbottom, Forest Hill, Worksop; *m* 1962, Anita, *d* of G. Trapani and

Mrs Basil Mavroleon; two *d*. *Educ:* Uppingham. Contested (C) Stockton-on-Tees, 1955; MP (C) York, 1959–66; Parly Private Secretary to Mr Iain Macleod, Leader of the House, 1961–63. Barrister, Inner Temple, 1958; Chairman: Austin & Pickersgill, Shipbuilders, Sunderland, 1966–72; A&P Appledore International Ltd, 1970–79; Seascope Holdings Ltd, 1970–82; Seascope Sale & Purchase, 1970–87; Seascope Shipping Ltd, 1982–87; Seascope Insurance Holdings Ltd, 1984–86; Seascope Insurance Services Ltd, 1984–87; Illingworth Morris Pension Trustees Ltd, 1990–94; Director: Henry Ansbacher Hldgs Ltd, 1982–87; Henry Ansbacher & Co., 1982–87; Ansbacher (Guernsey) Ltd, 1982–87; British Shipbuilders, 1986–2002; Kelt Energy plc, 1988–95; MC Shipping Inc., 1989–2007 (Chm., 2004–07); Newman Martin & Buchan, 1992–2000. Member: General Advisory Council, BBC, 1965–75; Community Relations Commn, 1968–70. Trustee, 1983–2002, Chm., 1988–2001, Acorn Christian Healing Trust, then Acorn Christian Foundn. *Recreations:* golf, travel. *Address:* 66 Kingston House North, Princes Gate, SW7 1LN. *Clubs:* White's, Carlton; Berkshire. *Died 5 Feb. 2013.*

LONGFIELD, Dr Michael David; Vice-Chancellor, University of Teesside, 1992 (Director, Teesside Polytechnic, 1980–92); *b* 28 April 1928; *s* of late Edric Douglas Longfield and Dorothy Longfield (*née* Hennessey); *m* 1st, 1952, Ann McDonnell; two *s* two *d*; 2nd, 1970, June Shirley, *d* of late Levi and Esther Beman; two *s*. *Educ:* Prince Henry's Grammar Sch., Otley; Leeds Univ. BSc, PhD; CEng, MIMechE. Lectr in Mech. Engrg, Univ. of Leeds, 1960–68; Manager, Leeds Univ. Industrial Unit of Tribology, 1968–70; Head of Dept of Mech., Marine and Production Engrg, Liverpool Polytechnic, 1970–72; Asst Dir, Teesside Poly., 1972–80. Hon. DSc Teesside, 1996. *Recreation:* the genealogy of the Longfields. *Address:* 16 Firs Road, Harrogate HG2 8RD. *Died 17 July 2014.*

LOOP, Bernadine P., (Mrs Floyd Loop); *see* Healy, B. P.

LORAM, Vice-Adm. Sir David (Anning), KCB 1979; CVO 1994 (LVO 1957); Deputy Supreme Allied Commander Atlantic, 1977–80; Gentleman Usher to The Queen, 1982–94, Extra Gentleman Usher, since 1994; *b* 24 July 1924; *o* surv. *s* of late Mr and Mrs John A. Loram; *m* 1st, 1958, Fiona Beloe (marr. diss. 1981); three *s*; 2nd, 1983, Diana Keigwin (marr. diss. 1990; she *d* 2008); 3rd, 1996, Sara Stead-Ellis (*née* Strickland Goodall). *Educ:* Royal Naval Coll., Dartmouth (1938–41). Awarded King's Dirk. Served War: HMS Sheffield, Foresight, Anson, Zealous, 1941–45. ADC to Governor-Gen. of New Zealand, 1946–48; specialised in Signal Communications, 1949; served in HMS Chequers, 1951; Equerry to the Queen, 1954–57; qualified helicopter pilot, 1955; commanded HMS Loch Fada, 1957; Directing Staff, JSSC, 1959–60; served in HMS Belfast, 1961; Naval Attaché, Paris, 1964–67; commanded HMS Arethusa, 1967; Dir, Naval Ops and Trade, 1970–71; commanded HMS Antrim, 1971; ADC to The Queen, 1972–73; Comdr British Forces, FO Malta, and NATO Comdr SE Mediterranean, 1973–75; Comdt, Nat. Defence Coll., 1975–77. Mem., RN Cresta Team, 1954–59. Fundraiser, CT Scanner Appeal, Royal Marsden Hosp., 1981–83. *Recreation:* fishing. *Address:* Hatherleigh House, Pettridge Lane, Mere, Wilts BA12 6DG. *T:* (01747) 860036. *Club:* Royal Over-Seas League. *Died 30 June 2011.*

LOSINSKA, Kathleen Mary, (Kate), OBE 1986; Senior Vice-President, Civil and Public Services Association, 1986–88 (President, 1979–82 and 1983–86, a Vice-President, 1982–83); *b* Croydon, Surrey, 5 Oct. 1924; *d* of late James Henry Conway, Border Regt and Dorothea Marguerite Hill; *m* 1942, Stanislaw Losinski (formerly serving Officer, Polish Air Force, subseq. 301 Bomber Sqdn, RAF, retd with rank of Sqdn Leader; awarded Polish Virtuti Militari Cross, Croix de Guerre, Cross of Lorraine, Yugoslav Cross of Valour, etc; he *d* 2002); one *s*. *Educ:* Selhurst Grammar Sch., Croydon (matriculation); university of life generally. Entered Civil Service, 1939; with Office of Population Censuses and Surveys. Delegate Mem., Council of Civil Service Unions, 1970–87 (Chm. 1980–81); Chm., CS Retirement Fellowship, 2000– (Vice-Chm., 1988–); Management Cttee, CS Benevolent Fund, 1991–. Commissioner: Trade Union TUC Nuclear Energy Review; CS Appeals Bd, 1988. Founder Mem. and Vice-Chm., Trade Union Cttee for European and Transatlantic Understanding. Chairman: White Eagle Trust, 1985; Solidarnosc Foundn. Held all honorary positions, CPSA. Founder Mem., Resistance Internat., 1983. Governor, Ruskin Coll., 1976, 1979–86. Silver Jubilee Medal, 1977. Kt Comdr, Order of Polonia Restituta, 1987. *Recreations:* journalism, reading, music, history, travel; work for the Christian Trade Union and Moderate Trade Union Movements. *Address:* Loretto, Baggottstown West, Bruff, Co. Limerick, Ireland. *T:* (61) 382225. *Club:* Civil Service. *Died 16 Oct. 2013.*

LOUDEN, Rt Rev. Mgr Stephen Henry, PhD; Research Associate, Centre for Theology and Education, Bangor University (formerly University of Wales, Bangor), since 1998; *b* 18 Nov. 1941; *s* of late Joseph Henry Louden and Sarah (*née* McNaughten). *Educ:* Upholland Coll. BA Open 1975; DipTh CNAA 1991; MTh Oxon 1993; PhD Wales 1998. Ordained priest, dio. Liverpool, 1968; Curate: All Saints, Anfield, 1968–73; St John's, Kirkdale, 1973–75; Our Lady's, Formby, 1975–78; Royal Army Chaplains' Department: TA Commn, 1973–78; Regular Army Commn, 1978; Dortmund Garrison, 1978–79; 8 Inf. Bde, 1979–80; Munster Garrison, 1980–82; Dhekelia Garrison, 1982–84; RC Chaplain, RMA Sandhurst, 1984–86; Berlin Inf. Bde, 1986–88; HQ NI, 1988; Hong Kong, 1988–90; Senior Chaplain RC: HQ BAOR, 1990–92; HQ NI, 1992–93; Principal RC Chaplain and VG (Army), 1993–97. Prelate of Honour, 1993. *Publications:* Chaplains in Conflict, 1996; (jtly) The Naked Parish Priest, 2003; contrib. to learned jls. *Recreations:* horology, photography, history. *Address:* Chapel House, 57 Chapel Lane, Netherton L30 7PF. *Died 17 Jan. 2013.*

LOUDOUN, 14th Earl of, *cr* 1633; **Michael Edward Abney-Hastings;** Lord Campbell of Loudoun, 1601; Lord Mauchline, 1638; *b* 22 July 1942; *s* of Countess of Loudoun (13th in line) and Captain Walter Strickland Lord; assumed, by deed poll, the surname of Abney-Hastings in lieu of his patronymic, 1946; *S* mother, 2002; *co-heir* (with aunt and cousins) to Baronies of Botreaux 1368, Stanley 1456 and Hastings 1461; *m* 1969, Noelene Margaret McCormick (*d* 2002), 2nd *d* of Mr and Mrs W. J. McCormick, Barham, NSW; two *s* three *d* (of whom one *s* one *d* were twins); *m* 2008, Margaret Ann Buntin, *e d* of late H. L. Thomas; three step *s* one step *d*. *Educ:* Ampleforth. *Heir:* *s* Lord Mauchline, *b* 29 Oct. 1974. *Died 30 June 2012.*

LOUGHEED, Hon. (Edgar) Peter, CC 1987; PC (Can.) 1982; QC (Can.) 1972; Counsel, Bennett Jones LLP, Barristers and Solicitors, Calgary, Edmonton and Toronto; *b* Calgary, 26 July 1928; *s* of late Edgar Donald Lougheed and Edna Bauld; *m* 1952, Jeanne Estelle Rogers, Edmonton; two *s* two *d*. *Educ:* public and secondary schs, Calgary; Univ. of Alberta (BA, LLB); Harvard Grad. Sch. of Business (MBA). Read law with Calgary firm of lawyers; called to Bar of Alberta, 1955, and practised law with same firm, 1955–56. Joined Mannix Co. Ltd, as Sec., 1956 (Gen. Counsel, 1958, Vice-Pres., 1959, Dir, 1960). Entered private legal practice, 1962. Chm. and Dir, Keyera Energy Mgt Ltd: Member: Adv. Bd, KERN Partners Ltd; Bd, MEG Energy Corp. Elected: Provincial Leader of Progressive Conservative Party of Alberta, also Member for Calgary West, 1965; Leader of the Official Opposition, 1967; Premier of Alberta, 1971–85 (re-elected 1975, 1979 and 1982). Mem., Trilateral Commn, 1999–2009; Co-Chair, N American Forum. Mem. Bd, Historical Foundn of Canada, 1999–2009. Chancellor, Queen's Univ., Ontario, 1996–2002, then Chancellor Emeritus (John Orr Award, 2008). Hon. LLD: St Francis Xavier, 1983; Alberta, 1986; Calgary, 1986; Windsor, Lethbridge, 1988; Dalhousie, 1995; Queen's, 1996; Toronto, 1997. *Recreation:* golf. *Address:* (office) 4500 Bankers Hall East, 855 2nd Street SW, Calgary, AB T2P 4K7, Canada. *Died 13 Sept. 2012.*

LOUISY, Rt Hon. Sir Allan (Fitzgerald Laurent), KCMG 2005; CBE 1983; PC 1981; barrister; *b* Laborie, St Lucia, 5 Sept. 1916. Clerk, Educn Dept, St Lucia; called to the Bar, Middle Temple and St Lucia, 1949; first Supervisor of Elections, St Lucia, 1950; Crown Attorney, Magistrate, then Registrar of the Supreme Court and Court of Appeal,

Jamaica; Judge of the Supreme Court, Windward and Leeward Islands, until 1973. Chm., Nat. Insurance Scheme. Mem. (St Lucia Lab) Laborie, House of Assembly, 1974–82; Leader, St Lucia Labour Party, 1974–82; Prime Minister of St Lucia, and Minister of Finance, Home Affairs, Inf. and Tourism, 1979–81; Minister without Portfolio, 1981–82; Attorney Gen., 1982. Gen. Sec., Seamen and Waterfront Workers Trade Union. Pres., St Lucia Civil Service Assoc. St Lucia Cross, 1998. *Address:* Laborie, St Lucia, West Indies. *Died 2 March 2011.*

LOUTH, 16th Baron *cr* 1541; **Otway Michael James Oliver Plunkett;** *b* 19 Aug. 1929; *o s* of Otway Randal Percy Oliver Plunkett, 15th Baron, and Ethel May, *d* of Walter John Gallichan, Jersey, Channel Islands; *S* father, 1950; *m* 1951, Angela Patricia Cullinane (*d* 2011), Jersey; three *s* two *d*. *Heir: s* Hon. Jonathan Oliver Plunkett, BSc, AMIEE [*b* 4 Nov. 1952; *m* 1981, Jennifer, *d* of Norman Oliver Hodgetts, Weston-super-Mare; one *s* one *d*]. *Died 6 Jan. 2013.*

LOVELL, Sir (Alfred Charles) Bernard, Kt 1961; OBE 1946; FRS 1955; Founder and Director of Jodrell Bank Experimental Station, Cheshire, subseq. Nuffield Radio Astronomy Laboratories, 1951–81 (renamed Jodrell Bank Observatory, 2000); Professor of Radio Astronomy, University of Manchester, 1951–80, then Emeritus Professor; *b* 31 Aug. 1913; *s* of G. Lovell, Oldland Common, Gloucestershire; *m* 1937, Mary Joyce Chesterman (*d* 1993); two *s* three *d*. *Educ:* Kingswood Grammar Sch., Bristol; University of Bristol. Asst Lectr in Physics, Univ. of Manchester, 1936–39; Telecommunication Res. Establishment, 1939–45; Physical Laboratories, Univ. of Manchester and Jodrell Bank Experimental Station, Cheshire; Lectr, 1945, Sen. Lectr, 1947, Reader, 1949, in Physics. Reith Lectr, 1958; Lectures: Condon, 1962; Guthrie, 1962; Halley, 1964; Queen's, Berlin, 1970; Brockington, Kingston, Ont, 1970; Bickley, Oxford, 1977; Crookshank, RCR, 1977; Angel Meml, Newfoundland, 1977; Blackett Meml, Operational Res. Soc., 1987. Vis. Montague Burton Prof. of Internat. Relations, Univ. of Edinburgh, 1973. Member: Air Navigation Cttee, 1953–56 (Vice-Chm., 1955–56); Air Warfare Cttee, 1954–60; ARC, 1955–58; Radar & Signals Adv. Bd, 1956–59; Sci. Adv. Council, 1957–60; Guided Weapons Adv. Bd, 1958–60; SRC, 1965–70; Amer. Philosophical Soc., 1974–. Pres., RAS, 1969–71; Vice-Pres., Internat. Astronomical Union, 1970–76; Pres., British Assoc., 1975–76. Pres., Guild of Church Musicians, 1976–89; Jun. Warden, 1984–85, Sen. Warden, 1985–86, Master, 1986–87, Musicians' Co. Hon. Freeman, City of Manchester, 1977. Hon. Fellow, Society of Engineers, 1964; Hon. Foreign Member American Academy of Arts and Sciences, 1955; Hon. Life Member, New York Academy, 1960; Hon. Member: Royal Swedish Academy, 1962; RNCM, 1981; Manchester Lit. & Philos. Soc., 1988. Hon. LLD: Edinburgh, 1961; Calgary, 1966; Liverpool, 1999; Hon. DSc: Leicester, 1961; Leeds, 1966; London, 1967; Bath, 1967; Bristol, 1970; Manchester, 2008; DUniv: Stirling, 1974; Surrey, 1975; Hon. FIET (Hon. FIEE, 1967); Hon. FInstP, 1976. Duddell Medal, 1954; Royal Medal, 1960; Daniel and Florence Guggenheim International Astronautics Award, 1961; Ordre du Mérite pour la Recherche et l'Invention, 1962; Churchill Gold Medal, 1964; Maitland Lecturer and Silver Medallist, Institution of Structural Engineers, 1964; Second RSA American Exchange Lectr, Philadelphia, 1980; Benjamin Franklin Medal, RSA, 1980; Gold Medal, Royal Astronomical Soc., 1981; Rutherford Meml Lectr, Royal Soc., 1984; John Dalton Medal, Eur. Geoscis Union, 2009. Commander's Order of Merit, Polish People's Republic, 1975. *Publications:* Science and Civilisation, 1939; World Power Resources and Social Development, 1945; Radio Astronomy, 1951; Meteor Astronomy, 1954; The Exploration of Space by Radio, 1957; The Individual and The Universe, (BBC Reith Lectures, 1958); The Exploration of Outer Space (Gregynog Lectures, 1961); Discovering the Universe, 1963; Our Present Knowledge of the Universe, 1967; (ed with T. Margerison) The Explosion of Science: The Physical Universe, 1967; The Story of Jodrell Bank, 1968; The Origins and International Economics of Space Exploration, 1973; Out of the Zenith, 1973; Man's Relation to the Universe, 1975; P. M. S. Blackett: a biographical memoir, 1976; In the Centre of Immensities, 1978; Emerging Cosmology, 1981; The Jodrell Bank Telescopes, 1985; Voice of the Universe, 1987; (with Sir Francis Graham Smith) Pathways to the Universe, 1988; Astronomer by Chance (autobiog.), 1990; Echoes of War, 1991; many publications in Physical and Astronomical journals. *Recreations:* cricket, gardening, music. *Address:* The Quinta, Swettenham, Cheshire CW12 2LD. *T:* (01477) 571254. *E:* acbl@jb.man.ac.uk. *Clubs:* Athenæum, MCC; Lancashire County Cricket (Pres., 1995–96). *Died 6 Aug. 2012.*

LOVELOCK, Sir Douglas (Arthur), KCB 1979 (CB 1974); First Church Estates Commissioner, 1983–93; Chairman, Central Board of Finance of the Church of England, 1983–92; *b* 7 Sept. 1923; *s* of late Walter and Irene Lovelock; *m* 1961, Valerie Margaret (*née* Lane); one *s* one *d*. *Educ:* Bec Sch., London. Entered Treasury, 1949; Min. of Supply, 1952; Private Sec. to Permanent Sec., 1953–54; Principal, 1954; Private Sec. to successive Ministers of Aviation (Rt Hon. Peter Thorneycroft and Rt Hon. Julian Amery), 1961–63; Asst Sec., 1963; Under-Sec. (Contracts), Min. of Technology, subseq. Min. of Aviation Supply, 1968–71; Asst Under-Sec. of State (Personnel), MoD, 1971–72; Dep. Sec., DTI, 1972–74, Depts of Trade, Industry, Prices and Consumer Protection, 1974–77; Chm., Bd of Customs and Excise, 1977–83. Chm., Civil Service Benevolent Fund, 1980–83. Chm., Review of Citizens' Advice Bureaux Service, 1983–84. Governor, Whitgift Foundn (Whitgift Sch., Trinity Sch., Old Palace Sch.), 1986–93 and 1998– (Chm., 1993–98). *Publications:* While I Remember, 1998. *Recreations:* walking, gardening, outdoor activities generally. *Address:* 154 Chaldon Way, Coulsdon, Surrey CR5 1DF. *T:* (01737) 555211. *Died 30 July 2014.*

LOW, Brian Buik, CBE 1994; HM Diplomatic Service, retired; High Commissioner to Papua New Guinea, 1994–97; *b* 15 Nov. 1937; *s* of Robert James Low and Helen Duncan Low; *m* 1960, Anita Joan Allum; three *d*. *Educ:* Arbroath High Sch. Served RAF, 1956–61. Joined Diplomatic Service, 1962; FO, 1962–65; Sofia, 1965–67; Sydney, 1967–69; Kuala Lumpur, 1969–73; Moscow, 1973–74; FCO, 1974–78; Singapore, 1978–81; Commercial Consul, British Trade Develt Office, NY, 1981–84; First Sec., FCO, 1984–88; Head of Chancery, Lima, 1988–91; Ambassador to Estonia, 1991–94. *Recreations:* music, reading, golf, watching sport. *Clubs:* Carnoustie Golf; Singapore Cricket. *Died 29 Oct. 2015.*

LOW, Prof. Donald Anthony, AO 2005; DPhil, LittD; FRHistS, FAHA, FASSA; President of Clare Hall, 1987–94, Smuts Professor of the History of the British Commonwealth, 1983–87, and Deputy Vice-Chancellor, 1990–94, University of Cambridge; *b* Nainital, India, 22 June 1927; *o s* of late Canon Donald Phillip Low and Winifred (*née* Edmunds); *m* 1952, Isobel Smails; one *s* two *d*. *Educ:* Haileybury and ISC; Exeter Coll., Oxford (Open Scholar in Modern History, 1944; Amelia Jackson Sen. Student, 1948; MA, DPhil; Hon. Fellow, 1992); PhD 1983, LittD 1998, Cantab. Lectr, subseq. Sen. Lectr, Makerere Coll., University Coll. of E Africa, 1951–58; Uganda corresp., The Times, 1952–58; Fellow, subseq. Sen. Fellow in History, Res. Sch. of Social Sciences, ANU, 1959–64; Founding Dean of Sch. of African and Asian Studies, and Prof. of Hist., Univ. of Sussex, 1964–72; Australian National University: Prof. of History, 1973–83; Dir, Res. Sch. of Pacific Studies, 1973–75; Vice Chancellor, 1975–82; University Fellow, 1997–2000; University of Cambridge: Fellow, Churchill Coll., 1983–87; Dir, Centre of Internat. Studies, 1985–87; Mem., Council of Senate, 1985–88. Sen. Visitor Nuffield Coll., Oxford, 1956–57; Smuts Fellow and Vis. Fellow, Clare Hall, Cambridge, 1971–72 (Hon. Fellow, 1999). Chm., Educn Adv. Cttee, Aust. Develt Assistance Bureau, 1979–82; Mem. Exec., 1976–82, Dep. Chm., 1980, Aust. Vice-Chancellors' Cttee; Member: Council, Univ. of Papua New Guinea, 1974–82; Standing Cttee, Aust. Univs Internat. Develt Program, 1975–82; Council, ACU, 1980–82; Cttee, Australian Studies Centre, London Univ., 1983–94; Governing Body: Inst. of Develt Studies, Sussex Univ., 1966–72 and 1984–91; SOAS, 1983–94; Haileybury, 1985–94; Chm., Cttee of Management, Inst. of Commonwealth Studies, London Univ., 1984–94. Hon. Fellow: Inst. of Develt

Studies, UK, 1972; University House, ANU 1983. President: African Studies Assoc. of Aust. and Pacific, 1979–82; Asian Studies Assoc. of Aust., 1980–82; British Australian Studies Assoc., 1984–86; Chm., Co-ordinating Council, Area Studies Assoc., 1988–91; Vice-Pres., Australian Acad. of Humanities, 1996–98. Chm., Round Table Moot, 1992–94. Commander of the Order of Civil Merit (Spain), 1984. *Publications:* Buganda and British Overrule, 1900–1955 (with R. C. Pratt), 1960; (ed) Soundings in Modern South Asian History, 1968; (with J. C. Iltis and M. D. Wainwright) Government Archives in South Asia, 1969; Buganda in Modern History, 1971; The Mind of Buganda, 1971; Lion Rampant, 1973; (ed) Congress and the Raj 1917–1947, 1977; Oxford History of East Africa: (contrib.) Vol. I, 1963 and Vol. II, 1965; (contrib. and ed jtly) Vol. III, 1976; (ed) Constitutional Heads and Political Crises, 1988; (ed) The Indian National Congress, 1988; (ed jtly) Sovereigns and Surrogates, 1990; Eclipse of Empire, 1991; (ed) Political Inheritance of Pakistan, 1991; The Egalitarian Moment: Asia and Africa 1950–80, 1996; Britain and Indian Nationalism, 1997; (ed) Keith Hancock: legacies of an historian, 2001; Fabrication of Empire, 2009; articles on internat. history in jls. *Address:* H114 Goodwin Village, 35 Bonney Street, Ainslie, ACT 2602, Australia. *Died 12 Feb. 2015.*

LOW, Sir James (Richard) Morrison-, 3rd Bt *cr* 1908; DL; DFH, CEng, MIET; Director, Osborne & Hunter Ltd, Glasgow, 1956–89 (Electrical Engineer with firm, since 1952); *b* 3 Aug. 1925; *s* of Sir Walter John Morrison-Low, 2nd Bt and Dorothy Ruth de Quincey Quincey (*d* 1946); *S* father, 1955; *m* 1953, Ann Rawson Gordon (*d* 2006); one *s* three *d*. *Educ:* Ardvreck; Harrow; Merchiston. Served Royal Corps of Signals, 1943–47; demobilised with rank of Captain. Faraday House Engineering Coll., 1948–52. Chm., Scottish Cttee, Nat. Inspection Council for Electrical Installation Contracting, 1982–88; Pres., Electrical Contractors Assoc. of Scotland, 1982–84. Chm., Fife Area Scout Council, 1966–84. Hon. Pipe-Major, Royal Scottish Pipers Soc., 1981–83. Eur Ing, 1990. DL Fife, 1978. *Recreations:* shooting, piping. *Heir:* *s* Richard Walter Morrison-Low [*b* 4 Aug. 1959; *m* 1994, Sandra Scott; one *s* one *d*]. *Address:* Kilmaron House, Cupar, Fife KY15 4NE. *T:* (01334) 652248. *Clubs:* New, Royal Scottish Pipers Society (Edinburgh). *Died 14 Oct. 2012.*

LOW, Prof. Martin Geoffrey, PhD; FRS 1996; Professor of Physiology and Cellular Biophysics, Columbia University, New York, since 1994; *b* 27 July 1950; *s* of Kenneth Douglas Low and Joan Elizabeth Low; *m* 1979, Eileen Ann Whalen; two *s*. *Educ:* Univ. of Newcastle upon Tyne (BSc Biochem.); Univ. of Birmingham (PhD Biochem. 1975). Postdoctoral Research Fellow: Univ. of Birmingham, 1974–77; Cornell Univ., 1977–79; Instructor, Med. Coll. of Va, 1979–81; Oklahoma Medical Research Foundation: Asst Mem., 1981–86; Associate Mem., 1986–87; Associate Prof., Columbia Univ., NY, 1987–94. *Publications:* contrib. original research and review articles in scientific jls incl. Science, Nature, Jl Biol Chem., Biochem. Jl. *Recreations:* reading, listening to music, fell walking, gardening. *Address:* Department of Physiology and Cellular Biophysics, Columbia University, 630 W 168th Street, New York, NY 10032, USA. *Died 6 Aug. 2013.*

LOWDEN, Gordon Stuart; President, Institute of Chartered Accountants of Scotland, 1989–90 (Senior Vice-President, 1988–89); Chairman, Dundee Port Authority, 1979–92; *b* 22 May 1927; *s* of James Soutar Lowden and Jean Lowden; *m* 1953, Kathleen Arnot; two *s* one *d*. *Educ:* Dundee High Sch.; Strathallan Sch.; St John's Coll., Cambridge (MA); Univ. of St Andrews (LLB). CA. Moody Stuart & Robertson, later Peat Marwick McLintock: training, 1949–53; Partner, 1959; Office Managing Partner, 1985; retired 1988. University of Dundee: Lectr, Sen. Lectr, 1955–83; Hon. Vis. Prof., Dept of Accountancy and Business Finance, 1987. *Recreations:* golf, watching sport, bridge. *Address:* 169 Hamilton Street, Barnhill, Dundee DD5 2RE. *T:* (01382) 778360. *Club:* Royal and Ancient Golf. *Died 21 Nov. 2012.*

LOWDEN, Richard Purdie; His Honour Judge Lowden; DL; a Circuit Judge, North Eastern Circuit, since 1994; *b* 23 April 1948; *s* of late Thomas Geoffrey Lowden, FRCS and Margaret Lowden (*née* Purdie); *m* 1973, Patricia (*d* 2002); one *s* two *d*. *Educ:* Sedbergh Sch.; Keble Coll., Oxford (MA). Called to the Bar, Inner Temple, 1971; a Recorder of the Crown Court, 1988–94; Resident Judge, Durham Crown Court, 2001–09; Hon. Judicial Recorder, City of Durham, 2005–10. DL Co. Durham, 2009. *Recreations:* fishing, fell walking, theatre. *Address:* Newcastle upon Tyne Combined Court Centre, Quayside, Newcastle upon Tyne NE1 2LA. *Died 5 July 2012.*

LOWE, Geoffrey Colin; aviation consultant, 1980–88; *b* 7 Sept. 1920; *s* of late Colin Roderick and Elsie Lowe; *m* 1948, Joan Stephen (*d* 1985); one *d*; *m* 1988, Jean Marion Bailey (*née* Wigginton) (*d* 2007). *Educ:* Reigate Grammar Sch. GPO, 1937; Exchequer and Audit Dept, 1939. Served War, RAFVR, 1941–46 (Flt-Lt). Asst Principal, Min. of Civil Aviation, 1947; Private Sec. to Permanent Sec., MCA, 1950; Principal, 1950; Colonial Office, 1954–57; Min. of Transport and Civil Aviation, 1957–61; Civil Air Attaché, SE Asia, 1961–64; Asst Sec., Overseas Policy Div., Min. of Aviation, 1964–68; Investment Grants Div., Bd of Trade, 1968–71; Counsellor (Civil Aviation), British Embassy, Washington, 1971–73, Counsellor (Civil Aviation and Shipping), Washington, 1973–74; Under Sec. (Management Services and Manpower), Depts of Industry and Trade, 1974–80. *Recreations:* theatre, crossword puzzles. *Address:* 13 Highwood, Sunset Avenue, Woodford Green, Essex IG8 0SZ. *T:* (020) 8504 7035. *Club:* Civil Service. *Died 14 Nov. 2011.*

LOWES, Peter Donald; Director, Anti-Slavery Society for Protection of Human Rights, 1987–89; *b* 13 Sept. 1926; *s* of Col J. H. Lowes and Queenie Frances Lowes (*née* Bowyer); *m* 1954, Linnea Newton (marr. diss. 1980); one *s* two *d*. *Educ:* Bradfield Coll.; Emmanuel Coll., Cambridge (MA); Univ. of British Columbia (LLB); Geneva Univ. (PhD). Served with Royal Engineers, 1946–48. Master, Wanganui Collegiate Sch., NZ, 1949, Upper Canada Coll., Toronto, 1950–51; practised law, Vancouver, 1953–55; UNRWA, Jordan, 1955–58; journalist, Canadian Broadcasting Corp., 1958; UN Narcotic Drugs, Geneva, 1959–65; External Aid, Canadian Govt, Ottawa, 1965–66; Resident Representative, United Nations Development Programme: Lesotho, 1966–68; Swaziland, 1968–71; Malaŵi, 1971–74; HQ, NY, 1974–75; Morocco, 1975–79; Co-ordinator, Internat. Drinking Water Supply and Sanitation Decade, Geneva, 1979–86. Mem. Bd, 1980–86, Consultant, 1987, Internat. Reference Centre, The Hague; UNDP and World Bank Consultant, 1987–97. Adviser: CARE (UK), 1987–93; Help the Aged, 1987–93; Crisis at Christmas, 1989–99; St Ethelburga's Project, 1995–99. *Publications:* The Genesis of International Narcotics Control, 1965. *Recreations:* walking, mountaineering, history. *Address:* Apartment 34, 4 Clos Belmont, Geneva 1208, Switzerland. *T:* 7350313. *Clubs:* Alpine, Climbers'. *Died 24 June 2012.*

LOWSON, Prof. Martin Vincent, FREng; FRAeS; President, ULTraPRT (formerly Advanced Transport Systems) Ltd, since 2010 (Chief Executive Officer, 1995–2007; Deputy Chairman, 2007–10); Senior Research Fellow, University of Bristol, since 2003; *b* 5 Jan. 1938; *s* of Alfred Vincent Lowson and Irene Gertrude Lowson; *m* 1961, Ann Pennicutt; one *s* one *d*. *Educ:* King's Sch., Worcester; Univ. of Southampton (BScEng, PhD). Apprentice, Vickers Armstrong (Aircraft), 1955; Res. student and Assistant, Univ. of Southampton, 1960; Head, Applied Physics, Wyle Labs, Huntsville, USA, 1964; Rolls-Royce Reader, Loughborough Univ., 1969; Westland Helicopters: Chief Scientist, 1973; Div. Dir, Corporate Develt, 1979; Bristol University: Sir George White Prof. of Aerospace Engrg, 1986–2001; Prof. of Advanced Transport, 2001–03. Chm., Flow Solutions Ltd, 1986–97. Fellow, Acoustical Soc. of America, 1971; FREng (FEng 1991); FAIAA 1996. Viva Award, Carmen's Co., 2009; Aeroacoustics Award, AIAA, 2011. *Publications:* numerous papers in learned jls, and patents. *Recreations:* research, squash, bluegrass music. *Address:* Alpenfels, North Road, Leigh Woods, Bristol BS8 3PJ. *T:* (0117) 973 6497. *Died 14 June 2013.*

LOWTHER, Sir John (Luke), KCVO 1997; CBE 1983; JP; Lord Lieutenant for Northamptonshire, 1984–98; *b* 17 Nov. 1923; *s* of Col J.G. Lowther, CBE, DSO, MC, TD and the Hon. Mrs Lowther; *m* 1952, Jennifer Jane Bevan; one *s* two *d*. *Educ:* Eton; Trinity College, Oxford. MA 1949. Served King's Royal Rifle Corps, 1942–47. Worked for Singer Sewing Co., USA, 1949–51; Managing Dir, own manufacturing Co., 1951–60; farmer, 1960–. CC Northants, 1970–84 (Leader of Council, 1977–81); High Sheriff 1971, DL 1977, JP 1984, Northants. Hon. Colonel: Royal Anglian Regt (Northamptonshire), TA, 1986–89; Northants ACF, 1991–96. *Recreations:* shooting, countryman. *Address:* Nortoft Grange, Guilsborough, Northants NN6 8QB. *T:* (01604) 740289. *Club:* Boodle's. *Died 11 April 2011.*

LOYD, Christopher Lewis, MC 1943; *b* 1 June 1923; 3rd and *o* surv. *s* of late Arthur Thomas Loyd, OBE, JP, Lockinge, Wantage, Berks, and Dorothy, *d* of late Paul Ferdinand Willert, Headington, Oxford; *m* 1957, Joanna (marr. diss.), *d* of Captain Arthur Turberville Smith-Bingham, Milburn Manor, Malmesbury, Wilts; two *s* one *d*. *Educ:* Eton; King's Coll., Cambridge (MA). Served 1942–46, with Coldstream Guards, Captain. ARICS 1952, FRICS 1955. Mem., Jockey Club, 1968–2008. Trustee, Wallace Collection, 1973–90. JP 1950, DL 1954, Oxfordshire (formerly Berks); High Sheriff of Berkshire, 1961. *Address:* Betterton Farm House, Ardington, Wantage, Oxfordshire OX12 8QP. *T:* (01235) 833265. *Club:* Boodle's. *Died 14 July 2013.*

LUCAS, Keith Stephen; artist; *b* 28 Aug. 1924; *m* Pamela Izzard (marr. diss.); two *s*; *m* 1969, Rona Stephanie Lucas (*née* Levy); (one *d* decd), and two step *s*. *Educ:* Royal Coll. of Art (ARCA). London Press Exchange, 1956–64; Prof. of Film and Television, Royal Coll. of Art, 1964–72 (first holder of Chair); Dir, British Film Institute, 1972–78; Television Consultant, BFI, 1979–84; Hd of Radio, Film and Television Studies, Christ Church Coll., Canterbury, 1984–89. Artistic Dir, Commonwealth Film and TV Fest. and supporting arts prog., Cyprus, 1980. Exhibitions: retrospective 1956–86, Poor Priests Hosp., Canterbury, 1986; John Nevill Gall., Canterbury, 1988; Royal Mus., Canterbury, 1990; Anna Mei Chadwick Gall., 1993, 1995; Cleary Gall., Canterbury, 1993. Chairman: Canterbury New Theatre Ltd, 1979–83; Canterbury Theatre and Festival Trust, 1983–86 (Pres., 1986); Vice-Pres., Centre Internat. de Liaison des Ecoles de Cinéma et de Télévision, 1970–72. Governor: North East London Poly., 1971–72; Canterbury Coll. of Art (formerly Canterbury Sch. of Art), 1971–74, 1981–87; Maidstone Coll. of Art, 1982–87; Kent Inst. of Art and Design, 1987–89. Hon. Fellow, Royal Coll. of Art, 1972. *Recreations:* writing, listening to music. *Address:* The Penthouse, 88 Valiant House, Vicarage Crescent, SW11 3LX. *T:* (020) 7228 5289. *Club:* Chelsea Arts. *Died 23 March 2012.*

LUCAS, Prof. Raleigh Barclay; Professor of Oral Pathology, University of London, 1954–79, then Emeritus; Consultant Pathologist, Royal Dental Hospital of London, 1950–79; *b* 3 June 1914; *s* of H. Lucas; *m* 1942, Violet Sorrell; one *d* (one *s* decd). *Educ:* George Watson's Coll.; Univ. of Edinburgh. MB, ChB (Edinburgh) 1937; DPH 1939; MD 1945; MRCP 1946; FRCPath 1963; FRCP 1974; FDS RCS 1974. Asst Bacteriologist, Edinburgh Royal Infirmary, 1939–40; Pathologist, Stoke Mandeville Hosp. and Royal Buckinghamshire Hospital, 1947–49; Reader in Pathology, University of London, 1950–54; Dean, Sch. of Dental Surgery, Royal Dental Hospital of London, 1958–73. Examiner in Pathology and Bacteriology for dental degrees, Univs of London, Glasgow, Birmingham, Sheffield, Liverpool and Wales. Served War of 1939–45, Major RAMC. FRSocMed; Fellow and Past Pres., Royal Medical Society; Mem. Pathological Soc. of Great Britain and Ireland; Mem. BMA. *Publications:* (jtly) Bacteriology for Students of Dental Surgery, 1954; Pathology of Tumours of the Oral Tissues, 1964; (jtly) Tumors of the Major Salivary Glands, 1974; (jtly) Atlas of Oral Pathology, 1985; various articles in medical and scientific journals. *Died 11 Oct. 2011.*

LUDLOW, Her Honour Caroline Mary; a Circuit Judge, 1997–2013; Designated Family Judge, Ipswich, 2003–13; *b* 25 Sept. 1947; *d* of William George Hughes Woodward and Mary Josephine Woodward; *m* 1st, 1970, Brian Ludlow (marr. diss. 1976); 2nd, 1987, John Warwick Everitt; one *d*. *Educ:* Hillingdon Court; St Mary's Grammar Sch.; Queen Mary Coll., London Univ. (LLM). Called to the Bar, Inner Temple, 1970; practised on South Eastern Circuit, 1979–97; a Recorder, 1995–97. Designated Family Judge, Chelmsford County Court, 2000–04. Chm., Children's Legal Centre, 2002–09. Mem., Law Sch. Adv. Cttee, 1992–, Court, 1999–, Essex Univ. (Bar Co-ordinator, Law in Action course, 1992–97). Trustee: SAFEchild, 2005–; Pact, 2006–14 (Chair, 2010–14); Porch Project, 2011–14; Suffolk Foundn, 2013–14. Patron, Ipswich Blind Soc., 2007–. Guardian of the Foyer, Ipswich, 2004–14. *Recreations:* reading, gardening. *Died 10 Dec. 2014.*

LUKE, 3rd Baron *cr* 1929, of Pavenham, Co. Bedford; **Arthur Charles St John Lawson Johnston;** fine art dealer, since 1972; an Opposition Whip, House of Lords, 1997–2010; *b* 13 Jan. 1933; *e s* of 2nd Baron Luke and Barbara, *d* of Sir FitzRoy Hamilton Anstruther-Gough-Calthorpe, 1st Bt; *S* father, 1996; *m* 1st, 1959, Silvia Maria (marr. diss. 1971), *yr d* of Don Honorio Roigt, Argentina; one *s* two *d*; 2nd, 1971, Sarah Louise, *d* of Richard Hearne, OBE; one *s*. *Educ:* Eton; Trinity Coll., Cambridge (BA Hons Hist.). Elected Mem., H of L, 1999–2015; Opposition spokesman on defence, and on culture, media and sport, 2004–10; Chm., Works of Art Cttee, 2010–14. Mem., Beds CC, 1965–70 (Chm., Staffing Cttee, 1967–70). President: Nat. Assoc. of Warehousekeepers, 1962–78; Internat. Assoc. of Book-Keepers, 1997–2001. Comdr, St John Ambulance, Beds, 1985–90 (Comr, 1972–85). Member Court: Corp. of Sons of the Clergy, 1980–2005; Drapers' Co., 1993– (Master, 2001–02). High Sheriff, Beds, 1969–70, DL Beds, 1989–2004. KStJ 1988. *Recreations:* shooting, fishing. *Heir:* *s* Hon. Ian James St John Lawson Johnston [*b* 3 Oct. 1963; *m* 1998, Rowena Jane, *y d* of John Aldington; two *s* one *d*]. *Address:* The Hollies, Gretton, Corby, Northants NN17 3DL. *Died 2 Oct. 2015.*

LUMET, Sidney; film director; *b* Philadelphia, 25 June 1924; *o s* of Baruch and Eugenia Lumet; *m* Rita Gam (marr. diss.); *m* 1956, Gloria Vanderbilt (marr. diss. 1963); *m* 1963, Gail Jones (marr. diss. 1978); two *d*; *m* 1980, Mary Gimbel. *Educ:* Professional Children's Sch., NY; Columbia Univ. Served US Army, SE Asia, 1942–46. Appeared as child actor: Dead End; The Eternal Road; Sunup to Sunday; Schoolhouse on the Lot; My Heart's in the Highlands; Dir, Summer Stock, 1947–49; taught acting, High Sch. of Professional Arts; Associate Dir, CBS, 1950, Dir, 1951–57. *TV shows include:* Danger; Your Are There; Alcoa: The Sacco and Vanzetti Story; Goodyear Playhouse; Best of Broadway; Omnibus. *Films directed include:* Twelve Angry Men, 1957; Stage Struck, 1958; That Kind of Woman, 1959; The Fugitive Kind, 1960; A View from the Bridge, Long Day's Journey into Night, 1962; Fail Safe, 1964; The Pawnbroker, The Hill, 1965; The Group, 1966; The Deadly Affair, 1967; Bye Bye Braverman, Last of the Mobile Hot Shots, Child's Play, The Seagull, 1969; The Anderson Tapes, 1971; The Offence, 1973; Serpico, Murder on the Orient Express, 1974; Dog Day Afternoon, 1975; Network, 1977; Equus, 1977; The Wiz, 1979; Just Tell Me What You Want, 1979; Prince of the City, 1980; Deathtrap, 1981; The Verdict, 1982; Daniel, 1983; Garbo Talks, 1984; Power, 1985; The Morning After, 1987; Family Business, 1990; Q & A, 1991; A Stranger Among Us, 1992; Guilty as Sin, 1993; Night Falls on Manhattan, 1996; Gloria, 1999; Before the Devil Knows You're Dead, 2008; *play:* Caligula, 1960. Hon. Acad. Award for Lifetime Achievement, 2005. *Died 9 April 2011.*

LUMSDEN, George Innes, FRSE; CGeol, FGS; consultant in geology and scientific staff recruitment, 1991–2001; *b* 27 June 1926; *s* of George Lumsden and Margaret Ann Frances Lumsden (*née* Cockburn); *m* 1958, Sheila Thomson; two *s* one *d*. *Educ:* Banchory Academy; Aberdeen University (Lyon Prize in Geol.; BSc). Geological Survey of GB, 1949; District Geologist S Scotland, 1970, Asst Dir and Sen. Officer Scotland, 1980, Inst. of Geol Scis; British Geological Survey: CSO and Dep. Dir, 1982–85; Dir, 1985–87; Mem., CS Commn Sci. Div.'s Panel of

Chairmen, 1988–91; Chm. Recruitment Bds, DRA, then DERA, 1991–2001. Member: Council of Management, Macaulay Inst. for Soil Research, 1980–87; Engineering and Sci. Adv. Cttee, Derby Coll. of Higher Educn, 1983–87; Geol. Museum Adv. Panel, 1985–87; Chm., Dirs of Western European Geol Surveys' Standing Gp on Envmtl Geology, 1984–87, Hon. Pres., 1987–, Hon. Sec., 1988–95; Sec., Forum of European Geol Surveys, 1996–2002. *Publications:* (ed) Geology and the Environment in Western Europe, 1992, 2nd edn 1994; maps, papers and books on geol topics in official Geol Survey. *Recreations:* music, theatre, sport, gardening. *Address:* 5 Churchill Place, Yarnton, Oxford OX5 1GQ. *Died 4 Sept. 2012.*

LUMSDEN, James Alexander, MBE 1945; TD 1962; DL; Partner, Maclay, Murray & Spens, Solicitors, Glasgow and Edinburgh, 1947–82; *b* 24 Jan. 1915; *s* of late Sir James Robert Lumsden and Lady (Henrietta) Lumsden (*née* Macfarlane Reid); *m* 1947, Sheila (decd), *d* of late Malcolm Cross and Evelyn Cross (*née* Newlands); three *s*. *Educ:* Rugby Sch.; Corpus Christi Coll., Cambridge (BA, MA 1995; LLB). Director: Bank of Scotland, 1958–85; Weir Group PLC, 1957–84; William Baird PLC, 1959–84; Murray Growth Trust PLC and other companies in Murray Johnstone Group, 1967–85 (Chm., 1971–84); Scottish Provident Instn, 1968–85 (Chm., 1977–83); Burmah Oil Co. Ltd, 1957–76 (Chm., 1971–75). Mem. Jenkins Cttee on Company Law. Mem., Queen's Body Guard for Scotland, Royal Company of Archers, 1963–. DL Dunbartonshire, 1966. *Address:* Arden-Beag, 7 Station Road, Craigendoran, Helensburgh G84 7BG. *T:* (01436) 676204. *Clubs:* New (Edinburgh); Western (Glasgow). *Died 31 March 2013.*

LUNCH, John, CBE 1975; VRD 1965; FCA, FCILT; Director-General of the Port of London Authority, and Board Member, 1971–76; Chairman: Comprehensive Shipping Group, 1973–75; Transcontinental Air Ltd, 1973–75; *b* 11 Nov. 1919; *s* of late Percy Valentine Lunch and Amy (*née* Somerville); *m* 1st, 1943, Joyce Barbara Clerke (*d* 1989), *d* of late Arnold Basil O'Connell Clerke and Norah Buckley (*née* Browne); two *s*; 2nd, 1995, Fiona Charis Elizabeth Fleck, *d* of late Arthur Axel Miller, MC and Charis Harrison Martin (*née* Petty), and *widow* of Peter Hugo Fleck. *Educ:* Roborough Sch., Eastbourne. FCA 1946; FCILT (FCIT 1965). Served War, Lt RNVR, Medit. and Home Fleets, 1939–46 (N Atlantic convoys, Crete, N Africa, Malta convoys, Sicily D-Day landings; Torpedo specialist, 1944), subseq. Permanent RNVR, later RNR; Lt-Comdr RNR, retd list, 1969; Lt-Col RE (TA), Engr and Logistic Staff Corps (formerly Engr and Transport Staff Corps), 1971, Col, 1976, retd list, 1994. In business in City, 1946–48: Asst Man. Dir, Tokenhouse Securities Corp. Ltd, 1947, and dir several cos; British Transport Commn, 1948–61: road and rail transport and ancillary businesses; PLA, 1961; Dir of Finance, also Dir of Commerce, 1966; Asst Dir-Gen., responsible docks and harbour, 1969; Chairman: (and founder) PLA Port Users Consultative Cttee, 1966–71; Internat. Port Develt Cttee, Internat. Assoc. of Ports and Harbors, 1972–76; Pres., Inst. of Freight Forwarders, 1972–73. Chm., London Industrial Chartered Accountants, 1971–72; Member Council: Inst. of Chartered Accountants, 1970–77; Chartered Inst. of Transport, 1973–76; MInstRE, 2007. Mem. Cttee of Management (a Trustee), 1977–94, a Vice-Pres., 1987–94, a Life Vice-Pres., 1994, RNLI; Founder Chm., RNLI Manhood Br., 1976–78; Pres., RNLI, Hayling Island Lifeboat Station, 1978–88; Hon. Art Adviser, RNLI, 1981–99. Hon. Life Mem. Internat. Assoc. of Airport and Seaport Police, 1974. CCMI (FBIM 1971); FCIM (FInstM 1973); FILT 1999; FRSA (Council nominee) 1976; Hon. FIFP 1986. Freeman: City of London, 1970; Watermen & Lightermen's Co. of River Thames, 1970 (Court Mem., 1976–80, Hon. Court Mem., 1980–). ADC to Governor of Louisiana, with rank Adm., 1971–. Malta GC 50th Anniv. Medal, 1992. *Publications:* The Chartered Accountant in Top Management, 1965; A Plan for Britain's Ports, 1975. *Recreations:* art, opera, horse racing, sailing. *Address:* Martins, East Ashling, Chichester, West Sussex PO18 9AX. *T:* (01243) 575252. *Clubs:* Army and Navy; Itchenor Sailing (West Sussex). *Died 10 May 2011.*

LUND, John Walter Guerrier, CBE 1975; DSc, PhD; FRS 1963; FSB, FCIWEM; Botanist, at Windermere Laboratory of Freshwater Biological Association, 1945–78; Deputy Chief Scientific Officer; *b* 27 Nov. 1912; *s* of George E. Lund and Kate Lund (*née* Hardwick); *m* 1949, Hilda M. Canter; one *s* one *d*. *Educ:* Sedbergh Sch.; Univ. of Manchester; London Univ. (PhD 1939; DSc 1951). Demonstrator in Botany, Univ. of Manchester, also Queen Mary Coll. and Chelsea Polytechnic, Univ. of London, 1935–38; Temp. Lectr in Botany, Univ. of Sheffield, 1936; Staff Biologist, W Midland Forensic Science Laboratory, Birmingham, 1938–45. Hon. DSc Buckingham, 1988. *Publications:* (ed with Elizabeth Howarth) Lake Sediments and Environmental History: studies in palaeolimnology and palaeoecology in honour of Winifred Tutin, 1984; (with Hilda Canter-Lund) Freshwater Algae: their microscopic world explored, 1995; papers and articles in scientific jls, symposium vols, etc. *Recreations:* gardening, Russian. *Address:* Ellerbeck, Ellerigg Road, Ambleside, Cumbria LA22 9EU. *T:* (015394) 32369. *Died 21 March 2015.*

LUND, Rodney Cookson; Chairman: Short Brothers, 1988–90 (Director, 1988–99); National Bus Co., 1986–88 (part-time Member, 1989–92); *b* 16 June 1936; *s* of late Arthur and Doris Lund; *m* 1st, Lynda Brooks (marr. diss.); one *s*; 2nd, Hyacinth, (Miki), Wallace. *Educ:* Wallasey Grammar School; Liverpool University (BCom Hons). Served RAPC, 1957–59. Evans Medical, 1959; Carreras Rothmans, 1960–64; Partner, Urwick Orr & Partners, 1964–66 and 1969–73; Man. Dir, The Mace Voluntary Gp, 1966–69; Vice-Chm., Produce Importers Alliance, 1966–69; Executive Director: Rank Radio International, 1973–75; British Sugar Corp., 1976–82; Woolworth Holdings, 1982–86; Hazlewood Foods, 1991–2001. Mem., Nationalised Industries Chairmen's Gp, 1986–88; Chm., The Enterprise Support Gp, 1991–94. CCMI. *Recreations:* travel, opera, cooking. *Address:* 28 Chelsea Crescent, Chelsea Harbour, SW10 0XB. *T:* (020) 7352 2641. *Died 17 Jan. 2011.*

LUNN, Peter Northcote, CMG 1957; OBE 1951; Government Service, 1939–86; *b* 15 Nov. 1914; *e s* of late Sir Arnold Lunn; *m* 1939, Hon. (Eileen) Antoinette (*d* 1976), *d* of 15th Viscount Gormanston; two *s* two *d* (and one *s* one *d* decd); partner, Christa Palmer. *Educ:* Eton. Joined Govt Service, 1939; SIS, 1941; Malta, 1939–44; Italy, 1944–45; W Germany, 1945–46; London, 1946–48; Vienna, 1948–50; Bern, 1950–53; Berlin, 1953–56; London, 1956–57; Bonn, 1957–62; Beirut, 1962–67; London, 1967–86. Mem., Brit. International Ski team, 1931–37, Capt. 1934–37; Capt. British Olympic Ski team, 1936; competitor, Inferno downhill ski race, 1978–86, 1988–89, 1995–2005. *Publications:* High-Speed Ski-ing, 1935; Evil in High Places, 1947; A Ski-ing Primer, 1948, rev. edn 1951; The Guinness Book of Ski-ing, 1983. *Clubs:* Ski Club of Great Britain; Denham Water Ski. *Died 30 Nov. 2011.*

LUNNY, William Francis; Sheriff of South Strathclyde, Dumfries and Galloway, 1984–98; *b* 10 Dec. 1938; *s* of James F. Lunny and Sarah Ann Crawford or Lunny; *m* 1967, Elizabeth McDermott; two *s* one *d*. *Educ:* Our Lady's High School, Motherwell; Glasgow Univ. (MA, LLB). Solicitor, 1961–67; Depute Procurator Fiscal, 1967–74; Crown Counsel/Legal Draftsman, Antigua, 1974–76; Advocate, 1977. Barrister, Antigua, 1981. KHS 1989. *Recreations:* walking, travelling. *Died 2 May 2015.*

LUSH, Christopher Duncan, CMG 1983; HM Diplomatic Service, retired; Governor, British Institute of Human Rights, since 1988; Editor, Human Rights Case Digest, since 1989; *b* 4 June 1928; *s* of late Eric Duncan Thomas Lush and Iris Leonora (*née* Greenfield); *m* 1967, Marguerite Lilian (*d* 2005), *d* of Frederick Albert Bolden; (one *s* decd). *Educ:* Sedbergh; Magdalen Coll., Oxford. Called to Bar, Gray's Inn, 1953. Asst Legal Adviser, FO, 1959–62; Legal Adviser, Berlin, 1962–65, Dep. Political Adviser, Berlin, 1965–66; FO (later FCO), 1966–69; Head of Chancery, Amman, 1969–71; Head of Aviation and Telecommunications Dept, FCO, 1971–73; Canadian Nat. Defence Coll., 1973–74; Counsellor, Paris, 1974–78; Counsellor, Vienna, 1978–82; Ambassador and UK Perm. Rep. to Council of Europe, Strasbourg, 1983–86.

Médaille de Vermeil, Société d'Encouragement au Progrès, 1978. *Publications:* articles in Internat. and Compar. Law Qly, Connoisseur. *Address:* 53 Cheyne Court, Royal Hospital Road, SW3 5TS. *Clubs:* Travellers, Chelsea Arts. *Died 23 Feb. 2012.*

LUXMOORE, Rt Rev. Christopher Charles; Bishop of Bermuda, 1984–89; Assistant Bishop of Chichester and Canon Emeritus of Chichester Cathedral, since 1991; *b* 9 April 1926; *s* of Rev. William Cyril Luxmoore and Constance Evelyn Luxmoore; *m* 1955, Judith, *d* of late Canon Verney Johnstone; four *s* one *d*. *Educ:* Sedbergh School, Yorks; Trinity Coll., Cambridge; Chichester Theol Coll. Deacon 1952, priest 1953; Asst Curate, St John the Baptist, Newcastle upon Tyne, 1952–55; Priest-in-Charge, St Bede's Ecclesiastical Dist, Newsham, 1955–57; Vicar of Newsham, 1957–58; Rector of Sangre Grande, Trinidad, 1958–66; Vicar of Headingley, Leeds, 1967–81; Proctor in Convocation and Mem. Gen. Synod, 1975–81; Hon. Canon of Ripon Cathedral, 1980–81; Precentor and Canon Residentiary of Chichester Cathedral, 1981–84; Dean of Bermuda Cathedral, 1984–89; Archdeacon of Lewes and Hastings, 1989–91. Commissary for Bishop of Trinidad and Tobago, 1968–84. Provost, Woodard Schools Southern Div., 1989–96. *Recreations:* opera, church history. *Address:* 42 Willowbed Drive, Chichester, W Sussex PO19 8JB. *T:* (01243) 784680. *Died 24 Feb. 2014.*

LYCETT GREEN, Candida; writer; *b* 22 Sept. 1942; *d* of Sir John Betjeman, CBE and Penelope, *d* of Field Marshal Lord Chetwode, GCB, OM, GCSI; *m* 1963, Rupert Lycett Green; two *s* three *d*. *Educ:* St Mary's, Wantage. TV documentary films: The Front Garden, 1979; The English Woman and the Horse, 1981; A Cottage in the Country, 1983. Mem., Historic Bldgs and Monuments Commn for England (English Heritage), 1992–2001. Vice Pres., Churches Conservation Trust. Mem., PRS. Patron, Dance Scholarship Trust. *Publications:* Hadrian the Hedgehog, 1969; Hadrian in the Orient, 1971; (with Christopher Booker) Goodbye London, 1972; The Front Garden, 1974; English Cottages, 1984; Brilliant Gardens, 1989; The Perfect English Country House, 1991; John Betjeman: Letters, Vol. I, 1994, Vol. II, 1995; England: travels through an unwrecked landscape, 1996; (ed) Coming Home: an anthology of prose by John Betjeman, 1997; (ed) Betjeman's Britain, an anthology of prose and verse, 1999; Country Life's 100 Favourite Houses, 1999; (with HRH Prince of Wales) The Garden at Highgrove, 2000; Over the Hills and Far Away, 2002; The Dangerous Edge of Things, 2005; Unwrecked England, 2009; Seaside Resorts, 2011. *Recreation:* touring England by horse. *Address:* c/o Aitken Alexander Associates, 18–21 Cavaye Place, SW10 9PT. *Died 19 Aug. 2014.*

LYDDON, (William) Derek (Collier), CB 1984; Chief Planning Officer, Scottish Development Department, 1967–85; *b* 17 Nov. 1925; *s* of late A. J. Lyddon, CBE, and E. E. Lyddon; *m* 1949, Marian Louise Kaye Charlesworth (*d* 2013), *d* of late Prof. J. K. Charlesworth, CBE; two *d*. *Educ:* Wrekin Coll.; University Coll., London. BA (Arch.) 1952; ARIBA 1953; DipTP 1954; AMTPI 1963; FRTPI 1973. Depute Chief Architect and Planning Officer, Cumbernauld Development Corp., 1962; Chief Architect and Planning Officer, Skelmersdale Development Corp., 1963–67. Gov., Edinburgh Coll. of Art, 1988–96; Chm., Planning Exchange, 1991–96 (Vice-Chm., 1984–88); Vice-Chairman: Edinburgh Old Town Renewal Trust, 1991–99; Edinburgh World Heritage Trust, 1999–2004. Pres., Internat. Soc. of City and Regional Planners, 1981–84. Hon. Prof., Heriot-Watt Univ., 1986; Vis. Prof., Strathclyde Univ., 1986–89. FRSGS 1996. Hon. Fellow: Univ. of Edinburgh, 1986–89; Duncan of Jordanstone Coll. of Art, Dundee, 1986–. Hon. DLitt Heriot-Watt, 1981. *Recreations:* walking, reading. *Address:* 31 Blackford Road, Edinburgh EH9 2DT. *T:* (0131) 667 2266. *Died 7 Feb. 2015.*

LYGO, Adm. Sir Raymond (Derek), KCB 1977; aerospace, defence and industrial consultant; *b* 15 March 1924; *s* of late Edwin T. Lygo and of Ada E. Lygo; *m* 1st, 1950, Pepper Van Osten (*d* 2004), USA; two *s* one *d*; 2nd, 2009, Janette Brown. *Educ:* Valentine's Sch., Ilford; Ilford County High Sch.; Clark's Coll., Bromley. The Times, 1940; Naval Airman, RN, 1942; Naval Pilot, 1943; CO, HMS Ark Royal, 1969–71; Vice Chief of Naval Staff, 1975–78 and Chief of Naval Staff, 1978. British Aerospace: Man. Dir, Hatfield/Lostock Div., 1978–79, Group Dep. Chm., 1980; Bd Mem., 1980–89; Chm. and Chief Exec., Dynamics Gp, 1980–82; Man. Dir, 1983–86; Chief Exec., 1986–89; Chairman: BAe Inc., 1983–88; Royal Ordnance, 1987–88; BAe Enterprises Ltd, BAe (Space Systems) Ltd, BAe Hldgs Inc., 1988–89; TNT Europe Ltd and TNT Express (UK), 1992–97; Rutland Trust PLC, 1992–99; River and Mercantile First UK Investment Trust, then Liontrust, 1997–2004; Mem., Supervisory Bd, Airbus Industrie, 1987–89. Director: James Capel Corporate Finance, 1990–92; LET, 1990–92. Dir, CBI Educn Foundn, 1985–92; Member: Council, Industrial Soc., 1985–2001; NEDC, 1989–91; Council, Foundn for Management Educn, 1992–2004. Conducted review of the management of prison service, 1991. Appeal Pres., SENSE (Nat. Deafblind & Rubella Assoc.), 1983–2001; Appeal Chm., Industrial Soc., 1989–91; Dir, Southern Counties, Prince's Youth Business Trust, 1993–97; Patron, Youth Sports Trust, 1996–. Pres., FAA Officers Assoc., 1990–2009; Patron, Nat. FAA Assoc., 1989–. Pres., St Vincent Assoc. Freeman, City of London, 1985; Liveryman: Coachmakers' and Coach Harness Makers' Co., 1986–; Shipwrights' Co., 1988–. Life Mem., Royal Soc. of St George, 1984. FRSA; MInstD; CCMI. Hon. FRAeS; Hon. Fellow, Univ. of Westminster (formerly Poly. of Central London), 1989. *Publications:* Collision Course, 2002. *Recreations:* flying, building, gardening, joinery. *Address:* c/o Barclays Premier Banking, 1 Churchill Place, E14 5HP. *Clubs:* City Livery (Pres., 1996–97), Ambassadeurs; Royal Naval and Royal Albert Yacht (Portsmouth). *Died 7 March 2012.*

LYLES, John, CVO 2004; CBE 1987; JP; Lord-Lieutenant of West Yorkshire, 1992–2004; *b* 8 May 1929; *yr s* of Percy George Lyles and Alice Maud Mary (*née* Robinson); *m* 1953, Yvonne (*née* Johnson); two *s* two *d*. *Educ:* Giggleswick Sch.; Leeds Univ. (BSc Textiles 1950). Chm., S. Lyles plc, 1972–95; non-exec. Dir, Hillards plc, 1983–87. Chairman: Assoc. of Yorks and Humberside Chambers of Commerce, 1975–76; Yorks and Humberside CBI, 1983–85; Industry Year 86: Yorks and Humberside Reg.; CBI Mem., Speaker's Commn on Citizenship, 1988–90; Mem., Nat. Employers' Liaison Cttee for Volunteer and Reserve Forces, 1986–92. Mem., Yorks Cttee, NT, 1988–98. Member, Court: Leeds Univ., 1988–2010; Bradford Univ., 1992–2004. Pres., Shrievalty Assoc., 1999–2010 (Chm., 1993–95). President: Calderdale Community Foundn, 1994–2004; N of England Horticl Soc., 2002–04; Chairman: W Yorks Police Community Trust, 1996–2004; Northern Trng Centre Appeal, Hearing Dogs for Deaf People, 2007–09. Hon. Colonel: 8th Bn, (Yorks) LI (Vols), 1993–96; King's Own Yorks Yeomanry (LI), 1996–99; Vice Pres., Yorks and Humberside TAVRA, 1992–97, 1999–2002 (Pres., 1997–99). JP Batley and Dewsbury, 1967; High Sheriff, W Yorks, 1985–86; DL W Yorks, 1987. DUniv Bradford, 1995. KStJ 1993. *Recreations:* gardening, photography, music, opera. *Address:* Thimbleby House, Hampsthwaite, Harrogate HG3 2HB. *Club:* Lansdowne. *Died 14 June 2013.*

LYNN, Maurice Kenneth, MA; Head of French, Westminster School, 1983–88 and 1999–2008; *b* 3 March 1951. *Educ:* Thornleigh Salesian College, Bolton; Magdalen College, Oxford (Open Scholar; BA Hons 1973; MA 1977). Asst Master, Oratory Sch., 1973–79; Asst Master, Radley Coll., 1979–83; Headmaster, The Oratory Sch., 1989–91; Westminster School: Asst Master, 1992–95; Hd, Mod. Langs, 1995–99. Dir of Eur. interests for The Oratory Sch. Assoc., 1992. *Recreations:* English Catholic poetry, twentieth century French drama, soccer, ski-ing, cricket, acting and producing, cycling, travel. *Address:* 10 impasse Molière, 34300 Agde, France. *Died 14 July 2015.*

LYON, Mary Frances, ScD; FRS 1973; Deputy Director, Medical Research Council Radiobiology Unit, Harwell, 1982–90; *b* 15 May 1925; *e d* of Clifford James Lyon and Louise Frances Lyon (*née* Kirby). *Educ:* King Edward's Sch., Birmingham; Woking Grammar Sch.; Girton Coll., Cambridge (ScD 1968; Hon. Fellow 1985). MRC Scientific Staff, Inst. of Animal Genetics, Edinburgh,

1950–55; MRC Radiobiology Unit, Harwell, 1955–90, Hd Genetics Div., 1962–87. Clothworkers Visiting Research Fellow, Girton Coll., Cambridge, 1970–71. Foreign Hon. Mem., Amer. Acad. Arts and Scis, 1980 (Amory Prize, 1977). Foreign Associate, US Nat. Acad. of Scis, 1979. Hon. FIBiol 2006. Royal Medal, Royal Soc., 1984; Prize for Genetics, Sanremo, Italy, 1985; Gairdner Foundn Award, 1985; Allan Award, Amer. Soc. of Human Genetics, 1986; Wolf Prize for medicine, Wolf Foundn, 1996; March of Dimes Prize in Develtl Biol., 2004; Pearl Meister Greengard Award, Rockefeller Univ., 2006; Rosenstiel Award, Brandeis Univ., 2007. *Publications:* papers on genetics in scientific jls. *Address:* MRC Mammalian Genetics Unit, Harwell, Oxon OX11 0RD. *T:* (01235) 841000. *Died 25 Dec. 2014.*

LYON, Victor Lawrence, QC 2002; Senior Counsel, Attride-Stirling & Woloniecki, Bermuda, since 2007; *b* 10 Feb. 1956; *s* of Dr J. B. Lyon; *m* 1986, Rosalind Sara Compton Burnett; two *s*; partner, Abo Wales Davids. *Educ:* Marlborough Coll.; Trinity Coll., Cambridge (BA Hons 1979). Called to the Bar: Gray's Inn, 1980; Bermuda, 2008. Essex Ct Chambers, 1981–2007; Asst Recorder, 1999–2000; Recorder, 2000–07. *Publications:* Practice and Procedure of the Commercial Court, 1st edn 1981 to 6th edn 2008. *Recreations:* tennis, swimming, golf. *Address:* Attride-Stirling & Woloniecki, PO Box HM 2879, Hamilton HM LX, Bermuda. *T:* (441) 2956500, *Fax:* (441) 2956566. *E:* victor.lyon@aswlaw.com, vlyon@essexcourt.net; c/o Essex Court Chambers, 24 Lincoln's Inn Fields, WC2A 3EG. *T:* (020) 7813 8000. *Died 29 Jan. 2013.*

LYONS, Dennis John, CB 1972; CEng, FRAeS; Director General of Research, Department of the Environment, 1971–76; *b* 26 Aug. 1916; *s* of late John Sylvester Lyons and of Adela Maud Lyons; *m* 1939, Elisabeth (*d* 2009), *d* of Arnold and Maria Friederika Müller Haefliger, Weggis, Switzerland; five *s* two *d*. *Educ:* Grocers' Company School; Queen Mary Coll., London Univ. (Fellow, 1969). Aerodynamics Dept, Royal Aircraft Estabt, 1937; RAFVR, 1935–41; Aerodynamics Flight Aero Dept, RAE, 1941–51; Head of Experimental Projects Div., Guided Missiles Dept, RAE, 1951; Head of Ballistic Missile Group, GW Dept, 1956; Head of Weapons Dept, RAE, 1962; Dir, Road Research Laboratory, 1965–71. Member: Adv. Board for Res. Councils, 1973–76; SRC, 1973–76; Engineering Bd, SRC, 1970–76; Natural Environment Res. Council, 1973–76. Pres. OECD Road Research Unit, 1968–72. Hon. Mem., Instn Highway Engineers. *Publications:* papers in scientific jls. *Recreations:* ski-ing, pottery-making, philately. *Address:* 115 Clare Park, Crondall, Farnham, Surrey GU10 5DT. *Died 29 March 2011.*

M

MAATHAI, Wangari Muta, PhD; MP (National Rainbow Coalition) Tetu, Kenya, 2002–07; founding Member, Nobel Women's Initiative, 2006; Founder and Chair, Green Belt Movement, since 1977; *b* 1 April 1940; *d* of Muta Njugi and Wanjiru Kibicho; *m* 1969, Mwangi Mathai (marr. diss.); one *s* two *d*. *Educ:* Mount St Scholastica Coll., Kansas (BS 1964); Univ. of Pittsburgh (MS 1966); Univ. of Nairobi (PhD 1971). Hd, Dept of Veterinary Anatomy, 1976, Associate Prof., 1977, Univ. of Nairobi. Dir, Kenya Red Cross, 1973–80. Mem. Bd, Nat. Council of Women of Kenya (Chm., 1981–87). Asst Minister for Envmt, Natural Resources and Wildlife, Kenya, 2003–06. Hon. FRIBA 2008. Nobel Peace Prize, 2004. *Publications:* The Canopy of Hope: my life campaigning for Africa, women and the environment, 2002; The Green Belt Movement: sharing the approach and experience, 2002; Unbowed: one woman's story, 2007; The Challenge for Africa: a new vision, 2009; Replenishing the Earth: spiritual values for healing ourselves and the world, 2010. *Address:* c/o Green Belt Movement, Adams Arcade, Kilimani Lane off Elgeyo Marakwet Road, PO Box 67545–00200, Nairobi, Kenya. *Died 25 Sept. 2011.*

MAAZEL, Lorin; conductor; Music Director: Munich Philharmonic Orchestra, 2012–14; Palau de les Arts Reina Sofia, Valencia, 2006–11; *b* 6 March 1930; *s* of Lincoln Maazel and Marie Varencove; *m* 1st, 1952, Miriam Sandbank; two *d*; 2nd, 1969, Israela Margalit; one *s* one *d*; 3rd, 1986, Dietlinde Turban; two *s* one *d*. *Educ:* Pittsburgh University. FRCM 1981. Début as a conductor at age of 9, as violinist a few years later; by 1941 had conducted foremost US Orchestras, including Toscanini's NBC; European début as conductor, 1953; active as conductor in Europe, Latin America, Australia, Japan and USA, 1954–; performances at major festivals, including Edinburgh, Bayreuth, Salzburg and Lucerne; in USA: conducted Boston Symphony, New York Philharmonic, Philadelphia Orchestra, and at Metropolitan, 1960 and 1962; Covent Garden début, 1978. Artistic Director of Deutsche Oper Berlin, 1965–71; Chief Conductor, Radio Sinfonie Orchester, Berlin, 1965–75; Associate Principal Conductor, Philharmonia (formerly New Philharmonia) Orchestra, 1970–72, Principal Guest Conductor, 1976–80; Music Director, Cleveland Orchestra, 1972–82, Conductor Emeritus, 1982; Principal Guest Conductor, 1977–88, Music Director, 1988–90, Orchestre National de France; Director, Vienna State Opera, 1982–84; Music Director: Pittsburgh SO, 1988–96; Bayerischer Rundfunk SO, Munich, 1993–2002; New York Philharmonic, 2002–09. Composer and conductor, 1984 (opera), Royal Opera House, 2005. Founder, Pres. and Artistic Dir, Châteauville Foundn, 1997–. Made over 300 recordings. Hon. Dr of Music Pittsburgh Univ., 1968; Hon. Dr of Humanities Beaver Coll., 1973; Hon. Dr of Fine Arts, Carnegie-Mellon Univ., Pennsylvania; Hon. Dr of Music, RCM, 1984; Hon. DCL Univ. of South, Sewanee, 1988; Hon. Dr Indiana Univ., 1988. Sibelius Medal, Finland, 1969. Commander's Cross of Order of Merit, Federal Republic of Germany, 1977; Officier, Légion d'Honneur, France, 1981. *Died 13 July 2014.*

McALISTER, Michael Ian, FCA; Managing Director, The Tam Programme, European Bank for Reconstruction and Development, 1993–2002; *b* Leeds, Yorkshire, 23 Aug. 1930; *s* of S. McAlister, CBE, and J. A. McAlister (*née* Smith); *m* 1st, 1953, Patricia (*née* Evans) (marr. diss. 1983); four *s* three *d*; 2nd, 1984, Elizabeth Anne, *o d* of Mr and Mrs Ludwig Hehn. *Educ:* Brazil; France; St John's Coll., Oxford (MA). National Service, Lieut, Intelligence Corps (MI8), 1950–51 (Acting Capt). Articled Clerk, Price Waterhouse, London, 1954–58; Private Sec. to the Duke of Windsor, 1959–61; Investment Manager, Ionian Bank Ltd, London, 1961–67; Managing Dir, Ionian Bank Trustee Co., London, 1967–68; Slater Walker Securities (Australia): Dep. Chm., 1969–70, Chm., 1970–72; Pres., Aust. Associated Stock Exchanges, 1972–74; Director: (Middle East), Lester B. Knight and Associates, USA, 1975–79; Cluff Oil Holdings, subseq. Cluff Resources, 1979–89. Chm., Woking Cons. Assoc., 1967–68. *Recreations:* carpentry, DIY. *Address:* Kempshott, off Wilderness Road, Onslow Village, Guildford, Surrey GU2 7QP. *T:* (01483) 577258. *E:* mielmcalister@aol.com. *Died 5 April 2011.*

McALISTER, Maj.-Gen. Ronald William Lorne, CB 1977; OBE 1968 (MBE 1959); *b* 26 May 1923; 2nd *s* of late Col R. J. F. McAlister, OBE and Mrs T. M. Collins, Bath; *m* 1964, Sally Ewart Marshall; two *d*. *Educ:* Dreghorn Castle Sch., Edinburgh; Sedbergh School. Commnd 3rd QAO Gurkha Rifles, 1942; Adjt 1/3 GR Burma, 1945 (despatches); Adjt 2/10 GR Malaya, 1950–52 (despatches); Instructor, Sch. of Infantry, 1953–55; psc 1956; Bde Major 99 Gurkha Bde, Malaya, 1957–59 (MBE); jssc 1961–62; Asst Sec., Chiefs of Staff Cttee, 1962–64; 2nd in comd and CO 10th PMO Gurkha Rifles, Borneo, 1964–66 (despatches); Internal Security Duties, Hong Kong, 1967–68 (OBE); Instructor, Jt Services Staff Coll., 1968; comd Berlin Inf. Bde, 1968–71; ndc, Canada, 1971–72; Exercise Controller UK Cs-in-C Cttee, 1972–75; Dep. Commander Land Forces Hong Kong and Maj.-Gen. Brigade of Gurkhas, 1975–77; retired 1977. Col, 10th Princess Mary's Own Gurkha Rifles, 1977–85; Chm., Gurkha Brigade Assoc., 1980–90. Bursar, Wellesley House Sch., Broadstairs, 1977–88. Chm., Buckmaster Meml Home, Broadstairs, 1980–2009. *Publications:* (ed and contrib.) Bugle and Kukri, Vol. 2, 1986. *Recreations:* golf, gardening. *Address:* The Chalet, 41 Callis Court Road, Broadstairs, Kent CT10 3AU. *T:* (01843) 862351. *Clubs:* Army and Navy; Royal St George's Golf (Captain, 1989–90; Hon. Treas., 1991–96; Pres., 2004–08), Senior Golfers' Society. *Died 8 Sept. 2015.*

McALPINE OF WEST GREEN, Baron *cr* 1984 (Life Peer), of West Green in the County of Hampshire; **Robert Alistair McAlpine;** Director, Sir Robert McAlpine & Sons Ltd, 1963–95; *b* 14 May 1942; *s* of Lord McAlpine of Moffat and Ella Mary Gardner Garnett (*d* 1987); *m* 1st, 1964, Sarah Alexandra Baron (marr. diss. 1979); two *d*; 2nd, 1980, Romilly (marr. diss.), *o d* of A. T. Hobbs, Cranleigh, Surrey; one *d*; 3rd, 2002, Athena Malpas, *d* of Capt. Malpas. *Educ:* Stowe. Joined Sir Robert McAlpine & Sons Ltd, 1958. Hon. Treasurer: Eur. Democratic Union, 1978–88; Eur. League for Econ. Co-operation, 1974–75 (Vice Pres., 1975–); Conservative and Unionist Party, 1975–90 (Dep. Chm., 1979–83). Director: George Weidenfeld Holdings Ltd, 1975–83; ICA, 1972–73. Mem., Arts Council of GB, 1981–82; Vice-President: Friends of Ashmolean Museum, 1969–; Greater London Arts Assoc., 1971–77; Vice-Chm., Contemporary Arts Soc., 1973–80. Pres., British Waterfowl Assoc., 1978–81, Patron 1981–. Member: Friends of V&A Museum, 1976–; Council, English Stage Co., 1973–75. Trustee, Royal Opera House Trust, 1974–80; Dir, Theatre Investment Fund, 1981–90 (Chm., 1985–90). Governor: Polytechnic of the South Bank, 1981–82; Stowe Sch., 1981–84; Pres., St Bartholomew's Hosp. Med. Coll., 1993–95. Mem., H of L, 1984–2010. Hon. Freeman, Municipality of Broome, Australia. *Publications: as Alistair McAlpine:* The Servant, 1992; Journal of a Collector, 1994; Letters to a Young Politician, 1995; Once a Jolly Bagman (memoirs), 1997; The New Machiavelli, 1997; (jtly) Collecting and Display, 1998 Australian Memoirs, 2000; The Ruthless Leader, 2000; (jtly) The Essential Guide to Collectables, 2003. *Recreations:* the arts, horticulture, aviculture, agriculture. *Club:* Garrick. *Died 17 Jan. 2014.*

McALPINE, Alistair; *see* Baron McAlpine of West Green.

MACARA, Sir Alexander (Wiseman), Kt 1998; FRCP, FRCGP, FFPH; Consultant Senior Lecturer in Epidemiology and Public Health Medicine, University of Bristol and Hon. Visiting Consultant, Bristol Royal Infirmary, 1976–97; Chairman of Council, British Medical Association, 1993–98; *b* 4 May 1932; *s* of late Rev. Alexander Macara, MA Hons and Marion Wiseman Macara (*née* Mackay); *m* 1964, Sylvia May Williams, BSc

Hons, DipEd, *d* of late Edward Brodbeck and Ellen Florence Williams; one *s* one *d*. *Educ:* Irvine Royal Acad.; Glasgow Univ. (Carnegie Bursar; MB ChB 1958); LSHTM. DPH (Hecht Prize) 1960; FFPH (FFPHM 1989; FFCM 1973; MFCM 1972), Hon. FFPH 2008; FRSPH (FRIPHH 1973); FRCGP (*ad eundem gradum*) 1983; FRCP 1991; FRCPE 1997. House Physician and House Surgeon posts in Glasgow Teaching Hosps, 1958–59; General Practice experience, London and Glasgow, 1959–60; Asst MOH and Sch. MO, City and Co. of Bristol, 1960–63, then Hon. Community Physician, 1963–74; Lectr then Sen. Lectr, Univ. of Bristol, 1963–76 (Actg Head, Dept of Public Health, 1974–76). Sir Wilson Jameson Travelling Scholar, LSHTM, 1967; Vis. Prof., Univ. of Malaya, 1980; Vis. Prof. and Ext. Examr for higher degrees, Univ. of Khartoum, 1983; Hon. Vis. Prof. in Health Studies, York Univ., 1998–2002; Ext. Examr in Community Med. (Human Ecology), Univ. of Glasgow, 1979–82; Ext. Examr, Inst. of Population Studies, Univ. of Exeter, 1993–97. Jt Chm., Jt Wkg Party of Med. Profession and DoH on Med. Services for Children, 1991–92, and Chm., Jt Wkg Party on Child Protection, 1993–94. General Medical Council: Mem., 1979–2002; mem. various cttees. Faculty of Community Medicine (later of Public Health Medicine): Mem. Bd, 1973–79; Treasurer, 1979–84. British Medical Association: Chm., Med. Ethics Cttee, 1982–89; Dep. Chm., 1987–89, Chm., 1989–92, Representative Body; Rep. on Standing Cttee, Doctors in the EC, 1980–2010 (Vice-Pres., Cttee on Public Health and the Envmt, 2001–09); Chm. or Mem., numerous working parties, incl. Bd of Science and Educn; Fellow, 1978. Sec.-Gen., World Fedn for Educn and Res. in Public Health, 1988–96; Dir, WHO Collaborating Centre in Envmtl Health Promotion and Ecology, 1989–97; Advr and Consultant on Educn, Trng and Health Manpower Develt, WHO, 1970–; Sec., European Collaborative Health Services Studies, 1977–89; Pres., Nat. Heart Forum, 2007– (Chm., 1998–2007). Mem. Court of Govs, LSHTM, 1993–2008; Gov., Redland High Sch. for Girls, Bristol, 1998–. Lectures: Long Fox Meml, Bristol Univ., 1995; Harben, RIPH & H, 1996; Gregg Meml, AMA, 1997. Founder FMedSci 1998. Hon. Member: Hungarian Soc. Social Medicine, 1989; Italian Soc. Hygiene, Preventive Medicine and Public Health (Gold Medallist), 1991; Hon. Life Fellow, Soc. Public Health, 1991; Hon. FFOM 2000. Hon. Dr Public Health and Gerasimos Alivizatos Award, Sch. of Public Health, Athens, 1992; Hon. DSc UWE, 1998. Public Health Award, 1992, John Kershaw Award, 1994, Soc. of Public Health; James Preston Meml Award, Soc. of Public Health and BMA, 1993; Médaille d'or de l'Ordre de Médecin Français, 1998; Gold Medal, BMA, 1999; Andrija Stampar Medal, Assoc. of Schs of Public Health in Eur. Reg., 2002. *Publications:* (jtly) Personal Data Protection in Health and Social Services, 1988; chapters in various books and articles and reports in med. jls on epidemiology, public health, envmtl health and ethics in medicine. *Recreations:* gardening, reading, music. *Address:* Elgon, 10 Cheyne Road, Stoke Bishop, Bristol BS9 2DH. *T:* (0117) 968 2838, *Fax:* (0117) 968 4602. *Club:* Athenæum. *Died 21 June 2012.*

MACAULAY OF BRAGAR, Baron *cr* 1989 (Life Peer), of Bragar in the county of Ross and Cromarty; **Donald Macaulay;** *m* Mary; two *d*. *Educ:* Univ. of Glasgow (MA, LLB). Admitted to Faculty of Advocates, 1963; QC (Scot.) 1975. Contested (Lab) Inverness, 1970. Opposition spokesman on Scottish legal affairs until 1997. Chm., SACRO, 1993–96. *Address:* House of Lords, SW1A 0PW. *Died 12 June 2014.*

MACBEATH, Prof. (Alexander) Murray, PhD (Princeton, NJ); MA (Cantab); Professor of Mathematics and Statistics, University of Pittsburgh, 1979–90; *b* 30 June 1923; *s* of late Prof. Alexander Macbeath, CBE; *m* 1951, Julie Ormrod, Lytham St Anne's; two *s*. *Educ:* Royal Belfast Academical Instn; Queen's Univ., Belfast; Clare Coll., Cambridge. Entrance Schol., Dixon Prize in Maths, Purser Studentship, 1st class hons in Maths, BA, QUB. Bletchley Park (centre for work on breaking German Enigma codes), 1943–45. Cambridge, 1945–48; Maj. Entrance Schol., Wrangler Math. Tripos, Part II, dist. Part III, BA, Owst Prize. Commonwealth Fund Fellowship, Princeton, NJ, 1948–50; Smith's Prize, 1949; PhD Princeton, 1950. Research Fellow, Clare Coll., Cambridge, 1950–51; MA Cambridge, 1951. Lectr in Maths, Univ. Coll. of North Staffordshire, 1951–53; Prof. of Maths, Queen's Coll., Dundee, 1953–62; Mason Prof. of Pure Maths, Univ. of Birmingham, 1962–79. Visiting Professor: California Inst. of Technology, 1966–67; Univ. of Pittsburgh, 1974–75; Hon. Professor: Univ. of St Andrews, 1990–94; Univ. of Warwick, 1994–2003. *Publications:* Elementary Vector Algebra, 1964; papers in: Jl London Mathematical Soc.; Proc. London Math. Soc.; Proc. Cambridge Philosophical Soc.; Quarterly Jl of Mathematics; Annals of Mathematics; Canadian Jl of Mathematics. *Recreation:* Scottish country dancing. *Died 14 May 2014.*

McCABE, John, CBE 1985; professional musician; composer and pianist; *b* 21 April 1939; *s* of Frank and Elisabeth McCabe; *m* 1974, Monica Christine Smith. *Educ:* Liverpool Institute High Sch. for Boys; Manchester Univ. (MusBac); Royal Manchester Coll. of Music (ARMCM); Hochschule für Musik, Munich. Pianist-in-residence, University Coll., Cardiff, 1965–68; freelance musical criticism, 1966–71. Dir, London Coll. of Music, 1983–90. Career as composer and pianist: many broadcasts and recordings as well as concert appearances in various countries. Prizewinner in Gaudeamus Competition for Interpreters of Contemporary Music, Holland, 1969. Recordings incl. 12-CD set of complete piano music by Haydn; complete piano music of Nielsen (2 records). Awarded Special Citation by Koussevitsky Internat. Recording Foundn of USA, for recording of Symph. No 2 and Notturni ed Alba, 1974; Special Award by Composers' Guild of Gt Brit. (services to Brit. music), 1975; Ivor Novello Award (TV theme tune, Sam), 1977; Distinguished Musician Award, ISM, 2003; Classical Music Award, Ivor Novello Awards, 2014. Pres., ISM, 1983–84; Chm., Assoc. of Professional Composers, 1984–85. Hon. FRMCM; Hon. FLCM 1983; Hon. FRCM 1984; Hon. RAM 1985; Hon. FTCL 1989. Hon. DPhil Thames Valley, 2001; Hon. DMus Liverpool, 2006. *Compositions* include: seven symphonies; two operas; five ballets, incl. Edward II, and Arthur, Pts 1 and 2; concerti, incl. Horn Concerto, Trumpet Concerto (Primavera) and Cello Concerto; orchestral works incl. The Chagall Windows and Hartmann Variations, Notturni ed Alba, for soprano and orch., Fire at Durilgai for orch., Cloudcatcher Fells for brass band; chamber music, incl. The Woman by the Sea, for piano and string quartet; Les Martinets noirs, for two violins and string orchestra; keyboard works; vocal compositions. *Publications:* Rachmaninov (short biog.), 1974; Bartok's Orchestral Music (BBC Music Guide), 1974; Haydn Piano Sonatas (Ariel Music Guide), 1986; Alan Rawsthorne: portrait of a composer, 1998. *Recreations:* cricket, snooker, books, films. *Address:* c/o Novello & Co. Ltd, Music Sales, 14–15 Berners Street, W1T 3LJ. *Died 13 Feb. 2015.*

McCABE, Thomas; Member (Lab) Hamilton South, Scottish Parliament, 1999–2011; *b* Hamilton, Lanarks, 28 April 1954; *m* 2006, Shuming Kong; one *d*; one *s* one *d* from former marriage. *Educ:* St Martin's Secondary Sch., Hamilton; Bell Coll. of Technology, Hamilton (Dip. Public Sector Mgt). Light engrg, Hoover Factory, Cambuslang, 1974–93; Welfare Rights Officer, Strathclyde Regl Council and N Lanarks Council, 1993–98. Member (Lab): Hamilton DC, 1988–96 (Chm., Housing, 1990–92; Leader, 1992–96); S Lanarks Council, 1996–99 (Leader, 1996–99). Scottish Executive: Minister for Parlt and Chief Govt Whip, 1999–2001; Dep. Minister for Health and Community Care, 2003–04; Minister for Finance and Public Service Reform, 2004–07. Contested (Lab) Hamilton, Larkhall and Stonehouse, Scottish Parlt, 2011. *Recreations:* sport, golf, reading, walking, cinema. *Died 19 April 2015.*

McCAFFREY, Anne Inez; writer; *b* 1 April 1926; *d* of George H. McCaffrey and Anne Dorothy McElroy-McCaffrey; *m* 1950, H. Wright Johnson (marr. diss. 1970; he *d* 2009); two *s* one *d*. *Educ:* Stuart Hall Secondary Sch.; Radcliffe Coll., Harvard Univ. (BA *cum laude* 1947). Advertising copywriter and layout artist, Liberty Music Shops, NYC, 1948–50; copywriter, then Sec. to Sales Manager, Helena Rubinstein, 1950–52. Established Equine Centre, Dragonhold Stables, Co. Wicklow, 1977. Numerous awards, including: Golden Pen Award, 1982;

Science Fiction Book Club Awards, 1986, 1989, 1990, 1992, 1993, 1994, 1997; Margaret A. Edwards Award for Lifetime Literary Achievement, Amer. Liby Assoc., 1999; Grand Master, Science Fiction and Fantasy Writers of America, 2005. *Publications:* Restoree, 1967; Dragonflight, 1968; (ed) Alchemy & Academe, 1970; Mark of Merlin, 1971; Dragonquest, 1971; Ring of Fear, 1971; To Ride Pegasus, 1973; Out of This World Cookbook, 1973; The White Dragon, 1975; Kilternan Legacy, 1975; Dragonsong, 1976; Dragonsinger, 1977; Get off the Unicorn, 1977; Dragondrums, 1979; Crystal Singer, 1982; The Coelura, 1983; Moreta, Dragonlady of Pern, 1983; Stitch in Snow, 1984; Killashandra, 1985; Chronicles of Pern: First Fall, 1985; The Girl who Heard Dragons, 1986; The Year of the Lucy, 1986; Nerilka's Story, 1986; The Carradyne Touch, 1988 (US edn as The Lady); Dragonsdawn, 1988; Pern Portrait Gallery, 1988; (jtly) Guidebook to Pern, 1989, 2nd edn as The Dragonlover's Guide to Pern, 1997; Renegades of Pern, 1989; Pegasus in Flight, 1990; The Rowan, 1990; All the Weyrs of Pern, 1991; Damia, 1992; Crystal Line, 1992; Damia's Children, 1993; Lyon's Pride, 1994; The Dolphins of Pern, 1994; An Exchange of Gifts, 1995; Freedom's Landing, 1995; Black Horses for the King, 1996; A Diversity of Dragons, 1997; Dragonseye (UK title: Red Star Rising), 1997; Freedom's Choice, 1997; Masterharper of Pern, 1998; Freedom's Challenge, 1998; If Wishes Were Horses, 1998; Nimisha's Ship, 1999; The Tower & The Hive, 1999; Pegasus in Space, 2000; Skies of Pern, 2001; A Gift of Dragons, 2002; (with Todd McCaffrey) Dragon's Kin, 2003; (ed jtly) Serve it Forth: cooking with Anne McCaffrey, 2004; *variously with Margaret Ball, Jody-Lynn Nye, Elizabeth Ann Scarborough and others:* Dinosaur Planet, 1978; Dinosaur Planet Survivors, 1984; Doona series: Decision at Doona, 1969; Crisis on Doona, 1992; Treaty Planet (reissued as Treaty at Doona), 1994; Ship series: The Ship Who Sang, 1970; The Partner Ship, 1992; The Ship who Searched, 1992; The City who Fought, 1993; The Ship Who Won, 1994; The Ship Avenged, 1997; Petaybee series: Power Play, 1992; Powers that Be, 1993; Power Lines, 1994; Changelings, 2005; Acorna series: Acorna: the unicorn girl, 1997; Acorna's People, 1997; Acorna's Quest, 1998; Acorna's World, 1999; Acorna's Search, 2002; Acorna's Rebels, 2003; Acorna's Triumph, 2004; books trans. into numerous foreign langs and Braille. *Recreations:* equine events, raising Maine Coon cats, quilting. *Address:* Dragonhold-Underhill, Newcastle, Co. Wicklow, Ireland. *Club:* Sloane. *Died 21 Nov. 2011.*

MacCALLUM, Prof. Charles Hugh Alexander, RIBA; ARIAS; Professor of Architecture, Glasgow University, and Head, Mackintosh School of Architecture, Glasgow School of Art, 1994–2000, then Emeritus Professor; architect in private practice, since 1973; *b* Glasgow, 24 June 1935; *s* of Alister Hugh McCallum, Pitlochry, and Jessie McLean (*née* Forsyth), Perth; *m* 1963, Andrée Simone Tonnard; two *d.* *Educ:* Hutchesons' Grammar Sch.; Glasgow Sch. of Architecture (DA); Massachusetts Inst. of Technol. (MCP 1969). RIBA 1961; ARIAS 1986. Architect, Gillespie Kidd & Coia, Glasgow, 1957–67; Sen. Architect, Dept of Architecture and Planning, Clydebank, 1969–70; Statutory Lectr, later Exec. Dir, Sch. of Architecture, University Coll., Dublin, 1969–73; Prof. of Architectural Design, Welsh Sch. of Architecture, Univ. of Wales Coll. of Cardiff, 1986–94. Architectural consultant, Scots Kirk, Paris, 2000–04. Mem. Cttee and UK rep. on Educn, Franco-British Union of Architects, 2000–. Médaille de la Formation, Académie d'Architecture, Paris, 2003. *Publications:* (with Françoise Hamon) Louis Visconti 1791–1853, 1991; articles on architecture and engrg, in UK, France and Russia. *Recreations:* gardening, watercolours. *Address:* 11A Charlbury Road, Oxford OX2 6UT. *Club:* Caledonian. *Died 15 Sept. 2013.*

McCALLUM, Sir Donald (Murdo), Kt 1988; CBE 1976; DL; FREng; FRSE; General Manager, Scottish Group, 1968–85, and Director, 1970–87, Ferranti plc; Chairman, Laser Ecosse Ltd, 1990–95; *b* 6 Aug. 1922; *s* of Roderick McCallum and Lillian (*née* McPhee); *m* 1st, 1949, Barbara Black (*d* 1971); one *d*; 2nd, 1974, Mrs Margaret Illingworth (*née* Broadbent) (*d* 1997); 3rd, 2007, Mrs Jill Morgan (*née* Maxwell). *Educ:* George Watson's Boys' Coll.; Edinburgh Univ. (BSc). FIET (FIEE 1969); FREng (FEng 1982); FRAeS 1986. Admiralty Signal Establishment, 1942–46; Standard Telecommunication Laboratories, 1946; Ferranti Ltd, 1947: Chairman: Ferranti Defence Systems Ltd, 1984–87 (Hon. Pres., 1987–90); Ferranti Industrial Electronics, 1984–87 (Hon. Pres., 1987–90). Dir, Short Bros Ltd, 1981–89; Chairman: Scottish Tertiary Education Adv. Council, 1984–87; Scottish Council Develt & Industry, 1985–91 (Pres., 1991–93; Fellow, 1993). Scottish Sub-Cttee, UGC, 1987–88; Member: UFC, 1989–91 (Chm., Scottish Cttee, 1989–91); Scottish Econ. Council, 1983–92. Mem., Leeds Churches Together in Mission, 2002–07. Member: Court, Heriot-Watt Univ., 1979–85; Governing Body, Napier Polytechnic, 1988–93; Court, Napier Univ., 1993–95; Governing Body, Edinburgh Coll. of Art, 1988–93; Bd of Trustees, Nat. Liby of Scotland, 1990–96. Hon. Life Mem., Edinburgh Univ. Students' Assoc., 1984. Liveryman, Company of Engineers, 1984; Freeman, City of London. DL City of Edinburgh, 1984. CCMI (CBIM 1983). Hon. FRSGS 1993. Hon. Fellow, Paisley Coll. of Technol., 1987; Fellow, SCOTVEC, 1988. DUniv Stirling, 1985; Hon. DSc: Heriot-Watt, 1986; Napier Coll. of Commerce and Technology, Edinburgh, 1986; Hon. LLD: Strathclyde, 1987; Aberdeen, 1989. British Gold Medal, RAeS, 1985. *Recreations:* photography, reading. *Address:* Brackenhill, Newland, Ulverston LA12 7QD. *T:* (01229) 583187. *Club:* New (Edinburgh). *Died 18 Oct. 2011.*

McCALLUM, Googie, (Mrs John McCallum); *see* Withers, G. L.

McCARRAHER, His Honour David, VRD 1964; a Circuit Judge, 1984–95; *b* 6 Nov. 1922; *s* of Colin McCarraher and Vera Mabel McCarraher (*née* Hickley); *m* 1950, Betty Johnson (*née* Haywood) (*d* 1990); one *s* three *d.* *Educ:* King Edward VI Sch., Southampton; Magdalene Coll., Cambridge (MA Law). RN, 1941–45. Called to the Bar, Lincoln's Inn, 1948; practised Western Circuit until 1952, disbarred at own request to be articled; admitted solicitor, 1955; Sen. Partner in private practice, 1960–84; a Recorder, 1979–84. Mem. Panel, Dep. Circuit Judges, 1973–79. Pres., Hampshire Incorporated Law Soc., 1982–83. Founder Mem. and Past Pres., Southampton Junior Chamber of Commerce. Governor, King Edward VI Sch., Southampton, 1961–84 (Chm., 1983–84; Fellow, 1986). Sub-Lieut, RNVR, 1943–45, RNVSR, 1946–52; served to Captain RNR, 1969; CO Solent Div., RNR, 1969–72; ADC to the Queen, 1972–73; retired 1975. Hon. Sec., RNR Benevolent Fund, 1973–84. *Recreations:* family, golf. *Clubs:* Naval; Stoneham Golf (Southampton); Royal Naval Sailing Association (Portsmouth); Southampton Police (Hon. Mem.) (Southampton). *Died 13 Dec. 2013.*

McCARTHY, Baron *cr* 1975 (Life Peer), of Headington in the City of Oxford; **William Edward John McCarthy,** DPhil; Emeritus Fellow of Nuffield College and sometime Associate Fellow of Templeton College, Oxford; engaged in Industrial Arbitration and Chairman of Committees of Inquiry and Investigation; *b* 30 July 1925; *s* of E. and H. McCarthy; *m* 1957, Margaret, *d* of Percival Godfrey. *Educ:* Holloway County; Ruskin Coll.; Merton Coll.; Nuffield Coll. MA (Oxon), DPhil (Oxon). Trade Union Scholarship to Ruskin Coll., 1953; Research Fellow of Nuffield Coll., 1959; Research Dir, Royal Commn on Trade Unions and Employers' Assocs, 1965–68; Sen. Economic Adviser, Dept of Employment, 1968–71. Chm., Railway Staff Nat. Tribunal, 1973–86; Special Advisor on Industrial Relations to Sec. of State for Social Services, 1975–77; Member: Houghton Cttee on Aid to Political Parties, 1975–76; TUC Independent Review Cttee, 1976; CS Arbitration Tribunal, 1983–; Pres., British Univ. Industrial Relations Assoc., 1975–78; Special Comr, Equal Opportunities Commn, 1977–80; Dep. Chm., Teachers' Nat. Conciliation Cttee, 1979–. Chairman: TUC Newspaper Feasibility Adv. Study Gp, 1981–83; Independent Inquiry into Rover Closure Proposals, 1989–90. Adjudicator, Nursing and Midwifery Staffs Negotiating Council, 1994–. Mem., H of L Select Cttee on Unemployment, 1980–82; Opposition front bench spokesman on employment, 1980–97. Mem., All Party Motor Industry Gp, 1989–; Vice Chairman: All Party Friends of Music Gp, 1992–; All Party Theatre Gp, 2002–. Pres., Oxford Assoc. of Univ. Teachers, 1999–. FIPD 1995. *Publications:* The Closed Shop in Britain, 1964; The Role of Shop Stewards in British Industrial Relations, 1966; (with

V. L. Munns) Employers' Associations, 1967; (with A. I. Marsh) Disputes Procedures in Britain, 1968; The Reform of Collective Bargaining at Plant and Company Level, 1971; (ed) Trade Unions, 1972, 2nd edn, 1985; (with A. I. Collier) Coming to Terms with Trade Unions, 1973; (with N. D. Ellis) Management by Agreement, 1973; (with J. F. O'Brien and V. E. Dowd) Wage Inflation and Wage Leadership, 1975; Making Whitley Work, 1977; (jtly) Change in Trade Unions, 1981; (jtly) Strikes in Post-War Britain, 1983; Freedom at Work 1985; The Future of Industrial Democracy, 1988; (with C. Jennings and R. Undy) Employee Relations Audits, 1989; (ed) Legal Intervention in Industrial Relations, 1992; New Labour at Work, 1997; Fairness at Work: past comparisons and future problems, 1999; (contrib.) Legal Regulation of the Employment Relation, 2000; articles in: Brit. Jl of Industrial Relns; Industrial Relns Jl 1995. *Recreations:* gardening, theatre, ballet, opera. *Address:* 4 William Orchard Close, Old Headington, Oxford OX3 9DR. *T:* (01865) 762016. *Club:* Reform. *Died 18 Nov. 2012.*

McCARTHY, His Honour David Laurence; a Circuit Judge, 1995–2009; *b* 7 April 1947; *s* of Laurence Alphonsus McCarthy and Vera May McCarthy; *m* 1981, Rosalind Marguerite Stevenson; two *s*. *Educ:* St Philip's Grammar Sch., Birmingham; Christ Church, Oxford (MA). Called to the Bar, Middle Temple, 1970; a Recorder, 1992; Midland and Oxford Circuit. *Recreations:* science fiction, playing the organ. *Died 21 April 2013.*

McCARTHY, Peter Herbert; Grants and Oversight Director, Motability, since 2011; *b* 9 Oct. 1953; *s* of Adolf and Ursula McCarthy; *m* 2000, Angela Fleming; one *d*. *Educ:* Bedales Sch.; Merton Coll., Oxford (BA PPE). Joined DTI, 1979; transferred to Dept for Transport, 1983; Private Sec. to Sec. of State, 1989–92; Head: Rail Privatisation Legislation Div., 1992–96; Local Transport Policy Div., 1996–2002; Transport Finance Directorate, 2002–05; Dir, Rail Customer and Stakeholder Relns, 2005–07; ind. consultant, 2008–10; Performance and Planning Dir, Motability, 2010–11. *Recreations:* reading, cycling, motoring, music, theatre. *Address:* 176 Wimbledon Park Road, SW18 5RL. *T:* (020) 8870 5710. *E:* petermccarthy@talktalk.net. *Died 30 April 2012.*

McCLARTY, David; Member, East Londonderry, Northern Ireland Assembly, since 1998 (UU, 1998–2010, Ind, since 2011); *b* 23 Feb. 1951; *s* of Douglas and Helen McClarty; *m* 1973, (Alma) Norma (Yvonne) Walls; two *s*. *Educ:* Coleraine Academical Instn; Magee Coll., Londonderry. Sales Asst, NI Electricity, 1973; General Accident: Trainee Fire Underwriter, 1973; Dep. Manager, Fire Insurance Dept, 1978–84; Fire Underwriter, 1973–78; Insurance Consultant, D. McClarty & Co., 1984–98. Mem., Coleraine BC, 1989– (UU, 1989–2010, Ind, 2011–); Mayor of Coleraine Borough, 1993–95. Freeman, City of London, 1995. *Recreations:* amateur dramatics, choral singing, sport in general. *Address:* 22 Slievebanna, Coleraine, Co. Londonderry BT51 3JG. *T:* (028) 7035 6734. *Died 18 April 2014.*

McCLELLAND, George Ewart, CB 1986; Solicitor, Department of Employment, 1982–87; *b* 27 March 1927; *s* of George Ewart McClelland and Winifred (*née* Robinson); *m* 1956, Ann Penelope, *yr d* of late Judge Arthur Henry Armstrong; one *s* two *d*. *Educ:* Stonyhurst Coll.; Merton Coll., Oxford (Classical Scholar; MA). Called to the Bar, Middle Temple, 1952. Entered Solicitor's Dept, Min. of Labour, 1953; Asst Solicitor, 1969; Principal Asst Solicitor, 1978. *Died 7 Jan. 2015.*

McCLELLAND, Prof. (William) Grigor, CBE; former business executive and academic; *b* 2 Jan. 1922; *oc* of Arthur and Jean McClelland, Gosforth, Newcastle upon Tyne; *m* 1st, 1946, Diana Avery Close (*d* 2000); two *s* two *d*; 2nd, 2003, Caroline Mary (*née* Kent), *widow* of Tristram Spence. *Educ:* Leighton Park; Balliol Coll., Oxford (First Class PPE, 1948; MA). Friends' Ambulance Unit, 1941–46. Man. Dir, Laws Stores Ltd, 1949–65, 1978–85 (Chm., 1966–85); Sen. Res. Fellow in Management Studies, Balliol Coll., 1962–65; Dir, Manchester Business Sch., 1965–77, and Prof. of Business Administration, 1967–77, Univ. of Manchester; Dep. Chm., Nat. Computing Centre, 1966–68; Chm., Washington Develt Corp., 1977–88. Founding Editor, Jl of Management Studies, 1963–65. Chm., EDC for the Distributive Trades, 1980–84 (Mem., 1965–70); Member: The Consumer Council, 1963–66; Economic Planning Council, Northern Region, 1965–66; IRC, 1966–71; NEDC, 1969–71; SSRC, 1971–74; North Eastern Industrial Develt Bd, 1977–86. Hon. Vis. Prof., 1977–, and Gov., 1986–98, Durham Univ. Business Sch. Chairman: Tyne Tees Telethon Trust, 1987–93; Community Foundn serving Tyne & Wear and Northumberland (formerly Tyne and Wear Foundn), 1988–93 (a Vice-Pres., 1994–); NE Adv. Panel, Nat. Lottery Charities Bd, 1995–97. Dir, Oxford Res. Gp, 2001–05. Trustee: Joseph Rowntree Charitable Trust, 1956–94 (Chm., 1965–78); Anglo-German Foundn for the Study of Industrial Soc., 1973–79; Millfield House Foundn, 1976–; Employment Inst., 1985–92; Governor: Nat. Inst. of Econ. and Social Research; Leighton Park Sch., 1952–60 and 1962–66. Mem., Soc. of Friends, 1942–. DL Tyne and Wear, 1988. MBA Manchester 1971. Hon. DCL Dunelm, 1985. CBE 1994 (returned in protest at invasion of Iraq, 2003–09). *Publications:* Quakers Visit China (ed), 1957; Studies in Retailing, 1963; Costs and Competition in Retailing, 1966; And a New Earth, 1976; Washington: over and out, 1988; Embers of War, 1997; (ed) From Tyne to Tsar, 2007; occasional pamphlets and contribs to books. *Recreations:* family, friends, current affairs. *Address:* 50 Reid Park Road, Jesmond, Newcastle upon Tyne NE2 2ES. *E:* grigor@gmcclelland.co.uk. *Died 6 Nov. 2013.*

McCLUNEY, Ian, CMG 1990; HM Diplomatic Service, retired; High Commissioner, Sierra Leone, 1993–97; *b* 27 Feb. 1937; *s* of John McCluney and Annie McCluney (*née* Currie); *m* 1962; two *s* one *d*. *Educ:* Edinburgh Univ. (BSc). Served HM Forces, 1958–62. Joined FO, 1964; Addis Ababa, 1964–67; FCO, 1969–70; Baghdad, 1972–74; FCO, 1975–78; Kuwait, 1979–82; Consul-Gen., Alexandria, 1982–86; FCO, 1986–88; Ambassador to Somalia, 1989–90; Dep. High Comr, Calcutta, 1991–93. Reference Sec., Competition Commn, 2000–03. Dir, St Thomas Foundn, Jamaica, 2006–. *Recreations:* sailing, farming in Jamaica. *Died 17 July 2015.*

McCLURE, Joseph Robert, MBE 2000; *b* 21 Oct. 1923; *s* of Thomas Render McClure and Catherine Bridget McClure; *m* 1943, Evelyn Joyce; one *d*. *Educ:* Prior Street Sch.; Oakwellgate Sch., Gateshead. Served War, Royal Marines, 1941–46. Elected Councillor (Lab): County Borough of Gateshead, 1964–73, Dep. Mayor, 1973–74; Tyne and Wear CC, 1974–82 (Chm., 1977–78). President: Tyneside Br., 1996–2001, Durham Br., 2003–, Royal Marine Assoc.; Gateshead RBL, 1971–; Vice Pres., Northumberland/Tyne and Wear County, RBL, 1997–. JP Gateshead and Blaydon, 1979–93. *Recreation:* bowls. *Address:* 104 Greenford, Kibblesworth, Gateshead, Tyne and Wear NE11 0TW. *T:* (0191) 670 6523. *Died 23 March 2013.*

McCORD, Brig. Mervyn Noel Samuel, CBE 1978 (OBE 1974); MC 1951; Commander, Ulster Defence Regiment, 1976–78; *b* 25 Dec. 1929; *s* of late Major G. McCord, MBE and Muriel (*née* King); *m* 1953, Annette Mary, *d* of C. R. W. Thomson; two *s* (and one *s* decd). *Educ:* Coleraine, NI; RMA Sandhurst. Commissioned Royal Ulster Rifles, 1949; Korea, 1950–51; School of Infantry, 1958–60; Staff Coll., Camberley, 1961–62; DAQMG, Eastern Command, Canada, 1963–65; BM, HQ 6 Infantry Brigade, 1967–69; JSSC, 1969; GSO1, HQNI, 1970–71; CO, 1st Bn The Royal Irish Rangers, 1971–74; Brig. 1975; Dep. Comdr, Eastern Dist, 1978–81; Brig. King's Div., 1981–84. ADC to the Queen, 1981–84. Col, The Royal Irish Rangers, 1985–90 (Dep. Col, 1976–81). Chairman: SHAA, 1986–93; SHAA Retirement Homes plc, 1986–93; Dir, Sussex Housing and Care, 1994–2001. *Recreations:* cricket, athletics, country sports, gardening. *Address:* c/o Drummonds, 49 Charing Cross, SW1A 2DX. *Club:* Army and Navy. *Died 8 Feb. 2013.*

MacCORMAC, Sir Richard Cornelius, Kt 2001; CBE 1994; RA 1993; PPRIBA; Chairman, MJP Architects (formerly MacCormac Jamieson Prichard Ltd, a Partnership, incorporated in 2002), 1972–2010; President, Royal Institute of British Architects, 1991–93; *b* 3 Sept. 1938; *s* of late Henry MacCormac, CBE, MD, FRCP and Marion Maud, *d* of B. C. Broomhall, FRCS; *m* 1964, Susan

Karin Landen (separated 1983); one *s* (and one *s* decd). *Educ:* Westminster Sch.; Trinity Coll., Cambridge (BA 1962; Hon. Fellow, 2006); University College London (MA 1965). RIBA 1967. Served RN, 1957–59. Proj. Archt, London Bor. of Merton, 1967–69; estabd private practice, 1969. Major works include: Cable & Wireless Coll., Coventry (Royal Fine Art Commn/Sunday Times Bldg of the Year Award, 1994); Garden Quadrangle, St John's Coll., Oxford (Ind. on Sunday Bldg of the Year Award, 1994); Bowra Bldg, Wadham Coll., Oxford; Burrell's Fields, Trinity Coll., Cambridge (RIBA Regl Award, Civic Trust Award, 1997); Ruskin Liby, Lancaster Univ. (Ind. on Sunday Bldg of the Year Award, 1996; Royal Fine Art Commn/BSkyB Bldg of the Year, Univs Winner, 1998; Millennium Product status, Design Council, 1999); Southwark Stn, Jubilee Line Extension (Millennium Bldg of the Year Award, Royal Fine Art Commn Trust/BSkyB, 2000); Wellcome Wing, Science Mus. (Celebrating Construction Achievement, Regl Award for Gtr London, 2000); Kendrew Quadrangle, St John's Coll., Oxford, 2010. Taught in Dept of Arch., Cambridge Univ., 1969–75 and 1979–81, Univ. Lectr, 1976–77; Studio Tutor, LSE 1998. Visiting Professor: Univ. of Edinburgh (Dept of Architecture), 1982–85; Hull Univ., 1998–99. Dir, Spitalfields Workspace, 1981–. Chm., Good Design in Housing Awards, RIBA London Region, 1977; Mem., Royal Fine Art Commn, 1983–93; Comr, English Heritage, 1995–98. Royal Academy: Chairman: RA Forum, 1995–; Architecture Cttee, 1998–2008. Advisor: British Council, 1993–; Urban Task Force, 1998–. Pres., London Forum of Amenity and Civic Socs, 1997–; Trustee: Greenwich Foundn for RNC, 1998–2002; Sir John Soane Mus., 1998–. FRSA 1982. *Publications:* Building Ideas, 2010; Two Houses in Spitalfields, 2014; articles in Architectural Review and Archts Jl. *Recreations:* sailing, music, reading. *Address:* 9 Heneage Street, E1 5LJ. *T:* (020) 7377 9262. *Died 26 July 2014.*

MacCORMICK, Iain Somerled MacDonald; Database and IT Controller, Nationwide Trade Hospitality Ltd, 2005–09; *b* Glasgow, 28 Sept. 1939; *er s* of John MacDonald MacCormick, MA, LLB, LLD and Margaret Isobel MacCormick, MA, BSc; *m* 1st, 1964, Micky Trefusis Elsom (marr. diss. 1987); two *s* three *d*; 2nd, 1988, Carole Burnett (*née* Story) (marr. diss. 1991); 3rd, 2009, Riona Taylor MacInnes. *Educ:* Glasgow High Sch.; Glasgow Univ. (MA). Queen's Own Lowland Yeomanry, 1957–67 (Captain). Major Account Manager, 1982, Dir Liaison Manager, 1984, BT plc; Trade Consultant, Bartering Co. Ltd, 1993–95; Agent, DataLocator Ltd, 2000. Contested (SNP) Argyll, 1970; MP (SNP) Argyll, Feb. 1974–1979; introduced, as private member's bill, Divorce (Scotland) Act, 1976. Founder Mem., SDP, 1981. Mem., Argyll and Bute District Council, 1979–80. *Recreations:* Rugby football, sailing, local history. *Address:* 2 Tower View, Villa Road, Oban, Argyll PA34 4NA. *T:* (01631) 562926. *Club:* Glasgow Art (Glasgow). *Died 19 Sept. 2014.*

McCULLOCH, Prof. Ernest Armstrong, OC 1988; OOnt 2006; MD; FRSC 1974; FRS 1999; Senior Scientist Emeritus, Ontario Cancer Institute, and Princess Margaret Hospital, since 1991; University Professor, University of Toronto, 1982–91, then Emeritus; *b* 27 April 1926; *s* of Dr Albert Ernest McCulloch and Letitia Riddell McCulloch (*née* Armstrong); *m* 1953, Ona Mary Morganty; four *s* one *d*. *Educ:* Univ. of Toronto (MD Hons 1948). FRCPC 1954. Res. Fellow, Lister Inst., London, 1948–49 (Ellen Mickle Fellow); University of Toronto: Clin. Teacher, Dept of Medicine, 1954–60; Asst Prof., 1959–64, Associate Prof., 1964–66, Prof., 1966–91, Dept of Med. Biophysics; Asst Prof., 1967–68, Associate Prof., 1968–70, Prof., 1970–91, Dept of Medicine; Graduate Sec., 1969–75, Dir, 1975–79, Inst. of Med. Sci.; Asst Dean, Sch. of Graduate Studies, 1979–82; Physician, Toronto Gen. Hosp., 1960–67; Ontario Cancer Institute: Scientific Staff, 1957–91; Head, Div. of Biological Res., 1982–89; Head, Div. of Cellular and Molecular Biology, 1989–91. Vis. Prof. of Lab Medicine and Pathology, Univ. of Texas, MD Anderson Cancer Center, 1991–93; Hon. Prof., Shanxi Cancer Inst., China, 1991–. Pres., Acad. of Sci., RSC, 1987–90 (Eadie Medal, 1991). Hon. DSc Toronto, 2004. (Jtly) Annual Gairdner Award, 1969; (jtly) Albert Lasker Award, Lasker Foundn, 2005. Silver Jubilee Medal, 1977. *Publications:* more than 275 papers and reviews in med. jls. *Recreations:* sailing, gardening. *Address:* (office) 610 University Avenue, Toronto, ON M5G 2M9, Canada; (home) Grenadier, 2100 Bloor Street West, Apt 412, Toronto, ON M6S 1M7, Canada. *Club:* Badminton and Racquet (Toronto). *Died 20 Jan. 2011.*

McDERMID, Ven. Norman George Lloyd Roberts; Archdeacon of Richmond, 1983–93, then Emeritus; *b* 5 March 1927; *s* of Lloyd Roberts McDermid and Annie McDermid; *m* 1953, Vera Wood; one *s* three *d*. *Educ:* St Peter's School, York; St Edmund Hall, Oxford (MA); Wells Theological Coll. Deacon 1951, priest 1952; Curate of Leeds, 1951–56, in charge of St Mary, Quarry Hill, Leeds, 1953–56; Vicar of Bramley, Leeds, 1956–64; Rector of Kirkby Overblow, 1964–80; Stewardship Adviser, Ripon Diocese, 1964–76, Bradford and Wakefield, 1973–76; Vicar of Knaresborough, 1980–83. Hon. Canon of Ripon Cathedral, 1972–93, Emeritus 1993–; RD of Harrogate, 1977–83. Member: General Synod, 1970–93; Church of England Pensions Bd, 1972–78; Redundant Churches Fund, 1977–89; Central Bd of Finance of C of E, 1985–93. Church Commissioner, 1978–83. Chairman: Ripon Diocesan House of Clergy, 1981–93; Ripon Diocesan Bd of Finance, 1988–93 (Mem., 1957–93); Mem., Ripon Cathedral Fabric Cttee, 1990–2008. Mem., N Yorks County Educn Cttee, 1993–97. Chm., Bedale Probus 25 Club, 2000–03. *Recreations:* investment, historic churches, pedigree cattle, gardening. *Address:* Greystones, 10 North End, Bedale, N Yorks DL8 1AB. *T:* (01677) 422210. *Died 30 Sept. 2014.*

McDONALD, Alistair; Economic Development Officer, Wandsworth Borough Council, 1983–89; *b* 13 March 1925; *e s* of late John Bell McDonald and Mary McDonald; *m* 1954, Isabel Margaret Milne; two *d*. *Educ:* Fraserburgh Academy; Aberdeen Univ. (BSc 1st Cl. Hons Natural Philosophy). Served RAF and Fleet Air Arm, 1943–46. Malayan Meteorological Service, 1950–56; ICI, 1956–66; Min. of Technology, 1966–70; Dept of Trade and Industry, 1970–74; Dept of Industry, 1974–77; Director, British Shipbuilders (on secondment), 1977–79; Regional Dir, NW Region, Dept of Industry, 1979–83. *Recreation:* golf. *Died 1 May 2014.*

MACDONALD, Dame Anne M.; *see* Maxwell Macdonald.

MacDONALD, Hon. Flora Isabel, CC 1999 (OC 1993); PC (Can.) 1979; Chairperson: HelpAge International, 1997–2001; Future Generations Canada, 2007–09; *b* N Sydney, Nova Scotia, 3 June 1926; *d* of George Frederick MacDonald and Mary Isabel MacDonald (*née* Royle). *Educ:* schools in North Sydney, Nova Scotia; Empire Business Coll., Sydney, NS; Canadian Nat. Defence Coll. With Nat. HQ, Progressive Cons. Party, 1957–66 (Exec. Dir, 1961–66); Nat. Sec., Progressive Cons. Assoc. of Canada, 1966–69; Administrative Officer and Tutor, Dept of Political Studies, Queen's Univ., Kingston, 1967–73; MP (Progressive C) Kingston, Ontario, 1972–88; Sec. of State for External Affairs, Canada, 1979–80; Minister of Employment and Immigration, 1984–86; Minister for Communications, 1986–88. Vis. Scholar, Centre for Canadian Studies, Univ. of Edinburgh, 1989. Special Advr, Commonwealth of Learning, 1990–91; Chairperson, Internat. Develt Res. Centre, 1992–97. Dir, C. T. Financial Services, 1989–97. Director: Care Canada, 1993–2002; Partnership Africa Canada, 1997–2004 (Hon. Pres.); Future Generations, Franklin, WV, 1996. Chairman: Canadian Co-ordinating Cttee, UN Internat. Year of Older Persons, 1999; Shastri Indo-Canada Adv. Council, 1996–2004. Pres., World Federalists of Canada, 2001–04. Patron, Commonwealth Human Rights Initiative. Mem., Carnegie Commn on Preventing Deadly Conflict, Washington, 1994–98. Pres., Assoc. of Canadian Clubs, 1999–2003. Presenter, North/South (weekly TV prog.), 1990–94. Hon. degrees from Univs in Canada, US and UK. Padma Shri (India), 2004. *Publications:* papers on political subjects. *Recreations:* speedskating, mountain climbing. *Address:* #1103, 350 Queen Elizabeth Driveway, Ottawa, ON K1S 3N1, Canada. *Died 26 July 2015.*

MACDONALD, John B(arfoot), OC 1991; DDS, MS, PhD; Chairman, Addiction Research Foundation, 1981–87 (President and Chief Executive Officer, 1976–81); Executive Director, Council of Ontario Universities, 1968–76; Professor of Higher Education, University of Toronto, 1968–76; *b* 23 Feb. 1918; *s* of Arthur A. Macdonald and Gladys L. Barfoot; *m*; two *s* one *d*; *m* 1967, Liba Kucera; two *d*. *Educ:* Univ. of Toronto, University of Illinois, Columbia Univ. DDS (with hons) Toronto, 1942; MS (Bact) Ill, 1948; PhD (Bact) Columbia, 1953. Lectr, Prev. Dentistry, University of Toronto, and private practice, 1942–44. Canadian Dental Corps, 1944–46 (Capt.). Instr, Bacteriol., University of Toronto, and private practice, 1946–47; Res. Asst, Univ. of Illinois, 1947–48; Kellogg Fellow and Canadian Dental Assoc. Res. Student, Columbia Univ., 1948–49; University of Toronto: Asst Prof. of Bacteriol., 1949–53; Assoc. Prof. of Bacteriol., 1953–56; Chm., Div. of Dental Res., 1953–56; Prof. of Bacteriol., 1956; Cons. in Dental Educn, University of BC, 1955–56; Dir, Forsyth Dental Infirmary, 1956–62 (Cons. in Bacteriol., 1962); Prof. of Microbiol., Harvard Sch., of Dental Med., 1956–62 (Dir of Postdoctoral Studies, 1960–62); President, Univ. of British Columbia, 1962–67. Consultant: Dental Med. Section of Corporate Research Div. of Colgate-Palmolive Co., 1958–62; Donwood Foundn, Toronto, 1967 (Chm. of Bd, 1972–75); Science Council of Canada, 1967–69; Addiction Research Foundn of Ontario, 1968–74 (Mem., 1974–76); Nat. Inst. of Health, 1968– (Mem., Dental Study Sect., 1961–65). Chm., Commn on Pharmaceutical Services of the Canadian Pharmaceutical Assoc., 1967; Mem. and Vice-Chm., Ontario Council of Health, 1981–84; Councillor-at-Large, Internat. Assoc. for Dental Research, 1963, Pres. 1968–69. Fellow, Mem. or Chm. of numerous assocs etc, both Canadian and international. FACD 1955; Hon. FICD 1965. Hon. AM, Harvard Univ., 1956; Hon. LLD: Univ. of Manitoba, 1962; Simon Fraser Univ., 1965; Hon DSc Univ. of British Columbia, 1967; Hon. LLD: Wilfred Laurier, 1976; Brock, 1976; W Ontario, 1977; Hon. DSc: Windsor, 1977; Toronto, 2000. *Publications:* Higher Education in British Columbia and a Plan for the Future, 1962 etc.; numerous contribs to learned jls. *Recreations:* golf, fishing. *Clubs:* University of BC Faculty (Vancouver); Faculty (University of Toronto). *Died 23 Dec. 2014.*

MacDONALD, Margo, (Mrs James Sillars); Member, Lothian, Scottish Parliament, since 2011 (Lothians, 1999–2011) (SNP 1999–2003, Ind since 2003); journalist; *b* 19 April 1943; *d* of Robert and Jean Aitken; *m* 1st, 1965, Peter MacDonald (marr. diss. 1980); two *d*; 2nd, 1981, James Sillars. *Educ:* Hamilton Academy; Dunfermline Coll. (Diploma of Physical Educn). Contested (SNP) Paisley, Gen. Elecn, 1970; MP (SNP) Glasgow (Govan), Nov. 1973–Feb. 1974; contested (SNP): Glasgow (Govan), Gen. Elecn, Feb. 1974 and Oct. 1974; Hamilton, By-elecn, May 1978. Vice-Chm., Scottish National Party, 1972–79 (Senior Vice-Chm., 1974–79); Mem., SNP Nat. Exec., 1980–81; Chm., SNP '79 Group, 1978–81. Director of Shelter (Scotland), 1978–81. *Recreations:* swimming, aquarobics, country music, Hibs FC. *Address:* Scottish Parliament, Edinburgh EH99 1SP. *Died 4 April 2014.*

MACDONALD, Mary Elizabeth; Registrar, Judicial Committee of the Privy Council, 2005–09; *b* 2 Aug. 1958; *d* of Malcolm A. Macdonald and Anne E. Macdonald; *m* 1988, Iain MacVay (separated); one *s*. *Educ:* Univ. of British Columbia (BA 1st Cl. Hons Hist. 1981); Univ. of Victoria (LLB 1986); Darwin Coll., Cambridge (LLM Internat. Law and Civil Liberties 1989). Legal researcher, Peace Tax Fund, Victoria, 1983; TEFL, Cambridge Sch., Lisbon, 1983–84; legal researcher, Hanan, Gordon & Co., Victoria, 1985; called to the Bar, British Columbia, 1987; articled law student, then lawyer, Harris, Campbell, Threlfall & O'Neill, barristers and solicitors, Burnaby, 1986–87; Crown Counsel for Province of British Columbia, 1988; Department of Justice: lawyer, Admin. Law Reform Unit, Ottawa, 1989–90; historical researcher on behalf of Justice Res. Unit (native land claims), London, 1990–91; admitted solicitor, 1991; Section Manager and Human Rights Co-ordinator, Criminal Appeal Office, Royal Courts of Justice, 1991–93, 1994–99; Sen. Crown Prosecutor, Policy Gp, Crown Prosecution Service HQ, 1993–94; Hd, Policy Initiatives Team, Women's Unit, Cabinet Office, 1999; Hd (Human Rights and Codification) Br., Criminal Justice Div., and Hd, Criminal Justice Br., Human Rights and Constitution Div., LCD, 1999–2001; Managing Lawyer, Criminal Law Team, Law Commn, 2002; Sen. Lawyer, Law Enforcement and Internat. Adv. Div., Solicitor's Office, HM Customs and Excise, 2002–04; Sen. Lawyer and Team Leader, Litigation D2a, Office of Treasury Solicitor, 2004–05. *Publications:* (jtly) Crown Law, 1991. *Recreations:* cinema, gym, literature. *Died 11 Feb. 2012.*

McDONALD, Very Rev. William James Gilmour; Moderator of the General Assembly of the Church of Scotland, 1989–90; Parish Minister of Mayfield, Edinburgh, 1959–92; *b* 3 June 1924; *s* of Hugh Gilmour McDonald and Grace Kennedy Hunter; *m* 1952, Margaret Patricia Watson; one *s* two *d*. *Educ:* Daniel Stewart's College, Edinburgh; Univ. of Edinburgh (MA, BD); Univ. of Göttingen. Served Royal Artillery and Indian Artillery, 1943–46. Parish Minister, Limekilns, Fife, 1953–59. Convener, Assembly Council, 1984–87. Chaplain, Edinburgh Merchant Co., 1982–2002. Warrack Lectr, Edinburgh and Aberdeen Univs, 1992, Glasgow and St Andrews Univs, 1995; Turnbull Trust Preacher, Scots Ch, Melbourne, 1993. Hon. DD Edinburgh, 1987. *Publications:* Words Thought and Said: prayers and reflections, 2014. *Address:* 7 Blacket Place, Edinburgh EH9 1RN. *T:* (0131) 667 2100. *Died 9 Dec. 2015.*

MACDONALD, Prof. William Weir, PhD, DSc; FSB; Selwyn Lloyd Professor of Medical Entomology, 1980–94, then Professor Emeritus, and Dean, 1983–88, Liverpool School of Tropical Medicine; *b* 5 Dec. 1927; *s* of William Sutherland Macdonald and Ina Weir; *m* 1950, Margaret Lawrie; two *d*. *Educ:* Univ. of Glasgow (BSc 1948). MSc 1964, PhD 1965, Univ. of Liverpool; DSc 1973, Univ. of Glasgow. FSB (FIBiol 1966). Strang-Steel Scholar, Glasgow Univ., 1948; Colonial Office Res. Scholar, 1949–50; Entomologist, E African Fisheries Res. Org., Uganda, 1950–52; Res. Fellow, Inst. for Med. Res., Kuala Lumpur, 1953–60; Lectr, Sen. Lectr, and Reader, Liverpool Sch. of Trop. Medicine, 1960–76; Prof. of Med. Entomology, London Sch. of Hygiene and Trop. Medicine, 1977–80. Consultant: WHO; various overseas govts. Chalmers Medal, Royal Soc. of Trop. Medicine and Hygiene, 1972. *Publications:* papers on med. entomology in scientific jls. *Recreations:* golf, gardening. *Address:* 10 Headland Close, West Kirby, Wirral CH48 3JP. *T:* (0151) 625 7857. *Died 30 April 2015.*

MACDONALD-BUCHANAN, John, MC 1945; Vice Lord-Lieutenant of Northamptonshire, 1991–2000; *b* 15 March 1925; *s* of Major Sir Reginald Macdonald-Buchanan, KCVO, MBE, MC and Hon. Lady Macdonald-Buchanan, OStJ, *oc* of 1st Baron Woolavington, GCVO; *m* 1st, 1950, Lady Rose Fane (marr. diss. 1969; she *d* 1984), *d* of 14th Earl of Westmorland; one *s* two *d*; 2nd, 1969, Mrs Jill Rosamonde Trelawnay, *d* of Maj.-Gen. Cecil Benfield Fairbanks, CB, CBE; two *d*. *Educ:* Eton; RMC, Sandhurst; RAC, Cirencester. 2nd Lt, Scots Guards, 1943; served War, 1944–45, NW Europe; Malaya, 1948–50; retired, 1952. Mem., Horserace Betting Levy Bd, 1973–76. Steward of Jockey Club, 1969–72, Sen. Steward 1979–82. High Sheriff 1963–64, DL 1978, Northants. *Address:* The Stables House, Cottesbrooke, Northampton NN6 8PH. *T:* (01604) 505732; Clunie House, Hans Place, SW1X 0EY. *T:* (020) 7581 7951. *Clubs:* White's, Turf. *Died 11 Oct. 2014.*

MACDONALD-SMITH, Maj.-Gen. Hugh, CB 1977; *b* 8 Jan. 1923; *s* of Alexander and Ada Macdonald-Smith; *m* 1st, 1947, Désirée Violet (*née* Williamson) (*d* 2004); one *s* one *d* (and one *d* decd); 2nd, 2008, Lucy Margaret Woollett (*née* Maxwell). *Educ:* Llanelli Grammar Sch.; Llandovery Coll.; Birmingham Univ. BSc. CEng, FIET. Commissioned REME, 1944; served: India, 1945–47; Singapore, 1956–58; BAOR, 1961–63; Technical Staff Course, 1949–51; Staff Coll., Camberley, 1953; Lt-Col, 1963; Asst Dir, Electrical and Mechanical Engineering, HQ Western Comd, 1963–65; Asst Mil. Sec., MoD, 1965–66; Comd REME, 1 (BR) Corps Troops, 1966–67; Technical Gp, REME, 1967–72; Col, 1967; Brig. 1970; Dep. Dir, Electrical and Mechanical Engineering (Eng. Pol.), (Army), 1972–75; Dir, later Dir Gen., Electrical and Mech. Engrg (Army), 1975–78; retired 1978. Col Comdt, REME, 1978–83; Rep. Col Comdt, REME, 1979–80. Dir, TEMA, 1981–87

(Sec. to Council, 1979–80). Mem., Cttee of Inquiry into Engrg Profession, 1977–79. Mem. Council, IMechE, 1975–76. *Recreations:* golf, gardening, photography. *Address:* c/o TSB, Bridport DT6 3QL. *Died 18 March 2014.*

McDOWELL, George Roy Colquhoun, CBE 1988; CEng, FIET; Chairman, British Standards Institution, 1985–88; *b* 1 Sept. 1922; *s* of Robert Henry McDowell and Jean McDowell; *m* 1948, Joan Annie Bryan; two *s*. *Educ:* Coleraine Academical Instn; Queen's Univ., Belfast (BSc Eng). Signals Officer, RAF, 1942–46. Works Manager, Distribn Transformer Div., subseq. Works Manager, Power Transformer Div., Ferranti Ltd, 1950–69; Dir, 1969–87, Man. Dir Designate, 1969–72, Chm. and Man. Dir, 1972–87, George H. Scholes. Director: Clipsal (UK), 1983–98 (Chm., 1985–98); Clipsal Ltd, 1997–98; Elbocks Ltd, 1997–98. Chairman: Electrical Installation Equipment Manufacturers' Assoc., 1977–80; British Electrotechnical Cttee, BSI; Electrotechnical Council, BSI, 1982–85; President: British Electrical and Allied Manufacturers' Assoc., 1981–82; Internat. Electrotechnical Commn, 1987–90; IEEIE; Institution of Electrical Engineers: Chm., Power Bd; Chm., Finance Cttee; Mem. Council. Hon. FIIE. Grand Decoration of Honour for Services to the Republic of Austria, 1978. *Recreations:* golf, Rugby, cricket. *Address:* 11 Abbey Mill, Shirleys Drive, Prestbury, Macclesfield, Cheshire SK10 4XY. *T:* (01625) 827750. *Club:* Army and Navy. *Died 2 July 2013.*

McEWAN, Geraldine, (Mrs Hugh Cruttwell); actress; *b* 9 May 1932; *d* of Donald and Norah McKeown; *m* 1953, Hugh Cruttwell (*d* 2002); one *s* one *d*. *Educ:* Windsor County Girls' School. Acted with Theatre Royal, Windsor, 1949–51; Who Goes There, 1951; Sweet Madness, 1952; For Better For Worse, 1953; Summertime, 1955; Love's Labour's Lost, Stratford-on-Avon, 1956; The Member of the Wedding, Royal Court Theatre, 1957; The Entertainer, Palace, 1957–58; Stratford-on-Avon, 1958: Pericles; Twelfth Night; Much Ado About Nothing; 1961: Much Ado About Nothing; Hamlet; Everything in the Garden, Arts and Duke of York's, 1962; School for Scandal, Haymarket, and USA, 1962; The Private Ear, and The Public Eye, USA, 1963; Loot, 1965; National Theatre, Old Vic, 1965–71: Armstrong's Last Goodnight; Love For Love; A Flea in Her Ear; The Dance of Death; Edward II; Home and Beauty; Rites; The Way of the World; The White Devil; Amphitryon 38; Dear Love, Comedy, 1973; Chez Nous, Globe, 1974; The Little Hut, Duke of York's, 1974; Oh Coward!, Criterion, 1975; On Approval, Haymarket, 1975; Look After Lulu, Chichester, and Haymarket, 1978; A Lie of the Mind, Royal Court, 1987; Lettice and Lovage, Globe, 1988; Hamlet, Riverside Studio, 1992; The Bird Sanctuary, Abbey, Dublin, 1994; Grace Note, Old Vic, 1997; The Chairs, Royal Court Downstairs, 1997, USA 1998; Hay Fever, Savoy, 1999; Royal National Theatre: The Browning Version and Harlequinade, 1980; The Provok'd Wife, 1980; The Rivals, 1983; Two Inches of Ivory, 1983; You Can't Take It With You, 1983; The Way of the World, 1995. Directed: As You Like It, Birmingham Rep., transf. Phoenix, 1988; Treats, Hampstead, 1989; Waiting for Sir Larry, Edinburgh, 1990; Four Door Saloon, Hampstead, 1991; Keyboard Skills, Bush, 1993. *Television includes:* The Prime of Miss Jean Brodie, 1978; The Barchester Chronicles, 1982; Mapp and Lucia, 1985, 1986; Oranges are not the only Fruit, 1990; Mulberry, 1992, 1993; The Red Dwarf, 1999; Thin Ice, 2000; Carrie's War, 2004; Agatha Christie's Marple, 2004, 2005, 2006. *Films:* The Adventures of Tom Jones, 1975; Escape from the Dark, 1978; Foreign Body, 1986; Henry V, 1989; Robin Hood, Prince of Thieves, 1991; Moses, 1996; The Love Letter, 1999; Titus, Love's Labour's Lost, 2000; The Magdalene Sisters, 2002; Pure, 2003; The Lazarus Child, 2004; Vanity Fair, 2005. *Address:* c/o Independent Talent Group Ltd, 40 Whitfield Street, W1T 2RH. *Died 30 Jan. 2015.*

MACEY, Rear-Adm. David Edward, CB 1984; *b* 15 June 1929; *s* of Frederick William Charles Macey and Florence May Macey; *m* 1st, 1958, Lorna Therese Verner (decd), *o d* of His Honour Judge Oliver William Verner; one *s* one *d*, and one step *s* two step *d*; 2nd, 1982, Fiona (marr. diss. 1994), *o d* of Vice-Adm. Sir William Beloe, KBE, CB, DSC; 3rd, 1996, Rosemary Bothway, *o d* of Percy Crotch. *Educ:* Sir Joseph Williamson's Mathematical Sch., Rochester; Royal Naval Coll., Dartmouth. Midshipman, 1948; Cruisers, Carriers, Destroyers, 1950–63; Comdr, 1963; Amer. Staff Coll., 1964; Comdr, RNC Dartmouth, 1970; Captain, 1972; Directorate Naval Plans, 1972–74; RCDS, 1975; Dir, RN Staff Coll., 1976–78; Dir, Naval Manpower, 1979–81; Rear-Adm., 1981; Dep. Asst Chief of Staff (Ops), SACEUR, 1981–84. ADC to HM the Queen, 1981. Order of the Bath: Gentleman Usher of the Scarlet Rod, 1985–90; Registrar and Sec., 1990–2001. Receiver-Gen., Canterbury Cathedral, 1984–98; Mem., Archbps' Commn on Cathedrals, 1992–94. Chm., Canterbury Choral Soc., 1992–2002. *Recreations:* walking, cricket, cooking. *Address:* Bell Tower House, Painter's Forstal, Faversham, Kent ME13 0EL. *Clubs:* MCC; Royal Thames Yacht; Band of Brothers (Kent). *Died 23 Jan. 2013.*

McFARLANE OF LLANDAFF, Baroness *cr* 1979 (Life Peer), of Llandaff in the County of South Glamorgan; **Jean Kennedy McFarlane;** Professor and Head of Department of Nursing, University of Manchester, 1974–88, then Professor Emeritus; *b* 1 April 1926; *d* of late James and Elvina Alice McFarlane. *Educ:* Howell's Sch., Llandaff; Bedford Coll., London (BScSoc); Birkbeck Coll., London (MA; Fellow, 1997). SRN, SCM, HV Tutor's Cert.; FRCN 1976; FCNA 1984. Staff Nurse, St Bartholomew's Hosp., 1950–51; Health Visitor, Cardiff CC, 1953–59; Royal Coll. of Nursing: Organising Tutor, Integrated Course, Educn Div., London, 1960–62; Educn Officer, Birmingham, 1962–66; Res. Project Ldr (DHSS sponsored), London, 1967–69; Dir of Educn, Inst. of Advanced Nursing Educn, London, 1969–71; Univ. of Manchester: Sen. Lectr in Nursing, Dept of Social and Preventive Medicine, 1971–73; Sen. Lectr and Head of Dept of Nursing, 1973–74. Member: Royal Commn on NHS, 1976–79; Commonwealth War Graves Commn, 1983–88. Chm., English Bd for Nursing, Midwifery and Health Visiting, 1980–83. Mem., Gen. Synod of C of E, 1990–95. Hon. FRCP 1990. Hon. MSc Manchester, 1979; Hon. DSc: Ulster, 1981; City, 2005; Hon. DEd CNAA, 1983; Hon. MD Liverpool, 1990; Hon. DLit Glamorgan, 1995; Hon. LLD Manchester, 1998. *Publications:* The Problems of Developing Criteria of Quality for Nursing Care (thesis), 1969; The Proper Study of the Nurse, 1970; (with G. Castledine) The Practice of Nursing using the Nursing Process, 1982. *Recreations:* music, walking, travelling, photography. *Died 13 May 2012.*

McFARLANE, James Sinclair, CBE 1986; CEng, FIMMM; Director General, Engineering Employers' Federation, 1982–89; *b* 8 Nov. 1925; *s* of John Mills McFarlane and Hannah McFarlane; *m* 1951, Ruth May Harden; three *d*. *Educ:* Manchester Grammar Sch.; Emmanuel Coll., Cambridge (MA, PhD). CEng 1961; FIMMM (FIM 1961). ICI Ltd, 1949–53; Henry Wiggin & Co. Ltd, 1953–69; Chm. and Man. Dir, Smith-Clayton Forge Ltd (GKN Ltd), 1969–76; Man. Dir, Garringtons Ltd (GKN Ltd), 1976–77; Guest Keen & Nettlefolds Ltd: Gen. Man., Personnel, 1977–79; Exec. Dir, 1979–82. Mem., NEDC, 1982–89; a Civil Service Comr (pt-time), 1983–88. CCMI. *Publications:* contrib. scientific and technical jls. *Recreation:* music. *Address:* 24 Broad Street, Ludlow, Shropshire SY8 1NJ. *T:* (01584) 872495. *Club:* Caledonian. *Died 18 Feb. 2012.*

MacFARLANE, Maj.-Gen. Robert Goudie, MBE 1952; FRCP, FRCPE; Deputy Secretary, Scottish Council for Postgraduate Medical Education, 1975–84; *b* 1 March 1917; *s* of late Archibald Forsyth MacFarlane and Jessie Robertson Goudie; *m* 1945, Mary Campbell Martin (*d* 2010); three *s*. *Educ:* Hillhead High Sch., Glasgow; Glasgow Univ. MB, ChB, 1940; MD 1955; FRCPE 1964; MRCP 1970; FRCP 1979. Served War: commissioned RAMC, 1941; in Madagascar, India, Burma, 1941–45. Specialist in Medicine and Consultant Physician, 1948–; CO, British Mil. Hosp., Iserlohn, 1968–70; Prof. of Mil. Med., Royal Army Medical Coll., 1970–71; Consulting Physician, BAOR, 1971–73. Dir of Army Medicine and Consulting Physician to the Army, 1973–74. QHP 1973. *Address:* 6 Redholm, Greenheads Road, North Berwick, East Lothian EH39 4RA. *Died 18 March 2011.*

McGILL, Angus, MBE 1990; journalist; *b* 26 Nov. 1927; *s* of Kenneth and Janet McGill; civil partnership 2006, Robert Jennings. *Educ:* Warehousemen, Clerks' and Drapers' Schools, Addington, Surrey. Reporter, Shields Gazette, 1944; Army service; feature writer, Evening Chronicle, Newcastle, 1948; Londoner's Diary, Evening Standard, 1957; columnist, Evening Standard, 1961–92. Chm., Knobs & Knockers, 1964–77. British Press Award, descriptive writer of the Year, 1968. *Publications:* Augusta, comic strip (drawn by Dominic Poelsma), 1968–; Yea Yea Yea (novel), 1969; Pub: an anthology, 1969; (with Kenneth Thomson) Live Wires, 1982; London Pub Guide, annually 1995–97. *Address:* 83 Winchester Court, Vicarage Gate, W8 4AF. *T:* (020) 7937 2166. *Died 16 Oct. 2015.*

McGILL, Maj.-Gen. Nigel Harry Duncan, CB 1966; Chief of Staff to Commandant-General, Royal Marines, 1967–68; *b* 15 Oct. 1916; *s* of Lt-Col H. R. McGill; *m* 1944, Margaret Constance Killen; two *s* one *d. Educ:* Victoria Coll., Jersey. Commissioned 2nd Lt RM 1934; Maj.-Gen. 1964; Comdr, Portsmouth Group, RM, 1964–67. Representative Col Comdt RM, 1977–78. Exec., Rolls Royce Ltd, 1968–78. *Address:* Alderwood, Manor Farm Road, Fordingbridge, Hants SP6 1DY. *Died 1 Feb. 2013.*

McGOVERN, George Stanley; United States Senator, 1963–81; US Permanent Representative to United Nations Food and Agriculture Organisation, 1998–2001; United Nations Global Ambassador on Hunger, since 2001; *b* Avon, S Dakota, 19 July 1922; *s* of Rev. Joseph C. McGovern and Francis (*née* McLean); *m* 1943, Eleanor Faye Stegeberg (*d* 2007); three *d* (and one *s* one *d* decd). *Educ:* Dakota Wesleyan Univ. (BA); Northwestern Univ. (MA, PhD). Served World War II, USAAF (DFC). Prof. of History and Govt, Dakota Wesleyan Univ., 1950–53. Exec. Sec., S Dakota Democratic Party, 1953–56; Mem., 1st Dist, S Dakota, US House of Reps, 1957–61; Dir, Food for Peace Programme, 1961–62; Senator from South Dakota, 1963–81. Democratic nominee for US President, 1972. Visiting Professor: Columbia Univ., 1977; Univ. of Pa, 1978; Northwestern Univ., 1981; Univ. of New Orleans, 1982; University Coll., Dublin, 1982; Duke Univ., 1985; Univ. of Munich, 1987. Mem., Amer. Hist. Assoc. Presidential Medal of Freedom, 2000. *Publications:* The Colorado Coal Strike 1913–14, 1953; War Against Want, 1964; Agricultural Thought in the Twentieth Century, 1967; A Time of War, A Time of Peace, 1968; (with Leonard F. Guttridge) The Great Coalfield War, 1972; An American Journey, 1974; Grassroots, an Autobiography, 1978; Terry: my daughter's life-and-death struggle with alcoholism, 1996; The Third Freedom: ending hunger in our time, 2001; The Essential America, 2004; What It Means to Be a Democrat, 2011. *Died 21 Oct. 2012.*

McGRADY, Edward Kevin; *b* 3 June 1935; *y s* of late Michael McGrady and Lilian Leatham; *m* 1959, Patricia (*d* 2003), *d* of William Swail and Margaret Breen; two *s* one *d. Educ:* St Patrick's High Sch., Downpatrick. ACA 1957, FCA 1962. Former Partner, M. B. McGrady & Co., chartered accountants and insurance brokers. Councillor, Downpatrick UDC, 1961–89; Chm. of UDC, 1964–73; Vice-Chm., Down District Council, 1973, 1975–76, 1977, Chm. 1974, 1976, 1978, 1981, 1982. 1st Chm. of SDLP, 1971–73; 1st Chm. of SDLP Assembly Party; Chief Whip, SDLP, 1979–2010; SDLP Parly Chief Whip, 1987–2010; SDLP Party Assembly Chief Whip, 1998–2003; Chm., SDLP, 2007–09. Member (SDLP): S Down: NI Assembly, 1973–75 (Head of Office of Exec. Planning and Co-ordination (Minister for Co-ordination, Jan.–May 1974)); NI Constitutional Convention, 1975–76; NI Assembly, 1982–86; Down S, NI Assembly, 1998–2003. Contested (SDLP) Down S, gen. elections, 1979, 1983 and 1986. MP (SDLP) South Down, 1987–2010. Mem., NI Affairs Cttee, H of C, 1994–2005. Mem., NI Policing Bd, 2001–05. *Recreations:* golf, badminton, choral work. *Died 11 Nov. 2013.*

McGRATH, William Joseph; Founder and Chief Executive Officer, Greenfield Services Ltd, since 1996; Managing Director, British Gas Energy Centres, since 1999; *b* 30 Sept. 1940; *s* of William George McGrath and Wallis (*née* Reinwold); *m* 1963, Mary Teresa Bridget Galvin; two *d. Educ:* St John's RC Sch., Tamworth, Staffs; Open Univ. (BA Hons). With Cunard Steamship Co. Ltd, 1956–68; G. J. Keddie & Sons Ltd, 1968–75; Director: Asda Stores Ltd, 1975–81; Comet PLC, 1981–84; Founder and Chief Exec. Officer, Builders Mate, 1984–87; Dir, Wickes PLC, 1990–93 (Dep. Chm., 1993); Chief Exec. Officer, Pentos Gp, 1994–95; Chm. and CEO, British Home Doors, 2000–04 (non-exec. Dir, 1995–2000; non-exec. Chm., 1997–2000). Non-executive Chairman: Gasflair Ltd, 1999–2003; Hiatt Ltd, 2000–; Lease 360 plc, 2006–; non-executive Director: Cashbuild, South Africa, 1995–2002; Gainsborough Building Soc., 2000–02. MInstD 1984; MCIM 1989. FRSA 1994. Wine and Spirit Educn Trust (Cert., Higher Cert. Dist. and Dip.). Compagnon de Beaujolais, 1976. KSC 1962. *Recreations:* chess, walking, gardening. *Address:* Manor House, Gringley on the Hill, Notts DN10 4RG. *T:* (01777) 817716. *Club:* East India. *Died 12 Sept. 2011.*

McGREGOR, Harvey, CBE 2014; QC 1978; DCL; in practice as a barrister; Warden, New College, Oxford, 1985–96 (Fellow, 1972–85; Hon. Fellow, 1996); *b* 25 Feb. 1926; *s* of late William Guthrie Robertson McGregor and Agnes (*née* Reid). *Educ:* Inverurie Acad.; Scarborough Boys' High Sch.; Queen's Coll., Oxford (Hastings Scholar; BA 1951, BCL 1952, MA 1955, DCL 1983); Dr of Juridical Science, Harvard, 1962. Flying Officer, RAF, 1946–48. Called to the Bar, Inner Temple, 1955, Bencher, 1985; admitted to Faculty of Advocates, 1995. Bigelow Teaching Fellow, Univ. of Chicago, 1950–51; Visiting Professor: New York Univ. and Rutgers Univ., 1963–69 (various times); Univ. of Edinburgh, 1998–. Consultant to Law Commn, 1966–73. Pres., Harvard Law Sch. Assoc. of UK, 1981–2001; Mem., Acad. of European Private Lawyers, 1994–; Associate Mem., Soc. of WS, 2002–. Ind. Chm., London Theatre Council and The Theatre Council (formerly Provincial Theatre Council), 1992– (Dep. Ind. Chm., 1971–92); Pres., Oxford Stage Co., 1992–; Trustee: Oxford Union Soc., 1977–2004 (Chm. Trustees, 1994–2004); Harlech Scholars' Trust, 1985–2010; Chalet Trust, 1985– (Chm., 1994–). Fellow, Winchester Coll., 1985–96. Mem., Vice-Chancellor's Circle, Univ. of Oxford, 2015. Trustee, Migraine Trust, 1999–2012. Mem. Editorial Cttee, 1967–86, Mem., Editorial Bd, 1986–, Modern Law Review. Hon. Fellow: St Hilda's Coll., Oxford, 2008 (Privilegiate, 2001–08); Queen's Coll., Oxford, 2010. *Publications:* McGregor on Damages, 12th edn 1961 to 19th edn 2014; Contract Code, 1993; (contrib.) International Encyclopedia of Comparative Law, 1972; articles in legal jls. *Recreation:* giving concerts at home. *Address:* (chambers) Hailsham Chambers, 4 Paper Buildings, Temple, EC4Y 7EX. *T:* (020) 7353 3366; (residence) Gray's Inn Chambers, Gray's Inn, WC1R 5JA. *T:* (020) 7242 4942; 29 Howard Place, Edinburgh EH3 5JY. *T:* (0131) 556 8680. *Clubs:* Garrick; New (Edinburgh). *Died 27 June 2015.*

McGREGOR, Sir James David, Kt 1997; OBE 1976; ISO 1973; Member, Executive Council, Hong Kong, 1995–97; *b* 30 Jan. 1924; *s* of David Nelson McGregor and Ann Horsburgh McGregor; *m* 1st, 1947, Doreen Davis (marr. diss.); one *d*; 2nd, 1963, Christine K. C. Hung; one *s* one *d. Educ:* Morgan Acad., Dundee; No 1 Sch. of Tech. Trng, Halton (RAF). RAF service, 1940–54 (armament specialist and aeronautical inspector). Hong Kong Government: Exec. Officer, 1954; Dep. Dir, Commerce and Industry Dept and Dep. Comr of Customs, 1972–75; Dir, Hong Kong General Chamber of Commerce, 1975–88; elected MLC, Hong Kong, 1988–95. JP Hong Kong, 1967–97. Hon. LLD Napier, 1995. *Publications:* Life and Death (short stories), 1995; numerous articles on politics, economics, Hong Kong and Asian affairs. *Recreations:* golf, snooker, writing, embroidery. *Clubs:* Hong Kong, Hong Kong Jockey; Tsawwassen Beach Grove Golf (Vancouver). *Died 16 July 2014.*

McGREGOR, Peter, CEng, FIET; writer and consultant; Director General, Export Group for the Constructional Industries, 1984–91 (Consultant, 1991–94); *b* 20 May 1926; *s* of Peter McGregor and Margaret Thomson McGregor (*née* McAuslan); *m* 1st, 1954, Marion (*d* 2001), *d* of H. T. Downer; one *s* (one *d* decd); 2nd, 2006, Sheena Macmillan, *d* of George Lorimer McCubbin. *Educ:* Cardiff High Sch.; Univ. of Birmingham; London Sch. of Economics (BSc

(Econs)). National Service, RE, 1946–48. Various appointments, Ferranti Ltd, 1950–74, incl. Works Manager, Distribution Transformer Dept, Sales Manager, Transformer Div., Gen. Manager, Power Div.; Dir, Industrie Elettriche di Legnano (Italy), 1970–74; Associate Dir, Corporate Renewal Associates Ltd, 1988–93. Dir, Oxford Univ. Business Summer Sch., 1972; first Sec. Gen., Anglo-German Foundn for Study of Industrial Soc., 1974–81; Industrial Dir (Dep. Sec.), NEDO, 1981–84. Chm., Textile Machinery EDC, 1982–86; Dir, Templeton Technol. Seminar, 1985. Member: N American Adv. Gp, BOTB, 1968–74; Eur. Trade Cttee, BOTB, 1981–83; Adv. Bd, Public Policy Centre, 1984–88; Cttee on Exchange Rate, Public Policy Centre, 1984–87. Industrial Advr to Liberal Party, 1960–73; an Industrial Advr to Social and Liberal Democrats, 1988–90; Chm., Hazel Grove Liberal Assoc., 1971–74; contested (L) Ilford South, 1964. Mem., Königswinter Conf. steering cttee, 1976–90. Hon. Treasurer, Anglo-German Assoc., 1983–91. Elder and Hon. Treas., St Columba's Ch, Oxford, 1992–97. MCIM; FCMI. *Publications:* The Retreat (novel), 1997; Lessons in Duplicity (novel), 2005; various articles and pamphlets especially on industrial relations, company structure, market economy. *Recreations:* walking, reading, listening to music, writing, conversation, gardening, drawing attention to the Emperor's lack of clothes. *Club:* Caledonian. *Died March 2014.*

McHUGH, James, CBE 1989; FREng; Chairman, British Pipe Coaters Ltd, 1991–96; *b* 4 May 1930; *s* of late Edward McHugh and Martha (*née* Smith); *m* 1953, Sheila (*née* Cape) (decd); two *d*. *Educ:* Carlisle Grammar Sch.; various colls. FREng (FEng 1986); FIMechE, FIGEM, FInstPet. Served Army, National Service. Entered Gas Industry, 1947; technical and managerial appts in Northern and E Midlands Gas Bds; Prodn Engr 1967, Dir of Engrg 1971, W Midlands Gas Bd; British Gas Corporation, subseq. British Gas plc: Dir of Ops, 1975; Mem., 1979; Man. Dir, Prodn and Supply, 1982; Man. Dir, 1986; Gp Exec. Mem., 1986–91. Director: Lloyd's Register Quality Assurance Ltd, 1985–2002; UK Accreditation Service, 1995–2000. Member: Meteorological Cttee, MoD, 1981–85; Engrg Council, 1989–92; President: IGasE, 1986–87; Inst. of Quality Assurance, 1992–97; World Quality Council, 1997–2002. Hon. FCQI (Hon. FIQA 1997); CCMI; FRSA. Freeman, City of London, 1984; Liveryman, Engineers' Co., 1984–. *Recreations:* mountaineering, dinghy sailing. *Club:* Anglo-Belgian. *Died 8 Sept. 2012.*

McINNES, John Colin; DL; QC (Scot.) 1990; Sheriff Principal of South Strathclyde, Dumfries and Galloway, 2000–05; *b* 21 Nov. 1938; *s* of late Mr I. W. McInnes, WS, and Mrs Lucy McInnes, Cupar, Fife; *m* 1966, Elisabeth Mabel Neilson; one *s* one *d*. *Educ:* Cargilfield Sch., Edinburgh; Merchiston Castle Sch., Edinburgh; Brasenose Coll., Oxford (BA); Edinburgh Univ. (LLB). 2nd Lieut 8th Royal Tank Regt, 1957–58; Lieut Fife and Forfar Yeomanry/Scottish Horse (TA), 1958–64. Advocate, 1963. In practice at Scottish Bar, 1963–73; Tutor, Faculty of Law, Edinburgh Univ., 1965–73; Sheriff of the Lothians and Peebles, 1973–74, of Tayside Central and Fife, 1974–2000. Member and Vice-President: Security Service Tribunal, 1989–2001; Intelligence Services Tribunal, 1994–2001; Mem., Investigatory Powers Tribunal, 2000–. Member: Cameron Gp on Shrieval Trng, 1995–96; Scottish Criminal Justice Forum, 1996–2000; Judicial Studies Cttee (Scotland), 1996–2000; Parole Bd for Scotland, 2005–11; Chairman: Summary Justice Review Cttee, Scotland, 2001–04; Youth Court Project Gp (Scotland), 2002. Comr of Northern Lighthouses, 2000–05. Pres., Sheriffs' Assoc., 1995–97. Director: R. Mackness & Co. Ltd, 1963–70; Fios Group Ltd, 1970–72 (Chm., 1970–72). Chm., Fife Family Conciliation Service, 1988–90. Mem. Court, St Andrews Univ., 1983–91. DL Fife, 1997. Hon. LLD St Andrews, 1994. Contested (C) Aberdeen North, 1964. *Publications:* Divorce Law and Practice in Scotland, 1990. *Recreations:* shooting, fishing, ski-ing, photography. *Died 12 Oct. 2011.*

MACINTOSH, Joan, CBE 1978; *b* 23 Nov. 1919; *d* of Leonard Burbidge and Edith Cockin; *m* 1952, Ian Gillies Macintosh (*d* 1992); one *s* two *d* (and one *s* decd). *Educ:* Amer. and English schs; Oxford Univ. (MA Modern History). BBC, 1941–42; Amer. Div., Min. of Inf., 1942–45; HM Foreign Service, 1945–52; retd on marriage. Voluntary work in India, 1953–69; CAB Organiser, Glasgow, 1972–75. Chm. Council, Insurance Ombudsman Bureau, 1981–85; Lay Observer for Scotland (Solicitors (Scotland) Act), 1981–89; Chm., Scottish Child Law Centre, 1989–92; Mem., Royal Commn on Legal Services in Scotland, 1975–80; Mem., Scottish Constitutional Commn, 1994. Chm., Scottish Consumer Council, 1975–80; Vice-Chm., National Consumer Council, 1976–84; Vice-Pres., Nat. Fedn of Consumer Gps, 1982–97; Member: Council, Victim Support Scotland, 1992–96; Auchterarder Community Council, 1995–98. Hon. Pres., Scottish Legal Action Group, 1990. Hon. LLD: Dundee, 1982; Strathclyde, 1991; DUniv Stirling, 1988. *Publications:* (as Joan Cockin): Curiosity Killed the Cat, 1947; Villainy at Vespers, 1949; Deadly Earnest, 1952; (as Joan Macintosh): various educational books and adaptations of children's classics. *Recreations:* writing, local history. *Address:* Wynd End, Auchterarder, Perthshire PH3 1AD. *T:* (01764) 662499. *Died 28 May 2014.*

McINTYRE, Air Vice Marshal Ian Graeme; former consultant in dental and public health for Warwickshire, and Solihull; Chief Executive, Defence Dental Agency, 1997–2001; *b* 9 July 1943; *s* of Arthur McIntyre and Eileen McIntyre (*née* Patmore); *m* 1966, Joan; two *s*. *Educ:* Royal Masonic Sch. for Boys; Durham Univ. (BDS); BPMF, Inst. of Dental Surgery, London Univ. (MSc). MGDS RCS, DDPH RCS; FDSRCSE *ad hominem* 1998. Commnd RAF, 1961; Triservice Advr in Gen. Dental Practice, 1989; Asst Dir, Dental Service, RAF, 1991; CO, RAF Inst. of Dental Health and Trng, 1994; Dir, Clinical Services, Defence Dental Agency and Dir, RAF Dental Branch, 1995; QHDS, 1995–2001. Pres., BDA, 2003–04. *Recreations:* hill walking, gardening, watching Rugby. *Address:* Dunelm, 8 Walton Fields, Kineton, Warwicks CV35 0JP. *Club:* Royal Air Force. *Died 8 May 2011.*

McINTYRE, Ian James; writer and broadcaster; *b* Banchory, Kincardineshire, 9 Dec. 1931; *y s* of late Hector Harold McIntyre, Inverness, and late Annie Mary Michie, Ballater; *m* 1954, Leik Sommerfelt (*d* 2012), 2nd *d* of late Benjamin Vogt, Kragerø, Norway; two *s* two *d*. *Educ:* Prescot Grammar Sch.; St John's Coll., Cambridge (Scholar; Med. and Mod. Langs Tripos, Pts I and II; BA 1953; MA); Coll. of Europe, Bruges. Pres., Cambridge Union, 1953. Commnd, Intelligence Corps, 1955–57. Current affairs talks producer, BBC, 1957; Editor, At Home and Abroad, 1959; Man. Trng Organiser, BBC Staff Trng Dept, 1960; Programme Services Officer, ITA, 1961; staff of Chm., Cons. Party in Scotland, 1962; Dir of Inf. and Res., Scottish Cons. Central Office, 1965; contested (C) Roxburgh, Selkirk and Peebles, 1966; long-term contract, writer and broadcaster, BBC, 1970–76; presenter and interviewer, Analysis, and other programmes on politics, for. affairs and the arts; travelled widely in Europe, N America, Africa, Asia and ME; Controller: BBC Radio 4, 1976–78; BBC Radio 3, 1978–87. Associate Ed., The Times, 1989–90. *Publications:* The Proud Doers: Israel after twenty years, 1968; (ed and contrib.) Words: reflections on the uses of language, 1975; Dogfight: the transatlantic battle over Airbus, 1992; The Expense of Glory: a life of John Reith, 1993; Dirt and Deity: a life of Robert Burns, 1995; Garrick, 1999 (Annual Book Prize, Soc. for Theatre Res., 2000); Joshua Reynolds: the life and times of the first president of the Royal Academy, 2003; Hester: the remarkable life of Dr Johnson's 'Dear Mistress', 2008; contrib. Oxford DNB, 2004; articles and book reviews in The Listener, The Times, The Independent, The Spectator. *Recreation:* family life. *Address:* Spylaw House, Newlands Avenue, Radlett, Herts WD7 8EL. *T:* (01923) 853532. *E:* ian.mcintyre@waitrose.com. *Club:* Union (Cambridge). *Died 19 April 2014.*

McKAY, Allen; JP; *b* 5 Feb. 1927; *s* of Fred and Martha Anne McKay; *m* 1949, June Simpson (*d* 1997); one *s*. *Educ:* Hoyland Kirk Balk Secondary Modern School; extramural studies, Univ. of Sheffield. Clerical work, Steel Works, 1941–45; general mineworker, 1945–47; Mining Electrical Engineer, 1947–65; NCB Industrial Relations Trainee, 1965–66; Asst Manpower Officer, Barnsley Area, NCB, 1966–78. MP (Lab) Penistone, July 1978–1983; Barnsley West and Penistone, 1983–92. Opposition Whip, 1981. JP

Barnsley, 1971. *Recreation:* reading. *Address:* 24 Springwood Road, Hoyland, Barnsley, South Yorks S74 0AZ. *T:* (01226) 743418. *Died 2 May 2013.*

MACKAY, His Honour David Ian; a Circuit Judge, 1992–2010; *b* 11 Nov. 1945; *s* of David and Jessie Mackay; *m* 1974, Mary Elizabeth Smith; one *s* two *d*. *Educ:* Birkenhead Sch.; Brasenose Coll., Oxford (Schol.; MA 1992). Called to the Bar, Inner Temple, 1969; practised on Northern Circuit, 1970–92; Asst Recorder, 1986–89; Recorder, 1989–92. Official Referee's business, 1993–98; Provincial Judge, Technology and Construction Court, 1998–2010. Fellow, Soc. of Advanced Legal Studies. 2001. Vice Pres., Birkenhead Sch., 2008– (Gov., 1979–2001; Chm., 1991–2001); Chm., Birkenhead Sch. Foundn Trust, 1998–2004. *Recreations:* history, transport, France. *Club:* Athenæum (Liverpool). *Died 20 April 2012.*

McKAY, Rt Hon. Sir Ian (Lloyd), KNZM 1998; PC 1992; Chartered Arbitrator; Judge of the Court of Appeal of Samoa, since 2001; Judge of the Court of Appeal of New Zealand, 1991–97; *b* 7 March 1929; *s* of Neville James McKay and Kathleen Mary (*née* McGrath); *m* 1958, Ruth Constance Younger (*d* 2010); four *s* two *d*. *Educ:* Victoria Coll., Univ. of NZ (BA, LLB). FCIArb; FAMINZ(Arb). Barrister and Solicitor, High Court of NZ, 1952; in practice as barrister and solicitor with Swan Davies & McKay, Wellington, later Swan Davies McKay & Co., then Young Swan McKay & Co., subseq. Young Swan Morison McKay, and Kensington Swan, 1953–91; Sen. Partner, 1967–91. Chm., various govt law reform cttees, 1971–87. Dir, public and private cos, 1970–91. Fellow, Internat. Acad. Trial Lawyers, USA, 1982–. Hon. Mem., Amer. Bar Assoc., 1981. *Publications:* contrib. Defamation, to Laws of New Zealand, 1994; The Art of Piobaireachd, 1997; The Wellington Gaelic Club 75 Years, 2006; papers to nat. confs and jls of various professional bodies. *Recreations:* Highland bagpipe music, tennis. *Address:* PO Box 17028, Wellington 6147, New Zealand. *T:* (4) 4768950, *Fax:* (4) 4767950. *Club:* Wellington (Wellington, NZ). *Died 20 Feb. 2014.*

McKAY, Dr John Henderson, CBE 1987; JP; DL; Tutor and Associate Lecturer, Open University, 1993–2001; Hon. Vice President, Royal Caledonian Horticultural Society, since 1997 (Vice President, 1993–97); *b* 12 May 1929; *s* of Thomas Johnstone McKay and Patricia Madeleine Henderson; *m* 1964, Catherine Watson Taylor; one *s* one *d*. *Educ:* West Calder High School; BA Hons, PhD, Open Univ. Labourer, clerk, Pumpherston Oil Co. Ltd, 1948–50; National Service, Royal Artillery, 1950–52; Officer and Surveyor, Customs and Excise, 1952–85. Mem., 1974–77 and 1978–88, Lord Provost and Lord Lieutenant, 1984–88, City of Edinburgh DC; Chm., Edinburgh Internat. Fest. Soc., 1984–88; Jt Chm., Edinburgh Mil. Tattoo Policy Cttee, 1984–88; Councillor, Royal Caledonian Horticultural Soc., 1974–78, 1980–81, 1984–88 (Sec. and Treas., 1988–93). Convener, Business Cttee, 1992–96, Assessor on Univ. Court, 1996–99, Gen. Council of Edinburgh Univ. Chm., Scottish Wkg People's History Trust, 1992–2000; Trustee: Inst. of Occupnl Medicine Res. Trust, 1992–2002; Almond Valley Collections Trust, 1994–2007; Edinburgh Quartet Trust, 1994–2002 (Chm., 1995–2000); Hon. Pres., Scottish Craftsmanship Assoc., 1987–2000; Hon. Vice-Pres., St Andrew Soc., 1989–2004; Patron, Scotland Yard Adventure Centre, 1988–2002. JP 1984, DL 1988, Edinburgh. Dr *hc* Edinburgh, 1989. *Publications:* (jtly) Pumpherston: the story of a shale oil village, 2002; contributed: A Sense of Place: studies in Scottish local history, 1988; Participating in the Knowledge Society, 2005; Women's Work in Industrial England, 2007; Caledonian Gardener, 2009; contrib. Local Population Studies. *Recreations:* gardening, listening to music. *Address:* 2 Buckstone Way, Edinburgh EH10 6PN. *T:* (0131) 445 2865. *Died 1 Nov. 2011.*

McKEAN, Prof. Charles Alexander, FRSE; FSAScot, FRHistS; Professor of Scottish Architectural History, 1998–2011, then Emeritus, and Senior Research Fellow, since 2011, Dundee University (Professor of Architecture, 1995–98); *b* 16 July 1946; *s* of John Laurie McKean and Nancy Burns Lendrum; *m* 1975, Margaret Elizabeth Yeo; two *s*. *Educ:* Fettes Coll., Edinburgh; Univ. of Bristol (BA Hons); Univ. of Poitiers (certificat d'études supérieures). Regional Secretary, RIBA, 1968–79; Sec. and Treas., RIAS, 1979–94; Architectural Correspondent: The Times, 1977–83; Scotland on Sunday, 1988–89; Trustee, Thirlestane Castle Trust, 1983–92; Director, Workshops and Artists Studios Scotland (WASPS), 1980–85; Member: Scottish Arts Council Exhibitions Panel, 1980–83; Adv. Council for the Arts in Scotland, 1984–87; Edinburgh Common Purpose Adv. Cttee, 1990–94; Scottish Cttee, Heritage Lottery Fund, 2003–09; Historic Envmt Adv. Council for Scotland, 2003–06; Chm., Edinburgh World Heritage Trust, 2006–12; Mem. Council, and Chm. Buildings Cttee, Nat. Trust for Scotland, 1995–2003. Lectures: Bossom, RSA, 1986; RCS Prestigious, 1992. Hon. Mem., Saltire Soc. FRSE 1999; FRHistS 2010; FRSA 1980. Hon. FRIBA 1989; Hon. FRIAS 1994; Hon. FRSGS 2002. Hon. DLitt Robert Gordon, 1993. General Editor, RIAS/Landmark Trust series to Scotland, 1982–2008. Architectural Journalist of the Year, 1979 and 1983; Building Journalist of the Year, 1983. *Publications:* (with David Atwell) Battle of Styles, 1974; Guide to Modern Buildings in London 1965–75, 1976; Fight Blight, 1977; Architectural Guide to Cambridge and East Anglia 1920–80, 1980; Edinburgh—an illustrated architectural guide, 1982, 3rd edn 1983; (with David Walker) Dundee—an illustrated introduction through its buildings, 1984, 2nd edn 1986; Stirling and the Trossachs, 1984; The Scottish Thirties, 1987; The District of Moray—an illustrated introduction, 1987; (jtly) Central Glasgow—an illustrated architectural guide, 1989; Banff and Buchan—an illustrated architectural guide, 1990; For a Wee Country, 1990; Edinburgh: portrait of a city, 1991; Edinburgh—an illustrated architectural guide, 1992; (with David Walker) Dundee—an illustrated architectural guide, 1993; Value or Cost, 1994; Claim, 1998; The Making of the Museum of Scotland, 2001; The Scottish Château, 2001; Battle for the North, 2006; (with Pat Whatley) Lost Dundee, 2008; (ed jtly) Dundee—Renaissance to Enlightenment, 2009. *Recreations:* gardening, travel, topography, books, architecture and glass collecting, history, architectural analysis. *Address:* 10 Hill Park Road, Edinburgh EH4 7AW. *T:* (0131) 336 2753. *Club:* Scottish Arts. *Died 29 Sept. 2013.*

MACKENZIE, Archibald Robert Kerr, CBE 1967; HM Diplomatic Service, retired; *b* 22 Oct. 1915; *s* of James and Alexandrina Mackenzie; *m* 1963, Virginia Ruth Hutchison. *Educ:* Glasgow, Oxford, Chicago and Harvard Universities. Diplomatic Service, with duty at Washington, 1943–45; United Nations, 1946–49; Foreign Office, 1949–51; Bangkok, 1951–54; Cyprus, 1954; Foreign Office, 1955–57; OEEC, Paris, 1957–61; Commercial Counsellor, HM Embassy, Rangoon, 1961–65; Consul-General, Zagreb 1965–69; Ambassador, Tunisia, 1970–73; Minister (Econ. and Social Affairs), UK Mission to UN, 1973–75. Brandt Commission, 1978–80. *Publications:* Faith in Diplomacy, 2002. *Recreation:* golf. *Address:* Strathcashel Cottage, Rowardennan, near Glasgow G63 0AW. *T:* (01360) 870262. *Died 15 April 2012.*

MACKENZIE, Rear-Adm. David John, CB 1983; FNI; Royal Navy, retired 1983; Director, Atlantic Salmon Trust, 1985–97 (Life Vice-President, 1998); *b* 3 Oct. 1929; *s* of late David Mackenzie and of Alison Walker Lawrie; *m* 1965, Ursula Sybil Balfour; two *s* one *d*. *Educ:* Cargilfield Sch., Barnton, Edinburgh; Royal Naval Coll., Eaton Hall, Cheshire. Cadet to Comdr, 1943–72: served in East Indies, Germany, Far East, Home and Mediterranean Fleets, and commanded: HMML 6011, HM Ships: Brinkley, Barrington, Hardy, Lincoln, Hermione; Captain 1972; Senior Officers War Course, 1972; commanded HMS Phoenix (NBCD School), 1972–74; Captain F8 in HMS Ajax, 1974–76; Director of Naval Equipment, 1976–78; Captain: HMS Blake, 1979; HMS Hermes, 1980; Rear Admiral 1981; Flag Officer and Port Admiral, Gibraltar, Comdr Gibraltar Mediterranean, 1981–83. Younger Brother of Trinity House, 1971–. Member, Queen's Body Guard for Scotland (Royal Company of Archers), 1976–. Vice Pres., Nautical Inst., 1985–93. Vice Pres., Seafarers UK (formerly King George's Fund for Sailors) (Scotland), 2009– (Pres., 1996). *Recreations:* shooting, fishing. *Address:* Easter Meikle Fardle, Meikleour, Perthshire PH2 6EF. *Club:* New (Edinburgh). *Died 26 Nov. 2015.*

McKENZIE, John Cormack, FREng; FICE; Hon. Secretary, Overseas Affairs, Royal Academy of Engineering, 1988–92; Vice-Chairman, Thomas Telford Ltd, 1982–90; Director, H. R. Wallingford plc, 1990–95; *b* 21 June 1927; *s* of William Joseph McKenzie and Elizabeth Frances Robinson; *m* 1954, Olga Caroline Cleland; three *s* one *d*. *Educ:* St Andrew's Coll.; Trinity Coll., Dublin (MA, MAI); Queen's Univ., Belfast (MSc). FREng (FEng 1984); FIPM, FIEI, FIE(Aust). McLaughlin & Harvey, and Sir Alexander Gibb & Partners, 1946–48; Asst Lectr, QUB, 1948–50; Edmund Nuttall Ltd, 1950–82, Dir, 1967–82; Chm., Nuttall Geotechnical Services Ltd, 1967–82; Dir, British Wastewater Ltd, 1978–82. Secretary: ICE, 1982–90; Commonwealth Engineers' Council, 1983–90; Advr to Pres., World Fedn of Engrg Orgs, 2001– (Sec. Gen., 1987–97; Treas., 1997–2001); Vice-Pres., Register of Engrs for Disaster Relief. Pres., Beaconsfield Adv. Centre, 1978–2007. Hon. DSc: Tajikistan, 1993; Nottingham, 1997. *Publications:* papers: Research into some Aspects of Soil Cement, 1952; Engineers: Administrators or Technologists?, 1971; (contrib.) Civil Engineering Procedure, 3rd edn 1979; Comparison of the Market and Command Economics, 1990; Wealth Creation, 1992; Sustainable Development and the Maintenance of Economic Viability, 1994; The Contribution of Engineers to the UN International Decade for Natural Disaster Reduction, 1994; International Application of Ethics for Engineers, 1996; Beyond the Bottom Line, 1996; Quo Vadis, 1997; The Complete Engineer, 1997. *Recreations:* philately, collecting ancient pottery. *Address:* The Cottage (Annex), 20 Ledborough Lane, Beaconsfield, Bucks HP9 2PZ. *Club:* Athenæum. *Died 30 March 2012.*

McKENZIE, Rear-Adm. John Foster, CB 1977; CBE 1974 (OBE 1962); Chief of Naval Staff, and Member, Defence Council, New Zealand, 1975–77; *b* Waiuku, 24 June 1923; *s* of Dr J. C. McKenzie; *m* 1st, 1945, Doreen Elizabeth (*d* 1996), *d* of Dr E. T. and Dr G. M. McElligot; one *s* one *d*; 2nd, 1996, Jocelyn Elva McIntosh. *Educ:* Timaru Boys' High Sch.; St Andrew's Coll., Christchurch, NZ. Served War of 1939–45: Royal Navy; transferred to Royal New Zealand Navy, 1947; Head, Defence Liaison Staff, London, 1966–68; Imperial Defence Coll., 1969; Asst Chief of Defence Staff (Policy), Defence HQ, NZ, 1970–71; Deputy Chief of Naval Staff, 1972; Commodore, Auckland, 1973–75; retired 1977. ADC 1972–75. *Recreations:* gardening, fishing. *Address:* 1/38 Seaview Road, Remuera, Auckland 1005, New Zealand. *Died 28 March 2013.*

MACKESY, Dr Piers Gerald, FRHistS; FBA 1988; Fellow of Pembroke College, Oxford, 1954–87, then Emeritus; *b* 15 Sept. 1924; *s* of Maj.-Gen. Pierse Joseph Mackesy, CB, DSO, MC and Dorothy (*née* Cook), (novelist as Leonora Starr); *m* 1st, 1957, Sarah Davies; one *s* two *d*; 2nd, 1978, Patricia Timlin (*née* Gore). *Educ:* Wellington Coll.; Christ Church, Oxford (1st cl. Hons Modern Hist., 1950; DPhil 1953; DLitt 1978). FRHistS 1965. Lieut, The Royal Scots Greys (NW Europe, 1944–47); Captain, TA, 1950–57. Robinson Schol., Oriel Coll., Oxford, 1951–53; Harkness Fellow, Harvard Univ., 1953–54; Vis. Fellow, Inst. for Advanced Study, Princeton, 1962–63; Vis. Prof., CIT, 1966; Huntington Liby, San Marino, Calif, 1967. Lectures: Lees-Knowles, Cambridge, 1972; American Bicentennial, at Williamsburg, Va, Clark Univ., Naval War Coll., US Mil. Acad., Nat. War Coll., Peabody Mus., N Eastern Univ., Capitol Historical Soc. Member, Council: Inst. for Early Amer. Hist. and Culture, 1970–73; Nat. Army Mus., 1983–92; Soc. for Army Historical Res., 1985–94 (Vice-Pres., 2003–). Chm., N of Scotland Br., Royal Scots Dragoon Guards Assoc., 1993–2007. *Publications:* The War in the Mediterranean 1803–10, 1957; The War for America 1775–83, 1964, 2nd edn 1993; Statesmen at War: the Strategy of Overthrow 1798–99, 1974; The Coward of Minden: the affair of Lord George Sackville, 1979; War without Victory: the downfall of Pitt 1799–1802, 1984; British Victory in Egypt, 1801: the end of Napoleon's conquest, 1995 (Templer Medal, Soc. for Army Histl Res., 1995), 2nd edn 2010; contribs to various books and jls. *Address:* Westerton Farmhouse, Dess, by Aboyne, Aberdeenshire AB34 5AY. *T:* (013398) 84415. *Died 30 June 2014.*

MACKEY, Most Rev. John, CBE 1983; Bishop of Auckland, NZ, (RC), 1974–83; *b* Bray, Co. Wicklow, 11 Jan. 1918; *s* of Malachy Mackey and Kathleen (*née* Byrne). *Educ:* Auckland Univ. (MA, DipEd); Notre Dame Univ., USA (PhD). Emigrated to NZ, 1924. Ordained priest, 1941; Adminr for Auckland Diocesan Schs, 1951–71; Lectr, Holy Cross Seminary, 1972–74; formerly Professor in Theological Faculty, National Seminary of Mosgiel, Dunedin. *Publications:* The Making of a State Education System, 1967; Reflections on Church History, 1975; Looking at Ourselves, 1994. *Address:* 3 Karaka Street, Takapuna, Auckland, New Zealand. *Died 20 Jan. 2014.*

MACKEY, William Gawen; Partner, 1952, Managing Partner UK Operations, 1981–86, Ernst & Whinney; *b* 22 Sept. 1924; *s* of William Gawen Mackey and Jane Mackey; *m* 1948, Margaret Reeves Vinycomb; two *s*. *Educ:* Dame Allan's Sch., Newcastle upon Tyne. Qualified Chartered Accountant, 1949. Served RN, 1942–45 (Sub-Lt). Joined Ernst & Whinney, 1952, Newcastle; transf. London, 1973, with responsibility for corporate restructuring and insolvency services in UK. Receiver: Airfix; British Tanners; Laker; Stone-Platt. Chm., Insolvency Sub Cttee, CCAB, 1978–82; Dir, Inst. Corporate Insolvency Courses, 1974–80. *Publications:* articles and lectures on corporate management, restructuring and insolvency. *Recreations:* opera, gardening, France. *Address:* Eynesse, Ste Foy La Grande 33220, France. *T:* 557410042, *Fax:* 557410070. *Died 12 May 2015.*

MACKIE OF BENSHIE, Baron *cr* 1974 (Life Peer), of Kirriemuir; **George Yull Mackie,** CBE 1971; DSO 1944; DFC 1944; Chairman: Caithness Glass Ltd, 1966–84; Caithness Pottery Co. Ltd, 1975–84; The Benshie Cattle Co. Ltd, 1975–89; Land and Timber Services Ltd, since 1986; *b* 10 July 1919; *s* of late Maitland Mackie, OBE, Hon. LLD; *m* 1st, 1944, Lindsay Lyall Sharp (*d* 1985), *y d* of late Alexander and Isabella Sharp, OBE, Aberdeen; three *d* (one *s* decd); 2nd, 1988, Jacqueline, *widow* of Andrew Lane, and *d* of late Col Marcel Rauch. *Educ:* Aberdeen Grammar Sch.; Aberdeen Univ. Served War of 1939–45, RAF; Bomber Command, (DSO, DFC); Air Staff, 1944. Farming at Ballinshoe, Kirriemuir, 1945–89. Contested (L) South Angus, 1959; MP (L) Caithness and Sutherland, 1964–66; contested (L) Scotland NE, European Parliamentary election, 1979. Pres., Scottish Liberal Party, 1983–88 (Chm., 1965–70); Member: EEC Scrutiny Cttee (D), House of Lords; Liberal Shadow Admin; Exec., IPU; Council of Europe, 1986–97 (Mem. and Rapporteur, Cttee on Agricl and Rural Develt, 1990–97); WEU, 1986–; Liberal, then Lib Dem, Spokesman, House of Lords, 1975–2000: Devolution, Agriculture, Scotland, Industry. Chm., Cotswold Wine Co. (UK) Ltd, 1983–85. Dir, Scottish Ballet, 1986–88. Rector, Dundee Univ., 1980–83. Hon. LLD Dundee, 1982. *Publications:* Policy for Scottish Agriculture, 1963; Flying, Farming and Politics (memoir), 2004. *Address:* Benshie Cottage, Oathlaw, by Forfar, Angus DD8 3PQ. *T:* (01307) 850376. *Clubs:* Farmers, Royal Air Force. *Died 17 Feb. 2015.*

McKINLEY, John Key; Chairman and Chief Executive Officer, Texaco Inc., 1980–86 (President, 1971–83); *b* Tuscaloosa, Ala, 24 March 1920; *s* of Virgil Parks McKinley and Mary Emma (*née* Key); *m* 1946, Helen Grace Heare (decd); two *s*. *Educ:* Univ. of Alabama (BS Chem. Engrg, 1940; MS Organic Chemistry, 1941); Harvard Univ. (Graduate, Advanced Management Program, 1962). Served War, AUS, Eur. Theatre of Ops, 1941–45 (Major; Bronze Star). Texaco Inc., 1941–86: Asst Dir of Res., Beacon, NY, 1957–59; Asst to the Vice-Pres., 1959–60; Manager of Commercial Develt Processes, 1960; Gen. Man., Worldwide Petrochemicals, NYC, 1960–67, Vice-Pres., Petrochem. Dept, 1967–71 (also Vice-Pres. i/c Supply and Distribution); Sen. Vice-Pres., Worldwide Refining, Petrochems, Supply and Distribn, 1971, Pres. and Dir, 1971–83; Director: Texaco Inc., 1971–92; Merck & Co., Inc., 1982–90; Manufacturers Hanover Corp., 1980–90; Hanover Trust Co., 1980–90; Martin Marietta, 1985–90; Apollo Computer, 1987–89; Burlington Industries Inc., 1977–87; Federated Dept Stores, Inc., 1990–. Hon. Dir, Amer. Petroleum Inst. Man. Dir, Met. Opera Assoc., 1980–; National Chm., Met. Opera Centennial Fund, 1980. Dir, Americas Soc. Member: Bd of Overseers, Meml

Sloan-Kettering Cancer Center, 1981–91; Brookings Council, 1986; Business Council. Fellow, Amer. Inst. of Chem. Engrs; Sesquicentennial Hon. Prof., Univ. of Alabama; Hon. LLD: Univ. of Alabama, 1972; Troy State Univ., 1974. *Address:* Tuscaloosa, AL, USA; Darien, CT 06820, USA; Buffalo, Wyoming, USA. *Clubs:* Brook (NYC); Wee Burn Country (Darien); Augusta National Golf (Georgia); Blind Brook (Purchase, NY); North River Yacht (Tuscaloosa). *Died 12 June 2014.*

MACKINTOSH, (John) Malcolm, CMG 1975; HM Diplomatic Service, retired; *b* 25 Dec. 1921; *s* of late James Mackintosh, MD, LLD, FRCP, and Marjorie Mackintosh; *m* 1946, Elena Grafova; one *s* one *d* (and one *s* decd). *Educ:* Mill Hill; Edinburgh Academy; Glasgow Univ. MA (Hons) 1948. Served War, Middle East, Italy and Balkans, 1942–46; Allied Control Commn, Bulgaria, 1945–46. Glasgow Univ., 1946–48. Programme Organiser, BBC Overseas Service, 1948–60; Foreign Office, engaged on research, 1960–68; Asst Sec., Cabinet Office, 1968–87. Sen Fellow in Soviet Studies, IISS, 1989–91; Hon. Sen. Res. Fellow, KCL, 1987–91; Hon. Lectr in Internat. Relns, St Andrews Univ., 1991–97; Hon. Vis. Fellow, SSEES, 1994–2001. *Publications:* Strategy and Tactics of Soviet Foreign Policy, 1962, 2nd edn 1963; Juggernaut: a history of the Soviet armed forces, 1967. *Recreations:* walking, climbing. *Address:* 3 Silverbell Court, 2 Hoptree Close, N12 8LP. *T:* (020) 8445 9714. *Clubs:* Garrick, Royal Over-Seas League. *Died 20 Nov. 2011.*

MACKINTOSH, Prof. Nicholas John, DPhil; FRS 1987; Professor of Experimental Psychology, University of Cambridge, 1981–2002; Fellow of King's College, Cambridge, 1981–2005; *b* 9 July 1935; *s* of Dr Ian and Daphne Mackintosh; *m* 1st, 1960, Janet Ann Scott (marr. diss. 1978); one *s* one *d*; 2nd, 1978, Bundy Wilson (marr. diss. 1989); two *s*; 3rd, 1992, Leonora Caroline Brosan, *d* of late Dr George Stephen Brosan, CBE, TD; one *s*. *Educ:* Winchester; Magdalen Coll., Oxford (BA 1960; MA; DPhil 1963). Univ. Lectr, Univ. of Oxford, 1964–67; Res. Fellow, Lincoln Coll., Oxford, 1966–67; Res. Prof., Dalhousie Univ., 1967–73; Prof., Univ. of Sussex, 1973–81. Visiting Professor: Univ. of Pennsylvania, 1965–66; Univ. of Hawaii, 1972–73; Bryn Mawr Coll., 1977; Univ. of NSW, 1990; Univ. de Paris-Sud, Orsay, 1993–94; Yale Univ., 2002. Editor: Qly Jl of Experimental Psychology, 1977–84; Animal Behaviour Processes sect., Jl of Experimental Psychology, 2003–09. *Publications:* (ed with W. K. Honig) Fundamental Issues in Associative Learning, 1969; (with N. S. Sutherland) Mechanisms of Animal Discrimination Learning, 1971; The Psychology of Animal Learning, 1974; Conditioning and Associative Learning, 1983; Animal Learning and Cognition, 1994; Cyril Burt: fraud or framed?, 1995; IQ and Human Intelligence, 1998, 2nd edn 2011; papers in psychological journals. *Address:* Department of Experimental Psychology, Downing Street, Cambridge CB2 3EB. *T:* (01223) 764194. *Died 8 Feb. 2015.*

MACKLEY, Ian Warren, CMG 1989; CVO 1999; HM Diplomatic Service, retired; Clerk, Select Committee on the Constitution, House of Lords, 2002–06; *b* 31 March 1942; *s* of late Harold William Mackley and Marjorie Rosa Sprawson (*née* Warren); *m* 1st, 1968, Jill Marion (*née* Saunders) (marr. diss. 1988); three *s*; 2nd, 1989, Sarah Anne Churchley; one *s* one *d*. *Educ:* Ardingly College. FO, 1960; Saigon, 1963; Asst Private Sec. to Ministers of State, FCO, 1967; Wellington, 1969; First Sec., 1972; FCO 1973; Head of Inf. Services, New Delhi, 1976; Asst Head, UN Dept, FCO, 1979; seconded to ICI, 1982; Counsellor, Dep. Hd of UK Delegn to Conf. on Confidence- and Security-Building Measures and Disarmament in Europe, Stockholm, 1984–86; Chargé d'Affaires, Kabul, 1987–89; Dep. High Comr, Canberra, 1989–93; Head of Training, FCO, 1993–96; High Comr to Ghana and Ambassador (non-res.) to Togo, 1996–2000. Pres., Kabul Golf and Country Club, Afghanistan, 1987–89. *Recreation:* armchair sport. *Died 2 Jan. 2014.*

MACKLIN, David Drury, CBE 1989; DL; *b* 1 Sept. 1928; *s* of Laurence Hilary Macklin and Alice Dumergue (*née* Tait); *m* 1955, Janet Smallwood; four *s*. *Educ:* Felsted Sch., Essex; St John's Coll., Cambridge. MA. Articled to Baileys Shaw & Gillett, Solicitors, 1951–54; Assistant Solicitor: Coward Chance & Co., 1954–56; Warwickshire CC, 1956–61; Devon CC, 1961–69; Dep. Clerk, Derbyshire CC, 1969–73; Chief Executive: Lincolnshire CC, 1973–79; Devon CC, 1979–88. Mem., Boundary Commn for England, 1989–99. Chm., Community Council of Devon, 1992–96; Mem., Devon and Cornwall Housing Assoc., 1989–98. Founder Mem., ViRSA Educnl Trust (Chm., 1994–98). DL Devon, 1991. *Recreations:* music, theatre, croquet. *Address:* The Garden Cottage, Station Road, Topsham, Exeter EX3 0DT. *T:* (01392) 873160. *Died 29 March 2015.*

MACKLIN, Prof. John Joseph, PhD; Professor of Hispanic Studies, and Head of School of Modern Languages and Cultures, University of Glasgow, 2010–13 (Hon. Professorial Research Fellow, 2009–10); *b* 9 Oct. 1947; *s* of James and Mary Macklin; *m* 1969, Pauline Ruben; one *s* two *d*. *Educ:* Queen's Univ., Belfast (BA 1st cl. French, 1st cl. Spanish; PhD 1976). University of Hull: Lectr in Hispanic Studies, 1973–85; Sen. Lectr, 1985–87; Hd of Dept, 1986–87; University of Leeds: Cowdray Prof. of Spanish, 1988–2001; Dean, Faculty of Arts, 1992–94; Dean for Res. in Humanities, 1994–99; Pro-Vice-Chancellor, 1999–2001; Principal and Vice-Chancellor, Univ. of Paisley, 2001–05; Prof. of Spanish, Univ. of Strathclyde, 2006–09. Vis. Prof., Univ. of Ulster, 2007–. Director: Scottish Enterprise, Renfrewshire, 2002–05; Council, ILT, 2003–05. FHEA 2007. Acad. Corresp. de la Real Academia Alfonso X el Sabio, 2007. Comdr, Orden de Isabel la Católica (Spain), 1994. *Publications:* Tigre Juan and El curandero de su honra, 1980; The Modernist Fictions of Ramón Pérez de Ayala, 1988; Tres novelas ejemplares by Miguel de Cervantes (bilingual edn), 1992; The Scripted Self, 1995; Ábel Sánchez by Miguel de Unamuno (bilingual edn), 2009; contrib. to Bull. Hispanic Studies, Bull. Spanish Studies, MLR, Hispanic Rev., Cuadernos Hispano-americanos, Neophilologus, Anales de la literatura española contemporánea. *Recreations:* gardening, cinema, current affairs, art history. *Died 9 Aug. 2014.*

McKUEN, Rod; poet, composer, author, performer, columnist, classical composer; *b* Oakland, Calif, 29 April 1933. Appeared in numerous films, TV, concerts, nightclubs, and with symphony orchestras. Composer: modern classical music; scores for motion pictures and TV. President: Stanyan Records; Discus Records; New Gramophone Soc.; Mr Kelly Prodns; Montcalm Prodns; Stanyan Books; Cheval Books; Biplane Books; Rod McKuen Enterprises; Vice-Pres., Tamarack Books; Dir, Animal Concern; Member, Advisory Board: Fund for Animals; Internat. Educn; Market Theatre, Johannesburg; Member, Board of Directors: National Ballet Theatre; Amer. Dance Ensemble; Amer. Guild of Authors and Composers; Exec. Pres., Amer. Guild of Variety Artists; Member: Amer. Soc. of Composers, Authors and Publishers; Writers' Guild; Amer. Fedn of TV and Radio Artists; Screen Actors' Guild; Equity; Modern Poetry Assoc.; Amer. Guild of Variety Artists; AGAC; Internat. Platform Assoc. Mem., Bd of Governors, National Acad. of Recording Arts and Sciences; Trustee: Univ. of Nebraska; Freedoms Foundn. Nat. spokesperson for Amer. Energy Awareness; Internat. spokesperson for Cttee for Prevention of Child Abuse (also Nat. Bd Mem.). Numerous awards, including: Grand Prix du Disc, Paris, 1966, 1974, 1975 and 1982; Golden Globe Award, 1969; Grammy for best spoken word album, Lonesome Cities, 1969; Entertainer of the Year, 1975; Man of the Year Award, Univ. of Detroit, 1978; awards from San Francisco, LA, Chattanooga, Topeka, Lincoln and Nebraska; Freedoms Foundn Patriot Medal, 1981; Salvation Army Man of the Year, 1982. Over 200 record albums; 41 Gold and Platinum records internationally; nominated Pulitzer Prize in classical music for The City, 1973. *Publications: poetry:* And Autumn Came, 1954; Stanyan Street and Other Sorrows, 1966; Listen to the Warm, 1967; Lonesome Cities, 1968; Twelve Years of Christmas, 1968; In Someone's Shadow, 1969; A Man Alone, 1969; With Love, 1970; Caught in the Quiet, 1970; New Ballads, 1970; Fields of Wonder, 1971; The Carols of Christmas, 1971; And to Each Season, 1972; Pastorale, 1972; Grand Tour, 1972; Come to Me in Silence, 1973; America: an Affirmation, 1974; Seasons in the Sun, 1974; Moment to Moment, 1974; Beyond the Boardwalk, 1975; The Rod McKuen Omnibus, 1975; Alone, 1975;

Celebrations of the Heart, 1975; Finding my Father: one man's search for identity (prose), 1976; The Sea Around Me, 1977; Hand in Hand, 1977; Coming Close to the Earth, 1978; We Touch the Sky, 1979; Love's Been Good to Me, 1979; Looking for a Friend, 1980; An Outstretched Hand (prose), 1980; The Power Bright and Shining, 1980; Too Many Midnights, 1981; Rod McKuen's Book of Days, 1981; The Beautiful Strangers, 1981; The Works of Rod McKuen: Vol. 1, Poetry, 1950–82, 1982; Watch for the Wind…, 1982; Rod McKuen—1984 Book of Days, 1983; The Sound of Solitude, 1983; Suspension Bridge, 1984; Another Beautiful Day, 1984, vol. 2, 1985; Valentines, 1986; Intervals, 1987; A Safe Place to Land, 2001; Rusting in the Rain, 2004; *major classical works:* Symphony No One; Concerto for Guitar and Orchestra; Concerto for Four Harpsichords; Concerto for Cello and Orch.; Concerto for Bassoon and Orch.; Seascapes; Concerto for Piano and Orchestra; Adagio for Harp and Strings; Piano Variations; The Black Eagle (opera); Birch Trees (Concerto for Orch.); various other classical commns; numerous lyrics; *film and television scores:* Joanna, 1968; Travels with Charley, 1968; The Prime of Miss Jean Brodie (Academy Award Nomination), 1969; Me, Natalie, 1969; The Loner, 1969; A Boy Named Charlie Brown (Academy Award Nomination), 1970; Come to your Senses, 1971; Scandalous John, 1971; Wildflowers, 1971; The Borrowers, 1973; Lisa Bright and Dark, 1973; Hello Again, 1974; Emily, 1975; The Unknown War, 1979; Man to Himself, 1980; Portrait of Rod McKuen, 1982; The Beach, 1984. *Address:* 1155 Angelo Drive, Beverly Hills, CA 90210–2703, USA. *Died 29 Jan. 2015.*

McLEAN, Denis Bazeley Gordon, CMG 1989; writer; *b* Napier, NZ, 18 Aug. 1930; *s* of John Gordon McLean and Renée Maitland Smith; *m* 1958, Anne Davidson, Venado Tuerto, Argentina; two *s* one *d. Educ:* Nelson Coll., NZ; Victoria Univ. Coll., NZ (MSc); Rhodes Schol. 1954; University Coll., Oxford (MA). Jun. Lectr in Geology, Victoria UC, 1953–54; joined Dept of External Affairs of NZ Govt, London, 1957; served in: Wellington, 1958–60; Washington, 1960–63; Paris, 1963–66; Kuala Lumpur, 1966–68; Asst Sec. (Policy), MoD, Wellington, 1969–72; RCDS, 1972; Dep. High Comr, London, 1973–77; Dep. Sec. of Defence, NZ, 1977, Sec. of Defence, 1979–88; Ambassador to US, 1991–94; Warburg Prof. in Internat. Relns, Simmons Coll., Boston, Mass, 1995–98. Visiting Fellow: Strategic and Defence Studies Centre, ANU, Canberra, 1989; Guest Scholar, Woodrow Wilson Center, and Sen. Associate, Carnegie Endowment for Internat. Peace, Washington, 1990–91; Distinguished Fellow, US Inst. of Peace, 1994–95. Mem., NZ Press Council, 2000–09. Pres., Wellington Br., NZ Inst. of Internat. Affairs, 2002–05. Chair, Te Araroa Wellington Regl Trust, 2002–. *Publications:* The Long Pathway: Te Ara Roa, 1986; Peace Operations and Commonsense, 1996; The Prickly Pair: making nationalism in Australia and New Zealand, 2003; (with Maj.-Gen. W. B. Thomas) Pathways to Adventure: a memoir of Major-General W. B. Thomas, CB, DSO, MC and Bar, 2004; Howard Kippenberger: dauntless spirit, 2008. *Recreations:* reading, looking at art, writing, geology. *Address:* 11 Dekka Street, Khandallah, Wellington 6035, New Zealand. *Club:* Wellington (NZ). *Died 30 March 2011.*

MACLEAN, Rear-Adm. Euan, CB 1986; Director General Fleet Support, 1983–86; *b* 7 July 1929; *s* of John Fraser Maclean and Dorothy Mary Maclean; *m* 1954, Renée Shaw; two *d. Educ:* BRNC Dartmouth; RNEC Keyham/Manadon. Joined Exec. Br., RN, 1943; transf. to Engr Br., 1947; sea service in HMS Sirius, Illustrious, St Kitts, Gambia, Ocean, Indefatigable, Defender, Hermes, Eagle and Ark Royal, 1950–72; on loan to Royal Malaysian Navy, 1965–68; Prodn Dept, Portsmouth Dockyard, 1968–71; HMS Ark Royal, 1971–72; Exec. Officer, HMS Sultan, 1973; Dep. Prodn Man., Devonport Dockyard, 1974–77; Fleet Marine Engr Officer, 1977–79; student, RCDS, 1980; Prodn Man., Portsmouth Dockyard, 1981–83. ADC to the Queen, 1982. Comdr 1965, Captain 1974, Rear-Adm. 1983. *Recreations:* cycling, writing limericks (sometimes coincident). *Died 2 June 2012.*

MACLEAN, Hector Ronald; Sheriff of Lothian and Borders, at Linlithgow, 1988–2003; *b* 6 Dec. 1931; *s* of Donald Beaton Maclean and Lucy McAlister; *m* 1967, Hilary Elizabeth Jenkins; three *d. Educ:* High Sch. of Glasgow; Glasgow Univ. Admitted to Faculty of Advocates, 1959. Sheriff of N Strathclyde (formerly Renfrew and Argyll), 1968–88. *Recreation:* golf. *Address:* Barrfield, Houston, Johnstone, Renfrewshire PA6 7EL. *T:* (01505) 612449. *Died 3 April 2011.*

McLENNAN, Gordon; General Secretary, Communist Party of Great Britain, 1975–89; *b* Glasgow, 12 May 1924; *s* of a shipyard worker; *m* Mary; three *s* one *d. Educ:* Hamilton Crescent Sch., Partick, Glasgow. Engineering apprentice, Albion Motors Ltd, Scotstoun, 1939, later engineering draughtsman. Elected Glasgow Organiser, Communist Party, 1949; Sec., Communist Party in Scotland, 1957; Nat. Organiser, Communist Party of GB, 1966. *Recreations:* golf and other sports; cultural interests. *Address:* c/o Unlock Democracy, 9 Cynthia Street, N1 9JF. *Died 21 May 2011.*

MacLEOD, Calum Alexander, CBE 1991; Chairman, Grampian Television, later stv north, 1993–2007 (Deputy Chairman, 1982–93); *b* 25 July 1935; *s* of Rev. Lachlan Macleod and Jessie Mary Morrison; *m* 1962, Elizabeth Margaret Davidson; two *s* one *d. Educ:* Nicolson Inst., Stornoway; Glenurquhart High Sch.; Aberdeen Univ. Partner, Paull & Williamsons Advocates, Aberdeen, 1964–80; Chairman: Aberdeen Petroleum, 1982–92; Harris Tweed Assoc. Authority, 1984–93 (Vice-Chm., 1993–95); Aberdeen Develt Capital plc, 1986–2005; Deputy Chairman: Scottish Eastern Investment Trust, 1988–99; Britannia Life, 1992–94 (Chm., 1990–92); Britannia Building Society, 1993–94 and 1999–2000 (Chm., 1994–99); Scottish Media Group, then SMG plc, 1997–2005 (acting Chm., 1998–99); Martin Currie Portfolio Investment Trust plc, 1999–2002; Director: North Bd, Bank of Scotland, 1980–2000; Bradstock Gp, 1994–98; Macdonald Hotels, 1995–2003. Member: White Fish Authy, 1973–80; N of Scotland Hydro-Electric Bd, 1976–84; Highlands and Islands Develt Bd, 1984–91; Chm., Grampian Health Bd, 1993–2000. Chairman: Chancellor's Assessor, Aberdeen Univ., 1979–90; Robert Gordon's Coll., 1981–94; SATRO North Scotland, 1986–90; Scottish Council of Ind. Schs, 1992–97; Trustee, Carnegie Trust for the Univs of Scotland, 1997–2008; Governor: Caledonian Res. Foundn, 1990–94; UHI Millennium Inst., 2000–08. Hon LLD Aberdeen, 1986. *Recreations:* golf, fishing, motoring, Hebridean coastal walking, reading, music. *Address:* 6 Westfield Terrace, Aberdeen AB25 2RU. *T:* (01224) 641614. *Clubs:* Royal Northern and University (Aberdeen); Royal Aberdeen Golf; Nairn Golf. *Died 27 Oct. 2013.*

McLEOD, Sir Charles Henry, 3rd Bt *cr* 1925; *b* 7 Nov. 1924; *o surv. s* of Sir Murdoch Campbell McLeod, 2nd Bt, and Annette Susan Mary (*d* 1964), *d* of Henry Whitehead, JP, 26 Pelham Crescent, SW7; *S* father, 1950; *m* 1957, Gillian (*d* 1978), *d* of Henry Bowlby, London; one *s* two *d. Educ:* Winchester. Diploma Master Brewer, 1950. Member, London Stock Exchange, 1955–. Part-time in-house proof-reader and freelancer, 1998–. Represented India, Squash Rackets Internat., 1956–58. *Heir: s* James Roderick Charles McLeod [*b* 26 Sept. 1960; *m* 1990, Helen M. Cooper, *d* of Captain George Cooper, OBE, RN; one *s* one *d*]. *Clubs:* MCC; I Zingari, Free Foresters, Jesters. *Died 26 Dec. 2012.*

MACLEOD, Ian Buchanan, FRCSE; Hon. Secretary, Royal College of Surgeons of Edinburgh, 1993–96; Consultant Surgeon, Royal Infirmary, Edinburgh, and Hon. Senior Lecturer, Department of Clinical Surgery, University of Edinburgh, 1969–93; Surgeon to the Queen in Scotland, 1987–93; *b* 20 May 1933; *s* of Donald Macleod, MB, ChB, and Katie Ann Buchanan; *m* 1961, Kathleen Gillean Large; one *s* one *d. Educ:* Wigan Grammar Sch.; Univ. of Edinburgh (BSc Hons; MB ChB Hons). FRCSE 1962. Resident appts, Royal Inf., Edinburgh, 1957–59. National Service, MO RAMC, 1959–61. Res. Fellow, Lectr and Sen. Lectr, Univ. of Edinburgh, 1962–93; Hon. and Cons. Surg., Royal Inf., Edinburgh, 1969–93. Editor, Journal of Royal College of Surgeons of Edinburgh, 1982–87. *Publications:* Principles and Practice of Surgery (with A. P. M. Forrest and D. C. Carter), 1985; (contrib.) A Companion to Medical Studies, 1968, 3rd edn 1985; (contrib.) Farquharson's Textbook of Operative Surgery, 1986; papers in surgical jls. *Recreations:* golf, photography. *Address:* 1 Southbank, Easter Park Drive, Edinburgh EH4 6SG. *T:* (0131) 336 1541. *Club:* Bruntsfield Links Golfing Society (Edinburgh). *Died 2 Dec. 2013.*

McLEOD, Prof. John Bryce, DPhil; FRS 1992; Professor of Mathematics, University of Pittsburgh, 1988–2007, then Emeritus; *b* 23 Dec. 1929; *s* of John McLeod and Adeline Annie (*née* Bryce); *m* 1956, Eunice Martin Third; three *s* one *d*. *Educ:* Aberdeen Grammar Sch.; Univ. of Aberdeen (MA 1950); Oxford Univ. (BA 1952, MA, DPhil 1958). Rotary Foundn Fellow, Univ. of BC, 1952–53; Educn Officer, RAF, 1953–55; Harmsworth Sen. Scholar, Merton Coll., Oxford, 1955–56; Jun. Lectr in Maths, Oxford Univ., 1956–58; Lectr, Univ. of Edinburgh, 1958–60; University of Oxford: Fellow, Wadham Coll., 1960–91; Lectr in Maths, 1960–88; Jun. Proctor, 1963–64; Sen. Fellow, SERC, 1986–91. Vis. Prof., Univ. of Oxford, 2007–. *Publications:* numerous papers in mathematical jls. *Recreations:* travel, music, gardening. *Address:* 49 Northcourt Road, Abingdon, Oxon OX14 1PJ. *T:* (01235) 520239. *Died 20 Aug. 2014.*

McLETCHIE, David William, CBE 2013; Member (C) Lothian, Scottish Parliament, since 2011 (Lothians, 1999–2003, Edinburgh Pentlands, 2003–11); *b* 6 Aug. 1952; *s* of James Watson McLetchie and Catherine Alexander McLetchie (*née* Gray); *m* 1st, 1977, Barbara Gemmell Baillie (*d* 1995); one *s*; 2nd, 1998, Sheila Elizabeth Foster. *Educ:* Leith Acad.; George Heriot's Sch., Edinburgh; Edinburgh Univ. (LLB Hons). Admitted solicitor, 1976; joined Tods Murray, WS, Edinburgh, 1976, Partner, 1980–2005; specialised in trusts, estates and tax. Scottish Parliament: Leader, 1999–2005, Chief Whip and Business Manager, 2007–11, Cons. Gp; spokesman on justice and constitutional affairs, 2011–. *Recreations:* golf, watching football, music, reading crime fiction and political biographies. *Address:* Scottish Parliament, Edinburgh EH99 1SP. *T:* (0131) 348 5659. *Clubs:* New (Edinburgh), Bruntsfield Links Golfing Society. *Died 12 Aug. 2013.*

MACLURE, (John) Stuart, CBE 1982; Editor, Times Educational Supplement, 1969–89; *b* 8 Aug. 1926; *s* of Hugh and Bertha Maclure, Highgate, N6; *m* 1951, Constance Mary Butler; one *s* two *d*. *Educ:* Highgate Sch.; Christ's Coll., Cambridge (BA 1948; MA 1951). Joined The Times, 1950; The Times Educational Supplement, 1951; Editor, Education, 1954–69. Hon. Prof. of Educn, Keele Univ., 1981–84; Dist. Vis. Fellow, PSI, 1989–90; Associate Fellow, Centre for Educn and Industry, Warwick Univ., 1991–94. President: Br. Sect., Comparative Educn Soc. in Europe, 1979; Educnl Sect., BAAS, 1983; Member: Educnl Adv. Council, IBA, 1979–84; Consultative Cttee, Assessment of Performance Unit, 1974–82. Regents' Lecturer, Univ. of California, Berkeley, 1980. Gov., Commonwealth Inst., 1991–97. Hon. Fellow, City of Sheffield Polytechnic, 1976; Hon. FCP 1985; Hon. Fellow, Westminster Coll., 1990. DUniv Open, 1991. *Publications:* Joint Editor (with T. E. Utley) Documents on Modern Political Thought, 1956; Editor, Educational Documents, 1816–1963, 1965; A Hundred Years of London Education, 1970; (with Tony Becher) The Politics of Curriculum Change, 1978; (ed with Tony Becher) Accountability in Education, 1979; Education and Youth Employment in Great Britain, 1979; Educational Development and School Building, 1945–1973, 1984; Education Re-formed, a guide to the Education Reform Act, 1988; A History of Education in London 1870–1990, 1990; Missing Links—The Challenge to Further Education, 1991; (ed with Peter Davies) Learning to Think—Thinking to Learn, 1992; The Inspectors' Calling—HMI and the Shaping of Educational Policy, 2001. *Address:* 109 College Road, Dulwich, SE21 7HN. *Club:* MCC. *Died 14 June 2011.*

MacMANUS, Dr Bernard Ronald; Vice-Chancellor, Bournemouth University, 1992–94; *b* 25 April 1936; *s* of Ronald MacManus and Doris Evelyn MacManus (*née* Sherriff); *m* 1959, Patricia Mary Greet; one *s* one *d*. *Educ:* St Boniface's Coll., Devon; Plymouth Poly.; Univ. of Birmingham (BScEng, PhD). Head, Dept of Mech. Production and Aeronautical Engrg, Manchester Poly., 1972–73; Dean, Faculty of Engrg, Sunderland Poly., 1973–78; Dep. Dir, Glasgow Coll. of Technology, 1978–83; Director: Dorset Inst. of Higher Educn, 1983–91; Bournemouth Poly., 1991–92. Hon. DEd Bournemouth, 2007. *Publications:* contribs to learned jls on manufacturing systems. *Recreations:* swimming, classic cars, music. *Address:* Thurlstone, Chapel Lane, Osmington, Dorset DT3 6ET. *Died 10 March 2013.*

MACMILLAN, Sir (Alexander McGregor) Graham, Kt 1983; Director, Scottish Conservative Party, 1975–84; *b* 14 Sept. 1920; *s* of James Orr Macmillan and Sarah Dunsmore (*née* Graham); *m* 1947, Christina Brash Beveridge (*d* 1998); two *s* two *d*. *Educ:* Hillhead High Sch., Glasgow. Served War, RA, 1939–46. Conservative Agent: W Lothian, 1947–50; Haltemprice, 1950–53; Bury St Edmunds, 1953–60; Dep. Central Office Agent, NW Area, 1960–61; Central Office Agent, Yorks Area, 1961–75. Chairman: M & P Financial Services Ltd, 1986–87 (Dir, 1984–87); Mid-Anglian Enterprise Agency Ltd, 1988–92 (Gov., 1987–97); Exec. Sec., YorCan Communications Ltd, 1989–94. Chairman: Bury St Edmunds Round Table, 1959–60 (Pres., 1997–2001); Bury St Edmunds Br., Multiple Sclerosis Soc., 1987–95. Mem., Transport Users' Consultative Cttee for E England, 1987–95. Hon. Sec., Suffolk Assoc. of Boys' Clubs, 1986–88. Governor, Leeds Grammar Sch., 1968–75. *Recreations:* fishing, watching cricket and rugby. *Address:* 46 Crown Street, Bury St Edmunds, Suffolk IP33 1QX. *T:* (01284) 704443. *Died 17 March 2011.*

MacMILLAN, Prof. Andrew, OBE 1992; RSA 1990; RIBA; FRIAS; Professor of Architecture, Glasgow University, and Head, Mackintosh School of Architecture, 1973–94, then Emeritus Professor; *b* 11 Dec. 1928; *s* of Andrew Harkness MacMillan of Murlaggan and Mary Jane McKelvie; *m* 1955, Angela Lillian McDowall; one *s* three *d*. *Educ:* Maryhill Public Sch.; North Kelvinside Sen. Secondary Sch., Glasgow; Glasgow Sch. of Architecture (MA 1973). FRIAS 1973. Apprenticeship, Glasgow Corp. Housing Dept, 1945–52; Architectural Asst, East Kilbride New Town Develt Corp., 1952–54; Asst Architect, 1954–63, Partner, 1966–88, Gillespie Kidd & Coia; consultant architect in private practice, 1988–. Davenport Vis. Prof., Yale Univ., 1986. Mem., Scottish Arts Council, 1978–82; Vice-Pres. for Educn, RIBA, 1981–85; Vice President: Prince and Princess of Wales Hospice, 1981–; Charles Rennie Mackintosh Soc., 1984–; Patron, Arts Educn Trust, 1988–. Hon. Vice Pres., Glasgow Sch. of Art, 1999. DUniv: Paisley, 1999; Strathclyde, 2000; Hon. LLD Glasgow, 2008. Royal Scottish Acad. Gold Medal, 1975; RIBA Bronze Medal, 1985; RIBA Award for Arch., 1966, 1967, 1968 and 1982; Lifetime Achievement Award, RIAS, 2008; Lifetime Achievement Award, Scottish Design Awards, 2008; Annie Spinks Award for Excellence in Architectural Teaching, 2008; Saltire awards and Civic Trust awards at various times. *Publications:* Gillespie Kidd & Coia Architecture 1956–87, 2007; books, papers and articles mainly dealing with urban design, urban building, architectural educn, Glasgow arch. of 20th century, and Charles Rennie Mackintosh. *Recreations:* travel, sailing, watercolours. *Address:* The Penthouse, 28 Wilson Street, Glasgow G1 1SS. *T:* (0141) 552 2481. *Died 16 Aug. 2014.*

MACMILLAN, Sir Graham; *see* Macmillan, Sir A. McG. G.

MacMILLAN, Prof. John, (Jake), PhD Glasgow; DSc Bristol; FRS 1978; CChem, ARIC; Alfred Capper Pass Professor of Organic Chemistry, 1985–90, and Head of Department of Organic Chemistry, 1983–90, University of Bristol, then Professor Emeritus and Senior Research Fellow; *b* 13 Sept. 1924; *s* of John MacMillan and Barbara Lindsay; *m* 1952, Anne Levy; one *s* two *d*. *Educ:* Lanark Grammar Sch.; Glasgow Univ. Res. Chemist, Akers Res. Labs, ICI Ltd, 1949; Associate Res. Manager, Pharmaceuticals Div., ICI Ltd, 1962; Lectr in Org. Chemistry, Bristol Univ., 1963, Reader 1968, Prof. 1978. Pres., Internat. Plant Growth Substance Assoc., 1973–76. For. Associate, Nat. Acad. of Scis, USA, 1991. *Publications:* (ed) Encyclopedia of Plant Physiology, New Series vol. 9, 1980; (ed jtly) Gibberellins, 1991; (jtly) GC-MS of Gibberellins and Related Compounds: methodology and a library of reference spectra, 1991; research papers in learned jls on natural organic products, esp. plant growth hormones. *Recreations:* gardening, theatre, music. *Address:* 7 Burrough Way, Winterbourne, S Glos BS36 1LF. *T:* (01454) 775244. *Died 12 May 2014.*

MACMILLAN, Dr Robert Hugh; Professor of Vehicle Design and Head of School of Automotive Studies, 1977–82, Dean of Engineering, 1980–82, Cranfield Institute of Technology; *b* Mussoorie, India, 27 June 1921; *s* of H. R. M. Macmillan and E. G. Macmillan (*née* Webb); *m* 1950, Anna Christina Roding (*d* 2012), Amsterdam; one *s* two *d*. *Educ:* Felsted Sch.; Emmanuel Coll., Cambridge. Technical Branch, RAFVR, 1941; Flt Lt, 1945; Dept of Engrg, Cambridge Univ., 1947; Asst Prof. and Fulbright Fellow, MIT, 1950–51; Prof. of Mech. Engrg, Swansea, 1956; Dir, Motor Industry Res. Assoc., 1964–77; Associate Prof., Warwick Univ., 1965–77. 20th Leonardo Da Vinci Lectr, 1973. Chm. Council, Automobile Div., IMechE, 1976–77; Member: Noise Adv. Council, 1970–77; Internat. Technical Commn, FIA, 1975–88; FISITA: Mem. Council, 1970–80; Chm., London Congress, 1972. Approved Lectr for NADFAS, 1985–98; official guide, Winslow Hall, 1985–97, Ascott, 1988–93; Steward, Bath Abbey, 2000–01. Member: Council, Loughborough Univ., 1966–81, 1988–91; Court, Bath Univ., 2002–. Editor, The Netherlands Philatelist, 1984–88. MIET; FIMechE; FRPSL. Hon. DTech Loughborough, 1992. Gold Medal, FISITA, 1970. *Publications:* Theory of Control, 1951; Automation, 1956; Geometric Symmetry, 1978; Dynamics of Vehicle Collisions, 1983; Netherlands Stamps 1852–1939, 1996. *Recreations:* music, philately, national heritage. *Address:* 8 Portland Drive, Willen, Bucks MK15 9JU. *T:* (01908) 672417. *Club:* Royal Air Force. *Died 10 May 2015.*

McMINN, Prof. Robert Matthew Hay; Emeritus Professor of Anatomy, Royal College of Surgeons and University of London; *b* 20 Sept. 1923; *o s* of Robert Martin McMinn, MB, ChB, Auchinleck and Brighton, and Elsie Selene Kent; *m* 1948, Margaret Grieve Kirkwood (*d* 2011), MB, ChB, DA; one *s* one *d*. *Educ:* Brighton Coll. (Schol.); Univ. of Glasgow (Scottish Univ. Champion, 440 yds hurdles, 1944). MB, ChB 1947, MD (commendation) 1958, Glasgow; PhD Sheffield 1956; FRCS 1978. Hosp. posts and RAF Med. Service, 1947–50; Demonstrator in Anatomy, Glasgow Univ., 1950–52; Lectr in Anatomy, Sheffield Univ., 1952–60; Reader, 1960–66, Prof. of Anatomy, 1966–70, King's Coll., London Univ.; Sir William Collins Prof. of Human and Comparative Anatomy, RCS, Conservator, Hunterian Museum, RCS, and Prof. of Anatomy, Inst. of Basic Med. Scis, London Univ., 1970–82, prematurely retd. Late Examr to RCS, RCPSG and Univs of London, Cambridge, Edinburgh, Belfast, Singapore, Malaya and Makerere. Arris and Gale Lectr, RCS, 1960; Arnott Demonstrator, RCS, 1970. Former Treas., Anatomical Soc. of Gt Britain and Ireland (Special Presentation Award, 2000); Foundn Sec., British Assoc. of Clinical Anatomists; FRSocMed; Member: Amer. Assoc. of Anatomists; Amer. Assoc. of Clinical Anatomists; BMA; Trustee, Skin Res. Foundn. *Publications:* Tissue Repair, 1969; The Digestive System, 1974; The Human Gut, 1974; (jtly) Colour Atlas of Human Anatomy, 1977, 6th edn 2008; (jtly) Colour Atlas of Head and Neck Anatomy, 1981, 4th edn 2010; (jtly) Colour Atlas of Foot and Ankle Anatomy, 1982, 4th edn 2012; (jtly) Colour Atlas of Applied Anatomy, 1984; (jtly) Picture Tests in Human Anatomy, 1986; (jtly) The Human Skeleton, 1987; (ed) Last's Anatomy, 8th edn 1990, 9th edn 1994; (jtly) McMinn's Functional and Clinical Anatomy, 1995; (jtly) Concise Handbook of Human Anatomy, 1998; articles in various med. and sci. jls. *Recreations:* motoring, photography, archaeology, short-wave radio; deputy organist, Craignish Parish Church. *Address:* Achnafuaran, Ardfern, Lochgilphead, Argyll PA31 8QN. *T:* (01852) 500274. *Died 11 July 2012.*

McMULLAN, His Honour Michael Brian; a Circuit Judge, 1980–95; *b* 15 Nov. 1926; *s* of late Joseph Patrick McMullan and Frances McMullan (*née* Burton); *m* 1960, Rosemary Jane Margaret, *d* of late Stanley Halse deL. de Ville; one *s* two *d*. *Educ:* Manor Farm Road Sch.; Taunton's Sch., Southampton; The Queen's College, Oxford (MA). Called to the Bar, Gray's Inn, 1960. National Service, Army, 1946–48. Colonial Administrative Service: Gold Coast and Ghana, Political Administration, Ashanti, Min. of Finance, Accra, Agricl Development Corp., 1949–60. In practice as Barrister, SE Circuit, 1961–80; a Recorder of the Crown Court, 1979. *Club:* Oxford and Cambridge. *Died 8 Aug. 2013.*

McMULLEN, His Honour Jeremy John; QC 1994; QC (NI) 1996; a Circuit Judge, and Judge of the Employment Appeal Tribunal, 2001–13; a Senior Circuit Judge, 2006–13; a Deputy High Court Judge, Queen's Bench Division, 2007–13; *b* 14 Sept. 1948; *s* of John Ezra McMullen and late Irene McMullen; *m* 1973, Deborah Cristman; one *s* one *d*. *Educ:* William Hulme's Grammar Sch., Manchester; Brasenose Coll., Oxford (MA); LSE (MSc). Called to the Bar: Middle Temple, 1971, Bencher, 2010; NI, 1994; Associate Attorney, New York, 1971–73; General, Municipal, Boilermakers' Union: Legal Officer, 1973–77; Regl Officer, London, 1977–84; in practice at the Bar, 1985–2001; an Asst Recorder, 1998–2000; a Recorder, 2000–01; Sports Arbitrator, 2000–. Chm. (part-time), Employment (formerly Industrial) Tribunals, 1993–2002. Chair: Industrial Law Soc., 1989–93; Employment Law Bar Assoc., 1994–95; ILO Jt Panel, 2001–02. Vis. Prof., Middlesex Univ., 2009–. Pres., Brasenose Soc., 2006–. *Publications:* Rights at Work, 1978, 2nd edn 1983; (contrib.) Penguin Guide to Civil Liberties, 1989; Employment Tribunal Procedure, 1996, 3rd edn 2005; (ed jtly) Employment Precedents and Company Policy Documents, 1996–2013. *Recreations:* rowing, cycling, allotment. *Address:* c/o Employment Appeal Tribunal, Fleetbank House, Salisbury Square, EC4Y 8JX. *Clubs:* Reform, MCC; Leander (Henley-on-Thames); Vincent's (Oxford). *Died 10 Feb. 2015.*

McMURRAY, David Bruce, MA; Headmaster, Oundle School, 1984–99; *b* Edinburgh, 15 Dec. 1937; *s* of late James McMurray, CBE, and Kathleen McMurray (*née* Goodwin); *m* 1962, Antonia Murray; three *d*. *Educ:* Loretto Sch.; Pembroke Coll., Cambridge (BA, MA). National service, Royal Scots, 1956–58, 2nd Lieut. Pembroke Coll., Cambridge, 1958–61; Asst Master, Stowe Sch., 1961–64; Fettes College: Asst Master, 1964–72; Head of English, 1967–72; Housemaster, 1972–76; Headmaster, Loretto Sch., 1976–84. Mem., Edinburgh Fest. Council, 1980–84. HM Comr, Queen Victoria Sch., Dunblane, 1977–87; Chm. of Govs, Fettes Coll., 2006–12. FRSA 1989. CCF Medal, 1976, and Bar, 1984. *Recreations:* golf, pétanque, poetry. *Address:* 7 Amisfield Park, Haddington, East Lothian EH41 4QE. *T:* (01620) 825474; Apt No 1, La Punta, Los Cristianos, 38650 Arona, Tenerife, Canary Islands. *Clubs:* MCC, Free Foresters; New (Edinburgh). *Died 7 June 2015.*

MACNAB of Macnab, James Charles; The Macnab; 23rd Chief of Clan Macnab; *b* 14 April 1926; *e s* of late Lt-Col James Alexander Macnabb, OBE, TD (*de jure* 21st of Macnab), London, SW3, and Mrs Ursula Walford (*née* Barnett), Wokingham, Berks; *S* gt uncle Archibald Corrie Macnab of Macnab, (*de facto*) 22nd Chief, 1970; *m* 1959, Hon. Diana Mary (*d* 2012), DL, *er d* of Baron Kilmany, MC, PC, and Monica Helen, (Lady Kilmany), OBE, JP, *oc* of late Geoffrey Lambton, 2nd *s* of 4th Earl of Durham; two *s* two *d*. *Educ:* Cothill House; Radley Coll.; Ashbury Coll., Ottawa. Served in RAF and Scots Guards, 1944–45; Lieut, Seaforth Highldrs, 1945–48. Asst Supt, then Acting Dep. Supt, Fedn of Malaya Police Force, 1948; retd, 1957. Mem., Western DC of Perthshire, 1961–64; CC, Perth and Kinross Jt County Council, 1964–75; Mem., Central Regional Council, 1978–82. Exec., subseq. Sen., Consultant, Hill Samuel Investment Services, 1982–92. Member, Royal Company of Archers, Queen's Body Guard in Scotland. Capt., Seaforth Highldrs, TA, 1960–64. JP Perthshire, 1968–75, Stirling, 1975–86. *Recreations:* shooting, travel. *Heir: s* James William Archibald Macnab, younger of Macnab [*b* 22 March 1963; *m* 1994, Dr Jane Mackintosh, *d* of late Dr David Mackintosh; one *s* one *d*]. *Address:* Leuchars Castle Farmhouse, Leuchars, St Andrews, Fife KY16 0EY. *T:* (01334) 838777. *Club:* New (Edinburgh). *Died 11 Jan. 2013.*

McNAIR, Archibald Alister Jourdan, (Archie); Co-founder, 1955, and Chairman, 1955–88, Mary Quant Group of Companies; Founder, 1971, and Chairman,

1971–88, Thomas Jourdan plc; *b* 16 Dec. 1919; *s* of late Donald McNair and Janie (*née* Jourdan); *m* 1954, Catherine Alice Jane (*d* 2014), *d* of late John and Margaret Fleming; one *s* one *d*. *Educ:* Blundell's. Served War, 1939–45: River Thames Formation. Photographer, 1950–57. *Recreations:* sculpting, chess. *Address:* c/o McNair & Co., EBC House, Ranelagh Gardens, SW6 3PA. *Club:* Hurlingham. *Died 2 July 2015.*

McNALLY, Joseph, (Joe), CVO 2011; Chief Executive, 1984–2001, Vice President, 1989–2001, Compaq Computer Ltd; *b* 17 July 1942; *s* of Joseph McNally and Emily McNally; *m* 1968, Anne Buglass; one *s* one *d*. *Educ:* Gateshead GS; King's Coll., Newcastle. Programmer, ICL, 1966–68; sales manager, Honeywell, 1968–79; Chief Exec. Designate, FMC/Harris, 1979–83; Founder Man. Dir, Compaq Computer UK, 1984. Non-exec. Dir, In Technology plc, 2000–. Trustee, Duke of Edinburgh's Award Scheme, 1999–2010. MInstD 1984. *Recreations:* shooting, fishing, gardening. *Address:* Compaq Computer Ltd, Hotham House, 1 Heron Square, Richmond, Surrey TW9 1EJ. *Clubs:* Farmers, St James's, Royal Automobile. *Died 1 March 2012.*

McNAMARA, Air Chief Marshal Sir Neville (Patrick), KBE 1981 (CBE 1972); AO 1976; AFC 1961; Chief of Defence Force Staff, Royal Australian Air Force, 1982–84; *b* Toogoolawah, Qld, 17 April 1923; *s* of late P. F. McNamara; *m* 1950, Dorothy Joan Miller; two *d*. *Educ:* Christian Brothers Coll., Nudgee, Qld. Enlisted RAAF, 1941; commnd 1944; Fighter Pilot WWII with No 75 Sqdn, Halmaheras and Borneo; served with No 77 Sqdn in Japan on cessation of hostilities; Air Traffic Control duties, HQ NE Area, 1949; Flying Instructor, Central Flying Sch., 1951–53; operational tour with No 77 Sqdn in Korean War; Pilot Trng Officer, HQ Trng Comd, 1954–55; Staff Officer, Fighter Operations Dept Air, 1955–57; CO No 25 Sqdn W Australia, 1957–59; CO No 2 Operational Conversion Unit, 1959–61; CO and Sen. Air Staff Officer, RAAF Staff, London, 1961–63; Director of Personnel (Officers), Dept Air, 1964–66; OC RAAF Contingent, Thailand, 1966–67; Air Staff Officer, RAAF Richmond, 1967–69; Dir-Gen., Organisation Dept Air, 1969–71; Comdr RAAF Forces Vietnam, 1971–72; Aust. Air Attaché, Washington, 1972–75; Dep. Chief of Air Staff, 1975–79; Chief of Air Staff, 1979–82. RAAF psc, pfc, jssc. *Publications:* The Quiet Man (autobiog.), 2005. *Died 7 May 2014.*

McNAUGHTON, Lt-Col Ian Kenneth Arnold; Chief Inspecting Officer of Railways, Department of Transport, 1974–82; *b* 30 June 1920; *er s* of late Brig. F. L. McNaughton, CBE, DSO and Betty, *d* of late Rev. Arnold Pinchard, OBE; *m* 1946, Arthea, *d* of late Carel Begeer, Voorschoten, Holland; two *d*. *Educ:* Loretto Sch.; RMA Woolwich; RMCS Shrivenham. BScEng, CEng, FIMechE, FIRSE. 2nd Lieut RE, 1939; served War of 1939–45, NW Europe (Captain) (despatches); GHQ MELF, 1949 (Major); Cyprus, 1955; OC 8 Rly Sqdn, 1958; Port Comdt Southampton, 1959 (Lt-Col); SO I Transportation HQ BAOR, 1960; retd 1963. Inspecting Officer of Rlys, Min. of Transport, 1963. Chm., Rlys Industry Adv. Cttee, Health and Safety Commn, 1978–82. *Recreations:* gardening, foreign travel. *Address:* Chawton Glebe, Alton, Hants GU34 1SH. *T:* (01420) 83395. *Died 22 April 2011.*

McNEIL, (David) John, CBE 1988; WS; NP; Partner, Morton Fraser (formerly Morton Fraser Milligan), 1968–2002; President, Law Society of Scotland, 1986–87; *b* 24 March 1937; *s* of Donald S. McNeil and Elizabeth (*née* Campbell); *m* 1962, Georgina Avril Sargent (*d* 2005); one *s* two *d*. *Educ:* Daniel Stewart's Coll., Edinburgh; Edinburgh Univ. (MA Hons, LLB). Apprenticed to Davidson & Syme, WS, Edinburgh, 1959–62; admitted Solicitor in Scotland, 1962; WS 1964; Partner, Fraser, Stodart and Ballingall, 1964–68. Mem. Council, Law Soc. of Scotland, 1972–92. Mem., Warnock Inquiry into Aspects of Human Infertility and Embryology, 1982–84. *Recreations:* golf, snooker, music and opera, theatre. *Died 25 Jan. 2012.*

McNEIL, Ian Robert, MBE 2004; JP; FCA; Partner, Moores Rowland, Chartered Accountants, 1958–98; *b* 14 Dec. 1932; *s* of Robert and Doris Mary McNeil; *m* 1963, Ann Harries-Rees; two *d*. *Educ:* Brighton Coll. ACA 1955. Partner, Nevill Hovey Gardner (later amalgamated into Moores Rowland), 1958. Dep. Chm., Financial Reporting Council, 1991–92; Mem., Takeover Panel, 1991–92. Member: Lord Chancellor's Adv. Cttee on Legal Educn and Conduct, 1994–99; Legal Services Consultative Panel, 2000–03. Institute of Chartered Accountants in England and Wales: Vice-Pres., 1989–90; Dep. Pres., 1990–91; Pres., 1991–92. Chm., Audit Cttee, Archbishops' Council, C of E, 1999–2004. Governor, Hurstpierpoint Coll., 1999–2002. Trustee and Hon. Treas., Action Research, 1999–2000. Liveryman: Curriers' Co., 1959 (Master, 1994–95); Chartered Accountants' Co., 1989–2002. JP Hove 1967 (Chm., Hove Bench, 1988–89); Mem. Council, Magistrates' Assoc., 1983–89. *Address:* 6 The Daisycroft, Henfield, West Sussex BN5 9LH. *T:* (01273) 492606. *Club:* Athenæum. *Died 5 Aug. 2013.*

McNEIL, John; *see* McNeil, D. J.

McNEILL, Peter Grant Brass; QC (Scot.) 1988; PhD; Sheriff of Lothian and Borders at Edinburgh, 1982–96, temporary Sheriff, 1996–98; writer and lecturer; *b* Glasgow, 3 March 1929; *s* of late William Arnot McNeill and late Lillias Philips Scrimgeour; *m* 1959, Matilda Farquhar Rose, *d* of late Mrs Christina Rose; one *s* three *d*. *Educ:* Hillhead High Sch., Glasgow; Morrison's Academy, Crieff; Glasgow Univ. MA (Hons Hist.) 1951; LLB 1954; Carnegie Fellowship, 1955; Faulds Fellowship, 1956–59; PhD, 1961. Law apprentice, Biggart Lumsden & Co., Glasgow, 1952–55; called to Scottish Bar, 1956. Hon. Sheriff Substitute of Lanarkshire, and of Stirling, Clackmannan and Dumbarton, 1962; Standing Junior Counsel to Scottish Development Dept (Highways), 1964; Advocate Depute, 1964–65; Sheriff of Lanarks, subseq. redesignated Glasgow and Strathkelvin, at Glasgow, 1965–82. Pres., Sheriffs' Assoc., 1982–85. Chm., Review Bd, Chinook Helicopter Accident, 1988. Mem., Scottish Records Adv. Council, 1989–95. Mem. Council, Scottish Nat. Dictionary Assoc. Ltd, 1987–2002 (Chm., 1997–2001); Chairman: Scottish Legal History Gp, 1990–97; Council, Stair Soc., 1990–98 (Vice Pres., 2007–); Trustee, Scottish Medievalists, 2007. *Publications:* (ed) Balfour's Practicks (Stair Society), 1962–63; (ed jtly) An Historical Atlas of Scotland *c* 400–*c* 1600, 1975; Adoption of Children in Scotland, 1982, (jtly) 4th edn 2010; (ed jtly) Atlas of Scottish History to 1707, 1996; legal and historical articles in Encyclopaedia Britannica, Juridical Review, Scots Law Times, Glasgow Herald, DNB, Oxford DNB, etc. *Recreations:* legal history, gardening, bookbinding. *Address:* 31 Queensferry Road, Edinburgh EH4 3HB. *T:* (0131) 332 3195. *Died 22 April 2011.*

McNICOL, Prof. George Paul, CBE 1992; FRSE 1984; Principal and Vice-Chancellor, University of Aberdeen, 1981–91; *b* 24 Sept. 1929; *s* of Martin and Elizabeth McNicol; *m* 1959, Susan Ritchie; one *s* two *d*. *Educ:* Hillhead High Sch., Glasgow; Univ. of Glasgow (MD 1964, PhD 1965). FRCPG 1967; FRCPE 1968; FRCP 1977; FRCPath 1977. House Surg., Western Infirmary, Glasgow, 1952; House Phys., Stobhill Gen. Hosp., Glasgow, 1953; Regimental MO, RAMC, 1953–55; Glasgow Medical Sch., 1955–71: various posts in clinical acad. med., 1955–65; Hon. Cons. Phys., 1966–71; Reader in Medicine, 1970–71; Prof. of Medicine and Hon. Cons. Phys., Leeds Gen. Infirmary, 1971–81; Chm., Bd of Faculty of Medicine, Leeds Univ., 1978–81. Harkness Fellow, Commonwealth Fund, Dept of Internal Medicine, Washington Univ., 1959–61; Hon. Clinical Lectr and Hon. Cons. Phys., Makerere UC Med. Sch. Extension, Kenyatta Nat. Hosp., Nairobi (on secondment from Glasgow Univ.), 1965–66. Chm. Med. Adv. Cttee, Cttee of Vice-Chancellors and Principals, 1985–90; Member: British Council Cttee on Internat. Co-op. in Higher Educn, 1985–91; Council, ACU, 1988–91; former Mem., Adv. Council on Misuse of Drugs. Chm., Part I Examining Bd, Royal Colls of Physicians (UK). Vice-Chm., Raigmore Hosp. NHS Trust, 1993–95. Chm., Bd of Governors, Rowett Res. Inst., 1981–89; Mem., Bd of Governors, N of Scotland Coll. of Agriculture, 1981–91; Co-Pres., EU Standing Cttee for Med. Trng, 1990–93. Mem., Exec. Cttee, Scottish Council (Develt and Industry), 1989–91. Mem. Aberdeen Local Bd, Bank of

Scotland, 1983–92. Hon. FACP. Hon. DSc Wabash Coll., Indiana, 1989; Hon. LLD Aberdeen, 1992. *Publications:* papers in sci. and med. jls on thrombosis and bleeding disorders. *Address:* 17 The Old Tannery, Downton, Salisbury, Wilts SP5 3FB. *Died 28 July 2014.*

McPHERSON, Ann, CBE 2000; FRCP, FRCGP; Principal in General Practice, Oxford, 1979–2008; Fellow, Green Templeton (formerly Green) College, Oxford, since 2000; *b* 22 June 1945; *d* of late Max Egelnick and of Sadie Egelnick; *m* 1968, Prof. Klim McPherson; one *s* two *d. Educ:* Copthall Co. Grammar Sch.; St George's Hosp. Med. Sch., London (MB BS 1968); DCH 1972; MRCGP (with dist.) 1978, FRCGP 1993; FRCP 2001. Pt-time trng posts in paediatrics and gen. practice, London, Harvard and Oxford, 1968–76; Department of Primary Care, Oxford University: pt time Lectr, 2001–; Med. Dir, Health Experiences Res. Gp, 2001–. Active in res. in women's health, teenage health and patients' experiences of illness. Co-Founder: Healthtalkonline.org (formerly www.dipex.org); www.youthhealthtalk.org; www.teenagehealthfreak.org. *Publications:* (with A. Anderson) Women's Problems in General Practice, 1983; (jtly) Miscarriage, 1984, 2nd edn 1990; Cervical Screening: a practical guide, 1985, 2nd edn (jtly) 1992; Fresher Pressure: how to survive as a student, 1994; (ed with D. Waller) Women's Health in General Practice, 5th edn 2003; (with N. Durham) Women's Health: by women, for women, about women, 1998; (with A. Macfarlane): Mum I Feel Funny, 1982; Diary of a Teenage Health Freak, 1987, 3rd edn 2002; I'm a Health Freak Too, 1989, 3rd edn as The Diary of the Other Health Freak, 2002; Me and My Mates, 1991; The Virgin Now Boarding, 1992; Adolescents: the Agony, the Ecstasy, the Answers: a book for parents, 1999; Healthcare of Young People: promotion in primary care, 2002; Sex: the facts, 2003; Drugs: the facts, 2003; Bullying: the facts, 2004; Relationships: the facts, 2004; The Truth: a teenager's survival guide, 2007. *Recreations:* swimming, playing tennis, reading, walking, chatting. *Address:* 25 Norham Road, Oxford OX2 6SF. *T:* (01865) 558743, *T:* (office) (01865) 289328. *Died 28 May 2011.*

McPHERSON, James Alexander Strachan, CBE 1982; JP; FSA (Scot.); Lord-Lieutenant of Banffshire (formerly Grampian Region (Banffshire)), 1987–2002; Solicitor, since 1954; *b* 20 Nov. 1927; *s* of Peter John McPherson and Jean Geddie Strachan; *m* 1960, Helen Marjorie Perks, MA; one *s* one *d. Educ:* Banff Academy; Aberdeen Univ. MA, BL, LLB. National Service, 1952–54; commissioned RA. Solicitor; Partner, Alexander George & Co., Macduff, 1954–95 (Senior Partner, 1986–95; Consultant, 1995–2001). Macduff Town Council: Mem., 1958–75; Treasurer, 1965–72; (last) Provost, 1972–75; Banff County Council: Mem., 1958–75; Chm., Educn Cttee, 1967–70; Chm., Management and Finance Cttee, 1970–75; (last) Convener, County Council, 1970–75; Member: Assoc. of County Councils for Scotland, 1965–75; COSLA, 1974–86; Grampian Regional Council, 1974–90 (Chm., Public Protection Cttee, 1974–86); Police Adv. Bd for Scotland, 1974–86. Mem., Scottish Solicitors Discipline Tribunal, 1990–95; Pres., Banffshire Soc. of Solicitors, 1976–79. Former mem., numerous Scottish Cttees and Boards. Vice-Pres., Highland RFCA (formerly TAVRA), 1987–2002. Director: Banffshire Partnership, 2003–09; NE Scotland Preservation Trust, 2003–09; Deveron Care Services, 2003–07. Governor, Scottish Police Coll., 1974–86. Mem. Court, Aberdeen Univ., 1993–97. Elder, and Free Will Offering Treas., Macduff Parish Church. Chairman: Banff and Buchan JP Adv. Cttee, 1987–98; Aberdeenshire JP Adv. Cttee, 1998–2002; Hon. Sheriff, Grampian Highland and Islands at Banff, 1972–. JP Banff and Buchan, subseq. Aberdeenshire, 1974. *Recreations:* sailing, swimming, reading, local history. *Address:* Dun Alastair, Macduff, Banffshire AB44 1XD. *T:* (home) (01261) 832377, (office) (01261) 832201. *Clubs:* Royal Northern and University (Aberdeen); Banff Town and County. *Died 12 Aug. 2012.*

MACPHERSON of Biallid, Sir (Ronald) Thomas (Stewart), (Tommy), Kt 1992; CBE (mil.) 1968; MC 1943, Bars 1944 and 1945; TD 1960; DL; Chairman: Boustead plc, 1986–2008; Annington Holdings PLC, 1996–2007; *b* 4 Oct. 1920; 5th *s* of Sir Thomas Stewart Macpherson, CIE, LLD, and Lady (Helen) Macpherson (*née* Cameron); *m* 1953, Jean Henrietta, *d* of late David Butler Wilson; two *s* one *d. Educ:* Cargilfield; Fettes Coll. (scholar); Trinity Coll., Oxford (1st open classical scholar; MA 1st Cl. Hons PPE; Hon. Fellow, 2011). Athletics Blue and Scottish International; British Team World Student Games, Paris, 1947; represented Oxford in Rugby football and hockey, 1946–47; played Rugby for London Scottish, 1945–55; played hockey for Mid Surrey and Anglo Scots, 1956–59. Reader Middle Temple. 2nd Lieut Queen's Own Cameron Highlanders TA, 1939; Scottish Commando, parachutist, 1940; POW, 1941–43, escaped 1943; Major 1943 (despatches). Consultant, Italo-Yugoslav Border Commn, 1946. 21 SAS TA, 1947–52; CO 1st Bn London Scottish TA, 1961–64; Col TA London Dist, 1964–67. Mem., Queen's Body Guard for Scotland (Royal Co. of Archers). Chairman: Mallinson-Denny Gp, 1981–82 (Dir, 1948–82; Man. Dir, 1967–81); Birmid Qualcast, 1982–88; Cosmopolitan Textile Co., 1983–91; Allstate Reinsurance Ltd, 1983–96; Employment Conditions Abroad Ltd, 1983–93; Webb-Bowen Internat. Ltd, 1984–94; SNTC (France), 1985–95; Owl Creek Investments plc, 1989–91; Wineworld (London) PLC, 1996–2000; Internet Network Services Ltd, 1995–99; Entuity Ltd, 2000–; Nexus Investments Ltd, 2001–07; XchangePoint Ltd, 2001–05; EMAC Ltd, 2005–09; Dep. Chm., Keller Group plc, 1991–99. Exec. Dir, Brooke Bond Gp plc, 1981–82; Director: Transglobe Expedition Ltd, 1976–83; Scottish Mutual Assurance Soc., 1982–91; C. H. Industrials PLC, 1983–91; NCB, 1983–86 (Vice Chm., 1983–85); English Architectural Glazing Ltd, 1985–99; TSB Scotland, 1986–91; Independent Insurance plc, 1987–93; Fitzwilton (UK) plc, 1990–2008; Soc. Générale Merchant Bank, 1991–93; Architectural Glazing (Scotland) Ltd, 1998–99; Deutsche Annington Immobilien GmbH, 2001–07; UK Consultant, Sears Roebuck & Co., Chicago, 1984–98; Consultant: Bain & Co., 1987–99; Candover Investment plc, 1989–95. Member: Adv. Council, Terra Firma Capital Partners, 2001–08; UK Adv. Bd, Kanbay Inc., 2006–09. Founder Chm., Nat. Employment Liaison Cttee for TA and Reserves, 1986–94; Chm., ABCC, 1986–88; Pres., Eurochambres (Assoc. of European Chambers of Commerce), 1992–94, then Hon. Pres.; Vice-Pres., London Chamber of Commerce, 1985–97 (Chm., Council, 1980–82). Member: Council, CBI (Chm., London and SE Reg., CBI, 1975–77); Scottish Council Develt and Industry, London; Prices and Incomes Bd, 1968–69; Council, GBA, 1979–83; Council, Strathclyde Univ. Business Sch., 1982–86. Foundn Trustee, Acad. of European Law, Germany, 1994–2011. Chm., 1961–79, Pres., 1979–, Achilles Club; Vice-Pres., Newtonmore Camanachd Club; President: Commando Assoc., 2000–05; Friends of Scottish Rugby, 2000–09 (then Hon. Life Pres.); Highland Soc. of London, 2001–05; Royal Scottish Corp., 2003–09; Badenoch Br., RBL Scotland, 2014. Chieftain, Newtonmore Highland Games, 1999–. Vice Patron, POW Reserve Forces Ulysses Trust. Governor, Fettes Coll., 1984–92; Pres., London Old Fettesians, 1999–2006. Prime Warden, Co. of Dyers, 1985–86; Hon. Mem. of Court, Carpenters' Co. FRSA, FCMI. DL 1977, High Sheriff, 1983–84, Greater London. Chevalier, Légion d'Honneur, and Croix de Guerre with 2 palms and star, France; Medaglia d'Argento and Resistance Medal, Italy; Kt of St Mary of Bethlehem. *Publications:* (with Richard Bath) Behind Enemy Lines, 2010. *Recreation:* outdoors as much as possible. *Address:* Speyville House, Newtonmore, Inverness-shire PH20 1AR. *T:* 07736 958280, *T:* and *Fax:* (01540) 673224. *Clubs:* Hurlingham, MCC; New (Edinburgh). *Died 6 Nov. 2014.*

MACREADY, Sir Nevil (John Wilfrid), 3rd Bt *cr* 1923; CBE 1983; Chairman, Mental Health Foundation, 1993–97; *b* 7 Sept. 1921; *s* of Lt-Gen. Sir Gordon (Nevil) Macready, 2nd Bt, KBE, CB, CMG, DSO, MC, and Elisabeth (*d* 1969), *d* of Duc de Noailles; *S* father, 1956; *m* 1949, Mary, (Emma), (*d* 2007), *d* of late Sir (John) Donald (Balfour) Fergusson, GCB; one *s* three *d. Educ:* Cheltenham; St John's Coll., Oxford. Served in RA (Field), 1942–47 (despatches); Staff Captain, 1945. BBC European Service, 1947–50. Vice-Pres. and Gen. Manager, Mobil Oil Française, 1972–75; Man. Dir, Mobil Oil Co. Ltd,

1975–85. Pres., Inst. of Petroleum, 1980–82. Chairman: Crafts Council, 1984–91; Horseracing Adv. Council, 1986–93; Dep. Chm., British Horseracing Bd, 1993–95. Pres., Royal Warrant Holders' Assoc., 1979–80; Trustee, V&A Museum, 1985–95. *Recreations:* racing, fishing, theatre, music. *Heir:* *s* Charles Nevil Macready [*b* 19 May 1955; *m* 1st, 1981, Lorraine McAdam (marr. diss. 1994); one *s* one *d*; 2nd, 2001, Gillian Simms]. *Address:* The White House, Odiham, Hants RG29 1LG. *T:* (01256) 702976. *Clubs:* Boodle's; Jockey (Paris). *Died 27 Sept. 2014.*

MacSWEEN, Sir Roderick (Norman McIver), Kt 2000; MD; FRCPE, FRCPGlas, FRCPath, FMedSci; FRSB; FRSE; Professor of Pathology, University of Glasgow, 1984–99, then Emeritus; President, Royal College of Pathologists, 1996–99; *b* 2 Feb. 1935; *s* of Murdo MacLeod MacSween and Christina (*née* McIver); *m* 1961, Dr Marjory Pentland Brown; one *s* one *d*. *Educ:* Inverness Royal Acad.; Glasgow Univ. (BSc Hons 1956; MD 1973). FRCPGlas 1972; FRCPE 1974; FRCPath 1976; FRSB (FIBiol 1987); FRSE 1985. University of Glasgow: Lectr, then Sen. Lectr in Pathology, 1965–78; Titular Prof. in Pathology, 1978–84. Instructor in Pathology, Univ. of Colo, Denver, 1968–69; Otago Savings Bank Vis. Prof., Univ. of Otago, NZ, 1983. Ed., Histopathology, 1984–95. Mem., GMC, 2000–04. Chm., Unrelated Live Transplant Regulatory Authy, 2000–06. President: Royal Medico-Chirurgical Soc. of Glasgow, 1978–79; British Div., Internat. Acad. of Pathology, 1989–91; Chm., Acad. of Med. Royal Colls, 1998–2000. Hon. Librarian, RCPSG, 1985–95. Chm., Tenovus Scotland, 2006–11. Pres., Royal Philosophical Soc. of Glasgow, 2009–12. Chm., Sen. Fellows' Club, RCPSG, 2011–. Founder FMedSci 1998. Hon. Fellow, Coll. of Pathologists of S Africa, 1998; Hon. FRCP 1999; Hon. FRCS 2013; Hon. FRCSE 2000. Hon. DSc Glasgow, 2007. *Publications:* (ed jtly) Pathology of the Liver, 1979, 5th edn 2007 as MacSween's Pathology of the Liver; (ed with P. P. Anthony) Recent Advances in Histopathology Nos 11–16, 1992–94; (ed with K. Whaley) Muir's Textbook of Pathology, 13th edn 1992. *Recreations:* golf, gardening, hill-walking… and more golf! *Address:* 23 Lochbroom Drive, Newton Mearns, Glasgow G77 5PF. *Clubs:* Athenæum; Glasgow Golf, Dunaverty Golf (Past Capt.), Machrihanish Golf (Past Capt.). *Died 11 Dec. 2015.*

MACVICAR, Neil; QC (Scot.) 1960; Sheriff of Lothian and Borders (formerly the Lothians and Peebles), at Edinburgh, 1968–85; *b* 16 May 1920; *s* of late Neil Macvicar, WS; *m* 1949, Maria, *d* of Count Spiridon Bulgari, Corfu; one *s* two *d*. *Educ:* Loretto Sch.; Oriel Coll., Oxford; Edinburgh Univ. (MA, LLB). Served RA, 1940–45. Called to Scottish Bar, 1948. Chm., Med. Appeal Tribunals, 1961–67 and 1987–94. Chancellor, Dio. of Edinburgh, 1961–74. Chm. of Govs, Dean Orphanage and Cauvin's Trust, 1967–85. *Publications:* A Heart's Odyssey (memoirs), 1991; Grace Notes: variations on a Greek theme, 1995. *Address:* 25 Blackford Road, Edinburgh EH9 2DT. *T:* (0131) 667 2362; Kapoutsi, Gastouri, Corfu, Greece. *T:* (661) 56110. *Clubs:* New (Edinburgh); Anagnostiki Etairia (Corfu). *Died 3 May 2011.*

MacWILLIAM, Very Rev. Alexander Gordon; Dean of St Davids Cathedral, 1984–90, then Dean Emeritus; *b* 22 Aug. 1923; *s* of Andrew George and Margaret MacWilliam; *m* 1951, Catherine Teresa (*née* Bogue); one *s*. *Educ:* Univ. of Wales (BA Hons Classics, 1943); Univ. of London (BD 2nd Cl. Hons, 1946, PhD 1952, DipEd 1962). Deacon 1946, priest 1947; Curate of Penygroes, Gwynedd, 1946–49; Minor Canon, Bangor Cathedral, 1949–55; Assistant Curate: St Mary's, Bangor, 1950–53; St James's, Bangor, 1953–55; Rector: Llanfaethlu, Gwynedd, 1955–58; Llanfairynghornwy with Llanrhwydrus, 1956–58; Head of Dept of Theology, Trinity Coll., Carmarthen, Dyfed, 1958–74; Head of School of Society Studies, Trinity Coll. (Inst. of Higher Education, Univ. of Wales), 1974–84; Canon of St Davids Cathedral and Prebendary of Trefloden, 1978–84. Examining Chaplain to Bishop of St Davids, 1969. Vis. Prof. of Philosophy and Theology, Central Univ. of Iowa, USA, 1983–84. Prov. Grand Master, S Wales Western Div., United Grand Lodge of England, 1992. Chm., Myrddin Probus Club, Carmarthen, 2003. *Publications:* contribs to Learning for Living (Brit. Jl of Religious Education), UCW Jl of Educn. *Recreations:* travel to archaeological sites and art centres, classical music, food and wine. *Address:* Pen Parc, Smyrna Road, Llangain, Carmarthen, Carmarthenshire SA33 5AD. *Died 24 Oct. 2014.*

MADARIAGA, Prof. Isabel Margaret de, FRHistS; FBA 1990; Professor of Russian Studies, University of London at School of Slavonic and East European Studies, 1981–85, then Professor Emerita; *b* 27 Aug. 1919; *d* of late Salvador de Madariaga and Constance Archibald, MA; *m* 1943, Leonard Bertram Schapiro, CBE, FBA (marr. diss. 1976; he *d* 1983). *Educ:* Ecole Internationale, Geneva; Instituto Escuela, Madrid and fifteen other schools; SSEES, Univ. of London (BA, PhD). FRHistS 1967. BBC Monitoring Service, 1940–43; Min. of Information (later COI), 1943–47; Economic Information Unit, HM Treasury, 1947–48; Editl Asst, Slavonic and East European Review, 1951–64; Asst Lectr and Lectr, LSE, intermittently, 1951–66; Lectr in Modern History, Univ. of Sussex, 1966–68; Sen. Lectr in Russian Hist., Univ. of Lancaster, 1968–71; Reader in Russian Studies, SSEES, Univ. of London, 1971–81. Corresp. Mem., Royal Spanish Acad. of History, 1991. Member, Editorial Boards: Government and Opposition, 1965–2004; Slavonic and E European Review, 1971–86; European History Qly, 1971–2004. *Publications:* Britain, Russia and the Armed Neutrality, 1963; (with G. Ionescu) Opposition, 1968; Russia in the Age of Catherine the Great, 1981 (trans. French 1986, Italian 1988, Russian 2002); Catherine the Great: a short history, 1990 (trans. German 1993, Spanish 1994, Portuguese 1996, Turkish 1997, Russian 2006); Politics and Culture in Eighteenth-Century Russia, 1998; Ivan the Terrible, 2005 (trans. Italian 2006, Russian and Finnish 2007, Swedish and Latvian 2008, Turkish, 2012); articles in learned jls. *Recreation:* music. *Address:* 25 Southwood Lawn Road, Highgate, N6 5SD. *T:* (020) 8341 0862. *Died 16 June 2014.*

MADDEN, (Albert) Frederick (McCulloch), DPhil, DLitt; Reader in Commonwealth Government, Oxford, 1957–84; Professorial (Charter) Fellow of Nuffield College, 1958–84, Emeritus Fellow since 1984, Pro-Proctor, 1988–89; *b* 27 Feb. 1917; *e s* of A. E. and G. McC. Madden; *m* 1941, Margaret (*d* 2004), *d* of Dr R. D. Gifford; one *s* one *d*. *Educ:* privately, by mother; Bishop Vesey's Grammar Sch.; Christ Church, Oxford (Boulter and Gladstone exhibns; BA 1938, BLitt 1939); DPhil 1950, DLitt 2005, Oxon. Dep. Sup., Rhodes House Library, 1946–48; Beit Lectr, 1947–57; Sen. Tutor to Overseas Service Courses, 1950–; Co-Dir, Foreign Service Course, 1959–72; Dir, Inst. of Commonwealth Studies, 1961–68; Vice-Chm., History Bd, 1968–73. Co-founder, Oxford Samaritans, 1961. Canadian Vis. Fellow, 1970; Vis. Prof., Cape Town, 1973; Vis. Fellow, Res. Sch., ANU, 1974. Dir, Hong Kong admin. course, 1975–86. Dir, Prospect Theatre, 1963–66. Author and actor in pageants: Marcham, 1951; Stanford, 1999; nativity and passion plays, 1995–96. FRHistS 1952. *Publications:* (with V. Harlow) British Colonial Developments, 1774–1834, 1953; (with K. Robinson) Essays in Imperial Government, 1963; chapter in Cambridge History of British Empire III, 1959; Imperial Constitutional Documents, 1765–1965, 1966; (with W. Morris-Jones) Australia and Britain, 1980; (with D. K. Fieldhouse) Oxford and the Idea of Commonwealth, 1982; Perspectives on Imperialism and Decolonisation (Festschrift), 1984; Select Documents on the Constitutional History of the British Empire: Vol. I, The Empire of the Bretaignes 1165–1688, 1985; Vol. II, The Classical Period of the First British Empire 1689–1783, 1986; Vol. III, Imperial Reconstruction 1763–1840, 1987; Vol. IV, Settler Self-government 1840–1900, 1989; Vol. V, The Dependent Empire and Ireland 1840–1900, 1991; Vol. VI, The Dominions and India since 1900, 1993; Vol. VII, The Dependent Empire 1900–48, 1994; Vol. VIII, The End of Empire 1948–97, 2000; articles and reviews in English Historical Review, etc. *Recreations:* acting (Cranmer in Quatercentenary, St Mary's, Oxford, and 186 other parts); photographing islands and highlands, hill towns, country houses, churches; Renaissance art; writing music and listening; taking services. *Address:* 1 Penstones Court, Marlborough Lane, Stanford-in-the-Vale, Oxfordshire SN7 8SW. *T:* (01367) 718068. *Died 10 Sept. 2011.*

MÁDL, Ferenc, Hon. GCMG 2002; PhD; President of Hungary, 2000–05; *b* 29 Jan. 1931; *s* of A. Mádl; *m* 1955, Dalma Némethy; one *s*. *Educ:* Loránd Eötvös Univ., Budapest (law degree, 1955); Univ. of Strasbourg; PhD 1974. Inst. of State and Legal Scis, Hungarian Acad. of Scis; Lectr, 1973, Dir, Inst. of Civil Law, 1978–85, Dir, Faculty of Internat. Pvte Law, 1985, Loránd Eötvös Univ., Budapest. Minister: without portfolio, 1990–93; of Culture and Educn, 1993–94. *Publications:* 20 books on law of internat. econ. relations, internat. investment law, EEC law, etc; articles on law. *Address:* c/o Office of the President, Sándor Palace, Szent György tér 1, 1014 Budapest, Hungary. *Died 29 May 2011.*

MAGUIRE, Hugh, FRAM; violinist and conductor; Director of Strings, Britten-Pears School for Advanced Music Studies, 1978–2002; Professor of Violin, Royal Academy of Music, 1957–83; *b* 2 Aug. 1926; *m* 1st, 1953, Suzanne Lewis (marr. diss. 1987), of International Ballet; two *s* three *d*; 2nd, 1988, Tricia Catchpole (*d* 2013). *Educ:* Belvedere Coll., SJ, Dublin; Royal Academy of Music, London (David Martin); Paris (Georges Enesco). Leader: Bournemouth Symphony Orchestra, 1952–56; London Symphony Orchestra, 1956–62; BBC Symphony Orchestra, 1962–67; Cremona String Quartet, 1966–68; Allegri String Quartet, 1968–76; Melos Ensemble, 1972–85; Orch. of Royal Opera House, Covent Garden, 1983–91. Artistic Dir, Irish Youth Orch., 1970–91; String coach, European Community Youth Orch., 1980–88. Mem., Irish Arts Council, 1980–90. Hon. MMus Hull, 1975; Hon. DLitt Univ. of Ulster, 1986; Hon. DMus NUI, 1992. Harriet Cohen Internat. Award, 1963; Councils Gold Medal (Ireland), 1963; Cobbett Medal, Musicians' Co., 1982. *Address:* Chapel Cottage, Peasenhall, Suffolk IP17 2JD. *Died 14 June 2013.*

MAHON, Sir (John) Denis, CH 2003; Kt 1986; CBE 1967; FBA 1964; art historian; Trustee of the National Gallery, 1957–64 and 1966–73; Member, Advisory Panel, National Art-Collections Fund, since 1975; *b* 8 Nov. 1910; *s* of late John FitzGerald Mahon (4th *s* of Sir William Mahon, 4th Bt) and Lady Alice Evelyn Browne (*d* 1970), *d* of 5th Marquess of Sligo. *Educ:* Eton; Christ Church, Oxford (MA 1936; Hon. Student, 1996). Specialised in the study of 17th-Century painting in Italy and formed a collection of pictures of the period (exhibited Nat. Gall., 1997); Mem. Cttee of the Biennial Exhibitions at Bologna, Italy; long campaigned for fiscal measures to encourage support from private individuals for art galls and museums. Awarded Medal for Benemeriti della Cultura by Pres. of Italy for services to criticism and history of Italian art, 1957; Archiginnasio d'Oro, City of Bologna, 1968; Serena Medal for Italian Studies, British Acad., 1972. Elected Accademico d'Onore, Clementine Acad., Bologna, 1964; Sen. Fellow, RCA, 1988; Corresp. Fellow: Accad. Raffaello, Urbino, 1968; Deputazione di Storia Patria per le provincie di Romagna, 1969. Ateneo Veneto, 1987. Hon. Citizen, Cento, 1982. Hon. FRA 2002. FRSA. Hon. DLitt: Newcastle, 1969; Oxford, 1994; Rome (La Sapienza), 1998; Bologna, 2002. *Publications:* Studies in Seicento Art and Theory, 1947; Mostra dei Carracci, Catalogo critico dei Disegni, 1956 (1963); Poussiniana, 1962; Catalogues of the Mostra del Guercino (Dipinti, 1968; Disegni, 1969); (with Nicholas Turner) The Drawings of Guercino in the Collection of Her Majesty the Queen at Windsor Castle, 1989; catalogues of exhibitions for 4th centenary of Guercino's birth, 1991–92; contributed to: Actes of Colloque Poussin, 1960; Friedlaender Festschrift, 1965; Problemi Guardeschi, 1967; (consultant) Luigi Salerno, I Dipinti del Guercino, 1988; articles, including a number on Caravaggio and Poussin, in art-historical periodicals, *eg*, The Burlington Magazine, Apollo, The Art Bulletin, Journal of the Warburg and Courtauld Institutes, Bulletin of the Metropolitan Museum of New York, Gazette des Beaux-Arts, Art de France, Paragone, Commentari, Zeitschrift für Kunstwissenschaft; collaborated in the compilation of catalogues raisonnés of exhibitions, *eg*, Artists in 17th Century Rome (London, 1955), Italian Art and Britain (Royal Academy, 1960), L'Ideale Classico del Seicento in Italia (Bologna, 1962), Omaggio al Guercino (Cento, 1967). *Address:* 33 Cadogan Square, SW1X 0HU. *T:* (020) 7235 7311, 7235 2530. *Died 24 April 2011.*

MAHY, Margaret May, ONZ 1993; writer; *b* 21 March 1936; *d* of Francis George Mahy and Helen May Penlington; two *d*. *Educ:* Whakatane Primary and High Schs; Univ. of NZ (BA). Asst Librarian, Petone Public Library, 1959; Asst Children's Librarian, Christchurch Public Library, 1960; Librarian i/c of school requests, Sch. Library Service (Christchurch Br.), 1967; Children's Librarian, Christchurch Public Library, 1977; full time writer, 1980–. Hon. DLitt Canterbury, 1993. Carnegie Medal, 1982, 1984; Esther Glen Medal. *Publications: picture books:* The Dragon of an Ordinary Family, 1969; A Lion in the Meadow, 1969; Mrs Discombobulous, 1969; Pillycock's Shop, 1969; The Procession, 1970; The Little Witch, 1970; Sailor Jack and the Twenty Orphans, 1970; The Princess and the Clown, 1971; The Boy with Two Shadows, 1971; The Man whose Mother was a Pirate, 1972; The Railway Engine and the Hairy Brigands, 1973; Rooms for Rent/Rooms to Let, 1974; The Witch in the Cherry Tree, 1974; The Rare Spotted Birthday Party, 1974; Stepmother, 1974; The Ultra-Violet Catastrophe, 1975; The Great Millionaire Kidnap, 1975; The Wind Between the Stars, 1976; David's Witch Doctor, 1976; Leaf Magic, 1976; The Boy who was Followed Home, 1977; Jam, 1985; The Great White Man-Eating Shark, 1989; The Tin Can Band and Other Poems, 1989; Making Friends, 1990; The Pumpkin Man and the Crafty Creeper, 1990; The Seven Chinese Brothers, 1990; The Dentist's Promise, 1991; Keeping House, 1991; The Queen's Goat, 1991; The Horrendous Hullabaloo, 1992; The Three-Legged Cat, 1993; A Busy Day for a Good Grandmother, 1993; The Christmas Tree Tangle, 1994; The Rattlebang Picnic, 1994; The Big Black Bulging Bump, 1995; Boom, Baby, Boom, Boom!, 1996; Beaten by a Balloon, 1997; Summery Saturday Morning, 1998; Simply Delicious!, 1999; Dashing Dog, 2002; Down the Back of the Chair, 2006; Bubble Trouble, 2008; *collections of stories:* three Margaret Mahy Story Books, 1972, 1973, 1975; A Lion in the Meadow, 1976; Nonstop Nonsense, 1977; The Great Piratical Rumbustification and The Librarian and the Robbers, 1978; The Chewing-Gum Rescue, 1982; The Birthday Burglar and a Very Wicked Headmistress, 1984; The Downhill Crocodile Whizz, 1986; Mahy Magic, 1986; The Three Wishes, 1986; The Door in the Air, 1988; Bubble Trouble, 1991; Tick Tock Tales, 1993; *junior novels:* Clancy's Cabin, 1974; The Bus Under the Leaves, 1975; The Pirate Uncle, 1977; Raging Robots and Unruly Uncles, 1981; The Pirates' Mixed-Up Voyage, 1983; The Blood and Thunder Adventure on Hurricane Peak, 1989; The Cousins Quartet, books 1–4, 1994; The Greatest Show off Earth, 1994; Tingleberries, Tuckertubs and Telephones: a tale of love and ice-cream, 1995; The Five Sisters, 1996; The Horribly Haunted School, 1997; Dinsmore Down in the Dump, 1999; A Villain's Night Out, 1999; *novels for older readers:* The Haunting, 1982; The Changeover, 1984; The Catalogue of the Universe, 1985; Aliens in the Family, 1986; The Tricksters, 1986; Memory, 1987; Dangerous Spaces, 1991; Underrunners, 1992; The Other Side of Silence, 1995; Operation Terror, 1997; Alchemy, 2002; *for schools:* The Crocodile's Christmas Jandals, 1982; The Bubbling Crocodile, 1983; Mrs Bubble's Baby, 1983; Shopping with a Crocodile, 1983; Going to the Beach, 1984; The Great Grumbler and the Wonder Tree, 1984; Fantail Fantail, 1984; A Crocodile in the Garden, 1985; The Crocodile's Christmas Thongs, 1985; Horrakapotchkin, 1985; *for emergent readers:* Ups and Downs, 1984; Wibble Wobble, 1984; The Dragon's Birthday, 1984; The Spider in the Shower, 1984; The Adventures of a Kite, 1985; Sophie's Singing Mother, 1985; The Earthquake, 1985; The Cake, 1985; The Catten, 1985; Out in the Big Wide World, 1985; A Vary Happy Bathday, 1985; Clever Hamburger, 1985; Muppy's Ball, 1986; Baby's Breakfast, 1986; The Tree Doctor, 1986; The Garden Party, 1986; The Man who Enjoyed Grumbling, 1986; The Trouble with Heathrow, 1986; The Pop Group, 1986; Feeling Funny, 1986; A Pet to the Vet, 1986; The New House Villain, 1986; Tai Taylor is Born, 1986; The Terrible Topsy-Turvy Tissy-Tossy Tangle, 1986; Trouble on the Bus, 1986; Mr Rumfitt, 1986; My Wonderful Aunt, 1986; The Funny, Funny Clown Face, 1986; The Haunting of Miss Cardamon, 1987; The Girl Who Washed by Moonlight, 1987; The King's Jokes, 1987; The Mad Puppet, 1987; *verse:* Seventeen Kings and

Forty-Two Elephants, 1972; The Word Witch, 2009; *non-fiction:* Look Under 'V', 1977. *Recreations:* reading, gardening. *Address:* No 1 RD, Lyttelton, New Zealand. *T:* (3) 299703. *Died 23 July 2012.*

MAIDEN, (James) Dennis, CEng; Director General, Federation of Master Builders, 1991–97; *b* 28 June 1932; *s* of James William Maiden and Elsie (*née* Brotherton); *m* 1953, Irene Harris; one *s* one *d*. *Educ:* Wath-upon-Dearne Grammar Sch. CEng 1966; MIMechE 1966; FFB 1987–2003. Engrg Consultant, Husband & Co., 1958–63; Chief Engr, British Shoe Corp., 1963–67; Construction Industry Training Board: Develt Manager, 1967–73; Gen. Manager, 1973–76; Dir of Trng, 1976–85; Chief Exec., 1985–90; Dir-Gen. designate, Fedn of Master Builders, 1990–91. Chief Exec., Construction Ind. Services Ltd, 1991–97; Managing Director: Nat. Register of Warranted Builders Ltd, 1991–97; Trade Debt Recovery Service Ltd, 1991–97. Pres., Kings Lynn Inst. of Mgt, 1988. Chm., Park House Hotel for Disabled People, 1983–88 and 1995–99. Trustee, Leonard Cheshire Foundn, 1987–92; Pres., Norfolk Outward Bound Assoc., 1988. Hon. Mem., C & G, 1981; CCMI (CIMgt 1986); MIPM 1971; FRSA 1987. Freeman, City of London, 1988; Liveryman, Co. of: Constructors, 1988; Plumbers, 1989. *Recreations:* art, gardening, theatre. *Address:* Micklebring, Church Lane, Bircham, Kings Lynn, Norfolk PE31 6XS. *T:* (01485) 578336. *Died 26 Oct. 2015.*

MAIS, Francis Thomas; Secretary, Royal Northern College of Music, 1982–90; *b* 27 June 1927; *s* of Charles Edward Mais and Emma (*née* McLoughlin); *m* 1st, Margaret Edythe Evans (*d* 1984); one *d*; 2nd, 1987, Joan Frost-Smith. *Educ:* Barnsley Grammar Sch.; Christ's Coll., Cambridge (MA). Northern Ireland Civil Service, 1951–82: Permanent Secretary: Dept of Commerce, 1979–81; Dept of Manpower Services, 1981–82. Governor, Associated Bd, Royal Schs of Music, 1985–92. Hon. RNCM 1987. *Address:* No 2 Applegarth, Fairybead Lane, Stainton, Penrith, Cumbria CA11 0DD. *T:* (01768) 210531. *Died 22 Sept. 2014.*

MAISONROUGE, Jacques Gaston; management consultant; *b* Cachan, Seine, 20 Sept. 1924; *s* of Paul Maisonrouge and Suzanne (*née* Cazas); *m* 1948, Françoise Andrée Féron; one *s* four *d*. *Educ:* Lycée Voltaire and Saint Louis, Paris. Studied engineering; gained dip. of Ecole Centrale des Arts et Manufactures. Engineer, 1948; various subseq. appts in IBM Corp., France; Chm. and Chief Exec. Officer, IBM World Trade Europe/ME/Africa Corp., 1974–81; Pres., IBM Europe, 1974–81; Sen. Vice-Pres., 1972–84, and Mem. Bd of Dirs, 1983–84, IBM Corp.; Chm., IBM World Trade Corp., 1976–84; Vice Chm., Liquid Air Corp., 1984–86; Dir-Gen. of Industry, France, 1986–87; Chm. of Bd, French Centre for Foreign Trade, 1987–89. Director: L'Air Liquide, 1964–94; IBM Europe/ME/Africa, 1987–94. Chm., Bd of Trustees, Ecole Centrale des Arts et Manufactures, 1976–87; Chancellor, Internat. Acad. of Management, 1987–93. Hon. Gov., American Hosp. of Paris (Gov., 1988). Nat. Pres., France-US Assoc., 1994–2000. Grand Officier, Ordre de la Légion d'Honneur; Commander: Ordre National du Mérite; des Palmes Académiques; Order of Merit of the Italian Republic; Order of Saint Sylvester; Order of Star of North (Sweden); Grand Officer, Order of Malta. *Publications:* Inside IBM: a European's story, 1985. *Address:* 3 boulevard Flandrin, 75116 Paris, France. *Clubs:* Automobile of France, Cercle Interallié. *Died 25 Jan. 2012.*

MAITLAND, Alastair George, CBE 1966; Consul-General, Boston, 1971–75; *b* 30 Jan. 1916; *s* of late Thomas Douglas Maitland, MBE, and Wilhelmina Sarah Dundas; *m* 1st, 1943, Betty Hamilton (*d* 1981); two *s* one *d*; 2nd, 1986, Hazel Margaret Porter. *Educ:* George Watson's Coll., Edinburgh; Universities of Edinburgh (MA First Class Hons), Grenoble and Paris, Ecole des Sciences Politiques. Vice-Consul: New York, 1938; Chicago, 1939; New York, 1939; Los Angeles, 1940; apptd to staff of UK High Commissioner at Ottawa, 1942; apptd to Foreign Office, 1945; Brit. Middle East Office, Cairo, 1948; Foreign Office, 1952; UK Delegation to OEEC, Paris, 1954; Consul-General: at New Orleans, 1958–62; at Jerusalem, 1962–64; at Cleveland, 1964–68; Dir-Gen., British Trade Develt Office, NY, 1968–71. Hon. LLD Lake Erie Coll., Ohio, 1971. CStJ. *Recreations:* music, golf, gardening, reading. *Address:* Box 31, Heath, MA 01346–0031, USA. *Died 21 Dec. 2011.*

MAITLAND, David Henry, CVO 1988; Chief Executive, 1966–81, and Chairman, 1979–81, Save & Prosper Group; *b* 9 May 1922; *s* of George and Mary Annie Maitland; *m* 1955, Judeth Mary Gold; three *d*. *Educ:* Eton; King's College, Cambridge. FCA. Army, 1941–46, Captain, Oxf. & Bucks Light Inf. Articled Whinney Smith & Whinney, 1946; qualified ACA 1950; Mobil Oil Co., 1952–60; Save & Prosper Group: Comptroller, 1960; Managing Dir, 1966; non-exec. Dir, 1981; retired 1987. Dir, HFC Bank, 1989–95. Chm., Unit Trust Assoc., 1973–75; Member: City Capital Markets Cttee, 1975–84; Inflation Accounting Steering Group, 1976–80; Council, Duchy of Lancaster, 1977–87; Bethlem Royal Hosp. and Maudsley Hosp. SHA, 1982–90; Royal Commn for 1851 Exhibn, 1984–97; Treloar Trust (formerly Lord Mayor Treloar Trust), 1984–2002. Vice-Chm., Crafts Council, 1989–90 (Mem., 1984–90). Mem., Cttee of Management, Inst. of Psychiatry, 1984–96 (Chm., 1987–90). *Address:* Angel House, 4 High Street, Odiham, Hants RG29 1LG. *Died 18 April 2013.*

MAITLAND SMITH, Geoffrey; chartered accountant; *b* 27 Feb. 1933; *s* of late Philip John Maitland Smith and Kathleen (*née* Goff); *m* 1st, 1956, Winifred Patricia Lane (marr. diss. 1967); three *s* one *d*; 2nd, 1967, Gabriella Armandi (marr. diss. 1981); one *s* one *d*; 3rd, 1986, Lucinda Enid, *d* of late Lt-Col Gerald Owen Whyte. *Educ:* University Coll. Sch., London. Partner, Thornton Baker & Co., Chartered Accountants, 1960–70; Sears plc: Dir, 1971–95; Dep. Chm., 1978–84; Jt Chm., 1984; Chief Exec., 1978–88; Chm., 1985–95; Chairman: Selfridges Ltd, 1985–93; Mallett plc, 1986–89; Hammerson plc, 1993–99 (Dir, 1990–99); W. and F. C. Bonham and Sons Ltd, 1996–2000; Fiske plc, 2000–04; Dep. Chm., Midland Bank plc, 1992–96 (Dir, 1986–96); Director: Asprey plc, 1980–93; Central Independent Television plc, 1983–85; Courtaulds plc, 1983–90; Imperial Group plc, 1984–86; HSBC Holdings plc, 1992–96. Mem. Bd, Financial Reporting Council, 1990–98. Chm., 1996 British Olympic Games Appeal, 1994–97. Hon. Vice Pres., Inst. of Marketing, 1987–94. Chm. Council, University Coll. Sch., 1987–96. *Recreation:* opera. *Address:* (office) Manor Barn, Fifield, Chipping Norton, Oxon OX7 6HF. *Died 6 May 2014.*

MAKGILL CRICHTON MAITLAND, Major John David; Lord-Lieutenant of Renfrewshire, 1980–94; *b* 10 Sept. 1925; *e s* of late Col Mark Edward Makgill Crichton Maitland, CVO, DSO, DL, JP, The Island House, Wilton, Salisbury, Wilts, and late Patience Irene Fleetwood Makgill Crichton Maitland (*née* Fuller); *m* 1st, 1954, Jean Patricia (*d* 1985), *d* of late Maj.-Gen. Sir Michael Creagh, KBE, MC, Pigeon Hill, Homington, Salisbury; one *s* one *d*; 2nd, 1987, Mary Ann Vere, *o d* of late Major Charles Herbert Harberton Eales, MC, and *widow* of Capt. James Quintin Penn Curzon. *Educ:* Eton. Served War, 1944–45, Grenadier Guards. Continued serving until 1957 (temp. Major, 1952; retd 1957), rank Captain (Hon. Major). Renfrew CC, 1961–75. DL Renfrewshire 1962, Vice-Lieutenant 1972–80. *Address:* Daluaine, Rhynie, Huntly, Aberdeenshire AB54 4WA. *T:* (01464) 861638. *Died 7 May 2015.*

MAKINSON, William, CBE 1977; former engineering management consultant; *b* 11 May 1915; *s* of Joshua Makinson and Martha (*née* Cunliffe); *m* 1952, Helen Elizabeth Parker; one *s* three *d*. *Educ:* Ashton-in-Makerfield Grammar Sch.; Manchester Univ. Asst Lecturer, Electronics, Manchester Univ., 1935–36; Education Officer, RAF Cranwell, 1936–39; RAE Farnborough, 1939–52; Hon. Squadron-Ldr, RAF, 1943–45; Superintendent, Blind Landing Experimental Unit, 1952–55; Defence Research Policy Staff, 1955–56; Managing Director, General Precision Systems Ltd, 1956–64; Group Jt Managing Director, Pullin, 1964–65; Mem., NRDC, 1967–80 (Man. Dir, 1974–80, Chief Exec., Engrg Dept, 1965–74). *Publications:* papers to Royal Aeronautical Society. *Recreation:* golf. *Address:* 2 Miller Place, West Common, Gerrards Cross, Bucks SL9 7QQ. *T:* (01753) 893219. *Died 19 April 2011.*

MALCOLM, Prof. Hon. David Kingsley, AC 1992; QC 1980; Professor of Law, University of Notre Dame, Australia, 2006–11, then Emeritus; Lieutenant Governor of Western Australia, 1990–2009; Judge of the Supreme Court of Fiji, since 2004; *b* Bunbury, WA, 6 May 1938; *s* of Colin Kingsley Malcolm and Jeanne (*née* Cowan); *m* 1st, 1965, Jennifer Birney (marr. diss. 1997); (one *s* decd); 2nd, 1997, Kaaren Brizland; one *d*. *Educ:* Guildford Grammar Sch.; Univ. of Western Australia (LLB 1st Cl. Hons); Wadham Coll., Oxford (Rhodes Schol.; BCL 1st Cl. Hons; Hon. Fellow, 2002). Partner, Muir Williams Nicholson, 1964–67; Counsel, Asst Gen. Counsel, Dep. Gen. Counsel, Asian Development Bank, Manila, 1967–70; Partner, Muir Williams Nicholson & Co., 1970–79; Independent Bar, 1980–88; Chief Justice, WA, 1988–2006. QC: WA, 1980; NSW, 1983. Member: Law Reform Commn of WA, 1966–67 and 1975–82 (Chm., 1976, 1979–82); Copyright Tribunal, 1978–86; Chm., Town Planning Appeal Tribunal, 1979–86. Mem., Council of Law Soc. of WA, 1966–67, 1985–88 (Vice-Pres., 1986–88); Pres., WA Bar Assoc., 1982–84; Vice Pres., Aust. Bar Assoc., 1984; Dep. Chm., 1990–95, Chm., 1995–2006, Judicial Sect., Law Assoc. for Asia and Pacific; Chm. WA Br., Internat. Commn of Jurists, 1994–2002; Chm., Conf. of Chief Justices of Asia and Pacific, Perth, 1991, Beijing, 1995, Manila, 1997, Seoul, 1999, Christchurch, 2001, Tokyo, 2003, Gold Coast, Qld, 2005. Mem. Council, Internat. Soc. for the Reform of Criminal Law, 1992–. Chairman, Advisory Board: Neuromuscular Res. Inst. of Aust., 1989–95; Crime Res. Centre, Univ. of WA, 1991–2006; Chm., Bd of Trustees, Francis Burt Legal Educn Centre and Law Mus., 1995–2006; Member: Council, Guildford Grammar Sch., 1971–98 (Dep. Chm., 1974–80; Chm., 1980–83); Senate, Univ. of WA, 1988–94; Constitutional Centenary Foundn Council, 1991–2000. Chm., Bd of Trustees, Special Airborne Services Resources Trust, 1996–. Patron, various community and sporting orgns. Hon. FRAPI 1984. Hon. Bencher, Lincoln's Inn, 1999. Paul Harris Fellow, Rotary Internat., 1997. Hon. PhD Law Western Australia, 2008. Citizen of the Year, WA, 2000. KCSJ 2006. *Publications:* articles in various learned jls, incl. Aust. Law Jl, Aust. Bar Rev., Aust. Business Law Rev., Univ. of WA Law Rev., LAWASIA Jl. *Recreations:* Rugby Union 'Soaks', windsurfing. *Address:* PO Box 538, Cottesloe, WA 6911, Australia. *Club:* Weld (Perth, WA). *Died 20 Oct. 2014.*

MALCOLM, Sir James (William Thomas Alexander), 12th Bt *cr* 1665 (NS), of Balbedie and Innertiel, Co. Fife; DL; *b* 15 May 1930; *s* of Lt-Col A. W. A. Malcolm, CVO (*d* 1989) and Hester Mary Malcolm (*née* Mann) (*d* 1992); *S* cousin, 1995; *m* 1955, Gillian Heather (*née* Humpherus); two *s* two *d*. *Educ:* Eton Coll.; RMA Sandhurst; Staff Coll., Camberley (psc). CO 1st Bn Welsh Guards, 1970–72; Regimental Col, Welsh Guards, 1972–76. Appeals Dir, British Heart Foundn, 1976–89. High Sheriff, 1991–92, DL 1991, Surrey. *Recreations:* golf, cricket. *Heir: s* Col Alexander James Elton Malcolm, OBE [*b* 30 Aug. 1956; *m* 1982, Virginia (*née* Coxon); two *s* one *d*]. *Address:* Grove House, Wrecclesham Hill, Wrecclesham, Farnham, Surrey GU10 4JN. *T:* (01252) 712167. *Clubs:* MCC; Royal St George's Golf (Sandwich); Berkshire Golf (Ascot). *Died 4 Sept. 2012.*

MALLET, Philip Louis Victor, CMG 1980; HM Diplomatic Service, retired; *b* 3 Feb. 1926; *e s* of late Sir Victor Mallet, GCMG, CVO and Christiana Jean, *d* of Herman A. Andreae; *m* 1953, Mary Moyle Grenfell Borlase; three *s*. *Educ:* Winchester; Balliol Coll., Oxford. Army Service, 1944–47. Entered HM Foreign (subseq. Diplomatic) Service, 1949; served in: FO, 1949; Baghdad, 1950–53; FO, 1953–56; Cyprus, 1956–58; Aden, 1958; Bonn, 1958–62; FO, 1962–64; Tunis, 1964–66; FCO, 1967–69; Khartoum, 1969–73; Stockholm, 1973–76; Head of Republic of Ireland Dept, FCO, 1977–78; High Comr in Guyana and non-resident Ambassador to Suriname, 1978–82. *Address:* Wittersham House, Wittersham, Kent TN30 7ED. *Club:* Brooks's. *Died 1 Dec. 2011.*

MALLETT, Conrad Richard, FRICS; Member, Lands Tribunal, 1980–92; *b* 11 May 1919; *s* of Captain Raymond Mallett, OBE, MN and Joyce Mallett (*née* Humble); *m* 1942, Elisabeth (Paulina) Williams; one *s* two *d*. *Educ:* Wellingborough Sch. Ordinary Airman to Lieut Comdr (A), RNVR, 1939–46 (despatches 1941). Partner, Montagu Evans and Son, Chartered Surveyors, London and Edinburgh, 1950–80. *Recreation:* cruising under sail. *Address:* 2 Hadley Hurst Cottages, Hadley Common, Barnet, Herts EN5 5QF. *T:* (020) 8449 5933. *Died 26 Feb. 2012.*

MANDELA, Nelson Rolihlahla, Hon. OM 1995; President of South Africa, 1994–99; President, African National Congress, 1991–97 (Deputy President, 1990–91); *b* 1918; *s* of Chief of Tembu tribe; *m* 1st, 1944, Evelyn Mase (marr. diss. 1957; she *d* 2004); one *d* (and two *s* one *d* decd); 2nd, 1958, Winnie Mandela (marr. diss. 1996); two *d*; 3rd, 1998, Graça (Hon. DBE 2007), *widow* of Samora Machel. *Educ:* Univ. Coll., Fort Hare; Univ. of Witwatersrand. Legal practice, Johannesburg, 1952. On trial for treason, 1956–61 (acquitted); sentenced to five years' imprisonment, 1962; tried for further charges, 1963–64, and sentenced to life imprisonment; released, 1990. Holds hon. degrees from Oxford, Cambridge and other UK univs. Hon. QC 2000. Jawaharlal Nehru Award, India, 1979; Simon Bolivar Prize, UNESCO, 1983; Sakharov Prize, 1988; (with F. W. De Klerk) Nobel Peace Prize, 1993. *Publications:* No Easy Walk to Freedom, 1965; Long Walk to Freedom, 1994; Conversations with Myself, 2010. *Address:* c/o President's Office, Private Bag X 1000, Cape Town 8000, South Africa. *Died 5 Dec. 2013.*

MANDUCA, John Alfred; High Commissioner for Malta in London, 1987–90; (concurrently) Ambassador to Norway, Sweden and Denmark, 1988–90, and to Ireland, 1990; *b* 14 Aug. 1927; *s* of Captain Philip dei Conti Manduca and Emma (*née* Pullicino); *m* 1954, Sylvia Parnis; two *s* two *d*. *Educ:* St Edward's Coll., Malta. Served 11 HAA Regt, Royal Malta Artillery (T), 1952–55 (commnd 1953). Joined Allied Malta Newspapers Ltd, 1945, Dep. Editor, 1953–62; Malta Correspondent, The Daily Telegraph and The Sunday Telegraph, 1946–62; joined Broadcasting Authority, Malta, 1962; BBC attachment, 1963; Chief Exec., Broadcasting Authority, Malta, 1963–68; Dir and Manager, Malta Television Service Ltd, 1968–71; Man. Dir, Rediffusion Gp of Cos in Malta, 1971–76; Chm., Tourist Projects Ltd, 1976–83; Dir Gen., Confedn of Private Enterprises, 1983–87; Dir, RTK Radio, 1991–93. Chairman: Malta Br., Inst. of Journalists, 1957, 1959 and 1961; Hotels and Catering Establishments Bd, 1970–71; Hon. Treas., Malta Br., Inst. of Dirs, 1975; Member: Tourist Bd, 1969–70; Broadcasting Authority, 1979–81. Trustee: Lady Strickland Trust for Malta, 1991–2005; Lady Strickland Trust for St Edward's Coll., 1997–2008. Chm. Bd of Governors, St Edward's Coll., 1995–98 (Mem., 1966–75, 1991–94). Editor, Treasures of Malta, 1994–2005. Order of Merit (Malta), 2010. *Publications:* Tourist Guide to Malta and Gozo, 1967, 7th edn 1980; Tourist Guide to Harbour Cruises, 1974, 3rd edn 1981; Connoisseur's Guide to City of Mdina, 1975, 3rd edn 1985; Gen. Ed., Malta Who's Who, 1987; (ed) Antique Maltese Clocks, 1992; (ed) Antique Furniture in Malta, 2002; Welcome Travel Guide to City of Mdina and Rabat, 2003; Welcome Travel Guide to Malta & Gozo—Sun, Sea & History, 2003; The Bonham-Carter Diaries: what the British Governor thought of Malta and the Maltese, 2004; The Bride of Mosta: a ballad by Francis Berry, 2005; The Three Cities—Vittoriosa, Senglea and Cospicua, 2005; City of Valletta and Floriana, 2006; The Flavour of the Mintoff Era: secret negotiations made public, 2008; The Pens That Felled the Mighty: 100 years of cartoons on Malta published in Britain, 2009. *Recreations:* collecting Melitensia, current affairs, gardening. *Address:* Beaulieu, Bastion Square, Citta Vecchia (Mdina) MDN 1150, Malta. *T:* 21454009, *Fax:* 21452608. *Clubs:* Royal Over-Seas League; Casino Maltese (Malta). *Died 6 Nov. 2014.*

MANGHAM, Maj.-Gen. William Desmond, CB 1978; Director, The Brewers' Society, 1980–90; *b* 29 Aug. 1924; *s* of late Lt-Col William Patrick Mangham and Margaret Mary Mangham (*née* Donnachie); *m* 1960, Susan, *d* of late Col Henry Brabazon Humfrey; two *s* two *d*. *Educ:* Ampleforth College. 2nd Lieut RA, 1943; served India, Malaya, 1945–48; BMRA 1st Div. Egypt, 1955; Staff, HQ Middle East, Cyprus, 1956–58; Instructor, Staff Coll., Camberley and Canada, 1962–65; OC 3rd Regt Royal Horse Artillery, 1966–68; Comdr RA 2nd Div., 1969–70;

Royal Coll. of Defence Studies, 1971; Chief of Staff, 1st British Corps, 1972–74; GOC 2nd Div., 1974–75; VQMG, MoD, 1976–79. Colonel Commandant: RA, 1979–88; RHA, 1983–88. Advisory Governor, Ampleforth Coll., 1990–98. Mem., Gordon Foundn, 1980–2003. *Recreations:* shooting, golf. *Address:* 12 The Grange, Enborne, Newbury, Berks RG14 6RJ. *Club:* Army and Navy. *Died 23 Nov. 2014.*

MANLEY, Brian William, CBE 1994; FREng, FInstP; FCGI; Managing Partner, Manley Moon Associates, 1988–2001; President, Institute of Physics, 1996–98; *b* 30 June 1929; *s* of late Gerald William Manley and Ellen Mary Manley (*née* Scudder); *m* 1954, Doris Winifred Dane; one *d* (one *s* decd). *Educ:* Shooters Hill Sch.; Woolwich Poly.; Imperial Coll. of Science and Technology (BSc, DIC); Harvard Business Sch. (SMP). FInstP 1967; FIEE 1974, Hon. FIET (Hon. FIEE 1999); FREng (FEng 1984); FCGI 1990. Served RAF, 1947–49. Represented England at swimming, 1947–50. Mullard Research Labs, 1954–68; Commercial Gen. Manager, Mullard Ltd, 1969–75; Managing Director: Pye Business Communications, 1975–77; TMC Ltd, 1977–82; Philips Data Systems, 1979–82; Gp Man. Dir, Philips Business Systems, 1980–83; Chm. and Man. Dir, MEL Defence Systems, 1983–86; Dir, Philips Electronic & Associated Industries Ltd, 1983–87; Chairman: AT&T Network Systems (UK) Ltd, 1986–89; Moondisks Ltd, 1994–2001. Mem. Bd, Teaching Co. Scheme, 1996–98. Pres., IEE, 1991–92; Sen. Vice Pres., Royal Acad. of Engrg, 1993–96. Centenary Fellow, Univ. of Greenwich, 1991. Sen. Pro-Chancellor and Chm. Council, Univ. of Sussex, 1995–2001. Trustee: RC dio. Arundel and Brighton, 1999–2009; Daphne Jackson Trust, 1999–2007. Hon. DSc: Loughborough, 1995; City, 1998; Sussex, 2002. KSG 2009. *Publications:* many papers on electronics, communications and engrg educn; some 30 patents in the field of electronics. *Recreations:* gardening, second-hand bookshops, searching for my Irish roots. *Address:* Hopkins Crank, Ditchling Common, Hassocks, Sussex BN6 8TP. *T:* (01444) 233734. *Club:* Athenæum. *Died 20 Dec. 2014.*

MANN, Eric John; Controller, Capital Taxes Office, 1978–81; *b* 18 Dec. 1921; *s* of Percival John Mann and Marguerite Mann; *m* 1960, Gwendolen Margaret Salter (*d* 2003); one *d* (one *s* decd). *Educ:* University Coll. Sch., Hampstead; Univ. of London (LLB). Entered Inland Revenue, 1946; Dep. Controller, Capital Taxes Office, 1974. *Publications:* (ed jtly) Green's Death Duties, 5th–7th edns, 1962–71. *Address:* Lawn Gate, Moccas, Herefordshire HR2 9LF. *Died 2 Nov. 2013.*

MANN, Dr Felix Bernard; medical practitioner; *b* 10 April 1931; *s* of Leo and Caroline Mann; *m* 1986, Ruth Csorba von Borsa. *Educ:* Shrewsbury House; Malvern Coll.; Christ's Coll., Cambridge; Westminster Hosp. MB, BChir, LMCC. Practised medicine or studied acupuncture in England, Canada, Switzerland, France, Germany, Austria and China. Founder, Medical Acupuncture Soc., 1959. *Publications:* Acupuncture; the ancient Chinese art of healing, 1962, 2nd edn 1971; The Treatment of Disease by Acupuncture, 1963; The Meridians of Acupuncture, 1964; Atlas of Acupuncture, 1966; Acupuncture: cure of many diseases, 1971; Scientific Aspects of Acupuncture, 1977; Textbook of Acupuncture, 1987; Reinventing Acupuncture, 1992, 2nd edn 2000; also edns in Italian, Spanish, Dutch, Finnish, Portuguese, German, Japanese and Swedish; contrib. various jls on acupuncture. *Recreation:* walking in the country and mountains. *Address:* Caynham Hill House, Caynham, Ludlow, Shropshire SY8 4JY. *T:* (01584) 878965. *Club:* Royal Society of Medicine. *Died 2 Oct. 2014.*

MANN, Rt Rev. Michael Ashley, KCVO 1989; Assistant Bishop, Diocese of Gloucester, since 1989; Dean of Windsor, 1976–89; Chairman, St George's House, 1976–89; Register, Order of the Garter, 1976–89; Domestic Chaplain to the Queen, 1976–89; Prelate, Order of St John, 1980–2000; *b* 25 May 1924; *s* of late H. G. Mann and F. M. Mann, Harrow; *m* 1st, 1949, Jill Joan Jacques (*d* 1990); one *d* (one *s* decd); 2nd, 1991, Elizabeth Pepys (*d* 2009). *Educ:* Harrow Sch.; RMC Sandhurst; Wells Theological Coll.; Graduate School of Business Admin, Harvard Univ. Served War of 1939–45: RMC, Sandhurst, 1942–43; 1st King's Dragoon Guards, 1943–46 (Middle East, Italy, Palestine). Colonial Admin. Service, Nigeria, 1946–55. Wells Theological Coll., 1955–57; Asst Curate, Wolborough, Newton Abbot, 1957–59; Vicar: Sparkwell, Plymouth, 1959–62; Christ Church, Port Harcourt, Nigeria, 1962–67; Dean, Port Harcourt Social and Industrial Mission; Home Secretary, The Missions to Seamen, 1967–69; Residentiary Canon, 1969–74, Vice-Dean, 1972–74, Norwich Cathedral; Adviser to Bp of Norwich on Industry, 1969–74; Bishop Suffragan of Dudley, 1974–76. Church Comr, 1977–85; Comr, Royal Hospital Chelsea, 1985–91. Dep. Chm., Imperial War Museum, 1990–96 (Trustee, 1980–96); Trustee: Army Museums Ogilby Trust, 1984–96; British Library, 1990–93; Military Records Soc., 1992–2003. Pres., Soc. of Friends of Nat. Army Mus., 1989– (Chm., 1989–97). Governor: Harrow Sch., 1976–91 (Chm., 1980–88); Atlantic Coll., 1987–91. Nat. Chaplain, Royal British Legion, 1991–2001. CCMI. GCStJ 1997 (KStJ 1990). *Publications:* A Windsor Correspondence, 1984; And They Rode On, 1984; A Particular Duty, 1986; China 1860, 1989; Some Windsor Sermons, 1989; Survival or Extinction, 1989; Regimental History of 1st Queen's Dragoon Guards, 1993; The Trucial Oman Scouts, 1994; The Veterans, 1997; Sermons for Soldiers, 1998. *Recreations:* military history, philately, ornithology. *Address:* The Cottage, Lower End Farm, Eastington, Northleach, Glos GL54 3PN. *T:* (01451) 860767. *Club:* Cavalry and Guards. *Died 31 Dec. 2011.*

MANNERS, Elizabeth Maude, TD 1962; MA; Headmistress of Felixstowe College, Suffolk, 1967–79; Member, East Anglia Regional Health Authority, 1982–85; *b* 20 July 1917; *d* of William George Manners and Anne Mary Manners (*née* Sced). *Educ:* Stockton-on-Tees Sec. Sch.; St Hild's Coll., Durham Univ. (BA 1938; MA 1941). Teacher of French at: Marton Grove Sch., Middlesbrough, 1939–40; Ramsey GS, IOM, 1940–42; Consett Sec. Sch., Durham, 1942–44; Yarm GS, Yorks, 1944–54; Deputy Head, Mexborough GS, Yorks, 1954–59; Head Mistress, Central GS for Girls, Manchester, 1959–67. Vice-President: Girl Guides Assoc., Co. Manchester, 1959–67; Suffolk Agric. Assoc., 1967–82. Member: Educn Cttee, Brit. Fedn of Univ. Women, 1966–68; Council, Bible Reading Fellowship, 1973–81; Cttee, E Br., RSA, 1974–90; Cttee, ISIS East, 1974–79. Mem. (C), Suffolk CC, 1977–85 (Member: Educn Cttee, 1977–85; Staff Joint and Personnel Cttees, 1981–85; Vice-Chm., Secondary Educn Cttee, 1981–85); Mem. (C), Felixstowe Town Council, 1991–95; Mem., Suffolk War Pensions Cttee, 1980–90. Sponsor, the Responsible Society, 1982–90. Chm. Governors, Felixstowe Deben High Sch., 1985–88. Enlisted ATS (TA), 1947; commissioned, 1949. FRSA 1972. Coronation Medal, 1953. *Publications:* The Vulnerable Generation, 1971; The Story of Felixstowe College, 1980. *Recreations:* narrow boating, choral singing, theatre, motoring, good food and wine. *Address:* 6 Graham Court, Hamilton Gardens, Felixstowe, Suffolk IP11 7ES. *Died 17 May 2012.*

MANNING, Prof. Susan Lindsay, PhD; FRSE; Grierson Professor of English Literature, since 1999, and Director, Institute for Advanced Studies in the Humanities, since 2005, University of Edinburgh; *b* 24 Dec. 1953; *d* of James Moncur Valentine and Honora Margaret Struan Valentine; *m* 1976, Howard John Manning; three *d*. *Educ:* Newnham Coll., Cambridge (BA 1976; PhD 1986). Res. Fellow, 1981–83, Coll. Lectr in English, 1984–99, Newnham Coll., Cambridge; Faculty of English, University of Cambridge: Univ. Asst Lectr, 1989–94; Univ. Lectr, 1994–99; Asst Chm., 1997–99. FRSE 2005; FRSA 2006. *Publications:* The Puritan-Provincial Vision: Scottish and American literature in the nineteenth century, 1990; Fragments of Union: making connections in Scottish and American writing, 2002; (ed jtly) The Edinburgh History of Scottish Literature, 3 vols, 2006; Transatlantic Literary Studies, 2007; (ed jtly) The Atlantic Enlightenment, 2008; edns of works by Walter Scott, Henry Mackenzie, Nathaniel Hawthorne, Washington Irving, Hector St John de Crèvecoeur. *Address:* Institute for Advanced Studies, University of Edinburgh, Hope Park Square, Edinburgh EH8 9NW. *T:* (0131) 650 4671. *E:* susan.manning@ed.ac.uk. *Died 15 Jan. 2013.*

MANSFIELD AND MANSFIELD, 8th Earl of, *cr* 1776 (and 9th Earl of, *cr* 1792) (GB); **William David Mungo James Murray;** JP, DL; Baron Scone, 1605; Viscount Stormont, 1621; Baron Balvaird, 1641; (Earl of Dunbar, Viscount Drumcairn, and Baron Halldykes in the Jacobite Peerage); Hereditary Keeper of Bruce's Castle of Lochmaben; First Crown Estate Commissioner, 1985–95; *b* 7 July 1930; *o s* of 7th Earl of Mansfield and Mansfield, and of Dorothea Helena (*d* 1985), *y d* of late Rt Hon. Sir Lancelot Carnegie, GCVO, KCMG; *S* father, 1971; *m* 1955, Pamela Joan, *o d* of W. N. Foster, CBE and Millicent Agnes Mary Foster, later Lady Cochrane of Cults; two *s* one *d*. *Educ:* Eton; Christ Church, Oxford. Served as Lieut with Scots Guards, Malayan campaign, 1949–50. Called to Bar, Inner Temple, 1958; Barrister, 1958–71. Mem., British Delegn to European Parlt, 1973–75; an opposition spokesman in the House of Lords, 1975–79; Minister of State: Scottish Office, 1979–83; NI Office, 1983–84. Mem., Tay Salmon Fisheries Bd, 1971–79. Director: General Accident, Fire and Life Assurance Corp. Ltd, 1972–79, 1985–98; American, then US Tracker, Trust, 1985–2002; Pinneys of Scotland, 1985–89; Ross Breeders Ltd, 1989–90. Ordinary Dir, Royal Highland and Agricl Soc., 1976–79. President: Fédn des Assocs de Chasse de l'Europe, 1977–79; Scottish Assoc. for Care and Resettlement of Offenders, 1974–79; Scottish Assoc. of Boys Clubs, 1976–79; Royal Scottish Country Dance Soc., 1977–2007; Chm., Scottish Branch, Historic Houses Assoc., 1976–79. Mem., Perth CC, 1971–75; Hon. Sheriff for Perthshire, 1974–; JP 1975, DL 1980, Perth and Kinross. Hon. Mem., RICS, 1994. *Publications:* articles on agriculture, land management and wine. *Heir: s* Viscount Stormont, *b* 17 Oct. 1956. *Address:* Logie House, Logiealmond, Perth PH1 3SD; 16 Thorburn House, Kinnerton Street, SW1X 8EX. *Clubs:* Pratt's, Turf. *Died 21 Oct. 2015.*

MANZIE, Sir (Andrew) Gordon, KCB 1987 (CB 1983); Second Permanent Secretary, Department of the Environment, and Chief Executive, Property Services Agency, 1984–90; *b* Edinburgh, 3 April 1930; *s* of late John Mair and Catherine Manzie; *m* 1955, Rosalind Clay (*d* 2008); one *s* one *d*. *Educ:* Royal High Sch. of Edinburgh; London Sch. of Economics and Political Science (BScEcon; Hon. Fellow, 2003). Joined Civil Service as Clerical Officer, Scottish Home Dept, 1947. National Service, RAF, 1949. Min. of Supply: Exec. Officer (Higher Exec. Officer, 1957). Private Sec. to Perm. Sec., Min. of Aviation, 1962; Sen. Exec. Officer, 1963; Principal, 1964; Sec. to Cttee of Inquiry into Civil Air Transport (Edwards Cttee), 1967; Asst Sec., Dept of Trade and Industry, on loan to Min. of Posts and Telecommunications, 1971; Dept of Industry, 1974; Under-Sec., Dir, Office for Scotland, Depts of Trade and Industry, 1975; Under Sec., Scottish Economic Planning Dept, 1975–79; Dir, Industrial Develt Unit, 1980–81, Dep. Sec., 1980–84, Dept of Industry (Dept of Trade and Industry, 1983–84). Chairman: Anglo Japanese Construction Ltd, 1990–95; Forthspan Ltd, 1993–97; Thistle Water, 1995–97; Yorkshire Link Ltd, 1996–97; Director: Altnacraig Shipping, 1990–96; Motherwell Bridge Hldgs, 1990–97; Trafalgar House Construction Hldgs Ltd, later Kvaerner Construction, 1991–97; Trafalgar House, later Kvaerner, Corporate Develt Ltd, 1991–97; Altnamara Shipping plc, 1994–2002; Mem., Adv. Bd, LEK Partnership, 1992–2000. Gov., LSE, 1994–2005, then Emeritus (Mem., Standing Cttee and Council, 1995–2001). Trustee, Stort Trust, 1990–2001; Pres., Bishop's Stortford Caledonian Soc., 1987–93. CCMI (CBIM 1987); Hon. FCIOB 1990. *Recreations:* reading, watching Rugby football. *Address:* 28 Manor Links, Bishop's Stortford, Herts CM23 5RA. *T:* (01279) 651960. *Club:* Caledonian. *Died 24 Sept. 2014.*

MAOATE, Sir (Tuamure) Terepai, KBE 2007; Deputy Prime Minister, Cook Islands, 2005–09; *b* Rarotonga, Cook Is, 1 Sept. 1934; *m* 1959, Marito Mapu; five *s* one *d*. *Educ:* Fiji Sch. of Medicine (Med. Officer 1954); Auckland Univ. (Dip. Obstetrics 1973); Amsterdam Univ. (MA Public Health 1976). Gen. surgeon and Dir, Clin. Services, 1976–82. MP, Cook Is, 1983–2010; Minister of Health and Agric., 1983–89; Dep. Prime Minister, 1985–89; Leader of Opposition, 1998–99; Prime Minister, 1999–2002; Leader of Opposition, 2002–03; Dep. Prime Minister, 2003–04; Leader of Opposition, 2004–05. Pres., Cook Is Golden Oldies Rugby Assoc. Patron: Ngatangiia/Matavera Sports Assoc.; Ngatangiia Cook Is Christian Ch Youth. *Recreations:* Rugby, cricket, fishing, reading, tennis, table tennis, sailing. *Died 9 July 2012.*

MAPLES, Baron *cr* 2010 (Life Peer), of Stratford-upon-Avon in the County of Warwckshire; **John Cradock Maples;** *b* 22 April 1943; *s* of late Thomas Cradock Maples and Hazel Mary Maples; *m* 1986, Jane Corbin; one *s* one *d*. *Educ:* Marlborough Coll., Wiltshire; Downing Coll., Cambridge; Harvard Business Sch., USA. Called to the Bar, Inner Temple, 1965. Chm. and Chief Exec., Saatchi & Saatchi Govt Communications Worldwide, 1992–96; Chm., Rowland Sallingbury Casey, 1994–96. MP (C) W Lewisham, 1983–92; contested (C) W Lewisham, 1992; MP (C) Stratford-on-Avon, 1997–2010. PPS to Financial Sec. to HM Treasury, 1987–90; Econ. Sec. to HM Treasury, 1990–92; Opposition front bench spokesman on health, 1997–98, on defence, 1998–99, on foreign affairs, 1999–2000; a Dep. Chm., Cons. Party, 1994–95 and 2006–10. *Recreations:* sailing, ski-ing. *Address:* House of Lords, SW1A 0PW. *Died 9 June 2012.*

MARGERISON, Thomas Alan; author, journalist and broadcaster on scientific subjects; *b* 13 Nov. 1923; *s* of late Ernest Alan Margerison and Isabel McKenzie; *m* 1950, Pamela Alice Tilbrook (*d* 2009); two *s*; partner, Marjorie Shiona Douglas Wallace, CBE; one *d*. *Educ:* Huntingdon Grammar Sch.; Hymers Coll., Hull; King's Sch., Macclesfield; Sheffield University. Research Physicist, 1949; film script writer, Film Producers Guild, 1950; Scientific Editor, Butterworths sci. pubns, Ed. Research, 1951–56; Man. Editor, Heywood Pubns and National Trade Press, 1956. First Scientific Editor, The New Scientist, 1956–61; Science Corresp., Sunday Times, 1961; Dep. Editor, Sunday Times Magazine, 1962; Man. Dir, Thomson Technical Developments Ltd, 1964; Dep. Man. Dir, 1967–69, Chief Exec., 1969–71, London Weekend Television; Dir, 1966, Chm., 1971–75, Computer Technology Ltd. Formerly Dir, Nuclear Electricity Information Gp. Consultant, British Nuclear Forum, 1989. Chm., Communications Cttee, UK Nat. Commn for UNESCO. Worked for many years with Tonight team on BBC. Responsible for applying computers to evening newspapers in Reading and Hemel Hempstead. *Publications:* articles and television scripts, scientific papers; (ed) popular science books. *Address:* 26 Bisham Gardens, N6 6DD. *Died 25 Feb. 2014.*

MARGESSON, 2nd Viscount *cr* 1942, of Rugby; **Francis Vere Hampden Margesson;** *b* 17 April 1922; *o s* of 1st Viscount Margesson, PC, MC, and Frances H. Leggett (*d* 1977), New York; *S* father, 1965; *m* 1958, Helena, *d* of late Heikki Backstrom, Finland; one *s* three *d*. *Educ:* Eton; Trinity Coll., Oxford. Served War of 1939–45, as Ordinary Seaman and Sub-Lt, RNVR. A Director of Thames & Hudson Publications, Inc., New York, 1949–53. ADC to Governor of the Bahamas, 1956; Information Officer, British Consulate-General, NY, 1964–70. *Heir: s* Major the Hon. Richard Francis David Margesson, late Coldstream Guards [*b* 25 Dec. 1960; *m* 1st, 1990, Wendy Maree, *d* of James Hazelton; one *d*; 2nd, 2003, Rosa Ita Escalona (*née* Rowlands)]. *Address:* 63 The Hills, Port Ewen, New York, NY 12466, USA. *Died 11 Nov. 2014.*

MARKL, Prof. Hubert, Dr rer. nat.; Professor of Biology, University of Konstanz, 1974–2003, then Emeritus; *b* 17 Aug. 1938; *m* Eva-Maria Markl; one *s*. *Educ:* Univ. of Munich (Dr rer. nat. 1962). Scientific Assistant: Zoological Inst., Univ. of Munich, 1962–63; Zoological Inst., Univ. of Frankfurt, 1963–67; Res. Associate, Biological Labs, Harvard Univ. and Rockefeller Univ., 1965–66; Associate Prof., Zoological Inst., Univ. of Frankfurt, 1967–68; Prof. of Zoology and Dir, Zoological Inst., Technical Univ. of Darmstadt, 1968–74. Heinrich-Hertz Vis. Prof., Univ. of Karlsruhe, 1994–95. Vice Pres., Alexander von Humboldt Foundn, 1986–91; President: Deutsche Forschungsgemeinschaft, 1986–91 (Mem. Senate, 1974–77; Vice Pres., 1977–83); Ges. Deutscher Naturforscher und Ärzte, 1993–94; Berlin-Brandenburg Acad. of Scis, 1993–95; Max Planck Ges., 1996–2002. Member: Deutsche Akad. der Naturforscher Leopoldina, 1985; Berlin-Brandenburg Acad. of Scis, 1993; MAE 1988;

FAAAS 1981; Corresponding Member: Bayer. Akad. der Wissenschaften, 1985; Nordrhein-Westfäl. Akad. der Wissenschaften, 1987; Akad. der Wissenschaften zu Göttingen, 1996; Foreign Member: Amer. Philos. Soc., 2000; Royal Soc., 2002; Hon. Member: Ges. Deutscher Chemiker, 1997; Max Planck Ges., 2002; Foreign Hon. Member: Amer. Acad. Arts and Scis, 1985; Indian Acad. Sci., 1991. Hon. Dr rer. nat.: Saarland, 1992; Dublin, 1997; Potsdam, 1999; Hon. DHL Jewish Theol Seminary, NY, 2000; Hon. DPhil: Tel Aviv, 2001; Hebrew Univ. of Jerusalem, 2001; Weizman Inst. Sci., 2002. Bayerische Verdienstorden, 2001. *Publications:* Biophysik, 1977 (trans. English 1983); Evolution of Social Behaviour, 1980; Natur und Geschichte, 1983; Neuroethology and Behavioral Physiology, 1983; Evolution, Genetik und menschliches Verhalten, 1986; Natur als Kulturaufgabe, 1986; Wissenschaft: zur Rede gestellt, 1989; Wissenschaft im Widerstreit, 1990; Die Fortschrittsdroge, 1992; Wissenschaft gegen Zukunftsangst, 1998; Schöner neuer Mensch?, 2002. *Address:* Universität Konstanz, Fachbereich Biologie, 78457 Konstanz, Germany. *T:* (7531) 882725. *E:* hubert.markl@uni-konstanz.de. *Died 8 Jan. 2015.*

MARKS, Bernard Montague, OBE 1984; Life President, Alfred Marks Bureau Group of Companies, 1985 (Managing Director and Chairman, 1946–84); *b* 11 Oct. 1923; *s* of Alfred and Elizabeth Marks; *m* 1956, Norma Renton (*d* 1990); one *s* (and one *s* decd). *Educ:* Highgate Public Sch.; Royal Coll. of Science. Served Somerset LI, seconded to RWAFF (Staff Capt.), 1944–46. Chm. or Vice-Chm., Fedn of Personnel Services of GB, 1965–79, 1983–84. Mem., Equal Opportunities Commn, 1984–86. *Publications:* Once Upon A Typewriter, 1974. *Recreations:* bridge, golf, theatre. *Address:* 5 Monarch Point, Lensbury Avenue, Imperial Wharf, SW6 2HW. *Clubs:* St George's Hill Golf, Coombe Hill Golf. *Died 4 Feb. 2013.*

MARKS, Dennis Michael; broadcaster, lecturer, writer and film-maker, since 1997; *b* 2 July 1948; *s* of Samuel Marks and Kitty Ostrovsky; *m* 1st, 1972, Deborah Cranston (marr. diss. 1992); one *s* one *d*; 2nd, 1992, Sally Hilary Groves, MBE. *Educ:* Haberdashers' Aske's Sch., Elstree; Trinity Coll., Cambridge (1st Cl. Hons English Tripos). British Broadcasting Corporation, 1969–81: TV researcher, 1969–71; Dir, TV music and arts, 1972–78; Dir/Producer, Bristol Arts Unit, 1978–81; Dir/Producer, 3rd Eye Prodns, 1981–85; BBC TV: Editor, music progs, 1985–88; Asst Head of Music and Arts Dept, 1988–91; Hd of Music Progs, 1991–93; Gen. Dir, ENO, 1993–97; Man. Dir, Directors Cut Ltd, 1999–2003. Pres., Internat. Music Centre, Vienna, 1989–92. For Celebrating Gershwin, (with Humphrey Burton) Internat. Emmy, 1988; for Bartok, Bluebeard's Castle, (with Leslie Megahey) Italia Prize, 1989. *Publications:* Great Railway Journeys, 1981; Repercussions, 1985; Wandering Jew: the search for Joseph Roth, 2011. *Recreations:* cooking, travel. *Address:* 50 Walkerscroft Mead, West Dulwich, SE21 8LJ. *Died 2 April 2015.*

MARKS, Frederick Charles, OBE 1983; Commissioner for Local Administration in Scotland, 1994–2000; *b* 3 Dec. 1934; *s* of James Marks and Elizabeth (*née* McInnes); *m* 1959, Agnes Miller Bruce; two *s* one *d* (and one *s* decd). *Educ:* Wishaw High Sch.; Univ. of Glasgow (MA Hons; LLB). Admitted solicitor, 1960. Legal Asst, Burgh of Motherwell and Wishaw, 1957–61; Solicitor, Burgh of Kirkcaldy, 1961–63; Depute Town Clerk, City and Royal Burgh of Dunfermline, 1963–68; Town Clerk, Burgh of Hamilton, 1968–75; Chief Exec., Motherwell Dist, 1974–83; Gen. Manager, Scottish Special Housing Assoc., 1983–89; Dep. Chm., Local Govt Boundary Commn for Scotland, 1989–94. Vice-Chairman: Queen Margaret Hosp. NHS Trust, Dunfermline, 1994–99; Fife Acute Hosps NHS Trust, 1999–2001. *Address:* 5 Queen Margaret Fauld, Dunfermline, Fife KY12 0UY. *Died 28 June 2012.*

MARLBOROUGH, 11th Duke of, *cr* 1702; **John George Vanderbilt Henry Spencer-Churchill;** DL; Baron Spencer, 1603; Earl of Sunderland, 1643; Baron Churchill, 1685; Earl of Marlborough, 1689; Marquis of Blandford, 1702; Prince of the Holy Roman Empire; Prince of Mindelheim in Suabia; late Captain Life Guards; *b* 13 April 1926; *s* of 10th Duke of Marlborough and Hon. Alexandra Mary Hilda Cadogan, CBE (*d* 1961), *d* of late Henry Arthur, Viscount Chelsea; *S* father, 1972; *m* 1st, 1951, Susan Mary (marr. diss. 1960; she *m* 1962, Alan Cyril Heber-Percy), *d* of Michael Hornby; one *s* one *d* (and one *s* decd); 2nd, 1961, Mrs Athina Livanos (marr. diss. 1971; she *d* 1974), *d* of late Stavros G. Livanos, Paris; 3rd, 1972, Rosita Douglas (marr. diss. 2008); one *s* one *d* (and one *s* decd); 4th, 2008, Lily Mahtani. *Educ:* Eton. Lieut Life Guards, 1946; Captain, 1953; resigned commission, 1953. Chairman: Martini & Rossi, 1979–96; London Paperweights Ltd, 1974–88. Member: Council, Winston Churchill Meml Trust, 1966–; Trusthouse Charitable Trust (formerly Forte Council), 1994–2013. Chm., Badminton Conservation Trust, 1997–2001; Mem., Woodland Cttee, Countryside Foundn for Educn, 2001–. President: Thames and Chilterns Tourist Board, 1974–85; Oxfordshire Branch, CLA, 1978–; Oxfordshire Assoc. for Young People, 1972–2009; Oxford Br., SSAFA, 1977–2009; Sports Aid Foundn (Southern), 1981–; Oxford United Football Club, 1964–2003; Oxfordsailability; Dep. Pres., Nat. Assoc. of Boys' Clubs, 1987–. Patron: Oxfordshire Br., BRCS; Heart UK; Katharine House Hospice; Soldiers for Oxfordshire; Oxford Homeless Medical Fund; Vice Patron, Nat. Assoc. of Almshouses. CC 1961–64, Oxfordshire; JP 1962; DL 1974. *Heir:* *s* Marquess of Blandford, *b* 24 Nov. 1955. *Address:* Blenheim Palace, Woodstock, Oxon OX20 1PX. *Clubs:* Portland, White's. *Died 16 Oct. 2014.*

MARLER, Dennis Ralph Greville, FRICS; Chairman, Falcon Property Trust, 1988–95; *b* 15 June 1927; *s* of late Greville Sidney Marler, JP, FRICS and Ivy Victoria (*née* Boyle); *m* 1952, Angela (*née* Boundy); one *s* one *d*. *Educ:* Marlborough. Served Royal Lincolnshire Regt, Palestine, 1945–48; articled pupil, Knight, Frank & Rutley, 1948–50; Partner, Marler & Marler, 1950–83; Jt Man. Dir, 1966–76, Man. Dir, 1976–85, Chm., 1985–90, Capital & Counties plc; Chairman: Knightsbridge Green Hotel Ltd, 1966–2007; Pension Fund Property Unit Trust, 1987–89. Member: NEDO Working Party for Wood Report (Public Client and Construction Industry), 1974–75; Adv. Bd, Dept of Construction Management, Univ. of Reading, 1981–88; DHSS Nat. Property Adv. Gp, 1984–91; FCO *ad hoc* Adv. Panel on Diplomatic Estate, 1985–90; RIBA Art for Architecture Panel, 1990–93. A Vice-Pres., TCPA, 1983–97; Pres., British Property Fedn, 1983–84. A Vice-Pres., RNIB, 1994–99. Mem. Ct of Assistants, Merchant Taylors' Co., 1984–. CCMI; FRSA. *Recreations:* reading, golf, gardening. *Address:* Windrush, Cocklawelva, Rock, Wadebridge, Cornwall PL27 6LW. *T:* (01208) 862141. *Clubs:* Royal Thames Yacht, Roehampton; St Enodoc Golf. *Died 12 Nov. 2014.*

MARMION, Prof. Barrie Patrick, AO 1994; Visiting Professor, Department of Pathology, University of Adelaide (Adelaide Medical School), 1985–2005; *b* Alverstoke, 19 May 1920; *s* of Joseph P. and Melita Hannah Marmion, Alverstoke, Hants; *m* 1953, Diana Ray Newling, *d* of Dr P. Ray Newling, Adelaide, SA; one *d*. *Educ:* University Coll. and University Coll. Hosp., London. MD London 1947, DSc London 1963; FRCPath 1962, FRCPA 1964, FRCPE 1970, FRACP 1984; FRSE 1976. House Surg., UCH, 1942; Bacteriologist, Public Health Laboratory Service, 1943–62; Rockefeller Trav. Fellow, at Walter and Eliza Hall Inst., Melbourne, 1951–52; Foundation Prof., Microbiology, Monash Univ., Melbourne, Australia, 1962–68; Robert Irvine Prof. of Bacteriology, Univ. of Edinburgh, 1968–78; Dir, Div. of Virology, Inst. of Med. and Vet. Science, Adelaide, 1978–85. Vis. Fellow, Clare Hall, Cambridge, 2004 (Life Mem., 2005). Hon. Life Member: Australian Soc. Infectious Diseases, 1985 (Pres., 1985); Australian Soc. Microbiol., 1987 (Pres., 1987); Australian Vet. Assoc., 1988; American Soc. for Rickettsiology, 2003. DUniv Adelaide, 1990. Distinguished Fellow Award (Gold Medal), RCPath Australia, 1986. *Publications:* (ed) Mackie and McCartney's Medical Microbiology, 12th edn 1975 to 14th edn 1996; numerous papers on bacteriology (Qfever and Mycoplasmas) and virology. *Recreation:* enjoying classical music. *Address:* 14 Birksgate Drive, Urrbrae, Adelaide, SA 5064, Australia. *Died 12 July 2014.*

MAROWITZ, Charles; Founding Artistic Director: Malibu Stage Company, since 1990; Texas Stage Company, since 1994; Director and Dramaturge, California Repertory Theatre, Long Beach, since 1996; *b* 26 Jan. 1932; Austrian mother, Russian father; *m* 1982, Jane Elizabeth Allsop; one *s*. *Educ:* Seward Park High Sch.; University Coll. London. Dir, In-Stage Experimental Theatre, 1958; Asst Dir, Royal Shakespeare Co., 1963–65; Artistic Director: Traverse Theatre, 1963–64; Open Space Theatre London, 1968–81; Open Space Theatre of Los Angeles, 1982; Associate Dir, LA Theater Center, 1984–89. Drama Critic: Encore Magazine, 1956–63; Plays and Players, 1958–74; The Village Voice, 1955–; The NY Times, 1966–; West Coast critic: Theatre Week magazine, 1990–97; In-Theater magazine, 1997–; Official Drama critic, Jewish Jl, 1998–; columnist: LA View, 1994–; SWANS.com, 2005–. *West End* Director: Loot, Criterion, 1967; The Bellow Plays, Fortune, 1966; Fortune and Men's Eyes, Comedy, 1969; productions *abroad:* Woyzeck, 1965, The Shrew, 1979, Nat. Theatre, Bergen; Hedda, 1978, Enemy of the People, 1979, Nat. Theatre, Oslo; Measure for Measure, Oslo New Theatre, 1981; The Father, Trondheim, 1981; Ah Sweet Mystery of Life, Seattle, 1981; A Midsummer Night's Dream, Odense, Denmark, 1983; Tartuffe, Molde, Norway, 1985; Marat/Sade, Rutgers, 1993; Merry Wives of Windsor, Dallas Shakespeare Fest., 1993; Bashville in Love, Texas, 1995; Death of Ophelia, Copenhagen, 2006; productions in *Los Angeles:* Artaud at Rodez, 1982; Sherlock's Last Case, 1984; The Petrified Forest, 1985; The Fair Penitent, 1986; The Shrew, 1986; Importance of Being Earnest, 1987; What the Butler Saw, 1988; Wilde West, 1989; Variations on Measure for Measure, 1990; A MacBeth, 1991; Murdering Marlow, 2002; Silent Partners, 2006. Order of the Purple Sash, 1969. *Publications:* The Method as Means, 1960; The Marowitz Hamlet, 1967; A Macbeth, 1970; Confessions of a Counterfeit Critic, 1973; Open Space Plays, 1974; Measure for Measure, 1975; The Shrew, 1975; Artaud at Rodez, 1976; Variations on The Merchant of Venice; The Act of Being, 1977; The Marowitz Shakespeare, 1978; New Theatre Voices of the 50s and 60s, 1981; Sex Wars, 1982; Prospero's Staff, 1986; Potboilers (collection of plays), 1986; Recycling Shakespeare, 1991; Burnt Bridges, 1991; Directing The Action, 1992; (trans.) Cyrano de Bergerac, 1995; Alarums and Excursions, 1996; The Other Way, 1997; Boulevard Comedies, 1999; Stage Fright, 2000; Stagedust (collection of reviews), 2001; Roar of the Canon (collection of Shakespeare criticism), 2001; The Other Chekhov: biography of Michael Chekhov, 2004; Murdering Marlowe, 2004; Silent Partners; How to Stage a Play, Make a Fortune, Win a Tony and Become a Theatrical Icon, 2006; Sounds of Music: early recording artists, 2008; Lost Silents, 2010; Losers. *Recreation:* balling. *Address:* 3058 Sequit Drive, Malibu, CA 90265, USA. *Died 2 May 2014.*

MÁRQUEZ, Gabriel García; Colombian novelist; *b* 6 March 1928; *m* 1958, Mercedes García Márquez; two *s*. *Educ:* Univ. of Bogotá; Univ. of Cartagena. Corresp., El Espectador, Rome and Paris; formed Cuban Press Agency, Bogotá; worked for Prensa Latina, Cuba, later as Dep. Head, NY office, 1961; lived in Venezuela, Cuba, USA, Spain, Mexico; returned to Colombia, 1982; divides time between Mexico and Colombia. Rómulo Gallegos Prize, 1972; Nobel Prize for Literature, 1982. *Publications:* La hojarasca, 1955 (Leaf Storm, 1973); El coronel no tiene quien le escriba, 1961 (No One Writes to the Colonel, 1971); La mala hora, 1962 (In Evil Hour, 1980); Los funerales de la Mamá Grande, 1962; Cien años de soledad, 1967 (One Hundred Years of Solitude, 1970); La increíble y triste historia de la cándida Eréndira, 1972 (Innocent Erendira and other stories, 1979); El otoño del patriarca, 1975 (The Autumn of the Patriarch, 1977); Crónica de una muerte anunciada, 1981 (Chronicle of a Death Foretold, 1982; filmed, 1987); (with P. Mendoza) El olor de la guayaba, 1982 (Fragrance of Guava, ed T. Nairn, 1983); El amor en los tiempos del cólera, 1984 (Love in the Time of Cholera, 1988; filmed, 2008); Amores difíciles, 1989 (Of Love and Other Demons, 1995); El general en su laberinto, 1989 (The General in his Labyrinth, 1991); Collected Stories, 1991; Doce cuentos peregrinos, 1992 (Strange Pilgrims, 1993); Memoria de mis putas tristes, 2004 (Memories of My Melancholy Whores, 2005); *non-fiction:* Relato de un náufrago, 1970 (The Story of a Shipwrecked Sailor, 1986); La aventura de Miguel Littín, clandestina en Chile (Clandestine in Chile: adventures of Miguel Littín), 1986; Noticia de un secuestro, 1996 (News of a Kidnapping, 1997); Vivir para contarla (autobiog.), 2002 (Living to Tell the Tale, 2003). *Address:* c/o Agencia Literaria Carmen Balcells, Avenida Diagonal 580, Barcelona 08021, Spain. *Died 17 April 2014.*

MARRACK, Rear-Adm. Philip Reginald, CB 1979; CEng, FIMechE, FIMarEST; Director, Dockyard Production and Support, 1977–81; *b* 16 Nov. 1922; *s* of Captain Philip Marrack, RN and Annie Kathleen Marrack (*née* Proud); *m* 1954, Pauline Mary (*née* Haag) (decd); two *d*. *Educ:* Eltham Coll.; Plymouth Coll.; RNC Dartmouth; RN Engineering Coll., Manadon. War service at sea, HM Ships Orion and Argus, 1944–45; Advanced Engineering Course, RNC Greenwich, 1945–47; HM Submarines Templar and Token, 1947–50; served in Frigate Torquay, Aircraft Carriers Glory and Hermes, and MoD; Captain 1965; Commanded Admiralty Reactor Test Estab., Dounreay, 1967–70; CSO (Mat.) on Staff of Flag Officer Submarines, and Asst Dir (Nuclear), Dockyard Dept, 1970–74; Rear-Adm. 1974; Dir, Naval Ship Production, 1974–77. *Recreations:* fly fishing, gardening. *Died 29 May 2014.*

MARRIOTT, Arthur Leslie; QC 1997; barrister; a Deputy High Court Judge, since 1997; a Recorder, since 1998; *b* 30 March 1943; *s* of Arthur Leonard Marriott and Helen Gracie Marriott (*née* Patterson); *m*; two *d*. *Educ:* Selhurst Grammar Sch. for Boys, Croydon; Gymnasium Christian Ernestinum, Bayreuth, Germany; Coll. of Law. FCIArb 1990; Chartered Arbitrator, 2001. Admitted Solicitor, England and Wales, 1966, Hong Kong, 1976; with Wilmer, Cutler & Pickering, 1988–97; Debevoise & Plimpton, 1997–2005; Dewey & LeBoeuf (formerly LeBoeuf Lamb Greene & MacRae) LLP, 2005–10. Hon. Bencher, Gray's Inn, 2001. *Publications:* (with Henry Brown) Alternative Dispute Resolution: principles and practice, 1993, 2nd edn 1999. *Recreations:* fishing, music. *Address:* 4–5 Gray's Inn Square, WC1R 5AH. *Clubs:* Athenæum, Royal Automobile. *Died 4 Sept. 2015.*

MARRIOTT, Sir Hugh Cavendish S.; *see* Smith-Marriott.

MARRIS, Prof. Robin Lapthorn; Professor of Economics, 1981–86, and Head of Department of Economics, 1983–86, Birkbeck College, University of London, then Professor Emeritus; *b* 31 March 1924; *s* of Eric Denyer Marris, CB, and late Phyllis, *d* of T. H. F. Lapthorn, JP; *m* 1st, 1949, Marion Ellinger; 2nd, 1954, Jane Evelina Burney Ayres; one *s* two *d*; 3rd, 1972, Anne Fairclough Mansfield; one *d*. *Educ:* Bedales Sch.; King's Coll., Cambridge (BA 1946; ScD 1968). Asst Principal, HM Treasury, 1947–50; UN, Geneva, 1950–52; Fellow of King's Coll., Cambridge, 1951–76; Lectr, 1951–72, Reader, 1972–76, in Econs, Univ. of Cambridge; Prof. 1976–81 and Chm., 1976–79, Dept of Economics, Univ. of Maryland. Visiting Professor: Univ. of California, Berkeley, 1961; Harvard, 1967; Trento Univ., Italy, 1989–91. Dir, World Economy Div., Min. of Overseas Develt, 1964–66. Consultant: Home Office, 2001–05; DfES, 2001–05; Mem., Econs Adv. Panel, Home Office, 2005–. Mem., Vis. Cttee, Open Univ., 1982–. *Publications:* Economic Arithmetic, 1958; The Economic Theory of Managerial Capitalism, 1964; The Economics of Capital Utilisation, 1964; (with Adrian Wood) The Corporate Economy, 1971; The Corporate Society, 1974; The Theory and Future of the Corporate Economy and Society, 1979; The Higher Education Crisis, 1987; Reconstructing Keynesian Economics with Imperfect Competition, 1991; Economics, Bounded Rationality and the Cognitive Revolution, 1992; How to Save the Underclass, 1996; Managerial Capitalism in Retrospect, 1998; Ending Poverty, 1999; contrib. Econ. Jl, Rev. Econ. Studies, Economica, Jl Manchester Stat. Soc., Jl Royal Stat. Soc., Amer. Econ. Rev., Qly Jl of Econs, Jl of Economic Literature, etc. *Recreations:* cooking, scuba diving, sailing. *Address:* Lingard House, Chiswick Mall, W4 2PJ. *E:* robinmarris@btinternet.com. *Died 25 Sept. 2012.*

MARSDEN, Sir Simon (Neville Llewelyn), 4th Bt *cr* 1924, of Grimsby, co. Lincoln; fine art photographer; author; *b* 1 Dec. 1948; *s* of Sir John Denton Marsden, 2nd Bt and Hope (later Dowager Lady Marsden), *yr d* of late G. E. Llewelyn; *S* brother, 1997; *m* 1st, 1970, Catherine Thérèsa Windsor-Lewis (marr. diss. 1978); 2nd, 1984,

Caroline Stanton; one *s* one *d.* *Educ:* Ampleforth Coll., Yorks; Sorbonne Univ., Paris. Photographer, 1969–; group exhibns, 1972–, include: London, NY, Paris, European and USA tour; one-man exhibns, 1975–, include: London, NY, Dublin, Paris, Brussels, Tokyo; work in collections including: Arts Council of GB, V & A Mus., Saatchi Collection, London; Bibliothèque Nationale, Paris; J. Paul Getty Mus., Malibu, Cleveland Mus. of Art, USA. Radio and TV appearances, 1986–, incl. Ghosthunter (docu-drama), Granada TV, 1992. Arts Council of GB Awards, 1975 and 1976. *Publications:* In Ruins: the once great houses of Ireland, 1980; The Haunted Realm: ghosts, witches and other strange tales, 1986; Visions of Poe, 1988; Phantoms of the Isles: further tales from the haunted realm, 1990; The Journal of a Ghosthunter: in search of the undead from Ireland to Transylvania, 1994; Beyond the Wall: the lost world of East Germany, 1999; Venice, City of Haunting Dreams, 2001; The Twilight Hour: Celtic visions from the past, 2003; This Spectred Isle: a journey through haunted England, 2005; Ghosthunter: a journey through haunted France, 2006; Memento Mori: churches and churchyards of England, 2007. *Recreations:* sport, walking, historic buildings, reading. *Heir:* *s* Tadgh Orlando Denton Marsden, *b* 25 Dec. 1990. *Address:* The Presbytery, Hainton, Market Rasen, Lincs LN8 6LR. *T:* (01507) 313646. *Club:* Chelsea Arts. *Died 22 Jan. 2012.*

MARSH, Baron *cr* 1981 (Life Peer), of Mannington in the County of Wiltshire; **Richard William Marsh,** Kt 1976; PC 1966; FZS; FCIT; Chairman: Mannington Management Services, 1989–99; Laurentian Financial Group plc, 1986–95; *b* 14 March 1928; *s* of William Marsh, Belvedere, Kent; *m* 1st, 1950, Evelyn Mary (marr. diss. 1973), *d* of Frederick Andrews, Southampton; two *s*; 2nd, 1973, Caroline Dutton (*d* 1975); 3rd, 1979, Hon. Felicity, *d* of Baron McFadzean of Kelvinside. *Educ:* Jennings Sch., Swindon; Woolwich Polytechnic; Ruskin Coll., Oxford. Health Services Officer, National Union of Public Employees, 1951–59; Mem., Clerical and Administrative Whitley Council for Health Service, 1953–59; MP (Lab) Greenwich, Oct. 1959–April 1971; promoted Offices Act 1961; Member: Select Cttee Estimates, 1961; Chm. Interdepartmental Cttee to Co-ordinate Govt Policy on Industrial Training, 1964; Parly Sec., Min. of Labour, 1964–65; Joint Parly Sec., Min. of Technology, 1965–66; Minister of Power, 1966–68; Minister of Transport, 1968–69. Chairman: British Railways Bd, 1971–76; Newspaper Publishers' Assoc., 1976–90; British Iron and Steel Consumers' Council, 1977–82; Allied Investments Ltd, 1977–81; Member: NEDC, 1971; Freight Integration Council, 1971; Council, CBI, 1970 Chairman: Allied Medical Group, 1977–81; Vivat Hldgs PLC, 1982–88; TV-am, 1983–84 (Dep. Chm., 1980–83); Lopex PLC, 1986–97 (Dir, 1985–97); China & Eastern Investments Trust, Hong Kong, 1990–98 (Dir, 1987–98); Gartmore British Income & Growth Trust, 1994–; Dep. Chm., United Medical Enterprises Ltd, 1978–81; Director: Imperial Life of Canada UK, 1983–97; Imperial Life Assurance Co. of Canada, 1983–97; Charles Church Developments, 1987–97; Laurentian Group Corp. (Montreal), 1990–94; Advisor: Nissan Motor Co., 1981–; Fujitec, 1982–. Pres., Council ECSC, 1968. Governor: British Transport Staff Coll. (Chm.); London Business Sch. FCMI; FInstD; FInstM. *Publications:* Off the Rails (autobiog.), 1978. *Address:* House of Lords, SW1A 0PW. *Died 29 July 2011.*

MARSH, Rear-Adm. Geoffrey Gordon Ward, CB 1985; OBE 1969; Project Manager, NATO Frigate 90, Hamburg, 1988–90; *b* Hertford, 4 Feb. 1929; *m* 1953, Mary Millington-Limb (*d* 2008); one *s* one *d.* *Educ:* St Albans Sch.; Queens' Coll., Cambridge. Britannia Royal Naval Coll., 1947; jssc; served on HM Ships: Indefatigable; Victorious; Carron; Norfolk; Girdle Ness; Bristol; involved in develt of Sea Dart missile; Hd of Propulsion Machinery Control, Ship Dept; Asst Dir (Surface Warfare), Naval Op. Req.; Dir, Weapons Co-ordination and Acceptance (Naval), MoD, 1978–80; i/c HMS Thunderer, 1980–82; ACNS (Op. Req.), 1982–84; Dep. Controller, Warships Equipment, MoD (Navy), 1984–87; Chief Naval Engr Officer, 1985–87. *Address:* c/o Naval Secretary, Fleet Headquarters, Whale Island, Portsmouth PO2 8BY. *Died 24 Oct. 2014.*

MARSH, Prof. Leonard George, OBE 1992; MEd; DPhil; Principal, Bishop Grosseteste College, 1974–96; *b* 23 Oct. 1930; third *c* of late Ernest Arthur Marsh and Anne Eliza (*née* Bean); *m* 1953, Ann Margaret Gilbert; one *s* one *d.* *Educ:* Ashford (Kent) Grammar Sch.; Borough Road Coll., London Inst. of Educn (London Univ. Teachers' Certif. and Academic Dip.); Leicester Univ. (MEd); DPhil York, 1988. Lectr in Educn and Mathematics, St Paul's Coll., Cheltenham, 1959–61; Lectr, 1961–63, Sen. Lectr, 1963–65, Principal Lectr and Head of Postgraduate Primary Educn Dept, 1965–74, Goldsmiths' Coll., London. Hon. Prof., Hull Univ., 1987–96. Visiting Lectr, Bank Street Coll., New York, and Virginia Commonwealth Univ.; former Consultant, OECD, Portugal; Educnl Consultant, Teacher Trng Proj., Botswana, 1981; Dir, Sindh Pakistan Primary Educn Develt Prog., 1992–96; Specialist tour to India for British Council; Mem., SCAA, 1993–97. Dir (non-exec.), A & C Black plc, 1994–2000. Member: Gen. Adv. Council, IBA, 1977–82; N Lincolnshire AHA, 1984–90; Chm., Nat. Assoc. for Primary Educn, 1981–83. Gov., Canterbury Christ Church Coll., 1997–2001. FRSA. Hon. FCP (FCP 1989). Hon. DLitt Hull, 1996. *Publications:* Let's Explore Mathematics, Books 1–4, 1964–67; Children Explore Mathematics, 1967, 3rd edn 1969; Exploring Shapes and Numbers, 1968, 2nd edn 1970; Exploring the Metric System, 1969, 2nd edn 1969; Exploring the Metric World, 1970; Approach to Mathematics, 1970; Alongside the Child in the Primary School, 1970; Let's Discover Mathematics, Books 1–5, 1971–72; Being A Teacher, 1973; Helping your Child with Maths—a parents' guide, 1980; The Guinness Mathematics Book, 1980; The Guinness Book for Young Scientists, 1982. *Recreations:* photography, theatre, walking, films. *Address:* Broomfields, 16 The Meadow, Chislehurst, Kent BR7 6AA. *T:* (020) 8467 6311. *Club:* Athenæum. *Died 3 Oct. 2014.*

MARSHALL OF KNIGHTSBRIDGE, Baron *cr* 1998 (Life Peer), of Knightsbridge in the City of Westminster; **Colin Marsh Marshall,** Kt 1987; Chairman, Pirelli UK Ltd, since 2003; non-executive Director, Nomura Holdings, Inc., since 2010 (Chairman: Nomura International, 2004–11; Nomura Europe Holdings plc, 2009–11); *b* 16 Nov. 1933; *s* of Marsh Edward Leslie and Florence Mary Marshall; *m* 1958, Janet Winifred (*née* Cracknell); one *d.* *Educ:* University College Sch., Hampstead. Progressively, cadet purser to Dep. Purser, OSNC, 1951–58; Hertz Corp., 1958–64: management trainee, Chicago and Toronto, 1958–59; Gen. Man., Mexico, Mexico City, 1959–60; Asst to Pres., New York, 1960; Gen. Manager: UK London, 1961–62; UK Netherlands and Belgium, London, 1962–64; Avis Inc., 1964–79: Reg. Man./Vice-Pres., Europe, London, 1964–66; Vice-Pres. and Gen. Man., Europe and ME, London, 1966–69; Vice-Pres. and Gen. Man., International, London, 1969–71; Exec. Vice-Pres. and Chief Operating Officer, New York, 1971–75; Pres. and Chief Operating Officer, New York, 1975–76; Pres. and Chief Exec. Officer, New York, 1976–79; Co-Chm., 1979–81; Exec. Vice-Pres., Norton Simon Inc., New York, 1979–81; Dir and Dep. Chief Exec., Sears Holdings plc, 1981–83; British Airways, 1983–2004: Chief Exec., 1983–95; Dep. Chm., 1989–93; Chm., 1993–2004. Chairman: Inchcape plc, 1996–2000; Siebe, subseq. BTR Siebe, then Invensys, plc, 1998–2003; Dep. Chm., British Telecommunications plc, 1996–2001. Board Member: HSBC Holdings, 1992–2004; US Air, 1993–96; Qantas, 1993–96 and 2000–01; NY Stock Exchange, 1994–2000; Royal Automobile Club Ltd, 1998–99. Sen. Advr, FSA, 2010–. Chm., Visit Britain, 2005–06. Dep. Chm., Financial Reporting Council, 1996–99. Chm. Trustees, Conference Bd, NY, 2000–04. Member: Council, Inst. of Dirs, 1982–2006; Chartered Inst. of Marketing, 1989–96 (Pres., 1989–94); Marketing Council, 1995–2004 (Chm., 1995–96); Vice Pres., Advertising Assoc., 1988–; Pres., 1996–98, Dep. Pres., 1998–99, CBI. Vice Chm., World Travel & Tourism Council, 1990–99; Pres., Commonwealth Youth Exchange Council, 1998–. Chm., London Development Partnership, 1998–2000. Chm., RIIA (Chatham House), 1999–2003. President: Knightsbridge Assoc., 2003–; Westminster City Academy, 2007–. Mem., Hong Kong Assoc., 1996–2000. Trustee, RAF Museum, 1991–2000. Chm. of Govs, Birkbeck Coll.,

London Univ., 2003–10. Hon. DHL Suffolk, Boston, USA, 1984; Hon. LLD: Bath, 1989; American Univ. in London, Richmond Coll., 1993; Lancaster, 1997; Hon. DSc: Buckingham, 1990; Cranfield, 1997; Hon. DCL Durham, 1997; Hon. LittD Westminster, 1999; Hon. Dr Business London Guildhall, 2000. *Recreation:* tennis. *Address:* Nomura International plc, One Angel Lane, EC4R 3AB. *T:* (020) 7102 2912. *E:* blanche.murphy@nomura.com. *Clubs:* Royal Automobile, All England Lawn Tennis and Croquet, Queen's (Chm., 2007–10). *Died 5 July 2012.*

MARSHALL, Prof. Christopher John, DPhil; FRS 1995; Director of Research, since 2008, and Head, Division of Cancer Biology, since 2011, Institute of Cancer Research; *b* 19 Jan. 1949; *s* of Lillian and James Marshall; *m* 1st, 1973, Vivien Roma Morrall (marr. diss. 1997); two *s* one *d*; 2nd, 2005, Lesley Ford. *Educ:* King Henry VIII Sch., Coventry; Churchill Coll., Cambridge (MA); Lincoln Coll., Oxford (DPhil). Postdoctoral Fellow: ICRF, 1973–78; Sidney Farber Cancer Inst., Boston, USA, 1978–80; Institute of Cancer Research: Research Scientist, 1980–; Dir, CRUK (formerly CRC) Centre for Cell and Molecular Biol., 1980–2008; Dir, CRUK Tumour Cell Signalling Unit, 2008–13. Gibb Life Fellow, CRC (later Cancer Res. UK), 1992. Choh Hao Li Meml Lectr, Univ. of Calif, Berkeley, 2002. Mem., EMBO, 1993; Founder FMedSci 1998; Fellow, Eur. Acad. of Cancer Scis, 2010. Novartis Prize and Medal, Biochemical Soc., 1999; Buchanan Medal, Royal Soc., 2008; Lifetime Achievement in Cancer Res. Award, CRUK, 2011. *Publications:* contribs to learned jls. *Recreation:* cycling. *Address:* Chester Beatty Laboratories, Institute of Cancer Research, 237 Fulham Road, SW3 6JB. *T:* (020) 7352 9772. *Club:* Norwood Paragon Cycling. *Died 8 Aug. 2015.*

MARSHALL, Prof. (Ian) Howard, PhD; Professor of New Testament Exegesis, University of Aberdeen, 1979–99, then Professor Emeritus; *b* 12 Jan. 1934; *s* of Ernest Ewart Marshall and Ethel Marshall (*née* Curran); *m* 1st, 1961, Joyce Elizabeth Proudfoot (*d* 1996); one *s* three *d*; 2nd, 2011, Maureen Wing Sheung Yeung. *Educ:* Univ. of Aberdeen (MA 1955; BD 1959; PhD 1963); Fitzwilliam Coll., Cambridge (BA 1959); Univ. of Göttingen. Asst Tutor, Didsbury Coll., Bristol, 1960–62; pastoral work, Darlington, 1962–64; University of Aberdeen: Lectr, 1964–70; Sen. Lectr, 1970–77; Reader, 1977–79. Hon. DD Asbury, Kentucky, 1996. *Publications:* Eschatology and the Parables, 1963, 2nd edn 1978; Pocket Guide to Christian Beliefs, 1963, 3rd edn 1978, repr. 1989; The Work of Christ, 1969, 2nd edn 1994; Kept by the Power of God, 1969, 3rd edn 1995; Luke: historian and theologian, 1970, 3rd edn 1989; The Origins of New Testament Christology, 1976; (ed) New Testament Interpretation, 1977, 2nd edn 1979; I Believe in the Historical Jesus, 1977; The Gospel of Luke, 1978; The Epistles of John, 1978; Acts, 1980; Last Supper and Lord's Supper, 1980; Biblical Inspiration, 1982, 2nd edn 1995; 1 and 2 Thessalonians, 1983; (ed) Christian Experience in Theology and Life, 1988; Jesus the Saviour: studies in New Testament theology, 1990; 1 Peter, 1991; The Acts of the Apostles, 1992; The Epistle to the Philippians, 1992; (with K. P. Donfried) The Theology of the Shorter Pauline Letters, 1993; (ed with D. Peterson) Witness to the Gospel: the theology of the Book of Acts, 1998; (with P. H. Towner) A Critical and Exegetical Commentary on the Pastoral Epistles, 1999; (contrib.) Exploring the New Testament: Vol. 2: The Letters and Revelation, 2002; (ed) Moulton and Geden: Concordance to the Greek New Testament, 6th edn 2002; New Testament Theology: many witnesses, one Gospel, 2004; (jtly) Beyond the Bible: moving from scripture to theology, 2004; Aspects of the Atonement, 2007; A Concise New Testament Theology, 2008. *Recreations:* hill walking, gardening, music, reading. *Died 12 Dec. 2015.*

MARSHALL, James; Assistant Auditor General, National Audit Office, 1993–2002; *b* 16 March 1944; *s* of James Marshall and late Winifred Marshall (*née* Hopkins); *m* 1980, Patricia Anne Smallbone; one *s*. *Educ:* Sacred Heart Coll., Droitwich; King Charles I Grammar Sch., Kidderminster; Jesus Coll., Cambridge (MA). Joined Inland Revenue, 1966: Asst Principal, 1966–69; Private Sec. to Chm. of Bd, 1969–70; Principal, 1970–74; First Sec., Budget and Fiscal, UK Repn to EC, Brussels, 1974–77; First Asst, UK Mem. of Court, European Court of Auditors, 1977–80; Asst Sec., Inland Revenue, 1980–88; Consultant, CJA Mgt Recruitment, 1988–89; Dir, Nat. Audit Office, 1989–93. *Recreations:* reading, walking, Medieval churches, entertaining, music. *Address:* 56 Melody Road, SW18 2QF. *T:* (020) 8870 3308. *Club:* Oxford and Cambridge. *Died 25 May 2014.*

MARSHALL, Prof. John, CBE 1990; FRCP, FRCPE; Professor of Clinical Neurology in the University of London, 1971–87, then Emeritus; *b* 16 April 1922; *s* of James Herbert and Bertha Marshall; *m* 1946, Margaret Eileen Hughes (*d* 2010); two *s* three *d*. *Educ:* Univ. of Manchester (MB ChB 1946, MD 1951, DSc 1981). FRCPE 1957, FRCP 1966; DPM 1952. Sen. Registrar, Manchester Royal Infirmary, 1947–49; Lt-Col RAMC, 1949–51; MRC research worker, 1951–53; Sen. Lectr in Neurology, Univ. of Edinburgh, 1954–56; Reader in Clinical Neurology, Univ. of London, 1956–71. Chm., Disability Living (formerly Attendance) Allowance Bd, 1982–93. Knight of the Order of St Sylvester (Holy See), 1962, KCSG 1986 (KSG 1964). Auenbrugger Medal, Univ. of Graz, 1983. *Publications:* The Management of Cerebrovascular Disease, 1965, 3rd edn 1976; The Infertile Period, Principles and Practice, 1963, 2nd rev. edn 1969; Love One Another, 1995. *Recreations:* gardening, walking. *Address:* Flat 15, 85 Worple Road, SW19 4JH. *T:* (020) 8247 3513. *Died 21 Feb. 2014.*

MARSHALL, John Alexander, CB 1982; General Secretary, Distressed Gentlefolk's Aid Association, 1982–89; *b* 2 Sept. 1922; *s* of James Alexander Marshall and Mena Dorothy Marshall; *m* 1947, Pauline Mary (*née* Taylor); six *s*. *Educ:* LCC elem. sch.; Hackney Downs School. Paymaster General's Office, 1939; FO, 1943; HM Treasury, 1947: Principal, 1953; Asst Sec., 1963; Under-Sec., 1972; Cabinet Office, 1974–77; Northern Ireland Office, 1977–82, Dep. Sec., 1979–82. *Recreations:* literature, music. *Address:* 48 Long Lane, Ickenham, Middx UB10 8TA. *T:* (01895) 672020. *Died 29 March 2013.*

MARSHALL, His Honour Laurence Arthur; a Circuit Judge, 1991–2003; *b* 1 June 1931; *s* of Reginald Herbert Marshall and Nora Marshall; *m* 1st, 1959, Marian Charlotte Mowlem Burt (marr. diss. 1979); two *s* two *d*; 2nd, 1980, Gloria Elizabeth Kindersley (*d* 2007). *Educ:* Ardingly Coll.; King's Coll., London (LLB). Called to the Bar, Gray's Inn, 1956. *Recreation:* building. *Address:* The Old Post Office, Stourton, Shipston on Stour, Warwicks CV36 5HG. *T:* (01608) 686363. *Club:* Royal London Yacht. *Died 31 May 2011.*

MARSHALL, Prof. Sir (Oshley) Roy, Kt 1974; CBE 1968; High Commissioner for Barbados in the United Kingdom, 1989–91; Vice-Chancellor, Hull University, 1979–85, Emeritus Professor since 1985; *b* 21 Oct. 1920; *s* of Fitz Roy and Corene Carmelita Marshall; *m* 1st, 1945, Eirwen Lloyd (*d* 1998); one *s* three *d*; 2nd, 2000, Hon. Marie Elizabeth Bourne Hollands, CHB. *Educ:* Harrison Coll., Barbados, WI; Pembroke Coll., Cambridge (Barbados Scholar, 1938; BA 1945, MA 1948); University Coll., London (PhD 1948; Fellow, 1985). Barrister-at-Law, Inner Temple, 1947. University Coll., London: Asst Lecturer, 1946–48; Lecturer, 1948–56; Sub-Dean, Faculty of Law, 1949–56; Prof. of Law and Head of Dept of Law, Univ. of Sheffield, 1956–69, Vis. Prof. in Faculty of Law, 1969–80; on secondment to University of Ife, Ibadan, Nigeria, as Prof. of Law and Dean of the Faculty of Law, 1963–65; Vice-Chancellor, Univ. of West Indies, 1969–74; Sec.-Gen., Cttee of Vice-Chancellors and Principals, 1974–79. Chairman: Commonwealth Educn Liaison Cttee, 1974–81; Cttee on Commonwealth Legal Co-operation, 1975; Commonwealth Standing Cttee on Student Mobility, 1982–94; Council for Educn in the Commonwealth, 1985–91; Review Cttee on Cave Hill Campus, Univ. of WI, 1986; Constitutional Commn on the Turks and Caicos Islands, 1986; Barbados National Commn on Law and Order, 2002–; Member: Police Complaints Bd, 1977–81; Council, RPMS, 1976–83; Council, ACU, 1979–85; Management Cttee, Universities Superannuation Scheme Ltd, 1980–85; UGC for Univ. of S Pacific, 1987; Chm., Bd of Governors, Hymers Coll., Hull, 1985–89; Vice-Chm., Governing Body of Commonwealth

Inst., 1980–81; Mem., Bd of Governors, Commonwealth of Learning, 1988–91; Trustee, Commonwealth Foundn, 1981. Hon. LLD: Sheffield, 1972; West Indies, 1976; Hull, 1986; Hon. DLitt CNAA, 1992. *Publications:* The Assignment of Choses in Action, 1950; A Casebook on Trusts (with J. A. Nathan), 1967; Theobald on Wills, 12th edn, 1963. *Recreation:* racing and cricket. *Address:* Evanston, Nelson Road, Navy Gardens, Christ Church BB 14031, Barbados, West Indies. *T:* 426 2474. *Died 2 Feb. 2015.*

MARSHALL, Peter David, CMG 2002; OBE 1990; Consultant, Forensic Seismology and Arms Control Research Programmes, Atomic Weapons Establishment, Blacknest, since 2002; *b* 13 June 1937; *s* of Jonathan Marshall and Grace Florence Marshall (*née* Mayes); *m* 1957, Pamela Margaret Rose Champion (*d* 2012); one *d. Educ:* Dagenham Co. High Sch.; Durham Univ. (MSc Geophysics). Min. of Supply, AERE Harwell, 1953; AWE Foulness, UKAEA, 1955; with Forensic Seismology Gp, AWE Blacknest, UKAEA, 1963–72; MoD, 1972–92 (PSO, 1980; SPSO, 1992); Vis. Scientist, Lawrence Livermore Nat. Lab., Calif., 1975–76; Tech. Advr to UK Delegn, Trilateral Test Ban Negotiations, 1977–81; Dep. Hd, 1982–2001, Hd, 2001–02, Forensic Seismology Gp, AWE Blacknest; Dist. Scientist, AWE, 2000. UK Delegate, UN Conf. of Disarmament (CD) Gp of Scientific Experts, Geneva, 1976–93; Technical Advisor: on verification techniques to UK CD Delegn, 1971–96; UK CD Delegn to negotiate a Comprehensive Nuclear Test Ban Treaty, and Chm., Gp of Scientific Experts, during negotiations, 1994–96. Consultant, CTBTO, Vienna, 1997–. Hon. Treas., 2006–07, Chm., 2007–, Oxford Transplant Foundn. *Publications:* contrib. numerous peer-reviewed papers on technical issues related to solving problems of detecting, locating and identifying nuclear test explosions. *Recreations:* reading, cryptic crosswords, philately, gardening. *Address:* 2 Appletree Close, Newbury, Berks RG14 6HR. *E:* petermpam@aol.com. *Died 5 Oct. 2012.*

MARSHALL, Sir Roy; *see* Marshall, Sir Oshley R.

MARTIN, (Arthur) Bryan, CB 1987; Member of Health and Safety Executive, 1985–88, and Director, Resources and Planning Division, 1977–88; Head of UK Delegation, and Alternate Chairman, Channel Tunnel Safety Authority, 1989–92; *b* 16 July 1928; *s* of Frederick Arthur Martin and Edith Maud Martin; *m* 1953, Dyllis Naomi Eirne Johnstone-Hogg; two *s. Educ:* Bristol Grammar Sch.; Royal Mil. Coll. of Science (BSc). Joined Army, REME, 1948; commnd, 1948; Lt-Col, 1967–69; served in UK, Germany, Malaya (despatches, 1959), Cyprus and Aden; joined Civil Service (Dept of Employment), 1969, as direct entrant principal; Asst Sec., Factory Inspectorate, 1973; Under Sec., HSE, 1977. Director: Docklands Light Railway, 1993–98; Angel Train Contracts, 1996–99. *Died 30 Dec. 2014.*

MARTIN, Christopher Jon, CB 2014; CVO 2015; Principal Private Secretary to the Prime Minister and Director General, Prime Minister's Office, since 2012; *b* West Bromwich, 15 May 1973; *s* of Peter and Gwenda Martin; *m* 2005, Christina Scott (marr. diss.); *m* 2015, Zoe Conway. *Educ:* Univ. of Bristol (BSc Hons Pols, BSc Physics 1996). Private Sec. to Financial Sec. to HM Treasury, 1999–2002; Sen. Manager, London Bor. of Hackney, 2002; HM Treasury: Asst Sec., Gen. Expenditure Policy, 2003–04; Hd, Productivity Team, 2004–06; Press Sec. to the Chancellor of the Exchequer and Head of Communications, 2006–07; Dir, Public Services and Envmt, 2007–10; interim Dir, Corporate Services, 2009; Dir, Nat. Security Secretariat, Cabinet Office, 2011. *Recreations:* cooking, running, entertaining. *Address:* 10 Downing Street, SW1A 2AA. *Club:* Arsenal Football. *Died 25 Nov. 2015.*

MARTIN, Vice-Adm. Sir John (Edward Ludgate), KCB 1972 (CB 1968); DSC 1943; FNI; Lieutenant-Governor and Commander-in-Chief of Guernsey, 1974–80; *b* 10 May 1918; *s* of late Surgeon Rear-Admiral W. L. Martin, OBE, FRCS and Elsie Mary Martin (*née* Catford); *m* 1942, Rosemary Ann Deck; two *s* two *d. Educ:* RNC, Dartmouth. Sub Lt and Lt, HMS Pelican, 1938–41; 1st Lt, HMS Antelope, 1942; navigation course, 1942; Navigation Officer, 13th Minesweeping Flotilla, Mediterranean, 1943–44, including invasions N Africa, Sicily, Pantelleria, Salerno; RNAS Yeovilton, 1944; Navigation Officer: HMS Manxman and HMS Bermuda, 1944–46; HMS Nelson, 1947; HMS Victorious, 1948; Staff Coll., 1949; Navigation Officer, HMS Devonshire, 1950–51; Dirg Staff, Staff Coll., 1952–54; Jt Services Planning Staff, Far East, 1954–55; Exec. Off., HMS Superb, 1956–57; Jt Services Staff Coll., 1958; Dep. Dir Manpower Planning and Complementing Div., Admty, 1959–61; Sen. Naval Off., W Indies, 1961–62; Comdr Brit. Forces Caribbean Area, 1962–63; Capt. Britannia Royal Naval Coll., Dartmouth, 1963–66; Flag Officer, Middle East, 1966–67; Comdr, British Forces Gulf, 1967–68 (despatches); Dir-Gen., Naval Personal Services and Training, 1968–70; Dep. Supreme Allied Comdr, Atlantic, 1970–72. Comdr 1951; Captain 1957; Rear-Adm. 1966; Vice-Adm. 1970. Pres., Nautical Inst., 1975–78. *Recreations:* fishing, shooting, beagling (Jt Master Britannia Beagles, 1963–66), sailing. *Clubs:* Army and Navy; Royal Naval Sailing Association; Royal Yacht Squadron. *Died 31 May 2011.*

MARTIN, Peter; *see* Martin, R. P.

MARTIN, Peter Anthony; Financial Adviser to Association of Police Authorities, 2005–10; *b* 8 Dec. 1946; *s* of Frank and Renie Martin; *m* 1970, Jennifer Margaret (*née* Shaw); one *s* four *d. Educ:* Nottingham High Sch.; St John's Coll., Oxford (BA Hons); Univ. of Kent at Canterbury (MA Management). CIPFA 1973. Accountant, Derbyshire CC, 1969–76; Asst County Treasurer, W Sussex CC, 1976–81; Kent County Council: Dep. County Treas., 1981–86; County Treas., later Finance Dir, 1986–97; Dir, Peter Martin Consultancy Ltd, 1997–2001. Treasurer: Kent Police Authy, 1995–2000; Metropolitan Police Authy, 2000–05. Pres., Police Authy Treasurers Soc., 2004–05. Local Authy Assocs' Revenue Support Grant Principal Negotiator, 1991–94. Pres., Soc. of Co. Treasurers, 1996–97. *Recreations:* cricket, reading, family. *Address:* Woodside, Hadlow Park, Hadlow, Tonbridge, Kent TN11 0HZ. *Died 19 June 2013.*

MARTIN, Richard Graham; Vice-Chairman, Allied-Lyons, 1988–92 (Director, 1981–92; Chief Executive, 1989–91); *b* 4 Oct. 1932; *s* of Horace Frederick Martin, MC and Phyllis Jeanette Martin; *m* 1958, Elizabeth Savage; two *s* one *d. Educ:* Sherborne School; St Thomas's Hosp. Med. Sch., 1953–54. 2nd Lt, RA, 1951–52. Joined Friary Holroyd & Healy's Brewery, 1955, Dir, 1959; Dir, Friary Meux, 1963–66; Managing Dir, Ind Coope (East Anglia), 1966–69; Director: Joshua Tetley & Son, 1969–72; Allied Breweries, 1972–92; Chief Exec., Joshua Tetley & Son, 1972–78; Vice-Chm., Joshua Tetley & Son and Tetley Walker, 1978–79; Chm., Ind Coope, 1979–85; Man. Dir, 1985–86, Chm. and Chief Exec., 1986–88, Allied Breweries; Chairman: J. Lyons & Co. Ltd, 1989–91; Hiram Walker, 1991 (Dir, 1989–91); Allied-Lyons, later Allied-Domecq, Pensions and Trustee Services, 1992–95; non-exec. Dir, Gibbs Mew plc, 1995–98. Chm., Brewers' Soc., 1991–92 (Vice-Chm., 1989–91). Pres., Shire Horse Soc., 1981–82. *Recreations:* travel, music, food. *Died 6 Oct. 2015.*

MARTIN, (Roy) Peter, MBE 1970; author and critic; *b* 5 Jan. 1931; *s* of Walter Martin and Annie Mabel Martin; *m* 1st, 1951, Marjorie Peacock (marr. diss. 1960); 2nd, Joan Drumwright (marr. diss. 1977); two *s*; 3rd, 1978, Catherine Sydee. *Educ:* Highbury Grammar Sch.; Univ. of London (BA 1953, MA 1956); Univ. of Tübingen. Nat. Service (RAF Educn Branch), 1949–51. Worked as local govt officer, schoolteacher and tutor in adult educn; then as British Council officer, 1960–83; service in Indonesia, Hungary (Cultural Attaché) and Japan (Cultural Counsellor). *Publications:* (with Joan Martin) Japanese Cooking, 1970; The Chrysanthemum Throne, 1997; (as James Melville): The Wages of Zen, 1979; The Chrysanthemum Chain, 1980; A Sort of Samurai, 1981; The Ninth Netsuke, 1982; Sayonara, Sweet Amaryllis, 1983; Death of a Daimyo, 1984; The Death Ceremony, 1985; Go Gently Gaijin, 1986; The Imperial Way, 1986; Kimono For A Corpse, 1987; The Reluctant Ronin, 1988; A Haiku for Hanae, 1989; A Tarnished Phoenix, 1990; The Bogus Buddha, 1990; The Body Wore Brocade, 1992; Diplomatic Baggage, 1994; The Reluctant Spy, 1995; (as Hampton Charles): Miss Seeton At The Helm, 1990; Miss

Seeton, By Appointment, 1990; Advantage Miss Seeton, 1990. *Recreations:* music, books. *Address:* c/o Curtis Brown, 28/29 Haymarket, SW1Y 4SP. *Clubs:* Travellers, Detection. *Died 2014.*

MARTIN-JENKINS, Christopher Dennis Alexander, MBE 2009; cricket writer, The Times; BBC cricket commentator, since 1972; *b* 20 Jan. 1945; *s* of late Dennis Frederick Martin-Jenkins, TD and Dr Rosemary Clare Martin-Jenkins (*née* Walker); *m* 1971, Judith Oswald Hayman; two *s* one *d*. *Educ:* Marlborough; Fitzwilliam Coll., Cambridge (BA (Modern Hist.); MA). Dep. Editor, The Cricketer, 1967–70; sports broadcaster, 1970–73, Cricket Correspondent, 1973–80, 1984–91, BBC; Editor, 1981–88, Editl Dir, 1988–91, The Cricketer International; Cricket Corresp., Daily Telegraph, 1991–99; Chief Cricket Corresp., The Times, 1999–2008. President: Rugby Fives Assoc., 1993–95; W Sussex Assoc. of Umpires and Scorers, 1995–; Cricket Soc., 1998–2008. Chm., Arundel Castle Cricket Foundn, 2012–. Trustee, Brian Johnston Meml Trust, 1995– (Chm., 1998–2000). *Publications:* Testing Time, 1974; Assault on the Ashes, 1975; MCC in India, 1977; The Jubilee Tests and the Packer Revolution, 1977; In Defence of the Ashes, 1979; Cricket Contest, 1980; The Complete Who's Who of Test Cricketers, 1980; The Wisden Book of County Cricket, 1981; Bedside Cricket, 1981; Twenty Years On: Cricket's years of change, 1984; Cricket: a way of life, 1984; (ed) Cricketer Book of Cricket Eccentrics, 1985; (ed) Seasons Past, 1986; (ed jtly) Quick Singles, 1986; Grand Slam, 1987; Cricket Characters, 1987; Sketches of a Season, 1989; Ball by Ball, 1990; (jtly) Summers Will Never Be the Same, 1994; The Spirit of Cricket (anthology), 1994; World Cricketers, 1996; (jtly) An Australian Summer, 1999; Men For All Seasons, 2001; The Top 100 Cricketers of All Time, 2009; CMJ: a cricketing life (autobiog.), 2012. *Recreations:* cricket, golf, music, theatre, walking. *E:* cmartinjenkins@googlemail.com. *Clubs:* East India, MCC (Pres., 2010–11); I Zingari, Free Foresters, Arabs, Marlborough Blues, Cranleigh Cricket, Albury Cricket, Rudgwick Cricket, Horsham Cricket; West Sussex Golf, Royal St George's Golf. *Died 1 Jan. 2013.*

MARTINI, His Eminence Cardinal Carlo Maria, SJ; Archbishop of Milan, 1980–2002, then Emeritus; *b* 15 Feb. 1927; *s* of Leonardo and Olga Maggia. *Educ:* Pontifical Gregorian Univ. (DTheol); Pontifical Biblical Inst. (Doctorate in holy scripture). Ordained priest, 1952; Rector, Pontifical Biblical Inst., 1969–78; Rector, Gregorian Univ., 1978–79. Cardinal 1983. Pres., Consilium Conferentiarum Episcopalium Europae, 1987–93. *Died 31 Aug. 2012.*

MASON OF BARNSLEY, Baron *cr* 1987 (Life Peer), of Barnsley in South Yorkshire; **Roy Mason;** PC 1968; DL; *b* 18 April 1924; *s* of Joseph and Mary Mason; *m* 1945, Marjorie, *d* of Ernest Sowden; two *d*. *Educ:* Carlton Junior Sch.; Royston Senior Sch.; London Sch. of Economics (TUC Scholarship). Went underground at 14 years of age, 1938–53; NUM branch official, 1947–53; Mem. Yorks Miners' Council, 1949. MP (Lab): Barnsley, March 1953–1983; Barnsley Central, 1983–87. Labour party spokesman on Defence and Post Office affairs, 1960–64; Minister of State (Shipping), Bd of Trade, 1964–67; Minister of Defence (Equipment), 1967–April 1968; Postmaster-Gen., April–June 1968; Minister of Power, 1968–69; President, Bd of Trade, 1969–70; Labour party spokesman on Civil Aviation, Shipping, Tourism, Films and Trade matters, 1970–74; Secretary of State for: Defence, 1974–76; Northern Ireland, 1976–79; opposition spokesman on agriculture, fisheries and food, 1979–81. Mem., Council of Europe and WEU, 1973. Chm., Yorkshire Gp of Labour MPs, 1972–74; Chm., Miners Gp of MPs, 1974, Vice-Chm., 1980. Chairman: Prince's Trust, S Yorks, 1985–; Barnsley Business and Innovation Centre, 1990–. DL South Yorks, 1992. DUniv Sheffield Hallam, 1993; Hon. DCL Northumbria, 2005. *Recreations:* work, provided one stays on top of it, fly-fishing, cravatology (tie-designing). *Address:* 12 Victoria Avenue, Barnsley, S Yorks S70 2BH. *Club:* Lords and Commons Fly-Fishing (founder, and Pres., 1983–). *Died 20 April 2015.*

MASON, Sir (Basil) John, Kt 1979; CB 1973; FRS 1965; DSc (London); Director-General of the Meteorological Office, 1965–83; Chancellor, University of Manchester Institute of Science and Technology, 1994–96 (President, 1986–94); *b* 18 Aug. 1923; *s* of late John Robert and Olive Mason, Docking, Norfolk; *m* 1948, Doreen Sheila Jones; two *s*. *Educ:* Fakenham Grammar Sch.; University Coll., Nottingham. Commissioned, Radar Branch RAF, 1944–46. BSc 1st Cl. Hons Physics (London), 1947, MSc 1948; DSc (London) 1956. Shirley Res. Fellow, Univ. of Nottingham, 1947; Asst Lectr in Meteorology, 1948, Lectr, 1949, Imperial Coll.; Warren Res. Fellow, Royal Society, 1957; Vis. Prof. of Meteorology, Univ. of Calif, 1959–60; Prof. of Cloud Physics, Imperial Coll. of Science and Technology (Univ. of London), 1961–65. Dir, Royal Soc. prog. on Acidification of Surface Waters, 1983–90; Sen. Advr, Centre for Envmtl Technol. (formerly Global Envmt Res. Centre), Imperial Coll., 1990–2000; Chairman: WMO/ICSU Scientific Cttee, World Climate Res. Prog., 1984–88; Co-ordinating Cttee, Marine Science and Technol., 1988–91. Hon. Gen. Sec. British Assoc., 1965–70; President: Physics Section, British Assoc., 1965; Inst. of Physics, 1976–78; BAAS, 1982–83; Nat. Soc. for Clean Air, 1989–91; Assoc. for Science Educn, 1992; Pres., 1968–70, Hon. Mem., 1985, Royal Meteorol. Soc.; Sen. Vice-Pres., 1976–86, and Treasurer, 1976–86, Royal Soc.; Pres., Soc. of Envmtl Engrs, 1999–2003. UK Perm. Rep., World Meteorological Orgn, 1965–83 (Mem. Exec. Cttee, 1966–75 and 1977–83). Member: ABRC, 1983–87; Astronomy, Space Radio Bd, SERC, 1981–85. Chm. Council, 1970–75, Pro-Chancellor, 1979–85, Surrey Univ. Lectures: James Forrest, ICE, 1967 and 1993; Kelvin, IEE, 1968; Dalton, RIC, 1968; Bakerian, Royal Soc., 1971; Hugh MacMillan, IES, 1975; Symons, Royal Meteorol. Soc., 1976; Halley, Oxford, 1977; Jesse Boot, Nottingham, 1987; Rutherford, Royal Soc., Larmor, Cambridge and Belfast, Linacre, Oxford, H. L. Welch, Toronto, and Cockcroft, Manchester, 1990; Loretto, Edinburgh, 1993; Sir Henry Tizard, Westminster Sch., 1999. Mem., Academia Europaea, 1989; Hon. Mem., Amer. Meteorol Soc., 1988; Foreign Mem., Norwegian Acad. of Sci. and Letters, 1993. Hon. Fellow: Imperial Coll. of Science and Technology, 1974; UMIST, 1979; Hon. FInstP, 2009. Hon. DSc: Nottingham, 1966; Durham, 1970; Strathclyde, 1975; City, 1980; Sussex, 1983; Plymouth Polytechnic, 1990; Heriot-Watt Univ., 1991; UMIST, 1994; Reading, 1998; Hon. ScD East Anglia, 1988. Hugh Robert Mill Medal, Royal Meteorol. Soc., 1959; Charles Chree Medal and Prize, Inst. Physics and Phys. Soc., 1965; Rumford Medal, Royal Soc., 1972; Glazebrook Medal, Inst. Physics, 1974; Symons Meml Gold Medal, Royal Meteorol. Soc., 1975; Royal Medal, Royal Soc., 1991. *Publications:* The Physics of Clouds, 1957, 2nd edn 1971; Clouds, Rain and Rain-Making, 1962, 2nd edn 1975; The Surface Waters Acidification Programme, 1990; Acid Rain, 1992; more than 250 papers in physics and meteorological journals. *Recreations:* foreign travel, music, gardening. *Address:* 64 Christchurch Road, East Sheen, SW14 7AW. *Died 6 Jan. 2015.*

MASON, (James) Stephen, CB 1988; Counsel to the Speaker, House of Commons, 1994–2000; *b* 6 Feb. 1935; *s* of Albert Wesley Mason and Mabel (*née* Topham); *m* 1961, (Tania) Jane Moeran; one *s* two *d*. *Educ:* Windsor County Grammar Sch.; Univ. of Oxford (MA, BCL). Called to the Bar, Middle Temple, 1958; in practice, 1961–67; Office of Parly Counsel, 1967–94: Parly Counsel, 1980–94. *Recreations:* reading, playing the piano, compulsory gardening. *Address:* Amberley House, Church Street, Amberley, West Sussex BN18 9NF. *Died 20 Oct. 2012.*

MASON, Sir John; *see* Mason, Sir B. J.

MASON, Sir John (Peter), Kt 1994; CBE 1989; DL; solicitor; Chairman, National Union of Conservative and Unionist Associations, 1992–93 (Vice Chairman, 1989–92); *b* 25 Dec. 1940; *m* Margaret Jehu; one *s* two *d*. *Educ:* Scunthorpe GS. Admitted solicitor, 1964; Sen. Partner, Mason Baggott & Garton, solicitors, Scunthorpe, 1976–. Chairman: Scunthorpe HA, 1981–93; Scunthorpe and Goole Hosps NHS Trust, 1993–2001; N Lincs PCT, 2001–06. Conservative Party: Chm., E Midlands Area, 1985–89; Dep. Chm., Bd of Finance, 1994–; Mem., Nat.

Union Exec. Cttee, 1977–98 (Chm., European Cttee, 1989–92). Chm., Humberside ProHelp Gp, 2006–. Board Member: N Lincs Local Strategic Partnership, 2007–; Lincs Wildlife Trust, 2007– (Chm., 2010–). President: Scunthorpe and Dist Choral Soc., 1978–; Scunthorpe and Dist Scouts Assoc., 1989–. DL Lincs, 2006. *Address:* Mason, Baggott & Garton, 13/19 Wells Street, Scunthorpe, N Lincs DN15 6HN. *Died 27 June 2014.*

MASON, Stephen; *see* Mason, J. S.

MASSE, Hon. Marcel, OQ 1995; PC (Can.) 1984; Président, Société Héritage de Champlain, since 2004; *b* 27 May 1936; *s* of Rosaire Masse and Angeline Masse (*née* Clermont); *m* 1960, Cécile, *d* of René and Clementine Martin; one *s* one *d*. *Educ:* Ecole Normale Jacques-Cartier, Montréal; Univ. de Montréal; Inst. of Pol Sci., Paris; Sorbonne, Paris; City of London Coll.; Inst. Européen d'Admin des Affaires, Fontainebleau. History teacher, Joliette, Québec, 1962–66; Mem., Québec Nat. Assembly, 1966–73 (Minister, 1966–70); Dir, Lavalin Inc., Montréal, 1974–84; MP (Progressive C) Frontenac, Québec, 1984–93; Minister of Communications, Canada, 1984–86, 1989–91; Minister of Energy, Mines and Resources, 1986–89; Minister of National Defence, 1991–93; Quebec Deleg. Gen. in Paris, 1996–97. Président: Commn des biens culturels du Québec, 1997–2000; Commn franco-québécoise sur les lieux de mémoire communs, 1997–2007. Officer, Legion of Honour (France), 1999. *Recreations:* reading, music, fishing, ski-ing. *Address:* CP 1030, Saint-Donat, QC J0T 2C0, Canada. *Club:* Garnison (Quebec). *Died 25 Aug. 2014.*

MASSEY, Anna (Raymond), CBE 2005; actress; *b* 11 Aug. 1937; *d* of late Raymond Massey and Adrianne Allen; *m* 1st, 1958, Jeremy Huggins, (actor, as Jeremy Brett) (marr. diss. 1963; he *d* 1995); one *s*; 2nd, 1988, Uri Andres. *Educ:* London; New York; Switzerland; Paris; Rome. *Plays:* The Reluctant Debutante, 1955; Dear Delinquent, 1957; The Elder Statesman, 1958; Double Yolk, 1959; The Last Joke, 1960; The Miracle Worker, 1961; The School for Scandal, 1962; The Doctor's Dilemma, 1963; The Right Honourable Gentleman, 1964; The Glass Menagerie, 1965; The Prime of Miss Jean Brodie, 1966; The Flip Side, 1967; First Day of a New Season, 1967; This Space is Mine, 1969; Hamlet, 1970; Spoiled, 1971; Slag, 1971; Jingo, 1975; Play, 1976; The Seagull, 1981; Broadway Bound, 1991; A Hard Heart, 1992; Grace, 1992; Moonlight, 1993; *at National Theatre:* Heartbreak House, 1975; Close of Play, 1979; Summer; The Importance of Being Earnest; A Kind of Alaska, and Family Voices, in Harold Pinter trio Other Places, 1982; King Lear, 1986; Mary Stuart, 1996. *Films:* Gideon's Day, 1957; Peeping Tom, 1960; Bunny Lake is Missing, 1965; The Looking Glass War, 1969; David Copperfield, 1969; De Sade, 1971; Frenzy, 1972; A Doll's House, 1973; Sweet William, 1979; The Corn is Green, 1979; Five Days One Summer, 1982; Another Country, 1984; The Chain, 1985; Le Couleur du Vent, 1988; The Tall Guy, 1989; Haunted, 1995; The Grotesque, 1995; The Slab Boys, 1997; Déjà Vu, 1997; Captain Jack, 1999; Mad Cows, 1999; Room to Rent, 2001; Dark Blue World, 2002; The Importance of Being Earnest, 2002; The Machinist, 2004; The Oxford Murders, 2008; *films for television:* Journey into the Shadows, Sakharov, 1984; Sacred Hearts, 1985; Hotel du Lac, 1986; The Christmas Tree, 1987; Sunchild, 1988; A Tale of Two Cities, 1989; Man From the Pru, 1990; The Sleeper, 2000; numerous appearances in TV plays, including Shalom, Joan Collins, 1990; A Respectable Trade (series), 1998; He Knew He Was Right (series), 2004; The Web of Belonging, 2004; The Robinsons (series), 2005; A Good Murder, 2006; Pinochet in Suburbia, 2006; Oliver Twist, 2007; Affinity, 2008. *Publications:* Telling Some Tales (autobiog.), 2006. *Address:* c/o Markham, Froggatt & Irwin Ltd, 4 Windmill Street, W1T 2HZ. *Died 3 July 2011.*

MASTER, (Humphrey) Simon Harcourt; Group Managing Director, 1989–90, Group Deputy Chairman, 1989–2004, Chairman, General Books Division, 1992–2004, and non-executive Director, 2004–11, Random House (formerly Random Century) Group; *b* 10 April 1944; *s* of Humphrey Ronald Master and Rachel Blanche Forshaw (*née* Plumbly); *m* 1969, Georgina Mary Cook Batsford, *d* of Sir Brian Batsford; two *s*. *Educ:* Ardingly Coll.; Univ. de La Rochelle. Hatchards Booksellers, 1963; Pan Books Ltd, 1964, Sen. Editor, 1967; Sen. Editor, B. T. Batsford Ltd, 1969; Pan Books Ltd: Editorial Dir, 1971; Publishing Dir, 1973; Man. Dir, 1980–87; Chief Exec., Random House UK Ltd, 1987–89; Vice Pres., Internat. Random House Inc., 1987–90; Chm. and Chief Exec., Arrow, 1990–92; Vice Pres., Random House (Delaware) Ltd, 1997–99. Non-exec. Dir, HMSO, 1990–95; non-exec. Chm., London Book Fair, 2006–12; Mem., British Book Awards Acad. Bd, 2006–08. Publishers Association: Mem. Council, 1989–95, Mem. Bd, 1997–98; Vice Pres., 1995–96 and 2000–01; Pres., 1996–97 and 2001–02. *Recreations:* gardening, golf, old cars, shooting, woodland management. *Address:* c/o Random House Group, 20 Vauxhall Bridge Road, SW1V 2SA. *Clubs:* Groucho; Sherborne Golf; AC Owners. *Died 16 Jan. 2015.*

MASUR, Kurt; German conductor; Principal Conductor, London Philharmonic Orchestra, 2000–07; Music Director, Orchestre National de France, 2002–08, then Hon. Music Director; *b* 18 July 1927; *m* 3rd, Tomoko Sakurai, soprano; one *s*; four *c* by previous marriages. *Educ:* Nat. Music Sch., Breslau; Leipzig Conservatory. Orch. Coach, Nat. Theatre of Halle, Saxony, 1948–51; Conductor: Erfurt City Theatre, 1951–53; Leipzig City Theatre, 1953–55; Dresden Philharmonic Orch., 1955–58; Music Director: Mecklenburg State Theatre, Schwerin, 1958–60; Komische Oper, E Berlin, 1960–64; Chief Conductor, Dresden Philharmonic Orch., 1967–72; Artistic Dir, Gewandhaus Orch. of Leipzig, 1970–96 (Hon. Mem., 1981; Conductor Laureate, 1996); Music Dir, NY Philharmonic Orch., 1992–2002, now Emeritus (Guest Conductor, 1982–92); Guest Conductor: Cleveland Orch., 1974; Philadelphia Orch.; Boston SO; Berlin Philharmonic Orch.; Leningrad Philharmonic Orch.; l'Orchestre de Paris; RPO. Prof., Leipzig Acad. of Music, 1975–. *Died 19 Dec. 2015.*

MATACA, Most Rev. Petero; Archbishop of Suva, (RC), 1976–2012; *b* 28 April 1933; *s* of Gaberiele Daunivucu and Akeneta Taina. *Educ:* Holy Name Seminary, Dunedin, NZ; Propaganda Fidei, Rome. Priest, Rome, 1959; Vicar-Gen. of Archdiocese of Suva, 1966; Rector of Pacific Regional Seminary, 1973; Auxiliary Bishop of Suva, 1974. Pres., Episcopal Conf. of South Pacific, 1981. *Died 30 June 2014.*

MATHER, Richard Martin; Principal, Rick Mather Architects, since 1973; *b* 30 May 1937; *s* of late Richard John Mather and Opal Mather (*née* Martin). *Educ:* Sch. of Architecture and Allied Arts, Univ. of Oregon (BArch); Dept of Urban Design, Architectural Assoc. Teacher, UCL, Univ. of Westminster, and Harvard Grad. Sch. of Design, 1967–88; RIBA External Examiner to univs and colls in England and Scotland, 1986– (Mem. Council, RIBA, 1998–2000). Consultant Architect: Architectural Assoc., 1978–92 (Mem. Council, 1992–96); UEA, 1988–92; Univ. of Southampton, 1996–2006. Trustee, V & A Mus., 2000–09. Thomas Jefferson Prof., Univ. of Virginia, 2003. Projects include: Times Newspaper HQ, London (RIBA Award, 1992); further UEA buildings (RIBA Award, 1994; Civic Trust Award, 1995); All Glass Structure, London (RIBA Nat. Award, 1994); ARCO Building, Keble Coll., Oxford (RIBA Award, 1996; Civic Trust Award, 1997); The Priory, Hampstead (RIBA Nat. Award, 1998; AIA Award, 1997; Civic Trust Award, 1998); ISMA Centre, Univ. of Reading (RIBA Award, Civic Trust Award, 1999); Neptune Court, Nat. Maritime Mus. (Civic Trust Award, 2000); Wallace Collection, 2000; Dulwich Picture Gall. (RIBA Conservation Award, 2001; AIA Business Week/Arch. Record Award, 2001; Civic Trust Award, 2002); London South Bank Centre Masterplan, 2000–; Lindley Library, RHS, 2001; Sloane Robinson Bldg, Keble Coll., Oxford, 2002; Central Milton Keynes Residential Quarter, 2002–; Ashmolean Mus., Oxford Masterplan, 2002; Greenwich World Heritage Site Masterplan, 2002; Lincoln Sch. of Architecture, 2004; Lyric Th., Hammersmith, 2004; new Girls' Boarding House, Stowe Sch., 2008; Acland Hosp. Site, Keble Coll., Oxford, 2008–; Art & Design Acad., John Moores Univ., Liverpool, 2009 (RIBA Award 2010; Civic Trust Award, 2011); Towner, Eastbourne, 2009 (RIBA Award 2010; Civic Trust Award, 2011); Corpus Christi Coll. Auditorium, 2009 (RIBA

Award 2010); Ashmolean Mus. expansion, 2009 (RIBA Award 2010; Civic Trust Award, 2011); Virginia Mus. of Fine Arts, 2010 (AIA Excellence in Arch. Award, 2010; RIBA Internat. Award, 2011); New Library, Christ's Coll., Cambridge, 2010–. *Recreations:* gardens, food, ski-ing. *Address:* Rick Mather Architects, 123 Camden High Street, NW1 7JR. *T:* (020) 7284 1727. *Died 20 April 2013.*

MATHERS, Sir Robert (William), Kt 1981; *b* 2 Aug. 1928; *s* of William Mathers and Olive Ida (*née* Wohlsen); *m* 1957, Betty Estelle Greasley; three *d*. *Educ:* Church of England Grammar Sch., E Brisbane. FAIM; FRMIA 1982. Chm. and Man. Dir, Mathers Enterprises Ltd, 1973–88; Chm., Kinney Shoes (Australia) Ltd, 1988–90; Dep. Chm., Bligh Coal Ltd, 1981–88; Director: Finlayson Timber & Hardware Pty Ltd, 1986–98; Nat. Mutual Life Assoc. of Australasia, 1988–96; Kidston Gold Mines, 1988–96; Buderim Ginger, 1989–95; Coles Myer, 1992–96; Leutenegger, 1992–95; Touraust Funds Management, 1994–96; Australian Tourism Co., 1994–96. Mem., Aust. Adv. Bd, Kmart Corp., USA, 1991–94. Life Mem., Retailers Assoc. of Qld, 1990 (Mem. Council, 1952–90); Pres., Footwear Retailers Assoc., 1960–63. Member: Council, Australian Bicentennial Authority, 1980–89; Finance Adv. Cttee for XII Commonwealth Games, 1979; Australiana Fund, 1980–94; Brisbane Adv. Bd, Salvation Army, 1990–96; Adv. Bd, Bond Univ. Sch. of Business, 1991–96; Councillor: Griffith Univ., 1978–88; Enterprise Australia, 1983–92; Deputy Chairman: Nat. Finance Cttee, Australian Stockman's Hall of Fame and Outback Heritage Centre, 1984–89; Organising Cttee, Brisbane Bid for 1992 Olympics, 1985–88. Liberal Party: Treas., Qld Br., 1976–90; Member: State Exec., Qld, 1976–90; Federal Council, 1977–90; Life Member: Qld Div., 1984; Young Liberal Movt, Qld Div., 1984. Trustee: WWF, Australia, 1981–87; Queensland Art Gall., 1983–87 (Founding Cttee Mem., Qld Art Gall. Foundn, 1979). Hon. FAMI 1984; FRSA 1989. DUniv Griffith, 1992. Cavaliere, Order of Merit (Italy), 1983. *Recreations:* golf, tennis, swimming. *Address:* Unit 2 Waterford, 88 Macquarie Street, St Lucia, Qld 4067, Australia. *T:* (7) 38703339. *Clubs:* Rotary, Royal Queensland Yacht Squadron, Tattersalls, Brisbane Polo, Queensland Rugby Union, Indooroopilly Golf (Brisbane). *Died 8 Jan. 2011.*

MATOKA, Dr Peter Wilfred, GCCF 2006; Chancellor, Copperstone University, Kitwe, Zambia, since 2010; *b* 8 April 1930; *m* 1957, Grace Joyce; two *s* one *d*. *Educ:* Mwinilunga Sch.; Munali Secondary Sch.; University Coll. of Fort Hare (BA Rhodes); American Univ., Washington (Dipl. Internat. Relations); Univ. of Zambia (MA); Univ. of Warwick (PhD 1994). MP Mwinilunga, Parlt of Zambia, 1964–78; Minister: of Information and Postal Services, 1964–65; of Health, 1965–66; of Works, 1967; of Power, Transport and Works, 1968; of Luapula Province, 1969; High Comr for Zambia in UK and Ambassador to the Holy See, 1970–71; Minister of Health, 1971–72; Minister of Local Govt and Housing, 1972–77; Minister of Economic and Technical Co-operation and Pres., Africa, Caribbean and Pacific Gp of States, 1977; retd from active politics, 1992; Sen. Regl Advr, Econ. Commn for Africa, UN, Addis Ababa, 1979–83; High Comr in Zimbabwe, 1984–89; Sen. Lectr, Dept of Social Develt Studies, Univ. of Zambia, 1995. Mem. Central Cttee, United National Independence Party, 1971–78 and 1984–91 (Chairman: Social and Cultural Cttee, 1989–90; Sci. and Technol. Cttee, 1990–91). Life Mem., CPA, 1974. Pres., AA of Zambia, 1969–70. Kt of St Gregory the Great, 1964; Mem., Knightly Assoc. of St George the Martyr, 1986–. *Publications:* Child Labour in Zambia, 1999. *Recreations:* reading, walking, watching television. *Address:* Copperstone University, Plot 8122, Copperhouse, Central Street, PO Box 22041, Kitwe, Zambia; (home) 26D Ibex Hill Township, Lusaka, Zambia. *Died 12 Sept. 2014.*

MATTHEW, Chessor Lillie, FRIBA, FRIAS; Principal, Duncan of Jordanstone College of Art, Dundee, 1964–78; *b* 22 Jan. 1913; *s* of William Matthew and Helen Chessor Matthew (*née* Milne); *m* 1939, Margarita Ellis (*d* 2010); one *s*. *Educ:* Gray's School of Art; Robert Gordon's Coll., Aberdeen. Diploma in Architecture; MRTPI 1948; FRIBA 1958; FRIAS 1958. Lectr, Welsh Sch. of Architecture, Cardiff, 1936–40. Served RAF, 1940–46, Flt-Lt. Sen. Lectr, Welsh Sch. of Architecture, Cardiff, 1946–57; Head of Sch. of Architecture, Duncan of Jordanstone Coll. of Art, Dundee, 1958–64. Mem., Royal Fine Art Commn for Scotland, 1966–78. JP 1974. *Recreations:* hill walking, foreign travel. *Address:* Craigmhor, 36 Albany Road, West Ferry, Dundee DD5 1NW. *T:* (01382) 778364. *Died 15 Sept. 2011.*

MATTHEWS, Geoffrey Vernon Townsend, OBE 1986; Director of Research and Conservation, 1955–88, and Deputy Director, 1973–88, Wildfowl Trust, Slimbridge; *b* 16 June 1923; *s* of Geoffrey Tom Matthews and Muriel Ivy Townsend; *m* 1st, 1946, Josephine (marr. diss. 1961), *d* of Col Alured Charles Lowther O'Shea Bilderbeck; one *s* one *d*; 2nd, 1964, Janet Kear (marr. diss. 1978; she *d* 2004); 3rd, 1980, Mary Elizabeth, *d* of William Evans; one *s* one *d*. *Educ:* Bedford Sch.; Christ's Coll., Cambridge (MA, PhD). RAF Operational Res., Bomber and SE Asia Comds (Sci. Officer/Flt Lieut), 1943–46. Post-doctoral res., Cambridge Univ., 1950–55; Special Lectr, Bristol Univ., 1965–88; Hon. Lectr 1966–69, Professorial Fellow 1970–90, UC, Cardiff. Dir, Internat. Waterfowl Res. Bureau, 1969–88, Counsellor of Honour, 1989–. Served on numerous non-govtl and govtl cttees; travelled widely. Pres., Assoc. for the Study of Animal Behaviour, 1971–74; Vice-Pres., British Ornithologists' Union, 1972–75, Union Medal, 1980. FSB (FIBiol 1974); Corresp. Fellow, Amer. Ornithologists' Union, 1969–. RSPB Medal, 1990. Officer, Dutch Order of Golden Ark, 1987. *Publications:* Bird Navigation, 1955, 2nd edn 1968; The Ramsar Convention on Wetlands, 1993 (trans. German and Japanese); chapters contributed to 45 multi-authored books; more than 100 papers in sci. and conservation jls. *Recreations:* fossil hunting, collecting zoological stamps, reading, household maintenance. *Address:* 32 Tetbury Street, Minchinhampton, Glos GL6 9JH. *T:* (01453) 884769. *Club:* Victory. *Died 21 Jan. 2013.*

MATTHEWS, Michael Gough; pianist, teacher, adjudicator and consultant; Director, 1985–93, Vice President, since 1994, Royal College of Music, 1985–93; *b* 12 July 1931; *s* of late Cecil Gough Matthews and Amelia Eleanor Mary Matthews. *Educ:* Chigwell School; Royal College of Music (Open Scholarship, 1947; Hopkinson Gold Medal, 1953; ARCM, FRCM 1972); ARCO; Diploma del Corso di Perfezionamento St Cecilia, Rome. Diploma of Honour and Prize, Chopin Internat. Piano Competition, 1955; Italian Govt Scholarship, 1956; Chopin Fellowship, Warsaw, 1959. Pianist; recitals, broadcasts, concerts, UK, Europe and Far East. Supervisor Junior Studies, RSAMD, 1964–71; Royal College of Music: Dir, Junior Dept, and Prof. of Piano, 1972–75; Registrar, 1975; Vice-Dir, 1978–84. Teacher and adjudicator of internat. competitions; Chm. Adjudicators, Royal Over-Seas League Competition, 2005–07. Hon. Dir, Royal Music Foundn, Inc., USA, 1985–. Member: NYO GB; Royal Philharmonic Soc., 1985–; Music Study Gp, EEC, 1989–; Comité d'Honneur, Presence de l'Art, Paris, 1990–; Council, Purcell Tercentenary Trust, 1992. Vice-President: RCO, 1985–; Nat. Youth Choir, 1986–; Herbert Howells Soc., 1987–; Hon. Vice-Pres., Royal Choral Soc., 1992–. Chm., Parkhouse Award, 1997–99. Consultant to HM the Sultan of Oman, 1993–2000, to Jaguar Cars, 1993–. Hon. FLCM 1976; Hon. RAM 1979; FRSAMD 1986; FRNCM 1991; Hon. GSM 1987. Hon. DMus RCM, 2010. Recordings of piano music by Fauré, 1995 and 1997, and Brahms, 1999. *Publications:* various musical entertainments; arranger of educational music. *Recreation:* gardening. *Address:* 608 The Bridge, 334 Queenstown Road, Battersea, SW8 4NP. *T:* (020) 7720 3235. *Club:* Athenæum. *Died 11 April 2013.*

MATTHEWS, Rev. Canon William Andrew; Vicar of Bradford-on-Avon, 1981–2009; Chaplain to the Queen, since 2001; *b* 8 Jan. 1944; *s* of Charles and Olive Matthews; *m* 1969, Jean Elizabeth McNicholas; one *s*. *Educ:* Malmesbury Grammar Sch.; Univ. of Reading (BA 1965; MA 1994); St Stephen's House, Oxford. Ordained deacon, 1967, priest, 1968; Curate: St Alban's, Westbury Park, Bristol, 1967–70; Marlborough, 1970–73; Priest i/c, 1973–75, Vicar, 1975–81, Winsley. RD, Bradford-on-Avon, 1984–94; Canon and Preb., Salisbury Cath., 1988–2009, then Canon Emeritus. *Address:* 21 Williams

Lane, Fernwood, Newark, Notts NG24 3FN. *T:* (01636) 646927. *E:* wajematthews@gmail.com.
Died 24 Nov. 2013.

MATTINGLY, Dr Stephen, TD 1964; FRCP; Consultant Physician, Middlesex Hospital, 1958–81, then Emeritus; Consultant Physician, 1956–82 and Medical Director, 1972–82, Garston Manor Rehabilitation Centre; Hon. Consultant in Rheumatology and Rehabilitation to the Army, 1976–81; *b* 1 March 1922; *s* of Harold Mattingly, CBE and Marion Grahame Meikleham; *m* 1945, Brenda Mary Pike; one *s*. *Educ:* Leighton Park Sch.; UCH (MB, BS); Dip. in Physical Med., 1953. FRCP 1970. House-surg., UCH, 1947; Regtl MO, 2/10 Gurkha Rifles, RAMC Far East, 1947–49; House-surg. and Registrar, UCH, 1950–55; Sen. Registrar, Middx Hosp., 1955–56. Reg. Med. Consultant for London, S-Eastern, Eastern and Southern Regions, Dept of Employment, 1960–74. Mem., Attendance Allowance Bd, 1978–83. Lt-Col RAMC TA, 1952–67. *Publications:* (contrib.) Progress in Clinical Rheumatology, 1965; (contrib.) Textbook of Rheumatic Diseases, ed Copeman, 1969; (contrib.) Fractures and Joint Injuries, ed Watson Jones, 5th edn 1976, 6th edn 1982; (ed) Rehabilitation Today, 1977, 2nd edn 1981; Aspects of Brington: a Northamptonshire Country Parish, 1997, 3rd edn 2010. *Recreation:* gardening. *Address:* Highfield House, Steeple Lane, Little Brington, Northants NN7 4HN. *T:* (01604) 770271. *Died 19 Jan. 2011.*

MAUD, Hon. Sir Humphrey (John Hamilton), KCMG 1993 (CMG 1982); FRCM; HM Diplomatic Service, retired; Chairman, Commonwealth Disaster Management Agency Ltd, since 1999; *b* 17 April 1934; *s* of Baron Redcliffe-Maud, GCB, CBE and Jean, *yr d* of late J. B. Hamilton, Melrose; *m* 1963, Maria Eugenia Gazitua; three *s*. *Educ:* Eton (Oppidan Scholar); King's Coll., Cambridge (Scholar; Classics and History); MA. Mem., NYO, 1949–52. Instructor in Classics, Univ. of Minnesota, 1958–59; entered Foreign Service, 1959; FO, 1960–61; Madrid, 1961–63; Havana, 1963–65; FO, 1966–67; Cabinet Office, 1968–69; Paris, 1970–74; Nuffield Coll., Oxford (Econs), 1974–75; Head of Financial Relations Dept, FCO, 1975–79; Minister, Madrid, 1979–82; Ambassador, Luxembourg, 1982–85; Asst Under Sec. of State, FCO, 1985–88; High Comr, Cyprus, 1988–90; Ambassador to Argentina, 1990–93. Dep. Sec. Gen. (Econ. and Social Affairs) of the Commonwealth, 1993–99. Chairman: Emerging Markets Partnership—Financial Advisors, 1999–2002; Pall Mall Initiatives, 2001–. Member, Council: British Diabetic Assoc., 1986–90; RCM, 1987–2002. Dir, Orchestra of St John's, 1997–2002. Trustee: Parkhouse Award, 1994–; Musequality, 2008– (Chm., 2008–). Mem., Queen's Medal for Music Cttee, 2004–. FRCM 2002. *Recreations:* music ('cellist), golf. *Address:* 31 Queen Anne's Grove, W4 1HW. *Clubs:* Oxford and Cambridge, Garrick; Royal Mid-Surrey Golf.
Died 10 Nov. 2013.

MAUNSELL, Susan Pamela; Policy Co-ordinator, 2002–05, Inquiry Secretary, 2007, Competition Commission; *b* 30 Jan. 1942; *d* of George Cruickshank Smith and Alice Monica Smith (*née* Davies); *m* 1965, Michael Brooke Maunsell (marr. diss. 1986). *Educ:* Nottingham High Sch. for Girls (GPDST); Girton Coll., Cambridge (schol.; BA classics; MA). Ministry of Health: Asst Principal, 1964; Private Sec. to Perm. Sec., 1967, to Parly Sec., 1968; Department of Health and Social Security: Principal, 1969; Asst Sec., 1976; Regl Controller, London S Social Security Reg., 1981–85; various HQ policy posts, 1985–89; Under Sec., Policy Div. A, DSS, 1989–92; Dir, Office of Parly Comr for Admin, 1993–2001. Mem., CSAB, 1993–99. Chair, Age Concern Bromley, 1997–2001. FRSA 1995. *Recreations:* travel, books, theatre, riding, food, wine. *Address:* 27 Longton Avenue, SE26 6RE. *T:* (020) 8778 5605. *E:* SusanMaunsell@live.co.uk.
Died 4 Aug. 2015.

MAUROY, Pierre; Senator, Nord, 1992–2011; *b* 5 July 1928; *s* of Henri Mauroy and Adrienne Mauroy (*née* Bronne); *m* 1951, Gilberte Deboudt; one *s*. *Educ:* Lycée de Cambrai; Ecole normale nationale d'apprentissage de Cachan. Joined Young Socialists at age of 16 (Nat. Sec., 1950–58); teacher of technical educn, Colombes, 1952; Sec.-Gen., Syndicat des collèges d'enseignement technique de la Fédération de l'Education nationale, 1955–59; Sec., Fedn of Socialist Parties of Nord, 1961; Mem., Political Bureau, 1963, Dep. Gen. Sec., 1966, Socialist Party; Mem. Exec. Cttee, Fédération de la gauche démocratique et socialiste, 1965–68; First Sec., Fedn of Socialist Parties of Nord and Nat. Co-ordination Sec., Socialist Party, 1971–79; First Sec., Socialist Party, 1988–92. Member, from Le Cateau, and Vice-Pres., Conseil Gen. du Nord, 1967–73; Town Councillor and Deputy Mayor of Lille, 1971, Mayor, 1973–2001, Vice-Pres., Town Corp., 1971–81; Deputy, Nord, 1973–81, 1986–92; Prime Minister of France, 1981–84. Pres., Regional Council, Nord-Pas-de-Calais, 1974–81; Socialist Rep. and Vice-Pres., Political Commn, EEC, 1979–81. Political Dir, Action Socialiste Hebdo, 1979–81; President: Communauté Urbaine de Lille, 1989–2008; Fédération nationale Léo Lagrange; Fédération Nationale des Elus Socialistes et Républicains, 1987–90; Socialist International, 1992–99; Fondation Jean Jaurès, 1992–. *Publications:* Héritiers de l'avenir, 1977; C'est ici le chemin, 1982; A gauche, 1985; Parole de Lillois, 1994; Léo Lagrange, 1996; Mémoires, 2003. *Address:* 17–19 rue Voltaire, 59800 Lille, France. *Died 7 June 2013.*

MAWSON, David, OBE 1990; JP; DL; FSA; Partner, Feilden and Mawson, Architects, Norwich, 1957–90, Consultant, since 1990; *b* 30 May 1924; *s* of John William Mawson and Evelyn Mary Mawson (*née* Bond); *m* 1951, Margaret Kathlyn Norton; one *s* one *d*. *Educ:* Merchant Taylors' Sch., Sandy Lodge; Wellington Coll., NZ; Auckland Univ., NZ; Kingston-upon-Thames Coll. of Art. Royal Navy, 1945–47. Architect, 1952–. Architect: Norwich Cathedral, 1977–90; St Giles Cathedral, Edinburgh, 1977–81. Chairman: Norfolk Soc. (CPRE), 1971–76 (Vice Pres., 1976–96, 2001–; Pres., 1996–2000); 54 Gp, 1982–; Norfolk ProHelp (formerly Norfolk Professional Firms Gp), BITC, 1994–2004; Friends of Norwich Museums, 1985–2000 (Vice-Pres., 2002–); Founder and Chm., British Assoc. of Friends of Museums, 1973–89 (Vice-Pres., 1989–); Founder Pres., World Fedn of Friends of Museums, 1975–81, Past Pres., 1981–; Pres., Costume and Textile Assoc. for Norfolk Museums, 1989–2013. Mem., Cttee of Nat. Heritage, 1973–89; Trustee: Norfolk Historic Bldgs Trust, 1975–90 (Dir, 1990–); Theatre Royal, Norwich, 1991–99; Dep. Pres., Norfolk Gardens Trust, 2005– (Founder, and Chm., 1988–91; Vice-Pres., 1991–2005); Council Mem., Assoc. of Gardens Trusts, 1994–98. Mem., Norfolk Assoc. of Architects, 1952–94 (Pres., 1979–81); Hon. Treas., Heritage Co-ordination Gp, 1981–87. Trustee, Wymondham Bridewell Preservation Trust, 1994–. First Gov., Wymondham Coll., 1991–99. Pres., Norwich Venta Probus Club, 2001–02. Chm., Townclosians (Alumni of Town Close House Sch., Norwich), 2003–07. JP Norwich, 1972; DL Norfolk, 1986. FSA 1983. Hon. MA UEA, 1995. Cert. of Merit, World Fedn of Friends of Museums, 2011. *Publications:* paper on British Museum Friends Socs in Proc. of First Internat. Congress of Friends of Museums, Barcelona, 1972; contrib. Jl of Royal Soc. of Arts. *Recreations:* gardening, sailing. *Club:* Norfolk (Norwich) (Pres., 1986–87). *Died 21 Nov. 2013.*

MAXEY, Peter Malcolm, CMG 1982; HM Diplomatic Service, retired 1986; *b* 26 Dec. 1930; *m* 1st, 1955, Joyce Diane Marshall; two *s* two *d*; 2nd, Christine Irene Spooner. *Educ:* Bedford Sch.; Corpus Christi Coll., Cambridge. Served HM Forces, 1949–50. Entered Foreign Office, 1953; Third Sec., Moscow, 1955; Second Sec., 1956; First Sec., Helsinki, 1962; Moscow, 1965; First Sec. and Head of Chancery, Colombo, 1968; seconded to Lazard Bros, 1971; Inspector, 1972; Deputy Head UK Delegation to CSCE, Geneva, 1973; Head of UN Dept, FCO, 1974; NATO Defence Coll., Rome, 1977; Dublin, 1977; on secondment as Under Sec., Cabinet Office, 1978–81; Ambassador, GDR, 1981–84; Ambassador and Dep. Perm. Rep. to UN, NY, 1984–86. Editorial Dir, Global Analysis Systems, 1986–88. *Died 23 Oct. 2014.*

MAXWELL, David Campbell F.; *see* Finlay-Maxwell.

MAXWELL-HYSLOP, (Kathleen) Rachel, FSA; FBA 1991; archaeologist; *b* 27 March 1914; *d* of Sir Charles Clay, CB, FBA and Hon. Lady Clay; *m* 1938, Aymer Robert Maxwell-Hyslop (*d* 1993); one *s* two *d*. *Educ:* Downe

House Sch.; Sorbonne; London Univ. (Acad. Postgrad. Dip. in Archaeology of Western Asia). FSA 1950. Institute of Archaeology, University of London: Asst Lectr, 1947–52; Lectr in W Asiatic Archaeology, 1952–66. Archaeol research and travel in Turkey, Cyprus, Iraq, Jordan, Israel, 1950–89; lectured in Philadelphia, MIT, Teheran, Amman; excavations in British Isles, Turkey, Cyprus, Iraq and Iran, 1936–90. *Publications:* Western Asiatic Jewellery *c.* 3000–612 BC, 1971; articles in Iraq, Levant, Jl of Archaeol Science, Anatolian Studies and jls in USA and Turkey. *Recreations:* gardening, painting, piano. *Address:* Water Lane House, Little Tew, Chipping Norton, Oxon OX7 4JG. *T:* (01608) 683226. *Died 9 May 2011.*

MAXWELL MACDONALD, Dame Anne, Btss (11th in line), *cr* 1682 (NS), of Pollok, Renfrewshire; *b* 8 Sept. 1906; *o d* of Sir John Maxwell Stirling-Maxwell, 10th Bt, KT and Ann Christian, *d* of Rt Hon. Sir Herbert Maxwell, 7th Bt; *S* father who *d* 1956, after which Btcy was dormant until succession recognised by Lyon Court in 2005 under the terms of the 1707 special remainder; *m* 1930, John Moreton Macdonald (later Maxwell Macdonald) (*d* 1995); two *s*. *Heir: er s* John Ronald Maxwell Macdonald [*b* 22 May 1936; *m* 1964, Eleanor Ruth (*née* Laird); two *s* one *d*]. *Died 21 April 2011.*

MAY, Gordon Leslie, OBE 1982; retired solicitor; *b* 19 Nov. 1921; *s* of A. Carveth May and Isobella May; *m* 1945, Nina Cheek (*d* 2002); one *s* two *d*. *Educ:* Worcester College for the Blind; Manchester Univ. War service, 1939–45. Admitted Solicitor, 1947; South Eastern Gas Board: Solicitor, 1956; Secretary, 1961; Executive Board Member, 1968; British Gas Corporation: Dep. Chairman, SW Region, 1974; Corp. Sec., 1977–84; Mem. Executive, 1982–84. Consultant, Keene Marsland, solicitors, 1984–87. Mem. Exec. Council, RNIB, 1975–89. Chm. Bd of Governors, Worcester Coll. for the Blind, 1980–87. Liveryman, Solicitors' Co., 1963. *Recreation:* sailing. *Clubs:* Medway Yacht (Upnor); Alderney Sailing. *Died 24 Nov. 2013.*

MAY, Graham; Under Secretary, Department of the Environment, 1972–81; *b* 15 Dec. 1923; *s* of Augustus May; *m* 1952, Marguerite Lucy Griffin (*d* 2009); four *s*. *Educ:* Gravesend County Sch. for Boys; Balliol Coll., Oxford (BA). War Service, Royal Artillery, 1942–46. Asst Principal, Min. of Works, 1948, Principal 1952; seconded to Treasury, 1961–63; Asst Sec., MPBW, 1963. *Died 24 Feb. 2014.*

MAY, Valentine Gilbert Delabere, CBE 1969; *b* 1 July 1927; *s* of Claude Jocelyn Delabere May and Olive Gilbert; *m* 1st, 1955, Penelope Sutton; one *d*; 2nd, 1980, Petra Schroeder; one *d*. *Educ:* Cranleigh Sch.; Peterhouse Coll., Cambridge. Trained at Old Vic Theatre Sch. Director: Ipswich Theatre, 1953–57; Nottingham Playhouse, 1957–61; Bristol Old Vic Company, 1961–75; plays directed at Bristol which transf. to London incl.: War and Peace, 1962; A Severed Head, 1963; Love's Labour's Lost, 1964 (also British Council European tour); Portrait of a Queen, 1965; The Killing of Sister George, 1965; The Italian Girl, 1968; Mrs Mouse, Are You Within, 1968; Conduct Unbecoming, 1969; It's a Two-Foot-Six Inches Above the Ground World, 1970; Poor Horace, 1970; Trelawny, 1972; The Card, 1973. Directed at Old Vic: Richard II, 1959; Mourning Becomes Electra, 1961; Tribute to the Lady, 1974–75. Dir, Yvonne Arnaud Theatre, Guildford, 1975–92; plays directed which transferred to London: Baggage, 1976; Banana Ridge, 1976; The Dark Horse, 1978; House Guest, 1981. Directed: Little Me, Prince of Wales, 1984; Royal Baccarat Scandal, Chichester Fest., 1988, London, 1989; Henry IV (by Pirandello), London, 1990; The Accused, Haymarket Theatre Royal, 2000. Dir, Ludlow Festival, 1993–96: The Taming of the Shrew, Richard III, King Lear. Overseas prodns include: Romeo and Juliet, and Hamlet (NY and USA tour); The Taming of the Shrew (Hong Kong Fest. and Latin America tour); Broadway prodns: A Severed Head; Portrait of a Queen; The Killing of Sister George; Conduct Unbecoming; Murder Among Friends; Pygmalion. Hon. MA Bristol, 1975. *Recreations:* reading, architecture, music, astronomy. *Address:* Manor House Farm, Peasmarsh, Guildford, Surrey GU3 1LY. *T:* (01483) 563547. *Died 6 April 2012.*

MAYHEW-SANDERS, Sir John (Reynolds), Kt 1982; MA; FCA; Chief Executive, 1975–83, and Chairman, 1978–83, John Brown PLC (Director, 1972–83); *b* 25 Oct. 1931; *e s* of Jack Mayhew-Sanders, FCA; *m* 1958, Sylvia Mary (*d* 1995), *d* of George S. Colling; three *s* one *d*. *Educ:* Epsom Coll.; RNC, Dartmouth; Jesus Coll., Cambridge (MA Engrg). FCA 1958. RN, 1949–55. Mayhew-Sanders & Co., Chartered Accountants, 1955–58; P-E Consulting Gp Ltd, 1958–72 (Dir, 1968–72). Director: Dowty Gp, 1982–85; Rover Gp (formerly BL plc), 1980–89; Chm., Heidrick and Struggles UK, 1985–87; Chief Exec., Samuelson Gp, 1987. Member: Management Bd, Engineering Employers' Fedn, 1977–81; BOTB, 1980–83; BBC Consultative Gp on Industrial and Business Affairs, 1981–83; Chm., Overseas Projects Bd, 1980–83; Pres., British-Soviet Chamber of Commerce, 1982–88; Vice-Pres., Inst. of Export, 1982. Governor, Sadler's Wells Foundn, 1983–89. CCMI (CBIM 1980); FRSA 1983. *Recreations:* fishing, shooting, astronomy, music. *Address:* Great Deptford House, High Bickington, Umberleigh, N Devon EX37 9BP. *Died 1 Nov. 2013.*

MAYNE, John Fraser, CB 1986; Principal Establishment and Finance Officer, Department of Health and Social Security, then Department of Health, 1986–90; *b* 14 Sept. 1932; *s* of late John Leonard Mayne and Martha Laura (*née* Griffiths); *m* 1958, Gillian Mary (*née* Key); one *s* one *d*. *Educ:* Dulwich Coll.; Worcester Coll., Oxford. National Service, Royal Tank Regt, 1951–53. Air Min., 1956–64; HM Treasury, 1964–67; MoD, 1967–70; Asst Private Sec. to Sec. of State for Defence, 1968–70; Cabinet Office and Central Policy Rev. Staff, 1970–73; MoD, 1973–78; Private Sec. to Sec. of State for Def., 1975–76; Asst Under-Sec. of State (Air Staff), 1976–78; Principal Establishments and Finance Officer, NI Office, 1979–81; Dir Gen. of Management Audit, MoD, 1981–83; Dep. Sec., Cabinet Office (MPO), 1984–86. Non-exec. Mem., Hampstead HA, 1991–93. Associate, PA Consulting Group, 1990–95; Dir, Carnegie Young People Initiative, 1996–98. Member: Council, RUSI, 1986–89; Public Policy Unit, 1992–97. Trustee, Nat. AIDS Trust, 1992–2007. Chm., Friends of Scottish Opera, 2004–09; Mem. Bd, Scottish Opera, 2004–11. Freeman, City of London, 1983. *Recreations:* listening to music, restoring furniture, cooking. *Address:* 4/1 Carlton Terrace, Edinburgh EH7 5DD. *Club:* New (Edinburgh). *Died 18 April 2014.*

MAZRUI, Prof. Ali Al'Amin, DPhil; Albert Schweitzer Professor in the Humanities, since 1989, and Director, Institute of Global Cultural Studies, State University of New York, Binghamton; *b* Kenya, 24 Feb. 1933; *s* of Al'Amin Ali Mazrui, Judge of Islamic Law, and Safia Suleiman Mazrui; *m* 1st, 1962, Molly Vickerman (marr. diss. 1982); three *s*; 2nd, 1991, Pauline Uti; two *s* and one adopted *d*. *Educ:* Univ. of Manchester (BA with distinction 1960); Columbia Univ. (MA 1961); Nuffield Coll., Oxford (DPhil 1966). Makerere University, Kampala, Uganda: Lectr, 1963–65; Prof. and Head of Dept of Political Science, 1965–73; Dean, Faculty of Social Sciences, 1967–69; Res. Prof., Univ. of Jos, Nigeria, 1981–86; Prof. of Pol Science and of Afroamerican and African Studies, Univ. of Michigan, 1974–91; Andrew D. White Prof.-at-Large, Cornell Univ., 1986–92, Emeritus and Sen. Scholar, 1992–; Ibn Khaldun Prof.-at-Large, Sch. of Islamic and Social Scis, Leesburg, 1997–. Vis. Prof., Univs of London, Manchester, Sussex, Leeds, Harvard, Calif (LA), Northwestern, Stanford, Colgate, Ohio State, Bridgewater State Coll., Mass, Denver, Pennsylvania State, McGill, Canada, Nairobi, Cairo, Baghdad, Singapore and Australian National, 1965–; Walter Rodney Vis. Prof., Univ. of Guyana, 1997–98. Expert Adviser: World Bank, 1988–91; UN Commn on Transnational Corps, 1987–92. Member: Adv. Cttee, Trans-Africa Run for Wildlife Foundn, Inc., 1987–; Adv. Bd of Dirs, Detroit Chapter, AFRICARE, 1987–; Pan-African Adv. Council to UNICEF, 1988–. Pres., African Studies Assoc. of USA, 1978–79; Vice-President: Internat. Congress of African Studies, 1978–; Internat. African Inst., 1987–; World Congress of Black Intellectuals, 1988–. BBC Reith Lectr, 1979; Presenter, The Africans (BBC TV series), 1986. *Publications:* Towards a Pax Africana, 1967; The Anglo-African Commonwealth, 1967; On Heroes and Uhuru-Worship, 1967; Violence and Thought, 1969; (with R. I. Rotberg) Protest and Power in

Black Africa, 1970; The Trial of Christopher Okigbo (novel), 1971; Cultural Engineering and Nation-Building in East Africa, 1972; (with Hasu Patel) Africa in World Affairs: the next thirty years, 1973; World Culture and the Black Experience, 1974; Soldiers and Kinsmen in Uganda, 1975; The Political Sociology of the English Language: an African perspective, 1975; A World Federation of Cultures: an African perspective, 1976; Africa's International Relations, 1977; The Warrior Tradition in Modern Africa, 1978; Political Values and the Educated Class in Africa, 1978; The African Condition (The Reith Lectures), 1980; (with Michael Tidy) Nationalism and New States of Africa, 1984; The Africans: a triple heritage, 1986; Cultural Forces in World Politics, 1990; Africa since 1935 (Vol. VIII, UNESCO General History of Africa), 1993; (with A. M. Mazrui) The Power of Babel: language and governance in Africa's experience, 1998; (ed jtly) The African Diaspora, 1999; (with A. M. Mazrui) Political Culture of Language, 1999; Africanity Redefined, collected essays, vol. 1, 2002; Africa and Other Civilizations, collected essays, vol. 2, 2002; The Titan of Tanzania: Julius K. Nyerere's legacy, 2002; (with A. M. Mazrui) Black Reparations in the Era of Globalization, 2002; The African Predicament and the American Experience, 2004; A Tale of Two Africas, 2006; Euro-Jews and Afro-Arabs: the great semitic divergence in world history, 2007; The Politics of War and the Culture of Violence, 2008; (ed jtly) Africa's Islamic Experience: history, culture and politics, 2009. *Address:* Institute of Global Cultural Studies, Binghamton University, PO Box 6000 LNG–100, Binghamton, NY 13902, USA. *T:* (607) 7774494; 313 Murray Hill Road, Vestal, NY 13850, USA. *Died 12 Oct. 2014.*

MBEKEANI, Nyemba W.; Chief Executive, Mkulumadzi Farm Bakeries Ltd, since 1981; Chairman, Spearhead Holdings Ltd, since 1987; *b* 15 June 1929; Malawi parentage; *m* 1950, Lois Moses (*née* Chikankheni); two *s* three *d*. *Educ:* Henry Henderson Institute, Blantyre; London Sch. of Economics (Economic and Social Administration, 1963). Local Government Officer, 1945–58; political detention in Malawi and Southern Rhodesia, 1959–60; Business Executive, 1960–61; Local Govt Officer, 1963–64; Foreign Service, 1964; High Commissioner for Malawi in London, 1964–67; Ambassador to USA and Permanent Rep. at the UN, 1967–72; Ambassador to Ethiopia, 1972–73; Gen. Manager, Malaŵi Housing Corp., 1973–81. Farmer, company director, tea broker, baker, confectioner. Chm., Petroleum Control Commn, 1987–93; Comr, Malaŵi Electoral Commn, 1998–99. Board Member: Lingadzi Farming Co., 1987–; Sable Farming Co., 1987–. Trustee, Small Farmers Fertilizer Revolving Fund, 1988–. Counsellor, Malaŵi Univ. Council, 1984–93; Chm., Malaŵi Polytechnic Bd of Govs, 1988–93. *Recreation:* flower gardening. *Address:* PO Box 2095, Blantyre, Malaŵi. *T:* 08831060; *Telex:* 44847 Lumadzi MI. *Died 2 Sept. 2015.*

MEACHER, Rt Hon. Michael (Hugh); PC 1997; MP (Lab) Oldham West and Royton, since 1997 (Oldham West, 1970–97); *b* 4 Nov. 1939; *s* of late George Hubert and Doris May Meacher; *m* 1st, 1962, Molly Christine (*née* Reid) (*see* Baroness Meacher) (marr. diss. 1987); two *s* two *d*; 2nd, 1988, Mrs Lucianne Sawyer. *Educ:* Berkhamsted Sch., Herts; New College, Oxford (Greats, Class 1 1962); LSE (DSA 1963). Sec. to Danilo Dolci Trust, 1964; Research Fellow in Social Gerontology, Univ. of Essex, 1965–66; Lecturer in Social Administration: Univ. of York, 1967–69; London Sch. of Economics, 1970. Parly Under-Secretary of State: DoI, 1974–75; DHSS, 1975–76; Dept of Trade, 1976–79; Mem., Shadow Cabinet, 1983–97; chief opposition spokesman on health and social security, 1983–87, on employment, 1987–89, on social security, 1989–92, on development and co-operation, 1992–93, on Citizen's Charter, 1993–94, on transport, 1994–95, on employment, 1995–96, on envmtl protection, 1996–97; Minister of State (Minister for the Envmt), DETR, 1997–2001, DEFRA, 2001–03. Mem., Treasury Select Cttee, 1980–83 (a Chm. of its sub-cttee). Chm., Labour Co-ordinating Cttee, 1978–83; Member: Campaign for Press Freedom; Labour Party NEC, 1983–88. Vis. Prof., Univ. of Surrey, Dept of Sociology, 1980–87. *Publications:* Taken for a Ride: Special Residential Homes for the Elderly Mentally Infirm, a study of separatism in social policy, 1972; Fabian pamphlets incl. The Care of the Old, 1969; Wealth: Labour's Achilles Heel, in Labour and Equality, ed P. Townsend and N. Bosanquet, 1972; Socialism with a Human Face, 1981; Diffusing Power: the key to Socialist revival, 1992; Destination of the Species: the riddle of human existence, 2010; The State We Need: keys to the renaissance of Britain, 2013; numerous articles. *Recreations:* music, sport, reading. *Address:* House of Commons, SW1A 0AA; 34 Kingscliffe Gardens, SW19 6NR. *Died 20 Oct. 2015.*

MEAD, Prof. William Richard, FBA 1994; Professor and Head of Department of Geography, University College, London, 1966–81, then Emeritus Professor; *b* 29 July 1915; *s* of William Mead and Catharine Sarah Stevens; unmarried. *Educ:* Aylesbury Gram. Sch. (Foundation Governor, 1981–2010); London Sch. of Economics (Hon. Fellow 1979). PhD 1946, DSc(Econ) 1968, London. Served RAF, 1940–46. Asst Lectr and Lectr, University of Liverpool, 1947–49; Rockefeller Fellowship, held in Finland, 1949–50; Lectr, 1950, Reader, 1953, University Coll., London. Chm. Council, Sch. of Slavonic and E European Studies, 1978–80. Chm., Anglo-Finnish Soc., 1966–95; President: Inst. of British Geographers, 1971 (Hon. Mem., 1989); Geog. Assoc., 1981–82 (Hon. Mem., 1991); Bucks Archaeol. Soc., 2001–08; Hon. Sec., Royal Geographical Society, 1967–77 (Vice Pres., 1977–81, Hon. Vice-Pres., 1981–). Pres., Crabtree Foundn, 1997–98. Brown Meml Lectr, Univ. of Minnesota, 1983. Hon. Member: Finnish Geog. Soc.; Fenno-Ugrian Soc.; Porthan Soc.; Sydsvenska geografiska sällskapet; Det norske Videnskaps. Akademi, 1976; Det Norske Geografiske Selskab; Foreign Mem., Finnish Acad. of Science and Letters. Gill Memorial Award, 1951, Founder's Medal, 1980, RGS; Wahlberg Gold Medal, Swedish Geographical Soc., 1983; Fennia Medal, Finnish Geographical Soc., 1988; Res. Medal, RSGS, 1988. Dr *hc*: University of Uppsala, 1966; Turku, 2003; DPhil *hc* Univ. of Helsinki, 1969; PhD *hc* Lund, 1987. Chevalier, Swedish Order of Vasa, 1962; Comdr, Orders of: Lion of Finland, 1963 (Chevalier, 1953); White Rose of Finland, 1976; Polar Star of Sweden, 1977. *Publications:* Farming in Finland, 1953; Economic Geography of Scandinavian States and Finland, 1958; (with Helmer Smeds) Winter in Finland, 1967; Finland (Modern Nations of the World Series), 1968; (with Wendy Hall) Scandinavia, 1972; The Scandinavian Northlands, 1973; (with Stig Jaatinen) The Åland Islands, 1974; An Historical Geography of Scandinavia, 1981; An Experience of Finland, 1993; Aylesbury: a personal memoir from the 1920s, 1996, 2nd edn 2009; Aylesbury Grammar School 1598–1998, 1997; A Celebration of Norway, 2002; Pehr Kalm: a Finnish visitor to the Chilterns 1748, 2003; Adopting Finland, 2006; The Anglo-Finnish Society 1911–2011, 2011; Introducing the Finnish Economic Society, 2013; other books on Norway, Sweden, Canada and USA. *Recreation:* music. *Address:* 6 Lower Icknield Way, Aston Clinton, near Aylesbury, Bucks HP22 5JS. *Died 20 July 2014.*

MEADE, Richard John Hannay, OBE 1974; equestrian consultant; Bureau Member, and Chairman of Northern European Group of Nations, International Equestrian Federation, 1990–98; *b* Chepstow, 4 Dec. 1938; *s* of late John Graham O'Mahony Meade and Phyllis Brenda Meade (*née* Watts); *m* 1977, Angela Dorothy Farquhar; two *s* one *d* (and one *s* decd). *Educ:* Lancing College; Magdalene College, Cambridge (Engineering Degree). Competed for GB in 3-day equestrian events, 1963–82; won 3 Olympic gold medals: team gold, 1968; team and individual gold, Munich, 1972; World Championships individual medals include: silver, Burghley, 1996; silver, Punchestown, 1970; World Championships team medals include: gold, Punchestown, 1970; gold, Luhmühlen, 1982; European Championships team medals include: gold, Punchestown, 1967; gold, Burghley, 1971; gold, Horsens, 1981; won Burghley 1964 and Badminton 1970 and 1982. Mem., 3-day Event Cttee, Internat. Equestrian Fedn, 1977–80; Pres., British Equestrian Fedn, 1989–92; Chairman: British Horse Foundn, 1991–; Internat. Eventing Officials Club, 2003–. *Publications:* Fit for Riding, 1984. *Address:* Church Farm, West Littleton, Chippenham, Wilts SN14 8JB. *T:* (01225) 891226. *Died 8 Jan. 2015.*

MEARS, Rt Rev. John Cledan; Bishop of Bangor, 1983–92; *b* 8 Sept. 1922; *s* of Joseph and Anna Lloyd Mears; *m* 1949, Enid Margaret (*d* 2011); one *s* one *d*. *Educ:* Univ. of Wales, Aberystwyth (BA Philosophy 1943); Wycliffe Hall, Oxford; St Deiniol's Library, Hawarden. MA Wales 1948 (research, Blaise Pascal). Deacon 1947, priest 1948, St Asaph; Curate: Mostyn, 1947–49; Rhosllannerchrugog, 1949–55; Vicar of Cwm, 1955–58; Lecturer, St Michael's Coll., Llandaff and Univ. of Wales, Cardiff, 1959–73; Chaplain, 1959–67; Sub-warden, 1967–73; Vicar of St Mark's, Gabalfa, Cardiff, 1973–82. Examining Chaplain, 1960–73; Hon. Canon of Llandaff Cathedral, 1981–82; Sec. of Governing Body, Church in Wales, 1977–82. *Publications:* reviews in Theology, articles in Efrydiau Athronyddol, Diwynyddiaeth, and Barn. *Recreations:* hiking, mountaineering. *Address:* 25 Avon Ridge, Thornhill, Cardiff CF14 9AU. *T:* (029) 2061 5505. *Died 13 July 2014.*

MEDAWAR, His Honour Nicholas Antoine Macbeth; QC 1984; a Circuit Judge, 1987–2005; *b* 25 April 1933; *e s* of Antoine Medawar and Innes (*née* Macbeth); *m* 1st, 1962, Joyce Catherine (*née* Crosland-Boyle) (marr. diss. 1977); one *s* (one *d* decd); 2nd, 1977, (Caroline) Mary, *d* of Harry Samuel Collins, of Nottingham and Buckley. *Educ:* Keswick Grammar School; Trinity College, Dublin (BA Mod., LLB); Hague Acad. of Internat. Law (dip.). Called to the Bar, Gray's Inn, 1957. Nat. Service, RASC, 1957–59, 2nd Lieut. In practice at the common law bar, 1959–87; Recorder of the Crown Court, 1985–87; authorised to sit as a Judge of the High Ct in Family, Queen's Bench and Chancery Divs, 1987–2005. A Legal Assessor, Gen. Optical Council, 1984–87. Mem. Ethnic Minorities Adv. Cttee, Judicial Studies Bd, 1993–96. Non-exec. Dir, Cine Tele Sound Ltd, 1959–72. *Recreation:* divers. *Address:* 2/11 Wedderburn Road, Hampstead, NW3 5QS. *Died 30 Jan. 2015.*

MEEK, Marshall, CBE 1989; RDI 1986; FREng, FRINA; Chairman, Argonautics Maritime Technologies Ltd, 1995–2002; Director, North of England (formerly European) Microelectronics Institute, 1996–2002; President, Royal Institution of Naval Architects, 1990–93 (Vice President, 1979–90); *b* 22 April 1925; *s* of Marshall Meek and Grace R. Smith; *m* 1957, Elfrida M. Cox; three *d*. *Educ:* Bell Baxter School, Cupar; Glasgow University (BSc Naval Arch. 1946). FIES 1963; FREng (FEng 1990). Caledon Shipbuilding Co., 1942–49; Asst Naval Architect, BSRA, 1949–53; Naval Architect, Ocean Fleets (formerly Alfred Holt & Co.), 1953–79 (Dir, 1964–79); Head of Ship Technology, British Shipbuilders, 1979–84; Managing Dir, National Maritime Inst., 1984–85; Dep. Chm., British Maritime Technology, 1985–86. Visiting Professor in Naval Architecture: Strathclyde Univ., 1972–83; UCL, 1983–86. Mem., Lloyds Register of Shipping Technical Cttee, 1979–2001. Chm., Marine Technology Bd, 1984–88; Member: Defence Scientific Adv. Council, 1989–94; Marine and Coastguard Agency (formerly Surveyor General's, then Marine Safety Agency) Res. Cttee, Dept of Transport, 1992–98; Cadland (Royal Yacht replacement) Cttee, 1996–2000. Pres., NECInst, 1984–86. Chm., NE Coast Engrg Trust, 1994–96. Master, RDI, 1997–99. Mem., Northumberland Br., Gideons International in UK, 1986– (Chm., 2000–03, 2009–12); Trustee, Northumberland and Newcastle upon Tyne Police Court Mission Fund, 1990–2008. JP City of Liverpool, 1977–79. FRSA 1968 (Mem. Council, 1995–99; Vice Pres., 1997–99; Mem., Design Adv. Gp, 1997–99; Chm., Student Engrg Design Award Panel, 1997–2000; Chm., NE Reg., 1992–97). Hon. DSc Strathclyde, 2005. *Publications:* There Go the Ships (memoirs), 2003, 2nd edn 2007; numerous papers to RINA and other marine jls. *Recreations:* gardening, reading, church activities. *Address:* 12 Meadowcroft Park, Thropton, Morpeth, Northumberland NE65 7HR. *T:* (01669) 622270. *Died 7 Aug. 2013.*

MEERES, Norman Victor, CB 1963; Under-Secretary, Ministry of Defence, 1971–73; *b* 1 Feb. 1913; *m* 1938, Elizabeth Powys Fowler (*d* 1998); two *s* one *d*. *Educ:* Sloane Sch., Chelsea; Magdalene Coll., Cambridge. Asst Principal, Air Ministry, 1935; Principal, 1940, Asst Sec., 1944, Ministry of Aircraft Prodn; Asst Sec., Min. of Supply, 1946; Under Secretary: Min. of Supply, 1956; Min. of Aviation, 1959–67; seconded to Diplomatic Service in Australia, with title Minister (Defence Research and Civil Aviation), 1965–68; Under-Sec., Min. of Technology, 1969–70. ARCM (piano teaching), 1974. *Recreations:* music, lawn tennis. *Address:* 89 Grove Way, Esher, Surrey KT10 8HF. *T:* (020) 8398 1639. *Died 2 Nov. 2011.*

MEINERTZHAGEN, Peter Richard; Chairman, Hoare Govett, 1991–2004 and 2005–07; *b* 16 April 1946; *s* of late Daniel Meinertzhagen and Marguerite Meinertzhagen (*née* Leonard); *m* 1967, Nikki Phillips; four *d* (and one *d* decd). *Educ:* Eton College; Sorbonne. Hoare & Co.: joined 1965; Partner, 1973; Dir, Institutional Sales, 1973–90. Dir, London Stock Exchange, 1998–2008. Non-exec. Dir, Oriel Securities, 2010–. *Recreations:* golf, tennis, horse-racing, music. *T:* (020) 7352 6806. *Club:* White's. *Died 28 Nov. 2012.*

MELLAART, James, FBA 1980; Lecturer in Anatolian Archaeology, Institute of Archaeology, University of London, 1964–91; *b* 14 Nov. 1925; *s* of J. H. J. Mellaart and A. D. Van Der Beek; *m* 1954, Arlette Meryem Cenani; one *s*. *Educ:* University College, London. BA Hons (Ancient Hist. and Egyptology) 1951. Archaeol field surveys in Anatolia as Scholar and Fellow of British Inst. of Archaeol. at Ankara, 1951–56; excavations at Hacilar, 1957–60; Asst Dir, British Inst. of Archaeol. at Ankara, 1959–61; excavations at Çatal Hüyük, Turkey, 1961–63 and 1965; Foreign Specialist, Lectr at Istanbul Univ., 1961–63. Corresp. Mem., German Archaeol Inst., 1961. *Publications:* Earliest Civilisations of the Near East, 1965; The Chalcolithic and Early Bronze Ages in the Near East and Anatolia, 1966; Çatal Hüyük, a Neolithic Town in Anatolia, 1967; Excavations at Hacilar, 1970; The Neolithic of the Near East, 1975; The Archaeology of Ancient Turkey, 1978; Çatal Hüyük and Anatolian Kilims, 1989; (with Ann Murray) Beycesultan, vol. III 2, 1995; chapters in Cambridge Ancient History; numerous articles in Anatolian Studies, etc. *Recreations:* geology, Turkish ceramics, clan history, Gaelic and classical music, Seljuk art. *Address:* 13 Lichen Court, 79 Queen's Drive, N4 2BH. *T:* (020) 8802 6984. *Died 29 July 2012.*

MELLOR, Hugh Wright; Secretary and Director, National Corporation for Care of Old People (later Centre for Policy on Ageing), 1973–80; *b* 11 Aug. 1920; *s* of late William Algernon and Katherine Mildred Mellor; *m* 1944, (Winifred) Joyce Yates. *Educ:* Leys Sch., Cambridge; London Univ. (BScEcon). Friends Relief Service, 1940–45; Sec., St Albans Council of Social Service, 1945–48; Community Develt Officer, Hemel Hempstead Develt Corp., 1948–50; Asst Sec., Nat. Corp. for Care of Old People, 1951–73. Pres., Hanover Housing Assoc., 1994–99 (Chm., 1980–85). *Publications:* The Role of Voluntary Organisations in Social Welfare, 1985; (with Joyce Mellor) Quakers in High Wycombe 1650–2000: a brief history, 2003. *Recreations:* walking, reading, music. *Address:* Swarthmore Residential Home, 31 Marsham Lane, Gerrards Cross, Bucks SL9 8HB. *Club:* Royal Commonwealth Society. *Died 13 April 2013.*

MELVILLE, 9th Viscount *cr* 1802; **Robert David Ross Dundas;** Baron Duneira 1802; *b* 28 May 1937; *s* of Hon. Robert Maldred St John Melville Dundas (2nd *s* of 7th Viscount) (killed in action, 1940), and of Margaret Connell (who *m* 2nd, 1946, Gerald Bristowe Sanderson), *d* of late Percy Cruden Ross; *S* uncle, 1971; *m* 1982, Fiona Margaret Stilgoe, *d* of late Roger and of Mrs Stilgoe, Stogumber, Som; two *s*. *Educ:* Wellington College. District Councillor, Lasswade, Midlothian; Mem., Midlothian CC, 1964–67. Pres., Lasswade Civic Soc. Lieutenant, Ayrshire Yeomanry; Captain (Reserve), Scots Guards. *Recreations:* fishing, shooting, golf, chess. *Heir:* *s* Hon. Robert Henry Kirkpatrick Dundas, *b* 23 April 1984. *Address:* Bridges Court, Luckington, Wilts SN14 6NT. *Clubs:* Cavalry and Guards; House of Lords Motor; Midlothian County; Bonnyrigg and Lasswade District Ex-Servicemen's. *Died 21 July 2011.*

MELVILLE, James; *see* Martin, R. P.

MELVYN HOWE, Prof. George; *see* Howe.

MENTZ, Donald, AM 1994; Chief Executive Officer, Mentz International Trading, 2004; *b* 20 Oct. 1933; *s* of Stanley Mentz and Marie Agnes (*née* Bryant); *m* 1959, Mary Josephine (*née* Goldsworthy); one *s* two *d*. *Educ:* Hampton High School, Victoria; Dookie Agricultural College, Victoria (DDA); Melbourne Univ. (BAgrSc); Australian Nat. Univ. (BEcon). Dept of External Territories, Australia, 1969–73; Aust. Develt Assistance Bureau, Dept of Foreign Affairs, 1973–77; Dept of Business and Consumer Affairs, 1977–78; Dir of Operations, Asian Develt Bank, Philippines, 1979–81; Dep. Sec., Dept of Business and Consumer Affairs, Aust., 1981–82; Dep. Sec., Dept of Territories and Local Govt, 1983–84; Dir Gen., Commonwealth Agricl Bureaux, later CAB Internat., 1985–92; Man. Dir, Mentz Internat. Trading, 1993–99; Exec. Dir, Crawford Fund for Internat. Agricl Res., Aust., 1999–2001; Man. Dir, Mentak Granite and Marble Pty Ltd, 2000–03. *Recreations:* ski-ing, gardening. *Address:* 10 Bonwick Place, Garran, ACT 2605, Australia. *Clubs:* Athenæum; Commonwealth (Canberra). *Died 30 Oct. 2015.*

MENZIES-WILSON, William Napier, CBE 1985; Chairman, Ocean Transport & Trading plc, Liverpool, 1980–86 (Director, 1973–88); *b* 4 Dec. 1926; *s* of James Robert Menzies-Wilson and Jacobine Napier Williamson-Napier; *m* 1953, Mary Elizabeth Darnell Juckes; two *s* one *d*. *Educ:* Winchester; New Coll., Oxford (MA); Northwestern Univ., Chicago. Joined Stewarts & Lloyds Ltd, 1950; Managing Director, Stewarts & Lloyds of South Africa Ltd, 1954–61, Chairman, 1961; Director, Stewarts & Lloyds Ltd, 1964; Dir, Supplies & Transport, British Steel Corporation, 1967–73; Chairman: Wm Cory & Son Ltd, 1973–77; Viking Resources Trust, 1986–89; Director: Overseas Containers Holdings, 1979–86; Dunlop Holdings, 1982–84; NFC, 1986–95. Pres., Gen. Council of British Shipping, 1984–85; Mem. Exec. Bd, Lloyd's Register of Shipping, 1984–87. Trustee, Help the Aged, 1984– (Chm., Bd of Trustees, 1988–95). *Recreations:* shooting, golf, gardening. *Address:* Chaftonhop, Wacton Lane, Bredenbury, Bromyard, Herefords HR7 4TF. *T:* (01885) 483267. *Club:* Hon. Co. of Edinburgh Golfers. *Died 9 June 2011.*

MEREDITH DAVIES, (James) Brian; *see* Davies, James B. M.

MERTHYR, Barony of (*cr* 1911); title disclaimed by 4th Baron; *see under* Lewis, Trevor Oswin.

MERTON, John Ralph, MBE (mil.) 1942; draughtsman, portrait painter, inventor (of military, domestic and fun inventions), engineer; *b* 7 May 1913; *s* of late Sir Thomas Merton, KBE, FRS; *m* 1939, Viola Penelope von Bernd (*d* 2009); two *d* (and one *d* decd). *Educ:* Eton; Balliol Coll., Oxford. Served War of 1939–45 in Far East (MBE); Asst to Mountbatten's Scientific Advr in Kandy, Ceylon; Air Photo reconnaissance research, Lieut-Col 1944. Works include: Mrs Daphne Wall, 1948; The Artist's daughter, Sarah, 1949; Altar piece, 1952; The Countess of Dalkeith, at Drumlanrig, 1958; A myth of Delos, 1959; Clarissa, 1960; Mrs Julian Sheffield, 1970; Sir Charles Evans, 1973; Iona Colquhoun Duchess of Argyll, 1982; Triple Portrait of Sir David Piper, 1984 (in Nat. Portrait Gall.); James Meade, 1987; Triple Portrait of HRH The Princess of Wales (for Cardiff City Hall), 1987; HM The Queen (at Buckingham Palace), 1989; Paul H. Nitze (in Johns Hopkins Univ.), 1991; Triple Portrait of Duke of Grafton (for Nat. Portrait Gall.), 1992; Peregrine Churchill, 1993; John Lewis (Chm. of the Trustees, Wallace Collection), 1995, his daughter Lily Lewis, 2003; Lord and Lady Romsey with a mirror reflecting Broadlands, 1997; double portrait drawing of two children, 1999 (exhibited RA, 2000); two paintings, from own photos, of coral trees under S China Sea off Tioman Is, N Malaysia: vertical tree (a mile offshore), 2000; horizontal tree (in shallower water), 2001; retrospective exhibn, Fine Art Soc., London, 2003; Lyndsay Wicksham, age 6, USA; Roy Bohana; large paintings from own 35mm transparencies, incl. S of France, Scotland, John Dory fish underwater in Kimmeridge Bay (Dorset), Paleokrastritsa (Corfu), Pound House pond; small paintings from underwater slides in Tioman Island, Malaysia. Legion of Merit (USA), 1945. *Publications:* A Journey Through an Artist's Life, 1994, part 2, 2003. *Recreations:* music, making things. *Address:* Pound House, Oare, near Marlborough, Wilts SN8 4JA. *T:* (01672) 563539. *Died 16 Feb. 2011.*

MERVYN DAVIES, David Herbert; *see* Davies, Hon. Sir David H. M.

MESSER, Cholmeley Joseph; Chairman, Hamilton Insurance, 1995–2000; Director, HFC Bank plc, 1993–99; *b* 20 March 1929; *s* of late Col Arthur Albert Messer, DSO. CBE, FRIBA, and Lilian Hope Messer (*née* Dowling); *m* 1956, Ann Mary Power; two *d*. *Educ:* Wellington Coll. Served KRRC, 2nd Lieut, 1948–49. Articled Lawrance Messer & Co., Solicitors, London 1949–54; Partner, 1957–66; Save & Prosper Group: Exec. Dir, 1967–72; Dep. Man. Dir, 1973–80; Man. Dir, 1980–84; Chm., 1981–89. Chm., Code of Advertising Practice Cttee, Advertising Standards Authority, 1977–78; Vice-Chm., Internat. Bar Assoc. Cttee on Investment Cos Funds and Trusts, 1978–81; Chm., Unit Trust Assoc., 1981–83; Mem., 1989–92, Chm., 1992–98, London Pension Funds Authy. Chm., British Bobsleigh Assoc., 1989–92. *Recreations:* armchair sport, gardening, golf, collecting military postcards. *Address:* 66 Glaziers Lane, Normandy, Guildford, Surrey GU3 2DQ. *T:* (01483) 810910. *Clubs:* City of London, MCC. *Died 21 July 2015.*

METCALF, Prof. Donald, AC 1993 (AO 1976); FRS 1983, FRACP, FRCPA, FAA; Assistant Director and Head of Cancer Research Unit, Walter and Eliza Hall Institute of Medical Research, Melbourne, 1965–96; Research Professor of Cancer Biology, University of Melbourne, 1986–96, then Professor Emeritus; *b* 26 Feb. 1929; *s* of Donald Davidson Metcalf and Enid Victoria Metcalf (*née* Thomas); *m* 1954, Josephine Emily Lentaigne; four *d*. *Educ:* Sydney University. MD, BSc (med). Resident MO, Royal Prince Alfred Hosp., Sydney, 1953–54; Surgeon-Lt, RANR, 1953–58; Carden Fellow in Cancer Res., Walter and Eliza Hall Inst. of Med. Res., 1954–65. Vis. Fellow, Harvard Med. Sch., 1956–58; Visiting Scientist: Roswell Park Meml Inst., Buffalo, 1966–67; Swiss Inst. for Experimental Cancer Res., Lausanne, 1974–75; Radiobiological Res. Inst., Rijswijk, 1980–81; Royal Soc. Guest Res. Fellow, Cambridge Univ., 1981. *Publications:* The Thymus, 1966; (with M. A. S. Moore) Haemopoietic Cells, 1971; Hemopoietic Colonies, 1977; Hemopoietic Colony Stimulating Factors, 1984; The Molecular Control of Blood Cells, 1988; (with N. A. Nicola) The Hemopoietic Colony Stimulating Factors, 1995; Summon Up the Blood (autobiog.), 2000; numerous scientific papers on cancer and leukaemia. *Recreations:* music, tennis. *Address:* 268 Union Road, Balwyn, Victoria 3103, Australia. *T:* (3) 98361343. *Died 15 Dec. 2014.*

METCALF, Malcolm, MC 1944; DL; Chairman, Surrey County Council, 1978–81; *b* 1 Dec. 1917; *s* of Charles Almond Metcalf and Martha Fatherly Atkins Metcalf; *m* 1945, Charis Thomas (*d* 2003); two *s*. *Educ:* Merchant Taylors' Sch., Crosby. ACIS. Army service, 1939–46. Contested (C) Barrow-in-Furness, 1959; Mem., Surrey CC, 1965–89 (Leader, 1973–77; Vice-Chm., 1977–78); Member: Metrop. Water Board, 1965–74 (Vice-Chm. 1971–72); Thames Conservancy, 1970–74; Thames Water Authority, 1973–78, 1981–87. Mem., Assoc. of County Councils, 1975–88. DL Surrey, 1979. *Clubs:* MCC; Burhill Golf (Walton-on-Thames). *Died 7 Jan. 2011.*

METCALF, Ven. Robert Laurence; Archdeacon of Liverpool, 1994–2002, then Emeritus; *b* 18 Nov. 1935; *s* of late Victor Noel Metcalf and Phyllis Maud Metcalf (*née* Dunwell); *m* 1964, Rachel Margaret Herring; two *s* three *d*. *Educ:* St John's Coll., Durham Univ. (BA 1960; rowing colours, 1960); Cranmer Hall, Durham (DipTheol 1962); Cardiff Univ. (LLM 2002). Nat. Service, REME, 1955–57. Ordained deacon, 1962, priest, 1963; Curate: Christ Church, Bootle, 1962–65; i/c St John's, Widnes, 1965–67; Vicar, St Catharine, Wigan, 1967–75; Dir, Wigan Br., Samaritans, 1970–75; Rector, Holy Trinity, Wavertree, 1975–94; Chaplain: Liverpool Royal Sch. for the Blind, 1975–94; Blue Coat Sch., Liverpool, 1975–94; Diocesan Dir of Ordinands, Liverpool, 1982–94; Hon. Canon, Liverpool Cathedral, 1988. Priest-in-Charge, St Michael, Garston, 2004–06. Chm., Pre-theol Educn Panel, Ministry Div., Archbps' Council, 1999–2006. Mem., Toxteth

Rotary Club, 1985–98 (Pres., 1995–96). Chm., Liverpool Welsh Choral, 2005–08 (Vice-Pres., 2008–). Occasional broadcaster, BBC Radio Merseyside. *Publications:* contrib.: Prayers for Today's Church, 1972; For All the Family, 1984; Celebration of Creation, 1992; Prayers for Today's World, 1993; Reconciliation. *Recreations:* walking, rowing, reading novels (political intrigue!), holidaying, leading pilgrimages to the Holy Land and biblical countries, leading quiet days and retreats, singing. *Address:* 32 Storrsdale Road, Liverpool L18 7JZ. *T:* (0151) 724 3956, 07931 309103. *E:* bob.metcalf@uwclub.net. *Died 26 Dec. 2014.*

METHUEN, 7th Baron *cr* 1838; **Robert Alexander Holt Methuen;** electrical engineer, with Rolls-Royce plc, 1975–94; *b* 22 July 1931; *y s* of 5th Baron Methuen and Grace (*d* 1972), *d* of Sir Richard Durning Holt, 1st Bt; *S* brother, 1994; *m* 1st, 1958, Mary Catharine Jane (marr. diss. 1993), *o d* of late Ven. C. G. Hooper; two *d*; 2nd, 1994, Margrit Andrea, *o d* of Friedrich Hadwiger. *Educ:* Shrewsbury; Trinity Coll., Cambridge. Elected Mem., H of L, 1999. Member: EC sub-cttee B, 1995–99; Admin and Works sub-cttee, 1997–2000; Sci. and Technol. Cttee, 2000–03 and 2007–; Library and Computers sub-cttee, 2000–03; Merits of Statutory Instruments Cttee, 2003–07. *Heir: cousin* James Paul Archibald Methuen-Campbell, *b* 25 Oct. 1952. *Died 9 July 2014.*

MEYER, Rev. Mgr Canon Conrad John Eustace; *b* 2 July 1922; *s* of William Eustace and Marcia Meyer; *m* 1960, Mary Wiltshire; no *c*. *Educ:* Clifton Coll.; Pembroke Coll., Cambridge; Westcott House. BA 1946, MA 1948. Served War of 1939–45: Royal Navy (commissioned from lower deck), 1942–46. Lieut (S) RNVR, post war, until apptd Chaplain, RNVR, 1950–54. Deacon, 1948; Priest, 1949; Asst Curate: St Francis, Ashton Gate, Bristol, 1948–51; Kenwyn, Truro, 1951; Falmouth Parish Church, 1954; Vicar of Devoran, Truro, 1956–65; Diocesan Youth Chaplain, 1956; Asst Dir of Religious Educn, 1958; Diocesan Sec. for Educn, 1960–69; Archdeacon of Bodmin, 1969–79; Hon. Canon of Truro, 1966–79; Examining Chaplain to Bishop of Truro, 1973–79; Bishop Suffragan of Dorchester, 1979–87 (Area Bishop, 1985–87); Hon. Asst Bishop, dio. of Truro, 1990–94. Received into RC Ch, 1994; ordained priest, 1995; Hon. Canon, Plymouth RC Cathedral, 2001. Hon. Diocesan Sec., Nat. Soc., 1960–69. Society for Promoting Christian Knowledge: Mem. Governing Body, 1972–90; Chairman: Projects Cttee, 1973–87; Appeals Cttee, 1987–90; Vice Chm., 1988–90; Vice-Pres., 1990–. Chairman: Federation of Catholic Priests, 1976–79; Church Union Exec. Cttee, 1979–84; The Churches' Group on Funerals at Cemeteries and Crematoria, 1980–89. Fellow, Woodard Corp. of Schools, 1967–92; Provost, Western Div., Woodard Corp., 1970–92 (Hon. Fellow, 1993–94). Hon. Fellow, Inst. of Civil Protection and Emergency Mgt. Prelate of Honour, 2009; Freedom of the City of St John's, Newfoundland, 2009. *Recreations:* swimming, walking, military history, civil defence, archaeology. *Address:* Hawk's Cliff, 38 Praze Road, Newquay, Cornwall TR7 3AF. *Club:* Royal Commonwealth Society. *Died 23 July 2011.*

MEYJES, Sir Richard (Anthony), Kt 1972; DL; President, Association of Optometrists, 1995–2000; *b* 30 June 1918; *s* of late Anthony Charles Dorian Meyjes and Norah Isobel Meyjes; *m* 1939, Margaret Doreen Morris; three *s*. *Educ:* University College School, Hampstead. War Service, RASC, Sept. 1939–Jan. 1946 (temp. Captain). Qualified as Solicitor, June 1946; Legal Dept, Anglo-Saxon Petroleum Co., 1946–56; Manager, Thailand and Vietnam Division, Shell International Petroleum Co., 1956–58; Marketing Manager, Shell Co. of Philippines, Ltd, Manila, 1958–61; President, 1961–64; Head of Regional Marketing Div., Shell International Petroleum Co., London, 1964–66; Marketing Coordinator, 1966–70; seconded to HM Govt (Mr Heath's Admin) as Head of Business Team, 1970–72; Dir and Group Personnel Co-ordinator, Shell International Petroleum Co. Ltd, 1972–76. Director: Foseco Minsep, later Foseco plc, 1976–89 (Dep. Chm., 1986–89); Coates Bros plc, 1976–83 (Chm., 1978–83); Portals Hldgs, 1976–88. Vice-Pres., Assoc. of Optometrists, 1988–95. Chm. Council, Univ. of Surrey, 1980–85. DL, 1983, High Sheriff, 1984, Surrey. Master, Worshipful Co. of Spectacle Makers, 1985–87. CCMI; FInstD; Hon. FCOptom; FRSA. DUniv Surrey, 1988. Officer of Philippine Legion of Honour, 1964. *Recreations:* gardening, walking. *Died 9 March 2013.*

MICHAEL, Ian (Lockie), CBE 1972; Deputy Director, Institute of Education, University of London, 1973–78; *b* 30 Nov. 1915; 4th *c* of late Reginald Warburton Michael and Margaret Campbell Kerr; *m* 1942, Mary Harborne Bayley (*d* 2007), *e c* of late Rev. William Henry Bayley; one *s* one *d*. *Educ:* St Bees Sch.; private study. BA (London) 1938; PhD (Bristol) 1963. Schoolmaster: St Faith's Sch., Cambridge, 1935–40; Junior Sch., Leighton Park, 1941–45, Headmaster, 1946–49; Lectr in Educn, Bristol Univ., 1950–63; Prof. of Educn, Khartoum Univ., 1963–64; Vice-Chancellor, Univ. of Malaŵi, 1964–73. Leverhulme Emeritus Fellowship, 1978–79, 1979–80; Vis. Prof. of Educn, Univ. of Cape Town, 1981. Hon. DLitt Malaŵi, 1974. *Publications:* English Grammatical Categories and the Tradition to 1800, 1970; The Teaching of English from the Sixteenth Century to 1870, 1987; Early Textbooks of English, 1993; Literature in School 1700–1830, 1999. *Address:* 6 Jessop Crescent, Westbury Fields, Westbury-on-Trym, Bristol BS10 6TQ. *T:* (0117) 950 5621. *Died 24 Oct. 2014.*

MICHELL, Keith; actor, since 1948; *b* Adelaide, 1 Dec. 1928; *s* of Joseph Michell and Alice Maud (*née* Aslat); *m* 1957, Jeannette Sterke; one *s* one *d*. *Educ:* Port Pirie High Sch.; Adelaide Teachers' Coll.; Sch. of Arts and Crafts; Adelaide Univ.; Old Vic Theatre Sch. Formerly taught art. *Stage:* First appearance, Playbox, Adelaide, 1947; Young Vic Theatre Co., 1950–51; first London appearance, And So To Bed, 1951; Shakespeare Meml Theatre Co., 1952–56, inc. Australian tour, 1952–53 (Henry IV Part 1, As You Like It, Midsummer Night's Dream, Troilus and Cressida, Romeo and Juliet, Taming of the Shrew, All's Well That Ends Well, Macbeth, Merry Wives of Windsor); Don Juan, Royal Court, 1956; Old Vic Co., 1956 (Antony and Cleopatra, Much Ado about Nothing, Two Gentlemen of Verona, Titus Andronicus); Irma La Douce, Lyric, 1958, Washington, DC, 1960 and Broadway, 1960–61; The Chances, Chichester Festival, 1962; The Rehearsal, NY, 1963; The First Four Hundred Years, Australia and NZ, 1964; Robert and Elizabeth, Lyric, 1964; The King's Mare, 1966; Man of La Mancha, 1968–69, NY, 1970; Abelard and Heloise, 1970, Los Angeles and NY, 1971; Hamlet, Globe, 1972; Dear Love, Comedy, 1973; The Crucifer of Blood, Haymarket, 1979; On the Twentieth Century (musical), Her Majesty's, 1980; Pete McGynty and the Dreamtime (own adap. of Peer Gynt), Melbourne Theatre Co., 1981; Captain Beaky Christmas Show, Lyric, Shaftesbury Ave., 1981–82; The Tempest, Brisbane, 1982; opened Keith Michell Theatre, Port Pirie, with one-man show, 1982; Amadeus (UK tour), 1983; La Cage Aux Folles, San Francisco and NY, 1984, Sydney and Melbourne, 1985; Portraits, Malvern Fest. and Savoy, 1987; Aspects of Love, Edmonton and Toronto, 1991–92, Chicago, 1992; Scrooge, Melbourne, 1993; Caesar and Cleopatra, Edmonton, 1994; Brazilian Blue, Brisbane, 1995; various one-man shows, Family Matters, and All the World's a Stage, UK tour, S Australia Adelaide Fest. and Keith Michell Th., Port Pirie, 2000–04; Bernardino Ramazzini - The Artisan's Archangel, RSocMed London, 2005; *Chichester Festival Theatre:* Artistic Director, 1974–77; Tonight We Improvise, Oedipus Tyrannus, 1974; Cyrano de Bergerac, Othello, 1975; (dir and designed) Twelfth Night, 1976; Monsieur Perrichon's Travel, 1976; The Apple Cart, 1977; (dir and designed) In Order of Appearance, 1977; Murder in the Cathedral (Chichester Cathedral), 1977; Henry VIII, 1991; toured Australia with Chichester Co., 1978 (Othello, The Apple Cart); acted in: On the Rocks, 1982; Jane Eyre, 1986; The Royal Baccarat Scandal, 1988, transf. Theatre Royal Haymarket, 1989; Henry VIII, 1991; Monsieur Amilcar (Minerva), 1995. *Films include:* Dangerous Exile; The Hell Fire Club; Seven Seas to Calais; The Executioner; House of Cards; Prudence and the Pill; Henry VIII and his Six Wives; Moments, The Deceivers; Love/Lost. *Television includes:* Henry VIII in the Six Wives of Henry VIII (series), 1972; Keith Michell at Chichester, 1974; My Brother Tom, 1986; Captain James Cook, 1987; Murder She Wrote (series), 1990. Many recordings. First exhibn of paintings, 1959; subseq. one-man exhibns at John Whibley Gall., London, Wright

Hepburn and Webster Gall., NY, Century Gall., Henley-on-Thames, Wylma Wayne Gall., London, Vincent Gall., Adelaide. Many awards. *Publications:* (ed and illus.) Twelve Shakespeare Sonnets (series of lithographs produced 1974), 1981; illus. and recorded Captain Beaky series, 1975; (compiled and illus.) Practically Macrobiotic, 1987, 3rd edn 2000. *Recreations:* gardening, photography, swimming, cooking. *Died 20 Nov. 2015.*

MICHIE, Prof. David Alan Redpath, OBE 1997; RSA 1972 (ARSA 1964); RGI 1984; Head, School of Drawing and Painting, Edinburgh College of Art, 1982–90; Professor Emeritus, Heriot-Watt University, 1991; *b* 30 Nov. 1928; *s* of late James Michie and Anne Redpath, OBE, ARA, RSA; *m* 1951, Eileen Anderson Michie (*d* 2003); two *d*. *Educ:* Edinburgh Coll. of Art (DA; Hon. Fellow, 2009). National Service, 1947–49; Edinburgh Coll. of Art, 1949–53 (studied painting); travelling scholarship, Italy, 1953–54; Lectr in Painting, Gray's Sch. of Art, Aberdeen, 1958–62; Lectr in Painting, Edinburgh Coll. of Art, 1962–82, Vice-Principal, 1974–77. Visiting Professor of Painting: Acad. of Fine Art, Belgrade, 1979; Univ. of Calif, Santa Barbara, 1992. Member: Gen. Teaching Council for Scotland, 1976–80; Edinburgh Festival Soc., 1976–; Museums and Galls Commn, 1991–96. Mem. Court, Heriot-Watt Univ., 1979–82. Pres., Soc. of Scottish Artists, 1961–63. One Man Exhibitions: Mercury Gallery, London, 1967, 1969, 1971, 1974, 1980, 1983, 1992, 1996, 1999; Mercury Gall., Edinburgh, 1986; Lothian Region Chambers, 1977; Scottish Gall., Edinburgh, 1980, 1994, 1998, 2003, 2008; Kasteel de Hooge Vuursche, Baarn, Netherlands, 1991; Scott Gall., Hawick, 2009; Scottish Art Club, 2010; Michie Family, Scottish Gall., 2012; Border Boys, Peebles, 2013; Anne Redpath and Family, Scott Gall., Hawick, 2015. RWA 1991–2000. FRSA 1990; FFCS 2000. *Recreation:* music. *Address:* 17 Gilmour Road, Edinburgh EH16 5NS. *T:* (0131) 667 2684. *Died 24 Aug. 2015.*

MIDDLEMAS, Prof. Robert Keith; Professor of History, University of Sussex, 1986–98, then Emeritus; *b* 26 May 1935; *s* of late Robert James Middlemas, Solicitor and of Eleanor Mary (*née* Crane), Howick, Northumberland; *m* 1958, Susan Mary, *d* of Laurence Edward Paul Tremlett and Marjorie Isobel Derrington Bell; one *s* three *d*. *Educ:* Stowe Sch.; Pembroke Coll., Cambridge (Exhibnr, scholar, BA 1st cl. History 1958); DPhil 1972, DLitt 1982, Sussex. 2nd Lieut, Northumberland Fusiliers, 1954–55 (served in Kenya); Clerk, House of Commons, 1958–66; Lectr in History, Univ. of Sussex, 1966–76, Reader, 1976–86. Visiting Professor: Stanford Univ. and Hoover Instn, Stanford, 1984; Univ. of Beijing, 1989. Member: UK Nat. Cttee, Unesco, 1980–86; Council, Inst. of Contemporary British History; Council and Res. Cttee, Foundn for Manufg and Industry, 1993–96; Conseil de Surveillance, ESL and Network, Paris, 1997–2006; Chm., ESL and Network (UK) Ltd, 2002–06. FRSA. Co-Founder and Editor, Catalyst: a jl of public debate, 1985–87. *Publications:* The Master Builders, 1963; The Clydesiders, 1965; (with John Barnes) Baldwin, 1969; Diplomacy of Illusion, 1972; (ed) Thomas Jones: Whitehall Diary, vols I and II, 1969–70, vol. III, 1972; Politics in Industrial Society, 1979; Cabora Bassa, 1975; Power and the Party, 1980; Industry, Unions and Government, 1984; Power, Competition and the State, vol. I, Britain in Search of Balance 1940–61, 1986, vol. 2, Threats to the Post-War Settlement: Britain 1961–74, 1990; vol. 3, The End of the Post-War Era: Britain since 1974, 1991; Orchestrating Europe: informal politics of the European Community since 1973, 1995; Kinship and Survival, 2009; As They Really Were: citizens of Alnwick 1831, 2011; articles and reviews in learned jls. *Recreations:* sports, sailing, fishing, landscape gardening; Member, UK Nat. Rifle Team, Canadian tour, 1958. *Address:* West Burton House, West Burton, Pulborough, West Sussex RH20 1HD. *T:* (01798) 831516. *Club:* Flyfishers'. *Died 10 July 2013.*

MIDDLETON, 12th Baron *cr* 1711; **Digby Michael Godfrey John Willoughby,** MC 1945; DL; Bt 1677; *b* 1 May 1921; *er s* of 11th Baron Middleton, KG, MC, TD, and Angela Florence Alfreda (*d* 1978), *er d* of Charles Hall, Eddlethorpe Hall, Malton, Yorks; *S* father, 1970; *m* 1947, Janet, *o d* of General Sir James Marshall-Cornwall, KCB, CBE, DSO, MC; three *s*. *Educ:* Eton; Trinity Coll., Cambridge. BA 1950; MA 1958. Served War of 1939–45: Coldstream Guards, 1940–46; NW Europe, 1944–45 (despatches, MC, Croix de Guerre); Hon. Col, 2nd Bn Yorkshire Volunteers, TAVR, 1976–88. Mem., H of L Select Cttee on Eur. Communities, 1985–97; Chm., H of L Sub-Cttee D, Agriculture and Food, 1989–92, 1994–97. Pres., CLA, 1981–83; Member: Yorks and Humberside Econ. Planning Council, 1968–79; Nature Conservancy Council, 1986–89. DL 1963, JP 1958, CC 1964–74, ER of Yorks; CC N Yorks, 1974–77. *Heir: s* Hon. Michael Charles James Willoughby [*b* 14 July 1948; *m* 1974, Hon. Lucy Sidney, *y d* of 1st Viscount De L'Isle, VC, KG, GCMG, GCVO, PC; two *s* three *d*]. *Address:* Birdsall House, Malton, N Yorks YO17 9NR. *Died 27 May 2011.*

MIDDLETON, Donald King, CBE 1981; HM Diplomatic Service, retired; Chairman, Leominster Abbeyfield Society, 1993–97; *b* 24 Feb. 1922; *s* of late Harold Ernest Middleton and Ellen Middleton; *m* 1st, 1945, Marion Elizabeth Ryder (*d* 1988); one *d*; 2nd, 1996, Mary Elaine Aston. *Educ:* King Edward's Sch., Birmingham; Saltley College. Min. of Health, 1958–61; joined Commonwealth Relations Office, 1961; First Sec., British High Commn, Lagos, 1961–65; Head of Chancery, British Embassy, Saigon, 1970–72; British Dep. High Commissioner, Ibadan, 1973–75; HM Chargé d'Affaires, Phnom Penh, 1975; seconded to NI Office, Belfast, 1975–77; High Comr, Papua New Guinea, 1977–82. *Died 21 Jan. 2015.*

MIDDLETON, Rear Adm. Linley Eric, CB 1986; DSO; FRAeS; Flag Officer, Naval Air Command, 1984–87; *b* 17 Aug. 1929; *m* 1965, Pamela Mannerings (*née* Lewis); three *s*. *Educ:* Dale Coll., Kingwilliamstown. Qualified as FAA pilot, 1952; served HMS Indefatigable, HMS Centaur, HMS Bulwark, HMS Eagle, HMS Mounts Bay, HMS Victorious and HMS Ark Royal, 1952–63; BRNC Dartmouth, 1964–65; CO, 809 Naval Air Squadron in HMS Hermes, 1966–67; Naval Staff, MoD, 1968–69; CO, HMS Whitby, 1970–71; Staff of Flag Officer, Naval Air Comd, 1971–73; Capt. 2nd Frigate Sqn and CO, HMS Undaunted, 1973–74, and CO, HMS Apollo, 1974–75; Chief Staff Officer to Flag Officer Carriers & Amphibious Ships, 1975–77; Dir, Naval Air Warfare, 1978–79; CO, HMS Hermes, 1980–82; Asst Chief of Naval Staff (Ops), 1983–84. Man. Dir, British Internat. Helicopters, 1987–92. Liveryman: Coach Makers' and Coach Harness Makers' Co., 1983; GAPAN, 1993. *Died 3 Dec. 2012.*

MIDDLETON, Peter James; Chairman, GTL Resources plc, 2002–07 (Director, 2000–07); *b* 10 Feb. 1940; *s* of Roy and Freda Middleton; *m* 1st, 1968, Yvonne Summerson (marr. diss. 1996); two *s* one *d*; 2nd, 1996, Anita Mehra; two *s* one *d* (of whom one *s* one *d* are twins). *Educ:* Univ. of Paris; Univ. of Hull (BA Hons). HM Diplomatic Service, 1969–85: Second Sec., Jakarta, 1969–71; First Sec., Dar-es-Salaam, 1973–74; Paris, 1978–82; Midland Bank, 1985–87, Head of Banking Ops, 1986–87; Gp Chief Exec., Thomas Cook Gp, 1987–92; Chief Executive: Lloyd's of London, 1992–95; Salomon Brothers Internat., later Salomon Smith Barney, 1995–98; Chm., Football League, 1998–2000; Chief Exec., World Snooker Assoc., 1999–2000; Transaction Dir, Nomura Internat. plc, 2000–02. Chairman: London Luton Airport, 1999–2000; Rockingham Motor Speedway, 2000–02; Tees Valley Urban Regeneration Co., 2002–05; Harvey and Thompson plc, 2004–08. Non-exec. Dir, Thomas Cook Gp, 2009–12. *Recreations:* soccer, horse-racing, music. *Died 15 March 2014.*

MIDWINTER, Stanley Walter, CB 1982; Chief Planning Inspector (Director of Planning Inspectorate), Departments of the Environment and Transport, 1978–84; *b* 8 Dec. 1922; *s* of late Lewis Midwinter and Beatrice (*née* Webb); *m* 1954, Audrey Mary Pepper (*d* 1988); one *d*. *Educ:* Regent Street Polytechnic Sch.; Sch. of Architecture (DipArch, ARIBA 1948); Sch. of Planning and Res. for Regional Develt (AMTPI 1952, FRTPI 1965); Dip. in Sociol., Univ. of London, 1976. Served War, RE, 1942–46: N Africa, Italy, Greece. Planning Officer, LCC, 1949–54; Bor. Architect and Planning Officer, Larne, NI, 1955–60; joined Housing and Planning Inspectorate, 1960; Dep. Chief Inspector, 1976. Assessor at Belvoir Coalfield Inquiry,

1979. Town Planning Institute: Exam. Prize, 1952; Thomas Adams Prize, 1955; President's Prize, 1958. *Publications:* articles in TPI Jl. *Died 17 Dec. 2015.*

MILBURN, Donald B.; *see* Booker-Milburn.

MILES, Prof. Charles William Noel, CBE 1980; Head of Department of Land Management and Development, 1968–81, Dean of Faculty of Urban and Regional Studies, 1972–75, and Professor Emeritus, 1981, University of Reading; Chairman, Agricultural Wages Board for England and Wales, 1972–81; *b* 3 Nov. 1915; 2nd *s* of late Lt-Col Sir Charles William Miles, 5th Bt; *heir-presumptive* to nephew, Sir Philip John Miles, 7th Bt; *m* 1940, Jacqueline, (Dickie), Cross (*d* 1998); one *d* (one *s* decd). *Educ:* Stowe Sch.; Jesus Coll., Cambridge (MA). FRICS. Army Service, 1939–46; Univ. Demonstrator and Univ. Lectr, Dept of Estate Management, Cambridge, 1946–54; Chief Agent to Meyrick Estates in Hants and Anglesey, 1954–68; Agent to Bisterne Estate, 1957–68. Pres., Chartered Land Agents Soc., 1965–66; Mem., Cambs AEC, 1953–54; Mem., SE Region Adv. Cttee of Land Commn, 1967–70. Mem., Yates Cttee on Recreation Management Trng, 1977–82. Leverhulme Trust Emeritus Fellowship, 1982–84. *Publications:* Estate Finance and Business Management, 1953, 4th edn 1981; Estate Accounts, 1960; Recreational Land Management, 1977, 2nd edn 1992; (co-ed) Walmesley's Rural Estate Management, 6th edn, 1978; Running an Open house, 1986; Going Public, 1991; (jtly) Aspects of Rural Estate Management, 1995. *Recreations:* walking, gardening, theatre. *Address:* Brownstones, 49 The Quarry, Cam, Glos GL11 6JA. *Club:* Farmers. *Died 1 Feb. 2013.*

MILES, (Frank) Stephen, CMG 1964; HM Diplomatic Service, retired; *b* 7 Jan. 1920; *s* of Harry and Mary Miles; *m* 1953, Margaret Joy (*née* Theaker); three *d*. *Educ:* Hermitage Sch., Helensburgh; John Watson's Sch., Edinburgh; Daniel Stewart's Coll., Edinburgh; St Andrews Univ. (MA; Sec., Students' Rep. Council); Harvard Univ. (Commonwealth Fellowship; MPA). Served with Fleet Air Arm, 1942–46 (Lt (A) RNVR). Scottish Home Dept, 1948; FCO (previously CRO), 1948–80; served in: New Zealand, 1949–52; E and W Pakistan, 1954–57; Ghana, 1959–62; Uganda, 1962–63; British Dep. High Commissioner, Tanzania, 1963–65 (Acting High Commissioner, 1963–64); Acting High Commissioner in Ghana, March–April 1966; Consul-Gen., St Louis, 1967–70; Dep. High Comr, Calcutta, 1970–74; High Comr, Zambia, 1974–78; High Comr, Bangladesh, 1978–79. A Dir of Studies, Overseas Services Unit, RIPA, 1980–83. Councillor: Tandridge DC, Surrey, 1982–90; Limpsfield Parish Council, 1983–95 (Chm., 1987–89). *Recreations:* cricket, tennis, golf. *Address:* 25 Sycamore Court, Hoskins Road, Oxted, Surrey RH8 9JQ. *T:* (01883) 713132. *Clubs:* Royal Commonwealth Society, MCC; Tandridge Golf. *Died 26 April 2013.*

MILES, Sir Peter (Tremayne), KCVO 1986; an Extra Equerry to HM the Queen, since 1988; *b* 26 June 1924; *er s* of late Lt-Col E. W. T. Miles, MC; *m* 1956, Philippa Helen Tremlett; two *s* one *d*. *Educ:* Eton Coll.; RMC, Sandhurst. First The Royal Dragoons, 1944–49; J. F. Thomasson & Co., 1949–59; Gerrard & National Discount Co. Ltd, 1959–80 (Managing Director, 1964–80). Director: P. Murray-Jones Ltd, 1966–75; Astley & Pearce Holdings Ltd, 1975–80 (Chm., 1978–80). Keeper of the Privy Purse and Treas. to the Queen, 1981–87; Receiver-Gen., Duchy of Lancaster, 1981–87; Mem., Prince of Wales' Council, 1981–87. *Clubs:* Cavalry and Guards, Pratt's, White's. *Died 15 Oct. 2013.*

MILES, Raymond Reginald; Chief Executive, CP Ships Ltd, 1988–2005; *b* 2 Aug. 1944; *s* of Reginald Gonville Miles and Ellen Mary Miles (*née* Gower); *m* 1966, Susan Georgina Barrow, *d* of George Barrow; two *d*. *Educ:* Lanchester Poly. (BA Econs); London Business Sch. (MBA 1972). Ocean Group plc, Liverpool: Corporate Planner, 1972–75; Divl Finance Dir, 1975–78; Wilh. Wilhelmsen, Norway, USA and London: Exec. Vice Pres., Barber Blue Sea, 1978–86; Man. Dir, Global Equipt Mgt, 1986–88. Sen. Ind. Dir, Provident Financial plc, 2003–06; Sen. Ind. Dir, 2006–08, Chm., 2008–11, Southern Cross Healthcare Gp plc; Lead Ind. Dir, Stelmar Shipping Ltd, USA, 2004–05; Adv. Dir, Stena AB, Sweden, 2006–; Dep. Chm., Internat. Personal Finance plc, 2006–10; Adv. Dir, Survitec Gp, 2012–. Chm., World Shipping Council, 2001–05. Dir, W of England Protection and Indemnity Club, 1994–2004; Chm., Box Club, 2003–05. Trustee: Nat. Maritime Mus., Greenwich, 1998–2006; Nat. Maritime Mus., Cornwall, 2001–08; Garden Opera, 2003–10; Country Holidays for Inner City Kids, 2006–11; Chm., Devon Community Foundn, 2006–09. *Recreations:* Chelsea FC, opera, theatre, shooting. *E:* ray.miles@woodtown.org. *Club:* Reform. *Died 6 Nov. 2015.*

MILES, Roy; dealer in British fine paintings and writer; *b* 9 Feb. 1935; *s* of Edward Marsh and Elsa McKinley (who later *m* George Miles); *m* 1970, Christine Rhodes (*d* 1997). *Educ:* Bembridge Sch., Isle of Wight; Sorbonne, Paris. Gold Medal for painting, Liverpool Watercolour Soc., 1945. Set world record prices for British paintings, such as Stubbs and Canaletto, 1970; subseq. instrumental in creation of Victorian art market. Dir and prop., Roy Miles Gall., 1975–98; first dealer to put on exhibitions of Russian art, early 1980s. Encouraged young artists; worked with various charities. *Publications:* Priceless: a life in art (autobiog.), 2003; articles in magazines, newspapers and jls. *Recreation:* classical music. *Address:* 10 Ennismore Gardens, SW7 1NP. *T:* (020) 7581 7969. *Died 10 Dec. 2012.*

MILES, Stephen; *see* Miles, F. S.

MILLAN, Rt Hon. Bruce; PC 1975; Member, Commission of the European Communities, 1989–95; *b* 5 Oct. 1927; *s* of David Millan; *m* 1953, Gwendoline May Fairey; one *s* one *d*. *Educ:* Harris Academy, Dundee. Chartered Accountant, 1950–59. Contested: West Renfrewshire, 1951, Craigton Div. of Glasgow, 1955. MP (Lab): Glasgow, Craigton, 1959–83; Glasgow, Govan, 1983–88; Parly Under-Sec. of State: for Defence, (RAF), 1964–66, for Scotland, 1966–70; Minister of State, Scottish Office, 1974–76; Sec. of State for Scotland, 1976–79; opposition spokesman on Scotland, 1979–83. *Address:* 1 Torridon Avenue, Glasgow G41 5LA. *T:* (0141) 427 6483. *Died 21 Feb. 2013.*

MILLARD, Sir Guy (Elwin), KCMG 1972 (CMG 1957); CVO 1961; HM Diplomatic Service, retired; *b* 22 Jan. 1917; *s* of Col Baldwin Salter Millard, and Phyllis Mary Tetley; *m* 1st, 1946, Anne (marr. diss. 1963), *d* of Gordon Mackenzie; one *s* one *d*; 2nd, 1964, Mary Judy, *d* of late James Dugdale and Pamela Dugdale (*née* Coventry, later Pamela, Countess of Aylesford); two *s*. *Educ:* Charterhouse; Pembroke Coll., Cambridge. Served RN, World War II. HM Diplomatic Service, 1939–76: Ambassador to Hungary, 1967–69; Minister, Washington, 1970–71; Ambassador to Sweden, 1971–74; Ambassador to Italy, 1974–76. Chm., British-Italian Soc., 1977–83. Grand Officer, Order of Merit, Italy, 1981. *Address:* Fyfield Manor, Southrop, Glos GL7 3NZ. *T:* (01367) 850234. *Died 26 April 2013.*

MILLEN, Brig. Anthony Tristram Patrick; Defence Advisor to British High Commissioner, Ottawa, Canada, 1980–83; *b* 15 Dec. 1928; *s* of Charles Reginald Millen and Annie Mary Martin; *m* 1954, Mary Alice Featherston Johnston (*d* 2008); three *s* two *d* (and two *s* decd). *Educ:* Mount St Mary's Coll. 5th Royal Inniskilling Dragoon Guards, 1948; served in Germany, Korea, Cyprus, N Ireland, Hong Kong, USA. *Publications:* articles in US military jls. *Recreation:* sailing. *Address:* Finchley House, Crakehall, Bedale, N Yorks DL8 1HJ. *T:* (01677) 425922. *Died 20 March 2013.*

MILLER OF HENDON, Baroness *cr* 1993 (Life Peer), of Gore in the London Borough of Barnet; **Doreen Miller,** MBE 1989; JP; *b* 13 June 1933; *d* of Bernard Henry Feldman and Hetty Feldman; *m* 1955, Henry Miller; three *s*. *Educ:* Brondesbury and Kilburn High Sch.; LSE; Univ. of Hull (MA). Chairman and Managing Director, 1971–88: Universal Beauty Club Ltd (UK); Cosmetic Club International GmbH (Germany); Universal Beauty Club (Pty) Ltd (Australia). Nat. Chm. and Exec. Dir, The 300 Group, 1985–88; Chm., Women Into Public Life Campaign, 1987–; Human Rights Advr, Soroptimist International, 1987–90. A Baroness in Waiting (Govt Whip), 1994–97; an Opposition Whip, 1997–99; Opposition spokesman on trade and industry, 1999–2007.

Crown Agent, 1990–94. Chairman: Barnet FHSA, 1990–94; Nat. Assoc. of Hosp. and Community Friends (formerly Nat. Assoc. of Leagues of Hosp. Friends), 1997–2003. Mem., Monopolies and Mergers Commn, 1992–93. Trustee, Menerva Educnl Trust, 1992–. Jt Treas., 1990–93, Chm., 1993–96, Pres., 1996–98, Greater London Area, Nat. Union of Conservative & Unionist Party. FRSA. JP Brent, 1971. *Publications:* Let's Make Up, 1975. *Recreations:* politics, reading, football, sitting by sunlit swimming pools given the opportunity. *Address:* House of Lords, SW1A 0PW. *Died 21 June 2014.*

MILLER, Bruce; *see* Miller, J. D. B.

MILLER, Sir Hilary Duppa, (Sir Hal), Kt 1988; DL; Chairman, Cosmopolitan Holdings Ltd, 1991–2005; *b* 6 March 1929; *s* of late Lt-Comdr John Bryan Peter Duppa-Miller, GC, and Hon. Barbara Miller, *y d* of 1st Viscount Buckmaster; *m* 1st, 1956, Fiona Margaret McDermid; two *s* two *d*; 2nd, 1976, Jacqueline Roe, *d* of T. C. W. Roe and Elizabeth Ann Roe (later Lady Londesborough); one *s* one *d*. *Educ:* Eton; Merton Coll., Oxford (MA 1956); London Univ. (BSc (Estate Management) 1962). With Colonial Service, Hong Kong, 1955–68. Company Director. Chief Exec., SMMT, 1991–93. Contested: (C), Barrow-in-Furness, 1970; Bromsgrove by-elecn, May 1971; MP (C) Bromsgrove and Redditch, Feb. 1974–1983, Bromsgrove, 1983–92. PPS to Sec. of State for Defence, 1979–81, to Chancellor of the Duchy of Lancaster, 1981, resigned; Vice-Chm., Conservative Party Orgn, and PPS to the Chm., 1984–87; Mem., UK delegn to Council of Europe, 1974–76. Jt Chm., All Party Motor Industry Gp, 1978. Chm., Nat. Clubs Assoc., 2001–09. Mem. Council, RFU, 2003–09. Fellow, Econ. Develt Inst. of World Bank, Washington. Trustee, Age UK, Hereford and localities, 2009–13. DL Worcs, 2000. *Recreations:* sailing, fell walking, cricket, Rugby. *Address:* Moorcroft Farm, Sinton Green, Worcester, Worcs WR2 6NW. *Clubs:* Oxford and Cambridge; Vincent's (Oxford); Eton Ramblers, Free Foresters, Blackheath Football (Pres., 1999–2003). *Died 21 March 2015.*

MILLER, Prof. J(ohn) D(onald) Bruce; Executive Director, Academy of the Social Sciences in Australia, 1989–91; Professor of International Relations, Research School of Pacific Studies, Australian National University, 1962–87, then Emeritus; *b* 30 Aug. 1922; *s* of Donald and Marion Miller, Sydney, Australia; *m* 1st, 1943, Enid Huthnance; one *s*; 2nd, 1957, Margaret Martin; one *s*; 3rd, 1990, Judith Bennet. *Educ:* Sydney High Sch.; University of Sydney (BEc, 1944; MEc 1951); MA Cantab 1978. Announcer and Talks Officer, Australian Broadcasting Commission, Sydney and Canberra, 1939–46; Staff Tutor, Department of Tutorial Classes, University of Sydney, 1946–52; Asst Lecturer in Political Science and International Relations, London Sch. of Economics, 1953–55; Lecturer in Politics, University Coll., Leicester, 1955–57; Prof. of Politics, University of Leicester, 1957–62; Dean of Social Sciences, 1960–62; Public Orator, 1961–62. Res. Associate, Chatham House, 1965, 1969, 1973. Visiting Professor: Indian Sch. of International Studies, 1959; Columbia Univ., New York, 1962, 1966, 1981; Yale, 1977; Princeton, 1984, 1986; Overseas Vis. Fellow, St John's Coll., and Smuts Vis. Fellow, Cambridge Univ., 1977–78; Macrossan Lectr, University of Queensland, 1966. Member: Aust. Population and Immigration Council, 1975–81; Aust. Res. Grants Cttee, 1975–81. Joint Editor, Journal of Commonwealth Political Studies, 1961–62; Editor, Australian Outlook, 1963–69; Chm., Editorial Adv. Bd for Austr. documents on foreign relations, 1971–77; Austr. Nat. Commn for UNESCO, 1982–84, 1990–93. Canberra correspondent, The Economist, 1962–87. FASSA 1967 (Treas., 1979–83). *Publications:* Australian Government and Politics, 1954, 4th edn with B. Jinks 1970; Richard Jebb and the Problem of Empire, 1956; Politicians (inaugural), 1958; The Commonwealth in the World, 1958; The Nature of Politics, 1962; The Shape of Diplomacy (inaugural), 1963; Australia and Foreign Policy (Boyer Lectures), 1963; (ed with T. H. Rigby) The Disintegrating Monolith, 1965; Britain and the Old Dominions, 1966; Australia, 1966; The Politics of the Third World, 1966; (ed) India, Japan, Australia: Partners in Asia?, 1968; Survey of Commonwealth Affairs: problems of expansion and attrition 1953–1969, 1974; (ed) Australia's Economic Relations, 1975; The EEC and Australia, 1976; The World of States, 1981; Ideology and Foreign Policy, 1982; Norman Angell and the Futility of War, 1986; (ed) Australians and British, 1987; (ed with L. J. Evans) Policy and Practice, 1987; (ed with R. J. Vincent) Order and Violence, 1990. *Recreation:* staying alive. *Address:* Morling Lodge, Redhill, ACT 2603, Australia. *T:* (2) 62952339. *Died 16 Jan. 2011.*

MILLER, Prof. Karl Fergus Connor; Lord Northcliffe Professor of Modern English Literature, University College London, 1974–92; Editor, 1979–89, and Co-Editor, 1989–92, London Review of Books; *b* 2 Aug. 1931; *s* of William and Marion Miller; *m* 1956, Jane Elisabeth Collet; two *s* one *d*. *Educ:* Royal High School, Edinburgh; Downing Coll., Cambridge. Asst Prin., HM Treasury, 1956–57; BBC TV Producer, 1957–58; Literary Editor, Spectator, 1958–61; Literary Editor, New Statesman, 1961–67; Editor, Listener, 1967–73. FRSL 1992. *Publications:* (ed) Poetry from Cambridge, 1952–54, 1955; (ed, with introd.) Writing in England Today: The Last Fifteen Years, 1968; (ed) Memoirs of a Modern Scotland, 1970; (ed) A Listener Anthology, August 1967–June 1970, 1970; (ed) A Second Listener Anthology, 1973; (ed) Henry Cockburn, Memorials of his Time, 1974; Cockburn's Millennium, 1975; (ed, with introd.) Robert Burns, 1981; Doubles: studies in literary history, 1985; Authors, 1989; Rebecca's Vest (autobiog.), 1993; Boswell and Hyde, 1995; Dark Horses: an experience of literary journalism (autobiog.), 1998; Electric Shepherd: a likeness of James Hogg, 2003; Tretower to Clyro (essays), 2011. *Recreation:* watching football. *Address:* 26 Limerston Street, SW10 0HH. *Died 24 Sept. 2014.*

MILLER, Keith William, FICE, FCIHT; Director, Keith Miller Consultants Ltd, 2007–11; *b* 25 Sept. 1952; *s* of late William George Ernest Miller and Doris Julia Miller (*née* Stapleton); *m* 1973, Vivien Jean Holding; one *s* one *d*. *Educ:* Luton Grammar Sch.; Luton Sixth Form Coll.; Univ. of Salford (BSc Civil Engrg 1973). CEng 1979; MICE 1980, FICE 2004; MIHT 1980, FCIHT (FIHT 2004). Norwest Holst, 1973–74; Luton BC, 1974–79; Department of Transport: Project Engr, 1979–86; Principal Private Sec. to Minister of State for Transport, 1986–88; Principal Engr, 1988–93; Projects Dir, 1993–96; Highways Agency: IT Dir, 1996–2000; Divl Dir, 10-Year Strategy, 2000, Lands and Ops Mgt, 2000–03, Dir of Major Projects, 2003–07. Mem. Council, ICE, 2005–08. *Publications:* minor contribs in technical press and jls. *Recreations:* meeting friends, painting muddy watercolours, playing games with my grandsons. *Address:* 1 Hartham Close, Grafham, Huntingdon, Cambs PE28 0ED. *Died 16 Oct. 2014.*

MILLER, Dr Kenneth Allan Glen, CBE 1988; FREng, FIMechE; Director General, Engineering Council, 1982–88; *b* 27 July 1926; *s* of Dr Allan Frederick Miller and Margaret Hutchison (*née* Glen); *m* 1st, 1954, Dorothy Elaine Brown (marr. diss. 1999); two *s* (and one *s* decd); 2nd, 1999, Betty Nanette Hatton (*née* Bridgwater). *Educ:* Upper Canada Coll., Toronto; Trinity Hall, Cambridge (BA 1946; MA 1950; Hon. Fellow, 1992); PhD Wales, 1949. FIMechE 1965; FREng (FEng 1981). Res. Asst to Prof. of Physics, Aberystwyth, 1946; joined ICI, Billingham, 1949; various posts on production and design, 1949–59; seconded to BTC, 1959–60; Asst Tech. Manager, 1960, Engrg Manager, 1963, Engrg Dir, 1965, HOC Div., ICI; Engrg Advr, ICI, 1971; Managing Director: APV Co., 1974; APV Holdings, 1977–82. Chm., Pollution Control and Measurement (Europe), subseq. PCME, Ltd, 1993–2002. Deputy Chairman: ECCTIS 2000 Ltd, 1990–96; standing Conf. on Schs' Sci. and Technology, 1990–96. Member: Cttee for Industrial Technol., 1972–76; UGC, 1981–83; Chm., Steering Cttee for Manufg Adv. Service, 1977–82. Member Council: Fellowship of Engrg, 1982–85; CRAC, 1987–96. FInstD 1974; CCMI (CIMgt 1985). *Publications:* The Outspoken Dr Miller (memoirs), 2006. *Recreations:* theatre, photography. *Address:* 66 Trematon Place, Broom Road, Teddington, Middx TW11 9RH. *T:* (020) 8943 3561. *Club:* Leander. *Died 5 April 2015.*

MILLER, Martin John; Chairman, City Diaries, since 1997; Co-Founder and Managing Director, Milroy Estates Ltd, since 1983; Founder, Martin Miller Foundation, since 2012; *b* 24 Nov. 1946; *s* of Marcus and Phyllis Miller; *m* 1st, 1966, Elaine (marr. diss. 1975); three *d*; 2nd, 1978, Judith Henderson Cairns (marr. diss. 1992); two *d*; 3rd, 2001, Ioana Beju. *Educ:* West Tarring Secondary Modern Sch., Worthing. Freelance photographer, 1965–68; Co-Founder, Lyle Publications, 1968–74; semi-retirement, 1974–79; Co-Founder, MJM Publications, 1979; Co-Founder, and Publisher, Miller's Magazine, 1991–95; Co-Founder, Martin Miller's Gin, 1999; with Judith Miller opened Chilston Park Hotel, 1985; opened: Miller's Residence, Notting Hill, 1997; Miller's Academy of Arts and Science, 2006; Glencot House Hotel, Somerset, 2007; (with Tanya Miller) Miller's at The Anchor Hotel, Somerset, 2009; Great Brampton House, Herefordshire, 2011; Down Stairs (contemp. art gall.), Herefordshire, 2011; Miller's at Tors, Lynmouth, 2012; Miller's Bistro and Hotel, 2012; The Arts Hotel, Lynmouth, 2012. Founder, Stay Historic website, Miller's Assoc. of Historic Hotels, Inns and Hideaways, 2009. *Publications:* Miller's Collectables Price Guide (with Judith Miller, annually, 1989–98); Antiques Source Book (annually, 2000–06); Antiques: furniture, 2002; Antiques Collectables, 2002; 20th Century Antiques, 2003; The Complete Guide to Antiques, 2003; Disjointed Noughts: collected poems, 2006; with Judith Miller: Miller's Antiques Price Guide, annually, 1979–98; The Antiques Directory—Furniture, 1985; Period Details, 1987; Miller's Antique Pocket Fact File, 1988; Period Style, 1989; Understanding Antiques, 1989; Country Style, 1990; Miller's Collectors Cars Price Guide, annually 1991–98; Miller's Art Deco Checklist, 1991; Furniture Checklist, 1991; Period Finishes and Effects, 1992; Victorian Style, 1993. *Recreations:* shooting, indulging in fine wines and gourmet food. *Club:* Groucho. *Died 24 Dec. 2013.*

MILLER, Terence George, TD 1960; MA Cantab; Director, Polytechnic of North London, 1971–80; *b* 16 Jan. 1918; *o s* of late George Frederick Miller, Cambridge, and Marion Johnston, Port William, Wigtownshire; *m* 1944, Inga Catriona (*d* 2012), 3rd *d* of Austin Priestman, MD, Folkestone, Kent; one *s* three *d*. *Educ:* Perse (foundn schol.); Jesus Coll., Cambridge (schol.; Nat. Sci. Tripos, pt 1 cl. 1, pt 2 cl. 1). Wiltshire Prizeman, 1939. Served War of 1939–45: RA, Glider Pilot Regt; RE (TA), 1947–67 (Lt-Col 1964). Harkness Scholar, 1948; Research Fellow, Jesus Coll., 1949–54. University Demonstrator, 1948; Lectr in Geology, Univ. of Keele, 1953; Sen. Lectr, 1963, Prof. of Geography, Univ. of Reading, 1965–67; Principal, University Coll. of Rhodesia, 1967–69; Vis. Prof., Reading Univ., 1969–71. *Publications:* Geology, 1950; Geology and Scenery in Britain, 1953; scientific papers in various jls. *Recreations:* studying command problems in war, listening. *Address:* Plough House, Docking Road, Sedgeford, Norfolk PE36 5LR. *Died 17 Jan. 2015.*

MILLING, Michael Crowley C.; *see* Crowley-Milling.

MILLS, Dame Barbara (Jean Lyon), DBE 1997; QC 1986; QC (NI) 1991; The Adjudicator, 1999–2009; Member, Financial Reporting Council, since 2008; *b* 10 Aug. 1940; *d* of John and Kitty Warnock; *m* 1962, John Angus Donald Mills; one *s* three *d*. *Educ:* St Helen's Sch., Northwood; Lady Margaret Hall, Oxford (Gibbs Scholar, 1961; MA; Hon. Fellow, 1991). Called to the Bar, Middle Temple, 1963, Bencher, 1990. Jun. Treasury Counsel, Central Criminal Court, 1981–86; a Recorder, 1982–92; Dir, Serious Fraud Office, 1990–92; DPP, 1992–98. Member: Criminal Injuries Compensation Bd, 1988–90; Parole Bd, 1990; Legal Assessor to GMC and GDC, 1988–90; DVO Complaints Assessor, 2001–04. Member: Gen. Adv. Council, BBC, 1991–92; Reporting Panel, Competition Commn, 2001–. Chairman: Forum UK, 1999–2001; Women's Liby Council, 2000–07; Professional Oversight Board, 2008–. Non-exec. Dir, Royal Free Hampstead NHS Trust, 2000–07. Governor, London Metropolitan (formerly London Guildhall) Univ., 1999–2007. Trustee, Victim Support, 1999–2004. Hon. Fellow, Soc. for Advanced Legal Studies, 1997. Hon. LLD: Hull, 1993; Nottingham Trent, 1993; London Guildhall, 1994. *Recreation:* my family. *Address:* Financial Reporting Council, 5th Floor, Aldwych House, 71–91 Aldwych, WC2B 4HN. *T:* (020) 7492 2341, *Fax:* (020) 7492 2359. *E:* b.mills@frc-pob.org.uk. *Died 28 May 2011.*

MILLS, Prof. Bernard Yarnton, AC 1976; DSc Eng; FRS 1963; FAA 1959; Professor of Physics (Astrophysics), University of Sydney, 1965–85, Emeritus Professor, 1986; *b* 8 Aug. 1920; *s* of Ellice Yarnton Mills and Sylphide Mills; *m* 1st, 1942, Lerida Karmalsky (*d* 1969); one *s* two *d*; 2nd, 1970, Crystal Davidson. *Educ:* King's Sch., New South Wales; University of Sydney. BSc 1940, DSc Eng 1959 (Sydney). Joined the then Council for Scientific and Industrial Research and worked on Develt of mil. radar systems; after working for many years on radioastronomy he joined Sydney Univ. to form a radioastronomy group in Sch. of Physics, 1960; Reader in Physics, 1960–65; responsible for Mills Cross radio-telescope, near Hoskinstown, NSW. Lyle Medal of Australian Academy of Science, 1957. *Publications:* (jtly) A Textbook of Radar, 1946; many contribs to sci. jls in Australia, England and America, mainly on subjects of radioastronomy and astrophysics. *Address:* 52 Victoria Street, Roseville, NSW 2069, Australia. *Died 25 April 2011.*

MILLS, Prof. Eric William, AM 1986; CChem, FRSC; FRACI; Director, South Australian Institute of Technology, 1978–85; *b* 22 April 1920; *s* of William and Lucy Margaret Mills; *m* 1st, 1945, Inge Julia Königsberger (*d* 1986); three *d*; 2nd, 1993, Natalya Bakaeva; one *d*. *Educ:* Liverpool Institute; Univ. of Liverpool (BSc, PhD). Chemist, British Insulated Cables, 1941–45; Research Chemist, British Oxygen Co., 1948–49; Sen. Lectr, Birmingham College of Advanced Technology, 1949–52; Head of Dept, Rutherford Coll. of Technology, 1952–57; Principal: Carlisle Technical Coll., 1958–60; Chesterfield Coll. of Technology, 1960–63; Asst Dir, SA Inst. of Technology, 1964–77. *Address:* 220 Greenhill Road, Eastwood, SA 5063, Australia. *T:* (8) 82741870. *Died 11 Jan. 2013.*

MILLS, Maj.-Gen. Giles Hallam, CB 1977; CVO 1984; OBE 1964; Major and Resident Governor, HM Tower of London, and Keeper of the Jewel House, 1979–84; *b* 1 April 1922; 2nd *s* of late Col Sir John Digby Mills, TD, Bisterne Manor, Ringwood, Hampshire, and Lady Mills; *m* 1947, Emily Snowden Hallam (*d* 2005), 2nd *d* of late Captain W. H. Tuck, Perrywood, Maryland, USA, and Mrs Tuck; two *s* one *d*. *Educ:* Eton Coll. Served War: 2nd Lieut, KRRC, 1941; 1st Bn, KRRC, N Africa, Italy (Adjt, despatches), 1943–47. Staff Coll., 1951; Armed Forces Staff Coll. (US), 1959; Mil. Asst to CIGS, 1961–63; CO, 2 Green Jackets, KRRC, 1963–65; Admin. Staff Coll., Henley, 1965; Regtl Col, Royal Green Jackets, 1966–67; Comd, 8 Infty Bde, 1968–69; IDC 1970; Comd, British Army Staff and Mil. Attaché, Washington, 1971–73; Divl Brig., The Light Div., 1973–74; Dir of Manning (Army), 1974–77, retd. *Publications:* Annals of The King's Royal Rifle Corps, vol. VI (with Roger Nixon), 1971, vol. VII, 1979. *Died 12 Sept. 2011.*

MILNE, Alasdair David Gordon; Director-General, BBC, 1982–87; *b* 8 Oct. 1930; *s* of late Charles Gordon Shaw Milne and Edith Reid Clark; *m* 1954, Sheila Kirsten Graucob (*d* 1992); two *s* one *d*. *Educ:* Winchester Coll.; New Coll., Oxford (Hon. Mods Oxon 1952; BA Oxon Mod. Langs, 1954; Hon. Fellow, 1985). Commnd into 1st Bn Gordon Highlanders, 1949. Joined BBC, 1954; Dep. Editor, 1957–61, Editor, 1961–62, of Tonight Programme; Head of Tonight Productions, 1963–65; Partner, Jay, Baverstock, Milne & Co., 1965–67; rejoined BBC, Oct. 1967; Controller, BBC Scotland, 1968–72; Dir of Programmes, 1973–77, Man. Dir, 1977–82, BBC TV; Dep. Dir-Gen., BBC, 1980–82. Chm., Darrell Waters Ltd, 1988–90. Chm., Gaelic Broadcasting Task Force, 1999–2000. Vis. Prof., Univ. of Miami, 1989. Vice-Pres., RTS, 1986–87. Chm., John MacFadyen Meml Trust, 1980–93. DUniv Stirling, 1983. Cyril Bennett Award, RTS, 1987. *Publications:* DG: the memoirs of a British broadcaster, 1988. *Recreations:* piping, salmon fishing, golf. *Address:* 30 Holland Park Avenue, W11 3QU. *Club:* Travellers. *Died 8 Jan. 2013.*

MILNE, Peter Alexander, PhD; Eur Ing, CEng, FIMechE, FIMarEST; Senior Consultant, AMRIE, 1996–2000 (Director, 1994–96); *b* 23 April 1935; *s* of late Alexander Ogston Milne and of Lilian Winifred Milne (*née* Murray); *m* 1961, Beatrice Taylor Reid; two *d*. *Educ:* Tynemouth Sch.; Harwell Reactor Sch.; BSc Marine Engrg Univ. of Durham 1957; PhD Applied Sci. Univ. of Newcastle 1960. Practical experience with apprenticeship at Wallsend Slipway & Engineering and at sea with Union Castle Mail Steamship; Trainee Manager, Swan Hunter Gp, 1961; Technical Dir, Swan Hunter Shipbuilders, 1970–74, Man. Dir, 1974–77; British Shipbuilders HQ at formation of Corp., 1977; Man. Dir, Shipbuilding Ops, 1978–80, Mem. Bd, 1981–90 (Bd Mem. for Engrg, 1981–83, for Merchant Ship and Enginebuilding, 1985–90), Man. Dir, Merchant and Composite Div., 1984, British Shipbuilders; Man. Dir, BMT Cortec, 1990–94. Director: Vosper Thornycroft, 1978–80; Tyneside Maritime and Engrg, 1996–98. Bd Mem., SMRTB, 1971–75; Chm., BSI Ind. Cttee, 1972–76; Dir, Lloyds Register of Shipping, 1984–91; Chm., Northern Engrg Centre, 1990–94. Vis. Lectr in Marine Engrg, Newcastle Univ., 1970–75. Pres., NECInst, 1986–88. Freeman, City of London, 1984; Liveryman, Shipwrights' Co., 1984–98. *Publications:* papers related to science and industry. *Recreations:* watching Rugby, cricket, hill-walking, enjoying grandchildren. *Address:* 14 Woodland Close, Earsdon Village, Whitley Bay, Tyne and Wear NE25 9LL. *T:* (0191) 252 2708. *Died 11 April 2013.*

MILNES, Rodney; *see* Blumer, Rodney Milnes.

MILTON, Sir Simon (Henry), Kt 2006; Deputy Mayor of London, Policy and Planning, since 2008; Chief of Staff to Mayor of London, since 2009; *b* 2 Oct. 1961; *s* of Clive Milton and Ruth Milton (*née* Klein); civil partnership 2007, Robert Jonathan Davis. *Educ:* Gonville and Caius Coll., Cambridge (BA Hons Hist 1983); Cornell Univ. (Master Professional Studies). Man. Dir, 1995–99, Chm., 1999–2001, Apco UK Ltd. Mem. (C), Westminster CC, 1988–2008 (Leader, 2000–08). Dep. Chm., Central London Partnership, 2002–. Dep. Chm., 2005–07, Chm., 2007–08, Sen. Advr, Planning, 2008, LGA; Bd Mem., Leadership Centre for Local Govt, 2005–. *Recreation:* city management. *Address:* Greater London Authority, City Hall, Queen's Walk, SE1 2AA. *Died 11 April 2011.*

MILTON-THOMPSON, Surg. Vice-Adm. Sir Godfrey (James), KBE 1988; FRCP; Warden, St Katharine's House, Wantage, 1993–98; Medical Director General (Naval), 1985–90; Surgeon General, Ministry of Defence, 1988–90; *b* 25 April 1930; *s* of Rev. James Milton-Thompson and May LeMare (*née* Hoare); *m* 1952, Noreen Helena Frances, *d* of Lt-Col Sir Desmond Fitzmaurice, CIE; three *d*. *Educ:* Eastbourne Coll.; Queens' Coll., Cambridge (MA); St Thomas' Hosp. (MB BChir); FRCP 1974 (MRCP 1961); DCH 1963. Joined Royal Navy, 1955; after general service and hosp. appts at home and abroad, Cons. Phys., RN Hosp., Plymouth, 1967–70 and 1972–75; Hon. Research Fellow, St Mark's Hosp., London, 1969–71; Prof. of Naval Medicine, 1975–80; RCDS 1981; Dep. Medical Director General (Naval), 1982–84; Surg. Rear-Adm. (Operational Med. Services), 1984–85; Dep. Surg. Gen. (Research and Trng), MoD, 1985–87. QHP, 1982–90. Chm., Cornwall Community Healthcare Trust, 1991–93. Member: Medical Research Soc., 1971–; British Soc. of Gastroenterology, 1972–; Vice Pres., British Digestive Foundn, 1993–2012. Hon. Col, 211 (Wessex) Field Hosp., RAMC(V), 1990–95. Chm., Liskeard DFAS, 2001–06. Gov., St Mary's Sch., Wantage, 1995–2006 (Chm., 1996–2006). Errol-Eldridge Prize, 1974; Gilbert Blane Medal, 1976. KStJ 1989 (Mem., Chapter Gen., 1988–95; Hospitaller, 1991–95; Chm., St John Council, Cornwall, 2000–10; Mem., English Priory Chapter, 2000–12; Nat. Chm., St John Fellowship, 2009–12). *Publications:* on clinical pharmacology of the gastro-intestinal tract and therapy of peptic ulcer, etc, in med. jls. *Recreations:* fishing, paintings and painting, literature, archery. *Address:* Pool Hall, Menheniot, Liskeard, Cornwall PL14 3QT. *Club:* Naval and Military. *Died 23 Sept. 2012.*

MINOGUE, Prof. Kenneth Robert; Professor of Political Science, London School of Economics and Political Science, University of London, 1984–95, then Emeritus; freelance writer; *b* 11 Sept. 1930; *s* of Denis Francis Minogue and Eunice Pearl Minogue (*née* Porter); *m* 1st, 1954, Valerie Pearson Hallett (marr. diss. 2001); one *s* one *d*; 2nd, Beverly Cohen (decd). *Educ:* Sydney Boys' High Sch.; Sydney Univ. (BA); London School of Economics (BScEcon; Hon. Fellow, 2002). Asst Lectr, Univ. of Exeter, 1955–56; London School of Economics: Asst Lectr, 1956; Sen. Lectr, 1964; Reader, 1971. Trustee, Civitas, 2000–. Centenary Medal for services to political science (Australia), 2003. *Publications:* The Liberal Mind, 1961; Nationalism, 1967; The Concept of a University, 1974; Alien Powers: the pure theory of ideology, 1985; Politics: a very short introduction, 1995; (ed and contrib.) Conservative Realism, 1996; The Silencing of Society, 1997; Waitangi Morality Reality, 1998; The Servile Mind: how democracy erodes the moral life, 2010; numerous contribs to learned jls. *Recreations:* opera, walking. *Address:* 93 Hamlet Gardens, W6 0SX. *T:* (020) 8741 8471. *Club:* Garrick. *Died 28 June 2013.*

MINTOFF, Hon. Dominic, (Dom), BSc, BE&A, MA, A&CE; Prime Minister of Malta, 1971–84; Leader of Malta Labour Party, 1949–84; *b* Cospicua, 6 Aug. 1916; *s* of Lawrence Mintoff and late Concetta (*née* Farrugia); *m* 1947, Moyra de Vere Bentinck (*d* 1997); two *d*. *Educ:* Govt Elem. Sch., Seminary and Lyceum, Malta; Univ. of Malta (BSc 1937; BE&A, A&CE 1939); Hertford Coll., Oxford (Govt Travelling Scholar; Rhodes Scholar; MA Engrg Science). Practised as civil engineer in Britain, 1941–43, and as architect in Malta, 1943–. Gen. Sec. Malta Labour Party, 1936–37; Mem., Council of Govt and Exec. Council, 1945; MP (Lab) Malta, 1947–98 (did not seek re-election following disagreement with Lab Party policies); Dep. Prime Minister and Minister for Works and Reconstruction, 1947–49 (resigned); Prime Minister and Minister of Finance, 1955–58; resigned office in 1958 to lead the Maltese Liberation Movement; Leader of Opposition, 1962–71; Minister of Foreign Affairs, 1971–81; Minister of the Interior, 1976–81 and 1983–84. Mem., Labour delegns to UK, 1945, 1947, 1948 and 1949. Negotiated removal of British Military base, 1971 and other foreign mil. bases by 1979. Co-Chairman: Malta Peace Movement, 2003–; Malta Arise Front, 2003–. Dr *hc* Univ. of Pol Studies, Ponterios, Greece, 1976. Order of the Republic, Libya, 1971; Grand Cordon: Order of the Republic, Tunisia, 1973; Order of Ouissam Alaouite, 1978. *Publications:* scientific, literary and artistic works. *Recreations:* horse-riding, swimming, water ski-ing, boċċi. *Address:* The Olives, Tarxien, Malta. *Died 20 Aug. 2012.*

MINTON, Kenneth Joseph, CBE 1995; Executive Chairman, 4 Imprint plc, 2004–10; Director: Solvay SA, 1996–2006; Pay Point plc, 2004–08; *b* 17 Jan. 1937; *s* of late Henry Minton and Lilian Minton (*née* Moore); *m* 1961, Mary Wilson; one *s*. *Educ:* Leeds Univ. (BSc 1st cl. Hons Mining Engrg). Management positions with: Unilever, UK and France, 1960–68; Laporte plc, 1968–95 (Chief Exec. and Man. Dir, 1979–95); Chm., SGB Gp plc, 1997–2000 (non-exec. Dir, SGB, 1997–2000); Executive Chairman: Arjo Wiggins Appleton plc, 1997–2001; Inveresk plc, 2001–02; non-executive Director: Caradon plc, 1991–99; Jeyes Gp plc, 1989–98 (Chm., 1993–96); John Mowlem & Co. PLC, 1994–98 (Chm., 1995–98); Sentrachem Ltd, 1996–97; Tomkins plc, 2000–06. Mem. Bd, CEFIC, 1991–95. Trustee, Industry and Parlt Trust, 1998– (Founder Mem., 1977; Chm., Mgt Council, 1993–96). Pres., SCI, 1996–98. SCI Centenary Medal, 1994. KSG 2006. *Recreations:* gardens, fine art, walking, South Africa, charities. *Address:* 7 Midway, St Albans, Herts AL3 4BD. *Died 19 Nov. 2015.*

MIRRLEES, Robin Ian Evelyn Stuart de la Lanne-; Richmond Herald of Arms, 1962–67; *b* Paris, 13 Jan. 1925; *s* of Duncan Gribbell-Milne and Countess Frances de la Lanne (later Mirrlees); grandson of Ambassador La Lanne; godson of 11th Duke of Argyll; one *s*. *Educ:* Cairo; Merton Coll., Oxford (MA). Several language diplomas. Served India, 1942–46; Captain RA, 1944; Gen. Staff, New Delhi, 1946; Embassy Attaché, Tokyo, 1947; Rouge Dragon Pursuivant of Arms, 1952–62 (and as such attended Coronation). Co-editor, Annuaire de France, 1966–. ADC to HM the King of Yugoslavia, 1963–70. Raised substantial funds for humanitarian organisations (incl. own private donations); undertook restoration of Inchdrewer Castle, Scotland, and others; Laird of Island of Bernera, pop. *c* 250. Freeman of City of London, 1960. Patrician of San Marino, 1964. Succeeded to the title of Comte de Lalanne (France), 1962 and titular Prince of Coronata. Various foreign orders of knighthood. *Recreations:* piloting, travelling, painting, mystic philosophy, fox-hunting. *Address:* Bernera Lodge, Great Bernera Island, by Stornoway, Outer Hebrides, Scotland. *Clubs:* Lansdowne; Travellers (Paris). *Died 23 June 2012.*

MITCHELL, Prof. Basil George, DD; FBA 1983; Nolloth Professor of the Philosophy of the Christian Religion, Oxford University, 1968–84; Fellow of Oriel College, 1968–84, then Emeritus; *b* 9 April 1917; *s* of George William Mitchell and Mary Mitchell (*née* Loxston); *m* 1950, Margaret Eleanor Collin; one *s* three *d. Educ:* King Edward VI Sch., Southampton; Queen's Coll., Oxford (Southampton Exhibitioner. 1st cl. Lit Hum 1939). Served Royal Navy, 1940–46; Lt RNVR 1942, Instructor Lt RN 1945. Lectr, Christ Church, Oxford, 1946–47; Fellow and Tutor in Philosophy, Keble Coll., Oxford, 1947–67, Emeritus Fellow, 1981; Sen. Proctor, 1956–57; Hebdomadal Council, 1959–65. Visiting Professor: Princeton Univ., 1963; Colgate Univ., 1976. Lectures: Stanton, in Philosophy of Religion, Cambridge Univ., 1959–62; Edward Cadbury, University of Birmingham, 1966–67; Gifford, Glasgow Univ., 1974–76; Nathaniel Taylor, Yale, 1986; Martin, Univ. of Hong Kong, 1987; Norton, Southern Baptist Theol Seminary, Louisville, 1989; Sarum, Oxford Univ., 1992. Member: C of E Working Parties on Ethical Questions, 1964–78; Doctrine Commn, 1978–84. Hon. DD Glasgow, 1977; Hon. DLitHum Union Coll., Schenectady, 1979. *Publications:* (ed) Faith and Logic, 1957; Law, Morality and Religion in a Secular Society, 1967; Neutrality and Commitment, 1968; (ed) The Philosophy of Religion, 1971; The Justification of Religious Belief, 1973; Morality: Religious and Secular, 1980; How to Play Theological Ping Pong, 1990; Faith and Criticism, 1994; (with J. R. Lucas) Engaging with Plato's Republic, 2003; Looking Back on Faith, Philosophy and Friends in Oxford, 2009; articles in philosophical and theological periodicals. *Recreations:* gardening, flower arrangement. *Address:* Bartholomew House, 9 Market Street, Woodstock, Oxford OX20 1SU. *T:* (01993) 811265. *Died 23 June 2011.*

MITCHELL, Sir David (Bower), Kt 1988; DL; *b* 20 June 1928; *er s* of James Mitchell, Naval Architect; *m* 1954, Pamela Elaine Haward (*d* 2005); two *s* one *d. Educ:* Aldenham. Farming, 1945–50; businessman, wine merchant, 1951–79. Chm., El Vino Co. Ltd, 1992–2001. MP (C) Basingstoke, 1964–83, Hampshire North West, 1983–97. An Opposition Whip, 1965–67; PPS to Sec. of State for Social Services, 1970–74; Parly Under Sec. of State, DoI, 1979–81, NI Office, 1981–83, Dept of Transport, 1983–85; Minister of State for Transport, 1986–88. Chm., Cons. Parly Smaller Business Cttee, 1974–79. Founder, Small Business Bureau, 1976. DL Hants, 1994. *Recreations:* gardening, walking, wine-tasting, travel. *Club:* Carlton. *Died 30 Aug. 2014.*

MITCHELL, Rear-Adm. Geoffrey Charles, CB 1973; Director, The Old Granary Art and Craft Centre, Bishop's Waltham, Hants, 1975–86; *b* 21 July 1921; *s* of William C. Mitchell; *m* 1st, 1955, Jocelyn Rainger (*d* 1987), Auckland, NZ; one *s* two *d*; 2nd, 1990, Dr Hilary Gardiner. *Educ:* Marlborough College. Joined RN 1940; Captain 1961; Director Officer Recruiting, 1961–63; Captain (F), 2nd Frigate Sqdn, 1963–65; Director Naval Ops and Trade, 1965–67; Comdr, NATO Standing Naval Force Atlantic, 1968–69; Director Strategic Policy, to Supreme Allied Comdr Atlantic, 1969–71; Rear Adm. 1971; Dep. Asst Chief of Staff (Ops), SHAPE, 1971–74; Chm., RNR and Naval Cadet Forces Review Bd, 1974–75. *Recreations:* golf, painting, music, languages, sailing. *Address:* 10 Nelson Close, Stockbridge, Hants SO20 6ES. *T:* (01264) 810365. *Died 15 Oct. 2015.*

MITCHELL, Prof. Joan Eileen, (Mrs James Cattermole); Professor of Political Economy, University of Nottingham, 1978–85; *b* 15 March 1920; *d* of late Albert Henry Mitchell, Paper Merchant, and Eva Mitchell; *m* 1956, James Cattermole (*d* 2007); one *s* one *d. Educ:* Southend-on-Sea High Sch.; St Hilda's Coll., Oxford. Economist, Min. of Fuel and Power, 1942; Tutor, St Anne's Coll., Oxford, 1945; Economist, BoT, 1947; Research Officer, Labour Party, 1950; Lectr in Econs, Nottingham Univ., 1952, Reader in Econs, 1962. Mem., NBPI, 1965–68; personal economic adviser to Sec. of State for Prices and Consumer Protection, 1974–76. Member: Cttee to Review the Functioning of Financial Institutions, 1977–80 (Chm. Res. Panel); Standing Commn on Pay Comparability, 1979–81. *Publications:* Britain in Crisis 1951, 1963; Groundwork to Economic Planning, 1966; The National Board for Prices and Incomes, 1972; Price Determination and Prices Policy, 1978. *Recreations:* gardening, cooking. *Address:* c/o 34 Streatham Common South, SW16 3BX. *Died 13 Feb. 2014.*

MITCHELL, His Honour Nicolas John; a Circuit Judge, 1996–2010; *b* 12 May 1940; *s* of Leslie George Tudor Mitchell and Emma Mitchell; *m* 1962, Marion Davies; two *s. Educ:* Bancroft's Sch. Admitted solicitor, 1962; in private practice, 1962–96; a Recorder, 1992–96. Sheffield Prize, Law Soc., 1962. *Recreations:* walking, gardening, outdoor pursuits, reading, opera. *Died 17 Sept. 2012.*

MITCHELL, Warren; actor; *b* 14 Jan. 1926; *s* of Montague and Annie Misell, later Mitchell; *m* 1952, Constance Wake; one *s* two *d. Educ:* Southgate Co. Sch.; University Coll., Oxford; RADA. Demobbed RAF, 1946. First professional appearance, Finsbury Park Open Air Theatre, 1950; Theophile in Can-Can, Coliseum, 1954; Crookfinger Jake in The Threepenny Opera, Royal Court and Aldwych, 1956; Mr Godboy in Dutch Uncle, Aldwych, 1969; Satan in Council of Love, Criterion, 1970; Herbert in Jump, Queen's, 1971; Ion Will in The Great Caper, Royal Court, 1974; The Thoughts of Chairman Alf, Stratford E, 1976; Willie Loman in Death of a Salesman, Nat. Theatre, 1979 (Best Actor, Olivier Awards, 1979); Ducking Out, Duke of York's, 1983; Harpagon in The Miser, Birmingham Rep., 1986; Max in The Homecoming, 1991; West Yorkshire Playhouse: King Lear, 1996; Visiting Mr Green, 2000; Art, Wyndhams, 2000; The Price, Tricycle, 2002, Apollo, 2003 (Best Supporting Actor, Olivier Awards, 2004); *films include:* Diamonds Before Breakfast; Assassination Bureau; Best House in London; Till Death Us Do Part; Moon Zero Two; Whatever Happened to Charlie Farthing; Jabberwocky; Stand Up Virgin Soldiers; Meetings with Remarkable Men; Norman Loves Rose; The Chain; *television:* Alf Garnett in Till Death Us Do Part, BBC, 1966–78, and In Sickness and in Health, BBC, 1985, 1986; The Thoughts of Chairman Alf (series), 1998; Shylock in Merchant of Venice, BBC, 1981; Till Death (series), ITV, 1981; The Caretaker, BBC, 1981; So You Think You've Got Troubles (series), BBC, 1994; Wall of Silence, BBC, 1995; Death of a Salesman, BBC, 1996; Gormenghast, BBC, 2000. TV Actor of the Year Award, Guild of Film and TV Producers, 1966; Actor of Year Award: Evening Standard, 1979; Soc. of West End Theatres, 1979; Plays and Players, 1979. *Recreations:* sailing, tennis, playing clarinet. *Address:* c/o The Artists Partnership, 101 Finsbury Pavement, EC2A 1RS. *Died 14 Nov. 2015.*

MITCHISON, Prof. (John) Murdoch, ScD; FRS 1978; FRSE 1966; Professor of Zoology, University of Edinburgh, 1963–88, then Professor Emeritus and Hon. Fellow; *b* 11 June 1922; *s* of Baron Mitchison, CBE, QC, and late Naomi Margaret Mitchison, CBE, writer; *m* 1947, Rosalind Mary Wrong (*d* 2002); one *s* three *d. Educ:* Winchester Coll.; Trinity Coll., Cambridge (BA 1943; PhD 1951; ScD 1967). Army Operational Research, 1941–46; Sen. and Research Scholar, Trinity Coll., Cambridge, 1946–50; Fellow, Trinity Coll., Cambridge, 1950–54; Edinburgh University: Lectr in Zoology, 1953–59; Reader in Zoology, 1959–62; Dean, Faculty of Science, 1984–85; Mem. of Court, 1971–74, 1985–88. J. W. Jenkinson Memorial Lectr, Oxford, 1971–72. Member: Council, Scottish Marine Biol. Assoc., 1961–67; Exec. Cttee, Internat. Soc. for Cell Biology, 1964–72; Biol Cttee, SRC, 1972–75; Royal Commn on Environmental Pollution, 1974–79; Science Bd, SRC, 1976–79; Working Gp on Biol Manpower, DES, 1968–71; Adv. Cttee on Safety of Nuclear Installations, Health and Safety Exec., 1981–84. Pres., British Soc. for Cell Biology, 1974–77. Mem., Academia Europaea, 1989. FInstBiol 1963.

Publications: The Biology of the Cell Cycle, 1971; papers in scientific jls. *Address:* Great Yew, Ormiston, East Lothian EH35 5NJ. *T:* (01875) 340530. *Died 17 March 2011.*

MOFFAT, Lt-Gen. Sir (William) Cameron, KBE 1985 (OBE 1975); FRCS; *b* 8 Sept. 1929; *s* of William Weir Moffat and Margaret Garrett; *m* 1953, Audrey Watson (*d* 2014); one *s*. *Educ:* King's Park Sch., Glasgow; Univ. of Glasgow, Western Infirmary (MB ChB). DTM&H. House Surgeon, Western Inf., Glasgow, 1952; Ship's Surg., Anchor Line, 1953; MO Seaforth Highlanders, 1954; SMO Edinburgh, 1956–57; Hammersmith Hosp., 1962; Birmingham Accident Hosp., 1964; Surg., RAAF Hosp. Malaya, 1965–67; Cons. Surg., BMH Rinteln, 1968–70; Prof. Military Surgery, RAM Coll. and RCS, 1970–75; CO BMH Rinteln, 1978–80; Comd MED HQ 1 (Br) Corps, 1980–83; PMO, UKLF, 1983–84; Surg. Gen./Dir Gen. Army Med. Servs, MoD, 1985–87. QHS 1984–88. Chief Med. Advr, BRCS, 1988–94. Hon. DSc Glasgow, 1991. CStJ 1985. *Publications:* contribs to surgical text books and jls on missile wounds and their management. *Recreations:* golf, travel, bird-watching. *Address:* Kippax, Pound Green, Camp Road, Freshwater, Isle of Wight PO40 9HH. *Died 29 June 2014.*

MOFFATT, John, MA, DPhil; Provost, The Queen's College, Oxford, 1987–93, Hon. Fellow, 1993; *b* 12 Oct. 1922; *s* of Jacob and Ethel Moffatt; *m* 1949, Una Lamorna Morris (*d* 1992); one *d*. *Educ:* Keighley Boys' Grammar Sch.; Magdalen Coll., Oxford (MA, DPhil). Radar research with British Thomson-Houston Co. Ltd, Rugby, 1942–46; Oxford University: Sen. Res. Officer, Clarendon Lab., 1950; Lectr, Dept of Nuclear Physics, 1965; The Queen's College: Fellow and Praelector in Physics, 1950; Sen. Tutor, 1972–76. *Publications:* articles on physics in various scientific jls. *Address:* 2 Cumnor Rise Road, Cumnor Hill, Oxford OX2 9HD. *Died 23 Dec. 2013.*

MOGG; *see* Rees-Mogg.

MOLLISON, Prof. Patrick Loudon, CBE 1979; MD; FRCP, FRCPath, FRCOG; FRS 1968; Professor of Hæmatology, St Mary's Hospital Medical School, London University, 1962–79, then Emeritus Professor; *b* 17 March 1914; *s* of William Mayhew Mollison, Cons. Surgeon (ENT), Guy's Hospital; *m* 1st, 1940, Dr Margaret D. Peirce (marr. diss. 1964); three *s*; 2nd, 1973, Dr Jennifer Jones. *Educ:* Rugby Sch.; Clare Coll., Cambridge; St Thomas' Hosp., London. MD Cantab 1944; FRCP 1959; FRCPath 1963; FRCOG *ad eund.*, 1980. House Phys., Medical Unit, St Thomas' Hosp., 1939; Medical Officer, S London Blood Supply Depot, 1939–43; RAMC, 1943–46; Dir, MRC Blood Transfusion Res. Unit, Hammersmith Hosp., 1946–60; part-time Dir, MRC Experimental Hæmatology Unit, 1960–79; Hon. Lectr, then Sen. Lectr, Dept of Medicine, Post-grad. Medical Sch., 1948; Consultant Hæmatologist: Hammersmith Hosp., 1947–60; St Mary's Hosp., 1960–79; Hon. Consultant Immunohaematologist, N London Blood Transfusion Centre, 1983–2000. Hon. FRSocMed 1979; Landsteiner Meml Award, USA, 1960; P. Levine Award, USA, 1973; Oehlecker Medal, Germany, 1974. *Publications:* Blood Transfusion in Clinical Medicine, 1951, 10th edn (jtly) 1997; papers on red cell survival and blood group antibodies. *Recreations:* music, gardening. *Address:* 60 King Henry's Road, NW3 3RR. *T:* (020) 7722 1947. *Died 26 Nov. 2011.*

MOLONY, (Thomas) Desmond; (3rd Bt *cr* 1925 of the City of Dublin); *b* 13 March 1937; *s* of Sir Hugh Francis Molony, 2nd Bt and Alexandra Campbell Molony (*née* Todd); *S* father, 1976, but did not use the title; *m* 1962, Doris Foley; four *d*. *Educ:* Ampleforth; Trinity Coll., Dublin. *Heir: cousin* Peter John Molony [*b* 17 Aug. 1937; *m* 1964, Elizabeth Mary Chaytor; three *s* one *d* (and one *s* decd)]. *Died 3 Oct. 2014.*

MOLYNEAUX OF KILLEAD, Baron *cr* 1997 (Life Peer), of Killead in the co. of Antrim; **James Henry Molyneaux,** KBE 1996; PC 1983; Leader, Ulster Unionist Party, 1979–95; *b* 27 Aug. 1920; *s* of late William Molyneaux, Seacash, Killead, Co. Antrim; unmarried. *Educ:* Aldergrove Sch., Co. Antrim. RAF, 1941–46. Vice-Chm., Eastern Special Care Hosp. Mgt Cttee, 1966–73; Chm. Antrim Br., NI Assoc. for Mental Health, 1967–70; Hon. Sec., S Antrim Unionist Assoc., 1964–70; Vice-Pres., Ulster Unionist Council, 1974–79. MP (UU): Antrim S, 1970–83; Lagan Valley, 1983–97. Leader, UU Party, House of Commons, 1974–95. Mem. (UU) S Antrim, NI Assembly, 1982–86. Dep. Grand Master of Orange Order and Hon. PGM of Canada. JP Antrim, 1957–87; CC Antrim, 1964–73. *Recreations:* gardening, music. *Address:* Aldergrove, Crumlin, Co. Antrim, N Ireland BT29 4AR. *Died 9 March 2015.*

MOLYNEUX, James Robert M.; *see* More-Molyneux.

MONCK, Sir Nicholas (Jeremy), KCB 1994 (CB 1988); Permanent Secretary, Employment Department Group, 1993–95; *b* 9 March 1935; *s* of Bosworth Monck and Stella Mary (*née* Cock); *m* 1960, Elizabeth Mary Kirwan; three *s*. *Educ:* Eton; King's Coll., Cambridge; Univ. of Pennsylvania; LSE. Asst Principal, Min. of Power, 1959–62; NEDO, 1962–65; NBPI, 1965–66; Senior Economist, Min. of Agriculture, Tanzania, 1966–69; HM Treasury, 1969–92: Asst Sec., 1971; Principal Private Sec. to Chancellor of the Exchequer, 1976–77; Under Sec. (Nationalised Industries, Home Finance), 1977–84; Dep. Sec. (Industry), 1984–90; Second Perm. Sec. (Public Expenditure), 1990–92. Dir, Standard Life, 1997–2005. Member: BSC, 1978–80; IMRO, 1995–2000; Council of Mgt, NIESR, 2002– (Pres., 2011–). Chm., British Dyslexia Assoc., 1995–2000. Member: Finance Cttee, Nat. Trust, 1990–2005; UCL Hosps NHS Foundn Trust, 2005–12. Trustee: Glyndebourne Arts Trust, 1996–2004; Better Govt Initiative, 2005–. *Address:* 31 Lady Margaret Road, NW5 2NG. *T:* (020) 7485 8474. *Died 14 Aug. 2013.*

MONEY, Ernle (David Drummond), CBE 1996; Barrister-at-Law; *b* 17 Feb. 1931; *s* of late Lt-Col E. F. D. Money, DSO, late 4th Gurkha Rifles, and Sidney, *o d* of D. E. Anderson, Forfar; *m* 1st, 1960, Susan Barbara (marr. diss. 1985), *d* of Lt-Col D. S. Lister, MC, The Buffs; two *s* two *d*; 2nd, Bella Maharaj (*d* 1993), barrister-at-law. *Educ:* Marlborough Coll.; Oriel Coll., Oxford (open scholar; MA Hons (2nd cl.) Mod. Hist. 1954). Served in Suffolk Regt, 1949–51, and 4th Bn, Suffolk Regt (TA), 1951–56. Tutor and lecturer, Swinton Conservative Coll., 1956. Called to Bar, Lincoln's Inn (Cholmeley Scholar), 1958. Mem., Bar Council, 1962–66. MP (C) Ipswich, 1970–Sept. 1974; Opposition Front Bench Spokesman on the Arts, 1974; Sec., Parly Cons. Arts and Amenities Cttee, 1970–73, Vice-Chm., 1974; Vice-Pres., Ipswich Cons. Assoc., 1979–81. Regular columnist, East Anglian Daily Times, for some years. Governor, Woolverstone Hall Sch., 1967–70; co-opted Mem., GLC Arts Cttee, 1972–73; Member: GLC Arts Bd, 1974–76; Cttee, Gainsborough's Birthplace, Sudbury; Acquisitions sub-cttee, 2001–, Exec. cttee, 2002–, Patrons of British Art, Tate Gall. Fine Arts Correspondent, Contemporary Review, 1968–88. Pres., Ipswich Town Football Club Supporters, 1974–80; Vice-Pres., E Suffolk and Ipswich Branch, RSPCA, 1974–77. Mem., Primrose League. *Publications:* (with Peter Johnson) The Nasmyth Family of Painters, 1970; Margaret Thatcher, First Lady of the House, 1975; regular contrib. various periodicals and newspapers on antiques and the arts. *Recreations:* music, pictures and antiques, watching Association football. *Clubs:* Carlton, Beefsteak, Dinosaurs; Norfolk (Norwich). *Died 14 April 2013.*

MONEY-COUTTS, Sir David (Burdett), KCVO 1991; Chairman, Coutts & Co., 1976–93; *b* 19 July 1931; *s* of late Hon. Alexander B. Money-Coutts (2nd *s* of 6th Baron Latymer, TD), and Mary E., *er d* of Sir Reginald Hobhouse, 5th Bt; *m* 1958, Penelope Utten Todd; one *s* two *d*. *Educ:* Eton (Hon. Fellow, 1996); New Coll., Oxford (MA). National Service, 1st Royal Dragoons, 1950–51; Royal Glos Hussars, TA, 1951–67. Joined Coutts & Co., 1954; Dir, 1958–96; Man. Dir, 1970–86. Director: National Discount Co., 1964–69; Gerrard Gp (formerly Gerrard & National), 1969–99 (Dep. Chm. 1969–89); United States & General Trust Corp., 1964–73; Charities Investment Managers (Charifund), 1964–2000 (Chm., 1984–2000); Dun & Bradstreet, 1973–87; National Westminster Bank, 1976–90 (Regl Dir, 1969–92, Chm., SE Reg., 1986–88; Chm., S Adv. Bd, 1988–92; Mem., UK Adv. Bd, 1990–92); Phoenix Assurance, 1978–85 (Dep. Chm., 1984–85); Sun Alliance & London Insurance, 1984–90; M & G Gp, 1987–97 (Chm., 1990–97). Member: Kensington and Chelsea and Westminster AHA, 1974–82 (Vice-Chm., 1978–82); Bloomsbury HA, 1982–90 (Vice-Chm., 1982–88); Health Educn Council, 1973–77. Middlesex Hospital: Governor, 1962–74 (Dep. Chm. Governors, 1973–74); Chm., Finance Cttee, 1965–74; Mem., Med. Sch. Council, 1963–88 (Chm., 1974–88; Special Trustee, 1974–2000 (Chm., 1974–97)). Chm., Inst. of Sports Medicine, 1997–2006. Mem., Council, UCL, 1987–97. Trustee: Multiple Sclerosis Soc., 1967–99; Scout Foundn, 1992–2001 (Chm., 1994–2001). Hon. Treas., Nat. Assoc. of Almshouses, 1960–92; Hon. Sec., Old Etonian Trust, 1969–76, Chm. Council, 1976–2001; Trustee, Mansfield Coll., Oxford, 1988–95. *Recreations:* odd jobs, living in the country. *Address:* Magpie House, Peppard Common, Henley-on-Thames, Oxon RG9 5JG. *T:* (01491) 628005. *Club:* Leander (Henley-on-Thames). *Died 25 June 2012.*

MONIER-WILLIAMS, His Honour Evelyn Faithfull; a Circuit Judge, 1972–92; continued sitting in Crown and County Courts until 1995; *b* 29 April 1920; *o s* of late R. T. Monier-Williams, OBE, Barrister-at-Law, and Mrs G. M. Monier-Williams; *m* 1948, Maria-Angela Oswald (*d* 1983); one *s* one *d*. *Educ:* Charterhouse; University Coll., Oxford (MA). Admitted to Inner Temple, 1940; served Royal Artillery, 1940–46 in UK, Egypt, Libya, Tunisia, Sicily (8th Army), France, Low Countries and Germany; called to Bar, Inner Temple, 1948; South Eastern Circuit; Master of the Bench, Inner Temple, 1967, Reader, 1987, Treas., 1988; Mem. Senate of Four Inns of Court, 1969–73; Mem. Council, Selden Soc., 1970– (Vice Pres., 1990–96); Mem., Council of Legal Educn, 1971–87, Vice Chm., 1974–87; Mem., Lord Chancellor's Adv. Cttee on Legal Educn, 1979–87; Mem., Council of the Inns of Court, 1987–88. Patron of Temple, Mahatma Gandhi Soc., 2011–. Livery, Glaziers' Company, 1974. *Recreation:* collecting old books. *Address:* Inner Temple, EC4Y 7HL. *Died 30 June 2015.*

MONK, Arthur James; Director, Components, Valves and Devices, Ministry of Defence, 1981–84; *b* 15 Jan. 1924; *s* of late Rev. Arthur S. Monk, AKC, and Lydia E. Monk; *m* 1953, Murial V. Peacock; one *s* two *d*. *Educ:* Latymer Upper School, Hammersmith; London Univ. (BSc Hons Physics 1953). FIET 1964. Served RAF, 1943–48. Services Electronic Research Labs, 1949–63; Asst Director (Co-ord. Valve Development), MoD, 1963–68; Student, Imperial Defence Coll., 1969; idc 1970; Admiralty Underwater Weapons Establishment, 1970–73; Dep. Director, Underwater Weapons Projects (S/M), MoD, 1973–76; Counsellor, Def. Equipment Staff, Washington, 1977–81. *Publications:* papers on electronics in jls of learned societies. *Recreations:* photography, family history and genealogy. *Address:* 65 Wyke Road, Weymouth, Dorset DT4 9QN. *T:* (01305) 782338. *Died 29 June 2014.*

MONSON, 11th Baron *cr* 1728; **John Monson;** Bt *cr* 1611; *b* 3 May 1932; *e s* of 10th Baron and of Bettie Northrup (who *m* 1962, Capt. James Arnold Phillips), *d* of late E. Alexander Powell; *S* father, 1958; *m* 1955, Emma, *o d* of late Anthony Devas, ARA, RP; three *s*. *Educ:* Eton; Trinity Coll., Cambridge (BA). Elected Mem., H of L, 1999. Pres., Soc. for Individual Freedom. *Heir: s* Hon. Nicholas John Monson [*b* 19 Oct. 1955; *m* 1st, 1981, Hilary (marr. diss. 1996), *o d* of Kenneth Martin, Nairobi and Diani Beach; one *s* one *d*; 2nd, 2002, La Ilustrisima Maria Victoria Nicklin Perez; *m* 2010, Silvana Fernandes, *widow* of Nicholas Jessen]. *Address:* The Manor House, South Carlton, Lincoln LN1 2RN. *T:* (01522) 730263. *Died 12 Feb. 2011.*

MONTAGU OF BEAULIEU, 3rd Baron *cr* 1885; **Edward John Barrington Douglas-Scott-Montagu;** Chairman, Historic Buildings and Monuments Commission, 1983–92; *b* 20 Oct. 1926; *o s* of 2nd Baron Montagu of Beaulieu and Pearl (who *m* 2nd, 1936, Captain Hon. Edward Pleydell-Bouverie, RN, MVO, *s* of 6th Earl of Radnor; she *d* 1996), *d* of late Major E. B. Crake, Rifle Brigade, and Mrs Barrington Crake; *S* father, 1929; *m* 1st, 1959, Elizabeth Belinda (marr. diss. 1974), *o d* of late Capt. the Hon. John de Bathe Crossley and Hon. Mrs Crossley; one *s* one *d*; 2nd, 1974, Fiona Herbert; one *s*. *Educ:* St Peter's Court, Broadstairs; Ridley Coll., St Catharines, Ont; Eton Coll.; New Coll., Oxford. Late Lt Grenadier Guards; released Army, 1948. Elected Mem., H of L, 1999. Founded Montagu Motor Museum, 1952 and World's first Motor Cycle Museum, 1956; created Nat. Motor Museum Trust, 1970, to administer new Nat. Motor Museum at Beaulieu, opened 1972. Mem., Develt Commn, 1980–84. President: Assoc. of British Transport and Engrg Museums, 1964–; Historic Houses Assoc., 1973–78; Southern Tourist Bd, 1977–2004; Union of European Historic Houses, 1978–81; Fédération Internationale des Voitures Anciennes, 1980–83; Museums Assoc., 1982–84; Fedn of British Historic Vehicle Clubs, 1989–; Tourism Soc., 1991–2000 (then Pres. Emeritus); UK Vineyards Assoc., 1996–; Millennium Pres., Inst. of Journalists, 2000; All-Pty Parly Historic Vehicles Gp, 2003–; Hon. Fellow, Inst. of Motor Industry, 1996; Chancellor, Wine Guild of UK, 1983–; Patron, Assoc. of Independent Museums, 1978–. Pres., Disabled Motoring UK (formerly Disabled Drivers Motor Club, then Mobilise). Freeman, City of London, 2003. FRSA 1981; FCIPR (FIPR 1998). Hon. FMA, 1988. Cdre, Nelson Boat Owners' Club; Vice Cdre, H of L Yacht Club. Founder and Editor, Veteran and Vintage Magazine, 1956–79. Hon. DTech Nottingham Trent, 1998. *Publications:* The Motoring Montagus, 1959; Lost Causes of Motoring, 1960; Jaguar, A Biography, 1961, rev. edn, 1986; The Gordon Bennett Races, 1963; Rolls of Rolls-Royce, 1966; The Gilt and the Gingerbread, 1967; Lost Causes of Motoring: Europe, vol. i, 1969, vol. ii, 1971; More Equal than Others, 1970; History of the Steam Car, 1971; The Horseless Carriage, 1975; Early Days on the Road, 1976; Behind the Wheel, 1977; Royalty on the Road, 1980; Home James, 1982; The British Motorist, 1987; English Heritage, 1987; The Daimler Century, 1995; Wheels Within Wheels (autobiog.), 2000. *Heir: s* Hon. Ralph Douglas-Scott-Montagu [*b* 13 March 1961; *m* 2005, Ailsa, *e d* of Kenneth Camm, Brecht, Belgium]. *Address:* Palace House, Beaulieu, Hants SO42 7ZN. *T:* (01590) 614701, *Fax:* (01590) 612623; Flat 11, Wyndham House, 24 Bryanston Square, W1H 2DS. *T:* (020) 7262 2603, *Fax:* (020) 7724 3262. *Clubs:* Historical Commercial Vehicle (Pres.), and mem. of many historic vehicle clubs. *Died 31 Aug. 2015.*

MONTAGUE BROWNE, Sir Anthony (Arthur Duncan), KCMG 2000; CBE 1965 (OBE 1955); DFC 1945; HM Diplomatic Service, retired; a Managing Director, Gerrard and National PLC, 1970–83 (Director, 1967–70); *b* 8 May 1923; *s* of late Lt-Col A. D. Montague Browne, DSO, OBE, Bivia House, Goodrich, Ross-on-Wye, and Violet Evelyn (*née* Downes); *m* 1st, 1950, Noel Evelyn Arnold-Wallinger (marr. diss. 1970); one *d*; 2nd, 1970, Shelagh Macklin (*née* Mulligan). *Educ:* Stowe; Magdalen Coll., Oxford (William Doncaster Schol.); abroad. Pilot RAF, 1941–45. Entered Foreign (later Diplomatic) Service, 1946; Resident Clerk, Foreign Office, 1947–49; Second Sec., British Embassy, Paris, 1949–52; seconded as Private Sec. to Prime Minister, 1952–55; seconded as Private Sec. to Rt Hon. Sir Winston Churchill, 1955–65; Counsellor, Diplomatic Service, 1964; seconded to HM Household, 1965–67. Dir, Columbia (British) Productions, 1967–77. Trustee, Winston Churchill Memorial Trust; Vice-Pres., Univs Fedn for Animal Welfare, 1987–93 (Mem., Council, 1985–91). Freeman, City of London, 1987. Hon. DL Westminster Coll., Fulton, Missouri, 1988. *Publications:* Long Sunset: memoirs of Winston Churchill's last Private Secretary, 1995. *Address:* Podkin Wood, High Halden, Ashford, Kent TN26 3HS. *T:* (01580) 291902. *Clubs:* Boodle's, Pratt's. *Died 1 April 2013.*

MONTEAGLE OF BRANDON, 6th Baron *cr* 1839; **Gerald Spring Rice;** late Captain, Irish Guards; one of HM Body Guard, Hon. Corps of Gentlemen-at-Arms, 1978–96; *b* 5 July 1926; *s* of 5th Baron and Emilie de Kosenko (*d* 1981), *d* of Mrs Edward Brooks, Philadelphia, USA; *S* father, 1946; *m* 1949, Anne, *d* of late Col G. J. Brownlow, Ballywhite, Portaferry, Co. Down; one *s* three *d* (of whom two are twins). *Educ:* Harrow. Member: London Stock Exchange, 1958–76; Lloyd's, 1978–98. *Heir: s* Hon. Charles James Spring Rice [*b* 24 Feb. 1953; *m* 1987, Mary Teresa Glover; four *d*]. *Address:* 28 Abbey Mews, Amesbury, Wilts SP4 7EX. *Clubs:* Cavalry and Guards, Pratt's; Kildare Street and University (Dublin). *Died 17 Nov. 2013.*

MONTEITH, Prof. John Lennox, FRS 1971; FRSE 1972; Emeritus Professor of Environmental Physics, University of Nottingham, 1989; *b* 3 Sept. 1929; *s* of Rev. John and Margaret Monteith; *m* 1955, Elsa Marion Wotherspoon; four *s* one *d*. *Educ:* George Heriot's Sch.; Univ. of Edinburgh (BSc 1951; Hon. DSc 1989); Imperial Coll., London. DIC, PhD. FInstP, FSB. Mem. Physics Dept Staff, Rothamsted Experimental Station, 1954–67; Prof. of Environmental Physics, 1967–86, Dean of Faculty of Agricl Sci., 1985–86, Nottingham Univ.; Dir, Resource Management Programme, Internat. Crops Res. Inst. for the Semi-Arid Tropics, 1987–91 (Vis. Scientist, 1984); Sen. Vis. Fellow, NERC, 1992–94. Adjunct Prof., Depts of Agricl Engrg and Agronomy, Univ. of Florida, 1991–; Vis. Prof., Reading Univ., 1992–95; Hon. Prof., Edinburgh Univ., 1992–. Governor: Grassland Res. Inst., 1976–83; Silsoe Res. Inst., 1993–97. Vice Pres., British Ecological Soc., 1977–79; Pres., Royal Meteorol Soc., 1978–80; Fellowship Sec., RSE, 1997–99. Member: NERC, 1980–84; British Nat. Cttee for the World Climate Programme, 1980–86; Lawes Agricl Trust Cttee, 1983–86. Nat. Res. Council Senior Res. Associate, Goddard Space Flight Center, Md, USA, 1985; Clive Behrens Lectr, Leeds Univ., 1986; York Distinguished Lectr, Univ. of Florida, 1991. Buchan Prize, 1962, Symon's Meml Medal, 1995, RMetS; Solco Tromp Award, Internat. Soc. of Biometeorology, 1983; Rank Fund Nutrition Prize, 1989. *Publications:* Instruments for Micrometeorology (ed), 1972; Principles of Environmental Physics, 1973, 3rd edn (with M. H. Unsworth), 2007; (ed with L. E. Mount) Heat Loss from Animals and Man, 1974; (ed) Vegetation and the Atmosphere, 1975; (ed with C. Webb) Soil Water and Nitrogen, 1981; (ed with R. K. Scott and M. H. Unsworth) Resource Capture by Crops, 1994; papers on Micrometeorology and Crop Science in: Quarterly Jl of RMetSoc.; Jl Applied Ecology, etc. *Recreations:* music, photography. *Address:* 34 St Alban's Road, Edinburgh EH9 2LU. *Died 20 July 2012.*

MONTGOMERY, Sir (William) Fergus, Kt 1985; *b* 25 Nov. 1927; *s* of late William Montgomery and Winifred Montgomery; *m* 1971, Joyce, *d* of George Riddle. *Educ:* Jarrow Grammar Sch.; Bede Coll., Durham. Served in Royal Navy, 1946–48; Schoolmaster, 1950–59. Nat. Vice-Chm. Young Conservative Organisation, 1954–57, National Chm., 1957–58. Contested (C) Consett Division, 1955; MP (C): Newcastle upon Tyne East, 1959–64; Brierley Hill, April 1967–Feb. 1974; contested Dudley W, Feb. 1974; MP (C) Altrincham and Sale, Oct. 1974–1997. PPS to Sec. of State for Educn and Science, 1973–74, to Leader of the Opposition, 1975–76. Chm., H of C Cttee of Selection, 1992–97; Mem. Exec. Cttee, British American Parly Gp, 1991–97. Mem. Executive, CPA, 1983–97. Councillor, Hebburn UDC, 1950–58. Lectured extensively in the USA. *Recreations:* bridge, reading, going to theatre. *Address:* 181 Ashley Gardens, Emery Hill Street, SW1P 1PD. *T:* (020) 7834 7905; 6 Groby Place, Altrincham, Cheshire WA14 4AL. *T:* (0161) 928 1983. *Died 19 March 2013.*

MOON, Brenda Elizabeth, FRSE; FCLIP; University Librarian, University of Edinburgh, 1980–96; *b* 11 April 1931; *d* of Clement Alfred Moon and Mabel (*née* Berks). *Educ:* King Edward's Grammar Sch. for Girls, Camp Hill, Birmingham; St Hilda's Coll., Oxford (MA); MPhil Leeds; PhD Hull 2002. FCLIP (FLA 1958); FRSE 1992. Asst Librarian, Univ. of Sheffield, 1955–62; Sub-Librarian, 1962–67, Dep. Librarian, 1967–79, Univ. of Hull. Curator, Royal Soc. of Edinburgh, 2002–05. *Publications:* Mycenaean Civilisation: publications since 1935, 1957; Mycenaean Civilisation: publications 1956–1960, 1961; Periodicals for South-East Asian Studies: a union catalogue of holdings in British and selected European libraries, 1979; More Usefully Employed: Amelia B. Edwards (biography), 2006; articles in prof. and other jls. *Recreation:* travel and the history of travel. *Address:* 4 Cobden Road, Edinburgh EH9 2BJ. *T:* (0131) 667 0071. *Died 7 March 2011.*

MOORE, John Royston, CBE 1983; CChem, FRSC; Chairman, Bradford Health Authority, 1982–88; *b* 2 May 1921; *s* of late Henry Roland and Jane Elizabeth Moore; *m* 1947, Dorothy Mackay Hick (*d* 2005), *d* of late Charles and Edith Mackay Hick; two *s*. *Educ:* Manchester Central Grammar Sch.; Univ. of Manchester (BSc Hons). War service, research and manufacture of explosives. Lecturer in schools and college, Manchester; Principal, Bradford Technical Coll., 1959–75; Sen. Vice Principal and Dir of Planning and Resources, Bradford Coll., 1975–80. Chm., Wool, Jute and Flax ITB, 1981–83. Leader, Baildon Urban DC, 1965–68; Councillor, West Riding CC, until 1973; West Yorkshire MCC: Member, 1973–86; Leader, 1978–81; Leader of the Opposition, 1981–86. Dir, Yorkshire Enterprise Ltd, 1981–90. President, Yorks Conservative Adv. Cttee on Educn, 1975–89; past Chm., Conservative Nat. Adv. Cttee on Educn. Hon. Mem., and Councillor, City and Guilds of London Inst., 1977–92. Hon. MA Bradford, 1986. *Publications:* (series) The Carroll Family Saga: lives of Carroll families in American colonies of United States, 1687–1870, 2009–10; (as Royston Moore) Makere: the female Pharaoh-Queen of Sheba, 2008. *Recreations:* music, history, bridge. *Address:* Bicknor, 33 Station Road, Baildon, Shipley, West Yorkshire BD17 6HS. *T:* (01274) 581777. *Died 3 Feb. 2014.*

MOORE, (Sir) Norman Winfrid, (3rd Bt *cr* 1919; has established his claim but does not use the title); Senior Principal Scientific Officer, Nature Conservancy Council, 1965–83 (Principal Scientific Officer, 1958–65); Visiting Professor of Environmental Studies, Wye College, University of London, 1979–83; *b* 24 Feb. 1923; *s* of Sir Alan Hilary Moore, 2nd Bt; *S* father, 1959; *m* 1950, Janet (*d* 2014), PhD, *o d* of late Mrs Phyllis Singer; one *s* two *d*. *Educ:* Eton; Trinity Coll., Cambridge (MA); Univ. of Bristol (PhD). Served War, 1942–45, Germany and Holland (wounded, POW). *Publications:* The Bird of Time, 1987; Oaks, Dragonflies and People, 2002; scientific papers and articles. *Heir: s* Peter Alan Cutlack Moore [*b* 21 Sept. 1951; *m* 1989, Pamela Edwardes; one *s* one *d*. *Educ:* Eton; Trinity Coll., Cambridge (MA); DPhil Oxon]. *Address:* The Farm House, 117 Boxworth End, Swavesey, Cambridge CB24 4RA. *Died 21 Oct. 2015.*

MOORE, Sir Patrick (Alfred) Caldwell-, Kt 2001; CBE 1988 (OBE 1968); free-lance author, since 1968; *b* 4 March 1923; *s* of late Capt. Charles Caldwell-Moore, MC, and Gertrude Lilian Moore. *Educ:* privately (due to illness). Served with RAF, 1940–45: Navigator, Bomber Command. Concerned in running of a school, 1945–52; free-lance author, 1952–65; Dir of Armagh Planetarium, 1965–68. TV Series, BBC, The Sky at Night, 1957–; radio broadcaster. Composed and performed in Perseus and Andromeda (opera), 1975, Theseus, 1982, and Galileo, 2000. Pres., British Astronomical Assoc., 1982–84. Honorary Member: Astronomic-Geodetic Soc. of USSR, 1971; Royal Astronomical Soc. of New Zealand, 1983; Royal Astronomical Soc. of Canada, 1994. Editor, Year Book of Astronomy, 1962–. Lorimer Gold Medal, 1962; Goodacre Gold Medal, 1968; Arturo Gold Medal (Italian Astronomical Socs), 1969; Jackson-Gwilt Medal, RAS, 1977; Roberts-Klumpke Medal, Astronom. Soc. of Pacific, 1979. Fellow, QMW. Hon. FRS 2001. Hon. DSc: Lancaster, 1974; Hatfield Polytechnic, 1989; Birmingham, 1990; Leicester, Keele, 1995; Portsmouth, 1998; Glamorgan, 2001; TCD, 2002. *Publications:* More than 100 books, mainly astronomical, including The Amateur Astronomer, 1970, rev. edn 2006; Atlas of the Universe, 1970, rev. edn 2007; Guide to the Planets, 1976; Guide to the Moon, 1976; Can You Speak Venusian?, 1977; Guide to the Stars, 1977; Guide to Mars, 1977; (jtly) Out of the Darkness: the Planet Pluto, 1980; The Unfolding Universe, 1982; Travellers in Space and Time, 1983; (jtly) The Return of Halley's Comet, 1984; Stargazing, 1985; Exploring the Night Sky with Binoculars, 1986; The A–Z of Astronomy, 1986; TV Astronomer, 1987; Astronomy for the Under-Tens, 1987; Astronomers' Stars, 1987; (jtly) The Planet Uranus, 1988; The Planet Neptune, 1989; Space Travel for the Under Tens, 1989; Mission to the Planets, 1990; A Passion for Astronomy, 1991; The Earth for Under Tens, 1992; Fireside Astronomy, 1992; The Starry Sky, 1994; The Great Astronomical Revolution, 1994; Stars of the Southern Skies, 1994; Guinness Book of Astronomy, 1995; Teach Yourself Astronomy, 1995, rev. edn 2008; Eyes on the Universe, 1997; Sun in Eclipse, 1999; West Country Eclipse, 1999; Patrick Moore on Mars, 1999; The Wandering Astronomer, 2000; Patrick Moore on the Moon, 2000, new edn 2006; The Star of Bethlehem, 2001;

The Data Book of Astronomy, 2001; 80 Not Out (autobiog.), 2003; Patrick Moore: the autobiography, 2005; (with Arthur C. Clarke) Asteroid, 2005; Stars of Destiny, 2005; Venus, 2006; (jtly) Bang! The Complete History of the Universe, 2006; Ancient Lights, 2008; Can You Play Cricket on Mars?, 2009; Legends of the Stars, 2009; Countdown, 2009; The Twitmarsh File, 2010; The New Astronomy Data Book, 2011; First Book of Stars, 2011; (jtly) The Cosmic Tourist, 2012. *Recreations:* cricket, chess, tennis, music, xylophone playing (composer of music in recordings The Ever Ready Band Plays Music by Patrick Moore, 1979, The Music of Patrick Moore, 1986, Moore Music, 1999). *Address:* Farthings, 39 West Street, Selsey, West Sussex PO20 9AD. *Clubs:* Athenæum, Lord's Taverners; Sussex County Cricket. *Died 9 Dec. 2012.*

MOORES, John, CBE 1993; Director, The Littlewoods Organisation, 1950–96; *b* 22 Nov. 1928; *s* of Sir John Moores, CBE; *m* 1st, 1949, Helen Sheila Moore; three *s* one *d*; 2nd, 1963, Jane Staveley-Dick; four *s* one *d*. *Educ:* Eton Coll.; Syracuse Univ., USA. Joined The Littlewoods Organisation, 1946, Dep. Chm., 1968–71; Chm., Medaillon Mode GmbH, 1968–71; Chm., Littlewoods Equal Opportunities, 1982–96. Mem. Council, Britain in Europe, 2000–05. Liverpool Polytechnic, later Liverpool John Moores University: Chm. Bd of Govs, 1988–92; Pro-Chancellor, 1992–94; Chancellor, 1994–99, then Emeritus. Associated with the Liverpool Motorists' Annual Outing, 1956–2008; President: Aberdeen Angus Cattle Soc., 1986–87; Roy Castle Lung Cancer Foundn, 1996–2001. DL Merseyside, 1993–2003. Hon. Freeman, City of Liverpool, 1994. *Recreations:* equal opportunities, languages, regionalisation, Europe, cattle breeding. *Address:* South Lodge, North Moss Lane, Formby, Liverpool L37 0AQ. *Club:* Boodle's. *Died 22 May 2012.*

MOORHOUSE, (Cecil) James (Olaf); *b* 1 Jan. 1924; *s* of late Captain Sidney James Humphrey Moorhouse and Anna Sophie Hedvig de Løvenskiold; *m* 1958, Elizabeth Clive Huxtable (marr. diss. 1995), Sydney, Aust.; one *s* one *d*; *m* 1997, Catherine Hamilton Peterson, New Mexico, USA. *Educ:* St Paul's School; King's Coll. and Imperial Coll., Univ. of London (BSc (Eng); DIC (Advanced Aeronautics)). CEng. Designer with de Havilland Aircraft Co., 1946–48; Project Engr, BOAC, 1948–53; Technical Advr, 1953–68, and Environmental Conservation Advr, 1968–72, Shell International Petroleum; Environmental Advr, Shell Group of Companies in UK, 1972–73; Group Environmental Affairs Advr, Rio-Tinto Zinc Corp., 1973–80, Consultant, 1980–84. Dir, Project Development International, 1985–90. Mem., Clean Air Council, 1974–80. Contested (C) St Pancras North, 1966 and 1970. MEP (C 1979–98, Lib Dem 1998–99), London S, 1979–84, London S and Surrey E, 1984–99. European Parliament: spokesman on transport for EDG, 1979–84 and 1987–89; spokesman on external economic relations for EDG, 1984–87 and 1989–92; Rapporteur, trade and economic relns between EU and Japan, 1985–99; dep. co-ordinator on external economic relations for EPP, 1992–94; co-ordinator on human rights for EPP and British Cons, 1994–98; spokesman on foreign affairs, defence and human rights for British Cons, 1997–98; Chm., delegn to N Europe and Nordic Council, 1979–84; First Vice-Chm., delegn to EFTA Parliamentarians, 1984–86; Vice-Pres., External Econ. Relations Cttee, 1989–92; Mem., EPP Bureau, 1994–98. Founder Mem., Bow Gp, 1950. Pres., Help Tibet, 1995–. Jt Founder, Lib Dem Human Rights Gp, 2001. Mem., Bd of Govs, ESU, 1952–59, 1981–87. Sir Evelyn Wrench Lectr, USA, 1999. Hon. Editor, Inst. of Petroleum, 1965–75. Polish Parlt Medal for work on human rights, 1997. *Publications:* (with Anthony Teasdale) Righting the Balance: a new agenda for Euro-Japanese trade, 1987; numerous articles and papers on aviation. *Recreations:* reading, travel, watching cricket, filmgoer. *Address:* 180 Piccadilly, W1J 9HF. *Clubs:* Sloane; University (Washington). *Died 6 Jan. 2014.*

MOORHOUSE, Peter William; Chairman, Police Complaints Authority, 1996–99 (Deputy Chairman, 1991–96); *b* 25 Dec. 1938; *s* of Francis and Dorothy Moorhouse; *m* 1962, Jane Catton; two *s* one *d*. *Educ:* Stonyhurst Coll. Joined Schweppes Group, 1961, Divl Dir, 1980–87; Mem., Police Complaints Authy, 1988–2000. Mem., Local Review Cttee, Parole Bd, 1973–88 (Chm., 1977–79, 1986–88). Complaints Convenor, Beds and Herts HA, 2002–05. Gov., Stonyhurst Coll., 1991–94. FRSA 1995. *Recreations:* opera, art, walking, inland boating. *Address:* c/o HSBC, 1 High Street, Harpenden, Herts AL5 2RS. *Died 11 April 2014.*

MORAN, 2nd Baron *cr* 1943; **Richard John McMoran Wilson,** KCMG 1981 (CMG 1970); *b* 22 Sept. 1924; *er s* of 1st Baron Moran, MC, MD, FRCP, and Dorothy (*d* 1983), MBE, *d* of late Samuel Felix Dufton, DSc; *S* father, 1977; *m* 1948, Shirley Rowntree Harris (*d* 2012); two *s* one *d*. *Educ:* Eton; King's Coll., Cambridge. Served War of 1939–45 (Arctic Star 2013); Ord. Seaman in HMS Belfast, 1943; Sub-Lt RNVR in Motor Torpedo Boats and HM Destroyer Oribi, 1944–45. Foreign Office, 1945; Third Sec., Ankara, 1948; Tel-Aviv, 1950; Second Sec., Rio de Janeiro, 1953; First Sec., FO, 1956; Washington, 1959; FO 1961; Counsellor, British Embassy in S Africa, 1965; Head of W African Dept, FCO, 1968–73, concurrently Ambassador to Chad (non-resident), 1970–73; Ambassador to Hungary, 1973–76, to Portugal, 1976–81; High Comr in Canada, 1981–84. Cross Bencher, H of L, 1984–; Mem., Industry sub cttee, 1984–86, Envmt sub cttee, 1986–91, Agric. sub cttee, 1991–95, 1997–2000, EC Cttee; sub cttee on the 1996 Inter-governmental Conf., 1995–96; Mem. Science and Technol. Cttee sub cttees on scientific base of Nature Conservancy Council, 1990, on fish stocks, 1995; Chm., All Party Parly Conservation Gp, 1992–2000 (Vice-Chm., 1989–92); elected Mem., H of L, 1999. Chm., Jt Fisheries Policy and Legislation Wkg Gp (Moran Cttee), 1997–. Vice-Chm., Atlantic Salmon Trust, 1988–95 (Mem. Management Cttee, 1984–; Vice-Pres., 1995–); Chm., Fisheries Adv. Cttee for Welsh Region, Nat. Rivers Authy, 1989–94; Mem., Regl Fisheries Adv. Cttee, Welsh Water Authority, 1987–89; Pres., Welsh Salmon and Trout Angling Assoc., 1988–95, 2000–; Chm., Salmon and Trout Assoc., 1997–2000 (Exec. Vice Pres., 2000–). Chm., Wildlife and Countryside Link, 1992–95; Pres., Radnorshire Wildlife Trust, 1993–2012; Vice-Pres., RSPB, 1997–98 (Mem. Council, 1989–94). Grand Cross, Order of the Infante (Portugal), 1978. *Publications:* (as John Wilson): C. B.: a life of Sir Henry Campbell-Bannerman, 1973 (Whitbread Award for biography, 1973); Fairfax, 1985; (with William and James Wilson) William Robert Grove: the lawyer who invented the fuel cell, 2007. *Recreations:* fishing, fly-tying, bird-watching. *Heir:* *s* Hon. James McMoran Wilson [*b* 6 Aug. 1952; *m* 1980, Hon. Jane Hepburne-Scott, *y d* of 10th Lord Polwarth, TD; two *s*]. *Address:* House of Lords, SW1A 0PW. *Clubs:* Beefsteak, Flyfishers' (Pres., 1987–88). *Died 14 Feb. 2014.*

MORAY, 20th Earl of, *cr* 1562; **Douglas John Moray Stuart;** Lord Abernethy and Strathearn, 1562; Lord Doune, 1581; Baron of St Colme, 1611; Baron Stuart (GB), 1796; *b* 13 Feb. 1928; *e s* of 19th Earl of Moray and Mabel Helen Maud Wilson (*d* 1968); *S* father, 1974; *m* 1964, Lady Malvina Murray, *er d* of 7th Earl of Mansfield and Mansfield; one *s* one *d*. *Educ:* Trinity Coll., Cambridge (BA), FLAS 1958. *Heir:* *s* Lord Doune, *b* 29 Aug. 1966. *Club:* New (Edinburgh). *Died 23 Sept. 2011.*

MORBY, Grainne; Head of Patient Advice and Liaison Service and Patient and Public Involvement (formerly Manager and Family Advocate, Patient Advice and Liaison Service), Great Ormond Street Hospital for Children and UCL Institute of Child Health, since 2004; *b* 26 June 1951; *d* of late Geoffrey Morby and of Dympna Morby. *Educ:* Essex Univ. (BA Hons). Dir, Community Information Project, LA, 1980–89; Dir of Communications, London Bor. of Hackney, 1989–95; acting Chief Exec., London Lighthouse, 1995–2001; Dir of London Services, Terrence Higgins Trust & Lighthouse, 2001–04. *Publications:* Knowhow: a guide to your rights, 1986. *Recreations:* gardening, Irish music. *Address:* Pals, Great Ormond Street Hospital for Children, Great Ormond Street, WC1N 3JH. *Died 7 Aug. 2014.*

MORE, Norman, FRICS; Managing Director, Redditch Development Corporation, 1979–85; *b* 20 Dec. 1921; *s* of Herbert and Anna More; *m* 1952, Kathleen Mary Chrystal; two *s* one *d*. *Educ:* Royal High Sch., Edinburgh; Edinburgh Univ. FRICS 1970 (ARICS 1951). Served in Royal Engineers, Middle East, N Africa, Italy, Greece and

Germany, Major, 1941–48. Surveyor, Directorate of Lands and Accommodation, Min. of Works, 1948–58; Sen. Valuer, City Assessor's Office, Glasgow Corporation, 1958–63; Valuation and Estates Officer, East Kilbride Development Corp., 1963–65; Chief Estates Officer, Redditch Development Corp., 1965–79. Consultant Chartered Surveyor, to Grimley J. R. Eve, London and Birmingham, 1985–90. Mem., W Midlands Regl Bd, TSB Gp, 1984–89. Chairman, West Midlands Br., Royal Instn of Chartered Surveyors, 1974–75. Chm., Friendship Project for Children, 1992–99. Pres., Stratford-upon-Avon circle, Catenian Assoc., 1972–73. *Publications:* press articles and contribs to jls. *Recreations:* music, sport. *Address:* Mead Cottage, 192 Loxley Road, Stratford-upon-Avon, Warwickshire CV37 7DU. *T:* (01789) 293763. *Clubs:* East India, Devonshire, Sports and Public Schools. *Died 27 Sept. 2011.*

MORE-MOLYNEUX, James Robert, OBE 1983; DL; Vice Lord-Lieutenant of Surrey, 1983–96; *b* 17 June 1920; *s* of Brig. Gen. Francis Cecil More-Molyneux-Longbourne, CMG, DSO and Gwendoline Carew More-Molyneux; *m* 1948, Susan Bellinger; one *s. Educ:* Eton; Trinity Hall, Cambridge. War service in 4/7th Royal Dragoon Guards and 14th PWO The Scinde Horse, 1941–46; Founder Chm., Guildway Ltd, 1947–85 (introduced first manufactured timber frame houses with brick cladding to UK, 1960); founded Loseley Co-Partnership, 1950; Chm., Loseley Park Farms, 1950–92; opened Loseley House to public, 1950–; founded Loseley Dairy Products, 1967; part-time Dir, Seeboard, 1975–84. Founder: Loseley & Guildway Charitable Trust, 1973; Loseley Christian Trust, 1983. Mem. Exec. Cttee, Industrial Participation Assoc., 1952–77. Mem., Lambeth Partnership, 1992–2004. Lay Pastoral Asst, 1986–. High Sheriff of Surrey, 1974; DL Surrey 1976. Bledisloe Gold Medal for Landowners, RASE, 1984. *Publications:* The Loseley Challenge, 1995; The Spark of God, 2000. *Recreations:* countryside, Christian Healing Ministry, photography, writing. *Address:* Nursery Wing, Loseley Park, Guildford, Surrey GU3 1HS. *T:* (01483) 566090. *Club:* Farmers. *Died 19 July 2013.*

MORETON, Sir John (Oscar), KCMG 1978 (CMG 1966); KCVO 1976; MC 1944; HM Diplomatic Service, retired; *b* 28 Dec. 1917; *s* of Rev. C. O. Moreton; *m* 1945, Margaret Katherine, *d* of late Sir John Fryer, KBE, FRS; three *d. Educ:* St Edward's Sch., Oxford; Trinity Coll., Oxford (MA). War Service with 99th (Royal Bucks Yeomanry) Field Regt RA, 1939–46: France, Belgium, 1940; India, Burma, 1942–45. Asst Master, Uppingham Sch., 1946; Colonial Office, 1948; Private Sec. to Perm. Under-Sec. of State, 1949–50; seconded to Govt of Kenya, 1953–55; Private Sec. to Sec. of State for Colonies (Rt Hon. Alan Lennox-Boyd), 1955–59; transf. to CRO, 1960; Counsellor, British High Commn, Lagos, 1961–64; IDC 1965; Asst Under-Sec. of State, CRO, 1965–66, CO 1966–68, FCO 1968–69; Ambassador to Vietnam, 1969–71; High Comr, Malta, 1972–74; Dep. Perm. Representative, with personal rank of Ambassador, UK Mission to UN, NY, 1974–75; Minister, British Embassy, Washington, 1975–77. Dir, Wates Foundn, 1978–87. Gentleman Usher of the Blue Rod, Order of St Michael and St George, 1979–92. Governor, St Edward's Sch., Oxford, 1980–92. Hon. DL Hanover Coll., Indiana, 1976. *Recreations:* most outdoor activities, formerly athletics (Oxford Blue and International, 880 yds, 1939). *Address:* Weston House, Leigh Place, Cobham, Surrey KT11 2HL. *Club:* Army and Navy. *Died 14 Oct. 2012.*

MORGAN, Rt Rev. Alan Wyndham, OBE 2005; Bishop Suffragan of Sherwood, 1989–2004; *b* 22 June 1940; *s* of A. W. Morgan; *m* 1965, Margaret Patricia, *d* of W. O. Williams; one *s* one *d. Educ:* Boys' Grammar School, Gowerton; St David's Coll., Lampeter (BA 1962); St Michael's Coll., Llandaff. Deacon 1964, priest 1965; Assistant Curate: Llangyfelach with Morriston, 1964–69; Cockett, 1969–72; St Mark with St Barnabas, Coventry, 1972–73; Team Vicar, St Barnabas, Coventry East, 1973–77; Bishop's Officer for Social Responsibility, Diocese of Coventry, 1978–83; Archdeacon of Coventry, 1983–89. Mem., Gen. Synod, 1980–89. Chairman: Dio. of Southwell Ministry Gp, 1989–97; Dio. of Southwell Social Housing Gp, 1990–97; Lay Training Partnership, Dio. of Southwell, 1998–2001; E Midlands Churches Forum, 1998–. Chm., 1986–89, Vice-Pres., 1989–93, NCVO; Chairman: Wkg Pty on Future of the Family, Bd of Social Responsibility, 1993–95; Notts Child Care Forum, 1993–99; Mansfield Social Strategy Gp, 1994–2003; Regl Awards Cttee, Nat. Lottery Charities Bd, 1999–2000 (Chm., E Midlands Regl Adv. Panel, 1995–99); Coalfields Regeneration Trust, 1999–; Notts Community Foundn, 2001–; Member: N Notts HA Local Res. Ethics Cttee, 1990–97; Governing Council, Family Policy Studies Gp, 1994–99; Dep. Prime Minister's Coalfield Task Force, 1997–98; Mansfield Area Strategic Partnership (formerly Mansfield Partnership Task Force), 1998–2002; President: Notts Help the Homeless, 1990–2001; Mansfield Disabled Inf. Advice Line, 1994–; Framework Housing, 2001–. Director: Greater Nottingham TEC, 1991–95; N Notts TEC, 1995–2001; Notts Enterprise, 2001–03. Trustee, Charities Aid Foundn, 1997–2002. *Died 24 Oct. 2011.*

MORGAN, Bill; *see* Morgan, J. W. H.

MORGAN, Rear-Adm. Brinley John, CB 1972; *b* 3 April 1916; *s* of Thomas Edward Morgan and Mary Morgan (*née* Parkhouse); *m* 1945, Margaret Mary Whittles (*d* 2011); three *s. Educ:* Abersychan Grammar Sch.; University Coll., Cardiff (BSc 1937). Entered Royal Navy as Instr Lt, 1939. Served War of 1939–45: Cruisers Emerald and Newcastle, 1939–41; Aircraft Carrier Formidable, 1941–43; Naval Weather Service (Admty Forecast Section), 1943–45. Staff of C-in-C Medit., 1945–48; HQ, Naval Weather Service, 1948–50; Staff of Flag Officer Trng Sqdn in HM Ships Vanguard, Indefatigable and Implacable, 1950–52; Instr Comdr, 1951; Lectr, RN Coll., Greenwich, 1952–54; Headmaster, RN Schools, Malta, 1954–59; Instr Captain, 1960; Staff of Dir, Naval Educn Service, 1959–61 and 1963–64; Sen. Officers' War Course, 1961; HMS Ganges, 1961–63; Dean, RN Engineering Coll., Manadon, 1964–69; Instr Rear-Adm., 1970; Dir, Naval Educn Service, 1970–75. Freeman, City of London, 1982. *Club:* Naval. *Died 2 Sept. 2013.*

MORGAN, Clifford Isaac, CVO 1986; OBE 1977; Head of Outside Broadcasts Group, BBC Television, 1975–87; *b* 7 April 1930; *m* 1st, 1955, Nuala Martin (*d* 1999); one *s* one *d*; 2nd, 2001, Patricia Ewing. *Educ:* Tonyrefail Grammar School, South Wales. Played International Rugby Union as fly-half for Wales (29 caps), British Lions and Barbarians, 1951–57. Joined BBC, 1958, as Sports Organiser, Wales; Editor, Sportsview and Grandstand, 1961–64; Producer, This Week, 1964–66; freelance writer and broadcaster, 1966–72; Editor, Sport Radio, 1972–74; Head of Outside Broadcasts, Radio, 1974–75; Presenter, Sport on 4, 1987–98. President: London Glamorgan Soc., 1974–2009; London Welsh Male Voice Choir, 1990–2010; Welsh Rugby Former Internat. Players' Assoc. (formerly Welsh Rugby Internats Benevolent Assoc.), 2001–; Welsh Pres., Cystic Fibrosis Res. Trust, 1987–97; Vice-President: Sequal, 1976–96; Welsh Sports Assoc. for Mental Handicap, 1988–92; London Welsh Trust, 1999–; Patron, Headline, Southampton head and neck cancer charity, 2006–. Chm., Saints and Sinners Club, 1984–85. Hon. Fellow, Polytechnic of Wales, 1989. Hon. MA Wales, 1988; DUniv: Keele, 1989; Central England, 1998; Hon. LLD Bristol, 1996. *Publications:* Beyond the Fields of Play (autobiog.), 1996. *Recreation:* music. *Address:* Glenford, Ducie Avenue, Bembridge, Isle of Wight PO35 5NE. *Died 29 Aug. 2013.*

MORGAN, (David) Dudley; Consultant, Theodore Goddard & Co., Solicitors, 1980–83 (Senior Partner, 1974–80); *b* 23 Oct. 1914; *y s* of Thomas Dudley Morgan; *m* 1948, Margaret Helene (*d* 2012), *o d* of late David MacNaughton Duncan, Loanhead, Midlothian; two *d. Educ:* Swansea Grammar Sch.; Jesus Coll., Cambridge (MA, LLM). War Service with RAF in Intell. Br., UK, 1940–42 and Legal Br., India, 1942–46; Wing Comdr 1945. Admitted Solicitor, 1939, with Theodore Goddard & Co.; Partner 1948. *Address:* St Leonard's House, St Leonard's Road, Nazeing, Waltham Abbey, Essex EN9 2HG. *T:* (01992) 892124. *Club:* Carlton. *Died 17 Nov. 2013.*

MORGAN, Sir John (Albert Leigh), KCMG 1989 (CMG 1982); HM Diplomatic Service, retired; Chairman: Celtic Development Co. (formerly East European Development Trust), since 1994; Ceiba Investments Ltd (formerly Beta Gran Caribe, then Ceiba Finance Ltd), Cuba, since 2002; *b* 21 June 1929; *s* of late John Edward Rowland Morgan, Bridge, Kent; *m* 1st, 1961, Hon. Fionn Frances Bride O'Neill (marr. diss. 1975), *d* of 3rd Baron O'Neill, Shane's Castle, Antrim; one *s* two *d*; 2nd, 1976, Angela Mary Eleanor, *e d* of Patrick Warre Rathbone, MBE, Woolton, Liverpool; one *s* one *d*. *Educ:* Chingford County High Sch.; London School of Economics (BScEcon Hons Econs and Law; Hon. Fellow, 1984). Served in Army, 1947–49: commnd 1948; interpreter with French Army, 1949. Entered Foreign Service, 1951; FO, 1951–53; 3rd Sec. and Private Sec. to HM Ambassador, Moscow, 1953–56; 2nd Sec., Peking, 1956–58; FO, 1958–63 (attended Geneva Conf. of Foreign Ministers on Berlin, 1959, and on Laos (interpreter in Russian and Chinese), 1961; interpreter for Mr Khrushchev's visit to UK, 1956, for Mr Macmillan's visit to Soviet Union, 1959, and for Summit Conf. in Paris, 1960); 1st Sec., 1960; Head of Chancery, Rio de Janeiro, 1963–64; FO, 1964–65; Chargé d'Affaires, Ulan Bator, 1965; Moscow, 1965–67; Dep. Hd, Econ. Relns Dept, subseq. Export Promotion Dept, FO, 1968; Head of Far Eastern Dept, FCO, 1970–72; Head of Cultural Relations Dept, FCO, 1972–80 (Member: Reviewing Cttee on Export of Works of Art; Fulbright Scholarship Commn; Selection Cttee, US Bicentennial Scholarships Prog.); Ambassador and Consul Gen. to Republic of Korea, 1980–83; Ambassador to Poland, 1983–86; Ambassador to Mexico, 1986–89. Man. Dir (Internat. Relations), Maxwell Communications Corp., 1989–90; Chairman: Invesco (formerly Drayton) Korea Trust plc, 1993–99 (Dir, 1991); Gulf Internat. Minerals (Vancouver), 1997–2003; Director: The European, 1990–91; Christies, 1993–95; Invesco Europe Ltd, 1994–99; Japan Discovery Trust, 1994–2005; Pres., Actions Asie Emergents, Paris, 1996–2001; Dir and Co. Sec., Global Tote, 1999–2010. Pres., IFPI, 1990–93. Served on Earl Marshal's Staff for State Funeral of Sir Winston Churchill, 1965, and for Investiture of Prince of Wales, 1969. Trustee, BM, 1991–99, then Emeritus (Trustee, BM Develt Trust, 1991–). Governor, LSE, 1971–94, 1997–2003; Chm., LSE Foundn, 1994–97. Chairman: Anglo-Korean Soc., 1990–96 (Hon. Pres., 2002–06); UK-Korea Forum for the Future, 1991–99; Member: Internat. Council, United World Colleges, 1990–; Internat. and Current Affairs Cttee, ESU, 1993–2000. Royal Philharmonic Orchestra: Dir, 1993–96; Hon. Life Mem. 1979; Chm., Development Trust, 1993–96; Vice Chm., South Bank Foundn Ltd, 1997–2003. FRSA; Fellow, Royal Asiatic Soc.; Hon. Life Mem., GB-China Centre. Hon. DSc (Politics) Korea Univ., 1983; Hon. LLD Mexico Acad. of Internat. Law, 1987. Order of the Aztec Eagle, 1st cl. (Mexico), 1994; Order of Diplomatic Merit, 1st cl. (Korea), 1999. *Publications:* (contrib.) Travellers' Tales, 1999; Martinis, Guns and Girls, 2002; (contrib.) More Tales from the Travellers, 2005; various works of French and Chinese literary criticism. *Recreations:* ornithology, oriental art. *Address:* Apartment 7.1, 20 Gillingham Street, SW1V 1AG. *T:* (020) 7630 1806; Beaumont Cottage, South Brewham, near Bruton, Somerset BA10 0JZ. *T:* (01749) 850606. *Club:* Travellers. *Died 24 June 2012.*

MORGAN, John William Harold, (Bill), CBE 1998; FREng; Chairman, Trafford Park Urban Development Corporation, 1990–98; Director: AMEC plc, 1983–91 (Chairman, 1984–88); Hill Samuel & Co., 1983–89; *b* 13 Dec. 1927; *s* of John Henry and Florence Morgan; *m* 1952, Barbara (*née* Harrison); two *d*. *Educ:* Wednesbury Boys' High Sch.; Univ. of Birmingham (BScEng, 1st Cl. Hons). FIMechE, MIET. National Service commn with RAF, 1949–51. Joined English Electric Co., Stafford, as design engr, subseq. Chief Development Engr (Machines), 1953; Chief Develt Engr (Mechanical), 1957; Chief Engr (DC Machines), 1960; Product Div. Manager, 1962; Gen. Manager, Electrical Machines Gp, 1965; Man. Dir, English Electric-AEI Machines Gp (following merger with GEC/AEI), 1968; Asst Man. Dir and main board dir, GEC plc, 1973–83. Chm., Staffordshire Cable, 1989–93; Dep. Chm., Petbow Holdings, 1983–86; Director: Simon Engineering, 1983–88; Pitney Bowes, 1989–92; Tekdata, 1989–99; UMIST Ventures, 1989–2001. Additional Mem., Monopolies and Mergers Commn (Electricity Panel), 1992–98. FREng (FEng 1978; Mem. Council, 1987–90). FRSA 1988. Hon. DSc Salford, 1997. S. G. Brown award for an outstanding contrib. to promotion and development of mechanical inventions, Royal Society, 1968. *Recreations:* craft activities, particularly woodworking. *Address:* Sparrows, Shelley, Ipswich, Suffolk IP7 5RQ. *T:* (01206) 337552. *Died 18 Sept. 2015.*

MORGAN, Prof. Keith John, DPhil; FRACI, FRSC; FAIM; Research Fellow, Research Institute for Higher Education, Hiroshima University, since 2003; *b* 14 Dec. 1929; *s* of C. F. J. Morgan and Winifred Burman (formerly Morgan, *née* Allen); *m* 1957, Hilary Chapman (marr. diss. 1999); one *d*. *Educ:* Manchester Grammar Sch.; Brasenose Coll., Oxford (MA, BSc, DPhil). Senior Research Fellow, Min. of Supply, 1955–57; ICI Res. Fellow, 1957–58; Lectr, Univ. of Birmingham, 1958–64; AEC Fellow, Purdue Univ., 1960–61; Lectr, Sen. Lectr, Prof., Dept of Chemistry, Univ. of Lancaster, 1964–86 (Pro-Vice-Chancellor, 1973–78; Sen. Pro-Vice-Chancellor, 1978–86; Emeritus Prof.); Vice-Chancellor, Univ. of Newcastle, NSW, 1987–93 (Emeritus Prof.); Prof., Univ. of Electro-Communications, Tokyo, 1993–95. Visiting Professor: Hiroshima Univ., 1995–99, 2007–08, 2009–10; Nagoya Univ., 2002. Chm., Hunter Foundn for Cancer Res., 1992–93; Dep. Chm., Hunter Technol. Develt Centre, 1987–93; Member: Hunter Econ. Develt Council, 1989–93; Hunter Federal Task Force, 1991–93; Hunter Area Health Service Bd, 1992–93; Dir, Hunter Orch., 1991–93. Chm., Regl Council, AIM, 1989–93. Chm. of Govs, Newcastle Grammar Sch., 1991–93; Member: UCNS, 1980–86; Council, Lancashire Polytechnic, 1985–86. Mem., NSW Envmtl Res. Trust, 1990–93. Hon. DSc Newcastle, NSW, 1993. *Publications:* scientific and economic papers in various jls. *Recreations:* mountains, Mozart, cricket. *Address:* 9B Castle Hill, Lancaster LA1 1YS. *T:* (01524) 68619. *Died 6 May 2012.*

MORGAN, Kenneth, OBE 1978; journalist; consultant on Press ethics; Director: Press Council, 1980–90; Press Complaints Commission, 1991; *b* 3 Nov. 1928; *s* of Albert E. and Lily M. Morgan; *m* 1950, Margaret Cynthia, *d* of Roland E. Wilson; two *d* (and one *d* decd). *Educ:* Stockport Grammar School. Reporter, Stockport Express, 1944; Army, 1946, commissioned, 1947 (served Palestine, Egypt, GHQ MELF, British Army newspaper unit); journalism, 1949; Central London Sec., NUJ, 1962; Nat. Organiser, NUJ, 1966; Gen. Sec., NUJ, 1970–77, Mem. of Honour, 1978. Press Council: Consultative Mem., 1970–77; Jt Sec., 1977–78; Dep. Dir and Conciliator, 1978–79; Consultant, Press Complaints Commn, 1992. Director: Journalists in Europe Ltd, 1982–97; Reuters Founder's Share Co., 1984–99. Mem. Exec. Cttee: Printing and Kindred Trades Fedn, 1970–73; Nat. Fedn of Professional Workers, 1970–77; Fedn of Broadcasting Unions, 1970–77; Confedn of Entertainment Unions, 1970–77; Bureau, Internat. Fedn of Journalists, 1970–78. Member: NEDC for Printing and Publishing Industry, 1970; Printing Industries Cttee, TUC, 1974–77; Printing and Publishing Industries Trng Bd, 1975–77; Jt Standing Cttee, Nat. Newspaper Industry, 1976–77; British Cttee, Journalists in Europe, 1977–2003; C of E General Synod Cttee for Communications Press Panel, 1981–90; CRE Media Gp, 1981–85; Judge, Samuel Storey Editl Awards, 1981–98; Internat. Ombudsman Inst., 1983; Trustee, Reuters, 1984–99. Consultant: Nat. Media Commn, Ghana, 1995–99; Fiji Media Council, 1998; Media Trust Bd, Mauritius, 1998; Ind. Media Commn, Sierra Leone, 2003; Botswana Press Council, 2004; (with John Prescott Thomas) conducted Cabinet review of media legislation, Fiji, 1996–97; Advr, Minister of Information and Culture, Sierra Leone, 1998. Vice Pres. (former Chm.), Dulwich UNA, 1989–. Gov., 1992–99, Hon. Sec., 1993–99, ESU. Associate Mem. IPI, 1980; FRSA 1980. Methodist Recorder Lectr, 1989; British Council and Council of Europe lectures in Central and W Africa, Papua New Guinea, Fiji, Spain, Greece, Germany, Russia and Japan. Associate Press Fellow, Wolfson Coll., Cambridge, 1998–. *Publications:* Press Conduct in the Sutcliffe Case, 1983; (with David Christie) New Connexions: the power to inform, 1989; (jtly) Future Media Legislation and

Regulation for the Republic of the Fiji Islands, 1996; A Press Council for Mauritius?: freedom, responsibility and redress for Mauritius and its media, 1999; *contributed to:* El Poder Judicial en le Conjunto de los Poderes del Estado y de la Sociedad, 1989; Media Freedom and Accountability, 1989; The Independence of the Journalist, Is de Klant of de Krant Koning, 1990; Beyond the Courtroom: alternatives for resolving press disputes, 1991; Sir Zelman Cowen: a life within the law, 1997; Arsenal for Democracy, 2002. *Recreations:* theatre, military history, inland waterways, travel. *Address:* 151 Overhill Road, Dulwich, SE22 0PT. *T:* (020) 8693 6585. *Died 5 Aug. 2015.*

MORGAN, Michael Hugh, CMG 1978; HM Diplomatic Service, retired; *b* 18 April 1925; *s* of late H. P. Morgan; *m* 1957, Julian Bamfield; two *s.* *Educ:* Shrewsbury Sch.; Downing College, Cambridge; School of Oriental and African Studies, London Univ. Army Service 1943–46. HMOCS Malaya, 1946–56. Foreign Office, 1956–57; First Secretary, Peking, 1957–60; Belgrade, 1960–64; attached to Industry, 1964; First Secretary, FCO, 1964–68; Counsellor and Head of Chancery, Cape Town/Pretoria, 1968–72; Counsellor, Peking, 1972–75; Inspector, FCO, 1975–77; High Comr, Sierra Leone, 1977–81; Ambassador to the Philippines, 1981–85. Consultant, British Rail Engrg, 1986–88; Dir, Swansea Overseas Trust, 1988–91. *Address:* 1 Silkmill Lane, Ludlow, Shropshire SY8 1BJ. *Died 4 Dec. 2012.*

MORGAN, Prof. Roger Pearce; Professor, 1988–96, External Professor, 1996–2006, of Political Science, European University Institute, Florence; *b* 3 March 1932; *s* of Donald Emlyn Morgan and Esther Mary Morgan (*née* Pearce); *m* 1st, 1957, Annie-Françoise, (Annette) Combes (marr. diss. 1988); three *s* one *d*; 2nd, 1988, Mrs Catherine Howell. *Educ:* Wolverton Grammar Sch.; Leighton Park Sch.; Downing Coll., Cambridge (MA 1957; PhD 1959); Univs of Paris and Hamburg. Staff Tutor, Dept of Extra-Mural Studies, London Univ., 1957–59; Asst Lectr and Lectr in Internat. Politics, UCW, Aberystwyth, 1959–63; Lectr in Hist. and Internat. Relations, Sussex Univ., 1963–67; Asst, then Dep. Dir of Studies, RIIA, 1968–74; Prof. of European Politics, 1974–78, and Dean, Sch. of Human and Environmental Studies, 1976–78, Loughborough Univ.; Head of European Centre for Political Studies, PSI, 1978–86; Vis. Fellow, Centre for Internat. Studies, LSE, 1987–88. Visiting Professor: Columbia Univ., 1965; Johns Hopkins Univ., 1969–70, 1988–89, 1995; Cornell Univ., 1972; Surrey Univ., 1980–84; UCLA, 1993, 2001; Univ. of Bonn, 1996–97; pt-time Prof., Dept of War Studies, KCL, 2000; Res. Associate, Center for Internat. Affairs, Harvard, 1965–66; Visiting Lecturer: Cambridge Univ., 1967; LSE, 1974, 1980–88; Associate Mem., Nuffield Coll., Oxford, 1980–83; Hon. Professorial Fellow, UCW, Aberystwyth, 1980–84, Hon. Prof., 1985–95; Sen. Associate Mem., St Antony's Coll., Oxford, 1996–97; Vis. Fellow, European Inst., LSE, 1998–2000. Lectr at RCDS, CS Coll., RNC, etc. Member: Council, RIIA, 1976–85, 1986–92 and 1997–2003; Academic Council, Wilton Park, 1982–83; Exec. Cttee and Bd, Wiener Liby Inst. of Contemporary History, 1985–2012. Trustee, Gilbert Murray Trust, 1973–88. Officer's Cross, Order of Merit (Germany), 2002. *Publications:* The German Social Democrats and the First International 1864–72, 1965, reprinted 2008; Modern Germany, 1966; (ed jtly) Britain and West Germany: changing societies and the future of foreign policy, 1971 (German edn 1970); West European Politics since 1945, 1972; (ed) The Study of International Affairs, 1972; High Politics, Low Politics: toward a foreign policy for Western Europe, 1973; The United States and West Germany 1945–1973: a study in alliance politics, 1974 (German edn 1975); West Germany's Foreign Policy Agenda, 1978; (ed jtly) Moderates and Conservatives in Western Europe, 1982 (Italian edn 1983); (ed jtly) Partners and Rivals in Western Europe: Britain, France and Germany, 1986; (ed) Regionalism in European Politics, 1986; (ed jtly) New Diplomacy in the Post-Cold War World, 1993; (ed jtly) The Third Pillar of the European Union, 1994; (ed jtly) Parliaments and Parties: the European Parliament in the political life of Europe, 1995; (ed jtly) New Challenges to the European Union: policies and policy-making, 1997; (ed jtly) Choice and Representation in the European Union, 2003; contribs to symposia and jls. *Recreations:* music, watching cricket. *Address:* Highgate Nursing Home, 12 Hornsey Lane, N6 5LX. *T:* (020) 7281 3511. *E:* rpm32@btinternet.com. *Club:* Reform. *Died 19 Feb. 2015.*

MORGAN-GILES, Rear-Adm. Sir Morgan (Charles), Kt 1985; DSO 1944; OBE 1943 (MBE 1942); GM 1941; DL; *b* 19 June 1914; *e s* of late F. C. Morgan-Giles, OBE, MINA, Teignmouth, Devon; *m* 1946, Pamela (*d* 1966), *d* of late Philip Bushell, Sydney, New South Wales; two *s* four *d*; *m* 1968, Marigold (*d* 1995), *d* of late Percy Lowe. *Educ:* Clifton Coll. Entered Royal Navy, 1932; served on China Station, and in destroyers. War Service: Atlantic convoys and Mediterranean; Tobruk garrison and Western Desert, 1941; with RAF, 1942; Sen. Naval Officer, Vis. (Dalmatia) and liaison with Commandos and Marshal Tito's Partisan Forces, 1943–44. Captain 1953; Chief of Naval Intelligence, Far East, 1955–56; Captain (D) Dartmouth Training Sqdn, 1957–58; HMS Belfast, in command, 1961–62; Rear-Adm. 1962; Adm. Pres., Royal Naval Coll., Greenwich, 1962–64; retd 1964. MP (C) Winchester, May 1964–79. Vice-Chm., Conservative Defence Cttee, 1965–75. Chm., HMS Belfast Trust, 1971–78; Life Vice-Pres., RNLI, 1989. Prime Warden, Shipwrights' Company, 1987–88. DL Hants, 1983. *Recreations:* sailing, country pursuits. *Address:* Anchor House, Little Sodbury Manor, Glos BS37 6QA. *T:* (01454) 327485. *Club:* Royal Yacht Squadron. *Died 4 May 2013.*

MORLEY, 6th Earl of, *cr* 1815; **John St Aubyn Parker,** KCVO 1998; JP; Lt-Col, Royal Fusiliers; Lord-Lieutenant of Devon, 1982–98; *b* 29 May 1923; *e s* of Hon. John Holford Parker (*y s* of 3rd Earl), Pound House, Yelverton, Devon; *S* uncle, 1962; *m* 1955, Johanna Katherine, *d* of Sir John Molesworth-St Aubyn, 14th Bt, CBE; one *s* one *d*. *Educ:* Eton. 2nd Lt, KRRC, 1942; served NW Europe, 1944–45; Palestine and Egypt, 1945–48; transferred to Royal Fusiliers, 1947; served Korea, 1952–53; Middle East, 1953–55 and 1956; Staff Coll., Camberley, 1957; Comd, 1st Bn Royal Fusiliers, 1965–67. Director: Lloyds Bank Ltd, 1974–78; Lloyds Bank UK Management Ltd, 1979–86; Chm., SW Region, Lloyds Bank, 1989–91 (Chm., Devon and Cornwall Regl Bd, 1974–89). Chm., Plymouth Sound Ltd, 1974–94. Mem., Devon and Co. Cttee, Nat. Trust, 1969–84; President: Plymouth Incorporated Chamber of Trade and Commerce, 1970–2008; Cornwall Fedn of Chambers of Commerce and Trader Assocs, 1972–79; West Country Tourist Bd, 1971–89. Governor: Seale-Hayne Agricl Coll., 1973–93; Plymouth Polytechnic, 1975–82 (Chm., 1977–82). Pres., Council of Order of St John for Devon, 1979–98. DL 1973, Vice Lord-Lieutenant, 1978–82, Devon. JP Plymouth, 1972. Hon. Colonel: Devon ACF, 1979–87; 4th Bn Devonshire and Dorset Regl, 1987–92. *Heir:* *s* Viscount Boringdon, *b* 22 Aug. 1956. *Address:* Pound House, Yelverton, Devon PL20 7LJ. *T:* (01822) 853162. *Died 20 Sept. 2015.*

MORLEY, Leslie Sydney Dennis, DSc; FRS 1992; FREng, FIMA, FRAeS; Hon. Associate Professorial Research Fellow, Brunel University, 1985–94; *b* 23 May 1924; *s* of Sydney Victor Morley, RN (Chief Petty Officer (Gunnery), HMS Hood, killed in action with the Bismarck, 1941) and Doris May Huntley (*née* Evans); *m* 1951, Norma Baker; two *s* one *d*. *Educ:* Portsmouth Northern Secondary Sch.; Portsmouth Municipal Tech. Sch.; Southampton Univ. Coll. (HNC 1945); Coll. Aeronautics, Cranfield (DCAe 1948; DSc 1971); Univ. of Cambridge (Post-Grad. Dip. Structures and Materials 1959). FRAeS 1962; FIMA 1964; FREng (FEng 1982). Airspeed Ltd: apprentice toolroom fitter, Portsmouth, 1940–45; Stress Office, Christchurch, 1945–46; Res. Officer, Nat. Luchtvaartlab., Amsterdam, 1948–49; Tech. Asst, Bristol Aeroplane Co., Filton, 1949–50; Structures Dept, RAE, 1950–84, DCSO, 1976; Professorial Res. Fellow, Inst. of Computational Maths, Brunel Univ., 1985–98. *Publications:* Skew Plates and Structures, 1963; numerous articles on structural mechanics, esp. finite element method, plate and shell theory, in learned jls in Britain and abroad. *Recreations:* family, British heritage, gardening. *Died 16 June 2011.*

MORPETH, Sir Douglas (Spottiswoode), Kt 1981; TD 1959; FCA; FRCM; Partner, Touche Ross & Co., 1958–85 (Senior Partner, 1977–85); *b* 6 June 1924; *s* of late Robert Spottiswoode Morpeth and Louise Rankine

Morpeth (*née* Dobson); *m* 1951, Anne Rutherford, *yr d* of Ian C. Bell, OBE, MC, Edinburgh; two *s* two *d*. *Educ:* George Watson's Coll., Edinburgh; Edinburgh Univ. (BCom). Commissioned RA; served 1943–47, India, Burma, Malaya. Mem., Inst. of Chartered Accountants in England and Wales, 1952, Fellow, 1957, Pres., 1972. Chm., Clerical Med. and Gen. Life Assce Soc., later Clerical Med. Investment Gp, 1978–94. Chairman: (of Trustees), British Telecom Staff Superannuation Scheme, 1983–92; British Borneo Petroleum Syndicate, 1985–95; Deputy Chairman: Brixton Estate plc, 1983–94; Leslie Langton Hldgs, 1987–91; Director: Allied-Irish Banks, 1986–91; First Ireland Investment Trust, 1992–99 (Chm., 1997–99). Mem., Investment Grants Advisory Cttee, 1968–71; Chm., Inflation Accounting Steering Gp, 1976–80; Vice-Chm., Accounting Standards Cttee, 1970–82. Mem. Council and Chm., Taxation Cttee, 1973–76, CBI. Honourable Artillery Company: Member, 1949–; Lt-Col, comdg 1st Regt HAC (RHA), 1964–66; Master Gunner within the Tower of London, 1966–69. Master, Co. of Chartered Accountants in England and Wales, 1977–78. FRCM (Hon. Treasurer, RCM, 1983–96). *Recreations:* golf, gardening, fishing. *Clubs:* Athenæum, Caledonian. *Died 26 Aug. 2014.*

MORPHET, Sarah Francis, (Sally), CMG 2002; Research Counsellor, Foreign and Commonwealth Office, 1998–2000; *b* 8 July 1940; *d* of Sir John Christopher Blake Richmond and Diana Richmond (*née* Galbraith); *m* 1965, Richard Edward Morphet, CBE; two *d*. *Educ:* Mayfield Convent, Sussex; Univ. of St Thomas, Houston, Texas; Newnham Coll., Cambridge (BA 1962, MA). COI, 1963–66; researcher, FCO, 1966–2000, covered major non-aligned meetings, 1979–2000. Vis. Prof., Univ. of Kent at Canterbury, 2001–06. *Publications:* contrib. chapters in books, including: United Nations, Divided World, 2nd edn 1993; The Conscience of the World, 1996; Human Rights and Comparative Foreign Policy, 2000; The United Nations at the Millennium, 2000; (jtly) The South in World Politics, 2009; contrib. articles to Global Governance, Internat. Peacekeeping, Rev. of Internat. Studies, Security Dialogue. *E:* sally.morphet@ntlworld.com. *Died 22 April 2014.*

MORPURGO DAVIES, Anna Elbina; *see* Davies, Anna E.

MORRELL, Prof. David Cameron, OBE 1982; FRCP, FRCGP; Wolfson Professor of General Practice, United Medical and Dental Schools of Guy's and St Thomas' Hospitals, 1974–93, Emeritus Professor of General Practice, 1993; *b* 6 Nov. 1929; *s* of William and Violet Morrell; *m* 1953, Alison Joyce Morrell; three *s* two *d*. *Educ:* Wimbledon Coll.; St Mary's Hosp. Med. Sch. (MB BS). DObstRCOG; FFPH. Phys., RAF Med. Br., 1954–57; Principal in Gen. Practice, Hoddesdon, Herts, 1957–63; Lectr in Gen. Practice, Univ. of Edinburgh, 1963–67; Sen. Lectr, then Reader, in Gen. Practice, St Thomas' Hosp. Med. Sch., 1967–74. Pres., BMA, 1994–95. KSG 1982. *Publications:* The Art of General Practice, 1966, 4th edn 1991; An Introduction to Primary Medical Care, 1976, 2nd edn 1981; (with J. Cormack and M. Marinker) Practice: a handbook of general practice, 1976, 2nd edn 1987. *Recreations:* gardening, walking. *Address:* 14 Higher Green, Ewell KT17 3BA. *T:* (020) 8786 9270. *Died 19 March 2012.*

MORRIS, 3rd Baron *cr* 1918; **Michael David Morris;** *b* 9 Dec. 1937; *er* twin *s* of 2nd Baron Morris and Jean Beatrice (later Lady Salmon; she *d* 1989), *d* of late Lt-Col D. Maitland-Makgill-Crichton; *S* father, 1975; *m* 1st, 1959, Denise Eleanor (marr. diss. 1962), *o d* of Morley Richards; 2nd, 1962, Jennifer (marr. diss. 1969), *o d* of Squadron Leader Tristram Gilbert; two *d*; 3rd, 1980, Juliet (marr. diss. 1996), twin *d* of Anthony Buckingham; two *s* one *d*; 4th, 1999, Nicola Mary, *o d* of Colin Morgan Watkins. *Educ:* Downside. *Heir:* *s* Hon. Thomas Anthony Salmon Morris, *b* 2 July 1982. *Died 5 May 2011.*

MORRIS OF MANCHESTER, Baron *cr* 1997 (Life Peer), of Manchester in the co. of Greater Manchester; **Alfred Morris;** AO 1991; QSO 1989; PC 1979; *b* 23 March 1928; *s* of late George Henry Morris and Jessie Morris (*née* Murphy); *m* 1950, Irene (*née* Jones); two *s* two *d*. *Educ:* elem. and evening schs, Manchester; Ruskin Coll., Oxford; St Catherine's, Univ. of Oxford (MA); Univ. of Manchester (Postgrad. certif. in Educn). Employed in office of a Manchester brewing firm from age 14 (HM Forces, 1946–48); Teacher and Lectr, Manchester, 1954–56; Industrial Relations Officer, The Electricity Council, London, 1956–64. Nat. Chm., Labour League of Youth, 1950–52; Observer, Council of Europe, 1952–53. Contested Liverpool, Garston, 1951. MP (Lab and Co-op) Manchester, Wythenshawe, 1964–97. PPS to Minister of Agric., Fisheries and Food, 1964–67, and to Lord President of the Council and Leader of House of Commons, 1968–70; Opposition front bench spokesman on social services, specialising in the problems and needs of disabled people, 1970–74 and 1979–92; Parly Under-Sec. of State, DHSS, as Britain's first-ever Minister for Disabled People, 1974–79. Treasurer, British Gp, IPU, 1971–74; Mem., UK Delegn to UN Gen. Assembly, 1966; Chm., Food and Agriculture Gp of Parly Lab. Party, 1971–74; Representative of Privy Council on Council of RCVS, 1969–74; promoted Chronically Sick and Disabled Persons Act, 1970, Food and Drugs (Milk) Act, 1970, Police Act, 1972, as a Private Member; Parly Advr to the Police Fedn, 1971–74; Hon. Parly Advr to Royal British Legion, 1989–; Chm., Co-operative Parly Group, 1971–72 and 1983–85; Vice-Chm., All-Party Parly Retail Trade Gp, 1972–74; Vice-Pres., Parly and Scientific Cttee, 1991–95 (Chm., 1988–91); Chairman: Managing Trustees, Parly Pensions Fund, 1983–97 (Man. Trustee, 1980–83); Managing Trustees, H of C Members' Fund, 1983–97; Anzac Gp of MPs and Peers, 1982–97 (Pres., 1997–); Jt Treasurer, British-Amer. Parly Gp, 1983–97. Mem., US Congressional Cttee of Inquiry into Gulf War illnesses, 2002–; architect of ind. public Inquiry into Gulf War Illnesses (report 2004). Mem., Gen. Adv. Council, BBC, 1968–74, 1983–95; Patron: Disablement Income Group, 1970–; Motability, 1978–; Royal Schools for Deaf Children, 1995–; Life Patron, Rehabilitation International (RI), 1999; Mem., Exec. Cttee, Nat. Fund for Research into Crippling Diseases, 1970–74. Chm., World Cttees apptd to draft "Charter for the 1980s" for disabled people worldwide, 1980–81, and "Charter for the New Millennium", 2000; President: N of England Regional Assoc. for the Deaf, 1980–; Co-operative Congress, 1995–96; Soc. of Chiropodists and Podiatrists, 1997–; Haemophilia Soc., 1999–; Vice-Pres., Crisis at Christmas, 1995– (Trustee, 1982–95). Trustee, Hallé Orch., 2002. FABE 2000. Hon. Fellow, Manchester Metropolitan Univ. (formerly Poly.), 1990. Hon. FRCPSGlas 2009; Hon. FRCP 2009. Hon. MA Salford, 1997; Hon. LLD Manchester, 1998. Field Marshal Lord Harding Award, 1971, for services to the disabled; Grimshaw Meml Award of Nat. Fedn of the Blind, 1971; Paul Harris Fellowship, Rotary Internat., for services to disabled people internationally, 1992; AA Award, 1997; Earl Snowdon Award, 1998; Lifetime Achievement Award, People of the Year, 2000; Henry H. Kessler Award, Rehabilitation Internat., 2000; Lifetime Achievement Award, ePolitix Charity Champions Awards, 2005. *Publications:* Value Added Tax: a tax on the consumer, 1970; The Growth of Parliamentary Scrutiny by Committee, 1970; (with A. Butler) No Feet to Drag, 1972; Ed. lectures (Human Relations in Industry), 1958; Ed. Jl (Jt Consultation) publ. Nat. Jt Adv. Coun. Elec. Supply Ind., 1959–61. *Recreations:* gardening, tennis, snooker, chess. *Address:* House of Lords, SW1A 0PW. *Died 12 Aug. 2012.*

MORRIS, Rt Hon. Charles Richard; PC 1978; DL; Chairman, Ponti's Group Ltd, 2001–05 (Deputy Chairman, 1987–2001); *b* 14 Dec. 1926; *s* of late George Henry Morris, Newton Heath, Manchester; *m* 1950, Pauline, *d* of Albert Dunn, Manchester; two *d*. *Educ:* Brookdale Park Sch., Manchester. Served with Royal Engineers, 1945–48. Pres., Clayton Labour Party, 1950–52. Mem. of Manchester Corporation, 1954–64: Chm. of Transport Cttee, 1959–62; Dep. Chm. of Establishment Cttee, 1963–64. Mem., Post Office Workers Union (Mem. Nat. Exec. Council, 1959–63). Contested (Lab) Cheadle Div. of Cheshire, 1959. MP (Lab) Manchester, Openshaw, Dec. 1963–1983; PPS to the Postmaster-General, 1964; Govt Asst Whip, 1966–67; Vice-Chamberlain, HM Household, 1967–69; Treasurer, HM Household (Deputy Chief Whip),

1969–70; PPS to Rt Hon. H. Wilson, MP, 1970–74; Minister of State: DoE, March–Oct. 1974; CSD, 1974–79; Dep. Shadow Leader of the House, 1980–83. Sec., NW Gp of Labour MPs, 1979–83. Chm., Oldham-Rochdale Groundwork Trust, 1984–99; Chm., Covent Garden Tenants' Adv. Gp, 1990–2005; Gov., Disley Sch., 1992–97. DL Greater Manchester, 1985. *Address:* Derwent Reach, Aston Lane, Oker, Matlock DE4 2JP. *T:* (01629) 732738. *Died 8 Jan. 2012.*

MORRIS, Christopher; Senior Partner, Corporate Recovery, Deloitte & Touche, 1980–2000; *b* 28 April 1942; *s* of Richard Archibald Sutton Morris, MC and Josephine Fanny Mary Morris (*née* Galliano); *m* 1968, Isabel Claire Ramsden Knowles (marr. diss. 1985); two *s*. *Educ:* privately. FCA 1967. Partner, Touche Ross & Co., later Deloitte & Touche, 1970–2000; Nat. Dir, Corporate Special Services, 1975; Chm., 1992. Major insolvency assignments: Banco Ambrosiano; Laker Airways; Rush & Tomkins; Polly Peck, BCCI. Chm., Insolvency Management Ltd, subseq. IM Litigation Funding Ltd, 2002–; Dir, Begbies Traynor, 2004–. *Recreations:* racing, music, travel, food and wine, countryside. *Clubs:* Turf, Garrick; New Frontier (Lincs). *Died 11 March 2015.*

MORRIS, David Elwyn; a District Judge (formerly Registrar) of the Principal Registry of the Family Division of the High Court of Justice, 1976–91; *b* 22 May 1920; *s* of Rev. S. M. Morris and K. W. Morris; *m* 1st, 1947, Joyce Hellyer (*d* 1977); one *s* one *d*; 2nd, 1978, Gwendolen Pearce (*d* 1988), *widow* of Dr John Pearce; 3rd, 1990, Mrs Clova M. Tudor. *Educ:* Mill Hill Sch.; Brasenose Coll., Oxford (Hulme Exhibnr; MA). With Friends' Ambulance Unit in China, 1942–44; served British Army in India, 1944–46. Called to Bar, Inner Temple, 1949; admitted Solicitor of the Supreme Court, 1955; Mem., Matrimonial Causes Rule Cttee, 1967–75. Partner, Jaques & Co. until 1975. Adv. Editor, Atkin's Encyclopaedia of Court Forms in Civil Proceedings, 1982–88. *Publications:* China Changed My Mind, 1948; The End of Marriage, 1971; contrib. Marriage For and Against, 1972; Pilgrim through this Barren Land, 1974. *Recreation:* reading. *Address:* 42 Frenchay Road, Oxford OX2 6TG. *T:* (01865) 558390. *Club:* Oxford and Cambridge. *Died 29 April 2015.*

MORRIS, John Evan A.; *see* Artro Morris.

MORRIS, Prof. Terence Patrick Michael; JP; Emeritus Professor of Criminology and Criminal Justice, University of London, since 1994 (Professor of Social Institutions, 1981–94); *b* 8 June 1931; *s* of Albert and Norah Avis Morris; *m* 1st, 1954, Pauline Jeannette Peake (*née* Morris) (marr. diss. 1973) one *d*; 2nd, 1973, Penelope Jane, *y d* of Stanley and Alexandra Tomlinson. *Educ:* John Ruskin Grammar Sch., Croydon; LSE, Univ. of London (Leverhulme Schol.; BSc (Soc) 1953, PhD (Econ) 1955). Lectr in Sociology, LSE, 1955–63; Reader, 1963–69, Prof., 1969–81, Sociology (with special ref. to Criminology), London Univ.; Founder Dir, Mannheim Centre for Criminology and Criminal Justice, LSE, 1990. Visiting Professor of Criminology: Univ. of California, 1964–65; Univ. of Manitoba, 1996. Mem., Adv. Mission on Treatment of Offenders (Western Pacific, British Honduras, Bahamas), 1966. Vice-Pres., Howard League for Penal Reform, 1986–2004; Mem., Magistrates' Assoc. Treatment of Offenders Cttee (co-opted), 1969–77; Founder Mem., Inst. for Study of Drug Dependence. Man. Editor, British Jl of Sociology, 1965–74. JP Inner London, 1967. *Publications:* The Criminal Area, 1957; (with Pauline Morris) Pentonville: a sociological study of an English prison, 1963; (with L. J. Blom-Cooper) A Calendar of Murder, 1964; Deviance and Control: the secular heresy, 1976; Crime and Criminal Justice since 1945, 1989; (with L. J. Blom-Cooper) With Malice Aforethought: a study of the crime and punishment for homicide, 2004; (with L. J. Blom-Cooper) Fine Lines and Distinctions: murder, manslaughter and the unlawful taking of human life, 2011; contribs to Brit. Jl Criminology, Brit. Jl Sociology, Encyc. Britannica, Crim. Law Review. *Recreations:* cycling, photography. *Address:* Christmas Cottage, Lower Road, South Wonston, Winchester, Hants SO21 3ER. *Club:* Cyclists' Touring. *Died 8 July 2013.*

MORRIS, Very Rev. William James, KCVO 1995; JP; Minister of Glasgow Cathedral, 1967–2005; a Chaplain to the Queen in Scotland, 1969–96, an Extra Chaplain, since 1996; Dean of the Chapel Royal in Scotland, 1991–96; *b* Cardiff, 22 Aug. 1925; *o s* of William John Morris and Eliza Cecilia Cameron Johnson; *m* 1952, Jean Daveena Ogilvy Howie, CBE, LLD (*d* 2005), *oc* of Rev. David Porter Howie and Veena Christie, Kilmarnock; one *s*. *Educ:* Cardiff High Sch.; Univ. of Wales; Edinburgh Univ. BA 1946, BD 1949, Wales; PhD Edinburgh, 1954. Ordained, 1951. Asst, Canongate Kirk, Edinburgh, 1949–51; Minister, Presbyterian Church of Wales, Cadoxton and Barry Is, 1951–53; Buckhaven (Fife): St David's, 1953–57; Peterhead Old Parish, 1957–67; Chaplain to the Lord High Comr to the General Assembly of the Church of Scotland, 1975–76; Chaplain: Peterhead Prison, 1963–67; Glasgow DC, 1967; Trades House of Glasgow, 1967–2005; W of Scotland Engrs Assoc., 1967–2005; The High Sch. of Glasgow, 1974–76; Glasgow Acad., 1976–2005; Strathclyde Police, 1977–2005; Queen's Body Guard for Scotland, Royal Co. of Archers, 1994–2007; Soc. of Friends of Glasgow Cathedral, 2002–05 (Chm. Council, 1967–2002); Hon. Chaplain, The Royal Scottish Automobile Club; Moderator, Presbytery of Deer, 1965–66; Convener Adv. Bd, Church of Scotland, 1977–80; Vice-Chm., Bd of Nomination to Church Chairs, Church of Scotland, 1978–81. Mem. IBA, 1979–84 (Chm. Scottish Adv. Cttee). President: Rotary Club of Peterhead, 1965–66; Peterhead and Dist Professional and Business Club, 1967; St Andrew's Soc., Glasgow, 1992–2005 (Vice-Pres., 1967–82); Chairman: Iona Cath. Trust, 1976–2005 (Trustee, 1967); Club Service Cttee, Dist 101, RIBI, 1964–66; Prison Chaplaincies Bd (Church of Scotland Home Bd), 1969–83; Member: Scottish Cttee, British Sailors' Soc., 1967–83; Bd of Management, W of Scotland Convalescent Home, 1967–75; Gen. Convocation, Strathclyde Univ., 1967–2005; Council of Management, Quarriers' Homes, 1968–88; Bd of Management, Glasgow YMCA, 1973–88; Scottish Council on Crime, 1974–76; Church of Scotland Bd of Practice and Procedure, 1981–85; Bd of Governors, Jordanhill Coll. of Educn, Glasgow, 1983–91; Hon. Pres., Glasgow Soc. of Social Services Inc., 1984–. Hon. Member: Scottish Ambulance Assoc., 1981; Royal Faculty of Procurators in Glasgow, 1997. JP: Co. of Aberdeen, 1963–71; Co. of City of Glasgow, 1971. ChStJ 1991. FRCPS(Hon.) 1983. Hon. LLD Strathclyde, 1974; Hon. DD Glasgow, 1979; Hon. DLitt Glasgow Caledonian, 2003. Lord Provost's Award, Glasgow, 1996; Paul Harris Fellow, Rotary Internat., 1997. *Publications:* A Walk Around Glasgow Cathedral, 1986; Amazing Graces, 2001. *Recreations:* fishing, gardening. *Address:* 1 Whitehill Grove, Newton Mearns, Glasgow G77 5DH. *T:* (0141) 6396327. *Clubs:* New (Edinburgh); RNVR (Scotland) (Hon.); University of Strathclyde Staff (Hon.); Rotary of Dennistoun (Hon.); Rotary of Glasgow (Hon.). *Died 31 Oct. 2013.*

MORRISON, His Honour Alexander John Henderson; a Circuit Judge, 1980–98; *b* 16 Nov. 1927; *yr s* of late Dr Alexander Morrison and Mrs A. Morrison; *m* 1978, Hon. Philippa, *y d* of 1st Baron Hives. *Educ:* Derby Sch.; Emmanuel Coll., Cambridge (MA, LLB). Called to the Bar, Gray's Inn, 1951. Mem. of Midland Circuit; Dep. Chm., Derbyshire QS, 1964–71; Regional Chm. of Industrial Tribunals, Sheffield, 1971–80; a Recorder of the Crown Court, 1971–80. A Pres., Mental Health Review Tribunals, 1983–98. Pres., Derbys Union of Golf Clubs, 1977–79. *Recreations:* golf, schools football. *Address:* c/o Derby Combined Court, Morledge, Derby DE1 2XE. *Died 28 June 2012.*

MORRISON, Donald Alexander Campbell; Assistant Under-Secretary of State, Home Office, 1972–76; *b* 30 Nov. 1916; *s* of late George Alexander Morrison, sometime MP for Scottish Univs, and Rachel Brown Morrison (*née* Campbell); *m* 1st, 1951, Elma Margaret Craig (*d* 1970); one *s* one *d* (and one *s* decd); 2nd, 1973, Jane Margaret Montgomery (*d* 2006); one step *s*. *Educ:* Fettes Coll.; Christ Church, Oxford (BA). Home Office, 1939; Asst Sec., 1955. A Senior Clerk (acting), House of Commons, 1976–81. War Service, 1940–45: 79th (Scottish Horse) Medium Regt, RA, 1942–45. *Publications:* Haps and Such (poems), 1986; *children's operas:* The Granite and the Heather, 1990 (perf. Aboyne, 1990); Little Jenny Nobody, 1991 (perf. Aboyne, 1990, Canterbury Fest., 1992); The Golden Slave, 1992 (perf. Aboyne, 1992); Afternoon in Jericho, 1993 (perf. Wingham Fest., 1993); Smugglers at Bay, 1993 (perf. Canterbury Fest., 1993); Remember David, 1995 (perf. Wingham Fest., 1995). *Recreation:* music. *Address:* 27 High Street, Wingham, near Canterbury, Kent CT3 1AW. *T:* (01227) 720774. *Died 25 March 2012.*

MORRISON, Sir (William) Garth, KT 2007; CBE 1994; Lord-Lieutenant, East Lothian, since 2001; *b* 8 April 1943; *s* of late Walter Courtenay Morrison and Audrey Elizabeth Morrison (*née* Gilbert); *m* 1970, Gillian Cheetham; two *s* one *d*. *Educ:* Pangbourne Coll.; Pembroke Coll., Cambridge (BA 1966). CEng 1973; MIET (MIEE 1973). Service in RN, retiring as Lieut, 1961–73; farming in family partnership, 1973–. Scouting: Area Comr, E Lothian, 1973–81; Chief Comr of Scotland, 1981–88; Chief Scout, 1988–96; Mem., World Scout Cttee, 1991–2002. Chairman: East and Midlothian NHS Trust, 1994–97; Royal Infirmary of Edinburgh NHS Trust, 1997–99; Lothian Primary Care NHS Trust, 1999–2004. Member: Lothian Region Children's Panel, 1976–83; Scottish Community Educn Council, 1988–95 (Fellow, 1995); Nat. Lottery Charities Bd, 1995–99. Chm., SE Regl Cttee, 1996–2000, Pres., 2001–04, Scottish Landowners' Fedn; Pres., RHASS, 2009–10. Vice-Pres., Commonwealth Youth Exchange Council, 1997–. Trustee: The MacRobert Trusts, 1998– (Chm., 2007–); Lamp of Lothian Collegiate Trust, 1978– (Chm., 2001–). DL E Lothian, 1984. Hon. DBA Napier, 2001; DUniv Queen Margaret, 2011. Argentine Gold Medal, 1962. *Publications:* chapter in The Scottish Juvenile Justice System, 1982. *Recreations:* golf, sailing, scouting. *Address:* West Fenton, North Berwick, East Lothian EH39 5AL. *T:* (01620) 842154. *Died 24 May 2013.*

MORRISON-LOW, Sir James; *see* Low.

MORT, Rev. (Margaret) Marion; Non-Stipendiary Curate, St Barnabas, Swanmore, 1997–2007; *b* 10 May 1937; *d* of Rev. Ivan H. Whittaker and Margaret Whittaker; *m* 1959, Colin James Mort; one *s* two *d*. *Educ:* St Mary's Sch., Wantage; Queen's Coll., Harley St; Edinburgh Univ.; Southern Dios MTS. Nat. Sec., World Development Movement, 1970–72; Licensed Lay Reader, 1983–97; Mem. Gen. Synod, 1985–90 (rep. in Partners in Mission consultation for Church in Kenya, 1988). World Develt Educn Adviser, Dio. Portsmouth, 1984–91; Co-ordinator, then Officer, Decade of Evangelism (C of E), 1990–93; Mission and Evangelism Sec., Bd of Mission, Gen. Synod, 1993–94; ordained deacon, 1997, priest, 1998; permission to officiate, dio. Portsmouth, 2007–. Dir, Ocean Sound (ILR), 1985–92; Member: Bd of Christian Aid, 1987–90; Gen. Cttee, British and Foreign Bible Soc., 1993–95; Convenor, World Church Forum, dio. of Portsmouth, 2004–. Hon. Canon, Portsmouth Cathedral, 2001–07, then Emeritus. *Publications:* (jtly) Mission Audit, 1983; (jtly) Called to Order, 1988; (jtly) Building Bridges, 1995; (jtly) A Time for Sharing, 1995; church educnl papers; contribs to Church press. *Recreations:* gardening, good beer, good conversation. *Address:* Rivendell, High Street, Shirrell Heath, Southampton SO32 2JN. *T:* and *Fax:* (01329) 832178. *Died 8 Sept. 2014.*

MORTENSEN, Prof. Dale T., PhD; Professor of Economics, since 1975, Professor of Managerial Economics and Decision Sciences, Kellogg School of Management, since 1980 and Board of Trustees Professor, since 2011, Northwestern University (Ida C. Cook Professor of Economics, 1985–2011); *b* Enterprise, Oregon, 2 Feb. 1939; *s* of late Thomas and Verna Mortensen; *m* 1963, Beverley Paiton; one *s* one *d*. *Educ:* Willamette Univ. (BA Econs 1961); Carnegie Mellon Univ. (PhD Econs 1967). Asst Prof. of Econs, 1965–71, Associate Prof., 1971–75, Northwestern Univ.; Res. Fellow, Inst. for Study of Labor, Bonn, 2001–; Res. Associate, Nat. Bureau of Econ. Res., 2005–. Visiting Professor of Economics: Cornell Univ., 1984; Univ. of Essex, 1993; CIT, 1994; Morgenstern Vis. Prof., NYU, 1985; Niels Bohr Vis. Prof. of Econs, Aarhus Univ., 2006–10; Vis. Economist, Central Inst. of Maths-Econs, USSR, 1989; Vis. Fellow, Econs Prog., ANU, 1996; Vis. Researcher, Centre for Labor Mkt and Social Res., Aarhus Univ., 1998. Fellow: Econometric Soc., 1979; Amer. Acad. Arts and Scis, 2000; Eur. Econ. Assoc., 2005; Soc. for Labor Econs, 2005; Dist. Fellow, Amer. Econ. Assoc., 2008. Labor Econs Prize, Inst. for Study of Labor, Bonn, 2005; Mincer Prize, Soc. of Labor Econs, 2007; (jtly) Nobel Prize in Econ. Scis, 2010. *Publications:* (contrib.) Microeconomic Foundations of Employment and Inflation Theory, 1970; (contrib.) The Economics of Information and Uncertainty, 1982; Wage Dispersion: why are similar people paid differently, 2003; (jtly) Jobs Matching, Wage Dispersion, and Unemployment, 2011; contribs to Econ. Rev., Internat. Econ. Rev., Econometrica. *Address:* Department of Economics, Northwestern University, 2003 Sheridan Road, Evanston, IL 60208, USA. *T:* (847) 4918230, *Fax:* (847) 4917001. *E:* d-mortensen@northwestern.edu. *Died 9 Jan. 2014.*

MORTIMER, James Edward; General Secretary of the Labour Party, 1982–85; *b* 12 Jan. 1921; *m* 1st, Renee Mabel Horton (decd); two *s* one *d*; 2nd, Pat Mortimer. *Educ:* Junior Techn. Sch., Portsmouth; Ruskin Coll., Oxford; London Sch. of Economics. Worked in Shipbuilding and Engrg Industries as Ship Fitter Apprentice, Machinist and Planning Engr; TUC Schol., Oxford, 1945–46; TUC Economic Dept, 1946–48; full-time Trade Union Official, Draughtsmen's and Allied Technicians' Assoc., 1948–68. Dir, London Co-operative Soc., 1968–71. Mem., NBPI, 1968–71; Mem., Bd, LTE, 1971–74. Chm., ACAS (formerly Conciliation and Arbitration Service), 1974–81. Member: Wilberforce Ct of Inquiry into the power dispute, 1970; Armed Forces Pay Review Body, 1971–74; EDC for Chemical Industry, 1973–74; Chm. EDC for Mechanical and Electrical Engineering Construction, 1974–82. Vis. Fellow, Admin. Staff Coll., Henley, 1976–82; Sen. Vis. Fellow, Bradford Univ., 1977–82; Vis. Prof., Imperial Coll. of Sci. and Technol., London Univ., 1981–83; Ward-Perkins Res. Fellow, Pembroke Coll., Oxford, 1981. Chm. Editl Cttee, Socialist Campaign Group News, 1987–2008; Mem. Exec. Cttee, Inst. of Employment Rights, 1989–2002, Vice-Pres., 2002–10, Hon. Pres., 2010–12. Hon. DLitt Bradford, 1982. *Publications:* A History of Association of Engineering and Shipbuilding Draughtsmen, 1960; (with Clive Jenkins) British Trade Unions Today, 1965; (with Clive Jenkins) The Kind of Laws the Unions Ought to Want, 1968; Industrial Relations, 1968; Trade Unions and Technological Change, 1971; History of the Boilermakers' Society, vol. 1, 1973, vol. 2, 1982, vol. 3, 1993; (with Valerie Ellis) A Professional Union: the evolution of the Institution of Professional Civil Servants, 1980; In Defence of Trade Unionism, 1998; A Life on the Left, 1999; The Formation of the Labour Party: lessons for today, 2000; The Trade Disputes Act 1906, 2005. *Address:* Flat 38, Garricks House, Wadbrook Street, Kingston-upon-Thames, Surrey KT1 1HS. *T:* (020) 8547 1885. *Died 23 April 2013.*

MOSELEY, Sir George (Walker), KCB 1982 (CB 1978); Chairman, British Cement Association, 1987–96; *b* 7 Feb. 1925; *oc* of late William Moseley, MBE, and Bella Moseley; *m* 1st, 1950, Anne Mercer (*d* 1989); one *s* one *d*; 2nd, 1990, Madge James. *Educ:* High Sch., Glasgow; St Bees Sch., Cumberland; Wadham Coll., Oxford (MA). Pilot Officer, RAF Levies, Iraq, 1943–48. Asst Principal, Min. of Town and Country Planning, 1950; Asst Private Sec. to Minister of Housing and Local Govt, 1951–52; Private Sec. to Parly Sec., 1952–54; Principal Private Sec. to Minister of Housing and Local Govt, 1963–65; Asst Sec. 1965; Under-Sec. 1970–76; Dep. Sec., DoE, 1976–78, CSD, 1978–80; Second Permanent Sec., DoE, 1980–81, Perm. Sec., 1981–85. Chm., Cement Makers' Fedn, 1987–88. Member: Adv. Council on Public Records, 1989–91; Ancient Monuments Adv. Cttee, 1986–91; Historic Buildings and Monuments Commn for England, 1986–91. Trustee, Civic Trust, 1987–2000 (Chm. Trustees, 1990–2000). *Address:* Churchmead, Church Lane, Widdington, Saffron Walden, Essex CB11 3SF. *Died 2 Oct. 2011.*

MOSER, Baron *cr* 2001 (Life Peer), of Regents Park in the London Borough of Camden; **Claus Adolf Moser,** KCB 1973; CBE 1965; FBA 1969; Chairman, British Museum Development Trust, 1993–2003, then Trustee Emeritus; Chancellor, Open University of Israel, 1994–2004 (Hon.

Fellow, 2002; Member Council, since 2004); Chairman, Askonas Holt (formerly Harold Holt) Ltd, 1990–2002; *b* Berlin, 24 Nov. 1922; *s* of late Dr Ernest Moser and Lotte Moser; *m* 1949, Mary Oxlin; one *s* two *d*. *Educ:* Frensham Heights Sch.; LSE, Univ. of London. RAF, 1943–46. London Sch. of Economics: Asst Lectr in Statistics, 1946–49; Lectr, 1949–55; Reader in Social Statistics, 1955–61; Prof. of Social Statistics, 1961–70; Vis. Prof. of Social Statistics, 1970–75; Oxford University: Vis. Fellow, Nuffield Coll., 1972–80; Warden, Wadham Coll., 1984–93 (Hon. Fellow, 1993); Pro-Vice Chancellor, 1991–93. Dir, Central Statistical Office and Hd of Govt Statistical Service, 1967–78. Statistical Adviser, Cttee on Higher Educn, 1961–64. Chm., Economist Intelligence Unit, 1979–83; Director: N. M. Rothschild & Sons, 1978–90 (Vice-Chm., 1978–84); The Economist Newspaper, 1979–93; Equity & Law Life Assurance Soc., 1980–87; International Medical Statistics Inc., 1982–88; Octopus Books Ltd, 1982–87; Property & Reversionary Investments plc, 1983–86. Mem., Nat. Commn on Educn, 1991–95; Chm., Basic Skills Agency, 1997–2002. Chairman: Royal Opera House, 1974–87; Adv. Bd, Music at Oxford, 1985–2009; Oxford Playhouse, 1992–2004 (Pres., 2004–09); Member: Governing Body, Royal Academy of Music, 1967–79; BBC Music Adv. Cttee, 1971–83; Adv. Bd, LSO, 1996–2013; Pilgrim Trust, 1982–99; Wigmore Hall Develt Cttee, 2007–10. Trustee: BM, 1988–2001; LPO, 1988–94; Glyndebourne Opera Arts Trust, 1989–93; Paul Hamlyn Foundn, 1991–; Soros Foundn, 1993–99; Rayne Foundn, 1995–. President: Royal Statistical Soc., 1978–80; BAAS, 1989–90; British Fedn of Fests for Music, Dance and Speech, 1990–99. Chancellor, Univ. of Keele, 1986–2002. Gov., Yehudi Menuhin Sch., 2000–11. Hon. FRAM 1970; Hon. FRIBA 2005; Hon. FZS 2012. Hon. Fellow: LSE, 1976; Inst. of Educn, Univ. of London, 1997; Birkbeck Coll., 1998. Hon. DSocSci Southampton, 1975; Hon. DSc: Leeds, 1977; City, 1977; Sussex, 1980; Wales, 1990; Liverpool, 1991; South Bank, 1994; Hon. DSc(Econ) London, 1991; Hull, 1994; DUniv: Surrey, 1977; Keele, 1979; York, 1980; Open, 1992; Hon. DTech Brunel, 1981; Dr *hc* Edinburgh, 1991; Heriot-Watt, 1995; Hon. DLitt: W of England, 1993; Brighton, 1994; Hon. DCL Northumbria, 1995. Albert Medal, RSA, 1996. Comdr de l'Ordre National du Mérite (France), 1976; Commander's Cross, Order of Merit (FRG), 1985. *Publications:* Measurement of Levels of Living, 1957; Survey Methods in Social Investigation, 1958; (jtly) Social Conditions in England and Wales, 1958; (jtly) British Towns, 1961; papers in statistical jls. *Recreation:* music. *Address:* 3 Regent's Park Terrace, NW1 7EE. *T:* (020) 7485 1619; 7 Ethelred Court, Old Headington, Oxford OX3 9DA. *T:* (01865) 761028. *Club:* Garrick. *Died 4 Sept. 2015.*

MOSS, Jane Hope; *see* Bown, J. H.

MOSS, (John) Michael, CB 1996; Command Secretary to Second Sea Lord and Commander-in-Chief Naval Home Command, 1994–96, and Assistant Under-Secretary of State (Naval Personnel), 1989–96, Ministry of Defence; *b* 21 April 1936; *s* of late Ernest and Mary Moss. *Educ:* Accrington Grammar Sch.; King's Coll., Cambridge (Foundn Scholar; MA Math. Tripos, Pt I Cl. I, Pt II Wrangler, Pt III Hons with Dist.). National Service, RAF Educn Branch: Pilot Officer 1958; Flying Officer 1959; Flt Lieut 1960; RAF Technical Coll., Henlow, 1959–60. Asst Principal, Air Min., 1960–63; Private Sec. to Air Member for Supply and Orgn, 1962–63; Principal, Air Min., 1963–64, and MoD, 1964–70; Private Sec. to Parly Under-Sec. of State for Defence for the RAF, 1969–70; Asst Sec., MoD, 1971–72; Estab. Officer, Cabinet Office, 1972–75; Sec., Radcliffe Cttee of Privy Counsellors on Ministerial Memoirs, 1975; returned to MoD as Asst Sec., 1976–83; RCDS, 1983; Asst Under-Sec. of State (Air), MoD (PE), 1984–88; Fellow, Center for Internat. Affairs, Harvard Univ., 1988–89. Chm., Greenwich Hosp. Adv. Panel, 1989–96. Choirman, 1968–2000, Sen. Sidesman, 2000–10, St Bartholomew the Gt, Smithfield; Hon. Steward, Westminster Abbey, 1996–. *Recreations:* travel, photography, choral singing. *Address:* c/o Royal Bank of Scotland, Admiralty Arch, 49 Charing Cross, SW1A 2DX. *Clubs:* Royal Air Force, Oxford and Cambridge. *Died 13 Aug. 2013.*

MÖSSBAUER, Rudolf L., PhD; Professor of Experimental Physics, Technische Universität München, 1977–97, then Emeritus; *b* Munich, 31 Jan. 1929; *m* 1957, Elisabeth Pritz; one *s* two *d*; *m* Christel (*née* Braun). *Educ:* High Sch. and Technische Hochschule, München (equiv. Bachelor's and Master's degrees). PhD (München) 1958. Thesis work, Max Planck Inst., Heidelberg, 1955–57; Research Fellow: Technische Hochschule, München, 1958–59, and at Caltech, 1960–61; Prof. of Physics, CIT, 1962–64; Prof. of Experimental Physics, München, 1965–71; Dir, Institut Max von Laue-Paul Langevin, and French-German-British High-Flux-Reactor at Grenoble, 1972–77. Member: Bavarian Acad. of Sci.; Nat. Acad. of Scis, Washington; Amer. Acad. of Arts and Scis; Pontifical Acad.; Soviet Acad. of Sci.; Acad. Leopoldina, etc. Hon. degrees Oxford, Leeuwen, Madrid, Grenoble, etc. Nobel Prize for Physics (jtly), 1961, and numerous other awards. Bavarian Order of Merit, 1962; Order of Merit for Scis and the Arts (Germany), 1996. *Publications:* on gamma resonance spectroscopy (Mössbauer effect) and on neutrino physics. *Recreations:* photography, music, mountaineering. *Address:* Technische Universität München, Physik-Department E 15, James-Franck-Strasse, 85748 Garching, Germany. *Died 14 Sept. 2011.*

MOSTYN, 6th Baron *cr* 1831, of Mostyn, co. Flint; **Llewellyn Roger Lloyd Mostyn;** Bt 1778; *b* 26 Sept. 1948; *o s* of 5th Baron Mostyn, MC and Yvonne Margaret (*née* Johnson); *S* father, 2000; *m* 1974, Denise Suzanne Duvanel; one *s* one *d*. *Educ:* Eton Coll. Directorate of Army Legal Services, 1974. Called to the Bar, Middle Temple, 1973; in practice, 1975–76 and 1985–89; with Kingsbury and Turner, Solicitors, 1976–78; part-time teacher, Bromley Coll. of Technology, 1981–85. *Recreations:* sport, cinema, theatre, classical music, Rugby, tennis. *Heir: s* Hon. Gregory Philip Roger Lloyd Mostyn, *b* 31 Dec. 1984. *Address:* 9 Anderson Street, SW3 3LU. *Club:* Lansdowne. *Died 22 March 2011.*

MOTT, Sir John (Harmar), 3rd Bt *cr* 1930; Regional Medical Officer, Department of Health and Social Security, 1969–84; *b* 21 July 1922; *s* of Sir Adrian Spear Mott, 2nd Bt and Mary Katherine (*d* 1972), *d* of late Rev. A. H. Stanton; *S* father, 1964; *m* 1950, Elizabeth, *d* of late Hugh Carson, FRCS; one *s* two *d*. *Educ:* Radley Coll.; New Coll., Oxford (MA 1948; BM, BCh, 1951). MRCGP 1958. Served War of 1939–45: Pilot, Royal Air Force, 1943–46. Middlesex Hospital: House Physician, 1951; House Surgeon, 1952; GP, Southport, Merseyside, 1952–69. *Recreation:* photography. *Heir: s* David Hugh Mott [*b* 1 May 1952; *m* 1st, 1980, Amanda Jane (marr. diss. 2007), *d* of Lt-Comdr D. W. P. Fryer, RN; two *s*; 2nd, 2013, Vivian Nanzhou Yuan, *d* of Chen Shangren]. *Address:* Staniford, Brookside, Kingsley, Cheshire WA6 8BG. *T:* (01928) 788123. *Died 15 May 2015.*

MOTTISTONE, 4th Baron *cr* 1933, of Mottistone; **David Peter Seely,** CBE 1984; Lord Lieutenant for Isle of Wight, 1986–95; Governor of the Isle of Wight, 1992–95; *b* 16 Dec. 1920; 4th *s* of 1st Baron Mottistone; *S* half brother, 1966; *m* 1944, Anthea Christine (*d* 2010), *er d* of T. V. W. McMullan, Cultra, Co. Down, N Ireland; two *s* two *d* (and one *d* decd). *Educ:* RN Coll., Dartmouth. Convoy escorting, Atlantic and Mediterranean, 1941–44; qualified in Communications, 1944; Served in Pacific, 1945; in comd HMS Cossack, FE Flt, 1958–59; in comd HMS Ajax and 24th Escort Sqdn, FE Flt (offensive ops against Indonesian confrontation) (despatches), 1963–65; Naval Advr to UK High Comr, Ottawa, 1965–66; retired at own request as a Captain, 1967. Dir of Personnel and Training, Radio Rentals Gp, 1967–69; Director: Distributive Industry Trng Bd, 1969–75; Cake and Biscuit Alliance, 1975–81; Export Secretary: Biscuit, Cake, Chocolate and Confectionery Alliance, 1981–83. FIET; FIPD. DL Isle of Wight, 1981. Hon. DLitt Bournemouth, 1993. KStJ 1989. *Recreation:* yachting. *Heir: s* Hon. Peter John Philip Seely [*b* 29 Oct. 1949; *m* 1st, 1972, Joyce Cairns (marr. diss. 1975); one *s*; 2nd, 1982, Linda (marr. diss. 2001), *d* of W. Swain, Bulphan Fen, Essex; one *s* three *d*]. *Address:* The Old Parsonage, Mottistone, Isle of Wight PO30 4EE. *Clubs:* Royal Commonwealth Society, House of Lords Yacht (Cdre, 1985–98); Royal Yacht Squadron, Royal Cruising, Island Sailing, Royal Navy Sailing Association. *Died 24 Nov. 2011.*

MOTTISTONE, 5th Baron *cr* 1933, of Mottistone, Southampton; **Peter John Philip Seely;** *b* 29 Oct. 1949; *er s* of 4th Baron Mottistone, CBE and Anthea Christine, *d* of Victor McMullan; *S* father, 2011; *m* 1st, Joyce Cairns (marr. diss. 1975); one *s*; 2nd, 1982, Linda Swain (marr. diss. 2001); one *s* three *d*. *Educ:* Uppingham. *Heir: s* Hon. Christopher David Peter Seely, *b* 1 Oct. 1974. *Address:* The Old Parsonage, Mottistone, Isle of Wight PO30 4EE. *Died 23 Jan. 2013.*

MOULTON, Alexander Eric, CBE 1976; RDI; FREng; Managing Director, Moulton Developments Ltd, since 1956; *b* 9 April 1920; *s* of John Coney Moulton, DSc, The Hall, Bradford-on-Avon, and Beryl Latimer Moulton. *Educ:* Marlborough Coll.; King's Coll., Cambridge (MA). Bristol Aeroplane Co., 1939–44: Engine Research Dept; George Spencer, Moulton & Co. Ltd, 1945–56; became Techn. Dir; estab. Research Dept (originated work on rubber suspensions for vehicles, incl. own design Flexitor); formed Moulton Developments Ltd, 1956 to do develt work on own designs of rubber suspensions for BLMC incl. Hydrolastic and Hydragas (Queen's Award to Industry, 1967); formed Moulton Bicycles Ltd to produce own design Moulton Bicycle, 1962 (Design Centre Award, 1964); designer of Moulton Coach, 1968–70; Chm., Moulton report on engrg design educn, Design Council, 1975–76; launched Alex Moulton Bicycle, 1983. Dir, SW Regional Bd, National Westminster Bank, 1982–87. RDI 1968 (Master, 1982–83); FRSA 1968; FREng (FEng 1980). Hon. Dr: RCA, 1967; Cranfield, 1994; Loughborough, 2006; Hon. DSc Bath, 1971. SIAD Design Medal, 1976; (jointly): James Clayton Prize, Crompton-Lanchester Medal, and Thomas Hawksley Gold Medal, IMechE, 1979; MacRobert Award (mem., jt winning team), FEng, 1991. *Publications:* numerous articles and papers on engineering and education. *Recreations:* cycling, canoeing, shooting. *Address:* The Hall, Bradford-on-Avon, Wilts BA15 1AJ. *Club:* Brooks's. *Died 9 Dec. 2012.*

MOUNTEVANS, 3rd Baron *cr* 1945, of Chelsea; **Edward Patrick Broke Evans;** *b* 1 Feb. 1943; *s* of 2nd Baron Mountevans and Deirdre Grace (*d* 1997), *d* of John O'Connell, Cork; *S* father, 1974; *m* 1973, Johanna Keyzer, *d* of late Antonius Franciscus Keyzer, The Hague. *Educ:* Rugby; Trinity Coll., Oxford. Reserve Army Service, 1961–66; 74 MC Regt RCT, AER; Lt 1964. Joined management of Consolidated Gold Fields Ltd, 1966; British Tourist Authority, 1972: Manager, Sweden and Finland, 1973; Head of Promotion Services, 1976; Asst Mkting Mgr, 1982–89; Advr, 1989. *Heir: b* Hon. Jeffrey Richard de Corban Evans, *b* 13 May 1948. *Died 21 Dec. 2014.*

MOUNTFIELD, Sir Robin, KCB 1999 (CB 1988); Permanent Secretary, Cabinet Office, 1998–99; *b* 16 Oct. 1939; *s* of late Alexander Stuart Mountfield and Agnes Elizabeth (*née* Gurney); *m* 1963, Anne Newsham; two *s* one *d*. *Educ:* Merchant Taylors' Sch., Crosby; Magdalen Coll., Oxford (BA). Assistant Principal, Ministry of Power, 1961, Principal, 1965; Private Sec. to Minister for Industry, 1973–74; Asst Sec., Dept of Industry, 1974, seconded to Stock Exchange, 1977–78; Under Sec., DoI, later, DTI, 1980–84; Deputy Secretary: DTI, 1984–92; HM Treasury, 1992–95; Permanent Sec., OPS, Cabinet Office, 1995–98. Non-exec. Dir, 2000–02, Consultant, 2002–10, Innogy Hldgs plc, subseq. RWE npower; Ind. Nat. Dir, Times Newspapers Hldgs Ltd, 2001–; non-exec. Dir, Medical Defence Union Ltd, 2004–06. Non-exec. Dir, Lending (formerly Banking Code) Standards Bd, 2006–; Lloyd's Members' Ombudsman, 2007–10. Chairman: St Katharine and Shadwell Trust, 1999–2009; Property Trustees, CS Benevolent Fund, 2000–08; Trustee, BHF, 2000–10. Mem. Council, 1999–2008, Hon. Fellow 2008, Univ. of Essex. *T:* (020) 8293 0359. *E:* rmountfield@hotmail.com. *Died 9 Nov. 2011.*

MTESA, Love; Chairman, Executive Board, and Adviser, CUTS International, Lusaka, 2010–13; *b* 9 July 1942; *s* of late William Mutesa and Olive Mutesa; *m* Marie Madeleine; two *s* two *d*. *Educ:* Inst. of Public Relations, Paris (Dip. Internat. Relations 1974); Mercy Coll., NY (BSc Pol Sci 1985); Univ. of Westminster (MA Diplomatic Studies). Teacher, Ndola, Zambia, 1962–64; 2nd Sec., Zambian Embassy, Kinshasa, 1966–70; 1st Sec., Addis Ababa, 1970–73; Counsellor, Kinshasa, 1974–75; Dir, Africa and Middle East, Foreign Affairs, Lusaka, 1975–79; Dep. High Comr, Harare, 1980–82; Dep. Perm. Rep., UN, NY, 1982–85; resigned from Govt, June 1986; Chm. of Opposition Party, Movement for Multi-Party Democracy for Lusaka Dist, 1990–92; Sec., Internat. Relations Cttee, MMD, 1991–92; High Comr for Zambia in London, 1992–97; Chm., Inf. and Publicity, United Party for Nat. Develt, Zambia, 2001–02; Ambassador of Zambia to UN, Geneva, 2002–09. Chm., Exec. Cttee, UNHCR, 2007. Part-time Lecturer: Zambia Inst. of Diplomacy and Internat. Studies, 2008–; Dag Hammarskjöld Inst. of Peace and Conflict Studies, Copperbelt Univ., Zambia, 2012–; Univ. of Lusaka, 2013–. Hon. Fellow, Univ. of Westminster, 1997. *Recreations:* table tennis, watching soccer. *Died 17 Nov. 2014.*

MULLER, Billie, (Mrs Robert Muller); *see* Whitelaw, Billie.

MULLIGAN, Christopher James; Director General, Passenger Transport Executive, Greater Manchester, 1991–2007; *b* 24 Feb. 1950; *s* of James Frederick Mulligan and Dorothy Mulligan (*née* Kneill); *m* 1989, Rowena May Burns. *Educ:* Hull Univ. (BA Hons 1971). Mem., CIPFA. Manchester CC, 1971–73; Gtr Manchester CC, 1973–77; Greater Manchester Passenger Transport Executive, 1977–2007: Dir of Finance, 1987–91. *Recreations:* reading, walking, good food. *Died 24 Nov. 2012.*

MUNDAY, John, FSA; Keeper of Weapons and Antiquities, National Maritime Museum, Greenwich, 1976–84, then Keeper Emeritus; *b* 10 Aug. 1924; *s* of Rodney H. J. Munday and Ethel Emma Cutting; *m* 1953, Brenda Warden; two *s*. *Educ:* Portsmouth Northern Grammar Sch.; King's Coll., Newcastle; Durham Univ. (BA 1950; MA 1961). FSA 1972. Assistant, Portsmouth Public Libraries and Museums Dept, 1940–42. Served RN, 1942–46; Sub Lieut (Ex. Sp.), RNVR. National Maritime Museum, Greenwich: Asst Keeper, Librarian, 1951; Curator of Presentation, 1964; Dep. Keeper, 1969; Curator of Weapons and Antiquities, 1971. Hon. Vice Pres., Soc. for Nautical Res., 1985 (Hon. Sec., 1979–84); Member: Develt Cttee, SS Great Britain Project, 1980–86; HMS Victory Adv. Technical Cttee, 1985–2003. Chm. Trustees, Deal Maritime & Local Hist. Mus., 1997–2003. *Publications:* For Those in Peril… lifesaving, then and now, 1963; Oar Maces of Admiralty, 1966; Dress of the British Sailor, rev. edn 1977; Heads & Tails—the Necessary Seating (with drawings), 1978; Naval Cannon, 1987; E. W. Cooke, RA, FRS: a man of his time, 1996. *Recreations:* painting, collecting, considering. *Address:* 8 Langtons Court, Sun Lane, Alresford, Hants SO24 9UE. *T:* (01962) 736 393. *E:* jb_munday@yahoo.co.uk. *Died 20 May 2012.*

MUNRO of Lindertis, Sir Alasdair (Thomas Ian), 6th Bt *cr* 1825; *b* 6 July 1927; *s* of Sir Thomas Torquil Alfonso Munro, 5th Bt and Beatrice Maude (*d* 1974), *d* of Robert Sanderson Whitaker; *S* father, 1985; *m* 1954, Marguerite Lillian, *d* of late Franklin R. Loy, Dayton, Ohio, USA; one *s* one *d*. *Educ:* Georgetown Univ., Washington, DC (BSS 1946); Univ. of Pennsylvania (MBA 1951); IMEDE, Lausanne. 2nd Lieut, USAF (previously US Army), 1946–53. Senior Vice-Pres., McCann-Erickson, New York, 1952–69; Pres., Jennings Real Estate, Waitsfield, Vermont, 1970–83. Founder, Dir (and Past Pres.), St Andrew's Soc. of Vermont, 1972–; Vice-Chm., Assoc. Bd of Directors, Howard Bank, Waitsfield, 1974–84; Founder, sometime Dir and Pres., Valley Area Assoc., Waitsfield, 1972–80. Chairman: Munro, Jennings & Doig, 1983–90; Highland Develt Gp, 1987–91. *Publications:* Scottish Antiques, 2004. *Recreations:* gardening, travel, collector/dealer in Scottish antiques, Scottish heritage matters. *Heir: s* Keith Gordon Munro [*b* 3 May 1959; *m* 1989, Jada Louise Elwell; one *s* one *d*]. *Address:* RiverRidge, Box 940, Waitsfield, VT 05673, USA. *Died 13 March 2014.*

MUNRO, Colin William Gordon R.; *see* Ross-Munro.

MUNRO, John Farquhar; JP; Member (Lib Dem) Ross Skye and Inverness West, Scottish Parliament, 1999–2011; *b* 26 Aug. 1934; *m* 1962, Cecilia; one *s* one *d*. *Educ:* Plockton High Sch.; Sea Trng Coll., Gloucester. Merchant Marine Service, 1951–61; Plant Fitter, Kings Road Construction, 1961–65; Manager, contracting co., 1965–75; heavy haulage, bus operation, civil engrg, and quarrying contractor, 1975–93; crofter, 1971–97. Member: Local Council, 1966–74; Skye and Lochalsh DC, 1974–90 (Convenor, 1984–95); Highland Regl Council, 1978–82 (Chair, Gaelic Cttee, 1978–82); Highland Council, 1995–99. Chair, Ross, Cromarty and Skye Scottish Liberal Democrats, 1984–98. Non-executive Director: Highland Opportunities Ltd; Acair Publishing; Skye and Lochalsh Enterprise; former Mem., Electricity Consultative Council; Chair: Rail Develt Partnership; Fishery Harbours Mgt; Shipping Service Adv. Cttee, Caledonian MacBrayne. Trustee, Gaelic Coll., Skye. *Recreations:* sailing, fishing, the company of my grandchildren. *Address:* Glomach House, Aultnachruinne, Glenshiel, Kyle of Lochalsh, Wester Ross IV40 8HN. *T:* (01599) 511222. *Died 26 Jan. 2014.*

MURDOCH, Dame Elisabeth (Joy), AC 1989; DBE 1963 (CBE 1961); *b* 8 Feb. 1909; *d* of Rupert Greene and Marie (*née* de Lancey Forth); *m* 1928, Sir Keith (Arthur) Murdoch (*d* 1952); one *s* three *d*. *Educ:* Clyde Sch., Woodend, Victoria. Mem., 1933–65, Pres., 1953–65, Mgt Cttee, Royal Children's Hospital, Melbourne. Trustee: National Gallery, Victoria, 1968–76, then Emeritus Trustee; McClelland Regl Art Gall., 1972. Founding Mem., Bd of Mgt, Victorian Tapestry Workshop, 1976– (Chm., 1986–88). Patron, Murdoch Children's Res. Inst., 1962–. Fellow, Trinity Coll., Univ. of Melbourne, 2000. Freeman, Victorian Coll. of the Arts, 1986; Freewoman, Melbourne, 2012. Hon. LLD: Melbourne, 1982; Monash, 2008. *Recreation:* gardening. *Address:* Cruden Farm, Langwarrin, Victoria 3910, Australia. *Clubs:* Alexandra, Lyceum (Melbourne). *Died 5 Dec. 2012.*

MURLEY, John Tregarthen, CB 1988; DPhil; *b* 22 Aug. 1928; *s* of John Murley and Dorothea Birch; *m* 1954, Jean Patricia Harris; one *d*. *Educ:* University College, London (BA 1st Cl. Hons History); St Antony's Coll., Oxford (DPhil). Entered FO, 1955; Counsellor, Washington, 1976–80. *Publications:* The Origin and Outbreak of the Anglo-French War of 1793, 1959. *Recreations:* tennis, golf, piano. *Died 12 Jan. 2012.*

MURPHY, Rev. Canon (John) Gervase (Maurice Walker), LVO 1987; MA; Chaplain of the Chapel Royal of St Peter ad Vincula, Tower of London, 1991–96; a Chaplain to the Queen, 1987–96, an Extra Chaplain, since 1996; *b* 20 Aug. 1926; *s* of William Stafford and Yvonne Iris Murphy; *m* 1957, Joy Hilda Miriam Livermore; five *d*. *Educ:* Methodist Coll., Belfast; Trinity Coll., Dublin (BA 1952, MA 1955; Rugby football team, 1947–52 (Capt., 1951–52); cricket colours); Birkbeck Coll., Univ. of London (BA Hons Classics, 2000). Guardsman, Irish Guards, 1944–45; commissioned Royal Ulster Rifles, 1945–47. TCD, 1947–52 and Divinity Sch., TCD, 1949–52. Ordained, deacon, 1952, priest, 1953; Curate, Shankill Parish, Lurgan, 1952–55; Royal Army Chaplains' Dept, 1955; served: Korea, 1955–57; Woolwich, 1957–59; Aden, 1959–62; Infantry Junior Leaders, Oswestry, 1962–64; Bagshot, 1964–65; Worthy Down, 1965; Commonwealth Bde Sen. Chaplain, 1965–67; Sen. Chaplain, Guards Depot, Pirbright, 1967–69; DACG, Rhine Area, 1969–72; Sen. Chaplain, RMA Sandhurst, 1972–74; Asst Chaplain General: BAOR, 1974–75; South East, 1975–77; Vicar of Ranworth and RD of Blofield, 1977–79; Chaplain for Holidaymakers on Norfolk Broads, 1977–79; Domestic Chaplain to the Queen, Rector of Sandringham and Leader of Sandringham Group of Parishes, 1979–87; RD of Heacham and Rising, 1985–87; Hon. Canon of Norwich Cathedral, 1986, Emeritus, 1987–; Rector, Christ Church Cathedral, Falkland Is, 1987–91; Chaplain, Lord Mayor of London, 1993–94. Vice-Pres., British Assoc. for Physical Trng, 1988– (Hon. Fellow, 1988). Played: Internat. Rugby football for Ireland, 1952, 1954 and 1958; Rugby football for British Army 1957, and for Barbarians, 1958. *Publications:* Christ Church Cathedral, Falkland Islands: its life and times 1892–1992, 1992; The Very Reverend Dean Lowther Edward Brandon 1846–1933, 2005. *Recreations:* sport, walking, gardening, interior decorating. *Address:* Saffron Close, 17 Ringstead Road, Heacham, Norfolk PE31 7JA. *T:* (01485) 572351. *Clubs:* East India (Hon. Chaplain Emeritus, 2007–), London Irish RFC, Public School Wanderers RFC; Leprechauns Cricket (Ireland); Mid-Ulster Cricket. *Died 7 Jan. 2014.*

MURRAY, John; *see* Dervaird, Hon. Lord.

MURRAY, Prof. Joseph Edward, MD, DSc; plastic surgeon; Professor of Surgery, Harvard University, 1970–86, then Emeritus; *b* 1 April 1919; *s* of William Andrew Murray and Mary Murray (*née* DePasquale); *m* 1945, Virginia Link; three *s* three *d*. *Educ:* Holy Cross Coll., Worcester, Mass (AB 1940); Harvard Univ. (MD 1943). US Army, 1944–47. Chief Plastic Surgeon: Peter Bent Brigham Hosp., 1951–86, Surgeon Emeritus, 1986; Children's Hosp., Boston, 1972–85. Hon. FRCS; Hon. FRCSI; Hon. FRACS. Hon. DSc: Holy Cross Coll., 1965; Rockford Coll., 1966; Roger Williams Coll., 1986. Numerous honours and awards from US sci. instns; (jtly) Nobel Prize for Medicine, 1990. *Publications:* Surgery of the Soul: reflections on a curious career (autobiog.), 2001. *Address:* 108 Abbott Road, Wellesley Hills, MA 02481–6104, USA. *Died 26 Nov. 2012.*

MURRAY, Sir Kenneth, Kt 1993; PhD; FRCPath; FRS 1979; FRSE; Biogen Professor of Molecular Biology, University of Edinburgh, 1984–98; *b* 30 Dec. 1930; *yr s* of Allen and Elizabeth Ann Murray; *m* 1958, Noreen Elizabeth Parker (Prof. N. E. Murray, CBE, FRS) (*d* 2011). *Educ:* Birmingham Univ. FRCPath 1991. Dept of Molecular Biology, Univ. of Edinburgh: Sen. Lecturer, 1967–73; Reader, 1973–76; Prof., 1976–98. Member: Biochemical Soc.; European Molecular Biology Organisation; Academia Europaea. Chm., Darwin Trust, Edinburgh, 1984– (Founder, 1983). FRSE 1989. *Publications:* papers on nucleic acid biochem., molecular genetics, genetic engineering and viral hepatitis. *Address:* c/o Institute of Cell Biology, University of Edinburgh, Edinburgh EH9 3JR. *Clubs:* Athenæum; New (Edinburgh). *Died 7 April 2013.*

MURRAY, Kenneth Alexander George, CB 1977; MA, EdB; Special Adviser to the Home Office on Police Service, Prison Service, and Fire Service selection, 1977–80; Director, Civil Service Selection Board, and Civil Service Commissioner, 1964–77; *b* 16 June 1916; *s* of late George Dickie Murray and Isabella Murray; *m* 1942, Elizabeth Ward Simpson (*d* 1999); one *d*. *Educ:* Skene Street and Central Schools, Aberdeen; Aberdeen Univ. (MA English (1st Cl. Hons), EdB Psychol. (1st Cl. Hons)). RAMC and War Office Selection Bd, 1940–45, Captain. Psychological Adviser, Govt of India, 1945–47; Lectr in Psychology, Univ. of Hull, 1948–50; Principal Psychologist and Chief Psychologist, CS Selection Bd, 1951–63. Adviser to Police Service in high-grade selection, 1963, also to Fire and Prison Services, to Church of Scotland and C of E; Adviser (earlier) to Govts of Pakistan and Western Nigeria through their Public Service Commns. FBPsS 1984. *Recreations:* reading, walking, bridge, watching cricket and Rugby League. *Clubs:* MCC, Royal Commonwealth Society. *Died 11 May 2012.*

MURRAY, Prof. Noreen Elizabeth, (Lady Murray), CBE 2002; PhD; FRS 1982; FRSE; Professor of Molecular Genetics, Institute of Cell and Molecular Biology (formerly Department of Molecular Biology), University of Edinburgh, 1988–2001, then Emeritus; *b* 26 Feb. 1935; *d* of John and Lilian Grace Parker; *m* 1958, Sir Kenneth Murray, FRS. *Educ:* King's College London (BSc; FKC 2006); Univ. of Birmingham (PhD). Research Associate: Stanford Univ., California, 1960–64; Univ. of Cambridge, 1964–67; Mem., MRC Molecular Genetics Unit, Edinburgh, 1968–74; Lectr, 1974, later Sen. Lectr, Reader, 1978–88, Dept of Molecular Biology, Univ. of Edinburgh; scientist in European Molecular Biol. Lab., Heidelberg, 1980–82. Member: Sci. Scholarships Cttee, Royal Commn for 1851, 2002–07; Sci. and Technol. Hons Cttee, Cabinet Office, 2005–. Mem., BBSRC, 1994–97; Pres., Genetical Soc., 1987–90. Mem., EMBO, 1981. Trustee, Darwin Trust of Edinburgh, 1990–. FRSE 1989. Hon. DSc: UMIST, 1995; Birmingham, 1995; Warwick, 2001; Lancaster, 2008;

Sheffield, 2010; Edinburgh, 2011. Gabor Medal, Royal Soc., 1989; AstraZeneca Award, Biochem. Soc., 2005; Royal Medal, RSE, 2011. *Publications:* original research papers and reviews in field of genetics and molecular biology. *Recreation:* gardening. *Address:* c/o Institute of Cell Biology, University of Edinburgh, Mayfield Road, Edinburgh EH9 3JR. *T:* (0131) 650 5374. *Club:* Athenæum. *Died 12 May 2011.*

MURTA, Prof. Kenneth Hall, FRIBA; Professor of Architecture, University of Sheffield, 1974–94, then Emeritus; *b* 24 Sept. 1929; *s* of John Henry Murta and Florence (*née* Hall); *m* 1955, Joan Wilson (*d* 2008); two *s* two *d*. *Educ:* Bede Collegiate GS, Sunderland; King's Coll., Univ. of Durham (BArch, DipArch). Architect in private practice and public service, 1954–59; Sen. Lectr, Nigerian Coll. of Arts, Science and Technology, then Ahmadu Bello Univ., 1959–62; University of Sheffield: Lectr, then Sen. Lectr, 1962–74; Dean, Faculty of Architectural Studies, 1974–77, 1984–88. Major designs: Anglican Cathedral, Kaduna, Nigeria; St John, Sheffield Park; All Saints, Denaby Main; St Laurence, Heanor; St Lawrence, Frodingham; Christ Church, Pitsmoor; St Mary the less, St John's Coll., Univ. of Durham; Christ Church, Stannington; St Luke, Lodge Moor, Sheffield; St Leonard, Thrybergh, Rotherham; All Saints, Totley, Sheffield; All Saints, Breadshall, Derbys; St Edward the Confessor, Barnsley; Pilgrims, Fordcombe, Kent; Turangi, West Malvern; Clowance, Praze, Cornwall; Stable Block, Brodsworth Hall, Doncaster. Chm., Working Commn 88, Building Pathology, Internat. Council for Bldg Studies and Res., 1973–94. Council Mem., Inst. of Liturgy and Architecture, Univ. of Birmingham, 1972–86; Mem., Sheffield Cathedral Fabric Adv. Cttee, 2007– (Chm., 1992–2007). Mem. and Hon. Officer, ARCUK, 1991–97 (Mem., 1986–97, Vice-Chm., 1990–91, Chm., 1991–97, Bd of Architectural Educn); Chm., RIBA Yorks Reg., 1984–85. Gov., Sheffield Teaching Hospital NHS Foundn Trust, 2004–. Hon. Sec., Ecclesiological Soc., 1991–2000. Editor, The Ecclesiologist, 1991–97. *Publications:* contribs to Architectural Rev., Ecclesiologist, Churchbuilding, Trans RIBA, Architects' Jl, RIBA Jl. *Recreations:* cricket, soccer, churchwatching, travel, walking in cities on Sundays. *Clubs:* Royal Over-Seas League; Ford & Hylton Lane Working Men's (Sunderland). *Died 13 Aug. 2014.*

MUSGROVE, Prof. Frank, DLitt; Sarah Fielden Professor of Education, University of Manchester, 1970–82, then Emeritus; Dean of the Faculty of Education, 1976–78; *b* 16 Dec. 1922; *e s* of late Thomas and Fanny Musgrove; *m* Dorothy Ellen (*née* Nicholls); one *d*. *Educ:* Henry Mellish Grammar Sch., Nottingham; Magdalen Coll., Oxford (MA); Univ. of Nottingham (PhD); Univ. of Manchester (MEd); Open Univ. (DLitt 1982). Served War, RAFVR, 1941–45; Navigator, Bomber Command (commnd), Ops 149 Sqdn (tour of bombing missions completed 1944). Educational appts in England and in the Colonial Educn Service, E Africa, 1947–57; Lectureships in Univs of Leicester and Leeds, 1957–65; Foundn Chair of Research in Educn, Univ. of Bradford, 1965–70. Visiting Professor: of Educn, Univ. of BC, 1965; of Sociology, Univ. of California (Davis), 1969; Guest lectr, Inst. of Sociology, Univ. of Utrecht, 1968; The Chancellor's Lectr, Univ. of Wellington, NZ, 1970. Hon. Prof., Univ. of Hull, 1985–88. Co-editor, Research in Education, 1971–76. FRSA 1971. *Publications:* The Migratory Elite, 1963; Youth and the Social Order, 1964; The Family, Education and Society, 1966; Society and the Teacher's Role (with P. H. Taylor), 1969; Patterns of Power and Authority in English Education, 1971; Ecstasy and Holiness, 1974, new edn 1994; Margins of the Mind, 1977; School and the Social Order, 1979; Education and Anthropology, 1982; The North of England: from Roman to present times, 1990; Dresden and the Heavy Bombers, 2005; research papers in: Africa; Sociological Review; Brit. Jl of Sociology; Brit. Jl of Educational Psychology; Economic History Review; Brit. Jl of Social and Clinical Psychology, etc. *Recreation:* fly fishing. *Address:* Dib Scar, The Cedar Grove, Beverley, E Yorks HU17 7EP. *T:* (01482) 868799. *Died 29 Aug. 2011.*

MUSTILL, Baron *cr* 1992 (Life Peer), of Pateley Bridge in the County of North Yorkshire; **Michael John Mustill,** Kt 1978; PC 1985; FBA 1996; a Lord of Appeal in Ordinary, 1992–97; *b* Leeds, 10 May 1931; *o s* of late Clement William and Marion Mustill; *m* 1st, 1960, Beryl Reid Davies (marr. diss. 1983; she *d* 2012); 2nd, 1991, Caroline Phillips; two *s*, and one step *d*. *Educ:* Oundle Sch.; St John's Coll., Cambridge (Hon. Fellow, 1992); LLD Cantab 1992. Royal Artillery, 1949–51 (commissioned, 1950). Called to Bar, Gray's Inn, 1955, Bencher, 1976. QC 1968. Dep. Chm., Hants QS, 1971; a Recorder of the Crown Court, 1972–78; Judge of High Court, QBD, 1978–85; a Lord Justice of Appeal, 1985–92. Presiding Judge, NE Circuit, 1981–84. Chairman: Civil Service Appeal Tribunal, 1971–78; Judicial Studies Board, 1985–89; Deptl Cttee on Law of Arbitration, 1985–90; Adv. Bd, Inst. of Criminology, Cambridge Univ., 1992–99. Hon. Prof. of Law, Birmingham Univ., 1995–; Yorke Dist. Vis. Fellow, 1996–, Arthur Goodhart Vis. Prof. of Legal Sci., and Fellow of St John's Coll., 2003–04, Cambridge Univ.; Sen. Fellow, Lauterpacht Centre for Internat. Law, 2006–. President: British Maritime Law Assoc., 1995–2003; CIArb, 1995–98; Assoc. of Average Adjusters, 1996–97; London Shipping Law Centre, 1996–; Seldon Soc., 1997–2000; Expert Witness Inst., 1997–2002; Internat. Law Assoc., 2000–02 (Pres., British Br., 1997–2004); Vice-Pres., Court of Arbitration, Internat. Chamber of Commerce, 1997–2005. Member: Comité Maritime Internat., 1996–; Amer. Law Inst. Hon. LLD Birmingham; DUniv Leeds Metropolitan. *Publications:* The Law and Practice of Commercial Arbitration in England (with S. C. Boyd, QC), 1982, 2nd edn 1989, 2001 Companion; Anticipatory Breach of Contract, 1990; Joint Editor: Scrutton on Charterparties and Bills of Lading; Arnould on Marine Insurance; articles in legal periodicals. *Club:* Travellers. *Died 24 April 2015.*

MUTCH, Dr William Edward Scott, OBE 1989; FRSE; forestry and land use consultant, 1989–99; Member of Board and Chairman, South East Region, Scottish Natural Heritage, 1992–94; *b* 14 Aug. 1925; *s* of Wilfred Ernest Mutch and Helen Anderson Mutch (*née* Bannerman); *m* 1950, Margaret Isobel McKay (*d* 2010); one *d*. *Educ:* Royal High Sch., Edinburgh; Edinburgh Univ. (BSc Forestry, PhD); St John's Coll., Oxford. FICFor. Colonial Service Forest Dept, Nigeria, 1946–52; University of Edinburgh: Lectr in Forestry, 1953; Sen. Lectr, 1963; Head of Dept of Forestry and Natural Resources, 1981–87. Dir, Central Scotland Woodlands Ltd, subseq. Central Scotland Countryside Trust, 1989–97. Member: Countryside Commn for Scotland, 1988–92; Nat. Forestry Res. Adv. Cttee, 1982–96; Nature Conservancy Council, 1989–91; Nature Conservancy Council for Scotland, 1991–92. Institute of Chartered Foresters: Pres., 1982–84; Inst. Medal, 1986. Editor, Scottish Forestry, 1957–62. *Publications:* Public Recreation in National Forests, 1967; The Interaction of Forestry and Farming, 1980; Farm Woodland Management, 1987; Tall Trees and Small Woods, 1998, 2nd edn 2008; *novels*: Steal me a Duchess, 2001; Eskdale Shoot, 2006; contribs to professional jls. *Recreations:* cabinet making, travel, painting. *Address:* Forestview, Knockstocks, Newton Stewart, Wigtownshire DG8 6RA. *T:* (01671) 402370. *Died 8 April 2014.*

MYERS, Geoffrey Morris Price; Under-Secretary, Agricultural and Food Research Council, 1973–87; *b* 8 May 1927. *Educ:* Reigate Grammar Sch.; King's Coll., London. Civil Service, 1950; UKAEA, 1959–67; Nat. Econ. Develt Office, 1967–69; Agric. Research Council, 1970. Chm., Croydon Soc., 2003–07. *Address:* 56 Northampton Road, Croydon CR0 7HT. *T:* (020) 8655 3158. *Died 20 Oct. 2013.*

MYERS, Sir Philip (Alan), Kt 1985; OBE 1977; QPM 1972; DL; one of Her Majesty's Inspectors of Constabulary, 1982–93; *b* 7 Feb. 1931; *s* of John and Catherine Myers; *m* 1951, Hazel Gittings; two *s*. *Educ:* Grove Park, Wrexham. RAF, 1949–50. Shropshire Constabulary, 1950–67; West Mercia Police, 1967–68; Dep. Chief Constable, Gwynedd Constabulary, 1968–70; Chief Constable, North Wales Police, 1970–81. OStJ 1972. DL Clwyd, 1983. *Died 21 June 2014.*

N

NAIRNE, Rt Hon. Sir Patrick (Dalmahoy), GCB 1981 (KCB 1975; CB 1971); MC 1943; PC 1982; Master, St Catherine's College, Oxford, 1981–88 (Hon. Fellow, 1988); Chancellor, Essex University, 1983–97; *b* 15 Aug. 1921; *s* of late Lt-Col C. S. and Mrs E. D. Nairne; *m* 1948, Penelope Chauncy Bridges, *d* of late Lt-Col R. F. and Mrs L. C. Bridges; three *s* three *d*. *Educ:* Radley Coll.; University Coll., Oxford (Exhibnr; 1st cl. hons Mod. Hist., 1947; MA 1947; Hon. Fellow, 1981). Seaforth Highlanders, 1941–45 (Capt.). Entered Civil Service and joined Admty, Dec. 1947; Private Sec. to First Lord of Admty, 1958–60; Asst Sec., 1960; Private Sec. to Sec. of State for Defence, 1965–67; Assistant Under-Sec. of State (Logistics), MoD, 1967–70; Dep. Under-Sec. of State, MoD, 1970–73; Second Perm. Sec., Cabinet Office, 1973–75; Perm. Sec., DHSS, 1975–81. Mem., Falkland Isles Review Cttee, 1982; Govt Monitor, Hong Kong, 1984; Chm., Commn on Conduct of Referendums, 1996. Central Independent TV: Mem. Bd, 1990–92; Dep. Chm., 1986–90, Chm., 1990–92, W Regl Bd. Church Comr, 1993–98; Chairman: Irene Wellington Educnl Trust, 1987–2002; Nuffield Council on Bioethics, 1991–96; President: Oxfordshire Craft Guild, 1993–97; Modern Art Oxford (formerly Oxford Mus. of Modern Art), 1998– (Chm. Adv. Bd, 1988–98); Vice-President: Soc. for Italic Handwriting, 1987– (Chm., 1981–87); Oxford Art Soc., 1990–; Trustee: Nat. Maritime Museum, 1981–91; Joseph Rowntree Foundn, 1983–96; Nat. AIDS Trust, 1987–95; Oxford Sch. of Drama, 1998–; Member: Radley Coll. Council, 1975–99; Council, Ditchley Foundn, 1988–2004; President: Assoc. of CS Art Clubs, 1976–89 (Vice-Pres., 1999–); Radleian Soc., 1980–83; Seamen's Hosp. Soc., 1982–2002. FRSA 1978–2000. Hon. LLD: Leicester, 1980; St Andrews, 1984; DU Essex, 1983. *Recreations:* watercolour painting, calligraphy. *Address:* Tulip Tree House, Church Street, Chipping Norton, Oxon OX7 3PP. *Club:* Oxford and Cambridge (Trustee, 1989–95). *Died 4 June 2013.*

NAKAJIMA, Hiroshi, MD, PhD; Director-General of the World Health Organization, 1988–98, then Director-General Emeritus; President, International Research Institute of Health and Welfare, 1998–2001; *b* Japan, 16 May 1928; *m* Martha Ann (*née* De Witt); two *s*. *Educ:* Nat. Sen. High Sch., Urawa; Tokyo Med. Coll. (MD 1955; PhD 1960); Faculty of Medicine, Univ. of Paris. Research, Nat. Inst. of Health and Med. Res., Paris, 1958–67; Dir of Res. and Admin, Nippon Roche Res. Centre, Tokyo, 1967–73; Scientist, Evaluation and Control of Drugs, 1973–76, Chief, Drug Policies and Management, 1976–79, WHO HQ, Geneva; Regional Dir, Western Pacific Region, WHO, 1979–88. Perm. Hon. Advr, World Fedn of Acupuncture and Moxybustion Socs, Beijing, 1998–. Vis. Prof. in Public Health, Tokyo Med. Coll., 1987; Vis. Prof., Univ. of Tokyo, 1991; Hon. Prof., Universidad Nacional Mayor de San Marcos, Peru, 1992. Corresp. Mem., Acad. de Pharmacie, France, 1988; Assoc. Foreign Mem., Acad. Nat. de Médecine de France, 1989; Hon. Member: Japanese Pharmacological Soc., 1990; Amer. Urological Assoc., 1995; Foreign Mem., Russian Acad. of Med. Scis, 1995; Hon. Foreign Mem., Acad. Royale de Médecine de Belgique, 1991. FCPS(Pak) 1990; Hon. FRCP 1992. DM (*hc*): Med. Univ., Ulan Bator, Mongolia, 1991; Univ. Nat. du Benin, 1997; Hon. DSc Mahidol Univ., Bangkok, 1994; Dr *hc* Bucharest, 1994. Kojima Prize, Japan, 1984; Okamoto Award, Japan, 1989; Polio Eradication Champion Award, Rotary Internat., 1999. First Order of Merit (Japan), 2000; Order of Merit (Poland), 1990; Chevalier de la Légion d'Honneur (France), 1991; Commandeur, Ordre Nat. du Lion (Senegal), 1991; Equestrian Order of St Agatha (San Marino), 1995. *Publications:* articles and reviews in Japanese, French and English pubns. *Address:* La Cognaquerie, 86800 Pouillé, France. *T:* (5) 49565950. *Died 26 Jan. 2013.*

NAMBU, Prof. Yoichiro, ScD; Harry Pratt Judson Distinguished Service Professor, Department of Physics and Enrico Fermi Institute, University of Chicago, 1976–91, then Emeritus; *b* Tokyo, 18 Jan. 1921; *m* 1945, Chieko Hida; one *s*. *Educ:* Univ. of Tokyo (MS 1942; ScD 1952). Prof., Osaka City Univ., 1950–56; Mem., Inst. of Advanced Study, Princeton Univ., 1952–54; University of Chicago: Res. Associate, 1954–56; Associate Prof., 1956–58; Prof., 1958–71; Dist. Service Prof., 1971–76; Chm., Dept of Physics, 1973–76. Member: NAS, 1971; Amer. Acad. of Arts and Scis, 1971; Hon. Mem., Japan Acad., 1984. Max Planck Medal, 1985; Sakurai Prize, APS, 1994; N. Bogoliubov Prize, Jt Inst. for Nuclear Res., 2003; Benjamin Franklin Medal, 2005; (jtly) Nobel Prize for Physics, 2008. *Publications:* articles in jls. *Address:* Department of Physics, University of Chicago, 5720 South Ellis Avenue, Chicago, IL 60637, USA. *Died 5 July 2015.*

NANKIVELL, Owen; JP; economic and business consultant; Director, Hinksey Network (formerly Hinksey Centre), since 1982 (Executive Director, 1982–2002); *b* 6 April 1927; *s* of John Hamilton Nankivell and Sarah Ann Mares; *m* 1956, Mary Burman Earnshaw; one *s* two *d*. *Educ:* Torquay Grammar Sch.; Univ. of Manchester. BA (Econ) 1951, MA (Econ) 1963. FRSS. Admty, 1951–52; Colonial Office, 1952–55; Central Statistical Office, 1955–65; DEA, 1965–69; HM Treasury, 1969–72; Asst Dir, Central Statistical Office, 1972–79; Gp Chief Economist, Lucas Industries, 1979–82. JP Worcester, 1983–89, Torbay, 1989. *Publications:* All Good Gifts, 1978; Economics, Society and Values, 1995. *Recreations:* Christian, tennis, choral music, singing. *Address:* 3 Thorne Park Road, Torquay TQ2 6RX. *T:* and *Fax:* (01803) 690147. *E:* owenmary@blueyonder.co.uk. *Died 14 May 2012.*

NAPIER, 14th Lord *cr* 1627 (Scotland), **AND ETTRICK,** 5th Baron *cr* 1872 (UK); **Francis Nigel Napier,** KCVO 1992 (CVO 1985; LVO 1980); DL; Bt of Thirlestane (NS) 1666; Chief of the Name of Napier; Major, Scots Guards (Reserve of Officers); Private Secretary, Comptroller and Equerry, 1973–98, then Treasurer, 1998–2002, to HRH the Princess Margaret, Countess of Snowdon; *b* 5 Dec. 1930; *e s* of 13th Baron Napier and 4th Ettrick, TD, and Muir (*d* 1992), *e d* of Sir Percy Newson, Bt; *S* father, 1954; *m* 1958, Delia Mary, *yr d* of late A. D. B. Pearson; two *s* two *d*. *Educ:* Wellesley House; Eton; RMA, Sandhurst. Commissioned, 1950; served Malaya, 1950–51 (invalided); Adjt 1st Bn Scots Guards, 1955–57. Equerry to His late Royal Highness The Duke of Gloucester, 1958–60, retd, 1960. Deputy Ceremonial and Protocol Secretary, CRO, 1962–66; Purple Staff Officer at State Funeral of Sir Winston Churchill, 1966. Sat in House of Lords, 1954–99 (a Cons. Whip, 1970–71). On behalf of HM The Queen, handed over Instruments of Independence to Tuvalu (formerly Ellice Is), 1978. Member: Royal Co. of Archers (Queen's Body Guard for Scotland), 1953–; Exec. Cttee, Standing Council of the Baronetage, 1985–98. Standing Council of Scottish Chiefs. Mem., Rolls-Royce Enthusiasts Club. Pres., St John Ambulance Assoc. and Brigade for County of London, 1975–83. DL Selkirkshire, 1974, Ettrick and Lauderdale, 1975–94. Freeman, City of London; Liveryman, Worshipful Company of Grocers. Hon. DLitt Napier Univ., 1993. KStJ 1991 (CStJ 1988). *Heir: s* Master of Napier, *b* 3 Nov. 1962. *Address:* Down House, Wylye, Wilts BA12 0QN. *Clubs:* Turf, Pratt's, Pitt. *Died 15 March 2012.*

NAPIER, Sir Oliver John, Kt 1985; Senior Partner, Napier & Sons, Solicitors, 1976–2000; Chairman, Standing Advisory Commission on Human Rights, 1988–92; *b* 11 July 1935; *e s* of James J. and Sheila Napier; *m* 1961, Brigid (*née* Barnes); three *s* five *d* (and one *s* decd). *Educ:* Ballycruttle Public Elem. Sch., Downpatrick; St Malachy's Coll., Belfast; Queen's Univ., Belfast (LLB). Qual. Solicitor, NI, 1959; Lectr and Mem. Bd of Examrs, Incorp. Law Soc. of NI, 1965–71. Mem. Exec., Ulster Liberal Party, 1962–69; Founder Mem., New Ulster Movt, 1969;

Founder Mem., Alliance Party, 1970, Leader 1973–84, Pres., 1989–92. Mem. (Alliance), E Belfast, NI Assembly, 1973–75; Minister of Legal Affairs, NI Executive, Jan.-May 1974; Mem. (Alliance), N Ireland Constitutional Convention for E Belfast, 1975–76; Mem. (Alliance) Belfast E, NI Assembly, 1982–86. Contested (Alliance): E Belfast, 1979, 1983; N Down, 1997. Councillor for E Belfast, Belfast CC, 1977–89; Mem. for N Down, NI Forum, 1996–98. Mem. (Alliance), Negotiation Team for Good Friday Agreement, 1996–98. Member: Lawyers Insolvency Assoc., 1991–2000; Council, Soc. of Practitioners of Insolvency, 1993–2000. *Recreation:* many and varied. *Address:* 83 Victoria Road, Holywood, Co. Down BT18 9BG. *Died 2 July 2011.*

NARJES, Karl-Heinz; Member, Commission of the European Communities, 1981–89 (Vice-President, 1985–89); *b* 30 Jan. 1924; *s* of Heinrich Narjes; *m* 1951, Eva-Maria Rahe; one *s* one *d*. *Educ:* Hamburg Univ. Entered Foreign Service, 1955; Chef du Cabinet, Pres. of EEC, 1963; Dir-Gen., Press and Inf. Directorate, EEC, 1968–69; Minister of Econs and of Transport, Schleswig-Holstein, 1969–73. Mem., Bundestag, 1972–81; Mem., For. Affairs Cttee, 1976–80; Pres., Econ. Affairs Cttee, 1972–76. *Died 26 Jan. 2015.*

NEALE, Sir Gerrard Anthony, (Sir Gerry), Kt 1990; *b* 25 June 1941; *s* of Charles Woodhouse Neale and Phyllis Muriel Neale; *m* 1st, 1965, Deirdre Elizabeth McCann (marr. diss. 2013); one *s* two *d*; 2nd, 2013, Susan Lorraine Harper. *Educ:* Bedford Sch. Articled to Solicitors, Bedford, 1961; admitted, 1966; Partner, Public and Parly Affairs Dept, Radcliffes & Co., Solicitors, 1991–2002. Councillor, Borough of Milton Keynes, 1973–79, Mayor, 1976–77. Chm., Buckingham Constituency Cons. Assoc., 1974–76. Contested (C) N Cornwall, Oct. 1974, 1992; MP (C) N Cornwall, 1979–92. PPS to Minister for Consumer Affairs, 1981–82, to Minister of State for Trade, 1981–83, to Sec. of State for Transport, 1985–86, to Sec. of State for the Environment, 1986–87, to Sec. of State for Defence, 1987–89. *Publications:* novels: Squaring Circles, 2011; If You Want To Say Yes, Say Yes, 2013; Win Some Lose Some, 2014. *Recreations:* sailing, golf, painting, writing and lyric writing. *Died 28 Oct. 2015.*

NEGUS, Richard; consultant designer; Senior Partner, Negus & Negus, 1967–87; *b* 29 Aug. 1927; *s* of Bertie and Kate Negus; *m* 1949, Pamela Wheatcroft-Hancock (*d* 2000); two *s* one *d*; *m* 2011, Aurea Whittingham. *Educ:* Battersea Grammar Sch.; Camberwell Sch. of Arts and Crafts. FSTD. Staff designer, Festival of Britain, 1948–51; Partner, Negus & Sharland, 1951–67; Lecturer, Central Sch. of Art, 1951–53. Consultant to: Cotton Board Design Centre, 1960–67; BNEC, 1969–75; British Airways, 1973–84, 1990–; Pakistan Airlines, 1975–79 and 1989–92; Rank Organisation, 1979–86; City of Westminster, 1973–75; National Exhibition Centre, 1974–77; Lloyds Bank, 1972–75; Godfrey Davis, 1971–80; John Laing, 1970–73; Andry Montgomery, 1967–; Celltech, 1980–83; Vickers Ltd, 1980–83; SDP, 1981–88; Historic Buildings and Monuments Commn, 1984–93; Nat. Maritime Mus., 1984–; Royal Armouries, 1984–; The Emirates (Airline), 1985–88; Tower of London, 1986–91; Science Museum, 1987–92; Northern Foods, 1986–91; Waterford/Wedgwood, 1987; DoE Royal Parks, 1987–88; Nature Conservation Council, 1987–89; John Lewis Partnership, 1987–89; Nat. Theatre, 1989–91; Internat. Youth Hostels, 1989; Dubai Tourist Bd, 1990–95; Blue Circle Properties, 1990–92. Member: Design Council Poster Awards Cttee, 1970–72; PO Stamps Adv. Cttee, 1977–2002; CNAA, 1980–85; Design Council, 1981–86; Art and Design Cttee, Technician Educn Council, 1981–86. Advisor, Norwich Sch. of Art, 1969–71; External Assessor: Birmingham and Bradford Colls of Art, 1969–73; Medway Coll. of Design, 1989–95; Governor: Camberwell Sch. of Art, 1964–78; Chelsea Sch. of Art, 1977–85; Mem. Court, RCA, 1979–82. PPCSD (Pres., SIAD, 1977–79, Vice Pres. 1966–68). Hon. RCM 1995. *Publications:* Designing for Export Printing, 1972; Display of Text in Museums, 1989; contribs to: Design Mag., The Designer, Graphis, Gebrauchgraphick, Architectural Review, Rolls Royce Mag., Creative Review, Art and Artists. *Recreations:* painting, the countryside, sailing. *Address:* 73 Hemingford Road, N1 1BY. *T:* (020) 7607 8642. *Died 22 April 2011.*

NEIGHBOUR, Oliver Wray, FBA 1982; Music Librarian, Reference Division of the British Library, 1976–85; *b* 1 April 1923; *s* of Sydney William Neighbour, OBE, TD, and Gwenydd Joyce (*née* Prentis). *Educ:* Eastbourne Coll.; Birkbeck Coll., London (BA 1950). Entered Dept of Printed Books, BM, 1946; Asst Keeper in Music Room, 1951; Dep. Keeper, 1976. *Publications:* (with Alan Tyson) English Music Publishers' Plate Numbers, 1965; The Consort and Keyboard Music of William Byrd, 1978; (ed) Music and Bibliography: essays in honour of Alec Hyatt King, 1980; article on Schoenberg in New Grove Dictionary of Music and Musicians, 1980, rev. edn 2001; editor of first publications of works by Schumann, Schoenberg and Byrd. *Address:* 12 Treborough House, 1 Nottingham Place, W1U 5LA. *T:* (020) 7935 1772. *Died 20 Jan. 2015.*

NEUBERGER, Michael Samuel, PhD; FRS 1993; Member, Scientific Staff, since 1980, Joint Head, Division of Protein and Nucleic Acid Chemistry, since 2002, and Deputy Director, since 2012, Medical Research Council Laboratory of Molecular Biology, Cambridge; Fellow, Trinity College, Cambridge, since 1985; *b* 2 Nov. 1953; *s* of Prof. Albert Neuberger, CBE, FRS and Lilian Ida (*née* Dreyfus); *m* 1991, Gillian Anne, *d* of late James and Anne Pyman; two *s* two *d*. *Educ:* Westminster Sch.; Trinity Coll., Cambridge (BA 1974; MA); Imperial Coll., University of London (PhD 1978). Teacher of Sci., Marlborough House Sch., Hawkhurst, 1970–71; Res. Fellow, Trinity Coll., Cambridge, 1977–81; SRC Postdoctoral Fellow, Imperial Coll., London, 1977–79; EMBO Postdoctoral Fellow, Inst. of Genetics, Cologne, 1979–80. Internat. Res. Scholar, Howard Hughes Med. Inst., 1992–97. Mem., EMBO, 1989; Founder FMedSci 1998. Hon. Prof., Univ. of Cambridge, 2002. For. Associate, US Nat. Acad. of Scis, 2013. Novartis Medal, Biochem. Soc., 2001; William Bate Hardy Prize, Cambridge Philos. Soc., 2001; Prix J.-P. Lecocq, Acad. des Scis, Inst de France, 2002; GlaxoSmithKline Prize, Royal Soc., 2003; Dannie-Heineman Prize, Akad. der Wissenschaften zu Göttingen, 2003. *Publications:* articles in learned jls on molecular biol. and immunology. *Address:* Medical Research Council Laboratory of Molecular Biology, Francis Crick Avenue, Cambridge CB2 0QH. *T:* (01223) 267091; Trinity College, Cambridge CB2 1TQ. *T:* (01223) 338400. *Died 26 Oct. 2013.*

NEUBERT, Sir Michael (Jon), Kt 1990; *b* 3 Sept. 1933; *s* of Frederick Henry and Mathilda Marie Louise Neubert; *m* 1959, Sally Felicity Bilger; one *s*. *Educ:* Queen Elizabeth's Sch., Barnet; Bromley Grammar Sch.; Royal Coll. of Music; Downing Coll., Cambridge (MA (Cantab) Modern and Medieval Langs). Travel and industrial consultant. Councillor, Borough of Bromley, 1960–63; London Borough of Bromley: Councillor, 1964–68; Alderman, 1968–74; Leader of the Council, 1967–70; Mayor, 1972–73. Contested (C): N Hammersmith, 1966; Romford, 1970. MP (C) Havering, Romford, Feb. 1974–1983, Romford, 1983–97; contested (C) same seat, 1997. PPS to: Minister for Social Security and for the Disabled, 1980; Ministers of State, NI Office, 1981; Minister of State for Employment, 1981–82; Sec. of State for Trade, 1982–83; Asst Govt Whip, 1983–86; a Lord Comr of HM Treasury, 1986–88; Vice-Chamberlain of HM Household, 1988; Parly Under-Sec. of State for the Armed Forces, 1988–89, for Defence Procurement, 1989–90, MoD. Chm., Cons. Back bench Employment Cttee, 1992–95; Joint Chm., Cons. Back bench Educn and Employment Cttee, 1995–97; Mem., 1922 Exec. Cttee, 1992–97. Chm., Bromley Conservative Assoc., 1968–69. Rector's Warden, St Margaret's, Westminster, 1997–2007 (Parly Warden, 1995–97). Chm., IoW Internat. Oboe Competition, 1997–2002. *Publications:* Running Your Own Society, 1967. *Recreations:* music, literature, cinema, theatre, the countryside. *Club:* Carlton. *Died 3 Jan. 2014.*

NEVILLE, John, CM 2006; OBE 1965; actor, stage and film; Hon. Professor in Drama, Nottingham University, since 1967; Artistic Director, Festival Theatre, Stratford,

Ontario, 1985–89; *b* Willesden, 2 May 1925; *s* of Reginald Daniel Neville and Mabel Lillian (*née* Fry); *m* 1949, Caroline Hooper; three *s* three *d*. *Educ:* Willesden and Chiswick County Schools; Royal Academy of Dramatic Art. Worked as a stores clerk before studying at RADA. First appearance on stage, walking-on part in Richard II; subseq. parts at Open Air Theatre, in repertory at Lowestoft, and with Birmingham Repertory Co.; Bristol Old Vic Co., 1950–53; Old Vic Co., London, 1953–61; Nottingham Playhouse, 1961–63; Theatre Director, Nottingham Playhouse, 1963–68; Dir, Park Theatre Co., Fortune, 1969; Theatre Director: Citadel Theatre, Edmonton, Canada, 1973–78; Neptune Theatre, Halifax, NS, 1978–83. Parts with Old Vic include: Ferdinand in The Tempest, Macduff, Richard II, Orlando in As You Like It, Henry Percy in Henry IV, Part I, Mark Antony; during Old Vic tour of Europe, 1958, Hamlet, Sir Andrew Aguecheek. Played lead in Irma La Douce, Lyric, 1959–60; produced Henry V, Old Vic, 1960; The Lady From the Sea, Queen's, 1961; The School for Scandal, Haymarket, 1962; Alfie, Mermaid and Duchess, 1963. Acted in: The Chichester Festival Theatre, 1962; Beware of the Dog, St Martin's, 1967; Iago in Othello, Nottingham Playhouse, 1967; Mr and Mrs, Palace, 1968; The Apple Cart, Mermaid, 1970; The Beggar's Opera, The Doctor's Dilemma, Chichester, 1972; Sherlock Holmes, NY, 1975; Happy Days, Nat. Theatre, 1977; Grand Theatre, London, Ontario: acted in Dear Antoine and Arsenic and Old Lace, directed Hamlet, 1983; Stratford, Ontario: acted in Love's Labour's Lost, 1983, Merchant of Venice, 1984, Intimate Admiration, 1987, My Fair Lady, 1988; directed Mother Courage, and Othello, 1987, Three Sisters, 1989; acted in: The School for Scandal, NT, 1990; The Dance of Death, Almeida, 1995; Beethoven's Tenth, Chichester, 1996; Krapp's Last Tape, Nottingham Playhouse, 1999. Tour W Africa (Jt Dir and acting), 1963. *Films:* Oscar Wilde; Topaze; Billy Budd; A Study in Terror; Adventures of Baron Munchausen; The X-Files. Television appearances, incl. The First Churchills, series for BBC 2. Hon. Dr Dramatic Arts Lethbridge Univ., 1979; Hon. DFA Nova Scotia Coll. of Art and Design, 1981; Hon. LLD Ryerson Univ., 1999. *Address:* 24 Wellesley Street West, #511, Toronto, ON M4Y 2X6, Canada. *Clubs:* Royal Over-Seas League; Arts and Letters (Toronto). *Died 19 Nov. 2011.*

NEVIN, Prof. Norman Cummings, OBE 2003; MD; FRCP, FRCPE, FRCPath, FFPH; Professor of Medical Genetics, Queen's University of Belfast, 1975–2000, then Emeritus (Personal Chair, 1975–78); Consultant Clinical Geneticist and Head, Northern Ireland Regional Genetics Service, Belfast City Health Trust, 1968–2000; *b* 10 June 1935; *s* of Joseph and Sarah Nevin; *m* 1961, Jean Hamilton; one *s* one *d*. *Educ:* Queen's Univ. of Belfast (BSc 1957; MB BCh; BAO 1960; MD 1964). FRCPE 1976; FFPH (FFPHM 1981); FRCPath 1981; FRCP 1990. House physician and surgeon, Royal Victoria Hosp., Belfast, 1960–61; John Dunville Fellow in Pathology, QUB, 1961–64; Registrar in Medicine, Royal Victoria Hosp., 1964–65; MRC Fellow, MRC Clinical Genetics Unit, Inst. of Child Health, London and MRC Population Genetics Res. Unit, Oxford, 1965–67; Lectr in Human Genetics, QUB, 1967–75. Mem., Gene Therapy Adv. Cttee, 1993–2006 (Chm., 1996–2006). Mem., Assoc. Physicians of GB and Ireland, 1986–. President: Clinical Genetics Soc., 1991–92; Ulster Paediatric Soc., 1989. *Publications:* numerous contribs on congenital abnormalities in learned medical jls. *Recreations:* walking (hill), painting, medical ethics. *Address:* 17 Ogles Grove, Hillsborough, Co. Down, Northern Ireland BT26 6RS. *Died 28 June 2014.*

NEWALL, Sir Paul (Henry), Kt 1994; TD 1967; JP; DL; Lord Mayor of London, 1993–94; *b* 17 Sept. 1934; *s* of late Leopold Newall and Frances Evelyn Newall (*née* Bean); *m* 1969, Penelope Moyra (MBE 2008), *o d* of Sir Julian (Errington) Ridsdale, CBE and Lady Ridsdale (Dame Paddy Ridsdale, DBE); two *s*. *Educ:* Harrow; Magdalene Coll., Cambridge (MA Econs). Nat. Service, commnd Royal Fusiliers, 1953–55; TA 1955–70, Major. Partner, Loeb Rhoades & Co. (mem., NY Stock Exchange), 1971; Overseas Director: Shearson Loeb Rhoades Inc., 1978; Shearson Lehman American Express (UK) Hldgs, 1981; Exec. Dir, Lehman Brothers Securities, 1990; Dir, Lehman Brothers Ltd (formerly Shearson Lehman International Ltd), 1985–94 (Sen. Advr, 1993–98); non-exec. Dir, Guardian Royal Exchange plc, 1995–99. Member: Adv. Cttee, Energy Internat. NV, 1978–98; Korea Advisers Gp, 1997–, Asia Pacific Advisers Gp, 2000–02, Trade Partners UK; UK-Japan 21st Century Gp, 1997–. Vice-Pres., Inst. of Export, 1995–2002. City of London: Mem., Court of Common Council (Ward of Cripplegate), 1980–81; Alderman, Ward of Walbrook, 1981–2005; Sheriff, 1989–90; Chm., City of London TAVRA, 1986–89; Vice-Chm., TA&VRA for Gtr London, 1989–95; Hon. Col, The London Regt, 1995–2001; Master, Bakers' Co., 1990–91; Founder Master, Guild of Internat. Bankers, 2001; Member: Guild of Freemen, 1988– (Court, 1988–91); Court, HAC, 1980–2005; Incorp. of Bakers of Glasgow, 1995–; Hon. Liveryman, Marketors' Co., 1995; Hon. Freeman, Fuellers' Co., 1995. Vice-Pres., City of London Sector, British Red Cross, 1986–; Member: Friends of St Paul's Cathedral; City Heritage Soc.; Samuel Pepys Club. Fellow, Coll. of Advocates, St Paul's Cathedral, 2013–. Pro-Chancellor and Chm. Council, City Univ., 1997–2003; Governor: MENCAP City Foundn, 1982–97; City of London Freemen's Sch., 1987–88; City of London Girls' Sch., 1997–98; City of London Boys' Sch., 1999–2001; Trustee: Morden Coll., 1991–2004; City of London Endowment Trust for St Paul's Cathedral, 1996–2004; Temple Bar Trust, 1996–2004; Internat. Bankers Charitable Trust, 1992–2008; Exec. Trustee, Army Benevolent Fund, 1998–2007; Pres., Fedn of Old Comrades Assocs of London Territorial and Auxiliary Units, 2003–. Patron: Samaritans Nat. Appeal, 1989–98; Internat. Centre for Child Studies, 1989–93. Hon. Rep., City of Seoul, 1996–; Chm., UK-Korea Forum for the Future, 1999–2008. Churchwarden, St Stephen's, Walbrook, 1981–2005. Burgess, City of Glasgow, 1995. One of HM Lieutenants of City of London, 1975–; DL Gtr London, 1977; JP City of London, 1981; Hon. Vis. Magistrate, HM Tower of London, 1988–. Hon. DLitt City, 1993. KStJ 1993. Hon. Citizen, Georgia, USA, 1994. Order of Diplomatic Merit (First Class) (Korea), 1999. *Publications:* Japan and the City of London, 1996. *Recreations:* fencing, fly fishing, shooting, water-ski-ing, tennis, trees. *Address:* Grove Park, Yoxford, Suffolk IP17 3HX. *Clubs:* East India, City Livery, United Wards, Walbrook Ward, MCC, Pilgrims. *Died 28 July 2015.*

NEWMAN, Frederick Edward Fry, CBE 1986; MC 1945; Chairman: Dan-Air Services, 1953–89; Davies & Newman Holdings, 1971–90; *b* 14 July 1916; *s* of Frank Newman and Katharine Newman; *m* 1947, Margaret Helen (*née* Blackstone) (*d* 2002); two *s* one *d*. *Educ:* The Leys School, Cambridge. Joined Davies & Newman, 1937; served HAC and 9th Field Regt, RA, 1939–46; formed Dan-Air Services, 1953. *Address:* Cranstone, Hook Heath Road, Woking, Surrey GU22 0DT. *T:* (01483) 772605. *Died 19 Oct. 2012.*

NEWMAN, Prof. Ronald Charles, PhD; FRS 1998; FInstP; Professor of Physics, University of London, 1989–99, then Emeritus; Senior Research Fellow, Centre for Semiconductor Materials and Devices, Department of Physics, Imperial College, London, 1999–2006; *b* 10 Dec. 1931; *s* of Charles Henry Newman and Margaret Victoria May Newman (*née* Cooper); *m* 1956, Jill Laura Weeks; two *d*. *Educ:* Imperial Coll. of Sci. and Technol. (BSc 1st Cl. Hons, ARCS; DIC 1954; PhD 1955). FInstP 1971. Research scientist, AEI Central Res. Lab., Aldermaston Court, 1955–63; Sen. Res. Scientist, AEI Rugby, 1963–64; University of Reading: Lectr, Dept of Physics, 1964–69; Reader, 1969–75; Prof., 1975–89; Vis. Prof., 1989–2009; Associate Dir, IRC for Semiconductor Materials, ICSTM, 1989–99. Vis. Prof., Dept of Electrical Engrg and Electronics, UMIST, 2000–05. Numerous consultancies. *Publications:* Infra-Red Studies of Crystal Defects, 1973; (contrib.) Semiconductors and Semimetals, 1993; (contrib.) Handbook on Semiconductors, 1994; numerous contribs to learned jls. *Recreations:* music, foreign travel. *Address:* 23 Betchworth Avenue, Earley, Reading, Berks RG6 7RH. *T:* (0118) 966 3816. *Died 30 July 2014.*

NEWTON OF BRAINTREE, Baron *cr* 1997 (Life Peer), of Coggeshall in the co. of Essex; **Antony Harold Newton,** OBE 1972; PC 1988; DL; economist; Chairman, Suffolk Mental Health Partnership NHS Trust, since 2009; *b* Aug.

1937; *m* 1st, 1962, Janet Huxley (marr. diss. 1986); two *d*; 2nd, 1986, Mrs Patricia Gilthorpe; one step *s* two step *d*. *Educ:* Friends' Sch., Saffron Walden; Trinity Coll., Oxford. Hons PPE. President: OU Conservative Assoc., 1958; Oxford Union, 1959. Formerly Sec. and Research Sec., Bow Group. Head of Conservative Research Dept's Economic Section, 1965–70; Asst Dir, Conservative Research Dept, 1970–74. Chm. Coningsby Club, 1965–66. Contested (C) Sheffield, Brightside, 1970. MP (C) Braintree, Feb. 1974–1997; contested (C) same seat, 1997. An Asst Govt Whip, 1979–81; a Lord Comr of HM Treasury, 1981–82; Parly Under-Sec. of State for Social Security, 1982–84, and Minister for the Disabled, 1983–84, Minister of State (Minister for Social Security and the Disabled), 1984–86, Minister of State (Minister for Health) and Chm., NHS Management Bd, 1986–88, DHSS; Chancellor of Duchy of Lancaster and Minister of Trade and Industry, 1988–89; Sec. of State for Social Security, 1989–92; Lord Pres. of the Council and Leader of H of C, 1992–97. Vice-Chm., Fedn of Univ. Conservative and Unionist Assocs, 1959. Mem. (and latterly Chm.), FEFC, 1998–2001 (Chm., E Region Cttee, 1998–2001). Chairman: Council on Tribunals, later Admin. Justice and Tribunals Council, 1999–2009; Privy Counsellors' Cttee on Anti-Terrorism, Crime and Security Act 2001, 2002–04; Buncefield Major Incident Investigation Bd, 2006–09; Tax Law Rewrite Steering Cttee, 2007–10; Honours Cttee for Community, Voluntary and Local Service, 2005–. Professional Standards Dir, Inst. of Dirs, 1998–2004. Chair, Standing Conf. on Drug Abuse, 1997–2001; Chairman: NE Essex Mental Health NHS Trust, 1997–2001; Royal Brompton and Harefield NHS Trust, 2001–08; E Anglia's Children's Hospices, 1998–2002; Help the Hospices, 2002–10. Interested in health and social services, social security, access to justice. DL Essex, 2002. *Address:* House of Lords, SW1A 0PW. *Died 25 March 2012.*

NEWTON, Sir (Charles) Wilfrid, Kt 1993; CBE 1988; Chairman and Chief Executive, London Regional Transport, 1989–94; Chairman, London Underground Ltd, 1989–94; *b* 11 Dec. 1928; *s* of late Gore Mansfield Newton and Catherine Knox Newton; *m* 1954, Felicity Mary Lynn Thomas; two *s* two *d*. *Educ:* Orange Prep. Sch., Johannesburg; Highlands North High Sch., Johannesburg; Univ. of Witwatersrand, Johannesburg. FCILT (FCIT 1989). Chartered Accountant (South Africa). Articled clerk, 1947–52, Audit Senior, 1952–55, Saml Thomson & Young, Chartered Accountants, Johannesburg; Territory Accounting Manager, Vacuum Oil Co. Ltd, SA, 1955–58; Territory Accounting and Finance Manager, Mobil Oil Ltd, S Africa, 1958–62; Actg Controller, Mobil Sekiyu KK, Tokyo, 1962–63; Finance Manager and Dep. Gen. Manager, Mobil, E Africa, Nairobi, 1963–65; Finance Dir, Mobil Sekiyu KK, Tokyo, and Chief Financial Officer, Mobil Interests in Japan, 1965–68; Turner & Newall plc: Finance Dir, 1968–71; Man. Dir of Finance and Planning, 1971–75; Gp Man. Dir, Mining, Plastics and Chemicals, 1975–82; Gp Chief Exec., 1982–83; Chm. and Chief Exec., Mass Transit Railway Corp., Hong Kong, 1983–89; Chm., Hong Kong Futures Exchange Ltd, 1986–89; non-executive Chairman: Jacobs Hldgs plc, 1992–99; Mountcity Investments Ltd, 1992–; Raglan Properties plc, 1994–98; Guy Maunsell Internat. Ltd, 1994–2001; non-executive Director: Hongkong & Shanghai Banking Corp. Ltd, Hong Kong, 1989–92; Sketchley plc, 1990–99; HSBC Hldgs plc, 1992–99; Midland Bank plc, subseq. HSBC Bank plc, 1992–99. CCIM (CBIM 1977); FRSA 1986. Hon. FREng (Hon. FEng 1993); Hon. FHKIE 1994. JP Hong Kong, 1994–89. *Recreations:* sailing, reading. *Address:* Newtons Gate, 12 Ramley Road, Pennington, Lymington, Hants SO41 8GQ. *T:* (01590) 679750. *Clubs:* Carlton; Wanderers (Johannesburg); Hong Kong, Aberdeen Yacht, Royal Hong Kong Yacht (Hong Kong); Royal Lymington Yacht. *Died 28 Nov. 2012.*

NEWTON, Richard James; Chairman, National and Provincial Building Society, 1988–93; *b* 17 Nov. 1927; *s* of Alfred Richard Newton and Rosamond Newton (*née* Tunstill); *m* 1961, Elizabeth Seraphine Meuwissen (*d* 1986); four *s*. *Educ:* Clifton; St John's College, Cambridge (MA). Managerial positions at: Courtaulds, 1951–58; Midland Silicones, 1959–62; Chemstrand, 1963–66; Keith Shipton & Co., 1967–69; Man. Dir, Bury & Masco (Holdings), 1970–77; non-executive Director: Sketchley, 1978–87 (Chm., 1983–87); National & Provincial Building Soc., 1985–93. Fellow and Bursar, Trinity Hall, Cambridge, 1977–89. Gov., Clifton Coll., 1990– (Mem. Council, 1993–98). *Recreations:* music, playing the piano. *Address:* 15 Valiant House, Vicarage Crescent, SW11 3LU. *Died 2 Feb. 2012.*

NEWTON, Sir Wilfrid; *see* Newton, Sir C. W.

NGATA, Sir Henare Kohere, KBE 1982 (OBE); chartered accountant; *b* Waiomatatini, 19 Dec. 1917; *s* of Sir Apirana Ngata and Arihia, *d* of Tuta Tamati; *m* 1940, Rora Lorna, *d* of Maihi Rangipo Mete Kingi; one *s*. *Educ:* Waiomatatini Sch.; Te Aute Coll., Victoria Univ. of Wellington, BA; BCom; FCA (NZ Soc. of Accountants). Served 28th Maori Bn, 1939–45: POW, Greece; Germany, 1941–45. Director: Fieldair Ltd, 1960–79; Gisborne Sheepfarmers Mercantile Co. Ltd; Gisborne Sheepfarmers Freezing Co. Ltd. Member: Gisborne Reg. Commn, NZ Historic Places Trust, 1962–70; NZ Maori Council, 1962–85; C of E Provincial Commn on Maori Schs, 1964–66; Gisborne/East Coast Regional Develt Council, 1973–78; Finance Cttee, Bishopric of Aotearoa. Nat. Pres., 28th Maori Bn Assoc., 1964–66. Vice-Pres., NZ Nat. Party, 1967–69. JP Gisborne, 1965. Hon. LLD, Victoria Univ. of Wellington, 1979. *Address:* 10 Grant Road, Gisborne 4010, New Zealand. *Died 11 Dec. 2011.*

NICHOL, Comdt (Daphne) Patricia, CBE 1986; Director, Women's Royal Naval Service, 1982–86; *b* 25 Sept. 1932; *d* of Captain Ralph Geoffrey Swallow, RN and Daphne Lucy Regina Swallow (*née* Parry); *m* 1991, Capt. Peter Dale Nichol, RN. *Educ:* St George's Sch., Ascot; Portsmouth Polytechnic (Hon. Fellow, 1983). Joined WRNS as Signal Wren, 1950; qualified as WRNS Communications Officer, 1955; served in HMS Drake and Malta, 1956–58; Oslo, Portsmouth, HMS Mercury, Northwood and Gibraltar, 1958–67; HMS Pembroke and HMS Heron, 1968–71; passed Naval Staff Course, 1972; HMS Dauntless, 1973–74; Staff of C-in-C Naval Home Comd and MoD, 1974–76; National Defence College Latimer Course, 1976–77; Staff of Naval Secretary, 1977; Command Personnel Officer to C-in-C Naval Home Comd, 1977–79; Dep. Dir, WRNS, 1979–81; Staff Officer Training Co-ordination and Comd WRNS Officer to C-in-C Naval Home Comd, 1981–82; Hon. ADC to the Queen, 1982–86. Asst Sec., Benevolent Dept, Officers' Assoc., 1987–89; Case Sec., DGAA, 1989–90. Member: Nat. Exec. Cttee, Forces Help Soc. and Lord Roberts Workshops, 1986–95; Council and Exec. Cttee, Shipwrecked Fishermen and Mariners Royal Benevolent Soc., 1991–96, 1998–2002; Council, Soc. of Friends of RN Mus. and HMS Victory, Portsmouth, 1994–97. Hon. Fellow, Univ. of Portsmouth, 1993. *Recreations:* tennis, dressmaking and needlework, reading, theatre, opera, music. *Address:* c/o Lloyds TSB, 23 Elm Grove, Hayling Island, Hants PO11 9EA. *Died 7 April 2014.*

NICHOLSON, Brian Thomas Graves, CBE 1998; Chairman, Advertising Standards Board of Finance, 1989–99; *b* 27 June 1930; *s* of late Ivor Nicholson, CBE, and Mrs Alan McGaw; *m* 1959, Henrietta, *d* of late Nevill Vintcent, OBE, DFC, and Mrs Ralph Dennis; two *s* (and one *s* decd). *Educ:* Charterhouse. Reporter, Newcastle Evening Chronicle, 1949–53; Montreal Star, Toronto Telegram, and Victoria Times, 1953–54; Manchester Evening Chronicle, 1954–56; Sunday Graphic, 1956–57; Advertisement Manager, Sunday Times, 1957–65; Director: Sunday Times, 1963–65; Beaverbrook Newspapers plc, 1967–77; Man. Dir, Evening Standard, 1972–77; Jt Man. Dir, Observer, 1977–84; Hd of Public Affairs, Lloyd's of London, 1990–92; Director: CompAir, 1977–85; Center for Communication (USA), 1981–95; Lloyd's of London Press, 1982–93; London Broadcasting Co., 1983–90; Royal Opera House Covent Garden, 1984–89; Royal Ballet, 1984–92 (Mem., Bd of Govs, 1995–2006); News (UK), 1985–87; CCA Galleries plc, 1986–89; Logie Bradshaw Media, 1986–97; Messenger Newspapers Gp, 1986–89; Aurora Productions, 1987–91; Messenger Television Ltd, 1989–2000; Whitespace Software Ltd, 1990–2004; Home Counties Newspaper

Holdings plc, 1991–98; Messenger Leisure Ltd, 1994–2003; Benesh Inst., 1995–98; Birmingham Royal Ballet, 2001–06; Chairman: Audit Bureau of Circulation, 1975–77; Marlar Internat. Ltd, 1985–90; Carthusian Trust, 1987–2000; SE Arts Bd (formerly Assoc.), 1989–95; Publicitas Hldg (UK) Ltd, 1989–99; Adv. Cttee on Advertising, COI, 1993–98; Charterhouse Sports Centre Ltd, 1995–2001; Dance Teachers' Benevolent Fund, 1999–2003. Vice President: CAM Foundn, 1975–2000; Royal Theatrical Fund (formerly Royal Gen. Theatrical Fund Assoc.), 1986– (Vice-Chm., 1996–2000); Pres., History of Advertising Trust, 2000–09; Member: Council of Commonwealth Press Union, 1975–99; Adv. Bd, New Perspective Fund (USA), 1984–97; Trustee, Glyndebourne Opera Co., 1977–2000; Gov., British Liver Foundn, 1989–99. Mem., Editorial Adv. Bd, Focus in Education Ltd, 1986–90. Churchwarden, St Bride's Church, Fleet Street, 1978–2002. Mackintosh Medal, Advertising Assoc., 2000. *Recreations:* travelling, listening, playing games. *Address:* 6 Laxford House, Cundy Street, SW1W 9JU. *Clubs:* Beefsteak, Brooks's, MCC. *Died 12 Aug. 2015.*

NICHOLSON, Rev. Prof. Ernest Wilson, DD; FBA 1987; Provost of Oriel College, Oxford, 1990–2003; Pro-Vice-Chancellor, University of Oxford, 1993–2003; *b* 26 Sept. 1938; *s* of Ernest Tedford Nicholson and Veronica Muriel Nicholson; *m* 1962, Hazel (*née* Jackson); three *d* (one *s* decd). *Educ:* Portadown Coll.; Trinity Coll., Dublin (Scholar; BA 1960; MA 1964; Hon. Fellow, 1992); Glasgow Univ. (PhD 1964); MA (by incorporation) 1967, BD 1971, DD 1978, Cambridge; DD Oxford (by incorporation) 1979. Lectr in Hebrew and Semitic Languages, TCD, 1962–67; Univ. Lectr in Divinity, Cambridge Univ., 1967–79; Fellow: University Coll. (later Wolfson Coll.), Cambridge, 1967–69 (Hon. Fellow, 1992); Pembroke Coll., Cambridge, 1969–79; Chaplain, Pembroke Coll., Cambridge, 1969–73, Dean, 1973–79; Oriel Prof. of the Interpretation of Holy Scripture, and Fellow of Oriel Coll., Oxford Univ., 1979–90. At various times vis. prof. at univs and seminars in Europe, USA, Canada and Australia. Pres., SOTS, 1988. Chm., Jardine Foundn, 1993–2000. Hon. Fellow: St Peter's Coll., Oxford, 1994; Oriel Coll., Oxford, 2003. Hon. MRIA 2010. Burkitt Medal for Biblical Studies, British Acad., 2009. Comdr, Order of Merit (Italian Republic), 1990. *Publications:* Deuteronomy and Tradition, 1967; Preaching to the Exiles, 1971; Exodus and Sinai in History and Tradition, 1973; (with J. Baker) The Commentary of Rabbi David Kimhi on Psalms 120–150, 1973; Commentary on Jeremiah 1–25, 1973; Commentary on Jeremiah 26–52, 1975; God and His People: covenant and theology in the Old Testament, 1986; The Pentateuch in the Twentieth Century: the legacy of Julius Wellhausen, 1997; (ed) A Century of Theological and Religious Studies in Britain, 2003; articles in biblical and Semitic jls. *Recreations:* music, the English countryside. *Address:* 39A Blenheim Drive, Oxford OX2 8DJ. *Died 22 Dec. 2013.*

NICHOLSON, Dr Howard, FRCP; Physician, University College Hospital, since 1948; Physician, Brompton Hospital, 1952–77; Fellow of University College, London, since 1959; *b* 1 Feb. 1912; *s* of Frederick and Sara Nicholson; *m* 1941, Winifrid Madeline Piercy (*d* 2001). *Educ:* University Coll., London, and University Coll. Hospital. MB, BS, London, 1935; MD London 1938; MRCP 1938, FRCP 1949. House appointments and Registrarship, UCH, 1935–38; House Physician at Brompton Hosp., 1938. Served War, 1940–45, RAMC; Physician to Chest Surgical Team and Officer i/c Medical Div. (Lt-Col). Registrar, Brompton Hosp., and Chief Asst, Inst. of Diseases of Chest, 1945–48. Goulstonian Lecturer, RCP, 1950. *Publications:* sections on Diseases of Chest in The Practice of Medicine (ed J. S. Richardson), 1961, and in Progress in Clinical Medicine, 1961; articles in Thorax, Lancet, etc. *Recreations:* reading, going to the opera. *Address:* Chelwood, Laughton, Lewes, E Sussex BN8 6BE. *Died 11 Feb. 2014.*

NICHOLSON, Margaret Beda; *see* Yorke, M.

NICOLL, Douglas Robertson, CB 1980; *b* 12 May 1920; *s* of James George Nicoll and Mabel Nicoll (*née* Styles); *m* 1st, 1949, Winifred Campion (*d* 1987); two *s*; 2nd, 1992, Mrs Cathryn Sansom. *Educ:* Merchant Taylors' School; St John's College, Oxford (MA 1946). FO (Govt Code & Cipher Sch., Bletchley Pk, deciphering German Enigma machine), 1941–45; FCO (GCHQ), 1946–80; Joint Services' Staff College, 1953; Under Secretary, 1977–80; Cabinet Office, 1980–81 (produced Nicoll Report on performance of Jt Intelligence Cttee which remains classified but conclusions published in *Cold War History*, 7:4, 2007). *Publications:* contrib. to DNB and Oxford DNB. *Recreations:* chess, bridge, National Hunt racing, politics. *Address:* c/o National Westminster Bank, 31 The Promenade, Cheltenham, Glos GL50 1LH. *Club:* Travellers. *Died 29 Sept. 2015.*

NIEMEYER, Oscar; architect; *b* Rio de Janeiro, 15 Dec. 1907; *s* of Oscar Niemeyer Soares; *m* 1st, Anita Niemeyer (*d* 2004); (one *d* decd); 2nd, 2006, Vera Lucia Cabreira. *Educ:* Escola Nacional de Beles Artes, Univ. of Brazil. Joined office of Lúcio Costa, 1935; worked on Min. of Education and Health Building, Rio de Janeiro, Brazilian Pavilion, NY World Fair, etc., 1936–41. Designed more than 500 buildings; major projects include: Pamphulha, Belo Horizonte, 1941–43; also Quitandinha, Petrópolis; Exhibition Hall, São Paulo, 1953; Brasilia (Dir of Architecture), 1957–60; French Communist Party HQ, Paris, 1971; Mus. of Contemporary Art, Niteroi, Brazil, 1996; summer pavilion, Serpentine Gall., 2003. Brazilian Rep., UN Bd of Design Consultants, 1947. Lenin Peace Prize, 1963; Prix Internat. de l'Architecture Aujourd'hui, 1966; Royal Gold Medal for Architecture, RIBA, 1998; Praemium Imperiale, Japan Art Assoc., 2004. *Publications:* The Curves of Time: the memoirs of Oscar Niemeyer, 2001. *Address:* 3940 Avenida Atlântica, CEP 22070–002, Rio de Janeiro, Brazil. *Died 5 Dec. 2012.*

NINIS, Ven. Richard Betts; Archdeacon of Lichfield (formerly Stafford), 1974–98; Canon Treasurer of Lichfield Cathedral, 1974–98; *b* 25 Oct. 1931; *s* of late George Woodward Ninis and Mary Gertrude Ninis; *m* 1967, Penelope Jane Harwood; two *s* one *d*. *Educ:* Lincoln Coll., Oxford (MA); Bishop's Hostel, Lincoln (GOE). Curate, All Saints, Poplar, 1955–62; Vicar of: St Martins, Hereford, 1962–71; Bullinghope and Dewsall with Callow, 1966–71. Preb., Hereford Cathedral, 1970–74; Diocesan Missioner for Hereford, 1971–74. Chm., USPG, 1988–91. Chm., Derbyshire Coll. of Higher Educn, 1978–90; Vice Chm., Univ. of Derby, 1992–98. Hon. Dr Derby, 1999. *Recreations:* gardening, travel. *Address:* 47 Golf Drive, Nuneaton, Warwickshire CV11 6ND. *Died 15 Oct. 2014.*

NISBET, Prof. John Donald, OBE 1981; MA, BEd, PhD; FEIS; Professor of Education, Aberdeen University, 1963–88; *b* 17 Oct. 1922; *s* of James Love Nisbet and Isabella Donald; *m* 1952, Brenda Sugden (*d* 1995); one *s* one *d*. *Educ:* Dunfermline High Sch.; Edinburgh Univ. (MA, BEd); PhD (Aberdeen); Teacher's Certif. (London). Royal Air Force, 1943–46. Teacher, Fife, 1946–48; Lectr, Aberdeen Univ., 1949–63. Editor: British Jl of Educnl Psychology, 1967–74; Studies in Higher Education, 1979–84; Chairman: Educnl Research Bd, SSRC, 1972–75; Cttee on Primary Educn, 1974–80; Scottish Council for Research in Educn, 1975–78; President: British Educnl Research Assoc., 1975; Scottish Inst. of Adult and Continuing Educn, 1991. FEIS 1975. Hon. DEd Edinburgh, 2004. *Publications:* Family Environment, 1953; Age of Transfer to Secondary Education, 1966; Transition to Secondary Education, 1969; Scottish Education Looks Ahead, 1969; Educational Research Methods, 1970; Educational Research in Action, 1972; Impact of Research, 1980; Towards Community Education, 1980; (ed) World Yearbook of Education, 1985; Learning Strategies, 1986; Curriculum Reform: assessment in question, 1993; Educational Disadvantage, 1994; Pipers and Tunes: a decade of educational research in Scotland, 1995; Thirty Years On, 2005; papers in jls on educnl psychology and curriculum develt. *Recreation:* golf. *Address:* 7 Lawson Avenue, Banchory AB31 5TW. *T:* (01330) 823145. *Died 5 Oct. 2012.*

NISBET, Prof. Robin George Murdoch, FBA 1967; Corpus Christi Professor of Latin, Oxford, 1970–92; Fellow of Corpus Christi College, Oxford, 1952–92, Hon. Fellow 1992; *b* 21 May 1925; *s* of R. G. Nisbet, Univ.

Lecturer, and A. T. Husband; *m* 1969, Anne (*d* 2004), *d* of Dr J. A. Wood. *Educ:* Glasgow Academy; Glasgow Univ.; Balliol Coll., Oxford (Snell Exhibitioner; Hon. Fellow, 1989). Tutor in Classics, Corpus Christi College, Oxford, 1952–70. Kenyon Medal, British Acad., 1997. *Publications:* Commentary on Cicero, *in Pisonem*, 1961; (with M. Hubbard) on Horace, *Odes I*, 1970; *Odes II*, 1978; Collected Papers on Latin Literature, 1995; (with N. Rudd) Commentary on Horace, *Odes III*, 2004. *Recreation:* 20th century history. *Address:* 80 Abingdon Road, Cumnor, Oxford OX2 9QW. *T:* (01865) 862482. *Died 14 May 2013.*

NIVEN, Peter Ashley Robertson, FRCS, FRCOG; Consultant Obstetrician and Gynaecologist, United Bristol Hospitals, 1976–2003; *b* 3 March 1938; *s* of late Harold Robertson Niven and Elizabeth Isobel Robertson Niven (*née* Mair); *m* 1964, Sarah Peta Callaway; three *s*. *Educ:* Dulwich Coll.; Gonville and Caius Coll., Cambridge (Open Exhibnr 1955; BA 1959; MA 1963); St Bartholomew's Hosp. (MB BChir 1962). FRCS 1966; MRCOG 1969, FRCOG 1981. Eden Travelling Fellow, RCOG, 1972; Purdue Frederick Award, Amer. Coll. of Obstetricians and Gynecologists, 1975; Sen. Registrar, St Bartholomew's Hosp., 1971–74; Consultant, Newcastle Gen. and Hexham Gen. Hosps, 1975–76. Chm., Higher Trng Cttee, and Mem. Council, RCOG, 1992–95; Pres., SW Obstetrical and Gynaecol Soc., 1997–98; Mem., Gynaecol Vis. Soc. of GB and Ireland, 1978. FRSocMed 1971. *Recreations:* ski-ing, golf, Rugby, cricket, history, travel, long distance walking. *Address:* 21 Clifton Park, Clifton, Bristol BS8 3BZ. *T:* (0117) 973 8446. *Clubs:* MCC; Clifton. *Died 7 March 2013.*

NOBBS, David Gordon; writer; *b* 13 March 1935; *s* of Gordon and Gwen Nobbs; *m* 1st, 1968, Mary Blatchford (marr. diss. 1998); two step *s* one step *d*; 2nd, 1998, Susan Sutcliffe; one step *d*. *Educ:* Marlborough; St John's Coll., Cambridge (BA English). Wrote scripts for: That Was the Week That Was, BBC TV, 1963; The Frost Report, The Two Ronnies, The Fall and Rise of Reginald Perrin, 1976–78; BBC TV: The Hello Goodbye Man, 1984; Dogfood Dan and The Carmarthen Cowboy, 1988; Love on a Branch Line, 1994; Gentlemen's Relish, 2000; Reggie Perrin, 2009; Yorkshire TV: Sez Les; Cupid's Darts, 1981; A Bit of a Do, 1989, 1990; Rich Tea and Sympathy, 1991; Stalag Luft, 1993; Granada: Our Young Mr Wignall, 1976; The Glamour Girls, 1980, 1982; Channel 4: Fairly Secret Army, 1984, 1986; The Life and Times of Henry Pratt, 1992. *Publications:* The Itinerant Lodger, 1965; Ostrich Country, 1968; A Piece of the Sky is Missing, 1969; The Fall and Rise of Reginald Perrin, 1975; The Return of Reginald Perrin, 1977; The Better World of Reginald Perrin, 1978; Second From Last in the Sack Race, 1983; A Bit of a Do, 1986; Pratt of the Argus, 1988; Fair Do's, 1990; The Cucumber Man, 1994; The Legacy of Reginald Perrin, 1995; The Reginald Perrin Omnibus, 1999; Going Gently, 2000; I Didn't Get Where I Am Today: an autobiography, 2003; Sex and Other Changes, 2004; Pratt à Manger, 2006; Cupid's Dart, 2007; Obstacles to Young Love, 2010; It Had to Be You, 2011; The Fall and Rise of Gordon Coppinger, 2012; The Second Life of Sally Mottram, 2014. *Recreations:* cricket, football, bird-watching, travel, food, drink, bridge, theatre. *Address:* c/o Jonathan Clowes, Iron Bridge House, Bridge Approach, NW1 8BD. *Died 9 Aug. 2015.*

NOBLE, Barrie Paul; Chairman, 2004–08, Vice President, since 2008, West Oxfordshire Conservative Association; *b* 17 Oct. 1938; *s* of late Major and Mrs F. A. Noble; *m* 1965, Alexandra Helene Giddings; one *s*. *Educ:* Hele's, Exeter; New Coll., Oxford (BA Jurisprudence); Univ. of Dakar. RAF, 1957–59. HM Diplomatic Service, 1962–93: Third, later Second Sec., (Leopoldville) Kinshasa, 1965–67; Second Sec. (Commercial), Kaduna, 1967–69; FCO, 1969–72; First Sec., 1972–75 and Head of Chancery, 1975, Warsaw; FCO, 1976–80; Counsellor, UK Mission to UN, Geneva, 1980–84; Counsellor: FCO, 1984–89; Paris, 1989–93; Chm., CSSB Panel, 1993–97; Chm. and Assessor, CSSB Preliminary (Disabled) Interview Bd, 1997–99. Mem., Student Sporting and Cultural Develt Awards Cttee, New Coll., Oxford, 2009–12 (Chm., 2011). *Publications:* Droit Coutumier, Annales Africaines, 1965. *Recreations:* grass cutting, bridge, ski-ing, archery. *Clubs:* Royal Air Force, Ski Club of Great Britain. *Died 11 Oct. 2013.*

NOEL, Geoffrey Lindsay James; Metropolitan Stipendiary Magistrate, 1975–93; *b* 19 April 1923; *s* of Major James Noel and Maud Noel; *m* 1st, 1947, Beryl MacGregor; two *d*; 2nd, 1966, Eileen Pickering (*née* Cooper) (*d* 2008); two step *s*. *Educ:* Crewkerne Sch., Somerset. Enlisted Royal Regt of Artillery, 1941; commnd, 1942; attached 9th Para Bn, 6 Airborne Div., 1944, Captain; POW Oflag 79; RWAFF, 1952–55; Major 1957; retd 1960. Called to Bar, Middle Temple, 1962; practised London and SE circuit. Chm., Juvenile Courts, 1977–79; Dep. Circuit Judge, 1980–82. *Recreations:* gardening, golf. *Address:* Loja, Albourne Road, Hurstpierpoint, Hassocks, W Sussex BN6 9ES. *Died 1 Aug. 2014.*

NOEL-BUXTON, 3rd Baron *cr* 1930; **Martin Connal Noel-Buxton;** *b* 8 Dec. 1940; *s* of 2nd Baron Noel-Buxton and Helen Nancy (*d* 1949), *yr d* of late Col K. H. M. Connal, CB, OBE, TD; *S* father, 1980; *m* 1st, 1964, Miranda Mary (marr. diss. 1968), *er d* of H. A. Chisenhale-Marsh; 2nd, 1972, Sarah Margaret Surridge (marr. diss. 1982), *o d* of N. C. W. Barrett, TD; one *s* one *d*; 3rd, 1986, Abigail Marie, *yr d* of E. P. R. Clent; one *d*. *Educ:* Bryanston School; Balliol College, Oxford (MA). Admitted a Solicitor, 1966. *Heir:* *s* Hon. Charles Connal Noel-Buxton, *b* 17 April 1975. *Died 1 Dec. 2013.*

NOON, Baron *cr* 2011 (Life Peer), of St John's Wood in the London Borough of Camden; **Gulam Kaderbhoy Noon,** Kt 2002; MBE 1996; Founder, Noon Products Ltd, 1989 (Chairman, 1989–2005, non-executive Chairman, since 2005); Chairman, Noon Group, since 1995; *b* Bombay, 24 Jan. 1936; *s* of Kaderbhoy Ebrahimjee and Safiabai Kaderbhoy; *m* Raeka Abdulali (marr. diss.); two *d*; *m* 1998, Mohini Kent. Joined family business, Royal Sweets, Bombay, 1953; Founder, Chm. and Man. Dir, Bombay Halwa Ltd, London, 1972–. Founder, Asian Business Assoc., 1995 (Chm.); Mem. Bd, 1998–, Pres., 2002–, London Chamber of Commerce and Ind.; Chm., London Internat. Trade Forum, 2002–. Director: Covent Garden Market Authy, 1995–2000; Britain in Europe, 2004–07; Transport for London, 2004–; Good Relations (India) Pvt Ltd, 2006–; Zee Telefilms Ltd, 2006–; Zee Entertainment Studios Ltd, 2008–; non-executive Director: Obento Ltd (Subway Restaurants), 2004–; NeutraHealth plc, 2004–; Casualty Plus Ltd, 2005–; Member, Advisory Board: Bridges Community Ventures Ltd, 2007– (non-exec. Dir, 2005–07); British Olympic Assoc., 2007–; Member: Adv. Council, Prince's Trust, 1996–; Ethnic Minority Business Forum, 2000–03; Adv. Bd on Naturalisation and Integration, Home Office, 2004–08. Founder Mem., Cancer Res. UK, 2002–; Mem. Bd, Care Internat. UK, 2002–06; Trustee: Noon Foundn, 1995–; Arpana Charitable Trust UK, 1996–; Memorial Gates Trust, 1998–; British Food Trust, 1999–; Maimonides Foundn, 2002–; Co-Existence Trust; Founder and Chief Trustee, Noon Hosp. and Res. Centre, 2008–. Hon. Life Vice-Pres., Surrey Cricket Club, 2005. Chancellor, Univ. of E London, 2012–. Fellow, Birkbeck, Univ. of London, 2012. MUniv Surrey, 1998; Hon. DBA: London Guildhall, 2001; Kingston, 2005; E London, 2009; DUniv: Middlesex, 2002; UCE, 2002; W London, 2011; Hon. LLD Warwick, 2010; Hon. DLitt De Montfort, 2011. Asian of the Year, 1994; Multicultural Achievement Award, Carlton TV, 2002; Best Business Leader, Sage Business Awards, 2003; Asian Business Award, 2004; Gold Medal, Pravasi Bharatiya Samman Award, 2006; Global Indian, Rajiv Gandhi Awards, 2007; Platinum Award for Lifetime Achievement, Asian Achievers Awards, 2012. *Recreations:* cricket, current affairs, cinema. *Address:* 25 Queen Anne's Gate, St James's Park, SW1H 9BU. *Clubs:* Reform, MCC. *Died 27 Oct. 2015.*

NORMAN, Sir Arthur (Gordon), KBE 1969 (CBE 1966); DFC 1943 (and Bar 1944); Chairman, The De La Rue Company, 1964–87; *b* North Petherton, Som, 18 Feb. 1917; *m* 1944, Margaret Doreen Harrington (*d* 1982); three *s* two *d*. *Educ:* Blundell's Sch. Joined Thomas De La Rue & Co., 1934. RAF, 1939–45; Wing-Comdr, 1943. Rejoined Thomas De La Rue & Co., 1946; Director, 1951;

Managing Director, 1953–77. Vice-Chm., Sun Life Assurance Society, 1984–87 (Dir, 1966–87); Director: SKF (UK) Ltd, 1970–87; Kleinwort, Benson, Lonsdale plc, subseq. Kleinwort Benson Gp, 1985–88. Pres., CBI, 1968–70. Bd Mem., Internat. Inst. for Environment and Develt, 1982–92; Chairman: WWF UK, 1977–84, 1987–90; UK CEED, 1984–96; Mem., Nature Conservancy Council, 1980–86. *Recreations:* golf, country life. *Address:* Fir Tree Cottage, Hammoon, Sturminster Newton, Dorset DT10 2DB. *Died 30 Sept. 2011.*

NORMAN, Gailene Patricia S.; *see* Stock-Norman.

NORMAN, Sir Mark (Annesley), 3rd Bt *cr* 1915; DL; farmer; *b* 8 Feb. 1927; *s* of Sir Nigel Norman, 2nd Bt, CBE, and Patricia Moyra (*d* 1986) (who *m* 2nd, 1944, Sir Robert Perkins), *e d* of late Colonel J. H. A. Annesley, CMG, DSO; *S* father, 1943; *m* 1st, 1953, Joanna Camilla (*d* 2009), *d* of late Lt-Col I. J. Kilgour; two *s* one *d*; 2nd, 2009, Mrs Jonette Lois Surridge. *Educ:* Winchester Coll.; RMA. Coldstream Guards, 1945–47; Flying Officer, 601 (County of London) Sqdn, RAuxAF, 1953–56. Hon. Air Cdre, No 4624 (County of Oxford) Movements Sqdn, RAuxAF, 1984–2000. Chm., Anglo-US Cttee, RAF Upper Heyford, 1984–91. Director: Gotaas-Larsen Shipping Corp., 1979–88. Chm., IU Europe Ltd, 1973–87. Mem., Council, St Luke's, Oxford, 1985–91 (Chm., 1986–88). Patron and Churchwarden, St Peter's, Wilcote, 1972–2006. High Sheriff, 1983–84, DL 1985, Oxon. *Recreations:* gardening, workshop, offshore cruising. *Heir:* *s* Nigel James Norman, late Major 13/18th Royal Hussars (Queen Mary's Own) [*b* 5 Feb. 1956; *m* 1994, Mrs Juliet Marriott, *e d* of R. Baxendale; three *s* one *d*]. *Address:* Wilcote Manor, Wilcote, Chipping Norton, Oxon OX7 3EB. *T:* (01993) 868357, *Fax:* (01993) 868032. *Clubs:* Royal Air Force; St Moritz Tobogganing; Royal Southern Yacht. *Died 9 Sept. 2013.*

NORRIS, John Hallam Mercer, CBE 1987; Crown Estate Commissioner, 1991–99; Vice Lord-Lieutenant of Essex, 1992–2003; *b* 30 May 1929; *s* of late William Hallam Norris and Dorothy Edna Norris (*née* Mercer); *m* 1954, Maureen Joy Banyard; two *d*. *Educ:* Brentwood School. Mem., BSES Expedn, Newfoundland, 1947. Partner, W. H. Norris & Sons, 1963–. Chm., Essex River Authy, 1971–74; Member: Anglian Water Authy, 1974–85; Adv. Cttee, 1988, Board, 1989–94, NRA; Adv. Cttee, Envmt Agency, 1994–96; Founder Mem., Envmt Agency Bd, 1996–97; Chairman: Essex Land Drainage Cttee, 1974–89; Crouch Harbour Authy, 1981–88. President: CLA, 1985–87 (Mem., Exec. Cttee, 1973–; Chm., 1983–85); Essex Agricl Soc., 1989; Soc. of Old Brentwood, 2003–04. Chm., Chelmsford Cathedral Council, 2000–. FRAgS 1992; Hon. FIWEM 1992. DL Essex, 1989. *Recreations:* fishing, sailing. *Address:* Mountnessing Hall, Brentwood, Essex CM13 1UN. *T:* (01277) 352152. *Clubs:* Boodle's, Farmers. *Died 4 Oct. 2015.*

NORTH, Prof. Douglass Cecil, PhD; Spencer T. Olin Professor in Arts and Sciences, Washington University, St Louis, since 1995; Bartlett Burnap Senior Fellow, Hoover Institution, Stanford University, since 2001; *b* 5 Nov. 1920; *s* of Henry North and Edith Saitta; *m* 1st, 1944, Lois Heister; three *s*; 2nd, 1972, Elisabeth Case. *Educ:* Univ. of California at Berkeley (BA, PhD). Acting Asst Prof., Asst Prof., Associate Prof. and Prof., Univ. of Washington, Seattle, 1950–83; Washington University, St Louis: Henry R. Luce Prof. of Law and Liberty and Prof. of Econs and of History, 1983–90. Peterkin Prof. of Political Economy, Rice Univ., 1979; Pitt Prof. of American Instns, Cambridge, 1981–82. Fellow, Amer. Acad. of Arts and Scis; Corresp. FBA, 1996; Dist. Fellow, AEA, 2009. Hon. degrees: Cologne 1988; Zürich 1993; Stockholm 1994; Colombia, 1998; St Louis, Missouri, 2003. (Jtly) Nobel Prize for Economics, 1993. *Publications:* The Economic Growth of the United States 1790–1860, 1961; Growth and Welfare in the American Past, 1966; (with Roger Miller) The Economics of Public Issues, 1971; (with Lance Davis) Institutional Change and American Economic Growth, 1971; (with Robert Thomas) The Rise of the Western World, 1973; Structure and Change in Economic History, 1981; Institutions, Institutional Change and Economic Performance, 1990; Understanding the Process of Economic Change, 2004; (with John Wallace and Barry Weingast) Violence and Social Orders: a conceptual framework for interpreting recorded human history, 2009. *Recreations:* tennis, hiking, music, photography. *Address:* Department of Economics, Seigle Hall 391, Washington University, Campus Box 1208, One Brookings Drive, St Louis, MO 63130–4899, USA. *Died 23 Nov. 2015.*

NORTHARD, John Henry, CBE 1987 (OBE 1979); FREng; Director of Operations, 1985–88, Deputy Chairman, 1988–92, British Coal Corporation; Chairman, British Coal Enterprise Ltd, 1991–93; *b* 23 Dec. 1926; *s* of William Henry Northard and Nellie Northard; *m* 1952, Marian Josephine Lay; two *s* two *d*. *Educ:* St Bede's Grammar School, Bradford; Barnsley Mining and Technical College (Certificated Colliery Manager, first class). CEng, FREng (FEng 1983). Colliery Manager, Yorks, 1955–57, Leics, 1957–63; Group Manager, Leics Collieries, 1963–65; Dep. Chief Mining Engineer, NCB, Staffs Area, 1965–70; Area Dep. Dir (Mining), NCB, N Derbyshire Area, 1970–73; Area Dir, NCB, N Derbyshire Area, 1973–81, Western Area, 1981–85; Bd Mem., NCB, 1986–92. Pres., IMinE, 1982. CCMI. Hon. FIMMM. SBStJ 1981. *Publications:* contribs to mining engineering instns and tech. jls. *Died 3 Oct. 2012.*

NORTHFIELD, Baron *cr* 1975 (Life Peer), of Telford, Shropshire; **(William) Donald Chapman;** Chairman: Telford Development Corporation, 1975–87; Consortium Developments Ltd, 1986–92; *b* 25 Nov. 1923; *s* of Wm H. and Norah F. E. Chapman, Barnsley. *Educ:* Barnsley Grammar Sch.; Emmanuel Coll., Cambridge (Sen. Schol.; BA 1st Cl. Hons (Economics) 1945, MA 1948, also degree in Agriculture; Hon. Fellow, 2003). Research in Agric. Economics, Cambridge, 1943–46. Cambridge City Councillor, 1945–47; Sec., Trades Council and Labour Party, 1945–57; MP (Lab) Birmingham (Northfield), 1951–70. Research Sec. of the Fabian Soc., 1948–49, Gen. Sec., 1949–53. Gwilym Gibbon Fellow, Nuffield Coll., Oxford, 1971–73; Vis. Fellow, Centre for Contemporary European Studies, Sussex Univ., 1973–79. Special Adviser to EEC Commn, 1978–84; Chairman: Rural Develt Commn, 1974–80; Inquiry into recent trends in acquisition and occupancy of agric. land, 1977–79. *Publications:* The European Parliament: the years ahead, 1973; The Road to European Union, 1975; articles and Fabian pamphlets. *Recreation:* travel. *Address:* House of Lords, SW1A 0PW. *Died 18 April 2013.*

NUGEE, Edward George, TD 1964; QC 1977; *b* 9 Aug. 1928; *o s* of late Brig. George Travers Nugee, CBE, DSO, MC, RA, and Violet Mary (*née* Richards, later Brooks); *m* 1955, Rachel Elizabeth Makower; four *s*. *Educ:* Brambletye; Radley Coll. (Open Scholar); Worcester Coll., Oxford (Open Exhibnr; Law Mods, Distinction, 1950; 1st Cl. Hons Jurisprudence, 1952; Eldon Law Scholar, 1953; MA 1956). National Service, RA, 1947–49 (Office of COS, GHQ, FARELF); service with 100 Army Photographic Interpretation Unit, TA, 1950–64 (retd Captain, Intell. Corps, 1964). Read as pupil with Lord Templeman and Lord Brightman; called to the Bar, Inner Temple, 1955, Bencher 1976, Treas. 1996; *ad eundem* Lincoln's Inn, 1968. Jun. Counsel to Land Commn (Chancery and Conveyancing), 1967–71; Counsel for litigation under Commons Registration Act, 1965, 1968–77; Conveyancing Counsel to Treasury, WO, MAFF, Forestry Commn, MoD (Admiralty), and DoE, 1972–77; Conveyancing Counsel of Court, 1976–77. Poor Man's Lawyer, Lewisham CAB, 1954–72. Member: CAB Adv. Cttee, Family Welfare Assoc., 1969–72; Mgt Cttee, Greater London Citizens Advice Bureaux Service Ltd, 1972–74; Mgt Cttee, Forest Hill Advice Centre, 1972–76; Bar Council, 1962–66 (Mem., External Relations Cttee, 1966–71); Council of Legal Educn, 1967–90 (Vice-Chm. 1976–82, and Chm. of Bd of Studies, 1976–82); Adv. Cttee on Legal Educn, 1971–90; Common Professional Exam. Bd, 1976–89 (Chm., 1981–87); Lord Chancellor's Law Reform Cttee, 1973–; various working parties and consultative groups of Law Commn, 1966–; Inst. of Conveyancers, 1971– (Pres., 1986–87); Chm., Cttee of Inquiry into Management Problems of Privately Owned Blocks of Flats, 1984–85. Church Comr, 1990–2001 (Mem., Bd of Govs, 1993–2001); Mem., C of E Legal Adv.

Commn, 2001–. Trustee, Temple Music Trust, 1997–. Chm. Governors, Brambletye Sch., 1972–77; Mem. Council, Radley Coll., 1975–95. Lifetime Achievement Award, Chambers and Partners, 2011. *Publications:* (jtly) Nathan on the Charities Act 1960, 1962; (ed jtly) Halsbury's Laws of England, titles Landlord and Tenant (3rd edn 1958), Real Property (3rd edn 1960 to 4th edn reissue 1998); contribs to legal jls. *Recreations:* travel, cooking, church and family life. *Address:* Wilberforce Chambers, 8 New Square, Lincoln's Inn, WC2A 3QP. *T:* (020) 7306 0102; 35 The Panoramic, 12 Pond Street, Hampstead, NW3 2PS. *T:* (020) 7435 9204. *Died 30 Dec. 2014.*

NUGEE, Rachel Elizabeth, MA; *b* 15 Aug. 1926; *d* of John Moritz Makower and Adelaide Gertrude Leonaura Makower (*née* Franklin); *m* 1955, Edward George Nugee, TD, QC (*d* 2014); four *s*. *Educ:* Roedean Sch., Brighton; Lady Margaret Hall, Oxford; MA (Eng. Lang. and Lit.); Reading Univ. (Dip. Soc. Studies). FO, Bletchley Park (Station X), 1944–45. Joined Mothers' Union, 1956; Diocesan Pres., London Dio., 1974–76; Internat. Pres., 1977–82; MU rep. on Women's Nat. Commn, 1983–88. Chm., Edmonton Area Social Responsibility Policy Cttee, 1987–90; Member: Royal Free Hosp. (Hampstead Gen. Hosp.) House Cttee and Patients' Services Cttee, 1961–72; London Diocesan Bd for Social Responsibility, 1984–85, 1987–90; Law of Marriage Gp, General Synod, 1985–88; Lord Chancellor's Adv. Cttee on Conscientious Objectors, 1986–2000. Trustee: Mothers' Union, London Dio., 1983–2013; One plus One - the Marriage and Partnership res. charity, subseq. One plus One Marriage and Partnership Research, 1984–94; King's Cross Furniture Project, 1996–98; Grandparents' Assoc., 2001–07. Voluntary Worker: Witness Service, CCC, Old Bailey, 1997–2000; Personal Support Unit, Royal Cts of Justice, 2001–03. JP Inner London (Thames), 1971–96; Dep. Chm. of Bench, 1985–91; Court Chm., Inner London Family Panel, 1991–96. *Publications:* several religious articles and booklets. *Recreations:* active support of Church and family life, reading, especially history, visiting friends, criminal and family law. *Died 11 Aug. 2015.*

NUNAN, Manus; lecturer; *b* 26 March 1926; *s* of Manus Timothy Nunan, Dist Justice, and Nan (*née* FitzGerald); *m* 1987, Valerie (*née* Robinson); one *s* one *d* by previous marriages. *Educ:* St Mary's Coll., Dublin; Trinity Coll., Dublin (BA, LLB). Called to the Irish Bar, King's Inns, 1950; called to the English Bar, Gray's Inn, 1956. Asst d'Anglais, Lycée Masséna, Nice, 1949–50; practised at Irish Bar, 1950–53; entered Colonial Legal Service, 1953; Crown Counsel, Nigeria, 1953–59; legal draftsman, Northern Nigeria, 1959–62; Solicitor-Gen., Northern Nigeria, 1962–64; Minister of Govt, Northern Nigeria, 1962; QC (Nigeria) 1962; practised at English Bar, 1965–85; a Recorder, 1978–84; from 1985 lectured throughout English-speaking world on the life and trials of Oscar Wilde, Dr Samuel Johnson and his circle, Talleyrand, Bernard Shaw, Oliver Gogarty; autobiog. lect., Never Listen to an Irishman; Evelyn Wrench Lectr, E-SU of USA, 1988; Vis. Lectr, Broward Community Coll., Fla, 1989; Lecturer: Amer. Irish Historical Soc., NY, 1990; Nat. Portrait Gall., 1991–94; Bournemouth Internat. Festival, QE2, Oxford Univ. E-SU Soc., and Mus. of Modern Art, Oxford, 1992; Shirley Soc., Cambridge Univ., 1993; Centre Culturel Irlandais, Paris, 1994. Hon. Mem., Univ. Philos. Soc., TCD, 1987. *Address:* 53 Stonecrop, Colchester, Essex CO4 5UG. *Club:* Kildare Street and University (Dublin). *Died 4 Aug. 2015.*

NUNNELEY, John Hewlett, MBE 2001; Chairman, AMF Microflight Ltd, 1987–93; *b* Sydney, NSW, 26 Nov. 1922; *o s* of Wilfred Alexander Nunneley and Audrey Mary (*née* Tebbitt); *m* 1st, 1945, Lucia Ceruti (*d* 2011); one *s* one *d*; 2nd, Carolyn Jane (*née* Oxton). *Educ:* Lawrence Sheriff Sch. Served War of 1939–45: Somerset LI, seconded KAR; Abyssinia, Brit. Somaliland, 1942; Burma campaign, 1944–45 (wounded, despatches); Captain and Adjt. Various management posts in aircraft, shipping, printing and publishing industries, 1946–55. Dir of Publicity, Beaverbrook Newspapers, 1955–62; joined BTC, 1962: Chief Publicity Officer, 1962–63; Chief Development Officer (Passenger) BR Bd, 1963–64; Chief Passenger Manager, 1964–69, introd. BR Corporate Identity, 1964 and Inter-City concept, 1965; Pres. and Chm., BR-Internat. Inc., New York, USA, 1966–69; Man. Dir, British Transport Advertising Ltd, 1969–87. Principal Advertising Consultant, Hong Kong Govt, 1981–83. Member: Passenger Co-ordination Cttee for London, 1964–69; Outdoor Advertising Council, 1969–88. Pres., European Fedn of Outdoor Advertising (FEPE), 1984–87 (Life Pres., 1987). Hon. Mem., All-Burma Veterans Assoc. of Japan, 1991–; Chm., Burma Campaign Fellowship Gp, 1996–2002. FRSA; FCILT. Freeman, GAPAN, 1990. Commemorative Medal, Internat. Union of Railways, 1973; City of Paris Medal, 1986. *Publications:* Tales from the King's African Rifles, 1997; (ed) Tales from the Burma Campaign 1942–1945, 1998; (with K. Tamayama) Tales by Japanese Soldiers, 2000; articles on aviation, military and transport subjects. *Recreations:* gliding (FAI Gold C and Two Diamonds), powered flight. *Address:* 6 Ashfield Close, Petersham, Surrey TW10 7AF. *Died 27 July 2013.*

NURSTEN, Prof. Harry Erwin, PhD, DSc; CChem, FRSC; FIFST; FSLTC; Professor of Food Science, Reading University, 1976–92, Professor Emeritus 1992; *s* of Sergius Nursten and Helene Nursten; *m* 1950, Jean Patricia Frobisher. *Educ:* Ilkley Grammar Sch.; Leeds Univ. (BSc 1st Cl. Hons Colour Chemistry, 1947; PhD 1949; DSc 1973). FRIC 1957; FIFST 1972; FSLTC 1986. Bradford Dyers Assoc. Res. Fellow, Dept of Colour Chem. and Dyeing, Leeds Univ., 1949–52; Lectr in Textile Chem. and Dyeing, Nottingham and Dist Tech. Coll., 1952–54; Lectr 1955–65, Sen. Lectr 1965–70, and Reader 1970–76, Procter Dept of Food and Leather Science, Leeds Univ.; Head of Dept of Food Sci., 1976–86, Head of Dept of Food Science and Technology, 1986–89, Head of Sub-Dept of Food Sci., 1989–91, Reading Univ. Res. Associate, Dept of Nutrition, Food Science and Technol., MIT, 1961–62; Visiting Professor: Univ. of Calif, Davis, 1966; Univ. of Zimbabwe, 1994. Chief Examiner, Mastership in Food Control, 1982–90. Pres., Soc. of Leather Technologists and Chemists, 1974–76. Bill Littlejohn Memorial Medallion Lectr, Brit. Soc. of Flavourists, 1974; Sen. Medal, Food Chemistry Gp, RSC, 1996; Distinguished Service Award, SCI, 2011. *Publications:* (ed jtly) Progress in Flavour Research, 1979; (contrib.) Rothe and Kruse, Aroma, Perception, Formation, Evaluation, 1995; (contrib.) Schubert and Spiro, Chemical and Biological Properties of Tea Infusions, 1997; (ed jtly) The Maillard Reaction in Foods and Medicine, 1998; (contrib.) Caffeinated Beverages: health benefits, physiological effects, and chemistry, 2000; (jtly) Capillary Electrophoresis for Food Analysis: method development, 2000; (contrib.) Rothe, Flavour 2000: perception, release, evaluation, formation, acceptance, nutrition/health, 2001; The Maillard Reaction: chemistry, biochemistry, and implications, 2005; (contrib.) Bredie and Petersen, Flavour Science: recent advances and trends, 2006; (jtly) The University of Reading, Department of Dairying: the history of an unusual university department over its first hundred years, 2009; papers mainly in Jl Sci. Food Agric. and Jl Chromatog. *Address:* Department of Food and Nutritional Sciences, School of Chemistry, Food and Pharmacy, University of Reading, Whiteknights, PO Box 226, Reading RG6 6AP. *T:* (0118) 378 6725. *Died 20 Dec. 2011.*

PARLIAMENTARY ARCHIVES

O

OAKLEY, Brian Wynne, CBE 1981; *b* 10 Oct. 1927; *s* of Bernard and Edna Oakley; *m* 1953, Marian Elizabeth (*née* Woolley); one *s* three *d*. *Educ:* Exeter Coll., Oxford (MA). FInstP, FBCS. Telecommunication Res. Establishment, 1950; Head, Industrial Applications Unit, RRE, 1966–69; Head, Computer Systems Branch, Min. of Technology, 1969–72; Head, Res. Requirements Div., DTI, 1972–78; Sec., SRC, later SERC, 1978–83; Dep. Sec., DTI, and Dir, Alvey Programme, 1983–87. Dir, Logica (Cambridge) Ltd. Pres., BCS, 1988. DUniv York, 1988. *Publications:* (with Kenneth Owen) Alvey, 1990. *Recreations:* theatre, sailing. *Address:* 120 Reigate Road, Ewell, Epsom, Surrey KT17 3BX. *T:* (020) 8393 4096. *Died 17 Aug. 2012.*

OAKSEY, 2nd Baron *cr* 1947 (properly **TREVETHIN,** 4th Baron *cr* 1921, **AND OAKSEY); John Geoffrey Tristram Lawrence,** OBE 1985; Racing Correspondent to Daily Telegraph, 1957–94; racing commentator: ITV, 1970–2002; Channel Four Racing, 1984–2002; *b* 21 March 1929; *o s* of 1st Baron Oaksey and 3rd Baron Trevethin and Marjorie (*d* 1984), *d* of late Commander Charles N. Robinson, RN; *S* father, 1971; *m* 1st, 1959, Victoria Mary (marr. diss. 1987), *d* of late Major John Dennistoun, MBE; one *s* one *d*; 2nd, 1988, Rachel Frances Crocker, *d* of late Alan Hunter. *Educ:* Horris Hill; Eton; New College, Oxford (BA); Yale Law School. As an amateur jockey rode more than 200 winners incl. Whitbread Gold Cup and Hennessey Gold Cup on Taxidermist, 1958; 2nd in Grand National on Carrickbeg, 1963; retired 1975. Racing Correspondent: Horse and Hound, 1959–88; Sunday Telegraph, 1960–88; columnist, Racing Post, 1988–90. Director: HTV, 1980–91; Elite Racing Club, 2000–08. Founding Trustee, Injured Jockeys Fund, 1964– (Chm., 1982–2002; Pres., 2002–). JP Malmesbury, 1978–99. *Publications:* History of Steeplechasing (jointly), 1967; The Story of Mill Reef, 1974; Oaksey on Racing, 1991; Mince Pie for Starters (autobiog.), 2003. *Recreations:* ski-ing, riding. *Heir:* *s* Hon. Patrick John Tristram Lawrence, *b* 29 June 1960. *Address:* Hill Farm, Oaksey, Malmesbury, Wilts SN16 9HS. *T:* (01666) 577303, *Fax:* (01666) 577962. *Club:* Brooks's. *Died 5 Sept. 2012.*

OAKSHOTT, Hon. Sir Michael Arthur John, 3rd Bt *cr* 1959, of Bebington, co. Palatine of Chester; *b* 12 April 1932; *yr s* of Baron Oakshott (Life Peer), 1st Bt, MBE and Joan (*née* Withington); *S* brother, 2002; *m* 1st, 1957, Christina Rose Methuen (*née* Banks) (*d* 1985); three *s*; 2nd, 1988, Helen Clare Jones (*née* Ravell) (marr. diss. 1996). *Heir:* *s* Thomas Hendrie Oakshott, *b* 12 June 1959. *Died 20 June 2014.*

OATES, Sir Thomas, Kt 1972; CMG 1962; OBE 1958 (MBE 1946); Governor and Commander-in-Chief of St Helena, 1971–76; *b* 5 Nov. 1917; *er s* of late Thomas Oates, Wadebridge, Cornwall; unmarried. *Educ:* Callington Grammar School, Cornwall; Trinity College, Cambridge (Mathematical Tripos (Wrangler); MA). Admiralty Scientific Staff, 1940–46; HMS Vernon, Minesweeping Section, 1940–42; British Admiralty Delegn, Washington, DC, 1942–46; Temp. Lieut, RNVR. Colonial Administrative Service, Nigeria, 1948–55; seconded to HM Treasury, 1953–55; Adviser to UK Delegn to UN Gen. Assembly, 1954. Financial Sec. to Govt of: British Honduras, 1955–59, Aden, 1959–63; Dep. High Comr, Aden, 1963–67; Permanent Sec., Gibraltar, 1968–69; Dep. Governor, Gibraltar, 1969–71. *Recreation:* reading. *Address:* Windmill Court, St Minver, Wadebridge, Cornwall PL27 6RD. *Clubs:* East India, Devonshire, Sports and Public Schools. *Died 28 June 2015.*

O'BRIEN, Sir Frederick (William Fitzgerald), Kt 1984; QC (Scot.) 1960; Sheriff Principal of Lothian and Borders, 1978–89; Hon. Sheriff at Edinburgh and Paisley, since 1990; *b* 19 July 1917; *s* of Dr Charles Henry Fitzgerald O'Brien and Helen Jane O'Brien; *m* 1950, Audrey Muriel Owen (*d* 2012); two *s* one *d*. *Educ:* Royal High Sch.; Univ. of Edinburgh; MA 1938; LLB 1940. Admitted Faculty o Advocates, 1947. Comr, Mental Welfare Commission o Scotland, 1962–65; Home Advocate Depute, 1964–65 Sheriff-Principal of Caithness, Sutherland, Orkney an Shetland, 1965–75; Interim Sheriff-Principal of Aberdeen Kincardine and Banff, 1969–71; Sheriff Principal of N Strathclyde, 1975–78. Hon. Mem., Sheriffs' Assoc., 1990– Member: Scottish Medical Practices Cttee, 1973–76 Scottish Records Adv. Council, 1974–83; Convener o Sheriffs Principal, 1972–89; Chm., Sheriff Court Rule Council, 1975–81. Chm., Northern Lighthouse Bd 1983–84 and 1986–87. Convener, Gen. Council Busines Cttee, Edinburgh Univ., 1980–84. Hon. Pres., Royal Hig Sch. Former Pupils Club, 1982–92 (Pres. 1975–76); Chm Edinburgh Sir Walter Scott Club, 1989–92. *Recreation*: golf, music. *Address:* 22 Arboretum Road, Edinburgh EH 5PN. *T:* (0131) 552 1923. *Clubs:* New (Edinburgh Bruntsfield Golf (Hon. Mem.); Scottish Bench and Bar Go (former Captain). *Died 29 Dec. 2012*

O'BRIEN, Prof. John W., PhD; Professor of Economic 1965–96, Rector and Vice Chancellor, 1974–84, the Rector Emeritus, Concordia University (incorporatin Loyola College and Sir George Williams Universit Montreal); *b* 4 Aug. 1931; *s* of Wilfred Edmond O'Brie and Audrey Swain; *m* 1956, Joyce Helen Bennett; two *Educ:* McGill Univ., Montreal, Que; BA 1953, MA 195 PhD 1962. Sir George Williams University, Montrea Lectr in Economics, 1954; Asst Prof. of Economics, 195 Associate Prof. of Economics and Asst Dean, 1961; Dea Faculty of Arts, 1963; Vice-Principal (Academic), 1968–6 Principal, 1969–74. Hon. DCL Bishop's, 1976; Hon. LLI McGill, 1976; Concordia, 2004. *Publications:* Canadia Money and Banking, 1964 (2nd edn, with G. Lerme 1969). *Died 16 Dec. 201*

O'BRIEN, Prof. Michael, PhD; FBA 2008; Professor American Intellectual History, University of Cambridg since 2005; Fellow, Jesus College, Cambridge, since 2002; Plymouth, 13 April 1948; *s* of John McCarthy O'Brien ar Lilian Isabella O'Brien; *m* 1969, Patricia Caroline Ma Bacon. *Educ:* Trinity Hall, Cambridge (BA 1969; Ph 1976); Vanderbilt Univ. (MA). Jun. Fellow, Michigan So of Fellows, 1976–79; University of Arkansas: Asst Pro 1980–82; Associate Prof., 1982–85; Prof., 1985–87; Shriv Prof., Miami Univ., Ohio, 1987–2002; University Cambridge: Sen. Mellon Schol., 1993–2002; Lec 2002–03; Reader in American Intellectual Hist., 2003–0 Fellow Commoner, Jesus Coll., 1993–2002. Visiti Professor: Univ. of S Carolina, 1980; Univ. of Alabam 1985. Fellow: Huntington Liby, 1987; Liguria Stu Center, 2008; Mass Histl Soc., 2012. Mem., Ame Antiquarian Soc., 2010. Bancroft Prize, Columbia Uni 2005; Woodward-Franklin Prize, Fellowship of Southe Writers, 2013. *Publications:* The Idea of the Americ South, 1920–1941, 1979; (ed) All Clever Men, Who Ma Their Way: critical discourse in the Old South, 1982; Character of Hugh Legaré, 1985; (ed with D. Moltk Hansen) Intellectual Life in Antebellum Charleston, 198 Rethinking the South: essays in intellectual history, 198 (ed) An Evening When Alone: four journals of sing women in the South, 1827–67, 1993; Conjectures Order: intellectual life and the American Sou 1810–1860, 2 vols, 2004 (Bancroft Prize, Columbia Uni Merle Curti Award, Orgn of American Historians; Hu Holman Award, Soc. for the Study of Southern L Owsley Award, Southern Historical Soc.; Amer. Stud Network Book Prize, Eur. Assoc. for American Studie Henry Adams and the Southern Question, 20 Cosmopolitismo e Località, 2006; Placing the South, 20 Mrs Adams in Winter: a journey in the last days Napoleon, 2010; Intellectual Life and the American Sou 1810–1860: an abridgement of Conjectures of Order, 201 (ed) The Letters of C. Vann Woodward, 2013. *Recreatio* golf, squash, supporting Tottenham Hotspur. *Address:* Je

College, Cambridge CB5 8BL. *T:* (01223) 339317, *Fax:* (01223) 324910. *E:* mo10003@cam.ac.uk. *Club:* Gog Magog Golf. *Died 6 May 2015.*

O'CONNOR, Prof. Daniel John; Professor of Philosophy, University of Exeter, 1957–79, then Emeritus; *b* 2 April 1914; *m* 1st, 1948, Kathleen Kemsley (*d* 2000); no *c*; 2nd, 2003, Maureen Castle. *Educ:* Birkbeck Coll., University of London. Entered Civil Service, 1933; Commonwealth Fund Fellow in Philosophy, University of Chicago, 1946–47; Professor of Philosophy, University of Natal, SA, 1949–51; Professor of Philosophy, University of the Witwatersrand, Johannesburg, 1951–52; Lecturer in Philosophy, Univ. Coll. of North Staffordshire, 1952–54; Professor of Philosophy, University of Liverpool, 1954–57. Visiting Professor, University of Pennsylvania, 1961–62. *Publications:* John Locke, 1952; Introduction to Symbolic Logic (with A. H. Basson), 1953; Introduction to the Philosophy of Education, 1957; A Critical History of Western Philosophy (ed), 1964; Aquinas and Natural Law, 1968; Free Will, 1971; (ed jtly) New Essays in the Philosophy of Education, 1973; The Correspondence Theory of Truth, 1975; various papers in philosophical journals. *Address:* 101a Pennsylvania Road, Exeter EX4 6DT. *Died 12 Aug. 2012.*

O'CONNOR, Rory, CBE 1991; Member, Gibraltar Court of Appeal, 1991–97; Judge of the High Court of Hong Kong, 1977–90; *b* Co. Down, 26 Nov. 1925; *s* of late James O'Connor and Mary (*née* Savage); *m* 1963, Elizabeth, *d* of late Frederick Dew; one *s* two *d*. *Educ:* Blackrock Coll., Dublin; Univ. Coll., Dublin (BCom). Called to Irish Bar, King's Inns, 1949. Resident Magistrate, Kenya, 1956–62; Hong Kong: Magistrate, 1962–70; District Judge, 1970–77. *Address:* 12 Windermere Crescent, Bangor, Co. Down, N Ireland BT20 4QH. *Died 10 Aug. 2015.*

ODDIE, Prof. Guy Barrie; Robert Adam Professor of Architecture, 1968–82, then Emeritus, and Head of Department of Architecture, 1968–80, University of Edinburgh; *b* 1 Jan. 1922; *o s* of Edward Oddie and Eleanor Pinkney; *m* 1952, Mabel Mary Smith (*d* 1990); two step *d*. *Educ:* state schools in London and Co. Durham; King's Coll., Univ. of Durham (later Univ. of Newcastle upon Tyne) (BArch Dunelm). Local Defence Volunteer, later Home Guard, 1939–45; commnd Univ. of Durham STC. Demonstrator, Univ. of Newcastle upon Tyne, 1944–45; Asst, public offices, Glasgow and Coventry, 1945–47; Research Architect, Building Res. Stn, 1947–50; Sen. Lectr, Birmingham Sch. of Architecture, 1950–52; Develt Gp, Min. of Educn, 1952–58; Staff architect, UGC, 1958–63 (designed innovative hall of residence, Reading Univ.); Consultant to OECD, 1963–66; Dir, Laboratories Investigation Unit, DES, 1966–68. Sen. Res. Advr to OECD Prog. on Educnl Bldg, 1972–84. Participant in and advocate for 1950s architectural movement led by school-designers and aimed at producing quality buildings on time, in the number needed and at a politically acceptable cost; involved in campus develt for new univs recommended by Robbins report, 1963. *Publications:* School Building Resources and their Effective Use, 1966; Development and Economy in Educational Building, 1968; Industrialised Building for Schools, 1975; Inspired by Lutyens: a life in and out of architectural practice at the centre of the Post-War Movement (autobiog.), 2010; contrib. Architects Jl, Architectural Rev., RIBA Jl. *Recreations:* slamming political correctness, writing light verse while anticipating promoting sales of my memoirs, yet still revelling in the company of friends. *Address:* 29 The Causeway, Edinburgh EH15 3QA. *Died 29 June 2011.*

ODDY, Christine Margaret; consultant; Lecturer (part-time): in European Union and International Political Economy, Warwick University Open Studies, since 2000; in Financial Studies, London Metropolitan (formerly London Guildhall) University, since 2000; *b* 20 Sept. 1955; *d* of Eric Lawson Oddy and Audrey Mary Oddy. *Educ:* Stoke Park Sch., Coventry; University Coll. London (LLB Hons); Licence Spéciale en droit européen, Inst. d'Etudes européennes, Brussels; Birkbeck Coll., London (MSc (Econ)). Stagiaire (grad. trainee) in EC, 1979–80; Articled Clerk, Clifford Turner, 1980–82; admitted Solicitor, 1982; Lectr in Law, City of London Poly., 1984–89. MEP (Lab) Midlands Central, 1989–94, Coventry and N Warwicks, 1994–99; European Parliament: Member: Legal Affairs Cttee, 1989–99; Social Affairs Cttee, 1989–99; Women's Rights Cttee, 1989–99; Central America Delegn, 1989. Sec., Anti-Racism Wkg Gp, 1989–99, and Treas., Eur. Parly Labour Pty, 1994–99. Contested (Ind.) Coventry NW, 2001. Non-executive Director: Coventry Univ., 2002–; Coventry Refugee Centre, 2002–. Law Soc. rep., Home Office Adv. Gp on Rehabilitation of Offenders Act, 2001–02. Member: RIIA, 1990; Law Soc., 1982 (Mem., Employment Law Cttee); ESU, 1987; Inst. for Employment Rights. Co-Chair, S Asia Assoc. for Regl Co-operation, 1998 (Chair, Saving Sight in S Asia, 1998). Vice Patron, Vocaleyes, 2003–. FRSA 1992. *Recreations:* travel, wine, theatre, cinema. *Address:* 33 Longfellow Road, Coventry CV2 5HD. *T:* (024) 7645 6856. *Died 26 July 2014.*

ODDY, Revel, FSA; Keeper, Department of Art and Archaeology, Royal Scottish Museum, Edinburgh, 1974–83; *b* 11 April 1922; *s* of Sidney Oddy and Muriel Barnfather; *m* 1949, Ariadne Margaret (decd), *d* of late Sir Andrew Gourlay Clow, KCSI, CIE; two *s* two *d*. *Educ:* Worksop Coll.; Pembroke Coll., Cambridge (MA). FSA 1982. Served War, Loyal Regt and King's African Rifles, 1941–46. Mod. langs master, Dr Challoner's Grammar Sch., Amersham, 1949; Res. Asst, V&A Mus., London, 1950–55; Asst Keeper, Royal Scottish Mus., Edinburgh, 1955–74. *Recreations:* mild gardening, reading. *Address:* 44 Findhorn Place, Edinburgh EH9 2NT. *T:* (0131) 667 5815. *Club:* Civil Service. *Died 22 March 2011.*

OGILVIE-LAING of Kinkell, Gerald, NDD; FRBS 1993 (ARBS 1987); sculptor; *b* 11 Feb. 1936; *s* of Gerald Francis Laing and Enid Moody (*née* Foster), and *g s* of Capt. Gerald Ogilvie Laing; adopted name of Ogilvie-Laing by Deed Poll, 1968; *m* 1st, 1962, Jenifer Anne Redway; one *d*; 2nd, 1969, Galina Vassilovna Golikova; two *s*; 3rd, 1988, Adaline Havemeyer Frelinghuysen; two *s*. *Educ:* Berkhamsted Sch.; RMA, Sandhurst; St Martin's Sch. of Art, London (NDD) 1964). Served Royal Northumberland Fusiliers, 1955–60, resigned; lived in NYC, 1964–69; Pop painting, 1962–65, abstract sculpture, 1965–73; Artist in Residence, Aspen Inst., 1966; restored Kinkell Castle, Scotland, 1969–70 (Civic Trust Award, 1971); established Tapestry Workshop, 1970–74; changed to figurative sculpture, 1973. Vis. Prof. of Painting and Sculpture, Univ. of New Mexico, 1976–77; Prof. of Sculpture, Columbia Univ., 1986–87. Installed: Callanish sculpture, Strathclyde Univ., 1971; Frieze of Wise and Foolish Virgins, Edinburgh, 1979; Fountain of Sabrina, Bristol, 1980; Conan Doyle Meml, and Axis Mundi, Edinburgh, 1991; Bank Station Dragons, 1995; four figures on Rowland Hill Gate, Twickenham Rugby Stadium, 1996; St George and Dragon sequence, Harrow, 1996; Cricketer, Wormsley, Bucks, 1998; Fire Icon, Bluewater, Kent, 1999; Glass Virgins, Edinburgh, and Fifth Fusilier Meml, Badajoz, Spain, 2000; Batsman, MCC, Lord's Ground, 2001; Wormsley Sundial, 2001; Falcon Square Mercat Cross, Inverness, 2003; series of anti-war paintings inspired esp. by Iraq conflict, exhibited King's Coll., Cambridge, NY and Paris, 2005, London, 2007 and 2008; Lineout Sculpture, Twickenham Stadium, 2010; frequent exhibitions; work in many public and private collections worldwide, including Tate Gall., V&A, Nat. Portrait Gall., London and Edinburgh, Nat. Gall. (portrait bust of Sir Paul Getty, 1997), Nat. Army Mus., London, Scottish Nat. Gall. of Modern Art, Mus. of Modern Art, NY, Whitney Mus., NY, and Smithsonian Instn. Member: Art Cttee, Scottish Arts Council, 1978–80; Royal Fine Art Commn for Scotland, 1987–95. Chm., Black Isle Civic Trust, 1991–93. *Publications:* Kinkell—the Reconstruction of a Scottish castle, 1974, 2nd edn 1984. *Address:* Kinkell Castle, Ross and Cromarty IV7 8AT. *T:* (01349) 861485. *E:* kinkell@btinternet.com; (London studio) Flat 1, 33 Tite Street, SW3 4JP. *T:* (020) 7378 8538. *Clubs:* Chelsea Arts, Academy, Frontline, Ivy, Groucho. *Died 23 Nov. 2011.*

O'HARA, Bill; JP; National Governor of the BBC for Northern Ireland, 1973–78; *b* 26 Feb. 1929; *s* of William P. O'Hara and Susanna Agnes O'Hara (*née* Gill); *m* 1953, Anne Marie Finn; two *s* two *d*. *Address:* Summer

Cottage, 12 Raglan Road, Bangor, Co. Down, N Ireland BT20 3TL. *Clubs:* Royal Ulster Yacht, Royal Belfast Golf. *Died 10 April 2011.*

O'HARA, Prof. Michael John, PhD; FRS 1981; FRSE 1969; FLSW; Professor of Geology, 1978–93, Hon. Professor, 2004, University of Wales, Aberystwyth; *b* 22 Feb. 1933; *s* of Michael Patrick O'Hara, OBE, and Winifred Dorothy O'Hara; *m* 1st, 1962, Janet Tibbits; one *s* two *d*; 2nd, 1977, Susan Howells; two *s* one *d*. *Educ:* Dulwich Coll. Prep. Sch.; Cranleigh; Peterhouse, Cambridge (MA, PhD). Asst, Lectr, Reader and Prof. (1971), Edinburgh Univ., 1958–78; Dist. Res. Prof., UWCC, 1994–2003. Principal Investigator, NASA Lunar Science Prog., 1968–75; Prof. of Geology, Sultan Qaboos Univ., Oman, 1988–90. Sherman-Fairchild Vis. Scholar, Calif Inst. of Technology, 1984–85; Visiting Professor: Harvard Univ., 1986; North West Univ., Xi'an, 2004; Concurrent Prof., Nanjing Univ., 2004; Honorary Professor: China Inst. of Geoscis, Beijing, 2004; of Geol., Durham Univ., 2005. Member: Council, NERC, 1986–88; UGC, 1987–89. Associate Mem., Geol Soc. of France; Geochemistry Fellow, Geochemical Soc. and Eur. Assoc. for Geochem., 1997; Fellow, Amer. Geophys. Union, 2004; FLSW 2010. Murchison Medal, Geol Soc., 1983; Bowen Award, 1984, Hess Medal, 2007, Amer. Geophys. Union. *Publications:* numerous in learned jls. *Recreations:* mountaineering, postal history. *Died 24 Nov. 2014.*

OLINS, Wallace, (Wally), CBE 1999; MA Oxon; FCSD; Founder, Wolff Olins; Chairman, Saffron Brand Consultants, London, Madrid, New York and Mumbai, since 2001; *b* 19 Dec. 1930; *s* of Alfred Olins and Rachel (*née* Muscovitch); *m* 1st, 1957, Maria Renate Olga Laura Steinert (marr. diss. 1989); two *s* one *d*; 2nd, 1990, Dornie Watts; one *d*. *Educ:* Highgate Sch.; St Peter's Coll., Oxford (Hons History, MA; Hon. Fellow 2012). National Service, Army, in Germany, 1950–51. S. H. Benson Ltd, London, 1954–57; Benson, India, 1957–62; Caps Design Group, London, 1962–65; Wolff Olins, London, 1965–2001. Vis. Lectr, Design Management, London Business Sch., 1984–89; Visiting Professor, Management School: Imperial Coll., 1987–89; Lancaster Univ., 1992–; Visiting Professor: Copenhagen Business Sch., 1993–; DUXX (formerly Centro de Excelencia Empresarial), Mexico, 1995–2002; Saïd Business Sch., Oxford Univ., 2002–. Non-exec. Dir, HEA, 1996–99; Dir, Glasgow Year of Design and Architecture, 1999. Vice-Pres., SIAD, 1982–85. Chm., Design Dimension Educnl Trust, 1987–93; Mem. Devlt Trust, RPO, 1994–99. Mem., Council, RSA, 1989–95. Bicentenary Medal, RSA, 2000; D&AD President's Award, 2003. *Publications:* The Corporate Personality, 1978; The Wolff Olins Guide to Corporate Identity, 1983; The Wolff Olins Guide to Design Management, 1985; Corporate Identity, 1989; International Corporate Identity, vol. 1, 1995; The New Guide to Identity, 1996; Trading Identities, 1999; On Brand, 2003; The Brand Handbook, 2008; Brand New: the shape of brands to come, 2014; numerous articles in Design and Management publications. *Recreations:* looking at buildings, shopping for books, theatre. *Address:* 3 Holford Yard, WC1X 9HD. *W:* www.wallyolins.com. *Died 14 April 2014.*

OLIVE, Prof. David Ian, CBE 2002; FRS 1987; Research Professor of Physics, University of Wales Swansea (formerly University College of Swansea), 1994–2002, then Emeritus Professor; *b* 16 April 1937; *s* of Ernest Edward Olive and Lilian Emma Olive (*née* Chambers); *m* 1963, Jenifer Mary Tutton; two *d*. *Educ:* Royal High Sch., Edinburgh; Univ. of Edinburgh (MA); Univ. of Cambridge (BA, PhD). Fellow of Churchill Coll., 1963–70; Lectr, Univ. of Cambridge, 1965–71; Staff Mem., CERN, 1971–77; Imperial College: Lectr, 1977; Reader, 1980; Prof. of Theoretical Physics, 1984–92; Res. Prof. of Maths, Univ. Coll. of Swansea, 1992–94. Visiting Professor: Univ. of Virginia, 1982–83; Univ. of Geneva, 1986; Inst. for Advanced Studies, Princeton, 1987–88; Newton Inst. for Math. Scis, Cambridge, 1992, 1997; Kramers Prof., Univ. of Utrecht, 2000. Founding FLSW 2010. Foreign Mem., Royal Soc. of Arts and Scis, Göteborg, 2007. Dirac Medal and Prize, Abdus Salam Internat. Centre for Theoretical Physics, Trieste, 1997. *Publications:* (jtly) The Analytic S-Matrix, 1966; (jtly) Kac-Moody and Virasoro Algebras, 1988; (jtly) Paul Dirac: the man and his work, 1998; many articles on theoretical physics in learned jls. *Recreation:* listening to music. *Address:* 63 King's Grove, Barton, Cambs CB23 7AZ. *Died 7 Nov. 2012.*

OLIVER, Prof. Michael Francis, CBE 1985; MD; FRCP, FRCPEd, FFPH; FRSE; Duke of Edinburgh Professor of Cardiology, University of Edinburgh, 1979–89, Emeritus Professor, 1990; *b* Borth, Aberystwyth, 3 July 1925; *s* of late Captain Wilfrid Francis Lenn Oliver, MC (DLI), and Cecilia Beatrice Oliver (*née* Daniel, later Leishman); *m* 1st, Margaret Yool Abbey (marr. diss.); two *s* one *d* (and one *s* decd); 2nd, 1985, Helen Louise Daniel (*d* 2014). *Educ:* Marlborough Coll.; Univ. of Edinburgh (MB, ChB 1947, MD (Gold Medal) 1957). FRSE 1987. General Practice in Leith, 1948–50. Edinburgh University: Consultant Physician, Royal Infirmary and Sen. Lectr in Medicine, 1961; Reader in Medicine, 1973; Personal Prof. of Cardiology, 1977; Dir, Wynn Inst. for Metabolic Res., 1989–93; Hon. Prof., Nat. Heart and Lung Inst., 1989–93. Fellow, Rockefeller Inst., NY, 1969. Dist. Res. Fellow, Imperial Coll., London, 2000–. Sen. Ed., European Jl Clin. Investigation, 1968–75. Ext. Examr, Univs of Cambridge, Wales, Leeds and Dundee, 1970–85. Mem., Cardiovascular Panel, Govt Cttee on Medical Aspects of Food Policy, 1971–74, 1982–84; UK Rep. Mem., Adv. Panel for Cardiovascular Disease, WHO, 1972–2001; Chm., BBC-Medical Adv. Gp in Scotland, 1975–81; Mem. Scientific Bd, Internat. Soc. of Cardiology, 1968–78 (Chm., Council on Atherosclerosis and Ischaemic Heart Disease, 1968–75); Chairman: Brit. Atherosclerosis Discussion Gp, 1970–75; Science Cttee, Fondation Cardiologique Princess Lilian, Belgium, 1976–85; MoT Panel on driving and cardiovascular disease, 1985–90; Jt Cttee on Higher Medical Training, 1987–90. Convener, Cardiology Cttee, Scottish Royal Colls, 1978–81; Council Mem., Brit. Heart Foundn, 1976–85. Pres., British Cardiac Soc., 1981–85; Pres., RCPEd, 1986–88. FESC 1986. Hon. FRCPI 1988; Hon. FRACP 1988. Bishop Lectr and Fellow, 1968, Hon. Fellow, 1973, Amer. Coll. of Cardiology. Hon. MD: Karolinska Inst., Stockholm, 1980; Univ. Bologna, 1985. Purkinje Medal, 1981; Polish Cardiac Soc. Medal, 1984; Lifetime Achievement Award, Scottish Cardiac Soc., 2011; Cullen Prize and Medal, RCPE, 2012. *Publications:* Acute Myocardial Infarction, 1966; Intensive Coronary Care, 1970, 2nd edn 1974; Effect of Acute Ischaemia on Myocardial Function, 1972; Modern Trends in Cardiology, 1975; High-Density Lipoproteins and Atherosclerosis, 1978; Coronary Heart Disease in Young Women, 1978; Strategy for Screening of Coronary Heart Disease, 1986; 425 contribs to sci. and med. jls on causes of coronary heart disease, biochemistry of fats, myocardial metabolism, mechanisms of sudden death, clinical trials of drugs, and population studies of vascular diseases. *Recreations:* Italy and the italians, art history, 20th century English painting, writing. *Address:* Keepier Wharf, 12 Narrow Street, E14 8DH. *T:* (020) 7790 4203. *Clubs:* Athenæum, Garrick; Medical Pilgrims. *Died 7 June 2015.*

OLIVER, Prof. Roland Anthony, MA, PhD (Cantab); FBA 1993; Professor of the History of Africa, London University, 1963–86; *b* Srinagar, Kashmir, 30 March 1923; *s* of late Major D. G. Oliver and Lorimer Janet (*née* Donaldson); *m* 1st, 1947, Caroline Florence (*d* 1983), *d* of late Judge John Linehan, KC; one *d*; 2nd, 1990, Suzanne Doyle, *widow* of Brig. Richard Miers. *Educ:* Stowe; King's Coll., Cambridge. Attached to Foreign Office (Bletchley Park), 1942–45; R. J. Smith Research Studentship, King's Coll., Cambridge, 1946–48; Lecturer, School of Oriental and African Studies, 1948–58, Hon. Fellow, 1992; Reader in African History, University of London, 1958–63. Francqui Prof., University of Brussels, 1961; Visiting Professor: Northwestern Univ., Illinois, 1962; Harvard Univ., 1967; travelled in Africa, 1949–50 and 1957–58; org. international Conferences on African History and Archæology, 1953–61. President: African Studies Assoc., 1967–68; British Inst. in Eastern Africa, 1981–93. Vice-Pres., Royal African Soc., 1965– (Mem. Council, 1959–65); Mem., Perm. Bureau, Internat. Congress of Africanists, 1973–78; Chm., Minority Rights Group, 1973–91. Corresp. Member, Académie Royale des Sciences d'Outre-Mer, Brussels. Editor (with J. D. Fage) Jl of African

History, 1960–73. Haile Selassie Prize Trust Award, 1966; Distinguished Africanist Award: American African Studies Assoc., 1989; African Studies Assoc. of UK, 2004. *Publications:* The Missionary Factor in East Africa, 1952; Sir Harry Johnston and the Scramble for Africa, 1957; (ed) The Dawn of African History, 1961; (with J. D. Fage) A Short History of Africa, 1962; (ed with Gervase Mathew) A History of East Africa, 1963; (with A. E. Atmore) Africa since 1800, 1967; (ed) The Middle Age of African History, 1967; (with B. M. Fagan) Africa in the Iron Age, 1975; (with A. E. Atmore) The African Middle Ages, 1400–1800, 1981; The African Experience, 1991; In the Realms of Gold: pioneering in African history, 1997; (with A. E. Atmore) Medieval Africa, 2001; Gen. Editor (with J. D. Fage), Cambridge History of Africa, 8 vols, 1975–86. *Address:* Frilsham Woodhouse, Thatcham, Berks RG18 9XB. *T:* (01635) 201407. *Died 9 Feb. 2014.*

OLLERENSHAW, Dame Kathleen (Mary), DBE 1971; DL; MA, DPhil; FIMA, FCP, CMath; Chairman, Council for St John Ambulance in Greater Manchester, 1974–89; Member, Manchester City Council, 1956–81, Leader of Conservative Opposition, 1977–80; Alderman, 1970–74, Hon. Alderman since 1981; Lord Mayor, 1975–76, Deputy Lord Mayor, 1976–77; *b* 1 Oct. 1912; *d* of late Charles Timpson, JP, and late Mary Elizabeth Timpson (*née* Stops); *m* 1939, Robert Ollerenshaw (*d* 1986); (one *s* decd one *d* decd). *Educ:* Ladybarn House Sch., Manchester; St Leonard's Sch., St Andrews; (open schol. in maths) Somerville Coll., Oxford (BA (Hons) 1934, MA 1943, DPhil 1945; Hon. Fellow, 1978). Foundation Fellow, Institute of Mathematics and its Applications (FIMA), 1964 (Mem. Council, 1973–94, Vice-Pres., 1976–77, Pres., 1978–79; Hon. Fellow 1986). Research Assistant, Shirley Institute, Didsbury, 1937–40. Hon. Res. Fellow, Dept of Computer Sci., Univ. of Manchester, 1999–2003. Chairman: Educn Cttee, Assoc. of Municipal Corporations, 1968–71; Assoc. of Governing Bodies of Girls' Public Schs, 1963–69; Manchester Educn Cttee, 1967–70 (Co-opted Mem., 1954–56); Manchester Coll. of Commerce, 1964–69; Council, Science and Technology Insts, 1980–81; first Chm., Court, Royal Northern Coll. of Music, Manchester, 1971–86 (CRNCM 1978); Member: Central Adv. Council on Educn in England, 1960–63; CNAA, 1964–74; SSRC, 1971–75; Tech. Educn Council, 1973–75; (Vice-Pres.) British Assoc. for Commercial and Industrial Educn (Mem. Delegn to USSR, 1963); Exec., Assoc. of Educn Cttees, 1967–71; Nat. Adv. Council on Educn for Industry and Commerce, 1963–70; Gen. Adv. Council of BBC, 1966–72; Schools Council, 1968–71; Management Panel, Burnham Cttee, 1968–71; Nat. Foundn of Educnl Res., 1968–71; Layfield Cttee of Inquiry into Local Govt Finance, 1974–76; Court, Univ. of Salford, 1967– (Mem. Council, 1967–89; a Pro-Chancellor, 1983–89); Court, Univ. of Manchester, 1964–; Manchester Polytechnic, 1968–86 (first Chm., 1969–72; Dep.-Chm., 1972–75; Hon. Fellow, 1979); Court, UMIST, 1971–87 (Vice-Pres., 1976–86; Hon. Fellow, 1987); Court, Lancaster Univ., 1991– (Mem. Council, 1975–91; a Dep. Pro-Chancellor, 1978–91); Council, CGLI, 1972–84 (Hon. Fellow, 1978; Vice-Pres., 1979–84); Rep. Governor, Royal Coll. of Advanced Technol., Salford, 1959–67; Governor: St Leonard's Sch., St Andrews, 1950–72 (Pres., 1980–2003); Manchester High Sch. for Girls, 1959–69; Ladies' Coll., Cheltenham, 1966–68; Chetham's Hosp. Sch., Manchester, 1967–77; Further Educn Staff Coll., Blagdon, 1960–74. Sen. Res. Fellow (part-time), 1972–75, Hon. Res. Fellow, 1975–77, Lancaster Univ.; Hon. Res. Fellow, Dept of Computer Science, Univ. of Manchester, 1998–2001. Member: Manchester Statistical Soc., 1950– (Mem. Council, 1977–; Vice-Pres., 1977, Pres., 1981–83); Manchester Astronomical Soc., 1990– (Hon. Vice-Pres., 1994–); Hon. Member: Manchester Technology Assoc., 1976– (Pres., 1982); Manchester Literary and Philosophical Soc., 1982–; Hon. Col, Manchester and Salford Univs OTC, 1977–81; Mem., Mil. Educn Cttee, 1979–. Dir, Greater Manchester Independent Radio, Ltd, 1972–83. Winifred Cullis Lecture Fellow to USA, 1965; Fourth Cockroft Lecture, UMIST and Manchester Tech. Assoc., 1977. DL Greater Manchester, 1987. Hon. LLD CNAA, 1975; Hon. DSc Salford, 1975; Hon LLD Manchester, 1976; Hon. DSc Lancaster, 1992; Hon. LLD Liverpool, 1994. Freeman of the City of Manchester, 1984. Mancunian of the Year, Jun. Chamber of Commerce, 1977; Pick of the Year, BBC Woman's Hour, 2004. DStJ 1983 (CStJ 1978) (Mem., Chapter Gen., 1974–96). Catherine Richards Award, IMA, 2006. *Publications:* Education of Girls, 1958; Education for Girls, 1961; The Girls' Schools, 1967; Returning to Teaching, 1974; The Lord Mayor's Party, 1976; First Citizen, 1977; (with Prof. David Brée) Most-Perfect Pandiagonal Magic Squares: their construction and enumeration, 1998; To Talk of Many Things (autobiog.), 2004; Constructing Magic Squares of Arbitrarily Large Size, 2006; papers in mathematical journals, 1945–54 and 1977–, incl. Proc. RI 1981 (on form and pattern), Phil. Trans Royal Soc. 1982 (on magic squares), and Proc. Royal Soc. 1986 (on pandiagonal magic squares); articles on education and local govt in national and educational press. *Recreations:* research mathematics, astronomy. *Address:* 2 Pine Road, Didsbury, Manchester M20 6UY. *T:* (0161) 445 2948. *Club:* English-Speaking Union. *Died 10 Aug. 2014.*

O'LOGHLEN, Sir Colman (Michael), 6th Bt *cr* 1838; *b* 6 April 1916; *s* of Henry Ross O'Loghlen (*d* 1944), 6th *s* of 3rd Bt, and of Doris Irene, *d* of late Major Percival Horne, RA; *S* uncle, 1951; *m* 1939, Margaret, *d* of Francis O'Halloran, Melbourne, Victoria; six *s* two *d*. *Educ:* Xavier Coll., Melbourne; Melbourne Univ. (LLB). Formerly Captain AIF. Sometime Magistrate and Judge of Supreme Court, PNG. *Heir: s* Michael O'Loghlen, *b* 21 May 1945. *Died 6 March 2014.*

OLSEN, Noel David Lyche, FRCP, FFPH; independent consultant public health physician, since 1996; Chairman, Alcohol Education and Research Council, UK, 2002–08; *b* 20 Jan. 1946; *s* of Frank Olsen and late Dora (*née* Wyatt); *m* 1982, Nicky Tewson; two *d*. *Educ:* Mill Hill Sch.; St George's Hosp. Med. Sch. (MB BS 1969); London Sch. of Hygiene and Tropical Medicine (MSc 1978); Henley Mgt Coll. MRCP 1972, FRCP 1993; MFPHM 1979, FFPH (FFPHM 1986). Instructor, Outward Bound Trust, and Watch Officer, Sail Trng Schooner, Malcolm Miller, (intermittent periods) 1966–75; jun. med. posts at St George's Hosp., the Brompton Hosp., Edinburgh Univ. and Royal Free Hosp., 1969–74; Consultant Chest Physician, Barking, London, 1974–76; Sen. Registrar and Lectr, LSHTM and KCH Med. Sch., 1977–79; Dist Community Physician, Cambridge, 1979–82; Dist MO, Hampstead HA, 1982–91; Dir, Public Health, Plymouth, 1991–95. Hon. Associate Lectr, Univ. of Cambridge, 1979–82; Hon. Sen. Lectr, Royal Free Hosp. Sch. of Medicine, 1982–92; Sen. Vis. Res. Fellow, Plymouth Univ., 1994–96. Temp. Consultant Advr, Poverty and Health, WHO, Geneva and Bangladesh, 1999. Member: Nat. Taskforce for Physical Activity, DoH, 1993–96; Air Quality Strategy Forum, DEFRA, 1998–2010; Fuel Poverty Adv. Gp, DEFRA/DTI, then DECC, 2002–. Chm., Public Health Medicine Consultative Cttee, UK, 1994–98; Mem., Jt Consultants' Cttee, 1994–98. Hon. Sec., Internat. Agency on Tobacco and Health, 1991–2010. Mem. Council, 1993–98, Mem., Bd of Sci., 1994–2002, BMA; Mem. Cttee, BMJ, 1995–2002. Chm., WaterVoice SW, 2001–06. Nat. Hon. Sec., ASH, 1975–94; Chm., Policy Cttee, Alcohol Concern, 1987–90; Trustee, Nat. Heart Forum, 1988– (Nat. Hon. Sec., 1988–94). Ind. Gov., Univ. of Plymouth, 2006–11. Hon. DH Plymouth, 2011. Inaugural Gold Medal, RSPH, 2008. *Publications:* Smoking Prevention: a health promotion guide for the NHS, 1980; contrib. articles on medical audit, preventive medicine, social, envmtl and health policy, fuel poverty and health effects of inequality. *Recreations:* sailing, ski-ing, family. *Address:* Oakdale, Courtwood, Newton Ferrers, Devon PL8 1BW. *T:* (01752) 873054. *Clubs:* Royal Ocean Racing; Yealm Yacht (Newton Ferrers). *Died 2 Sept. 2013.*

OLVER, Sir Stephen (John Linley), KBE 1975 (MBE 1947); CMG 1965; HM Diplomatic Service, retired; *b* 16 June 1916; *s* of late Rev. S. E. L. Olver and Mrs Madeleine Olver (*née* Stratton); *m* 1953, Maria Morena, Gubbio, Italy; one *s*. *Educ:* Stowe. Indian Police, 1935–44; Indian Political Service, Delhi, Quetta, Sikkim and Bahrain, 1944–47; Pakistan Foreign Service, Aug.–Oct. 1947; Foreign Service, Karachi, 1947–50; Foreign Office, 1950–53; Berlin,

1953–56; Bangkok, 1956–58; Foreign Office, 1958–61; Washington, 1961–64; Foreign Office, 1964–66; The Hague, 1967–69; High Comr, Freetown, 1969–72; High Comr, Nicosia, 1973–75. *Recreations:* photography, painting. *Address:* 6 Saffrons Court, Compton Place Road, Eastbourne, Sussex BN21 1DX. *Died 22 June 2011.*

O'NEILL, Prof. Patrick Geoffrey, BA, PhD; Professor of Japanese, School of Oriental and African Studies, University of London, 1968–86, then Emeritus; *b* 9 Aug. 1924; *m* 1951, Diana Howard; one *d*. *Educ:* Rutlish Sch., Merton; Sch. of Oriental and African Studies, Univ. of London. Lectr in Japanese, Sch. of Oriental and African Studies, Univ. of London, 1949. Vis. Prof., Univ. of Michigan, 1961–62. Chm., Organizing Cttee, Eur. Assoc. for Japanese Studies, 1973 (Sec., 1974–79); Pres., British Assoc. for Japanese Studies, 1980–81. First Sakura Award, Nihon Zenkoku Gakushikai, 1976. Order of the Rising Sun (Japan), 1987. *Publications:* A Guide to Nō, 1954; Early Nō Drama, 1958; (with S. Yanada) Introduction to Written Japanese, 1963; A Programmed Course on Respect Language in Modern Japanese, 1966; Japanese Kana Workbook 1967; A Programmed Introduction to Literary-style Japanese, 1968; Japanese Names, 1972; Essential Kanji, 1973; (ed) Tradition and Modern Japan, 1982; (with H. Inagaki) A Dictionary of Japanese Buddhist Terms, 1984; A Reader of Handwritten Japanese, 1984; (trans.) Japan on Stage, by T. Kawatake, 1990; annotated plate supplement, in H. Plutschow, Matsuri, 1996; P. G. O'Neill—Collected Writings, 2001. *Died 19 Jan. 2012.*

ONSLOW, 7th Earl of, *cr* 1801; **Michael William Coplestone Dillon Onslow;** Bt 1660; Baron Onslow, 1716; Baron Cranley, 1776; Viscount Cranley, 1801; *b* 28 Feb. 1938; *s* of 6th Earl of Onslow, KBE, MC, TD, and Hon. Pamela Louisa Eleanor Dillon (*d* 1992), *o d* of 19th Viscount Dillon, CMG, DSO; *S* father, 1971; *m* 1964, Robin Lindsay, *o d* of Major Robert Lee Bullard III, US Army, and of Lady Aberconway; one *s* two *d*. *Educ:* Eton; Sorbonne. Life Guards, 1956–60, served Arabian Peninsula. Farmer. Governor, Royal Grammar Sch., Guildford; formerly Governor, University Coll. at Buckingham. High Steward of Guildford. Mem., Communications Select Cttee, H of L. Elected Mem., H of L, 1999. *Heir: s* Viscount Cranley, *b* 16 June 1967. *Address:* Temple Court, Clandon Park, Guildford, Surrey GU4 7RQ. *Clubs:* Garrick, Beefsteak. *Died 14 May 2011.*

ORD, Andrew James B.; *see* Blackett-Ord.

O'REILLY, Francis Joseph; Chancellor, University of Dublin, Trinity College, 1985–98 (Pro-Chancellor, 1983–85; Hon. Fellow, 1999); Chairman, Ulster Bank Ltd, 1982–89 (Deputy Chairman, 1974–82; Director, 1961–90); Director, National Westminster Bank, 1982–89; *b* 15 Nov. 1922; *s* of Lt-Col Charles J. O'Reilly, DSO, MC, MB, KSG and Dorothy Mary Martin; *m* 1950, Teresa Mary, *e d* of Captain John Williams, MC; three *s* seven *d*. *Educ:* St Gerard's Sch., Bray; Ampleforth Coll., York; Trinity Coll., Dublin (BA, BAI). Served HM Forces, RE, 1943–46. John Power & Son, 1946–66 (Dir, 1952–66, Chm., 1955–66); Chm., Player & Wills (Ire.) Ltd, 1964–81; Chm., 1966–83, Dir, 1983–88, Irish Distillers Gp. President: Marketing Inst. of Ireland, 1983–85; Inst. of Bankers in Ireland, 1985–86. President: Equestrian Fedn of Ireland, 1963–79; Royal Dublin Soc., 1986–89 (Mem. Cttees, 1959–80; Chm. of Soc., 1980–86); Chm., Collège des Irlandais, Paris, 1987–2000. Hon. Life Delegate, Fédn Equestre Internationale, 1979–. MRIA 1987–. LLD *hc:* Univ. of Dublin, 1978; NUI, 1986. GCLJ 1992. KCSG 2001. *Recreations:* fox-hunting, racing, gardening. *Address:* Rathmore, Naas, Co. Kildare, Ireland. *T:* (45) 862136. *Clubs:* Kildare Street and University (Dublin); Irish Turf (The Curragh, Co. Kildare). *Died 11 Aug. 2013.*

ORMEROD, Alec William; Deputy Judge and Prison Adjudicator, 2003–08; *b* 19 July 1932; *s* of William and Susan Ormerod; *m* 1976, Patricia Mary Large. *Educ:* Nelson Grammar Sch.; Christ's Coll., Cambridge (Major Scholar; MA, LLM). Solicitor. Mil. Service, Staff of GOC London Dist, 1956–58. Asst Lectr in Law, Burnley Coll., 1953–55; Local Govt Service, 1958–64; Sen. Partner, Boyle and Ormerod, Solicitors, Aylesbury, 1964–88; Metropolitan Stipendiary Magistrate then Dist Judge (Magistrates' Cts), 1988–2003; Chm., Family Ct, 1991–2003; AJAG, 1996–2003; Judge, Summary Appeals Ct, 2000–03. Councillor, Aylesbury Borough Council, 1966–72. Freeman, City of London, 1973. *Publications:* A Judge's Jottings, 2009; The Duo, 2010. *Recreations:* travel, fine art, gardening. *Address:* 7 The Cloisters, Long Street, Sherborne, Dorset DT9 3BS. *Club:* Naval and Military. *Died 22 Nov. 2011.*

ORR, Dr James Henry; consultant in forensic psychiatry, 1982–98; *b* 2 Feb. 1927; *s* of Hubert Orr and Ethel Maggs; *m* 1950, Valerie Elizabeth Yates; two *s* one *d*. *Educ:* Bristol Grammar Sch.; Bristol Univ. (MB, ChB 1955). DPM; FRCPsych. Enlisted, 1944; commnd RE, 1947; demobilised, 1949. Hosp. appts, 1955–56; gen. practice, 1956–58; Medical Officer, HM Prison: Leeds, 1958; Winchester, 1962; Lincoln, 1966; SMO, Leeds, 1967; Asst Dir, Prison Med. Services, 1973; Dir, Prison Med. Services, and Mem., Prisons Bd, 1976–82; Mem., Parole Bd, 1983–86. *Recreation:* gardening. *Died 7 Oct. 2014.*

ORR-EWING, Hamish; Chairman, Rank Xerox Ltd, 1980–86; *b* 17 Aug. 1924; *o s* of Hugh Eric Douglas Orr-Ewing and Esme Victoria (*née* Stewart), Strathgarry, Killiecrankie, Perthshire; *m* 1st, 1947, Morar Margaret Kennedy; one *s* (one *d* decd); 2nd, 1954, Ann Mary Teresa Terry. *Educ:* Heatherdown, Ascot; Eton. Served War, Captain Black Watch. Salesman, EMI, 1950; Ford Motor Co., 1954; Ford Light Car Planning Manager, 1959–63; Leyland Motor Corp. Ltd, 1963–65; joined Rank Xerox, 1965; apptd to Bd as Dir of Product Planning, 1968; Dir of Personnel, 1970; Man. Dir, Rank Xerox (UK) Ltd, 1971; Reg. Dir for Rank Xerox Ops in UK, France, Holland, Sweden and Belgium, 1977; Chairman: Jaguar plc, 1984–85; White Horse Hldgs, 1987–91; Dir, Tricentrol PLC, 1975–86. Chairman: Work and Society, 1982–85; European Govt Business Relations Council, 1980–84; Member: MSC, 1983–85; Engrg Council, 1984–87; Envmt Awards Panel, RSA, 1987–94; President: Inst. of Manpower Studies, 1986–89; Inst. of Training and Develt, 1987–89. CBI: Member: Bd, Educn Foundn (UBI), 1982–87; Council, 1985–87; Chm., Educn and Trng Cttee, 1985–87. Trustee: Shaw Trust, 1985– (Pres., 2003–09); Roman Res. Trust, 1990–97. Governor: Interphil, 1985–94; New Coll., Swindon, 1984–95 (Chm. of Govs, 1986–92); Bradon Forest Sch., 1989–92. CCMI (CBIM 1981). *Recreations:* anything mechanical, country life, the Roman Empire. *Address:* Fox Mill Farm, The Fox, Purton, near Swindon, Wilts SN5 4EF. *T:* (01793) 770496. *Died 17 Nov. 2015.*

ORSON, Rasin Ward, CBE 1985; FIET; consultant; Member, The Electricity Council, 1976–89; *b* 16 April 1927; *s* of Rasin Nelson Orson and Blanche Hyre; *m* 1st, 1950, Marie Goodenough; two *s*; 2nd, 1979, Lesley Jean Vallance. *Educ:* Stratford Grammar Sch.; London School of Economics (BScEcon 1948). Asst Statistician, Min. of Civil Aviation, 1948, Statistician, 1953; Electricity Council: Head of Economics and Forecasting Branch, 1963; Dep. Commercial Adviser, 1968; Commercial Adviser, 1972. Dir, Chloride Silent Power, 1974–89. *Recreations:* music, photography. *Address:* The Old Garden, Dunorlan Park, Tunbridge Wells, Kent TN2 3QA. *T:* (01892) 524027. *Died 9 Nov. 2011.*

ORTIZ DE ROZAS, Carlos; career diplomat, retired; Professor of International Relations, University of Belgrano, Buenos Aires, since 1995; *b* 26 April 1926; *m* 1952, María del Carmen Sarobe (decd). *Educ:* School of Diplomacy, Min. of Foreign Affairs, Buenos Aires (grad. 1949). Lawyer, Faculty of Law, Univ. of Buenos Aires, 1950. Entered Argentine Foreign Service, 1948; served Bulgaria, Greece, UAR and UK (Minister); Ambassador to Austria, 1967–70; Permanent Rep. to UN, 1970–77; Pres. UN Security Council, 1971–72; Chairman: First (Polit. and Security) Cttee of 29th Gen. Assembly, 1974; Preparatory Cttee of Special Session on Disarmament, 1977–78; Cttee on Disarmament, Geneva, 1979; Mem. Adv. Bd on Disarmament Studies, New York, 1978–92; Ambassador to UK, 1980–82; Head, Argentine Special Mission to the Holy See, 1982–83; Ambassador to France, 1984–89; Dep. Foreign Minister, 1990; Ambassador to USA, 1991–93; retd Foreign Service, 1994. Universidad del Salvador, Buenos

Aires: Prof. of History and Constitutional Law, and Prof. of Political Science, Faculty of Law, 1958–80; Prof. of Internat. Relations, School of Political Sciences, and at School of Diplomacy, 1962–80. Mem. Bd of Dirs, Bunge and Born SA, 1995–99; President: Bunge and Born Foundn, 1994–99; Alliance Française, Buenos Aires, 2000–02. Mem., Nat. Acad. of Moral and Political Scis, 2005. Holds many foreign decorations incl. Grand Cross, Order of Pius IX, 1985, and Commandeur, Légion d'Honneur, 1985. *Publications:* Confidencias diplomáticas, 2011. *Address:* Gelly y Obes 2263, 1425 Buenos Aires, Argentina. *Clubs:* Jockey, Círculo de Armas, Club Francés (Buenos Aires). *Died 13 March 2014.*

OSBORN, Sir John (Holbrook), Kt 1983; scientist, soldier, industrialist and politician; *b* 14 Dec. 1922; *s* of late Samuel Eric Osborn and Aileen Decima, *d* of Colonel Sir Arthur Holbrook, KBE, MP; *m* 1st, 1952, Molly Suzanne (*née* Marten) (marr. diss.); two *d*; 2nd, 1976, Joan Mary MacDermot (*née* Wilkinson) (*d* 1989); 3rd, 1989, Patricia Hine (*née* Read). *Educ:* Rugby; Trinity Hall, Cambridge (Part 2 Tripos in Metallurgy; MA); Diploma in Foundry Technology, Nat. Foundry Coll., 1949. Served in Royal Corps of Signals, 1943–47 (West Africa, 1944–46; Captain); served in RA (TA) Sheffield, 1948–55, Major. Joined 1947, and Technical Dir, 1951–79, Samuel Osborn & Co. Ltd, and associated companies. Chairman, Hillsborough Divisional Young Conservative and Liberal Association, 1949–53. MP (C) Hallam Div. of Sheffield, 1959–87 (NL and U, 1959–64); PPS to the Secretary of State for Commonwealth Relations and for the Colonies, 1963–64. Chairman: Cons. Parly Transport Cttee, 1970–74; Anglo-Swiss Parly Gp, 1981–87; (or Vice-Chm.) Anglo-Soviet Parly Gp, 1968–87; Vice Chm., Parly and Scientific Cttee, 1963–66, 1982 (Officer, 1959–87; Life Mem., 1987); Jt Sec., 1922 Cttee, 1968–87; Member: Science and Technol. Select Cttee, 1970–73; Educn, Science and Arts Select Cttee, 1979–83; Chm., All Party Channel Tunnel Gp, 1985–87; Individual Mem., Parly Gp for Energy Studies, 1987 (Chm., 1985–87; Vice-Chm., Cons. Parly Energy Cttee, 1979–81). Mem., UK Delegn to Council of Europe and WEU, 1973–75, 1980–87 (Hon. Associate, Council of Europe, 1987, WEU, 1990); Council of Europe: Vice Chm., Science and Technol. Cttee, 1981–87; Chm., Eur. Scientific Contact Gp, 1982–87. Chm., Econ. Affairs and Develt Sub-Cttee (North/South: Europe's role), 1985–87. Mem., European Parlt, 1975–79. Life Member, British Branch: CPA, 1987 (Mem., 1959–87); IPU, 1987 (Mem. Exec., 1968–75, 1979–83). Mem. Council, European Atlantic Gp, 1990. Mem., Interim (formerly Voluntary) Licensing Authy, MRC/RCOG, 1987–91. Chairman: Friends of Progress, 1989–95; Business and Develt Cttee, UK Chapter, Soc. for Internat. Develt, 1990–95. Mem., RIIA, 1985–. Freeman Co. of Cutlers in Hallamshire, 1987 (Asst Searcher, 1951–65; Searcher, 1965–70 and 1973–87). Fellow, Institute of British Foundrymen, 1948–72 (Member Council, Sheffield Branch, 1954–64); FIMMM (FIM 1986; MISI 1947); Fellow, Institute of Directors; Member Council: Sheffield Chamber of Commerce, 1956–89 (Hon. Life Mem., 1989); Assocs British Chambers of Commerce, 1960–62 (Hon. Secretary, 1962–64); British Iron and Steel Res. Association, 1965–68; CBI and Yorks and WR Br., CBI, 1968–79; Industrial Soc., 1963–79 (Life Mem.). Hon. Patron, Sheffield Inst. of Advanced Motorists, 1996– (Pres., 1960–96); Chm., H of C Motor Club, 1979–84. Mem., Court and Council Sheffield Univ., 1951–79. Trustee: Talbot Trust, 1950–98; Zackery Merton Trust, 1951–2002 (Chm., 1988–98). FRSA 1966. Travelled widely in business and politics. *Recreations:* golf, photography, gardening, walking. *Clubs:* Carlton, Royal Over-Seas League. *Died 2 Dec. 2015.*

OSBORNE, Denis Gordon, CMG 1990; adviser on governance and development, since 1992; *b* 17 Sept. 1932; *s* of A. Gordon Osborne and Frances A. Osborne (*née* Watts); *m* 1970, Christine Susannah, *d* of P. Rae Shepherd and C. Elaine Shepherd; two *d*. *Educ:* Dr Challoner's Grammar Sch., Amersham; University Coll., Durham (BSc 1st Cl. Hons Physics, PhD). FInstP 1966. Lectr in Physics, Univ. of Durham, 1957; Lectr, Fourah Bay Coll., Sierra Leone, 1957–58; Lectr, 1958–63, Sen. Lectr, 1963–64, Univ. of Ghana; Reader in Physics, 1964–66, Prof., 1966–71, Dean of Science, 1968–70, Univ. of Dar es Salaam; Res. Fellow, UCL, 1971–72; Cons. for World Bank missions to Malaysia and Ethiopia, 1971, 1972; Overseas Development Administration: Multilateral Aid Dept, 1972–75; Mediterranean and Near East Dept, 1975–77; Sci. and Technology Dept, 1977–80; Hd of Dept in Natural Resources Div., 1980–84; Hd of E and W Africa Dept, 1984–87; HM Diplomatic Service, High Comr in Malaŵi, 1987–90; RIPA Internat., 1990–92. Reader, C of E, 1975–, at local parish church, 1980–. *Publications:* Way Out: some parables of science and faith, 1977; research papers on develt, corruption and governance, and until 1978 on geophysics, particularly the equatorial ionosphere and envmt. *Address:* The Arc, North Elham, Canterbury CT4 6NH. *E:* do@governance.org.uk. *Club:* Athenæum. *Died 3 Sept. 2014.*

OSTROM, Prof. Elinor, PhD; Arthur F. Bentley Professor of Political Science, since 1991, Distinguished Professor, since 2010, and Senior Research Director, Workshop in Political Theory and Policy Analysis, since 2009, Indiana University, Bloomington; *b* Los Angeles, 7 Aug. 1933; *d* of Adrian Awan and Leah Awan (*née* Hopkins); *m* 1963, Vincent Ostrom. *Educ:* Beverly Hills High Sch., Calif; Univ. of Calif, Los Angeles (BA Hons Pol Sci. 1954; MA Pol Sci. 1962; PhD Pol Sci. 1965). Employment Interviewer and Asst Employee Relns Manager, Godfrey L. Cabot, Inc., Boston, Mass, 1955–57; Personnel Analyst III, UCLA, 1957–61; Indiana University: Vis. Asst Prof., 1965–66, Asst Prof. and Graduate Advr, 1966–69, Dept of Govt; Associate Prof., 1969–74, Prof., 1974–91, Chair, 1980–84, Actg Chair, 1989–90, Dept of Pol Sci.; Co-Director: Workshop in Pol Theory and Policy Analysis, 1973–2009; Center for Study of Instns, Popn and Envmtl Change, 1996–2006; Prof. (pt-time), Sch. of Public and Envmtl Affairs, 1984–. Founding Dir, Center for Study of Instnl Diversity, Arizona State Univ., Tempe, 2006–. Member: Adv. Panel for Div. of Policy Res. and Analysis, 1977–78, Pol Sci. Panel, 1983–84, Panel on Instnl Develt, 1985, Nat. Sci. Foundn; Panel on Common Property Resource Mgt, 1985–86, Cttee on Nat. Urban Policy, 1985–88, Scientific Cttee on Problems of Envmt, 1995–98, NAS/Nat. Res. Council; Local Govt Res. Adv. Bd, US Adv. Commn on Intergovtl Relns, 1985–88; Res. Adv. Cttee, US Agency for Internat. Develt, 1989–91; Adv. Bd, Inst. for Policy Reform, 1993–96; Cttee on Human Dimensions of Global Change, NAS, 1997–2000; Bd of Dirs, Beijer Internat. Inst. of Ecol Econs, 1997–2001; Cttee on Grand Challenges in Envmtl Scis, Nat. Res. Council, 1998–2000; Scientific Adv. Bd, Max-Planck Inst. for Res. on Collective Goods, 2000–09; Scientific Cttee, Internat. Human Dimensions of Global Change Prog., 2000–05; Bd of Advrs, Inst. of Mathematical Econs, Univ. of Bielefeld, 2002–06; Div. Cttee for Behavioral and Social Scis and Educn, Nat. Academies, 2003–04; Expert Gp on Develt Issues, Min. of For. Affairs, Sweden, 2003–04; Nat. Adv. Bd, Long Term Ecol Res. Network, 2005–07; Scientific Cttee, Regl Develt Proj., FAO/Regl Office for Latin America, 2005–06; Ext. Adv. Cttee for Strategic Assessment, Sch. of Natural Resources and Envmt, Univ. of Michigan, 2005–07; Acad. Adv. Council, Romanian Center for Instnl Analysis and Develt, 2006–; Bd of Dirs, Stockholm Resilience Centre, 2007–10; Bd of Sci., Resilience Alliance, 2000–. Fellow: Amer. Acad. of Arts and Scis, 1991; Amer. Acad. of Pol and Social Sci., Philadelphia, 2008; FAAAS 2001; MNAS 2001; Mem., Amer. Philosophical Soc., 2006; Beijer Fellow, Beijer Inst. of Ecol Econs, Stockholm, 2007. Member: Amer. Pol Sci. Assoc.; Assoc. for Pols and Life Scis; Internat. Assoc. for Study of Common Property; Midwest Pol Sci. Assoc.; Phi Beta Kappa Soc.; Policy Studies Orgn; Public Choice Soc.; Resilience Alliance. Hon. Dr Econs Zurich, 1999; Hon. Dr: Inst. of Social Studies, The Hague, 2002; Luleå Univ. of Technol., 2005; in Commemoration of Carl Linnaeus, Uppsala, 2007; Humboldt, Berlin, 2007; McGill, 2008; Norwegian Univ. of Sci. and Technol., Trondheim, 2008; Dr of Humane Letters Michigan, 2006. Donald Campbell Award, 1986, Miriam Mills Award, 1996, Thomas R. Dye Service Award, 1997, Policy Studies Orgn; Harold and Margaret Sprout Award, Internat. Studies Assoc., 1992; Frank E. Seidman Dist. Award in Pol Econ., 1997; Johan Skytte Prize in Pol Sci., Uppsala Univ., 1999; John J. Carty Award, NAS, 2004; James Madison Award, 2005, William

Riker Award, 2006, Amer. Pol Sci. Assoc.; Cozzarelli Prize, Procs of NAS, 2006; William H. Riker Prize, Univ. of Rochester, NY, 2008; Galbraith Award, Amer. Agricl Econs Assoc., 2008; Jonathan M. Tisch Prize, Tufts Univ., 2009; (jtly) Nobel Prize for Economics, 2009; Sagamore of Wabash Award, State of Indiana, 2009; Univ. Medal, Indiana Univ., 2010. *Publications:* (jtly) Community Organization and the Provision of Police Services, 1973; (ed) The Delivery of Urban Services: outcomes of change, 1976; (jtly) Policing Metropolitan America, 1977; (jtly) Patterns of Metropolitan Policing, 1978; (jtly) Basic Issues in Police Performance, 1982; (ed) Strategies of Political Inquiry, 1982; (jtly) Il governo locale negli Stati Uniti, 1984; (jtly) Local Government in the United States, 1988; Governing the Commons: the evolution of institutions for collective action, 1990; Crafting Institutions for Self-Governing Irrigation Systems, 1992; (jtly) Institutional Incentives and Sustainable Development: infrastructure policies in perspective, 1993; (ed jtly) From Farmers' Fields to Data Fields and Back: a synthesis of participatory information systems for irrigation and other resources, 1994; (jtly) Rules, Games and Common-Pool Resources, 1994; (ed with Robert Keohane) Local Commons and Global Interdependence: heterogeneity and cooperation in two domains, 1995; (ed jtly) Competition and Cooperation: conversations with Nobelists about economics and political science, 1999; (ed jtly) People and Forests: communities, institutions and governance, 2000; (ed jtly) Institutions, Ecosystems and Sustainability, 2001; (ed jtly) Protecting the Commons: a framework for resource management in the Americas, 2001; (ed with Ganesh Shivakoti) Improving Irrigation Governance and Management in Nepal, 2002; (ed jtly) The Drama of the Commons, 2002; (ed with James Walker) Trust and Reciprocity: interdisciplinary lessons from experimental research, 2003; (ed with Nives Dolšak) The Commons in the New Millennium: challenges and adaptations, 2003; (ed with T. K. Ahn) Foundations of Social Capital, 2003; Understanding Institutional Diversity, 2005; (ed with Emilio Moran) Seeing the Forest and the Trees: human-environment interactions in forest ecosystems, 2005; (jtly) The Samaritan's Dilemma: the political economy of development aid, 2005; (ed jtly) Asian Irrigation in Transition: responding to challenges, 2005; (ed jtly) Linking the Formal and Informal Economy: concepts and policies, 2006; (ed with Charlotte Hess) Understanding Knowledge as a Commons: from theory to practice, 2007; (jtly) Working Together: collective action, the commons and multiple methods in practice, 2010; contrib. articles in many learned jls. *Recreation:* growing flowering plants. *Address:* Workshop in Political Theory and Policy Analysis, Indiana University, 513 North Park Avenue, Bloomington, IN 47408–3895, USA. *T:* (812) 8550441, *Fax:* (812) 8553150. *E:* ostrom@indiana.edu. *Died 12 June 2012.*

O'SULLEVAN, Sir Peter (John), Kt 1997; CBE 1991 (OBE 1977); Racing Correspondent: Daily Express, 1950–86; Today, 1986–87; BBC Television Commentator, 1946–97; *b* 3 March 1918; *o s* of late Col John Joseph O'Sullevan, DSO, formerly Resident Magistrate, Killarney, and Vera, *o d* of Sir John Henry, DL, JP; *m* 1951, Patricia (*d* 2009), *o d* of Frank Duckworth, Winnipeg, Manitoba, Canada. *Educ:* Hawtreys; Charterhouse; Collège Alpin, Switzerland. Specialised in ill-health in early life and not accepted for fighting forces in 1939–45 war, during which attached to Chelsea Rescue Services. Subsequently worked for John Lane, the Bodley Head, on editorial work and MSS reading. Joined Press Assoc. as Racing Correspondent, 1945, until appointed Daily Express, 1950, in similar capacity. Race-broadcasting 1946–97 (incl. Australia, S Africa, Italy, France, USA); in 1953 became first regular BBC TV and horse-racing commentator to operate without a race-reader; commentated: first television Grand National, 1960; world's first televised electronic horse race from Atlas computer at Univ. of London, transmitted by BBC TV Grandstand, 1967; first horse race transmitted live via satellite, from NY, to invited audience in London, 1980; completed 50th Grand National broadcast, 1997. Director: Internat. Racing Bureau, 1979–93; Racing Post Ltd, 1985–95. Mem., Jockey Club, 1986–. Chm., Osborne Studio Gall., 1999–. Patron: Brooke Hosp. for Animals; Internat. League for Protection of Horses; Thoroughbred Rehabilitation Centre. Derby Award for Racing Journalist of the Year, 1971 (with late Clive Graham), 1986; Racehorse Owner of the Year Award, Horserace Writers' Assoc., 1974; Clive Graham Meml Award for services to racing, Press Club, 1978, 1985; Evening News Sports Commentator of the Year, 1978; William Hill Golden Spurs for services to racing, 1985; Par Excellence Award, Racing Club of Ireland, 1993; Sport on TV Award, Daily Telegraph, 1994; Media Award, Variety Club of GB, 1995; Services to Racing Award, Daily Star, 1995; Lesters Award, Jockeys' Assoc., 1996; TV Sports Award, RTS, 1996; George Ennor Trophy, Horserace Writers and Photographers Assoc., 1997; Special Award, TRIC, 1998. *Publications:* Calling the Horses: a racing autobiography, 1989; Peter O'Sullevan's Horse Racing Heroes, 2004; Calling the Horses: a racing autobiography, 25 years on, 2014. *Recreations:* racehorse owning, in minor way (happiest broadcasting experience commentating success of own horses, Be Friendly, 1966–67, and Attivo, 1974); travel, reading, art, food and wine. *Address:* 37 Cranmer Court, SW3 3HW. *T:* (020) 7584 2781. *Died 29 July 2015.*

OSWALD, Adm. of the Fleet Sir (John) Julian (Robertson), GCB 1989 (KCB 1987); Director, Marine and General Mutual Life Insurance (International), 2004–08; *b* 11 Aug. 1933; *s* of George Hamilton Oswald and Margaret Elliot Oswald (*née* Robertson), Newmore, Invergordon; *m* 1958, Veronica Therese Dorette Thompson; two *s* three *d*. *Educ:* Beaudesert Park, Minchinhampton; Britannia RNC, Dartmouth. Junior Officer, 1951; served in HM Ships Devonshire, Vanguard, Verulam, Newfoundland, Jewel, Victorious, Naiad; specialised in Gunnery, 1960; Commanded HMS Yarnton, 1962–63, HMS Bacchante, 1971–72; MoD, 1972–75; RCDS, 1976; Commanded HMS Newcastle, 1977–79; RN Presentation Team, 1979–80; Captain, Britannia RNC, 1980–82; ACDS (Progs), 1982–84; ACDS (Policy and Nuclear), 1985; Flag Officer, Third Flotilla, and Comdr, Anti-Submarine Warfare, Striking Fleet, 1985–87; C-in-C, Fleet, Allied C-in-C, Channel, and C-in-C, E Atlantic, 1987–89; First Sea Lord and Chief of Naval Staff, and First and Principal Naval ADC to the Queen, 1989–93. Chairman: Aerosystems Internat., 1995–2005; Green Issues Communications, 1999–2008; non-exec. Dir, Marine and Gen. Mutual Life Insurance, 1994–2006. Vice-Chm., S and W RHA, 1993–96. Vice President: RUSI, 1992–; World Ship Trust, 1997–; Mem., European Atlantic Gp, 1988–. Chairman: Nat. Historic Ships Cttee, 1995–2004; Ends of the Earth, 1996–2004; Maritime Trust, 1994–2006; Naval Rev., 1999–2006. Trustee, Nat. Maritime Mus., 1995–2004. President: Jellicoe Sea Cadets, Newcastle, 1979–96; Invergordon Br., RBL, 1992–; Assoc. of Royal Naval Officers, 1993–2003; Sea Cadet Assoc., 1994–2003; Trident Trust, 1993–2003; Officers' Assoc., 1994–2003; Frinton Soc., 1993–99. Member: Mensa, 1964–84; Catholic Union, 1987–. Book reviewer for various publications. FRSA 1995. Hon. Mem., Krewe Rex, New Orleans, 1990. Hon. DBA CNAA, 1992; Hon. LLD Portsmouth, 2000. *Publications:* The Royal Navy—Today and Tomorrow, 1993; articles on strategy and defence policy. *Recreations:* walking, stamp collecting, family, fishing. *Address:* c/o Naval Secretary, Fleet Headquarters, Whale Island, Portsmouth PO2 8BY. *Died 19 July 2011.*

O'TOOLE, (Seamus) Peter; actor; *b* 2 Aug. 1932; *s* of Patrick Joseph O'Toole; *m* 1960, Siân Phillips, CBE (marr. diss. 1979); two *d*; *m* 1983, Karen Brown (marr. diss.); one *s*. *Educ:* Royal Academy of Dramatic Art. With Bristol Old Vic Company, 1955–58; first appearance on London stage as Peter Shirley in Major Barbara, Old Vic, 1956. Associate Dir, Old Vic Co., 1980. *Plays include:* Oh, My Papa!, Garrick, 1957; The Long and the Short and the Tall, Royal Court and New, 1959; season with Shakespeare Memorial Theatre Company, Stratford-on-Avon, 1960; Baal, Phœnix, 1963; Hamlet, National Theatre, 1963; Ride a Cock Horse, Piccadilly, 1965; Juno and the Paycock, Man and Superman, Pictures in the Hallway, Gaiety, Dublin, 1966; Waiting for Godot, Happy Days (dir.), Abbey, Dublin, 1969; Uncle Vanya, Plunder, The Apple Cart, Judgement, Bristol Old Vic, 1973; Uncle Vanya, Present Laughter, Chicago, 1978; Macbeth, Old Vic, 1980; Man and Superman, Haymarket, 1982; Pygmalion, Shaftesbury,

1984, Yvonne Arnaud, Guildford, and NY, 1987; The Apple Cart, Haymarket, 1986; Jeffrey Bernard is Unwell, Apollo, 1989, Shaftesbury, 1991, Old Vic, 1999; Our Song, Apollo, 1992. *Films include:* Kidnapped, 1959; The Day They Robbed the Bank of England, 1959; The Savage Innocents, 1960; Lawrence of Arabia, 1962; Becket, 1963; Lord Jim, 1964; What's New, Pussycat, 1965; How to Steal a Million, 1966; The Bible… in the Beginning, 1966; The Night of the Generals, 1967; Great Catherine, 1968; The Lion in Winter, 1968; Goodbye Mr Chips, 1969; Brotherly Love, 1970; Murphy's War, 1971; Under Milk Wood, 1971; The Ruling Class, 1972; Man of La Mancha, 1972; Rosebud, 1975; Man Friday, 1975; Foxtrot, 1975; The Stunt Man, 1977; Coup d'Etat, 1977; Zulu Dawn, 1978; Power Play, 1978; The Antagonists, 1981; My Favorite Year, 1981; Supergirl, 1983; Club Paradise, 1986; The Last Emperor, 1987; High Spirits, 1988; Creator, 1990; King Ralph, 1991; Wings of Fame, 1991; Rebecca's Daughters, 1992; Fairytale: the true story, 1997; Bright Young Things, 2003; Troy, 2004; Lassie, 2005; Venus, 2006; Dean Spanley, 2008; *television:* Rogue Male, 1976; Strumpet City, 1979; Masada, 1981; Svengali, 1982; Pygmalion, 1983; Kim, 1983; Banshee, 1986; The Dark Angel, 1989; Civvies, 1992; Coming Home (serial), 1998; Casanova, 2005. Hon. Academy Award, 2003. *Publications:* Loitering With Intent: the Child (autobiog.), 1992; Loitering With Intent: the Apprentice (autobiog.), 1996. *Address:* c/o Steve Kenis & Co., Royalty House, 72–74 Dean Street, W1D 3SG. *Club:* Garrick. *Died 14 Dec. 2013.*

OVERBURY, (Henry) Colin (Barry), CBE 1993 (OBE (mil.) 1974); independent lecturer in EC Law, 1993–2007; Consultant in EC Law, Allen & Overy, Solicitors, 1993–2007; *b* 13 Jan. 1931; *s* of Daisy Victoria and step *s* of Stanley Overbury; *m* 1st, 1954, Dawn Rhodes Dade (marr. diss. 1981); three *s*; 2nd, 1989, Louise Jane Rosewarne. *Educ:* Dragon Sch., Oxford; Eastbourne Coll.; Law Society's Coll. of Law. Admitted Solicitor of the Supreme Court, 1955. HM Army Legal Services, 1955–74: progressively, Captain, Major, Lt-Col; Retired List, Lt-Col, 1974. European Commission: Prin. Administrator, 1974–82; Adviser, 1982–84; Hd of Div., 1984–86; Dir, Directorate-Gen. for Competition, 1986–93, retd; Hon. Dir Gen., 1993. Sen. Fellow of the Salzburg Seminar, 1984. *Publications:* articles in Common Market Law Rev., 1977, Fordham Univ. Law Inst. Jl, 1984, 1989. *Recreations:* travel, boating, good living. *Club:* Lansdowne. *Died 23 March 2015.*

OVEREND, Prof. (William) George; Professor of Chemistry in the University of London, 1957–87, then Professor Emeritus; Master, Birkbeck College, 1979–87 (Vice-Master, 1974–79; Hon. Fellow, 1988); *b* 16 Nov. 1921; *e s* of late Harold George Overend, Shrewsbury, Shropshire; *m* 1949, Gina Olava, *y d* of late Horace Bertie Cadman, Birmingham; two *s* one *d*. *Educ:* Priory School, Shrewsbury; Univ. of Birmingham (BSc (Hons) 1943; PhD 1946; DSc 1954). CChem; FRSC (FRIC 1955); CSci 2004. Asst Lecturer, Univ. Coll., Nottingham, 1946–47; Research Chemist with Dunlop Rubber Co. Ltd and subsequently British Rubber Producers' Assoc., 1947–49; Hon. Research Fellow, 1947–49, Lecturer in Chemistry, 1949–55, Univ. of Birmingham; Vis. Associate Prof., Pennsylvania State Univ., 1951–52; Reader in Organic Chemistry, Univ. of London, 1955–57; Hd of Dept of Chem., Birkbeck Coll., London, 1957–79. Univ. of London: Mem., Academic Council, 1963–67, 1976–79 and 1984–87; Mem., Collegiate Council, 1979–87; Mem., University Entrance and Schools Examination Council, 1966–67 and 1985–87; Mem., F and GP Cttee, 1976–87; Mem., External Cttee, 1984–87; Chm., Bd of Studies in Chemistry, 1974–76; Mem., Senate, 1976–87; Mem., Jt Cttee of Court and Senate for collective planning, 1976–79; Dean, Faculty of Science, 1978–79; Chm., Acad. Adv. Bd in Sci., 1978–79; Mem., Extra-Mural Council, 1979–87, Chm., 1983–84; Chm., Cttee for Extra-Mural Studies, 1984–87. Mem. Council, Inst. of Educn, 1979–82; Leverhulme Emeritus Fellow, 1987–89. Mem., Lewisham Council for Tertiary Educn, 1980; Member Council: National Inst. of Adult Continuing Educn, 1983–88; London and E Anglian Gp for GCSE, 1986–87; Mem. Chem. Bd, 1981–84, Mem. Adv. Bd on Credit Accumulation and Transfer, 1986–87, CNAA. Rep. of South Bank Poly., Assoc. of Colls of Further and Higher Educn, 1981–91. Royal Institute of Chemistry: Examiner, 1958–62; Assessor, 1959–72; Mem., Institutions and Examinations Cttee, 1969–75 (Chm., 1976–85); Mem. Council, 1977–80; Mem. Qual. and Admissions Cttee, 1977–80; Mem. Qual. and Exam. Bd, RSC, 1980–85; Chemical Society (subseq. Royal Society of Chemistry): Mem. Council, 1967–70, 1972–77; Mem. Publications Bd, 1967–78; Hon. Sec. and Hon. Treasurer, Perkin Div., 1972–75; Vice-Pres., 1975–77; Mem., Interdivisional Council, 1972–75; Mem., Educn and Trng Bd, 1972–78; Soc. of Chemical Industry: Mem., Council, 1955–65; Mem., Finance Committee, 1956–65; Mem., Publications Cttee, 1955–65 (Hon. Sec. for publications and Chairman of Publications Committee, 1958–65); Member: Brit. Nat. Cttee for Chemistry, 1961–66, 1973–78; Brit. Nat. Cttee for Biochemistry, 1975–81; Chemical Council, 1960–63 and 1964–69 (Vice-Chm. 1964–69); European Cttee for Carbohydrate Chemists, 1970–85 (Chm.); Hon. Sec., Internat. Cttee for Carbohydrate Chemistry, 1972–75 (Pres., 1978–80); Mem., Jt IUPAC-IUB Commn on Carbohydrate Nomenclature, 1971–. Jubilee Memorial Lecturer, Society of Chemical Industry, 1959–60; Lampitt Medallist, Society of Chemical Industry, 1965; Member: Pharmacopœia Commission, 1963–81; Home Office Poisons Board, 1973–94. Governor: Polytechnic of the South Bank, 1970–91 (Chm., 1980–89; Chm., Audit Cttee, 1989–91; Hon. Fellow 1989); Thomas Huxley Coll., 1971–77; Mem., Council of Governors, Queen Elizabeth Coll., Univ. of London, 1983–85. Mem., Cttee of Management, Inst. of Archaeology, 1980–86. FCMI (FBIM 1988). Hon. FCollP 1986. DUniv Open, 1988. *Publications:* The Use of Tracer Elements in Biology, 1951; papers in Nature, and Jl of Chemical Soc. *Recreation:* gardening (rose grower). *Address:* The Retreat, Nightingales Lane, Chalfont St Giles, Bucks HP8 4SR. *Clubs:* Athenæum, Royal Automobile. *Died 18 Sept. 2012.*

OWEN, Alun, MC 1945; Under-Secretary, Land Use Planning Group, Welsh Office, 1975–79; *b* 14 March 1919; *s* of Evan Thomas Owen and Gwladys Owen (*née* David); *m* 1946, Rhona Evelyn Griffiths; one *s* four *d*. *Educ:* West Monmouth Grammar Sch.; Bridgend Grammar Sch.; LSE (BScEcon). Mil. Service, 1939–46: Ches. Regt, 1940–46 (Captain) (despatches, Normandy, 1944). Civil Service, Min. of Labour NW Region, 1946–48; Min. of Fuel and Power, 1948–50; Customs and Excise, 1950–59; Welsh Office, Min. of Housing and Local Govt, 1959–62; Welsh Bd of Health, 1962–69; Welsh Office, 1969–79. *Address:* 12 Knowbury Avenue, Penarth, South Glam CF64 5RX. *Died 23 March 2012.*

OWEN, Prof. John V.; *see* Vallance-Owen.

OWENS, John Ridland; artist; Chairman, Owens Associates, independent consultancy specialising in strategic advice and government relations, 1993–2004; *b* 21 May 1932; *s* of Dr Ridland Owens and late Elsie Owens; *m* 1st, 1958, Susan Lilian (*née* Pilcher); two *s* one *d*; 2nd, 1985, Cynthia Rose (*née* Forbes); one *s*. *Educ:* Merchant Taylors' Sch.; St John's Coll., Oxford (MA). National Service, RA (Lieut), 1951–52. ICI, 1955–67; Managing Dir, Cape Asbestos Fibres, 1967–73; Dir Gen., Dairy Trade Fedn, 1973–83; Dep. Chm., Assilec, Paris, 1973–83; Exec. Dir, Nat. Dairy Council, 1975–83; Dep. Dir Gen., CBI, 1983–90; Dir Gen., Building Employers Confederation, 1990–92; Dir, UK Skills Ltd, 1990–92. Chm., Haringey Healthcare NHS Trust, 1993–99. Vice-Chm., EEC Adv. Cttee on Milk and Milk Products; Member: Food and Drink Industry Council, 1973–83; RSA Industry Cttee for Industry Year, 1986; Council, Assoc. of Business Sponsorship of the Arts, 1985–94; Exec. Cttee, PRO NED, 1983–90; Council, CBI, 1990–92; NHS Supplies Policy Steering Gp, 1995–97; Mem. Trust Council, 1995–97, Chm., Procurement and Facilities Mgt Gp, 1995–97, NAHAT, then NHS Confedn. Member: Council, CGLI, 1988–93; Court, City Univ., 1988–2005. Founder: Stokesley Soc.; Civic Trust for NE; Nat. Mus. of Dairying. FRSA (Mem. Council, 1995–2001). Mem. Court, Merchant Taylors' Co., 1982 (Master, 2002–03, First Upper Warden, 2007–08); Freeman, Painter Stainers' Co., 2005. Governor: Merchant Taylors' Sch., 1996–2005 (Vice-Chm. Govs, 1999–2005); Middx Univ., 1999–2002.

Member: Armed Forces Art Soc., 2005–; Painters Fine Art Soc., 2005–. Practising painter-etcher; paintings and etchings based upon drawings made on the spot. *Publications:* Marketing for the NHS—Putting Patients First, 1993; Strategic Procurement for the NHS: working with suppliers, 1996; articles for The Times Review of Industry. *Recreations:* painting, etching, walking. *W:* www.johnowensgallery.com. *Club:* Reform.
Died 8 March 2014.

OXFORD AND ASQUITH, 2nd Earl of, *cr* 1925; **Julian Edward George Asquith,** KCMG 1964 (CMG 1961); Viscount Asquith, *cr* 1925; Governor and Commander-in-Chief, Seychelles, 1962–67; Commissioner, British Indian Ocean Territory, 1965–67; *b* 22 April 1916; *o s* of late Raymond Asquith and Katharine Frances (*d* 1976), *d* of late Sir John Horner, KCVO; *S* grandfather, 1928; *m* 1947, Anne Mary Celestine, CStJ (*d* 1998), *d* of late Sir Michael Palairet, KCMG; two *s* three *d*. *Educ:* Ampleforth; Balliol Coll., Oxford (Scholar), 1st Class Lit. Hum., 1938. Lieut, RE, 1941; Assistant District Commissioner, Palestine, 1942–48; Dep. Chief Secretary, British Administration, Tripolitania, 1949; Director of the Interior, Government of Tripolitania, 1951; Adviser to Prime Minister of Libya, 1952; Administrative Secretary, Zanzibar, 1955; Administrator of St Lucia, WI, 1958. KStJ. *Heir: s* Viscount Asquith, *b* 24 Aug. 1952. *Address:* The Manor House, Mells, Frome, Somerset BA11 3PN. *T:* (01373) 812324. *Club:* Naval and Military. *Died 16 Jan. 2011.*

P

PACKER, Jane, (Mrs G. Wallis); floral artist; Founder and Chair, Jane Packer Ltd, since 1982; *b* 22 Sept. 1959; *d* of Maurice and Brenda Packer; *m* 1990, Gary Wallis; one *s* one *d*. First Jane Packer Flowers shop opened James St, London W1, 1981; stores opened in NY, Seoul and Tokyo, 2001; estabd Jane Packer Flower Sch., London, 1989, sister sch. in Minato-ku, Tokyo, 1990. Consultant, M&S Horticulture, 1987–; designer Marks and Spencer Garden, Hampton Court Flower Show, 1991 (award from RHS), 1992 (award from RHS), 1993 (Gold Medal), 1994 (Gold Medal), 1995 (Gold Medal), 1996 (Gold Medal), 1997 (Gold Medal), 1998 (Silver Medal); Silver Medal, RHS Hampton Court, 2010. Lecture tours in Europe, USA, Japan and UK. Prince Philip Medal, C&G, 2005. *Publications:* Celebrating with Flowers, 1986; Flowers For All Seasons, 4 books, Spring, Summer, Autumn, Winter, 1989; New Flower Arranging, 1993; Complete Guide to Flower Arranging, 1995, 10th edn 2005; Living With Flowers, 1996, 2nd edn 1997; Fast Flowers, 1998, 5th edn 2005; Flowers, Design, Philosophy, 2000, 3rd edn 2005; World Flowers, 2003, 2nd edn 2006; Colour, 2007; Flower Course, 2008; At Home with Flowers, 2011. *Recreations:* family, garden, cooking. *Address:* Jane Packer Ltd, 32–34 New Cavendish Street, W1G 8UE. *T:* (020) 7935 0787. *Died 9 Nov. 2011.*

PACKSHAW, Robin David; Chairman, International City Holdings, Money and Securities Brokers, 1985–89; *b* 20 March 1933; *s* of late Savil Packshaw and Fay Mary Packshaw; *m*; three *s* one *d*. *Educ:* Diocesan Coll., Cape Town; Bradfield Coll., Berks. Served RM, 1951–53; commnd and served in Special Boat Service; RMFVR, 1953–58. Iraq Petroleum Co. Ltd, 1953–63; Long Till and Colvin Ltd, 1963–69; founded Packshaw & Associates Ltd, Sterling Money Brokers, 1969, became Fulton Packshaw Ltd, 1973; Chairman: Charles Fulton (UK) Ltd, Internat. For. Exch. and Currency Deposit Brokers, 1982; Manex Sterling Brokers Ltd, 1993; Consultant: BITC, 1990–92; London First, 1992–93; Sterling, then Sterling Internat., Brokers Ltd, 1993–99. Dep. Chm., Partners in the Countryside, 1996–2001. Chm., Radionic Assoc., 1991–99. Chm., Stours Br., N Dorset Conservation Assoc., 1989–95. Church Warden, All Saints, Stour Row, Dorset, 1984–95. Gov., Stour Provost Co. Primary Sch., 1992–95. Freeman, City of London, 1983; Life Mem., Guild of Freemen of City of London. FZS 1972; FRGS 1997; FRSA 1997. Hon. Fellow, Radionic Assoc., 1999. *Recreations:* travel, people, voluntary work. *Address:* 5 Hurlingham Court, Ranelagh Gardens, SW6 3SH. *T:* (020) 7736 6832. *Died 19 May 2011.*

PAGE, Maj.-Gen. John Humphrey, CB 1977; OBE 1967; MC 1952; *b* 5 March 1923; *s* of late Captain W. J. Page, JP, Devizes and Alice Mary Page (*née* Richards); *m* 1956, Angela Mary Bunting; three *s* one *d*. *Educ:* Stonyhurst. Commnd into RE, 1942; served in NW Europe, India, Korea, Middle East and UK, 1942–60; Instr, Staff Coll., Camberley, 1960–62; comd 32 Armd Engr Regt, 1964–67; idc 1968; CCRE 1st Br. Corps, 1969–70; Asst Comdt, RMA Sandhurst, 1971–74; Dir of Personal Services (Army), MoD, 1974–78, retd. Col Comdt, RE, 1980–85. Dir, London Law Trust, 1979–88. Dir, RBM (Holdings), 1980–86. Member Council: REOWS, 1980–92 (Chm., 1990–92; Chm. Investment Cttee, 1990–95); Officers' Pension Soc., 1979–96; Vice-Chm., SSAFA, 1983–87. Chm. Trustees, Home-Start Consultancy, 1982–90; Mem., Management Cttee, Stackpole Trust, 1981–92; Chm. for Wilts, Winged Fellowship Trust, 1997–2000; Chm., The Trust For Devizes, 1999–2002. Chm., Bd of Governors, St Mary's Sch., Shaftesbury, 1985–93 (Trustee, St Mary Sch. Shaftesbury Trust, 1990–99); Mem., Bd of Governors, Stonyhurst Coll., 1980–90 (Trustee, Stonyhurst Charitable Fund, 1983–97). KSG 1993. *Recreations:* rough gardening, watercolour painting, military history, English cathedrals and churches, the family, including fifteen grandchildren. *Address:* c/o Lloyds TSB, Devizes, Wiltshire. *Died 21 Sept. 2011.*

PAGE, Oliver, OBE 2004; financial services consultant, since 2006; *b* 29 April 1946; *s* of Sir Harry Robertson Page and Lady Elsie Page (*née* Dixon); *m* 1968, Jennifer Jane Murphy; one *d*. *Educ:* Trinity Coll., Cambridge (BA 1967; DipEcon 1968). Bank of England, 1968–98: posts included: Chief Manager, Reserves Management, 1984–90; Hd of Banking Supervision, 1996–98; Director, Financial Services Authority: 1998–2006: posts incl. Dir, Complex, then Financial, later Major Retail Gps Div., Sector Leader for Financial Stability and Dir responsible for ARROW2 and Treating Customers Fairly. UK Alternate Dir, EIB, 1989–95. Non-exec. Dir, Mitsubishi UFJ Securities Internat. Ltd, 2006–. Mem., Basel Cttee on Banking Supervision, 1998–2006 (Chm., Capital Gp, 1999–2005; Co-Chm., Jt Basel/IOSCO Trading Book Review, 2004–05). *E:* jennandoliver.page@ntlworld.com. *Died 3 June 2012.*

PAGE, Prof. Raymond Ian, LittD; Fellow, Corpus Christi College, Cambridge, since 1962; Elrington and Bosworth Professor of Anglo-Saxon, University of Cambridge, 1984–91, then Professor Emeritus; *b* 25 Sept. 1924; *s* of Reginald Howard Page and Emily Louise Page; *m* 1953, Elin Benedicte Hustad, *d* of Tormod Kristoffer Hustad and Anne Margarethe Hustad, Oslo; two *d* (one *s* decd). *Educ:* King Edward VII Sch., Sheffield; Rotherham Technical Coll.; Univ. of Sheffield. LittD Cambridge 1974. Assistant Lecturer and Lecturer, Univ. of Nottingham, 1951–61; Cambridge University: successively Lectr, Reader and Professor, Dept of Anglo-Saxon, Norse and Celtic, 1961–91; Sandars Reader in Bibliography, 1989–90; Corpus Christi College: Librarian, 1965–91; Dir, Leverhulme Trust Res. Gp on MS Evidence, Parker Liby, 1989–94. Special Prof. in Anglo-Saxon Studies, Univ. of Nottingham, 1992–97; Hon. Sen. Res. Fellow, Dept of Eng. Lang., Univ. of Glasgow, 1993–; Hon. Res. Fellow, Dept of Anglo-Saxon, Norse and Celtic, Univ. of Cambridge, 2007–. Hon. LittD Sheffield, 1994; Hon. Dr phil Trondheim, 1996. Dag Strömbäck prize, Royal Gustav Adolfs Acad., Uppsala, 1995. *Address:* Ashton House, Newnham Road, Cambridge CB3 9EY. *Died 10 March 2012.*

PAHL, Prof. Raymond Edward, PhD; FBA 2008; Visiting Research Professor in Sociology, Institute of Social and Economic Research, University of Essex, since 1999; Professor, University of Kent, 1972–96, then Emeritus; *b* London, 17 July 1935; *s* of Ronald Herman Pahl and Jean Fleming Pahl (*née* Heron); *m* 1959, Janice Mary Cockburn (marr. diss. 1997); two *s* one *d*. *Educ:* St Albans Sch.; St Catharine's Coll., Cambridge (BA 1959); London Sch. of Econs (PhD 1964). Extra-Mural Tutor, Univ. of Cambridge, 1959–65; Lectr, 1965–68, Sen. Lectr, 1968–72, Univ. of Kent. Pt-time Prof. of Sociol., Univ. of Essex, 1994–99; Hon. Vis. Prof., Univ. of Keele, 1999–2010. Assessor to Gtr London Develt Plan Inquiry, 1970–72. Member: Social Studies Sub-Cttee, Univ. Grants Cttee, 1979–89; Archbishop of Canterbury's Commn on Urban Priority Areas, 1983–85. President: RC21, Internat. Sociological Assoc., 1974–78; Section N, BAAS, 1975. AcSS 2004. Lifetime Achievement Award, British Sociological Assoc., 2011. *Publications:* Whose City?, 1970; (with J. M. Pahl) Managers and Their Wives, 1971; Divisions of Labour, 1984 (trans. Spanish 1991); After Success: fin-de-siècle anxiety and identity, 1995 (trans. Portuguese 1997); On Friendship, 2000 (trans. Spanish 2003); (with L. Spencer) Rethinking Friendship, 2006. *Recreations:* collecting Italian and British art, choral singing, hill walking, pottering in house and garden. *Address:* Institute of Social and Economic Research, University of Essex, Wivenhoe Park, Colchester, Essex CO4 3SQ. *T:* (01206) 872645, *Fax:* (01206) 873151. *E:* rpahl@essex.ac.uk. *Died 3 June 2011.*

PAIBA, His Honour Denis Anthony; a Circuit Judge, 1982–98; *b* 10 Dec. 1926; *e s* of late Geoffrey Paiba and Geraldine Paiba; *m* 1955, Lesley Patricia Dresden; two *s*. *Educ:* University Coll. Sch. (Junior); Magdalen Coll. Sch., Oxford; Jesus Coll., Cambridge. 44 Royal Marine Commando, 1945–47. Financial Times, 1957–58. Called to the Bar, Gray's Inn, 1958; a Dep. Circuit Judge and a Dep. Family Div. Judge, 1969–80; a Recorder of the Crown Court, 1980–82. *Recreations:* theatre, music, gardening, study of English ceramics up to 1850, watching Rugby and cricket, wining and dining. *Address:* 11 Angel Mews, Roehampton High Street, SW15 4HU. *T:* and *Fax:* (020) 8788 4674. *Died 19 Feb. 2011.*

PAIGE, Victor Grellier, CBE 1978; Chairman, National Health Service Management Board, and Second Permanent Secretary, Department of Health and Social Security, 1985–86; *b* 5 June 1925; *s* of Victor Paige and Alice (*née* Grellier); *m* 1948, Kathleen Winifred, 3rd *d* of Arthur and Daisy Harris; one *s* one *d*. *Educ:* East Ham Grammar Sch.; Univ. of Nottingham. CIPD, FCILT, FAIM. Roosevelt Mem. Schol. 1954. Dep. Personnel Manager, Boots Pure Drug Co. Ltd, 1957–67; Controller of Personnel Services, CWS Ltd, 1967–70; Dir of Manpower and Organisation, 1970–74, Exec. Vice-Chm. (Admin), 1974–77, Nat. Freight Corp.; Dep. Chm., Nat. Freight Corp., later Nat. Freight Co., 1977–82; Dir, 1977–88 (non-exec., 1985–88), and Dep. Chm., 1982–85, Nat. Freight Consortium; Chm., Iveco (UK), 1984–85. Chm., PLA, 1980–85; Member: Manpower Services Commn, 1974–80; Thames Water Authy, 1983–85. Member: Notts Educn Cttee, 1957–63; Secondary Schs Examn Council, 1960–63; UK Adv. Council for Educn in Management, 1962–65; Careers Adv. Bd, Univ. of Nottingham, 1975–81; Chairman: Regional Adv. Council for Further Educn, E Mids, 1967; Exec. Council, British Assoc. for Commercial and Industrial Educn, 1974 (Vice-Pres. 1980); Pres., Inst. of Admin. Management, 1984–90; Vice-Pres., Chartered Inst. of Transport, 1984–85 (Mem. Council, 1976–79); Mem. Council, CBI, 1983–85 (Chm., Educn and Trng Cttee, 1983–85). Mem. Court, Henley, The Management College, 1985–94. Governor, British Liver Trust, 1990–98. Vice-Pres., London Fedn of Boys' Clubs. Freeman, Co. of Watermen and Lightermen of the River Thames; Freeman, City of London, 1981. Commander, Order of Orange Nassau, The Netherlands, 1982. *Publications:* contrib. techn. press on management. *Recreations:* reading, sport generally, athletics in particular (Pres. Notts Athletic Club, 1962–67). *Address:* 7 Benningfield Gardens, Castle Village, Berkhamsted, Herts HP4 2GW. *T:* (01442) 865030. *Club:* MCC. *Died 1 April 2012.*

PAINE, Peter Stanley, CBE 1981; DFC 1944; Chairman, Oracle Teletext Ltd, 1984–93; *b* 19 June 1921; *s* of Arthur Bertram Paine and Dorothy Helen Paine; *m* 1st, 1942, Sheila Mary (*d* 1994), *d* of Frederick Wigglesworth, MA; two *s* two *d*; 2nd, 1999, Marion Dyason Strong (*née* Hunter). *Educ:* King's Sch., Canterbury. Served 1940–46, 2 Gp RAF (Flt-Lt). Worked in Punch Publishing Office, 1945–47; Sales Promotion Man., Newnes Pearson, 1948–52, Odhams Press, later Sales Dir and Dir of Tyne Tees Television, 1958–67; Sales Dir and Dir of Yorkshire Television, 1967–74; Managing Director: Tyne Tees Television, 1974–83; Tyne Tees Television Holdings, 1981–84. Director: Trident Television, 1970–81; Independent Television News Ltd, 1982–83; Independent Television Publications Ltd, 1977–83; Broadcasters Audience Res. Bd, 1980–86; Member: Council, Independent Television Companies Assoc., 1974–83 (4 yrs Chm. Marketing Cttee); Cable Authority, 1984–90. *Recreations:* golf, fishing, theatre, music, reading. *Address:* Briarfield, Ashwood Road, Woking, Surrey GU22 7JW. *T:* (01483) 773183. *Club:* Worplesdon Golf. *Died 7 Feb. 2012.*

PALLISER, Rt Hon. Sir (Arthur) Michael, GCMG 1977 (KCMG 1973; CMG 1966); PC 1983; HM Diplomatic Service, retired; Vice-Chairman, Board of Salzburg Global Seminar (formerly Board of Salzburg Seminar), 1995–2008; *b* 9 April 1922; *s* of late Admiral Sir Arthur Palliser, KCB, DSC, and Lady Palliser (*née* Margaret Eva King-Salter); *m* 1948, Marie Marguerite (*d* 2000), *d* of late Paul-Henri Spaak; three *s*. *Educ:* Wellington Coll.; Merton Coll., Oxford (Hon. Fellow 1987). Served with Coldstream Guards, 1942–47 (despatches); Capt. 1944. Entered HM Diplomatic Service, 1947; SE Asia Dept, Foreign Office, 1947–49; Athens, 1949–51; Second Sec., 1950; Foreign Office: German Finance Dept, 1951–52; Central Dept, 1952–54; Private Sec. to Perm. Under-Sec., 1954–56; First Sec., 1955; Paris, 1956–60; Head of Chancery, Dakar, 1960–62 (Chargé d'Affaires in 1960, 1961 and 1962); Counsellor, and seconded to Imperial Defence College, 1963; Head of Planning Staff, Foreign Office, 1964; a Private Sec. to PM, 1966; Minister, Paris, 1969; Ambassador and Head of UK Deleg. to European Communities, Brussels, 1971; Ambassador and UK Permanent Representative to European Communities, 1973–75; Permanent Under-Sec. of State, FCO and Head of Diplomatic Service, 1975–82; Special Advr to PM during Falklands Campaign, 1982. Fellow, Center for Internat. Affairs, Harvard, 1982; Chm., Samuel Montagu & Co., 1984–85, 1986–93 (Dir, 1983–96; Vice Chm., 1988, 1993–96); Deputy Chairman: Midland Montagu (Hldgs), 1987–93; Midland Bank, 1987–91. Director, 1983–92: BAT Industries plc; Booker plc; Eagle Star Hldgs; Shell Transport & Trading Co. plc; Director: United Biscuits (Hldgs), 1983–89; Arbor Acres Farm Inc., 1985–91; UK-Japan 2000 Gp, 1987–96; XCL Ltd, 1994–2000. Dep. Chm., BI (formerly BIEC), 1987–95. Pres., China-Britain Trade Gp, 1992–96; Member: Council, IISS, 1982–91 (Chm., 1983–90; Vice-Pres., 1999–); Trilateral Commn, 1982–96; Security Commn, 1983–92; Council, British N American Cttee and Res. Assoc., 1987–95 (British Chm., 1990–92); BOTB, 1993–96; Adv. Bd, RAND Europe, 1995–2003 (Chm., 1999–2003); Adv. Council, British Consultants Bureau, 1997–2002. Mem., Royal Nat. Theatre Bd, 1988–96. Pres., Internat. Social Service of UK, 1982–96; Chairman: City and E London Confedn of Medicine and Dentistry, 1989–95; Major Projects Assoc., 1994–98. Trustee, The Tablet, 1989–2011. Governor, Wellington Coll., 1982–92. FRSA 1983. Hon. Fellow, QMW, 1990. Chevalier, Order of Orange Nassau, 1944; Commandeur, Légion d'Honneur, 1996 (Chevalier, 1957). *Address:* 12B Wedderburn Road, NW3 5QG. *T:* (020) 7794 0440, *Fax:* (020) 7916 2163. *Club:* Buck's. *Died 19 June 2012.*

PALMER, Rev. Preb. Francis Harvey; Prebendary of Sawley in Lichfield Cathedral, 1986–89; Prebendary Emeritus, since 1989; *b* 13 Jan. 1930; *s* of Harry Hereward North Palmer and Ada Wilhelmina Annie Utting; *m* 1955, Mary Susan Lockhart; three *d*. *Educ:* Nottingham High Sch.; Jesus Coll., Cambridge (Exhibnr); Wycliffe Hall, Oxford. MA. Deacon, 1955; Priest, 1956. Asst Curate: Knotty Ash, Liverpool, 1955–57; St Mary, Southgate, Crawley, 1958–60; Chaplain, Fitzwilliam House, Cambridge, 1960–64; Vicar of Holy Trinity, Cambridge and Chaplain to Cambridge Pastorate, 1964–71; Principal, Ridley Hall, Cambridge, 1971–72; Rector of Worplesdon, Surrey, 1972–80; Diocesan Ecumenical Officer, Guildford, 1974–80; Diocesan Missioner, Lichfield, 1980–89. *Publications:* (contrib.) New Bible Dictionary, 1959. *Died 28 Jan. 2014.*

PALMER, Joe; *see* Palmer, T. J.

PALMER, Michael Julian Barham, CMG 1990; writer; Advisor to the Governor, Luxembourg Central Bank, 2000–09; *b* 2 Feb. 1933; *s* of Cecil Barham Palmer and Phyllis Palmer; *m* 1983, Dr Karin Reichel. *Educ:* Corpus Christi College, Oxford (MA). Research Officer, Political and Economic Planning, 1957–61; Sec., Political Cttee, Council of Europe, 1961–66; Councillor for Defence and Armaments, WEU, 1966–68; Dir of Cttees, N Atlantic Assembly, 1968–72; Dir-Gen. of Research, European Parlt, 1972–90. Jean Monnet Prof., European Univ. Inst., Florence, 1989. Economic Consultant, Inst. for East-West Studies, NY and Prague, 1992–98. Chm., East-West Cttee, European League for Economic Co-operation, 1996–2006. Austrian Order of Merit, 1990; Order of Oak Leaf Crown (Luxembourg), 1990; Order of Leopold (Belgium), 2011. *Publications:* European Organisations, 1959; European Unity, 1968; Prospects for a European Security Conference, 1971; The European Parliament, 1981; From Ensor to Magritte, 1994; Belgian paintings in the Simon collection, 1997; Liliane Heidelberger-Sculptrice, 1999;

The Central Bank of Luxembourg, 2001; Belgian Art 1940–2000, 2002; 500 Belgian Masterpieces, 2006; Brief History of Belgian Art, 2007; articles in The World Today, Foreign Policy, The Times, Christie's International, EIU publications. *Recreations:* music, art, cooking, mountain walking. *Address:* 8 rue des Franciscaines, 1539 Luxembourg Grand Duchy. *Died 4 July 2014.*

PALMER, Thomas Joseph, (Joe), CBE 1990; Chairman, Personal Investment Authority, 1993–2000; *b* 11 Sept. 1931; *m* 1955, Hilary Westrup; two *s* two *d*. *Educ:* King's School, Bruton; Trinity College, Cambridge. MA. Asst Gen. Manager (Planning), Legal and General Assurance Soc., 1969–72, Dir and Gen. Man. (Admin.), 1972–78; Legal & General Group plc: Dir, 1978–91; Gen. Man. (Internat.), 1978–83; Group Chief Exec., 1984–91. Chm., Laser Richmount, 1991–93; Director: SIB, 1991–93; Halifax BS, 1991–93; National Power plc, 1991–96; Sedgwick Gp, 1992–93; ProShare, 1992–94. Chairman: London Business Sch. Assoc., 1974–78; Assoc. of British Insurers, 1989–91; Pres., Insurance Inst. of London, 1982–83; Dir, Investors' Compensation Scheme, 1992–93. Gov., King's Sch., Bruton, 1989–2005 (Jun. Warden, 2001–03). Hon. Fellow, London Business Sch., 1990. *Recreations:* gardening, long-distance walking. *Died 15 Aug. 2015.*

PANTON, Dr Francis Harry, CBE 1997 (MBE (mil.) 1948); FSA; Consultant, Ministry of Defence, 1984–99; Director, Royal Armament Research and Development Establishment, Ministry of Defence, 1980–83; *b* 25 May 1923; 3rd *s* of George Emerson Panton and Annie Panton; *m* 1st, 1952, Audrey Mary Lane (*d* 1989); two *s*; 2nd, 1995, Pauline Joyce Dean. *Educ:* City Sch., Lincoln; University College and Univ. of Nottingham; PhD (Chem.) Nottingham, 1952; PhD (History) Kent, 1999. Served War of 1939–45: commissioned, Bomb Disposal, Royal Eng., 1943–47. Pres., Univ. of Nottingham Union, 1950–51; Vice-Pres., Nat. Union of Students, 1952–54; Technical Officer, ICI, Billingham, 1952–53; Permanent Under-Secretary's Dept, FO, 1953–55; Office of Political Adviser, Berlin, 1955–57; Dep. Head, Technical Research Unit, MoD, 1957–58; Attaché, British Embassy, Washington, DC, 1958–59; Technical Adviser, UK Delegn to Conf. on Discontinuance of Nuclear Tests, Geneva, 1959–61; Permanent Under-Secretary's Dept, FO, 1961–63; Counsellor (Defence), British Embassy, Washington, DC, 1963–66; Head of Defence Science 6, MoD, 1966–68; Asst Chief Scientific Adviser (Nuclear), MoD, 1969–76; Dir Gen., Estabs, Resources and Programmes (B), MoD, April–Sept. 1976; Dir, Propellants, Explosives and Rocket Motor Estabt, and Head, Rocket Motor Exec., MoD, 1976–80. Consultant, Cabinet Office, 1985–97. Chairman: Mgt Cttee, Canterbury Archaeol Trust, 1985–2000; Dover Bronze Age Boat Trust, 1995–2006 (Hon. Pres., 2007–); Mem. Council, Kent Archaeol Soc., 1990– (Hon. Librarian, 1999–; Vice-Pres., 2005–). FRSC (FRIC 1961); FRSA 1973; FRAeS 1982; FSA 2012. *Recreations:* archaeology, local history. *Address:* Grove End, Tunstall, Sittingbourne, Kent ME9 8DY. *T:* (01795) 472218. *Club:* Reform. *Died 8 April 2013.*

PARDOE, John George Magrath, CBE 1975; FRAeS; Director-General, Airworthiness, Civil Aviation Authority, 1972–79; *b* 2 April 1914. *Educ:* Coll. of Aeronautical Engineering. Entered design work in Aircraft Industry, 1935; joined Accidents Inspection Br. of Air Ministry, 1942; joined Staff, Air Registration Bd, 1945; Chief Technical Officer, 1969. Médaille de l'aéronautique, 1980. *Died 2 Sept. 2011.*

PARIZEAU, Jacques, PhD; Member, Québec National Assembly (Parti Québécois) for Assomption, 1976–84 and 1989–96; Prime Minister of Québec, 1994–96; *b* Montreal, 9 Aug. 1930; *s* of Gerard Parizeau and Germaine Parizeau (*née* Biron); *m* 1st, 1956, Alicja Poznanska (decd); one *s* one *d*; 2nd, 1992, Lisette Lapointe. *Educ:* Ecole des Hautes Etudes Commerciales, Montreal; Institut d'Etudes Politiques, Paris (Dip. 1952); London Sch. of Econs (PhD 1955). Prof., Ecole des Hautes Etudes Commerciales, Montreal, 1955–65, 1967–76 and 1985–89 (Dir, Applied Econs Inst., 1973–75). Econs and financial advr to Prime Minister and Cabinet of Québec, 1961–69; Minister of Finance, 1976–84; also Pres., Treasury Bd and Minister of Revenue and of Financial Instns; Leader, Official Opposition, 1989–94. Parti Québécois: Mem., 1969–; Chm., Nat. Exec., 1970–73; Pres., 1988–96. Pres., Québec Financial Instns Task Force, 1967–69; Chm., Québec Municipalities Study Commn, 1985. *Publications:* The Terms of Trade of Canada, 1956; Initiation à l'économie du Québec, 1975; Pour un Québec souverain, 1997; numerous articles. *Recreations:* reading, music, gardening. *Died 1 June 2015.*

PARKER, Sir Eric (Wilson), Kt 1991; FCA; Chairman, Caradon plc, 1998–99 (Director, Metal Box plc, then MB-Caradon, later Caradon plc, 1985–99); *b* 8 June 1933; *s* of late Wilson Parker and Edith Gladys (*née* Wellings); *m* 1955, Marlene Teresa (*née* Neale); two *s* two *d*. *Educ:* The Priory Grammar Sch. for Boys, Shrewsbury. FCA 1967 (ACA 1956). Articled Clerk with Wheeler, Whittingham & Kent, Shrewsbury, 1950–55; National Service, Pay Corps, 1956–58; Taylor Woodrow Gp, 1958–64; Trafalgar House Gp, 1965–93: Finance/Admin Dir, 1969; Dep. Man. Dir, 1973; Gp Man. Dir, 1977; Chief Exec., 1983–92; Dep. Chm., 1988–93; Chm., Graham Consulting, 1993–97. Non-exec. Chm., Albert Goodwin plc, 2003–10; non-executive Director: European Assets Trust NV, 1972–85; Sealink UK Ltd, 1979–81; British Rail Investments Ltd, 1980–84; Evening Standard Co. Ltd, 1982–85; Touche Remnant Hldgs Ltd, 1985–89; The Royal Automobile Club (formerly The Automobile Pty Ltd), 1986–95; Hardy Oil & Gas, later British Borneo, plc, 1989–2000; Internat. Real Estates (formerly Criterion Properties) plc, 1998–2009; Job Partners Ltd, 2000–02. Mem., Lloyds, 1978–. Advr, Phoenix Develt Capital Fund, 1992–97; Mem. Adv. Bd, QMG, MoD, 1997–2000. Director: Trafalgar House Pension Trust Ltd (formerly Kvaerner Trustee (KPF) Ltd), 2001–12; Nameco Ltd, 2009–. Director: British Horseracing Bd, 1999–2004; Horserace Betting Levy Bd, 2000–04; Horserace Totaliser Bd, 2002–08; National Stud, 2005–08; Pres., Race Horse Owners' Assoc., 1998–2001 (Dir, 1994–). Proprietor, Crimbourne Stud, 1991–. Patron, Teenage Cancer Trust. CCMI (CBIM 1983). *Recreations:* sports (including golf and horseracing), wines. *Address:* Crimbourne House, Crimbourne Lane, Wisborough Green, Billingshurst, W Sussex RH14 0HR. *Clubs:* Royal Automobile, MCC; West Sussex Golf. *Died 21 Aug. 2014.*

PARKER, (James) Geoffrey, CBE 1996; High Master, Manchester Grammar School, 1985–94; Chairman, Teacher Training Agency, 1994–97; *b* 27 March 1933; *s* of late Ian Sutherland Parker and Kathleen Lilian Parker; *m* 1956, Ruth Major (*d* 2005); two *d*. *Educ:* Alderman Newton's Sch., Leicester; Christ's Coll., Cambridge (Exhibnr); Wadham Coll., Oxford. National Service, RA, 1954–56. Asst Master, Bedford Modern Sch., 1957–66; Head of History Dept, Tonbridge Sch., 1966–75; Headmaster, Queen Elizabeth Grammar Sch., Wakefield, 1975–85. Chairman: HMC, 1991; ISIS, 1994–97. Gov., Charterhouse, 1993–2005; Trustee: St George's English Sch., Rome, 1992–97; Berlin British Sch., 1994–2005. *Address:* 20 South Street, Partridge Green, W Sussex RH13 8EL. *T:* (01403) 711716. *Died 29 Feb. 2012.*

PARKER, Rt Hon. Sir Roger (Jocelyn), Kt 1977; PC 1983; a Lord Justice of Appeal, 1983–92; *b* 25 Feb. 1923; *s* of Captain Hon. T. T. Parker, DSC, RN (Retired) and Marie Louise Leonie (*née* Kleinwort); *m* 1948, Ann Elizabeth Frederika (*née* White); one *s* three *d*. *Educ:* Eton; King's Coll., Cambridge (BA 1948). Served Rifle Bde, 1941–46. Called to Bar, Lincoln's Inn, 1948, Bencher, 1969; QC 1961. Dep. Chm., Herts QS, 1969–71; Judge of the Courts of Appeal, Jersey and Guernsey, 1974–83; a Judge of the High Court, QBD, 1977–83. Member, Bar Council, 1968–69, Vice-Chm., 1970–72, Chm., 1972–73. Vice-Pres., Senate of Four Inns of Court, 1972–73. Treas., Lincoln's Inn, 1990–91. Conducted Windscale Nuclear Fuel Reprocessing Inquiry, 1977. Chm., Court of Inquiry into Flixborough Explosion, 1974. *Clubs:* Lansdowne; Leander. *Died 21 May 2011.*

PARKES, John Hubert, CB 1984; Permanent Secretary, Department of Education, Northern Ireland, 1979–90; *b* 1 Oct. 1930; 2nd *s* of Frank Hubert Parkes and Mary Edith (*née* Barnes), Birmingham; *m* 1956, Elsie Griffiths Henderson; two *s*. *Educ:* George Dixon Sch., Birmingham; Magdalen Coll., Oxford (MA). Joined NI Civil Service, 1953; Asst Sec. 1966; RCDS 1972; Dep. Sec., 1973. Hon. DLitt Ulster, 1991. *Address:* 193 Woodbury Road, Halesowen, W Midlands B62 9AG. *Club:* Oxford and Cambridge. *Died 23 Nov. 2013.*

PARKES, Prof. Malcolm Beckwith, DLitt; FSA; FRHistS; FBA 1993; Professor of Palaeography, University of Oxford, 1996–97, then Emeritus; Lyell Reader in Bibliography, Oxford, 1998–99; Fellow, Keble College, Oxford, 1965–97, then Emeritus; *b* 26 June 1930; *s* of Edward James Lennard Parkes and Clara Parkes (*née* Beckwith); *m* 1954, Ann Winifred Dodman (*d* 2009); two *s*. *Educ:* Colfe's Grammar Sch.; Strasbourg Univ.; Hertford Coll., Oxford (BA Eng. Lang. and Lit. 1953; MA 1957; BLitt 1959; Gordon-Duff Prize 1959; DLitt 1985). FSA 1971; FRHistS 1977. Archivist, Lambeth Palace Library, 1957–58; Lectr in English Lang., Keble and Mansfield Colls, Oxford, 1961–65; Tutor in Eng. Lang., Keble Coll., Oxford, 1965–97; Lectr, Faculty of English, 1964–71, Lectr in Palaeography, 1971–93, Reader, 1993–96, Univ. of Oxford. Vis. Prof., Universität Konstanz, 1974 and 1980; James J. Hill Prof., Univ. of Minn (Twin Cities), 1991; Vis. Prof. of Latin, Harvard, 1998; Vis. Fellow, Princeton Univ., 1996; Mem., Inst. for Advanced Study, Princeton, 1997. Special Lecturer: in Palaeography and Diplomatic, Univ. of Durham, 1972; in Palaeography, Univ. of London, 1976; Lectures: Jarrow, 1982; Mont Follick, Univ. of Manchester, 1986; Robert F. Metzdorf, Univ. of Rochester, NY, 1987; James L. Rosier, Univ. of Pennsylvania, 1995; Fellows', Medieval Acad. of America, 2000. Mem., Standing Conf. of Nat. and Univ. Libraries, Adv. Cttee on MSS, 1977–86. Member: Wolfenbütteler Mediävistischen Arbeitskreis, 1986–2004; Comité Internat. de Paléographie Latine, 1986–; Council, EETS, 1995–. Corresp. Fellow, Medieval Acad. of America, 1992. *Publications:* English Cursive Book Hands 1250–1500, 1969, rev. edn 1979; (ed with A. G. Watson) Medieval Scribes, Manuscripts and Libraries: essays presented to N. R. Ker, 1978; Medieval Manuscripts of Keble College, Oxford, a descriptive catalogue, 1979; Scribes, Scripts and Readers, 1991; Pause and Effect: an introduction to the history of punctuation in the West, 1992; Their Hands Before Our Eyes: a closer look at scribes, 2008; Pages from the Past: medieval writing skills and manuscript books, 2012; introductions to facsimile edns of various manuscripts; articles and chapters on topics in palaeography, book production and ownership, and history of reading in learned jls and series. *Recreation:* growing fuchsias. *Address:* 460 Banbury Road, Oxford OX2 7RG. *Died 10 May 2013.*

PARKINSON, Ronald Dennis; Assistant Curator, Victoria and Albert Museum, 1978–98; *b* 27 April 1945; *s* of Albert Edward Parkinson and Jennie Caroline Clara Meager. *Educ:* St Dunstan's Coll.; Clare Coll., Cambridge (MA). Res. Assistant: Paul Mellon Foundn for British Art, 1971–72; V&A Mus., 1972–74; Asst Keeper, Tate Gall., 1974–78. *Publications:* (ed jtly) Richard Redgrave, 1988; Catalogue of British Oil Paintings 1820–1860 in the Victoria and Albert Museum, 1990; British Watercolours at the Victoria and Albert Museum, 1998; Constable, the man and his art, 1998; articles in Apollo, Burlington Mag., Cambridge Res., Connoisseur, Country Life, Times Higher Educn Sup. *Recreations:* reading, shopping. *Address:* 13 Childebert Road, SW17 8EY. *Club:* Algonquin. *Died 20 Nov. 2012.*

PARNABY, Dr John, CBE 1987; FREng; Chairman and Chief Executive Officer, BPSE Ltd, since 1998; Chairman, Aston University Day Hospital (formerly Academy of Life Sciences Ltd), since 2003; *b* 10 July 1937; *s* of John Banks Parnaby and Mary Elizabeth Parnaby; *m* 1959, Lilian Armstrong; three *s* one *d*. *Educ:* Durham Univ. (BSc Mech. Engrg, 1961); Glasgow Univ. (PhD Control Systems Engrg, 1966). MIEE 1966, Hon. FIET (Hon. FIEE 1989); FIProdE 1978; FIMechE 1978 (Hon. FIMechE 1998); FREng (FEng 1986). Technical Apprentice, 1954–58, Ironworks Develt Engr, 1961–62, United Steel Co.; Res. Asst, Univ. of Durham, 1962–63; Lectr in Mech. Engrg, Univ. of Glasgow, 1963–66; Sen. Projects Engr, Albright & Wilson Ltd, 1966–67; Works Man., Solway Chemicals Ltd, 1967–70; University of Bradford: Sen. Lectr, 1970–73; Prof. of Manufg Systems Design, 1973–80 (Chm., Sch. of Manufacturing Systems Engrg, 1975–80); Technical and Marketing Dir, subseq. Jt Man. Dir, Rieter Scragg Ltd, 1980–82; Gen. Man., Dunlop Ltd, 1982–83; Gp Dir, Technology, Lucas Industries, 1983–90; Man. Dir and CEO, Lucas Electronic Systems Products (formerly Lucas Applied Technology Sector), 1990–96; Gp Dir, LucasVarity plc, 1996–98; Chairman: Lucas Metier, later Lucas Mgt Systems, 1990–96; Lucas Engrg and Systems Ltd, 1990; Lucas Gp Dir, Develt, 1995–96; Knowledge Process Software plc, 2000–05; Think Digital Solutions plc, 2001–04; Amchem Ltd, 2001–03. Dir and CEO, Geared Systems Inc., 1996–98; Director: Scottish Power plc, 1994–2001; Molins plc, 1998–2003; Jarvis plc, 1999–2001. Chm., Anglo-German Res. Cttee, British Council, 1990–. Chm., Link Bd, DTI/OST, 1993–96; Mem., DTI/EPSRC Innovative Manufrs Initiative Mgt Cttee, 1998–. Vis. Hon. Prof. of Manufacturing Systems Engrg, Univ. of Birmingham, 1984–2000; Vis. Hon. Prof. of Engrg, Univ. of Cambridge, 1999–. President: IProdE, 1989; IEE, 1995–96 (Dep. Pres., 1993–95); Mem. Council, Royal Acad. of Engrg, 1997–2001; Senator, Engrg Council, 1997–2001. Mem., Queen's Anniversary Award Cttee, 1996–2002. Aston University: Mem. Council, 1999–; Treas. and Chm. Finance Cttee, 2002–. Hon. Fellow: Coventry Poly., 1989; Sheffield Poly., 1991; Univ. of Wales, 1995. Hon. DTech: Liverpool Poly., 1990; CNAA 1990; Loughborough, 1991; Napier, 1997; Hon. DSc Hull, 1991; DUniv Open, 1992; Hon. DEng: Bradford, 1993; Newcastle, 2000; Aston, 2002. Gold Medal, Instn of Manufg Engrs, 1987; Silver Medal, 1990, Faraday Medal, 1994, IEE. *Publications:* Minicomputers and Microcomputers in Engineering and Manufacture, 1986; Manufacturing Systems Engineering Miniguide Handbook, 1989, 2nd edn 1992; Managing by Projects for Business Success, 2003; over 80 papers in engrg and management jls on manufg systems, control engrg, process engrg, business process systems engrg, hospital and business systems process, organisation design and management and machinery design. *Recreations:* hockey, sailing, golf. *Address:* Crest Edge, Beechnut Lane, Solihull, W Midlands B91 2NN. *T:* (0121) 705 4348. *E:* drjparnaby@aol.com. *Died 5 Jan. 2011.*

PARR, John Robert; an Hon. Director, General Secretariat, Council of Ministers of European Union (formerly Council of Ministers of European Communities), since 1989; *b* 25 Sept. 1934; *s* of Henry George Parr and Hilda Frances Parr (*née* Pattison); *m* 1993, Prof. (Margaret) Dolores O'Reilly; one *d*. *Educ:* Dulwich Coll.; Merton Coll., Oxford (Postmaster; MA). Joined British Iron and Steel Fedn as Admin. Asst, 1959, Dep. Sec., 1963–65; Principal, Industrial Policy Div., Dept of Economic Affairs, 1965–68 (Sec., Inter-Deptl cttees on industrial productivity and on govt sharehldgs in the private sector, 1966–68); British Steel Corp., 1968–73, Co-ordinator, EC Affairs, 1972–73 (responsible for preparing entry into ECSC); Dir-Gen., British Footwear Manufacturers Fedn, 1973–76; Divl Hd, Gen. Secretariat, Council of Ministers of European Communities, 1976–89 (responsible for EC legislation to liberalise air transport within internal market); Dir Gen., Air Transport Users Council, 1989–96. Chm., Airline-Consumer Forum, IATA, Geneva, 1995–99. Dir, Ulster Orch. Soc., 2007–; Chm., Friends of Ulster Orch., 2007–. *Recreations:* political history of 19th and 20th centuries, opera and other forms of classical music, Irish country life. *Address:* 7 Culmore Square, Derry BT48 8GF. *Died 3 Dec. 2011.*

PARRY, Morgan; Member, Board: Natural Resources Wales, since 2013; Joint Nature Conservation Committee, since 2013; *b* Liverpool, 15 Dec. 1957; *s* of Jonathan Morgan Parry and Joan Charles Parry; *m* 2001, Wendi Jones; one *s* one *d*. *Educ:* Liverpool Poly. (BSc Applied Biol. 1981); Coleg Normal, Bangor (Countryside Mgt Dip. 1982). Country Parks Manager, Gwynedd Council, 1984–94; Dir, N Wales Wildlife Trust, 1994–2000; Hd, Worldwide Fund for Nature Cymru, 2000–09; Chair, Countryside Council for Wales, 2010–13. Mem. Bd, Friends of the Earth, 1986–89. *Recreations:* sitting on top of mountains, reading history, listening to music, speaking Welsh, watching Rugby. *Address:* Natural Resources Wales, Maes y ffynnon, Bangor, Gwynedd LL57 2DW. *Died 4 Jan. 2014.*

PARSONS, Susie; Managing Director, Susie Parsons Management Solutions, since 2005; Joint Managing Director, Lasting Transformation Ltd, since 2011; *b* 29 April 1950; *d* of Alfred Parsons and late Dorothy Parsons (*née* Barratt); partner, Dave Perry; one *s*. *Educ:* E Grinstead Co. Grammar Sch.; Univ. of Lancaster (BA Hons French Studies); King's Coll. London (PGCE). Teacher of French, John Kelly Girls' High Sch., LB of Brent, 1973–74; Dir, Community Educn, Shelter, 1974–77; Housing Projects Officer, N Kensington Law Centre, 1977–81; Sec., Paddington and N Kensington CHC, 1981–84; Gen. Manager, London Energy and Employment Network, 1984–87; Hd, Press and Publicity, London Borough of Hackney, 1987–94; Exec. Dir, 1994–97, Chief Exec., 1997–99, London Lighthouse; Chief Exec., CRE, 1999–2001; ind. mgt consultant, 2001–02; Chief Exec., Campaign for Learning, 2002–05. *Publications:* (jtly) Workout, 1979; The Right Side of the Law, 1993; (jtly) Learning to Learn in Schools, 2005; (jtly) Learning to Learn for Life, 2005; (contrib.) Reinventing Education, 2005; numerous reports, pamphlets, articles etc on health, social care, quality, equality, women in mgt and lifelong learning. *Recreations:* friendship, swimming, voluntary work, the arts. *Address:* 131a Kilburn Park Road, NW6 5LD. *E:* susie@lastingtransformation.co.uk. *Died 6 June 2015.*

PASCO, Richard Edward, CBE 1977; actor; Hon. Associate Artist, Royal Shakespeare Company; *b* Barnes, 18 July 1926; *s* of Cecil George Pasco and Phyllis Irene Pasco; *m* 1st, Greta (*née* Watson) (marr. diss.); one *s*; 2nd, 1967, Barbara Leigh-Hunt. *Educ:* Colet Court; King's Coll. Sch., Wimbledon; Central Sch. of Speech and Drama (Gold Medallist). Served HM Forces, 1944–48. 1st stage appearance, She Stoops to Conquer, 1943; 1st London appearance, Zero Hour, Lyric, 1944; 1st New York appearance, The Entertainer, 1958. London appearances include: leading roles, English Stage Co., Royal Court, 1957; The Entertainer, Palace, 1957; The Lady from the Sea, Queen's, 1961; Teresa of Avila, Vaudeville, 1961; Look Homeward, Angel, Phoenix, 1962; The New Men, Strand, 1962; The Private Ear and the Public Eye, Globe, 1963; Bristol Old Vic: Henry V (title role), Berowne in Love's Labour's Lost, 1964; Peer Gynt (title role), Angelo in Measure for Measure, Hamlet (title role), 1966 (and world tour); Ivanov, Phoenix, 1965; The Italian Girl, Wyndham's, 1968. Joined RSC, 1969; leading roles include: Becket, Murder in the Cathedral, Aldwych, 1972; (alternated with Ian Richardson) Richard and Bolingbroke in Richard II, Stratford-on-Avon, 1973, and Stratford and Aldwych, 1974; Jacques in As You Like It, 1973; tour of Amer. univs; Jack Tanner in Man and Superman, Malvern Festival, tour and Savoy, 1977; Timon in Timon of Athens, Clarence in Richard III, Arkady Schatslivtses in The Forest, Stratford, 1980–81; La Ronde, Aldwych, 1982; Soren in The Seagull, Stratford, tour and Barbican, 2000; National Theatre: The Father in Six Characters in Search of an Author, Pavel in Fathers and Sons, 1987; Rt Rev. Charlie Allen in Racing Demon, 1990, 1993; Sir Peter Edgecombe in Murmuring Judges, 1991, 1993; Birling in An Inspector Calls, 1992; Malcolm Pryce in Absence of War, 1993; Boss Findley in Sweet Bird of Youth, 1994. Many foreign tours; accompanied HSH Princess Grace of Monaco at Edinburgh, Stratford and Aldeburgh Festivals and on tour of USA, 1977–78. Frequent appearances at Aldeburgh, Brighton, Windsor and Harrogate festivals, Stratford-upon-Avon Poetry Festival etc. Recent films: A Watcher in the Woods; Wagner; Mrs Brown. Countless TV and radio appearances; recent television series: Sorrell & Son; Drummonds; Hannay; Inspector Morse; Absence of War; Kavanagh QC, Hetty Wainthropp Investigates, etc. Many recordings of poems, plays, recitals, etc. Life Trustee, Shakespeare Birthplace Trust, 1992. *Publications:* (contrib.) Shakespeare in Perspective, 1982; (contrib.) Time and Concord: Aldeburgh Festival recollections, 1997; (contrib.) Acting in Stratford, 1997. *Recreations:* music, gardening, reading. *Address:* c/o Michael Whitehall, Whitehall Artists Ltd, 10 Lower Common South, SW15 1BP. *Club:* Garrick. *Died 12 Nov. 2014.*

PASCO, Rowanne, (Mrs William FitzGerald); writer and broadcaster; *b* 7 Oct. 1938; *d* of John and Ann Pasco; *m* 1994, Rev. William FitzGerald (*d* 2004). *Educ:* Dominican Convent, Chingford; Ursuline Convent, Ilford; Open Univ. (BA Hons). Reporter, 1956–57, Editor, 1957–58, Chingford Express; Publicity Officer, NFU, 1958–59; Account Exec., Leslie Frewin PR, 1959–60; Travel Rep., Horizon Holidays, 1960–64; Publicity Asst, Paramount Pictures Corp., Hollywood, 1964–66; Publicity Officer, Religious Progs, Radio and TV, BBC, 1966–71; Reporter, BBC Radio London, 1971–72; TV Editor, Ariel, BBC Staff Newspaper, 1972–74; Radio 4 Reporter, 1974–76; Researcher, Religious Progs, BBC TV, 1976–77; Producer and Presenter, Religious Progs, BBC Radio, 1977–78; Dep. Editor, 1979–81, Editor, 1981–87, The Universe; Religious Editor, TV-am, 1987–92; religious correspondent, GMTV, 1993–94; Editl Advr, CCJ, 1994–2006; Presenter, Daily Service, BBC Radio 4, 2005–. *Publications:* (ed with Fr John Redford) Faith Alive, 1988, New Catechism edn, 1994; Answers to One Hundred & One Questions on the Catechism, 1995; Why I am a Catholic, 1995. *Recreations:* cats, gardening, Italy, creative cooking. *Address:* 12 The Dell, Blockley, Glos GL56 9DB. *Died 14 March 2015.*

PASHA, Dr Syed Aziz, OBE 2005; Secretary General, Union of Muslim Organisations of the UK and Eire, since 1970; *b* 10 July 1930; *s* of Prof. Syed Rauf Pasha and Azmatunnisa Begum. *Educ:* Madras Univ. (BSc, BL); Wisconsin Univ. (LLM); New York Univ. Law Sch. (SJD). Advr to Indian Delegn to UN, 1961–62; Internat. Law Consultant to Matthew Bender, NY, 1963–64; Advocate, Madras High Court, 1964–65; post-doctoral res. on Islamic law, SOAS, Univ. of London, 1965–70. *Recreations:* debating, lecturing, sports. *Address:* Union of Muslim Organisations of UK and Eire, 109 Campden Hill Road, W8 7TL. *T:* (020) 7221 6608. *Died 23 Nov. 2011.*

PASQUA, Charles Victor; Joint Founder and President, Rassemblement pour la France, 1999–2012; *b* 18 April 1927; *s* of late André Pasqua and Françoise (*née* Rinaldi); *m* 1947, Jeanne Joly; (one *s* decd). *Educ:* Grasse High Sch.; Law Inst., Nice; Univ. of Aix-en-Provence (degree in Law). Sales Rep., then Sales Dir, 1962–63; Dir for sales in France and exports, 1963–68. Deputy (UDR) for Hauts-de-Seine, 1968–73; President: Centre National de la Libre Enterprise; Amicale Parlementaire Présence et Action du Gaullisme, 1972–73; Nat. Sec., then Dep. Gen. Sec., UDR, 1974–76; Senator: (RPR) for Hauts-de-Seine, 1977–86, 1988–93 and 1995–99; (UMP) for Hauts-de-Seine, 2004–11; Pres., RPR in Senate, 1981–86 and 1988–93; Minister of Interior, 1986–88; Minister of State and Minister for the Interior and Town and Country Planning, 1993–95. Pres., Gen. Council for Hauts-de-Seine, 1973–76 and 1988–2004. Mem. (RPF) for France, 1999–2004, and Pres., Union pour l'Europe des Nations Gp, 1999–2006, EP. Croix du Combattant volontaire de la Résistance; Médaille de la France Libre; Officier de la Légion d'Honneur. *Publications:* La Libre enterprise un état d'esprit, 1964; L'ardeur nouvelle, 1985; Que demande le peuple, 1992. *Recreation:* travel. *Died 29 June 2015.*

PASTON-BEDINGFELD, Sir Edmund George Felix, 9th Bt *cr* 1661; Major late Welsh Guards; Managing Director, Handley Walker (Europe) Ltd, 1969–80; *b* 2 June 1915; *s* of Sir Henry Edward Paston-Bedingfeld, 8th Bt and Sybil (*d* 1985), *e d* of late H. Lyne Stephens of Grove House, Roehampton; *S* father, 1941; *m* 1st, 1942, Joan Lynette (*née* Rees) (*d* 1965); one *s* one *d*; 2nd, 1957, Agnes Kathleen (*d* 1974), *d* of late Miklos Gluck, Budapest; 3rd, 1975, Mrs Peggy Hannaford-Hill (*d* 1991), Fort Victoria, Rhodesia; 4th, 1992, Sheila Riddell (*née* Finlayson Douglas). *Educ:* Oratory School; New College, Oxford. Under-Sec., Head of Agricultural Div., RICS, 1966–69. Liveryman, Bowyers' Co., 1988–. *Heir: s* Henry Edgar Paston-Bedingfeld, *b* 7 Dec. 1943. *Address:* 4 Finsbury Place, Bury St Edmunds, Suffolk IP33 1NU. *T:* (01284) 788160. *Died 24 May 2011.*

PATEMAN, Prof. John Arthur Joseph, FRS 1978; FRSE 1974; Professor of Genetics, Australian National University, 1979–88, then Emeritus (Executive Director, Centre for Recombinant DNA Research, 1982–88); *b* 18 May 1926; *s* of John and Isobel May Pateman; *m* 1952, Mary Phelps; one *s* two *d*. *Educ:* Clacton County High Sch., Essex; University Coll., Leicester. BSc, PhD(Lond); MA(Cantab). Lectr, Univ. of Sheffield, 1954–58; Sen. Lectr, Univ. of

Melbourne, Australia, 1958–60; Lectr, Univ. of Cambridge, 1960–67; Prof., Flinders Univ., S Australia, 1967–70; Prof. of Genetics, Univ. of Glasgow, 1970–79. Fellow, Churchill Coll., Cambridge, 1961–67. *Publications:* scientific papers in genetical, biochemical and microbiological jls. *Recreations:* reading, music, walking. *Address:* 1 Abberbury Road, Oxford OX4 4ET. *T:* (01865) 748275. *Club:* Oxford and Cambridge. *Died 18 May 2011.*

PATERSON, His Honour Frank David; a Circuit Judge (formerly County Court Judge), 1968–93; *b* 10 July 1918; *yr s* of late David Paterson and Dora Paterson, Liverpool; *m* 1953, Barbara Mary, 2nd *d* of late Oswald Ward Gillow and Alice Gillow, Formby; one *s* two *d*. *Educ:* Calderstones Preparatory Sch. and Quarry Bank High Sch., Liverpool; Univ. of Liverpool (LLB). Called to Bar, Gray's Inn, 1941; Warden, Unity Boys' Club, Liverpool, 1941; Asst Warden, Florence Inst. for Boys, Liverpool, 1943. Practised on Northern Circuit. Chairman: Min. of Pensions and Nat. Insce Tribunal, Liverpool, 1957; Mental Health Review Tribunal for SW Lancashire and Cheshire, 1963. Asst Dep. Coroner, City of Liverpool, 1960. Pres., Merseyside Magistrates' Assoc., 1978–93; Jt Pres., Council of HM Circuit Judges, 1987. Hon. LLD Liverpool, 1993. *Address:* Vailima, 2 West Lane, Formby, Liverpool L37 7BA. *T:* (01704) 874345. *Club:* Athenæum (Liverpool). *Died 22 April 2014.*

PATNICK, Sir (Cyril) Irvine, Kt 1994; OBE 1980; Chairman, Watt Solutions Ltd, 2004–09; *b* 29 Oct. 1929; *m* 1960, Lynda Margaret (*née* Rosenfield); one *s* one *d*. *Educ:* Sheffield Poly. FCIOB. Member: Sheffield City Council, 1967–70; Sheffield MDC, 1971–88; S Yorks CC, until abolition in 1986 (Opposition Leader, 1973–86); Dep. Chm., S Yorks Residuary Body, 1985–87; Chm., Cons. Party Local Govt Adv. Cttee, 1989–90. Contested (C) Sheffield, Hillsborough, 1970, 1979. MP (C) Sheffield, Hallam, 1987–97; contested (C) same seat, 1997. An Asst Govt Whip, 1989–90; a Lord Comr of HM Treasury (Govt Whip), 1990–94. Member: Envmt Select Cttee, 1994–97; Cttee of Selection, 1997; Dep. Chm., Channel Tunnel Rail Link Bill Select Cttee, 1995–96. Vice-Chm., Cons. Party Back Bench Envmt Cttee, 1988–89. Member: Council of Europe, 1995–97; WEU, 1995–97. Mem., Cons. Party NEC, 1987–89. Chm., Yorks and Humberside Council for Sport and Recreation, 1979–85; Member: Sheffield Community Health Council, 1974–75; Yorks and Humberside Tourist Bd, 1977–79; Governor, Sports Aid Foundn, Yorks and Humberside, 1980–85. Chm., Keyturn Solutions Ltd, 1997–2004. Hon. Life Vice-Pres., ACC Ltd, 2003. Patron, Home Business Alliance, 1999–. Freeman, City of London, 1996. *Died 30 Dec. 2012.*

PATTEN, (Hilda Elsie) Marguerite, CBE 2010 (OBE 1991); freelance cookery writer, broadcaster and lecturer, since 1952; *b* Bath, 4 Nov. 1915; *d* of Wallace and Elsie Ann Brown; *m* 1942, Sqdn Ldr Charles Alfred Patten (*d* 1997); one *d*. *Educ:* Queen Elizabeth Girls' Grammar Sch., Barnet; cookery courses, Barnet, 1932; N Metropolitan Coll. (trng as Home Economist 1932). Jun. Home Economist, N Metropolitan Electric Power Supply Co., 1935–38; Sen. Home Economist, Frigidaire, 1938–39; Sen. Food Advr, Yorkshire Power Co., 1939–41; Advr, Min. of Food, 1941–44; Food Advr, Harrods, 1944–52. *Publications:* books include: Harrods Cookery Book, 1947; The Creda Housecraft Manual, 1958; Cookery in Colour, 1960; Marguerite Patten's Book of Cakes and Baking, 1961; Step-by-step Cooking, 1963; Round the World Cookery, 1964; Marguerite Patten's Family Cookbook, 1964; Marguerite Patten's Make a Menu Book, 1965; Everyday Cook Book in Colour, 1968; Junior Cook Book, 1971; Cooking Today in Colour, 1972; Family Cooking, 1973; Recipes for Two, 1973; Family Cook Book, 1975; Successful Baking, 1984; 1000 Favourite Recipes, 1985; We'll Eat Again, 1985; What's Cooking: recipes of a lifetime, 1992; Classic British Dishes, 1994; Soups, 1996; Post-War Kitchen, 1998; Marguerite Patten's Century of British Cooking, 1999; Spam: the cookbook, 2000; (with J. Ewin) Eat to Beat Arthritis, 2001; The Basic Basics Jams, Preserves and Chutney, 2001; The Basic Basics Soups Handbook, 2002; The Basic Basics Baking Handbook, 2002; Victory Cookbook: nostalgic food and facts from 1940–1954, 2002; Coronation Cookbook, 2002; The War-Time Kitchen, 2004; (with J. Ewin) The Healthy Gut Cookbook, 2004; Feeding the Nation: nostalgic recipes and facts from 1940–1954, 2005; Marguerite Patten's 100 Top Teatime Treats, 2005; Marguerite Patten's Best British Dishes, 2008; The Basic Basics Pressure Cooker Book, 2010. *Recreations:* gardening, music, especially opera. *Died 4 June 2015.*

PAUNCEFORT-DUNCOMBE, Sir Philip; *see* Duncombe.

PAWSON, Prof. Anthony James, CH 2006; OC 2000; PhD; FRS 1994; FRSC 1994; Senior Scientist, since 1985, and Director, 2002–05, Samuel Lunenfeld Research Institute, Mount Sinai Hospital, Toronto; Professor, Department of Molecular Genetics, University of Toronto, since 1985; *b* 18 Oct. 1952; *s* of late Henry Anthony Pawson, OBE and Hilarie Anne Pawson (*née* Bassett); *m* 1975, Margaret Anne Luman (*d* 2011); two *s* one *d*. *Educ:* Clare Coll., Cambridge (BA); London Univ. (PhD). Grad. Student, ICRF, London, 1973–76; Postdoctoral Fellow, Univ. of Calif, Berkeley, 1976–80; Asst Prof., Univ. of BC, 1981–85. Sen. Scientist, 1985–88, Terry Fox Cancer Res. Scientist, 1988–98, Nat. Cancer Inst. of Canada; Internat. Res. Schol., Howard Hughes Med. Inst., 1991–2001; Apotex Prof. of Molecular Oncology, Mt Sinai Hosp., 1991–. Associate Mem., EMBO, 2003; Foreign Associate, US NAS, 2004; For. Mem., Amer. Acad. of Arts and Scis, 2004; Fellow, Amer. Acad. of Microbiol., 2004; Hon. Mem., Japanese Biochem. Soc., 2005. Hon. DSc: Alberta, 2008; McMaster, 2010; MD *hc* Karolinska Inst., 2010. Gairdner Foundn Internat. Award, 1994; Robert L. Noble Prize, Nat. Cancer Inst. of Canada, 1995; Amer. Assoc. for Cancer Res. Inc./Pezcoller Internat. Award, 1998; Dr H. P. Heineken Prize for Biochem. and Physics, Royal Netherlands Acad. of Arts and Scis, 1998; Flavelle Medal, RSC, 1998; Dist. Scientist Award, MRC of Canada, 1998; Henry Friesen Award, Canadian Soc. for Clinical Investigation, 1998; Killam Prize for Health Scis, Canada Council for the Arts, 2000; J. Allyn Taylor Internat. Prize in Medicine, Univ. of Western Ont., 2000; Michael Smith Prize for Health Res., CIHR, 2002; Louisa Gross Horwitz Prize, Columbia Univ., 2004; Poulsson Medal, Norwegian Soc. of Pharmacol. and Toxicol., 2004; Ernst W. Bertner Meml Award, MD Anderson Cancer Center, 2004; Wolf Prize in Medicine, Wolf Foundn, Israel, 2005; Royal Medal, Royal Soc., 2005; Daniel Nathans Meml Award, Van Andel Res. Inst., 2005; Howard Taylor Ricketts Award, Univ. of Chicago, 2007; Herbert Tabor/Jl of Biol Chem. Lectureship Award, Amer. Soc. for Biochem. and Molecular Biol., 2007; Jubilee Lecture Award, Biochemical Soc., 2007; Diamond Jubilee Award, Nat. Cancer Inst. of Canada, 2007; Kyoto Prize in Basic Sciences, Inamori Foundn, 2008; inaugural Hon. Medal, Signal Transduction Soc., 2010; Award, Canadian Cancer Res. Alliance, 2011; Dist. Researcher Award, Canadian Nat. Proteomics Network, 2013. Mem., Order of Ontario, 2004. *Publications:* papers in Nature, Cell, Science, Molecular and Cell Biol., Proc. Nat. Acad. of Sci. (USA), Jl Virology, EMBO Jl, Jl Biol Chem., Oncogene and other learned jls. *Recreations:* reading, theatre, fly-fishing, ski-ing, baseball. *Address:* Samuel Lunenfeld Research Institute, Mount Sinai Hospital, 600 University Avenue, Toronto, ON M5G 1X5, Canada. *T:* (416) 5868262; 34 Glenwood Avenue, Toronto, ON M6P 3C6, Canada. *T:* (416) 7632266. *Died 7 Aug. 2013.*

PEACOCK, Prof. Sir Alan (Turner), Kt 1987; DSC 1945; MA; FBA 1979; FRSE; Hon. Research Professor in Public Finance, Heriot-Watt University, since 1987; *b* 26 June 1922; *s* of late Professor A. D. Peacock, FRSE and of Clara Mary (*née* Turner); *m* 1944, Margaret Martha Astell Burt (*d* 2011); two *s* one *d*. *Educ:* Grove Acad.; Dundee High School; University of St Andrews (1939–42, 1945–47). Royal Navy, 1942–45 (Lieut RNVR). Lecturer in Economics: Univ. of St Andrews, 1947–48; London Sch. of Economics, 1948–51 (Hon. Fellow, 1980); Reader in Public Finance, Univ. of London, 1951–56; Prof. of Economic Science, Univ. of Edinburgh, 1957–62; Prof. of Economics, Univ. of York, 1962–78; Prof. of Economics, and Principal-designate, University Coll. at Buckingham, 1978–80, Principal, 1980–83; Vice-Chancellor, Univ. of Buckingham, 1983–84, Professor Emeritus, 1985–; Exec.

Dir, David Hume Inst., Edinburgh, 1985–90 (Hon. Pres., 2002–05). Seconded from Univ. of York as Chief Economic Advr, Depts of Industry and Trade, 1973–76. Visiting Prof. of Economics, Johns Hopkins Univ., 1958. Keynes Lectr, British Acad., 1994. Mem., 1959–87, Chm., 1991–93, Adv. Council, IEA (Trustee, 1987–93; Hon. Fellow, 1994); Member: Commission of Enquiry into land and population problems of Fiji, 1959; Departmental Committee on Electricity in Scotland, 1961; Council, REconS, 1961–78; Cttee of Enquiry on impact of rates, 1964; Commn on the Constitution, 1970–73; SSRC, 1972–73; Cttee of Inquiry on Retirement Provision, 1984; Chm., Rowntree Inquiry into Corporate Takeovers, 1990–91. Chm., UN Adv. Mission to Russian Fedn on Social Protection, 1992. Pres., Internat. Inst. of Public Finance, 1966–69. Mem., Arts Council, 1986–92; Chairman: Arts Council Enquiry on Orchestral Resources, 1969–70; Cttee on Financing the BBC, 1985–86; Scottish Arts Council, 1986–92. Non-executive Director: Economist Intelligence Unit Ltd, 1977–84; Caledonian Bank plc, 1991–96. FRSE 1989. Corresp. Fellow, Accademia Nazionale dei Lincei, Rome, 1996. Hon. Mem., Royal Soc. of Musicians, 1996. DUniv: Stirling, 1974; Brunel, 1989; York, 1997; Hon. DEcon Zürich, 1984; Hon. DSc: Buckingham, 1986; Edinburgh, 1990; Hon. LLD: St Andrews, 1990; Dundee, 1990; Dr *hc*: Catania, 1991; Lisbon, 1999; Turin, 2001. *Publications:* Economics of National Insurance, 1952; (ed) Income Redistribution and Social Policy 1954; National Income and Social Accounting (with H. C. Edey), 1954, 3rd imp. 1967; The National Income of Tanganyika (1952–54) (with D. G. M. Dosser), 1958; The Growth of Public Expenditure in the UK, 1890–1955 (with J. Wiseman), 1961; Economic Theory of Fiscal Policy (with G. K. Shaw), 1971, 2nd edn, 1976; The Composer in the Market Place (with R. Weir), 1975; Welfare Economics: a liberal re-interpretation (with C. K. Rowley), 1975; Economic Analysis of Government, 1979; (ed and contrib.) Structural Economic Policies in West Germany and the UK, 1980; (ed jtly) Political Economy of Taxation, 1981; (ed and contrib.) The Regulation Game, 1984; (ed jtly) Public Expenditure and Government Growth, 1985; Waltz Contrasts (for piano solo), 1988; Public Choice Analysis in Historical Perspective, 1992; (with G. Bannock) Corporate Takeovers and the Public Interest, 1991; Paying the Piper, 1993; (ed jtly) Cultural Economics and Cultural Policies, 1994; Political Economy of Economic Freedom, 1997; (ed) The Political Economy of Heritage, 1998; (with B. Main) What Price Civil Justice?, 2000; Calling the Tune, 2001; The Enigmatic Sailor, 2003; Public Broadcasting Without the BBC?, 2004; (with I. Rizzo) The Heritage Game: economics, policy and practice, 2008; Anxious to Do Good, 2010; Defying Decrepitude, 2013; articles on applied economics in Economic Jl, Economica and other journals. *Recreations:* trying to write music, wine spotting. *E:* pavone@blueyonder.co.uk. *Club:* Reform. *Died 2 Aug. 2014.*

PEAKE, David Alphy Edward Raymond; Chairman, BNP Paribas (formerly Banque Nationale de Paris) UK Hldgs Ltd, 1997–2005 (Director, since 1974); Director, BNP Paribas (formerly Banque Nationale de Paris) SA, 1998–2004; *b* 27 Sept. 1934; *s* of Sir Harald Peake, AE and Mrs Resy Peake, OBE; *m* 1962, Susanna Kleinwort; one *s* one *d*. *Educ:* Ampleforth Coll.; Christ Church, Oxford (MA History, 1958). 2nd Lieut Royal Scots Greys, 1953–55. Banque Lambert, Brussels, 1958–59; J. Henry Schroder Wagg & Co. Ltd, 1959–63; Kleinwort Benson Ltd, 1963–93: Dir, 1971–93; Vice-Chm., 1985–87; Chm., 1988–89; Chm., Kleinwort Benson Group plc, 1989–93 (Dir, 1986–96); Hargreaves Group, 1964–86: Dir, 1964–86; Vice-Chm., 1967–74; Chm., 1974–86; Dir, M&G Gp, 1979–87. Pt-time Mem. of Bd, British Liby, 1990–96. Chairman: City and Inner London N TEC, 1990–93; 21st Century Learning Initiative (UK) (formerly Educn 2000 Trust), 1994–2010; Mem., BOTB, 1993–96. Chm., Chipping Norton Theatre Ltd, 1995–2010. Trustee, Harefield Hosp. Fund, 1994–95. Mem. Council, Goldsmiths Coll., Univ. of London, 1997–2004. Mem. Ct of Assts, Goldsmiths' Co., 1992– (Prime Warden, 2003–04). *Recreations:* reading, country sports. *Address:* Home Farm, Bourton-on-the-Hill, Moreton-in-Marsh GL56 9AF. *Clubs:* Brooks's, Pratt's, Cavalry and Guards. *Died 7 Sept. 2015.*

PEARCE, Most Rev. George Hamilton, SM; Archbishop Emeritus of Suva (RC); *b* 9 Jan. 1921; *s* of George H. Pearce and Marie Louise Duval. *Educ:* Marist Coll. and Seminary, Framingham Center, Mass, USA. Entered Seminary, 1940; Priest, 1947; taught in secondary sch. in New England, USA, 1948–49; assigned as missionary to Samoa, 1949; consecrated Vicar Apostolic of Samoa, 1956; first Bishop of Apia, 1966; Archbishop of Suva, 1967–76, retired 1976. *Address:* Cathedral Rectory, 30 Fenner Street, Providence, RI 02903, USA. *T:* (401) 3312434. *Died 30 Aug. 2015.*

PEARSON, Maj.-Gen. Ronald Matthew, CB 1985; MBE 1959; Director, Army Dental Service, 1982–85; *b* 25 Feb. 1925; *s* of Dr John Pearson and Sheila Pearson (*née* Brown); *m* 1956, Florence Eileen Jack; two *d*. *Educ:* Clifton Hall Sch., Ratho, Midlothian; Glasgow Acad.; Glasgow Univ./Glasgow Dental Hosp. LDS RFPS(Glas) 1948; FBIM 1979. Civilian Dental Practice, 1948–49. Commnd RADC, 1949; served: RWAFF, 1950–53; UK, 1953–57; BAOR, 1957–60; UK, 1961–67; CO No 1 Dental Gp, BAOR, 1967–70; CO Army Dental Centres, Cyprus, 1970–73; CO No 8 Dental Gp, UK, 1973–75; CO No 4 Dental Gp, UK, 1975–76; Dep. Dir Dental Service, UKLF, 1976–78; Dep. Dir Dental Service, BAOR, 1978–82. QHDS, 1978–85. CStJ 1983. *Recreations:* trout fishing, photography, gardening, caravanning. *Address:* 27 Glenearn Court, Pittenze Street, Crieff, Perthshire PH7 3LE. *Died 14 Dec. 2011.*

PECK, Stanley Edwards, CBE 1974; BEM 1954; QPM 1964; DL; HM Inspector of Constabulary, 1964–78; *b* 24 Jan. 1916; *er s* of late Harold Edwards Peck, Edgbaston and Shanghai; *m* 1st, 1939, Yvonne Sydney Edwards (*d* 1994), *er d* of late John Edwards Jessop, LDS; two *s* two *d*; 2nd, 1996, Elizabeth Beddows; one step *s* one step *d*. *Educ:* Solihull School; Birmingham University. Served with RAF, 1941–45 (Flt-Lt). Joined Metropolitan Police, 1935; Chief Inspector and Supt, New Scotland Yard, 1950–54; Asst Chief Constable, Staffs, 1954–61; Chief Constable, Staffs, 1961–64. DL Staffs, 1962. Pres., Royal Life Saving Soc., UK, 1969–74 (Chm., East Midlands Region, RLSS, 1968–80). OStJ. *Address:* April Cottage, Butchers Hill, Ickleton, Saffron Walden, Essex CB10 1SR. *Club:* Royal Air Force. *Died 24 Jan. 2014.*

PEEL, Prof. John David Yeadon, FBA 1991; Professor of Anthropology and Sociology, with reference to Africa, School of Oriental and African Studies, University of London, 1989–2007, then Professor Emeritus; *b* 13 Nov. 1941; *e s* of late Prof. Edwin Arthur Peel and Nora Kathleen Yeadon; *m* 1st, 1969, Jennifer Christine Ferial (marr. diss. 2000), *d* of K. N. Pare, Leicester; three *s*; 2nd, 2014, Anne Ogbigbo. *Educ:* King Edward's Sch., Birmingham; Balliol Coll., Oxford (Scholar; BA 1963, MA 1966); LSE (PhD 1966); DLit London 1985. Asst Lectr, then Lectr in Sociology, Nottingham Univ., 1965–70; Lectr in Sociology, LSE, 1970–73; Charles Booth Prof. of Sociology, 1975–89, Dean, Faculty of Social and Envmtl Studies, 1985–88, Univ. of Liverpool; Dean of Undergraduate Studies, SOAS, 1990–94. Vis. Reader in Sociology and Anthropology, Univ. of Ife, Nigeria, 1973–75; Vis. Prof. in Anthropology and Sociology, Univ. of Chicago, 1982–83; Marett Lectr, 1993, Associate, Inst. of Develt Studies, 1973–94. Pres., African Studies Assoc. of UK, 1996–98; Vice-Pres., British Acad., 1999–2000. Chm. Trustees, Internat. African Inst., 2006– (Editor, Africa, and Officer, 1979–86); Gen. Editor, Internat. African Library, 1986–. Frazer Lectr, Univ. of Oxford, 2000; Galton Lectr, 2003; Roy H. Rappaport Lectr, 2003; Birkbeck Lectr in Ecclesiastical History, Univ. of Cambridge, 2009; Winchester Lectr in World Religions, Univ. of Oxford, 2011. Hon. DLitt Birmingham, 2012. Amaury Talbot Prize, RAI, 1983, 2000; Herskovits Award, African Studies Assoc., USA, 1984, 2001. *Publications:* Aladura: a religious movement among the Yoruba, 1968; Herbert Spencer: the evolution of a sociologist, 1971; (ed) Herbert Spencer on Social Evolution, 1972; Ijeshas and Nigerians, 1983; Religious Encounter and the Making of the Yoruba, 2000;

articles in anthropological, sociological and Africanist jls; *Festschrift:* Christianity and Social Change in Africa: essays in honour of J. D. Y. Peel, ed Toyin Falola, 2005; Christianity, Islam and the Orisa: comparative studies of Three Religions in interaction and transformation, 2015. *Recreations:* gardening, fell-walking, French church architecture. *Address:* 80 Archway Road, N19 3TT. *T:* (020) 7272 9487. *Died 2 Nov. 2015.*

PEEL, Rev. Jonathan Sidney, CBE 1994; MC 1957; Vice Lord-Lieutenant of Norfolk, 1981–2005; Ordained Local Minister, Horning Benefice, Diocese of Norwich, since 2001; *b* 21 June 1937; *s* of Major D. A. Peel, MC (killed in action 1944) and Hon. Mrs David Peel (*née* Vanneck); *m* 1965, Jean Fulton Barnett, *d* of Air Chief Marshal Sir Denis Barnett, GCB, CBE, DFC; one *s* four *d*. *Educ:* Norwich Sch.; Eton; St John's Coll., Cambridge (BA Land Economy; MA 1970); Norwich Dio. OLM Scheme. Commnd, Rifle Bde, Royal Green Jackets, 1956; served Malaya, 1956–57; UN forces, Congo (Zaire), 1960–61; Cyprus, 1962–63; resigned, 1966. Dir, Norwich Union Insce Gp, 1973–98; Chm., Pleasureworld plc, 1986–89. Vice Pres., Norfolk Naturalists Trust, 1984–2000; National Trust: Mem. Exec. Cttee, 1982–2002; Mem. Council, 1984–2002; Dep. Chm., 1992–2002; Chm., Cttee for East Anglia, 1981–90; Chm., Properties Cttee, 1990–2000. Norfolk Scouts Association: Dist Comr, 1971–75; Comr for Norwich, 1975–77; County Comr, 1977–81. Chairman: E Anglian Br., Royal Forestry Soc., 1979–81; Norfolk Police Authority, 1983–89; Norfolk Churches Trust, 1983–85; The Broads Authority, 1985–97; Norwich Sch., 1985–2003; How Hill Trust, 1987–2007; Pres., Norfolk Assoc. for the Advancement of Music, 1978–93. Mem., Norfolk CC, 1973–97 (Chm., Planning and Transportation Cttee, 1990–93). JP North Walsham, 1973–86. High Sheriff, Norfolk, 1984. Ordained deacon, 2000, priest, 2001, C of E. Hon. DCL UEA, 2005. *Publications:* (with M. J. Sayer) Towards a Rural Policy for Norfolk, 1973. *Recreations:* forestry, music. *Address:* Barton Hall, Barton Turf, Norwich NR12 8AU. *T:* (01692) 536250. *Clubs:* Boodle's; Norfolk (Norwich). *Died 11 Dec. 2014.*

PEIRSE, Sir Henry Grant de la Poer B.; *see* Beresford-Peirse.

PEIRSE, Air Vice-Marshal Sir Richard (Charles Fairfax), KCVO 1988; CB 1984; Registrar and Secretary, Order of the Bath, 2002–06; *b* 16 March 1931; *s* of late Air Chief Marshal Sir Richard Peirse, KCB, DSO, AFC and late Lady Peirse; *m* 1st, 1955, Karalie Grace Cox (marr. diss. 1963); two *d*; 2nd, 1963, Deirdre Mary O'Donovan (*d* 1976); (one *s* decd); 3rd, 1977, Anna Jill Margaret Long (*née* Latey). *Educ:* Bradfield Coll.; RAF Coll., Cranwell. Commnd 1952; 2nd TAF No 266 Sqdn and HQ 2 Gp, 1952; Flying Instructor, Cranwell, 1956; Air Staff No 23 Gp, 1960; Staff Coll., 1962; Flt Comdr No 39 Sqdn and OC Ops Wg, Luqa, Malta, 1963; Air Sec.'s Dept, 1965; jssc 1968; OC No 51 Sqdn, 1968; Dep. Captain, The Queen's Flight, 1969; RCDS 1972; OC RAF Waddington, 1973; Dep. Dir, Op Requirements, 1976; Dir of Personnel (Air), 1977; Dir of Op Requirements, 1980; AOC and Comdt, RAF Coll. Cranwell, 1982; Defence Services Sec., 1985–88, retd. Gentleman Usher of the Scarlet Rod, Order of the Bath, 1990–2002. *Recreations:* theatre, archaeology. *Address:* Bemerton House, Lower Bemerton, Salisbury, Wilts SP2 9NH. *T:* (01722) 321921. *Club:* Royal Air Force. *Died 8 Feb. 2014.*

PELIZA, Sir Robert (John), KBE 1998 (OBE 1989); ED 1955; company director, since 1962; Speaker, House of Assembly, Gibraltar, 1989–96; *b* 16 Nov. 1920; *s* of late Robert Peliza; *m* 1950, Irma Risso; three *s* three *d* (and one *d* decd). *Educ:* Christian Brothers' Coll., Gibraltar. Served in Gibraltar Defence Force (later Royal Gibraltar Regt), 1939–61. Founder Mem., Integration with Britain Party (first leader), 1967; Chief Minister, 1969–72, apptd following Gen. Elections, 1969; elected MHA, 1969–84; Leader of the Opposition, 1972–73. Pres., Gibraltar Br., CPA, 1989. Hon. Col, Gibraltar Regt, 1993–98. *Recreations:* walking, painting, reading, jogging, cycling, rowing. *Address:* 125 Beverley Drive, Edgware, Middlesex HA8 5NH. *T:* and *Fax:* (020) 8952 1712. *Died 12 Dec. 2011.*

PELLEREAU, Maj.-Gen. Peter John Mitchell, MA, CEng, FIMechE, FIMgt; Secretary, Association of Consulting Engineers, 1977–87; *b* Quetta, British India, 24 April 1921; *s* of late Col J. C. E. Pellereau, OBE and Mrs A. N. V. Pellereau (*née* Betham); *m* 1949, Rosemary, *e d* of late S. R. Garnar; two *s*. *Educ:* Wellington Coll.; Trinity Coll., Cambridge (BA 1942, MA 1957). Commnd into Royal Engrs, 1942; War Service in NW Europe, 1944–45; OC 26 Armd Engr Sqdn, RE, 1946; ptsc, psc, 1950–51; Sec., Defence Research Policy Cttee, 1960; Asst Mil. Sec., WO, 1961; CO 131 Parachute Engr Regt RE TA, 1963; Mil. Dir of Studies, RMCS, 1965; Asst Dir RE Equipment Develt, 1967; Sen. Mil. Officer, Royal Armament R&D Estabt, 1970; Vice-Pres., 1973–75, Pres., 1975–76, Ordnance Board; retired 1976. Hon. Col, RE (Vol.) (Explosive Ordnance Disposal), 1980–86. Liveryman: Worshipful Co. of Plumbers, 1977–92; Worshipful Co. of Engineers, 1984–92. Mem., Smeatonian Soc. of Civil Engineers, 1981– (Pres., 2002). Vice-Pres., Surrey Hockey Umpires' Assoc., 1979–85; Pres., Oxted Hockey Club, 1975–84. Mem., Wolfe Soc. Cttee, 1970– (Vice Pres., 2007–); Chm., Westerham Motorway Action Gp, 1993–2001. *Address:* Woodmans Folly, Crockham Hill, Edenbridge, Kent TN8 6RJ. *T:* and *Fax:* (01732) 866309. *Died 15 Feb. 2014.*

PELLY, Derek Roland, (Derk); Deputy Chairman, Barclays Bank PLC, 1986–88 (Vice Chairman, 1984–85); *b* 12 June 1929; *s* of late Arthur Roland Pelly and Elsie Pelly; *m* 1953, Susan Roberts; one *s* two *d*. *Educ:* Marlborough; Trinity Coll., Cambridge. Served RA, 1947–49 (2nd Lieut). Entered Barclays Bank, 1952; Local Director: Chelmsford, 1959; Luton, 1969; Vice Chm., 1977–85, Chm., 1986–87, Barclays Internat. Ltd. Dir, The Private Bank & Trust Co., 1989–94. Member: Milton Keynes Develt Corp., 1976–85; Council, ODI, 1984–89. Mem. Cttee, Family Assce Soc., 1988–91. Dir, Chelmsford Dio. Bd of Finance, 1989–96. Governor: London House for Overseas Graduates, 1985–91; Chelmsford Coll., 1994–95. *Recreation:* painting. *Address:* 2 Swallow Field, Earls Colne, Colchester CO6 2RW. *T:* (01787) 223389. *Died 14 Feb. 2015.*

PEMBERTON, Sir Francis (Wingate William), Kt 1976; CBE 1970; DL; FRICS; company director; *b* 1 Oct. 1916; *s* of late Dr William Warburton Wingate (assumed Arms of Pemberton, by Royal Licence, 1921) and Viola Patience Campbell Pemberton; *m* 1st, 1941, Diana Patricia (*d* 1999), *e d* of late Reginald Salisbury Woods, MD, and Irene Woods, CBE, TD; two *s*; 2nd, 2002, Mrs Mary Dadd. *Educ:* Eton; Trinity Coll., Cambridge (MA). Senior Consultant, Bidwells, Chartered Surveyors, 1980–89. Director: Agricultural Mortgage Corp. Ltd, 1969–91; Barclays Bank UK Ltd, 1977–81; Severn Trent Property Ltd, 1990–95. Chm. Adv. Cttee, Inst. of Animal Physiology and Genetics Res. (Cambridge and Edinburgh), 1983–90; Hon. Dir, Royal Show, 1963–68; Royal Agricultural Society of England: Mem. Council, 1951– (Pres., 1974–75, Dep. Pres., 1975–76); Chm. Exec. Bd, 1969–71; Trustee, 1969–; Gold Medal for distinguished services to agric., 1989. Trustee, Robinson Coll., Cambridge, 1973–85. Member: Water Resources Board, 1964–74; Winston Churchill Meml Trust, 1965–80; Economic Planning Council for East Anglia, 1965–74; National Water Council, 1974–81; Water Authorities Superannuation Pension Fund (Dep. Chm., Fund Management and Policy Cttee), 1983–89. High Sheriff, Cambridgeshire and Isle of Ely, 1965–66; DL Cambs, 1979. *Address:* The Flat, Trumpington Hall, Cambridge CB2 9LH. *T:* (01223) 841941. *Club:* Farmers. *Died 2 Nov. 2011.*

PENFOLD, Maj.-Gen. Robert Bernard, CB 1969; LVO 1957; *b* 19 Dec. 1916; *s* of late Bernard Hugh Penfold, Selsey, and Ethel Ives Arnold; *m* 1940, Ursula (*d* 2010), *d* of late Lt-Col E. H. Gray; two *d*. *Educ:* Wellington; RMC, Sandhurst. 2nd Lieut, Royal Leics Regt, 1936; commnd into 11th Sikh Regt, Indian Army, 1937; served in NWFP and during War of 1939–45 in Middle East, Central Mediterranean Forces; Instructor, Staff Coll., Quetta,

1946–47; transf. to British Army, RA, 1947; RN Staff Coll., 1953; Secretary, British Joint Services Mission, Washington, 1957–59; comdg 6 King's African Rifles, Tanganyika, 1959–61; Comdr 127 Inf. Bde (TA), 1962–64; Security Ops Adviser to High Commissioner, Aden, 1964–65; Imperial Defence Coll., 1966; Chief of Defence Staff, Kenya, 1966–69; GOC South East District, 1969–72. Gen. Manager and Chief Exec., Royal Hong Kong Jockey Club, 1972–80. Chm., Horseracing Adv. Council, 1980–86. *Recreations:* shooting, golf, gardening. *Address:* Park House, Amport, Andover, Hants SP11 8BW. *Club:* Army and Navy. *Died 22 April 2015.*

PENRY-DAVEY, Hon. Sir David (Herbert), Kt 1997; a Judge of the High Court of Justice, Queen's Bench Division, 1997–2010; *b* 16 May 1942; *s* of late Watson and Lorna Penry-Davey; *m* 1970, Judy Walter; two *s* one *d.* *Educ:* Hastings Grammar Sch.; King's Coll., London (LLB Hons; FKC 1998). British Univs debating tour of Canada, 1964. Called to the Bar, Inner Temple, 1965, Bencher, 1993; a Recorder, 1986–97; QC 1988; Leader, S Eastern Circuit, 1992–95; a Dep. High Court Judge, 1994–97; Presiding Judge, Northern Circuit, 2000–03. Dep. Chm., Security Vetting Appeals Panel, 2004–13. Chm., Gen. Council of the Bar, 1996 (Vice-Chm., 1995). *Recreations:* music, golf, cycling, hill-walking. *Died 10 Oct. 2015.*

PENTECOST, Prof. Brian Leonard, OBE 2000; MD; FRCP; Medical Director, British Heart Foundation, 1993–99; *b* 12 March 1934; *s* of Leonard Austin Pentecost and Florence Pentecost; *m* 1958, Janice Morgan Jones; one *s* two *d* (and one *d* decd). *Educ:* Erith Grammar Sch.; St Mary's Med. Sch., Univ. of London (MB BS 1957; MD 1965). FRCP 1972. Jun. appts, St Mary's, Brompton and Hammersmith Hosps; Jun. Med. Specialist, RAMC, 1959–61; Consultant Physician and Cardiologist, United Birmingham Hosps, 1965–93; Dean of Postgraduate Med. and Dental Educn, 1987–91, Hon. Prof. of Medicine, 1991–96, then Emeritus, Univ. of Birmingham. Consultant Advr in Cardiology to CMO, 1986–93. Member: Med. Subcttee, UGC, 1985–89; Cttee on Safety of Medicines, 1984–89, 1996–98. Royal College of Physicians: Examr, 1977–92; Mem. Council, 1979–82; Censor, 1982–84; Linacre Fellow, 1991–94; Med. Co-ordinator, Jt Cttee on Higher Med. Educn, 1991–94. Mem. Council, 1973–77, Sec., 1976–80, British Cardiac Soc. Chm. Trustees, Royal Medical Benevolent Fund, 2001–07. Gov., The Health Foundation (formerly PPP Medical Healthcare Trust), 1998–2004. Hon. DSc Aston, 1998. *Publications:* contribs on cardiovascular medicine to books and scientific jls. *Recreations:* gardening, theatre, golf. *Address:* 37 Farquhar Road, Edgbaston, Birmingham B15 3RA. *Club:* Army and Navy. *Died 16 Jan. 2015.*

PERCIVAL, John, MBE 2002; freelance dance critic, since 1950; Joint Dance Critic, The Independent, since 1996; *b* 16 March 1927; *s* of Cecil Ernest Percival and Mua Phoebe Margaret Mary Percival (*née* Milchard); *m* 1954, Freda Betty Margaret Thorne-Large (marr. diss. 1972); *m* 1972, Judith Alymer Cruickshank. *Educ:* Sir George Monoux Grammar Sch., Walthamstow; St Catherine's Coll., Oxford (MA). On admin. staff, LCC, then GLC and ILEA, 1951–90. Archivist, Ballet Annual, 1960–64; ballet critic, New Daily, 1960–65; Associate Editor, 1964–81, Editor, 1981–94, Dance & Dancers; Chief Dance Critic, The Times, 1965–94; London correspondent: Dance Mag. (NY), 1965–89; German annual, Ballett, 1966–87; London dance critic, NY Times; Chm. and Dir, Dance & Dancers Ltd, 1991–94; Eur. correspondent, Ballet Review (NY), 1996–. Advr, Nureyev Foundn, 1993–. Mem. Cttee, Gulbenkian Foundn. Broadcaster on radio and TV in Britain, Europe, America and Australia. *Publications:* Antony Tudor, 1963; Modern Ballet, 1970, rev. edn 1980; The World of Diaghilev, 1971, rev. edn 1979; Experimental Dance, 1971; Nureyev: aspects of the dancer, 1975, rev. edn 1979 (trans. Italian 1981, Japanese 1983); The Facts about a Ballet Company, 1979; Theatre in My Blood: a biography of John Cranko, 1983 (trans. German 1985); (with Alexander Bland) Men Dancing, 1984; contributed to: Enciclopedia dello Spettacolo, 1966; Marcia Haydee, Ballerina, 1975; Encyclopaedia of Dance and Ballet, 1977; Das Ballett und die Künste, 1981; John Neumeier und das Hamburger Ballett, 1983, 2nd edn 1993. *Recreations:* watching dance and writing and talking about it, reading thrillers, eating with friends. *Address:* 13 Great James Street, WC1N 3DN. *T:* (020) 7405 0267. *Club:* Critics' Circle (Past Pres.). *Died 20 June 2012.*

PERCIVAL SMITH, Ven. (Anthony) Michael; Archdeacon of Maidstone, 1979–89; *b* 5 Sept. 1924; *s* of Kenneth and Audrey Smith; *m* 1950, Mildred Elizabeth; two *d.* *Educ:* Shrewsbury; Gonville and Caius Coll., Cambridge (MA); Westcott House Theological Coll. Served Army, Rifle Brigade, 1942–46. Cambridge, 1946–48; Westcott House, 1948–50. Deacon 1950, priest 1951; Curate, Holy Trinity, Leamington, 1950–53; Domestic Chaplain to Archbishop of Canterbury, 1953–57; Vicar of All Saints, Upper Norwood, 1957–66; Vicar of Yeovil, 1966–72; Prebendary of Wells Cathedral, 1968–72; RD of Murston, 1968–72; Vicar of St Mildred's, Addiscombe, Croydon, 1972–80; Hon. Canon of Canterbury Cathedral, 1980–89, then Canon Emeritus; Diocesan Dir of Ordinands, 1980–89; RD of Rye, 1991–93. *Recreations:* reading, walking. *Address:* Halliwell Nursing Home, Kingswood Road, Tunbridge Wells TN2 4UN. *Died 27 Sept. 2013.*

PERHAM, Prof. Richard Nelson, ScD; FRS 1984; FMedSci; Master, St John's College, Cambridge, 2004–07 (Fellow, since 1964); *b* 27 April 1937; *s* of Cyril Richard William Perham and Helen Harrow Perham (*née* Thornton); *m* 1969, Nancy Jane Lane, OBE; one *s* one *d.* *Educ:* Latymer Upper School; St John's College, Cambridge (BA 1961, MA 1965, PhD 1965, ScD 1976; Scholar; Slater Studentship, 1961–64; Henry Humphreys Prize, 1963). Nat. Service RN, 1956–58. Cambridge University: MRC Scholar, Lab. of Molecular Biol., 1961–64; Univ. Demonstrator in Biochem., 1964–69, Lectr, 1969–77; Reader in Biochemistry of Macromolecular Structures, 1977–89; Head, Dept of Biochem., 1985–96; Prof. of Structural Biochem., 1989–2004; Res. Fellow, St John's Coll., 1964–67, Tutor, 1967–77, Pres., 1983–87. Helen Hay Whitney Fellow, Dept of Molecular Biophysics, Yale Univ., 1966–67; EMBO Fellow, Max-Planck-Institut für Medizinische Forschung, Heidelberg, 1971; Drapers' Vis. Prof., Univ. of New South Wales, 1972; Biochem. Soc. Visitor, Aust. and NZ, 1979; Fogarty Internat. Scholar, NIH, USA, 1990–93. Member: EMBO, 1983; SRC Enzyme Chem. and Tech. Cttee, 1973–75; Enzyme Panel, Biol. Scis Cttee, 1975–76; SERC Science Bd, 1985–90; Biochem. Soc. Cttee, 1980–84; British Nat. Cttee for Biochem., 1982–87; Dir's Adv. Gp, AFRC Inst. of Animal Physiology, 1983–86; Exec. Council, Novartis (CIBA) Foundn, 1989–2002 (Trustee, 2002–08); Chm., Biol Scis Cttee, SERC, 1987–90 (Mem., 1983–85); Pres., Section D (Biological Scis), BAAS, 1987–88. Founder Chm., Cambridge Centre for Molecular Recognition, 1988–92. Chm., Scientific Adv. Cttee, Lister Inst. of Preventive Medicine, 2000–06 (Mem., 1992–98). Mem., Marshall Aid Commemoration Commn, FCO, 1999–2005 (Vice-Chm., 2004–05). Chm. Govs, Latymer Upper Sch., 2005–10 (Gov., 1990–2010). Mem., Academia Europaea, 1992. Syndic, CUP, 1988–2004. FRSA 1988; FMedSci 2005. Max Planck Res. Prize, 1993; Novartis Medal and Prize, 1998; Silver Medal, Italian Biochem. Soc., 2000; Edman Prize, Internat. Assoc. of Protein Structure Analysis and Proteomics, 2008; Diplôme d'Honneur, Fedn of Eur. Biochem. Socs, 2011. *Publications:* (ed) Instrumentation in Amino Acid Sequence Analysis, 1975; papers in sci. jls. *Recreations:* gardening, rowing (Lady Margaret BC), theatre, nosing around in antique shops. *Address:* St John's College, Cambridge CB2 1TP. *T:* (01223) 338600. *Clubs:* Oxford and Cambridge; Hawks (Cambridge). *Died 14 Feb. 2015.*

PERL, Prof. Martin Lewis, PhD; FInstP; Professor of Physics, Stanford Linear Accelerator Center, Stanford University, California, 1963–2004, then Emeritus; *b* Brooklyn, NY, 24 June 1927; *s* of Oscar Perl and Fay Rosenthal Perl; *m* 1948, Teri Hoch (marr. diss.); three *s* one *d.* *Educ:* Polytechnic Univ., NY (BE Chem. 1948); Columbia Univ., NY (PhD Physics 1955). FInstP 1998. Chemical Engr, General Electric Co., 1948–50; Research Asst, Columbia Univ., 1950–55; Instructor, Asst Prof. and Associate Prof., Univ. of Michigan, 1955–63; Chm. of Faculty, Stanford Univ., 1991. Mem., US Nat. Acad. of Scis, 1980–. Hon. DSc Chicago, 1990. Wolf Prize in

Physics, Wolf Foundn, Israel, 1982; Nobel Prize in Physics, 1995. *Publications:* High Energy Hadron Physics, 1974; Physics Careers, Employment and Education, 1977; The Search for New Elementary Particles, 1992; The Tau-Charm Factory, 1994; Reflections on Experimental Science, 1996; numerous in physics and in science education. *Recreations:* collecting mechanical antiques, swimming, gardening. *Address:* Stanford Linear Accelerator Laboratory, 2575 Sand Hill Road, Menlo Park, CA 94025, USA. *T:* (650) 9262652. *Died 30 Sept. 2014.*

PERRY, Rev. Canon Michael Charles, MA; Canon Residentiary, 1970–98, then Canon Emeritus, and Sub-Dean, 1985–98, Durham Cathedral; Senior Chaplain to the Bishop of Durham, 1993–98; *b* 5 June 1933; *o s* of late Charlie Perry; *m* 1963, Margaret, *o d* of late John Middleton Adshead; two *s* one *d*. *Educ:* Ashby-de-la-Zouch Boys' Grammar Sch.; Trinity Coll., Cambridge (Sen. Schol.); Westcott House, Cambridge. Asst Curate of Berkswich, Stafford, 1958–60; Chaplain, Ripon Hall, Oxford, 1961–63; Chief Asst for Home Publishing, SPCK, 1963–70; Archdeacon of Durham, 1970–93. Examining Chaplain to Bishop of Lichfield, 1965–74. Sec., Archbishops' Commn on Christian Doctrine, 1967–70. Diocesan Chm., 1970–81, Mem. Council, 1975–81, USPG; Mem., 1981–88, Vice-Chm., 1982–88, Hosp. Chaplaincies Council, Gen. Synod; Mem. Council for the Deaf, Gen. Synod, 1986–90. Mem., Durham HA, 1982–88. Trustee, 1970–96, Chm., 1982–96, Lord Crewe's Charity; Chm., Churches' Fellowship for Psychical and Spiritual Studies, 1986–95 (Pres., 1998–2008). Lectures: Selwyn, NZ, 1976; Marshall Meml, Melbourne, 1976; Beard Meml, London, 1977; Maurice Elliott Meml, London, 1986; Shepherd Meml, Worcester, 1988. DD Lambeth, 2003. Editor: Church Quarterly, 1968–71; Christian Parapsychologist, 1978–2008. *Publications:* The Easter Enigma, 1959; The Pattern of Matins and Evensong, 1961; (co-author) The Churchman's Companion, 1963; Meet the Prayer Book, 1963; (contrib.) The Miracles and the Resurrection, 1964; (ed) Crisis for Confirmation, 1967; (co-author) Declaring The Faith: The Printed Word, 1969; Sharing in One Bread, 1973; The Resurrection of Man, 1975; The Paradox of Worship, 1977; A Handbook of Parish Worship, 1977, 2nd edn 1989; (contrib.) Yes to Women Priests, 1978; (co-author) A Handbook of Parish Finance, 1981, 3rd edn 1992; Psychic Studies: a Christian's view, 1984; Miracles Then and Now, 1986; (ed) Deliverance, 1987, reissue of 2nd edn 2012; Gods Within: a critical guide to the New Age, 1992; Psychical and Spiritual, 2003. *Address:* 57 Ferens Park, Durham DH1 1NU. *T:* (0191) 386 1891. *Died 22 Jan. 2015.*

PERSKE, Betty Joan; *see* Bacall, B. J.

PESKETT, Stanley Victor, MA; Principal, Royal Belfast Academical Institution, 1959–78; *b* 9 May 1918; *o s* of Sydney Timber and Mary Havard Peskett; *m* 1948, Prudence Eileen, OBE 1974, *o d* of C. R. A. and M. A. Goatly; two *s* one *d* (and one *d* decd). *Educ:* Whitgift Sch.; St Edmund Hall, Oxford. Served War, 1939–46 (despatches) in Royal Marines, Norway, Shetland, Normandy, India and Java; Lt-Col, 1944; two Admiralty awards for inventions. Senior English Master, 1946–59, Housemaster 1954–59, The Leys School. Mem. Cttee, Headmasters' Conf., 1976; Mem. Council, Headmasters' Assoc., and Pres., Ulster Headmasters' Assoc., 1973–75; Chm., Northern Ireland Cttee, Voluntary Service Overseas, 1969–78; Founder Pres., Irish Schools Swimming Assoc., 1968–69 (Chm., Ulster Branch, 1968–78); Chm., NI Branch, School Library Assoc., 1964–73; Governor, Belfast Sch. of Music, 1974–77; Mem. Adv. Council, UDR, 1975–78. *Publications:* The Metfield Clock, 1980; (contrib.) People, Poverty and Protest in Hoxne Hundred 1780–1880, 1982; Only For a Day, 1984; Our Names, 1985; Wheelock 'Founder of Medfield', 1992; Monumental Inscriptions, Metfield, Suffolk, 1992; Metfield Parish and Poor in the late 18th Century, 2011; articles in educational jls. *Address:* Huntsman and Hounds Cottage, Metfield, Harleston, Norfolk IP20 0LB. *T:* (01379) 586425. *Died 31 March 2012.*

PESTELL, Catherine Eva; *see* Hughes, C. E.

PETERS, Prof. Richard Stanley, BA (Oxon), BA (London), PhD (London); Professor of the Philosophy of Education, University of London Institute of Education, 1962–82, then Emeritus Professor; Dean, Faculty of Education, London University, 1971–74; *b* 31 Oct. 1919; *s* of late Charles Robert and Mabel Georgina Peters; *m* 1943, Margaret Lee Duncan (decd); one *s* two *d*. *Educ:* Clifton Coll., Bristol; Queen's Coll., Oxford; Birkbeck Coll., University of London. War service with Friends' Ambulance Unit and Friends' Relief Service in E London, 1940–44. Classics Master, Sidcot School, Somerset, 1944–46; Birkbeck Coll., University of London: Studentship and part-time Lecturer in Philos. and Psychol., 1946–49; full-time Lecturer in Philos. and Psychol., 1949–58; Reader in Philosophy, 1958–62. Visiting Prof. of Education: Grad. School of Education, Harvard Univ., 1961; Univ. of Auckland, 1975; Visiting Fellow, Australian National Univ., 1969. Part-time lectureships, Bedford Coll., LSE; Tutor for University of London Tutorial Classes Cttee and Extension Cttee. Member, American National Academy of Education, 1966. *Publications:* (revised) Brett's History of Psychology, 1953; Hobbes, 1956; The Concept of Motivation, 1958; (with S. I. Benn) Social Principles and the Democratic State, 1959; Authority, Responsibility and Education, 1960; Ethics and Education, 1966; (ed) The Concept of Education, 1967; (ed) Perspectives on Plowden, 1969; (with P. H. Hirst) The Logic of Education, 1970; (ed with M. Cranston) Hobbes and Rousseau, 1971; (ed with R. F. Dearden and P. H. Hirst) Education and the Development of Reason, 1972; Reason and Compassion (Lindsay Meml Lectures), 1973; (ed) The Philosophy of Education, 1973; Psychology and Ethical Development, 1974; (ed) Nature and Conduct, 1975; (ed) The Role of the Head, 1976; Education and the Education of Teachers, 1977; (ed) John Dewey Reconsidered, 1977; Essays on Educators, 1981; Moral Development and Moral Education, 1981. *E:* Bengtrans@aol.com. *Died 30 Dec. 2011.*

PETERS, William, CMG 1981; LVO 1961; MBE 1959; HM Diplomatic Service, retired; *b* 28 Sept. 1923; *o s* of John William Peters and Louise (*née* Woodhouse), Morpeth, Northumberland; *m* 1st, 1944, Catherine B. Bailey (*d* 1997); no *c*; 2nd, 2004, Gill Rosemary Casebourne. *Educ:* King Edward VI Grammar Sch., Morpeth; Balliol Coll., Oxford (MA Lit. Hum. 1948); LSE and SOAS. War Service, Queen's Royal Rifles, KOSB, and 9th Gurkha Rifles, 1942–46. Joined HMOCS as Asst District Comr, Gold Coast, 1950; served in Cape Coast, Bawku and Tamale; Dep. Sec., Regional Comr, Northern Region, 1958–59; apptd to CRO as Asst Prin., 1959; Prin., 1959; 1st Sec., Dacca, 1960–63; 1st Sec., Cyprus, 1963–67; Head of Zambia and Malaŵi Dept, CRO, 1967–68; Head of Central African Dept, FCO, 1968–69; Dir, Internat. Affairs Div., Commonwealth Secretariat, 1969–71; Counsellor and Head of Chancery, Canberra, 1971–73; Dep. High Comr, Bombay, 1974–77; Ambassador to Uruguay, 1977–80; High Comr in Malaŵi, 1980–83. Member: Royal African Soc., 1980–85 (Hon. Treas., 1983–85); RSAA, 1987– (Mem., Editl Bd, 1990–2003); Exec., S Atlantic Council, 1985– (Vice Chm., 1997–2002); Churches Refugee Network, 2002–05; Chairman: Exec. Cttee, Lepra, 1984–92; Tibet Soc. of UK, 1986–94; Ethnic Minorities Sub-Cttee, Abbeyfield Soc., 1991–95; Vice-Pres., Us (formerly USPG), 1994– (Mem. Council and Exec. Cttee, 1991–94; Gov., 1996–2004); Co-Founder, Jubilee 2000, 1994; Vice-Pres., Jubilee 2000 Coalition, 1997–2000 (Bd Mem., 1998–2000); Bd Mem., Jubilee Debt Campaign, 2001–06; Trustee, Tibet Relief Fund of UK, 1985–93 (Vice-Pres., 1994–); President: Downs Br., Royal British Legion, 1986–2003; Rotary Club of Deal, 1989–90; Dover Dist Assoc., Neighbourhood Watch, 2000–. Chm. of Govs, Walmer Sch., later Walmer Science Coll., 1996–2006. FCMI (FBIM 1984); FRSA 2000. MLitt Lambeth, 2001. Alchemist Award, Common Purpose, 2000; Gandhi Internat. Peace Award, Gandhi Foundn, 2001. *Publications:* Diplomatic Service: Formation and Operation, 1971; (with M. Dent) Confronting a Global Crisis, 1998; (with M. Dent) The Crisis of Poverty and Debt in the Third World, 1999; contribs to Jls of Asian Affairs and of African Administration; Illustrated Weekly of India; Noticias (Uruguay); Army Qly and Defence

Review; Bull. of Assoc. of Christian Economists, USA; Christian Aid; Oxford; Round Table. *Recreation:* music. *Address:* 12 Crown Court, Middle Street, Deal, Kent CT14 7AG. *T:* (01304) 365640. *E:* peterslvo@aol.com. *Clubs:* Oxford and Cambridge, Royal Commonwealth Society. *Died 29 March 2014.*

PETERSON, Col Sir Christopher (Matthew), Kt 1994; CBE 1983; TD 1952; Chairman, Cardiff Health Foods Ltd, since 1988; *b* 22 Feb. 1918; *s* of Oscar Peterson and Minnie Dee; *m* 1945, Grace Winifred McNeil (*d* 2000); one *s* one *d* (and one *s* decd). *Educ:* St Illtyd's Coll., Cardiff; Cardiff Tech. Coll. Shipbroker Office, Cardiff Docks, 1936–39; served RASC, 1940–46 (Capt.). Joined S Wales India Rubber Co., subseq. SWIRCO-Newton Gp, 1952, Chm., 1968–79; Dir, Dorada Hlgs plc, 1979–83; Chairman: Wales Local Bd, Commercial Union Assce Co., 1972–77; J. McNeil (Cameras), 1983–92; Randall Cox (Photographic), 1984–92; Cox & Tarry Ltd, 1984–89; Stanton-King Orgn, 1985–89; Taff Ely Enterprise Partnership, 1989–91; SWIRCO-Hall, 1990–92. Member: Cardiff City Council, 1968–71; S Glam CC, 1973–85. JP City of Cardiff, 1973; DL 1977, High Sheriff 1981–82, S Glam. Served TA, 1946–65; CO, 1961–65 (Lt-Col), Hon. Col, 1972–77, 157 Regt RCT. Mem., Imperial Soc. of Knights Bachelors. CStJ 1997. *Recreation:* walking. *Address:* 6 Cranbourne Way, Pontprennau, Cardiff CF23 8SL. *T:* (029) 2073 3793. *Clubs:* Army and Navy; Cardiff and County. *Died 8 Sept. 2011.*

PETIT, Roland; Commandeur de la Légion d'honneur 2004; Officier des Arts et des Lettres 1978; Commandeur de l'Ordre National du Mérite, 2002; French choreographer and dancer; Artistic Director and Choreographer, Ballet National de Marseille, 1972–97; *b* Villemomble, 13 Jan. 1924; *m* 1954, Renée, (Zizi) Jeanmaire; one *d*. *Educ:* Ecole de Ballet de l'Opéra de Paris. L'Opéra de Paris, 1940–44; founded Les Vendredis de la Danse, 1944, Les Ballets des Champs-Elysées, 1945, Les Ballets de Paris de Roland Petit, 1948. Choreographic works include: Les Forains, 1945; Le Jeune Homme et la Mort, 1946; Les Demoiselles de la nuit, 1948; Carmen, 1949; Deuil en 24 heures, 1953; Le Loup, 1953; Les Chants de Maldoror, 1962; Notre Dame de Paris, 1965; L'éloge de la Folie, 1966; Paradise Lost, 1967; Les Intermittences du coeur, 1974; L'Arlésienne, 1974; La Symphonie fantastique, 1975; La Dame de Pique, 1978 (new version, 2001); Die Fledermaus, Le Chat Botté, 1985; Coppelia, The Blue Angel, 1985; Pink Floyd Ballet; Ma Pavlova, 1986; Charlot Danse Avec Nous, 1991; Clavigo, 1999; Duke Ellington Ballet, 2001, etc; choreographer and dancer: La Belle au Bois Dormant; Cyrano de Bergerac. Appeared in films: Hans Christian Andersen; Un, Deux, Trois, Quatre (arr. ballets, for film, and danced in 3); 4 ballets, Black Tights. *Publications:* J'ai dansé sur les flots (autobiog.). *Address:* c/o ATER, Via Giardini 466/G, 41100 Modena, Italy. *Died 10 July 2011.*

PETRE, His Honour Francis Herbert Loraine; a Circuit Judge, 1972–97; Chairman, Police Complaints Authority, 1989–92; *b* 9 March 1927; *s* of late Maj.-Gen. R. L. Petre, CB, DSO, MC and Mrs Katherine Sophia Petre; *m* 1958, Mary Jane, *d* of late Everard C. X. White and Sydney Mary Carleton White (*née* Holmes); three *s* one *d*. *Educ:* Downside; Clare Coll., Cambridge. Called to Bar, Lincoln's Inn, 1952; Dep. Chm., E Suffolk QS, 1970; Dep. Chm., Agricultural Lands Tribunal (Eastern Area), 1972; a Recorder, 1972; Regular Judge, Central Criminal Court, 1982–93. Mem., Parole Bd, 1997–2000. *Address:* Malting Cottage, High Street, Bures, Suffolk CO8 5JG. *Died 25 Feb. 2015.*

PETRIE, David Dick; Member (C) Highlands and Islands, Scottish Parliament, April 2006–2007; *b* 10 Dec. 1946; *s* of David and Beatrice Petrie; *m* 1974, Grace Munro; one *d*. *Educ:* Trinity Acad., Edinburgh; Heriot-Watt Univ., Edinburgh (BSc Civil Engrg 1971); Moray House Sch. of Educn, Edinburgh (PGCE Maths 2004). CEng 1975–2003. Engr, Roads Dept, Argyll CC, 1971–75; Chartered Engr and Manager, Roads and Water Services, Strathclyde Regl Council, 1975–96; Manager, W of Scotland Water, 1996–2002; Community Relns Manager, Scottish Water, 2002–03; Maths Probationer, Oban and Lochaber High Sch., 2004–06. Mem., Highlands and Is Regl Cttee, Scottish Cons. and Unionist Party, 1999–2002; Chm. Oban Br., and Exec. Mem., Argyll and Bute Scottish Cons. and Unionist Assoc., 1999–2002. Contested (C): Argyll and Bute, Scottish Parlt, 1999, 2003; Argyll and Bute, 2001; Western Isles, Scottish Parlt, 2007. *Recreations:* family, politics, current affairs, travel, golf, swimming. *Address:* Ardbeg, Duncraggan Road, Oban, Argyll PA34 5DU. *T:* and *Fax:* (01631) 564145. *E:* petriedave@hotmail.com. *Clubs:* Oban Lorne Rugby Football (Capt., 1974–75; Pres., 1997–99); Glencruitten Golf; Rotary (Oban) (Pres., 1994–95). *Died 31 Aug. 2011.*

PETTIGREW, Sir Russell (Hilton), Kt 1983; FInstD; FCILT; Chairman, Chep Handling Systems NZ Ltd, 1980–93; *b* 10 Sept. 1920; *s* of Albert and Bertha Pettigrew; *m* 1965, Glennis Olive Nicol; one *s* one *d*. *Educ:* Hangatiki Sch., King Country; Te Kuiti Dist High Sch. Served War, Naval Service, 1941–44 (Service Medals). Hawkes Bay Motor Co., 1935–40; Pettigrews Transport, 1946–63; formed Allied Freightways (later Freightways Holdings Ltd), 1964. Chairman: NZ Maritime Holdings Ltd, 1981–89; AGC NZ, 1984–88; Dep. Chm., NZ Forest Products, 1980–88 (Dir, 1975–90). FCILT (FCIT 1972) (Life Mem. 1995); Fellow, NZ Inst. of Dirs, 1972; Life Mem., NZ Road Transport Assoc., 1981. Paul Harris Fellow, Rotary Internat., 2003. Freedom, City of Napier, 2004. Knighthood for services to the Transport Industry. *Publications:* article in The Modern Freight Forwarder and the Road Carrier, 1971. *Recreations:* farming, Rugby, horse racing. *Club:* Hawkes Bay (New Zealand). *Died 20 March 2015.*

PETTITT, Sir Dennis, Kt 1998; Leader, Nottinghamshire County Council, 1981–2001; *b* 21 Aug. 1925; *m* 1949, Dorothy Mary; two *s* one *d* (and one *d* decd). Served War of 1939–45. Electrician; trade unionist; Kenya, 1950–60; Vice Chm., Kenya League, 1952–53. Member (Lab): Birmingham CC, 1962–68; Broxtowe BC, 1974–99 (Leader, Lab Gp, 1974–77; Hon. Alderman, 2003); Notts CC, 1977–2001 (Leader, Lab Gp, 1979–2001; Hon. Alderman, 2001). Chm., ACC, 1988–89, 1991–92. Mem., Cttee of the Regions, EU, 1993–2001. Contested (Lab) Carlton, Oct. 1974. Hon. Citizen, Poznan, Poland, 2001. Commander's Cross, Order of Merit (Poland), 1993. *Address:* 32 Scalby Close, Eastwood, Notts NG16 3QQ. *Died 16 Jan. 2011.*

PETTY, William Henry, CBE 1981; County Education Officer, Kent, 1973–84; *b* 7 Sept. 1921; *s* of Henry and Eveline Ann Petty, Bradford; *m* 1948, Margaret Elaine, *o d* of Edward and Lorna Bastow, Baildon, Yorks; one *s* two *d*. *Educ:* Bradford Grammar Sch.; Peterhouse, Cambridge; London Univ. MA 1950, BSc 1953. Served RA, India and Burma, 1941–45. Admin, teaching and lectrg in London, Doncaster and N R Yorks, 1946–57; Sen. Asst Educn Officer, W R Yorks CC, 1957–64; Dep. County Educn Officer, Kent CC, 1964–73. Member: Council and Court, Univ. of Kent at Canterbury, 1974–84, 1992–; Local Govt Trng Bd, Careers Service Trng Cttee, 1975–84; Careers Service Adv. Council, 1976–84; Trng and Further Educn Cons. Gp, 1977–83; Vital Skills Task Gp, 1977–78; Manpower Services Commn, SE Counties Area Bd, 1978–83; Bd of Dirs, Industrial Trng Service, 1978–97; Exec. Mem. and Sec. for SE Reg., Soc. of Educn Officers, 1978–82; Pres., Soc. of Educn Officers, 1980–81; Chm., Assoc. of Educn Officers, 1979–80 (Vice-Chm., 1978–79); Member: JNC for Chief Officers, Officers' side, 1974–84 (Chm., 1981–84); C of E Bd of Educn, Schs Cttee, 1981–86; County Educn Officers' Soc., 1974–84 (Chm., 1982–83); Youth Trng Task Gp, 1982; National Youth Trng Bd, 1983–84; Kent Area Manpower Bd, 1983–84; Canterbury Diocesan Bd of Educn, 1984–92 (Vice-Chm., 1989–92); Consultant, Further Educn Unit, 1984–90. Dir, Sennocke Services Ltd, 1989–97. Governor: Christ Church Coll., Canterbury, 1974–94 (Chm., 1992–94; Vice-Chm., 1988–92); Sevenoaks Sch., 1974–97; YMCA Nat. Coll., 1992–94. Hon. DLitt Kent, 1983. Prizewinner: Cheltenham Fest. of Lit., 1968; Camden Fest. of Music and Arts, 1969; Swanage Fest. of the Arts, 1995; Greenwood Prize, 1978; Lake Aske Meml Award, 1980; Kent Fedn of Writers Prize, 1995; White Cliffs Prize, Cruse Bereavement Care, 2000; Envoi Prize, Envoi mag., 2004; Essex Poetry Fest. Prize, 2006; Newark Poetry Soc. Prize, 2007.

Publications: No Bold Comfort, 1957; Conquest, 1967; (jtly) Educational Administration, 1980; Executive Summaries (booklets), 1984–90; Springfield, 1994; (with Robert Roberts) Genius Loci, 1995; The Louvre Imperial, 1997; Interpretations of History, 2000; No-one Listening, 2002; Breaking Time, 2005; Hijacked over China with Jane Austen, 2006; But Someone Liked It, 2008; contrib. educnl and lit. jls and anthologies. *Recreations:* literature, travel. *Address:* Willow Bank, Moat Road, Headcorn, Kent TN27 9NT. *T:* (01622) 890087. *Club:* Oxford and Cambridge. *Died 19 April 2011.*

PHELAN, His Honour Andrew James; a Circuit Judge, 1974–95; *b* 25 July 1923; *e s* of Cornelius Phelan, Kilganey House, Clonmel, Eire; *m* 1950, Joan Robertson McLagan; one *s* two *d*. *Educ:* Clongowes Wood, Co. Kildare; National Univ. of Ireland (MA); Trinity Coll., Cambridge. Called to: Irish Bar, King's Inns, 1945; English Bar, Gray's Inn, 1949. Jun. Fellow, Univ. of Bristol, 1948–50; in practice at English Bar, 1950–74. *Publications:* The Law for Small Boats, 2nd edn, 1970; Ireland from the Sea, 1998; Turning Tides: a voyage through the Irish Sea, 2003. *Recreations:* sailing, mountain walking. *Clubs:* Royal Cruising, Bar Yacht. *Died 23 Feb. 2013.*

PHELPS, Anthony John, CB 1976; Deputy Chairman, Board of Customs and Excise, 1973–82; *b* 14 Oct. 1922; *s* of John Francis and Dorothy Phelps, Oxford; *m* 1st, 1949, Sheila Nan Rait (*d* 1967), *d* of late Colin Benton Rait, Edinburgh; one *s* two *d*; 2nd, 1971, Janet M. T. Dawson (*d* 2008), *d* of late Charles R. Dawson, Edinburgh. *Educ:* City of Oxford High Sch.; University Coll., Oxford. HM Treasury, 1946; Jun. Private Sec. to Chancellor of the Exchequer, 1949–50; Principal, 1950; Treasury Rep. in Far East, 1953–55; Private Sec. to the Prime Minister, 1958–61; Asst Sec., 1961; Under-Sec., 1968. Freeman, City of Oxford, 1971. *Publications:* (with Sir Richard Hayward) A History of Civil Service Cricket, 1993. *Recreations:* music, watching sport. *Address:* 1 Woodsyre, Sydenham Hill, SE26 6SS. *T:* (020) 8670 0735. *Clubs:* City Livery, MCC. *Died 9 Nov. 2014.*

PHELPS, Howard Thomas Henry Middleton; Chairman, Brewery Court Ltd, 1990–94 (Vice-President, 2004); *b* 20 Oct. 1926; *s* of Ernest Henry Phelps, Gloucester, and Harriet (*née* Middleton); *m* 1st, 1949, Audrey (*née* Ellis) (*d* 2005); one *d*; 2nd, 2008, Mrs Carolyn Sibbald. *Educ:* Crypt Grammar Sch., Gloucester; Hatfield Coll.; Durham Univ. (BA Hons Politics and Econs 1951). National Coal Board, Lancs, Durham and London, 1951–72, finally Dep. Dir-Gen. of Industrial Relations; Personnel Dir, BOAC, 1972; British Airways: Gp Personnel Dir, 1972; Bd Mem., 1973–83; Dir of Operations, 1979–86. Dir, P&OSN Co., 1986–89; Chairman: Sutcliffe Catering Gp, 1986–88; Sterling Guards Ltd, 1986–89; Earls Court and Olympia Ltd, 1986–89; Niccol Centre Ltd, 1989–90. Non-exec. Chm., QA Training Ltd, Cirencester, 1989–94; non-exec. Dir, Alden Press Ltd, Oxford, 1990–97. FRAeS; FCILT (FCIT 1975; FILT 1980). Chm., Alice Ruston Housing Assoc., 1973–84; President: Durham Univ. Soc., 1988–99 (Chm., 1975–88); Hatfield Assoc., 1983–90. Chm. Council, Durham Univ., 1992–97 (Mem., 1985–88); Dep. Chm., Governing Body, Middlesex Polytechnic, 1987–89 (Vis. Prof., 1987–); Chairman: Cirencester Tertiary Coll., 1990–99; Rendcomb Coll., Cirencester, 1986–91; Assoc. of Colleges, 1996–98. Pres., Brewery Arts, Cirencester, 1985–. Hon. DCL Durham, 1995. *Recreations:* gardening, musical appreciation. *Address:* Tall Trees, Chedworth, near Cheltenham, Glos GL54 4AB. *T:* (01285) 720324. *Club:* Bull (Cirencester). *Died 9 Feb. 2011.*

PHILIPSON, Garry, DFC 1944; Managing Director, Aycliffe and Peterlee Development Corporation, 1974–85; *b* 27 Nov. 1921; *s* of George and Marian Philipson; *m* 1949, June Mary Miller Somerville (*d* 1997); one *d*. *Educ:* Stockton Grammar Sch.; Durham Univ. (BA(Hons)). Jubilee Prize, 1947. Served War, RAFVR (2 Gp Bomber Comd), 1940–46. Colonial Service and Overseas Civil Service, 1949–60. Various Dist and Secretariat posts, incl. Clerk, Exec. Council and Cabinet Sec., Sierra Leone; Principal, Scottish Develt Dept, 1961–66; Under Sec., RICS, 1966–67; Dir, Smith and Ritchie Ltd, 1967–70; Sec., New Towns Assoc., 1970–74; Vice-Chm. (NE), North Housing Assoc., 1985–92. Trustee, Dales-Care, 1988–91. *Publications:* Aycliffe and Peterlee New Towns 1946–88, 1988; press articles and contribs to various jls. *Recreations:* country pursuits, history. *Address:* Little Lodge, Fletching Common, North Chailey, East Sussex BN8 4JH. *T:* (01825) 723027. *Club:* Royal Air Force. *Died 7 July 2013.*

PHILLIPS, Sir Fred (Albert), Kt 1967; CVO 1966; QC (Barbados) 1991; *b* 14 May 1918; *s* of Wilbert A. Phillips, Brighton, St Vincent; *m* Gloria; four *s* two *d* by a previous marriage. *Educ:* London Univ. (LLB); Toronto Univ.; McGill Univ. (MCL); Hague Acad. of International Law. Called to the Bar, Middle Temple. Legal Clerk to Attorney-General of St Vincent, 1942–45; Sen. Officer, Secretariat, 1945–47; Windward Island: Chief Clerk, Governor's Office, 1948–49; District Officer/Magistrate of District III, 1949–53; Magistrate, Grenada, and Comr of Carriacou, 1953–56; Asst Administrator and MEC, Grenada, 1957–58 (Officer Administrating the Govt, April 1958); Senior Asst Sec., Secretariat, Fedn of W Indies (dealing with constitutional development), 1958–60; Permanent Sec. (Sec. to Cabinet), 1960–62 (when Fedn dissolved); actg Administrator of Montserrat, 1961–62; Sen. Lectr, Univ. of W Indies and Sen. Resident Tutor, Dept of Extra-mural Studies, Barbados, 1962–63; Sen. Asst Registrar, Coll. of Arts and Science, Univ. of W Indies, 1963–64; Sen. Res. Fellow, Faculty of Law and Centre for Developing Area Studies, McGill Univ., 1964–65; Guggenheim Fellow, 1965; Administrator of St Kitts, 1966–67; Governor, St Kitts/Nevis/Anguilla, 1967–69; Chief Legal Advr for Cable & Wireless in the Caribbean, 1969–97. Chairman, Constitutional Review Commission: Grenada, 1984; St Kitts and Nevis, 1998; Antigua and Barbuda, 1999, 2000 and 2001. Attended numerous conferences as a Legal or Constitutional Adviser. KStJ 1968. Hon. LLD West Indies, 1989. *Publications:* Freedom in the Caribbean: a study in constitutional change, 1977; The Evolving Legal Profession in the Commonwealth, 1978; West Indian Constitutions: post-Independence reforms, 1985; Caribbean Life and Culture: a citizen reflects, 1991; Commonwealth Caribbean Constitutional Law, 2002; Ethics of the Legal Profession, 2004; The Death Penalty and Human Rights, 2009; The Modern Judiciary: challenges, stresses and strains, 2010; papers in various jls. *Recreations:* reading, legal writing. *Address:* Sandy Lane, Hodges Bay, PO Box 3298, St John's, Antigua. *Died 20 Feb. 2011.*

PHILLIPS, Ian, FCA; Chairman, Investment Advisory Committee, PanEuropean Property Unit Trust, since 2008 (Member, since 1996); *b* 16 July 1938; *s* of Wilfrid and Dorothy Phillips; *m* 1961, Fay Rosemary Stoner; two *s*. *Educ:* Whitgift Sch., South Croydon. Articled clerk, Hatfield Dixon Roberts Wright & Co., Accountants, 1955–61; Robert J. Ward & Co., Accountants, 1961–65; John Lewis' Partnership, 1965–69; London Transport Executive: Director of Corporate Planning, 1969–75; Chief Business Planning Officer, 1975–78; Group Planning Director, 1978–80; Mem. Board, LTE, later LRT, 1980–84; Dir, Finance and Planning, BRB, 1985–88; Finance Dir, BBC, 1988–93; Chief Exec., BBC Pension Services Ltd, 1990–96; Chm., BBC Enterprises Ltd, 1991–93; Director: Schroder UK Growth Fund, 1994–2008; M & G Equity Investment Trust, 2000–11. Chairman: OUP Pension Fund, 1995–2006; Severn Trent Pension Fund, 1998–2004. Bd Mem., Gloucestershire Hosps NHS Foundn Trust, 2002–09. Dir, Hothouse Fiction Ltd, 2009–. Non-exec. Dir, RAF Trng Gp Defence Agency, 1998–2001. *Recreations:* sport, politics, reading, family. *Address:* 5 The Croft, Carpenters Lane, Cirencester, Glos GL7 1EE. *Died 20 May 2013.*

PHILLIPS, (Mervyn) John, AO 2004 (AM 1987); Chancellor, University of Western Sydney, 2001–10, then Emeritus Chancellor; *b* 1 April 1930; *m* 1956, Moya, *d* of A. C. Bleazard; one *s* one *d*. *Educ:* De La Salle Coll., Ashfield; Univ. of Sydney (BEc). Commonwealth Bank of Australia, 1946–60; Reserve Bank of Australia, 1960–92: Manager for PNG, 1962–64; Chief Manager, Internat. Dept, 1976–79, Securities Markets Dept, 1980–82, Financial Markets Group, 1983–85; Adviser, 1982; Chief Admin. Officer, 1985–87; Dep. Gov. and Dep. Chm., 1987–92; Chm., I. B.

J. Australia Bank Ltd, 1992–2002; Dir, CBOA Credit Union, 1964–73 (Chm., 1967–72); Chm., Note Printing Australia, 1990–93; Director: QBE Insce Gp, 1992–2002; Alcoa of Australia, 1992–96; Aust. Gas Light Co., 1992–2003 (Chm., 1996–); O'Connell Street Associates Pty, 1992–; Woolworths Ltd, 1993–2001; GRW Property Ltd, 1994–98; WMC Ltd, 1996–2002. Chairman: For. Investment Review Bd, 1997–; Aust. Charities Fund, 2001–07. Member: PNG Currency Conversion Commn, 1965–66; NSW Credit Union Adv. Cttee, 1968–72; Govt Cttees on PNG Banking, 1971–73; Off-shore Banking in Australia, 1984; Prime Minister's Task Force on Internat. Monetary Reform, 2000; Medical Indemnity Policy Reform Panel, 2003. Nat. Treas., Australian Catholic Relief, subseq. Caritas Australia, 1993–2001. Mem., Finance Cttee, Archdio. Sydney, 2002–. Chm. Council, St John's Coll., 2012–13. Member: Senate, Australian Catholic Univ., 1991–98; Adv. Council, Australian Grad. Sch. of Management, 1991–2001. Mem., Pontifical Council, Cor Unum, 1994–2000. FAICD 1992; Sen. Fellow, Fin. Services Inst. of Australasia, 1990–. Hon. DLitt Western Sydney, 2011. GCSG 2004. Centenary Medal (Australia) 2003. *Address:* O'Connell Street Associates Pty Ltd, 6 O'Connell Street, Sydney, NSW 2000, Australia. *T:* (2) 92231822. *Died 3 Nov. 2014.*

PHILLIPS, Robin, OC 2005; actor and director; *b* Haslemere, Surrey, 28 Feb. 1940; *s* of James William Phillips and Ellen Anne (*née* Barfoot). *Educ:* Midhurst Grammar School, Sussex. Trained as director, actor and designer, Bristol Old Vic Co.; first appearance, Bristol, as Mr Puff in The Critic, 1959; Associate Dir, Bristol Old Vic, 1960–61; played at Lyric, Hammersmith, 1961, Chichester Fest., 1962, and with Oxford Playhouse Co., 1964. Asst Dir, Timon of Athens and Hamlet, Royal Shakespeare Co., Stratford upon Avon, 1965; Dir or Associate Dir, Hampstead, Exeter, (Thorndike) Leatherhead, 1966–69; Artistic Dir, Stratford Festival, Canada, 1974–80; Artistic Dir, Grand Theatre Co., London, Ontario, 1982; Dir, Young Company, Stratford Festival Theatre, 1986; Dir Gen., The Citadel Theatre, Edmonton, Canada, 1990–95. Hon. Dr Univ. of Western Ontario, 1982. Guild Shield, Conestoga Coll., 1982. Governor General's Award for Lifetime Achievement, Canada Council for the Arts, 2010. *London productions include:* Tiny Alice, RSC, Aldwych, 1970; Abelard and Heloise, Wyndhams and Broadway; The Two Gentlemen of Verona, Stratford and Aldwych, 1970; Miss Julie, for RSC (also directed film); Virginia, Haymarket, 1981; Long Day's Journey Into Night, Lyric, 2000; Ghosts, Comedy, 2001; *Chichester:* Caesar and Cleopatra and Dear Antoine, 1971; played Dubedat in The Doctor's Dilemma and directed The Lady's Not for Burning and The Beggar's Opera, 1972; The Jeweller's Shop, 1982; Antony and Cleopatra, 1985; *Greenwich:* formed Company Theatre and apptd Artistic Dir, 1973: plays directed include: The Three Sisters, Rosmerholm, Zorba; *Stratford Festival productions include:* 1975: The Two Gentlemen of Verona and The Comedy of Errors (both also Nat. tour), Measure for Measure, Trumpets and Drums and The Importance of Being Earnest; 1976–78: Hamlet, The Tempest, Antony and Cleopatra, A Midsummer Night's Dream, The Way of the World, Richard III, The Guardsman, As You Like It, Macbeth, The Winter's Tale, Uncle Vanya, The Devils, Private Lives, Hay Fever, Judgement; 1979: Love's Labours Lost, The Importance of Being Earnest, King Lear; 1980: Virginia, Long Day's Journey into Night; 1986: Cymbeline; 1987: The School for Scandal, As You Like It, Romeo and Juliet, Journey's End; 1988: Twelfth Night, King Lear, Oedipus, The Critic; 1993: King John; *Edmonton productions include:* A Midsummer Night's Dream, The Crucible, 1989; The Philadelphia Story, 1990; Never the Sinner, The Mousetrap, Romeo and Juliet, Democracy, 1991; Lend Me A Tenor, Fallen Angels, Oedipus, Man of La Mancha (also Toronto, 1993), Black Comedy, Invisible Friends, The Royal Hunt of the Sun, Hamlet, As You Like It, 1992; La Bête, The Two of Us, She Stoops to Conquer, Saint Joan, Oliver!, Aspects of Love (also Toronto, US tour), 1993; Cyrano de Bergerac, Macbeth, Hay Fever (also Winnipeg), Caesar and Cleopatra, A Man for All Seasons, The Music Man, 1994; Richard III, The Cherry Orchard, The Beggar's Opera, The Alberta Quilt, 1995; *other productions include:* The Marriage of Figaro, 1993, Beatrice and Benedict, 1996, Canadian Opera Co., Toronto; Owen Wingrave, Glyndebourne Touring Opera, 1995; Jekyll and Hyde, NY, 1997; Don Carlos, The Misanthrope, Soulpepper Th. Co., 1998; The Elephant Man, Toronto, 2007; Long Day's Journey Into Night, Kreeger Th., Arena Stage's Mead Center for Amer. Th., 2012. *Films:* as actor: Decline and Fall, David Copperfield (title part), Tales from the Crypt; as director: The Wars, Miss Julie, Waiting for the Parade. *Television:* Wilfred Desert in The Forsyte Saga; Constantin in The Seagull. *Address:* Wildwood House, RR3, Lakeside, ON N0M 2G0, Canada. *Died 25 July 2015.*

PHYSICK, John Frederick, CBE 1984; DrRCA; FSA; Deputy Director, Victoria and Albert Museum, 1983; *b* 31 Dec. 1923; *s* of Nino William Physick and Gladys (*née* Elliott); *m* 1954, Eileen Mary Walsh; two *s* one *d.* *Educ:* Battersea Grammar Sch. Home Guard, 1940–42; Royal Navy, 1942–46 (Petty Officer Airman) (volunteer, 1941); 1832 Air Squadron RNVR, 1947–56; London Scottish Regt TA, 1957–69. Joined Victoria and Albert Museum, as Museum Asst, Dept of Engraving, Illustration and Design, 1948; Research Asst, 1949; Sen. Research Asst, 1965; Asst Keeper, Dept of Public Relations and Educn, 1967; Keeper, Dept of Museum Services, 1975–83; Sec. to Adv. Council, 1973–83; Asst to Dir, 1974–83. Leverhulme Trust Emeritus Fellow, 1984–86. Pres., Church Monument Soc., 1984–86, 1996–2001 (Hon. Vice-Pres., 2001–); Vice-Pres., Public Monuments and Sculpture Assoc., 1999– (Mem. Adv. Cttee, 1991–98); Chm., Monuments Sub-Cttee, 1984–2001 (Mem., 1978–2001), Conservation Cttees, 1993–2001 (Mem., 1984–93), Council for Care of Churches; Member: Council, Working Men's Coll., 1952–54; Rochester DAC for the Care of Churches, 1964–91 (Vice-Chm., 1987–91; Consultant, 1991–); RIBA Drawings Cttee, 1975; Cathedrals Adv. Cttee, 1977–81; Council, British Archaeol Assoc., 1985–88; Westminster Abbey Architectural Adv. Panel, 1985–98; Rochester Cathedral Fabric Cttee, 1987–2011 (Vice-Chm., 1992–); Jt Diocesan Archaeol Survey Cttee, 1994–2005, Jt Diocesan Books and Documents Cttee, 1994–2005, Canterbury and Rochester; Guildford Cath. Fabric Adv. Cttee, 1999–2004. Mem. Council, Soc. of Antiquaries, 1991–93. Trustee, London Scottish Regt, 1977–87. Mem., Cttee of Mgt, Gunnis Dictionary of British Sculptors, 1999–2007. Freeman, City of London, 1997. DLitt Lambeth, 1996. Silver Jubilee Medal, 1977. *Publications:* Catalogue of the Engravings of Eric Gill, 1963; (ed) Handbook to the Departments Prints and Drawings and Paintings, 1964; The Duke of Wellington in caricature, 1965; Designs for English Sculpture 1680–1860, 1969; The Wellington Monument, 1970; (jtly) Victorian Church Art, 1971; Five Monuments from Eastwell, 1973; (with M. D. Darby) Marble Halls, 1973; Photography and the South Kensington Museum, 1975; (with Sir Roy Strong) V&A Souvenir Guide, 1977; The Victoria and Albert Museum—the history of its building, 1982; (ed) V&A Album II, 1983; (ed) Sculpture in Britain 1530–1830, 2nd edn 1988; (contrib.) Change and Decay, the Future of our Churches, 1977; (contrib.) Westminster Abbey, 1986; (contrib.) The Royal College of Art, 1987; (introd.) Westminster Abbey: the monuments, 1989; (contrib.) Design of the Times, 1996; (contrib.) The Dictionary of Art, 1996; (contrib.) The Albert Memorial, 2000; (contrib.) Kensal Green Cemetery, 2001; (contrib.) Westminster Abbey: the Lady Chapel of Henry VII, 2003; (contrib.) Biographical Dictionary of British Sculptors 1660–1851, 2009. *Recreations:* photography, genealogy. *Address:* 49 New Road, Meopham, Kent DA13 0LS. *T:* (01474) 812301. *Died 14 Oct. 2013.*

PICKFORD, Michael Alan, CB 1994; FIA; Directing Actuary, Supervision of Insurance Companies and Friendly Societies, Government Actuary's Department, 1989–95; *b* 22 Aug. 1937. *Educ:* City of Oxford Sch. Govt Actuary's Dept, 1958–95. *Died 4 June 2012.*

PIKE, Sir Philip Ernest Housden, Kt 1969; Chief Justice of Swaziland, 1970–72; *b* 6 March 1914; *s* of Rev. Ernest Benjamin Pike and Dora Case Pike (*née* Lillie); *m* 1st, 1943, Phyllis Kelvin Calder; one *s* one *d*; 2nd, 1959, Millicent Locke Staples (*d* 1996); 3rd, 2004, Patricia Ethne Hodson. *Educ:* De Carteret School, and Munro Coll., Jamaica;

Middle Temple, London. Barrister at Law, 1938. Crown Counsel, Jamaica, 1947–49; Legal Draftsman, Kenya, 1949–52; Solicitor General, Uganda, 1952–58; QC (Uganda) 1953; Attorney General, Sarawak, 1958–65; QC (Sarawak) 1958; Chief Justice, High Court in Borneo, 1965–68; Judge, High Court of Malawi, 1969–70, Actg Chief Justice, 1970. Coronation Medal, 1953. PNBS-Sarawak, 1965; Malaysia Commemorative Medal, 1967; PMN Malaysia 1968. *Recreations:* golf, gardening. *Address:* 3 Earlewood Court, 180/184 Ron Penhaligon Way, Robina, Qld 4226, Australia. *Died 20 March 2011.*

PIKE, Dr Richard Andrew, CEng, CSci; FRSC; FInstP; FIMechE; FIChemE; FIET; FEI; Chief Executive, Royal Society of Chemistry, since 2006; *b* 2 April 1950; *s* of Tudor Morgan Pike and Eileen Mary (*née* Oxley); *m* 1986, Fiona Elizabeth Henry; one *s* two *d*. *Educ:* Gosport Co. Grammar Sch.; Downing Coll., Cambridge (BA 1st Cl. Engrg; MA; PhD 1977). CEng 1987; FIMechE 1988; FIChemE 1991; FEI 1992; FIET (FIEE 1996); CSci 2004; FRSC 2006; FInstP 2009. Joined British Petroleum as univ. apprentice, 1968; Maintenance Engr, BP Llandarcy, 1971–72; res. student, Cambridge, 1972–75; Develt Engr, BP Engrg, London, 1975–80; Area Commissioning Engr, Sullom Voe Terminal, Shetland, 1980–82; Business Develt Co-ordinator, Jt Ventures, London, 1982–83; Develt Supt, Pipelines and Facilities, Aberdeen, 1984–85; Offshore Prodn Engr, Forties, North Sea, 1985–86; Manager Technical, Sullom Voe Terminal, 1986–88; Manager, Jt Venture, Japan, 1988–89; Gen. Manager, Chems, BP Far East, Tokyo, 1989–93; Pres., BP Chems, Japan, 1991–93; Dir, Samsung-BP Chems, S Korea, 1989–91; Dir Gen., IMechE, 1993–98; Exec. Vice-Chm., Professional Engineering Publishing, 1993–98; Ops Manager, Cambridge Management Consulting, 1998–2000; Sen. Associate, Gaffney, Cline & Associates, 2000–06. Chm., Chemistry and Energy Wkg Party, Eur. Assoc. for Molecular and Chem. Scis, 2006–. Director: Chemistry Innovation Ltd, 2009–; Howard Partnership Trust, 2010–. Freeman, City of London, 2007; Liveryman, Engineers' Co., 2009. *Publications:* articles in jls, magazines and newspapers on engrg, sci. and educn, incl. boiling in zero gravity, oil and gas reserves, and school examination standards. *Recreations:* reading, swimming (first person to swim from Yell to Mainland and Yell to Unst, Shetland Is, 1980), languages, travel. *Address:* Royal Society of Chemistry, Burlington House, Piccadilly, W1J 0BA. *T:* (020) 7437 8656. *Died 23 July 2011.*

PILDITCH, Sir Richard (Edward), 4th Bt *cr* 1929; *b* 8 Sept. 1926; *s* of Sir Philip Harold Pilditch, 2nd Bt, and Frances Isabella, *d* of J. G. Weeks, JP, Bedlington, Northumberland; *S* brother, Sir Philip John Frederick Pilditch, 3rd Bt, 1954; *m* 1950, Pauline Elizabeth Smith; one *s* one *d*. *Educ:* Charterhouse. Served War of 1939–45, RNVR and RN, 1944–46, incl. service in India and Ceylon. *Recreation:* fishing. *Heir: s* John Richard Pilditch, *b* 24 Sept. 1955. *Died 30 June 2012.*

PILKINGTON OF OXENFORD, Baron *cr* 1995 (Life Peer), of West Dowlish in the county of Somerset; **Rev. Canon Peter Pilkington;** Chairman, Broadcasting Complaints Commission, 1992–96; Hon. Canon of Canterbury Cathedral, 1975–90, then Canon Emeritus; *b* 5 Sept. 1933; *s* of Frank and Doris Pilkington; *m* 1966, Helen (*d* 1997), *d* of Charles and Maria Wilson; two *d*. *Educ:* Dame Allan's Sch., Newcastle upon Tyne; Jesus Coll., Cambridge (BA 1955; MA 1958). Schoolmaster, St Joseph's Coll., Chidya, Tanganyika, 1955–57; ordained 1959; Curate in Bakewell, Derbys, 1959–62; Schoolmaster, Eton College, 1962–75, Master in College, 1965–75; Headmaster, King's Sch., Canterbury, 1975–86; High Master, St Paul's Sch., 1986–92. Mem., Parole Bd, 1990–95. *Address:* Oxenford House, near Ilminster, Somerset TA19 0PP. *T:* (01460) 52813. *Clubs:* Beefsteak, Garrick, Pratt's. *Died 14 Feb. 2011.*

PILKINGTON, Air Vice-Marshal Michael John, CB 1991; CBE 1982; Air Officer Commanding Training Units, Royal Air Force Support Command, 1989–92; *b* 9 Oct. 1937; *s* of David and Mary Pilkington; *m* 1960, Janet Rayner; one *d* (and one *s* decd). *Educ:* Bromley Grammar Sch. psc rcds. Commnd Royal Air Force, 1956; Bomber Sqdns, No 35, No 83, No 27, 1959–70; RAF sc 1971; HQ Near East Air Force, 1972–73; CO No 230 Vulcan OCU, 1974–75; Defence Policy Staff, 1977–78; CO RAF Waddington, 1979–81; RCDS 1982; Branch Chief Policy, SHAPE, 1982–85; DG of Trng, RAF, 1986–89. *Recreations:* golf, gardening, theatre, wine. *Club:* Royal Air Force. *Died 29 Jan. 2015.*

PILLAR, Rt Rev. Kenneth Harold; Bishop Suffragan of Hertford, 1982–89; an Assistant Bishop, diocese of Sheffield, since 1990; *b* 10 Oct. 1924; *s* of Harold and Mary Pillar; *m* 1955, Margaret Elizabeth Davies; one *s* three *d*. *Educ:* Devonport High School; Queens' Coll., Cambridge (MA); Ridley Hall, Cambridge. Asst Curate, Childwall, Liverpool, 1950–53; Chaplain, Lee Abbey, Lynton, N Devon, 1953–57; Vicar: St Paul's, Beckenham, 1957–62; St Mary Bredin, Canterbury, 1962–65; Warden of Lee Abbey, Lynton, N Devon, 1965–70; Vicar of Waltham Abbey, Essex, 1970–82; RD of Epping Forest, 1976–82. *Recreations:* walking, music, reading. *Address:* 75 Dobcroft Road, Millhouses, Sheffield S7 2LS. *T:* (0114) 236 7902. *Died 21 Feb. 2011.*

PILLINGER, Prof. Colin Trevor, CBE 2003; PhD; FRS 1993; Professor of Planetary Science, Open University, since 1990; *b* 9 May 1943; *s* of Alfred Pillinger and Florence (*née* Honour); *m* 1975, Judith Mary Hay; one *s* one *d*. *Educ:* Kingswood Grammar Sch.; University Coll. Swansea, Univ. of Wales (BSc Hons Chem. 1965; PhD 1968; Hon. Fellow, 2003). Department of Chemistry, University of Bristol: Post Doctoral Fellow, 1968–72; BSC Fellow, 1972–74; Res. Associate, 1974–76; Res. Associate and Sen. Res. Associate, Dept of Earth Sci., Cambridge, 1976–84; Sen. Res. Fellow, Dept of Earth Sci., Open Univ., 1984–90. Gresham Prof. of Astronomy, 1996–2000. Lead Scientist, British-led Beagle 2 mission to land on Mars, 1997–. FRAS 1981 (Mem. Council, 1989–91); Fellow, Meteoritical Soc., 1986; FRGS 1993; Founder Mem., British Mass Spectrometry Soc. (Aston Medal, 2003). Fellow, UC Swansea, 2003. Hon. DSc Bristol, 1985. A. C. Clarke Award, British Rocketry Oral Hist. Prog., 2005; Space Achievement Medal, BIS, 2005; Reginald Mitchell Medal, Stoke-on-Trent Assoc. of Engrs, 2006; Faraday Medal, IET, 2012. Asteroid 15614 named Pillinger, 2005. *Publications:* Beagle: from Darwin's epic voyage to the British mission to Mars, 2003; Space is a Funny Place, 2007; My Life on Mars: the Beagle 2 diaries, 2010; numerous papers in learned jls and contribs to radio and TV, UK and abroad. *Recreations:* farming, animals, soccer. *Address:* Department of Physical Sciences, Open University, Milton Keynes MK7 6AA. *T:* (01908) 652119, *Fax:* (01908) 655667. *Died 7 May 2014.*

PIMENTA, His Eminence Cardinal Simon Ignatius; Archbishop of Bombay (RC), 1978–97, then Emeritus; *b* 1 March 1920; *s* of late Joseph Anthony Pimenta and Rosie E. Pimenta. *Educ:* St Xavier's Coll., Bombay (BA with Maths); Propaganda Univ., Rome (Degree in Canon Law). Secretary at Archbishop's House, and Vice-Chancellor and Defensor Vinculi, Bombay, 1954; Vice Rector of Cathedral, 1960; Visiting Prof. of Liturgy, Bombay Seminary, 1960; Episcopal Vicar for Liturgy and Pastoral Formation of Junior Clergy, 1968; Rector of the Cathedral, 1967, Rector of Seminary, 1971; Auxiliary Bishop, 1971; Coadjutor Archbishop with right of succession, 1977. President: Catholic Bishops' Conf. of India, 1982–88; (Latin Rite), Conf. of Catholic Bishops of India, 1994–96. Cardinal, 1988. *Publications:* (edited) The Catholic Directory of Bombay, 1960 and 1964 edns; Circulars and Officials of the Archdiocese of Bombay, vols I and II, 1964, vol. III, 1971; booklet on the Cathedral of the Holy Name, 1964; Priest for Ever (homilies), 1999; Memoirs and Milestones (autobiog.), 2000; Cardinal Valerian Gracias: his life and ministry, 2002. *Address:* Archbishop's House, 21 Nathalal Parekh Marg, Mumbai 400 001, India. *T:* 2021093, 2021193, 2021293, (personal) 22049696. *Died 19 July 2013.*

PINCHER, (Henry) Chapman; freelance journalist, novelist and business consultant; Assistant Editor, Daily Express, and Chief Defence Correspondent, Beaverbrook Newspapers, 1972–79; *b* Ambala, India, 29 March 1914; *s* of Major Richard Chapman Pincher, E Surrey Regt, and

Helen (*née* Foster), Pontefract; *m* 1965, Constance, (Billee), Wolstenholme; one *s* one *d* (by previous *m*). *Educ:* Darlington Gram. Sch.; King's Coll., London (FKC 1979); Inst. Educn; Mil. Coll. of Science. Carter Medallist, London, 1934; BSc (hons Botany, Zoology), 1935. Staff Liverpool Inst., 1936–40. Joined Royal Armoured Corps, 1940; Techn SO, Rocket Div., Min. of Supply, 1943–46; Defence, Science and Medical Editor, Daily Express, 1946–73. Academician, Russian Acad. for Defence, Security and Internal Affairs, 2005. Hon. DLitt Newcastle upon Tyne, 1979. Granada Award, Journalist of the Year, 1964; Reporter of the Decade, 1966. Order of the Great Victory (Russia), 2006 (for war service). *Publications:* Breeding of Farm Animals, 1946; A Study of Fishes, 1947; Into the Atomic Age, 1947; Spotlight on Animals, 1950; Evolution, 1950; (with Bernard Wicksteed) It's Fun Finding Out, 1950; Sleep, and how to get more of it, 1954; Sex in Our Time, 1973; Inside Story, 1978; (jtly) Their Trade is Treachery, 1981; Too Secret Too Long, 1984; The Secret Offensive, 1985; Traitors—the Labyrinths of Treason, 1987; A Web of Deception, 1987; The Truth about Dirty Tricks, 1991; One Dog and Her Man, 1991; Pastoral Symphony (autobiog.), 1993; A Box of Chocolates, 1993; Life's a Bitch!, 1996; Tight Lines!, 1997; Treachery, 2011; Dangerous to Know: a life (autobiog.), 2014; *novels:* Not with a Bang, 1965; The Giantkiller, 1967; The Penthouse Conspirators, 1970; The Skeleton at the Villa Wolkonsky, 1975; The Eye of the Tornado, 1976; The Four Horses, 1978; Dirty Tricks, 1980; The Private World of St John Terrapin, 1982; Contamination, 1989; original researches in genetics, numerous articles in scientific, agricultural and sporting jls. *Recreations:* fishing, natural history, country life; spy-hunting, ferreting in Whitehall and bolting politicians. *Address:* The Church House, 16 Church Street, Kintbury, near Hungerford, Berks RG17 9TR. *T:* (01488) 658397. *Died 5 Aug. 2014.*

PINCOTT, Leslie Rundell, CBE 1978; Managing Director, Esso Petroleum Co. Ltd, 1970–78; *b* 27 March 1923; *s* of Hubert George Pincott and Gertrude Elizabeth Rundell; *m* 1st, 1944, Mary Mae Tuffin (*d* 1996); two *s* one *d*; 2nd, 1997, Elaine Sunderland. *Educ:* Mercers' Sch. FCA. Served War, Royal Navy, 1942–46 (Lieut, RNVR). Broads Paterson & Co. (Chartered Accountants), 1946–50; joined Esso Petroleum Co. Ltd, 1950; Comptroller, 1958–61; Asst Gen. Manager (Marketing), 1961–65; Dir and Gen. Manager, Cleveland Petroleum Co. Ltd, 1966–68; Standard Oil Co. (NJ), 1968–70; Vice-Chm., Remploy Ltd, 1979–87 (Dir, 1975–87); Chairman: Canada Permanent Trust Co. (UK) Ltd, 1978–80; Stone-Platt Industries PLC, 1980–82; Edman Communications Gp PLC, 1982–87; BR Southern Bd, 1986–89 (Dir, 1977–86). Director: George Wimpey PLC, 1978–85; Highlands Fabricators Ltd, 1984–91. A Dep. Chm., 1978–79, Chm., 1979–80, Price Commn; Chairman: Hundred Gp of Chartered Accountants, 1978–79; Oxford Univ. Business Summer Sch., 1975–78; Printing Industries EDC, NEDO, 1982–88; Mem., Investment Cttee, London Develt Capital Fund (formerly part of Guinness Mahon), 1985–99. Chm., Wandle Housing Assoc., 1996–2000; Dir, Hurlingham Ct Ltd, 1999– (Chm., 2000–05, 2008–). Pres., District Heating Assoc., 1977–79. Vice-Pres., English Schs Athletics Assoc., 1977–; Mem. Council, ISCO, 1982–97. Mem., The Pilgrims, 1971–. *Recreations:* tennis, bowls, travel. *Address:* 53 Hurlingham Court, Ranelagh Gardens, SW6 3UP. *Club:* Hurlingham (Chm., 1988–92; Trustee, 1996–98). *Died 22 June 2014.*

PINDER, John Humphrey Murray, OBE 1973; Professor, 1970–99, Hon. Professor, since 1999, College of Europe; *b* 20 June 1924; *s* of Harold Pinder and Lilian Pinder (*née* Murray); *m* 1964, Pauline Hawtayne Lewin (*d* 2012). *Educ:* Marlborough Coll.; King's Coll., Cambridge. Served RA, W African Artillery, 1943–47. Press Officer, Federal Union, 1950–52; EIU, 1952–64, Internat. Dir, 1957–64; Dir, PEP, then PSI, 1964–85. Member, Editorial Board: Government and Opposition, 1975–2001; Jl Common Mkt Studies, 1979–92. Pres., Union of Eur. Federalists, 1984–90 (Hon. Pres., 1990–); Vice-President: Eur. Movement (Internat.), 1990–2000; Eur. Movement (UK), 2001– (Vice Chm., 1975–90; Dep. Chm., 1990–98; Mem. Bd, 1998–2007); Member, Board: Inst. Eur. Envmtl Policy, 1990–2001; Trans Eur. Policy Studies Assoc., 1995–98; Action for a Global Climate Community, 2004–; Member, Council: ODI, 1972–99; Hansard Soc., 1973–99; RIIA, 1985–91. Chairman: Federal Trust, 1985–2008; Pinder Centre Trustees, Pinder Trust, 1998–2006; James Madison Trust, 2001–; Trustee, One World Trust, 1993–2000. *Publications:* Britain and the Common Market, 1961; Europe against de Gaulle, 1963; (jtly) Europe after de Gaulle, 1969; (ed) The Economics of Europe, 1971; (ed) Fifty Years of PEP: looking forward 1931–1981, 1981; (jtly) Policies for a Constrained Economy, 1982; (ed) National Industrial Strategies and the World Economy, 1982; (ed jtly) One European Market?: a critical analysis of the Commission's internal market strategy, 1988; (ed jtly) Pacifism is not Enough: collected lectures and speeches of Lord Lothian, 1990; (jtly) Federal Union: the pioneers, 1990; The European Community and Eastern Europe, 1991; The Building of the European Union, 1991, 3rd edn 1998; (ed jtly) Maastricht and Beyond: building the European Union, 1994; (ed) Altiero Spinelli and the British Federalists, 1999; (ed) Foundations of Democracy in the European Union, 1999; The European Union: a very short introduction, 2001, (jtly) 2nd edn 2007; (jtly) The EU and Russia: the promise of partnership, 2002; (ed jtly) Multinational Federations, 2007. *Recreations:* music, walking, foreign languages and literature. *Address:* 26 Bloomfield Terrace, SW1W 8PQ. *Club:* Brooks's. *Died 7 March 2015.*

PININFARINA, Sergio; Cavaliere del Lavoro, 1976; engineer; Member, European Parliament (Liberal and Democratic Group), 1979–88; Chairman, Pininfarina SpA, 1966–2006, then Hon. Chairman; *b* 8 Sept. 1926; *s* of Battista Pininfarina and Rosa Copasso; *m* 1951, Giorgia Gianolio; one *s* one *d* (and one *s* decd). *Educ:* Polytechnic of Turin; graduated in Mech. Eng., 1950. Joined Pininfarina, 1950; Gen. Manager, 1960; Man. Dir, 1961–2003. President: Federpiemonte, 1983–88; OICA, 1987–89; Confindustria, 1988–92; Comitato Promotore Alta Velocità, 1991–2001; Vice-Pres., UNICE, 1990–94. Chm., Fidia; Board Member: Ferrari; Banca Passadore; Banca Brignone; Toro Assicurazioni; Edison; Ind. Internat. Univ. of Social Studies, Rome. Life Senator, Italian Republic, 2005. Foreign Mem., Royal Swedish Acad. of Engrg Scis, 1988. Hon. Dr Econs, Ind. Internat. Univ. of Social Studies, Rome, 1993. Chevalier, Légion d'Honneur, 1979. Hon. RDI 1983. Compasso d'Oro, Assoc. for Industrial Design, 1995. *Recreation:* golf. *Address:* PO Box 295, 10100 Turin, Italy. *T:* (11) 70911. *Clubs:* Società Whist Accademia Filarmonica, Rotary, Subalpino, Artisti (Turin); Golf Torino, Golf Garlenda, Associazione Sportiva I Roveri. *Died 3 July 2012.*

PINKERTON, Prof. John Henry McKnight, CBE 1983; Professor of Midwifery and Gynæcology, Queen's University, Belfast, 1963–85, then Emeritus; Gynæcologist: Royal Victoria and City Hospitals, Belfast, 1963–85; Ulster Hospital for Women and Children, 1963–85; Surgeon, Royal Maternity Hospital, Belfast, 1963–85; *b* 5 June 1920; *s* of late William Ross Pinkerton and Eva Pinkerton; *m* 1947, Florence McKinstry, MB, BCh, BAO; four *s*. *Educ:* Royal Belfast Academical Institution; Queen's Univ., Belfast. Hyndman Univ. Entrance Scholar, 1939; MB, BCh, BAO Hons; Magrath Scholar in Obstetrics and Gynæcology, 1943. Active service in HM Ships as Surg.-Lt, RNVR, 1945–47. MD 1948; MRCOG 1949; FRCOG 1960; FZS 1960; FRCPI 1977. Sen. Lectr in Obstetrics and Gynæcology, University Coll. of the West Indies, and Consultant Obstetrician and Gynæcologist to University Coll. Hosp. of the West Indies, 1953–59; Rockefeller Research Fellow at Harvard Medical Sch., 1956–57; Prof. of Obstetrics and Gynæcology, Univ. of London, at Queen Charlotte's and Chelsea Hosps and the Inst. of Obstetrics and Gynæcology, 1959–63; Obstetric Surgeon to Queen Charlotte's Hosp.; Surgeon to Chelsea Hosp. for Women. Vice-Pres., RCOG, 1977–80; Chm., Inst. of Obstetrics and Gynæcol., RCPI, 1984–87 (Hon. Fellow, 2007). Hon. DSc NUI, 1986. *Publications:* various papers on obstetrical and gynæcological subjects. *Address:* 41c Sans Souci Park, Belfast BT9 5QZ. *T:* (028) 9068 2956. *Died 22 Sept. 2013.*

PINSENT, Sir Christopher (Roy), 3rd Bt *cr* 1938, of Selly Hill, City of Birmingham; Lecturer and Tutor, Camberwell School of Art, 1962–86; *b* 2 Aug. 1922; *s* of Sir Roy

Pinsent, 2nd Bt, and Mary Tirzah Pinsent (*d* 1951), *d* of Dr Edward Geoffrey Walls, Spilsby, Lincs; *S* father, 1978; *m* 1951, Susan Mary, *d* of John Norton Scorer, Fotheringhay; one *s* two *d*. *Educ:* Winchester College. *Heir: s* Thomas Benjamin Roy Pinsent [*b* 21 July 1967; *m* 2007, Angelika Waltraud Heinkel]. *Address:* Ramblers, The Cricket Green, Woodside Road, Chiddingfold, Surrey GU8 4UG. *Died 19 Aug. 2015.*

PITAKAKA, Sir (Puibangara) Moses, GCMG 1995; Governor-General, Solomon Islands, 1994–99; *b* 24 Jan. 1945; *s* of Isaiah Puibangara and Lilian Tanaquana; *m* 1967, Lois Qilariava; three *s* four *d*. *Educ:* Goldie Coll., Western Prov., Solomon Is; Solomon Is Teachers' Coll.; Univ. of Birmingham; Univ. of S Pacific, Fiji; Univ. of Manchester; Queen Elizabeth House, Oxford Univ. School teacher, Solomon Is, 1964–66; Educn Officer, 1969–71; Dist Officer, Lands Officer and Magistrate, 1972–75; Honiara Town Clerk, Jan.–May 1976; Hd of Foreign Affairs, Prime Minister's Office, 1977–79; managed family business, 1980–81; Chm., N New Georgia Timber Co-op. Commn of Inquiry, 1982; Human Resources Develt Manager, Unilever Gp in Solomon Is, 1983–85; Leadership Code Commission: Comr, 1987–88; Chm., 1989–94. Chairman: Solomon Is Citizenship Commn, 1978–88; Nat. Educn Bd, 1980–86; Comr to Judicial and Legal Services Commn, 1981–83. Deacon, World Wide Church of God, 1993–. *Recreations:* reading, canoeing, swimming, jogging, table tennis. *Address:* c/o PO Box 52, Gizo, Western Province, Solomon Islands. *Died 25 Dec. 2011.*

PLATT OF WRITTLE, Baroness *cr* 1981 (Life Peer), of Writtle in the County of Essex; **Beryl Catherine Platt,** CBE 1978; DL; FREng; Chairman, Equal Opportunities Commission, 1983–88; *b* Leigh-on-Sea, 18 April 1923; *d* of Ernest and Dorothy Myatt; *m* 1949, Stewart Sydney Platt (*d* 2003); one *d* (and one *s* decd). *Educ:* Westcliff High School; Girton Coll., Cambridge (MA; Fellow, 1988). CEng, FREng (FEng 1987); FRAeS (Hon. FRAeS 1994). Technical Assistant, Hawker Aircraft, 1943–46; BEA, 1946–49. Mem. Bd, British Gas, 1988–94. Member: Engineering Council, 1981–90; Engrg Training Authy, 1990–92; Meteorological Office Adv. Cttee (UK), 1992–99 (Chm., 1995–99). Member, Chelmsford RDC, 1958–74. Essex County Council: Mem., 1965–85; Alderman, 1969–74, Hon. Alderman, 2005; Vice-Chm., 1980–83; Chm., Education Cttee, 1971–80. Mem., H of L Select Cttee for Science and Technology, 1982–85, 1990–94, 1996–2001 and 2003–07, on Relationships between Central and Local Govt, 1995–96, on Stem Cell Res., 2001–02; Vice Pres., Parly Scientific Cttee, 1996–2000. Mem., Adv. Cttee on Women's Employment, 1984–88. Vice-Chairman: Technician Education Council, 1979–81; London Regional Adv. Council for Technology Education, 1975–81. President: Chelmsford Engrg Soc., 1979–80; Cambridge Univ. Engrs Assoc., 1987–2001; Assoc. for Sci. Educn, 1988; Pipeline Industries Guild, 1994–96; Vice-President: UMIST, 1985–92; Engrg Section, BAAS (Pres., 1988); ACC, 1992–97 (Mem. Educn Cttee, 1974–80); Member: CNAA, 1973–79; Council, CGLI, 1974–94; Cambridge Univ. Appointments Bd, 1975–79; Council, Careers Research and Adv. Centre, 1983–93; Council, RSA, 1983–88; COPUS, 1990–93; Council, Foundn for Sci. and Technology, 1991–97. Patron, Women into Sci. and Engrg, 1995–2010. Member of Court: Essex Univ., 1964–99; City Univ., 1969–78; Brunel Univ., 1985–92; Cranfield Inst. of Technology, 1989–2003; Chancellor, Middlesex Univ., 1993–2000. Trustee, Homerton Coll., 1970–81. Liveryman, Engineers' Co., 1988–2010 (Mem., Ct of Assistants, 1995–2002, then Emeritus). DL Essex, 1983. Freeman, City of London, 1988. Fellow, 1987, Dir, 1989–94, Smallpeice Trust; Fellow, Manchester Polytechnic, 1989. FIGEM (FIGasE 1990); CInstE 1993; CIPD 1995; FRSA. Hon. FIMechE 1984; Hon. FITD 1994; Hon. FCP 1987; Hon. FIStructE 1991; Hon. FICE 1991; Hon. Fellow: Polytechnic of Wales, 1985; Women's Engrg Soc., 1988; UMIST, 1992. Hon. DSc: City, 1984; Salford, 1984; Cranfield, 1985; Nottingham Trent, 1993; Westminster, 1997; Sheffield, 2000; Anglia Ruskin, 2007; Southampton, 2008; DUniv: Open Univ., 1985; Essex, 1985; Middlesex, 1993; Sheffield Hallam, 2001; Hon. DEng Bradford, 1985; Hon. DTech: Brunel, 1986; Loughborough, 1993; Hon. LLD Cantab, 1988. European Engr, FEANI, 1987; Insignia Award *hc*, CGLI, 1988; RSC Parliamentary Award, 2007. *Recreations:* cooking, reading. *Address:* House of Lords, SW1A 0PW. *Died 1 Feb. 2015.*

PLATT, Prof. Colin Peter Sherard; Professor of History, Southampton University, 1983–99, then Emeritus; *b* Canton, China, 11 Nov. 1934; twin *s* of late James Westlake Platt and Veronica Norma Hope Arnold; *m* 1st, 1963, Valerie Ashforth (marr. diss. 1996); two *s* two *d*; 2nd, 1996, Claire Donovan. *Educ:* Collyer's Grammar School, Horsham; Balliol College, Oxford (BA 1st cl., MA); Leeds University (PhD). Research Assistant in Medieval Archaeology, Leeds Univ., 1960–62, Lectr, 1962–64; Lectr, Sen. Lectr and Reader in History, Southampton Univ., 1964–83. *Publications:* The Monastic Grange in Medieval England, 1969; Medieval Southampton: the port and trading community AD 1000–1600, 1973; (with Richard Coleman-Smith) Excavations in Medieval Southampton 1953–1969, 2 vols, 1975; The English Medieval Town, 1976; Medieval England: a social history and archaeology from the Conquest to 1600 AD, 1978; The Atlas of Medieval Man, 1979; The Parish Churches of Medieval England, 1981; The Castle in Medieval England and Wales, 1982; The Abbeys and Priories of Medieval England, 1984; Medieval Britain from the Air, 1984; The Traveller's Guide to Medieval England, 1985; The National Trust Guide to late Medieval and Renaissance Britain, 1986; The Architecture of Medieval Britain: a social history (Wolfson Prize for History), 1990; The Great Rebuildings of Tudor and Stuart England: revolutions in architectural taste, 1994; King Death: the Black Death and its aftermath in late medieval England, 1996; Marks of Opulence: the why, when and where of western art 1000–1914, 2004; A Concise History of Jersey, 2009. *Recreations:* reading novels, visiting medieval antiquities. *Address:* The Old Rectory, Littlehempston, Totnes, Devon TQ9 6LY. *T:* (01803) 862598. *Died 23 July 2015.*

PLOURDE, Most Rev. Joseph Aurèle; Archbishop of Ottawa (RC), 1967–89, then Emeritus; *b* 12 Jan. 1915; *s* of Antoine Plourde and Suzanne Albert. *Educ:* Bathurst Coll.; Bourget Coll., Rigaud; Major Seminary of Halifax; Inst. Catholique, Paris; Gregorian Univ., Rome. Auxiliary Bishop of Alexandria, Ont., 1964. Hon. DEd Moncton Univ., 1969. *Address:* Jean-Paul II Residence, 1243 Kilborn Avenue, Ottawa, ON K1H 6K9, Canada. *Died 5 Jan. 2013.*

PLUNKET, 8th Baron *cr* 1827; **Robin Rathmore Plunket;** *b* 3 Dec. 1925; *s* of 6th Baron Plunket (*d* 1938) and Dorothé Mabel (*d* 1938), *d* of late Joseph Lewis and *widow* of Captain Jack Barnato, RAF; *S* brother, 1975; *m* 1951, Jennifer, *d* of late Bailey Southwell, Olivenhoutpoort, S Africa. *Educ:* Eton. Formerly Captain, Rifle Brigade. *Heir: nephew* Tyrone Shaun Terence Plunket [*b* 5 Feb. 1966; *m* 2000, Lucy Marguerite Curry; two *s* (twins)]. *Address:* 39 Lansdowne Gardens, SW8 2EL. *Died 16 Nov. 2013.*

PLUNKETT, William Joseph; Valuer and Estates Surveyor, Greater London Council, 1977–81; *b* 8 Nov. 1921; *s* of John Joseph Archer and Marjorie Martin Plunkett; *m* 1949, Gwendoline Innes Barron; two *s* five *d*. *Educ:* Finchley Catholic Grammar Sch.; Coll. of Estate Management. BSc(Est. Man.). FRICS. RN, 1941–46; commnd, 1942; Lt RNVR. Dep. County Valuer, Middlesex CC, 1962–65; Asst Valuer, Valuation and Estates Dept, GLC, 1965–73; Dep. Valuer and Estates Surveyor, GLC, 1973–74; Dir of Valuation and Estates Dept, GLC, 1974–77. Mem., South Bank Polytechnic Adv. Cttee on Estate Management, 1973–76; Chm., Covent Garden Officers' Steering Gp, 1977–81. Mem. General Council, RICS, 1978–80 (Pres. Planning and Develt Div., 1978–79; Chm., S London Br. Cttee, 1976–77); Pres., Assoc. of Local Authority Valuers and Estate Surveyors, 1980–81. *Publications:* articles on Compensation, Valuation and Development. *Died 16 April 2014.*

POGO, Most Rev. Ellison Leslie, KBE 2000; Archbishop of Melanesia and Bishop of Central Melanesia, 1994–2008; *b* 9 Dec. 1947; *s* of Stephen Zaku and Sarah Duri; *m* 1978, Roslyn (*née* Kairopo); one *s* two *d*. *Educ:* Bishop Patteson Theol Coll., Kohimarama, Solomon Is; St John's Theol Coll., Auckland, NZ (LTh). Asst Priest, Anderson's Bay, Dunedin, 1979–81; Bishop of Ysabel, Solomon Is,

1981–94. Mem., Exec. Cttee, Pacific Conf. of Churches, 1984; Comr for Pacific Region, Unit IV (Sharing and Service), WCC, 1989; Ex Officio Mem., Pacific Ecumenical Regl Gp, 1989. Chm., Bd of Govs, Pacific Theol Coll., Suva, Fiji, 1994–2008. *Recreations:* reading, gardening. *Died 13 May 2013.*

PÖHL, Karl Otto; Grosskreuz des Verdienstordens der Bundesrepublik Deutschland; Member, Shareholder Committee, Sal. Oppenheim Jr & Cie, 1998 (Partner, 1992–98); Governor, Deutsche Bundesbank and German Governor, International Monetary Fund and Bank for International Settlements, 1980–91; *b* 1 Dec. 1929; *m* 1974; two *s* two *d.* *Educ:* Göttingen Univ. (Econs; Diplom.-Volkswirt). Div. Chief for Econ. Res., IFO-Institut, Munich, 1955–60; econ. journalist, Bonn, 1961–67; Mem. Exec., Fed. Assoc. of German Bank, Cologne, 1968–69; Div. Chief in Fed. Min. of Econs, Bonn, 1970–71; Dept Chief in Fed. Chancellery (Head, Dept for Econ. and Fiscal Policy), Bonn, 1971–72; Sec. of State in Fed. Min. of Finance, 1972–77; Dep. Governor, Deutsche Bundesbank, 1977–79; Chairman: EEC Monetary Cttee, 1976–77; Deputies of Gp of Ten, 1978–80; Gp of Ten, 1983–89; Cttee of Governors, Central Banks of EC Member States, 1990–91. Hon. DHL Georgetown Univ., 1983; Hon. DEconSc Ruhr Univ., 1985; Hon. DPhil Tel Aviv, 1986; Hon. Dr of Laws Univ. of Md, 1987; Hon. DSc: Buckingham, 1992; London, 1992; Hon. Dr Science Econ. Frankfurt, 2000. *Publications:* miscellaneous. *Died 9 Dec. 2014.*

POLAK, Dame Julia (Margaret), DBE 2003; FRCPath, FMedSci; Professor of Endocrine Pathology, London University, at Imperial College School of Medicine, 1984–2006, then Emeritus; Head, Imperial College Interdisciplinary Group on Tissue Engineering, 1997–2006; Director, Centre for Tissue Engineering and Regenerative Medicine, Chelsea and Westminster Hospital, 1999–2006; *b* 26 June 1939; *d* of Carlos and Rebeca Polak; *m* 1961, Prof. Daniel Catovsky; two *s* (one *d* decd). *Educ:* Univ. of Buenos Aires (MD 1964; Dip Histopath. 1966); DSc London, 1980. Hospital appts, Buenos Aires, 1961–67; Royal Postgraduate Medical School, London: Research Assistant in Histochemistry, 1968–69; Asst Lectr, Lectr, and Sen. Lectr, 1970–82; Reader, 1982–84; Dep. Dir, Dept of Histopathol., Hammersmith Hosp., 1988–99; Member: Exec. Cttee, Acad. Bd, RPMS, 1990–97; Med. Exec. Unit, Hammersmith Hosp., 1990–; Sub-Cttee in Biotech., London Univ., 1988–. Chm., British Endocrine Pathologists Gp, 1988–; Mem., Exec. Cttee of Council, Amer. Heart Assoc., 1989–. Mem., editl bds of med. jls. FMedSci 1999. Benito de Udaondo Cardiology Prize, 1967; Medal, Soc. of Endocrinology, 1984; Sir Eric Sharpe Prize for Oncology, Cable and Wireless, 1986–87. *Publications:* contribs to Nature and numerous professional jls. *Address:* Department of Chemical Engineering, Tissue Engineering and Regenerative Medicine, Imperial College, South Kensington Campus, SW7 2AZ. *T:* (020) 8237 2670, *Fax:* (020) 8746 5619. *E:* julia.polak@imperial.ac.uk. *Died 11 Aug. 2014.*

POLAND, Rear-Adm. Edmund Nicholas, CB 1967; CBE 1962; Chief of Staff to Commander-in-Chief Home Fleet, 1965–68; *b* 19 Feb. 1917; 2nd *s* of late Major Raymond A. Poland, RMLI and Mrs F. O. Bayly Jones; *m* 1941, Pauline Ruth Margaret Pechell; three *s* one *d* (and one *d* decd). *Educ:* Royal Naval Coll., Dartmouth. Served at sea during Abyssinian and Palestine crises, Spanish Civil War; War of 1939–45: convoy duties, Norwegian waters; Motor Torpedo Boats, Channel and Mediterranean; Torpedo Specialist, 1943; Staff Officer Ops to Naval Force Comdr, Burma; Sqdn T. Officer, HMS Royalist; HMS Hornet, 1946; Flotilla Torpedo and Anti-Submarine Officer of Third Submarine Flotilla, HMS Montclare; Air Warfare Div., Admiralty, 1950; British Naval Staff, Washington, 1953; jssc 1955; Directorate of Tactics and Ship Requirements, Admiralty; comd RN Air Station, Abbotsinch, 1956; Nato Standing Gp, Washington; Director of Under Sea Warfare (Naval), Ministry of Defence, 1962. Commander, 1950; Capt., 1956; Rear-Adm., 1965. Vice-Pres., Internat. Prisoners' Aid Assoc., 1978, Chm. (UK), 1979; Vice-Pres., Scottish Assoc. for Care and Resettlement of Offenders, 1979 (Dir, 1974–79). *Publications:* The Torpedomen, 1992; Majumba's Survival Trail, 1992. *Recreation:* gardening. *Address:* 39 Limmer Lane, Felpham, Bognor Regis, West Sussex PO22 7HD. *Died 10 March 2012.*

POLLARD, Bernard, CB 1988; Deputy Secretary and Director General (Technical), Board of Inland Revenue, 1985–88; *b* 24 Oct. 1927; *s* of late Isaac Polak and Sarah Polak (*née* Bloom); adopted surname Pollard, 1952; *m* 1961, Regina (*née* Stone); one *s* one *d.* *Educ:* Tottenham Grammar Sch.; London Univ. (BSc Econ; Gladstone Meml Prize (Econs), 1949). Called to the Bar, Middle Temple, 1968. Served RAF (Flying Officer), 1949–53. Entered Tax Inspectorate, Inland Revenue, 1953; Principal Inspector of Taxes, 1969; Asst Sec., 1973; Under Sec., 1979; Dir of Counter Avoidance and Evasion Div., 1981–85. *Recreations:* reading biographies, watching cricket and National Hunt racing. *Address:* 1 Albany House, 3 Balcombe Road, Poole, Dorset BH13 6DX. *T:* (01202) 763488. *Died 28 July 2012.*

POLLARD, Prof. Roger David, PhD; CEng, FREng, FIET, FIEEE; Professor of High Frequency Measurements, 1995–2010, then Emeritus, and Dean, Faculty of Engineering, 2003–10, University of Leeds; Research and Development Engineer (part-time), Agilent Technologies, Santa Rosa, California, since 2011; *b* 1 June 1946; *s* of late Mendel Pollard and Tilley Pollard (*née* Addess); *m* 1970, Anne Clara Price; two *d.* *Educ:* Hendon Co. Grammar Sch.; Univ. of Leeds (BSc 1972, PhD 1980). CEng 1979; FIEEE 1997; FIET (FIEE 2000); FREng 2005. University of Leeds: Lectr, 1974–85; Sen. Lectr, 1985–95; Hd, Sch. of Electronic and Electrical Engrg, 1999–2003. Consulting Engr, Agilent Technols (formerly Hewlett-Packard), 1981–. Pres., Microwave Theory and Techniques Soc., 1998, Vice-Pres., Technical Activities, 2010, IEEE. Measurement Prize, IEE, 1999; Millennium Medal, IEEE, 2000. *Publications:* papers, book chapters and patents on microwave active devices, circuits and measurements. *Recreations:* family, travel, reading, flying light aircraft. *Address:* 65 Albany, Manor Road, Bournemouth BH1 3EJ. *T:* (01202) 949104. *Died 3 Dec. 2011.*

PONCET, Jean André F.; *see* François-Poncet.

PONTIFEX, Brig. David More, CBE 1977 (OBE 1965; MBE 1956); General Secretary, Army Cadet Force Association and Secretary, Combined Cadet Force Association, 1977–87; *b* 16 Sept. 1922; *s* of Comdr John Weddall Pontifex, RN, and Monica Pontifex; *m* 1968, Kathleen Betsy (*née* Matheson); one *s* four *d.* *Educ:* Worth Preparatory Sch.; Downside Sch. Commnd The Rifle Brigade, 1942; served War, Italy (despatches); Staff Coll., Camberley, 1951; HQ Parachute Brigade, 1952–54; Kenya, 1954–56; War Office, 1956–58; Armed Forces Staff Coll., USA, 1958–59; Brigade Major, 63 Gurkha Brigade, 1961–62; CO 1st Bn Federal Regular Army, Aden, 1963–64; GSO1 2nd Div., BAOR, 1965–66; Col GS, Staff Coll., Camberley, 1967–69; Divisional Brig., The Light Div., 1969–73; Dep. Dir, Army Staff Duties, MoD, 1973–75; Dep. Comdr and COS, SE District, 1975–77, retired 1977. ADC to the Queen, 1975–77. *Address:* 68 Shortheath Road, Farnham, Surrey GU9 8SQ. *T:* (01252) 723284. *Club:* Naval and Military. *Died 19 Feb. 2011.*

POOT, Dr Anton, Hon. CBE 1989; Officer, Order of Oranje-Nassau (Netherlands), 1989; Managing Director, 1983–88, Chairman, 1983–89, Philips Electronics & Associated Industries Ltd; Chairman, Philips UK Ltd, 1985–89; *b* 23 Nov. 1929; *m* 1983, Jesmond Masters; one *s* one *d* by a former marriage. *Educ:* High School in Holland; electronics and economics, Holland and Johannesburg; Univ. of Surrey (BA 2002); Royal Holloway and Bedford New Coll., Univ. of London (MA 2004; PhD 2013). NV Philips' Gloeilampenfabrieken, Hilversum, Utrecht, Eindhoven, 1946–51; Philips S Africa, Fedn of Rhodesia and Nyasaland, 1951–63; NV Philips' Gloeilampenfabrieken, Eindhoven, 1963–66; Chairman and Man. Dir, Philips East Africa, 1965–71; Man. Dir, Ada (Halifax) Ltd and Philips Electrical Ltd UK, 1971–76; Man. Dir, NV Philips' Gloeilampenfabrieken, Eindhoven, 1976–78; Chm. and Man. Dir, Philips Appliances Div.,

1978–83. Hon. Freeman, Co. of Information Technologists, 1992. FRSA. *Recreations:* music, golf, political philosophy. *Died 23 Aug. 2013.*

POPE, Sir Joseph (Albert), Kt 1980; DSc, PhD (Belfast), WhSc; Director, since 1960, Consultant, since 1988, TQ International (formerly TecQuipment Group), Nottingham (Chairman, 1974–88); *b* 18 Oct. 1914; *s* of Albert Henry and Mary Pope; *m* 1940, Evelyn Alice Gallagher (*d* 2010); one *s* one *d* (and one *d* decd). *Educ:* School of Arts and Crafts, Cambridge; King's College, London. Apprentice, Boulton & Pauls, Norwich, 1930–35. Whitworth Scholarship, 1935. Assistant Lecturer in Engineering: Queen's Univ., Belfast, 1938–44; Univ. of Manchester, 1944–45; Lecturer, then Senior Lecturer, Univ. of Sheffield, 1945–49; Professor of Mechanical Engineering, Nottingham University, 1949–60; Research Dir, Mirrlees Nat. Research Div., Stockport, and Dir, Mirrlees National Ltd, 1960–69; Vice-Chancellor, Univ. of Aston in Birmingham, 1969–79. Director: John Brown & Co. Ltd, 1970–82; Midlands Electricity Bd, 1975–80; Royal Worcester Ltd, 1979–83; Chm., W Midlands Econ. Planning Council, 1977–79. Gen. Treasurer, British Assoc., 1975–82; Pres., Whitworth Soc., 1978–79; Chm., Birmingham Civic Soc., 1978–79. Hon. LLD Birmingham, 1979; DUniv Heriot-Watt, 1979; Hon. DSc: Aston, 1979; Belfast, 1980; Salford, 1980; Nottingham, 1987. *Publications:* papers on the impact of metals and metal fatigue published in Proc. of Inst. of Mech. Engineers and Jl of Iron and Steel Inst. *Address:* 3 Mapperley Hall Drive, Nottingham NG3 5EP. *T:* (0115) 962 1146. *Died 24 March 2013.*

PORTER, Andrew Brian; writer on music; Music Critic, Times Literary Supplement, 1997–2009; *b* Cape Town, SA, 26 Aug. 1928; *s* of Andrew Ferdinand Porter and Vera Sybil (*née* Bloxham). *Educ:* University Coll., Oxford (MA). Music Critic, Financial Times, 1952–72; Editor, Musical Times, 1960–67; Music Critic: New Yorker, 1972–92; The Observer, 1992–97. Vis. Fellow, All Souls Coll., Oxford, 1972–73; Bloch Prof., Univ. of Calif, Berkeley, 1980–81. Corresp. Mem., Amer. Musicol Soc., 1994. *Publications:* A Musical Season, 1974; The Ring of the Nibelung, 1976; Music of Three Seasons, 1978; Music of Three More Seasons, 1981; (ed with D. Rosen) Verdi's Macbeth: a sourcebook, 1984; The Tempest (opera libretto), 1985; Musical Events 1980–1983, 1987; Musical Events 1983–1986, 1989; The Song of Majnun (opera libretto), 1991; A Music Critic Remembers, 2000; *festschrift:* Words on Music (ed. C. Brook and D. Rosen), 2003; many opera translations; contrib. Music & Letters, Musical Qly, etc. *Address:* 9 Pembroke Walk, W8 6PQ. *Died 3 April 2015.*

PORTER, Ivor Forsyth, CMG 1963; OBE (mil.) 1944; HM Diplomatic Service, retired; *b* 12 Nov. 1913; *s* of Herbert and Evelyn Porter; *m* 1951, Ann, *o d* of late Dr John Speares (marr. diss., 1961); *m* 1961, Katerina, *oc* of A. T. Cholerton; one *s* one *d*. *Educ:* Barrow Grammar Sch.; Leeds Univ. (BA, PhD). Lecturer at Bucharest Univ., 1939–40; Temp. Secretary, at Bucharest Legation, 1940–41; SOE, 1941–45 (Major). Joined Foreign (subseq. Diplomatic) Service, May 1946, as 2nd Secretary in Sen. Branch; 1st Secretary 1948; transferred to Washington, 1951; Foreign Office, 1953; UK Delegation to NATO Paris as Counsellor and Head of Chancery, 1956; Nicosia, 1959 (Deputy Head UK Mission), Deputy High Commissioner, 1961–62, Cyprus; Permanent Rep. to Council of Europe, Strasbourg, 1962–65 (with personal rank of Minister); Dep. High Commissioner, Eastern India, 1965–66; Ambassador, UK Delegn to Geneva Disarmament Conf., 1968–71 (Minister, 1967–68); Ambassador to Senegal, Guinea, Mali and Mauritania, 1971–73; later Dir, Atlantic Region, Research Dept, FCO. Comdr, Order of Cultural Merit (Romania), 2005; Cross of Royal House of Romania, 2008. *Publications:* (as Ivor Crane) The Think Trap (novel), 1972; Operation Autonomous: with SOE in wartime Roumania, 1989; Michael of Romania: the King and the Country, 2005. *Recreations:* writing, walking. *Address:* 17 Redcliffe Road, SW10 9NP. *Clubs:* Travellers, PEN. *Died 29 May 2012.*

PORTER, James Forrest, CBE 1991; Director General (formerly Director) of the Commonwealth Institute, 1978–91; Leverhulme Research Fellow, 1991–99, Visiting Fellow, 1991–93, Head of International Development, 1993–95 and Acting Dean for New Initiatives, 1995–96, London University Institute of Education; *b* Frodsham, Cheshire, 2 Oct. 1928; *s* of Ernest Porter and Mary Violetta Porter; *m* 1952, Dymphna (*d* 2006), *d* of Leo Francis Powell, London; two *d*. *Educ:* Salford Grammar Sch.; LSE (BSc Sociol.); Univ. of London Inst. of Educn (MA). Asst Master, St George in the East Sec. Sch., Stepney, 1948–50; Leverhulme Scholar, Univ. of London, 1950–55; Lectr in Sociol. and Educn, Worcester Coll., 1955–60; Head of Educn Dept, Chorley Coll., 1960–62; Dep. Principal, Coventry Coll., 1962–67; Principal, Bulmershe Coll. of Higher Educn, Reading, 1967–78. Director: bi-annual internat. courses on teacher educn, Brit. Council, 1975, 1977, 1979, on Museum Educn, 1982; Adult Literacy Support Services Fund, 1977–81. Consultant: Finland, 1976; Unesco, Paris, 1979–; Commonwealth Fellow, Australia, 1977. Chm., Newsconcern Foundn, 1984–91; Member: Nat. Cttee of Inquiry into Teacher Educn and Trng (James Cttee), 1971; Educn Cttee, UGC, 1970–78; Educnl Adv. Council, IBA, 1970–80; Nat. Council for Dance Educn, 1978; Exec. Cttee, Internat. Council of Museums, 1981–87; Educn Council, BBC, 1987–92; President: British Comparative Educn Soc., 1983–84; World Educn Fellowship, 1989– (Chm., 1979–82). Member: UK Delegn to Unesco, Geneva, 1975 (Vice-Pres., Commn on Changing Role of Teacher); Unesco Missions to Morocco and Senegal, 1982, to Jordan, 1983. Mem., Educn Council, Royal Opera House, Covent Garden, 1985–91; Gov., Henley Coll. Corp., 2008–. Mem., Editorial Bd, Higher Education Review, 1974–; Chm., Editorial Bd, Commonwealth Today, 1985–89 (Mem., 1982). FRSA 1978; Hon. FCP 1978; FRGS 1984. *Publications:* (ed) Rural Development and the Changing Countries of the World, 1969; (with N. Goble) The Changing Role of the Teacher, Paris 1977; Reschooling and the Global Future: politics, economics and the English experience, 1999. *Recreations:* writing, river watching. *Address:* The Garden Flat, The Hermitage, 29 Vicarage Road, Henley-on-Thames RG9 1HT. *Died 27 Oct. 2012.*

PORTER, Sir John Simon H.; *see* Horsbrugh-Porter.

PORTER, Rt Hon. Sir Robert (Wilson), Kt 1971; PC (NI) 1969; QC (NI) 1965; County Court Judge, Northern Ireland, 1978–95; *b* 23 Dec. 1923; *s* of late Joseph Wilson Porter and late Letitia Mary (*née* Wasson); *m* 1953, Margaret Adelaide (decd), *y d* of late F. W. Lynas; one *s* one *d* (and one *d* decd). *Educ:* Model Sch. and Foyle Coll., Londonderry; Queen's Univ., Belfast. RAFVR, 1942–46; Royal Artillery (TA), 1950–56. Foundation Schol., Queen's Univ., 1947 and 1948; LLB 1949. Called to Bar: N Ireland, 1950; Ireland, 1975; Middle Temple, 1988. Lecturer in Contract and Sale of Goods, Queen's Univ., 1950–51; Jun. Crown Counsel, Co. Londonderry, 1960–63, Co. Down, 1964–65; Counsel to Attorney-General for N Ireland, 1963–64 and 1965; Recorder: of Londonderry, 1979–81; of Belfast, 1993–95. Vice-Chairman, 1959–61, Chairman, 1961–66, War Pensions Appeal Tribunal for N Ireland. MP (U) Queen's Univ. of Belfast, 1966–69, Lagan Valley, 1969–73, Parlt of N Ireland; Minister of Health and Social Services, N Ireland, 1969; Parly Sec., Min. of Home Affairs, 1969; Minister of Home Affairs, Govt of NI, 1969–70. Hon. Col, OTC, QUB, 1988–93. *Recreations:* gardening, golf. *Address:* Cullo Hill, 12 Clogher Road, Hillsborough, Co. Down BT26 6PJ. *Clubs:* Royal Air Force; Malone Golf (Belfast). *Died 25 May 2014.*

POSTGATE, Prof. John Raymond, FRS 1977; FSB; Director, AFRC Unit of Nitrogen Fixation, 1980–87 (Assistant Director, 1963–80), and Professor of Microbiology, University of Sussex, 1965–87, then Emeritus; *b* 24 June 1922; *s* of Raymond William Postgate and Daisy Postgate (*née* Lansbury); *m* 1948, Mary Stewart (*d* 2008); three *d*. *Educ:* principally Woodstock Sch., Golders Green; Kingsbury County Sch., Middx; Balliol Coll., Oxford. BA, MA, DPhil, DSc. Research in chemical microbiology: with D. D. Woods on action of sulfonamide drugs, 1946–48, with K. R. Butlin on sulphate-reducing bacteria, 1948–59. Research on bacterial death, 1959–63, incl. Visiting Professor: Univ. of Illinois, 1962–63, working on sulphate-reducing bacteria; Oregon State Univ., 1977–78. President: Inst. of Biology, 1982–84; Soc. for Gen. Microbiology, 1984–87. Hon. DSc Bath, 1990; Hon. LLD Dundee, 1997. *Publications:* Microbes and Man, 1969, 4th edn 2000; Biological Nitrogen Fixation, 1972; A Plain Man's Guide to Jazz, 1973; Nitrogen Fixation, 1978, 3rd edn 1998; The Sulphate-Reducing Bacteria, 1979, 2nd edn 1984; The Fundamentals of Nitrogen Fixation, 1982; The Outer Reaches of Life, 1994; (with Mary Postgate) A Stomach for Dissent: the life of Raymond Postgate, 1994; Lethal Lozenges and Tainted Tea: a biography of John Postgate (1820–1881), 2001; Microbes, Music and Me: a life in science, 2013; ed, 4 scientific symposia; regular columnist in Jazz Monthly, 1952–72; numerous scientific papers in microbiol/biochem. jls; many jazz record reviews in specialist magazines; articles on jazz. *Recreation:* listening to jazz and attempting to play it. *Address:* 1 Houndean Rise, Lewes, Sussex BN7 1EG. *T:* (01273) 472675. *Died 22 Oct. 2014.*

POSTLETHWAITE, Peter William, OBE 2004; actor; *b* 16 Feb. 1945; *m* 2003, Jacqueline Morrish; one *s* one *d*. *Educ:* Bristol Old Vic Theatre Sch. *Stage* includes: Troilus and Cressida, Bristol Old Vic; Royal Shakespeare Company: Richard III; Cyrano de Bergerac; King Lear; Fair Maid of the West; a Midsummer Night's Dream; Macbeth, Bristol Old Vic and tour, 1997; The Homecoming, Royal Exchange Th., Manchester, 2002; King Lear, Everyman, Liverpool, 2008; *television* includes: The Muscle Market; Coast to Coast, 1987; The Bill; Martin Chuzzlewit, 1994; Between the Lines; Lost for Words, 1999; Alice in Wonderland, 2000; The Sins, 2000; *films* include: A Private Function, 1985; Distant Voices, Still Lives, 1988; The Dressmaker, 1989; The Last of the Mohicans, 1991; Alien 3, 1992; In the Name of the Father, 1993; Usual Suspects, 1995; Dragonheart, 1996; Brassed Off, 1996; Romeo and Juliet, 1997; The Lost World: Jurassic Park, 1997; Amistad, 1997; Serpent's Kiss, 1997; Among Giants, 1998; The Shipping News, 2002; Dark Water, The Constant Gardener, 2005; The Omen, 2006; Closing the Ring, 2007; The Age of Stupid, 2009. *Address:* c/o Markham & Froggatt Ltd, 4 Windmill Street, W1P 1HF. *Died 2 Jan. 2011.*

POTTER, Ernest Frank; Director, Finance, Cable & Wireless plc, 1979–87 (Director of Finance and Corporate Planning, 1977–79); *b* 29 April 1923; *s* of Frank William and Edith Mary Potter; *m* 1st, 1945, Madge (*née* Arrowsmith) (*d* 1990); one *s*; 2nd, 1992, Barbara (*née* Brewis-Levie). *Educ:* Dr Challoner's Grammar Sch., Amersham. FCMA, FCIS, MIMC. Commissioned Pilot and Navigator, RAF, 1941–49. Chief Accountant, Bulmer & Lumb Ltd, 1950–58; Director, Management Consulting, Coopers & Lybrand, 1959–71; British Steel Corporation, Cammell Laird Shipbuilders Ltd, 1972–77; Director (non-executive): Cable & Wireless (West Indies) Ltd, 1977–87; Bahrain Telecommunications Corp., 1982–89; Cable & Wireless North America Inc., 1980–87; Cable & Wireless Hongkong Ltd, 1982–87; Cable & Wireless (Leasing) Ltd, 1982–87; Bahrain Telecommunications Corp., 1982–89; Cable & Wireless Marine Ltd, 1984–87; Mercury Communications Ltd, 1985–87; Cable & Wireless (Bermuda) Ltd, 1986–87; General Hybrid Ltd, 1987–91; Cable Corp. Ltd, 1988–97; Windsor Cable Ltd, 1988–97; Telephone Corp. Ltd, 1988–92; Micrelec Gp, 1989–92; Chairman: Clebern Internat. Ltd, 1988–89; Holmes Protection Inc., 1990–91; Themes Internat., 1991–92. Mem., Accounting Standards Cttee, 1985–90. *Recreations:* golf, sailing. *Address:* 11 Ridgeway, St Ann's Park, Virginia Water, Surrey GU25 4TE. *T:* (01344) 842178. *Clubs:* Royal Air Force; Foxhills (Surrey); St Mawes Sailing. *Died 19 April 2011.*

POTTER, John Herbert, MBE 1974; HM Diplomatic Service, retired; *b* 11 Jan. 1928; *s* of Herbert George and Winifred Eva Potter; *m* 1953, Winifred Susan Florence Hall (*d* 2000); one *d*. *Educ:* elementary education at various state schools. Electrical Engineering jobs, 1942–45; served HM Forces, 1945–48; GPO, 1948–53; Foreign Office, 1953–55; Commercial Attaché, Bangkok, 1955–57; FO, 1957–60; Istanbul, 1960; Ankara, 1960–64; Second Secretary, Information, 1962; Second Sec., Information, Addis Ababa, 1964; Vice-Consul, Information, Johannesburg, 1964–66; DSAO, later FCO, 1966–70; First Sec. (Administration): Brussels, 1970–74; Warsaw, 1974–76; FCO (Inspectorate), 1976–80; Counsellor (Admin) and Consul-Gen., Moscow, 1980–81; Counsellor (Admin), Bonn, 1981–82. *Recreations:* reading, languages. *Address:* The Penthouse Flat, 37 Park Road, Bexhill-on-Sea, E Sussex TN39 3HX. *Died 14 Feb. 2015.*

POTTER, Rev. Philip Alford; General Secretary, World Council of Churches, 1972–84; *b* 19 Aug. 1921; *s* of Clement Potter and Violet Peters, Roseau, Dominica, Windward Is, WI; *m* 1st, 1956, Ethel Olive Doreen Cousins (*d* 1980), Jamaica, WI; 2nd, 1984, Rt Rev. Barbel von Wartenberg (former Bishop of Holstein-Lübeck). *Educ:* Dominica Grammar Sch.; United Theological Coll., Jamaica; London Univ. BD, MTh. Methodist Minister. Overseas Sec., British SCM, 1948–50; Superintendent, Cap Haïtien Circuit, Methodist Church, Haiti, 1950–54; Sec., later Dir, Youth Dept, WCC, 1954–60; Sec. for WI and W Africa, Methodist Missionary Society, London, 1961–66; Dir, Commn on World Mission and Evangelism, and Associate Gen. Sec., WCC, 1967–72. Chaplain, Univ. of WI and Lectr, United Theol Coll. of WI, 1985–90. Mem., then Chm., Youth Dept Cttee, WCC, 1948–54; Chm., World Student Christian Fedn, 1960–68. Editor: Internat. Review of Mission, 1967–72; Ecumenical Rev., 1972–84. Hon. Doctor of Theology: Hamburg Univ., Germany, 1971; Geneva, 1976; Theol Inst. of Rumanian Orthodox Church, 1977; Humboldt Univ., Berlin, 1982; Uppsala, 1984; Hon. LLD W Indies, 1974; Hon. DD Birmingham, 1985; Hon. Dr Cape Town, 1998; Vienna, 2001. Niwano Peace Prize, Japan, 1986. *Publications:* (with Prof. Hendrik Berkhof) Key Words of the Gospel, 1964; The Love of Power or the Power of Love, 1974; Life in all its Fullness, 1981; (with Barbel von Wartenberg) Freedom is for Freeing, 1990; (jtly) Seeking and Serving the Truth: first hundred years of the World Student Christian Federation, 1997; chapter in Explosives Lateinamerika (ed by T. Tschuy), 1969; essays in various symposia; contrib. various jls, incl. Ecumenical Rev., Internat. Rev. of Mission, Student World. *Recreations:* swimming, hiking, music, geology. *Address:* Plönniesstrasse 6, 23560 Lübeck, Germany. *Died 30 March 2015.*

POTTS, Sir (Francis) Humphrey, Kt 1986; a Judge of the High Court of Justice, Queen's Bench Division, 1986–2001; *b* 18 Aug. 1931; *er s* of late Francis William Potts and Elizabeth Hannah (*née* Humphrey), Penshaw, Co. Durham; *m* 1971, Philippa Margaret Campbell, *d* of the late J. C. H. Le B. Croke and Mrs J. F. G. Downes; two *s* and two step *s*. *Educ:* Royal Grammar Sch., Newcastle upon Tyne; St Catherine's Society, Oxford (BCL 1954, MA 1957; Hon. Fellow, St Catherine's Coll., 2002). Barrister-at-Law, Lincoln's Inn, 1955 (Tancred Student, 1953; Cholmeley Scholar, 1954), Bencher, 1979; North Eastern Circuit, 1955; practised in Newcastle upon Tyne, 1955–71; QC 1971; a Recorder, 1972–86; admitted to Hong Kong Bar, 1984; Presiding Judge, NE Circuit, 1988–91. Member: Mental Health Review Tribunal, 1984–86; Criminal Injuries Compensation Bd, 1985–86; Parole Bd, 1992–96 (Vice-Chm., 1995–96); Chm., Special Immigration Appeals Commn, 1997–2001. Trustee, Mental Health Foundn, 1990–96. Pres., Norcare, 1997–99. *Address:* c/o Royal Courts of Justice, Strand, WC2A 2LL; Third Floor North, 4 Stone Buildings, Lincoln's Inn, WC2A 3XT. *Died 2 Dec. 2012.*

POWELL, Prof. Michael James David, FRS 1983; John Humphrey Plummer Professor of Applied Numerical Analysis, University of Cambridge, 1976–2001, then Emeritus; Fellow of Pembroke College, Cambridge, 1978–2001, then Emeritus; *b* 29 July 1936; *s* of William James David Powell and Beatrice Margaret (*née* Page); *m* 1959, Caroline Mary Henderson; two *d* (one *s* decd). *Educ:* Eastbourne Coll.; Peterhouse, Cambridge (Schol.; BA 1959; ScD 1979). Mathematician at Atomic Energy Research Estabt, Harwell, 1959–76; special merit research appt to banded level, 1969, and to senior level, 1975. For. Associate, NAS, US, 2001; Corresp. Mem., Australian Acad. of Sci., 2007. Hon. DSc UEA, 2001. George B. Dantzig Prize in Mathematical Programming, 1982;

Naylor Prize, 1983, Sen. Whitehead Prize, 1999, London Math. Soc.; Gold Medal, IMA, 1996. *Publications:* Approximation Theory and Methods, 1981; papers on numerical mathematics, especially approximation and optimization calculations. *Recreations:* golf, sudokus, walking. *Address:* 134 Milton Road, Cambridge CB4 1LE. *Died 19 April 2015.*

POWELL-JONES, John Ernest, CMG 1974; HM Diplomatic Service, retired; Ambassador to Switzerland, 1982–85; *b* 14 April 1925; *s* of late Walter James Powell-Jones and Gladys Margaret (*née* Taylor); *m* 1st, 1949, Ann Murray (marr. diss. 1967); one *s* one *d* (and one *s* decd); 2nd, 1968, Pamela Sale. *Educ:* Charterhouse; University Coll., Oxford (1st cl. Modern Hist.). Served with Rifle Bde, 1943–46. HM Foreign (later Diplomatic) Service, 1949; 3rd Sec. and Vice-Consul, Bogota, 1950–52; Eastern and later Levant Dept, FO, 1952–55; 2nd, later 1st Sec., Athens, 1955–59; News Dept, FO, 1959–60; 1st Sec., Leopoldville, 1961–62; UN Dept, FO, 1963–67; ndc Canada 1967–68; Counsellor, Political Adviser's Office, Singapore, 1968–69; Counsellor and Consul-General, Athens, 1970–73; Ambassador at Phnom Penh, 1973–75; RCDS 1975; Ambassador to Senegal, Guinea, Mali, Mauritania and Guinea-Bissau, 1976–79, to Cape Verde, 1977–79; Ambassador and Perm. Rep., UN Conf. on Law of the Sea, 1979–82. Chm., Inter Counsel UK Ltd, 1986–93. Member: Waverley BC, 1987–95; Wonersh Parish Council, 1987–99 (Vice-Chm., 1990–99). Chm., Wonersh United Charities, 1999–2005. Member: Bd, Surrey Historic Bldgs Trust, 1989–92; Council, SE England Agricl Soc., 1991–95. *Recreations:* gardening, walking. *Address:* Gascons, Gaston Gate, Cranleigh, Surrey GU6 8QY. *T:* (01483) 274313. *Club:* Travellers. *Died 13 Jan. 2012.*

POWERSCOURT, 10th Viscount *cr* 1743; **Mervyn Niall Wingfield;** Baron Wingfield, 1743; Baron Powerscourt (UK), 1885; *b* 3 Sept. 1935; *s* of 9th Viscount Powerscourt and Sheila Claude (*d* 1992), *d* of late Lt-Col Claude Beddington; *S* father, 1973; *m* 1st, 1962, Wendy Ann Pauline (marr. diss. 1974), *d* of R. C. G. Slazenger; one *s* one *d*; 2nd, 1979, Pauline (marr. diss. 1995), *d* of W. P. Van, San Francisco. *Educ:* Stowe; Trinity Coll., Cambridge. Formerly Irish Guards. *Heir: s* Hon. Mervyn Anthony Wingfield, *b* 21 Aug. 1963. *Died 25 July 2015.*

POWNALL, John Harvey; Director, DTI-North West, 1988–93; *b* 24 Oct. 1933; *s* of late Eric Pownall and Gladys Mary Pownall (*née* Baily); *m* 1958, Pauline M. Marsden, *o d* of William Denton Marsden; one *s* two *d*. *Educ:* Tonbridge School; Imperial College, London (BSc Eng Met). ARSM. Scientific Officer, Atomic Energy Research Estab., Harwell, 1955–59; Warren Spring Lab., DSIR, 1959–64; Dept of Economic Affairs, 1964–66; Board of Trade/Dept of Trade and Industry, 1966–83; Dir-Gen., Council of Mechanical and Metal Trade Assocs, 1983–85; Hd of Electricity Div., Dept of Energy, 1985–87; Under Sec., DTI, 1987, on secondment to CEGB, 1987–88. Mem. Council, 1989–2004, Pro-Chancellor, 2001–04, Salford Univ. (Chm., Estates Cttee, 1993–2003). *Died 6 June 2014.*

PRACY, Robert, FRCS; Dean of the Institute of Laryngology and Otology, University of London, 1981–85; a Medical Chairman, Pensions Appeal Tribunals, since 1984 (Medical Member, since 1982); *b* 19 Sept. 1921; *s* of Douglas Sherrin Pracy and Gwendoline Blanche Power; *m* 1946, Elizabeth Patricia Spicer (*d* 2008); one *s* two *d* (and one *s* decd). *Educ:* Berkhamsted Sch.; St Bartholomew's Hosp. Med. Coll. (MB BS 1945); MPhil (Lond.) 1984. LRCP 1944; MRCS, FRCS 1953. Former Captain, RAMC. House Surgeon appts, St Bartholomew's Hosp.; formerly: Registrar, Royal Nat. Throat, Nose and Ear Hosp.; Consultant Surgeon: Liverpool Regional Board, 1954; United Liverpool Hosps, 1959; Alder Hey Children's Hosp., 1960; Royal Nat. Throat, Nose and Ear Hosp.; Hosp. for Sick Children, Gt Ormond St; Dir, Dept of Otolaryngology, Liverpool Univ. Mem. Ct of Examnrs, RCS and RCSI. Lectures: Yearsley, 1976; Joshi, 1978; Wilde, 1979; Semon, London Univ., 1980. Pres., British Assoc. of Otolaryngologists; FRSocMed (Pres., Sect. of Laryngology, 1982–83). Hon. FRCSI 1982; Hon. Fellow: Irish Otolaryngol Assoc.; Assoc. of Otolaryngologists of India; Polish Otolaryngological Assoc. *Publications:* (jtly) Short Textbook: Ear, Nose and Throat, 1970, 2nd edn 1974 (trans. Italian, Portuguese, Spanish); (jtly) Ear, Nose and Throat Surgery and Nursing, 1977; contribs to learned jls. *Recreations:* painting, engraving, theatre. *Address:* Ginkgo House, New Road, Moreton-in-Marsh, Glos GL56 0AS. *T:* (01608) 650740. *Died 7 Oct. 2015.*

PRAIS, Prof. Sigbert Jon, FBA 1985; Senior Research Fellow, National Institute of Economic and Social Research, London, since 1970; *b* Frankfurt am Main, Germany, 19 Dec. 1928; *s* of Samuel and Bertha Prais; came to England as refugee, 1934; UK citizen, 1946; *m* 1971, Vivien Hennessy, LLM, solicitor; one *s* three *d*. *Educ:* King Edward's School, Birmingham; Univ. of Birmingham (MCom); Fitzwilliam Coll., Cambridge (PhD 1953; ScD 1974). Dept of Applied Economics, Cambridge, 1950–57; post-doctoral Fellow, Univ. of Chicago, 1953–54; research officer, NIESR, 1953–59; UN Tech. Assistance Orgn, 1959–60; IMF Washington, 1960–61; Finance Dir, Elbief Co., 1961–70. Vis. Prof. of Econs, City Univ., 1975–84. Mem. Council, Royal Economic Soc., 1979–83. Mem. Council, City Univ., 1990–94. Hon. DLitt City, 1989; Hon. DSc Birmingham, 2006. *Publications:* Analysis of Family Budgets (jtly), 1955, 2nd edn 1971; Evolution of Giant Firms in Britain, 1976, 2nd edn 1981; Productivity and Industrial Structure, 1981; Productivity, Education and Training, 1995; (jtly) From School to Productive Work in Britain and Switzerland, 1997; Social Disparities and the Teaching of Literacy, 2001; articles in economic and statistical jls, esp. on influence of educn on economic progress. *Address:* 83 West Heath Road, NW3 7TN. *T:* (020) 8458 4428, (office) (020) 7654 1939. *Died 22 Feb. 2014.*

PRATCHETT, Sir Terence (David John), Kt 2009; OBE 1998; author; *b* 28 April 1948; *s* of David and Eileen Pratchett; *m* 1968, Lyn Purves; one *d*. *Educ:* High Wycombe Tech. High Sch.; Beaconsfield Public Library. Assorted journalism, 1965–80; Press Officer, CEGB, 1980–87. Chm., Soc. of Authors, 1994–95. Hon. DLitt: Warwick, 1999; Portsmouth, 2001; Bath, 2003; Bristol, 2004; Dublin, 2008; Bradford, 2009; Winchester, 2009; Hon. Dr Buckinghamshire New, 2008; DUniv Open, 2013. *Publications:* The Carpet People, 1971; The Dark Side of the Sun, 1976; Strata, 1981; The Colour of Magic, 1983; The Light Fantastic, 1986; Equal Rites, 1987; Mort, 1987; Sourcery, 1988; Wyrd Sisters, 1988; Pyramids, 1989; Truckers, 1989; Guards! Guards!, 1989; The Unadulterated Cat, 1989; Eric, 1989; (with N. Gaiman) Good Omens, 1990; Moving Pictures, 1990; Diggers, 1990; Wings, 1990; Reaper Man, 1991; Witches Abroad, 1991; Small Gods, 1992; Only You Can Save Mankind, 1992; Lords and Ladies, 1992; Johnny and the Dead, 1993; Men At Arms, 1993; Soul Music, 1994; (with S. Briggs) The Discworld Companion, 1994, rev. edn 2003; Interesting Times, 1994; Maskerade, 1995; Johnny and the Bomb, 1996; Feet of Clay, 1996; Hogfather, 1996; Jingo, 1997; The Last Continent, 1998; Carpe Jugulum, 1998; The Fifth Elephant, 1999; (jtly) The Science of Discworld, 1999; (jtly) Nanny Ogg's Cookbook, 1999; The Truth, 2000; Thief of Time, 2001; The Last Hero, 2001; The Amazing Maurice and his Educated Rodents, 2001 (Carnegie Medal, 2002); (jtly) The Science of Discworld II: The Globe, 2002; Night Watch, 2002; The Wee Free Men, 2003; Monstrous Regiment, 2003; A Hat Full of Sky, 2004; Going Postal, 2004; (jtly) The Science of Discworld III: Darwin's Watch, 2005; Thud!, 2005; Wintersmith, 2006; Making Money, 2007; Nation, 2008; (with J. Simpson) The Folklore of Discworld, 2008; Unseen Academicals, 2009; I Shall Wear Midnight, 2010; (with Josh Kirby) The Illustrated Eric, 2010; Snuff, 2011; Dodger, 2012; A Blink of the Screen, 2012; (with S. Baxter) The Long Earth, 2012; (with S. Briggs) Turtle Recall, 2012; Raising Steam, 2013; (jtly) The Science of Discworld IV: Judgement Day, 2013; (with S. Baxter) The Long War, 2013; (with S. Baxter) The Long Mars, 2014; A Slip of the Keyboard: collected non-fiction, 2014; *posthumous publication:* The Shepherd's Crown, 2015. *Recreation:* letting the mind wander. *Address:* c/o Colin Smythe, 38 Mill Lane, Gerrards Cross, Bucks SL9 8BA. *T:* (01753) 886000. *Died 12 March 2015.*

PRATT, (Arthur) Geoffrey, CBE 1981; Hon. Secretary, Institution of Gas Engineers, 1982–87; *b* 19 Aug. 1922; *s* of William Pratt, Willington, Co. Durham; *m* 1st, 1946, Ethel, (Effie), Luck (*d* 1997); two *s* twin *d*; 2nd, 1998, Mrs Mavis Scargill (*d* 2002). *Educ:* King James I Grammar Sch., Bishop Auckland. CEng, FIGasE. Joined E Mids Gas Bd, 1951: Chief Engr, 1964; Dir of Engrg, 1967; Dep. Chm., S Eastern Gas Bd, 1970–72; Chm., SE Gas Region, 1972–81; part-time Mem., British Gas Corp., 1981–82. Chm., Metrogas Building Soc., 1977–85. Pres., IGasE, 1974–75; Hon. FIGEM (Hon. FIGasE 1987). *Recreations:* keep-fit, motoring. *Address:* 3 Hither Chantlers, Langton Green, Tunbridge Wells, Kent TN3 0BJ. *Died 20 July 2014.*

PRATT, Michael John; QC 1976; a Recorder of the Crown Court, 1974–94; *b* 23 May 1933; *o s* of W. Brownlow Pratt; *m* 1960, Elizabeth Jean Hendry; two *s* three *d. Educ:* West House Sch., Edgbaston; Malvern Coll. LLB (Birmingham). Army service, 2nd Lieut, 3rd Carabiniers (Prince of Wales's Dragoon Guards); Staff Captain. Called to the Bar, Middle Temple, 1954, Bencher, 1986; a Dep. High Court Judge, 1982–94. Chm. Govs, West House Sch., Edgbaston, 1975–2000; Gov., Malvern Coll., 1976–. *Recreations:* music, theatre, sport generally. *Address:* 9 Moorland Road, Edgbaston, Birmingham B16 9JP. *T:* (0121) 454 1071. *Clubs:* Cavalry and Guards; Edgbaston Golf. *Died 21 June 2011.*

PRATT, Timothy Jean Geoffrey, CB 1993; Counsel to the Speaker (European Legislation), House of Commons, 1993–97; *b* 25 Nov. 1934; *s* of Geoffrey Cheeseborough Pratt and Elinor Jean (*née* Thomson); *m* 1963, Pamela Ann Blake; two *d. Educ:* Brighton College; Trinity Hall, Cambridge (MA). Called to the Bar, Middle Temple, 1959; in practice, 1959–61; joined Treasury Solicitor's Dept, 1961; Law Officers' Dept, 1972; DTI, 1974; Legal Advisor: Dir-Gen. of Fair Trading, 1979; Cabinet Office (European Secretariat), 1985; Dep. Treasury Solicitor, 1990–93. Vis. Fellow, 1998, Sen. Fellow, 1999–2001, Cambridge Univ. Centre for European Legal Studies. Advr on EU Law to BSE Inquiry, 1998–2000. *Address:* Game Keepers Cottage, Melton Park, Melton Constable, Norfolk NR24 2NG. *T:* (01263) 861577. *Club:* Oxford and Cambridge. *Died 23 Nov. 2011.*

PRAWER, Prof. Siegbert Salomon, FBA 1981; Taylor Professor of German Language and Literature, University of Oxford, 1969–86, then Professor Emeritus; Professorial Fellow, 1969–86, Supernumerary Fellow, 1986–90, Hon. Fellow, 1990, The Queen's College, Oxford (Dean of Degrees, 1978–93); *b* 15 Feb. 1925; *s* of Marcus Prawer and Eleonora Prawer (*née* Cohn); *m* 1949, Helga Alice (*née* Schaefer); one *s* two *d* (and one *s* decd). *Educ:* King Henry VIII Sch., Coventry; Jesus Coll., Cambridge (Charles Oldham Shakespeare Scholar, 1945–46, MA 1950; Hon. Fellow, 1996); PhD Birmingham, 1953; LittD Cantab 1962; MA 1969, DLitt 1969, Oxon. Adelaide Stoll Res. Student, Christ's Coll., Cambridge, 1947–48; Asst Lecturer, Lecturer, Sen. Lecturer, University of Birmingham, 1948–63; Prof. of German, Westfield Coll., London Univ., 1964–69. Fulbright Exchange Schol., 1956; Visiting Professor: City Coll., NY, 1956–57; University of Chicago, 1963–64; Harvard Univ., 1968; Hamburg Univ., 1969; Univ. of Calif, Irvine, 1975; Otago Univ., 1976; Pittsburgh Univ., 1977; Visiting Fellow: Knox Coll., Dunedin, 1976; Humanities Research Centre, ANU, 1980; Tauber Inst., Brandeis Univ., 1981–82; Russell Sage Foundn, NY, 1988. Hon. Director, London Univ. Inst. of Germanic Studies, 1966–68. President: British Comp. Lit. Assoc., 1984–87 (Hon. Fellow, 1989); English Goethe Soc., 1990–94 (Vice-Pres., 1994–). Hon. Fellow, London Univ. Inst. Germanic Studies, 1987; Corresp. Fellow, Deutsche Akademie für Sprache und Dichtung, 1989. Hon. Mem., Modern Language Assoc. of America, 1986. Hon. Dr phil. Cologne, 1984; Hon. DLitt Birmingham, 1988. Goethe Medal, 1973; Friedrich Gundolf Prize, 1986; Gold Medal, German Goethe Soc., 1995. Co-editor: Oxford German Studies, 1971–75; Anglica Germanica, 1973–79. *Publications:* German Lyric Poetry, 1952; Mörike und seine Leser, 1960; Heine's Buch der Lieder: A Critical Study, 1960; Heine: The Tragic Satirist, 1962; The Penguin Book of Lieder, 1964; The Uncanny in Literature (inaug. lect.), 1965; (ed, with R. H. Thomas and L. W. Forster) Essays in German Language, Culture and Society, 1969; (ed) The Romantic Period in Germany, 1970; Heine's Shakespeare, a Study in Contexts (inaug. lect.), 1970; (ed) Seventeen Modern German Poets, 1971; Comparative Literary Studies: an Introduction, 1973; Karl Marx and World Literature, 1976 (Isaac Deutscher Meml Prize, 1977); Caligari's Children: the film as tale of terror, 1980; Heine's Jewish Comedy: a study of his portraits of Jews and Judaism, 1983; A. N. Stencl: poet of Whitechapel (Stencl Meml Lect.), 1984; Coalsmoke and Englishmen (Bithell Meml Lecture), 1984; Frankenstein's Island: England and the English in the writings of Heinrich Heine, 1986; Israel at Vanity Fair: Jews and Judaism in the writings of W. M. Thackeray, 1992; (introd) Das Kabinett des Dr Caligari (first printing of original screenplay), 1996; Breeches and Metaphysics: Thackeray's German discourse, 1997; W. M. Thackeray's European Sketch Books: a study of literary and graphic portraiture, 2000; Sternberg's The Blue Angel, 2002; Werner Herzog's Nosferatu: Phantom of the Night, 2004; Between Two Worlds: the Jewish presence in German and Austrian film, 1910–1933, 2005; A Cultural Citizen of the World: Sigmund Freud's knowledge and use of British and American writings, 2009; articles on German, English and comparative literature in many specialist periodicals and symposia. *Recreation:* portrait drawing. *Address:* 9 Hawkswell Gardens, Oxford OX2 7EX. *Died 5 April 2012.*

PRAWER JHABVALA, Ruth; *see* Jhabvala.

PRENDERGAST, John Barry, (John Barry), OBE 1999; composer; *b* York, 3 Nov. 1933; *s* of late Jack Prendergast; *m* 1978, Laurie; one *s*; two *d* by previous marriages and one *d* by previous relationship. Founder, trumpeter and vocalist, John Barry Seven, 1957–62. Composer of stage musical, Billy, 1974; music for musical, Brighton Rock, 2004; film scores include: Beat Girl, 1960; Dr No, 1962; From Russia with Love, 1963; Zulu, 1964; Goldfinger, 1964; Thunderball, 1965; Born Free, 1966 (2 Acad. Awards); You Only Live Twice, 1967; The Lion in Winter, 1968 (Acad. Award); Midnight Cowboy, 1969; On Her Majesty's Secret Service, 1969; Mary, Queen of Scots, 1971; Diamonds Are Forever, 1971; A Doll's House, 1973; The Man with the Golden Gun, 1974; Moonraker, 1979; Body Heat, 1981; Octopussy, 1983; Out of Africa, 1985 (Acad. Award); A View to a Kill, 1985; Jagged Edge, 1985; Peggy Sue Got Married, 1986; The Living Daylights, 1987; Dances with Wolves, 1990 (Acad. Award); Chaplin, 1992; Indecent Proposal, 1993; The Specialist, 1994; The Scarlet Letter, 1995; Cry, the Beloved Country, 1995; Playing By Heart, 1998; Mercury Rising, 1998; Enigma, 2001. *Albums:* The Beyondness of Things, 1999; Eternal Echoes, 2001. *Address:* c/o Kraft-Engel Management, 15233 Ventura Boulevard, Sherman Oaks, CA 91403, USA. *Died 30 Jan. 2011.*

PRENDERGAST, Dame Simone (Ruth), DBE 1986 (OBE 1981); JP, DL; *b* 2 July 1930; *d* of late Mrs Neville Blond, OBE and Norman Laski; *m* 1st, 1953, Albert Kaplan (marr. diss. 1957); 2nd, 1959, Christopher Anthony Prendergast, CBE (*d* 1998); one *s. Educ:* Queen's College; Cheltenham Ladies' College. Lady Mayoress of Westminster, 1968–69; Member: Lord Chancellor's Adv. Cttee for Inner London, 1981–91; Solicitors' Disciplinary Tribunal, 1986–2002; E London and Bethnal Green Housing Assoc., 1988–90; Exec. Cttee, Westminster Children's Soc., 1970–97 (Chm., 1980–90); Chairman: Jewish Refugees Cttee, 1980–96; Greater London Area Nat. Union of Conservative Assocs, 1984–87; E Grinstead Med. Res. Trust, 1984–; Blond McIndoe Centre for Med. Research, 1986–2004; Vice-Chm., Age Concern, Westminster, 1986–2002; Comr (part-time), CRE, 1996–98. Jt Treas., 1991–, Vice Pres., 1997–, Central British Fund for World Jewish Relief (Mem. Council, 1969–97); Life Patron, British Fedn of Women Zionists, 1994. Trustee, Kennedy Inst. of Rheumatology, 2003–09. Comdt, Jewish Lads' and Girls' Bde, 1996–2000. Court of Patrons, RCS, 1987. FRSA 1988. JP Inner London 1971; DL Greater London 1982. Associate CStJ 1982. *Recreations:* reading, walking. *Died 11 Aug. 2012.*

PRICE, (Arthur) Leolin, CBE 1996; QC 1968; *b* 11 May 1924; 3rd *s* of late Evan Price and Ceridwen Price (*née* Price), Hawkhurst, Kent; *m* 1963, Hon. Rosalind Helen

Penrose Lewis, CBE (*d* 1999), *er d* of 1st Baron Brecon, PC, and Mabel, Baroness Brecon, CBE, JP; two *s* two *d*. *Educ:* Judd Sch., Tonbridge; Keble Coll., Oxford (Schol.; MA). War service, 1943–46 with Army: Capt., RA; Adjt, Indian Mountain Artillery Trng Centre and Depot, Ambala, Punjab, 1945–46. Treas., Oxford Union, 1948; Pres., Oxford Univ. Cons. Assoc., 1948. Tutor, Keble Coll., Oxford, 1951–59. Called to Bar, Middle Temple, 1949, Bencher, 1970–, Treas. 1990; Barrister of Lincoln's Inn, 1959. QC (Bahamas) 1969; QC (NSW) 1987; Barrister: BVI, 1994; Gibraltar, 1996. Member: Editorial Cttee, Modern Law Review, 1954–65; Bar Council Law Reform Cttee, 1969–75; Cttee, Soc. of Cons. Lawyers, 1971– (Vice-Chm., 1987–90). Pres., SR Europe Investment Trust plc (formerly Child Health Res. Investment Trust, then Thornton, later SR Pan-Eur. Investment Trust), 1999– (Dir, 1980–99; Chm., 1987–99); Director: Marine Adventure Sailing Trust plc, 1981–89; Thornton Asian Emerging Markets Investment Trust plc, 1989–95. Institute of Child Health: Chairman, 1976–2007; Fellow, 1996. Chm., Child Health Res. Appeal Trust, 1976–2007. Governor, Gt Ormond St Hosp. for Sick Children, 1972–92 (Trustee, 1992–2007); Mem., Falkland Islands Cttee, 1972–. Governor, Christ Coll., Brecon, 1977–. Chancellor, Diocese of Swansea and Brecon, 1982–99. Hon. Fellow UCL, 2001. *Publications:* articles and notes in legal jls. *Recreations:* conversation, politics, reading, sending letters to The Times. *Address:* 32 Hampstead Grove, NW3 6SR. *T:* (020) 7435 9843; 10 Old Square, Lincoln's Inn, WC2A 3SU. *T:* (020) 7405 0758, *Fax:* (020) 7831 8237. *E:* leolinprice@tenoldsquare.com; Moor Park, Llanbedr, near Crickhowell, Powys NP8 1SS. *T:* (01873) 810443, *Fax:* (01873) 810659; Selborne Chambers, 174 Phillip Street, Sydney, NSW 2000, Australia. *T:* (2) 92335188. *Clubs:* Carlton, Garrick. *Died 24 March 2013.*

PRICE, Barry David Keith, CBE 1991; QPM 1981; intelligence consultant, since 1993; Co-ordinator, National Drugs Intelligence Unit, 1987–92; *b* 28 June 1933; *s* of John Leslie Price and Lena Price; *m* 1953, Evelyne Jean Horlick; three *d*. *Educ:* Southall Grammar Sch. Metropolitan Police, 1954–75: Constable, uniform and CID, then through ranks to Det. Chief Supt; Asst Chief Constable, Northumbria Police, 1975–78; Dep. Chief Constable, Essex Police, 1978–80; Chief Constable, Cumbria Constabulary, 1980–87. Member: Adv. Council on the Misuse of Drugs, 1982–87; Drugs Intelligence Steering Gp, 1987–; Advr to ACPO Crime Cttee on drugs matters, 1985–88 (past Chm. and Sec.). President: English Police Golf Assoc., 1981–92; Northern Police Cricket League, 1983–87; Patron, NW Counties Schoolboys ABA, 1980–87. CCMI (FBIM 1975). SBStJ 1982 (County Dir, St John Amb. Assoc., 1981–87). Police Long Service and Good Conduct Medal, 1976. *Publications:* various articles in law enforcement and med. pubns. *Recreations:* golf, painting, gardening. *Died 10 Feb. 2013.*

PRICE, (Benjamin) Terence; Secretary-General, Uranium Institute, 1974–86; *b* 7 Jan. 1921; *er s* of Benjamin and Nellie Price; *m* 1947, Jean Stella Vidal (*d* 2006); one *s* one *d*. *Educ:* Crypt School, Gloucester; Queens' College, Cambridge (Scholar). Naval electronics res., 1942–46; Lieut RNVR, 1945–46; Atomic Energy Research Establishment, Harwell (Nuclear Physics Division), 1947–59; Head of Reactor Development Division, Atomic Energy Estabt, Winfrith, 1959–60; Ministry of Defence: Chief Scientific Officer, 1960–63; Assistant Chief Scientific Adviser (Studies), 1963–65; Director, Defence Operational Analysis Establishment, 1965–68; Chief Scientific Adviser, Min. of Transport, 1968–71; Dir of Planning and Development, Vickers Ltd, 1971–73. Chairman: OECD Transport Res. Gp, 1969–71; NEDO Mechanical Handling Sector Working Party, 1976–80. Mem., MRC Review Cttee on Industrial Psychology Res., 1964–66. Reviewer, CET, 1984–85. *Publications:* Radiation Shielding, 1957; Political Electricity, 1990; Political Physicist, 2004; MS in the Family, 2008. *Recreations:* making music, writing. *Address:* Seers Bough, Wilton Lane, Jordans, Beaconsfield, Bucks HP9 2RG. *T:* (01494) 874589. *Club:* Athenæum. *Died 7 Jan. 2013.*

PRICE, Hon. Charles Harry, II; Director, Mercantile Bancorporation, St Louis, 1991–96; *b* 1 April 1931; *s* of Charles Harry Price and Virginia (*née* Ogden); *m* 1969, Carol Ann Swanson; two *s* three *d*. *Educ:* University of Missouri. Chairman: Price Candy Co., 1969–81; American Bancorpn, 1973–81; American Bank & Trust Co., 1973–81; American Mortgage Co., 1973–81; Ambassador: to Belgium, 1981–83; to UK, 1983–89; Chm. Bd, Mercantile Bank, Kansas City, 1990–96. Non-executive Director: Hanson PLC, 1989–95; New York Times Co., 1989–95; Texaco Inc., 1989–2001; non-exec. Chm., Midwest Res. Inst., 1990–99 (Vice-Chm. and Mem. Exec. Cttee, 1978–81); Mem. Bd of Dirs, Civic Council, Greater Kansas City, 1979–80. Member: Young Presidents Orgn; IISS; World Business Council. Hon. Fellow, Regent's Coll., London, 1986. Hon. Dr Westminster Coll., Missouri, 1984; Hon. Dr of Laws Missouri, 1988. Salvation Army's William Booth Award, 1985; Kansas City Mayor's World Citizen of the Year, 1985, Trustee Citation Award, Midwest Res. Inst., 1987; Distinguished Service Award, Internat. Relations Council, 1989; Mankind Award, Cystic Fibrosis Foundn, 1990; Gold Good Citizen Award, Sons of the American Revolution, 1991; William F. Yates Medallion for Distinguished Service, 1996. *Recreations:* golf, shooting. *Address:* 1 West Armour Boulevard, Ste 300, Kansas City, MO 64111, USA. *Clubs:* White's, Mark's; Swinley Forest Golf; Eldorado Country (Palm Springs); Kansas City Country, River (Kansas City); Los Angeles Country (Los Angeles); Cypress Point (Monterey); Vintage (Palm Springs). *Died 12 Jan. 2012.*

PRICE, Christopher; *b* 26 Jan. 1932; *s* of Stanley Price and Katherine (*née* Thornton); *m* 1956, Annie Grierson Ross; two *s* one *d*. *Educ:* Leeds Grammar School; Queen's College, Oxford. Sec., Oxford Univ. Labour Club, 1953; Chm., Nat. Assoc. of Labour Student Organisations, 1955–56. Sheffield City Councillor, 1962–66; Dep. Chm., Sheffield Educn Cttee, 1963–66. Contested (Lab): Shipley, 1964; Birmingham, Perry Barr, 1970; Lewisham W, 1983. MP (Lab): Perry Barr Division of Birmingham, 1966–70; Lewisham W, Feb. 1974–1983; PPS to Secretary of State for Education and Science, 1966–67 and 1975–76; Chm., H of C Select Cttee on Educn, Science and the Arts, 1980–83. Mem., European Parlt, 1977–78. Dir, London Internat. Festival of Theatre Ltd, 1982–86; Pro-Asst Dir, The Polytechnic of the South Bank, 1983–86; Dir, Leeds Poly., 1986–92, Principal, Leeds Metropolitan Univ., 1992–94; Dir, 1991–95, Chm., 1994–95, Statesman & Nation Publishing Co. Ltd. Chm., Council, Nat. Youth Bureau, 1977–80; Member: Council, Inst. for Study of Drug Dependence, 1984–86; Bd, Phoenix House Ltd (Britain's largest gp of drug rehabilitation houses), 1986–87 (Chm., 1980–86); Council, Public Concern at Work, 1994–; Arts Council of England, 1997–98. Co-Chm., Campaign for Freedom of Information, 1990–94; Chair: Yorks and Humberside, then Yorks, Arts, 1997–2000 (Mem. Bd, 1994–2000; Chm., Audit Cttee, 1995–97); LGA Commn on Organisation of Sch. Year, 2000–03. Pres., BEMAS, 1992–94; Member: Delegacy, Univ. of London Goldsmiths' Coll., 1981–86; Court, Polytechnic of Central London, 1982–86; London Centre for Biotechnology Trust, 1984–86; Council, Open Univ., 1996–; Fellow, Internat. Inst. of Biotechnology, 1984. Vis. Sen. Fellow, Office of Public Management, 1994–96; Vis. Fellow, Centre for Policy Studies in Educn, Univ. of Leeds, 1994–97; Vis. Prof., UCE, 1996–. Vice Chm., Cttee for the Reunification of the Parthenon Marbles (formerly Cttee for the Restitution of the Parthenon Marbles), 1997–. FRSA 1988. Editor, New Education, 1967–68; Founding Editor, The Stakeholder (Editor, 1997–2000); Educn corresp., New Statesman, 1969–74; Columnist: TES, 1983–85; THES, 1990–92. DUniv Leeds Metropolitan, 1994. Ambassador of Hellenism, Athens Prefecture, 2009. Independence Medal (Vanuatu), 1982. *Publications:* (contrib.) A Radical Future, 1967; Crisis in the Classroom, 1968; (ed) Your Child and School, 1968; Which Way?, 1969; (contrib.) Life and Death of the Schools Council, 1985; (contrib.) Police, the Constitution and the Community, 1985. *Address:* 9 Pickwick Road, SE21 7JN. *Died 20 Feb. 2015.*

PRICE, Sir David (Ernest Campbell), Kt 1980; DL; *b* 20 Nov. 1924; *o s* of Major Villiers Price; *m* 1960, Rosemary

Eugénie Evelyn (*d* 2006), *o d* of late Cyril F. Johnston, OBE; one *d*. *Educ:* Eton; Trinity College, Cambridge; Yale University, USA; Rosebery Schol., Eton; Open History Schol., Trinity College, Cambridge. Served with 1st Battalion Scots Guards, CMF; subsequently Staff Captain (Intelligence) HQ, 56 London Div., Trieste, 1942–46. Trin. Coll., Cambridge, BA Hons, MA. Pres. Cambridge Union; Vice-Pres. Fedn of Univ. Conservative and Unionist Assocs, 1946–48; Henry Fellow of Yale Univ., USA, 1948–49. Industrial Consultant. Held various appts in Imperial Chemical Industries Ltd, 1949–62. MP (C) Eastleigh Div. of Hampshire, 1955–92; Parly Sec., Board of Trade, 1962–64; Opposition Front-Bench spokesman on Science and Technology, 1964–70; Parly Sec., Min. of Technology, June–Oct. 1970; Parly Sec., Min. of Aviation Supply, 1970–71; Parly Under-Sec. of State, Aerospace, DTI, 1971–72. Member: Public Accounts Cttee, 1974–75; Select Cttee on Transport, 1979–83; Select Cttee on Social Services, 1983–90; Select Cttee on Health, 1990–92; Vice-Pres., Parly and Scientific Cttee, 1975–79 and 1982–86 (Vice-Chm., 1965–70, Chm., 1973–75 and 1979–82). Vice-Chm., Cons. Arts and Heritage Cttee, 1979–81 and 1983–87; Chm., Cons. Shipping and Ship-Building Cttee, 1985–91; President: Wessex Area Cons. and Unionist Party, 1986–89 (Life Vice-Pres., 1991); Romsey and Waterside Cons. Assoc., 1993–99; Itchen Test and Avon Cons. Euro-Forum, 1994–99. British Representative to Consultative Assembly of the Council of Europe, 1958–61. Dir, Assoc. British Maltsters, 1966–70. Gen. Cons. to IIM (formerly IWM), 1973–90; Cons. to Union International Ltd, 1974–92; Non-exec. Dir, Southampton Univ. Hosps Trust, 1993–97. Vice-Pres., IIM, 1980–92. President: Wessex Glyndebourne Assoc., 1990–2001; Wessex Rehabilitation Assoc., 1990–2000; Chm., Hants CC Community Care Forum, 1993–96; Trustee: Wessex Medical Trust, 1988–96; Nuffield Theatre, 1990–; Mayflower Theatre, 1990–. Governor, Middlesex Hospital, 1956–60. FCMI. DL Hants, 1982. *Recreations:* swimming, arts and heritage, wine, cooking, gardening. *Address:* Forest Lodge, Moonhills Lane, Beaulieu, Hampshire SO42 7YW. *T:* (01590) 612537. *Clubs:* Beefsteak, Sloane. *Died 31 Jan. 2014.*

PRICE, Geoffrey Alan; DL; Chairman, Herefordshire Community Health Trust, 1997–2000; *m* Helen; two *s* one *d*. Local Govt finance posts in Glos CC, Cheshire CC, Southend-on-Sea and W Sussex CC, 1952–70; Dep. Co. Treas., 1970–76, Co. Treas., 1976–83, Hants CC; Chief Exec., 1983–93, Co. Treas., 1988–93, Hereford and Worcester CC; Clerk: to Lord Lieutenant, Hereford and Worcester, 1983–93; to West Mercia Police Authority, 1983–93; non-exec. Dir, Herefordshire HA, 1993–97. DL Hereford and Worcester, 1993. *Died 20 Jan. 2011.*

PRICE, Rt Hon. George (Cadle), OCC 2001; PC 1982; Senior Minister, 1998–2003, and former Minister of Defence and National Emergency Management, Belize; *b* 15 Jan. 1919; *s* of William Cadle Price and Irene Cecilia Escalante de Price. *Educ:* Holy Redeemer Primary Sch., Belize City; St John's Coll., Belize City. Private Sec. to late Robert S. Turton; entered politics, 1944; City Councillor, 1947–65 (Mayor of Belize City several times); founding Mem., People's United Party, 1950; Party Sec., 1950–56; Leader, 1956–96; Mem., National Assembly, subseq. House of Reps, 1954–84, 1989–2003; under 1961 Ministerial System, led People's United Party to 100% victory at polls and became First Minister; under 1964 Self-Govt Constitution, title changed to Premier; Premier, 1964 until Independence, 1981; Prime Minister of Belize, 1981–84 and 1989–93; Leader of the Opposition, 1993, then Leader Emeritus (second term, 1996), People's United Party. Hon. DLaws West Indies, 2006. National Hero Award, Belize, 2000. Led delegns to Central American and Caribbean countries; spearheaded internationalization of Belize problem at internat. forums; addressed UN's Fourth Cttee, 1975, paving way for overwhelming victory at UN when majority of nations voted in favour of Belize's right to self-determination and territorial integrity. *Address:* c/o House of Representatives, Belmopan, Belize. *Died 19 Sept. 2011.*

PRICE, Leolin; *see* Price, A. L.

PRICE, Dame Margaret (Berenice), DBE 1993 (CBE 1982); opera singer; with Bayerische Staatsoper München, until 1999; *b* Tredegar, Wales, 13 April 1941; *d* of late Thomas Glyn Price and of Lilian Myfanwy Richards. *Educ:* Pontllanfraith Secondary Sch.; Trinity Coll. of Music, London. Debut as Cherubino in Marriage of Figaro, Welsh Nat. Opera Co., 1962; debut, in same rôle, at Royal Opera House, Covent Garden, 1963; subseq. sang many principal rôles at Glyndebourne, San Francisco Opera Co., Cologne Opera House, Munich State Opera, Hamburg State Opera, Vienna State Opera, Lyric Opera, Chicago, Paris Opera; La Scala, Milan; Metropolitan Opera House, NY. Major rôles include: Countess in Marriage of Figaro; Pamina in The Magic Flute; Fiordiligi in Così Fan Tutte; Donna Anna in Don Giovanni; Konstanze in Die Entführung; Amelia in Simone Boccanegra; Agathe in Freischütz; Desdemona in Otello; Elisabetta in Don Carlo; Amelia in Un Ballo In Maschera; title rôles in Aida, Norma and Ariadne auf Naxos. BBC recitals and concerts, also TV appearances and recordings. Hon. FTCL; Hon. DMus Wales, 1983. Elisabeth Schumann Prize for Lieder; Ricordi Prize for Opera; Silver Medal, Worshipful Co. of Musicians; Bayerische Kammersängerin. *Recreations:* cooking, driving, reading, walking, swimming. *Address:* c/o Stefan Hahn, Artist Management HRA, Sendlinger Strasse 56, 80331 München, Germany. *Died 28 Jan. 2011.*

PRICE, Michael Anthony, LVO 1991; HM Diplomatic Service, retired; High Commissioner, Fiji, 2000–02, also (non-resident) to Kiribati, Tuvalu and Nauru; *b* 13 Aug. 1944; *s* of Francis George and Lena Beatrice Price; *m* 1968, Elizabeth Anne Cook; one *s* one *d*. *Educ:* Forest Grammar Sch. Bd of Trade, 1964; Diplomatic Service, 1966–; served New Delhi, Freetown, Paris, Montreal; JSDC, 1983–84; Dep. Head of News Dept, FCO, 1984; First Sec. (Press and Public Affairs), Washington, 1988; Counsellor and HM Consul-Gen., Tokyo, 1992; on loan to No 10 Downing St, 1994–95; Counsellor, Paris, 1995–2000. *Recreations:* cricket, Gilbert and Sullivan, cooking. *Address:* Kasauli, Church Field, Monks Eleigh, Suffolk IP7 7JH. *Died 22 Oct. 2013.*

PRICE, Pamela Joan V.; *see* Vandyke Price.

PRICE, Terence; *see* Price, B. T.

PRICE, Vivian William Cecil; QC 1972; *b* 14 April 1926; 4th *s* of late Evan Price, Hawkhurst, Kent; *m* 1961, Elizabeth Anne, *oc* of late Arthur Rawlins and Georgina (*née* Guinness); three *s* two *d*. *Educ:* Judd Sch., Tonbridge, Kent; Trinity Coll., Cambridge (BA); Balliol Coll., Oxford (BA). Royal Navy, 1946–49, Instructor Lieut. Called to the Bar: Middle Temple, 1954 (Bencher, 1979); Hong Kong, 1975; Singapore, 1979. Dep. High Court Judge (Chancery Div.), 1975–85; a Recorder of the Crown Court, 1984. Sec., Lord Denning's Cttee on Legal Educn for Students from Africa, 1960; Junior Counsel (Patents) to the Board of Trade, 1967–72; Mem., Patents Procedure Cttee, 1973. Mem., Incorporated Council of Law Reporting for England and Wales, 1980–85. *Address:* Redwall Farmhouse, Redwall Lane, Linton, Maidstone, Kent ME17 4AX. *T:* (01622) 743682. *Club:* Travellers. *Died 11 Nov. 2012.*

PRIDEAUX, Sir Humphrey (Povah Treverbian), Kt 1971; OBE 1945; DL; Chairman, Morland & Co., 1983–93 (Director, 1981–93; Vice Chairman, 1982); Chairman, Lord Wandsworth Foundation, 1966–92; *b* 13 Dec. 1915; 3rd *s* of Walter Treverbian Prideaux and Marion Fenn (*née* Arbuthnot); *m* 1939, Cynthia (*d* 2008), *er d* of late Lt-Col H. Birch Reynardson, CMG; four *s*. *Educ:* St Aubyn's, Rottingdean; Eton; Trinity Coll., Oxford (MA). Commissioned 3rd Carabiniers (Prince of Wales's Dragoon Guards) 1936; DAQMG Guards Armd Div., 1941; Instructor, Staff Coll., 1942; AQMG 21 Army Gp, 1943; AA QMG Guards Armd Div., 1944; Joint Planning Staff, War Office, 1945; Naval Staff Coll., 1948; Commandant School of Administration, 1948; Chiefs of Staff Secretariat, 1950; retired, 1953. Director, NAAFI, 1956–73 (Man. Dir, 1961–65; Chm., 1963–73); Dir, London Life Association Ltd, 1964–88 (Vice-Pres., 1965–72; Pres., 1973–84); Chm., Brooke Bond Liebig Ltd, 1972–80 (Dir, 1968; Dep. Chm., 1969–71); Vice-Chm., W. H. Smith & Son Ltd, 1977–81 (Dir, 1969–77); Dir, Grindlays, 1982–85. DL Hants 1983.

Recreation: country pursuits. *Address:* Kings Cottage, Buryfields, Odiham, Hants RG29 1NE. *T:* (01256) 703658. *Club:* Cavalry and Guards. *Died 7 May 2014.*

PRIDHAM, Kenneth Robert Comyn, CMG 1976; HM Diplomatic Service, retired; *b* 28 July 1922; *s* of late Colonel G. R. Pridham, CBE, DSO, and Mignonne, *d* of late Charles Cumming, ICS; *m* 1965, Ann Rosalind (decd), *d* of late E. Gilbert Woodward, Metropolitan Magistrate, and of Mrs Woodward. *Educ:* Winchester; Oriel Coll., Oxford. Lieut, 60th Rifles, 1942–46; served North Africa, Italy, Middle East (despatches). Entered Foreign (subseq. Diplomatic) Service, 1946; served at Berlin, Washington, Belgrade and Khartoum, and at the Foreign Office; Counsellor: Copenhagen, 1968–72; FCO, 1972–74; Asst Under Sec. of State, FCO, 1974–78; Ambassador to Poland, 1978–81. Vis. Res. Fellow, RIIA, 1981–82. *Address:* c/o Lloyds Bank, 8/10 Waterloo Place, SW1Y 4BE. *Club:* Travellers. *Died 15 Nov. 2015.*

PRIESTLEY, Clive, CB 1983; Chairman, St Bartholomew's Hospital Medical College Trust, since 1997 (Member, 1996–97); *b* 12 July 1935; *s* of late Albert Ernest and Annie May Priestley; *m* 1st, 1961, Barbara Anne Wells (marr. diss. 1984); two *d*; 2nd, 1985, Daphne June Challis Loasby, OBE, JP, DL, *o d* of late W. Challis and Dorothy Franks. *Educ:* Loughborough Grammar Sch.; Nottingham Univ. BA 1956; MA 1958. Nat. Service, RA, RAEC, 1958–60. Joined HM Home Civil Service, 1960; Min. of Educn, later DES, 1960–65; Schools Council, 1965–67; Harkness Commonwealth Fund Fellow, Harvard Univ., 1967–68; CSD, 1969–79; Prime Minister's Office, 1979–83 (Chief of Staff to Sir Derek Rayner); Under Sec., 1979–83; MPO, 1982–83; Div. Dir, British Telecom plc, 1983–88. Consultant: Corp. of London, 1988–90; Metropolitan Police Comr, 1989–91; LDDC, 1990–91; NEDC, 1992–93. Chm., Review of structure of arts funding in NI for govt, 1992, of responsibilities and gradings of chief officers of nat. museums, galleries and libraries, 1994; Assessor, Review of museums policy in NI, 1995. Member: Council, Univ. of Reading, 1984–86; Develt Trust, Univ. of Nottingham, 1994–97; Council, QMW, 1995–2002; Philharmonia Trust, 1985–87; Univ. of Cambridge Careers Service Syndicate, 1986–90; Adv. Council, Buxton Festival, 1987–97; Arts Council, of GB, 1991–94, of England, 1994–95 and 1996–97; British Soc. of Gastroenterology, 2000–05; Sec., Fundraising Cttee, Thiepval Proj., 2000–05; Chairman: London Arts Bd, 1991–97; Trafalgar Square 2000, 1996–98; Council for Dance Educn and Trng, 1997–2000. Vice-Pres., St Bartholomew's Hosp. Med. Coll., 1993–95 (Mem. Council, 1990–95). Governor: Royal Shakespeare Co., 1984–2004; City Lit. Inst., 1995–96; Trinity Coll. of Music, 1997–2005. Wandsman, St Paul's Cathedral, 1983–97; jt planner, Millennial Service for London, St Paul's Cathedral, 1998–2000. Hon. Perpetual Student, St Bartholomew's Hosp. Medical Coll., 1995; Hon. FTCL 1996; Hon. Fellow, QMUL, 2007. Freeman, City of London, 1989; Liveryman, Worshipful Co. of Glaziers and Painters of Glass, 1989–2002. *Publications:* financial scrutinies of the Royal Opera House, Covent Garden Ltd, and of the Royal Shakespeare Co., 1984. *Address:* Field House, Ham, Wilts SN8 3QR. *T:* and *Fax:* (01488) 669094. *E:* ClivPrs@aol.com. *Club:* Army and Navy. *Died 24 Jan. 2012.*

PRIESTLEY, Prof. Maurice Bertram, MA, PhD; Professor of Statistics, University of Manchester Institute of Science and Technology, 1970–96 (Head of Department of Mathematics, 1973–75, 1977–78, 1980–85 and 1987–89), then Professor Emeritus, University of Manchester; *b* 15 March 1933; *s* of Jack and Rose Priestley; *m* 1959, Nancy, *d* of late Ralph and Hilda Nelson; one *s* one *d*. *Educ:* Manchester Grammar Sch.; Jesus Coll., Cambridge. BA (Wrangler, 1954), MA, DipMathStat (Cambridge); PhD (Manchester). Scientific Officer, RAE, 1955–56; Asst Lectr, Univ. of Manchester, 1957–60, Lectr, 1960–65; Vis. Professor, Princeton and Stanford Univs, USA, 1961–62; Sen. Lectr, UMIST, 1965–70; Dir, Manchester-Sheffield Sch. of Probability and Stats, and Hon. Prof. of Probability and Stats, Sheffield Univ., 1976–79, 1988–89, 1991–92. Mem. Court and Council, UMIST, 1971–74 and 1989–96. FIMS; FSS; Member Council: Royal Statistical Soc., 1971–75; Manchester Statistical Soc., 1986–96; Mem., ISI. Editor-in-chief, Jl of Time Series Analysis, 1980–. *Publications:* Spectral Analysis and Time Series, Vols I and II, 1981; Non-linear and non-stationary time series analysis, 1988; papers and articles in Jl RSS, Biometrika, Technom., Automatica, Jl of Sound and Vibration. *Recreations:* music, hi-fi and audio, golf. *Address:* School of Mathematics, University of Manchester, Oxford Road, Manchester M13 9PL. *T:* (0161) 306 3668. *Died 15 June 2013.*

PRINGLE, Air Marshal Sir Charles (Norman Seton), KBE 1973 (CBE 1967); MA; FREng; *b* 6 June 1919; *s* of late Seton Pringle, OBE, FRCSI, Dublin; *m* 1946, Margaret, *d* of late B. Sharp, Baildon, Yorkshire; (one *s* decd). *Educ:* Repton; St John's Coll., Cambridge. Commissioned, RAF, 1941; served India and Ceylon, 1942–46. Air Ministry, 1946–48; RAE, Farnborough, 1949–50; attached to USAF, 1950–52; appts in UK, 1952–60; STSO No 3 Group, Bomber Comd, 1960–62, and Air Forces Middle East, 1962–64; Comdt RAF St Athan and Air Officer Wales, 1964–66; MoD, 1967; IDC, 1968. Dir-Gen. of Engineering (RAF) MoD, 1969–70; Air Officer Engineering, Strike Command, 1970–73; Dir-Gen. Engineering (RAF), 1973; Controller, Engrg and Supply (RAF), 1973–76; Sen. Exec., Rolls Royce Ltd, 1976–78; Dir, Hunting Engineering Ltd, 1976–78; Dir and Chief Exec., SBAC, 1979–84. Director: FR Group plc, 1985–89; Aeronautical Trusts Ltd, 1987–97. President: RAeS, 1975–76; IMGTechE, 1979–82; Smeatonian Soc. of Civil Engrs, 2006; Vice-Chm., 1976–77, Chm., 1977–78, CEI. Mem., Defence Industries Council, 1978–84. Member Council: Air League, 1976–92; CBI, 1979–84; RSA, 1978–83 and 1986–92. Chm. Governors, Repton Sch., 1985–92. Liveryman, Coachmakers' and Coach Harness Makers' Co., 1981–. FREng (FEng 1977). Hon. FRAeS 1989. Hon. Secretary: Cambridge Univ. Auto Club, 1938–40; Irish Motor Racing Club, 1939–40. *Recreations:* photography, ornithology, motor sport. *Address:* Appleyards, Fordingbridge, Hants SP6 3BP. *T:* (01425) 652 357. *Club:* Royal Air Force. *Died 15 April 2012.*

PRINGLE, Lt Gen. Sir Steuart (Robert), 10th Bt *cr* 1683, of Stichill, Roxburghshire; KCB 1982; Commandant General Royal Marines, 1981–84; Chairman and Chief Executive, Chatham Historic Dockyard Trust, 1984–91; *b* 21 July 1928; *s* of Sir Norman H. Pringle, 9th Bt and Lady (Oonagh) Pringle (*née* Curran) (*d* 1975); *S* father, 1961; *m* 1953, Jacqueline Marie Gladwell (*d* 2012); one *s* two *d* (and one *s* decd). *Educ:* Sherborne. Royal Marines: 2nd Lieut, 1946; 42 Commando, 1950–52; 40 Commando, 1957–59; Chief Instructor, Signal Trng Wing, RM, 1959–61; Bde Signal Officer, 3 Commando Bde, RM, 1961–63; Defence Planning Staff, 1964–67; Chief Signal Officer, RM, 1967–69; 40 Commando, Far East, 1969–71; CO 45 Commando Group, 1971–74; HQ Commando Forces, 1974–76; RCDS, 1977; Maj.-Gen. RM Commando Forces, 1978–79; Chief of Staff to Comdt Gen., RM, 1979–81. Col Comdt, RM, 1989–90, Representative Col Comdt, 1991–92. President: St Loye's Coll., 1984–2000; City of London Br., RM Assoc., 1984–2004; Vice-Pres., Officers Pensions Soc., 1984–99; Mem. Council, Union Jack Club, 1982–85; Vice-Patron, Royal Naval Benevolent Trust, 1984–. Liveryman, Plaisterers' Co., 1984. Hon. DSc City, 1982; Hon. LLD Exeter, 1994. Hon. Admiral, Texas Navy; Hon. Mem., Co. of Bear Tamers. *Publications:* (contrib) Peace and the Bomb, 1982; The Future of British Seapower, 1984; contribs to RUSI Jl, Navy International, etc. *Heir:* *s* Simon Robert Pringle [*b* 6 Jan. 1959; *m* 1992, Pamela Margaret, *d* of George Hunter; one *s* one *d*]. *Address:* 76 South Croxted Road, Dulwich, SE21 8BD. *Clubs:* Army and Navy, Royal Thames Yacht. *Died 18 April 2013.*

PRIOR, Peter James, CBE 1980; DL; Chairman, H. P. Bulmer Holdings PLC, 1977–82 (Director, 1977–85; Managing Director, H. P. Bulmer Ltd, 1966–77); *b* 1 Sept. 1919; *s* of Percy Prior; *m* 1957, Prinia Mary (*d* 2001), *d* of late R. E. Moreau, Berrick Prior, Oxon; two *s*. *Educ:* Royal Grammar Sch., High Wycombe; London Univ. BScEcon. FCA, FIMC. Royal Berks Regt, 1939; Intell. Corps, 1944–46 (Captain) (Croix-de-Guerre 1944). Company Sec., Saunders-Roe (Anglesey) Ltd, 1948; Consultant, Urwick, Orr & Partners, 1951; Financial Dir, International

Chemical Co., 1956; Financial Dir, British Aluminium Co., 1961; Dep. Chm., Holden Hydroman, 1984–88; Dir, Trebor, 1982–86. Member: English Tourist Bd, 1969–75; Midlands Electricity Bd, 1973–83; Chairman: Inquiry into Potato Processing Industry, 1971; Motorway Service Area Inquiry, 1977–78; Home Office Deptl Inquiry into Prison Discipline, 1984–85. Pres., Incorp. Soc. of British Advertisers' Council, 1980–83. FCMI (Mem. Council, BIM, 1974–82). Chm. Trustees, Leadership Trust, 1975–79; Member: Council, Regular Forces Employment Assoc., 1981–86; Council, Operation Raleigh, 1984–89. DL Hereford and Worcester, 1983. FRSA. Communicator of the Year Award, British Assoc. of Industrial Editors, 1982. *Publications:* Leadership is not a Bowler Hat, 1977; articles on management and leadership. *Recreations:* flying, motor-cycling, swimming, mountain walking, formerly parachuting (UK record for longest delayed drop (civilian), 1981). *Address:* Highland, Holbach Lane, Sutton St Nicholas, Hereford HR1 3DF. *T:* (01568) 797222. *Club:* Special Forces. *Died 15 April 2011.*

PRIOR, William Johnson, CBE 1979; CEng, FIET; Chairman, Manx Electricity Authority, 1984–85; *b* 28 Jan. 1924; *s* of Ernest Stanley and Lilian Prior; *m* 1945, Mariel (*née* Irving); two *s* one *d*. *Educ:* Goole and Barnsley Grammar Schs. Barugh, Mexborough, Stuart Street (Manchester) and Stockport Power Stations, 1944–52; Keadby, 1952–56, Supt, 1954–56; Supt, Berkeley, 1957–58; Supt, Hinkley Point Generating Station, 1959–66; CEGB and predecessors: Asst Reg. Dir (Generation), NW Region, 1967–70; Dir (Generation), SW Region, 1970–72; Dir-Gen., SE Region, 1972–76; Mem., Electricity Council, 1976–79; Chm., Yorks Electricity Bd, 1979–84. Member: NCB, 1977–83; Adv. Cttee on Safety of Nuclear Installations, 1980–87. *Recreation:* country walking. *Address:* Apartment 3, Coach House Court, 14 Deighton Road, Wetherby, W Yorks LS22 7TE. *T:* (01937) 584434. *Died 25 Jan. 2011.*

PRITCHARD, Rear-Adm. Gwynedd Idris, CB 1981; *b* 18 June 1924; *s* of Cyril Idris Pritchard and Lily Pritchard; *m* 1975, Mary Thérèsa (*née* Curtin); three *s* by a previous marriage. *Educ:* Wyggeston Sch., Leicester. FCMI. Joined Royal Navy, 1942; Sub-Lieut 1944; Lieut 1946; Lt-Comdr 1954; Comdr 1959; Captain 1967; Rear-Adm. 1976; Flag Officer Sea Training, 1976–78; Flag Officer Gibraltar, 1979–81; retired list, 1981. Chm., SW Regl Planning Conf., 1990–93. Mem., Dorset CC, 1985–2001. *Recreations:* gardening, golf. *Address:* Hoofprints, Beach Road, Burton Bradstock, Dorset DT6 4RF. *Died 19 June 2012.*

PRITCHARD, Kenneth John, CB 1982; Director, Greenwich Hospital, 1987–92; *b* 18 March 1926; *s* of William Edward Pritchard and Ethel Mary Pritchard (*née* Cornfield); *m* 1st, 1949, Elizabeth Margaret Bradshaw (*d* 1978); two *d*; 2nd, 1979, Angela Madeleine Palmer; one *s* two *d*. *Educ:* Newport High Sch.; St Catherine's Coll., Oxford (MA 1951). Served Army, 1944–48; Indian Mil. Acad., Dehra Dun, 1945; served with 8th/12th Frontier Force Regt and 2nd Royal W Kent Regt. Asst Principal, Admiralty, 1951; Private Sec. to Sec. of State for Wales, 1964; Asst Sec., Min. of Aviation, 1966; RCDS, 1972; Principal Supply and Transport Officer (Naval), Portsmouth, 1978, Exec. Dir 1980; Dir Gen. of Supplies and Transport (Naval), MoD, 1981–86, retd. Vice Patron, Royal Naval Benevolent Trust, 1992–. Chairman: Beckington Music Hall, 1985–2012; Frome Tourist Information Ltd, 1996–2010. Almoner, Christ's Hosp. Sch., 1988–92. Freeman, City of London, 1988; Liveryman, Coopers' Co., 1988. Mem., Cousinerie de Bourgogne, 1997 (Ambassadeur, 2009–). FCIPS (FInstPS 1986). *Recreations:* tennis, music hall, good wine. *Address:* Pickford House, Beckington, Som BA11 6SJ. *T:* (01373) 830329. *Died 15 Oct. 2015.*

PROBERT, David Henry, CBE 1996; FCIS, FCMA, FCCA; Chief Executive, 1976–86, Executive Chairman, 1986–98, W. Canning plc (Director, 1976); *b* 11 April 1938; *s* of William David Thomas Probert and Doris Mabel Probert; *m* 1968, Sandra Mary Prince; one *s* one *d*. *Educ:* Bromsgrove High School. A Crown Agent for Oversea Govts and Admins, 1981–98 (Dep. Chm., 1985–90; Chm., 1990–98); Crown Agent for Holdings and Realisation Bd, 1981–98. Dir, Private Patients Plan Ltd, 1988–96; Chm., PPP Healthcare Group plc, 1996–98; Gov., PPP Medical Trust, 1998–99. Chairman: Leigh Interests plc, 1996–98 (Dir, 1995–98); Saville Gordon Estates plc, 1999–2001 (Dir, 1998–2001); Ash & Lacy plc, 1998–2000; Director: BSA Ltd, 1971–73; Mills and Allen International Ltd, 1974–76; HB Electronics plc, 1977–86; British Hallmarking Council, 1983–91; Linread Public Limited Company, 1983–90; ASD plc, 1985–90; Sandvik Ltd, 1985–90; Rockwool Ltd, 1988–90, 1992–94; Richard Burbridge Ltd, 1990–91; William Sinclair plc, 1994–2001; Hampson Industries plc, 1994–2002. Pres., Birmingham Chamber of Commerce and Industry, 1994–95 (Vice Pres., 1992–94). Gov., UCE, 1998–2001. Liveryman: Chartered Secretaries and Administrators' Co., 1984; Founders' Co., 1997. CCMI. *Recreations:* theatre, music, sport. *Address:* 4 Blakes Field Drive, Barnt Green, Worcs B45 8JT. *Club:* Lord's Taverners (Regl Chm., 1996–99). *Died 11 Oct. 2014.*

PROSSER, Rt Hon. Lord; William David Prosser; PC 2000; a Senator of the College of Justice in Scotland and Lord of Session, 1986–2001; *b* 23 Nov. 1934; *yr s* of David G. Prosser, MC, WS, Edinburgh; *m* 1964, Vanessa, *er d* of Sir William O'Brien Lindsay, KBE, Nairobi; two *s* two *d*. *Educ:* Edinburgh Academy; Corpus Christi Coll., Oxford (MA); Edinburgh Univ. (LLB). Advocate, 1962; QC (Scotland) 1974; Standing Junior Counsel in Scotland, Board of Inland Revenue, 1969–74; Advocate-Depute, 1978–79; Vice-Dean, Faculty of Advocates, 1979–83; Dean of Faculty, 1983–86. Mem., Scottish Cttee, Council on Tribunals, 1977–84. Chm., Royal Fine Art Commn for Scotland, 1990–95. Chairman: Royal Lyceum Theatre Co., 1987–92; Scottish Historic Buildings Trust, 1988–98; Chamber Gp of Scotland, 1993–98; Edinburgh Sir Walter Scott Club, 1993–96; Scottish Architectural Educn Trust, 1994–2007; Mem., Franco-British Council, 1997–2007 (Trustee, 2002–07); Pres., Franco-British Lawyers' Soc., 1999–2002. Gov., UHI (formerly UHI Millennium Inst.), 2001–13. Hon. FRIAS 1995. Officier, Ordre des Arts et des Lettres (France), 2007. *Address:* 7 Randolph Crescent, Edinburgh EH3 7TH. *T:* (0131) 225 2709; 6 cité Pigalle, 75009 Paris, France. *T:* 40230433. *Clubs:* New, Scottish Arts (Edinburgh). *Died 22 March 2015.*

PROTHEROE, Alan Hackford, CBE (mil.) 1991 (MBE (mil.) 1980); TD 1981; DL; journalist and media consultant; *b* 10 Jan. 1934; *s* of Rev. B. P. Protheroe and R. C. M. Protheroe; *m* 1st, 1956, Anne Miller (*d* 1999); one *s* (and one *s* decd); 2nd, 2004, Mrs Rosemary Margaret Louise Tucker. *Educ:* Maesteg Grammar Sch., Glamorgan. FCMI; MCIPR. Nat. Service, 2nd Lieut The Welch Regt, 1954–56; Lt-Col, Royal Regt of Wales (TA), 1979–84; Col, 1984–90. Reporter, Glamorgan Gazette, 1951–53; BBC Wales: Reporter, 1957–59; Industrial Correspondent, 1959–64; Editor, News and Current Affairs, 1964–70; BBC TV News: Asst Editor, 1970–72; Dep. Editor, 1972–77; Editor, 1977–80; Asst Dir, BBC News and Current Affairs, 1980–82; Asst Dir Gen., BBC, 1982–87. During BBC career wrote, produced, directed and presented films and radio programmes, reported wars, and travelled widely; seconded to Greek Govt to assist in reorganisation of Greek TV, 1973. Man. Dir, Services Sound and Vision Corp., 1988–94; Director: Visnews Ltd, 1982–87; Defence Public Affairs Consultants Ltd, 1987–93. Mem., Steering Cttee, EBU News Gp, 1977–87. Mem. Council, RUSI, 1984–87; Association of British Editors: Founder Mem., 1984–; Dep. Chm., 1984–87; Chm., 1987. Chm., Eastern Wessex Reserve Forces Assoc., 1991–99 (Dep. Chm., 1990–91). St James's Vice Pres., 1990–, and Mem. Bd of Mgt, 1992–, RBL; Dir, RBL Training, 1992–99. Hon. Col, TA Information Officers, 1991–96. DL Bucks, 1993. *Publications:* contribs to newspapers and specialist jls on industrial, media and defence affairs. *Recreations:* wine, travel, photography. *Address:* 2 Lord Reith Place, Hedgerley Lane, Beaconsfield, Bucks HP9 2GE. *T:* and *Fax:* (01494) 730410. *Club:* Army and Navy. *Died 6 April 2013.*

PROUDFOOT, (George) Wilfred; owner, self-service stores; consultant in distribution; professional hypnotist and hypnotherapist, Master Practitioner of Neuro-Linguistic

Programming; owner, Proudfoot School of Hypnosis and Hypnotherapy; *b* 19 Dec. 1921; *m* 1950, Margaret Mary, *d* of Percy Clifford Jackson, Pontefract, Yorks; two *s* one *d*. *Educ:* Crook Council Sch.; Scarborough Coll. Served War of 1939–45, NCO Fitter in RAF, 1940–46. Served Scarborough Town Council, 1950–58 (Chm. Health Cttee, 1952–58). Contested (C): Hemsworth, 1951; Cleveland, 1955, 1964 and 1966; MP (C) Cleveland Division of Yorkshire, 1959–64; PPS to Minister of State, Board of Trade, Apr.–July 1962, to Minister of Housing and Local Govt and Minister for Welsh Affairs (Rt Hon. Sir Keith Joseph, Bt, MP), 1962–64; MP (C) Brighouse and Spenborough, 1970–Feb. 1974; Minister of State, Dept of Employment, 1970; contested (C) Brighouse and Spenborough, Feb. and Oct. 1974. Man. Dir, Radio 270, 1965–. Chm., Scarborough Cons. Assoc., 1978–80; Chm., Cleveland European Constituency Cons. Assoc., 1979–. Professional hypnotist; face lifted by Dr John Williams, USA, 1978. Chm., UK Guild of Hypnotist Examiners, 1983–; Mem., Virginia Satir Internat. Avanta Network, 1987–. *Publications:* The Two Factor Nation, or How to make the people rich, 1977; The Consumer Guide to Hypnosis, 1990. *Recreations:* reading, photography, caravanning, travel, walking, jogging. *Address:* 278 Scalby Road, Scarborough, North Yorkshire YO12 6EB. *T:* (01723) 367027. *Died 19 July 2013.*

PRYER, (Eric) John, CB 1986; Chief Land Registrar, 1983–90; Assistant Secretary, Council for Licensed Conveyancers, 1991–92; *b* 5 Sept. 1929; *s* of late Edward John and Edith Blanche Pryer; *m* 1962, Moyra Helena Cross; one *s* one *d*. *Educ:* Beckenham and Penge County Grammar Sch.; Birkbeck Coll., London Univ. (BA Hons). Called to the Bar, Gray's Inn, 1957. Exec. Officer, Treasury Solicitor's Dept, 1948; Legal Asst, HM Land Registry, 1959; Asst Land Registrar, 1965; Dist Land Registrar, Durham, 1976; Dep. Chief Land Registrar, 1981–83. Hon. Associate Mem., RICS, 1986. *Publications:* (ed) Ruoff and Roper, The Law and Practice of Registered Conveyancing, 5th edn 1986, 6th edn 1991; Land Registration Handbook, 1990; official pubns; articles in jls. *Recreation:* reading. *Died 24 Feb. 2014.*

PUGH, Andrew Cartwright; QC 1988; *b* 6 June 1937; *s* of late Lewis Gordon Pugh and Erica Pugh; *m* 1984, Chantal Hélène Langevin; two *d*. *Educ:* Tonbridge; New Coll. Oxford (MA 1966). Served Royal Sussex Regt, 1956–57. Bigelow Teaching Fellow, Law Sch., Univ. of Chicago, 1960–61. Called to the Bar, Inner Temple, 1961, Bencher, 1989. Recorder, 1990–2003. Legal Assessor: GMC, 1991–2007; GDC, 1991–2009. Pres., Mental Health Review Tribunals, 2003–07. *Recreations:* gardening, reading, tennis. *Address:* Blackstone Chambers, Blackstone House, Temple, EC4Y 9BW. *T:* (020) 7583 1770. *Clubs:* Oxford and Cambridge; Waldron Cricket. *Died 6 June 2011.*

PUGH, John Arthur, OBE 1968; HM Diplomatic Service, retired; Chairman and Director, Numjai Restaurants, 1998; *b* 17 July 1920; *er s* of late Thomas Pugh and Dorothy Baker Pugh. *Educ:* Brecon Grammar Sch.; Bristol Univ. RN, 1941–45. Home CS, 1950–54; Gold Coast Admin. Service, 1955–58; Adviser to Ghana Govt, 1958–60; First Sec., British High Commn, Lagos, 1962–65; First Sec. (Economic), Bangkok, and British Perm. Rep. to Economic Commn for Asia and Far East, 1965–68; British Dep. High Comr, Ibadan, 1971–73; Diplomatic Service Inspector, 1973–76; High Comr to Seychelles, 1976–80. *Publications:* The Friday Man, 1992; editorial and other contributions to jls etc on political affairs, travel and history. *Recreations:* Oriental ceramics, travel. *Address:* Penybryn House, Hay on Wye, Hereford HR3 5RS. *T:* (01497) 820695. *Club:* Royal Commonwealth Society. *Died 6 Sept. 2012.*

PUGH, Peter David S.; *see* Storie-Pugh.

PULFORD, Richard Charles; consultant in cultural policy and arts management; *b* 14 July 1944; *s* of late Charles Edgar Pulford and Grace Mary Pulford (*née* Vickors). *Educ:* Royal Grammar Sch., Newcastle upon Tyne; St Catherine's Coll., Oxford (BA Jurisprudence). Voluntary service in the Sudan, 1966–67; Home Civil Service, 1967–79: Department of Education and Science: Asst Principal, 1967–72, Principal, 1972–75; HM Treasury, 1975–77; Asst Secretary, DES, 1977–79. Arts Council of GB: Dep. Sec.-Gen., 1979–85; South Bank Planning Dir, 1985–86; Gen. Dir (Admin), South Bank Centre, 1986–92; consultant on cultural policy and admin, 1993–2001, including work with/for Min. of Culture, Bulgaria, Min. of Culture, Hungary, Arts Council of GB, Arts Council of England, British Council, Millennium Commn, London Arts Bd, Royal Opera House, Wales Millennium Centre, Birmingham Rep. Theatre; Chief Exec. Soc. of London Theatre, and TMA, 2002–10. Bd Mem., Internat. Soc. of Performing Arts Administrators, 1988–92 (Pres., 1990–91); Member: South Bank Theatre Bd, 1985–92; Council, English Stage Co., 1989–2001; Dolphin Square Trust, 2000–11; Bd, Nat. Campaign for the Arts, 2001–06 (Chm., 1992–96; Vice-Pres., 1996–2001); V&A Museum Cttee for Theatre Museum, 2002–07; Dolphin Square 2005 Ltd, 2005–. Pres., Performing Arts Employers League Europe, 2005–09. Director: Stage One, 2002–10; Stage One Club, 2004–05. Trustee, Crusaid and STAR Foundn, 1993–2001. *Publications:* articles in various newspapers and specialist magazines. *Recreations:* trying to avoid respectability, white Burgundy, cooking for friends. *Address:* 905 Beatty House, Dolphin Square, SW1V 3PN. *T:* (020) 7798 8308, 07984 343340. *E:* richard_pulford@hotmail.com. *Died 7 Aug. 2011.*

PULLEIN-THOMPSON, Denis; *see* Cannan, D.

PULLEIN-THOMPSON, Josephine Mary Wedderburn, MBE 1984; writer; General Secretary, English Centre, International PEN, 1976–93; *b* 3 April 1924; *e d* of H. J. Pullein-Thompson, MC and Joanna Cannan, novelist. *Educ:* briefly at Wychwood Sch., Oxford. Horsewoman and writer; Vis. Comr, 1960–68, Dist Comr, 1970–76, Pony Club; Member: Cttee, Crime Writers' Assoc., 1971–73; Cttee, Children's Writers' Gp, Soc. of Authors, 1973–79 (Dep. Chm., 1978–79); English Centre of International PEN: Cttee, 1974–76; Pres., 1993–97; Vice Pres., 1997–. *Publications:* How Horses are Trained, 1961; (jtly) Ponies in Colour, 1962; Learn to Ride Well, 1966; Horses and Their Owners (anthology), 1970; Ride Better and Better, 1974; (with sisters) Fair Girls and Grey Horses: memories of a country childhood, 1996; *fiction:* It Began with Picotee (with sisters), 1946; Six Ponies, 1946; I had Two Ponies, 1947; Plenty of Ponies, 1949; Pony Club Team, 1950; The Radney Riding Club, 1951; Prince Among Ponies, 1952; One Day Event, 1954; Show Jumping Secret, 1955; Patrick's Pony, 1956; Pony Club Camp, 1957; The Trickjumpers, 1958; All Change, 1961, new edn as The Hidden Horse, 1982; Race Horse Holiday, 1971; Proud Riders (anthology), 1973; Black Ebony, 1975; Star Riders of the Moor, 1976; Fear Treks the Moor, 1978; Black Nightshade, 1978; Ride to the Rescue, 1979; Ghost Horse on the Moor, 1980; The No Good Pony, 1981; Treasure on the Moor, 1982; The Prize Pony, 1982; Black Raven, 1982; Pony Club Cup, 1982; Save the Ponies, 1984; Mystery on the Moor, 1984; Pony Club Challenge, 1984; Pony Club Trek, 1985; Suspicion Stalks the Moor, 1986; Black Swift, 1991; A Job with Horses, 1994; *crime:* Gin and Murder, 1959; They Died in the Spring, 1960; Murder Strikes Pink, 1963; (as J Mann) A Place with Two Faces, 1972; contrib. Oxford DNB. *Recreations:* gardening; formerly travelling, reading, theatre going. *Address:* 16 Knivet Road, SW6 1JH. *Died 19 June 2014.*

PULLEYBLANK, Prof. Edwin George, PhD; FRSC; Professor of Chinese, University of British Columbia, 1966–87, then Emeritus; *b* Calgary, Alberta, 7 Aug. 1922; *s* of William George Edwin and Ruth Elizabeth Pulleyblank, Calgary; *m* 1st, 1945, Winona Ruth Relyea (*d* 1976), Arnprior, Ont; one *s* two *d*; 2nd, 2002, Yihong Pan, Beijing. *Educ:* Central High School, Calgary; University of Alberta (BA Hons Classics 1942); University of London. Nat. Research Council of Canada, 1943–46. School of Oriental and African Studies, Univ. of London: Chinese Govt Schol., 1946; Lectr in Classical Chinese, 1948; PhD in Classical Chinese, 1951; Lectr in Far Eastern History, 1952; Professor of Chinese, University of Cambridge, 1953;

Head, Dept of Asian Studies, Univ. of British Columbia, 1968–75. Fellow of Downing Coll., Cambridge, 1955–66. Corresp. Fellow, Italian Inst. for the Middle and Far East, 1993. *Publications:* The Background of the Rebellion of An Lu-Shan, 1955; Middle Chinese, 1984; Lexicon of Reconstructed Pronunciation in Early Middle Chinese, Late Middle Chinese and Early Mandarin, 1991; Outline of Classical Chinese Grammar, 1995; articles in Asia Major, Bulletin of School of Oriental and African Studies, etc. *Address:* c/o Department of Asian Studies, University of British Columbia, Vancouver, BC V6T 1Z2, Canada. *Died 13 April 2013.*

PURCELL, (Robert) Michael, CMG 1983; HM Diplomatic Service, retired; Adviser and Secretary, East Africa Association, 1984–87; *b* 22 Oct. 1923; *s* of late Lt-Col Walter Purcell and Constance (*née* Fendick); *m* 1965, Julia Evelyn, *o d* of late Brig. Edward Marsh-Kellett; two *d*. *Educ:* Ampleforth Coll. Served 60th Rifles (Greenjackets), 1943–47 (Italian Campaign, 1944–45). Colonial Admin, Uganda, 1949–62, retd; 1st Sec., CRO, later FCO, 1964–68; 1st Sec. (Commercial/Economic), Colombo, 1968–69; FCO, 1969–71; 1st Sec. (Aid), Singapore, 1971–73; Head of Chancery, HM Legation to the Holy See, 1973–76; Counsellor and Dep. High Comr, Malta, 1977–80; Ambassador to Somali Democratic Republic, 1980–83. KCSG 1976. *Recreations:* country life, books, bridge. *Address:* French Mill Cottage, Shaftesbury, Dorset SP7 0LT. *T:* (01747) 853615. *Died 18 June 2014.*

PUSACK, George Williams, MS; Chief Executive, Mobil Oil Australia Ltd, 1980–85; *b* 26 Sept. 1920; *s* of George F. Pusack and Winifred (*née* Williams); *m* 1942, Marian Preston (decd); one *s* one *d* (and one *s* decd). *Educ:* Univ. of Michigan; Univ. of Pennsylvania. BSE (AeroEng), BSE (Eng.Math), MS (MechEng). Aero Engr, US Navy, 1942–45; Corporal, US Air Force, 1945–46; Mobil Oil Corp.: Tech. Service and Research Manager, USA, 1946–53; Product Engrg Manager, USA, 1953–59; International Supply Manager, USA, 1959–69; Vice-Pres., N Amer. Div., USA, 1969–73; Regional Exec., Mobil Europe, London, 1973–76; Chm. and Chief Exec., Mobil Oil Co. Ltd, 1976–80. Pres., County Hospice, York, SC, 1989–91. Trustee, Victorian State Opera Foundn, 1983–85. Teacher, layreader, vestryman and warden of Episcopal Church (Trustee, York, SC, 1992–). *Recreations:* golf, travel. *Address:* 400 Avinger Lane #431, Davidson, NC 28036, USA. *T:* (704) 8961431. *Clubs:* River Hills Country (Pres., 1991) (Clover, USA); River Run Country (Davidson, NC). *Died 26 Feb. 2011.*

Q

QUAYLE, Maj.-Gen. Thomas David Graham, CB 1990; Vice Chairman, Salisbury NHS Foundation Trust, 2006–08; *b* 7 April 1936; *s* of Thomas Quayle and Phyllis Gwendolen Johnson; *m* 1962, Susan Jean Bradford; three *d*. *Educ:* Repton; Trinity College, Oxford. Commissioned RA 1958; Student, Indian Staff Coll., 1968; Comdr, The Chestnut Troop, 1971–72; Instructor, Staff Coll., Camberley, 1974–76; Comdr, 40 Field Regt (The Lowland Gunners), 1976–79; Comdr Artillery, 4th Armoured Div., 1981–83; Defence Attaché, Bonn, 1983–86; Comdr Artillery, 1st British Corps, 1987–90, retd. Ombudsman for Estate Agents (formerly for Corporate Estate Agents), 1990–99. Non-exec. Dir, Salisbury Health Care NHS Trust, 1999–2006. Mem., Mortgage Code Compliance Bd, 1999–2004. *Recreations:* fishing, bridge. *Address:* Oriole House, Figheldean, Salisbury, Wilts SP4 8JJ. *E:* tdg.quayle@tiscali.co.uk. *Died 25 June 2015.*

QUIGLEY, Sir (William) George (Henry), Kt 1993; CB 1982; PhD; Chairman: Short Brothers, since 1999 (Director, since 1989); Ulster Bank Ltd, 1989–2001 (Deputy Chairman, 1988–89); *b* 26 Nov. 1929; *s* of William George Cunningham Quigley and Sarah Hanson Martin; *m* 1971, Moyra Alice Munn, LLB. *Educ:* Ballymena Academy; Queen's Univ., Belfast (BA (1st Cl. Hons), 1951; PhD, 1955). Apptd Asst Principal, Northern Ireland Civil Service, 1955; Permanent Secretary: Dept of Manpower Services, NI, 1974–76; Dept of Commerce, NI, 1976–79; Dept of Finance, NI, 1979–82; Dept of Finance and Personnel, NI, 1982–88. Director: Irish-American Partnership, 1989–; Nat. Westminster Bank, 1990–99; Independent News and Media (UK), 2001–10; Chm., Natwest Pension Trustees Ltd, 1998–2002. Chairman: Co-operation North, 1994–96; NI Economic Council, 1994–98. Chm., Royal Group of Hospitals Trust, NI, 1992–95. Chm., NI Div., Inst. of Dirs, 1990–94; Member: Fair Employment Commn for NI, 1989–93; Council, NI Chamber of Commerce and Industry, 1989–92; Council, NI Div., CBI, 1990–95; Chm., Review of Parades Commn of NI, 2001–02. Chm., Scottish Fee Support Review, 1998–2000; Member: Nat. Cttee of Inquiry into Higher Educn, 1996–97; Qualifications and Curriculum Authority, 1997–99. Chm., Lothbury Property Trust, 2001–. President: Econ. and Social Res. Inst., 1999–2002; Inst. of Internat. Trade of Ireland, 1999–2001. Chm. Bd, Inst. of British-Irish Studies, UCD, 2006–. Professorial Fellow, QUB, 1989–93. Fellow, Inst. of Bankers in Ireland, 1989. MRIA 2007. CCMI. Hon. Fellow, IMgtI. Hon. LLD QUB, 1996; DUniv: Ulster, 1998; Open, 2005. Compaq Lifetime Achievement Award, 1997. *Publications:* (ed with E. F. D. Roberts) Registrum Iohannis Mey: The Register of John Mey, Archbishop of Armagh, 1443–1456, 1972. *Recreations:* historical research, reading, music, gardening. *Address:* Short Brothers Ltd, PO Box 241, Airport Road, Belfast BT3 9DZ. *Died 3 March 2013.*

QUILTER, Sir Anthony (Raymond Leopold Cuthbert), 4th Bt *cr* 1897; landowner since 1959; *b* 25 March 1937; *s* of Sir (John) Raymond (Cuthbert) Quilter, 3rd Bt and Margery Marianne (*née* Cooke); *S* father, 1959; *m* 1964, Mary Elise (*d* 2013), *er d* of late Colonel Brian (Sherlock) Gooch, DSO, TD; one *s* one *d*. *Educ:* Harrow. Engaged in farming. *Recreations:* shooting, golf. *Heir: s* Guy Raymond Cuthbert Quilter [*b* 13 April 1967; *m* 1992, Jenifer, *o d* of John Redvers-Cox; three *s*]. *Address:* Cliff Farm, Sutton, Woodbridge, Suffolk IP12 3JJ. *T:* (01394) 411246. *Died 28 Aug. 2014.*

QUINCE, Peter; *see* Thompson, John W. McW.

QUINN, Niall Peter; QC 2006; a Recorder, since 1999; *b* 16 June 1950; *s* of late Michael Quinn and Sheelagh Quinn (*née* O'Hare); *m* 1st, 1970, Mary O'Flynn (*d* 1997); one *s* two *d*; 2nd, 2001, Linda Bamford (*née* Austin); two step *s*. *Educ:* Emanuel Sch.; Univ. of Manchester (LLB Hons 1971); Coll. of Law, London. Admitted solicitor, 1974; Foinette Quinn, then Woodfine Foinette Quinn, later Woodfines LLP, solicitors: Partner, 1975; Sen. Partner, 1984; Partner, 2000–. Asst Recorder, 1995–99. *Recreations:* Times crossword, karaoke. *Address:* Woodfines LLP, Regency Court, Milton Keynes MK9 2HR. *T:* (01908) 202150, *Fax:* (01908) 644096. *E:* nquinn@woodfines.co.uk. *Died 14 Aug. 2013.*

QUINTON, Sir John (Grand), Kt 1990; Chairman, Barclays Bank PLC, 1987–92 (Deputy Chairman, 1985–87); *b* 21 Dec. 1929; *s* of William Grand Quinton and Norah May (*née* Nunn); *m* 1954, Jean Margaret Chastney; one *s* one *d*. *Educ:* Norwich Sch.; St John's Coll., Cambridge (MA 1954); FCIB (FIB 1964). Joined Barclays Bank, 1953: Manager, King's Cross, 1965; seconded to Min. of Health as Principal, Internat. Div. and UK Deleg., World Health Assembly, 1966; Asst Gen. Manager, 1968; Local Dir, Nottingham, 1969; Reg. Gen. Manager, 1971; Gen. Manager, 1975; Dir and Sen. Gen. Man., 1982–84; Vice-Chm., 1985. Dep. Chm., Mercantile Credit Co. Ltd, 1975–79; Chairman: FA Premier League, 1992–99; George Wimpey PLC, 1993–95; non-exec. Dir, Norwich and Peterborough BS, 1993–99 (Dep. Chm., 1996–99). Chairman: Chief Exec. Officers, Cttee of London Clearing Bankers, 1982–83; Adv. Council, London Enterprise Agency, 1986–90; Office of the Banking Ombudsman, 1987–92; Cttee of London and Scottish Bankers, 1989–91; Metropolitan Police Cttee, 1995–2000. Member: City Capital Markets Cttee, 1981–86; NE Thames RHA, 1974–87; Accounting Standards Cttee, 1982–85; Econ. and Financial Policy Cttee, CBI, 1985–88 (Chm., 1987–88); Metropolitan Police Authy, 2000–04. Treasurer, Chartered Inst. of Bankers, 1980–86 (Pres., 1989–90); Hon. Treas. and Bd Mem., Business in the Community, 1986–91. Chairman: British Olympic Appeal, 1988; Royal Anniversary Trust Appeal, 1992. Trustee: Royal Acad. Trust, 1987–93; Westminster Abbey Trust, 1991–98; Thrombosis Res. Inst., 1993–2001; Chm. Bd of Trustees, Botanic Gdns Conservation Internat., 1991–99. Pres., East of England Show, 1992. Chm., Motability Finance Ltd, 1978–85; Gov., Motability, 1985–2010 (Hon. Treas., 1998–2003); Vice-Chm., Motability Tenth Anniversary Trust Ltd, 1995–2010. Gov., Ditchley Foundn, 1987–92; Member: Court of Governors, Royal Shakespeare Theatre, 1986–2000; Court, Henley Coll., 1987–92. FRSA 1988. Chm., Chenies Parish Council, 2007–. Freeman: Norwich, 1952; City of London, 1989. *Recreations:* gardening, music, golf. *Address:* Chenies Place, Chenies, Bucks WD3 6EU. *Club:* Reform. *Died 28 April 2012.*

QUIRK, John Stanton S.; *see* Shirley-Quirk.

R

RABIN, Prof. Brian Robert; Professor of Biochemistry, 1988–93, then Emeritus, Fellow since 1984, University College, London; *b* 4 Nov. 1927; *s* of Emanuel and Sophia Rabin, both British; *m* 1954; one *s* one *d*. *Educ:* Latymer Sch., Edmonton; University Coll., London. BSc 1951, MSc 1952, PhD 1956. University College, London: Asst Lectr, 1954–57; Lectr, 1957–63; Reader, 1963–67; Prof. of Enzymology, 1967–70; Hd of Dept of Biochemistry, 1970–88. Rockefeller Fellow, Univ. of California, 1956–57. Founder Dir, London Biotechnology Ltd, 1985–. Invented prosthetogen-based diagnostic detection technol., and reverse polarity ADEPT for cancer treatment. *Publications:* numerous in Biochem. Jl, European Jl of Biochem., Nature, Proc. Nat. Acad. Sciences US, etc. *Recreations:* travel, listening to music, carpentry. *Address:* 22 Leaf House, Catherine Place, Harrow, Middx HA1 2JW. *T:* (020) 8861 5278. *Died 30 Oct. 2012.*

RABINOVITCH, Prof. Benton Seymour, FRS 1987; Professor of Chemistry, University of Washington, Seattle, 1957–86, then Emeritus; *b* 19 Feb. 1919; *s* of Samuel Rabinovitch and Rachel Schachter; *m* 1st, 1949, Marilyn Werby; two *s* two *d*; 2nd, 1980, Flora Reitman. *Educ:* McGill Univ. (BSc, PhD). Served Canadian Army overseas, Captain, 1942–46. Milton Fellow, Harvard Univ., 1946–48; University of Washington: Asst Prof., 1948–53; Associate Prof., 1953–57. Guggenheim Fellow, 1961–62. Fellow: Amer. Acad. of Arts and Scis, 1979; APS. Hon. Liveryman, Goldsmiths' Co., 2000. Hon. DSc Technion, Haifa, 1991. Sigma Xi Dist. Res. Award, 1981; Peter Debye Award, ACS, 1984; Michael Polanyi Medal, RSC, 1984. *Publications:* Physical Chemistry, 1964; Antique Silver Servers, 1990; Contemporary Silver, 2000; Contemporary Silver Pt II, 2005; (ed) annual reviews Phys. Chem., 1975–85; over 200 contribs to jls. *Recreation:* silversmithing. *Address:* Department of Chemistry, Box 351700, University of Washington, Seattle, WA 98195, USA. *T:* (206) 5431636. *Died 2 Aug. 2014.*

RACKHAM, Dr Oliver, OBE 1998; FBA 2002; FSA; Fellow, since 1964, and Master 2007–08, Corpus Christi College, Cambridge; *b* 17 Oct. 1939; *s* of Geoffrey Herbert Rackham and Norah Kathleen Rackham (*née* Wilson). *Educ:* Norwich Sch.; Norwich City Coll.; Corpus Christi Coll., Cambridge (Natural Scis Tripos, BA 1961, MA 1964, PhD 1964). FSA 2010. Jun. Proctor, 1996–97, Hon. Prof., 2006–10, Cambridge Univ. DU Essex, 2000. Hon. Mem., British Ecol. Soc., 2009. *Publications:* Hayley Wood, its history and ecology, 1975; Trees and Woodland in the British Landscape, 1976, 2nd edn 1990; Ancient Woodland: its history, vegetation and uses in England, 1980, 2nd edn 2003; The History of the Countryside, 1986; Ancient Woodland of England: the woods of South-East Essex, 1986; The Last Forest: the story of Hatfield Forest, 1989; The Illustrated History of the Countryside, 1994; (with J. A. Moody) The Making of the Cretan Landscape, 1996; (with A. T. Grove) The Nature of Southern Europe: an ecological history, 2001; Treasures of Silver at Corpus Christi College, Cambridge, 2002; Woodlands, 2006; The Ash Tree, 2014. *Recreations:* archaeology, especially of carpentry. *Address:* Corpus Christi College, Cambridge CB2 1RH. *T:* (01223) 360144. *E:* or10001@cam.ac.uk. *Died 12 Feb. 2015.*

RADCLIFFE, Anthony Frank, FSA; Hon. Keeper of Renaissance and Baroque Sculpture, Fitzwilliam Museum, since 1996; *b* Wivenhoe, Essex, 23 Feb. 1933; *s* of late Dr Walter Radcliffe and Muriel Laure Radcliffe (*née* Brée); *m* 1960, Enid Clair Cawkwell; two *s*. *Educ:* Oundle Sch.; Gonville and Caius Coll., Cambridge (BA 1955; MA 1959). Victoria and Albert Museum: joined Dept of Circulation, 1958; transferred to Dept of Architecture and Sculpture, 1960; Res. Asst, Dept of Circulation, 1961–67; Asst to Dir, 1967–74; Asst Keeper, Dept of Architecture and Sculpture, 1974–79; Keeper of Sculpture, 1979–89; Head of Res., 1989–90; Keeper Emeritus, 1990–96. Mellon Sen. Vis. Curator, Nat. Gall. of Art, Washington, 1990; Guest Scholar, J. Paul Getty Mus., 1991, 1995; Samuel H. Kress Prof., CASVA, Nat. Gall. of Art, Washington, 1993–94. Member: Adv. Council, NACF, 1993–; Consultative Cttee, Burlington Magazine, 1990–. Medal, Accademia delle Arti del Disegno, Florence, 1986. Cavaliere Ufficiale al Merito della Repubblica Italiana, 2003. *Publications:* European Bronze Statuettes, 1966; Jean-Baptiste Carpeaux, 1968; (with J. Pope-Hennessy and T. Hodgkinson) The Frick Collection: an illustrated catalogue, III, IV, 1970; (with C. Avery) Giambologna, sculptor to the Medici, 1978; (with M. Baker and M. Maek Gérard) The Thyssen-Bornemisza Collection: Renaissance and later sculpture, 1992; The Robert H. Smith Collection: Bronzes 1500–1650, 1994; (jtly) The Robert H. Smith Collection: Art of the Renaissance Bronze 1500–1650, 2004; contribs to Burlington Mag., Apollo, Connoisseur, etc. *Address:* 203 Waller Road, SE14 5LX. *T:* (020) 7639 4605. *Died 1 Jan. 2011.*

RADJI, Parviz Camran; diplomat; Ambassador of Iran to the Court of St James's, 1976–79; *b* 1936; *m* 1986, Golgoun Partovi. *Educ:* Trinity Hall, Cambridge (MA Econs). National Iranian Oil Co., 1959–62; Private Sec. to Minister of Foreign Affairs, 1962–65; Private Sec. to Prime Minister, subseq. Personal Asst, 1965–72; Special Adviser to Prime Minister, 1972–76. *Publications:* In the Service of the Peacock Throne: the diaries of the Shah's last Ambassador to London, 1983. *Died 23 March 2014.*

RAHTZ, Prof. Philip Arthur; Professor of Archaeology, University of York, 1978–86, then Emeritus; *b* 11 March 1921; *s* of Frederick John Rahtz and Ethel May Rahtz; *m* 1st, 1940, Wendy Hewgill Smith (*d* 1977); three *s* two *d*; 2nd, 1978, Lorna Rosemary Jane Watts; one *s*. *Educ:* Bristol Grammar Sch. MA Bristol 1964. FSA. Served RAF, 1941–46. Articled to accountant, 1937–41; photographer (Studio Rahtz), 1946–49; schoolteacher, 1950–53; archaeological consultant, 1953–63; Univ. of Birmingham: Lectr, 1963–75; Sen. Lectr, later Reader, 1975–78. Pres., Council for British Archaeology, 1986–89. Hon. MIFA. Hon. DLitt Bristol, 2002. Frend Medal, Soc. of Antiquaries of London, 2003. *Publications:* Rescue Archaeology, 1973; Chew Valley Lake Excavations, 1978; Saxon and Medieval Palaces at Cheddar, 1979; Invitation to Archaeology, 1985, 2nd edn 1991; Tamworth Saxon Watermill, 1992; Glastonbury, 1993, 2nd edn 2003; Cannington Cemetery, 2000; Living Archaeology, 2001; contrib. nat. and regional jls in England, W Africa and Poland. *Recreations:* swimming, sunbathing, music. *Died 2 June 2011.*

RAIKES, Vice-Adm. Sir Iwan (Geoffrey), KCB 1976; CBE 1967; DSC 1943; DL; Flag Officer Submarines, and Commander Submarines, Eastern Atlantic Area, 1974–76; retired 1977; *b* 21 April 1921; *s* of late Adm. Sir Robert Henry Taunton Raikes, KCB, CVO, DSO and bar, and Lady (Ida Guinevere) Raikes; *m* 1947, Cecilia Primrose Hunt; one *s* one *d*. *Educ:* RNC Dartmouth. Entered Royal Navy, 1935; HMS Sussex, 1939–40; HMS Repulse, 1940; HMS Beagle, 1941; specialised in Submarines, 1941; comd HM Submarines: Sealion, 1941–42; Saracen, 1942–43; H43, 1943; Varne, 1944; Virtue, 1946; Talent, 1948–49; Aeneas, 1952; Logistics Div., Allied Forces Mediterranean, 1953–55; Comdr SM Third Submarine Sqn, 1958–60; Capt. 1960; comd HM Ships: Loch Insh, 1961; Kent, 1968; Exec. Officer, HMS Newcastle, 1955–57; Dep. Dir, Undersurface Warfare, 1962–64; Dir, Plans & Operations, Staff of C-in-C Far East, 1965–66; JSSC, 1957; IDC, 1967. Rear-Adm., 1970; Naval Sec., 1970–72; Vice-Adm., 1973; Flag Officer, First Flotilla, 1973–74. Chm., United Usk Fisherman's Assoc., 1978–93. Mem., Governing Body, 1979–93, Rep. Body, 1982–93, Church in Wales. DL Powys, 1983. *Recreations:* shooting, fishing, gardening. *Address:* Aberyscir Court, Brecon, Powys LD3 9NW. *Died 27 Dec. 2011.*

RAINER, Luise; actress and painter; *b* Vienna, 12 Jan. 1910; *d* of Heinz Rainer; *m* 1937, Clifford Odets (from whom she obtained a divorce, 1940; he *d* 1963); *m* 1945, Robert (*d* 1989), *s* of late John Knittel; one *d*. *Educ:* Austria, France, Switzerland and Italy. Started stage career at age of sixteen under Max Reinhardt in Vienna; later was discovered by Metro-Goldwyn-Mayer talent scout in Vienna; came to Hollywood; starred in: Escapade, 1935; The Great Ziegfeld, 1936; The Good Earth, Emperor's Candlesticks, Big City, 1937; Toy Wife (Frou Frou), The Great Waltz, Dramatic School, 1938; Hostages, 1942; The Gambler, 1997; Poetry, 2001; received Motion Picture Academy of Arts and Sciences Award for the best feminine performance in 1936 (for The Great Ziegfeld) and 1937 (for The Good Earth). One-man exhibn of paintings at Patrick Seale Gallery, SW1, 1978. US tour in dramatised recitation of Tennyson's Enoch Arden with music by Richard Strauss, 1983–84. TV film (wrote and starred), By herself—a dancer, 1986. George Eastman Award, George Eastman Inst., Rochester, NY, 1982. Grand Cross 1st class, Order of Merit (Federal Republic of Germany), 1985. *Recreations:* formerly mountain climbing, later writing, painting. *Died 30 Dec. 2014.*

RAINS, Prof. Anthony John Harding, CBE 1986; MS, FRCS; Professor of Surgery, Charing Cross Hospital Medical School, University of London, and Hon. Consultant Surgeon, Charing Cross Hospital, 1959–81; *b* 5 Nov. 1920; *s* of late Dr Robert Harding Rains and Mrs Florence Harding Rains; *m* 1943, Mary Adelaide Lillywhite (*d* 2011); three *d*. *Educ:* Christ's Hospital School, Horsham; St Mary's Hospital, London. MB, BS London 1943; MS London 1952; MRCS; LRCP 1943; FRCS 1948. Ho. Surg. and Ho. Phys. St Mary's, 1943. RAF, 1944–47. Ex-Service Registrar to Mr Handfield-Jones and Lord Porritt, 1947–48; Res. Surgical Officer, Bedford County Hosp., 1948–50; Lectr in Surgery, Univ. of Birmingham, 1950–54, Sen. Lectr, 1955–59; Asst Dir, BPMF, Univ. of London, and Postgraduate Dean, SW Thames RHA, 1981–85. Hon. Consulting Surgeon, United Birmingham Hospitals, 1954–59; Hon. Consultant Surgeon to the Army, 1972–82. Royal College of Surgeons of England: Mem. Court of Examiners, 1968–74; Mem. Council, 1972–84; Dean, Inst. of Basic Med. Scis, 1976–82; Hunterian Trustee, 1982–95; Vice-President, 1983–84; Hon. Librarian, 1984–95. Chm., Med. Commn on Accident Prevention, 1974–83. Pres., Nat. Assoc. of Theatre Nurses, 1979–81. Trustee, Smith and Nephew Foundn, 1972–95. Sir Arthur Keith medal, RCS. Editor: Annals of RCS; Jl of RSocMed, 1985–94. *Publications:* (ed with Dr P. B. Kunkler) The Treatment of Cancer in Clinical Practice, 1959; Gallstones: Causes and Treatment, 1964; (ed) Bailey and Love's Short Practice of Surgery, 13th edn (ed with W, M. Capper), 1965, 20th edn (ed with C. V. Mann), 1988; Edward Jenner and Vaccination, 1975; Emergency and Acute Care, 1976; Lister and Antisepsis, 1977; 1,001 Multiple Choice Questions and Answers in Surgery, 1978, 4th edn 1996; (contrib.) A Millennium of Archdeacons, 2003; articles on the surgery of the gall bladder, on the formation of gall stones, inguinal hernia and arterial disease. *Recreations:* gardening, poetry. *Address:* 2 Stable Courtyard, Flete House, Ermington, Devon PL21 9NZ. *T:* (01752) 830167. *Died 21 June 2014.*

RAISON, Dr John Charles Anthony, MA, MD; FFPH; Consultant in Public Health Medicine, Wessex Regional Health Authority, 1982–91; *b* 13 May 1926; *s* of late Cyril A. Raison, FRCS, Edgbaston, Birmingham, and of Ceres Raison; *m* 1st, 1951, Rosemary Padmore (marr. diss. 1982); one *s* two *d*; 2nd, 1983, Ann Alexander, *d* of Captain Faulkner, MM and Mrs J. H. R. Faulkner, Southampton; three step *d*. *Educ:* Malvern Coll.; Trinity Hall, Cambridge (MD); Birmingham Univ. Consultant Clinical Physiologist in Cardiac Surgery, Birmingham Reg. Hosp. Bd, 1962; Hon. Associate Consultant Clinical Physiologist, United Birmingham Hosps, 1963; Sen. Physiologist, Dir of Clinical Res. and Chief Planner, Heart Research Inst., Presbyterian-Pacific Medical Center, San Francisco, 1966; Chief Scientific Officer and Sen. Prin. Medical Officer, Scientific Services, DHSS, 1974–78; Dep. Dir, Nat. Radiological Protection Bd, 1978–81. Vis. Consultant, Civic Hosps, Lisbon (Gulbenkian Foundn), 1962; Arris and Gale Lectr, Royal College of Surgeons, 1965. Councillor, Southam RDC, 1955–59. *Publications:* chapters in books, and papers in medical jls on open-heart surgery, extracorporeal circulation, intensive care, scientific services in health care, and computers in medicine. *Recreations:* gardening, golf, singing. *Address:* 15 The Woodlands, Church Lane, Kings Worthy, near Winchester, Hants SO23 7QQ. *T:* (01962) 885722. *Died 6 March 2014.*

RAISON, Rt Hon. Sir Timothy (Hugh Francis), Kt 1991; PC 1982; Chairman: Advertising Standards Authority, 1991–94; Aylesbury Vale Community Healthcare NHS Trust, 1992–98; *b* 3 Nov. 1929; *s* of late Maxwell and Celia Raison; *m* 1956, Veldes Julia Charrington; one *s* three *d*. *Educ:* Dragon Sch., Oxford; Eton (King's Schol.); Christ Church, Oxford (Open History Schol.). Editorial Staff: Picture Post, 1953–56; New Scientist, 1956–61; Editor: Crossbow, 1958–60; New Society, 1962–68. Member: Youth Service Develt Council, 1960–63; Central Adv. Council for Educn, 1963–66; Adv. Cttee on Drug Dependence, 1966–70; Home Office Adv., Council on Penal System, 1970–74; (co-opted) Inner London Educn Authority Educn Cttee, 1967–70; Richmond upon Thames Council, 1967–71. MP (C) Aylesbury, 1970–92; PPS to Sec. of State for N Ireland, 1972–73; Parly Under-Sec. of State, DES, 1973–74; Opposition spokesman on the Environment, 1975–76; Minister of State, Home Office, 1979–83; Minister of State, FCO, and Minister for Overseas Develt, 1983–86. Chm., Select Cttee on Educn, Science and the Arts, 1987–89. Sen. Fellow, Centre for Studies in Soc. Policy, 1974–77; Mem. Council, PSI, 1978–79; Vice-Chm. Bd, British Council, 1987–92. Trustee, BM, 1991–99. Mem. Council, Nat. Trust, 1997–2000. Nansen Medal (for share in originating World Refugee Year), 1960. *Publications:* Why Conservative?, 1964; (ed) Youth in New Society, 1966; (ed) Founding Fathers of Social Science, 1969; Power and Parliament, 1979; Tories and the Welfare State, 1990; various political pamphlets. *Recreations:* gardening, history of art. *Club:* Beefsteak. *Died 3 Nov. 2011.*

RALPHS, Enid Mary, (Lady Ralphs), CBE 1984; JP; DL; Chairman of the Council, 1981–84, Vice-President, since 1984, Magistrates' Association; *b* 20 Jan. 1915; *d* of Percy William Cowlin and Annie Louise Cowlin (*née* Willoughby); *m* 1938, Sir (Frederick) Lincoln Ralphs, Kt 1973 (*d* 1978); one *s* two *d*. *Educ:* Camborne Grammar Sch.; University Coll., Exeter (BA); DipEd Cambridge. Pres., Guild of Undergrads, Exeter, 1936–37; Vice-Pres., NUS, 1937–38. Teacher, Penzance Grammar Sch., 1937–38; Staff Tutor, Oxford Univ. Tutorial Classes Cttee, 1942–44; pt-time Sen. Lectr, Keswick Hall Coll. of Educn, 1948–80. Member: Working Party on Children and Young Persons Act 1969, 1977–78; Steering Cttee on Community Alternatives for Young Offenders, NACRO, 1979–82; Consultative Cttee on Educn in Norwich Prison, 1982–87; Home Office Adv. Bd on Restricted Patients, 1985–91; Chairman: Working Party on the Victim in Court, 1988; Working Party on Sentencing, a way ahead, 1989. Member: Religious Adv. Council, BBC Midland Reg., 1963–66; Guide Council for GB, 1965–68. President: Norwich and Dist Br., UNA, 1973–2002; Norfolk Guides (formerly Girl Guides), 1987–2002. Visitor, Wymondham Coll., 1991–. Trustee, Norfolk Children's Projects, 1982–2002. JP Norwich 1958; Chairman: Norwich Juvenile Panel, 1964–79; Norwich Bench, 1977–85; former Mem., Licensing Cttee; Mem., Domestic Panel, 1981–85; Vice-Pres., Norfolk Br., Magistrates' Assoc., 1986–; Dep. Chm., Norfolk Magistrates' Courts Cttee, 1978–85 (Chm., Trng Sub-Cttee); Mem., Central Council, Magistrates' Courts Cttees, 1974–81. DL Norfolk 1981. Hon. DCL East Anglia, 1989. *Publications:* (jtly) The Magistrate as Chairman, 1987; contribs to various jls. *Recreations:* gardening, travel. *Address:* Jesselton, 218 Unthank Road, Norwich NR2 2AH. *T:* (01603) 453382. *Clubs:* Royal Over-Seas League; Norfolk (Norwich). *Died 28 Jan. 2014.*

RAMAGE, (James) Granville (William), CMG 1975; HM Diplomatic Service, retired; *b* 19 Nov. 1919; *s* of late Rev. George Granville Ramage and Helen Marion (*née* Middlemass); *m* 1947, Eileen Mary Smith; one *s* two *d*. *Educ:* Glasgow Acad.; Glasgow University. Served in HM Forces, 1940–46 (despatches). Entered HM Foreign Service, 1947; seconded for service at Bombay, 1947–49;

transf. to Foreign Office, 1950; First Sec. and Consul at Manila, 1952–56; South-East Asia Dept, FO, 1956–58; Consul at Atlanta, Ga, 1958–62; Gen. Dept, FO, 1962–63; Consul-General, Tangier, 1963–67; High Comr in The Gambia, 1968–71; Ambassador, People's Democratic Republic of Yemen, 1972–75; Consul General at Boston, Massachusetts, 1975–77. *Recreation:* music. *Address:* King's Head Court, London Road, Sawbridgeworth, Herts CM21 9JT. *T:* (01279) 860740. *Died 4 March 2011.*

RAMSDEN, Prof. Herbert, MA, Dr en Filosofía y Letras; Professor of Spanish Language and Literature, University of Manchester, 1961–82, then Emeritus; *b* 20 April 1927; *s* of Herbert and Ann Ramsden; *m* 1953, Joyce Robina Hall, SRN, ONC, CMB; three *s* (incl. twin *s*) twin *d*. *Educ:* Sale Grammar Sch.; Univs of Manchester, Strasbourg, Madrid and Sorbonne. National Service, Inf. and Intell. Corps, 1949–51 (commnd). Travel, study and research abroad (Kemsley Travelling Fellow, etc), 1951–54; University of Manchester: Asst Lectr in Spanish, 1954–57; Lectr in Spanish, 1957–61; Pres., Philological Club, 1966–68. British Hispanists' rep., Nat. Council for Modern Languages, 1972–73; British rep., Asociación Europea de Profesores de Español, 1975–80. *Publications:* An Essential Course in Modern Spanish, 1959; Weak-Pronoun Position in the Early Romance Languages, 1963; (ed with critical study) Azorín, La ruta de Don Quijote, 1966; Angel Ganivet's Idearium español: A Critical Study, 1967; The Spanish Generation of 1898, 1974; The 1898 Movement in Spain, 1974; (ed with critical study) Lorca, Bodas de sangre, 1980; Pío Baroja: La busca, 1982; Pío Baroja: La busca 1903 to La busca 1904, 1982; (ed with critical study) Lorca, La casa de Bernarda Alba, 1983; Lorca's Romancero gitano, 1988; (ed, with critical study) Lorca, Romancero gitano: eighteen commentaries, 1988; articles in Bulletin of Hispanic Studies, Modern Language Review, Modern Languages, etc. *Recreations:* family, hill-walking, foreign travel. *Address:* 7 Burford Avenue, Bramhall, Stockport, Cheshire SK7 1BL. *T:* (0161) 439 4306. *Died 27 Sept. 2011.*

RAMSEY, Prof. Norman Foster; Higgins Professor of Physics, Harvard University, since 1947; Senior Fellow, Harvard Society of Fellows, since 1971; *b* 27 Aug. 1915; *s* of Brig.-Gen. and Mrs Norman F. Ramsey; *m* 1940, Elinor Stedman Jameson (*d* 1983); four *d*; *m* 1985, Ellie A. Welch. *Educ:* Columbia Univ.; Cambridge Univ. (England). Carnegie Fellow, Carnegie Instn of Washington, 1939–40; Assoc., Univ. of Ill, 1940–42; Asst Prof., Columbia Univ., 1942–45; Research Assoc., MIT Radiation Laboratory, 1940–43; Cons. to Nat. Defense Research Cttee, 1940–45; Expert Consultant to Sec. of War, 1942–45; Gp Leader and Assoc. Div. Head, Los Alamos Lab. of Atomic Energy Project, 1943–45; Chief Scientist of Atomic Energy Lab. at Tinian, 1945; Assoc. Prof., Columbia Univ., 1945–47; Head of Physics Dept, Brookhaven Nat. Lab., 1946–47; Assoc. Prof., Harvard Univ., 1947–50; John Simon Guggenheim Fell., Oxford Univ., 1953–54; George Eastman Vis. Prof., Oxford Univ., 1973–74; Luce Prof. of Cosmology, Mt Holyoke, 1982–83; Prof., Univ. of Virginia, 1983–84. Dir, Harvard Nuclear Lab., 1948–50, 1952; Chm., Harvard Nuclear Physics Cttee, 1948–60; Science Adviser, NATO, 1958–59; Fellow: Amer. Phys. Soc. and Amer. Acad. of Arts and Sciences; Nat. Acad. of Sciences; Amer. Philos. Soc.; Foreign Associate, French Acad. of Science; Sigma Xi; Phi Beta Kappa; Amer. Assoc. for Advancement of Science, 1940– (Chm., Phys. Sect., 1976). Bd of Directors, Varian Associates, 1964–66; Bd of Trustees: Associated Univs; Brookhaven Nat. Lab., 1952–55; Carnegie Endowment for Internat. Peace; Univ. Research Assoc. (Pres., 1966–81, Pres. Emeritus, 1981–); Rockefeller Univ., 1976–; Air Force Sci. Adv. Bd, 1948–54; Dept of Defense Panel on Atomic Energy, 1953–59; Bd of Editors of Review of Modern Physics, 1953–56; Chm. Exec. Cttee for Camb. Electron Accelerator, 1956–63; Council, Amer. Phys. Soc., 1956–60 (Vice-Pres., 1977; Pres., 1978); Chm., Bd of Governors, Amer. Inst. of Physics, 1980–86. Gen. Adv. Cttee, Atomic Energy Commn, 1960–72. Chm., High Energy Accelerator Panel of President's Sci. Adv. Cttee and AEC, 1963. Chm. Bd, Physics and Astronomy Nat. Res. Council, 1986–89. Pres., Phi Beta Kappa, 1985 (Vice-Pres., 1982). Presidential Certificate of Merit, 1947; E. O. Lawrence Award, 1960; Davisson-Germer Prize, 1974; Award for Excellence, Columbia Univ. Graduate Alumni, 1980; Medal of Honor, IEEE, 1984; Rabi Prize, Frequency Control Symposium, IEEE, 1985; Monie Ferst Prize, Sigma Xi, 1985; Compton Award, Amer. Inst. of Physics, 1985; Rumford Premium, Amer. Acad. of Arts and Scis, 1985; Oersted Medal, Amer. Assoc. of Physics Teachers, 1988; Nat. Medal of Science, 1988; (jtly) Nobel Prize for Physics, 1989; Pupin Medal, Columbia Univ., 1992; Erice Science for Peace Prize, 1992; Einstein Medal, Optical and Quantum Electronics Soc., 1993; Vannevar Bush Award, US Nat. Sci. Bd, 1995; Alexander Hamilton Award, Columbia Univ., 1995. Hon. MA Harvard, 1947; Hon. ScD Cambridge, 1953; Hon. DSc: Case Western Reserve, 1968; Middlebury Coll., 1969; Oxford, 1973; Rockefeller Univ., 1986; Chicago, 1989; Houston, 1992; Michigan, 1993; Harvard, 2006; Hon. DCL Oxford, 1990. *Publications:* Experimental Nuclear Physics, 1952; Nuclear Moments, 1953; Molecular Beams, 1956; Quick Calculus, 1965; Spectroscopy with Coherent Radiation, 1999; and numerous articles in Physical Review and other scientific jls. *Recreations:* tennis, ski-ing, walking, sailing, etc. *Address:* 24 Monmouth Court, Brookline, MA 02446, USA. *T:* (617) 2772313. *Died 4 Nov. 2011.*

RANDALL OF ST BUDEAUX, Baron *cr* 1997 (Life Peer), of St Budeaux in the co. of Devon; **Stuart Jeffrey Randall;** *b* 22 June 1938; *m* 1963, Gillian Michael; three *d*. *Educ:* University Coll., Cardiff (BSc Elect. Engrg). English Electric Computers and Radio Corp. of America, USA, 1963–66; Marconi Automation, 1966–68; Inter-Bank Res. Orgn, 1968–71; BSC, 1971–76; BL, 1976–80; Nexos Office Systems, 1980–81; Plessey Communications Systems, 1981–83. MP (Lab) Hull West, 1983–97. PPS to Shadow Chancellor of the Exchequer, 1984–85; Opposition front bench spokesman on Agricl, Food and Fisheries Affairs, 1985–87, on Home Affairs, 1987–92. *Recreations:* sailing, flying, jazz, opera. *Address:* House of Lords, SW1A 0PW. *Died 11 Aug. 2012.*

RANDOLPH, Denys, BSc; CEng, MRAeS, FIProdE, FIET, FInstD; Director, Partnership Wines Ltd, 1995–2000; *b* 6 Feb. 1926; *s* of late Harry Beckham Randolph and Margaret Isabel Randolph; *m* 1951, Marjorie Hales; two *d*. *Educ:* St Paul's School; Queen's Univ., Belfast (BSc). Served Royal Engineers, 1944–48 (Captain). Queen's Univ., Belfast, 1948–52; post-grad. apprenticeship, Short Bros & Harland, 1952–55; Wilkinson Sword Ltd: Prodn Engr/Prodn Dir, Graviner Div., 1955–66; Man. Dir, Hand Tools Div., 1966–69; Chm., Graviner Div., 1969–79; Chm., 1972–79; Pres., 1980–85; Wilkinson Match Ltd: Dir, 1974–80; Chm., 1976–79. Chairman: Woodrush Investments Ltd, 1980–93; Poitires Eyots Ltd, 1972–93; Dir, Henley Distance Learning Ltd, 1985–94. Proprietor, Clapcot Vineyards, 1986–98. Institute of Directors: Chm., 1976–79; Vice-Pres., 1979–96. Past Master: Worshipful Co. of Scientific Instrument Makers, 1977; Cutlers' Co., 1986. Mem. Council, Brunel Univ., 1986–91; Governor, Henley Admin. Staff Coll., 1979–91. CIMgt; FRSA (Manufactures and Commerce). *Publications:* From Rapiers to Razor Blades—The Development of the Light Metals Industry (paper, RSA). *Recreation:* viticulture. *Died 27 Jan. 2015.*

RANGER, Prof. Terence Osborn, DPhil; FBA 1988; Rhodes Professor of Race Relations, and Fellow of St Antony's College, University of Oxford, 1987–97, then Emeritus Professor and Fellow; *b* 29 Nov. 1929; *s* of Leslie Ranger and Anna Ranger (*née* Bradford); *m* 1953, Shelagh Campbell Clarke; two *d* (and one *d* decd). *Educ:* Highgate Sch.; Queen's Coll., Oxford (BA, MA; DPhil 1960). Lecturer: RNC, Dartmouth, 1955–56; UC of Rhodesia and Nyasaland, 1957–63; Prof. of History, UC, of Dar es Salaam, 1963–69; Prof. of African History, Univ. of Calif, LA, 1969–74; Prof. of Modern History, Univ. of Manchester, 1974–87; Chm., Oxford Univ. Cttee on African Studies, 1987–94. Vis. Prof., Univ. of Zimbabwe, 1998–2001. Chm., Jl of Southern African Studies, 1976–92; Vice-Chm., Past and Present, 1987–. Hon. DLitt Zimbabwe, 1995. *Publications:* Revolt in Southern Rhodesia 1896–7, 1967; The African Voice in Southern Rhodesia 1898–1930, 1970; Dance and Society in Eastern Africa, 1975; Peasant Consciousness and Guerrilla War in

Zimbabwe, 1985; Are We Not Also Men?, 1995; Voices From the Rocks: nature, culture and history in the Matopos mountains in Zimbabwe, 1999; (jtly) Violence and Memory: one hundred years in the dark forests of Matabeleland, 2000; Bulaway Burning: the social history of a Southern African city, 1893–1960, 2010; Writing Revolt: encounters with African Nationalism, 1957–67, 2013. *Recreations:* theatre, opera, walking. *Address:* Ground Floor, 100 Woodstock Road, Oxford OX2 7NE. *E:* terence.ranger@sant.ox.ac.uk. *Died 3 Jan. 2015.*

RANKIN, Andrew; QC 1968; a Recorder of the Crown Court, 1972–97; *b* 3 Aug. 1924; *s* of William Locke Rankin and Mary Ann McArdle, Edinburgh; *m* 1st, 1944, Winifred (marr. diss. 1963), *d* of Frank McAdam, Edinburgh; one *s* two *d* (and two *s* decd); 2nd, 1964, Veronica (*d* 1990), *d* of George Aloysius Martin, Liverpool; 3rd, 1991, Jenifer Margaret, *d* of Alfred George Hodges Bebington, Wirral. *Educ:* Royal High Sch., Edinburgh; Univ. of Edinburgh (BL 1946); Downing Coll., Cambridge (BA 1st cl. hons Law Tripos 1948). Served War of 1939–45: Sub-Lt, RNVR, 1943. Royal Commonwealth Soc. Medal, 1942; Cecil Peace Prize, 1946; Lord Justice Holker Exhibn, Gray's Inn, 1947–50; Lord Justice Holker Schol., Gray's Inn, 1950–53; Univ. Blue, Edin., 1943 and 1946 and Camb., 1948. Lectr in Law, Univ. of Liverpool, 1948–52. Called to Bar, Gray's Inn, 1950. *Publications:* (ed, 4th edn) Levie's Law of Bankruptcy in Scotland, 1950; various articles in UK and foreign legal jls. *Recreations:* swimming, travel by sea, racing (both codes), watching soccer (especially Liverpool FC). *Address:* Chelwood, Pine Walks, Prenton, Birkenhead, Merseyside CH42 8LQ. *T:* (0151) 608 2987. *Died 11 Feb. 2015.*

RANNIE, Prof. Ian, FRCPath; FSB; Professor of Pathology (Dental School), University of Newcastle upon Tyne, 1960–81, Professor Emeritus 1981; *b* 29 Oct. 1915; *o s* of James Rannie, MA, and Nicholas Denniston McMeekan; *m* 1943, Flora Welch (decd); two *s*. *Educ:* Ayr Academy; Glasgow Univ. (BSc 1935; MB, ChB 1938; BSc Hons Pathology and Bacteriology 1939; Hutcheson Research Schol. (Pathology) 1940). FRCPath 1964; FSB (FIBiol 1964). Assistant to Professor of Bacteriology, Glasgow, 1940–42; Lecturer in Pathology, 1942–60, King's College, Univ. of Durham. Consultant Pathologist, United Newcastle upon Tyne Hospitals, 1948–81, Hon. Consultant, 1981–. Pres., International Soc. of Geographical Pathology, 1969–72; Vice-President: Assoc. of Clinical Pathologists, 1978–80; Internat. Union of Angiology. Hon. Mem., Hungarian Arteriosclerosis Res. Soc. *Publications:* papers on various subjects in medical journals. *Address:* Apartment G, 8 Osborne Villas, Newcastle upon Tyne NE2 1JU. *T:* (0191) 281 3163. *Club:* Royal Over-Seas League. *Died 30 Aug. 2013.*

RAPER, (Alfred) Graham, CBE 1988; PhD; FREng; Chairman, Projecta, consulting engineers, 1987–99; Chief Executive and Deputy Chairman, Davy Corporation, 1985–87; *b* 15 May 1932; *s* of Hilda and Alfred William Raper; *m* 1st, Elizabeth Williams (marr. diss. 1975); two *s* one *d*; 2nd, Valerie Benson; one *s*. *Educ:* Lady Manners School, Bakewell; Univ. of Sheffield (BScTech Hons, PhD). FREng (FEng 1986); FIChemE. Asst Lectr, Univ. of Sheffield, 1955–57; Research Engineer, Head Wrightson Co., 1957–59; Technical Manager, Davy United Engineering, 1959–65; Steel Plant Manager, Highveld Steel & Vanadium, S Africa, 1965–69; joined Davy Corp., 1969; Vice-Chm., Kvaerner Davy, 1995–97. Non-exec. Dir, Vosper Thornycroft (UK) Ltd, 1995–2001. *Publications:* articles in jls of Iron & Steel Institute and British Association. *Recreations:* golf, gardening. *Address:* 54 Golf Links Road, Ferndown, Wimborne, Dorset BH22 8BZ. *T:* (01202) 873512. *Died 14 Nov. 2013.*

RAPHAEL, Prof. David Daiches, DPhil, MA; Emeritus Professor of Philosophy, University of London, since 1983; *b* 25 Jan. 1916; 2nd *s* of late Jacob Raphael and Sarah Warshawsky, Liverpool; *m* 1942, Sylvia (*d* 1996), *er d* of late Rabbi Dr Salis Daiches and Flora Levin, Edinburgh; two *d*. *Educ:* Liverpool Collegiate School; University College, Oxford (scholar). 1st Class, Classical Moderations, 1936; Hall-Houghton Junior Septuagint Prizeman, 1937; 1st Class, Literae Humaniores, 1938; Robinson Senior Scholar of Oriel College, Oxford, 1938–40; Passmore Edwards Scholar, 1939. Served in Army, 1940–41. Temporary Assistant Principal, Ministry of Labour and National Service, 1941–44; temp. Principal, 1944–46. Professor of Philosophy, University of Otago, Dunedin, NZ, 1946–49; Lecturer in Moral Philosophy, Univ. of Glasgow, 1949–51; Senior Lecturer, 1951–60; Edward Caird Prof. of Political and Social Philosophy, Univ. of Glasgow, 1960–70; Prof. of Philosophy, Univ. of Reading, 1970–73; Prof. of Philosophy, Imperial Coll., Univ. of London, 1973–83 (Acad. Dir of Associated Studies, 1973–80; Head of Dept of Humanities, 1980–83; Hon. Fellow 1987). Visiting Professor of Philosophy, Hamilton Coll., Clinton, NY (under Chauncey S. Truax Foundation), and Univ. of Southern California, 1959; Mahlon Powell Lectr, Indiana Univ., 1959; Vis. Fellow, All Souls Coll., Oxford, 1967–68; John Hinkley Vis. Prof. of Political Sci., Johns Hopkins Univ., 1984. Independent Member: Cttee on Teaching Profession in Scotland (Wheatley Cttee), 1961–63; Scottish Agricultural Wages Board, 1962–84; Agricultural Wages Bd for England and Wales, 1972–78. Mem. Academic Adv. Cttee, Heriot-Watt Univ., Edinburgh, 1964–71; Mem. Cttee on Distribution of Teachers in Scotland (Roberts Cttee), 1965–66; Independent Member Police Advisory Board for Scotland, 1965–70; Member Social Sciences Adv. Cttee, UK Nat. Commission, UNESCO, 1966–74; Vice-Pres., Internat. Assoc. Philosophy of Law and Social Philosophy, 1971–87; Pres., Aristotelian Soc., 1974–75. Academic Mem., Bd of Govs, Hebrew Univ. of Jerusalem, 1969–81, Hon. Gov., 1981–. Chm., Westminster Synagogue, 1987–89. *Publications:* The Moral Sense, 1947; Edition of Richard Price's Review of Morals, 1948; Moral Judgement, 1955; The Paradox of Tragedy, 1960; Political Theory and the Rights of Man, 1967; British Moralists 1650–1800, 1969; Problems of Political Philosophy, 1970, 2nd edn 1990; (ed jtly) Adam Smith's Theory of Moral Sentiments, 1976; Hobbes: Morals and Politics, 1977; (ed jtly) Adam Smith's Lectures on Jurisprudence, 1978; (ed jtly) Adam Smith's Essays on Philosophical Subjects, 1980; Justice and Liberty, 1980; Moral Philosophy, 1981, 2nd edn 1994; (trans. jtly with Sylvia Raphael) Richard Price as Moral Philosopher and Political Theorist, by Henri Laboucheix, 1982; Adam Smith, 1985; Concepts of Justice, 2001; The Impartial Spectator, 2007; articles in jls of philosophy and of political studies. *Address:* 54 Sandy Lane, Petersham, Richmond, Surrey TW10 7EL. *Died 22 Dec. 2015.*

RASHBASS, Dr Barbara, FRCP; Director and Secretary: Wolfson Foundation, 1990–97; Wolfson Family Charitable Trust, 1989–97; *d* of late Leonard Cramer and Sarina (*née* Klinger); *m* 1956, Cyril Rashbass (*d* 1982); two *s* one *d*. *Educ:* Godolphin Sch., Salisbury; University Coll. London (MB, BS; Fellow 1999). DCH 1961; DPH 1968; FRCP 1995. Called to the Bar, Middle Temple, 1969. PMO, MRC, 1983–87. Dep. Chm., Harrow HA, 1982–84; non-exec. Dir, Harrow and Hillingdon Healthcare NHS Trust, 1998–2001. Mem., Med. Legal Soc., 1970–2002. FRSocMed 1989–2007. Trustee, Ronald Raven Cancer Res. Trust, 2000–02. *Died 6 April 2013.*

RATTRAY, Hon. (Raphael) Carl, OJ 1994; President, Court of Appeal, Jamaica, 1993–99; *b* 18 Sept. 1929; *s* of late Benjamin Bruce Rattray and Agnes Agatha Rattray (*née* Wright); *m* 1951, Audrey Elaine Da Costa; two *s* two *d*. *Educ:* Beckford Smith's High Sch., Jamaica; Univ. of London (ext. LLB). Called to the Bar, Lincoln's Inn, 1956; Stipendiary Magistrate, Cayman Is, 1957–58; in private practice at Jamaican Bar, 1958–75; QC (Jamaica) 1969; Senator, Jamaican Parlt, 1975–83; Attorney Gen. and Minister of Justice, 1976–80; Leader: Govt Business in Senate, 1975–80; Opposition Business in Senate, 1980–83; Founding Mem., Rattray, Patterson, Rattray, 1981; in practice at Bar, 1981–89; MP (PNP), 1989–93; Attorney Gen. and Minister of Legal Affairs, 1989–92. Vice-Pres., Jamaican Bar Council, 1988–89. Hon. LLD Capital, Columbus, Ohio, 1990. *Publications:* Firstlings: a collection of poems, 1951; contrib. to Caribbean Law Rev., Jamaican Law Jl. *Recreations:* reading, writing, walking. *Address:* 4 Rockhampton Drive, Kingston 8, Jamaica. *T:* 9252723. *Died 14 March 2012.*

RAVEN, John Armstrong, CBE 1982; Director-General, International Express Carriers' Conference, 1991–93 and 1995–99 (Director (Facilitation), 1993–94); Adviser: World Bank, 1983–2005; International Air Cargo Association, since 2000; *b* 23 April 1920; *s* of late John Colbeck Raven; *m* 1st, 1945, Megan Humphreys (*d* 1963); one *s* one *d*; 2nd, 1965, Joy Nesbitt (*d* 1983); one step *d*; 3rd, 2011, Lucienne Sabatier. *Educ:* High Sch., Cardiff; Downing Coll., Cambridge (MA). Called to Bar, Gray's Inn, 1955. Dir, British Coal Exporters' Fedn, 1947–68; Section Head, Nat. Economic Develt Office, 1968–70. Dir-Gen., Assoc. of British Chambers of Commerce, 1972–74; Vice-Chm., SITPRO, 1974–82. *Recreation:* wondering. *Address:* 215 Avenue de Messidor, 1180 Brussels, Belgium. *T:* (2) 3457620. *Club:* Oxford and Cambridge. *Died 6 Nov. 2011.*

RAWCLIFFE, Rt Rev. Derek Alec, OBE 1971; Bishop of Glasgow and Galloway, 1981–91; *b* 8 July 1921; *s* of James Alec and Gwendoline Rawcliffe; *m* 1977, Susan Speight (*d* 1987). *Educ:* Sir Thomas Rich's School, Gloucester; Univ. of Leeds (BA, 1st cl. Hons English); College of the Resurrection, Mirfield. Deacon 1944, priest 1945, Worcester; Assistant Priest, Claines St George, Worcester, 1944–47; Asst master, All Hallows School, Pawa, Solomon Islands, 1947–53; Headmaster, 1953–56; Headmaster, S Mary's School, Maravovo, Solomon Is, 1956–58; Archdeacon of Southern Melanesia, New Hebrides, 1959–74; Assistant Bishop, Diocese of Melanesia, 1974–75; First Bishop of the New Hebrides, 1975–80; Asst Bishop, dio. of Ripon, 1991–96. New Hebrides Medal, 1980; Vanuatu Independence Medal, 1980. *Publications:* The Meaning of it All is Love (articles and essays), 2000; Pilgrimage to Melanesia, 2005; Gethsemane to Calvary, 2006; *poems:* The Stone and the Hazel Nut, 2000; Seasons of the Spirit, 2003; The White Blackbird, 2005. *Recreations:* music, poetry. *Address:* 7 Dorset Avenue, Leeds LS8 3RA. *T:* (0113) 249 2670. *Died 1 Feb. 2011.*

RAWLEY, Alan David; QC 1977; a Recorder of the Crown Court, 1972–99; Fellow Commoner, Magdalene College, Cambridge, since 1991; *b* 28 Sept. 1934; *er s* of late Cecil David Rawley and of Theresa Rawley (*née* Pack); *m* 1964, Ione Jane Ellis; two *s* one *d*. *Educ:* Wimbledon Coll.; Brasenose Coll., Oxford. Nat. Service, 1956–58; commnd Royal Tank Regt. Called to the Bar, Middle Temple, 1958; Bencher, 1985; Autumn Reader, 2004. Dep. Chairman, Cornwall Quarter Sessions, 1971. Member: CICB, 1999–2000; CICAP, 2000–08. *Address:* Outer Temple Chambers, 222 Strand, WC2R 1BA. *T:* (020) 7353 6381. *Clubs:* Garrick, Pilgrims, MCC. *Died 26 Aug. 2014.*

RAWLINS, Surg. Vice-Adm. Sir John (Stuart Pepys), KBE 1978 (OBE 1960; MBE 1956); *b* 12 May 1922; *s* of Col S. W. H. Rawlins, CB, CMG, DSO and Dorothy Pepys Cockerell; *m* 1944, Diana Margaret Freshney Colbeck (*d* 1992); one *s* three *d*. *Educ:* Wellington Coll.; University Coll., Oxford (Hon. Fellow, 1991); St Bartholomew's Hospital. BM, BCh 1945; MA, FRCP, FFPH, FRAeS. Surg. Lieut RNVR, HMS Triumph, 1947; Surg. Lieut RN, RAF Inst. Aviation Med., 1951; RN Physiol Lab., 1957; Surg. Comdr RAF Inst., Aviation Med., 1961; HMS Ark Royal, 1964; US Navy Medical Research Inst., 1967; Surg. Captain 1969; Surg. Cdre, Dir of Health and Research (Naval), 1973; Surg. Rear-Adm. 1975; Dean of Naval Medicine and MO i/c, Inst. of Naval Medicine, 1975–77; Actg Surg. Vice-Adm. 1977; Medical Dir-Gen. (Navy), 1977–80. QHP 1975. Chairman: Deep Ocean Engineering Inc., 1983–89; Medical Express Ltd, 1984–; Trident Underwater Engrg (Systems) Ltd, 1985–; General Offshore Corp. (UK) Ltd, 1988–91; Director: Diving Unlimited International Ltd, 1980–; Deep Ocean Technology Inc., 1989– (Chm., 1983–89); Deep Ocean Engrg, 1989–91. Pres., Soc. for Underwater Technology, 1980–84 (Hon. Fellow, 1986); Vice-Pres., Underseas Med. Soc.; Hon. Life Mem., British Sub-Aqua Club, 1983; Founder-Mem. European Underseas Biomed. Soc.; Fellow Aerospace Med. Soc. (Armstrong Lectr, 1980); FRAeS 1973; FRSocMed. Hon. Fellow, Lancaster Univ., 1986. Hon. DTech Robert Gordon's Inst. of Technology, 1991. Erroll-Eldridge Prize 1967; Sec. of US Navy's Commendation 1971; Gilbert Blane Medal 1971; Tuttle Meml Award 1973; Chadwick Medal and Prize 1975; Nobel Award, Inst. of Explosives Engrs, 1987; NOGI Award, US Acad. of Underwater Arts and Scis, 1998; Colin McLeod Award, British Sub-Aqua Club, 2000; Lowell Thomas Award, Explorers' Club, 2000; Man of the Year, British Council for Rehabilitation of the Disabled, 1964. *Publications:* papers in fields of aviation and diving medicine. *Recreations:* diving, fishing, stalking, riding. *Address:* Little Cross, Holne, Newton Abbot, S Devon TQ13 7RS. *T:* (01364) 631249. *Club:* Vincent's (Oxford). *Died 27 July 2011.*

RAWLINSON, Dennis George Fielding, OBE 1978; JP; FCILT; company director; *b* 3 Sept. 1919; *s* of George and Mary Jane Rawlinson; *m* 1943, Lilian Mary; one *s* one *d*. *Educ:* Grocers' Co. Sch. Army, 1939–46. Various progressive positions in omnibus industry; Mem. Bd, Nat. Bus Co., 1979–84 (Northern Regl Dir, 1974–84). Mem., Transport Tribunal, 1986–91. JP Darlington, 1971. *Recreations:* theatre, music, golf and various lesser sports. *Address:* 62 Cleveland Avenue, Darlington, Co. Durham DL3 7HG. *T:* (01325) 461254. *Club:* Army and Navy. *Died 10 June 2013.*

RAY, Philip Bicknell, CMG 1969; Ministry of Defence, 1947–76; *b* 10 July 1917; *s* of late Basil Ray and Clare (*née* Everett); *m* 1946, Bridget Mary Robertson (decd); two *s* one *d*. *Educ:* Felsted Sch.; Selwyn Coll., Cambridge (MA). Indian Police, 1939–47 (Indian Police Medal, 1944). *Publications:* Jesus Through the Spyglass, 2005, rev. edn publd posthumously as The Committed Carpenter, 2012. *Address:* 3 South Green Road, Newnham, Cambridge CB3 9JP. *Died 23 Oct. 2011.*

RAYCHAUDHURI, Prof. Tapan Kumar, DPhil, DLitt; Professor of Indian History and Civilisation, University of Oxford, 1992–93; Fellow, St Antony's College, Oxford, 1973–93, then Emeritus; *b* 8 May 1926; *s* of Amiya Kumar and Prativa Raychaudhuri; *m* 1960, Pratima Sen-Roy; one *d*. *Educ:* Presidency Coll., Calcutta; Balliol Coll., Oxford. MA, DPhil Calcutta; MA, DPhil, DLitt Oxon. Lectr, Calcutta Univ., 1948–55; Dep. Dir, Nat. Archives of India, 1957–59 (Acting Dir, 1957–58); Delhi School of Economics: Reader in Econ. History, 1959–64; Prof., 1964–70; Dir, 1965–67; Prof. of History, Delhi Univ., 1971–72; Reader in Mod. S Asian History, Univ. of Oxford, 1973–92. Visiting Professor: Duke Univ., 1964; Univ. of Calif., Berkeley, 1964; Univ. of Penn., 1969; Harvard, 1969–70; El Colegio de México, 1981; Univ. of Sydney, 1986. Fellow: Woodrow Wilson Center, 1993–94; Wissenschaftskolleg zu Berlin, 1997–98; Nat. Res. Prof., 2011. Gen. Ed (with D. Kumar), Cambridge Economic History of India, 1982–83. Hon. DLitt: Burdwan, 1998; Calcutta, 2003; Vidyasagar, 2007. Padma Bhushan, 2007. *Publications:* Bengal under Akbar and Jahangir: an introductory study in social history, 1953, 2nd edn 1969; Jan Company in Coromandel 1605–1690: European trade and Asia's traditional economies, 1962; (ed with I. Habib) Cambridge Economic History of India, vol. I, 1982, vol. II, 1983; Europe Reconsidered: perceptions of the West in Nineteenth Century Bengal, 1986, 2nd edn 2003; Perceptions, Sensibilities, Emotions: essays on India's Colonial and post-Colonial experiences, 1999; (with G. Forbes) Memoirs of Dr Haimavati Sen: from child widow to lady doctor, 2000; The World in our Time—a memoir, 2012; (in Bengali): Romanathan, 1993; Bangalnama (memoirs), 2007; Pravandha-Samgraha (essays), 2009; contrib. Desh mag. *Recreations:* travel, cinema, reading. *Address:* 1 Hawkswell Gardens, Oxford OX2 7EX. *T:* (01865) 559421. *E:* tapanraychaudhuri2010@gmail.com. *Died 26 Nov. 2014.*

RAYMOND, William Francis, CBE 1978; FRSC; agricultural science consultant; *b* 25 Feb. 1922; *m* 1949, Amy Elizabeth Kelk; three *s* one *d*. *Educ:* Bristol Grammar Sch.; The Queen's Coll., Oxford (MA). Research Officer, MRC, 1943–45; Head of Animal Science Div. and later Asst Dir, Grassland Research Inst., Hurley, 1945–72; Dep. Chief Scientist, 1972–81, Chief Scientist (Agriculture and Horticulture), 1981–82, MAFF. Mem., ARC, 1981–82. Sec., 8th Internat. Grassland Congress, 1960; President: Brit. Grassland Soc., 1974–75; Brit. Soc. Animal Production, 1981–82. Vis. Prof. in Agriculture, Wye Coll., 1978–83. Chm., Stapledon Meml Trust, 1983–93;

Member: Policy Cttee, CPRE, 1993–96; Cttee, Family Farmers' Assoc., 1996– (Vice-Chm., 1998); Hon. Treas., RURAL, 1984–2009; Chm., Internat. Agricl Res. Review, Council for Res. Policy, Denmark, 1992; Mem., Internat. Agricl Res. Review, Min. of Agric. and Forestry, Finland, 1996. Chm., Henley and Mapledurham Dist, CPRE, 2001–06. *Publications:* (with Shepperson and Waltham) Forage Conservation and Feeding, 1972, 5th edn 1996; EEC Agricultural Research Framework Programme, 1983; Research in Support of Agricultural Policies in Europe, FAO Regional Conf., Reykjavik, 1984; over 250 papers in scientific jls. *Recreation:* gardening. *Address:* Periwinkle Cottage, Christmas Common, Watlington OX49 5HR. *T:* (01491) 612942. *Died 2 Aug. 2012.*

READ, Miss; *see* Saint, D. J.

READ, Air Marshal Sir Charles (Frederick), KBE 1976 (CBE 1964); CB 1972; DFC 1942; AFC 1958; Chief of the Air Staff, RAAF, 1972–75; *b* Sydney, NSW, 9 Oct. 1918; *s* of J. F. Read, Bristol, England; *m* 1946, Betty E. (*d* 2005), *d* of A. V. Bradshaw; three *s*. *Educ:* Sydney Grammar Sch. Former posts include: OC, RAAF Base, Point Cook, Vic., 1965–68; OC, RAAF, Richmond, NSW, 1968–70; Dep. Chief of Air Staff, 1969–72. *Recreation:* yachting. *Address:* 18 Ocean Drive, Safety Beach, Woolgoolga, NSW 2456, Australia. *T:* (2) 66540883. *Died 17 Sept. 2014.*

READ, Brig. Gregory, CBE 1984; Clerk to Vintners' Company, 1984–96; *b* 11 Oct. 1934; *s* of Edward Charles Read and Margaret Florence Maud Holdsworth; *m* 1957, Rosemary Patricia Frost; three *s*. *Educ:* Sherborne Sch.; RMA Sandhurst; RMCS Shrivenham (BSc Eng 1959); Open Univ. (BA Hons 2001). Commnd RTR, 1955; Comd 3 RTR, 1973–76; Comd RAC 1 (BR) Corps, 1979–81; Dir, Combat Develt, 1981; Dir, Battlefield Doctrine, 1982–84. Mem., Wine Standards Board, 1984–96; Trustee, Wine and Spirit Educn Trust, 1989–92. Vice-Chm., Riverpoint Charity, 1996–98 (Trustee, 1994–2001); Chm., S Wilts MENCAP, 2004–13 (Pres., 2000–04); Dir, Wessex Community Action, 2005–. *Recreations:* marathons, European history, travel. *Address:* The Girnel, Broad Chalke, Salisbury, Wilts SP5 5EN. *T:* (01722) 780276. *Died 7 Oct. 2014.*

READ, Sir John (Emms), Kt 1976; FCA 1947; President, Charities Aid Foundation, 1994–98 (Trustee, 1985–98; Chairman of Trustees, 1990–94); *b* 29 March 1918; *s* of late William Emms Read and of Daysie Elizabeth (*née* Cooper); *m* 1942, Dorothy Millicent Berry (*d* 2004); two *s*. *Educ:* Brighton, Hove and Sussex Grammar Sch. Served Royal Navy, 1939–46 (rank of Comdr (S) RNVR); Admiral's Secretary: to Asst Chief of Naval Staff, Admty, 1942–45; to Brit. Admty Technical Mission, Ottawa, Canada, 1945–46. Ford Motor Co. Ltd, 1946–64 (Admin. Staff Coll., Henley, 1952), Dir of Sales, 1961–64; Dir, Electric and Musical Industries Ltd, 1965–87; EMI Group: Jt Man. Dir, 1967; Chief Exec., 1969–79; Dep. Chm., 1973–74; Chm., 1974–79; Thorn EMI: Dep. Chm., 1979–81, Dir, 1981–87. Director: Capitol Industries-EMI Inc., 1970–83; Dunlop Holdings Ltd, 1971–84; Thames Television, 1973–88 (Dep. Chm., 1981–88); Wonderworld plc, 1984–97; Hill Samuel Gp, 1987–88; Caflash (formerly Cafman) Ltd, 1990–98; Chairman: TSB Holdings Ltd, 1980–86; Trustee Savings Banks Central Bd, 1980–88; Central TSB Ltd, 1983–86; TSB England and Wales, 1983–86; TSB Gp plc, 1986–88; UDT, 1981–85; Target Gp plc, 1987–88; FI Group plc, 1989–93. Chm., EDC for Electronics Industry, 1977–80. Member: (part time), PO Bd, 1975–77; Engineering Industries Council, 1975–80; BOTB, 1976–79; Armed Forces Pay Review Body, 1976–83; Nat. Electronics Council, 1977–80; Groupe des Présidents des Grandes Enterprises Européennes, 1977–80. Vice-Pres., Inst. of Bankers, 1982–89. Gen. Partner, Midland Enterprise Bd for SE, 1991–98; Member: RN Film Corp., 1975–83; Brighton Festival Soc. Council of Management, 1977–82; CBI Council, 1977–90 (Mem., Presidents' Cttee, 1977–84; Chm., F&GP Cttee, 1978–84); White Ensign Assoc. Council of Management, 1979–95; Council, The Prince's Youth Business Trust, 1987–89; Nat. Theatre Develt Council, 1987–90; Court, Surrey Univ., 1986–96; Governing Body and F&GP Cttee, BPMF, London Univ., 1982–96 (Dep. Chm., 1987–96); Governing Council, Business in the Community, 1985–89; Council, British Heart Foundn, 1986–89; Chm., Inst. of Neurology Council of Management, 1980–97; Trustee: Westminster Abbey Trust, 1978–85; Brain Res. Trust, 1982–2002 (Chm., 1986–2002); Crimestoppers Trust (formerly Community Action Trust), 1987–2001; Eyeless Trust, 1991–2002; Dir and Trustee, Brighton Fest. Trust, 1977–92; Dir, NCVO Ltd, 1990–94. President: SABC Clubs for Young People (formerly Sussex Assoc. of Boys' Clubs), 1982–97; Cheshire Homes, Seven Rivers, Essex, 1979–85; Governor, Admin. Staff Coll., Henley, 1974–92 (Hon. Fellow 1993). CCMI (FBIM 1974); CompIERE 1974; FIB 1982. Hon. Fellow, UCL, 1999. DUniv Surrey, 1989; Hon. DBA Internat. Management Centre, Buckingham, 1990. *Recreations:* music, arts, sports, various charities. *Club:* MCC. *Died 4 April 2015.*

READ, Lionel Frank; QC 1973; a Recorder of the Crown Court, 1974–98; a Deputy High Court Judge, 1989–98; *b* 7 Sept. 1929; *s* of late F. W. C. Read and Lilian (*née* Chatwin); *m* 1956, Shirley Greenhalgh; two *s* one *d*. *Educ:* Oundle Sch.; St John's Coll., Cambridge (MA). Mons OCS Stick of Honour; commnd 4 RHA, 1949. Called to Bar, Gray's Inn, 1954, Bencher, 1981 (Treas., 2001); Mem., Senate of the Inns of Court and the Bar, 1974–77. A Gen. Comr of Income Tax, Gray's Inn Div., 1986–90. Chm., Local Government and Planning Bar Assoc., 1990–94 (Vice-Chm., 1986–90); Member: Bar Council, 1990–94; Council on Tribunals, 1990–96. *Recreations:* reading, travel. *Address:* Cedarwood, Church Road, Ham Common, Surrey TW10 5HG. *T:* (020) 8940 5247. *Clubs:* Garrick; Hawks (Cambridge). *Died 9 Nov. 2015.*

READING, Peter Gray, FRSL; writer, since 1970; *b* 27 July 1946; *s* of Wilfred Gray Reading and Ethel Mary Reading; *m* 1st, 1968, Diana Joy Gilbert (marr. diss. 1996); one *d*; 2nd, 1996, Deborah Joyce Jackson (marr. diss. 2002); 3rd, 2002, Penelope Anne Hamblen. *Educ:* Liverpool Coll. of Art (BA Fine Art and Painting). Art Teacher, Ruffwood Sch., 1967–68; Lectr, Liverpool Coll. of Art, 1968–70; animal feedmill worker, 1970–92. FRSL 1988. *Publications: poetry:* Water and Waste, 1970; For the Municipality's Elderly, 1974; The Prison Cell and Barrel Mystery, 1976; Nothing for Anyone, 1977; Fiction, 1979; Tom o'Bedlam's Beauties, 1981; Diplopic, 1983; 5x5x5x5x5, 1983; C, 1984; Ukulele Music, 1985; Going On, 1985; Stet, 1986; Final Demands, 1988; Perduta Gente, 1989; Shitheads, 1989; Evagatory, 1992; Last Poems, 1994; Eschatological, 1996; Collected Poems, vol. 1, 1995, vol. 2, 1996, vol. 3, 2003; Work in Regress, 1997; Chinoiserie, 1997; Ob, 1998; Apothegmatic, 1999; Marfan, 2000; untitled, 2001; Faunal, 2002; –273.15, 2005; Vendange Tardive, 2010. *Recreations:* ornithology, natural sciences. *Address:* c/o Bloodaxe Books, Highgreen, Tarset, Northumberland NE48 1RP. *Died 17 Nov. 2011.*

REAY, 14th Lord *cr* 1628, of Reay, Caithness; **Hugh William Mackay;** Bt (NS), 1627; Baron Mackay of Ophemert and Zennewijnen, Holland; Chief of Clan Mackay; *b* 19 July 1937; *s* of 13th Lord Reay and Charlotte Mary Younger; *S* father, 1963; *m* 1st, 1964, Hon. Annabel Thérèse Fraser (marr. diss. 1978); two *s* one *d*; 2nd, 1980, Hon. Victoria Isabella Warrender, *d* of 1st Baron Bruntisfield, MC; two *d*. *Educ:* Eton; Christ Church. Mem., European Parlt, 1973–79 (Vice-Chm., Cons. Gp); Delegate, Council of Europe and WEU, 1979–86. Lord in Waiting (Govt Whip), 1989–91; Parly Under-Sec. of State, DTI, 1991–92; Mem., Select Cttee on European Communities, H of L, 1993–99 (Chm., Sub-Cttee on Food and Agric., 1996–99); elected Mem., H of L, 1999. *Heir: s* Master of Reay, *b* 20 March 1965. *Address:* House of Lords, SW1A 0PW. *Died 10 May 2013.*

REAY, Lt-Gen. Sir (Hubert) Alan (John), KBE 1981; FRCP, FRCPE; Chairman, Lambeth Health Care (formerly West Lambeth Community Care) NHS Trust, 1992–97; Director General, Army Medical Services, 1981–85; *b* 19 March 1925; *s* of Rev. John Reay; *m* 1960, Ferelith Haslewood Deane, artist and printmaker; two *s* two *d* (and one *s* decd). *Educ:* Lancing College; Edinburgh Univ. MB, DTM&H, DCH. FRCPE 1968; FRCP 1972. Field Medical Services, Malaya, 1949–52 (despatches); Exchange Physician, Brooke Hosp., San Antonio, Texas,

1957; Command Paediatrician: Far East, 1962; BAOR, 1965; Adviser in Paediatrics, MoD (Army), 1968; Hon. Out-patient Consultant, Great Ormond Street Hosp., 1975–79, 1985–87; QHP 1976–85; Postgraduate Dean and Comdt, Royal Army Med. Coll., 1977–79; DMS, HQ BAOR, 1979–81. Hon. Col, 217 (London) General Hosp. RAMC (Volunteers) TA, 1986–90. Chm., Med. Cttee, Royal Star and Garter Home, 1986–92. Member Council: SSAFA, 1986–93; RSocMed, 1987–91 (Pres., Paediatric Section, 1984–85). Pres., Friends of St Thomas' Hosp., 1993–2003. Vice-Chm., Thames Reach Homelessness Project, 1992–94; Chm., Mosaic Clubhouse for people with mental illness, 1997–2001; Trustee: Children's Hospice for Eastern Reg., Cambridge, 1988–97; Buttle Trust, 1991–2002. Chief Hon. Steward, Westminster Abbey, 1985–97. Inaugural Lectr, Soc. of Armed Forces Med. Consultants, Univ. of Health Scis, Bethesda, 1984. FRCPCH 1997 (Hon. Mem., BPA, 1988); Hon. FRCGP 1985. CStJ 1981 (OStJ 1979). *Publications:* paediatric articles in med. jls. *Address:* 63 Madrid Road, Barnes, SW13 9PQ. *Died 4 Feb. 2012.*

RECKERT, Prof. (Frederick) Stephen, FBA 1994; Camoens Professor of Portuguese, University of London, 1967–82, then Emeritus; Co-Founder, Institute for Study of Symbology, New University of Lisbon, 1980; Hon. Senior Research Fellow, School of Advanced Study, University of London, since 1995; *b* 31 May 1923; *oc* of Frederick Carl Reckert and Aileen Templeton Adams Reckert; *m* 1st, 1946, Olwen Roberts (*d* 1963); two *s* one *d*; 2nd, 1965, Dídia Mateus Marques. *Educ:* Phillips Exeter Acad., USA; Saybrook Coll., Yale (BA *summa cum laude* 1945, ranked first in class); Trinity Coll., Cambridge (MLitt 1948); Berkeley Coll., Yale (PhD 1950). Japanese translator with RAF, Bletchley, 1943–45; Fellow, Berkeley Coll. and Asst Prof. of Spanish, Yale, 1948–58; Prof. and Head of Hispanic Studies, Univ. of Wales, 1958–66; Head, Portuguese and Brazilian Studies, Univ. of London, 1967–82. Visiting Professor: Univ. of Madrid, 1971; New Univ., Lisbon, 1974–78; Univ. of Rome, 1985; Kate Elder Lectr, London Univ., 1996; Guest Lectr, Univs of Lisbon, Coimbra, Oporto, Évora, Seville, Warsaw, Jagiellonian Univ. of Cracow. Corresp. Fellow: Hispanic Soc. of America; Acad. of Scis, Lisbon (formerly Portuguese Acad. of Scis); Royal Spanish Acad. Hon. Fellow, Asociación Hispánica de Literatura Medieval. Mem., Phi Beta Kappa. Nobiling Medal for Medieval Studies, Brazil, 1978. Comendador, Order of Southern Cross (Brazil), 1979; Grand Cross, Order of Henry the Navigator (Portugal), 1990. *Publications:* (with Dámaso Alonso) Vida y Obra de Medrano, 1958; (with H. Macedo) Do Cancioneiro de Amigo, 1976, 3rd edn 1996; Gil Vicente, 1977; (with Y. K. Centeno) Fernando Pessoa, 1978; Espírito e Letra de Gil Vicente, 1986; Um Ramalhete para Cesário, 1987; Beyond Chrysanthemums, 1993; Play it Again, Sam, 1997; From the Resende Songbook, 1998; Más allá de las neblinas de noviembre, 2001; Presence of East Asia in Some Modern Portuguese Poets, 2001; Gil Terrón lletrudo está, 2001; The Sign of the City: visions of mythic space, 2003; Al alba venid, buen amigo, 2004; Cantigas Mínimas of a Pan-Iberian Poet, 2005; Itinerario de un iberista, 2006; The Other Latin, 2008; Identidade, Interioridade e Mutação na Poesia de Yvette Centeno, 2011; Time is of the Essence: essence, existence and reminiscence in Camões and Sá de Miranda, 2013; as Frederick Carlson: A Perfeição, Musée de l'Homme, Contos da Palma da Mão, 1994; Brasil e Alguns Poemas, 1999; contribs to jls and collective vols. *Recreations:* poetry, music, conviviality, ailurophilia. *Address:* Rua das Janelas Verdes 17–4°, 1200–690 Lisbon, Portugal. *T:* 213962292; Ayot Weir, Weybridge, Surrey KT13 8HR. *T:* (01932) 843589. *Clubs:* Oxford and Cambridge; PEN (Portuguese centre). *Died 17 Jan. 2013.*

REDDISH, Prof. Vincent Cartledge, OBE 1974; PhD, DSc; FRSE; Regius Professor of Astronomy, Edinburgh University, Director, Royal Observatory, Edinburgh, and Astronomer Royal for Scotland, 1975–80, then Professor Emeritus; *b* Leigh, Lancs, 28 April 1926; *s* of William H. M. Reddish and Evelyn Reddish; *m* 1951, Elizabeth Waltho; two *s*. *Educ:* Wigan Techn. Coll.; London Univ. (BSc Hons, PhD, DSc). Lectr in Astronomy, Edinburgh Univ., 1954; Lectr in Radio Astronomy, Manchester Univ., 1959; Royal Observatory, Edinburgh: Principal Scientific Officer, 1962; Sen. Principal Sci. Off., 1966; Dep. Chief Sci. Off., 1974. FRSE 1965. Governor, Rannoch Sch., 1981–97. *Publications:* Evolution of the Galaxies, 1967; The Physics of Stellar Interiors, 1974; Stellar Formation, 1978; The D-Force, 1993; The Field of Rotating Masses, 2010; numerous sci. papers in Monthly Notices RAS, Trans RSE, Nature and other jls. *Recreations:* gardening, sailing, ornithology, research into basic fields. *Address:* Limecroft Care Home, Templar Rise, Livingston, West Lothian EH54 6PJ. *Died 2 Jan. 2015.*

REDGRAVE, Maj.-Gen. Sir Roy Michael Frederick, KBE 1979; MC 1945; FRGS; Commander, British Forces, Hong Kong, and Major-General Brigade of Gurkhas, 1978–80; *b* 16 Sept. 1925; *s* of late Robin Roy Redgrave and Michelene Jean Capsa; *m* 1953, Caroline Margaret Valerie (*d* 2010), *d* of Major Arthur Wellesley and Margaret Baker-Kirby; two *s*. *Educ:* Sherborne Sch. Served War of 1939–45: enlisted Trooper, Royal Horse Guards, 1943; Lieut, 1st Household Cavalry Regt, NW Europe, 1944–45. GSO III Intell., HQ Rhine Army, 1950; Canadian Army Staff Coll., 1955; GSO II Ops HQ, London Dist, 1956; Recce, Sqn Ldr, Cyprus, 1959 (despatches); Mil. Assistant to Dep. SACEUR, Paris, 1960–62; JSSC 1962; Comd Household Cavalry Regt (Mounted), 1963–64; Comd Royal Horse Guards (The Blues), 1965–67; AAG PS12, MoD, 1967–68; Chief of Staff, HQ 2nd Div., 1968–70; Comdr, Royal Armoured Corps, 3rd Div., 1970–72; Nat. Defence Coll., Canada, 1973; Comdt Royal Armoured Corps Centre, 1974–75; British Comdt, Berlin, 1975–78. Hon. Col 31st Signal Regt (V), 1983–88. Dir Gen., Winston Churchill Meml Trust, 1980–82. Member: Council, Charing Cross and Westminster Med. Sch., 1981–85; Hammersmith SHA, 1981–85; Council, Victoria League for Commonwealth Friendship; Britain Nepal Soc., 1982–. Chairman: Hammersmith and Fulham HA, 1981–85; Lambrook Appeal, 1984–85; Charing Cross and West London Hosps, 1988–97 (Special Trustee, 1981–99); Trustee: Westminster and Roehampton Hosps, 1988–93; Governor General's Horse Guards, Canada, 1987–; Chelsea and Westminster Hosp., 1993–97; Governor, Commonwealth Trust, 1989–97. Guest Lectr, tours to N Cyprus, Mexico, NZ, Albania, High Arctic, N Africa, 1982–2002. Grand Master, OSMTH, Order of Knights Templar, 1998–2005. *Publications:* Balkan Blue, 2000; The Adventures of Colonel Daffodil, 2007. *Recreations:* native peoples, wildlife, archaeology, philately. *Address:* 44 Slaidburn Street, Chelsea, SW10 0JW. *Club:* Cavalry and Guards. *Died 3 July 2011.*

REDMAN, Maurice; Chairman, Scottish Region, British Gas Corporation, 1974–82 (Deputy Chairman, 1970–74); *b* 30 Aug. 1922; *s* of Herbert Redman and Olive (*née* Dyson); *m* 1960, Dorothy (*née* Appleton); one *d* (and one *d* decd). *Educ:* Hulme Grammar Sch., Oldham; Manchester Univ. BSc(Tech), 1st cl. Hons. Joined staff of Co. Borough of Oldham Gas Dept, 1943; Asst, later Dep. Production Engr, North Western Gas Bd, 1951; Chief Develt Engr, NW Gas Bd, 1957; Chief Engr, Southern Gas Bd, 1966; Dir of Engrg, Southern Gas Bd, 1970. Mem., Internat. Gas Union Cttee on Manufactured Gases, 1961–82. *Publications:* papers to Instn of Gas Engrs, Inst. of Fuel, various overseas conferences, etc. *Recreations:* gardening, music, photography. *Address:* Avington, 3 Cramond Regis, Edinburgh EH4 6LW. *T:* (0131) 312 6178. *Club:* New (Edinburgh). *Died 28 Sept. 2011.*

REECE, Alan Richard, PhD; Owner Director, Pearson Engineering Ltd, Newcastle upon Tyne, since 1985; *b* London, 7 March 1927; *s* of Richard Reece and Olive Reece; *m* 1948, Doreen Harrison; two *s* one *d*. *Educ:* Harrow Co. Sch. for Boys; Durham Univ. (BSc Mech. Engrg 1947; MSc Agricl Engrg 1950); Univ. of Newcastle upon Tyne (PhD 1964). MIMechE 1957; MIAgrE 1960. Grad. apprentice, Vickers Armstrong Ltd, Newcastle upon Tyne, 1947–48; mgt trainee, Ford Motor Co., Dagenham, 1950–52; Product Engr, International Harvester Co., Doncaster, 1952–56; Lectr, Sen. Lectr, then Reader in Agricl Engrg, Univ. of Newcastle upon Tyne, 1956–84. Founder and owner, Soil Machine Dynamics Ltd, 1971–84. Vis. Scientist, US Army Tank Automotive Centre, Detroit, 1962–63. Ed., Jl of Terramechanics, 1963–73. Founder Mem. and first Pres., Internat. Soc. for Terrain Vehicle

Systems, 1964–67. Lectr, Strategic Leadership Prog., Templeton Coll., Oxford, 1984–92. Founder and Chm. of Trustees, Reece Foundn, Univ. of Cambridge, 2007–. Hon. DSc Newcastle upon Tyne, 2006. Lifetime Achievement Award, Entrepreneurs' Forum, 2009. *Publications:* Reviving British Industry, 2011; over 50 articles in jls, 1956–89. *Recreation:* cycling. *Address:* Woodside, The Crescent, Wylam, Northumberland NE41 8HU. *T:* (01661) 852112. *E:* alanr@pearson-eng.com. *Died 31 Dec. 2012.*

REES, Prof. David, FRS 1968; Professor of Pure Mathematics, University of Exeter, 1958–83, then Emeritus; *b* 29 May 1918; *s* of David and Florence Gertrude Rees; *m* 1952, Joan Sybil Cushen; four *d*. *Educ:* King Henry VIII Grammar School, Abergavenny; Sidney Sussex College, Cambridge. Manchester University: Assistant Lecturer, 1945–46, Lecturer, 1946–49; Cambridge University: Lecturer, 1949–58; Fellow of Downing College, Cambridge, 1950–58, Hon. Fellow, 1970–. Mem. Council, Royal Soc., 1979–81. Hon. DSc Exeter, 1993. Polya Prize, London Mathematical Soc., 1993. *Publications:* papers on Algebraic topics in British and foreign mathematical journals. *Recreation:* reading and listening to music. *Address:* Dove Tree House, 89–91 Heavitree Road, Exeter EX1 2ND. *Died 16 Aug. 2013.*

REES, Rt Rev. (John) Ivor; Bishop of St Davids, 1991–95; *b* 19 Feb. 1926; *o s* of David Morgan Rees and Cecilia Perrott Rees; *m* 1954, Beverley Richards; three *s*. *Educ:* Llanelli Gram. Sch.; University Coll. of Wales (BA 1950); Westcott House, Cambridge. Served RN, Coastal Forces and British Pacific Fleet, 1943–47. Ordained deacon 1952, priest 1953, Dio. of St David's; Curate: Fishguard, 1952–55; Llangathen, 1955–57; Priest-in-Charge, Uzmaston, 1957–59; Vicar: Slebech and Uzmaston, 1959–65; Llangollen, 1965–74; Rural Dean of Llangollen, 1970–74; Rector of Wrexham, 1974–76; Dean of Bangor, 1976–88; Vicar of Cathedral Parish of Bangor, 1979–88; Archdeacon of St Davids and Asst Bp, Dio. of St Davids, 1988–91. Canon of St Asaph, 1975–76; Chaplain, Order of St John for County of Clwyd, 1974–76, County of Gwynedd, 1976–88. Hon. Fellow, Trinity Coll., Carmarthen, 1996. KStJ 2006 (SBStJ 1975, OStJ 1981, Sub-Prelate, 1993–2002). *Publications:* Monograph—The Parish of Llangollen and its Churches, 1971; Keeping 40 Days—Sermons for Lent, 1989. *Recreation:* music and good light reading. *Address:* Llys Dewi, 45 Clover Park, Uzmaston Road, Haverfordwest, Pembs SA61 1UE. *T:* (01437) 764846. *E:* jir.1926@hotmail.co.uk. *Died 11 Jan. 2012.*

REES, Rt Rev. Leslie Lloyd; Bishop Suffragan of Shrewsbury, 1980–86; *b* 14 April 1919; *s* of Rees Thomas and Elizabeth Rees; *m* 1944, Rosamond Smith (*d* 1989); one *s* (and one *s* decd). *Educ:* Pontardawe Grammar Sch.; Kelham Theological College. Asst Curate, St Saviour, Roath, 1942; Asst Chaplain, HM Prison, Cardiff, 1942; Chaplain, HM Prison: Durham, 1945–48; Dartmoor, 1948–55; Vicar of Princetown with Postbridge and Huccaby Chapels, 1948–55; Chaplain, HM Prison, Winchester, 1955; Chaplain General of Prisons, Home Office Prison Dept, 1962–80. Chaplain to the Queen, 1971–80. Mem., Parole Bd, 1987–90. Hon. Canon of Canterbury, 1966–80, of Lichfield, 1980–86; Hon. Asst Bishop, Dio. of Winchester, 1987–2004. Freeman, City of London. ChStJ 1985. *Recreation:* music. *Address:* Blackwater Mill Retirement Home, Blackwater, Newport, Isle of Wight PO30 3BJ. *Died 4 July 2013.*

REES-MOGG, Baron *cr* 1988 (Life Peer), of Hinton Blewitt in the County of Avon; **William Rees-Mogg,** Kt 1981; Chairman: Pickering & Chatto (Publishers) Ltd, since 1983; Fleet Street Publications, since 1995; *b* 14 July 1928; *s* of late Edmund Fletcher Rees-Mogg and Beatrice Rees-Mogg (*née* Warren), Temple Cloud, Somerset; *m* 1962, Gillian Shakespeare Morris, *d* of T. R. Morris; two *s* three *d*. *Educ:* Charterhouse; Balliol Coll., Oxford (Brackenbury Scholar). President, Oxford Union, 1951. Financial Times, 1952–60: Chief Leader Writer, 1955–60; Asst Editor, 1957–60; Sunday Times: City Editor, 1960–61; Political and Economic Editor, 1961–63; Deputy Editor, 1964–67; Editor, The Times, 1967–81; columnist, 1992–; Mem., Exec. Bd, Times Newspapers Ltd, 1968–81; Director: The Times Ltd, 1968–81; Times Newspapers Ltd, 1978–81. Columnist, Mail on Sunday, 2004–11. Chairman: Sidgwick & Jackson, 1985–89; NewsMax Media Inc., 2000–06; Director: GEC, 1981–97; E. F. G. Private Bank, 1993–2005; Private Financial Holdings, 1995–2005. Vice-Chm., Bd of Governors, BBC, 1981–86; Chairman: Arts Council of GB, 1982–89; Broadcasting Standards Council, 1988–93; IBC plc, 1994–98. Contested (C) Chester-le-Street, Co. Durham, By-election 1956; General Election, 1959. Treasurer, Institute of Journalists, 1960–63, 1966–68, Pres., 1963–64; Vice-Chm. Cons. Party's Nat. Advisory Cttee on Political Education, 1961–63. Pres., English Assoc., 1983–84. Mem., Internat. Cttee, Pontifical Council for Culture, 1983–87. Vis. Fellow, Nuffield Coll., Oxford, 1968–72. High Sheriff, Somerset, 1978. Hon. LLD Bath, 1977. *Publications:* The Reigning Error: the crisis of world inflation, 1974; An Humbler Heaven, 1977; How to Buy Rare Books, 1985; Picnics on Vesuvius: steps toward the millennium, 1992; (with James Dale Davidson): Blood in the Streets, 1988; The Great Reckoning, 1991; The Sovereign Individual, 1997; Memoirs, 2011. *Recreation:* collecting. *Address:* 17 Pall Mall, SW1Y 5LU. *Club:* Garrick. *Died 29 Dec. 2012.*

REEVE, Sir Anthony, KCMG 1992 (CMG 1986); KCVO 1995; HM Diplomatic Service, retired; High Commissioner (formerly Ambassador) to South Africa, 1991–96; *b* 20 Oct. 1938; *s* of Sidney Reeve and Dorothy (*née* Mitchell); *m* 1st, 1964, Pamela Margaret Angus (marr. diss. 1988); one *s* two *d*; 2nd, 1997, Susan Doull (*née* Collins), Durban, S Africa. *Educ:* Queen Elizabeth Grammar Sch., Wakefield; Marling Sch., Stroud; Merton Coll., Oxford (MA); Open Univ. (MA). Lever Brothers & Associates, 1962–65; joined HM Diplomatic Service, 1965; Middle East Centre for Arab Studies, 1966–68; Asst Political Agent, Abu Dhabi, 1968–70; First Secretary, FCO, 1970–73; First Sec., later Counsellor, Washington, 1973–78; Head of Arms Control and Disarmament Dept, FCO, 1979–81; Counsellor, Cairo, 1981–84; Head of Southern Africa Dept, FCO, 1984–86; Asst Under Sec. of State (Africa), FCO, 1986–87; Ambassador to Jordan, 1988–91. Dir, Barclays Private Bank Ltd, 1997–2001; Dep. Chm., 1998–2007, Chm., 2007–, Curzon Corp. (formerly Union-Castle Travel). *Recreations:* golf, music, the Open University. *Address:* Box Tree Cottage, Horsley, Stroud, Glos GL6 0QB. *Clubs:* Oxford and Cambridge; Leander (Henley-on-Thames); Minchinhampton Golf. *Died 6 Nov. 2014.*

REEVES, Nicholas Philip, OBE 2011; CEnv; Executive Director, Chartered Institution of Water and Environmental Management, since 1998; Managing Director, CIWEM Services Ltd, since 2008; artist and writer; *b* 11 Sept. 1952; *s* of late Philip George Reeves and Rachel Reeves (*née* Rivers); *m* 2001, Janet Maureen Eade; two *d*, and one step *s* one step *d*. *Educ:* Birmingham Coll. of Art and Design (DipAD 1973); University Coll. London (BA 1974; DMS 1980). Chartered Water and Envmt Manager. Artist and freelance journalist, 1973–88; one-man exhibn of paintings and drawings, Compendium Galls and Warwick Gall., 1973; group exhibitions of paintings and drawings: Ikon Gall., 1975; Middlesbrough Mus. and Art Gall., 1981; Royal Birmingham Soc. of Artists, 1976, 1977, 1978, 2011, 2012. Man. Dir, Land Technology Ltd, 1989–92; Hd, Envmt and Recreation, Broxbourne BC, 1992–94; Dir of Policy and Dep. Dir, Inst. of Leisure and Amenity Mgt, 1994–98. Non-exec. Dir, Force 3 Leisure Ltd, 1989–92. Chm., Centre for Amenity and Leisure Contracting Study and Research, Writtle Coll., Univ. of Essex, 1996–98. Mem., Council for Travel and Tourism, 1996–98; Advr, Southern Arts Bd, 1997–99; Member Board: Science Council, 1999–; Soc. for the Envmt, 2000– (Chm., Ext. Affairs Cttee, 2004); Green Flag Adv. Bd, DCLG, 2005–; Sustainable Organic Resources Partnership, 2006–; Mem. Cttee, Thames Recreation, Fisheries, Ecology Adv. Cttee, Envmt Agency, 2005–. Trustee: Brumcan, 2005–10; Population Matters, 2010. Co-Founder, Green Flag Parks Award Scheme, 1995 (Chm., Green Flag Awards Steering Gp, 2002–05); Founder, Arts and the Envmt Network, 2007. Mem., Envmt Awards Cttee, RSA, 2004. Mem., Surrealists of London Action Gp, 2008. Co-Founder, John Wilkes Soc. Dining Club, 2007.

FIHort 1990; FRSA 2004; FLS 2010. Hon. FCIWEM 2000; Hon. FSE 2008. Freeman, City of London, 2000; Court Asst, Co. of Water Conservators, 2006–. *Publications:* A Guide to Business Planning for Leisure and Environment Managers, 2002; various papers on envmt and cultural affairs in learned jls and pubns; articles in the press. *Recreations:* collecting contemporary art, Richard III Society, pubs and real ale, thinking out loud. *Address:* Chartered Institution of Water and Environmental Management, 15 John Street, WC1N 2EB. *T:* (020) 7831 3110, *Fax:* (020) 7405 4967. *E:* nick@ciwem.org; Sunnyside Cottage, Stanwell Road, Horton, Berks SL3 9PE. *T:* (01753) 682900. *E:* ecoreeves@btinternet.com. *Club:* Reform. *Died 7 July 2013.*

REEVES, Rt Rev. Sir Paul Alfred, ONZ 2007; GCMG 1985; GCVO 1986; QSO 1990; Kt 1985; Governor-General, New Zealand, 1985–90; Chancellor, Auckland University of Technology, since 2005; *b* 6 Dec. 1932; 2nd *s* of D'Arcy Lionel and Hilda Mary Reeves; *m* 1959, Beverley Gwendolen Watkins; three *d. Educ:* Wellington Coll., New Zealand; Victoria Univ. of Wellington (MA); St John's Theol Coll., Auckland (LTh); St Peter's Coll., Univ. of Oxford (MA; Hon. Fellow, 1980). Deacon, 1958; Priest, 1960; Curate: Tokoroa, NZ, 1958–59; St Mary the Virgin, Oxford, 1959–61; Kirkley St Peter, Lowestoft, 1961–63; Vicar, St Paul, Okato, NZ, 1964–66; Lectr in Church History, St John's Coll., Auckland, NZ, 1966–69; Dir of Christian Educn, Dio. Auckland, 1969–71; Bishop of Waiapu, 1971–79; Bishop of Auckland, 1979–85; Primate and Archbishop of New Zealand, 1980–85; Anglican Observer at UN, and Assisting Bishop, Episcopal Dio. of NY, 1991–93; Dean, Te Rau Kahikatea Theol Coll., Auckland, 1994–95. Chairman: Environmental Council, 1974–76; Bioethics Council, 2002–04; Queen Elizabeth II Nat. Trust, 2000–03. Dep. Leader, Commonwealth Observers, S African elections, 1994; Leader, Commonwealth Observers, Ghanaian elections, 1996; Special Envoy of Commonwealth Sec. Gen. to Guyana, 2002–06; Special Rep. of Commonwealth Sec. Gen. to Fiji, 2007–. Chm., Fijian Constitutional Review Commn, 1995–96. Visiting Professor: Univ. of Auckland, 1997–2000; Auckland Univ. of Technol., 2000–05. KStJ 1986. Hon. DCL Oxford, 1985; Hon LLD Wellington, 1989; Hon. DD: Gen. Theol Seminary, NY, 1992; Church Divinity Sch. of Pacific, San Francisco, 1994; Hon. Dr Edinburgh, 1994. Hon. CF (Fiji), 1999. *Recreations:* jogging, sailing, swimming. *Address:* 14B Victoria Avenue, Remuera, Auckland, New Zealand. *Died 14 Aug. 2011.*

REGAN, Charles Maurice; Clerk to the Trustees, Hampstead Wells and Campden Trust, 1985–93; Under-Secretary, Department of Health and Social Security, 1972–79 and 1981–85; *b* 31 Oct. 1925; *m* 1961, Susan (*née* Littmann) (*d* 1972); one *s* one *d. Educ:* Taunton Sch.; London Sch. of Economics and Political Science (BScEcon). Academic research, 1950–52. Asst Principal, Min. of National Insurance, 1952; Principal Private Sec. to Minister of Pensions and National Insurance, 1962–64; Asst Sec., 1964; Treasury/Civil Service Dept, 1967–70; Under-Sec., DES, 1979–81. *Recreations:* walking, travel. *Address:* 35 Crediton Hill, NW6 1HS. *T:* (020) 7794 6404. *Club:* Athenæum. *Died 31 March 2015.*

REICHMANN, Paul; Executive Director, Canary Wharf Group plc, until 2004 (Chairman, until 2003); Chief Executive, Reichmann Group of Companies; President, Olympia & York California Capital Corp.; *b* Vienna, Sept. 1930; *s* of Samuel and Renee Reichmann; *m* Lea Feldman; two *s* three *d.* Moved to Toronto, 1954; with brothers, formed Olympia and York Develts Ltd; completed First Canadian Place, Toronto (offices), 1975; purchased 8 office buildings in Manhattan, NY, 1976; completed building of World Financial Centre, NY, 1986; responsible for concept and realisation of Canary Wharf project, 1987. Trustee: Retirement Residences Real Estate Investment Trust; CPL Long Term Care Real Estate Investment Trust; former Trustee, IPC US Income Commercial Real Estate Investment Trust. *Address:* c/o Canary Wharf Group, One Canada Square, Canary Wharf, E14 5AB. *Died 25 Oct. 2013.*

REID, Sir Hugh, 3rd Bt *cr* 1922; farmer; *b* 27 Nov. 1933; *s* of Sir Douglas Neilson Reid, 2nd Bt, and Margaret Brighton Young (*d* 1992), *d* of Robert Young Maxtone, MBE, JP; *S* father, 1971. *Educ:* Loretto. Royal Air Force, 1952–56; RAFVR, 1956–78 (Flying Officer, Training Branch, 1965–78). *Recreations:* ski-ing, travel. *Heir:* none. *Address:* Caheronaun Park, Loughrea, Co. Galway, Ireland; 4772 Vouni Village, Limassol District, Cyprus. *Died 20 Nov. 2012 (ext).*

REID, William, CBE 1987; FSA; Director, National Army Museum, 1970–87; Consultative Director, The Heralds' Museum, 1988–92; *b* Glasgow, 8 Nov. 1926; *o s* of Colin Colquhoun Reid and Mary Evelyn Bingham; *m* 1958, Nina Frances Brigden. *Educ:* Glasgow and Oxford. Commnd RAF Regt, 1946–48. Joined staff of Armouries, Tower of London, 1956. Organising Sec., 3rd Internat. Congress of Museums of Arms and Military History, London, Glasgow and Edinburgh, 1963; Sec.-Gen., Internat. Assoc. of Museums of Arms and Military History, 1969–81, Pres., 1981–87, Hon. Life Pres., 1987; Member: British Nat. Cttee, ICOM, 1973–88; Council, Chelsea Soc., 1979–85; Founding Council, Army Records Soc., 1983–88. FSA 1965 (Mem. Council, 1975–76); FMA 1974–88, resigned. Trustee: The Tank Museum, 1970–87; RAEC Museum, 1985–99; Museum of Richmond, 1987–2003 (Patron, 2003–); Florence Nightingale Museum Trust, 1987–2000; Royal Hants Regt Mus., 1990–97; Lord Brock Meml Trust, 1994–2000; AGC Mus., 1999–2003. Mem., Conservative Adv. Cttee on the Arts and Heritage, 1988–2005. Vice Pres., Arms and Armour Soc., 2000–. Hon. Life Mem., Friends of the Nat. Army Mus., 1987; Hon. Member: Amer. Soc. of Arms Collectors, 1975; Indian Army Assoc., 1981–2007. Freeman, Scriveners' Co., 1989–98 (Liveryman, 1990); Freeman, City of London, 1989. *Publications:* (with A. R. Dufty) European Armour in the Tower of London, 1968; The Lore of Arms, 1976 (Military Book Society choice) (also trans. Chinese, French, German, Danish, Italian, Spanish and Swedish); We're certainly not afraid of Zeiss: Barr & Stroud binoculars and the Royal Navy, 2002; contribs to British and foreign jls. *Recreations:* the study of armour and arms, military history, music, bird-watching. *Address:* 66 Ennerdale Road, Richmond, Surrey TW9 2DL. *T:* (020) 8940 0904. *Club:* Athenæum. *Died 19 June 2014.*

REITH, Douglas, CBE 1994; TD 1994; QC (Scot.) 1957; a Social Security (formerly National Insurance) Commissioner, 1960–92; *b* 29 June 1919; *s* of William Reith and Jessie McAllan; *m* 1949, Elizabeth Archer Stewart (decd); one *s* one *d. Educ:* Aberdeen Grammar School; Aberdeen University (MA, LLB). Became Member of Faculty of Advocates in Scotland, 1946. Served in Royal Signals, 1939–46. Standing Junior Counsel in Scotland to Customs and Excise, 1949–51; Advocate-Depute, Crown Office, Scotland, 1953–57; Pres., Pensions Appeal Tribunal (Scotland), 1958–64; Chm., Nat. Health Service Tribunal (Scotland), 1963–65. *Address:* 2 Ravelston Court, Ravelston Dykes, Edinburgh EH12 6HQ. *T:* (0131) 337 0332. *Club:* New (Edinburgh). *Died 15 April 2013.*

RENDELL OF BABERGH, Baroness *cr* 1997 (Life Peer), of Aldeburgh in the co. of Suffolk; **Ruth Barbara Rendell,** CBE 1996; crime novelist, since 1964; *b* 17 Feb. 1930; *d* of Arthur Grasemann and Ebba Kruse; *m* 1950, Donald Rendell (marr. diss. 1975; remarried, 1977; he *d* 1999); one *s. Educ:* Loughton County High School. FRSL. Arts Council National Book Award for Genre Fiction, 1981; Sunday Times Award for Literary Excellence, 1990. *Publications:* From Doon with Death, 1964; To Fear a Painted Devil, 1965; Vanity Dies Hard, 1966; A New Lease of Death, 1967; Wolf to the Slaughter, 1967 (televised 1987); The Secret House of Death, 1968; The Best Man to Die, 1969; A Guilty Thing Surprised, 1970; One Across Two Down, 1971; No More Dying Then, 1971; Murder Being Once Done, 1972; Some Lie and Some Die, 1973; The Face of Trespass, 1974 (televised, as An Affair in Mind, 1988); Shake Hands for Ever, 1975; A Demon in my View, 1976 (film 1991); A Judgement in Stone, 1977; A Sleeping Life, 1978; Make Death Love Me, 1979; The Lake of Darkness, 1980 (televised, as Dead Lucky, 1988); Put on by Cunning, 1981; Master of the Moor, 1982 (televised 1994); The Speaker of Mandarin, 1983; The Killing Doll, 1984;

The Tree of Hands, 1984 (film 1989); An Unkindness of Ravens, 1985; Live Flesh, 1986; Heartstones, 1987; Talking to Strange Men, 1987; (ed) A Warning to the Curious—The Ghost Stories of M. R. James, 1987; The Veiled One, 1988 (televised 1989); The Bridesmaid, 1989 (film 2005); Ruth Rendell's Suffolk, 1989; (with Colin Ward) Undermining the Central Line, 1989; Going Wrong, 1990; Kissing the Gunner's Daughter, 1992; The Crocodile Bird, 1993; Simisola, 1994; (ed) The Reason Why, 1995; The Keys to the Street, 1996; Road Rage, 1997; A Sight for Sore Eyes, 1998; Harm Done, 1999; Adam and Eve and Pinch Me, 2001; The Babes in the Wood, 2002; The Rottweiler, 2003; Thirteen Steps Down, 2004; End in Tears, 2005; The Water's Lovely, 2006; Not in the Flesh, 2007; Portobello, 2008; The Monster in the Box, 2009; Tigerlily's Orchids, 2010; The Vault, 2011; Archie and Archie, 2013; No Man's Nightingale, 2013; The Girl Next Door, 2014; *short stories:* The Fallen Curtain, 1976; Means of Evil, 1979; The Fever Tree, 1982; The New Girl Friend, 1985; Collected Short Stories, 1987; The Copper Peacock, 1991; Blood Linen, 1995; Piranha to Scurfy, 2000; Collected Stories, 2007; (as Barbara Vine): A Dark-Adapted Eye, 1986 (televised 1994); A Fatal Inversion, 1987 (televised 1992); The House of Stairs, 1988; Gallowglass, 1990; King Solomon's Carpet, 1991; Asta's Book, 1993; No Night Is Too Long, 1994; The Brimstone Wedding, 1996; The Chimney Sweeper's Boy, 1998. *Recreations:* reading, walking, opera. *Address:* House of Lords, SW1A 0PW. *Clubs:* Groucho, Detection. *Died 2 May 2015.*

RENDLE, Michael Russel; Managing Director, British Petroleum plc, 1981–86; Chairman: Forestry Investment Management, since 1992 (Director since 1989); Willis Pension Trustees, since 1998 (Director, since 1986); Director, Willis Ltd, since 2005; *b* 20 Feb. 1931; *s* of late H. C. R. Rendle and Valerie Patricia (*née* Gleeson); *m* 1957, Heather, *d* of J. W. J. Rinkel; two *s* two *d*. *Educ:* Marlborough; New College, Oxford (MA 1959). Joined Anglo-Iranian Oil Co. (later BP), 1954; Man. Dir, BP Trinidad, 1967–70; Man. Dir, BP Australia, 1974–78; Dir, BP Trading Ltd, 1978–81; Chairman: BP Chemicals Internat., 1981–83; BP Coal, 1983–86; BP Nutrition, 1981–86; Dep. Chm., British-Borneo Petroleum Syndicate plc, 1986–2000. Deputy Chairman: Imperial Continental Gas Assoc., 1986–87; Tace, 1991; Chairman: Markheath, later TBI, 1991–95; Campbell & Armstrong PLC, 1996–98 (Dir, 1992–); Director: London Adv. Bd, Westpac Banking Corp. (formerly Commercial Bank of Australia), 1978–89; Willis Faber, then Willis Corroon plc, 1985–98; Petrofina SA, 1986–87; OIS International Inspection plc, 1993–96 (Chm., 1995–96); Medical Defence Union, 1998–2001. Mem. BOTB, 1982–86; Chm., European Trade Cttee, 1982–86. Chm. Social Affairs Cttee, UNICE, 1984–87; Mem. Internat. Council and UK Adv. Bd, INSEAD, 1984–86. Mem. Council, Marlborough Coll., 1987–95. *Recreations:* golf, music, outdoor sports, gardening. *Address:* c/o Willis Group Ltd, 51 Lime Street, EC3M 7DQ. *T:* (020) 3124 7431. *Clubs:* Vincent's (Oxford); Australian (Melbourne). *Died 8 April 2011.*

RENDLE, Peter Critchfield; Under-Secretary (Principal Finance Officer), Scottish Office, 1978–80; *b* Truro, 31 July 1919; *s* of late Martyn and Florence Rendle; *m* 1944, Helen Barbara Moyes; three *s*. *Educ:* Queen Elizabeth's Sch., Hartlebury. Clerical Officer, Min. of Transport, 1936–49. Served War, Royal Navy, 1940–46 (Lieut RNVR). Min. of Town and Country Planning, 1949; Dept of Health for Scotland, 1950–59 (Sec., Guest Cttee on Bldg Legislation in Scotland); Scottish Home and Health Dept, 1959–63 and 1972–73; Scottish Educn Dept, 1963–72; Under Sec., Housing, Scottish Development Dept, 1973–78. Member: Legal Aid Central Cttee for Scotland, 1980–87; Scottish Is Councils Cttee of Inquiry, 1982–84; Scottish Legal Aid Bd, 1987–89. *Publications:* Rayner Report, Scrutiny of HM Inspectors of Schools in Scotland, 1981. *Recreations:* theatre, taking photographs. *Address:* 3/6 Caithness Place, Clark Road, Edinburgh EH5 3AE. *T:* (0131) 552 8024. *Club:* Royal Scots (Edinburgh). *Died 16 Dec. 2011.*

RENNIE, Alexander Allan, CBE 1980; QPM 1971; Chief Constable, West Mercia Constabulary, 1975–81; *b* 13 June 1917; *s* of late Charles Rennie and Susan Parsons Rennie; *m* 1941, Lucy Brunt; one *s* one *d*. *Educ:* Ellon Acad., Aberdeenshire. Armed Services, 1941–45: commnd 30 Corps Royal Northumberland Fusiliers; active service in Europe (mentioned in despatches, 1945). Joined Durham County Constab., 1937; Chief Supt, 1963; Dep. Chief Constable, Shropshire, 1963–67; Dir, Sen. Comd Course, Police Coll., Bramshill, 1967–69; Asst Chief Constable, West Mercia, 1969–72, Dep. Chief Constable, 1973–75. OStJ 1975. *Recreations:* golf, hill walking. *Address:* 1 Rowan Court, Droitwich Spa, Worcs WR9 8AH. *Died 8 July 2011.*

REPORTER, Sir Shapoor (Ardeshirji), KBE 1973 (OBE 1969); Consultant on Economic and Political Matters concerning Iran, since 1962; *b* 26 Feb. 1921; *s* of Ardeshirji Reporter and Shirin Reporter; *m* 1952, Assia Alexandra; one *s* one *d*. *Educ:* Zoroastrian Public Sch., Teheran; matriculated in Bombay (specially designed course in Political Science under Cambridge Univ. Tutors, UK). PRO, British Legation, Teheran, 1941–43; in charge of Persian Unit of All India Radio, New Delhi, 1943–45; Teaching English, Imperial Staff Coll., Teheran, 1945–48; Political Adviser, US Embassy, Teheran, 1948–54; Free-lance Correspondent, 1954–62; Economic Consultant to major British interests in Iran, 1962–73. *Publications:* English-Persian Phrases, 1945 (Delhi); Dictionary of English-Persian Idioms, 1956 (Teheran); Dictionary of Persian-English Idioms, 1972 (Teheran Univ.). *Recreations:* tennis, walking, travelling. *Died 23 Dec. 2013.*

RESNAIS, Alain; French film director; *b* Vannes, 3 June 1922; *s* of Pierre Resnais and Jeanne (*née* Gachet). *Educ:* Institut des Hautes Etudes Cinématographiques. Assistant to Nicole Védrée for film Paris 1900, 1947–48; directed his own films (many of which have won prizes), 1948–. Short films, 1948–59, include: Van Gogh, 1948; Guernica (jtly with Robert Hessens), 1950; Les statues meurent aussi (jtly with Chris Marker), 1952; Nuit et brouillard, 1955. Full length films include: Hiroshima mon amour, 1959; L'année dernière à Marienbad, 1961; Muriel, 1963; La guerre est finie, 1966; Je t'aime, je t'aime, 1968; Stavisky, 1974; Providence, 1977; Mon Oncle d'Amérique, 1980; La vie est un roman, 1983; L'amour à Mort, 1984; Mélo, 1986; Je veux rentrer à la maison, 1989; Smoking/No Smoking, 1993; On connaît la chanson, 1998; Pas sur la bouche, 2003; Coeurs, 2006 (UK as Private Fears in Public Places, 2007); Les herbes folles, 2009 (Lifetime Achievement Award, Cannes, 2009); Aimer, Boire et Chanter, 2014. *Address:* c/o Intertalent, 16 rue Henri Barbusse, 75005 Paris, France. *Died 1 March 2014.*

RETTIE, (James) Philip, CBE 1987; TD 1962; farmer, since 1964; Director, Rettie & Co., since 1992; *b* 7 Dec. 1926; *s* of James Rettie and Rachel Buist; *m* 1st, 1955, Helen Grant; two *s* one *d*; 2nd, 1980, Mrs Diana Harvey (*née* Ballantyne). *Educ:* Trinity College, Glenalmond. Royal Engineers, 1945–48; RE (TA), 1949–65. Wm Low & Co. plc, 1948–85 (Chm., 1980–85); Mem., TSB Scotland Area Bd, 1983–88; Partner, Crossley & Rettie, 1989–95. Dir, Edinburgh and Glasgow Investment Co., 1989–2003. Chm., Sea Fish Industry Authority, 1981–87. Director: Unicorn Preservation Soc., 1990–2001; Tayside Conservation Trust, 1992–. Chm., Scottish Soc. for Employment of ex-Regular Sailors, Soldiers and Airmen, 1995–2010. Trustee, Scottish Civic Trust, 1983–2002. Hon. Col, Northern Gp Field Sqns, RE (T), 1982–89. MInstRE 2008. *Recreations:* shooting, gardening, hill-walking, fishing. *Address:* Hill House, Ballindean, Inchture, Perthshire PH14 9QS. *T:* (01828) 686337. *Died 28 Aug. 2013.*

REVELSTOKE, 6th Baron *cr* 1885, of Membland, co. Devon; **James Cecil Baring;** *b* 16 Aug. 1938; *yr s* of 4th Baron Revelstoke and Hon. Florence Fermor-Hesketh, 2nd *d* of 1st Baron Hesketh; *S* brother, 2003; *m* 1st, 1968, Aneta (marr. diss.), *yr d* of Erskine A. H. Fisher; two *s*; 2nd, 1983, Sarah (marr. diss. 1990), *d* of William Edward Stubbs, MBE; two *d*. *Educ:* Eton. *Heir:* *s* Hon. Alexander Rupert Baring, *b* 9 April 1970. *Died 7 Feb. 2012.*

REX, Prof. John Arderne; Research Professor on Ethnic Relations, 1984–90, then Emeritus, and Associate Director, Centre for Research in Ethnic Relations, 1974–90, University of Warwick; *b* 5 March 1925; *s* of Frederick Edward George Rex and Winifred Natalie Rex; *m* 1st,

1949, Pamela Margaret Rutherford (marr. diss. 1963); two *d*; 2nd, 1965, Margaret Ellen Biggs; two *s*. *Educ:* Grey Institute High Sch. and Rhodes University Coll., S Africa. BA (S Africa), PhD (Leeds). Served War, Royal Navy (Able Seaman), 1943–45. Graduated, 1948; Lecturer: Univ. of Leeds, 1949–62; Birmingham, 1962–64; Prof. of Social Theory and Institutions, Durham, 1964–70; Prof. of Sociology, Univ. of Warwick, 1970–79; Dir, SSRC Research Unit on Ethnic Relations, Univ. of Aston in Birmingham, 1979–84. Visiting Professor: Univ. of Toronto, 1974–75; Univ. of Cape Town, 1991; NY Univ., 1996. *Publications:* Key Problems of Sociological Theory, 1961; (with Robert Moore) Race Community and Conflict, 1967, 2nd edn 1973; Race Relations in Sociological Theory, 1970; Discovering Sociology, 1973; Race, Colonialism and the City, 1974; (ed) Approaches to Sociology, 1974; Sociology and the Demystification of the Modern World, 1974; (with Sally Tomlinson) Colonial Immigrants in a British City, 1979; Social Conflict, 1980; (ed) Apartheid and Social Research, 1981; Race and Ethnicity, 1986; The Ghetto and the Underclass, 1988; Ethnic Identity and Ethnic Organisation in Britain, 1991; (with Beatrice Drury) Ethnic Mobilisation in a Multicultural Europe, 1994; Ethnic Minorities in the Modern Nation State, 1996; (with Montserrat Guibernau) The Ethnicity Reader, 1997; (ed with Gurharpal Singh) Governance in Multicultural Societies, 2004; Ethnicité et Citoyenneté: la sociologie des sociétés multiculturelles, 2006. *Recreations:* politics, race relations work. *Address:* 33 Arlington Avenue, Leamington Spa, Warwicks CV32 5UD. *Died 20 Dec. 2011.*

REYNOLDS, Alan (Munro); painter, maker of reliefs, and printmaker; *b* 27 April 1926; *m* 1957, Vona Darby. *Educ:* Woolwich Polytechnic Art School; Royal College of Art (Scholarship and Medal). One man exhibitions: Redfern Gall., 1952, 1953, 1954, 1956, 1960, 1962, 1964, 1966, 1970, 1972, 1974; Durlacher Gall., New York, 1954, 1959; Leicester Galleries, 1958; Aldeburgh, Suffolk, 1965; Arnolfini Gall., Bristol, 1971 (graphics); Annely Juda Fine Art, 1978, 1991, 2006; Juda Rowan Gall., 1982, 1986; Thomas Agnew, Albemarle Street Gall., 1982; Gall. Wack, Kaiserslautern, 1986, 1990, 1995, 1999, 2004, 2008; Galerie Lahumière, Paris, 1990; Galerie Art, Nürnberg, 1992; Gal. Konstruktiv Tendens, Stockholm, 2002; Galerie Gimpel & Müller, Paris, 2009, 2012; retrospective exhibitions: Wilhelm-Hack Mus., Ludwigshafen am Rhein, 1996; Städtische Galerie, Wolfsburg, 1996; Kettle's Yard, Cambridge, 2003, 2010; Musée des Ursulines Macon, 2009; Museum Liner, Appenzell, 2009; work in exhibitions: Carnegie (Pittsburgh) Internat., USA, 1952, 1955, 1958, 1961; Internat. Exhibn, Rome, (awarded one of the three equal prizes), subsequently Musée d'Art Moderne, Paris, and Brussels; British Council Exhibn, Oslo and Copenhagen, 1956; Redfern Gall., 1971; Spectrum, Arts Council of GB, 1971; British Painting 1952–77, Royal Academy, 1977; Galerie Loyse Oppenheim, Nyon, Switzerland, 1977; Galerie Renée Ziegler, Zürich, 1981; group exhibitions: Scottish Nat. Gall. of Modern Art, Edinburgh, 1984; Annely Juda Fine Art and Juda Rowan Gall., London, 1985; Galeries Renée Ziegler, Zürich, 1985–86; Annely Juda Fine Art, 1986, 1991, 1996, 2011; Wilhelm-Hack Mus., Ludwigshafen am Rhein, 1987; Stiftung für Konkrete Kunst, Reutlingen, 1992–93. Works acquired by: Tate Gall.; V&A; National Galleries of: S Aust.; Felton Bequest, Vic., Aust.; NZ; Canada; City Art Galleries of: Birmingham; Bristol; Manchester; Wakefield; Mus. of Modern Art, NY; Contemporary Art Soc.; British Council; Arts Council of GB; Rothschild Foundn; The Graves Art Gall., Sheffield; Nottingham Castle Mus.; Fitzwilliam Mus., Cambridge; Mus. of Modern Art, São Paulo, Brazil; Leeds Art Gall.; Toledo Art Gall., Ohio, USA; Oriel Coll., Oxford; Warwick Univ.; Mus. and Art Galls, Brighton and Plymouth; Texas Univ., Austin, USA; Berlin Nat. Gall.; McCrory Corp., NY; Wilhelm-Hack Mus., Ludwigshafen am Rhein; Louisiana Mus., Denmark; Tel Aviv Mus., Israel; Musée des Beaux Arts de Grenoble; Mus. Pfalzgalerie, Kaiserslautern, W Germany; Inst. für Kultur, Kunstsammlung Nordrhein-Westfalen, Düsseldorf. CoID Award, 1965; Arts Council of GB Purchase Award, 1967. *Relevant publication:* The Painter, Alan Reynolds, by J. P. Hodin, 1962; Alan Reynolds, by Michael Harrison, 2011. *Address:* Briar Cottage, High Street, Cranbrook, Kent TN17 3EN. *Died 28 Aug. 2014.*

REYNOLDS, Albert; Member of the Dáil (TD) (FF), 1977–2003; Taoiseach (Prime Minister of Ireland), 1992–94; President, Fianna Fáil, 1992–94 (Vice-President, 1983–92); *b* Rooskey, Co. Roscommon, 3 Nov. 1932; *m* Kathleen Coen; two *s* five *d*. *Educ:* Summerhill Coll., Sligo. Minister: for Posts and Telegraphs, and for Transport, 1979–81; for Industry and Energy, March–Dec. 1982; Opposition spokesperson: for Industry and Employment, 1983–85; for Energy, 1985–87; Minister for: Industry and Commerce, 1987–88; Finance, 1988–91. Mem., Oireachtas Jt Cttee on Commercial State-Sponsored Bodies, 1983–87. Mem., Longford CC, 1974–79. Pres., Longford Chamber of Commerce, 1974–78. *Publications:* Albert Reynolds: my autobiography, 2009. *Address:* 18 Ailesbury Road, Dublin 4, Ireland. *Died 21 Aug. 2014.*

REYNOLDS, (Arthur) Graham, CVO 2000; OBE 1984; FBA 1993; Keeper of the Department of Prints and Drawings, 1961–74 (of Engraving, Illustration and Design, 1959–61), and of Paintings, Victoria and Albert Museum, 1959–74; *b* Highgate, 10 Jan. 1914; *o s* of late Arthur T. Reynolds and Eva Mullins; *m* 1943, Daphne, painter and engraver (*d* 2002), *d* of late Thomas Dent and Florence Haskett, Huddersfield. *Educ:* Highgate School; Queens' College, Cambridge. Joined staff of Victoria and Albert Museum, 1937. Seconded to Ministry of Home Security, 1939–45. Hon. Keeper of Portrait Miniatures, Fitzwilliam Mus., Cambridge, 1994–. Member: Adv. Council, Paul Mellon Centre for Studies in British Art, 1977–84; Reviewing Cttee on the Export of Works of Art, 1984–90. Trustee, William Morris Gallery, Walthamstow, 1972–75; Chm., Gainsborough's House Soc., Sudbury, 1977–79. Leverhulme Emeritus Fellowship, 1980–81. *Publications:* Twentieth Century Drawings, 1946; Nicholas Hilliard and Isaac Oliver, 1947, 2nd edn 1971; Van Gogh, 1947; Nineteenth Century Drawings, 1949; Thomas Bewick, 1949; An Introduction to English Water-Colour Painting, 1950, rev. edn 1988; Gastronomic Pleasures, 1950; Elizabethan and Jacobean Costume, 1951; English Portrait Miniatures, 1952, rev. edn 1988; Painters of the Victorian Scene, 1953; Catalogue of the Constable Collection, Victoria and Albert Museum, 1960, rev. edn 1973; Constable, the Natural Painter, 1965; Victorian Painting, 1966, 2nd edn 1987; Turner, 1969; A Concise History of Water Colour Painting, 1972; Catalogue of Portrait Miniatures, Wallace Collection, 1980; Constable's England, 1983; The Later Paintings and Drawings of John Constable, 2 vols, 1984 (Mitchell Prize); The Earlier Paintings and Drawings of John Constable, 2 vols, 1996; Catalogue of Portrait Miniatures, Metropolitan Museum of Art, 1996; The Sixteenth and Seventeenth Century Miniatures in the Collection of Her Majesty the Queen, 1999; Daphne Reynolds: a memoir, 2007; Editor of series English Masters of Black and White; contribs to Burlington Magazine, Apollo, etc. *Address:* The Old Manse, Bradfield St George, Bury St Edmunds, Suffolk IP30 0AZ. *T:* (01284) 386610. *Club:* Athenæum. *Died 13 Oct. 2013.*

REYNOLDS, Barbara, PhD; author, lexicographer; Reader in Italian Studies, University of Nottingham, 1966–78; *b* 13 June 1914; *d* of late Alfred Charles Reynolds; *m* 1st, 1939, Prof. Lewis Thorpe (*d* 1977); one *s* one *d*; 2nd, 1982, Kenneth Imeson (*d* 1994). *Educ:* St Paul's Girls' Sch.; University Coll., London (BA Hons; PhD). MA Cantab 1946. Asst Lectr in Italian, LSE 1937–40. Chief Exec. and Gen. Editor, The Cambridge Italian Dictionary, 1948–81; Man. Editor, Seven, an Anglo-American Literary Review, 1980–2004. Mem. Council Senate, Cambridge Univ., 1961–62. University Lecturer in Italian Literature and Language, Cambridge, 1945–62 (Faculty Assistant Lecturer, 1940–45); Warden of Willoughby Hall, Univ. of Nottingham, 1963–69. Vis. Professor: Univ. of Calif., Berkeley, 1974–75; Wheaton Coll., Illinois, 1977–78, 1982; Trinity Coll., Dublin, 1980, 1981; Hope Coll., Mich., 1982. Hon. Reader in Italian, Univ. of Warwick, 1975–80. Pres., Dorothy L. Sayers Soc., 1995– (Chm., 1986–94). Hon. DLitt: Wheaton Coll., Illinois, 1979; Hope Coll., Mich., 1982; Durham Univ., 1995. Silver Medal for Services to Italian culture (Italian Govt), 1964;

Edmund Gardner Prize, 1964; Silver Medal for services to Anglo-Veneto cultural relations, Prov. Admin of Vicenza, 1971; Cavaliere Ufficiale al Merito della Repubblica Italiana, 1978. *Publications:* (with K. T. Butler) Tredici Novelle Moderne, 1947; The Linguistic Writings of Alessandro Manzoni: a Textual and Chronological Reconstruction, 1950; rev. edn with introd., Dante and the Early Astronomers, by M. A. Orr, 1956; The Cambridge Italian Dictionary, Vol. I, Italian-English, 1962, Vol. II, English-Italian, 1981; (with Dorothy L. Sayers) Paradise: a translation into English triple rhyme, from the Italian of Dante Alighieri, 1962, 3rd edn 2004; (with Lewis Thorpe) Guido Farina, Painter of Verona, 1967; La Vita Nuova (Poems of Youth); trans. of Dante's Vita Nuova, 1969, 2nd edn 2004; Concise Cambridge Italian Dictionary, 1975; Orlando Furioso, trans. into rhymed octaves of Ariosto's epic, Vol. I, 1975 (Internat. Literary Prize, Monselice, Italy, 1976) Vol. II, 1977; (ed) Cambridge-Signorelli Dizionario Italiano-Inglese, Inglese-Italiano, 1986; (ed jtly) The Translator's Art, 1987; The Passionate Intellect: Dorothy L. Sayers' encounter with Dante, 1989; Dorothy L. Sayers: her life and soul, 1993; (ed) The Letters of Dorothy L. Sayers, Vol. I, 1995, Vol. II, 1997, Vol. III, 1998, Vol. IV, 2000, Vol. V, 2002; Dante: the poet, the political thinker, the man, 2006; numerous articles on Italian literature in learned jls. *Address:* 220 Milton Road, Cambridge CB4 1LQ. *T:* (01223) 565380, *Fax:* (01223) 424894. *Clubs:* University Women's (Chm., 1988–90), Royal Air Force.
Died 29 April 2015.

REYNOLDS, Sir David James, 3rd Bt *cr* 1923, of Woolton, Co. Lancaster; *b* 26 Jan. 1924; *er s* of Sir John Francis Roskell Reynolds, 2nd Bt, MBE, JP and Milicent (*d* 1931), *d* of late Major James Orr-Ewing and Lady Margaret Orr-Ewing, *d* of 7th Duke of Roxburghe; *S* father, 1956; *m* 1966, Charlotte Baumgartner; one *s* two *d*. *Educ:* Downside. Active service in Army, 1942–47, Italy, etc; on demobilisation, Captain 15/19 Hussars. *Recreation:* sport. *Heir: s* James Francis Reynolds [*b* 10 July 1971; *m* 2004, Camilla Anne Stewart; one *s* one *d*]. *Address:* Jersey, CI.
Died 13 Feb. 2015.

REYNOLDS, Eva Mary Barbara; *see* Reynolds, Barbara.

REYNOLDS, Graham; *see* Reynolds, A. G.

REYNOLDS, Maj.-Gen. Michael Frank, CB 1983; author (military history); *b* 3 June 1930; *s* of Frank Reynolds and Gwendolen Reynolds (*née* Griffiths); *m* 1955, Anne Bernice (*née* Truman); three *d*. *Educ:* Cranleigh; RMA Sandhurst (Infantry Prize). Commnd Queen's Royal Regt, 1950 (last Adjt, 1959); served Germany, Korea (severely wounded), Cyprus (EOKA emergency), Canada (exchange officer), Persian Gulf, Netherlands, Belgium; psc 1960; GSO 1 Ops, HQ AFCENT, 1970–71; CO 2 Queen's, BAOR and Ulster, 1971–73; GSO 1 Ops, N Ireland, 1973–74; Comdr 12 Mech. Bde, BAOR, 1974–76; RCDS, 1977; Dep. Adjt Gen., BAOR, 1978–80; Comdr, Allied Command Europe Mobile Force (Land), 1980–83; Asst Dir, IMS (Plans and Policy), HQ NATO, 1983–86. Col Comdt, The Queen's Division, 1984–86; (Last) Col, The Queen's Regt, 1989–92. Pres., E Anglian Aviation Soc., 1996–98. Comdr First Cl., Order of the Dannebrog (Denmark), 1990; Grand Cross, Order of Orange-Nassau (Netherlands), 1992. *Publications:* The Devil's Adjutant, 1995; Steel Inferno, 1997; Men of Steel, 1999; Sons of the Reich, 2002; Eagles and Bulldogs in Normandy 1944, 2003; Monty and Patton - Two Paths to Victory, 2005; Soldier at Heart - Private to General, 2012; Soldier at Heart: from Private to General, 2013. *Recreations:* military history (especially Normandy and Battle of the Ardennes, 1944), writing. *Died 21 Oct. 2015.*

RHODES, John Ivor McKinnon, CMG 1971; Minister, UK Mission to UN, 1966–74; *b* 6 March 1914; *s* of late Joseph Thomas Rhodes and Hilda (*née* McKinnon); *m* 1939, Eden Annetta Clark (*d* 1990); one *s* one *d*. *Educ:* Leeds Modern School. Exec. Officer, WO, 1933; Financial Adviser's Office, HQ British Forces in Palestine, 1938; Major 1940; Asst Comd Sec., Southern Comd, 1944. Financial Adviser, London District, 1946; Principal 1947, Asst Sec. 1959, HM Treasury. Member: UN Pension Board, 1966–71; UN Cttee on Contributions, 1966–71, 1975–77; Chm., UN Adv. Cttee on Admin. and Budgetary Questions, 1971–74; Senior Adviser (Asst Sec.-Gen.) to Administrator, UNDP, 1979–80. *Recreations:* gardening, playing the electronic organ. *Address:* Quintins, Watersfield, Pulborough, W Sussex RH20 1NE. *T:* (01798) 831634.
Died 17 May 2011.

RICE, His Honour Gordon Kenneth; a Circuit Judge, 1980–2000; *b* 16 April 1927; *m* 1967. *Educ:* Brasenose Coll., Oxford (MA). Called to the Bar, Middle Temple, 1957. *Address:* 4 Kings Road, Westcliff-on-Sea, Essex SS0 8BH.
Died 19 Jan. 2014.

RICE, Michael Penarthur Merrick, CMG 2002; FCIPR; Chairman, The Michael Rice Group Ltd, 1957–2005; *b* 21 May 1928; *s* of late Arthur Vincent Rice, Penarth, Glam, and Dora Kathleen (*née* Blacklock). *Educ:* Challoner Sch. Dir, Eastern England Television Ltd, 1964–83; Consultant/Advr, Govts of Egypt, Jamaica, Bahrain, Saudi Arabia and Oman; planner and designer, museums in Bahrain, Qatar, Saudi Arabia and Oman. Co-Founder, Public Relations Consultants Assoc. (Chm., 1978–81; Hon. Fellow, 1985); Advr, Bahrain British Foundn, 1980–2005; Chm., Bahrain Soc., 1997–2008; Mem., Internat. Assoc. of Egyptologists, 1990. FCIPR (FIPR 1975). Aga Khan Award for Architecture, 1980; Rawabi Prize, Saudi Arabia, 2009. Order of Bahrain, 1st Cl., 2003. *Publications:* The Temple Complex at Barbar, Bahrain, 1983; Dilmun Discovered: the first hundred years of the archaeology of Bahrain, 1984; (ed jtly) Bahrain Through the Ages, 1986; Egypt's Making, 1990; The Archaeology of the Arabian Gulf, 1993; False Inheritance: Israel in Palestine and the search for a solution, 1996; The Power of the Bull, 1998; Egypt's Legacy: the archetypes of Western Civilization, 1997; Who's Who in Ancient Egypt, 1999; Traces of Paradise: the archaeology of Bahrain 2500 BC–300 AD (exhibition catalogue), 2000; (ed jtly) Consuming Ancient Egypt, 2003; (ed jtly) Swifter than the Arrow: the golden hunting hounds of Ancient Egypt, 2006. *Recreations:* collecting paintings, listening to music, the Eighteenth Century. *Address:* The North Wing, The Mansion House, Burley on the Hill, Oakham, Rutland LE15 7FH. *T:* (01572) 770696, *Fax:* (01572) 770694. *E:* michaelricecmg@icloud.com. *Club:* Athenæum.
Died 1 Oct. 2013.

RICE, Peter Anthony Morrish; stage designer; *b* 13 Sept. 1928; *s* of Cecil Morrish Rice and Ethel (*née* Blacklaw); *m* 1954, Patricia Albeck; one *s*. *Educ:* St Dunstan's Coll., Surrey; Royal Coll. of Art (ARCA 1951). Designed first professional prodn, Sex and the Seraphim, Watergate Theatre, London, 1951, followed by The Seraglio, Sadler's Wells Opera, 1952, and Arlecchino, Glyndebourne, 1954; subsequently designed over 100 plays, operas and ballets, including: *plays:* Time Remembered, 1954; The Winter's Tale, and Much Ado About Nothing, Old Vic, 1956; Living for Pleasure, 1956; A Day in the Life of…, 1958; The Lord Chamberlain Regrets, and Toad of Toad Hall, 1961; The Farmer's Wife, The Italian Straw Hat, and Heartbreak House, Chichester, 1966; Flint, and Arms and the Man, 1970; Happy Birthday, 1977; Private Lives, Greenwich and West End, 1980; Present Laughter, Greenwich and West End, 1981; Cavell, and Goodbye Mr Chips, Chichester, 1982; The Sleeping Prince, Chichester and West End, 1983; Forty Years On, Chichester and West End, 1984; Thursday's Ladies, Apollo, 1987; Hay Fever, Chichester, and Re: Joyce!, Fortune, 1988; Don't Dress for Dinner, Apollo, 1990; Night Must Fall, Haymarket, 1996; The Importance of Being Earnest, Chichester, transf. Haymarket, 1999; *operas:* Count Ory, Sadler's Wells, 1962; Arabella, Royal Opera, 1964, Paris Opera, 1981, Chicago, 1984, and Covent Garden, 1986; The Thieving Magpie, and The Violins of St Jacques, Sadler's Wells, 1967; La Bohème, Scottish Opera, 1970; The Magic Flute, Ottawa, 1974; Tosca, Scottish Opera, 1980; The Secret Marriage, Buxton Fest., 1981; The Count of Luxembourg, Sadler's Wells, 1982, 1987; Death in Venice, Antwerp, and Die Fledermaus, St Louis, USA, 1983; Manon, Covent Garden, 1987; Così Fan Tutte, Ottawa, 1990, Hong Kong, 1991; Carmen, Hong Kong, 1992; Ottone, Tokyo, 1992, QEH, 1993; Madama Butterfly, Holland, 1993; L'Infedelta Delusa, Garsington, 1993; L'Etoile, La Bohème, Carmen, 1995–97, Martha, 2000, Castleward Opera, NI; Un Ballo in Maschera, Iris, Eugene Onegin, 1996–97, Così fan tutte,

The Yeomen of the Guard, 2000, The Merry Widow, 2006, Lakmé, 2007, Orpheus in the Underworld, 2009, Opera Holland Park; Tosca (revival), Opera di Orviedo, 2009; *ballets:* Romeo and Juliet, Royal Danish Ballet, 1955, new prodn 1995, and London Festival Ballet, 1985; Sinfonietta, Royal Ballet, 1966; The Four Seasons, Royal Ballet, 1974. Theatre interiors: Vaudeville Theatre, London; Grand Theatre, Blackpool; His Majesty's Theatre, Aberdeen; Minerva Studio Theatre, Chichester. *Publications:* The Clothes Children Wore, 1973; Farming, 1974; Narrow Boats, 1976. *Recreation:* ancient films. *Club:* Garrick. *Died 24 Dec. 2015.*

RICHARDS, Arthur Cyril, FIA; consultant; *b* 7 April 1921; *s* of Ernest Arthur Richards and Kate Richards (*née* Cooper); *m* 1st, 1944, Joyce Bertha Brooke (marr. diss. 1974); two *s* two *d*; 2nd, 1975, Els Stoyle; two step *s* one step *d*. *Educ:* Tollington Sch., London. FIA 1949; FSVA 1962. Insurance, 1937–41. Served RAF, 1941–46. Insurance, consulting actuary, steel manufacture, investment banking, internat. property develt, 1946–64; Advr, Samuel Montagu & Co. Ltd, 1965–67; Gp Finance Dir, Bovis Ltd, 1967–71; United Dominions Trust Ltd: Gp Finance Dir, 1971–76; Gp Man. Dir, 1976–80; Chief Exec., 1981–83; Dir, 1978–88, Chm., 1983–88, Blackwood Hodge plc. Chm., Federated Land, 1982; Director: MSL Gp Internat., 1970–81; TSB Trust Co., 1981–88; Combined Lease Finance PLC, 1985–89; Hermes Gp, 1990–2002. *Recreations:* sailing, antiques. *Died 13 June 2011.*

RICHARDS, Prof. Peter, FMedSci; President, Hughes Hall, Cambridge, 1998–2006; *b* 25 May 1936; *s* of William and Barbara Richards; *m* 1st, 1959, Anne Marie Larsen (marr. diss. 1986); one *s* three *d*; 2nd, 1987, Prof. Carol Anne Seymour. *Educ:* Monkton Combe Sch.; Emmanuel Coll., Cambridge (BA 1957; MB BChir 1960; MA 1961; MD 1971; Hon. Fellow, 2002); St George's Hosp. Medical Sch.; Royal Postgraduate Medical Sch. (PhD 1966); FRCP 1976. Consultant Physician, St Peter's Hosp., Chertsey and Hon. Sen. Lectr in Medicine, St Mary's Hosp. Med. Sch., 1970–73; Sen. Lectr in Medicine, St George's Hosp. Med. Sch., 1973–79; Dean and Prof. of Medicine, 1979–95, Emeritus Prof., 1995, St Mary's Hosp. Med. Sch. (part of ICSTM, 1988–), Univ. of London; Pro-Rector (Medicine), Imperial Coll., 1988–95; Med. Dir, Northwick Park and St Mark's NHS Trust, 1995–98. Non-exec. Dir, W Suffolk Hosps NHS Trust, 2001–06. Chm., Council of Deans of UK Med. Schs and Faculties, 1994–95. Mem., Septemviri, Univ. of Cambridge, 2000–05. Med. Advr to Health Service Ombudsman, 1999–2001. Member: GMC, 1994–2003 (Dep. Chm., 1999–2002, Chm., 2002, Professional Conduct Cttee); Council, RCP, 1994–97. Mem. Council, Anglo-Finnish Soc., 1984–. Freeman, City of London, 1985; Liveryman, Soc. of Apothecaries, 1984–. Hon. Fellow, Hughes Hall, Cambridge, 2006. Founder FMedSci 1998. Kt, Order of White Rose (Finland), 2001. *Publications:* The Medieval Leper, 1977; (ed jtly) Clinical Medicine and Therapeutics, Vol. I, 1977, Vol. II, 1979; Understanding Water, Electrolyte and Acid/Base Metabolism, 1983; Learning Medicine, 1983, 17th edn 2006; Living Medicine, 1990; UCAS Guide to Entry to Medicine, 1996, 2nd edn 1997; (with S. Stockhill) The New Learning Medicine, 1997 (Soc. of Authors Prize for best gen. med. book, 1998); Harvest of a Quiet Eye, 2010; scientific papers esp. concerning kidney disease and criteria for selection of medical students in Lancet, BMJ, etc. *Recreations:* walking, listening to music, Finland, social history, cycling. *Address:* Barefords, 78 Commercial End, Swaffham Bulbeck, Cambs CB25 0NE. *T:* (01223) 812007. *E:* pr229@cam.ac.uk. *Clubs:* Garrick; Hawks (Cambridge). *Died 29 Sept. 2011.*

RICHARDSON, George Taylor, CM 2002; OM 2000; Hon. Chairman, James Richardson & Sons, Limited, Winnipeg, Canada, since 2000 (Chairman, 1993–2000; President 1966–93; Vice-President 1954); *b* 22 Sept. 1924; *s* of late James Armstrong Richardson and Muriel (*née* Sprague); *m* 1948, Tannis Maree Thorlakson; two *s* one *d*. *Educ:* Grosvenor Sch. and Ravenscourt Sch., Winnipeg; Univ. of Manitoba (BComm). Joined family firm of James Richardson & Sons Ltd, 1946. Hon. LLD: Manitoba; Winnipeg. *Recreations:* hunting, helicopter flying. *Clubs:* MB, St Charles (Winnipeg); Bear's Paw (Naples, Fla). *Died 14 May 2014.*

RICHARDSON, Rt Hon. Sir Ivor (Lloyd Morgan), Kt 1986; PCNZM 2002; PC 1978; SJD; President, Court of Appeal of New Zealand, 1996–2002 (Judge, 1977–96); Non-Permanent Judge, Hong Kong Court of Final Appeal, 2003–09; *b* 24 May 1930; *s* of W. T. Richardson; *m* 1955, Jane, *d* of I. J. Krchma; three *d*. *Educ:* Canterbury Univ. (LLB); Univ. of Mich (LLM, SJD). Partner, Macalister Bros, Invercargill, 1957–63; Crown Counsel, Crown Law Office, Wellington, 1963–66; Victoria University of Wellington: Prof. of Law, 1967–73; Dean of Law Faculty, 1968–71; Pro-Chancellor, 1979–84; Chancellor, 1984–86; Dist. Vis. Fellow, 2002–; Partner, Watts & Patterson, Wellington, 1973–77. Chm., Cttees of Inquiry into Inflation Accounting, 1975–76, into Solicitors Nominee Cos, 1983. Chairman: Council of Legal Educn, 1983–92; Royal Commn on Social Policy, 1986–88; Orgnl Rev. of Inland Revenue Dept, 1993–94. Hon. LLD: Canterbury, 1987; Victoria, 1989. *Publications:* books and articles on legal subjects. *Address:* 16/127 Molesworth Street, Wellington 6011, New Zealand. *T:* (4) 4728826. *Club:* Wellington (Wellington, NZ). *Died 29 Dec. 2014.*

RICHARDSON, John Francis; Director and Chief Executive, National & Provincial Building Society, 1985–86; *b* 16 June 1934; *s* of Francis and Stella Richardson; *m* 1960, Jacqueline Mary Crosby; two *d*. *Educ:* Wadham College, Oxford (PPE). FCBSI. Burnley Building Society, 1959–82; Chief General Manager, 1980–82; Dep. Chief Executive, National & Provincial Building Society, 1983–85. Pres., CBSI, 1985. *Recreations:* gardening, military history. *Address:* Low Gables, Spofforth Hill, Wetherby, West Yorks LS22 6SF. *Died 21 July 2011.*

RICHARDSON, Prof. Robert Coleman, PhD; Floyd Newman Professor of Physics, Cornell University, since 1987; *b* 26 June 1937; *s* of Robert Franklin Richardson and Lois Richardson (*née* Price); *m* 1962, Betty Marilyn McCarthy; one *d* (and one *d* decd). *Educ:* Virginia Poly. Inst. and State Univ.; Duke Univ. Served US Army, 1959–60. Cornell University: Res. Associate, 1966–67; Asst Prof., 1968–71; Associate Prof., 1972–74; Prof. of Physics, 1975–86; Dir, Lab. of Atomic and Solid State Physics, 1990–97; Vice Provost for Res., 1998–2007; Emeritus Sen. Vice Provost for Res., 2008–; Sen. Sci. Advr to Pres. and Vice Provost, 2007–09. Chm., C-5 Cttee, IUPAP, 1981–84; Mem., Bd of Assessment, Nat. Bureau of Standards, 1983–. FAAAS. (Jtly) Nobel Prize for Physics, 1996. *Publications:* (jtly) Discovering Complexity: decomposition and localization as strategies in scientific research, 1993; (jtly) Experimental Techniques in Condensed Matter Physics at Low Temperatures, 1998; articles in learned jls. *Address:* Department of Physics, Cornell University, 517 Clark Hall, Ithaca, NY 14853, USA. *Died 19 Feb. 2013.*

RICHARDSON, Lt-Gen. Sir Robert (Francis), KCB 1982; CVO 1978; CBE 1975 (OBE 1971; MBE 1965); Lieutenant of the Tower of London, 1992–95; Administrator, MacRobert Trusts, 1985–95; *b* Leith, 2 March 1929; *s* of late Robert Buchan Richardson and Anne (*née* Smith); *m* 1st, 1956, Maureen Anne Robinson (*d* 1986); three *s* one *d*; 2nd, 1988, Alexandra Inglis (*née* Bomford); two step *s*. *Educ:* George Heriot's Sch., Edinburgh; RMA Sandhurst. Commnd into The Royal Scots, 1949; served in BAOR, Korea, and Middle East with 1st Bn The Royal Scots until 1960; Defence Services Staff Coll., India, 1960–61; psc 1961; GSO II MO4, MoD, 1961–64; jssc 1964; Brigade Major Aden Bde, 1967 (Despatches); GSO II ACDS (Ops), MoD, 1968–69; CO 1st Bn The Royal Scots, 1969–71; Col Gen. Staff, Staff Coll. Camberley, 1971–74; Comdr 39 Infantry Bde, Northern Ireland, 1974–75; Deputy Adjutant General, HQ BAOR, 1975–78; GOC Berlin (British Sector), 1978–80; Vice Adjutant Gen. and Dir of Army Manning, 1980–82; GOC NI, 1982–85. Col, The Royal Scots (The Royal Regt), 1980–90. Chairman: Greencastle Farming plc, 1995–2004; RSC Mgt Ltd, 1999–2012. Man. Trustee, BLESMA, 1995–2002 (Mem., National Adv. Cttee, 2000–04); Trustee, Scottish Civic Trust, 1997–2003. OStJ

1988. *Recreations:* golf, shooting, gardening, supporter of Rugby playing grandsons. *Address:* c/o Bank of Scotland, PO Box 23688, The Mound, Edinburgh EH1 1WG. *Clubs:* Royal Scots (Trustee, 1995–2012) (Edinburgh); Hon. Co. of Edinburgh Golfers (Muirfield). *Died 21 Nov. 2014.*

RICHARDSON, Maj.-Gen. Thomas Anthony, (Tony), CB 1976; MBE 1960; Secretary, Christmas Tree Growers Association of Western Europe, 1989–2003; *b* 9 Aug. 1922; *s* of late Maj.-Gen. T. W. Richardson, Eaton Cottage, Unthank Road, Norwich, and Mrs J. H. Boothby, Camberley; *m* 1st, 1945, Katharine Joanna Ruxton Roberts (*d* 1988), Woodland Place, Bath; one *s* one *d*; 2nd, 1991, Anthea Rachel Fry, Wimbledon. *Educ:* Wellington Coll., Berks. Technical Staff Course, psc, Fixed Wing Pilot, Rotary Wing Pilot, Parachutist. War of 1939–45: enlisted, Feb. 1941; commissioned, RA, March 1942; Essex Yeomanry (France and Germany), 1942–45; Air Observation Post, 1945–46. Tech. Staff/G Staff, 1949–52, 1954–55, 1959–60, 1963–64; Regt duty, 1942–45, 1952–54, 1957–58, 1961–62. Instr, Mil. Coll. Science, 1955–56; CO, 7th Para, RHA, 1965–67; CRA, 2 Div., 1967–69; Dir, Operational Requirements (Army), 1969–71; Dir, Army Aviation, 1971–74; Defence and Military Advr, India, 1974–77. Col Comdt, RA, 1978–83. Asst Sec., 1978–80, Sec. 1980–84, Timber Growers England and Wales Ltd; Sec., British Christmas Tree Growers Assoc., 1980–98; Dep. Chm., 1984–86, Chm., 1986–88, Tree Council. Chm., Queen Mary's Roehampton Trust, 2001–02. President: Essex Yeomanry Assoc., 1982–2006 (Vice-Pres., 2006–); Surrey Normandy Veterans Assoc., 1993–; Normandy Veterans Assoc., 2007–12 (Vice-Patron, 2012–); Pres./Chm., Air Observation Post Officers' Assoc., 2002–12. *Recreations:* sailing, fishing. *Address:* The Lodge, 7 Woodhayes Road, Wimbledon, SW19 4RJ. *Club:* Army and Navy. *Died 26 March 2015.*

RICKUS, Gwenneth Margaret, CBE 1981; Director of Education, London Borough of Brent, 1971–84; *b* 1925; *d* of Leonard William Ernest and Florence Rickus. *Educ:* Latymer Sch., Edmonton; King's Coll., Univ. of London. BA, PGCE. Teaching, 1948–53; Asst Sec., AAM, 1953–61; Education Administration: Middx CC, 1961–65; London Borough of Brent, 1965–84. Cllr (Lib Dem), New Forest DC, 1991–99. Co-opted Mem. Educn Cttee, Hampshire CC, 1985–97. Comr for Racial Equality, 1977–80. *Recreations:* reading, crafts, music. *Died 28 Jan. 2015.*

RIDDELL, (John) Alistair, OBE 1988; Treasurer, British Medical Association, 1987–96; *b* 11 Feb. 1930; *s* of Alexander Riddell and Mamie McFarlane MacKintosh; *m* 1st, 1956, Elizabeth Park McDonald Davidson (*d* 1999); one *s* three *d*; 2nd, 1999, Susan Anne Fraser, MD, FRCPGlas. *Educ:* Glasgow Acad.; Glasgow Univ. (MB ChB). FRCGP 1983; FRCPGlas 1996. GP E Glasgow, 1956–95; Clinical Asst, Geriatrics, Lightburn Hosp., 1968–78. Member: Glasgow Local Med. Cttee, 1964–95 (Med. Sec., 1978–91); Scottish GDC, 1975–82; Gen. Med. Services Cttee, 1972–96 (Negotiator, 1982–87; Vice-Chm., 1985–87); Chairman: Scottish Gen. Med. Services Cttee, 1983–86; Glasgow Area Med. Cttee, 1974–90. Mem. Council, BMA, 1983– (Chm., Community Care Cttee, 1991–94; Mem., 1982–2003, Chm., 2001–03, Scottish Council; Mem., 1982–2005, Chm., 2001–05, Charities Cttee); Mem., GMC, 1994–99 (Chm., Assessment Referral Cttee, 1997–99); Treas., Commonwealth Med. Assoc., 1989–2001. Dir, GP Finance Corp., 1975–90 (Vice-Chm., 1989–90); Dir, BMA Services, 1987–97; Chm., BMA Prof. Services, 1994–96. Dir, Silver Birch (Scotland) Ltd, 1996– (Chm., 1997–2002). Assessor, Scottish Community Foundn, 1997–2003. Mem., CAB Easter House, 1974–77. Mem., Bonnetmakers' Craft and Grand Antiquity Soc., Glasgow. *Publications:* contrib. BMJ and Scottish Med. Jl. *Recreations:* golf, ski-ing, sailing. *Address:* 27 Upper Glenburn Road, Bearsden, Glasgow G61 4BN. *T:* (0141) 942 0235. *Died 19 March 2012.*

RIDLEY, 4th Viscount *cr* 1900; **Matthew White Ridley,** KG 1992; GCVO 1994; TD 1960; JP; DL; Baron Wensleydale, 1900; Bt 1756; Lord-Lieutenant and Custos Rotulorum of Northumberland, 1984–2000; Lord Steward of HM Household, 1989–2001; *b* 29 July 1925; *e s* of 3rd Viscount Ridley; *S* father, 1964; *m* 1953, Lady Anne Lumley (*d* 2006), 3rd *d* of 11th Earl of Scarbrough, KG, GCSI, GCIE, GCVO, PC; one *s* three *d*. *Educ:* Eton; Balliol College, Oxford. MRICS (ARICS 1951). Coldstream Guards (NW Europe), 1943–46, Captain, 1946; Northumberland Hussars, 1947–64 (Lt-Col 1961, Bt Col 1964); ADC to Sir Evelyn Baring, Gov. of Kenya, 1952–53; Hon. Colonel: Northumberland Hussars Sqdn, Queen's Own Yeomanry, 1979–86; Queen's Own Yeomanry RAC TA, 1984–86; Northumbrian Univs OTC, 1986–90; Col Comdt, Yeomanry RAC TA, 1982–86. Director: Northern Rock Building Soc., 1962– (Chm., 1987–92); Tyne Tees Television, 1964–90; Barclays Bank (NE) Ltd, 1964–90; Municipal Mutual Insurance, 1982–93. Chm., NE Housing Assoc., 1970–74; Member: Layfield Cttee of Enquiry into Local Govt Finance, 1974–; Commonwealth War Graves Commn, 1991–99. Chm., Internat. Dendrology Soc., 1988–93; President: British Deer Soc., 1970–73; Natural Hist. Soc. of Northumbria, 1997–2005. Chm., N of England TA Assoc., 1980–84; Pres., TA & VRA Council, 1984–95 (Patron, 1995–); Vice-Pres., SSAFA. Chm., Newcastle Univ. Develt Trust, 1981–84; Chancellor, 1978–80, Hon. Fellow, 1980, Newcastle upon Tyne Polytechnic; Chancellor, Newcastle Univ., 1989–99. Hon. FRHS 1986; Hon. FRICS 1986. JP 1957, CC 1958, CA 1963, DL 1968, Northumberland; Chm., Northumberland CC, 1967–74, Chm., new Northumberland CC, 1974–79; Pres., ACC, 1979–84. Pres., Blyth Spartans FC, 2000. KStJ 1984; Hon. DCL Newcastle, 1989. Order of Merit, West Germany, 1974. *Heir:* *s* Hon. Matthew White Ridley, *b* 7 Feb. 1958. *Address:* Boston House, Blagdon, Seaton Burn, Newcastle upon Tyne NE13 6DB. *T:* (01670) 789236. *Clubs:* Boodle's, Pratt's; Northern Counties (Newcastle upon Tyne). *Died 22 March 2012.*

RISK, Sir Thomas (Neilson), Kt 1984; FRSE; Governor of the Bank of Scotland, 1981–91 (Director, 1971; Deputy Governor, 1977–81); *b* 13 Sept. 1922; *s* of late Ralph Risk, CBE, MC, and Margaret Nelson Robertson; *m* 1949, Suzanne Eiloart (*d* 2011); three *s* (and one *s* decd). *Educ:* Kelvinside Academy; Glasgow Univ. (BL). Flight Lieut, RAF, 1941–46; RAFVR, 1946–53. Partner, Maclay Murray & Spens, Solicitors, 1950–81; Director: Standard Life Assurance Co., 1965–88 (Chm., 1969–77); British Linen Bank, 1968–91 (Governor, 1977–86); Howden Group, 1971–87; Merchants Trust, 1973–94; MSA (Britain) Ltd, 1958–98; Shell UK Ltd, 1982–92; Barclays Bank, 1983–85; Bank of Wales, 1986–91; Chm., Scottish Financial Enterprise, 1986–89. Member: Scottish Industrial Develt Bd, 1972–75; Scottish Econ. Council, 1983–91; NEDC, 1987–91. Chm., Edinburgh Internat. Festival Endowment Fund, 1987–96. Chm., Univ. of Glasgow Trust, 1992–2004. Hon. Pres., Citizens Th., Glasgow, 1995–2002. FRSE 1988. Hon. LLD Glasgow, 1985; Dr *hc* Edinburgh, 1990. *Address:* 29/31 Inverleith Place, Edinburgh EH3 5QD. *T:* (0131) 552 0571. *Clubs:* Royal Air Force; New (Edinburgh). *Died 27 June 2012.*

RITCHESON, Prof. Charles Ray; University Professor of History, Dean and University Librarian Emeritus, University of Southern California, since 1991; *b* 26 Feb. 1925; *s* of Charles Frederick and Jewell Vaughn Ritcheson; *m* 1st, 1953, Shirley Spackman (marr. diss. 1964); two *s*; 2nd, 1965, Alice Luethi; four *s*. *Educ:* Univs of Harvard, Zürich, Oklahoma and Oxford. DPhil (Oxon). FRHistS. Prof. and Chm. of History, Kenyon Coll., 1953–65; Chm. and Dir, Graduate Studies, Southern Methodist Univ., 1966–70; Lovell Prof. of History, Univ. of Southern Calif., 1971–74; Cultural Attaché, US Embassy, 1974–77; University of Southern California: Lovell Distinguished Prof. of History, 1977–84; Univ. Prof., Univ. Librarian, Dean and Special Advr to Pres., 1984–91; Dist. Emeritus Prof., 2000. Vis. Prof., Univs of Edinburgh and Cambridge, 1965–66. Chm., British Inst. of the US, 1979–81; Exec. Sec., American Conf. on British Studies, 1971–74. Vice-Pres., Board of Dirs, Amer. Friends of Covent Garden, 1978–84; Exec. Vice Pres., Fund for Arts and Culture in Central and Eastern Europe, 1992–96; Member: National Council for the Humanities, 1983–87 and 1988–91; US Bd of Foreign Scholarships, 1987–88; Adv. Council, Amer. Ditchley Foundn, 1977–2001; Adv. Council, Univ. of

Buckingham (formerly UC Buckingham), 1977–90; Examination Jury, Ecole Nat. de l'Admin, 1998–2000; Bd of Dirs, Trust for Mus. Exhibitions, 2003–05; Sen. Advr, Libya Project, 2005–. Member: Assoc. pour le Rayonnement de l'Opéra à Paris, 1993–; French Archaeol Soc., 1998–; French Heritage Soc., 2002–. Hon. DLitt Leicester, 1976. *Publications:* British Politics and the American Revolution, 1954; Aftermath of Revolution: British policy toward the United States 1783–1795, 1969 (paperback 1971); The American Revolution: the Anglo-American relation, 1969; (with E. Wright) A Tug of Loyalties, 1971; contrib. articles and reviews. *Recreations:* horseback riding, swimming, opera. *Address:* 2801 New Mexico Avenue NW, The Colonnade, Washington, DC 20007, USA. *Clubs:* Beefsteak, Brooks's; Cosmos (Washington). *Died 8 Dec. 2011.*

RITCHIE OF BROMPTON, Baroness *cr* 2010 (Life Peer), of Brompton in the Royal Borough of Kensington and Chelsea; **Shireen Olive Ritchie;** Member (C) Royal Borough of Kensington and Chelsea Council, since 1998 (Deputy Mayor, 2008–09); *b* 22 June 1945; one *s* by a former marriage; *m* 1982, John Ritchie; one step *s* one step *d.* Cabinet Mem. for Social Services and Health, 2003–05, for Family and Children's Services, 2005–, RBK&C Council. Chm., Children and Young People's Bd, LGA. Chm., Candidates Cttee, Cons. Party, 2006–10. Member: Kensington and Chelsea Cons. Assoc. (former Chm.); Cons. Councillors Assoc. Mem. Bd, CAFCASS; Vice Pres., UK Youth, 1996–; Pres., Nat. Children's Bureau, 2010–. *Address:* House of Lords, SW1A 0PW. *Died 24 April 2012.*

RITCHIE, Rear-Adm. George Stephen, CB 1967; DSC 1942; writer; hydrographer; *b* 30 Oct. 1914; *s* of Sir (John) Douglas Ritchie, MC and Margaret Stephen, OBE 1946, JP, Officer of the Order of Orange-Nassau, *d* of James Allan, Methlick, Aberdeenshire; *m* 1942, Mrs Disa Elizabeth Smith (*née* Beveridge) (*d* 2000); two *s* one *d* (and one *s* decd). *Educ:* RNC, Dartmouth. Joined RN Surveying Service, 1936; attached Eighth Army, 1942–43; served in HM Survey Ship Scott for invasion of Europe, 1944; comd HMS Challenger on scientific voyage round world, 1950–51; comd HM New Zealand Survey Ship Lachlan and NZ Surveying Service, 1953–56; comd HM Surveying Ship Dalrymple, Persian Gulf, 1959; comd HM Surveying Ship Vidal, West Indies and Western Europe, 1963–65; ADC to the Queen, 1965; Hydrographer of the Navy, 1966–71; Vis. Research Fellow, Southampton Univ., 1971–72; Pres., Directing Cttee, Internat. Hydrographic Bureau, Monaco, 1972–82; Founder Pres., 1972–73, Emeritus Mem., 1988–, Hydrographic Soc. Hon. Member: Canadian Hydrographic Assoc., 1981; Hydrographic Soc. of SA, 1985; Challenger Soc., 1992 (Hon. Life Mem., 1993). Chm., Collieston Harbour Trustees, 1991–96. Columnist, Hydro Internat. jl, 1997–2007. Founder's Medal, RGS, 1972; Prix Manley-Bendall, Académie de Marine, Paris, 1977; Gold Medal, Royal Inst. of Navigation, 1978; Dalrymple Trophy, Internat. Hydrographic Orgn, 2006. *Publications:* Challenger, 1957; The Admiralty Chart, 1967, new edn 1995; No Day Too Long, 1992; As It Was - Highlights of Hydrographic History, 2003; papers on navigation and oceanography in various jls, including Developments in British Hydrography since days of Captain Cook (RSA Silver Medal, 1970). *Recreations:* conserving Collieston, boules, sea-fishing. *Address:* Sea View, Collieston, Ellon, Aberdeenshire AB41 8RS. *Clubs:* Reform; Royal Northern and University (Aberdeen) (Hon. Mem.); Collieston Boules; Monte Carlo (Emeritus Mem.). *Died 8 May 2012.*

RIX, Timothy John, CBE 1997; Chairman, Longman Group Ltd, 1984–90 (Chief Executive, 1976–89); *b* 4 Jan. 1934; *s* of late Howard Terrell Rix and Marguerite Selman Rix; *m* 1st, 1960, Wendy Elizabeth Wright (marr. diss. 1967); one *d*; 2nd, 1967, Gillian Diana Mary Greenwood; one *s* one *d. Educ:* Radley Coll.; Clare Coll., Cambridge (BA); Yale Univ., USA. Sub-Lieut, RNVR, 1952–54. Mellon Fellow, Yale, 1957–58; joined Longmans, Green & Co. Ltd, subseq. Longman Gp, 1958; Overseas Educnl Publisher, 1958–61; Publishing Manager, Far East and SE Asia, 1961–63; Head of English Language Teaching Publishing, 1964–68; Divl Man. Dir, 1968–72; Jt Man. Dir, 1972–76. Director: Pearson Longman Ltd, 1979–83; Goldcrest Television, 1981–83; Yale Univ. Press, London, 1984–2010; ECIC (Management) Ltd, 1990–92; Blackie and Son Ltd, 1990–93; B. H. Blackwell Ltd, 1990–95; Blackwell Ltd, 1993–95; HEA Publishing Adv. Bd, 1993–95; Geddes and Grosset Ltd, 1996–98; Jessica Kingsley Publishers Ltd, 1997–2008; Frances Lincoln Ltd, 1997–2009; Meditech Media Ltd, 1997–2003; Scottish Book Source, 1999–2008. Chairman: Book Marketing Ltd, 1990–2003; Edinburgh University Press, 2001–07; Senior Consultant: Pofcher Co., 1990–95; van Tulleken Co., 1996–2007. Chm., Pitman Examns Inst., 1987–90. Publishers Association: Chm., Trng Cttee, 1974–78; Chm., Book Develt Council, 1979–81; Vice-Pres., 1980–81 and 1983–84; Pres., 1981–83. Chairman: Book Trust, 1986–88; Book House Training Centre, 1986–89; British Library Centre for the Book, 1990–96; Society of Bookmen, 1990–92; British Library Publishing, 1992–2003; Book Aid International, 1994–2006; Nat. Book Cttee, 1997–2003. Member: Exec. Cttee, NBL, 1979–86 (Dep. Chm., 1984–86); Publishers Adv. Panel, British Council, 1978–98 (Chm., 1994–98); Arts Council Literature Panel, 1983–86; British Library Adv. Council, 1982–86; British Library Bd, 1986–96; British Council Bd, 1988–97; Finance Cttee, Delegacy of OUP, 1992–2002; Bd, HEA, 1996–99; Adv. Council, Inst. of English Studies, London Univ., 1999–2008. Hon. Pres., Independent Publishers' Guild, 1993–2008. Governor: Bell Educnl Trust, 1990–2004 (Chm. Govs, 1995–2001); ESU, 1999–2005. CCMI (CBIM 1981); FRSA 1986. Hon. MA Oxford, 1992; DUniv Stirling, 2006. *Publications:* articles on publishing in trade jls. *Recreations:* reading, landscape, wine. *Address:* Flat 1, 29 Barrington Road, N8 8QT. *T:* (020) 8348 4143. *Club:* Garrick. *Died 8 Nov. 2012.*

ROACH, Prof. Gary Francis, FRSE; Professor of Mathematics, University of Strathclyde, 1979–96, then Emeritus; *b* 8 Oct. 1933; *s* of John Francis Roach and Bertha Mary Ann Roach (*née* Walters); *m* 1960, Isabella Grace Willins Nicol. *Educ:* University Coll. of S Wales and Monmouthshire (BSc 1955); Univ. of London (MSc 1960); Univ. of Manchester (PhD 1964). FRAS, FIMA, CMath. RAF (Educn Branch), Flying Officer, 1955–58; Research Mathematician, BP, 1958–61; Lectr, UMIST, 1961–66; Vis. Prof., Univ. of British Columbia, 1966–67; University of Strathclyde: Lectr, 1967; Sen Lectr, 1970; Reader, 1971; Prof., 1979; Dean, Faculty of Science, 1982–87. Mem., Edinburgh Mathematical Soc. (Past Pres.). Deacon, Incorp. of Bonnetmakers and Dyers of Glasgow, 1997–98. FRSA 1991. Hon. Fellow, Solvay Inst., 1998. Hon. DSc Manchester, 1991; Hon. ScD Lodz, 1993. OStJ 1992. *Publications:* Green's Functions, 1970, 2nd edn 1982; An Introduction to Linear and Nonlinear Scattering Theory, 1997; Wave Scattering by Time-Dependent Perturbations: an introduction, 2007; An Introduction to Echo Analysis, 2010; (jtly) Mathematical Analysis of Deterministic and Stochastic Problems in Complex Media Electromagnets, 2012; articles in learned jls. *Recreations:* mountaineering, photography, philately, gardening, music. *Address:* 11 Menzies Avenue, Fintry, Glasgow G63 0YE. *T:* (01360) 860335. *Died 17 March 2012.*

ROADS, Peter George, MD; FFPH; Regional Medical Officer, South West Thames Regional Health Authority, 1973–82; *b* 14 Nov. 1917; *s* of Frank George Roads and Mary Dee Hill Roads (*née* Bury); *m* 1949, Evelyn Clara (*née* Daniel) (*d* 2014); one *s* one *d. Educ:* Bedford Sch.; St Mary's Hosp. Med Sch., London Univ. (MD); Hon. Society of Inner Temple. FFPH (FFCM 1974; FFPHM 1989). Served War, in China, 1944–46. MRC, Pneumoconiosis Unit, 1949–50; Dep. MOH, etc, City and Co. of Bristol, 1956–59; MOH, Principal Sch. Med. Officer and Port Med. Officer for City and Port of Portsmouth, 1959–73; Med. Referee to Portchester Crematorium, 1959–73, to Chilterns Crematorium, 1980–2005. Mem., Central Midwives Bd, 1964–76; Adviser on Health Services, Assoc. of Municipal Corporations, 1966–74. FRSocMed; Fellow, Soc. of Public Health (formerly of Community Medicine) (Pres., 1988–89). Chairman: Bucks Br., Historical Assoc., 1987–93; Bucks Family History Soc., 1990–93; Bucks Management Cttee, Oxford Diocesan Council for the Deaf, 1991–93. Mem. Deanery Synod, and Church Warden, Stone Dinton and Hartwell, 1988–91.

Publications: Care of Elderly in Portsmouth, 1970; Medical Importance of Open Air Recreation (Proc. 1st Internat. Congress on Leisure and Touring), 1966. *Recreations:* open air, walking, forestry, history, touring. *Address:* c/o Duchray House, Aberfoyle, Stirlingshire FK8 3XL. *T:* (01877) 389373. *Died 2 June 2015.*

ROBERTS OF CONWY, Baron *cr* 1997 (Life Peer), of Talyfan in the co. of Gwynedd; **Ieuan Wyn Pritchard Roberts,** Kt 1990; PC 1991; *b* 10 July 1930; *s* of late Rev. E. P. Roberts and Margaret Ann Roberts; *m* 1956, Enid Grace Williams; two *s* (and one *s* decd). *Educ:* Harrow; University Coll., Oxford. Sub-editor, Liverpool Daily Post, 1952–54; News Asst, BBC, 1954–57; TWW Ltd: News, Special Events and Welsh Language Programmes Producer, 1957–59; Production Controller, 1959–60; Exec. Producer, 1960–68; Welsh Controller, 1964–68; Programme Exec., Harlech TV, 1969. MP (C) Conway, 1970–83, Conwy, 1983–97. PPS to Sec. of State for Wales, 1970–74; opposition front bench spokesman on Welsh Affairs, 1974–79; Parly Under-Sec. of State, 1979–87, Minister of State, 1987–94, Welsh Office. Opposition front bench spokesman on Welsh Affairs, H of L, 1997–2007. Vice-Pres., Assoc. of District Councils, 1975–79. Mem. of Gorsedd, Royal National Eisteddfod of Wales, 1966. Member, Court of Governors: Nat. Library of Wales, 1970–91; Nat. Museum of Wales, 1970–91; University Coll. of Wales, Aberystwyth, 1970–91. Pres., Univ. of Wales Coll. of Medicine, 1997–2004; Vice Pres., Univ. of Cardiff, 2005–07. Hon. Fellow: Univ. of Wales, Bangor, 1995, Aberystwyth, 1997. Hon. LLD Wales, 2005. *Recreation:* gardening. *Address:* Tan y Gwalia, Conwy, Gwynedd LL32 8TY. *T:* (01492) 650371. *Died 13 Dec. 2013.*

ROBERTS, Prof. Benjamin Charles; Professor of Industrial Relations, London School of Economics, University of London, 1962–84, then Emeritus; *b* 1 Aug. 1917; *s* of Walter Whitfield Roberts and Mabel Frances Roberts; *m* 1945, Veronica Lilian (*d* 2001), *d* of George Frederick and Vera Lilian Vine-Lott; two *s*. *Educ:* London Sch. of Economics (Hon. Fellow, 1988); New Coll., Oxford (MA 1953). Research Student, Nuffield Coll., Oxford, 1948–49; Part-time Lectr, Ruskin Coll., Oxford, 1948–49; London Sch. of Economics: Lectr in Trade Union Studies, 1949–56; Reader in Industrial Relations, 1956–62; Mem. Ct of Govs, 1964–69, 1979–83. Visiting Professor: Princeton Univ., 1958; MIT 1959; Univ. of Calif., Berkeley, 1965. Assoc., Internat. Inst. of Labour Studies, Geneva, 1966; Member: Council, Inst. Manpower Studies; British-N American Cttee; Nat. Reference Tribunal of Coal Mining Industry, 1970–93; Council, ACAS, 1979–86; Bruges Gp, 1990–. Editor, British Jl of Industrial Relations, 1963–89, Hon. Editor, 1990–. Pres., British Univs Industrial Relations Assoc., 1965–68; Pres., Internat. Industrial Relations Assoc., 1967–73. Consultant to EEC, 1976–79. Chm., Economists' Bookshop, 1979–87. Wincott Lecture, IEA, 1987. *Publications:* Trade Unions in the New Era, 1947; Trade Union Government and Administration in Great Britain, 1956; National Wages Policy in War and Peace, 1958; The Trades Union Congress, 1868–1921, 1958; Trade Unions in a Free Society, 1959; (ed) Industrial Relations: Contemporary Problems and Perspectives, 1962; Labour in the Tropical Territories of the Commonwealth, 1964; (ed) Manpower Planning and Employment Trends 1966; (with L. Greyfié de Bellecombe) Collective Bargaining in African Countries, 1967; (ed) Industrial Relations: Contemporary Issues, 1968; (with John Lovell) A Short History of the TUC, 1968; (with R. O. Clarke and D. J. Fatchet) Workers' Participation in Management in Britain, 1972; (with R. Loveridge and J. Gennard) Reluctant Militants: a study of industrial technicians, 1972; (with H. Okomoto and G. Lodge) Collective Bargaining and Employee Participation in Western Europe, North America and Japan, 1979; also Evidence to Royal Commn on Trade Unions, 1966, and Report to ILO on Labour and Automation: Manpower Adjustment Programmes in the United Kingdom, 1967; Industrial Relations in Europe: the imperatives of change, 1985; (with T. Kochan and N. Meltz) New Departures in Industrial Relations: developments in USA, the UK and Canada, 1988; Europe—Uniformity or Freedom?: the real EC questions, 1991. *Address:* 28 Temple Fortune Lane, NW11 7UD. *T:* (020) 8458 1421. *Clubs:* Reform, Political Economy. *Died 17 May 2011.*

ROBERTS, Bernard, FRCM; concert pianist; Piano Professor, Royal College of Music, 1962–99; *b* 23 July 1933; *s* of William Wright Roberts and Elsie Alberta Roberts (*née* Ingham); *m* 1st, 1955, Patricia May Russell (marr. diss. 1988); two *s*; 2nd, 1992, Caroline Ireland. *Educ:* William Hulme's Grammar Sch., Manchester; Royal Coll. of Music (ARCM 1951; FRCM 1982). Début as concert pianist, Wigmore Hall, 1957; recital, concerto and chamber music pianist, 1957–; appeared with major British orchestras as soloist, incl. Promenade Concerts, 1979; recitals in UK and abroad, incl. master classes in major centres; broadcasts on BBC Radio 3. Member: Parikian-Fleming-Roberts Trio, 1975–84; Piano Trio with sons, 1991–2004. Piano Tutor, Chetham's Sch. of Music, Manchester, 2000–. FRWCMD 2004. DUniv Brunel, 1989. *Recreations:* philosophy, religion, model railways. *Address:* Uwchlaw'r Coed, Llanbedr, Gwynedd LL45 2NA. *T:* (01341) 241532. *E:* caroline.ireland@btinternet.com. *Died 3 Nov. 2013.*

ROBERTS, Rear-Adm. Cedric Kenelm, CB 1970; DSO 1952; Flag Officer, Naval Flying Training, 1968–71; *b* 19 April 1918; *s* of F. A. Roberts; *m* 1940, Audrey, *d* of T. M. Elias; four *s*. *Educ:* King Edward's Sch., Birmingham. Joined RN as Naval Airman 2nd Cl., 1940; commnd Temp. Sub-Lt (A), RNVR, 1940; sunk in HMS Manchester, 1942, Malta Convoy; interned in Sahara; released, Nov. 1942; Personal Pilot to Vice-Adm. Sir Lumley Lyster, 1943; HMS Trumpeter, Russian Convoys, 1944; perm. commn as Lt RN, HMS Vindex, Pacific, 1945; CO 813 Sqdn, 1948; Naval Staff Coll., 1949; CO 767 Sqdn, 1950–51; CO 825 Sqdn, 1951–52: served Korean War; shot down, rescued by US Forces; lent to RAN as Dep. Dir, Air Warfare, 1953–55; CO, RNAS Eglinton, 1958–59; Chief Staff Officer: FONFT, 1959–61; FOAC, 1961–62; Capt., HMS Osprey, 1962–64; Capt., RNAS Culdrose, 1964–65; Chief Staff Officer (Ops), Far East Fleet, 1966–67; retired RN 1971; farmed in Somerset, 1971–79; emigrated to Australia, 1979. Comdr 1952; Capt. 1958; Rear-Adm. 1968. Arctic Emblem, 2006. *Recreations:* sitting in the sun, drinking plonk, and watching the sheilas go by. *Address:* 11 Collins Street, Merimbula, NSW 2548, Australia. *T:* (2) 64951754. *Died 29 July 2011.*

ROBERTS, Sir Denys (Tudor Emil), KBE 1975 (CBE 1970; OBE 1960); *b* 19 Jan. 1923; *s* of William David and Dorothy Elizabeth Roberts; *m* 1st, 1949, Brenda Marsh (marr. diss. 1973); one *s* one *d*; 2nd, 1985, Anna Fiona Dollar Alexander; one *s*. *Educ:* Aldenham; Wadham Coll., Oxford, 1942 and 1946–49 (MA 1948, BCL 1949; Hon. Fellow, 1984). Served with Royal Artillery, 1943–46, France, Belgium, Holland, Germany, India (Captain). English Bar, 1950–53; Crown Counsel, Nyasaland, 1953–59; QC Gibraltar 1960; QC Hong Kong 1964; Attorney-General, Gibraltar, 1960–62; Solicitor-General, Hong Kong, 1962–66; Attorney-General, Hong Kong, 1966–73; Chief Secretary, Hong Kong, 1973–78; Chief Justice, Hong Kong, 1979–88; Pres., Court of Appeal, Bermuda, 1988–94; Chief Justice, 1979–2001, Pres., Ct of Appeal, 2002–03, Negara Brunei Darussalam. Hon. Bencher, Lincoln's Inn, 1978. SPMB (Negara Brunei Darussalam), 1984. *Publications:* Smuggler's Circuit, 1954; Beds and Roses, 1956; The Elwood Wager, 1958; The Bones of the Wajingas, 1960; How to Dispense with Lawyers, 1964; Doing them Justice, 1986; I'll Do Better Next Time, 1995; Yes Sir But, 2000; Another Disaster, 2006. *Recreations:* cricket, walking, writing. *Address:* The Grange, North Green Road, Pulham St Mary, Norfolk IP21 4QZ. *Clubs:* MCC (Pres., 1989–90), Royal Commonwealth Society. *Died 20 May 2013.*

ROBERTS, Prof. Geoffrey Frank Ingleson, CBE 1978; FREng; Chairman, British Pipe Coaters Ltd, 1978–88; Professor of Gas Engineering, University of Salford, 1983–89, Professorial Fellow, 1989–91; *b* 9 May 1926; *s* of late Arthur and Laura Roberts; *m* 1st, 1949, Veronica (*d* 1993), *d* of late Captain J. Busby, Hartlepool; two *d*; 2nd, 1995, Patricia, *widow* of Neville H. H. Johnson, Ilkley. *Educ:* Cathedral Sch., and High Sch. for Boys, Hereford; Leeds Univ. (BSc Hons). FIChemE; FInstE; FREng (FEng

1978). Pupil engr, Gas Light & Coke Co., and North Thames Gas Bd, 1947–50; North Thames Gas Board: Asst Engr, 1950–59; Stn Engr, Slough, 1959–61; Dep. Stn Engr, Southall Stn, 1961–66; Group Engr, Slough Group, 1966–68; Dep. Dir (Ops) Gas Council, 1968–71; Mem. for Production and Supply, Gas Council, later British Gas Corp., 1972–78; Mem. for External Affairs, British Gas Corp., 1979–81. President: IGasE, 1980–81 (Hon. FIGEM 1983); Inst. of Energy, 1983–84. *Recreation:* woodwork. *Address:* 2 Birchwood Court, South Parade, Ilkley, West Yorks LS29 9AW. *T:* (01943) 601671. *Died 24 March 2013.*

ROBERTS, John Arthur, CEng, FIET; Under-Secretary, Department of Energy, 1974–77; *b* 21 Dec. 1917; *s* of late John Richard and Emily Roberts; *m* 1st, 1944, Winifred Wilks Scott (*d* 1976); two *s* one *d*; 2nd, 1977, Rosetta Mabel Price (*d* 2009). *Educ:* Liverpool Institute; Liverpool Univ. (BEng). Apprentice, Metropolitan-Vickers Electrical Co. Ltd, 1939. Served War, Royal Signals, 1940–46, Major. Sen. Lectr, Applied Science, RMA, Sandhurst, 1947–49; SSO and PSO, RAE, Farnborough, 1949–59; Head, Control and Computers Section, Applications Br., Central Electricity Generating Bd, 1959–62; Project Ldr, Automatic Control, CEGB, 1962–67; DCSO, Min. of Tech. and DTI, 1967–72; Under-Sec., DTI, 1972–74. *Address:* Court House, Church Street, Cheddar BS27 3RA. *T:* (01934) 741637. *Died 2 Sept. 2013.*

ROBERTS, Prof. Lewis Edward John, CBE 1978; FRS 1982; Wolfson Professor of Environmental Risk Assessment, University of East Anglia, 1986–90, Emeritus Professor, since 1990; *b* 31 Jan. 1922; *s* of William Edward Roberts and Lilian Lewis Roberts; *m* 1948, Eleanor Mary Luscombe; one *s*. *Educ:* Swansea Grammar Sch.; Jesus Coll., Oxford (MA, DPhil). Clarendon Laboratory, Oxford, 1944; Scientific Officer, Chalk River Res. Estabt, Ont, Canada, 1946–47; AERE, Harwell, 1947, Principal Scientific Officer, 1952; Commonwealth Fund Fellow, Univ. of Calif, Berkeley, 1954–55; Dep. Head, Chemistry Div., 1966, Asst Dir, 1967, Dir, 1975–86, AERE. Mem., UKAEA, 1979–86. Pres., British Nuclear Energy Soc., 1985–87; Mem. Council and Vice Pres., Royal Instn, 1991–94. R. M. Jones Lectr, QUB, 1981; Rutherford Meml Lectr, Royal Soc., 1992. Governor, Abingdon Sch., 1978–86. *Publications:* Nuclear Power and Public Responsibility, 1984; Power Generation and the Environment, 1990; papers in qly revs and in scientific journals and IAEA pubns. *Recreations:* reading, gardening. *Address:* Penfold Wick, Chilton, Didcot OX11 0SH. *T:* (01235) 834309. *Died 10 April 2012.*

ROBERTS, Michael Guist, MBE 2011; FCA; Founder, Chief Executive Officer and Winemaker, Ridgeview Wine Estate, since 1994; *b* Colwyn Bay, N Wales, 1 Dec. 1943; *s* of Lionel and Barbara Roberts; *m* 1965, Christine Pamela Parson; one *s* one *d*. *Educ:* Purley Co. Grammar Sch. for Boys. FCA 1966. Analyst, Esso Chemical, Fawley Refinery, 1967–69; Financial Controller, Bowthorpe plc, 1969–74; Gp Finance Dir, Ofrex Gp plc, 1974–83; Founder and CEO, Michael Business System plc, 1983–94. Chm., English Wine Producers, 2005–. *Recreations:* sailing, learning French, my grandsons, working with my family. *Address:* Ridgeview Estate Winery Ltd, Fragbarrow Lane, Ditchling Common, Sussex BN6 8TP. *T:* (01444) 241441. *E:* mike@ridgeview.co.uk. *Club:* Royal Ocean Racing. *Died 14 Nov. 2014.*

ROBERTS, Prof. Simon Arthur, PhD; Professor of Law, London School of Economics and Political Science, 1986–2010, then Emeritus; *b* 13 April 1941; *s* of Arthur and Margaret Roberts; *m* 1965, Marian Bernadt; one *s* one *d*. *Educ:* Tonbridge Sch.; London Sch. of Econs and Pol Sci. (LLB 1962; PhD 1968; Hon. Fellow 2012). Lectr, Inst. of Public Admin, Blantyre, Malaŵi, 1963–64; London School of Economics: Asst Lectr, 1965–68; Lectr, 1968–77; Sen. Lectr, 1977–81; Reader, 1981–86. Prof. Invité, Aix-en-Provence, 1990. Gen. Ed., Modern Law Rev., 1988–95. Advr on Customary Law, Govt of Botswana, 1968–73. Member: Lord Chancellor's Adv. Bd on Family Law, 1997–2002; Adv. Cttee on Civil Costs, 2007–09. *Publications:* Order and Dispute, 1979; (with J. L. Comaroff) Rules and Processes, 1981; (with W. T. Murphy and T. Flessas) Understanding Property Law, 1987, 4th edn 2004; (with M. Palmer) Dispute Processes, 1998, 3rd edn 2014; A Court, 2013. *Recreations:* art, architecture, countryside. *Address:* London School of Economics, Houghton Street, WC2A 2AE. *T:* (020) 7955 7253. *E:* simon.roberts@lse.ac.uk. *Club:* Surrey. *Died 30 April 2014.*

ROBERTS, Sir William (James Denby), 3rd Bt *cr* 1909; *b* 10 Aug. 1936; *s* of Sir James Denby Roberts, 2nd Bt, OBE, and of Irene Charlotte D'Orsey, *yr d* of late William Dunn, MB, CM; *S* father, 1973. *Educ:* Rugby; Royal Agricultural Coll., Cirencester. MRAC, FRICS. Farmed at Strathallan Castle. *Recreation:* swimming. *Heir: nephew* James Elton Denby Roberts-Buchanan [*b* 12 July 1966; *m* 1994, Lisa Jane Stirling; one *s* three *d*]. *Address:* Strathallan Castle, Auchterarder, Perthshire PH3 1JZ. *T:* (01764) 662131. *Died 23 Nov. 2012.*

ROBERTSON, Donald Buchanan; QC (Scot.) 1973; Temporary Judge, Court of Session, Scotland, 1991–2002; *b* 29 March 1932; *s* of Donald Robertson, yachtbuilder, Sandbank, Argyll, and Jean Dunsmore Buchanan; *m* 1st, 1955, Louise Charlotte, *d* of Dr J. Linthorst-Homan; one *s* one *d*; 2nd, 1965, Daphne Jean Black Kincaid, (D. J. B. Robertson, WS). *Educ:* Dunoon Grammar Sch.; Glasgow Univ. (LLB). Admitted Solicitor, 1954; Royal Air Force (National Service), 1954–56. Passed Advocate, 1960; Standing Junior to Registrar of Restrictive Practices, 1970–73. Member: Sheriff Court Rules Council, 1972–76; Royal Commn on Legal Services in Scotland, 1976–80; Legal Aid Central Cttee, 1982–85; Criminal Injuries Compensation Bd, 1986–2002; Chm., VAT Tribunal, 1978–85. Hon. Sheriff, Lothian and Peebles, 1982–. FSA (Scot.) 1982. *Recreations:* shooting, numismatics, genealogy. *Address:* 11 Grosvenor Crescent, Edinburgh EH12 5EL. *T:* (0131) 337 5544. *Club:* New (Edinburgh). *Died 9 April 2012.*

ROBERTSON, Hamish, CB 1992; MBE 1966; Under Secretary, Scottish Office Education Department (formerly Scottish Education Department), 1987–92; *b* 6 April 1931; *s* of James and Elizabeth Robertson, Huntly; *m* 1955, Barbara Suzanne Taylor, *d* of late Dr G. C. and I. H. McL. Taylor, Peterhead; two *s* two *d*. *Educ:* The Gordon Schs, Huntly; Aberdeen Univ. (MA). RA, 1952–54. Joined Colonial Admin. Service; Nyasaland, 1954–64; HMOCS, Malawi, 1964–67; Scottish Office: Principal, 1967; Asst Sec., 1973. *Recreation:* country pursuits. *Address:* 14 Harviestoun Road, Dollar FK14 7HG. *T:* (01259) 742374. *Died 10 Sept. 2013.*

ROBERTSON, Rear-Adm. Ian George William, CB 1974; DSC 1944; *b* 21 Oct. 1922; *s* of late W. H. Robertson, MC, and Mrs A. M. Robertson; *m* 1947, Barbara Irène Holdsworth; one *s* one *d*. *Educ:* Radley College. Joined RNVR, 1941; qual. Pilot; Sub-Lt 1943; air strike ops against enemy shipping and attacks against German battleship Tirpitz, 1944 (DSC); Lieut, RN, 1945; flying and instructional appts, 1944–53; Comdr (Air): RNAS Culdrose, 1956; HMS Albion, 1958; in command: HMS Keppel, 1960; HMS Mohawk, 1963; RNAS Culdrose, 1965; idc 1968; in comd, HMS Eagle, 1970; Admiral Comdg Reserves, 1972–74; retd 1974. Comdr 1954; Captain 1963; Rear-Adm. 1972. Dir-Gen., Navy League, 1975–76; Scoutreach Resources Organiser, Scout Assoc., 1976–79. Pres., Craft Club, 1992–99. *Recreations:* golf, sailing, fishing. *Address:* The Studio, Bedford Place, Uckfield, E Sussex TN22 1LW. *T:* (01825) 764682. *Clubs:* Naval; Piltdown Golf. *Died 22 Feb. 2012.*

ROBERTSON, John Davie Manson, CBE 1993 (OBE 1978); DL; FRSE; Chairman, S. & J. D. Robertson Group, 1979–2010; *b* 6 Nov. 1929; *s* of late John Robertson and Margaret Gibson (*née* Wright); *m* 1959, Elizabeth Amelia Macpherson; two *s* two *d*. *Educ:* Kirkwall Grammar Sch.; Univ. of Edinburgh (BL). Anglo Iranian Oil Co., later BP, UK and ME, 1953–58; S. & J. D. Robertson Gp, 1958–. Dir, Stanley Services, Falkland Is, 1987–; Founder Chm., Orkney Today, 2003–10; Chm., Orkney Media Gp, 2007–10. Chairman: Kirkwall Ba' Cttee, 1977–2010; Orkney Health Bd, 1983–91 (Mem., 1974–79, Vice-Chm., 1979–83); Highland Health Bd, 1991–97; N of Scotland Water Authy, 1995–98. Member: Bd of Mgt, Orkney Hosps, 1970–74; Highlands and Is Consultative Council,

1988–91; Highlands and Is Enterprise, 1990–95; NHS Tribunal, 1990–2012; Chairman: Children's Panel, Orkney, 1971–76 (Chm., Adv. Cttee, 1977–82); Highlands and Is Savings Cttee, 1975–78; Scottish Health Mgt Efficiency Gp, 1985–95; Chm. and Vice-Chm., Scottish Health Bds Chairmen's Gp, 1995–97. Chm., Lloyds TSB Foundn for Scotland, 1997–99 (Trustee, 1989–99). Hon. Sheriff, Grampian Highland and Islands, 1977–. Hon. Vice Consul for Denmark, 1972–2004; Hon. Consul for Germany, 1976–2007. DL Sutherland, 1999. FRSE 2000; FRSA 1993. Hon. FCIWEM 1996. Knight, Order of Dannebrog (Denmark), 1982; Officer's Cross, Order of Merit (Germany), 1999 (Cavalier's Cross, 1986). *Publications:* Uppies and Doonies, 1967; (ed) An Orkney Anthology, vol. I, 1991, vol. II, 2012; Spinningdale and its Mill 1791–2000, 2000; The Kirkwall Ba', 2004; The Island of Fara 1739–2008, 2009; The Press Gang in Orkney and Shetland, 2011. *Recreations:* history, art. *Address:* S. & J. D. Robertson Gp, Dunkirk, Shore Street, Kirkwall, Orkney KW15 1LG; Spinningdale House, Spinningdale, Sutherland IV24 3AD. *T:* (01862) 881240. *Club:* New (Edinburgh). *Died 2 Nov. 2015.*

ROBERTSON, John Windeler; Senior Partner, Wedd Durlacher Mordaunt, 1979–86; *b* 9 May 1934; *s* of late John Bruce Robertson and Evelyn Windeler Robertson; *m* 1st, 1959, Jennifer-Ann Gourdou (marr. diss.; she *d* 2010); one *s* one *d*; 2nd, 1987, Rosemary Helen Jane Banks. *Educ:* Winchester Coll. National Service, RNVR, 1953–55. Joined Wedd Jefferson & Co. (Members of Stock Exchange), 1955; Partner, 1961. Dep. Chm., Barclays de Zoete Wedd Securities Ltd (BZW), 1986–88. Dep. Chm., Stock Exchange, 1976–79 (Mem. Council, 1966–86); Dir, Securities Assoc., 1986–88. Mem., City Capital Markets' Cttee, 1981–88. Trustee, Lloyds TSB (formerly TSB) Foundn, 1991–98. Mem. Council, GDBA, 1989–2000 (Chm., 1993–2000). *Recreations:* marine art, bell ringing, walking. *Address:* Eckensfield Barn, Compton, near Chichester, West Sussex PO18 9NT. *T:* (023) 9263 1239. *Club:* City of London. *Died 18 June 2012.*

ROBERTSON, Sholto David Maurice, (Toby), OBE 1978; director and actor, theatre, opera and television; *b* 29 Nov. 1928; *s* of David Lambert Robertson and Felicity Douglas (*née* Tomlin); *m* 1963, Teresa Jane McCulloch (marr. diss. 1981); two *s* two *d*. *Educ:* Stowe; Trinity Coll., Cambridge (BA 1952, MA 1981). Formerly an actor. Dir. first prof. prodn, The Iceman Cometh, New Shakespeare, Liverpool, 1958. Dir. plays, London, Pitlochry and Richmond, Yorks, and for RSC, 1959–63. Member: Bd, Prospect Productions Ltd, 1964– (Artistic Dir, Prospect Theatre Co., 1964–79); Bd, Cambridge Theatre Co., 1970–74; Director: Old Vic Theatre, 1977–80, Old Vic Co., 1979–80; Acting Co., Kennedy Centre, Washington, 1983; Associate Dir, Circle Rep., New York, 1983–84; Dir, Theatr Clwyd, Mold, 1985–92. Drama Advr, Argo Records, 1979–; Prof. of Theatre, Brooklyn Coll., City Univ. NY, 1981–82; Hon. Prof. of Drama, 1987–90, Hon. Prof. of English, 1990–92, Fellow, 1996, UCNW. Lectures: Wilson Meml, Cambridge Univ., 1974; Hamlet, Athens Univ., 1978; Rikstheatre, Stockholm, 1980; Hamlet, Gulbenkian Foundn, Lisbon, 1987. Director of over 40 prodns for *Prospect Theatre Co.*, many staged in London and Edinburgh, 1964–79, including: The Soldier's Fortune; You Never Can Tell; The Confederacy; The Importance of Being Earnest; The Square; Howard's End; The Man of Mode; Macbeth; The Tempest; The Gamecock; A Murder of No Importance; A Room with a View; No Man's Land; The Beggar's Opera; The Servant of Two Masters; Edward II; Much Ado About Nothing; Boswell's Life of Johnson; Venice Preserved; King Lear and Love's Labour's Lost (Australian tour); Alice in Wonderland; Richard III; Ivanov; The Grand Tour; Twelfth Night, Pericles and The Royal Hunt of the Sun (internat. fests, Moscow, Leningrad and Hong Kong); The Pilgrim's Progress; A Month in the Country (Chichester Fest.); directed for *Old Vic Co.*: War Music; Antony and Cleopatra; Smith of Smiths; Buster; The Lunatic, The Lover and The Poet; Romeo and Juliet; The Government Inspector; The Padlock; Ivanov; Hamlet (Elsinore, and first visit by a British co., China, 1980); directed for *Theatr Clwyd*: Medea (also Young Vic), 1986; Barnaby and the Old Boys, 1987 (also Vaudeville, 1989); Edward III (jtly adapted, attrib. William Shakespeare) (also Cambridge and Taormina Fests), 1987; Captain Carvallo, 1988, transf. Greenwich; Revenger's Tragedy, 1988; The Old Devils, 1989; Othello, 1989; The Importance of Being Earnest, 1990; Enemy of the People, 1991, transf. Lyric Hammersmith; The Cherry Orchard, 1991 (also Brighton Festival); Marching Song, 1992; Hamlet (also Nat. Tour), 1991–92; The Seagull, 1992; Loot, 1995; directed *other productions*, including: Next Time I'll Sing to You, Greenwich, 1980; Beggar's Opera, Lyric, Hammersmith, 1980; Measure for Measure, People's Arts Theatre, Peking, 1981; Pericles, NY, 1981 (Obie award, 1982); Night and Day (opening prodn), 1982 and The Taming of the Shrew, 1983, Huntingdon Theatre Co., Boston; The Tempest (opening prodn), New Cleveland Playhouse, 1983; Love's Labour's Lost, Shakespeare Workshop, 1983, Circle Rep., 1984, NYC; York Cycle of Mystery Plays, York Fest., 1984; Midsummer Night's Dream, Open Air Theatre, Regent's Park, 1985; (jt dir) Antony and Cleopatra, The Taming of the Shrew, Haymarket, 1986; Coriolanus, festivals in Spain, 1986; You Never Can Tell, Haymarket, 1988; Richard II, Folger Theatre, Washington; Trelawny of the 'Wells', Comedy, 1992; The Old Devils, Philadelphia, 1993; The Taming of the Shrew, Regent's Park, 1993; Macbeth, Tel Aviv, 1994; Hamlet, Oberlin Coll., Ohio, 1997. *Opera:* for Scottish Opera, incl.: A Midsummer Night's Dream, 1972; Hermiston, 1975; Marriage of Figaro, 1977; for Opera Co. of Philadelphia: Elisir d'Amore (with Pavarotti and winners of Pavarotti competition), Dido and Aeneas, Oedipus Rex, 1982; Faust, 1984; Wiesbaden: A Midsummer Night's Dream, 1984; NY City Opera: Barber of Seville, 1984; Wexford Opera: The Kiss, 1984. Asst Dir, Lord of the Flies (film), 1961. Dir of more than 25 television prodns, incl.: The Beggar's Opera; Richard II; Edward II. *Recreation:* painting. *Address:* 32 Stamford Brook Road, W6 0XL. *Club:* Garrick. *Died 4 July 2012.*

ROBERTSON, Vernon Colin, OBE 1977; self employed consultant, specialising in environmental issues in developing countries; *b* 19 July 1922; *s* of Colin John Trevelyan Robertson and Agnes Muriel Robertson (*née* Dolphin). *Educ:* Imperial Service College, Windsor; Univ. of Edinburgh (BSc Agr subs. Forestry); Univ. of Cambridge (Dip Agr 1950; MA). Joined Home Guard, 1940; enlisted RA, 1941, commissioned 1942; served 12th HAC Regt RHA, N Africa, Italy, Austria, 1942–45 (despatches 1945); with 1st Regt RHA, Italy, 1945–46 (Adjutant). Staff, Sch. of Agric., Cambridge, 1950; joined Hunting Aerosurveys Ltd, 1953, as ecologist heading new natural resources survey dept; developed this into overseas land and water resource consultancy, renamed Hunting Technical Services Ltd (Managing Director, 1959–77; after retirement continuing as Director and Consultant until 1987), development planning in Africa, Asia and Latin America. Director: Hunting Surveys and Consultants Ltd, 1962–77; Groundwater Development Consultants (International) Ltd, 1975–85; Vice-Chm. and acting Chm., Environmental Planning Commn, Internat. Union for Conservation of Nature, 1972–78; Chm., Trop. Agric. Assoc. (UK), 1981–85; Mem. Bd, Commonwealth Develt Corp., 1982–90. *Publications:* articles in learned jls. *Recreations:* natural history, esp. plants and birds, gardening, painting, photography, music, sailing. *Address:* Brickfields, Quay Lane, Kirby-le-Soken, Essex CO13 0DP. *T:* (01255) 674585. *Club:* Honourable Artillery Company. *Died 27 March 2012.*

ROBINS, William Edward Charles; Metropolitan Stipendiary Magistrate, 1971–89; *b* 13 March 1924; *s* of late E. T. and late L. R. Robins; *m* 1946, Jean Elizabeth, *yr d* of Bruce and Flora Forsyth, Carlyle, Saskatchewan, Canada; one *s* one *d*. *Educ:* St Albans Sch. Served War: commissioned as Navigator, RAF, 1943–47. Admitted as a Solicitor, 1948; joined Metropolitan Magistrates' Courts' service, 1950; Dep. Chief Clerk, 1951–60; Chief Clerk, 1960–67; Sen. Chief Clerk, Thames Petty Sessional Div., 1968–71. Sec., London Magistrates' Clerks' Assoc., 1953–60 (Chm. 1965–71). Member, Home Office working parties, on: Magistrates' Courts' Rules; Legal Aid; Motor Vehicle Licences; Fines and Maintenance Orders Enforcement, 1968–71; Member: Lord Chancellor's Sub-Cttee on Magistrates' Courts' Rules, 1969–70; Adv.

Council on Misuse of Drugs, 1973–86. Fellow Commoner, Corpus Christi Coll., Cambridge, Michaelmas 1975. *Died 26 Jan. 2013.*

ROBINSON, Arthur Alexander; Director of Computing Centre, University of Wales College of Cardiff (formerly at University of Wales Institute of Science and Technology), 1976–91; *b* 5 Aug. 1924; *o s* of Arthur Robinson and Elizabeth (*née* Thompson); *m* 1956, Sylvia Joyce Wagstaff; two *s* one *d*. *Educ:* Epsom Coll.; Clare Coll., Cambridge (MA); Univ. of Manchester (PhD). English Electric Co. Ltd, 1944; Ferranti Ltd, 1950; Dir and Gen. Man., Univ. of London Atlas Computing Service, 1962; Dir, Univ. of London Computer Centre, 1968; Dir, National Computing Centre Ltd, 1969–74. *Publications:* papers in Proc. IEE. *Recreations:* travel, gardening. *Address:* 6 Portland Close, Penarth, Vale of Glamorgan CF64 3DY. *Died 4 Nov. 2012.*

ROBINSON, Hon. (Arthur Napoleon) Raymond, SC; President, Trinidad and Tobago, 1997–2003; *b* 16 Dec. 1926; *s* of late James Alexander Andrew Robinson, Headmaster, and Emily Isabella Robinson; *m* 1961, Patricia Rawlins (*d* 2009); one *s* one *d*. *Educ:* Bishop's High Sch., Tobago; St John's Coll., Oxford (Hon. Fellow 1988). LLB (London); MA (PPE) Oxon. Called to Bar, Inner Temple; in practice, 1957–61. Treas., People's Nat. Movt (governing Party) 1956; Mem. Federal Parlt, 1958; MHR for Tobago East, 1961–71 and 1976–80; Minister of Finance, 1961–66; Dep. Political Leader of Party, 1966; Actg Prime Minister (during his absence), April and Aug. 1967; Minister of External Affairs, Trinidad and Tobago, 1967–70; Chm., Democratic Action Congress, 1971–86; Chm., Tobago House of Assembly, 1980–86; Leader, Nat. Alliance for Reconstruction, 1986–92; Prime Minister of Trinidad and Tobago, 1986–91. Member: Legal Commn on US Leased Areas under 1941 Agreement, 1959; Industrial Develt Corp., 1960; Council, Univ. of West Indies, 1960–62. Dir, Foundn for establishment of an Internat. Criminal Court, 1972–87. Member: UN Expert Gp on Crime and the Abuse of Power, 1979; Adv. Council, Nuclear Age Peace Foundn, 1994–; Pres. and Exec. Mem., Parliamentarians for Global Action, 1993–95. Hon. DCL Obafemi Awolowo Univ., Nigeria, 1991. Dist. Internat. Criminal Law Award, Internat. Criminal Court Foundn, 1977; Dist. Human Develt Award, Internat. Conf. on Human Rights and Humanitarian Law, UN Affiliate, 1983; Commendation Award, and Freeman, City of a Thousand Oaks, Calif, 1987; Dist. Service Award, Calif Lutheran Univ., 1987; Individual of the Year Award, Friends of Tobago Liby Cttee, 1995. Freeman: LA, 1988; Caracas, 1990. KStJ 1992. Gran Cordon, Orden de El Libertador (Venezuela), 1990; Chief of Ile Ife (Nigeria), 1991. *Publications:* The New Frontier and the New Africa, 1961; Fiscal Reform in Trinidad and Tobago, 1966; The Path of Progress, 1967; The Teacher and Nationalism, 1967; The Mechanics of Independence, 1971; Caribbean Man, 1986; In the Midst of It (memoir), 2012; articles and addresses. *Address:* 21 Ellerslie Park, Maraval, Trinidad and Tobago. *Died 9 April 2014.*

ROBINSON, Derek, CBE 1979; Fellow of Magdalen College, Oxford, 1969–99, then Emeritus; Senior Research Officer, Oxford Institute of Economics and Statistics, 1961–99; *b* 9 Feb. 1932; *s* of Benjamin and Mary Robinson; *m* 1956, Jean Evelyn (*née* Lynch); one *s* one *d*. *Educ:* Barnsley Holgate Grammar Sch.; Ruskin Coll., Oxford; Lincoln Coll., Oxford. MA (Oxon), DipEcPolSci (Oxon). Civil Service, 1948–55. Sheffield Univ., 1959–60; Senior Research Officer, Oxford Inst. of Economics and Statistics, 1961–99. Economic Adviser, Nat. Bd for Prices and Incomes, 1965–67; Sen. Economic Adviser, Dept of Employment and Productivity, 1968–70; Dep. Chm., Pay Bd, 1973–74; Chm., SSRC, 1975–78. Mem., British Library Bd, 1979–82. Visiting Professor: Cornell Univ., 1983; Univ. of Hawaii, 1983. Chairman: Oxfordshire Dist Manpower Cttee, 1980–83 (Oxf. and S Bucks, 1975–79); Cttee of Inquiry into the remuneration of members of local authorities, 1977; Chilterns Area Bd, Manpower Services Commn Special Programmes, 1978–79. Inter-regional Adviser on Wage Policy, ILO, 1986–88. Mem., Internat. Reference Panel to Presidential Comprehensive Labour Market Commn, S Africa, 1995–96. *Publications:* Non-Wage Incomes and Prices Policy, 1966; Wage Drift, Fringe Benefits and Manpower Distribution, 1968; Workers' Negotiated Savings Plans for Capital Formation, 1970; (ed) Local Labour Markets and Wage Structures, 1970; Prices and Incomes Policy: the Austrian Experience (with H. Suppanz), 1972; Incomes Policy and Capital Sharing in Europe, 1973; (with J. Vincens) Research into Labour Market Behaviour, 1974; (with K. Mayhew *et al*) Pay Policies for the Future, 1983; Introduction to Economics, 1986; Monetarism and the Labour Market, 1986; Civil Service Pay in Africa, 1990; contributor to Bulletin of Oxford Univ. Inst. of Economics and Statistics, Industrial Relations Jl, etc. *Address:* 56 Lonsdale Road, Oxford OX2 7EP. *T:* (01865) 552276. *Died 1 Sept. 2014.*

ROBINSON, Eric Embleton; Director, Lancashire Polytechnic (formerly Preston Polytechnic), 1982–90; *b* 12 March 1927; *s* of Cyril Robinson and Florence Mary Embleton. *Educ:* local authority schools, Nelson and Colne, Lancs; London Univ. (MSc). Teaching, Prescot Grammar Sch., 1948, Acton Tech. Coll., 1949–56, Brunel Coll., 1956–62, Enfield Coll., 1962–70; Dep. Dir, NE London Polytechnic, 1970–73; Principal, Bradford Coll., 1973–82. Pres., Assoc. of Teachers in Tech. Instns, 1962; Exec. Mem., Nat. Union of Teachers, 1961–67; Member: Burnham Cttees, 1961–67; Nat. Council for Training and Supply of Teachers, 1964–66; Minister's Working Party on Polytechnics, 1965–66; Equal Opportunities Commn, 1976–81; CNAA, 1976–82; UNESCO Nat. Commn, 1975–78. Vice Pres., Socialist Educn Assoc., 1966–. Hon. Advr, Beijing Inst. of Business, 1987–; Hon. Vis. Prof., Wolverhampton University (formerly Wolverhampton Polytechnic), 1990–. Hon. Fellow, Sheffield Hallam Univ. (Sheffield City Polytechnic, 1990). Hon. DEd CNAA (E London), 1990; DUniv Central Lancs, 2006. *Publications:* The New Polytechnics, 1968; numerous articles and papers. *Address:* 8 Roundwood Avenue, Reedley, Burnley BB10 2LH. *T:* (01282) 447320. *Club:* Savile. *Died 16 Jan. 2011.*

ROBINSON, Peter Damian, CB 1983; Deputy Secretary, Lord Chancellor's Department, 1980–86; *b* 11 July 1926; *s* of late John Robinson and Jill Clegg (*née* Easten); *m* 1st, 1956, Mary Katinka Bonner (*d* 1978), Peterborough; one *d* (and one *d* decd); 2nd, 1985, Mrs Sheila Suzanne Gibbins (*née* Guille). *Educ:* Corby Sch., Sunderland; Lincoln Coll., Oxford. MA. Royal Marine Commandos, 1944–46. Called to Bar, Middle Temple, 1951; practised common law, 1952–59; Clerk of Assize, NE Circuit, 1959–70; Administrator, NE Circuit, 1970–74; Circuit Administrator, SE Circuit, 1974–80; Dep. Clerk of the Crown in Chancery, Lord Chancellor's Dept, 1982–86. Advr on Hong Kong Judiciary, 1986. Member, Home Office Departmental Cttee on Legal Aid in Criminal Proceedings (the Widgery Cttee), 1964–66; Chm., Interdeptl Cttee on Conciliation, 1982–83. *Recreations:* reading, the countryside, antiques. *Died 29 Sept. 2012.*

ROBINSON, Hon. Raymond; *see* Robinson, Hon. A. N. R.

ROBINSON, Robert Henry; writer and broadcaster; *b* 17 Dec. 1927; *o s* of Ernest Redfern Robinson and Johanna Hogan; *m* 1958, Josephine Mary Richard; one *s* two *d*. *Educ:* Raynes Park Grammar Sch.; Exeter Coll., Oxford (MA). Editor of Isis, 1950. TV columnist, Sunday Chronicle, 1952; film and theatre columnist, Sunday Graphic, and radio critic, Sunday Times, 1956; editor Atticus, Sunday Times, 1960; weekly column, Private View, Sunday Times, 1962; film critic, Sunday Telegraph, 1965. Writer and presenter of TV programmes: Picture Parade, 1959; Points of View, 1961; Divided We Stand, 1964; The Look of the Week, 1966; Reason to Believe?, The Fifties, 1969; Chm., Call My Bluff, Ask The Family, 1967; The Book Programme, Vital Statistics, 1974; Word for Word, 1978; The Book Game, 1983 and 1985; Behind The Headlines, 1989–; films for TV: Robinson's Travels - the Pioneer Trail West, 1977; B. Traven: a mystery solved, 1978; From Shepherd's Bush to Simla, 1979; Robinson Cruising, 1981; The Auden Landscape, 1982; Robinson Country, 1983, 1987, 1993; In Trust—Houses and Heritage, 1986; The Magic Rectangle, 1986; presenter of: BBC radio current affairs programme Today, 1971–74; Chm., Brain of Britain, 1973–2010; Chm., Stop the Week,

1974–92; Ad Lib, 1989–; devised and presented: Conversations with Strangers, 1997; Divided We Stand, 1998; Odd Obits, 1999. Mem., Kingman Cttee on the teaching of the English Language, 1987–88. Pres., Johnson Soc. of Lichfield, 1982. Radio Personality of the Year: Radio Industries Club, 1973; Variety Club of GB, 1980. *Publications:* (ed) Poetry from Oxford, 1951; Landscape with Dead Dons, 1956; Inside Robert Robinson (essays), 1965; (contrib.) To Nevill Coghill from Friends, 1966; The Conspiracy, 1968; The Dog Chairman, 1982; (ed) The Everyman Book of Light Verse, 1984; Bad Dreams, 1989; Prescriptions of a Pox Doctor's Clerk, 1990; Skip All That, 1996; The Club, 2000. *Address:* 16 Cheyne Row, SW3 5HL. *Club:* Garrick. *Died 12 Aug. 2011.*

ROBINSON, Sir Wilfred (Henry Frederick), 3rd Bt *cr* 1908; Staff, Diocesan College School, Rondebosch, South Africa, 1950–77, Vice-Principal, 1969–77; *b* 24 Dec. 1917; *s* of Wilfred Henry Robinson (*d* 1922) (3rd *s* of 1st Bt), and Eileen (*d* 1963), *d* of Frederick St Leger, Claremont, SA; *S* uncle, Sir Joseph Benjamin Robinson, 2nd Bt, 1954; *m* 1946, Margaret Alison Kathleen, *d* of late Frank Mellish, MC, Cape Town, SA; one *s* two *d*. *Educ:* Diocesan Coll., Rondebosch; St John's Coll., Cambridge (MA 1944). Served War of 1939–45, Devonshire Regt and Parachute Regt, Major. Finance Officer, Soc. of Genealogists, 1980–92. *Heir: s* Peter Frank Robinson [*b* 23 June 1949; *m* 1988, Alison Jane, *e d* of D. Bradley, Rochester, Kent; three *d*]. *Address:* 102 Riverview Gardens, Barnes, SW13 8RA. *Died 3 Dec. 2012.*

ROBINSON, William Rhys Brunel; Under Secretary, Overseas Division, Department of Employment, 1980–89; *b* 12 July 1930; *s* of late William Robinson and Elizabeth Myfanwy Robinson (*née* Owen); *m* 1988, Pamela Mary Hall (*d* 2006). *Educ:* Chepstow Secondary Grammar Sch.; St Catherine's Soc., Oxford (MA, BLitt). Entered Min. of Labour, 1954; Asst Private Sec. to Minister, 1958–59; Principal, Min. of Labour, 1959; Asst Sec., 1966; London Sch. of Economics, 1972–73 (MSc Industrial Relations, 1973); Asst Sec., Trng Services Agency, 1973–75; Dep. Chief Exec., Employment Service Agency, 1975–77; Under-Sec. and Dir of Establishments, Dept of Employment, 1977–80. Chm., Governing Body, ILO, 1986–87. FSA 1978; FRHistS 1991. *Publications:* Early Tudor Gwent 1485–1547, 2002; (contrib.) Gwent County History, vol. 2, 2008, vol. 3, 2009; articles in historical jls. *Recreation:* historical research. *Address:* 7 Shere Avenue, Cheam, Surrey SM2 7JU. *T:* (020) 8393 3019. *Died 18 Dec. 2011.*

ROBOROUGH, 3rd Baron *cr* 1938, of Maristow; **Henry Massey Lopes;** Bt 1805; *b* 2 Feb. 1940; *s* of 2nd Baron Roborough and Helen (*d* 1998), *o d* of Lt-Col E. A. F. Dawson; *S* father, 1992; *m* 1st, 1968, Robyn Zenda Carol (marr. diss. 1986), *e d* of John Bromwich; two *s* two *d*; 2nd, 1986, Sarah Anne Pipon, 2nd *d* of Colin Baker; two *d*. *Educ:* Eton. MRICS. Late Lt Coldstream Guards. Farmer, managing Maristow Estate, Plymouth. Racehorse owner and breeder. *Heir: s* Hon. Massey John Henry Lopes [*b* 22 Dec. 1969; *m* 1996, Jean, *d* of Peter George Underwood, Supreme Court of Tasmania; two *s* one *d*]. *Club:* Turf. *Died 8 Feb. 2015.*

ROCHDALE, 2nd Viscount *cr* 1960; **St John Durival Kemp;** Baron 1913; *b* 15 Jan. 1938; *s* of 1st Viscount Rochdale, OBE and Elinor Dorothea Pease, CBE, JP (*d* 1997); *S* father, 1993; *m* 1st, 1960, Serena Jane Clark-Hall (marr. diss. 1974); one *s* two *d* (and one *s* decd); 2nd, 1976, Elizabeth Anderton. *Educ:* Eton. *Heir: s* Hon. Jonathan Hugo Durival Kemp [*b* 10 June 1961; *m* 1994, Mingxian Zhu; one *d*]. *Died 27 Feb. 2015.*

ROCKLEY, 3rd Baron *cr* 1934; **James Hugh Cecil;** Director, Kleinwort Benson Group, 1986–98 (Chairman, 1993–96); *b* 5 April 1934; *s* of 2nd Baron Rockley, and Anne Margaret (*d* 1980), *d* of late Adm. Hon. Sir Herbert Meade-Featherstonhaugh, GCVO, CB, DSO; *S* father, 1976; *m* 1958, Lady Sarah Primrose Beatrix, *e d* of 7th Earl Cadogan, MC; one *s* two *d*. *Educ:* Eton; New Coll., Oxford. Wood Gundy & Co. Ltd, 1957–62; Kleinwort Benson Ltd, 1962–96. Chairman: Dartford River Crossing, 1988–93; Kleinwort Develt Fund, 1990–93; Midland Expressway, 1992–93; Hall & Woodhouse Ltd, 2000–10; Adv. Bd, Lambert Energy, 2000–; Director: Equity and Law, 1980–91; Christies Internat., 1989–98; Cobham (formerly FR Gp), 1990–2002; Abbey National, 1990–99; Foreign and Colonial Investment Trust, 1992–2003; Cadogan Gp Ltd, 1996–; Dusco (UK) Ltd, 1996–2000; Hypo Foreign & Colonial Mgt (Hldgs) Ltd, 1996–99. Mem., Design Council, 1987–93; Trustee, Nat. Portrait Gall., 1981–88. Chm. of Govs, Milton Abbey Sch., 2000–04. *Heir: s* Hon. Anthony Robert Cecil [*b* 29 July 1961; *m* 1988, Katherine Jane, *d* of G. A. Whalley; one *s* two *d*]. *Address:* The Bell House, Ellisfield, Basingstoke, Hants RG25 2QD. *T:* (01256) 381212. *Died 5 Dec. 2011.*

RODDIE, Prof. Ian Campbell, CBE 1988; TD 1967; Dunville Professor of Physiology, Queen's University, Belfast, 1964–87, then Emeritus; *b* 1 Dec. 1928; *s* of Rev. J. R. Wesley Roddie and Mary Hill Wilson; *m* 1st, 1958, Elizabeth Ann Gillon Honeyman (decd); one *s* three *d*; 2nd, 1974, Katherine Ann O'Hara (marr. diss.); one *s* one *d*; 3rd, 1987, Janet Doreen Saville (*née* Lennon). *Educ:* Methodist Coll., Belfast; Queen's Univ., Belfast. Malcolm Exhibnr, 1951, McQuitty Schol., 1953; BSc (1st cl. Hons Physiol.), MB BCh, BAO, MD (with gold medal), DSc; MRCPI, FRCPI; MRIA. Major RAMC (T&AVR); OC Med. Sub-unit, QUB OTC, retd 1968. Resident MO, Royal Victoria Hosp., Belfast, 1953–54; Queen's University, Belfast: Lectr in Physiology, 1954–60; Sen. Lectr, 1961–62; Reader, 1962–64; Dep. Dean, 1975–76, Dean, 1976–81, Faculty of Medicine; Pro-Vice-Chancellor, 1983–87; Head of Med. Educn, 1990–94, and Dep. Med. Dir, 1991–94, King Khalid Nat. Guard Hosp., Jeddah. Consultant Physiologist: NI Hosps Authority, 1962–72; Eastern Health Bd, NI, 1972–88. Staff Consultant, Asian Develt Bank, Manila, 1987–88; part-time consultant, IFC/African Project Develt Facility/World Bank, Washington, 1989–2004. Harkness Commonwealth Fund Fellow, Univ. of Washington, Seattle, 1960–61; Visiting Professor: Univ. of NSW, 1983–84; Chinese Univ. of Hong Kong, 1988–90; Res. Fellow, Japan Soc. for Promotion of Science, Matsumoto, Japan, 1984. External Examiner: Univs of Aberdeen, Baghdad, Benghazi, Birmingham, Bristol, Glasgow, Ireland, Jeddah, Jos, Lagos, Leeds, London, Sheffield, Southampton, Zimbabwe; RCS, RCSE, RCPGlas, RCSI. Chief Reg. Sci. Advr for Home Defence, NI, 1977–88; Member: Home Defence Sci. Adv. Conf., 1977–88; Eastern Area Health and Social Services Bd, NI, 1976–81; Physiol Systems Bd, MRC, 1974–76; Med. Adv. Cttee, Cttee of Vice-Chancellors and Principals, 1976–81; GMC, 1979–81; GDC, 1979–81. President: Royal Acad. of Medicine in Ireland, 1985–88; Biol Scis Sect., Royal Acad. of Medicine in Ireland, 1964–66; Ulster Biomed. Engrg Soc., 1979–83; Chm. Cttee, Physiol Soc., 1985–88 (Mem. Cttee, 1966–69; Hon. Mem., 1989). Arris and Gale Lectr, RCS, 1962. Conway Bronze Medal, Royal Acad. of Medicine in Ireland, 1977. *Publications:* Physiology for Practitioners, 1971, 2nd edn 1975; Multiple Choice Questions in Human Physiology, 1971, 6th edn 2004; The Physiology of Disease, 1975; papers on physiology and pharmacology of vascular, sudorific and lymphatic systems. *Address:* 32a Hazlewell Road, Putney, SW15 6LR. *T:* (020) 8789 1848. *E:* ian.roddie@gmail.com. *Club:* Reform. *Died 28 May 2011.*

RODERICK, Caerwyn Eifion; Councillor, South Glamorgan County Council, 1980–96; *b* 15 July 1927; *m* 1952, Eirlys Mary Lewis; one *s* two *d*. *Educ:* Maes-y-Dderwen County Sch., Ystradgynlais; University Coll. of North Wales, Bangor. Asst Master, Caterham Sch., Surrey, 1949–52; Sen. Master, Chartesey Sch., LCC, 1952–54; Sen. Maths Master, Boys' Grammar Sch., Brecon, 1954–57; Method Study Engineer, NCB, 1957–60; Sen. Maths Master, Hartridge High Sch., Newport, Mon, 1960–69; Lecturer, Coll. of Educn, Cardiff, 1969–70. MP (Lab) Brecon and Radnor, 1970–79; PPS to Rt Hon. Michael Foot. Dist Officer, NUT, 1980–91. Mem. Council: UC, Cardiff; formerly Mem. Council, RCVS. *Address:* 29 Charlotte Square, Rhiwbina, Cardiff CF14 6NE. *T:* (029) 2062 8269. *Died 16 Oct. 2011.*

RODGER OF EARLSFERRY, Baron *cr* 1992 (Life Peer), of Earlsferry in the District of North East Fife; **Alan Ferguson Rodger;** PC 1992; FBA 1991; a Justice of the Supreme Court of the United Kingdom, since 2009 (a Lord of Appeal in Ordinary, 2001–09); *b* 18 Sept. 1944; *er s* of Prof. Thomas Ferguson Rodger and Jean Margaret Smith Chalmers. *Educ:* Kelvinside Acad., Glasgow; Glasgow Univ. (MA, LLB); New Coll., Oxford (MA (by decree), DPhil; DCL; Hon. Fellow, 2005). Dyke Jun. Res. Fellow, Balliol Coll., Oxford, 1969–70 (Hon. Fellow, 1999); Fellow, New Coll., Oxford, 1970–72; Mem., Faculty of Advocates, 1974; Clerk of Faculty, 1976–79; QC (Scot.) 1985; Advocate Depute, 1985–88, Home Advocate Depute, 1986–88; Solicitor-Gen. for Scotland, 1989–92; Lord Advocate, 1992–95; a Senator of the Coll. of Justice in Scotland, 1995–96; Lord Justice Gen. of Scotland and Lord President of the Court of Session, 1996–2001. Member: Mental Welfare Commn for Scotland, 1981–84; UK Delegn to CCBE, 1984–89; Acad. of European Private Lawyers, 1994–. Maccabaean Lectr, British Acad., 1991. Visitor, St Hugh's Coll., Oxford, 2003–; High Steward, Oxford Univ., 2008–. FRSE 1992. Hon. Bencher: Lincoln's Inn, 1992; Inn of Court of NI, 1998. Hon. Mem., SPTL, subseq. SLS, 1992; Corresp. Mem., Bayerische Akad. der Wissenschaften, 2001. Pres., Holdsworth Club, 1998–99. Hon. Fellow, American Coll. of Trial Lawyers, 2008. Hon. LLD: Glasgow, 1995; Aberdeen, 1999; Edinburgh, 2001; Hon. Dr Erasmus Univ., Rotterdam, 2011. *Publications:* Owners and Neighbours in Roman Law, 1972; (asst editor) Gloag and Henderson's Introduction to the Law of Scotland, 10th edn, 1995; (ed jtly) Mapping the Law, 2006; The Courts, the Church and the Constitution, 2008; articles mainly on Roman Law. *Recreation:* walking. *Address:* Supreme Court of the United Kingdom, Parliament Square, SW1P 3BD. *Club:* Athenæum. *Died 26 June 2011.*

RODNEY, 10th Baron *cr* 1782; **George Brydges Rodney;** Bt 1764; *b* 3 Jan. 1953; *o s* of 9th Baron Rodney and Régine (*d* 2003), *d* of Chevalier Pangaert d'Opdorp, Belgium; *S* father, 1992; *m* 1996, Jane, *d* of Hamilton Rowan Blakeney; one *s*. *Educ:* Eton. *Heir: s* Hon. John George Brydges Rodney, *b* 5 July 1999. *Address:* 38 Pembroke Road, W8 6NU. *Died 13 Feb. 2011.*

ROE, Dame Raigh (Edith), DBE 1980 (CBE 1975); JP; Director, Airlines of Western Australia, 1981–90; World President, Associated Country Women of the World, 1977–80; *b* 12 Dec. 1922; *d* of Alwyn and Laura Kurts; *m* 1941, James Arthur Roe; three *s*. *Educ:* Perth Girls' Sch., Australia. Country Women's Association: State Pres., 1967–70; National Pres., 1969–71. World Ambassador, WA Council, 1978–; Hon. Ambassador, State of Louisiana, USA, 1979–. Comr, ABC, 1978–83; Nat. Dir (Aust.), Queen Elizabeth II Silver Jubilee Trust for Young Australians, 1978–94. JP Western Australia, 1966. Australian of the Year, 1977; Brooch of Merit, Deutscher Landfrauenverband, Fed. Republic of Germany, 1980. *Died Nov. 2014.*

ROGERS, Maj.-Gen. Anthony Peter Vernon, OBE 1985; Director, Army Legal Services, 1994–97; military lawyer as writer and teacher (part-time), 1997–2011; *b* 10 July 1942; *s* of Kenneth David Rogers, ICS, and Eileen (*née* Emmott); *m* 1965, Anne-Katrin Margarethe, *d* of Dr Ewald Lembke; two *d*. *Educ:* Highgate Sch.; Coll. of Law; Liverpool Univ. (LLM 1994). Admitted Solicitor, 1965. Commnd as Capt., Army Legal Services, 1968; served HQ BAOR, Command Legal Aid Section, BAOR, MoD, SHAPE, HQ UKLF, 3 and 1 Armoured Divs; Col Army Legal Services 2, MoD, 1989–92; Brig. Legal, HQ BAOR, 1992–94. Vice Pres., Internat. Soc. for Mil. Law and Law of War, 1994–97 (Hon. Pres., 1997–); Member: Internat. Inst. of Humanitarian Law, 1992–99 (Chm., Cttee for Mil. Instruction, 1993–97); Internat. Humanitarian Fact-Finding Commn, 2001–06 (Vice-Pres., 2004–06). Fellow: Lauterpacht Res. Centre for Internat. Law, Univ. of Cambridge, 1999–2011 (Sen. Fellow, 2006–11); Human Rights Centre, Univ. of Essex, 1999–2004 (Vis. Fellow, 2005–08); Affiliated Lectr, 1999–2008, Yorke Dist. Vis. Fellow, 2003–09, Faculty of Law, Univ. of Cambridge. Founder Mem. and Chm., Army Legal Services Assoc., 2010–. Mem., Bd of Govs, Halliford Sch., 2004–. FRSA 1995. *Publications:* Law on the Battlefield, 1996, 3rd edn 2012; (jtly) ICRC Model Manual on The Law of Armed Conflict, 1999; (co-ed) UK MoD Manual of The Law of Armed Conflict, 2004; articles on law of war. *Recreations:* music, the arts, playing the piano (especially as accompanist) and bassoon, walking, cricket. *Address:* c/o Directorate of Army Legal Services, Andover, Hants SN9 6BE. *T:* (01264) 382477. *Died 16 April 2015.*

ROGERS, Surgeon Rear-Adm. (D) Brian Frederick, CB 1980; Director of Naval Dental Services, 1977–80; *b* 27 Feb. 1923; *s* of Frederick Reginald Rogers, MIMechE, MIMarE, and Rosa Jane Rogers; *m* 1946, Mavis Elizabeth (*née* Scott); one *s* two *d*. *Educ:* Rock Ferry High Sch.; Liverpool Univ. (LDS 1945). House Surgeon, Liverpool Dental Hosp., 1945; joined RNVR, 1946; transf. to RN, 1954; served HMS Ocean, 1954–56 and HMS Eagle, 1964–66; Fleet Dental Surg. on staff of C-in-C Fleet, 1974–77; Comd Dental Surg. to C-in-C Naval Home Comd, 1977. QHDS 1977. *Recreations:* European touring, photography, DIY. *Address:* 22 Trerieve, Downderry, Torpoint, Cornwall PL11 3LY. *T:* (01503) 250526; Montana Roja, Lanzarote, Canary Islands. *T:* (28) 517150. *Died 16 Sept. 2013.*

ROGERS, Martin Hartley Guy; HM Diplomatic Service, retired; *b* 11 June 1925; *s* of late Rev. Canon T. Guy Rogers and Marguerite Inez Rogers; *m* 1959, Jean Beresford Chinn; one *s* three *d*. *Educ:* Marlborough Coll.; Jesus Coll., Cambridge. CRO, 1949; 2nd Sec., Karachi, 1951–53; CRO, 1953–56 and 1958–60; seconded to Govt of Fedn of Nigeria, 1956–57; ndc 1960–61; 1st Sec., Ottawa, 1961–62; Adviser to Jamaican Min. of External Affairs, 1963; CRO, later Commonwealth Office, 1963–68; Dep. High Comr, Bombay, 1968–71, Kaduna, 1972–75; High Comr, The Gambia, 1975–79; on loan to CSSB as Asst Dir, 1979–85. *Recreation:* bridge. *Address:* Rydal, Tower Road, St Helier, Jersey JE2 3HR. *T:* (01534) 731429. *Died 28 Dec. 2012.*

ROGERS, Maj.-Gen. Norman Charles, FRCS 1949; Director, Army Surgery, 1969–73; consultant surgeon, retired 1986; *b* 14 Oct. 1916; *s* of Wing Comdr Charles William Rogers, RAF, and Edith Minnie Rogers (*née* Weaver); *m* 1954, Pamela Marion (*née* Rose); two *s* one *d*. *Educ:* Imperial Service Coll.; St Bartholomew's Hosp. MB, BS London; MRCS, LRCP 1939. Emergency Commn, Lieut RAMC, Oct. 1939; 131 Field Amb. RAMC, Dunkirk (despatches, 1940); RMO, 4th Royal Tank Regt, N Africa, 1941–42; Italy, 1942–43 (POW); RMO 1st Black Watch, NW Europe, 1944–45 (wounded, despatches twice). Ho. Surg., St Bartholomew's Hosp., 1946–47; Registrar (Surgical) Appts, Norwich, 1948–52; Sen. Registrar Appts, Birmingham, 1952–56; granted permanent commn, RAMC, 1956; surgical appts in mil. hospitals: Chester, Dhekelia (Cyprus), Catterick, Iserlohn (BAOR), 1956–67; Command Consultant Surgeon, BAOR, 1967–69; QHS, 1969–73. Clin. Supt, 1975–80, and Consultant, 1973–81, Accident and Emergency Dept, Guy's Hosp.; Civilian Consultant Surgeon: BMH Iserlohn, 1983–86; BMH Munster, 1986. *Publications:* contribs on surgical subjects. *Address:* 110 Mill Street, Kidlington OX5 2EF. *Died 19 Feb. 2011.*

ROGERS, Paul; actor; *b* Plympton, Devon, 22 March 1917; *s* of Edwin and Dulcie Myrtle Rogers; *m* 1st, 1939, Jocelyn Wynne (marr. diss. 1955); two *s*; 2nd, 1955, Rosalind Boxall (*d* 2004); two *d*. *Educ:* Newton Abbot Grammar School, Devon. Michael Chekhov Theatre Studio, 1936–38. First appearance on stage as Charles Dickens in Bird's Eye of Valour, Scala, 1938; Stratford-upon-Avon Shakespeare Memorial Theatre, 1939; Concert Party and Colchester Rep. Co. until 1940. Served Royal Navy, 1940–46. Colchester Rep. Co. and Arts Council Tour and London Season, Tess of the D'Urbervilles, 1946–47; Bristol Old Vic, 1947–49; London Old Vic (incl. tour S Africa and Southern Rhodesia), 1949–53; also at Edinburgh, London and in USA, 1954–57; London, 1958; tour to Moscow, Leningrad and Warsaw, 1960. Roles with Old Vic include numerous Shakespearean leads; Gloucester, in King Lear, 1989. Other parts include: Sir Claude Mulhammer in The Confidential Clerk, Edinburgh Festival and Lyric, London, 1953; Lord Claverton in The Elder Statesman, Edinburgh Fest. and Cambridge Theatre, London, 1958; Mr Fox in Mr Fox of Venice, Piccadilly, 1959; Johnny Condell in One More River, Duke of York's and Westminster, 1959; Nickles in JB, Phœnix, 1961; Reginald Kinsale in Photo

Finish, Saville, 1962; The Seagull, Queen's, 1964; Season of Goodwill, Queen's, 1964; The Homecoming, Aldwych, 1965; Timon of Athens, Stratford-upon-Avon, 1965; The Government Inspector, Aldwych, 1966; Henry IV, Stratford-upon-Avon, 1966; Max in The Homecoming, New York, 1967 (Tony Award and Whitbread Anglo-American Award); Plaza Suite, Lyric, 1969; The Happy Apple, Apollo, 1970; Sleuth, St Martin's, 1970, NY, 1971; Othello, Bristol Old Vic, 1974; Heartbreak House, Nat. Theatre, 1975; The Marrying of Ann Leete, Aldwych, 1975; The Return of A. J. Raffles, Aldwych, 1975; The Zykovs, Aldwych, 1976; Volpone, The Madras House, Nat. Theatre, 1977; Eclipse, Royal Court, 1978; You Never Can Tell, Lyric, Hammersmith, 1979; The Dresser, New York, 1981, 1982; The Importance of Being Earnest, A Kind of Alaska, Nat. Theatre, 1982; The Apple Cart, Theatre Royal, Haymarket, 1986; Danger: Memory!, Hampstead, 1988; Other People's Money, Lyric, 1990. Appears in films and television. *Publications:* a Preface to Folio Soc. edition of Shakespeare's Love's Labour's Lost, 1959. *Recreations:* gardening, carpentry, books. *Address:* 9 Hillside Gardens, Highgate, N6 5SU. *T:* (020) 8340 2656. *Died 6 Oct. 2013.*

ROGERS, Col Richard Annesley C.; *see* Coxwell-Rogers.

ROHRER, Dr Heinrich; IBM Research Division, Zurich Research Laboratory, 1963–97, and IBM Fellow, 1986–97; *b* 6 June 1933; *s* of Heinrich and Katharina Rohrer; *m* 1961, Rose-Marie Egger; two *d. Educ:* Federal Inst. of Technology, ETH, Zürich (Dr. sc. nat); PhD 1960. Post-doctoral Fellow, Rutgers Univ., 1961–63; joined IBM Res. Div. as Res. Staff Mem., 1963; then various managerial posts. Vis. Scientist, Univ. of Calif. at Santa Barbara, 1974–75. Mem. Bd, Swiss Fed. Insts of Technol., 1993–2003. Mem., Swiss Acad. of Technical Scis, 1988; For. Associate, US Acad. of Sci., 1988; Hon. Member: Swiss Physical Soc., 1990; Swiss Assoc. of Engrs and Architects, 1991; Zurich Physical Soc., 1992. Hon. Fellow, RMS, 1988. Hon. Dr: Rutgers, 1987; Marseille, 1988; Madrid, 1988; Tsukuba, Japan, 1994; Wolfgang Goethe Univ., Frankfurt, 1996; Tohoku, Japan, 2000. (Jtly) King Faisal Internat. Prize for Science, 1984; (jtly) Hewlett Packard Europhysics Prize, 1984; (jtly) Nobel Prize in Physics, 1986; (jtly) Cresson Medal, Franklin Inst., Philadelphia, 1987. *Recreations:* ski-ing, hiking, gardening. *Died 16 May 2013.*

ROMANES, Prof. George John, CBE 1971; PhD; Professor of Anatomy, 1954–84, and Dean of Faculty of Medicine, 1979–83, Edinburgh University; Professor of Anatomy, Royal Scottish Academy, since 1983; *b* 2 Dec. 1916; *s* of George Romanes, BSc, AMICE, and Isabella Elizabeth Burn Smith; *m* 1945, Muriel Grace Adam (*d* 1992), Edinburgh; four *d. Educ:* Edinburgh Academy; Christ's College, Cambridge (BA, PhD); Edinburgh University (MB, ChB). Marmaduke Sheild Scholar in Human Anatomy, 1938–40; Demonstrator in Anatomy, Cambridge, 1939; Beit Memorial Fellow for Medical Research, Cambridge, 1944–46; Lectr in Neuroanatomy, Edinburgh Univ., 1946–54. Commonwealth Fund Fellow, Columbia Univ., NY, 1949–50. Chm., Bd of Management, Edinburgh Royal Infirmary, 1959–74. Mem. Anatomical Soc. of Gt Brit. and Ireland; Mem. Amer. Assoc. of Anatomists; Assoc. Mem. Amer. Neurological Assoc. FRSE 1955; FRCSE 1958. Hon. DSc Glasgow, 1983. *Publications:* (ed) Cunningham's Textbook and Manuals of Anatomy; various papers on the anatomy and development of the nervous system in Jl of Anatomy and Jl of Comparative Neurology. *Recreations:* angling, curling. *Address:* Camus na Feannag, Kishorn, Strathcarron, Ross-shire IV54 8XA. *T:* (01520) 733273. *Died 9 April 2014.*

RONE, Ven. James; Archdeacon of Wisbech, 1995–2002; *b* 28 Aug. 1935; *s* of James and Bessie Rone; *m* 1st, 1956, Ivy Mylchreest (*née* Whitby) (*d* 1970); one *s* one *d*; 2nd, 1976, Mary Elizabeth (*née* Angove). *Educ:* Skerry's Coll., Liverpool; St Stephen's House, Oxford. FSCA 1971. RAMC, 1953–56. Accountant, ICI Ltd, 1957–64; Hawker Siddeley Dynamics, 1964–65; Subsidiary co. dir and Sec., Reed International, 1965–71; Gp Chief Accountant, Leigh & Sillavan, 1971–73; Finance Officer, Oxford Diocesan Bd of Finance, 1973–79. Ordained deacon 1980, priest 1981; Curate, Stony Stratford, dio. of Oxford, 1980–82; Vicar, SS Peter and Mary Magdalene, Fordham and Rector of Kennett, 1982–89; Canon Residentiary, 1989–95, Treasurer, 1992–95, Hon. Canon, 1995–2002, Ely Cathedral. Mem., Gen. Synod of C of E, 1995–2002. Bishop's Advr for Hosp. Chaplaincy, 1996–2002. *Recreations:* walking, Rugby (now non-playing), cricket (Middlesex CCC), classical music, theatre, good food and wine. *Address:* 69 Deacons Lane, Ely, Cambs CB7 4PS. *T:* (01353) 667088. *Died 26 Jan. 2014.*

ROOKE, James Smith, CMG 1961; OBE 1949; Grand Decoration of Honour in Gold, of the Austrian Republic, 1981; Chief Executive, British Overseas Trade Board, 1972–75; HM Diplomatic Service, retired; Lecturer, Diplomatic Academy, Vienna, 1980–97; *b* 6 July 1916; *s* of Joseph Nelson Rooke and Adeline Mounser (*née* Woodgate); *m* 1938, Maria Theresa Rebrec, Vienna; one *s* two *d. Educ:* Workington Grammar Sch.; University College, London; Vienna Univ. Apptd to Dept of Overseas Trade, 1938. Military service, 1940–45, KRRC and AEC. Second Secretary (Commercial), British Embassy, Bogotá, 1946; UK Delegation to ITO Conf., Havana, 1947; Dep. UK Commercial Rep., Frankfurt, 1948; First Secretary (Commercial), British Embassy, Rome, 1951; Consul (Commercial), Milan, 1954; Deputy Consul-General (Commercial), New York, 1955–59; HM Counsellor (Commercial) British Embassy, Berne, 1959–63, Rome, 1963–66; Minister (Commercial), British High Commn, Canberra, 1966–68; Minister (Economic), British Embassy, Paris, 1968–72. *Publications:* Trade and the Diplomat, 2006. *Recreations:* walking, swimming. *Address:* Flotowgasse 26/3/1, 1190 Vienna, Austria. *Clubs:* East India, Devonshire, Sports and Public Schools. *Died 2011.*

ROPNER, (William Guy) David; Director, Ropner PLC, 1953–94 (Chairman, 1973–85); *b* 3 April 1924; *s* of late Sir William Guy Ropner and Lady (Margarita) Ropner; *m* 1st, 1955, Mildred Malise Hare Armitage (marr. diss. 1978); one *d* three *s*; 2nd, 1985, Hon. Mrs Charlotte M. Taddei; one *s. Educ:* Harrow. FICS 1953. Served War, 1942–47: 2nd Lieut RA, Essex Yeomanry; Captain 3rd Regt, RHA. Joined Sir R. Ropner and Co. Ltd, 1947; dir of various Ropner PLC gp cos, 1953–94. Member: Lloyd's, 1952–91; Gen. Cttee, Lloyd's Register of Shipping, 1961–94; Pres., Gen. Council of British Shipping, 1979–80; Chairman: Deep Sea Tramp Section, Chamber of Shipping, 1970–72; Lights Adv. Cttee, GCBS, 1978–87; Merchant Navy Welfare Bd, 1980–94; Cleveland & Durham Industrial Council, 1980–94; Dir, British Shipowners Assoc., 1954–89. *Recreation:* country and garden pursuits. *Address:* Dolphin House, 99 Windsor Road, Chobham, Surrey GU24 8LE. *Club:* St Moritz Tobogganing. *Died 16 April 2015.*

ROSE, Christine B.; *see* Brooke-Rose.

ROSE, Clifford; *see* Rose, F.C.

ROSE, Donald Henry Gair, LVO 1982; HM Diplomatic Service, retired; Consul-General, Jedda, 1983–86; *b* 24 Sept. 1926; *m* 1950, Sheila Munro; three *s*. HM Forces, 1944–48; Scottish Office, 1948–66; Commonwealth Office, 1966; Nairobi, 1967; Tripoli, 1971; First Sec., Cairo, 1974–77; FCO, 1977–79; High Comr, Kiribati, 1979–83. *Address:* 11 Buckstone Gardens, Edinburgh EH10 6QD. *Died 4 Dec. 2012.*

ROSE, Dr F(rank) Clifford, FRCP; Hon. Consulting Neurologist, Charing Cross Hospital, since 1991; *b* 29 Aug. 1926; *s* of James and Clare Rose; *m* 1963, Angela Juliet Halsted; three *s. Educ:* King's Coll., London; Westminster Hosp. Med. Sch.; Univ. of California, San Francisco; Hôpital de la Salpêtrière, Paris. MB BS London; DCH; MRCS; FRCP 1971 (LRCP 1949, MRCP 1954). Medical Registrar, Westminster Hosp., 1955; Resident MO, National Hosp., Queen Square, 1957; Sen. Registrar, Dept of Neurology, St George's Hosp., 1960; Consultant Neurologist: Medical Ophthalmology Unit, St Thomas' Hosp., 1963–85; Moor House Sch. for Speech Disorders, 1965–70; Physician i/c, Dept of Neurology, Regl Neuroscis Centre, Charing Cross Hosp., 1965–91; Dir, Academic Unit of Neuroscis, Charing Cross and

Westminster Med. Sch., 1985–91; Dir, London Neurological Centre, 1991–2005; Prof. Associate, Dept of Health Scis, Brunel Univ., 1991–97. PMO, Allied Dunbar (formerly Hambro Life) Assurance Co., 1970–96. Mem., Wkg Pty on Stroke, RCP, 1988; Chairman: European Stroke Prevention Study, 1981–88; Res. Adv. Cttee, Assoc. for Res. in Multiple Sclerosis, 1987–91; Internat. Amyotrophic Lateral Sclerosis/Motor Neurone Disease Res. Foundn, 1987–90; Motor Neurone Disease Assoc., 1988–90 (Med. Patron, 1978–90; Scientific Advr, 1990–91); Ind. Doctors Forum, 1994–96 (Chm., Specialists' Cttee, 2003–05); Ciba Epilepsy Res. Award, 1997. Sen. Editor, Neuroepidemiology, 1991–96 (Dep. Editor, 1982–83; Editor, 1984–90); Editor: World Neurology, 1990–98; Jl of Hist. of Neuroscis, 1992–96; Co-editor, Headache Qly, 1991–95. President: Med. Soc. London, 1983–84 (Lettsomian Lectr, 1979; Treas., 1984–89; Internat. Sec., 1995–2007); Assurance Med. Soc., 1983–85; Section of Neurology, RSM, 1990–91; Sec.-Treas. Gen., World Fedn of Neurology, 1989–98. Trustee: Migraine Trust (Chm., 1988–96); The Way Ahead Appeal, 1986–91. Examr in Clinical Pharmacology and Therapeutics, Univ. of London. Guest Lectr, Scandinavian Migraine Soc., 1983. Hon. Member: Neurol Soc. of Thailand, 1992; Austrian Soc. of Neurol., 1992; Hon. Life Mem., Internat. Headache Soc., 1997. Harold Wolff Award, 1981 and 1984, and Distinguished Clinician Award, 1986, Amer. Assoc. for the Study of Headache; Louis Boshes Award, Northwestern Univ., Chicago, 1994; Lifetime Award, Internat. Soc. for the History of Neuroscis, 2003. *Publications:* (jtly) Hypoglycaemia, 1965, 2nd edn, 1981 (trans. Japanese 1988); (jtly) Basic Neurology of Speech, 1970, 3rd edn 1983; (ed) Physiological Aspects of Clinical Neurology, 1976; (ed) Medical Ophthalmology, 1976; (ed) Motor Neurone Disease, 1977; (ed) Clinical Neuroimmunology, 1978; (ed) Paediatric Neurology, 1979; (jtly) Optic Neuritis and its Differential Diagnosis, 1979; (ed jtly) Progress in Stroke Research 1, 1979; (ed jtly) Progress in Neurological Research, 1979; (jtly) Migraine: the facts, 1979 (trans. Spanish 1981); (ed) Clinical Neuroepidemiology, 1980; (ed) Animal Models of Neurological Disorders, 1980; (ed jtly) Research Progress in Parkinson's Disease, 1981; (ed) Metabolic Disorders of the Nervous System, 1981; (ed jtly) Progress in Migraine Research 1, 1981; (jtly) Stroke: The Facts, 1981 (trans. Dutch 1982); (ed jtly) Historical Aspects of the Neurosciences, 1982; (ed jtly) Cerebral Hypoxia in the Pathogenesis of Migraine, 1982; (ed) Advances in Stroke Therapy, 1982; (ed) Advances in Migraine Research and Therapy, 1982; (ed) Research Progress in Epilepsy, 1982; (ed jtly) Immunology of Nervous System Infections, 1983; (ed) The Eye in General Disease, 1983; (ed jtly) Progress in Stroke Research 2, 1983; (ed) Research Progress in Motor Neurone Disease, 1984; (ed) Progress in Migraine Research 2, 1984; (ed) Progress in Aphasiology, 1985; (ed) Modern Approaches to the Dementias (2 vols), 1985; (ed jtly) Neuro-oncology, 1985; (ed) Migraine: clinical and research advances, 1985; Handbook of Clinical Neurology: headache, 1986; (ed) Stroke: epidemiological, therapeutic and socio-economic aspects, 1986; (jtly) Atlas of Clinical Neurology, 1986 (trans. Japanese 1989); (ed jtly) Multiple Sclerosis: diagnostic, immunological and therapeutic aspects, 1987; (ed) Advances in Headache Research, 1987; (ed) Parkinson's Disease: clinical and research advances, 1987; (ed jtly) Physiological Aspects of Clinical Neuro-ophthalmology, 1987; (jtly) Answers to Migraine, 1987; (ed jtly) Aphasia, 1988; (ed) The Management of Headache, 1988; (ed jtly) Neuromuscular Stimulation, 1989; (ed) James Parkinson, his life and times, 1989; (ed) Control of the Hypothalamic-Pituitary-Adrenal Axis, 1989; (ed) New Advances in Headache Research, 1989; (ed) Neuroscience across the Centuries, 1989; (ed jtly) Clinical Trial Methodology in Stroke, 1989; (ed jtly) Amyotrophic Lateral Sclerosis: new advances in toxicology and epidemiology, 1990; (ed) Progress in Clinical Neurologic Trials: amyotrophic lateral sclerosis, 1990; (ed) New Advances in Headache Research 2, 1991; (ed) Parkinson's Disease and the Problems of Clinical Trials, 1992; (ed) Molecular Genetics and Neurology, 1992; (ed) Advances in Clinical Neuropharmacology, 1993; (ed) ALS: from Charcot to the present and into the future, 1994; (ed) New Advances in Headache Research 3, 1994; (ed) Tropical Neurology, 1996; Towards Migraine 2000, 1996; A Short History of Neurology: the British contribution 1660–1910, 1999; Multiple Sclerosis at Your Fingertips, 2000; Twentieth Century Neurology: the British contribution, 2001; (jtly) Motor Neurone Disease at your fingertips, 2003; (ed) Neurology of the Arts, 2004; (jtly) Migraine, 2004; (jtly) Managing Your Multiple Sclerosis, 2004; The Neurobiology of Painting, 2006; Neurology of Music, 2010; History of British Neurology, 2011; papers in neurological and gen. med. jls. *Recreations:* reading, wine. *Address:* 7–8 Church Street, Little Bedwyn, Marlborough, Wilts SN8 3JQ. *T:* (01672) 870303. *Club:* Royal Society of Medicine. *Died 1 Nov. 2012.*

ROSE, Irwin A., (Ernie), PhD; Researcher, Department of Physiology and Biophysics, University of California, Irvine, 1997, then Distinguished Professor Emeritus; *b* 16 July 1926; *s* of Harry Royze and Ella Greenwald; *m* 1955, Dr Zelda Budenstein; three *s* (incl. twins) (one *d* decd). *Educ:* Univ. of Chicago (BS 1948; PhD 1952). Instructor in Biochem., Yale Univ. Med. Sch., 1954–63; Scientist, Fox Chase Cancer Center, Philadelphia, 1963–95. (Jtly) Nobel Prize in Chemistry, 2004. *Publications:* articles in learned jls. *Address:* Department of Physiology and Biophysics, College of Medicine, University of California, Irvine, CA 92697–4560, USA. *Died 1 June 2015.*

ROSE, Joyce Dora Hester, CBE 1981; JP, DL; Chairman, Council and Executive, Magistrates' Association, 1990–93; *b* 14 Aug. 1929; *d* of late Abraham (Arthur) Woolf and Rebecca Woolf (*née* Simpson); *m* 1953, Cyril Rose; two *s* one *d*. *Educ:* King Alfred Sch., London; Queen's Coll., London; in N America. Chm., Watford Magistrates' Court, 1990–94 (Dep. Chm., Juvenile Panel, 1968–91, Family Proceedings (formerly Domestic) Panel, 1982–99 (Chm., 1979–82)); Member: Herts Magistrates' Courts Cttee, 1973–95; Herts Probation Cttee, 1971–95. Pres., 1979–80, Chm., 1982–83, Liberal Party; Pres. and Chm., Women's Liberal Fedn, 1972, 1973; Mem., Lib Dem Federal Appeals Panel, 1994–2005. Mem., Women's Nat. Commn, 1981–87 (Mem. Exec., 1985–87); former Mem., Nat. Exec., UK Cttee for UNICEF (Vice-Chm., 1968–70). Board Member: Apex Trust, 1994–2004; Herts Care Trust, 1995–99; SW Herts Hospice Charitable Trust (Peace Hospice), 1996–2003; Herts Family Mediation Service, 1996–2002. JP Herts, 1963; DL Herts, 1990. Hon. LLD Hertfordshire, 1992. *Address:* 2 Oak House, 101 Ducks Hill Road, Northwood, Middx HA6 2WQ. *T:* (01923) 821385. *Club:* National Liberal. *Died 3 Nov. 2013.*

ROSE, Kenneth Vivian, CBE 1997; FRSL; writer; *b* 15 Nov. 1924; *s* of Dr J. Rose, MB, ChB. *Educ:* Repton Sch.; New Coll., Oxford (scholar; MA). Served Welsh Guards, 1943–46; attached Phantom, 1945. Asst master, Eton Coll., 1948; Editorial Staff, Daily Telegraph, 1952–60; founder and writer of Albany column, Sunday Telegraph, 1961–97. Vice-Pres., London Liby, 2012–. *Publications:* Superior Person: a portrait of Curzon and his circle in late Victorian England, 1969; The Later Cecils, 1975; William Harvey: a monograph, 1978; King George V, 1983 (Wolfson Award for History, 1983; Whitbread Award for Biography, 1983; Yorkshire Post Biography of the Year Award, 1984); Kings, Queens and Courtiers: intimate portraits of the Royal House of Windsor, 1985; (contrib.) Founders and Followers: literary lectures on the London Library, 1992; Elusive Rothschild: the life of Victor, Third Baron, 2003; contribs to Dictionary of National Biography. *Address:* 38 Brunswick Gardens, W8 4AL. *T:* (020) 7221 4783. *Clubs:* Beefsteak, Pratt's. *Died 28 Jan. 2014.*

ROSE, Paul (Bernard); HM Coroner, London Southern District, 1988–2002; *b* 26 Dec. 1935; *s* of Arthur and Norah Rose; *m* 1957, Eve Marie-Thérèse; two *s* one *d*. *Educ:* Bury Gram. Sch.; Manchester Univ.; Gray's Inn. LLB (Hons) Manch., 1956; Barrister-at-Law, 1957. Legal and Secretarial Dept, Co-op. Union Ltd, 1957–60; Lectureship, Dept of Liberal Studies, Royal Coll. of Advanced Technology, Salford, 1961–63; Barrister-at-Law, 1963–88; Asst Recorder (formerly Dep. Circuit Judge), 1974–88; Immigration Adjudicator (part-time), Hatton Cross, 1987– (Special Adjudicator, 1993–). MP (Lab) Manchester, Blackley, 1964–79; PPS to Minister of Transport, 1967–68; Opposition Front Bench Spokesman, Dept of

Employment, 1970–72. Chairman: Parly Labour Home Office Group, 1968–70; Parly Labour Employment Group, 1974–79; Campaign for Democracy in Ulster, 1965–73. Delegate to Council of Europe and WEU, 1968–69; Vice-Chm., Labour Cttee for Europe, 1977–79. Mem., Campaign for Electoral Reform, 1975–. Founder Mem., SDP (Brent Area Sec., 1981–82). Chm., NW Regional Sports Council, 1966–68. Member: Coroners' Soc. (Pres., SE Coroners Soc., 1996–97); Medico-Legal Soc. AIL. *Publications:* Handbook to Industrial and Provident Societies Act, 1960; Guide to Weights and Measures Act 1963, 1965; The Manchester Martyrs, 1970; Backbencher's Dilemma, 1981; The Moonies Unmasked, 1981; (jt) A History of the Fenian Movement in Britain, 1982; contrib. to many periodicals on political and legal topics. *Recreations:* sport, theatre, languages, travel, computers. *Address:* Lynnden, 70 Amersham Road, Chalfont St Peter, Bucks SL9 0PB. *Died 3 Nov. 2015.*

ROSEN, Charles; pianist and writer; International Chair in Performance and Musicology, Royal Northern College of Music, 2007–09; *b* New York, 5 May 1927; *s* of Irwin Rosen and Anita Gerber. *Educ:* studied piano with Mr and Mrs Moriz Rosenthal; Princeton Univ. (PhD). Début, NY, 1951. His many recordings include: first complete recording of Debussy Etudes, 1951; late keyboard works of Bach, 1969; last six Beethoven Sonatas, 1970; Schumann piano works; Diabelli Variations; also works by Liszt, Elliott Carter, Boulez, etc. Eliot Norton Prof. of Poetry, Harvard Univ., 1980; George Eastman Vis. Prof., Oxford Univ., 1987–88; Prof. of Music, Univ. of Chicago, 1991–96. Corresp. FBA 2002. Hon. MusD: Trinity Coll., Dublin, 1976; Cambridge, 1992; Hon. DMus Durham, 1980. *Publications:* The Classical Style, 1971; Schoenberg, 1976; Sonata Forms, 1980; (with H. Zerner) Romanticism and Realism: the mythology of nineteenth century art, 1984; The Romantic Generation, 1995; Piano Notes: the hidden world of the pianist, 2003; Music and Sentiment, 2010; Freedom and the Arts, 2012. *Recreations:* music, books. *Address:* c/o Owen/White Management, 22 Brunswick Terrace #6, Hove, East Sussex BN3 1HJ. *T:* (01273) 727127, *Fax:* (05601) 527038. *Died 9 Dec. 2012.*

ROSENTHAL, Thomas Gabriel, PhD; publisher, writer and broadcaster; Chairman: André Deutsch Ltd, 1984–98 (joined as Joint Chairman and Joint Managing Director, 1984; Chief Executive, 1987–96); Bridgewater Press Ltd, since 1997; *b* 16 July 1935; *o s* of late Dr Erwin I. J. Rosenthal and Elisabeth Charlotte (*née* Marx); *m* 1967, Ann Judith Warnford-Davis; two *s*. *Educ:* Perse Sch., Cambridge; Pembroke Coll., Cambridge (Exhibnr, MA, PhD 2005). Served RA, 1954–56, 2nd Lieut; subseq. Lieut Cambridgeshire Regt (TA). Joined Thames and Hudson Ltd, 1959; Man. Dir, Thames & Hudson Internat., 1966; joined Martin Secker & Warburg Ltd as Man. Dir, 1971; Dir, Heinemann Gp of Publishers, 1972–84; Man. Dir, William Heinemann International Ltd, 1979–84; Chairman: World's Work Ltd, 1979–84; Heinemann Zsolnay Ltd, 1979–84; William Heinemann Ltd, 1980–84; Martin Secker & Warburg Ltd, 1980–84; Kaye & Ward Ltd, 1980–84; William Heinemann, Australia and SA, 1981–82; Frew McKenzie (Antiquarian Booksellers), 1985–93; Pres., Heinemann Inc., 1981–84. Art Critic: The Listener, 1963–66; The New Statesman, 2001. Chm., Soc. of Young Publishers, 1961–62; Member: Cambridge Univ. Appts Bd, 1967–71; Exec. Cttee, NBL, 1971–74; Trans. Panel, Arts Council, 1988–94; Cttee of Management, Amateur Dramatic Club, Cambridge (also Trustee); Council, RCA, 1982–87; Exec. Council, ICA, 1987–99 (Chm., 1996–99); Council, Friends of ENO, 1997–2001; Trustee: Phoenix Trust, 1970–79; Fitzwilliam Mus., Cambridge, 2003–09. Mem. Editl Bd, Logos, 1989–93. *Publications:* Monograph on Jack B. Yeats, 1964; (with Alan Bowness) Monograph on Ivon Hitchens, 1973; (with Ursula Hoff) Monograph on Arthur Boyd, 1986; A Reader's Guide to European Art History, 1962; A Reader's Guide to Modern American Fiction, 1963; The Art of Jack B. Yeats, 1993; Sidney Nolan, 2002; Paula Rego: the complete graphic work, 2003, rev. and enlarged edn 2012; Josef Albers Formulation: articulation, 2006; L. S. Lowry: the art and the artist, 2010; On Art and Artists, 2013; introdns to paperback edns of Theodore Dreiser's The Financier, The Titan and Jennie Gerhardt; programme essays for Royal Opera House, ENO and WNO; articles in The Times, Guardian, TLS, THES, Punch, Music Magazine, London Magazine, Encounter, New Statesman, Jl of Brit. Assoc. for Amer. Studies, Studio Internat., Modern Painters, Art Rev., DNB, Bookseller, Nature, Prospect, Opera Now, Opera News, Opera-Opera, etc. *Recreations:* opera, bibliomania, looking at pictures, reading other publishers' books, watching cricket. *Address:* Flat 7, Huguenot House, 19 Oxendon Street, SW1Y 4EH. *T:* (020) 7839 3589. *Clubs:* Garrick, MCC. *Died 3 Jan. 2014.*

ROSOMAN, Leonard Henry, OBE 1981; RA 1969 (ARA 1960); FSA; Tutor, Royal College of Art, 1957–78; *b* 27 Oct. 1913; *s* of Henry Rosoman; *m* 1st, 1963, Jocelyn (marr. diss. 1969; she *d* 2005), *d* of Bertie Rickards, Melbourne, Australia; 2nd, 1994, Roxanne, *d* of Dr Milton Wruble, Michigan, USA. *Educ:* Deacon's Sch., Peterborough; Durham Univ. Teacher of Drawing and Painting, Reimann Sch. of Art, London, 1938–39; Official War Artist to Admiralty, 1943–45; Teacher: Camberwell Sch. of Art, London, 1948–56; (Mural Painting) Edinburgh Coll. of Art, 1948–56; Chelsea School of Art, 1956–57. One Man Shows: St George's Gallery, London, 1946 and 1949; Roland, Browse and Delbanco Gallery, London, 1954, 1957, 1959, 1965 and 1969; Fine Art Soc., 1974, 1978, 1983, 1990, 2003. Works bought by: HM Govt, Arts Council, British Council, York Art Gall., Contemporary Art Soc., Adelaide Art Gallery, V&A Museum, Lincoln Center, NY. Executed large mural paintings for: Festival of Britain, 1951; British Pavilion, Brussels World Fair, 1958; Harewood House, 1959; Lambeth Palace Chapel, 1988, 1992. HRSW; FRPS; Hon. ARCA; Hon. Fellow, Edinburgh Coll. of Art, 2005. *Recreation:* travelling as much as possible. *Address:* 7 Pembroke Studios, Pembroke Gardens, W8 6HX. *T:* (020) 7603 3638. *Clubs:* Arts, Chelsea Arts. *Died 21 Feb. 2012.*

ROSS, Donald Nixon, FRCS; Consultant Thoracic Surgeon, Guy's Hospital, 1958–78, then Emeritus; Consultant Surgeon, National Heart Hospital, 1963–93 (Senior Surgeon, 1967); *b* 4 Oct. 1922; *m* 1st, 1956, Dorothy Curtis (marr. diss. 2001); one *d*; 2nd, 2001, Barbara Cork. *Educ:* Boys' High Sch., Kimberley, S Africa; Univ. of Cape Town (BSc, MB, ChB 1st Cl. Hons, 1946). FRCS 1949; FACC 1973; FACS 1976. Sen. Registrar in Thoracic Surgery, Bristol, 1952; Res. Fellow, 1953, Sen. Thoracic Registrar, 1954, Guy's Hosp.; Dir, Dept of Surgery, Inst. of Cardiology, 1970. Introduced: aortic homograft, 1962; Ross procedure (pulmonary autograft), 1967. Pres., Soc. for Cardiothoracic Surgery in GB and Ireland, 1984. Hon. FRSocMed 1996; Hon. FRCSI 1984; Hon. FRCS Thailand, 1987. Hon. DSc CNAA, 1982. Clement Price Thomas Award, RCS, 1983; Lifetime Achievement Award, Soc. for Cardiothoracic Surgery in GB and Ireland, 2008; Bourakovski Premium, Bakoulev Scientific Center for Cardiovascular Surgery, Russian Acad. of Medical Scis, 2012. Order of Cedar of Lebanon, 1975; Order of Merit (1st cl.) (West Germany), 1981; Royal Order (Thailand), 1994. *Publications:* A Surgeon's Guide to Cardiac Diagnosis, 1962; (jtly) Medical and Surgical Cardiology, 1968; (jtly) Biological Tissue in Heart Valve Replacement, 1972; contrib. BMJ, Lancet, Proc. RSM, Annals Royal Coll. Surg., Amer. Jl Cardiol. *Recreations:* Arabian horse breeding, horse riding, gardening, music, racing. *Address:* 35 Cumberland Terrace, Regent's Park, NW1 4HP. *T:* (020) 7935 0756. *Clubs:* Garrick; Kimberley (SA). *Died 6 July 2014.*

ROSS, William Mackie, CBE 1987; TD 1969; DL; MD; FRCS; FRCSE; FRCR; Consultant Radiotherapist, Northern Regional Health Authority, 1953–87; Lecturer in Radiotherapy, University of Newcastle upon Tyne, 1973–87; *b* 14 Dec. 1922; *s* of Harry Caithness Ross and Catherine Ross; *m* 1948, Mary Burt (decd); one *s* two *d*. *Educ:* Durham and Newcastle. MB, BS 1945; MD 1953. FRCS 1956; FRCR 1960; FRCSE 1994. Trainee in Radiotherapy, 1945–51; National Service, 1951–53; RAMC TA, 1953–72; Col, CO 201 Gen. Hosp., 1967–72, Hon. Col, 1977–82. President: Section of Radiology, RSM, 1978; British Inst. of Radiology, 1979; North of England Surgical Soc., 1983; Royal Coll. of Radiologists, 1983–86. Hon. FACR, 1986. DL Northumberland, 1971–74, Tyne and Wear, 1974.

Publications: articles on cancer, its causation and treatment. *Address:* 62 Archery Rise, Durham City DH1 4LA. *T:* (0191) 3869256. *Died 15 March 2011.*

ROSS-MUNRO, Colin William Gordon; QC 1972; *b* 12 Feb. 1928; *s* of late William Ross-Munro and of Adela Chirgwin; *m* 1958, Janice Jill Pedrana (*d* 2010); one step *d*. *Educ:* Lycée Français de Londres; Harrow Sch.; King's Coll., Cambridge. Served in Scots Guards and in Army Education Corps. Called to the Bar, Middle Temple, 1951 (Master of the Bench, 1983). *Recreations:* tennis, travel. *Address:* (home) 22 Rivermead Court, SW6 3RU; Blackstone Chambers, Blackstone House, Temple, EC4Y 9BW. *Died 5 Sept. 2015.*

ROSSI, Marie-Louise Elizabeth; international regulatory adviser, since 2005; *b* 18 Feb. 1956; *d* of Sir Hugh Alexis Louis Rossi and Philomena Elizabeth Jennings. *Educ:* St Paul's Girls' Sch.; St Anne's Coll., Oxford (BA Hons Lit. Hum., MA; Treas., Oxford Union, 1978). Hogg Robinson Gp plc, 1979–87; Asst Dir, Sedgwick Gp plc, 1987–90; Consultant, Tillinghast-Towers Perrin, mgt consultants and actuaries, 1990–93; Chief Executive: London Internat. Insurance and Reinsurance Market Assoc., 1993–98; Internat. Underwriting Assoc. of London, 1998–2005; Dep. Chm., 2004–06, Acting Chm., 2006, Chm., 2006–07, European Movement UK; Hd, Insce and Risk Mgt, and Mem., Adv. Bd, New Security Foundn, 2007–; expert witness in ICC arbitration, 2011–. Member: Lloyd's, 1985–97 (Underwriting Mem., 1985–91); Gen. Cttee, Lloyd's Register of Shipping, 2000–04. Mem. (C), Westminster CC, 1986–94 (Chm., Educn Cttee, 1989–92). Chairman: Bow Gp, 1988–89 (Trustee, 1996–99); Foreign Affairs Forum, Conservative Party, 1993–96; Chm., Pro Euro Cons. Party, 1999–2001. Liberal Democrats: Chm., The Peel Gp, 2005–09; Member: Federal Exec., 2005, 2007–08; Internat. Relns Cttee, 2005–10. Trustee and Director: Foundn for Young Musicians, 1990–2005; Orch. of St John's Ltd, 1995–99. Mem., LSC London Central, 2000–04. Mem. Governing Council, Nottingham Univ., 2001–05. Contested (Lib Dem) Cities of London and Westminster, 2005; Parly Spokesman (Lib Dem) for Buckingham, General Election campaign, 2010. MIEx 1991; FIRM 2004. FRSA 1993. Hon. Citizen, City of Baltimore, Md, 1994. *Clubs:* Athenæum, Special Forces. *Died 27 Oct. 2014.*

ROTHSCHILD, Leopold David de, CBE 1985; Director, Rothschild (formerly N M Rothschild & Sons Limited), since 1970 (Partner, 1956–70); *b* 12 May 1927; *yr s* of late Lionel Nathan de Rothschild and Marie Louise Beer. *Educ:* Bishop's Coll. Sch., Canada; Harrow; Trinity Coll., Cambridge. Director of Bank of England, 1970–83. Chm., Exbury Gdns Ltd, 1989–. Chairman: Anglo Venezuelan Soc., 1975–82; English Chamber Orchestra and Music Soc. Ltd, 1963–2001 (Pres., 2001–); Bach Choir, 1976–99 (Pres., 2002–); Music Adv. Cttee, British Council, 1986–93; Council, RCM, 1988–99 (FRCM 1977). Trustee, Science Mus., 1987–98; Mem. Council, Winston Churchill Meml Trust, 1990–2000. DUniv York, 1991. Order of Francisco de Miranda, 1st cl. (Venezuela), 1978; Gran Oficial, Order of Merit (Chile), 1993; Ordem Nacional do Cruzeiro do Sul (Brazil), 1993; Order of Aztec Eagle, Encomienda (Mexico), 1994. *Recreations:* music, walking, industrial archaeology. *Address:* New Court, St Swithin's Lane, EC4P 4DU. *T:* (020) 7280 5000. *Clubs:* Brooks's; Royal Yacht Squadron. *Died 19 April 2012.*

ROUSSEL, (Philip) Lyon, OBE 1974; Controller, Arts Division, British Council, 1979–83; *b* 17 Oct. 1923; *s* of late Paul Marie Roussel and Beatrice (*née* Cuthbert; later Lady Murray); *m* 1959, Elisabeth Mary (*d* 2007), *d* of Kenneth and Kathleen Bennett; one *s* one *d*. *Educ:* Hurstpierpoint Coll.; St Edmund Hall, Oxford (MA, Cert. Public and Social Admin); Chelsea Sch. of Art. Served Indian Army in Parachute Regt, 1942–46 (Major); Parachute Regt (TA), 1946–50. Sudan Political Service, 1950–55; Principal, War Office, 1955–56; Associated Newspapers, 1956–57; British Council, 1960–83: India, 1960–67 (Regional Rep., Western and Central India, 1964–67); Dir, Scholarships, 1967–71; Rep. and Cultural Attaché, British Embassy, Belgium and Luxembourg, 1971–76; Europalia-Great Britain Festival Cttee, 1973; Cultural Attaché (Counsellor), British Embassy, Washington, 1976–79. Sponsorship Consultant, National Theatre, 1983–84. Member: Fest. of India Cttee, 1981–82; British Adv. Cttee, Britain Salutes New York, 1981–83; Bd, The Hanover Band, 1984–87; Common Room, Wolfson Coll., Oxford, 1988 (Chm., Arts Soc., 2000–10). Hon. Organiser, Poppy Appeal, Woodstock Br., Royal British Legion, 1991–97 (Cert. of Appreciation, 1997). FRGS 1981; FRSA 1979. *Recreations:* painting, looking at pictures, reading and a barn in France. *Address:* Flat 27, Chartwell House, 12 Ladbroke Terrace, W11 3PG. *Clubs:* Athenæum; Oxford Union. *Died 22 Jan. 2011.*

ROWE, Prof. Peter Noël, DSc(Eng); FREng, FIChemE; Ramsay Memorial Professor of Chemical Engineering, and Head of Department, University College London, 1965–85, then Professor Emeritus; *b* 25 Dec. 1919; *e s* of Charles Henry Rowe and Kate Winifred (*née* Storry); *m* 1952, Pauline Garmirian; two *s*. *Educ:* Preston Grammar Sch.; Manchester Coll. of Technology; Imperial Coll., London. Princ. Scientific Officer, AERE, Harwell, 1958–65. Crabtree Orator, 1980. Vis. Prof., Univ. Libre de Bruxelles, 1988, 1995. Advr, HEFCE, 1992– (Chm., Assessment Panel, 1992, 1996). Consultant, SERC, 1990–. Pres., IChemE, 1981–82; Hon. Sec., Fellowship of Engrg, 1982–85. FCGI 1983. Hon. Fellow, UCL, 1993. Hon. DSc Brussels, 1978. *Publications:* scientific articles in Trans IChemE, Chem. Eng. Science, etc. *Address:* Pamber Green, Upper Basildon, Reading, Berks RG8 8PG. *T:* (01491) 671382. *Died 27 April 2014.*

ROWLAND, Prof. F(rank) Sherwood, PhD; Donald Bren Research Professor of Chemistry, University of California at Irvine, since 1994 (Professor of Chemistry, since 1964); *b* 28 June 1927; *m* 1952, Joan Lundberg; one *s* one *d*. *Educ:* Ohio Wesleyan Univ. (AB 1948); Univ. of Chicago (MS 1951; PhD 1952). Chemistry Instr, Princeton Univ., 1952–56; Asst Prof., 1956–58, Associate Prof., 1958–63, Prof., 1963–64, of Chemistry, Univ. of Kansas; Chm. of Chemistry Dept, 1964–70, Daniel G. Aldrich, Jr Prof. of Chemistry, 1985–89, Donald Bren Prof. of Chemistry, 1989–94, Univ. of Calif at Irvine. Discovered (with Dr Mario J. Molina) that chlorofluorocarbon gases deplete the ozone layer of the stratosphere. Mem., Acid Rain Peer Review Panel, US Office of Science and Tech., 1982–84. International Association of Meteorology and Atmospheric Physics: Member: Commn on Atmospheric Chemistry and Global Pollution, 1979–91; Ozone Commn, 1980–88 (Hon. Life Mem., 1996); Jt Chm., Dahlem Conf. on Our Changing Atmosphere, Germany, 1987. Member: Amer. Acad. of Arts and Scis, 1977; NAS, 1978 (Foreign Sec., 1994–2002); AAAS (Pres., 1992; Chm. Bd, 1993; Fellow); Amer. Philosophical Soc., 1995–; Founding Mem., Academia Bibliotheca Alexandrinae, Egypt, 2004–; Fellow: APS; Amer. Geophysical Union. For. Mem., Royal Soc., 2004. Numerous hon. degrees and awards; (jtly) Nobel Prize for Chemistry, 1995. *Publications:* on atmospheric chemistry, radio-chemistry and chemical kinetics. *Address:* Department of Chemistry, University of California, 571 Rowland Hall, Irvine, CA 92697–2025, USA. *T:* (949) 8246016, *Fax:* (949) 8242905. *Died 10 March 2012.*

ROWLANDS, Sir David, KCB 2006 (CB 1991); FCILT; Chairman: Angel Trains Group Ltd, since 2010; Semperian PPP Investment Partners Group Ltd, since 2012; *b* 31 May 1947; *s* of George and Margaret Rowlands; *m* 1975, Louise Marjorie Brown; two *s*. *Educ:* St Mary's Coll., Crosby; St Edmund Hall, Oxford. Entered Civil Service, 1974; Private Sec. to Minister of State for Industry, 1978–80; Principal, Dept of Trade, then of Transport, 1980–84; Asst Sec., 1984–90, Under Sec., 1990–93, Dept of Transport; Dep. Sec. (Dir Gen.), Dept of Transport, later DETR, then DTLR, then DfT, 1993–2003; Perm. Sec., DfT, 2003–07. Chairman: High Speed Two, 2009–10; Gatwick Airport Ltd, 2009–13. Sen. Advr, Global Infrastructure Partners, 2008–12; Advr, Capita Gp plc, 2009. Chm., Remuneration Panel, Essex CC, 2012–. Mem., Adv. Panel, Regl Growth Fund, 2010–. Mem., Public Policy Cttee, RAC Foundn, 2009–. Gov., Anglia Ruskin Univ., 2008–. FCILT 2010. *Address:* 22 Lyon Close, Chelmsford, Essex CM2 8NY. *Died 11 May 2014.*

ROWLEY, Frederick Allan, CMG 1978; OBE 1959; MC 1945; Major (retd); HM Diplomatic Service, retired; *b* 27 July 1922; *m* 1951, Anne Crawley (*d* 2014); one *s* three *d*. *Educ:* Haig Sch., Aldershot. Served War of 1939–45: Ranks, 8th Worcs Regt (TA), 1939–40; Emergency Commnd Officer, 5th Bn, 10th Baluch Regt (KGVO), Jacob's Rifles, Indian Army, Burma Campaign (MC), June 1941–Nov. 1948. At partition of India, granted regular commn (back-dated, 1942) in Worcestershire Regt, but retd (wounded), sub. Major. Joined HM Diplomatic Service, Nov. 1948: served (with brief periods in FO) in: Egypt; Ethiopia; Turkey; Burma; Singapore; Australia; Malaysia; FCO 1971–72; Under-Sec., N Ireland Office (on secondment), 1972–73; Counsellor, FCO, 1973–79. Joint Services Staff College (jssc), 1959. *Recreations:* cricket, golf. *Clubs:* Army and Navy; MCC. *Died 28 July 2014.*

ROYDS, Rev. John Caress, MA; Headmaster, Uppingham School, 1965–75; *b* 1920; 3rd *s* of Rev. Edward Thomas Hubert Royds, BA. *Educ:* Monkton Combe School, Bath; Queens' College, Cambridge (BA II 1 hons History, 1947; MA 1950). Military service with British and Indian Armies, 1940–46. Assistant master, Bryanston School, Dorset, 1947–61, House-master, 1951–61; Headmaster, General Wingate School, Addis Ababa, 1961–65. Deacon, 1974; Priest, 1975; Dir of Educn for Peterborough diocese, 1976–81; Vicar of St James's, Northampton, 1981–85; with CMS, Peshawar, Pakistan, 1985–86. *Address:* 16B Donaldson Road, Salisbury SP1 3DA. *Died 31 March 2011.*

RUBINSTEIN, Hilary Harold; Chairman, Hilary Rubinstein Books (Literary Agents), since 1992; *b* 24 April 1926; *s* of H. F. and Lina Rubinstein; *m* 1955, Helge Kitzinger; three *s* one *d*. *Educ:* Cheltenham Coll.; Merton Coll., Oxford (MA). Editorial Dir, Victor Gollancz Ltd, 1952–63; Special Features Editor, The Observer, 1963–64; Dep. Editor, The Observer Magazine, 1964–65. Partner, later Director, 1965–92, Chm. and Man. Dir, 1983–92, A. P. Watt Ltd. Mem. Council, ICA, 1976–92; Trustee, Open Coll. of the Arts, 1987–96. Founder-editor, The Good Hotel Guide (published in USA as Europe's Wonderful Little Hotels and Inns), 1978–2000. *Publications:* The Complete Insomniac, 1974; Hotels and Inns, an Oxford anthology, 1984. *Recreations:* hotel-watching, reading in bed. *Address:* 32 Ladbroke Grove, W11 3BQ. *T:* (020) 7727 9550. *E:* hilaryrubinstein@pobox.com. *Died 22 May 2012.*

RUCK-KEENE, John Robert, CBE 1977 (MBE 1946); TD 1950; Secretary General, Royal Society of Chemistry, 1980–81; *b* 2 Jan. 1917; *s* of late Major Robert Francis Ruck Keene, OBE, and Dorothy Mary (*née* Chester); *m* 1951, Beryl M Manistre (*d* 2004); two *s*. *Educ:* Eton; Trinity Coll., Cambridge (BA 1938, MA 1955). Commissioned TA, Oxford and Bucks LI, 1939; served UK and NW Europe, 1939–45 (Major 1944, MBE 1946). First appointment with Chemical Society, 1946; General Secretary, 1947–80, when the Royal Society of Chemistry was formed by unification under Royal Charter of The Chemical Society and The Royal Institute of Chemistry, 1 June 1980. Hon. FRSC, 1982. *Address:* Flat 28, Archer Court, 43 Chesham Road, Amersham, Bucks HP6 5UL. *T:* (01494) 727123. *Died 29 March 2014.*

RUDD-JONES, Derek, CBE 1981; PhD; Director, Glasshouse Crops Research Institute, Littlehampton, Sussex, 1971–86; *b* 13 April 1924; 2nd *s* of late Walter Henry Jones and Doris Mary, *er d* of H. Rudd Dawes; *m* 1948, Joan, 2nd *d* of late Edward Newhouse, Hong Kong, and Malvern, Worcs; two *s* one *d*. *Educ:* Whitgift; Repton; Emmanuel Coll., Cambridge. BA, MA, PhD (Cantab); FSB; FIHort. Agricultural Research Council, postgrad. student, Botany Sch., Univ. of Cambridge, 1945–48; Plant Pathologist, E African Agric. and Forestry Research Orgn, Kenya, 1949–52; Nat. Research Council, Postdoctoral Fellow, Univ. of Saskatchewan, Saskatoon, Canada, 1952–53. ICI Ltd, Akers Research Laboratory, The Frythe, Welwyn, Herts, 1953–56; Jealott's Hill Research Station, Bracknell, Berks, 1956–59; Scientific Adviser to Sec., Agricl Research Council, 1959–71; Foundn Chm., 1968–72, Managing Editor, 1986–93, British Crop Protection Council (Mem., 1968–86); Pres., Section K, BAAS, 1981–82; Mem., Scientific Cttee, RHS, 1985–96; formerly Mem., Adv. Cttee on Pesticides and Other Toxic Chemicals. Vis. Fellow, Univ. of Southampton, 1975–86. Governor, Chichester (formerly W Sussex) Inst. of Higher Educn, 1980–95; Trustee, Thomas Phillips Price Trust, 1988–93. *Publications:* papers in scientific journals. *Recreations:* gardening, riding, fly-fishing. *Address:* Corner Cottage, Austin Street, Stamford PE9 2QP. *Club:* Farmers. *Died 22 Nov. 2011.*

RUDDEN, Prof. Bernard (Anthony), LLD; FBA 1995; Professor of Comparative Law, University of Oxford, 1979–99, then Emeritus; Fellow of Brasenose College, Oxford, 1979–99, then Emeritus; *b* Carlisle, Cumbria, 21 Aug. 1933; *s* of John and Kathleen Rudden; *m* 1957, Nancy Campbell Painter; three *s* one *d*. *Educ:* City of Norwich Sch.; St John's Coll., Cambridge. LLD Cantab; DCL Oxon; PhD Wales. Solicitor. Fellow and Tutor, Oriel Coll., Oxford, 1965–79. Hon. LLD McGill, 1991. *Publications:* Soviet Insurance Law, 1966; The New River, 1985; Basic Community Cases, 1987, 2nd edn 1997; co-author or editor of: The Law of Mortgages, 1967; Source-Book on French Law, 1973, 3rd edn 1991; Basic Community Laws, 1980, 7th edn 1999; The Law of Property, 1982, 3rd edn 2002; Comparing Constitutions, 1995; contrib. periodical pubns. *Address:* 15 Redinnick Terrace, Penzance TR18 4HR. *T:* (01736) 360395. *Club:* Oxford and Cambridge. *Died 4 March 2015.*

RUDKIN, Walter Charles, CBE 1981; Director of Economic Intelligence, 1973–81, of Economic and Logistic Intelligence, 1982, Ministry of Defence; *b* 22 Sept. 1922; *e s* of Walter and Bertha Rudkin; *m* 1950, Hilda Mary Hope (*d* 2009); two *s*. *Educ:* Carre's Grammar Sch., Sleaford; UC Hull. BSc (Econ) London. Served with RAF, 1942–46. Lectr, Dept of Econs and Econ. History, Univ. of Witwatersrand, 1948–52. Entered Min. of Defence, 1954; appts incl. Hong Kong, 1956–59; Junior Directing Staff, Imperial Defence Coll., 1962–64; Cabinet Office, 1968–71. *Died 21 Feb. 2014.*

RUDOE, Wulf, CB 1975; *b* 9 March 1916; *m* 1942, Ellen Trilling; one *s* one *d*. *Educ:* Central Foundation School; Peterhouse, Cambridge (Open Schol. and Research Schol.). Mathematics Tripos Pt III, 1938, Distinction. Royal Aircraft Establishment, 1939. Operational Research, RAF, 1939–45. Operational Research in Building Industry, Min. of Works, 1946–48, Principal Scientific Officer 1948; Board of Trade, Statistician 1948, Chief Statistician 1952; Dir of Statistics and Research, DHSS (formerly Min. of Health), 1966–76; Asst Sec., Price Commn, 1976–79; Adviser to Govt of Ghana, 1980–81. Fellow Inst. of Statisticians; Mem. Council, 1962–78, Hon. Treasurer, 1965–74, Vice-Pres., 1974–75 and 1976–77, Royal Statistical Soc. *Recreations:* walking, travel, languages. *Address:* 72 North End Road, NW11 7SY. *T:* (020) 8455 2890. *Died 26 Sept. 2013.*

RUGGIERO, Renato, Hon. KCMG 1980; *b* Naples, 9 April 1930; *s* of Antonio Ruggiero and Lucia (*née* Rubinacci); *m* 1956, Paola Tomacelli Filomarino; two *s* one *d*. *Educ:* Univ. of Naples (degree in law 1953). Joined Italian diplomatic service; served São Paulo, Moscow, Washington, Belgrade and Brussels; Chef de Cabinet of Pres., 1969–73, Dir-Gen. for Regional Policies, 1973–77, Spokesman of the Pres., 1977–78, EC; Foreign Ministry, Rome, 1978–80; Ambassador to EEC, 1980–84; Dir-Gen. for Econ. Affairs, 1984–85, Sec. Gen., 1985–87, Foreign Ministry; Foreign Trade Minister, 1987–91; Dir-Gen., WTO, 1995–99; Vice-Chm., Salomon Smith Barney Internat., 2000–01; Foreign Minister, Italy, 2001–02; Chm., Citigroup in Switzerland, and Vice-Chm., Citigroup European Investment Bank, 2002. Dir and adviser, various Italian, European and American cos, 1991–95. KCSG 1997. Cavaliere di Gran Croce (Italy), 1985; Grand Cordon, Order of the Sacred Treasure (Japan), 1991. *Recreations:* sailing, hiking. *Died 4 Aug. 2013.*

RULE, Margaret Helen, (Mrs A. W. Rule), CBE 1983; FSA; Consultant, Mary Rose Trust, 1994–98 (Research Director, 1983–94); *b* 27 Sept. 1928; *d* of Ernest Victor and Mabel Martin; *m* 1949, Arthur Walter Rule (*d* 2014); one *s*. *Educ:* Univ. of London. FSA 1967. Dir of Excavations, Chichester Civic Soc., 1961–79; Hon. Curator, Fishbourne

Roman Palace and Museum, 1968–79; Archaeol Dir, Mary Rose Trust, 1979–82. Hon. Fellow, Portsmouth Polytechnic, 1982. Hon. DLitt Liverpool, 1984; Hon. DSc Portsmouth, 1999. Reginald Mitchell Medal, Stoke-on-Trent Assoc. of Engrs, 1983. *Publications:* Chichester Excavations 1, 1967; The Mary Rose, 1982; A Gallo-Roman Trading Vessel from Guernsey, 1993; Life at Sea: Tudors and Stuarts, 1994; many papers in jls in Britain and USA. *Recreation:* anything in or on the water. *Address:* Crofton, East Bracklesham Drive, Bracklesham Bay, W Sussex PO20 8JW. *Died 9 April 2015.*

RUNDLE, Christopher John Spencer, OBE 1983; HM Diplomatic Service, retired; Research Counsellor, Foreign and Commonwealth Office, 1991–98; *b* 17 Aug. 1938; *s* of late Percy William and Ruth Rundle (*née* Spencer); *m* 1970, Qamar Said; one *d. Educ:* Cranbrook Sch.; St John's Coll., Cambridge (MA). Served HM Forces, 1957–59. Central Asian Res. Centre, 1962–63; joined Diplomatic Service, 1963; Tehran, 1967–68; Oriental Sec., Kabul, 1968–70; FCO, 1970–75; seconded to Cabinet Office, 1975–77; First Secretary: FCO, 1977–81; Tehran, 1981–84; FCO, 1985. Member Council, British Inst. of Persian Studies, 1990–2003. Hon. Fellow, Inst. for Middle Eastern and Islamic Studies, Durham Univ., 2001. Mem., Editl Bd, Asian Affairs, 2006–11. *Publications:* From Colwyn Bay to Kabul: an unexpected journey, 2004; papers in academic jls, incl. Durham Middle East Papers. *Recreations:* sports, foreign films and literature. *Died 24 March 2012.*

RUNDLE, John Louis, AM 1981; JP; Agent-General for South Australia, 1980–85; *b* 11 Jan. 1930; *s* of late J. A. Rundle; *m* Elizabeth Phillipa, *d* of John P. Little, Melbourne; one *s* one *d. Educ:* Rostrevor Coll. Formerly Senior Partner, J. C. Rundle & Co., and Rundle, Parsons & Partners; Former Chairman: J. C. Rundle Holdings Pty Ltd; Seacliff Investments Pty Ltd; Thevenard Hotel Pty Ltd; former Director: Commonwealth Accommodation & Catering Service Ltd; Mallen & Co. Ltd; Commercial & Domestic Finance Ltd. Former Member: Nat. Employers Ind. Council (Dep. Chm., 1979–80); Confedn of Aust. Industry (Mem. Bd, 1978–80); State Develt Council, SA; Ind. Relations Adv. Council, SA; Adv. Curriculum Bd, SA; Council, Royal AA of SA. Pres., Junior Chambers, Adelaide, 1957, SA, 1958, Australia, 1959; Vice-Pres., JCI, 1960, 1963, Exec. Vice-Pres., 1964, World Pres., 1965, Pres. Senate, 1966; Councillor, Adelaide Chamber of Commerce, 1956–57, 1961–72, Vice-Pres., 1968–70, Dep. Pres., 1970–72; Vice-Pres., Chamber of Commerce & Industry, SA, 1973–75, Dep. Pres., 1975–77, Pres. 1977–79 (Chm., Commerce Div., 1973, 1974; Chm., Ind. Matters Cttee); Exec. Mem., Aust. Chamber of Commerce, 1980. Councillor: Red Cross Soc., SA Div., 1957–63 (Chm., Junior Red Cross, 1961–62); Burnside City Council, 1962–64; President: Assoc. of Ind. Schools of SA, 1972–75; Nat. Council of Ind. Schools, 1975–77; Chm., Bd of Governors, Rostrevor Coll., 1967–77. Mem. Central Council, Royal Over-Seas League, 1988–93. Freeman, City of London, 1981. JP SA, 1956. KHS 1989. *Address:* Southern Cross Care, 18 Cross Road, Myrtle Bank, SA 5064, Australia. *Clubs:* East India; Naval Military and Air Force (Adelaide). *Died 22 Nov. 2013.*

RUSBY, Vice-Adm. Sir Cameron, KCB 1979; LVO 1965; *b* 20 Feb. 1926; *s* of late Captain Victor Evelyn Rusby, CBE, RN, and Mrs Irene Margaret Rusby; *m* 1948, Marion Elizabeth Bell; two *d. Educ:* RNC, Dartmouth. Midshipman 1943; specialised in communications, 1950; CO HMS Ulster, 1958–59; Exec. Officer, HM Yacht Britannia, 1962–65; Dep. Dir, Naval Signals, 1965–68; CO HMS Tartar, 1968–69; Dep. ACOS (Plans and Policy), staff of Allied C-in-C Southern Europe, 1969–72; Sen. Naval Officer, WI, 1972–74; Rear-Adm. 1974; ACDS (Ops), 1974–77; Vice-Adm. 1977; Flag Officer Scotland and N Ireland, 1977–79; Dep. Supreme Allied Comdr, Atlantic, 1980–82. Chief Exec., Scottish SPCA, 1983–91; former Chm., British Wildlife Rehabilitation Council. Dir, World Soc. for the Protection of Animals, 1986–98 (Hon. Vice Pres., 1998–2005). Dir, Freedom Food Ltd, 1994–2000. Vice Pres., Seafarers UK (formerly King George's Fund for Sailors), 1996–2012. *Recreations:* sailing, country pursuits. *Club:* New (Edinburgh). *Died 6 Sept. 2013.*

RUSSELL, 6th Earl *cr* 1861; **Nicholas Lyulph Russell;** Viscount Amberley 1861; *b* 12 Sept. 1968; *s* of 5th Earl Russell, FBA and Elizabeth Franklyn Russell (*née* Sanders); *S* father, 2004. *Heir: b* Hon. John Francis Russell [*b* 19 Nov. 1971; *m* 2002, Jane Elizabeth Swann; one *d*]. *Died 17 Aug. 2014.*

RUSSELL, Alexander William, (Sandy), CB 1996; Commissioner, 1985–98, and Deputy Chairman, 1993–98, HM Customs and Excise; *b* 16 Oct. 1938; *s* of late William and Elizabeth W. B. Russell (*née* Russell); *m* 1st, 1962, Elspeth Rae (*d* 1996); 2nd, 1999, Patricia Sebbelov. *Educ:* Royal High Sch., Edinburgh; Edinburgh Univ. (MA Hons); Manitoba Univ. (MA). Assistant Principal, Scottish Development Dept, 1961–64; Private Sec. to Parliamentary Under Secretary of State, Scottish Office, 1964–65; Principal, Regional Development Div. and Scottish Development Dept, 1965–72; Principal Private Sec. to Secretary of State for Scotland, 1972–73; Asst Secretary: Scottish Development Dept, 1973–76; Civil Service Dept, 1976–79; Under-Secretary: Management and Personnel Office (formerly CSD), 1979–82; Hd of Treasury MPO Financial Management Unit, 1982–85; Dir Orgn, 1985–90, Dir Customs, 1990–93, HM Customs and Excise. Advr on efficiency matters to Cabinet Sec., 1999–2002. Mem., Council on Tribunals, 2002–05. Chm., Europro, 1999–2001 (Mem. Council, 2001–03); Dir and Mem. Bd, SITPRO, 1999; Mem., Steering Gp, Tax Mgt Res. Network (Univs of Nottingham and Bath, and UK Revenue Depts), 2000–03. *Address:* 1/18 Fidra Road, North Berwick EH39 4NG. *Died 23 Nov. 2012.*

RUSSELL, Rt Rev. David Hamilton; Bishop of Grahamstown, 1987–2004; *b* 6 Nov. 1938; *s* of James Hamilton Russell and Kathleen Mary Russell; *m* 1980, Dorothea Madden; two *s. Educ:* Diocesan College, Rondebosch; Univ. of Cape Town (BA, PhD); Univ. of Oxford (MA). Assistant Priest, 1965–75; Chaplain to migrant workers, 1975–86; banned and house arrested by SA Government, 1977–82; Suffragan Bishop, Diocese of St John's, 1986; Dean, Province of Anglican Church of Southern Africa, 2000–03. Mem. Bd, Inclusive and Affirming Ministries, Cape Town, 2004–12. *Address:* 3 Pillans Road, Rosebank, Cape Town 7700, South Africa. *T:* and *Fax:* (21) 6862721. *Died 17 Aug. 2014.*

RUSSELL, Edwin John Cumming, FRBS 1978; sculptor; *b* 4 May 1939; *s* of Edwin Russell and Mary Elizabeth Russell; *m* 1964, Lorne McKean; two *d. Educ:* Brighton Coll. of Art and Crafts; Royal Academy Schs (CertRAS). *Works:* Crucifix, limewood, pulpit, St Paul's Cathedral, 1964; St Catherine, lead, Little Cloister, Westminster Abbey, 1966; St Michael, oak, Chapel of St Michael and St George, St Paul's Cath., 1970; Bishop Bubwith, W Front Wells Cath., 1980; sundials: Jubilee Dolphin Dial, bronze, Nat. Maritime Mus., Greenwich, 1978; 3m, Sultan Qaboos Univ., Oman, 1986; Botanical Armillary, Kew Gardens, 1987; 5m, bronze, Parliament Square, Dubai, 1988; Forecourt sculpture, Rank Xerox Internat. HQ, 1989; shopping centre sculpture: Mad Hatter's Tea Party play sculpture, granite, Warrington, 1984; Lion and Lamb, teak, Farnham, 1986; public works: Suffragette Meml, 1968; 1st Gov. of Bahamas, Sheraton Hotel, Nassau, 1968; Lewis Carroll commemorative sculpture, Alice and the White Rabbit, Guildford, 1984; Panda, marble, WWF Internat. HQ, 1988; private collections: Goodwood House; Sir Robert McAlpine & Sons Ltd; Rosehaugh Stanhope Developments; Arup Associates; Bovis; YRM International; Trafalgar House plc; Cementation International; John Laing Construction; John Mowlem & Co.; ARC; Worshipful Co. of Stationers; City of London Grammar School. Royal Academy Gold Medal for Sculpture, 1960; Otto Beit Medal for sculpture, RBS, 1991. *Recreation:* philosophy. *Address:* Lethendry, Polecat Valley, Hindhead, Surrey GU26 6BE. *T:* (01428) 605655. *Died 16 Feb. 2013.*

RUSSELL, His Honour James Francis Buchanan, (Frank); QC (NI) 1968; County Court Judge of Northern Ireland, 1978–97; *b* 7 July 1924; *e s* of John Buchanan Russell and Margaret Bellingham Russell; *m* 1946, Irene McKee; two *s* one *d* (and one *d* decd). *Educ:* King's Sch., Worcester; St Andrews Univ.; Queen's

Univ., Belfast (LLB). Served Royal Air Force, 1941–47. Called to Bar, NI, 1952; Crown Prosecutor: Co. Fermanagh, 1970; Co. Tyrone, 1974; Co. Londonderry, 1976; Recorder of Belfast, 1995–97. Bencher, Inn of Court, N Ireland, 1972–78 and 1988–, Treasurer, 1977. Member, Standing Advisory Commn on Human Rights, 1974–78; Chairman, Pensions Appeal Tribunal, N Ireland, 1970–99. *Recreations:* golf, gardening. *Address:* 5 Grey Point, Helen's Bay, Co. Down, Northern Ireland BT19 1LE. *T:* (028) 9185 2249. *Clubs:* Royal Air Force; Royal Belfast Golf. *Died 28 Jan. 2013.*

RUSSELL, Ken; film director, since 1958; *b* 3 July 1927; *m* 1958, Shirley Kingdom (marr. diss. 1978; she *d* 2002); four *s* one *d*; *m* 1984, Vivian Jolly; one *s* one *d; m* 1992, Hetty Baines (marr. diss. 1997); one *s*; *m* 2001, Elize Tribble. Merchant Navy, 1945; RAF, 1946–49. Ny Norsk Ballet, 1950; Garrick Players, 1951; free-lance photographer, 1951–57; Film Director, BBC, 1958–66; free-lance film director, 1966–; started new film movt on mini-DV, Les Garagistes, 2004. Vis. Prof. of Film Studies, Southampton Solent Univ. (formerly Southampton Inst.), 1996–. *Films for TV:* Elgar; Bartok; Debussy; Henri Rousseau; Isadora Duncan; Delius; Richard Strauss; Clouds of Glory; The Planets; Vaughan Williams; ABC of British Music (Emmy award); The Mystery of Dr Martinù; The Secret Life of Arnold Bax; Classic Widows; Elgar: fantasy on a composer on a bicycle, 2002; *television serial:* Lady Chatterley, 1993; *films:* French Dressing, 1964; The Billion Dollar Brain, 1967; Women in Love, 1969; The Music Lovers, 1970; The Devils, 1971; The Boy Friend, 1971; Savage Messiah, 1972; Mahler, 1973; Tommy, 1974; Lisztomania, 1975; Valentino, 1977; Altered States, 1981; Crimes of Passion, 1985; Gothic, 1987; (jtly) Aria, 1987; Salome's Last Dance, 1988; Lair of the White Worm, 1989; The Rainbow, 1989; Whore, 1991; Lion's Mouth, 2000; Fall of the Louse of Usher, 2001; Hot Pants: 3 Sexy Shorts (Revenge of the Elephant Man, The Mystery of Mata Hari, The Good Ship Venus), 2005; *opera:* The Rake's Progress, Florence, 1982; Madam Butterfly, Spoleto, 1983; La Bohème, Macerata, 1984; Faust, Vienna, 1985; Princess Ida, ENO, 1992; Salome, Bonn, 1993. Screen Writers Guild Award for TV films Elgar, Debussy, Isadora and Dante's Inferno; Achievement Awards: Telluride Film Fest., 2001; Dallas Film Fest., 2002; Belgrade Film Fest., 2003; Istanbul Film Fest., 2003; Mar del Plata Film Fest., 2004. *Publications:* A British Picture (autobiog.), 1989; Fire Over England, 1993; Mike and Gaby's Space Gospel (novel), 1999; Directing Film: the director's art from script to cutting room, 1999; Violation (novel), 2006; Elgar: the erotic variations, 2006; Delius: a moment with Venus, 2006; Beethoven Confidential and Brahms Gets Laid, 2006. *Recreations:* music, walking. *Died 27 Nov. 2011.*

RUSSELL, Most Rev. Philip Welsford Richmond; Archbishop of Cape Town and Metropolitan of Southern Africa, 1981–86, then Archbishop Emeritus; *b* 21 Oct. 1919; *s* of Leslie Richmond Russell and Clarice Louisa Russell (*née* Welsford); *m* 1945, Violet Eirene (decd), *d* of Ven. Dr O. J. Hogarth, sometime Archdeacon of the Cape; one *s* three *d*. *Educ:* Durban High Sch.; Rhodes Univ. College (Univ. of South Africa), BA 1948; LTh 1950. Served War of 1939–45; MBE 1943. Deacon, 1950; Priest, 1951; Curate, St Peter's, Maritzburg, 1950–54; Vicar: Greytown, 1954–57; Ladysmith, 1957–61; Kloof, 1961–66; Archdeacon of Pinetown, 1961–66; Bishop Suffragan of Cape Town, 1966–70; Bishop of Port Elizabeth, 1970–74; Bishop of Natal, 1974–81. *Recreation:* walking. *Address:* Roselin Court, 251 Payneham Road, Joslin, SA 5070, Australia. *Died 25 July 2013.*

RUSSELL, Rudolf Rosenfeld; a Recorder of the Crown Court, 1980–97; *b* 5 Feb. 1925; *s* of Robert and Johanna Rosenfeld; *m* 1952, Eva Maria Jaray; one *s*. *Educ:* Bryanston Sch.; Worcester Coll., Oxford (MA). Service in RAF, 1943–46. Called to the Bar, Middle Temple, 1950. *Recreations:* walking, music, ski-ing. *Address:* 197 Roehampton Lane, SW15 4HN. *T:* (020) 8788 9925. *Died 23 Nov. 2012.*

RUSSELL, Terence Francis; Sheriff of North Strathclyde at Kilmarnock, 1983–2002; *b* 12 April 1931; *s* of Robert Russell and Catherine Cusker Russell; *m* 1965, Mary Ann Kennedy; two *d*. *Educ:* Glasgow Univ. (BL). Qualified as Solicitor, 1955; practised in Glasgow, 1955–58 and 1963–81; Solicitor in High Court, Bombay, 1958–63. Sheriff of N Strathclyde, and of Grampian, Highland and Islands, 1981–83. *Recreations:* gardening, travel. *Died 24 April 2014.*

RUTHNASWAMY, Elizabeth Kuanghu; *see* Han Suyin.

RUTT, Rev. Mgr Canon (Cecil) Richard, CBE 1973; *b* 27 Aug. 1925; *s* of Cecil Rutt and Mary Hare Turner; *m* 1969, Joan Mary Ford (*d* 2007). *Educ:* Huntingdon Grammar School; Kelham Theol Coll.; Pembroke Coll., Cambridge (BA 1954; MA 1958). RNVR, 1943–46. Deacon, 1951; Priest, 1952. Asst Curate, St George's, Cambridge, 1951–54; Dio. of Korea, 1954; Parish Priest of Anjung, 1956–58; Warden of St Bede's House Univ. Centre, Seoul, 1959–64; Rector of St Michael's Seminary, Oryu Dong, Seoul, 1964–66; Archdeacon, West Kyonggi (Dio. Seoul), 1965–66; Asst Bishop of Taejon, 1966–68; Bishop of Taejon, 1968–74; Bishop Suffragan of St Germans, 1974–79; Hon. Canon, St Mary's Cathedral, Truro, 1974–79; Bishop of Leicester, 1979–90. Received into RC Ch, 1994, ordained priest, 1995; Hon. Asst, St Mary Immaculate, Falmouth; Hon. Canon, Plymouth Cathedral Chapter, 2001–. Associate Gen. Sec., Korean Bible Soc., 1964–74; Episcopal Sec., Council of the Church of SE Asia, 1968–74; Commissary, dio. of Taejon, 1974–90; Pres., Roy. Asiatic Soc., Korea Br., 1974. Chairman: Adv. Council on Relations of Bishops and Religious Communities, 1980–90; Bishop of Truro's Adv. Gp on Services in Cornish, 1975–79 and Ecumenical Adv. Gp (formerly Adv. Gp on Services in Cornish), 1990–2005; Mem., Anglican/Orthodox Jt Doctrinal Discussions, 1983–89. Bard of the Gorsedd of Cornwall, Cornwhylen, 1976 (Chaplain, 1993–97). Hon. Fellow, Northumbrian Univs' E Asia Centre, 1990. Hon. DLitt Confucian Univ., Seoul, 1974. Tasan Cultural Award (for writings on Korea), 1964. ChStJ 1978. Order of Civil Merit, Peony Class (Korea), 1974. Prelate of Honour, 2009. *Publications:* (ed) Songgonghoe Songga (Korean Anglican Hymnal), 1961; Korean Works and Days, 1964; P'ungnyu Han'guk (in Korean), 1965; (trans.) An Anthology of Korean Sijo, 1970; The Bamboo Grove, an introduction to Korean Sijo poetry, 1971; James Scarth Gale and his History of the Korean People, 1972; The Green People (translations of Korean poet, Yi Unsang), 1973; Virtuous Women, three masterpieces of traditional Korean fiction, 1974; A History of Handknitting, 1987; The Book of Changes (Zhouyi): a Bronze Age document translated with introduction and notes, 1996; (with K. L. Pratt) Korea: an historical and cultural dictionary, 1999; The Song of a Faithful Wife: Ch'unhyang, 1999; (contrib.) The Path to Rome, ed D. Longenecker, 1999; Martyrs of Korea, 2002; contribs on Korean classical poetry and history to Trans Royal Asiatic Soc. (Korea Br.) and various Korean publications. *Address:* 3 Marlborough Court, Falmouth, Cornwall TR11 2QU. *T:* (01326) 312276. *Died 27 July 2011.*

RYAN, (Christopher) Nigel (John), CBE 1977; television executive; Chairman, TV-am News, 1989–92 (Director, 1985–92); *b* 12 Dec. 1929; *s* of late Brig. C. E. Ryan, MC, RA; *m* 1st, 1984, Susan Anne Crewe (marr. diss.); 2nd, 2014, Hélène Celier Geoffroy. *Educ:* Ampleforth Coll.; Queen's Coll., Oxford (MA). Joined Reuters, London, 1954; Foreign Corresp., 1957–60; joined Independent Television News, 1961, Editor, 1968–71, Editor and Chief Executive, 1971–77; Vice-Pres., NBC News, America, 1977–80; Dir of Progs, Thames Television, 1980–82. Silver Medal, Royal Television Soc., 1970; Desmond Davis Award, 1972. *Publications:* A Hitch or Two in Afghanistan, 1983; (jtly) The Scholar and the Gypsy, 1992; Paramaribo! (novel), 2012; trans. novels from French by Georges Simenon and others. *Address:* 4 Cleveland Square, W2 6DH. *T:* (020) 7723 8552. *Club:* Beefsteak. *Died 17 July 2014.*

RYLE, Michael Thomas; Clerk of Committees, House of Commons, 1987–89; *b* 30 July 1927; *s* of Peter Johnston Ryle and Rebecca Katie (*née* Boxall); *m* 1952, Bridget Moyes; one *s* two *d*. *Educ:* Newcastle upon Tyne Royal Grammar Sch.; Merton Coll., Oxford (1st Cl. Hons PPE, 1951; MA). Served RA, 1946–48 and TA, 1950–57. Entered Clerk's Dept, House of Commons, 1951; served in various offices; Clerk of Overseas Office, 1979–83; Principal Clerk, Table Office, 1983–84; Clerk of the Journals, 1985–87; attached Nova Scotia Legislature, 1976. Consultant/advr, Belarus, Slovakian, Ukrainian and other parlts in E Europe, 1995–97. Chm., Lib Dem Wkg Gp on Reform of H of C, 1996. Member: Study of Parlt Gp, 1964– (Founding Mem.; Chm., 1975–78; Pres., 1986–94); Council, Hansard Soc., 1974–94 (Mem. and Sec., Commn on the Legislative Process, 1991–93); Council, RIPA, 1982–88; Lambeth HMC, 1960–64. Governor, St Thomas' Hosp., 1964–74. Hon. Res. Fellow, Univ. of Exeter, 1990–. Exmoor Society: Mem., Exec. Cttee, 1991–2005; Vice-Chm., 2000–05; Vice-Pres. *Publications:* (ed with S. Walkland) The Commons in the Seventies, 1977, 2nd edn, as The Commons Today, 1981; (contrib.) The House of Commons in the Twentieth Century, 1979; (ed with P. G. Richards) The Commons Under Scrutiny, 1988; (with J. A. G. Griffith) Parliament, 1989, (contrib.) 2nd edn (ed R. Blackburn and A. Kennon), 2003; (contrib.) The Future of Parliament, 2006; contrib. to books on parly practice and procedure; articles in Pol Qly, Parly Affairs, The Table, etc. *Recreations:* watching cricket, golf, birds, playing bridge. *Address:* Jasmine Cottage, Winsford, Minehead, Somerset TA24 7JE. *T:* and *Fax:* (01643) 851317. *E:* michaelryle@tiscali.co.uk. *Died 7 Dec. 2013.*

RYRIE, Sir William (Sinclair), KCB 1982 (CB 1979); Chairman, Baring Emerging Europe Trust plc, 1994–2002; *b* 10 Nov. 1928; *s* of Rev. Dr Frank Ryrie and Mabel Moncrieff Ryrie (*née* Watt); *m* 1st, 1953, Dorrit Klein (marr. diss. 1969); two *s* one *d*; 2nd, 1969, Christine Gray Thomson; one *s*. *Educ:* Mount Hermon Sch., Darjeeling; Heriot's Sch., Edinburgh; Edinburgh Univ. (MA 1st cl. hons History, 1951). Nat. Service, 1951–53: Lieut, Intell. Corps, Malaya, 1952–53 (despatches). Colonial Office, 1953; seconded to Uganda, 1956–58; Principal 1958; transf. to Treasury, 1963; Asst Sec., internat. monetary affairs, 1966–69; Principal Private Sec. to Chancellor of Exchequer, 1969–71; Under-Sec., Public Sector Gp, HM Treasury, 1971–75; Econ. Minister, Washington, and UK Exec. Dir, IMF and IBRD, 1975–79; 2nd Perm. Sec. (Domestic Economy Sector), HM Treasury, 1980–82; Permanent Sec., ODA, FCO, 1982–84; Exec. Vice-Pres. and Chief Exec., IFC at World Bank, 1984–93; Dir, Commonwealth Develt Corp., 1994–98 (Dep. Chm., 1995–98). Vice Chm., ING Barings Hldg Co., 1995–98. Director: Barings plc, 1994–95; First NIS Regl Fund, 1994–99; W. S. Atkins plc, 1994–2001; Ashanti Goldfields Co. Ltd, 1995–2000. Dir, CARE Britain, 1994–2001. Pres., Edinburgh Univ. Develt Trust, 1994–99. Mem., Gp of 30, 1992–98. FRSA 1993. *Publications:* First World, Third World, 1995. *Recreations:* photography, walking. *Address:* Hawkwood, Hawkwood Lane, Chislehurst, Kent BR7 5PW. *Club:* Reform. *Died 6 July 2012.*

S

SACHS, Prof. Leo, PhD; FRS 1997; Otto Meyerhof Professor of Molecular Biology, Weizmann Institute of Science, Rehovot, Israel, since 1968; *b* 14 Oct. 1924; *s* of Elias and Louise Sachs; *m* 1970, Pnina Salkind; one *s* three *d*. *Educ:* City of London Sch.; Univ. of Wales, Bangor (BSc 1948; Hon. Fellow, 1999); Trinity Coll., Cambridge (PhD 1951). Research Scientist in Genetics, John Innes Inst., 1951–52; Weizmann Institute of Science, Rehovot, Israel: Res. Scientist, 1952–; estabd Dept of Genetics and Virology, 1960; Head, Dept of Genetics, 1962–89; Dean, Faculty of Biol., 1974–79. Fogarty Internat. Scholar, US NIH, 1972; Harvey Lecture, Rockefeller Univ., 1972; Ham-Wasserman Lecture, Amer. Soc. of Hematology, 2000. Member: EMBO, 1965; Israel Acad. of Scis and Humanities, 1975. Foreign Associate, NAS, 1995; Foreign MAE, 1998; Hon. Life Mem., Internat. Cytokine Soc., 2001. Hon. Dr Bordeaux, 1985; Hon. DMed Lund, 1997. Israel Prize for Natural Scis, 1972; Rothschild Prize in Biol Scis, 1977; Wolf Prize in Medicine, 1980; Bristol-Myers Award for Distinguished Achievement in Cancer Res., 1983; Wellcome Foundn Prize, Royal Soc., 1986; Alfred P. Sloan Prize, General Motors Cancer Res. Foundn, 1989; Warren Alpert Foundn Prize, Harvard Med. Sch., 1997; EMET Prize for Life Scis, AMN Foundn, Israel, 2002. *Publications:* published papers on stem cells, blood cells, develt and cancer res. in various scientific jls. *Recreations:* music, museums. *Address:* Department of Molecular Genetics, Weizmann Institute of Science, Rehovot 76100, Israel. *T:* (8) 9344068, *Fax:* (8) 9344108. *Died 12 Dec. 2013.*

SACKS, Oliver Wolf, CBE 2008; neurologist and writer; Professor of Neurology, and Consulting Neurologist, Comprehensive Epilepsy Center, New York University, since 2012; *b* London, 9 July 1933; *s* of Samuel Sacks and Muriel Elsie Landau Sacks. *Educ:* St Paul's Sch.; Queen's Coll., Oxford (BA 1954; BM BCh 1958; Hon. Fellow, 1999); Middlesex Hosp. Med. Sch. (MA 1956). Jun. med. posts, Middlesex Hosp., 1959–60, Mount Zion Hosp., San Francisco, 1961–62; Resident in Neurology and Neuropathology, UCLA, 1962–65; Fellow, Neurology and Neurochemistry, 1965–66, Instructor in Neurology, 1966–75, Albert Einstein Coll. of Medicine, NY; Consulting Neurologist: Headache Unit, Montefiore Hosp., NY, 1966–68; Bronx Psychiatric Center, NY, 1966–91; Beth Abraham Hosp., NY, 1966–2006; Little Sisters of the Poor Hosp., NY, 1971–; Asst Prof., 1975–78, Associate Prof., 1978–85, in Neurology, Clinical Prof. of Neurology, 1985–2007, Albert Einstein Coll. of Medicine; Adjunct Prof. of Neurology, NY Univ. Med. Center, 1992–2007; Columbia Univ. Artist and Prof. of Neurology and Psychiatry, Columbia Univ., 2007–12. Member: Amer. Acad. of Neurology, 1962– (Presidential Citation, 1991); NY Inst. for the Humanities, 1984–; Soc. for Neurosci., 1992–. Guggenheim Fellow, 1989; Fellow: Amer. Acad. of Arts and Letters, 1996; NY Acad. of Scis, 1999. Hon. Fellow, Cowell Coll., Univ. of Calif, 1987; Hon. Mem. Amer. Neurological Assoc., 1992. Hon. DHumLit: Georgetown Univ., Washington, DC, 1990; Coll. of Staten Island, NY, 1991; Hon. DSc: Tufts Univ., Mass, 1991; NY Med. Coll., 1991; Bard Coll., NY, 1992; Hon. LLD Queen's Univ. at Kingston, Ont, 2001; Hon. MD Karolinska Inst., Stockholm, 2003; Hon. DCL Oxon, 2005. Oskar Pfisker Award, Amer. Psychiatric Assoc., 1988; Harold D. Vursell Meml Award, Amer. Acad. and Inst. of Arts and Letters, 1989; Communicator of the Year Award, RNID, 1991; George S. Polk Award, 1994; Lewis Thomas Prize, Rockefeller Univ., 2002. *Publications:* Migraine, 1970, 2nd edn 1993; Awakenings, 1973, 2nd edn 1990 (Hawthornden Prize, 1975; filmed, 1990); A Leg to Stand On, 1984, 2nd edn 1993; The Man Who Mistook His Wife For a Hat, 1985; Seeing Voices: a journey into the world of the deaf, 1989; An Anthropologist on Mars: seven paradoxical tales, 1995; The Island of the Colorblind, and Cycad Island, 1996; Uncle Tungsten: memories of a chemical boyhood, 2001; Oaxaca Journal, 2002; Musicophilia: tales of music and the brain, 2007; Th Mind's Eye, 2010; Hallucinations, 2012; On the Move: life (autobiog.), 2015; papers, contribs to books and j chiefly on neurology and neuroscience. *Address:* 2 Horati Street #3G, New York, NY 10014, USA. *T:* (21 6338373, *Fax:* (212) 6338928. *E:* mail@oliversacks.com. *Died 30 Aug. 2015*

SADLER, Anthony John, CBE 2004; Archbishop Appointments Secretary, 1996–2003; *b* 2 Oct. 1938; *s* David James Sadler and Joan Sybil (*née* Alt); *m* 1966, Mari José Lucas; three *d*. *Educ:* Bedford Sch.; Magdalene Col Cambridge (MA). Personnel Manager, Hawker Siddel Aviation, Hatfield, 1964–75; Asst Personnel Controlle Rank Orgn, 1975–78; Employee Relns Manager, Lloy Bank Internat., 1978–83; Dir, Gp Human Resource Minet plc, 1983–92. Vice-Pres., Internat. IPM, 1981–8 Chm., Staff Mgt Assoc., 1989–91. Chm., Southwa Welcare Centenary Appeal Cttee, 1993–95. Chm., London Industrial Mission, 1980–82. Church Warden, Luke, Kew, 1976–88. CCIPD (CIPM 1983). *Publication* Human Resource Management: developing a strateg approach, 1995. *Recreations:* cycling, bird-watching, classic music. *Address:* 14 Venelle de la Clef des Champs, 175 Ars en Ré, France. *T:* (5) 46424518. *Clubs:* Lansdown MCC. *Died 1 Oct. 201*

SAINSBURY, Jeffrey Paul, FCA; chartered accountar Executive Vice-President, Computershare Ltd (forme General Manager, Computershare Investor Services pl 2000–12; Lord Mayor of Cardiff, 1991–92; *b* 27 June 194 *s* of Capt. Walter Ronald Sainsbury and Joan Margar Slamin; *m* 1967, Janet Elizabeth Hughes; one *s* one *d*. *Edi* Cardiff High Sch. FCA 1966. Partner, Pannell Kerr Forst 1969–94; Man. Dir, Exchange Registrars Ltd, 1994–200 Mem., Cardiff CC, 1969–96. Member: S Glamorgan H 1987–91; Bd, Cardiff Bay Develt Corp., 1991–2000. Chn New Theatre, Cardiff, 1983–87. Chm., S Glam TE 1996–99; Dep. Chm., TEC SE Wales, 1999–2000. Go WCMD, 1995–2001. OStJ 1997. *Recreations:* computir cooking, music, theatre, sport. *Address:* 6 Druidsto House, Druidstone Road, St Mellons, Cardiff CF3 6X *Club:* Cardiff and County. *Died 2 Dec. 201*

SAINT, Dora Jessie, MBE 1998; (*pen name* Miss Rea writer, since 1950; *b* 17 April 1913; *d* of Arthur Gun Shafe and Grace Lilian Shafe; *m* 1940, Douglas Edwa John Saint (*d* 2004); one *d*. *Educ:* Bromley County Sc Homerton Coll., Cambridge. Teaching in Middlese 1933–40; occasional teaching, 1946–63. *Publications:* Villa School, 1955, reissue, 2005; Village Diary, 1957, reissu 2005; Storm in the Village, 1958, reissue, 2005; Thru Green, 1959; Fresh from the Country, 1960; Winter Thrush Green, 1961; Miss Clare Remembers, 196 Chronicles of Fairacre, 1963; Over the Gate, 1964; Mark Square, 1965; Village Christmas, 1966; Fairacre Festiv 1968; News from Thrush Green, 1970; Tiggy, 1971; Em Davis, 1971; Tyler's Row, 1972; The Christmas Mou 1973; Farther Afield, 1974; Battles at Thrush Green, 197 No Holly for Miss Quinn, 1976; Village Affairs, 197 Return to Thrush Green, 1978; The White Robin, 197 Village Centenary, 1980; Gossip from Thrush Green, 198 Affairs at Thrush Green, 1983; Summer at Fairacre, 198 At Home in Thrush Green, 1985; The School at Thru Green, 1987; The World of Thrush Green, 1988; M Pringle, 1989; Friends at Thrush Green, 1990; Celebratic at Thrush Green, 1992; Farewell to Fairacre, 1993; Ta from a Village School, 1994; Early Days, 1995; The Year Thrush Green, 1995; A Peaceful Retirement, 199 Christmas at Fairacre, 2005; Christmas at Thrush Gree 2009; *for children*: Hobby Horse Cottage, 1958; Hob and Horse-Bat, 1965; The Red Bus Series, 1965; *non-ficti* Country Bunch (anthology), 1963; Miss Read's Coun Cooking, 1969; *autobiography:* A Fortunate Grandchi 1982; Time Remembered, 1986. *Recreations:* theatre-goi reading. *Address:* c/o Michael Joseph Ltd, Penguin Gro (UK), 80 Strand, WC2R 0RL. *Died 7 April 201*

ST AUBYN, Major Thomas Edward, CVO 1993; DL; FRGS; Lieutenant, HM Body Guard of Honourable Corps of Gentlemen at Arms, 1990–93 (Clerk of the Cheque and Adjutant, 1986–90); *b* 13 June 1923; *s* of Hon. Lionel Michael St Aubyn, MVO, and Lady Mary St Aubyn; *m* 1953, Henrietta Mary, *d* of Sir Henry Studholme, 1st Bt; three *d*. *Educ:* Eton. Served in King's Royal Rifle Corps, 1941–62; Italian Campaign, 1944–45; Adjt 1st KRRC, 1946–48; seconded to Sudan Defence Force in rank of Bimbashi, 1948–52; leader of Tibesti Mountain Expedn in Chad, 1957; Bde Adjt Green Jackets Bde, 1960–62. Mem., HM Body Guard, 1973–93. High Sheriff of Hampshire, 1979–80; DL Hampshire, 1984. FRGS 1959. *Recreations:* shooting, fishing. *Address:* West Leigh House, Nether Wallop, Stockbridge, Hants SO20 8EY. *T:* (01264) 782914. *Club:* Army and Navy. *Died 29 Nov. 2012.*

ST CLAIR-FORD, Sir Colin (Anson), 8th Bt *cr* 1793, of Ember Court, Surrey; *b* 19 April 1939; *s* of Lt-Comdr Drummond St Clair-Ford, RN and Nora Elizabeth (*née* Maberly, later Buckley); *S* cousin, 2009; *m* 1964, Gillian Mary, *er d* of Rear-Adm. Peter Skelton, CB; two *d*. *Educ:* Nautical Coll., Pangbourne. *Heir: b* Robin Sam St Clair-Ford [*b* 6 June 1941; *m* 1980, Alison Frances Dickson; two *s*]. *Died 3 Dec. 2012.*

ST JOHN OF FAWSLEY, Baron *cr* 1987 (Life Peer), of Preston Capes in the County of Northamptonshire; **Norman Antony Francis St John-Stevas;** PC 1979; FRSL 1966; Master, Emmanuel College, Cambridge, 1991–96, Life Fellow, 1996; Chairman: Royal Fine Art Commission, 1985–99; Royal Fine Art Commission Educational Trust, since 1985; Sky Arts, 2007–10; Grand Bailiff and Head of the Military and Hospitaller Order of St Lazarus of Jerusalem in England and Wales, since 2000; author, barrister and journalist; *b* London, 18 May 1929; *o s* of late Stephen S. Stevas, civil engineer and company director, and Kitty St John O'Connor; unmarried. *Educ:* Ratcliffe; Fitzwilliam, Cambridge (Hon. Fellow 1991); Christ Church, Oxford; Yale. Scholar, Clothworkers Exhibnr, 1946, 1947; BA (Cambridge) (1st cl. hons in law), 1950, MA 1954; President, Cambridge Union, 1950; Whitlock Prize, 1950; MA 1952, BCL 1954 (Oxon); Sec. Oxford Union, 1952; DLitt Oxon 1994; LittD Cantab, 1994. Barrister, Middle Temple, 1952; Blackstone and Harmsworth schol., 1952; Blackstone Prize, 1953. Lecturer, Southampton University, 1952–53, King's Coll., London, 1953–56, tutored in jurisprudence, Christ Church, 1953–55, and Merton, 1955–57, Oxford. Founder member, Inst. of Higher European Studies, Bolzano, 1955; PhD (Lond.) 1957; Yorke Prize, Cambridge Univ., 1957; Fellow Yale Law School, 1957; Fulbright Award, 1957; Fund for the Republic Fellow, 1958; Dr of Sc. of Law (Yale), 1960; Lecture tours of USA, 1958–68. Regents' Prof., Univ. of California at Santa Barbara, 1969; Regents' Lectr, Univ. of Calif at La Jolla, 1984. Legal Adviser to Sir Alan Herbert's Cttee on book censorship, 1954–59; joined The Economist, 1959, to edit collected works of Walter Bagehot and became legal, ecclesiastical and political correspondent. Contested (C) Dagenham, 1951; MP (C) Chelmsford, 1964–87. Mem. Shadow Cabinet, 1974–79, and Opposition Spokesman on Educn, 1975–78, Science and the Arts, 1975–79; Shadow Leader of the House, 1978–79; Parly Under-Sec. of State, DES, 1972–73; Min. of State for the Arts, DES, 1973–74; Chancellor of the Duchy of Lancaster, Leader of the House of Commons and Minister for the Arts, 1979–81. Sec., Cons. Parly Home Affairs Cttee, 1969–72; Vice-Chm., Cons. Parly N Ireland Cttee, 1972–74; Mem. Executive, Cons. Parly 1922 Cttee, 1971–72 and 1974; Vice Chm., Cons. Group for Europe, 1972–75; Member: Cons. Nat. Adv. Cttee on Policy, 1971; Fulbright Commission, 1961; Parly Select Cttee: on Race Relations and Immigration, 1970–72; on Civil List, 1971–73; on Foreign Affairs, 1983–89; Deleg., Council of Europe and WEU, 1967–71; Head, British delegn to Helsinki Cultural Forum, Budapest, 1985. Chm., New Bearings for the Re-Establishment, 1970–. Dir, Sky TV, 1991; Advr on Arts, Religion and the Constitution to Chm. and Chief Exec., Sky plc, 2010–. Hon. Sec., Fedn of Cons. Students, 1971–73, Hon. Vice-Pres. 1973. Chm., Booker McConnell Prize, 1985. Mem. Council: RADA, 1983–88; Nat. Soc. for Dance, 1983–; Nat. Youth Theatre, 1983– (Patron, 1984–); RCA, 1985–; Mem., Pontifical Council for Culture, 1987–92; Patron, Medieval Players, 1984–89; Dir, N. M. Rothschild Trust, 1990–98; Trustee: Royal Philharmonic Orch., 1985–88; Philharmonic Orch., 1988–; Royal Soc. of Painters in Watercolours, 1984; Decorative Arts Soc., 1984–. Editor, The Dublin (Wiseman) Review, 1961. Vice Pres., Les Amis de Napoléon III, 1974; Mem., Académie du Second Empire, 1975. Hon. FRIBA 1990; Presidential Fellow, Aspen Inst., 1980; Hon. Fellow, St Edmund's College, Cambridge, 1985. Romanes Lectr, Oxford, 1987. DD (*hc*) Univ. of Susquehanna, Pa, 1983; DLitt (*hc*): Schiller Univ., 1985; Bristol Univ., 1988; Hon. LLD: Leicester, 1991; Notre Dame, 1999; Hon. DArts De Montfort, 1996. Silver Jubilee Medal, 1977. SBStJ. Gran Ufficiale, Order of Merit (Italian Republic), 1989 (Commendatore, 1965). GCLJ 1976 (KLJ 1963). *Publications:* Obscenity and the Law, 1956; Walter Bagehot, 1959; Life, Death and the Law, 1961; The Right to Life, 1963; Law and Morals, 1964; The Literary Works of Walter Bagehot, vols I, II, 1966, The Historical Works, vols III, IV, 1968, The Political Works, vols V, VI, VII and VIII, 1974, The Economic Works, vols IX, X and XI, 1978, Letters and Miscellany, vols XII, XIII, XIV and XV, 1986; The Agonising Choice, 1971; Pope John Paul II, his travels and mission, 1982; The Two Cities, 1984; contrib. to: Critical Quarterly, Modern Law Review, Criminal Law Review, Law and Contemporary Problems, Twentieth Century, Times Lit. Supp., Dublin Review. *Recreations:* reading, talking, listening (to music), travelling, walking, appearing on television, sleeping. *Address:* Chacombe House, Chacombe Park, Banbury, Oxon OX17 2SL; Emmanuel College, Cambridge CB2 3AP; House of Lords, SW1A 2PW. *T:* (020) 7219 3199. *Clubs:* Garrick, Pratt's, Arts (Hon. Mem., 1980), The Other; Hawks (Cambridge) (Hon. Mem., 1993); Emmanuel Boat (Pres., 1993–2006). *Died 2 March 2012.*

ST LEVAN, 4th Baron *cr* 1887; **John Francis Arthur St Aubyn,** OBE 2004; DSC 1942; DL; Bt 1866; Vice Lord-Lieutenant of Cornwall, 1992–94; *b* 23 Feb. 1919; *s* of 3rd Baron St Levan, and Hon. Clementina Gwendolen Catharine Nicolson (*d* 1995), *o d* of 1st Baron Carnock; *S* father, 1978; *m* 1970, Susan Mary Marcia (*d* 2003), *d* of late Maj.-Gen. Sir John Kennedy, GCMG, KCVO, KBE, CB. *Educ:* Eton Coll.; Trinity Coll., Cambridge (BA). Served RNVR, 1940–46 (Lieut). Admitted a Solicitor, 1948. Administrator for Nat. Trust, St Michael's Mount, 1976–2003. Vice President: Royal Bath and West and Southern Counties Soc., 1984– (Pres., 1983); Royal Cornwall Agricl Assoc., 1980– (Pres., 1979); Minack Theatre, 1989–; Pres., London Cornish Assoc., 1987–97; Jt Pres., Cornwall Community Foundn, 2005–; Patron: Truro Naval Assoc., 1995–; West Country Writers' Assoc., 1999–; Penlee Lifeboat Station, 2008–. High Sheriff of Cornwall, 1974; DL Cornwall, 1977. Bard of Cornwall, 1995. FRSA 1974. KStJ 1998. *Publications:* Illustrated History of St Michael's Mount, 1974. *Recreation:* sailing. *Heir: nephew* James Piers Southwell St Aubyn [*b* 6 June 1950; *m* 1981, Mary Caroline, *yr d* of late Peter Ward Bennett, OBE; two *s* two *d*]. *Address:* 8 St Mary's Terrace, Penzance, Cornwall TR18 4DZ. *Clubs:* Brooks's; Royal Yacht Squadron. *Died 7 April 2013.*

ST OMER, Sir Dunstan (Gerbert Raphael), KCMG 2010; MBE 1984; SLC 2004; artist, painter and art specialist, 1971–2000; *b* Castries, St Lucia, 24 Oct. 1927; *s* of Gerald and Louisa St Omer; *m* 1952, Cynthia St Croix; four *s* five *d*. *Educ:* St Mary's Coll. Extra-mural Tutor, UWI, 1951–56; Ed., Voice of St Lucia, 1959–62; Sec., St Lucia Chamber of Commerce, 1967–71; Curriculum Officer for Art, Min. of Educn, 1971–2000. Designer, St Lucia nat. flag, 1979. Hon. DLitt West Indies, 2009. *Publications:* essays for regl and local pubns. *Recreations:* lawn tennis, reading. *Address:* PO Box 716, Castries, St Lucia, West Indies. *T:* 4502044. *E:* cynthia_st.omer@hotmail.com. *Club:* St Lucia Racquet. *Died 5 May 2015.*

SAINZ MUÑOZ, Most Rev. Faustino; Apostolic Nuncio to the Court of St James's, 2005–10; *b* 5 June 1937; *s* of Manuel Sainz and Luisa Muñoz. *Educ:* Colegio de Nuestra Señora del Prado, Ciudad-Real; Colegio de Nuestra Señora del Pilar, Madrid; Univ. Central de Madrid (Lic. in Law 1958); Pontifical Univ., Salamanca (Lic. in Theology 1965); Pontifical Lateran Univ. (DCnL 1969).

Ordained priest, 1964; priest, dio. of Madrid, 1965–67: parish priest, Somosierra, 1965–66; Prof. of Religion, Faculty of Law, 1965–67; asst priest, Parish of Conception of Our Lady, Madrid, 1966–67; Counsellor to young Catholic students at the univ., 1966–67; trng, Pontifical Ecclesiast. Acad., Rome, 1967–69; entered Diplomatic Service of Holy See, 1970; served in: Senegal, for French speaking W Africa, 1970–72; Denmark, and other countries of Scandinavia, 1972–75; Secretariat of State, 1975–88; Titular Archbishop of Novaliciana and Apostolic Pro-Nuncio to Cuba, 1988–92; Apostolic Nuncio: Zaire, 1992–97, then Dem. Rep. of Congo, 1997–99; EC, Brussels, 1999–2004. *Died 31 Oct. 2012.*

SALEM, Daniel Laurent Manuel; Chairman, The Condé Nast Publications Ltd, London, 1968–97; *b* 29 Jan. 1925; *s* of Raphael Salem and Adriana Gentili di Giuseppe; *m* 1950, Marie-Pierre Arachtingi. *Educ:* Harvard Univ., Cambridge, Mass (BA, MA). Served Free French Forces, 1943–45. Exec. Asst, Lazard Frères & Co., New York, 1946–50; exec. positions, The Condé Nast Publications Inc., New York, 1950–60, Vice-Pres., 1965–86, Dep. Chm., 1986–92; Vice Pres., Banque Paribas, Paris, 1961–65; Chm., Condé Nast International Inc., 1971–91. Chairman: Mercury Selected Trust, 1974–96; Mercury Offshore Selected Trust, 1979–96; Philharmonia Trust Ltd, 1985–92 (Chm. Emeritus, 2011). Officier: Legion of Honour (France), 1997; Ordre des Arts et des Lettres (France), 1997; Commendatore, Order of Merit (Italy), 1988. *Recreations:* music, bridge, chess, golf. *Clubs:* White's, Portland; Harvard (New York). *Died 21 April 2012.*

SALMON, Very Rev. Thomas Noel Desmond Cornwall; Dean of Christ Church, Dublin, 1967–88; *b* Dublin, 5 Feb. 1913; *s* of Francis Allen Cornwall Salmon, BDS, and Emma Sophia, *d* of Dr Hamilton Jolly, Clonroche, Co. Wexford; unmarried. *Educ:* privately; Trinity College, Dublin; BA 1935, MA, BD. Deacon 1937; Priest 1938. Curate Assistant: Bangor, Co. Down, 1937–40; St James' Belfast, 1940–42; Larne, Co. Antrim, 1942–44; Clerical Vicar, Christ Church Cathedral, 1944–45; Curate Assistant, Rathfarnham, Dublin, 1945–50; Incumbent: Tullow, Carrickmines, 1950–62; St Ann, Dublin, 1962–67. Asst Lectr in Divinity School, TCD, 1945–63; Examining Chaplain to Archbishop of Dublin, 1949–96. *Recreations:* in younger days Rugby football (Monkstown FC Dublin) and swimming; then walking, gardening and reading. *Address:* Brabazon House, Gilford Road, Sandymount, Dublin 4, Ireland. *T:* 2800101. *Died 20 July 2013.*

SAMUEL, 3rd Viscount *cr* 1937, of Mount Carmel and of Toxteth, Liverpool; **David Herbert Samuel,** OBE 1996; Professor of Physical Chemistry, Weizmann Institute of Science, Rehovot, Israel, 1967–87, then Emeritus; *b* 8 July 1922; *s* of 2nd Viscount Samuel, CMG, and Hadassah (*d* 1986), *d* of Judah Goor (Grasovsky); *S* father, 1978; *m* 1st, 1950, Esther Berelowitz (marr. diss. 1957); one *d*; 2nd, 1960, Rinna Dafni (*née* Grossman) (marr. diss. 1979); one *d*; 3rd, 1980, Veronika Engelhardt Grimm (marr. diss. 1993); 4th, 1997, Eve Black (marr. diss. 2006); 5th, 2007, Ruth Eden (*née* Weisser). *Educ:* Balliol Coll., Oxford (MA 1948); Hebrew Univ. (PhD 1953). Served War of 1939–45 (despatches); Captain RA, in India, Burma and Sumatra. Weizmann Institute of Science, Rehovot, Israel: Member of Scientific Staff, 1949–, of Isotope Dept, 1949–86, of Dept of Neurobiology, 1986–; Dir, Center for Neurosciences and Behavioural Research, 1978–87; Head, Chemistry Gp, Science Teaching Dept, 1967–83; Dean, Faculty of Chemistry, 1971–73; Chm., Bd of Studies in Chemistry, Feinberg Grad. Sch., 1968–74. Post-doctoral Fellow, Chem. Dept, UCL, 1956; Res. Fellow, Chem. Dept, Harvard Univ., 1957–58; Res. Fellow, Lab. of Chemical Biodynamics (Lawrence Radiation Lab.), Univ. of California, Berkeley, 1965–66; Vis. Prof., Sch. of Molecular Scis, Univ. of Warwick, 1967; Royal Soc. Vis. Prof., MRC Neuroimmunology Unit, Zoology Dept, UCL, 1974–75; Vis. Prof., MIT, 1982; Vis. Prof., Pharmacol. Dept, Yale Sch. of Medicine, 1983–84; McLaughlin Prof., Sch. of Medicine, McMaster Univ., 1984; Vis. Prof., Dept of Chemistry, Univ. of York, 1995–96, 1997. Member: Adv. Bd, Bat-Sheva de Rothschild Foundn for Advancement of Science in Israel, 1970–83; Bd, US-Israel Educnl (Fulbright) Foundn, 1969–74 (Chm., 1974–75); Bd, Israel Center for Scientific and Technol Information, 1970–74; Scientific Adv. Cttee and Bd of Trustees of Israel Center for Psychobiol., 1973–; Acad. Adv. Cttee, Everyman's (Open) Univ., 1976–83; Bd of Govs, Bezalel Acad. of Arts and Design, 1977–; Council, Israel Chemical Soc., 1977–83; Internat. Brain Res. Org. (IBRO), 1977–; Israel Exec. Cttee, America-Israel Cultural Foundn, 1978–89 (Chm., 1986–89); Bd of Governors, Tel Aviv Museum of Art, 1980–; Cttee on Teaching of Chemistry, IUPAC, 1981–89; Anglo-Israel Assoc., 1985– (Chm., Colloquia, 1997–); British Israel Arts Foundn, 1986–98; Bd of Trustees, Menninger Foundn, USA, 1988–; Soc. of Manufacturing Engrs, 1989–94; Fibre Soc., 1990–94. Pres., Shenkar Coll. of Textile Technology and Fashion, 1987–94. Former Member, Editorial Board: Jl of Labelled Compounds & Radiopharmaceuticals; Alzheimer Disease and Associated Disorders; Brain Behaviour and Immunity. Hon. Fellow, Shenkar Coll. of Engrg and Design, 2002. Scopus Award, Hebrew Univ. of Jerusalem, 2000; Tercentenary Medal, Yale Univ., 2001. *Publications:* Memory: how we use it, lose it and can improve it, 1999; more than 300 papers, reviews and parts of collective volumes on isotopes, physical chemistry, reaction mechanisms, neurochemistry, psychopharmacology, animal behavior, education and the history and teaching of science. *Heir:* *b* Hon. Dan Judah Samuel [*b* 25 March 1925; *m* 1st, 1957, Nonni (Esther) (marr. diss. 1977), *d* of late Max Gordon, Johannesburg; one *s* two *d*; 2nd, 1981, Heather (marr. diss. 1992), *d* of Angus and Elsa Cumming, Haywards Heath; one *s* one *d*]. *Address:* 25 Motzkin Street, Apt 1, Tel Aviv 62288, Israel. *T:* (3) 6023507. *Died 7 Oct. 2014.*

SAMUEL, 4th Viscount *cr* 1937, of Mount Carmel and of Toxteth, Liverpool; **Dan Judah Samuel;** *b* 25 March 1925; *s* of 2nd Viscount Samuel, CMG and Hadassah Samuel (*née* Goor); *S* brother, Oct. 2014; *m* 1st, 1957, Nonni Esther Gordon (marr. diss. 1977); one *s* two *d*; 2nd, 1981, Heather Cumming (marr. diss. 1992); one *s* one *d*. *Heir:* *s* Hon. Jonathan Herbert Samuel [*b* 17 Dec. 1965; *m* 1995, Bridget Elizabeth Mahoney; two *d*]. *Died 7 Nov. 2014.*

[This entry did not appear in Who's Who.]

SAMUEL, Richard Christopher, CMG 1983; CVO 1983; HM Diplomatic Service, retired; Ambassador to Latvia, 1991–93; *b* Edinburgh, 8 Aug. 1933; *m* 1986, Frances Draper (*d* 2007); one *s* one *d*. *Educ:* Durham Sch.; St John's Coll., Cambridge (BA). Royal Navy, 1952–54. FO, 1957–58; Warsaw, 1958–59; Rome, 1960–63; FO, 1963; Private Sec. to Parly Under-Sec. of State, 1965–68; Hong Kong, 1968–69; 1st Sec. and Head of Chancery: Singapore, 1969–71; Peking, 1971–73; Counsellor, Washington, 1973–76; Head of Far Eastern Dept, FCO, 1976–79; Counsellor (Commercial), Moscow, 1980–82; Minister and Dep. High Comr, New Delhi, 1982–85; Under-Sec. for Asia and the Oceans, ODA, FCO, 1986–88; on loan to Inter-Amer. Develt Bank, Washington, as Exec. Dir for UK/Western Europe, 1988–91. Hd, CSCE Resident Mission, Moldova, 1994; Head, OSCE Resident Mission: Estonia, 1995; Latvia, 1997–98. Diplomatic Adviser: to UN Special Envoy, Inter-Tajik negotiations in Ashkhabad, 1995–96; to EU Justice and Home Affairs Mission to Central Asia, 1997; Consultant to OSCE, Vienna, 2002–03. Founder and Chm., British-Latvian Assoc., 2004–09. Comdr, Order of the Three Stars (Latvia), 1999. *Recreations:* classical music, the arts. *Address:* 36 Northumberland Place, W2 5AS. *T:* and *Fax:* (020) 7229 8357. *Died 2 Sept. 2012.*

SANCTUARY, Gerald Philip; Secretary, National Union of Journalists Provident Fund, 1984–95; *b* 22 Nov. 1930; *s* of late John Cyril Tabor Sanctuary, MD and Maisie Toppin Sanctuary (*née* Brooks); *m* 1956, Rosemary Patricia L'Estrange, Dublin; three *s* two *d*. *Educ:* Bryanston Sch.; Law Soc.'s Sch. of Law. National Service Pilot, 1953–55; Asst Solicitor, Kingston, 1955–56; Partner in Hasties, Solicitors, Lincoln's Inn Fields, 1957–62; Field Sec., Nat. Marriage Guidance Council, 1963–65, Nat. Secretary 1965–69; Exec. Dir, Sex Information and Educn Council of US, 1969–71; Sec., Professional and Public Relations, The Law Soc., 1971–78; Exec. Dir, Internat. Bar Assoc., 1978–79; Legal Adviser and Regional and Local Affairs Dir, Mencap, 1979–84. Regl PR Consultant, E of England

Reg., Prince's Trust, 2000–. Hon. Treas., GAPAN, 1986–. Editor, Law Soc. series, It's Your Law, 1973–79. Regular broadcaster on radio. *Publications:* Marriage Under Stress, 1968; Divorce—and After, 1970, 2nd edn 1976; Before You See a Solicitor, 1973, 2nd edn 1983; After I'm Gone—what will happen to my Handicapped Child?, 1984, 2nd edn 1991; contrib., Moral Implications of Marriage Counselling, 1971; Vie Affective et Sexuelle, 1972; Loss Prevention Manual, 1978; The English Legal Heritage, 1979; booklets: Fishpool Street—St Albans, 1984; Tudor St Albans; St Albans and the Wars of the Roses, 1985; The Romans in St Albans, 1986; The Monastery at St Albans, 1987; Shakespeare's Globe Theatre, 1992; Abbey Theatre, St Albans, 1993. *Recreations:* amateur drama, organising murder mystery weekends. *Address:* 99 Beechwood Avenue, St Albans, Herts AL1 4XU. *T:* (01727) 842666. *Died 5 Aug. 2011.*

SANDARS, Nancy Katharine, FBA 1984; FSA; archaeologist; *b* 29 June 1914; *d* of Edward Carew Sandars and Gertrude Annie Sandars (*née* Phipps). *Educ:* at home; Wychwood School, Oxford; Inst. of Archaeology, Univ. of London (Diploma 1949); St Hugh's College, Oxford (BLitt 1957). Archaeological research and travel in Europe, 1949–69; British School at Athens, 1954–55; Elizabeth Wordsworth Studentship, St Hugh's College, Oxford, 1958–61; travelled in Middle East, 1957, 1958, 1962, 1966; conferences, lectures (Prague, Sofia, McGill Univ.); excavations in British Isles and Greece. *Publications:* Bronze Age Cultures in France, 1957; The Epic of Gilgamesh, an English version, 1960, rev. edn 1972; Prehistoric Art in Europe, 1967, rev. edn 1985; Poems of Heaven and Hell from Ancient Mesopotamia, 1971; The Sea-Peoples: warriors of the ancient Mediterranean, 1978; Grandmother's Steps: poems, 2001; articles on David Jones, painter and poet. *Recreations:* walking, translating, looking at pictures. *Address:* The Manor House, Little Tew, Chipping Norton, Oxford OX7 4JF. *Club:* University Women's. *Died 20 Nov. 2015.*

SANDARS, Prof. Patrick George Henry; Professor of Experimental Physics and Student of Christ Church, Oxford University, 1978–2000; *b* 29 March 1935; *s* of late P. R. and A. C. Sandars; *m* 1959, P. B. Hall; two *s*. *Educ:* Wellington Coll.; Balliol Coll., Oxford (MA, DPhil). Oxford University: Weir Junior Research Fellow, University Coll., and ICI Research Fellow, Clarendon Laboratory, 1960–63; Tutorial Fellow, Balliol Coll., and Univ. Lectr, 1964–72; Reader in Physics, 1972–77; Head of Clarendon Lab., 1987–90; Hd, Atomic and Laser Physics, 1990–95; Junior Proctor, 1971–72. *Address:* 3 Hawkswell Gardens, Oxford OX2 7EX. *T:* (01865) 558535. *Died 26 April 2013.*

SANDERLING, Kurt; conductor; *b* 19 Sept. 1912; *m* 1st, 1941, Nina Bobath; one *s*; 2nd, 1963, Barbara Wagner; twin *s*. *Educ:* privately. Conductor: Leningrad Philharmonic Orch., 1941–60; East Berlin Symphony Orch., 1960–95; Philharmonia, 1980, then Conductor Emeritus. Guest conductor of many orchs in Europe and N America. *Address:* Am Iderfenngraben 47, 13156 Berlin, Germany. *Died 17 Sept. 2011.*

SANDERS, Sir John Reynolds M.; *see* Mayhew-Sanders.

SANDERS, Kate Emily Tyrrell, (Mrs C. W. Sanders); *see* Boyes, K. E. T.

SANDFORD, Rear-Adm. Sefton Ronald, CB 1976; Flag Officer, Gibraltar, 1974–76; *b* 23 July 1925; *s* of Col H. R. Sandford and Mrs Faye Sandford (*née* Renouf); *m* 1st, 1950, Mary Ann Prins (*d* 1972); one *s*; 2nd, 1972, Jennifer Rachel Newell; two *d*; 3rd, 2001, Susan Elizabeth Capstick. *Educ:* St Aubyn's, Rottingdean, 1934–38; Royal Naval Coll., Dartmouth, 1939–42. Served War: went to sea, July 1942; commanded HMMTB 2017, Lieut, 1946–47; ADC to Comdr British Forces, Hong Kong (Lt-Gen. Sir Terence Airey), 1952–53; commanded HMS Teazer (rank Comdr), 1958; Staff of Imperial Defence Coll., 1963–65; comd HMS Protector, Captain, 1965–67; Naval Attaché, Moscow, 1968–70; comd HMS Devonshire, 1971–73; ADC to the Queen, 1974. Master Mariner. A Younger Brother of Trinity House, 1968. *Recreations:* cricket, messing about in boats, fishing, photography. *Address:* Rozel, Le Bourg, 47700 Anzex, France. *T:* (5) 53846839. *Clubs:* MCC; Royal Yacht Squadron (Cowes). *Died 11 Nov. 2012.*

SANDLER, Prof. Merton, MD; FRCP, FRCPath, FRCPsych; Professor of Chemical Pathology, Royal Postgraduate Medical School, Institute of Obstetrics and Gynaecology, University of London, 1973–91, Professor Emeritus, since 1991; Consultant Chemical Pathologist, Queen Charlotte's Maternity Hospital, 1958–91; *b* 28 March 1926; *s* of late Frank Sandler and Edith (*née* Stein), Salford, Lancs; *m* 1961, Lorna Rosemary, *d* of late Ian Michael and Sally Grenby, Colindale, London; two *s* two *d*. *Educ:* Manchester Grammar Sch.; Manchester Univ. (MB ChB 1949; MD 1962). FRCPath 1970 (MRCPath 1963); FRCP 1974 (MRCP 1955); FRCPsych 1986. Jun. Specialist in Pathology, RAMC (Captain), 1951–53. Research Fellow in Clin. Path., Brompton Hosp., 1953–54; Lectr in Chem. Path., Royal Free Hosp. Sch. of Med., 1955–58. Visiting Professor: Univ. of New Mexico, 1983; Chicago Med. Sch., 1984; Univ. of S Fla, 1988. Recognized Teacher in Chem. Path., 1960–91; extensive examining experience for various Brit. and for. univs and Royal Colls; Mem. Standing Adv. Cttee, Bd of Studies in Path., Univ. of London, 1972–76 (also Mem. Chem. Path. Sub-Cttee, 1973–91); Chm., Academic Bd, 1972–73, Bd of Management, 1975–84, Inst. of Obst. and Gyn.; Governor: Brit. Postgrad. Med. Fedn, 1976–78; Queen Charlotte's Hosp. for Women, 1978–84; Council Mem. and Meetings Sec., Assoc. of Clin. Pathologists, 1959–70; Mem. Council, Collegium Internat. Neuro-Psychopharmacologicum, 1982–90. Various offices in: RSM, incl. Hon. Librarian, 1987–93, and Pres. Section of Med. Exper. Med. and Therapeutics, 1979–80; Brit. Assoc. for Psychopharm., incl. Pres., 1980–82 (Hon. Mem., 1993); British Assoc. for Postnatal Illness (Pres., 1980–); office in many other learned socs and grant-giving bodies, incl. Med. Adv. Councils of Migraine Trust, 1975–80 (Chm., Scientific Adv. Cttee, 1985–91; Trustee, 1987–91), Schizophrenia Assoc. of GB, 1975–78, Parkinson's Disease Soc., 1981–97 (Trustee, 1994–97); Chm. of Trustees, Nat. Soc. for Res. into Mental Health, 1983–. Pres., W London Medico-Chirurgical Soc., 1996–97. Chm. and Sec., Biol Council Symposium on Drug Action, 1979; Sec., Mem. Bd of Management and Chm. Awards Subcttee, Biological Council, 1983–91; Member, Executive Committee: Marcé Soc., 1983–86; Med. Council on Alcoholism, 1987–90; Sec. and Mem. Council, Harveian Soc. of London, 1979–89 (Vice Pres., 1990; Pres., 1991–92); Mem. Council of Management and Patron, Helping Hand Orgn, 1981–87. Organiser or Brit. rep. on org. cttees of many nat. and internat. meetings incl. Internat. Chm., 6th Internat. Catecholamine Congress, 1987. For. Corresp. Mem., Amer. Coll. of Neuropsychopharm., 1975; Hon. Member: Indian Acad. of Neuroscis, 1982; Hungarian Pharmacological Soc., 1985. Jt Editor: British Jl of Pharmacology, 1974–80; Clinical Science, 1975–77; Jl of Neural Transmission, 1979–82; Jt Editor-in-Chief, Jl of Psychiatric Research, 1982–93, and present or past Mem. Editorial Bds of 17 other sci. jls; eponymous lectures to various learned socs incl. 1st Cumings Meml, 1976, James E. Beall II Meml, 1980, Biol Council Lecture and Medal, 1984; F. B. Smith Meml, 1995; Jane Chomet Meml, 1997; Marcia Wilkinson, 2001; provision of Nat. Monoamine Ref. Laboratory Service, 1976–91. Dr *hc* Semmelweis Univ. of Medicine, Budapest, 1992. Anna Monika Internat. Prize (jtly), for Res. on Biol Aspects of Depression, 1973; Gold Medal, Brit. Migraine Assoc., 1974; Senator Dr Franz Burda Internat. Prize for Res. on Parkinson's Disease, 1988; Arnold Friedman Distinguished Clinician Researcher Award, 1991; British Assoc. for Psychopharmacology/Zeneca Lifetime Achievement Award, 1999; Pfizer Pioneer in Psychopharmacology Award, Collegium Internat. Neuro-Psychopharmacologicum, 2006. *Publications:* Mental Illness in Pregnancy and the Puerperium, 1978; The Psychopharmacology of Aggression, 1979; Enzyme Inhibitors as Drugs, 1980; Amniotic Fluid and its Clinical Significance, 1980; The Psychopharmacology of Alcohol, 1980; The Psychopathology of Anticonvulsants, 1981; Nervous Laughter, 1990; Parkinson's Disease, 1993; *jointly:* The Adrenal Cortex, 1961; The Thyroid Gland, 1967; Advances in Pharmacology, 1968; Monoamine Oxidases,

1972; Serotonin—New Vistas, 1974; Sexual Behaviour: Pharmacology and Biochemistry, 1975; Trace Amines and the Brain, 1976; Phenolsulphotransferase in Mental Health Research, 1981; Tetrahydroisoquinolines and β-Carbolines, 1982; Progress towards a Male Contraceptive, 1982; Neurobiology of the Trace Amines, 1984; Psychopharmacology and Food, 1985; Neurotransmitter Interactions, 1986; Progress in Catecholamine Research, 1988; Design of Enzyme Inhibitors as Drugs, Vol. 1, 1989, Vol. 2, 1994; Migraine: a spectrum of ideas, 1990; 5-Hydroxytryptamine in Psychiatry, 1991; Monoamine Oxidase: basic and clinical aspects, 1993; Genetic Research in Psychiatry, 1992; Migraine-Pharmacology and Genetics, 1996; Wine: a scientific exploration, 2003; numerous research pubns on aspects of biologically-active monoamine metabolism. *Recreations:* reading, listening to music, travel. *Address:* 33 Park Road, Twickenham, Middlesex TW1 2QD. *T:* (020) 8892 9085, *Fax:* (020) 8891 5370. *Club:* Athenæum. *Died 24 Aug. 2014.*

SANDYS, 7th Baron *cr* 1802; **Richard Michael Oliver Hill;** DL; Captain of the Yeomen of the Guard (Deputy Government Chief Whip, House of Lords), 1979–82; Landowner; *b* 21 July 1931; *o s* of 6th Baron Sandys, Lt-Col, RE, and Cynthia Mary (*d* 1990), *o d* of late Col F. R. T. T. Gascoigne, DSO; *S* father, 1961; *m* 1961, Patricia Simpson Hall, *d* of late Captain Lionel Hall, MC. *Educ:* Royal Naval College, Dartmouth. Lieutenant in The Royal Scots Greys, 1950–55. A Lord in Waiting, 1974; an Opposition Whip, H of L, 1974–79. FRGS. DL Worcestershire, 1968. *Heir:* (*presumptive*) 9th Marquess of Downshire. *Address:* Ombersley Court, Droitwich, Worcestershire WR9 0HH. *T:* (01905) 620220. *Club:* Cavalry and Guards. *Died 11 Feb. 2013.*

SANGER, Frederick, OM 1986; CH 1981; CBE 1963; PhD; FRS 1954; on staff of Medical Research Council, 1951–83; *b* 13 Aug. 1918; *s* of Frederick Sanger, MD, and Cicely Sanger; *m* 1940, M. Joan Howe; two *s* one *d*. *Educ:* Bryanston; St John's College, Cambridge (Hon. Fellow, 2010). BA 1939; PhD 1943. From 1940, research in Biochemistry at Cambridge University; Beit Memorial Fellowship for Medical Research, 1944–51; at MRC Lab. of Molecular Biol., Cambridge, 1961–83; Fellowship at King's College, Cambridge, 1954 (Hon. Fellow 1983). For. Hon. Mem., Amer. Acad. of Arts and Sciences, 1958; Hon. Mem. Amer. Society of Biological Chemists, 1961; Foreign Assoc., Nat. Acad. of Sciences, 1967. Hon. DSc: Leicester, 1968; Oxon, 1970; Strasbourg, 1970; Cambridge, 1983. Corday-Morgan Medal and Prize, Chem. Soc., 1951; Nobel Prize for Chemistry, 1958, (jointly) 1980; Alfred Benzon Prize, 1966; Royal Medal, Royal Soc., 1969; Sir Frederick Gowland Hopkins Meml Medal, 1971; Gairdner Foundation Annual Award, 1971, 1979; William Bate Hardy Prize, Cambridge Philosophical Soc., 1976; Hanbury Meml Medal, 1976; Copley Medal, Royal Soc., 1977; Horwitz Prize, Albert Lasker Award, 1979; Biochem. Analysis Prize, German Soc. Clin. Chem., 1980; Gold Medal, RSM, 1983. *Publications:* papers on Chemistry of Insulin and Nucleic Acid Structure in Biochemical and other journals. *Died 19 Nov. 2013.*

SAOUMA, Edouard; Director-General of the Food and Agriculture Organization of the United Nations, Rome, 1976–93; agricultural engineer and international official; *b* Beirut, Lebanon, 6 Nov. 1926; *s* of Victor Youssef Saouma and Evelyne Tyan; *m* 1951, Inés Forero; one *s* two *d*. *Educ:* St Joseph's University Sch. of Engineering, Beirut; École Nat. Supérieure d'Agronomie, Montpellier, France. Director: Tel Amara Agric. Sch., 1952–53; Nat. Centre for Farm Mechanization, 1954–55; Sec. Gen., Nat. Fedn of Lebanese Agronomists, 1955; Dir-Gen., Nat. Inst. for Agricl Res., 1957–62; Mem. Gov. Bd, Nat. Grains Office, 1960–62; Minister of Agric., Fisheries and Forestry, 1970. Food and Agric. Organization of UN: Dep. Regional Rep. for Asia and Far East, 1962–65; Dir, Land and Water Develt Div., 1965–75; Dir-Gen., 1976, re-elected 1981, 1987. Hon. Prof. of Agronomy, Agricl Univ. of Beijing, China. Said Akl Prize, Lebanon; Chevalier du Mérite Agricole, France; Grand Cross: Order of the Cedar, Lebanon; Ordre National du Chad; Ordre Nat. du Ghana; Ordre National de Haute Volta; Mérito Agrícola of Spain; Orden Nacional al Mérito, Colombia; Kt Comdr, Order of Merit, Greece; Order of Agricl Merit, Colombia; Gran Oficial, Orden de Vasco Nuñez de Balboa, Panamá; Orden al Mérito Agrícola, Peru; Order of Merit, Egypt; Order of Merit, Mauritania; Grand Officier: Ordre de la République, Tunisia; Ordre National, Madagascar; Ordre de Commandeur, Ouissan Alouite, Morocco. Dr (*hc*): Univ. of Bologna, Italy; Agric. Univ. La Molina, Peru; Univ. of Seoul, Republic of Korea; Univ. of Uruguay; Univ. of Jakarta, Indonesia; Univ. of Warsaw; Univ. of Los Baños, Philippines; Punjab Agricultural Univ., India; Faisalabad Agricultural Univ., Pakistan; Univ. of Agricl Scis of Gödöllö, Hungary; Univ. Nacional Autónoma, Nicaragua; Univ. of Florence, Italy; Univ. of Gembloux, Belgium; Univ. of Prague, Czechoslovakia; Catholic Univ. of America; Univ. of Bologna, Italy; Agricl Inst., Mongolia. Accademico Corrispondente, Accademia Nazionale di Agricoltura, Bologna, Italy. *Publications:* technical publications on agriculture. *Address:* POB 40210, Baabda, Lebanon. *Died 1 Dec. 2012.*

SAREI, Sir Alexis Holyweek, Kt 1987; CBE 1981; PhD; Premier of North Solomons Provincial Government, Papua New Guinea, 1976–80 and 1985–88; *b* 25 March 1934; *s* of late Joseph Nambong and Joanna Mota; *m* 1972, Claire Dionne (*d* 2011); three *s* three *d* (all adopted). *Educ:* PNG Primary to Tertiary, 1949–66; Rome Univ., 1968–71 (PhD Canon Law). RC Priest, 1966–72; Secretary to Chief Minister, PNG, 1972–73; District Comr, 1973–75; Advisor to Bougainville people, 1975–76; High Comr in UK, 1980–84. Following revolution on Bougainville, went to USA, 1990; Security Guard, 1992–93; retired 1994; left Calif, USA in 2008 to establish revival govt, Hanate Soing, in Peit Solos, Buka Island; elected Mem., Autonomous Bougainville Govt, 2010. PNG Independence Medal 1977; CBE for work in Provincial Govt, pioneering work in the system in PNG. Successor to his uncle, Gregory Moah, as Chief of Clan, Petisuun. *Publications:* The Practice of Marriage Among the Solos, Buka Island, 1971. *Recreations:* music, sketching, golf, swimming, sports. *Address:* Petisuun Notukou Village, PO Box 28, Buka Island, Bougainville Region, Papua New Guinea. *Died 22 Sept. 2014.*

SARGENT, Prof. Wallace Leslie William, FRS 1981; Ira S. Bowen Professor of Astronomy, California Institute of Technology, since 1981; *b* 15 Feb. 1935; *s* of Leslie William Sargent and Eleanor (*née* Denniss); *m* 1964, Anneila Isabel Cassells, PhD; two *d*. *Educ:* Scunthorpe Tech. High Sch. (first pupil to go to univ., 1953); Manchester Univ. (BSc Hons, MSc, PhD). Research Fellow in Astronomy, California Inst. of Tech., 1959–62; Sen. Research Fellow, Royal Greenwich Observatory, 1962–64; Asst Prof. of Physics, Univ. of California, San Diego, 1964–66; California Institute of Technology: Asst Prof. of Astronomy, 1966–68, Associate Prof., 1968–71, Professor, 1971–81; Executive Officer for Astronomy, 1975–81 and 1996–97; Dir, Palomar Observatory, 1997–2000. Lectures: George Darwin, RAS, 1987; Thomas Gold, Cornell Univ., 1995; Sackler Dist., Harvard Univ., 1995; Sackler Prize, Univ. of California, Berkeley, 1996; Henry Norris Russell, AAS, 2001; Icko Iben, Univ. of Illinois, 2002. Vice-Pres., American Astronomical Soc., 2004–07. Mem., Nat. Acad. of Scis, USA, 2005; Fellow, American Acad. of Arts and Sciences, 1977; Associate, RAS, 1998. Warner Prize, American Astronomical Soc., 1968; Dannie Heineman Prize, 1991; Bruce Gold Medal, Astronomical Soc. of the Pacific, 1994; Institut d'Astrophysique de Paris Medal, 2009. *Publications:* many papers in learned jls. *Recreations:* reading, gardening, mountain walking, watching sports. *Address:* Astronomy Dept 249–17, California Institute of Technology, Pasadena, CA 91125, USA. *T:* (626) 3954055; 400 South Berkeley Avenue, Pasadena, CA 91107, USA. *T:* (626) 7956345. *Club:* Athenæum (Pasadena). *Died 29 Oct. 2012.*

SASSOON, Vidal, CBE 2009; hairdresser, entrepreneur and businessman; *b* London, 17 Jan. 1928; *s* of late Jack Sassoon and Elizabeth Bellin; *m* 1st, 1956, Elaine Wood; 2nd, 1967, Beverly Adams (marr. diss. 1980); one *s* one *d* one adopted *s* (and one *d* decd); 3rd, Jeanette Hartford-Davis; 4th, 1992, Rhonda Holbrook. Salon owner; first salon opened, 1954; subseq. salons opened in UK and internationally; moved to US, 1980; former owner of Vidal Sassoon brand product co., salons and academies; TV series, Your New Day,

1970s. Founder, Vidal Sassoon Internat. Center for Study of Antisemitism, Hebrew Univ. of Jerusalem, 1982. Hon. PhD Hebrew Univ. of Jerusalem. *Publications:* Sorry I Kept You Waiting, Madam, 1967; (with Beverly Adams) A Year of Health and Beauty, 1976; Vidal (autobiog.), 2010. *Recreations:* philanthropist, art collector. *Club:* Chelsea Arts. *Died 9 May 2012.*

SATTERTHWAITE, Rt Rev. John Richard, CMG 1991; Bishop of Gibraltar in Europe, 1980–93; an Assistant Bishop, Diocese of Carlisle, since 1994; *b* 17 Nov. 1925; *s* of William and Clara Elisabeth Satterthwaite. *Educ:* Millom Grammar Sch.; Leeds Univ. (BA); Coll. of the Resurrection, Mirfield. History Master, St Luke's Sch., Haifa, 1946–48; Curate: St Barnabas, Carlisle, 1950–53; St Aidan, Carlisle, 1953–54; St Michael Paternoster Royal, London, 1955–59, Curate-in-Charge, 1959–65; Guild Vicar, St Dunstan-in-the-West, City of London, 1959–70. Gen. Sec., Church of England Council on Foreign Relations, 1959–70 (Asst Gen. Sec., 1955–59); Gen. Sec., Archbp's Commn on Roman Catholic Relations, 1965–70; Bishop of Gibraltar and Bishop Suffragan of Fulham, 1970, known as Bishop of Fulham and Gibraltar until creation of new diocese, 1980. Hon. Canon of Canterbury, 1963–71; ChStJ 1972 (Asst ChStJ 1963); Hon. Canon of Utrecht, Old Catholic Church of the Netherlands, 1969. Holds decoration from various foreign churches. *Recreations:* fell walking, music. *Address:* 25 Spencer House, St Paul's Square, Carlisle, Cumbria CA1 1DG. *T:* (01228) 594055. *Club:* Athenæum. *Died 22 May 2014.*

SAVILE, Sir James (Wilson Vincent), Kt 1990; OBE 1971; TV and radio personality; *b* 31 Oct. 1926. *Educ:* St Anne's, Leeds. Presenter: Radio One Weekly Show, 1969–89; Independent Radio weekly show, 1989–; television: Jim'll Fix It, making dreams come true, No 1 in the ratings every year, 1975–94; Jim'll Fix It Strikes Again, 2007; Mind How You Go, road safety show; Top of the Pops. Man of many parts but best known as a voluntary helper at Leeds Infirmary, Broadmoor Hospital, and Stoke Mandeville where he raised twelve million pounds to rebuild the National Spinal Injuries Centre. Fellow of Cybernetics, Reading Univ., 1990. Hon. FRCR 1997. Hon. LLD Leeds, 1986; Hon. DArts Bedfordshire, 2009. Hon. KCSG (Holy See), 1982; Bronze and Gold medals, SMO, St John of Jerusalem. *Publications:* As It Happens (autobiog.), 1975; Love is an Uphill Thing (autobiog.), 1975; God'll Fix It, 1978. *Recreations:* running, cycling, wrestling. *Address:* General Infirmary at Leeds, Great George Street, Leeds LS1 3EX. *T:* (0113) 392 2620; National Spinal Injuries Centre, Stoke Mandeville Hospital, Aylesbury, Bucks HP21 8AL. *Club:* Athenæum. *Died 29 Oct. 2011.*

SAVILL, His Honour David Malcolm; QC 1969; a Senior Circuit Judge and Resident Judge, Leeds Combined Court Centre, 1991–96 (a Circuit Judge, 1984–91); *b* 18 Sept. 1930; *s* of late Lionel and Lisbeth Savill; *m* 1955, Mary Arnott (*née* Eadie), JP, *d* of late Lady Hinchcliffe and step *d* of late Hon. Sir (George) Raymond Hinchcliffe; one *s* two *d*. *Educ:* Marlborough Coll. (Pres., Marlburian Club, 1996–97); Clare Coll., Cambridge (BA Hons 1953). 2nd Lieut Grenadier Guards, 1949–50. Called to the Bar, Middle Temple, 1954 (Bencher, 1977); Mem., Senate of Inns of Court and the Bar, 1976, 1980–83. A Recorder, 1972–84 (Hon. Recorder, Leeds, 1993–96); Chancellor: diocese of Bradford, 1976–99; diocese of Ripon, 1987–92; Leader, NE Circuit, 1980–83. Chairman: Adv. Cttee on Conscientious Objectors, 1978–91; W Yorks Criminal Justice Liaison Cttee, 1992–96. *Recreations:* travel, golf, gardening. *Address:* Priory Cottage, Abbey Road, Knaresborough, N Yorks HG5 8HX. *Club:* MCC. *Died 22 Feb. 2011.*

SAWARD, Rev. Canon Michael John; Treasurer and Canon Residentiary of St Paul's Cathedral, 1991–2000, Canon Emeritus, since 2001; *b* 14 May 1932; *s* of late Donald and Lily Saward; *m* 1956, Jackie (*d* 2009), *d* of late Col John Atkinson, DSO, OBE, TD, and Eileen Atkinson, MBE; one *s* three *d*. *Educ:* Eltham Coll.; Bristol Univ. (BA Theology); Tyndale Hall, Bristol. 2nd Lieut, RA, 1950–52, RWAFF (Nat. Service). Deacon 1956, priest 1957; curacies in Croydon, 1956–59, and Edgware, 1959–64; Sec., Liverpool Council of Churches, 1965–67; C of E Radio and Television Officer, 1967–72; Hon. Curate, St John, Beckenham, 1969–72; Vicar: St Matthew, Fulham, 1972–78; Ealing, 1978–91; Priest in Charge, St Paul, Northfields, Ealing, 1986–89; Prebendary of St Paul's Cathedral, 1985–91. Canon Theologian, St Michael Sanibel, Florida, 2001–02. Mem., General Synod, 1975–95 (Mem., House of Clergy Standing Cttee, 1981–86); a Church Comr, 1978–93 (Member: Redundant Churches Cttee, 1978–81; Houses Cttee, 1981–88; Bd of Govs, 1986–93; Pastoral Cttee, 1988–93); Chairman: C of E Pensions Measure Revision Cttee, 1987–88; Care of Cathedrals (Supplementary Provisions) Measure Revision Cttee, 1992–93; Billy Graham Mission '89 Media Task Gp, 1988–89; Member: Lambeth Conf., Preparatory Cttee, 1967–68; Archbishops' Council on Evangelism, 1975–78; C of E Evangelical Council, 1976–93; Nat. Partners in Mission Wkg Party, 1979–81; Dioceses Commn, 1981–89; Council, CPAS, 1992–98; Cttee, Hymn Soc., 2000–06, 2007–10. Sec., Gen. Synod Broadcasting Commn, 1970–73. Trustee: Hartlebury Castle Trust, 1983–88; Church Urban Fund, 1989–90; Christian Evidence Soc., 1992–98. Member, Council: Tyndale Hall, 1968–72; Trinity Theol Coll., 1974–78; Member: BCMS, 1964–76; RTS, 1970–72. Gov., St Paul's Cathedral (formerly Choir) Sch., 1991–2000. Chm., Jubilate Hymns Ltd, 1999–2001. Religious Advr, Cromwell (film), 1971. Journalist, broadcaster (650 progs), lectr, reviewer. Winston Churchill Travelling Fellowship, 1984. Freeman, City of London, 1993; Liveryman, Co. of Gardeners, 1997–2001. Words Editor: Hymns for Today's Church, 1974–82; Sing Glory, 1997–99; Sing to the Lord, 2000; Come Celebrate, 2009. Chairman, Panel of Judges: St Paul's Cathedral Millennium Hymn Competition, 1997–99; The Times Preacher of the Year Comp., 2000. Prizewinner: Southern TV Hymn for Britain competition, 1966; BBC-TV Songs of Praise new hymn competition, 1985; Polly Bond journalism award (USA), 1990. *Publications:* Leisure, 1963 (Norwegian edn 1971); Christian Youth Groups, 1965; Task Unfinished, 1973; Cracking the God-Code, 1974, 3rd edn 1989 (USA edn 1974, Chinese and Swedish edns 1976); And So To Bed?, 1975; God's Friends, 1978; All Change, 1983; Evangelicals on the Move, 1987; These Are The Facts, 1997; A Faint Streak of Humility, 1999; Jubilate Everybody, 2003; Signed, Sealed, Delivered, 2004; Christ Triumphant (hymns), 2006; contribs to books including: Broadcasting, Society and the Church, 1973; Christian Initiation, 1991; Prayers for Today's World, 1993; Has Keele Failed?, 1995; The Post Evangelical Debate, 1997; 366 Graces, 1999; Come Celebrate: contemporary hymns, 2009, and to 325 hymnbooks worldwide; author of 112 hymns, incl. Christ Triumphant, publd in 216 books and regularly sung on Songs of Praise. *Recreations:* reading (esp. military history), music, cricket, travel, food and drink, writing hymns. *Address:* 6 Bromley College, London Road, Bromley, Kent BR1 1PE. *T:* (020) 8464 3185. *Club:* Athenæum (Mem., General Cttee, 1997–2000). *Died 31 Jan. 2015.*

SAWDY, Peter Bryan; Director: Griffin International Ltd, 1988–2007 (Consultant, 2007–09); Yule Catto PLC, 1990–2002; Lazard Birla Indian Investment Fund plc, 1994–2002; *b* 17 Sept. 1931; *s* of Alfred Eustace Leon Sawdy and Beatrice Sawdy; *m* 1st, 1955, Anne Stonor (marr. diss. 1989; she *d* 1995); two *d*; 2nd, 1989, Judith Mary Bowen. *Educ:* Ampleforth Coll.; Regent St Polytechnic; LSE. Trainee, Brooke Bond Ltd, 1952; Chm., Brooke Bond Ceylon Ltd, 1962–65; Director: Brooke Bond Ltd, 1965–68; Brooke Bond Liebig Ltd, 1968–75; Brooke Bond Group: Man. Dir, 1975–77; Gp Chief Exec., 1977–81; Dep. Chm. and Gp Chief Exec., 1981–85. Chm., Costain Gp, 1990–93; Dep. Chm., Hogg Gp, 1992–94 (Dir, 1986–96). *Recreations:* golf, opera, collecting modern first editions. *Address:* 20 Smith Terrace, SW3 4DL. *Clubs:* Naval and Military; Royal Mid-Surrey Golf (Richmond). *Died 20 March 2015.*

SAWKO, Prof. Felicjan, DSc; Professor of Civil Engineering and Head of Department: University of Liverpool, 1967–86; Sultan Qaboos University, Oman, 1986–95, then Emeritus Professor; *b* 17 May 1937; *s* of Czeslaw Sawko and Franciszka (*née* Nawrot); *m* 1960, Genowefa Stefania (*née* Bak); four *s* one *d*. *Educ:* Leeds

Univ. (BSc Civil Engrg, 1958; MSc 1960; DSc 1973). Engr, Rendel Palmer & Tritton, London, 1959–62; Lectr, 1962–67, Reader, 1967, Leeds University. Henry Adams Award, IStructE, 1980. *Publications:* (ed) Developments in Prestressed Concrete, Vols 1 and 2, 1968; (with Cope and Tickell) Numerical Methods for Civil Engineers, 1981; some 70 papers on computer methods and structural masonry. *Recreations:* travel, bridge, numismatics. *Address:* 23 Floral Wood, Liverpool L17 7HR. *T:* (0151) 727 0913. *E:* fsawko@hotmail.com. *Died 2 May 2013.*

SCHAPIRO, Isabel Margaret; *see* Madariaga, I. M. de.

SCHEELE, Sir Nicholas Vernon, KCMG 2001; President, Ford Motor Company, 2001–05 (Chief Operating Officer, 2001–04); Chairman: Key Safety Systems Inc., USA, since 2007; Metalsa SA, Mexico, since 2010; Stackpole International, since 2013; *b* 3 Jan. 1944; *s* of late Werner James Scheele and Norah Edith Scheele (*née* Gough); *m* 1967, Rosamund Ann Jacobs; two *s* one *d*. *Educ:* Durham Univ. (BA). Purchasing, Supply, Procurement, Ford of Britain, 1966–78; Ford of US: Purchasing, Supply, Procurement Management, 1978–83; Dir, Supply Policy and Planning, 1983–85; Dir, Body and Chassis Parts Purchasing, 1985–88; Pres., Ford of Mexico, 1988–91; Vice-Chm., Jan.–April 1992, Chm. and Chief Exec., 1992–99, Jaguar Cars; Sen. Vice-Pres., April–July 1999, Chm., July 1999–2001, Ford of Europe; Mem. Supervisory Bd, Ford Werke AG, 1999–2001; Vice-Pres. for N America, Ford Motor Co., 2001. Dir, W Midlands Radio, 2000–. Member Council: Midlands Region, Inst. of Dirs, 1994–99; SMMT, 1992–99; President: Motor and Allied Trades Benevolent Fund, 1996–97; Coventry and Warwicks Partnership; Midlands Business of the Year, 1996; Chm., Business in the Arts, West Midlands, 1997–99. Chairman: Prince of Wales Business and Envmt Cttee, 1999–2006; Manufacturing Theme Gp, Foresight, 2020, 1999–2002; (non-exec.) CMI (Cambridge/MIT jt commercial venture), 2005–. Non-executive Director: BAT, 2005–13; Grupo Proeza (Mexico), 2005–; Pegasus Gp Hldgs (USA), 2005–09; Caparo Gp Ltd, 2006–09; Mem. Bd, Reynolds American Inc., 2014–. Member, Advisory Board: British American Chamber of Commerce, 1995–99; Fulbright Commn, 1995–99. Member, Board of Advisors: Coventry Univ., 1995–; Durham Univ., 1996–. Chancellor, Warwick Univ., 2002–08. Pres., Coventry Mus. of Transportation, 2006–. Life Mem., NSPCC (Chm., Coventry Centenary Appeal, 1994–96); mem. charity bds and cttees devoted to children's welfare, community relns and indust. regeneration. Hon. RCM. Hon. FIMechE 2000. Gold Medal: IMI Castrol, 1999; IMechE, 2000; Carmen's Co., 2000. 6 hon. doctorates. *Publications:* articles on manufg efficiency, quality, envmtl affairs, and youth employment and trng. *Recreations:* reading, classical music, golf, tennis, squash. *Clubs:* Royal Automobile; Catawba Island (Great Lakes); Bloomfield Hills Country (Bloomfield Hills); Loblolly (Florida). *Died 18 July 2014.*

SCHERER, Paul Joseph; Managing Director, 1982–95, Chairman, 1995–96, Transworld Publishers Ltd; *b* 28 Dec. 1933; *s* of François Joseph Scherer and Florence (*née* Haywood); *m* 1959, Mary Fieldus; one *s* three *d*. *Educ:* Stonyhurst Coll. National Service, commnd BUFFS (Royal E Kent Regt), 1952–54. Bailey Bros & Swinfen, 1954–56; Jun. Editor, G. Bell & Sons, 1956–58; Sales Man., Penguin Books, 1958–63; Gp Sales Dir, Paul Hamlyn, 1963–68; William Collins Sons & Co.: Man. Dir, Internat. Div., 1968–77; Pres., Collins & World USA, 1974–75; Man. Dir, Mills & Boon, 1977–82; Sen. Vice Pres., Bantam Doubleday Dell Publishing Gp Inc., 1990–98; Chm., Curtis Brown Gp, 1996–2004. Director: Bloomsbury Publishing plc, 1993–2006 (Vice-Chm., 2004–06); Book Tokens Ltd, 1995–2002. Member Board: Book Develt Council, 1971–74; Book Marketing Council, 1977–84 (Chm., 1982–84); British Library, 1996–2000; Mem. Council, Publishers Assoc., 1982–84 and 1989–94 (Pres., 1991–93); Pres., Book Trade Benevolent Soc., 1995–99. Trustee, Whizz-Kidz, 1996–2001 (Chm., 1998–2000). Founding Chm., Unicorn Sch., Kew, 1970–73; Gov., Worth Sch., 1993–96. *Recreation:* laughing at my own jokes. *Address:* 18 Carlyle Mansions, Cheyne Walk, SW3 5LS. *T:* (020) 7376 7570. *Clubs:* Garrick, Hurlingham. *Died 28 Oct. 2013.*

SCHMIDT, Helmut H. W.; Chancellor, Federal Republic of Germany, 1974–82; Member of Bundestag, Federal Republic of Germany, 1953–61, and 1965–87; Publisher, Die Zeit, since 1983; *b* 23 Dec. 1918; *s* of Gustav Lentfält Schmidt and Ludovica Schmidt; *m* 1942, Hannelore Glaser (*d* 2010); one *d*. *Educ:* Univ. of Hamburg. Diplom-Volkswirt, 1949. Manager of Transport Administration, State of Hamburg, 1949–53; Social Democratic Party: Member, 1946–; Mem. Federal Executive, 1958–83; Chm., Parly Gp, 1967–69; Vice-Chm. of Party, 1968–84; Senator (Minister) for Domestic Affairs in Hamburg, 1961–65; Minister of Defence, 1969–72; Minister of Finance and Economics, 1972; Minister of Finance, 1972–74. Hon. LLD: Newberry Coll., S Carolina, 1973; Johns Hopkins Univ., 1976; Cambridge, 1976; Hon. DCL Oxford, 1979; Hon. Doctorate: Harvard, 1979; Sorbonne, 1981; Georgetown, 1986; Scranton, Pennsylvania, 1987; Bergamo, 1989; Keio, Tokyo, 1991; Nat. Chung-Hsing, Taipei, 1992; Potsdam, Haifa, 2000. Athinai Prize for Man and Mankind, Onassis Foundn, Greece, 1986. *Publications:* Defence or Retaliation, 1962; Beiträge, 1967; Balance of Power, 1971; Auf dem Fundament des Godesberger Programms, 1973; Bundestagsreden, 1975; Kontinuität und Konzentration, 1975; Als Christ in der politischen Entscheidung, 1976; (with Willy Brandt) Deutschland 1976—Zwei Sozialdemokraten im Gespräch, 1976; Der Kurs heisst Frieden, 1979; Freiheit verantworten, 1980; Pflicht zur Menschlichkeit, 1981; A Grand Strategy for the West, 1985; Menschen und Mächte, 1987 (trans. as Men and Powers, 1989); Die Deutschen und ihre Nachbarn, 1990; Handeln für Deutschland, 1993; Das Jahr der Entscheidung, 1994; Weggefährten, 1996; Jahrhundertwende, 1998; Allgemeine Erklärung der Menschenpflichten, 1998; Globalisierung, 1998; Auf der Suche nach einer öffentlichen Moral, 1998; Die Selbstbehauptung Europas, 2000; Hand aufs Herz, 2002; Die Mächte der Zukunft, 2004; Auf dem Weg zur deutschen Einheit, 2005; (with Frank Sieren) Nachbar China, 2007; Ausser Dienst, 2008; (with Fritz Stern) Unser Jahrhundert: ein gespräch, 2010; Religion in der Verantwortung, 2011; (with Peer Steinbrück) Zug um Zug, 2012; Ein Letzer Besuch: begegnungen mit der weltmacht China, 2013. *Recreations:* sailing, chess, playing the organ. *Address:* c/o Deutscher Bundestag, Platz der Republik 1, 11011 Berlin, Germany. *Died 10 Oct. 2015.*

SCHNEIDER, Dr William George, OC 1977; FRS 1962; FRSC 1951; Research Consultant, National Research Council of Canada, Ottawa, since 1980 (President, 1967–80); *b* Wolseley, Saskatchewan, 1 June 1915; *s* of Michael Schneider and Phillipina Schneider (*née* Kraushaar); *m* 1940, Jean Frances Purves; two *d*. *Educ:* University of Saskatchewan (BSc 1937; MSc 1939); McGill University (PhD (in physical chem.) 1941); Harvard University. Research physicist at Woods Hole Oceanographic Inst., Woods Hole, Mass, USA, 1943–46 (US Navy Certificate of Merit, 1946). Joined Nat. Research Council, Division of Pure Chemistry, Ottawa, 1946; Vice-President (Scientific), 1965–67. Pres., Internat. Union of Pure and Applied Chemistry, 1983–85. Chemical Inst. of Canada Medal, 1961, Montreal Medal, 1973; Henry Marshall Tory Medal, RSC, 1969; Queen's Diamond Jubilee Medal, 2012. Hon. DSc: York, 1966; Memorial, 1968; Saskatchewan, 1969; Moncton, 1969; McMaster, 1969; Laval, 1969; New Brunswick, 1970; Montreal, 1970; McGill, 1970; Acadia, 1976; Regina, 1976; Ottawa, 1978; Hon. LLD: Alberta, 1968; Laurentian, 1968. *Publications:* (with J. A. Pople and H. J. Bernstein) High Resolution Nuclear Magnetic Resonance, 1959; scientific papers in chemistry and physics research jls. *Recreations:* tennis, skiing. *Address:* 100 Island Lodge Road, Apt 806, Ottawa, ON K1N 0A2, Canada. *Died 18 Feb. 2013.*

SCHOLEY, Sir Robert, Kt 1987; CBE 1982; FREng; Chairman, British Steel plc (formerly British Steel Corporation), 1986–92; *b* 8 Oct. 1921; *s* of Harold and Eveline Scholey; *m* 1946, Joan Methley; two *d*. *Educ:* King Edward VII Sch. and Sheffield Univ. Associateship in Mech. Eng; FREng (FEng 1990). United Steel Companies,

1947–68; British Steel Corporation, 1968–92: Dir and Chief Executive, 1973–86; Dep. Chm., 1976–86. Dir, Eurotunnel Bd, 1987–94. Mem., HEFCE, 1992–95. Pres., Eurofer, 1985–90. Chm., Internat. Iron and Steel Inst., 1989–90; Pres., Inst. of Metals, 1989–90. Hon. DEng Sheffield, 1987; Hon. DSc Teesside, 1995. *Recreations:* outdoor life, history. *Died 12 Jan. 2014.*

SCHOUVALOFF, Alexander, MA; Founder Curator, Theatre Museum, Victoria & Albert Museum, 1974–89; *b* 4 May 1934; *s* of Paul Schouvaloff (professional name Paul Sheriff) and Anna Schouvaloff (*née* Raevsky); *m* 1st, Gillian Baker (marr. diss.); one *s*; 2nd, 1971, Daria Chorley (*née* de Mérindol). *Educ:* Harrow Sch.; Jesus Coll., Oxford (MA). Asst Director, Edinburgh Festival, 1965–67; Dir, North West Arts Assoc., 1967–74. Director: Rochdale Festival, 1971; Chester Festival, 1973. Sec. Gen., Société Internat. des Bibliothèques et des Musées des Arts du Spectacle, 1980–90; Committee Member: for Jerome Robbins Dance Div., NY Public Liby for Performing Arts, 1993–; Scientific Cttee, Inst nat. d'histoire de l'art, Paris, 2002–06. Trustee, London Archives of the Dance, 1976–2008. BBC Radio plays: Summer of the Bullshine Boys, 1981; No Saleable Value, 1982. Cross of Polonia Restituta, 1971. *Publications:* Place for the Arts, 1971; Summer of the Bullshine Boys, 1979; (with Victor Borovsky) Stravinsky on Stage, 1982; (with April FitzLyon) A Month in the Country, 1983; (with Catherine Haill) The Theatre Museum, 1987; Theatre on Paper, 1990; Léon Bakst: The Theatre Art, 1991; catalogues: Thyssen-Bornemisza Collection (set and costume designs), 1987; The Art of Ballets Russes (the Serge Lifar collection of theater designs, costumes, and paintings at the Wadsworth Atheneum), 1998. *Recreations:* France, Italy. *Address:* 10 Avondale Park Gardens, W11 4PR. *T:* (020) 7727 7543. *Club:* Garrick. *Died 30 Dec. 2012.*

SCHRAM, Prof. Stuart Reynolds; Professor of Politics (with reference to China) in the University of London, School of Oriental and African Studies, 1968–89, then Emeritus; Research Associate, Harvard University, 1989–2008; *b* Excelsior, Minn, 27 Feb. 1924; *s* of Warren R. Schram and Nada Stedman Schram; *m* 1972, Marie-Annick Lancelot; one *s*. *Educ:* West High Sch., Minneapolis, Minn; Univ. of Minnesota (BA, 1944); Columbia Univ. (PhD 1954). Dir, Soviet and Chinese Section, Centre d'Etude des Relations Internationales, Fondation Nationale des Sciences Politiques, Paris, 1954–67; Head, Contemporary China Inst., SOAS, 1968–72. *Publications:* Protestantism and Politics in France, 1954; The Political Thought of Mao Tse-Tung, 1963, rev. edn 1969; Le marxisme et l'Asie 1853–1964, 1965, rev. and enl. English edn 1969; Mao Tse-tung, 1966; Ideology and Policy in China since the Third Plenum, 1978–84, 1984; (ed) The Scope of State Power in China, 1985; (ed) Foundations and Limits of State Power in China, 1987; The Thought of Mao Tse-tung, 1989; (ed) Mao's Road to Power: Revolutionary Writings 1912–1949, vol. I 1992, vol. II 1994, vol. III 1995, vol. IV 1997, vol. V 1999, vols VI and VII, 2004. *Recreations:* concert- and theatre-going, walking in the country, fishing. *Died 8 July 2012.*

SCHREIER, Sir Bernard, Kt 2000; mechanical engineer; Chairman, CP Holdings Ltd; President, IIC Industries Inc., NY; *b* 28 March 1918; *m* 1943, Lily Geckts; one *d* (one *s* decd). Chm., Danubius Hotels RT, Hungary; Dep. Chm., Bank Leumi (UK) plc. Hon. Fellow, UCL. Queen's Award for Export, 1976; Jubilee Award, Israel, 1998. Officer's Cross, Order of Hungarian Republic, 1998; Third Class, Order of White Two-Arm Cross (Slovak Republic). *Address:* CP Holdings Ltd, CP House, Otterspool Way, Watford, Herts WD25 8JJ. *Died 1 June 2013.*

SCHULTZ, Rt Rev. Bruce Allan; Bishop of Grafton, NSW, 1985–98; *b* 24 May 1932; *s* of Percival Ferdinand and Elsie Amelia Schultz; *m* 1962, Janet Margaret Gersbach; two *s* two *d* (and one *s* decd). *Educ:* Culcairn High School; St Columb's Hall and St John's Coll., Morpeth. ThL (ACT) 1960. Sheep and wheat property, Manager-Owner, 1950–57. Theolog. student, 1957–60; deacon 1959, priest 1960, dio. Riverina; Asst Priest, Broken Hill, 1961–63; Priest-in-charge, Ariah Park, Ardlethan and Barellan with Weethalle, 1964–67; Rector: Deniliquin, 1967–73; Gladstone, dio. Rockhampton, 1973–79; Archdeacon and Commissary of Rockhampton, 1975–79; Rector of Grafton and Dean of Christ Church Cathedral, 1979–83; Asst Bishop of Brisbane (Bishop for the Northern Region), 1983–85. Nat. Chm., Anglican Boys' Soc. in Australia, 1987–94; Episcopal overseer, Cursillo Movement in Australia, 1987–95; Chm., NSW Provincial Commn on Christian Educn, 1988–94; Bd Mem., Australian Bd of Missions, 1988–95; Chm., Nat. Home Mission Fund, 1999–2002. *Recreations:* family, fishing, gardening. *Address:* Unit 52, 405 Mooloolaba Road, Buderim, Qld 4556, Australia. *Clubs:* Mooloolaba Surf Life Saving, Mooloolaba Bowls (Mooloolaba). *Died 27 July 2012.*

SCHWARZKOPF, Gen. H. Norman, Hon. KCB 1991; Commander, Allied Forces, Gulf War, Jan.–Feb. 1991; Commander in Chief, US Central Command, MacDill Air Force Base, Florida, 1988–91; *b* 22 Aug. 1934; *s* of Herbert Norman Schwarzkopf and Ruth (*née* Bowman); *m* 1968, Brenda Holsinger; one *s* two *d*. *Educ:* Bordentown Mil. Inst.; Valley Forge Mil. Acad. (football schol.); US Mil. Acad., West Point; Univ. of S Calif (MME 1964). Commnd 2nd Lieut. Inf. and airborne trng, Fort Benning, Ga; 101st Airborne Div., Fort Campbell, Ky; Teacher, Mil. Acad., West Point, 1964 and 1966–68; Task-Force Advr, S Vietnamese Airborne Div., 1965; Comdr, 1st Bn, 6th Inf., 198th Inf. Bde, Americal Div., 1969–73; Dep. Comdr, 172nd Inf. Bde, Fort Richardson, Alaska, 1974–76; Comdr, 1st Bde, 9th Inf. Div., Fort Lewis, Wash, 1976–78; Dep. Dir of Plans, US Pacific Comd, Camp Smith, Hawaii, 1978–80; Asst Div. Comdr, 8th Mechanized Inf. Div., W Germany, 1980–82; Dir, Military-Personnel Management, Office of Dep. Chief of Staff for Personnel Management, Office of Dep. Chief of Staff for Personnel, Washington, DC, 1982–83; Comdr, 24th Mechanized Inf. Div., Fort Stewart, Ga, 1983–85; Comdr, US Ground Forces and Dep. Comdr, Jt Task Force, Grenada op. Oct. 1983; Asst Dep. Chief of Staff, Army Ops, Washington DC, 1985–86; Comdr, I Corps, Fort Lewis, Wash, 1986–87; Dep. Chief for Ops and Plans, Washington, DC, 1987–88. DSM with oak leaf cluster; DFC; Silver Star with 2 oak leaf clusters; Bronze Star with 3 oak leaf clusters; Purple Heart with oak leaf cluster; Congressional Gold Medal, 1991. *Publications:* (with Peter Petre) It Doesn't Take a Hero (autobiog.), 1992. *Address:* c/o Marvin Josephson, International Creative Management, 40 West 57th Street, New York, NY 10019–4001, USA. *Died 27 Dec. 2012.*

SCOON, Sir Paul, GCMG 1979; GCVO 1985; OBE 1970; Governor General of Grenada, 1978–92; *b* 4 July 1935; *m* 1970, Esmai Monica McNeilly (*née* Lumsden) (*d* 2004); two step *s* one step *d*. *Educ:* St John's Anglican Sch., Grenada; Grenada Boys' Secondary Sch.; Inst. of Education, Leeds; Toronto Univ. BA, MEd. Teacher, Grenada Boys' Secondary Sch., 1953–67. Chief Educn Officer, 1967–68, Permanent Sec., 1969, Secretary to the Cabinet, 1970–72, Grenada; Dep. Director, Commonwealth Foundn, 1973–78. Governor, Centre for Internat. Briefing, Farnham Castle, 1973–78; Vice-Pres., Civil Service Assoc., Grenada, 1968; Co-founder and former Pres., Assoc. of Masters and Mistresses, Grenada. *Publications:* Survival for Service, 2003. *Recreations:* reading, tennis. *Address:* PO Box 180, St George's, Grenada. *T:* 4402180. *Died 2 Sept. 2013.*

SCOTT, Rt Rev. Colin John Fraser; Bishop Suffragan of Hulme, 1984–98; Hon. Assistant Bishop of Leicester, 1999–2011; *b* 14 May 1933; *s* of late Kenneth Miller Scott and Marion Edith Scott; *m* 1958, Margaret Jean MacKay; one *s* two *d*. *Educ:* Berkhamsted School; Queens' College, Cambridge (MA); Ridley Hall, Cambridge. Curate: St Barnabas, Clapham Common, 1958–61; St James, Hatcham, 1961–64; Vicar, St Mark, Kennington, 1964–71; Rural Dean of Lambeth, 1968–71; Team Rector, Sanderstead Team Ministry, 1977–84. Vice-Chm., Southwark Diocesan Pastoral Cttee, 1971–77; Chm., Council for the Care of Churches, 1994–98. Hon. Chaplain to Bishop of Southwark, 1967–80; Hon. Canon, Southwark Cathedral, 1973–84. *Address:* The Priest House, Prior Park Road, Ashby de la Zouch, Leics LE65 1BL. *T:* (01530) 564403. *Died 1 April 2014.*

SCOTT, Derek John; Adviser, Europe Economics, since 2005; *b* 17 Jan. 1947; *s* of John William Scott and Alice Isabel Scott (*née* Heal); *m* 1st, 1985, Elinor Mary Goodman, freelance journalist (marr. diss. 2007); 2nd, 2010, Gisela Gschaider Stuart, MP. *Educ:* Liverpool Univ. (BA Hons); London Sch. of Econs (MSc Econ); Birkbeck Coll., Univ. of London (MSc Econ). Mem. (Lab) RBK&C, 1974–78. Special Advr to Denis Healey, 1977–79; Econ. Advr to James Callaghan, 1979–81; Internat. Policy Advr, Shell Internat., 1982–86; Dir, European Economics, Barclays de Zoete Wedd, 1986–97; Econ. Advr to Prime Minister, 1997–2003; Economic Consultant, KPMG, 2004–. Non-exec. Dir, Liberty Syndicates Ltd, 2008–; Mem. Adv. Bd, Vestra Wealth LLP, 2009–. *Publications:* Off Whitehall, 2004. *Address:* 80 Denbigh Street, SW1V 2EX. *Died 1 Aug. 2012.*

SCOTT, (Ian) Jonathan, CBE 1995; FSA; Deputy Chairman, 1997–2003 and Trustee, 1996–2003, Victoria & Albert Museum; *b* 7 Feb. 1940; *s* of late Col Alexander Brassey Jonathan Scott, DSO, MC and Rhona Margaret Scott; *m* 1965, Annabella Constance Loudon; two *s* one *d*. *Educ:* Harrow Sch.; Balliol Coll., Oxford (BA). FSA 1980. Director: Charterhouse Japhet, 1973–80; Barclays Merchant Bank, subseq. Barclays de Zoete Wedd, 1980–92. Chairman: Reviewing Cttee on Export of Works of Art, 1985–95; Acceptance in Lieu Panel, 2000–10. Mem. Panel, Nat. Heritage Meml Fund, 2011–. Trustee, Imperial War Mus., 1984–98. *Publications:* Piranesi, 1975; Salvator Rosa, 1995; The Pleasures of Antiquity, 2003. *Recreations:* horses, trees. *Address:* Lasborough Manor, Tetbury, Glos GL8 8UF. *Club:* Brooks's. *Died 28 Dec. 2012.*

SCOTT, Sir John; *see* Scott, Sir P. J.

SCOTT, John Gavin, LVO 2004; FRCO; Organist and Director of Music, St Thomas, Fifth Avenue, New York City, since 2004; *b* 18 June 1956; *s* of Douglas Gavin Scott and Hetty Scott (*née* Murphy); *m* 1st, 1979, Carolyn Jane Lumsden (marr. diss. 2010); one *s* one *d*; 2nd, 2013, Lily Isabel Ardalan; one *s* born posthumously. *Educ:* Queen Elizabeth Grammar Sch., Wakefield; St John's Coll., Cambridge (MA, MusB). Asst Organist, Wakefield Cath., 1970–74; Organ Scholar, St John's Coll., Cambridge, 1974–78; Asst Organist, Southwark Cath., 1978–85; St Paul's Cathedral: Asst Organist, 1978–85; Sub-Organist, 1985–90; Organist and Dir of Music, 1990–2004. Prof., Royal Acad. of Music, 1988–91. Accompanist, Bach Choir, 1979–91. Hon. RAM 1990; Hon. FGCM 1996; Hon. FTCL 2002; Hon. FRSCM 2005. Hon. DMus Nashotah House, 2007. First Prizewinner: Manchester Internat. Organ Fest., 1978; Leipzig Internat. J. S. Bach Competition, 1984. *Recreations:* reading, travel, ecclesiastical architecture. *Address:* 202 West 58th Street, New York, NY 10019, USA. *Died 12 Aug. 2015.*

SCOTT, Jonathan; *see* Scott, I. J.

SCOTT, Oliver Lester Schreiner; Emeritus Consultant: Skin Department, Charing Cross Hospital, since 1985 (Physician-in-Charge, 1956–84); South West Metropolitan Regional Hospital Board, since 1985 (Consultant Dermatologist, 1951–84); *b* London, 16 June 1919; *s* of Ralph Lester Scott, FRCSE, and Ursula Hester Schreiner; *m* 1943, Katherine Ogle Branfoot (*d* 1987); two *d*. *Educ:* Diocesan College, Cape Town; Trinity College, Cambridge; St Thomas's Hospital, London. MRCS, LRCP 1942; MA, MB, BChir, (Cantab) 1943; MRCP (London) 1944. FRCP 1964. Med. Specialist, RAF Med. Branch, 1943–46 (Sqn Leader). Consultant, Medical Insurance Agency, 1976–93; Hon. Consultant: Dispensaire Français, 1960–86; King Edward VII Hosp. for Officers, London, 1975–84. Hon. Treas., RSocMed, 1978–82 (Pres., Dermatology Section, 1977–78); Vice-Pres., Royal Medical Foundn of Epsom Coll., 1992– (Hon. Treas., 1978–93); Hon. Mem., British Assoc. of Dermatologists (Pres., 1982–83). Chevalier, l'Ordre National du Mérite, France. *Publications:* section on skin disorders in Clinical Genetics, ed A. Sorsby; medical articles in Lancet, British Journal of Dermatology, etc. *Recreations:* fishing, gardening. *Address:* South Lodge, 7 South Side, Wimbledon Common, SW19 4TL. *T:* (020) 8946 6662. *Died 25 May 2012.*

SCOTT, Sir (Philip) John, KBE 1987; FRCP; FRACP; FRSNZ; Professor of Medicine, University of Auckland, 1975–97, then Emeritus; *b* 26 June 1931; *s* of Horace McD. Scott and Doris A. Scott (*née* Ruddock); *m* 1st, 1956, Elizabeth Jane MacMillan (*d* 2002); one *s* three *d*; 2nd, 2003, Margaret Fernie Wann (*d* 2007); 3rd, 2011, Alison Rhona Roberton. *Educ:* Univ. of Otago (BMedSci; MB, ChB); Univ. of Birmingham (MD). Qual. in medicine, Dunedin, 1955; hosp. and gen. practice experience, Auckland, 1956–58; postgrad. trng, RPMS, London, 1959–60; Queen Elizabeth Hosp. and Univ. of Birmingham, 1960–62; Med. Res. Fellowships, Auckland, 1962–68; Sen. Lectr, Univ. of Otago, based on Auckland Hosp., 1969–72; University of Auckland: Sen. Lectr, 1970–72; Associate Prof., 1973–75; Hd, Dept of Medicine, the Univ.'s Sch. of Medicine, 1979–87. Pres., Royal Soc. of NZ, 1998–2000. Res. interests in lipoprotein metabolism, arterial disease, human nutrition, med. econs and educn, professional ethics. *Publications:* (first author/co-author) articles in sci./med. jls and in press, on aspects of coronary artery disease, atherosclerosis, lipoprotein metabolism, human nutrition, ethical issues, medical history and educn, health service orgn. *Recreations:* music, pottery, gardening. *Address:* 64 Temple Street, Meadowbank, Auckland 1072, New Zealand. *T:* (9) 5215384. *Died 20 Oct. 2015.*

SCOTT, Prof. William, RSA 1984; FRBS; Post-Graduate Course Leader, Edinburgh College of Art, 1997–2000 (Head of Sculpture, 1989–97); President, Royal Scottish Academy, since 2008 (Secretary, 1998–2008); *b* 16 Aug. 1935; *s* of George Barclay Scott and Jeanie Stuart Scott (*née* Waugh); *m* 1961, Phyllis Owen Fisher; one *s* two *d*. *Educ:* Edinburgh Coll. of Art (DA 1959); Ecole des Beaux Arts, Paris. FRBS 1994. Prof., Heriot-Watt Univ., 1994–2000, then Prof. Emeritus. Contributor to: annual exhibns in Scotland; British Art Show, 1979–80; Fifth Biennial of Small Sculptures, Budapest, 1981; Chelsea Harbour Show, 1993; Städtische Gal. im Park, Viersen, 1999; Transistors, Iwate Arts Fest., 1999, Trondheim, 2000; Südbahnhof Gall., Krefeld, 2000; Internat. Medaillen Kunst, Weimar, 2000; Kunst Transfer Heinsberg, 2003; Insiders: Boxart, Oriel Davies Gall., 2003; Canterbury Mus., 2005; Demarco Romania exhibn, Sibiu, 2007; *one-person exhibitions* in galleries and museums, 1971–, including: New 57 Gall., Edinburgh, 1979; Kirkcaldy Mus. and Gall., 1985; Talbot Rice Gall., Edinburgh Univ., 1994; Fettes Coll. Gall., 2002; Demarco Roxy Gall., 2003; Kunst Verein, Heinsberg, 2004; RBS Gall., London. 2005; Gracefield Art Centre, Dumfries, 2008; Inverness Mus. and Gall., 2009; *commissions* include: public sculptures, St Andrews, 1970, Cumbernauld, 1980, Glasgow, 1985 and 1998; sculpture for Sir Alec Douglas-Home at The Hirsel, Coldstream, 1998; Elizabeth Crichton Sculpture, Crichton campus, Dumfries, 2000; portrait of Sorley Maclean, Edinburgh Park, 2003; sculptures and drawings in *public collections*, including: Aberdeen Art Gall.; Royal Scottish Acad.; Kirkcaldy Gall. and Mus.; Leeds City; Edinburgh City; also work in private collections. Mem., Bd of Dirs, Fruit Mkt Gall., Edinburgh, 1981–92; Chm., Edinburgh Sculpture Workshop, 1998–. Mem., Selection Cttee for British Sch. at Rome, 1985–90; Chm., Scottish Arts Council Awards Panel, 1990–93. Hon. RA 2008; Hon. RWA 2008; Hon. Mem. RHA 2008. *Recreations:* walking, reading, travel. *Address:* 45 St Clair Crescent, Roslin, Midlothian EH25 9NG. *T:* (0131) 440 2544. *Died 22 March 2012.*

SCOTT-BOWDEN, Maj.-Gen. Logan, CBE 1972 (OBE 1964); DSO 1944; MC 1944 and Bar 1946; farmer; *b* 21 Feb. 1920; *s* of late Lt-Col Jonathan Scott-Bowden, OBE, TD, and Mary Scott-Bowden (*née* Logan); *m* 1950, Helen Jocelyn (*d* 2010), *d* of late Major Sir Francis Caradoc Rose Price, 5th Bt, and late Marjorie Lady Price; three *s* three *d*. *Educ:* Malvern Coll.; RMA Woolwich. Commissioned Royal Engineers, 1939; served in War of 1939–45: Norway, 1940; Adjt, 53rd (Welsh) Div. RE, 1941; Liaison Duties in Canada and USA, 1942; Normandy Beach Reconnaissance Team (Major), 1943; OC 17 Fd Co. RE, NW Europe, 1944; psc 1945; Singapore, Burma (Bde Maj. 98 Indian Inf. Bde), Palestine, Libya, 1946–51; Korea, 1953; jssc 1956; Arabia, 1958–60 (Lt-Col 1959); CRE 1st Div., BAOR, 1960; Head, UK Land Forces Planning Staff, 1963; Asst Dir, Def. Plans MoD (Col), 1964; Comd Trng Bde RE (Brig.), 1966; Nat. Defence Coll. (India), 1969;

Comd Ulster Defence Regiment, 1970–71; Head of British Defence Liaison Staff, India, 1971–74, retd 1974. Col Comdt RE, 1975–80. *Recreations:* ski-ing, travel. *Died 9 Feb. 2014.*

SCOTT-JOYNT, Rt Rev. Michael Charles; Bishop of Winchester, 1995–2011; an Honorary Assistant Bishop: Diocese of Europe, since 2011; Diocese of Chichester, since 2011; *b* 15 March 1943; *m* 1965, Mary Louise White; twin *s* one *d*. *Educ:* King's College, Cambridge (BA 1965, MA 1968); Cuddesdon Theological College. Deacon 1967, priest 1968; Curate, Cuddesdon, 1967–70; Tutor, Cuddesdon Coll., 1967–71, Chaplain 1971–72; Team Vicar, Newbury, 1972–75; Priest-in-charge: Caversfield, 1975–79; Bicester, 1975–79; Bucknell, 1976–79; Rector, Bicester Area Team Ministry, 1979–81; RD of Bicester and Islip, 1976–81; Canon Residentiary of St Albans, 1982–87; Dir of Ordinands and In-Service Training, Diocese of St Albans, 1982–87; Suffragan Bishop of Stafford, 1987–95. *Address:* Easter House, Funtington, Chichester PO18 9LJ. *E:* michael.scottjoynt11@gmail.com. *Died 27 Sept. 2014.*

SCRIVENER, Anthony Frank Bertram; QC 1975; *b* 31 July 1935; *s* of late Frank Bertram Scrivener and of Edna Scrivener; *m* 1964, Irén Becze (marr. diss.); one *s* one *d*; *m* 1993, Ying Hui Tan. *Educ:* Kent Coll., Canterbury; University Coll. London (LLB). Called to Bar, Gray's Inn, 1958 (Holt Scholar); a Recorder, 1976–92; Bencher, Lincoln's Inn, 1985. Lectr in Law, Ghana, 1959–61; practice as Junior, 1961–75. Chm., Gen. Council of Bar, 1991 (Vice-Chm., 1990). Lifetime Achievement Award, Chambers UK Directories, 2008. *Recreations:* tennis, chess, cricket, car racing, taking the dog for a walk. *Died 27 March 2015.*

SCROGGS, Cedric Annesley; Chief Executive, Fisons plc, 1992–93; *b* 2 Jan. 1941; *s* of Richard B. H. Scroggs and Vera Wesley Shutte (*née* Coombs); *m* 1964, Patricia Mary Sutherland Ogg; two *s* one *d*. *Educ:* Reading Sch.; St John's Coll., Oxford (Sir Thos White Scholar; BA 1962). Marketing posts: AEI-Hotpoint Ltd, 1962–67; General Foods Ltd, 1967–73; Cadbury Ltd, 1973–76 (Mkting Dir, 1974–76); Mkting Dir, Leyland Cars, 1976–78; Fisons plc: Man. Dir, Scientific Equipment Div., 1979–81; Dir and Div. Chm., 1981. Dep. Chm., Sarginsons plc, 1999–2010; non-executive Director: Caradon plc, 1988–89; Montpellier Group plc (formerly Y. J. Lovell (Hldgs) plc, then YJL plc), 1990–2004 (Chm., 1999–2004); Hillingdon Hosp. NHS Trust, 1991–92; Genus plc, 1994–2000 (Dep. Chm., 1995–2000); Huntsworth (formerly Holmes & Marchant Gp) plc, 1997–2000. Advr, Müller Gp, 1997–2003. Director: Oxfordshire Mental Healthcare NHS Trust, 1995–2001; Oxford Health NHS Foundation Trust (formerly Oxon & Bucks Mental Health Partnership NHS Trust, later Oxon & Bucks Mental Health NHS Foundn Trust), 2006– (Vice Chm., 2008–); Chm., SE Oxon Primary Care Trust, 2001–02. President: BEAMA, 1991–92; CBI Nat. Mfg Council, 1992–94; Mem., Milk Mktg Bd, 1991–94. Vis. Fellow, Nuffield Coll., Oxford, 1993–2001. Gov., Reading Sch., 2010–11. Pres., Old Redingensians Assoc., 2008. *Recreations:* boating, golf, diving. *Address:* Sotwell Priory, Wallingford, Oxon OX10 0RH. *Clubs:* Leander (Henley); Huntercombe Golf (Oxon). *Died 11 Feb. 2015.*

SCRUBY, Ven. Ronald Victor, MA; Archdeacon of Portsmouth, 1977–85, then Emeritus; *b* 23 Dec. 1919; 6th *s* of late Thomas Henry Scruby and Florence Jane Scruby, Norwood Green, Southall, Middx; *m* 1955, Sylvia Tremayne Miles (*d* 1995), *e d* of late Rear-Adm. Roderic B. T. Miles, Trotton, Sussex; two *s* one *d*. *Educ:* Southall Technical Coll.; Trinity Hall, Cambridge (BA 1948; MA 1952). Engineering Apprentice, London Transport, 1936–39. Royal Engineers, 1939–45; Capt. 1943. Cuddesdon Coll., Oxford, 1948–50. Asst Curate, Rogate, Sussex, 1950–53; Chaplain, King Edward VII Hosp., Midhurst, 1950–53; Chaplain, Saunders-Roe, Osborne, E Cowes, 1953–58; Vicar of Eastney, Portsmouth, 1958–65; Rural Dean of Portsmouth, 1960–65; Archdeacon of the Isle of Wight, 1965–77. *Address:* Church House, Rogate, Petersfield, Hants GU31 5EA. *T:* (01730) 821784. *Died 31 Jan. 2011.*

SCULLARD, Geoffrey Layton, OBE 1971; HM Diplomatic Service, retired; *b* 5 July 1922; *s* of late William Harold Scullard and late Eleanor Mary Scullard (*née* Tomkin); *m* 1945, Catherine Margaret Pinington (*d* 2003); three *d*. *Educ:* St Olave's Grammar Sch. Joined Foreign Office, 1939. Served War (RAF Signals), 1942–46. Diplomatic service at Stockholm, Washington, Baghdad, Los Angeles, Moscow and in FCO. *Recreation:* birdwatching. *Address:* Albury House, 6 Albury Road, Guildford, Surrey GU1 2BT. *T:* (01483) 539915. *Clubs:* Civil Service; Bramley Golf. *Died 15 March 2014.*

SCULLY, Hugh; television presenter and producer; Founder and Chairman, Fine Art Productions, since 1988; *b* Bradford on Avon, Wilts, 5 March 1943; *s* of Wing Comdr Hugh Scully and Edith Scully; *m* 1966, Barbara Dean, Lusaka; two *s*. *Educ:* British mil. schs, Malta and Egypt; Prior Park Coll., Bath. Artists liaison, Steinway & Sons, 1960–61; Paris sabbatical, 1962–63; freelance presenter and reporter, BBC Plymouth, 1963–78; Chm., Talking About Antiques, BBC Radio 4, 1968–78; Presenter: Collectors World, BBC 2, 1970–72; Nationwide, BBC 1, 1977–84; Antiques Roadshow, BBC 1, 1980–99; The Story of English Furniture, BBC 2, 1993; Melodies for You, BBC Radio 2, 1996–99; Britain's Finest Stately Homes, ITV, 2003; Executive Producer: The Falklands War, Channel 4, 1992; Thatcher: the Downing Street Years, BBC 1, 1993; The Gulf War, BBC 1, 1995. *Recreations:* music, fine claret and long lingering lunches in France. *E:* hugh.scully@btinternet.com. *Clubs:* Athenæum; Royal Cornwall Yacht. *Died 8 Oct. 2015.*

SCURR, Dr Cyril Frederick, CBE 1980; LVO 1952; FRCS, FRCA; Hon. Consulting Anaesthetist, Westminster Hospital, since 1985 (Consultant Anaesthetist, 1949–85); Hon. Anaesthetist, Hospital of SS John and Elizabeth, 1952–94, then Emeritus; *b* 14 July 1920; *s* of Cyril Albert Scurr and Mabel Rose Scurr; *m* 1947, Isabel Jean Spiller; three *s* one *d*. *Educ:* King's Coll., London; Westminster Hosp. MB, BS. Served War of 1939–45: RAMC, 1942–47, Major, Specialist Anaesthetist. Faculty of Anaesthetists: Mem. Bd, 1961–77; Dean, 1970–73; Mem. Council, RCS, 1970–73; Pres., Assoc. of Anaesthetists of GB and Ireland, 1976–78; Mem. Health Services Bd, 1977–80; Chm., Scientific Programme, World Congress of Anaesthetists, London, 1968; Pres., 1978–79, Hon. Mem., 1988, Anaesthetics Section, RSocMed; Mem. Adv. Cttee on Distinction Awards, 1973–84; Vice-Chm., Jt Consultants Cttee, 1979–81; past Member: Cttee, Competence to Practise; Standing Med. Adv. Cttee, DHSS. Mem. d'Honneur, Société Française d'Anesthésie et de Réanimation, 1978; Academician, European Acad. of Anaesthesiology, 1978. Frederick Hewitt Lectr, RCS, 1971; Magill Centenary Oration, RCS, 1988. Dudley Buxton Prize, RCS, 1977; Gold Medal, Faculty of Anaesthetists, 1983; John Snow Medal, Assoc. of Anaesthetists of GB and Ireland, 1984. Hon. FFARCSI 1977. *Publications:* Scientific Foundations of Anaesthesia, 1970, 4th edn 1990; (jtly) Drug Mechanisms in Anaesthesia, 1987, 2nd edn 1993. *Recreations:* photography, gardening. *Address:* 16 Grange Avenue, Totteridge Common, N20 8AD. *T:* (020) 8445 7188. *Died 6 July 2012.*

SEAMAN, Gilbert Frederick, AO 1981; CMG 1967; Chairman, State Bank of South Australia, 1963–83; Deputy Chairman, Electricity Trust of SA, 1970–84; Trustee, Savings Bank of SA, 1973–81; *b* 7 Sept. 1912; *s* of Eli S. Seaman, McLaren Vale, South Australia; *m* 1935, Avenal Essie Fong; one *s* one *d*. *Educ:* University of Adelaide. BEc, Associate of University of Adelaide, 1935, High School Teacher, Port Pirie and Unley, 1932–35; South Australian Public Service, 1936–41; Seconded to Commonwealth of Australia as Assistant Director of Manpower for SA, 1941–46; Economist, SA Treasury, 1946–60; Under Treasurer for SA, 1960–72. *Address:* 27 William Street, Hawthorn, SA 5062, Australia. *T:* (8) 82714271. *Died 22 Feb. 2011.*

SEAMAN, Sir Keith (Douglas), KCVO 1981; OBE 1976; Governor of South Australia, 1977–82; *b* 11 June 1920; *s* of late E. S. and E. M. Seaman; *m* 1946, Joan (*d* 2008), *d* of F. Birbeck; one *s* one *d*. *Educ:* Unley High Sch.; Univ. of Adelaide (BA, LLB); Flinders Univ. (MA, DipHum). South

Australian Public Service, 1937–54; RAAF Overseas HQ, London, 1941–45, Flt-Lieut. Entered Methodist Ministry, 1954: Renmark, 1954–58; Adelaide Central Methodist Mission, 1958–77 (Supt, 1971–77). Sec., Christian Television Assoc. of S Australia, 1959–73; Mem. Executive, World Assoc. of Christian Broadcasting, 1963–70; Director, 5KA, 5AU and 5RM Broadcasting Companies, 1960–77; Chm., 5KA, 5AU and 5RM, 1971–77. Mem., Australian Govt Social Welfare Commn, 1973–76. KStJ 1978. *Recreations:* reading, gardening. *Address:* 28 Ruth Drive, Lenah Valley, Tas 7008, Australia. *Died 30 June 2013.*

SEARLE, Ronald William Fordham, CBE 2004; RDI 1988; AGI; artist; *b* Cambridge, 3 March 1920; *s* of William James Searle and Nellie Hunt; *m* 1st, Kaye Webb, editor and publisher (marr. diss. 1967; she *d* 1996); one *s* one *d*; 2nd, 1967, Monica Koenig (*d* 2011). *Educ:* Cambridge School of Art. Served with 287 Field Co. RE, 1939–46; captured by the Japanese at fall of Singapore, 1942; Prisoner of War in Siam and Malaya, 1942–45; Dept of Psychological Warfare, Allied Force HQ Port Said Ops, 1956. Creator of the schoolgirls of St Trinian's, 1941 (abandoned them in 1953); Cartoonist to Tribune, 1949–51; to Sunday Express, 1950–51; Special Feature artist: News Chronicle, 1951–53; Life Mag., 1955–62; Weekly Cartoonist, News Chronicle, 1954; Punch Theatre artist, 1949–62; Contributor: New Yorker and New York Times, 1966–; Le Monde, 1995–. Designer of commemorative medals for: the French Mint, 1974–; British Art Medal Soc., 1983–. FRSA 1990. DUniv Anglia Ruskin, 2007. Chevalier de la Légion d'Honneur (France), 2006; Niedersachsen Order of Merit (Germany), 2009. *One man exhibitions include:* Leicester Galls, 1948, 1950, 1954, 1957; New York, 1959, 1963, 1969, 1976; Galerie La Pochade, Paris, 1966, 1967, 1968, 1969, 1971; Galerie Gurlitt, Munich, 1967, 1968, 1969, 1970, 1971, 1973, 1976; Grosvenor Gall., London, 1968; Bibliothèque Nat., Paris, 1973; Galerie Carmen Cassé, Paris, 1975, 1976, 1977; Staatliche Mus., Berlin, 1976; Rizzoli Gall., NY, Gal. Bartsch & Chariau, Munich, 1981; Cooper-Hewitt Museum, NY, 1984; Neue Galerie Wien, 1985, 1988; Imperial War Museum, BM, 1986; Fitzwilliam Museum, Cambridge, 1987; Mus. of Fine Arts, San Francisco, 1987–88; Heineman Galls, NY, 1994; Wilhelm-Busch Mus., Hanover, 1996, (with Monica Searle), 2001, 2010; Galerie Martine Gossieaux, Paris, 2000; Forbes Galls, NY, 2007, 2010; (retrospective) Cartoon Mus., London, 2010–11; Olaf Gulbransson Mus., Tegernsee, 2011. *Works in permanent collections:* V&A, BM, Imperial War Museum, Tate Gall.; Bibliothèque Nat., Paris; Wilhelm-Busch Museum, Hanover; Staatlische Mus., Berlin; Cooper-Hewitt Museum, NY; Univ. of Texas, Austin; Mus. of Fine Arts, San Francisco; Liby of Congress, Washington, DC. *Films based on the characters of St Trinian's:* The Belles of St Trinian's, 1954; Blue Murder at St Trinian's, 1957; The Pure Hell of St Trinian's, 1960; The Great St Trinian's Train Robbery, 1966; The Wildcats of St Trinian's, 1980; St Trinian's, 2007; St Trinian's: The Legend of Fritton's Gold, 2009. *Films designed:* John Gilpin, 1951; On the Twelfth Day, 1954 (Acad. Award Nomination); Energetically Yours (USA), 1957; Germany, 1960 (for Süddeutschen RTV); The King's Breakfast, 1962; Those Magnificent Men in their Flying Machines (Animation Sequence), 1965; Monte Carlo or Bust (Animation Sequence), 1969; Scrooge (Animation Sequence), 1970; Dick Deadeye, 1975. *Publications:* Forty Drawings, 1946; Le Nouveau Ballet Anglais, 1947; Hurrah for St Trinian's!, 1948; The Female Approach, 1949; Back to the Slaughterhouse, 1951; John Gilpin, 1952; Souls in Torment, 1953; Rake's Progress, 1955; Merry England, etc, 1956; A Christmas Carol, 1961; Which Way Did He Go?, 1961; Searle in the Sixties, 1964; From Frozen North to Filthy Lucre, 1964; Pardong M'sieur, 1965; Searle's Cats, 1967; The Square Egg, 1968; Take one Toad, 1968; Baron Munchausen, 1960; Hello—where did all the people go?, 1969; Hommage à Toulouse-Lautrec, 1969; Secret Sketchbook, 1970; The Addict, 1971; More Cats, 1975; Drawings from Gilbert and Sullivan, 1975; The Zoodiac, 1977; Ronald Searle (Monograph), 1978; The King of Beasts, 1980; The Big Fat Cat Book, 1982; Illustrated Winespeak, 1983; Ronald Searle in Perspective (monograph), 1984; Ronald Searle's Golden Oldies 1941–61, 1985; To the Kwai—and Back, 1986, facsimile edn 2006; Something in the Cellar, 1986; Ah Yes, I Remember It Well…, 1987; Ronald Searle's Non-Sexist Dictionary, 1988; Slightly Foxed—but still desirable, 1989; Carnet de Croquis: le plaisir du trait, 1992; The Curse of St Trinian's, 1993; Marquis de Sade meets Goody Two-Shoes, 1994; Ronald Searle dans Le Monde, 1998; The Scrapbook Drawings, 2005; More Scraps & Watteau Revisited, 2008; What? Already?: Searle at ninety, 2010; Les Très Riches Heures de Mrs Mole, 2011; *in collaboration:* (with D. B. Wyndham Lewis) The Terror of St Trinian's, 1952; (with Geoffrey Willans) Down with Skool, 1953; How to be Topp, 1954; Whizz for Atomms, 1956; The Compleet Molesworth, 1958; The Dog's Ear Book, 1958; Back in the Jug Agane, 1959; (with Kaye Webb) Paris Sketchbook, 1950 and 1957; Looking at London, 1953; The St Trinian's Story, 1959; Refugees 1960, 1960; (with Alex Atkinson) The Big City, 1958; USA for Beginners, 1959; Russia for Beginners, 1960; Escape from the Amazon!, 1964; (with A. Andrews & B. Richardson) Those Magnificent Men in their Flying Machines, 1965; (with Heinz Huber) Haven't We Met Before Somewhere?, 1966; (with Kildare Dobbs) The Great Fur Opera, 1970; (with Irwin Shaw) Paris! Paris!, 1977; (with Sarah Kortum) The Hatless Man, 1995; (with Simon Rae) The Face of War, 1999; Le théâtre à Paris (1954–1962), 2000; (with Monica Searle) Searle & Searle, 2001; (with Robert L. Forbes) Beastly Feasts, 2007; Let's Have a Bite!, 2010; *relevant publications:* Ronald Searle: a biography, by Russell Davies, 1990; Ronald Searle: monograph, ed Gisela Vetter-Liebenow, 1996; Ronald Searle: graphic master, ed Anita O'Brien, 2010. *Address:* Sayle Literary Agency, 1 Petersfield, Cambridge CB1 1BB. *T:* (01223) 303035. *E:* rachel@sayleliteraryagency.com. *Club:* Garrick. *Died 30 Dec. 2011.*

SEBAG-MONTEFIORE, Harold Henry; barrister-at-law; Deputy Circuit Judge, 1973–83; *b* 5 Dec. 1924; *e s* of late John Sebag-Montefiore and Violet, *oc* of late James Henry Solomon; *m* 1968, Harriet, *o d* of late Benjamin Harrison Paley, New York; one *d*. *Educ:* Stowe; Lower Canada Coll., Montreal; Pembroke Coll., Cambridge (MA). Served War of 1939–45, RAF. Called to Bar, Lincoln's Inn, 1951. Mem., Disciplinary Tribunal, Bar Council. Contested (C) North Paddington, Gen. Elecn, 1959; Chm., Conservative Parly Candidates Assoc., 1960–64. Member: LCC, 1955–65 (last Alderman, Co. of London, 1961–65); GLC, for Cities of London and Westminster, 1964–73, First Chm., GLC Arts and Recreation Cttee, 1968–73; Sports Council, 1972–74. Pres., Anglo-Jewish Assoc., 1966–71; Jt Pres., Barkingside Jewish Youth Centre, 1988–94; Mem. Council, Anglo-Netherlands Soc., 1988–2001. Freeman, City of London, and Liveryman, Spectacle Makers' Co. Trustee: Royal Nat. Theatre Foundn; Internat. Festival of Youth Orchestras; Whitechapel Art Gall.; Touro National Heritage, RI; Mem., Cttee of Honour: RAH Centenary; "Fanfare for Europe"; William and Mary Tercentenary; Centenary of Montefiore Hosp., NY. Rode winner of Bar Point-to-Point, 1957 and 1959; Pres., Greater London Horse Show, 1970–73. Chevalier, Légion d'Honneur, 1973. *Publications:* obituaries; book reviews and articles on Polo under *nom-de-plume* of "Marco II". *Recreations:* theatre, travel, collecting conductors' batons. *Clubs:* Garrick, Hurlingham, Pegasus (Pres., 1979). *Died 5 Oct. 2011.*

SECCOMBE, Sir (William) Vernon (Stephen), Kt 1988; JP; Chairman, Plymouth Hospitals NHS Trust, 1993–98; former electrical contractor; *b* 14 Jan. 1928; *s* of Stephen Seccombe and Edith Violet (*née* Smith); *m* 1950, Margaret Vera Profit; four *s*. *Educ:* Saltash Grammar Sch.; Plymouth and Devonport Tech. Coll. Mem., E Cornwall Water Bd, 1960–74 (Vice-Chm., 1963–66; Chm., 1966–69); Chairman: Cornwall and Isles of Scilly DHA, later AHA, 1981–82; S Western RHA, 1983–90; Plymouth HA, 1990–93; Dep. Comr, 1970–79, Comr, 1979–82, Western Area Traffic Comrs. Member: Saltash BC, 1953–74 (Chairman: Works Cttee, 1956–62; Finance and Estabs Cttee, 1963–74; Mayor, 1962–63); Caradon DC, 1973–79 (Vice-Chm., 1973–76; Chm., 1976–78). Governor, Saltash Comprehensive Sch., 1970–81 (Chm., 1974–78). JP SE Cornwall, 1970. *Recreations:* industrial and local archaeology, genealogy (Pres., Cornwall Family History Soc., 1995–2010). *Address:* Hawks Park House, 42 Hawks Park, Saltash, Cornwall PL12 4SP. *Died 6 Dec. 2014.*

SEDGEMORE, Brian Charles John; *b* 17 March 1937; *s* of Charles John Sedgemore, fisherman; *m* 1964, (Mary) Audrey Reece (marr. diss.; remarried 2002); one *s*. *Educ:* Newtown Primary Sch.; Hele's Sch.; Corpus Christi Coll., Oxford Univ. (MA; Foundn Fellow, 2009). Diploma in public and social administration. Called to Bar, Middle Temple, 1966. RAF, 1956–58; Oxford, 1958–62. Administrative Class, Civil Service, Min. of Housing and Local Govt, 1962–66 (Private Sec. to R. J. Mellish, MP, then junior Minister of Housing, 1964–66). Practising barrister, 1966–74. MP (Lab): Luton West, Feb. 1974–1979; Hackney South and Shoreditch, 1983–2005. PPS to Tony Benn, MP, 1977–78. Researcher, Granada TV, 1980–83. *Publications:* The How and Why of Socialism, 1977; Mr Secretary of State (fiction), 1979; The Secret Constitution, 1980; Power Failure (fiction), 1985; Big Bang 2000, 1986; Pitiless Pursuit (fiction), 1994; Insider's Guide to Parliament, 1995; one time contributor to Britain's top satirical magazine. *Recreations:* art, Mozart. *Address:* 17 Sutton Square, E9 6EQ. *Club:* National Liberal. *Died 5 May 2015.*

SEED, John Junior, CEng, FIET; Chief Executive, South Western Electricity plc, 1992–95; *b* 25 Oct. 1938; *s* of John Seed and Elizabeth (*née* Earley); *m* 1961, Maureen Syder; two *d*. *Educ:* City of Norwich Grammar Sch.; Norwich City Coll. CEng 1972; FIET (FIEE 1986). Eastern Electricity: Dist Manager, Bury St Edmunds, 1976–80; Area Manager, Suffolk, 1980–82; Dir of Engrg, 1982–86; Dep. Chm., S Western Electricity Bd, 1986–90; Man. Dir, S Western Electricity plc, 1990–92. Director: Royal United Hosp. Trust, 1991–97; United Utilities plc, 1996–2005; British Smaller Companies VCT plc, 1996–2004; Prism Rail plc, 1996–2000; Rebus Gp plc, 1997–99; Weston Attenas Ltd, 2001–02; Frazer-Nash Consultancy Ltd, 2002–04; Chairman: Great Western Assured Growth plc, 1991–97; Windelectric Ltd, 1996–99; Warren Associates Ltd, 1998–2001. CCMI (FBIM 1980). *Recreations:* golf, walking, bridge. *Died 2 April 2012.*

SEGAL, Hanna Maria, FRCPsych; psycho-analyst in private practice; teacher; *b* Poland, 20 Aug. 1918; *d* of Czeslaw and Isabella Poznanski; *m* 1946, Paul Segal (*d* 1996); three *s*. *Educ:* Warsaw and Geneva; Polish Medicine Sch. in Edinburgh. Vis. Prof., Freud Meml Chair, UCL, 1987–88. Pres., 1977–80, Actg Pres., 1981–82, British Soc. Psycho-Analysis; Vice-Pres., Internat. Psychoanalytical Assoc. Founder Member: Psychoanalysts for Prevention of Nuclear War, 1983; Internat. Psychoanalysts Against Nuclear Weapons, 1985. Sigourney Award for Services to Psychoanalysis, 1992. *Publications:* Introduction to the Work of Melanie Klein, 1964, repr. 1988; Melanie Klein, 1979; The Work of Hanna Segal (collected papers), 1981, repr. 1986; (contrib.) Do I Dare Disturb the Universe? A Memorial to Wilfrid R. Bion, ed James S. Grotstein, 1981; (contrib.) Models of the Mind: their relationships to clinical work, ed Arnold Rothstein, 1985; Dream, Phantasy and Art, 1990; (contrib.) Psychoanalysis, Mind and Art: Perspectives on Richard Wollheim, 1992; (contrib.) Psychoanalysis in Contexts: paths between theory and modern culture, 1995; Psychoanalysis, Literature and War (collected papers, ed John Steiner); (contrib.) Terrorism and War: unconscious dynamics of political violence, 2002; Yesterday, Today and Tomorrow (collected papers, ed N. Abel-Hirsch), 2007; contribs to jls incl. Internat. Jl Psycho-Analysis, Internat. Rev. Psycho-Analysis, Psychoanalysis in Europe, Jl Amer. Psychoanalytic Soc., Jl de la psychoanalyse de l'enfant. *Recreations:* swimming and snorkelling, family, politics and aesthetics. *Address:* c/o Melanie Klein Trust, 21 Goodwyns Vale, N10 2HA. *T:* (020) 8883 1700. *E:* KleinTrust@aol.com. *Died 5 July 2011.*

SEIPP, Walter, Dr jur; Chairman, Supervisory Board, Commerzbank AG, 1991–99, then Hon. Chairman; *b* 13 Dec. 1925; *m* 1954, Marianne Zimmermann; two *s*. *Educ:* Univ. of Frankfurt (Law studies); final legal examination and doctorate in Law, 1950–53. Military Service, 1943–45. Deutsche Bank AG, 1951–74: Exec. Vice Pres., 1970–74; Vice Chm., UBS-DB Corp., New York, 1972–74; Westdeutsche Landesbank Girozentrale, 1974–81: Mem. Bd, 1974–81, and Dep. Chm. of the Bd, 1977–81; Chm., Bd of Man. Dirs, Commerzbank AG, 1981–91. Pres., Internat. Monetary Conf., 1987–88. *Publications:* multiple. *Address:* (office) Kaiserplatz, 60311 Frankfurt am Main, Germany. *T:* (69) 13620. *Died 4 Feb. 2015.*

SELIGMAN, Sir Peter (Wendel), Kt 1978; CBE 1969; BA; FIMechE; *b* 16 Jan. 1913; *s* of late Dr Richard Joseph Simon Seligman and of Hilda Mary Seligman; *m* 1st, 1937, Elizabeth Lavinia Mary Wheatley (*d* 2005); two *s* three *d* (and one *d* decd); 2nd, 2006, Joan Bruins. *Educ:* King's Coll. Sch., Wimbledon; Harrow Sch.; Kantonsschule, Zürich; Caius Coll., Cambridge. Joined APV Co. Ltd, as Asst to Man. Dir, 1936; appointed Dir, 1939; Man. Dir, 1947; Dep. Chm., 1961; Chm., APV Holdings Ltd, 1966–77. Director: St Regis International Ltd, 1973–83 (Vice-Chm., 1981–83); EIBIS International Ltd, 1980–90; Bell Bryant Pty Ltd, 1976–80; St Regis ACI Pty Ltd, 1980–84. Mem., Engineering Industries Council, 1975–77. Mem., Retired Chartered Engrs Assoc., 2003–05. Chm., Nat. Ski Fedn of GB, 1977–81. *Recreation:* travelling. *Address:* Church View, The Street, Thakehan, W Sussex RH20 3EP. *T:* (01798) 815726. *Clubs:* Athenæum; Hawks (Cambridge); Ski of Great Britain (Invitation Life Mem.); Kandahar Ski (Chm., 1972–77; Hon. Mem.). *Died 12 July 2012.*

SELLERS, Robert Firth, ScD; FRSE; MRCVS; consultant on foreign animal diseases; *b* 9 June 1924; *s* of Frederick Sellers and Janet Walkinshaw Shiels; *m* 1951, Margaret Peterkin; one *s* one *d*. *Educ:* Christ's Hospital; Gonville and Caius Coll., Cambridge (MA, ScD); Royal (Dick) School of Veterinary Studies, Edinburgh (PhD, BSc). FSB. Served War, Royal Artillery, 1943–46. Research Institute (Animal Virus Diseases), Pirbright, 1953–58; Wellcome Research Laboratories, Beckenham, 1958–62; Instituto Venezolano de Investigaciones Científicas, Venezuela, 1962–64; Animal Virus Research Institute, Pirbright, 1964–84, Dep. Dir, 1964–79, Dir, 1979–84; Consultant, Foreign Animal Disease Unit, Agriculture, Canada, 1985–88. J. T. Edwards Meml Medal, 1976. *Publications:* papers on animal viruses in scientific jls. *Recreation:* archaeology. *Address:* 4 Pewley Way, Guildford, Surrey GU1 3PY. *Died 25 June 2011.*

SEMPLE, Prof. Andrew Best, CBE 1966; VRD 1953; Professor of Community and Environmental Health (formerly of Public Health), University of Liverpool, 1953–77, then Professor Emeritus; *b* 3 May 1912; *m* 1941, Jean (*née* Sweet) (*d* 2013); one *d*. *Educ:* Allan Glen's School, Glasgow; Glasgow Univ. MB, ChB 1934, MD 1947, DPH 1936, Glasgow. FFCM 1972. Various hospital appointments, 1934–38; Asst MOH and Deputy Medical Superintendent, Infectious Diseases Hosp., Portsmouth, 1938–39; Asst MOH and Asst School Medical Officer, Blackburn, 1939–47 (interrupted by War Service); Senior Asst MOH, Manchester, 1947–48; Deputy MOH, City and Port of Liverpool, 1948–53, MOH and Principal Sch. Med. Officer, 1953–74; Area MO (teaching), Liverpool AHA, 1974–77. Served War of 1939–46; Surgeon Commander, RNVR; Naval MOH, Western Approaches, Malta and Central Mediterranean. Chm. Council and Hon. Treasurer, RSH, 1963. QHP 1962. *Publications:* various regarding infectious disease, port health, hygiene, etc. *Died 15 Nov. 2013.*

SENDAK, Maurice Bernard; writer and illustrator of children's books; theatrical designer; Artistic Director, The Night Kitchen, national children's theater; *b* 10 June 1928; *yr s* of Philip Sendak and Sarah (*née* Schindler). *Educ:* Lafayette High School, Brooklyn; Art Students' League, NY. Worked part-time at All American Comics; window display work with Timely Service, 1946–48, F. A. O. Schwartz, 1948–50; illustrated over 50 books by other writers, 1951–. Retrospective one-man exhibitions: Sch. of Visual Arts, NY, 1964; Ashmolean, Oxford, 1975; Amer. Cultural Center, Paris, 1978; Rosenbach Mus. and Liby, Philadelphia, 2008. *Stage designs:* The Magic Flute, Houston, 1980; The Cunning Little Vixen, NY, 1981; The Love of Three Oranges, Glyndebourne, 1982; Where the Wild Things Are, NT, 1984; L'enfant et les sortilèges, L'Heure espagnole, Glyndebourne, 1987. Hon. RDI 1986. Nat. Medal of Arts (USA), 1996. *Publications:* Kenny's Window, 1956; Very Far Away, 1957; The Sign on Rosie's

Door, 1960; Nutshell Library set, 1962; Where the Wild Things Are, 1963 (Amer. Liby Assoc. Caldecott Medal, 1964; opera, by Oliver Knussen, Glyndebourne, 1984, film, by Spike Jonze, 2009); Higglety Pigglety Pop!, 1967; Hector Protector, 1967; In the Night Kitchen, 1971; (with Charlotte Zolotow) Rabbit and the Lovely Present, 1971; Pictures, 1972; Maxfield Parrish Poster Book, 1974; (with Matthelo Margolis) Some Swell Pup, 1976; Charlotte and the White Horse, 1977; (ed) Disney Poster Book, 1977; Seven Little Monsters, 1977; (with Doris Orgel) Sarah's Room, 1977; Outside Over There, 1981; (with Frank Corsaro) The Love for Three Oranges, 1984; (with Ralph Manheim) Nutcracker, 1984; (illus.) Dear Mili, 1988; Caldecott and Company (essays), 1989; (illus.) We are all in the Dumps with Jack and Guy, 1993; (illus.) Swine Lake, 1999; (with T. Kushner) Brundibar, 2003; (with J. Sendak) The Happy Rain, 2004; (with R. Krauss) Bears, 2005; (with A. Yorinks) Mommy?, 2006; Bumble-Ardy, 2011. *Address:* c/o HarperCollins Children's Books, 1350 Avenue of the Americas, New York, NY 10019, USA. *Died 8 May 2012.*

SENIOR, Olive Edith; JP; MPhil; SRN; consultant in clinical risk, 1995–2000; Regional Nursing Officer, Trent Regional Health Authority, 1973–86; Fellow, Nottingham University, 1988–95; *b* 26 April 1934; *d* of Harold and Doris Senior, Mansfield, Notts. *Educ:* Harlow Wood Orthopaedic Hosp., 1949–52; St George's Hosp., Hyde Park Corner, 1952–56; City Hosp., Nottingham (Pt I, CMB 1956); Nottingham Univ. (HV Cert. 1957, MPhil 1978). Health Visitor, Notts CC, 1958–60; St George's Hosp., London (Ward Sister), 1960–63; S Africa, June–Dec. 1963; Forest Gate Hosp., London (SCM), 1964; St Mary's Hosp., Portsmouth (Asst Matron/Night Supt), 1964–66; NE Metropolitan Regional Hosp. Bd (Management Services), 1966–71; Chief Nursing Officer, Nottingham and Dist HMC, 1971–73. Member: Local Res. Ethics Cttee, N Notts HA, 1998–; N Notts CHC, 2001–03. Secretary of State Fellow, 1973. JP Nottingham Guildhall, 1973. *Publications:* An Analysis of Nurse Staffing Levels in Hospitals in the Trent Region (1977 Data), 1978; Dependency and Establishments, 1979; contrib. to Nursing Times (Determining Nursing Establishments). *Address:* 94 Oak Tree Lane, Mansfield, Notts NG18 3HL. *Club:* Nottingham University (Nottingham). *Died 4 Jan. 2012.*

SERENY, Gitta, Hon. CBE 2003; writer; *b* 13 March 1921; *d* of Gyula and Margit Serényi; *m* 1948, Donald Honeyman (*d* 2011); one *s* one *d*. *Educ:* Vienna Realgymnasium Luithlen; Stonar House Sch., Sandwich, Kent; Reinhardt-Seminar, Vienna; Sorbonne, Univ. of Paris. *Publications:* The Medallion (novel), 1957; *non-fiction:* The Case of Mary Bell, 1972; Into That Darkness, 1974; The Invisible Children, 1984; Albert Speer, His Battle With Truth, 1995; Cries Unheard, 1998; The Healing Wound: experiences and reflections 1938–2001, 2001; contrib. features and series to newspapers and periodicals, incl. The Times, Sunday Times and The Independent, Die Zeit, Dagens Nyheter, and NY Review of Books. *Recreation:* reading. *Address:* c/o Sayle Literary Agency, 1 Petersfield, Cambridge CB1 1BB. *Died 14 June 2012.*

SERVICE, Alastair Stanley Douglas, CBE 1995; MVO 2007; writer, historian and campaigner; *b* 8 May 1933; *s* of late Douglas William Service and Evelyn Caroline (*née* Sharp); *m* 1st, 1959, Louisa Anne Hemming (OBE 1997) (marr. diss. 1984); one *s* one *d*; 2nd, 1992, Zandria Madeleine Pauncefort. *Educ:* Westminster Sch.; Queen's Coll., Oxford. Midshipman, RNR, 1952–54. Trainee, Lazard Bros, 1956–58; Director: McKinlay, Watson and Co. Ltd, Brazil, USA and London, 1959–64 (export finance); Seeley, Service and Co. Ltd (publishers), 1965–79; Municipal Journal Ltd, 1970–78. Hon. Parly Officer: Abortion Law Reform Assoc., organising MPs' and Peers' support of Abortion Act, 1964–67; Divorce Law Reform Union, organising support of Divorce Reform Act, 1967–69; Chm., Birth Control Campaign, organising support of NHS (Family Planning) Amendment Act, 1972, and NHS Reorganisation Act, 1973 (made vasectomy and contraception available free from NHS); involved in other parly campaigns, incl.: Town and Country Amenities Act, 1974; Children's Act, 1975; Public Lending Right for Authors; One-Parent Families. Nat. Chm., 1975–80, Gen. Sec., 1980–89, FPA; Vice-Chm., Health Educn Council, 1976–87; Dep. Chm. (Sec. of State appointee), Health Educn Authy, 1987–89. Chairman: Wilts and Bath Health Commn, 1992–96; Wessex RHA, 1993–94 (non-exec. Dir, 1989–93; Vice-Chm., 1992–93); Wilts HA, 1996–2000; Wilts NHS and Local Govt Strategic Forum, 1996–2000. Vice-Pres., Interact World Wide (formerly Population Concern), 2004– (Mem., Nat. Cttee, 1973–2004; Chm., 1975–79); Mem., Adv. Panel, Population Matters (formerly Optimum Population Trust), 2005–. Mem., Nat. Cttee, Victorian Soc., 1975–95 (Chm., Publications Cttee, 1982–89); Co-Founder, Action for River Kennet, 1991– (Hon. Sec., 1991–2002). Trustee, Prince of Wales's Foundn, 1999–2002; Chm., Prince's Regeneration Through Heritage Gp, 2000–02. Chm., Avebury Soc., 2002–. Mem. Judging Panel, Patron's Award, Almshouse Assoc., 2000–05; Chm., Judging Cttee, Prince of Wales' Craft Scholarships, 2000–07. Life Member: FPA; SPAB; Victorian Soc. *Publications:* A Birth Control Plan for Britain (with Dr John Dunwoody and Dr Tom Stuttaford), 1972; The Benefits of Birth Control—Aberdeen's Experience, 1973; Edwardian Architecture and its Origins, 1975; Edwardian Architecture, 1977; The Architects of London from 1066 to Present Day, 1979; London 1900, 1979; (with Jean Bradbery) Megaliths of Europe, 1979; Lost Worlds, 1981; Edwardian Interiors, 1982; series editor, The Buildings of Britain, 1981–84, and author, Anglo-Saxon and Norman Buildings vol., 1982; Victorian and Edwardian Hampstead, 1989; The Standing Stones of Europe, 1993; Sky Speaker (opera libretto; music by James Harpham), 1999; An Avebury Carol (Christmas carol; music by Robin Nelson), 2002; The Angel Cantata (cantata; music by Robin Nelson), 2003; Brunel's Kingdom (cantata; music by Robin Nelson), 2005; articles in Arch. Rev., Guardian, Independent, Oldie, etc. *Recreations:* Italy, Greece, Scotland, looking at buildings (old, new and megalithic), opera (esp. Verdi and Bellini), cycling, Dalmatian dogs, et al. *Address:* Swan House, Avebury, Wilts SN8 1RA. *Club:* Garrick. *Died 20 March 2013.*

SEVERN, Prof. Roy Thomas, CBE 1992; FREng, FICE; Professor of Civil Engineering, Bristol University, 1968–95, then Emeritus; *b* 6 Sept. 1929; *s* of Ernest Severn and Muriel Woollatt; *m* 1957, Hilary Irene Saxton; two *d*. *Educ:* Deacon's School, Peterborough; Imperial College (DSc). Lectr, Imperial College, 1949–54; Royal Engineers (Survey), 1954–56; Bristol University: Lectr, 1956–65; Reader, 1965–68; Dean of Faculty of Engrg, 1970–73 and 1991–94; Pro-Vice Chancellor, 1981–84. Pres., ICE, 1991. FREng (FEng 1981). *Publications:* (ed) Engineering Structures: developments in the twentieth century, 1983; The Development of the Faculty of Engineering at the University of Bristol, 1909–2009: a history to mark its centenary, 2009; contribs to Procs of ICE, Jl Earthquake Eng. and Structural Dynamics. *Recreations:* sailing, gardening, cricket. *Address:* 49 Gloucester Road, Rudgeway, Bristol BS35 3SF. *T:* (01454) 412027. *Died 25 Nov. 2012.*

SEVERNE, Air Vice-Marshal Sir John (de Milt), KCVO 1988 (LVO 1961); OBE 1968; AFC 1955; Extra Equerry to the Queen, since 1984; *b* 15 Aug. 1925; *s* of late Dr A. de M. Severne, Wateringbury, Kent; *m* 1951, Katharine Veronica, *d* of late Captain V. E. Kemball, RN (Retd); three *d*. *Educ:* Marlborough. Joined RAF, 1944; Flying Instr, Cranwell, 1948; Staff Instr and PA to Comdt CFS, 1950–53; Flt Comdr No 98 Sqdn, Germany, 1954–55; Sqdn Comdr No 26 Sqdn, Germany, 1956–57; Air Min., 1958; Equerry to Duke of Edinburgh, 1958–61; psa 1962; Chief Instr No 226 Operational Conversion Unit (Lightning), 1963–65; jssc 1965; Jt HQ, ME Comd, Aden, and Air Adviser to the South Arabian Govt, 1966–67; DS, JSSC, 1968; Gp Captain Organisation, HQ Strike Comd, 1968–70; Stn Comdr, RAF Kinloss, 1971–72; RCDS 1973; Comdt, Central Flying School, RAF, 1974–76; Air Cdre Flying Trng, HQ RAF Support Comd, 1976–78; Comdr, Southern Maritime Air Region, Central Sub-Area Eastern Atlantic Comd, and Plymouth Sub-Area Channel Comd, 1978–80; retd 1980; recalled as Captain of the Queen's Flight, 1982–89. ADC to The Queen, 1972–73. Hon. Air Cdre, No 3 (Co. of Devon) Maritime HQ Unit, RAuxAF, 1990–95. President: SW Area Council, RAFA, 1981–95; Queen's Flight Assoc., 1990–2000; CFS Assoc.,

1993–98; Taunton and dist Br., ESU, 1996–2009. Pres., RAF Equitation Assoc., 1976–79 (Chm. 1973); Chm., Combined Services Equitation Assoc., 1977–79 (Vice-Chm., 1976). Won King's Cup Air Race, British Air Racing Champion, 1960. DL Somerset, 1991–2001. *Publications:* Silvered Wings (memoirs), 2007. *Address:* Ashley House, Alhampton, Shepton Mallet, Somerset BA4 6PY. *Club:* Royal Air Force. *Died 4 Oct. 2015.*

SHACKLETON, Keith Hope, MBE 2012; artist and naturalist; President, Society of Wildlife Artists, 1978–83; Chairman, Artists League of Great Britain; *b* 16 Jan. 1923; *s* of W. S. Shackleton; *m* 1951, Jacqueline Tate; two *s* one *d*. *Educ:* Oundle. Served RAF, 1941–46. Civil Pilot and Dir, Shackleton Aviation Ltd, 1948–63; natural history programmes for television, 1964–68; joined naturalist team aboard MS Lindblad Explorer, 1969. Pres., Royal Soc. of Marine Artists, 1973–78. Member: RGS; Zool Soc. of London; NZ Antarctic Soc. Vice Pres., Wildfowl and Wetlands Trust, 1994–. Trustee, UK Antarctic Heritage Trust, 1997–2000. Hon. LLD Birmingham, 1983. *Publications:* Tidelines, 1951; Wake, 1953; Wild Animals in Britain, 1959; Ship in the Wilderness, 1986; Wildlife and Wilderness, 1986; Keith Shackleton: an autobiography in paintings, 1998; Shakewell Afloat, 2004; illustrations for books. *Recreations:* small Boat Sailing, exploration field work. *Address:* 39 Holmead Walk, Poundbury, Dorchester DT1 3GE. *Club:* Itchenor Sailing. *Died 17 April 2015.*

SHAKERLEY, Sir Geoffrey (Adam), 6th Bt *cr* 1838; Chairman, Photographic Records Ltd, since 1972; *b* 9 Dec. 1932; *s* of Sir Cyril Holland Shakerley, 5th Bt, and Elizabeth Averil (MBE 1955; *d* 1990), *d* of late Edward Gwynne Eardley-Wilmot; *S* father, 1970; *m* 1st, 1962, Virginia Elizabeth (*d* 1968), *d* of W. E. Maskell; two *s*; 2nd, 1972, Lady Elizabeth Georgiana (marr. diss. 2009), *d* of late Viscount Anson and Princess Georg of Denmark; one *d*; 3rd, 2010, Virginia, *widow* of Richard Elworthy. *Educ:* Harrow; Trinity College, Oxford. *Publications:* Henry Moore Sculptures in Landscape, 1978; The English Dog at Home, 1986. *Heir: s* Nicholas Simon Adam Shakerley, *b* 20 Dec. 1963. *Address:* Brent House, North Warnborough, Hants RG29 1BE. *Died 3 Dec. 2012.*

SHALIKASHVILI, Gen. John Malchase David; Chairman, Joint Chiefs of Staff, USA, 1993–97; Visiting Professor, Center for International Security and Co-operation, Stanford University; *b* Poland, 27 June 1936; *s* of Dimitri Shalikashvili and Maria Shalikashvili (*née* Ruediger); *m* 1st, 1963, Gunhild Bartsch (*d* 1965); 2nd, 1966, Joan Zimpelman; one *s*. *Educ:* Bradley Univ. (BS Mech. Eng 1958); George Washington Univ. (MS Internat. Affairs 1970); Officer Candidate Sch. Commissioned Artillery, 1959; served USA, Germany, Vietnam, Korea, Italy; Office of DCS for Ops, 1981–84 and 1986–87; Asst Div. Comdr, 1st Armd Div., 1984–86; Commanding Gen., 9th Inf. Div., 1987–89; Dep. C-in-C, US Army Europe and 7th Army, 1989–91; Asst to Chm., Jt Chiefs of Staff, 1991–92; Supreme Allied Comdr, Europe, and C-in-C, US European Command, 1992–93. *Address:* 55 Chapman Loop, Steilacoom, WA 98388–1731, USA. *Died 23 July 2011.*

SHAMS-UD DOHA, Aminur Rahman; Minister for Foreign Affairs, Government of the People's Republic of Bangladesh, 1982–84; Publisher and Editor-in-Chief: Dialogue Publications Ltd, Dhaka; Dialogue, international English weekly, since 1988; *b* 24 Jan. 1929; *m* 1950, Shahnaz Begum; two *s*; *m* 1981, Wajiha Moukaddem. *Educ:* Calcutta and Dacca Univs (BSc Hons; BA). Commnd 2nd Lieut, Pakistan Artillery, 1952; Sch. of Artillery and Guided Missiles, Ft Sill, Okla, USA, 1957–58; Gen. Staff Coll., Quetta, 1962; GS Inf. Bde HQ, 1963; RMCS, Shrivenham, 1964–65; Sen. Instr, Gunnery, 1965; GS GHQ, 1965–66; retired, 1968 (Major). Editor and Publisher, Inter-Wing, Rawalpindi, 1968–71; Gen. Sec., Awami League, Rawalpindi, 1969–71, and Mem. Working Cttee; Ambassador of Bangladesh to: Yugoslavia and Roumania, 1972–74; Iran and Turkey, 1974–77; High Comr for Bangladesh in UK, 1977–82; Minister for Information, Bangladesh, March–June 1982. Member and Leader of Bangladesh delegns to numerous internat., Islamic and Commonwealth meetings. Associate Mem., Inst. of Strategic Studies, London. C-in-C's Commendation, 1964; several military awards and decorations. Order of the Lance and Flag, Cl. 1 (Yugoslavia); Order of Diplomatic Service, Gwanghwa Medal (S Korea). *Publications:* Arab-Israeli War, 1967; The Emergence of South Asia's First Nation State; Aryans on the Indus (MS); In the Shadow of the Eagle and the Bear (MS). *Recreations:* sport (selected for all India Trials, London Olympics, 1948), writing, gardening. *Clubs:* English-Speaking Union, Royal Over-Seas League. *Died 3 March 2012.*

SHAND, Rt Rev. David Hubert Warner; Assistant Bishop and Bishop in Geelong, Diocese of Melbourne, Archbishop's Provincial Assistant, 1985–88; *b* 6 April 1921; *s* of late Rev. Canon Rupert Warner Shand and Madeleine Ethel Warner Shand; *m* 1946, Muriel Jean Horwood Bennett; one *s* three *d*. *Educ:* The Southport Sch., Queensland; St Francis' Theological Coll., Brisbane (ThL, 2nd Cl. Hons); Univ. of Queensland (BA, 2nd Cl. Hons). Served War, AIF, 1941–45: Lieut, 1942. St Francis' Coll., Brisbane, 1946–48. Deacon, 1948; priest, 1949; Asst Curate, Lutwyche. Served in Parishes: Moorooka, Inglewood, Nambour, Ipswich; Org. Sec., Home Mission Fund, 1960–63; Rural Dean of Ipswich, 1963–66; Dio. of Brisbane: Chaplain CMF, 1950–57; Vicar, Christ Church, South Yarra, 1966–69; St Andrew's, Brighton, 1969–73; Rural Dean of St Kilda, 1972–73; Dio. of Melbourne: consecrated Bishop, St Paul's Cathedral, Melbourne, Nov. 1973; Bishop of St Arnaud, 1973–76 (when diocese amalgamated with that of Bendigo); Vicar of St Stephen's, Mt Waverley, 1976–78; Bishop of the Southern Region, 1978–85. Chm., Gen. Bd of Religious Educn, 1974–84. *Recreation:* carpentry. *Address:* 27 Weerona Way, Mornington, Vic 3931, Australia. *Died 8 July 2011.*

SHANKAR, Ravi, Hon. KBE 2001; Presidential Padma Vibhushan Award, 1980; Bharat Ratna, 1999; musician and composer; MP (Member of Rajya Sabha) India, since 1986; *b* 7 April 1920; *m* 1989, Sukanya Rajan; one *d*, and one *d* by Sue Jones (one *s* decd). *Educ:* Studied with brother Uday Shankar in Paris, 1930, with Ustad Allaudin Khan in Maihar, 1938–. Music Dir, All-India Radio, 1949–56; music and choreography for ASIAD 82 (Asian Games, New Delhi, 1982). Fellow, Sangeet Natak Akademi, 1977 (President's Award, 1962); Member, Nat. Acad. for Recording Arts and Sciences, 1966. Over 50 recordings, including recordings with Yehudi Menuhin, Jean-Pierre Rampal, Philip Glass, and others. Received 17 hon. doctorates in letters and arts including Harvard Univ., Univ. of Calcutta. Deshikottam Award, 1982; Praemium Imperiale, 1997; Juliet Hollister Award, 1997; Polar Music Prize, Sweden, 1998; Fellowship Award, Asian Awards, 2011. Commandeur de la Legion d'Honneur (France), 2000. *Compositions:* Indian ragas; music for ballet, and films incl. Gandhi, 1983; Concertos for sitar and orch., No 1, 1971, No 2, 1981, No 3, 2008; Ghanashyam—A Broken Branch, 1989. *Publications:* My Music My Life, 1968; Raga Mala (autobiog.), 1997. *Recreations:* films, people, music, theatre. *Address:* c/o Sulivan Sweetland, 1 Hillgate Place, Balham Hill, SW12 9ER; Ravi Shankar Institute for Music and Performing Arts, 7 Chanakyapuri, New Delhi 110021, India. *Died 11 Dec. 2012.*

SHANNON, 9th Earl of, *cr* 1756; **Richard Bentinck Boyle;** Viscount Boyle, Baron of Castle-Martyr, 1756; Baron Carleton (GB), 1786; late Captain Irish Guards; Director of companies; *b* 23 Oct. 1924; *o s* of 8th Earl of Shannon; *S* father, 1963; *m* 1st, 1947, Catherine Irene Helen (marr. diss. 1955), *d* of the Marquis Demetrio Imperiali di Francavilla; 2nd, 1957, Susan Margaret (marr. diss. 1979), *d* of late J. P. R. Hogg; one *s* two *d*; 3rd, 1994, Almine, *d* of late Rocco Catorsia de Villiers, Cape Town. *Educ:* Eton College. A Dep. Speaker and Dep. Chm. of Cttees, House of Lords, 1968–78; Chm., British-Armenian All-Party Parly Gp, 1992–99. Dir, Cttee of Dirs of Res. Assocs, 1969–85; Sec. and Treas., Fedn of Eur. Indust. Co-operative Res. Orgns, 1971–86; President: Architectural Metalwork Assoc., 1966–74; Kent Br., BIM, 1970–87; Vice-President: Aslib, 1974; British Hydromechanics Res. Assoc., 1975–87; Foundn for Sci. and Tech. (founding Chm., 1977–83); IWA. FRSA, FCMI, FBHI. Provincial Grand Master, Masonic Province of Surrey, 1967–99. Patron, Freemen of England and Wales, 2000–. *Heir: s*

Viscount Boyle, *b* 19 Jan. 1960. *Address:* Pimm's Cottage, Man's Hill, Burghfield Common, Berks RG7 3BD. *Club:* White's. *Died 9 May 2013.*

SHARON, Maj. Gen. Ariel; Prime Minister of Israel and Minister of Immigrant Absorption, 2001–06; Leader, Likud Party, 1999–2005; founded Kadima Party, 2005; Member, Knesset, 1973–74 and 1977–2006; *b* 27 Feb. 1928; *s* of Schmuel and Devorah Sharon; *m* 1st 1953, Margalit Zimmerman (*d* 1962) (one *s* decd); 2nd, 1963, Lili Zimmerman (*d* 2000); two *s*. *Educ:* Hebrew Univ.; Tel Aviv Univ. (LLB). Joined Haganah, 1942; Instructor, Haganah Police units, 1947; Platoon Comdr, Alexandroni Bde, 1948; Regtl Intelligence Officer, Israeli Army, 1948; Co. Comdr, 1949; Comdr, Bde Reconnaissance Unit, 1949–50; Intelligence Officer, Central and Northern Comds, 1951–52; Hd, Commando Unit 101, 1953–57; Comdr, Paratroopers Bde 202, Sinai Campaign, 1956; staff coll., Camberley, UK, 1957–58; Trng Comdr, Gen. Staff and Hd, Infantry Sch., 1958–62; Comdr, Armoured Bde, 1962; Chief of Northern Comd, 1964; Chief of Gen. HQ Trng Dept, 1966; Comdr, Armoured Reserve Div. 138, Six-Day War, 1967; Chief of Southern Comd, 1969; resigned from Army, 1973; recalled as Comdr, Armd Reserve Div. 143, Yom Kippur War, 1973. Founder Mem., Likud Front, 1973; Security Advr to Prime Minister of Israel, 1975–77. Minister: of Agriculture, 1977–81; of Defence, 1981–83; without portfolio, 1983–84; of Trade and Industry, 1984–90; of Construction and Housing, 1990–92; of Nat. Infrastructure, 1996–99; of Foreign Affairs, 1998–99. Mem., Foreign Affairs and Defence Cttee, Knesset, 1992–96. *Publications:* Warrior (autobiog.), 1989; articles in newspapers. *Address:* c/o Office of the Prime Minister, PO Box 187, 3 Rehov Kaplan, Kiryat Ben-Gurion, Jerusalem 91919, Israel. *Died 11 Jan. 2014.*

SHARPE, Thomas Ridley; novelist; *b* 30 March 1928; *s* of Rev. George Coverdale Sharpe and Grace Egerton Sharpe; *m* 1969, Nancy Anne Looper; three *d*. *Educ:* Lancing College; Pembroke Coll., Cambridge (MA). National service, Royal Marines, 1946–48. Social worker 1952, teacher 1952–56, photographer 1956–61, in S Africa; Lecturer in History, Cambridge Coll. of Arts and Technology, 1963–71; full time novelist, 1971–. Lauréat, Le Grand Prix de l'Humour Noir, Paris, 1986; Légion de l'Humour, Assoc. for Promotion of Humour in Internat. Affairs, Paris, 1986. *Publications:* Riotous Assembly, 1971; Indecent Exposure, 1973; Porterhouse Blue, 1974 (televised, 1987); Blott on the Landscape, 1975 (televised, 1985); Wilt, 1976 (filmed, 1989); The Great Pursuit, 1977; The Throwback, 1978; The Wilt Alternative, 1979; Ancestral Vices, 1980; Vintage Stuff, 1982; Wilt on High, 1984; Grantchester Grind, 1995; The Midden, 1996; Wilt in Nowhere, 2004; The Gropes, 2009; The Wilt Inheritance, 2010. *Recreations:* gardening, photography, conversation. *Address:* c/o Sheil Land Associates Ltd, 52 Doughty Street, WC1N 2LS. *Died 6 June 2013.*

SHAW, Maj.-Gen. Anthony John, CB 1988; CBE 1985; Director General, Army Medical Services, 1988–90; *b* 13 July 1930; *s* of late Lt Col W. A. Shaw, MC and Mrs E. Shaw (*née* Malley); *m* 1961, Gillian Shaw (*née* Best); one *s* one *d*. *Educ:* Epsom College; Clare College, Cambridge (MA; MB BChir); Westminster Hosp. MRCS; LRCP 1954; D(Obst)RCOG 1956; DTM&H 1961; FFCM 1983; FRCP 1989. Casualty Officer, Westminster Hosp.; House Surgeon and Obst. House Officer, Kingston Hosp., 1955–56; Commissioned Lieut RAMC, 1956; Staff College, 1963; served in UK, Malta, Berlin, BAOR, MoD, Malaya, Nepal, Penang, Cameron Highlands; CO 28 Field Ambulance, 1969–70; Chief Instructor, RAMC Training Centre, 1970–72; Nat. Defence Coll., 1973; ADGMS, MoD, 1973–76; CO Cambridge Mil. Hosp., 1977–79; Comdr Med. 2 Armd Div., BAOR, 1979–81; Comdr Med. SE Dist, 1981; Dir of Med. Supply, MoD, 1981–83; DDGAMS, 1983–84; Dir, Army Community and Occupational Medicine, 1983–87; Comdr Medical Servs, UKLF, 1984–87. QHP 1983–90. Member: BMA; Board of Faculty of Community Medicine, 1983–87. Pres., Standing Med. Bd, Aldershot, 1995–2005. Fellow, Med. Soc. of London, 1988. Freeman, City of London, 1990. CStJ 1989. *Died 27 July 2015.*

SHAW, Sir Brian (Piers), Kt 1986; Chairman, Port of London Authority, 1993–2000 (Member, 1987–2000); *b* 21 March 1933; *s* of Percy Augustus Shaw and Olive Shaw (*née* Hart); *m* 1962, Penelope Reece; three *s*. *Educ:* Wrekin Coll.; Corpus Christi Coll., Cambridge (BA 1956; MA 1960). National Service (2nd Lieut, Cheshire Regt), 1951–53. Called to Bar, Gray's Inn, 1957, Bencher, 1992. Joined Pacific Steam Navigation Co., Liverpool, 1957; Company Secretary, 1960; Company Sec., Royal Mail Lines, London, 1961; Dir, Royal Mail Lines, 1968–87; Furness Withy & Co.: Manager, 1969; Dir, 1973; Man. Dir, 1977–87; Chm., 1979–90; Chairman: Shaw Savill & Albion Co., 1973–87; ANZ Grindlays Bank, 1987–95; Director: Overseas Containers Ltd, 1972–80; Nat. Bank of NZ, 1973–77 (London Board, 1977–80; Chm., London Adv. Cttee, 1980–84); New Zealand Line, 1974–79; Grindlays Bank, 1977–85; Orient Overseas (Holdings), 1980–91; ANZ Holdings (UK), 1985–87; Enterprise Oil, 1986–98; Walter Runciman, 1988–90; Andrew Weir, 1991–2003; Henderson plc, 1998–2000; Centrica plc, 1999–2003. Mem., Gen. Cttee, Lloyd's Register of Shipping, 1974–2000; Chairman: Internat. Chamber of Shipping, 1987–92; Council of European and Japanese Nat. Shipowners' Assocs (CENSA), 1979–84; Pres., Gen. Council of British Shipping, 1985–86. Automobile Association: Mem. Cttee, 1988–99; Treas., 1990–93; Vice-Chm., 1992–95; Chm., 1995–99; Chm., Motoring Trust, 2002–05. Pres., New Zealand Soc., 1979–80; Chm., Cook Soc., 1995. Pres., Seamen's Hosp. Soc., 2003–. Prime Warden, Shipwrights' Co., 1993–94; Freeman, Watermen and Lightermen's Co., 1994; Elder Brother, Trinity House, 1989–. *Recreations:* golf, music, theatre, cricket. *Address:* The Coach House, Biddestone, Wilts SN14 7DQ. *T:* (01249) 713112; 3A Lansdowne Road, W11 3AL. *T:* (020) 7221 4066. *Clubs:* Brooks's, MCC; Denham Golf. *Died 5 Feb. 2011.*

SHAW, Prof. C(harles) Thurstan, CBE 1972; FBA 1991; Professor of Archaeology, University of Ibadan, 1963–74; *b* 27 June 1914; 2nd *s* of late Rev. John Herbert Shaw and Grace Irene (*née* Woollatt); *m* 1st, 1939, Gilian Ione Maud (*d* 1992), *e d* of late Edward John Penberthy Magor and Gilian Sarah (*née* Westmacott); two *s* three *d*; 2nd, 2004, Pamela Jane Smith, PhD, *d* of Loren Reed Smith and Agnes (*née* Palmer). *Educ:* Blundell's Sch.; Sidney Sussex Coll., Cambridge (1st cl. hons Arch. and Anthrop. Tripos 1936; MA; PhD; Hon. Fellow 1994); Univ. of London Inst. of Education (DipEd). FRAI 1938; FSA 1947. Curator, Anthropology Museum, Achimota Coll., Gold Coast, 1937–45; Cambs Educn Cttee, 1945–51; Cambridge Inst. of Educn, 1951–63; Dir of Studies, Archaeol. and Anthrop., Magdalene Coll., Cambridge, 1976–79. Vis. Fellow, Clare Hall, Cambridge, 1973; Vis. Prof., Northwestern Univ., USA, 1969; Vis. Res. Prof., Ahmadu Bello Univ., 1975–78; Visiting Lecturer: Harvard, 1975; Yale, 1979; Calgary, 1980; Hans Wolff Meml Lectr, Indiana Univ., 1984. Founder and Editor: W African Archaeological Newsletter, 1964–70; W African Jl of Archaeology, 1971–75. Mem. Perm. Council, Internat. Union of Pre- and Proto-historic Sciences, 1965–74; Vice-Pres., Panafrican Congress on Prehistory and Study of Quaternary, 1966–77; Dir, and Mem. Exec. Cttee, World Archaeol Congress, 1986–89. Founder, and Chm., Icknield Way Assoc., 1984–89, Pres., 1989–; Pres., Prehistoric Soc., 1986–90. Mem. Council, Univ. of Ibadan, 1969–71. Hon. DSc: Univ. of Nigeria, 1982; Ibadan, 1989. Amaury Talbot Prize, Royal Anthrop. Inst., 1970 and 1978; Gold Medal, Soc. of Antiquaries, 1990. Onuna-Ekwulu Ora of Igbo-Ukwu, 1972; Onyofuonka of Igboland, 1989; Onuna Ekwulu Nri, 1989; Olokun-Ayala of Ife, 1991. *Publications:* Excavation at Dawu, 1961; Archaeology and Nigeria, 1964; (with J. Vanderburg) Bibliography of Nigerian Archaeology, 1969; (ed) Nigerian Prehistory and Archaeology, 1969; Igbo-Ukwu: an account of archaeological discoveries in eastern Nigeria, 2 vols, 1970; Discovering Nigeria's Past, 1975; Why 'Darkest' Africa?, 1975; Unearthing Igbo-Ukwu, 1977; Ancient People and Places: Nigeria, 1978; (with S. G. H. Daniels) Excavations at Iwo Eleru, Ondo State, Nigeria, 1988; (with K. D. Aiyedun) Prehistoric Settlement and Subsistence in the Kaduna Valley, Nigeria, 1989; (ed jtly) The Archaeology of Africa, 1993; *festschrift:* (ed jtly) Africa:

the challenge of archaeology, 1998; numerous articles on African archaeology and prehistory in jls. *Recreations:* walking, music, calligraphy. *Address:* 3 Brooklyn Court, Cherry Hinton Road, Cambridge CB1 7HF. *T:* (01223) 413669. *Clubs:* Athenæum; Explorers (New York). *Died 8 March 2013.*

SHAW, Colin Don, CBE 1993; writer and lecturer; Director, Broadcasting Standards Council, 1988–96; *b* 2 Nov. 1928; *s* of late Rupert M. Shaw and Enid F. Shaw (*née* Smith); *m* 1955, Elizabeth Ann, *d* of late Paul Bowker; one *s* twin *d*. *Educ:* Liverpool Coll.; St Peter's Hall, Oxford (MA). Called to the Bar, Inner Temple, 1960. Nat. Service, RAF, 1947–49. Joined BBC as Radio Drama Producer, North Region, 1953; Asst, BBC Secretariat, 1957–59; Asst Head of Programme Contracts Dept, 1959–60; Sen. Asst, BBC Secretariat, 1960–63; special duties in connection with recruitment for BBC2, 1963; Asst Head of Programmes, BBC North Region, 1963–66; various posts in TV Programme Planning, ending as Head of Group, 1966–69; Secretary to the BBC, 1969–72, Chief Secretary, 1972–76; Dir of Television, IBA, 1977–83; Dir, Programme Planning Secretariat, ITCA, 1983–87. Vis. Fellow, Eur. Inst. for the Media, Düsseldorf, 1985–98; Vis. Lectr, Annenberg Sch. of Communications, Univ. of Pa, 1988; Manchester University: Hon. Lectr in Educn, 1994–96; Hon. Prof., 1996–99. Member: Arts Council of GB, 1978–80 (Chairman: Arts Council Research Adv. Gp, 1978–80; Housing the Arts Cttee, 1979–80; Touring Cttee, 1980); Home Office Working Party on Fear of Crime, 1990. Trustee, Internat. Inst. of Communications, 1983–89; Chm., Voice of the Listener Trust, 2004–05. Governor, E-SU of the Commonwealth, 1976–83; Chm., Bd of Governors, Hampden House Sch., 1972–77. FRTS 1987. *Publications:* Deciding what we watch: taste, decency and media ethics in the UK and the USA, 1999; (with A. Millwood Hargrave) Accountability and the Public Interest in Broadcasting, 2009; several radio plays and a stage-play for children. *Recreations:* going to the theatre, reading. *Address:* Lesters, Little Ickford, Aylesbury, Bucks HP18 9HS. *T:* (01844) 339225. *Died 18 Sept. 2014.*

SHAW, Maj.-Gen. Dennis, CB 1991; CBE 1983 (OBE 1978); FIMechE; Director General Electrical and Mechanical Engineering (Army), 1988–91; *b* 11 May 1936; *s* of Nathan Shaw and Frances Ellen (*née* Cookson); *m* 1955, Barbara Tate; two *d*. *Educ:* Humberstone Foundn Sch.; Scunthorpe Grammar Sch.; Royal Military Coll. of Science. BScEng 1st Cl. Hons, London. Commd into REME, 1956; served in Cyprus, 1957–58, and with 3 Commando Bde, Far East, 1963–66; sc Shrivenham and Camberley, 1967–68; Staff of High Commn, Ottawa, 1969–70; comd 1 Corps Troops Workshop, W Germany, 1971–72; Dep. Asst Adjt Gen., MoD, 1972–74; NDC Latimer, 1974–75; comd Commando Logistic Regt, RM, 1975–78; Instr, Ghana Armed Forces Staff Coll., Accra, 1978–80; ACOS in Comd HQ, 1981–83; served Logistic Executive (Army), 1983; RCDS 1984; ACOS, HQ UKLF, 1985–87. Col Comdt, REME, 1991–95. Dir, Greig Fester Group Services Ltd, 1994–96 (Gp Advr, 1992–96). Hon. Mem., RM Officers' Dining Club. Liveryman, Turners' Co., 1990– (Clerk, 1996–97). Freeman, City of London, 1990. *Recreations:* golf, motoring. *Address:* c/o Royal Bank of Scotland, Laurie House, Victoria Road, Farnborough, Hants GU14 7NR. *Club:* Gainsborough Golf. *Died 20 Jan. 2011.*

SHAW, Rev. Canon Geoffrey Norman; Principal, Wycliffe Hall, Oxford, 1979–89; Hon. Canon Emeritus of Christ Church Cathedral, Oxford, since 1989 (Hon. Canon, 1985–89); *b* 15 April 1926; *s* of Samuel Norman Shaw and Maud Shaw; *m* 1st, 1948, Cynthia Brown (*d* 1997); one *s* two *d*; 2nd, 1998, Margaret Dorothy Thurlow. *Educ:* Holgate Grammar Sch., Barnsley; Jesus Coll., Oxford (MA); Wycliffe Hall, Oxford. Asst Curate, St Mary, Rushden, 1951–54; Vicar of St Paul, Woking, 1954–62; Rector of St Leonards-on-Sea, Sussex, 1962–68; Asst Master, Ecclesfield Grammar Sch., Sheffield, 1968–69; Head of Religious Educn and Classics, Silverdale Sch., Sheffield, 1969–72; Vice-Principal, Oak Hill Theol Coll., Southgate, 1972–79. Hon. Asst Chaplain, Kingham Hill Sch., 1992–2008. *Recreations:* bird watching, walking, golf, music. *Address:* 15A West Street, Kingham, Oxon OX7 6YQ. *T:* (01608) 658006. *E:* canonshaw@aol.com. *Died 12 Feb. 2011.*

SHAW, Geoffrey Peter; QC 1991; *b* 19 April 1944; *s* of late James Adamson Shaw and Hilda Gargett Shaw (*née* Edwards); *m* 1985, Susan Cochrane. *Educ:* Worksop College, Notts; Worcester College, Oxford (BA, BCL). Teaching Fellow, Univ. of Chicago Law Sch., 1966; Arden Scholar of Gray's Inn, 1967; called to the Bar, Gray's Inn, 1968; defamation specialist. CEDR accredited mediator, 2003. *Recreations:* walking, travel, gardening. *Address:* 1 Brick Court, Temple, EC4Y 9BY. *T:* (020) 7353 8845. *E:* clerks@onebrickcourt.com. *Died 12 Oct. 2014.*

SHAW, Sir (George) Neville B.; *see* Bowman-Shaw.

SHAW, Sir John Michael Robert B.; *see* Best-Shaw.

SHAW, Sir Neville B.; *see* Bowman-Shaw.

SHAW, Captain Peter Jack, CBE 1990; RN (retd); General Secretary, British Group Inter-Parliamentary Union, 1979–90; Consultant to President, Interparliamentary Council, 1991–93; *b* Geelong, Australia, 27 Oct. 1924; *s* of late Jack and Betty Shaw; *m* 1951, Pauline, *e d* of Sir Frank Madge, 2nd Bt, and Lady (Doris) Madge, East Grinstead; one *s* one *d*. *Educ:* Watford Grammar School; RNC Dartmouth; RN Staff Coll. Greenwich; NATO Defence Coll., Paris. FCIL (FIL 1957). War service in HM Ships Kenya, Resolution, Quadrant, Kelvin, incl. Malta and Russian Convoys and D-Day landings; comd HM Ships Venus, Carron, Vigilant, 1958–61; Staff, C-in-C Portsmouth and MoD, 1961–65; SHAPE, Paris and Mons, 1966–68; Comdr, RN Coll. Greenwich, 1968–70; Defence and Naval Attaché, The Hague, 1971–73; Captain of Port and Queen's Harbourmaster, Plymouth, 1973–76; Captain of Port, Chatham, 1976–79. *Recreations:* international relations, foreign languages, domestic pursuits. *Address:* Woodside, Rogate, Petersfield, Hants GU31 5DJ. *T:* (01730) 821344. *Died 10 Feb. 2015.*

SHAW, Sir Roy, Kt 1979; Secretary General of the Arts Council of Great Britain, 1975–83; *b* 8 July 1918; *s* of Frederick and Elsie Shaw; *m* 1946, Gwenyth Baron; five *s* two *d*. *Educ:* Firth Park Grammar School, Sheffield; Manchester Univ. BA(Hons). Newspaper printing department 'copy-holder', 1937; newspaper publicity, 1938; Library Asst, Sheffield City Library, 1939; Cataloguer, Manchester Univ. Library, 1945; Organizing Tutor, WEA, 1946; Adult Educn Lectr, Leeds Univ., 1947; Warden, Leeds Univ. Adult Educn Centre, Bradford, 1959; Professor and Dir of Adult Educn, Keele Univ., 1962. Vis. Prof., Centre for Arts, City Univ., London, 1977–83. Theatre critic, The Tablet, 1990–2000. Hon. DLitt: City, 1978; Southampton, 1984; DUniv Open, 1981. *Publications:* The Arts and the people, 1987; (ed) The Spread of Sponsorship, 1993; contrib. chapters to: Trends in English Adult Education, 1959; The Committed Church, 1966; Your Sunday Paper, 1967; (jtly) Cambridge Guide to the Arts in Britain, vol. 9: since the second world war, 1988; over 170 articles and book chapters on cultural policy, adult education and the mass media. *Recreations:* reading, theatre, opera, films, concerts and art galleries, swimming, watching the best of television—and sometimes, for clinical reasons, the worst. *Address:* Flat Four, 6 Grand Avenue, Hove BN3 2LF. *T:* (01273) 724051. *Club:* Arts. *Died 15 May 2012.*

SHAW, Sir Run Run, Kt 1977; CBE 1974; Founder and Chairman, Shaw Organisation, since 1963; Founder and Chairman, Shaw Foundation, since 1973; *b* 14 Oct. 1907; *m* 1st, 1932, Lily Wong Mee Chun (*d* 1987); two *s* two *d*; 2nd, 1997, Lee Mong-lan (Mona Fong). Left China for Singapore and began making films and operating cinemas, 1927; left Singapore for Hong Kong and built Shaw Movietown, making and distributing films, 1959. Pres., Hong Kong Red Cross Soc., 1972–98. Chairman: Hong Kong Arts Festival, 1974–88; Bd of Governors, Hong Kong Arts Centre, 1978–88; Television Broadcasts Ltd, 1980– (non-exec. Chm., 2010–). Chinese University of Hong Kong: Mem. Council, 1977–92; Chm., Bd of Trustees, United Coll., 1983–92; Founder, Shaw Coll., 1986.

Appointed by Govt of People's Republic of China, Hong Kong Advr, 1992–97, Mem., Preparatory Cttee, 1995–98. Est. Shaw Prize, 2003. Hon. LLD Hong Kong Univ., 1980; Hon. Dr Soc. Scis: Chinese Univ. of Hong Kong, 1981; Univ. of E Asia, Macau, 1985; Hon. DLitt: Sussex, 1987; Hong Kong Baptist Coll., 1990; Hon. DSc City Poly., Hong Kong, 1988; Hon. DHL SUNY at Stony Brook, 1989; Hon. DCL Oxford, 1992; Hon. DBA Hong Kong Poly., 1991. Queen's Badge, Red Cross, 1982; Montblanc de la Culture Award, 1993. BAFTA Special Award, 2013. Comdr, Order of the Crown of Belgium, 1989; Chevalier, Légion d'Honneur (France), 1991. *Address:* Shaw House, Lot 220 Clear Water Bay Road, Kowloon, Hong Kong. *T:* 27198371. *Died 7 Jan. 2014.*

SHAW, Thurstan; *see* Shaw, C. T.

SHEARING, Sir George (Albert), Kt 2007; OBE 1996; jazz pianist and composer; *b* 13 Aug. 1919; *s* of James Philip Shearing and Ellen Amelia Shearing (*née* Brightman); *m* 1st, 1941, Beatrice Bayes (marr. diss. 1973); one *d*; 2nd, 1975, Eleanor Geffert. *Educ:* Linden Lodge Sch. for the Blind, London. Founded George Shearing Quintet, 1949; also led other jazz ensembles. Composed Lullaby of Birdland, 1952, and many other popular songs. Made many recordings, 1939–. Hon. DMus: Westminster Coll., Salt Lake City, 1975; Hamilton Coll., NY, 1994; DePauw, 2002. Golden Plate Award, American Acad. of Achievement, 1968. *Publications:* Lullaby of Birdland, 2003. *Address:* c/o IVI Management, 25864 Tournament Road, Suite L, Valencia, CA 91355, USA. *Died 14 Feb. 2011.*

SHEFFIELD; 8th Baron. *See under Stanley of Alderley, 8th Baron.*

SHEFTON, Prof. Brian Benjamin, FBA 1985; FSA 1980; Professor of Greek Art and Archaeology, 1979–84, then Emeritus, and Hon. Fellow 2005, University of Newcastle upon Tyne; *b* 11 Aug. 1919; *yr s* of late Prof. I. Scheftelowitz (Cologne, Germany, until 1933 and Oxford) and Frieda (*née* Kohn); *né* Bruno Scheftelowitz; *m* 1960, Jutta Ebel of Alingsås, Sweden; one *d*. *Educ:* Apostelgymnasium, Cologne; St Lawrence Coll., Ramsgate; Magdalen Coll. Sch., Oxford; Oriel Coll., Oxford (Open Scholar, 1938; Hon. Mods Greek and Latin Lit. 1940; Lit Hum 1947, Class I). War service, HM Forces (change of name), 1940–45. Sch. Student, British Sch. at Athens, 1947; Derby Scholar, Oxford, 1948; Bishop Fraser Scholar, Oriel Coll., Oxford, 1949, in Aegean to 1950; excavated at Old Smyrna; Lectr in Classics, University Coll., Exeter, 1950–55; Lectr in Greek Archaeology and Ancient History, 1955, Sen. Lectr, 1960, Reader, 1974–79, King's Coll., Univ. of Durham (later Univ. of Newcastle upon Tyne). Established and directed Univ.'s Greek Museum (renamed Shefton Mus. of Greek Art and Archaeology, 1994; incorporated as Shefton Gall. into Great North Mus., Newcastle upon Tyne, 2009), 1956–84, Hon. Advr, 1985–; Trustee, Oriental Mus., Durham Univ., 1989–93. Vis. Res. Fellow, Merton Coll., Oxford, 1969; British Acad. Vis. Scholar to Albania, 1973; Munro Lectr, Edinburgh Univ., 1974; British Acad. European Exchange Fellow, Marburg Univ., 1975; German Academic Exchange Fellow, Marburg and Cologne, 1976; Leverhulme Res. Fellow, 1977; Webster Meml Lectr, Stanford Univ., 1981; Vis. Prof. of Classical Archaeology, Vienna Univ. (winter), 1981–82; British Council Vis. Scholar to Soviet Union, 1982, to Spain, 1985; Jackson Knight Meml Lectr, Exeter Univ., 1983; Leverhulme Emeritus Fellow, 1984–86; Balsdon Sen. Fellow, British Sch. at Rome, 1985; Vis. Scholar, J. Paul Getty Museum, 1987; British Academy Exchange Fellow, Jerusalem, 1993; Lorant Meml Lectr, BM, 2009. Mem., German Archaeological Inst., 1961; Foreign Mem., Inst. of Etruscan and Italic Studies, Florence, 1990. Hon. Dr phil Cologne, 1989. Aylwin Cotton Award, 1977; Kenyon Medal, British Acad., 1999. *Publications:* History of Greek Vase Painting (with P. Arias and M. Hirmer), 1962; Die rhodischen Bronzekannen, 1979; *chapters in:* Perachora II, 1962; Phoenizier im Westen, 1982; The Eye of Greece, 1982; Das Kleinaspergle, 1988; Cyprus and the East Mediterranean in the Iron Age, 1989; The Rogozen Treasure, 1989; Kotinos, 1992; Cultural Transformations and Interactions in Eastern Europe, 1993; The Archaeology of Greek Colonization, 1994; Social Complexity and the Development of Towns in Iberia, 1995; Italy in Europe: economic relations 700BC–AD50, 1995; Sur les traces des Argonautes, 1996; Céramique et peinture grecques: modes d'emploi, 1999; I Piceni, 1999; Periplous, 2000; Heuneburg XI, 2000; Piceni e l'Italia medio-adriatica, 2003; Die Hydria von Grächwil 1851–2001, 2004; Complessi archeologici di Trestina e di Fabbrecce nel Museo Archeologico di Firenze, 2009; Gli Umbri in età preromana, 2012; articles in British and foreign periodicals. *Recreations:* music, travel. *Address:* 24 Holly Avenue, Jesmond, Newcastle upon Tyne NE2 2PY. *T:* (0191) 281 4184. *Died 25 Jan. 2012.*

SHELDON, Harold; Chairman, Batley Sports Development Council, 1965–2000; Vice Chairman, Kirklees District Sports Council, 1974–2000; *b* 22 June 1918; *s* of Charles Edwin Sheldon and Lily Sheldon (*née* Taylor); *m* 1941, Bessie Sheldon (*née* Barratt); two *s* one *d*. HM Forces, 1939–45 (Sgt; wounded D Day landings). Local Government: elected Batley Borough Council, 1953; Mayor of Batley, 1962–63; W Yorkshire County Council, 1973–86 (Chm., 1976–77), re-elected 1977, 1981; Mem., Kirklees MDC, 1987–98 (Mayor, 1994–95). Mem., W Yorks Police Authy, 1989–95 (Vice-Chm., 1992–95). Mem., Yorks and Humberside Council for Sport and Recreation, 1977–86 and 1991–98; President: Batley Boys' Club (Founder Mem.), 1975–2000; Batley CAB, 1987–92; Batley Sports for the Disabled Assoc., 1987–96. *Died 24 March 2013.*

SHELDON, Mark Hebberton, CBE 1997; President of The Law Society, 1992–93; Senior Partner, 1988–91, Joint Senior Partner, 1991–93, Linklaters & Paines; *b* 6 Feb. 1931; *s* of late George Hebberton Sheldon and Marie Sheldon (*née* Hazlitt); *m* 1971, Catherine Ashworth; one *s* one *d*. *Educ:* Wycliffe Coll.; Corpus Christi Coll., Oxford (BA Jurisprudence (Hons), MA; Hon. Fellow, 1995). National Service, 1949–50, TA, 1950–54, Royal Signals (Lieut). Linklaters & Paines: articled clerk, 1953–56; Asst Solicitor, 1957–59; Partner, 1959–93; Resident Partner, NY, 1972–74; Consultant, 1994–96. Dir, Coutts & Co., 1996–98; Chm., PPP healthcare medical trust, subseq. PPP Foundn, 1999–2001 (Gov., 1998–2002). Mem. Council 1978–96, Treas. 1981–86, Vice-Pres., 1991–92, Law Soc.; Mem. Court 1975–, Master 1987–88, City of London Solicitors' Co.; Pres., City of London Law Soc., 1987–88. Bar Council: Mem., Collyear Cttee on Educn and Trng for the Bar, 1998–2000; Ind. Chm., Working Party on Barristers' Rights to Conduct Litigation, 1999–2000; Glidewell Working Pty on Judicial Appts and Silk, 2002–03. Nominated Mem., Council of Corp. of Lloyd's, 1989–90 (Chm., Wkg Party on Members' Voting Rights, 1993); Member: Financial Reporting Council, 1990–98; Cadbury Cttee on Financial Aspects of Corporate Governance, 1991–95; Financial Law Panel, 1993–98; Council, Justice, 1993–2005; Sen. Salaries Rev. Body, 1994–99; Panel of Conciliators, Internat. Centre for Investment Disputes, 1995–2003; Adv. Panel, Centre for Socio-Legal Studies, Univ. of Oxford, 1995–2003. Hon. Bencher, Inner Temple, 1993; Hon. Member: Canadian Bar Assoc., 1993–; SLS (formerly SPTL), 1993–. Trustee/Director: Oxford Inst. of Legal Practice, 1993–2009; Court Based Personal Support, Royal Courts of Justice, 2002–11. Gov., Yehudi Menuhin Sch., 1996–2011. Chm., Corpus Assoc., 1983–89. *Recreations:* music, English water-colours, wine, swimming. *Address:* 5 St Albans Grove, W8 5PN. *T:* (020) 7460 7172, *Fax:* (020) 7938 4771. *Clubs:* Travellers, City of London, Hurlingham. *Died 3 May 2013.*

SHELLEY, Dr Alan John; Senior Partner, Knight, Frank & Rutley, 1983–92; *b* 7 Aug. 1931; *s* of Stanley and Ivy Shelley; *m* 1958, Josephine Flood, MBE (*d* 2007); one *s* one *d*. *Educ:* People's College, Nottingham; SOAS, London (MA 1994); Nottingham Trent Univ. (PhD 2006). FRICS. Senior Partner, Knight, Frank & Rutley (Nigeria), 1965. General Commissioner of Income Tax, 1984–2007. Chairman: W Africa Cttee, 1985–97; Mansfield Settlement, 1992–2000; Vice-Chm., Aston Mansfield, 2000–. Mem. Ct of Governors, Royal Shakespeare Theatre, 1990–2001. *Publications:* Athol Fugard: his plays, people and politics, 2008; *novels:* The Colour was Red, 2008; I Never Met Ernest Hemingway, 2009; Not So Private Lives, 2009; A Place in the Country, 2010; The Unseen, 2010; The Fall,

2011. *Recreations:* theatre, memories of squash. *Address:* Thatch Farm, Glaston, Rutland LE15 9BX. *T:* (01572) 822396. *Clubs:* Oriental, MCC. *Died 14 April 2012.*

SHEPHERD, John Dodson, CBE 1979; Regional Administrator, Yorkshire Regional Health Authority, 1977–82, retired; *b* 24 Dec. 1920; *s* of Norman and Elizabeth Ellen Shepherd; *m* 1948, Marjorie Nettleton (*d* 2006); one *s* two *d. Educ:* Barrow Grammar School. RAF, 1940–46: N Africa, Italy, Middle East, 1943–46. Asst Sec., Oxford RHB, 1956–58; Dep. Sec., Newcastle upon Tyne HMC, 1958–62; Sec., East Cumberland HMC, 1962–67; Sec., Liverpool RHB, 1967–73; Reg. Administrator, Mersey RHA, 1973–77. Pres., Inst. of Health Service Administrators, 1974–75 (Mem. Council, 1969–78). Trustee, Leonard Cheshire Foundn, 1989–95. *Recreations:* reading, music. *Club:* Harrogate Golf. *Died 25 March 2013.*

SHEPHERD, Rt Rev. Ronald Francis; Bishop of British Columbia, 1985–92; *b* 15 July 1926; *s* of Herbert George Shepherd and Muriel Shepherd (*née* Grant); *m* 1952, Ann Alayne Dundas, *d* of Rt Hon. R. S. Dundas; four *s* two *d. Educ:* Univ. of British Columbia (BA Hons 1948); King's Coll., London (AKC 1952). Fellow, Coll. of Preachers, Washington, DC, 1972. Curate, St Stephen's, Rochester Row, London SW, 1952–57; Rector: St Paul's, Glanford, Ont, 1957–59; All Saints, Winnipeg, 1959–65; Dean and Rector: All Saints Cathedral, Edmonton, 1965–69; Christ Church Cathedral, Montreal, 1970–83; Rector, St Matthias, Victoria, 1983–84. Hon. Assisting Bishop for Develt of Mission in Borrego Reg., Dio. of San Diego, Calif, 2000. Hon. DD St John's Coll., Winnipeg, 1988. *Recreations:* reading, writing. *Address:* Parkwood Place, Suite 311, 3051 Shelbourne Street, Victoria, BC V8R 6T2, Canada. *Died 24 Oct. 2012.*

SHEPHERDSON, Prof. John Cedric, ScD; FBA 1990; FIMA; H. O. Wills Professor of Mathematics, Bristol University, 1977–91, then Emeritus; *b* 7 June 1926; *s* of Arnold Shepherdson and Elsie (*née* Aspinall); *m* 1957, Margaret Smith; one *s* two *d. Educ:* Manchester Grammar Sch.; Trinity Coll., Cambridge (BA, MA, ScD). Asst Experimental Officer, Aerodynamics and Maths Div., NPL, 1946; Bristol University: Asst Lectr in Maths, 1946–49; Lectr, 1949–55; Reader, 1955–63; Prof. of Pure Maths, 1964–77. Mem., Inst. for Advanced Study, Princeton, 1953–54; Vis. Associate Prof., 1958–59, Vis. Prof., 1966–67, Univ. of Calif at Berkeley; Vis. Prof., Monash Univ., 1971, 1986, 1991, 1992, 1994, 1996; Vis. Scientist, IBM Res. Labs, Yorktown Heights, NY, 1973, 1975, 1979; Guest, Technische Hochschule, Zürich, 1988. *Publications:* papers in mathematical, logical and computer sci. jls. *Recreations:* walking, cycling. *Address:* Oakhurst, North Road, Leigh Woods, Bristol BS8 3PN. *T:* (0117) 973 5410. *E:* john.shepherdson@bris.ac.uk. *Clubs:* Fell & Rock Climbing (Lake District); Bristol Corinthian Yacht. *Died 8 Jan. 2015.*

SHEPPARD OF DIDGEMERE, Baron *cr* 1994 (Life Peer), of Roydon in the County of Essex; **Allen John George Sheppard,** KCVO 1998; Kt 1990; Chairman, Grand Metropolitan plc, 1987–96 (Chief Executive, 1986–93); *b* 25 Dec. 1932; *s* of John Baggott Sheppard and Lily Marjorie Sheppard (*née* Palmer); *m* 1st, 1959, Peggy Damaris (*née* Jones) (marr. diss. 1980); 2nd, 1980, Mary (*née* Stewart). *Educ:* Ilford County School; London School of Economics (BSc Econ). FCMA, FCIS, ATII. Ford of Britain and Ford of Europe, 1958–68; Rootes/Chrysler, 1968–71; British Leyland, 1971–75; Grand Metropolitan, 1975–96. Non-exec. Dir, later Chm., UBM Gp, 1981–85; Chm., Mallinson-Denny Gp, 1985–87. Chairman: McBride Ltd, 1993–2007; Group Trust (formerly Group Development Capital Trust) PLC, 1994–2001; Unipart, 1996–2012; GB Railways, 1996–2004; OneClickHR PLC (formerly Visual Business Tools), 1999–2010; Namibian Resources Ltd, 2004–; Deputy Chairman: Meyer Internat., 1992–94 (non-exec. Dir, 1989–94); Brightreasons Group PLC, 1994–96; part time Mem., BR Board, 1985–90; Director: Bowater, 1993–94; High-Point Rendel Gp plc, 1997–2003; Gladstone PLC, 1999–2001; Nyne (formerly Zolon) plc, 1999–2007; Transware plc, 2001–03. Chm., Adv. Bd, British American Chamber of Commerce, 1991–94; Vice-Pres., BITC (Dep. Chm., 1989–94; Chm., 1994–97); Dep. Chm., Internat. Business Leaders Forum, 1990–95; Member: Nat. Trng Task Force, 1989–92; NEDC, 1990–92. Chairman: Bd of Trustees, Prince's Youth Business Trust, 1990–94; Prince's Trust Council, 1995–98; Mem. Exec. Cttee, Animal Health Trust. Pres., London First, 2002– (Chm., 1992–2002); Co-Chair, London Pride Partnership, 1994–99; Dir, London Develt Partnership, 1997–2000. Vice-President: Blue Cross; United Response; Brewers & Licensed Retailers' Assoc. Mem., Bd of Management, Conservative Party, 1993–98. Governor, LSE, 1989–; Chancellor, Middlesex Univ., 2000–13. CCMI (CBIM 1982; Gold Medal, 1994); FRSA. Hon. FCGI 1993; Hon. Fellow, London Business Sch., 1993. Hon. Dr: Internat. Management Centre, 1989; South Bank Univ., 1994; Brunel, 1994; East London, 1997; Westminster, 1998; Middlesex, 1999; LSE, 2001. *Publications:* Your Business Matters, 1958; Maximum Leadership, 1995; articles in professional jls. *Recreations:* gardens, reading, red setter dogs. *Address:* House of Lords, SW1A 0PW. *Died 25 March 2015.*

SHEPPARD, Prof. Norman, FRS 1967; Professor of Chemical Sciences, University of East Anglia, Norwich, 1964–86, then Emeritus; *b* 16 May 1921; *s* of Walter Sheppard and Anne Clarges Sheppard (*née* Finding); *m* 1949, Kathleen Margery McLean (*d* 2005); two *s* one *d* (and one *s* decd). *Educ:* Hymers Coll., Hull; St Catharine's Coll., Cambridge. BA Cantab 1st cl. hons 1943; PhD and MA Cantab 1947. Vis. Asst Prof., Pennsylvania State Univ., 1947–48; Ramsay Memorial Fellow, 1948–49; Senior 1851 Exhibn, 1949–51; Fellow of Trinity Coll., Cambridge and Asst Dir of Research in Spectroscopy, Cambridge Univ., 1955–64. *Publications:* scientific papers on spectroscopy and surface chemistry in Proc. Roy. Soc., Faraday Trans., Jl Chem. Soc., Spectrochimica Acta, etc. *Recreations:* architecture, classical music, philosophy of science, walking. *Address:* 5 Hornor Close, Norwich NR2 2LY. *T:* (01603) 453052. *E:* kandnsheppard@dsl.pipex.com. *Died 10 April 2015.*

SHERIDAN, Roderick Gerald, OBE 1978; MVO 1968; HM Diplomatic Service, retired; Consul-General, Barcelona and Andorra, 1977–80; *b* 24 Jan. 1921; *s* of late Sir Joseph Sheridan; *m* 1942, Lois Mary (*née* Greene); one *s* one *d. Educ:* Downside Sch.; Pembroke Coll., Cambridge. Served War, Coldstream Guards, N Africa and Italy, 1940–46. HM Overseas Colonial Service: Zanzibar and Cyprus, 1946–60; retd as District Comr, Nicosia; HM Diplomatic Service, 1960–80: First Sec., Cyprus, 1960–63; Foreign Office, 1964–66; First Sec., Brasilia, 1966–69; FO, 1969–70; Head of Chancery, Oslo, 1970–73; Consul, Algeciras, 1973–77. Hon. Vice-Consul, Menorca, 1983–93. *Recreations:* tennis, golf, ski-ing. *Died 30 March 2013.*

SHERRARD, Michael David, CBE 2003; QC 1968; Director, Middle Temple Advocacy, 1994–2004, then Emeritus; a Recorder of the Crown Court, 1974–93; *b* 23 June 1928; *er s* of late Morris and Ethel Sherrard; *m* 1952, Shirley, *d* of late Maurice and Lucy Bagrit; two *s. Educ:* King's Coll., London (LLB 1949). Called to Bar, Middle Temple, 1949 (Bencher 1977; Treas., 1996); Mem., Inner Temple, 1980; Mem. Senate, 1977–80. Mem., SE Circuit, 1950. Mem., Winn Cttee on Personal Injury Litigation, 1966; Mem. Council, Justice, British Section, Internat. Commn of Jurists, 1974–2000; Dept of Trade Inspector, London Capital Group, 1975–77; Chm., Normansfield Hosp. Inquiry, 1977–78; Comr for trial of local govt election petitions (under Representation of the People Act 1949), 1978–80. Mem., Bar Assoc. of NYC, 1986–94. FRSA 1991. *Publications:* (with Linda Goldman) Wigs and Wherefores, 2008. *Recreations:* oriental art, travel, listening to opera. *Address:* 26 Eton Avenue, Hampstead, NW3 3HL. *T:* (020) 7431 0713. *Died 30 Nov. 2012.*

SHERRINGTON, Prof. David Colin, PhD; FRS 2007; FRSE, FRSC; Professor of Polymer Chemistry, and Head, Department of Pure and Applied Chemistry, University of Strathclyde, 1987–2010, then Professor Emeritus; *b* Liverpool, 5 March 1945; *m* 1972, Valerie. *Educ:* Waterloo Grammar Sch.; Univ. of Liverpool (Sir W. H. Tate Schol.; BSc 1st Cl. Hons 1966; PhD 1969; DSc 1992). FRSC 1981. Lectr, 1972–83, Sen. Lectr, 1983–87, Reader, 1987,

Dept of Pure and Applied Chem., Univ. of Strathclyde; on secondment as Polymer Sci. Area Hd, Unilever Res., Port Sunlight, 1984–87. Vis. Prof., Univs of Pisa, Tanta, Egypt, Nankai, China, Bombay, Oulu, Finland, Bordeaux, Gyeongsang, S Korea and Tokyo Inst. of Technol. Internat. Ed., Jl Reactive Polymers, 1987–96. FRSE 1990. Beilby Medal, 1993, J. B. Goodenough Award, 2009, RSC; Macrogp Medal, RSC/Soc. Chem. Industry, 2004. *Publications:* (with P. Hodge) Polymer-supported Reactions in Organic Synthesis, 1980; (with P. Hodge) Synthesis and Separations Using Functional Polymers, 1988; (ed with T. Riste) Phase Transitions in Soft Condensed Matter: proceedings, 1990; contribs to jls incl. Jl Polymer Sci., Polymer, Jl Chem. Soc., Eur. Polymer Jl, Jl Chromatography. *Address:* Department of Pure and Applied Chemistry, Thomas Graham Building, University of Strathclyde, 295 Cathedral Street, Glasgow G1 1XL. *Died 4 Oct. 2014.*

SHEVARDNADZE, Eduard Amvrosiyevich, Hon. GCMG 2000; President of Georgia, 1995–2003; *b* Georgia, 25 Jan. 1928; christened Georgi, 1992, but known as Eduard; *m* Nanuli Tsagareishvili (*d* 2004); one *s* one *d*. *Educ:* Pedagogical Institute, Kutaisi. Mem., CPSU, 1948–91; Sec., Komsomol Cttee in Kutaisi, 1952–56, of Georgia, 1956–61; 1st Sec., Regional Party Cttee, Mtsheta, 1961–63, Tbilisi, 1963–64; Minister of Internal Affairs, Georgia, 1964–72; 1st Sec., Republican Party Cttee, Georgia, 1972–85; Mem., Politburo, 1985–91; Minister of Foreign Affairs, USSR, 1985–90, 1991; founder, Movement for Democratic Reform, 1991; Chm., Georgian State Council, 1992; Chm., Supreme Council and Head of State, Georgia, 1992–95. Hon. doctorates from Harvard, Boston, Emory and Providence, USA and Trieste, Italy. Order of Lenin (five times); Hero of Socialist Labour (twice); Order of Red Banner of Labour. *Publications:* The Future Belongs to Freedom, 1991. *Died 7 July 2014.*

SHIELDS, Hon. Dame Margaret (Kerslake), DNZM 2009 (DCNZM 2008); QSO 1996; Cabinet Minister, New Zealand, 1984–90; *b* Wellington, NZ, 18 Dec. 1941; *d* of (Ernest) Blake Porter and Dorothy Bessie Porter (*née* Levy); *m* 1960, Patrick John Shields; one *d* (and one *d* decd). *Educ:* Victoria Univ., Wellington (BA). Co-founder, Soc. for Res. on Women in NZ, 1966; Researcher, Consumers' Inst., 1966–71; Res. Officer, NZ Dept of Statistics, 1973–81; MP (Lab) Kapiti, 1981–90. Dir, UN Internat. Res. and Trng Inst. for the Advancement of Women, 1991–94. Mem., Wellington Regl Council, 1995–2007; Chm., Gtr Wellington Regl Council, 2001–04. Vice Pres., Local Govt NZ, 1997–2004. *Recreations:* reading, theatre, narrow boating. *Address:* 23 Haunui Road, Pukerua Bay, Porirua 5026, New Zealand. *T:* (4) 2399949. *E:* marg.shields@xtra.co.nz. *Died 29 May 2013.*

SHIERLAW, Norman Craig; Senior Partner, N. C. Shierlaw & Associates (Stock and Sharebrokers), 1968–87; Chairman, Swiss Partners (Stock and Sharebrokers), 1987–91; *b* 17 Aug. 1921; *s* of Howard Alison Shierlaw and Margaret Bruce; *m* 1st, 1944, Patricia Yates (*d* 1987); two *d*; 2nd, 1989, Barbara Jean Lacey. *Educ:* Pulteney Grammar Sch., Adelaide; St Peter's Coll., Adelaide; Univ. of Adelaide (BE). Mem. Australian Inst. Mining and Metallurgy; FSASM; Mining Manager's Certificate. War Service, AIF, 1941–45 (War Service medals). Mining Engr with North Broken Hill Ltd, 1949–58; Sharebroker's Clerk, 1959–60; Partner, F. W. Porter & Co. (Sharebrokers), 1960–68. Chairman: Australian Development Ltd, 1981–83 (Dir, 1959–81); Burmine Ltd, 1990–92 (Dir, 1985–90); Director: Poseidon Ltd, 1968–77; North Flinders Mines Ltd, 1969–77; Nobelex NL, 1974–80; Palm Springs Ltd, 1987–2001; Gympie Eldorado Gold Mines, 1993–97; Cooper's Brewery Ltd, 1995–97. FAIM 1971. *Recreations:* golf, tennis. *Clubs:* Kooyonga Golf (Adelaide); Victoria Racing (Melbourne). *Died 26 Sept. 2013.*

SHIPLEY, Jane; Her Honour Judge Shipley; a Circuit Judge, since 2000; *b* 5 Jan. 1952; *m* 1977, David; two *d*. *Educ:* Maltby Grammar Sch. (Head Girl); St Hugh's Coll., Oxford (Pres., Law Soc.; MA). Called to the Bar, Gray's Inn, 1974; in practice, Leeds, NE Circuit, 1974–2000. Asst Recorder, 1991–95; Recorder, 1995–2000. *Recreation:* gardening. *Address:* Sheffield Combined Court Centre, 50 West Bar, Sheffield S3 8PH. *Died 3 Feb. 2014.*

SHIRLEY-QUIRK, John Stanton, CBE 1975; bass-baritone singer; visiting teacher, Bath Spa University, since 2012; *b* 28 Aug. 1931; *s* of Joseph Stanley and Amelia Shirley-Quirk; *m* 1st, 1955, Patricia Hastie (*d* 1981); one *s* one *d*; 2nd, 1981, Sara V. Watkins (*d* 1997); one *s* one *d* (and one *d* decd); 3rd, 2009, Teresa May Perez (*née* Cardoza). *Educ:* Holt School, Liverpool; Liverpool University. Violin Scholarship, 1945; read Chemistry, Liverpool Univ., 1948–53; BSc (Hons), 1952; Dipl. in Educn 1953; became professional singer, 1961. Officer in Education Br., RAF, 1953–57. Asst Lectr in Chemistry, Acton Technical Coll., 1957–61; Lay-clerk in St Paul's Cathedral, 1961–62. First Appearance Glyndebourne Opera in Elegy for Young Lovers, 1961; subseq. 1962, 1963. Sang in first performance of Curlew River, 1964, The Burning Fiery Furnace, 1966, The Prodigal Son, 1968, Owen Wingrave, 1970, Death in Venice, 1973, Confessions of a Justified Sinner, 1976, The Ice Break, 1977. Sang world wide. First American tour, 1966; Australian tour, 1967; first appearance Metropolitan Opera, NY, 1974. Made numerous recordings: operas, songs, cantatas, etc. Member, Voice Faculty: Peabody Conservatory, Baltimore, 1991–2012; Carnegie-Mellon Univ., Pittsburgh, 1994–98. Mem. Court, Brunel Univ., 1977–81. Hon. RAM 1972; Hon. DMus Liverpool, 1976; DUniv Brunel, 1981. Liverpool Univ. Chem. Soc. Medal, 1965; Sir Charles Santley Meml Gift, Worshipful Co. of Musicians, 1969. *Recreations:* trees, canals, clocks. *Died 7 April 2014.*

SHOOTER, Prof. Reginald Arthur, CBE 1980; Emeritus Professor of Medical Microbiology, London University, since 1981; *b* 4 April 1916; *s* of Rev. A. E. Shooter, TD and M. K. Shooter; *m* 1946, Jean Wallace, MB, ChB (*d* 2012); one *s* three *d*. *Educ:* Mill Hill Sch.; Caius Coll., Cambridge; St Bartholomew's Hosp. BA 1937; MB, BChir 1940; MRCS, LRCP 1940; MA 1941; MD 1945; MRCP 1961; FRCP 1968; FRCS 1977; FRCPath 1963 (Vice-Pres., 1971–74). After various Hosp. appts became Surgeon Lieut, RNVR. Appointments at St Bartholomew's Hospital from 1946; Rockefeller Travelling Fellow in Medicine, 1950–51; Reader in Bacteriology, 1953–61, Prof. of Medical Microbiology, 1961–81, Univ. of London; Bacteriologist to St Bartholomew's Hosp., 1961–81 and Dean, Medical Coll., 1972–81. Member: City and E London AHA (T), 1974–81; Gloucester HA, 1981–85; Chm., Regional Computing Policy Steering Gp, SW RHA, 1983–85. Mem., Public Health Lab. Service Bd, 1970–82; Chm., Dangerous Pathogens Adv. Gp, 1975–81. Mem., Scientific Adv. Council, Stress Foundn, 1981–90. Governor: St Bartholomew's Hosp., 1972–74; Queen Mary Coll., 1972–81; Trustee: Mitchell City of London Trust, 1958–82; Jenner Trust, 1989–2001 (Smallpox Archivist, 2001–). Mem. Court, City Univ., 1972–81. Pybus Medal, N of England Surg. Soc., 1979. Asst Editor, British Jl of Exp. Pathology, 1953–58; Hon. Editor, RSocMed, 1960–65. *Publications:* books, and articles in medical journals. *Recreations:* archaeology, gardening, fishing. *Address:* Blackmore Gardens, Blackmore Park, Hanley Swan, Worcs WR8 0EF. *Died 24 Dec. 2013.*

SHORT, Rt Rev. Kenneth Herbert, AO 1988; Dean of Sydney (St Andrew's Cathedral), 1989–92; *b* 6 July 1927; *s* of Cecil Charles Short and Joyce Ellen Begbie; *m* 1950, Gloria Noelle Funnell; one *s* two *d*. *Educ:* Moore Theological Coll. (ThL and Moore Coll. Dipl.). Commissioned AIF, 1946; with BCOF, 1946–48; theological training, 1949–52; ordained Anglican Ministry, 1952; Minister in Charge, Provisional Parish of Pittwater, 1952–54; with CMS in Tanzania, E Africa, 1955–64; Chaplain, Tabora 1955, Mwanza 1955–59; founding Principal, Msalato Bible School, 1961–64; Gen. Secretary, CMS NSW Branch, 1964–71, including Sec. for S America; Canon of St Andrew's Cathedral, Sydney, 1970–75; Exam. Chaplain to Archbishop of Sydney, 1971–82; Rector of St Michael's, Vaucluse, 1971–75; Bishop of Wollongong, Dio. of Sydney, 1975–82 (Acting Bishop, 1993 and 1999); Archdeacon of Wollongong and Camden, 1975–79; Chaplain Gen. (CE), Australian

Army, 1979–81; Anglican Bishop to Aust. Defence Force (Army, Navy and Air Force), 1979–89; Bishop of Parramatta, Dio. of Sydney, 1982–89; Assistant, St John's Shaughnessy, Vancouver, Dio. of New Westminster, 1992–93 and 1995–96. Acting Gen. Sec., CMS Victoria, 1997, NSW, 1998. ChStJ 1989. *Publications:* Guidance, 1969; (contrib.) Evangelism and Preaching in Secular Australia, 1989. *Recreation:* reading. *Address:* 2/5 Brown Street, Kiama, NSW 2533, Australia. *T:* (2) 42321261. *Died 19 Oct. 2014.*

SHOVELTON, Prof. David Scott, FDSRCS; Professor of Conservative Dentistry, University of Birmingham, 1964–89, Professor Emeritus, since 1990; *b* 12 Sept. 1925; *s* of Leslie Shovelton, LDSRCS, and Marion de Winton (*née* Scott); *m* 1949, Pearl Holland (*d* 2008); two *s*. *Educ:* The Downs Sch., Colwall; King's Sch., Worcester; Univ. of Birmingham (BSc, LDS, BDS). House Surg., Birmingham Dental Hosp., 1951; gen. dental practice, Evesham, Worcs, 1951; Dental Officer, RAF, 1951–53; Birmingham University: Lectr in Operative Dental Surg., 1953–60; Sen. Lectr, 1960–64; Dir, 1974–78, Dep. Dir, 1982–84, Dental Sch.; Consultant Dental Surgeon, Utd Birmingham Hosps, subseq. Central Birmingham HA, 1960–89. Vis. Asst Prof. of Clin. Dentistry, Univ. of Alabama, 1959–60. Hon. Cons. Dental Surg., Birmingham Reg. Hosp. Bd, 1962–74; Hon. Consultant in Conservative Dentistry, Central Birmingham HA, 1989–2004. Pres., British Soc. for Restorative Dentistry, 1970–71 (Vice-Pres., 1968–70 and 1971–72). Consultant, Commn on Dental Practice, Fédn Dentaire Internat., 1972–79; Consultant Adviser in Restorative Dentistry, DHSS, 1983–89. Member: Gen. Dental Council, 1974–89; Birmingham Area Health Authority (Teaching), 1973–79; Cttee of Management, Sch. for Dental Therapists, 1977–80; Jt Cttee for Higher Trng in Dentistry, 1979–84 (Chm., Specialist Adv. Cttee in Restorative Dentistry, 1979–84); Standing Dental Adv. Cttee, 1982–88; Bd, Faculty of Dental Surgery, RCS, 1983–91; Jt Dental Cttee of MRC, Health Depts and SERC, 1984–87; Cttee of Enquiry into unnecessary dental treatment, 1984–85. Ext. Examr in dental subjects, univs and colls, 1968–94. *Publications:* Inlays, Crowns and Bridges (jtly), 1963, 5th edn 1993 (trans. Portuguese 1991); articles in med. and dental jls, 1957–89. *Recreations:* music, learning about wine, gardening. *Address:* c/o 73 Cornwall Road, Harrogate, N Yorks HG1 2NB. *T:* (01423) 502718. *Club:* Royal Air Force. *Died 17 Nov. 2012.*

SHOVELTON, (Walter) Patrick, CB 1976; CMG 1972; FCILT; Director-General, General Council of British Shipping, 1978–85; *b* 18 Aug. 1919; *s* of late S. T. Shovelton, CBE, and May Catherine (*née* Kelly), cousin of Patrick and Willie Pearse, Irish patriots; *m* 1st, 1942, Marjorie Lucy Joan Manners (marr. diss. 1967); one *d*; 2nd, 1968, Helena Richards, (Dame Helena Shovelton, DBE). *Educ:* Charterhouse; Keble Coll., Oxford (scholar of both). Rep. Oxford Univ. at Eton Fives. Served in RA and RHA (HAC), 1940–46; DAAG, War Office, 1945–46. Entered Administrative Civil Service as Asst Principal, Min. of War Transport, 1946; Principal 1947; Admin. Staff College, 1951; Private Sec. to Secretary of State for Co-ordination of Transport, Fuel and Power, 1951–53; Asst Sec., Road Transport, 1957; transferred to Min. of Aviation, 1959; IDC, 1962; Under Secretary, 1966; transferred to Min. of Technology, 1966, and to DTI, 1970; Mem., UK Negotiating Team for entry into EEC, 1970–72; Deputy Secretary: DTI, 1972–74; Dept of Prices and Consumer Protection, 1974–76; Dept of Trade, 1976–78; led UK Negotiating Team for Bermuda 2, 1977 and 2A, 1978; Dir, British Airports Authy, 1982–85. Chm., Birmingham Executive, later European, Airways, 1988–93; Director: Maersk Co., 1985 (Vice-Chm., 1987–95); Kent Line, 1987–90; Maersk Air Ltd, 1993–95. William and Mary Tercentenary Trust: Chairman: Maritime Cttee, 1985–89; Finance and Sponsorship Cttee, 1988–89. Council, CIT, 1982–85; Advr, Inquiries into EEC Maritime Transport Policy H of L, 1985–86, into Merchant Shipping, H of C, 1986–88. Brancker Lectr (civil aviation), 1979; Grout Lectr (shipping), 1985. Founder and Chm., 1991–98, Pres., 1998–, Friends of Tunbridge Wells and Rusthall Commons. Officer, Order of Orange-Nassau (Netherlands), 1989. *Recreations:* attending funerals, writing obituaries, regretting golf, theatre and opera going, playing bridge, reading. *Address:* Garden Lodge, Bayham Abbey, near Lamberhurst, Tunbridge Wells, Kent TN3 8BG. *T:* (01892) 891598, (020) 7226 9353. *Clubs:* Brooks's; Jesters; Royal Ashdown Forest Golf, Hampstead Golf, Seniors Golf. *Died 20 Jan. 2012.*

SHRIVER, (Robert) Sargent; Partner, 1971–86, Lawyer Of Counsel, Fried, Frank, Harris, Shriver & Jacobson, since 1986; Chairman, Special Olympics International, 1990–2003, then Emeritus (President, 1984–90); *b* Westminster, Md, 9 Nov. 1915; *s* of Robert Sargent and Hilda Shriver; *m* 1953, Eunice Mary Kennedy (*d* 2009); four *s* one *d*. *Educ:* parochial schools, Baltimore; Canterbury School, New Milford, Conn.; Yale College; Yale University (BA (*cum laude*) 1938; LLB 1941; LLD 1964). Apprentice Seaman, USNR, 1940; Ensign, 1941. Served War of 1941–45: Atlantic and Pacific Ocean Areas aboard battleships and submarines; Lt-Comdr, USNR. Admitted to: New York Bar, 1941; Illinois Bar, (retd) 1959; US Supreme Court, 1966; District of Columbia Bar, 1971. With legal firm of Winthrop, Stimson, Putnam & Roberts, NYC, 1940–41; Asst Editor, Newsweek, 1945–46; associated with Joseph P. Kennedy Enterprises, 1946–48; Asst Gen. Man., Merchandise Mart, 1948–61; President: Chicago Bd of Educn, 1955–60; Catholic Interracial Council of Chicago, 1954–59; Dir, Peace Corps, Washington, 1961–66; Dir, Office of Economic Opportunity (resp. for develt of Head Start, Job Corps, VISTA Community Action, Legal Services for the Poor, etc), and Special Asst to Pres. Johnson, 1964–68; US Ambassador to France, 1968–70. Vice-Presidential candidate (Democrat), Nov. 1972. Democrat; Roman Catholic. US Presidential Medal of Freedom, 1994; Franklin D. Roosevelt Freedom From Want Award, 1994. *Address:* (office) 1001 Pennsylvania Avenue, NW, Washington, DC 20004, USA. *Died 18 Jan. 2011.*

SHUCKBURGH, Sir Rupert (Charles Gerald), 13th Bt *cr* 1660, of Shuckburgh, Warwickshire; *b* 12 Feb. 1949; *s* of Sir Charles Gerald Stewkley Shuckburgh, 12th Bt, TD and Nancy Diana Mary, OBE (*d* 1984), *o d* of late Captain Rupert Lubbock, RN; *S* father, 1988; *m* 1st, 1976, Judith (marr. diss. 1987), *d* of W. G. Mackaness; two *s*; 2nd, 1987, Margaret Ida, *d* of late W. Evans. *Heir: s* James Rupert Charles Shuckburgh, *b* 4 Jan. 1978. *Address:* Shuckburgh Hall, Daventry, Northants NN11 6DT. *Club:* Farmers. *Died 24 Jan. 2012.*

SHURMAN, Laurence Paul Lyons; Banking Ombudsman, 1989–96; Member, Executive Board, The Accountancy and Actuarial Discipline Board Ltd (formerly Accountancy Investigation and Discipline Board Ltd), 2004–09 (a Director, 2001–04); *b* 25 Nov. 1930; *s* of Joseph and Sarah Shurman; *m* 1963, Mary Seamans (*née* McMullan); two *s* one *d*. *Educ:* Newcastle upon Tyne Royal Grammar Sch.; Magdalen Coll., Oxford (MA). Solicitor. Articles, John H. Sinton & Co., Newcastle, 1954–57; Assistant Solicitor: Haswell Croft, Newcastle, 1957–58; Hall Brydon, London, 1958–60; Kaufman & Siegal, London, 1960–61; Partner: Shurman & Bindman, Solicitors, London, 1961–64; Shurman & Co., London, 1964–67; Kingsley Napley, London, 1967–89 (Managing Partner, 1975–89). Legal Mem., Mental Health Review Tribunal, 1976–94; Chm., Portman Gp (drinks industry) Complaints Panel, 1997–2001; Mem. Council, Justice, 1973– (Mem., Exec. Bd, 2003–). Lectures: Gilbart, 1990; Ernest Sykes Meml, 1991. Pres., City of Westminster Law Soc., 1980–81; Chm., British and Irish Ombudsman Assoc., 1993–95. Vice-Chm., Disciplinary Cttee, Assoc. of Chartered Certified Accountants, 1998–2000. Member: Mgt Cttee, Care and Repair England, 1998– (Vice-Chm., 2001–); Council, RSAS AgeCare, 1998–2007 (Vice-Pres., 2008–). Governor: Channing Sch., 1985–2007 (Vice-Chm., 1988–2007); Newcastle upon Tyne Royal Grammar Sch., 1991–2001. Trustee, Highgate Literary and Scientific Inst., 2002–09 (Pres., 1998–2002). *Publications:* The Practical Skills of the Solicitor, 1981, 2nd edn 1985; contributor on Mental Health Tribunals in Vol. 26 of Atkin's Encyc. of Court Forms, 2nd edn 1985. *Recreations:* reading, fell walking, swimming, law reform. *Address:* 14 Southwood Avenue, N6 5RZ. *T:* (020) 8348 5409. *Club:* Leander (Henley). *Died 27 July 2012.*

SIDAWAY, Ven. Geoffrey Harold; Archdeacon of Gloucester, 2000–12; Canon Residentiary, Gloucester Cathedral, 2007–12; Priest-in-charge, Highnam, Lassington, Rudford, Tibberton and Taynton, 2012–13; *b* 28 Oct. 1942; *s* of Harold and Margaret Sidaway; *m* 1970, Margaret Bates; two *s* one *d*. *Educ:* Kelham Theol Coll. Ordained deacon, 1966, priest, 1967; Curate: Beighton, Derby, 1966–70; St Mary and All Saints, Chesterfield, 1970–72; Vicar, St Bartholomew, Derby, 1972–77; Chaplain to E Midlands Ordination Course, 1974–77; Vicar: St Martin, Maidstone, 1977–86; Bearstead and Thurnham, 1986–2000. Rural Dean, Sutton, 1992–99; Hon. Canon, Canterbury Cathedral, 1994–2000. Mem., Gen. Synod of C of E, 1995–2000, 2005–07. *Recreations:* cooking, gardening, walking, showing labradors. *Address:* Corner House, Over Old Road, Hartpury, Gloucester GL19 3BJ. *T:* (01452) 700456. *Died 20 April 2014.*

SIDDELL, Sir Peter (Graham), KNZM 2009 (DCNZM 2008); QSO 1991; painter (full-time), since 1971; *b* Ngawha, 31 July 1935; *s* of Joseph and Dorothy Siddell; *m* 1960, Sylvia Grace Bartlett; two *d*. *Educ:* Richmond Road and Newton Central Prim. Schs; Mount Albert Grammar Sch.; Auckland Teachers' Coll. Former electrician and teacher. Arts Laureate, Waitakere City Council, 2008. *Recreations:* reading, exploring bush and beach, mountaineering, snorkelling. *Address:* 27 Fairview Road, Mount Eden, Auckland 1024, New Zealand. *T:* (9) 6301130. *E:* siddell@xtra.co.nz. *W:* http://siddell.co.nz. *Died 24 Oct. 2011.*

SIDDIQI, Prof. Obaid, Padma Vibhushan 2006 (Padma Bhushan 1984); FRS 1984; FIASc 1968; FNA 1977; Professor of Molecular Biology, Tata Institute of Fundamental Research, National Centre for Biological Sciences, Bangalore, 1972–95, then Emeritus; *b* 7 Jan. 1932; *s* of M. A. Qadeer Siddiqi and Umme Kulsum; *m* 1955, Asiya Siddiqi; two *s* two *d*. *Educ:* Univ. of Aligarh (MSc); Univ. of Glasgow (PhD). Lecturer, Aligarh Univ., 1954–57; Indian Agricl Res. Inst., 1957–58; Dept of Genetics, Glasgow Univ., 1958–61; Cold Spring Harbor Lab., NY, 1961; Univ. of Pennsylvania, 1961–62; Tata Inst. of Fundamental Research: Fellow, 1962; Dir, Nat. Centre for Biol Scis, Bangalore, 1992–99. Vis. Associate, Yale Univ., 1966; Vis. Prof., MIT, 1970–71; CIT Gosney Fellow, 1971–72; Sherman Fairchild Distinguished Scholar, 1981–82; Fellow, Third World Acad. of Sciences, Trieste, 1986; Vis. Fellow, 1997, and Life Mem., Clare Hall, Cambridge. Foreign Associate, NAS, USA, 2003. Hon. DSc: Aligarh, 1984; Banaras Hindu, 1986. *Publications:* (co-ed) Development and Neurobiology of Drosophila, 1981; several papers in learned jls on genetics and neurobiology. *Recreations:* music, tennis, photography. *Address:* Tata Institute of Fundamental Research, National Centre for Biological Sciences, GKVK Campus, Bangalore 560065, India. *T:* (80) 3636420, ext. 2110, *Fax:* (80) 3636662. *E:* osiddiqi@ncbs.res.in; (home) 1280 3d Main, 9th Cross, BEL Layout 1st Block, Vidyaranyapura, Bangalore 560097, India. *T:* (80) 3648507. *Died 26 July 2013.*

SILBERSTON, Prof. (Zangwill) Aubrey, CBE 1987; Professor of Economics, University of London, at Imperial College, 1978–87, then Emeritus, and Head of Department of Social and Economic Studies, 1981–87; *b* 26 Jan. 1922; *s* of Louis and Polly Silberston; *m* 1st, 1945, Dorothy Marion Nicholls, MBE (marr. diss.; she *d* 2006); (one *s* decd and one *d* decd); 2nd, 1985, Michèle Ledić. *Educ:* Hackney Downs Sch., London; LSE; Jesus Coll., Cambridge. MA (Cantab); MA (Oxon). Served war of 1939–45, Royal Fusiliers, Lieut, 1942–45. Courtaulds Ltd, 1946–50; Kenward Res. Fellow in Industrial Admin, St Catharine's Coll., Cambridge, 1950–53; University Lectr in Economics, Cambridge, 1951–71; Fellow, 1958–71, Dir of Studies in Econs, 1965–71, St John's Coll., Cambridge; Chm., Faculty Bd of Econs and Politics, Cambridge, 1966–70; Official Fellow in Econs, 1971–78, and Dean, 1972–78, Nuffield Coll., Oxford. Sen. Res. Fellow, Business Sch. (formerly Management Sch., then Tanaka Business Sch.), Imperial Coll. London, 1987–2005. Rockefeller Fellow, Univ. of Calif, Berkeley, 1959–60; Visiting Professor: Queensland Univ., 1977; Univ. of the South, Sewanee, 1984. Member: Monopolies Commn, 1965–68; Board of British Steel Corp., 1967–76; Departmental Cttee on Patent System, 1967–70; Econs Cttee, SSRC, 1969–73; Royal Commn on the Press, 1974–77; Restrictive Practices Ct, 1986–92; Royal Commn on Environmental Pollution, 1986–96; Biotechnol. Adv. Commn, Stockholm Envmt Inst., 1993–97; Council of Experts, Intellectual Property Inst., 1992–2013. Sen. Advr, London Economics, 1992–2004; Economic Adviser, CBI, 1972–74; Specialist Advr, Eur. Communities Cttee, H of L, 1993; Chm., Assoc. of Learned Societies in the Social Sciences, 1985–87; President: Section F, British Assoc., 1987; Confedn of European Economic Assocs, 1988–90 (Vice-Pres., 1990–92); Vice-Pres., REconS, 1992– (Sec.-Gen., 1979–92). *Publications:* Education and Training for Industrial Management, 1955; (with G. Maxcy) The Motor Industry, 1959; (jtly) Economies of Large-scale Production in British Industry, 1965; (jtly) The Patent System, 1967; (with C. T. Taylor) The Economic Impact of the Patent System, 1973; (ed) Industrial Management: East and West, 1973; (with A. Cockerill) The Steel Industry, 1974; (jtly) Microeconomic Efficiency and Macroeconomic Performance, 1983; The Multi-Fibre Arrangement and the UK Economy, 1984; (jtly) British Manufacturing Investment Overseas, 1985; The Economic Importance of Patents, 1987; (ed) Technology and Economic Progress, 1989; Patent Policy: is the pharmaceutical industry a special case?, 1989; (with Michèle Ledić) The Future of the Multi-Fibre Arrangement, 1989; (ed with Gianna Boero) Environmental Economics, 1995; (jtly) Beyond the Multifibre Arrangement, 1995; (with C. Raymond) The Changing Industrial Map of Europe, 1996; PR China's Textile and Clothing Sector and its Export Potential, 1999; (with Philip Bentley) Anti-dumping and Countervailing Action: limits imposed by economic and legal theory, 2007; articles in Econ. Jl, Bulletin of Oxford Inst. of Statistics, Oxford Economic Papers, Jl of Royal Statistical Society. *Recreations:* music, reading. *Address:* Rue Jules Lejeune 2, 1050 Brussels, Belgium. *Club:* Fondation Universitaire (Brussels). *Died 24 March 2015.*

SILKE, William James; Non-Permanent Judge, Court of Final Appeal, Hong Kong, 1997–2006; Judge of the Court of Appeal, Brunei Darussalam, 1998–2005; *b* 21 Sept. 1929; *s* of William Joseph Silke and Gertrude (*née* Delany). *Educ:* Dominican Convent, Wicklow; Xavier Sch., Donnybrook; King's Inns, Dublin. Called to Irish Bar (South Eastern Circuit, Leinster Bar), 1955; Magistrate, North Borneo/ Malaysia, 1959; Registrar, High Court in Borneo (Sabah-Sarawak), 1965; Puisne Judge, 1966; retired under compensation scheme during Malaysianisation, 1969; Hong Kong: Magistrate, 1969; President, Tenancy Tribunal, 1971; Acting Asst Registrar, High Court, 1972; President, Lands Tribunal, 1974; Judge, District Court, 1975; Judge of the High Court, 1979; Justice of Appeal, Supreme Court, 1981–94; Vice-Pres., Court of Appeal, 1987–94; Judicial Comr, State of Brunei, 1978–91. Mem., Royal Dublin Soc., 1996–. *Recreations:* horse racing/breeding, music, travel. *Address:* 16 Seabank Court, Marine Parade, Sandycove, Co. Dublin, Ireland. *T:* (1) 2808739, *Fax:* (1) 2808372. *Clubs:* Royal Over-Seas League; Stephen's Green (Dublin); Royal Sabah Turf (Sabah, Malaysia); Hong Kong, Hong Kong Jockey (Hong Kong). *Died 17 Jan. 2012.*

SILLARS, Margo; *see* MacDonald, M.

SIMEON, Sir Richard (Edmund Barrington), 8th Bt *cr* 1815, of Grazeley, Berkshire; PhD; FRSC; Professor of Political Science and Law, University of Toronto, 1990–2010, then Emeritus; *b* 2 March 1943; *s* of Sir John Simeon, 7th Bt and of Anne Robina Mary (*née* Dean); *S* father, 1999, but his name does not appear on the Official Roll of the Baronetage; *m* 1st, 1966, Agnes Joan Weld (marr. diss. 1990); one *s* one *d*; 2nd, 1992, Maryetta Cheney. *Educ:* Univ. of British Columbia (BA Hons 1964); Yale Univ. (MA 1966; PhD 1968). FRSC 2005. Queen's University, Kingston, Ont: Asst Prof., 1968; Assoc. Prof., 1972–76; Dir, Inst. of Intergovtl Relns, 1976–83; Prof. of Political Studies, 1976–90; Dir, Sch. of Public Admin, 1985–90. Res. Co-ordinator, Royal Commn on the Econ. Union and Canada's Develt Prospects, 1983–85; Vice Chm., Ontario Law Reform Commn, 1988–96. Vis. Prof., Essex Univ., 1975–76; Vis. Prof. of Public Law, Univ. of Cape Town, 1997 and 2000; William Lyon Mackenzie

King Prof. of Canadian Studies, Harvard Univ., 1998 and 2006–08. *Publications:* Federal-Provincial Diplomacy: the making of recent policy in Canada, 1972; (jtly) Small Worlds: provinces and parties in Canadian political life, 1983; (jtly) State, Society and the Development of Canadian Federalism, 1991; (jtly) Degrees of Freedom: Canada and the United States in a changing world, 1997; ed numerous other works; contribs to jls. *Recreations:* walking, canoeing. *Heir:* *s* Stephen George Barrington Simeon [*b* 29 Oct. 1970; *m* 1996, Michelle Owens; one *s* one *d*]. *Address:* (home) #906, 21 Dale Avenue, Toronto, ON M4W 1K3, Canada. *T:* (416) 9618314. *Died 11 Oct. 2013.*

SIMEONS, Charles Fitzmaurice Creighton, MA; DL; formerly Consultant: Environmental Control, Market and Behavioural Studies, Health and Safety at Work, Communications with Government, technical programmes for conferences and annual events in international chemical control, London and Washington; *b* 22 Sept. 1921; *s* of Charles Albert Simeons and Vera Hildegarde Simeons; *m* 1st, 1945, Rosemary (*née* Tabrum) (*d* 1991); one *s* one *d*; 2nd, 1991, Constance Anne Dowson (*née* Restell). *Educ:* Oundle; Queens' Coll., Cambridge. Royal Artillery with 8th Indian Div., 1942–45, HQ RA E African Comd and Northern Comd (Major). Man. Dir, supplier to photographic industry, 1957–70. MP (C) Luton, 1970–Feb. 1974. Dir, Action Learning Trust, 1978–82. Chm., Luton Cons. Assoc., 1960–63. President: Luton, Dunstable and District Chamber of Commerce, 1967–68; Rotary Club of Luton, 1960 (Mem., 1951–91); District Gov., Rotary International, 1967–68; Mem., Rotary Club of Holt, 1992; Advisor, Eastern Area, Prince's Youth Business Trust, 1994–2000; Chm. of cttees raising funds for disabled and cancer research and for National Children's Homes, 1969–78; Chm., Kelling Hosp. Gala, 1996–97, 2000; Member: Nat. Appeals Cttee, Cancer Res. Campaign, 1977–78; Children in Danger Campaign, 1985–90. Chm., Adv. Cttee, Rotary Internat. Bd on Environmental Research and Resources, 1973–74; Vice Pres., Nat. Industrial Material Recovery Assoc., 1972–77; Member: Internat. Cttee, Water Pollution Control Federation, Washington, DC, 1974–77; Customer Consultative Cttee, Anglian Water, 1984–89, Thames Water, 1986–89; Eastern Customer Services Cttee, Water Services, 1990–96; Council, Smaller Business Assoc., 1974–76; ABCC Small Firms Panel; Chm., Central Govt Cttee, Union of Independent Cos. Member: N Norfolk Public Plenary Gp, 1998–2000; N Norfolk Healthwatch, 2000–03; Co-ordinator, Kelling Hosp. Ambulance Appeal, 2003–04. Founder Chm., Friends of Pensthorpe Waterfowl Trust, 1993–95 (Founder Patron of Trust, 1990). Hon. Mem., Inst. of Water Pollution Control, 1973. Liveryman: Co. of Feltmakers (Master, 1987–88); Co. of Water Conservators, 2000 (Mem., 1991). Guild of Freemen of City of London. FIIM. Hon. FIWEM. Pres., Old Oundelian Club, 1976–77; Hon. Secretary: 8th Indian Clover Club, 1984–2003; Manchester Artillery 52nd Field Regt RA Officers' Reunion, 1998–2003. Patron, Luton Area, Dunkirk Veterans, 1995–2000 (Pres., 1965–95). JP Luton, 1959–74; DL Beds, 1987. *Publications:* Energy Research in Western Europe, 1976; Coal: its role in tomorrow's technology, 1978; Water as a Source of Energy, 1980; A Review of Chemical Response Data Bases in Europe and the United States, 1985; Studies on Incidents Involving Chemicals on Board Ship, in Port, and at Sea in Europe and the United States, 1985; Data Bases capable of response to Chemical Incidents Worldwide, 1986; Kelling Hospital Centenary Book, 2003. *Recreations:* watching football, cricket, gardening. *Address:* Mill Leet, High Street, Cley-next-the-Sea, Norfolk NR25 7RR. *T:* (01263) 740772. *E:* charles.simeons@btinternet.com. *Clubs:* Achilles, City Livery. *Died 3 Aug. 2014.*

SIMMONS, Peter Patrick; High Commissioner for Barbados in the United Kingdom, 1995–2003; *b* 13 April 1942; *s* of late Kenneth G. Simmons and of Sybil Louise Simmons; *m* 1968, Rosalind Cecelia Hinds; one *s* one *d*. *Educ:* London Sch. of Journalism (Diploma); New York State Univ. (BA); Univ. of WI, St Augustine (Cert Govt Admin). Sub-Editor, Barbados Advocate, 1961–73; Min. of Foreign Affairs, London, NY, Bridgetown, 1963–76; Asst Registrar, Univ. of WI, Cave Hill Campus, 1976–79; Dep. Perm. Rep. and Chargé d'Affaires, Barbados Mission to UN, 1979–82; Chief Develt Planner, Min. of Finance and Planning, 1982–84; Dir of Communications, Barbados, 1984–86; Political Specialist, US Embassy, Bridgetown, 1986–91; Chm., SBG Develt Corp., 1991–94. ITV documentary: The Red Legs of Barbados, 1986. *Publications:* Red Legs: class and colour contradictions in Barbados, 1976; (with Sir Garfield Sobers) The Changing Face of Cricket, 1995. *Recreations:* reading, public affairs, cricket, cooking, walking. *Died 28 Oct. 2014.*

SIMONET, Sir (Louis Marcel) Pierre, Kt 1985; CBE 1980 (OBE 1972); Director and Proprietor, Pharmacie Simonet, since 1955 (founded by father, 1926); *b* 6 March 1934; *s* of Marcel Simonet and Marguerite Simonet. *Educ:* Collège du St Esprit up to Higher School Certificate. Town Council of Curepipe: Mem., 1960; Vice-Chm., 1962; Chm., 1964; Mayor, 1980; 1st Mem. for Curepipe, Legislative Assembly, 1976–82. Judge Assessor, Permt Arbitration Tribunal, 1984. Dir, Central Electricity Bd, 1972. Chm., Central Housing Authority, 1986–88. Mem., Ex-servicemen's Assoc., 1977; Pres., Widows and Orphans Pension Fund, 1978; Pres., Lions Club of Curepipe, 1979; Chm., Centre Culturel d'Expression Française, 1983–96 (Founder Mem., 1960). Pres., Soc. of St Vincent de Paul. Testimonial, Royal Humane Soc. for life saving, 1962; Chevalier de l'Ordre National du Mérite (France), 1980. *Address:* Queen Mary Avenue, Floreal, Mauritius. *T:* (office) 6763532, *T:* (residence) 6865240. *Club:* Mauritius Racing. *Died 14 July 2015.*

SIMPSON, Prof. (Alfred William) Brian; JP; DCL; FBA 1983; Charles F. and Edith J. Clyne Professor of Law, University of Michigan, 1987–2009, then Emeritus; Professor of Law, University of Kent, 1973–85, then Emeritus; *b* 17 Aug. 1931; *s* of Rev. Canon Bernard W. Simpson and Mary E. Simpson; *m* 1st, 1954, Kathleen Anne Seston (marr. diss. 1968); one *s* one *d*; 2nd, 1969, Caroline Elizabeth Ann Brown; one *s* two *d*. *Educ:* Oakham Sch., Rutland; The Queen's Coll., Oxford (MA 1958, DCL 1976). Nat. Service with Nigeria Regt, RWAFF, 1950–51; E Yorks Regt, TA, 1951–57 (Capt.). Junior Research Fellow, St Edmund Hall, Oxford, 1954–55; Fellow and Tutor, Lincoln Coll., Oxford, 1955–73; Dean: Faculty of Law, Univ. of Ghana, 1968–69; Faculty of Social Sciences, Univ. of Kent, 1975–78; Prof. of Law, Univ. of Chicago, 1984–86. Called to the Bar, Gray's Inn, 1994. Visiting Professor: Dalhousie Univ., 1964; Univ. of Chicago, 1979, 1980, 1982, 1984; Univ. of Michigan, 1985; Goodhart Prof. of Legal Sci., Univ. of Cambridge, 1993–94; Univ. of Toronto, 2009. Hon. Dep. District Attorney, Denver City, 1982. Member, Deptl Cttee on Obscenity and Film Censorship, 1977–79. Fellow, Amer. Acad. of Arts and Scis, 1993. JP Canterbury and St Augustine's, 1968–. Hon. QC 2001. Hon. Fellow, Lincoln Coll., Oxford, 1995. Hon. DLitt Ghana, 1993; Hon. LLD: Dalhousie, 2003; Kent, 2003. *Publications:* Introduction to the History of the Land Law, 1961, new edn as A History of the Land Law, 1986; (ed) Oxford Essays in Jurisprudence, 2nd Series, 1973; A History of the Common Law of Contract, 1975; Pornography and Politics, 1983; Cannibalism and the Common Law, 1984; (ed) A Biographical Dictionary of the Common Law, 1984; Legal Theory and Legal History: essays on the common law, 1987; Invitation to Law, 1988 (trans. Chinese 2008); In the Highest Degree Odious: detention without trial in wartime Britain, 1992; Leading Cases in the Common Law, 1995; Human Rights and the End of Empire: Britain and the genesis of the European Convention, 2001; articles in legal jls. *Recreation:* gardening. *Address:* 3 The Butchery, Sandwich, Kent CT13 9DL. *T:* (01304) 612783, 07703 444664. *E:* bsimpson@umich.edu. *Died 10 Jan. 2011.*

SIMPSON, Ian; artist and writer; Course Director, Open College of the Arts, 1996–99, Consultant, 1999–2010 (East Regional Organizer and Visual Arts Course Leader, 1992–96); *b* 12 Nov. 1933; *s* of Herbert William and Elsie Simpson; *m* 1st, 1958, Joan (*née* Charlton) (marr. diss. 1982); two *s* one *d*; 2nd, 1982, Birgitta Willcocks (*née* Brädde) (decd). *Educ:* Bede Grammar Sch., Sunderland; Sunderland Coll. of Art; Royal Coll. of Art. ARCA 1958. Freelance artist and illustrator, 1958–63; Hornsey Coll. of Art: Lectr, 1963–66; Head, Dept of Visual Research, 1966–69; Head, Dept of Co-ordinated Studies, 1969–72;

Principal, 1972–86, Head, 1986–88, St Martin's Sch. of Art; Asst Rector, London Inst., 1986–88. Exhibited various exhibns, Britain, USA, etc; one-man exhibn, Cambridge, 1975, Durham, 1977, Blandford, 1985, Chappel, Colchester, 1994. Mem. Council, CNAA, 1974–80 (Chm., Fine Art Bd, 1976–81). Pres., Nat. Soc. for Art Educn, 1976. Consultant, Leisure Study Group Ltd, 1986–87. FSAE 1976; FRSA 1983. *Publications:* Eyeline, 1968; Drawing: seeing and observation, 1973; Picture Making, 1973; Guide to Painting and Composition, 1979; Painters Progress, 1983, repr. as Practical Art School, 1995; Encyclopedia of Drawing Techniques, 1987; The Challenge of Landscape Painting, 1990; The New Guide to Illustration, 1990; Anatomy of Humans, 1991; Collins Complete Painting Course, 1993; Collins Complete Drawing Course, 1994. *Television Programmes:* Eyeline (10 programmes), 1968, 1969; Picture Making (10 programmes), 1973, 1976; Reading the Signs (5 programmes), 1977–78. *Recreations:* reading, music. *Address:* 20A The Paddocks, Bures, Suffolk CO8 5DF. *Died 15 Dec. 2011.*

SIMPSON, Malcolm Carter; Director of Finance, Leeds City Council, 1978–82; *b* 15 June 1929; *s* of Arthur and Rhoda Simpson; *m* 1st, 1952, Doreen Patricia Wooler; two *d*; 2nd, 1980, Andrea Gillian Blythe. *Educ:* Stanningley Council Sch. DPA; CIPFA. Employed by Leeds CC for whole of working life, 1943–82: Asst Dir of Finance, 1968; Dep. Dir of Finance, 1973. Board Member: Yorks Water Authority, 1983–88; S Yorks Residuary Body, 1985–89. *Recreations:* golf, bridge. *Address:* Swiss Cottage, 44 Millbeck Green, Collingham Bridge, Leeds LS22 5AJ. *T:* (01937) 573917. *Died 11 March 2013.*

SIMPSON, His Honour Peter Robert; a Circuit Judge, 1989–2008; Second Judge, Mayor's and City of London Court, 1994–2008; *b* 9 Feb. 1936; *o s* of late Surg. Capt. (D) Donald Lee Simpson, RN and of Margaret Olive Simpson (*née* Lathan); *m* 1st, 1968, Mary Elizabeth (marr. diss. 1994; she *d* 2003), *y d* of late Thomas Kirton and Frances Florence Cecilia Kirton; two *s*; 2nd, 1995, Megan Elizabeth, *o d* of late Kenneth John Dodd and Melva Dodd. *Educ:* St John's Coll., Southsea, Hants. Admitted Solicitor, 1960; called to the Bar, Inner Temple, 1970, admitted *ad eundem* Lincoln's Inn, 1972. Practised on S Eastern Circuit, then at Chancery Bar, mainly in property and conveyancing matters; an Asst Recorder, 1983–87; a Recorder, 1987–89; London County Courts, 1989–94. Former Mem., Herts and Essex Sessions Bar mess; a Judicial Mem., S Eastern Circuit Bar mess, 2007–08. Freeman, City of London, 2007; Liveryman, Fan Makers' Co., 2007–. *Recreations:* playing chess, reading legal and political biographies, dipping into books of history, listening to music, browsing through the law reports, dining out. *Address:* Mayor's and City of London Court, Guildhall Buildings, Basinghall Street, EC2V 5AR. *T:* (020) 7796 5400; New Square Chambers, 12 New Square, Lincoln's Inn, WC2A 3SW. *T:* (020) 7405 3808. *Clubs:* Guildhall, Sloane. *Died 10 Jan. 2014.*

SIMPSON-JONES, Peter Trevor, CBE 1971; Président d'Honneur, Société Française des Industries Lucas, since 1980 (Président-Directeur Général, 1957–80); *b* 20 March 1914; *s* of Frederick Henry Jones and Constance Agnès Simpson; *m* 1948, Marie-Lucy Sylvain; one *s* one *d*. *Educ:* Royal Navy School. Served War, RN and SOE. British Chamber of Commerce, France: Vice-Pres., 1967–68 and 1970–72; Pres., 1968–70. Mem., RNSA, 1955–. Chevalier de la Légion d'Honneur, 1948, Officier 1973. *Recreation:* yachting. *Address:* 11 rue Max Blondat, 92 Boulogne-sur-Seine, France. *T:* 48250120. *Club:* Special Forces. *Deceased.*

SINCLAIR, Prof. David Cecil; first Professor of Anatomy, University of Western Australia, 1957–64, then Emeritus; *b* 28 Aug. 1915; *s* of Norman James Sinclair and Annie Smart Sinclair; *m* 1945, Grace Elizabeth Simondson (*d* 1973), Melbourne, Vic.; one *s* one *d*. *Educ:* Merchiston Castle Sch.; St Andrews Univ. (MB, ChB (Commendation) 1937; MD (Hons and Rutherford Gold Medal) 1947); MA Oxon, 1948; DSc Western Australia, 1965. Served in RAMC, 1940–46: AMF, 1943–45; Head of Physiology Sect., Aust. Chem. Warfare Research and Experimental Stn, 1943–44; Dep. Chief Supt, Aust. Field Experimental Stn, 1944–45. Sen. Res. Off., Dept of Human Anatomy, Oxford, 1946–49; Univ. Demonstrator in Anatomy, Oxford, 1949–56; Lectr in Anatomy, Pembroke Coll., Oxford, 1950–56; Lectr in Anatomy, Ruskin Sch. of Fine Art, 1950–56; Dean of Med. Sch., Univ. of Western Australia, 1964; Regius Prof. of Anatomy, Univ. of Aberdeen, 1965–75; Dir of Postgrad. Med. Educn, Queen Elizabeth II Med. Centre, WA, 1975–80. FRCSE 1966; Fellow, Anatomical Soc., 2012. Life Governor, Aust. Postgrad. Fedn in Medicine, 1983. *Publications:* Medical Students and Medical Sciences, 1955; An Introduction to Functional Anatomy, 1957, 5th edn 1975; A Student's Guide to Anatomy, 1961; Cutaneous Sensation, 1967, Japanese edn 1969; Human Growth after Birth, 1969, 6th edn 1998; Muscles and Fascia (section in Cunningham's Anatomy), 11th edn 1972, 12th edn 1981; Basic Medical Education, 1972; The Nerves of the Skin (section in Physiology and Pathophysiology of the Skin, ed Jarrett), 1973; Growth, section in Textbook of Human Anatomy (ed Hamilton), 1976; Mechanisms of Cutaneous Sensation, 1981; Not a Proper Doctor (autobiog.), 1989; Outside the Dissecting Room, 1989; papers on chemical warfare, neurological anatomy, experimental psychology, and medical education; Editor, Jl of Anatomy, 1970–73. *Recreations:* reading, writing, photography, chess problems. *Address:* Flat 3, Netherby, Netherby Road, Cults, Aberdeen AB15 9HL. *Died 30 April 2013.*

SINCLAIR, Sir Ian (McTaggart), KCMG 1977 (CMG 1972); QC 1979; Barrister-at-Law, practising public international law, 1984–2005; Visiting Professor of International Law, King's College, London, 1989–93; *b* 14 Jan. 1926; *s* of late John Sinclair, company director; *m* 1954, Barbara Elizabeth (*née* Lenton) (*d* 2013); two *s* one *d*. *Educ:* Merchiston Castle Sch. (Scholar); King's Coll., Cambridge; BA 1948, LLB 1949 (1st cl. hons). Served Intelligence Corps, 1944–47. Called to the Bar, Middle Temple, 1952; Bencher, 1980. Asst Legal Adviser, Foreign Office, 1950–56; Legal Adviser, HM Embassy, Bonn, 1957–60; Asst Legal Adviser, FO, 1960–64; Legal Adviser, UK Mission to the UN, New York, and HM Embassy, Washington, 1964–67; Foreign and Commonwealth Office: Legal Counsellor, 1967–71; Dep. Legal Advr, 1971–72; Second Legal Advr, 1973–75; Legal Advr, 1976–84. Legal Adviser to UK delegn at numerous internat. confs, incl. Geneva Conf. on Korea and Indo-China, 1954, and Brussels negotiations for UK entry into the EEC, 1961–63; Dep. Chm., UK delegn to Law of Treaties Conf., Vienna, 1968–69; Legal Adviser to UK delegn on negotiations for UK entry into EEC, 1970–72; Member: Bureau of European Cttee on Legal Co-operation, Council of Europe, 1979–81; Panel of Conciliators, Annex to Vienna Convention on Law of Treaties, 1981–; Internat. Law Commn, 1981–86; Panel of Arbitrators, Internat. Centre for Settlement of Investment Disputes, 1988–94; Panel of Legal Experts under INTELSAT Convention, 1990–96; Perm. Ct of Arbitration, 1992–2003. Mem., Committee of Management: British Inst. of Internat. and Comparative Law, 1976–; Inst. of Advanced Legal Studies, 1980–84. Associate Mem., Inst de Droit Internat., 1983, elected Mem., 1987, Emeritus Mem., 2006; Hon. Mem., Amer. Soc. of Internat. Law, 1987. *Publications:* Vienna Convention on the Law of Treaties, 1973, 2nd edn 1984; International Law Commission, 1987; articles in British Yearbook of International Law, International and Comparative Law Qly and other legal jls. *Recreations:* theatre, watching sea-birds. *Address:* Lassington, Chithurst, Petersfield, Hants GU31 5EU. *Died 8 July 2013.*

SINCLAIR, Sir Patrick (Robert Richard), 10th Bt *cr* 1704 (NS), of Dunbeath, Caithness-shire; barrister; *b* 21 May 1936; *s* of Alexander Robert Sinclair (Robin) (*d* 1972) (*b* of 8th Bt) and Vera Mabel (*d* 1981), *d* of late Walter Stephings Baxendale; *S* cousin, 1990; *m* 1974, Susan Catherine Beresford Davies, *e d* of Geoffrey Clive Davies, OBE; one *s* one *d*. *Educ:* Winchester; Oriel Coll., Oxford (MA 1963). Nat. Service, RNVR, 1954–56 (Actg Sub-Lieut). Called to the Bar, Lincoln's Inn, 1961, Bencher, 1994; retired Mem., Chancery Bar. *Recreation:* reading. *Heir:* *s* William Robert Francis Sinclair, *b* 27 March 1979. *Address:* 5 New Square, Lincoln's Inn, WC2A 3RJ. *T:* (020) 7404 0404. *Club:* Pin Mill Sailing (Suffolk). *Died 6 March 2011.*

SINDEN, Sir Donald (Alfred), Kt 1997; CBE 1979; actor; *b* 9 Oct. 1923; *s* of Alfred Edward Sinden and Mabel Agnes (*née* Fuller), Sussex; *m* 1948, Diana (*d* 2004), *d* of Daniel and Muriel Mahony; one *s* (and one *s* decd). First appearance on stage, 1942, in Charles F. Smith's Co., Mobile Entertainments Southern Area; Leicester Repertory Co., 1945; Memorial Theatre Co., Stratford upon Avon, 1946 and 1947; Old Vic and Bristol Old Vic, 1948; The Heiress, Haymarket, 1949–50; Bristol Old Vic, 1950; Red Letter Day, Garrick, 1951. Under contract to Rank Organisation, 1952–60, appearing in 23 films including The Cruel Sea, Doctor in the House, etc. Returned to theatre, appearing in Odd Man In, St Martin's, 1957; Peter Pan, Scala, 1960; Guilty Party, St Martin's, 1961; Royal Shakespeare Co., playing Richard Plantagenet in Henry VI (The Wars of the Roses), Price in Eh!, etc, 1963 and 1964; British Council tour of S America in Dear Liar and Happy Days, 1965; There's a Girl in my Soup, Globe, 1966; Lord Foppington in The Relapse, RSC, Aldwych, 1967; Not Now Darling, Strand, 1968; RSC, Stratford, 1969 and Aldwych, 1970 playing Malvolio; Henry VIII; Sir Harcourt Courtly in London Assurance, revived at New Theatre, 1972, tour of the USA, 1974 (Drama Desk Award); In Praise of Love, Duchess, 1973; Stockmann in An Enemy of the People, Chichester, 1975; Habeas Corpus, USA, 1975; Benedick in Much Ado About Nothing, King Lear, RSC, Stratford, 1976, Aldwych, 1977 (Variety Club of GB Stage Actor of 1976; Evening Standard Drama Award, Best Actor, 1977); Shut Your Eyes and Think of England, Apollo, 1977; Othello, RSC, Stratford, 1979, Aldwych, 1980; Present Laughter, Vaudeville, 1981; Uncle Vanya, Haymarket, 1982; The School for Scandal, Haymarket and Duke of York's (Eur. tour, 1984), 1983; Ariadne auf Naxos, Coliseum, 1983, 1992, 1997; Two Into One, Shaftesbury, 1984; The Scarlet Pimpernel, Chichester transf. to Her Majesty's, 1985; Major Barbara, Chichester, 1988; Over My Dead Body, Savoy, 1989; Oscar Wilde, Playhouse, 1990; Out of Order, Shaftesbury, 1990, nat. tour, 1990–91, Australia, 1992–93; Venus Observed, Chichester, 1992; She Stoops to Conquer, Queen's, 1993; Polonius, Gielgud, 1994; Quartet, Albery, 1999; The Hollow Crown, RSC, Australia and NZ, 2002, Australia, 2003, Canada, 2004; dir, The Importance of Being Earnest, Royalty, 1987; *television series include:* Our Man at St Mark's; Two's Company; Discovering English Churches; Never the Twain; Judge John Deed; Great West End Theatres; appeared in many films. Assoc. Artist, RSC, 1967–. Member: Council, British Actors' Equity Assoc., 1966–77 (Trustee, 1988–2004); Council, RSA, 1972; Adv. Council, V&A Museum, 1973–80; Arts Council Drama Panel, 1973–77; Leicestershire Educn Arts Cttee, 1974–2004; BBC Archives Adv. Cttee, 1975–78; London Acad. of Music and Dramatic Art Council, 1976–; Kent and E Sussex Reg. Cttee, National Trust, 1978–82; Arts Council of GB, 1982–86; Chairman: British Theatre Museum Assoc., 1971–77; Theatre Museum Adv. Council, 1973–80; President: Fedn of Playgoers Socs, 1968–93; Royal Theatrical Fund, 1983–2013; Green Room Benevolent Fund, 1998–2005; Vice-President: London Appreciation Soc., 1960–; Ecclesiological Soc., 2000–. FRSA 1966. Freeman, City of London, 1997. Hon. DLitt Leicester, 2005; Hon. DArts Kent, 2011. *Publications:* A Touch of the Memoirs (autobiog.), 1982; Laughter in the Second Act (autobiog.), 1985; (ed) The Everyman Book of Theatrical Anecdotes, 1987; The English Country Church, 1988; (ed) The Last Word, 1994. *Recreations:* theatrical history, architecture, ecclesiology, genealogy, serendipity. *Address:* Tenterden, Kent TN30 7HX. *Clubs:* Garrick (Trustee, 1980–2000), Beefsteak. *Died 12 Sept. 2014.*

SINGH, Prof. Ajit, PhD; Manmohan Singh Professor, Punjab University, Chandigarh, since 2012; Professor of Economics, Cambridge University, 1995–2007, then Emeritus; Fellow of Queens' College, Cambridge, 1965–2007, then Life Fellow (Senior Fellow, 1992); *b* Lahore, 11 Sept. 1940; *s* of Gurbachan Singh and Pushpa Singh; *m* 1993, Josephine Bradley (marr. diss. 2012); *m* Ann Zammit. *Educ:* Punjab Univ. (BA); Howard Univ. (MA); Univ. of California at Berkeley (PhD). Queens' College, Cambridge: Asst Lectr, 1965; Dir of Studies in Econs, 1972–94; Univ. Lectr, then Reader, Econs Faculty, Cambridge Univ. Scholl Vis. Prof. of Internat. Econs, Univ. of Notre Dame, USA, 1987–95; Prof. of Econs, Univ. of Birmingham Business Sch., 2007–08; Tun Ismail Ali Prof., Univ. of Malaya, 2010–11. Research Consultant: UN Univ., World Inst. of Develt Econ. Res., 1986–92; ILO, 1988–; UNCTAD, 1988–; IFC, 1989–; South Commn, later South Centre, Geneva, 1990–; other adv. positions in Switzerland, Mexico, Tanzania. Founding Editor, Cambridge Jl of Economics, 1977–. Glory of India Award, Indo-British Friendship Soc., 2010. *Publications:* (with G. Whittington) Growth, Profitability and Valuation, 1968; Takeovers, 1971; (ed jtly) The State, Markets and Development, 1994; Corporate Financial Patterns in Industrialising Countries, 1995; (jtly) The Effects of Hyper-Inflation on Accounting Ratios, 1997; (ed with C. Howes) Competitiveness Matters: industry and economic performance in the US, 2000; over 200 articles in learned jls incl. Economic Jl, Rev. of Econ. Studies, Eur. Econ. Review, Cambridge Jl of Econs, Jl of Econ. Literature, World Develt. *Recreations:* table tennis, hiking, travel, friends. *Address:* Queens' College, Cambridge CB3 9ET. *T:* (01223) 335200. *Died 23 June 2015.*

SINGH, Khushwant; Padma Vibhushan 2007 (Padma Bhushan, 1974); Barrister-at-law; writer; Member, Rajya Sabha, India, 1980–86; *b* 2 Feb. 1915; *m* Kaval (*née* Malik) (decd); one *s* one *d*. *Educ:* King's Coll., London (LLB). Called to the Bar, Inner Temple. Practising Lawyer, High Court, Lahore, 1939–47; Min. of External Affairs, of India; PRO Ottawa and London, 1947–51; UNESCO, 1954–56. Visiting Lectr: Oxford (Spalding Trust); USA: Rochester, Princeton, Hawaii, Swarthmore; led Indian Delegn to Writers' Conf., Manila, Philippines, 1965; Guest Speaker at Montreal 'Expo 67'. Wrote for many nat. dailies and foreign jls: New York Times; Observer and New Statesman (London); Harper's (USA); Evergreen Review (USA); London Magazine. Editor, The Illustrated Weekly of India, Bombay, 1969–78; Chief Editor, New Delhi, 1979–80; increased circulation of Illustrated Weekly of India from 80,000 to 410,000 in 9 yrs; Editor-in-chief, The Hindustan Times and Contour, New Delhi, 1980–83. *Broadcasting and television:* All India Radio, BBC, CBC; LP recordings. Awards include: from Punjab Govt: 5,000 rupees and Robe of Honour, for contrib. to Sikh literature; Mohan Singh Award: 1,500 rupees for trans. of Sikh hymns, etc. *Publications: Sikh history and religion:* The Sikhs, 1953; A History of the Sikhs: vol. i, 1469–1839, 1964; vol. ii, 1839–1964, 1967; Ranjit Singh, Maharajah of the Punjab, 1780–1839, 1963; Fall of the Kingdom of the Punjab; Sikhs Today; (ed) Sunset of the Sikh Empire, by Dr Sita Ram Kohli (posthumous); Hymns of Nanak The Guru; The End of India, 2003; *fiction:* The Mark of Vishnu and other stories, 1951; Train to Pakistan, 1956; I Shall Not Hear the Nightingale, 1961; Delhi, 1990; The Company of Women, 2000; Burial at Sea, 2004; The Sunset Club, 2010; *stories:* The Voice of God and other stories; Black Jasmine and other stories; A Bride for the Sahib and other stories; Paradise and other stories, 2004; (*co-author*): Sacred Writing of the Sikhs; (with Arun Joshi) Shri Ram: a biog., 1969; (with Satindra Singh) Ghadr Rebellion; (with Suneet Veer Singh) Homage to Guru Gobind Singh; *miscellaneous:* Love and Friendship (editor of anthology); Khushwant Singh's India—collection of articles (ed Rahul Singh); Shri Ram—a biography; Delhi—a Profile, 1982; The Sikhs, 1984; (with Kuldip Nayar) Punjab Tragedy, 1984; Truth, Love and a Little Malice (autobiog.), 2002; Death at My Doorstep (obituaries), 2005; Khushwantnama: the lessons of my life (autobiog.), 2014; *translations:* Umrao Jan Ada, Courtesan of Lucknow, by Mohammed Ruswa (with M. A. Husaini); The Skeleton (by Amrita Pritam); Land of the Five Rivers; I Take This Woman, by Rajinder Singh Bedi; Iqbal's Dialogue with Allah (Shikwah and Jawab-e-Shikwah); We Indians. *Recreation:* bird watching. *Address:* 49E Sujan Singh Park, New Delhi 110003, India. *T:* (11) 690159. *Clubs:* Imperial Gymkhana (New Delhi); Bombay Gymkhana (Bombay). *Died 20 March 2014.*

SINGH, Marsha; *b* 11 Oct. 1954; *s* of Harbans Singh and late Kartar Kaur; *m* 1971, Sital Kaur (*d* 2001); one *s* one *d*; *m* 2006, Kuldip Mann; one step *s* one step *d*. *Educ:* Loughborough Univ. (BA Hons Pols and Econs of Modern Europe). With Lloyds Bank, 1976–79; Bradford Community Relations Council, 1979–80; Bradford Law Centre, 1980–83; Directorate of Educn, Bradford Council,

1983–90; Bradford Community Health Trust, 1990–97. MP (Lab) Bradford W, 1997–March 2012. *Recreations:* reading, chess, bridge. *Died 17 July 2012.*

SIRS, William; JP; General Secretary, Iron and Steel Trades Confederation, 1975–85; *b* 6 Jan. 1920; *s* of Frederick Sirs and Margaret (*née* Powell); *m* 1941, Joan (*née* Clark) (*d* 2010); one *s* one *d*. *Educ:* Middleton St Johns, Hartlepool; WEA. Steel Industry, 1937–63; Iron and Steel Trades Confedn: Organiser, 1963; Divisional Officer, Manchester, 1970; Asst Gen. Sec., 1973. Member: Iron and Steel Industry Trng Bd, 1973; TUC Gen. Council, 1975–85; Trade Union Steel Industry Cons. Cttee, 1973 (Chm., 1975) and Jt Accident Prevention Adv. Cttee, 1973; Employment Appeal Tribunal, 1976; Jt Sec., Jt Industrial Council for Slag Industry, 1973; Exec. Mem., Paul Finet Foundn, European Coal and Steel Community, 1974; Hon. Sec. (British Section), Internat. Metalworkers Fedn, 1975. Mem., Management Cttee, BSC (Industry) Ltd, 1975. Pres., Northern Home Counties Productivity Assoc., 1985–93; Mem. RIIA, 1973. Mem. Council, Winston Churchill Meml Trust, 1985–90. Director (formerly Governor), Oaklands Coll., Herts, 1991–. JP Hartlepool, Co. Durham, later Knutsford, Cheshire, then Herts, 1963. Freeman, City of London, 1984. *Publications:* Hard Labour (autobiog.), 1985. *Recreations:* sailing, squash, swimming, running. *Address:* Hatfield, Hertfordshire. *Died 16 June 2015.*

SKINNER, Prof. Andrew Stewart, FBA 1993; FRSE; Adam Smith Professor of Political Economy, University of Glasgow, 1994–97, then Emeritus (Daniel Jack Professor, 1985–94); *b* 11 Jan. 1935; *s* of late Andrew Paterson Skinner and Isabella Bateman (*née* Stewart); *m* 1966, Margaret Mary Dorothy Robertson. *Educ:* Glasgow Univ. (MA 1958; BLitt 1960). FRSE 1988. Tutor and Asst Lectr, QUB, 1959–62; Lectr, Queen's Coll., Dundee, Univ. of St Andrews, 1962–64; University of Glasgow: Lectr, 1964–70; Sen. Lectr, 1970–75; Reader, 1975–77; Prof., 1977–85; Dean, Faculty of Social Scis, 1980–83; Clerk of Senate, 1983–90; Vice-Principal, 1991–96. DUniv Glasgow, 2001. *Publications:* (ed) Sir James Steuart, Principles of Political Economy, 1966; (ed with R. H. Campbell and W. B. Todd) Adam Smith, The Wealth of Nations, 1976; A System of Social Science: papers relating to Adam Smith, 1979, 2nd edn 1996; (with R. H. Campbell) Adam Smith: a short biography, 1982; (ed with P. Jones) Adam Smith Reviewed, 1992; (with K. Haakonssen) Index to Smith's Works, 2001. *Recreation:* gardening. *Address:* Department of Political Economy, The University, Glasgow G12 8RT. *T:* (0141) 330 4657; Glen House, Cardross, Dumbarton, Dunbartonshire G82 5ES. *T:* (01389) 841603. *Died 22 Nov. 2011.*

SLACK, His Honour John Kenneth Edward, TD 1964; DL; a Circuit Judge, 1977–99; *b* 23 Dec. 1930; *o s* of late Ernest Edward Slack, formerly Chief Clerk Westminster County Court, and Beatrice Mary Slack (*née* Shorten), Broadstairs; *m* 1959, Patricia Helen, MA Cantab, *o d* of late William Keith Metcalfe, Southport; two *s*. *Educ:* University College Sch., Hampstead; St John's Coll., Cambridge (MA). Captain, RAEC, 1950. Admitted Solicitor, 1957; Partner, Freeborough Slack & Co., 1958–76; Mem. No 1 (later No 14) Legal Aid Area, 1966–69; Deputy Registrar, County Courts, 1969–72; a Recorder of the Crown Court, 1972–77; Pres., Wireless Telegraphy Appeals Tribunal, 1974–77. Captain Club Cricket Conf., 1962–66; Captain Bucks County Cricket Club, 1967–69 (Minor County Champions 1969); Active Vice-Pres., Club Cricket Conf., 1969–77, Pres., 1978. Chm. Council, University Coll. Sch., 1980–87 (Mem., 1974–90). DL Bucks, 1995. *Recreations:* cricket (Cambridge Blue 1954), golf. *Address:* c/o Crown Court, Aylesbury, Bucks HP20 1XD. *Clubs:* Hawks (Cambridge); Beaconsfield Golf. *Died 6 May 2012.*

SLACK, Timothy Willatt, LVO 1995; MA; Principal, St Catharine's Foundation at Cumberland Lodge, 1985–95; *b* 18 April 1928; *yr s* of late Cecil Moorhouse Slack, MC, and Dora Willatt, Beverley, Yorks; *m* 1st, 1957, Katharine (*d* 1993), 2nd *d* of late Walter Norman Hughes, MA, and Jean Sorsbie, Chepstow, Mon; one *s* three *d*; 2nd, 1996, Shuna Ann Black (marr. diss. 2003; she *d* 2006). *Educ:* Winchester Coll.; New Coll., Oxford. Hons. PPE, 1951. Asst, Lycée de Rennes, France, 1951; Asst master, the Salem School, Baden, Germany, 1952; Assistant master, Repton School, 1953–59; Headmaster of Kambawsa College, Taunggyi, Shan State, Burma, 1959–62; Headmaster, Bedales Sch., 1962–74. Chairman, Society of Headmasters of Independent Schools, 1968–70. Dep. Dir, 1975–77, Dir, 1977–83, Wiston House FCO Conf. Centre (incorp. Wilton Park Confs), Steyning; Headmaster, Hellenic Coll. of London, 1983–84. Kurt Hahn Meml Lectr, 1982. Dir, Nat. Tenants Resource Centre, 1993–2008; Chm., Sir Heinz Koeppler Trust, 2001–05. Chm. Governors, The Royal Sch., Windsor Great Park, 1988–95. Chm., Round Table Moot, 1994–2001. Contested (L): Petersfield, Feb. and Oct. 1974; Enfield, Southgate, Dec. 1984; (L/Alliance) Fareham, 1987. *Address:* Greenlands, Stoner Hill, Steep, Petersfield, Hampshire GU32 1AG. *Died 29 June 2013.*

SLATER, James Derrick, FCA; Chairman, Salar Properties Ltd, since 1983; Deputy Chairman, Agrifirma Services Ltd, since 2008; *b* 13 March 1929; *o s* of Hubert and Jessica Slater; *m* 1965, Helen Wyndham Goodwyn; two *s* two *d*. *Educ:* Preston Manor County Sch. Accountant and then Gen. Man. to a gp of metal finishing cos, 1953–55; Sec., Park Royal Vehicles Ltd, 1955–58; Dep. Sales Dir, Leyland Motor Corp. Ltd, 1963; Chm., Slater Walker Securities Ltd, 1964–75; Dir, BLMC, 1969–75. Dep. Chm., Galahad Gold, 2003–08. FCA 1963 (ACA 1953). *Publications:* Return to Go, 1977; The Zulu Principle, 1992; Investment Made Easy, 1994; Pep Up Your Wealth, 1994; Beyond the Zulu Principle, 1996; How to Become a Millionaire, 2000; *for children:* Goldenrod, 1978; A. Mazing Monsters, 1979; Grasshopper and the Unwise Owl, 1979; The Boy Who Saved Earth, 1979. *Recreations:* bridge, salmon fishing. *Died 18 Nov. 2015.*

SLATYER, Prof. Ralph Owen, AC 1993 (AO 1982); FRS 1975; Visiting Fellow, Australian National University, since 1992; *b* 16 April 1929; *s* of Thomas Henry and Jean Slatyer; *m* 1953, June Helen Wade; one *s* two *d*. *Educ:* Univ. of Western Australia (DSc (Agric.). CSIRO Res. Scientist, subseq. Chief Res. Scientist, 1951–67; Prof., Inst. of Advanced Studies, 1967–89, Dir, Res. Sch. of Biol Scis, 1984–89, ANU; Chief Scientist, Dept of Prime Minister and Cabinet, Australia, 1989–92; Mem. and Exec. Officer, Prime Minister's Science Council, 1989–92. Aust. Amb. to UNESCO, 1978–81. Vis. Prof., Duke Univ., 1963–64; Ford Foundn Fellow and Vis. Prof., UCSB, 1973–74. Member: Australian Res. Grants Cttee, 1969–72; Nat. Capital Planning Cttee, 1973–76; Aust. Nat. Commn for UNESCO, 1975–78 (Chm., 1976–78); Policy Adv. Council and Bd of Management, Aust. Centre for Internat. Agricl Research, 1981–85; President: Ecol Soc. of Austr., 1969–71; UNESCO Man and the Biosphere Programme, 1977–81; UNESCO World Heritage Cttee, 1981–83; ICSU Sci. Cttee on Problems of the Environment, 1982–85; ANZAAS, 1983; Chairman: Aust. Biol. Resources Study, 1981–84; Australian Science and Technology Council, 1982–87; Co-ordination Cttee on Sci. and Technol., 1989–92; Co-op. Res. Centres Cttee, 1990–93; Co-op. Res. Centre for Rainforest Ecology and Mgt, 1993–2001; Dep. Chm., Nat. Greenhouse Adv. Cttee, 1989–93. FAA 1967; Fellow, Aust. Acad. of Technol Scis and Engrg, 1992. For. Associate, US Nat. Acad. of Sciences, 1976; Hon. For. Mem., Amer. Acad. of Arts and Scis, 1981; For. Mem., Korean Acad. of Scis and Technol., 1996. Hon. DSc: WA, 1983; Duke, 1986; Qld, 1992; Charles Sturt, 1999; James Cook, 2003; Newcastle, 2003. Edgeworth David Medal, Royal Soc. of NSW, 1960; Austr. Medal of Agric. Sci., 1968; ANZAAS Medal, 1991; Centenary Medal, Australia, 2003. *Publications:* (with I. C. McIlroy) Practical Microclimatology, 1961; Plant-Water Relationships, 1967; (ed with R. A. Perry) Arid Lands of Australia, 1969; (ed jtly) Photosynthesis and Photorespiration, 1971; (ed) Plant Response to Climatic Factors, 1974; papers in learned jls. *Recreations:* bushwalking, golf. *Died 26 July 2012.*

SLIGO, 11th Marquess of, *cr* 1800; **Jeremy Ulick Browne;** Baron Mount Eagle 1760; Viscount Westport 1768; Earl of Altamont 1771; Earl of Clanricarde 1543 and 1800; Baron Monteagle (UK) 1806; *b* 4 June 1939; *s* of 10th Marquess of Sligo and of José Gauche; *S* father, 1991; *m* 1961, Jennifer June, *d* of Major Derek Cooper, Dunlewey, Co. Donegal, and Mrs C. Heber Percy, Pophleys, Radnage; five *d. Educ:* St Columba's College, Eire; Royal Agricultural College, Cirencester. *Heir: cousin* Sebastian Ulick Browne [*b* 27 May 1964; *m* 1984, Christina Maria (marr. diss. 1992), *d* of late Luis Suanzbar; one *s* one *d*]. *Address:* Westport House, Co. Mayo, Eire. *Died 13 July 2014.*

SLIVE, Prof. Seymour; Gleason Professor of Fine Arts at Harvard University, 1973–91, then Emeritus; Director, Fogg Art Museum, 1975–82, sometime Elizabeth and John Moors Cabot Director of Harvard Art Museums; *b* Chicago, 15 Sept. 1920; *s* of Daniel Slive and Sonia (*née* Rapoport); *m* 1946, Zoya Gregorovna Sandomirsky; one *s* two *d. Educ:* Univ. of Chicago (BA 1943; PhD 1952). Served US Navy, Lieut, CO Small Craft, 1943–46. Instructor in Art History, Oberlin Coll., 1950–51; Asst Prof. and Chm. of Art Dept, Pomona Coll., 1952–54; Asst Prof. 1954–57, Assoc. Prof. 1957–61, Prof. 1961–73, Chm. of Dept 1968–71, Fine Arts, Harvard Univ.; Exchange Prof., Univ. of Leningrad, 1961. Ryerson Lectr, Yale, 1962. Slade Prof. of Fine Art, Univ. of Oxford, 1972–73. Trustee, Solomon R. Guggenheim Foundn, 1978–2008. FAAAS 1964; Corresp. FBA 1995. For. Mem., Netherlands Soc. of Sciences, 1971. Hon. MA Harvard, 1958; Hon. MA Oxford, 1972; Hon. PhD 2014. Officer, Order of Orange Nassau, 1962. *Publications:* Rembrandt and His Critics: 1630–1730, 1953; Drawings of Rembrandt, 1965; (with J. Rosenberg and E. H. ter Kuile) Dutch Art and Architecture: 1600–1800, 1965, 2nd edn, 1978; Frans Hals, 3 vols, 1970–74, 2nd rev. edn 2014; Jacob van Ruisdael, 1981; Frans Hals, 1989; Dutch Painting: 1600–1800, 1995, 2nd edn 1998; Jacob van Ruisdael: a complete catalogue of his paintings, drawings and etchings, 2001; Jacob van Ruisdael: master of landscape, 2005; Rembrandt Drawings: a new study, 2009; Jacob van Ruisdael: windmills and water mills, 2011; Windmill at Wijk bij Duurstede, Jacob van Ruisdael, 2013; contribs to learned jls. *Address:* 1 Walker Street Place, Cambridge, MA 02138, USA. *Died 14 June 2014.*

SLOMAN, Sir Albert (Edward), Kt 1987; CBE 1980; DPhil; Vice-Chancellor, University of Essex, 1962–87; *b* Launceston, Cornwall, 14 Feb. 1921; *y s* of Albert Sloman; *m* 1948, Marie-Bernadette, *d* of Leo Bergeron, Cognac, France; three *d. Educ:* Launceston Coll., Cornwall; Wadham Coll., Oxford (Pope Exhibitioner, 1939; Hon. Fellow, 1982). BA Mediæval and Mod. Langs, 1941; MA (Oxon and Dublin); DPhil (Oxon). Served War of 1939–45 (despatches): night-fighter pilot with 219 and 68 squadrons; Flt-Lieut. Lecturer in Spanish, Univ. of California, Berkeley, USA, 1946–47; Reader in Spanish, in charge of Spanish studies, Univ. of Dublin, 1947–53; Fellow TCD, 1950–53; Gilmour Professor of Spanish, University of Liverpool, 1953–62; Dean, Faculty of Arts, 1961–62. Editor of Bulletin of Hispanic Studies, 1953–62. Reith Lecturer, 1963. Chairman: Dept of Education, subseq. British Acad., Studentship Cttee, 1965–87; Cttee of Vice-Chancellors and Principals of UK Univs, 1981–83 (Vice-Chm., 1979–81); Overseas Research Students Fees Support Scheme, 1980–87; Univs' Council for Adult and Continuing Educn, 1984–86; Inter-Univ. and Polytechnic Council, 1985–88; Cttee for Internat. Co-operation in Higher Educn, 1985–88; Selection Cttee of Commonwealth Scholarship Commn, 1986–; Internat. Bd, United World Colls, 1988–92 (Mem., 1985–92); Bd, Univ. of London Inst. of Latin American Studies, 1990–92; Member: Council of Europe Cttee for Higher Educn and Research, 1963–72; Inter-Univ. Council for Higher Educn Overseas, 1964–81; Conf. of European Rectors and Vice-Chancellors, 1965–85 (Pres., 1969–74); Admin. Bd, Internat. Assoc. of Univs, 1965–75 (Vice-Pres., 1970–75); Economic and Social Cttee, EEC, 1973–82; Council, ACU, 1981–87 (Vice-Chm., 1985–87); Commonwealth Scholarship Commn, 1984–93; Bd, British Council, 1985–88. Chm. Bd of Governors, Centre for Inf. on Lang. Teaching and Res., 1979–87; Member: Bd of Governors, Guyana Univ., 1966–92; Cttee of Management, British Inst. in Paris, 1982–97. Pres., Penzance Library, 1990–97. Director: Isys Ltd, 1987–98; Close Brothers Business Expansion Secure Share Account cos, 1992–99. Hon. Doctorate: Nice, 1974; Essex, 1988; Liverpool, 1989. *Publications:* The Sources of Calderón's El Principe constante, 1950; The Dramatic Craftsmanship of Calderón, 1958; A University in the Making, 1964; articles and reviews in Modern Language Review, Bulletin of Hispanic Studies, Hispanic Review, Romance Philology and other journals. *Recreations:* travel, walking. *Address:* 19 Inglis Road, Colchester CO3 3HU. *Died 28 July 2012.*

SLOMAN, (Margaret) Barbara; Under Secretary, Management and Personnel Office (formerly Civil Service Department), 1975–84; *b* 29 June 1925; *d* of Charles and Margaret Pilkington-Rogers; *m* 1950, Peter Sloman (*d* 2003); one *s* one *d. Educ:* Cheltenham Ladies' Coll.; Girton Coll., Cambridge (BA Hons Classics). Asst Principal, Treasury, 1947, Principal 1954–65; Asst Sec., DES, 1965–69; Asst Sec., Civil Service Dept, 1970–75. FCMI. *Address:* 11 Lowther Road, SW13 9NX. *T:* (020) 8748 2196. *Died 11 Sept. 2014.*

SMALE, John Gray; Chairman, Executive Committee of Board of Directors, General Motors Corporation, 1996–2000; *b* 1 Aug. 1927; *s* of Peter John Smale and Vera Gladys (*née* Gray); *m* 1950, Phyllis Anne Weaver (*d* 2006); two *s* two *d. Educ:* Miami Univ., Oxford, Ohio (BS 1949). Procter & Gamble Company, 1952–90: Pres., 1974–81; Pres. and Chief Exec., 1981–86; Chm. Bd and Chief Exec., 1986–90; Chm., Exec. Cttee of Bd of Dirs, 1990; General Motors: Dir, 1981–92; Chm., 1992–96. Hon. LLD: Kenyon Coll., 1974; Miami, 1979; Xavier, 1986; Hon. DSc DePauw, 1983; Hon. DCL St Augustine's Coll., 1985. *Address:* Procter & Gamble, PO Box 599, Cincinnati, OH 45201–0599, USA. *T:* (513) 9831100. *Clubs:* Queen City, Commercial, Cincinnati Country (Cincinnati). *Died 19 Nov. 2011.*

SMALL, David Purvis, CMG 1988; MBE 1966; HM Diplomatic Service, retired; High Commissioner to Guyana and non-resident Ambassador to Suriname, 1987–90; *b* 17 Oct. 1930; *s* of Joseph Small and Ann (*née* Purvis); *m* 1st, 1957, Patricia Kennedy (*d* 1998); three *s*; 2nd, 2003, Pauline L. Alexander. *Educ:* Our Lady's High Sch., Motherwell. National Service, RAF Transport Comd, 1949–51. Metropolitan Vickers, 1951–53; Clerical Officer, Admiralty, Bath, 1953–55; Exec. Officer, HM Dockyard, Rosyth, 1955–58 and Singapore, 1958–60; Admiralty, London, 1960–61; CRO, 1961; Chief Clerk, Madras, 1962–64; Second Sec., Ibadan, 1964–68; Second, later First Sec. and Head of Chancery, Quito, 1968–73; FCO, 1973–76; Head of Chancery, Dacca, 1976–80; First Sec. (Commercial), Stockholm, 1980–82; Counsellor (Economic and Commercial), Copenhagen, 1982–87. *Recreations:* golf, soccer. *Address:* Linden Lea, 31 Royal Crescent, Dunoon, Argyll PA23 7AQ. *T:* (01369) 702620. *Club:* Innellan Golf. *Died 3 Sept. 2015.*

SMALLMAN, Barry Granger, CMG 1976; CVO 1972; HM Diplomatic Service, retired; Founder, Granger Consultancies, 1984; *b* 22 Feb. 1924; *s* of late C. Stanley Smallman, CBE, ARCM, and Ruby Marian Granger; *m* 1952, Sheila Knight (*d* 2009); two *s* one *d. Educ:* St Paul's School; Trinity College, Cambridge (Major Scholar, MA). Served War of 1939–45, Intelligence Corps, Australia 1944–46. Joined Colonial Office, 1947; Assistant Private Secretary to Secretary of State, 1951–52; Principal, 1953; attached to United Kingdom Delegation to United Nations, New York, 1956–57, 1958, 1961, 1962; seconded to Government of Western Nigeria, Senior Assistant Secretary, Governor's Office, Ibadan, 1959–60; transferred to CRO, 1961; British Deputy High Comr in Sierra Leone, 1963–64; British Dep. High Comr in NZ, 1964–67; Imp. Defence Coll., 1968; FCO, 1969–71; Counsellor and Consul-Gen., British Embassy, Bangkok, 1971–74; British High Comr to Bangladesh, 1975–78; Resident Diplomatic Service Chm., Civil Service Selection Bd, 1978–81; High Comr to Jamaica and non-resident Ambassador to Haiti, 1982–84. Mem. Governing Council: SPCK, 1984–99 (Vice Chm., 1993–99); Leprosy Mission, 1985–97; St Lawrence Coll., Ramsgate, 1984–97 (Vice-Pres., 1997–2005); Benenden Sch., 1985–92 (Chm., 1986–92). Reader, C of E, 1996–. *Recreations:* reading, crosswords, making and listening to music, light verse, bird watching. *Address:* Beacon Lodge, Benenden, Kent TN17 4BU. *T:* (01580) 240625. *Died 13 Oct. 2015.*

SMALLMAN, Prof. Raymond Edward, CBE 1992; FRS 1986; FREng; Emeritus Professor of Metallurgy and Materials Science, University of Birmingham, since 2001 (Feeney Professor, 1969–88, Professor, 1988–96; Hon. Professor, 1996–2001); *b* 4 Aug. 1929; *s* of David Smallman and Edith French; *m* 1952, Joan Doreen Faulkner; one *s* one *d*. *Educ:* Rugeley Grammar Sch.; Univ. of Birmingham (BSc, PhD, DSc). FIMMM (FIM 1964); FREng (FEng 1991). AERE Harwell, 1953–58; University of Birmingham: Lectr in Dept of Physical Metallurgy, 1958, Sen Lectr, 1963; Prof. of Phys. Metall., 1964; Head of Dept of Phys. Metall. and Sci. of Materials, 1969–81, of Metallurgy and Materials, 1981–88; Dean of Faculty of Sci. and Eng., 1984–85, of Faculty of Eng., 1985–87; Pro-Vice-Chancellor and Vice-Principal, 1987–92. Visiting Professor: Pennsylvania, 1961; Stanford, 1962; NSW, 1974; Calif, Berkeley, 1978; Cape Town, 1982; Hon. Prof., 1990–, Dist. Lectr, 1999, Univ. of Hong Kong; Van Horn Dist. Lectr, Case Western Reserve Univ., 1978; Edwin Liddiard Lectr, Inst. of Metals, 1991. IUC Consultant, Hong Kong, 1979. Academic Adviser: Ghulam Ishaq Khan Inst. of Engrg Scis and Technol., Topi, Pakistan, 1996–2001; Hong Kong Univ., 1997–2000. Member: Inter-Services Cttee, MoD, 1965; Metals and Materials Cttee, SRC, 1968–71; Materials Adv. Cttee, MoD, 1971; Cttee, Engrg Profs Conf., 1985; Materials Commn, 1988–91, Council, 1992–94, SERC. President: Birmingham Metallurgical Assoc., 1972–73; Fedn of European Materials Socs, 1994–96 (Vice-Pres., 1992–94); Vice-Pres., Metals Soc., 1980–84 (Chm., Metals Sci Cttee, 1974–84); Member: Council, Inst. of Materials (Vice Pres., 1995–99; Chm., Internat. Affairs Cttee, 1993–96); Lunar Soc., 1991–99; Steering Cttee, Industry '96, W Midlands Festival of Industry and Enterprise, 1993–96. Advr, ACU, 1985–91. Warden, Birmingham Assay Office, 1994–97 (Guardian, 1992–94). Dir, Univ. Hosps Birmingham NHS Trust, 1995–99. Gov., Tettenhall Coll., 1979–2009. Foreign Associate, NAE, US, 2005. Hon. Foreign Member: China Ordinance Soc., 1992; Czech Soc. for Metal Sci., 1995. Hon. DSc: Wales, 1990; Univ. of Novi Sad, Yugoslavia, 1990; Cranfield, 2001. Sir George Beilby Gold Medal, Inst. of Metals and Chem. Soc., 1969; Rosenhain Medal, Inst. Metals, 1972; Elegant Work Prize, Metals Soc., 1979; Platinum Medal, Inst. of Metals, 1989; Acta Materialia Gold Medal, 2004. *Publications:* Modern Physical Metallurgy, 1962, 8th edn (jtly) 2013; (jtly) Modern Metallography, 1966; (jtly) Structure of Metal and Alloys, 1969; (jtly) Defect Analysis in Electron Microscopy, 1975; (jtly) Metals and Materials: science, processing and applications, 1994; (jtly) Modern Physical Metallurgy and Materials Engineering, 1999; (jtly) Physical Metallurgy and Advanced Materials, 2007; sci. papers on relationship of microstructure of materials to their properties in learned jls. *Recreations:* writing, travel, friendly golf, bridge. *Address:* The Snippet, Foredraught Lane, Tibberton, Droitwich, Worcester WR9 7NH. *E:* (home) ray.smallman@btopenworld.com, (office) R.E.Smallman@bham.ac.uk. *Club:* South Staffordshire Golf. *Died 25 Feb. 2015.*

SMART, Prof. (Arthur David) Gerald, CBE 1991; FRTPI; Emeritus Professor of Urban Planning, University of London, since 1984; Professor of Urban Planning at University College London, 1975–84 and part-time, 1984–87 (Head of Bartlett School of Architecture and Planning, University College London, 1975–80); *b* 19 March 1925; *s* of Dr A. H. J. Smart and A. O. M. Smart (*née* Evans); *m* 1955, Anne Patience Smart (*née* Baxter); one *d* (and one *d* decd). *Educ:* King's Coll. Choir Sch., Cambridge (chorister); Rugby Sch.; King's Coll., Cambridge; Regent St Polytechnic. MA, DipTP; MRICS, FRSA. Served in The Rifle Brigade, 1943–47 (Captain). Appts in local govt (planning), London, NE England, E Midlands, 1950–63; County Planning Officer, Hants CC, 1963–75; Member: Planning Adv. Gp, 1964–65, Cttee on Public Participation in Planning, 1968–69, Min. of Housing and Local Govt; Planning and Transportation Res. Adv. Council, DoE, 1975–79; Working Party on alternative uses of Historic Buildings, Historic Bldgs Council and BTA, 1979–81; Council, TCPA, 1983–89; Council, RSPB, 1985–90; Governing Body, British Assoc. for Central and East Europe (formerly GB/E Europe Centre), 1985–96; Council, Solent Protection Soc., 1986– (Soc. rep. on Solent Forum); House Builders' Fedn Commn on Inner Cities, 1986–87; occasional Chm., Structure Plans Exams in Public for DoE; Consultant for review of Areas of Outstanding Natural Beauty, Countryside Commn, 1989–90. Chm., Milford-on-Sea Parish Council, 1989–93 (Councillor, 1987–99); Mem. Cttee, Lymington Choral Soc., 1994–2002. Bowland Award, Nat. Assoc. for Areas of Outstanding Natural Beauty, 1999. *Publications:* (with Dr M. Anderson) Planning and Management of Areas of Outstanding Natural Beauty, 1990; (jtly) Landscapes at Risk?, 2001; (jtly) The Future of the South Downs, 2007; articles, conf. papers, chapters in books, professional and other jls, booklets and reports. *Recreations:* sailing, ornithology, music, walking. *Address:* 10 Harewood Green, Keyhaven, Lymington, Hants SO41 0TZ. *T:* (01590) 645475. *Clubs:* Royal Lymington Yacht, Keyhaven Yacht (Lymington). *Died 5 April 2012.*

SMILLIE, (William) John (Jones); Managing Director, Gatehouse Records, since 1992; *b* 18 Feb. 1940; *s* of late John Smillie and Emily Mary Caroline (*née* Jones). *Educ:* Lauriston Sch., Falkirk; Territorial Sch., Stirling; Stirling High Sch. Scottish hotel family background; trained in all hotel depts in Scotland and Paris, with extensive kitchen work; progressed to management with Edward R. Barnett & Co. Ltd, industrial caterers (Asst Gen. Man., 1964–67); joined House of Commons Catering Dept as Personnel Manager, 1967: Personnel Manager and Asst to Catering Manager, 1970; Gen. Man., 1971; Head of Dept, 1980–91. Mem., Newbury Community Radio Assoc., 1996–2000. Member: British Inst. of Cleaning Science, 1976–; Hine Soc., 1979–; Craft Guild of Chefs, 1985–; FIH (FHCIMA 1979); Fellow, Cookery and Food Assoc., 1967; Founder Mem., Wine Guild of UK, 1984–; Mem., Restaurateurs Assoc. of GB, 1983–; Hon. Member: Assoc. Culinaire Française, 1972; Conseil Culinaire Française de Grande Bretagne, en Reconnaissance des Services Rendus à l'Art Culinaire, 1987. *Publications:* articles for catering trade papers. *Recreations:* theatre, ballet, music, piano, motoring, boating, radio presenting, travel, gourmandise, intervals at the opera, jazz music. *Address:* The Gatehouse, 90 Wimbledon Parkside, SW19 5LT. *T:* (020) 8780 9232, *Fax:* (020) 7823 8905. *Died 15 Sept. 2011.*

SMITH, Sir Alan, Kt 1982; CBE 1976; DFC 1941, and Bar 1942; DL; President, Dawson International plc, since 1982; *b* 14 March 1917; *s* of Alfred and Lilian Smith; *m* 1st, 1943, Margaret Stewart Todd (*d* 1971); three *s* one *d* (and one *d* decd); 2nd, 1977, Alice Elizabeth Moncur. *Educ:* Bede College, Sunderland. Self employed, 1931–36; Unilever Ltd, 1937–39; RAF, 1939–45; Man. Dir, Todd & Duncan Ltd, 1946–60; Chm. and Chief Exec., Dawson International, 1960–82. DL Kinross, 1967. *Recreations:* sailing, swimming. *Address:* Ardgairney House, Cleish, by Kinross, Scotland KY13 0LG. *T:* (01577) 850265. *Club:* Lansdowne. *Died 1 March 2013.*

SMITH, Alistair; *see* Smith, Edward A.

SMITH, Sir Andrew Colin H.; *see* Hugh Smith.

SMITH, Anthony (John Francis); writer, broadcaster; *b* 30 March 1926; 2nd *s* of late Hubert Smith (formerly Chief Agent, National Trust) and Diana Watkin; *m* 1st, 1956, Barbara Dorothy Newman (marr. diss. 1983); one *s* two *d*; 2nd, 1984, Margaret Ann Holloway (marr. diss. 2007); one *s*. *Educ:* Dragon School, Oxford; Blundell's School, Devon; Balliol College, Oxford. MA Oxon, 1951. Served with RAF, 1944–48. Oxford University, 1948–51. Manchester Guardian, 1953 and 1956–57; Drum, Africa, 1954–55; Science Correspondent, Daily Telegraph, 1957–63. Founded British Balloon and Airship Club, 1965 (Pres., 1970–); Chm., 1997–2010, Pres., 2010–, Airship Heritage Trust. Voyaged across Atlantic by raft, 2011. Scientific Fellow of Zoological Society. Glaxo Award for Science Writers, 1977; Cherry Kearton Medal and Award, RGS, 1978. TV series include: Balloon Safari, Balloons over the Alps, Great Zoos of the World, Great Parks of the World, Wilderness; radio series include: A Sideways Look, 1977–89; High Street Africa Revisited, 1983–84; Truth to Tell, 1990–93. *Publications:* Blind White Fish in Persia, 1953, repr. 1990; Sea Never Dry, 1958; High Street Africa, 1961; Throw Out Two Hands, 1963; The Body, 1968, new edn 1985; The Seasons, 1970; The Dangerous Sort,

1970; Mato Grosso, 1971; Beside the Seaside, 1972; Good Beach Guide, 1973; The Human Pedigree, 1975; Animals on View, 1977; Wilderness, 1978; A Persian Quarter Century, 1979; A Sideways Look, 1983; The Mind, 1984; Smith & Son, 1984; Which Animal Are You?, 1988; The Great Rift, 1988; Explorers of the Amazon, 1990; Swaps, 1992; The Free Life, 1994; Sex, Genes and All That, 1997; The Human Body, 1998; Survived, 1998; Ballooning, 1998; The Weather, 2000; Machine Gun, 2002; The Lost Lady of the Amazon, 2003. *Recreations:* travel, lighter-than-air flying. *Address:* 52 Mayfield Road, W12 9LU. *T:* (020) 8743 0551; St Aidan's, Bamburgh, Northumberland NE69 7BJ. *T:* (01668) 214944. *Died 7 July 2014.*

SMITH, Ven. (Anthony) Michael P.; *see* Percival Smith.

SMITH, Bryan Crossley, CBE 1982; CEng, FIGEM; Member for Marketing, British Gas Corporation, 1977–82; Chairman: C.S.E. (Wendover) Ltd, Business Consultants, since 1981; Turbine Power Ltd (formerly Power Generation), 1988–2002; *b* 28 Feb. 1925; *s* of Frank Riley Smith and Fanny Smith; *m* 1948, Patricia Mabbott; one *s* one *d*. *Educ:* Hipperholme Grammar Sch.; Bradford Technical Coll. CEng, FIGEM (FIGasE 1944). Articled pupil to John Corrigan, 1941; Operating Engr, Humphreys & Glasgow, 1944; Works Engr, Middlesbrough Corp. Gas Dept, 1948; N Eastern Gas Board: Asst Works Manager, Huddersfield, 1952; Engr and Man., Dewsbury, 1956; Group Sales Man., Wakefield, 1961; Conversion Man., 1966; Dep. Commercial Man., 1968; Chief Service Man., Gas Council, 1970; Service Dir, British Gas Corp., 1973. Senior Vice-Pres., IGasE, 1980–81. Pres., Wendover Soc., 2002– (Chm., 1985–2002). *Recreation:* gardening. *Address:* 28a Dobbins Lane, Wendover, Aylesbury, Bucks HP22 6DH. *T:* (01296) 622742. *Died 29 Feb. 2012.*

SMITH, Charles; Sheriff of Tayside, Central and Fife at Cupar and Dundee, 1991–97; *b* 15 Aug. 1930; *s* of late Charles Smith and Mary Allan Hunter or Smith; *m* 1959, Janet Elizabeth Hurst (*d* 1999); one *s* one *d*. *Educ:* Kinnoull Primary Sch.; Perth Academy; St Andrews University. MA, LLB. Solicitor 1956. Practised as principal with Campbell Brooke and Myles, Perth, 1961–82; Interim Depute Procurator Fiscal, 1975–82; Temporary Sheriff, 1977–82 and 1997–2002; Sheriff (floating appointment): of Glasgow and Strathkelvin, 1982–86; of Tayside, Central and Fife at Perth, 1986–91. Tutor, Dept of Law, Dundee Univ., 1979–82. Member Council: Law Soc. of Scotland, 1977–82 (Convener, various cttees); Sheriffs' Assoc., 1987–90. Mem., Perth Town Council, 1966–68. *Recreations:* tennis, golf, croquet. *Address:* c/o Brodies, LLP, 15 Atholl Crescent, Edinburgh EH3 8HA. *T:* (0131) 228 3777. *Clubs:* Western (Glasgow); Kinnoull Lawn Tennis. *Died 14 Nov. 2011.*

SMITH, Sir Colin S.; *see* Stansfield Smith.

SMITH, His Honour David Arthur; QC 1982; a Circuit Judge, 1986–2004; *b* 7 May 1938; *s* of late Arthur Heber Smith and Marjorie Edith Pounds Smith; *m* 1967, Clementine Smith, JP (*née* Urquhart); two *s*. *Educ:* Lancing College; Merton Coll., Oxford (MA Hons Jurisprudence). Called to Bar, Middle Temple, 1962; Official Principal of Archdeaconry of Hackney, 1973–; a Recorder, 1978–86. Mem., Parole Bd, 1989–94. Wine Treasurer, Western Circuit, 1980–86; Pres., Council of HM Circuit Judges, 2000 (Treas., 1991–98). *Publications:* John Evelyn's Manuscript on Bees from Elysium Britannicum, 1966; (jtly) Bibliography of British Bee Books, 1979; (with David Frimston) Beekeeping and the Law—Swarms and Neighbours, 1993. *Recreations:* acting (Mem., Old Stagers, 1982–), bees (Sec. of Internat. Bee Research Assoc., 1963–), books, canals, Rossini. *Died 30 March 2015.*

SMITH, David Buchanan, FSAScot; Sheriff of North Strathclyde at Kilmarnock, 1975–2001; *b* 31 Oct. 1936; *s* of William Adam Smith and Irene Mary Calderwood Hogarth; *m* 1961, Hazel Mary Sinclair; one *s* one *d* (and one *s* decd). *Educ:* Paisley Grammar Sch.; Glasgow Univ. (MA); Edinburgh Univ. (LLB). Harry Dalgety Scholarship, 1961, 1962. Advocate, 1961; Standing Junior Counsel to Scottish Educn Dept, 1968–75. Tutor, Faculty of Law, Univ. of Edinburgh, 1964–72. Res. Associate, Nat. Mus of Scotland, 2002–. Member Council: Stair Soc., 1994– (Vice Chm. Council, 1998–); Scottish Nat. Dictionary Assoc., 1994–2002; Sheriffs' Assoc., 1998–2001 (Treas., 1979–89; archivist, 1989–); Scottish Language Dictionaries, 2002–; Mem., Scottish Records Adv. Council, 2001–08. Trustee: The Scottish Curling Museum Trust, 1980–; Scottish Curling Trust (formerly Royal Caledonian Curling Club Charitable Trust); President: Ayr Curling Club, 1995–96; Eglinton County Curling Game, 2000–04. Lifetime Achievement Award, Royal Caledonian Curling Club, 2005. *Publications:* Curling: an illustrated history, 1981; The Roaring Game: memories of Scottish curling, 1985; (contrib.) The Laws of Scotland: Stair Memorial Encyclopedia, vol. 6, 1988; George Washington Wilson in Ayrshire, 1991; (contrib.) Atlas of Scottish History to 1707, 1996; (contrib.) Macphail, Sheriff Court Practice, 2nd edn 1999; (contrib.) Sport, Scotland and the Scots, 2000; (contrib.) Oxford Companion to Scottish History, 2001; (contrib.) Encyclopaedia of Traditional British Rural Sports, 2005; articles in Scots Law Times, Juridical Rev., Jl of Law Soc. of Scotland, Scottish Book Collector, The Medal, Rev. of Scottish Culture, Scottish Curler, Procs of Soc. of Antiquaries of Scotland, Book of the Old Edinburgh Club, and newspapers. *Recreations:* history of the law and institutions of Scotland, curling, collecting curliana, music, architecture, grandchildren. *Address:* 72 South Beach, Troon, Ayrshire KA10 6EG. *T:* (01292) 312130. *E:* dvdsmith1936@gmail.com. *Died 2 Dec. 2015.*

SMITH, David Gerard G.; *see* Gordon-Smith.

SMITH, David Grahame G.; *see* Grahame-Smith.

SMITH, David John Harry, CBE 1998; PhD; FRSC; Director, Research and Development, 1994–2001, Board Member, 1995–2001 and Chief Executive Officer, 1996–2001, Whatman plc; *b* 5 Aug. 1941; *s* of Harry Nelson Smith and Mabel Freda Smith (*née* Stanford); *m* 1963, Dorothy Patricia Evans; one *s* one *d*. *Educ:* Univ. of Aston (BSc Chem. 1963); Univ. of Western Ontario (PhD Organic Chem. 1967). FRSC 1982. Univ. Lectr, Chem. Dept, Univ. of Leicester, 1969–80; Res. Dir, Biosynth AG, Zürich, 1978–82; joined BP, 1980; Vice-Pres., R&D, BP America, 1987; Head, BP Gp Res. and Engrg, 1992. Non-executive Director: Murphy Oil Corp., 2001–; Idatech plc, 2007–. Member: Strategic Allocations Cttee, Nat. Sci. and Engrg Council, Canada, 1993–96; Technology Foresight Steering Cttee, 1994–96; EPSRC, 1994–2000; Chairman: LINK TCS (formerly LINK) Bd, 1996–2001; LINK Review, 2001–02; Vet. Lab. Agency Ownership Bd, DEFRA, 2006–10. *Publications:* numerous scientific papers and patents. *Recreations:* educating palate, golf. *Address:* Iverston House, 20 Fitzroy Road, Fleet, Hants GU51 4JJ. *Died 1 Sept. 2015.*

SMITH, Derek B.; *see* Bryce-Smith.

SMITH, Dick K.; *see* King-Smith.

SMITH, Ven. Donald John; Archdeacon of Sudbury, 1984–91, then Emeritus; Hon. Canon of St Edmundsbury and Ipswich, 1973–91, then Emeritus; *b* 10 April 1926; *s* of Dr John Arthur Smith and Evelyn Peggy Smith; *m* 1948, Violet Olive Goss (*d* 1999); two *s* (one *d* decd). *Educ:* Clifton Theological Coll.; Cardiff Law Sch., Univ. of Wales (LLM 1996). Deacon, 1953; priest, 1954; Assistant Curate: Edgware, 1953–56; St Margaret's, Ipswich, 1956–58; Vicar of St Mary, Hornsey Rise, Islington, 1958–62; Rector of Whitton, Ipswich, 1962–75; Rector of Redgrave cum Botesdale with The Rickinghalls, 1975–79; Archdeacon of Suffolk, 1975–84. HCF 1964. *Publications:* A Confirmation Course, 1974; (ed) Tourism and the Use of Church Buildings, 1983; Covenanting for Disunity, 1981; Thank you Lord for Alison, 1987; Straightforward and Simple: a guide for churchwardens, 1989; Fourteen Charges - and The Rest, 2006; (ed) Poems by Violet Smith, 2010. *Recreations:* foreign travel, chess, photography, gardening, good food, dining out. *Address:* 1 Manor Lane, Shipton-on-Stour, Warwicks CV36 4EF. *T:* (01608) 663828. *Died 22 Aug. 2014.*

SMITH, Ven. Douglas Leslie B.; *see* Bartles-Smith.

SMITH, Dr (Edward) Alistair, CBE 1982; Director, University of Aberdeen International Office, 1990–2002; *b* 16 Jan. 1939; *s* of Archibald Smith and Jean Milne Johnston. *Educ:* Aberdeen Grammar Sch.; Univ. of Aberdeen (MA, PhD); Univ. of Uppsala, Sweden. Lectr, Univ. of Aberdeen, 1963–88. Dir, Univ. of Aberdeen Develt Trust, 1982–90; Mem., Grampian Health Bd, 1983–91. Pres., Scottish Conservative and Unionist Assoc., 1979–81; Dep. Chm., Scottish Conservative Party, 1981–85. Member: Exec., Aberdeen and NE Council on Disability; Exec., Grampian ASH; Scottish Cttee, 1989–91, NE Scotland Regl Bd, 1991–92, NCC; SCOTVEC, 1989–92. *Publications:* (with R. E. H. Mellor) Europe: a geographical survey of the Continent, 1979; articles on Scandinavia, Europe and Scotland. *Recreations:* travel, photography, music. *Address:* Villa Little Paradise, Dharmavijayarama Mawatha, Pitaramba, Bentota, Sri Lanka. *T:* 776144989. *E:* aberdeensmith@aol.com. *Died 25 July 2012.*

SMITH, Eric Norman, CMG 1976; HM Diplomatic Service, retired; British High Commissioner in The Gambia, 1979–81; *b* 28 Jan. 1922; *s* of late Arthur Sidney David Smith; *m* 1955, Mary Gillian Horrocks. *Educ:* Colfe's Sch., London. Served War, Royal Corps of Signals, 1941–46. Foreign Office, 1947–53; HM Embassy, Cairo, 1953–55; UK Delegn to the UN, New York, 1955–57; FO, 1957–60; HM Embassy, Tehran, 1960–64; FO, 1964–68; British Information Services, New York, 1968–71; FCO, 1971–75; Singapore, 1975–79. *Recreations:* music, photography. *Address:* Troodos, Castle Lane, Budleigh Salterton, Devon EX9 7AN. *Died 29 July 2011.*

SMITH, Geoffrey M.; *see* Maitland Smith.

SMITH, Prof. Harry, CBE 1993; PhD, DSc; FRCPath; FRS 1979; FSB; Professor and Head, Department of Microbiology, University of Birmingham, 1965–88, then Emeritus Professor; *b* 7 Aug. 1921; *s* of Harry and Annie Smith; *m* 1947, Janet Mary Holmes; one *s* one *d*. *Educ:* Northampton Grammar Sch.; University Coll. (of London) at Nottingham. BPharm, BScChem (1st Cl. Hons), PhD, DSc London. Analyst, Boots Pure Drug Co., Nottingham, 1942–45; Asst Lectr, then Lectr, Dept of Chemistry, UCL at Nottingham, 1945–47; Microbiological Research Establishment, Porton: Sen. Scientific Officer, 1947; Principal Sci. Officer, 1951; Sen. Prin. Sci. Officer (Research Merit), 1956; Dep. Chief Sci. Officer (Res. Merit), 1964. Visiting Professor: Dept of Bacteriology, Univ. of Calif, Berkeley, USA, 1964, UCLA, 1972; (summer) Dept of Microbiol., Univ. of Washington, Seattle, USA, 1977, Univ. of Michigan, Ann Arbor, 1981, TCD, 1991. Society for General Microbiology: Mem. Council, 1960–64; Meetings Sec., 1964–68; Treas., 1968–75; Pres., 1975–78; Hon. Mem., 1986; Treas., Fedn of Eur. Microbiol Socs, 1975–82; Pres. and Chm., Organising Cttee, 14th (1986) Internat. Congress of Microbiology, Manchester. Member: Adv. Cttee on Dangerous Pathogens, 1985–88; PHLS Bd, 1985–89; Defence Scientific Adv. Council, 1987–93; Council, Royal Soc., 1989–91; NATO Adv. Panel, Security-related Civil Sci. and Tech., 1999–2004; Assessor, AFRC, 1990–94. Lectures: Amer. Soc. for Microbiol., 1984; Australian Soc. for Microbiol., 1985; Fred Griffith, 1989, Jubilee (50 yrs), 1995, Soc. for Gen. Microbiol.; Leeuwenhoek, Royal Soc., 1991. Hon. MRCP 1986; Hon. ARCVS 1993. Hon. DSc: Leicester, 1992; Nottingham, 2001. Bledisloe Vet. Award, RASE, 1992; Stuart Mudd Award, Internat. Union of Microbiol. Socs, 1994. *Publications:* over 350 papers in jls and books, mainly on mechanisms of microbial (bacterial, viral and fungal) pathogenicity. *Recreation:* interest in farming. *Address:* The Medical School, University of Birmingham, Birmingham B15 2TT. *T:* (0121) 414 6920. *E:* hsmithcbefrsbham@btopenworld.com. *Club:* Athenæum. *Died 10 Dec. 2011.*

SMITH, Prof. Harry, FRS 2000; Professor of Botany, University of Leicester, 1978–2001, then Emeritus; Special Professor in Photobiology, University of Nottingham, 2001–09; *b* 19 Sept. 1935; *s* of Joseph and Alice Smith; *m* 1961, Elinor Anne Chandler; one *s* two *d*. *Educ:* Univ. of Manchester (BSc 1959; DSc 1976); Univ. of Wales (PhD 1962). Theresa Seessel Res. Fellow, Yale Univ., 1962–64; Asst Lectr, Birkbeck Coll., London Univ., 1964–65; Lecturer in Botany: Queen Mary Coll., London Univ., 1965–68; Manchester Univ., 1968–71; Prof. of Plant Physiology, Nottingham Univ., 1971–78. Miller Foundn Fellow, Univ. of California, Berkeley, 1995. Corresp. Life Mem., Amer. Soc. Plant Physiologists, 1998. Hon. DSc: Marseilles, 1978; Teesside, 2001. Chief Ed., Plant, Cell and Envmt, 1975–2001; Founding Editor: Molecular Ecology, 1990–; Global Change Biology, 1995–. *Publications:* Phytochrome and Photomorphogenesis, 1975. *Recreations:* garden design, painting in acrylics and watercolour. *Died 9 Feb. 2015.*

SMITH, Maj.-Gen. Hugh M.; *see* Macdonald-Smith.

SMITH, Jack, ARCA 1952; artist; *b* 18 June 1928; *s* of John Edward and Laura Smith; *m* 1956, Susan Craigie Halkett. *Educ:* Sheffield College of Art; St Martin's School of Art; Royal College of Art. Exhibitions: Whitechapel Art Gallery, 1959, 1970, 1971; Beaux Arts Gallery, 1952–58; Matthiesen Gallery, 1960, 1963; Catherine Viviano Gallery, New York, 1958, 1961; Pittsburgh International, 1955, 1957, 1964; Grosvenor Gallery, 1965; Marlborough Gallery, 1968; Konsthallen, Gothenburg, Sweden, 1968; Hull Univ., 1969; Bear Lane Gallery, Oxford, 1970; Redfern Gall., 1973 and 1976; Serpentine Gall., 1978; Fischer Fine Art, London, 1981, 1983; British Painting, Museo Municipal, Madrid, 1983; Flowers East Gall., London, 1990, 1991, 1992, 1994, 1996, 2000, 2009 (retrospective); Flowers Central, 2003, 2007. Designer, sets and costumes: Carmen Arcadiae Mechanicae Perpetuum, Ballet Rambert, 1986; Pursuit, Royal Ballet, 1987. Guggenheim Award (Nat.), 1960. Work in permanent collections: Tate Gallery; Arts Council of Great Britain; Contemporary Art Society; British Council. *Relevant publications:* Jack Smith: a painter in pursuit of marvels, by Norbert Lynton, 2000; The Art of Jack Smith, by Robert Heller, 2007; Jack Smith: retrospective, by Sam Chatterton Dixon, 2008. *Address:* 29 Seafield Road, Hove, Sussex BN3 2TP. *T:* (01273) 738312. *Died 11 June 2011.*

SMITH, James S.; *see* Stuart-Smith.

SMITH, Air Vice-Marshal John Edward, CB 1979; CBE 1972; AFC 1957; Air Officer Administration, Headquarters Strike Command, 1977–81; *b* 8 June 1924; *m* 1944, Roseanne Margurite (*née* Eriksson); four *s* two *d* (and one *s* decd). *Educ:* Tonbridge Sch. Served in Far East, ME, USA and Germany as well as UK Stations from joining the Service in Nov. 1941. *Recreations:* sailing, travel. *Address:* 1 Butlers Grove, Great Linford, Bucks MK14 5DT. *Died 22 June 2013.*

SMITH, Melvyn Kenneth; actor, writer, director; *b* 3 Dec. 1952; *s* of Kenneth and Vera Smith; *m* 1988, Pamela Gay-Rees. *Educ:* Latymer Upper Sch., Hammersmith; New Coll., Oxford. Asst Dir, Royal Court Th., 1973; freelance Dir, Bristol Old Vic, 1973, Liverpool Everyman, 1974, Bush Th., 1975; Associate Director: Crucible Th., Sheffield, 1975–78; Young Vic, 1978–79; actor: Hairspray (musical), Shaftesbury, 2007; actor/writer, TV series: Not The Nine O'Clock News, Muck and Brass, Alas Smith and Jones, 1979–81; Smith & Jones, 1982–92, 1995, 1997, 1998; actor, Dancing on the Edge, 2013; appeared in Small Doses (series of short plays), 1989; Milner, 1994. Films: The Tall Guy, 1989 (Dir); Wilt, 1989; Radioland Murders, 1995 (Dir); Twelfth Night, 1996; Bean, 1997 (Dir); High Heels and Low Lifes, 2001 (Dir); Blackball, 2003 (Dir). Director: TalkBack Prodns, 1982–; Playback Training Films, 1987–; Smith Jones Campbell (formerly Smith Jones Brown and Cassie Commercials) Ltd, 1988–99; Lola Prodns, 1998–. *Publications:* Not the book, 1981; Not the Nine O'Clock News Diary, 1982; (jtly) The Smith and Jones World Atlas, 1983; (jtly) The Lavishly Tooled Smith and Jones, 1986; (jtly) Janet Lives with Mel and Griff, 1988; (jtly) Smith & Jones Head to Head, 1992. *Address:* c/o The Rights House, Drury House, 34–43 Russell Street, WC2B 5HA. *Club:* Groucho. *Died 19 July 2013.*

SMITH, Peter, FSA; Secretary, Royal Commission on Ancient Monuments in Wales, 1973–91, retired; *b* 15 June 1926; *s* of late L. W. Smith, HMI, and Mrs H. Smith (*née* Halsted); *m* 1954, Joyce Evelyn, *d* of late J. W. Abbott and of Alice Abbott (*née* Lloyd); two *s* one *d*. *Educ:* King

Edward VI Sch., Southampton; Peter Symonds' Sch., Winchester; Oriel Coll. and Lincoln Coll. (Open Scholar), Oxford (BA, Hons Mod. Hist. 1947); Hammersmith Sch. of Building (Inter ARIBA 1950). Royal Commission on Ancient Monuments in Wales: Jun. Investigator, 1949; Sen. Investigator, 1954; Investigator in Charge of Nat. Monuments Record, 1963. President: Cambrian Archaeological Assoc., 1979; Vernacular Architecture Gp, 1983–86. Hon. Mem., Soc. of Architects in Wales, 1993. Hon. DLitt Wales, 1991. G. T. Clark Prize, 1969; Alfred Davis Hitchcock Medallion, Soc. of Architectural Historians of GB, 1978. *Publications:* Houses of the Welsh Countryside, 1975, 2nd edn 1988; contribs to Agrarian History of England; periodical literature on historic domestic architecture. *Recreations:* reading, drawing, learning Welsh. *Address:* Tŷ-coch, Lluest, Llanbadarn Fawr, Aberystwyth, Ceredigion SY23 3AU. *T:* (01970) 623556. *Died 12 March 2013.*

SMITH, Peter Vivian Henworth, CB 1989; Government legal adviser, 1990–99; Legal Adviser, Broadcasting Standards Council, later Broadcasting Standards Commission, 1989–98; *b* 5 Dec. 1928; *s* of Vivian and Dorothea Smith; *m* 1955, Mary Marjorie, *d* of Frank John Willsher and Sybil Marjorie Willsher; five *d*. *Educ:* Clacton County High Sch.; Brasenose Coll., Oxford (MA, BCL). Called to the Bar, Lincoln's Inn, 1953. HM Overseas Civil Service: Resident Magistrate, Nyasaland, 1955–63; Registrar, High Court, Nyasaland, 1963–64; Sen. Resident Magistrate, Malaŵi, 1964–69; Puisne Judge, Malaŵi, 1969–70; HM Customs and Excise: Legal Asst, 1970–72; Sen. Legal Asst, 1972–76; Asst Solicitor, 1976–82; Prin. Asst Solicitor, 1982–85; Solicitor, 1986–89. Legal Advr, Bldg Socs Commn, 1990–92. Mem. Cttee, Friends of Malaŵi. *Recreations:* classical music, bridge, computers. *Address:* Likabula, 14 St Albans Road, Clacton-on-Sea CO15 6BA. *T:* (01255) 422053. *E:* pvhsmith@aol.com. *Died 25 May 2011.*

SMITH, Richard John, AM 1997; Director-General, Office of National Assessments, Canberra, 1996–98; *b* 14 Dec. 1934; *s* of C. A. Smith and T. A. O'Halloran; *m* 1958, Janet Campbell; two *s* two *d*. *Educ:* Sydney High Sch.; Sydney Univ. (BA, LLB Hons I 1958). Teacher, London, 1958–59; Solicitor, NSW, 1959–61; Foreign Affairs Trainee, 1961; First Sec., Australian Embassy, Washington, 1967–70; Dep. Perm. Rep., Australian Mission to UN, Geneva, 1972–74; Asst Sec., Internat. Legal Branch, 1974–75; Ambassador to Israel, 1975–77; First Assistant Secretary: Legal & Treaties Div., 1977–81; Management & Foreign Service Div., 1981–83; Actg Dep. Sec., Dept of Foreign Affairs, 1983–85; Ambassador to Thailand, 1985–88; Dep. Sec., Dept of Foreign Affairs and Trade, Canberra, 1988–90; High Comr for Australia in the UK, 1991–94; Ambassador to the Philippines, 1994–96. *Recreations:* walking, reading, travel. *Address:* 11 Glebe Street, Edgecliff, NSW 2027, Australia. *T:* (2) 93620504. *Died 26 July 2015.*

SMITH, Stanley Frank, MA; CEng, FIMechE; Vice-President (Technology), Urban Transport Development Company, Kingston, Ontario, 1985–86; *b* 15 Dec. 1924; *s* of Frederick and Edith Maria Smith; *m* 1st, 1946, Margaret (*née* Garrett) (*d* 1984); two *s* three *d*; 2nd, 1987, Catherine Cooke Murphy. *Educ:* Purley Sch.; Hertford Coll., Oxford (MA). Served War, RAF Pilot, 1943–46. Oxford Univ., 1946–49. Rolls-Royce Ltd, 1949–65 (Chief Research Engineer, 1963); British Railways, 1965–71 (Dir of Engineering Research, 1965; Dir of Research, 1966); joined London Transport, 1971: Dir-Gen. of Research and Develt, 1971–72; Chief Mech. Engr, 1972–81; Gen. Manager, Res. Develt, Urban Transport Development Co., 1981–85. *Recreations:* tennis, windsurfing, cycling, walking, ski-ing, sailing. *Address:* 6789 Highway 33, Bath, ON K0H 1G0, Canada. *T:* (613) 3527429. *Died 20 Jan. 2012.*

SMITH, Stewart Ranson, CBE 1986; Controller, Europe Division, British Council, 1989–90; *b* 16 Feb. 1931; *s* of John Smith and Elizabeth Smith; *m* 1960, Lee Tjam Mui, (Amy), Singapore. *Educ:* Bedlington Grammar Sch., Northumberland; Nottingham Univ. (BA, MA); Yale Univ., USA (MA). British Council: Asst Rep., Singapore, 1957–59; Reg. Officer, Overseas A, 1959–61; Dir, Curitiba, Brazil, 1961–65; Asst Rep., Sri Lanka, 1965–69; Planning Officer, London, 1969–70; seconded Min. of Overseas Develt, 1970–73; Rep., Kenya, 1973–76; Controller, Overseas B, 1976–80; Rep., Spain, 1980–87; Controller, Higher Educn Div., 1987–89. Chm., Consortium for Madrid Capital City of Culture 1992, 1990–92; Consultant, Internat. Relations, Complutense Univ. of Madrid, 1993–95. Cross, Order of Isabella la Católica (Spain). *Recreations:* music, cricket. *Address:* Flat 10, Wellington Place, London Road, Cheltenham, Glos GL52 6EW. *Club:* Athenæum. *Died 25 Nov. 2013.*

SMITH, Stuart Brian, OBE 2004; FMA; Secretary, International Committee for Conservation of Industrial Heritage, 1986–2012, then Honorary Secretary; international consultant on industrial world heritage, since 2002; *b* 19 Aug. 1944; *s* of Jack Fearnly Smith and Edith Dorothy Turner; *m* 1969, Jacqueline Slater; two *s* one *d*. *Educ:* Rochdale Grammar Sch.; Univ. of Surrey (BSc); Univ. of Manchester (MSc). Curator of Technology, Sunderland Museum, 1968–72; Ironbridge Gorge Museum: Curator of Technology, 1972; Dep. Dir, 1977–83; Dir, 1983–92; Chief Exec., Trevithick Trust, 1993–2002. Hon. Lectr, Univ. of Birmingham, 1981–92. Vice Pres., Assoc. for Industrial Archaeology, 1992– (Asst Sec., 1975–92). Member: Royal Commn on Ancient and Historical Monuments in Wales, 1991–96; Industrial Archaeology Panel, English Heritage, 1993–2002. Pres., Midlands Fedn of Museums and Galls, 1991–92 (Vice-Pres. 1989); Mem. Cttee, Icomos UK, 1987–2011. Mem. Council, Trevithick Soc., 1993–2002. Mem., Cornish Mining Consultative Forum, 2012–. Freedom of City of London, 1984; Freeman, Pewterers' Co., 2003. *Publications:* A View from the Ironbridge, 1979; (with Michael Sagar-Fenton) Serpentine, 2005; articles in learned jls. *Recreations:* collecting, industrial archaeology (especially of Asia and Norway). *Address:* Chygarth, 5 Beacon Terrace, Camborne, Cornwall TR14 7BU. *T:* and *Fax:* (01209) 612142. *Died 13 April 2014.*

SMITH, William Jeffrey, CB 1976; Under-Secretary, Northern Ireland Office, 1972–76; *b* 14 Oct. 1916; 2nd *s* of Frederick Smith, Sheffield, and Ellen Hickinson, Ringinglow, Derbyshire; *m* 1942, Marie Hughes (*d* 2007); one *s* one *d*. *Educ:* King Edward VII Sch., Sheffield; University Coll., Oxford (Schol.) (MA). Employed by Calico Printers' Assoc., Manchester, 1938–40 and in 1946. Served War, Army: enlisted Sept. 1939, embodied, 1940; RA and York and Lancaster Regt (Captain), 1940–46. Dominions Office (subseq. CRO), 1946; Principal, 1948; Office of UK High Commissioner in South Africa, 1953–56; Asst Sec., 1959; sundry internat. confs; Dept of Technical Co-operation, 1961–64; Min. of Overseas Development, 1964–70; Overseas Develt Admin, 1970–72; UK Rep. to UNESCO, 1969–72. Sec. to Widgery Tribunal on loss of life in Londonderry, 1972; Northern Ireland Office, 1972. *Recreations:* formerly scrambling up mountains, theatre, bell ringing. *Died 19 Oct. 2011.*

SMITH-DODSWORTH, Sir John (Christopher), 8th Bt *cr* 1784; *b* 4 March 1935; *s* of Sir Claude Smith-Dodsworth, 7th Bt, and Cyrilla Marie Louise von Sobbe, (*d* 1984), 3rd *d* of William Ernest Taylor, Linnet Lane, Liverpool; *S* father, 1940; *m* 1st, 1961, Margaret Anne (*née* Jones) (marr. diss. 1971); one *s* one *d*; 2nd, 1972, Margaret Theresa (*d* 1990) (*née* Grey), Auckland, NZ; one *s*; 3rd, 1991, Lolita (marr. diss. 2004), *d* of Romeo Pulante; one *s* one *d*; 4th, 2006, Nerrisa, *d* of Mateo Feratero. *Educ:* Ampleforth Coll., Yorks. Resided in Coromandel, New Zealand. *Publications:* (jtly) New Zealand Ferns and Allied Plants, 1989; New Zealand Native Shrubs and Climbers, 1991. *Heir:* *s* David John Smith-Dodsworth [*b* 23 Oct. 1963; *m* 1996, Elizabeth Anne Brady, Thirsk, N Yorks; one *s* one *d*]. *Died 21 Sept. 2012.*

SMITH-MARRIOTT, Sir Hugh Cavendish, 11th Bt *cr* 1774, of Sydling St Nicholas, Dorset; Public Relations and Marketing Executive Director, since 1987; Director, H.S.M. Marketing Ltd, Bristol, since 1988; *b* 22 March 1925; *s* of Sir Ralph George Cavendish Smith-Marriott, 10th Bt and Phyllis Elizabeth (*d* 1932), *d* of Richard Kemp; *S* father, 1987; *m* 1953, Pauline Anne (*d* 1985), *d* of F. F. Holt; one *d*. *Educ:* Bristol Cathedral School. Man. Dir, Drawing Office Co., 1956; Group Marketing Executive,

Bryan Brothers Group, 1976. Dir, Bristol Fest. of Remembrance, RBL, 1966–2006; Mem., Royal Marines Assoc., Bristol. Pres., Bristol Musical Comedy Club. *Recreations:* hockey (county level), cricket, painting, theatre. *Heir:* *b* Peter Francis Smith-Marriott [*b* 14 Feb. 1927; *m* 1961, Jean Graham Martin, *d* of James Sorley Ritchie; five *s* (including twin *s*)]. *Clubs:* MCC; Gloucestershire CC, Durham CC, Bristol Savages, Bristol RF. *Died 19 July 2013.*

SMITHIES, His Honour Kenneth (Charles Lester); a Circuit Judge, 1975–90; *b* 15 Aug. 1927; *s* of late Harold King Smithies and Kathleen Margaret (*née* Walsh); *m* 1st, 1950, Joan Winifred (*née* Ellis) (*d* 1983); one *s* two *d*; 2nd, 1996, Kathleen Mary, (Kitty), Floyd (*née* Stevens). *Educ:* City of London Sch. (Corporation Scholar); University College London (LLB). Volunteered 60th Rifles, 1945, later commnd in Royal Artillery, in India; demobilised, 1948. Called to Bar, Gray's Inn, 1955. *Recreations:* music, bridge, pedantry. *Address:* Apartment 13, Richmond Village, Stroud Road, Painswick, Glos GL6 6UH. *T:* (01452) 810721. *Club:* Bath and County (Bath). *Died 23 Nov. 2013.*

SNAITH, George Robert, FRINA; Partner, Pi-Sigma Technology and Systems Advisers, 1990–97; *b* 9 July 1930; *s* of late Robert and Clara Snaith; *m* 1953, Verna Patricia (*née* Codling); one *s* one *d*. *Educ:* University of Durham. BSc Applied Science (Naval Architecture), 1952. A. Kari & Co., Consulting Naval Architects, Newcastle, 1952–57; Northern Aluminium Co. Ltd, Banbury, 1957–59; Burness, Corlett & Partners, Consulting Naval Architects, Basingstoke, 1959–64; British Ship Research Association, 1964–77, Dir of Research, 1976–77; British Shipbuilders: Dir of Research, 1977–81; Technol. and Systems Adviser (formerly Production Systems Adviser), 1981–85; Consultant, Computervision Ltd, 1985–90. Vis. Prof., 1980–96, Vis. Lectr, 1997–2000, Vis. Fellow, 2000–02, Dept of Marine Technology (formerly Naval Architecture and Shipbldg), Univ. of Newcastle upon Tyne. FNECInst 1992. Member: Council, RINA, 1977–87; Ship and Marine Technol. Requirements Bd, Dept of Industry, 1978–81; Bd, National Maritime Inst., 1978–82. *Recreations:* ships and shipbuilding, technology, education. *Address:* 10 Fieldhouse Close, Hepscott, Morpeth, Northumberland NE61 6LU. *T:* (01670) 515319. *Died 15 Oct. 2013.*

SNEATH, Prof. Peter Henry Andrews, MD; FRS 1995; Professor of Clinical Microbiology, Leicester University, 1975–89, then Emeritus Professor, Department of Infection, Immunity and Inflammation (formerly Microbiology and Immunology); *b* 17 Nov. 1923; *s* of Rev. Alec Andrews Sneath and Elizabeth Maud Adcock; *m* 1953, Joan Sylvia Thompson; one *s* two *d*. *Educ:* Wycliffe Coll., Stonehouse, Glos; King's Coll., Cambridge (BA 1944; MB BChir 1948, MD 1959); King's Coll. Hosp.; London Sch. of Hygiene and Trop. Med. (Dip. Bact. 1953). MRCS, LRCP 1947. RAMC, Captain and Temp. Major, 1950–52. Mem., Sci. Staff, MRC, 1953–75 and Dir, Microbial Systematics Res. Unit, 1964–75; Hon. Consultant Microbiologist, Leics HA, 1975–89. Hon. mem., microbiol. and bacteriol. socs, UK, France, USA. Hon. DSc Ghent, 1969. *Publications:* (with R. R. Sokal) Principles of Numerical Taxonomy, 1963; Planets and Life, 1970; (with R. R. Sokal) Numerical Taxonomy, 1973; papers in learned jls on microbiology and computing. *Recreations:* reading, gardening, music. *Address:* 22 Barnsdale Close, Great Easton, Leics LE16 8SQ. *T:* (01536) 771071; Department of Infection, Immunity and Inflammation, The University, Leicester LE1 7RH. *T:* (0116) 252 2951. *Died 9 Sept. 2011.*

SNELL, Maeve, (Mrs Gordon Snell); *see* Binchy, M.

SNOW, Rear-Adm. Kenneth Arthur, CB 1987; Deputy High Bailiff of Westminster, 1998–2008; *b* 14 April 1934; *s* of Arthur Chandos Pole Snow (*né* Pole-Soppitt) and Evelyn (*née* Joyce); *m* 1956, Pamela Elizabeth Terry (*née* Sorrell); one *s* two *d*. *Educ:* St Andrew's College, Grahamstown; South African Nautical College. Joined RN, 1952; commanded HMS Kirkliston, 1962; qualified navigation specialist, 1963; commanded: HMS Llandaff, 1970; HMS Arethusa, 1979; HMS Hermes, 1983; Dep. Asst Chief of Staff (Ops), SACEUR, 1984–87. Receiver-Gen. and Chapter Clerk, Westminster Abbey, 1987–98. FNI 1992. *Recreations:* reading, painting. *Address:* 49B Queens Road, Cowes, Isle of Wight PO31 8BW. *Club:* Army and Navy. *Died 5 Dec. 2011.*

SNOW, Philip Albert, OBE 1985 (MBE 1979); JP; MA; FRSA; FRAI; author, bibliographer and administrator; *b* 7 Aug. 1915; *s* of William Edward Snow, FRCO and Ada Sophia Robinson; *m* 1940, Anne Harris (*d* 2005); one *d*. *Educ:* Newton's Sch., Leicester; Christ's Coll., Cambridge (MA Hons). FRAI 1952. HM Colonial Administrative Service: Provincial Comr, Magistrate, Establishment and Protocol Officer, and Asst Colonial Sec., Fiji and Western Pacific, 1937–52; ADC to Governor and C-in-C, Fiji and High Comr for Western Pacific, 1939–40; Dep. Sheriff, Fiji, 1940–52; Official Mem., Legislative Council, Fiji, 1951; Fiji Govt Liaison Officer, US and NZ Forces, 1942–44. Bursar, Rugby Sch., 1952–76. Mem., Jt Cttee, Governing Bodies of Schools' Assoc., 1959–65. President: Public Schs Bursars' Assoc., 1962–65 (Vice-Pres., 1959–62); The Worthing Soc., 1983– (Jt Founder); Vice-Pres., Fiji Soc., 1944–52; Trustee, Fiji Museum, 1950–52. Founder Member Committee: Union Club, Suva, 1944; Fiji Arts Club, 1945. Founder, Suva Cricket Assoc., Nadi Cricket Assoc. and six other dist cricket assocs, 1939–49; Founder, Fiji Cricket Assoc., 1946, Vice-Patron, 1952–; Captain, Fiji Cricket Team, NZ first-class tour, 1948; Liaison Officer/Manager, first Fiji Cricket Team in England, 1979; Liaison Officer, Fiji teams in England, 1982–86. International Cricket Conference: Perm. Rep. of Fiji, 1965–90; Mem., first Cricket World Cup Cttee, 1971–75; first Chm., Associate Member Countries, 1982–87; Perm. Rep. of Fiji, Internat. Cricket Council, 1990–94; Gold Centenary Medal, 2010. Organiser, Rugby Sch. 400th anniv. celebrations and visit of the Queen, 1967; designer, Fiji Govt stamps for centenary of Fiji cricket, 1974. Broadcasts on Fiji radio, BBC and in NZ, 1948–; question setter on Pacific, Mastermind, BBC, 1975–. Literary Executor of Lord Snow of Leicester. JP Warwicks, 1967–76, and W Sussex, 1976–. FRSA 1984. Foreign Specialist Award, USA Govt, 1964; Independence Silver Jubilee Medal, Fiji, 1995. *Publications:* Air Raids Precautions Services, Lautoka, 1943; (ed with G. K. Roth) Sources Describing Fijian Customs for Fijian Examination Candidates, 1944; (ed) Civil Service Journal, 1945; Cricket in the Fiji Islands, 1949; Rock Carvings in Fiji, 1950; Report on the Visit of Three Bursars to the United States of America and Canada in 1964, 1965; Best Stories of the South Seas, 1967; Bibliography of Fiji, Tonga and Rotuma, vol. 1, 1969; (with Stefanie Snow Waine) The People from the Horizon: an illustrated history of the Europeans among the South Sea Islanders, 1979; Stranger and Brother: a portrait of C. P. Snow, 1982; The Years of Hope: Cambridge, colonial administrator in the South Seas and cricket (autobiog.), 1997; A Time of Renewal: clusters of characters, C. P. Snow and coups (autobiog.), 1998; contrib. to books and jls incl. TLS, Sunday Times, Daily Telegraph, The Times, Jls of RAI, RGS, Fiji Museum, Pacific History, Fiji Soc., Polynesian Soc., and Rupert Brooke Soc., Jl de la Société des Océanistes, Amer. Anthropologist, Wisden's Almanack, Barclays World of Cricket, Dictionary of Nat. Biog.; numerous reviews of, and introductions to, Pacific and general books. *Recreations:* taming robins; formerly cricket (Capt., Leics 2nd XI, 1936–38, Leics, 1946, Cambridge Crusaders, Googlies, MCC (Capt., 1955–65), Authors, Fiji first-class), chess (half-Blue), table-tennis (half-Blue and Cambs), deck-tennis, tennis. *Address:* 46 Bennett Court, Station Road, Letchworth, Herts SG6 3WA. *T:* (01462) 677556. *Clubs:* MCC (Hon. Life Mem. for services to internat. cricket, 1970), Stragglers of Asia (Hon. Mem.); De Flamingos (Hon. Mem.) (Holland); Mastermind; Hawks (Cambridge). *Died 5 June 2012.*

SNOW, Surg. Rear-Adm. Ronald Edward, CB 1991; LVO 1972; OBE 1977; Surgeon Rear Admiral (Operational Medical Services), 1989–91; *b* 17 May 1933; *s* of Arthur Chandos Pole Snow (formerly Soppitt) and Evelyn Dorothea Snow (*née* Joyce); *m* 1959, Valerie Melian French; two *d*. *Educ:* St Andrew's Coll., Grahamstown, S Africa; Trinity Coll., Dublin (MA, MB, BCh, BAO); FFOM, DA, LMCC. HMS Victorious, 1966; HMS

Dolphin, 1967; HMY Britannia, 1970; MoD, 1973 and 1977; Inst. of Naval Medicine, 1975 and 1984; Staff of Surg. Rear Adm. (Naval Hosps), 1980; Staff of C-in-C Fleet, 1982; Asst Surg. Gen. (Service Hosps), 1985; Surg. Rear Adm. (Support Med. Services), 1987. QHP 1984–91. Vice Patron, Cerebral Palsy Centre, Portsmouth, 2003–06. OStJ 1986. *Recreation:* National Hunt racing. *Died 13 Aug. 2011.*

SOAME, Sir Charles (John) Buckworth-Herne-, 12th Bt *cr* 1697; *b* 28 May 1932; *s* of Sir Charles Burnett Buckworth-Herne-Soame, 11th Bt, and Elsie May (*d* 1972), *d* of Walter Alfred Lloyd; *S* father, 1977; *m* 1958, Eileen Margaret Mary, *d* of Leonard Minton; one *s*. *Heir: s* Richard John Buckworth-Herne-Soame, *b* 17 Aug. 1970. *Address:* Sheen Cottage, Coalbrookdale, Telford, Salop TF8 7EQ. *Died 28 July 2013.*

SOAMES, Lady; Mary Soames, LG 2005; DBE 1980 (MBE (mil.) 1945); FRSL; Member of Council, 1978–97, and Chairman of Trustees, 1991–2002, Winston Churchill Memorial Trust; Chairman, Royal National Theatre Board, 1989–95; *b* 15 Sept. 1922; *y d* of Rt Hon. Sir Winston Churchill, KG, OM, CH, FRS, and Baroness Spencer-Churchill, GBE; *m* 1947, Captain Christopher Soames, Coldstream Guards, later Baron Soames, GCMG, GCVO, CH, CBE, PC (*d* 1987); three *s* two *d*. *Educ:* privately. Served War: Red Cross and WVS, 1939–41; ATS, 1941–46, with mixed anti-aircraft batteries in UK and Europe (Jun. Comdr). Accompanied father on various journeys; campaigned with husband through six elections whilst he was Conservative MP for Bedford, 1950–66; accompanied husband to Paris where he was Ambassador, 1968–72, and to Brussels where he was first British Vice Pres. of Eur. Commn, 1973–76; accompanied husband when he was appointed last British Governor of Southern Rhodesia, Dec. 1979–April 1980. Chm., UK Assoc. for Internat. Year of the Child, 1979. Governor, Harrow Sch., 1980–95. Freeman, City of London, 1994; Hon. Freewoman, Skinners' Co., 1994. JP E Sussex, 1960–74. FRSL 2000. Hon. Fellow, Churchill Coll., Cambridge, 1983. Hon. DLitt: Sussex, 1989; Kent, 1997; Univ. of the South, Tennessee, 2004; Hon. LLD Alberta, 2004. Franklin Delano Roosevelt Freedom Medal, Franklin and Eleanor Roosevelt Inst., 2005. Chevalier de la Légion d'Honneur (France), 1995. *Publications:* Clementine Churchill by Her Daughter Mary Soames, 1979 (a Wolfson Prize for History, and Yorkshire Post Prize for Best First Work, 1979), rev. and updated edn, 2002; A Churchill Family Album—A Personal Anthology Selected by Mary Soames, 1982; The Profligate Duke: George Spencer-Churchill 5th Duke of Marlborough and his Duchess, 1987; Winston Churchill: his Life as a Painter: a memoir by his daughter Mary Soames, 1990; Speaking for Themselves—The Personal Letters of Winston & Clementine Churchill: edited by their daughter Mary Soames, 1998; A Daughter's Tale, 2011. *Recreations:* reading, sight-seeing, gardening. *Died 31 May 2014.*

SOMERLEYTON, 3rd Baron *cr* 1916; **Savile William Francis Crossley,** GCVO 1999 (KCVO 1994); DL; Bt 1863; farmer; Master of the Horse, 1991–98; *b* 17 Sept. 1928; *er s* of 2nd Baron Somerleyton, MC; *S* father, 1959; *m* 1963, Belinda Maris Loyd (OBE 1997), *d* of late Vivian Loyd and of Mrs Gerald Critchley; one *s* four *d*. *Educ:* Eton Coll. Captain Coldstream Guards, 1948; retired, 1956. Royal Agricultural Coll., Cirencester, 1958–59; farming, 1959–. A Lord in Waiting to the Queen, 1978–91. Dir, Essex & Suffolk Water plc, 1994–97. DL Suffolk, 1964. *Heir: s* Hon. Hugh Francis Savile Crossley [*b* 27 Sept. 1971; *m* 2009, Lara Kate, *d* of Richard Bailey; one *s*]. *Address:* Blocka Hall Farm, Herringfleet, Lowestoft, Suffolk NR32 5NW. *Club:* White's. *Died 24 Jan. 2012.*

SOMERS, Dame Phyllis, DBE 2013; philanthropist; *b* April 1922; *née* Webber; *m* 1946, John Nathaniel, (Nat), Somers (*d* 1998); one *s*. Charitable services include donations to medical res. and social welfare charities. Hon. Fellow, Birkbeck, Univ. of London, 2005. *Died 5 March 2014.*

SOMERSET, David Henry Fitzroy, FCIB; Chief of Banking Department and Chief Cashier, Bank of England, 1980–88; *b* 19 June 1930; *s* of late Brig. Hon. Nigel Somerset, CBE, DSO, MC and Phyllis Marion Offley (*née* Irwin); *m* 1955, Ruth Ivy, *d* of late W. R. Wildbur; one *s* one *d*. *Educ:* Wellington Coll.; Peterhouse, Cambridge (MA). Entered Bank of England, 1952; Personal Asst to Managing Director, International Monetary Fund, Washington DC, 1959–62; Private Secretary to Governor of Bank of England, 1962–63; Asst Chief Cashier, 1968–69; Asst Chief of Establishments, 1969–73; Dep. Chief Cashier, 1973–80; Fellow and Financial Advr, Peterhouse, Cambridge, 1988–97, Emeritus Fellow, 1997–. Dir, Yamaichi Bank (UK) PLC, 1988–95; Consultant, Bank Julius Baer, 1997–2000 (Chm. London Adv. Bd, 1991–97). Comr, English Heritage, 1988–91. Mem. Council, Friends of Peterhouse, 1982–2007; Pres., Old Wellingtonian Soc., 2003–08 (Chm., 1988–97); Gov., Wellington Coll., 1989–2000. *Recreations:* gardening, racing, shooting. *Address:* 15 Willicombe Park, Tunbridge Wells, Kent TN2 3US. *T:* (01892) 522454. *Died 25 Oct. 2014.*

SOMERVILLE, Philip Douglas Frank; milliner; Managing Director, Philip Somerville, 1972–2011; *b* Winchester, 12 Feb. 1930; *s* of Ivie Frank Somerville and Elinor Anne Somerville. *Educ:* St Thomas's High Sch., Winchester; afterwards largely self-educated. Work in theatre, Australia, 1950–52; milliner, NZ, 1952–61; milliner/director, London, 1961–72. Royal Warrant Holder to The Queen, 1994–2011; milliner to: Duchess of Kent; Duchess of Gloucester; Queen Silvia of Sweden; the late Diana Princess of Wales. *Recreations:* theatre, country pursuits, charity functions. *Address:* Penthouse D, Kingsley Lodge, 23 New Cavendish Street, W1G 9UG. *T:* (020) 7487 4661. *Club:* Bishopsgate Ward. *Died 14 Sept. 2014.*

SOMERVILLE, Most Rev. Thomas David; Archbishop of New Westminster and Metropolitan of Ecclesiastical Province of British Columbia, 1975–80; Anglican Chaplain, Vancouver School of Theology, 1981–84; *b* 11 Nov. 1915; *s* of Thomas Alexander Somerville and Martha Stephenson Scott; *m* 1985, Frances Best (*d* 2007). *Educ:* King George High Sch., Vancouver; Univ. of British Columbia (BA 1937); Anglican Theological Coll. of BC (LTh 1939, BD 1951). Deacon, 1939; priest, 1940; Incumbent of: Princeton, 1940–44; Sardis with Rosedale, 1944–49; Curate of St James, Vancouver, 1949–52, Rector, 1952–60; Chapter Canon, Dio. of New Westminster, 1957; Dean of Residence, Anglican Theological Coll. of BC, 1960–65; Gen. Sec., Gen. Bd of Religious Education, Anglican Church of Canada, 1965–66; Director of Planning and Research, Anglican Church of Canada, 1966–69; Coadjutor Bishop of New Westminster, 1969–71; Bishop of New Westminster, 1971. Hon. DD: Anglican Theol. Coll. of BC, 1969; Vancouver Sch. of Theology, 1981. *Recreations:* music, botany. *Address:* 980 Lynn Valley Road, North Vancouver, BC V7J 3V7, Canada. *Died 25 July 2011.*

SOMJEE, Shamoon; a District Judge (Magistrates' Courts) (formerly Metropolitan Stipendiary Magistrate), since 1995 (Stipendiary Magistrate, Middlesex, 1991–95); *b* 13 Nov. 1943; *s* of Rahim Somjee, former Sessions Judge, Pakistan, and Khairunissah Somjee; *m* 1970, Isabel Fonfria Fernandez; one *s*. *Educ:* St Lawrence's Sch., Karachi; Univ. of Karachi (BA 1963; LLB 1965). Came to UK, 1965. Called to the Bar, Lincoln's Inn, 1967. Mem., editl team, Halsbury's Statutes of England, and Annotated Legislation Service, Butterworths, 1967–68; Magistrates' Clerk, Inner London, 1968–91: Dep. Chief Clerk: Bow Street, 1968–75; Juvenile Courts, 1976–77; Horseferry Road, 1977–80; Chief Clerk: Wells Street, 1980–84; Old Street, 1984–90; Horseferry Road, 1990–91; Sen. Chief Clerk, S Westminster PSD, 1990–91. Chm., London Magistrates' Clerks Assoc., 1985–87. Member: Home Office Working Party on Magistrates' Courts, 1983–87; Home Office sub-group on Procedure at Substantive Hearings, 1990–91 and Appeals, Warrants and Forms, 1991. *Recreations:* travelling, music. *Address:* c/o Tower Bridge Magistrates' Court, 211 Tooley Street, SE1 2JY. *T:* (020) 7805 6706. *Died 27 Dec. 2011.*

SONNABEND, Yolanda; painter, portraitist and theatre designer; *b* 26 March 1935; *d* of Dr Henry Sonnabend and Dr Fira Sonnabend (*née* Sandler). *Educ:* Eveline High Sch., Bulawayo; Slade Sch. of Fine Art (Dip.). Lectr in Theatre

Design, Slade Sch. of Fine Art, 1989–2001. Fellow, UCL, 2002. *Painting: exhibitions* include: Whitechapel Art Gall. (solo), 1975; Serpentine Gall. (solo), 1986; Amphitheatre, ROH, 2000; portraits of Stephen Hawking and others, Nat. Portrait Gall.; portrait for Pembroke Coll., Cambridge; portrait of Lord Rees for Royal Soc.; *theatre design: installations:* Japan, Denmark, Poland; *ballet* productions: for Royal Ballet, incl. Swan Lake and works for Kenneth Macmillan (Requiem, My Brother My Sister); for La Scala, Milan; for K Ballet Co., Tokyo: Swan Lake, 2003; The Nutcracker, 2005; Le Corsaire, 2007; The Beethoven, with symphony and symphonic ballet, 2008; Romeo and Juliet, 2010; Strasbourg; Lisbon; Stuttgart; Hong Kong; Nice; Chicago; Boston; *opera* productions: Aldeburgh; Sadler's Wells; Italy; *theatre* includes: Oxford Playhouse; RSC; Old Vic; *film:* The Tempest, 1980. Garrick Milne Prize for Theatrical Portraiture, 2000. *Recreation:* usual diversions. *Address:* 30 Hamilton Terrace, NW8 9UG. *T:* (020) 7286 9616. *Died 9 Nov. 2015.*

SORLEY WALKER, Kathrine; freelance writer; *b* 5 March 1920; *d* of James Sorley Walker and Edith Jane Sorley Walker (*née* Robertson). *Educ:* St Margaret's Sch. for Girls, Aberdeen; Crouch End Coll., London; King's Coll. London; Univ. of Besançon; Trinity Coll. of Music. Geographical Magazine, 1951–56; Helga Greene Literary Agency, 1961–86; freelance critic and historian; dance critic, Daily Telegraph, 1969–94. *Publications:* (ed) Raymond Chandler Speaking, 1962; Eyes on the Ballet, 1963; Eyes on Mime, 1969; Saladin, Sultan of the Holy Sword, 1971; Dance and its Creators, 1972; (ed) Writings on Dance, by A. V. Coton, 1975; Emotion and Atmosphere (verse), 1975; Ballet for Boys and Girls, 1979; The Royal Ballet: a picture history, 1981; De Basil's Ballets Russes, 1982; (ed) Remembering Helga, 1986; Ninette de Valois: idealist without illusions, 1987; Late Century Poems (verse), 1999; New Century Reflections (verse), 2004; Cyril W. Beaumont: dance writer and publisher, 2006; Thoughts and Impressions (verse), 2008; Robert Helpmann: a rare sense of the theatre, 2009; contribs to Dancing Times, Dance Chronicle, Dance Now, Dance International, Choreologica, Dance Research, Encyclopedia Britannica, International Encyclopedia of Dance, Enciclopedia dello Spettacolo, Encyclopedia of Dance and Ballet, International Dictionary of Ballet, Oxford DNB. *Recreations:* travel, art exhibitions, theatre-going. *Died 15 April 2015.*

SOUHAMI, Mark; Chairman, Codic International SA, 1998–2005 and 2008–12; *b* 25 Sept. 1935; *s* of late John Souhami and Freda Souhami (*née* Harris); *m* 1964, Margaret Austin; two *d. Educ:* St Marylebone Grammar School. Lieut RA, 1954–60; early career in City and timber industry; joined Dixons, 1970: Group Marketing Dir, 1970; Man. Dir, 1973; Gp Man. Dir, 1986–92, Dep. Chm., 1992–2003, Dixons Gp plc. Dir, Thomson Travel Group plc, 1998–2000. Chm., British Retail Consortium, 1994–98. Mem. Econ. Affairs Cttee, CBI, 1978–94 (Mem. Council, 1978–91 and 1996–2000). Mem., Metropolitan Police Cttee, 1995–99. Trustee, Photographers' Gall., 1978–90. Founder Mem., Marketors' Co., 1975. *Recreations:* fishing, shooting. *Club:* Savile. *Died 1 April 2014.*

SOUTHALL, Kenneth Charles; Under-Secretary, Inland Revenue, 1975–82; *b* 3 Aug. 1922; *s* of Arthur and Margarette Jane Southall; *m* 1947, Audrey Kathleen Skeels; one *s. Educ:* Queen Elizabeth's Grammar Sch., Hartlebury, Worcs. Inland Revenue, 1939; RAF, 1942–46; Administrative Staff College, 1962. *Address:* The Green, Brill, Bucks HP18 9RU. *Died 24 Jan. 2011.*

SOUTHAMPTON, 6th Baron *cr* 1780; **Charles James FitzRoy;** *b* 12 Aug. 1928; *o s* of Charles FitzRoy (5th Baron, disclaimed peerage for life, 1964) and Margaret (*d* 1931), *d* of Rev. Preb. Herbert Mackworth Drake; *S* father, 1989; *m* 1st, 1951, Pamela Anne (*d* 1997), *d* of Edward Percy Henniker; one *s* one *d* (and one *s* decd); 2nd, 1997, Alma Slater (*née* Pasqual); one *s* one *d. Educ:* Stowe. Master: Easton Harriers, 1968–71; Blaikney Foxhounds, 1971–72. *Recreations:* shooting, fishing, golf. *Heir: s* Hon. Edward Charles FitzRoy [*b* 8 July 1955; *m* 1978, Rachel Caroline Vincent, 2nd *d* of Peter John Curnow Millett; one *s* three *d*]. *Address:* Stone Cross, Stone Lane, Chagford, Newton Abbot, Devon TQ13 8JU. *Died 10 Jan. 2015.*

SOUTHAN, His Honour Robert Joseph; a Circuit Judge, 1986–2001; *b* 13 July 1928; *s* of late Thomas Southan and of Kathleen Southan; *m* 1960, Elizabeth Andreas Evatt (AC 1995); one *d* (one *s* decd). *Educ:* Rugby; St Edmund Hall, Oxford (MA); University Coll., London (LLM); Open Univ. (BA Hons 2008). Called to the Bar, Inner Temple, 1953; called to the Bar of NSW, 1976; a Recorder, 1983–86. *Recreations:* theatre, opera, sailing, tennis. *Clubs:* Royal Corinthian Yacht, Bar Yacht; Cumberland Lawn Tennis. *Died 30 Sept. 2015.*

SOUTHGATE, Air Vice-Marshal Harry Charles, CB 1976; CBE 1973 (MBE 1950); Director General of Engineering and Supply Policy and Planning, Ministry of Defence (Air), 1973–76; *b* 30 Oct. 1921; *s* of George Harry Southgate and Lily Maud (*née* Clarke); *m* 1945, Violet Louise Davies (*d* 1991); one *s. Educ:* St Saviour's Sch., Walthamstow. Entered RAF, 1941; India, 1942–45; HQ 90 Gp, 1946–50; RAF Stafford, 1950–52; Air Min., 1952–53; transf. to Equipment Br., 1953; RAF Tangmere, 1953–55; Singapore, 1955–57; psc 1957; Air Min., 1958–60; jssc 1961; Dirg Staff, RAF Staff Coll., Bracknell, 1961–64; CO 35 MU RAF Heywood, 1965–66; SESO, RAF Germany, 1967–68; idc 1969; Dir Supply Management, MoD Air, 1970–73. Pres., Ripon Arts, 2001–11 (Chm., 1989–2000); Patron, Yorkshire Air Mus., 1990. *Recreations:* travel, golf, painting, bird-watching. *Club:* Royal Air Force. *Died 4 June 2013.*

SOUTHGATE, Malcolm John, OBE 1995; Deputy Managing Director, Eurostar UK (formerly European Passenger Services Ltd), 1990–2000; *b* 11 Nov. 1933; *s* of Harold Edwin Southgate and Mary (*née* Kelleher); *m* 1959, Anne Margaret Yeoman; two *s. Educ:* Royal Grammar Sch., Colchester; Corpus Christi Coll., Cambridge (BA). British Railways: Divl Manager, S Eastern Div., 1972; Chief Operating Manager, 1975, Dep. Gen. Man., 1977, Southern Region; Dir of Ops, 1980, Dir of Policy Unit, 1983, BRB; Gen. Man., LMR, 1983; Dir, Channel Tunnel, BRB, 1986. *Recreations:* Rugby, education administration, transport affairs. *Address:* 4 Langdale Rise, Maidstone, Kent ME16 0EU. *T:* (01622) 753792. *Died 23 Dec. 2013.*

SOUTHWELL, Ven. Roy; Archdeacon of Northolt, 1970–80, Archdeacon Emeritus, since 1980; Warden of the Community of All Hallows, Ditchingham, Norfolk, 1983–89; *b* 3 Dec. 1914; *s* of William Thomas and Lilian Southwell; *m* 1948, Nancy Elizabeth Lindsay Sharp; two *d. Educ:* Sudbury Grammar Sch.; King's Coll., London (AKC 1942). Curate: St Michael's, Wigan, 1942–44; St John the Divine, Kennington, 1944–48; Vicar of Ixworth, 1948–51; Vicar of St John's, Bury St Edmunds, 1951–56; Rector of Bucklesham with Brightwell and Foxhall, 1956–59; Asst Director of Religious Education, Diocese of St Edmundsbury and Ipswich, 1956–58, Director, 1959–67. Hon. Canon of St Edmundsbury, 1959–68; Vicar of Hendon, 1968–71. *Recreations:* reading, singing, watching TV. *Address:* 397 Sprowston Road, Norwich NR3 4HY. *T:* (01603) 405977. *Died 23 July 2011.*

SPAFFORD, Rev. Christopher Garnett Howsin; Provost and Vicar of Newcastle, 1976–89; *b* 10 Sept. 1924; *s* of late Rev. Canon Douglas Norman Spafford and Frances Alison Spafford; *m* 1953, Stephanie Peel; three *s. Educ:* Marlborough Coll.; St John's Coll., Oxford (MA 2nd Cl. Hons Modern History); Wells Theological Coll. Curate of Brighouse, 1950–53; Curate of Huddersfield Parish Church, 1953–55; Vicar of Hebden Bridge, 1955–61; Rector of Thornhill, Dewsbury, 1961–69; Vicar of St Chad's, Shrewsbury, 1969–76. *Recreations:* reading, gardening. *Address:* Low Moor, Elm Close, Leominster, Herefordshire HR6 8JX. *T:* (01568) 614395. *Died 29 April 2011.*

SPALDING, John Oliver, CBE 1988; Chief Executive and Director, Halifax Building Society, 1982–88; *b* 4 Aug. 1924; *s* of John and Winifred Ethel Spalding; *m* 1952, Mary Whitworth Hull (*d* 2010); one *s* one *d. Educ:* William Hulme's Grammar School, Manchester; Jesus College,

Cambridge (MA). Served War: Capt. RA, attached IA; served India, Burma, Singapore, Java. Admitted a Solicitor, 1952; service with Manchester Corporation and Hampshire CC, 1952–62; Halifax Building Society, 1962–88. Chm., NHBC, 1988–92. Chm., Future Constitution and Powers of Bldg Socs Working Party (Spalding Cttee), 1981–83; Mem., Farrand Cttee investigating Conveyancing, 1984. *Recreation:* boats and bird-watching. *Address:* Pembroke, 22 Thamesfield Court, Henley-on-Thames, Oxfordshire RG9 2LX. *Died 16 April 2012.*

SPANKIE, (Hugh) Oliver; HM Diplomatic Service, retired; *b* 11 Dec. 1936; *s* of late Col Hugh Vernon Spankie and Elizabeth Ursula (*née* Hills); *m* 1st, 1963, Anne Bridget Colville (marr. diss. 1981); one *s* one *d*; 2nd, 1988, Leena Marjatta Paloheimo. *Educ:* Tonbridge Sch. RM Officer, 1955–66; HM Diplomatic Service, 1967–86: Helsinki, 1968–71; FCO, 1971–74; Helsinki, 1974–77; FCO and CSD, 1977–81; Counsellor, Copenhagen, 1981–85. *Address:* c/o Barclays Bank plc, 1–3 Broad Street, Hereford HR4 8BH. *Died 4 April 2012.*

SPARKS, Ian Leslie, OBE 1999; Chief Executive, Haven House Children's Hospice, 2008–11; *b* 26 May 1943; *s* of Ronald Leslie and Hilda Sparks; *m* 1967, Eunice Jean; one *d*. *Educ:* Whitefield Road Primary School, Liverpool; Holt High School, Liverpool; Brunel Univ. (MA); Kingston Univ. (DMS). AIB. Bank clerk, 1959–68; social worker, Liverpool, 1971–75; Asst Divl Dir, Barnardo's, 1975–80; Social Work Dir, 1981–86, Chief Exec., 1986–2002, The Children's Soc. Chairman: British Agencies for Adoption and Fostering, 1996–2000; End Child Poverty Campaign, 2002–04; Consultation Organiser, Internat. Anglican Family Network, 2002– (Chm., 1989–2001 and 2012–). Trustee: NCVCCO, 1995–2002; Frontier Youth Trust, 2000– (Chm., 2004–); Haven House Foundn, 2003–08 and 2011– (Chm., 2007–08 and 2011–); Tyn-y-Nant Christian Centre, 2004–; ChildAid to Russia and the Republics, 2007–. *Recreations:* piano playing, gardening in miniature. *Address:* 16 Frating Crescent, Woodford Green, Essex IG8 0DW. *Died 18 Jan. 2014.*

SPEDDING, Sir Colin (Raymond William), Kt 1994; CBE 1988; Professor of Agricultural Systems, 1975–90, and Pro-Vice-Chancellor, 1986–90, University of Reading, then Professor Emeritus; *b* 22 March 1925; *s* of Robert Kewley Spedding and Ilynn Spedding; *m* 1952, Betty Noreen George (*d* 1988); one *s* one *d* (and one *s* decd). *Educ:* London Univ. (External) (BSc 1951; MSc 1953; PhD 1955; DSc 1967). FZS 1962; FSB (FIBiol 1967), CBiol 1984; FRASE 1984; FIHort 1986; FRAgS 1986; FLS 1995. Ilford Ltd, 1940–43; RNVR, 1943–46; Allen & Hanbury, 1948–49; Grassland Research Institute: joined 1949; Head of Ecology Div., 1967–75; Asst Dir, 1969–72; Dep. Dir, 1972–75; University of Reading: Visiting, then part-time Prof. of Agric. Systems, 1970–75; Head of Dept of Agric. and Hortic., 1975–83; Dean, Faculty of Agriculture and Food, 1983–86; Dir, Centre for Agricl Strategy, 1981–90, Consultant Dir, 1990–99. Commonwealth Prestige Fellow, NZ, 1977; Vis. Prof., Univ. of Guelph, Canada, 1978. Editor, Agricultural Systems, 1976–88. Mem., Programme Cttee, Internat. Livestock Centre for Africa, Addis Ababa, 1976–80, Vice Chm., 1980–83; Chm., Nat. Equine Forum Organising Cttee, 1992–. Special Advr, H of C Select Cttee on Agric., 1980–83; Chairman: UK Register of Organic Food Standards Bd, 1987–99; Farm Animal Welfare Council, 1988–98; Apple and Pear Res. Council, 1989–97; Science Council (formerly CSTI), 1994–2000; Assured Chicken Production Ltd, 2000–04; Dir, Assured Food Standards, 2001–08. Dir, Lands Improvement Hldgs PLC (formerly Gp Ltd), 1986–99 (Dep. Chm., 1990–99). Adv. Dir, 1998–2003, Special Scientific Advr to Dir-Gen., 2003, WSPA; Advr, Companion Animal Welfare Council, 1999–; Specialist Advr, H of L Select Cttee on EC, Sub-Cttee D (Agric., Fisheries and Food), 1999; Hd, UK Delegn to Internat. Whaling Commn, Grenada, 1999, Berlin, 2003. President: European Assoc. of Animal Production Study Commn for Sheep and Goat Production, 1970–76; British Soc. for Animal Production, 1979–80; Vice-Pres., Inst. of Biology, 1997–99 (Pres., 1992–94). Governor: Royal Agricl Coll., 1982–88; Inst. of Grassland and Envmtl Res. (formerly Inst. for Grassland and Animal Production), 1987–91; Mem., Council of Management, PDSA, 1988–2007 (Dep. Chm., 1996–2003); Vice Pres., RSPCA, 2002–. Chm. Trustees, FAWT, 2003–. Chm. Editl Bd, World Agriculture, 2010–. Mem., Inst. of Dirs, 1992–98. FRSA 1988. Hon. Life Mem., BSAS, 1990; Hon. FIBiol 1994; Hon. Associate, RCVS, 1994; Hon. MRSocMed, 1998. Hon. DSc Reading, 1995. George Hedley Award, 1971; Canadian Inst. of Agric. Recognition Award, 1971; Wooldridge Meml Medal, BVA, 1982; Hawkesbury Centenary Medal of Honour, Univ. of Western Sydney, 1991; Massey Ferguson Nat. Agricl Award, 1991; Victory Medal, Central Vet. Soc., 2000; Special Award, Poultry Industry, 2009. *Publications:* Sheep Production and Grazing Management, 1965, 2nd edn 1970; Grassland Ecology, 1971; (ed with E. C. Diekmahns) Grasses and Legumes in British Agriculture, 1972; The Biology of Agricultural Systems, 1975; An Introduction to Agricultural Systems, 1979, 2nd edn 1988; (ed) Vegetable Productivity, 1981; (with J. M. Walsingham and A. M. Hoxey) Biological Efficiency in Agriculture, 1981; (ed) Fream's Agriculture, 1983; (ed) Fream's Principles of Food and Agriculture, 1992; Agriculture and the Citizen, 1996; Animal Welfare, 2000; The Natural History of a Garden, 2003; The Second Mouse Gets the Cheese: proverbs and their uses, 2005; What's in Your Garden, 2010; over 250 sci papers in learned jls. *Address:* Vine Cottage, Orchard Road, Hurst, Berks RG10 0SD. *Clubs:* Athenæum, Farmers. *Died 17 Dec. 2012.*

SPEIRS, John Garrett, CBE 1996; LVO 2003; Member, Royal Commission on Environmental Pollution, 2002–08; *b* 17 June 1937; *s* of William Blair Speirs and Margaret Sarah Garrett Speirs; *m* 1963, Susan Elizabeth Seyler, Dayton, Ohio; two *s*. *Educ:* Glenalmond Coll.; Exeter Coll., Oxford (MA Lit.Hum.); Cornell Univ., NY (MBA). Tube Investments Gp, 1962–76: industrial engr, British Aluminium Co., Falkirk, 1962–66; corporate planning exec., London, 1966–69; Prodn Manager, Gen. Manager and Dir, TI Stainless Tubes, Walsall, 1969–74; Dir, Ops Secretariat, 1974–76; Divl Dir, NEB, 1976–81; Man. Dir, Norsk Hydro (UK) Ltd, London, 1981–2002. Chm., Merton, Sutton & Wandsworth FHSA, 1989–95. Mem., British Cttee, Det Norsk Veritas, 1987–2001. Advr, Kleinwort Capital Ltd, 1991–2007; Chm., Dramgate Ltd, 1991–. Member: Adv. Cttee on Business and the Envmt, 1991–95; Business in the Envmt, 1991–99; SERC, 1993–94. Mem. Council, Aluminium Fedn, 1992–2003 (Pres., 1997–98); Pres., Nat. Soc. for Clean Air and Envmtl Protection, 2002–03. Non-exec. Dir, Carbon Trust, 2001–07. Chm., UK Faculty, Prince of Wales's Business and Envmt Prog., 1993–2002 (Mem., Mgt Cttee, 1997–2004). *Recreations:* opera, theatre, visual arts and architecture, Munro-bagging, gardening, incompetent golf. *Address:* 20 Dunstall Road, SW20 0HR. *T:* (020) 8879 1308. *Died 27 Dec. 2014.*

SPELLER, Antony; Senior Associate (Europe), Resource Planning and Management Systems Ltd, 1992–2000; *b* 12 June 1929; *s* of late John and Ethel Speller; *m* 1st, Margaret Lloyd-Jones (marr. diss.); two *s* one *d*; 2nd, 1960, Maureen R. McLellan; one *s* one *d*. *Educ:* Loreto; Calcutta; Exeter Sch., Devon; Univ. of London (BScEcon); Univ. of Exeter (BA Social Studies). FIH. Nat. Service, Subaltern, Devonshire Regt, 1951; Major, Devonshire and Dorset Regt TA, 1965. Nigerian Produce Marketing Boards, 1952–54; Dir, Atlas Ltd, Nigeria, 1955–61. Chairman: Exeter Photo-Copying, 1963–93; EuroSpeedy Printing Centres UK, 1988–93; Copyshops of SW England, 1989–93. Vice Chairman: E Devon Water Bd, 1965–73; Devon River Authority, 1970–73. Councillor, Exeter CC, 1963–74 (Chairman: Public Works Cttee, 1965–69; Education Cttee, 1971–72). MP (C) N Devon, 1979–92; contested (C) N Devon, 1992. Mem., Select Cttee on Energy, 1982–88; Chairman: All-Party Alternative Energy Gp, 1984–92; W Africa Cttee, 1987–92. Chm., W Country Cons. MPs, 1983–87; Pres., 1996–99, Vice-Pres., 2000–08, N Devon Cons. Assoc.; Vice-Chm., Tiverton and Honiton Cons. Assoc., 1997–99. Mem., Newton St Cyres Parish Council, 2007–10. Hon. Pres., Nat. Outdoor Events Assoc., 1992–98; Hon. Commercial Advr, The Keep, Mil. Mus. of Devon and Dorset, 2001–02; Regtl Advr, History Park, Mus. of Barnstaple and N Devon, 2002–08. Vice-Pres., Railway Develt Soc., 1992–. Mem. Cttee, Duke of

Edinburgh Award Scheme, Devon, 2000–04. *Address:* 11 Newton House, Newton St Cyres, Exeter, Devon EX5 5BL. *E:* tonyspeller@hotmail.com. *Died 15 Feb. 2013.*

SPELLER, Maj.-Gen. Norman Henry, CB 1976; Government Relations Adviser, ICL, 1976–86; *b* 5 March 1921; *s* of late Col Norman Speller and Emily Florence Speller (*née* Lambert); *m* 1950, Barbara Eleanor (*née* Earle); two *s*. *Educ:* Wallingford Grammar School. Commnd RA, 1940; War Service N Africa; transf. to RAOC, 1945; psc 1952; DAA&QMG 39 Inf. Bde, 1953–55; Dirg Staff, Staff Coll., 1955–58; OC 20 Ordnance Field Park, 1958–60; Admin. Staff Coll., 1961; AA&QMG N Ireland, 1961–63; D/SPO COD Donnington, 1964–65; Col AQ 54 (EA) Div./District, 1965–66; AAG AG9, MoD, 1967; DDOS 1 British Corps, 1968–69; idc 1970; Dir of Systems Coordination, MoD, 1971–73; Dir of Ordnance Services, MoD, 1973–76. Col Comdt, RAOC, 1978–83. Chm. Management Cttee, The Royal Homes for Officers' Widows and Daughters (SSAFA), 1987–94. *Recreations:* sailing, golf. *Address:* 1 Steeple Close, SW6 3LE. *Club:* Roehampton. *Died 7 April 2013.*

SPENCE, Prof. Alastair Andrew, CBE 1993; MD; FRCA, FRCSE, FRCPG, FRCPE, FRCS; Professor of Anaesthetics, University of Edinburgh, 1984–98, then Emeritus; *b* 18 Sept. 1936; *s* of James Glendinning Spence and Margaret Macdonald; *m* 1963, Maureen Isobel Aitchison; two *s*. *Educ:* Ayr Acad.; Glasgow Univ. FRCA (FFARCS 1964); FRCPG 1980; FRCSE 1991; FRCPE 1994; FRCS 1994. Western Infirmary, Glasgow, 1961–65; MRC Res. Fellow, Univ. of Glasgow Dept of Surgery, 1965–66; Steinberg Res. Fellow and Clinical Asst to Prof. of Anaesthesia, Univ. of Leeds, 1966–69; Sen. Lectr and Head of Dept of Anaesthesia, later Reader and Prof., Western Infirmary, Glasgow, 1969–84. Hon. Consultant Anaesthetist, Lothian Health Bd, then Royal Infirmary of Edinburgh Trust, 1984–98. Lewis H. Wright Meml Lect., Amer. Soc. of Anesthesiologists, 2006. Member: Clinical Standards Adv. Gp, 1994–99; Adv. Cttee on Distinction Awards, 1992–2000 (Dir and Med. Vice-Chm., Scottish Sub-Cttee, 1995–98); Scottish Adv. Cttee on Distinction Awards, 1998–2000. Pres., Royal Coll. of Anaesthetists, 1991–94 (Vice-Pres., 1988–91). Hon. FDS 1994; Hon. FRCEM (Hon. FFAEM 1997). Editor, British Jl of Anaesthesia, 1973–83 (Chm. Bd, 1983–91). *Publications:* books, chapters and papers on anaesthesia and respiratory care. *Recreations:* golf, gardening. *Address:* Harewood, Kilmacolm, Renfrewshire PA13 4HX. *T:* (01505) 872962. *Died 30 Nov. 2015.*

SPENCE, Most Rev. Francis John; Archbishop of Kingston (Ontario), (RC), 1982–2002, then Archbishop Emeritus; *b* Perth, Ont, 3 June 1926; *s* of William John Spence and Rose Anna Spence (*née* Jordan). *Educ:* St Michael's Coll., Toronto (BA 1946); St Augustine's Seminary, Toronto; St Thomas Univ., Rome (JCD 1955). Ordained priest, 1950; Bishop, 1967; Auxiliary to Mil. Vicar, Canadian Forces, 1967–82; Bishop of Charlottetown, PEI, 1970–82; Mil. Vicar, 1982–88. Pres., Canadian Conf. of Catholic Bishops, 1995–97. *Address:* 390 Palace Road, Kingston, ON K7L 4T3, Canada. *Died 27 July 2011.*

SPENCE, Ian Richard; international tax consultant and adviser to developing countries, since 1998; *b* 15 Oct. 1938; *s* of John Jack Spence and Floretta Spence (*née* Bate); *m* 1971, Anne Kiggell; two *d*. *Educ:* Dulwich Coll.; Jesus Coll., Cambridge (BA Hist.). Joined Inland Revenue, 1962; seconded to DEA, 1966; Principal, 1967; seconded to CSSB, 1972; Asst Sec., 1975; Under Sec., and Dir, Internat. Div., Bd of Inland Revenue, 1991–98. Mem., Permanent Scientific Cttee, Internat. Fiscal Assoc., 1993–99. Sen. Res. Fellow, Internat. Tax and Investment Centre, 1999–2002. *Recreations:* theatre, opera, tennis, sailing, golf. *Address:* 98 Burbage Road, SE24 9HE. *T:* and *Fax:* (020) 7274 6198. *E:* Ian_spence@btinternet.com. *Clubs:* Athenæum; Dulwich Sports; Dulwich and Sydenham Golf; Old Fogeys Golfing Soc. *Died 2 Aug. 2012.*

SPENCER, Comdt Anne Christine, CBE 1994; Director, Women's Royal Naval Service, 1991–93; *b* 15 Dec. 1938; *d* of late Ernest Spencer and Dora Harrie (*née* Hauxwell). *Educ:* Newlands High Sch.; Yorks Coll. of Housecraft (HCIMA 1959). Direct Entry Officer, WRNS, 1962; commnd 1963; HMS Victory, 1963–64; HMS Dauntless, 1964–66; HMS Terror, Singapore, 1966–68; HMS St Vincent, 1968–69; HMS Nelson, 1969–70; Officer i/c WRNS, HMS Excellent, 1970–73; HMS Pembroke, 1973–74; Mess Manager, RNC, Greenwich, 1974–76; Defence Intelligence Staff, MoD, 1976–78; RNSC, 1978; Directorate of Naval Service Conditions, MoD, 1978–79; Terminology Co-ordinator, NATO HQ Brussels, 1979–81; WRNS Officers Appointer, MoD, 1981–83; Dep. Dir, WRNS, MoD, 1984–86; Naval Dir, NAAFI Bd of Management, 1986–88; Chief Staff Officer (Admin) to Flag Officer, Plymouth, 1988–91. ADC to HM Queen, 1991–93. *Recreations:* theatre, art, food, friends, Yorkshire. *Address:* 6 Wilkinson House, Gunners Row, Marine Gate, Southsea, Hants PO4 9XQ. *Died 15 July 2012.*

SPENCER, Cyril Charles, CMG 1951; First Deputy Executive Director, International Coffee Organisation, London, 1964–68; *b* 1 Feb. 1912; *s* of late Albert Edward Spencer, CBE, and Elsie Maud Spencer; *m* 1st, 1938; (one *d* decd); 2nd, 1949, Catherine Dewar Robertson (*d* 1995); 3rd, 1998, Phyllis Steele (*née* Rees) (*d* 1999); 4th, 2001, Penny Adames (*née* Salvidge). *Educ:* Royal Grammar Sch., Worcester; St John's Coll., Cambridge (BA 1934). Uganda: Asst Treas., 1935; Asst District Officer, 1937; Asst Financial Sec., 1946; Economic Sec., E Africa High Commission, 1948; Financial Sec., 1948; Acting Chief Sec. at various dates; Acting Governor, July 1951; Chairman: Uganda Lint Marketing Bd; Uganda Coffee Marketing Board; Member: Uganda Electricity Board; Uganda Development Corp.; Comr on Special Duty, Uganda, 1953–61; Sec.-Gen., Inter-African Coffee Organisation, Paris, 1961–64. *Recreations:* golf, fishing. *Died 30 April 2011.*

SPENDLOVE, Peter Roy, CVO 1981; HM Diplomatic Service, retired; consultant in development and public administration; Chairman, East Anglia Regional Ambulance Service NHS Trust, 1993–95; *b* 11 Nov. 1925; *s* of H. A. Spendlove and Florence (*née* Jackson); *m* 1952, Wendy Margaret Valentine (*d* 2010); two *s* three *d*. *Educ:* Chichester High Sch.; London Sch. of Economics; Edinburgh and Cambridge Univs. BScEcon Hons 1951. Called to Bar, Middle Temple, 1964. Served HM Forces, 1943–47: commnd, Indian Army/Royal Indian Artillery. LSE, 1948–51; Internat. Law Scholar at The Hague, 1951; Univ. of Cambridge, 1951–52. Apptd District Officer, Kenya, 1952; retired after serving in Provincial Admin and Central Govt, 1964. First Secretary, FCO, 1964; served in E Malaysia, Washington, Manila, FO, Jamaica; Counsellor, Economic, Commercial and Aid, Jakarta, 1977–80; Deputy High Comr, Sri Lanka, 1981–82; Dep. Chief Administrator, Broads Authority (E Anglia), 1983–86. Chm., Norfolk Ambulance Service NHS Trust, 1990–94. *Recreation:* riding. *Address:* 7 Wrenshaw Court, The Downs, Wimbledon, SW20 8HZ. *T:* (020) 8946 2767. *Died 9 March 2014.*

SPERRY, Rt Rev. John Reginald, CM 2002; CD 1987; Bishop of The Arctic, 1974–90; National President, Canadian Bible Society, since 1990; Vice President, United Bible Societies (Americas Region), since 1992; *b* 2 May 1924; *s* of William Reginald Sperry and Elsie Agnes (*née* Priest); *m* 1952, Elizabeth Maclaren (*d* 2001); one *s* one *d* (and one *d* decd). *Educ:* St Augustine's Coll., Canterbury; King's Coll., Halifax (STh). Deacon, 1950; priest, 1951; St Andrew's Mission, Coppermine, NWT, 1950–69; Canon of All Saints' Cathedral, Aklavik, 1957–59; Archdeacon of Coppermine, 1959–69; Rector of St John's, Fort Smith, NWT, 1969–73; Rector of Holy Trinity, Yellowknife, NWT, 1974. Hon. DD: Coll. of Emmanuel, St Chad, 1974; Wycliffe Coll., Toronto, 1979. Queen's Diamond Jubilee Medal, 2012. *Publications:* translations into Copper Eskimo: Canadian Book of Common Prayer (1962), 1969; Four Gospels and Acts of the Apostles, 1972; Igloo Dwellers Were My Church (memoirs), 2001. *Address:* 1 Dakota Court, Yellowknife, NT X1A 2A4, Canada. *T:* (867) 8736163. *Died 11 Feb. 2012.*

SPICER, Sir James (Wilton), Kt 1988; company director; *b* 4 Oct. 1925; *s* of James and Florence Clara Spicer; *m* 1954, Winifred Douglas Shanks (MBE 2008) (*d* 2010); two *d*. *Educ:* Latymer. Regular army, 1943–57, retd (Major);

commnd Royal Fusiliers, 1944; Para. Regt, 1951–57. Nat. Chm., CPC, 1968–71. Mem. (C) European Parlt, 1975–84 (elected Mem. for Wessex, 1979–84); Chief Whip, European Democratic Gp, 1975–79; Chairman: Cons. Group for Europe, 1975–78 (Dir, 1972–74); Conservatives Abroad, 1986–93. MP (C) Dorset West, Feb. 1974–1997. Mem., Select Cttee on Agriculture, 1984–85. A Vice Chm., Cons. Party Orgn, and Chm., Internat. Office, 1985–92. Chairman: Westminster Foundn for Democracy, 1992–97; Agricl and Rural Parlt Trust, 1998–2000. Chairman: Inglewood Health Hydro, 1999–2001; St James Security, 2003–06; Airborne Initiative, 2012–. Patron, Dorset/Somerset, Marie Curie Cancer Care, 2000–06 (Chm., Dorset Br., 1998–2000); Chm., Dorset Br., Action Res., 1999–2000. Order of Golden Eagle (Austria), 1988. *Recreations:* swimming, tennis. *Address:* Whatley, Beaminster, Dorset DT8 3SB. *T:* (01308) 862337. *Died 21 March 2015.*

SPINK, Prof. Ian Walter Alfred; Professor of Music, London University at Royal Holloway College, later Royal Holloway and Bedford New College, 1974–97, then Emeritus; *b* 29 March 1932; *s* of William James Spink and Margaret Hamilton (*née* Anderson); *m* 1960, Margaret Storry Walton; three *s* four *d*. *Educ:* Mercers' Sch.; Trinity Coll. of Music (BMus 1952); Barber Inst. of Fine Arts, Univ. of Birmingham (MA 1957). Nat. Service, 1953–55, 2nd Lieut, RA. Overseas Examiner for Trinity Coll. of Music in Canada, NZ and Australia, 1958–59; Dir of Music, Westlain GS, Brighton, Sussex, 1960–62; Lectr, then Sen. Lectr, Univ. of Sydney, NSW, 1962–69; RHC, later RHBNC, University of London: Head of Music Dept, 1969–92; Sen. Lectr, 1969–72; Reader, 1972–74; Dean, Fac. of Arts, 1973–75 and 1983–85; Dean, Fac. of Music, and Mem. Senate, Univ. of London, 1974–78. Leverhulme Res. Fellowship, 1996. *Publications:* English Song: Dowland to Purcell, 1974, 2nd edn 1986; The Seventeenth Century, Blackwell History of Music in Britain, vol. 3, 1992; Restoration Cathedral Music 1660–1714, 1995; Henry Lawes: Cavalier songwriter, 2000; editions of music in: The English Lute-songs, 2nd series, vol. 17, 1961, 2nd edn 1974, vol. 18, 1962, vol. 19, 1966; Musica Britannica, vol. 33, 1971, 2nd edn 1977, vol. 42, 1978; The Works of Henry Purcell, vol. 2, 1990, vol. 4, 1994, vol. 20, 1998, vol. 22a, 2000, vol. 22b, 2007; (contrib.) The New Grove, 1980, 2nd edn 2001; (contrib.) The New Oxford History of Music, vol. 6, 1986; (contrib.) Purcell Studies, 1995; articles in Acta Musicologica, Music and Letters, Proc. Royal Musical Assoc., Early Music, etc. *Address:* Bridge House, Trumps Green Road, Virginia Water, Surrey GU25 4JA. *T:* (01344) 843039. *Died 29 Oct. 2011.*

SPORBORG, Christopher Henry, CBE 2001; Chairman, Countrywide plc (formerly Hambro Countrywide, then Countrywide Assured Group), 1986–2007; *b* 17 April 1939; *s* of late H. N. Sporborg and Mary (*née* Rowlands); *m* 1961, Lucinda Jane (*née* Hanbury) (*d* 2010); two *s* two *d*. *Educ:* Rugby School; Emmanuel College, Cambridge (BA Hons). Nat. Service, Coldstream Guards, 1957–59 (Lieut). Hambros Bank, 1962–95: Dir, 1970; Dep. Chm., 1983–95; Hambros PLC: Vice-Chm., 1986–90; Dep. Chm., 1990–98. Chairman: United Racecourses (Hldgs), 1994–96; Racecourse Hldgs Trust, 1998–2003 (Dir, 1994–2003); Chesnara plc, 2004–08; Dep. Chm., C. E. Heath PLC, 1994–97; Director: Getty Images Inc., 1997–2008; Cunningham Lindsey Inc. (formerly Lindsay Morden Ltd), 1999–2007. Mem., Jockey Club, 1982–; Dir, Jockey Club Estates, 1985–2002; Mem., Horserace Totalisator Bd, 1993–2005. Trustee: Develt Trust (for the Mentally Handicapped); Nat. Hosp. Develt Foundn; Corporate Action Trust; Sir Jules Thorn Charitable Trust; Fitzwilliam Family Trusts. *Recreations:* hunting, shooting, racing (owner), bridge. *Address:* The West Wing, Brooms Farm, Upwick Green, Albury, Ware, Herts SG11 2JX. *T:* (01279) 771444. *Club:* Boodle's. *Died 2 Jan. 2015.*

SPOTTISWOOD, Air Vice-Marshal James Donald, CB 1988; CVO 1977; AFC 1971; *b* 27 May 1934; *s* of James Thomas Spottiswood and Caroline Margaret Spottiswood; *m* 1957, Margaret Maxwell (*née* Harrison); two *s* one *d*. *Educ:* West Hartlepool Grammar School; Boston Univ., USA (MA). Enlisted RAF, 1951, commissioned, 1952; 617 Sqn, 1962–64; Royal Naval Staff Coll., 1965; PSO to C-in-C Middle East, 1966–67; Commanded 53 Sqn, 1968–70; JSSC, 1970; Commanded: RAF Thorney Island, 1972–75; RAF Benson, 1975–76; Dep. Captain, the Queen's Flight, 1975–76; RCDS, 1978; Secretary to IMS, HQ NATO, 1980–83; DG of Trng, RAF, 1983–85; Air Officer Trng, RAF Support Comd, 1985–89. ADC to the Queen, 1971–76. Man. Dir, Airwork Ltd, Bournemouth Internat. Airport, 1989–97; Vice Pres., Support Services Div., Short's, 1994–97. Chm., British Gliding Assoc., 1989–97. FCMI (FBIM 1983). *Recreations:* gliding, sailing. *Address:* Royal Bank of Scotland, 49–51 Old Christchurch Road, Bournemouth BH1 1EG. *Club:* Royal Air Force. *Died 28 Dec. 2013.*

SPRACKLING, Maj.-Gen. Ian Oliver John, OBE 1977; *b* 3 Oct. 1936; *m* 1959, Ann Vonda (*née* Coote); two *s*. *Educ:* Bristol Grammar School; RMCS (BSc Eng); psc, RCDS. RMA Sandhurst, 1955; 2nd Lieut, Royal Corps of Signals, 1957; RMCS, 1958–61; served Far East, UK, BAOR, 1961–75; Staff Officer, Sultan of Oman's Armed Forces, 1975–77; CO, Electronic Warfare Regt, BAOR, 1977–79; Col, Cabinet Office, 1979–81; Comdr, Catterick Garrison, 1982–84; RCDS 1984; Dir, Mil. Assistance Overseas, 1985–86; Dir Gen., Management and Support of Intelligence, MoD, 1986–89. Defence Advr, 1989–92, Hd of Russian practice, Moscow, 1993–96, Andersen Consulting. Non-exec. Dir, i Ventures Capital, 2000–03; Chm., ITT Defence Ltd, 2004–10. Master of Signals, 1997–2003. *Recreations:* bridge, socialising, keep fit, watching Rugby. *Clubs:* Army and Navy; Fadeaways. *Died 28 March 2014.*

SPRATT, Sir Greville (Douglas), GBE 1987; TD 1962, Bar 1968; JP; DL; Underwriting Member of Lloyd's, 1950–98; Lord Mayor of London, 1987–88; *b* 1 May 1927; *e s* of Hugh Douglas Spratt and Sheelah Ivy (*née* Stace); *m* 1954, Sheila Farrow Wade (*d* 2002); three *d*. *Educ:* Leighton Park; Charterhouse; Sandhurst. Served Coldstream Guards, 1945–46; commnd Oxfordshire and Bucks LI, 1946; seconded to Arab Legion; served Palestine, Trans Jordan and Egypt, 1946–48; GSO III (Ops and Intell.), 1948. Lloyd's, 1948–61; joined J. & N. Wade Gp of Electrical Distributors, 1961; Dir, 1969–76 and Man. Dir, 1972–76. Dir, 1989–92, Chm., 1991–92, City and West End Regl Adv. Bd, National Westminster Bank; Chairman: Forest Mere Ltd, 1993–96 (Dir, 1991–96); Claremount Underwriting Agency, 1994–97; Kingsmead Underwriting Agency, 1997–99; Director: Williams Lea Gp, 1989–96; Charterhouse Enterprises Ltd, 1991–95; Craigie Taylor Internat., 1995–96. Lieut of the City of London, 1972; Life Mem., Guild of Freemen, 1977 (Mem. Court, 1982–90); Liveryman, Ironmongers' Co., 1977– (Mem. Ct, 1982–; Master, 1995–96); Alderman, Castle Baynard Ward, 1978–95; JP 1978, Sheriff, 1984–85, City of London; DL Greater London, 1986; Mem., Police Cttee, 1989–91, Planning and Communications Cttee, 1990–91, Corp. of City of London. Joined HAC Infantry Bn as private, 1950; re-commnd 1950; CO, 1962–65; Regtl Col, 1966–70; Mem., Ct of Assts, HAC, 1960–70 and 1978–95; ADC to the Queen, 1973–78; Mem., City TA&VRA, 1960– (Vice Chm., 1973–77, Chm., 1977–82); Vice Pres., TA&VRA for Greater London, 1994 (Chm., 1991–94; Mem., Exec. and Finance Cttee, 1977–94); Hon. Colonel: City and NE sector, London ACF, 1983–99; 8th Bn, The Queen's Fusiliers (City of London), 1988–92; The London Regt, 1992–95. Chm., Action Res. for the Crippled Child, 1989–99 (Mem. Council, 1982–; Mem. Haslemere Cttee, 1971–82); President: Alzheimer's Soc., Haslemere, 1995–; Royal British Legion, Haslemere (St James Vice Pres., 1991–); London Fedn of Old Comrades Assocs, 1983–; Vice President: Not Forgotten Assoc., 1990–; British Red Cross, 1993– (Dep. Pres., London, 1983–91); Mem. Council, Reserve Forces Assoc., 1981–84. Chm., Anglo Jordanian Soc., 1990–97; Member: Cttee, Guildhall Sch. of Music and Drama, 1978–80 (Hon. Mem., 1988–); Court, City Univ., 1981–88 (Chancellor, 1987–88); Governing Bodies of Girls' Schs Assoc., 1982–90; Governor: St Ives Sch., 1976– (Vice Chm., 1977–86; Chm., 1986–90); King Edward's Sch., Witley, 1978–96 (Vice-Pres., 1989–96); Christ's Hosp., 1978–95; Bridewell Royal Hosp., 1978–96; City of London Sch. for Girls, 1981–82; Malvern Girls' Coll., 1982–90; St Paul's Cathedral Choir Sch., 1985–99; Charterhouse, 1985–99 (Chm. Governing Body, 1989–95);

City of London Freemen's Sch., 1992–95; Life Governor, Corp. of the Sons of the Clergy, 1985–; Patron: Internat. Centre for Child Studies, 1985–; Surrey Charity Gp, 1989–; Emily Appeal, 1992–98; Vice Patron, Almshouse Assoc., 1997–; Chm., David Shepherd Conservation Foundn, 1996–2000. Church Comr. 1993–96; Mem., St Paul's Cathedral Court of Advisers, 1993–99. Member: Blackdown Cttee, Nat. Trust, 1977–87; Surrey Scout Council, 1990–. Trustee: Chichester Theatre; Chichester Cathedral; Endowment of St Paul's Cathedral; Children's Research Internat. Carthusian Trust; Charterhouse Soc.; Castle Baynard Educnl Trust; Special Trustee, St Bartholomew's Hosp., 1989–96. FRSA; FRGS. Hon. DLitt City Univ., 1988. KStJ 1987 (OStJ 1985). Chevalier de la Légion d'Honneur, 1961; Commandeur de l'Ordre National du Mérite, 1984; Commander, Order of the Lion, Malaŵi, 1985; Mem., Nat. Order of Aztec Eagle, Mexico, 1985; Order of St Olav, Norway, 1988; Order of Merit, Senegal, 1988. *Recreations:* tennis, music, military history. *Clubs:* City Livery, Guildhall, United Wards. *Died 13 Dec. 2012.*

SPROAT, Iain Mac Donald; Chairman, European Cultural Foundation-UK, since 2006; *b* Dollar, Clackmannanshire, 8 Nov. 1938; *s* of late William Bigham Sproat and Lydia Bain Sproat (*née* Mac Donald); *m* 1979, Judith Mary Kernot (*née* King); one step *s*. *Educ:* St Mary's Sch., Melrose; Winchester Coll.; Univ. of Aix-en-Provence; Magdalen Coll., Oxford (MA). Served RGJ (4th Bn), 1972–76; TA Volunteers Reserve Course, RMA, 1973. Chm., Milner and Co., 1981, 1983–93, and 1997–; Founder and Proprietor, 1980–2005, Chm., 1980–93, 1997–2005, Cricketers' Who's Who Ltd. Contested (C) Roxburgh and Berwickshire, 1983. MP (C): Aberdeen South, 1970–83; Harwich, 1992–97; contested (C) Harwich, 1997, 2001. PPS to Sec. of State for Scotland, 1973–74; Parly Under-Sec. of State, Dept of Trade, 1981–83 (Minister: of Aviation and Shipping; of Tourism; responsible for: Govt Statistics; Retail Trade; Distributive Trades; Video, Cinema and Film Industry); Parly Under-Sec. of State, 1993–95, Minister of State, 1995–97, DNH (Minister for Sport, 1993–97). Special Advr to Prime Minister, Gen. Election, 1987. Leader, Cons. Gp, Scottish Select Cttee, 1979–81; Chm., Scottish Cons. Cttee, 1979–81; Chm., Soviet and E European Gp, Cons. Foreign Affairs Cttee, 1975–81. Member: British Parly Delegn to oversee S Vietnamese Elections, 1973; British Parly Delegn to Soviet Union, 1974; Leader, British Parly Delegn to Austria, 1980. Dist. Vis. Prof., Texas Univ., 1992. Lecturer: on guerilla warfare, RCDS, 1973; on Kurdish guerilla warfare in Iran/Iraq, RUSI, 1975; on works of Alexander Pushkin, in Russia, USA and UK, 2002–07; lecture tour in USA on special relationship between UK and USA, 1979. Trustee: African Med. and Res. Foundn (Flying Doctors), 1986–91; Scottish Self-Governing Schools Trust, 1989–2006. Mem., Churchill Archives Cttee, Churchill Coll., Cambridge, 2003–. Chairman, Editorial Board: Oxford Univ. Press Hist. of the British Empire, 1987–92; Complete Works of Pushkin, 1987–93, 1997– (Moscow Internat. Book Fair prize for trans., 1999). Cricket Writer of the Year, Wombwell Cricket Lovers' Soc., 1983. *Publications:* (ed) Cricketers' Who's Who, 1980–93; Wodehouse at War, 1981; (contrib.) The British Prime Ministers; contrib. Oxford DNB. *Recreations:* collecting books, Rugby football, cricket. *Address:* c/o Coutts & Co., 440 Strand, WC2R 0QS. *Clubs:* Cavalry and Guards, Oxford and Cambridge, MCC, Drones; Sir Walter Scott (Edinburgh). *Died 29 Sept. 2011.*

SPUFFORD, Prof. (Honor) Margaret, OBE 1996; PhD, LittD; FRHistS; FBA 1995; Research Professor in Social and Local History, University of Roehampton (formerly Roehampton Institute, later University of Surrey, Roehampton), 1994–2001, then Emeritus Professor; *b* 10 Dec. 1935; *d* of Leslie Marshall Clark and Mary (*née* Johnson); *m* 1962, Peter Spufford, (Prof. Peter Spufford, FBA); one *s* (one *d* decd). *Educ:* Univ. of Leicester (MA with Dist. 1963; PhD 1970); LittD Cantab 1986. FRHistS 1974. Calouste Gulbenkian Res. Fellow, Lucy Cavendish Coll., Cambridge, 1968–72; University of Keele: Hon. Lectr, 1974–79; Sen. Res. Fellow, 1978–79; Sen. Res. Associate, Faculty of Hist., Univ. of Cambridge, 1979–81; Fellow, Newnham Coll., Cambridge, 1980–92. Vis. Res. Fellow, 1992–93, Guest of the Rector, 2005, Netherlands Inst. for Advanced Study; Vis. Prof., Rikkyo Univ., Tokyo, 1994; Guest, Japan Acad., 2003. Earl Lectr, Univ. of Keele, 1993; James Ford Special Lectr, Univ. of Oxford, 1994. Founder and first Dir, British Acad. Hearth Tax Project, Roehampton, 1996–2006. Founder, Bridget's Hostel for Disabled and Chronically Sick Students, Cambridge, 1987 (Chm., Bridget's Trustees, 1999–2000). DUniv Open, 2002; Hon. LittD Keele, 2005. A Woman of the Year, Women of the Year Assembly and Lunch, 1998. *Publications:* (with P. Spufford) Eccleshall: the story of a Staffordshire market town, 1964; A Cambridgeshire Community: Chippenham from settlement to enclosure, 1966; Contrasting Communities: the English villager in the sixteenth and seventeenth centuries, 1974, 2nd edn 2000; Small Books and Pleasant Histories: popular fiction and its readership in seventeenth century England, 1981; The Great Reclothing of Rural England: petty chapmen and their wares in the seventeenth century, 1984; Celebration, 1989 (trans. Dutch, 1994, French, 1995, Slovene, 2001; USA edn, 1996); (ed) The World of Rural Dissenters, 1995; Poverty Portrayed: Gregory King and Eccleshall, Staffordshire, 1995; Figures in the Landscape: rural society in England, 1500–1700, 1999; contrib. chapters in edited books, including: Literacy and Social Development in the West, 1981; Order and Disorder in Early Modern England, 1985; English Rural Society 1500–1800, 1990; A Miracle Mirror'd: the Dutch Republic in European Perspective, 1995; Spiritual Classics of the late Twentieth Century, 1995; Opening the Nursery Door, 1997; The English Rural Landscape, 2000; Cambridge History of Early Modern English Literature, 2002; Christianity: a complete guide, 2004; (contrib.) Cambridge History of Libraries in Britain and Ireland, vol. 1, 2006; contrib. articles in learned jls incl. Albion, Econ. Hist. Review, Textile History, Proc. Cambridge Antiquarian Soc., Agricl Hist. Rev., Studies in Church Hist., Jl Eccl Hist., Theology. *Recreations:* Benedictine Anglican oblate, exploring countryside, vernacular architecture, listening to people. *Address:* The Guildhall, North Road, Whittlesford, Cambridge CB22 4XF. *Died 6 March 2014.*

SPURGEON, Maj.-Gen. Peter Lester, CB 1980; Chief Executive, Royal Agricultural Benevolent Institution, 1982–91; *b* 27 Aug. 1927; *s* of Harold Sidney Spurgeon and Emily Anne (*née* Bolton); *m* 1959, Susan Ann (*née* Aylward); one *s* one *d*. *Educ:* Merchant Taylors' Sch., Northwood. Commnd, 1946; 1949–66: HMS Glory; Depot, RM Deal; 40 Commando RM; ADC to Maj.-Gen. Plymouth Gp RM; DS Officers' Sch., RM; RAF Staff Coll., Bracknell; Staff of Comdt Gen. RM; 40 Commando RM; Jt Warfare Estab.; GSO2 HQ: ME Comd, Aden, 1967; Army Strategic Comd, 1968–69; Second-in-Comd, 41 Commando RM, 1969–71; DS National Defence Coll., Latimer, 1971–73; CO RM Poole, 1973–75; Dir of Drafting and Records, RM, 1975–76; Comdr, Training Gp, RM, 1977–79 and Training and Reserve Forces, RM, 1979–80; retd 1980. Col Comdt, RM, 1987–90. Pres., RM Assoc., 1986–90. *Recreations:* golf, gardening. *Address:* c/o Lloyds TSB, 1 High Street, Oxford OX1 4AA. *Club:* Army and Navy. *Died 6 Jan. 2014.*

SRIVASTAVA, Chandrika Prasad, Padma Vibhushan 2009 (Padma Bhushan 1972); Hon. KCMG 1990; Secretary-General, International Maritime Organization (formerly IMCO), 1974–89, then Emeritus; Founding Chancellor, World Maritime University, 1983–91, then Emeritus; *b* 8 July 1920; *s* of B. B. Srivastava; *m* 1947, Nirmala Salve (*d* 2011); two *d*. *Educ:* Lucknow, India. 1st cl. BA 1940, 1st cl. BA Hons 1941, 1st cl. MA 1942, 1st cl. LLB 1944; gold medals for proficiency in Eng. Lit. and Polit. Science. Under-Sec., Min. of Commerce, India, 1948–49; City Magistrate, Lucknow, 1950; Addnl Dist Magistrate, Meerut, 1951–52; Directorate-Gen. of Shipping, 1953; Dep. Dir-Gen. of Shipping, 1954–57; Dep. Sec., Min. of Transport, and Pvte Sec. to Minister of Transport and Communications, 1958; Sen. Dep. Dir-Gen. of Shipping, 1959–60; Man. Dir, Shipping Corp. of India, 1961–64; Jt Sec. to Prime Minister, 1964–66; Chm. and Man. Dir, Shipping Corp. of India, 1966–73. Director: Central Inland Water Transport Corp., 1967; Central Bd, Reserve Bank of India, 1972–73; Chm., Mogul Line Ltd, 1967–73. Chm., Indian Register of Shipping, 1991. Chm.,

Cttee on Maritime Educn and Trng, Govt of India, 1992. Vice-Pres., Sea Cadet Council, 1970–73. President: Indian Nat. Shipowners' Assoc., 1971–73; Inst. of Marine Technologists, India, 1972–89 (Hon. Mem., 1981); UN Conf. on Code of Conduct for Liner Confs, 1973–74; Internat. Maritime Lectrs' Assoc., 1980–91; Chm., Cttee of Invisibles, 3rd UN Conf. on Trade and Develt, 1972; Member: Nat. Shipping Bd, 1959–73; Merchant Navy Trng Bd, 1959–73; Nat. Welfare Bd for Seafarers, 1966–73; Amer. Bureau of Shipping, 1969; Governing Body, Indian Inst. of Foreign Trade, 1970; State Bd of Tourism, 1970; Nat. Harbour Bd, 1970–73; Gen. Cttee, Bombay Chamber of Commerce and Ind., 1971; Governing Body, Indian Inst. of Management, 1972–73; Adv. Bd, Seatrade Acad., 1978–89 (Chm. Awarding Body, Seatrade Annual Awards for Achievement, 1988); Europort Internat. Cttee of Honour, 1980–89; Bd, Internat. Maritime Bureau, ICC, 1981–89; Bd of Dirs, ICC Centre for Maritime Co-operation, 1985–89; Hon. Adv. Cttee, Internat. Congress on The Port—an Ecological Challenge, Hamburg, 1989–90; Chairman: Gov. Bd, IMO Internat. Maritime Law Inst., 1989; Gov. Council, Tolani Maritime Inst., Pune, India, 1998, then Emeritus; Chm., Nat. Maritime Day Awards Cttee, India, 2000. Life Gov., Marine Soc., 1984. Vice Pres., Welsh Centre for Internat. Affairs, 1989. FRSA 1981; Fellow: Inst. Marine Engrs, India, 1998; Co. of Master Mariners, India, 1998. Hon. Member: Master Mariners' Co., UK, 1978–89; Royal Inst. of Navigation, 1984; Internat. Fedn of Shipmasters' Assocs, 1985; The Warsash Assoc., 1988; Internat. Maritime Pilots' Assoc., 1988; Hon. Fellow: Plymouth Polytech., 1979; Nautical Inst., 1985. Hon. LLD: Bhopal, 1984; Wales, 1987; Malta, 1988. Admiral Padilla Award, Colombia, 1978; Gran Amigo del Mar Award, Colombia, 1978; Gold Mercury Internat. Award Ad Personam, 1984; Award, Seatrade Acad., 1988; Gold Medal of Honour and Hon. Citizen, Malmö, Sweden, 2003; Lal Bahadur Shastri Nat. Award for Excellence in Public Admin, Academics and Mgt, India, 2005. Commandeur du Mérite Maritime, France, 1982; Comdr, Order of St Olav, Norway, 1982; Grande Ufficiale dell'Ordine al Merito, Italy, 1983; Comdr, Order of Prince Henry the Navigator, Portugal, 1983; Gold Order of Distinguished Seafarers, Poland, 1983; Nautical Medal, 1st cl., Greece, 1983; Gran Cruz Distintivo Blanco, Orden Cruz Peruana al Mérito Naval, Peru, 1984; Gran Cruz, Orden de Manuel Amador Guerrero, Panama, 1985; Grande-Oficial, Ordem do Mérito Naval, Brazil, 1986; Commander's Cross, Order of Merit, Poland, 1986; Silver Medal of Honour, Malmö, Sweden, 1988; Kt Great Band, Order of Humane African Redemption, Liberia, 1989; Comdr's Cross of Order of Merit, FRG, 1989; Comdr Grand Cross, Royal Order of the Star of the North, Sweden, 1989; Order of Merit, First Grade, Egypt, 1990; Encomienda de Numero de la Order de Isabel la Católica, Spain, 1994; Comendador, Orden Naval Almirante Padilla, Colombia, 2004. *Publications:* Lal Bahadur Shastri: Prime Minister of India 1964–1966—a life of truth in politics, 1995; Corruption: India's Enemy Within, 2001; World Maritime University: first twenty years-background and concept, establishment and progress, 2 vols, 2003; articles on shipping in newspapers and jls. *Recreations:* music, tennis, reading. *Address:* Palazzo Doria, Cabella Ligure, 15060 Allessandria, Italy; International Maritime Organisation, 4 Albert Embankment, SE1 7SR. *Clubs:* Willingdon Sports (Bombay); Pune (Pune). *Died 22 July 2013.*

STACEY, Rear Adm. Michael Lawrence, CB 1979; private consultant in marine pollution; Life Vice President, Royal National Lifeboat Institution, since 1997; *b* 6 July 1924; *s* of Maurice Stacey and Dorice Evelyn (*née* Bulling); *m* 1955, Penelope Leana (*née* Riddoch); two *s*. *Educ:* Epsom Coll. Entered RN as Cadet, 1942; Normandy landings, HMS Hawkins, 1944; served in HM Ships Rotherham, Cambrian, Shoreham, Hornet, Vernon, Euryalus, Bermuda, Vigilant; Comdr 1958; staff of RN Staff Coll.; in comd HMS Blackpool, 1960–62; JSSC; Captain 1966; Chief Staff Officer to Admiral Commanding Reserves, 1966–68; in comd HMS Andromeda and Captain (F) Sixth Frigate Sqdn, 1968–70; Dep. Dir of Naval Warfare, 1970–73; in comd HMS Tiger, 1973–75; Asst Chief of Naval Staff (Policy), 1975–76; Flag Officer, Gibraltar, 1976–78. ADC to the Queen, 1975. Dir, Marine Emergency Ops, Marine Div., Dept of Trade, later Dept of Transport, 1979–87. Mem., Adv. Cttee on Protection of the Sea, 1988–2008. FNI; FCMI. Younger Brother, Trinity House, 1979. Liveryman, Shipwrights' Co., 1991; Mem., Master Mariners' Co., 1999. *Recreations:* fishing, yachting. *Address:* Flat 6, Headon Court, The Close, Tilford Road, Farnham, Surrey GU9 8DR. *T:* (01252) 713032. *Clubs:* Army and Navy, Royal Navy of 1765 and 1785, Royal Naval Sailing Association. *Died 15 July 2013.*

STACK, Neville; international editorial consultant and syndicated political columnist, in South and South East Asia, Africa and the Caribbean, since 1989; *b* 2 Sept. 1928; *m* 1953, Molly Rowe; one *s* one *d*. *Educ:* Arnold School. Reporter: Ashton-under-Lyne Reporter, 1948; Express & Star, 1950; Sheffield Telegraph, and Kemsley National Papers, 1955; Northern News Editor, IPC national papers, 1971; Sub-editor, Daily Express, 1973; Editor, Stockport Advertiser, 1974; Editor, Leicester Mercury, 1974–87; Dir, F. Hewitt and Co. (1927) Ltd (Mercury Publishers), 1982–88; Editorial Consultant, Straits Times, Singapore, 1988–89; Consultant: New Paper, Singapore, 1990–; Trinidad Daily Express, 1990–; Independent Newspapers Gp, SA, 1998–99; Columnist: The Hindu, Chennai, 1990–2004; Indian Business Leaders mag., Mumbai, 1990–; Today, Singapore, 1999–2003; political commentator, Singapore Straits Times, 1990–99. Hon. Press Fellow, Wolfson Coll., Cambridge, 1987–88. Evaluator, RSA journalism qualification, 1992–; Co-organiser and Mem., Wolfson Coll. Regl Seminar for Editors, 1992–. Mem. Court, Leicester Univ., 1999. Hon. MA Leicester, 1988. *Publications:* The Empty Palace, 1976; Editing for the Nineties, 1988. *Recreations:* writing, computers, travel. *Address:* Letter-na-Caight, Letterbarrow, Donegal Town, Co. Donegal, Ireland. *T:* 0857546260. *Died 27 Oct. 2012.*

STACPOOLE, John Wentworth; Deputy Secretary, Department of Health and Social Security, 1979–82; *b* 16 June 1926; *s* of late G. W. Stacpoole and of Mrs M. G. Butt; *m* 1954, Charmian, *d* of late J. P. Bishop and Mrs E. M. Bishop; one *s* one *d*. *Educ:* Sedbergh; Magdalen Coll., Oxford (Demy; MA). Army, 1944–47 (Lieut, Assam Regt). Colonial Office, 1951–68, Private Sec. to Sec. of State, 1964–65; transf. to Min. of Social Security, 1968; Under-Sec., DHSS, 1973. Mem., Maidstone HA, 1982–91. Chm., Maidstone Hospice Appeal, 1987–92. *Publications:* (ed) Sedbergh School 1900–2000: a celebration, 2000. *Recreations:* reading, sketching. *Address:* 25 Offham Road, West Malling, Kent ME19 6RB. *T:* (01732) 847162. *Died 22 March 2012.*

STAFFORD, Godfrey Harry, CBE 1976; PhD; FRS 1979; FInstP; Master of St Cross College, Oxford, 1979–87; *b* 15 April 1920; *s* of Henry and Sarah Stafford; *m* 1950, Helen Goldthorp (*née* Clark) (*d* 2003); one *s* twin *d*. *Educ:* Rondebosch Boys' High Sch., S Africa; Univ. of Cape Town (MSc 1941); Gonville and Caius Coll., Cambridge (Ebden Scholar, PhD 1950); MA Oxon 1971. South African Naval Forces, 1941–46. Harwell, 1949–51; Head of Biophysics Subdiv., CSIR, Pretoria, 1951–54; Cyclotron Gp, AERE, 1954–57; Rutherford Laboratory: Head of Proton Linear Accelerator Gp, 1957; Head of High Energy Physics Div., 1963; Dep. Dir, 1966; Dir, Rutherford Lab., Chilton, 1969–79; Dir Gen., 1979–81, Hon. Scientist, 1987–, Rutherford Appleton Laboratory; Fellow, St Cross Coll., Oxford, 1971–79 (Hon. Fellow, 1987). CERN appointments: UK deleg. to Council, 1973; Vice-Pres., Council, 1973; Scientific Policy Cttee, 1973, Vice-Chm., 1976, Chm., 1978. Vice-Pres. for meetings, Inst. of Physics, 1976; President: European Physical Soc., 1984–86 (Vice-Pres., 1982–84); Inst. of Physics, 1986–88. Governor: Oxford Centre for Post-Graduate Hebrew Studies, 1983–93; Westminster Coll., 1987–93. Glazebrook Prize and Medal, Inst. of Physics, 1981. Hon. DSc Birmingham, 1980. *Publications:* papers and articles in learned jls on: biophysics, nuclear physics, high energy physics. *Recreations:* walking, foreign travel, music. *Address:* Ferry Cottage, North Hinksey Village, Oxford OX2 0NA. *T:* (01865) 247621. *Died 29 July 2013.*

STAINTON, Sir (John) Ross, Kt 1981; CBE 1971; Member, 1971, Deputy Chairman and Chief Executive, 1977–79, Chairman, 1979–80, British Airways Board; *b* 27

May 1914; *s* of late George Stainton and Helen Ross; *m* 1939, Doreen Werner (*d* 2001); three *d*. *Educ:* Glengorse, Eastbourne; Malvern Coll., Worcestershire. Joined Imperial Airways as Trainee, 1933; served in Italy, Egypt, Sudan. Served with RAF in England, West Indies and USA, 1940–46. Man. N America, BOAC, 1949–53; General Sales Man. BOAC, and other Head Office posts, 1954–68; Dep. Man. Dir, 1968–71; Man. Dir, 1971–72; Mem., BOAC Bd, 1968, Chm. and Chief Exec., 1972, until merged into British Airways, 1974. Vice Pres., Private Patients Plan, 1986– (Dir, 1979–86). Hon. Treasurer, Air League Council, 1986–91. FCILT (Pres., 1970–71); CRAeS 1978. *Clubs:* Royal Air Force; Royal and Ancient Golf (St Andrews); Sunningdale Golf. *Died 5 Dec. 2011.*

STALLWORTHY, Prof. Jon Howie, FBA 1990; FRSL; Professor of English Literature, Oxford University, 1992–2000, then Emeritus; Senior Research Fellow, Wolfson College, Oxford, since 2000 (Fellow, since 1986; Acting President, 2006–08); *b* 18 Jan. 1935; *s* of Sir John (Arthur) Stallworthy and late Margaret Wright (*née* Howie); *m* 1960, Gillian Meredith (*née* Waldock) (*d* 2013); two *s* one *d*. *Educ:* The Dragon Sch., Oxford; Rugby Sch.; Magdalen Coll., Oxford (MA, BLitt; Newdigate Prize, 1958 (runner-up, 1957)). Served RWAFF (pre-Oxford). Joined Oxford Univ. Press, 1959, Dep. Head, Academic Div., 1975–77; John Wendell Anderson Prof. of English Lit., Cornell Univ., 1977–86; Reader in English Lit., Oxford Univ., 1986–92. Chatterton Lectr on an English Poet, British Academy, 1970; during a sabbatical year, 1971–72, was a Visiting Fellow at All Souls Coll., Oxford. FRSL 1971. *Publications: poems* (collections): The Astronomy of Love, 1961; Out of Bounds, 1963; Root and Branch, 1969; Positives, 1969; The Apple Barrel: selected poems, 1955–63, 1974; Hand in Hand, 1974; A Familiar Tree, 1978; The Anzac Sonata: new and selected poems, 1986; The Guest From the Future, 1995; Rounding the Horn: collected poems, 1998; Body Language, 2004; War Poet, 2009; *criticism:* Between the Lines, W. B. Yeats's Poetry in the Making, 1963; Vision and Revision in Yeats's Last Poems, 1969; Survivors' Songs from Maldon to the Somme, 2008; *biography:* Wilfred Owen, 1974 (winner of Duff Cooper Meml Prize, W. H. Smith Literary Award and E. M. Forster Award); Louis MacNeice (Southern Arts Lit. Prize), 1995; *autobiography:* Singing School: the making of a poet, 1998; *translations:* (with Peter France) Alexander Blok: The Twelve and other poems, 1970; (with Jerzy Peterkiewicz) poems for 2nd edn of Five Centuries of Polish Poetry, 1970; (with Peter France) Boris Pasternak: Selected Poems, 1983; *edited:* The Penguin Book of Love Poetry, 1973; Wilfred Owen: Complete Poems and Fragments, 1983; The Oxford Book of War Poetry, 1984, rev. edn as The New Oxford Book of War Poetry, 2014; The Poems of Wilfred Owen, 1985; First Lines: poems written in youth, from Herbert to Heaney, 1987; Henry Reed: Collected Poems, 1991; The War Poems of Wilfred Owen, 1994; (jtly) The Norton Anthology of Poetry, 4th edn, 1996; Anthem for Doomed Youth: twelve soldier poets of the First World War, 2002; The New Penguin Book of Love Poetry, 2003; (jtly) The Norton Anthology of English Literature, 8th edn, 2006; (with Jane Potter) Three Poets of the First World War: Ivor Gurney, Isaac Rosenberg, Wilfred Owen, 2011. *Address:* Wolfson College, Oxford OX2 6UD; Long Farm, Elsfield Road, Old Marston, Oxford OX3 0PR. *Died 19 Nov. 2014.*

STAMER, Sir (Lovelace) Anthony, 5th Bt *cr* 1809; MA; AMIMI; *b* 28 Feb. 1917; *s* of Sir Lovelace Stamer, 4th Bt, and Eva Mary (*d* 1974), *e d* of R. C. Otter; *S* father, 1941; *m* 1st, 1948, Stella Huguette (marr. diss. 1953), *d* of late Paul Burnell Binnie, Brussels; one *s* one *d*; 2nd, 1955, Margaret Lucy (marr. diss. 1959), *d* of late Major Belben; 3rd, 1960, Marjorie June (marr. diss. 1968), *d* of late T. C. Noakes, St James, Cape; 4th, 1983, Elizabeth Graham Smith (*d* 1992), *widow* of G. P. H. Smith, Colyton, Devon; 5th, 1997, Pamela Grace (*née* Hawkins), *widow* of P. B. Cheston. *Educ:* Harrow; Trinity Coll., Cambridge; Royal Agricultural Coll., Cirencester. BA 1947; MA 1963; AMIMI 1963. Served RAF 1939–41; Officer in ATA 1941–45. Executive Director: Bentley Drivers Club Ltd, 1969–73; Bugatti & Ferrari Owners Club, 1973–75; Hon. Treasurer, Ferrari Owners' Club, 1975–81. *Heir: s* Peter Tomlinson Stamer, Sqn Leader, RAF, retd [*b* 19 Nov. 1951; *m* 1979, Dinah Louise Berry (marr. diss. 1989); one *s* one *d*; *m* 1999, Věra Řeháková (marr. diss. 2002)]. *Address:* Old Timbers, Church Street, Moreton-in-Marsh, Glos GL56 0LN. *Died 30 April 2012.*

STAMMERS, Michael Kingsley; Keeper of Merseyside Maritime Museum, 1986–2003, Curator Emeritus, 2004; *b* 30 Aug. 1943; *s* of John Kingsley Stammers and late Thelma Marjorie Stammers (*née* Gooch); *m* 1971, Pauline Birch (*d* 2012); one *s* one *d*. *Educ:* Norwich Sch.; Univ. of Bristol (BA Hons History). AMA. Curator of Folk Life, Warwick County Museum, 1966–69; Keeper of Shipping, Liverpool City Museum, 1969–74; Curator of Maritime History, Merseyside County Museums, 1974–86. Mem., Nat. Historic Ships Cttee, 1990–2000. Trustee: Internat. Congress of Maritime Museums, 2002–; Nat. Maritime Mus., Cornwall, 2002–. FRHistS 2000; FSA 2002. *Publications:* West Coast Shipping, 1976, 2nd edn 1989; The Passage Makers, 1978; Liverpool: the port and its ships, 1991; (with J. Kearon) The Jhelum: a Victorian merchant ship, 1992; Mersey Flats and Flatmen, 1993; (with J. G. Read) A Guide to the Records of Merseyside Maritime Museum, 1995; A Maritime Fortress, 2001; Norfolk Shipping, 2002; Charles Cooper: the last emigrant ship, 2003; Suffolk Shipping, 2003; End of Voyages, 2004; Figureheads and Ship Carving, 2005; Crosby Curiosities, 2006; The Industrial Archaeology of Docks and Harbours, 2007; Sailing Barges of the British Isles, 2008; Shipbuilding at Wells, 2011; contribs to learned jls. *Recreations:* going to sea, gardening, music. *Address:* 55 Kimberley Drive, Great Crosby L23 5TA. *Clubs:* Liverpool Artists'; Royal Mersey Yacht. *Died 30 Jan. 2013.*

STANBRIDGE, Ven. Leslie Cyril; Archdeacon of York, 1972–88, then Archdeacon Emeritus; *b* 19 May 1920. *Educ:* Bromley County Grammar Sch., Kent; St John's Coll., Durham Univ. (MA, DipTheol). Asst Curate of Erith Parish Church, Kent, 1949–51; Tutor and Chaplain, St John's Coll., Durham, 1951–55; Vicar of St Martin's, Hull, 1955–64; Examining Chaplain to the Archbishop of York, 1962–74; Rector of Cottingham, Yorks, 1964–72; Canon of York, 1968–2000, then Emeritus; Succentor Canonicorum, 1988–2000; Rural Dean of Kingston-upon-Hull, 1970–72; Warden, York Diocesan Readers' Assoc., 1988–95. *Address:* 32 The Oaks, Hartrigg Oaks, New Earswick, York YO32 4DY. *T:* (01904) 750812. *Died 19 March 2015.*

STANLEY OF ALDERLEY, 8th Baron *cr* 1839 (UK); **Thomas Henry Oliver Stanley;** DL; Bt 1660; Baron Sheffield (Ire), 1783; Baron Eddisbury, 1848; Captain, Coldstream Guards; Tenant Farmer of New College, Oxford, since 1954; *b* 28 Sept. 1927; *s* of Lt-Col The Hon. Oliver Hugh Stanley, DSO, JP (3rd *s* of 4th Baron) (*d* 1952), and Lady Kathleen Stanley (*d* 1977), *e d* of 5th Marquess of Bath; *S* cousin (known as Baron Sheffield), 1971; *m* 1955, Jane Barrett, *d* of Ernest George Hartley; three *s* one *d*. *Educ:* Wellington College, Berks. Coldstream Guards, 1945–52; Guards Parachute Battalion and Independent Company, 1947–50; Northamptonshire Institute of Agriculture, 1952–53. Mem., Cttee of Management, RNLI, 1981–2003; Chm., Fund Raising Cttee, RNLI, 1985–94. Governor, St Edward's Sch., Oxford, 1979–98. FRAgS 2005. DL Gwynedd, 1985. *Recreations:* sailing, ski-ing, fishing. *Heir: e s* Hon. Richard Oliver Stanley, BSc [*b* 24 April 1956; *m* 1983, Carla, *er d* of Dr K. T. C. McKenzie, Solihull; three *d* (one *s* decd)]. *Address:* Trysglwyn Fawr, Amlwch, Anglesey LL68 9RF. *T:* (01407) 830364; Rectory Farm, Stanton St John, Oxford OX33 1HF. *T:* (01865) 351214. *Clubs:* Farmers, Pratt's. *Died 19 Nov. 2013.*

STANLEY, (Geoffrey) Colin; Director General, British Printing Industries Federation, 1988–95; *b* 3 May 1937; *s* of Harold Bertram Smerdon Stanley and Ruth Mary (*née* Dunn); *m* 1962, Lesley Shadrach McWilliam; one *s* one *d*. *Educ:* Wallasey Grammar Sch. Joined Wiggins Teape, 1957: Director and General Manager: Wiggins Teape Toys & Crafts, 1976–78; Wiggins Teape Stationery Ltd, 1979–82; Dir and Manager, Wiggins Teape Paper Ltd, 1982–87; Dir, Wiggins Teape (UK) plc, 1983–85. Dir, John Howitt Gp, 1995–99. Man. Dir, Wessex Childcare Ltd, 1996–98; Chm., Wessex Children's Hospice Trust, 1997–99. Pres.,

Nat. Assoc. of Paper Merchants, 1986–88. Mem., Council, CBI, 1988–95 (Chm., Industrial Relns, Wages and Conditions Cttee, 1992–95; Mem., Employment Affairs Cttee, 1992–95). FRSA 1991. Freeman, City of London, 1985; Liveryman, Co. of Stationers & Newspaper Makers, 1987–2009. *Recreations:* golf, gardening, music, reading. *Address:* 2 Abbey Hill Close, Winchester, Hants SO23 7AZ. *Died 18 April 2013.*

STANLEY, Michael Edward; Director, Modern Art Oxford, since 2009; *b* Widnes, 23 July 1975; *s* of Eric Stanley and Janet Stanley; *m* 1998, Carrina Robson; two *s* one *d*. *Educ:* Saints Fisher and More RC High Sch.; Ruskin Sch. of Drawing and Fine Art, Univ. of Oxford (BA Fine Art). Curator: Compton Verney, 1999–2002; Ikon Gall., 2002–04; Dir, Milton Keynes Gall., 2004–09. *Publications:* George Shaw, What I Did this Summer, 2003; Marcel Broodthaers, 2007; Thomas Houseago, 2010. *Recreations:* family, gardening, running. *Address:* Modern Art Oxford, 30 Pembroke Street, Oxford OX1 1BP. *T:* (01865) 722733. *E:* michael.stanley@modernartoxford.org.uk. *Died 21 Sept. 2012.*

STANSFIELD SMITH, Sir Colin, Kt 1993; CBE 1988; consultant architect; Professor of Architectural Design, University of Portsmouth (formerly Portsmouth Polytechnic), 1990–2001, then Professor Emeritus; *b* 1 Oct. 1932; *s* of Stansfield Smith and Mary (*née* Simpson); *m* 1961, Angela Jean Earnshaw; one *s* one *d*. *Educ:* William Hulme's Grammar Sch., Manchester; Cambridge Univ. Sch. of Architecture (MA, DipArch). ARIBA. Schools Div., LCC, 1958–60; Sen. Asst then Associate Partner, Emberton Frank & Tardrew, Architects, 1960–65; Partner, Emberton Tardrew & Partners, 1965–71; Dep. County Architect, Cheshire CC, 1971–73; County Architect, Hants CC, 1973–92. Mem., Royal Fine Art Commn, 1997–99. RIBA Royal Gold Medal, 1991. *Publications:* Hampshire Architecture (1974–1984), 1985; Schools of Thought, Hampshire Architecture (1974–1991), 1991; articles in Architects' Jl and Architectural Review. *Recreations:* golf, painting. *Address:* 8 Christchurch Road, Winchester, Hants SO23 9SR. *T:* (01962) 851970. *Club:* Hockley Golf (Twyford, Hants). *Died 19 June 2013.*

STANSGATE, 2nd Viscount; *see* Benn, Rt Hon. A. N. W.

STANTON, Rev. John Maurice, MA; Rector of Chesham Bois, 1973–83; *b* 29 Aug. 1918; *s* of Frederick William Stanton, MInstCE and Maude Lozel (*née* Cole); *m* 1947, Helen Winifred (decd) (*née* Bowden); one *s* two *d*. *Educ:* King's School, Rochester; University College, Oxford (Gunsley Exhibnr; 2nd Class Hons, Final Hon. Sch. of Nat. Science, 1947; MA 1947). Commissioned Royal Artillery, 1940, 92nd Field Regt, RA, 1940–43. Inter Services Liaison Detachment, Central Med. Force, 1943–46. Assistant Master, Tonbridge School, 1947–59; Headmaster, Blundell's School, 1959–71; Curate, St Matthew's, Exeter, 1972. Ordained Deacon, 1952; Priest, 1953. Sec., Oxford Diocesan Bd of Patronage, 1984–90. *Recreations:* water colour painting, gardening. *Address:* 16 Emden House, Barton Lane, Headington, Oxford OX3 9JU. *T:* (01865) 765206. *Died 14 March 2013.*

STAPLES, Sir Richard Molesworth, 17th Bt *cr* 1628, of Lissan, co. Tyrone; *b* 11 June 1914; 3rd *s* of Thomas Staples and Mary Ussher Staples (*née* Greer); *S* brother, 1999; *m* 1954, Marjory Charlotte (*née* Jefcoate) (*d* 1998). *Educ:* St Andrew's Coll., Dublin. RAF, 1940–52 (Burma Star, 1943); RNZAF, 1952–59. Teachers' Trng Coll., Christchurch, NZ, 1959–74. *Publications:* John Cain Mole, Airman, WW2, 1998; A Wild Gosling's Footprints, 2008. *Recreations:* travel, reading, gardening, writing, watching tennis on TV. *Club:* Union Jack. *Died 8 Nov. 2013 (dormant or ext).*

STAPLETON, Guy, CB 1995; Chief Executive, Intervention Board Executive Agency (formerly Intervention Board for Agricultural Produce), 1986–95; *b* 10 Nov. 1935; *s* of William Algernon Swann Stapleton and Joan Denise Stapleton (*née* Wilson). *Educ:* Malvern Coll. Clerical Officer, Min. of Transport and Civil Aviation, 1954–58; Exec. Officer, 1958; transf. to Min. of Aviation, 1959; Civil Aviation Asst, British Embassy, Rome, 1960–63; Private Sec. to Controller of National Air Traffic Control Services, 1963–65; Asst Principal, MAFF, 1965; Private Sec. to Jt Parly Sec., 1967–68; Principal, 1968; Asst Sec., 1973; Dept of Prices and Consumer Protection, 1974–76; Under Sec., 1981; European Secretariat, Cabinet Office, 1982–85; Dir of Establishments, MAFF, 1985–86. *Publications:* A Walk of Verse, 1961; (compiled) Poet's England: 2, Gloucestershire, 1977, 2nd edn 1982; 4, Avon and Somerset, 1981; 7, Devon, 1986; 9, Hertfordshire, 1988; 12, Leicestershire and Rutland, 1992; 13, Nottinghamshire, 1993; 19, Dorset, 1996; Vale of Moreton Churches, 1989, revd edn 2002; (ed) Memories of Moreton, 1989; Four Shire Memories, 1992; Moreton & Batsford Roll of Honour, 2000; History of Moreton-in-Marsh Hospital, 2001. *Recreations:* local and family history, topographical verse. *Club:* Royal Over-Seas League. *Died 11 Sept. 2012.*

STARKER, Janos; concert cellist, recording artist; Distinguished Professor of Cello, Indiana University, since 1958; *b* Budapest, 5 July 1924; *s* of F. Sandor and M. Margit; *m* 1944, Eva Uranyi; one *d*; *m* 1960, Rae D. Busch; one *d*. *Educ:* Franz Liszt Academy of Music, Budapest; Zrinyi Gymnasium, Budapest. Professional solo cellist, 1939–; Budapest Opera and Philh., 1945–46; Dallas Symphony, 1948–49; Metropolitan Opera, 1949–53; Chicago Symphony, 1953–58; concert tours on all continents in recitals and as soloist with orchestras; numerous recordings (Grand Prix du Disque, 1948; Grammy Award, 1998). Member: Amer. Fedn Musicians; Indiana Acad. of Arts and Scis; Amer. Acad. of Arts and Scis, 1999; Hon. RAM 1981. Invented the Starker Bridge. Hon. DMus: Chicago Conservatory Coll., 1961; Cornell, 1978; East-West Univ., 1982; Williams Coll., 1983; Lawrence Univ., 1990; New England Conservatory of Music, 2006. George Washington Award, 1972; Sanford Fellowship Award, Yale, 1974; Herzl Award, Israel, 1978; Ed Press Award, 1983; Kodály Commemorative Medallion, NY, 1983; Arturo Toscanini Award, Toscanini Foundn, 1986; Tracy Sonneborn Award, Indiana Univ., 1986; Pro Cultura Hungarica, 1992; Indiana Governors Award, 1995; La Médaille de la ville de Paris, 1995; Pres.'s Medal for Excellence, Indiana Univ., 1999; Pres. of Hungary's Gold Medal, 1999; Isaac Stern Award, 2005. Chevalier, l'Ordre des Arts et des Lettres (France), 1997. *Publications:* Cello Method: an organised method of string playing, 1963; Bach Suites, 1971; Concerto Cadenzas, 1976; Beethoven Sonatas, 1978; Beethoven Variations, 1979; Bach Sonatas, 1979; Schubert-Starker Sonatina, 1980; Dvorak Concerto, 1981; Bottermund-Starker Variations, 1982; Encores, 1985; many articles and essays. *Recreations:* writing, swimming, staying alive. *Address:* Indiana University Music Department, Bloomington, IN 47405, USA; c/o Colbert Artists, 111 West 57th Street, New York, NY 10019, USA. *Died 28 April 2013.*

STATHATOS, Stephanos; Commander, Order of Phoenix; Officer, Order of George I; *b* 30 Sept. 1922; *s* of Gerassimo and Eugenia Stathatos; *m* 1947, Thalia Mouzina. *Educ:* Law School, Athens Univ.; post graduate studies: Ecole des Sciences Politiques, Paris; LSE. Entered Greek Diplomatic Service, 1953; served Cairo, NATO, Paris, Athens, Washington; Dep. Perm. Rep. to UN, NY, 1968–72; Dir, Middle East Political Affairs, Min. of Foreign Affairs, 1972–74; Ambassador, Perm. Rep. to EEC, 1974–79; Ambassador, Paris, 1979–82; non-resident Ambassador to Holy See, 1981–82; Dep. Political Dir, 1982–84, Political Dir, 1984–85, Min. of Foreign Affairs; Ambassador to UK, 1986–89, and non-resident Ambassador to Iceland; Head of Prime Minister's Diplomatic Office, 1989–90. Pres., EU *ad hoc* Gp on Stability Pact, 1994; Nat. Rep. to Reflexion Gp for revision of Maastricht Treaty, 1995. Mem., Hon. Council, Hellenic Foundn for Eur. and Foreign Policy. Holds numerous foreign orders and decorations. *Publications:* Greece's Stance Towards EU Evolution, 2001; Forty Years in the Diplomatic Arena, 2007. *Address:* 24 Raviné Street, Athens 11521, Greece. *T:* (1) 7222004. *Club:* Athenæum. *Died 18 June 2013.*

STAUGHTON, Rt Hon. Sir Christopher (Stephen Thomas Jonathan Thayer), Kt 1981; PC 1988; FCIArb; arbitrator; a Lord Justice of Appeal, 1987–97; Judge of the Court of Appeal, Gibraltar, 2000–06 (President, 2005–06);

b 24 May 1933; *yr s* of late Simon Thomas Samuel Staughton of Melbourne, Australia and Edith Madeline Jones of Halifax, Canada; *m* 1960, Joanna Susan Elizabeth, OBE, DL, *er d* of late George Frederick Arthur Burgess; two *d*. *Educ:* Eton Coll. (Scholar); Magdalene Coll., Cambridge (Scholar; George Long Prize for Roman Law, 1955; BA 1956; MA 1961; Hon. Fellow 1988). 2nd Lieut, 11th Hussars PAO, 1952–53. Called to Bar, Inner Temple, 1957, Bencher, 1978, Reader, 1996, Treasurer, 1997; QC 1970; a Recorder of the Crown Court, 1972–81; a Judge of the High Court of Justice, QBD, 1981–87. Appeal Adjudicator, enemy property claims, 2001–11. Mem., Senate of the Inns of Court and the Bar, 1974–81; Chm., Code of Conduct sub-cttee, 1979–80. Member: Adv. Bd, British Library, 1999–2002; Police Surveillance Commn, 1999–2000. Chm., St Peter's Eaton Square Church of England Sch., 1974–83. Hon. LLD Hertfordshire, 1996. *Publications:* (Jt Editor) The Law of General Average (British Shipping Laws vol. 7), 1964, new edn, 1975; (jtly) Profits of Crime and their Recovery, 1984; articles on plain English in the law. *Recreations:* bridge, growing dahlias. *Address:* 20 Essex Street, WC2R 3AL. *T:* (020) 7842 1200, *Fax:* (020) 7842 1270. *E:* jstaughton@care4free.net.
Died 15 Oct. 2014.

STAVELEY, Maj.-Gen. Robert; Chief of Staff, Logistic Executive (Army), 1979–82; *b* 3 June 1928; *s* of Brig. Robin Staveley, DSO, and Ilys (*née* Sutherland); *m* 1958, Airlie, *d* of Maj.-Gen. W. H. Lambert, CB, CBE; one *s* one *d*. *Educ:* Wellington. RMA Sandhurst, 1947; Staff Colls India and Camberley; commissioned RA, 1948; served BAOR, 1949–51; ADC to GOC Malta, 1951–53; Air OP pilot, Malaya, 1954–57 (despatches); ADC to GOC-in-C Northern Command, 1957–58; Indian Staff Coll., 1959; Staff Officer and Missile Battery Comdr, BAOR, 1960–65; Instructor, Staff Coll., 1966–68; commanded 47 Lt Regt RA, UK and Hong Kong, 1969–71; MoD, 1972; CRA 2nd Div., BAOR, 1973–74; RCDS 1975; Director of Operational Requirements, MoD, 1976–79. Admin. Controller, Norton Rose, solicitors, 1983–91. Col Comdt, RA, 1982–87. Chm., Bd of Govs, Royal Sch., Hampstead, 1993–98. FCMI (FBIM 1983). *Recreations:* good food, sailing, ski-ing, music, not gardening. *Address:* c/o Lloyds TSB (Cox's & King's Branch), 7 Pall Mall, SW1Y 5NA. *Clubs:* Army and Navy, Royal Ocean Racing; Royal Artillery Yacht (Commodore, 1980–83; Admiral, 1991–97). *Died 21 Sept. 2012.*

STEEDMAN, Martha, (Mrs R. R. Steedman); *see* Hamilton, M.

STEEL, Rupert Oliver; *b* 30 April 1922; *s* of Joseph Steel and Beatrice Elizabeth Courage; *m* 1st, Marigold Katharine (*d* 1995), *d* of Percy Lowe; two *s*; 2nd, Lucinda Evelyn Tennant (*d* 2013), *d* of Arthur James; one *s* one *d*. *Educ:* Eton. Served War of 1939–45 (despatches), Pilot, RNVR, Fleet Air Arm, 1941–46. Courage & Co. Ltd, 1946–78; Imperial Group Ltd, 1975–78; Chm., Everards Brewery Ltd, 1978–81; Director: Lloyds Bank UK Management, 1970–85; Lloyds Bank Ltd, 1977–79; Umeco plc, 1979–95; South Uist Estates Ltd, 1980–94. High Sheriff, Berks, 1985–86. *Recreation:* country. *Address:* Winterbourne Holt, Newbury, Berks RG20 8AP. *T:* (01635) 248220.
Died 17 Nov. 2013.

STEELE, John Hamilton; Vice President, Esso Norge AS, 1997; *b* Lenoir, NC, 13 March 1941; *s* of late Joe Jones Steele and Sue Mae Hickman Steele; *m* Merida Hathorn Steele; one *s* one *d*. *Educ:* North Carolina State Univ. (BS Civil Engr, MS Engr). MInstPet. Exxon Corp., USA: joined 1965; Oil & Gas Production; Calif. Dist Manager, 1976–78; Production Manager, Esso Production Malaysia Inc., Malaysia, 1978–82; Dir, Esso Exploration, Stavanger, 1982–85; Exxon Company, USA: Div. Manager, New Orleans, 1985–92; Production Ops Manager, Houston, 1992–93; Vice-Pres., Production, Houston, 1993–94; Man. Dir, Esso Exploration and Prodn UK, 1995–97. Mem., Soc. of Petroleum Engineers. *Recreations:* golf, ballet, opera.
Died 17 Jan. 2015.

STEELE, Dr John Hyslop, FRS 1978; FRSE; President, Woods Hole Oceanographic Institution, Mass, 1986–92, then President Emeritus (Director, 1977–89); *b* 15 Nov. 1926; *s* of Adam Steele and Annie Hyslop Steele; *m* 1956, Margaret Evelyn Travis; one *s*. *Educ:* George Watson's Boys' Coll., Edinburgh (Higher Cert. of Educn); University Coll., London Univ. (BSc, DSc). FRSE 1968. Marine Lab., Aberdeen, Scotland: Marine Scientist, 1951–66; Sen. Principal Scientific Officer, 1966–73; Dep. Dir, 1973–77. Dir, Exxon Corp., 1989–97. Mem., Cttee for Res. and Exploration, Nat. Geographic Soc., 1987–2000. Trustee, Robert Wood Johnson Foundn, 1991–2001. Fellow, Amer. Acad. of Arts and Sciences, 1980; FAAAS 1985. Hon. Prof., Aberdeen Univ., 1993–. Agassiz Medal, Nat. Acad. of Sciences, USA, 1973. *Publications:* Structure of Marine Ecosystems, 1974; over 100 pubns in oceanographic and ecological jls. *Recreation:* sailing. *Address:* Woods Hole Oceanographic Institution, Woods Hole, MA 02543, USA. *T:* (508) 2892220. *E:* jsteele@whoi.edu.
Died 4 Nov. 2013.

STEELE, John Roderic, CB 1979; Chairman, Prisma Consulting Group (formerly Prisma Transport Consultants), 1987–2008; *b* 22 Feb. 1929; *s* of late Harold Graham Steele and Doris Steele (*née* Hall); *m* 1956, Margaret Marie, *d* of late Joseph and Alice Stevens; two *s* two *d*. *Educ:* Queen Elizabeth Grammar Sch., Wakefield; Queen's Coll., Oxford (MA). Asst Principal, Min. Civil Aviation, 1951; Private Sec. to Parly Sec., MTCA, 1954; Principal, Road Trans. Div., 1957; Sea Transport, 1960; Shipping Policy, 1962; Asst Sec., Shipping Policy, BoT, 1964; Counsellor (Shipping), British Embassy, Washington, 1967; Asst Sec., Civil Aviation Div., DTI, 1971; Under-Secretary, Department of Trade: Space Div. (Dep. Chm., ESA), 1973, Shipping Policy Div. (Chm., Maritime Gp of Nations for Negotiation of UN Convention on Law of the Sea; Chm., NATO Planning Bd for Ocean Shipping), 1974, Gen. Div., 1975; Dep. Sec., Dept of Trade (Chm., Policy Cttee, European Civil Aviation Conf.), 1976–80, Dept of Industry, 1980–81; Dir-Gen. for Transport, EEC, 1981–86. Chm., P & O European Transport Service, 1989–95; Director: P & O Containers Ltd, 1987–96; P&OSN Co., 1992–99. Mem., Dover Harbour Bd, 1990–92. Dir, Business Aircraft Users Assoc., 1999–2004. *Recreation:* normal. *Address:* 4 Wickham Court, Bristol BS16 1DQ. *Clubs:* Oxford and Cambridge; Philippics.
Died 8 Nov. 2011.

STEER, Prof. John Richardson, FSA 1981; Emeritus Professor of the History of Art, University of London; art-historian and director; *b* 14 Oct. 1928; *s* of Walter Wallis Steer and Elsie Gertrude (*née* Colman). *Educ:* Clayesmore Sch., Dorset; Keble Coll., Oxford (MA); Courtauld Inst. of Art, Univ. of London (BA). Gen. Asst, City Art Gall., Birmingham, 1953–56; Asst Lectr, Dept of Fine Art, Univ. of Glasgow, 1956–59; Lectr in Hist. of European Art, Univ. of Bristol, 1959–67; Prof. of Fine Arts, Univ. of St Andrews, 1967–80; Prof. of Hist. of Art, Birkbeck Coll., Univ. of London, 1980–84. Chm., Adv. Cttee on Validation, Heriot-Watt Univ./Edinburgh Coll. of Art, 1978–91; Chm., Art Historians Assoc. of GB, 1980–83; Vice-Chm., Scottish Theatre Ballet, 1969–71; Mem., Cttee for Art and Design, CNAA, 1977–82 (Chm., Hist. of Art/Design and Complementary Studies Bd, 1977–79); Member: Theatre Museum Adv. Council, 1981–83; Theatre Museum Cttee, V&A Mus., 1984–2001; Exec., Genius of Venice Exhibn, RA, 1983–84; Royal Fine Art Commn, 1992–99. Chm., Theatre Manoeuvres Ltd, 1991–2000. Trustee, V&A Mus., 1991–99. Adjudicator, National Student Drama Festival, 1977. Theatrical prodns include: The Seagull, St Andrews, 1971; And When Love Speaks, Edinburgh, 1975; The Privacy of the Patients, Edinburgh Fringe, 1977, ICA, 1978; Waiting for Godot, St Andrews, 1978; Minna von Barnhelm, plc, Theatre Co., Young Vic Studio, 1987. Hon. FRCA 1996. Hon. DLitt: St Andrews, 1990; Heriot-Watt, 1991. *Publications:* A Concise History of Venetian Painting, 1967; Mr Bacon's Titian (Selwyn Brinton Lecture, RSA), 1977; Alvise Vivarini, 1982; (with A. White) Atlas of Western Art History, 1994; contribs to Burlington Magazine, Apollo, Art History. *Recreation:* travel. *Address:* 1 Cheriton Square, SW17 8AE. *Died 20 Feb. 2012.*

STEER, Wilfred Reed; QC 1972; *b* 23 Aug. 1926; *s* of George William and Dorothy Steer; *m* 1953, Jill Park; one *s* one *d*, and two step *s*. *Educ:* Bede Collegiate Sch., Sunderland, Co. Durham; London Sch. of Economics. LLB

(Lond.) 1949. Called to the Bar, Gray's Inn, 1950. *Address:* Park Court Chambers, 16 Park Place, Leeds LS1 1SJ. *T:* (0113) 243 3277. *Died 25 April 2011.*

STEERE, Sir Ernest Henry L.; *see* Lee-Steere.

STEIN, Cyril; Chairman: St James's Club Ltd, 1995–2005; Ladbroke Group PLC, 1966–93; *b* 20 Feb. 1928; *s* of late Jack Stein and Rebecca Stein (*née* Selner); *m* 1949, Betty Young; two *s* one *d.* *Died 15 Feb. 2011.*

STEINBERG, Gerald Neil, (Gerry); *b* Durham, 20 April 1945; *s* of Harry and Esther Steinberg; *m* 1969, Margaret Cruddace Thornton; one *s* one *d.* *Educ:* St Margaret's Primary Sch.; Whinney Hill Secondary Sch.; Durham Johnston Sch.; Sheffield Coll. of Education; Newcastle Polytechnic. Cert. of Educn for Backward Children. Teacher, Dukeshouse Wood Camp Sch., Hexham, 1966–69; Teacher, Elemore Hall, 1969–75, Dep. Head, 1975–79; Head Teacher, Whitworth House Special Sch., 1979–87. Mem., Durham City Council, 1975–87 (Sec., Labour Gp, 1981–87). MP (Lab) City of Durham, 1987–2005. Member, Select Committee: on Education, 1987–96; on Educn and Employment, 1996–98; on Public Accounts, 1998–2005; on Catering, 1998–2001; Vice Chm., Labour Educn Cttee, 1997–98 (Chm., 1990–96). *Recreations:* Sunderland AFC supporter, all sport (Vice Pres., Brandon AFC). *Clubs:* Sherburn Workman's, Brandon Workman's, Nevilles Cross Workman's. *Died 21 Aug. 2015.*

STEINBERG, Saul Phillip; Chairman, Reliance Group Holdings Inc. (formerly Leasco Data Processing Equipment Corp.), 1961–2001 (Chief Executive Officer, 1961–2000); *b* 13 Aug. 1939; *s* of Julius and Anne Cohen Steinberg; *m* 3rd, 1984, Gayfryd McNabb; one *d*, one step *s*, and three *s* one *d* by previous marriages. *Educ:* Wharton School of Univ. of Pennsylvania (BScEcon). Founder, Ideal Leasing Co., later Leasco Data Processing Equipment Corp., 1961. Director: Zenith National Insurance Corp.; Symbol Technologies Inc. Dir, Long Island Jewish Medical Center. Mem., Bd of Overseers, Cornell Univ. Medical Coll.; Chm., Wharton Bd of Overseers; Trustee: Univ. of Pennsylvania; NY Public Library. *Died 7 Dec. 2012.*

STEINER, Prof. Robert Emil, CBE 1979; Professor of Diagnostic Radiology, University of London, Royal Postgraduate Medical School, 1961–83, then Emeritus; *b* 1 Feb. 1918; *s* of Rudolf Steiner and Clary (*née* Nordlinger); *m* 1945, Gertrude Margaret Konirsch; two *d.* *Educ:* University of Vienna; University College, Dublin. Dep. Director, Dept of Radiology, Hammersmith Hosp.; Lecturer Diagnostic Radiology, Postgraduate Med. School of London, 1950, Sen. Lecturer, 1955, Director, 1955. Vice-Chm., Nat. Radiological Protection Bd, 1972–83. Past Consultant Adviser in Radiology to DHSS; Past Civil Consultant in Radiology to Med. Dir-Gen., Navy. Warden of Fellowship, Faculty of Radiologists. Former Mem. Council, RCS; Past Pres., British Inst. Radiology; Pres., RCR, 1977–80. Hon. Fellow: Amer. Coll. of Radiology; Australian Coll. of Radiology; Faculty of Radiologists, RCSI. Hon. Mem., Radiological Socs of Finland, N America, Switzerland and Austria; Amer. Roentgen Ray Soc.; Germany Roentgen Soc. Barclay Medal, British Inst. of Radiology; Gold Medal, RCR, 1986; Gold Medal, European Radiology Assoc., 2007. Former Editor, British Jl of Radiology. *Publications:* Clinical Disorders of the Pulmonary Circulation, 1960; Recent Advances of Radiology, vols 4–8, 1979–85; contrib. to British Journal of Radiology, Clinical Radiology, British Heart Jl, Lancet, BMJ, etc. *Address:* 12 Stonehill Road, East Sheen, SW14 8RW. *T:* (020) 8876 4038. *Club:* Hurlingham. *Died 12 Sept. 2013.*

STEPHEN, David; Chief Executive, Student Awards Agency for Scotland, 1999–2009; *b* 21 Nov. 1947; *s* of John and Margaret Stephen; *m* 1970, Rosalyn Slater; one *s* one *d.* *Educ:* Aberdeen Grammar Sch.; Univ. of Aberdeen. Chartered FCIPD 2003. Asst Dir of Manpower, NHS Mgt Exec., 1988–91; Hd, Personnel Policy, Scottish Office, 1991–98; Dir of Ops, Student Awards Agency for Scotland, 1998–99. *Recreations:* golf, swimming, travel. *Address:* 3 Muirhead Place, Penicuik, Midlothian EH26 0LE. *Club:* Glencorse Golf. *Died 18 Dec. 2012.*

STEPHENS, Christopher Wilson Treeve; *see* Stephens, W. T.

STEPHENS, Prof. Kenneth Gilbert, CEng, FIET; CPhys, FInstP; Professor of Electronic and Electrical Engineering, 1978–96, then Emeritus, and Dean of the Faculty of Engineering, 1992–96, University of Surrey; *b* 3 May 1931; *s* of George Harry Stephens and Christiana Stephens; *m* 1980, Elizabeth Carolynn (*née* Jones); one *s* one *d*, and two step *s.* *Educ:* Bablake Sch., Coventry; Birmingham Univ. (BSc, PhD). Nuclear Reactor Res. Physicist, AEI Ltd, Aldermaston, 1955–62; Sen. Res. Engr, Pye Ltd, Cambridge, 1963–66; University of Surrey: Lectr 1966; Reader 1967; Head, Dept of Electronic and Electrical Engrg, 1983–91. Chm., Bd of Govs, Royal Grammar Sch., Guildford, 1996–2004. *Publications:* (ed jtly) Low Energy Ion Beams (conf. procs), 1978, 1980; (ed jtly) Ion Implantation Technology (conf. procs), 1991; articles on ion beam effects on semiconductors in learned jls. *Recreations:* reading, music, gardening, watching sport, especially cricket. *Address:* 10 Brockway Close, Merrow, Guildford, Surrey GU1 2LW. *T:* (01483) 575087. *Clubs:* MCC; Blackheath Cricket. *Died 26 June 2013.*

STEPHENS, Prof. Philip John, DPhil; FRS 2008; Professor of Chemistry, University of Southern California, Los Angeles, 1976, then Emeritus; *b* West Bromwich, 9 Oct. 1940; *s* of Frank Stephens and Christine Mary Stephens; *m*; one *d.* *Educ:* Christ Church, Oxford (BA 1st Cl. Chem. 1962); DPhil Oxon 1964; Univ. of Copenhagen; Univ. of Chicago. University of Southern California, Los Angeles: Asst Prof. of Chemistry, 1967–70; Associate Prof., 1970–76; Chair, Dept of Chem., 1992–98. Alfred P. Sloan Res. Fellow, 1968; Vis. Fellow, Res. Sch. of Chem., ANU, 1975; SRC Sen. Vis. Fellow, UEA, 1977; John Simon Guggenheim Fellow, ARC Nitrogen Fixation Unit, Univ. of Sussex, 1984. Visiting Professor: Univ. of Copenhagen, 1978; Ecole Supérieure de Physique et Chimie Industrielle, Paris, 1998; Univ. degli Studi, Florence, 1999. Schatz Lectr, Univ. of Virginia, 1999. *Publications:* (contrib.) Optical Activity and Chiral Discrimination, 1979; (contrib.) Computational Medicinal Chemistry for Drug Discovery, 2003; contribs to jls incl. Jl Chem. Physics, Nature, Jl American Chem. Soc., Jl Phys. Chem., Biochemistry. *Address:* Department of Chemistry, University of Southern California, Los Angeles, CA 90089–0482, USA. *T:* (213) 7404119, *Fax:* (213) 7403972. *E:* pstephen@usc.edu. *Died 31 July 2012.*

STEPHENS, Wilson (Treeve); Editor of The Field, 1950–77, Consultant 1987–90; Consultant, Country Illustrated (formerly Countryweek), 1991–2002; *b* 2 June 1912; *s* of Rev. Arthur Treeve Stephens, Shepton Beauchamp, Somerset, and Margaret Wilson; *m* 1st, 1934, Nina, *d* of Arthur Frederick Curzon, Derby; two *d*; 2nd, 1960, Marygold Anne, *o d* of Major-General G. O. Crawford, CB, CBE; two *d.* *Educ:* Christ's Hosp. Served War of 1939–45, Royal Artillery. Formerly on editorial staffs of several provincial newspapers, and of The Daily Express. *Publications:* The Guinness Guide to Field Sports, 1979; Gundog Sense and Sensibility, 1982, 4th edn 2004; Pigeon Racing, 1983; A Year Observed, 1984; Rivers of Britain (series) 1985–; contribs to numerous publications. *Recreations:* fly-fishing, shooting. *Address:* c/o Blake, Friedmann, 122 Arlington Road, NW1 7HP. *Died 21 Sept. 2012.*

STEPHENSON, His Honour Jim; a Circuit Judge, 1983–98; *b* 17 July 1932; *s* of late Alex and Norah Stephenson, Heworth, Co. Durham; *m* 1964, Jill Christine, *d* of late Dr Lindeck, Fairwarp, Sussex; three *s.* *Educ:* Royal Grammar Sch. and Dame Allan's Sch., Newcastle; Exeter Coll., Oxford (Exhibnr, BA). Pres., Oxford Univ. Law Society, Michaelmas, 1955. Called to Bar, Gray's Inn, 1957. Mem., General Council of the Bar, 1961–64; Junior, NE Circuit, 1961; a Recorder of the Crown Court, 1974–83. Pres., NE Br., Magistrates' Assoc., 1988–92. Additional Mem. of Bd, Faculty of Law, Newcastle Univ., 1984–90. Gov., Newcastle Prep. Sch., 1985–92. Trustee, Senhouse Mus., Maryport, 2004–12. *Recreations:* music, travel, history. *Address:* Garth House, Wetheral, Carlisle CA4 8JN. *T:* (01228) 560986. *Died 29 July 2015.*

STEPHENSON, Maj.-Gen. John Aubrey, CB 1982; OBE 1971; defence consultant, 1981–93; Managing Director, Weapon Systems Ltd, 1982–91; Deputy Master General of the Ordnance, 1980–81; *b* 15 May 1929; *s* of Reginald Jack Stephenson and Florence Stephenson; *m* 1953, Sheila Colbeck; two *s* one *d*. *Educ:* Dorchester Grammar School. Commnd RA, 1948; served Malaya (despatches, 1951), Libya, Canal Zone and Germany, 1949–58 (student pilot, 1953–54); student, RMCS, 1958–60; 39 Missile Regt, 1960–61; student, RMCS and Staff Coll., 1961–62; served UK and Germany, 1962–67; Staff, RMCS, 1967–69; CO 16 Light Air Defence Regt RA, 1969–71; Project Manager, 155mm Systems, Woolwich, 1971–73; student, RCDS, 1974; Comdr, 1st Artillery Bde, Germany, 1975–77; Sen. Mil. Officer, RARDE, 1977–78; Dir Gen. Weapons (Army), 1978–80. Dir, ATX Ltd, 1984–91. Col Comdt, RA, 1984–89; Hon. Regtl Col, 16 Regt (formerly 16 Light Air Defence Regt), RA, 1989–95. Governor, The Dorchester Thomas Hardye Sch. (formerly Hardye's Sch.), 1984–96. Pres., Houghton and District Br., RBL, 1987–2000, 2002–. Vice Pres., Stockbridge FC, 2002–. FCMI. *Recreations:* fishing, sailing, gardening, bridge, golf, military history. *Address:* Collingwood, 27 Trafalgar Way, Stockbridge, Hants SO20 6ET. *T:* (01264) 810458. *Died 24 May 2015.*

STEPHENSON, Margaret Maud; *see* Tyzack, M. M.

STEPHENSON, Stanley, CMG 1987; HM Diplomatic Service, retired; *b* 30 Sept. 1926; *s* of George Stephenson and Margaret Jane (*née* Nicholson); *m* 1957, Grace Claire Lyons (*d* 1987); one *s* one *d*. *Educ:* Bede Sch., Sunderland. Inland Revenue, 1942; Royal Navy, 1944–48; Foreign (later Diplomatic) Service, 1948–: Cairo, Jedda, Damascus, Curaçao, Ciudad Trujillo (later Santo Domingo), San José, Seoul, Santiago de Cuba, Bogotá (twice), Asunción, San Francisco, FCO; Diplomatic Service Inspector, 1978–80; Ambassador to Panama, 1981–83; Consul-Gen., Vancouver, 1983–86. *Recreations:* watching most sports, theatre, gardening. *Address:* Marymount, Raggleswood, Chislehurst, Kent BR7 5NH. *T:* (020) 8467 6066. *Club:* Civil Service. *Died 23 Dec. 2014.*

STEPTOE, (Frances) Jane; *see* Wardle, F. J.

STEVENS, Sir Jocelyn (Edward Greville), Kt 1996; CVO 1993; Chairman: Prince of Wales's Phoenix Trust, 2000–04; The Prince's Regeneration through Heritage Trust, 2002–04; *b* 14 Feb. 1932; *s* of late Major C. G. B. Stewart-Stevens and Mrs Greville Stevens (*née* Hulton); *m* 1st, 1956, Jane Armyne Sheffield (marr. diss. 1979); one *s* two *d* (and one *s* decd); 2nd, 2008, Emma, *o d* of Sir Iain Tennant. *Educ:* Eton; Cambridge. Military service in Rifle Bde, 1950–52; Journalist, Hulton Press Ltd, 1955–56; Chairman and Managing Dir, Stevens Press Ltd, and Editor of Queen Magazine, 1957–68; Personal Asst to Chairman of Beaverbrook Newspapers, May–Dec. 1968; Director, 1971–81; Managing Director: Evening Standard Co. Ltd, 1969–72; Daily Express, 1972–74; Beaverbrook Newspapers, 1974–77; Express Newspapers, 1977–81 (Dep. Chm. and Man. Dir); Editor and Publisher, The Magazine, 1982–84; Dir, Centaur Communications, 1982–84; Rector and Vice Provost, RCA, 1984–92; Dep. Chm., ITC, 1991–96; Dir, TV Corp., 1996–2002. Chairman: English Heritage, 1992–2000; RCHME, 1999–2000. Personal Special Advr on Stonehenge to Sec. of State for Culture, Media and Sport, 2000–. Chm., Silver Trust, 1990–93; Trustee: Mental Health Foundn, 1972–94; Eureka! The Museum for Children, 1986–2000; Butrint Foundn, 2000–; Vice-Chm., Prince's Foundn, 2000–02; Pres., Cheyne Walk Trust, 1989–93. Governor: Imperial Coll. of Science, Technology and Medicine, 1985–92; Winchester Sch. of Art, 1986–89. FRSA 1984; Senior Fellow RCA, 1990. Hon. FCSD 1990. Hon. DLitt: Loughborough, 1989; Buckingham, 1998. *Address:* Field Place, Newtown, Hungerford, Berks RG17 0PR. *Clubs:* Buck's, Beefsteak, White's. *Died 9 Oct. 2014.*

STEVENSON, (Arthur) William, TD 1980; QC 1996; a Recorder, 1992–2011; *b* 17 Oct. 1943; *s* of late Arthur John Stevenson, TD, MA and Olivia Diana Stevenson (*née* Serocold); *m* 1969, Bridget Laura York; two *s* one *d*. *Educ:* Marlborough Coll.; Trinity Coll., Oxford (MA). Called to the Bar, Lincoln's Inn, 1968, Bencher, 2001; in practice, 1968–2012. *Recreations:* country sports, ski-ing, sailing. *Clubs:* Boodle's, Bar Yacht. *Died 9 Dec. 2012.*

STEVENSON, Rt Rev. Kenneth William, PhD, DD; FRHistS; Bishop of Portsmouth, 1995–2009; an Honorary Assistant Bishop, Diocese of Chichester, since 2009; *b* 9 Nov. 1949; *s* of Frederik Robert and Margrete Stevenson; *m* 1970, Sarah Julia Mary (*née* Glover); one *s* three *d*. *Educ:* Edinburgh Acad.; Edinburgh Univ. (MA 1970); Southampton Univ. (PhD 1975); Manchester Univ. (DD 1987). FRHistS 1990. Ordained deacon, 1973, priest, 1974; Asst Curate, Grantham with Manthorpe, 1973–76; Lectr, Boston, 1976–80; part-time Lectr, Lincoln Theol Coll., 1975–80; Chaplain and Lectr, Manchester Univ., 1980–86; Team Vicar, 1980–82, Team Rector, 1982–86, Whitworth, Manchester; Rector, Holy Trinity and St Mary's, Guildford, 1986–95. Member: C of E Liturgical Commn, 1986–96; Faith and Order Advisory Gp, 1991–96; C of E Doctrine Commn, 1996–2003; Chm., C of E Bd of Educn and Nat. Soc. Council, 2003–09. Chairman: Anglo-Nordic-Baltic Theol Conf., 1997–2009 (Sec., 1985–97); Porvoo Panel, 2005– (Vice-Chm., 1999–2005). Vis. Prof., Univ. of Notre Dame, Indiana, 1983. Seat in H of L, 1999–2009. Hon. LLD Portsmouth, 2008. Comdr, Order of the Dannebrog (Denmark), 2006. *Publications:* Nuptial Blessing, 1982; Eucharist and Offering, 1986; Jerusalem Revisited, 1988; The First Rites, 1989; Covenant of Grace Renewed, 1994; (with H. R. McAdoo) The Mystery of the Eucharist in the Anglican Tradition, 1995; Handing On, 1996; The Mystery of Baptism in the Anglican Tradition, 1998; All the Company of Heaven, 1998; Abba Father: understanding and using the Lord's Prayer, 2000; (ed jtly) Love's Redeeming Work: The Anglican quest for holiness, 2001; Do This: the shape, style and meaning of the eucharist, 2002; The Lord's Prayer: a text in tradition, 2004; Rooted In Detachment: living the transfiguration, 2007; Watching and Waiting: a guide to the celebration of Advent, 2007; Take, Eat: reflections on the eucharist, 2008; (ed and contrib.) A Fallible Church: Lambeth essays, 2008; contribs to Scottish Jl of Theology, Ephemerides Liturgicae, Theology, etc. *Recreations:* historical biographies, Chinese cooking, piano, Denmark. *Address:* 18 Melbourne Road, Chichester PO19 7NE. *Club:* Nobody's Friends. *Died 11 Jan. 2011.*

STEVENSON, Prof. Olive, CBE 1994; DLitt; Professor of Social Work Studies, University of Nottingham, 1984–94 (Head, School of Social Studies, 1987–91), then Professor Emeritus; Fellow, St Anne's College, University of Oxford, since 1970; *b* 13 Dec. 1930; *d* of John and Evelyn Stevenson. *Educ:* Purley County Grammar Sch. for Girls; Lady Margaret Hall, Oxford (BA EngLitt, MA 1955); London Sch. of Economics (Dip. in Social Studies, Dip. in Child Care); DLitt Nottingham, 1992. Tavistock Clinic; Child Care Officer, Devon CC, 1954–58; Lecturer in Applied Social Studies: Univ. of Bristol, 1959–61; Univ. of Oxford, 1961–68; Social Work Adviser, Supplementary Benefits Commn, 1968–70; Reader in Applied Social Studies, Univ. of Oxford, 1970–76; Prof. of Social Policy and Social Work: Univ. of Keele, 1976–82; Univ. of Liverpool, 1983–84. Member: Royal Commn on Civil Liability, 1973–78; Social Security Adv. Cttee, 1982–2002; Registered Homes Tribunal, 1985–90; Chairman: Adv. Cttee, Rent Rebates and Rent Allowances, 1977–83; Age Concern England, 1980–83; Councils of Voluntary Service Nat. Assoc., 1985–88; Care and Repair, 1993–97; Peterborough, Cambridge, Leicester City, Leics and Rutland County Area Child Protection Cttees, 1997–2000; Serious Case Review, 1999–2003; Fostering Options Adv. Cttee, 2004–. Research Report on Sexual Abuse of Elderly People, Anne Craft Trust, 2003. Series Ed., Working Together for Children, Young People and Families, 1996–99. Hon. Professor: Kingston Univ., 2003; Hong Kong Poly Univ., 2004. Hon. LittD: East Anglia, 1996; Kingston, 2004. *Publications:* Someone Else's Child, 1965, rev. edn 1977; Claimant or Client?, 1970; Social Service Teams: the practitioner's view, 1978; Child Abuse: interprofessional communication, 1979; Specialisation in Social Service Teams, 1981; (with Fuller) Policies, Programmes and Disadvantage, 1983; Age and Vulnerability, a guide to better care, 1988; (ed) Child Abuse: public policy and professional practice, 1989; (jtly)

Community Care and Empowerment, 1993; Neglected Children: issues and dilemmas, 1998, 2nd edn 2007; (jtly) Child Welfare in the UK, 1998; Reflections on a Life in Social Work (memoir), 2013. *Recreations:* music, cookery, conversation. *Address:* c/o Centre for Social Work, University of Nottingham, Nottingham NG7 2RD. *Died 30 Sept. 2013.*

STEVENSON, Sir Simpson, Kt 1976; DL; *b* 18 Aug. 1921; *s* of T. H. Stevenson, Greenock; *m* 1945, Jean Holmes Henry (*d* 1999), JP, Port Glasgow. *Educ:* Greenock High Sch. Member: Greenock Town Council, 1949–67 and 1971–74 (Provost of Greenock, 1962–65); Inverclyde DC, 1974–99 (Provost, 1984–88); Vice-Chm., Clyde Port Authority, 1966–69; Chm., Greater Glasgow Health Bd, 1973–83; Chm., Scottish Health Services Common Service Agency, 1973–77, 1983–87. Member: Western Regional Hosp. Bd (Scotland), 1959–; Scottish Hosp. Administrative Staffs Cttee, 1965–74 (Chm., 1972–74); Chm., W Regional Hosp. Bd (Scotland), Glasgow, 1967–74; Member: Scottish Hosp. Endowments Commn, 1969–70; Scottish Health Services Planning Council; Royal Commn on the NHS, 1976–79. Chm., Consortium of Local Authorities Special Programme (CLASP), 1974. DL Renfrewshire, 1990. Hon. LLD Glasgow, 1982. *Recreations:* football, reading, choral singing. *Address:* 3F Cragburn Gate, Albert Road West, Gourock PA19 1NZ. *Died 4 May 2015.*

STEVENSON, William; *see* Stevenson, A. W.

STEWART, Andrew Struthers, (Andy); farmer; Chairman, Agricultural Training Board, 1992–98; *b* 27 May 1937; *s* of late James Stewart and of Elizabeth Stewart; *m* 1961, Louise Melvin (*née* Skimming); one *s* one *d*. *Educ:* Strathaven Acad., Scotland; West of Scotland Agricl Coll. Farming Beesthorpe Manor Farm, 1961–. Mem., Caunton Parish Council, 1973–83; Conservative Mem., Notts CC, 1975–83 and 2002–; Cons. spokesman on leisure services, 1981–83. MP (C) Sherwood, 1983–92; contested (C) Sherwood, 1992. PPS to Minister of Agriculture, Fisheries and Food, 1987–89, to Sec. of State for Educn and Science, 1989–90, to Lord Pres. of Council and Leader of H of C, 1990–92. Comr, Rural Develt Commn, 1993–99. Chairman: Strathaven Br., Young Conservatives, 1957 and 1958; Caunton, Maplebeck and Kersall Cons. Br., 1970–73 (Founder Mem.). Chairman: Lantra, NTO for land based industries, 1998–2000; Lantra Trust, 2000–; Member: Newark Br., NFU, 1961– (Mem., County Exec. Cttee, 1966–); Newark and Notts Agricl Soc.; Adv. Mem., Nottingham University Coll. of Agriculture, 1977–82 (formerly Chm., Notts Coll. of Agriculture Brackenhurst); formerly Chm., Governing Bd, Rufford Comprehensive Sch. Youth Club Leader, 1965–76; Life Vice President: Southwell Rugby Club; Caunton Cricket Club; Trustee, Southwell Recreation Centre, 1979–83. Hon. Assoc. Mem., BVA, 1991–2009. *Address:* Beesthorpe Manor Farm, Caunton, Newark, Notts NG23 6AT. *T:* (01636) 636270. *Clubs:* Farmers; Bentinck Conservative (Hucknall, Notts). *Died 6 Oct. 2013.*

STEWART, Brian Thomas Webster, CMG 1969; Hon. Lecturer, Hong Kong University, 1986–98; *b* 27 April 1922; *s* of late Redvers Buller Stewart and Mabel Banks Sparks, Broich, Crieff; *m* 1946, Millicent Peggy Pollock (marr. diss. 1970); two *d*; *m* 1972, Sally Nugent; one *s* one *d*. *Educ:* Trinity Coll., Glenalmond; Worcester Coll., Oxford (MA). Commnd The Black Watch (RHR), 1942; served Europe and Far East (Capt.). Joined Malayan Civil Service, 1946; studying Chinese Macau, 1947; Asst Sec., Chinese Affairs, Singapore, 1949; Devonshire Course, Oxford, 1950; Asst Comr for Labour, Kuala Lumpur, 1951; Sec. for Chinese Affairs, Supt of Chinese Schs, Malacca and Penang, 1952–57; joined HM Diplomatic Service, 1957; served Rangoon, Peking, Shanghai, Manila, Kuala Lumpur, Hanoi; Asst Sec., Cabinet Office, 1968–72; Counsellor, Hong Kong, 1972–74; FCO, 1974–78. Special Rep., Rubber Growers Assoc., Malaysia, 1979–82; Dir of Ops (China), Racal Electronics, 1982–96. *Publications:* All Men's Wisdom (anthology of Chinese Proverbs), 1957; Scrapbook of a Roving Highlander (memoirs), 2002; Smashing Terrorism in Malaya, 2003; Fiji Jottings, 2005; Call to Arms, 2006; Chinese Without Tears, 2010; Why Spy?, 2015; Cracking the Chinese Code, 2015. *Recreations:* walking, chamber music, orientalia particularly chinoiserie. *Address:* c/o Royal Bank of Scotland, Crieff, Perthshire PH7 3RX. *Clubs:* Athenæum, Special Forces; Hong Kong. *Died 16 Aug. 2015.*

STEWART, (George Robert) Gordon, OBE 1984; Secretary, 1976–83, Legal Adviser 1983–87, Institute of Chartered Accountants of Scotland; *b* 13 Oct. 1924; *s* of David Gordon Stewart and Mary Grant Thompson or Stewart; *m* 1952, Rachel Jean Morrison; two *s* one *d*. *Educ:* George Watson's Coll., Edinburgh; Edinburgh Univ. (MA 1947, LLB 1949). WS. Mem., Law Soc. of Scotland, 1949–92. Served War, 1943–46: Captain, Royal Signals; Burma and SEAC. In practice as WS, Melville & Lindesay, WS, Edinburgh, 1950–59; Asst Sec., subseq. Sec., and Dir, Ideal-Standard Ltd, Hull, 1959–75. *Recreation:* gardening. *Died 2 Feb. 2012.*

STEWART, Hugh Parker, FCA; Chairman: Demaglass Ltd, 1994–99; Image Precision International Ltd, 1997–99; *b* 23 May 1934; *s* of George and Barbara Stewart; *m* 1960, Marion Gordon Cairns; one *s* one *d*. *Educ:* Sullivan Upper Sch., Holywood, Co. Down; Queen's Univ., Belfast (LLB Hons). Audit Manager, Hill Vellacott & Bailey, Belfast, 1959–62; Financial Comptroller, STC (NI) Ltd, Monkstown, 1962–67; Admin. Manager, AMF Beaird, Belfast, 1967–70; Gp Financial Controller, Brightside Engrg Hldgs, Sheffield, 1970–71; SMM Ltd, Greenwich: Financial Dir, 1971–74; Overseas Dir, 1974–78; Man. Dir, SMM Foundries Ltd, Greenwich, 1978–79; Finance Dir, Westland plc, 1979–81; Finance Dir, Westland plc, and Exec. Dir, Westland Technologies Ltd, 1981–84; Man. Dir, Westland Technologies Ltd, 1984–85; Chief Exec., Westland Gp plc, 1985–88. Chm., Scheduling Technology Gp Ltd, 1989–90; Practice Chm., Aaron & Partners, Solicitors, 1989–91; Chairman: Programming Research Ltd, 1990–91; Wootton Jeffreys Consultants Ltd, 1991–94; Aerospace Systems & Technologies, 1993–95; Western Computer Gp, 1993–95; Wellmann plc, 1995–98 (Dir, 1992–98); Director: DSK Systems Ltd, 1989–91; Cityflyer Express Ltd, 1991–99; Chessington Computer Centre, 1995–96 (Mem., Ministerial Adv. Bd, 1995–96). Governor, Sherborne Sch., 1982–2004. *Recreations:* golf, gardening. *Club:* Sloane. *Died 5 May 2011.*

STEWART, James Robertson, CBE 1971 (OBE 1964); Principal, University of London, 1978–83; *b* 25 July 1917; *s* of James and Isabella Stewart; *m* 1941, Grace Margaret Kirsop (*d* 1992); two *s* one *d*. *Educ:* Perth Acad.; Whitley and Monkseaton High Sch.; Armstrong Coll. (later King's Coll.), Newcastle, Univ. of Durham. BA Dunelm (1st cl. hons Mod. History) 1937; DThPT (1st cl.) 1938; research in Canada (Canada Co.), 1938–39; awarded Holland Rose Studentship, Cambridge, and William Black Noble Fellowship, Durham, 1939; admitted to Christ's Coll., Cambridge, 1939; MA Dunelm 1941. Served Army, 1939–46: Royal Artillery (BEF); Combined Ops HQ; Directorate of Combined Ops, India and SE Asia; Major (Actg Lt-Col); Certif. of Good Service. Dep. Clerk of Court, Univ. of London, 1946–49, Clerk of Court, 1950–82. Dir, Charterhouse Venture Fund Management, 1984–94. Mem., Sec. of State's Adv. Gp on London Health Services, 1980–81. Member, governing bodies: RPMS, 1983–89; Sch. of Pharmacy, London Univ., 1983–99 (Hon. Treas., 1984–99); Wye Coll., 1983–91; Inst. of Educn, 1983–93; RVC, 1983–2001 (Hon. Treas., 1984–96); LSE, 1984–89; Brunel Univ., 1984–89; Inst. of Germanic Studies, 1984–92 (Chm.); Roedean Sch., 1984–99; Sussex Univ., 1985–97; Westfield Coll., London, 1985–89. Hon. Fellow: KCL, 1982; Sch. of Pharmacy, London Univ., 1982; Birkbeck Coll., London, 1982; LSE, 1982; UCL, 1982; Wye Coll., 1987; Queen Mary and Westfield Coll., London, 1989 (Westfield Coll., 1981); Inst. of Germanic Studies, 1993. Hon. LLD: London, 1983; Western Ontario, 1984. Symons Medal, ACU, 1983; Betts Prize, RVC, 1994. *Recreations:* military history, gardening, watching soccer and cricket. *Address:* 2 Hilltop, Dyke Road Avenue, Brighton, E Sussex BN1 5LY. *T:* (01273) 551039. *Club:* Athenæum. *Died 9 July 2013.*

STEWART, Mary (Florence Elinor), (Lady Stewart); *b* 17 Sept. 1916; *d* of Rev. Frederick A. Rainbow, Durham Diocese, and Mary Edith (*née* Matthews), NZ; *m* 1945, Sir Frederick Henry Stewart, FRS (*d* 2001); no *c*. *Educ:* Eden Hall, Penrith, Cumberland; Skellfield School, Ripon, Yorks; St Hild's Coll., Durham Univ. BA 1938; MA 1941. Asst Lectr in English, Durham Univ., 1941–45; Part-time Lectr in English, St Hild's Training Coll., Durham, and Durham Univ., 1948–56. Hon. Fellow, Newnham Coll., Cambridge, 1986. Hon. DLitt Dunelm, 2009. *Publications: novels:* Madam, Will You Talk?, 1954; Wildfire at Midnight, 1956; Thunder on the Right, 1957; Nine Coaches Waiting, 1958; My Brother Michael, 1959; The Ivy Tree, 1961; The Moonspinners, 1962; This Rough Magic, 1964; Airs Above the Ground, 1965; The Gabriel Hounds, 1967; The Wind Off The Small Isles, 1968; The Crystal Cave, 1970 (Frederick Niven Award); The Little Broomstick, 1971; The Hollow Hills, 1973; Ludo and the Star Horse, 1974 (Scottish Arts Council Award); Touch Not the Cat, 1976; The Last Enchantment, 1979; A Walk in Wolf Wood, 1980; The Wicked Day, 1983; Thornyhold, 1988; Frost on the Window and Other Poems, 1990; Stormy Petrel, 1991; The Prince and the Pilgrim, 1995; Rose Cottage, 1997; also articles, radio plays. *Recreations:* gardening, music, painting. *Died 9 May 2014.*

STEWART, Robin Milton; QC 1978; a Recorder of the Crown Court, 1978–99; *b* 5 Aug. 1938; *s* of late Brig. Guy Milton Stewart and Dr Elaine Oenone Stewart, MD, BS; *m* 1962, Lynda Grace Medhurst; three *s*. *Educ:* Winchester; New Coll., Oxford (MA 1965). Called to the Bar, Middle Temple, 1963, Bencher, 1988; called to the Irish Bar, King's Inns, Dublin, 1975. Prosecuting Counsel to Inland Revenue, NE Circuit, 1976–78. Dir, Bar Mutual Indemnity Fund, 1988–93. Mem., Professional Conduct Cttee, Bar Council, 1991–93; (first) Chm., Professional Negligence Bar Assoc., 1991–93. Contested (C) Newcastle upon Tyne West, Feb. and Oct. 1974. Freeman, City of London, 1966; Liveryman, Co. of Glaziers, 1966–98. Trustee, Parkinson's Disease Soc., 1999–2002. Confrère des Chevaliers du Fromage de Livarot, 2002. *Recreations:* pictures, gardening, Scottish family history. *Address:* Springfield, 150 Front Street, Sowerby, Thirsk, N Yorks YO7 1JN. *T:* (01845) 522922. *Club:* Oriental. *Died 31 Aug. 2011.*

STEWART, William Ian; *see* Allanbridge, Hon. Lord.

STEWART-WILSON, Lt-Col Sir Blair (Aubyn), KCVO 1994 (CVO 1989 LVO 1983); Deputy Master of the Household and Equerry to Her Majesty, 1976–94, an Extra Equerry, since 1994; *b* 17 July 1929; *s* of late Aubyn Wilson and late Muriel Stewart Stevens; *m* 1962, Helen Mary Fox; three *d*. *Educ:* Eton; Sandhurst. Commnd Scots Guards, 1949, Atholl Highlanders, 1952 (Major, 1996; Lt-Col Comdg, 2003–11); served with Scots Guards in UK, Germany and Far East; Adjutant 2nd Bn, 1955–57; ADC to Viscount Cobham, Governor General and C-in-C, New Zealand, 1957–59; Equerry to late Duke of Gloucester, 1960–62; Regtl Adjutant, 1966–68; GSO1, Foreign Liaison Sect. (Army), MoD, 1970–73; Defence, Military and Air Attaché, British Embassy, Vienna, 1975–76. HM's Rep. Trustee, Bd of Royal Armouries, 1995–2004. Somerset County Patron, Cancer Res. UK (formerly Cancer Res. Campaign), 1999–; Vice-Pres., March Foundn, 2009–; Trustee, Wells Cathedral Preservation Trust, 1997–2010. *Address:* c/o Royal Bank of Scotland, 84 Atholl Road, Pitlochry PH16 5BJ. *T:* (home) (01823) 490111. *Club:* Pratt's. *Died 24 May 2011.*

STIBBON, Gen. Sir John (James), KCB 1988; OBE 1979; CEng, FICE; Chief Royal Engineer, 1993–99; *b* 5 Jan. 1935; *s* of Jack Stibbon and Elizabeth Matilda Stibbon (*née* Dixon); *m* 1957, Jean Fergusson Skeggs, *d* of John Robert Skeggs and Florence Skeggs (*née* Hayes); two *d*. *Educ:* Portsmouth Southern Grammar School; Royal Military Academy; Royal Military College of Science. BSc (Eng). CEng 1989; FICE 1989. Commissioned RE, 1954; CO 28 Amphibious Engineer Regt, 1975–77; Asst Military Secretary, 1977–79; Comd 20 Armoured Brigade, 1979–81; rcds 1982; Comdt, RMCS, 1983–85; ACDS Operational Requirements (Land Systems), 1985–87; Master Gen. of the Ordnance, 1987–91. Dir, Chemring Gp plc, 1993–2005; Chm., ITT Defence, 1993–2004. Colonel Commandant: RAPC, 1985–92; RPC, 1986–91; RE, 1987–99. Vice Pres., Royal Star & Garter Home, 1996–; Chm., Gordon Foundn, 1992–2002; Comr, Duke of York's Royal Mil. Sch., 1993–99. Hon. DSc: Cranfield Inst. of Technology, 1989; Greenwich, 2001. *Recreations:* Association football, athletics, painting, palaeontology. *Club:* Army and Navy. *Died 9 Feb. 2014.*

STINSON, His Honour David John; a Circuit Judge (formerly County Court Judge), 1969–86; *b* 22 Feb. 1921; *er s* of late Henry John Edwin Stinson, MC, MA, LLB, Beckenham, Kent (sometime Chief Commoner of City of London, solicitor) and Margaret Stinson (*née* Little); *m* 1950, Eleanor Judith, *er d* of K. M. Chance, DSO, Cumberland; two *s* two *d* (and one *s* decd). *Educ:* Eastbourne Coll.; Emmanuel Coll., Cambridge. MA 1946; Jesters Club, 1949 (Rugby Fives). Served War of 1939–45: Essex Yeomanry, Captain, RA, and Air OP, 1941–46 (despatches). Called to Bar, Middle Temple, 1947 (Harmsworth Schol., 1948); Dep. Chm., Herts QS, 1965–71; Suffolk and Essex County Court Circuit, 1973–86. Chancellor, Dio. of Carlisle, 1971–90. Chm., Ipswich Family Conciliation Service, 1982–88; Pres., Parents' Conciliation Trust, 1988–99. *Recreations:* bird-watching, gardening. *Address:* Barrack Row, Fishpond Road, Waldringfield, Woodbridge, Suffolk IP12 4QX. *T:* (01473) 736280. *Died 5 Oct. 2011.*

STIRLING, Sir Alexander (John Dickson), KBE 1981; CMG 1976; HM Diplomatic Service, retired; Council Member, SOS Sahel International—UK, since 1987 (Chairman, 1993–97); *b* 20 Oct. 1926; *e s* of late Brig. A. Dickson Stirling, DSO, MB, ChB, DPH, and Isobel Stirling, MA, DipEd, DipPsych, *d* of late Rev. J. C. Matthew (former senior Presidency Chaplain, Bombay); *m* 1955, Alison Mary, *y d* of Gp Capt. A. P. Campbell, CBE; two *s* two *d*. *Educ:* Edinburgh Academy; Lincoln Coll., Oxford (MA). RAFVR, 1945–48 (Egypt, 1945–47). Entered Foreign Office, 1951; Lebanon, 1952; British Embassy, Cairo, 1952–56 (Oriental Sec., 1955–56); FO, 1956–59; First Sec., British Embassy, Baghdad, 1959–62; First Sec. and Consul, Amman, 1962–64; First Sec., British Embassy, Santiago, 1965–67 (led UK Delegn to Fourth Antarctic Treaty Consultative Meeting, 1966); FO, 1967–69; British Political Agent, Bahrain, 1969–71, Ambassador, 1971–72; Counsellor, Beirut, 1972–75; RCDS 1976; Ambassador to Iraq, 1977–80, to the Tunisian Republic, 1981–84, to the Sudan, 1984–86. Chm., 1989–92, Mem. Council, 1994–2000, Soc. for Protection of Animals Abroad (formerly Soc. for Protection of Animals in N Africa). *Died 16 July 2014.*

STOCK-NORMAN, Gailene Patricia, CBE 2013; AM 1997; Director, Royal Ballet School, since 1999; *b* 28 Jan. 1946; *d* of Roy Keith Stock and Sylvia May Stock; *m* 1976, Gary William Norman; one *d*. *Educ:* Convent of Mercy, Melbourne; RMIT (Grad. DipEd Visual and Performing Arts); Royal Acad. of Dancing (Overseas Schol. at Royal Ballet Sch.; ARAD). Soloist and Principal Artist, Australian Ballet, 1962–74; Principal Artist: Nat. Ballet Canada, 1974–76; Royal Winnipeg Ballet, 1976–77; Australian Ballet, 1977–78; Dir, Nat. Ballet Sch., Vic, Australia, 1979–85; Lectr in Classical Dance, Vic Coll. of Arts, 1985–88; Administrator, Nat. Ballet Sch., Vic, 1988–90; Dir, Australian Ballet Sch., 1990–98. Mem., Exec. Cttee, RAD, 1999–2009. *Recreations:* reading, gardening, travelling, welfare of animals. *Address:* Royal Ballet School, 46 Floral Street, Covent Garden, WC2E 9DA. *T:* (020) 7836 8899. *Died 29 April 2014.*

STOKER, Sir Michael (George Parke), Kt 1980; CBE 1974; FRCP 1979; FRS 1968; FRSE 1960; President of Clare Hall, Cambridge, 1980–87 (Fellow, 1978; Hon. Fellow 1995); *b* 4 July 1918; *e s* of Dr S. P. Stoker, Maypole, Monmouth; *m* 1942, Veronica Mary English (*d* 2004); three *s* two *d*. *Educ:* Oakham Sch.; Sidney Sussex Coll., Cambridge (Hon. Fellow 1981); St Thomas' Hosp., London. MRCS, LRCP 1942; MB, BChir 1943; MD 1947. RAMC, 1942–47; Demonstrator in Pathology, Cambridge Univ., 1947–48; Univ. Lecturer in Pathology, 1948–50; Huddersfield Lecturer in Special Pathology, 1950–58; Asst Tutor and Dir of Medical Studies, Clare

Coll., 1949–58; Fellow of Clare College, 1948–58, Hon. Fellow, 1976; Prof. of Virology, Glasgow Univ., and Hon. Dir, MRC Experimental Virus Research Unit, 1959–68; Dir, Imperial Cancer Res. Fund Laboratories, 1968–79. Hon. Consultant, ICRF Cell Interactions Lab., Cambridge Univ. Med. Sch., 1980–90. WHO Travel Fellow, 1951; Rockefeller Foundn Travel Fellow, 1958; Vis. Prof., UCL, 1968–79. Royal Society: For. Sec., 1977–81; a Vice-Pres., 1977–81; Leeuwenhoek Lecture, 1971, Blackett Meml Lecture, 1980; Mendel Gold Medal, 1978. Dir, Celltech Ltd, 1980–86. Member: European Molecular Biology Organisation; Council for Scientific Policy, DES, 1970–73; Gen. Cttee, Internat. Council of Scientific Unions, 1977–81; Eur. Acad. of Arts, Scis and Humanities, 1980; Med. Res. Council, 1982–86; Chairman: UK Co-ordinating Cttee, Cancer Res., 1983–86; Scientific Cttee, Ludwig Inst. Cancer Res., 1985–93. Foreign Hon. Member: Amer. Acad. of Arts and Scis, 1973; Czech Acad. of Scis, 1980. Chm. of Trustees, Strangeways Res. Lab., Cambridge, 1981–93. Hon. DSc Glasgow, 1982. *Publications:* various articles on cell biology and virology. *Recreation:* painting. *Died 13 Aug. 2013.*

STOKES, Harry Michael; HM Diplomatic Service, retired; Counsellor, Foreign and Commonwealth Office, 1979–81; *b* 22 July 1926; *s* of late Wing Comdr Henry Alban Stokes, RAF, and Lilian Frances (*née* Ede); *m* 1951, Prudence Mary Watling; two *s* one *d*. *Educ:* Rossall Sch.; Worcester Coll., Oxford (BA, Dip. Slavonic Studies). Served RAF, 1944–47. Joined Foreign Service, 1951; attached Control Commission, Germany, 1952–55; Foreign Office, 1955; Singapore, 1958; FO, 1959; Washington, 1961; Copenhagen, 1963; FO 1965; New Delhi, 1976; FO, 1977. Chm., British Assoc. for Cemeteries in S Asia, 1985–92. Dir, Indo-British Review, 1988–92. *Recreations:* walking, racquet games, photography, music. *Club:* Royal Commonwealth Society. *Died 10 March 2011.*

STOLLERY, Prof. John Leslie, CBE 1994; DScEng; FREng; FCGI; FAIAA; Professor of Aerodynamics, 1973–95, then Emeritus, and Head, College of Aeronautics, 1976–86, and 1992–95, Cranfield University (formerly Cranfield Institute of Technology); *b* 21 April 1930; *s* of George and Emma Stollery; *m* 1956, Jane Elizabeth (*d* 2009), *d* of Walter and Mildred Reynolds; four *s*. *Educ:* East Barnet Grammar Sch.; Imperial Coll. of Science and Technol., London Univ. (BScEng 1951, MScEng 1953, DScEng 1973). DIC; CEng, FREng (FEng 1992); FCGI 1984; FAIAA 1988. Aerodynamics Dept, De Havilland Aircraft Co., 1952–56; Lectr, 1956, Reader, 1962, Aeronautics Dept, Imperial Coll., London; Dean, Faculty of Engrg, 1976–79, Pro Vice-Chancellor, 1982–85, Cranfield Inst. of Technol. Chairman: Aerospace Technology Bd, MoD, 1986–89; Aviation Cttee, DTI, 1986–94; Mem., Airworthiness Requirements Bd, 1990–2000. Pres., RAeS, 1987–88. Visiting Professor: Cornell Aeronautical Labs, Buffalo, USA, 1964; Aeronaut. Res. Lab., Wright Patterson Air Force Base, 1971; Nat. Aeronaut. Lab., Bangalore, India, 1977; Univ. of Queensland, 1983. Hon. FRAeS (FRAeS 1975). *Publications:* (Chief Editor) Shock Tube Research, 1971; papers in Jl of Fluid Mechanics, and various other aeronautical jls. *Recreations:* watching football, travelling. *Address:* 28 The Embankment, Bedford MK40 3PE. *T:* (01234) 406773. *Died 28 June 2013.*

STONE, Prof. (Francis) Gordon (Albert), CBE 1990; FRS 1976; Head of Department of Inorganic Chemistry, and Professor, Bristol University, 1963–90, then Professor Emeritus; Robert A. Welch and University Distinguished Professor of Chemistry, Baylor University, Texas, 1990–2010; *b* 19 May 1925; *s* of Sidney Charles and Florence Stone; *m* 1956, Judith M. Hislop (*d* 2008), Sydney, Australia; three *s*. *Educ:* Exeter Sch.; Christ's Coll., Cambridge (BA 1948, MA and PhD 1952, ScD 1963). Fulbright Schol., Univ. of Southern Calif., 1952–54; Instructor and Asst Prof., Harvard Univ., 1954–62; Reader, Queen Mary Coll., London, 1962–63. Visiting Professor: Monash Univ., 1966; Princeton Univ., 1967; Univ. of Arizona, 1970; Carnegie-Mellon Univ., 1972; Texas A&M Univ., 1980; ANU, 1982; Guggenheim Fellow, 1961; Sen. Vis. Fellow, Australian Acad. of Sciences, 1966; A. R. Gordon Distinguished Lectr, Univ. of Toronto, 1977; Misha Strassberg Vis. Lectr, Univ. of WA, 1982. Lectures: Boomer, Univ. of Alberta, 1965; Firestone, Univ. of Wisconsin, 1970; Tilden, Chem. Soc., 1971; Ludwig Mond, RSC, 1982; Reilly, Univ. of Notre Dame, 1983; Waddington, Univ. of Durham, 1984; Sir Edward Frankland Prize, RSC, 1987; G. W. Watt, Univ. of Texas (Austin), 1988. Member: Council, Royal Soc. of Chemistry (formerly Chemical Soc.), 1968–70, 1981–83; Dalton Div. Council, 1971–74, 1981–85 (Vice-Pres. 1973 and 1984–85; Pres., 1981–83); Chemistry Cttee, SERC, 1982–85 (Mem., Chem. Cttee, SRC, 1971–74); Council, Royal Soc., 1986–88 (Vice-Pres., 1987–88). Hon. DSc: Exeter, and Waterloo, Canada, 1992; Durham, Salford, 1993; Zaragoza, 1994. Organometallic Chemistry Medal, 1972, Transition Metal Chemistry Medal, 1979, RSC; Chugaev Medal, Inst. of Inorganic Chem., USSR Acad. of Sciences, 1978; Amer. Chem. Soc. Award in Inorg. Chem., 1985; Davy Medal, Royal Soc., 1989; Longstaff Medal, RSC, 1990. *Publications:* Leaving No Stone Unturned (autobiog.), 1993; (Editor) Advances in Organometallic Chemistry, vols 1–47, 1964–2000; (ed) Comprehensive Organometallic Chemistry, 1985–1995 (14 vols), 1995; numerous papers in Jl Chem. Soc., Jl Amer. Chem. Soc., etc. *Recreations:* work, world travel. *Address:* St Oswalds Orchard, Oswaldkirk, York YO62 5XT; 88 Hackberry Avenue, Waco, TX 76706, USA. *T:* (254) 7523617. *Died 6 April 2011.*

STONE, Frederick Alistair, CBE 1988; DL; Clerk and Chief Executive, Surrey County Council, 1973–88; *b* 13 Sept. 1927; *s* of Cyril Jackson and Elsie May Stone; *m* 1963, Anne Teresa Connor; one *s* one *d*. *Educ:* William Hulme's Grammar Sch.; Dulwich Coll.; Brasenose Coll., Oxford (BCL, MA). Asst Solicitor: Norwich City Council, 1954–58; Hampshire CC, 1958–60; Sen. Solicitor, CC of Lincoln (Parts of Lindsey), 1960–63; Asst Clerk, Hampshire CC, 1963–65; Dep. Clerk, Cheshire CC, 1965–73. Chairman: RIPA, 1979–81; Assoc. of County Chief Executives, 1986–87. Chm., Surrey Bd, Prince's Youth Business Trust, 1989–96; Dep. Chm., Anchor Housing Assoc. and Trust, 1990–97. Chm. of Govs, Worth Sch., 1990–99. DL Surrey, 1988. *Recreations:* music, walking, gardening. *Address:* Stables Cottage, Kiln Lane, Brockham, Betchworth RH3 7LZ. *T:* (01737) 842178. *Died 31 Jan. 2014.*

STONE, Gordon; *see* Stone, F. G. A.

STONE, Marcus; Sheriff of Lothian and Borders, 1984–93; Advocate; *b* 22 March 1921; *s* of Morris and Reva Stone; *m* 1956, Jacqueline Barnoin; three *s* two *d*. *Educ:* High Sch. of Glasgow; Univ. of Glasgow (MA 1940, LLB 1948). Served War of 1939–45, RASC: overseas service, West Africa, attd RWAFF. Admitted Solicitor, 1949; Post Grad. Dip., Psychology, Univ. of Glasgow, 1953; admitted Faculty of Advocates, 1965; apptd Hon. Sheriff Substitute, 1967, Sheriff, 1971–76, of Stirling, Dunbarton and Clackmannan, later N Strathclyde at Dumbarton; Sheriff of Glasgow and Strathkelvin, 1976–84. Accredited Mediator, Centre for Dispute Resolution, London, 1993; Principal: The Mediation Bureau; M. B. Publishing; practising mediator, 1994–; Founder and Hon. Pres., Assoc. of Mediators, 1997–2001. E-book Publisher, Courtroom and Mediation E-books, 2011–. *Publications:* Proof of Fact in Criminal Trials, 1984; Cross-examination in Criminal Trials, 1988, 3rd edn 2009; Fact-finding for Magistrates, 1990; Representing Clients in Mediation, 1998. *Recreations:* swimming, jazz piano. *Died 31 July 2012.*

STONEHAM, Prof. (Arthur) Marshall, PhD; FRS 1989; Massey Professor of Physics, and Director, Centre for Materials Research, 1995–2005, then Emeritus Professor, University College London (Honorary Fellow, 2006); *b* 18 May 1940; *s* of Garth Rivers Stoneham and Nancy Wooler Stoneham (*née* Leslie); *m* 1962, Doreen Montgomery; two *d*. *Educ:* Univ. of Bristol (BSc 1961; PhD 1964). CPhys, FInstP 1981; FIMMM (FIM 1996). Harwell Laboratory, UKAEA, 1964–95: Group Leader, 1974; Individual Merit promotions to Band level, 1974, and Sen. level, 1979; Hd of Materials Physics and Metallurgy Div., 1989–90; Hd of Technical Area, Core and Fuel Studies, UKAEA, 1988–90; Dir of Res., AEA Industrial Technology, 1990–93; Chief Scientist, UKAEA, 1993–97 (pt-time based at UCL, 1995–97). Wolfson Industrial Fellow, Oxford Univ.,

1985–89; Fellow, Wolfson Coll., Oxford, 1989–95; Sen. Fellow, BT Labs, subseq. Corning Res. Centre, 1998–2000. Visiting Professor: Univ. of Illinois, 1969; Univ. of Connecticut, 1973; Univ. of Keele, 1988–; Univ. of Salford, 1992–; visiting scientist: Gen. Electric, Schenectady, 1969; Centre d'Etudes Nucléaires Grenoble, 1970; KFA Julich, 1973; IBM Yorktown Heights, 1982; PTB Braunschweig, 1985, etc. Member, Council: Royal Soc., 1994–96; Inst. of Physics, 1994–2001 (Vice Pres., 1997–2001; Pres., 2010–). Dir, Oxford Authentication, 1997–. Fellow: APS, 1997; World Innovation Foundn, 2001. Royal Soc. Zeneca Prize, 1995; Guthrie Prize, Inst. of Physics, 2006. Dir, Inst. of Physics Publications, 1987–2001; Editor, Jl of Physics C: Solid State Physics, 1983–88; Divl Associate Ed., Physical Review Letters, 1992–96; Ed. in Chief, Jl Physics of Condensed Matter, 2002–06; mem. editl bds of other learned jls. *Publications:* Theory of Defects in Solids, 1975, new edn 1985, repr. as Oxford Classic, 2001 (Russian edn 1978); (with W. Hayes) Defects and Defect Processes in Non-Metallic Solids, 1985; Current Issues in Semiconductor Science, 1986; Current Issues in Condensed Matter Structure, 1987; (with M. G. Silk and J. A. G. Temple) Reliability of Non-Destructive Inspection, 1987; Ionic Solids at High Temperatures, 1989; Current Issues in Condensed Matter Spectroscopy, 1990; Materials Modelling: from theory to technology, 1992; (with S. C. Jain) GeSi Strained Layers and their Applications, 1995; (with J. A. Gillaspie and D. L. Clark) Wind Ensemble Sourcebook, 1997 (C. B. Oldman Prize, IAML, 1999); (with J. A. Gillaspie and D. L. Clark) The Wind Ensemble Catalog, 1998; (with N. Itoh) Materials Modification by Electronic Excitation, 2000; research papers on defect properties of the solid state, quantum diffusion, and ordered structures in Jl Phys C: Solid State Phys, Phys Rev., Phys Rev. Lett., Procs of Royal Soc., etc. *Recreations:* music, esp. horn playing in orchestral and chamber music, musical scholarship, reading. *Address:* 14 Bridge End, Dorchester-on-Thames, Wallingford, Oxon OX10 7JP. *T:* (01865) 340066. *E:* ucapams@ucl.ac.uk.
Died 18 Feb. 2011.

STOPFORD, Prof. John Morton; Professor of International Business, London Business School, 1974–2002, then Emeritus; *b* 16 Sept. 1939; *s* of Rt Rev. and Rt Hon. Robert Wright Stopford, KCVO, CBE, DD and Winifred Sophia Stopford (*née* Morton); *m* 1966, Sarah Woodman; two *s. Educ:* Sherborne Sch.; Hertford Coll., Oxford (BA 1961); MIT (SM); Harvard Univ. (DBA). Apprentice fitter, Baker Perkins, 1958; Engineer, Shell Chemicals, 1962–64; Acting Man. Dir, Guyana Stockfeeds, 1965; Sen. Lectr, Manchester Business Sch., 1968–70; Vis. Prof., Harvard Business Sch., 1970–71; Reader, London Business Sch., 1971–74. Non-exec. Dir, Shell UK, 1973–77; Chairman: The Learning Partnership Inc., 1997–; Strategic Partnership, 2000–02 (Dir, 1994–99). Pres., Eur. Internat. Business Assoc., 1978–79; Vice-Pres., Acad. of Internat. Business, 1994–96; Sen. Staff Officer, UN Centre on Transitional Corps, NY, 1977–78. Visiting Professor: MIT, 1993; Stockholm Sch. of Econs, 1994–95; Aoyama Gakuin Univ., Tokyo, 1994–95; Murmann Sch., Kiel, 2008; Harry Reynolds Vis. Prof., Wharton Sch., Univ. of Penn., 1999–2000. Governor, Goodenough Coll., 2005–10. Mem., Steering Cttee, Order of St John, 2004–. US Acad. of Management Book Prize, 1992. CStJ 2010. *Publications:* (with L. T. Wells) Managing the Multinational Enterprise, 1972; (with B. Garratt) Breaking down Barriers, 1980; Growth and Organisational Change, 1980; The Directory of Multinationals, 1980, 2nd edn, 1992; (with J. H. Dunning) Multinationals, 1983; (with L. Turner) Britain and the Multinationals, 1985; (with S. Strange) Rival States, Rival Firms, 1991; (with C. Baden-Fuller) Rejuvenating the Mature Business, 1992, rev. edn 1994; (ed jtly) Handbook of Organizational Learning, 2000; (ed jtly) The Future of the Multinational Company, 2003; contribs to learned jls. *Recreations:* hill-walking, tennis, reading. *Address:* 6 Chalcot Square, NW1 8YB. *Died 13 Aug. 2011.*

STORIE-PUGH, Col Peter David, CBE 1981 (MBE 1945); MC 1940; TD 1945 and 3 clasps; DL; Lecturer, University of Cambridge, 1953–82; Fellow of Wolfson College, Cambridge, 1967–82, then Emeritus; *b* 1 Nov. 1919; *s* of late Prof. Leslie Pugh, CBE, BSc, MA, FRCVS and Paula Storie; *m* 1st, 1946, Alison (marr. diss. 1971), *d* of late Sir Oliver Lyle, OBE; one *s* two *d;* 2nd, 1971, Leslie Helen, *d* of Earl Striegel; three *s* one *d. Educ:* Malvern; Queens' Coll., Cambridge (Hon. Foundn Scholar; MA, PhD); Royal Veterinary Coll., Univ. of London. FRCVS; CChem, FRSC. Served War of 1939–45, Queen's Own Royal W Kent Regt (escaped from Spangenberg and Colditz); comd 1st Bn, Cambs Regt, comd 1st Bn Suffolk and Cambs Regt; Col, Dep. Comdr, 161 Inf. Bde, ACF County Comdt. Wellcome Res. Fellow, Cambridge, 1950–52. Mem. Council, RCVS, 1956–84 (Chm. Parly Cttee, 1962–67; Pres., 1977–78); President: Cambridge Soc. for Study of Comparative Medicine, 1966–67; Internat. Pig Vet. Soc., 1967–69 (Life Pres., 1969); British Veterinary Assoc., 1968–69 and 1970–71 (Hon. Life Mem., 1984; Dalrymple-Champneys Cup and Medal, 1986); Mem. Exec. Cttee, Cambridgeshire Farmers Union, 1960–65; UK delegate, EEC Vet. Liaison Cttee, 1962–75 (Pres., 1973–75); UK Rep., Fedn of Veterinarians of EEC, 1975–83 (Pres. of Fedn, 1975–79); Chm., Eurovet, 1971–73; Mem. Jt RCVS/BVA Cttee on European Vet. Affairs, 1971–92; Observer, European Liaison Gp for Agric., 1972–80; Jt Pres., 1st European Vet. Congress, Wiesbaden, 1972; Permanent Mem. EEC Adv. Vet. Cttee, 1976–82; Mem. Council, Secrétariat Européen des Professions Libérales, 1976–80; Mem. Permanent Cttee, World Vet. Assoc., 1964–75. Member: Parly and Sci. Cttee, 1962–67; Home Sec.'s Adv. Cttee (Cruelty to Animals Act, 1876), 1963–80; Nat. Agric. Centre Adv. Bd, 1966–69; Production Cttee, Meat and Livestock Commn, 1967–70; Min. of Agriculture's Farm Animal Adv. Cttee, 1970–73; Econ. and Social Cttee, EEC, 1982–90. Chm., Nat. Sheep Breeders' Assoc., 1964–68; Vice-Pres., Agric. Section, British Assoc., 1970–71. Corresp. Mem., Bund Deutscher Veterinäroffiziere, 1979–. Robert von Ostertag Medal, German Vet. Assoc., 1972. DL Cambs, 1963. *Publications:* (and ed jtly) Eurovet: an Anatomy of Veterinary Europe, 1972; Eurovet-2, 1975. *Address:* Fort Mahon, 81630 Salvagnac, France. *T:* 563335427.
Died 20 Oct. 2011.

STOTT, Rev. John Robert Walmsley, CBE 2006; DD; Director, London Institute for Contemporary Christianity, 1982–86, then President; Chaplain to the Queen, 1959–91, Extra Chaplain, since 1991; *b* 27 April 1921; *s* of late Sir Arnold W. Stott, KBE, physician, and Emily Caroline Holland. *Educ:* Rugby Sch.; Trinity Coll., Cambridge (BA 1943; MA 1947); Ridley Hall, Cambridge. Curate of All Souls, Langham Place, 1945; Rector of All Souls, 1950–75 (with St Peter's, Vere Street, 1952), then Rector Emeritus. DD Lambeth, 1983; Hon. DD: Trinity Evangelical Divinity Sch., Deerfield, USA, 1971; Wycliffe Coll., Toronto, 1993; Brunel, 1997; Trinity Episcopal Sch. for Ministry, 2003. *Publications:* Men with a Message, 1954, rev. edn with Stephen Motyer, 1994; What Christ Thinks of the Church, 1958; Basic Christianity, 1958, new edn 2008; Your Confirmation, 1958, 2nd edn 1991; Fundamentalism and Evangelism, 1959; The Preacher's Portrait, 1961; Confess Your Sins, 1964; The Epistles of John, 1964; Canticles and Selected Psalms, 1966; Men Made New, 1966; Our Guilty Silence, 1967; The Message of Galatians, 1968; One People, 1969; Christ the Controversialist, 1970; Understanding the Bible, 1972; Guard the Gospel, 1973; Balanced Christianity, 1975; Christian Mission in the Modern World, 1975; Baptism and Fullness, 1975; The Lausanne Covenant, 1975; Christian Counter-Culture, 1978; Focus on Christ, 1979, 2nd edn as Life in Christ, 1991; God's New Society, 1979; I Believe in Preaching, 1982; The Bible Book for Today, 1982; Issues Facing Christians Today, 1984, 4th edn 2006; The Authentic Jesus, 1985; The Cross of Christ, 1986; (with David Edwards) Essentials, 1988; The Message of Acts, 1990; The Message of I and II Thessalonians, 1991; The Contemporary Christian, 1992; The Message of Romans, 1994; The Message of Timothy and Titus, 1996; Evangelical Truth, 1999; The Birds Our Teachers: Biblical lessons from a lifelong bird-watcher, 1999; The Incomparable Christ, 2001; Calling Christian Leaders, 2002; People My Teachers: around the world in 80 years, 2002; Why I am a Christian: this is my story, 2003; Through the Bible Through the Year, 2006; The Living Church: convictions of a lifelong pastor, 2007; The Last Word: reflections on a lifetime of preaching, 2008; John

Stott at Keswick: six Bible expositions given at Keswick, 2008; The Radical Disciple: wholehearted Christian living, 2010. *Recreation:* bird watching. *Address:* The College of St Barnabas, Blackberry Lane, Lingfield, Surrey RH7 6NJ. *Died 27 July 2011.*

STOUT, David Ker; Director, Centre for Business Strategy, and Professor of Economics, London Business School, 1992–97; Hon. Research Fellow in Economics, University College London, since 2001; *b* Bangor, N Wales, 27 Jan. 1932; *s* of late Prof. Alan Ker Stout, FAHA, FASSA and of Evelyn Roberts; *m* 1956, Margaret Sugden; two *s* two *d*. *Educ:* Sydney High Sch.; Sydney Univ., NSW (BA 1st Cl. English Lit, Econs, and University Medal in Econs, 1953); NSW Rhodes Scholar 1954; Magdalen Coll., Oxford; George Webb Medley Jun. Scholar 1955, Sen. Scholar 1956; PPE 1st Cl. 1956; Nuffield Coll., Oxford (Studentship 1956); Magdalen Prize Fellow by Examination, 1958–59. Fellow and Lectr in Econs, University Coll., Oxford, 1959–76; Economic Dir, NEDO, 1971–72 and 1976–80; Tyler Prof. of Econs, Leicester Univ., 1980–82; Head of Econs, Unilever, 1982–92. Adviser on tax structure to Syrian Govt, 1965, and New Hebrides Condominium, 1966; Sen. Econ. Adviser to Monopolies Commn, 1969; Consultant on VAT, Nat. Bureau of Econ. Res., NY, 1970; Adviser to Australian Govt on Prices Justification, 1973, and on Wage Indexation, 1975–76. Member: Exec. Cttee, NIESR, 1974–82, 1992–98 (Gov., 1974–); EEC Expert Gp on Community Planning, 1976–78, and on Adjustment Policy, 1979–80; ESRC, 1989–92 (Mem., Econ. Affairs Cttee, 1980–86; Chm., Industry, Economics and Envmt Cttee, 1989–92); Manufacturing Foresight Panel, OST, 1994–98; Technology Interaction Bd, BBSRC, 1994–96; Bd of Trustees, Strategic Planning Inst., Cambridge, Mass, 1983–87. Editor, Business Strategy Review, 1994–98. FRSA. *Publications:* papers on taxation policy, VAT, investment, incomes policy, trade performance, indust. policy, de-industrialisation, and European planning. *Recreations:* music, chess, bivalves. *T:* (01732) 884279. *E:* davidkerstout@gmail.com. *Died 10 May 2013.*

STOW, Ralph Conyers, CBE 1981; FCIS, FCIB; President and Chairman, Cheltenham & Gloucester Building Society, 1982–87 (Managing Director, 1973–82); *b* 19 Dec. 1916; *s* of Albert Conyers Stow and Mabel Louise Bourlet; *m* 1943, Eleanor Joyce Appleby (*d* 2002); one *s* one *d*. *Educ:* Woodhouse Sch., Finchley. FCIS 1959; FBS 1952. Supt of Branches, Temperance Permanent Bldg Soc., 1950, Asst Manager 1958; Gen. Man. and Sec., Cheltenham & Gloucester Bldg Soc., 1962, Dir 1967. Pres., Bldg Socs Inst., 1971–72; Chm., Midland Assoc. of Bldg Socs, 1973–74; Chm., Bldg Socs Assoc., 1977–79. Mem., Glos AHA, 1973–81; Chm., Cheltenham DHA, 1981–88. *Recreations:* photography, oil painting. *Club:* Rotary (Cheltenham). *Died 14 June 2012.*

STOWE, Sir Kenneth (Ronald), GCB 1986 (KCB 1980; CB 1977); CVO 1979; Trustee and Member of Council, Cancer Research UK, 2001–08 (Council Member, Cancer Research Campaign, 1987–2002); *b* 17 July 1927; *er s* of Arthur and Emily Stowe; *m* 1949, Joan Frances Cullen (*d* 1995); two *s* one *d*. *Educ:* County High Sch., Dagenham; Exeter Coll., Oxford (MA; Hon. Fellow, 1989). Asst Principal, Nat. Assistance Board, 1951; Principal, 1956; seconded UN Secretariat, New York, 1958; Asst Sec., 1964; Asst Under-Sec. of State, DHSS, 1970–73; Under Sec., Cabinet Office, 1973–75, Dep. Sec., 1976; Principal Private Sec. to the Prime Minister, 1975–79; Permanent Under Sec. of State, NI Office, 1979–81; Perm. Sec., DHSS, 1981–87. Member: President's Commn to review Public Service, Zimbabwe, 1987–89; Pres. Mandela's Commn on Public Service of SA, 1996–98. Mem., Bd of Dirs, Commonwealth Assoc. for Public Admin and Management, 1994–98, then Emeritus Dir (Chm., Founding Conf., PEI, 1994); Advr on admin. reform to HM Govt, UN Develt Prog., and Commonwealth Secretariat; Chm., wkg gp of voluntary-community sector on compact with Lab. govt, 1997–2002; Chm., HM Treasury reference gp on future builders fund for voluntary sector develt, 2002–03. Chairman: Inst. of Cancer Res., 1987–97 (Fellow, 1999); Thrombosis Res. Inst., 1998–2000; Dir, Royal Marsden Hosp. NHS Trust, 1994–97; Trustee: CHASE Children's Hospice, 1999–2004; Carnegie UK Trust, 1988–99; Chairman: Carnegie Inquiry into The Third Age, 1989–93; Carnegie Young People Project, 1996–99. Hon. DSc Inst. of Cancer Res., 2009. *Recreation:* listening and thinking. *Club:* Athenæum. *Died 29 Aug. 2015.*

STRACHAN, Alexander William Bruce, OBE 1971; HM Diplomatic Service, retired; *b* 2 July 1917; *s* of William Fyfe and Winifred Orchar Strachan; *m* 1940, Rebecca Prince MacFarlane (*d* 2011); one *s* one *d*. *Educ:* Daniel Stewart's Coll., Edinburgh; Allan Glen's High Sch., Glasgow. Served Army, 1939–46 (dispatches). GPO, 1935; Asst Postal Controller, 1949–64; Postal Adviser to Iraq Govt, 1964–66; First Sec., FCO, 1967–68; Jordan, 1968–72; Addis Ababa, 1972–73; Consul General, Lahore, 1973–74; Counsellor (Economic and Commercial) and Consul General, Islamabad, 1975–77. Order of Istiqlal, Hashemite Kingdom of Jordan, 1971. *Died 26 Dec. 2013.*

STRACHAN, Hon. Sir Curtis (Victor), Kt 1996; CVO 1985; Speaker, House of Representatives, Grenada, West Indies, 1995–2002; *b* 29 May 1926; *s* of Walter and Rosanna Strachan; *m* 1959, Etheline Robertson (decd); one *s* one *d*. *Educ:* Constantine Methodist Sch.; Grenada Boys' Secondary Sch.; Univ. of W Indies. Public Officer, Grenada, 1946, then Perm. Sec.; Clerk of Parlt, Grenada, 1959. *Publications:* Mainly for Parliamentary Freshmen; Assisting the New Member; The Basic Procedure. *Recreations:* tennis, swimming. *Address:* Bloomsbury, PO Box 681, 5 Tanteen Terrace, Grenada, West Indies. *T:* 4402687. *Died 26 April 2011.*

STRACHEY, Charles; former local government officer; *b* 20 June 1934; *s* of Rt Hon. Evelyn John St Loe Strachey (*d* 1963) and Celia (*d* 1980), 3rd *d* of late Rev. Arthur Hume Simpson; *S* to baronetcy of cousin, 2nd Baron Strachie, 1973 as 6th Bt *cr* 1801, but does not use the title, and his name does not appear on the Official Roll of the Baronetage; *m* 1973, Janet Megan, *d* of Alexander Miller; one *d*. *Heir: kinsman* Henry Leofric Benvenuto Strachey, *b* 17 April 1947. *Address:* 31 Northchurch Terrace, N1 4EB. *T:* (020) 7684 5479. *Died 23 Jan. 2014.*

STRAKER, Major Ivan Charles; Chairman, Seagram Distillers plc, 1984–93 (Chief Executive, 1983–90); *b* 17 June 1928; *s* of Arthur Coppin Straker and Cicely Longueville Straker; *m* 1st, 1954, Gillian Elizabeth Grant (marr. diss. 1971); one *s* one *d* (and one *s* decd); 2nd, 1976, Sally Jane Hastings (marr. diss. 1986); one *s*; 3rd, 1998, Rosemary Ann Whitaker. *Educ:* Harrow; RMA, Sandhurst. Commissioned 11th Hussars (PAO), 1948; served Germany, N Ireland, Middle East and Mil. Intell. Staff, War Office; left HM Armed Forces, 1962. Man. Dir, D. Rintoul & Co., 1964; Man. Dir, The Glenlivet and Glen Grant Agencies, 1964–71; apptd Main Board, The Glenlivet and Glen Grant Distillers, 1967; Chief Exec., The Glenlivet Distillers Ltd, 1971. Dir, Lothian Racing Syndicate Ltd, 1986–2008. Council Mem., Scotch Whisky Assoc., 1978–90 (Chm., Public Affairs Cttee, 1986–90). *Recreations:* fishing, shooting, racing. *Address:* Oaktree Cottage, Acomb, Hexham, Northumberland NE46 4PL. *T:* (01434) 604509. *Clubs:* Jockey, Cavalry and Guards. *Died 20 May 2013.*

STRANG, 2nd Baron *cr* 1954, of Stonesfield; **Colin Strang;** Professor of Philosophy, 1975–82, and Dean of the Faculty of Arts, 1976–79, University of Newcastle upon Tyne; *b* 12 June 1922; *s* of 1st Baron Strang, GCB, GCMG, MBE, and Elsie Wynne (*d* 1974), *d* of late J. E. Jones; *S* father, 1978; *m* 1st, 1948, Patricia Marie, *d* of Meiert C. Avis, Johannesburg; 2nd, 1955, Barbara Mary Hope Carr (*d* 1982); one *d*; 3rd, 1984, Mary Shewell (*née* Miles) (*d* 2012). *Educ:* Merchant Taylors' School; St John's Coll., Oxford (MA, BPhil). *Heir:* none. *Address:* Sheean View, Brodick, Isle of Arran KA27 8DH. *Died 19 Dec. 2014 (ext).*

STRATHEDEN, 6th Baron *cr* 1836, **AND CAMPBELL,** 6th Baron *cr* 1841; **Donald Campbell;** *b* 4 April 1934; *s* of 5th Baron Stratheden and Campbell and of Evelyn Mary Austen, *d* of late Col Herbert Austen Smith, CIE; *S* father, 1987; *m* 1st, 1957, Hilary Ann Holland (*d* 1991), *d* of Lt-Col William D. Turner; one *s* three *d*; 2nd, 2001, Elaine Margaret Fogarty. *Educ:* Eton. *Heir: s* Hon. David Anthony Campbell [*b* 13 Feb. 1963; *m* 1993, Jennifer Margaret

Owens; two *d*]. *Address:* Yalara, 120 Happy Jack Creek Road, Ridgewood, Cooroy, Qld 4563, Australia. *Died 23 Oct. 2011.*

STRATHIE, Dame Lesley (Ann), DCB 2010; Chief Executive and Permanent Secretary, HM Revenue and Customs, 2008–11; *b* Stranraer, 24 Sept. 1955; *d* of Rumold Francis Cooke and Agnes Elizabeth Cooke; *m* 1974, David George Strathie (marr. diss. 1996); one *d* (one *s* decd). *Educ:* Stranraer Acad. Entered CS, 1971: DHSS, 1971–74; Department of Employment, 1974–2000: Unemployment Benefit Service, London, then Employment Service, 1984–2000; Department of Work and Pensions: Field Dir, London, 2001–03, Chief Operating Officer, 2003–05, Jobcentre Plus; Chief Exec. and Second Perm. Sec., 2005–08. *Recreations:* theatre, especially the RSC and the National, supporter of Arsenal FC for most of adult life, good food and wine, travel. *Died 14 Jan. 2012.*

STRAWSON, Maj.-Gen. John Michael, CB 1975; OBE 1964; idc, jssc, psc; Senior Military Adviser, Westland Aircraft Ltd, 1978–85 (Head of Cairo Office, 1976–78); *b* 1 Jan. 1921; *s* of late Cyril Walter and Nellie Dora Strawson; *m* 1960, Baroness Wilfried von Schellersheim; two *d*. *Educ:* Christ's Coll., Finchley. Joined Army, 1940; commnd, 1941; served with 4th QO Hussars in Middle East, Italy, Germany, Malaya, 1942–50, 1953–54, 1956–58; Staff Coll., Camberley, 1950; Bde Major, 1951–53; Instructor, Staff Coll. and Master of Drag Hounds, 1958–60; GSO1 and Col GS in WO and MoD, 1961–62 and 1965–66; comd QR Irish Hussars, Malaysia and BAOR, 1963–65; comd Inf. Bde, 1967–68; idc 1969; COS, Live Oak, SHAPE, 1970–72; COS, HQ UKLF, 1972–76. Col, Queen's Royal Irish Hussars, 1975–85. US Bronze Star, 1945. *Publications:* The Battle for North Africa, 1969; Hitler as Military Commander, 1971; The Battle for the Ardennes, 1972; The Battle for Berlin, 1974; (jtly) The Third World War, 1978; El Alamein, 1981; (jtly) The Third World War: the untold story, 1982; A History of the SAS Regiment, 1984; The Italian Campaign, 1987; Gentlemen in Khaki: the British Army 1890–1990, 1989; Beggars in Red: the British Army 1789–1889, 1991; The Duke and the Emperor, 1994; Churchill and Hitler: in victory and defeat, 1997; On Draghunting, 1999; If By Chance, 2002; Hussars, Horses and History, 2007; Gentlemen in Khaki and Camouflage, 2009. *Recreations:* equitation, shooting, reading. *Club:* Cavalry and Guards (Chm., 1984–87). *Died 21 Feb. 2014.*

STREATFEILD, Maj.-Gen. Timothy Stuart Champion, CB 1980; MBE 1960; Director, Royal Artillery, 1978–81; *b* 9 Sept. 1926; *s* of Henry Grey Champion and Edythe Streatfeild; *m* 1951, Annette Catherine, *d* of Sir John Clague, CMG, CIE, and Lady Clague; two *s* one *d*. *Educ:* Eton; Christ Church, Oxford (MA). Commnd into RA, 1946; Instructor, Staff Coll., Camberley, 1963–65; Chief Instructor, Sudan Armed Forces Staff Coll., 1965–67; Commander, 7th Parachute Regt, RHA, 1967–69; Col Adjt and QMG, 4 Div., 1969–70; Commander, RA 2 Div., 1971–72; RCDS, 1973; Brigadier Adjt and QMG, 1st Corps, 1974–75; COS, Logistic Exec., MoD, 1976–78. Regtl Comptroller, RA, 1986–89. Colonel Commandant: RA, 1980–91; RHA, 1981–91. FCMI. *Recreations:* fishing, sporting, the countryside, music. *Address:* Toatley Farm, Chawleigh, Chulmleigh, N Devon EX18 7HW. *T:* (01363) 83363. *Club:* Army and Navy. *Died 15 Aug. 2011.*

STREET, Prof. Robert, AO 1985; DSc; Vice-Chancellor, University of Western Australia, 1978–86, Hon. Research Fellow, since 1986; *b* 16 Dec. 1920; *s* of late J. Street, Allerton Bywater, Yorkshire, UK; *m* 1943, Joan Marjorie Bere; one *s* one *d*. *Educ:* Hanley High Sch.; New Coll., Oxford (Open Exhibnr 1939); King's Coll., London. BSc, MSc, PhD, DSc (London). MIET, FInstP, FAIP, FAA. Scientific Officer, Dept of Supply, UK, 1942–45; Lectr, Dept of Physics, Univ. of Nottingham, 1945–54; Sen. Lectr, Dept of Physics, Univ. of Sheffield, 1954–60; Foundn Prof. of Physics, Monash Univ., Melbourne, Vic., 1960–74; Dir, Research Sch. of Physical Sciences, Aust. Nat. Univ., 1974–78. Former President: Aust. Inst. of Nuclear Science and Engrg; Aust. Inst. of Physics; Mem. and Chm., Aust. Research Grants Cttee, 1970–76; Chm., Nat. Standards Commn, 1967–78; Member: State Energy Adv. Council, WA, 1981–86; Australian Science and Technology Council, 1977–80; Council, Univ. of Technology, Lae, Papua New Guinea, 1982–84; Bd of Management, Royal Perth Hosp., 1978–85. Fellow, Aust. Acad. of Science, 1973 (Treas., 1976–77). Hon. DSc: Sheffield, 1986; Western Australia, 1988. Jt Special Award, Insts of Physics, UK and Australia, 2000. *Publications:* research papers in scientific jls. *Recreation:* swimming. *Address:* Department of Physics, University of Western Australia, 35 Stirling Highway, Crawley, WA 6009, Australia. *Club:* Weld (Perth). *Died 4 July 2013.*

STRICKLAND, Frank, OBE 1986; Vice-President, The Building Societies Association, since 1992 (Deputy Chairman, 1987–89; Chairman, 1989–91); *b* 4 Feb. 1928; *s* of Robert and Esther Strickland; *m* 1953, Marian Holt; one *d*. *Educ:* Harris Inst., Preston, Lancs. Asst Sec., Chorley and District Building Soc., 1952; Branch Manager, Hastings and Thanet Building Soc., 1955; Asst Sec., later Jt Sec., Corporation and Eligible Building Soc., 1965; Sunderland and Shields Building Society, later North of England Building Society: Gen. Manager, 1969; Chief Exec., 1975–89; Dir, 1982–92; Exec. Dep. Chm., 1989–91. Pres., European Fedn of Bldg Socs, 1989–91. *Recreations:* bowls, cricket. *Address:* 15 Glyne Hall, De La Warr Parade, Bexhill-on-Sea, East Sussex TN40 1LY. *T:* (01424) 734020. *Club:* MCC. *Died 19 Dec. 2012.*

STRONG, Air Cdre David Malcolm, CB 1964; AFC 1941; Officer Commanding, RAF Halton, 1964–66; *b* 30 Sept. 1913; *s* of Theo Strong; *m* 1941, Daphne Irene Warren-Brown (*d* 2008); two *s* one *d*. *Educ:* Cardiff High School. Pilot, under trng, 1936; Bomber Sqdn, 1937–41; POW, 1941–45. Station Commander, RAF Jurby, RAF Driffield, 1946–48; Staff Coll. (psa), 1949; Staff Officer, Rhodesian Air Trng Gp, 1949–51; Directing Staff, Staff Coll., 1952–55; Air Warfare Coll. (pfc), 1956; Station Comdr, RAF Coningsby, 1957–59; Dir of Personnel, Air Min., 1959–61; Senior Air Staff Officer, RAF Germany, 1962–63. Chairman: RAF Rugby Union, 1954–56; RAF Golf Soc., 1964–66. *Recreation:* golf. *Club:* Royal Air Force. *Died 21 Aug. 2011.*

STRONG, Dr John Anderson, CBE 1978 (MBE (mil.) 1942); MD; FRCP; FRCPE; FRSE; President, Royal College of Physicians of Edinburgh, 1979–82; *b* 18 Feb. 1915; *s* of Charles James Strong and Mabel Emma Strong (*née* Anderson); *m* 1939, Anne Frances Moira Heaney (*d* 1997); one *s* two *d*. *Educ:* Monkton Combe Sch., Bath; Trinity Coll., Dublin (MB 1937, MA, MD). Served RAMC, UK, India and Burma, 1939–46 (despatches, Burma, 1945); Hon. Lt-Col RAMC, 1946. Senior Lecturer, Dept of Medicine, Univ. of Edinburgh, 1949; Hon. Cons. Phys., Western General Hosp., Edinburgh, 1949; Hon. Physician, MRC Clinical and Population Cytogenetics Unit, 1959–80; Professor of Medicine, Univ. of Edinburgh, 1966–80, Professor Emeritus, 1981. Mem., Medicines Commn, 1976–83; Chm., Scottish Health Educn Co-ordinating Cttee, 1986–88. Hon. FACP 1980; Hon. FRCPI 1980; Hon. Fellow: Coll. of Physicians of Philadelphia, 1981; TCD, 1982; Coll. of Physicians of S Africa, 1982; Fellow *ad eundem*, RCGP, 1982; Mem., Acad. of Medicine, Singapore, 1982. *Publications:* chapter on Endocrinology in Principles and Practice of Medicine, ed L. S. P. Davidson, 1952, 12th edn 1977; articles in general medical and endocrinological jls. *Recreations:* fishing, golf, stalking, natural history. *Died 15 Dec. 2012.*

STRONG, Hon. Maurice Frederick; PC (Can.) 1993; OC 1976; FRSC 1987; Senior Advisor to the President, World Bank, since 1995; Special Advisor to Secretary-General of the United Nations, 1998–2005; *b* 29 April 1929; *s* of Frederick Milton Strong and late Mary Fyfe Strong; *m* 1st, 1950 (marr. diss. 1980); two *s* two *d*; 2nd, 1981, Hanne Marstrand; one foster *d*. *Educ:* Public and High Sch., Oak Lake, Manitoba, Canada. Served in UN Secretariat, 1947; worked in industry and Pres. or Dir, various Canadian and internat. corporations, 1948–66; Dir-Gen., External Aid Office (later Canadian Internat. Devel Agency), Canadian Govt, 1966–71; Under-Sec.-Gen. with responsibility for envmtl affairs, and Sec.-Gen. of 1972 Conf. on the Human Environment, Stockholm, 1971–72; Exec. Dir, UN Envmtl Programme, 1972–75; Pres., Chm.

of Bd and Chm. of Exec. Cttee, Petro-Canada, 1976–78; Chm. of Bd, AZL Resources Inc., USA, 1978–83; Under-Sec.-Gen., UN, 1985–87 and 1989–92; Exec. Co-ordinator, UN Office for Emergency Ops in Africa, NY, 1985–87; Sec.-Gen., UN 1992 Conf. on Envmt and Develt, 1990–92; Under-Sec. Gen. and Exec. Co-ordinator for UN Reform, 1997. Chm. and CEO, Ontario Hydro, 1992–95; Chairman: Quantum Energy Technols Corp., subseq. Super Critical Combustion; Technology Development Corp.; Strovest Hldgs Inc.; formerly: Dir, Massey Ferguson, Canada; Dir, Mem. Exec. Cttee and Vice Chm., Canada Develt Corp., Toronto; Chm., Canada Develt Investment Corp., Vancouver. Chairman: Centre for Internat. Management Studies, Geneva, 1971–78; American Water Development, Denver, 1986; Internat. Energy Develt Corp., Geneva (also Special Advr); Bd of Govs, Internat. Develt Res. Centre, 1977–78; Co-Chm., Interaction Policy Bd, Vienna; Vice-Chm. and Dir, Soc. Gén. pour l'Energie et les Ressources, Geneva, 1980–86; Foundn Dir, World Economic Forum. Chm., Internat. Adv. Gp, CH2M Hill Cos Ltd; Member: Internat. Adv. Bd, Toyota Motor Corp.; Adv. Bd, Lamont-Doherty Observatory; Bd, Bretton Woods Cttee, Washington; World Commn on Envmt and Develt; Alt. Gov., IBRD, ADB, Caribbean Develt Bank. President: World Fedn of UN Assocs, 1987; Better World Soc., 1988; Chairman: North South Energy Roundtable, Washington; North South Energy Roundtable, Rome; World Resources Inst.; Earth Council; Stockholm Envmt Inst.; Adv. Cttee, UN Univ., Tokyo, Japan; Pres. Council and Rector, UN Univ. for Peace; Mem., and Chm. Exec. Cttee, UN Foundn. Director: Leadership for Envmt and Develt; Lindisfarne Assoc.; Mem., Internat. Asia Soc., NY. Trustee: Rockefeller Foundn, 1971–78; Aspen Inst., 1971; Internat. Foundn for Develt Alternatives. Hon. Prof., Peking Univ., 2004. FRSA. Holds numerous hon. degrees from univs and colls in Canada, USA and UK. First UN Internat. Envmt Prize. Order of the Star of the North (Sweden); Comdr, Order of the Golden Ark (Netherlands). *Publications:* Where on Earth are We Going?, 2000; articles in various jls, including Foreign Affairs Magazine, Natural History Magazine. *Recreations:* swimming, skin-diving, farming, reading. *Clubs:* Yale (New York); University (Toronto). *Died 28 Nov. 2015.*

STROUD, Derek H.; *see* Hammond-Stroud.

STROUD, Ven. Ernest Charles Frederick; Archdeacon of Colchester, 1983–97, then Emeritus; *b* 20 May 1931; *s* of Charles Henry and Irene Doris Stroud; *m* 1959, Jeanne Marguerite Evans; two *d*. *Educ:* Merrywood Grammar School; Merchant Venturers' Technical College; St Chad's Coll., Univ. of Durham. BA (Hons Theology), Diploma in Theology, Diploma in Rural Ministry and Mission. Esso Petroleum Co. Ltd, 1947–55. Deacon 1960, priest 1961, dio. Wakefield; Asst Curate, All Saints, S Kirkby, Yorks, 1960–63; Priest-in-Charge, St Ninian, Whitby, 1963–66; Minister of Conventional District, and first Vicar, All Saints, Chelmsford, 1966–75; Vicar of St Margaret of Antioch, Leigh on Sea, 1975–83; Asst RD of Southend, 1976–79; RD of Hadleigh, 1979–83; Hon. Canon of Chelmsford, 1982–83. Member: General Synod, 1981–96; C of E Pensions Bd, 1984– (Vice-Chm., 1990–94, Chm., 1994–96, Finance and Investment Cttee). Chairman: Additional Curates Soc., 1988–98; Church Union, 1989–96; Dr George Richard's Charity, 1990–97. *Publications:* contrib. on ministry of healing to Christian. *Recreations:* travel, music, theatre. *Address:* St Thérèse, 67 London Road, Hadleigh, Benfleet, Essex SS7 2QL. *Died 18 June 2014.*

STRUDWICK, Air Cdre Arthur Sidney Ronald, CB 1976; DFC 1945; *b* 16 April 1921; *s* of Percival and Mary Strudwick; *m* 1941, Cissily (*d* 1983); two *s* one *d*. *Educ:* Guildford Tech. Coll.; RAF Colls. Joined RAF 1940; War Service as Fighter Pilot, 1941–43; POW Germany, 1944; Test Flying, Canada, 1948–50; CO No 98 Sqdn, 1951–53; Staff Coll., Camberley, 1954; Commanded Jt Services Trials Unit, Woomera, 1956–59; JSSC, 1959–60; MoD Planning Staff, 1960–62; Dir of Plans, Far East, 1962–64; Commanded RAF Leuchars, 1965–67; Air Cdre Plans, Strategic Comd, 1967–69; IDC 1969; Dir of Flying (R&D), MoD PE, 1970–73; AOC Central Tactics and Trials Orgn, 1973–76, retired 1976. Defence Liaison Officer, Singer Co., Link-Miles Div., 1976–86. *Recreations:* golf, gardening. *Club:* Royal Air Force. *Died 11 June 2013.*

STUART, Andrew Christopher, CMG 1979; CPM 1961; HM Diplomatic Service, retired; President, CfBT Education Trust (formerly Centre for British Teachers), since 2011 (Chairman, 1991–2005; Vice President, 2005–11); *b* 30 Nov. 1928; *s* of late Rt Rev. Cyril Edgar Stuart and Mary Summerhayes; *m* 1st, 1959, Patricia Kelly (*d* 2009); two *s* one *d*; 2nd, 2011, Susan Lines. *Educ:* Bryanston; Clare Coll., Cambridge (MA). Royal Navy, 1947–49. Colonial Admin. Service, Uganda, 1953; retd from HMOCS as Judicial Adviser, 1965. Called to Bar, Middle Temple, 1965. Entered HM Diplomatic Service, 1965; 1st Sec. and Head of Chancery, Helsinki, 1968; Asst, S Asian Dept, FCO, 1971; Head of Hong Kong and Indian Ocean Dept, FCO, 1972–75; Counsellor, Jakarta, 1975–78; British Resident Comr, New Hebrides, 1978–80; Ambassador to Finland, 1980–83. Principal, United World Coll. of the Atlantic, 1983–90. Consultant, VSO, 1990–96. Order of the Lion (Finland), 1990. *Publications:* Of Cargoes, Colonies and Kings, 2001. *Recreations:* sailing, gliding. *Address:* Long Hall, North Street, Wareham, Dorset BH20 4AG. *T:* (01929) 551658. *E:* andrew@astuart.eclipse.co.uk. *Clubs:* Oxford and Cambridge, Royal Commonwealth Society, Alpine; Jesters; Royal Naval Sailing Association. *Died 27 Jan. 2014.*

STUART-BROWN, Her Honour Gillian Margaret; a Circuit Judge, 2006–09; *b* 11 Oct. 1947; *d* of Joseph Moss and Margaret Gladys Moss; *m* 1970, Malcolm Stuart-Brown. *Educ:* Newbury Girls Grammar Sch.; London Univ. (LLB 1969 ext.). Admitted Solicitor, 1974; private practice, Bath, 1974–84; Partner, Stuart-Brown Practice, Calne, 1984–90; a District Judge, 1990–2006. *Recreation:* ski-ing in the afternoon winter sunshine from Scheidegg to Brandegg for apple doughnuts. *Died 16 Nov. 2011.*

STUART-SMITH, James, CB 1986; QC 1988; Judge Advocate General, 1984–91 (Vice Judge Advocate General, 1979–84); a Recorder, 1985–91; *b* 13 Sept. 1919; *s* of James Stuart-Smith and Florence Emma (*née* Armfield); *m* 1957, Jean Marie Therese Young Groundsell (*d* 2012), *d* of Hubert Young Groundsell, Newport, IoW; one *s* one *d*. *Educ:* Brighton Coll.; London Hospital. Medical student, 1938. Served War of 1939–45: commnd KRRC, 1940; served ME and Italy, and staff appointments in UK; demobilised 1947. Called to Bar, Middle Temple, 1948; practised in London, 1948–55; Legal Asst, JAG's Office, 1955; Dep. Judge Advocate, 1957; Asst Judge Advocate General, 1968; Dep. Judge Advocate, Middle East Comd (Aden), 1964–65; Dep. Judge Advocate General, British Forces Germany, 1976–79. Hon. Pres., Internat. Soc. for Military Law and the Law of War, 1991– (Vice-Pres., 1979–85; Pres., 1985–91). *Publications:* contribs to Internat. Soc. for Military Law and Law of War Rev. and Law Qly Rev., on history and practice of British military law. *Recreations:* composing letters, inexpert carpentry. *Address:* 3 Marine Parade, Bognor Regis PO21 2LT. *T:* (01243) 842255. *Club:* Royal Air Force. *Died 15 May 2013.*

SUCKLING, Dr Charles Walter, CBE 1989; FRS 1978; FRSC; *b* 24 July 1920; *s* of Edward Ernest and Barbara Suckling (*née* Thomson); *m* 1946, (Eleanor) Margaret Watterson; two *s* one *d*. *Educ:* Oldershaw Grammar Sch., Wallasey; Liverpool Univ. (BSc, PhD). ICI: joined Gen. Chemicals Div., 1942; R&D Director, Mond Div., 1967; Dep. Chairman, Mond Div., 1969; Chairman, Paints Div., 1972; Gen. Man., Res. and Technol., 1977–82; Chm., Bradbury, Suckling and Partners, 1982–93; Dir, Albright and Wilson, 1982–89. Hon. Visiting Professor: Univ. of Stirling, 1968–93; UEA, 1977–83. Member: BBC Science Consultative Gp, 1980–85; Royal Commn on Environmental Pollution, 1982–92; Electricity Supply Res. Council, 1983–90; ABRC/NERC Gp into Geol Surveying, 1985–87; Cttee of Inquiry into Teaching of English Language, 1987–88; Nat. Curriculum English Working Gp, 1988–89; Nat. Curriculum Mod. For. Langs Wkg Gp, 1989–90; Council, RCA, 1981–90 (Treasurer, 1984–90); Chm., Roy. Soc. Study Gp on Pollution Control Priorities, 1988–92; Member: Nat. Adv. Gp on Eco-labelling, 1990–92; Adv. Cttee on Dangerous

Pathogens Microbiol Risk Assessment Wkg Gp, 1993–95. Bicentennial Lecture, Washington Coll., Maryland, 1981; Robbins Lecture, Stirling Univ., 1990; Joseph Clover Lecture, Royal Coll. of Anaesthetists, 1994. Senior Fellow, RCA, 1986. Hon. DSc Liverpool, 1980; DUniv Stirling, 1985. Liverpool Univ. Chem. Soc. Medal, 1964; John Scott Medal, City of Philadelphia, 1973; Medal, Royal Coll. of Anaesthetists, 1992. *Publications:* (with A. Baines and F. R. Bradbury) Research in the Chemical Industry, 1969; (with C. J. Suckling and K. E. Suckling) Chemistry through Models, 1978; papers on anaesthetics, industrial research and strategy in journals. *Recreations:* music, gardening, languages, writing. *Address:* 1 Desborough Drive, Tewin, Welwyn, Herts AL6 0HQ. *T:* (01438) 798250. *Died 31 Oct. 2013.*

SUFFIELD, 11th Baron *cr* 1786; **Anthony Philip Harbord-Hamond,** Bt 1745; MC 1950; Major, retired, 1961; *b* 19 June 1922; *o s* of 10th Baron and Nina Annette Mary Crawfuird (*d* 1955), *e d* of John Hutchison of Laurieston and Edingham, Stewartry of Kirkcudbright; *S* father, 1951; *m* 1952, Elizabeth Eve (*d* 1995), *er d* of late Judge Edgedale; three *s* one *d*. *Educ:* Eton. Commission, Coldstream Guards, 1942; served War of 1939–45, in North African and Italian campaigns, 1942–45; Malaya, 1948–50. One of HM Hon. Corps of Gentlemen-at-Arms, 1973–92 (Harbinger, 1990–92). *Recreation:* artist. *Heir: s* Hon. Charles Anthony Assheton Harbord-Hamond [*b* 3 Dec. 1953; *m* 1st, 1983, Lucy (marr. diss. 1990), *yr d* of Comdr A. S. Hutchinson; 2nd, 1999, Mrs Emma Louise Royds, *er d* of Sir Lawrence Williams, 9th Bt; two *d*. Commissioned Coldstream Guards, 1972, RARO 1979]. *Address:* Gardeners Cottage, Gunton Park, Hanworth, Norfolk NR11 7HL. *T:* (01263) 768423. *Club:* Pratt's. *Died 8 Dec. 2011.*

SUGDEN, John Goldthorp, MA; ARCM; Headmaster, Wellingborough School, 1965–73; *b* 22 July 1921; *s* of A. G. Sugden, Brighouse, Yorkshire; *m* 1954, Jane Machin; two *s*. *Educ:* Radley; Magdalene College, Cambridge. War Service, Royal Signals, 1941–46. Asst Master, Bilton Grange Prep. School, 1948–52; Asst Master, The King's School, Canterbury, 1952–59; Headmaster, Foster's School, Sherborne, 1959–64. *Publications:* Niccolo Paganini, 1980; Sir Arthur Bliss, 1997. *Recreations:* music, golf. *Address:* Woodlands, 2 Linksview Avenue, Parkstone, Poole, Dorset BH14 9QT. *T:* (01202) 707497. *Died 27 Dec. 2014.*

SULLIVAN, David Douglas Hooper; QC 1975; author and historian; *b* 10 April 1926; *s* of Michael and Maude Sullivan; *m* 1st, 1951, Sheila, *d* of Henry and Georgina Bathurst; three *d*; 2nd, 1981, Ann Munro, *d* of Malcolm and Eva Betten. *Educ:* Haileybury (schol.); Christ Church, Oxford (schol.). MA 1949, BCL 1951. Served War, with RNVR (Sub-Lieut), 1944–46. Called to Bar, Inner Temple, 1951, Bencher, 1984, retired 1988. Mem., Central Policy Cttee, Mental Health Act Commn, 1983–86. Chm., Burgh House Trust, 1978–95; compiler, resource collection of John Constable's pictures of Hampstead Heath, Burgh House Mus., 2013. Author of various plays and media programmes, including: radio: Shadows are Realities to me; A right-royal Burglary; Straw and Steel; stage: John Constable and Maria. *Publications:* The Westminster Corridor, 1994; The Westminster Circle 1086–1307, 2006. *Recreations:* painting, medieval history. *Address:* 18 Greenhill, Prince Arthur Road, NW3 5UB. *T:* (020) 7431 3433. *Died 9 July 2015.*

SULLIVAN, Prof. (Donovan) Michael; Professor of Oriental Art, 1966–85, Christensen Professor, 1975–85, Stanford University, California; Fellow, St Catherine's College, Oxford, 1979–90, then Emeritus Fellow; *b* 29 Oct. 1916; *s* of Alan Sullivan and Elisabeth Hees; *m* 1943, Khoan, *d* of Ngo Eng-lim, Kulangsu, Amoy, China; no *c*. *Educ:* Rugby School; Corpus Christi College, Cambridge (MA); Univ. of London (BA Hons); Harvard Univ. (PhD); LittD Cambridge, 1966; MA, DLitt Oxon, 1973. Chinese Govt Scholarship, Univ. of London, 1947–50; Rockefeller Foundn Travelling Fellowship in USA, 1950–51; Bollingen Foundn Research Fellowship, 1952–54; Curator of Art Museum and Lectr in the History of Art, Univ. of Malaya (later Univ. of Singapore), Singapore, 1954–60; Lectr in Asian Art, Sch. of Oriental and African Studies, Univ. of London, 1960–66. Vis. Prof. of Far Eastern Art, Univ. of Michigan (Spring Semester), 1964; Slade Prof. of Fine Art, Oxford Univ., 1973–74, Cambridge Univ., 1983–84; Guggenheim Foundn Fellowship, 1974; Vis. Fellow, St Antony's Coll., Oxford, 1976–77; Nat. Endowment for the Humanities Fellowship, 1976–77; Professorial Fellow, Corpus Christi Coll., Cambridge, 1983–84; Vis. Fellow, Humanities Centre, ANU, 1987; Fellow, Ashmolean Museum, 2006–. Mem., Amer. Acad. of Arts and Sciences, 1977. Hon. Fellow, Chinese Australian Arts and Culture Res. Centre, Sun Yat-sen (Zhongshan) Univ., 2007. Hon. DLitt Nottingham, 2005. *Publications:* Chinese Art in the Twentieth Century, 1959; An Introduction to Chinese Art, 1961; The Birth of Landscape Painting in China, 1962; Chinese Ceramics, Bronzes and Jades in the Collection of Sir Alan and Lady Barlow, 1963; Chinese and Japanese Art, 1965; A Short History of Chinese Art, 1967, 3rd edn as The Arts of China, 1973, 5th edn 2008; The Cave Temples of Maichishan, 1969; The Meeting of Eastern and Western Art, 1973, rev. and expanded edn 1989; Chinese Art: recent discoveries, 1973; The Three Perfections, 1975, 2nd edn 1999; Chinese Landscape Painting, vol. II, The Sui and T'ang Dynasties, 1979; Symbols of Eternity: the art of landscape painting in China, 1979; Studies in the Art of China and South-East Asia, vol. 1, 1991, vol. 2, 1992; Art and Artists of Twentieth Century China, 1996; A Biographical Dictionary of Modern Chinese Artists, 2006; The Night Entertainments of Han Xizai, 2008; contrib. to learned journals, Encyclopedia Britannica, Chambers's Encyclopædia, etc. *Address:* St Catherine's College, Oxford OX1 3UJ. *Club:* Athenæum. *Died 28 Sept. 2013.*

SULZBERGER, Arthur Ochs; Chairman and Chief Executive Officer, New York Times Co., 1992–97, then Chairman Emeritus; Publisher of The New York Times, 1963–92; *b* 5 Feb. 1926; *s* of late Arthur Hays Sulzberger; *m* 1st, 1948, Barbara Grant (marr. diss. 1956); one *s* one *d*; 2nd, 1956, Carol Fox Fuhrman (*d* 1995); one *d*, and one adopted *d*; 3rd, 1996, Allison Stacey Cowles (*d* 2010). *Educ:* Browning School, New York City; Loomis School, Windsor, Conn; Columbia University, NYC. Reporter, Milwaukee Journal, 1953–54; Foreign Correspondent, New York Times, 1954–55; Asst to the Publisher, New York Times, 1956–57; Asst Treasurer, New York Times, 1957–63. Chm. Emeritus, Metropolitan Mus. of Art; Trustee Emeritus, Columbia Univ. Hon. LLD: Dartmouth, 1964; Bard, 1967; Hon. LHD: Montclair State Coll.; Tufts Univ., 1984. *Recreation:* fishing. *Address:* 229 West 43rd Street, New York, NY 10036, USA. *T:* (212) 5561771. *Clubs:* Overseas Press, Explorers (New York); Metropolitan, Army and Navy (Washington, DC). *Died 29 Sept. 2012.*

SUMNER, Sir Christopher (John), Kt 1996; a Judge of the High Court of Justice, Family Division, 1996–2008; *b* 28 Aug. 1939; *s* of His Honour Donald Sumner, OBE, QC and late Muriel Sumner; *m* 1970, Carole Ashley Mann; one *s* two *d*. *Educ:* Charterhouse; Sidney Sussex Coll., Cambridge (MA). Called to the Bar, Inner Temple, 1961, Bencher, 1994; Asst Recorder, 1983; Recorder, 1986; a Circuit Judge, 1987–96. Mem., Judicial Studies Bd, 1991–96, 1999–2005 (Jt Dir of Studies, 1995–96). *Recreations:* reading, music, sports poorly performed. *Clubs:* Hurlingham; Burnham Overy Staithe Sailing. *Died 12 Aug. 2013.*

SUNLEY, John Bernard; Chairman, Sunley Holdings plc, since 1979; *b* 31 May 1936; *s* of late Bernard and Mary Sunley; *m* 1st, 1961, Patricia Taylor (marr. diss. 1975); three *s* one *d*; 2nd, 1978, Anne Crosby (marr. diss. 1989); 3rd, 1992, Fiona Bateman; one *s* one *d*. *Educ:* Elstree Sch.; Harrow Sch.; Columbia Univ. Nat. Service, RM, 1954–56. Trainee Accountant, Allan Charlesworth, Chartered Accountants, 1956–57; Trainee Surveyor, Weatherall Green and Smith, Chartered Surveyors, 1957–58; joined family business as jun. exec., 1960; Director: Bernard Sunley Investment Trust Co. Ltd, 1962–; Blackwood Hodge Ltd, 1962–; Chairman: Bernard Sunley and Sons Ltd, 1964– (Dir, 1962–90); Sunley Homes Ltd, 1964– (Dir, 1962–). Chm., Bernard Sunley Charitable Foundn, 1964–. High Sheriff, Kent, 1999. *Recreations:* golf, tennis, squash, thoroughbred horse racing, farming, ski-ing. *Address:*

Sunley Holdings, 20 Berkeley Square, W1J 6LH. *T:* (020) 7499 8842. *Clubs:* MCC, Royal Thames Yacht; Royal and Ancient Golf; Royal St George's Golf. *Died 14 Feb. 2011.*

SUPHAMONGKHON, Dr Konthi, Kt Grand Cordon of the White Elephant, Kt Grand Cordon, Order of the Crown of Thailand; Kt Grand Commander, Order of Chula Chom Klao; Hon. GCVO 1972; *b* 3 Aug. 1916; *m* 1951, Dootsdi Atthakravi; two *s* one *d*. *Educ:* Univ. of Moral and Political Sciences, Bangkok (LLB); Univ. of Paris (Dr-en-Droit). Joined Min. of Foreign Affairs, 1941; Second Sec., Tokyo, 1942–44; Chief of Pol Div., 1944–48; Dir-Gen., Western Affairs Dept, 1948–50; UN Affairs Dept, 1950–52; Minister to Australia, 1952–56, Ambassador, June 1956–59, and to New Zealand, Oct. 1956–59; Dir-Gen. of Internat. Organizations, 1959–63; Adviser on Foreign Affairs to the Prime Minister, 1962–64; Sec.-Gen., SEATO, 1964–65; Ambassador to Federal Republic of Germany, 1965–70, and to Finland, 1967–70; Ambassador to Court of St James's, 1970–76. Frequent Lecturer, 1944–; notably at Thammasat Univ., 1944–52, at National Defence Coll., 1960–62, and at Army War Coll., Bangkok, 1960–63. Member: Internat. Law Assoc.; IISS; RIIA. Foreign decorations, incl. Grosskreuz des Verdienstordens (Germany), 1970. *Publications:* Thailand and her relations with France, 1940 (in French); Account of a return journey from Marseilles to Singapore, 1965 (in French); Thai Foreign Policy, 1984 (in Thai). *Recreations:* tennis, golf, swimming. *Address:* Kanta Mansion, 73 Soi 26, Sukhumvit Road, Bangkok, Thailand; 60 Kensington Court, Kensington, W8 5DG. *Clubs:* Siam Society, Royal Sport of Bangkok, Royal Turf (Bangkok). *Died 27 Dec. 2011.*

SUTTON, Air Marshal Sir John (Matthias Dobson), KCB 1986 (CB 1981); *b* 9 July 1932; *s* of late Harry Rowston Sutton and Gertrude Sutton; *m* 1st, 1954, Cherry Woodward (marr. diss. 1968); one *s* one *d*; 2nd, 1969, Angela Faith Gray; one *s* (and one *s* decd). *Educ:* Queen Elizabeth's Grammar Sch., Alford, Lincs. Joined RAF, 1950; pilot trng, commnd, 1951; served on Fighter Sqdns, UK and Germany; Staff Coll., 1963; OC 249 Sqdn, 1964–66; Asst Sec., Chiefs of Staff Cttee, 1966–69; OC 14 Sqdn, 1970–71; Asst Chief of Staff (Policy and Plans), HQ 2 ATAF, 1971–73; Staff, Chief of Def. Staff, 1973–74; RCDS, 1975; Comdt Central Flying Sch., 1976–77; Asst Chief of Air Staff (Policy), 1977–79; Dep. Comdr, RAF Germany, 1980–82; ACDS (Commitments), 1982–84; ACDS (Overseas), 1985; C-in-C, RAF Support Comd, 1986–89; Lt-Gov. and C-in-C, Jersey, 1990–95. Pres., RAFA, 2002–05. Chm., Bd of Governors, UC Northampton (formerly Nene Coll.), 1996–2000. KStJ 1990. *Recreations:* golf, gardening. *Address:* Garden House, Stretton, Rutland LE15 7QZ. *Clubs:* Royal Air Force; Colonels; Greetham Valley Golf; Luffenham Heath Golf. *Died 21 Nov. 2014.*

SUTTON, Rt Rev. Peter (Eves), CBE 1990; Bishop of Nelson, New Zealand, 1965–90; Senior Anglican Bishop, 1979–90; Acting Primate, New Zealand, 1985–86; *b* Wellington, NZ, 7 June 1923; *m* 1956, Pamela Cherrington, *e d* of R. A. Dalley, Patin House, Kidderminster; one *s* one *d*. *Educ:* Wellesley Coll.; Nelson Coll.; University of New Zealand. BA 1945; MA 1947; LTh 1948. Deacon, 1947; Priest, 1948 (Wellington); Curate of Wanganui, New Zealand, 1947–50; St John the Evangelist, Bethnal Green, 1950–51; Bishops Hatfield, Diocese of St Albans (England), 1951–52; Vicar of St Cuthbert's, Berhampore (NZ), 1952–58; Whangarei, Diocese of Auckland, New Zealand, 1958–64; Archdeacon of Waimate, 1962–64; Dean of Dunedin and Vicar of St Paul's Cathedral, Dunedin, 1964–65. Mem. Bd, 1965–93, Chm., 1977–90, Cawthron Inst. Founding Mem., Nelson Civic Trust; Founder: Protect our Heritage, Nelson; Friends of Nelson City; Life Mem., Founder's Mus., Nelson; Rep., Nelson Provincial Mus. Cttee, 1989–95; Patrons' Rep., Suter Art Gall. Bd, 1990–93; NZ Co-ordinator, All Religions, Amnesty Internat., 1989–2003; NZ Rep., St Deiniol's Library, Hawarden, 1988–90; Trustee, Nelson Civic Heritage Protection, 1995–2003. Governor, St John's Coll., Auckland, 1965–90. ChStJ 1986; Sub-Prelate, Order of St John, NZ, 1987–. Silver Jubilee Medal, 1977; NZ Commemoration Medal, 1990. *Publications:* Freedom for Convictions, 1971. *Recreation:* golf (Canterbury Univ. Blue). *Address:* 3 Ngatiawa Street, Nelson, New Zealand. *Died 23 March 2013.*

SUTTON, Dr Peter Morgan; Director, Public Health Laboratory Service Centre for Applied Microbiology and Research, Porton Down, 1979–92; *b* 21 June 1932; *s* of Sir Graham Sutton, CBE, FRS and late Lady Sutton (*née* Doris Morgan); *m* 1959, Helen Ersy Economides; two *s* two *d*. *Educ:* Bishop Wordsworth Sch., Salisbury; Wrekin Coll., Wellington; University Coll. (Fellow, 1985) and University Coll. Hosp. Med. Sch., London. House Surgeon and House Physician, UCH, 1956–57; Graham Scholar in Pathology, Univ. of London, 1958–59; on academic staff of UCH Med. Sch., 1960–65; Vis. Asst Prof. of Pathology, Univ. of Pittsburg, USA, 1966–67; Hon. Consultant Pathologist, UCH, 1967–79; Reader in Pathology, Univ. of London, 1971–79; Vice-Dean, UCH Med. Sch., 1973–78. Vis. Prof., Dept of Biochemical Pathology, UCL, 1983–. Sometime Examr in Pathology, Univ. of London and RCS. *Publications:* The Nature of Cancer, 1962; various papers on fibrinolytic enzymes and novel antiviral compounds. *Recreations:* English literature, history of science. *Address:* Manderley, 34 Bower Gardens, Salisbury, Wilts SP1 2RL. *T:* (01722) 323902. *Died 10 Feb. 2014.*

SUYIN; *see* Han Suyin.

SWAFFIELD, Sir James (Chesebrough), Kt 1976; CBE 1971; RD 1967; Chairman, British Rail Property Board, 1984–91; solicitor; *b* 16 Feb. 1924; *s* of Frederick and Kate Elizabeth Swaffield, Cheltenham; *m* 1950, Elizabeth Margaret Ellen, 2nd *d* of A. V. and K. E. Maunder, Belfast; two *s* two *d*. *Educ:* Cheltenham Grammar Sch.; Haberdashers' Aske's Hampstead Sch.; London Univ. (LLB); MA Oxon 1974. RNVR, 1942–46. Articled Town Clerk, Lincoln, 1946–49; Asst Solicitor: Norwich Corp., 1949–52; Cheltenham Corp., 1952–53; Southend-on-Sea Corp., 1953–56; Dep. Town Clerk, subseq. Town Clerk and Clerk of Peace, Blackpool, 1956–62; Sec., Assoc. of Municipal Corps, 1962–73; Dir-Gen. and Clerk to GLC, Clerk to ILEA and Clerk of Lieutenancy for Greater London, 1973–84. Chm., London Marathon Charitable Trust, 1980–2006; Vice-Pres., Maritime Volunteer Service; Trustee, Jubilee Walkway Trust. Lt Comdr RNR retd. DL Greater London, 1978–99. OStJ. Dist. Service Award (Internat. City Management Assoc.), 1984. *Address:* 2 Andrew Court, 68 Wickham Road, Beckenham, Kent BR3 6RG. *Club:* Naval. *Died 4 July 2015.*

SWAINE, Sir John (Joseph), Kt 1995; CBE 1987 (OBE 1980); QC (Hong Kong) 1975; JP; President, Legislative Council, Hong Kong, 1993–95; *b* 22 April 1932; *s* of Henry Edward Swaine, MBE and Gladys Elizabeth Luke Swaine; *m* 1959, Fatima Gwendoline Jorge Cotton; four *s* one *d*. *Educ:* Univ. of Hong Kong (BA). Admin. Officer, Hong Kong Govt, 1952–57; called to the Bar, Lincoln's Inn, 1960, Hong Kong, 1960; in practice, 1960–. Non-exec. Dir, Hong Kong & Shanghai Banking Corp. Ltd, 1986–97. JP Hong Kong, 1975. Hon. LLD: Baptist, HK, 1992; City, HK, 1993; Hon. PhD (Hum) Lingnan Coll., HK, 1994; Hon. DLitt Open, HK, 1996. *Recreation:* breeding and racing thoroughbred horses. *Clubs:* Hong Kong Jockey (Chm., 1993–96), Country (Hong Kong). *Died 7 Aug. 2012.*

SWAINSON, Eric, CBE 1981; Vice-Chairman, Fairey Group, 1987–97; Director, Lloyds TSB Group plc, 1996–97; *b* 5 Dec. 1926; *m* 1953, Betty Heywood; two *d*. *Educ:* Sheffield Univ. (BMet 1st cl. Hons; W. H. A. Robertson medal, 1959). Joined Imperial Chemical Industries Metals Div. (later IMI), 1946; Technical Officer, Res. Dept, 1946–53; Manager, Titanium Melting Plant, 1953–56; Asst Manager, Technical Dept, 1956–59; Gen. Manager and Man. Dir, Lightning Fasteners, 1961–69; Dir, IMI, 1969–86; Asst Man. Dir, 1972–74; Man. Dir, 1974–86; Dep. Chm., Pegler-Hattersley plc, 1986; Lloyds Bank plc: Dir, 1986–95; Vice-Chm., 1992–95. Director: Birmingham Broadcasting, 1973–92; AMEC, 1987–95; Midlands Radio Hldgs, 1988–92; Lloyds Merchant Bank Hldgs, 1989–93; Cheltenham & Gloucester Bldg Soc., 1995–97; Chm., Birmingham and West Midlands Reg. Bd, Lloyds Bank, 1985–91 (Reg. Dir, 1979–91). Chm., W Midlands Industrial Develt Bd, 1985–90; Member: Review

Bd for Govt Contracts, 1978–93; NEDC Cttee on Finance for Industry, 1978–86; Council, CBI, 1975–86; W Midlands Reg. Council, CBI, 1973–83 (Chm. 1976–78); Industrial Develt Adv. Bd, 1982–88. Pro-Chancellor, Aston Univ., 1981–86. FRSA 1985. Hon. DSc Aston, 1986. *Address:* Paddox Hollow, Norton Lindsey, Warwick CV35 8JA. *Died 15 Dec. 2014.*

SWALLOW, Comdt Patricia; *see* Nichol, Comdt D. P.

SWALLOW, Sydney; Senior Director, Procurement, Post Office, 1977–81; Chief Procurement Officer, British Telecommunications, 1981–83; *b* 29 June 1919; *s* of William and Charlotte Lucy Swallow; *m* 1950, Monica Williams (*d* 2007); one *s*. *Educ:* Woking County Sch.; St Catharine's Coll., Cambridge (Scholar; BA 1st cl. Hons 1940, MA). Mines Dept, Board of Trade, 1940–42. Served War: Royal Engineers (Survey), 1942–46. Nat. Coal Bd, 1946–59; Central Electricity Generating Bd, 1959–65; Associated Electrical Industries Ltd, 1965–68; General Electric Co. Ltd, 1968; Dir of Supplies, GLC, 1968–77. Chm., Educn Cttee, Inst. of Purchasing and Supply, 1967–77; Visiting Prof., Univ. of Bradford Management Centre, 1972–75; Vis. Fellow, ASC, 1976–80. FCIPS. *Publications:* various articles on purchasing and supply in professional jls. *Recreation:* watching cricket. *Address:* 17 Garricks House, Wadbrook Street, Charter Quay, Kingston upon Thames, Surrey KT1 1HS. *T:* (020) 8541 3407. *Died 28 June 2012.*

SWARBRICK, William Alfred; DL; CEng; Chief Executive, Cumbria County Council, 1997–2000; *b* 30 Sept. 1940; *s* of William and Agnes Swarbrick; *m* 1963, Catherine Lamey; one *s* one *d*. *Educ:* Manchester Grammar Sch.; Manchester Univ. (BSc Tech.). CEng, MICE 1968; Dip. in Traffic Engrg, IMunE, 1971; FCIHT (FIHT 1991). Cumberland CC, later Cumbria CC, 1963–2000; Gen. Manager, County Contracting, 1987–92; Dir, Cumbria Contract Services, 1992–97. Chm., PAC Ltd, 2000–. Chairman: Victim Support Cumbria, 2001–08 (Mem., Nat. Council); Carlisle RFC, 2000–. Pres., Cumbria Youth Orch., 2004–08. MCMI (MIMgt 1987). DL Cumbria, 2006. *Recreations:* cooking, gardening, viola and timpani playing. *Address:* 5 St Aidan's Road, Carlisle CA1 1LT. *Died 7 Oct. 2011.*

SWEETNAM, Sir (David) Rodney, KCVO 1992; CBE 1990; MA; FRCS; FRCP; Orthopaedic Surgeon to the Queen, 1982–92; President: Royal College of Surgeons of England, 1995–98 (Vice-President, 1992–94); Royal Medical Benevolent Fund, 1998–2002; *b* 5 Feb. 1927; second *s* of late Dr William Sweetnam and Irene (*née* Black); *m* 1959, Patricia Ann, *er d* of late A. Staveley Gough, OBE, FRCS; one *s* one *d*. *Educ:* Clayesmore; Peterhouse, Cambridge (Titular Scholar; BA 1947, MA 1951; Hon. Fellow, 2003); Middlesex Hosp. Med. Sch. (MB, BChir 1950). FRCS 1955; FRCP 2013. Surg. Lieut RNVR, 1950–52. Jun. appts, Middx Hosp., London Hosp. and Royal National Orthopaedic Hosp.; Consultant Surgeon to: The Middlesex Hospital, 1960–92; King Edward VII Hospital for Officers, London, 1964–97; UCH, 1990–92. Hon. Civil Consultant in Orth. Surgery to the Army, 1974–92; Hon. Consultant Orthopaedic Surgeon, Royal Hosp., Chelsea, 1974–92. Consultant Advisor in Orth. Surgery to DHSS, 1981–90; Hon. Consultant Surgeon, Royal Nat. Orthopaedic Hosp., 1983–92. Dir, Medical Sickness Annuity and Life Assce Soc. Ltd, 1982–97; Dir and Vice-Chm., Permanent Insurance Co., 1989–95. Chairman: DHSS Adv. Gp on Orthopaedic Implants, 1973–81; MRC's Working Party on Bone Sarcoma, 1980–85. Royal College of Surgeons: Mem. Council, 1985–98; Jacksonian Prize, 1966; Hunterian Prof., 1967; Gordon Taylor Meml Lectr, 1982; Stanford Cade Meml Lectr, 1986; Bradshaw Lectr, 1992; Robert Jones Lectr, 1993. President: Combined Services Orthopaedic Soc., 1983–86; British Orthopaedic Assoc., 1984–85 (Hon. Fellow, 1998). Trustee: Frances and Augustus Newman Foundn, 1989– (Chm., 2000–); Hunterian Collection, 1998– (Chm., 2005–08). Fellow, UCL, 1993. Chm., British Editorial Soc. of Bone and Joint Surgery, 1992–95 (Sec. and Treas., 1975–92). Hon. FRCSGlas 1997; Hon. FRCSI 1997; Hon. FCSSA 1998; Hon. FACS 1998; Hon. FDS RCS 1998; Hon. FRCSE 1999. *Publications:* (jtly) Essentials of Orthopaedics, 1965; (ed jtly) The Basis and Practice of Orthopaedics, 1980; contrib. med. books and jls in field of gen. orth. surgery, trauma and bone tumours. *Recreation:* gardening. *Address:* 25 Woodlands Road, Bushey, Herts WD23 2LS. *T:* (01923) 223161. *Died 17 May 2013.*

SWIFT, Lionel; QC 1975; JD; a Recorder of the Crown Court, and Deputy High Court Judge, 1979–96; *b* Bristol, 3 Oct. 1931; *s* of late Harris and Bessie Swift, Hampstead; *m* 1966, Elizabeth (*née* Herzig) (Liz E, London fashion writer); one *d*. *Educ:* Whittingehame Coll., Brighton; University Coll., London (LLB 1951); Brasenose Coll., Oxford (BCL 1959); Univ. of Chicago (Juris Doc, 1960). Solicitor, Natal, S Africa, 1954; called to the Bar, Inner Temple, 1959, Bencher, 1984; in practice as barrister, 1961–2006. British Commonwealth Fellow, Univ. of Chicago Law Sch., 1960; Amer. Social Science Res. Council Grant for work on admin of criminal justice, 1960. Jun. Counsel to Treasury in Probate Matters, 1974. Chm., Inst. of Laryngology and Otology, 1985–86. *Publications:* The South African Law of Criminal Procedure (Gen. Editor, A. B. Harcourt, QC), 1957. *Address:* c/o 4 Paper Buildings, Temple, EC4Y 7EX. *Died 24 March 2011.*

SWINDELLS, Maj.-Gen. (George) Michael (Geoffrey), CB 1985; Controller, Army Benevolent Fund, 1987–97; *b* 15 Jan. 1930; *s* of late George Martyn Swindells and Marjorie Swindells; *m* 1955, Prudence Bridget Barbara Tully; two *d* (and one *s* decd). *Educ:* Rugby School. Nat. Service Commission, 5th Royal Inniskilling Dragoon Guards, 1949; served in Germany, Korea and Canal Zone; Adjutant, Cheshire Yeomanry, 1955–56; Staff Coll., 1960; transfer to 9th/12th Royal Lancers, to command, 1969–71; Comdr 11th Armd Brigade, 1975–76; RCDS course, 1977; Dir of Op. Requirements (3), MoD, 1978–79; Chief of Jt Services Liaison Organisation, Bonn, 1980–83; Dir of Management and Support of Intelligence, 1983–85. Col, 9th/12th Royal Lancers, 1990–95. Chairman: Royal Soldiers' Daughters Sch., 1985–89; BLESMA, 1991–96; Pres., British Korean Veterans Assoc., 2006–15. Mem. Council, Wilts Wildlife Trust, 1998–2004; Trustee, Royal Soc. for Asian Affairs, 1999–2005. *Recreations:* country life, gardening. *Club:* Oriental. *Died 13 Oct. 2015.*

SYKES, Eric, CBE 2005 (OBE 1986); actor, writer, director, producer; *b* 4 May 1923; *s* of Vernon and Harriet Sykes; *m* 1952, Edith Eleanore Milbrandt; one *s* three *d*. Wireless Operator, Mobile Signals Unit, RAF, 1941–49. *Films* include: actor: Orders are Orders; Watch Your Stern; Very Important Person; Heavens Above; Shalako; Those Magnificent Men in their Flying Machines, 1964; Monte Carlo or Bust!, 1969; The Boys in Blue, 1982; Absolute Beginners, 1986; The Others, 2001; Harry Potter and the Goblet of Fire, 2005; Son of Rambow, 2008; *radio* includes: writer: Educating Archie; Variety Bandbox; *television* includes: actor: Sykes and A…, 1960–80 (also writer); Charley's Aunt, 1977; If You Go Down to the Woods Today (also prod. and dir), 1980; The 19th Hole, 1989; *silent films:* (actor, writer and dir): The Plank, 1980 (Press Award, Montreux Fest.); Mr H is Late; It's Your Move, 1984; The Big Freeze; Rhubarb, Rhubarb; *theatre* includes: actor: Big Bad Mouse, tour of Australia, 1977–78; A Hatful of Sykes, tour of Australia, Canada, Rhodesia, UK, 1977–78; Run For Your Wife, Shaftesbury, Criterion, and tour of Canada; The 19th Hole, nat. tour, 1992; Two of a Kind, nat. tour, 1995; Fools Rush In, nat. tour, 1996; The School for Wives, Kafka's Dick, 1998, Piccadilly; Charley's Aunt, nat. tour, 2001; Caught in the Net, Vaudeville, 2001; The Three Sisters, Playhouse, 2003; As You Like It, Th. Royal, Bath, 2003. Freeman, City of London, 1988. Hon. Fellow, Univ. of Lancashire, 1999. Lifetime Achievement Award, Writers' Guild, 1992. *Publications:* Sykes of Sebastopol Terrace, 1981, 2nd edn 2000; The Great Crime of Grapplemick (novel), 1985; UFOs are coming Wednesday, 1995; Smelling of Roses, 1997; Eric Sykes' Comedy Heroes, 2003; If I Don't Write It, Nobody Else Will, 2005. *Address:* c/o Eric Sykes Ltd, 9 Orme Court, W2 4RL. *T:* (020) 7727 1544. *Club:* Royal and Ancient Golf. *Died 4 July 2012.*

SYKES, Rt Rev. Prof. Stephen Whitefield; Principal, St John's College, and Professor of Theology, University of Durham, 1999–2006; an Honorary Assistant Bishop, Diocese of Durham, since 1999; *b* 1 Aug. 1939; *m* 1962, Marianne Joy Hinton (*d* 2014); one *s* two *d*. *Educ:* St John's Coll., Cambridge (BA 1961; MA 1964; Hon. Fellow, 2009). Univ. Asst Lectr in Divinity, Cambridge Univ., 1964–68, Lectr, 1968–74; Fellow and Dean, St John's Coll., Cambridge, 1964–74; Van Mildert Canon Prof. of Divinity, Durham Univ., 1974–85; Regius Prof. of Divinity, and Fellow, St John's College, Cambridge, 1985–90; Bishop of Ely, 1990–99. Mem., Archbishop's Cttee on Religious Educn, 1967. Chairman: Doctrine Commn of C of E, 1997–2005; Inter Anglican Theol and Doctrinal Commn, 1999–. Hon. Canon of Ely Cathedral, 1985–90. Examining Chaplain to Bishop of Chelmsford, 1970–75. Edward Cadbury Lectr, Univ. of Birmingham, 1978; Hensley Henson Lectr, Univ. of Oxford, 1982–83. Chm., North of England Inst. for Christian Educn, 1980–85. Pres., Council of St John's Coll., Durham, 1984–94. *Publications:* Friedrich Schleiermacher, 1971; Christian Theology Today, 1971; (ed) Christ, Faith and History, 1972; The Integrity of Anglicanism, 1978; (ed) Karl Barth: studies in his theological method, 1980; (ed) New Studies in Theology, 1980; (ed) England and Germany, Studies in Theological Diplomacy, 1982; The Identity of Christianity, 1984; (ed) Authority in the Anglican Communion, 1987; (ed) The Study of Anglicanism, 1988; (ed) Karl Barth: Centenary Essays, 1989; (ed) Sacrifice and Redemption, 1991; Unashamed Anglicanism, 1995; The Story of Atonement, 1997; Power and Christian Theology, 2006. *Recreations:* walking (especially relearning how to walk), retirement cookery. *Address:* Ingleside, Whinney Hill, Durham DH1 3BE. *T:* (0191) 384 6465. *Died 24 Sept. 2014.*

SYMONDS, Jane Ursula; *see* Kellock, J. U.

SYNGE, Sir Robert Carson, 8th Bt *cr* 1801; Manager and Owner, Bob's Furniture Store, Langley, BC; *b* 4 May 1922; *s* of late Neale Hutchinson Synge (2nd *s* of 6th Bt) and Edith Elizabeth Thurlow (*d* 1933), Great Parndon, Essex; *S* uncle, 1942; *m* 1944, Dorothy Jean Johnson, *d* of T. Johnson, Cloverdale; two *d*. *Heir: cousin* Allen James Edward Synge, *b* 15 Jan. 1942. *Died 17 Aug. 2011.*

SYNNOTT, Sir Hilary (Nicholas Hugh), KCMG 2002 (CMG 1997); HM Diplomatic Service, retired; Consulting Fellow, International Institute of Strategic Studies, since 2004; *b* 20 March 1945; *s* of late Commander Jasper Nicholas Netterville Synnott, DSC, RN and Florence England Synnott (*née* Hillary); *m* 1973, Anne Penelope Clarke; one *s* decd. *Educ:* Beaumont College; Dartmouth Naval College (scholar); Peterhouse, Cambridge (MA; Hon. Fellow, 2011); RN Engineering College. CEng; MIEE. RN 1962–73 (HM Submarines, 1968–73). Joined HM Diplomatic Service, FCO, 1973; UK Delegn to OECD, Paris, 1975; Bonn, 1978; FCO, 1981; Head of Chancery, Amman, 1985; Head of Western European Dept, FCO, 1989; Head of Security Co-ordination Dept, FCO, 1991; Minister and Dep. High Comr, New Delhi, 1993–96; Dir (S and SE Asia), FCO, 1996–98; Vis. Fellow, Inst. of Developing Studies, Univ. of Sussex, and IISS, 1999–2000; High Comr to Pakistan, 2000–03; Coalition Provisional Administrator, Southern Iraq, 2003–04. Mem., Atlantic Council Wkg Gp on Pakistan, 2008–09. Patron, Asian Studies Gp, Islamabad, 2001–03; Trustee, Impact Foundn, 2004–07. Chm., Peterhouse Soc., 2007–10. Eric Lane Fellow, Clare Coll., Cambridge, 2007. *Publications:* The Causes and Consequences of South Asia's Nuclear Tests, 1999; State Building in Southern Iraq, 2005; Bad Days in Basra: my turbulent time as Britain's man in southern Iraq, 2008; Transforming Pakistan: ways out of instability, 2009. *Address:* Long Barrow, Barrow Hill, Goodworth Clatford, Hants SP11 7SE. *Club:* Oxford and Cambridge. *Died 8 Sept. 2011.*

SZYMBORSKA, Wisława; Polish poet, translator, literary critic; *b* 2 July 1923; *d* of Wincenty Szymborski and Anna Rottermund; *m* 1948, Adam Włodek (marr. diss. 1954; he *d* 1986). *Educ:* Jagiellonian Univ., Cracow. Editorial Staff, Zycie Literackie, 1953–67. Mem., 1952–83, Mem. Gen. Bd, 1978–83, Polish Writers' Assoc. Nobel Prize for Literature, 1996. Gold Cross of Merit (Poland), 1955; Kt Cross, Order of Polonia Restituta (Poland), 1974; Order of the White Eagle (Poland), 2011. *Publications:* Dlatego żyjemy, 1952; Pytania zadawanie sobie, 1954; Wołanie do Yeti, 1957; Sól, 1962; Wiersze wybrane, 1964; Poezje wybrane, 1967; Sto pociech, 1967; Poezje, 1970; Wszelki wypadek, 1972; Wybór wierszy, 1973; Tarsjusz i inne wiersze, 1976; Wielka liczba, 1976; Poezje wybrane II, 1983; Ludzie na moście, 1986; People on a Bridge, 1990; Koniec i początek, 1993; View with a Grain of Sand, 1995; Widok z ziarnkiem piasku, 1996; Poems New and Collected 1957–1997, 1998; Wiersze wybrane, 2000; Chwila, 2002; Rymowanki dla duzych dzieci, 2003; Dwukropek, 2005; Tutaj, 2009. *Address:* (office) ul. Kanonicza 7, 31–002 Kraków, Poland. *Fax:* (12) 4224773. *Died 1 Feb. 2012.*

T

TABONE, Dr Vincent, (Censu), FRCSE; President of Malta, 1989–94; *b* 30 March 1913; *s* of Elisa Calleja and Nicolo Tabone; *m* 1941, Maria Wirth; three *s* five *d* (and one *s* decd). *Educ:* St Aloysius Coll.; Univ. of Malta. Dip. Ophth. Oxford 1946; FRCSE 1948; Dip. RCP; Dip. RCS; Dip. in Med. Jurisp., Soc. of Apothecaries of London, 1963. Surgeon Captain, Royal Malta Artillery (campaign medals), 1939–45 War. WHO Consultant on Trachoma in Taiwan, Indonesia, Iraq; Dep., Internat. Panel of Trachoma Experts, WHO, 1956; Lectr in Clinical Ophthalmology, Dept of Surgery, Univ. of Malta, 1960. MP, 1966–89; Minister of Labour, Employment and Welfare, 1966–71; Minister of Foreign Affairs, 1987–89. Mem., Council of Europe Cttees; Chm., Council of Ministers, 1988. Founded Medical Officers Union of Malta, 1954. Vis. Prof., Univ. of Malta, 1995–. Hon. LLD Univ. of Malta, 1989. Awarded UN Testimonial for service to UN Programme on Aging, 1989. *Recreations:* reading, watch repairing, travel. *Address:* 33 Carmel Street, St Julian's, Malta. *Clubs:* Casino Maltese (1852), Sliema Band. *Died 14 March 2012.*

TAIT, Andrew Wilson, OBE 1967; Deputy Chairman, Barratt plc, 1991–96 (Director, 1988–96); Chairman, National House-Building Council, 1984–87 (Director-General, 1964–84); *b* 25 Sept. 1922; *s* of late Dr Adam and Jenny Tait; *m* 1954, Elizabeth Isobel Maclennan; three *d*. *Educ:* George Watson's Coll., Edinburgh; Edinburgh Univ. (MA 1st Class Hons History). Served Army, 1942–45. Leader writer, The Scotsman, 1947–48; Scottish Office, 1948–64. Chairman: Housing Res. Foundn, 1969–85; Internat. Housing and Home Warranty Assoc., 1984–87; Jt Land Requirements Cttee, 1981–87; Home Buyers Adv. Service, 1985–; Bridging the Gap, 1986–; New Homes Mktg Bd, 1988–89; Johnson Fry Property, 1988–95; New Homes Envmtl Gp, 1988–91; Cost Reduction Partnership, 1995–2000. Mem., Lloyd's, 1985–98. *Recreations:* golf, tennis, chess. *Address:* Orchard Croft, Grimmshill, Great Missenden, Bucks HP16 9BA. *T:* (01494) 862061. *Club:* Caledonian. *Died 13 March 2011.*

TAIT, Prof. James Francis, PhD; FRS 1959; biophysicist and endocrinologist; engaged in making photographic guide to North Yorkshire and writing scientific history; Emeritus Professor, University of London, since 1982; *b* 1 Dec. 1925; *s* of Herbert Tait and Constance Levinia Brotherton; *m* 1956, Sylvia Agnes Simpson (*née* Wardropper), FRS (*d* 2003). *Educ:* Darlington Queen Elizabeth Grammar Sch.; Leeds Univ. (BSc 1st Cl. Hons Physics; PhD). Lectr in Medical Physics, Middlesex Hospital Medical School, 1948–55; External Scientific Staff, Medical Research Council, Middlesex Hospital Medical School, 1955–58; Senior Scientist, Worcester Foundation for Experimental Biology, USA, 1958–70; Joel Prof. of Physics as Applied to Medicine, Univ. of London, 1970–82; Co-Dir, Biophysical Endocrinology Unit, Physics Dept, Middlesex Hosp. Med. Sch., 1970–85. (With S. A. S. Tait) discovered electrocortin, later renamed aldosterone, 1947–53; (with T. Reichstein, S. A. S. Tait and Ciba Gp) isolated and arrived at structure of aldosterone, 1953–54. (With S. A. S. Tait) R. Douglas Wright Lectr and Medallion, Univ. of Melbourne, 1989. Hon. DSc Hull, 1979. Society for Endocrinology: Medal, 1969 and Sir Henry Dale Medal, 1979; Tadeus Reichstein Award, Internat. Soc. of Endocrinology, 1976; CIBA Award, Amer. Heart Assoc. for Hypertension Research, 1977. *Publications:* papers on medical physics, biophysics and endocrinology. *Recreations:* photography, touring in Yorkshire. *Address:* Granby Court, Granby Road, Harrogate, N Yorkshire HG1 4SR. *T:* (01423) 563627. *E:* jftait@globalnet.co.uk. *Died 2 Feb. 2014.*

TALBOT, Commandant Mary (Irene), CB 1975; Director, Women's Royal Naval Service, 1973–76; *b* 17 Feb. 1922. *Educ:* Bristol Univ. (BA Hons Philosophy and Economics). Joined WRNS as a Naval recruiting asst, Nov. 1943; Officer training course, 1944, and apptd to HMS Eaglet, in Liverpool, as an Educn and Resettlement Officer; served on staffs of C-in-Cs: Mediterranean; the Nore; Portsmouth, 1945–61; First Officer, and apptd to staff of Dir Naval Educn Service, 1952; subseq. served HMS Condor, Dauntless and Raleigh; Chief Officer, and apptd Sen. WRNS Officer, the Nore, 1960; on staff of Dir Naval Manning, 1963–66, and then became Asst Dir, WRNS; Superintendent, and served on staff of C-in-C Naval Home Command, 1969; Supt in charge, WRNS training estabt, HMS Dauntless, near Reading, 1972–73. Hon. ADC, 1973–76. Hon. LLD Bristol, 1993. *Recreations:* bridge, gardening, racing. *Address:* Sonning Cottage, Pound Lane, Sonning-on-Thames RG4 6XE. *T:* (0118) 969 4309. *Died 11 May 2012.*

TALBOYS, Rt Hon. Sir Brian (Edward), Hon. AC 1982; CH 1981; KCB 1991; PC 1977; *b* Wanganui, 7 June 1921; *s* of Francis Powell Talboys and Katherine Janet (*née* Balfour); *m* 1950, Patricia Floyd Adamson, *d* of Adam Laurence Adamson and Alice Floyd Harrington; two *s*. *Educ:* Wanganui Collegiate Sch.; Univ. of Manitoba; Victoria Univ., Wellington (BA). Served war of 1939–45, RNZAF. MP for Wallace, NZ, 1957–81; Dep. Leader, National Party, 1974–81; Parly Under-Sec. to Minister of Trade and Industry, 1960; Minister of Agriculture, 1962–69; Minister of Science, 1964–72; Minister of Education, 1969–72; Minister of Overseas Trade and Trade and Industry, 1972; Minister of Nat. Develt, 1975–77; Dep. Prime Minister and Minister of For. Affairs and Overseas Trade, 1975–81. Leader of a number of NZ delegns to overseas confs; NZ Rep., Standing Cttee of Pacific Economic Co-operation Conf., 1983–90. Grand Cross 1st Class, Order of Merit, Fed. Republic of Germany, 1978. Hon. DSc Massey Univ., 1981; Hon. DLitt Chung-Ang Univ., Seoul, 1981. *Address:* Winton, New Zealand. *Died 3 June 2012.*

TALLBOYS, Richard Gilbert, CMG 1981; OBE 1974; FCA; FCIS; FCPA; speaker on international affairs, since 1996; *b* 25 April 1931; *s* of late Harry Tallboys; *m* 1954, Margaret Evelyn, *d* of late Brig. H. W. Strutt, DSO, ED, Hobart; two *s* two *d*. *Educ:* Palmer's Sch.; LLB (London); BCom (Tasmania). Merchant Navy apprentice, 1947–51; Third/Second Mate, Australian coast, 1952–55; Lt-Comdr, RANR (ASM (FESR) 1945–75, AASM (Malaysia)), retd 1991. Accounting profession in Australia, 1955–62; Australian Govt Trade Commissioner, Johannesburg, Singapore, Jakarta, 1962–68. HM Diplomatic Service, 1968–88: First Secretary i/c Brasilia, 1969; Head of Chancery, Phnom Penh, 1972 (Chargé d'Affaires *ai* 1972, 1973); FO, 1973; Counsellor Commercial, Seoul, 1976–80 (Chargé d'Affaires *ai* 1977, 1978, 1979); Consul-General, Houston, 1980–85; Ambassador to Vietnam, 1985–87; Chief Exec., World Coal Inst., London, 1988–93. Mem., Internat. Trade Cttee, and Mem. Council, London Chamber of Commerce and Industry, 1990–93, 1995–98. Mem. Council, RIIA, 1995–2001. Alderman, Hobart City Council, 1958–62; Councillor (C), City of Westminster, 1998–2002. Freeman: City of London, 1985; Chartered Secretaries and Administrators' Co., 1999–. FRAS 2001. *Publications:* (ed) Developing Vietnam, 1995; (jtly) 50 Years of Business in Indonesia 1945–1995, 1995; (contrib.) Travellers' Tales & More Travellers' Tales, 2005; Encounters of a Diplomatic Kind, 2009. *Recreations:* travel, cautious adventuring, formerly sailing. *Address:* PO Box 1060, Sandy Bay, Tas 7006, Australia. *Clubs:* Tasmanian, Royal Yacht of Tasmania (Hobart), Derwent Sailing Squadron. *Died 2 Nov. 2013.*

TAMBLIN, Air Cdre Pamela Joy, CB 1980; Director, Women's Royal Air Force, 1976–80; *b* 11 Jan. 1926; *d* of late Albert Laing and Olga Victoria Laing; *m* 1970, Douglas Victor Tamblin (*d* 2006); one step *s* one step *d*. *Educ:* James Gillespie's High Sch., Edinburgh; Heaton High Sch., Newcastle upon Tyne; Durham Univ. (BA Hons). ATS, Intelligence Corps (Bletchley Park), 1943–45. Essex County Council Planning Officer, 1949–51. Joined Royal Air Force, 1951; served Education Branch, 1951–55: RAF

Locking; RAF Stanmore Park; RAF Wahn, Germany; Secretarial subseq. Administrative, Branch, 1955–76; Schools Liaison Recruiting, 1955–59; Accountant Officer, RAF St Mawgan and RAF Steamer Point, Aden, 1959–61; Staff College, 1962–63; MoD, Air Secretary's Dept, 1963–66; Sen. Trng Officer, RAF Spitalgate, 1966–68; Admin. Plans Officer, HQ Maintenance Comd, 1968–69; Command WRAF Admin. Officer, HQ Strike Comd, 1969–71; Station Comdr, RAF Spitalgate, 1971–74; Command Accountant, HQ Strike Comd, 1974–76. Chm., Cttee on Women in NATO Forces, 1977–79. Pres., E Cornwall Branch, RAFA, 1984–2009; Chm., S Western Area Council, RAFA, 1991–93 (Mem., 1986–93; Vice-Chm., 1988–91). FCMI (FBIM 1977, CBIM 1979); FRSA 1979. *Recreations:* various charitable works, tapestry work, church choir. *Address:* Trecairne, 3 Plaidy Park Road, Looe, Cornwall PL13 1LG. *Club:* Royal Air Force. *Died 8 March 2015.*

TAMUNO, Prof. Tekena Nitonye, CON 2003; OFR 2002; DLit; Emeritus Professor, University of Ibadan, since 1994; Distinguished Fellow, National Institute for Policy and Strategic Studies, Kuru, Nigeria, 1992–94 (Research Professor in History, 1990–92); *b* 28 Jan. 1932; *s* of late Chief Mark Tamuno Igbiri and Mrs Ransoline I. Tamuno; *m* 1963, Olu Grace Tamuno (*née* Esho); two *s* two *d. Educ:* University Coll. Ibadan; Birkbeck Coll., Univ. of London; Columbia Univ., New York City. BA (Hons) History, PhD History, DLit (London). University of Ibadan: Professor of History, 1971; Head, Dept of History, 1972–75; Dean of Arts, 1973–75; Chairman, Cttee of Deans, 1974–75; Vice-Chancellor, 1975–79; Res. Prof. in History, Inst. of African Studies, 1979–90. Principal, University Coll., Ilorin, Oct.–Nov. 1975; Pro-Chancellor and Chm. Council, Rivers State Univ. of Sci. and Technol., Port-Harcourt, 1981–88; Vis. Prof. in History, Nigerian Defence Acad., Kaduna, 1989–90. Member: Nat. Univs Commn Bd, 2002–05; Presidential Cttee on Reform of Nigeria Police Force, 2008. Chairman: Presidential Panel on Nigeria Since Independence History Project, 1980–2000; Panel on Policing Nigeria Project, 1992–93; Presidential Panel on Nat. Security, 2001–02; Okrika Community Peace Cttee, Port Harcourt, Rivers State, Nigeria, 2005–07; Presidential Cttee on Nigeria's Centenary Book, 2012–. Chm. Bd of Dirs, New Nigerian Newspapers Ltd, 1984–89. Pres. and Chm., Bd of Trustees, Bells Univ. of Technol., Ota, Nigeria, 2005–11; Chancellor, Redeemer's Univ., Redemption City, Ogun, Nigeria, 2009–. Nat. Vice-Pres., Historical Soc. of Nigeria, 1974–78 (Fellow, 1992). Nigerian Academy of Letters: Fellow, 2000; Vice-Pres., 2000–02; Pres., 2002–04. Gen. Ed., African Leadership Forum Biographical Series, 1991. JP Ibadan, 1976. *Publications:* Nigeria and Elective Representation, 1923–1947, 1966; The Police in Modern Nigeria, 1961–1965, 1970; The Evolution of the Nigerian State: The Southern Phase, 1898–1914, 1972; (ed with Prof. J. F. A. Ajayi) The University of Ibadan, 1948–1973: A History of the First Twenty-Five Years, 1973; History and History-makers in Modern Nigeria, 1973; Herbert Macaulay, Nigerian Patriot, 1975; (ed with E. J. Alagoa) Eminent Nigerians of the Rivers State, 1980; (ed) Ibadan Voices: Ibadan University in Transition, 1981; Songs of an Egg-Head (poems), 1982; (ed) National Conference on Nigeria since Independence: addresses at the formal opening, 1983; (ed) Proceedings of the National Conference on Nigeria since Independence, Zaria, March 1983, Vol. III: The Civil War Years, 1984; Nigeria Since Independence: The First Twenty-Five Years: (ed with J. A. Atanda) Vol. III, Education, 1989; (ed with J. A. Atanda) Vol. IV, Government and Public Policy, 1989; (ed with S. C. Ukpabi) Vol. VI, The Civil War Years, 1989; (ed with E. J. Alagoa) Land and People of Nigeria: Rivers State, 1989; Peace and Violence in Nigeria, 1991; (ed jtly) Policing Nigeria: past, present and future, 1993; Festival of Songs & Drums (poems), 1999; The Niger Delta Question, 2000; Lamentations of Yeske: poems in honour of HRH Professor Egbe Ifie, 2005; Wisdom of the Elders: joy of Nigerian proverbs, 2007; (ed) History of the Chapel of the Resurrection, University of Ibadan, 2008; (ed jtly) The Izon of the Niger Delta, 2009; Oil Wars in the Niger Delta 1849–2009, 2011; Stakeholders at War in Nigeria: from Lord Lugard to President Goodluck Jonathan, 2 vols, 2012. *Recreations:* music, gardening, domestic pets. *Address:* Institute of African Studies, University of Ibadan, Ibadan, Nigeria. *Died 11 April 2015.*

TAPSELL, Hon. Sir Peter (Wilfred), KNZM 1997; MBE 1968; FRCSE, FRCS; Speaker, House of Representatives, New Zealand, 1994–96; *b* Rotorua, 21 Jan. 1930; *s* of Peter and May Tapsell; *m* 1956, Margaret Diane Bourke (*d* 2008); two *s* two *d. Educ:* Rotorua High Sch.; Otago Univ. Med. Sch. (MB ChB 1954). FRCSE 1959; FRCS 1961. Hse surgeon, Waikato Hosp., 1955; demonstrator in anatomy, Sch. of Medicine, Dunedin, 1956; Resident Surgical Officer, Dunedin Public Hosp., 1957–58; post-grad. trng, Royal Infirmary, Edinburgh and London, 1958–61; Resident Surgeon, Woolwich, 1959; Orthopaedics Specialist, Orthopaedic Hosp., Oswestry, 1960–61; Orthopaedic Surgeon, Rotorua and Queen Elizabeth Hosps, 1961–81. MP (Lab) Eastern Maori, NZ, 1981–96; Minister of Internal Affairs, Civil Defence, Minister for the Arts and Associate Minister for Local Govt and Tourism, 1984–87; Minister: of Police, 1987–89; of Forestry and Recreation and Sport, 1987–90; of Lands, Survey and Land Inf. and in charge of Valuation Dept, 1987–90; of Science and DSIR, 1989; of Defence, 1990. Dep. Mayor, Rotorua City, 1979–83. Chm., NZ Maori Arts and Crafts Inst., 1973–82. Member Council: Univ. of Waikato, 1975; Waikato Teachers' Trng Coll., 1976. Hon. Fellow, Inst. Architects of NZ, 1986. Played Rugby for Otago and NZ Univs; Vice-Capt., Maori All Blacks tour to Fiji, 1954. Hon. LLD Otago, 1996; Hon. Dr Waikato, 1997. *Recreations:* hunting, shooting, fishing. *Address:* 2 Ngahu Street, Rotorua, New Zealand. *Died 5 April 2012.*

TATE, Brian; *see* Tate, R. B.

TATE, Sir (Henry) Saxon, 5th Bt *cr* 1898, of Park Hill, Streatham; CBE 1991; Chairman, London Futures and Options Exchange (formerly London Commodity Exchange Co. Ltd), 1985–91; Director, Tate & Lyle Ltd, 1956–99; *b* 28 Nov. 1931; *er s* of Lt-Col Sir Henry Tate, 4th Bt, TD and his 1st wife, Nairne (*d* 1984), *d* of Saxon Gregson-Ellis, JP; *S* father, 1994; *m* 1st, 1953, Sheila Ann (marr. diss. 1975; she *d* 1987), *e d* of Duncan Robertson; four *s* (incl. twin *s*); 2nd, 1975, Virginia Sturm. *Educ:* Eton; Christ Church, Oxford. National Service, Life Guards (Lieut), 1949–50. Joined Tate & Lyle Ltd, 1952, Director, 1956; Pres. and Chief Executive Officer, Redpath Industries Ltd, Canada, 1965–72; Tate & Lyle Ltd: Chm., Executive Cttee, 1973–78; Man. Dir, 1978–80; Vice Chm., 1980–82. Chief Executive, Industrial Development Bd of NI, 1982–85. Fellow, Amer. Management Assoc., 1972; FCMI (FBIM 1975). *Recreation:* various. *Heir: s* Edward Nicholas Tate, *b* 2 July 1966. *Address:* 26 Cleaver Square, SE11 4EA. *Died 11 July 2012.*

TATE, Prof. (Robert) Brian, FBA 1980; FRHistS; Professor and Head of Department of Hispanic Studies, Nottingham University, 1958–83, then Emeritus Professor; *b* 27 Dec. 1921; *s* of Robert and Jane Grantie Tate; *m* 1951, Beth Ida Lewis; one *s* one *d. Educ:* Royal Belfast Academical Instn; Queen's Univ. Belfast (MA, PhD). FRHistS 1990. Asst Lectr, Manchester Univ., 1949–52; Lectr, QUB, 1952–56; Reader in Hispanic Studies, Nottingham Univ., 1956–58. Vis. Prof., Univs of Harvard, Cornell, SUNY at Buffalo, Texas and Virginia. Corresponding Fellow: Institut d'Estudis Catalans, Barcelona, 1964; Real Academia de Historia, Madrid, 1974; Real Academia de Buenas Letras de Barcelona, 1980. Hon. DArts Girona, 2004. *Publications:* Joan Margarit i Pau, Cardinal Bishop of Gerona: a biographical study, 1954; Ensayos sobre la historiografia peninsular del siglo XV, 1970; The Medieval Kingdoms of the Iberian Peninsula, in P. E. Russell, Spain: a companion to Spanish studies, 1973; El Cardenal Joan Margarit, vida i obra, 1976; (trans.) Pierre Vilar, A Brief History of Spain, 1978; (with Marcus Tate) The Pilgrim Route to Santiago, 1987; Pilgrimages to St James of Compostella from the British Isles during the Middle Ages, 1990; *edited:* (with A. Yates) Actes del Colloqui internacional de llengua i literatura catalanes, 1976; Essays on Narrative Fiction in the Iberian Peninsula, 1982; (with T. Turville Petre) Two Pilgrim Itineraries of the Later Middle Ages, 1995; *edited with introduction and notes:* Fernán Pérez de Guzmán, Generaciones y

Semblanzas, 1965; Fernando del Pulgar, Claros varones de Castilla, 1971, rev. edn 1985; (with I. R. Macpherson) Don Juan Manuel, Libro de los estados, 1974, rev. edn 1991; Anon, Directorio de príncipes, 1977; Alfonso de Palencia, Epistolario, 1983; (with J. H. N. Lawrance) Alfonso de Palencia, Gesta Hispaniensia, vols 1 and 2, 1998, vol. 3, 2008; contrib. articles in numerous learned jls. *Recreations:* architecture and the history of art, jazz. *Address:* 11 Hope Street, Beeston, Nottingham NG9 1DJ. *T:* (0115) 925 1243. *Died 21 Feb. 2011.*

TATE, Sir Saxon; *see* Tate, Sir H. S.

TAVARÉ, Sir John, Kt 1989; CBE 1983; CEng; Chairman, Luxonic Lighting plc, 1986–2000; *b* 12 July 1920; *s* of Leon Alfred Tavaré and Grace Tavaré; *m* 1949, Margaret Daphne Wray (*d* 2012); three *s* (and one *s* decd). *Educ:* Chatham House, Ramsgate; Bromley Grammar Sch.; King's Coll., London (BScEng 1946). FInstD 1983; FIWEM 1991; FIMechE 1996. Trainee, Thames Board Mills Ltd, 1938–43; Works Manager, Wm C. Jones Ltd, 1946–48; Personnel Administration Ltd, UK, Australia and NZ, 1949–58; Thames Board Mills Ltd (Unilever), 1958–68: Sales and Marketing Dir, 1960–65; Vice-Chm., 1966–68; Paper, Plastics and Packaging Bd, Unilever, 1968–70; Whitecroft plc, 1970–85: Gp Man. Dir, 1973–76; Chm. and Gp Man. Dir, 1976–85. Chm., Mersey Basin Campaign, DoE, 1985–92. Member: Nat. Council, CBI, 1978–85 (Chm., NW Reg., 1980–82); Nat. Rivers Authy Adv. Bd, NW Region, 1989–92. *Recreations:* garden, environment, business. *Address:* The Gables, 4 Macclesfield Road, Prestbury, Macclesfield, Cheshire SK10 4BN. *T:* (01625) 829778. *Died 23 Aug. 2014.*

TAVENER, Sir John (Kenneth), Kt 2000; composer; *b* 28 Jan. 1944; *m* 1991, Maryanna (*née* Schaefer); one *s* two *d*. *Educ:* Highgate Sch.; Royal Academy of Music (LRAM). Prof. of Composition, Trinity Coll. of Music, London, 1968–. Hon. FRAM, Hon. FTCL, Hon. FRSCM. Russian Orthodox religion. Apollo Award, Friends of Greek Nat. Opera, 1993. *Compositions include: orchestral:* Grandma's Footsteps; Theophany; Towards the Son: Ritual Procession; *solo instrument/voice and orchestra:* Eternal Memory; Ikon of Eros; Palintropos; Piano Concerto; The Protecting Veil; The Repentant Thief; Tears of the Angels; Lalishri; Popule Meus; *choral and orchestra:* Akhmatova Requiem; Eternity's Sunrise; Agraphon; In Alium; The Immurement of Antigone; Lament for Jerusalem; Sappho; Lyrical Fragments; 16 Haiku of Seferis; Three Holy Sonnets; Akathist of Thanksgiving; The Apocalypse; Celtic Requiem; Ikon of St Seraphim; Introit for March 27th, the Feast of St John Damascene; Kyklike Kinesis; The Last Discourse; Resurrection; Ultimos Ritos; The Veil of the Temple; We Shall See Him As He Is; The Whale; Risen!; Agraphon; Let's Begin Again; Total Eclipse; Fall and Resurrection; Requiem; *choral:* Annunciation; Canticle of the Mother of God; A Christmas Round; Eonia; The Great Canon of St Andrew of Crete; Ikon of Light; Ikon of St Cuthbert of Lindisfarne; Ikon of the Trinity; The Lamb; Lament of the Mother of God; Let Not the Prince be Silent; Liturgy of St John Chrysostom; O, Do Not Move; Orthodox Vigil Service; Panikhida; Prayer for the World; Psalm 121, I Will Lift Up Mine Eyes Unto The Hills; Song for Athene; Thunder Entered Her; Today the Virgin; Two Hymns to the Mother of God; The Tyger; The Uncreated Eros; A Village Wedding; The World is Burning; Three Antiphons; Innocence; Svyati (O Holy One); Amen; As One Who Has Slept; Hymn of the Unwaning Light; Notre Père; Prayer to the Holy Trinity; Wedding Prayer; Three Shakespeare Sonnets; *choral and instruments:* The Myrrh-Bearer; Hymns of Paradise; Responsorium in Memory of Annon Lee; Akhmatova Songs; The Child Lived; Lamentation, Last Prayer and Exaltation; Let's Begin Again; Meditation on the Light; Six Abbasid Songs; Three Sections from T. S. Eliot's 'The Four Quartets'; Three Surrealist Songs; Feast of Feasts; Schuon Lieder, 2004; *chamber:* Greek Interlude; The Hidden Treasure; In Memoriam Igor Stravinsky; The Last Sleep of the Virgin; Trisagion; Mandelion; Mandoodles; Palin; Thrinos; Lament for Phaedra; Chant for Solo Cello; Akhmatova Songs; Diodia; Vlepondas; Samaveda; Kaleidoscopes; *opera:* Cain and Abel (1st Prize, Monaco); The Cappemakers; Eis Thanaton; A Gentle Spirit; Mary of Egypt; Thérèse. *Publications:* (jtly) Ikons: meditations in words and music, 1994; (ed Brian Keeble) The Music of Silence: a composer's testament, 1999. *Address:* c/o Chester Novello, 14–15 Berners Street, W1T 3LJ. *Died 12 Nov. 2013.*

TAYLOR, Sir (Arthur) Godfrey, Kt 1980; DL; Chairman, The Shrievalty Association, 1995–98; *b* 3 Aug. 1925; *s* of Fred and Lucy Taylor; *m* 1945, Eileen Dorothy Daniel; one *s* two *d* (and one *d* decd). *Educ:* Stockport Secondary School. Sutton and Cheam Borough Council: Councillor, 1951–62; Alderman, 1962–65; London Bor. of Sutton: Alderman, 1964–78; Councillor, 1978–82; Hon. Freeman, 1978. Managing Trustee, Municipal Mutual Insurance Ltd, 1979–86; Chairman: Southern Water Authority, 1981–85; London Residuary Body, 1985–96. Chm., Assoc. of Metropolitan Authorities, 1978–80. Chm., London Bor. Assoc., 1968–71. High Sheriff, 1984, DL, 1988, Greater London. *Recreation:* golf. *Address:* 23 Somerhill Lodge, Somerhill Road, Hove, E Sussex BN3 1RU. *T:* (01273) 776161. *Died 31 May 2014.*

TAYLOR, Arthur Ronald, MBE (mil.) 1945; DL; Chairman, Willis Faber plc, 1978–81; Vice-Chairman, Legal and General Group plc, 1984–86 (Director, 1982–86); *b* 13 June 1921; *yr s* of late Arthur Taylor and Kathleen Frances (*née* Constable Curtis); *m* 1949, Elizabeth Josephine Kiek; three *s*. *Educ:* Winchester Coll.; Trinity Coll., Oxford. Served Grenadier Guards, 1940–53 (despatches); sc; Bde Major 32nd Guards Bde. Laurence Philipps & Co. (Insurance) Ltd, 1953–58; Member of Lloyd's, 1955; Director, Willis, Faber and Dumas Ltd, 1959; Dep. Chm., Willis Faber Ltd, 1974. Vice-President: Corporation of Insurance Brokers, 1967–78; British Insurance Brokers Assoc., 1978–81. DL Hants, 1994. *Recreations:* golf, shooting. *Address:* Coutts & Co., 440 Strand, WC2R 0QS. *Died 21 March 2011.*

TAYLOR, Brian William; Under Secretary, Civil Service Commission, retired; Resident Chairman, Recruitment and Assessment Services, Office of Minister for Civil Service, 1990–93; *b* 29 April 1933; *s* of late Alan Taylor and Betty Taylor; *m* 1959, Mary Evelyn Buckley; two *s* two *d*. *Educ:* Emanuel School. Entered Ministry of Nat. Insurance (subseq. DHSS, then DSS) as Exec. Officer, 1952; Higher Exec. Officer, 1963; Principal, 1968; Asst Sec., 1976; Under Sec., 1982; on loan from DSS, 1990–93. *Recreations:* music, theatre, literature, walking, grandchildren, trying to keep fit. *Died 28 Aug. 2012.*

TAYLOR, Douglas Hugh Charles, PhD; FREng; independent consultant on internal combustion engines, since 1992; *b* 4 April 1938; *s* of Richard Hugh Taylor and Alice Mary Davies; *m* 1st, 1970, Janet Elizabeth Scott (marr. diss.); two *d*; 2nd, 2001, Thea Caroline Lilian Vinter. *Educ:* King Edward VI Grammar Sch., Lichfield; Loughborough University of Technology. PhD, BTech. FREng (FEng 1987); FIMechE. Ruston & Hornsby/GEC Ruston Diesels, 1962–72, Chief Research Engineer, 1968; Ricardo Consulting Engineers, 1972–90: Head of Large Engines, 1973; Dir, 1977; Man. Dir, 1984–90; Chm., 1987–90; Gp Man. Dir, Ricardo Internat., 1990–91. Vis. Prof., Loughborough Univ., 1994–. Hon. DTech Loughborough, 2007. *Recreations:* campanology, flying. *Died 5 May 2012.*

TAYLOR, Dame Elizabeth (Rosemond), DBE 2000; film actress; *b* London, 27 Feb. 1932; *d* of late Francis Taylor and Sara (*née* Sothern); *m* 1st, 1950, Conrad Nicholas Hilton, Jr (marr. diss. 1951; he *d* 1969); 2nd, 1952, Michael Wilding (marr. diss. 1957; he *d* 1979); two *s*; 3rd, 1957, Mike Todd (*d* 1958); one *d*; 4th, 1959, Eddie Fisher (marr. diss. 1964; he *d* 2010); 5th, 1964, Richard Burton, CBE (marr. diss. 1974; remarried 1975; marr. diss. 1976; he *d* 1984); 7th, 1976, Senator John Warner (marr. diss. 1982); 8th, 1991, Larry Fortensky (marr. diss. 1996). *Educ:* Byron House, Hampstead; Hawthorne School, Beverly Hills; Metro-Goldwyn-Mayer School; University High School, Hollywood. First film, There's One Born Every Minute, 1942. *Films include:* Lassie Come Home, The White Cliffs of Dover, 1943; Jane Eyre, National Velvet, 1944; Courage of Lassie, Life with Father, 1946; Cynthia, 1947; A Date With Judy, 1948; Julia Misbehaves, 1948; The Big Hangover, 1949; Father's Little Dividend, Little Women, The Conspirator, Father of the Bride, 1950;

A Place in the Sun, Love is Better than Ever, 1951; Ivanhoe, 1952; Beau Brummel, Elephant Walk, Rhapsody, 1954; Last Time I Saw Paris, 1955; Giant, 1956; Raintree County, 1957; Cat on a Hot Tin Roof, 1958; Suddenly Last Summer, 1959; Holiday in Spain, Butterfield 8 (Academy Award for Best Actress), 1960; Cleopatra, The VIPs, 1963; The Sandpiper, 1965; Who's Afraid of Virginia Woolf? (Academy Award for Best Actress), 1966; The Taming of the Shrew, Doctor Faustus, 1967; Boom!, The Comedians, Reflections in a Golden Eye, Secret Ceremony, 1968; The Only Game in Town, 1970; Under Milk Wood, Zee and Co., Hammersmith is Out, 1972; Night Watch, 1973; Ash Wednesday, 1974; The Driver's Seat, Blue Bird, 1975; A Little Night Music, 1977; Winter Kills, 1979; The Mirror Crack'd, 1980; Between Friends, 1983; Young Toscanini, 1988; The Flintstones, 1994. Stage debut as Regina in The Little Foxes, NY, 1981, London stage debut, Victoria Palace, 1982; Private Lives, NY, 1983. Fellow, BAFTA, 1999. Initiated Elizabeth Taylor-Ben Gurion Univ. Fund for Children of the Negev, 1982; founded American Foundn for AIDS Res., 1985, Internat. Fund, 1985, Elizabeth Taylor AIDS Foundn, 1991. Aristotle S. Onassis Foundn Award, 1988; Humanitarian Award, American Academy, 1993. Comdr of Arts and Letters (France), 1985; Legion of Honour (France), 1987. *Publications:* (with Richard Burton) World Enough and Time, 1964; Elizabeth Taylor, 1966; Elizabeth Takes Off, 1988; Elizabeth Taylor: my love affair with jewellery, 2002. *Address:* PO Box 55995, Sherman Oaks, CA 91413, USA. *Died 23 March 2011.*

TAYLOR, Sir Godfrey; *see* Taylor, Sir A. G.

TAYLOR, John Ashley; His Honour Judge John Taylor; a Circuit Judge, since 2006; *b* 11 July 1946; *s* of late Cyril Ernest Taylor and of Mary Taylor; *m* 1968, Anne C. M. Walker; one *s* two *d* (and one *d* decd). *Educ:* Leeds City High Sch. Admitted solicitor, 1980; in private practice, 1974–98; Dist Judge, 1998–2006. *Recreations:* sailing, cycling, travel, listening to music. *Address:* Leeds Combined Court Centre, 1 Oxford Row, Leeds LS1 3BG. *Died 9 Jan. 2012.*

TAYLOR, John Charles; QC 1983; *b* 22 April 1931; *s* of late Sidney Herbert and Gertrude Florence Taylor, St Ives, Cambs; *m* 1964, Jean Aimée Monteith; one *d*. *Educ:* Palmers Sch., Grays, Essex; Queens' Coll., Cambridge (MA, LLB); Harvard Law School (LLM). Called to the Bar, Middle Temple, 1958. Mem., Stephens Cttee on Minerals Planning Control, 1972–74; Chm., Examn in Public Panel, Leics and Rutland Structure Plan, 1985; Insp., County Hall (London) Inquiries, 1990, 1991. Contested: (C) Kettering, 1970; (Referendum) NE Beds, 1997. *Recreations:* country pursuits, art. *Address:* The Grange, Grange Street, Clifton, Shefford, Beds SG17 5EW. *Clubs:* Travellers, Royal Ocean Racing. *Died 7 May 2014.*

TAYLOR, Prof. John Gerald; Professor of Mathematics, King's College, University of London, 1971–96, then Emeritus; *b* 18 Aug. 1931; *s* of William and Elsie Taylor; *m* Pamela Nancy (*née* Cutmore); two *s* three *d*. *Educ:* King Edward VI Grammar Sch., Chelmsford; Mid-Essex Polytechnic, Chelmsford; Christ's Coll., Cambridge. Fellow, Inst. for Advanced Study, Princeton, NJ, USA, 1956–58 (Mem., 1961–63); Fellow, Christ's Coll., Cambridge, 1958–60; Asst Lectr, Faculty of Mathematics, Univ. of Cambridge, 1959–60; Member: Inst. des Hautes Etudes Scient., Paris, 1960; Res. Inst. Advanced Study, Baltimore, Md, USA, 1960. Sen. Res. Fellow, Churchill Coll., Cambridge, 1963–64; Prof. of Physics, Rutgers Univ., New Brunswick, NJ, 1964–66; Fellow, Hertford Coll., Oxford, and Lectr, Math. Inst., Oxford, 1966–67; Reader in Particles and Fields, Queen Mary Coll., London, 1967–69; Prof. of Physics, Univ. of Southampton, 1969–71. Guest Scientist, Inst. of Medicine, Res. Centre, Juelich, Germany, 1996–99. Dir, Centre for Neural Networks, KCL, 1990–2001; Consultant Dir of Res., ECONOSTAT Ltd, 1991–2002. Chm., 1982–87, Vice-Chm., 1988–91, Mathematical Physics Gp, Inst. of Physics. Chm., Jt European Neural Net Initiative, 1990–91; Convener, British Neural Networks Soc., 1989–94; President: European Neural Network Soc., 1993–94 (Vice-Pres., 1991–93); Internat. Neural Network Soc., 1995–96 (Past Pres., 1996–97; Fellow, 2009); Dir, NEURONET, 1994–95; Co-ordinator, EC GNOSYS Cognitive Robot Proj., 2004–07. Institute of Physical and Chemical Research, Tokyo: Mem. Adv. Council, Human Sci. Frontiers Program, 1995–97; Mem. Adv. Bd, Brain Scis Inst., 1998–2003. European Editor-in-Chief, Neural Networks, 1991–. Pioneer Award in Neural Networks, IEE, 2009. *Publications:* Quantum Mechanics, an Introduction, 1969; The Shape of Minds to Come, 1970; The New Physics, 1972; Black Holes: the end of the Universe?, 1973; Superminds, 1975; Special Relativity, 1975; Science and the Supernatural, 1980; The Horizons of Knowledge, 1982; Finite Superstrings, 1992; The Promise of Neural Networks, 1993; When the Clock Struck Zero, 1994; The Race for Consciousness, 1999; The Mind: a user's manual, 2006; *edited:* Supergravity, 1981; Supersymmetry and Supergravity, 1982; Tributes to Paul Dirac, 1987; Recent Developments in Neural Computation, 1990; Coupled Oscillating Neurons, 1992; Theory and Applications of Neural Networks, 1992; Mathematical Approaches to Neural Networks, 1993; Neural Networks, 1995; Concepts for Neural Networks, 1997; also scientific papers in Proc. Royal Soc., Phys. Rev., Proc. Camb. Phil. Soc., Jl Math. Phys., Neural Networks, Neural Computation, etc. *Recreations:* listening to music, theatre, walking. *Address:* 33 Meredyth Road, Barnes, SW13 0DS. *T:* (020) 8876 3391. *Died 10 March 2012.*

TAYLOR, Kenneth, OBE 1981; FREng, FIMechE, FIET; consultant on railway mechanical and electrical engineering; Director of Mechanical and Electrical Engineering, British Railways Board, 1977–82; *b* 29 Sept. 1921; *s* of Charles Taylor and Amy (*née* Booth); *m* 1945, Elsie Armitt; one *d*. *Educ:* Manchester Coll. of Technol. FIMechE; FIET (FIEE 1971); FREng (FEng 1981). Principal appts with British Railways: Electric Traction Engr, Manchester, 1956; Electrical Engr, LMR, 1963; Chief Mech. and Elec. Engr, LMR, 1970; Traction Engr, BR Bd HQ, 1971. *Recreations:* golf, gardening. *Address:* 137 Burley Lane, Quarndon, Derby DE22 5JS. *T:* (01332) 550123. *Died 2 Oct. 2011.*

TAYLOR, Len Clive, (Kim); Director, Calouste Gulbenkian Foundation (UK Branch), 1982–88; *b* 4 Aug. 1922; *s* of late L. S. Taylor, Calcutta, India; *m* 1951, Suzanne Dufault (decd), Spencer, Massachusetts, USA; one *s* two *d*. *Educ:* Sevenoaks School; New College, Oxford (1st Cl. Hons Mod. Hist.; Commonwealth Fund Fellowship); Chicago University. Assistant Master, St Paul's School, Darjeeling, India, 1940–42 and 1945–46; Indian Army Intelligence Corps, 1942–45; New College, Oxford, 1946–49; Chicago University, 1949–50; Senior History Master, Repton School, 1950–54; Headmaster, Sevenoaks School, 1954–68; Dir, Nuffield Foundn 'Resources for Learning' Project, 1966–72; Principal Administrator, Centre for Educnl Res. and Innovation, OECD, Paris, 1972–77; Head of Educnl Prog. Services, IBA, 1977–82. Comdr, Order of Henry the Navigator (Portugal), 1989. *Publications:* Experiments in Education at Sevenoaks, 1965; Resources for Learning, 1971; (ed) Camões, Epic and Lyric, 1990; (ed) They Went to Portugal Too, 1990; (ed) A Centenary Pessoa, 1995; (ed) A Companion History of Portugal, 1997. *Address:* 8 Litten Terrace, Chichester, W Sussex PO19 7SA. *T:* (01243) 528091. *Died 20 July 2013.*

TAYLOR, Martin Gibbeson, CBE 1993; FCA; Vice Chairman, Hanson plc, 1988–95; *b* 30 Jan. 1935; *s* of late Roy G. Taylor and Vera Constance (*née* Farmer); *m* 1960, Gunilla Chatarina Bryner; two *s*. *Educ:* Haileybury; St Catharine's Coll., Cambridge (MA 1962). Company Sec., Dow Chemical (UK), 1963–69; joined Hanson plc, 1969, Dir 1976–95. Chm., National Westminster Life, 1992–2000; Dep. Chm., Charter plc, 1995–2002. Non-executive Director: Vickers plc, 1986–99; National Westminster Bank plc, 1990–2000; Securities Assoc., 1987–90; UGI plc, 1979–82; Millennium Chemicals Inc., 1996–2003. Confederation of British Industry: Mem. Council, 1981–96; Member: Companies Cttee, 1981–94 (Chm., 1990–94); City/Industry Task Force, 1987; President's Cttee, 1990–94; Steering Gp on Long Termism & Corporate Governance, 1990–92; Takeover Panel, 1989–95. Mem., Industrial Develt Adv. Bd, 1993–97. Hon. Treas., Snapshot Appeal, Nat. Assoc. for Epilepsy, 1992–95.

Governor, Mall Sch. Trust, 1987–2000. *Recreations:* art, books, sport, theatre. *Clubs:* MCC, Oxford and Cambridge. *Died 30 April 2014.*

TAYLOR, Phyllis Mary Constance, MA; Honorary Associate, Institute of Education, London, 1983–85; *b* 29 Sept. 1926; *d* of Cecil and Constance Tedder; *m* 1949, Peter Royston Taylor; one *s*. *Educ:* Woodford High Sch.; Sudbury High Sch., Suffolk; Girton Coll., Cambridge (State Scholar; BA Hons History, 1948; MA 1951). Asst Hist. Mistress, Loughton High Sch., 1948–51, Head of Hist., 1951–58; Teacher of Hist. and Religious Educn, Lancaster Royal Grammar Sch. for Boys, 1959; Head of Hist., Casterton Sch. (private boarding), Kirby Lonsdale, 1960; Teacher of Gen. Subjects, Lancaster Girls' Grammar Sch., 1960–61, Head of Hist., 1961–62; Dep. Headmistress, Carlisle Sch., Chelsea, 1962–64; Headmistress: Walthamstow High Sch. for Girls, 1964–68; Walthamstow Sen. High Sch., 1968–75; Wanstead High Sch., London Borough of Redbridge, 1976–82. Consultant Head to NE London Polytechnic (Counselling/Careers sect.), 1974–78; Moderator, Part-time Diploma, Pastoral Care and Counselling, 1979–85. Pres., Essex Sector, Secondary Heads' Assoc., 1978–79. Member: UGC, 1978–83 (Mem., Educn Sub-Cttee, 1978–85, and Wkg Party on Continuing Educn, 1983); Teacher Trng Sub-Cttee, Adv. Cttee on Supply and Educn of Teachers, 1980–85; former Mem., Nat. Exec., Assoc. of Head Mistresses. Mem., RAM Foundn Appeals Cttee, 1985–86. Parish Councillor, High Roding, 1995–2010. Chm., Dunmow Liberals, 1986–88. Governor, Rodings Primary Sch., 1988–90. *Publications:* (as Julianne Royston) The Penhale Saga: The Penhale Heiress, 1988; The Penhale Fortune, 1989. *Recreations:* music, theatre, bridge, horses, country life, ecology. *Address:* White Horses, High Roding, Great Dunmow, Essex CM6 1NS. *T:* (01371) 873161. *Died 21 Oct. 2014.*

TAYLOR THOMPSON, (John) Derek, CB 1985; Commissioner of Inland Revenue, 1973–87; Secretary, Churches' Main Committee, 1990–2007; *b* 6 Aug. 1927; *o s* of late John Taylor Thompson and Marjorie (*née* Westcott); *m* 1954, Helen Laurie Walker; two *d*. *Educ:* St Peter's Sch., York; Balliol Coll., Oxford. MA. Inland Revenue: Asst Principal, 1951; Private Sec. to Chm., 1954; Private Sec. to Minister without Portfolio (Rt Hon. William Deedes), 1962–64; Asst Sec., 1965; Dir of Manpower & Organisation, 1973–75; Dir, Personal Tax, 1975–81; Dir, Internat. Div., 1981–87. Chm., Fiscal Affairs Cttee, OECD, 1984–89. Chm., Legislation-Monitoring Service for Charities, 1991–2007. *Recreations:* rural pursuits, reading, historical writing. *Address:* Jessops, Bell Lane, Nutley, Sussex TN22 3PD. *Club:* Oxford and Cambridge. *Died 28 April 2014.*

TEAR, Robert, CBE 1984; concert and operatic tenor; first Professor of International Singing, Royal Academy of Music, since 1985; *b* 8 March 1939; *s* of Thomas Arthur and Edith Tear; *m* 1961, Hilary Thomas; two *d*. *Educ:* Barry Grammar Sch.; King's Coll., Cambridge (BA 1960; MA 1964; Hon. Fellow 1989). Hon. RCM, RAM. Mem., King's Coll. Choir, 1957–60; subseq. St Paul's Cathedral and solo career; joined English Opera Group, 1964. By 1968 had worked with world's leading conductors, notably Karajan, Giulini, Bernstein and Solti; during this period created many rôles in operas by Benjamin Britten. Appeared in all major festivals; close association with compositions of Sir Michael Tippett, 1970–; Covent Garden: début, The Knot Garden, 1970, closely followed by Lensky in Eugène Onégin; Fledermaus, 1977; Peter Grimes, 1978; Rake's Progress, 1979; Thérèse, 1979; Loge in Rheingold, 1980; Admetus in Alceste, 1981; David in Die Meistersinger, 1982; Captain Vere in Billy Budd, 1982; appeared regularly with Royal Opera. Glyndebourne: début, Aschenbach in Death in Venice, 1989; Marriage of Figaro, and Rake's Progress, 1994; The Makropoulos Case, 1997. Started relationship with Scottish Opera (singing in La Traviata, Alceste, Don Giovanni), 1974. Paris Opera: début, 1976; Lulu 1979. Début as conductor with Thames Chamber Orchestra, QEH, 1980. Conducted Minneapolis Orch., ECO, LSO, Philharmonia, London Mozart Players. Worked with every major recording co. and made numerous recordings (incl. solo recital discs). Sermon, King's Coll. Chapel, Cambridge Univ., 1990. *Publications:* Victorian Songs and Duets, 1980; Tear Here (autobiog.), 1990; Singer Beware, 1995. *Recreations:* any sport; interested in 18th and 19th century English water colours. *Club:* Arts. *Died 29 March 2011.*

TEELOCK, Dr Boodhun, GOSK 1997; High Commissioner for Mauritius in London, 1989–92; *b* 20 July 1922; *s* of Ramessur Teelock and Sadny Teelock; *m* 1956, Riziya Sahay (*d* 2004); three *d*. *Educ:* Edinburgh Univ. (MB ChB 1950); Liverpool Univ. (DTM&H 1951). DPH. Ministry of Health, Mauritius: School MO, 1952–58; Senior School MO, 1958–59; Principal MO, 1960–68; World Health Organisation: Regional Adviser, Public Health Administration, Brazzaville, 1968–71; Chief of Mission, Tanzania, 1971–74, Kenya and Seychelles, 1974–79; Immunisation MO, Air Mauritius, 1980–88. *Recreation:* reading. *Address:* 12 Labourdonnais Avenue, Quatre Bornes, Mauritius. *Died 23 May 2012.*

TELITO, Rev. Sir Filoimea, GCMG 2007; MBE 1997; Governor-General of Tuvalu, 2005–10; *b* 19 March 1945; *s* of Telogo Telito and Moti Silaati; *m* 1978, Pepapeti Tilafolau; one *s* two *d*. *Educ:* Vaitupu Primary Sch., Tuvalu; King George V Secondary Sch., Kiribati; Ardmore Teachers' Coll., NZ; Trinity Theol Coll., NZ (Dip. Christian Educn); Univ. of S Pacific, Fiji (DipEd (Secondary)); Pacific Theol Coll., Fiji (BD). Principal, 1968–70, 1974–76 and 2002–05, Chaplain, 1983–87, Motufoua Secondary Sch.; Parson, Funafuti Parish, Tuvalu, 1989–91; Principal, Fituvalu Secondary Sch., Tuvalu, 1991–94; Gen. Sec., Christian Ch of Tuvalu, 1995–98; Tuvalu Chaplaincy, Suva, Fiji Is, 1999–2002. Mem., Boys' Bde. *Recreations:* reading, table-tennis, gardening. *Address:* c/o Government House, PO Box 30, Funafuti, Tuvalu. *T:* 20715, *Fax:* 20709. *Died 11 July 2011.*

TEMPLE OF STOWE, 8th Earl *cr* 1822; **Walter Grenville Algernon Temple-Gore-Langton;** *b* 2 Oct. 1924; *s* of Comdr Hon. Evelyn Arthur Temple-Gore-Langton, DSO, RN (*d* 1972) (*y s* of 4th Earl) and Irene (*d* 1967), *d* of Brig.-Gen. Cavendish Walter Gartside-Spaight; *S* cousin, 1988; *m* 1st, 1954, Zillah Ray (*d* 1966), *d* of James Boxall; two *s* one *d*; 2nd, 1968, Margaret Elizabeth Graham, *o d* of late Col H. W. Scarth of Breckness. *Heir:* *s* Lord Langton, *b* 11 Sept. 1955. *Died 17 Sept. 2013.*

TEMPLEMAN, Baron *cr* 1982 (Life Peer), of White Lackington in the County of Somerset; **Sydney William Templeman,** Kt 1972; MBE 1946; PC 1978; a Lord of Appeal in Ordinary, 1982–94; *b* 3 March 1920; *s* of late Herbert William and Lilian Templeman; *m* 1st, 1946, Margaret Joan (*née* Rowles) (*d* 1988); two *s*; 2nd, 1996, Mrs Sheila Barton Edworthy (*d* 2008). *Educ:* Southall Grammar School; St John's College, Cambridge (Schol.; MA 1944; Hon. Fellow 1982). Served War of 1939–45: commnd 4/1st Gurkha Rifles, 1941; NW Frontier, 1942; Arakan, 1943; Imphal, 1944; Burma with 7 Ind. and 17 Ind. Divisions, 1945 (despatches; Hon. Major). Called to the Bar, 1947; Harmsworth and MacMahon schols; Mem., Middle Temple and Lincoln's Inn; Mem., Bar Council, 1961–65, 1970–72; QC 1964; Bencher, Middle Temple, 1969 (Treasurer, 1987). Attorney Gen. of the Duchy of Lancaster, 1970–72; a Judge of the High Court of Justice, Chancery Div., 1972–78; a Lord Justice of Appeal, 1978–82. Member: Tribunal to inquire into matters relating to the Vehicle and General Insurance Co., 1971; Adv. Cttee on Legal Education, 1972–74; Royal Commn on Legal Services, 1976–79; Chm., Bishop of London's Commn on City Churches, 1992–94. Treasurer, Senate of the Four Inns, 1972–74; Pres., Senate of the Inns of Court and the Bar, 1974–76. President: Bar Assoc. for Commerce, Finance and Industry, 1982–85; Bar European Gp, 1987–95; Assoc. of Law Teachers, 1997–2000. Pres., Holdsworth Club, 1983–84. Hon. Member: Canadian Bar Assoc., 1976; Amer. Bar Assoc., 1976; Newfoundland Law Soc., 1984. Hon. DLitt Reading, 1980; Hon. LLD: Birmingham, 1986; CNAA, 1990; Exeter, 1991; W of England, 1993; Nat. Law Sch. of India, 1994. *Address:* Mellowstone, 1 Rosebank Crescent, Exeter EX4 6EJ. *T:* (01392) 275428. *Died 4 June 2014.*

TEMPLEMAN, Michael; Member, First-tier Tax Tribunal, since 2009; *b* 6 May 1943; *s* of late Dr Geoffrey Templeman, CBE, founding Vice-Chancellor, Univ. of

Kent at Canterbury, and Dorothy May Templeman (*née* Heathcote); *m* 1970, Jane Margaret Willmer Lee; four *d*. *Educ:* King Edward's Sch., Birmingham; Selwyn Coll., Cambridge (MA). Inland Revenue, 1965–93: Inspector of Taxes, 1965; Dist Inspector, Cannock, 1971–72; Head Office Specialist, Oil Taxation, 1972–78; Dist Inspector, Luton, 1978–81; Head Office Specialist, Financial Concerns, 1981–89; Controller, Oil Taxation Office, 1989–92; Dir, Financial Institutions Div., 1992–93; J. Henry Schroder Wagg, then J. Henry Schroder, & Co., later Schroders PLC: Gp Tax Dir, 1994–2008. *Recreations:* cricket, classical music, cooking, cliff walking. *Died 24 Jan. 2012.*

TEMPLETON, John Marks, Jr; MD; FACS; President, since 1987, and Chairman, since 2006, John Templeton Foundation; *b* New York, 19 Feb. 1940; *s* of Sir John Marks Templeton; *m* 1970, Josephine Gargiulo; two *d*. *Educ:* Yale Univ. (BA 1962); Harvard Med. Sch. (MD 1968). FACS 1980. Intern in Surgery, 1968–69, Surgical Resident, 1969–73, Med. Coll. of Virginia; Pediatric Surgical Resident, Children's Hosp. of Philadelphia, 1973–75; Instructor in Pediatric Surgery, Univ. of Pennsylvania, 1973–75; Asst Prof., Dept of Surgery, Eastern Virginia Med. Sch., 1975–77; Asst Prof., 1978–86, Associate Prof., 1986–95, Prof. of Pediatric Surgery, 1995, Adjunct Prof., 1995–, Univ. of Pennsylvania; Barclay Fellow, Templeton Coll., Oxford, 1995. Hd of Pediatric Surgery, Naval Regl Med. Center, Portsmouth, Va, 1975–77; Children's Hospital of Philadelphia: Asst Surgeon, 1977–83; Associate Surgeon, 1983–95; Co-Chm., Emergency Services Cttee, 1978–85; Chm., Trauma Cttee, 1985–95; Co-Dir, Trauma Service, 1986–88; Trauma Prog. Dir, 1988–95; Pediatric Surgical Cons., Pennsylvania Hosp., 1980–95. Member: Amer. Med. Assoc.; Amer. Pediatric Surgical Assoc.; Eastern Assoc. for Surgery of Trauma; Amer. Assoc. for Surgery of Trauma; Bd, Amer. Trauma Soc.; Assoc. for Advancement of Automotive Med.; Internat. Assoc. for Surgery of Trauma and Surgical Intensive Care. Mem., Health and Safety Cttee, Univ. of Penn, 1984–90. Mem., Editl Adv. Bd, Trauma Quarterly, 1990–93. Member: Bd, Eastern Univ.; Foreign Policy Res. Inst.; Cradle of Liberty Council, Boy Scouts of Amer.; Melmark Foundn; Nat. Recreation Foundn; Nat. Bible Assoc. Hon. LLD Beaver Coll., Glenside, Penn, 1989; Hon. DHumLit: Buena Vista Univ., 1998; Commonwealth Univ., Richmond, Va, 2000; Alvernia Coll., Reading, Penn, 2001; Hon. Dr Sacred Theol., Florida Center for Theol Studies, 2001. I. A. Bigger Award, Med. Coll. of Va, 1973; Silver Beaver Award, Philadelphia Council, Boy Scouts of Amer., 1987; Curtis Artz Award, Amer. Trauma Soc., 1995; Heroes of Liberty Award, Nat. Liberty Mus., 2006; Three Faiths Forum Interfaith Gold Medallion, 2006; Canterbury Medal, Becket Fund for Religious Liberty, 2006. *Publications:* (ed jtly) Textbook of Pediatric Emergency Medicine, 1983, 2nd edn 1993; (contrib.) Textbook of Penetrating Trauma, 1996; A Searcher's Life, 1999; Thrift and Generosity: the joy of giving, 2004. *Address:* c/o Barbara McGraw, 601 Pembroke Road, Bryn Mawr, PA 19010, USA. *T:* (610) 5251961, *Fax:* (610) 5254943. *E:* bmcgraw@templeton.org. *Clubs:* Athenæum, Royal Over-Seas League, Oxford and Cambridge, White's; Lyford Cay (Bahamas); Merion Cricket (Haverford, Penn); Union League (Philadelphia, Penn). *Died 16 May 2015.*

TEMPLETON-COTILL, Rear-Adm. John Atrill, CB 1972; Flag Officer, Malta, and NATO Commander, South East Area Mediterranean, 1971–73; *b* 4 June 1920; *s* of late Captain Jack Lionel Cottle, Tank Corps; *m* Anna Wright (marr. diss. 1961); partner, Geneviève Denise (*d* 2009). *Educ:* Canford Sch.; New Coll., Oxford (MA 1946). Joined RNVR, 1939; served war 1939–45; HMS Crocus, 1940–41; British Naval Liaison Officer, French warship Chevreuil, 1941–42; staff, GOC New Caledonia (US), 1942; US Embassy, London, 1943; Flag Lieutenant to Vice-Adm., Malta, 1943–44; 1st Lieut, MTB 421, 1944–45; ADC to Governor of Victoria, 1945–46; served in HMS London, Loch Quoich, Whirlwind, Jutland, Barrosa and Sparrow, 1946–55; Comdr 1955; comd HMS Sefton and 108th Minesweeping Sqdn, 1955–56; jssc 1956; Comdr-in-Charge, RN School of Work Study, 1957–59; HMS Tiger, 1959–61; Captain 1961; British Naval Attaché, Moscow, 1962–64; comd HMS Rhyl and Captain (D), 23rd Escort Sqdn, 1964–66; Senior Naval Mem., Defence Operational Analysis Estabt, 1966–68; comd HMS Bulwark, 1968–69; Rear-Adm. Jan. 1970; Chief of Staff to Comdr Far East Fleet, 1970–71; Comdr, British Forces Malta, 1972–73. Director: Sotheby Parke Bernet (France), 1974–81; Sotheby Parke Bernet (Monaco), 1975–81. *Recreations:* gardening, riding, shooting, travel, ski-ing. *Address:* Moulin de Fontvive, Ribas, par 30290 Laudun, France. *T:* 66794737. *Died 23 May 2011.*

TENCH, David Edward, OBE 1987; Head of Legal Department, 1988–94, Director of Legal Affairs, 1991–94, Consumers' Association (publishers of Which?); consultant on public policy and consumer law, since 1994; *b* 14 June 1929; *s* of late Henry George Tench and Emma Rose (*née* Orsborn); *m* 1st, 1957, Judith April Seaton Gurney (*d* 1986); two *s* one *d*; 2nd, 1988, Elizabeth Ann Irvine Macdonald. *Educ:* Merchant Taylors' Sch., Northwood, Middx. Solicitor, 1952. Private practice, 1954–58; Office of Solicitor of Inland Revenue, 1958–69. Chm., Domestic Coal Consumers' Council, 1976–87; Energy Comr, 1977–79. Broadcaster on consumer affairs, 1964–. *Publications:* The Law for Consumers, 1962; The Legal Side of Buying a House, 1965, 2nd edn 1974; Wills and Probate, 1967, 6th edn 1977; How to Sue in the County Court, 1973; Towards a Middle System of Law, 1981. *Recreations:* music, bland gardening. *Address:* Crown Meadow, The Platt, Amersham, Bucks HP7 0HX. *T:* (01494) 724974. *Died 23 Jan. 2011.*

TENNANT, Sir Anthony (John), Kt 1992; Senior Adviser, Morgan Stanley UK Group, 1993–2000; Deputy Chairman, Arjo Wiggins Appleton plc, 1996–2000; *b* 5 Nov. 1930; *s* of late Major John Tennant, TD and Hon. Antonia, *d* of 1st Baron Charnwood (she later *m* 1st Viscount Radcliffe, GBE, PC, FBA); *m* 1954, Rosemary Violet Stockdale; two *s*. *Educ:* Eton; Trinity College, Cambridge (BA 1953). National Service, Scots Guards (Malaya). Mather & Crowther, 1953–66 (Dir, 1959); Marketing Consultancy, 1966–70; Dir, 1970, then Dep. Man. Dir, Truman Ltd; Dir, Watney Mann & Truman Brewers, 1972–76; Man. Dir, 1976–82, Chm., 1983–87, International Distillers & Vintners Ltd; Gp Chief Exec., 1987–89, Chm., 1989–92, Guinness plc; Deputy Chairman: Forte plc, 1992–96; Wellcome plc, 1994–95; Chm., Christie's Internat. plc, 1993–96 (Dir, 1993–98); Director: Exploration Co. plc, 1967–89; El Oro Mining and Exploration Co. plc, 1967–89; Grand Metropolitan PLC, 1977–87; Close Brothers Group plc, 1980–90; Guardian Royal Exchange, 1989–99; Guardian Assurance, 1989–94; BNP UK Hldgs, subseq. BNP Paribas UK Hldgs Ltd, 1990–2002; Savoy Hotel, 1995–96; Mem., Supervisory Bd, LVMH Moet Hennessy Louis Vuitton, Paris, 1988–92. Dir (non-exec.), Internat. Stock Exchange of UK and Republic of Ireland Ltd, 1991–94. Chm., Priorities Bd for R & D in Agric. and Food, 1992–93; Mem. Council, Food From Britain, 1983–86. Chairman: RA Trust, 1996–2002 (Trustee, 1994–2002); Southampton Univ. Develt Trust, 1996–2002 (Trustee, 1992–2002); Trustee, Cambridge Foundn, 1992–2000. Hon. DBA Nottingham Trent, 1996; DUniv Southampton, 2000. Médaille, Ville de Paris, 1989. Chevalier, Légion d'Honneur (France), 1991. *Address:* 18 Hamilton House, Vicarage Gate, W8 4HL. *T:* (020) 7937 6203. *Club:* Boodle's. *Died 4 Aug. 2011.*

TETTENBORN, Richard Garstin, OBE 1993; Treasurer: Staffordshire County Council, 1992–2003; Staffordshire Police Authority, 1995–2008; Stoke on Trent and Staffordshire Combined Fire Authority, 1997–2003; *b* 23 Sept. 1940; *s* of Philip Arthur de Gleichen Tettenborn and Helena Louise Tettenborn (*née* Sharpe); *m* 1983, Susan Margaret Wrigley (*née* Crew); one *s*. *Educ:* Herbert Strutt Sch., Belper; Brasenose Coll., Oxford (MA). IPFA 1967. Trainee accountant, Derbyshire CC, 1963–67; Sen. Accountant, London Borough of Sutton, 1967–70; Asst Treas., W Sussex CC, 1970–76; Dep. Treas., Mid Glamorgan CC, 1976–79; Treas., S Glamorgan CC, 1980–92. Financial Advr, Welsh Counties Cttee, 1984–91; Comr, Public Works Loan Bd, 1991–95. Mem. Bd, Police IT Orgn, 1998–2000. President: Soc. of Co. Treasurers, 1992–93; CIPFA, 1994–95; Police Authy Treasurers Soc., 2006–07. *Recreations:* family, golf, watching sport, theatre. *Address:* Sweetbriar, 68 Weeping Cross, Stafford ST17 0DL. *T:* (01785) 604613. *Club:* Oxford and Cambridge. *Died 10 Feb. 2011.*

TEW, Prof. John Hedley Brian, OBE 1988; PhD; Midland Bank Professor of Money and Banking, University of Nottingham, 1967–82; *b* 1 Feb. 1917; *s* of Herbert and Catherine Mary Tew; *m* 1944, Marjorie Hoey Craigie (*d* 2008); one *s* one *d*. *Educ:* Mill Hill School, Leicester; University College, Leicester; Peterhouse, Cambridge. BSc (Econ.) London; PhD Cantab. Iron and Steel Control, 1940–42; Ministry of Aircraft Production, 1942–45; Industrial and Commercial Finance Corp., 1946; Professor of Economics, Univ. of Adelaide (Australia), 1947–49; Professor of Economics, University of Nottingham, 1950–67. External Prof., Dept of Econs, Univ. of Loughborough, 1982–99. Part-time Member: Iron and Steel Board, 1964–67; East Midlands Electricity Board, 1965–76; Tubes Div., BSC, 1969–73; Mem., Cttee of Enquiry on Small Firms, Dept of Trade and Industry, 1969–71. *Publications:* Wealth and Income, 1950; International Monetary Co-operation 1952; (jt editor) Studies in Company Finance, 1959; Monetary Theory, 1969; The Evolution of the International Monetary System, 1977. *Died 12 Oct. 2013.*

THATCHER, Baroness *cr* 1992 (Life Peer), of Kesteven in the County of Lincolnshire; **Margaret Hilda Thatcher,** LG 1995; OM 1990; PC 1970; FRS 1983; *b* 13 Oct. 1925; *d* of late Alfred Roberts, Grantham, Lincs; *m* 1951, Denis Thatcher, later Sir Denis Thatcher, 1st Bt (*d* 2003); one *s* one *d* (twins). *Educ:* Kesteven and Grantham Girls' School; Somerville College, Oxford (BSc, MA; Hon. Fellow, 1970). Research Chemist, 1947–51; called to the Bar, Lincoln's Inn, 1954, Hon. Bencher, 1975. MP (C) Finchley, 1959–92; Joint Parly Sec., Min. of Pensions and National Insurance, Oct. 1961–64; Sec. of State for Educn and Sci., 1970–74; Leader of the Opposition, 1975–79; Prime Minister and First Lord of the Treasury, 1979–90. Co-Chm., Women's Nat. Commn, 1970–74. Chancellor: Univ. of Buckingham, 1992–98; William and Mary Coll., Virginia, 1993–2000. Chm. Bd, Inst. of US Studies, London Univ., 1994–2002. Freedom of Borough of Barnet, 1980, of City of London, 1989. Donovan Award, USA, 1981. *Publications:* In Defence of Freedom, 1986; The Collected Speeches of Margaret Thatcher, 1997; Statecraft: strategies for a changing world, 2002; *memoirs:* The Downing Street Years 1979–90, 1993; The Path to Power, 1995. *Recreations:* music, reading. *Address:* House of Lords, SW1A 0PW. *Club:* Carlton. *Died 8 April 2013.*

THEOBALD, George Peter; JP; company director, 1958–2009; *b* 5 Aug. 1931; *s* of late George Oswald Theobald and Helen (*née* Moore); *m* 1955, Josephine Mary (*née* Boodle); two *s* three *d*. *Educ:* Betteshanger Sch.; Harrow. National Service commission, 5 Regt RHA, 1950–52; 290 (City of London) RA (TA), 1953–59. Robert Warner Ltd, 1953–74: Director, 1958; Man. Dir, Chm. Gp subsidiaries, 1965; private company director, 1974–2008; Tea Clearing House, 1959–72 (Chm., 1970–72); Moran Holdings (formerly Moran Tea Holdings) plc, 1980–2005 (Chm., 1992–2005); Moran Tea Co. (India) plc, 1981–2005 (Chm., 1992–2005). City of London (Queenhithe Ward): Chm., Ward Club, 1966–68; Common Councilman, 1968–74; Alderman, 1974–79. Member: Transport Users' Consultative Cttee for London, 1969–84 (Dep. Chm. 1978); London Regional Passengers Cttee, 1984–90. Governor: Bridewell Royal Hosp., 1974–93; King Edward's Sch., Witley, 1974–93 (Trustee, Educational Trust, 1977–95); Donation Governor, Christ's Hosp., 1976–91; Governor, St Leonards-Mayfield Sch., 1982–88; Chm., St John's Sch., Northwood, 1989–97; Mem. Cttee, Langford Cross Children's Home, 1976–90; Trustee: National Flood and Tempest Distress Fund, 1977–; Harrow Mission, 1978–2001. Church Commissioner for England, 1978–79. Master, Merchant Taylors' Co., 1989–90, 1991–92. JP City of London, 1974. *Recreations:* gardening, transport, family. *Clubs:* Oriental, City Livery, Guildhall, MCC. *Died 26 Sept. 2013.*

THÉODORE, Jean-François; Director, NYSE Euronext, 2007–11 (Deputy Chief Executive Officer, 2007–09; Chief Executive, Euronext, 2000–07); *b* 5 Dec. 1946; *m* 1976, Claudine Lefebvre; one *s* two *d*. *Educ:* Univ. of Paris (Licencé); Institut d'Etudes Politiques; Ecole Nationale d'Administration. Asst Hd, State Holdings Bureau, French Treasury, 1974–78; seconded to Credit National, as Mem., Exec. Bd, 1978–80; Treasury: Hd, African States-Franc Zone Bureau, 1980–82; Hd, Foreign Investment Bureau, 1982–84; Dep. Dir i/c, Banking Dept, 1984–86; Dep. Dir, Investments, State Participations and Public Corps Dept, 1986–90; CEO, 1990–99, Chm., 1991–99, SBF-Paris Bourse; Chm., MATIF, 1998–99; CEO and Chm., Paris Bourse, 1999–2000. Chm., SICOVAM, 1993–2000. President: Internat. Fedn of Stock Exchanges, 1993–94; Fedn European Stock Exchanges, 1998–2000. Chm. Steering Cttee, Paris Europlace; Pres., Supervisory Bd, Mandel Partners, 2011–; Mem., Supervisory Bd, Moody's Investors Service Ltd, Moody's Deutschland, Moody's France, 2010–. Chevalier, Légion d'Honneur, 1994. *Clubs:* Paris-Europlace, Bourse (Paris). *Died 18 May 2015.*

THIRSK, Dr (Irene) Joan, CBE 1994; FBA 1974; Reader in Economic History in the University of Oxford, and Professorial Fellow of St Hilda's College, Oxford, 1965–83 (Hon. Fellow, 1983); *b* 19 June 1922; *d* of William Henry Watkins and Daisy (*née* Frayer); *m* 1945, James Wood Thirsk; one *s* one *d*. *Educ:* Camden School for Girls, NW5; Westfield Coll., Univ. of London (BA; Hon. Fellow, QMW, 1996); PhD London; MA Oxford. Subaltern, ATS, Intelligence Corps (Bletchley Park), 1942–45. Asst Lectr in Sociology, LSE, 1950–51; Sen. Res. Fellow in Agrarian History, Dept of English Local History, Leicester Univ., 1951–65. Ford Lectr in English History, Oxford, 1975. Sen. Mellon Fellow, Nat. Humanities Centre, 1986–87. Member: Royal Commn on Historical Monuments (England), 1977–86; Econ. and Social Hist. Cttee, SSRC, 1978–82; Royal Commn on Historical Manuscripts, 1989–96. Mem. Council, Economic Hist. Soc., 1955–83; Vice-Chm., Standing Conf. for Local Hist., 1965–82; President: British Agricl Hist. Soc., 1983–86, 1995–98 (Mem. Exec. Cttee, 1953–83, Chm. Exec. Cttee, 1974–77); Edmonton Hundred Historical Soc., 1978–96; Oxfordshire Local Hist. Assoc., 1981–86 (Vice-Pres., 1980–81); Conf. of Teachers of Regional and Local Hist. in Tertiary Educn, 1981–82; British Assoc. for Local Hist., 1986–92; Kent Hist. Fedn, 1990–99; Vice-President: Soc. for Lincs Hist. and Archaeol., 1979–; Past and Present Soc., 2003–. Foreign Mem., Amer. Philos. Soc., 1982–. Editor, Agricultural History Review, 1964–72; Gen. Editor, The Agrarian History of England and Wales, 1974–2000 (Dep. Gen. Ed., 1966–74); Mem. Editorial Bd, Past and Present, 1956–92. FRHistS 1954. Hon. Fellow, Kellogg Coll., Oxford, 1998. Hon. DLitt: Leicester, 1985; East Anglia, 1990; Kent, 1993; Sussex, 1994; Southampton, 1999; Greenwich, 2001; DUniv Open, 1991; Hon. DAgr Wageningen Agricl Univ., Netherlands, 1993. *Publications:* English Peasant Farming, 1957; Suffolk Farming in the Nineteenth Century, 1958; Tudor Enclosures, 1959; The Agrarian History of England and Wales: vol. IV, 1500–1640, 1967; vol. V, 1640–1750, 1984; (with J. P. Cooper) Seventeenth-Century Economic Documents, 1972; The Restoration, 1976; Economic Policy and Projects, 1978; The Rural Economy of England (collected essays), 1985; England's Agricultural Regions and Agrarian History 1500–1750, 1987; Alternative Agriculture: a history from the Black Death to the present day, 1997; The English Rural Landscape, 2000; Food in Early Modern England, 2007; Hadlow: life, land and people in a Wealden parish 1460–1600, 2007; articles in Economic History Rev., Agric. History Rev., Past and Present, History, Jl Modern History, etc. *Recreations:* gardening, sewing. *Address:* 1 Hadlow Castle, Hadlow, Tonbridge, Kent TN11 0EG. *E:* jthirsk@onetel.com. *Died 3 Oct. 2013.*

THOMAS, Caroline Jane H.; *see* Harry Thomas.

THOMAS, Prof. (Edward) Donnall, MD; Member, Fred Hutchinson Cancer Research Center, Seattle, 1974, then Member Emeritus (Director, Medical Oncology, 1974–89; Associate Director, Clinical Research Programs, 1982–89); Professor of Medicine, University of Washington School of Medicine, Seattle, 1963–90, then Emeritus; *b* Mart, Texas, 15 March 1920; *m* 1942, Dorothy Martin; two *s* one *d*. *Educ:* Univ. of Texas, Austin (BA 1941; MA 1943); Harvard Medical Sch. (MD 1946). Assignments in internal medicine, US Army, 1948–50; Nat. Res. Council Postdoctoral Fellow in Medicine, Dept of Biol., MIT, 1950–51; Chief Med. Resident and Sen. Asst Resident, Peter Bent Brigham Hosp., Boston, 1951–53, Hematologist, 1953–55; Instructor in Medicine, Harvard Med. Sch. and Res. Associate, Cancer Res. Foundn, Children's Med. Center, Boston, 1953–55; Physician-in-Chief, Mary Imogene Bassett Hosp., Cooperstown, NY and Associate Clinical Prof. of Medicine, Coll. of Physicians and Surgeons, Columbia Univ., NY, 1955–63; Hd, Div. of Oncology, Univ. of Washington Sch. of Medicine, Seattle, 1963–85. Consulting Physician, Children's Orthopedic Hosp. and Med. Center, Seattle, 1963–90; Attending Physician, Seattle: Univ. of Washington Hosp., 1963–90; Harborview Med. Center, 1963–90; Veterans Admin Hosp., 1963–90; Providence Med. Center, 1973–90; Swedish Hosp., 1975–90. Member Editorial Board: Blood, 1962–75, 1977–82; Transplantation, 1970–76; Procs Soc. Exptl Biol. and Medicine, 1974–81; Leukemia Res., 1977–87; Hematological Oncology, 1982–87; Jl Clinical Immunology, 1982–87; Amer. Jl Hematology, 1985–; Bone Marrow Transplantation, 1986–. Member: Amer. Assoc. Cancer Res.; Amer. Assoc. Physicians; Amer. Fedn Clinical Res.; Amer. Soc. Clinical Oncology; Amer. Soc. Clinical Investigation; Amer. Soc. Hematology (Pres., 1987–88); Nat. Acad. Scis and other foreign socs on related subjects. Lectures in US and UK on hematology and cancer res. Numerous awards from instns in N America and abroad incl. Nobel Prize for Physiology or Medicine, 1990; Presidential Medal of Science, 1990. *Recreations:* hunting, fishing, hiking. *Address:* c/o Fred Hutchinson Cancer Research Center, 1100 Fairview Avenue N, D5–100, PO Box 19024, Seattle, WA 98109–1024, USA. *Died 20 Oct. 2012.*

THOMAS, Keith Henry Westcott, CB 1982; OBE 1962; FREng, FRINA; RCNC; Chief Executive, Royal Dockyards, and Head of Royal Corps of Naval Constructors, 1979–83; *b* 20 May 1923; *s* of Henry and Norah Thomas; *m* 1946, Brenda Jeanette Crofton; two *s*. *Educ:* Portsmouth Southern Secondary Sch.; HM Dockyard Sch., Portsmouth; RNC, Greenwich. Asst Constructor, Admiralty Experiment Works, Haslar, 1947–49; Constructor: Admty, London, 1949–56; Large Carrier Design Section, Admty, Bath, 1956–60; Submarines and New Construction, HM Dockyard, Portsmouth, 1960–63; Project Leader, Special Refit HMS Hermes, Devonport, 1963–66; Dep. Planning Manager, HM Dockyard, Devonport, 1966–68; Project Manager, Ikara Leanders, MoD(N), 1968–70; Dir-Gen. of Naval Design, Dept of Navy, Canberra, Aust. (on secondment), 1970–73; Planning Manager, 1973–75, Gen. Manager, 1975–77, HM Dockyard, Rosyth; Gen. Manager, HM Dockyard, Devonport, 1977–79. Member: Portsmouth Royal Dockyard Historical Trust, 1995– (Chm., 1995–2006; Pres., Portsmouth Royal Dockyard Historical Soc., 1988–95); Nat. Historic Ships Cttee, 1996–2000. *Recreations:* music, lapidary, painting. *Address:* 6 Wyborn Close, Hayling Island, Hants PO11 9HY. *T:* (023) 9246 3435. *Died 30 Dec. 2015.*

THOMAS, Leslie John, OBE 2005; author; *b* 22 March 1931; *s* of late David James Thomas and late Dorothy Hilda Court Thomas, Newport (Mon); *m* 1st, 1956, Maureen Crane (marr. diss.); two *s* one *d*; 2nd, 1970, Diana Miles; one *s*. *Educ:* Dr Barnardo's, Kingston-upon-Thames; Kingston Technical Sch.; SW Essex Technical Coll., Walthamstow. Local Newspapers, London area, 1948–49 and 1951–53; Army, 1949–51 (rose to Lance-Corporal); Exchange Telegraph News Agency, 1953–55; Special Writer, London Evening News, 1955–66; subseq. author. Vice Pres., Barnardo's, 1998–. Hon. MA Wales, 1995; Hon. DLitt Nottingham, 1998. *Publications: autobiography:* This Time Next Week, 1964; In My Wildest Dreams, 1984; *novels:* The Virgin Soldiers, 1966; Orange Wednesday, 1967; The Love Beach, 1968; Come to the War, 1969; His Lordship, 1970; Onward Virgin Soldiers, 1971; Arthur McCann and All His Women, 1972; The Man with Power, 1973; Tropic of Ruislip, 1974; Stand up Virgin Soldiers, 1975; Dangerous Davies, 1976; Bare Nell, 1977; Ormerod's Landing, 1978; That Old Gang of Mine, 1979; The Magic Army, 1981; The Dearest and the Best, 1984; The Adventures of Goodnight and Loving, 1986; Dangerous in Love, 1987; Orders For New York, 1989; The Loves and Journeys of Revolving Jones, 1991; Arrivals and Departures, 1992; Dangerous by Moonlight, 1993; Running Away, 1994; Kensington Heights, 1996; Chloë's Song, 1997; Dangerous Davies and the Lonely Heart, 1998; Other Times, 1999; Waiting for the Day, 2003; Dover Beach, 2005; Soldiers and Lovers, 2007; *non-fiction:* Some Lovely Islands, 1968; The Hidden Places of Britain, 1981; A World of Islands, 1983; Short Singles, 1986; Almost Heaven: tales from a cathedral, 2010; TV plays and documentaries, etc, incl. Channel Four series, Great British Isles (also presented), 1989; The Last Detective (series, adaptation of Dangerous Davies novels), 2003, 2004, 2005; also short stories. *Recreations:* islands, antiques, cricket. *Address:* De Vaux House, De Vaux Place, Salisbury, Wilts SP1 2SN. *Clubs:* MCC, Lord's Taverners. *Died 6 May 2014.*

THOMAS, Meyric Leslie, OBE 1987; Vice Lord-Lieutenant of West Glamorgan, 1997–2001; Consultant, Hutchinson Thomas (formerly L. C. Thomas and Son, later Hutchinson Thomas), Solicitors, since 1990 (Partner, 1956–90); *b* 17 Nov. 1928; *s* of Charles Leslie Thomas and Edith Annie Thomas; *m* 1956, Jillian Hamilton Armstrong (decd); two *s* one *d*. *Educ:* Beaudesert Park; Clifton Coll.; Jesus Coll., Oxford (Mem., Univ. Boat Race crew, 1952, 1953; Pres., OUBC, 1953; MA Jurisprudence). Admitted Solicitor, 1956. Nat. Service, Glos Regt, 1947–49 (Belt of Honour, Eaton Hall, 1948). Mem. (Ind.), Neath BC, 1957–74 (Mayor, 1967). Pres., Neath RFC, 1973–78. DL W Glamorgan, 1993. *Recreations:* Rugby Union (spectator), bowls. *Address:* Braye Lea, Val Reuters, Alderney, Channel Islands GY9 3XE. *T:* (01481) 823465. *Club:* Alderney Bowls. *Died 12 May 2013.*

THOMAS, Susan Kanter; Managing Partner, ST Partnership Ltd, 2006–12; *b* NYC, 29 Feb. 1952; *d* of Capt. Marvin W. Kanter and Miriam Graboys Kanter; *m* 1974, Stewart Thomas. *Educ:* Nasson Coll., Maine (BA Pol Sci.). FCIPD 1994. Personnel Director posts, London Borough of Hackney, 1976–82; Hd of Personnel, S Bank Poly., 1982–86; Asst Chief Personnel Officer, 1986–93, Dir, Personnel and Admin, 1993–99, London Borough of Lewisham; Interim Dir, Corporate Services, GLA, 1999–2000; Dir-Gen., Corporate Services and Develt, and Bd Mem., DfES, 2000–06. Non-exec. Dir, Housing Ombudsman Service, 2006–. Mem. Council, St George's, Univ. of London, 2010–. Mem., Warner Cttee, DoH. Pres., Soc. of Chief Personnel Officers, 1997–98. FRSA. *Died 5 Sept. 2012.*

THOMAS, His Honour William Fremlyn Cotter; a Circuit Judge, 1990–2005; *b* 18 March 1935; *s* of Stephen Kerr Thomas and Nâdine Dieudonnée Thomas (*née* March); *m* 1st, 1960, Mary Alanna Mudie (decd); one *d*; 2nd, 1968, Thalia Mary Edith Myers (marr. diss. 1975); 3rd, 1978, Hon. Ursula Nancy Eden, *d* of 7th Baron Henley and of Nancy, Lady Henley; one *s* one *d*. *Educ:* Bryanston Sch.; University Coll., Oxford. National Service, 2nd Lieut, 1954–56. Called to the Bar, Inner Temple, 1961; SE Circuit; a Recorder, 1986. *Recreations:* music, architecture, gardening. *Address:* c/o Kingston-upon-Thames Crown Court, 6–8 Penrhyn Road, Kingston-upon-Thames, Surrey KT1 2BB. *Club:* Reform. *Died 22 June 2013.*

THOMPSON, Alan, CB 1978; Chairman, Review Group on the Youth Service, 1981–82; *b* 16 July 1920; *s* of Herbert and Esther Thompson; *m* 1944, Joyce Nora Banks (*d* 2000); two *s* one *d*. *Educ:* Carlisle Grammar Sch.; Queen's Coll., Oxford. Joined Min. of Education, 1946; Private Sec. to Minister of Education, 1954–56; Asst Sec., Further Education Br., 1956–64; Under Sec., UGC, 1964–71; Under Sec., Science Br., DES, 1971–75; Dep. Sec., DES, 1975–80. *Address:* 1 Haven Close, Wimbledon, SW19 5JW. *Died 27 March 2012.*

THOMPSON, Aubrey Gordon D.; *see* Denton-Thompson.

THOMPSON, Christopher Ronald; Senior Partner, Aldenham Business Services Ltd, since 1984; *b* 14 Dec. 1927; *s* of late Col S. J. Thompson, DSO, DL and Margaret Thompson (*née* Green); *m* 1st, 1949, Rachael Meynell (*d*

2003); one *s* one *d* (and one *s* decd); 2nd, 2006, Lucy Carolyn (*née* Fisher), *widow* of Charles Shakerley. *Educ:* Shrewsbury School; Trinity College, Cambridge. 1st Bn KSLI (Lieut), 1946–48. Dir, John Thompson Ltd, 1954–68, Chm., 1969; Dir, Rockwell-Thompson Ltd, 1973–74; Vice-Pres., Rockwell Europe, 1974–78. Chairman: NEI Internat., 1979–84; Wynn Electronics, 1983–87; Filtermist Internat. plc, 1985–97; John Sutcliffe Shipping Ltd, 1986–89; Director: Saraswati Syndicate pte India, 1954–; Barclays Bank Birmingham Bd, 1974–87; G. T. Japan Investment Trust, 1983–; Isotron plc, 1984–2003; Craven Grain Storage Ltd, 1984–95; Plessey Co. plc, 1988–89. Member: Overseas Projects Bd, BOTB, 1981–84; Sino-British Trade Council, 1983–85; Indo-British Industrial Forum, 1987–93. Pres., BEAMA, 1984–85. Chm., CLA Cttee for Shropshire, 1996–. Mem. Council, HHA, 1992–2004. Chm., Anglo-Venezuelan Soc., 1981–85. Trustee: Hereford Cathedral Trust, 1984–98; Mappa Mundi Trust, 1990–98. High Sheriff, Shropshire, 1984–85. *Recreations:* fly fishing, shooting, forestry. *Address:* Aldenham Park, near Bridgnorth, Shropshire WV16 4RN. *T:* (01746) 714218. *Club:* Boodle's. *Died 6 April 2015.*

THOMPSON, Denis P.; *see* Pullein-Thompson, D.

THOMPSON, Sir Gilbert (Williamson), Kt 1993; OBE 1985; Chairman: British Airports Group, 1995–2001; Alltram, 1997–2001; Chief Executive, 1981–93, and Board Member, 1986–93, Manchester Airport plc; *b* 1 March 1930; *s* of Henry Gordon Thompson and Isabella Thompson; *m* 1954, Dorothy Millar; two *d*. *Educ:* London Business Sch.; Manchester Business Sch. British European Airways, later British Airways: mgt trainee, Belfast, 1950; Regl Manager, Los Angeles, 1965–67; Manager, Irish Republic, 1967–69; General Manager: USA, 1969–72; Scotland, 1972–74; N of England, 1974–81. Dep. Chm., Campbell & Armstrong, 1996–2001. Pres., British Amer. Business Gp, 1995–2001; Member: British Amer. Business Council, 1995–2001; Bd, Nimtech, 1996–2001; BOTB, 1997–2001. Hon. DLitt Salford, 1993. *Recreations:* golf, bridge, soccer, jogging, keep fit. *Address:* Arncliffe, The Penthouse, Apartment 5, 66 South Downs Road, Bowdon, Cheshire WA14 3DR. *Died 1 Oct. 2013.*

THOMPSON, Sir Godfrey James M.; *see* Milton-Thompson.

THOMPSON, James, FCLIP; University Librarian, University of Birmingham, 1987–95; *b* 11 Jan. 1932; *s* of James Thompson and Mary Margaret Thompson (*née* Harland); *m* 1st, 1958, Mary Josephine McAndrew (marr. diss. 1987); one *s* one *d*; 2nd, 1988, Susan Lesley Challans. *Educ:* St Cuthbert's Grammar Sch.; Univ. of Durham (BA 1st Cl. Hons English). FCLIP (FLA 1963). Newcastle City Libraries, 1948–59; Nottingham Univ. Liby, 1959–63; Sen. Asst Librarian, UEA, 1963–65; Dep. Librarian, Univ. of Glasgow, 1965–67; Univ. Librarian, Univ. of Reading, 1967–87. Member: Council, LA, 1972–74; Berks Co. Liby Sub-cttee, 1973–87; SCONUL Council, 1983–86. Pres., Reading AUT, 1981–83. Project Hd, Location Register of Twentieth Century English Literary MSS and Letters, 1982–87. *Publications:* The Librarian and English Literature, 1968, 2nd edn as English Studies, 1971; Books: an anthology, 1968; An Introduction to University Library Administration, 1970, 4th edn 1987 (Spanish edn 1989); Library Power, 1974; A History of the Principles of Librarianship, 1977; (ed) University Library History, 1980; The End of Libraries, 1982; Redirection in Academic Library Management, 1991; A Centennial History of the Library of the University of Birmingham, 2000; contribs to books, conf. proceedings and jls. *Recreation:* gardening. *Address:* 35 Meadow Rise, Bournville, Birmingham B30 1UZ. *T:* (0121) 472 1735. *Died 30 Jan. 2015.*

THOMPSON, John; DL; *b* 27 Aug. 1928; *s* of Nicholas and Lilian Thompson; *m* 1952, Margaret Clarke; one *s* one *d*. *Educ:* Bothal Sch.; Ashington Mining Coll. Electrical Engr, 1966–83. Councillor: Wansbeck DC, 1974–79; Northumberland CC, 1974–85 (Leader, and Chm., Policy and Resources, and Employment Cttees, 1981–83). MP (Lab) Wansbeck, 1983–97. An Opposition Whip, 1990–97. Mem., Select Cttee on Educn, Science and Arts, 1985–87; Chm., Northern Labour MPs, 1991–92 (Sec., 1985–90). Member: Council of Europe (Chm., Fisheries Sub Cttee, 1995–97); WEU (Chm., Rules and Privileges Cttee, 1992–97). Chm., Ashington Educn Achievement Zone, 1999–2002. DL Northumberland, 1996. *Address:* 20 Falstone Crescent, Ashington, Northumberland NE63 0TY. *T:* (01670) 817830. *Died 21 July 2011.*

THOMPSON, (John) Derek T.; *see* Taylor Thompson.

THOMPSON, John Leonard C.; *see* Cloudsley-Thompson.

THOMPSON, John William McWean, CBE 1986; Editor, Sunday Telegraph, 1976–86; *b* 12 June 1920; *s* of Charles and Charlotte Thompson; *m* 1947, Cynthia Ledsham; one *s* one *d*. *Educ:* Roundhay Sch., Leeds. Previously on staffs of Yorkshire Evening News, Evening Standard, London, and The Spectator (Dep. Editor); joined Sunday Telegraph, 1970; Asst Editor, 1975. *Publications:* (as Peter Quince) Country Life, 1975; articles and reviews in many jls. *Address:* Corner Cottage, 1 Marsh Lane, Burnham Norton, Norfolk PE31 8DS. *T:* (01328) 738396. *Club:* Travellers. *Died 24 Nov. 2013.*

THOMPSON, Josephine Mary Wedderburn P.; *see* Pullein-Thompson.

THOMPSON, (Rupert) Julian (de la Mare); Chinese art consultant; *b* 23 July 1941; *s* of Rupert Spens Thompson and Florence Elizabeth (*née* de la Mare); *m* 1965, Jacqueline Mary Ivimy (marr. diss. 2008); three *d*; *m* 2009, Li Fan; one *s*; one *d* by Jenny Lu. *Educ:* Eton Coll.; King's Coll., Cambridge (MA). Joined Sotheby's, 1963: appointed a Director, 1969; Chm., 1982–86; Dep. Chm., 1987–92; Chm., Sotheby's International, 1982–85, 1987–88; non-exec. Chm., Sotheby's Asia, 1992–2003. *Address:* Crossington Farm, Upton Bishop, Ross-on-Wye, Herefordshire HR9 7UE. *T:* (01989) 780471. *Died 16 Jan. 2011.*

THOMSON, Prof. Andrew William John, PhD; OBE 1993; Professor, School of Management, Open University, 1988–2001, Professor Emeritus, 2006; *b* 26 Jan. 1936; *s* of Andrew Edward Thomson and Helen Thomson; *m* 1st, 1966, Joan Marjorie Hughes (marr. diss. 1980); two *s*; 2nd, 1992, Rosemary Joy Hetherington Smith (*d* 1998); 3rd, 2001, Prof. Angela Marilyn Bowey. *Educ:* St Bees Sch.; St Edmund Hall, Oxford (BA Hons PPE 1959); Cornell Univ. (MS 1961; PhD 1968). 2nd Lieut, RA, 1954–56; Lieut, Parachute Regt TA, 1958–63; Brand Manager, Lever Brothers, 1961–65; University of Glasgow: Lectr, Sen. Lectr and Reader, 1968–78; Prof. of Business Policy, 1978–87; Dean: Scottish Business Sch., 1983–87; Sch. of Management, Open Univ., 1988–93. Prof., Univ. of Chicago, 1973, 1977. Dir, Scottish Transport Gp, 1977–84; Mem., Scottish Agricl Wages Bd, 1985–99; Vice-Chairman: Mgt and Industrial Relations Cttee, SSRC, 1982–85; Industry and Employment Cttee, ESRC, 1985–88; Chm., Jt Cttee, ESRC-SERC, 1987–90. Chairman: Council of Univ. Mgt Schs, 1985–87; British Acad. of Mgt, 1990–93. Mem., Focus Paihia Community Trust. *Publications:* (with L. C. Hunter) The Nationalised Transport Industries, 1973; (with S. R. Engleman) The Industrial Relations Act, 1975; (with V. V. Murray) Grievance Procedures, 1976; (with P. B. Beaumont) Collective Bargaining in the Public Sector, 1978; (ed with M. Warner) The Behavioural Sciences and Industrial Relations, 1981; (ed with M. B. Gregory) A Portrait of Pay, 1990; (jtly) Changing Patterns of Management Development, 2001; (with J. Wilson) The Making of Modern Management: British management in historical perspective, 2006; (with E. Brech and J. Wilson) Lyndall Urwick Management Pioneer: a biography, 2010. *Recreations:* golf, walking, bridge. *Address:* PO Box 113, Paihia 0247, New Zealand. *T:* (9) 4028416. *Clubs:* Waitangi Golf; Bay of Islands Rotary. *Died 26 Dec. 2014.*

THOMSON, Prof. Derick Smith, FBA 1992; FRSE; Professor of Celtic, University of Glasgow, 1963–91, then Emeritus; *b* 5 Aug. 1921; *s* of James and Christina Thomson; *m* 1952, Carol Mac Michael Galbraith; five *s* one *d*. *Educ:* Nicolson Inst., Stornoway; Univ. of Aberdeen (MA); University College of North Wales, Bangor; Emmanuel Coll., Cambridge (BA 1948). Asst in Celtic, Univ. of Edinburgh, 1948–49; Lectr in Welsh, Univ. of

Glasgow, 1949–56; Reader in Celtic, Univ. of Aberdeen, 1956–63. Chm., Gaelic Books Council, 1968–91; Pres., Scottish Gaelic Texts Soc., 1964–96. Editor: Scottish Gaelic Studies, 1962–76; Gairm, 1952–2002. Hon. DLitt: Wales, 1987; Aberdeen, 1994; Glasgow, 2007. First recipient, Ossian Prize, FVS Foundn, Hamburg, 1974. *Publications:* The Gaelic Sources of Macpherson's Ossian, 1952; Branwen Verch Lyr, 1961, 2nd edn 1968; An Introduction to Gaelic Poetry, 1974, 2nd edn 1990; The Companion to Gaelic Scotland, 1983, 3rd edn 1994; The MacDiarmid MS Anthology, 1992; Gaelic Poetry in the Eighteenth Century, 1993; Alasdair Mac Mhaighstir Alasdair, Selected Poems, 1996; *poetry:* Creachadh Na Clàrsaich (Plundering the Harp), Collected Poems, 1982; Smeur an Dòchais (Bramble of Hope), 1992; Meall Garbh (The Rugged Mountain), 1995; Suil air Fàire (Surveying the Horizon), 2007. *Recreations:* writing, travel, politics, gardening. *Address:* 15 Struan Road, Cathcart, Glasgow G44 3AT. *T:* (0141) 637 3704. *Clubs:* Glasgow Art, Town and Gown (Glasgow). *Died 21 March 2012.*

THOMSON, Nigel Ernest Drummond, CBE 1993; Sheriff of Lothian and Borders, at Edinburgh and Peebles, 1976–96; *b* 19 June 1926; *y s* of late Rev. James Kyd Thomson and Joan Drummond; *m* 1964, Snjólaug Magnússon, *yr d* of late Consul-General Sigursteinn Magnússon; one *s* one *d*. *Educ:* George Watson's College, Edinburgh; Univs of St Andrews and Edinburgh. Served with Scots Guards and Indian Grenadiers, 1944–47. MA (St Andrews) 1950; LLB (Edin.) 1953. Called to Scottish Bar, 1953. Standing Counsel to Scottish Educn Dept, 1961–66; Sheriff of Lanarkshire, later S Strathclyde, Dumfries and Galloway, at Hamilton, 1966–76. Chm., Music Cttee, Scottish Arts Council, 1978–83; Chm., Edinburgh Youth Orchestra, 1986–92. Convenor, Council for Music in Hosps in Scotland, 1992–2001. Pres., Speculative Soc., Edinburgh, 1960; Vice President: Tenovus-Scotland, 1985–2001; British Assoc. for Counselling, 1992–2002. Hon. Texas Ranger, 1994. *Publications:* In and Out of Court (memoirs), 2001. *Recreations:* music, woodwork, golf. *Address:* 17/1 Wyvern Park, Edinburgh EH9 2JY. *Clubs:* New (Edinburgh); Bruntsfield Golf (Edinburgh). *Died 28 Dec. 2011.*

THOMSON, Sir Thomas (James), Kt 1991; CBE 1984 (OBE 1978); FRCPGlas, FRCP, FRCPEd, FRCPI; Chairman, Greater Glasgow Health Board, 1987–93; Consultant Physician and Gastroenterologist, Stobhill General Hospital, Glasgow, 1961–87; Hon. Lecturer, Department of Materia Medica, University of Glasgow, 1961–87; *b* 8 April 1923; *s* of Thomas Thomson and Annie Jane Grant; *m* 1948, Jessie Smith Shotbolt; two *s* one *d*. *Educ:* Airdrie Acad.; Univ. of Glasgow (MB, ChB 1945). FRCPGlas 1964 (FRFPSG 1949); FRCP 1969 (MRCP 1950); FRCPEd 1982; FRCPI 1983. Lectr, Dept of Materia Medica, Univ. of Glasgow, 1953–61; Postgrad. Adviser to Glasgow Northern Hosps, 1961–80. Sec., Specialist Adv. Cttee for Gen. Internal Medicine for UK, 1970–74; Chairman: Medico-Pharmaceutical Forum, 1978–80 (Chm., Educn Adv. Bd, 1979–84); National Med. Consultative Cttee for Scotland, 1982–87; Conf. of Royal Colls and Faculties in Scotland, 1982–84; Hon. Sec., 1965–73, Pres., 1982–84, RCPSGlas. Active participation in postgrad. med. educnl cttees, locally, nationally, in EEC and in Libya, Kuwait, Jordan and Oman. Mem. Ct, Strathclyde Univ., 1993–97. Hon. FACP 1983. Hon. LLD Glasgow, 1988; DUniv Strathclyde, 1997. *Publications:* (ed jtly) Dilling's Pharmacology, 1969; Gastroenterology—an integrated course, 1972, 3rd edn 1983; pubns related to gen. medicine, gastroent. and therapeutics. *Recreations:* swimming, golfing. *Address:* 1 Varna Road, Glasgow G14 9NE. *T:* (0141) 959 5930. *Club:* Royal Air Force. *Died 20 July 2013.*

THORNE, Rear-Adm. Edward Courtney, CB 1975; CBE 1971; Chairman, New Zealand Fire Service Commission, 1976–86; Chief of Naval Staff, New Zealand, 1972–75; *b* 29 Oct. 1923; *s* of Ernest Alexander Thorne and Ethel Violet Thorne; *m* 1949, Fay Bradburn (*née* Kerr) (*d* 2006); three *s*. *Educ:* Rongotai Coll.; Nelson Coll., NZ. IDC 1966. Chm., Nat. Council, United World Colls, 1982–94; Mem., Nat. Council, Duke of Edinburgh Award Scheme, 1976–89; Pres., Sea Cadet Assoc. of NZ, 1990–98. Hon. FIFireE 1983. *Recreations:* gardening, walking. *Address:* 119/57 Richard Farrell Avenue, Remuera, Auckland 1050, New Zealand. *Died 23 Oct. 2013.*

THORNING-PETERSEN, Rudolph; Knight Commander, Order of the Dannebrog, 1994; Ambassador; Chamberlain to the Queen of Denmark, since 1998; *b* 17 July 1927; *s* of Erik Thorning-Petersen, FRDanAA, architect, and Helga (*née* Westergaard); *m* 1949, Britta Leyssac; one *d* (one *s* decd). *Educ:* Copenhagen Univ. (LLM 1952). Entered Royal Danish Foreign Service, 1952; alternating service, Min. of Foreign Affairs and at Danish Embassies in Cairo, Moscow and Stockholm, 1952–75; Ambassador: to Lebanon, Syria, Jordan, Iraq and Cyprus (resident Beirut), 1975; to People's Republic of China, 1980; to USSR, 1983–89; to UK, 1989–96; Ambassador at large, 1996–97 (missions on behalf of Chm., OSCE, to Minsk and Belgrade; Hd, OSCE Assistance Gp to Chechnya, May–Dec. 1997). Comdr, Order of Polar Star (Sweden), 1971; Knight Grand Cross: Order of Cedar (Lebanon), 1980; Order of Independence (Jordan), 1980; Kt Comdr, Order of White Rose (Finland), 2001. *Recreations:* modern history, genealogy, history of art. *Address:* Jaegersborg Alle 23,2, 2920 Charlottenlund, Denmark. *Died 10 May 2012.*

THORNTON, Sir Peter (Eustace), KCB 1974 (CB 1971); Permanent Secretary, Department of Trade, 1974–77; *b* 28 Aug. 1917; *s* of Douglas Oscar Thornton and Dorothy (*née* Shepherd); *m* 1946, Rosamond Hobart Myers, US Medal of Freedom, Sewanee, Tennessee; two *s* one *d*. *Educ:* Charterhouse; Gonville and Caius Coll., Cambridge. Served with RA, mainly in Middle East and Italy, 1940–46. Joined Board of Trade, 1946. Secretary, Company Law Cttee (Jenkins Cttee), 1959–62; Assistant Under-Secretary of State, Department of Economic Affairs, 1964–67; Under-Sec., 1967–70, Dep. Sec., 1970–72, Cabinet Office, with central co-ordinating role during British negotiations for membership of EEC; Dep. Sec., DTI, March–July 1972; Sec. (Aerospace and Shipping), DTI, 1972–74; Second Permanent Sec., Dept of Trade, 1974. Director: Hill Samuel Gp, 1977–83; Rolls Royce, 1977–85; Courtaulds, 1977–87; Laird Gp, 1978–92; Superior Oil, 1980–84. Mem., Megaw Cttee of Inquiry into Civil Service Pay, 1981–82. Pro-Chancellor, Open Univ., 1979–83 (DUniv 1984). Governor, Sutton's Hosp., Charterhouse, 1980–89. *Died 13 July 2013.*

THORNTON, Sir Richard (Eustace), KCVO 1997; OBE 1980; JP; HM Lord Lieutenant of Surrey, 1986–97; *b* 10 Oct. 1922; *m* 1954, Gabrielle Elizabeth Sharpe; three *d* (and one *d* decd). *Educ:* Eton Coll.; Trinity Coll., Cambridge (MA). Member: Thames Conservancy, 1968–74; TWA, 1974–80; Royal Commission on Environmental Pollution, 1977–84. Chm., Mount Alvernia Management Trust, 1992–2002. Chm. Govs, Bishop Reindorp Sch., 1985–98; Mem. Governing Body, Charterhouse Sch. (Chm., 1981–89). Surrey: DL; High Sheriff 1978–79; JP. KStJ 1986. *Address:* Hampton, Seale, near Farnham, Surrey GU10 1JE. *T:* (01483) 810208. *Died 7 Jan. 2014.*

THORNTON, Robert John, CB 1980; Assistant Under Secretary of State and Director General of Supplies and Transport (Naval), Ministry of Defence, 1977–81; *b* 23 Dec. 1919; *s* of Herbert John Thornton and Ethel Mary Thornton (*née* Dunning); *m* 1944, Joan Elizabeth Roberts; three *s*. *Educ:* Queen Elizabeth Grammar School, Atherstone. MBIM 1970. Joined Naval Store Dept, Admiralty, as Asst Naval Store Officer, 1938; Singapore, 1941; Dep. Naval Store Officer, Colombo, 1942; Support Ship Hong Siang, 1943; Naval Store Officer, Admiralty, 1945; Gibraltar, 1951; Asst Dir of Stores, 1955; Superintending Naval Store Officer, Portsmouth, 1960; Dep. Dir of Stores, 1964; Dir of Victualling, 1971; Dir of Supplies and Transport (General Stores and Victualling), 1971. *Recreations:* bowls, fly fishing, gardening. *Died 17 Jan. 2011.*

THORPE, Rt Hon. (John) Jeremy; PC 1967; Chairman, Jeremy Thorpe Associates (Development Consultants in the Third World), since 1984; *b* 29 April 1929; *s* of late John Henry Thorpe, OBE, KC, MP (C) Rusholme, and Ursula, *d* of Sir John Norton-Griffiths, 1st Bt, KCB, DSO, sometime MP (C); *m* 1st, 1968, Caroline (*d* 1970), *d* of late Warwick Allpass, Kingswood, Surrey; one *s*; 2nd, 1973, Marion (CBE 2008) (*d* 2014), *d* of late Erwin Stein. *Educ:* Rectory Sch., Connecticut, USA; Eton Coll.; Trinity Coll., Oxford (Hon. Fellow, 1972). President, Oxford Union Society, Hilary, 1951; Barrister, Inner Temple, 1954. Member Devon Sessions. Contested (L) N Devon, 1955; MP (L) Devon N, 1959–79. Hon. Treasurer, Liberal Party Organisation, 1965–67; Leader, Liberal Party, 1967–76; Pres., N Devon Liberal Democrats (formerly N Devon Liberal Assoc.), 1987–. United Nations Association: Chm., Exec., 1976–80; Chm., Political Cttee, 1977–85. FRSA. Hon. LLD Exeter, 1974. *Publications:* (jtly) To all who are interested in Democracy, 1951; Europe: the case for going in, 1971; In My Own Time, 1999; contrib. to newspapers and periodicals. *Recreations:* music; collecting Chinese ceramics. *Clubs:* National Liberal (Hon. Mem.); N Devon Liberal. *Died 4 Dec. 2014.*

THURLOW, 8th Baron *cr* 1792; **Francis Edward Hovell-Thurlow-Cumming-Bruce,** KCMG 1961 (CMG 1957); Governor and C-in-C of the Bahamas, 1968–72; *b* 9 March 1912; *s* of 6th Baron Thurlow and Grace Catherine, *d* of Rev. Henry Trotter; *S* brother, 1971; *m* 1949, Yvonne Diana Aubyn Wilson, CStJ 1969 (*d* 1990); one *s* two *d* (and one *s* decd). *Educ:* Shrewsbury Sch.; Trinity Coll., Cambridge. Asst Principal, Dept of Agriculture for Scotland, 1935; transferred to Dominions Office, 1937; Asst Private Sec. to Sec. of State, 1939; Asst Sec., Office of UK High Comr in NZ, 1939; Asst Sec., Office of UK High Comr in Canada, 1944; Secretariat, Meeting of Commonwealth Prime Ministers in London, 1946; served with UK Delegn at Paris Peace Conf., 1946, and at UN Gen. Assemblies, 1946 and 1948; Principal Private Sec. to Sec. of State, 1946; Asst Sec., CRO, 1948; Head of Political Div., Office of UK High Comr in New Delhi, 1949; Establishment Officer, CRO, 1952; Head of Commodities Dept, CRO, 1954; Adviser on External Affairs to Governor of Gold Coast, 1955; Deputy High Comr for the UK in Ghana, 1957; Asst Under-Sec. of State, CRO, April 1958; Deputy High Comr for the UK in Canada, 1958; High Comr for UK: in New Zealand, 1959–63; in Nigeria, 1964–67; Dep. Under-Sec. of State, FCO, 1964. KStJ 1969. *Heir: s* Hon. Roualeyn Robert Hovell-Thurlow-Cumming-Bruce [*b* 13 April 1952; *m* 1980, Bridget Anne, *o d* of H. B. Ismay Cheape, Fossoway Lodge, Kinross; two *s* two *d*]. *Address:* 102 Leith Mansions, Grantully Road, W9 1LJ. *T:* (020) 7289 9664. *Club:* Travellers. *Died 24 March 2013.*

THURSBY, Peter Lionel, FRBS; sculptor; President, Royal West of England Academy, 1995–2000; *b* 23 Dec. 1930; *s* of Lionel Albert Thursby and Florence Bessie Thursby (*née* Macey); *m* 1956, Maureen Suzanne Aspden. *Educ:* Bishop Wordsworth Sch., Salisbury; Mons Officer Cadet Sch.; St Paul's Coll., Cheltenham; West of England Coll. of Art, Bristol; Exeter Coll. of Art (NDD Sculpture); Bristol Univ. (ATD). FRBS 1983 (ARBS 1973); RWA 1971. Nat. Service, 1949–51, RARO, 1951–57. Head of Art, Hele's Grammar Sch., Exeter, 1960–71; Head of Sch. of Art and Design, Exeter Coll., 1971–89. Invited Sculptor, Chichester Fest., 1994–96. *Solo exhibitions* include: Arnolfini, Bristol, 1963; AIA Gall., London, 1963; Marjorie Parr Gall., London, 1964, 1965, 1971; Sheviock Gall., Cornwall, 1969; Royal Albert Mus. and Art Gall., Exeter, 1969, Millennium Retrospective, 2000; Univ. of Exeter, 1974; Alwin Gall., London, 1976; RWA, 1981; Bruton Street Gall., London 1994, 1995, 1998; (retrospective) Salisbury Mus., 2003; Guernsey Mus. and Art Gall., 2005; Dorset County Mus., 2008; *public commissions:* Plymstock School, 1965; Raeburn House, Harrow, 1966; Randolph House, Croydon, 1966; Guildhall Square, Exeter, 1977 (to commemorate Silver Jubilee of HM Queen Elizabeth II); Bronze Fountain, Dallas, 1980; Bronze fountain and relief, Mazda head office, 1982; External bronze relief, City of Westminster, 1986 (Silver Medal, RBS); Bronze fountain, McDonald's Restaurants head office, 1988; Uxbridge, Coca-Cola Schweppes Beverages Ltd, 1988; Bath, NY State, 1996. Hon. DArt UWE, 1995. *Publications:* (illustrated) Roger Iredale, Turning Bronzes: an anthology of poetry, 1974; *relevant publication:* Peter Thursby (by V. Light and S. Olding), 2006. *Recreations:* genealogy, music, cinema, ornithology, swimming. *Address:* Oakley House, 28 Oakley Close, Pinhoe, Exeter, Devon EX1 3SB. *T:* and *Fax:* (01392) 467931. *E:* mo.thursby@btinternet.com. *Died 6 Jan. 2011.*

TICKELL, Kenneth Hugh, FRCO; Founder, Owner and Director, Kenneth Tickell & Co. Ltd, Organ Designers and Builders, since 1982; *b* 25 Aug. 1956; *s* of Gordon Hugh Tickell and Barbara Tickell (*née* Holmes); *m* 1977, Philippa Louise James; one *d*. *Educ:* Coventry Sch. of Music; Univ. of Hull (Organ Schol.; BA Hons Music 1978). FRCO 1977. Organbuilder, Grant Degens & Bradbeer Ltd, 1978–82. Major commissions include new organs designed and built for: Douai Abbey, 1993; St Barnabas, Dulwich, 1997; Nesbyen, Norway, 1998; Eton Coll., Lower Chapel, 2000; Cheltenham Ladies' Coll., 2006; Worcester Cathedral, 2008; Lincoln's Inn Chapel, 2009; Keble Coll., Oxford, 2011; St Mary's RC Cathedral, Newcastle upon Tyne, 2012; Rikkyo Gakuin, Tokyo, 2013; chamber organs for: Canterbury Cathedral, St Paul's Cathedral, Westminster Abbey, Christchurch, Oxford and cathedrals of Blackburn, Bristol, Exeter, Hereford, Lincoln, Liverpool Metropolitan, Peterborough, Portsmouth, St David's, Truro and Worcester. Organist and Choirmaster, St Mary the Virgin, Northampton, 1980–94. Pres., Inst. of British Organbuilding, 1996–2001. *Publications:* various technical contribs to Organbuilder, Organbuilding, ISO News (Jl of Internat. Soc. of Organbuilders). *Recreations:* photography, gardening. *Address:* (office) 16 Rothersthorpe Crescent, Northampton NN4 8JD. *T:* (01604) 768188. *E:* ken@tickell-organ.co.uk. *Died 24 July 2014.*

TIKARAM, Hon. Sir Moti, KBE 1980; CF 1996; Justice of the Court of Appeal, Fiji, 1988–2000; Judge of Supreme Court, Fiji, 2000–02; *b* 18 March 1925; *s* of Tikaram and Singari; *m* 1944, Satyawati (*d* 1981); two *s* one *d*. *Educ:* Marist Brothers High Sch., Suva; Victoria Univ., Wellington, NZ (LLB 1954). Started law practice, 1954; Stipendiary Magistrate, 1960; Puisne Judge, 1968; acted as Chief Justice, 1971, and thereafter on several occasions; Pres., Fiji Court of Appeal, 1994–2000. Ombudsman, Fiji, 1972–87. Patron, Fiji Lawn Tennis Assoc. Scouting Medal of Merit, 1986. *Publications:* articles in The Pacific Way and in Recent Law 131. *Recreation:* tennis. *Address:* Flat No 1, 65 Knolly Street, PO Box 514, Suva, Fiji. *T:* 3308415, *Fax:* 3308615. *Club:* Fiji (Suva). *Died 17 May 2012.*

TILEY, Prof. John, CBE 2003; LLD; FBA 2008; Professor of the Law of Taxation, University of Cambridge, 1990–2008, then Emeritus; Fellow, Queens' College, Cambridge, since 1967 (Vice-President, 1988–96); *b* 25 Feb. 1941; *s* of William Arthur Tiley, OBE and Audrey Ellen (*née* Burton); *m* 1964, Jillinda Millicent Draper; two *s* one *d*. *Educ:* Winchester Coll.; Lincoln Coll., Oxford (BA 1962; BCL 1963; MA 1967); LLD Cantab 1995. Called to the Bar, Inner Temple, 1964, Hon. Bencher, 1993; Asst Recorder, 1984–89; Recorder, 1989–99. Lecturer: Lincoln Coll., Oxford, 1963–64; Univ. of Birmingham, 1964–67; University of Cambridge: Asst Lectr, 1967–72; Lectr, 1972–87; Reader in Law of Taxation, 1987–90. Visiting Professor: Dalhousie Univ., 1972–73; Univ. of W Ontario, 1978–79; Univ. of Melbourne, 1979; Case Western Reserve Univ., 1985–86, 1996, 2002; Leverhulme Res. Fellow, 2009–11. Hon. QC 2009. Gen. Editor, Butterworth's Tax Guide, subseq. Tiley and Collison's UK Tax Guide, 1982–2008. *Publications:* A Casebook on Equity and Succession, 1968; Revenue Law, 1976, 6th edn 2008; (with Glen Loutzenhiser) Revenue Law, 7th edn, 2012; (with Glen Loutzenhiser) Advanced Topics in Revenue Law, 2013; contrib. to legal jls. *Recreations:* walking, cricket, music. *Address:* Queens' College, Cambridge CB3 9ET. *T:* (01223) 335511. *Died 30 June 2013.*

TILL, Barry Dorn; Principal of Morley College, London, 1965–86; Adviser, 1973–86, Director, 1986–92, Baring Foundation; *b* 1 June 1923; *s* of John Johnson and Hilda Lucy Till; *m* 1st, 1954, Shirley Philipson (marr. diss. 1965); two *s*; 2nd, 1966, Antonia, *d* of Sir Michael John Sinclair Clapham, KBE; two *d*. *Educ:* Harrow; Jesus College and Westcott House, Cambridge. 1st Class Theology Pt III, 1949; Lightfoot Scholar, 1949. Served War, Coldstream Guards, 1942–46; Italian campaign. Deacon, 1950; Priest, 1951; Asst Curate, Bury Parish Church, Lancs, 1950–53; Fellow of Jesus Coll., Cambridge, 1953–60, Chaplain,

1953–56, Dean, 1956–60, Tutor, 1957–60; Univ. Preacher, Cambridge, 1955; Examining Chaplain to Bishop of Lichfield, 1957–60; Dean of Hong Kong, 1960–64. Chm., Asia Christian Colleges Assoc., 1968–76, Vice-Pres., 1976–2002. Governor, British Inst. of Recorded Sound, 1967–72; Mem., Adv. Council, V&A Museum, 1977–83. Chairman: Greater London AACE, 1976–82; Work-Out, 1986–89; Mary Ward Settlement, 1987–98. Founder Mem., Exec. Cttee, Assoc. of Charitable Foundns, 1989–91. Governor, St Olaf's Grammar Sch., 1973–82 (Chm., 1980–82); Member: Cultural Cttee, European Culture Foundn, 1976–78; Council, London Sinfonietta, 1992–2002 (Trustee, 1998–2003). Trustee: Thomas Cubitt Trust, 1978–99; LentA Educnl Trust, 1987–92 (Chm., 1990–92); Open Coll. of the Arts, 1992–2002; Charity House, 1992–98; Transport 2000, 1992–2002; London Educn Business Partnership, 1992–99; Fitzwilliam Mus. Trust, 1993–2003. DD Lambeth, 2008. *Publications:* contrib. to The Historic Episcopate, 1954; Change and Exchange, 1964; Changing Frontiers in the Mission of the Church, 1965; contrib. to A Holy Week Manual, 1967; The Churches Search for Unity, 1972; contrib. Oxford DNB. *Recreations:* travel, gardening, opera. *Address:* 44 Canonbury Square, N1 2AW. *T:* (020) 7359 0708. *Club:* Brooks's. *Died 12 June 2013.*

TILL, Very Rev. Michael Stanley; Dean of Winchester, 1996–2005; *b* 19 Nov. 1935; *s* of Stanley Brierley Till and Mary Till; *m* 1965, Tessa, *d* of Capt. Stephen Roskill; one *s* one *d*. *Educ:* Brighton, Hove and Sussex Grammar School; Lincoln Coll., Oxford (BA, History 1960, Theology 1962; MA 1967); Westcott House, Cambridge. Curate, St John's, St John's Wood, NW8, 1964–67; Chaplain 1967–70, Dean and Fellow 1970–81, King's College, Cambridge; Vicar of All Saints', Fulham, 1981–86; Area Dean, Hammersmith and Fulham, 1984–86; Archdeacon of Canterbury, 1986–96. Chm., Petworth Fest., 2010–12. *Recreation:* writing and illustrating children's books. *Address:* Ryde House, Angel Street, Petworth, W Sussex GU28 0BG. *Died 4 Dec. 2012.*

TINDALE, Patricia Randall; architect; Chief Architect, Department of the Environment, 1982–86; *b* 11 March 1926; *d* of Thomas John Tindale and May Tindale (*née* Uttin). *Educ:* Blatchington Court, Seaford, Sussex; Architectural Assoc. Sch. of Architecture (AADip.). ARIBA. Architect, Welsh Dept, Min. of Educn, 1949–50; Min. of Educn Develt Gp, 1951–60; Min. of Housing and Local Govt R&D Gp, 1960–70; DoE Housing Develt Gp, 1970–72; Head, Building Regulations Professional Div., DoE, 1972–74; Dir, Housing Develt Directorate, DoE, 1974–81; Dir, Central Unit of Built Environment, DoE, 1981–82. Member: Building Regulations Adv. Cttee, 1993; British Bd of Agrément, 1993–99; Anchor Housing Assoc., 1993–98. Mem., AA Council, 1965–68. *Publications:* Housebuilding in the USA, 1966. *Recreations:* weaving, travelling. *Club:* Reform. *Died 13 May 2011.*

TINDEMANS, Leo; Member (Christian Democratic Party), House of Representatives, Belgium, 1961–89; *b* Zwijndrecht, 16 April 1922; *s* of Frans Tindemans and Margaret Tindemans (*née* Vercruyssen); *m* 1960, Rosa Naesens; two *s* two *d*. *Educ:* State Univ., Ghent; Catholic Univ., Louvain. Minister: for Community Relations, 1968–71; of Agriculture and Middle Class Affairs, 1972–73; Dep. Prime Minister and Minister for the Budget, 1973–74; Prime Minister of Belgium, 1974–78; Minister of Foreign Relations, 1981–89. MEP (EPP), 1979–81 and 1989–99. Mayor of Edegem, 1965–76. President: Christian Democratic Party, 1979–81; European People's Party, 1976–85; Gp of Eur. People's Party, EP, 1992–94. Prof., Faculty of Social Scis, Catholic Univ., Louvain, 1975–87, now Emeritus; first holder, Jacques Delors Chair, Maastricht, 1993. Pres., Internat. Commn on the Balkans, 1996–. Hon. DLitt: City Univ., 1976; Heriot-Watt Univ., 1978; Georgetown Univ., Washington, 1984; Univ. de Deusto, Bilbao, 1991. Charlemagne Prize, 1976; St Liborius Medaille für Einheit und Frieden, 1977; Stresemann Medaille, 1979; Schuman Prize, 1980; Médaille d'Or du Cercle Chateaubriand, 1992; Heinrich Brauns Prize, 1994. *Publications:* Ontwikkeling van de Benelux, 1958; L'autonomie culturelle, 1971; Regionalized Belgium: transition from the nation state to the multinational state, 1972; Een handvest voor woelig België, 1972; Dagboek van de werkgroep Eyskens, 1973; European Union, 1975; Europe, Ideal of our Generation, 1976; Atlantisch Europa, 1981; Europa zonder Kompas, 1987; L'Europe de l'Est vue de Bruxelles, 1989; Duel met de Minister, 1991; De toekomst van een idee, 1993; Kaïn in de Balkan, 1996; Memoires, 2002. *Recreations:* reading, writing, walking. *Address:* Jan Verbertlei 24, 2650 Edegem, Belgium. *Died 26 Dec. 2014.*

TINNISWOOD, Maurice Owen; Director of Personnel, BBC, 1970–77; *b* 26 March 1919; *y s* of late Robert Tinniswood, OBE; *m* 1946, Anne Katharine, *yr d* of late Rev. J. Trevor Matchett; one *s* one *d*. *Educ:* Merchant Taylors' School. Served with Royal Hampshire Regt, 1939–46 (Major). Joined PO, 1938 as Executive Officer, Principal, 1949; Asst Secretary, 1958; Imperial Defence College, 1963; Director of Establishments and Organisation, 1965; Director of Reorganization, 1966; Secretary to the Post Office, 1969–70. Chm., Kingston, Richmond and Esher Community Health Council, 1980–81; Mem., Kingston and Esher HA, 1982–85. CCMI. *Address:* 66 The Cloisters, Pegasus Grange, Whitehouse Road, Oxford OX1 4QQ. *T:* (01865) 721191. *Died 4 June 2014.*

TIZARD, Prof. Barbara, PhD; FBA 1997; FBPsS; Professor of Education, Institute of Education, University of London, 1982–90, then Emeritus; Director, Thomas Coram Research Unit, Institute of Education, 1980–90; *b* West Ham, 16 April 1926; *d* of late Herbert Parker and Elsie Parker (*née* Kirk); *m* 1947, Jack Tizard (*d* 1979); one *s* two *d* (and two *s* decd). *Educ:* St Paul's Girls' School; Somerville College, Oxford. BA Oxon, PhD London. Lectr, Dept of Experimental Neurology, Inst. of Psychiatry, 1963–67; Res. Officer then Senior Res. Fellow, Inst. of Education, 1967–77, Reader in Education, 1978–80. Chm., Assoc. of Child Psychology and Psychiatry, 1976–77. Hon. Mem., Assoc. for Child and Adolescent Mental Health, 2009. Co-editor, British Jl of Psychology, 1975–79; Member Editorial Board: Jl of Child Psychology and Psychiatry, 1979–90; Social Development, 1992–. *Publications:* Early Childhood Education, 1975; Adoption: a second chance, 1977; (with J. Mortimore and B. Burchell) Involving Parents in Nursery and Infant Schools, 1981; (with M. Hughes) Young Children Learning, 1984, 2nd edn 2002; (jtly) Young Children at School in the Inner City, 1988; (with A. Phoenix) Black, White or Mixed Race? Race and racism in the lives of young people of mixed parentage, 1993, revised edn 2002; articles on transracial and intercountry adoption, children in care, child development and early education. *Address:* Thomas Coram Research Unit, 27 Woburn Square, WC1H 0AA. *Died 4 Jan. 2015.*

TOBIAS, Prof. Phillip Vallentine, PhD, DSc; FRCP; FRS 1996; Professor Emeritus and Hon. Professorial Research Fellow, University of the Witwatersrand, since 1993 (Director, Palaeo-anthropology Research Unit, 1966–96); Director, Sterkfontein Research Unit, 1999–2007; *b* 14 Oct. 1925; *s* of Joseph Newman Tobias and Fanny Rosendorff. *Educ:* Univ. of the Witwatersrand, Johannesburg (BSc 1946; BSc Hons 1947; PhD 1953; MB BCh 1950; DSc 1967). FRCP 1992. University of the Witwatersrand Medical School: Lectr in Anatomy, 1951–52; Sen. Lectr, 1953–58; Prof., 1959–93; Hd, Dept of Anatomy, 1959–90; Dean, Faculty of Medicine, 1980–82. Visiting Professor: Univ. of Penn, 1992–94; Univ. of Florence, 1996; Andrew White Prof.-at-Large, Cornell Univ., 1996–2002; Hon. Professor: Univ. of Balearic Isles, 1996–; Univ. of Vienna, 1997–; Nanjing Normal Univ., 2002–; Inst. of Vertebrate Paleontology and Paleoanthropology, Chinese Acad. of Sci., Beijing, 2002–. For. Associate, NAS of USA, 1987; Mem., Amer. Philosophical Soc., 1996. Hon. FRSSAf 1987; Hon. Fellow, Coll. of Medicine, S Africa, 1998; Hon. Member: Amer. Assoc. of Anatomists, 1987; Canadian Assoc. of Anatomists, 1989; Anatomical Soc. of GB and Ireland, 1994; Geol Soc. of S Africa, 1999. Hon. DSc: Natal, 1980; Western Ont, 1986; Alberta, 1987; Cape Town, 1988; Guelph, 1990; S Africa, 1990; Durban-Westville, 1993; Witwatersrand, 1994; Musée Nat. d'Histoire Naturelle, Paris, 1996; Barcelona, 1997; Charles Univ., Prague, 1999; Stellenbosch, 1999; Transkei, 2003; Fribourg, 2003; Nelson

Mandela Metropolitan Univ., 2012; Hon. ScD: Cambridge, 1988; Penn, 1994; Hon. DMedChir Turin, 1998. Anisfield-Wolf Award in Race Relns, Cleveland Foundn, USA, 1978; Cert. of Honour, Univ. of Calif, Berkeley, 1983; Balzan Internat. Prize for Physical Anthropology, 1987; First L. S. B. Leakey Prize, 1991; Huxley Meml Medal, RAI, 1996; Charles R. Darwin Lifetime Achievement Award, Amer. Assoc. of Physical Anthropologists, 1997; Wood Jones Medal, RCS, 1997. CStJ 2003. Order of Meritorious Service, Gold Class (S Africa), 1992; Order of Southern Cross, Silver Class (S Africa), 1999; Hon. Cross for Sci. and Arts, 1st cl. (Austria), 2002; Commander: Nat. Order of Merit (France), 1998; Order of Merit (Italy), 1998. *Publications:* Chromosomes, Sex-cells and Evolution in a Mammal, 1956; (jtly) Man's Anatomy, 1963, 4th edn 1988; Olduvai Gorge, Vol. 2, 1967, Vols 4A and 4B, 1991; The Brain in Hominid Evolution, 1971; (ed) The Bushmen, 1978; Dart, Taung and the Missing Link, 1984; (ed) Hominid Evolution, Past, Present and Future, 1985; Images of Humanity, 1991; (ed) The Origins and Past of Modern Humans—towards Reconciliation, 1998; (ed) Humanity from African Naissance to Coming Millennia, 2001; Into the Past: a memoir, 2005; Tobias in Conversation, 2007. *Recreations:* people, music, books, philately, art, writing. *Address:* School of Anatomical Sciences, University of the Witwatersrand Medical School, 7 York Road, Parktown 2193, Johannesburg, South Africa. *T:* (2711) 7172516. *Club:* Explorers (New York). *Died 7 June 2012.*

TOBIAS, Richard David, OBE 1998; Chairman, Best Loved Hotels, since 2004; *b* 6 March 1945; *s* of late Gerald Joseph Tobias and Sylvia Tobias (*née* Pearlberg); *m* 1971, Brenda Margaret Anderson; two *s*. *Educ:* Clarkes Coll., London. Dir, subseq. Man. Dir, Kids International, 1966–79; Dir, Ardmore Adventure, 1979–88; British Incoming Tour Operators Association: Treas., 1988–90; Vice-Chm., 1990–91; Chm., 1992–93; Chief Exec., 1993–2003; Dir-Gen., Tourism Alliance, 2003–04. Chairman: World Media Publishing, 1999–; Right Connections Associates, 2003–; Yoga For Life, 2008–. Director: Here Is The City, 2007–13; Wells Tobias Recruitment, 2008–13. Founder Trustee, Just A Drop, 1998–. Frequent speaker, overseas travel and tourism orgns; occasional coll. lectr on tourism industry. FInstD 1994; FTS 1997; FInstTT 2004. *Publications:* contrib. to numerous tourism pubns. *Recreations:* reading, writing, music, golf, good food, Chelsea Football Club. *Address:* 11 Rodmell Slope, N12 7BX. *T:* (020) 8446 7791. *E:* richard@rtobias.co.uk. *Club:* Century. *Died 8 Jan. 2015.*

TODD, Rev. Alastair, CMG 1971; *b* 21 Dec. 1920; *s* of late Prof. James Eadie Todd, MA, FRHistS (formerly Prof. of History, Queen's University, Belfast) and Margaret Simpson Johnstone Maybin; *m* 1952, Nancy Hazel Buyers (*d* 2008); two *s* one *d* (and one *d* decd). *Educ:* Royal Belfast Academical Institution; Fettes Coll., Edinburgh; Corpus Christi Coll., Oxford; London Univ. (External); Salisbury and Wells Theological Coll. BA (Oxon), DipTheol (London). Served War, Army, 1940–46, Capt. RHA. Apptd Colonial Administrative Service, Hong Kong, 1946; Joint Services Staff Coll., 1950; Defence Sec., Hong Kong, 1957–60; Dep. Colonial Sec., Hong Kong, 1963–64; Dir of Social Welfare, also MLC, 1966–68; and, again, Defence Sec., 1968–71, retd. Ordained Deacon by Bishop of Chichester, 1973 and Priest, 1974; Asst Curate, Willingdon, 1973–77; Vicar, St Augustine's, Brighton, 1978–86. *Recreations:* reading, embroidery, gardening. *Address:* Ranworth Cottage, Sheath Lane, Oxshott KT22 0QU. *Died 27 March 2012.*

TODD, Sir Ian (Pelham), KBE 1989; FRCS; Consulting Surgeon: King Edward VII Hospital for Officers, since 1989 (Consultant Surgeon, 1972–89); St Bartholomew's Hospital, since 1981 (Consultant Surgeon, 1958–81); St Mark's Hospital, since 1986 (Consultant Surgeon, 1954–86); *b* 23 March 1921; *s* of Alan Herepath and Constance Todd; *m* 1946, Jean Audrey Ann Noble; two *s* three *d*. *Educ:* Sherborne Sch.; St Bartholomew's Hosp. Med. Coll.; Toronto Univ. (Rockefeller studentship, 1941–43; MD 1945; MS 1956). MRCS, LRCP 1944; DCH 1947; FRCS 1949. Served RAMC, Captain (AER Major). Wellcome Res. Fellow, 1955–56. Lectures: Wilson-Hay Meml, Perth, 1978; Howard H. Frykman Meml, Minneapolis, 1979; Patrick Hanley Meml, New Orleans, 1982; Gordon Watson, St Bart's Hosp., 1982; Purdue Frederick, New Orleans, 1984; Zachary Cope Meml, RCS, 1985; Henry Floyd Meml, Stoke Mandeville, 1986; John Clive Meml, Calif., 1986; Pybus Meml, Durham, 1988; Chesledon, St Thomas' Hosp., 1988; Cutait Oration, São Paulo, 1991. Visiting Professorships incl.: Montevideo; Ribeirao Preto; La Paz; Vellore; New Orleans; Minneapolis; Madras; Detroit. Examiner in Surgery: Univ. of London, 1958–64; Cambridge Univ., 1988; Dhaka, 1990; Ex-civilian Cons. (Proctology), RN, 1970–86. President: Sect. Colo-proctology, RSM, 1970–71; Med. Soc. of London, 1984–85; RCS, 1986–89 (Mem. Council, 1975–89; Hunterian Prof., 1953; Arris and Gale Lectr, 1957–58); British Colostomy Assoc., 1991–95; Vice-President: Imperial Cancer Res. Fund, 1986–89; Internat. Fedn of Surgical Colls, 1990–93. Founder, Leeds Castle Polyposis Gp, 1983. Fellow, Assoc. of Surgeons of GB and Ire., 1960; Founder Mem., Surgical Sixty Club; Hon. Member: Amer. Soc. of Colon and Rectal Surgs, 1974; RACS, 1974; Soc. Gastroent. Belge, 1964; Ileostomy Soc. of GB and Ire.; Surgical Res. Soc. of SA; Hellenic Surgical Assoc.; Assoc. of Surgs of India; Acad. of Medicine of Malaysia; NY State Surgical Soc., and S Amer. socs. Hon. FCSSA 1987; Hon. FRACS 1988; Hon. FACS 1988; Hon. FRCSCan 1989; Hon. FRCPSGlas 1989; FCPS (Bangladesh) 1990; Hon. Fellow, Colo-rectal Soc. of Sydney. Lister Prize in Surgery, Toronto, 1956. Star of Jordan, 1973. *Publications:* Intestinal Stomas, 1978; (ed) Rob and Smith, Operative Surgery, vol. 3, 1982; many articles on surgery of colon and rectum in Brit. and Amer. jls. *Recreations:* travel, music. *Address:* 4 Longmead Close, Farleigh Road, Norton St Philip, Bath BA2 7NS. *Died 21 April 2015.*

TODD, Prof. Malcolm; Principal, Trevelyan College, Durham, 1996–2000; *b* 27 Nov. 1939; *s* of Wilfrid and Rose Evelyn Todd; *m* 1964, Molly Tanner; one *s* one *d*. *Educ:* Univ. of Wales (BA, DLitt); Brasenose Coll., Oxford (Dip. Class. Archaeol (Dist.)). Res. Assistant, Rheinisches Landesmus., Bonn, 1963–65; Lectr 1965–74, Sen. Lectr 1974–77, Reader in Archaeology 1977–79, Univ. of Nottingham; Prof. of Archaeology, Univ. of Exeter, 1979–96. Vis. Prof., New York Univ., 1979; Visiting Fellow: All Souls Coll., Oxford, 1984; Brasenose Coll., Oxford, 1990–91; Sen. Res. Fellow, British Acad./Leverhulme Trust, 1990–91. Vice-Pres., Roman Soc., 1985–; Member: RCHM, 1986–92; Council, National Trust, 1987–91. Trustee: Roman Res. Trust, 1994–99; Trevelyan Trust, 1996–2000. Archaeological Consultant, Durham Cathedral, 1996–2000. Pres., Devon History Soc., 2006–. Corresp. Mem., German Arch. Inst., 1977–. Editor, Britannia, 1984–89. *Publications:* The Northern Barbarians, 1975, 2nd edn 1987; The Walls of Rome, 1978; Roman Britain, 1981, 3rd edn 1999; The South-West to AD 1000, 1987; (ed) Research on Roman Britain 1960–89, 1989; Les Germains: aux frontières romaines, 1990 (trans. Italian and German); The Early Germans, 1992 (trans. German, Italian, Czech and Turkish); Migrants and Invaders, 2001; (ed) A Companion to Roman Britain, 2004; Charterhouse-on-Mendip (Somerset), 2006; Die Zeit der Völkerwanderung, 2007; papers in Germania, Britannia, Antiquaries Jl, Antiquity, Amer. Jl of Arch. *Recreations:* reading, writing. *Died 6 June 2013.*

TOH CHIN CHYE; Nila Utama, 1st class, 1990; BSc, PhD, DipSc; *b* 10 Dec. 1921; *m* Yeap Sui Phek (decd); (one *d* decd). *Educ:* Raffles Coll., Singapore; University College, London; Nat. Inst. for Medical Research, London (PhD Physiology 1949). Reader in Physiology, 1958–64, Research Associate 1964, Vice-Chancellor, 1968–75, Univ. of Singapore. Chm., People's Action Party, 1954–81 (a Founder Mem.); MP, Singapore, 1959–88; Dep. Prime Minister of Singapore, 1959–68; Minister for Science and Technology, 1968–75; Minister for Health, 1975–81. Chm., Applied Res. Corp., 1973–75. Chairman, Board of Governors: Singapore Polytechnic, 1959–75; Regional Inst. of Higher Educn and Develt, 1970–75; Mem. Admin. Bd, Assoc. of SE Asian Insts of Higher Learning, 1968–75. DLitt (*hc*) Singapore, 1976. *Publications:* papers in Jl of Physiology and other relevant jls. *Address:* 23 Greenview Crescent, Singapore 1128. *Died 3 Feb. 2012.*

TOLLETT, Lorna Ann; *see* Casselton, L. A.

TOLLEY, Rev. Canon George, SOSc; Hon. Canon, 1976–98, Hon. Assistant, 1990–2007, then Canon Emeritus and Dean's Chaplain, since 2007, Sheffield Cathedral; *b* 24 May 1925; *s* of George and Elsie Tolley, Old Hill, Staffordshire; *m* 1947, Joan Amelia Grosvenor; two *s* one *d*. *Educ:* Halesowen Grammar Sch.; Birmingham Central Tech. Coll. (part-time); Princeton Univ., USA; Lincoln Theol Coll., 1965–67; Sheffield Univ. (MA). BSc, MSc, PhD (London); FRSC; FIMMM. Rotary Foundation Fellow, Princeton Univ., 1949–50. Head, Department of Chemistry, College of Advanced Technology, Birmingham, 1954–58; Head of Research and Experimental Dept, Allied Ironfounders Ltd, 1958–61; Principal, Worcester Tech. College, 1961–65; Senior Director of Studies, Royal Air Force Coll., Cranwell, 1965–66; Principal, Sheffield Coll. of Technology, 1966–69, Sheffield City Polytechnic, 1969–82; Manpower Services Commission: Dir, Open Tech Unit, 1983–84; Head, Quality Branch, 1984–85; Chief Officer, Review of Vocational Qualifications, 1985–86; Advr, NCVQ, 1986–88; Advr, Trng Commn, then Trng Agency, 1988–90. Ordained deacon, 1967, priest, 1968; Curate, St Andrew's, Sharrow, 1967–90. Chairman: Council, Plastics Inst., 1959–61; Further Educn Adv. Cttee, Food, Drink and Tobacco Ind. Trng Bd, 1974–78; Bd, Further Educn Curriculum Unit, 1978–82; BTec Continuing Educn Cttee, 1983–85; Council of the Selly Oak Colls, Birmingham, 1984–92; Adv. Bd, Pitman Exams Inst., 1987–92; Central Sheffield Univ. Hosps NHS Trust, 1992–95; Pres., Inst. of Home Economics, 1987–90; Vice-Pres., Educn 2000, 1990–92; Hon. Sec., Assoc. of Colleges of Further and Higher Educn, 1975–82; Member: CNAA (Chm., Cttee for Business and Management Studies, 1972–83); Yorks and Humberside Economic Planning Council, 1976–79; RAF Trng and Educn Cttee, 1975–80; Governing Body, Derbyshire Coll. of Higher Educn, 1984–87. Member Council: PSI, 1981–89; RSA, 1983–92. Dep. Chm., S Yorks Foundn, 1986–90. Hon. Treas., SOSc, 1995–2010. Sheffield Church Burgess. CCMI. Hon. FCP; Hon. Fellow: Sheffield City Polytechnic, 1982; CGLI, 1984; Inst. of Trng and Develt, 1989. Hon. DSc: Sheffield, 1984; CNAA, 1986; DUniv Open, 1984. *Publications:* Meaning and Purpose in Higher Education, 1976; A History of the Sheffield Church Burgesses, 1998; Bringing Prayer to Life, 2001; Julian of Norwich: saying 'yes' to God, 2010; many papers relating to plastics and education in British and foreign journals. *Recreation:* savouring remembered sounds. *Address:* 74 Furniss Avenue, Dore, Sheffield S17 3QP. *Died 21 Sept. 2015.*

TOMLINSON, Prof. (Alfred) Charles, CBE 2001; Professor of English, University of Bristol, 1982–92, then Emeritus, Senior Research Fellow, since 1996; *b* Stoke-on-Trent, 8 Jan. 1927; *s* of Alfred Tomlinson and May Lucas; *m* 1948, Brenda Raybould; two *d*. *Educ:* Longton High School; Queens' Coll., Cambridge (MA; Hon. Fellow, 1974); Royal Holloway and Bedford Colls, Univ. of London (MA; Hon. Fellow RHBNC, 1991). Lecturer, 1957–68, Reader in English poetry, 1968–82, Bristol Univ. Visiting Prof., Univ. of New Mexico, 1962–63; O'Connor Prof., Colgate Univ., NY, 1967–68 and 1989; Vis. Fellow, Princeton Univ., 1981; Lamont Prof., Union Coll., NY, 1987; Vis. Prof., McMaster Univ., Canada, 1987; Hon. Prof. of English, Keele Univ., 1989. Arts Council Poetry Panel, 1964–66. Lectures: Witter Bynner, Univ. of New Mexico, 1976; Clark, Cambridge, 1982; Edmund Blunden, Hong Kong, 1987; Stubbs, Toronto, 1992; St Jerome, London, 1995. Exhibition of Graphics: Ely House, OUP, London, 1972; Clare Coll., Cambridge, 1975; Arts Council touring exhibn, 1978–80; Poetry Soc., 1983; Regent's Coll. Gall., 1986; in Surrealism in English Art, touring exhibn, 1986–87; Colby Coll., Maine, USA, 1987; McMaster Univ. Gall., Canada, 1987. FRSL 1974. Hon. Foreign Fellow, Amer. Acad. of Arts and Scis, 1998; Hon. Fellow, MLA, 2003. Hon. DLitt: Keele, 1981; Colgate, 1981; New Mexico, 1986; Bristol, 2004; Gloucester, 2008. Cholmondeley Award, 1979; Wilbur Award, 1982; Cittadella Premio Europeo, 1991; Bennett Award, NY, 1993; Il Premio Internazionale di Poesia Ennio Flaiano, 2001; New Criterion Poetry Prize, NY, 2002; Premio Internazionale di Poesia Attilio Bertolucci, 2004. *Publications: poetry:* Relations and Contraries, 1951; The Necklace, 1955, repr. 1966; Seeing is Believing, 1960 (US 1958); A Peopled Landscape, 1963; Poems, 1964; American Scenes, 1966; The Poem as Initiation, 1968; The Way of a World, 1969; Poems, in Penguin Modern Poets, 1969; Renga, 1970, 1972, 1979; Written on Water, 1972; The Way In, 1974; Selected Poems, 1978; The Shaft, 1978; (with Octavio Paz) Air Born, 1981 (Mexico 1979); The Flood, 1981; Notes from New York and other Poems, 1984; Collected Poems, 1985, expanded repr., 1987; The Return, 1987; Nella pienezza del tempo, 1987; Annunciations, 1989; Selected Poems, 1989; The Door in the Wall, 1992; Poemas, 1992; Charles Tomlinson: sette poesie, 1993; Gedichte, 1994; La insistencia de las cosas, 1994; La huella del ciervo, 1994; En la plenitud del tiempo, 1994; Jubilation, 1995; In Italia, 1996; Portuguese Pieces, 1996; The Fox Gallery, 1996; Selected Poems 1955–97, 1997; The Vineyard Above the Sea, 1999; Luoghi Italiani, 2000; Skywriting, 2003; En la Plenitud del Tiempo: poemas 1955–2004, 2005; Cracks in the Universe, 2006; New Collected Poems, 2009; *prose:* Some Americans: a personal record, 1980 (US); Poetry and Metamorphosis, 1983; The Letters of William Carlos Williams and Charles Tomlinson, 1992, expanded edn, 1999; American Essays: making it new, 2001; Metamorphoses: poetry and translation, 2003; The Letters of Charles Tomlinson and George Oppen, 1963–1981, 2014; *graphics:* Words and Images, 1972; In Black and White, 1975; Eden, 1985; *translations:* (with Henry Gifford): Versions from Fyodor Tyutchev, 1960; Castilian Ilexes: Versions from Antonio Machado, 1963; Ten Versions from Trilce by César Vallejo, (US) 1970; Translations, 1983; Attilio Bertolucci: selected poems, 1993; *edited:* Marianne Moore: A Collection of Critical Essays, (US) 1969; William Carlos Williams: A Collection of Critical Essays, 1972; William Carlos Williams: Selected Poems, 1976, rev. edn (US) 1985; Octavio Paz: Selected Poems, 1979; The Oxford Book of Verse in English Translation, 1980; George Oppen: selected poems, 1990; Eros Englished: erotic poems from the Greek and Latin, 1992; John Dryden: poems selected by Charles Tomlinson, 2003; contribs to: Agenda, Essays in Criticism, Hudson Review, Modern Painters, New Criterion, Poetry (Chicago), Poetry Nation Review, Sewanee Review, Times Lit. Supp., Vuelta. *Recreations:* music, walking. *Address:* English Department, Bristol University, 3–5 Woodland Road, Bristol BS8 1TB. *Died 22 Aug. 2015.*

TONKS, Julian Matthew John; Senior Partner, Pinsent Masons (formerly Pinsent Curtis Biddle, later Pinsents) Solicitors, 2001–05; *b* 19 April 1953; *s* of John and Irene Tonks, Harborne, Birmingham; *m* 1980, Ann Miles Henderson; one *s*. *Educ:* Dudley GS; Trinity Coll., Oxford (Open Scholar; MA, MLitt). Admitted solicitor, 1982; Asst Solicitor, Freshfields, 1982–86; Tax Partner, 1987–94, Sen. Partner, 1994–95, Pinsent & Co.; Sen. Partner, Pinsent Curtis, 1995–2001. Mem. Regl Council, W Midlands, CBI, 1998. Chairman: Common Purpose, Birmingham, 1994–2001; W Midlands NSPCC Full Stop Appeal, 1999–2001. Trustee, Birmingham Royal Ballet Trust, 1996–2001. *Recreations:* visiting castles, wine, reading modern novels and medieval history. *Died 3 March 2014.*

TOOHEY, Hon. John Leslie, AC 1988 (AO 1986); Member, Bloody Sunday Inquiry Tribunal, 2000–10; *b* Perth, WA, 4 March 1930; *s* of Albert Leslie and Sylvia Josephine Toohey; *m* 1953, Loma Jean Buckenara; two *s* five *d*. *Educ:* Univ. of WA (BA, LLB 1st Cl. Hons). Admitted as Legal Practitioner, WA, 1952; QC (Aust.) 1968; Judge: Federal Court of Australia, 1977–87; Supreme Court of NT, 1977–87; Justice of High Court of Australia, 1987–98. Comr, Aboriginal Land, NT, 1977–87. Hon. LLD Murdoch, 1998; Hon. DLitt Western Australia, 2004. *Recreations:* music, tennis. *Address:* 13A Rosser Street, Cottesloe, WA 6011, Australia. *T:* (8) 93851783. *Died 9 April 2015.*

TOOK, John Michael Exton, (James), MBE 1964; Controller, Europe and North Asia Division, British Council, 1983–86; *b* 15 Sept. 1926; *s* of late George Took, Dover, and Ailsa Clowes (*née* Turner); *m* 1964, Judith Margaret, *d* of late Brig. and Mrs W. J. Birkle; two *d*. *Educ:* Dover Coll.; Jesus Coll., Cambridge. Served Indian Army, 1944–47. HM Colonial Admin. Service (later HMOCS), N

Rhodesia, 1950–57; Min. of External Affairs, Fedn of Rhodesia & Nyasaland, 1957–63; Min. of External Affairs, Republic of Zambia, 1964–65; joined British Council, 1965; Asst Reg. Dir, Frankfurt, 1965–67; Reg. Dir, Cape Coast, 1967–69; Rep., Cyprus, 1971–74; Cultural Attaché, British Embassy, Budapest, 1974–77; Dep. Controller, European Div., 1977–80; Rep., Greece, 1980–83. Dir, UK Cttee, Eur. Cultural Foundn, 1992–94. Chm., Romney Marsh Historic Churches Trust, 2001–05. *Publications:* Common Birds of Cyprus, 1973, 4th edn 1986; Birds of Cyprus, 1992; contribs to ornithological jls. *Recreations:* ornithology, fishing, natural history. *Address:* Downgate Lodge, Silverden Lane, Sandhurst, Cranbrook, Kent TN18 5NU. *T:* (01580) 851050. *Club:* Oxford and Cambridge. *Died 29 Dec. 2015.*

TOPLEY, (William) Keith, MA; Senior Master of the Supreme Court (Queen's Bench Division) and Queen's Remembrancer, 1990–96; Admiralty Registrar of the Supreme Court, 1986–92; *b* 19 Jan. 1936; *s* of late Bryan Topley and Grizel Hester (*née* Stirling); *m* 1980, Clare Mary Pennington; one *s* by former marriage. *Educ:* Bryanston School; Trinity Coll., Oxford (MA). Called to Bar, Inner Temple, 1959, Bencher, 1990; Master of Supreme Court, QBD, 1980–90. Mem., Bar Council, 1967–68. Mem. Adv. Bd, Coll. of Law, 1992–96. Freeman, City of London, 1993; Mem., Watermen and Lightermen's Co., 1993–. *Publications:* (ed jtly) Supreme Court Practice, 1988, 1991. *Recreations:* reading, writing, sailing. *Address:* 22 Queens Road, Cowes, Isle of Wight PO31 8BJ. *T:* (01983) 299742. *Clubs:* Royal Yacht Squadron, Royal London Yacht (Cdre, 1996–98) (Cowes); Bar Yacht (Cdre, 1992–95). *Died 18 May 2014.*

TOPOLSKI, Daniel; freelance writer, motivational speaker and broadcaster; photo-journalist; Oxford Boat-Race coach, 1973–87, consultant since 1995; *b* 4 June 1945; *s* of late Feliks Topolski and Marion Everall; *m* 1998, Susan Gilmore; one *s* two *d.* *Educ:* Lycée Français, London; Westminster Sch.; New Coll., Oxford (BA, Geography 1967; DipSoc Anthropology 1968, MA 1970; Hon. Fellow 2013). Writer and TV broadcaster on travel and sport; BBC TV Researcher and Producer, 1969–73; TV and Radio presenter and commentator, 1982–; expedition leader: Brazil, 1963; Iran (Marco Polo), 1973–74; travel in Africa, North and South America, India, Himalayas, China, Middle East, SE Asia, Australia. Rowing Competitor: Boat Race, Oxford, 1967, 1968; World Championships, 1969–78 (Gold medal 1977); Henley Regatta (4 victories); Rowing Coach: Oxford Boat Race Crew, 1973–87 (12 victories, record 10 in a row); Nat. Women's Squad, 1979–80, Olympics, 1980; Nat. Men's Pair and Women's Pair, 1982; Nat. Men's Pair, Olympics, 1984. Churchill Fellow, 1980. FRGS 1993. Radio Travel Prog. of the Year award for Topolski's Travels, 1993. *Publications:* Muzungu: one man's Africa, 1976; (with Feliks Topolski) Travels with my Father: journey through South America, 1983; Boat Race, 1985; (with Patrick Robinson) True Blue, 1989 (Sports Book of the Year, 1990), 2nd edn 1996 (filmed, 1998); Henley: the Regatta, 1989. *Recreations:* theatre, cinema, rowing (Steward, Henley Regatta), ski-ing, travel, family. *Address:* 69 Randolph Avenue, W9 1DW. *T:* (020) 7289 8939. *Clubs:* London Rowing (Putney); Leander (Henley). *Died 21 Feb. 2015.*

TORY, Sir Geofroy (William), KCMG 1958 (CMG 1956); HM Diplomatic Service, retired; *b* 31 July 1912; *s* of William Frank Tory and Edith Wreghitt; *m* 1st, 1938, Emilia Strickland; two *s* one *d*; 2nd, 1950, Hazel Winfield (*d* 1985). *Educ:* King Edward VII Sch., Sheffield; Queens' Coll., Cambridge. Apptd Dominions Office, 1935; Private Sec. to Perm. Under-Sec. of State, 1938–39; served War, 1939–43, in Royal Artillery; Prin. Private Sec. to Sec. of State, 1945–46; Senior Sec., Office of UK High Comr, Ottawa, 1946–49; Prin. Sec., Office of UK Rep. to Republic of Ireland, 1949–50; Counsellor, UK Embassy, Dublin, 1950–51; idc 1952; Dep. High Comr for UK in Pakistan (Peshawar), 1953–54, in Australia, 1954–57; Asst Under-Sec. of State, CRO, 1957; High Comr for UK in Fedn of Malaya, 1957–63; Ambassador to Ireland, 1964–66; High Commissioner to Malta, 1967–70. PMN (Malaysia) 1963. *Recreations:* painting, music. *Address:* Cliff Top, Harbour View, Kilbrittain, Co. Cork, Ireland. *Died 18 July 2012.*

TOULMIN, His Honour John Kelvin, CMG 1994; QC 1980; arbitrator and mediator; a Judge of the Technology and Construction Court of the High Court, 1998–2011; *b* 14 Feb. 1941; *s* of late Arthur Heaton Toulmin and B. Toulmin (*née* Fraser); *m* 1967, Carolyn Merton (*née* Gullick), barrister-at-law; one *s* two *d.* *Educ:* Winchester Coll.; Trinity Hall, Cambridge (Patterson Law Scholar, 1959; BA 1963, MA 1966); Univ. of Michigan (Ford Foundn Fellow and Fulbright Scholar, 1964; LLM 1965). Called to the Bar, Middle Temple, 1965 (Harmsworth Exhibnr, 1960; Astbury Scholar, 1965; Bencher, 1986, Sen. Bencher, 2011; Lent Reader, 2008); Western Circuit; a Recorder, 1984–97; a Dep. High Court Judge, 1994–97; an Official Referee and a Sen. Circuit Judge, 1997–98; called to Bar of NI, 1989, to Irish Bar, 1991. Commissary for Notarial Appeals, 2001–. Cambridge Univ. Debating Tour, USA, 1963. Chm., Young Barristers, 1973–75; Member: Bar Council, 1971–77, 1978–81 and 1987–90 (Chm., Internat. Practice Cttee, 1987); Supreme Court Rules Cttee, 1976–80; Council of Legal Educn, 1981–83; DHSS Enquiry into Unnecessary Dental Treatment in NHS (Report, 1986). Mem., Internat. Panel of Dist. Mediators, CPR Inst. for Dispute Resolution, NY, 1993; Panelist, WTO Disputes Settlement Body, 1996–; William W. Bishop Jr Fellow, Univ. of Michigan Law Sch., 1993. Council of Bars and Law Societies of Europe (CCBE): Mem. UK delegn, 1983–90, Leader, 1987–90; Mem. then Chm. of the cttee at European Courts of Justice, 1984–93; Vice-Pres., 1991–92; Pres., 1993. Senator, European Bar President's Conf., Vienna, 1994–. Member: Bd of Governors, Maudsley and Bethlem Royal Hosps, 1979–82; SHA, 1982–87; Cttee of Management, Inst. of Psychiatry, 1982–2002 (Chm., 1999–2002; Mem. Adv. Cttee, 2002–09); Bd of Visitors, Univ. of Michigan Law Sch., 1996–2006. Mem. Council, 1997–2009, Hon. Vis. Prof., Sch. of Law, 2009–, KCL. Trustee: Pro Corda, 1992–97; Temple Music Trust, 1993– (Chm., 2002–); Europäische Rechtsakademie, Trier, 1993– (Vice-Chm., 1994–97; Chm., 1997–2010; Hon. Life Pres., Bd of Trustees, 2011). Hon. Mem., Law Soc., 1994. FKC 2006; Helen Hudson Award for Distinguished Services to KCL, 2011. Grand Decoration for Merit (Austria), 1995. *Publications:* (contrib.) The Influence of Litigation in Medical Practice, 1977; European Ed., Encyclopaedia of Banking Law, 1990; Consulting Ed., European Legal Systems, 1992; EFTA Legal Systems, 1993; (contrib.) Practitioners' Handbook of EC Law, 1998; *festschrift:* A European Law Practitioner: Liber Amicorum John Toulmin. *Recreations:* cricket, music, theatre, Burgundy. *Address:* 3 Verulam Buildings, Gray's Inn, WC1R 3NT. *T:* (020) 7831 8441. *E:* chambers@3vb.com. *Clubs:* Pilgrims, MCC. *Died 2 July 2012.*

TOVEY, Sir Brian (John Maynard), KCMG 1980; independent art history scholar; Visiting Research Fellow, British Institute of Florence, since 2003; *b* 15 April 1926; *s* of Rev. Collett John Tovey (Canon, Bermuda Cathedral, 1935–38) and Kathleen Edith Maud Tovey (*née* Maynard); *m* 1989, Mary Helen (*née* Lane); one *s* two *d* (and one *d* decd) by previous marriage. *Educ:* St Edward's Sch., Oxford; St Edmund Hall, Oxford, 1944–45; School of Oriental and African Studies, London, 1948–50. BA Hons London. Service with Royal Navy and subseq. Army (Intelligence Corps and RAEC), 1945–48. Joined Government Communications Headquarters as Jun. Asst, 1950; Principal, 1957; Asst Sec., 1967; Under Sec., 1975; Dep. Sec., 1978; Dir, 1978–83. Defence Systems Consultant, 1983–85, and Defence and Political Adviser, 1985–88, Plessey Electronic Systems Ltd; Dir, Plessey Defence Systems Ltd, 1983–85. Chairman: IES Gp PLC, 1993–98; Cresswell Associates Ltd, 1988–2001; Fujitsu Europe Telecoms R & D Centre Ltd, 1990–2001. Vice-Pres. (Information and Communications Technology), Fedn of Electronics Industry, 1995–97. *Publications:* The Pouncey Index of Baldinucci's Notizie, 2005; contrib. Gazette des Beaux-Arts, Art Newspaper, Jl of Soc. for Renaissance Studies, Bull. of Soc. for Renaissance Studies. *Recreations:* music, history of art (espec. 16th and 17th

Century Italian, and historical methodology of Filippo Baldinucci). *Club:* Naval and Military (Vice-Pres., 1995–2005). *Died 23 Dec. 2015.*

TOWNES, Charles Hard; University Professor of Physics, 1967–86, Professor in the Graduate School, since 1994, University of California, USA; *b* Greenville, South Carolina, 28 July 1915; *s* of Henry Keith Townes and Ellen Sumter (*née* Hard); *m* 1941, Frances H. Brown; four *d*. *Educ:* Furman Univ. (BA, BS); Duke Univ. (MA); California Institute of Technology (PhD). Assistant in Physics, California Inst. of Technology, 1937–39; Member Tech. Staff, Bell Telephone Labs, 1939–47; Associate Prof. of Physics, Columbia Univ., 1948–50; Prof. of Physics, Columbia Univ., 1950–61; Exec. Director, Columbia Radiation Lab., 1950–52; Chairman, Dept of Physics, Columbia Univ., 1952–55; Vice-President and Director of Research, Inst. for Defense Analyses, 1959–61; Provost and Professor of Physics, MIT, 1961–66; Institute Professor, MIT, 1966–67. Guggenheim Fellow, 1955–56; Fulbright Lecturer, University of Paris, 1955–56, University of Tokyo, 1956; Lecturer, 1955, 1960, Dir, 1963, Enrico Fermi Internat. Sch. of Physics; Lectures: Scott, Univ. of Cambridge, 1963; Centennial, Univ. of Toronto, 1967; Rajiv Gandhi, India, 1997; Weinberg, Oak Ridge Nat. Lab., 1997; Henry Norris Russell, AAS, 1998; Sackler Leiden, 1999; Loeb, Harvard, 2000; Hamilton, Princeton, 2000; Bunyan, Stanford, 2000. Dir, Bulletin of Atomic Scientists, 1964–69. Board of Editors: Review of Scientific Instruments, 1950–52; Physical Review, 1951–53; Journal of Molecular Spectroscopy, 1957–60; Columbia University Forum, 1957–59. Fellow: American Phys. Society (Richtmyer Lecturer, 1959; Member Council, 1959–62, 1965–71; President, 1967); Inst. of Electrical and Electronics Engrs; Chairman, Sci. and Technology Adv. Commn for Manned Space Flight, NASA, 1964–69; Member: President's Science Adv. Cttee, 1966–69 (Vice-Chm., 1967–69); Scientific Adv. Bd, US Air Force, 1958–61; Soc. Française de Physique (Member Council, 1956–58); Nat. Acad. Scis (Mem. Council, 1969–72); American Acad. Arts and Sciences; American Philos. Society; American Astron. Society; American Assoc. of Physics Teachers; Société Royale des Sciences de Liège; Pontifical Acad., 1983; Nat. Acad. of Engrg, 1999; Foreign Member: Royal Society, 1976; Russian Acad. of Scis, 1994; Hon. Mem., Optical Soc. of America. Trustee: Salk Inst. for Biological Studies, 1963–68; Rand Corp., 1965–70; Carnegie Instn of Washington, 1965–; Calif Inst. of Technol., 1979–; California Acad. of Scis, 1987–96. Chairman: Space Science Bd, Nat. Acad. of Sciences, 1970–73; Science Adv. Cttee, General Motors Corp., 1971–73; Bd of Dirs, General Motors, 1973–86; Perkin-Elmer Corp., 1966–85. Trustee: Pacific Sch. of Religion, 1983–93; Center for Theol. and Natural Sci., 1989–; Grad. Theol Union, 1993–; California Vocations, 1994–; Enshrinee, Engrg and Sci. Hall of Fame, Ohio, 1983. Numerous honorary degrees. Research Corp. Annual Award, 1958; Comstock Prize, Nat. Acad. of Sciences, 1959; Stuart Ballantine Medal, Franklin Inst., 1959, 1962; Rumford Premium, Amer. Acad. of Arts and Sciences, 1961; Thomas Young Medal and Prize, Inst. of Physics and Physical Soc., England, 1963; Nobel Prize for Physics (jointly), 1964; Medal of Honor, Inst. of Electrical and Electronics Engineers, 1967; C. E. K. Mees Medal, Optical Soc. of America, 1968; Churchman of the Year Award, Southern Baptist Theological Seminary, 1967; Distinguished Public Service Medal, NASA, 1969; Michelson-Morley Award, 1970; Wilhelm-Exner Award (Austria), 1970; Medal of Honor, Univ. of Liège, 1971; Earle K. Plyler Prize, 1977; Niels Bohr Internat. Gold Medal, 1979; Nat. Medal of Sci., 1983; Commonwealth Award, 1993; Frederic Ives/James Quinn Medal, Optical Soc. of America, 1996; Frank Annunzio Award, Columbus Fellowship Foundn, 1999; Rabindranath Tagore Birth Centenary Plaque, Asiatic Soc., 1999; Best Book on Sci., American Inst. of Physics, 2000; Founders Award, NAE, 2000; Lomonosov Gold Medal, Russian Acad. of Scis, 2001; Karl Schwarzschild Medal, Astronomische Ges., 2002; Drake Award, SETI Inst., 2003; Templeton Prize, John Templeton Foundn, 2005; Vannevar Bush Award, Nat. Sci. Foundn, 2006. National Inventors Hall of Fame, 1976; S Carolina Hall of Fame, 1977. Hon. Citizen: Kwangju, Korea, 1996; Pusan, Korea, 1997. Officier, Légion d'Honneur (France), 1990. *Publications:* (with A. L. Schawlow) Microwave Spectroscopy, 1955; (ed) Quantum Electronics, 1960; (ed with P. A. Miles) Quantum Electronics and Coherent Light, 1964; Making Waves, 1995; How the Laser Happened: adventures of a scientist, 1999 (Best Book on Science, Amer. Inst. of Physics, 2000); many scientific articles on microwave spectroscopy, molecular and nuclear structure, quantum electronics, radio and infra-red astrophysics; fundamental patents on masers and (with A. L. Schawlow) lasers. *Address:* Department of Physics, University of California, Berkeley, CA 94720, USA. *T:* (510) 6421128. *Clubs:* Cosmos (Washington); Bohemian (San Francisco). *Died 27 Jan. 2015.*

TOWNSEND, Sir Cyril (David), Kt 1997; Director, Council for the Advancement of Arab-British Understanding, 1995–2002 (Joint Chairman, 1982–92); *b* 21 Dec. 1937; *s* of late Lt-Col Cyril M. Townsend and Lois (*née* Henderson); *m* 1976, Anita, MA, *d* of late Lt-Col F. G. W. Walshe and Mrs Walshe; two *s*. *Educ:* Bradfield Coll.; RMA Sandhurst. Commnd into Durham LI; served in Berlin and Hong Kong; active service in Cyprus, 1958 and Borneo, 1966; ADC to Governor and C-in-C Hong Kong, 1964–66; Adjt 1DLI, 1966–68. A Personal Assistant: to Edward Heath, 1968–70; to Sir Desmond Plummer, Ldr of GLC, 1970–73; Mem. Conservative Research Dept, 1970–74. MP (C) Bexleyheath, Feb. 1974–1997. PPS to Minister of State, DHSS, 1979; Member: Select Cttee on Violence in the Family, 1975; Select Cttee on Foreign Affairs, 1982–83; Vice-Chairman: Cons. Parly Defence Cttee, 1985–93 (Jt Sec., 1982–85); Cons. Parly Foreign Affairs Cttee, 1991–96; Chairman: Select Cttee on Armed Forces Bill, 1981; British-Cyprus Parly Gp, 1983–92; All-Party Freedom for Rudolf Hess Campaign, 1977–87; Bow Gp Standing Cttee on Foreign Affairs, 1977–84; (and Co-Founder) South Atlantic Council, 1983–95; Organizing Cttee, Argentine-British Conference, 1988–90; UN Parly Gp, 1992–96; Chm., Cons. ME Council, 1992–95 (Jt Vice-Chm., 1988–92); Vice-Chairman: Friends of Cyprus, 1980–92 (Mem., Exec. Cttee); Hansard Soc., 1988–97; Member: Exec. Cttee, UK Branch, CPA, 1992–93; Exec. Bd, UK Cttee, UNICEF, 1995–2000; Vice-Pres., UNA, 1996–2002; Pres., SW Reg., UNA, 1999–2002; Jt Hon. Pres., Islamic Res. Acad., 2000–08; Gov., Centre for World Dialogue, Nicosia, 1998–2013. Member: South Atlantic Council, 1983–2004; Nat. Cttee, British-Arab Univ. Assoc., 1995–2004. Mem., SE London Industrial Consultative Gp, 1975–83. Pres., Bexley Arthritis Care, 1990–96. Chm., Lord Caradon Lectures Trust, 2002–08. Patron, Forum Against Islamophobia and Racism, 2000–13. Trustee, Sir Heinz Koeppler Trust, Wilton Park, 2006–11. Fellow, Industry and Parliament Trust, 1982. Introduced Protection of Children Act, 1978. Parly Observer, Presidential Election, Lebanon, 1982; Ldr, Parly Delegn to Iran, 1988; Mem., British Delegn, CSCE, Moscow, 1991; EU Election Observer for elections in Palestine, 1996. Columnist: Al-Hayat, 1990–; Al-Ittihad, 2004–; Arab News, 2005–08; Western Morning News, 2010–. *Publications:* Helping Others to Help Themselves: voluntary action in the eighties, 1981; Cyprus and NATO's Southern Flank, 1986; contribs to Contemporary Review and political jls. *Recreations:* books, music, exercise, exploring Cornwall. *Address:* Chillaton House, Chillaton, Lifton, Devon PL16 0JD. *Died 20 Nov. 2013.*

TOWNSEND, Lady Juliet Margaret, DCVO 2014 (LVO 1981); Lord-Lieutenant of Northamptonshire, 1998–2014; *b* 9 Sept. 1941; *d* of 2nd Earl of Birkenhead, TD; *m* 1970, John Richard Townsend; three *d*. *Educ:* Westonbirt Sch.; Somerville Coll., Oxford. Lady in Waiting to Princess Margaret, 1965–71, Extra Lady in Waiting, 1971–2002. High Sheriff of Northamptonshire, 1991–92. *Publications:* The Shell Guide to Northamptonshire, 1968; Escape from Meerut, 1971. *Address:* Newbottle Manor, Banbury, Oxon OX17 3DD. *T:* (01295) 811295. *Died 29 Nov. 2014.*

TOWNSEND, Susan Lilian, (Sue); writer; *b* 2 April 1946; *m* Colin Broadway; one *d*; two *s* one *d* from a former marriage. *Educ:* South Wigston Girls' High Sch. FRSL 1994. Writer and Presenter, Think of England, BBC TV, 1991. *Publications:* The Secret Diary of Adrian Mole Aged

13¾, 1982; The Growing Pains of Adrian Mole, 1984; Bazaar and Rummage, Groping for Words, and Womberang (plays), 1984; The Great Celestial Cow (play), 1985; The Secret Diary of Adrian Mole (play), 1985; Rebuilding Coventry, 1988; Mr Bevan's Dream, 1989; Ten Tiny Fingers, Nine Tiny Toes (play), 1989; Adrian Mole From Minor to Major, 1991; The Queen and I, 1992 (adapted for stage, 1994); Adrian Mole—the Wilderness Years, 1993; Ghost Children, 1997; The Cappuccino Years, 1999; The Public Confessions of a Middle-Aged Woman Aged 55¾, 2001; Number Ten, 2002; Adrian Mole and the Weapons of Mass Destruction, 2004; Queen Camilla, 2006; The Lost Diaries of Adrian Mole 1999–2001, 2008; Adrian Mole: the prostrate years, 2009; The Woman Who Went to Bed for a Year, 2012. *Recreation:* listening. *Club:* Groucho. *Died 10 April 2014.*

TRACEY, Stanley William, CBE 2008 (OBE 1986); professional pianist, composer and arranger, since 1943; *b* 30 Dec. 1926; *s* of Stanley Clark Tracey and Florence Louise Tracey; *m* 1st, 1946, Joan; 2nd, 1954, Jean; 3rd, 1960, Florence Mary, (Jackie) (*d* 2009); one *s* (one *d* decd). *Educ:* Tooting, Graveney and Ensham Schools. Leading own small group, 1965–, orchestra, 1969–. Hon. RAM 1984. Fellow, City of Leeds Coll. of Music, 1993. Numerous records of own compositions and arrangements; compositions include: Under Milk Wood suite, 1965; Genesis, 1986; 500 other titles. Subject of BBC TV documentary, Stan Tracey: Godfather of British Jazz, 2003. Hon. DLitt Herts, 1997. Awards include: BASCA Award, 1984; voted best jazz composer, Wire/Guardian, 1989; voted best album of year, Big Band, 1989; pianist of the year, British Jazz Awards, 1992; best album of year, British Jazz Awards, 1993; best arranger/composer, British Jazz Awards, 1995, 1997, BT Jazz Awards, 1999; Jazz Medal, Co. of Musicians, 1997; Lifetime Achievement Award, BBC Jazz Awards, 2002; Ivors Jazz Award, Ivor Novello Awards, 2012; Services to Jazz Award, Parliamentary Jazz Awards, 2013. *Address:* 19 St Augusta Court, Batchwood View, St Albans, Herts AL3 5SS. *T:* (01727) 852595. *Died 6 Dec. 2013.*

TRAFFORD, Ian Colton, OBE 1967; Publisher, The Times Supplements, 1981–88; *b* 8 July 1928; *s* of late Dr Harold Trafford and Laura Dorothy Trafford; *m* 1st, 1949, Nella Georgara (marr. diss. 1964); one *d*; 2nd, 1972, Jacqueline Carole Trenque (*d* 2010). *Educ:* Charterhouse; St John's Coll., Oxford. Feature writer and industrial correspondent, The Financial Times, 1951–58; UK Correspondent, Barrons Weekly, New York, 1954–60; Director, Industrial and Trade Fairs Holdings Ltd, 1958–71, Managing Director, 1966–71; Director-General British Trade Fairs in: Peking, 1964; Moscow, 1966; Bucharest, 1968; São Paulo, 1969; Buenos Aires, 1970; Man. Dir, Economist Newspaper, 1971–81; Chm., Economist Intelligence Unit, 1971–79; Dep. Chm., Times Books Ltd, 1981–86. Local Dir, W London Board, Commercial Union Assce, 1974–83. OBE awarded for services to exports. *Address:* Grafton House, 128 Westhall Road, Warlingham, Surrey CR6 9HF. *T:* (01883) 622048. *Died 24 March 2011.*

TRAINOR, Roy; Senior Partner (formerly Chairman), ATM Consulting Ltd, 1990–2013; Chairman, Geneshall Ltd, since 1994; *b* 25 Jan. 1948; *s* of Thomas and Miriam Joyce Trainor; *m* 1972, Elizabeth Ann Evans; two *s*. *Educ:* Kingston Sch., Stafford; Staffordshire Poly. (DMS 1975); Univ. of Warwick (MA 1982). Mgt Trainee, Lotus Ltd, 1965–67; Personnel, Stoke-on-Trent City Council, 1967–68; Personnel Mgt, then Opnl Mgt, then Dir, NHS, 1968–89. Chm., Medistaff Health Gp, 1999–2003. Chm., Foundn NHS Trust, 1996–2001; non-exec. Dir, Corinth Healthcare Ltd, 2003–05. Pres., Stafford Chamber of Commerce and Industry, 1995–96. MIPD, MMS. *Recreations:* walking, reading, travel. *Address:* Vine Cottage, Coton Wood, Radmore Lane, Gnosall, Stafford ST20 0EG. *T:* (01785) 822097. *Club:* Naval and Military. *Died 11 Feb. 2015.*

TRAPNELL, Barry Maurice Waller, CBE 1982; DL; MA, PhD Cantab; Headmaster of Oundle School, 1968–84; Chairman, Cambridge Occupational Analysts, 1986–2003; *b* 18 May 1924; *s* of Waller Bertram and late Rachel Trapnell; *m* 1951, Dorothy Joan (*d* 2005), *d* of late P. J. Kerr, ICS; two *d*. *Educ:* University College Sch., Hampstead; St John's Coll., Cambridge (Scholar). Research in physical chemistry in Department of Colloid Science, Cambridge, 1945–46, and Royal Institution, London, 1946–50; Commonwealth Fund Fellow, Northwestern Univ., Ill., 1950–51; Lecturer in chemistry: Worcester Coll., Oxford, 1951–54; Liverpool Univ., 1954–57; Headmaster, Denstone Coll., 1957–68. Visiting Lecturer, American Association for Advancement of Science, 1961. Pres., Independent Schools Assoc. Inc., 1984–97; Member: Adv. Cttee on Supply and Training of Teachers; C of E Commn on Religious Education. E Anglian Regl Dir, Index, 1985–92. Mem. Governing Body, Roedean Sch., 1987–92. Director: Southend Estates Gp plc, 1984–86; Thomas Wall Trust, 1984–92. Hon. FCP, 1995. DL: Staffs, 1967; Northants, 1974–84. Hon. Liveryman, Worshipful Co. of Grocers, 1984. *Publications:* Chemisorption, 1955 (Russian edition, 1958; 2nd English edition, 1964); Learning and Discerning, 1966; papers in British and American scientific journals. *Recreations:* several games (represented Cambridge *v* Oxford at cricket and squash rackets, and Gentlemen *v* Players at cricket; won Amateur Championships at Rugby Fives), English furniture and silver. *Address:* 250 Kingston Road, Teddington, Middx TW11 9JF. *Clubs:* Oxford and Cambridge; Hawks (Cambridge); Vincent's (Oxford). *Died 1 Aug. 2012.*

TREADGOLD, Very Rev. John David, LVO 1990; Dean of Chichester, 1989–2001; Chaplain to the Queen, 1983–89; *b* 30 Dec. 1931; *s* of Oscar and Sybil Treadgold; *m* 1959, Hazel Rhona Bailey; two *s* one *d*. *Educ:* Nottingham Univ. (BA); Wells Theological College. Deacon 1959, priest 1960; Vicar Choral, Southwell Minster, 1959–64; Rector of Wollaton, Nottingham, 1964–74; Vicar of Darlington, 1974–81; Canon of Windsor and Chaplain to Windsor Great Park, 1981–89. Chaplain, TA, 1962–67; TAVR, 1974–78; Chaplain to High Sheriff: of Nottinghamshire, 1963–64 and 1975–76; of Durham, 1978–79; of W Sussex, 2002–03. Chairman: Chichester DAC for the Care of Churches, 1990–99; Trustees, Hosp. of St Mary, 1989–2001; Morse-Boycott Trust, 1995–2001. Trustee, Chichester Festival Theatre, 1989–2001; Vice Pres., Chichester Festivities, 1989–2001. Patron, Pallant Hse Gall., 1998. OStJ 2005 (Mem., Council, Order of St John, Sussex, 1994–2008). Chm. of Govs, Prebendal Sch., Chichester, 1989–2001; Governor: Slindon Coll., 1995–96; Wycombe Abbey Sch., 1995–2000; St Mary's Hall, Brighton, 2002–03. FRSA 1991–2002. *Recreations:* sculpting, musical appreciation, church architecture. *Address:* 43 Prior's Acre, Boxgrove, Chichester, W Sussex PO18 0ER. *T:* (01243) 782385. *E:* jandh@skymarket.org. *Club:* Sussex. *Died 15 Feb. 2015.*

TREMBLAY, Dr Marc-Adélard, OC 1980; GOQ 1995; Professor of Anthropology, Université Laval, Québec, 1956–94, then Emeritus; *b* Les Eboulements, Qué, 24 April 1922; *s* of Willie Tremblay and Lauretta (*née* Tremblay); *m* 1949, Jacqueline Cyr (decd); one *s* five *d*. *Educ:* Montréal Univ. (AB, LSA (Agricl Sci.)); Laval (MA Sociol.); Cornell Univ. (PhD Anthropol.). Research Associate, Cornell Univ., 1953–56; Université Laval: Vice-Dean, Faculty Social Scis, 1969–71; Head, Anthropology Dept, 1970; Dean, Graduate Sch., 1971–79. Pres., RSC, 1982–85. Comr, Nunavik Commn, 1999–2000. Pres. Council, Order of Quebec, 1998–2000. Hon. LLD: Ottawa, 1982; Guelph, 1984; Univ. of Northern BC, 1994; Carleton Univ., 1995; Univ. Ste Anne, 1997; McGill, 1998. Innis-Gerin Medal, RSC, 1979; Centennial Medal, RSC, 1982; Molson Prize, Canada Council, 1987; Marcel Vincent Medal, French Canadian Assoc. for Advancement of Science, 1988; Internat. Order of Merit, Internat. Biog. Inst., 1990; Esdras Minville Prize in Soc. Scis, Soc. St Jean-Baptiste, 1991. *Publications:* The Acadians of Portsmouth, 1954; (jtly) People of Cove and Woodlot, 1960; (jtly) Les Comportements économiques de la famille salariée, 1964; Les Fondements Sociaux de la Maturation chez l'enfant, 1965; (jtly) Rural Canada in Transition, 1966; (jtly) A Survey of Contemporary Indians of Canada, 1967; Initiation à la recherche dans les sciences humaines, 1968; (jtly) Etude sur les Indiens contemporains du Canada, 1969; (jtly) Les Changements socio-culturels à Saint-Augustin, 1969; (jtly) Famille et parenté en Acadie, 1971; (jtly)

Communautés et Culture, 1973 (Eng. trans. 1973); (jtly) Patterns of Amerindian Identity, 1976; (jtly) The Individual, Language and Society in Canada, 1977; L'Identité Québécoise en péril, 1983; (jtly) Conscience et Enquête, 1983; L'Anthropologie à l'Université Laval: fondements historiques, pratiques académiques, dynamismes d'évolution, 1989; Les fondements historiques et théoriques de la practique professionnelle en anthropologie, 1990; over one hundred and seventy-five scientific articles. *Recreations:* gardening, cross-country skiing. *Died 20 March 2014.*

TREVELYAN, (Adye) Mary; *see* Fedden, A. M.

TREVELYAN, Sir Geoffrey (Washington), 5th Bt *cr* 1874, of Wallington, Northumberland; *b* 4 July 1920; *s* of Rt Hon. Sir Charles Philips Trevelyan, 3rd Bt, PC and Mary Katharine Trevelyan (*d* 1966); *S* brother, 1996; found in 1999 to be rightful claimant to Trevelyan Baronetcy of Nettlecombe, Somerset, *cr* 1662, in abeyance since 1976, but chose not to prove claim nor be entered on the Official Roll of the Baronetage as 11th Bt; *m* 1947, Gillian Isabel Wood (MBE 1999) (*d* 2000); one *s* one *d. Educ:* Oundle; Trinity Coll., Cambridge (BA 1941; MA 1945). De Havilland Aircraft Co. Ltd, 1941–61; Dir, Chatto and Windus Ltd, 1962–77; Manager, Seatoller House, Keswick, 1978–81; Chm., The Lake Hunts Ltd, 1979–96; freelance technical writer, 1982–92. *Recreations:* hill-walking, gardening, cabinet-making. *Heir: s* Peter John Trevelyan [*b* 11 Sept. 1948; *m* 1996, Diane Terry; one *s*]. *Address:* Silkstead, 3 Abbey Mill End, St Albans, Herts AL3 4HN. *T:* (01727) 864866. *Died 28 Jan. 2011.*

TREVETHIN, 4th Baron, **AND OAKSEY,** 2nd Baron; *see under* Oaksey, 2nd Baron.

TREWIN, Ion Courtenay Gill; Literary Director (formerly Administrator), Man Booker annual and International prizes, since 2006; *b* 13 July 1943; *s* of late John Courtenay Trewin, OBE and Wendy Elizabeth Trewin (*née* Monk); *m* 1965, Susan Harriet Merry; one *s* one *d. Educ:* Highgate Sch., London. Journalist and editorial staff: The Independent & S Devon Times, 1960–63; Sunday Telegraph, 1963–67; The Times, 1967–79: Ed., The Times Diary, 1969–72; Literary Ed., 1972–79; Ed., Drama Magazine, 1979–81; Publisher: Hodder & Stoughton, 1979–92: Sen. Ed., 1979–85; Editl Dir, 1985–91; Publishing Dir, 1991–92; Orion Publishing Group, 1992–2006: Dir, 1994–2006; Weidenfeld & Nicolson imprint: Publishing Dir, 1992–96; Man. Dir, 1996–2001; Ed. in Chief, 2001–06. Man Booker (formerly Booker) Prize for Fiction: Chm. Judges, 1974; Mem. Adv. (formerly Mgt) Cttee, 1989– (Chm., 2006–); Dep. Administrator, 2004–06. Special Prof., Univ. of Nottingham, 2007–. Chairman: Library Cttee, Highgate Literary and Scientific Instn, 1974–90; Soc. of Bookmen, 1986–88; Cheltenham Fest. of Literature, 1997–2006; Library Cttee, Garrick Club, 2011–; Member: Literature Panel, Arts Council of GB, 1975–78; Arts and Library Cttee, MCC, 1988–96. Ronald Politzer Award for Innovation in Publishing, 1976; (jtly) Innovation in Teaching Politics award, Political Studies Assoc., 2011. *Publications:* Journalism, 1975; Norfolk Cottage, 1977; (ed) Alan Clark's Diaries: into politics, 2000, the last diaries, 2002; (ed) The Hugo Young Papers: thirty years of British politics - off the record, 2008 (Channel 4 Political Book of the Year); Alan Clark: the biography, 2009; (ed) Alan Clark: a life in his own words, the edited diaries, 1972–1999, 2010. *Recreations:* indulging grandchildren, gardening, watching cricket, gossip. *Address:* South Wing, Snettisham House, Snettisham, Norfolk PE31 7RZ. *E:* itrewin@aol.com. *Clubs:* MCC, Garrick. *Died 8 April 2015.*

TRICKETT, Anthony Robert, MBE 1998; General Medical Practitioner, Island of Hoy, Orkney, 1973–2010; Lord-Lieutenant of Orkney, since 2007 (Vice Lord-Lieutenant, 2005–07); *b* 16 Feb. 1940; *s* of late Robert Edward Trickett and Phyllis Trickett (*née* Grocott); *m* 1996, Elizabeth Jean Sadler; three *s* one *d. Educ:* Willaston Primary Sch.; Nantwich and Acton Grammar Sch.; Manchester Univ. Med. Sch. MRCS, LRCP 1964. Resident hosp. appts in Manchester, 1964–66; Demonstrator in Anatomy, Manchester Univ., 1966–67; GP, Pembroke, Dyfed, 1967–73. Director: Orkney Enterprise, 2001–06; Hoy & Walls Develt Assoc., 2004–. Longhope Lifeboat Station: Hon. Med. Advr, 1973–2010; Hon. Sec., subseq. Lifeboat Ops Manager, 1995–2010; Chm., 2010–; Med. Referee, 2003–05, Area Med. Advr, 2005–09, RNLI (Scotland); Mem., Med. and Survival Cttee, RNLI, 2003–09. Chairman: Longhope Lifeboat Mus. Trust, 2001–; Soc. of Friends of St Magnus Cath., 2007–; Orkney Children's Trust, 2007–; Orkney Heritage Property Trust, 2007–; Trustee: Hoy Trust, 1984– (Chm., 1992–); Pickaquay Centre, Kirkwall, 2004–07; Orkney Archaeol Trust, 2007–. Founder and Chm., Hoy Half-Marathon, 1985–. Dir, Gable End Th., Hoy, 2005–. DL Orkney, 1999. Silver Badge, 1994, Gold Badge, 2004, RNLI. *Recreations:* growing trees, hill walking, traditional dancing, ecology, almost all music, especially live, fitness promotion, exercising - ever more slowly, striving to ward off geriatric decrepitude. *Address:* Glebelands, Longhope, Hoy, Orkney KW16 3PA. *T:* (01856) 701460, *Fax:* (01856) 701294. *E:* tony@hoyorkney.co.uk. *Died 18 May 2013.*

TRITTON, Major Sir Anthony (John Ernest), 4th Bt *cr* 1905; *b* 4 March 1927; *s* of Sir Geoffrey Ernest Tritton, 3rd Bt, CBE, and Mary Patience Winifred (*d* 1960), *d* of John Kenneth Foster; *S* father, 1976; *m* 1957, Diana, *d* of Rear-Adm. St J. A. Micklethwait, CB, DSO, and of Clemence Penelope Olga Welby-Everard; one *s* one *d. Educ:* Eton. Commissioned 3rd Hussars, Oct. 1945; retired as Major, 1964, The Queen's Own Hussars. *Recreations:* shooting, fishing. *Heir: s* Jeremy Ernest Tritton [*b* 6 Oct. 1961; *m* 2007, Mary Catherine Claydon]. *Address:* River House, Heytesbury, Wilts BA12 0EE. *Club:* Cavalry and Guards. *Died 9 Aug. 2012.*

TROWELL, Prof. Brian Lewis, PhD; Heather Professor of Music and Fellow of Wadham College, University of Oxford, 1988–96, then Emeritus; *b* 21 Feb. 1931; *s* of Richard Lewis and Edith J. R. Trowell; *m* 1958, Rhianon James; two *d. Educ:* Christ's Hospital; Gonville and Caius Coll., Cambridge. MA 1959; PhD 1960. Asst Lectr, later Lectr, in Music, Birmingham Univ., 1957–62; freelance scholar, conductor, opera producer, lecturer and editor, 1962–67; Head of BBC Radio opera, 1967–70; Reader in Music, 1970, Professor of Music, 1973, King Edward Prof. of Music, 1974–88, KCL. Regents' Prof., Univ. of California at Berkeley, 1970; Vis. Gresham Prof. of Music, City Univ., 1971–74. Pres., Royal Musical Assoc., 1983–88. Hon. RAM 1972; Hon. FGSM 1972; FRCM 1977; FTCL 1978; Fellow: Curwen Inst., 1987; KCL, 1997. Chm., Editorial Cttee, Musica Britannica, 1983–93. *Publications:* The Early Renaissance, Pelican History of Music vol. ii, 1963; Four Motets by John Plummer, 1968; (ed jtly) John Dunstable: Complete Works, ed M. F. Bukofzer, 2nd edn, 1970; (ed) Invitation to Medieval Music, vol. 3 1976, vol. 4 1978; Elgar Complete Edition, vol. 16: solo songs with piano, 1901–1934, 2010; opera translations; contrib. dictionaries of music and articles in learned journals. *Recreations:* theatre, reading, gardening. *Address:* 5 Tree Lane, Iffley Village, Oxford OX4 4EY. *Died 13 Nov. 2015.*

TUCK, Clarence Edward Henry; Civil Service Commissioner, 1977–83; *b* 18 April 1925; *s* of Frederick and May Tuck; *m* 1950, Daphne Robinson; one *s* one *d. Educ:* Rendcomb Coll., Cirencester; Merton Coll., Oxford (BA 1949). Served in Royal Signals, 1943–47. Inland Revenue, 1950; Min. of Supply, 1950–55; seconded to Nigerian Federal Govt, Lagos, 1955–57; Ministry of: Supply, 1957–59; Aviation, 1959–60; Defence, 1960–62; Aviation, 1962–66; IDC, 1967; Min. of Technology, 1968–70; Trade and Industry, 1970; CSD, 1971; Trade and Industry, 1973; Dept of Energy, 1974; Civil Service Dept, 1976; Management and Personnel Office, 1981; Dir, Civil Service Selection Board, 1977–81. Asst Principal, 1950; Principal, 1953; Asst Sec., 1962; Under-Sec., 1970. *Died 29 March 2013.*

TUDHOPE, James Mackenzie, CB 1987; part-time Chairman of Social Security Appeal Tribunals, 1987–91; *b* 11 Feb. 1927; *m* Margaret Willock Kirkwood, MA Glasgow (*d* 2010); two *s. Educ:* Dunoon Grammar School; Univ. of Glasgow (BL 1951). Served Army, 1945–48. Admitted Solicitor, 1951. Private legal practice, 1951–55;

Procurator Fiscal Depute, 1955, Senior PF Depute, 1962, Asst PF, 1968–70, Glasgow; PF, Kilmarnock, 1970–73, Dumbarton, 1973–76; Regional Procurator Fiscal: S Strathclyde, Dumfries and Galloway at Hamilton, 1976–80; for Glasgow and Strathkelvin, 1980–87. Hon. Sheriff, N Strathclyde, 1989–. Mem. Council, Law Soc. of Scotland, 1983–86. *Recreations:* serendipity, living. *Address:* Point House, Dundonald Road, Kilmarnock, Ayrshire KA1 1TY. *Died 9 Jan. 2012.*

TUDOR EVANS, Sir Haydn, Kt 1974; a Judge of the High Court of Justice, Queen's Bench Division, 1978–94 (Family Division, 1974–78); *b* 20 June 1920; 4th *s* of John Edgar Evans and Ellen (*née* Stringer); *m* 1947, Sheilagh Isabella Pilkington; one *s*. *Educ:* Cardiff High Sch.; West Monmouth School; Lincoln College, Oxford. RNVR, 1940–41. Open Scholar, Lincoln Coll., Oxford (Mod. History), 1940; Stewart Exhibitioner, 1942; Final Hons Sch., Mod. History, 1944; Final Hons Sch., Jurisprudence, 1945. Cholmeley Scholar, Lincoln's Inn, 1946; called to the Bar, Lincoln's Inn, 1947, Bencher 1970. QC 1962; Dep. Chm., Kent QS, 1968–72; Recorder of Crown Court, 1972–74; a Judge, Employment Appeal Tribunal, 1982–88. *Recreations:* watching Rugby, racing and cricket. *Address:* 50 James Street, Louth, Lincs LN11 0JW. *Clubs:* Garrick, MCC. *Died 22 March 2012.*

TUNSTALL, Dr David Prestwich, FInstP; FRSE; Reader in Physics, University of St Andrews, 1978–2004; *b* 15 July 1939; *s* of Henry Brian Tunstall and Emmeline Grace Tunstall (*née* Denman); *m* 1963, Rosemarie Bebbington; two *s* one *d*. *Educ:* Sir John Talbot's Sch., Whitchurch; UCNW, Bangor (BSc *summa cum laude*; PhD). FInstP 1985; FRSE 1990. Post-doctoral Fellow: Zurich, 1963–64; Grenoble, 1964–66; Lectr, 1966–75, Sen. Lectr, 1975–78, Univ. of St Andrews. Visiting Fellow: Cornell Univ., 1973–74; UCLA, 1979. *Publications:* (jtly) Nuclear Magnetic Resonance, 1973; The Metal Non-Metal Transition in Disordered Systems, 1978; (ed jtly) High Temperature Superconductivity, 1991; contrib. to learned jls. *Recreations:* hill walking, skiing, tennis. *Address:* 10 The Circus, Bath BA1 2EW. *T:* (01225) 465064. *Died 26 Aug. 2012.*

TUPMAN, William Ivan, DPhil; Director General of Internal Audit, Ministry of Defence, 1974–81; *b* 22 July 1921; *s* of Leonard and Elsie Tupman; *m* 1945, Barbara (*née* Capel); two *s* one *d*. *Educ:* Queen Elizabeth's Hosp., Bristol; New Coll., Oxford (Exhibnr; MA, DPhil). Served War, 1942–45, RN (Lieut RNVR). Entered Admiralty as Asst Principal, 1948; Private Sec. to Parly Sec., 1950–52; Principal, 1952; Civil Affairs Adviser to C-in-C, Far East Station, 1958–61; Private Sec. to First Lord of the Admiralty, 1963; Asst Sec., 1964; IDC, 1967. *Died 29 June 2015.*

TURCOTTE, His Eminence Cardinal Jean-Claude; Archbishop of Montreal, (RC), 1990–2012; *b* 26 June 1936. Ordained priest, 1959; consecrated bishop, 1982; Cardinal, 1994. *Address:* c/o Office of the Archbishop, 2000 Sherbrooke Street West, Montreal, QC H3H 1G4, Canada. *Died 8 April 2015.*

TURNBULL, Jeffrey Alan, CBE 1991; FREng; FICE, FCIHT; Consultant, Mott MacDonald Group Ltd, 1994–96 (Chairman and Director, 1989–94); *b* 14 Aug. 1934; *s* of Alan Edward Turnbull and Alice May (*née* Slee); *m* 1957, Beryl (*née* Griffith); two *s* one *d*. *Educ:* Newcastle upon Tyne Royal Grammar Sch.; Liverpool Coll. of Technology. DipTE 1964; CEng; FCIHT (FIHT 1966); FICE 1973; FREng (FEng 1992). National Service, RE, 1956–58. Jun. Engr, Cheshire CC, 1951–55; Engr, Herefordshire CC, 1955–59; Resident Engr, Berks CC, 1959–66; Mott Hay & Anderson, 1966–88: Chief Designer (Roads), 1968; Associate, 1973; Dir, Mott Hay & Anderson International Ltd, 1975–88; Dir, Mott Hay & Anderson, 1978–88; Dir, 1983–88, Chief Exec., 1987–88, Mott Hay & Anderson Holdings Ltd. *Publications:* (contrib.) Civil Engineer's Reference Book, 4th edn 1988. *Recreation:* visiting France. *Address:* 63 Higher Drive, Banstead, Surrey SM1 1PW. *T:* (020) 8393 1054. *Club:* Royal Automobile. *Died 22 Feb. 2015.*

TURNBULL, John William; Chief Executive, Hereford and Worcester County Council, 1993–97; *b* 12 May 1934; *s* of Henry W. Turnbull and Janet Turnbull; *m* 1956, Sheila Batey; two *d*. *Educ:* Westminster Coll.; LSE (BScEcon); London Inst. of Educn (MA, DipEd). Teacher, 1957–68; Lectr, 1968–70; Educn Officer, 1970–76; Dep. County Educn Officer, Leics, 1977–83; County Educn Officer, Hereford and Worcester, 1984–93. Advr, ACC, 1985 (Advr, Soc. Services Cttee, 1995–97); Mem. Bd, Midlands Examining Gp, 1989–93; Chm., W Midlands Exam. Bd, 1991–93; Mem., Nat. Youth Bureau, 1990–93. Clerk to Lord Lieutenancy, 1993–97. Governor, Further Educn Staff Coll., 1990–93. JP S Worcs, 1998. *Publications:* articles on educn and administration. *Recreations:* reading, playing piano, bowls. *Died 17 March 2013.*

TURNER, Alan B.; *see* Brooke Turner.

TURNER, Christopher John, CBE 1990 (OBE 1977); Partner, DCGlobal, since 1998; consultant, EBRD TurnAround Management programme (Balkans); *b* 17 Aug. 1933; *s* of Arthur Basil Turner and Joan Meddows (*née* Taylor); *m* 1961, Irene Philomena de Souza; two *d* (one *s* decd). *Educ:* Truro Cathedral Sch.; Jesus Coll., Cambridge (MA). Served RAF, Pilot Officer (Navigator), 1951–53. Tanganyika/Tanzania: Dist Officer, 1958–61; Dist Comr, 1961–62; Magistrate and Regional Local Courts Officer, 1962–64; Sec., Sch. Admin, 1964–69; Anglo-French Condominium of New Hebrides: Dist Agent, 1970–73; Develt Sec., 1973; Financial Sec., 1975; Chief Sec., 1977–80; Admin. Officer (Staff Planning), Hong Kong, 1980–82; Governor: Turks and Caicos Islands, 1982–87; Montserrat, WI, 1987–90. Manager, Internat. Business Develt, 1990–92, consultant on regl business develt, Santa Domingo, 1990–91, McLane (Wal Mart), Texas; Man. Dir, McLane (UK), 1993; Vice Pres. Develt, McLane Internat., 1994–96; Dir of Mkting, Cambridge Myers (Strasburger Enterprises Inc.), Texas, 1996–98. Vanuatu Independence Medal, 1981. *Recreations:* ornithology, photography, diving, tropical gardening. *Address:* 98 Christchurch Road, Winchester SO23 9TE. *T:* (01962) 870775. *Died 30 Oct. 2014.*

TURNER, Sir Colin (William Carstairs), Kt 1993; CBE 1985; DFC 1944; President, The Colin Turner Group, International Media Representatives and Marketing Consultants, 1988–97 (Chairman, 1985–88); *b* 4 Jan. 1922; *s* of late Colin C. W. Turner, Enfield; *m* 1949, Evelyn Mary, *d* of late Claude H. Buckard, Enfield; three *s* one *d*. *Educ:* Highgate Sch. Served War of 1939–45 with RAF, 1940–45, Air observer; S. Africa and E Africa, 223 Squadron; Desert Air Force, N. Africa, 1942–44; commissioned, 1943; invalided out as Flying Officer, 1945, after air crash; Chm., 223 Squadron Assoc., 1975–93; Pres., Enfield Br., 1979–93, Chm., 1994–99, Pres., 2000–09, PR Officer, 2009–, Sheringham and Dist Br., RAFA. Mem., Enfield Borough Council, 1956–58. Pres., Overseas Press and Media Association, 1965–67, Life Pres., 1982 (Hon. Secretary, 1967; Hon. Treasurer, 1974–82; Editor, Overseas Media Guide, 1968, 1969, 1970, 1971, 1972, 1973, 1974); Chm., PR Cttee, Commonwealth Press Union, 1970–87; Chm., Cons. Commonwealth and Overseas Council, 1976–82 (Dep. Chm. 1975); Vice-Pres., Cons. Foreign and Commonwealth Council, 1985–2008; Mem., Nat. Exec., Cons. Party, 1946–53, 1968–73, 1976–82; President: Enfield North Cons. Assoc., 1984–93 (Chm., 1979–84); North Norfolk Cons. Assoc., 1996–99; Chm., Cons. Eur. Constituency Council, London N, 1984–89. Contested (C) Enfield (East), 1950 and 1951; MP (C) Woolwich West, 1959–64. Editor, The Cholmeleian, 1982–95 (Pres., Old Cholmeleian Soc., 1985–86). *Recreations:* gardening, do-it-yourself, fishing. *Address:* The Thatched House, Balfour Road, West Runton, Norfolk NR27 9QJ. *T:* (01263) 837229. *Died 21 March 2014.*

TURNER, Hugh Wason, CMG 1980; Director, National Gas Turbine Establishment, 1980–83; *b* 2 April 1923; *s* of Thomas W. Turner and Elizabeth P. Turner (*née* Pooley); *m* 1950, Rosemary Borley; two *s* two *d*. *Educ:* Dollar Academy; Glasgow University (BSc Hons (Mech. Eng)). CEng; FRAeS. Aeroplane and Armament Experimental Establishment, 1943–52; Chief Tech. Instructor, Empire

Test Pilots School, 1953; A&AEE (Prin. Scientific Officer), 1954–64; Asst Director, RAF Aircraft, Min. of Technology, 1965–68; Superintendent, Trials Management, A&AEE, 1968–69; Division Leader, Systems Engineering, NATO MRCA Management Agency (NAMMA), Munich, 1969–74; Chief Superintendent, A&AEE, 1974–75; DGA1 (Dir Gen., Tornado), MoD (PE), 1976–80. *Recreations:* ski-ing, model building, photography, DIY. *Address:* Lavender Cottage, 1 Highcliff Road, Lyme Regis, Dorset DT7 3EW. *T:* (01297) 442310. *Died 30 May 2011.*

TURNER, Prof. John Derfel; Sarah Fielden Professor of Education, University of Manchester, 1985–94, then Professor Emeritus; *b* 27 Feb. 1928; *s* of Joseph Turner and Dorothy Winifred Turner; *m* 1951, Susan Broady Hovey; two *s*. *Educ:* Manchester Grammar Sch.; Univ. of Manchester (BA 1948; MA 1951; Teacher's Diploma 1951). Education Officer, RAF, 1948–50; teacher, Prince Henry's Grammar Sch., Evesham, 1951–53; Lectr in English, 1953–56, Sen. Lectr in Educn, 1956–61, Nigerian Coll. of Arts, Science and Technology; Lectr in Educn, Univ. of Exeter Inst. of Education, 1961–64; Prof. of Educn and Dir, Sch. of Educn, 1964–70, and Pro-Vice-Chancellor, 1966–70, Univ. of Botswana, Lesotho and Swaziland, Emeritus Prof., 1970; University of Manchester: Prof. of Educn and Dir of Sch. of Educn, 1970–76; Dean, Faculty of Educn, 1972–74 and 1986–91; Prof. of Adult and Higher Educn, 1976–85; Pro Vice-Chancellor, 1991–94. Rector, University Coll. of Botswana, Univ. of Botswana and Swaziland, 1981–82 and Vice-Chancellor, Univ. of Botswana, 1982–84. Chairman: Univs Council for Educn of Teachers, 1979–81 and 1988–91 (Vice-Chm., 1976–79); Council of Validating Univs, 1990–94; Presidential Commn on Higher Educn in Namibia, 1991–92, on Education, Culture and Training in Namibia, 1999; Member: UK Nat. Commn for UNESCO, 1975–81; IUC Working Parties on East and Central Africa and on Rural Development, 1975–81; Educn Sub-Cttee, UGC, 1980–81; Educn Cttee and Further Educn Bd, CNAA, 1979–81; Chm., European Develt Fund/IUC Working Party on Academic Develt of Univ. of Juba, 1977–78; Chm. and Mem. Council, Social Studies Adv. Cttee, Selly Oak Colleges, 1975–81. Pres., 1994–2004, Patron, 2004–, Coll. of Teachers (formerly Coll. of Preceptors) (Hon. FCP 1985). Chm., Bd of Governors, Abbotsholme Sch., 1980–98. Chm. Editl Bd, Internat. Jl of Educn and Develt, 1978–81; Ed., Jl of Practice in Educn for Develt, 1994–99. FRSA 2000. Hon. Fellow, Bolton Inst. of Higher Educn, 1988. Hon. LLD Ohio Univ., 1982; Hon. DLitt Botswana, 1995; Hon. PhD Bolton, 2010. *Publications:* Introducing the Language Laboratory, 1963; (ed with A. P. Hunter) Educational Development in Predominantly Rural Countries, 1968; (ed with J. Rushton) The Teacher in a Changing Society, 1974; (ed with J. Rushton) Education and Deprivation, 1975; (ed with J. Rushton) Education and Professions, 1976; (ed) The Reform of Educational Systems to Meet Local and National Needs, 1994; (ed) The State and the School, 1996; school text books and contribs to edited works and to jls. *Recreations:* reading, music, theatre, walking; Methodist local preacher. *Address:* 13 Firswood Mount, Gatley, Cheadle, Cheshire SK8 4JY. *T:* (0161) 283 8429, *Fax:* (0161) 282 1022. *E:* johndturner@ntlworld.com. *Died 29 Nov. 2013.*

TURNER, Air Vice-Marshal Peter, CB 1979; MA; Bursar and Steward, Wolfson College, Cambridge, 1979–89; *b* 29 Dec. 1924; *s* of late George Allen and of Emma Turner; *m* 1949, Doreen Newbon; one *s*. *Educ:* Tapton House Sch., Chesterfield. Served War of 1939–45; 640 Sqdn, 1943–45; Nos 51, 242 and 246 Sqdns, 1945–48; psa 1961; NATO staff, 1963–67; jssc 1967; Chief Equipment and Secretarial Instructor, RAF Coll., Cranwell, 1967–68; Comd Accountant, HQ Air Support Comd, 1968–69; Station Comdr, RAF Uxbridge, 1969–71; RCDS, 1972; Dir of Personnel (Ground) (RAF), MoD, 1973–75; AOA, HQ RAF Support Command, 1975–79, and Head of RAF Admin. Branch, 1976–79. MA Cantab 1979. *Recreation:* retrospective contemplation. *Address:* Hedge End, Potton Road, Hilton, Huntingdon PE28 9NG. *Club:* Royal Air Force. *Died 22 March 2012.*

TURNER, Peter William; District Secretary, Hereford and Worcester, Transport and General Workers' Union, 1969–91; *m* Maureen Ann Turner (*née* Hill), Councillor, JP. *Educ:* Bordesley Green Infant and Junior Sch.; Saltley Grammar Sch. (until 1940); various Trade Union weekend courses. Appointed District Officer, TGWU, 1969; District Sec., CSEU, 1974–76; seconded as Industrial Advr to DoI, 1976–78. Member of various cttees including: Chemical Industry Area Productivity Cttee, 1969–76 (Vice-Chm., 1970–72, Chm., 1972–74); TUC Regional Educn Adv. Cttee, 1970–76; Birmingham Crime Prevention Panel, 1973–76; W Midlands Conciliation Cttee on Race Relations, 1974–76; DoE Working Party on Race Relations, 1974–76; Teaching Co. Management Cttee, 1977–82. Member: Birmingham Trades Council, 1956–76; Local Appeals Tribunal, 1969–74. *Recreations:* do-it-yourself, reading, electronics, amateur radio (M0CHY). *Address:* 2 Oakleigh Road, Droitwich, Worcs WR9 0RP. *Died 20 Nov. 2012.*

TURNER, Wilfred, CMG 1977; CVO 1979; HM Diplomatic Service, retired; Director, Transportation Systems and Market Research Ltd (Transmark), 1987–90; *b* 10 Oct. 1921; *s* of late Allen Turner and Eliza (*née* Leach); *m* 1947, June Gladys Tite; two *s* one *d*. *Educ:* Heywood Grammar Sch., Lancs; London Univ. (BSc 1942). Min. of Labour, 1938–42; recruited by C. P. Snow as Radar Maintenance Officer, 1942. Served War, Capt., REME, 1942–47, Staff 13th Infantry Bde, 1945–47. Min. of Labour, 1947–55; British High Commn, New Delhi (Asst Lab. Adviser), 1955–59; Senior Wages Inspector, Min. of Labour, 1959–60; Principal, Hosps Div., Min. of Health, 1960–66 (drafted report recommending standardisation of Hosp. Med. Records, 1962; Sec., Cttee on Safety of Drugs (Dunlop Cttee), 1963–66; initiated drafting of Medicines Bill; designed and introd Yellow Card for reporting adverse reactions to medicines); joined HM Diplomatic Service, 1966; Commonwealth Office, 1966; Head of Chancery: Kaduna, Nigeria, 1966–69; Kuala Lumpur, 1969–73 (administered British Special Aid to Malaysia); Dep. High Comr, and Commercial/Economic Counsellor, Accra, 1973–77; High Comr to Botswana, 1977–81. Dir and Chief Exec., Southern Africa Assoc., 1983–88. Member: Cttee, Zambia Soc., 1983–91; Central Council, Royal Commonwealth Soc., 1987–94; RIIA, 1987–; Royal African Soc., 1987–. *Recreation:* hill walking. *Address:* 44 Tower Road, Twickenham TW1 4PE. *T:* (020) 8892 1593. *Died 26 June 2015.*

TURVEY, Ralph, DSc (Econ); economist; Visiting Professor of Economics, London School of Economics, 1973–75 and 1990–2009; *b* 1 May 1927; *s* of John and Margaret Turvey; *m* 1st, 1957, Sheila Bucher (*d* 1987); one *s* one *d*; 2nd, 2006, Barbara Williams. *Educ:* Sidcot School; London School of Economics; Uppsala University. Lectr, then Reader, in Economics, at London School of Economics, 1948–64, with interruptions. Vis. Lectr, Johns Hopkins Univ., 1953; Ford Foundation Vis. Res. Prof., Univ. of Chicago, 1958–59; Economic Section, HM Treasury, 1960–62; Center of Economic Research, Athens, 1963. Chief Economist, The Electricity Council, 1964–67. Member, NBPI, 1967–71, Jt Dep. Chm. 1968–71; Economic Advr, Scientific Control Systems Ltd, 1971–75; Economic Advr, then Chief Statistician, ILO, 1975–89; Dir, Dept of Labour Information and Statistics, ILO, until 1989; Res. Fellow, Statistics Canada, 1989–90. Member: Nat. Water Council, 1974–75; Inflation Accounting Cttee, 1974–75; NZ Adv. Cttee on price indices, 1991; RPI Adv. Cttee, 1992–94; Canadian and Swedish adv. cttees on consumer price indices, 1992–2006. Chm., Centre for the Study of Regulated Industries, 1993–2009. Associate, Frontier Economics, 2003–07. Governor, Kingston Poly., 1972–75. Hon. Fellow, Weimer Sch. of Advanced Studies in Real Estate and Land Econs, 2008. *Publications:* The Economics of Real Property, 1957; Interest Rates and Asset Prices, 1960; (joint author) Studies in Greek Taxation, 1964; Optimal Pricing and Investment in Electricity Supply, 1968; Economic Analysis and Public Enterprises, 1971; Demand and Supply, 1971; (joint author) Electricity Economics, 1977; Consumer Price Indices, 1989; (ed and joint author) Developments in International Labour Statistics, 1989; Consumer Price Indexes, 1999; papers on economic hist. of Victorian

London and on electricity pricing. *Recreation:* walking. *Address:* 20 The Croft, Bishopstone, Salisbury SP5 4DF. *Club:* Reform. *Died 7 April 2012.*

TWINN, John Ernest; Director General Guided Weapons and Electronics, Ministry of Defence, 1978–81; *b* 11 July 1921; *s* of late Col Frank Charles George Twinn, CMG and Lilian May Twinn (*née* Tomlinson); *m* 1950, Mary Constance Smallwood; three *d. Educ:* Manchester Grammar Sch.; Christ's Coll., Cambridge (MA). FIET (FIEE 1981). Air Min., 1941; Telecommunications Research Estabt (later Royal Radar Estabt), 1943; Head of Guided Weapons Gp, RRE, 1965; Head of Space Dept, RAE, 1968; Head of Weapons Dept, RAE, 1972; Asst Chief Scientific Advr (Projects), MoD, 1973; Dir Underwater Weapons Projects (Naval), 1976. *Recreations:* sailing, music, genealogy. *Address:* Timbers, 9 Woodway, Merrow, Guildford, Surrey GU1 2TF. *T:* (01483) 568993. *Died 31 May 2013.*

TWISK, Russell Godfrey; writer; Editor-at-Large, British Reader's Digest, 2002–06 (Editor-in-Chief, 1988–2002); *b* 24 Aug. 1941; *s* of late K. Y. Twisk and of Joyce Brunning; *m* 1965, Ellen Elizabeth Banbury; two *d. Educ:* Salesian Coll., Farnborough. Harmsworth Press, Dep. Editor, Golf Illustrated, 1960; Sub Editor, Sphere; freelance journalist, 1962; joined BBC, editorial staff Radio Times, 1966; Deputy Editor, Radio Times, 1971; Development Manager, BBC, 1975; Editor, The Listener, 1981–87. Director: Reader's Digest, 1988–2002; Berkeley Magazines, 1990–2002. Edited numerous BBC publications; Publisher, BBC Adult Literacy Project; radio critic for The Observer, 1989–94; writer, daily Birthday column, The Times, 2003–; corresp., The Oldie. Mem., Press Complaints Commn, 1999–2002. Governor, London College of Printing, 1967–87 (Chm., 1974, 1978). Chm., Reader's Digest Trust, 1988–99. Chm., National Campaign Cttee, Charities Aid Foundn, 1991–94. Chm., BSME, 1990; Pres., 1993–95, Mem. Council, 1996–, Media Soc. Mem. Council, Next Century Foundn, 1987–. Trustee, Christian Responsibility in Public Affairs, 1997–. *Recreations:* golf, walking, watching horses race. *Address:* The Old Barn, East Harting, near Petersfield, Hants GU31 5LZ. *T:* (01730) 825769. *Clubs:* Garrick, Pilgrims. *Died 4 Aug. 2013.*

TWISS, (Lionel) Peter, OBE 1957; DSC 1942 and Bar 1943; marine consultant; Director and General Manager, Hamble Point Marina Ltd, 1978–88; formerly Chief Test Pilot of Fairey Aviation Ltd; *b* 23 July 1921; *m* 1st, 1944, Constance Tomkinson (marr. diss.; she *d* 1996); 2nd, 1950, Mrs Vera Maguire (marr. diss.); one *d* (and one *d* decd), one step *s* one step *d*; 3rd, 1960, Cherry (marr. diss.), *d* of late Sir John Huggins, GCMG, MC; one *d*; 4th, 1964, Mrs Heather Danby (*d* 1988), Titchfield; one step *s* one step *d*; 5th, 2002, Jane Mary de Lucey. *Educ:* Sherborne Sch. Joined Fleet Air Arm, 1939; served on catapult ships, aircraft-carriers, 1941–43; night fighter development, 1943–44; served in British Air Commn, America, 1944. Empire Test Pilots School, Boscombe Down, 1945; Test Pilot, Fairey Aviation Co. Ltd, 1946, Chief Test Pilot, 1957–60. Dir, Fairey Marine Ltd, 1968–78. Mem., Lasham Gliding Soc. Holder of World's Absolute Speed Record, 10 March 1956. *Publications:* Faster than the Sun, 1963, 2nd edn 2000. *Address:* Nettleworth, 33 South Street, Titchfield, Hants PO14 4DL. *T:* (01329) 843146. *Club:* Royal Southern Yacht. *Died 31 Aug. 2011.*

TYBULEWICZ, Albin, CPhys, FInstP; Scientific Editor, Quantum Electronics, 1994–2000; *b* Poland, 1 March 1929; *s* of Julian and Elżbieta Tybulewicz (*née* Świgost); *m* 1959, Tuliola Sylwina Bryl; one *s* one *d. Educ:* schools in Poland, Russia, Iran, India; St Mary's High Sch., Bombay. BSc London 1952. CPhys 1985; FInstP 1967. Research Officer, BICC, 1953–56; Asst Editor, 1956–63, Editor, 1963–67, Physics Abstracts and Current Papers in Physics; Editor: Soviet Physics—Semiconductors, 1967–92; Soviet Jl of Quantum Electronics, 1970–92; Soviet Physics—Solid State (jtly with Prof. L. Azaroff), 1982–92. Founder and Chm., Food for Poland Fund, 1980–84. Mem. Prog. Adv. Bd, Polish Satellite TV (Polonia), 1997–2010, Vice-Chm., 2002–10. Fellow, Amer. Phys. Soc.; Hon. Fellow, Inst. of Translation and Interpreting (Mem. Council, 1986–94, 1995–2001; Vice-Chm., 1999–2001). Natthorst Non-Literary Prize, Fedn Internat. des Traducteurs, 1990; John Sykes Prize for Excellence, Inst. of Translation and Interpreting, 2007. Officer's Cross, Order of Polonia Restituta (Poland), 2006. *Publications:* American Institute of Physics Translation Manual, 1983; trans of numerous Russian physics monographs; contribs to physics and professional jls on language and translation. *Recreations:* theatre, reading, politics in Poland. *Address:* 2 Oak Dene, West Ealing, W13 8AW. *Died 17 April 2014.*

TYREE, Sir (Alfred) William, Kt 1975; OBE 1971; electrical engineer, chief executive and chairman; *b* Auckland, NZ, 4 Nov. 1921; *s* of J. V. Tyree and A. Hezeltine (who migrated to Australia, 1938); *m* 1946, Joyce (*d* 2006), *d* of F. Lyndon; two *s* one *d. Educ:* Auckland Grammar School; Sydney Technical Coll. (Dip. in Elec. Engrg). FIE (Aust) 1968 (Peter Nicol Russell Mem. Award 1985); FIEE 1983. Founded Tyree Industries Ltd and Westralian Transformers and subsids, 1956; Founder, Tyree Hldgs gp of companies incl.: Tytronics Develts Australia Pty Ltd (formerly Technical Components Pty Ltd, then Tytronics Pty Ltd); Tycan Australia Pty Ltd; Tyree Holdings Pty Ltd; Tyree Industries Pty Ltd (formerly A. W. Tyree Transformers Pty Ltd, subseq. Tyree Transformers (Aust.) Pty Ltd); Wirex Pty Ltd; A. W. Tyree Foundation. Mem., Aust. Inst. of Co. Dirs; Emeritus Councillor, Australian Industry Gp, 2001. Founder and Dir, Sir William Tyree Foundn. Hon. Fellow, Univ. of Sydney, 1985; Hon. Life Governor, Aust. Postgrad. Fedn in Medicine, 1985. Hon. DSc Univ. of NSW, 1986; Hon. DEng Sydney, 2008. James N. Kirby Medal, IProdE, Australia, 1980; IEEE USA Centennial Medal, 1984; Award of Merit, Aust. Nat. Cttee, CIGRE, 2000; Centenary Medal, Australia, 2003; ATSE Clunies Ross Lifetime Contribn Award, 2012. *Recreations:* photography, music, computers. *Address:* (home) 3 Lindsay Avenue, Darling Point, NSW, Australia. *Clubs:* Royal Prince Alfred Yacht, Royal Motor Yacht, Cruising Yacht, Kosciusko Alpine, Australian Golf. *Died 25 Oct. 2013.*

TYRRELL, Alan Rupert; QC 1976; Barrister-at-Law; a Recorder of the Crown Court, 1972–98; a Deputy High Court Judge, 1990–98; *b* 27 June 1933; *s* of Rev. T. G. R. Tyrrell, and Mrs W. A. Tyrrell, MSc; *m* 1960, Elaine Eleanor Ware, LLB; one *s* one *d. Educ:* Bridport Grammar Sch.; London Univ. (LLB). Called to the Bar, Gray's Inn, 1956, Bencher, 1986. Mem., Criminal Injuries Compensation Bd, 1999–2000 (Mem., Appeal Panel, 2000–08). Chm. of the Bar Eur. Gp, 1986–88; Chm. of the Internat. Practice Cttee, Bar Council (co-opted to Bar Council), 1988. Lord Chancellor's Legal Visitor, 1990–2009; Arbitrator, Internat. Chamber of Commerce, Paris, 1999–2006. Dir, Papworth Hosp. NHS Trust, 1993–2000. Council Mem., Med. Protection Soc., 1990–98. Chm. London Reg., and Mem. Nat. Exec., Nat. Fedn of Self-Employed, 1978–79 (Chm., Employment Law Policy Unit, 2002–). Mem. (C) London E, European Parlt, 1979–84; contested same seat, 1984, 1989. FCIArb 1993–2006. *Publications:* (ed) Moore's Practical Agreements, 10th edn 1965; Students' Guide to Europe, 1984; The Legal Professions in the New Europe, 1992, 2nd edn 1996; Public Procurement in Europe: enforcement and remedies, 1997. *Recreation:* bridge. *Address:* 15 Willifield Way, Hampstead Garden Suburb, NW11 7XU. *T:* (020) 8455 5798; Tanfield Chambers, 2–5 Warwick Court, WC1R 5DJ. *T:* (020) 7421 5300. *E:* alantyrrell@ntlworld.com. *Club:* Athenæum. *Died 23 Oct. 2014.*

TYRRELL, Anne Elizabeth, MBE 2008; Founder and Managing Director, Anne Tyrrell Design, international design consultancy, since 1982; *b* Norwich, 26 Aug. 1938; *d* of John Baly Tyrrell and Leah Marjorie Tyrrell (*née* Chapman); partner, Paul Mason. *Educ:* Norwich High Sch.; Norwich Art Sch.; Sch. of Fashion and Textiles, RCA (DesRCA 1960). Design Dir, John Marks, 1963–82, own label collection, Anne Tyrrell@John Marks. Visiting Lecturer: Norwich Sch. of Art, 1960–63; Walthamstow Coll. of Art, 1963–67; Tutor, 1967–74, Sen. Tutor, 1974–95, Vis. Prof., 1995, Sch. of Fashion and Textiles, RCA. British Fashion Council: Chm., Colleges Council, 1992–; Vice Chm., 2000–07; Mem., Adv. Bd, 2007–. Dir, Skillfast UK, 2002–10; Mem., Fashion and Textile Council, Creative Skillset, 2010–. Mem., Mgt Council, Texprint, 1990–. FRCA 1979, Hon. FRCA 1998. Hon. FCSD 2001.

Hon. MA Univ. of Creative Arts Rochester, 2008; Hon. DArts Univ. of London/Norwich Univ. of Arts, 2013. *Recreations:* polo, sailing, antiques and interiors, charity work, British art education for fashion and textiles. *Address:* Anne Tyrrell Design, 9 Cheltenham Terrace, SW3 4RD. *T:* (020) 7730 7962. *E:* info@annetyrrelldesigns.com. *Clubs:* Sloane; Norfolk Broads Yacht. *Died 6 Feb. 2015.*

TYSOE, John Sidney; Chairman, Yorkshire Electricity Group, 1992–94; *b* 14 March 1932; *s* of Florence Alice Tysoe (*née* Gypps) and late Sidney George Tysoe; *m* 1953, Ann Dunham; two *s* one *d*. *Educ:* Harrow Weald County Grammar Sch.; City of London Coll. FCCA, CPFA, FIET. Nat. Service Commn, RN, 1950–52. Exchequer and Audit Dept, 1953–65; Southern Electricity Bd, 1966–67; Head, Special Investigations and Asst Management Accountant, BR, 1967–68; Asst and Dep. Financial Advr, Electricity Council, 1969–77; Chief Accountant and Financial Dir, Southern Electricity Bd, 1978–85; Dep. Chm., Yorkshire Electricity Bd, 1985–89; Gp Man. Dir, Yorkshire Electricity Gp, 1989–92. Mem. Council, CBI, 1993–94. *Recreations:* walking, woodcarving, theatre. *Died 5 Aug. 2015.*

TYZACK, Margaret Maud, CBE 2010 (OBE 1970); actress; *b* 9 Sept. 1931; *d* of Thomas Edward Tyzack and Doris Moseley; *m* 1958, Alan Stephenson; one *s*. *Educ:* St Angela's Ursuline Convent; Royal Academy of Dramatic Art (Gilbert Prize for Comedy). First engagement, Civic Theatre, Chesterfield. Vassilissa in The Lower Depths, Royal Shakespeare Co., Arts Theatre, 1962; Lady MacBeth, Nottingham, 1962; Miss Frost in The Ginger Man, Royal Court, London, 1964; Madame Ranevsky in The Cherry Orchard, Exeter and Tour, 1969; Jacqui in Find Your Way Home, Open Space Theatre, London, 1970; Queen Elizabeth in Vivat! Vivat Regina!, Piccadilly, 1971; Tamora in Titus Andronicus, Portia in Julius Caesar and Volumnia in Coriolanus, Royal Shakespeare Co., Stratford-on-Avon, 1972; Portia in Julius Caesar, and Volumnia in Coriolanus, RSC, Aldwych, 1973; Maria Lvovna in Summerfolk, RSC, Aldwych, and NY, 1974–75; Richard III, All's Well That Ends Well, Ghosts, Stratford, Ont., 1977; People Are Living There, Manchester Royal Exchange, 1979; Martha, in Who's Afraid of Virginia Woolf?, Nat. Theatre, 1981 (Best Actress, Olivier Award); Countess of Rousillon, in All's Well That Ends Well, RSC Barbican and NY, 1983; An Inspector Calls, Greenwich, 1983; Tom and Viv, Royal Court, 1984, also New York, 1985; Mornings at Seven, Westminster, 1984; Night Must Fall, Greenwich, 1986; Lettice and Lovage, Globe, 1987 (Variety Club of GB Award for Best Stage Actress), and New York, 1990 (Tony award); The Importance of Being Earnest, Aldwych, 1993; An Inspector Calls, Aldwych, 1994; Indian Ink, Aldwych, 1995; Talking Heads, Chichester, 1996, Comedy, 1996–97, Australian tour, 2004; The Family Reunion, RSC, 1999; Tartuffe, NT, 2002; Auntie and Me, Wyndham's, 2003; His Girl Friday, NT, 2003; As You Desire Me, Playhouse, 2005; Southwark Fair, NT, 2006; The Boy Friend, Regent's Park, 2007; The Chalk Garden, Donmar, 2008 (Olivier Award, Best Actress, 2009); Phèdre, NT, 2009; My Fair Lady, Le Chatelet Opera, Paris, 2010. *Films:* Ring of Spies, 2001: A Space Odyssey, The Whisperers, A Clockwork Orange, The Legacy, The King's Whore, Match Point. *Television series include:* The Forsyte Saga; The First Churchills; Cousin Bette, 1970–71; I, Claudius, 1976; Quatermass, 1979; The Winter's Tale; Young Indiana Jones, 1992. Actress of the Year Award (BAFTA) for Queen Anne in The First Churchills, 1969. *Address:* c/o Markham, Froggatt & Irwin, 4 Windmill Street, W1T 2HZ. *T:* (020) 7636 4412, *Fax:* (020) 7637 5233. *Died 25 June 2011.*

U

ULLENDORFF, Prof. Edward, DPhil; FBA 1965; Professor of Semitic Languages, School of Oriental and African Studies, University of London, 1979–82, then Professor Emeritus (Professor of Ethiopian Studies, 1964–79; Head of Africa Department, 1972–77); *b* 25 Jan. 1920; *s* of late Frederic and Cilli Ullendorff; *m* 1943, Dina Noack. *Educ:* Gymnasium Graues Kloster; Univ. of Jerusalem (MA); St Catherine's Coll., Oxford (DPhil 1952). Chief Examiner, British Censorship, Eritrea, 1942–43; Editor, African Publ., British Ministry of Information, Eritrea-Ethiopia, 1943–45; Assistant Political Secretary, British Military Admin, Eritrea, 1945–46; Asst Secretary, Palestine Government, 1947–48; Research Officer and Librarian, Oxford Univ. Inst. of Colonial Studies, 1948–49; Scarbrough Senior Research Studentship in Oriental Languages, 1949–50; Lectr, 1950–56, Reader in Semitic Languages, 1956–59, St Andrews Univ.; Professor of Semitic Languages and Literatures, Univ. of Manchester, 1959–64. Carnegie Travelling Fellow to Ethiopia, 1958; Research Journeys to Ethiopia, 1964, 1966, 1969, etc. Catalogued Ethiopian Manuscripts in Royal Library, Windsor Castle. Chairman: Assoc. of British Orientalists, 1963–64; Anglo-Ethiopian Soc., 1965–68 (Vice-Pres. 1969–77); Pres., Soc. for Old Testament Study, 1971; Vice-Pres., RAS, 1975–79, 1981–85. Joint Organizer, 2nd Internat. Congress of Ethiopian Studies, Manchester, 1963. Chm., Editorial Bd, Bulletin of SOAS, 1968–78; Mem., Adv. Bd, British Library, 1975–83. Vice-Pres., British Acad., 1980–82; Schweich Lectr, British Acad., 1967. FRAS; Hon. Fellow: SOAS, 1985–; Oxford Centre for Hebrew Studies, 1998–; Foreign Fellow, Accademia Lincei, Rome, 1998–. MA Manchester, 1962; Hon. DLitt St Andrews, 1972; Hon. Dr Phil Hamburg, 1990. Imperial Ethiopian Gold Medallion, 1960; Haile Sellassie Internat. Prize for Ethiopian studies, 1972; Festschriften to EU 1989, 2005. *Publications:* The definite article in the Semitic languages, 1941; Exploration and Study of Abyssinia, 1945; Catalogue of Ethiopian Manuscripts in the Bodleian Library, Oxford, 1951; The Semitic Languages of Ethiopia, 1955; The Ethiopians, 1959, 3rd edn 1973; (with Stephen Wright) Catalogue of Ethiopian MSS in Cambridge University Library, 1961; Comparative Semitics in Linguistica Semitica, 1961; (with S. Moscati and others) Introduction to Comparative Grammar of Semitic Languages, 1964; An Amharic Chrestomathy, 1965, 2nd edn 1978; The Challenge of Amharic, 1965; Ethiopia and the Bible, 1968; (with J. B. Pritchard and others) Solomon and Sheba, 1974; trans. and annotated, Emperor Haile Sellassie, My Life and Ethiopia's Progress (autobiog.), 1976; Studies in Semitic Languages and Civilizations, 1977; (with M. A. Knibb) Book of Enoch, 1978; The Bawdy Bible, 1979; (jtly) The Amharic Letters of Emperor Theodore of Ethiopia to Queen Victoria, 1979; (with C. F. Beckingham) The Hebrew Letters of Prester John, 1982; A Tigrinya Chrestomathy, 1985; Studia Aethiopica et Semitica, 1987; The Two Zions, 1988; From the Bible to Enrico Cerulli, 1990; H. J. Polotsky (1905–1991), 1992; From Emperor Haile Sellassie to H. J. Polotsky, 1995; Joint Editor of Studies in honour of G. R. Driver, 1962; Joint Editor of Ethiopian Studies, 1964; articles and reviews in journals of learned societies; contribs to Encyclopaedia Britannica, Encyclopaedia of Islam, DNB, etc; Joint Editor, Journal of Semitic Studies, 1961–64. *Recreation:* music. *Address:* 4 Bladon Close, Oxford OX2 8AD. *Died 6 March 2011.*

UNDERWOOD, Hon. Peter George, AC 2009 (AO 2002); Governor of Tasmania, since 2008; *b* 10 Oct. 1937; *s* of George Underwood; *m* 1st, 1965 (marr. diss. 1980); one *s* two *d*; 2nd, 1981, Frances, *d* of Col V. P. Northam; one *s*. *Educ:* Launceston High Sch.; Univ. of Tasmania (LLB 1960). Admitted to Bar, Supreme Ct of Tasmania, 1960; legal practitioner, 1960 and 1962–63; Partner, Murdoch Clarke Cosgrove & Drake, 1963–84; Supreme Court of Tasmania: Judge, 1984–2004; Chief Justice, 2004–08; Lieut Gov., Tasmania, 2005–08. Member: Tasmania Law Reform Commn, 1977–84; Supreme Ct Rules Ctte 1981–84; Tasmania Racing Appeal Bd, 1983–84; Chm Council of Law Reporting Tasmania, 1988–2005; Mem 1996–98, Dep. Chm., 1998–2008, Defence Forc Discipline Appeal Tribunal. Member: Bar Assoc. c Tasmania, 1964–74; Legal Assistance Cttee, 1964–6 Tasmanian Law Council, 1969–73; Law Soc. Disciplinar Cttee, 1980–84. Pres., Aust. Inst. of Judicial Admi 2002–04; Chm., Nat. Judicial Coll. of Australia, 2007–0 Dir, Nat. Heart Foundn, 1970–83; Mem., Tasmanian Ar Adv. Bd, 1981–84; Chairman: Bd, Tasmanian Theat Trust, 1984; Tasmanian Symphony Orch., 1997–200 Mem., Bd of Govs, Friends Sch., Hobart, 1984–86 (Chm 1989–94). Hon. LLD Tasmania, 2001. *Recreation* swimming, music, theatre. *Address:* Government Hous Lower Domain Road, Hobart, Tas 7000, Australi *Died 7 July 2014*

UNSWORTH, Barry Forster; author; *b* 10 Aug. 1930; *s* c Michael Unsworth and Elsie (*née* Forster); *m* 1st, 195 Valerie Irene Moor (marr. diss. 1991); three *d*; 2nd, 199 Aira Pohjanvaara-Buffa. *Educ:* Stockton Grammar Sch Manchester Univ. (BA Hons English). FRSL 1973. Ho LittD Manchester, 1998. *Publications:* The Partnershi 1966; The Greeks Have a Word for It, 1967; The Hid 1970; Mooncranker's Gift (Heinemann Award), 1973; Th Big Day, 1976; Pascali's Island, 1980; The Rage of th Vulture, 1982; Stone Virgin, 1985; Sugar and Rum, 198 Sacred Hunger (jtly, Booker Prize), 1992; Morality Pla 1995; After Hannibal, 1996; Losing Nelson, 1999; Th Songs of the Kings, 2002; The Ruby in Her Navel, 200 Land of Marvels, 2009; The Quality of Mercy, 201 *Recreations:* gardening, viticulture, bird-watching. *Addres* c/o Vivien Green, Sheil Land Associates, 52 Dought Street, WC1N 2LS. *Died 5 June 2012*

URMSON, James Opie, MC 1943; Emeritus Professor c Philosophy, Stanford University; Emeritus Fellow Corpus Christi College, Oxford; *b* 4 March 1915; *s* of Re J. O. Urmson; *m* 1940, Marion Joyce Drage (*d* 2010); on *d*. *Educ:* Kingswood School, Bath; Corpus Christi Colleg Oxford. Senior Demy, Magdalen College, 1938; Fellow b examination, Magdalen College, 1939–45. Served Arm (Duke of Wellington's Regt), 1939–45. Lecturer of Chri Church, 1945–46; Student of Christ Church, 1946–5 Professor of Philosophy, Queen's College, Dunde University of St Andrews, 1955–59; Fellow and Tutor i Philosophy, CCC, Oxford, 1959–78. Visiting Associat Prof., Princeton Univ., 1950–51. Visiting Lectr, Univ. c Michigan, 1961–62, 1965–66, and 1969; Stuart Prof. c Philosophy, Stanford, 1975–80. *Publications:* Philosophic Analysis, 1956; The Emotive Theory of Ethics, 196 Berkeley, 1982; Aristotle's Ethics, 1988; The Gree Philosophical Vocabulary, 1990; edited: Encyclopedia c Western Philosophy, 1960; J. L. Austin: How to Do Thin with Words, 1962; (with G. J. Warnock) J. L. Austi Philosophical Papers, 2nd edn, 1970; translations fro ancient Greek; articles in philosophical jls. *Recreation* gardening, music. *Died 29 Jan. 2012.*

URQUHART, James Graham, CVO 1983; FCILT FIMH; Chairman, Fiox Ltd, 1990–92 (Director, 1988–90 *b* 23 April 1925; *s* of James Graham Urquhart and Ma Clark; *m* 1949, Margaret Hutchinson; two *d*. *Edu* Berwickshire High Sch. Served War, RAF, 1941–4 Management Trainee, Eastern Region, BR, 1949–5 Chief Controller, Fenchurch Street, 1956–59; Dist Traff Supt, Perth, 1960–62; Divl Operating Supt, Glasgow 1962–64; Divl Manager, Glasgow and SW Scotlan 1964–67; Asst Gen. Man., Eastern Reg., 1967–69; BR B HQ: Chief Ops Man., 1969–72; Exec. Dir, Personne 1972–75; Gen. Manager, London Midland Reg., BR 1975–76; BR Bd: Exec. Mem., Operations an Productivity, 1977–83; Mem., Exports, 1983–8 Chairman: British Transport Police, 1977–86; BRE-Metr 1978–86; BR Engrg Ltd, 1979–85; Freightliners, 1983–8 Transmark, 1983–86. Director: Waterslides PLC, 1987–8

Park Air Electronics Ltd, 1987–91; Systems Connection Group PLC, 1988–92; CVC Ltd, 1988–91; Sonic Tape PLC, 1988–90. Mem., Industrial Tribunal, 1987–90. MIPM, MCIM, CCMI. *Recreations:* golf, travel, gardening. *Address:* 12 Durlston Point, 78 Park Road, Swanage, Dorset BH19 2AE. *T:* (01929) 421574. *Died 14 July 2015.*

URSELL, Prof. Fritz Joseph, FRS 1972; Emeritus Professor of Applied Mathematics, Manchester University, since 1990 (Beyer Professor of Applied Mathematics, 1961–90); *b* Düsseldorf, 28 April 1923; *m* 1959, Katharina Renate (*née* Zander); two *d. Educ:* Clifton; Marlborough; Trinity College, Cambridge (BA 1943; MA 1947; ScD 1958); MSc Manchester, 1965. Admiralty Service, 1943–47; ICI Fellow in Applied Mathematics, Manchester Univ., 1947–50. Fellow (Title A), Trinity Coll., Cambridge, 1947–51; Univ. Lecturer in Mathematics, Cambridge, 1950–61; Stringer Fellow in Natural Sciences, King's Coll., Cambridge, 1954–60. Georg Weinblum Lectr in Ship Hydrodynamics, Hamburg and Washington, 1986; Stewartson Lectr in Fluid Mechanics, 1991. FIMA 1964 (Gold Medal, 1994). *Publications:* Collected Papers 1946–1992, 1994. *Address:* 28 Old Broadway, Manchester M20 3DF. *T:* (0161) 445 5791. *E:* f.ursell@ntlworld.com. *Died 12 May 2012.*

UTLEY, (Clifton) Garrick; Professor of Journalism, State University of New York, since 2011 (President, Levin Institute, 2003–11); *b* Chicago, 19 Nov. 1939; *s* of late Clifton Maxwell Utley and Frayn Garrick Utley; *m* 1973, Gertje Rommeswinkel. *Educ:* Carleton Coll., Northfield, Minn, USA (BA 1961); Free Univ., Berlin. Correspondent, NBC News: Saigon, Vietnam, 1964–65; Berlin, Germany, 1966–68; Paris, France, 1969–71; NY, 1971–72; London (Senior European Correspondent), 1973–79; New York (Chief Foreign Correspondent), 1980–93; Chief Foreign Correspondent, ABC News, London, 1993–96; contributor, CNN, NY, 1996–2003. Numerous documentary films on foreign affairs. Hon. LLD: Carleton Coll., 1979; Pomona Coll., 2001. *Recreations:* music, conversation, languages. *Address:* 19 East 88th Street, New York, NY 10128, USA. *Club:* Century (New York). *Died 20 Feb. 2014.*

V

VALLANCE, Michael Wilson; Headmaster of Bloxham School 1982–91; *b* 9 Sept. 1933; *er s* of late Vivian Victor Wilson Vallance and Kate Vallance, Wandsworth and Helston; *m* 1970, Mary Winifred Ann, *d* of John Steele Garnett; one *s* two *d*. *Educ:* Brighton Coll.; St John's Coll., Cambridge (MA). On staff of United Steel Companies Ltd, 1952–53; awarded United Steel Companies Scholarship (held at Cambridge), 1953; Asst Master, Abingdon School, 1957–61; Asst Master, Harrow School, 1961–72; Headmaster, Durham Sch., 1972–82. Chairman: Cttee of Northern ISIS, 1976–77; NE Div., HMC, 1981–82. World Challenge Expeditions Ltd: Consultant, 1991–; Dir, 1992–96; Chm. Bd, 1995–96. Chm., Council for the Registration of Schools Teaching Dyslexic Pupils, (formerly Nat. Registration Council), 1992–96 (Chm., Trustees, 1996–98). Trustee, Bloxham Project, 1987–91. Oblate of Belmont Abbey (Benedictine), 1999–. FRSA 1997. *Recreations:* reading, cricket, gardens (sitting in), the sea. *Address:* 4 Chalmore Gardens, Wallingford, Oxon OX10 9EP. *T:* (01491) 837321. *Clubs:* MCC, Jesters.
Died 22 Oct. 2013.

VALLANCE-OWEN, Prof. John, MA, MD, FRCP, FRCPI, FRCPath; Visiting Professor, Imperial College of Science, Technology and Medicine, later Imperial College London Faculty of Medicine, at Hammersmith Hospital, since 1988; *b* 31 Oct. 1920; *s* of late Prof. E. A. Owen; *m* 1950, Renee Thornton; two *s* two *d*. *Educ:* Friars Sch., Bangor; Epsom Coll.; St John's Coll., Cambridge (de Havilland Schol. from Epsom; BA 1943; MA 1946; MB, BChir 1946; MD 1951); London Hosp. (Schol.). FRCP 1962; FRCPath 1971; FRCPI 1973. Various appts incl. Pathology Asst and Med. 1st Asst to Sir Horace Evans, London Hosp., 1946–51; Med. Tutor, Royal Postgrad. Med. Sch., Hammersmith Hosp., 1952–55 and 1956–58; Rockefeller Trav. Fellowship, at George S. Cox Med. Research Inst., Univ. of Pennsylvania, 1955–56; Cons. Phys. and Lectr in Medicine, Univ. of Durham, 1958–64; Cons. Phys., Royal Victoria Infirmary and Reader in Medicine, Univ. of Newcastle upon Tyne, 1964–66; Prof. of Medicine, QUB, 1966–82; Consultant Physician: Royal Victoria Hosp., Belfast, 1966–82 (Chm., Med. Div., 1979–81); Belfast City Hosp., 1966–82; Forster Green Hosp., Belfast, 1975–82 (Chm., Med. Staff Cttee, 1979–82); Dir of Med. Services, Maltese Is, 1981–82; Chinese University of Hong Kong: Foundation Prof. and Chm., Dept of Medicine, 1983–88, then Emeritus Professor of Medicine; Associate Dean, Faculty of Medicine, 1984–88; Hon. Consultant in Medicine: to Hong Kong Govt, 1984–88; to British Army in Hong Kong, 1985–88; Consultant Physician: London Ind. Hosp., 1988–99; Wellington Hosp., London, 1999–2002. Med. Advr on Clinical Complaints, NE Thames RHA, 1989–96, S Thames RHA, 1995–96. Member: Standing Med. Adv. Cttee, Min. of Health and Social Services, NI, 1970–73; Specialist Adv. Cttee (General Internal Medicine) to the Govt; Northern Health and Social Services Bd, Dept of Health and Soc. Services, NI; Mem., Exec. Cttee, Assoc. of Physicians of GB and Ireland, 1976–79; Regional Adviser for N Ire, to RCP, 1970–75 and Councillor, RCP, 1976–79 (Oliver-Sharpey Prize, RCP, 1976); Councillor, RCPI, 1978–82; Mem. Research Cttee, Brit. Diabetic Assoc.; Brit. Council Lectr, Dept Medicine, Zürich Univ., 1963; 1st Helen Martin Lectr, Diabetic Assoc. of S Calif, Wm H. Mulberg Lectr, Cincinnati Diabetes Assoc., and Lectr, Brookhaven Nat. Labs, NY, 1965; Brit. Council Lectr, Haile Selassie Univ., Makerere UC and S African Univs, 1966; Guest Lecturer: Japan Endocrinological Soc., 1968; Madrid Univ., 1969; Endocrine Soc. of Australia, 1970; Bologna Univ., 1976. Hon. FRCPI 1970; Hon. FHKCP 1996. *Publications:* Essentials of Cardiology, 1961, 2nd edn 1968; Diabetes: its physiological and biochemical basis, 1976; papers in biochem., med., and scientific jls on carbohydrate and fat metabolism and aetiology of diabetes mellitus and related conditions, with special reference to insulin antagonism. *Recreations:* tennis, golf, music. *Address:* 10 Spinney Driv Great Shelford, Cambridge CB2 5LY. *T:* (01223) 84276 17 St Matthews Lodge, Oakley Square, NW1 1NB. *T:* (020) 7388 3644; Cuildochart, Killin, Perthshire FK2 8S *T:* (01567) 820337. *Clubs:* East India (Life Mem.), Roy Society of Medicine (Life Mem.); United Servic Recreation (Hong Kong).
Died 23 July 2011

VANCE, Charles Ivan; actor, director and theatric producer; Chairman, Charles Vance Productions Ltd, sinc 1962; *b* 6 Dec. 1929; *s* of Eric Goldblatt and Sarah (*n* Freeman); *m* 1965, Hon. Imogen Moynihan, *d* of 2n Baron Moynihan, OBE, TD; one *d*. *Educ:* Royal Sch Dungannon; Queen's Univ., Belfast. FInstD 1972; FRS 1975. Early career as broadcaster; acting debut with Ane MacMaster Co., Gaiety, Dublin, 1949; dir, first prodn, Th Glass Menagerie, Arts, Cambridge, 1960; founded Civ Theatre, Chelmsford, 1962; i/c rep. cos, Tunbridge Well Torquay, Whitby and Hastings, 1962; as Dir of Charl Vance Prodns, created Eastbourne Theatre Co., 1969; di own adaptation of Wuthering Heights, 1972; wrote an staged four pantomimes, 1972–75; devised and dir. Th Jolson Revue, 1974 (staged revival, Australia, 1978; wor tour, 1981); played Sir Thomas More in A Man for A Seasons, and dir, Oh! What a Lovely War, Greenwoo 1975; purchased Leas Pavilion Theatre, Folkestone, 197 (HQ of own theatre organisation until 1985); prod and di world tour of Paddington Bear, 1978; *produced:* Cinderell Stafford, 1981 (also dir.); Aladdin, Bognor, 1981; (Londo and national tours): Stop the World—I Want to Get O (revival), 1976; Salad Days (revival), 1977; (also dir.) I Praise of Love, 1977; Witness for the Prosecution (revival 1979, 1992; Hallo Paris, 1980; This Happy Breed (revival 1980; Starlite Spectacular, 1981; The Kingfisher (revival 1981; The Hollow (revival), 1982 (also dir.); The Litt Hut, Australia (also dir.), 1982; Cinderella, 1982, 198 1984, 1992 (also dir.); Aladdin, 1982 (also wrote); Lad Chatterley's Lover, 1983; The Mating Game, 1983; Th Sleeping Beauty, The Gingerbread Man, The Wizard c Oz, 1983; Dick Whittington, Jack and the Beanstal Pinocchio, Jesus Christ Superstar (revival), 1984; M Cinders (revival), 1985; Policy for Murder, 1984 (also dir.) Jane Eyre, 1985 (also wrote and dir.), (revival) 1996; O Calcutta! (revival), 1985–86; Wuthering Heights (ow adaptation), 1987; The Creeper (revival tour), 1994; (als adapted) A Christmas Carol, Gala Th., Durham, 200 Who Killed Agatha Christie? (tour), 2002; Whisky Galor (tour), 2003; *directed:* Verdict (revival), 1984; Alice i Wonderland, 1985 (also wrote); Dick Whittingto Aladdin, Jack and the Beanstalk, Cinderella, 1986–87 (als wrote); Dénouement (also prod), 1988; Spiders We (Agatha Christie Centenary Prodn) (also prod), 1990; Th Mousetrap, USA (also prod), 1990; Daisy Pulls it Off (als prod), 1991; Gaslight (also prod), 1991; Time and Tim Again (also prod), 1991; My Cousin Rachel (also prod 1992; Godspell (also prod), 1993–94; Peter Pan, 1993; Dic Whittington, 1994, 1998, 2001; Brideshead Revisited (als prod), 1995; Cinderella, 1995, 1996, 1997, 2001, 200 Jack and the Beanstalk, 1995, 1998, 2000; Eye Witne (prod), 1996; Babes in the Wood, 1996; Aladdin, 199 1997, 1999, 2000; Lettice and Lovage (prod.), 197 Huckleberry Finn, 1997–98 (tour); Snow White, 199 1998, 1999; The Thirty-Nine Steps, 1998, 2000; Th Ladykillers, What the Butler Saw, 1999 (tour); Passport t Pimlico, 2000 (tour); The Lady Vanishes, 2001; Oh What Lovely War, 2001; Me and My Girl (revival), 2001; Bedsid Manners, 2001; The Lavender Hill Mob (also prod), 200 (tour); The Edge of Darkness, 2003 (tour); Goldilocks an the Three Bears, 2003; The Musical Celebration o Yorkshire TV's Heartbeat, 2004; Peter Pan, 2004; Aladdi 2005; Worms Eye View (revival; tour), 2005; The Titfie Thunderbolt, Queens Th., Hornchurch and Th. Roya Windsor, 2005; Kind Hearts and Coronets (revival; als prod; Pitlochry Fest. Th. and tour), 2005; Washingto Square (adaptation), 2006; Whisky Galore (tour), 200 celebration of Tennessee Williams' earlier short plays (tour)

2007. Controlled: Floral Hall Th., Scarborough, 1984–86; Beck Th., Hillingdon, 1986–90; Grand Opera House York, 1988–89; Summer Th., Manor Pavilion, Sidmouth, 1987–; rep. seasons: Harlow Playhouse, 1993–94; Grand Th., Wolverhampton, 1994–; Wyvern, Swindon, 1996–97, 2003–; Lyceum, Crewe, 1996–; Palace, Westcliff, 1997; Alhambra, Bradford, 1997; Middlesbrough Th., 2001–; Alexandra Th., Birmingham, 2003–; Brewhouse, Taunton, 2005–; Grand Opera House, Belfast, 2006–; launched first UK Dinner Theatre, Imperial Hotel, Torquay, 1990. Theatrical Management Association: Mem. Council, 1969; Pres., 1971–73 and 1973–76; Exec. Vice-Pres., 1976– (also of Council of Reg. Theatre). Advisor to Govt of Ghana on bldg Nat. Theatre, 1969. Director: Theatres Investment Fund, 1975–83; Entertainment Investments Ltd, 1980–82; International Holiday Investments, 1980–87; Southern Counties Television, 1980–87; Channel Radio, 1981–86; Gateway Broadcasting Ltd, 1982; Prestige Plays Ltd, 1987–; Operations Dir, Contemporary Theatre Ltd, 1992–94; Trustee Dir, Folkestone Theatre Co., 1979–85. Chairman: Provincial Theatre Council, 1971–87; Standing Adv. Cttee on Local Authority and the Theatre, 1977–90 (Vice-Chm., 1975–77); Gala and Fund-raising Cttee, British Theatre Assoc., 1986–89; Standing Adv. Cttee on Local Authority and the Performing Arts, 1990–93. Vice-Chairman: Theatres Adv. Council, resp. for theatres threatened by develt, 1974–; (also dir.) Festival of Brit. Theatre, 1975–; Irving Soc., 1972–. Member: Theatres Nat. Cttee, 1971–; Drama Adv. Panel, SE Arts Assoc., 1974–85; Prince of Wales' Jubilee Entertainments Cttee, 1977; Entertainment Exec. Cttee, Artists' Benev. Fund, 1980–; Court, Guild of Thespians, 1998; Adv. Bd, Manor Pavilion Th., Sidmouth, 2006–. Chm. of Trustees (formerly Govs), Acad. of Live and Recorded Arts, 2000–. Mem., Variety Club of GB, 1984–; Life Mem., Equity, 1995; Patron, Voluntary Arts Network, 1992–; Vice-Pres., E Sussex Br., RSPCA, 1975–; Member: Rotary Internat., 1971–; Rotary Club of London, 1986–; Life Pres., Green Room Club. Founded Vance Offord (Publications) Ltd, publishers of British Theatre Directory, British Theatre Review, and Municipal Entertainment, 1971; Chm., Platform Publications Ltd, 1987–; Editor in Chief, Team Publishing, 1986–87; Editor, Amateur Stage, and Preview, 1987–. Chambellan, Ordre des Coteaux de Champagne, 1993. *Publications:* British Theatre Directory, 1972, 1973, 1974, 1975; (ed) Amateur Theatre Yearbook, 1989, 1991, 1993, 1995, 1997, 2000; Agatha Christie, The Theatrical Celebration, 1990; Community Arts Directory, 2003; *plays:* Wuthering Heights, 1992; Jane Eyre, 1996. *Recreations:* sailing (crossed Atlantic single-handed, 1956), cooking (Cordon Bleu, 1957), travelling, animals. *Address:* Hampden House, 2 Weymouth Street, W1W 5BT. *Clubs:* Hurlingham, Royal Automobile, Royal Over-Seas League, Directors', Kennel (Mem. Cttee, 1989–), Groucho, Home House, Lord's Taverners. *Died 13 Jan. 2013.*

van CUTSEM, Hugh Bernard Edward; self-employed; farmer; *b* 21 July 1941; *s* of Bernard van Cutsem and Mary van Cutsem (*née* Compton); *m* 1971, Emilie Elise Christine Quarles van Ufford; four *s*. *Educ:* Sunningdale Sch.; Ampleforth Coll. Lieut Life Guards. Chm., Ecospray Ltd. Member, Council: NT, 1998–2008 (Mem., Exec. Cttee); English Nature, 2002–06; a Vice Pres., Game Conservancy Trust, 1998–. Chm., Norfolk CLA, 2003–05. Pres., SW Norfolk Cons. Assoc., 2004–. Knight of Honour and Devotion, SMO Malta (Chancellor, 2007–08). *Address:* Hilborough House, Thetford, Norfolk IP26 5BQ. *T:* (01760) 756586, *Fax:* (01760) 756587. *E:* vancutsem@hilborough.com. *Clubs:* White's, Pratt's, Jockey. *Died 2 Sept. 2013.*

van der MEER, Dr Simon; Ridder Nederlandse Leeuw, 1985; Senior Engineer, CERN, Geneva (European Organisation for Nuclear Research), 1956–90; *b* 24 Nov. 1925; *s* of Pieter van der Meer and Jetske Groeneveld; *m* 1966, Catharina M. Koopman; one *s* one *d*. *Educ:* Technical University, Delft, Netherlands; physical engineer. Philips Research Laboratories, Eindhoven, 1952–56. Hon. degrees: Univ. of Geneva, 1983; Amsterdam, 1984; Genoa, 1985. Nobel Prize for Physics (jtly), 1984. *Recreation:* literature. *Address:* 4 chemin des Corbillettes, 1218 Grand-Saconnex, Switzerland. *T:* (22) 7984305. *Died 4 March 2011.*

VANDYKE PRICE, Pamela Joan; freelance writer and lecturer on wine, since 1956; *b* 21 March 1923; *o c* of Harry Norman Walford, MBE, and Florence Amélie Halliday; *m* 1950, Alan Vandyke Price, MB BS, MRCP (*d* 1955). *Educ:* privately; Somerville Coll., Oxford (MA Hons); Central Sch. of Speech and Drama. Various odd jobs, 1943–53; occasional adult educn lects, S Wales, 1951–52; Household Ed., House & Garden, 1953–55; Ed., Wine & Food, 1967–69; formerly: consumer contributor to Spectator; wine correspondent: The Times; Sunday Times; Observer; contribs to The Guardian, provincial newspapers and trade jls. Made frequent radio broadcasts. Circle of Wine Writers: Mem.; formerly Cttee Mem., Programme Sec., Chm., and Pres.; Hon. Trustee in Perpetuity; Hon. Mem., Internat. Food & Wine Soc. Glenfiddich Gold Medal and Trophy, 1971, Silver Medal, 1973. Chevalier du Mérite Agricole (France), 1981. *Publications:* Cooking with Wine, Spirits, Beer and Cider, 1959; France: a food and wine guide, 1960; Casserole Cooking, 1961; The Art of the Table, 1962; Cooking with Spices, 1964; Century Companion to the Wines of Bordeaux, 1971, rev. edn 1982 (trans. French, German and Dutch); Eating and Drinking in France Today, 1972; Wine Lovers' Handbook, 1972; Wines and Spirits, 1972; A Dictionary of Wines and Spirits, 1974; The Taste of Wine, 1975 (trans. French, German, Dutch and Japanese); Entertaining with Wine, 1976; Century Companion to the Wines of Champagne, 1979 (trans. French, German and Dutch); The Penguin Book of Spirits and Liqueurs, 1979; Dictionary of Wines and Spirits, 1980, rev. edn 1987; Understanding Wines and Spirits, 1981; Enjoying Wine: a taster's companion, 1982; The Penguin Wine Book, 1984; (with C. Fielden) Alsace Wines and Spirits, 1984; Wine: lore, legends and traditions, 1985 (Book of Year: Wine Mag., 1986; Wine Guild, 1986); Wine's Company, 1986; French Vintage, 1986; France for the Gourmet Traveller, 1988; Wines of the Graves, 1988; (ed) Christie's Wine Companion, 1989; Woman of Taste (autobiog.), 1990; Curiosities of Wine, 2002. *Recreation:* making wine vinegar. *Address:* 8 Queen's Gate, SW7 5EL. *Died 12 Jan. 2014.*

van MAURIK, Ernest Henry, OBE 1944; HM Diplomatic Service, retired; *b* 24 Aug. 1916; *s* of late Justus van Maurik and Sybil van Maurik (*née* Ebert), BEM; *m* 1945, Winifred Emery Ritchie Hay (*d* 1984); one *s* one *d*. *Educ:* Lancing Coll.; Ecole Sup. de Commerce, Neuchatel, Switzerland. Worked in Tea Export, Mincing Lane, 1936–39. Commnd as 2nd Lt, in Wiltshire Regt, 1939; seconded to Special Ops Exec., 1941–46; demob. with hon. rank of Lt-Col (subst. Major), 1946. Joined Foreign Office, 1946; Moscow, 1948–50; West Germany and West Berlin, 1952–56; Buenos Aires, 1958–62; Copenhagen, 1965–67; Rio de Janeiro, 1968–71; FCO, 1971–75. Commemorative Medal (Czech Republic), 2005; Anniversary Medal (Slovak Republic), 2005. Officier de la Couronne (Belgium), 1944; Chevalier, Légion d'Honneur (France), 2002. *Recreations:* gardening, languages. *Address:* Little Cotchford, Cotchford Lane, Upper Hartfield, E Sussex TN7 4DN. *Clubs:* Special Forces, Civil Service. *Died 21 Jan. 2012.*

VASQUEZ, Hon. Sir Alfred (Joseph), Kt 1988; CBE 1974; QC (Gibraltar) 1986; *b* 2 March 1923; *s* of Alfred Joseph Vasquez and Maria Josefa (*née* Rugeroni); *m* 1950, Carmen, *o d* of Lt-Col Robert Sheppard-Capurro, OBE, JP; three *s* one *d*. *Educ:* Mount St Mary's Sch., Millfield; Fitzwilliam Coll., Cambridge (MA). Gibraltar Defence Force, 1943–45; The Gibraltar Regt, 1957–64, Captain. Called to the Bar, Inner Temple, 1950; called to Gibraltar Bar, 1950; Sen. Partner, Vasquez Benady & Co., 1950–91; Consultant, Triay & Triay, barristers and solicitors, 1995–. Speaker, Gibraltar Hse of Assembly, 1970–89; Mayor of Gibraltar, 1970–76. Vice-Chm., Gibraltar Bar Council, 1996–98. Pres., Gibraltar Oxford & Cambridge Soc. Hon. Fellow, World Innovation Foundn, 2000. KHS 1989. *Recreations:* golf, shooting, gardening, bridge. *Address:* St Vincent House, 4a Rosia Parade, Gibraltar. *T:* 73710. *Clubs:* Royal Gibraltar Yacht; Sotogrande Golf (Spain). *Died 3 July 2012.*

VAUX OF HARROWDEN, 11th Baron *cr* 1523; **Anthony William Gilbey;** *b* 25 May 1940; *e s* of 10th Baron Vaux of Harrowden and Maureen, *d* of Hugh Gilbey; *S* father, 2002; *m* 1964, Beverley Anne, *o d* of

Charles Alexander Walton; two *s* two *d*. *Educ:* Ampleforth. FCA. *Heir: s* Hon. Richard Hubert Gordon Gilbey [*b* 16 March 1965; *m* 1996, Elizabeth Worsley; two *s*]. *Died 16 Dec. 2014.*

VENABLES, (Harold) David (Spenser), CB 1993; Official Solicitor to the Supreme Court, 1980–93; *b* 14 Oct. 1932; *s* of late Cedric Venables and Gladys Venables (*née* Hall); *m* 1964, Teresa Grace, *d* of late J. C. Watts; one *s* one *d*. *Educ:* Denstone College. Admitted Solicitor, 1956. Pilot Officer, Royal Air Force, 1957–58. Legal Assistant, Official Solicitor's Office, 1960; Secretary, Lord Chancellor's Cttee on the Age of Majority, 1965–67; Asst Official Solicitor, 1977–80. *Publications:* A Guide to the Law Affecting Mental Patients, 1975; The Racing Fifteen-Hundreds: a history of voiturette racing 1931–40, 1984; Napier: the first to wear the Green, 1998; First Among Champions: the Alfa Romeo Grand Prix cars, 2000; Bugatti: a racing history, 2002; Brooklands: the official centenary history, 2007; British Racing Green, 2008; French Racing Blue, 2009; The Classic Motor-Racing Circuits of Europe, 2010; Bentley: a racing history, 2011; contributor, Halsbury's Laws of England, 4th edn. *Recreations:* vintage cars, motoring and military history. *Address:* 11 Onslow Road, Hove, Sussex BN3 6TA. *T:* (01273) 502374. *Died 3 Oct. 2014.*

VERMES, Prof. Geza, FBA 1985; Professor of Jewish Studies, 1989–91, then Professor Emeritus, and Fellow of Wolfson College, 1965–91, then Fellow Emeritus, Oxford University; Director, Oxford Forum for Qumran Research, since 1991, Hon. Fellow, 2013, Oxford Centre for Hebrew and Jewish Studies (formerly for Postgraduate Hebrew Studies); *b* 22 June 1924; *s* of late Ernö Vermes and Terézia Riesz; *m* 1st, 1958, Pamela Curle (*née* Hobson) (*d* 1993); two step *d*; 2nd, 1996, Margaret Unarska; one step *s*. *Educ:* Univ. of Budapest; Coll. St Albert de Louvain, Louvain Univ. Licencié en Histoire et Philologie Orientales (avec la plus grande distinction), 1952; DTheol 1953; MA Oxon 1965, DLitt 1988. Asst Editor, Cahiers Sioniens, Paris, 1953–55; research worker, CNRS, Paris, 1955–57; Lectr, later Sen. Lectr in Divinity, Newcastle Univ., 1957–65; Reader in Jewish Studies, Oxford Univ., 1965–89; Chm. of Curators of Oriental Inst., Oxford, 1971–74; Chm. Bd of Faculty of Oriental Studies, Oxford, 1978–80; Emeritus Governor, Oxford Centre for Postgrad. Hebrew Studies (Governor, 1972–92). Vis. Prof. in Religious Studies, Brown Univ., 1971; Rosenstiel Res. Fellow, Univ. of Notre Dame, 1972; Dist. Vis. Prof. in Judeo-Christian Studies, Tulane Univ., 1982; Vis. Prof. of History, Univ. of Calif, San Diego, 1995; Vis. Prof. in Hebrew Studies, Peter Pázmány Univ., Budapest, 1996. Lectures: Margaret Harris in Religion, Dundee Univ., 1977; Riddell Meml, Newcastle Univ., 1981; Igor Kaplan Visiting, Toronto Sch. of Theology, 1985, 1987; Inaugural, Geza Vermes Lectures in Hist. of Religions, Univ. of Leicester, 1997; Gunning, Univ. of Edinburgh, 1998. Pres., British Assoc. for Jewish Studies, 1975, 1988; Pres., European Assoc. for Jewish Studies, 1981–84. Editor, Jl of Jewish Studies, 1971–. Fellow, Eur. Acad. of Arts, Scis and Humanities, 2001. Hon. DD: Edinburgh, 1989; Durham, 1990; Hon. DLitt Sheffield, 1994; Hon. DPhil Central Eur., Budapest, 2008. W. Bacher Medallist, Hungarian Acad. of Scis, 1996; Meml Medallist, City of Mako, Hungary, 2008; Tribute of Recognition, US House of Representatives, 2009. *Publications:* Les manuscrits du désert de Juda, 1953; Discovery in the Judean Desert, 1956; Scripture and Tradition in Judaism, 1961; The Dead Sea Scrolls in English, 1962, 4th edn 1995 (trans. Portuguese); Jesus the Jew, 1973 (trans. Spanish, French, Japanese, Italian, Portuguese, German, Hungarian, Polish); Post-Biblical Jewish Studies, 1975; (with Pamela Vermes) The Dead Sea Scrolls: Qumran in perspective, 1977 (trans. Spanish), 3rd edn 1994; The Gospel of Jesus the Jew, 1981; (ed jtly) Essays in Honour of Y. Yadin, 1982; Jesus and the World of Judaism, 1983 (trans. Portuguese, Hungarian); (ed and rev., with F. G. B. Millar and M. D. Goodman) E. Schürer, The History of the Jewish People in the Age of Jesus Christ I–III, 1973–87 (trans. Spanish, Italian); (with M. D. Goodman) The Essenes according to the Classical Sources, 1989; The Religion of Jesus the Jew, 1993 (trans. Spanish, Portuguese, Italian); (ed) Pamela Vermes, The Riddle of the Sparks, 1993; The Complete Dead Sea Scrolls in English, 1997, rev. edn 2004 (trans. Turkish, Arabic); Providential Accidents (autobiog.), 1998 (trans. Hungarian); (ed with P. S. Alexander) Discoveries in the Judaean Desert, vol. 26, 1998; An Introduction to the Complete Dead Sea Scrolls, 1999; The Dead Sea Scrolls, 2000; The Changing Faces of Jesus, 2000 (trans. Italian, Hungarian, Dutch, French, Polish); Jesus in his Jewish Context, 2003; The Authentic Gospel of Jesus, 2003 (trans. Hungarian, Polish, Portuguese, Czech); The Passion, 2005 (trans. French, Hungarian, German, Portuguese); Who's Who in the Age of Jesus, 2005 (trans. French, German, Polish); The Nativity: history and legend, 2006 (trans. German, Czech); The Resurrection, 2008; Searching for the Real Jesus: Jesus, the Dead Sea Scrolls and other religious themes, 2010; The Story of the Scrolls, 2010 (trans. Japanese); Jesus: nativity—passion—resurrection, 2010; Jesus in the Jewish World, 2010; Christian Beginnings from Nazareth to Nicaea AD30–325, 2012. *Recreations:* watching wild life, correcting proofs. *Address:* Oriental Institute, Pusey Lane, Oxford OX1 2LE; West Wood Cottage, Foxcombe Lane, Boars Hill, Oxford OX1 5DH. *T:* (01865) 735384, *Fax:* (01865) 735034. *E:* geza.vermes@orinst.ox.ac.uk. *Died 8 May 2013.*

VERNEY, His Honour Sir Lawrence (John), Kt 1993; TD 1955; DL; Recorder of London, 1990–98; *b* 19 July 1924; *y s* of Sir Harry Verney, 4th Bt, DSO; *m* 1972, Zoë Auriel, *d* of Lt-Col P. G. Goodeve-Docker. *Educ:* Harrow; Oriel Coll., Oxford. Called to Bar, Inner Temple, 1952, Bencher, 1990. Dep. Chm., Bucks QS, 1962–71; Dep. Chm., Middlesex Sessions, then a Circuit Judge, 1971–90. Governor, Harrow Sch., 1972–87. Master, Co. of Pattenmakers, 1988. Hon. Col 1 (RBY) Signal Sqdn, 1997–99. DL Bucks 1967. Jun. Grand Warden, United Grand Lodge of England, 2001. Hon. LLD London Guildhall, 1998; DUniv Bucks Chilterns UC, 2003. OStJ 1992. *Address:* Windmill House, Church Lane, Oving, Aylesbury, Bucks HP22 4HL. *Died 25 July 2014.*

VERNON, Sir (William) Michael, Kt 1995; Chairman, Royal National Lifeboat Institution, 1989–96 (Deputy Chairman, 1980–89; Vice-President, 1975–2001, then Chairman Emeritus); *b* 17 April 1926; *o* surv. *s* of late Sir Wilfred Vernon and Nancy Elizabeth Vernon (*née* Jackson); *m* 1st, 1952, Rosheen O'Meara (marr. diss. 1977); one *s*; 2nd, 1977, Mrs Jane Colston (*née* Kilham-Roberts) (*d* 1998); 3rd, 2001, Mrs Penelope Cuddeford (*née* Skelton). *Educ:* Marlborough Coll.; Trinity Coll., Cambridge. MA 1948. Lieut, Royal Marines, 1944–46. Joined Spillers Ltd, 1948: Dir, 1960; Jt Man. Dir, 1962; Chm. and Chief Exec., 1968–80; Chm., Granville Meat Co. Ltd, 1981–94. Director: EMI Ltd, 1973–80; Strong & Fisher (Hldgs) plc, 1980–90; Chm., Famous Names Ltd, 1981–85. Pres., Nat. Assoc. of British and Irish Millers, 1965; Vice-Chm., Millers' Mutual Assoc., 1968–80; Pres., British Food Export Council, 1977–80. CCMI. Bronze Medal, RHS, 1956. *Recreations:* shooting, travel. *Address:* Fyfield Manor, Andover, Hants SP11 8EL. *Clubs:* Royal Ocean Racing (Cdre 1964–68); Royal Yacht Squadron. *Died 24 Jan. 2014.*

VEST, Prof. Charles Marstiller, PhD; President: National Academy of Engineering, USA, 2007–13; Massachusetts Institute of Technology, 1990–2004, then President Emeritus; *b* 9 Sept. 1941; *m* 1963, Rebecca McCue; one *s* one *d*. *Educ:* West Virginia Univ.; Univ. of Michigan (MSc 1964; PhD 1967). Asst Prof., then Associate Prof., 1968–77, Prof. of Mechl Engrg, 1977–90, Univ. of Michigan. Internat. FREng 2010. Nat. Medal of Technology (USA), 2006. *Publications:* Holographic Interferometry, 1979; Pursuing the Endless Frontier: essays on MIT and the role of research universities, 2004; The American Research University from World War II to World Wide Web: governments, the private sector, and the emerging meta-university, 2007. *Address:* c/o National Academy of Engineering, 500 Fifth Street NW, Washington, DC 20001, USA. *Died 12 Dec. 2013.*

VICARION, Count Palmiro; *see* Logue, Christopher.

VICKERS, Eric, CB 1979; Director of Defence Services, Department of the Environment, 1972–81; *b* 25 April 1921; *s* of late Charles Vickers and Ida Vickers; *m* 1945, Barbara Mary Jones; one *s* one *d*. *Educ:* King's School, Grantham. Joined India Office, 1938; RAF (Fl/Lt Coastal Command),

1941–46; Ministry of Works, 1948; Principal, 1950; Assistant Secretary, 1962; Imperial Defence College, 1969; Dir of Home Estate Management, DoE, 1970–72. *Recreations:* gardening, music, wine appreciation. *Address:* 46 Stamford Road, Oakham, Rutland LE15 6JA. *T:* (01572) 724166. *Died 4 Dec. 2012.*

VICKERS, Jon, CC (Can.) 1968; dramatic tenor; *b* Prince Albert, Saskatchewan, 29 Oct. 1926; *m* 1953, Henrietta Outerbridge (*d* 1991); three *s* two *d*; *m* 1993, Judith Stewart. Studied under George Lambert, Royal Conservatory of Music, Toronto. Made debut with Toronto Opera Company, 1952; Stratford (Ontario) Festival, 1956. Joined Royal Opera House, Covent Garden, 1957. First sang at: Bayreuth Festival, 1958; Vienna State Opera, San Francisco Opera, and Chicago Lyric, 1959; Metropolitan, New York, and La Scala, Milan, 1960; Buenos Aires, 1962; Salzburg Festival, 1966; appeared in other opera houses of Argentina, Austria, Brazil, France, Germany, Greece, Mexico and USA. *Films:* Carmen; Pagliacci; Otello; Norma; Peter Grimes; Fidelio; Samson et Delilah. Made many recordings. Presbyterian. Hon. Dr: University of Saskatchewan, 1963; Bishop's Univ., 1965; Univ. West Ontario, 1970; Brandon Univ., 1976; Laval Univ., 1977; Univ. of Guelph, 1978; Illinois, 1983; Queens, Canada, 1984; Toronto, 1987. RAM 1977. Canada Centennial Medal, 1967; Critics' Award, London, 1978; Grammy Award, 1979. *Died 10 July 2015.*

VIDAL, Gore; author; *b* 3 Oct. 1925; *s* of Eugene and Nina Gore Vidal. *Educ:* Phillips Exeter Academy, New Hampshire, USA (grad. 1943). Army of the US, 1943–46: Private to Warrant Officer (jg) and First Mate, Army FS-35, Pacific Theatre Ops. Democratic-Liberal candidate for US Congress, 1960; candidate for Democratic nomination for election to US Senate from California, 1982. Apptd to President Kennedy's Adv. Council of the Arts, 1961–63. Hon. DLitt Brown Univ., 1988, etc. Chevalier de l'Ordre des Arts et des Lettres (France), 1995. *Publications: novels:* Williwaw, 1946; In a Yellow Wood, 1947; The City and the Pillar, 1948; The Season of Comfort, 1949; A Search for the King, 1950; Dark Green, Bright Red, 1950; The Judgment of Paris, 1952; Messiah, 1954; Julian, 1964; Washington, DC, 1967; Myra Breckinridge, 1968 (filmed 1969); Two Sisters, 1970; Burr, 1973; Myron, 1975; 1876, 1976; Kalki, 1978; Creation, 1981; Duluth, 1983; Lincoln, 1984; Empire, 1987; Hollywood, 1989; Live from Golgotha, 1992; The Smithsonian Institution, 1998; The Golden Age, 2000; *essays:* Rocking the Boat, 1962; Reflections upon a Sinking Ship, 1969; Homage to Daniel Shays (collected essays 1952–72), 1972; Matters of Fact and of Fiction, 1977; The Second American Revolution (UK title, Pink Triangle and Yellow Star and other essays (1976–1982)), 1982; Armageddon?, 1987; At Home, 1988; A View from the Diner's Club, 1991; Screening History, 1992; United States: essays 1952–1992, 1993 (Nat. Book Award, 1994); Virgin Islands: essays 1992–1997, 1997; The Last Empire: essays 1992–2000, 2001; Imperial America, 2005; Selected Essays, 2007; *short stories:* A Thirsty Evil, 1956; Clouds and Eclipses, 2006; *travel:* Vidal in Venice, 1987; *memoirs:* Palimpsest, 1995; Point to Point Navigation, 2006; *biography:* Inventing a Nation: Washington, Adams, Jefferson, 2003; *plays:* Visit to a Small Planet (NY prod.), 1957; The Best Man (NY prod.), 1960, 2000; Romulus (adapted from F. Dürrenmatt) (NY prod.), 1962; Weekend (NY prod.), 1968; On the March to the Sea (German prod.), 1962; An Evening with Richard Nixon (NY prod.), 1972; *screenplays*: from 1955: Wedding Breakfast, 1957; Suddenly Last Summer, 1958; The Best Man (Critic's Prize, Cannes), 1964, etc; *television plays:* 1954–56: The Death of Billy the Kid (translated to screen as The Lefthanded Gun, 1959, and as Gore Vidal's Billy the Kid, 1989), etc; *literary and political criticism for:* NY Review of Books, New Yorker, Nation, TLS, etc. *Recreation:* as noted above. *Club:* Athenæum. *Died 31 July 2012.*

VINCENT, Prof. Ewart Albert; Professor of Geology, and Fellow of University College, Oxford, 1967–86, then Emeritus; *b* 23 Aug. 1919; *o s* of Albert and Winifred Vincent, Aylesbury; *m* 1944, Myrtle Ablett (*d* 2004); two *d*. *Educ:* Reading Sch.; Univ. of Reading. BSc (Reading) 1940; PhD 1951; MA (Oxon) 1952; MSc (Manch.) 1966. FGS. Chemist, Min. of Supply, 1940–45; Geologist, Anglo-Iranian Oil Co., 1945–46; Lectr in Mineralogy and Crystallography, Univ. of Durham, 1946–51; Lectr in Geology, Oxford Univ., 1951–56; Reader in Mineralogy, Oxford Univ., 1956–62; Prof. of Geology, Manchester Univ., 1962–66. Visiting Professor: Univ. of Kuwait, 1970; Washington and Lee Univ., Va, 1980. Mem. NERC, 1975–78. Vice-Pres., Internat. Assoc. of Volcanology, 1968–71; Pres., Mineralogical Soc. of GB, 1974–76; Mem. Council, Geol Soc., 1973–76. Fellow, Mineralogical Soc. of Amer. Hon. Corresp. Mem., Soc. Géol. de Belgique. Awarded Wollaston Fund, Geol Soc. London, 1961. *Publications:* scientific papers in learned jls. *Recreations:* music, photography. *Address:* Oaken Holt, Eynsham Road, Farmoor, Oxford OX2 9NL. *T:* (01865) 863737; Department of Earth Sciences, South Parks Road, Oxford OX1 3AN. *Died 24 Dec. 2012.*

VINCENT, Rev. Irvin James; Supernumerary Minister, Taunton Methodist Church, since 1999; *b* 22 July 1932; *s* of Amy Mary Catharine Vincent (*née* Nye) and Vince Thomas Vincent; *m* 1959, Stella Margaret (*née* Chaplin); one *s* two *d*. *Educ:* Mitcham Grammar School; Didsbury College (Methodist), Bristol. BA Open Univ. Accountancy, 1948; National Service, RAF, 1950–52; Local Govt, 1952–55; theological training, 1955–59; Methodist Circuit, Stonehouse and Dursley, 1959–61; entered RN as Chaplain, 1961; Malta, 1968–72; exchange with USN, 1976–78; Principal Chaplain, Church of Scotland and Free Churches (Navy), 1984–86; QHC, 1984–86; Minister, Temple Methodist Church, Taunton, 1986–97; Hon. Associate Minister, Westminster Central Hall, 1997–99. *Recreations:* all sport, reading, family. *Address:* 60 Queen's Drive, Sherford Brook, Taunton, Som TA1 4XD. *Died 20 April 2013.*

VINCENT, Robin Anthony, CMG 2006; CBE 2001; senior consultant, international criminal and transitional justice issues, since 2005; Assistant Secretary General, United Nations (Registrar of Special Tribunal for Lebanon), 2008–09; *b* 27 Feb. 1944; *s* of late John Kenneth Vincent and of Ivy Elizabeth Ann Vincent (*née* Grayer); *m* 1971, Hazel Ruth Perkins; two *s*. *Educ:* King's Sch., Worcester. Clerk, Worcs QS, 1962–70; Sen. Asst and Dep. Clerk, Worcs County Justices, 1970–72; Higher Executive Officer: Worcester Crown Court, 1972–76; Worcs County Court, 1976–77; Court Business Officer, 1977–79; Sen. Exec. Officer (Personnel), Circuit Administrator's Office, Birmingham, 1979–80; Chief Clerk, Worcester Crown Court, 1980–82; Principal Chief Clerk, Manchester Crown Court, 1982–86; Head of Division, Lord Chancellor's Department: Court Service Develt, London, 1986–91; Personnel Mgt, 1991–93; Judicial Appts, 1993; Circuit Administrator, Northern Circuit, LCD, then Court Service Agency, 1993–2001; Internat. Court Mgt Consultant, UN and British Council, 2001–02; Asst Sec. Gen., UN (Registrar of Special Court for Sierra Leone), 2002–05; Special Advr to Legal Counsel, Office of Legal Affairs, UN, NY, 2007–08. Hon. MA Worcester, 2008. *Recreations:* cricket (playing), music, drinking red wine with Steve Baines. *Address:* The Moorings, 33 Grange Road, Bramhall, Stockport, Cheshire SK7 3BD. *T:* (0161) 440 9526. *Clubs:* Old Vigornians (Worcester); Eggington Cricket (Leighton Buzzard); Stockport Georgians (Stockport). *Died 12 June 2011.*

VINE, Barbara; *see* Rendell of Babergh, Baroness.

VINE, Roy; Vice-Chairman, Barclays Bank UK Ltd, 1982–84; *b* 1923; *m* 1945, Dorothy A. Yates; one *s* one *d*. *Educ:* Taunton's Sch., Southampton. Served RAF (Flt Lieut), 1942–46 and 1951–53. Dir, Barclays Bank plc, 1979–84 (Gen. Man., 1972; Senior Gen. Man., 1979–81). Director: First Nat. Finance Corp. plc, 1984–93; First Nat. Bank Plc (formerly First Nat. Securities Ltd), 1985–90; First Nat. Commercial Bank Ltd, 1990–93. FCIB 1951. *Recreations:* golf, football, music. *Address:* Summerfold, Itchen Abbas, Winchester SO21 1AX. *Died 4 Aug. 2013.*

VINES, Sir William (Joshua), AC 1987; Kt 1977; CMG 1969; FASA, ACIS; psc; Chairman, ANZ Banking Group, 1982–89 (Director, since 1976); Director, Dalgety Australia Ltd, 1980–91 (Chairman, 1970–80); grazier at Tara, Queensland, 1965–82 and Cliffdale, Currabubula, NSW, 1982–97; *b* 27 May 1916; *s* of P. V. Vines, Canterbury,

Victoria, Australia; *m* 1st, 1939, Thelma J. (*d* 1988), *d* of late F. J. Ogden; one *s* two *d*; 2nd, 1990, Judith Anne Ploeg, *d* of late T. E. Raynsford. *Educ:* Haileybury College, Brighton Beach, Victoria. Served War of 1939–45 (despatches, C-in-C's commendation for gallantry, El Alamein), 2nd AIF, 2/23 Aust. Inf. Bn, Middle East, New Guinea and Borneo, Major. Managing Director: Internat. Wool Secretariat, 1961–69 (Board Mem., 1969–79); Berger, Jenson & Nicholson Ltd, 1960 (Dir, 1961–69); Dalgety Australia Ltd, 1971–76 (Chm., 1970–80); Group Managing Director, Lewis Berger & Sons Ltd, 1955–61; Director: Lewis Berger & Sons (Aust.) Pty Ltd & Sherwin Williams Co. (Aust.) Pty Ltd, 1952–55; Goodlass Wall & Co. Pty Ltd, 1947–49; Dalgety Ltd; Dalgety New Zealand Ltd, 1969–80; Port Phillip Mills Pty Ltd, 1969–88; Wiggins Teape Ltd (UK), 1970–79; Tubemakers of Australia Ltd, 1970–86 (Dep. Chm., 1973–86); Associated Pulp & Paper Mills Ltd, 1971–83 (Dep. Chm. 1977, Chm. 1979–83); Conzinc Rio Tinto of Australia, 1977–84; Grindlays Hldgs, subseq. ANZ UK Hldgs, 1985–89; Grindlays Bank, 1987–89; Chm., Thorn Holdings Pty Ltd, 1969–74. Vice-President Melbourne Legacy, 1949–51; Pres. Building Industry Congress, Vic., 1954–55. Chm., Aust. Wool Commn, 1970–72; Mem. Exec., CSIRO, 1973–78; Chm. Council, Hawkesbury Agric. Coll., 1975–85. Mem., Australia New Zealand Foundn, 1979–84. Chm., The Sir Robert Menzies Meml Trust, 1978–92. Hon. DSc Econ Sydney, 1993. *Address:* 1/10 West Street, Balgowlah, NSW 2093, Australia. *T:* (2) 99481147. *Died 6 Jan. 2011.*

VINING, Rowena Adelaide, OBE 1979 (MBE 1964); HM Diplomatic Service, retired; *b* 25 Sept. 1921; *er d* of late Col Percival Llewellyn Vining and Phyllis Servante Vining. *Educ:* privately, and at Chiddingstone Castle, Edenbridge, Kent. Foreign Office, 1941–52 (war service in Italy, Indonesia, 1943–45). Commonwealth Relations Office, 1952–55; Second Secretary: Karachi, 1955–58; Sydney, 1958–62; First Secretary: CRO, 1962–65; Canberra, 1965–67; Commonwealth Office (later Foreign and Commonwealth Office), 1967–71; Vienna, 1972–74; Consul, Florence and Consul-General, San Marino, 1974–78; Dep. UK Permanent Rep. to the Council of Europe, 1978–81; Consul-General, Strasbourg, 1979–80. Staff Assessor, FCO, 1983–86. *Recreations:* gardening, music. *Address:* Dorchester Cottage, Greywell, Hook, Hants RG29 1BT. *Died 17 April 2013.*

VIOT, Jacques Edmond; Commandeur de la Légion d'Honneur; Commandeur de l'Ordre National du Mérite; President: France-Great Britain Association, 1987–2000; French section, Franco-British Council, 1992–2006 (Hon. President, 2006); Alliance Française de Paris, 1994–2004; *b* 25 Aug. 1921; *m* 1950, Jeanne de Martimprey de Romécourt. *Educ:* Bordeaux and Paris Lycées; Ecole Normale Supérieure; Ecole Nationale d'Admin. Foreign Office (European Dept), 1951–53; Second Sec., London, 1953–57; First Sec., Rabat, 1957–61; Tech. Advisor to Foreign Minister, 1961–62; Head of Technical Co-operation, FO, 1962–68; Dir for Personnel and Gen. Admin, 1968–72; Ambassador to Canada, 1972–77; Gen. Inspector for Foreign Affairs, 1977–78; Directeur de Cabinet to Foreign Minister, 1978–81; Gen. Inspector for Foreign Affairs, 1981–84; Ambassador to the Court of St James's, 1984–86; Ambassadeur de France, 1986; Chm., Review Cttee on Foreign Affairs, Paris, 1986–87. Chm. Entrance Examination Bd, Ecole Nat. d'Admin, 1987. Fellow, St Antony's College, Oxford. *Address:* 19 rue de Civry, 75016 Paris, France. *Died 4 July 2012.*

VISHNEVSKAYA, Galina; soprano; Founder, Galina Vishnevskaya Opera Centre, Moscow, 2002; *b* 25 Oct. 1926; *m* 1955, Mstislav Rostropovich, Hon. KBE, 'cellist (*d* 2007); two *d*. *Educ:* studied with Vera Garina. Toured with Leningrad Light Opera Co., 1944–48, with Leningrad Philharmonic Soc., 1948–52; joined Bolshoi Theatre, 1952. Concert appearances in Europe and USA, 1950–; first appeared at Metropolitan Opera, NY, 1961. Rôles included: Leonora in Fidelio, Tatiana in Eugene Onegin, Iolanta, Butterfly in Madame Butterfly, Aida, Liza in Queen of Spades, Natasha Rostova in War and Peace, Marguerite in Faust, Violetta in La Traviata, Liù in Turandot, Katerina Izmailova, Tosca, Marfa in The Tsar's Bride, etc. Sang in Britain at Festival Hall, Aldeburgh Festival, Edinburgh Festival, Covent Garden, Rostropovich Festival, Snape; Dir, Iolanta, Aldeburgh Fest., 1988. Made concert tours with her husband and made many recordings. Awarded numerous prestigious internat. awards. *Publications:* Galina (autobiog.), 1984. *Address:* Galina Vishnevskaya Opera Centre, Ostozhenka str., 25 build. 1, Moscow 119034, Russia. *Died 11 Dec. 2012.*

VOCKLER, Most Rev. John Charles, (Most Rev. Brother John-Charles); Founder, and Superior, Franciscan Order of the Divine Compassion, since 1990; Archbishop and Metropolitan of the Anglican Catholic Church, 2001–05; Bishop of the Missionary Diocese of Australia, 2004–05, Vicar-General, until 2008; *b* 22 July 1924; *e s* of John Thomas Vockler and Mary Catherine Vockler (*née* Widerberg), Sydney, New South Wales. *Educ:* Sydney Boys' High Sch.; after studying accountancy, matriculated by private study and correspondence (Metropolitan Business Coll. and Internat. Correspondence Schs, Sydney) to the Univ. of Sydney; Moore Theol Coll.; St John's Theol College, Morpeth, NSW; Australian Coll. of Theology (LTh 1948; Hey Sharp Prize for NT Greek); Univ. of Queensland (BA (1st cl. Hons History) 1953; Univ. Gold Medal for outstanding achievement, 1953; Walter and Eliza Hall Foundn Travelling Scholarship, 1953); Fulbright Schol., 1953; BA Univ. of Adelaide, *aegr.*, 1961; Gen. Theol Seminary, NY (MDiv 1954; STM 1956). Junior Clerk, W. R. Carpenter & Co. Ltd, Sydney, NSW, 1939–43. Deacon, 1948; priest, 1948; Asst Deacon, Christ Church Cathedral, Newcastle, 1948; Asst Priest, 1948–50; Vice-Warden of St John's Coll., Univ. of Queensland, 1950–53; Acting Chaplain, C of E Grammar Sch. for Boys, Brisbane, 1953; Acting Vice-Warden, St John's Coll., Morpeth and Lectr in Old Testament, 1953; Asst Priest, Cathedral of S John the Divine, NY and Chaplain, St Luke's Home for Aged Women and the Home for Old Men and Aged Couples, 1953–54; Australian Delegate to Anglican Congress, 1954; Fellow and Tutor, GTS, 1954–56; Asst Priest, St Stephen's Church, West 69th Street, NY, 1955; Priest-in-charge, St Stephen's, New York, 1956; Asst Priest, parish of Singleton, NSW, 1956–59; Lecturer in Theology, St John's Theol Coll., Morpeth, NSW, 1956–59; Secretary, Newcastle Diocesan Board of Education, 1958–59; Titular Bishop of Mount Gambier and Assistant Bishop of Adelaide (Coadjutor, 1959; title changed to Assistant, 1961), until 1962; also Archdeacon of Eyre Peninsula, 1959–62; Vicar-General, Examining Chaplain to Bishop of Adelaide, 1960–62; Bishop of Polynesia, 1962–68. Society of St Francis: entered Soc., 1969; professed, 1972; Chaplain, Third Order, European Province, 1972–74; made life profession, 1975; Guardian, Friary of St Francis, Brisbane, 1975–77, Islington, NSW, 1978–79; Minister Provincial, Pacific Province, 1976–81; Archivist, Amer. Province, 1985–89; left SSF, 1990; Vicar, Trinity Church, Monmouth, Ill, 1990–93; Adjunct Prof. of Ascetical Theology, Nashotah House Seminary, 1991–93; received into Anglican Catholic Church, USA, 1994: Commissary in USA for Bishop of Australia, 1994–98; Hon. Asst Bishop, dio. of Australia, 1994; Asst Bp to the Metropolitan, 1995–97; Chm., Dept of Ministry, 1996, Dept of Evangelism, 1997; VG, dio. of Australia, 1998; Dean, Holyrood Seminary, Liberty, NY, 1995–97 (Sub-Dean for Acad. Affairs, 1994–95); Prof. of Ascetical and Pastoral Theol., 1997; Bishop of New Orleans, 1999–2002, Archbishop, 2001. Warden: Community of St Clare, Newcastle, NSW, 1975–80; Soc. of Sacred Advent, Qld, 1976–80 (Priest Associate, 1975–); Poor Clares of Reparation, Mt Sinai, NY, 1982–83 (Bishop Protector, 1987–93); Spiritual Dir, Community of the Holy Spirit, NY, 1988–89; Bishop Visitor, Order of the Incarnation, NY, 1990–93 (Spiritual Advr, 1988–89); Spiritual Dir to Bishops and Priests of the Catholic and Apostolic Church of N America, 1988–97; Confessor Extraordinary, Soc. of St John the Evangelist, Cambridge, Mass, 1987–89; Chaplain to Monmouth Community Hosp., 1990–93. Collegial Mem., House of Bishops, Episcopal Church, USA, 1983–93; Member: House of Bishops' Cttee on Religious Life, 1986–89; Episcopal Synod of America, 1989–93. President, Harry Charman's All Races Sports and Social Club, Suva, Fiji, 1962–68, Hon. Life Vice-Pres., 1968; Chairman: S Pacific Anglican Council, 1963–68; Council of Pacific Theol Coll.,

1963–68; President: Fiji Council of Social Services, 1964–68; Fiji Branch, Royal Commonwealth Soc., 1966–68. Writing Grant, Literature Bd of Australia Council, 1979, 1981. Member: Soc. of Authors; Australian Soc. of Authors; PEN (International), Sydney Br. and New York Br.; Guild of Writers Inc., NY; Christian Writers' Fellowship (USA); Aust. Professional Writers' Services; Penman Club (UK); National Writers' Club (USA); Federated Clerks Union of Aust., 1978–81; Internat. Center for Integrative Studies, NY, 1983–93; Internat. Ecumenical Fellowship; Guild of All Souls; Confraternity of the Blessed Sacrament; Soc. of Mary; Catholic and Evangelical Mission; Anglican Pacifist Fellowship; Fellowship of Reconciliation (England & Australia); Fellowship of S Alban and S Sergius; Anglican Fellowship of Prayer, USA; Fellowship of Three Kings, Haddington, Scotland; Amnesty Internat., USA (Mem., Urgent Action Gp); Soc. of the Holy Cross, 1992–94; The Living Rosary of Our Lady and St Dominic, 1992–. Priest Associate, Shrine of Our Lady, Walsingham and Priory of Our Lady of Pew, Westminster Abbey, 1978–96; Associate, Guild of St Vincent, 1985–93; Priest Mem., OGS, 1952–75. Sec., Adv. Council for Religious Communities in Aust. and Pacific, 1976–80. Permission to officiate in various dioceses, UK, NZ, USA, Australia, 1969–93. Vice-Pres. and Mem. Council, USPG, 1973–74; Vice-Pres., Missions to Seamen, 1963–69; Hon. Asst Bp of Worcester, 1972–73; Assistant Bishop: Chelmsford, 1973–74; Southwark, 1974–75; Assisting Bishop, dio. of Quincy, USA, 1990–93; Hon. Canon of Southwark, 1975, Canon Emeritus 1975; Hon. Mission Chaplain, dio. Brisbane, 1975–79. Examr for Aust. Coll. of Theology, 1975–76 and 1979. Patron: Monarchist League, 1993–; King Kigali V's Fund for Rwandan Children, 1993–; Mem., Australian Monarchist League, 1998–. ThD (*jure dig.*) ACT, 1961; STD (*hc*) Gen. Theological Seminary, NY, 1961; BD (*ad eund.*) Melbourne College of Divinity, 1960. Bronze Medal, Royal Aust. Life Saving Soc., 1939; Bishop's Cross, dio. of Long Is, 1989; La Croce d'Oro di S Ambrogio, 2003. *Publications:* Can Anglicans Believe Anything—The Nature and Spirit of Anglicanism, 1961 (NSW); Forward Day by Day, 1962; (ed) Believing in God (by M. L. Yates), 1962 (Australian edn), revd edn 1983 (US); One Man's Journey, 1972; St Francis: Franciscanism and the Society of St Francis, 1980; A School of Prayer, 1998; Seven Deadly Sins, Seven Grace-full Virtues, and Seven Mystical or Spiritual Gifts, 1999; Two Paths to Holiness, 2002; An Introduction to Some Spiritual Classics, 2004; contributions to: Preparatory Volume for Anglican Congress, Toronto, 1963; Anglican Mosaic, 1963; Mutual Responsibility: Questions and Answers, 1964; All One Body (ed T. Wilson), 1968; Australian Dictionary of Biography (4 articles); St Mark's Review, Australian Church Quarterly, The Anglican, The Young Anglican, Pacific Journal of Theology, New Zealand Theological Review, weekly feature, Newcastle Morning Herald, NSW; book reviews in Amer. theol jls; Aust. corresp. to New Fire, 1980–81; book review Editor, New York Episcopalians, 1986–91; Contributing Ed., The Trinitarian, 1995–. *Recreations:* classical music, detective stories, theatre, films, prints and engravings. *Address:* Room 767, Benhome, 30 Regent Street, Maitland, NSW 2320, Australia. *T:* (2) 49320105. *Clubs:* Tonga (Nukualofa); St John's Coll. (Brisbane) (Hon Mem., 1976–); Returned Services League (Toronto, NSW); Gallipoli Legion (Newcastle, NSW); Royal Commonwealth Society (NSW). *Died 6 Feb. 2014.*

VOELCKER, Christopher David, TD 1967; a District Judge (Magistrates' Courts) (formerly Metropolitan Stipendiary Magistrate), 1982–2001; *b* 10 May 1933; *s* of Eric Voelcker and Carmen Muriel Lyon Voelcker (*née* Henstock); *m* 1st, 1964, Sybil Russell Stoneham (marr. diss. 1985); two *d*; 2nd, 1991, Petrina Alexandra Keany (*née* Holdsworth). *Educ:* Wellington Coll., Berks. Called to Bar, Middle Temple, 1955. National Service, 8th King's Royal Irish Hussars, 1952–53. 3/4 County of London Yeomanry (Sharpshooters) TA, 1953–60; Kent and County of London Yeomanry (Sharpshooters) TA, 1960–67. An Asst Recorder, 1985–89; a Recorder, 1989–94. Member: Inner London Probation Cttee, 1986–92; Recruitment and Trng Cttee, Central Council of Probation for England and Wales, 1988–91. *Recreations:* military history, gardening, preserved railways. *Address:* 6 Pump Court, Temple, EC4Y 7AR. *T:* (020) 7353 7242. *Club:* Cavalry and Guards. *Died 23 Oct. 2014.*

von WEIZSÄCKER, Richard, Dr jur; President of the Federal Republic of Germany, 1984–94; *b* Stuttgart, 15 April 1920; *s* of late Ernst von Weizsäcker; *m* 1953, Marianne von Kretschmann; two *s* one *d* (and one *s* decd). *Educ:* Berlin and Bern; Univs of Oxford, Grenoble and Göttingen (Dr jur). Army service, 1938–45 (Captain, wounded). Formerly with: Mannesmann; Waldthausen & Co., Essen/Düsseldorf; Boehringer, Ingelheim. Pres., German Protestant Convention, 1964–70, 1979–81; Mem., Synod and Council, German Evangelical Church, 1967–84. Joined Christian Democratic Union, 1954: Mem., Fed. Board; Chm., Gen. Policy Commn, 1971–74; Chm., Basic Prog. Commn, 1974–77; Dep. Chm., CDU/CSU Parlt Gp, 1972–79; Presidential candidate, 1974; First Chm., Berlin CDU, 1981–83. Mem., Bundestag, 1969–81, Vice-Pres., 1979–81; Governing Mayor of West Berlin, 1981–84. Royal Victorian Chain, 1992. *Address:* (office) Am Kupfergraben 7, 10117 Berlin, Germany. *Died 31 Jan. 2015.*

VOWLES, Paul Foster; Academic Registrar, University of London, 1973–82; *b* 12 June 1919; *s* of late E. F. Vowles and G. M. Vowles, Bristol; *m* 1948, Valerie Eleanor Hickman (decd); one *s* two *d*. *Educ:* Bristol Grammar Sch.; Corpus Christi Coll., Oxford (schol.; MA). Served Gloucestershire Regt and King's African Rifles, 1939–46 (despatches, Major). Asst Secretary: Appts Bd, Univ. of Birmingham, 1947–48; Inter-University Council for Higher Educn Overseas, 1948–51; Registrar, Makerere University Coll., E Africa, 1951–63; Sen. Asst to Principal, Univ. of London, 1964–68; Warden, Lillian Penson Hall, 1965–69; External Registrar, 1968–73. Mem., 1983–89, Vice-Chm., 1986–89, Westfield Coll. Council. Hon. Fellow, QMW (Fellow, 1991). *Address:* Oaken Holt, Eynsham Road, Oxford OX2 9NL. *Died 4 Sept. 2011.*

W

WADDELL, Gordon Herbert; Chairman, Shanks Group plc (formerly Shanks & McEwan), 1992–2002; *b* Glasgow, 12 April 1937; *s* of late Herbert Waddell; *m* 1st, 1965, Mary (marr. diss. 1971), *d* of Harry Frederick Oppenheimer; two *d*; 2nd, 1973, Kathy May, *d* of W. S. Gallagher; three *c*. *Educ:* St Mary's Sch., Melrose; Fettes Coll., Edinburgh; Cambridge Univ. (BA); Stanford Univ. (MBA). Rugby Blue, Cambridge Univ., 1958, 1959, 1961; Member, British Isles Rugby Touring Team: to Australia and NZ, 1959; to South Africa, 1962; eighteen rugby caps for Scotland. MP (Progressive Party) for Johannesburg North, April 1974–Nov. 1977. Dir, E. Oppenheimer & Son Ltd, 1965–87; Exec. Dir, Anglo American Corp. of South Africa Ltd, 1971–87; Chairman: Johannesburg Consolidated Investment Co. Ltd, 1981–87; Rustenburg Platinum Mines Ltd, 1981–87; South African Breweries Ltd, 1984–87; Fairway Group plc (formerly Fairway (London)), 1989–98; Ryan Gp (formerly Digger), 1991–95; Gartmore Scotland Investment Trust, 1991–2001; Tor Investment Trust, 1992–96; Mersey Docks and Harbour Co., 1992–2006; Director: Cadbury Schweppes, 1988–97; Scottish Nat. Trust, 1988–96; London and Strathclyde Trust, 1989–96. *Recreation:* golf. *Address:* 1 Alexander Place, SW7 2SG. *Clubs:* Hawks (Cambridge); Honourable Company of Edinburgh Golfers; Royal and Ancient (St Andrews). *Died 13 Aug. 2012.*

WADDINGTON, Leslie; Chairman, Waddington Custot Galleries (formerly Waddington Galleries), since 1966; *b* Dublin, 9 Feb. 1934; *s* of late Victor and Zelda Waddington; *m* 1st, 1967, Ferriel Lyle (marr. diss. 1983); two *d*; 2nd, 1985, Clodagh Frances Fanshawe. *Educ:* Portora Royal School; Ecole du Louvre (Diplômé). Formed Waddington Galleries with father, 1957. Chm., Modern Painting Sect., 1994–2004, Pictura Sect., 1996–2000, Maastricht Art Fair. Sen. Fellow, RCA, 1993. Feaga Award, Eur. Fedn of Art Gall. Assocs, 2013. *Recreation:* reading. *Address:* 11 Cork Street, W1S 3LT. *T:* (020) 7851 2200. *Died 30 Nov. 2015.*

WADDS, Mrs Jean Casselman, OC 1982; Member, Royal Commission on Economic Union and Development Prospects for Canada, 1983–85; *b* 16 Sept. 1920; *d* of Hon. Earl Rowe and Treva Lennox Rowe; *m* 1st, 1946, (Arza) Clair Casselman, QC, MP; one *s* one *d*; 2nd, 1964, Robert Wadds (marr. diss. 1977). *Educ:* Univ. of Toronto (BA); Weller Business Coll. First elected to Canadian House of Commons (Riding Grenville-Dundas), 1958; re-elected: 1962, 1963, 1965; defeated (Riding Grenville-Carlton), 1968. Member, Canada's Delegn to United Nations, 1961; Parliamentary Sec. to Minister of Health and Welfare, 1962. National Sec., Progressive Conservative Party, 1971–75; Member, Ontario Municipal Bd, 1975–79. Canadian High Comr to UK, 1980–83. Former Director: Bell Canada; Royal Trustco Ltd; Air Canada; Celanese Canada Inc.; Canadian Pacific Ltd. Adv. Bd, Norman Paterson Sch. of Internat. Affairs, Carleton Univ., Ont. Freeman, City of London, 1981. Hon. DCL Acadia Univ., NS, 1981; Hon. LLD St Thomas Univ., NB, 1983; hon. degrees: Univ. of Toronto, 1985; Dalhousie Univ., NS, 1985. Hon. Fellowship Award, Bretton Hall Coll., W Yorks, 1982; Hon. Patron, Grenville Christian Coll., Brockville, 1981. *Recreations:* walking, swimming. *Address:* PO Box 579, Prescott, ON K0E 1T0, Canada. *Died 25 Nov. 2011.*

WADE, Prof. Kenneth, FRS 1989; CChem, FRSC; Professor of Chemistry, Durham University, 1983–98, then Emeritus; *b* Sleaford, Lincs, 13 Oct. 1932; 2nd *s* of Harry Kennington Wade and Anna Elizabeth Wade; *m* 1962, Gertrud Rosmarie Hetzel; one *s* two *d*. *Educ:* Carre's Grammar Sch., Sleaford; Nottingham Univ. (BSc, PhD; DSc 1970). Postdoctoral research assistant: Cambridge Univ., 1957–59; Cornell Univ., 1959–60; Lectr in Inorganic Chemistry, Derby Coll. of Technology, 1960–61; Durham University: Lectr 1961–71, Sen. Lectr 1971–77, Reader 1977–83, in Chemistry; Chm., Dept of Chemistry, 1986–89. Vis. Res. Fellow, Loker Hydrocarbon Res. Inst., USC, LA, 1979–. Visiting Professor: Technic Univ., Warsaw, 1974; Free Univ., Amsterdam, 1977–7 Univ. of S California, 1979 and 1984–85; Notre Dan Univ., 1983; McMaster Univ., 1984; Western Ontar Univ., 1991. Tilden Lectr, 1987–88, Mond Lectr, 1998–9 RSC; Emanuel Merck Lectr, Darmstadt, 1994. Pres Dalton Div., RSC, 1995–97. Main Gp Element Awar RSC, 1982; Chancellor's Medal, Durham Univ., 201 *Publications:* (jtly) Organometallic Compounds: the mai group elements, 1967; (jtly) Principles of Organometall Chemistry, 1968; Electron Deficient Compounds, 197 (jtly) The Chemistry of Aluminium, Gallium, Indium ar Thallium, 1973; (jtly) Organometallic Chemistry, 197 Hypercarbon Chemistry, 1987, 2nd edn 2011; Electro Deficient Boron and Carbon Clusters, 1990; Contempora Boron Chemistry, 2000; many papers (res. and rev. article in learned jls. *Recreations:* (a) musing, (b) musing, (walking. *Address:* Chemistry Department, Durha University Science Laboratories, South Road, Durha DH1 3LE. *T:* (0191) 334 2029. *Died 16 March 2014*

WADE, R(obert) Hunter; New Zealand diplomat; *b* 1 June 1916; *s* of R. H. Wade, Balclutha, NZ; *m* 194 Avelda Grace Petersen (*d* 1990); one *s* two *d* (and one decd). *Educ:* Waitaki; Otago Univ. NZ Treasury ar Marketing Depts, 1939; NZ Govt diplomatic appts, Delh Simla, Sydney, Canberra, 1941–49; Head of Easter Political Div., Dept of External Affairs, Wellington, NZ 1949; NZ Embassy, Washington, 1951; NZ High Comm Ottawa, 1956; Director of Colombo Plan Burea Colombo, 1957; Dir, External Aid, Wellington, 195 Comr for NZ in Singapore and British Borneo, 1962; Hig Comr in Malaya/Malaysia, 1963–67; Dep. High Comr i London, 1967–69; NZ Ambassador to Japan and Kore 1969–71; Dep. Sec.-Gen. of the Commonwealth, 1972–7 NZ Ambassador to Federal Republic of Germany and Switzerland, 1975–78. Represented New Zealand Independence of: Uganda, 1962; Botswana, 1966; Lesoth 1966. Pres., Asiatic Soc. of Japan, 1971. *Address:* 12 Pleasa Place, Howick, Auckland, New Zealand. *Club:* Northe (Auckland). *Died 7 July 2011*

WADE-GERY, Sir Robert (Lucian), KCMG 1983 (CM 1979); KCVO 1983; Fellow, All Souls College, Oxfor since 1997; *b* 22 April 1929; *o s* of late Prof. H. T. Wade Gery; *m* 1962, Sarah, *er d* of A. D. Marris, CMG; one *s* or *d*. *Educ:* Winchester; New Coll., Oxford (1st cl. Hon. Mo 1949 and Lit. Hum. 1951; Hon. Fellow, 1985). Fellow, A Souls Coll., Oxford, 1951–73, 1987–89. Joined H Foreign (later Diplomatic) Service, 1951; FO (Econom Relations Dept), 1951–54; Bonn, 1954–57; FO (Priva Sec. to Perm. Under-Sec., later Southern Dept), 1957–6 Tel Aviv, 1961–64; FO (Planning Staff), 1964–67; Saigo 1967–68; Cabinet Office (Sec. to Duncan Cttee), 1968–6 Counsellor 1969; on loan to Bank of England, 1969; Hea of Financial Policy and Aid Dept, FCO, 1969–70; Unde Sec., Central Policy Review Staff, Cabinet Offic 1971–73; Minister, Madrid, 1973–77; Minister, Moscov 1977–79; Dep. Sec. of the Cabinet, 1979–82; High Con to India, 1982–87. Dir, Barclays Capital (formerly BZW 1987–99 (Vice-Chm., 1994–99). Hon. Treas., IIS 1991–2005. Chm., Anglo-Spanish Soc., 1995–98. Chm. Govs, SOAS, 1990–99. *Recreations:* walking, sailing, trave history. *Address:* The Old Vicarage, Cold Asto Cheltenham GL54 3BW. *T:* (01451) 821115, *Fax:* (0145 822496; 14 Hill View, 2 Primrose Hill Road, NW3 3A *T:* (020) 7722 4754, *Fax:* (020) 7586 5966. *Clubs:* Boodle' Beefsteak. *Died 16 Feb. 2015*

WADSWORTH, David Grant; Chief Executive, Servic Children's Education, Ministry of Defence, 1997–2009; 30 Dec. 1944; *s* of Fred Wadsworth and Lona Wadswort (*née* Booth); *m* Marcia Armour (*née* Lyles); one step *s* on step *d*; partner, Dr Jocelyne Herrtage (*née* Lucas). *Edu* Hipperholme Grammar Sch., Yorks; Oriel Coll., Oxfor (MA 1970); Univ. of Newcastle upon Tyne (MPhil 1992 Corpus Christi Coll., Cambridge. Teacher, 1966–7

Educn Admin, Leeds CC, 1973–85; Dep. Dir of Educn, Northumberland CC, 1985–89; Chief Educn Officer, Bedfordshire CC, 1989–96. HM Comr, Duke of York's Royal Military Sch., Dover, 2008–10. Chm., Covington Parish Council, 2009–12. Mem., Exec. Cttee, Cambridge Univ. RUFC, 2011–. Hon. DEd De Montfort, 1996. Chevalier, l'Ordre des Palmes Académiques (France), 1992; Cavaliere della Ordine al Merito (Italy), 1994. *Recreations:* Rugby and cricket (passively), travel, music, European food and wine. *Address:* The Pentelows, Covington, Huntingdon, Cambs PE28 0RY. *T:* (01480) 860162. *Club:* Oxford and Cambridge. *Died 24 Dec. 2012.*

WAIARU, Rt Rev. Amos Stanley, OBE 2001; Archbishop of Melanesia, and Bishop of Central Melanesia, 1988–93; *b* 19 April 1944; *s* of late Stanley Qagora and Emma Kaifo; *m* 1976, Mary Marjorie Waiaru (*née* Mwele); one *s* three *d. Educ:* Bishop Patteson Theol Coll., Kohimarama, Solomon Is; Pacific Theol Coll., Suva, Fiji Is (DipTh). Tutor, Torgil Training Centre, Vanuatu, 1976; Chaplain, Vureas High School, Vanuatu, 1977–78, Head Master 1979–80; Bishop of Temotu, Solomon Is, 1981–87. Chm., S Pacific Anglican Council, 1991–93. Mem., Makira-Ulawa Provincial Assembly, 1997–2003. *Recreations:* gardening, fishing. *Address:* Ngafinuatoga Village, Santa Anna, Makira-Ulawa Province, Solomon Islands. *Died 2011.*

WAINE, Dr Colin, OBE 1990; FRCGP, FRCPath; Director of Health Programmes and Primary Care Development, Sunderland Health Authority, 1996–2002; Chairman, Council, Royal College of General Practitioners, 1990–93; *b* 12 March 1936; *m* 1959, Gwendoline Jameson; two *d. Educ:* King James I Grammar Sch., Bishop Auckland; Medical Sch., King's Coll., Univ. of Durham (MB BS Hons). MRCGP (dist.) 1975, FRCGP 1976, FRCPath 1993. Principal in general practice, Bishop Auckland, 1962–93; Hosp. Practitioner in Paediatrics, Bishop Auckland General Hosp., 1963–88; Gen. Manager, SW Durham HA, 1985–92; Dir of Primary Care, Sunderland Health Commn, 1993–96. Vis. Prof., Primary and Community Care, Univ. of Sunderland, 2002–. Chm., Nat. Obesity Forum, 2005–08. Course Organiser (Continuing Educn), Regional Post Grad. Inst., Newcastle upon Tyne, 1978–86. Consultant and UK Delegate, European Health Cttee, Primary Care and Prevention Gp, Council of Europe, Strasbourg, 1983–85. *Publications:* (contrib.) Handbook of Preventative Care for Pre-School Children, 1984; Organisation of Prevention in Primary Care, 1986; Why not care for your diabetic patients?, 1986; (contrib.) Chronic Disease in Medical Audit in General Practice, 1990; Obesity and Weight Management in Primary Care, 2002; contrib. to reports of working parties and papers and articles on diabetes, health care for children, asthma, etc in BMJ, The Practitioner, Cardiology in Practice, Members Reference Books, RCGP. *Recreations:* reading, gardening, music, cricket. *Address:* 42 Etherley Lane, Bishop Auckland, Co. Durham DL14 7QZ. *T:* (01388) 604429. *Died 4 Aug. 2014.*

WAKEFIELD, Derek John, CB 1982; Under Secretary, Government Communications Headquarters, 1978–82; *b* 21 Jan. 1922; *s* of Archibald John Thomas and Evelyn Bessie Wakefield; *m* 1951, Audrey Ellen Smith (*d* 2001); one *d. Educ:* The Commonweal School. Air Ministry, 1939–42 and 1947–52. Served War, Lieut, Royal Pioneer Corps, 1942–47. Government Communications Headquarters, 1952–82. Mem., Airship Assoc. Governor, Barnwood House Trust, Gloucester, 1973–90. *Recreation:* airships. *Club:* Naval and Military. *Died 3 March 2013.*

WAKELEY, Sir John (Cecil Nicholson), 2nd Bt *cr* 1952; FRCS; Consultant Surgeon, West Cheshire Group of Hospitals, 1961–88; *b* 27 Aug. 1926; *s* of Sir Cecil Pembrey Grey Wakeley, 1st Bt, KBE, CB, MCh, FRCS, and Elizabeth Muriel (*d* 1985), *d* of James Nicholson-Smith; *S* father, 1979; *m* 1954, June Leney; two *s* one *d. Educ:* Canford Sch.; MB, BS London 1950. LRCP 1950, FRCS 1955 (MRCS 1950); FACS 1973. Lectr in Anatomy, Univ. of London, 1951–52. Sqdn Ldr, RAF, 1953–54. Councillor, RCS, 1971–83; Member: Mersey Regional Health Authority, 1974–78; Editorial Bd, Health Trends, DHSS, 1968–71. Examiner for Gen. Nursing Council for England and Wales, 1954–59; Consultant Adviser in Surgery to RAF, 1981–89, Hon. Consultant Advr, 1990–. Freeman of City of London; Liveryman: Worshipful Soc. of Apothecaries; Worshipful Co. of Barbers. CStJ 1959. *Publications:* papers on leading med. jls, incl. British Empire Cancer Campaign Scientific Report, Vol. II: Zinc 65 and the prostate, 1958; report on distribution and radiation dosimetry of Zinc 65 in the rat, 1959. *Recreations:* music, photography, bird-watching. *Heir: s* Nicholas Jeremy Wakeley [*b* 17 Oct. 1957; *m* 1991, Sarah Ann, *d* of Air Vice-Marshal Brian Lewis Robinson]. *Address:* Croxton Green Cottage, Croxton Green, Cholmondley, Malpas, Cheshire SY14 8HG. *T:* (01829) 720530. *Club:* Council Club of Royal College of Surgeons. *Died 10 March 2012.*

WALDER, Edwin James, CMG 1971; NSW Civil Service, retired; *b* 5 Aug. 1921; *s* of Edwin James Walder and Dulcie Muriel Walder (*née* Griffiths); *m* 1944, Norma Cheslin (decd); two *d. Educ:* North Newtown High Sch.; Univ. of Sydney (BEc). FRAIPA 1983. Apptd NSW Civil Service, 1938; NSW State Treasury: 1945; Asst Under-Sec. (Finance), 1959–61; Dep. Under-Sec., 1961–63; Under-Sec. and Comptroller of Accounts, 1963–65; Pres., Metrop. Water, Sewerage and Drainage Bd, Sydney, 1965–81. Member: State Pollution Control Commn, 1971–81; Metropolitan Waste Disposal Authority (Sydney), 1971–81; management consultant and co. dir, 1981–92. *Recreations:* genealogy, internet browsing. *Clubs:* Central Coast Leagues (Gosford); Avoca Beach Bowling; Probus (Avoca Beach, and Broadwater, Central Coast). *Died 18 May 2015.*

WALES, Daphne Beatrice; Chairman, Board for Mission and Unity, General Synod of the Church of England, 1983–88; *b* 6 Dec. 1917; *d* of Frederick James Wales and Lilian Frederica (*née* Whitnall). Dep. Principal, Bank of England. Mem., General Synod, 1975–90 (Mem., Panel of Chairmen, 1983); Chm., St Albans Diocese House of Laity, 1979–85. Chm., Highway Trust, 1992–99 (Vice-Chm., 1983–92); Gov., Partnership for World Mission, 1978–90; Trustee, S American Missionary Soc., 1983–97 (Vice-Chm., 1989–97). Mem. Council, Oak Hill Theol Coll., 1981–91. *Address:* 3 Wildwood Court, Cedars Village, Dog Kennel Lane, Chorleywood, Herts WD3 5GG. *T:* (01923) 352072. *Died 20 March 2015.*

WALEY-COHEN, Hon. Joyce Constance Ina; (Joyce, Hon. Lady Waley-Cohen), MA; President, Independent Schools Information Service Council, 1981–85 (Member, 1972–80); *b* 20 Jan. 1920; *o d* of 1st Baron Nathan, PC, TD, and Eleanor Joan Clara, *d* of C. Stettauer; *m* 1943, Sir Bernard Nathaniel Waley-Cohen, 1st Bt (*d* 1991); two *s* two *d. Educ:* St Felix Sch., Southwold; Girton Coll., Cambridge (MA). Member: Governing Body, St Felix Sch., 1945–83 (Chm., 1970–83); Westminster Hosp. Bd of Governors, 1952–68; Chairman: Westminster Children's Hosp., 1952–68; Gordon Hosp., 1961–68; Governing Bodies of Girls' Schools' Assoc., 1974–79 (Mem., 1963); Ind. Schs Jt Council, 1977–80. Governor: Taunton Sch., 1978–90; Wellington Coll., 1979–90. JP Middx 1949–59, Somerset 1959–86. *Recreations:* hunting, spinning, family life. *Address:* Honeymead, Simonsbath, Minehead, Somerset TA24 7JX. *T:* (01643) 831242. *Died 30 June 2013.*

WALFORD, Sir Christopher (Rupert), Kt 1995; TEM 1972; Lord Mayor of London, 1994–95; *b* 15 Oct. 1935; *s* of late John Rupert Charles Walford, MBE and Gladys Irene Walford (*née* Sperrin); *m* 1st, 1967, Anne Elizabeth Viggars (*d* 2004); two *s* (and one *s* decd); 2nd, 2009, Denise Anne Powlett (*née* Hudson). *Educ:* Charterhouse; Oriel College, Oxford (MA; Hon. Fellow, 1995). Solicitor (Hons). National Service, commissioned RA, 1954–56; HAC 1957–72 (to Warrant Officer). Allen & Overy, 1959–96 (Partner, 1970–96). Councillor, Kensington, 1962–65, Kensington & Chelsea, 1964–82, Dep. Mayor, 1974–75, Mayor, 1979–80; Alderman, Ward of Farringdon Within, 1982–2002; Sheriff, City of London, 1990–91. Member: Council, CGLI, 1984–98; Council, and Policy and Exec. Cttees, Inst. of Directors, 1986–94; Court of Assistants and Finance Cttee, Corp. of Sons of the Clergy, 1989–98; Trustee: St Paul's Cathedral Choir Sch. Foundn, 1985–97; Guildhall Sch., Music and Drama Foundn, 1989–97; Morden Coll., 1991–2014. Vice-Pres., Bridewell

Royal Hosp., 1996–2002 (Gov., 1984–2002). Governor, Hon. Irish Soc., 1997–2000; Mem. Bd of Govs, London Guildhall Univ., 1997–2002. Freeman, City of London, 1964; Liveryman: Makers of Playing Cards Co., 1978 (Master, 1987; Hon. Liveryman, 2002); City of London Solicitors Co., 1983 (Master, 1993); Hon. Mem., Court of Assts, Builders Merchants' Co., 1992. FRSA. Hon. DCL City, 1994; Hon. LLD Ulster, 2000. *Recreations:* listening to music, watching Rugby football and cricket, horse racing. *Clubs:* Athenæum, East India, MCC. *Died 21 Oct. 2015.*

WALKER, Charls E., PhD; Consultant, Washington, DC, since 1973; *b* Graham, Texas, 24 Dec. 1923; *s* of Pinkney Clay and Sammye McCombs Walker; *m* 1949, Harmolyn Hart, Laurens, S Carolina; one *s* one *d*. *Educ:* Univ. of Texas (MBA); Wharton Sch. of Finance, Univ. of Pennsylvania (PhD). Instructor in Finance, 1947–48, and later Asst and Associate Prof., 1950–54, at Univ. of Texas, in the interim teaching at Wharton Sch. of Finance, Univ. of Pennsylvania; Associate Economist, Fed. Reserve Bank: of Philadelphia, 1953, of Dallas, 1954 (Vice-Pres. and Economic Advr, 1958–61); Economist and Special Asst to Pres. of Republic Nat. Bank of Dallas, 1955–56 (took leave to serve as Asst to Treasury Sec., Robert B. Anderson, April 1959–Jan. 1961); Exec. Vice-Pres., Amer. Bankers Assoc., 1961–69. Under-Sec. of the Treasury, 1969–72, Dep. Sec., 1972–73. Chm., American Council for Capital Formation; Co-founder, Cttee on the Present Danger; Mem. Council on Foreign Relations; Founder Chm., Bretton Woods Cttee. Adjunct Prof. of Finance and Public Affairs, Univ. of Texas at Austin, 1985–; Dist. Vis. Prof., Emory Univ., 2000–. Dist. Alumnus, Univ. of Texas, 1994. Hon. LLD Ashland Coll., 1970. Alexander Hamilton Award, US Treasury, 1973; Award for Outstanding Contribs to Minority Enterprise and Educn, Urban League, 1973; Baker Award, Nat. Council on Econ. Educn, 1991. Co-editor, The Banker's Handbook, 1988–. *Publications:* (ed) New Directions in Federal Tax Policy, 1983; (ed) The Consumption Tax, 1987; (ed) The US Savings Challenge, 1990; contribs to learned jls, periodicals. *Clubs:* Congressional Country, Burning Tree Golf (Bethesda, Md). *Died 2 June 2015.*

WALKER, Prof. David Alan, PhD, DSc; FRS 1979; FSB; Professor of Photosynthesis, University of Sheffield, 1988–93, then Emeritus; *b* 18 Aug. 1928; *s* of Cyril Walker and Dorothy Walker (*née* Dobson); *m* 1956, Shirley Wynne Walker (*née* Mason); one *s* one *d*. *Educ:* King's Coll., Univ. of Durham (BSc, PhD, DSc). Royal Naval Air Service, 1946–48. Lecturer, 1958–63, Reader, 1963–65, Queen Mary Coll., Univ. of London; Reader, Imperial Coll., Univ. of London, 1965–70; University of Sheffield: Prof. of Biology, 1970–84; Prof. and Dir, Res. Inst. for Photosynthesis, 1984–88. Leverhulme Emeritus Fellow, 1991–93. Corresp. Mem., Amer. Soc. Plant Physiol., 1979; MAE 1994. Hon. LittD Sheffield, 2006. Alexander von Humboldt Prize, Alexander von Humboldt Foundn, Bonn, 1991. *Publications:* Energy Plants and Man, 1979, 2nd edn 1992; (with G. E. Edwards) C3, C4—Mechanisms, Cellular and Environmental Regulation of Photosynthesis, 1983; The Use of the Oxygen Electrode and Fluorescence Probes in Simple Measurements of Photosynthesis, 1987, 2nd edn 1990; A Leaf in Time, 1999; Like Clockwork, 2006; A New Leaf in Time, 2007; papers, mostly in field of photosynthesis. *Recreations:* changing the Biddlestone landscape, singing the Sheffield Carols, philosophising in The Cross Keys. *Address:* 6 Biddlestone Village, Morpeth, Northumberland NE65 7DT. *T:* (01669) 630235. *E:* d.a.walker@sheffield.ac.uk. *Died 13 Feb. 2012.*

WALKER, David Bruce; Member (part-time), British Coal Corporation, 1988–95; *b* 30 Aug. 1934; *s* of Noel B. Walker and June R. Walker (*née* Sutherland); *m* 1961, Leonora C. Freeman; two *s*. *Educ:* Knox Grammar Sch., Wahroonga, NSW; Univ. of Sydney (BSc (Hons), MSc, Geology). Demonstrator in Geology: Univ. of Sydney, 1956–58; Bristol Univ., 1958–59; British Petroleum Co., 1959–85: worked as geologist in UK, Gambia, Algeria, Libya, Colombia, Kuwait, Iran and US; Vice-Pres., Production Planning, USA, 1974–77; Regional Coordinator, Western Hemisphere, 1977–79; Controller, BP Exploration, 1979–80; Chief Executive, BP Petroleum Development (UK), 1980–82; Dir, Resources Development, BP Australia, 1982–85; Chief Exec., Britoil plc, 1985–88. Chairman: Sun Internat. Exploration and Production Co., 1988–91; Sun Oil Britain, 1988–91. Distinguished Lectr, Soc. of Petroleum Engineers, 1976. President, UK Offshore Operators Assoc., 1982. *Recreations:* music, gardening. *Address:* Spring Cottage, Chetnole, Sherborne, Dorset DT9 6PF. *T:* (01935) 872604. *Died 19 Feb. 2014.*

WALKER, Prof. David Maxwell, CBE 1986; QC (Scot.) 1958; FBA 1976; FRSE 1980; Regius Professor of Law, Glasgow University, 1958–90, then Professor Emeritus and Senior Research Fellow; Dean of the Faculty of Law, 1956–59; Senate Assessor on University Court, 1962–66; *b* 9 April 1920; *o s* of James Mitchell Walker, Branch Manager, Union Bank of Scotland, and Mary Paton Colquhoun Irvine; *m* 1954, Margaret Knox, OBE, MA, *yr d* of Robert Knox, yarn merchant, Brookfield, Renfrewshire. *Educ:* High School of Glasgow (Mackindlay Prizeman in Classics); Glasgow, Edinburgh and London Universities. MA (Glasgow) 1946; LLB (Distinction), Robertson Schol., 1948; Faulds Fellow in Law, 1949–52; PhD (Edinburgh), 1952; Blackwell Prize, Aberdeen Univ., 1955; LLB (London), 1957; LLD (Edinburgh), 1960; LLD (London), 1968; LLD (Glasgow), 1985. Served War of 1939–45, NCO Cameronians; commissioned HLI, 1940; seconded to RIASC, 1941; served with Indian Forces in India, 1942, Middle East, 1942–43, and Italy, 1943–46, in MT companies and as Brigade Supply and Transport Officer (Captain). HQ 21 Ind. Inf. Bde, 8 Ind. Div. Advocate of Scottish Bar, 1948; Barrister, Middle Temple, 1957; QC (Scotland) 1958; practised at Scottish Bar, 1948–53; studied at Inst. of Advanced Legal Studies, Univ. of London, 1953–54; Prof. of Jurisprudence, Glasgow Univ., 1954–58. Dir, Scottish Univs' Law Inst., 1974–80. Trustee, Hamlyn Trust, 1954–93. Vice-Pres., RSE, 1985–88. Governor: Scottish College of Commerce, 1957–64; High School of Glasgow (and Chm., Educational Trust), 1974–2001. Hon. Sheriff of Lanarkshire at Glasgow, 1966–82. FSAScot 1966. Hon. LLD Edinburgh, 1974. *Publications:* (ed) Faculty Digest of Decisions, 1940–50, Supplements, 1951 and 1952; Law of Damages in Scotland, 1955; The Scottish Legal System, 1959, 8th edn 2001; Law of Delict in Scotland, 1966, 2nd edn 1981; Scottish Courts and Tribunals, 1969, 5th edn 1985; Principles of Scottish Private Law (2 vols), 1970, 4th edn (4 vols), 1988–89; Law of Prescription and Limitation in Scotland, 1973, 6th edn 2002; Law of Civil Remedies in Scotland, 1974; Law of Contracts in Scotland, 1979, 3rd edn 1995; Oxford Companion to Law, 1980; (ed) Stair's Institutions (6th edn), 1981; (ed) Stair Tercentenary Studies, 1981; The Scottish Jurists, 1985; Legal History of Scotland, 7 vols, 1988–2004; Scottish Part of Topham and Ivamy's Company Law, 12th edn 1955, to 16th edn 1978; contribs to collaborative works; articles in legal periodicals; *festschrift:* Obligations in Context, ed A. J. Gamble, 1990. *Recreations:* book collecting, Scottish history. *Address:* 1 Beaumont Gate, Glasgow G12 9EE. *T:* (0141) 339 2802. *Died 5 Jan. 2014.*

WALKER, George Alfred; Chief Executive: Walkers International, 1992; Premier Telesports Plc, since 1994; *b* 14 April 1929; *s* of William James Walker and Ellen (*née* Page); *m* 1957, Jean Maureen Walker (*née* Hatton); one *s* two *d*. *Educ:* Jubilee Sch., Bedford, Essex. Formerly boxer and boxing manager; Amateur Light Heavyweight Boxing Champion, GB, 1951. Man. Dir, Brent Walker Ltd, 1974; Chm. and Chief Exec., Brent Walker Group PLC, 1982. *Recreations:* ski-ing, ocean racing, climbing. *Died 22 March 2011.*

WALKER, John; Under Secretary, Scottish Development Department, 1985; *b* 16 Dec. 1929; *s* of John Walker and Elizabeth White Fish; *m* 1952, Rena Robertson McEwan; two *d*. *Educ:* Falkirk High School. Entered Civil Service, Min. of Labour, as clerical officer, 1946. National Service, RAF, 1948–50. Asst Principal, Dept of Health for Scotland, 1958; Scottish Home and Health Dept: Principal, 1960; Secretary, Cttee on General Medical Services in the Highlands and Islands, 1964–67; Asst Sec., 1969; Scottish Development Dept, 1975–78; Under Sec., Scottish Home and Health Dept, 1978–85. Asst Comr, Scottish Local Govt Boundary Commn, 1987–94. *Recreations:* greatgrandparenthood, being cared for by Rena. *Address:* 8/1 Back Dean, Ravelston Terrace, Edinburgh EH4 3UA. *T:* (0131) 343 3811. *Died 16 April 2011.*

WALKER, Kathrine S.; *see* Sorley Walker.

WALKER, Prof. Nigel David, CBE 1979; MA Oxon, PhD Edinburgh, DLitt Oxon; Wolfson Professor of Criminology and Fellow of King's College, Cambridge, 1973–84 (Director, Institute of Criminology, 1973–81); *b* 6 Aug. 1917; *s* of David B. Walker and Violet Walker (*née* Johnson); *m* 1939, Sheila Margaret Johnston (decd); one *d*. *Educ:* Tientsin Grammar Sch.; Edinburgh Academy; Christ Church, Oxford (Hon. Scholar). Served War, Infantry officer (Camerons and Lovat Scouts), 1940–46. Scottish Office, 1946–61; Gwilym Gibbon Fellow, Nuffield Coll., 1958–59; University Reader in Criminology and Fellow of Nuffield Coll., Oxford, 1961–73. Visiting Professor: Berkeley, 1965; Yale, 1973; Stockholm, 1978; Cape Town, 1984. Chairman: Home Secretary's Adv. Council on Probation and After-care, 1972–76; Study Gp on Legal Training of Social Workers, 1972–73; President: Nat. Assoc. of Probation Officers, 1980–84; British Soc. of Criminology, 1984–87; Member: Home Sec.'s TV Research Cttee, 1963–69; Adv. Council on Penal System, 1969–73; Cttee on Mentally Abnormal Offenders, 1972–75; Working Party on Judicial Training and Information, 1975–78; Floud Cttee on Dangerous Offenders; Hodgson Cttee on Profits of Crime; Parole Bd, 1986–89. Hon. LLD: Leicester, 1976, Edinburgh 1985. Hon. FRCPsych 1987. *Publications:* Delphi, 1936 (Chancellor's Prize Latin Poem); A Short History of Psychotherapy, 1957 (various trans); Morale in the Civil Service, 1961; Crime and Punishment in Britain, 1965; Crime and Insanity in England, 2 vols, 1968 and (jtly) 1972; Sentencing in a Rational Society, 1969 (various trans.); Crimes, Courts and Figures, 1971; Explaining Misbehaviour (inaug. lecture), 1974; Treatment and Justice (Sandoz lecture), 1976; Behaviour and Misbehaviour, 1977; Punishment, Danger and Stigma, 1980; Sentencing Theory Law and Practice, 1985, 2nd edn (jtly) 1997; Crime and Criminology, 1987; (jtly) Public Attitudes to Sentencing, 1988; Why Punish?, 1991; (jtly) Dangerous People, 1996; Aggravation, Mitigation and Mercy, 1999; A Man Without Loyalties, 2003; reports, articles, etc. *Recreation:* chess. *Address:* Flat 32, 5 Oswald Road, Edinburgh EH9 2HE. *T:* (0131) 667 1450. *Died 13 Sept. 2014.*

WALKER, Air Marshal Peter Brett, CB 2005; CBE 1995; Lieutenant Governor and Commander in Chief of the Bailiwick of Guernsey and its Dependencies, since 2011; *b* Sedgeley, Staffs, 29 Sept. 1949; *s* of Gp Captain S. Walker and Mrs S. Walker (*née* Brett); *m* 1978, Lynda Avril Masters; two *s* one *d*. *Educ:* Pocklington Sch.; RAF Coll., Cranwell; Durham Univ. (BA 1972). Joined RAF, 1968; Phantom pilot instructor, 1975–85; jsdc 1985–86; on staff, MoD, 1986–89; Officer Commanding: 111 Sqdn, 1989–92; RAF Mt Pleasant, Falkland Is, 1993–94; Dir, Air Staff Briefing, 1995–96; ACOS, Ops, HQ AFCENT, 1997–99; Dir, Operational Capability, MoD, 1999–2001; ACDS Ops, MoD, 2001–02; ACOS Policy and Planning, SHAPE, 2002–04; Dir, Jt Warfare Control, Stavanger, Norway, 2005–07. President: Aircrew Assoc., 2007–11; Overseas Br., RAFA, 2011–15. *Recreations:* golf, fly fishing, offshore sailing. *Club:* Royal Air Force. *Died 6 Sept. 2015.*

WALKER, Philip Andrew Geoffrey; Editor, Daily Star, 1994–98; *b* 28 July 1944; *m* 1st, 1966, Stella Kaspar; one *s* three *d*; 2nd, 1987, Sharon Ring. *Educ:* Howardian High Sch., Cardiff. South Wales Echo, 1962–64; Daily Sketch, 1964–65; Evening Post, Reading, 1966–68; Daily Mail, 1968–69; Asst Editor, Daily Mirror, 1969–80; Associate Editor, Daily Express, 1980–83; Dep. Editor, Daily Mirror, 1983–88; freelance journalist, 1988–90; Dep. Editor, Daily Star, 1990–94. *Recreation:* natural history. *E:* phil@pagwal.demon.co.uk. *Died 6 Oct. 2011.*

WALKER, Richard Alwyne F.; *see* Fyjis-Walker.

WALL, David (Richard), CBE 1985; Ballet Master, English National Ballet Co., 1994–2007; *b* 15 March 1946; *s* of Charles and Dorothy Wall; *m* 1967, Alfreda Thorogood, Royal Ballet dancer; one *s* one *d*. *Educ:* Royal Ballet Sch. Joined Royal Ballet Co., Aug. 1964. Promotion to: Soloist, Aug. 1966; Junior Principal Dancer, Aug. 1967; Senior Principal Dancer, Aug. 1968; during period of employment danced all major roles and had many created for him, notably Lescaut in Manon, 1974 and Crown Prince Rudolf in Mayerling, 1978; retired from dancing, 1984. Assoc. Dir, 1984–87, Dir, 1987–91, Royal Acad. of Dancing. Guest repetiteur, London City Ballet, 1992–94. Evening Standard Award for Ballet, 1977. *Recreations:* music, theatre. *Address:* 34 Croham Manor Road, South Croydon, Surrey CR2 7BE. *Died 18 June 2013.*

WALL, Rt Rev. Eric St Quintin; Hon. Assistant Bishop, Diocese of Gloucester, since 2002; *b* 19 April 1915; *s* of Rev. Sydney Herbert Wall, MA, and Ethel Marion Wall (*née* Wilkins); *m* 1942, Doreen Clare (*née* Loveley); one *s* one *d*. *Educ:* Clifton; Brasenose Coll., Oxford (MA); Wells Theol College. Deacon, 1938; priest, 1939; Curate of Boston, 1938–41; Chaplain, RAFVR, 1941–45; Vicar of Sherston Magna, 1944–53; Rural Dean of Malmesbury, 1951–53; Vicar of Cricklade with Latton, 1953–60; Hon. Chaplain to Bp of Bristol, 1960–66; Hon. Canon, Bristol, 1960–72; Diocesan Adviser on Christian Stewardship, Dio. Bristol, 1960–66; Proc. Conv., 1964–69; Vicar, St Alban's, Westbury Park, Bristol, 1966–72; Rural Dean of Clifton, 1967–72; Bp Suffragan of Huntingdon, and Canon Residentiary of Ely, 1972–80. *Recreation:* golf. *Address:* Forest House, Cinder Hill, Coleford, Glos GL16 8HQ. *T:* (01594) 832424. *Died 11 April 2011.*

WALLACE, Charles William, CMG 1983; CVO 1975; HM Diplomatic Service, retired; *b* 19 Jan. 1926; *s* of Percival Francis and Julia Wallace; *m* 1957, Gloria Sanz-Agero (*d* 2006). *Educ:* privately and abroad. HM Foreign (later Diplomatic) Service, 1949; served: Bari; Bahrain; Tegucigalpa; Guatemala; Panama; Foreign Office; Baghdad; Buenos Aires; Montevideo; FO, later FCO, Asst Head of American Dept; Counsellor 1969; Rome and Milan; Mexico City; Ambassador: Paraguay, 1976–79; Peru, 1979–83; Uruguay, 1983–86. Freeman, City of London, 1981. *Publications:* The Valedictory, 1992. *Recreations:* reading, walking. *Address:* c/o Lloyds Private Banking, 50 Grosvenor Street, W1K 3LF. *Died 20 April 2014.*

WALLACE, (Dorothy) Jacqueline H.; *see* Hope-Wallace.

WALLACE, Hon. Sir John (Hamilton), KNZM 1997; Judge of the High Court of New Zealand, 1982–96; *b* 9 Sept. 1934; *s* of G. H. and C. I. Wallace; *m* 1961, Elizabeth Ann Goodwin; one *s* one *d*. *Educ:* King's Coll., Auckland; Auckland Univ.; Merton Coll., Oxford (MA 1958; Hon. Fellow 2006). Called to the Bar, Gray's Inn, 1958; admitted as Barrister and Solicitor, NZ, 1959; QC 1974. Chairman: Equal Opportunities Tribunal, 1978–82; Human Rights Commn, 1984–89; Royal Commn on the Electoral System, 1985–86; Pres., Electoral Commn, 1994–96; Dep. Pres., Law Commn, 1991–96; Member: Contracts and Commercial Law Reform Cttee, 1974–85; Royal Commn on the Courts, 1976–78. Pres., Auckland Law Soc., 1980–81; Vice Pres., NZ Law Soc., 1981–82. Fellow, Internat. Acad. of Trial Lawyers, 1981. *Recreation:* reading. *Died 20 Sept. 2012.*

WALLACE, Reginald James, CMG 1979; OBE 1961; Chairman, Abbey National Gibraltar Ltd, 1987–2000; *b* 16 Aug. 1919; *s* of James Wallace and Doris (*née* Welch); *m* 1st, 1943, Doris Barbara Brown, MD, FRCS, MRCOG (decd); one *d*; 2nd, 1973, Maureen Coady (*d* 1983); 3rd, 1983, Marilyn Ryan (*née* Gareze); two *d*. *Educ:* John Gulson Sch., Coventry; Tatterford Sch., Norfolk; Leeds Univ. (BA); Queen's Coll., Oxford. Served War, 1939–46, 7th Rajput Regt, Indian Army (Major). Gold Coast/Ghana Admin. Service, 1947–58; Sen. District Comr, 1955; Asst Chief Regional Officer, Northern Region, 1957; Regional Sec., 1958; Financial Sec., British Somaliland, 1958–60; War Office, 1961–66; HM Treasury, 1966–78; seconded to Solomon Is, as Financial Sec. (later Financial Adviser), 1973–76; seconded, as British Mem., Anglo/French Mission on Admin. Reform in the Condominium of the New Hebrides, 1977; Governor of Gilbert Is, 1978 to Independence, July 1979; Financial and Develt Sec., Gibraltar, 1979–83. Chm., Norwich Union Fire Insurance Soc. (Gibraltar) Ltd,

1984–99. Former Chm., Community Care, Gibraltar. *Recreations:* walks, reading, music, crosswords. *Club:* Royal Commonwealth Society. *Died 10 Dec. 2012.*

WALLENBERG, Peter, Order of Wasa, 1974; King's Medal 12th Class, 1983; Hon. KBE 1989; First Vice Chairman, Skandinaviska Enskilda Banken, 1984–96 (Vice Chairman, 1980–84); Chairman: Investor AB, 1982–97; Wallenberg Foundation, since 1982; *b* Stockholm, 26 May 1926; *s* of Marcus Wallenberg and Dorothy (*née* Mackay); *m* (marr. diss.); two *s* one *d. Educ:* Stockholm Univ. (LLB 1953). Various positions within Atlas Copco Gp, 1953–68; Man. Dir, Atlas Copco MCT AB, 1968–70; Dep. Man. Dir, Atlas Copco AB, 1970–74; Industrial Advr to Skandinaviska Enskilda Banken, 1974–80. Mem. Bd, Stockholm Sch. of Econs, 1976–. Pres., ICC, 1989–90. Hon. Dr: Stockholm Sch. of Econ., 1984; Augustana Coll., Ill, 1985; Upsala Coll., NJ, 1989; Georgetown, Wash, 1990. Seraphime Medal, 2000. Orden de Isabel la Católica (Spain), 1979; Comdr, Légion d'Honneur (France), 1987; Comdr 1st Cl. Order of Lion of Finland, 1988; Comdr l'Ordre de Léopold (Belgium), 1989; Grand Cross, Ordem do Merito e Industrial (Portugal), 1990; Grand Cross, Order of Gregorius the Great (Vatican), 1991; Comdr 1st Cl., Royal Norwegian Order of Merit, 1992. *Recreations:* hunting, sailing, tennis. *Address:* Investor AB, Arsenalsgatan 8C, 103 32 Stockholm, Sweden. *Died 19 Jan. 2015.*

WALLER, Rt Rev. John Stevens; Bishop Suffragan of Stafford, 1979–87; Assistant Bishop, Diocese of Bath and Wells, 1987–2003; *b* 18 April 1924; *m* 1951, Pamela Peregrine; two *s* three *d. Educ:* St Edward's School, Oxford; Peterhouse, Cambridge (MA); Wells Theol Coll. War service with RNVR, 1942–46. Deacon 1950, priest 1951, London; Leader, Strood Gp of Parishes, 1967–72, Team Rector of Strood 1972–73; Rector of St Nicholas, Harpenden, Herts, 1973–79; Team Vicar, Long Sutton and Long Load, Som, 1987–89. *Address:* College of St Barnabas, Blackberry Lane, Lingfield, Surrey RH7 6NJ. *T:* (01342) 872818. *E:* wallers@collegeofstbarnabas.com. *Died 3 Sept. 2015.*

WALLEY, Dr Francis, CB 1978; FREng; consulting engineer; Consultant to the Arup Group (formerly Ove Arup Partnership); *b* 30 Dec. 1918; *s* of late Reginald M. Walley and Maria M. Walley; *m* 1946, Margaret, *yr d* of late Rev. Thomas and Margaret J. Probert; two *d. Educ:* Cheltenham Grammar Sch.; Bristol Univ. MSc, PhD. FICE; FIStructE; FREng (FEng 1985). Entered Min. of Home Security as Engr, 1941: reported to CIGS on allied bombing of Pantelleria, 1943; Member: British Bombing Survey Unit, France, 1944–45; Jt UK/USA Survey Unit of Nagasaki and Hiroshima, 1945. Min. of Works, 1945; Suptg Civil Engr, 1963; Dep. Dir of Building Develt, 1965; Dir of Estate Management Overseas, 1969; Dir of Post Office Services, 1971; Under-Sec., Dir of Civil Engineering Services, DoE, 1973–78. I/c of Civil Defence Structures, British Atomic Trials, Aust., 1954; Mem., British Govt team looking at building construction in USSR, 1966. Mem., Standing Cttee on Structural Safety, 1977–88; Chairman: BSI Code Cttee for Structural Use of Concrete, 1987–2002; ISO Cttee of Design of Concrete Structures, 1989–2002. Mem. Council, ICE, 1978–81; Vice-Pres., IStructE, 1982–83 (Hon. Treas., 1981; Hon. Sec., 1979–81). Diamond Jubilee Lecture, British Cement Assoc., 1995; Lewis Kent Award, 1985, James Sutherland Lecture, 2000, IStructE. *Publications:* Prestressed Concrete Design and Construction, 1954; (with Dr S. C. C. Bate) A Guide to the Code of Practice CP 115, 1960; (contrib.) Historic Concrete, 2000; several papers to ICE and techn. jls. *Recreations:* gardening, furniture-making. *Died 18 Oct. 2012.*

WALLIS, Jane; *see* Packer, J.

WALLIS, Jeffrey Joseph; retail consultant; *b* 25 Nov. 1923; *s* of Nathaniel and Rebecca Wallis; *m* 1948, Barbara Brickman; one *s* one *d. Educ:* Owen's; Coll. Aeronautical Engrg. Man. Dir, Wallis Fashion Group, 1948–80. Mem., Monopolies and Mergers Commn, 1981–85. Formerly Member: CNAA; Clothing Export Council; NEDC (Textiles). Involved in art educn throughout career; various governorships. *Recreations:* motor racing, motor boating, industrial design. *Address:* 37 Avenue Close, NW8 6DA. *T:* (020) 7722 8665. *Died 27 Oct. 2014.*

WALLIS-KING, Maj.-Gen. Colin Sainthill, CBE 1975 (OBE 1971); Director of Service Intelligence, 1977–80; *b* 13 Sept. 1926; *s* of late Lt-Col Frank King, DSO, OBE, 4th Hussars, and Colline Ammabel, *d* of late Lt-Col C. G. H. St Hill; *m* 1962, Lisabeth, *d* of late Swan Swanstrøm, Oslo, Norway; two *d. Educ:* Stowe. Commissioned Coldstream Guards, 1945; Liaison Officer with Fleet Air Arm, 1954; Staff Coll., 1960; Regtl Adjutant, Coldstream Guards, 1961; seconded to Para. Regt, 1963; ACOS HQ Land Norway, 1965; Comdr 2nd Bn Coldstream Guards, 1969; Dep. Comdr 8 Inf. Brigade, 1972; Comdr 3 Inf. Brigade, 1973; BGS Intell., MoD, 1975. Dir, Kongsberg Ltd, 1982–87; UK Agent for Norsk Forsvarsteknologi A/S, 1987–93. *Recreations:* equitation, sailing, music, cross-country ski-ing, fishing. *Address:* c/o Royal Bank of Scotland, Lawrie House, Victoria Road, Farnborough, Hants GU14 7NR. *Club:* Cavalry and Guards. *Died 10 April 2012.*

WALLS, Rev. Brother Roland Charles; Member, Community of the Transfiguration, since 1965; *b* 7 June 1917; *s* of late Roland William Walls and Tina Josephine Hayward. *Educ:* Sandown Grammar Sch.; Corpus Christi Coll., Cambridge (BA 1948; MA 1952); Kelham Theological Coll. Curate of St James', Crossgates, Leeds, 1940–42; Curate of St Cecilia's, Parson Cross, Sheffield, 1942–45; Licensed preacher, Diocese of Ely, 1945–48; Fellow of Corpus Christi Coll., Cambridge, 1948–62; Lecturer in Theology, Kelham Theological Coll., 1948–51; Chaplain and Dean of Chapel, Corpus Christi Coll., Cambridge, 1952–58; Canon Residentiary, Sheffield Cathedral, 1958–62; Chaplain of Rosslyn Chapel, Midlothian, 1962–68. Examining Chaplain to Bishop of Edinburgh. Lecturer at Coates Hall Theological Coll.; Lecturer in Dogmatics Dept, New Coll., Edinburgh, 1963–74. Received into RC Church, ordained priest, 1983. *Publications:* (contrib.) Theological Word Book (ed A. Richardson), 1950; Law and Gospel, 1980; (contrib.) Dictionary of Christian Spirituality, 1983; (contrib.) Dictionary of Pastoral Counsel, 1984; The Royal Mysteries, 1990. *Recreations:* botany, music, etc. *Address:* St Joseph's House, 43 Gilmore Place, Edinburgh EH3 9NG. *Died 7 April 2011.*

WALSH, Maj.-Gen. Michael John Hatley, CB 1980; CBE 1996; DSO 1968; Director of Overseas Relations, St John's Ambulance, 1989–95; *b* 10 June 1927; *s* of Captain Victor Michael Walsh, late Royal Sussex, and Audrey Walsh; *m* 1952, Angela, *d* of Col Leonard Beswick; two *d. Educ:* Sedbergh Sch. Commnd, KRRC, 1946; served in Italy, Malaya, Germany, Cyprus, Suez, Aden, Australia and Singapore; Bde Maj. 44 Parachute Bde, 1960–61; GSO1 Defence Planning Staff, 1966; CO 1 Para Bn, 1967–69; Col AQ 1 Div., 1969–71; Comdr, 28 Commonwealth Bde, 1971–73; BGS HQ BAOR, 1973–76; GOC 3rd Armoured Div., 1976–79; Dir of Army Training, MoD, 1979–81. Hon. Col, 1st Bn Wessex Regt, TA, 1981–89. Chief Scout of the UK and Dependent Territories, 1982–88; Vice Pres., Scout Assoc., 1988–. Council Mem., Operation Raleigh, 1984; Royal National Life-boat Institution: Member: Cttee of Management, 1988–2003; Search and Rescue Sub-cttee, 1989–99; Fund Raising Sub-cttee, 1991–2001; Vice Pres., 1998–. Kt Pres., Hon. Soc. of Knights of the Round Table, 1988–95 (Kt 1986–); Mem., St John Council, Wilts, 1989–99, London, 1995–2000. Pres., 1525 Soc., 2004–09; Vice Pres., Old Sedberghian Club, 2005–11. DL Greater London, 1986–99. Freeman, City of London, 1987. KStJ 1993 (Mem., Chapter Gen., 1989–99). Surgeon-Gen. John White Medal for Services to Health and Internat. Relns, 2008. *Publications:* One Man in his Time, 2007. *Recreations:* athletics, boxing (Life Pres., Army Boxing Assoc., 1986), parachuting (Pres., Army Parachute Assoc., 1979–81), sailing, Australian Rules football, photography (LRPS). *Address:* c/o Barclays Bank, James Street, Harrogate HG1 1QX. *Died 13 Oct. 2015.*

WALSHAM, Sir Timothy (John), 5th Bt *cr* 1831, of Knill Court, Herefordshire; horticulturalist; *b* 26 April 1939; *o s* of Rear Adm. Sir John Walsham, 4th Bt, CB, OBE and

Sheila Christina, *o d* of Comdr B. Bannerman, DSO; *S* father, 1992. *Educ:* Sherborne. Peninsular & Oriental Shipping Company, 1960–67; Royal Fleet Auxiliary Service, 1968–72. *Recreation:* horticulture. *Heir: cousin* Gerald Percy Robert Walsham [*b* 7 Feb. 1939; *m* 1984, Evelyn Niebes]. *Address:* c/o Trefelix, Trebetherick, Wadebridge, Cornwall PL27 6SA. *Died 14 July 2011.*

WALTERS, Michael Quentin; Senior Partner, Theodore Goddard, Solicitors, 1983–89; *b* 14 Oct. 1927; *s* of late Leslie Walters and Helen Marie Walters; *m* 1st, 1954, Lysbeth Ann Falconer (*d* 1999); 2nd, 2005, Jennifer Anne Burden. *Educ:* Merchant Taylors' School; Worcester College, Oxford (MA). Served Army, 1946–48, 2nd Lieut. Joined Theodore Goddard, 1951; admitted Solicitor, 1954. Chm., EIS Group plc, 1977–94; Deputy Chairman: Martonair International plc, 1980–86; Tilbury Douglas plc, 1991–96; Dir, Delta plc, 1980–95. Mem., Management Cttee, Inst. of Neurology, 1986–91. *Recreations:* fishing, gardening, reading. *Address:* Woodlarks, Rhinefield Road, Brockenhurst, Hants SO42 7SQ. *T:* (01590) 622340. *Died 20 March 2013.*

WANLESS, Sir Derek, Kt 2005; FCIB; Chairman, Northumbrian Water Group plc, since 2006 (Director, since 2003); *b* 29 Sept. 1947; *s* of Norman Wanless and Edna (*née* Charlton); *m* 1971, Vera West; one *s* four *d*. *Educ:* Royal Grammar Sch., Newcastle upon Tyne; King's Coll., Cambridge (BA 1st cl. Hons Maths, MA). MIS 1973; ACIB 1978. Joined National Westminster Bank, 1970; appts include: Dir of Personal Banking, 1986–88; Gen. Manager, UK Branch Business, 1989–90; Chief Exec., UK Financial Services, 1990–92; Dir, 1991–99; Dep. Gp Chief Exec., Feb.–March 1992; Gp Chief Exec., 1992–99. Dir, Mastercard Internat., 1989–90; Vice-Chm., Eurocard Internat., 1989–90. Dir, Northern Rock plc, 2000–07. Chairman: Adv. Cttee on Business and Envmt set up by Secs of State for Envmt and Trade and Ind., 1993–95 (Mem., 1991–93); NACETT, 1997–2000; Financial Services NTO, 2000–03; Longevity Sci. Adv. Panel, Legal and General plc, 2009–; Member: EC Consultative Forum, on the Envmt, 1994–96; World Business Council for Sustainable Develt (formerly World Industry Council for the Envmt), 1993–96; Statistics Commn, 2000–08 (Vice Chm., 2004–08); Bd for Actuarial Standards, Financial Reporting Council, 2006–. President: CIB, 1999–2000; Inst Internat. d'Etudes Bancaires, 1999. Dir, BITC, 1995–2004; Trustee, NESTA, 2000–06. Report on funding health service, Securing our Future Health: taking a long-term view, 2002; report on public health, Securing Good Health for the Whole Population, 2004; report on social care, Securing Good Care for Older People, 2006; report on funding health service, Our Future Health Secured?, 2007. FRSA 1991; CCMI (CBIM 1992). Freeman, City of London, 1992. Hon. DSc City, 1995; Hon. DCL Durham, 2005; Hon. DBA: Coventry, 2007; Sunderland, 2007. *Recreations:* all sports, chess, music, walking, gardening. *Club:* Reform. *Died 22 May 2012.*

WARBURTON, Dame Anne (Marion), DCVO 1979 (CVO 1965); CMG 1977; HM Diplomatic Service, 1957–85; President, Lucy Cavendish College, Cambridge, 1985–94; *b* 8 June 1927; *d* of Captain Eliot Warburton, MC and Mary Louise (*née* Thompson), US. *Educ:* Barnard Coll., Columbia Univ. (BA); Somerville Coll., Oxford (BA, MA; Hon. Fellow, 1977); MA Cantab 1985. Economic Cooperation Administration, London, 1949–52; NATO Secretariat, Paris, 1952–54; Lazard Bros, London, 1955–57; entered Diplomatic Service, Nov. 1957; 2nd Sec., FO, 1957–59; 2nd, then 1st Sec., UK Mission to UN, NY, 1959–62; 1st Sec., Bonn, 1962–65; 1st Sec., DSAO, London, 1965–67; 1st Sec., FO, then FCO, 1967–70; Counsellor, UK Mission to UN, Geneva, 1970–75; Head of Guidance and Information Policy Dept, FCO, 1975–76; Ambassador to Denmark, 1976–83; Ambassador and UK Permanent Rep. to UN and other internat. organisations, Geneva, 1983–85. Dep. Leader, UK Delegn to UN Women's Conf., Nairobi, 1985; Leader, EC Investigative Mission: Abuse of Bosnian Muslim Women, 1992–93; Mem., Cttee on Standards in Public Life, 1994–97. Member: Equal Opportunities Commn, 1986–88; British Library Bd, 1989–95; Council, UEA, 1991–97. Governor, ESU, 1992–96. Hon. LLD Arkansas, 1994. Verdienstkreuz, 1st Class (West Germany), 1965; Grand Cross, Order of Dannebrog, 1979; Lazo de Dama, Order of Isabel la Católica (Spain), 1988. *Recreation:* enjoying the arts and reminiscing about travel. *Address:* Ansted, Thornham Magna, Eye, Suffolk IP23 8HB. *Died 4 June 2015.*

WARD, (Albert Joseph) Reginald; Chief Executive, Reg Ward Associates, since 1993; *b* 5 Oct. 1927; *s* of Albert E. and Gwendolene M. E. Ward, Lydbook, Glos; *m* 1954, Betty Anne Tooze (*d* 2010); one *s* one *d*. *Educ:* East Dean Grammar Sch., Cinderford, Glos; Univ. of Manchester (BA Hons History). HM Inspector of Taxes, 1952–65; Chief Administrator, County Architects Dept, Lancashire CC, 1965–68; Business Manager, Shankland Cox & Associates, 1968–69; Corporation Secretary, Irvine New Town Development Corporation, 1969–72; Chief Executive: Coatbridge Borough Council, 1972–74; London Borough of Hammersmith, 1974–76; Hereford and Worcester CC, 1976–80; LDDC, 1981–88; Kent European Enterprise, 1988–89; ISLEF, Danish develt co., 1989–92; Whitegate Develt Corp., St Kitts, 1999–2002. Mem., Duke of Edinburgh's Commn into Housing, 1986–87. Hon. Fellow, QMC, 1987; Fellow, Univ. of London. FRSA. *Recreations:* walking, tennis, music, architecture and urban design. *Address:* Abbot's Court, Deerhurst, Gloucester GL19 4BX. *T:* (01684) 274881. *Died 6 Jan. 2011.*

WARD, Rev. David Conisbee; Non-Stipendiary Minister, St George's, Tolworth, 1995–2006; *b* 7 Jan. 1933; *s* of late Sydney L. Ward and Ivy A. Ward; *m* 1958, Patricia Jeanette (*née* Nobes); one *s* one *d*. *Educ:* Kingston Grammar Sch.; St John's Coll., Cambridge (Scholar; BA 1954; MA 1958). Asst Principal, Nat. Assistance Bd, 1956, Principal, 1961; Asst Sec., DHSS, 1970, Under Sec., 1976–83. Southwark Ordination Course, 1977–80; Deacon, 1980; Priest, 1981; Non-Stipendiary Curate, St Matthew, Surbiton, 1980–83; Curate, Immanuel Church, Streatham Common, 1983–84, parish priest, 1984–87; Vicar, St Paul's, Hook, Surrey, 1987–93; NSM, All Saints, Kingston, 1993–95. Councillor (Lib Dem) Kingston-upon-Thames, 1994–98 (Dep. Mayor, 1996–97). Governor, Kingston GS, 1988–2003. FRSA 2000. *Publications:* (with G. W. Evans) Chantry Chapel to Royal Grammar School: the history of Kingston Grammar School 1299–1999, 2000. *Recreations:* member Kingstonian FC; Pitcairn Islands Study Group (philately). *Address:* 50 Elgar Avenue, Tolworth, Surbiton, Surrey KT5 9JN. *T:* (020) 8399 9679. *Clubs:* Civil Service; Rotary (Kingston upon Thames). *Died 29 July 2011.*

WARD, Reginald; *see* Ward, A. J. R.

WARD, Susan Mary, (Mrs Fergus Jamieson); a Judge of the Upper Tribunal (Immigration and Asylum Chamber) and Senior Immigration Judge (formerly a Senior Immigration Judge, Asylum and Immigration Tribunal), since 2008; *d* of late Ronald and Vera Ward; *m* 1989, Fergus Jamieson; one *s* one *d*. *Educ:* Brentwood Co. High Sch. for Girls, Essex; Univ. of Bristol (LLB Hons); Inns of Court Sch. of Law. Called to the Bar: Inner Temple, 1976 (Bencher, 2002); NSW, 1981; Barrister of Supreme Court of NSW and Fed. Court of Australia; in practice as barrister, London and Australia, 1976–86; Lawyer, Govt Legal Service, 1987–88; Legal Advr, then Gen. Counsel, APACS, 1988–2000; Gen. Counsel, London Clearing House, 2000–03; Gen. Counsel and Gp Co. Sec., LCH Clearnet Ltd, 2004–06; Sen. Legal Advr and Dir (Legal), Newedge Gp, 2007–08. Immigration Adjudicator, 1995–2000; Chm., Immigration and Asylum Tribunal, 2000–05; Immigration Judge, 2005–08. Mem., Policy Holders Protection Bd, 1999–2001. Mem., Bar Council, 1996–2004; Chm., Bar Assoc. for Commerce, Finance and Industry, 1998–99 (Hon. Vice Pres., 1995–); Hon. Vice Pres., Assoc. of Women Barristers, 1999– (Founder Mem. and Chm., 1998–99). Mem., Academic Adv. Panel, BPP Law Sch., 1998–2000. Gov. and Dir, Chigwell Sch., Essex, 2002–. *Recreations:* European languages, travel, collecting Champagne labels. *Address:* Upper Tribunal (Immigration and Asylum Chamber), Field House, 15–25 Breams Buildings, EC4A 1DZ. *T:* (020) 7073 4231. *E:* susan.ward@judiciary.gsi.gov.uk. *Died 27 May 2011.*

WARD, William Alan H.; *see* Heaton-Ward.

WARDLE, Prof. (Frances) Jane, PhD; FBPsS; FMedSci; FBA 2013; Professor of Clinical Psychology, since 1996 and Director, Cancer Research UK Health Behaviour Research Centre, since 1997, University College London; *b* Oxford, 30 Oct. 1950; *d* of Peter Brian Wardle and Marcella Frances Wardle; *m* 1st, 1976, Nicholas Stirling (marr. diss. 1986); one *d*; 2nd, 1991, Prof. Andrew Patrick Arthur Steptoe; one *s*. *Educ:* St Anne's Coll., Oxford (BA 1973); Inst. of Psychiatry, Univ. of London (MPhil 1975; PhD 1986). FBPsS 1989. Institute of Psychiatry, University of London: Lectr in Clin. Psychol., 1976–86; Sen. Lectr in Clin. Psychol., 1987–91; Reader in Health Psychol. and Sen. Scientist, ICRF Health Behaviour Unit, 1991–95; Clin. Psychologist, Maudsley Hosp., London, 1976–96. Founder and Res. Dir, Weight Concern, 1990–. Associate Ed., British Jl Clin. Psychol., 1992–95; Ed., British Jl Health Psychol., 1995–2001. Chm., Health Psychol. Div., BPsS, 2000–01. Fellow: Soc. of Behavioral Medicine, 2003; Amer. Psychol Soc., 2011; FMedSci 2012. MAE 2007. *Publications:* Psychosocial Processes and Health: a reader, 1994; contrib. articles to scientific jls on health psychol., cancer screening, obesity. *Recreations:* reading, theatre, friends, family. *Address:* Department of Epidemiology and Public Health, University College London, 1–19 Torrington Place, WC1E 6BT. *T:* (020) 7679 1734, *Fax:* (020) 7679 8354. *E:* j.wardle@ucl.ac.uk. *Died 20 Oct. 2015.*

WARE, Cyril George, CB 1981; Under-Secretary, Inland Revenue, 1974–82; *b* 25 May 1922; *s* of Frederick George Ware and Elizabeth Mary Ware; *m* 1946, Gwennie (*née* Wooding); two *s* one *d*. *Educ:* Leyton County High Sch. Entered Inland Revenue as Tax Officer, 1939; Inspector of Taxes, 1949; Sen. Principal Inspector, 1969. *Recreations:* music, woodwork, gardening, swimming. *Address:* 86 Tycehurst Hill, Loughton, Essex IG10 1DA. *T:* (020) 8508 3588. *Died 8 Oct. 2014.*

WAREING, Robert Nelson; *b* 20 Aug. 1930; *s* of late Robert Wareing and Florence Wareing (*née* Mallon); *m* 1962, Betty Coward (*d* 1989). *Educ:* Ranworth Square Sch., Liverpool; Alsop High Sch., Liverpool; Bolton Coll. of Educn; BSc (Econ) London Univ., 1956. RAF, 1948–50. Administrative Asst, Liverpool City Bldg Surveyor's Dept, 1946–56; Lecturer: Brooklyn Technical Coll., Birmingham, 1957–59; Wigan and Dist Mining and Technical Coll., 1959–63; Liverpool Coll. of Commerce, 1963–64; Liverpool City Inst. of Further Educn, 1964–72; Central Liverpool Coll. of Further Educn, 1972–83. Merseyside County Council: Mem., 1981–86; Chief Whip, Labour Gp, 1981–83; Chm., Economic Develt Cttee, 1981–83; Chm., Merseyside Economic Develt Co. Ltd, 1981–86. A Vice-Pres., AMA, 1984–97. Joined Labour Party, 1947: Pres., Liverpool Dist Labour Party, 1974–81; Mem., MSF. MP Liverpool, West Derby, 1983–2010 (Lab, 1983–2007; Ind, 2007–10). Introduced Chronically Sick and Disabled Persons Bill, 1983; Asst Labour Whip, 1987–92, with responsibility for health and social security, employment, sport, environment and foreign affairs. Mem., Select Cttee on Foreign Affairs, 1992–97. Vice-Chairman: British-Yugoslav Parly Gp, 1985–94, 2001–02 (Chm., 1994–97); Serbia-Montenegro Parly Gp, 2003–10; Armenia Parly Gp, 2004–10; Sec., British-Russian Parly Gp, 1997–2010 (Vice Pres., 1992–97); Treasurer: British-Azerbaijan Parly Gp, 1997–2010; British-Ukranian Parly Gp, 1999–2010; British-German Parly Gp, 2005–10. *Recreations:* watching soccer (especially Everton FC), concert-going and ballet, motoring and travel. *Died 12 Feb. 2015.*

WARNER, Prof. Anne Elizabeth, FRS 1985; Professor of Developmental Biology, 1986–2009, then Emeritus, and Research Strategy Director, since 2005, Centre for Mathematics and Physics in the Life Sciences and Experimental Biology, University College London (Director, 1999–2005); *b* 25 Aug. 1940; *d* of late James Frederick Crompton Brooks and of Elizabeth Marshall; *m* 1963, Michael Henry Warner (*d* 2011). *Educ:* Pate's Grammar School for Girls, Cheltenham; University College London (BSc); Nat. Inst. for Med. Res. (PhD). Res. Associate, Middlesex Hosp. Med. Sch., 1968–71, Lectr in Physiology 1971–75, Sen. Lectr 1975–76, Royal Free Hosp. Sch. of Medicine; Sen. Lectr in Anatomy, 1976–80, Reader in Anatomy, 1980–86, Fellow, 1993, UCL; Royal Soc. Foulerton Res. Prof., 1986–2001. *Publications:* papers in scientific jls. *Address:* University College London, Gower Street, WC1E 6BT. *Died 16 May 2012.*

WARNER, Sir (Edward Courtenay) Henry, 3rd Bt, *cr* 1910; *b* 3 Aug. 1922; *s* of Col Sir Edward Courtenay Thomas Warner, 2nd Bt, DSO, MC and Hon. Nesta Douglas-Pennant, *d* of 2nd Baron Penrhyn; *S* father, 1955; *m* 1949, Jocelyn Mary, *d* of Sir Thomas Lubbock Beevor, 6th Bt; three *s*. *Heir:* *s* Philip Courtenay Thomas Warner, *b* 3 April 1951. *Died 8 April 2011.*

WARREN, Ian Scott; Senior Master of the Supreme Court (Queen's Bench Division) and Queen's Remembrancer, 1988–90 (Master, 1970–90); *b* 30 March 1917; *er s* of Arthur Owen Warren and Margaret Cromarty Warren (*née* Macnaughton); *m* 1st, 1943, Barbara (marr. diss.), *er d* of Walter Myrick, Tillsonburg, Ont.; four *s* one *d*; 2nd, Jeanne Hicklin (marr. diss.), *d* of late Frederick and Lydia Shaw, Crosland Moor; 3rd, 1987, Olive Sybil (*d* 2012), *d* of late James Charles Montgomerie Wilson. *Educ:* Charterhouse (Exhibnr); Magdalene Coll., Cambridge (Exhibnr); BA 1938, MA 1950. Colonial Administrative Service, 1938–41, serving Gold Coast (Asst DC, 1940); RAF, 1942–46; Flying Badge and commissioned, 1943; Flt Lieut, 1944. Called to Bar, Lincoln's Inn, 1947, Bencher 1967; practised at Common Law Bar, London, 1947–70. *Publications:* Verses from Lincoln's Inn (jtly), 1975; Aesop's Fables: a selection, 1982. *Recreations:* ski-ing, walking, poetry. *Clubs:* Garrick, MCC. *Died 23 Feb. 2015.*

WARREN, Maurice Eric; Chairman, Aggregate Industries plc, 1997–2000; *b* 21 June 1933; *s* of Frederick Leonard Warren and Winifred (*née* Gale); *m* 1954, Molly Slater; one *s* one *d*. *Educ:* St Brendan's Coll., Bristol. Certified Accountant, FCCA. Crosfield & Calthrop, 1958–74 (Dir, 1970–74); Managing Director: Dalgety Crosfields, 1974–76; Dalgety Agriculture Ltd, 1976–81; Dalgety UK Ltd, 1981–87; Dalgety PLC: Dir, 1982; Chief Exec., 1989–93; Chm., 1993–96. Chairman: S Western Electricity, 1993–95; CAMAS, 1994–97; Great Western Holdings, 1996–98. *Recreation:* golf. *Died 14 March 2015.*

WARREN, Prof. Michael Donald, MD, FRCP, FFPH; Emeritus Professor of Social Medicine, University of Kent, since 1983; *b* 19 Dec. 1923; *s* of late Charles Warren and Dorothy Gladys Thornton Reeks; *m* 1946, Joan Lavina Peacock; two *d* (one *s* decd). *Educ:* Bedford Sch.; Guy's Hosp.; London Sch. of Hygiene and Tropical Medicine. MB 1946, MD 1952; DPH 1952, DIH 1952. MRCP 1969, FRCP 1975; FFCM 1972; Hon. FFPH (Hon. FFPHM 1991). Sqdn Ldr RAF, Med. Branch, 1947–51; Dep. MOH, Metropolitan Borough of Hampstead, 1952–54; Asst Principal MO, LCC, 1954–58; Sen. Lectr and Hon. Consultant in Social Medicine, Royal Free Hosp. Sch., Royal Free Hosp. and London Sch. of Hygiene and Tropical Medicine, 1958–64; Sen. Lectr in Social Medicine, LSHTM, 1964–67; Reader in Public Health, Univ. of London, 1967–71; Dir, Health Services Res. Unit, and Prof. of Social Medicine, Univ. of Kent, 1971–83, jtly with Specialist in Community Medicine (Epidemiology and Health Services Res.), SE Thames RHA, 1980–83. Chm., Soc. of Social Medicine, 1982–83. Academic Registrar, Faculty of Community Medicine, Royal Colls of Physicians, 1972–77. Jt Editor, British Jl of Preventive and Social Medicine, 1969–72. *Publications:* (jtly) Public Health and Social Services, 4th edn 1957, 6th edn 1965; (ed jtly) Management and the Health Services, 1971; (jtly) Physiotherapy in the Community, 1977; (jtly) Physically Disabled People Living at Home, 1978; (ed jtly) Recalling the Medical Officer of Health, 1987; (jtly) Health Services for Adults with Physical Disabilities, 1990; The Genesis of the Faculty of Community Medicine, 1997; A Chronology of State Medicine, Public Health, Welfare and Related Services in Britain 1066–1999, 2000; contribs to BMJ, Lancet, Internat. Jl of Epidemiology. *Recreations:* enjoying gardens, genealogy, reading, listening to music. *Address:* 2 Bridge Down, Bridge, Canterbury, Kent CT4 5AZ. *T:* (01227) 830233. *Club:* Royal Society of Medicine. *Died 25 Jan. 2015.*

WASTELL, Cyril Gordon, CBE 1975; Secretary General of Lloyd's, 1967–76; *b* 10 Jan. 1916; *s* of Arthur Edward Wastell and Lilian Wastell; *m* 1947, Margaret Lilian (*née* Moore); one *d*. *Educ:* Brentwood Sch., Essex. Joined Staff of Corporation of Lloyd's, 1932; apart from war service (Lieut Royal Corps of Signals), 1939–46, progressed through various depts and positions at Lloyd's, until retirement. *Recreations:* reading, gardening under duress, walking, crosswords, various trivial pursuits. *Died 22 Dec. 2013.*

WATERFORD, 8th Marquess of, *cr* 1789; **John Hubert de la Poer Beresford;** Baron Le Poer, 1375; Baronet, 1668; Viscount Tyrone, Baron Beresford, 1720; Earl of Tyrone, 1746; Baron Tyrone (Great Britain), 1786; *b* 14 July 1933; *er s* of 7th Marquess and Juliet Mary (who *m* 2nd, 1946, Lieut-Colonel John Silcock), 2nd *d* of late David Lindsay; *S* father, 1934; *m* 1957, Lady Caroline Wyndham-Quin, *yr d* of 6th Earl of Dunraven and Mount-Earl, CB, CBE, MC; three *s* one *d*. *Educ:* Eton. Lieut, RHG Reserve. *Heir:* *s* Earl of Tyrone, *b* 23 March 1958. *Address:* Curraghmore, Portlaw, Co. Waterford, Ireland. *T:* (51) 387102, 08725 50054, *Fax:* (51) 387481. *Club:* White's. *Died 11 Feb. 2015.*

WATERHOUSE, Sir Ronald (Gough), GBE 2002; Kt 1978; Judge of the High Court of Justice, Family Division, 1978–88, Queen's Bench Division, 1988–96; *b* Holywell, Flintshire, 8 May 1926; *s* of late Thomas Waterhouse, CBE, and Doris Helena Waterhouse (*née* Gough); *m* 1960, Sarah Selina, *d* of late Captain E. A. Ingram and Diana Mary Ingram (*née* Leigh-Bennett); one *s* two *d*. *Educ:* Holywell Grammar Sch.; St John's Coll., Cambridge (McMahon Schol., 1949; BA 1949; MA, LLB 1951; LLM 1985). RAFVR, 1944–48. Pres., Cambridge Union Soc., 1950. Called to Bar, Middle Temple, 1952 (Harmsworth Schol.), Bencher, 1977, Treas., 1995; Wales and Chester Circuit, Leader, 1978; QC 1969; a Recorder of the Crown Court, 1972–77; Presiding Judge, Wales and Chester Circuit, 1980–84; a Judge, Employment Appeal Tribunal, 1979–87. Mem. Bar Council, 1961–65. Deputy Chairman: Cheshire QS, 1964–71; Flintshire QS, 1966–71. Contested (Lab) West Flintshire, 1959. Chairman: Inter-departmental Cttee of Inquiry on Rabies, 1970; Cttees of Investigation for GB and England and Wales, under Agricultural Mkting Act, 1971–78; Local Govt Boundary Commn for Wales, 1974–78; Tribunal of Inquiry into Child Abuse in N Wales Children's Homes, 1996–2000; Ind. Supervisory Authy for Hunting, 2000–05. Pres., CAB, Royal Courts of Justice, 1992–98 (Chm., 1981–92). A Vice-Pres., Zoological Soc. of London, 1981–84 and 1992–93 (Mem. Council, 1972–89, 1991–93). President: Llangollen Internat. Musical Eisteddfod, 1994–97; St John's Wood Soc., 1994–96. Hon. LLD Wales, 1986. *Recreations:* music, reading. *Address:* Greystone House, Walford, Ross-on-Wye, Herefordshire HR9 5RJ. *Clubs:* Garrick, Pilgrims. *Died 8 May 2011.*

WATERLOW, Sir (James) Gerard, 4th Bt *cr* 1930; former management consultant; *b* 3 Sept. 1939; *s* of Sir Thomas Gordon Waterlow, 3rd Bt, CBE and Helen Elizabeth (*d* 1970), *yr d* of Gerard A. H. Robinson; *S* father, 1982; *m* 1965, Diana Suzanne, *yr d* of Sir Thomas Skyrme, KCVO, CB, CBE, TD and Hon. (Barbara) Suzanne Lyle, *yr d* of 1st Baron Lyle of Westbourne; one *s* one *d*. *Educ:* Marlborough Coll.; Trinity Coll., Cambridge. *Recreations:* tennis, bridge. *Heir:* *s* (Thomas) James Waterlow [*b* 20 March 1970; *m* 1999, Theresa, *y d* of Captain Francis Walsh; two *d*]. *Address:* Rushall Lodge, Pewsey, Wilts SN9 6EN. *Club:* Lansdowne. *Died 8 Oct. 2013.*

WATERPARK, 7th Baron *cr* 1792; **Frederick Caryll Philip Cavendish;** Bt 1755; Director, D. T. Dobie (East Africa) Ltd, 1995–2000; *b* 6 Oct. 1926; *s* of Brig.-General Frederick William Laurence Sheppard Hart Cavendish, CMG, DSO (*d* 1931) and Enid, Countess of Kenmare (she *m* 3rd, 1933, as his 3rd wife, 1st Viscount Furness, who *d* 1940; 4th, as his 2nd wife, 6th Earl of Kenmare), *d* of Charles Lindeman, Sydney, New South Wales, and *widow* of Roderick Cameron, New York; *S* uncle, 1948; *m* 1951, Daniele, *e d* of Roger Guirche, Paris; one *s* two *d*. *Educ:* Eton; Royal Mil. Coll., Sandhurst (Medal of Honour). Lieut, 4th and 1st Bn Grenadier Guards, 1944–46. Served as Assistant District Commandant Kenya Police Reserve, 1952–55, during Mau Mau Rebellion. Man. Dir, Spartan Air Services, 1955–60; Dep. Chm. and Man. Dir, CSE International Ltd, 1984–90; Dep. Chm., 1984–90, Chief Exec., 1990, CSE Aviation Ltd; Director: Handley Page Ltd, 1968–70; Airborne Group plc, 1990–93. Trustee, RAF Mus., 1994–2000. Founder Mem., Air Sqdn. *Heir:* *s* Hon. Roderick Alexander Cavendish [*b* 10 Oct. 1959; *m* 1989, Anne, *d* of Hon. Luke Asquith; two *s*]. *Club:* Cavalry and Guards. *Died 16 Oct. 2013.*

WATERS, David Watkin; Lt-Comdr RN; Deputy Director, National Maritime Museum, 1971–78; *b* 2 Aug. 1911; *s* of Eng. Lt William Waters, RN, and Jessie Rhena (*née* Whitemore); *m* 1946, Hope Waters (*née* Pritchard) (*d* 2009); one step *d* (and one step *s* decd). *Educ:* RN Coll., Dartmouth. Joined RN, 1925; Cadet and Midshipman, HMS Barham, 1929; specialised in Aviation (Pilot), 1935. Served War of 1939–45: Fleet Air Arm, Malta (PoW, Italy, Germany, 1940–45). Admty, 1946–50; retd, 1950. Admty Historian (Defence of Shipping), 1946–60; Head of Dept of Navigation and Astronomy, Nat. Maritime Museum, 1960–76, and Sec. of Museum, 1968–71. Pres., British Soc. for Hist. of Sci., 1976–78 (Vice-Pres., 1972–74, 1978–81). Vis. Prof. of History, Simon Fraser Univ., Burnaby, BC, 1978; Regents' Prof., UCLA, 1979; Caird Res. Fellow, Nat. Maritime Museum, 1979–83; Alexander O. Victor Res. Fellow, John Carter Brown Library, Brown Univ., Providence, RI, 1990. Chm., Japan Animal Welfare Soc., 1972–80. Gold Medal, Admiralty Naval History, 1936, and Special Award, 1946; FRHistS 1951; Fellow, Inst. Internacional da Cultura Portuguesa, 1966; FSA 1970. Hon. Fellow, Royal Inst. of Navigation, 1989 (Fellow 1959); Hon. Member: Scientific Instrument Soc., 1989; Acad. de Marinha Portuguesa, 1989; Soc. for Nautical Res., 1996. *Publications:* The True and Perfect Newes of Syr Francis Drake, 1955; (with F. Barley) Naval Staff History, Second World War, Defeat of the Enemy Attack on Shipping, 1939–1945, 1957, 2nd edn 1997; The Art of Navigation in England in Elizabethan and Early Stuart Times, 1958, 2nd edn 1978; The Sea—or Mariner's Astrolabe, 1966; The Rutter of the Sea, 1967; (with Hope Waters) The Saluki in History, Art, and Sport, 1969, 2nd edn 1984; (with G. P. B. Naish) The Elizabethan Navy and the Armada of Spain, 1975; Science and the Techniques of Navigation in the Renaissance, 1976; (with Thomas R. Adams) English Maritime Books relating to ships and their construction and operation at sea printed before 1801, 1995; contrib.: Jl RIN; RUSI; Mariners' Mirror; American Neptune; Jl RN Scientific Service; Jl British Soc. of History of Science; Navy International; Revista da Universidade de Coímbra. *Recreations:* maritime history, history of technology (medieval, Renaissance and Scientific Revolution, and Chinese sailing craft). *Address:* Gatekeeper's Lodge, Rhodes Road, Otahuna Valley, RD2 Christchurch, New Zealand. *Club:* English-Speaking Union. *Died 28 Nov. 2012.*

WATERSTONE, David George Stuart, CBE 1991; UK Chairman, Ansaldo Ltd, 1995–98; Chairman, ADAS Holdings Ltd, 1997–98; *b* 9 Aug. 1935; *s* of Malcolm Waterstone and Sylvia Sawday; *m* 1st, 1960, Dominique Viriot (marr. diss.); one *s* two *d*; 2nd, 1988, Sandra Packer (*née* Willey). *Educ:* Tonbridge; St Catharine's Coll., Cambridge (MA). HM Diplomatic Service, 1959–70; Sen. Exec., IRC, 1970–71; BSC, 1971–81: Board Mem., 1976–81; Man. Dir, Commercial, 1972–77; subseq. Executive Chairman, BSC Chemicals, 1977–81, and Redpath Dorman Long, 1977–81; Chief Exec., Welsh Develt Agency, 1983–90; Chief Exec., Energy and Technical Services Gp plc, 1990–95. Director: Portsmouth and Sunderland Newspapers, 1983–99; Hunting, 1995–2000; Precoat Internat., 1995–2003. Chm., Combined Heat and Power Assoc., 1993–95. *Publications:* (ed) Waste in Wales: a national resource, 2000; (ed) World Best Practice in Economic Development, 2002. *Recreations:* sailing, walking, painting, furniture making. *Address:* 1 Prior Park Buildings, Prior Park Road, Bath BA2 4NP. *T:* (01225) 427346. *Died 1 Oct. 2014.*

WATKINS, David John; Director, Council for the Advancement of Arab-British Understanding, 1983–90 (Joint Chairman, 1979–83; Hon. Treasurer, 1983–2004); *b* 27 Aug. 1925; *s* of Thomas George Watkins and Alice Elizabeth (*née* Allen); unmarried. *Educ:* S Bristol Central and

Merrywood Grammar Sch., Bristol. National Service, RAF, 1945–48. Member: Bristol City Council, 1954–57; Bristol Educn Cttee, 1958–66; Labour Party, 1950–; UNITE (formerly Amalgamated Engineering Union, later AEEU, then AMICUS), 1942–; Sec., AEU Gp of MPs, 1968–77. Contested Bristol NW, 1964. MP (Lab) Consett, 1966–83; Mem., House of Commons Chairmen's Panel, 1978–83. Sponsored Employers Liability (Compulsory Insurance) Act, 1969, and Industrial Common Ownership Act, 1976 as Private Member's Bills; introd Drained Weight Bill, 1973, and Consett Steel Works Common Ownership Bill, 1980. Chm., Labour Middle East Council, 1974–83; Treas., Internat. Co-ord. Cttee, UN Meeting of Non-Governmental Organisations on Question of Palestine, 1985–90. Dir, 1987–2004, Chm., 1990–2004, Courtlands Estate (Richmond) Ltd (Vice Chm., 1988–90). Hon. Treas., Med. Aid for Palestinians, 1995–2004 (Trustee, 1984–2004). *Publications:* Labour and Palestine, 1975; Industrial Common Ownership, 1978; The World and Palestine, 1980; The Exceptional Conflict, 1984; Palestine: an inescapable duty, 1992; Seventeen Years in Obscurity, 1996; Class and Consequence, 2007. *Recreations:* reading, listening to music, study of stroke rehabilitation. *Address:* 1 Carisbrooke House, Courtlands, Sheen Road, Richmond, Surrey TW10 5AZ. *Club:* Royal Commonwealth Society. *Died 23 Aug. 2013.*

WATKINS, Prof. (Eric) Sidney, OBE 2002; MD; FRCSE; President, FIA Institute for Motor Sport Safety, since 2004; Consultant Neurosurgeon, Princess Grace Hospital, since 1999; Professor of Neurosurgery, University of London, 1972–93, then Emeritus; *b* 6 Sept. 1928; *s* of Wallace and Jessica Watkins; *m* Susan; four *s* two *d. Educ:* Prescot Grammar Sch.; Univ. of Liverpool Med. Sch. (BSc Hons Neurophysiol. 1949; MB ChB 1952; MD 1956); MD New York 1962. FRCSE 1969. House physician and house surgeon, Walton and Stanley Hosps, Liverpool, 1952–53; Capt., RAMC, 1953–56; Specialist in Physiol., W African Council for Med. Res., Lagos, 1954–56; Registrar in Gen. Surgery and Orthopaedic Surgery, Weston-super-Mare Gen. Hosp. and Winford Orthopaedic Hosp., Bristol, 1956–58; Registrar in Neurosurgery, Radcliffe Infirmary, Oxford, 1958–61; MRC Res. Fellow, Middx and Maida Vale Hosp., 1961–62; Prof. of Neurosurgery, SUNY, Upstate Med. Center, 1962–70; Consultant Neurosurgeon, London Hosp., 1970–93. Consultant Surgeon, Formula One Constructors' Assoc., 1978–2004. Pres., Med., Safety and Res. Commns, Fedn Internat. de l'Automobile (World Governing Body of Motor Sport), 1981–2004. Hon. FRCS 2009. Hon. DSc Liverpool, 2004. Prince Michael of Kent RAC Centennial Award for Contributions to Motor Sport, 1998. *Publications:* Stereotaxic Anatomy of Thalmus and Basal Ganglia, 1969; Stereotaxic Anatomy of Cerebellum and Brain Stem, 1976; Life at the Limit: triumph and tragedy in Formula One, 1996; Beyond the Limit, 2001. *Recreation:* fly fishing. *Address:* FIA Institute for Motor Sport Safety, 8 Place de la Concorde, 75008 Paris, France. *Clubs:* Athenæum, Royal Automobile. *Died 12 Sept. 2012.*

WATKINS, Rev. Gordon Derek; Secretary, London Diocesan Advisory Committee, 1984–94; *b* 16 July 1929; *s* of Clifford and Margaret Watkins; *m* 1957, Beryl Evelyn Whitaker. *Educ:* St Brendan's College, Clifton. Nat. Service, RAOC, 1947–49. Staff of W. D. & H. O. Wills, 1944–51; deacon 1953, priest 1954; Curate, Grafton Cathedral, NSW, 1953–56; Vicar of Texas, Qld, 1957–61; Curate, St Wilfrid's, Harrogate, 1961–63; Vicar of Upton Park, 1963–67; Rector: Great and Little Bentley, 1967–73; Great Canfield, 1973–78; Pastoral Sec., Dio. London, 1978–84; Vicar, St Martin-within-Ludgate, City and Dio. of London, 1984–89; Priest Vicar, Westminster Abbey, 1984–90; Priest in Ordinary to the Queen, 1984–96. Freeman, City of London, 1984. *Recreations:* reading, music, country life. *Address:* 21 Cramond Place, Dalgety Bay, Dunfermline, Fife KY11 9LS. *Club:* Royal Scots (Edinburgh). *Died 28 Oct. 2012.*

WATSON, (Daniel) Stewart, CB 1967; OBE 1958; *b* 30 Dec. 1911; *s* of Reverend Dr William Watson, DD, DLitt, and Mary Mackintosh Watson; *m* 1939, Isabel (*née* Gibson) (*d* 1991); one *s. Educ:* Robert Gordon's Coll.; Aberdeen University. Student Apprentice, British Thomson Houston, Rugby, 1933, Research Engr, 1936. Scientific Officer, Admiralty, 1938–; Dir, Admiralty Surface Weapons Establishment, 1961–68; Dep. Chief Scientist (Naval), MoD, 1968–72; Dir Gen. Establishments, Resources Programme A, MoD, 1972–73. *Publications:* contribs to IEEJ. *Recreations:* thoroughbred cars, caravanning. *Address:* 28 Longhope Drive, Wrecclesham, Farnham, Surrey GU10 4SN. *T:* (01252) 733126. *Died 15 March 2012.*

WATSON, Sir David (John), Kt 1998; Professor of Higher Education, University of Oxford, since 2010; Principal, Green Templeton College, Oxford, since 2010; *b* 22 March 1949; *s* of late Lewis James Watson and Berenice Nichols; *m* 1975, Betty Pinto Skolnick; one *s* one *d. Educ:* Cheshunt Grammar School; Eton College; Clare College, Cambridge (MA); Univ. of Pennsylvania (PhD). ITLM 1999; CCMI 2001; FHEA 2007; FCGI 2013; FSRHE 2013. Sen. Lectr, Principal Lectr in Humanities, Crewe and Alsager Coll. of Higher Educn, 1975–81; Dean, Modular Course, Asst Dir, Dep. Dir, Oxford Polytechnic, 1981–90; Dir, then Vice-Chancellor, and Prof. of Hist. of Ideas, Brighton Poly., later Univ. of Brighton, 1990–2005; Prof. of Higher Educn Mgt, Inst. of Educn, Univ. of London, 2005–10. Member: Council, CNAA, 1989–93 (Mem., 1977–93); PCFC, 1988–93; HEFCE, 1992–96; Paul Hamlyn Foundn Nat. Commn on Educn, 1991–93; Open Univ. Validation Bd, 1992–2001; Nat. Cttee of Inquiry into Higher Educn (Dearing Cttee), 1996–97; Council, ILT, 2000–02; Bd, QCA, 2003–09; Chairman: Univs Assoc. for Contg Educn, 1994–98; Steering Cttee for ESRC Teaching and Learning Prog., 1998–2003; SE England Cultural Consortium, 1999–2002; UUK Longer Term Strategy Gp, 1999–2005; Nat. Inquiry into Future of Lifelong Learning, 2007–09. Pres., SRHE, 2005–12. Trustee, Nuffield Foundn, 2005–. Chm., Brighton Fest. Soc., 2002–05. Hon. RCM 2007. Nat. Teaching Fellowship, 2008. Hon. Fellow, QMUL, 2010. DUniv: Open, 2002; Oxford Brookes, 2003; Hon. DSocSc Southampton, 2004; Hon. LLD Sussex, 2005; Hon. DEd Bath, 2005; Hon. DLitt: Manchester Metropolitan, 2006; Brighton, 2006; Keele, 2010. Times Higher Lifetime Achievement Award, 2009. *Publications:* Margaret Fuller, 1988; Managing the Modular Course, 1989; (jtly) Developing Professional Education, 1992; Arendt, 1992; (jtly) Managing the University Curriculum, 1994; (jtly) Continuing Education in the Mainstream, 1996; (jtly) Lifelong Learning and the University, 1998; Managing Strategy, 2000; (jtly) New Directions in Professional Higher Education, 2000; (jtly) Higher Education and the Lifecourse, 2003; (jtly) Managing Institutional Self-study, 2005; Managing Civic and Community Engagement, 2007; (jtly) The Dearing Report: ten years on, 2007; The Question of Morale, 2009; (jtly) Learning Through Life, 2009; (jtly) The Engaged University, 2011; (jtly) Learning Transitions in Higher Education, 2013; The Question of Conscience, 2014; papers on history of American and British ideas, higher education policy. *Recreations:* cricket, tennis, music (piano). *Address:* Green Templeton College, Woodstock Road, Oxford OX2 6HG. *T:* (01865) 274775. *Died 8 Feb. 2015.*

WATSON, Sir Duncan (Amos), Kt 1993; CBE 1986; Principal Assistant Treasury Solicitor, Common Law, 1978–86; Chairman, Executive Council, Royal National Institute for the Blind, 1975–90; *b* 10 May 1926; *m* 1st, 1954, Mercia Casey (*d* 2002), Auckland, NZ; 2nd, 2007, Anthea Nicholson-Cole. *Educ:* Worcester College for the Blind; St Edmund Hall, Oxford (BA). Solicitor. Chm., Access Cttee for England, 1989–93; Pres., World Blind Union, 1988–92. *Died 21 April 2015.*

WATSON, Richard (Eagleson Gordon) Burges, CMG 1985; HM Diplomatic Service, retired; Ambassador to Nepal, 1987–90; *b* 23 Sept. 1930; *er s* of late Harold Burges Watson and Marjorie Eleanor (*née* Gordon); *m* 1966, Ann Rosamund Clarke; two *s* three *d. Educ:* King Edward VI Sch., Bury St Edmunds; St John's Coll., Cambridge. RA, 1948–50. Joined HM Foreign (subseq. Diplomatic) Service, 1954; Tokyo, 1954–60; FO, 1960–63; Bamako (Mali), 1963–66; British Delegn to OECD, 1966–69; FCO, 1969–71; Vis. Student, Woodrow Wilson Sch., Princeton, 1971–72; Tokyo, 1972–76; Brussels, 1976–78; FCO, 1978–81; Foundn for Internat. Research and Studies, Florence, 1981–82; FCO, 1982–83; Minister (Commercial) and Consul-Gen., Milan, 1983–86.

Recreations: travel, bridge. *Address:* Highfield House, Gloucester Road, Painswick GL6 6QN. *T:* (01452) 814763. *Club:* Hurlingham. *Died 2 June 2014.*

WATSON, Stewart; *see* Watson, D. S.

WATSON, Victor Hugo, CBE 1987; DL; *b* 26 Sept. 1928; *s* of Norman Victor and Ruby Ernestine Watson; *m* 1952, Sheila May Bryan; two *d. Educ:* Clare Coll., Cambridge (MA). Served Royal Engineers (2nd Lieut), 1946–48. Joined John Waddington Ltd, 1951; Chm., 1977–93. Director: Leeds & Holbeck Building Soc., 1985–99 (Pres., 1989–91); Stylo PLC, 1993–99; Topps Tiles PLC, 1997–2009; Black i Ltd, 1998–2003; Swivel Technologies, 2001–04. President: Royal Warrant Holders Assoc., 1983–84; Inst. of Packaging, 1984–2004. DL West Yorks, 1991. Hon. LLD Leeds, 1994; DUniv Leeds Metropolitan, 2001. *Recreations:* music, golf. *Address:* 1 Lodge Court, Hollins Hall, Killinghall, Harrogate HG3 2WX. *Died 25 Feb. 2015.*

WATT, Very Rev. Alfred Ian; Dean of the United Diocese of St Andrews, Dunkeld and Dunblane, 1989–98, then Dean Emeritus; *b* 20 March 1934; *m* 1959, Rita McGill; one *s* two *d. Educ:* Edinburgh Theol Coll. Deacon, 1960, priest 1961, Diocese of Brechin; Curate, St Paul's Cathedral, Dundee, 1960–63; Precentor, 1963–66; Rector of Arbroath, 1966–69; Provost of St Ninian's Cathedral, Perth, 1969–82; Canon, 1982–89; Rector, St Paul's, Kinross, 1982–95. Convenor, Mission Bd of General Synod, 1982–87. *Address:* 33 Stirling Road, Milnathort, Kinross KY13 9XS. *Died 2 July 2012.*

WATT, Prof. Donald C.; *see* Cameron Watt.

WATT, Hamish; writer, politician; Rector of Aberdeen University, 1985–88; *b* 27 Dec. 1925; *s* of Wm Watt and Caroline C. Allan; *m* 1948, Mary Helen Grant (marr. diss. 1989; she *d* 2007); one *s* two *d*; *m* 2013, Sara Isabella Ross. *Educ:* Keith Grammar Sch.; St Andrews Univ. Engaged in farming (dairy and sheep), until 2007; sometime company director, quarries. Contested (C), Caithness, 1966; contested (SNP): Banff, 1970; Moray, 1983. MP (SNP) Banff, Feb. 1974–1979. Regional and Dist Councillor (SNP), Moray, 1985–90 (Chm., Educn Cttee, 1986–90). Columnist, after-dinner speaker, story writer. JP Moray, 1984. Hon. LLD Aberdeen, 1988. *Address:* Jorglyn, Richmond Place, Portgordon, Buckie, Banffshire AB56 5QX. *T:* (01542) 832591. *Clubs:* Farmers, Whitehall Court. *Died 12 April 2014.*

WAY, Col Anthony Gerald, MC 1944; Member, HM Body Guard of the Honourable Corps of Gentlemen at Arms, 1972–90 (Standard Bearer, 1988–90); *b* 5 Nov. 1920; *s* of Roger Hill Way and Brenda Lathbury; *m* 1st, 1946, Elizabeth Leslie Richmond (*d* 1986); one *s* one *d*; 2nd, 1989, Mrs Anthea Methven, St Martin's Abbey, by Perth. *Educ:* Stowe Sch.; RMC Sandhurst. Joined Grenadier Guards, 1939, 2nd Lieut; served in N Africa and Italy; CO, 3rd Bn, 1960–61; Lt-Col comdg Grenadier Guards, 1961–64. *Recreations:* shooting, gardening. *Address:* Kincairney, Dunkeld, Perthshire PH8 0RE. *T:* (01738) 710304. *Died 4 Jan. 2012.*

WEBB, Colin Thomas; Editor-in-Chief, Press Association, 1986–94 (Director, 1989–96; General Manager, 1994–96); *b* 26 March 1939; *e s* of late William Thomas and Ada Alexandra Webb; *m* 1970, Margaret Frances, *y d* of late Maurice George and Joan Rowden Cheshire; two *s* one *d. Educ:* Portsmouth Grammar School. Reporter, Portsmouth Evening News, Surrey Mirror, Press Assoc., Daily Telegraph, The Times; Royal Army Pay Corps Short Service Commission (to Captain), 1960–64; Home News Editor, The Times, 1969–74; Editor, Cambridge Evening News, 1974–82; Dep. Editor, The Times, 1982–86; Journalist Dir, Times Newspaper Holdings, 1983–86. Member: Core Cttee, British Executive Internat. Press Inst., 1984–96; Council, Commonwealth Press Union, 1985–96; Lord Chancellor's Adv. Bd on Family Law, 1997–2001; Consultative Council, 2000–08, Adv. Council, 2006–11, BBFC. Chair, UK Coll. of Family Mediators, 2003–06. Nat. Trustee, Lloyds TSB Foundn for England and Wales, 2000–05. Gov., Univ. of Portsmouth, 2001–08 (Hon. Fellow, 1991). Lay Reader, Dio. Chichester, 2005–10. *Publications:* (co-author with The Times News Team) Black Man in Search of Power, 1968. *Recreations:* family, walking, history books. *Address:* Fairfield House, Pine Grove, West Broyle, Chichester, West Sussex PO19 3PN. *T:* (01243) 771870. *Died 18 May 2013.*

WEBB, Prof. Joseph Ernest, PhD (London) 1944, DSc (London) 1949; CBiol, FSB; FLS; FZS; Professor of Zoology, 1960–80, and Vice-Principal, 1976–80, Westfield College, University of London, then Emeritus Professor; *b* 22 March 1915; *s* of Joseph Webb and Constance Inman Webb (*née* Hickox); *m* 1940, Gwenlilian Clara Coldwell (*d* 1994); three *s. Educ:* Rutlish School; Birkbeck College, London (BSc 1940). FZS 1943; CBiol, FSB (FIBiol 1963); FLS 1972. Research Entomologist and Parasitologist at The Cooper Technical Bureau, Berkhamsted, Herts, 1940–46; Lecturer, Univ. of Aberdeen, 1946–48; Senior Lecturer, 1948–50, Professor of Zoology, 1950–60, University Coll., Ibadan, Nigeria. Hon. Fellow, QMW (formerly Westfield Coll.), 1986. *Publications:* (jointly): Guide to Invertebrate Animals, 1975, 2nd edn 1978; Guide to Living Mammals, 1977, 2nd edn 1979; Guide to Living Reptiles, 1978; Guide to Living Birds, 1979; Guide to Living Fishes, 1981; Guide to Living Amphibians, 1981; various on insect physiology, insecticides, systematics, populations, tropical ecology, marine biology and sedimentology. *Recreations:* art, music, photography, gardening. *Address:* 43 Hill Top, NW11 6EA. *T:* (020) 8458 2571. *Club:* Athenæum. *Died 2 Dec. 2011.*

WEBB, Michael Alfred Healey, OBE 2002; Consultant in Occupational Medicine; Deputy Chief Commander, St John Ambulance, 1999–2002; *b* 10 Oct. 1934; *s* of Alfred Webb and Lily Margaret Webb (*née* Beeson); *m* 1962, Shirley Ann Parsons; one *s* one *d. Educ:* Sir Walter St John's Grammar Sch.; King's Coll., London; King's Coll. Hosp. Med. Sch. MRCS, LRCP 1961; DIH 1978; FFOM 1996. Various posts as occupational health physician to: EMAS, 1973–78; Commonwealth Smelting Ltd, 1978–81; Post Office, 1981–94. Med. Dir, St John Ambulance Assoc., 1991–96; Dir-Gen., St John Ambulance, 1996–99. KStJ 1996. *Publications:* (jtly) First Aid Manual, 7th edn 1997. *Recreations:* gardening, home maintenance. *Address:* 48 Offington Avenue, Worthing, W Sussex BN14 9PJ. *Died 25 April 2015.*

WEBSTER, Derek Adrian, CBE 1979; Chairman and Editorial Director, Scottish Daily Record and Sunday Mail Ltd, 1974–86; *b* 24 March 1927; *s* of James Tulloch Webster and Isobel Webster; *m* 1966, Dorothy Frances Johnson; two *s* one *d. Educ:* St Peter's, Bournemouth. Served RN, 1944–48. Reporter, Western Morning News, 1943; Staff Journalist, Daily Mail, 1949–51; joined Mirror Group, 1952; Northern Editor, Daily Mirror, 1964–67; Editor, Daily Record, 1967–72; Director: Mirror Gp Newspapers, 1974–86; Clyde Cable Vision, 1983–87. Mem., Press Council, 1981–84 (Jt Vice-Chm., 1982–83). Vice-Chm., Age Concern (Scotland), 1977–83; Hon. Vice-Pres., Newspaper Press Fund, 1983–; Mem. Council, CPU, 1984–86. *Recreations:* travel, photography. *Address:* 6 Park Circus Place, Glasgow G3 6AN. *T:* (0141) 353 6330. *Died 27 Dec. 2013.*

WEBSTER, Michael George Thomas; Chairman, DRG plc (formerly Dickinson Robinson Group), 1985–87 (Director, 1976–87; Deputy Chairman, 1983–85); *b* 27 May 1920; *s* of late J. A. Webster, CB, DSO and Constance A. Webster, 2nd *d* of Richard and Lady Constance Combe; *m* 1947, Mrs Isabel Margaret Bucknill (*d* 2002), *d* of late Major J. L. Dent, DSO, MC; three *d. Educ:* Stowe; Magdalen Coll., Oxford (MA). Commnd Grenadier Guards, 1940–46: NW Europe Campaign, 1944–45 (despatches). Joined Watney Combe Reid & Co. Ltd, 1946; Chm., Watney Combe Reid, 1963–68; Watney Mann Ltd: Vice-Chm., 1965–70; Chm., 1970–72; Chm., Watney Mann & Truman Holdings, 1974; Director: Grand Metropolitan Ltd, 1972–74; National Provident Instn, 1973–85; Chm., Fitch Lovell PLC, 1977–83. Master of Brewers' Co., 1964–65; a Vice-Pres., The Brewers' Soc., 1975–. Gov., Gabbitas Truman & Thring, 1986–90 (Chm., Truman and Knightley Educnl Trust, 1985–87). Chm., Aldenham Sch. Governing Body, 1977–84. High Sheriff, Berks, 1971; DL Berks, 1975–90. *Recreations:* fishing, golf. *Clubs:* Cavalry and Guards, MCC. *Died 26 Oct. 2012.*

WEDDERBURN OF CHARLTON, Baron *cr* 1977 (Life Peer), of Highgate; **(Kenneth) William Wedderburn;** QC 1990; FBA 1981; Cassel Professor of Commercial Law, London School of Economics, University of London, 1964–92, then Professor Emeritus and Hon. Fellow; *b* 13 April 1927; *o s* of Herbert J. and Mabel Wedderburn, Deptford; *m* 1st, 1951, Nina Salaman (marr. diss. 1962); one *s* two *d*; 2nd, 1962, Dorothy E. Cole (marr. diss. 1969); 3rd, 1969, Frances Ann Knight; one *s*. *Educ:* Aske's Hatcham School; Whitgift School; Queens' College, Cambridge (MA 1951; LLB 1949; George Long Prize for Jurisprudence; Chancellor's Medal for English Law). Royal Air Force, 1949–51. Called to the Bar, Middle Temple, 1953, Bencher, 2008. Fellow, 1952–64, Tutor, 1957–60, Hon. Fellow, 1997, Clare College, Cambridge; Asst Lectr, 1953–55, Lectr 1955–64, Faculty of Law, Cambridge University. Visiting Professor: UCLA Law Sch., 1967; Harvard Law Sch., 1969–70. Staff Panel Mem., Civil Service Arbitration Tribunal; Chm., Independent Review Cttee, 1976–; Mem., Cttee on Industrial Democracy, 1976–77. Independent Chm., London and Provincial Theatre Councils, 1973–93. Hon. Pres., Industrial Law Soc., 1997–. Hon. Fellow, Goldsmiths Coll., Univ. of London, 2009. Gen. Editor, Modern Law Review, 1971–88; Mem. Editl Bd, Internat. Labour Law Reports, 1975–. Hon. Doctor of Jurisprudence, Pavia, 1987; Hon. Doctor of Econs, Siena, 1991; Hon. LLD Stockholm, 1995. *Publications:* The Worker and the Law, 1965, 3rd edn 1986; Cases and Materials on Labour Law, 1967; (with P. Davies) Employment Grievances and Disputes Procedures in Britain, 1969; (ed) Contracts, Sutton and Shannon, 1956, 2nd edn 1963; (Asst Editor) Torts, Clerk and Lindsell, 1969, 1975, 1982, 1989, 1995, 2000; (ed with B. Aaron) Industrial Conflict, 1972; (with S. Sciarra *et al*) Democrazia Politica e Democrazia Industriale, 1978; (ed with Folke Schmidt) Discrimination in Employment, 1978; (with R. Lewis and J. Clark) Labour Law and Industrial Relations, 1983; (ed with W. T. Murphy) Labour, Law and the Community, 1983; (with S. Ghimpu and B. Veneziani) Diritto del Lavoro in Europa, 1987; Social Charter, European Company and Employment Rights, 1990; Employment Rights in Britain and Europe, 1991; (with M. Rood *et al*) Labour Law in the post-Industrial Era, 1994; Labour Law and Freedom, 1995; I Diritti del Lavoro, 1998; articles in legal and other jls. *Recreation:* Charlton Athletic Football Club. *Address:* 29 Woodside Avenue, N6 4SP. *T:* (020) 8444 8472. *Died 9 March 2012.*

WEDDERBURN, Prof. Dorothy Enid Cole; Senior Research Fellow, Imperial College, London, 1981–2003; Principal, Royal Holloway and Bedford New College, 1985–90, and a Pro-Vice-Chancellor, 1986–88, University of London; *b* 18 Sept. 1925; *d* of Frederick C. Barnard and Ethel C. Barnard; *m* 1st, 1947, William Alan Cole (marr. diss. 1960); 2nd, 1962, Kenneth William Wedderburn (later Baron Wedderburn of Charlton, QC, FBA) (marr. diss. 1969; he *d* 2012). *Educ:* Walthamstow High Sch. for Girls; Girton Coll., Cambridge (MA). Research Officer, subseq. Sen. Res. Officer, Dept of Applied Economics, Cambridge, 1950–65; Imperial College of Science and Technology: Lectr in Industrial Sociology, 1965–70, Reader, 1970–77, Prof., 1977–81; Dir, Industrial Sociol. Unit, 1973–81; Head, Dept of Social and Economic Studies, 1978–81; Principal, Bedford Coll., 1981–85. Mem. Court, Univ. of London, 1981–90. Vis. Prof., Sloan Sch. of Management, MIT, 1969–70. Mem. SSRC, 1976–82; Chm., SERC/SSRC Jt Cttee, 1980–82. Chm., Cttee of Inquiry into Women Imprisonment, Prison Reform Trust, 1998–2000. Member: Govt Cttee on the Pay and Condition of Nurses, 1974–75; (part-time), Royal Commn on the Distribution of Income and Wealth, 1974–78; Council, Advisory Conciliation and Arbitration Service, 1976–82; Cttee of Vice-Chancellors and Principals, 1988–90; Bd, Anglo-German Foundn, 1987–2004; Bd of Governors, London Guildhall Univ. (formerly City of London Polytechnic), 1989–99; Council, Loughborough Univ., 1990–93; Court, City Univ., 1992–; Council, Goldsmiths Coll., London Univ., 1993–2000. Mem., Kensington, Chelsea and Westminster DHA, 1993–2002. Hon. Pres., Fawcett Soc., 1986–2002. Hon. Fellow: Ealing Coll. of Higher Educn, 1985; RHBNC, 1991; Goldsmiths Coll., London Univ., 2001; Hon. FIC 1986. Hon. DLitt: Warwick, 1984; Loughborough, 1989; DUniv Brunel, 1990; Hon. LLD Cambridge, 1991; Hon. DSc City, 1991; Hon. DSocSc Southampton, 1999; Hon. PhD London Guildhall, 2000. *Publications:* White Collar Redundancy, 1964; Redundancy and the Railwayman, 1964; Enterprise Planning for Change, 1968; (with J. E. G. Utting) The Economic Circumstances of Old People, 1962; (with Peter Townsend) The Aged in the Welfare State, 1965; (jtly) Old Age in Three Industrial Societies, 1968; (with Rosemary Crompton) Workers' Attitudes and Technology, 1972; (ed) Poverty, Inequality and Class Structure, 1974; Justice for Women: the case for reform, 2000; contrib. Jl of Royal Statistical Soc.; Sociological Review; New Society, etc. *Recreations:* politics, cooking. *Address:* Flat 5, 65 Ladbroke Grove, W11 2PD. *Died 20 Sept. 2012.*

WEDDERSPOON, Very Rev. Alexander Gillan; Dean of Guildford, 1987–2001, then Emeritus; *b* 3 April 1931; *s* of Rev. Robert John Wedderspoon and Amy Beatrice Woolley; *m* 1968, Judith Joyce Wynne Plumptre; one *s* one *d*. *Educ:* Westminster School; Jesus Coll., Oxford (MA, BD); Cuddesdon Theological Coll. Nat. Service, 1949–51; commnd, RA. Ordained deacon 1961, priest 1962; Curate, Kingston Parish Church, 1961–63; Lectr in Religious Education, Univ. of London, 1963–66; Education Adviser, C of E Schools Council, 1966–69; Sec. of Commn on Religious Education, 1966–69; Priest in charge, St Margaret's, Westminster, 1969–70; Canon Residentiary, 1970–87, Canon Treasurer, 1980–85, Winchester Cathedral. *Publications:* A City Set on a Hill: a selection of sermons, 2001. *Recreations:* walking, travel. *Address:* 1 Ellery Close, Cranleigh GU6 8DF. *Died 10 June 2014.*

WEDGWOOD, 4th Baron *cr* 1942, of Barlaston; **Piers Anthony Weymouth Wedgwood;** *b* 20 Sept. 1954; *s* of 3rd Baron Wedgwood and of Lady Wedgwood (Jane Weymouth, *d* of W. J. Poulton, Kenjockety, Molo, Kenya); *S* father, 1970; *m* 1985, Mary Regina Margaret Kavanagh Quinn, *d* of late Judge Edward Thomas Quinn and of Helen Marie Buchanan Quinn of Philadelphia; one *d*. *Educ:* Marlborough College; RMA Sandhurst. Royal Scots, 1973–80. GSM for N Ireland, 1976. Dir, Waterford Wedgwood, 2000–09. Trustee, Wedgwood Mus., 2010–. Freeman, City of London, 2006. Hon. DLitt Chicago, 2000; DUniv Staffordshire, 2009. *Heir: cousin* Antony John Wedgwood [*b* 31 Jan. 1944; *m* 1970, Angela Margaret Mary Page; one *s* two *d*]. *Address:* WWRD, Wedgwood Drive, Barlaston, Stoke-on-Trent, Staffordshire ST12 9ER. *Died 29 Jan. 2014.*

WEEKES, Rt Rev. Ambrose Walter Marcus, CB 1970; FKC; Assistant Bishop, Diocese in Europe, since 1988; *b* 25 April 1919; *s* of Lt-Comdr William Charles Tinnoth Weekes, DSO, RNVR, and Ethel Sarah Weekes, JP. *Educ:* Cathedral Choir Sch., Rochester; Sir Joseph Williamson's Sch., Rochester; King's Coll., London (Plumptre prize, Barry prize; AKC 1941, FKC 1972); Scholae Cancellarii, Lincoln. Asst Curate, St Luke's, Gillingham, Kent, 1942–44; Chaplain, RNVR, 1944–46, RN 1946–72; HMS: Ganges, 1946–48; Ulster, 1948–49; Triumph, 1949–51; Royal Marines, Deal, 1951–53; 45 Commando, RM, 1953–55; HMS: Ganges, 1955–56; St Vincent, 1956–58; Tyne, 1958–60; Ganges, 1960–62; 40 Commando, RM, 1962–63; MoD, 1963–65; HMS: Eagle, 1965–66; Vernon, 1966–67; Terror, and Staff of Comdr Far East Fleet, 1967–68; HMS Mercury, 1968–69; Chaplain of the Fleet and Archdeacon for the Royal Navy, 1969–72; QHC, 1969–72; Chaplain of St Andrew, Tangier, 1972–73; Dean of Gibraltar, 1973–77; Assistant Bishop, Diocese of Gibraltar, 1977, until creation of new diocese, 1980; Suffragan Bishop of Gibraltar in Europe, 1980–86; Dean, Pro-Cathedral of the Holy Trinity, Brussels, 1980–86; Hon. Asst Bishop of Rochester, 1986–88; Hon. Canon of Rochester Cathedral, 1986–88; Chaplain at Montreux, Switzerland, 1988–92. Freeman, City of London, 2000. *Recreations:* yachting, music. *Address:* Charterhouse, Charterhouse Square, EC1M 6AN. *Club:* MCC. *Died 24 April 2012.*

WEEKES, Mark K.; *see* Kinkead-Weekes.

WEIDENBAUM, Murray Lew, PhD; Hon. Chairman, Weidenbaum Center on the Economy, Government and Public Policy, since 2001; Mallinckrodt Distinguished

University Professor, Washington University, since 1971; *b* 10 Feb. 1927; *m* 1954, Phyllis Green; one *s* two *d*. *Educ:* City Coll., NY; Columbia Univ. (MA); Princeton Univ. (PhD 1958). Fiscal Economist, Budget Bureau, Washington, 1949–57; Corp. Economist, Boeing Co., Seattle, 1958–63; Sen. Economist, Stanford Res. Inst., 1963–64; Washington University, St Louis, 1964–81, 1982–: Prof. and Chm. of Dept of Econs, 1966–69; Dir, 1975–81 and 1983–95, and Chm., 1995–2000, Center for the Study of Amer. Business (renamed Weidenbaum Center on the Economy, Govt and Public Policy, 2001). Asst Sec., Treasury Dept, Washington, 1969–71 (on secondment). Chairman: Council of Economic Advisers, USA, 1981–82; Congressional Commn on Trade Deficit, 1999–2000. Fellow, Amer. Acad. of Arts and Scis, 2007. Hon. LLD: Baruch Coll., 1981; Evansville, 1983. Mem., Free Market Hall of Fame, 1983. Nat. Order of Merit, Republic of France, 1985. *Publications:* Federal Budgeting, 1964; Economic Impact of the Vietnam War, 1967; Modern Public Sector, 1969; Economics of Peacetime Defense, 1974; Government-Mandated Price Increases, 1975; Business, Government, and the Public, 1977, 7th edn (as Business and Government in the Global Marketplace), 2004; The Future of Business Regulation, 1980; Rendezvous with Reality: the American economy after Reagan, 1988; Small Wars, Big Defense, 1992; The Bamboo Network, 1996; One-armed Economist, 2004; Advising Reagan: making economic policy 1981–82, 2005; The Competition of Ideas, 2008. *Address:* Weidenbaum Center, Washington University, Campus Box 1027, St Louis, MO 63130–4899, USA. *Died 20 March 2014.*

WEILER, Terence Gerard, OBE 1993; *b* 12 Oct. 1919; *s* of Charles and Clare Weiler; *m* 1952, Truda, *d* of Wilfrid and Mary Woollen; two *s* two *d*. *Educ:* Wimbledon College; University College, London. Army (RA and Queen's Royal Regiment, Chindit), 1940–45; UCL, 1937–39 and 1945–47; Home Office: Asst Principal, 1947; Principal, 1948; Asst Sec., 1958; Asst Under-Sec. of State, 1967–80; Mem., Prisons Board, 1962–66, 1971–80; Chm., Working Party: on Habitual Drunken Offenders, 1967–70; on Adjudication Procedures in Prisons, 1975. *Recreations:* cinema, crime fiction. *Address:* 4 Vincent Road, Isleworth, Middx TW7 4LT. *T:* (020) 8560 7822. *Died 28 Dec. 2011.*

WEINBERG, Prof. Felix Jiri, FRS 1983; CPhys, FInstP; Professor of Combustion Physics, 1967–93, then Emeritus, and Distinguished (formerly Senior) Research Fellow, since 1993, Imperial College, University of London (later Imperial College London); consultant to numerous industrial and government research organisations in UK and USA; *b* 2 April 1928; *s* of Victor Weinberg and Nelly Marie (*née* Altschul); *m* 1954, Jill Nesta (*née* Piggott) (*d* 2006); three *s*. *Educ:* Univ. of London (BSc ext.); Imperial Coll., London (PhD, DIC, DSc). Lecturer, 1956–60, Sen. Lectr, 1960–64, Reader in Combustion, 1964–67, Dept of Chemical Engrg and Chem. Technology, Imperial Coll., London. Director, Combustion Inst., 1978–88 (Chm. British Sect., 1975–80); Founder and first Chm., Combustion Physics Gp, Inst. of Physics, 1974–77, and Rep. on Watt Cttee on Energy, 1979–85; Mem. Council, Inst. of Energy, 1976–79; Mem., Royal Institution. Leverhulme Emeritus Fellow, 1994. FCGI 1998. Foreign Associate, Amer. NAE, 2001. DSc *hc* Israel Inst. of Technol., Haifa, 1990. Combustion Inst. Silver Combustion Medal 1972, Bernard Lewis Gold Medal 1980; Rumford Medal, Royal Soc., 1988; ItalGas Prize for Res. and Innovation in Energy Scis, Turin Acad., 1991; Lifetime Achievement Award, Inst. of Physics, 2005. *Publications:* Optics of Flames, 1963; Electrical Aspects of Combustion, 1969; (ed) Combustion Institute European Symposium, 1973; Advanced Combustion Methods, 1986; over 220 papers in Proc., jls and symposia of learned socs. *Recreations:* Eastern philosophies, travel, archery. *Address:* Department of Chemical Engineering, Imperial College London, SW7 2AZ. *T:* (020) 7594 5580; 59 Vicarage Road, SW14 8RY. *T:* (020) 8876 1540. *Died 5 Dec. 2012.*

WEIR, Rear-Adm. Alexander Fortune Rose, CB 1981; DL; Consultant, McMullen Associates (formerly Captain Colin McMullen and Associates), Marine Consultants, since 2006 (Senior Associate, 1982–2006); *b* 17 June 1928; *s* of late Comdr Patrick Wylie Rose Weir and Minna Ranken Forrester Weir (*née* Fortune); *m* 1953, Ann Ross Hamilton Crawford, Ardmore, Co. Londonderry; four *d*. *Educ:* Royal Naval Coll., Dartmouth. Cadet, 1945–46; Midshipman, 1946–47; Actg Sub-Lieut under trng, HMS Zephyr, Portland, 1947; Sub-Lieut professional courses, 1947–48; Sub-Lieut and Lieut, HMS Loch Arkaig, Londonderry Sqdn, 1949–51; ADC to Governor of Victoria, Aust., 1951–53; HMS Mariner, Fishery Protection Sqdn, Home waters and Arctic, 1953–54; qual. as Navigating Officer, 1954; HMS St Austell Bay, WI, Navigating Officer, 1955–56; HMS Wave, Fishery Protection Sqdn, Home, Arctic and Iceland, 1956–58; Lt-Comdr, advanced navigation course, 1958; Staff ND Officer, Flag Officer Sea Trng at Portland, Dorset, 1958–61; HMS Plymouth, Staff Officer Ops, 4th Frigate Sqdn, Far East Station, 1961–62; Comdr 1962; Trng Comdr, BRNC Dartmouth, 1962–64; Comd, HMS Rothesay, WI Station, 1965–66; Staff of C-in-C Portsmouth, Staff Officer Ops, 1966–68; 2nd in Comd and Exec. Officer, HMS Eagle, 1968–69; Captain 1969; jssc 1969–70; Pres., Far East Comd Midshipman's Bd, 1970; Asst Dir Naval Operational Requirements, MoD(N), 1970–72; Captain (F) 6th Frigate Sqdn (8 ships) and HMS Andromeda, 1972–74; NATO Def. Coll., Rome, 1974–75; ACOS Strategic Policy Requirements and Long Range Objectives, SACLANT, 1975–77; Captain HMS Bristol, 1977–78; Rear-Adm. 1978; Dep. Asst Chief of Staff (Ops) to SACEUR, 1978–81. FCMI (FBIM 1979); AVCM 1982. Member: Nautical Inst.; Royal Inst. of Navigation. Trustee: St James Trust, St Kew, 1995– (Chm., 1995–2003; Pres., 2003–); Nat. Lobster Hatchery, Padstow, 2003–11 (Chm., 2008–09); Bodmin Hosp., 2001–. President: TS St Petroc, Padstow, Sea Cadet Unit, 1995–; Delabole Br., Royal Naval Assoc., 1995–. Licensed Royal Naval Lay Reader, 1981; Licensed Lay Reader: Westbourne Parish, dio. Chichester, 1982; St Kew Parish, dio. Truro, 1984–; Warden of Readers, dio. Truro, 1995–2000; Lay Canon, Truro Cathedral, 1996–2001, then Emeritus. JP: Chichester, 1982–84; Bodmin, 1985–97; DL Cornwall, 1993. *Recreations:* sailing, shooting, golf. *Address:* Tipton, St Kew, Bodmin, Cornwall PL30 3ET. *T:* (01208) 841289. *E:* weiralec@madasafish.com. *Clubs:* Institute of Directors; Royal Yachting Association, Royal Naval Sailing Association. *Died 23 June 2014.*

WEITZ, Dr Bernard George Felix, OBE 1965; DSc; MRCVS; FSB; Chief Scientist, Ministry of Agriculture, Fisheries and Food, 1977–81; *b* London, 14 Aug. 1919; *m* 1945, Elizabeth Shine; one *s* one *d*. *Educ:* St Andrew, Bruges, Belgium; Royal Veterinary College, London. MRCVS 1942; DSc London, 1961. Temp. Research Worker, ARC Field Station, Compton, Berks, 1942; Research Officer, Veterinary Laboratory, Min. of Agric. and Fisheries, 1942–47; Asst Bacteriologist, Lister Inst. of Preventive Medicine, Elstree, Herts, 1947; Head of Serum Dept, 1952; Dir, Nat. Inst. for Res. in Dairying, Univ. of Reading, Shinfield, Berks, 1967–77. Vis. Prof., Dept of Agriculture and Horticulture, Univ. of Reading, 1980–88. Member: ARC, 1978–81; NERC, 1978–81. Hon. FRASE 1977. *Publications:* many contribs to scientific journals on immunology and tropical medicine. *Recreations:* music, croquet. *Died 12 Nov. 2011.*

WELCH, Rear Adm. John Edwin Nugent, CB 1996; Chief of Naval Staff, New Zealand, 1994–97; *b* 14 Jan. 1941; *s* of Robert Nugent Welch and Mary Helen Anne Welch; *m* 1966, Adrienne Sandford Cox; three *s*. *Educ:* King's High Sch., Dunedin, NZ; Britannia Royal Naval Coll., Dartmouth. Service at sea, Pacific and Far East, 1961–66; Long Gunnery Course, HMS Excellent, 1967–68; i/c HMNZS Mako, 1968–69; service at sea, Far East, 1969–70; ashore, 1971–72; service at sea, 1972–75; i/c HMNZS Inverell, 1976–77; jssc, Australia, 1978; i/c HMNZS Otago, Far East and USA, 1978–80; staff appts, 1981–82; i/c HMNZS Canterbury, 1983–84; Capt. 1985; staff appts, Wellington, 1985–87; NZ Defence Advr, Ottawa, 1988–90; staff appts, 1991–97; Cdre 1992; Rear Adm. 1994. Naval Gen. Service Medal, 1964; NZ Armed Forces Award, 1985. Silver Jubilee Medal, 1977. *Recreations:* trout fishing, golf, reading, sailing. *Address:* 9 Rangitira Avenue, Takapuna, Auckland, New Zealand. *T:* (9) 4891237. *Clubs:* Auckland Central Rotary; Waitemata Golf. *Died 12 Sept. 2014.*

WELCH, Prof. Robert Anthony, PhD; MRIA, FEA; Professor of English, University of Ulster, 1984, then Emeritus (Dean, Faculty of Arts, 2000–08); *b* 25 Nov. 1947; *s* of Patrick Welch and Kathleen Kearney; *m* 1970, Angela O'Riordan; two *s* one *d* (and one *s* decd). *Educ:* University Coll., Cork (BA Hons 1968; MA 1971); Univ. of Leeds (PhD 1974). Lecturer: Sch. of English, Univ. of Leeds, 1971–73; in English, Univ. of Ife, Nigeria, 1973–74; Sch. of English, Univ. of Leeds, 1974–84; Head of Dept of English, 1984–94, Dir, Centre for Irish Lit. and Bibliography, 1994–2000, Univ. of Ulster. Mem. 1990–96, Vice Chm. 1992–93, Arts Council of NI. Chm., Internat. Assoc. for Study of Ireland's Literatures, 1988–91. Founding FEA, 2000. MRIA 2008. *Publications:* Irish Poetry from Moore to Yeats, 1980; A History of Verse Translation from the Irish, 1988; Changing States: transformations in modern Irish literature, 1993; Muskerry (poems), 1993; The Kilcolman Notebook (novel), 1994; (ed) Oxford Companion to Irish Literature, 1996; Secret Societies (poems), 1997; Groundwork (novel), 1997; The Blue Formica Table (poems), 1998; The Abbey Theatre: 1899–1999, 1999; (ed) The Concise Oxford Companion to Irish Literature, 2000; (trans.) Forty Four: Dana Podracka - poems from the Slovak, 2005; The Evergreen Road (poems), 2006; Protestants (play), 2006; (gen. ed.) Oxford History of the Irish Book, vol. III, 2006, vol. V, 2011; Constanza (poems), 2010; Kicking the Black Mamba (memoir), 2012; *posthumous publication*: The Cold of May Day Monday: an approach to Irish literary history, 2014. *Recreations:* gardening, fishing. *Address:* Faculty of Arts, University of Ulster, Coleraine, Northern Ireland BT52 1SA. *Club:* Kildare Street and University (Dublin). *Died 3 Feb. 2013.*

WELLAND, Colin, (Colin Williams); actor, playwright; *b* 4 July 1934; *s* of John Arthur Williams and Norah Williams; *m* 1962, Patricia Sweeney; one *s* three *d*. *Educ:* Newton-le-Willows Grammar Sch.; Bretton Hall Coll.; Goldsmiths' Coll., London (Teacher's Dip. in Art and Drama; Hon. Fellow, 2000). Art teacher, 1958–62; entered theatre, 1962; Library Theatre, Manchester, 1962–64; television, films, theatre, 1962–. Freelance sports writer: The Observer; The Independent. Films (actor): Kes; Villain; Straw Dogs; Sweeney; Dancing through the Dark; (original screenplay): Yanks, 1978; Chariots of Fire, 1980 (won Oscar, Evening Standard and Broadcasting Press Guild Awards, 1982); Twice in a Lifetime, 1986; A Dry White Season, 1989; War of the Buttons, 1994; television (actor): Blue Remembered Hills; The Fix; Bramwell, 1998. Plays (author): Say Goodnight to Grandma, St Martin's, 1973; Roll on Four O'clock, Palace, 1981. Award winning TV plays include: Roll on Four O'clock, Kisses at 50, Leeds United, Jack Point, Your Man from Six Counties, Bambino Mio. Best TV Playwright, Writers Guild, 1970, 1973 and 1974; Best TV Writer, and Best Supporting Film Actor, BAFTA Awards, 1970; Broadcasting Press Guild Award (for writing), 1973. *Publications:* Northern Humour, 1982; plays: Roomful of Holes, 1972; Say Goodnight to Grandma, 1973. *Recreations:* sport, theatre, cinema, politics, dining out. *Address:* c/o United Agents, 12–26 Lexington Street, W1F 0LE. *Died 2 Nov. 2015.*

WELLBELOVED, James; commercial consultant; Director General, National Kidney Research Fund, 1984–93; *b* 29 July 1926; *s* of Wilfred Henry Wellbeloved, Sydenham and Brockley (London), and Paddock Wood, Kent; *m* 1948, Mavis Beryl Ratcliff; two *s* one *d*. *Educ:* South East London Technical College. Boy seaman, 1942–46; building maintenance operative, 1946–50; marketing electrical appliances, 1950–56; marketing, sales and merchandising, 1956–65. TU Branch Officer, activist in CLP and Mem. Jt Mgt Cttee, LCC, 1946–50; Mem., Erith BC, 1950–56 (Chm., Estabt Cttee); first Leader, Bexley LBC, 1965–66. MP (Lab 1965–81, SDP 1981–83) Erith and Crayford, Nov. 1965–1983; Parly Private Secretary: Minister of Defence (Admin), 1967–69; Sec. of State for Foreign and Commonwealth Affairs, 1969–70; an Opposition Whip, 1972–74; Parly Under-Sec. of State for Defence (RAF), MoD, 1976–79. UK Rep., North Atlantic Assembly, 1972–76, 1979–82. Dep. Chm., London MPs Parly Gp, 1970–81; Chairman: River Thames Gp; All Party Parly Camping and Caravanning Gp, 1967–74; Nat. Whitley Council, MoD, 1976–79; Member: Ecclesiastical Cttee, 1971–76; RACS Political Purposes Cttee, 1973–83; PLP Liaison Cttee, 1974–78; Defence Council, 1976–79; Unrelated Live Transplant Regulatory Authority, 1990–97; Vice Chm., Labour Party Defence Gp, 1970–81. Contested (SDP) 1983, (SDP/Alliance) 1987, Erith and Crayford. Dir, Greenwich and Bexley Cottage Hospice, 1998–2006. Pres., British Transplant Organ Donor Soc., 1992–97. Nat. Vice-Pres., Camping and Caravanning Club, 1974–. Former Governor, Greenwich Hosp. Sch. *Publications:* Local Government, 1971. *Recreations:* camping, travel. *Address:* 9 Woodstock Close, Bexley, Kent DA5 3JT. *Died 10 Sept. 2012.*

WELLER, Sir Arthur (Burton), Kt 1997; CBE 1988; Chairman, Citadel Reinsurance Company Ltd, since 1984; *b* 9 Nov. 1929; *s* of Thomas Burton Weller and Mary Johnston Weller (*née* Norman); *m* 1962, Margaret Marea Piper (*née* Callinan); one *s* one *d*. *Educ:* Trinity Acad., Edinburgh. Master Mariner, 1957. Chm., Sirius Insurance Co., 1969–91. Chairman: Britain-Australia Bicentennial Schooner Trust, 1986–2003; Maritime Trust, 1989–96 (Mem. Council, 1977; Hon. Warden, 1996–); HM Bark Endeavour Foundn, 1991–2000; Trustee, 1990–97, Hon. Cdre, 2006, Nat. Maritime Mus. *Recreation:* reading. *Address:* 1503 Quay Grand, 61–69 Macquarie Street, Sydney, NSW 2000, Australia. *E:* sirarthurweller@acenet.com.au. *Clubs:* Hong Kong Yacht (Hong Kong); Royal Sydney Yacht Squadron (Sydney). *Died 29 Nov. 2011.*

WELLER, Walter; Music Director, National Orchestra of Belgium, 2007–12; Principal Guest Conductor, National Orchestra of Spain, 1987–2004; *b* 30 Nov. 1939; *s* of Walter and Anna Weller; *m* 1966, Elisabeth Samohyl; one *s*. *Educ:* Realgymnasium, Vienna; Akademie für Musik, Vienna (degree for violin and piano). Founder of Weller Quartet, 1958–69; Member, Vienna Philharmonic, 1958–69. First Leader, 1960–69; Conductor, Vienna State Opera, 1969–75; Guest Conductor with all main European and American Orchestras, also in Japan and Israel, 1973–; Principal Conductor and Artistic Adviser, Royal Liverpool Philharmonic Orch., 1977–80; Principal Conductor, RPO, 1980–85; Principal Conductor and Music Dir, Royal Scottish Nat. Orch., 1992–97, then Conductor Emeritus; Artistic Dir, Allgemeine Musikges. Basel, 1994–95; Associate Dir, Orch. of Valencia; Conductor Laureate, Stuttgart Philharmonic Orch., 2004–. Many recordings (Grand Prix du disque Charles Cros). Outstanding People of the 20th Century Medal, Cambridge Biographical Centre, 1999. Medal of Arts and Sciences, Austria, 1968; Great Silver Cross of Honour, Austria, 1998. *Recreations:* magic, model railway, sailing, swimming, stamp-collecting, ski-ing. *Address:* Doblinger Hauptstrasse 40, 1190 Vienna, Austria. *Died 14 June 2015.*

WELLINGTON, 8th Duke of, *cr* 1814; **Arthur Valerian Wellesley,** KG 1990; LVO 1952; OBE 1957; MC 1941; DL; Baron Mornington, 1746; Earl of Mornington, Viscount Wellesley, 1760; Viscount Wellington of Talavera and Wellington, Somersetshire, Baron Douro, 1809; Earl of Wellington, Feb. 1812; Marquess of Wellington, Oct. 1812; Marquess Douro, 1814; Prince of Waterloo, 1815, Netherlands; Count of Vimeiro, Marquess of Torres Vedras and Duke of Victoria in Portugal; Duke of Ciudad Rodrigo 1812 and a Grandee of Spain, 1st class (title renounced in favour of heir, 2010); *b* 2 July 1915; *s* of 7th Duke of Wellington, KG, and Dorothy Violet (*d* 1956), *d* of Robert Ashton, Croughton, Cheshire; *S* father, 1972; *m* 1944, Diana Ruth (MBE 2007) (*d* 2010), *o d* of Maj.-Gen. D. F. McConnel; four *s* one *d*. *Educ:* Eton; New Coll., Oxford. Served War of 1939–45 in Middle East (MC), CMF and BLA. Lt-Col Comdg Royal Horse Guards, 1954–58; Silver Stick-in-Waiting and Lt-Col Comdg the Household Cavalry, 1959–60; Comdr 22nd Armoured Bde, 1960–61; Comdr RAC 1st (Br.) Corps, 1962–64; Defence Attaché, Madrid, 1964–67; Col-in-Chief, The Duke of Wellington's Regt, 1974–2007; Hon. Col 2nd Bn, The Wessex Regt, 1974–80; Dep. Col, The Blues and Royals, 1998–2002; Dep. Col-in-Chief, Yorks Regt, 2007–. Director: Massey Ferguson Holdings Ltd, 1967–89; Massey Ferguson Ltd, 1973–84. President: Game Conservancy, 1976–81 (Dep. Pres., 1981–87); SE Branch, Royal British Legion, 1978; BSJA, 1980–82; Rare Breeds Survival Trust, 1984–87; Council for Environmental Conservation, 1983–87;

Atlantic Salmon Trust, 1983–; Thames Salmon Trust, 1986–2002; Labrador Retriever Club, 1997–; Nat. Canine Defence League, 1999–; Vice-President: Zool Soc. of London, 1983–89; Kennel Club, 1985–; Mem. Council, RASE, 1976– (Dep. Pres., 1993). HM's Rep. Trustee, Bd of Royal Armouries, 1983–95; Trustee, WWF (UK), 1985–90. Hampshire CC 1967–74; DL Hants, 1975. Pres., Hampshire Assoc. of Parish and Town Councils, 1994–99. Governor of Wellington Coll., 1964–. Pres., Pitt Club. OStJ. Officier, Légion d'Honneur (France); Kt Grand Cross: Order of St Michael of the Wing (Portugal), 1984; Order of Isabel the Catholic (Spain), 1986. *Heir: s* Marquess of Douro, OBE, *b* 19 Aug. 1945. *Address:* Park Corner House, Heckfield, Hook, Hants RG27 0LJ; Apsley House, 149 Piccadilly, W1J 7NT. *Club:* Cavalry and Guards. *Died 31 Dec. 2014.*

WELLS, Malcolm Henry Weston, FCA; Director, Carclo Engineering Group PLC, 1982–97 (Deputy Chairman, 1987–93); *b* 26 July 1927; *s* of late Lt-Comdr Geoffrey Weston Wells; *m* 1952, Elizabeth A. Harland, *d* of late Rt Rev. Maurice Henry Harland, DD; one *s* one *d*. *Educ:* Eton Coll. ACA 1951, FCA 1961. Served RNVR, 1945–48. Peat, Marwick Mitchell, 1948–58; Siebe Gorman and Co. Ltd, 1958–63; Charterhouse Japhet, 1963–80 (Chm., 1973–80); Dir, Charterhouse Gp, 1971–80; Chairman: Charterhouse Petroleum PLC, 1977–82; Granville Business Expansion Funds, 1983–93; BWD Securities, 1987–95; London rep., Bank in Liechtenstein, 1981–85; Director: Bank in Liechtenstein (UK) Ltd, 1985–90; Nat. Home Loans Corp., 1989–93. Mem., CAA, 1974–77. Mem. Solicitors' Disciplinary Tribunal, 1975–81. *Recreation:* sailing. *Address:* Willow Cottage, The Wad, West Wittering, Chichester PO20 8AH. *Died 3 March 2014.*

WELSH, Michael Collins; *b* 23 Nov. 1926; *s* of Danny and Winnie Welsh; *m* 1950, Brenda Nicholson; two *s*. *Educ:* Sheffield Univ. (Dept of Extramural Studies, Day Release Course, three years); Ruskin Coll., Oxford. Miner from age of 14 years. Member, Doncaster Local Authority, 1962–69. MP (Lab) Don Valley, 1979–83, Doncaster North, 1983–92. *Club:* Carcroft Village Workingmen's (Carcroft, near Doncaster). *Died 24 Jan. 2012.*

WELSH, Maj.-Gen. Peter Miles, OBE 1983; MC 1967; President, Regular Commissions Board, 1983–85; *b* 23 Dec. 1930; *s* of William Miles Moss O'Donnel Welsh and Mary Edith Margaret Gertrude Louise Welsh (*née* Hearn); *m* 1974, June Patricia McCausland (*née* Macadam); two step *s* one step *d*. *Educ:* Winchester College; RMA Sandhurst. Commissioned, KRRC, 1951; Kenya Regt, 1958–60; student, Staff Coll., 1961; Malaya and Borneo, 1965–66; Royal Green Jackets, 1966; JSSC, 1967; Instructor, Staff Coll., 1968–71; CO 2 RGJ, 1971–73; Comd 5 Inf. Bde, 1974–76; RCDS, 1977; HQ BAOR, 1978–80; Brig., Light Div., 1980–83. *Recreations:* shooting, fishing, vegetable gardening, cooking, golf. *Clubs:* MCC, Free Foresters, I Zingari, Jesters; Berks Golf. *Died 17 April 2011.*

WEST, Christopher John, CBE 2002; Solicitor to HM Land Registry, 1991–2006; *b* 4 May 1941; *s* of late George William West and Kathleen Mary West; *m* 1978, Susan Elizabeth Kirkby; one *d*. *Educ:* Raynes Park County Grammar Sch.; Inns of Court Sch. of Law. Called to the Bar, Lincoln's Inn, 1966. Exec. Officer, Charity Commn, 1961; HM Land Registry, 1969–2006: Sen. Land Registrar, 1983; Dist Land Registrar, Tunbridge Wells Dist Land Registry, 1987. *Publications:* (contrib.) Land Registration (jtly) and Land Charges, to Halsbury's Laws of England, 4th edn, 1977; (contrib.) Atkin's Court Forms, 1978, 1987; (with T. B. F. Ruoff) Concise Land Registration Practice and Land Registration Forms, 1982; (ed jtly) Ruoff and Roper's Registered Conveyancing, 5th edn 1986, looseleaf edn updated bi-annually 1991–2003, 2nd looseleaf edn, 2003. *Recreations:* theatre, jazz, watching sport. *Address:* 1 Brooklands Park, Blackheath, SE3 9BN. *T:* (020) 8852 0667. *E:* cjwblackheath@gmail.com. *Died 22 April 2015.*

WEST, Dr John James; Member (Lab), 1981–2001, Leader, 1997–2001, Lancashire County Council (Deputy Leader, 1989–97); *b* 19 April 1939; *s* of John West and Teresa West (*née* Campbell); two *s*. *Educ:* St Mary's RC Sch., Dublin; Dublin Univ. (BA Econs and Hist. 1961); Harris Coll., Preston and Poole Tech. Coll. (Dip. Business Studies 1974); Open Univ. (PhD 2006). MInstTA 1976; MCIT 1978. Dep. Manager/Dep. Chm. of Bd, Preston Borough Transport Ltd, 1961–92. Freelance pt-time Lectr in Econs and History. Lancashire County Council: Chair: Superannuation Panel, 1984–2001; Finance Cttee, 1985–2001; Hon. Alderman, 2001. Exec. Mem., LGA, 1994–2001. Chairman: Lancashire Waste Services Ltd, 1991–2001; Lancashire Co-op Develt Agency, 1991–2001; non-executive Director: Preston and S Ribble Develt Agency, 1997–2001; Preston Acute Hosp. NHS Trust, 1997–2001; Lancashire Teaching Hosps NHS Trust, 2002–06. *Recreations:* reading (especially ancient history), watching most sports. *Address:* Apartment No 1, Cotton House, 127 Manchester Road, Preston PR1 4HL. *Died 27 April 2014.*

WEST, Martin Litchfield, OM 2014; DPhil, DLitt; FBA 1973; Senior Research Fellow, All Souls College, University of Oxford, 1991–2004, Emeritus Fellow, 2004–14, then Honorary Fellow; *b* 23 Sept. 1937; *s* of Maurice Charles West and Catherine Baker West (*née* Stainthorpe); *m* 1960, Stephanie Roberta Pickard (Dr Stephanie Roberta West, FBA); one *s* one *d*. *Educ:* St Paul's Sch.; Balliol Coll., Oxford (MA 1962; DPhil 1963; DLitt 1994; Hon. Fellow, 2004). Chancellor's Prizes for Latin Prose and Verse, 1957; Hertford and de Paravicini Schols, 1957; Ireland Schol., 1957; Conington Prize, 1965. Woodhouse Jun. Research Fellow, St John's Coll., Oxford, 1960–63 (Hon. Fellow 2007); Fellow and Praelector in Classics, University Coll., Oxford, 1963–74 (Hon. Fellow 2001); Prof. of Greek, Bedford Coll., then at RHBNC, London Univ., 1974–91. Corresp. Mem., Akademie der Wissenschaften zu Göttingen, 1991; MAE 1998; Foreign Mem., Accademia Nazionale dei Lincei, 2007; Internat. Mem., Amer. Philosophical Soc., 2010; Mem., Accademia Ambrosiana, Milan, 2015; Fellow, Acad. of Athens, 2009. Editor of Liddell and Scott's Greek-English Lexicon, 1965–81. Hon. DLitt: Cyprus, 2008; Urbino, 2011. Internat. Balzan Prize for Classical Antiquity, 2000; Kenyon Medal for Classical Studies, British Acad., 2002. *Publications:* (ed) Hesiod, Theogony, 1966; (ed with R. Merkelbach) Fragmenta Hesiodea, 1967; Early Greek Philosophy and the Orient, 1971; Sing Me, Goddess, 1971; (ed) Iambi et Elegi Graeci, 1971–72; Textual Criticism and Editorial Technique, 1973; Studies in Greek Elegy and Iambus, 1974; (ed) Hesiod, Works and Days, 1978; (ed) Theognidis et Phocylidis fragmenta, 1978; (ed) Delectus ex Iambis et Elegis Graecis, 1980; Greek Metre, 1982; The Orphic Poems, 1983; (ed) Carmina Anacreontea, 1984; The Hesiodic Catalogue of Women, 1985; (ed) Euripides, Orestes, 1987; Introduction to Greek Metre, 1987; Hesiod (trans.), 1988; (ed) Aeschyli Tragoediae, 1990; Studies in Aeschylus, 1990; Ancient Greek Music, 1992; Greek Lyric Poetry (trans.), 1993; The East Face of Helicon, 1997; (ed) Homeri Ilias, 2 vols, 1998 and 2000; Studies in the Text and Transmission of the Iliad, 2001; (with E. Pöhlmann) Documents of Ancient Greek Music, 2001; (ed and trans.) Homeric Hymns, Homeric Apocrypha, Lives of Homer, 2003; (ed and trans.) Greek Epic Fragments, 2003; Indo-European Poetry and Myth, 2007; The Hymns of Zoroaster, 2010; The Making of the Iliad, 2011; Old Avestan Syntax and Stylistics, 2011; Hellenica I, 2011; Hellenica II, 2013; Hellenica III, 2013; The Epic Cycle, 2013; The Making of the Odyssey, 2014; articles in classical periodicals. *Recreation:* strong music. *Address:* All Souls College, Oxford OX1 4AL. *Died 13 July 2015.*

WESTBROOK, Sir Neil (Gowanloch), Kt 1988; CBE 1981; Chairman and Managing Director: Central Manchester Holdings Ltd, 1960–2005; Trafford Park Estates PLC, 1963–98; *b* 21 Jan. 1917; *s* of Frank and Dorothy Westbrook; *m* 1st, 1945, Hon. Mary Joan Fraser (*d* 2004), *o d* of 1st Baron Strathalmond, CBE; one *s* one *d*; 2nd, 2005, Dorothy Lilian Stevenson. *Educ:* Oundle Sch.; Clare Coll., Cambridge (MA). FRICS. Served War of 1939–45: Sapper, 1939; Actg Lt-Col 1945 (despatches). Chm., NW Industrial Council, 1982–87; Member: Council, CBI North West Region, 1982–88 (Chairman: NW Inner Cities Studies Gp, 1985; NW Working Party on Derelict Land Clearance, 1986); Inst. of Directors Greater Manchester Branch Cttee, 1972–86. Treas., Manchester Conservative Assoc., 1964–73, Dep. Chm., 1973–74, Chm., 1974–83; Chairman: Greater Manchester Co-ordinating Cttee, NW Area Cons. Assoc., 1977–86; Exchange Div. Cons. Assoc., 1973; Manchester Euro South Cons. Assoc., 1978–84; Member: NW Area F and GP Cttee, Cons. Party, 1974–87; Nat. Union Exec. Cttee, 1975–81; Cons. Bd of Finance, 1984–87. Mem., Manchester City Council, 1949–71; Dep. Leader 1967–69; Lord Mayor 1969–70. Chm., North Western Art Galleries and Museums Service, 1965–68; Mem., Exec. Cttee, Museums Assoc., 1965–69. Pres., Central Manchester Br., Arthritis and Rheumatism Council, 1970. Member: Duke of Edinburgh's Award Scheme Cttee, Manchester Area, 1972–75; Bd, Manchester YMCA, 1960–73. Mem., Chartered Auctioneers & Estate Agents Agricl Cttee, 1949–70; Mem., ABCC Rating Cttee, 1971–74. Hon. Mem., Magdalene Coll., Cambridge. *Recreations:* football, fishing, horse racing. *Address:* Middlemede, Wigan Lane, Ballasalla, Isle of Man IM9 3EP. *Clubs:* Carlton, Jockey. *Died 13 Aug. 2014.*

WESTBURY, Prof. Gerald, OBE 1990; FRCP, FRCS; Professor of Surgery, 1982–89, then Professor Emeritus, and Dean, 1986–92, Institute of Cancer Research; Hon. Consultant Surgeon, Royal Marsden Hospital, 1982–89; *b* 29 July 1927; *s* of Lew and Celia Westbury; *m* 1965, Hazel Frame (*d* 2014); three *d. Educ:* St Marylebone Grammar Sch.; Westminster Med. Sch., Univ. of London (MB, BS (Hons) 1949); FRCS 1952; FRCP 1976. House Surg., Westminster and Royal Northern Hosps, 1949–50; RAF Med. Service, 1950–52; RSO, Brompton Hosp., 1952–53; Registrar and Sen. Registrar, Westminster Hosp., 1953–60; Fellow in Surgery, Harvard Med. Sch., 1957; Cons. Surg., Westminster Hosp., 1960–82 (Hon. Cons. Surgeon, 1982–89); Hon. Cons. in Surgery to the Army, 1980–89. Pres., British Assoc. of Surgical Oncology, 1989–92. Examiner, Univs of London, Edinburgh, Cambridge, Hong Kong; Hunterian Prof., RCS, 1963; Honyman Gillespie Lectr, Univ. of Edinburgh, 1965; Semon Lectr and Haddow Lectr, RSM, 1982; Gordon-Taylor Lectr, RCS, 1989. Fellow, Inst. of Cancer Res., 2000; Hon. FRCSE, 1993. Walker Prize, RCS, 1990. *Publications:* medical articles and contribs to text books. *Recreations:* music, bird watching. *Club:* Athenæum. *Died 12 June 2014.*

WESTCOTT, Prof. John Hugh, DSc(Eng), PhD, DIC; FRS 1983; FREng; FCGI, FInstD; Professor of Control Systems, Imperial College of Science and Technology, 1961–84, then Emeritus; Chairman, Feedback plc, 1958–99; *b* 3 Nov. 1920; *s* of John Stanley Westcott and Margaret Elisabeth Westcott (*née* Bass); *m* 1950, Helen Fay Morgan; two *s* one *d. Educ:* Wandsworth Sch.; City and Guilds Coll., London; Massachusetts Inst. of Technology. Royal Commission for the Exhibition of 1851 Senior Studentship; Apprenticeship BTH Co., Rugby. Radar Research and Develt Estabt, 1941–45; Imperial College, London: Lectr, 1950; Reader, 1956; Head of Computing and Control Dept, 1970–79; Sen. Res. Fellow, 1984–94. Control Commn for Germany, 1945–46. Consultant to: Bataafsche Petroleum Maatschappij (Shell), The Hague, Holland, 1953–58; AEI, 1955–69; ICI, 1965–69; George Wimpey & Son, 1975–80; Westland plc, 1983–85. Chm., Control and Automation Div., Instn of Electrical Engrs, 1968–69. Mem., Exec. Council of Internat. Fedn of Automatic Control, 1969–75; Chm., United Kingdom Automation Council, 1973–79; Pres., Inst. of Measurement and Control, 1979–80. Mem., Adv. Council, RMCS, 1986–2001; Governor, Kingston Polytechnic, 1974–80. FREng (FEng 1980). Hon. FIET; Hon. FInstMC. *Publications:* An Exposition of Adaptive Control, 1962; monographs and papers, mainly on Control Systems and related topics. *Recreations:* gardening, reading. *Address:* (home) 8 Fernhill, Oxshott, Surrey KT22 0JH; Department of Electrical Engineering, Imperial College, SW7 2BT. *T:* (020) 7594 6240. *Died 14 Oct. 2014.*

WHEELER, Sir Anthony; *see* Wheeler, Sir H. A.

WHEELER, Arthur William Edge, CBE 1979 (OBE 1967); Chairman, Foreign Compensation Commission, 1983–2001; a Social Security Commissioner, 1992–98; a Child Support Commissioner, 1993–98; *b* 1 Aug. 1930; *e s* of Arthur William Wheeler and Rowena (*née* Edge); *m* 1956, Gay; two *s* one *d. Educ:* Mountjoy Sch.; Trinity Coll., Dublin (Reid Prof.'s Prize, MA, LLB). Called to the Irish Bar, King's Inns, 1953; called to the Bar, Gray's Inn, 1960; practised at Irish Bar, 1953–55; Crown Counsel, Nigeria, 1955; Legal Sec. (Actg), Southern Cameroons, and Mem. Exec. Council and House of Assembly, 1958; Principal Crown Counsel, Fedn of Nigeria, 1961; Northern Nigeria: Dep. Solicitor Gen., 1964; Dir of Public Prosecutions, 1966; High Court Judge, 1967; Chief Judge (formerly Chief Justice), Kaduna State of Nigeria, 1975; Comr for Law Revision, northern states of Nigeria, 1980. Mem., Body of Benchers, Nigeria, 1975; Associate Mem., Commonwealth Parly Assoc. *Recreations:* sport (university colours for hockey and assoc. football; Nigerian hockey internat.), music. *Club:* MCC. *Died 3 Nov. 2013.*

WHEELER, Sir (Harry) Anthony, Kt 1988; OBE 1973; RSA, FRIBA, FRIAS; President, Royal Scottish Academy, 1983–90; Senior Partner, 1954–86, Consultant, 1986–89, Wheeler & Sproson, Architects and Planning Consultants, Edinburgh and Kirkcaldy; *b* 7 Nov. 1919; *s* of Herbert George Wheeler and Laura Emma Groom; *m* 1944, Dorothy Jean Campbell (decd); one *d. Educ:* Stranraer High Sch.; Royal Technical Coll., Glasgow; Glasgow School of Art; Univ. of Strathclyde (BArch). DipTP. Glasgow Sch. of Architecture, 1937–48 (war service, Royal Artillery, 1939–46); John Keppie Scholar and Sir Rowand Anderson Studentship, 1948; RIBA Grissell Gold Medallist, 1948, and Neale Bursar, 1949. Assistant: to City Architect, Oxford, 1948; to Sir Herbert Baker & Scott, London, 1949; Sen. Architect, Glenrothes New Town, 1949–51; Sen. Lectr, Dundee Sch. of Arch., 1952–58; commenced private practice in Fife, 1952. Principal works include: Woodside Shopping Centre and St Columba's Parish Church, Glenrothes; Reconstruction of Giles Pittenweem; Redevelopment of Dysart and of Old Buckhaven; Town Centre Renewal, Grangemouth; Students' Union, Univ. of St Andrews; Hunter Building, Edinburgh Coll. of Art; St Peter's Episcopal Ch, Kirkcaldy; Leonard Horner Hall, and Students' Union, Heriot-Watt Univ.; Bank of Scotland, and Royal Bank of Scotland, Dunfermline; Community and Outdoor Centre, Linlithgow. Member: Royal Fine Art Commn for Scotland, 1967–86; Scottish Housing Adv. Cttee, 1971–75; Trustee, Scottish Civic Trust, 1970–83; Pres., Royal Incorpn of Architects in Scotland, 1973–75; Vice-Pres., RIBA, 1973–75. FRSA; RSA 1975 (ARSA 1963; Treasurer, 1978–80; Sec., 1980–83); Hon. RA 1983; Hon. RHA 1983; Hon. RGI 1987. Hon. DDes Robert Gordon's Inst. of Technology, 1991. Hon. Pres., Saltire Soc., 1995. 22 Saltire Awards and Commendations for Housing and Reconstruction; 12 Civic Trust Awards and Commendations. *Publications:* articles on civic design and housing in technical jls. *Recreations:* making gardens, sketching and water colours, fishing, music and drama. *Address:* South Inverleith Manor, 31/6 Kinnear Road, Edinburgh EH3 5PG. *T:* (0131) 552 3854. *Clubs:* New, Scottish Arts (Edinburgh). *Died 19 Dec. 2013.*

WHELDON, Dame Juliet (Louise), DCB 2004 (CB 1994); Chief Legal Adviser and Adviser to the Governor of the Bank of England, 2006–08; *b* 26 March 1950; *d* of late John Wheldon and of Ursula Mabel Caillard. *Educ:* Sherborne School for Girls; Lady Margaret Hall, Oxford (1st Cl. Hons Mod. Hist.; Hon. Fellow 2006). Called to the Bar, Gray's Inn, 1975, Bencher 1999. Treasury Solicitor's Dept, 1976–83; Law Officers Dept, 1983–84; Treasury Solicitor's Dept, 1984–86; Asst Legal Sec. to the Law Officers, 1986–87; Legal Advr to HM Treasury, Treasury Solicitor's Dept, 1987–89; Legal Sec. to the Law Officers, 1989–97; Legal Advr to Home Office, 1997–2000; HM Procurator Gen., Treasury Solicitor and Hd of Govt Legal Service, 2000–06. Member: Nat. Security Forum, 2009–11; Adv. Cttee on Business Appts, 2009–11. Hon. QC 1997. *Died 2 Sept. 2013.*

WHICHER, Peter George, CEng; FRAeS; MIET; Principal, INECO, since 1994; *b* 10 March 1929; *o s* of late Reginald George Whicher and Suzanne (*née* Dexter); *m* 1st, 1962, Susan Rosemary Strong (*d* 1989); one *s* one *d*; 2nd, 1992, Margaret Rosemary (*née* Rickman). *Educ:* Chichester High Sch.; BScEng London 1948. CEng, MIET (MIEE 1957). STC, 1948–51; Flying Officer, RAF, 1951–53; Min. of Aviation, 1953; Principal Expert in Telecommunications, Eurocontrol Agency, Paris, 1962–64; Cabinet Office, 1964–66; Asst Dir, Telecommunications R

& D, and Manager, Skynet Satellite Communications Project, Min. of Technology, 1967–71; Superintendent, Communications Div., RAE, 1971–73; Dir, Air Radio, MoD(PE), 1973–76; RCDS, 1977; Dir, Defence Sci. (Electronics), MoD, 1978–81; Dep. Dir, RAE, 1981–84. Consultant, Logica, 1985–94. FRAeS 1985. *Publications:* reports and papers for professional instns. *Recreations:* sailing, innovation, arts. *Address:* Widgers Wood, Sheets Heath, Brookwood, Woking, Surrey GU24 0EJ. *Club:* Offshore Cruising. *Died 7 April 2012.*

WHICKER, Alan Donald, CBE 2005; television broadcaster (Whicker's World); writer; *b* 2 Aug. 1925; *o s* of late Charles Henry Whicker and late Anne Jane Cross. *Educ:* Haberdashers' Aske's Sch. Capt., Devonshire Regt; Dir, Army Film and Photo Unit, with 8th Army and US 5th Army. War Corresp. in Korea, Foreign Corresp., novelist, writer, television and radio broadcaster. Joined BBC TV, 1957: Tonight programme (appeared nightly in filmed reports from around the world, studio interviews, outside broadcasts, Eurovision, and Telstar, incl. first Telstar two-way transmission at opening of UN Assembly, NY, 1962); TV Series: Whicker's World, 1959–60; Whicker Down Under, 1961; Whicker on Top of the World!, 1962; Whicker in Sweden, Whicker in the Heart of Texas, Whicker Down Mexico Way, 1963; Alan Whicker Report series: The Solitary Billionaire (J. Paul Getty), etc; wrote and appeared in own series of monthly documentaries on BBC 2, subseq. repeated on BBC 1, under series title, Whicker's World, 1965–67 (31 programmes later shown around the world); BBC radio programmes and articles for The Listener, etc; left BBC, 1968. Various cinema films, incl. The Angry Silence. Mem., successful consortium for Yorkshire Television, 1967. Completed 16 Documentaries for Yorkshire TV during its first year of operation, incl. Whicker's New World series, and Specials on Gen. Stroessner of Paraguay, Count von Rosen, and Pres. Duvalier of Haiti; Whicker in Europe; Whicker's Walkabout; Broken Hill—Walled City; Gairy's Grenada; documentary series, World of Whicker; Whicker's Orient; Whicker within a Woman's World, 1972; Whicker's South Seas, Whicker way out West, 1973; Whicker's World, series on cities, 1974–77; Whicker's World—Down Under, 1976; Whicker's World: US, 1977 (4 progs); India, 1978 (7 progs); Indonesia, 1979; California, 1980 (6 progs); Peter Sellers Meml programme, 1980; Whicker's World Aboard the Orient Express, 1982; Around Whicker's World in 25 Years (3 YTV retrospect. progs), 1982; BBC TV, 1982–92; Whicker's World—the First Million Miles (6 retrospect. progs), 1982; Whicker's World—a Fast Boat to China (4 QE2 progs), 1984; Whicker! (10 talk shows), 1984; Whicker's World—Living with Uncle Sam (10 progs), 1985; Whicker's World—Living with Waltzing Matilda (10 progs), 1987–88; Whicker's World—Hong Kong (8 progs), 1990; Whicker's World—a Taste of Spain (8 progs), 1992; returned to ITV for: Around Whicker's World—the Ultimate Package! (4 progs), 1992; Whicker's World—The Absolute Monarch (the Sultan of Brunei), 1992; South Africa: Whicker's Miss World, and Whicker's World—The Sun King, 1993; South-East Asia: Whicker's World Aboard the real Orient Express; Whicker—the Mahathir Interview (Dr Mahathir Mohammed, PM of Malaysia); Pavarotti in Paradise, 1994; updated 27 progs for Travel Channel, 1996 and 4 for Yorkshire-Tyne Tees, 1997; Auntie's Greatest Hits, 1998, One-On-One, 2002, BBC TV; Whicker's War (2 progs), Channel 4, 2004; Comedy Map of Britain (12 progs), 2007, (6 progs), 2008, BBC TV; Whicker's World—Journey of a Lifetime (4 progs), BBC TV, 2009. BBC Radio: Chm., Start the Week; Whicker's Wireless World (3 series), 1983; Around Whicker's World (6 progs), 1998; Whicker's Week, 1999; Whicker's New World (7 progs), 1999; Whicker's World Down Under (6 progs), 2000; The Fabulous Fifties (4 progs), 2000; The History of Television—It'll Never Last! (6 progs), 2001; Fifty Royal Years (6 progs), Around Whicker's World, 3 essays, 2002; Archive Hour, 2005. FRSA 1970. Various awards, 1963–, incl. Screenwriters' Guild, best Documentary Script, 1963; Guild of Television Producers and Directors Personality of the Year, 1964; Silver Medal, Royal Television Soc., 1968; Dumont Award, Univ. of California, 1970; Best Interview Prog. Award, Hollywood Festival of TV, 1973; Dimbleby Award, BAFTA, 1978; TV Times Special Award, 1978; first to be named in RTS Hall of Fame for outstanding creative contribution to British TV, 1993; Travelex travel writers' Special Award for outstanding achievement in travel journalism, 1998; Grierson Documentary Award, BAFTA Tribute, 2001; NFT Tribute, 6 TV Fest., 2002; War Reporter of the Year and Lifetime Achievement Award, Official Airline Guide, 2006; Lifetime Contribution to Travel Award, Travel Press Awards, 2010. *Publications:* Some Rise by Sin, 1949; Away—with Alan Whicker, 1963; Best of Everything, 1980; Within Whicker's World: an autobiography, 1982; Whicker's Business Traveller's Guide (with BAA), 1983; Whicker's New World, 1985; Whicker's World Down Under, 1988; Whicker's World—Take 2, 2000; Whicker's War, 2005; Whicker's World—Journey of a Lifetime, 2009; Sunday newspaper columns; contrib. various internat. pubns. *Recreations:* people, photography, writing, travel, and reading (usually airline timetables). *Address:* Trinity, Jersey. *Died 12 July 2013.*

WHINERAY, Sir Wilson (James), KNZM 1998; OBE 1961; Chairman, National Bank of New Zealand Ltd, 1998–2004 (Director, 1993–2004); *b* 10 July 1935; *s* of Bruce Ludlow Whineray and Ida Cecilia Whineray (*née* Billany); *m* 1959, Elisabeth Eve Seymour; one *s* two *d*. *Educ:* Auckland GS; Auckland Univ. (BCom 1964); Grad. Sch. of Business Admin, Harvard Univ. (MBA 1969). Played Rugby for All Blacks, 1957–65, Capt., 1958–65; 32 Tests, 30 as Captain. State Advances Corp. of NZ, 1958–64; Dominion Breweries Ltd, 1964–67; joined Alex Harvey Industries Ltd, 1969 which became Carter Holt Harvey Ltd, 1985: Dir, 1987–2003; Dep. Man. Dir, 1987–93; Chm., 1993–2003. Chm., Hillary Commn, 1993–98. Gov., NZ Sports Fedn, 1981–95. Col Comdt, NZ SAS, 1997–2001. NZ Sportsman of the Year, 1965. *Address:* 2/422 Remuera Road, Remuera, Auckland, New Zealand. *Died 22 Oct. 2012.*

WHITAKER, Benjamin Charles George, CBE 2000; author; *b* 15 Sept. 1934; 3rd *s* of late Maj.-Gen. Sir John Whitaker, 2nd Bt, CB, CBE, and late Lady Whitaker (*née* Snowden), Babworth Hall, Retford, Notts; *m* 1964, Janet Alison Stewart, (Baroness Whitaker); two *s* one *d*. *Educ:* Eton; New Coll., Oxford (BA Modern History). Nat. Service, Coldstream Guards, 1952–54 (2nd Lt, 1953–54, Lt, 1954). Called to Bar, Inner Temple, 1959 (Yarborough-Anderson Scholar). Practised as Barrister, 1959–67. Extra-mural Lectr in Law, London Univ., 1963–64. Executive Director: Minority Rights Group, 1971–88; Gulbenkian Foundn (UK), 1988–99. MP (Lab) Hampstead, 1966–70; PPS to Minister of Overseas Development, 1966; Housing and Local Govt, 1966–67; Parly Sec., ODM, 1969–70. Member: UN Human Rights Sub-Commn, 1975–88 (Vice-Chm., 1979); Goodman Cttee on Charity Law Reform, 1974–76; UK Nat. Commn for UNESCO, 1978–85; Speaker's Commn on Citizenship, 1989–90; Nat. Lottery Charities Bd, subseq. Community Fund, 2000–04; Chm., SE Reg., Big Lottery (formerly Community) Fund, 2003–06; Chairman: UN Working Gp on Slavery, 1976–78; Defence of Literature and Arts Soc., 1976–82; City Poverty Cttee, 1971–83; Friends of Regent's Park, 1991–93; Foundns Forum, 1996–98. Judge: NCR Book Award, 1990; RIBA Architecture Awards, 1992. Gen. Service Medal (Canal Zone), 2004. Lieut, Order of Merit (Portugal), 1993. *Publications:* The Police, 1964; (ed) A Radical Future, 1967; Crime and Society, 1967; Participation and Poverty, 1968; Parks for People, 1971; (ed) The Fourth World, 1972; The Foundations, 1974; The Police in Society, 1979; (contrib.) Human Rights and American Foreign Policy, 1979; UN Report on Slavery, 1982; (ed) Teaching about Prejudice, 1983; A Bridge of People, 1983; (ed) Minorities: a question of human rights?, 1984; UN Report on Genocide, 1985; The Global Connection, 1987; (contrib.) The United Kingdom—The United Nations, 1990; Gen. Editor, Sources for Contemporary Issues series (7 vols), 1973–75. *Died 8 June 2014.*

WHITAKER, Sheila; Director, London Film Festival, 1987–96; *b* 1 April 1936; *d* of Hilda and Charles Whitaker. *Educ:* Cathays High Sch. for Girls, Cardiff; Kings Norton Grammar Sch. for Girls, Birmingham; Univ. of Warwick (BA Hons). Secretarial and admin. posts in commerce and industry, 1956–68; Chief Stills Officer, National Film

Archive, 1968–74; Univ. of Warwick, 1975–78; Dir, Tyneside Cinema, Tyneside Film Festival, Newcastle upon Tyne, 1979–84; Head, Programming: NFT, 1984–90; Article 27, 2000. Director: Film London Ltd, 1997–2001; Metropolis Films Ltd, 2002–03. Adv. Ed., I. B. Tauris Contemp. Cinema pubns, 2001–12. Mem., Programming Commn, Locarno Internat. Film Fest., 2002–05; Dir of Internat. Programming, Dubai Internat. Film Fest., 2004–; Mem., Bd of Dirs, Engaged Events (Palestine Fest. of Literature), 2007–. Dir, Free Form Arts Trust, 2000–09. Mem. Jury, Venice Internat. Film Festival, 1992. Co-Editor, Framework Jl, 1976–78; Founder and Co-Editor, Writing Women, 1981–84; Gen. Editor, Tyneside Publications, 1984; Dir, Vertigo Mag., 2007–10. Hon. DLitt Newcastle, 1997; Hon. LLD Warwick, 2005. Chevalier des Arts et des Lettres (France), 1996. *Publications:* (ed jtly) Life and Art: the new Iranian cinema, 1999; An Argentine Passion: Maria Luisa Bemberg and her films, 2000; contribs to Framework, Screen, Sight and Sound, Guardian, Observer, New Statesman, TES. *Recreations:* reading, watching movies. *Address:* Flat 401, 4 St John's Place, EC1M 4NP. *Died 29 July 2013.*

WHITE, Derek Leslie; HM Diplomatic Service, retired; *b* 18 April 1933; *s* of John William and Hilda White; *m* 1989, Elisabeth Denise Marcelle Lemoine; one *d* from previous marr. *Educ:* Catshill Secondary Sch., Bromsgrove; RAF Apprentice Sch. Served RAF, 1950–63. For. Office (later HM Diplomatic Service), 1963; served Helsinki, Sofia, Algiers; Vice Consul, Tripoli, 1970; FCO, 1972; Commercial Officer, Baghdad, 1975, Second Sec., 1977; Port Louis, 1979; Antananarivo, 1983; FCO, 1984, First Sec., 1985; Consul, Marseilles and Principality of Monaco, 1986; FCO, 1989; High Comr to Kiribati, 1990–93, and concurrently Ambassador to Federated States of Micronesia and to Marshall Is, 1992–93. *Recreations:* cooking, music, reading. *Address:* 1 Place Simon Bellon, 83470 Pourcieux, France. *T:* 494597879. *Died 6 July 2012.*

WHITE, Edward George, OBE 1976; HM Diplomatic Service, retired; *b* 30 June 1923; *s* of late George Johnson White, OBE, ISO, and Edith (*née* Birch); *m* 1st, 1945, Sylvia Shears; two *d*; 2nd, 1966, Veronica Pauline Crosling. *Educ:* Bec Secondary Sch., London SW. Served RAF, 1941–47. Various consular and diplomatic appts in Guatemala, USA, Madagascar, Burma, Thailand and India; Dep. Head of Finance Dept, FCO, 1976–78; Counsellor (Admin), Bonn, 1978–79. Specialist Adviser, Foreign Affairs Cttee, H of C, 1980–87. *Publications:* Nightfighter Navigator, 1994. *Address:* 13 Elvestone, Fore Street Hill, Budleigh Salterton, Devon EX9 6HD. *T:* (01395) 443008. *Died 15 Sept. 2013.*

WHITE, His Honour Sir Frank (John), Kt 1997; a Senior Circuit Judge, 1994–97 (a Circuit Judge, 1974–94); *b* 12 March 1927; *s* of late Frank Byron White and Marie-Thérèse Renée White (*née* Cachou); *m* 1953, Anne Rowlandson, MBE, *d* of Sir Harold Gibson Howitt, GBE, DSO, MC and Dorothy Howitt (*née* Radford); two *s* two *d*. *Educ:* Reading Sch.; King's Coll., London (LLB, LLM; FKC 1999). Sub-Lt, RNVR, 1945–47; called to the Bar, Gray's Inn, 1951, Bencher, 1997; Dep. Chm., Berkshire QS, 1970–72; a Recorder of the Crown Court, 1972–74. Pres., Council of HM Circuit Judges, 1990–91. Member: Lord Chancellor's Adv. Cttee on Legal Aid, 1977–83; Judicial Studies Bd, 1985–89; County Court Rule Cttee, 1991–97 (Chm., 1993–97). Mem., General Council of the Bar, 1969–73. Pres., KCL Assoc., 2000–02. Pres., Le Demi-Siècle de Londres, 1997–2002. *Publications:* Bench Notes and Exercises for Assistant Recorders, 1988. *Recreations:* walking, photography. *Address:* 49 Fairacres, Roehampton Lane, SW15 5LY. *T:* (020) 8876 3558. *Clubs:* Athenæum, Roehampton. *Died 23 Oct. 2012.*

WHITE, Air Vice-Marshal George Alan, CB 1984; AFC 1973; FRAeS; Commandant, Royal Air Force Staff College, 1984–87; *b* 11 March 1932; *s* of James Magee White and Evangeline (*née* Henderson); *m* 1955, Mary Esmé (*née* Magowan) (decd); two *d*. *Educ:* Wallace High Sch., Lisburn, NI; Queen's Univ., Belfast; University of London ext. (LLB). Pilot, 1956; served in RAF Squadrons and OCUs, 1956–64; RAF Staff College, 1964; HQ Middle East Command, 1966–67; 11 Sqn, 1968–70; 5 Sqn, 1970–72; Nat. Defence Coll., 1972–73; in command, RAF Leuchars, 1973–75; Royal Coll. of Defence Studies, 1976; Dir of Ops (Air Defence and Overseas), 1977–78; SASO No 11 Group, 1979–80; Air Cdre Plans, HQ Strike Comd, 1981–82; Dep. Comdr, RAF Germany, 1982–84. FRAeS 1985. *Publications:* Lightning Up, 2009; A Sojourn in Cyprus, 2012; Savannah And The Soldier, 2013. *Recreations:* writing, reading, bridge, gardening. *Address:* The Grange, Pulham St Mary, Diss, Norfolk IP21 4QZ. *Club:* Royal Air Force. *Died 8 June 2015.*

WHITE, Adm. Sir Hugo (Moresby), GCB 1995 (KCB 1991); CBE 1985; DL; Governor and Commander-in-Chief, Gibraltar, 1995–97; *b* 22 Oct. 1939; *s* of late Hugh Fortescue Moresby White, CMG and Betty Sophia Pennington White; *m* 1966, Josephine Mary Lorimer Pedler; two *s*. *Educ:* Dragon School; Nautical Coll., Pangbourne; Britannia RN Coll., Dartmouth. HMS Blackpool, 1960; submarine training, 1961; HM Submarines Tabard, Tiptoe, Odin, 1961–65; Long Navigation Course, HMS Dryad, 1966; Navigator, HMS Warspite, 1967; First Lieut, HMS Osiris, 1968–69; in Comd, HMS Oracle, 1969–70; Staff, BRNC Dartmouth, 1971–72; Submarine Sea Training, 1973–74; in Comd, HMS Salisbury (cod war), 1975–76; Naval Sec.'s Dept, 1976–78; Naval Plans, 1978–80; in Comd, HMS Avenger (Falklands) and 4th Frigate Sqn, 1980–82; Principal Staff Officer to Chief of Defence Staff, 1982–85; in Comd, HMS Bristol and Flag Captain, 1985–87; Flag Officer Third Flotilla, and Comdr Anti-Submarine Warfare Striking Force, 1987–88; ACNS, 1988–91; Flag Officer Scotland and NI, 1991–92; C-in-C Fleet, Allied C-in-C, Eastern Atlantic, 1992–95, also Allied C-in-C, Channel, 1991–94; Naval Comdr, NW Comd, 1994–95. DL Devon, 1999. *Recreations:* sailing, travelling, gardening, reading. *Address:* c/o Naval Secretary, Fleet Headquarters, Whale Island, Portsmouth PO2 8BY. *Club:* Army and Navy. *Died 1 June 2014.*

WHITE, Norman Arthur, PhD; CEng, FIMechE; Eur Ing; corporate executive, international consultant and management academic; *b* Hetton-le-Hole, Durham, 11 April 1922; *s* of late Charles Brewster White and Lillian Sarah (*née* Finch); *m* 1st 1944, Joyce Marjorie Rogers (*d* 1982); one *s* one *d*; 2nd, 1983, Marjorie Iris Rushton. *Educ:* Luton Tech. Coll. (HNC); Manchester Inst. of Sci. and Technol. (AMCT Hons); London Univ. (BSc Eng (Hons)); Univ. of Philippines (MSc); London Polytechnic (DMS); Harvard Business Sch. (grad. AMP 1968); LSE (PhD 1973). CEng; MRAeS; FEI; FIMechE; FIMMM. Industrial apprentice, George Kent, and D. Napier & Son, 1936–43; Flight Test Engr, Mil. Aircraft develt, 1943–45. Royal Dutch/Shell Gp, 1945–72: Petroleum Res. Engr, Thornton Res. Centre, 1945–51; Tech. Manager, Shell Co. of Philippines, 1951–55; Shell International Petroleum: Div. Hd, later Dep. Manager, Product Develt Dept, 1955–61; special assignments in various countries, 1961–63; Gen. Manager, Lubricants, Bitumen and LPG Divs, 1963–66; Dir of Marketing Develt, 1966–68; Chief Exec., New Enterprises Div., London and The Hague, 1968–72; Chm. and Dir, Shell oil and mining cos, UK and overseas, 1963–72. Established Norman White Associates (specialists in technology based enterprises and international resources), 1972, Director and Principal Executive, 1972–94; Energy Adviser: Hambros Bank, 1972–76; Tanks Consolidated Investments, Nassau, 1974–85; Chm./Dir, various petroleum exploration and prodn cos in UK, Netherlands, Canada and USA, 1974–92; Chairman: KBC Advanced Technologies, 1979–90; Tesel plc, 1983–85 (Dir, 1980–85); Ocean Thermal Energy Conversion Systems, 1982–2009; Process Automation and Computer Systems, 1985–94; Andaman Resources plc, 1986–90; Technology Transfer Centre Surrey Ltd, 1990–97; SpaceLink Learning Foundn (formerly Millennium Satellite Centre Ltd), 1995; Director: Environmental Resources, 1973–87; Henley Centre for Forecasting, 1974–92 (Dep. Chm., 1974–87); Proscyon Partners, 1992–2000 (Chm., 2000–04); Corporate Adviser: Placer Dome, Vancouver, 1973–78; Kennedy & Donkin Gp, 1986–94; Alcatel-Alsthom, Paris, 1993–96. Mem., Parly and Scientific Cttee, House of Commons, 1977–83, 1987–92. World Energy Council, Member: British Nat. Cttee, 1977–88; Conservation Commn, 1979–87; Internat. Exec. Assembly, 1987–94;

World Petroleum Congress: Chm., British Nat. Cttee, 1987–94 (Dep. Chm., 1977–87); Permanent Council, 1979–97; Treasurer, 1983–91, 1994–97; Chm., Develt Cttee, 1989–97; Vice-Pres., 1991–94; Presidential Award, 1997; Member: Bd and World Council, Internat. Road Fedn, Geneva and Washington, 1964–72; UK CAA Cttee of Enquiry on Flight Time Limitations (Bader Cttee), 1972–73; Internat. Energy/Petroleum Delegn to Russia, Rumania, E Germany, Hungary, Venezuela, Japan, Korea, People's Republic of China, Indonesia, India, Mexico, Argentina, Brazil, Iran and Southern Africa, 1979–97; Royal Soc./Inst. of Petroleum Delegn to People's Republic of China, 1985; Chm., China Technical Exchange Cttee, 1985–89. Visiting Professor: Arthur D. Little Management Educn Inst., Boston, USA, 1977–79; Henley Management Coll., 1979–89 (Vis. Fellow 1976–79); Manchester Business Sch., 1981–90 (Vis. Industrial Dir 1971–81); City Univ., 1990–96 (ext. examr, 1983–89); Vis. Lectr, RCDS, 1981–85. London University: Member: Senate, 1974–87; External Council, 1974–84; Governing Bd, Commerce Degree Bureau, 1975–84; Academic Adv. Bd in Engrg, 1976–85; Collegiate Council, 1984–87; Cttee of Mgt, Inst. of US Studies, 1984–92; Mem., Council of Mining and Metallurgical Instns, 1981–87; Member Council: Inst. of Petroleum, 1975–81 (Vice-Pres., 1978–81; Council Award for Meritorious Service, 1996); IMechE, 1980–85, 1987–91 (Chm., Engrg Management Div., 1980–85, Southern Br., 1987–89; Presidential Award for Meritorious Service, 1994); Founder Chm., Jt Bd for Engrg Management, 1990–93 (Chm. Academic Bd, 1994–97; Hon. DipEM 1997). FRSA 1944; FCMI; MRI; Mem., RIIA; Founder Mem., British Inst. of Energy Econs. Associate, St George's House, Windsor Castle, 1972. Governor: King Edward VI Royal Grammar Sch., Guildford, 1976–2002; Reigate Grammar Sch., 1976–93. Freeman, City of London, 1983; Liveryman: Worshipful Co. of Engineers, 1984; Co. of Spectacle Makers, 1986; Member: Guild of Freemen, 1986; Co. of World Traders, 1989. *Publications:* Financing the International Petroleum Industry, 1978; The International Outlook for Oil Substitution to 2020, 1983; (contrib.) Handbook of Engineering Management, 1988; Space-based Learning Service for Schools Worldwide, 2002; contribs to professional jls in UK, Philippines and Canada, on fluid mechanics, petroleum utilization, energy resources, R&D management, project financing and engrg management. *Recreations:* family and various others in moderation, country and coastal walking, wild life, browsing, international affairs, comparative religions, domestic odd-jobbing. *Died 13 Jan. 2015.*

WHITEHEAD, Ian Richard; HM Diplomatic Service, retired; Counsellor (Management), Paris, 1999–2003; *b* 21 July 1943; *s* of Alexander Guthrie Whitehead and Mary Helen (*née* Crosby-Milligan); *m* 2nd, 1996, Pamela Denise Mitchison; one *d*, and one *d* from previous marriage. *Educ:* Parmiter's Grammar Sch., London. Entered Foreign Office, 1960: 3rd Secretary: Addis Ababa, 1965–69; UK Delegn, NATO, Brussels, 1969–71; Consular Officer, Dubai, 1971–72; Vice Consul, Casablanca, 1972–75; FCO, 1975–78; 2nd Sec., Bridgetown, 1978–83; First Secretary: Paris, 1983–88; FCO, 1988–91; Dep. High Comr, Dar-es-Salaam, 1991–93; Head of Mission, Skopje, 1993–94; Counsellor, FCO, 1994–98; High Comr to Guyana and Ambassador to Suriname, 1998. *Recreations:* football, tennis, reading. *Address:* Ashview, 5 Lawrence's Lane, Cold Ash, Berks RG18 3LF. *Died 11 July 2014.*

WHITEHEAD, Sir John (Stainton), GCMG 1992 (KCMG 1986; CMG 1976); CVO 1978; HM Diplomatic Service, retired; Chairman, Daiwa Anglo-Japanese Foundation, 2008–12 (Trustee, 2004–12); *b* 20 Sept. 1932; *s* of late John William and Kathleen Whitehead; *m* 1964, Carolyn (*née* Hilton); two *s* two *d*. *Educ:* Christ's Hospital (Almoner, 2005–07); Hertford Coll., Oxford (MA; Hon. Fellow 1991); Open Univ. (BA Hons 2004). HM Forces, 1950–52; Oxford, 1952–55; FO, 1955–56; Tokyo, 1956–61; FO, 1961–64; 1st Sec., Washington, 1964–67; 1st Sec. (Economic), Tokyo, 1968–71; FCO, 1971–76, Head of Personnel Services Dept, 1973–76; Counsellor, Bonn, 1976–80; Minister, Tokyo, 1980–84; Dep. Under-Sec. of State (Chief Clerk), FCO, 1984–86; Ambassador to Japan, 1986–92. Chairman: Deutsche Morgan Grenfell Trust Bank Ltd (Japan), 1996–99; Japaninvest, 2004–09 (Hon. Pres., 2009–); non-executive Director: Cadbury Schweppes, 1993–2001; Serco Group, 1994–96; BPB, 1995–2002; Senior Adviser: Morgan Grenfell, later Deutsche Morgan Grenfell, Gp, 1992–99; Deutsche Asset Mgt Gp Ltd, 1996–2000; Adviser: Cable and Wireless plc, 1992–2002; Sanwa Bank Ltd, 1993–2000; Tokyo Electric Power Co. Inc., 1993–2002; Adviser to Board: Inchcape plc, 1992–96; Guinness plc, 1992–97; Mem. Adv. Bd, PowerGen International, 1996–2001. Exec. Consultant, WDA, 1992–94; Advr to Pres. of BoT, 1992–95; Mem. Adv. Panel, All Nippon Airways Co. Ltd, 2000–03. Member: UK-Japan 2000 Gp, 1992–2000, UK Japan 21st Century Gp, 2001– (Dir, 1995–2006); Council, Japan Soc., 1992–2006 (Mem. Exec. Cttee, 1996–2000, Jt Chm., 2000–04, Chm., 2004–06); Management Council, GB Sasakawa Foundn, 1993–96. Trustee, Monteverdi Choir and Orchestra, 1991–2000; Member: Royal Opera House Trust, 1992–93; Council, Buckingham Univ., 1992–95. Pres., Hertford Soc., 1991–97. Bundesverdienstkreuz (FRG), 1978; Grand Cordon, Order of Rising Sun (Japan), 2006. *Recreations:* new challenges, music, travel, golf, woodland management. *Address:* Bracken Edge, High Pitfold, Hindhead, Surrey GU26 6BN. *Clubs:* Oxford and Cambridge, London Capital, MCC; Liphook Golf (Hants). *Died 8 Nov. 2013.*

WHITEHOUSE, Dr David Bryn; Senior Scholar, The Corning Museum of Glass, Corning, USA, since 2011 (Director, 1992–99; Executive Director, 1999–2011); Trustee, The Rockwell Museum, since 1992; *b* 15 Oct. 1941; *s* of Brindley Charles Whitehouse and Alice Margaret Whitehouse; *m* 1st, 1963, Ruth Delamain Ainger (marr. diss.); one *s* two *d*; 2nd, 1975, Elizabeth-Anne Ollemans; one *s* two *d*. *Educ:* King Edward's Sch., Birmingham; St John's Coll., Cambridge (MA, PhD). FSA; FRGS. Scholar, British Sch. at Rome, 1963–65; Wainwright Fellow in Near Eastern Archaeology, Univ. of Oxford, 1966–73; Dir, Sīrāf Expedn, 1966–73; Dir, British Inst. of Afghan Studies, 1973–74; Dir, British Sch. at Rome, 1974–84; Chief Curator, 1984–88, Dep. Dir, 1988–92, Corning Mus. of Glass, Corning, USA. President: Internat. Union of Institutes, 1980–81; Internat. Assoc. for Hist. of Glass, 1991–95 (Mem. Management Cttee, 1988–95 and 1998–2012); Mem. Council, Internat. Assoc. for Classical Archaeology, 1974–84. Mem., Steering Cttee, Dublin Blaschka Congress, 2006. Trustee, Amer. Friends of Chartres Cathedral, 2005–12. Corresp. Mem., German Archaeological Inst.; Academician, Accademia Fiorentina dell'Arte del Disegno; Fellow: Pontificia Accademia Romana di Archeologia; Accademia di Archeologia, Lettere e Belle Arti, Naples. Ed., Jl of Glass Studies, 1988–2012. *Publications:* (jtly) Background to Archaeology, 1973; (jtly) The Origins of Europe, 1974; (with Ruth Whitehouse) Archaeological Atlas of the World, 1975; (ed jtly) Papers in Italian Archaeology I, 1978; Siraf III: The Congregational Mosque, 1980; (with David Andrews and John Osborne) Papers in Italian Archaeology III, 1981; (with Richard Hodges) Mohammed, Charlemagne and the Origins of Europe, 1983; (jtly) Glass of the Caesars, 1987; Glass of the Roman Empire, 1988; (jtly) Treasures from The Corning Museum of Glass, 1992; Glass: a pocket dictionary, 1993, rev. edn 2006; English Cameo Glass, 1994; Roman Glass in The Corning Museum of Glass, Vol. I, 1997, Vol. II, 2001, Vol. III, 2003; Ancient Glass from Ed-Dur, 1998; The Corning Museum of Glass: a decade of glass collecting 1990–1999, 2000; (with Stefano Carboni) Glass of the Sultans, 2001; Sasanian and Post-Sasanian Glass in The Corning Museum of Glass, 2005; (jtly) Drawing upon Nature: studies for the Blaschkas' glass models, 2007; Reflecting Antiquity, 2007; Siraf: history, topography and environment, 2009; Islamic Glass in the Corning Museum of Glass, vol. 1, 2010; Glass: a short history, 2012; many papers in Iran, Antiquity, Med. Archaeol., Papers of Brit. Sch. at Rome, Jl of Glass Studies, etc. *Address:* The Corning Museum of Glass, One Museum Way, Corning, NY 14830–2253, USA. *T:* (607) 9748424. *E:* whitehoudb@cmog.org. *Club:* Athenæum. *Died 17 Feb. 2013.*

WHITELAW, Billie Honor, CBE 1991; actress; *b* Coventry, 6 June 1932; *d* of Perceval and Frances Whitelaw; *m* 1st, 1952, Peter Vaughan (marr. diss. 1966); 2nd, 1967, Robert Muller (*d* 1998), writer; one *s*. *Educ:* Thornton Grammar Sch., Bradford. Appeared in: *plays:*

Hotel Paradiso, Winter Garden, 1954 and Oxford Playhouse, 1956; Progress to the Park, Theatre Workshop and Saville, 1961; England our England, Prince's, 1962; Touch of the Poet, Venice and Dublin, 1962; National Theatre, 1963–65: Othello, London and Moscow; Hobson's Choice; Beckett's Play; Trelawny of the Wells; The Dutch Courtesan; After Haggerty, Criterion, 1971; Not I, Royal Court, 1973 and 1975; Alphabetical Order, Mayfair, 1975; Footfalls, Royal Court, 1976; Molly, Comedy, 1978; Happy Days, Royal Court, 1979; The Greeks, Aldwych, 1980; Passion Play, Aldwych, 1981; Rockaby and Enough, NY, 1981, with Footfalls, 1984, NT 1982, Riverside, 1986, Adelaide Fest., 1986, Purchase Fest., NY, 1986; Tales from Hollywood, NT, 1983; Who's Afraid of Virginia Woolf?, Young Vic, 1987; *films:* No Love for Johnny; Charlie Bubbles; Twisted Nerve; The Adding Machine; Start the Revolution Without Me; Leo the Last; Eagle in a Cage; Gumshoe; Frenzy; Night Watch; The Omen; Leopard in the Snow; The Water Babies; An Unsuitable Job for a Woman; Slayground; Shadey; The Chain; The Dressmaker; Maurice; Joyriders; The Krays; Deadly Advice; Jane Eyre; Canterbury Tales (animated film); Quills; Hot Fuzz; *television:* No Trams to Lime Street; Lena Oh My Lena; Resurrection; The Skin Game; Beyond the Horizon; Anna Christie; Lady of the Camellias; The Pity of it all; Love on the Dole; A World of Time; You and Me; Poet Game; Sextet (8 plays); Napoleon and Love (9 plays: Josephine); The Fifty Pound Note (Ten from the Twenties); The Withered Arm (Wessex Tales); The Werewolf Reunion (2 plays); Ghost Trio, and But the Clouds, by Samuel Beckett; Not I; Eustace and Hilda (2 plays); The Serpent Son; Happy Days (dir. by Beckett); Private Schulz; Last Summer's Child; A Tale of Two Cities; Jamaica Inn; Camille; Old Girlfriends; The Secret Garden; Imaginary Friends (mini-series); The Picnic; Three Beckett plays; The 15 Streets; Lorna Doone; The Entertainer; A Murder of Quality; The Cloning of Joanna May; Firm Friends I and II (mini-series); Born to Run; Shooting the Past; A Dinner of Herbs; *radio plays:* The Master Builder; Hindle Wakes; Jane Eyre; The Female Messiah; Alpha Beta; The Cherry Orchard; Vassa Zheleznova; Filumena; The Wireless Lady. Lecturer on Beckett: in USA at univs of Santa Barbara, Stanford and Denver, 1985, Smith and Dartmouth Colls, 1992, Franklyn and Marshall Colls, 1993, Albany Univ., NY, 1997; at Balliol Coll., Oxford, 1986; An Informal Evening with Samuel Beckett and lecture tours, USA, 1992–95 and 1996; one-woman Beckett Evening, NY, 1997 and QEH, 1999. Annenberg/Beckett Fellow, Reading Univ., 1993. Silver Heart Variety Club Award, 1961; TV Actress of Year, 1961, 1972; British Academy Award, 1968; US Film Critics Award, 1968; Variety Club of GB Best Film Actress Award, 1977; Evening News Film Award as Best Actress, 1977; Sony Best Radio Actress Award, 1987; Evening Standard Film Award for Best Actress, 1988. Hon. DLitt: Bradford, 1981; St Andrews, 1997; Birmingham, 1997. *Publications:* Billie Whitelaw: who he? (autobiog.), 1995, USA 1996. *Recreation:* pottering about the house. *Address:* c/o Independent Talent Group Ltd, 40 Whitfield Street, W1T 2RH. *Died 21 Dec. 2014.*

WHITELEY, Sir Hugo Baldwin H.; *see* Huntington-Whiteley.

WHITFIELD, John Flett; JP; DL; Chairman: Surrey Police Authority, 1985–89; Police Committee, Association of County Councils, 1985–88; *b* 1 June 1922; *s* of John and Bertha Whitfield; *m* 1946, Rosemary Elisabeth Joan Hartman; two *d. Educ:* Epsom Coll., Surrey. Served War, King's Royal Rifle Corps, 1939–46. HM Foreign Service, 1946–57; Dir, Materials Handling Equipment (GB) Ltd, 1957–61; London Dir, Hunslet Holdings Ltd, 1961–64. Dir, Sunningdale Golf Club, 1973–77. Councillor: Berkshire CC, 1961–70; Surrey CC, 1970–89 (Chm., 1981–84). Contested (C) Pontefract, General Election, 1964. JP Berkshire 1971 (Chm., Windsor County Bench, 1978–80); DL Surrey 1982, High Sheriff, 1985–86. Chm., Surrey Univ. Council, 1986–88 (Vice-Chm., 1983–86). *Recreations:* golf, foreign languages, bookbinding. *Address:* Moor Cottage, Chobham Road, Sunningdale, Berks SL5 0HU. *T:* (01344) 620997. *Clubs:* Royal and Ancient Golf of St Andrews; Royal Cinque Ports Golf; Sunningdale Golf; Rye Golf; Woking Golf. *Died 15 July 2011.*

WHITHAM, Prof. Gerald Beresford, FRS 1965; Charles Lee Powell Professor of Applied Mathematics, at the California Institute of Technology, Pasadena, Calif, 1983–98, then Emeritus Professor of Applied Mathematics; *b* 13 Dec. 1927; *s* of Harry and Elizabeth Ellen Whitham; *m* 1951, Nancy (*née* Lord); one *s* two *d. Educ:* Elland Gram. Sch., Elland, Yorks; Manchester University (PhD Maths 1953). Lectr in Applied Mathematics, Manchester Univ., 1953–56; Assoc. Prof., Applied Mathematics, New York Univ., 1956–59; Prof., Mathematics, MIT, 1959–62; Prof. of Aeronautics and Maths, 1962–67, Prof. of Applied Maths, 1967–83, CIT. FAAAS 1959. Wiener Prize in Applied Mathematics, 1980. *Publications:* Linear and Nonlinear Waves, 1974; Lectures on Wave Propagation, 1979; research papers in Proc. Roy. Soc., Jl Fluid Mechanics, Communications on Pure and Applied Maths. *Died 26 Jan. 2014.*

WHITING, Alan; Managing Director, Merlan Financial, since 2004; *b* 14 Jan. 1946; *s* of Albert Edward and Marjorie Irene Whiting; *m* 1968, Annette Frances Pocknee; two *s* two *d. Educ:* Acklam Hall Grammar Sch., Middlesbrough; Univ. of East Anglia (BA Hons); University College London (MSc Econ). Research Associate and Asst Lectr, Univ. of East Anglia, 1967; Cadet Economist, HM Treasury, 1968; Economic Asst, DEA, and Min. of Technology, 1969; Economist, EFTA, Geneva, 1970; Economist, CBI, 1972; Economic Adviser, DTI, 1974; Sen. Econ. Adviser, 1979; Industrial Policy Div., Dept of Industry, 1983–85; Under Sec., Economics Div., DTI, 1985; Finance and Resource Management Div., DTI, 1989–92; Under Sec., Securities and Investment Services, later Financial Regulation, HM Treasury, 1992–97; Exec. Dir, Regulation and Compliance, London Metal Exchange, 1997–2004. Director: Nymex Europe Ltd, 2005–07; NYSE/Euronext/LIFFE, 2006– (Chm., 2012–14); Nymex London Ltd, 2008–09; ICE Europe Ltd 2013–. Dep. Chm., Mortgage Code Compliance Bd (formerly Council of Mortgage Code Register Intermediaries), 1999–2005; Mem., Gibraltar Financial Services Commn, 2005– (Chm., 2011–14); Dir, Lending Standards Bd (formerly Banking Code Standards Bd), 2005–14. *Publications:* (jtly) The Trade Effects of EFTA and the EEC 1959–1967, 1972; (ed) The Economics of Industrial Subsidies, 1975; articles in economic jls. *Recreations:* building, gardening, music, golf, sailing, tennis. *Address:* The Willows, Larges Lane, Bracknell RG12 9AN. *Clubs:* Bracknell Lawn Tennis; Mill Ride Golf (Ascot). *Died 14 June 2015.*

WHITLAM, Hon. (Edward) Gough, AC 1978; QC 1962; Member: Executive Board of Unesco, 1985–89 (Australian Ambassador to Unesco, 1983–86); Constitutional Commission, 1986–88; Prime Minister of Australia, 1972–75; *b* Melbourne, 11 July 1916; *s* of late H. F. E. Whitlam, Australian Crown Solicitor and Aust. rep. on UN Human Rights Commission and Martha Whitlam (*née* Maddocks); *m* 1942, Margaret Elaine, AO (*d* 2012), *d* of late Mr Justice Dovey, NSW Supreme Court; three *s* one *d. Educ:* University of Sydney. BA 1938; LLB 1946. RAAF Flight Lieut, 1941–45. Barrister, 1947; MP for Werriwa, NSW, 1952–78; Mem., Jt Parly Cttee on Constitutional Rev., 1956–59; Leader, 1973 and 1975, Dep. Leader, 1977, Const. Conventions; Deputy Leader, Aust. Labor Party, 1960, Leader, 1967–77; Leader of the Opposition, 1967–72 and 1976–77; Minister for Foreign Affairs, 1972–73. Vis. Fellow, 1978–79, First Nat. Fellow, 1980–81, ANU; Fellow, Univ. of Sydney Senate, 1981–83, 1986–89; Visiting Professor: Harvard Univ., 1979; Univ. of Adelaide, 1983. Chairman: Australia-China Council, 1986–91; Australian Nat. Gall., 1987–90. Pres., Australian Sect., Internat. Commn of Jurists, 1982–83. Founder, Hanoi Architectural Heritage Foundn, 1993. FAHA 1993. Corresp. Mem., Acad. of Athens, 1992. Hon. DLitt: Sydney, 1981; Wollongong, 1989; La Trobe, Wodonga, 1992; Univ. of Technol., Sydney, 1995; Univ. of Western Sydney, 2002; Hon. LLD Philippines, 1974. Silver Plate of Honour, Socialist Internat., 1976; Mem. of Honour, IUCN, 1988; Redmond Barry Award, Australian Library and Info. Assoc., 1994; Dunlop Asia Award, 2001; Friendship Ambassador, China, 2002. Grand Cross of Apostle Andrew, Greek Orthodox Archdio. of Australia, 2002. Grand Cross, Order of Makarios III (Cyprus), 1983; Grand Comdr, Order of Honour (Greece), 1996; Order of the Phoenix (Greece), 1998; Grand Officer, Order of Merit (Italy), 1999 (Comdr, 1997); Grand Comdr, Order of Logohu (PNG), 2005; Grand Cordon, Order of the Rising Sun (Japan), 2006. *Publications:* The Constitution *versus* Labor, 1957; Australian Foreign Policy, 1963; Socialism within the Constitution, 1965; Australia, Base or Bridge?, 1966; Beyond Vietnam: Australia's Regional Responsibility, 1968; An Urban Nation, 1969; A New Federalism, 1971; Urbanised Australia, 1972; Australian Public Administration and the Labor Government, 1973; Australia's Foreign Policy: New Directions, New Definitions, 1973; Road to Reform: Labor in Government, 1975; The New Federalism: Labor's Programs and Policies, 1975; Government of the People, for the People—by the People's House, 1975; On Australia's Constitution, 1977; Reform During Recession, 1978; The Truth of the Matter, 1979, 3rd edn 2005; The Italian Inspiration in English Literature, 1980; A Pacific Community, 1981; The Cost of Federalism, 1983; The Whitlam Government 1972–75, 1985; International Law-Making, 1989; Australia's Administrative Amnesia, 1990; Living with the United States: British Dominions and New Pacific States, 1990; National and International Maturity, 1991; Human Rights in One Nation, 1992; Abiding Interests, 1997; My Italian Notebook, 2002. *Address:* 100 William Street, Sydney, NSW 2011, Australia. *Died 21 Oct. 2014.*

WHITNEY, Sir Raymond (William), Kt 1997; OBE 1968; *b* 28 Nov. 1930; *o s* of late George Whitney, Northampton; *m* 1956, Sheila Margot Beswick Prince; two *s*. *Educ:* Wellingborough Sch.; RMA, Sandhurst; London Univ. (BA (Hons) Oriental Studies). Commnd Northamptonshire Regt, 1951; served in Trieste, Korea, Hong Kong, Germany; seconded to Australian Army HQ, 1960–63; resigned and entered HM Diplomatic Service, 1964; First Sec., Peking, 1966–68; Head of Chancery, Buenos Aires, 1969–72; FCO, 1972–73; Dep. High Comr, Dacca, 1973–76; FCO, 1976–78, Hd of Information Res. Dept and Hd of Overseas Inf. Dept, 1976–78. MP (C) Wycombe, April 1978–2001. PPS to Treasury Ministers, 1979–80; Parly Under-Sec. of State, FCO, 1983–84, DHSS, 1984–86. Vice-Chm., Cons. Employment Cttee, 1980–83; Chm., Cons. For. Affairs Cttee, 1981–83; Mem., Public Accounts Cttee, 1981–83; Vice-Chairman: Parly Latin-America Gp, 1997–2001 (Chm., 1987–97); All-Party China Gp, 1997–2001; All-Party Hospice Gp, 1997–2001; Sec., All-Party Parly Argentine Gp, 1997–2001; Chm., Positive European Gp, 1993–2001. Chm., Mountbatten Community Trust (formerly Mountbatten Training), 1987–. Chm., The Cable Corp., 1989–96. Licensed Lay Minister, Dio. of Oxford, 1999–. *Publications:* National Health Crisis—a modern solution, 1988; articles on Chinese and Asian affairs in professional jls. *Recreations:* theatricals, golf, bridge, walking. *Address:* The Dial House, Sunninghill, Berks SL5 0AG. *T:* (01344) 623164. *E:* ray.whitney@o2.co.uk. *Died 15 Aug. 2012.*

WHITTAKER, Geoffrey Owen, OBE 1974 (MBE 1962); Governor of Anguilla, 1987–89; *b* 10 Jan. 1932; *s* of late Alfred James Whittaker and Gertrude (*née* Holvey); *m* 1959, Annette Faith Harris; one *s* one *d*. *Educ:* Nottingham High Sch.; Bristol Univ. (BA). Auditor: Tanganyika, 1956–58; Dominica, 1958–60; Principal Auditor, Windward Is, 1960–64; Dir of Audit, Grenada, 1964–67; Audit Adviser, British Honduras, 1967–69; Colonial Treas., St Helena, 1970–75; Financial Sec. and Actg Governor, Montserrat, 1975–78; Financial Sec., British Virgin Is, 1978–80; Admin. Officer, Hong Kong, 1980–87; Finance Br., 1980–83; Principal Asst Sec., Lands and Works Br., 1983–85; Gen. Man., Hong Kong Industrial Estates Corp., 1985–87. *Recreations:* music, Basset hounds, heraldry. *Address:* Ashley, near Market Harborough, Leics. *Died 24 Feb. 2015.*

WHITTAKER, Nigel; corporate consultant; Chairman, ReputationInc Ltd, 2002–09; *b* 7 Nov. 1948; *s* of late Phillip Whittaker and Joan Whittaker; *m* 1972, Joyce Cadman; three *s*. *Educ:* Caterham Sch.; Clare Coll., Cambridge (BA 1971; MA 1977); Yale Law Sch. (JD). Called to the Bar, Middle Temple, 1974. Roche Products, 1974–77; British Sugar, 1977–82; Woolworth Holdings, subseq. Kingfisher plc, 1982–95 (Exec. Dir, 1983–95). Chairman: Retail Decisions (formerly Card Clear) plc, 1996–2006; Burson-Marsteller UK, 1997–99; MTI Partners Ltd, 1997–2002; Gourmet Hldgs (formerly City Gourmets Hldgs, later Madisons Coffee) plc, 1998–2007; Edelman Public Relations Worldwide, 1999–2002; Eagle Eye Telematics plc, 2000–04; Dir, Wickes plc, 1996–2000. Chm., CBI Distributive Trades Survey, 1986–94; Chm., British Retail Consortium (formerly Retail Consortium), 1995; Mem., UK Ecolabelling Bd (formerly Nat. Adv. Gp on Environmental Labelling), 1993–98. *Recreation:* cricket. *Address:* Sharps Farm, Bathealton, Taunton, Somerset TA4 2BJ. *Died 19 Feb. 2011.*

WHITTALL, (Harold) Astley, CBE 1978; CEng; Chairman: B.S.G. International Ltd, 1981–94; Ransomes plc (formerly Ransome, Sims & Jefferies Ltd), 1983–93 (Director 1979–93; Deputy Chairman, 1981–83); *b* 8 Sept. 1925; *s* of Harold and Margaret Whittall; *m* 1952, Diana Margharita Berner. *Educ:* Handsworth Grammar Sch., Birmingham; Handsworth and Birmingham Technical Colls. Gen. Manager, Belliss & Morcom, 1962; Managing Dir, Amalgamated Power Engineering, 1968, Chm., 1977–81; Director: LRC Internat., 1982–85; APV (formerly APV Baker and APV plc), 1982–95; R. Platnauer Ltd, 1984–2011; Sykes Pickervant, 1987–94; Inchcape Insurance Hldgs, 1988–90; Qualifications for Industry Ltd, 1997–; RTITB Ltd, 1999–2015 (Dep. Chm., 2005–15). Pres., Engineering Employers' Fedn, 1976–78; Chairman: Engrg ITB, 1985–91; ETA, 1990–94; British Iron and Steel Consumers Council, 1987–91. Freeman, City of London, 1984. Liveryman, Engineers' Co., 1984–. *Address:* Brook Farmhouse, Whelford, near Fairford, Glos GL7 4DY. *T:* (01285) 712393. *Clubs:* Royal Automobile, St James'. *Died 28 Aug. 2015.*

WHITTALL, Michael Charlton, CMG 1980; OBE 1963; HM Diplomatic Service, retired; First Secretary, then Counsellor, Foreign and Commonwealth Office, 1963–81; *b* 9 Jan. 1926; *s* of Kenneth Edwin Whittall and Edna Ruth (*née* Lawson); *m* 1953, Susan Olivia La Fontaine; one *d*. *Educ:* Rottingdean; Rugby; Trinity Hall, Cambridge. Served RAF, 1944–48. Foreign Office, 1949; Salonika, 1949; British Middle East Office, 1952; Vice-Consul, Basra, 1953; FO, 1955; Second Secretary, Beirut, 1956; FO, 1958; First Secretary, Amman, 1959. *Recreations:* railways (GWR), birdwatching, photography. *Died 9 Nov. 2014.*

WHITTINGHAM, Charles Percival, PhD; Head of Department of Botany, Rothamsted Experimental Station, 1971–82; *b* 1922; *m* 1946, Alison Phillips; two *d*. *Educ:* St John's College, Cambridge (BA 1943; PhD 1950). Professor of Botany, London University, at Queen Mary College, 1958–64; Head of Dept of Botany, 1967–71, and Prof. of Plant Physiology, 1964–71, Imperial Coll., Univ. of London; Dean, Royal Coll. of Science, 1969–71; Hon. Dir, ARC Unit for Plant Physiology, 1964–71. Vis. Prof., Univ. of Nottingham, 1978. *Publications:* Chemistry of Plant Processes, 1964; (with R. Hill) Photosynthesis, 1955; The Mechanism of Photosynthesis, 1974; contrib. to scientific journals. *Recreations:* music, travel. *Address:* Red Cottage, The Green, Brisley, Dereham, Norfolk NR20 5LN. *Died 31 Aug. 2011.*

WICKS, Rt Hon. Malcolm (Hunt); PC 2008; MP (Lab) Croydon North, since 1997 (Croydon North West, 1992–97); *b* 1 July 1947; *s* of Arthur Wicks and late Daisy (*née* Hunt); *m* 1968, Margaret Baron; one *s* two *d*. *Educ:* Norfolk House; Elizabeth Coll., Guernsey; NW London Poly.; LSE (BSc Hons Sociology). AcSS 2011. Fellow, Dept of Social Admin, York Univ., 1968–70; res. worker, Centre for Envmtl Studies, 1970–72; Lectr in Social Admin, Dept of Govt Studies, Brunel Univ., 1970–74; Social Policy Analyst, Urban Deprivation Unit, Home Office, 1974–77; Lectr in Social Policy, Civil Service Coll., 1977–78; Res. Dir and Sec., Study Commn on the Family, 1978–83; Dir, Family Policy Studies Centre, 1983–92; Co-Dir, European Family and Social Policy Unit, 1992. Parliamentary Under-Secretary of State: DFEE, 1999–2001; DWP, 2001–03; Minister of State: for Pensions, DWP, 2003–05; for Energy, DTI, 2005–06; for Science and Innovation, DTI, 2006–07; for Energy, BERR, 2007–08; Special Rep. of the Prime Minister on internat. energy issues, 2008–10. Sec., PLP Social Security Cttee, 1994–96. Mem., Family Policy Observatory, Eur. Commn, 1987–92. Chm., Winter Action on Cold Homes, 1986–92. Trustee, Nat. Energy

Foundn, 1987–94. Hon. DSSc Brunel, 2009. *Publications:* Old and Cold: hypothermia and social policy, 1978; (jtly) Government and Urban Policy, 1983; A Future for All: do we need a welfare state?, 1987; (jtly) Family Change and Future Policy, 1990; The Active Society: defending welfare, 1994; Energy Security: a national challenge in a changing world, 2009; contribs to books and periodicals. *Recreations:* walking, music, writing. *Address:* House of Commons, SW1A 0AA. *T:* (020) 7219 3000. *Club:* Ruskin House Labour (Croydon). *Died 29 Sept. 2012.*

WICKSTEAD, Cyril; Chairman, Eastern Electricity Board, 1978–82; Member, Electricity Council, 1978–82; *b* 27 Sept. 1922; *s* of John William and Mary Caroline Wickstead; *m* 1948, Freda May Hill (*d* 2008); two *s*. *Educ:* Rowley Regis Central Sch.; City of Birmingham Commercial Coll. FCIS. Served War, Royal Navy (Lieut RNVR), 1942–46. Midland Electric Corporation for Power Distribution Ltd: various positions, 1937–42; Asst Sec., 1946–48; Midlands Electricity Board: Sec., S Staffs and N Worcs Sub-Area, 1948–59; Dep. Sec. of Bd, 1959–63; Sec., 1964–72; Dep. Chm., 1972–77. Freeman, City of London, 1979. *Recreations:* music, reading, gardening, sport (spectator, alas). *Died 27 Nov. 2012.*

WIGGIN, Sir Alfred William, (Sir Jerry Wiggin), Kt 1993; TD 1970; *b* 24 Feb. 1937; *e s* of late Col Sir William H. Wiggin, KCB, DSO, TD, DL, JP, and Lady Wiggin, Worcestershire; *m* 1st, 1964, Rosemary Janet (marr. diss. 1982), *d* of David L. D. Orr; two *s* one *d*; 2nd, 1991, Morella Bulmer (*née* Kearton). *Educ:* Eton; Trinity Coll., Cambridge. 2nd Lieut, Queen's Own Warwickshire and Worcestershire Yeomanry (TA), 1959; Major, Royal Yeomanry, 1975–78. Contested (C) Montgomeryshire, 1964 and 1966. MP (C) Weston-super-Mare, 1969–97. PPS to Lord Balniel, at MoD, later FCO, 1970–74, and to Ian Gilmour, MoD, 1971–72; Parly Sec., MAFF, 1979–81; Parly Under-Sec. of State for Armed Forces, MoD, 1981–83. Chm., Select Cttee on Agriculture, 1987–97. Jt Hon. Sec., Conservative Defence Cttee, 1974–75; Vice-Chm., Conservative Agricultural Cttee, 1975–79; Chm., West Country Cons. Gp, 1978–79; Pres., Wells Cons. Assoc., 2000–06. Promoted Hallmarking Act, 1973. Chm., Economic Cttee, North Atlantic Assembly, 1990–94. Hon. Col, Warwickshire and Worcs Yeomanry (A) Sqn, Royal Mercian and Lancastrian Yeomanry, 1992–99. Pres., Worcs Hunt Club, 2013–. Mem. Ct of Assts, Goldsmiths' Co., 1995– (Prime Warden, 2006–07; London Assay Office Mgt Cttee, 2010–12). *Address:* The Square House, 36 Avenue Road, Malvern, Worcs WR14 3BJ. *T:* (01684) 565232. *E:* wigginjerry@aol.com. *Clubs:* Beefsteak, Pratt's; Royal Yacht Squadron. *Died 12 March 2015.*

WIGGIN, Sir Charles Rupert John, 5th Bt *cr* 1892, of Metchley Grange, Harborne, Staffs; *b* 2 July 1949; *s* of Sir John Wiggin, 4th Bt, MC and his 1st wife, Lady Cecilia Evelyn Anson (*d* 1963), *yr d* of 4th Earl of Lichfield; *S* father, 1992; *m* 1979, Mrs Mary Burnett-Hitchcock; one *s* one *d*. *Educ:* Eton. Civil Service; Major (retd), Grenadier Guards. *Heir:* *s* Richard Edward John Wiggin, *b* 1 July 1980. *Address:* c/o Child & Co., 1 Fleet Street, EC4Y 1BD. *Died 12 Oct. 2012.*

WIGGIN, Sir Jerry; *see* Wiggin, Sir A. W.

WIGHTWICK, (Charles) Christopher Brooke, MA; educational consultant, since 1991; *b* 16 Aug. 1931; *s* of Charles Frederick Wightwick and Marion Frances Wightwick (*née* Smith); *m* 1st, 1955, Pamela Layzell (marr. diss. 1986); one *s* two *d*; 2nd, 1986, Gillian Rosemary Anderson (*née* Dalziel). *Educ:* St Michael's, Otford Court; Lancing Coll.; St Edmund Hall, Oxford (BA 1954; MA 1958). Asst Master, Hurstpierpoint Coll., 1954–59; Head of German, Denstone Coll., 1959–65; Head of Languages, then Director of Studies, Westminster Sch., 1965–75; Head Master, King's College Sch., Wimbledon, 1975–80; HM Inspector of Schs, 1980–91; Staff Inspector for Mod. Langs, 1988–91. Series Editor, Berlitz Language Reference Handbooks, 1992–. *Publications:* (co-author) Longman Audio-Lingual German, 3 vols, 1974–78; Berlitz German Grammar Handbook, 1993; (jtly) Teaching and Learning Languages: a practical guide to learning by doing, 2012. *Recreations:* photography, computer programming, running, judo, language learning, inventing. *Address:* 19 Nottingham Road, SW17 7EA. *T:* and *Fax:* (020) 8767 6161. *E:* ccbwightwick@aol.com. *Died 20 March 2013.*

WILD, John Vernon, CMG 1960; OBE 1955; Colonial Administrative Service; *b* 26 April 1915; *m* 1st, 1942, Margaret Patricia Rendell (*d* 1975); one *d* (one *s* decd); 2nd, 1976, Marjorie Mary Lovatt Robertson. *Educ:* Taunton School; King's College, Cambridge. Senior Optime, Cambridge Univ., 1937; Cricket Blue, 1938. Colonial Administrative Service, Uganda: Assistant District Officer, 1938; Assistant Chief Secretary, 1950; Establishment Secretary, 1951; Administrative Secretary, 1955–60; Chairman, Constitutional Committee, 1959. Teacher and Lectr in Mathematics, 1960–76. *Publications:* The Story of the Uganda Agreement; The Uganda Mutiny; Early Travellers in Acholi; Uganda Long Ago. *Recreation:* gardening. *Club:* Hawks (Cambridge). *Died 21 July 2012.*

WILEMAN, Margaret Annie, MA; Honorary Fellow, Hughes Hall, Cambridge, since 1973 (President (formerly Principal), 1953–73); *b* 19 July 1908; *e d* of Clement Wileman and Alice (*née* Brinson). *Educ:* Lady Margaret Hall, Oxford, and the University of Paris. Scholar of Lady Margaret Hall, Oxford, 1927; First in Hons School of Mod. Langs, 1930; Zaharoff Travelling Scholar, 1931; Assistant, Abbey School, Reading, 1934; Senior Tutor, Queen's College, Harley Street, 1937; Lecturer, St Katherine's Coll., Liverpool, 1940; Resident Tutor, Bedford College, Univ. of London, 1944–53; Univ. Lectr, and Dir of Women Students, Dept of Educn, Cambridge Univ., 1953–73. Officier, Ordre des Palmes Académiques (France), 2000. *Address:* 5 Drosier Road, Cambridge CB1 2EY. *T:* (01223) 351846. *Club:* University Women's. *Died 12 Aug. 2014.*

WILKES, Gen. Sir Michael (John), KCB 1991; CBE 1988 (OBE 1980); Lieutenant-Governor and Commander-in-Chief, Jersey, 1995–2000; *b* 11 June 1940; *s* of late Lt-Col Jack Wilkes, OBE, MC and of Phyllis Wilkes; *m* 1966, Anne Jacqueline Huelin; two *s*. *Educ:* King's Sch., Rochester; RMA Sandhurst. Commnd RA, 1960; joined 7 Para Regt, RHA, 1961; Special Forces, 1964–67, Radfan, S Arabia, Borneo; Staff Coll., 1971–72; Bde Major RA, HQ3 Armd Div., 1973–74; Battery Comdr Chestnut Troop, 1 RHA (BAOR), 1975–76, CO 22 SAS Regt, 1977–79; Mil. Asst to CGS, 1980–81; COS, 3 Armd Div., 1982–83; Comdr, 22 Armd Bde, 1984–85; Dir Special Forces, MoD, 1986–88; GOC 3 Armd Div., 1988–90; Comdr UK Field Army and Inspector Gen., TA, 1990–93; ME Advr to MoD, 1992–95; Adjutant Gen., 1993–95. Col Comdt and Pres., HAC, 1992–98; Hon. Col, Field Sqn RE (Royal Jersey Militia), 2005–. Pres., ACFA, 1999–2005. Kermit Roosevelt Lectr, 1995. MInstD 2001. Freeman, City of London, 1993. KStJ 1995. Order of Mil. Merit, 1st class (Jordan), 1994. *Recreations:* sailing, ski-ing, military history. *Clubs:* Travellers; Royal Channel Islands Yacht, St Helier Yacht, Royal Artillery Yacht (Adm., 2002–07). *Died 27 Oct. 2013.*

WILKINSON, Prof. Christopher David Wicks, PhD; FRSE; James Watt Professor of Electrical Engineering, Glasgow University, 1992–2005, then Professor Emeritus; *b* 1 Sept. 1940; *s* of Charles Norman Wilkinson and Doris Margaret (*née* Wicks); *m* 1963, Dr Judith Anne Hughes; one *s* two *d*. *Educ:* Balliol Coll., Oxford (BA Physics; MA); Stanford Univ. (PhD Applied Physics). FRSE 1987. Engr, English Electric Valve Co., Chelmsford, 1968; Department of Electronics and Electrical Engineering, Glasgow University: Lectr, 1969–75; Sen. Lectr, 1975–79; Reader, 1979–82; Titular Prof., 1982–92. Vis. Scientist, IBM Res. Centre, Yorktown Heights, USA, 1975–76; Vis. Prof., NTT Labs, Tokyo, 1982. *Publications:* 325 papers on nanoelectronics, optoelectronics and bioelectronics, in learned jls. *Recreations:* hill walker, allotment holder, cooking, theatre. *Address:* 31 Hyndland Road, Glasgow G12 9UY. *T:* (0141) 357 0204. *Died 23 Feb. 2012.*

WILKINSON, David Lloyd; Chief Executive and General Secretary, Co-operative Union, 1975–99; *b* 28 May 1937; *m* 1960; one *s* one *d*. *Educ:* Royds Hall Grammar Sch. ACIS; CSD. *Address:* 2 Old House, Marsden, Huddersfield HD7 6AS. *T:* (01484) 844580. *Died 8 April 2014.*

WILKINSON, John Arbuthnot Du Cane; *b* 23 Sept. 1940; 2nd *s* of late Denys Wilkinson and Gillian Wilkinson, Eton College; *m* 1st, 1969 Paula Adey (marr. diss. 1987); one *d*; 2nd, 1987, Cecilia Cienfuegos, *d* of late Raul Cienfuegos Lyon, Santiago, Chile; one *s*. *Educ:* Eton (King's Scholar); RAF Coll., Cranwell; Churchill Coll., Cambridge (2nd cl. Hons Mod. Hist.; MA). Flight Cadet, RAF Coll., Cranwell, 1959–61 (Philip Sassoon Meml Prize, qualified French Interpreter); commnd 1961; Flying Instructor, No 8 FTS, Swinderby, 1962. Churchill Coll., Cambridge, Oct. 1962–65. Trooper, 21st Special Air Service Regt (Artists'), TA, 1963–65; rejoined RAF 1965; Flying Instructor, RAF Coll., Cranwell, 1966–67; Tutor, Stanford Univ.'s British Campus, 1967; ADC to Comdr 2nd Allied Tactical Air Force, Germany, 1967; resigned RAF, 1967. Head of Universities' Dept, Conservative Central Office, 1967–68; Aviation Specialist, Cons. Research Dept, 1969; Senior Administration Officer (Anglo-French Jaguar Project), Preston Div., British Aircraft Corp., 1969–70; Tutor, Open Univ., 1970–71; Vis. Lectr, OCTU RAF Henlow, 1971–75; Chief Flying Instructor, Skywork Ltd, Stansted, 1974–75; Gen. Manager, General Aviation Div., Brooklands Aviation Ltd, 1975–; PA to Chm., BAC, 1975–77; Senior Sales Executive, Eagle Aircraft Services Ltd, 1977–78; Sales Manager, Klingair Ltd, 1978–79. MP (C) Bradford W, 1970–Feb. 1974; contested same seat, Feb. and Oct. 1974; MP (C) Ruislip Northwood, 1979–2005. PPS to Minister of State for Industry, 1979–80, to Sec. of State for Defence, 1981–82. Chairman: Cons. Parly Aviation Cttee, 1983–85, and 1992–93 (Jt Sec., 1972–74; Vice-Chm., 1979); Cons. Parly Defence Cttee, 1993–94, 1996–97 (Vice-Chm., 1983–85, 1990–91, 1992–93; Sec., 1972–74 and 1980–81); Special Select Cttee on Armed Forces Bill, 1991; Member Select Committee on: Race Relations and Immigration, 1972–74; Sci. and Technol., 1972–74; Defence, 1987–90. Chairman: Anglo-Asian Cons. Soc., 1979–82; European Freedom Council, 1982–90; Cons. Space Sub Cttee, 1986–90 (Vice-Chm., 1983–85). Chm., Horn of Africa Council, 1984–88. Delegate to Council of Europe (Chm., Space Sub-Cttee, 1984–88, Migration Sub-Cttee, 2001–04; Chm., Cttee on Migration, Refugees and Demography, 2004–05) and WEU (Chm., Cttee on Scientific, Technological and Aerospace Questions, 1986–89), 1979–90, 2000–05; Leader, EDG/EPP Gp, Assembly of WEU, 2000–02; Chief Whip, EDG Gp, Council of Europe, 2001–04; Vice-Chm., British Gp, 2001–04, Vice-Pres., Cttee on Peace and Security, 2004–05, IPU; Chm., Defence Cttee, WEU, 2002–05. Parly Industrial Fellow, GKN plc, 1989–90; Postgrad. Fellow, TI plc, 1993; Parly Armed Forces Scheme attachment, RM, 1993–94; Metropolitan Police attachment, Parly Police Service Scheme, 2002–03. Mem., Commonwealth War Graves Commn, 1997–2003. Pres., London Green Belt Council, 1997–2005. CRAeS 1997. HQA (Pakistan), 1989; Order of Terra Mariana, 3rd cl. (Estonia), 1999; Order of Three Stars (Latvia), 2005; Order of Bernardo O'Higgins (Chile), 2005. *Publications:* (jtly) The Uncertain Ally, 1982; British Defence: a blueprint for reform, 1987; (novels as John Du Cane) The Cry of the Jets, 2012; The Huaso, 2013; pamphlets and articles on defence and politics. *Recreation:* writing. *Address:* c/o Barclays International Banking, PO Box 9, Barclays House, Douglas, Isle of Man IM99 1AJ. *Club:* Royal Air Force. *Died 1 March 2014.*

WILKINSON, Prof. Paul, CBE 2009; Professor of International Relations, 1990–2007, Emeritus Professor, 2008, and Chairman (formerly Director), Advisory Board, Centre for the Study of Terrorism and Political Violence, since 1999, University of St Andrews; *b* 9 May 1937; *s* of late Walter Ross Wilkinson and of Joan Rosemary (*née* Paul); *m* 1960, Susan Flook; two *s* one *d*. *Educ:* Lower School of John Lyon; University Coll., Swansea, Univ. of Wales (BA (jt Hons Mod. Hist. and Politics), MA; Hon. Fellow, 1986). Royal Air Force regular officer, 1959–65. Asst Lecturer in Politics, 1966–68, Lectr in Politics, 1968–75, Sen. Lectr in Politics, 1975–77, University Coll., Cardiff; Reader, Univ. of Wales, 1978–79; Prof., Internat. Relations, 1979–89, Hd, Dept of Politics and Internat. Relations, 1985–89, Univ. of Aberdeen; Dir, Res. Inst. for Study of Conflict and Terrorism, 1989–94; Hd, Sch. of History and Internat. Relations, Univ. of St Andrews, 1994–96. Vis. Fellow, Trinity Hall, Cambridge, 1997–98. Mem., IBA Scottish Adv. Cttee, 1982–85. Special Consultant, CBS Broadcasting Co., USA, 1986–91; Advr, Commonwealth Scholarships Commn, 2002–. FRSA 1995. Joint Editor: Terrorism and Political Violence Jl, 1988–2006; Cass Political Violence series, 1990–; Emeritus Editor, Handbook of Security, 1991–; Co-Chm., Praeger International series, 2004–08. *Publications:* Social Movement, 1971; Political Terrorism, 1974; Terrorism versus Liberal Democracy, 1976; Terrorism and the Liberal State, 1977, rev. edn 1986; (jtly) Terrorism: theory and practice, 1978; (ed) British Perspectives on Terrorism, 1981; The New Fascists, 1981, rev. edn 1983; Defence of the West, 1983; (jtly) Contemporary Research on Terrorism, 1987; Lessons of Lockerbie, 1989; Terrorist Targets and Tactics: new risks to world order, 1990; Northern Ireland: reappraising Republican violence, 1991; (ed) Technology and Terrorism, 1993; (ed) Terrorism: British perspectives, 1993; Lloyd Inquiry into Legislation against Terrorism, vol. 2 (research report), 1996; (jtly) Aviation Terrorism and Security, 1998; Terrorism Versus Democracy: the liberal state response, 2000, 3rd edn 2011; (jtly) Addressing the New International Terrorism, 2003; (ed) UK Homeland Security, 2007; International Relations - a very short introduction, 2007; (jtly) Terrorism and Human Rights, 2008; contribs to wide range of jls in Britain, USA and Canada. *Recreations:* modern art, poetry, walking. *Address:* School of International Relations, The Scores, St Andrews, Fife KY16 9AX. *T:* (01334) 462936. *Club:* Savile. *Died 11 Aug. 2011.*

WILKINSON, Prof. Tony James, FBA 2008; Professor of Archaeology, University of Durham, since 2006; landscape archaeologist; *b* Braintree, Essex, 14 Aug. 1948; *s* of James Wesley Wilkinson and Maggie Wilkinson; *m* 1995, Eleanor Rose Barbanes. *Educ:* Birkbeck Coll., London (BSc Geog.); McMaster Univ. (MSc Geog.). Consultant landscape archaeologist, 1972–89; Asst Dir, British Sch. of Archaeol. in Iraq, 1989–91; Res. Associate (Associate Prof.), Oriental Inst., Univ. of Chicago, 1992–2003; Lectr, 2003–05, Prof. of Near Eastern Archaeol., 2005–06, Univ. of Edinburgh. *Publications:* (with S. Duhon) Excavations at Franchthi Cave, Greece Franchthi Paralia, 1990; Town and Country in SE Anatolia, vol. 1, 1990; (with P. Murphy) The Archaeology of the Essex Coast, vol. 1, 1995; (with D. J. Tucker) Settlement Development in the North Jazira, Iraq, 1995; Archaeological Landscapes of the Near East, 2003 (Book Award, Soc. for Amer. Archaeol., 2004; James R. Wiseman Book Award, Archaeol. Inst. of America, 2005); Settlement and Land Use at Tell Sweyhat, and in the Upper Lake Tabqa, Syria, 2004. *Recreations:* blues: listening and playing (mem., Bamboo Beat Band, Lincoln, 1982–90), walking. *Address:* Department of Archaeology, Durham University, South Road, Durham DH1 3LE. *Died 25 Dec. 2014.*

WILKS, Jean Ruth Fraser, CBE 1977; Chairman of Council and Pro-Chancellor, Birmingham University, 1985–89; *b* 14 April 1917; *d* of Mark Wilks. *Educ:* North London Collegiate Sch.; Somerville Coll., Oxford (MA; Hon. Fellow, 1985). Assistant Mistress: Truro High Sch., 1940–43; James Allen's Girls' Sch., Dulwich, 1943–51; Head Mistress, Hertfordshire and Essex High Sch., Bishop's Stortford, Hertfordshire, 1951–64; Head Mistress, King Edward VI High Sch. for Girls, Birmingham, 1965–77. Pres., Assoc. of Head Mistresses, 1972–74; Member: Public Schools Commn, 1968–70; Governing Council of Schools Council, 1972–75; Adv. Council on Supply and Trng of Teachers, 1973–78; Educn Cttee, Royal Coll. of Nursing, 1973–79; University Authorities Panel, 1982–89. University of Birmingham: Mem. Council, 1971–89; Life Mem. Court, 1977; Chm., Academic Staffing Cttee, 1978–85; Dep. Pro-Chancellor, 1979–85. Pres., ASM, Somerville Coll., Oxford, 1982–85. Chm. Governors, Ellerslie, Malvern, 1982–89; Mem. Council, Malvern Coll., 1992–93. FCP 1978. Hon. LLD Birmingham, 1986. *Address:* 4 Hayward Road, Oxford OX2 8LW. *Died 15 July 2014.*

WILL, Ronald Kerr; Deputy Keeper of Her Majesty's Signet, 1975–83; formerly Senior Partner, Dundas & Wilson, CS, Edinburgh; *b* 22 March 1918; 3rd *s* of late James Alexander Will, WS and Bessie Kennedy Salmon,

Dumfries; *m* 1953, Margaret Joyce, *d* of late D. Alan Stevenson, BSc, FRSE; two *s*. *Educ:* Merchiston Castle Sch.; Edinburgh Univ. Commnd King's Own Scottish Borderers, 1940; served with 1st Bn and in Staff appts (despatches); psc; GSO II. Writer to the Signet, 1950. Director: Scottish Equitable Life Assce Soc., 1965–88 (Chm., 1980–84); Scottish Investment Trust PLC, 1963–88; Standard Property Investment PLC, 1972–87. Mem. Council on Tribunals, 1971–76 and Chm. of Scottish Cttee, 1972–76. Governor, Merchiston Castle Sch., 1953–76. *Recreation:* gardening. *Address:* 4 Waverley South, East Links Road, Gullane, East Lothian EH31 2AF. *T:* (01620) 845380. *Club:* New (Edinburgh). *Died 11 Sept. 2014.*

WILLCOCKS, Sir David (Valentine), Kt 1977; CBE 1971; MC 1944; conductor; Musical Director of the Bach Choir, 1960–98, Conductor Laureate, since 1998; General Editor, OUP Church Music, since 1961; *b* 30 Dec. 1919; *s* of late T. H. Willcocks; *m* 1947, Rachel Gordon, *d* of late Rev. A. C. Blyth, Fellow of Selwyn Coll., Cambridge; one *s* two *d* (and one *s* decd). *Educ:* Clifton Coll.; King's Coll., Cambridge (MA; MusB). Chorister, Westminster Abbey, 1929–33; Scholar, Clifton Coll., 1934–38; FRCO, 1938; Scholar at College of St Nicolas (RSCM), 1938–39; Organ Scholar, King's Coll., Cambridge, 1939–40; Open Foundation Scholarship, King's Coll., Cambridge, 1940; Stewart of Rannoch Scholarship, 1940. Served War of 1939–45, 5th Bn DCLI, 1940–45. Organ Scholar, King's Coll., Cambridge, 1945–47; Fellow of King's Coll., Cambridge, 1947–51, Hon. Fellow, 1979–; Organist of Salisbury Cathedral, 1947–50; Master of the Choristers and Organist, Worcester Cathedral, 1950–57; Fellow and Organist, King's Coll., Cambridge, 1957–73; Univ. Lectr in Music, Cambridge Univ., 1957–74; Univ. Organist, Cambridge Univ., 1958–74; Dir, RCM, 1974–84. Conductor: Cambridge Philharmonic Soc., 1947; City of Birmingham Choir, 1950–57; Bradford Festival Choral Soc., 1957–74; Cambridge Univ. Musical Soc., 1958–73. President: RCO, 1966–68; ISM, 1978–79; Old Cliftonian Soc., 1979–81; Nat. Fedn of Music Socs, 1980–89; Assoc. of British Choral Dirs, 1993–. Mem. Council, Winston Churchill Trust, 1980–90. Freeman, City of London, 1981. FRSCM 1965; FRCM 1971; FRNCM 1977; FRSAMD 1982; Hon. RAM 1965; Hon. FTCL 1976; Hon. GSM 1980; Hon. FRCCO 1967. Hon. MA Bradford, 1973; Hon. DMus: Exeter, 1976; Leicester, 1977; Westminster Choir Coll., Princeton, 1980; Bristol, 1981; St Olaf Coll., Minnesota, 1991; RCM, 1998; Victoria, BC, 1999; Rowan, 2007; Hon. DLitt: Sussex, 1982; Newfoundland, 2003; Hon. Dr of Sacred Letters, Trinity Coll., Toronto, 1985; Hon. Dr of Fine Arts, Luther Coll., Iowa, 1998; Hon. LLD Toronto, 2001. *Publications:* miscellaneous choral and instrumental works; *relevant publication*: A Life in Music: conversations with Sir David Willcocks and friends (ed by William Owen), 2008. *Address:* 13 Grange Road, Cambridge CB3 9AS. *T:* (01223) 359559. *Club:* Athenæum. *Died 17 Sept. 2015.*

WILLCOX, James Henry, CB 1988; Clerk of Public Bills, House of Commons, 1982–88; *b* 31 March 1923; *s* of George Henry and Annie Elizabeth Willcox; *m* 1st, 1950, Winsome Rosemarie Adèle Dallas Ross (*d* 1984); one *s* one *d*; 2nd, 1985, Pamela (*d* 2011), *widow* of Col John Lefroy Knyvett. *Educ:* St George's Coll., Weybridge; St John's Coll., Oxford (Schol.; MA). Served RNVR, HMS Laforey, 1942–43 and Offa, 1943–45. Assistant Clerk, House of Commons, 1947; Sen. Clerk, 1951; Clerk of Standing Committees, 1975–76; Clerk of Overseas Office, 1976–77; Clerk of Private Bills, Examiner of Petitions for Private Bills and Taxing Officer, 1977–82. *Recreations:* walking, gardening. *Address:* Lime Cottage, Horseshoe Lane, Ibthorpe, Andover, Hants SP11 0BY. *T:* (01264) 736552. *Club:* Garrick. *Died 6 May 2013.*

WILLETT, Allan Robert, CMG 1997; CVO 2011; Lord-Lieutenant of Kent, 2002–11; Chairman, Willett International Ltd, 1983–2002 (Chief Executive, 1983–91); *b* 24 Aug. 1936; *s* of Robert Willett and Irene Willett; *m* 1st, 1960, Mary Hillman (marr. diss. 1993); one *s* two *d*; 2nd, 1993, Anne Boardman (*née* Stead). *Educ:* Eastbourne Coll. Commnd Royal E Kent Regt, 1955–57; seconded, KAR, 1955–56. Man. Dir, G. D. Peters Ltd, 1969–71; Chm., Northampton Machinery Co., 1970–74; Dep. Chm., Rowen & Boden, 1973–74; formed Willett Cos, 1974. Chm., SE England Develt Agency, 1998–2002. President: Kent Br., SSAFA, 2002–11; County Cttee, Army Benevolent Fund, 2002–11; Assoc. of Men of Kent and Kentish Men, 2002–11; Patron: Kent Community Foundn, 2002–11; Kent Br., RBL, 2002–11; Trustee: Rochester Cathedral Trust, 2002–11; Canterbury Cathedral Trust Fund, 2002– (Chm., 2006–08). Hon. Fellow, Canterbury Christ Church Coll., 2003. Hon. DCL Kent, 2002; Hon. LLB Greenwich, 2003. *Recreations:* military history, golf, walking. *Address:* Cumberland Cottage, Chilham, Kent CT4 8BX. *T:* (01227) 738800, *Fax:* (01227) 738855. *E:* allan@allanwillett.org. *Died 18 July 2015.*

WILLIAMS, Rt Hon. Alan John; PC 1977; *b* Caerphilly, 14 Oct. 1930; *s* of Emlyn Williams, coalminer and Violet Williams (*née* Ross); *m* 1957, Mary Patricia Rees, Blackwood, Mon; two *s* one *d*. *Educ:* Cardiff High Sch.; Cardiff College of Technology; University College, Oxford. BSc (London); BA (Oxon). Flying Officer, RAF, 1956–58. Lecturer in economics, Welsh College of Advanced Technology; Free-lance Journalist. Joined Labour Party, 1950. Member: Fabian Society; Co-operative Party; National Union of Students delegation to Russia, 1954. Advr, Assoc. of First Div. Civil Servants, 1982–93. Contested (Lab) Poole, 1959. MP (Lab) Swansea W, 1964–2010. PPS to Postmaster General, 1966–67; Parly Under-Sec., DEA, 1967–69; Parly Sec., Min. of Technology, 1969–70; Opposition Spokesman on Consumer Protection, Small Businesses, Minerals, 1970–74; Minister of State: Dept of Prices and Consumer Protection, 1974–76; DoI, 1976–79; Opposition spokesman on Wales, 1979–80; Shadow Minister for CS, 1980–83; opposition spokesman on: trade and industry, 1983–87; Wales, 1987–89; Dep. Shadow Leader of the House, 1983–89 and 1988–89; Shadow Sec. of State for Wales, 1987–88; Father of the House, 2005–10. Member: Public Accts Cttee, 1966–67, 1990–2010 (Sen. Mem., 1997–2010); Standards and Privileges Cttee, 1994–95, 1997–2003; Lord Chancellor's Adv. Council on Public Records, 1995–2001; Jt Cttee on Parly Privilege, 1997–98; Chairman: Public Accounts Commn, 1997–2010; Liaison Cttee, 2001–10; Sec., British Amer. Parly Gp, 2001–08; Jt Chm., All-Party Minerals Cttee, 1979–86; Chairman, Welsh PLP, 1966–67; Delegate, Council of Europe and WEU, 1966–67. Sponsored by TSSA (Mem., 1984–95). *Died 21 Dec. 2014.*

WILLIAMS, Brynle; Member (C) North Wales, National Assembly for Wales, since 2003; *b* 9 Jan. 1949; *s* of George and Maenwen Williams; *m* 1970, Frances Mary Shawcross; one *s* one *d*. *Educ:* Ysgol Uwchradd Maes Garmon, Mold. Farmer. Chm., 2002–03, Pres., 2003–04, Flintshire County, Farmers Union of Wales; Council Member: Royal Welsh Agricl Soc., 1988–; Welsh Ponies and Cobs Soc., 1997–. *Recreation:* showing and judging cobs and ponies. *Address:* National Assembly for Wales, Cardiff Bay, Cardiff CF99 1ND. *T:* (029) 2089 8755, *Fax:* (029) 2089 8416. *E:* brynle.williams@wales.gov.uk. *Died 1 April 2011.*

WILLIAMS, Rear-Adm. Charles Bernard, CB 1980; OBE 1967; Flag Officer Medway and Port Admiral Chatham, 1978–80; *b* 19 Feb. 1925; *s* of Charles Williams and Elizabeth (*née* Malherbe); *m* 1946, Patricia Mary (*d* 2008), *d* of Henry Brownlow Thorp and Ellen Thorp; one *s* one *d*. *Educ:* Graeme Coll., Grahamstown, SA; Royal Naval Engineering Coll., Plymouth. Served in HM Ships Nigeria, Hornet, Triumph, 1946–53; in charge: Flight deck trials unit, 1953; Naval Wing, Nat. Gas Turbine Estabt, 1956; Sen. Engr, HMS Cumberland, 1958; in charge Admiralty Fuel Experimental Station, 1960; Comdr 1960; Engineer Officer, HMS London, 1962; Staff Engr, Flag Officer ME, 1964; Duty Comdr, Naval Ops MoD (N), 1967; Captain 1969; Dep. Manager, Portsmouth Dockyard, 1969; Supt, Clyde Submarine Base, 1972; Captain, HMS Sultan, 1975; Rear-Adm. 1978. Chairman: RYA Yachting Qualifications Cttee, 1976–86; Whitbread Round the World Race, 1978–90. *Recreations:* sailing, walking, music, bridge. *Address:* Parkes Meadows Care Home, Fareham, Hants PO16 0UD. *Clubs:* Royal Ocean Racing (Hon.

Mem.); Royal Naval Sailing Association (Life Vice Cdre); Royal London Yacht (Hon. Mem.); Royal Southern Yacht (Hon. Mem.); Hornet Sailing. *Died 11 June 2015.*

WILLIAMS, Colin; *see* Welland, C.

WILLIAMS, Colin Hartley; Partner, Williams & Williams, PR consultants, since 1992; *b* 7 Dec. 1938; *s* of late Gwilym Robert Williams and Margaret (*née* Hartley); *m* 1st, 1964, Carolyn (née Bulman) (*d* 1993); one *s* two *d*; 2nd, 1997, Shirley Ann (*née* Lavers). *Educ:* Grangefield Grammar Sch., Stockton-on-Tees; University College of Wales, Aberystwyth (BA). Journalist: Evening Gazette, Middlesbrough, 1960–63; Today Magazine, Odhams Press, 1964; Daily Sketch, 1964–66; Senior Lecturer, International Press Inst., Nairobi, 1967–68; Corporate and Public Relations Executive, 1969–74; Press Officer, Corporation of City of London, 1975–76; Asst Dir, City Communications Centre, 1977, Exec. Dir, 1979–83; Exec. Dir, Cttee on Invisible Exports, 1982–83; Chief Press Relations Manager, 1983–90, Hd of Corporate Communications, 1990–91, Hd of PR Gp, 1991–92, Nat. Westminster Bank. *Recreations:* writing, wine, golf, choral singing. *Address:* Goodacres House, Goodacres Lane, Lacey Green, Princes Risborough, Bucks HP27 0QD. *T:* (01844) 347271. *Died 28 Sept. 2013.*

WILLIAMS, Adm. Sir David, GCB 1977 (KCB 1975); DL; Governor and Commander-in-Chief, Gibraltar, 1982–85; a Gentleman Usher to The Queen, 1979–82, an Extra Gentleman Usher, since 1982; *b* 22 Oct. 1921; 3rd *s* of A. E. Williams, Ashford, Kent; *m* 1947, Philippa Beatrice Stevens; two *s*. *Educ:* Yardley Court Sch., Tonbridge; RN College, Dartmouth. Cadet, Dartmouth, 1935. Graduate, US Naval War Coll., Newport, RI. Served War of 1939–45 at sea in RN. Qual. in Gunnery, 1946; Comdr, 1952; Captain, 1960; Naval Asst to First Sea Lord, 1961–64; HMS Devonshire, 1964–66; Dir of Naval Plans, 1966–68; Captain, BRNC, Dartmouth, 1968–70; Rear-Adm. 1970; Flag Officer, Second in Command Far East Fleet, 1970–72; Vice-Adm. 1973; Dir-Gen. Naval Manpower and Training, 1972–74; Adm. 1974; Chief of Naval Personnel and Second Sea Lord, 1974–77; C-in-C Naval Home Comd, and ADC to the Queen, 1977–79. Pres., Ex Services Mental Welfare Soc., 1979–91; Chm. of Council, Missions to Seamen, 1989–93. Member: Commonwealth War Graves Commn, 1980–89 (Vice Chm., 1985–89); Museums and Galleries Commn, 1987–93. Hon. Liveryman, Fruiterers' Co.; KStJ 1982. DL Devon, 1981. *Recreation:* gardening. *Address:* Barnhill, Stoke Gabriel, Totnes, Devon TQ9 6SJ. *Clubs:* Army and Navy; Royal Dart Yacht; Royal Naval Sailing Association; Royal Yacht Squadron. *Died 16 July 2012.*

WILLIAMS, Sir David Innes, Kt 1985; MD; FRCS; Consulting Urologist: Hospital for Sick Children, Great Ormond Street (Urologist, 1952–78); St Peter's Hospital, London (Surgeon, 1950–78); *b* 12 June 1919; *s* of late Gwynne E. O. Williams, MS, FRCS; *m* 1944, Margaret Eileen Harding (*d* 2011); two *s*. *Educ:* Sherborne Sch.; Trinity Hall, Cambridge (MChir; MD); Univ. College Hospital (Hon. Fellow, 1986). RAMC, 1945–48 (Major, Surg. Specialist). Urologist, Royal Masonic Hosp., 1963–72; Civilian Consultant Urologist to RN, 1974–84; Dir, BPMF, 1978–86, Pro-Vice-Chancellor, 1985–87, Univ. of London. Mem., 1975–91, Chm., 1982–91, Council, ICRF; Chm., Council for Postgrad. Med. Educn in England and Wales, 1985–88. Mem., Home Sec's Adv. Cttee on Cruelty to Animals, 1975–79. Mem., GMC, 1979–89 (Chm., Overseas Cttee, 1981–88); Vice-Pres., RCS, 1983–85 (Mem. Council, 1974–86; Mem. Jt Consultants Cttee, 1983–85; Hon. Medal, 1987); President: BMA, 1988–89; RSocMed, 1990–92 (Past Pres., Urology Sect.). Pres., Friends of the Wellcome Inst. for History of Medicine, 1998–2003. Hon. Member: British Assoc. Paediatric Surgeons (Denis Browne Medal, 1977); British Assoc. Urological Surgeons (Past Pres.; St Peter's Medal, 1967); Assoc. Française d'Urologie; Amer. Surgical Assoc.; British Paediatric Assoc.; Amer. Acad. Pediatrics (Urology Medal, 1986). Hon. FACS 1983; Hon. FRCSI 1984; Hon. FDSRCS; Hon. FRSocMed 1993; Hon. FRCPCH 1996. *Publications:* Urology of Childhood, 1958; Paediatric Urology, 1968, 2nd edn 1982; Scientific Foundations of Urology, 1976, 2nd edn 1982; The London Lock, 1995; various contributions to medical journals. *Address:* 66 Murray Road, SW19 4PE. *T:* (020) 8879 1042. *Died 3 May 2013.*

WILLIAMS, David John; *b* 10 July 1914; *s* of late James Herbert Williams and Ethel (*née* Redman); unmarried. *Educ:* Lancing College; Christ Church, Oxford (MA). Called to Bar, Inner Temple, 1939. Postgrad. Dip. in Social Anthropology, LSE, 1965. Served War of 1939–45, Royal Artillery. Practised as Barrister, Norwich, 1946–51; Resident Magistrate, Tanganyika, 1951–56; Senior Resident Magistrate, 1956–60; Judge of High Court of Tanganyika, 1960–62; Lord Chancellor's Office, 1966–79. *Recreation:* the arts and travelling. *Clubs:* Travellers, Hurlingham. *Died 4 Aug. 2011.*

WILLIAMS, Prof. David Raymond, OBE 1993; Emeritus Professor of Chemistry, Cardiff University, since 2006; *b* 20 March 1941; *s* of Eric Thomas and Amy Gwendoline Williams; *m* 1964, Gillian Kirkpatrick Murray; two *d*. *Educ:* Grove Park Grammar Sch., Wrexham, Denbys; Univ. of Wales, Bangor (BSc (1st Cl. Hons Chemistry); PhD); DSc St Andrews. CChem, FRSC, 1976; EurChem 1992; FRSocMed 2005. NATO Postdoctoral Fellowship, Univ. of Lund, 1965–66; Lectr in Chemistry, Univ. of St Andrews, 1966–77; Prof. of Applied Chemistry, later Speciation and Analytical Chemistry, then Chemistry, UWIST, later UC Cardiff, then Cardiff Univ., 1977–2006. Chm., Sci. Adv. Cttee, British Council, 1986–94; Member: Radioactive Waste Management Adv. Cttee, DoE, 1980–95; Cttee on Medical Aspects of Radiation in the Environment, DHSS, later Dept of Health, 1985–89; Adv. Cttee on Hazardous Substances, DEFRA (formerly DETR), 2000–05. FRSA 1978. Jeyes Silver Medal, RSC, 1987; Wolfson Foundn Res. Award, 1988. *Publications:* The Metals of Life, 1970; An Introduction to Bioinorganic Chemistry, 1976; The Principles of Bioinorganic Chemistry, 1977; Laboratory Introduction to Bioinorganic Chemistry, 1979; Analysis Using Glass Electrodes, 1984; Trace Metals in Medicine and Chelation Therapy, 1995; What is Safe?: the risks of living in a nuclear age, 1998; 500 res. papers. *Recreations:* cycling, swimming, other outdoor pursuits, public speaking. *Address:* Cerrig Llwydion, St Fagans, Cardiff CF5 6EF. *T:* (029) 2056 8178. *Died 21 March 2013.*

WILLIAMS, Sir Denys (Ambrose), KCMG 1993; Kt 1987; Gold Crown of Merit, Barbados, 1981; Chief Justice of Barbados, 1987–2001; *b* 12 Oct. 1929; *s* of George Cuthbert and Violet Irene Williams; *m* 1954, Carmel Mary Coleman; two *s* four *d*. *Educ:* Combermere and Harrison College, Barbados; Worcester College, Oxford (BCL, MA). Called to the Bar, Middle Temple, 1954. Asst Legal Draftsman, Barbados, 1957; Asst to Attorney General, 1959; Asst Legal Draftsman, Fedn of West Indies, 1959; Senior Parly Counsel, Barbados, 1963; Judge of the Supreme Court, 1967. *Recreations:* horse racing, tennis, walking. *Address:* No 9, Garrison, St Michael, Barbados. *T:* 4271164. *Clubs:* Carlton, Barbados Turf (Barbados). *Died 7 Aug. 2014.*

WILLIAMS, Air Cdre Edward Stanley, CBE 1975 (OBE 1968); *b* 27 Sept. 1924; *s* of late William Stanley Williams and Ethel Williams; *m* 1947, Maureen Donovan; two *d*. *Educ:* Wallasey Central Sch.; London Univ. Sch. of Slavonic and E European Studies; St John's Coll., Cambridge (MPhil (Internat. Relations), 1982). Joined RAF, 1942; trained in Canada; service in flying boats, 1944; seconded BOAC, 1944–48; 18 Sqdn, Transport Comd, 1949; Instr, Central Navigation Sch., RAF Shawbury, 1950–52; Russian Language Study, 1952–54; Flying Appts MEAF, A&AEE, 216 Sqdn Transport Comd, 1954–61; OC RAF Element, Army Intell. Centre, 1961–64; Asst Air Attaché, Moscow, 1964–67; first RAF Defence Fellow, UCL, 1967–68; comd Jt Wing, Sch. of Service Intell., 1968–71; Chief, Target Plans, HQ Second ATAF, 1971–73; Chief Intell. Officer, HQ British Forces Near East, 1973–75; comd Jt Air Reconn. Intell. Centre, 1976–77; Defence and Air Attaché, Moscow, 1978–81, retired RAF, 1981. Vice-Chm. (Air), NW Area, TAVRA, 1988–93. *Publications:* The Soviet Military, 1986; Soviet Air Power: prospects for the future, 1990; Cold War, Hot Seat,

2000; various articles in professional jls. *Recreations:* Russian studies, photography. *Address:* c/o HSBC, 2 Liscard Way, Wallasey, Merseyside CH44 5TR. *Club:* Royal Air Force. *Died 12 March 2012.*

WILLIAMS, Evelyn Faithfull M.; *see* Monier-Williams.

WILLIAMS, Prof. Gareth Howel; Professor of Chemistry, University of London, 1967–84 (Head of Department of Chemistry, Bedford College, 1967–84), then Emeritus Professor; *b* 17 June 1925; *s* of Morgan John and Miriam Williams, Treherbert, Glam; *m* 1955, Marie, BA, *yr d* of William and Jessie Mary Mitchell, Wanlockhead, Dumfriesshire; one *d* (one *s* decd). *Educ:* Pentre Grammar Sch.; University Coll., London. BSc, PhD, DSc London; FRSC 1960. Asst Lectr, then Lectr in Chemistry, King's Coll., Univ. of London, 1947–60; Research Fellow, Univ. of Chicago, 1953–54; Reader in Organic Chemistry, Birkbeck Coll., Univ. of London, 1960–67. Vis. Lectr, Univ. of Ife, Nigeria, 1965; Rose Morgan Vis. Prof., Univ. of Kansas, 1969–70; Vis. Prof., Univ. of Auckland, NZ, 1977. External Examr: Univ. of Rhodesia, 1967–70; Univ. of Khartoum, 1967–73, 1976–80; City Univ., 1968–74; Univ. of Surrey, 1974–76; Brunel Univ., 1980–85. Chm., London Welsh Assoc., 1987–90. JP Brent, 1979 (Dep. Chm., 1989–91). *Publications:* Homolytic Aromatic Substitution, 1960; Organic Chemistry: a conceptual approach, 1977; (Editor) Advances in Free-Radical Chemistry, Vol. I, 1965, Vol. II, 1967, Vol. III, 1969, Vol. IV, 1972, Vol. V, 1975, Vol. VI, 1980; numerous papers in Jl Chem. Soc. and other scientific jls. *Recreation:* music. *Address:* 4 Dovey Court, North Common, Bristol BS30 8YX. *T:* (0117) 907 9092. *Club:* Athenæum. *Died 5 July 2012.*

WILLIAMS, (George Haigh) Graeme; QC 1983; barrister; a Recorder of the Crown Court, 1981–2002; *b* 5 July 1935; *s* of Dr Leslie Graeme Williams, MC, and Joan Haigh Williams (*née* Iago); *m* 1963, Anna Maureen Worrall, QC; two *d. Educ:* Tonbridge Sch. (Scholar); Brasenose Coll., Oxford (MA). Nat. Service, RA, England and Hong Kong, 1953–55. Called to the Bar, Inner Temple, 1959 (Entrance Scholar; Bencher, 1996); in practice at Common Law Bar, London, and on Oxford, later Midland and Oxford, Circuit. Hd of Chambers, 1988–98. Mem., No 3 Legal Aid Area Cttee, 1980–2000; Legal Pres., Mental Health Review Tribunals (Restricted Cases), 1996–2008. Legal Assessor, GMC and GDC, 1998–2007. *Publications:* Death of a Circuit, 2006. *Address:* 13 King's Bench Walk, Temple, EC4Y 7EN. *T:* (020) 7353 7204. *Died 23 Nov. 2013.*

WILLIAMS, George Mervyn, CBE 1977; MC 1944; TD; Vice Lord-Lieutenant of Mid Glamorgan, 1986–94; *b* 30 Oct. 1918; *yr s* of late Owain Williams and late Mrs Williams; *m* 1st, 1940, Penelope (marr. diss. 1946), *d* of Sir Frank Mitchell, KCVO; 2nd, 1950, Grizel Margaretta Cochrane, DStJ (*d* 2009), *d* of late Major Walter Stewart, DSO; one *s. Educ:* Radley Coll. Served Royal Fusiliers, N Africa and Italy, 1939–46; Major, British Military Mission to Greece, 1945. Great Universal Stores, 1946–49; Christie-Tyler PLC: Sales Dir, 1949; Man. Dir, 1950–80; Chm., 1959–85; Director: Lloyds Bank plc, 1972–77; Lloyds Bank UK Management Ltd, 1975–85; Chm., S Wales Regl Bd, Lloyds Bank, 1977–87. Governor, United World Coll. of Atlantic, 1980–88. JP 1965–70, High Sheriff 1966, DL 1967–86, Glamorgan. CStJ. *Address:* Tretower House, Tretower, near Crickhowell, Powys NP8 1RF. *T:* (01874) 730953; Llanharan House, Llanharan, Mid Glamorgan CF72 9NR. *T:* (01443) 226253. *Club:* Brooks's. *Died 7 Jan. 2013.*

WILLIAMS, Graeme; *see* Williams, George H. G.

WILLIAMS, Ven. Henry Leslie; Archdeacon of Chester, 1975–88; *b* 26 Dec. 1919; *m* 1949, Elsie Marie (*d* 2002); one *s. Educ:* Bethesda County Sch.; St David's Coll., Lampeter (BA); St Michael's Coll., Llandaff. Deacon 1943, priest 1944, Bangor; Curate of Aberdovey, 1943–45; St Mary's, Bangor, 1945–48; Chaplain, HMS Conway, 1948–49; Curate, St Mary-without-the-Walls, Chester, 1949–53; Vicar of Barnston, Wirral, 1953–84. RD of Wirral North, 1967–75; Hon. Canon of Chester Cathedral, 1972–75. Mem., General Synod, 1978–80, 1985–88. CF (TA), 1953–62. *Recreations:* fly-fishing, grandparenthood. *Address:* 1 Bartholomew Way, Westminster Park, Chester CH4 7RJ. *T:* (01244) 675296. *Died 29 Sept. 2013.*

WILLIAMS, Hilary a'Beckett E.; *see* Eccles-Williams.

WILLIAMS, John Melville; QC 1977; a Recorder, 1986–94; *b* 20 June 1931; *o s* of late Baron Francis-Williams and Lady (Jessie Melville) Francis-Williams; *m* 1955, Jean Margaret (*d* 1995), *d* of Harold and Hilda Lucas, Huddersfield; three *s* one *d. Educ:* St Christopher Sch., Letchworth; St John's Coll., Cambridge (BA). Called to the Bar, Inner Temple, 1955, Bencher, 1985. A legal assessor to GMC (and formerly to GDC), 1983–2007; first Pres., Assoc. of Personal Injury Lawyers, 1990–94; Co-Chm., Internat. Practice Sect., Assoc. of Trial Lawyers of Amer., 1991–92; Mem., Ind. Review Body Under New Colliery Review Procedure, 1985. Member: Criminal Injuries Compensation Bd, 1998–2000; Criminal Injuries Compensation Appeals Panel, 2000–08. Chm., The ClaimRoom.com Ltd, 2002–. Chm., Y2K Lawyers' Assoc., 1999. *Recreations:* mountain scrambling and walking, grandchildren, photography, travel. *Address:* 9 Nanhurst Park, Cranleigh, Surrey GU6 8JX. *T:* (01483) 274846. *E:* jmwqc@dial.pipex.com; Cnoclochan, Scourie, by Lairg, Sutherland IV27 4TE. *Died 7 Oct. 2011.*

WILLIAMS, Very Rev. Mgr John Noctor, CBE 1989; Prelate of Honour, 1985; Parish Priest, Our Lady and St John's, Heswall, 1993–2005; *b* 9 Aug. 1931; *s* of Thomas Williams and Anne Williams (*née* Noctor). *Educ:* St Anselm's Grammar School, Birkenhead; Ushaw College, Durham. Curate: St Laurence's, Birkenhead, 1956; St Joseph's, Sale, 1958; Sacred Heart, Moreton, 1958; Our Lady's, Birkenhead, 1959–66; Army, Chaplains' Dept, 1966–89: 7 Armd Bde, 1966; Singapore, 1969; 6 Armd Bde, 1971; UN, Cyprus, 1972; Senior Chaplain: Hong Kong, 1976; 1 Div., 1978; N Ireland, 1980; HQ BAOR, 1982; SE District, 1984; Prin. RC Chaplain, 1985–89, retd. VG 1986–89. *Recreations:* bridge, golf, motoring. *Club:* Conwy (Caernarvonshire) Golf. *Died 11 June 2014.*

WILLIAMS, Sir (Michael) Osmond, 2nd Bt *cr* 1909; MC 1944; JP; *b* 22 April 1914; *s* of late Captain Osmond T. D. Williams, DSO, 2nd *s* of 1st Bt, and Lady Gladys Margaret Finch Hatton, *o d* of 13th Earl of Winchilsea; *S* grandfather, 1927; *m* 1947, Benita Mary (*d* 2003), *yr d* of G. Henry Booker, and Mrs Michael Burn; two *d. Educ:* Eton; Freiburg Univ. Royal Scots Greys, 1935–37, and 1939–45; served Palestine, Africa, Italy and NW Europe. Chm., Quarry Tours Ltd (Llechwedd Slate Caverns), 1973–77. Vice-Chm., Amnesty Internat. (British Sect.), 1971–74. Mem., Merioneth Park Planning Cttee, 1971–74. Governor, Rainer Foundn Outdoor Pursuits Centre, 1964–76. MRI 1976. JP 1960 (Chairman of the Bench, Ardudwy-uwch-Artro, Gwynedd, 1974–84). Chevalier, Order of Leopold II with Palm; Croix de Guerre with Palm (Belgium), 1940. *Recreations:* music, travelling. *Heir:* none. *Address:* Borthwen, Penrhyndeudraeth, Gwynedd LL48 6EN. *Club:* Travellers. *Died 19 Dec. 2012 (ext).*

WILLIAMS, Nicholas James Donald; *b* 21 Oct. 1925; *s* of late Nicholas Thomas Williams and Daisy Eustace (*née* Hollow); *m* 1st, 1947, Dawn Vyvyan (*née* Hill); one *s* one *d*; 2nd, 1955, Sheila Mary (*née* Dalgety) (decd); two *s* one *d*; 3rd, Betty Edwards (*née* Danby). *Educ:* St Erbyn's Sch., Penzance; Rugby Sch. (Scholar). Admitted Solicitor 1949. Served Royal Marines, 1943–47 (Captain). Partner, Nicholas Williams & Co., Solicitors, London, 1950; Senior Partner, Surridge & Beecheno, Solicitors, Karachi, 1955; Burmah Oil Co. Ltd: Legal Adviser, 1961; Co-ordinator for Eastern ops, 1963; Dir, 1965; Asst Man. Dir, 1967; Man. Dir and Chief Exec., 1969–75; Man. Dir and Chief Exec., Don Engineering, 1977–84. Director: Flarebay Ltd, 1978–85; EBC Gp PLC, 1986–90; Ranvet Ltd, 1986–92. *Recreation:* sailing. *Club:* Royal Ocean Racing. *Died 25 Oct. 2011.*

WILLIAMS, Norman; *see* Williams, R. N.

WILLIAMS, Sir Osmond; *see* Williams, Sir M. O.

WILLIAMS, Penry Herbert; Fellow and Tutor in Modern History, New College, Oxford, 1964–92, Hon. Fellow, 1998; *b* 25 Feb. 1925; *s* of late Douglas Williams and Dorothy Williams (*née* Murray); *m* 1952, June Carey Hobson (*d* 1991), *d* of late George and Kathleene Hobson; one *s* one *d*. *Educ:* Marlborough Coll.; New Coll., Oxford, 1947–50; St Antony's Coll., Oxford, 1950–51. MA, DPhil Oxon. Served Royal Artillery, 1943–45, Royal Indian Artillery, 1945–47. Asst Lecturer in History, 1951–54, Lectr, 1954–63, Sen. Lectr, 1963–64, Univ. of Manchester. Sexual Harassment Officer and Dir, Graduate Studies, Faculty of Modern History, Univ. of Oxford, 1989–90. Fellow of Winchester Coll., 1978–93. Chairman: New Coll. Develt Cttee, 1992–97; Thomas Wall Trust, 1995–99. Jt Editor, English Historical Review, 1982–90; Editor, New College Record, 1993–2003. *Publications:* The Council in the Marches of Wales under Elizabeth I, 1958; Life in Tudor England, 1963; The Tudor Regime, 1979; (ed with John Buxton) New College, Oxford 1379–1979, 1979; The Later Tudors: England 1547–1603, 1995; (with Mark Nicholls) Sir Walter Raleigh in Life and Legend, 2010; contribs to learned jls. *Recreations:* travel, theatre. *Address:* Flat 3, Ockham Mews, 24 Bardwell Road, Oxford OX2 6SR. *T:* (01865) 554908, 558701. *Died 30 April 2013.*

WILLIAMS, Peter Keegan, CMG 1992; HM Diplomatic Service, retired; Chairman, Vietnam Enterprise Investments Ltd, since 1997; Director, Prudential Vietnam Ltd, since 1999; Senior Advisor: Prudential Corp. Ltd, since 1997; Tate & Lyle, since 1997; *b* 3 April 1938; *s* of William Edward Williams and Lilian (*née* Spright); *m* 1969, Rosamund Mary de Worms; two *d*. *Educ:* Calday Grange Grammar Sch.; Collège de Marcq-en-Baroeul (Nord); Univ. de Lille; Pembroke Coll., Oxford (MA). Joined Diplomatic Service, 1962; language student, MECAS, Lebanon, 1962; Second Sec., Beirut, 1963, Jedda, 1964; Commonwealth Office, 1967; First Sec., FCO, 1969; Director, Policy and Reference Div., British Information Services, New York, 1970; First Sec., FCO, 1973; First Sec., Head of Chancery and Consul, Rabat, 1976 (Chargé d'Affaires, 1978 and 1979); Counsellor, GATT, UK Mission, Geneva, 1979–83 (Chm. Panel, USA/Canada, 1980–81; Chm., Cttee on Finance, 1981–83); Ambassador, People's Democratic Republic of Yemen, 1983–85; Hd of UN Dept, FCO, 1986–89; RCDS, 1989; Ambassador to Socialist Republic of Vietnam, 1990–97. Sen. Advr, Scottish Enterprise, 1997–2002. Chm., Internat. Council, Christina Noble Children's Foundn, 1998–99. *Recreations:* wine, walking. *Clubs:* Travellers, Oxford and Cambridge. *Died 2 Dec. 2012.*

WILLIAMS, Dr Peter Orchard, CBE 1991; FRCP; Director: The Wellcome Trust, 1965–91; Wellcome Institute for the History of Medicine, 1981–83; *b* 23 Sept. 1925; *s* of Robert Orchard Williams, CBE, and Agnes Annie Birkinshaw; *m* 1949, Billie Innes Brown (*d* 2007); two *d*. *Educ:* Caterham Sch.; Queen's Royal College, Trinidad; St John's Coll., Cambridge (MA); St Mary's Hospital Medical School. MB, BChir 1950; MRCP 1952; FRCP 1970. House Physician, St Mary's Hospital, 1950–51; Registrar, Royal Free Hospital, 1951–52; Medical Specialist, RAMC, BMH Iserlohn, 1954; Medical Officer, Headquarters, MRC, 1955–60; Wellcome Trust: Asst and Dep. Scientific Secretary, 1960–64; Scientific Secretary, 1964–65. Vice-Pres., Royal Soc. of Tropical Med. and Hygiene, 1975–77, Pres., 1991–93; Member: Nat. Council of Soc. Services Cttee of Enquiry into Charity Law and Practice, 1974–76; BBC, IBA Central Appeals Adv. Cttee, 1978–83; DHSS Jt Planning Adv. Cttee, 1986–; Chairman: Foundations Forum, 1977–79; Assoc. of Med. Res. Charities, 1974–76, 1979–83; Hague Club (European Foundns), 1981–83. Hon. Vis. Fellow, Green Coll., Oxford, 1993. Hon. Fellow, LSHTM, 1986. Hon. DSc: Birmingham, 1989; West Indies, 1991; Glasgow, 1992; Hon. DM: Nottingham, 1990; Oxford, 1993. Mary Kingsley Medal for Services to Tropical Medicine, Liverpool Sch. of Trop. Med., 1983. *Publications:* Careers in Medicine, 1952; The Exotic Fruits of My Life (autobiog.), 2003; The Story of the Wellcome Trust, 2010; papers in scientific journals. *Recreations:* garden, history of science. *Address:* Courtyard House, Bletchingdon, Kidlington, Oxon OX5 3DL. *Died 25 July 2014.*

WILLIAMS, Raymond Lloyd, CBE 1987; DPhil, DSc; CChem, FRSC; Director, Metropolitan Police Laboratory, 1968–87; Visiting Professor in Chemistry, University of East Anglia, 1968–93; *b* Bournemouth, 27 Feb. 1927; *s* of late Walter Raymond Williams and Vera Mary Williams; *m* 1956, Sylvia Mary Lawson Whitaker; one *s* one *d*. *Educ:* Bournemouth Sch.; St John's Coll., Oxford (schol.). Gibbs Univ. Schol. 1948, BA 1st Cl. Hons Nat Sci-Chem, MA, DPhil, DSc Oxon. Research Fellow, Pressed Steel Co., 1951–53; Commonwealth Fund Fellow, Univ. of California, Berkeley, 1953–54; progressively, Sen. Res. Fellow, Sen. Scientific Officer, Principal Sci. Officer, Explosives R&D Estab., 1955–60; PSO, Admiralty Materials Lab., 1960–62; Explosives R&D Establishment: SPSO, 1962; Supt, Analytical Services Gp, 1962–65; Supt, Non-metallic Materials Gp, 1965–68. External Examiner: Univ. of Strathclyde, 1983–85; KCL, 1986–88. Vis. Lectr, Univ. of Lausanne, 1989; Lectures: Theophilus Redwood, RSC, 1984; Schools, RSC, 1988; Public, RSC, 1990; Dalton, RSC, 1995. Jt Editor: Forensic Science International, 1978–97; Forensic Science Progress, 1984–92. Pres., Forensic Science Soc., 1983–85; Hon. Mem., Assoc. of Police Surgeons of GB, 1980. FFSSoc 2008. Adelaide Medal, Internat. Assoc. of Forensic Scis, 1993. *Publications:* papers in scientific jls on spectroscopy, analytical chemistry, and forensic science. *Recreations:* lawn tennis (played for Civil Service and Oxfordshire: representative colours), carpentry. *Address:* 9 Meon Road, Bournemouth, Dorset BH7 6PN. *T:* (01202) 423446. *Died 19 Nov. 2012.*

WILLIAMS, (Reginald) Norman, CB 1982; Assistant Registrar of Friendly Societies, 1984–93; *b* 23 Oct. 1917; *s* of Reginald Gardnar Williams and Janet Mary Williams; *m* 1956, Hilary Frances West; two *s*. *Educ:* Neath Grammar Sch.; Swansea Univ. Served War: Captain RA and later Staff Captain HQ 30 Corps, 1940–46. Solicitor in private practice, 1947–48. Dept of Health and Social Security (formerly Min. of Nat. Insurance): Legal Asst, 1948; Sen. Legal Asst, 1959; Asst Solicitor, 1966; Principal Asst Solicitor, 1974; Under Sec., 1977–82. Member of Law Society. *Recreations:* golf, photography, reading. *Address:* Brecon, 23 Castle Hill Avenue, Berkhamsted, Herts HP4 1HJ. *T:* (01442) 865291. *Died 17 Dec. 2011.*

WILLIAMS, Prof. Robert Joseph Paton, MBE 2010; DPhil; FRS 1972; Emeritus Fellow, Wadham College, Oxford, since 1995 (Fellow, 1955–95, Senior Research Fellow, 1991–95); Royal Society Napier Research Professor at Oxford, 1974–91; *b* 25 Feb. 1926; *m* 1952, Jelly Klara (*née* Büchli); two *s*. *Educ:* Wallasey Grammar Sch.; Merton Coll., Oxford (MA, DPhil; Hon. Fellow, 1991). FRSC. Rotary Foundn Fellow, Uppsala, 1950–51; Jun. Res. Fellow, Merton Coll., Oxford, 1951–55; Lectr, 1955–72, Reader in Inorganic Chemistry, 1972–74, Univ. of Oxford. Associate, Peter Bent Brigham Hosp., Boston, USA; Commonwealth Fellow, Mass, 1965–66; Vis. Prof., Royal Free Hosp., London Univ., 1991–. Lectures: Buchman Meml, CIT, 1972; Liversidge, Chem. Soc., 1979; Commem., Biochem. Inst., Univ. of Zurich, 1981; Bakerian, 1981, Rutherford, 1996, Royal Soc.; Goodman, London, 1992; J. D. Bernal, Birkbeck Coll., Univ. of London, 1993; Cohn, Univ. of Philadelphia, 1997; Birchall, Univ. of Keele, 1999; Huxley, Univ. of Birmingham, 2000. President: Chem. Sect., BAAS, 1985–86; Dalton Div., RSC, 1991–93. Foreign Member: Acad. of Science, Portugal, 1981; Royal Soc. of Science, Liège, 1981; Royal Swedish Acad. of Sciences, 1983; Czechoslovak Acad. of Science, 1989. Hon. DSc: Liège, 1980; Leicester, 1985; East Anglia, 1992; Keele, 1993; Instituto Superior Técnico, Lisbon, 1997. Tilden Medal, Chem. Soc., 1970; Keilin Medal, Biochem. Soc., 1972; Hughes Medal, Royal Soc., 1979; Claire Bruylants Medal, Louvain, 1980; Krebs Medal, Eur. Biochem. Soc., 1985; Linderstrøm-Lang Medal, Carlsberg Foundn, Copenhagen, 1986; Sigillum Magnum (Medal), Univ. of Bologna, 1987; Heyrovský Medal, Internat. Union of Biochem., 1988; Frederick Gowland Hopkins Medal, Biochem. Soc., 1989; Royal Medal, Royal Soc., 1995; Longstaff Medal, Chem. Soc., 2002; Certificate of Honour, Oxford City, 2003. *Publications:* (with C. S. G. Phillips) Inorganic Chemistry, 1965; (jtly) Nuclear Magnetic Resonance in Biology, 1977; (ed jtly) New Trends in Bio-Inorganic Chemistry, 1978; (with S. Mann and J. Webb) Biomineralization, 1989; (ed jtly) Chemistry at Oxford, 1600–2005, 2009; (with R. E. M. Rockaby) Evolution's Destiny, 2012; with J. J. R. Frausto da Silva: The Biological Chemistry of the Elements, 1991, 2nd edn 2001; The Natural Selection of the Chemical Elements, 1996; Bringing Chemistry to Life, 1999; papers in Jl Chem. Soc., biochemical jls, etc. *Recreation:* walking in the country. *Address:* Wadham College, Oxford OX1 3QR. *T:* (01865) 242564. *Died 21 March 2015.*

WILLIAMS, Robert Martin, CB 1981; CBE 1973; Chairman, State Services Commission, New Zealand, 1975–81; *b* 30 March 1919; *s* of late Canon Henry Williams; *m* 1944, Mary Constance, *d* of late Rev. Francis H. Thorpe; one *s* two *d*. *Educ:* Christ's Coll., NZ; Canterbury University College, NZ; St John's Coll., Cambridge. MA. 1st Class Hons Mathematics, Univ. Sen. Schol., Shirtcliffe Fellow, NZ, 1940; BA, 1st Class Hons Mathematics Tripos, Cantab, 1947; PhD Math. Statistics, Cantab, 1949. Mathematician at Radar Development Laboratory, DSIR, NZ, 1941–44; Member UK Atomic Group in US, 1944–45; Member, 1949–53, Director, 1953–62, Applied Mathematics Laboratory, DSIR, NZ; Harkness Commonwealth Fellow and Vis. Fellow, at Princeton Univ., 1957–58; State Services Commissioner, NZ Public Service, 1963–67; Vice-Chancellor: Univ. of Otago, Dunedin, 1967–73; ANU, 1973–75. Mem., NZ Metric Adv. Bd, 1969–73. Mem., Internat. Statistical Inst., 1961–97. Chairman: Cttee of Inquiry into Educnl TV, 1970–72; Policy Cttee, Dictionary of NZ Biography, 1983–90. President: NZ Book Council, 1989–92; Nat. Liby Soc., 1992–95. Carnegie Travel Award, 1969. Hon. LLD Otago, 1972. *Publications:* papers mainly on mathematical statistics and related topics. *Address:* 21 Wadestown Road, Wellington, New Zealand. *Club:* Wellington (Wellington, NZ). *Died 18 March 2013.*

WILLIAMS, Sir Robin (Philip), 2nd Bt *cr* 1953, of Cilgeraint, co. Caernarvon; Insurance Broker, 1952–91; Lloyd's Underwriter, 1961–99; 2nd Lieut, retired, RA; *b* 27 May 1928; *s* of Sir Herbert Geraint Williams, 1st Bt, MP, MSc, MEngAssoc, MInstCE; *S* father, 1954; *m* 1955, Wendy Adèle Marguerite, *o d* of late Felix Joseph Alexander, London and Hong Kong; two *s*. *Educ:* Eton Coll.; St John's Coll., Cambridge (MA). 2nd Lieut, Royal Artillery, 1947. Vice-Chairman, Federation of Univ. Conservative and Unionist Assocs, 1951–52; Acting Chairman, 1952; Chairman of Bow Group (Conservative Research Society), 1954. Called to Bar, Middle Temple, 1954; Chm., Anti-Common Market League, 1969–84; Dir, Common Market Safeguards Campaign, 1973–76; Hon. Secretary: Safeguard Britain Campaign, 1976–89; Campaign for an Independent Britain, 1989–2008. Councillor, Haringey, 1968–74. *Publications:* Whose Public Schools?, 1957. *Heir: s* Anthony Geraint Williams [*b* 22 Dec. 1958; *m* 1990, Rachel Jane, *e d* of Norman Jennings; three *s* one *d*]. *Address:* 1 Broadlands Close, Highgate, N6 4AF. *Died 14 Sept. 2013.*

WILLIAMS, Ronald William; Senior Adviser (Global Human Resources), PricewaterhouseCoopers (formerly Coopers & Lybrand), 1986–2001; Director, Office of Manpower Economics, 1980–86 (on secondment); *b* 19 Dec. 1926; *yr s* of late Albert Williams and Katherine Teresa Williams (*née* Chilver). *Educ:* City of London Sch.; Downing Coll., Cambridge (MA, LLB). RN, 1945–48. Iraq Petroleum Co. Ltd, 1956–58; Philips Electrical Industries Ltd, 1958–64; Consultant, later Sen. Consultant, PA Management Consultants Ltd, 1964–69; Asst Sec., NBPI, 1969–71; Sen. Consultant, Office of Manpower Economics, 1971–73; Asst Sec., CSD, 1973–80 (UK Govt rep. and Chm., inter-govt negotiating cttee, ILO Tripartite Conf. on Public Servs, 1975); Under Sec. 1980; HM Treasury, 1982; Dept of Employment, 1986. Mem., Nat. Whitley Council for the Civil Service, 1975–77. *Recreations:* music, history. *Address:* 10 Pine Park Mansions, 1–3 Wilderton Road, Branksome Park, Poole, Dorset BH13 6EB. *T:* (01202) 769736. *Died 20 Nov. 2014.*

WILLIAMS, Susan Eva, MBE 1959; Lord-Lieutenant of South Glamorgan, 1985–90; *b* 17 Aug. 1915; *d* of Robert Henry Williams and Dorothy Marie Williams; *m* 1950, Charles Crofts Llewellyn Williams (*d* 1952). *Educ:* St James's, West Malvern. WAAF, 1939–45. JP 1961, High Sheriff 1968, DL 1973, Glamorgan; Lieut, S Glam, 1981–85. DStJ 1990. *Recreation:* National Hunt racing. *Address:* Caercady, Welsh St Donats, Cowbridge, Vale of Glamorgan CF71 7ST. *T:* (01446) 772346. *Died 7 Jan. 2011.*

WILLIAMSON OF HORTON, Baron *cr* 1999 (Life Peer), of Horton in the county of Somerset; **David Francis Williamson,** GCMG 1998; CB 1984; PC 2007; Secretary-General, Commission of the European Communities, 1987–97; *b* 8 May 1934; *s* of late Samuel Charles Wathen Williamson and Marie Eileen Williamson (*née* Denney); *m* 1961, Patricia Margaret Smith; two *s*. *Educ:* Tonbridge Sch.; Exeter Coll., Oxford (MA). Entered Min. of Agriculture, Fisheries and Food, 1958; Private Sec. to Permanent Sec. and to successive Parly Secs, 1960–62; HM Diplomatic Service, as First Sec. (Agric. and Food), Geneva, for Kennedy Round Trade Negotiations, 1965–67; Principal Private Sec. to successive Ministers of Agric., Fisheries and Food, 1967–70; Head of Milk and Milk Products Div., Marketing Policy Div. and Food Policy Div., 1970–74; Under-Sec., Gen. Agricultural Policy Gp, 1974–76, EEC Gp, 1976–77; Dep. Dir Gen., Agriculture, European Commn, 1977–83; Dep. Sec., Cabinet Office, 1983–87. Mem., Select Cttee on EU, H of L, 2001–04. Convenor of crossbench peers, 2004–07. Non-exec. Dir, Whitbread plc, 1998–2005; Chm., Somerset Strategic Partnership, 2001–04. Vis. Prof., Univ. of Bath, 1997–2000. Pres., Univs Assoc. for Contemp. Eur. Studies, 2001–03. Trustee, Thomson Foundn, 2001–06. Hon. DEconSc Limerick, 1996; Hon. DCL Kent, 1998; Hon. Dr of Laws: Robert Gordon, 1999; Bath, 1999. Kt Commander's Cross, Order of Merit (Germany), 1991; Commander Grand Cross, Royal Order of Polar Star (Sweden), 1998; Commandeur, Légion d'Honneur (France), 1999. *Address:* 58 St Joseph's Field, Taunton, Somerset TA1 3TF. *Died 30 Aug. 2015.*

WILLIAMSON, Prof. James, CBE 1985; FRCPE; Professor of Geriatric Medicine, University of Edinburgh, 1976–86, then Emeritus; *b* 22 Nov. 1920; *s* of James Mathewson Williamson and Jessie Reid; *m* 1945, Sheila Mary Blair; three *s* two *d*. *Educ:* Wishaw High Sch., Lanarkshire; Univ. of Glasgow (MB ChB 1943); FRCPE 1959 (MRCPE 1949). Training in general medicine, incl. two years in general practice, later specialising in respiratory diseases, then in medicine of old age; Consultant Physician, 1954–73; Prof. of Geriatric Medicine in newly established Chair, Univ. of Liverpool, 1973–76. Pres., British Geriatrics Soc., 1986–88; Chairman: Age Concern Scotland, 1987–90; Chest Heart Stroke Assoc., Scotland, 1993–98. Hon. DSc Rochester, USA, 1989. *Publications:* chapters in various textbooks; numerous articles in gen. med. jls and in jls devoted to subject of old age. *Recreations:* walking, reading. *Address:* 8 Chester Street, Edinburgh EH3 7RA. *T:* (0131) 477 0282. *Died 29 June 2013.*

WILLIAMSON, Nicol; actor; *b* Hamilton, Scotland, 14 Sept. 1938; *m* 1971, Jill Townsend (marr. diss. 1977); one *s*. Dundee Rep. Theatre, 1960–61; Royal Court: That's Us, Arden of Faversham, 1961; A Midsummer Night's Dream, Twelfth Night, 1962; Royal Shakespeare Company, 1962; Nil Carborundum, The Lower Depths, Women Beware Women; Spring Awakening, Royal Court, 1962; Kelly's Eye, The Ginger Man, Royal Court, 1963; Inadmissible Evidence, 1964, 1978, Royal Court, Wyndham's 1965 (Evening Standard Best Actor Award), NY 1965 (NY Drama Critics Award); A Cuckoo in the Nest, Waiting for Godot, Miniatures, 1964; Sweeney Agonistes, Globe, 1965; Diary of a Madman, Duchess, 1967; Plaza Suite, NY, 1968; Hamlet, Round House, 1969 (Evening Standard Best Actor Award), NY and US tour, 1969; Midwinter Spring, Queen's, 1972; Circle in the Square, Uncle Vanya, NY, 1973; Royal Shakespeare Company, 1973–75: Coriolanus, Midwinter Spring, Aldwych, 1973; Twelfth Night, Macbeth, Stratford 1974, Aldwych 1975; dir and title role, Uncle Vanya, Other Place, Stratford, 1974; Rex, NY, 1975; Inadmissible Evidence, NY, 1981; Macbeth, NY, 1983; The Entertainer, NY, 1983; The Lark, USA, 1983; The Real Thing, NY, 1985; Jack—A Night on the Town with John Barrymore, Criterion, 1994; King Lear, Clwyd Th. Cymru, 2001. *Films:* Inadmissible Evidence, 1967; The

Bofors Gun, 1968; Laughter in the Dark, 1968; The Reckoning, 1969; Hamlet, 1970; The Jerusalem File, 1971; The Wilby Conspiracy, 1974; The Seven Per Cent Solution, 1975; The Cheap Detective, The Goodbye Girl, Robin and Marion, 1977; The Human Factor, 1979; Excalibur, Venom, 1980; I'm Dancing as Fast as I Can, 1981; Return to Oz, 1984; Black Widow, 1986; The Hour of the Pig, 1994; The Wind in the Willows, 1996; Spawn, 1997; Return to Oz, 1998. *Television:* The Word, 1977; Macbeth, BBC Shakespeare series, 1982; Christopher Columbus, 1983; Lord Mountbatten—the Last Viceroy, 1985; Passion Flower, 1985. *Publications:* Ming's Kingdom, 1996. *Died 16 Dec. 2011.*

WILLIS, Norman David; General Secretary, Trades Union Congress, 1984–93; *b* 21 Jan. 1933; *s* of Victor J. M. and Kate E. Willis; *m* 1963, Maureen Kenning; one *s* one *d*. *Educ:* Ashford County Grammar Sch.; Ruskin and Oriel Colls, Oxford, 1955–59 (Hon. Fellow, Oriel Coll., 1984). Employed by TGWU, 1949; Nat. Service, 1951–53; PA to Gen. Sec., TGWU, 1959–70; Nat. Sec., Research and Educn, TGWU, 1970–74; TUC: Asst Gen. Sec., 1974–77, Dep. Gen. Sec., 1977–84. Councillor (Lab) Staines UDC, 1971–74. Member: NEDC, 1984–92; Council, ODI, 1985–93; Council, Motability, 1985–93; Employment Appeal Tribunal, 1995–2003; Chm., Nat. Pensioners' Convention Steering Cttee, 1979–93; Vice-President: IMS, 1985–93; ICFTU, 1984–93; WEA, 1985–93; Trades Union Adv. Cttee to OECD, 1986–93; Pres., ETUC, 1991–93 (Vice-Pres., 1984–91). Member: Exec. Bd, UNICEF, 1986–90; Council for Charitable Support, 1988–93; Trustee: Duke of Edinburgh's Commonwealth Study Conf., 1986–93; Anglo-German Foundn for the Study of Industrial Soc., 1986–95; Council, Prince of Wales Youth Business Trust, 1986–93; Patron, West Indian Welfare (UK) Trust, 1986–93. Member: Norfolk Naturalist Trust; Wildfowl and Wetlands Trust; Nat. Trust; Spelthorne Natural History Soc.; Thames Valley Horticultural Soc.; The Arthur Ransome Soc. (Pres., 2000–09); Cley Bird Club; New Chalet Club; Embroiderers' Guild; Cross Stitch Guild; Friends of Royal Sch. of Needlework; Fordbridge Centre, 2002–; Dir and Trustee, Royal Sch. of Needlework, 1999–2007; Trustee and Black Bin Bag Operative (Grade 2), Sunbury-on-Thames Millennium Embroidery Gallery, 2007–. Columnist, CrossStitcher magazine, 1998–2009. Hon. Member: Writers' Guild of GB; Poetry Soc. (former Vice-Pres.). Fellow, RSPB. Gold Star Award, Ashford (Middx) WI, 2003. *Recreations:* poetry, embroidery, birdwatching, snooker. *Address:* c/o Trades Union Congress, Congress House, Great Russell Street, WC1B 3LS. *Died 7 June 2014.*

WILLIS, His Honour Stephen Murrell; a Circuit Judge, 1986–95; *b* 21 June 1929; *s* of late John Henry Willis and late Eileen Marian (*née* Heard), Hadleigh, Suffolk; *m* 1st, 1953, Jean Irene Eve; one *s* three *d*; 2nd, 1975, Doris Florence Davies (*née* Redding); two step *d*. *Educ:* (chorister) Christ Church Cathedral, Oxford; Bloxham Sch. (scholar). Admitted solicitor, 1955; Partner: Chamberlin Talbot & Bracey, Lowestoft and Beccles, Suffolk, 1955–63; Pearless, de Rougemont & Co., East Grinstead, Sussex, 1964–85; a Recorder, 1980–85. Chm., Lord Chancellor's Adv. Cttee for SE London, 1987–95. Founder Chm., Friends' Hospice, Paphos, Cyprus, 2006–10; Founder Pres., Friends' Hospice Foundn, Paphos, 2010 (Vice-Pres., 2011–). Cavaliere dell'Ordine del Merito della Stella della Solidarietà italiana, 2010. Founded The Suffolk Singers, 1960; Founder and Director, The Prodigal Singers and Gallery Band, 1964–96; Chm., Renaissance Singers, 1969–95 (Vice-Pres., 1995–). *Compositions:* mediaeval song settings for radio and theatre plays. *Recording:* (with The Prodigal Singers) Christmas Tree Carols. *Recreations:* performing early music, travel, walking. *Address:* Villa Callisto, 49 Melissovounou Avenue, Tala Paphos, 8577, Cyprus. *Died 26 Sept. 2013.*

WILLS, Brian Alan, PhD; FRPharmS, CChem, FRSC; Chief Pharmacist, Department of Health (formerly of Health and Social Security), 1978–89; *b* 17 Feb. 1927; *s* of late William Wills and Emily (*née* Hibbert); *m* 1955, Barbara Joan Oggelsby; one *d*. *Educ:* Univ. of Nottingham (BPharm); PhD London 1955; MA Leeds 1997. FRPharmS (MPS 1949; FPS 1972); FRSC (ARIC 1957; FRIC 1967); CChem 1975. Lecturer in Pharmaceutics, Sch. of Pharmacy, Univ. of London, 1951–57; Head of Research and Control Dept, Allen & Hanburys (Africa) Ltd, Durban, S Africa, 1957–62; Head of Control Div., Allen & Hanburys Ltd, London, E2, 1962–78. Member: British Pharmacopoeia Commn, 1973–94; UK delegn to European Pharmacopoeia Commn, 1975–94; UK delegn to Council of Europe Public Health Cttee (Partial Agreement) on Pharmaceutical Questions, 1979–89; WHO Expert Adv. Panel on Internat. Pharmacopoeia and Pharmaceutical Preparations, 1979–89. Visiting Professor: Univ. of Bath, 1979–83; Univ. of Bradford, 1984–. Member: Jt Formulary Cttee for British Nat. Formulary, 1979–89; Pharmacy Working Party, Nat. Adv. Body for Local Authy Higher Educn, 1982–89; Bd of Studies in Pharmacy, London Univ., 1979–87; Council, Sch. of Pharmacy, London Univ., 1981–89. Hon. Auditor, RPSGB, 1990–2005. Mem. Ct of Assts, Soc. of Apothecaries of London, 1987–98, Emeritus Asst, 1998–. *Publications:* papers on sterilisation and disinfection and on the preservation, stability and quality control of pharmaceutical preparations. *Address:* 5 Spa Court, Park Street, Ripon, N Yorks HG4 2BX. *T:* (01765) 604469. *Died 24 July 2013.*

WILLS, Peter Gordon Bethune, TD 1967; Director: Hambro Clearing Ltd (formerly Sheppards and Chase Options Ltd), 1977–93 (Chairman, 1977–92); BCW Stock Lending Consultants Ltd, 1992–93; *b* 25 Oct. 1931; *s* of P. L. B. Wills and E. W. Wills (*née* Stapledon); *m* 1st, Linda Hutton; two *s* (one *d* decd); 2nd, Gloria Hart; 3rd, Faith Hines. *Educ:* Malvern Coll.; Corpus Christi Coll., Cambridge, 1952–55 (MA). National Service with Royal Inniskilling Fusiliers, N Ireland and Korea, 1950–52; TA, London Irish Rifles, 1952–67. Joined Sheppards & Co. (later Sheppards and Chase), 1955, Partner, 1960–85; Chm., Sheppards Moneybrokers Ltd, 1985–89. Mem., Stock Exchange Council, 1973–87 (Dep. Chm., 1979–82); Chm., Stock Exchange Money Brokers' Cttee, 1985–89. Director: Wills Group plc, 1969–87 (Vice Chm.); LIFFE, 1982; BAII Holding, 1986–89; The Securities Assoc., 1986–89 (Chm., Membership Cttee); London Clear, 1986–89; The Securities Inst., 1992–93 (Chm., Membership Cttee; Fellow, 1993). Specialist Advr to Social Security Cttee, H of C, 1993. Hon. FCSI 2010. *Address:* 5 Old Court, Long Melford, Sudbury, Suffolk CO10 9HA. *Died 11 Feb. 2014.*

WILLSON, Prof. (Francis Michael) Glenn; Vice-Chancellor, 1978–84, Emeritus Professor, since 1985, Murdoch University, Western Australia; *b* 29 Sept. 1924; *s* of late Christopher Glenn Willson and Elsie Katrine (*née* Mattick); *m* 1945, Jean (*née* Carlyle); two *d*. *Educ:* Carlisle Grammar Sch.; Manchester Univ. (BA Admin); Balliol and Nuffield Colls, Oxford (DPhil, MA). Merchant Navy, 1941–42; RAF, 1943–46; BOAC 1946–47. Research Officer, Royal Inst. of Public Admin, 1953–60; Res. Fellow, Nuffield Coll., Oxford, 1955–60; Lectr in Politics, St Edmund Hall, Oxford, 1958–60; Prof. of Govt, UC Rhodesia and Nyasaland, 1960–64; Dean, Faculty of Social Studies, UC Rhodesia and Nyasaland, 1962–64; University of California, Santa Cruz: Prof. of Govt/Politics, 1965–74; Provost of Stevenson Coll., 1967–74; Vice-Chancellor, College and Student Affairs, 1973–74; Vis. Prof., 1985–92; Warden, Goldsmiths' Coll., London, 1974–75; Principal of Univ. of London, 1975–78. *Publications:* (with D. N. Chester) The Organization of British Central Government 1914–56, 2nd edn 1914–64, 1968; Administrators in Action, 1961; A Strong Supporting Cast: the Shaw Lefevres 1789–1936, 1993; Our Minerva: the men and politics of the University of London 1836–1858, 1995; In Just Order Move: the progress of the Laban Centre for Movement and Dance, 1997; The University of London 1858–1900: the politics of Senate and Convocation, 2004; contrib. Public Admin, Polit. Studies, Parly Affairs, etc. *Address:* Galsworthy House, 177 Kingston Hill, Kingston-upon-Thames KT2 7LX. *Died 13 Aug. 2014.*

WILLSON, John Michael, CMG 1988; HM Diplomatic Service, retired; High Commissioner in Zambia, 1988–90; *b* 15 July 1931; *e s* of late Richard and Kathleen Willson; *m* 1954, Phyllis Marian Dawn, *oc* of late William and Phyllis Holman Richards, OBE; two *s* two *d*. *Educ:* Wimbledon Coll.; University Coll., Oxford (MA); Trinity Hall,

Cambridge. National Service, 1949–51. HM Colonial Service, N Rhodesia, 1955–64; Min. of Overseas Development, 1965–70 (seconded to British High Commn, Malta, 1967–70); joined HM Diplomatic Service, 1970; British Consulate-General, Johannesburg, 1972–75; FCO (W Indian and N American Depts), 1975–78; Special Counsellor for African Affairs, 1978; Secretary-General, Rhodesian Independence Conf., 1979; Salisbury (on staff of Governor of Rhodesia), 1979–80; Counsellor, Bucharest, 1980–82; Ambassador to Ivory Coast, Burkina (formerly Upper Volta) and Niger, 1983–87; seconded to RCDS, 1987. *Recreations:* gardening, photography, music. *Address:* 34 The Playing Close, Charlbury, Oxon OX7 3RJ. *Died 17 April 2013.*

WILMOT, Sir David, Kt 2002; QPM 1989; DL; Chief Constable, Greater Manchester Police, 1991–2002; *b* 12 March 1943; *m* Ann Marilyn (*née* Doyle). *Educ:* Southampton Univ. (BSc). Lancashire Constabulary, 1962; Merseyside Police, 1974; W Yorkshire Police, 1983; Deputy Chief Constable, Greater Manchester Police, 1987. Trustee, Broughton House, home for disabled ex-servicemen, 2005–13. Pres., Greater Manchester Fedn of Clubs for Young People, 2006–13. Hon. RNCM 2001. Greater Manchester: DL 1996; High Sheriff, 2005–06. Hon. DSc Salford, 2000. *Recreations:* wine, travel. *Club:* Army and Navy. *Died 13 June 2015.*

WILMOT, Sir Michael John Assheton E.; *see* Eardley-Wilmot.

WILSON, Andrew James; *see* Wilson, Snoo.

WILSON, Andrew Thomas, CMG 1982; Consultant, Agricultural Sciences Division, Rockefeller Foundation, 1987–98; Chief Natural Resources Adviser, Overseas Development Administration, 1983–87; *b* 21 June 1926; *s* of John Wilson, farmer, and Gertrude (*née* Lucas); *m* 1954, Hilda Mary (*née* Williams) (*d* 1996); two *d*. *Educ:* Cowley Sch.; Leeds Univ. (BSc); St John's Coll., Cambridge (DipAg); Imperial College of Tropical Agriculture (DTA). Colonial Service/HMOCS, Northern Rhodesia/Zambia, 1949–66: Agricultural Officer, 1949; Chief Agricl Officer, 1959; Chief Agricl Research Officer, 1961; Dep. Director of Agriculture, 1963; ODM/ODA: Agricl Adviser, British Development Div. in the Caribbean, 1967; FCO: Agricl Adviser, Nairobi and Kampala, 1969; ODM/ODA: Agricl Adviser, E Africa Development Div., 1974; Agricl Adviser, Middle East Development Div., 1976; Head of British Develt Div. in S Africa, 1979. *Recreations:* sport, gardening. *Address:* 16 Henley Court, Henley Road, Brighton, East Sussex BN2 5NA. *Clubs:* Farmers; Nairobi (Kenya). *Died 1 Aug. 2011.*

WILSON, Sir Anthony, Kt 1988; FCA; Head of Government Accountancy Service and Chief Accounting Adviser to HM Treasury, 1984–88; *b* 17 Feb. 1928; *s* of late Charles Ernest Wilson and Martha Clarice Wilson (*née* Mee); *m* 1955, Margaret Josephine Hudson; two *s* one *d*. *Educ:* Giggleswick School. Royal Navy, 1946–49. John Gordon Walton & Co., 1945–46 and 1949–52; Price Waterhouse, 1952, Partner, 1961–84; HM Treasury, 1984–88. Non-exec. Dir, Capita Gp plc, 1989–92. Chm., Jt Disciplinary Scheme of UK Accountancy Profession, 1990–93; Member: UK Govt Production Statistics Adv. Cttee, 1972–84; Accounting Standards Cttee, 1984–88; Auditing Practices Cttee, 1987–88; Rev. Body on Sen. Salaries, 1989–98; Council, Inst. of Chartered Accountants in England and Wales, 1985–88. Mem. Management Cttee, SW Regl Arts Assoc., 1983–91 (Chm., 1988–91); Member: English Ceramic Circle, 1983–2008; Northern Ceramic Soc., 1976–89. Pres., Chandos Chamber Choir, 1986–88; Chairman: Dorset Opera, 1988–93; Dorset Musical Instruments Trust, 1994–2009; Vice Chm., Sherborne House Trust, 1995–2000; Dir, Opera-80 Ltd, 1989–91. Liveryman, Chartered Accountants' Co., 1977–2004; Master, Needlemakers' Co., 1999–2000. FRSA 1983. *Recreations:* gardening, collecting pottery. *Address:* The Barn House, 89 Newland, Sherborne, Dorset DT9 3AG. *T:* (01935) 815674. *Club:* Reform. *Died 25 Feb. 2012.*

WILSON, Lt-Col Sir Blair Aubyn S.; *see* Stewart-Wilson.

WILSON, (Christopher) David, CBE 1968; MC 1945; Chairman: Southern Television Ltd, 1976–81 (Managing Director, 1959–76); Southstar Television International, 1976–81; Beaumont (UK) Ltd, 1979–81; *b* 17 Dec. 1916; *s* of late James Anthony Wilson, Highclere, Worplesdon, Surrey; *m* 1947, Jean Barbara Morton Smith (*d* 1997); no *c*. *Educ:* St George's Sch., Windsor; Aldenham. Served War of 1939–45: Captain RA, in India, Middle East and Italy. Business Manager, Associated Newspapers Ltd, 1955–57; Dir, Associated Rediffusion Ltd, 1956–57; Gen. Manager, Southern Television Ltd, 1957–59; Chm., ITN Ltd, 1969–71. Mem. Council, Southampton Univ., 1980–89; Trustee, Chichester Festival Theatre Trust Ltd. FCA 1947. *Recreations:* sailing, music. *Clubs:* MCC; Royal Southern Yacht. *Died 25 Feb. 2012.*

WILSON, Colin Henry; author; *b* Leicester, 26 June 1931; *s* of Arthur Wilson and Annetta Jones; *m* 1st, Dorothy Betty Troop; one *s*; 2nd, Joy Stewart; two *s* one *d*. *Educ:* The Gateway Secondary Technical School, Leicester. Left school at 16. Laboratory Asst (Gateway School), 1948–49; Civil Servant (collector of taxes), Leicester and Rugby, 1949–50; national service with RAF, AC2, 1949–50. Various jobs, and a period spent in Paris and Strasbourg, 1950; came to London, 1951; various labouring jobs, long period in plastic factory; returned to Paris, 1953; labouring jobs in London until Dec. 1954, when began writing The Outsider: thereafter made a living at writing. Visiting Professor: Hollins Coll., Va, 1966–67; Univ. of Washington, Seattle, 1967; Dowling Coll., Majorca, 1969; Rutgers Univ., NJ, 1974. Plays produced: Viennese Interlude; The Metal Flower Blossom; Strindberg. *Publications:* The Outsider, 1956; Religion and the Rebel, 1957; The Age of Defeat, 1959; Ritual in the Dark, 1960; Adrift in Soho, 1961; An Encyclopædia of Murder, 1961; The Strength to Dream, 1962; Origins of the Sexual Impulse, 1963; The Man without a Shadow, 1963; The World of Violence, 1963; Rasputin and the Fall of the Romanovs, 1964; The Brandy of the Damned (musical essays), 1964; Necessary Doubt, 1964; Beyond the Outsider, 1965; Eagle and Earwig, 1965; The Mind Parasites, 1966; Introduction to The New Existentialism, 1966; The Glass Cage, 1966; Sex and the Intelligent Teenager, 1966; The Philosopher's Stone, 1968; Strindberg (play), 1968; Bernard Shaw: A Reassessment, 1969; Voyage to a Beginning, 1969; Poetry and Mysticism, 1970; The Black Room, 1970; A Casebook of Murder, 1970; The God of the Labyrinth, 1970; Lingard, 1970; (jtly) The Strange Genius of David Lindsay, 1970; The Occult, 1971; New Pathways in Psychology, 1972; Order of Assassins, 1971; Tree by Tolkien, 1973; Hermann Hesse, 1973; Strange Powers, 1973; The Schoolgirl Murder Case, 1974; Return of the Lloigor, 1974; A Book of Booze, 1974; The Craft of the Novel, 1975; The Space Vampires, 1976 (filmed as Lifeforce, 1985); Men of Strange Powers, 1976; Enigmas and Mysteries, 1977; The Geller Phenomenon, 1977; Mysteries, 1978; Mysteries (play), 1979; The Quest for Wilhelm Reich, 1979; The War Against Sleep: the philosophy of Gurdjieff, 1980; Starseekers, 1980; Frankenstein's Castle, 1981; (ed with John Grant) The Directory of Possibilities, 1981; Poltergeist!, 1981; Access to Inner Worlds, 1982; The Criminal History of Mankind, 1983; (with Donald Seaman) Encyclopaedia of Modern Murder, 1983; Psychic Detectives, 1983; The Janus Murder Case, 1984; The Essential Colin Wilson, 1984; The Personality Surgeon, 1985; Spider World: the tower, 1987; (with Damon Wilson) Encyclopedia of Unsolved Mysteries, 1987; Spider World: the delta, 1987; (ed with Ronald Duncan) Marx Refuted, 1987; Aleister Crowley: the nature of the beast, 1987; (with Robin Odell) Jack the Ripper: summing up and verdict, 1987; The Magician from Siberia, 1988; The Misfits: a study of sexual outsiders, 1988; Beyond the Occult, 1988; Written in Blood, 1989; (with Donald Seaman) The Serial Killers, 1990; Mozart's Journey to Prague (play), 1991; Spider World: the magician, 1992, new edn 2002; The Strange Life of P. D. Ouspensky, 1993; From Atlantis to the Sphinx, 1996; Atlas of Sacred Sites and Holy Places, 1996; Alien Dawn, 1998; The Devil's Party, 2000; (with Rand Fle'math) Atlantis Blueprint, 2000; Spider World: shadowland, 2003; Dreaming to Some Purpose (autobiog.), 2004; Atlantis and the Neanderthals,

2006; The Angry Years: the rise and fall of the angry young men, 2007; Super Consciousness, 2009; contribs to: The Times, Daily Mail, etc. *Recreations:* collecting gramophone records, mainly opera; mathematics. *Club:* Savage. *Died 5 Dec. 2013.*

WILSON, Maj.-Gen. Dare; *see* Wilson, Maj.-Gen. R. D.

WILSON, David; *see* Wilson, C. D.

WILSON, Sir David, 3rd Bt *cr* 1920; *b* 30 Oct. 1928; *s* of Sir John Mitchell Harvey Wilson, 2nd Bt, KCVO, and Mary Elizabeth (*d* 1979), *d* of late William Richards, CBE; *S* father, 1975; *m* 1955, Eva Margareta, *e d* of Tore Lindell, Malmö, Sweden; two *s* one *d*. *Educ:* Deerfield Acad., Mass., USA; Harrow School; Oriel Coll., Oxford (Brisco Owen Schol.). Barrister, Lincoln's Inn, 1954–61; admitted Solicitor, 1962; Partner, Simmons & Simmons, EC2, 1963–92. *Heir: s* Thomas David Wilson [*b* 6 Jan. 1959; *m* 1st, 1984, Valerie Stogdale (marr. diss. 2002); two *s*; 2nd, 2006, Briony Jane Roberts (*née* Clark)]. *Address:* Tandem House, Queens Drive, Oxshott, Leatherhead, Surrey KT22 0PH. *Died 28 April 2014.*

WILSON, George; *see* Wilson, W. G.

WILSON, His Honour Harold, AE 1963; a Circuit Judge, 1981–2000 (Midland and Oxford Circuit); a Deputy Circuit Judge, 2001–03; *b* 19 Sept. 1931; *s* of late Edward Simpson Wilson; *m* 1st, Diana Marion (marr. diss.), *d* of late (Philip) Guy (Dudley) Sixsmith; two *s* one *d* (and one *s* decd); 2nd, 1973, Jill Ginever, *d* of late Charles Edward Walter Barlow; one step *s* one step *d*. *Educ:* St Albans Sch.; Sidney Sussex Coll., Cambridge (State Scholar; MA). Pilot Officer, RAF, 1950–51; Flying Officer, RAFVR, 1951–54; Flt Lt, RAuxAF, 1954–63. Administrative Trainee, KCH, 1954–56; Schoolmaster, 1957–59. Called to the Bar, Gray's Inn, 1958 (Holker Exhibnr; runner-up, Lee Essay Prize, 1959), Bencher, 1998; Oxford Circuit, 1960–70 (Circuit Junior, 1964–65); Midland and Oxford Circuit, 1971–75; Dep. Chm., Monmouthshire Quarter Sessions, 1969–70; a Recorder, Midland and Oxford Circuit, 1971–75; Chm. of Industrial Tribunals, Birmingham, 1976–81; Resident Judge, Coventry Crown Ct, 1983–92; Liaison Judge, 1986–92; Hon. Recorder of Coventry, 1986–93; designated Care Centre Judge, Coventry, 1991–92, Oxford, 1993–2000; Resident Judge, Oxford Crown Ct, 1993–2000; Liaison Judge to Oxfordshire Magistrates, 1993–96; Hon. Recorder of Oxford, 1999–2001; a Judge of the Employment Appeal Tribunal, 1999–2000; an Addnl Judge, Supreme Ct of Gibraltar, 2003. Pres., Transport Tribunal, 1991–96; Chairman: Coventry Reparation Unit Adv. Cttee, 1991–92; Thames Valley Area Criminal Justice Strategy (formerly Liaison) Cttee, 1996–2000. Member: Matrimonial Causes Rules Cttee, 1984–88; W Midlands Probation Cttee, 1985–92. Shrieval Remembrancer, Oxon, 2004–11. *Recreations:* watching Rugby football, reading and listening to music. *Address:* 2 Harcourt Buildings, Temple, EC4Y 9DB. *T:* (020) 7353 6961. *Club:* Royal Air Force (Trustee, 2005–10). *Died 5 Nov. 2011.*

WILSON, Prof. Henry Wallace, PhD; CPhys, FInstP; FRSE; physicist; Director, Scottish Universities' Research and Reactor Centre, 1962–85; Personal Professor of Physics, Strathclyde University, 1966–85, then Emeritus; *b* 30 Aug. 1923; *s* of Frank Binnington Wilson and Janet (*née* Wilson); *m* 1955, Fiona McPherson Martin, *d* of Alfred Charles Steinmetz Martin and Agnes Mary (*née* McPherson); three *s*. *Educ:* Allan Glen's Sch., Glasgow; Glasgow Univ. (BSc, PhD Physics). AInstP 1949, FInstP 1962; FRSE 1963. Wartime work as Physicist, Explosives Res. Div., ICI, Ardeer. Asst Lectr, Natural Philosophy Dept, Glasgow Univ., 1947–51; post-doctoral Res. Fellow, Univ. of Calif, Berkeley, 1951–52; Lectr, Nat. Phil. Dept, Glasgow Univ., 1952–55; Leader of Physical Measurements Gp, UKAEA, Aldermaston, 1955–62 (Sen. Principal Scientific Officer, 1958). Hon. Scientific Advr, Nat. Mus. of Antiquities of Scotland, 1969; Scientific Advr, Scottish Office, 1975–93. Mem., Nuclear Safety Cttee, SSEB, 1964–89; Mem., Radioactive Substances Adv. Cttee, 1966–70. Inst. of Physics: Mem. Council, 1970–71; Chm., Scottish Br., 1969–71; mem. several cttees; Royal Soc. of Edinburgh: Mem. Council, 1966–69, 1976–79; Vice Pres., 1979–81. Member: British Mass Spectrometry Soc. (formerly Mass Spectrometry Gp), 1958– (Chm., 1977–79); Nuclear Inst. (formerly Brit. Nuclear Energy Soc.), 1969–. FRSA 1996. *Publications:* contributions to: Alpha, Beta and Gamma-ray Spectroscopy, ed K. Siegbahn, 1965; Activation Analysis, ed Lenihan and Thomson, 1965; Modern Aspects of Mass Spectrometry, ed R. I. Reed, 1968; Encyclopaedic Dictionary of Physics, ed J. Thewlis, 1973; (ed) Nuclear Engineering sect., Chambers' Science and Technology Dictionary, 1988; papers on radioactivity, low energy nuclear physics, meson physics, mass spectrometry, isotope separation, effects of radiation, and reactor physics, in scientific jls. *Recreations:* walking, industrial archaeology, bookbinding, photography. *Address:* Ashgrove, The Crescent, Busby, Glasgow G76 8HT. *T:* (0141) 644 3107. *Died 7 Nov. 2014.*

WILSON, Ian D.; *see* Douglas-Wilson.

WILSON, John; *see* Moran, Baron.

WILSON, John Veitch D.; *see* Drysdale Wilson.

WILSON, Rt Rev. Dr John Warwick; Bishop of the Southern Region (Assistant Bishop, Diocese of Melbourne), 1985–2007; Vicar General, Diocese of Melbourne, 2001–07 (Bishop Administrator, 2006–07); Chairman, Acorn Press Ltd, since 1994; *b* 12 July 1937; *s* of Walter and Norma Wilson; *m* 1963, Jill Brady; two *d*. *Educ:* Bathurst Coll., NSW; Ridley Coll., Parkville, Victoria (ThL, ThSchol); London Univ. (BD (Hons)); Yale Univ. (STM); Duke Univ. (PhD). Educn Officer, Papua New Guinea, 1957–59. Ordained deacon and priest, 1964; Asst, St Cyprian's, Narrabri, 1964–67; Vicar, St Andrew, Tingha, 1967–68; Priest in charge, St John's Henderson, North Carolina, USA, 1969–72; Lectr in OT, Ridley Coll., 1973–85. *Publications:* The Old Testament and Christian Living, 1981, 2nd edn 1985; Ezekiel: God's Communicator, 1990; The Old Testament on the Way to the Cross, 1994; Christianity alongside Islam, 2010. *Recreations:* reading, music, cinema. *Address:* 3 Sunview Place, Berwick, Vic 3806, Australia. *T:* (3) 87869938, *Fax:* (3) 87869940. *Died 22 Jan. 2011.*

WILSON, Julian David Bonhôte; freelance journalist and broadcaster; Racing Correspondent, BBC Television, 1966–97; *b* 21 June 1940; *s* of Peter Jardine Bonhôte Wilson, OBE and Helen Angela Josephine Mann; *m* 1st, 1970, Carolyn Anne Michael (marr. diss. 1980); one *s*; 2nd, 1981, Alison Christian Findlay Ramsay. *Educ:* Harrow. Writer and reporter, Mirror Group Newspapers, 1958–64; Editor, Tote Racing Annual, 1965. *Publications:* Lester Piggott: the pictorial biography, 1985; 100 Greatest Racehorses, 1987; The Racing World, 1991; Some You Win (autobiog.), 1998. *Recreation:* cricket. *Address:* Home Farm Cottage, Burrough Green, Newmarket, Suffolk CB8 9ER; 10 Windsor Lane, Tokai 7945, Cape Town, South Africa. *Died 20 April 2014.*

WILSON, Prof. Kenneth Geddes, PhD; Professor of Physics, Ohio State University, 1988–2002; *b* 8 June 1936; *s* of Edgar Bright Wilson and Emily Fisher Buckingham; *m* 1982, Alison Brown. *Educ:* Harvard Univ. (AB); Calif Inst. of Technol. (PhD). Cornell University: Asst Prof. of Physics, 1963; Prof. of Physics, 1963–88; Dir, Center for Theory and Simulation in Sci. and Engrg, 1985–88. Co-Prin. Investigator, Nat. Sci. Foundn Statewide Systematic Initiative, Project Discovery, Ohio, to reform sci. and math. educn, 1991–96. Hon. PhD: Harvard, 1981; Chicago, 1976. Nobel Prize for Physics, 1982. *Publications:* (ed jtly) Broken Scale Invariance and the Light Cone, 1971; Quarks and Strings on a Lattice, 1975; (contrib.) New Pathways in High Energy Physics, Vol. II 1976; (contrib.) New Developments in Quantum Field Theory and Statistical Mechanics, 1977; (contrib.) Recent Developments in Gauge Theories, 1980; (with Bennett Daviss) Redesigning Education, 1994; contrib. Jl of Math. Phys, Nuovo Cimento, Acta Phys. Austriaca, Phys Rev., Jl of Chem. Phys, Comm. Math. Phys, Phys Reports, Advances in Maths, Rev. of Mod. Phys, Scientific American; symposia and conf. papers. *Address:* c/o Department of Physics, Ohio State University, 191 West Woodruff Avenue, Columbus, OH 43210–1117, USA. *Died 15 June 2013.*

WILSON, Prof. Louise, OBE 2008; Director, MA Fashion Course, Central Saint Martins College of Art and Design, since 1992; Professor, University of the Arts London (formerly London Institute), since 1999; *b* Cambridge, 23 Feb. 1962; *d* of William Wilson and Pamela Elizabeth, (Tebbs), Wilson; partner, Thomas Kwamina Aggrey; one *s*. *Educ:* Preston Poly. (BA Hons 1st cl. 1984); St Martins School of Art (MA Fashion with Distn 1986). Design Dir, Women's Collection and Licensing, Donna Karan International, NY, 1997–2002; Consultant to the fashion industry, 2002–10. Mem., British Fashion Council, 2007. Isabella Blow Award for Fashion Creator, British Fashion Awards, 2012. *Recreations:* going out, staying in, eating, sleeping, my profession, voicing one's opinion. *Address:* School of Fashion and Textile Design, Central Saint Martins College of Art and Design, University of the Arts London, Granary Building, 1 Granary Square, N1C 4AA. *T:* (020) 7514 7168. *E:* l.wilson@csm.arts.ac.uk. *Died 17 May 2014.*

WILSON, Ven. Mark John Crichton; self-employed psychotherapist, 2005–09; *b* 14 Jan. 1946; *s* of Rev. William Hubert Wilson and Gladys Margaret Wilson; *m* 1970, Rev. Canon Mavis Kirby Wilson; one *s* three *d*. *Educ:* St Paul's Cathedral Choir Sch.; St John's Sch., Leatherhead; Clare Coll., Cambridge (BA, MA 1970); Ridley Hall, Cambridge; Univ. of E London (Cert. Psychosynthesis Counselling 2003; Postgrad. Dip. Psychosynthesis Psychotherapy 2006). Ordained deacon, 1969, priest, 1970; Assistant Curate: Luton with East Hyde, 1969–72; Ashtead, Surrey, 1972–77; Chaplain, Epsom Coll., 1977–81; Vicar, Christ Church, Epsom Common, 1981–96; Archdeacon of Dorking, 1996–2005; Archdeacon Emeritus, 2011. Rural Dean of Epsom, 1987–92. Warden, St Peter's Convent, Woking, 2003–07. *Recreation:* gardening (growing fuchsias). *Address:* 48 Byrefield Road, Guildford, Surrey GU2 9UB. *Died 5 Oct. 2013.*

WILSON, Maj.-Gen. (Ronald) Dare, CBE 1968 (MBE 1949); MC 1945; DL; MA Cantab; Director, Army Aviation, Ministry of Defence, 1970–71; later interests farming, forestry and writing; *b* 3 Aug. 1919; *s* of Sydney E. D. Wilson and Dorothea, *d* of George Burgess; *m* 1973, Sarah, *d* of Sir Peter Stallard, KCMG, CVO, MBE; two *s*. *Educ:* Shrewsbury Sch.; St John's Coll. Cambridge (Part I 1939, BA 1972). Commissioned into Royal Northumberland Fusiliers, 1939; served War, 1939–45: BEF 1940, ME and NW Europe (MC, despatches 1945); 6th Airborne Div., Palestine, 1945–48; 1st Bn Parachute Regt, 1949; MoD, 1950; Royal Northumberland Fusiliers: Korea, 1951; Kenya, 1953; GSO2, Staff Coll., Camberley, 1954–56; Brevet Lt-Col 1958; AA&QMG, 3rd Div., 1958–59; comd 22 Special Air Service Regt, 1960–62; Canadian Nat. Defence Coll., 1962–63; Col GS 1(BR) Corps BAOR, 1963–65; comd 149 Infantry Bde (TA), 1966–67; Brig. 1966; Brig., AQ ME Comd, 1967; Maj.-Gen. 1968; Dir, Land/Air Warfare, MoD, 1968–69. Exmoor Nat. Park Officer, 1974–78. Formerly Consultant to Fedn of Nature and Nat. Parks of Europe. Speaker for ESU in USA. Church Warden, Church of St George, Morebath, Devon, 1980–93. Helicopter and light aircraft pilot; Mem., Army Cresta Run Team and Army Rifle VIII; captained British Free-Fall Parachute Team, 1962–65; Chm., British Parachute Assoc., 1962–65. Mem. Council, Cambridge Soc., 1989–2002 (Pres., Somerset br.). FRGS. DL Somerset, 1979. Royal Humane Soc. Award, 1953; Royal Aero Club Silver Medal, 1967. *Publications:* Cordon and Search, 1948, reissued USA, 1984, 2nd edn as With 6th Airborne Division in Palestine, 2008; Tempting the Fates (autobiog.), 2006; The General's Game Book, 2013; contribs to military jls. *Recreations:* country pursuits, music, travelling. *Address:* Combeland, Dulverton, Somerset TA22 9LJ. *Clubs:* Flyfishers'; Hawks (Cambridge); St Moritz Tobogganing. *Died 15 Aug. 2014.*

WILSON, Sandy; composer, lyric writer, playwright; *b* 19 May 1924; *s* of George Walter Wilson and Caroline Elsie (*née* Humphrey). *Educ:* Elstree Preparatory School; Harrow School; Oriel College, Oxford (BA Eng. Lit.). Contributed material to Oranges and Lemons, Slings and Arrows, 1948; wrote lyrics for touring musical play Caprice, 1950; words and music for two revues at Watergate Theatre, 1951 and 1952; (musical comedy) The Boy Friend for Players' Theatre, 1953, later produced in West End and on Broadway, 1954, revival, Comedy, 1967 (also directed), revival, Old Vic, 1984, 40th anniv. production, Players' Theatre, 1994; (musical play) The Buccaneer, 1955; Valmouth (musical play, based on Firbank's novel), Lyric, Hammersmith and Savile Theatre, 1959, New York, 1960, revival, Chichester, 1982; songs for Call It Love, Wyndham's Theatre, 1960; Divorce Me, Darling! (musical comedy), Players' Theatre, 1964, Globe, 1965, revival, Chichester, 1997; music for TV series, The World of Wooster, 1965–66; music for As Dorothy Parker Once Said, Fortune, 1969; songs for Danny la Rue's Charley's Aunt (TV), 1969; wrote and performed in Sandy Wilson Thanks the Ladies, Hampstead Theatre Club, 1971; His Monkey Wife, Hampstead, 1971; The Clapham Wonder, Canterbury, 1978; Aladdin, Lyric, Hammersmith, 1979. *Publications:* This is Sylvia (with own illustrs), 1954; The Boy Friend (with own illustrs), 1955; Who's Who for Beginners (with photographs by Jon Rose), 1957; Prince What Shall I Do (illustrations, with Rhoda Levine), 1961; The Poodle from Rome, 1962; I Could Be Happy (autobiog.), 1975; Ivor, 1975; Caught in the Act, 1976; The Roaring Twenties, 1977. *Recreations:* cinema, travel, reminiscing. *Address:* 2 Southwell Gardens, SW7 4SB. *T:* (020) 7373 6172. *Died 27 Aug. 2014.*

WILSON, Snoo; writer, since 1969; *b* 2 Aug. 1948; *s* of late Leslie Wilson and Pamela Mary Wilson; *né* Andrew James Wilson; *m* 1976, Ann McFerran; two *s* one *d*. *Educ:* Bradfield Coll.; Univ. of East Anglia (BA English and American Studies). Associate Director, Portable Theatre, 1970–75; Dramaturge, Royal Shakespeare Co., 1975–76; Script Editor, Play for Today, 1976; Associate Prof. of Theatre, Univ. of Calif at San Diego, 1987. Henfield Fellow, Univ. of E Anglia, 1978; US Bicentennial Fellow in Playwriting, 1981–82. Hon. Texan, 1992. *Filmscripts:* Shadey, 1986; The Touch, 1989; Eichmann, 2007; *opera:* (adapted) Gounod's La Colombe, 1983; *radio plays:* Poonsh, 1993; The Good Doctor, 1994; Johnson's Xmas Interlude, 1994; I'll be George, 2001; Hippomania, 2004; Pack Up Your Troubles (musical), 2006. *Publications: plays:* Layby (jtly), 1972; Pignight, 1972; The Pleasure Principle, 1973; Blowjob, 1974; Soul of the White Ant, 1976; England England, 1978; Vampire, 1978; The Glad Hand, 1978; A Greenish Man, 1978; The Number of the Beast, 1982; Flaming Bodies, 1982; Grass Widow, 1983; Loving Reno, 1983; Hamlyn, 1984; More Light, 1987; Lynchville, 1989; Callas, 1990; Erofeyev's Walpurgis Night (adaptation), 1991; HRH, 1994; Darwin's Flood, 1994; Bedbug (adaptation, after Mayakovsky), 1995; Framing Faust (adaptation, after Ernst), 1996; Sabina, 1998; Moonshine, 1999; Reclining Nude with Black Stockings, 2010; *novels:* Spaceache, 1984 (adapted for radio, 1990); Inside Babel, 1985; I, Crowley, 1997; The Works of Melmont, 2004; *opera:* Orpheus in the Underworld (new version), 1984; *musical:* 80 Days, 1988. *Recreations:* beekeeping, space travel. *Address:* 28 Middleton Road, E8 4BS. *Died 3 July 2013.*

WILSON, William Desmond, OBE 1964 (MBE 1954); MC 1945; DSC (USA) 1945; HM Diplomatic Service, retired; Deputy High Commissioner, Kaduna, Nigeria, 1975–81; *b* 2 Jan. 1922; *s* of late Crozier Irvine Wilson and Mabel Evelyn (*née* Richardson); *m* 1949, Lucy Bride; two *s*. *Educ:* Royal Belfast Academical Instn; QUB; Trinity Coll., Cambridge. Joined Indian Army, 1941; served with 10 Gurkha Rifles, India and Italy, 1942–46 (Major). Colonial Admin. Service: Northern Nigeria, 1948–63 (MBE for Gallantry, 1954); retd as Permanent Sec.; joined Foreign (subseq. Diplomatic) Service, 1963; First Sec., Ankara, 1963–67; UN (Polit.) Dept, FO, 1967; First Sec. and Head of Chancery, Kathmandu, 1969–74; Counsellor, 1975; Sen. Officers' War Course, RNC Greenwich, 1975. *Recreation:* boring friends. *Address:* 19 The Haven, Hythe, Kent CT21 4PJ. *T:* (01303) 260767. *Club:* East India. *Died 3 Jan. 2014.*

WILSON, (William) George, OBE 1960; Associate Director, PA Consulting Group, 1989–92; *b* 19 Feb. 1921; *s* of late William James Wilson and late Susannah Wilson; *m* 1948, Freda Huddleston (*d* 2010); three *s*. Min. of Health, 1939. Served War, Army, in India and Ceylon, 1940–46. Min. of Nat. Insurance, 1947; Asst Principal, Colonial Office, 1947; Principal, CO, 1950–57 (Adviser, UK Delegn to UN Gen. Assembly, 1951); Financial Sec., Mauritius, 1957–60; Asst Sec., MoH, 1962; Consultant, Hosp. Design and Construction, Middle East and Africa, 1968–70; Asst Sec., DHSS, 1971; Under-Sec., DHSS, 1972–81. Chm., Paul James & George Wilson Ltd, Health Service Develt Advrs, 1986–89 (Dir, 1983–86). *Recreation:* Border history and genealogy. *Address:* 8 Near Park, Scotby, Carlisle, Cumbria CA4 8AU. *Died 22 Jan. 2014.*

WILSON, William Napier M.; *see* Menzies-Wilson.

WILTON, Sir (Arthur) John, KCMG 1979 (CMG 1967); KCVO 1979; MC 1945; HM Diplomatic Service, retired; *b* 21 Oct. 1921; *s* of Walter Wilton and Annetta Irene Wilton (*née* Perman); *m* 1950, Maureen Elizabeth Alison Meaker; four *s* one *d*. *Educ:* Wanstead High School; Open Schol., St John's Coll., Oxford, 1940 (MA 1946). Commissioned, Royal Ulster Rifles, 1942; served with Irish Brigade, N Africa, Italy and Austria, 1943–46 (despatches). Entered HM Diplomatic Service, 1947; served Lebanon, Egypt, Gulf Shaikhdoms, Roumania, and Yugoslavia; Dir, Middle East Centre for Arabic Studies, Shemlan, 1960–65; Dep. High Comr, Aden, 1966–67; Ambassador to Kuwait, 1970–74; Asst Under-Sec. of State, FCO, 1974–76; Ambassador to Saudi Arabia, 1976–79. Dir, London House for Overseas Graduates, 1979–86. Chm., Arab-British Centre, 1981–86; Pres., Plymouth Br., ESU, 1991–2006 (Vice-Pres., 1988–91); Trustee, Arab-British Chamber Charitable Foundn, 1989–2009. Gov., Hele's Sch., Plympton, 1988–92. Churchwarden, St Maurice, Plympton, 1992–2004. Hon. LLD New England Coll., NH, 1986. *Recreations:* reading, gardening. *Address:* 25 Worcester Road, Chichester, W Sussex PO19 5DW. *Died 12 June 2011.*

WING, Dr Lorna Gladys, OBE 1995; FRCPsych; Consultant Psychiatrist to National Autistic Society, 1990–2008; *b* 7 Oct. 1928; *d* of Bernard Newbury Tolchard and Gladys Ethel Tolchard (*née* Whittell); *m* 1950, Prof. John Kenneth Wing, CBE, MD (*d* 2010); (one *d* decd). *Educ:* Chatham Grammar Sch.; University Coll. Hosp. (MD). Scientific Staff, MRC Social Psychiatry Unit, 1964–90; Hon. Consultant Psychiatrist, Maudsley Hosp., 1972–90; Hon. Sen. Lectr, Inst. of Psychiatry, 1974–90. *Publications:* Autistic Children, 1971, 2nd edn 1980; (ed) Early Childhood Autism, 1976; (ed) Aspects of Autism, 1988; Hospital Closure and the Resettlement of Residents, 1989; The Autistic Spectrum, 1996; papers in sci. jls. *Recreations:* reading, gardening, walking. *Address:* Elliot House, 113 Masons Hill, Bromley, Kent BR2 9HT. *T:* (020) 8466 0098. *Died 6 June 2014.*

WINKLEY, Dr Stephen Charles, MA; Headmaster, Rossall School, 2008–13; *b* 9 July 1944; *e s* of late George Winkley and Eunice Winkley (*née* Golding); *m* 1st, 1968, Georgina Smart; two *s*; 2nd, 1983, Jennifer Burt; two *d*. *Educ:* St Edward's School, Oxford; Brasenose College, Oxford (MA 1967; DPhil 1973). Asst Master, Cranleigh Sch., 1969–85; Second Master, Winchester College, 1985–91; Headmaster, Uppingham Sch., 1991–2006. *Recreations:* music, water colours. *Address:* 88 Rockingham Road, Kettering, Northants NN16 9AD; Le Peyré, 47170 St Pé St Simon, France. *Died 3 April 2014.*

WINNER, Michael Robert; Chairman: Scimitar Films Ltd, Michael Winner Ltd, Motion Picture and Theatrical Investments Ltd, since 1957; *b* 30 Oct. 1935; *s* of late George Joseph and Helen Winner; *m* 2011, Geraldine Lynton-Edwards. *Educ:* St Christopher Sch., Letchworth; Downing Coll., Cambridge Univ. (MA). Film critic and Fleet Street journalist and contributor to: The Spectator, Daily Express, London Evening Standard, Daily Mail, etc; columnist, Sunday Times. Panellist: Any Questions, BBC Radio; Question Time, BBC TV; presenter: Michael Winner's True Crimes, LWT; Michael Winner's Dining Stars, 2010. Entered Motion Pictures, 1956, as Screen Writer, Asst Director, Editor. Films directed include: Play It Cool, 1962; The Cool Mikado (and writer), 1962; West Eleven, 1963; The System (and prod.), 1963; You Must Be Joking (and prod., writer), 1965; The Jokers (and prod., writer), 1966; I'll Never Forget What's 'isname (and prod.), 1967; Hannibal Brooks (and prod., writer), 1968; The Games (and prod.), 1969; Lawman (and prod.), 1970; The Nightcomers (and prod.), 1971; Chato's Land (and prod.), 1971; The Mechanic, 1972; Scorpio (and prod.), 1972; The Stone Killer (and prod.), 1973; Death Wish (and prod.), 1974; Won Ton Ton The Dog That Saved Hollywood (and prod.), 1975; The Sentinel (and prod., writer), 1976; The Big Sleep (and prod., writer), 1977; Firepower (and prod.), 1978; Death Wish Two (and prod., writer), 1981; The Wicked Lady (and prod., writer), 1982; Scream for Help (and prod.), 1984; Death Wish Three (and prod.), 1985; Appointment with Death (and prod., writer), 1988; A Chorus of Disapproval (and prod., jt screenplay writer), 1989; Bullseye! (and prod., jt screenplay writer), 1990; Dirty Weekend (and prod., jt screenplay writer), 1993; Parting Shots (and prod., writer), 1997; appearances as actor include: For the Greater Good, 1990; Decadence, 1993; radio play: The Flump, 2000; actor/dir, several television commercials. Theatre productions: The Tempest, Wyndhams, 1974; A Day in Hollywood A Night in the Ukraine, 1978. Founder and Chm., Police Meml Trust, 1984–. *Publications:* Winner's Dinners, 1999, rev. edn 2000; Winner Guide, 2002; Winner Takes All (autobiog.), 2004; The Fat Pig Diet, 2007; Winner's Dinners: the restaurant and hotel guide, 2009; Unbelievable! (autobiog.), 2010; Tales I Never Told (autobiog.), 2011; Michael Winner's Hymie Joke Book, 2012. *Recreations:* walking around art galleries, museums, antique shops, eating, being difficult, making table mats, washing silk shirts, doing Pilates badly. *Address:* 219 Kensington High Street, W8 6BD. *T:* (020) 7734 8385. *Died 21 Jan. 2013.*

WINSTON, Very Rev. Jeremy Hugh; Dean of Monmouth, since 2011; *b* Harlington, Middx, 20 May 1954; *s* of Hugh Winston and Vera Winston. *Educ:* Croesyceiliog Grammar Sch.; Trinity Coll., Carmarthen (BEd 1976); St Stephen's House, Oxford (BA 1978). Cert Ed. Ordained deacon, 1979, priest, 1980; Asst Curate, St Basil, Bassaleg, 1979–83; Vicar: St Arvan's with Penterry, Itton, Devauden and Kilgwrrwg, 1983–93; Abergavenny and Area Dean, 1993–2011; Priest-in-charge, Christchurch, Govilon, 2009–11. Children's Advr, Dio. of Monmouth, 1982–90. Canon, St Woolas Cathedral, 2002–. Chm., Res. and Ethics Cttee, Gwent Area, 1998–2003. OStJ 2006. *Recreations:* composition, opera, gardening, entertaining, poetry, Benedictine spirituality. *Address:* The Deanery, 105 Stow Hill, Newport NP20 4ED. *T:* (01633) 663268. *E:* jeremy.winston@virgin.net. *Club:* Royal Over-Seas League. *Died 12 Nov. 2011.*

WINSTONE, Dame Dorothy (Gertrude), DBE 1990; CMG 1976; *b* 23 Jan. 1919; *d* of Stanley Fowler and Constance May Fowler (*née* Sherwin); *m* 1941, Wilfrid Frank Winstone (*d* 2000); three *s* one *d*. *Educ:* Auckland Girls' Grammar Sch.; Auckland Teachers' Coll.; Auckland University Coll. (BA 1940; DipEd 1943); Univ. of Auckland (BTh 1998). Primary School Teacher, 1938; Asst Mistress, Seddon Memorial Tech. Coll., 1939–45; voluntary community worker, 1945–. Mem., Royal Commn on Contraception, Sterilisation and Abortion, 1975–77. Foundn Mem., NZ Envmtl Council, 1970–81. Dir, Virginia Gildersleeve Fund, Internat. Fedn of Univ. Women, 1993–2002. Member Emerita, NZ Fedn of Univ. Women, 1973; Life Mem., Nat. Council of Women of NZ, 1980. Hon. LLD Univ. of Auckland, 1983. Adelaide Ristori Medal, Centro Culturale Italiano, 1975; New Zealand Suffrage Centennial Medal, 1993. *Publications:* Everyday Words and Phrases, 1975; A Century of Service, 1985; Wesley Methodist Church 1938–1993, 1996. *Recreations:* reading, gardening, 13 grandchildren, 11 great-grandchildren. *Address:* 2A, 416 Remuera Road, Remuera, Auckland 1050, New Zealand. *T:* (9) 5203407. *Died 3 April 2014.*

WINTON, Sir Nicholas (George), Kt 2003; MBE 1983; *b* 19 May 1909; *s* of Rudolf and Barbara Winton; *m* 1948, Grete Gjelstrup (*d* 1999); one *s* one *d* (and one *s* decd). *Educ:* Stowe Sch. (founder mem. 1923). Banking, 1928–31; Mem., Stock Exchange, 1931–39; Internat. Refugee Orgn, 1946–48; International Bank, 1948–49; company director, 1950–68. President: Maidenhead Mencap, 1972–; Abbeyfield Maidenhead, 1986–. Mem., Probus Club. Freedom of Borough, Windsor and Maidenhead, 1999. Order of Tomas Masaryk (Czech Republic), 1998. *Recreations:* gardening, music, tapestry, travelling. *Address:*

New Ditton, Pinkneys Green, Maidenhead SL6 6NT. *T:* (01628) 626613. *Club:* Rotary (Maidenhead) (Pres., 1972–73). *Died 1 July 2015.*

WISE, 2nd Baron *cr* 1951, of King's Lynn; **John Clayton Wise;** farmer; *b* 11 June 1923; *s* of 1st Baron Wise and Kate Elizabeth (*d* 1987), *e d* of late John Michael Sturgeon; *S* father, 1968; *m* 1st, 1946, Margaret Annie (marr. diss. 1986), *d* of Frederick Victor Snead, Banbury; two *s*; 2nd, 1993, Janice Harman Thompson (marr. diss. 1998). *Heir: s* Hon. Christopher John Clayton Wise, PhD [*b* 19 March 1949; *m* 1988, Rosalind Myrtle Reed; two *s*]. *Died 29 Oct. 2012.*

WISE, Prof. Michael John, CBE 1979; MC 1945; PhD; FRGS; Emeritus Professor of Geography, University of London; *b* Stafford, 17 Aug. 1918; *s* of Harry Cuthbert and Sarah Evelyn Wise; *m* 1942, Barbara Mary (*d* 2007), *d* of C. L. Hodgetts, Wolverhampton; one *s* one *d*. *Educ:* Saltley Secondary School, Birmingham; University of Birmingham (BA (Hons Geography) and Mercator Prize in Geography, 1939; DipEd 1940; PhD 1951). Served War, Royal Artillery, 80th LAA Regt, 1941–44, 5th Bn The Northamptonshire Regt, 1944–46, in Middle East and Italy; commissioned, 1941, Major, 1944. Assistant Lecturer, Univ. of Birmingham, 1946–48, Lecturer in Geography, 1948–51; London School of Economics: Lecturer in Geography, 1951–54; Sir Ernest Cassel Reader in Economic Geography, 1954–58; Prof. of Geography, 1958–83; Pro-Director, 1983–85; Hon. Fellow, 1988. Chm., Departmental Cttee of Inquiry into Statutory Smallholdings, 1963–67; Mem., Dept of Transport Adv. Cttee on Landscape Treatment of Trunk Roads, 1971–90 (Chm., 1981–90). Mem., UGC for Hong Kong, 1966–73. Recorder, Sect. E, Brit. Assoc. for Advancement of Science, 1955–60 (Pres., 1965); Founder Pres., Transport Studies Soc., 1962; President: Inst. of British Geographers, 1974 (Hon. Mem., 1989); IGU, 1976–80 (Vice-Pres., 1968–76); Geographical Assoc., 1976–77 (Hon. Treasurer, 1967–76, Hon. Mem., 1983); Vice-Pres., Nat. Assoc. for Envmtl Educn, 1977–; Mem., SSRC, 1976–82; Chm., Council for Extra-Mural Studies, Univ. of London, 1976–83; Chm., Exec. Cttee, Assoc. of Agriculture, 1972–83 (Vice-Pres., 1983–93); Mem. Adv. Cttees, UN Univ., 1976–82; Hon. Sec., RGS, 1963–73, Vice-Pres., 1975–78, Hon. Vice-Pres., 1978–80, 1983–, Pres., 1980–82. Chm., Birkbeck Coll., 1983–89 (Governor, 1968–89; Fellow, 1989); Mem. Delegacy, Goldsmiths' Coll., 1984–88. Chm., Dudley Stamp Meml Trust, 1988–2005 (Hon. Sec., 1966–88; Hon. Pres., 2006). Erskine Fellow, Univ. of Canterbury, NZ, 1970. Hon. Life Mem., Univ. of London Union, 1977. Hon. Member: Geog. Soc. of Russia, 1975; Assoc. of Japanese Geographers, 1980; Geog. Soc. of Mexico, 1984; Geog. Soc. of Poland, 1986; Membre d'Honneur, Société de Géographie, 1983. FIEnvSc 1980; FRSA 1983. Hon. FLI 1991. DUniv Open, 1978; Hon. DSc Birmingham, 1982. Received Gill Memorial award of RGS, 1958; RGS Founder's Medal, 1977; Alexander Körösi Csoma Medal, Hungarian Geographical Soc., 1980; Tokyo Geographical Soc. Medal, 1981; Lauréat d'Honneur, IGU, 1984. *Publications:* Hon. Editor, Birmingham and its Regional Setting, 1951; A Pictorial Geography of the West Midlands, 1958; General Consultant, An Atlas of Earth Resources, 1979; The Great Geographical Atlas, 1982; (consultant and contrib.) The Ordnance Survey Atlas of Great Britain, 1982; numerous articles on economic and urban geography. *Recreations:* music, gardening. *Address:* 45 Oakleigh Avenue, N20 9JE. *T:* (020) 8445 6057. *Club:* Athenæum. *Died 13 Oct. 2015.*

WISEMAN, Julian Paul Geoffrey, CMG 2000; Director, Penumbra Partners Ltd, since 2002; *b* 3 Oct. 1944; *s* of Norman William Thomas Wiseman and Joan Marion Allen Wiseman; *m* 1973, Diana Christine Spooner; two *d*. *Educ:* Cranleigh Sch.; Australian Nat. Univ. (Dip. in Mod. Langs, 1969). Royal Marines, 1963–75: Troop Comdr, 40 Cdo; ADC to Gov. of Qld, 1967–69; Adjt, 42 Cdo, 1972–74; Bde Signal Officer, 3 Cdo Bde, 1975; HM Diplomatic Service, 1976–99: First Secretary: FCO, 1976–78; UKMIS to UN, Geneva, 1978–82; SOAS, 1982–83; FCO, 1982–84; Dhaka, 1984–87; FCO, 1987–90; Counsellor: Islamabad, 1990–92; FCO, 1992–99. Dir, Retainagroup Ltd, 1999–2002. Mem., Sussex Cttee and London Reg. Adv. Cttee, Duke of Edinburgh's Award, 2000–. Trustee, Switchback, 2008–. Gov., Cranleigh Sch., 2010. Liveryman, Coachmakers' and Coach Harness Makers' Co., 2000. FRGS. *Recreations:* ski-ing, fishing, golf, music, travel. *Address:* Penumbra Partners Ltd, 51 Catherine Place, SW1E 6DY. *Clubs:* Boodle's, Army and Navy; Piscatorial Society; West Sussex Golf. *Died 18 May 2012.*

WISTRICH, Ernest, CBE 1973; Vice-President, European Movement (British Council), since 2000 (Director, 1969–86); *b* 22 May 1923; *s* of Dr Arthur and Mrs Eva Wistrich; *m* 1950, Enid Barbara (*née* Heiber); one *s* one *d* (and one *s* decd). *Educ:* Poland; University Tutorial Coll., London. Served in RAF, 1942–46; Timber Merchant, 1946–67; Dir, Britain in Europe, 1967–69; Councillor, Hampstead Borough Council, 1959–65; Camden Borough Council, Alderman 1964–71, Councillor 1971–74; Chm., Camden Cttee for Community Relations, 1964–68; Mem., Skeffington Cttee on Public Participation in Planning, 1968–69. Contested (Lab): Isle of Thanet, 1964; Hendon North, 1966; Cleveland, 1979; contested (SDP) London Central, 1984, European Parly elections. Editor of various jls, incl. The European, 1986–88. *Publications:* After 1992, 1989; The United States of Europe, 1994; contrib. Into Europe, Facts, New Europe and other jls. *Recreations:* music, walking. *Address:* 37B Gayton Road, NW3 1UB. *T:* (020) 7419 1686. *Died 7 May 2015.*

WITHERS, Georgette Lizette, (Googie), (Mrs John McCallum), AO 1980; CBE 2001; actress, since 1932; *b* Karachi, India, 12 March 1917; *d* of late Captain E. C. Withers, CBE, CIE, RIM, and Lizette Catherine Wilhelmina van Wageningen; *m* 1948, John Neil McCallum, AO, CBE (*d* 2010); one *s* two *d*. *Educ:* Fredville Park, Nonnington, Kent; Convent of the Holy Family, Kensington. Started as dancer in Musical Comedy. First film contract at age of 17; acted in over 50 pictures, starring in 30. *Films include:* One of our Aircraft is Missing, 1941; The Silver Fleet, 1941; On Approval, 1942; Loves of Joanna Godden, 1946; It Always Rains on Sunday, 1947; White Corridors, 1950; Nickel Queen, 1970; Country Life, 1994; Shine, 1995. *Plays include:* They Came to a City; Private Lives; Winter Journey; The Deep Blue Sea; Waiting for Gillian; Janus; Stratford on Avon Season, 1958: Beatrice in Much Ado About Nothing; Gertrude in Hamlet; The Complaisant Lover, New York, 1962; Exit the King, London, 1963; Getting Married, Strand, 1967; Madame Renevsky in The Cherry Orchard, Mrs Cheveley in An Ideal Husband, 1972; Lady Kitty in The Circle, Chichester Festival Theatre, 1976, Haymarket, 1977 (nominated for SWET best actress award), Toronto, 1978; Lady Bracknell in The Importance of Being Earnest, Chichester, 1979; Time and the Conways, Chichester, 1983; Lady Sneerwell in The School for Scandal, Duke of York's, 1984 (also European tour); The Chalk Garden, Chichester, 1986; Hay Fever, Ring Round the Moon, Chichester, 1988; An Ideal Husband, Old Vic, 1995–96, Australia, 1997–98; Lady Windermere's Fan, Chichester, 1997, Theatre Royal, Haymarket, 2002. Tours: Roar Like a Dove, The Constant Wife and Woman in a Dressing Gown, Australia and NZ, 1959; excerpts Shakespeare (Kate, Margaret of Anjou, Beatrice, Portia, Rosalind, Cleopatra), 1964; Beekman Place, Australia and NZ, 1965; Relatively Speaking, Australia, 1968; Plaza Suite, Australia and NZ, 1969–70; The Kingfisher, Australia, NZ and Far East, 1978–80, FE, ME and Gulf, 1987; The Cherry Orchard, The Skin Game, Dandy Dick, UK, 1981; Stardust, UK and Australia, 1984–85; The Cocktail Hour, Australia and UK, 1989–90; High Spirits, Australia, 1991, 1993; On Golden Pond, UK, 1992; The Chalk Garden, Australia, 1995; An Ideal Husband, Australia, 1998. *Television* appearances in drama including The Public Prosecutor; Amphitryon 38; The Deep Blue Sea (Best Actress, 1954); Last Year's Confetti, Court Circular, 1971; Knightsbridge, 1972; The Cherry Orchard, 1973; series Within These Walls, 1974–76 (Best Actress of the Year, 1974); Time after Time (TV film), 1985 (Best Actress ACE Award, USA, 1988); Hotel du Lac (TV film), 1985; Northanger Abbey (TV film), 1986; Ending Up, 1989. *Recreations:* music, travel, reading, interior decorating. *Address:* c/o Davenport, 80 St Albans Avenue, Chiswick, W4 5JR. *Died 15 July 2011.*

WITHERS, Rt Hon. Reginald (Greive); PC 1977; Senator (L) for Western Australia, 1966–87; Lord Mayor of Perth, Western Australia, 1991–93; *b* 26 Oct. 1924; *s* of late F. J. Withers and I. L. Greive; *m* 1953, Shirley Lloyd-Jones; two *s* one *d*. *Educ:* Bunbury; Univ. of WA (LLB). Barrister-at-law 1953. Served War, RAN, 1942–46. Councillor, Bunbury Municipal Council, 1954–56; Mem., Bunbury Diocesan Council, 1958–59, Treasurer, 1961–68. State Vice-Pres., Liberal and Country League of WA, 1958–61, State Pres., 1961–65; Mem., Federal Exec. of Liberal Party, 1961–65; Fed. Vice-Pres., Liberal Party, 1962–65. Govt Whip in Senate, 1969–71; Leader of Opposition in Senate, 1972–75; Special Minister of State, Minister for Capital Territory, Minister for Media, and Minister for Tourism and Recreation, Nov.–Dec. 1975; Vice-Pres. of Exec. Council, Leader of Govt in Senate, and Minister for Admin. Services, 1975–78. Sec., SW Law Soc., 1955–68. *Recreations:* swimming, reading, painting. *Address:* 23 Malcolm Street, West Perth, WA 6005, Australia. *T:* (8) 93241322. *E:* reg@withers.pn. *Died 15 Nov. 2014.*

WOLTERS, Gwyneth Eleanor Mary; a Commissioner of Inland Revenue, 1971–78; *b* 21 Nov. 1918; *d* of late Prof. and Mrs A. W. Wolters. *Educ:* Abbey Sch., Reading; Reading Univ.; Newnham Coll., Cambridge (Class. Tripos; Hilda Richardson Prize). Temp. Admin. Asst, Min. of Works, 1941–47; Asst Principal, 1947–49, Principal, 1949–57, Asst Sec., 1957–71, Inland Revenue. *Address:* 45 Albert Road, Caversham, Reading RG4 7AW. *T:* (0118) 947 2605. *Died 25 April 2015.*

WOLVERTON, 7th Baron *cr* 1869; **Christopher Richard Glyn,** FRICS; *b* 5 Oct. 1938; *s* of 6th Baron Wolverton, CBE and Audrey Margaret, *d* of late Richard Stubbs; *S* father, 1988; *m* 1st, 1961, Carolyn Jane (marr. diss. 1967), *yr d* of late Antony N. Hunter; two *d*; 2nd, 1975, Mrs Frances S. E. Stuart Black (marr. diss. 1989); 3rd, 1990, Gillian Konig (marr. diss. 1994). *Educ:* Eton. *Heir: nephew* Miles John Glyn, *b* 6 Jan. 1966. *Address:* 97 Hurlingham Road, SW6 3NL. *Died 24 Jan. 2011.*

WOOD, His Honour Frank; Deputy Senior Judge, Sovereign Base Areas of Akrotiri and Dhekelia, 1995–2006 (Resident Judge, 1986–95); *b* 10 June 1929; *s* of late Robert Wood and Marjorie Edith Park Wood (*née* Senior); *m* 1951, Diana Mae Shenton; two *s* one *d*. *Educ:* Berkhamsted; RMA Sandhurst. Called to the Bar, Lincoln's Inn, 1969. Commissioned RASC, 1949–52. Bechuanaland Protectorate Police, 1953–65 (Supt 1965), Acting Dist Comr, 1957–58, 1959–60; Crown Counsel, Bechuanaland, 1965–66, State Counsel, 1966–67; Magistrate, Seychelles, 1970, Sen. Magistrate, 1974; Puisne Judge and Justice of Appeal, Seychelles, 1977–85, Acting Chief Justice, 1982–84; Chief Justice and Justice of Appeal, Solomon Islands, 1985–86; Justice of Appeal, Vanuatu, 1985–87. Chancellor, Dio. of Seychelles, 1973–84. Mem. Council, Commonwealth Magistrates' Assoc., 1973–77. *Publications:* Sovereign Base Areas Law Reports 1960–87, 1988. *Recreations:* reading, philately. *Address:* Pooh Corner, 2 Erimi Gardens, Erimi 4630, Limassol, Cyprus. *Club:* Civil Service. *Died 15 Feb. 2014.*

WOOD, Maj.-Gen. Harry Stewart, CB 1967; TD 1950; President, Ordnance Board, 1966–67 (Vice-President, 1964–66); *b* 16 Sept. 1913; *e s* of late Roland and Eva M. Wood; *m* 1939, Joan Gordon (*d* 1999), *d* of Gordon S. King; two *s* (and one *s* decd). *Educ:* Nautical Coll., Pangbourne. Civil Engineer (inc. articled trng), 1931–39. Commnd RA (TA), 1937. Served War of 1939–45: Regimental Service, Sept. 1939–June 1944; subseq. Technical Staff. Dep. Dir of Artillery, Min. of Supply (Col), 1958–60; Dep. Dir, Inspectorate of Armaments (Brig.), 1960–62; Sen. Mil. Officer, Royal Armament Research and Development Estab. (Brig.), 1962–64. Maj.-Gen. 1964; retd, 1967. Legion of Merit, degree of Legionnaire (USA), 1947. *Recreations:* home and garden, motor sport. *Died 2 March 2013.*

WOOD, John, CBE 2007; actor; *m* Sylvia; one *s* two *d*, and one *s* by a previous marriage. *Educ:* Bedford Sch.; Jesus Coll., Oxford (Pres. OUDS). Old Vic Co., 1954–56; Camino Real, Phoenix, 1957; The Making of Moo, Royal Court, 1957; Brouhaha, Aldwych, 1958; The Fantasticks, Apollo, 1961; Rosencrantz and Guildenstern are Dead, NY, 1967; Exiles, Mermaid, 1970; joined Royal Shakespeare Company, 1971; Enemies, The Man of Mode, Exiles, The Balcony, Aldwych, 1971; The Comedy of Errors, Stratford, 1972; Julius Caesar, Titus Andronicus, Stratford, 1972, Aldwych, 1973; Collaborators, Duchess, 1973; A Lesson in Blood and Roses, The Place, 1973; Sherlock Holmes, Travesties (Evening Standard Best Actor Award, 1974; Tony Award, 1976), Aldwych, 1974, NY, 1974; The Devil's Disciple, Ivanov, Aldwych, 1976; Death Trap, NY, 1978; Undiscovered Country, Richard III, Nat. Theatre, 1979; The Provok'd Wife, Nat. Theatre, 1980; Royal Shakespeare Co.: The Tempest, 1988; The Man Who Came to Dinner, The Master Builder, 1989; King Lear, 1990 (Evening Standard Best Actor Award, 1991); Love's Labour's Lost, 1990; The Invention of Love, RNT, 1997, transf. Haymarket, 1998; No Man's Land, NT, 2001; Henry IV, Pts 1 and 2, NT, 2005. *Television:* A Tale of Two Cities, Barnaby Rudge, 1964–65; The Victorians, 1965; The Duel, 1966. *Films:* Nicholas and Alexandra, 1971; Slaughterhouse Five, 1972; War Games, 1983; The Madness of King George, 1994; Sabrina, Richard III, Jane Eyre, 1996; The Gambler, 1997; Chocolat, 2001; The Little Vampire, 2000; Imagining Argentina, 2004; The White Countess, 2005. *Died 6 Aug. 2011.*

WOOD, Rt Rev. Mark; *see* Wood, Rt Rev. S. M.

WOOD, Robert Noel; psychotherapist; *b* 24 Dec. 1934; *s* of Ernest Clement Wood, CIE and Lucy Eileen Wood; *m* 1st, 1962, Sarah Child (marr. diss. 1981); one *s* one *d*; 2nd, 2009, Wendy Joy Hartman. *Educ:* Sherborne Sch.; New Coll., Oxford (BA Hons PPE); LSE (Rockefeller Student; Certif. in Internat. Studies). Nat. Service Commn, RHA, 1953–55 (Best Cadet, Mons OCS). Dep. Res. Dir, Internat. Div., Economist Intelligence Unit Ltd, 1959–65; Inst. of Econs and Statistics, Oxford, 1965–70; Sen. Economist, Min. of Econ. Affairs and Develt Planning, Tanzania, 1966–69; Econ. Advr, ODM, 1970; Dir of Studies, Overseas Develt Inst., 1970–74; Adviser to House of Commons Select Cttee on Overseas Develt, 1973–74; Dir, Overseas Develt Inst., 1974–82. Jungian analysis, 1982–90; Psychotherapist Mem., Foundn for Psychotherapy and Counselling, 1989–2010. Chm., Friends of the Union Chapel, 1983–87; Mem., Religious Soc. of Friends (Quakers), 1982–. Gov., Quintin Kynaston Sch., 1974–86. *Publications:* contrib. Bull. Oxford Inst. of Econs and Statistics, ODI Rev. *Recreations:* Victorian artists, listening to music, singing, swimming, walking, Arsenal football club, poetry, Jung. *Address:* The Coach House, Parc-An-Dix Lane, Phillack, Cornwall TR27 5AB. *T:* (01736) 755484. *Died 14 July 2015.*

WOOD, Rt Rev. (Stanley) Mark; an Hon. Assistant Bishop, Diocese of Southwark, since 2002; *b* 21 May 1919; *s* of Arthur Mark and Jane Wood; *m* 1947, Winifred Ruth, *d* of Edward James Toase; three *s* two *d*. *Educ:* Pontypridd County School; University College, Cardiff (BA 2nd cl. Greek and Latin); College of the Resurrection, Mirfield. Curate at St Mary's, Cardiff Docks, 1942–45; Curate, Sophiatown Mission, Johannesburg, 1945–47; Rector of Bloemhof, Transvaal, 1947–50; Priest in charge of St Cyprian's Mission, Johannesburg, 1950–55; Rector of Marandellas, Rhodesia, 1955–65; Dean of Salisbury, Rhodesia, 1965–70; Bishop of Matabeleland, 1971–77; Asst Bishop of Hereford, 1977–81; Bishop Suffragan of Ludlow, 1981–87; Archdeacon of Ludlow, 1982–83. *Address:* College of St Barnabas, Lingfield, Surrey RH7 6NJ. *Died 28 Sept. 2014.*

WOODALL, Alec; *b* Hemsworth, 20 Sept. 1918; *m* 1950, Molly Scott; one *s* one *d*. *Educ:* South Road Elementary School, Hemsworth. Served War, KOYLI (Sergeant). Colliery official, South Kirby. MP (Lab) Hemsworth, Feb. 1974–1987. PPS to Sec. of State for Trade, 1976–78. Mem. Nat. Council, 1975–87, case worker, 1987–, SSAFA. *Address:* 2 Grove Terrace, Hemsworth, West Yorkshire WF9 4BQ. *T:* (01977) 613897. *Died 3 Jan. 2011.*

WOODCOCK, Sir John, Kt 1989; CBE 1983; QPM 1976; HM Chief Inspector of Constabulary, 1990–93; *b* 14 Jan. 1932; *s* of late Joseph Woodcock and of Elizabeth May Woodcock (*née* Whiteside); *m* 1953, Kathleen Margaret Abbott; two *s* one *d*. *Educ:* Preston, Lancs, elementary schs; Preston Technical Coll. Police cadet, Lancashire

Constabulary, 1947–50; Army Special Investigation Branch, 1950–52; Constable to Chief Inspector, Lancashire Constabulary, 1952–65; Supt and Chief Supt, Bedfordshire and Luton Constabulary, 1965–68; Asst Chief Constable, 1968–70, Dep. Chief Constable, 1970–74, Gwent Constabulary; Dep. Chief Constable, Devon and Cornwall Constabulary, 1974–78; Chief Constable: N Yorkshire Police, 1978–79; S Wales Constabulary, 1979–83; HM Inspector of Constabulary, Wales and Midlands, 1983–90. Conducted inquiry into escapes from Whitemoor Prison, reported 1994. Intermed. Comd Course, Police Coll., 1965, Sen. Comd Course, 1968; Study, Bavarian Police, 1977; European Discussion Centre, 1977; Internat. Police Course (Lectr), Sicily, Rome, 1978; FBI, Nat. Exec., Washington, 1981; Lectr, Denmark, 1983, Holland, 1990; Study, Royal Hong Kong Police, 1989. Adviser and Member: UK Atomic Energy Police Authy, 1993–99; MoD Police Cttee, 1995–2000. Dir, Capital Corp. plc, 1994–99; Advr, Control Risks Group Ltd, 1995–2002. Vice-Pres., Welsh Assoc. of Youth Clubs, 1981–87; Chm., South Wales Cttee, Royal Jubilee and Prince's Trusts, 1983–85; Member: Admin. Council, Royal Jubilee Trusts, 1981–85; Prince's Trust Cttee for Wales, 1981–85; Mem., Governing Body, World College of the Atlantic, 1980–85. Pres., Police Mutual Assurance Soc., 1990–94. Jt Vice Pres., The Choughs, Cornwall Wheelchair Dance Team, 2009–. St John Council, N Yorks, S Glam, Mid Glam (Chm.), Hereford and Worcs, 1979–90. Freeman, City of London, 1993. CCMI (CIMgt 1980). FRCA 1995. CStJ 1992; KSG 1984. *Recreation:* golf. *Address:* c/o Home Office, 2 Marsham Street, SW1P 4DF. *Clubs:* Swansea Lions (Hon. Mem.); Merlin Golf (Cornwall). *Died 21 Sept. 2012.*

WOODGATE, Joan Mary, CBE 1964; RRC 1959; Matron-in-Chief, Queen Alexandra's RN Nursing Service, 1962–66; *b* 30 Aug. 1912; *d* of Sir Alfred Woodgate, CBE, and Louisa Alice (*née* Digby). *Educ:* Surbiton High Sch., Surrey. Trained at St George's Hospital, 1932–36, Sister, 1937–38; Queen Charlotte's Hospital, 1936. Joined QARNNS, 1938; served Middle East and Far East; HM Hospital Ship, Empire Clyde, 1945–47; HM Hospital Ship, Maine, 1953–54; Principal Matron: RNH Haslar, 1959–61; RNH Malta, 1961–62. OStJ 1959; QHNS, 1962–64. Member, Commonwealth War Graves Commn, 1966–83. *Recreations:* gardening, country pursuits. *Address:* Laurel Cottage, Northover Lane, Tiptoe, near Lymington, Hants SO41 6FS. *Club:* English-Speaking Union. *Died 10 March 2013.*

WOODHEAD, Sir Christopher (Anthony), Kt 2011; Stanley Kalms Professor of Education, University of Buckingham, since 2002; Chairman, Cognita Group, 2004; *b* 20 Oct. 1946; *m* 2006, Christine Kensett; one *d* from former marriage. *Educ:* Wallington Grammar Sch.; Bristol Univ. (BA Sp. Hons English, PGCE); Univ. of Keele (MA). English Teacher, Priory Sch., Shrewsbury, 1969–72; Dep. Head of English, Newent Sch., Gloucester, 1972–74; Head of English, Gordano Sch., Avon, 1974–76; Tutor for English, Oxford Univ., 1976–82; English Advr, 1982–84, Chief Advr, 1984–88, Shropshire LEA; Dep. Chief Educn Officer, Devon LEA, 1988–90, Cornwall LEA, 1990–91; Dep. Chief Exec., 1991, Chief Exec., 1991–93, Nat. Curriculum Council; Chief Exec., SCAA, 1993–94; HM Chief Inspector of Schs, 1994–2000. Special Prof., Univ. of Nottingham, 1993–95. Hon. DLitt Buckingham, 2011. *Publications:* Class War, 2002; A Desolation of Learning, 2009. *Address:* University of Buckingham, Hunter Street, Buckingham MK18 1EG. *Died 23 June 2015.*

WOODHOUSE, Rt Hon. Sir (Arthur) Owen, ONZ 2007; KBE 1981; Kt 1974; DSC 1944; PC 1974; Founding President, Law Commission, New Zealand, 1986–91; a Judge of the Supreme Court, New Zealand, 1961–86; a Judge of the Court of Appeal, 1974–86, President of the Court of Appeal, 1981–86; *b* Napier, 18 July 1916; *s* of A. J. Woodhouse and W. J. C. Woodhouse (*née* Allen); *m* 1940, Margaret Leah Thorp; four *s* two *d*. *Educ:* Napier Boys' High Sch.; Auckland Univ. (LLB). Served War of 1939–45, Lt-Comdr in RNZNVR on secondment to RN; service in MTBs; liaison officer with Yugoslav Partisans, 1943; Asst to Naval Attaché, HM Embassy Belgrade, 1945. Joined Lusk, Willis & Sproule, barristers and solicitors, 1946; Crown Solicitor, Napier, 1953; appointed Judge of Supreme Court, 1961. Chm., Royal Commn on Compensation and Rehabilitation in respect of Personal Injury in NZ, 1966–67, and of inquiry into similar questions in Australia, 1973–74; Pres., NZ Sect., Internat. Commn of Jurists, 1986–93. Hon. LLD: Victoria Univ. of Wellington, 1978; Univ. of York, Toronto, 1981. *Publications:* A Personal Affair, 2004. *Recreations:* music, golf. *Address:* 244 Remuera Road, Auckland 1005, New Zealand. *Clubs:* Northern (Auckland); Hawkes Bay (Napier); Wellesley, Wellington (Wellington). *Died 15 April 2014.*

WOODHOUSE, Dr Frank, OBE 1998; Director, British Institute of Florence, 1988–97; *b* 29 April 1943; *s* of Samuel Woodhouse and Clarice (*née* Bache); *m* 1966, Melba Sterry; two *s*. *Educ:* King Edward VI Grammar Sch., Stourbridge; Birmingham Univ. (BCom); Trinity Hall, Cambridge (MA, PhD). Asst Lectr, later Lectr in Italian, Hull Univ., 1972–81; Lectr in Italian, Cambridge Univ., 1981–92; Fellow, 1983–92, Associate Dean, 1986–87, Darwin Coll., Cambridge. Co-dir (pt-time), S. Woodhouse & Sons (Investments) Ltd, 1998–2009. *Publications:* Language and Style in a Renaissance Epic, 1982; articles on Italian subjects. *Recreations:* reading, travel, Italy. *Address:* 16 Melbourne Place, Cambridge CB1 1EQ. *Club:* Travellers. *Died 4 July 2013.*

WOODHOUSE, Rt Hon. Sir Owen; *see* Woodhouse, Rt Hon. Sir A. O.

WOODROFFE, Most Rev. George Cuthbert Manning, KBE 1980 (CBE 1973); MA, LTh; Archbishop of West Indies, 1980–86; Bishop of Windward Islands, 1969–86; *b* 17 May 1918; *s* of James Manning Woodroffe and Evelyn Agatha (*née* Norton); *m* 1947, Aileen Alice Connell; one *s* one *d* (and one *s* decd). *Educ:* Grenada Boys' Secondary School; Codrington Coll., Barbados. Clerk in Civil Service, Grenada, 1936–41; Codrington Coll. (Univ. of Durham), 1941–44; Deacon 1944; Priest 1945; Asst Priest, St George's Cath., St Vincent, 1944–47; Vicar of St Simon's, Barbados, 1947–50; Rector: St Andrew, 1950–57; St Joseph, 1957–62; St John, 1962–67; Rural Dean of St John, Barbados, 1965–67; Sub-Dean and Rector of St George's Cathedral, St Vincent, Windward Islands, 1967–69. Vice-Chm., Anglican Consultative Council, 1974. Chm., Vis. Justices St Vincent Prisons, 1968–76. Mem., Prerogative of Mercy Cttee, St Vincent, 1969–86. Member: Bd of Educn, Barbados, 1964–67; National Trust of St Vincent, 1967–86 (Chm., 1972–82); Council, Univ. of the West Indies, 1980–83; Chm., Bd of Governors, Alleyne Sch., Barbados, 1951–57. Hon. DD Nashotah House, USA, 1980; Hon. LLD Univ. of the West Indies, 1981. *Recreations:* music, driving, detective tales and novels, military band music. *Address:* PO Box 919, VCO 100, Murray Road, St Vincent and the Grenadines, West Indies. *T:* 4561277. *Club:* Royal Commonwealth Society. *Died 29 Nov. 2012.*

WOODS, His Honour Brian; DL; a Circuit Judge, 1975–94; *b* 5 Nov. 1928; *yr s* of late E. P. Woods, Woodmancote, Cheltenham; *m* 1957, Margaret, *d* of late F. J. Griffiths, Parkgate, Wirral; three *d*. *Educ:* City of Leicester Boys' Sch.; Nottingham Univ. (LLB 1952). National Service, RAF, 1947–49. Called to the Bar, Gray's Inn, 1955; Midland Circuit; Dep. Chm., Lincs (Lindsey) QS, 1968. Chancellor, Diocese of Leicester, 1977–79; Reader, dio. of Leicester, 1970–79, dio. of Lichfield, 1978–2013. Member Council: S Mary and S Anne's Sch., Abbots Bromley, 1977–92; Ellesmere Coll., 1983–84. Mem., Law Adv. Cttee, Nottingham Univ., 1979–94; a Legal Mem., Mental Health Review Tribunals for Trent, W Midlands, Yorkshire, N and SW Thames Region, 1983–99. Fellow, Midland Div., Woodard Corp., 1979–92. DL Derbys, 1994. *Recreations:* daughters, musical music, taking photographs. *Died 22 Sept. 2013.*

WOODS, Prof. Robert Ivor, DPhil, LittD; FBA 2003; John Rankin Professor of Geography, University of Liverpool, since 1989; *b* 17 Sept. 1949; *s* of Ivor and Rhoda Woods; *m* 1977, Alison Cook; one *s* one *d*. *Educ:* Fitzwilliam Coll., Cambridge (BA 1971, MA 1975; LittD 2004); St Antony's Coll., Oxford (DPhil 1975). Lectr in Quantitative Social Sci., Univ. of Kent at Canterbury, 1974–75; Lectr, 1975–85, Sen. Lectr, 1985–88, Reader, 1988–89, in Geog., Univ. of Sheffield. Editor: Internat. Jl

Population Geog., 1995–2002; Population Studies, 2003–. Pres., British Soc. for Population Studies, 1991–93. *Publications:* The Demography of Victorian England and Wales, 2000; Children Remembered, 2006; Death before Birth, 2009. *Recreations:* books, red wine, tombstones, Rugby Union football. *Address:* Department of Geography, University of Liverpool, Liverpool L69 3BX. *T:* (0151) 794 2837, *Fax:* (0151) 794 2866. *E:* riwoods@liv.ac.uk. *Died 20 Feb. 2011.*

WOODWARD, Adm. Sir John (Forster), GBE 1989; KCB 1982; Commander-in-Chief, Naval Home Command, 1987–89; *b* Penzance, Cornwall, 1 May 1932; *s* of late T. Woodward and M. B. M. Woodward; *m* 1960, Charlotte Mary McMurtrie; one *s* one *d. Educ:* Royal Naval College, Dartmouth. Under training, Home Fleet, until 1953; Submarine Specialist, serving in HMS Sanguine, Porpoise, Valiant, and commanding HMS Tireless, Grampus and Warspite, from 1953; Min. of Defence and senior training posts, from 1971, plus comd HMS Sheffield, 1976–77; Director of Naval Plans, 1978–81; Flag Officer, First Flotilla, 1981–83, Sen. Task Gp Comdr, S Atlantic, during Falklands Campaign, Apr.–July 1982; Flag Officer, Submarines, and Comdr, Submarines Eastern Atlantic, 1983–84; Dep. Chief of Defence Staff (Commitments), 1985–87; Flag ADC to the Queen, 1987–89. Ind. Inspector, Lord Chancellor's Panel, 1994–96. Chm., Falklands Is Meml Chapel Trust, 1994–2000. Hon. Liveryman, Glass Sellers' Co., 1982. *Publications:* One Hundred Days: the memoirs of the Falklands Battle Group Commander, 1992; Strategy by Matrix, 2001. *Recreations:* sailing, bridge. *Address:* c/o The Naval Secretary, Fleet Headquarters, Mail Point 3.1, Sir Henry Leach Building, Whale Island, Portsmouth PO2 8BY. *Died 4 Aug. 2013.*

WOOLSEY, Rt Rev. Gary Frederick; National Director, Anglican Fellowship of Prayer, Canada, 2006–12; Assistant Bishop of Calgary, 1992–2002, and Rector of St Peter's, Calgary, 1991–2002; *b* 16 March 1942; *s* of William and Doreen Woolsey; *m* 1967, Marie Elaine Tooker; two *s* two *d. Educ:* Univ. of Western Ontario (BA); Huron Coll., London, Ont. (BTh); Univ. of Manitoba (Teacher's Cert.). Deacon, 1967; Priest-pilot, Diocese of Keewatin, 1967–68; Rector: St Peter's, Big Trout Lake, Ont, 1968–72; St Mark's, Norway House, Manitoba, 1972–76; St Paul's, Churchill, Man, 1976–80; Program Director and Archdeacon of Keewatin, 1980–83; Bishop of Athabasca, 1983–91. *Publications:* On a Wing and a Prayer: motorcycle meditations, 2013; Meditations from a Hospice Bed, 2013. *Recreations:* fishing, camping, photography, motorcycle touring. *Address:* 184 Cedar Ridge Crescent SW, Calgary, AB T2W 1X8, Canada. *T:* (403) 2519569. *Died 18 Oct. 2013.*

WOON, Peter William; Editor, BBC TV News, 1980–85; *b* 12 Dec. 1931; *s* of Henry William Woon and Gwendoline Constance Woon; *m* 1st, 1956, Elizabeth Hird (marr. diss. 1974); one *s*; 2nd, 1974, Diana Ward (marr. diss. 1993). *Educ:* Christ's Hospital. 2nd Lieut Royal Signals, 1954–56; Reporter, Bristol Evening Post, 1949–54 and 1956–58; air corresp., Daily Express, 1958–61; BBC: reporter, 1961–66; Asst Editor, TV News, 1966–69; Editor, Radio News, 1969–75; Head of Information, 1975–77; Editor, News and Current Affairs, radio, 1977–80; Head, Ops, N America, 1985–88. *Died 20 May 2014.*

WOOSNAM, Charles Richard, CBE 1993; a Forestry Commissioner, 1986–94; *b* 4 Aug. 1925; *s* of late Ralph William Woosnam and Kathleen Mary Woosnam (*née* Evan-Thomas); *m* 1950, Patricia Rodney Carruthers; two *s* two *d. Educ:* Winchester; Pembroke Coll., Cambridge. BA Estate Management. FRICS. Commissioned 15th/19th The King's Royal Hussars, 1943–47, served Europe and Palestine; with Land Agents Strutt & Parker, Builth Wells office, 1950–63; set up own Land Agency partnership, Woosnam & Tyler, 1964, merged with Strutt & Parker, 1996, Consultant, 1988–98. Member: Welsh Water Authy, 1973–76 (Chm., Fisheries Adv. Cttee); Exec. Cttee, Timber Growers UK (formerly Timber Growers England & Wales), 1976–86 (Dep. Chm., England and Wales; Chm., Finance Cttee); Chm., CLA Game Fair Local Cttee, 1976; Pres., Royal Forestry Soc. of England, Wales and NI, 1995–97. High Sheriff, Powys, 1985–86. *Recreations:* shooting, fishing. *Address:* Cefnllysgwynne, Llanynis, Builth Wells, Powys LD2 3HN. *T:* (01982) 552237. *Club:* Army and Navy. *Died 8 April 2012.*

WORSKETT, Prof. Roy, RIBA; consultant architect; Partner, Architectural Planning Partnership, Horsham, 1982–85; *b* Horsham, 3 Sept. 1932; *s* of Archibald Ellwood Worskett and Dorothy Alice Roffey; two *s* one *d. Educ:* Collyer's Sch., Horsham; Worthing Art Sch.; Portsmouth Sch. of Architecture. MRTPI 1975 (retd); RIBA 1955. Architect's Dept, LCC, 1957–60; Architect, Civic Trust, London, 1960–63; Historic Areas Div., DoE (formerly MPBW), 1963–74; City Architect and Planning Officer, Bath City Council, and Prof. of Urban Conservation, Sch. of Architecture, Bath Univ., 1974–79; Consultant Head, Conservation Section, Crafts Council, 1979–82. Consultant Architect: Bath CC, 1979–83; Salisbury DC, 1980–83; Brighton Palace Pier, 1987–2002; London borough of Greenwich, 1988–99; London boroughs of Lambeth, Kensington and Chelsea, and Richmond, 1988; Consultant: Ford Foundn in India, 1982–86; Council of Europe, 1984–86; Nat. Audit Office, 1987; evidence to Public Inquiries at: Mansion House, for City of London; County Hall, London, 1984; Thameslink, 2000; Advr, Urban Redevelt Authority, Singapore, 1992–93; Conservation Advr, Union Rlys and British Land, 1993–99; Advisor: Historic Royal Palaces, Tower of London Environs Scheme, 1996–98; King's Cross Station Proposals, London Borough of Camden, 1997–99; Cambridge City Centre, 1997–98; Nat. Film and TV Sch., 2001. Chairman: Conservation Cttees, Crafts Adv. Cttee, 1974–79; Design Panel, Spitalfields Develt Gp, 1990–96; Member: Heritage Educn Group, 1976–88; Council for Urban Study Centres, TCPA, 1977–80; Council of Management, Architectural Heritage Fund, 1977–2000. Pres., Urban Design Gp, 1983–84. Vis. Prof., Internat. Centre for Conservation, Rome, 1972–97. *Publications:* The Character of Towns, 1968; articles in architect. and planning magazines. *Recreation:* looking and listening in disbelief. *Address:* 1 Hampers Lane, Horsham, West Sussex RH13 6HB. *T:* (01403) 254208. *Died 23 Aug. 2014.*

WORSLEY, Sir Marcus; *see* Worsley, Sir W. M. J.

WORSLEY, Michael Dominic Laurence; QC 1985; *b* 9 Feb. 1926; *s* of Paul Worsley and Magdalen Teresa Worsley; *m* 1962, Pamela (*née* Philpot) (*d* 1980); one *s* (and one *s* decd); *m* 1986, Jane, *d* of Percival and Mary Sharpe. *Educ:* Bedford School; Inns of Court School of Law. RN 1944–45. Lived in Africa, 1946–52; called to the Bar, Inner Temple, 1955, Bencher, 1980; Standing Prosecuting Counsel to Inland Revenue, 1968–69; Treasury Counsel at Inner London Sessions, 1969–71; Junior Treasury Counsel, 1971–74, Senior Treasury Counsel, 1974–85, CCC. *Recreations:* music, travelling. *Clubs:* Garrick, Lansdowne. *Died 22 Dec. 2015.*

WORSLEY, Gen. Sir Richard (Edward), GCB 1982 (KCB 1976); OBE 1964; Chairman: Western Provident Assoc., 1989–96; Electro-Optical Division, Pilkington Brothers, 1984–86 (Chief Executive, 1982–86); Barr and Stroud, 1982–86; Pilkington PE, 1982–86; *b* 29 May 1923; *s* of H. H. K. Worsley, Grey Abbey, Co. Down; *m* 1st, 1959, Sarah Anne Mitchell (marr. diss.); one *s* one *d*; 2nd, 1980, Caroline, Duchess of Fife, *er d* of 3rd Baron Forteviot, MBE. *Educ:* Radley Coll. Served War: commissioned into Rifle Bde, 1942, Middle East and Italian Campaigns, 1942–45. Instr, RMA Sandhurst, 1948–51; Malayan Emergency, 1956–57; Instr, Staff Coll., Camberley, 1958–61; CO, The Royal Dragoons, 1962–65; Comdr, 7th Armoured Bde, 1965–67; Imperial Defence Coll., 1968; Chief of Staff, Far East Land Forces, 1969–71; GOC 3rd Div., 1972–74; Vice-QMG, MoD, 1974–76; GOC 1 (Br) Corps, 1976–78; QMG, 1979–82. Freeman, City of London, 1983. *Recreations:* shooting, ornithology. *Club:* Cavalry and Guards. *Died 23 Feb. 2013.*

WORSLEY, Sir (William) Marcus (John), 5th Bt *cr* 1838; JP; Lord-Lieutenant of North Yorkshire, 1987–99; *b* 6 April 1925; *s* of Colonel Sir William Arthington Worsley, 4th Bt, and Joyce Morgan (*d* 1979), *d* of Sir John Fowler Brunner, 2nd Bt; *S* father, 1973; *m* 1955, Hon. Bridget Assheton (*d* 2004), *d* of 1st Baron Clitheroe, PC, KCVO; two *s* one *d* (and one *s* decd). *Educ:* Eton; New Coll.,

Oxford (BA Hons Modern History 1949). Green Howards, 1943–47 (Lieut seconded to Royal West African Frontier Force). Programme Assistant, BBC European Service, 1950–53. Contested (C) Keighley, 1955; MP (C) Keighley, 1959–64, Chelsea, 1966–Sept. 1974; Parliamentary Private Secretary: to Minister of Health, 1960–61; to Minister without Portfolio, 1962–64; to Lord President of the Council, 1970–72. Second Church Estates Commissioner, 1970–74; a Church Commissioner, 1976–84. Pres., Royal Forestry Soc. of England, Wales and N Ireland, 1980–82 (Vice-Pres., 1976–80); National Trust: Dep. Chm., 1986–92; Chm., Yorks Reg. Cttee, 1969–80; Chm., Properties Cttee, 1980–90. Hon. Col, 2nd Bn, Yorkshire Volunteers, 1988–93. JP 1957 (Chm., Malton Bench, 1983–90), DL 1978, North Yorks; High Sheriff of North Yorks, 1982. KStJ 1987. *Recreations:* walking, reading. *Heir:* *s* William Ralph Worsley, FRICS [*b* 12 Sept. 1956; *m* 1987, Marie-Noëlle, *yr d* of Bernard H. Dreesmann; one *s* two *d*]. *Address:* Park House, Hovingham, York YO62 4JZ. *T:* (01653) 628002. *Club:* Boodle's. *Died 18 Dec. 2012.*

WORTH, Prof. Katharine Joyce; Professor of Drama and Theatre Studies in the University of London at Royal Holloway and Bedford New College, 1985–87, then Emeritus (at Royal Holloway College, 1978–85); *b* Newcastle upon Tyne, 4 Aug. 1922; *d* of George and Elizabeth Lorimer; *m* 1947, George Worth (decd); two *s* one *d*. *Educ:* Bedford Coll., Univ. of London (BA English, MA res. degree, PhD). Lectr in drama and theatre history (pt-time), Central Sch. of Speech and Drama and for Univ. of London Dept of Extra-Mural Studies, 1948 intermittently until 1963; Lectr 1964–74, Reader 1974–78, in English Lit., RHC; Hon. Fellow, RHBNC, 1990. Leverhulme Professorial Fellowship, 1987–89. Vis. Prof., KCL, 1987–96. Chm., Boilerhouse Fund-raising Cttee, 1999–2001, Mem., Boilerhouse Develt Cttee, 2001–, Royal Holloway. Consultant, London Centre for Th. Studies, 2001–. Hon. Pres., Consortium for Drama and Media in Higher Educn, 1975–87; Co-editor, Theatre Notebook, 1987–97; Member, Editorial Board: Yeats Annual, 1985–; Modern Drama, 1985–2000; Univ. of Michigan Press, 1988–. Hon. Life Mem., Soc. for Theatre Res., 1997. Prodns of Beckett's TV play, Eh Joe, and his radio plays, Words and Music, Embers and Cascando, 1972–84 (music for Words and Music and Cascando by Humphrey Searle); stage adaptation of Samuel Beckett's Company, perf. Edinburgh, Belfast, London and NY, 1987–88, Dublin, 1991; Dir, staged readings of the play behind the opera, Verdi Fest., Royal Opera House, 1995–99. *Publications:* Revolutions in Modern English Drama, 1973; (ed) Beckett the Shape Changer, 1975; The Irish Drama of Europe: from Yeats to Beckett, 1978; Oscar Wilde, 1983; Maeterlinck's Plays in Performance, 1985; (critical edn): W. B. Yeats: Where There is Nothing, and, W. B. Yeats and Lady Gregory: The Unicorn from the Stars, 1987; Waiting for Godot and Happy Days: text and performance, 1990; Sheridan and Goldsmith, 1992; Samuel Beckett's Theatre: life journeys, 1999; (contrib.) Samuel Beckett - 100 Years, ed. C. Murray, 2006; many articles and reviews on modern drama in symposia and in English, Irish and Amer. jls, incl. Modern Drama, TLS, Irish Univ. Rev., Th. Notebook, etc. *Recreations:* foreign travel, theatre, art galleries, walking in the country. *Address:* 48 Elmfield Avenue, Teddington, Middx TW11 8BT. *T:* (020) 8977 5778. *Died 28 Jan. 2015.*

WORTHINGTON, His Honour George Noel; a Circuit Judge, 1979–94; *b* 22 June 1923; *s* of late George Errol Worthington and Edith Margaret Boys Worthington; *m* 1954, Jacqueline Kemble Lightfoot, 2nd *d* of late G. L. S. Lightfoot and Mrs Lightfoot; one *s* one *d* (and one *s* decd). *Educ:* Rossall Sch., Lancashire. Served War of 1939–45 in Royal Armoured Corps, 1941–46. Admitted a solicitor, 1949; a Recorder of the Crown Court, 1972–79. Liveryman, Wax Chandlers' Co. *Recreations:* gardening, theatre. *Address:* 49 Temple Sheen Road, East Sheen, SW14 7QF. *Clubs:* Athenæum, Hurlingham. *Died 19 Nov. 2014.*

WRAITH, Prof. (James) Edmond, FRCP, FRCPCH; Professor of Paediatric Inherited Metabolic Disease, Department of Genetic Medicine, St Mary's Hospital, Manchester, since 2009; *b* S Shields, Tyne and Wear, 30 Oct. 1953; *s* of James Edmond Wraith and Victoria Wraith (*née* Vacher); *m* 1976, Elizabeth Susan Ellison; two *s* one *d*. *Educ:* S Shields Grammar Tech. Sch. for Boys; Sheffield Univ. Med. Sch. (MB ChB 1977). FRCP 1993; FRCPCH 1997. SHO in Paediatrics, Sheffield, 1978–80; Registrar in Paediatrics, Royal Manchester Children's Hosp., 1980–83; Sen. Registrar in Paediatrics, Salford and Wigan, 1983–88; Consultant Paediatrician, Royal Manchester Children's Hosp., 1988–2009. Best Doctor, Well Child Charity, 2009. *Publications:* book chapters; contrib. articles to learned jls. *Recreations:* watching Newcastle United FC, reading, music, computing. *Address:* Department of Genetic Medicine, St Mary's Hospital, Oxford Road, Manchester M13 9WL. *T:* (0161) 701 2138, *Fax:* (0161) 701 2303. *E:* ed.wraith@cmft.nhs.uk. *Club:* Newcastle United Supporters. *Died 10 April 2013.*

WRAN, Hon. Neville Kenneth, AC 1988; CNZM 2010; QC (NSW) 1968; Premier of New South Wales, 1976–86; *b* 11 Oct. 1926; *m* 1st, Marcia Oliver (marr. diss.); one *s* one *d*; 2nd, 1976, Jill Lesley Norton Hickson, AM; one *s* one *d*. *Educ:* Fort Street Boys' High Sch., Sydney; Sydney Univ. (LLB). Solicitor before admission to Bar of NSW, 1957. Joined Australian Labor Party, 1954, Nat. Pres., 1980–86. Elected to Legislative Council, 1970; Dep. Leader of Opposition, 1971; Leader of Opposition, Legislative Council, 1972; MLA for Bass Hill, Nov. 1973–1986; Leader of Opposition, Dec. 1973–1976. Chm., CSIRO, 1986–91. Especially interested in law reform, civil liberties, industrial relations, conservation and cultural matters. Exec. Chm., Wran Partners Pty Ltd, 1997–2010; Dir, Cabcharge Australia Ltd, 2000–10. Australian Mem., Eminent Persons' Gp, Asia-Pacific Econ. Co-operation, 1993–95. Patron, Victor Chang Cardiac Res. Inst., 2009–. FRSA 1990. Hon. LLD: Sydney, 1995; NSW, 2006. *Recreations:* reading, walking, swimming, tennis. *Address:* GPO Box 4545, Sydney, NSW 2001, Australia. *T:* (2) 92235151. *Club:* Sydney Labor (Hon. Life Mem.). *Died 20 April 2014.*

WRAY, James; *b* 28 April 1938; *m* 1st, Mary (marr. diss. 1981); one *s* two *d*; 2nd, Catherine (marr. diss. 1998); 3rd, 1999, Laura Walker; one *s*. Heavy goods vehicle driver. Mem., Strathclyde Regl Council, 1976. MP (Lab): Glasgow, Provan, 1987–97; Glasgow Baillieston, 1997–2005. President: Scottish Fedn of the Blind, 1987 (Vice Pres., 1986); St Enoch's Drug Centre; Scottish Ex-Boxers' Assoc.; Gorbals United FC. Mem., TGWU. *Died 25 May 2013.*

WRENBURY, 3rd Baron *cr* 1915; **Rev. John Burton Buckley;** Non-Stipendiary Minister, Dallington, since 1990, Warbleton and Bodle Street Green, since 2012, Diocese of Chichester; *b* 18 June 1927; *s* of 2nd Baron Wrenbury and Helen Malise (*d* 1981), 2nd *d* of late His Honour John Cameron Graham of Ballewan, Stirlingshire; *S* father, 1940; *m* 1st, 1956, Carolyn Joan Maule (marr. diss. 1961), *o d* of Lt-Col Ian Burn-Murdoch, OBE, of Gartincaber, Doune, Perthshire; 2nd, 1961, Penelope Sara Frances, *o d* of Edward D. Fort, The White House, Sixpenny Handley, Dorset; one *s* two *d*. *Educ:* Eton Coll.; King's Coll., Cambridge. Deputy Legal Adviser to the National Trust, 1955–56; Partner: Freshfield's, Solicitors, 1956–74; Thomson Snell and Passmore, 1974–90. Ordained deacon, 1990, priest, 1991; NSM, Brightling, Mountfield and Netherfield, Dio. of Chichester, 1990–2012. *Recreations:* golf, campanology (Royal Cumberland Youths, Cambridge Univ. Guild of Change Ringers), bagpipes (Founder Mem., Pinstripe Highlanders). *Heir:* *s* Hon. William Edward Buckley [*b* 19 June 1966; *m* 1996, Emma, *o d* of Peter Clementson; two *s*]. *Address:* Oldcastle, Dallington, near Heathfield, East Sussex TN21 9JP. *T:* (01435) 830400. *Clubs:* Oriental; Rye Golf. *Died 27 Sept. 2014.*

WRIGHT, (Arthur Robert) Donald, OBE 1984; *b* 20 June 1923; *s* of late Charles North Wright and Beatrice May Wright; *m* 1948, Helen Muryell Buxton, *d* of late Patrick Buxton, FRS; two *s* three *d*. *Educ:* Bryanston Sch.; Queens' Coll., Cambridge. War Service (commnd 1943), NW Europe (despatches) and India, 1942–46. Taught at: University Coll. Sch., 1948–50; The Hill School, Pennsylvania, 1950; Leighton Park School, 1951–52; Marlborough College (Housemaster), 1953–63;

Headmaster, Shrewsbury Sch., 1963–75. Chm., HMC, 1971. Appointments' Sec. to Archbishops of Canterbury and York, 1975–84 and Sec., Crown Appointments Commn, 1977–84. A Chm., Civil Service Comrs' Interview Panels, 1984–91. Chm., William Temple Foundn, 1976–85. Chm., Council, Benenden Sch., 1976–86; Governor, King's Coll. Sch., Wimbledon, 1981–93. *Publications:* (ed) Neville Cardus on Music: a centenary collection, 1988; (ed and contrib.) Walter Hamilton: a portrait, 1991. *Recreations:* musical, defending the rural environment, counting my blessings. *Address:* Mill Barn, Coulston, near Westbury, Wilts BA13 4NY. *Died 10 July 2012.*

WRIGHT, (Charles) Christopher; Costs Judge (formerly Master of Supreme Court Costs (formerly Taxing) Office), 1992–2010; *b* 15 July 1938; *s* of late Charles Gordon Wright, LDS RCS and Gwendoline Margaret Wright; *m* 1969, Angela Whitford. *Educ:* Emscote Lawn, Warwick; Rugby Sch.; New Coll., Oxford (MA 2nd Cl. Hons Jurisp. 1961). Solicitor of the Supreme Court, 1965; Partner, Lee & Pembertons, 1967–92. Sen. Vice-Pres., West London Law Society, 1991–92. Editor, Civil Legal Aid sect., Butterworths Costs Service, 1996–2009. *Recreations:* walking, swimming, holiday golf, reading. *Address:* 68 Eccleston Square, SW1V 1PJ. *Club:* Royal Automobile. *Died 1 Sept. 2014.*

WRIGHT, Clarissa Teresa D.; *see* Dickson Wright.

WRIGHT, David Stephen, OBE 1995; FRCP, FFOM; consultant occupational physician; Chief Medical Officer, British Petroleum Co. plc, 1989–95; *b* 4 Aug. 1935; *s* of Edward Alfred Wright and Winifred May Wright (*née* Oliver); *m* 1966, Caroline Auza; two *s* one *d*. *Educ:* Epsom Coll.; St Bartholomew's Hosp. Med. Coll. (MB BS 1959); MSc Salford 1973; DPH, DIH. FFOM 1983; FRCP 1989. MO, RN, 1960–85; Prof. of Naval Occupational Medicine, 1982–85; Head, BP Gp Occupational Health Centre, 1985–91. Vice-Dean, 1988–91, Dean, 1991–94, Faculty of Occupational Medicine. British Medical Association: Member: Armed Forces Cttee, 1966–88 (Chm., 1985–88); Council, 1985–88. OStJ 1984. *Publications:* (ed) 5th edn, Guidance on Ethics for Occupational Physicians, 1999; (contrib.) Fitness for Work, 2000; contribs on asbestos and noise to learned jls. *Recreations:* gardening, walking, golf. *Address:* 9 Ashburton Road, Alverstoke, Gosport, Hants PO12 2LH. *T:* (023) 9258 2459. *Died 8 Feb. 2011.*

WRIGHT, Donald; *see* Wright, A. R. D.

WRIGHT, Eric David, CB 1975; Deputy Under-Secretary of State, Home Office, and Director-General, Prison Service, 1973–77; *b* 12 June 1917; *s* of Charles Henry and Cecelia Wright; *m* 1944, Doris (*née* Nicholls) (decd); one *s*. *Educ:* Ealing County Grammar School. Joined War Office, 1935; Principal, 1945; seconded to Dept of the Army, Australia, 1951; Asst Secretary, 1955; Command Secretary, BAOR, 1955–58; Imperial Defence College, 1964; Asst Under-Sec. of State, MoD, 1965; on loan to Home Office, Police Dept, 1970–73. Mem., Parole Bd, 1978–83. Chm., Hillingdon CHC, 1988–90. *Address:* 3 The Cedars, Dog Kennel Lane, Chorleywood, Herts WD3 5GL. *Died 10 June 2012.*

WRIGHT, Gerard; QC 1973; *b* 23 July 1929; *s* of Leo Henry and Catherine M. F. Wright; *m* 1950, Betty Mary Fenn (*d* 2001); one *s* two *d*. *Educ:* Stonyhurst Coll.; Lincoln Coll., Oxford (BA, BCL). Served in Army, 1947–49, rank T/Captain. Called to Bar, Gray's Inn, 1954 (Arden Scholar, Barstow Scholar); Northern Circuit. KHS 1974; KCHS 1979; KCSHS 1992; Auxiliaire de l'Hospitalité de Notre Dame de Lourdes, 1982, Titulaire 1985. *Publications:* Test Tube Babies—a Christian view (with others), 1984. *Recreation:* reading. *Address:* Mimiju, Portfield, Langport, Somerset TA10 0NJ. *Died 5 Feb. 2011.*

WRIGHT, Hon. James Claude, Jr; Speaker, US House of Representatives, 1987–89; Senior Political Consultant, American Income Life Insurance Co., since 1989; *b* 22 Dec. 1922; *s* of James Claude Wright and Marie Wright (*née* Lyster); *m* 1972, Betty Hay; one *s* three *d* by former marr. *Educ:* Weatherford College, Univ. of Texas. Served US Army Air Force, 1941–45 (DFC, Legion of Merit). Mem., Texas Legislature, 1947–49; Mayor of Weatherford, Texas, 1950–54; Mem., US House of Representatives for Fort Worth, 1955–89; Dep. Democratic Whip to 1976; Majority Leader, 1976–87; former Mem. of Committees: Budget, Public Works and Transportation; Govt Operations; Highway Beautification (Chm.). Vis. Prof., Texas Christian Univ., 1991–. Former lay minister, Presbyterian Church. Columnist, Fort Worth Star-Telegram, 1992–. *Publications:* You and Your Congressman, 1965; The Coming Water Famine, 1966; Of Swords and Plowshares, 1968; (jtly) Congress and Conscience, 1970; Reflections of a Public Man, 1984; Worth It All, 1993; Balance of Power, 1996. *Died 6 May 2015.*

WRIGHT, Captain John, DSC 1944; RN (retd); General Manager, HM Dockyard, Devonport, 1972–77; *b* 30 April 1921; *s* of Percy Robert and Lucy Ada Wright; *m* 1946, Ethel Lumley Sunderland; one *s* two *d*. *Educ:* Liverpool Univ. (Part I for BSc). MIET; Silver Medal, City and Guilds. Served War: RNVR, 1942; 16th Destroyer Flotilla, 1942; HMS Birmingham, 1943; HMS Diadem, 1943. Devonport Gunnery Sch., 1946; HMS Collingwood, 1948; BJSM, USA, 1951; Admiralty Surface Weapons Estabt, 1952; HMS Cumberland, 1956; Naval Ordnance Div., 1958; British Naval Staff, USA, 1960; Polaris Technical Dept, 1964; HM Dockyard, Chatham, 1968; RN retd 1972. Gen. Manager, Marconi Space and Defence Systems Ltd, Portsmouth, 1981–82; Asst Man. Dir and Gen. Manager, Marconi Underwater Systems, 1982–84. *Recreations:* fishing, gardening, golf. *Address:* The Ferns, 15 Brook Meadow, Fareham, Hants PO15 5JH. *T:* (01329) 280512. *Died 1 Oct. 2013.*

WRIGHT, Prof. Michael Thomas, FREng; Professor of Mechanical Engineering, 1990–2006, then Emeritus, and Vice Chancellor, 1996–2006, Aston University; *b* 11 April 1947; *s* of William George and Lilly May Wright; *m* 1970, Patricia Eunice Cox; one *d*. *Educ:* Sheldon Heath Sch., Birmingham; Aston Univ. (BSc 1st Cl. Hons, PhD). Sen. Mem., IEEE 1980; FIET (FIEE 1981); FREng (FEng 1988); FIMechE 1989; FIMA 1994. Apprentice, Electrical Power Engineering Co., 1969–82: Redman Heenan Froude, Heenan Drives, Linear Motors, Parsons Peebles Motors and Generators, NEI Peebles, Scottish Engineering Training Scheme; Engrg Dir, GEC Large Machines, 1982–85; Man. Dir, Molins Tobacco Machinery, 1985–87; Man. Dir, 1988–90, non-exec. Dir, 1990–97, Molins; Aston University: Vis. Prof. of Electrical Engrg, 1986–90; Head, Dept of Mech. and Elect. Engrg, 1990–92; Sen. Pro-Vice-Chancellor, 1994–96. Chairman: Aston Business Sch., 1992–93; 600 Group plc, 1993–2007. Non-executive Director: ERA Technology Ltd, 1995–2004; Birmingham Technology Ltd, 1996–2008; Aston Science Park Ltd, 1996–; ERA Foundn, 2001–02; Director: W Midlands Develt Agency, 1997–2001; James Watt Foundn, 2005–. CCMI (CIMgt 1997). *Publications:* numerous papers on electrical machines and drives in learned jls; articles on shooting and ballistics. *Recreations:* shooting, history of film, travelling, reading, classic motorcycles. *Address:* Evesmere, Weston On Avon, Stratford-upon-Avon, Warwickshire CV37 8JY. *Died 10 Jan. 2015.*

WRIGHT, Peter, CBE 1988 (OBE 1982); Chief Constable, South Yorkshire Police, 1983–90; *b* Stockport, 21 July 1929; *s* of late Henry Wright and Elizabeth (*née* Burton); *m* 1950, Mary Dorothea (*née* Stanway); one *s*. *Educ:* Edgeley Roman Catholic Sch.; Stockport Technical School. RN, 1947–49. Manchester City Police, 1954, to Chief Superintendent, Greater Manchester, 1975; Asst Chief Constable, 1975–79, Dep. Chief Constable, 1979–82, Merseyside. Police Advr, MoD, 1990–93. Mem., Parole Review Cttee, 1987–88. Pres., ACPO, 1988–89. Freeman, City of London, 1992. *Recreations:* walking, gardening. *Address:* c/o South Yorkshire Police, Snig Hill, Sheffield S3 8LY. *Died 17 Sept. 2011.*

WRIGHT, Maj.-Gen. Richard Eustace John G.; *see* Gerrard-Wright.

WRIGHT, Rt Rev. Royston Clifford; Bishop of Monmouth, 1986–91; *b* 4 July 1922; *s* of James and Ellen Wright; *m* 1945, Barbara Joyce Nowell; one *s* one *d*. *Educ:* Univ. of Wales, Cardiff (BA 1942); St Stephen's House,

Oxford. Deacon 1945, priest 1946; Curate: Bedwas, 1945–47; St John Baptist, Newport, 1947–49; Walton-on-the-Hill, Liverpool, 1949–51; Chaplain RNVR, 1950; Chaplain RN, 1951–68; Vicar of Blaenavon, Gwent, 1968–74; RD of Pontypool, 1973–74; Canon of Monmouth, 1974–77; Rector of Ebbw Vale, Gwent, 1974–77; Archdeacon of Monmouth, 1977–88; Archdeacon of Newport, 1977–86. *Recreations:* four grandchildren; listening to Baroque music. *Address:* 58 Homevalley House, Bryngwyn Road, Newport NP20 4JQ. *T:* (01633) 250770. *Died 14 Feb. 2014.*

WRIGHT, Sheila Rosemary Rivers; *b* 22 March 1925; *d* of Daniel Rivers Wright and Frances Grace Wright; *m* 1949, Ronald A. Gregory; one *s* one *d*. Social Science Cert. 1951; BScSoc London External 1956. Personnel Officer, 1951–57; Social Worker, 1957–74. Councillor: Birmingham CC, 1956–78; West Midlands CC, 1973–81. MP (Lab) Birmingham, Handsworth, 1979–83. Member: Birmingham Reg. Hosp. Bd and W Midlands RHA, 1966–80; Birmingham Central DHA, 1981–90. *Address:* 1 Sorrento Court, 15 Wake Green Road, Birmingham B13 9HB. *Died 5 July 2013.*

WRIGLEY, Prof. Jack, CBE 1977; Professor of Education, 1967–88, and Deputy Vice-Chancellor, 1982–88, University of Reading, then Professor Emeritus; *b* 8 March 1923; *s* of Harry and Ethel Wrigley; *m* 1946, Edith Baron; two *s*. *Educ:* Oldham High Sch.; Manchester Univ. BSc, MEd (Manch.); PhD (Queen's, Belfast). Asst Mathematics Teacher: Stretford Grammar Sch., 1946–47; Chadderton Grammar Sch., 1948–50; Research Asst, Manchester Univ., 1950–51; Lectr in Educn: Queen's Univ., Belfast, 1951–57; Univ. of London Inst. of Educn, 1957–62; Research Adviser, Curriculum Study Gp in Min. of Educn, 1962–63; Prof. of Educn, Univ. of Southampton, 1963–67; Dir of Studies, Schools Council, 1967–75. Member: Bullock Cttee on Teaching of Reading and other uses of English, 1972–74; SSRC, Mem. Council and Chm. Educnl Res. Bd, 1976–81. Specialist Adviser, H of C Select Cttee on Educn, Sci., and Arts, 1989–90. *Publications:* (ed) The Dissemination of Curriculum Development, 1976; Values and Evaluation in Education, 1980; contrib. learned jls. *Recreations:* chess (Ulster Chess Champion, 1957), theatre, foreign travel. *Address:* Valley Crest, Thrushwood, Keswick, Cumbria CA12 4PG. *T:* (017687) 71146. *Died 15 May 2013.*

WRINTMORE, His Honour Eric George; a Circuit Judge, 1984–2000; *b* 11 June 1928; *s* of Rev. F. H. and Muriel Wrintmore; *m* 1951, Jean Blackburn; two *s* one *d*. *Educ:* Stationers' Company's Sch.; King's Coll. London (LLB Hons). Called to Bar, Gray's Inn, 1955; full-time Chm., Industrial Tribunals, 1971; Regional Chm., Industrial Tribunals, 1976–84; a Dep. Circuit Judge, 1980–83; a Recorder, 1983–84. *Recreations:* sailing, golf. *Club:* Chichester Yacht. *Died 31 Jan. 2013.*

WROE, David Charles Lynn, CB 1995; consultant, 1996–2011; Special Adviser to the European Commission, 1998–99; *b* 20 Feb. 1942; *m* 1966, Susan Higgitt; three *d*. *Educ:* Reigate Grammar Sch.; Trinity Coll., Cambridge (MA); Trinity Coll., Oxford (Cert. Statistics); Birkbeck Coll., London (MSc). Min. of Pensions and National Insurance, 1965–68; Central Statistical Office, 1968–70, 1973–75, 1976–82; secondment to Zambian Govt, 1971–72; Secretariat of Royal Commission on Distribution of Income and Wealth, 1975–76; Under Sec., Regional Policy Directorate, 1982–86, Dir of Stats, 1982–91, Under Sec., Housing Monitoring and Analysis, 1986–91, DoE; Dep. Dir, CSO, 1991–96 (Actg Dir, April–June 1996). Mem., Adv. Bd, UK Centre for Measurement of Govt Activity, 2005–12. Non-exec. Dir, John Laing Construction Ltd, 1994–96. Vice Pres., Royal Statistical Soc., 1995–98 (Mem. Council, 1993–98). Trustee: Community Links (formerly Bromley Centre for Voluntary Service), 1999–2005; Bromley Voluntary Sector Trust, 2000–03. *Recreations:* sailing, walking. *Died 2 Feb. 2014.*

WRONG, Prof. Oliver Murray, DM; FRCP, FRCPE; Professor of Medicine, University College London, 1972–90, then Emeritus Professor; *b* 7 Feb. 1925; *s* of Edward Murray Wrong and Rosalind Grace Wrong (*née* Smith); *m* 1956, Marilda Musacchio; two *d* (and one *d* decd). *Educ:* Upper Canada Coll., Toronto; Edinburgh Acad.; Magdalen Coll., Oxford (Demy; BM BCh 1947; DM 1964). FRCP 1968; FRCPE 1970. Junior hosp. appts, Oxford, 1947–51; RAMC, MO Singapore and Malaya, 1948–50; Toronto Gen. Hosp., 1951–52; Mass. Gen. Hosp., Boston, 1952–53; Univ. Tutor in Medicine, Manchester, 1954–58; Lectr and Sen. Lectr in Medicine, RPMS, 1961–69; Prof. of Medicine, Univ. of Dundee, 1969–72; Dir, Dept of Medicine, UCL, 1972–82. Teale Lectr, RCP, 1971; James Howard Means Vis. Physician, Mass. Gen. Hosp., 1974; Vis. Prof., Harvard and Sherbrooke Med. Schs, 1974; Toronto and McGill Med. Schs, 1976. Chm., Nat. Kidney Res. Fund, 1976–80. *Publications:* (with C. J. Edmonds and V. S. Chadwick) The Large Intestine: its role in mammalian nutrition and homeostasis, 1981; articles in med. jls on salt and water metabolism, kidney function, renal tubular diseases, the large intestine. *Recreations:* nature, travel, music (esp. baroque). *Address:* Flat 8, 96–100 New Cavendish Street, W1W 6XN. *T:* (020) 7637 4740; School House, West Dean, Salisbury, Wilts SP5 1JQ. *E:* oliverwrong@aol.com. *Died 24 Feb. 2012.*

WYATT, Arthur Hope, CMG 1980; HM Diplomatic Service, retired; re-employed in Foreign and Commonwealth Office, 1990–95; *b* 12 Oct. 1929; *s* of Frank and Maggie Wyatt, Anderton, Lancs; *m* 1957, Barbara Yvonne (*d* 2002), *d* of Major J. P. Flynn, late Indian Army; one *d* (and one *d* decd). *Educ:* Bolton School. Army, 1947–50; FO, 1950–52; 3rd Sec., Ankara, 1952–56; 2nd Sec., Phnom Penh, 1956–58; 2nd Sec., Ankara, 1958–61; FO, 1962–66; 1st Sec., Bonn, 1966–70; FCO, 1970–72; Counsellor and Head of Chancery, Lagos, 1972–75; Dep. High Comr, Valletta, 1975–76; Diplomatic Service Inspector, 1977–79; Counsellor (Econ. and Comm.) and Consul-Gen., Tehran, 1979–80; Counsellor, Ankara, 1981–84; Minister, Lagos, 1984–86; High Comr to Ghana and Ambassador (non-resident) to Togo, 1986–89. *Recreations:* golf, football, bridge, crosswords. *Address:* 44 Baronsmede, W5 4LT. *T:* (020) 8579 0782. *Died 4 March 2015.*

WYNN, Terence Bryan; freelance journalist and writer; *b* 20 Nov. 1928; *o s* of late Bernard Wynn and Elsie Wynn (*née* Manges); unmarried. *Educ:* St Cuthbert's Grammar Sch., Newcastle upon Tyne. Started as jun. reporter with Hexham Courant, Northumberland, 1945; Blyth News, 1947–48; Shields Evening News, 1948–50; Sunderland Echo, 1950–53; Reporter with Daily Sketch, 1953–58; News Editor, Tyne Tees Television, 1958, then Head of News and Current Affairs, 1960–66; Editorial Planning, BBC Television News, 1966–67; Sen. Press and Information Officer with Land Commn, 1967–71; Sen. Inf. Officer, HM Customs and Excise, 1971–72; Editor, The Universe, 1972–77; Editor, Liberal News, and Head of Liberal Party Orgn's Press Office, 1977–83; Regl Press Officer, MSC, COI, London and SE Region, 1983–85; Editor, Your Court (house jl of Lord Chancellor's Dept), 1985–88. Helped to found and first Editor of Roman Catholic monthly newspaper, Northern Cross. Editor, Brentwood News, 1990–2001. Chm., Catholic Writers' Guild, 1967–70 (Hon. Vice-Pres., 1970); Judge for British Television News Film of the Year Awards, 1961–64; Mem. Mass Media Commn, RC Bishops' Conf. of England and Wales, 1972–83. Hon. Life Pres., Editors' Forum (diocesan newspapers), 2000 (Chm., 1998–2000). KSG 2001. *Publications:* Walsingham, a modern mystery play, 1975. *Recreations:* reading, writing, talking, writing letters to The Times. *Address:* Bosco Villa, 30 Queen's Road, South Benfleet, Essex SS7 1JW. *T:* (01268) 792033. *Died 4 May 2011.*

WYNNE, David, OBE 1994; sculptor, since 1949; *b* Lyndhurst, Hants, 25 May 1926; *s* of Comdr Charles Edward Wynne and Millicent (*née* Beyts); *m* 1959, Gillian Mary Leslie Bennett (*née* Grant) (*d* 1990); one *s* (and one *s* decd), and one step *d* (one step *s* decd). *Educ:* Stowe Sch.; Trinity Coll., Cambridge. FZS; FRSA. Served RN, 1944–47: minesweepers and aircraft carriers (Sub-Lieut RNVR). No formal art training. First exhibited at Leicester Galls, 1950, and at Royal Acad., 1952. One-man Exhibitions: Leicester Galls, 1955, 1959; Tooth's Gall., 1964, 1966; Temple Gall., 1964; Findlay Galls, New York,

1967, 1970, 1973; Covent Garden Gall., 1970, 1971; Fitzwilliam Museum, Cambridge, 1972; Pepsico World HQ, New York, 1976; Agnew's Gall., 1983; Mall Galls, 1997; retrospective, Cannizaro House, 1980; also various mixed exhibns. Large works in public places: Magdalen Coll., Oxford; Malvern Girls' Coll.; Civic Centre, Newcastle upon Tyne; Lewis's, Hanley; Ely Cathedral; Birmingham Cath.; Church of St Paul, Ashford Hill, Berks; Ch of St Thomas More, Bradford-on-Avon; Mission Ch, Portsmouth; Fountain Precinct, Sheffield; Bowood House, Wilts; Risen Christ and 2 seraphim, west front of Wells Cathedral, 1985; Virgin Mary, Lady Chapel, Ely Cathedral, 2001; Abbey Gdns, Tresco, Isles of Scilly; Highgrove, Glos; London and environs: Albert Bridge; British Oxygen Co., Guildford; Cadogan Place Gardens and Cadogan Sq.; Crystal Palace Park; Guildhall; Longbow House; St Katharine-by-the-Tower; Taylor Woodrow; Wates Ltd, Norbury; also London Road, Kingston-upon-Thames; Elmsleigh Centre, Staines; IPC HQ, Sutton; St Raphael's Hospice, Cheam, Surrey; Central Park, Watford; Queen Elizabeth Gates, Hyde Park Corner; Hurlingham Club; Highgrove Gardens; USA: Ambassador Coll., Texas, and Ambassador Coll., Calif; Atlantic Richfield Oil Co., New Mexico; Lakeland Meml Hosp., Wis; First Fed. Savings, Mass; Pepsico World HQ, Purchase, NY; Playboy Hotel and Casino, Atlantic City, NJ; Sarasota, Fla; Mayo Foundation, Minn; Sherman, Texas; Ritz Carlton, Rancho Mirage, Calif; Mayo Clinic, Rochester, Minn; Grayson Bank, Sherman, Texas; also Perth, WA, and Place Camelotti, Geneva, 1988. Bronze portraits include: Sir Thomas Beecham, 1956; Sir John Gielgud, 1962; Yehudi Menuhin, 1963; The Beatles, 1964; Kokoschka, 1965; Sir Alec Douglas-Home, 1966; Robert, Marquess of Salisbury, 1967; The Prince of Wales, 1969; Lord Baden-Powell, 1971; Virginia Wade, 1972; The Queen, 1973; King Hassan of Morocco, 1973; Air Chief Marshal Lord Dowding, 1974; The Begum Aga Khan, 1975; Pele, 1976; Lord Hailsham, 1977; Prince Michael of Kent, 1977; Earl Mountbatten of Burma, 1981; Paul Daniels, 1982; Jackie Stewart, 1982; Elvis Presley; Victor Ubogu; Portrait Figures: Arnold Palmer, 1983; Björn Borg, 1984; Leonard Cheshire, for Stowe Sch., 1995; Bernard Gallacher, Wentworth Club, 1998; other sculptures: Fred Perry, AELTC, 1984; Shergar and jockey, 1981; Shareef Dancer and groom, 1984; Cresta Rider, St Moritz, 1985; Two Dolphins, Provence, France, 1986; Shergar and Sinndar, Kildare, Ireland. Designed: Common Market 50 pence piece of clasped hands, 1973; King Hassan, for Moroccan coinage, 1973; the Queen's Silver Jubilee Medal, 1977 (with new effigy of the Queen wearing St Edward's Crown). *Publications:* The Messenger, a sculpture by David Wynne, 1982; *relevant publications:* T. S. R. Boase, The Sculpture of David Wynne 1949–1967, 1968; Graham Hughes, The Sculpture of David Wynne 1968–1974, 1974; Jonathan Stone (ed), The Sculpture of David Wynne 1974–92, 1993. *Recreations:* active sports, poetry, music. *Address:* 5 Burlington Lodge Studios, Buer Road, SW6 4LA. *T:* (020) 7731 1071. *Clubs:* Garrick, Queen's, Hurlingham; Village (Wimbledon); Leander (Henley-on-Thames); 1st and 3rd Trinity Boat; St Moritz Tobogganing; The Royal Tennis Court (Hampton Court Palace).

Died 4 Sept. 2014.

YZ

YALOW, Rosalyn Sussman, PhD; Senior Medical Investigator, Veterans Administration, later Veterans Affairs, 1972–92, Senior Medical Investigator Emeritus, since 1992; *b* 19 July 1921; *d* of Simon Sussman and Clara (*née* Zipper); *m* 1943, Aaron Yalow (*d* 1992); one *s* one *d*. *Educ:* Hunter Coll., NYC (AB Physics and Chemistry, 1941); Univ. of Ill, Urbana (MS Phys. 1942, PhD Phys. 1945). Diplomate, Amer. Bd of Radiol., 1951. Asst in Phys., Univ. of Ill, 1941–43, Instr, 1944–45; Lectr and Temp. Asst Prof. in Phys., Hunter Coll., 1946–50. Veterans Admin Hospital, Bronx, NY: Consultant, Radioisotope Unit, 1947–50; Physicist and Asst Chief, Radioisotope Service, 1950–70 (Actg Chief, 1968–70); Chief, Nuclear Medicine Service, 1970–80; Dir, Solomon A. Berson Res. Lab., 1973–; Chm., Dept of Clin. Scis, Montefiore Hosp. and Med. Center, Bronx, NY, 1980–85; Chief, VA Radioimmunoassay Ref. Lab., 1969–. Consultant, Lenox Hill Hosp., NYC, 1952–62. Res. Prof., Dept of Med., Mt Sinai Sch. of Med., 1968–74, Distinguished Service Prof., 1974–79; Distinguished Prof.-at-Large, Albert Einstein Coll. of Med., Yeshiva Univ., NY, 1979–85, Prof. Emeritus, 1985–; Solomon A. Berson Distinguished Prof.-at-Large, Mt Sinai Sch. of Medicine, City Univ. of NY, 1986–. IAEA Expert, Instituto Energia Atomica, Brazil, 1970; WHO Consultant, Radiation Med. Centre, India, 1978; Sec., US Nat. Cttee on Med. Physics, 1963–67. Member: President's Study Gp on Careers for Women, 1966–67; Med. Adv. Bd, Nat. Pituitary Agency, 1968–71; Endocrinol. Study Sect., Nat. Insts of Health, 1969–72; Cttee for Evaluation of NPA, Nat. Res. Council, 1973–74; Council, Endocrine Soc., 1974–80 (Koch Award, 1972; Pres., 1978); Bd of Dirs, NY Diabetes Assoc., 1974–77. Member: Editorial Adv. Council, Acta Diabetologica Latina, 1975–77; Ed. Adv. Bd, Encyclopaedia Universalis, 1978–; Ed. Bd, Mt Sinai Jl of Medicine, 1976–79; Ed. Bd, Diabetes, 1976–79. Fellow: NY Acad. of Sciences (Chm., Biophys. Div., 1964–65; A. Cressy Morrison Award in Nat. Sci., 1975); Radiation Res. Soc.; Amer. Assoc. of Physicists in Med.; Biophys. Soc.; Amer. Diabetes Assoc. (Eli Lilly Award, 1961; Commemorative Medallion, 1972; Banting Medal, 1978; Rosalyn S. Yalow Res. and Develt Award estabd 1978); Amer. Physiol Soc.; Soc. of Nuclear Med. Associate Fellow in Phys., Amer. Coll. of Radiol. Member: Nat. Acad. of Sciences; Amer. Acad. Arts and Sciences; Foreign Associate, French Acad. of Medicine. Hon. DSc and Hon. DHumLett from univs and med. colls in the US, France, Argentina, Canada. Nobel Prize in Physiology or Medicine, 1977; VA Exceptional Service Award, 1975 and 1978; Nat. Medal of Sci., 1988. Gave many distinguished lectures and received many awards and prizes from univs and med. socs and assocs. *Publications:* over 500 papers and contribns to books, research reports, proceedings of conferences and symposia on radioimmunoassay of peptide hormones and related subjects, since 1950. *Address:* James J. Peters VA Medical Center, 130 West Kingsbridge Road, Bronx, NY 10468, USA. *T:* (718) 579 1644. *Died 30 May 2011.*

YAPP, Sir Stanley Graham, Kt 1975; Chairman, Birmingham International Airport, 1988–94; Chairman, West Midlands County Council, 1983–84 (Leader, 1973–77; Vice-Chairman, 1982–83); Member, Birmingham City Council, later Birmingham District Council, 1961–77 (Leader, 1972–74); *s* of late William and of Elsie Yapp; *m* 1961, Elisbeth Wise (marr. diss.); one *d*; *m* 1974, Carol Matheson (marr. diss.); one *s*; *m* 1983, Christine Horton, MBE, JP. Member, West Midlands Economic Planning Council (Chm., Transport Cttee); Member many bodies both local and national, inc.: Vice-Chm. LAMSAC; Member: Local Govt Trng Board; Nat. Jt Councils on pay and conditions; AMA; BR Adv. Bd, Midlands and N Western Reg., 1977–79; Chm., West Midlands Planning Authorities Conf., 1973–75, Vice-Chm. 1975–77. Governor, BFI, 1977–79. FCMI. *Publications:* contribs to Local Government Chronicle, Municipal Journal, Rating and Valuation. *Recreations:* astronomy reading, walking. *Address:* 134 Bushmore Road, Hal Green, Birmingham B28 9QZ. *Died 1 April 2012.*

YARDLEY, Sir David (Charles Miller), Kt 1994 Chairman, Commission for Local Administration ir England, 1982–94; a Complaints Commissioner, Financia Services Authority (formerly Securities and Investment Board), 1994–2001; *b* 4 June 1929; *s* of late Geoffrey Mille Yardley and Doris Woodward Yardley (*née* Jones); *m* 1954 Patricia Anne Tempest Olver; two *s* two *d*. *Educ:* The Ol Hall Sch., Wellington; Ellesmere Coll., Shropshire; Univ of Birmingham (LLB, LLD); Univ. of Oxford (MA, DPhil) Called to Bar, Gray's Inn, 1952. RAF Flying Officer (nat service), 1949–51. Bigelow Teaching Fellow, Univ. o Chicago, 1953–54; Fellow and Tutor in Jurisprudence, S Edmund Hall, Oxford, 1953–74, Emeritus Fellow, 1974– CUF Lectr, Univ. of Oxford, 1954–74; Sen. Proctor, Univ of Oxford, 1965–66; Barber Prof. of Law, Univ. o Birmingham, 1974–78; Head of Dept of Law, Politics an Economics, Oxford Poly., 1978–80; Rank Foundn Prof. o Law, University Coll. at Buckingham, 1980–82. Visitin Prof. of Law, Univ. of Sydney, 1971; Hon. Prof. of Law Univ. of Buckingham, 1994; Vis. Prof., Oxford Brooke Univ., 1995–2001. Constitutional Consultant, Govt of W Nigeria, 1956. Chm., Thames Valley Rent Tribuna 1963–82; Vice-Pres., Cambs Chilterns and Thames Ren Assessment Panel, subseq. Chilterns Thames and Easter Rent Assessment Panel, 1966–82, 1995–99; Oxford Cit Councillor, 1966–74; Chairman: Oxford Area Nat. Insc Local Appeal Tribunal, 1969–82; Oxford Preservatio Trust, 1989–2009 (Vice-Pres., 2010–); Examining Bd 1994–2006, Awards Panel, 1996–2001, IRRV; Ind Adjudicator, W Bromwich Building Soc., 1996–2001; Ind Reviewer, Millennium Commn, 1999–2005; Ind Complaints Reviewer for UK Lottery Distributor 2005–06. Chm. of Governors, St Helen's Sch., Abingdon 1967–81. FRSA 1991. Freeman, City of Oxford, 198 *Publications:* Introduction to British Constitutional Law 1960, 8th edn (as Introduction to Constitutional an Administrative Law), 1995; A Source Book of Englis Administrative Law, 1963, 2nd edn, 1970; The Future c the Law, 1964; Geldart's Elements of English Law, 7th edn 1966–10th edn (as Geldart's Introduction to English Law) 1991, 11th edn 1995; Hanbury's English Courts of Law, 4t edn, 1967; Hanbury and Yardley, English Courts of Law 5th edn, 1979; Principles of Administrative Law, 1981, 2n edn, 1986; (with I. N. Stevens) The Protection of Libert 1982; contrib. Halsbury's Laws of England, and Atkin Court Forms. *Recreations:* opera, cats. *Address:* Belbroughton Road, Oxford OX2 6UZ. *T:* (01865 554831. *Club:* Royal Air Force. *Died 3 June 2014.*

YATES, Ivan Ray, CBE 1982; FREng; Deputy Chie Executive, 1986–90, Director, 1981–90, British Aerospac PLC; *b* 22 April 1929; *s* of Ernest Ray and Ivy Ray (*ne* Nears, later Yates); *m* 1967, Jennifer Mary Holcombe; on *s* one *d*. *Educ:* Liverpool Collegiate Sch.; Liverpool Univ (BEng 1st Class Hons). FIMechE; FRAeS 1968; FREn (FEng 1983); FAIAA 1984. Graduate Apprentice, Englis Electric, Preston, 1950; Chief Project Engr, TSR-2, 195 Project Manager, Jaguar, 1966; British Aircra Corporation: Special Dir, Preston Div., 1970; Dir, Presto Warton Div., 1973; Dir, Aircraft Projects, 1974; Directo SEPECAT SA, 1976; Panavia GmbH, 1977; Eurofighte GmbH, 1986–90; British Aerospace: Man. Dir, Warto 1978; Dir of Engrg and Project Assessment, Aircraft G 1981; Chief Exec., Aircraft Gp, 1982–85; Dep. Man. D (Aircraft), 1985–86. Vis. Prof. in Design, Cambridge Univ 1991–2003; By-Fellow, Churchill Coll., Cambridg 1992–2000. Mem., Technology Requirements B 1985–89; Advr, H of C Sci. and Technol. Cttee, 1993–9 Pres., 1988–89, Dep. Pres., 1989–90, SBAC; Mem Council, RAeS, 1986–91. Member: Design Counci 1990–99; Council, RUSI, 1989–93. Commissioner, Roy Commn for Exhibn of 1851, 1990–99. Mem. Counci

Imperial Coll., 1991–99. CCMI; FRSA 1985. Foreign Mem., Royal Swedish Acad. of Engrg Scis, 1990. Hon. DSc: Loughborough, 1989; City, 1991. British Silver Medal, 1979, Gold Medal, 1985, RAeS. *Publications:* Innovation, Investment and Survival of UK Economy, 1993; numerous papers and lectures. *Recreations:* walking, sculpture, music. *T:* (office) (01273) 480469. *Clubs:* Athenæum, Royal Air Force. *Died 2 Aug. 2015.*

YATES, Peter (James); film director/producer and theatre director; *b* 24 July 1929; *s* of Col Robert L. Yates and Constance Yates; *m* 1960, Virginia Pope; two *s* one *d* (and one *d* decd). *Educ:* Charterhouse; Royal Academy of Dramatic Art. Entered film industry, 1956. *Films directed:* Summer Holiday, 1962; One Way Pendulum, 1964; Robbery, 1966; Bullitt, 1968; John and Mary, 1969; Murphy's War, 1970; The Hot Rock, 1971; The Friends of Eddie Coyle, 1972; For Pete's Sake, 1973; Mother, Jugs and Speed, 1975; The Deep, 1976; Breaking Away (dir and prod.), 1979 (nominated 1980 Academy Awards, Director and Producer); The Janitor (dir and prod.), 1980; Krull, 1982; The Dresser (dir and prod.), 1983 (nominated 1984 Academy Awards, Dir and Producer); Eleni, 1985; The House on Carroll Street (dir and prod.), 1986; Suspect, 1987; An Innocent Man, 1989; Year of the Comet, 1991; Roommates, 1993; The Run of the Country, 1996; Curtain Call, 1997; Don Quixote, 2000; A Separate Peace, 2002. *Theatre directed:* The American Dream, Royal Court, 1961; The Death of Bessie Smith, (London) 1961; Passing Game, (New York) 1977; Interpreters, (London) 1985. *Recreations:* tennis, sailing, ski-ing. *Address:* c/o Judy Daish Agency, 2 St Charles Place, W10 6EG. *Club:* Garrick. *Died 9 Jan. 2011.*

YERBURGH, John Maurice Armstrong; Vice Lord-Lieutenant of Dumfries and Galloway (District of Stewartry), 1990–98; President, Daniel Thwaites PLC, since 1993 (Director, since 1947; Chairman, 1966–93); *b* 23 May 1923; *e s* of late Major Guy Yerburgh (*d* 1926), OBE, Belgian Croix de Guerre, Italian Croce di Guerra and Lady (Hilda Violet Helena) Salisbury-Jones, *e d* of Rt Hon. Sir Maurice de Bunsen, Bt, GCMG, GCVO, CB; *m* 1973, Ann Jean Mary, *d* of N. P. Maclaren, Brooklands, Crocketford, Dumfries; one *s* four *d*. *Educ:* Eton; Magdalene College, Cambridge (BA). Commissioned Irish Guards 1943; served with 2nd Bn, France, Holland, Belgium, Germany; retired 1947 with rank of Captain. Contested (C) Blackburn, 1959 and 1963. Chm., S of Scotland Regional Adv. Cttee, Forestry Commn, 1972–87; Governor, Cumbria College of Agriculture and Forestry, 1975–89; Shire Horse Society: Pres., 1983–84; Dep. Pres., 1988. DL Dumfries and Galloway (Dist of Stewartry), 1989. *Recreations:* shooting, fishing, trees. *Address:* Barwhillanty, Parton, Castle Douglas, Kirkcudbrightshire DG7 3NS. *T:* (01644) 470237. *Died 17 June 2014.*

YONG NYUK LIN; Member, Presidential Council for Minority Rights, Singapore, 1979–91; *b* Seremban, Malaya, 24 June 1918; *s* of late Yong Thean Yong and Chen Shak Moi; *m* 1939, Kwa Geok Lan; two *d*. *Educ:* Raffles Coll., Singapore. Science Master, King George V Sch., Seremban, Malaya, 1938–41; with Overseas Assurance Corp., Singapore, 1941 (resigned, as Gen. Manager, 1958). Legislative Assemblyman, Singapore, 1959–65, MP 1965–79; Minister for Educn, 1959–63; Chm., Singapore Harbour Bd, 1961–62; Minister for: Health, 1963–68; Communications, 1968–75; Minister without Portfolio, 1975–76; High Comr in London, 1975–76. Chm., Singapore Land/Marina Centre Development Private Ltd, 1980–86. *Address:* 50 Oei Tiong Ham Park, Singapore 267055. *Died 29 June 2012.*

YORK, Susannah; actress and writer; *b* 9 Jan. 1942; *d* of late Simon William Fletcher and Joan Bowring; *m* 1960, Michael Wells (marr. diss. 1976); one *s* one *d*. *Educ:* Marr Coll., Troon, Scotland; RADA, London. *Films* include: The Greengage Summer, 1961; Freud, 1962; Tom Jones, 1963; A Man for All Seasons, 1966; The Killing of Sister George, 1968; They Shoot Horses, Don't They, 1969; X, Y and Zee, 1971; Images, 1972; Superman, 1978; Golden Gate Murders, 1979; Alice, 1980; Superman 2, 1984; A Christmas Carol, Mio My Mio, 1986; Bluebeard; Just Ask for Diamonds, 1988; Melancholia, 1989; Barbarblu Barbarblu; Little Women; The Gigolos, 2007. *Theatre* includes: Wings of a Dove, 1964; A Singular Man, 1965; The Maids, 1974; Peter Pan, 1977; The Singular Life of Albert Nobbs, 1978; Hedda Gabler, New York 1981, London 1982; Agnes of God, 1983; The Human Voice (own trans. of Cocteau), 1984; Fatal Attraction, Haymarket, 1985; The Apple Cart, Haymarket, 1986; The Women, Old Vic, 1986; The Glass Menagerie (tour), 1989; A Streetcar Named Desire, Octagon, Bolton, 1990; Noonbreak (own trans. of Claudel), London and Manchester, 1991; September Tide, London, 1993; The Merry Wives of Windsor, 1996, Hamlet, 1997, RSC; Camino Real, RSC, 1997; The Loves of Shakespeare's Women, Edinburgh and Adelaide Fests, 2001, US and UK tour, 2002–04; Quartet, Yvonne Arnaud Th., 2010. *TV series:* Second Chance, 1981; We'll Meet Again, 1982; The Prince Regent, 1983; Devices and Desires, 1990; Trainer, 1991, 1992; Holby City, 2003. Officier de l'Ordre des Arts et des Lettres (France), 1991. *Publications:* In Search of Unicorns, 1973, rev. edn 1984; Larks Castle, 1975, rev. edn, 1985; (ed) The Big One, 1984; The Loves of Shakespeare's Women, 2001; translated: Paul Claudel, Partage de Midi; Jean Cocteau, La Voix Humaine; Sacha Guitry, Un Sujet de Roman. *Recreations:* family, writing, gardening, reading, houses, riding, languages, travelling, theatre, cinema, walking. *Address:* c/o United Agents, 12–26 Lexington Street, W1F 0LE. *Died 15 Jan. 2011.*

YORKE, Margaret, (Margaret Beda Nicholson); writer; *b* 30 Jan. 1924; *d* of John Peel Alexander Larminie and Alison Yorke (*née* Lyle); *m* 1945, Basil Nicholson (marr. diss. 1957, he *d* 1987); one *s* one *d*. *Educ:* Prior's Field, Surrey. WRNS, 1942–45. Bookseller; School Sec.; Asst Librarian, St Hilda's Coll., Oxford, 1959–60; Library Asst (cataloguer), Christ Church, Oxford, 1963–65. Chm., Crime Writers' Assoc., 1979–80. CWA Cartier Diamond Dagger Award, 1999. *Publications:* Summer Flight, 1957; Pray Love Remember, 1958; Christopher, 1959; Deceiving Mirror, 1960; The China Doll, 1961; Once a Stranger, 1962; The Birthday, 1963; Full Circle, 1965; No Fury, 1967; The Apricot Bed, 1968; The Limbo Ladies, 1969; Dead in the Morning, 1970; Silent Witness, 1972; Grave Matters, 1973; Mortal Remains, 1974; No Medals for the Major, 1974; The Small Hours of the Morning, 1975; The Cost of Silence, 1977; The Point of Murder, 1978; Death on Account, 1979; The Scent of Fear, 1980 (Swedish Acad. of Detection Award, 1982); The Hand of Death, 1981; Devil's Work, 1982; Find Me a Villain, 1983; The Smooth Face of Evil, 1984; Intimate Kill, 1985; Safely to the Grave, 1986; Evidence to Destroy, 1987; Speak for the Dead, 1988; Crime in Question, 1989; Admit to Murder, 1990; A Small Deceit, 1991; Criminal Damage, 1992; Dangerous to Know, 1993; Almost the Truth, 1994; Pieces of Justice (short stories), 1994; Serious Intent, 1995; A Question of Belief, 1996; Act of Violence, 1997; False Pretences, 1998; The Price of Guilt, 1999; A Case to Answer, 2000; Cause for Concern, 2001. *Recreations:* theatre, reading, gardening, travel. *Address:* c/o Curtis Brown, 28/29 Haymarket, SW1Y 4SP. *Died 17 Nov. 2012.*

YOUARD, Richard Geoffrey Atkin; The Investment Ombudsman (formerly Investment Referee), 1989–96; *b* 27 Jan. 1933; *s* of Geoffrey Bernard Youard, MBE and Hon. Rosaline Joan Youard (*née* Atkin); *m* 1960, Felicity Ann Morton; one *s* two *d*. *Educ:* Bradfield Coll., Berks; Magdalen Coll., Oxford (BA Jurisprudence; MA 1998). Admitted Solicitor, 1959. Commnd (2nd Lieut) RA, 1952 (Nat. Service); Lieut TA, 1954. Slaughter and May, London: Articled Clerk, 1956–59; Asst Solicitor, 1959–68; Partner, 1968–89. Inspector, DTI, 1987. Ind. Investigator, SIB, 1994–97. Hon. Sen. Res. Fellow, KCL, 1988–. Chairman: Nat. Fedn of Consumers Groups, 1968; Cttee of Inquiry, Accountants Jt Disciplinary Scheme, 1989; Mem., Home Office Cttee on London Taxicab and Car Hire Trade, 1967. Clerk to Governors, Bradfield Coll., 1968–89, Governor, 1989–95. Mem., Chancellor's Court of Benefactors, Oxford Univ., 1995–2000. Mem. Council, Pali Text Soc., 1991–2000. Trustee, Elizabeth Garrett Anderson Hosp. Appeal, 1997–2005. *Publications:* (contrib.) Sovereign Borrowers, 1984; (contrib.) Current Issues of International Financial Law, 1985; (jtly) Butterworths Banking Documents, 1986; (contrib.) Butterworths Banking and Financial Law Review, 1987; contribs on legal aspects of internat. finance to Jl of Business Law, Euromoney and Internat. Financial Law Review. *Recreations:* gardening, electronics (holder of Amateur Transmitting Licence), map collecting, reading, jazz, Welsh language/history. *Address:* Hill Fort House, Ruckhall, Eaton Bishop, Herefordshire HR2 9QG. *T:* (01981) 251754; Cwm Mynach Ganol, Bontddu, Dolgellau, Gwynedd LL40 2TU. *Died 24 Oct. 2015.*

YOUD, Sam; writer, since 1958; *b* 16 April 1922; *s* of Sam and Harriet Youd; *m* 1st, 1946, Joyce Fairbairn (marr. diss. 1978); one *s* four *d*; 2nd, 1980, Jessica Ball (*d* 2001). *Educ:* Peter Symonds Sch., Winchester. Manager, Industrial Diamond Inf. Bureau, London, 1956–58. Chm., Children's Writers' Gp, Soc. of Authors, 1983–85. Atlantic Award in Literature, Rockefeller Foundn, 1947; George Stone Award, 1977. *Publications* include: as John Christopher: The Twenty Second Century (short stories), 1954; The Year of the Comet, 1955; The Death of Grass, 1956; The Caves of Night, 1958; A Scent of White Poppies, 1959; The Long Voyage, 1960; The World in Winter, 1962; Cloud on Silver, 1964; The Possessors, 1965; A Wrinkle in the Skin, 1965; The Little People, 1966; Pendulum, 1968; Bad Dream, 2003; for young adults: The Tripods trilogy (The White Mountains, 1967; The City of Gold and Lead, 1967; The Pool of Fire, 1968); The Lotus Caves, 1969; The Guardians, 1970 (Guardian Prize, and Christopher Medal, 1971; Jugendbuchpreis, 1976); The Sword trilogy (The Prince in Waiting, 1970; Beyond the Burning Lands, 1971; The Sword of the Spirits, 1972); Dom and Va, 1973; Wild Jack, 1974; Empty World, 1977; The Fireball trilogy (Fireball, 1981; New Found Land, 1983; Dragon Dance, 1986); When the Tripods Came, 1988; A Dusk of Demons, 1993; Bad Dream, 2003; also wrote as Hilary Ford, William Godfrey, Peter Graaf, Anthony Rye, Stanley Winchester, and Samuel Youd. *Address:* One Whitefriars, Conduit Hill, Rye, E Sussex TN31 7LE. *Died 3 Feb. 2012.*

YOUNG, Rt Rev. Clive; Bishop Suffragan of Dunwich, 1999–2013; an Honorary Assistant Bishop, Diocese of Hereford, since 2013; *b* 31 May 1948; *s* of late William Alfred Young and Dorothy Young; *m* 1971, Susan Elizabeth Tucker. *Educ:* King Edward VI Grammar Sch., Chelmsford; St John's Coll., Durham (BA Hons); Ridley Hall, Cambridge. Ordained: deacon, 1972; priest, 1973; Assistant Curate: Neasden cum Kingsbury St Catherine, London, 1972–75; St Paul, Hammersmith, 1975–79; Priest-in-charge, 1979–82, Vicar, 1982–92, St Paul with St Stephen, Old Ford; Area Dean, Tower Hamlets, 1988–92; Archdeacon of Hackney and Vicar of Guild Church of St Andrew, Holborn, 1992–99. *Recreations:* music, gardening. *Address:* The Sycamores, Ewyas Harold, Herefordshire HR2 0JD. *T:* (01981) 240776. *Died 7 Oct. 2015.*

YOUNG, (David) Junor; HM Diplomatic Service, retired; *b* 23 April 1934; *m* 1954, Kathleen Brooks; two *s* two *d*. *Educ:* Robert Gordon's College. Joined Foreign Office, 1951; served Berlin, Ankara, South Africa, DSAO, Port Louis, Belgrade, 1951–75; Consul (Comm.), Stuttgart, 1978–81; First Sec., Kampala, 1981–84; Consul Gen., Hamburg, 1984–86; Counsellor (Commercial), Bonn, 1986–88; High Comr, Solomon Is, 1988–90; Dep. High Comr, Karachi, 1991–94. *Recreation:* gardening. *Address:* Pine Cottage, Hintlesham, Suffolk IP8 3NH. *Died 18 June 2015.*

YOUNG, Donald Anthony, CEng, FIGEM; Managing Director, National Transmission, British Gas plc, 1991–93; *b* 23 June 1933; *s* of Cyril Charles Young and Sarah Young; *m* 1960, June (*née* Morrey); two *d*. *Educ:* Stockport Secondary Sch. FIGEM (FIGasE 1969). National Service, 2nd Lieut REME, 1953–55. North Western Gas Bd, 1949–60; E Midlands Gas Bd, 1960–68; Gas Council Terminal Manager, Bacton Natural Gas Reception Terminal, 1968–70; Gas Council Plant Ops Engr, 1970–73; Asst Dir (Ops), Prodn & Supply Div., British Gas HQ, 1973–77; Regional Dep. Chm., N Thames Gas, 1977–79; Dir (Operations), Prodn & Supply Div., British Gas HQ, 1979–83; Regional Chairman: Southern Reg., British Gas Corp., subseq. British Gas plc Southern, 1983–89; British Gas plc West Midlands, 1989–91. Pres., IGasE, 1988–89. CCMI (CBIM 1986). Freeman: City of London, 2006; Engineers' Co., 2006. *Recreations:* gardening, walking. *Address:* Georgian House, Penn Lane, Tanworth in Arden, Warwickshire B94 5HH. *Died 23 June 2011.*

YOUNG, Eric, OBE 1976; HM Diplomatic Service, retired; Editor, Control Risks Information Services, 1984–93; *b* 16 Nov. 1924; *s* of late Robert Young, MBE, MIMinE and Emily Florence Young, Doncaster; *m* 1949, Sheila Hutchinson; three *s* one *d*. *Educ:* Maltby Grammar Sch.; Sheffield Univ. (BA 1948). Served War, RN, 1943–46. Editorial staff: Sheffield Telegraph, 1948; Western Morning News, 1951; Daily Dispatch, 1952; Manchester Guardian, 1953; PRO, NCB, Manchester, 1958; Dep. Dir, UK Inf. Office, Tanganyika and Zanzibar, 1960; First Secretary: (Inf.), Dar es Salaam, 1961; (Aid), Kaduna, 1963; Commonwealth Office (later FCO), 1967; Madras, 1969; Head of Chancery, Reykjavik, 1973 (Hd of Brit. Interests Section, French Embassy, during breach of diplomatic relations, 1976); Dep. High Comr, Bombay, 1977; High Comr, Seychelles, 1980–83. *Recreations:* music, books, my family. *Address:* 3 West Hall, Sudbourne Park, Orford, Woodbridge, Suffolk IP12 2AJ. *Died 26 Dec. 2011.*

YOUNG, John Henderson, OBE 1980; JP, DL; Member (C) West of Scotland, Scottish Parliament, 1999–2003; *b* 21 Dec. 1930; *s* of late William W. Young and Jeannie Young (*née* Henderson); *m* 1956, Doris Paterson (*d* 2001); one *s*. *Educ:* Hillhead High Sch., Glasgow; Scottish Coll. of Commerce. Served RAF, 1949–51. Shipping Manager/Dep. Contracts Manager, Kelvin-Diesel Engines, 1959–77; Export Admin Sales Manager, Teachers Whisky, 1977–88; Chm., Allied-Lyons Shipping & Marine Insce Cttee, 1987–88; Public Relns Consultant, Proscot Ltd, 1989–92. Newspaper columnist, The Extra, 1997–. Mem., Local Govt Commn, 1998. Mem. (C) Glasgow City Council, 1964–99: Leader, 1977–79; Opposition Leader, 1979–80, 1988–92, 1996–98; Police Judge, 1970–72; Bailie, 1968–71, 1977–80, 1984–88, 1988–92; Vice-Chm., Glasgow Corp. Airport Cttee, 1968–71; Mem., Strathclyde PTA, 1995–99. Chm., Assoc. Scottish Cons. Councillors, 1991–94. Tspt spokesman, Scottish Cons. Party, 1998–99. Mem., Scottish Parly Corporate Body, 1999–2003; Dep. Convener, Nat. Galleries Bills Cttee, Scottish Parlt, 2003. Mem., Commonwealth Parly Delegn of Scottish Parlt, Quebec, Canada, 2002. Mem., All-Party Gp on Animal Welfare, Scottish Parlt, 1999–. Chm., Assoc. of Former MSPs, 2003–. Vice-Chm., Scottish Pakistani Assoc., 1981–84; Sec., Scottish/S African Soc., 1986–88. FCMI (FIMgt 2001). Contested (C): Rutherglen, 1966; Cathcart, 1992; Eastwood, Scottish Parlt, 1999. Life Mem., Cathcart Conservatives. JP Glasgow, 1968–2007; DL Glasgow, 1981. Gov., Hutcheson's Educnl Trust, 1991–97. KStJ. Life Mem., Merchants' House of Glasgow. *Publications:* A History of Cathcart Conservative Association 1918–93, 1993; contrib. articles to newspapers and magazines. *Recreations:* meeting people, history, writing, reading, animal welfare. *Address:* 4 Deanwood Avenue, Netherlee, Glasgow G44 3RJ. *T:* (0141) 637 9535. *Died 3 Nov. 2011.*

YOUNG, Junor; *see* Young, D. J.

YOUNG, Kenneth Middleton, CBE 1977; Chairman, Further Education Funding Council for Wales, 1999–2001 (Member, Council, and Quality Assurance Committee, 1998–2001); *b* 1 Aug. 1931; *s* of Cyril W. D. Young and Gwladys Middleton Young; *m* 1958, Brenda May Thomas; one *s* one *d*. *Educ:* Neath Grammar Sch.; University Coll. of Wales, Aberystwyth (Hon. Fellow, 1991); Coll. of Science and Technology, Univ. of Manchester. BA (Hons) 1952; Diploma in Personnel Management, 1954. Pilot Officer/Navigator, General Duties (Aircrew), RAF, 1952–54. Asst Personnel Manager, Elliott-Automation Ltd, 1955–59; Collective Agreements Manager, later Salary Administration Manager, Massey-Ferguson (UK) Ltd, 1959–64; Personnel Adviser, Aviation Div., Smiths Industries Ltd, 1964–66; Group Personnel Manager, General Electric Company Ltd, and Dir, GEC (Management) Ltd, 1966–71; Post Office Corporation, 1972–92: Bd Mem. for Personnel, 1972–84, for Personnel and Corporate Resources, 1984–90; Man. Dir, Royal Mail Parcels, 1987; Vice-Chm., 1986–90; Actg Chm., 1989; Dep. Chm., 1990–92; Chairman: Subscription Services, 1988–92; Girobank PLC, 1989–90; Post Office Counters,

1990–92. Chm., Student Loans Co. Ltd, 1992–96; Director: Courage (formerly FBG) Pensions Ltd, 1993–2002; Courage (formerly FBG) Pensions Investments Ltd, 1993–2002. Member: Management Bd, Engineering Employers Fedn, 1971; CBI Employment Policy Cttee, 1978–84; Employment Appeal Tribunal, 1985–2002; BIC Target Team on Business/Educn Partnerships, 1988–89; Trustee, Post Office Pension Funds, 1989–95. Chairman: Rev. Gp, Further Educn Funding Councils for England and Wales, 1993; Further Educn Develt Assoc., subseq. Agency, 1994–97. Member: Council, Inst. of Manpower Studies, 1980–86; London Business Sch. Liaison Cttee, 1982–89; Chairman: Bd of Govs, SW London Coll., 1991; Roehampton Inst., 1992–95; Vice-Pres., Univ. of Wales (formerly St David's UC), Lampeter, 1993–99; Member: Council, Univ. of Wales, Aberystwyth, 1994–97 (Pres., Old Students Assoc., 1998–2000); Ct of Govs, 1998–2000, Council, 1999–2000, Univ. of Wales. CCMI; FIPM. *Recreations:* photography, Wales Rugby, painting. *Address:* Bryn Aber, Northcliffe Drive, Penarth, South Glamorgan CF64 1DQ. *Died 7 Feb. 2015.*

YOUNGER, Hon. Robert Edward Gilmour; Sheriff of Tayside, Central and Fife, 1982–2004; *b* 25 Sept. 1940; *y s* of 3rd Viscount Younger of Leckie, OBE and Evelyn Margaret, MBE, *e d* of Alexander Logan McClure, KC; *m* 1972, Helen Jane Hayes; one *s* one *d*. *Educ:* Cargilfield Sch., Edinburgh; Winchester Coll.; New Coll., Oxford (MA); Edinburgh Univ. (LLB); Glasgow Univ. Advocate, 1968; Sheriff of Glasgow and Strathkelvin, 1979–82. *Recreation:* wondering. *Address:* Old Leckie, Gargunnock, Stirling, Scotland FK8 3BN. *T:* (01786) 860213. *Died 23 Dec. 2012.*

YOUNIE, Edward Milne, OBE 1978; HM Diplomatic Service, retired; *b* 9 Feb. 1926; *s* of John Milne and Mary Dickie Younie; *m* 1st, 1952, Mary Groves (*d* 1976); 2nd, 1979, Mimi Barkley (marr. annulled 1991); 3rd, 1994, Mrs Alyn Denholm. *Educ:* Fettes Coll. (Scholar); Gonville and Caius Coll., Cambridge (Scholar) (BA Hons 1949). RN, 1944–46. HM Colonial Service, Tanganyika, 1950–62; FCO, 1963; Johannesburg, 1964–67; Blantyre, 1967–69; First Secretary: Lagos, 1972–76; Nairobi, 1977–79; Salisbury, 1979–81 (Counsellor, 1980); FCO, 1981–82. Dir, Fairbridge (Scotland), 1996–. *Recreations:* golf, music. *Address:* Wester Corsehill, Thornhill, Stirling FK8 3QD. *Club:* Brooks's. *Died 25 June 2011.*

YOUNSON, Maj.-Gen. Eric John, OBE 1952; Eur Ing; CEng, FRAeS; President, Ordnance Board, 1972–73 (Vice-President, 1970–72); *b* 1 March 1919; *o s* of late Ernest M. Younson, MLitt, BCom, Jarrow; *m* 1946, Jean Beaumont Carter, BA; three *d*. *Educ:* Jarrow Grammar Sch.; Univ. of Durham (BSc); Royal Military Coll. of Science; Administrative Staff Coll. CEng 1970; FRAeS 1970; Eur Ing 1991. Served War of 1939–45: commissioned, RA, 1940; UK and NW Europe (despatches). Directing Staff, RMCS, 1953–55; Atomic Weapons Research Estab., 1957–58; Attaché (Washington) as rep. of Chief Scientific Adviser, 1958–61; Head of Defence Science 3, MoD, 1961–63; Dep. Dir of Artillery, 1964–66; Dir of Guided Weapons Trials and Ranges, Min. of Technology, 1967–69. Sen. Asst Dir, Central Bureau for Educnl Visits and Exchanges, 1973–74; Dep. Dir, SIMA, 1974–78; Sec.-Gen., EUROM, 1975–77; Clerk to Worshipful Co. of Scientific Instrument Makers, 1976–87 (Hon. Liveryman and Clerk Emeritus, 1987). FRSA 1944; FCMI 2001; MIET (MIEE 2002). Freeman, City of London, 1981. *Publications:* (ed jtly) UK/US Nuclear Weapons Classification Guide, 1963; The Worshipful Company of Scientific Instrument Makers: history, 1988; articles on gunnery and scientific subjects in Service jls. *Recreations:* photography, electronics, Talking Newspapers for the Blind. *Address:* 7 Pondwick Road, Harpenden, Herts AL5 2HG. *T:* (01582) 621691. *Died 14 Aug. 2013.*

ZAHIRUDDIN bin Syed Hassan, Tun Syed, SPCM 1987; SMN, PSM, DUNM; SPMP 1970; JMN, PJK; Hon. GCVO 1974; Orang Besar Empat, Perak, since 1984; *b* 11 Oct. 1918; *m* 1949, Toh Puan Halimah, *d* of Haji Mohamed Noh; five *s* five *d*. *Educ:* Malay Coll., Kuala Kangsar; Raffles Coll., Singapore (Dip.Arts). Passed Cambridge Sch. Cert. Malay Officer, Tanjong Malim, etc, 1945–47; Dep. Asst Dist Officer, 1948; Asst Dist Officer, 1951–54; 2nd Asst State Sec., Perak, 1955; Registrar of Titles and Asst State Sec. (Lands), Perak, 1956; Dist Officer, Batang Padang, Tapah, 1957; Dep. Sec., Public Services Commn, 1958; Principal Asst Sec. (Service), Fedn Estabt Office, Kuala Lumpur, 1960; State Sec., Perak, 1961; Permanent Sec.: Min. of Agric. and Co-operatives, Kuala Lumpur, 1963; Min. of Educn, Kuala Lumpur, 1966; Dir-Gen., Public Services Dept, Kuala Lumpur, 1970; retd, 1972. Chm., Railway Services Commn, Kuala Lumpur, 1972–73. High Comr for Malaysia in London, 1974–75; Governor of Malacca, 1975–84. Chairman: Special Cttee on Superannuation in the Public Services, 1972, and Statutory Bodies. Vice-Pres., Subang Nat. Golf Club, 1972–74. *Recreation:* golf. *Address:* No 60 Jalan Sultan Azlan Shah, 31400 Ipoh, Malaysia. *Died 20 April 2013.*

ZAPF, Hermann; freelance book and type designer, since 1938; *b* Nuremburg, 8 Nov. 1918; *s* of Hermann Zapf and Magdalene Zapf (*née* Schlamp); *m* 1951, Gudrun von Hesse; (one *s* decd). Type dir, D. Stempel AG, type foundry, Frankfurt, 1947–56; design consultant, Mergenthaler Linotype Co., NYC and Frankfurt, 1957–74; Consultant, Hallmark Internat., Kansas City, 1966–73; Vice-Pres., Design Processing Internat. Inc., NYC, 1977–86; Prof., Typographic Computer Programs, Rochester Inst. Technol., NY, 1977–87; Chm., Zapf, Burns & Co., NYC, 1987–91. Designer of types: Palatino, Melior, Optima, ITC Zapf Chancery, ITC Zapf Internat., Digiset-Marconi, Digiset-Edison, Digiset-Aurelia, Pan-Nigerian, URW (Roman and San Serif), Renaissance Roman, Zapfino Script. Mem., RSA. Hon. Mem., Soc. of Scribes and Illuminators. Hon. RDI 1985. Hon. DFA Illinois, 2003. Frederic W. Goudy Award, Rochester Inst. Technol., Rochester, NY, 1969; Gutenberg Prize, City of Mainz, 1974; Robert H. Middleton Award, Soc. Typographic Arts, Chicago, 1987; Euro Design Award, Design Biennial Oostende, 1994; Wadim Lazursky Award, Acad. Design, Moscow, 1996. *Publications:* William Morris, 1948; Pen and Graver, 1952; Manual Typographicum, 1954, 2nd edn 1968; About Alphabets, 1960, 2nd edn 1970; Typographic Variations, 1964; Orbis Typographicus, 1980; Hora fugit/Carpe diem, 1984; Hermann Zapf and his Design Philosophy, 1987; ABC-XYZapf, 1989; Poetry Through Typography, 1993; August Rosenberger, 1996; The Fine Art of Letters, 2000; The World of Alphabets, 2001; Calligraphic Type Design in the Digital Age, 2001; Alphabet Stories, 2007. *Address:* Seitersweg 35, 64287 Darmstadt, Germany. *T:* (6151) 76825, *Fax:* (6151) 717204. *Clubs:* Double Crown (Hon. Mem.), Wynkyn de Worde (Hon. Mem.); Type Directors (NY) (Hon. Mem.). *Died 4 June 2015.*

ZEMAN, Prof. Zbyněk Anthony Bohuslav; Research Professor in European History, 1982–96, then Emeritus, and Professorial Fellow of St Edmund Hall, 1983–96, Oxford University; *b* Prague, 18 Oct. 1928; *s* of late Jaroslav and Růžena Zeman; *m* 1st, 1956, Sarah Anthea Collins (*d* 1998); two *s* one *d*; 2nd, 1998, Dagmar Hájková. *Educ:* London and Oxford Universities. BA (Hons) London, DPhil Oxon. Research Fellow, St Antony's Coll., Oxford, 1958–61, and Mem. editorial staff, The Economist, 1959–62; Lectr in Modern History, Univ. of St Andrews, 1962–70; Head of Research, Amnesty International, 1970–73; Director, East-West SPRL (Brussels) and European Co-operation Research Gp, 1974–76; Prof. of Central and SE European Studies and Dir, Comenius Centre, Lancaster Univ., 1976–82. Vis. Prof. of Hist., Charles University, Prague, 1990–91. Hon. Fellow: Österreichisches Ost- und Südosteuropa-Institut, 1988–89; Inst. of History of Czech Army, Prague, 1994–95. *Publications* include: The Break-up of the Habsburg Empire 1914–1918, 1961; Nazi Propaganda, 1964; (with W. B. Scharlau) The Merchant of Revolution, A Life of Alexander Helphand (Parvus), 1965; Prague Spring, 1969; A Diplomatic History of the First World War, 1971; (ed jtly) International Yearbook of East West Trade, 1975; The Masaryks, 1976; (jtly) Comecon Oil and Gas, 1977; Selling the War: art and propaganda in the Second World War, 1978; Heckling Hitler: caricatures of the Third Reich, 1984; Pursued by a Bear: the making of Eastern Europe, 1989; The Making and Breaking of Communist Europe, 1991; (with A. Klimek) The Life of Edvard Beneš

1884–1948: Czechoslovakia in peace and war, 1997; Edvard Beneš: politický životopis, 2000, 2009; (with Rainer Karlsch) Uraniumgeheimnisse, Das Erzgebirge im Brennpunkt der Weltpolitik 1933–1960, 2002, English edn as Uranium Matters: Central European uranium in international politics 1900–1960, 2008. *Address:* Čínská 18, 160 00 Prague, Czech Republic. *Died 22 June 2011.*

ZETTERBERG, Christer; Chairman: IDI AB (Industrial Develt and Investment), since 1996; Carnegie AB, since 2001; Carnegie Investment Bank, since 2006; *b* 2 Nov. 1941; *m* 1966, Inger Mathson; three *d.* MBA 1967. Officer, Royal Swedish Navy Reserve, 1964. Svenska Cellulosa AB, 1968–76 (Manager, Pulp Sales and Head, Pulp Div.); President and Chief Executive Officer: Calor-Celsius, 1976–80; Tibnor, 1980–83; Holmens Bruk, 1983–88; PKBanken, 1988–90; AB Volvo, 1990–92. Chm., BooForssjö AB. Board Member: LE Lundberggroup; Camfil AB; Nike Hydraulics AB; Swedeship Marine AB. Member: Royal Swedish Acad. of Engrg Scis, 1990; Royal Acad. of Naval Scis, 1991. *Address:* IDI AB, Hovslagargatan 5B, 11148 Stockholm, Sweden; Granneberg, 61075 Västerljung, Sweden. *Died 5 April 2012.*

ZOCHONIS, Sir John (Basil), Kt 1997; DL; Chairman, Paterson Zochonis, 1970–93; Member, Commonwealth Development Corporation, 1992–95; *b* 2 Oct. 1929; *s* of Constantine and Octavia Nitza Zochonis; *m* 1990, Brigid Mary Evanson Demetriades. *Educ:* Rugby; Corpus Christi Coll., Oxford (BA Law). Joined Paterson Zochonis, 1953; Dir, 1957; retd, 1993. Founder, Zochonis Charitable Trust, 1977. Member Council: BESO, 1987–2005; Royal African Soc., 1984–. Mem., Court and Council, Manchester Univ., 1968–90 (Chm., Council, 1987–90); Chm. Govs, Withington Girls' Sch., 1995–98. Pres., Adventure Farm Trust, 1994–99; Vice-Pres., Manchester YMCA, 1993–. Freeman, City of London, 1978; Liveryman, Tallow Chandlers' Co., 1978–. DL 1989, High Sheriff, 1994–95, Greater Manchester. Hon. RNCM 1991. Hon. LLD Manchester, 1991. *Recreations:* reading, watching cricket. *Clubs:* Carlton, Travellers, MCC. *Died 30 Nov. 2013.*